WEBSTER'S COLOR DICTIONARY

Edited by

John Gage Allee, Ph.D.

Professor of English Philology,
The George Washington University

This book is not published by the original publishers
of WEBSTER'S DICTIONARY, or by their successors.

BONANZA BOOKS
New York

KEY TO THIS DICTIONARY

The entries in this Dictionary are arranged in groups, derived and related words being placed under the main entry.

A. Each main entry, in bold-faced type, is syllabized with the phonetic spelling and accented syllable shown in parentheses. The part of speech, in italics, follows; then the definition.
   Ex.: **cross** (kraws) *a.* intersecting; interchanged. . . .

B. Sub-entries are shown in bold-faced type following the definition of the main entry.
   1. If a hyphen precedes the sub-entry, the ending is added to the main entry.
   Ex.: **-ing** (crossing)
   2. If a dash precedes the sub-entry, a hyphenated word is indicated.
   Ex.: **—examination** (cross-examination)
   3. If a dash and a space precede the sub-entry, this indicates words that are commonly found together.
   Ex.: **—reference** (cross reference)
   4. If the sub-entry is spelled out and/or pronunciation shown, this may indicate differences from the main entry. (In some instances, sub-entries are spelled out where confusion may otherwise develop).

C. The etymology of the main-entry is found in brackets following the entry paragraph; lack of etymology indicates uncertain or unknown word origin.

Note: Irregularities of verb forms, plurals and comparisons are included as sub-entries to facilitate word usage.

ABBREVIATIONS USED IN THIS DICTIONARY

a. adjective
abbrev. abbreviation
ablat. ablative; ablatival
Aborig. Aboriginal
acc. accusative
A.D. Anno Domini (in the year of Our Lord)
adv. adverb
Aero. Aeronautics
Afr. Africa; African
Agric. Agriculture
Alg. Algebra
alt. alternative
Amer. America; American
Anat. Anatomy
Anglo-Ind. Anglo-Indian
Anthropol. Anthropology
Ar. Arabic
Arch. Archaic
Archaeol. Archaeology
Archit. Architecture
Arith. Arithmetic
Astrol. Astrology
Astron. Astronomy
aux. auxiliary
Aviat. Aviation

Bacter. Bacteriology
B.C. before Christ
Bib. Biblical
Biol. Biology
Bot. Botany
Br., Brit. British
Braz. Brazilian
Bret. Breton
Build. Building

c. about (L. = *Circa*)
C. Centigrade; Central
Can. Canada; Canadian
Cap. capital letter
Carib. Caribbean
Carp. Carpentry
Celt. Celtic
cent. century
Cent. Central
cf. compare (L. = *confer*)
ch. Chapter
Chem. Chemistry
Chin. Chinese
Class. Myth. Classical Mythology
Colloq. Colloquial; Colloquialism

Comm. Commerce; Commercial
comp. comparative
conj. conjunction
conn. connected
contr. contraction
corrupt. corruption

Dan. Danish
dat. dative
def. art. definite article
demons. demonstrative
der. derivation; derived
Dial. Dialect; Dialectal
Dict. Dictionary
dim. diminutive
Dut. Dutch
Dyn. Dynamics

E. East; English
Eccl. Ecclesiastical
e.g. for example (L. = *exemplia gratia*)
E.Ind. East Indian
Elect. Electricity
Embryol. Embryology
Engin. Engineering
Entom. Entomology
esp. especially
Ethnol. Ethnology
etym. etymology

F., Fahr. Fahrenheit
fem. feminine
fig. figuratively
Finn. Finnish
Flem. Flemish
Fort. Fortification
fr. from
Fr. French
freq. frequentative

Gael. Gaelic
gen. genitive
Geog. Geography
Geol. Geology
Geom. Geometry
Ger. German
Gk. Greek
Gk. Myth. Greek Mythology
Gram. Grammar

Heb. Hebrew
Her. Heraldry

Hind. Hindustani
Hist. History
Hort. Horticulture
Hung. Hungarian

i. intransitive
Ice. Icelandic
i.e. that is (L. = *id est*)
imit. imitation; imitative
imper. imperative
impers. impersonal
Ind. Indian
indef. art. indefinite article
indic. indicative
infin. infinitive
interj. interjection
interrog. interrogative
Ir. Irish
It. Italian

Jap. Japanese

L. Latin
l.c. lower case letter
L.Ger. Low German
lit. literally
Lit. Literature
L.L. Low (Late) Latin

masc. masculine
Math. Mathematics
M.E. Middle English
Mech. Mechanics
Med. Medicine
Metal. Metallurgy
Meteor. Meteorology
Mex. Mexican
M.H.Ger. Middle High German
Mil. Military
Min. Mineralogy
Mod. Modern
Mus. Music
Myth. Mythology

n. noun
N. North; Norse
Nat.Hist. Natural History
Naut. Nautical
neg. negative
neut. neuter
nom. nominative
Norw. Norwegian
n.pl. noun plural

n.sing. noun singular
N.T. New Testament

obj. object; objective
obs. obsolete
O.E. Old English
O.Fr. Old French
O.H.Ger. Old High German
O.L.Ger. Old Low German
O.N. Old Norse
Onomat. Onomatopoeic
opp. opposite; opposed
Opt. Optics
orig. originally
Ornith. Ornithology
O.T. Old Testament

Paint. Painting
pa.p. past participle
pass. passive
pa.t. past tense
Path. Pathology
perh. perhaps
pers. person
Pers. Persian
pert. pertaining
Peruv. Peruvian
Pharm. Pharmacy
Philol. Philology
Philos. Philosophy
Phon. Phonetics
Photog. Photography
Phys. Physics
Physiol. Physiology
pl. plural
Poet. Poetry; poetical
Pol. Polish
Port. Portuguese
poss. possessive
pref. prefix
prep. preposition
pres. present
Print. Printing
prob. probably
pron. pronoun
Pros. Prosody
Prov. Provincial
pr.p. present participle
Psych. psychology

q.v. which see (L. = *quod vide*)

R. River

R.C. Roman Catholic
recip. reciprocal
redup. reduplication
ref. reference; referring
refl. reflexive
rel related; relative
Rhet. Rhetoric
Rom. Roman
Rom.Myth. Roman Mythology
Russ. Russian

S. South
S.Afr. South African
S.Amer. South American
Sans. Sanskrit
Scand. Scandinavian
Scot. Scots; Scottish
Sculp. Sculpture
sing. singular
Singh. Singhalese
Slav. Slavonic
Sp. Spanish
St. Saint
superl. superlative
Surg. Surgery
Sw. Swedish
Syn. Synonym

t. transitive
Teleg. Telegraphy
Teut. Teutonic
Theat. Theatre
Theol. Theology
Trig. Trigonometry
Turk. Turkish

U.S.(A.) United States (of America)
usu. usually

v. verb
var. variant; variation
v.i. verb intransitive
v.t. verb transitive
vulg. vulgar

W. Welsh; West

Yid. Yiddish

Zool. Zoology

KEY TO PRONUNCIATION

These pronunciation symbols are used for the sounds indicated by the bold face letter or letters in the key words.

Vowels and diphthongs:

a—bat
à—botany
ạ—about, soda (unstressed)
ā—bait
aw—bought
e—bet
ē—beet
i—bit
i·—city (final syllable)

ī—bite
ō—boat
oo—book
ŏŏ—boot
oi—boil
ou—bout
u—but
ū—butte
ur—Bert (stressed)
er—blubber (unstressed)

Consonants:

b—bill
ch—church
d—dill
f—fill
g—get
h—hill
hw—wheel
j—judge
k—kill
l—lily

m—mill
n—nil
ng—sing
ngg—finger
p—pill
r—rill
s—sill
sh—shall, sure
t—till
th—thin

TH—then
v—villa
w—will
y—yet
z—zillion
zh—pleasure

This edition is published by Bonanza Books,
a division of Crown Publishers, Inc.
by arrangement with Ottenheimer Publishers, Inc.
a b c d e f g h

A

A (ā, ạ) *a*, the indefinite *article*, meaning *one*. A contraction of *an* (fr. O.E. *an*, *one*), used before vowels.

A-1 (ā wun) first-rate; excellent; physically fit.

aard·vark (ärd′·värk) *n.* animal resembling the ant-eater, found in parts of Africa. [Dut. *aarde*, earth; *vark*, a pig].

A.B. (ā bē) Bachelor of Arts [L. *Artium Baccalaureus*]

ab- (ab) *prefix* meaning from, away, off [L.].

a·ba·cá (ậb′·ậ·kä) *n.* Manila hemp, or the plant producing it [Malay].

a·back (ạ·bak′) *adv.* backwards; on the back; (*Naut.*) against the masts, of sails pressed back by the wind. **taken aback**, taken by surprise; disconcerted [O.E. *on bacc*].

ab·a·cus (ab′·ạ·kạs) *n.* an instrument with parallel wires on which arithmetical calculations are made with sliding balls or beads; a counting-frame; (*Archit.*) a tablet crowning a column and its capital [L., from Gk. *abax*, a reckoning-board].

a·baft (ạ·baft′) *adv.* and *prep.* (*Naut.*) at or towards the stern; behind [O.E. *baft*, behind].

ab·a·lone (ab·ạ·lō′·nē) *n.* the name of several species of limpet-like molluscs or "earshells," yielding mother-of-pearl [Sp.].

a·ban·don (ạ·ban′·dạn) *v.t.* to give up wholly and finally; to relinquish; to surrender; *n.* careless freedom; a yielding to unrestrained impulse; dash. **-ed** *a.* deserted; forsaken; unrestrained; given up entirely to, esp. wickedness. **-edly** *adv.* **-ment** *n.* the act of abandoning, or state of being abandoned; (*Law*) the relinquishing of an interest or claim [Fr. *abandonner*, to give up].

a·base (ạ·bās′) *v.t.* to bring low; to cast down; to humble. **-ment** *n.* humiliation [L. *ad*, to; L.L. *bassare*, to lower].

a·bash (ạ·bash′) *v.t.* to strike with shame or fear; to excite a consciousness of guilt, inferiority, etc. **-ment** *n.* confusion from shame, etc. [Fr. *ébahir*, to astound].

a·bate (ạ·bāt′) *v.t.* to beat down, lessen; (*Law*) to put an end to, as a nuisance; to annul, as a writ; *v.i.* to decrease, subside, decline. **-able** *a.* **-ment** *n.* **-r** *n.* [L. *ad*, and *batere*, for *batuere*, to strike].

a·bat·toir (a·bạ·twár′) *n.* a slaughter-house [Fr. *abattre*, to fell].

ab·ba·cy (ab′·ạ·si·) *n.* the office or dignity of an abbot; the building under the control of an abbot; an abbey. **abbatial** (ạ·bā′·shạl) *a.* pert. to an abbot, or an abbey. **abbé** (ab′·i·) *n.* designation of and mode of address for an R.C. priest in France; an abbot. **abbey** *n.* a church establishment forming the dwelling-place of a community of monks or nuns. **abbot** (*fem.* **abbess**) *n.* the head of an abbey or monastery. **abbotship** *n.* [Syriac *abba*, father; Heb. *ab*, father].

ab·bre·vi·ate (ạ·brē′·vi·āt) *v.t.* to shorten, reduce by contraction or omission. **abbreviation** *n.* the act of abbreviating; a shortened form. **abbreviator** *n.* **abbreviatory** *a.* [L. *abbreviare*, fr. *brevis*, short].

A·b·c (ā·bē·sē′) *n.* the first three letters of the alphabet; the alphabet; the rudiments of any subject; a primer.

ab·di·cate (ab′·di·kāt) *v.t.* and *i.* formally to give up power or office. **abdication** *n.* [L. *ab*, from; *dicare*, to proclaim].

ab·do·men (ab·dō′·mạn, ab′·dạ·mạn) *n.* the lower part of the trunk of the body; the belly. **abdominal** *a.* **abdominous** *a.* having a big belly; paunchy [L.].

ab·duct (ab·dukt′) *v.t.* to take away by fraud or force; to kidnap; (*Anat.*) to draw, e.g. a limb away from its natural position. **abducent** (ab·dōō·sent) *a.* (*Anat.*) abducting. **abduction** *n.* [L. *ab*, from; *ducere*, *ductum*, to lead].

a·beam (ạ·bēm′) *adv.* (*Naut.*) at right angles to a ship's length; hence, straight across a ship; abreast [E. *beam*].

a·bed (ạ·bed′) *adv.* in bed [E. *on bed*].

a·bele (ạ·bēl′) *n.* the white poplar-tree [L. *albus*, white].

ab·er·rate (ab′·ẹr·āt) *v.i.* to deviate from the right path or normal course. **aberrant** (ab··er′·ạnt) *a.* deviating from the normal. **aberration** (ab·ạ·rā′·shun) *n.* a wandering, esp. mental disorder, forgetfulness; mental instability or peculiarity; moral lapse [L. *ab*, from; *errare*, to wander].

a·bet (ạ·bet′) *v.t.* to encourage or aid, esp. in doing wrong. *pr.p.* **-ting.** *pa.p.* and *pa.t.* **-ted.** **-tment** *n.* **-ter, -tor** *n.* [O.Fr. *abeter*, to incite].

a·bey·ance (ạ·bā′·ạns) *n.* a state of suspension or temporary inactivity; the condition of not being in use or action. Also **abeyancy** [O.Fr. *abeer*, to gape at].

ab·hor (ab·hawr′) *v.t.* to hate extremely. *pr.p.* **-ring.** *pa.p.* and *pa.t.* **-red.** **-rence** *n.* detestation; loathing. **-rent** *a.* detestable; abominable; repugnant. **-rer** *n.* [L. *ab*, from; *horrere*, to shiver].

a·bide (ạ·bīd′) *v.i.* to stay; reside; continue firm or stable; *v.t.* to tolerate; bear; wait for; *pa.p.* and *pa.t.* **abode or abided. abidance** *n.* **abiding** *a.* lasting; enduring [O.E. *abidan*].

a·bil·i·ty (ạ·bil′·i·ti·) *n.* quality, state, or condition of being able; power to act; skill; capacity; competence. [L. *habilitas*, cleverness].

ab·i·o·gen·e·sis (ab·i·ō·jen′·ạ·sis) *n.* (*Biol.*) the theory of spontaneous generation from non-living matter [Gk. *a-*; neg.; *bios*, life; *genesis*, birth].

ab·ject (ab′·jekt) *a.* base; degraded; mean and worthless; contemptible; miserable. **-ly** *adv.* **-ion, -ness** *n.* degradation; abasement; servility [L. *ab*, away; *jacere*, *jactum*, to throw].

ab·jure (ab·jŏŏr′) *v.t.* to renounce upon oath;

to abandon allegiance to a cause, doctrine, or principle; repudiate; forswear. **abjuration** *n.* [L. *abjurare*, to deny on oath].

ab·la·tive (ab′·lạ·tiv) *a.* (used as *n.*) the sixth case of Latin nouns and pronouns expressing *time when*; originally implied *separation from*. **ablatival** *a.* [L. *ab*, from; *ferre*, *latum*, to carry].

ab·laut (ab′·lout) *n.* (*Philol.*) variation of root vowel in certain related words, as *sink*, *sank*, *sunk* [Ger. *ab*, from; *laut*, sound].

a·blaze (ạ·blāz′) *a.* on fire; aglow; gleaming.

a·ble (ā′·bl) *a.* having skill, strength to perform a task; competent; talented; vigorous. **—bodied** *a.* of sound body; robust; (of a seaman, *abbrev.* **A.B.**) having all-round knowledge of seamanship. **ability** *n.* being able. **-ness** *n.* **ably** *adv.* competently [L. *habilis*, manageable].

a·bloom (ạ·blóom′) *adv.* or *a.* in bloom.

ab·lu·tion (ab·lŏŏ′·shạn) *n.* cleansing or washing; (usually plural) the purification of the body or of sacred vessels before certain religious ceremonies, e.g., Eucharist; the wine and water used. **-ary** *a.* pert. to cleansing [L. *ab*, from; *luere*, *lutum*, to wash].

ab·ne·gate (ab′·ne·gāt) *v.t.* to deny; surrender; relinquish. **abnegation** *n.* denying; renunciation [L. *ab*, away; *negare*, to deny].

ab·nor·mal (ab·nawr′·mạl) *a.* contrary to rule, or system; deviating from a recognized standard; exceptional; psychologically maladjusted. Also **-ity, -ism** *n.* the state of being abnormal; deformity; idiosyncrasy. **-ly** *adv.* **abnormity** *n.* abnormality; monstrosity [L. *ab*, from; *norma*, rule].

a·board (ạ·bōrd′) *adv.* and *prep.* (*Naut.*) on board; within a vessel; on a train.

a·bode (ạ·bōd′) *n.* residence, permanent or temporary; a dwelling place [from *abide*].

a·bol·ish (ạ·bál′·ish) *v.t.* to do away with; to repeal; to obliterate. **-ment** *n.* [L. *abolescere*, to destroy].

ab·o·li·tion (ab·ạ·lish′·ạn) *n.* the act of abolishing, as of laws, taxes, etc. **-al** *a.* **-ist** *n.* **-ism** *n.* the policy of an abolitionist [L. *abolescere*, to destroy].

A-bomb (ā′·bám) *n.* atomic bomb.

a·bom·i·nate (ạ·bám′·i·nāt) *v.t.* to loathe; detest extremely; abhor. **abominable** *a.* loathsome; morally detestable; odious. **abominableness** *n.* **abominably** *adv.* **abomination** *n.* the act or object of loathing; a despicable practice [L. *abominari*, to detest].

ab·o·rig·ines (ab·ạ·rij′·i·nēz) *n.pl.* the original inhabitants of a country. **aboriginal** *a.* [L. *ab origine*, from the beginning].

a·bort (ab·awrt′) *v.i.* to miscarry in giving birth; (*Fig.*) to fail to come to fruition. **abortifacient** (ạ·bawr′·ti·fā·shạnt) *n.* a drug causing abortion; *a.* capable of producing abortion.

1

-ion *n.* miscarriage; one born permaturely. **-ionist** *n.* **-ive** *a.* prematurely produced; undeveloped; imperfect; rudimentary. **-ively** *adv.* [L. *aboriri, abortus*, to miscarry].

a·bound (a·bound′) *v.i.* to be in great plenty (used with preps. *with* and *in*). **-ing** *a.* plentiful [L. *abundare*, to overflow].

a·bout (a·bout′) *adv.* and *prep.* on every side; concerning; approximately; (before an infin.) on the point of. **to bring about**, to effect. **about face**, *n.* and *v.* turn in opposite direction [O.E. *būtan*, outside].

a·bove (a·buv′) *adv.* and *prep.* and *a.* higher than; more in number, quantity or degree. **above board**, open or openly; honorably. [O.E. *abufan*, upwards].

ab·ra·ca·dab·ra (ab′·ra·ka·dab′·ra) *n.* corruption of sacred Gnostic term, derived from ancient Egyptian magical formula; a catchword; gibberish.

a·brade (a·brād′) *v.t.* to rub or wear off; to scrape or grate off; to graze (of skin). **abradant** *n.* a substance, e.g. emery powder, for polishing. **abrading** *n.* soil-erosion. **abrasion** *n.* a rubbing or scraping off; a grazing of the skin. **abrasive** *a.* tending to abrade; scouring; *n.* something used for scouring. [L. *ab*, from; *radere, rasum*, to scrape].

ab·re·ac·tion (ab·rē·ak′·shan) *n.* in psychoanalysis, elimination of a morbid complex by expression through conscious association with the original cause. **abreact** *v.t.* [L. *ab*, from; and *reaction*].

a·breast (a·brest′) *adv.* side by side; on a line with [E.].

a·bridge (a·brij′) *v.t.* to shorten; curtail; reduce; diminish; epitomize. **-ment** *n.* a cutting-off; a summary; a précis; an abstract of evidence. **-r** *n.* [Fr. *abréger*; L. *abbreviare*, to shorten].

a·broad (a·brawd′) *adv.* and *a.* at large, over a wide space; beyond or out of a house, camp, or other enclosure; in foreign countries; overseas [E.].

ab·ro·gate (ab′·ra·gāt) *v.t.* to annul; repeal (a law); do away with; put an end to; cancel. **abrogation** *n.* [L. *ab*, away; *rogare*, to ask].

ab·rupt (a·brupt′) *a.* broken off; steep; precipitous; describing a sudden change of subject, etc. in speech or writing; curt; unceremonious; brusque; (*Bot.*) without a terminal leaf. **-ly** *adv.* **-ness** *n.* [L. *ab*, away; *rumpere, ruptum*, to break].

ab·scess (ab′·ses) *n.* gathering of pus in any infected organ or tissue of the body [L. *abscessus*, a going away].

ab·scind (ab·sind′) *v.t.* to cut off; pare away; separate; rend apart. **absciss, abscissa** *n.* (*Geom.*) the distance of a point from a fixed line measured horizontally; one of the elements of reference by which a point, as of a curve, is referred to a system of fixed rectilineal co-ordinate axes; *pl.* **abscissas, abscissae. abscission** *n.* act or process of cutting off [L. *ab*, away; *scindere, scissum*, to cut].

ab·scond (ab·skånd′) *v.i.* to take oneself off; to flee from justice. **-ence** *n.* **-er** *n.* [L. *abs*, away; *condere*, to hide].

ab·sence (ab′·sans) *n.* being absent; failure to appear when cited to a court of law; inattention to prevailing conditions. **absent** *a.* not present; inattentive. **absent** (ab·sent′) *v.t.* to withdraw (oneself); deliberately to fail to appear. **absentee** *n.* one who is not present. **absently** *adv.* casually; forgetfully. **absent-minded** *a.* abstracted; absorbed; pre-occupied [L. *ab*, away; *esse*, to be].

ab·sinthe, ab·sinth (ab′·sinth) *n.* a green-colored liqueur flavored with wormwood and other aromatics [L. *absinthium*, wormwood].

ab·so·lute (ab′·sa·lōōt) *a.* unconditional; without restraint; (*Gram.*) not dependent; pure. **-ly** *adv.* positively; very; entirely. **-ness** *n.* **absolution** *n.* a remission of sin after confession, pronounced by the R. C. Church; formal acquittal by a judge. **absolutism** *n.* unrestricted and unlimited rule; arbitrary government. **absolutist** *n.* **absolutory, absolvatory** *a.* **absolute alcohol**, alcohol free from water. **absolute pressure** (*Phys.*) pressure of gas, steam, or liquid measured as excess over zero pressure, i.e. over atmospheric pressure. **absolute zero** (*Phys.*) the lowest possible temperature —273.1° C. **nominative (ablative) absolute**, a grammatical construction consisting of a substantive and a participle independent of the main sentence [L. *absolutus*, freed].

ab·solve (ab·sålv′) *v.t.* to set free from an obligation, guilt, debt, penalty; to pardon; acquit. **-r** *n.* [L. *ab*, away; *solvere*, to loosen].

ab·sorb (ab·sawrb′) *v.t.* to swallow up; drink in; soak up; to engage one's whole attention. **-ability** *n.* **-able** *a.* **-ing** *a.* **-ent** *a.* absorbing; *n.* anything which absorbs. **-ency** *n.* [L. *ab*, away; *sorbere, sorptum*, to suck].

ab·sorp·tion (ab·sawrp′·shan) *n.* the act of absorbing. **absorptive** *a.* able to absorb [fr. *absorb*].

ab·stain (ab·stān′) *v.i.* to forbear; to refrain. **-er** *n.* one who abstains, esp. from alcohol [L. *abs*, from; *tenere*, to hold].

ab·ste·mi·ous (ab·stē′·mi·as) *a.* showing moderation in the use of food and drink. **-ly** *adv.* **-ness** *n.* [L. *abs*, from; *temetum*, strong drink].

ab·sten·tion (ab·sten′·shan) *n.* the act of abstaining or refraining from. **-ist** *n.* [L. *abs*, from; *tenere*, to hold].

ab·sti·nence (ab′·sti·nans) *n.* voluntary forbearance from using or doing something. Also **abstinency. abstinent** *a.* temperate; refraining from. **abstinently** *adv.* [L. *abs*, from; *tenere*, to hold].

ab·stract (ab·strakt′) *v.t.* to separate from; remove, summarize; reduce. **-ed** *a.* **-edly** *adv.* *a.* not concrete, theoretical. (ab′·strakt) *n.* that which comprises in itself the essential qualities of a larger thing, or of several things; a summary. **-ion** *n.* abstracting or separating; a theoretical idea. **in the abstract**, without reference to particular cases [L. *abs*, from; *trahere, tractum*, to draw].

ab·struse (ab·strōōs′) *a.* hidden; difficult or hard to be understood. **-ly** *adv.* **-ness** *n.* [L. *abs*, from; *trudere, trusum*, to thrust].

ab·surd (ab·surd′) *a.* contrary to reason; ridiculous; silly. **-ly** *adv.* **-ity** *n.* that which is absurd. Also **-ness** [L. *absurdus*, out of tune].

a·bun·dance (a·bun′·dans) *n.* ample sufficiency; great plenty. **abundant** *a.* fully sufficient; plentiful. **abundantly** *adv.* [L. *abundare*, to overflow].

a·buse (a·būz′) *v.t.* to make a wrong use of; to ill-treat; to violate; revile; malign. **abuse** (a·būs′) *n.* ill-usage; improper treatment; a corrupt practice; rude language. **abusive** *a.* practicing abuse; rude; insulting. **abusiveness** *n.* [Fr. *abuser*].

a·but (a·but′) *v.i.* to end; to touch with one end; to border on; to adjoin. *pr.p.* **-ting.** *pa.p.* **-ted. -ment** *n.* (*Archit.*) the support at end of an arch or bridge [O.Fr. *abouter*, to join at the end].

a·byss (a·bis′) *n.* any deep chasm; a gulf. formerly, **abysm** (a·bizm′) *n.* **abysmal** *a.* bottomless; vast; profound. **abysmally** *adv.* **abyssal** *a.* inhabiting, or characteristic of, the depths of the ocean; abysmal [Gk. *abussos*, bottomless].

a·ca·cia (a·kā′·sha) *n.* thorny, leguminous tree or shrub, yielding gum arabic [Gk. *akakia*, from *akē*, a sharp point].

a·cad·e·my (a·kad′·a·mi·) *n.* a place of education or specialized training; popularly a school; a society of men united for the promotion of the arts and sciences. **academic, academical** *a.* belonging to an academy or other institution of learning. **academician** (a·kad·a·mish′·an) *n.* a member of an academy or society for promoting the arts and sciences [Gk. *akademeia*].

a·can·thus (a·kan′·thas) *n.* a prickly plant, also called 'bear's breech' or 'brank-ursine'; (*Archit.*) an ornament like this leaf, esp. on the capitals of Corinthian pillars [Gk. *ake*, a point; *anthos*, a flower].

a cap·pel·la (á ka·pel′·a) *mus.* singing without instrumental accompaniment [It.].

a·cat·a·lec·tic (a·kat·a·lek′·tik) *a.* not stopping short; complete in syllables; *n.* a verse that has the complete number of syllables.

a·cat·a·lep·sy (a·kat·a·lep′·si·) *n.* incomprehensibility; **acatalepsia** *n.* (*Med.*) uncertainty in the diagnosis of a disease. **acataleptic** *a.* [Gk. *a-*, neg.; *kata*, down; *lepsis*, a seizing].

a·cat·a·pha·si·a (a·kat·a·fā′·zi·a) *n.* difficulty or inability in expressing ideas logically.

ac·cede (ak·sēd′) *v.i.* to agree; assent; consent; to arrive at a certain state or condition; to succeed as heir. **-r** *n.* [L. *ad*, to; *cedere*, to go].

ac·cel·er·an·do (ak·sel·a·ran′·dō) *a.* and *r.* (*Mus.*) a direction to quicken the time [It. fr. L. *celer*, swift].

ac·cel·er·ate (ak·sel′·a·rāt) *v.t.* and *i.* to cause to move faster; to become swifter. **acceleration** *n.* an increase in speed, action, etc.; the rate of increase in the velocity of a moving body. **accelerative** *a.* quickening. **accelerator** *n.* a mechanism for increasing speed. **acceleratory** *a.* [L. *celer*, swift].

ac·cent (ak′·sent) *n.* stress on a syllable or syllables of a word; a mark to show this; inflection of the voice; manner of speech; pronunciation and inflection of the voice peculiar to a country, town, or individual. **accent** (ak·sent′) *v.t.* to utter, pronounce, or mark with accent; to emphasize; to stress. **-ual** *a.* **-uate** *v.t.* to accent; to stress; to make more prominent. **-uation** *n.* [Fr. fr. L. *accentus*, a tone].

ac·cept (ak·sept′) *v.t.* to take; receive; admit; believe; to agree to; (*Comm.*) to agree to pay a bill. **-able** *a.* welcome; pleasing; agreeable. **-ably** *adv.* **-ability** *n.* **-ance** *n.* the act of accepting. **-ation** *n.* the usual meaning of a word, statement, etc. **-ed** *a.* **-er, -or** *n.* [L. *acceptare*].

ac·cess (ak′·ses) *n.* a coming to the means or

way of approach; admission; entrance; attack; fit. **-ary** *a.* (*Law.* See accessory). **-ible** *a.* easy of access or approach; approachable. **-ibility** *n.* **-ion** *n.* increase; a coming to, esp. to a throne, office, or dignity. **-ory** (ak·ses′·a·ri·), **-ary** *a.* aiding; contributing; additional; *n.* an additional, secondary piece of equipment; an accompaniment; (*Law*) one implicated in a felony (though not as a principal); a confederate [L. *accedere, accessum*, to go to].

ac·ci·dence (ak′·si·dans) *n.* the part of grammar dealing with changes in the form of words, e.g. plurals, etc. [fr. *accidents*].

ac·ci·dent (ak′·si·dent) *n.* chance; a mishap; a casualty; contingency; a quality not essential. **-al** *a.* **-ally** *adv.* [L. *ad*, to; *cadere*, to fall].

ac·claim (a·klām′) *v.t.* and *i.* to receive with applause, etc.; cheer; to hail as; **acclamation** (ak·la·mā′·shan) *n.* general applause. **acclamatory** (a·klam′·a·tōr·i·) *a.* [L. *acclamare*, to shout to].

ac·cli·ma·tize (a·klī′·ma·tiz) *v.t.* to accustom to a new climate. Also **acclimate** (a·klī′·mit). **acclimatization** *n.* Also **acclimation, acclimation** (ak·li·mā′·shun) *n.* [fr. *climate*].

ac·cliv·i·ty (a·kliv′·i·ti·) *n.* an upward slope [L. *ad*, to; *clivus*, a slope].

ac·co·lade (ak′·a·lād) *n.* a ceremony used in conferring knighthood, consisting now of a tap given on the shoulder; award, praise [L. *ad*, to; *collum*, the neck].

ac·com·mo·date (a·kam·a·dāt) *v.t.* to render fit or suitable; adapt; adjust; reconcile; provide room for. **accommodating** *a.* obliging. **accommodation** *n.* (usually pl.) a loan of money; convenience; room or space for; lodgings **accommodative** *a.* obliging; supplying accommodation; adaptive [L. *accommodare*, to fit].

ac·com·pa·ny (a·kum′·pa·ni·) *v.t.* to go with; (*Mus.*) to play the accompaniment. **accompaniment** *n.* that which goes with; (*Mus.*) the instrumental parts played with a vocal or other instrumental part. **accompanist** *n.* [Fr. *accompagner*].

ac·com·plice (a·kàm′·plis) *n.* a companion in evil deeds; an associate in crime [Earlier *complice*, fr. L. *complex*, woven together].

ac·com·plish (a·kàm′·plish) *v.t.* to carry out; to finish; to complete; to perform. **-ed** *a.* complete; perfect; having accomplishments; hence, talented. **-ment** *n.* completion; finish; that which makes for culture, elegant manners, etc. [L. *ad*, to; *complere*, to complete].

ac·cord (a·kawrd′) *n.* agreement; harmony; *v.t.* to grant; settle; compose; *v.i.* to agree; to agree in pitch and tone. **-ance** *n.* **-ant** *a.* corresponding. **-ing** *a.* in accordance; agreeing; suitable. **-ingly** *adv.* **of one's own accord**, of one's own free will; voluntarily [L. *ad*, to; *cor, cordis*, the heart].

ac·cor·di·on (a·kawr′·di·an) *n.* wind instrument fitted with bellows and button keyboards; in the **piano-accordion** the right hand keyboard is like that of a piano. **accordion-pleated** *a.* having narrow folds like those of the bellows of an accordion.

ac·cost (a·kawst′) *v.t.* to speak first to; to address; to approach [L. *ad*, to; *costa*, a rib].

ac·count (a·kount′) *n.* a reckoning; a record; a report; a description; a statement of debts and credits in money transactions; value; advantage; profit; *v.t.* to reckon, judge; *v.i.* to give a reason; to give a financial reckoning. **-able** *a.* liable to be held responsible; able to be explained. **-ably** *adv.* **-ability** *n.* **-ancy** *n.* the profession of an accountant. **-ant** *n.* one skilled in recording financial transactions, esp. as a profession. **-ing** *n.* or *a.* [O.Fr. *aconter*, to reckon].

ac·cou·ter (a·kōō′·ter) *v.t.* to furnish with dress or equipment, esp. military; to equip. **-ments** *n.pl.* dress; military dress and equipment [Fr. *accoutrer*, to dress].

ac·cred·it (a·kred′·it) *v.t.* to give trust or confidence to; to vouch for; to recommend; to furnish with credentials, as an envoy or ambassador. **-ed** *a.* **-ation** *n.* [Fr. *accréditer*].

ac·crete (a·krēt′) *v.i.* to grow together; *v.t.* to add by growth. **accretion** *n.* an increase in growth, esp. by an addition of parts externally. **accretive** *a.* [L. *ad*, to; *crescere*, to grow].

ac·crue (a·krōō′) *v.i.* to increase; to result naturally; to come as an addition, e.g. interest, profit, etc. **accrual** *n.* [Fr. *accrue*, an extension, from L. *ad*, to; *crescere*, to grow].

ac·cu·mu·late (a·kū′·mū·lāt) *v.t.* to heap up; to collect; *v.i.* to grow into a mass; to increase. **accumulation** *n.* a collection; a mass; a pile. **accumulative** *a.* **accumulatively** *adv.* **accumulator** *n.* one who, or that which, collects; an apparatus for the storage of electricity [L. *ad*, to; *cumulus*, a heap].

ac·cu·rate (ak′·ū·rit) *a.* correct. **-ly** *adv.* **-ness** *n.* **accuracy** *n.* correctness; exactness; precision [L. *ad*, to; *cura*, care].

ac·curse (a·kurs′) *v.t.* to doom to destruction; to curse. **-ed** *a.* under a curse. **-dness** *n.*

ac·cuse (a·kūz′) *v.t.* to charge with a crime or fault; to blame. **-d** *a.* charged with a crime; *n.* one so charged. **-r** *n.* **accusation** (a·kū·zā′·shun) *n.* a charge. **accusative** *a.* producing or containing accusations; (*Gram.*) of the case which forms the direct object of a transitive verb (the objective case); *n.* the accusative case. **accusatory** *a.* [L. *accusare*].

ac·cus·tom (ạ·kus′·tạm) v.t. to make familiar by use; to familiarize; to habituate. **-ed** a. often practiced; usual; ordinary [O.Fr. *acostumer*].

ace (ās) n. a card with only one spot; a single point; the best, highest; an outstanding fighter pilot; an expert player; an unreturnable service in tennis [L. *as*, a unit].

ac·er·bate (as′·ẹr·bāt) v.t. to make bitter; to exasperate; a. embittered; severe; exasperated. **acerbity** n. sourness of taste, with bitterness and astringency; hence bitterness, or severity in persons [L. *acerbus*, bitter].

a·ce·tic (ạ·set′·ik, ạ·sē′·tik) a. pert. to acetic acid, the acid in vinegar. **acetate** n. (Chem.) a salt formed by acetic acid; also a rayon material made from the acetic ester of cellulose. **acetify** v.t. and v.i. to turn into vinegar. **acetification** n. **acetous** (ạ·sē′·tạs) a. sour. [L. *acetum*, vinegar].

a·cet·y·lene (ạ·set′·i·lēn) n. a highly inflammable gas used as an illuminant [L. *acetum*, vinegar].

ache (āk) n. a continuous dull, heavy pain; often found compounded in such words as *ear-ache*, *headache*; v.i. to be in pain. **aching** a. and n. [O.E. *acan*].

a·chieve (ạ·chēv′) v.t. to bring to a successful end; to accomplish. **achievable** a. **-ment** n. performing; a performance; an exploit; a feat. **-r,** n. [O.Fr. *à chef*, to a head].

ach·ro·ma·si·a (ak·rō·mā′·zi·ạ) n. (Med.) absence of color. **achromate** a. without color; showing color-blindness [Gk. *a-,* neg.; *chroma*, color].

ach·ro·mat·ic (ak·rạ·mat′·ik) a. (Opt.) free from color; transmitting light without decomposing it; of a lens, giving an image free from color around the edges. **-ity** (ak·rō·mạ·ti′·si·ti) n. **achromatism** (ạ·krō′·mạ·tizm) n. **achromatize** v.t. to deprive of color. **achromatous** a. [Gr. *a-,* neg.; *chroma*, color].

ac·id (as′·id) a. sour; sharp to the taste; having the taste of vinegar; n. a sour substance; (Chem.) a substance which contains hydrogen replaceable by a metal, is generally sour and reacts with a base to form salt and water. **-ify** v.t. and i. to make or become sour; to turn into an acid. **-ity** n. the state or quality of being acid; sourness; sharpness. **-osis** (as·i·dō′·sis) n. (Med.) fatty-acid poisoning in the blood, due to over-production of acids in it. **-ulate** v.t. to make slightly acid or sour; (Fig.) to embitter. **-ulated, -ulous** a. slightly sour; sourish; severe. **acid test** (Fig.) a conclusive proof of genuineness (referring to the test of gold by acid) [L. *acidus*, sour].

ack-ack (ak′·ak) a. (Mil. slang) anti-aircraft; n. anti-aircraft fire.

ac·knowl·edge (ak·nál′·ij) v.t. to admit as true; to give a receipt for; to give thanks for; to reward. **-ment** n. [M.E. *knowlechen*, to perceive].

ac·me (ak′·mē) n. the highest point, the top; perfection [Gk. *akmē*, the top].

ac·ne (ak′·nē) n. a skin disease characterized by hard, reddish pimples often appearing as blackheads [fr. Gk. *akmē*, a point].

ac·o·lyte (ak′·ạ·līt) n. a candidate for priesthood in the R. C. Church; a lesser church officer; an assistant; a novice [Gk. *akolouthos*, a follower].

ac·o·nite (ak′·ạ·nīt) n. (Bot.) wolf's-bane or monk's-hood; a poisonous drug extracted from it [Gk. *akoniton*].

a·corn (ā′·kawrn) n. the seed or fruit of the oak. [O.E. *aecern*, fruit of the open country].

a·cous·tic (ạ·kóó′·stik, ạ·kou′·stik) a. pert. to the sense of hearing. **acoustics** n.pl. the science of sounds; the estimation of audibility in a theater, etc. [Gk. *akouein*, to hear].

ac·quaint (a·kwānt′) v.t. to make fully known or familiar; to inform. **-ance** n. familiar knowledge; a person known slightly. **-anceship** n. **-ed** a. [O.Fr. *acointier*; L. *cognoscere*, *cognitum*, to know].

ac·qui·esce (ak·wi·es′) v.i. to agree in silence; to assent without objection. **-nce** n. **-ent** a. submissive; consenting [L. *ad*, to; *quiescere*, to keep quiet].

ac·quire (ạ·kwīr′) v.t. to gain; to obtain; to get. **acquirable** a. **-ment** n. **acquisition** (ak·wi·zi′·shạn) n. the act of acquiring; the thing acquired. **acquisitive** a. grasping; greedy for gain. **acquisitiveness** n. [L. *ad*, to; *quaerere*, to seek].

ac·quit (ạ·kwit′) v.t. to set free; release; declare innocent; to conduct oneself; to discharge a debt. **pr.p. -ting.** pa.p. and pa.t. **-tal.** n. judicial release; declaration of 'not guilty.' **-tance** n. [Fr. *acquitter*, L. *quies*, rest].

a·cre (ā′·kẹr) n. a measure of land containing 4840 square yards. **-age** (ā′·crē·ij) n. extent of a piece of land in acres [O.E. *aecer*, a field].

ac·rid (ak′·rid) a. bitter; sharp; pungent; harsh; ill-tempered. **-ly** adv. **-ness, -ity** n. [L. *acer*, sharp].

ac·ri·mo·ny (ak′·ri·mōn·i·) n. bitterness of temper or of language. **acrimonious** (ak·ri·mō′·ni·us) a. sharp; bitter; stinging; sarcastic. **acrimoniously** adv. [L. *acer*, sharp].

ac·ro·bat (ak′·rạ·bat) n. one skilled in gymnastic feats; a rope-dancer; a tumbler. **-ic** a. **-ics** n.pl. skill of an acrobat. [Gk. *akrobatein*, to walk on tiptoe].

ac·ro·nym (ak′·rạ·nim) n. a word formed from initials, e.g., *radar*.

ac·ro·pho·bi·a (ak·rạ·fō′·bi·ạ) n. a morbid fear of heights. [Gk. *akros*, extreme; *phobia*, fear].

a·crop·o·lis (ạ·kráp′·ạ·lis) n. the fortified summit of a Greek city; a citadel, esp. the citadel of Athens, on which stands the Parthenon [Gk. *akros*, topmost; *polis*, city].

a·cross (ạ·kraws′) adv. and prep. from side to side; transversely; athwart; at an angle with [a, and *cross*].

a·cros·tic (ạ·kraws′·tik) n. a composition in verse, in which the first, and sometimes last, letters of the lines read in order form a name, a sentence, or title [Gk. *akros*, extreme; *stichos*, a line].

act (akt) v.t. to perform, esp. upon stage; to behave as; v.i. to exert energy; to fulfil a function; to operate. n. deed; performance; actuality; action; a decree, law, edict, or judgment; principal division of a play. **-ing** a. performing a duty; performing on the stage; serving for, as *Acting Captain*. **-or** n. one who performs. **-ress** n. a female actor [L. *agere*, *actum*, to do].

ACTH Adreno-corticotropic-hormone used in the treatment of rheumatic diseases.

ac·tin·i·a (ak·tin′·i·ạ) n. the sea anemone. pl. **actiniae** [Gk. *aktis*, a ray].

ac·tin·ism (ak′·ti·nizm) n. the radiation of light or heat; the property possessed by the sun's ray, of producing chemical changes, as in photography. **actinic** a. pert. to actinism. **actiniform** a. having a ray-like structure [Gk. *aktis*, a ray].

ac·tin·i·um (ak·tin′·i·um) n. a radio-active element; symbol **Ac** [Gk. *aktis*, a ray].

ac·ti·nol·o·gy (ak·ti·nál′·ạ·ji·) n. that branch of science concerned with chemical action of light [Gk. *aktis*, a ray; *logos*, word].

ac·ti·no·ther·a·py (ak·tin·ạ·ther′·ạ·pi·) n. the treatment of disease by natural or artificial light rays; often known as 'sunlight treatment' [Gk. *aktis*, a ray; *therapeia*, service].

ac·tion (ak′·shạn) n. a thing done; behavior; physical movement; function; a battle; the development of events in a play, etc.; legal proceedings; (Chem.) effect. **-able** a. affording grounds for legal proceedings. **-ably** adv. **reflex action**, an involuntary motor reaction to a sensory impulse [L. *agere*, *actum*, to do].

ac·ti·vate (ak′·ti·vāt) v.t. to make active. **activation** n.

ac·tive (ak′·tiv) a. having the power to act; agile; busy; alert; (Gram.) implying action by the subject. **-ly** adv. vigorously. **activism** n. policy of those who, by energetic action, seek to fulfil the promises of a political program. **activist** n. one who advocates or practices activism. **activity** **-ness** n. [L. *agere*, *actum*, to do].

ac·tu·al (ak′·choo·ạl) a. existing now or as a fact; real; effectual. **-ize** v.t. to make real in fact or by vivid description. **-ist** n. a realist. **-ity** (ak·choo·al′·ạ·ti·) n. reality, existence. **-ly** adv. [L. *actualis*, active].

ac·tu·a·ry (ak′·choo·ar·i·) n. registrar or clerk; an official who calculates for insurance companies. **actuarial** a. **actuarially** adv. [L. *actuarius*, a clerk].

ac·tu·ate (ak′·choo·āt) v.t. to put into action; incite; motivate; influence. **actuation** n. **actuator** n. [L. *actus*, action].

a·cu·men (ạ·kū′·mạn) n. quickness of perception or discernment; sharpness; penetration. **acuminous** a. [L. *acumen*, a point].

a·cute (ạ·kūt′) a. sharp; pointed; sagacious; subtle; penetrating; (Med.) of disease with severe symptoms and sharp crisis; (Geom.) less than a right angle. **-ly** adv. **-ness** n. **acute accent**, a mark (′) over a letter, as in French, to indicate pronunciation [L. *acutus*, sharp].

ad (ad) n. (Colloq.) advertisement.

A.D. (ā dē) in the year of our Lord [L. *anno Domini*].

ad·age (ad′·ij) n. saying or maxim that has obtained credit by long use; a proverb; a byword. **adagial** a. [L. *adagium*, proverb].

a·da·gio (ạ·dá′·jō) adv. (Mus.) slowly and expressively; n. a slow movement, in a symphony or sonata. **adagio cantabile**, slowly and in a singing manner [It.].

ad·a·mant (ad′·ạ·mạnt) n. a stone of impenetrable hardness; the diamond; a. very hard; unyielding. **adamantine** (ạ·dạ·man′·tin) a. [Gk. *a-,* neg.; *damaein*, subdue].

Ad·am's ap·ple (ad′·ạmz a′·pl) m. projection of cartilage at the front of one's throat.

a·dapt (ạ·dapt′) v.t. to make fit or suitable; to make to correspond. **-ability, -ableness** n. the quality of being adaptable. **-able** a. may be adapted; versatile. **-ation** (a·dap·tā′·shạn) n. the gradual process of adjustment to new physical conditions exhibited by living organisms. **-er** n. any appliance which makes possible a union of two different parts of an apparatus. **-ive** a. **-ively** adv. **-iveness** n. **-or** n. a device to make possible the use of a machine, tool, etc. with modification [L. *ad*, to; *aptare*, to fit].

add (ad) v.t. to join, unite to form one sum or whole; to annex; to increase; to say further. **-able, -ible -er** n. a machine which adds; a comptometer. **-ibility** n. **-ition** n. the act of adding; anything added; the branch of arithmetic which deals with adding. **-itional** a. supplementary; extra. **-itionally** adv. **-itive** a. to be added; of the nature of an addition [L. *ad*, to; *dare*, to give].

ad·dend (ad′·end) n. number to be added.

ad·den·dum (a·den′·dạm) n. a thing to be added; an appendix; pl. **addenda** [L.].

ad·der (ad′·ẹr) n. a venomous serpent [M.E. an *addere* for a *naddere*, fr. O.E. *naeddre*, snake].

ad·dict (ạ·dikt′) v.t. to apply habitually; habituate. **addict** (ad′·ikt) n. one addicted to evil habit, e.g. drug-taking. **-ed** a. devoted, wholly given over to. **-ion, -ness,** n. [L. *addicere*, to assign].

ad·dle (ad′·l) v.t. to corrupt; putrify; confuse; to make addled. **addle, addled,** a. diseased, e.g. an egg; putrid; unfruitful. **-brained, -headed, -pated** a. confused [O.E. *adela*, filth].

ad·dress (ạ·dres′) v.t. to direct in writing, as a letter; to apply (oneself); to make a speech; to present a congratulatory message or petition; accost; n. a formal speech; manner of speaking; direction of a letter; skill. **-es** n.pl. attentions in courtship. **-ee** n. person to whom a communication is sent. **-er** n. **-ograph** n. a machine for addressing envelopes, etc. [Fr. *adresser*].

ad·duce (ạ·dūs′) v.t. to bring forward as proof; to cite; to quote. **-nt** a. **-r** n. **adducible** a. **adduction** (ạ·duk′·shạn) n. drawing together or bringing forward. **adductive** a. tending to bring together. **adductor** n. adducent muscle [L. *ad*, to; *ducere*, to lead].

ad·en (o) - (ad′·n-(o)) a combining form. **-itis** n. inflammation of the lymphatic glands. **-oid, -oidal** a. glandular; gland-shaped. **-oids** n.pl. a swelling of tissue between nose and throat [fr. Gk. *aden*, a gland].

a·dept (ạ·dept′) n. one skilled in any art; an expert; a. well skilled; expert [L. *adeptus*, having attained].

ad·e·quate (ad′·ạ·kwit) a. equal to; sufficient. **adequacy -ness** n. **-ly** adv. [L. *adaequatus*, made equal to].

ad·here (ạd·hēr′) v.i. to stick fast; to be devoted to; to hold to (an opinion). **-nce** n. state of adhering; steady attachment. **-nt** a. united with or to; n. supporter of person or cause. **adhesion** n. act of adhering. **adhesive** a. sticky; tenacious; n. an agent which sticks things together. **adhesively** adv. **adhesiveness** n. [L. *ad*, to; *haerere*, to stick].

ad·hib·it (ạd·hib′·it) v.t. to use or apply; to attach [L. *adhibitus*, added to].

a·dieu (ạ·dū′) interj. good-bye; farewell; n. a farewell; a leave-taking. pl. **adieus, adieux** (ạ·dūz′) [Fr. meaning, "to God"].

ad in·fi·ni·tum (ad in·fạ·nī′·tạm) to infinity, without limit [L.].

ad in·ter·im (ad in′·tẹr·im) in the meantime [L.].

a·di·os (á·dōs′) good-bye [Sp.].

ad·i·pose (ad′·i·pōs) a. pert. to animal fat; fatty. **adiposity** (ad·i·pás′·i·ti·) n. fatness. **adipic** a. pert. to, or derived from, fatty substances [L. *adeps*, soft fat].

ad·it (ad′·it) *n.* horizontal or inclined entrance into a mine [L. *aditus,* an entrance].

ad·ja·cent (a·jā′·sant) *a.* lying close to; adjoining, bordering on. **-ly** *adv.* **adjacency** *n.* [L. *ad,* to; *jacere,* to lie].

ad·jec·tive (ad′·jik·tiv) *n.* a word used with a noun to qualify, limit, or define it; *a.* pert. to an adjective. **adjectival** (ad·jik·tī′·v'l) *a.* **adjectivally** *adv.* [L. *adjicere,* to add].

ad·join (a·join′) *v.t.* to join or unite to; to be next or contiguous to; *v.i.* to be next to. **-ing** *a.* [L. *adjungere,* to join to].

ad·journ (a·jurn′) *v.t.* to put off to another day; to postpone. **-ment** *n.* [L. *diurnus,* daily].

ad·judge (a·juj′) *v.t.* to settle judicially; to pronounce judgment; to award; to regard or deem. **adjudgment** *n.* **adjudicate** (a·jóō′·di·kāt) *v.t.* to settle judicially; *v.i.* to pronounce judgment. **adjudication** *n.* **adjudicator** *n.* a judge [L. *adjudicare,* to award as a judge].

ad·junct (ad′·jungkt) *n.* something joined to another thing, but not essential to it; *(Gram.)* a word or phrase added to modify meaning; *a.* added to; united with. **-ive, -ively** *adv.* [L. *adjunctus,* united to].

ad·jure (ad·jóor′) *v.t.* to charge or bind, under oath; to entreat earnestly. **adjuration** *n.* a solemn command on oath; an earnest appeal. **adjuratory** *a.* [L. *adjurare,* to confirm by oath].

ad·just (a·just′) *v.t.* to adapt; to put in working order; to accommodate. **-able** *a.* **-ment** *n.* **-er, -or** *n.* arrangement; settlement; adaptation [L. *ad,* to; *justus,* just].

ad·ju·tant (aj′·a·tant) *n.* an assistant; staff officer who helps the commanding officer issue orders. **adjutancy** *n.* the office of an adjutant. **adjutant bird** a species of Indian stork [L. *ad,* to; *juvare,* to help].

ad lib (ad lib′) *v.i.* and *v.t. (Colloq.)* to improvise something not in the script [L. abbrev. for *ad libitum,* at pleasure].

ad·min·is·ter (ad·min′·is·ter) *v.t.* to manage public affairs or an estate; to dispense, as justice or relief; to give, as medicine; to apply, as punishment or reproof; *(Law)* to settle the estate of one who has died intestate; *v.i.* to give aid (to). **administrable** *a.* **administrant** *a.* executive; *n.* one who administers. **administration** *n.* the executive part of a government: dispensation; direction. **administrative** *a.* **administrator** *n. (fem.* **administratrix**) one who directs; executes affairs of any kind [L. *ad,* to; *ministrare,* to give service].

ad·mi·ral (ad′·mi·ral) *n.* a naval officer of the highest rank (graded as—admiral, vice-admiral, or rear-admiral). **-ty** *n.* rank or authority of an admiral; maritime law [Fr. *amiral,* fr. Ar. *amir-al-bahr,* prince of the sea].

ad·mi·ral (ad′·mi·ral) *n.* a species of butterfly, esp. the red admiral.

ad·mire (ad·mīr′) *v.t.* to regard with wonder and approval, esteem, or affection; to prize highly; *v.i.* to wonder; to marvel. **-r** *n.* **admiring** *a.* **admiringly** *adv.* **admirable** (ad′·mi·ra·bl) *a.* excellent; praiseworthy. **admirably** *adv.* **admiration** *n.* wonder mingled with esteem, love, or veneration [L. *ad,* to; *mirari,* to wonder].

ad·mis·si·ble (ad·mis′·i·bl) *a.* allowable. **admissibly** *adv.* **admissibility** *n.* **admission** *n.* permission to enter; the price paid for this [L. (part.) *admissus,* allowed to go].

ad·mit (ad·mit′) *v.t.* to grant entrance; to concede as true' to acknowledge. *pr.p.* **-ting.** *pa.p.* and *pa.t.* **-ted. -tance** *n.* permission to enter [L. *ad,* to; *mittere,* to send].

ad·mix (ad·miks′) *v.t.* to mingle with something else. **-ture** *n.* [L. *admiscere,* to mix].

ad·mon·ish (ad·man′·ish) *v.t.* to reprove gently; to instruct or direct. **-er** *n.* **admonition** (ad·ma·ni′·shan) *n.* rebuke. **admonitory** *a.* [L. *ad,* to; *monere, monitum,* to warn].

ad nau·se·am (ad naw′·shi·am, also ·nawz·) to a sickening degree [L.].

a·do (a·doo′) *n.* fuss; bustle; trouble.

a·do·be (a·dō′·bi·) *n.* sun-dried brick [Sp.].

ad·o·les·cence (ad·a·les′·ens) *n.* stage between childhood and manhood; youth. **adolescent** *a.* growing up; *n.* a young man or woman [L. *adolescere,* to grow up].

a·dopt (a·dápt′) *v.t.* to receive the child of another and treat it as one's own; to select and accept as one's own, e.g. a view. **-er** *n.* **-able** *a.* **-ion** *n.* **-ive** *a.* that adopts or is adopted [L. *ad,* to; *optare,* to choose].

a·dore (a·dōr′) *v.t.* to worship; to love deeply;

-r *n.* a lover. **adorable** *a.* **adorably** *adv.* **adorableness** *n.* **adoration** (ad·a·rā′·shan) *n.* profound veneration; ardent devotion [L. *ad,* to; *orare,* to pray].

a·dorn (a·dawrn′) *v.t.* to decorate; to deck or ornament; to set off to advantage. **-ing** *a.* beautifying; ornamental. **-ment** *n.* ornament; embellishment [L. *ad,* to; *ornare,* to deck].

ad·re·nal (ad·rē′·nal) *n.* a small, ductless gland situated close to upper end of each kidney (same as *supra-renal;* *a.* (supra-renal). **adrenalin** (ad·ren′·al·in) *n.* the hormone of the adrenal glands; the most effective hemostatic agent known [L. *ad,* to; *renes,* kidneys].

a·drift (a·drift′) *adv.* and *a.* floating at random; at mercy of the wind and tide; *(Fig.)* at a loss.

a·droit (a·droit′) *a.* dexterous; skillful; ingenious; adept. **-ly** *adv.* **-ness** *n.* [Fr.].

ad·sorb (ad·sawrb′) *v.t.* said of solids, to condense and hold a gas on the surface. **adsorption** *n.* [L. *ad,* to; *sorbere,* to drink in].

ad·u·late (aj′·ū·lāt) *v.t.* to praise or flatter in a servile manner; to fawn; to cringe. **adulation** *n.* **adulator** *n.* **adulatory** (aj·a·la·tawr′·i·) *a.* excessively [L. *adulari,* to flatter].

a·dult (a·dult′, ad′·ult) *a.* grown to maturity, or to full size and strength; appropriate for a grown-up; *n.* a grown-up person. **-ness** *n.* **-hood** *n.* [L. *adultus,* grown up].

a·dul·ter·ate (a·dul′·ta·rāt) *v.t.* to debase by addition of inferior materials; to vitiate; to corrupt. *a.* debased; guilty of adultery. **adulteration** *n.* the act of debasing a substance [L. *adulterare,* to defile].

a·dul·ter·y (a·dul′·ter·i·) *n.* violation of the marriage vows. **adulterer** *n. (fem.* **adulteress). adulterous** *a.* pert. to or guilty of adultery. **adulterously** *adv.* [L. *adulterare,* to defile].

ad·um·brate (ad·um′·brāt) *v.t.* to shadow forth; to give faint outline of; to forecast; to typify. **adumbral** *a.* shady. **adumbrant** *a.* showing a slight resemblance. **adumbrative** *a.* **adumbration** *n.* [L. *ad,* to; *umbra,* a shade].

ad·vance (ad·vans′) *v.t.* to bring or push forward; to raise in status, price, or value; to propose as a claim; to supply beforehand, esp. money; *v.i.* to go forward; to improve; to rise in rank, etc. *a.* before the time, as in *advance-booking;* *n.* a forward movement; gradual approach; a paying out of money before due; an increase in price; expansion of knowledge. **-d** *a.* in the front rank; progressive; well on in years; beyond the elementary stage (in education). **-ment** *n.* promotion; improvement; success; the state of being progressive in opinion; a loan of money. **-r** *n.* a promoter [Fr. *avancer,* to go forward].

ad·van·tage (ad·van′·tij) *n.* any state or means favorable to some desired end; upperhand; profit; in tennis, a point gained after deuce; *v.t.* to benefit, to promote the interests of; to profit. **-able** *a.* able to be turned to advantage. **-ous** (ad·van·tā′·jus) *a.* beneficial; opportune; convenient. **-ously** (ad·van·tā′·jus·li·) *adv.* [Fr. *avantage*].

ad·vent (ad′·vent) *n.* arrival; approach; the anticipated coming of Christ; the four weeks from the Sunday nearest to St. Andrew's Day (30th Nov.) to Christmas. **-ual** *adv.* pertaining to the season of Advent [L. *ad,* to; *venire,* to come].

ad·ven·ti·tious (ad·ven·tish′·as) *a.* accidental; out of the proper place; extraneous. **-ly** *adv.* [L. *ad,* to; *venire,* to come].

ad·ven·ture (ad·ven′·cher) *n.* risk; bold undertaking; chance; trading enterprise of a speculative nature; *v.t.* to risk. *v.i.* to venture; to dare. **-r** *n. (fem.* **adventuress**). **-some** *a.* bold; daring; enterprising; facing risk. **-someness** *n.* **adventurous** *a.* inclined to take risks; perilous; hazardous. **adventurously** *adv.* [L. *adventurus,* about to arrive].

ad·verb (ad′·vurb) *n.* a word used to modify a verb, adjective, or other adverb. **-ial** *a.* **-ially** *adv.* [L. *ad,* to; *verbum,* a word].

ad·ver·sa·ry (ad′·ver·ser·i·) *n.* an opponent; one who strives against us; an enemy [L. *adversus,* opposite to].

ad·ver·sa·tive (ad·vers′·a·tiv) *a.* expressing opposition; not favorable [L. *adversus*].

ad·verse (ad·vurs′) *a.* contrary; opposite in position; unfortunate; opposed. **-ly** *adv.* **-ness** *n.* **adversity** *n.* adverse circumstances; misfortune [L. *adversus,* opposite to].

ad·vert (ad·vurt′) *v.i.* to turn the mind or attention to; to remark upon; allude; refer. **-ence, -ency** *n.* [L. *ad,* to; *vertere,* to turn].

ad·ver·tise (ad′·ver·tiz) *v.t.* and *v.i.* to give public notice of; to inform; to make known through agency of the press. **-ment** *n.* a public intimation in the press; legal notification. **-r** *n.* one who advertises; **advertising** *n.* and *a.* [Fr. *avertir,* from L. *ad,* to; *vertere,* to turn].

ad·vice (ad·vīs′) *n.* opinion offered as to what one should do; counsel; information [Fr. *avis*].

ad·vise (ad·vīz′) *v.t.* to give advice to; to counsel; to give information to; to consult (with). *v.i.* to deliberate. **advisability, advisableness** *n.* expediency. **advisable** *a.* prudent; expedient. **advisably** *adv.* **advised** *a.* acting with due deliberation; cautious; prudent; judicious. **advisedly** *adv.* purposely. **advisedness, -ment** *n.* deliberate consideration. **-r** or

advisor *n.* **advisory** *a.* having power to advise; containing advice [Fr. *avis*].

ad·vo·cate (ad′·va·kit) *n.* a vocal supporter of any cause; one who pleads or speaks for another. (ad′·va·kāt) *v.t.* to recommend; to maintain by argument. **advocacy** *n.* a pleading for; judicial pleading. **advocator** *n.* an intercessor; a pleader [L. *ad,* to; *vocare,* to call].

adz, adze (adz) *n.* a carpenter's tool for chipping, having a thin arching blade set at right angles to the handle [O.E. *adesa*].

ae·gis (ē′·jis) *n.* originally the shield of Jupiter; *(Fig.)* protection [Gk. *aigis*].

ae·on, eon (ē′·an) *n.* an infinitely long period of time; an age [Gk. *aion,* an age].

aer·ate (ā′·er·āt) *v.t.* to charge with carbon dioxide or other gas; to supply with air. **aeration** *n.* the act of exposing to the action of the air; saturation with a gas. **aerator** *n.* **aerated waters,** beverages charged with carbon dioxide [Gk. *aer,* air].

aer·i·al (ār′·i·al) *a.* pert. to, consisting of, air; *n.* and *a. (Radio and Television)* an insulated wire or wires, generally elevated above the ground and connected to a transmitting or receiving set. **-ly** *adv.* [Gk. *aēr,* air].

aer·i·al·ist (ār′·i·al·ist) *n.* high wire acrobat.

a·er·ie, a·er·y (ā′·ri·, e′·ri·) *n.* the nest of a bird of prey, esp. of the eagle [O.Fr. *aire*].

a·er·o (ā′·er·ō) a combining form from Gk. *aēr,* air, used in many derivatives.

a·er·o·dy·nam·ics (er·a·di·nam′·iks) *n.pl.* the science that treats of gases in motion [Gk. *aēr,* air; *dunamis,* power].

aer·o·lite (er′·a·līt) *n.* a meteorite; a meteoric stone. Also **aerolith, aerolithic** *a.* **aerology** *n.* the science which treats of the air and its phenomena [Gk. *aēr,* air; *lithos,* stone; *logos,* discourse].

a·er·o·me·ter (er·am′·a·ter) *n.* an instrument for measuring the weight or density of air and other gases. **aerometry** *n.* this science [Gk. *aēr,* air; *metron,* a measure].

aer·o·naut (ār′·a·nawt) *n.* a balloonist. **-ic** *a.* pert. to aeronautics. **-ics** *n.* the science of flight. [Gk. *aēr,* air; *nautes,* a sailor].

aer·o·sol (ār′·a·sal) *n.* a smoke, suspension of insoluble particles in a gas.

aer·o·stat (ār′·a·stat) *n.* a generic term for all lighter than air flying machines. **-ics** *n.* the science that treats of the equilibrium of gases, or of the buoyancy of bodies sustained in them; the science of air-navigation [Gk. *aēr,* air; *statos,* standing].

aes·thet·ics (es·thet′·iks) *n.* the laws and principles determining the beautiful in nature, art, taste, etc. **aesthetic, aesthetical** *a.* **aesthetically** *adv.* **aesthete** (es′·thēt) *n.* a disciple of aestheticism; a lover of the beautiful. **aestheticism** *n.* [Gk. *aisthanesthai,* to perceive].

a·far (a·far′) *adv.* from, at, or to a distance; far away [E. *far*].

af·fa·ble (af′·a·bl) *a.* ready to converse; easy to speak to; courteous; friendly. **affably** *adv.* **affability** *n.* [L. *ad,* to; *fari,* to speak].

af·fair (a·fār′) *n.* what is to be done; a business or matter; a concern; a thing; *(Mil.)* a minor engagement. **affairs** *n.pl.* public or private business; finances. **affair of honor,** a duel [L. *ad,* to; *facere,* to do].

af·fect (a·fekt′) *v.t.* to act upon; to produce a change in; to put on a pretense of; to influence. **-ed** *a.* inclined or disposed; not natural. **-edly** *adv.* **-edness** *n.* **-ing** *a.* moving; pathetic. **-ingly** *adv.* **-ation** *n.* a striving after artificial appearance or manners. **affective** *a.* **affectively** *adv.* [L. *affectare,* to apply onself to].

af·fec·tion (a·fek′·shan) *n.* disposition of

mind; good-will; tender attachment; disease. **-ate** *a.* loving. **-ately** *adv.* [L. *affectare*, to apply oneself to].

af·fer·ent (af′·ẽr·ant) *a.* conveying to, esp. of nerves carrying sensations to the centers [L. *ad*, to; *ferre*, to carry].

af·fi·ance (a·fī′·ans) *n.* plighted faith; betrothal; the marriage contract; reliance; confidence; *v.t.* to betroth [O.Fr. *afiance*, trust].

af·fi·da·vit (af·i·dā′·vit) *n.* (*Law*) a written statement of evidence on oath [L.L. = he pledged his faith, from L. *ad*, to; *fides*, faith].

af·fil·i·ate (a·fil′·i·āt) *v.t.* to adopt as a son; to receive into fellowship; to unite a society, firm, or political party with another, but without loss of identity. **affiliation** *n.* act of being affiliated; relationship. (a·fil′·i·at) *n.* one who affiliates [L. *ad*, to; *filius*, a son].

af·fin·i·ty (a·fin′·i·ti·) *n.* relationship by marriage; close agreement; resemblance; attraction; similarity. **affined** (a·find′) *a.* **affinitive** *a.* closely related [L. *affinis*, related].

af·firm (a·furm′) *v.t.* to assert positively; to confirm; to aver; to strengthen; to ratify a judgment; *v.i.* (*Law*) to make a solemn promise to tell the truth without oath; to ratify a law. **-able** *a.* **-ably** *adv.* **-ance** *n.* **-ant**, **-er** *n.* **-ative** *a.* ratifying; *n.* positive; speaking in favor of a motion or subject of debate. **in the affirmative**, yes. **-atively** *adv.* [L. *affirmare*, to assert].

af·fix (a·fiks′) *v.t.* to fasten to; to attach; to append to. **affix** (a′·fiks) *n.* addition to either end of word to modify meaning or use (includes *prefix* and *suffix*) [L. *affigere*].

af·fla·tus (a·flā′·tas) *n.* inspiration; impelling inner force [L. a blast].

af·flict (a·flikt′) *v.t.* to give continued pain to; to cause distress or grief to. **-ed** *a.* distressed in mind; diseased. **-ing** *a.* distressing. **-ingly** *adv.* **-ion** *n.* a cause of continued pain of body or mind. **-ive** *a.* causing distress. **-ively** *adv.* [L. *affligere*].

af·flu·ence (af′·lōō·ans) *n.* abundance, esp. riches. **affluent** *a.* wealthy; flowing to; *n.* tributary of river. **affluently** *adv.* **afflux, affluxion** *n.* flowing to; that which flows to [L. *ad*, towards; *fluere*, to flow].

af·ford (a·fōrd′) *v.t.* to yield, supply, or produce; to be able to bear expense [O.E. *geforthian*, to further].

af·for·est (a·fár′·est) *v.t.* to plant trees on a big scale. **-ation** *n.* [from *forest*].

af·fran·chise (a·fran′·chiz) *v.t.* to enfranchise; to free from slavery; to liberate. **-ment** *n.* [Fr. *affranchir*, make free].

af·fray (a·frā′) *n.* a noisy quarrel or fight in public; *v.t.* to frighten; to startle [Fr. *effrayer*, to frighten].

af·fright, af·fright·en (a·frīt′, -an) *v.t.* to impress with sudden and lively fear [O.E. *afyrhtan*, to terrify].

af·front (a·frunt′) *v.t.* to confront; to meet face to face; to insult one to the face; to abash. **-ed** *a.* [L. *ad*, to; *frons*, *frontis*, forehead].

a·field (a·fēld′) *adv.* to or in the field; abroad; off the beaten track; astray [E.].

a·fire (a·fīr′) *adv.* and *a.* on fire.

a·flame (a·flām′) *adv.* and *a.* flaming; on fire; glowing; ablaze [E.].

a·float (a·flōt′) *adv.* and *a.* borne on the water; not aground or anchored.

a·flut·ter (a·flut′·ẽr) *a.* fluttering

a·foot (a·foot′) *adv.* on foot; astir [E.].

a·fore (a·fōr′) *adv.* and *prep.* before. **-hand** *adv* beforehand; before; *a.* provided; prepared. **-mentioned** *a.* spoken of, or named before. **-said** *a.* said or mentioned before. **-thought** *a.* thought of beforehand; premeditated. **-time** *adv.* in times past; at a former time; previously [O.E. *on foran*, in front].

a·foul (a·foul′) *adv.* in collision, in a tangle.

a·fraid (a·frād′) *a.* filled with fear; frightened [orig. *affrayed*].

a·fresh (a·fresh′) *adv.* anew; over again.

aft (aft) *adv.* or *a.* (*Naut.*) toward, or at, the stern. **fore and aft**, lengthwise [O.E. *afta*, behind].

af·ter (af′·tẽr) *prep.* behind; later; in pursuit of; in imitation of; according to; *adv.* behind; *a.* in the rear; succeeding. **-birth** *n.* (*Med.*) the placenta, etc. expelled from uterus after childbirth. **-crop** *n.* a later crop in same year from same soil. **-damp** *n.* a gas formed in a mine after an explosion of fire-damp; choke-damp. **-deck** *n.* weather deck aft of midship house. **-effect** *n.* a secondary result, an effect coming after. **-glow** *n.* a glow in the sky after sunset. **-math** *n.* result; consequence. **-most** *a.* hindmost; nearest to stern. **-noon** *n.* time from noon to evening. **-pains** *n.pl.* pains succeeding childbirth. **-thought** *n.* reflection after an act; an idea occurring later. **-ward(s)** *adv.* later; subsequently [O.E. *aefter*, farther away].

a·gain (a·gen′) *adv.* another time; once more; in return; moreover [O.E. *ongean*].

a·gainst (a·genst′) *prep.* in contact with; opposite to; in opposition to; in preparation for; in exchange for [fr. *again*].

a·gape (a·gāp′) *a.* or *adv.* open-mouthed, as in wonder, expectation, etc.; gaping.

ag·ate (ag′·it) *n.* a precious stone, composed of layers of quartz of different colors [Gk. *Achatēs*, so called because found near the river *Achatēs*, in Sicily].

agate

age (āj) *n.* the length of time a person or thing has existed; a period of time; periods of history; maturity; (*Colloq.*) a long time; *v.t.* to cause to grow old; *v.i.* to grow old; *pr.p.* aging. **-d** *a.* of the age of. **aged** (āj′·ed) *a.* **agedness** *n.* **-less** *a.* **-long** *a.* to come of age, to attain one's 21st birthday [Fr. *âge*, from L. *aetas*, age].

a·gen·cy (ā′·jen·si·) *n.* instrumentality; a mode of exerting power; office or duties of an agent [L. *agere*, to do.]

a·gen·da (a·jen′·da) *n.* literally, things to be done; the items of business to be discussed at a meeting [L. *pl.* of *agendum*].

a·gent (ā′·jent) *n.* a person or thing that exerts power or has the power to act; one entrusted with the business of another; a deputy or substitute [L. *agere*, to do].

ag·glom·er·ate (a·glám′·a·rāt) *v.t.* and *i.* to collect into a mass; *a.* heaped up; *n.* (*Geol.*) a mass of compacted volcanic debris. **agglomeration** *n.* **agglomerative** *a.* [L. *ad*, to; *glomus*, mass or ball].

ag·glu·ti·nate (a·glōō′·ti·nāt) *v.t.* to unite with glue; *a.* united, as with glue. **agglutination** *n.* **agglutinative** *a.* having a tendency to cause adhesion; (*Phil.*) applied to languages which are non-inflectional [L. *ad*, to; *gluten*, glue].

ag·gran·dize (a·gran′·dīz) *v.t.* to make greater in size, power, rank, wealth, etc.; to promote; to increase; to exalt. **aggrandizement** *n.* [L. *ad*, to; *grandis*, great).

ag·gra·vate (ag′·ra·vāt) *v.t.* to make more grave, worse; (*Colloq.*) to irritate. **aggravating** *a.* making worse; provoking. **aggravatingly** *adv.* **aggravation** *n.* [L. *aggravare*, to make heavier].

ag·gre·gate (ag′·ra·gāt) *v.t.* to collect into a total; to accumulate into a heap; (ag′·ra·git) *n.* a sum or assemblage of particulars; the sum total; *a.* collected together. **aggregation** *n.* the act of aggregating; a combined whole. **aggregative** *a.* collective; accumulative [L. *aggregare*, to form into a flock, fr. *grex, gregis*, a flock].

ag·gress (a·gres′) *v.i.* to attack; to start a quarrel. **-ion** *n.* a first act of hostility; an unprovoked attack. **-ive** *a.* **-ively** *adv.* **-iveness** *n.* **-or** *n.* the one who first attacks [L. *aggredi*, to attack].

ag·grieve (a·grēv′) *v.t.* to give pain or sorrow to; to bear heavily upon; to vex; to afflict. **-d** *a.* [L. *aggravare*, to make heavier].

a·ghast (a·gast′) *a.* struck with amazement, horror, terror; transfixed with fright [earlier *agast*, fr. O.E. *gaestan*, to terrify].

ag·ile (aj′·il) *a.* having the power of quick motion; nimble. **-ly** *adv.* **-ness, agility** *n.* [L. *agilis*, fr. *agere*, to do.]

ag·i·tate (aj′·i·tāt) *v.t.* to throw into violent motion; to stir up; to disturb, excite, upset; to debate earnestly; *v.i.* to cause a disturbance. **agitatedly** *adv.* **agitation** *n.* violent and irregular motion; perturbation; inciting to public disturbance. **agitator** *n.* [L. *agitare*, to keep in motion].

a·gleam (a·glēm′) *adv.*, *a.* gleaming.

a·glow (a·glō′) *adv.*, *a.* glowing.

ag·nate (ag′·nāt) *n.* any male relation on the father's side. *a.* related on the father's side; akin; allied. **agnatic** *a.* **agnation** *n.* [L. *ad*, to; *natus*, born].

ag·no·men (ag·nō′·man) *n.* an additional name given by the Romans, generally because of some famous exploit, as Alexander the Great [L. *ad*, to; *nomen*, name].

ag·nos·tic (ag·nás′·tik) *n.* one who believes that God, life hereafter, etc., can neither be proved nor disproved, and who accepts material phenomena only; *a.* pert. to agnosticism. **-ism** *n.* [Gk. *a-*, neg.; *gnostikos*, knowing].

a·go, a·gone (a·gō′, a·gawn′) *adv.*, *a.* past; gone; in time past [O.E. *agan*, to pass away].

a·gog (a·gág′) *a.* and *adv.* eagerly excited; expectantly [Fr. *en gogues*, in a merry mood].

a·gon·ic (a·gán′·ik) *a.* not forming an angle [Gk. *a-*, neg.; *gonia*, an angle].

ag·o·ny (ag′·a·ni·) *n.* extreme physical or mental pain; the death struggle; throes; pang. **agonize** *v.t.* to distress with great pain; to torture. *v.i.* to writhe in torment. **agonizing** *a.* agonizingly *adv.* **agony column**, section of newspaper containing advertisements for lost relatives, personal messages, etc. [Gk. *agon*, a contest].

ag·o·ra (ag′·a·ra) *n.* forum, public square, or market of ancient Greek towns. **-phobia** *n.* fear of open spaces [Gk. *agora*, a market place; *phobia*, fear].

a·gou·ti (a·gōō′·ti·) *n.* a genus of rodents or gnawing animals, natives of S. America, allied to the guinea-pig [Native].

a·grar·i·an (a·grar′·i·an) *a.* relating to lands, their management and distribution; (*Bot.*) growing in a field. *n.* one who favors an equal division of property. **-ize** *v.t.* **-ism** *n.* an equal division of land or property [L. *ager*, a field].

a·gree (a·grē′) *v.i.* to be of one mind; to acquiesce; to resemble; (*Gram.*) to correspond in gender, case, or number. *pr.p.* **-ing**. *pa.p.* **-d**. **-able** *a.* consenting; favorable; suitable; pleasant; congenial. **-ably** *adv.* **-ableness** *n.* **-ment** *n.* agreeing; bargain; a written statement accepting certain conditions [L. *ad*, to; *gratus*, pleasing].

ag·ri·cul·ture (ag′·ri·kul·chẽr) *n.* the science and practice of the cultivation of the soil. **agricultural** *a.* **agriculturist** or **agriculturalist** *n.* one skilled in agriculture; a farmer [L. *ager*, a field; *colere, cultum*, to till].

a·gron·o·my (a·grán′·a·mi·) *n.* rural economy; husbandry. **agronomical, agronomic, agronomical** *a.* *n.pl.* the science of management of farms. **agronomist** *n.* [Gk. *agros*, field; *nemein*, to deal out].

a·ground (a·ground′) *adv.* and *a.* on the ground; stranded; run ashore; beached.

a·gue (ā′·gū) *n.* (*Med.*) intermittent malarial fever, marked by fits of shivering, burning, sweating. **agued, aguish** *a.* [L. *acuta febris*, acute fever].

a·head (a·hed′) *adv.* farther forward; in advance; in front; head foremost [E.].

a·hoy (a·hoi′) *interj.* used in hailing, as in *ship ahoy* [form of *interj.* hoy].

ai (á′·ē) *n.* the three-toed sloth of S. America, named from its cry [Braz.].

aid (ād) *v.t.* and *v.i.* to help; to relieve. *n.* help; assistance; the person or thing which aids; auxiliary; assistant. **aide** *n.* [Fr. *aider*].

aide-de-camp (ād·de·kamp′) *n.* an officer attached to the personal staff of a general to assist him in his military routine. *pl.* **aides-de-camp** [Fr.].

ai·grette (ā′·gret) *n.* a tuft or spray, as of feathers, diamonds, etc.; the small white heron; an egret [Fr.].

ai·guille (ā·gwēl′) *n.* (*Geol.*) a sharp, slender rock; a drill for boring rock. **aiguillette, aiguillet** (ā·gwē·let′) *n.* the tag of a shoe-lace; *pl.* ornamental spangles of a dancer's dress [Fr. = a needle].

ail (āl) *v.t.* to trouble; disturb; to pain; afflict. *v.i.* to feel pain; to be ill. **-ing** *a.* **-ment** *n.* illness. [O.E. *eglan*, to pain].

ai·le·ron (ā′·la·rán) *n.* adjustable flaps near the tips of the wings of an airplane for balance and lateral control [Fr.].

aim (ām) *v.t.* to point at; to direct; to endeavor after; to intend; *n.* direction; end; purpose; intention. **-less** *a.* without aim or purpose. **-lessly** *adv.* **-lessness** *n.* [O.Fr. *esmer*, esteem].

ain't (ānt) (*Colloq.*) contracted form of *am not*, extended to *is not*, or *are not*.

air (ār) *n.* the atmosphere; a gas; a light breeze; a tune; manner, bearing of a person; carriage; appearance; mien. *v.t.* to expose to air or heat, for drying or warming; to parade before the public. **airs** *n.pl.* an affected manner. **-ing** *n.* a ride or walk in the open air. **-y** *a.* of air; exposed to the air; light-hearted. **-ily** *adv.* gaily; merrily; lightly. **-iness** *n.* openness to the air; gaiety. **air base** *n.* a place for housing, or directing operations of, aircraft. **air-borne** *a.* carried by aircraft; supported by the air (of aircraft). **air brake** *n.* brake worked by compressed air. **air condenser** *n.* an electrical condenser insulated between the plates by air. **air-condition** *v.t.* to provide a building, etc. with air through a filtering apparatus. **air conditioning** *n.* **air cool** *v.t.* to cool by air, to air condition. **aircraft** *n.* all kinds of machines for flying. **aircraft carrier**, an armed vessel built to carry aircraft. **airdrome** *n.* an airport. **airfield** *n.* tract of land, used for accommodation and maintenance of aircraft. **airfoil** *n.* any surface wing, etc. to help in lifting or controlling an aircraft. **air force**, the whole of a nation's aircraft. **air gun** *n.* a gun discharged by elastic force of air. **air lift** *n.* large-scale transport operation by aircraft. **air line** *n.* a service of aircraft plying regularly; a telephone line above ground level. **air liner** *n.* a large passenger airplane flying on a definite route. **air load** *n.* cargo carried by aircraft. **air lock** *n.* the stoppage of the flow of liquid in a pipe caused by the presence of air; a small chamber to allow the passage of men or materials at the top of a caisson. **air mail** *n.* the transport of letters, parcels, etc., by airplane. **airman** *n.* an aviator. **air-minded** *adj.* interested in aviation. **airplane** *n.* a heavier than air aircraft. **airport** *n.* a terminal station for passenger airplanes. **air pressure** *n.* pressure of atmosphere. **air pump** *n.* a machine for exhausting the air from a closed vessel. **air raid** *n.* an attack by hostile aircraft. **air rifle** n. a rifled air gun. **air sacs** n. pl. air-cells in the bodies of birds. **air ship** n. lighter-than-air machine, developed from balloon. **airsick** adj. ill from air travel. **airstrip** n. concrete runway on an airfield. **airtight** a. admitting no air. **airway** n. a prepared route for travel by airplane; a ventilating passage [Gk. *aēr*, air].

aire-dale (ār'·dāl) n. a kind of large terrier, with a close, wiry coat of tan and black [originally fr. *Airedale*, Yorkshire].

aisle (il) n. the wing of a building; any lateral division of a church; the passage-ways between rows [L. *ala*, a wing].

aitch-bone (āch'·bōn) n. the rump bone of an ox; the cut of beef surrounding it [L. *natis*, the rump: E. bone].

a·jar (ạ·jār') adv. partly open, as a door [M.E. *on char*, on the turn].

a·kim·bo (ạ·kim'·bō) adv. with a crook; bent. **with arms akimbo**, with hands on hips and elbows turned outward [M.E. *in kenebow*, into a crooked bend].

a·kin (ạ·kin') a. related by blood; allied by nature; having the same properties.

-al (ạl) a suffix to n. to form a.; or to form n. from v.

à la (á·lá), according to [Fr.].

al·a·bas·ter (al'·ạ·bas·tẹr) n. gypsum; a semi-transparent kind of soft marble-like mineral; a. made of, or white as, alabaster. **albastrian, alabastrine** a. [Gk. *alabastros*].

a·lack (ạ·lak') interj. (Arch.) an exclamation expressive of sorrow. **alack-a-day** (ạ·lak'·ạ·dā) interj. an exclamation of regret [E.].

a·lac·ri·ty (ạ·lak'·ri·ti·) n. cheerful readiness; eagerness; briskness [L. *alacer*, brisk].

a·lar (ā'·lẹr) a. wing-like; pert. to wings; having wings [L. *ala*, a wing].

a·larm (ạ·lārm') n. sound giving notice of danger; a mechanical contrivance to rouse from sleep; a summons to arms; sudden fear or apprehension; dismay; trepidation. v.t. to fill with apprehension; to call to arms. **-ingly** adv. **-ist** n. one given to exciting alarm, esp. needlessly. **alarum** n. an old spelling of 'alarm' [O.Fr. *a l'arme*, to arms].

a·las (ạ·las') interj. an exclamation of sorrow, pity, etc. [O.Fr. *a las*, ah weary].

a·late (al'·āt) a. having wings; winged. Also **-d** a. [L. *ala*, a wing].

alb (alb) n. a vestment of white linen, reaching to the feet, worn by R.C. clergy officiating at the Eucharist [L. *albus*, white].

al·ba·core (al'·bạ·kōr) n. tunny fish [Ar. *al*, the; *bukr*, a young camel].

al·ba·tross (al'·bạ·traws) n. a large web-footed sea-bird commonest in the South Seas [fr. obsolete *alcatras*, a frigate-bird].

al·be·it (awl·bē'·it) conj. although; even though; notwithstanding that [E. *al* = although, *be*, and *it*].

al·bi·no (al·bī'·nō) n. a person, or animal, with an abnormal whiteness of the skin and hair, and a pink color in the eyes. **albinism** n. [L. *albus*, white].

al·bum (al'·bạm) n. a book for autographs, photographs, stamps, etc.; a book of selections [L. *album*, a white tablet].

al·bu·men (al·bū'·mạn) n. white of egg; a similar substance found in the tissues of animals and plants. **albumin** n. any of a class of proteins, necessary for growth in the body. **albuminoid** n. a substance resembling albumen. **albuminous** a. [L. *albumen*, white of egg].

al·bur·num (al·bur'·nạm) n. sapwood, part of tree under bark and outside heart up which sap rises [L. *albus*, white].

al·che·my (al'·kạ·mi·) n. the forerunner of modern chemistry. Its chief aims were (a) transmuting the baser metals into gold, and (b) discovery of an elixir of life. **alchemic** a. **alchemist** n. [Ar. *al*, the; *kimia* fr. Gk. *chumeia*, alloying of metals].

al·co·hol (al'·kạ·hál) n. pure spirit; a liquid of strong pungent taste, the intoxicating element in fermented or distilled liquor. **-ism** n. a morbid condition caused by over-indulgence in alcoholic liquor. **-ic** a. pert. to alcohol; n. one addicted to the immoderate use of alcohol; a habitual drunkard. **absolute alcohol**, alcohol entirely free from water [Ar. *al-koh'l*, powder of antimony to stain the eyelids].

al·cove (al'·kōv) n. a recess in a room; a covered seat in a garden [Sp. *alcoba*].

al·de·hyde (al'·dạ·hīd) n. a liquid produced by the oxidation of alcohol [fr. letters of *alcohol dehydro*genatum, i.e. alcohol without hydrogen].

al·der (awl'·dẹr) n. a tree of birch family, growing in marshy soil [O.F. *alor*].

al·der·man (awl'·dẹr·mạn) n. a civic dignitary. *pl.* **aldermen** [O.E. *ealdorman*].

ale (āl) n. liquor made from malt by fermentation; a festivity (from the amount of ale drunk at it. **alehouse** n. a place where ale is sold [O.E. *ealu*].

a·lem·bic (ạ·lem'·bik) n. a vessel of glass or metal formerly used in distillation; (*Fig.*) a refining medium, as in the *alembic of the mind* [Ar. *al-ambig*, a cup].

a·lert (ạ·lurt') a. watchful; vigilant; brisk; nimble; active; n. a signal by sirens of air attack; period of air-raid. **-ly** adv. **-ness** n. [It. *all' erta*, on the look-out].

a·lex·an·drine (al·eg·zan'·drin) n. a verse of six iambic feet, probably from O.Fr. poems dealing with Alexander the Great; found as ninth line of Spenserian Stanza.

a·lex·i·a (ạ·lek'·si·ạ) n. inability to understand written language.

al·fal·fa (al·fal'·fạ) n. plant of the pea family, valued as fodder [Sp. *alfalfa*, three-leaved grass].

al·fres·co (al·fres'·kō) a. and adv. in the fresh air, as an *alfresco* meal [It.].

al·ga (al'·gạ) n. (Bot.) one of the **algae** (al'·jē) pl. plants found in sea-water, and in slow-moving fresh or stagnant water. **algal, algoid, algous** a. **algology** n. scientific study of marine plants [L. *alga*, seaweed].

al·ge·bra (al'·je·brạ) n. a branch of mathematics in which calculations are made by using letters to represent numbers or quantities and symbols to denote arithmetical operations of these numbers; a kind of abstract arithmetic used in almost all branches of science. **-ic(al)** (al·je·brā'·ik(al)) a. **-ically** adv. **-ist** n. [Ar. *al'jebr*, joining together of fragment].

al·gid (al'·jid) a. cold. **algid cholera** Asiatic cholera. **-ity, -ness** n. coldness. **algific** a. causing cold [L. *algere*, to be cold].

a·li·as (ā'·li·ạs) adv. otherwise; n. an assumed name [L. *alias*, at another time].

al·i·bi (al'·i·bi) n. (*Law*) a plea that the prisoner was elsewhere when the crime was committed; excuse [L. *alibi*, elsewhere].

al·ien (āl'·yạn) a. of another country; foreign; different in nature; estranged; n. a non-naturalized foreigner. **-able** a. (of property) capable of being sold or handed over. **-ability** n. **-ate** v.t. to transfer to another; estrange; **-ation** n. (*Med.*) insanity. **-ator** n. **-ism** n. study of mental diseases. **-ist** n. a specialist in treatment of mental diseases; a psychiatrist [L. *alienus*, belonging to another].

a·lif·er·ous (al·if'·ẹr·ạs) a. having wings.

a·light (ạ·lit') adv. or a. on fire; illuminated; kindled [O.E. *on; lēoht*, light].

a·light (ạ·lit') v.i. to dismount; to finish one's journey; to fall; to descend. **-ing** n. [O.E. *alihtan*, to descend].

a·lign (ạ·lin') v.t. to adjust by a line; to line up; to range; v.i. to form in a line; to fall in, as troops. Also **aline, -ment** n. [Fr. *aligner*, to put in line].

a·like (ạ·lik') a. having likeness; similar; adv. similarly; equally [O.E. *gelic*, like].

al·i·ment (al'·i·mạnt) n. nourishment; nutriment; (*Law*) provision for maintenance. v.t. to maintain. **-al** a. **-ally** adv. **-ary** a. pert. to food; nutritive. **-ation** n. the process of introducing nutriment into the body. **-ary canal**, the large intestine [L. *alimentum*, nourishment].

al·i·mo·ny (al'·i·mō·ni·) n. means of living, esp. an allowance made to a wife out of her husband's income, after legal separation [L. *alimonia*, sustenance].

al·i·quant (a'·li·kwạnt) a. (of a number) not dividing without remainder [L. *aliquantus*, considerable].

al·i·quot (al'·i·kwạt) a. dividing exactly, or without remainder [L. *aliquot*, some].

a·live (ạ·liv') a. having life; existent; active; alert; thronged with [O.E. *on life*, living].

al·ka·li (al'·kạ·li) n. one of a class of chemical compounds which combine with acids to form salts—used with fats to form soap. **alkalify** (al'·kạ·li·fī), **alkalize** v.t. to render alkaline;

v.i. to become alkaline; pa.p. **-fied. -fiable** a. capable of being converted into an alkali. **-metry** (al·kạ·lim'·ạ·tri·) n. the quantitative estimation of the strength of alkalis. **-ne** a. pert. to alkali; with qualities of alkali. **-nity** (al·kạ·lin'·i·ti·) n. **alkaloid** n. nitrogenous organic compound which acts chemically like an alkali; a. resembling an alkali in properties [Ar. *al*, the; *qaliy*, calcined ashes].

all (awl) a. the whole of; every one of; n. whole amount; whole duration of; adv. wholly; entirely. **all-American** adj. chosen best in U.S.; n. player so chosen. **all-around** adj. versatile, having many abilities. **all-fours** n. hands and feet. **all-hail!** interj. welcome! good health! **all-in** a. exhausted. **all out** adj. total. **all-powerful** a. omnipotent. **all but**, nearly; almost. **all in all**, in all respects [O.E. *all. eall*].

al·lay (ạ·lā') v.t. to lighten; to make quiet; to lessen grief or pain. **-er** n. **-ment** n. [O.E. *alecgan*, to put down].

al·le·ga·tion (al·ạ·gā'·shạn) n. affirmation; that which is positively asserted; the act of alleging [L. *allegare*, to allege]. **allege** (ạ·lej') v.t. to bring forward with positiveness; to plea, or excuse; to declare; affirm; cite. **allegeable** a. **allegedly** adv. [L. *allegare*, to allege].

al·le·giance (ạ·lē'·jạns) n. the duty of a subject to his government or superior; loyalty; an oath of homage. **allegiant** a. loyal; n. one who owes allegiance [fr. O.Fr. *ligeance*].

al·le·go·ry (al'·ạ·gō·ri·) n. a narrative in which abstract ideas are personified; a description to convey a different meaning from that which is expressed; a continued metaphor. **allegoric, (-al)** a. **allegorically** adv. **allegorize** v.t. to write in allegorical form; v.i. to use figurative language. **allegorist** n. [Gk. *allos*, other; *agoreuein*, to speak].

al·le·gret·to (al·lạ·gret'·tō) a. (*Mus.*) livelier than *andante* but not so quick as *allegro* [It. dim. of *allegro*, gay].

al·le·gro (ạ·lā'·grō) a. (*Mus.*) brisk, gay, sprightly (movement). **allegro vivace** (vē·vátch'·e), allegro in an even more spirited manner [It. *allegro*, gay].

al·le·lu·ia (al·ạ·lōō'·ya) interj. hallelujah; n. song of praise to the Almighty [Heb.].

al·ler·gy (al'·ẹr·ji·) n. hyper-sensitivity to particular substances; susceptibility to ill-effects from eating some foods. **allergen** n. a substance which induces allergy. **allergic** a. [Gk. *allos*, other; *ergon*, work].

al·le·vi·ate (ạ·lē'·vi·āt) v.t. to make light; to lighten; to ease; to afford relief; to mitigate. **alleviation** n. **alleviative** a. **alleviator** n. [L. *alleviare* fr. *levis*, light].

al·ley (al'·i·) n. a narrow passage between buildings; a garden path; a long, narrow passage for bowling. **alley-way** n. an alley [Fr. *aller*, to go].

al·li·ance (ạ·li·ạns) n. persons, parties, or states allied together for a common purpose; union by marriage [Fr. *allier*].

al·li·ga·tor (al'·i·gā·tẹr) n. a reptile distinguished from crocodile by a broad flat head, depressed muzzle and unequal teeth [Sp. *el lagarto*, the lizard].

al·lit·er·ate (ạ·lit'·ẹr·āt) v.i. to begin each word with the same letter or sound. **alliteration** n. recurrence of a letter or letters at the beginning of words in close succession; head rhyme. **alliterative** adj. [L. *ad*, to; *littera*, letter].

al·lo·cate (al'·ō·kāt) v.t. to distribute; to assign to each his share; to place. **allocation** n. **allocatur** n. (*Law*) a certificate that costs have been allowed [L. *ad*, to; *locus*, a place].

al·lo·cu·tion (al·ō·kū'·shạn) n. a formal address, esp. of the Pope to his clergy [L. *ad*, to; *locutio*, a speech].

al·lot (ạ·lat') v.t. to divide by lot; to distribute as shares. pr.p. **-ting**. pa.p. and pa.t. **-ted. -ment** n. what is alloted; distribution; a share; a portion [L. *ad*, to; O.E. *hlot*, a share].

al·lot·ro·py (ạ·lát'·rạ·pi·) n. property of some chemical substances of being found in two or more different forms, e.g. coal, graphite, and diamond are all carbon. **allotropic** a. **allotropism** n. [Gk. *allos*, other; *tropos*, manner].

al·low (ạ·lou') v.t. to acknowledge; to permit; to give; to set apart; v.i. to provide. **-able** a. permissible; lawful; acceptable. **-ance** n. what is allowed; permission; a stated quantity to be added or deducted; a rebate; a grant. **-edly** adv. **to make allowance for**, to take into consideration [O.Fr. *allouer*].

al·loy (ạ·loi′) *v.t.* to melt together two or more metals; to reduce the purity of a metal by mixing with a less valuable one; to debase. **alloy** (al′·oi, ạ·loi′) *n.* any mixture of metals e.g. copper and zinc to form brass; a combination; an amalgam; (*Fig.*) evil mixed with good [L. *ad*, to; *ligare*, to join].

all right (awl rit) satisfactory, yes, certainly.

all·spice (awl′·spīs) *n.* a spice [E. *all*, and *spice*].

al·lude (ạ·lōōd′) *v.i.* to refer indirectly to; to hint at; to suggest; to mention lightly [L. *ad*, at; *ludere*, to play].

al·lure (ạ·loor′) *v.t.* to tempt by a lure, offer, or promise. **-ment** *n.* that which allures. **alluring** *a.* enticing; attractive; fascinating. **alluringly** *adv.* [L. *ad*, to; Fr. *leurre*, bait].

al·lu·sion (ạ·lōō′·zhun) *n.* a passing or indirect reference; a hint; a suggestion. **allusive** *a.* referring to indirectly; marked by allusions; symbolical. **allusively** *adv.* [fr. *allude*].

al·lu·vi·on (ạ·lōō′·vi·ạn) *n.* land formed by washed-up earth and sand. **alluvium** *n.* water-borne matter deposited on low-lying lands. [L. *alluvio*, an overflowing].

al·ly (ạ·li′) *v.t.* to join by treaty, marriage, or friendship; *pr.p.* **-ing**; *pa.p.* and *pa.t.* **allied**. **ally** (ạ·li′, or a′·li) *n.* a person, family, country, etc., bound to another; esp. of nations in war-time; a partner. *pl.* **allies** (ạ·liz′, or a′·liz) [L. *ad*, to; *ligare*, to bind].

al·ma ma·ter (al′·mạ mā′·ter) *n.* college or school one attended [L. fostering mother].

al·ma·nac (awl′·mạ·nak) *n.* a calendar of days, weeks and months, to which astronomical and other information is added [etym. uncertain].

al·might·y (awl·mīt′·i·) *a.* all-powerful; omnipotent. **The Almighty**, the Supreme Being; God; **almightiness** *n.* [O.E. *ealmihtig*].

al·mond (à′·mạnd) *n.* the kernel of the nut of the almond-tree [Gk. *amugdalē*, an almond].

al·mon·er (à′·, àl′·mạn·ẹr) *n.* one who distributes alms or bounty. **almonry** *n.* a place for distributing alms [O.Fr. *almosnier*].

al·most (awl′·mōst) *adv.* very nearly; all but [O.E. *eallmoest*].

alms (ámz) *n.* gift offered to relieve the poor; a charitable donation. **alms-house** *n.* a building, usually erected and endowed by private charity, for housing the aged poor [Gk. *eleēmosunē*, pity].

al·oe (al′·ō) *n.* a bitter plant used in medicine; a purgative drug, made from the juice of several species of aloe. — **wood** [Gk. *aloe*, a bitter herb].

a·loft (ạ·lawft′) *adv.* on high; (*Naut.*) on the yards or rigging [O.N. *a lopt*, in the air].

a·lo·ha (ạ·lō′·ạ, á·lō′·há) *n., interj.* greetings, farewell [Hawaiian].

a·lone (ạ·lōn′) *a.* solitary; single; *adv.* by oneself; singly [E. *all* and *one*].

a·long (ạ·lawng′) *adv.* in a line with; throughout the length of; lengthwise; onward; in the company of (followed by *with*); *prep.* by the side of. **-side** *adv.* by the side of, esp. of a ship [O.E. *andlang*].

a·loof (ạ·lōōf′) *a.* reserved in manner, almost unsociable; *adv.* at a distance; apart. **-ness** *n.* [fr. Dut. *to loef*, to windward].

al·o·pe·ci·a (al·ạ·pē′·shi·ạ) *n.* disease causing loss of hair [Gk. *alopekia*, fox-mange].

a·loud (ạ·loud′) *adv.* with a loud voice or noise; loudly; audibly [fr. E. *loud*].

alp (alp) *n.* a high mountain; mountain pastureland. **Alps** *n.pl.* the mountains of Switzerland. **alpine** *a.* pert. to the Alps; *n.* a plant that grows on high ground. **alpinist** (al′·pin·ist) *n.* [L. *Alpes*].

al·pac·a (al·pak′·a) *n.* a sheeplike animal of Peru; a species of llama; a thin kind of cloth made of the wool of the alpaca [Sp.].

al·pen·horn, alp·horn (al′·pen·hawrn, alp′·hawrn) *n.* a long wooden horn curving towards a wide mouth-piece, used by Swiss herds.

alpenstock *n.* a long, stout staff, shod with iron, used by mountaineers [Ger.=horn (stick) of the Alps].

al·pha (al′·fạ) *n.* the first letter of Greek alphabet. **alpha and omega**, the first and the last. **alpha particle**, a helium nucleus travelling at high speed, given out when atoms of Uranium, Radium, etc., undergo radioactive breakdown. **alpha rays**, streams of alpha particles [Gk.].

al·pha·bet (al′·fạ·bet) *n.* letters of a language arranged in order; first principles. **-ic, -al** *a.* **-ically** *adv.* **-ize** *v.* [Gk. *alpha, beta*, the first two Greek letters].

al·read·y (awl·red′·i·) *adv.* before this; even now; even then; previously to the time specified [E. *all ready*, prepared].

al·so (awl′·sō) *adv.* and *conj.* in like manner; likewise; further.

al·tar (awl′·tẹr) *n.* a table or raised structure in a place of worship, on which gifts and sacrifices are offered to a deity; the communion table [L. *altare*].

al·ter (awl′·tẹr) *v.t.* to change; *v.i.* to become different. **-ably** *adv.* **-ability** *n.* **-ation** *n.* the act of altering; change; modification [L. *alter*, other].

al·ter·cate (awl′·tẹr·kāt) *v.i.* to contend in words; to wrangle. **altercation** *n.* a dispute; a controversy [L. *altercari*, to wrangle].

al·ter·nate (awl·tẹr′·nit) *a.* occuring by turns; one following the other in succession. **-ly** *adv.* by turns. **alternate** (awl′·tẹr·nāt) *v.t.* to cause to follow by turns; *v.i.* to happen by turns. **alternation** *n.* **alternative** *a.* offering a choice of two things; *n.* a choice of two things. **alternatively** *adv.* **alternator** *n.* (*Elect.*) a dynamo for producing alternating current. **alternating current** (*Elect.*) a current which reverses its direction of flow at fixed periods. *Abbrev.* **A.C.** [L. *alternare*, fr. *alter*, other].

al·though (awl·THŌ′) *conj.* admitting that; notwithstanding that [E. *all* and *though*].

al·tim·e·ter (al·tim′·ạ·tẹr) *n.* an instrument for taking altitudes; in aviation, barometer to show height [L. *altus*, high; Gk. *metron*, a measure].

al·ti·tude (al′·ti·tūd) *n.* height; perpendicular elevation above a given level [L. *altitudo*].

al·to (al′·tō) *n.* (*Mus.*) part once sung by highest male voice or counter-tenor, now sung by lowest female voice; singer with voice higher than tenor, lower than soprano; contralto [L. *altus*, high].

al·to·geth·er (awl·tạ·geTH′·ẹr) *adv.* wholly, entirely, quite; on the whole [E.].

al·tru·ism (al′·trōò·izm) *n.* the principle of living for the good of others (opp. to *egoism*). **altruist** *n.* **altruistic** *a.* unselfish. **altruistically** *adv.* [L. *alter*, another].

al·um (al′·ạm) *n.* a double sulphate of alumina and potash; a mineral salt used as a styptic, astringent, etc., as a mordant in dyeing, and in tanning [L. *alumen*].

a·lu·mi·num (ạ·lōō′·mi·nạm) *n.* a whitish metal produced largely from bauxite; it is strong, light, malleable. **alumina, alumine** *n.* an oxide of aluminum; the clay, loam, etc., from which alum is obtained. **aluminate** *v.t.* to impregnate with alum. **aluminic** *a.* **aluminiferous** *a.* containing alum or alumina. **aluminite** *n.* a sulphate of alumina [L. *alumen*, alum].

a·lum·nus (ạ·lum′·nus) *n.* (*fem.* **alumna**, *pl.* **alumnae**) a graduate or former student of a school, college, or university. *pl.* **alumni** [L. *alumnus*, foster-child].

al·ve·o·lar (al·vē′·ō·lẹr) *a.* pert. to or resembling the sockets of the teeth. **alveolate** *a.* pitted; honeycombed. **alveolus** *n.* (*pl.* **alveoli**) a tooth socket; a cell in a honeycomb [L. *alveolus*, a small cavity].

al·ways (awl′·wāz) *adv.* at all times; perpetually; invariably; regularly [O.E. *ealne weg*, the whole way].

a·lys·sum (a′·li·sạm) *n.* a species of rock plant with white or yellow flowers; madwort [Gk. *alussos*, curing madness].

am (am) the *first person sing. pres. indic.* of the verb **to be**.

a. m. (ā em) before noon [L. *ante meridiem*].

a·mah (à′·mạ) *n.* a nurse, in the Orient [Port. *ama*].

a·main (ạ·mān′) *adv.* (*Arch.*) with all strength or force [E. *on; main*, strength].

a·mal·gam (ạ·mal′·gạm) *n.* a compound of mercury with another metal; a mixture of different substances. **-ate** *v.t.* to mix a metal with quicksilver; to compound; to consolidate; to combine (esp. of business firms); *v.i.* to coalesce; to blend; to fuse. **-ation** *n.* the act or results of amalgamating. **-ative** *a.* **-ator** *n.* [Gk. *malagma*, an emollient].

a·man·u·en·sis (ạ·man·ū·en′·sis) *n.* one who writes what another dictates, or copies what another has written; a secretary. *pl.* **amanuenses** [L. *ab*, from; *manus*, hand].

am·a·ranth (am′·ạ·ranth) *n.* an imaginary purple flower which never fades; 'love-lies-bleeding'; a purplish color; also a real flower. **amaranthine** *a.* never-fading; purplish [Gk. *amaranthos*, never-fading].

am·a·ryl·lis (a′·mạ·ril·ạs) *n.* a plant, the belladonna lily [Gk.].

a·mass (ạ·mas′) *v.t.* to heap up; to collect; accumulate [L. *ad*, to; *massa*, a lump].

am·a·teur (am′·ạ·tẹr) *n.* one who cultivates any study, art, or sport for the love of it, and not for money; *a.* like an amateur. **amateurish** *a.* unskilled; clumsy. **amateurism, amateurishness** *n.* [L. *amare*, to love].

am·a·tive (am′·ạ·tiv) *a.* pert. to love; amorous [L. *amare*, to love].

am·a·tol (am′·ạ·tāl) *n.* explosive of ammonium nitrate of trinitrotoluene (T.N.T.) [name from parts of names of ingredients].

am·a·to·ry (am′·ạ·tōr·i·) *a.* pert. to or causing love. **amatorial** *a.* amorous; affectionate. **amatorially** *adv.* [L. *amare*, to love].

a·maze (ạ·māz′) *v.t.* to fill with astonishment or wonder; to confound; to perplex. **-dly** (ạ·māz·ad·li′) *adv.* **-ment** *n.* astonishment, surprise. **amazing** *a.* causing amazement, wonder, or surprise. **amazingly** *adv.* [O.E. *amasian*, to confound].

Am·a·zon (am′·ạz·ạn) *n.* one of a mythical race of female warriors of Scythia; a masculine woman. **Amazonian** *a* [Gk. *a-*, neg. and *mazos*, breast].

am·bages (am′·bājz) *n.pl.* circumlocution; subterfuge; evasion; used in *pl.* [L. *ambages*, a winding].

am·bas·sa·dor (am·bas′·ạ·dẹr) *n.* an envoy of highest rank sent to a foreign country; (*Fig.*) an intermediary; a messenger. **ambassadress** *n. fem.* **ambassadorial** *a.* **-ship** *n.* [L. *ambactus*, vassal].

am·ber (am′·bẹr) *n.* a yellowish, brittle fossil resin of vegetable origin, used in making jewelry, etc.; *a.* of or like, amber [Ar. *anbar*, ambergris].

am·ber·gris (am′·bẹr·grēs) *n.* a fragrant, ash-colored. waxy substance, derived from a biliary secretion of the spermaceti whale [Fr. *ambre gris*, grey amber].

am·bi·dex·ter (am·bi·leks′·tẹr) *n.* one able to use either hand with equal dexterity; a double-dealer. **ambidexterity** *n.* **ambidextrous** *a.* able to use either hand equally skilfully. **ambidextrously** *adv.* [L. *ambo*, both; *dexter*, right hand].

am·bi·ent (am′·bi·ạnt) *a.* encompassing on all sides [L. *ambire*, to go round].

am·bi·gu·i·ty (am·bi·gū′·i·ti·) *n.* any statement that may be interpreted in more than one way. **ambiguous** *a.* doubtful or uncertain; equivocal; susceptible of two or more meanings. **ambiguously** *adv.* **ambiguousness** *n.* [L. *ambigere*, to waver].

am·bit (am′·bit) *n.* circuit or compass; sphere of action; scope [L. *ambire*, to go round].

am·bi·tion (am·bish′·ạn) *n.* an eager desire for the attainment of honor, fame, or power; aim; aspiration. **ambitious** *a.* ardently desirous of acquiring power, rank, office, etc. **ambitiously** *adv.* [L. *ambitio*, going about for votes].

am·biv·a·lence, am·biv·a·len·cy (am·biv′·ạ·lạns, -i·) *n.* in psychoanalysis, the simultaneous operation in the mind of two conflicting wishes. **ambivalent** *a.* [L. *ambo*, both; *valere*, to be strong].

am·ble (am′·bl) *v.i.* to move along easily and gently; *n.* a peculiar gait of a horse; a stroll. **ambler** *n.* **ambling** *a.* **amblingly** *adv.* [L. *ambulare*, to walk].

am·bro·sia (am·brō′·si·ạ) *n.* (*Myth.*) the food of the Ancient Greek gods which conferred immortality; an exquisite dish. **ambrosial** *a.* [Gk. *a-*, neg.; *brotos*, mortal].

am·bu·lance (am′·bū·lạns) *n.* a covered vehicle for the transport of the injured or sick; a hospital unit in the field [Fr. *ambulance*].

am·bu·lant (am′·bū·lạnt) *a.* walking. **ambulate** *v.i.* to walk backwards and forwards. **ambulation** *n.* walking. **ambulatory** *a.* having power of walking; used for walking; moving from place to place; *n.* a cloister for walking exercise [L. *ambulare*, to walk].

am·bush (am′·boosh) same as **ambuscade** (am·bạs·kād) *n.* a surprise attack; the place of ambush; the force concealed; *v.i.* to lie in wait; *v.t.* to attack from a concealed position [L. *in*; Late L. *boscus*, a wood].

a·me·ba. See **amoeba**.

a·me·lio·rate (ạ·mēl′·yẹr·āt) *v.t.* and *v.t.* to make better; to improve. **amelioration** *n.* **ameliorative** *a.* [L. *ad*, to; *melior*, better].

A·men (ā·men′, ả′·men) *adv.* or *interj.* so be it; verily; verily (uttered at the end of a prayer) [Heb. = certainly].

a·me·na·ble (ạ·mē′·nạ·bl, ạ·men′·ạ·bl) *a.* liable to be brought to account; easily led; willing to yield or obey. **amenability, -ness** n. the state of being amenable. **amenably** adv. [Fr. *amener*, to lead near].

a·mend (a·mend′) v.t. to change for the better; to improve; to alter in detail as a law, etc.; v.i. to grow better. **-able** a. **-atory** a. **-ment** n. the act of amending; a change for the better. **amends** n.pl. reparation for loss or injury; compensation [L. *emendare*, to remove a fault].

a·men·i·ty (a·men′·i·ti·) n. pleasantness in situation, climate, manners, or disposition. **amenities** n.pl. pleasant ways or manners; agreeable surroundings [L. *amoenus*, agreeable].

a·merce (a·murs′) v.t. to punish by a fine. **-able** a. liable to a fine. **-ment** n. a pecuniary penalty [L. *merces*, a fine].

A·mer·i·can (a·mer′·i·kan) n. in, of, or characteristic of the United States or America. n. a native, citizen or resident of America or the United States. **-a** n.pl. collection of facts, books, data pert. to America. **-ism** n. **-ize** v.t. and v.i. **-ization** n. [fr. *Amerigo* Vespucci, Italian navigator].

am·e·thyst (am′·a·thist) n. a kind of quartz; violet, purple, or blue color. **amethystine** a. pert. to amethyst; bluish-violet [Gk. *a-*, neg.; *methein*, to be drunken].

a·mi·a·ble (ā′·mi·a·bl) a. worthy of love or affection; sweet-tempered. **amiably** adv. **amiability** n. Also **-ness** [L. *amicabilis*, friendly].

am·i·ca·ble (am′·i·ka·bl) a. friendly; peaceable. **amicably** adv. **amicability** n. Also **-ness** [L. *amicabilis*, friendly].

a·mid, a·midst (a·mid′, a·midst′) prep. in the middle of; among [O.E. *on middan*].

a·mi·no ac·ids (a·mē′·nō as′·idz) a group of nitrogenous organic compounds, basic constituents of proteins.

a·miss (a·mis′) a. wrong; faulty; improper; adv. in a faulty manner [E. *miss*, a failure].

am·i·ty (am′·i·ti·) n. friendship [Fr. *ami*, a friend, fr. L. *amicus*].

am·me·ter (am′·mē·ter) n. an instrument used to measure the strength of an electric current in amperes [fr. *ampere*, and Gk. *metron*, a measure].

am·mo (am′·ō) n. (*Army Slang*) ammunition.

am·mo·ni·a (a·mō′·ni·a) n. a pungent, alkaline gas, very soluble in water; a solution of this gas in water, for household use. **ammoniac, ammoniacal** a. **ammoniated** a. combined with, containing, ammonia. **ammonium** n. hypothetical base of ammonia [fr. *sal ammoniac*].

am·mu·ni·tion (am·ū·nish′·an) n. military projectiles and missiles of all kinds; originally, military stores. a. [O.Fr. *l'amunition*, for *la munition*].

am·ne·sia (am·nē′·zhi·a) n. memory loss [Gk.]

am·nes·ty (am′·nes·ti·) n. an act of oblivion; a general pardon of political offenders [Gk. *amnesia*, a forgetting].

a·moe·ba (a·mē′·ba) n. a minute animalcule of the simplest structure constantly changing in shape. pl. **amoebae, amoebas. amoeboid, amoebic** a. [Gk. *amoibē*, change].

a·mok (a·mák′) See **amuck**.

a·mong, a·mongst (a·mung′, a·mungst′) prep. mixed with; making part of; amidst [M.E. *amonge*].

a·mor·al (ā·már′·al) a. non-moral; heedless of morals [Gk. *a-*, neg.; and E. *moral*].

am·o·rous (am′·er·as) a. having a propensity for love and sexual enjoyment; in love; pert. to love. **-ly** adv. **-ness** n. [L. *amor*, love].

a·mor·phous (a·mawr′·fas) a. without regular shape; shapeless; irregular; uncrystallized [Gk. *a-*, neg.; *morphe*, form].

a·mor·tize (am′·er·tīz) v.t. to pay off a debt usually by periodic payments. **amortization** n.

a·mount (a·mount′) v.i. to rise to; to result in; to come to (in value or meaning); to be equal to; n. the sum total; the whole, or aggregate [O.Fr. *amonter*, to mount up].

am·pere (am′·pir) n. the unit of electric current; (*Abbrev.* amp.). **amperage** n. strength of electric current in amperes [named after André *Ampère*, a French physicist, 1775-1836].

am·per·sand (am′·per·sand) n. the name given to the sign & [fr. *and per se and*, i.e. 'and' by itself = 'and.'].

Am·phib·i·a (am·fib′·i·a) n.pl. animals that can live either on land or in water, as frogs, toads, newts, etc. **amphibian** a. pert. to or having the qualities of Amphibia. n. an animal of the class Amphibia. **amphibious** a. [Gk. *amphi*, on both sides; *bios*, life].

---

amphibian

am·phi·brach (am′·fi·brak) n. in prosody, a foot of three syllables, the middle one long, the first and last short. (⏑—⏑). In English the term is applied to a foot of three syllables of which only the middle one is stressed. a. [Gk. fr. *amphi*, on both sides; *brachus*, short].

am·phi·the·a·ter (am′·fi·thē·a·ter) n. an edifice, having tiers of seats, encircling an arena, used for sports or spectacles; a rising gallery in a theater, concert-hall, etc. [Gk. *amphi*, on both sides: *theatron*, a theater].

am·pho·ra (am′·fa·ra) n. a two-handled earthenware vessel or jar, used by the ancient Greeks and Romans; 6 gallons [Gk. *amphi*, on both sides; *pherein*, to bear].

am·ple (am′·pl) a. of full dimensions; of adequate size; of sufficient quantity; abundant; copious. **amply** adv. **-ness** n. [L. *amplus*].

am·pli·fy (am′·pli·fī) v.t. to make larger; to extend; to enlarge; v.i. to dilate; to expatiate upon. **amplification** n. **amplifier** n. an apparatus which increases the volume of sound [L. *amplus*, large; *facere*, to make].

am·pli·tude (am′·pli·tūd) n. largeness; extent; abundance; (*Radio*) (of a wave) vertical distance between its highest and lowest levels; **amplitude modulation (AM)** radio transmission by changing the amplitude of waves (contrasted with frequency modulation, FM); (*Elect.*) maximum value of an alternating current [L. *amplus*, large].

am·poule (am′·pòòl) n. also **ampule** (am′·pūle), a small sealed glass container holding hypodermic dose [Fr.].

am·pul·la (am·pūl′·a) n.; pl. **-e**; a sacred vessel for holding oil; cruet holding wine and water for Mass [L. *ampulla*].

am·pu·tate (am′·pū·tāt) v.t. to cut off, as a limb of the body, or bough of a tree. **amputation** n. **amputee** n. one who has lost a limb through amputation [L. *amputare*, to cut off].

a·muck, a·mok (a·muk′, a·mák′) adv. to rush about frantically or murderously [Malay *amuq*, rushing in frenzy].

am·u·let (am′·ya·lit) n. a talisman; a charm; a. [Fr. *amulette*, fr. L. *amuletum*].

a·muse (a·mūz′) v.t. to entertain agreeably; to occupy pleasantly; to divert. **-ment** n. anything which entertains or pleases; a pastime. **amusing** a. [Fr. *amuser*, to entertain].

an (an) a. the form of the indefinite article used before a vowel sound. See **a**. Also *Arch. conj.* if = a form of and [O.E. *an*, one].

an·a·bap·tist (an·a·bap′·tist) n. one who denies the validity of infant baptism and advocates re-baptism of adults (by immersion) [Gk. *ana*, again; *baptizein*, to dip].

a·nab·a·sis (a·nab′·a·sis) n. a military expedition. pl. **anabases** [Gk.].

a·nab·o·lism (an·ab′·al·izm) n. (*Physiol.*) the constructive form of metabolism; the building-up of tissues by plant or animal which process alternates with the breaking down (katabolism) in the chemical routine [Gk. *ana*, up; *bole*, a throwing].

a·nach·ro·nism (an·ak′·ran·izm) n. a chronological error; post- or ante-dating of an event or thing. **anachronistic** a. **anachronous** a. [Gk. *ana*, back; *chronos*, time].

an·a·con·da (a·na·kán′·da) n. a gigantic, non-venomous snake of tropical S. America.

a·nae·mia See **anemia.**

an·aes·the·sia, anesthesia See **anesthesia.**

an·a·glyph (an′·a·glif) n. a figure or ornament cut in low relief; a cameo. **anaglyphic** a. [Gk. *ana*, up; *gluphein*, to engrave].

an·a·gram (an′·a·gram) n. a transposition of the letters of a word or phrase to form a new word or phrase. **anagrammatic, -al** a. **anagrammatically** adv. **anagrammatize** v.t. to

---

form anagrams. **anagrammatism** n. [Gk. *ana-*, again; *gramma*, letter].

a·nal (ā′·nal) a. pert. to or near the anus.

an·a·lects, an·a·lec·ta (an′·a·lekts, an·a·lek′·ta) n.pl. an anthology of short literary fragments. **analectic** a. [Gk. *analektos*, choice].

an·a·lep·sis (an·a·lep′·sis) n. (*Med.*) restoration of strength after disease. Also **analepsy. analeptic** a. [Gk. *ana*, up; *lepsis*, a taking].

an·al·ge·sia (an·al·jē′·zi·a) n. (*Med.*) absence of pain while retaining tactile sense; painlessness. **analgesic** a. insensible to or alleviating pain; n. a drug which relieves pain [Gk. *an-*, neg.; *algēsis*, pain].

a·nal·o·gy (a·nal′·a·ji·) n. resemblance in essentials between things or statements otherwise different; relationship; likeness; parallelism; correspondence. **analogic, -al** a. **analogically** adv. **analogize** v.t. to explain by analogy. **analogism** n. an argument proceeding from cause to effect; investigation by, or reasoning from, analogy. **analogist** n. **analogous** (a·nal′·a·gus) a. having analogy. **analogously** adv. **analogue** n. a word or thing resembling another [Gk. *analogia*, proportion].

a·nal·y·sis (a·nal′·i·sis) n. the resolution, separating, or breaking up of anything into its constituent elements; a synopsis; (*Chem.*) determination of elements comprising a compound or mixture; (*Gram.*) logical arrangement of a sentence into its component parts; (*Math.*) theory of real and complex numbers. pl. **analyses. analyzable** a. **analyzation** n. **analyze** v.t. to take to pieces; to examine critically part by part. **analyst** n. one skilled in analysis; an analytical chemist. **analytic, -al** a. **analytically** adv. **analytics** n.pl. the technique of logical analysis [Gk. *ana*, up; *lusis*, a loosening].

an·a·pest, an·a·paest (an′·a·pest) n. in prosody, a foot of three syllables, two short or unaccented followed by one long or accented syllable (⏑⏑—). **anapestic** a. [Gk. *anapaistos* reversed].

an·ar·chy (an′·er·ki·) n. want of government in society; lawless disorder in a country; a political theory, which would dispense with all laws, founding authority on the individual conscience. **anarchic, anarchically** adv. **anarchize** v.t. **anarchism** n. confusion, chaos. **anarchist** n. [Gk. *an-*, neg.; *archein*, to rule].

a·nath·e·ma (a·nath′·a·ma) n. the word used in the R.C. church as part of the formula in excommunication; something highly distasteful to one; accursed thing. **-tic** a. **-tization** n. **-ize** v.t. to pronounce a curse against; to excommunicate [Gk.].

a·nat·o·my (a·nat′·a·mi·) n., pl. **-mies**, art of dissecting an animal or a plant; study of form or structure of an animal; the body; a skeleton. **anatomic, -al** a. **anatomically** adv. **anatomize** v.t. to dissect; to lay open the interior structure for examining each part. **anatomist** n. [Gk. *ana*, up; *tome*, cutting].

an·ces·tor (an′·ses·ter) n. (*fem.* **ancestress**) forefather; progenitor; forebear. **ancestral** a. **ancestry** n. lineage [L. *ante*, before; *cedere*, *cessum*, to go].

an·chor (ang′·ker) n. a heavy iron instrument by which a ship is held fast to the sea-bottom; a molder's chaplet; v.t. to place at anchor; to weight down; v.i. to cast anchor; to stop; **anchorage** n. a sheltered place where a ship may anchor; dues chargeable on ships which wish to anchor in harbor. **anchored** a. at anchor; firmly fixed. **to cast anchor**, to let down anchor. **to weigh anchor**, to raise anchor preparatory to sailing [L. *ancora*].

an·cho·rite, an·chor·et (ang′·ke·rit, -ret) n. one who lives apart, renouncing the world for religious reasons; a hermit. **anchoress, anchoritess** n. a female hermit. **anchorage** n. home of anchorite [Gk. *anachorētes*, one who retires].

an·cho·vy (an′·chō·vi·; an·chō′·vi·) n. small fish of the herring family [Sp. *anchova*].

an·cient (ān′·shant) a. very old; antique; venerable; former; n. an aged or venerable person; one who lived in olden times. **-ly** adv. **-ness** n. **-ry** n. ancestry; seniority [L. *ante*, before].

an·cil·lar·y (an′·sal·er·i·) a. giving help to; attending upon; auxiliary; subordinate [L. *ancilla*, a maid-servant].

and (and) conj. added to; together with; a word that joins words, clauses, or sentences [O.E.].

an·dan·te (an·dan′·ti·, án·dán′·ti·) a. or adv. (*Mus.*) moving rather slowly, but in a steady, flowing manner, faster than *larghetto*, but slower than *allegretto*; n. a moderately slow, flowing movement [It. *andare*, to go].

and·i·ron (and'·ī·ẹrn) *n.* a utensil for supporting logs in a fireplace; a firedog [O.Fr. *andier*].

an·dro·gen (an'·drạ·jạn) *n.* male sex hormone [Gk. *andros* man, and *gen*].

an·drog·y·nous (an·dráj'·i·nus) *a.* having the characteristics of both sexes; hermaphrodite. Also **androgynal. androgyny** *n.* [Gk. *aner, andros,* a man; *kephale,* the head; *gune,* a woman].

an·ec·dote (an'·ik·dōt) *n.* a biographical incident; a brief account of any fact or happening (often amusing); **anecdotage** *n.* anecdotes collectively. **anecdotal** *a.* **anecdotist** *n.* a writer or teller of anecdotes [Gk. *anekdotos,* not published].

an·e·lec·tric (an·i·lek'·trik) *a.* non-electric; *n.* a body that does not become electric; a conductor of electricity [Gk. *an-,* neg., and *electric*].

a·ne·mi·a (a·nē'·mi·ạ) *n.* Also **anaemia** (a·nē'·mi·ạ) *n.* disease characterized by a deficiency of blood or of hemoglobin. **anemic** *a.* [Gk. *an-,* neg.; *haima,* blood].

a·nem·o·ne (ạ·nem'·ạ·nē) *n.* plant of crow-foot family; wind-flower. **sea-anemone** *n.* name given to certain plant-like marine animals [Gk. *anemos,* wind].

a·nent (ạ·nent') *prep.* concerning; about; in respect of; as to [O.E. *on; efen,* even].

an·e·roid (an'·e·roid) *a.* denoting a barometer depending for its action on the pressure of the atmosphere on a metallic box almost exhausted of air, without the use of mercury or other fluid [Gk. *a-,* neg.; *neres,* wet; *eidos,* form].

an·es·the·sia, an·aes·the·sia (an·ạs·thē'·zh·ạ) *n.* absence of sensibility to external impressions, particularly touch. Also **anesthesis. anesthetic** *n.* a drug which induces insensibility to pain; *a.* producing loss of feeling and sensation. **anesthetically** *adv.* **anesthetize** *v.t.* **anesthetist** *n.* [Gk. *an-,* not; *aisthesis,* feeling].

an·eu·rism (an'·yạ·rizm) *n.* (*Med.*) a local widening or dilatation in the course of an artery [Gk. *ana,* up; *eurus,* wide].

a·new (ạ·nū') *adv.* in a new form or manner; newly; over again; afresh [M.E. of *newe*].

an·gel (ān'·jel) *n.* a heavenly messenger; a spirit who conveys God's will to man; a guardian spirit; (*Colloq.*) a lovable person; a dear. **angel fish** *n.* a bright-colored tropical fish. **angel food cake** *n.* a spongy, light, white cake. **angelic(al)** (an·jel'·ic) *a.* like an angel. **angelically** *adv.* [Gk. *angelos,* a messenger].

an·ge·lus (an'·jạ·lạs) *n.* a short devotional service in the R.C. Church held morning, noon, and sunset; the bell rung to remind the faithful to recite the prayer [L.].

an·ger (ang'·gẹr) *n.* a strong passion or emotion excited by injury; rage; *v.t.* to excite to wrath; to enrage. **angry** (ang'·gri·) *a.* roused to anger; displeased; enraged; inflamed. **angrily** *adv.* **angriness** *n.* [O.N. *angr,* trouble].

an·gi·na (an·jī'·nạ, an'·ji·nạ) *n.* (*Med.*) inflammation of the throat, e.g., quinsy. **angina pectoris,** a heart disease characterized by attacks of agonizing pain [L.].

an·gi·o·sperm (an'·ji·ō·spurm) *n.* (*Bot.*) a plant whose seeds are enclosed in a seed-vessel [Gk. *nageion,* a vessel; *sperma,* a seed].

an·gle (ang'·gl) *n.* a fish-hook; a rod and line for fishing; *v.i.* to fish with rod, line, and hook; (*Fig.*) to use artifice. **angler** *n.* one who angles. **angling** *n.* [O.E. *angul*].

an·gle (ang'·gl) *n.* a corner; the point at which two lines meet; (*Geom.*) the amount of turning made by revolving a straight line in a plane, round a point in itself, from one direction to another. **acute angle,** one less than 90°. **obtuse angle,** greater than 90° but less than 180°. **right angle,** a quarter of a complete revolution, i.e. 90°. (*Fig.*) a point of view. [L. *angulus,* a corner].

An·gli·can (ang'·gli·cạn) *a.* English; of, or belonging to, Church of England; *n.* a member of Church of England. **Anglicanism** *n.* [L. *Angli,* the Angles].

an·gli·cize (ang'·glạ·sīz) *v.t.* to make or express in English idiom. **anglicism** *n.* an English idiom; an English custom or characteristic. **anglify** *v.t.* to make English [L. *Angli,* the Angles].

An·glo- (ang'·glō) *prefix* fr. L. *Anglus,* an Angle, combining to form many compound words. **Anglo-American** *a.* involving English and Americans. **Anglo-Saxon** *a.* pert. to Anglo-Saxons or their language; *n.* one of the nations formed by the union of the Angles, Saxons. **Anglophile** (ang'·glō·fil) *a.* favoring anything English; *n.* a supporter of English customs, manners, or policy.

An·go·ra (ang·gō'·rạ) *n.* a Turkish province in Asia minor, famous for a breed of goats; cloth made from hair of these goats.

an·guish (ang'·gwish) *n.* acute pain of body or of mind; grief; anxiety; moral torment. **-ment** *n.* [L. *angustia,* straitness].

an·gu·lar (ang'·gū·lạr) *a.* having angles; sharp-cornered; (of people) not plump; gawky; irascible. **angularity** *n.* **-ly** *adv.* **angulate** *v.t.* having angles [L. *angulus,* n. corner].

an·hy·dride (an·hī'·drid) *n.* (*Chem.*) a compound formed from an acid by evaporation of water. **anhydrous** *a.* entirely without water [Gk. *an-,* neg.; *hudor,* water].

an·il (an'·il) *n.* a West Indian shrub from the leaves and stalks of which indigo is made. **aniline** (an'·il·in, or -in) *n.* a product orig. obtained from indigo, now mainly from coal-tar, and used in the manufacture of brilliant dyes, colored inks, soaps, explosives, etc.; *a.* pert. to anil or aniline [Fr. fr. Sans. *nila,* dark blue].

an·ile (an'·īl) *a.* like an old woman; imbecile. **anility** *n.* senility [L. *anus,* an old woman].

an·i·mad·vert (an·i·mad·vurt') *v.t.* to turn the mind to; to consider disparagingly; to comment on censoriously; to reprove. **animadversion** *n.* [L. *animus,* the mind; *vertere,* to turn].

an·i·mal (an'·i·mạl) *n.* a living creature having sensation and power of voluntary motion; a living organism, distinct from plants; *a.* pert. to or got from animals. **-cule** *n.* a very minute animal (*pl.* **-cules** or **-cula**). **-culine** *a.* pert. to animalcula. **-ism** *n.* sensuality. — **magnetism,** mesmerism, hypnotism. — **spirits,** natural buoyance [L. *anima,* breath].

an·i·mate (an'·i·māt) *v.t.* to give natural life to; to endow with spirit or vigor; to energize; to inspire; to make alive; *a.* living or organic. **-d** *a.* **-dly** *adv.* **animating** *a.* inspiring. **animation** *n.* the state of possessing life or spirit; vivacity. **animator** *n.* one who or that which animates; a movie cartoonist [L. *animatus,* filled with life].

an·i·mism (an'·i·mizm) *n.* the belief that all forms of organic life have their origin in the soul; that all natural objects have a soul. **animist** *n.* **animistic** *a.* [L. *anima,* life or soul].

an·i·mos·i·ty (an·i·más'·i·ti·) *n.* violent hatred; active enmity; acrimony; orig. meant courage [L. *animosus,* full of spirit].

an·i·mus (an'·i·mạs) *n.* animosity; temper; grudge; (*Law*) intention, purpose [L. *animus,* spirit, temper].

an·ise (an'·is) *n.* an herb with pungent smell and bearing aromatic seeds. **aniseed** *n.* seed of anise used for flavoring and in manufacture of liqueurs [Gk. *anis*].

an·kle (ang'·kl) *n.* the joint connecting the foot with the leg. **anklet** *n.* a sock which reaches just above the ankle; an ornament for the ankle [M.E. *ancle*].

an·nals (an'·alz) *n.pl.* history of events recorded each year; a yearly chronicle. **annalize** *v.t.* to write annals; to record chronologically. **annalist** *n.* [L. *annus,* a year].

an·neal (ạ·nēl') *v.t.* to heat, and then cool slowly, for the purpose of rendering less brittle; to heat in order to fix colors. **-ing** *n.* [O.E. *an; aclan,* to kindle].

an·nex (an'·eks) *v.t.* to unite at the end; to subjoin; to bind to; to take additional territory under control; *n.* something joined on; building attached to, or sufficiently near, main building to be considered part of it. **annexation** *n.* the act of annexing; what is annexed. **annexion, annexment** *n.* [L. *ad,* to; *nectere,* to bind].

an·ni·hi·late (ạ·nī'·hil·āt) *v.t.* to reduce to nothing; to destroy; to make null and void.

annihilable *a.* **annihilation** *n.* **annihilator** *n.* [L. *ad,* to; *nihil,* nothing].

an·ni·ver·sa·ry (an·i·vur'·sạ·ri·) *a.* yearly; annual; *n.* day on which event is yearly celebrated [L. *annus,* year; *vertere,* to turn].

an·no·tate (an'·ō·tāt) *v.t.* to mark in writing; to write explanatory notes, etc. upon literary text. **annotation** *n.* a written commentary. **annotator** *n.* **annotatory** *a.* [L. *annotatus,* marked with notes].

an·nounce (ạ·nouns') *v.t.* to give first public notice of; to proclaim; to promulgate; to publish. **-ment** *n.* giving public notice; proclamation; declaration. **-r** *n.* a broadcasting official who gives the news, etc. [L. *ad,* to; *nuntiare,* to announce].

an·noy (ạ·noi') *v.t.* to injure, disturb continually; to torment; tease; vex; pester; molest; trouble. **-ance** *n.* [fr. L. *in odio,* in hatred].

an·nu·al (an'·ū·ạl) *a.* yearly; performed in the course of a year; *n.* a periodical published once a year; a plant which completes its life-cycle within a year. **-ly** *adv.* [L. *annus,* a year].

an·nu·i·ty (ạ·nū'·i·ti·) *n.* a fixed sum of money payable each year for a number of years, or for life. **annuitant** *n.* one in receipt of an annuity [L. *annus,* a year].

an·nul (ạ·nul') *v.t.* to make void; to nullify; repeal; cancel; *pr.p.* **-ling;** *pa.t.* and *pa.p.* **-led. -ment** *n.* [L. *ad,* to; *nullus,* none].

an·nu·lar (an'·ū·lạr) *a.* ring-shaped; like a ring. **annulated** *a.* having rings or belts. **annulet** *n.* a little ring. **annularly** *adv.* **annulose** *a.* ringed. **annulation** *n.* ring-like formation [L. *annulus,* a ring].

an·num (a'·nạm) *n.* year [L.].

an·nun·ci·ate (ạ·nun'·si·āt) *v.t.* to announce; to make known; to proclaim. **annunciation** *n.* an announcing; (*cap.*) a holy day (March 25) in R.C. Church. **annunciator** *n.* **annunciatory** *a.* [L. *ad,* to; *nuntiare,* to announce].

an·ode (an'·ōd) *n.* positive electrode of a voltaic current; (*Radio*) plate of an electron tube [Gk. *anodos,* way up].

an·o·dyne (an'·ō·dīn) *n.* a drug or measures which relieve pain [Gk. *an-,* neg.; *odunē,* pain].

a·noint (ạ·noint') *v.t.* to pour oil upon; to rub over with an ointment or oil; to consecrate by unction. **-ed** *a.* consecrated; *n.* a consecrated person. **-ment** *n.* consecration; a salve. **the Lord's anointed,** Christ [L. *in,* on; *ungere,* to anoint].

a·nom·a·ly (ạ·nám'·ạ·li·) *n.* deviation from the common rule or type; irregularity. **anomalism** *n.* **anomalistic** *a.* **anomalous** *a.* irregular; incongruous [Gk. *anomalos,* not even].

a·non (ạ·nán') *adv.* quickly; at once; forthwith; soon. **ever and anon,** every now and then [O.E. *on,* in; *an,* one].

a·non·y·mous (ạ·nán'·i·mạs) *a.* applied to a writing or work of which the author is not named. **anonym** *n.* one who remains anonymous. **-ly** *adv.* **anonymity** *n.* [Gk. *an-,* neg.; *onoma,* name].

a·noph·e·les (ạn·áf'·ạl·ēz) *n.* the mosquito carrying the parasite which causes malaria [Gk. *an-,* neg.; *ophelein,* benefit].

an·oth·er (ạ·nuTH'·ẹr) *a.* not the same; different; one more; *pron.* any one else [E.].

an·swer (an'·sẹr) *v.t.* to speak or write in return; to vindicate; to witness for; *v.i.* to reply; to suit; to suffer the consequence of; *n.* something said or written in return to a question, etc.; the solution of a problem; response. **-able** *a.* capable of being answered; responsible. **-er** *n.* to answer for, to be responsible for [O.E. *andswarian,* to swear back].

ant (ant) *n.* a small mebranous-winged insect living in colonies in wood or the ground; an emmet. **ant-bear** *n.* the great ant-eater of South America. **ant-eater** *n.* one of several quadrupeds, e.g. ant-bear, aardvark, that feed chiefly on ants. **ant-hill** *n.* a mound raised by a colony of ants or termites [O.E. *aemette*].

ant- (ant) a combining form fr. Gk. *anti,* against, used to form compounds. **-acid** (ant-as'·id) *a.* counteracting acidity; *n.* a remedy for acidity of the stomach.

an·tag·o·nize (an·tag'·ạ·nīz) *v.t.* to contend violently against; to act in opposition; to oppose; to make hostile. **antagonism** *n.* opposition; hostility; hatred; dislike. **antagonist** *n.* **antagonistic** *a.* **antagonistically** *adv.* [Gk. *anti,* against; *agon,* a contest].

ant·arc·tic (ant·árk'·tik) *a.* opposite to arctic pole; relating to southern pole or region near it [Gk. *anti,* against; E. *arctic*].

an·te (an'·te) *n.* in poker, a player's stake [L. *ante,* before].

an·te- (an′·te) *prefix* fr. L. *ante*, meaning *before* (place, time, or order), combining to form derivatives. **antebellum** *a.* [L.] before the war (esp. U.S. Civil War). **antecedent** (an·tạ·sēd′·ạnt) *a.* going before in time, place, rank, etc.; preceding; prior; *n.* that which goes before; (*Gram.*) the noun or pronoun to which a relative refers. **antechamber** *n.* a chamber leading to the chief apartment. **antecursor** *n.* a forerunner [L. *cedere*, to go; *camera*, a room; *currere*, to run].

an·te·date (an′·tạ·dāt) *v.t.* to date before the true time; to precede in time [L. *ante*, before, E. *date*].

an·te·di·lu·vi·an (an·te·di·lōō′·vi·ạn) *a.* pert. to before the Flood; ancient; antiquated [L. *ante*, before; *diluvium*, a flood].

an·te·lope (an′·tạ·lōp) *n.* (*pl.* **-lope, lopes**) a hoofed ruminant, notable for its graceful and agile movement [Gk. *antholops*].

an·te·me·rid·i·an (an·te·mẹ·rid′·i·ạn) *a.* before noon (abbrev. **a.m.**) [L. *ante meridiem* = before midday, the period of time between midnight and noon].

an·ten·na (an·ten′·ạ) *n.* feeler of an insect, crustacean, etc. *pl.* **antennae** (an·ten′·ē). **antenna** *n.* (*Radio*) a wire for sending or receiving electric waves; an aerial. *pl.* **antennas. -ry** *a.* [L. *antenna*, a sailyard].

an·te·pe·nult (an·te·pē′·nạlt) *n.* last syllable but two of word. **antepenultimate** *a.* [L. *ante*, before; *paene*, almost; *ultimus*, last].

an·te·ri·or (an·te′·ri·ẹr) *a.* before; occurring earlier. **anteriority** *n.* [L. *ante*, before].

an·te·room (an′·te·rōōm) *n.* a room giving entry to another [L. *ante*, before; E. *room*].

an·them (an′·tham) *n.* a hymn sung in alternate part; Church music adapted to passages from the Scriptures; song of praise [Gk. *antiphonon*, a response sung].

an·ther (an′·thẹr) *n.* the little sac in a flower, containing the pollen or fertilizing dust. **-al** *a.* [Gk. *antheros*, flowery].

an·thol·o·gy (an·thál′·ạ·ji·) *n.* orig. a collection of flowers; a collection of literary passages or poetry. **anthologist** *n.* [Gk. *anthos*, a flower; *legein*, to gather].

an·thra·cene (an′·thrạ·sēn) *n.* product from distillation of coal-tar, used in manufacture of dyes. **anthracite** *n.* coal, nearly pure carbon, burning without smoke or flame [Gk. *anthrax*, coal].

an·thrax (an′·thrax) *n.* a carbuncle; a malignant disease in cattle and sheep; a malignant pustule [Gk. *anthrax*, coal].

an·thro·po- (an′·thrạ·pō) *prefix* fr. Gr. *anthropos*, meaning man, combining to form derivatives. **anthropogency** (·poj′·en·i·) *n.* science of development of man. **anthropoid** *a.* man-like [Gk. *genesthai*, to be born; *graphein*, to write; *eidos*, form; *lithos*, a stone].

an·thro·pol·o·gy (an·thrạ·pál′·ạ·ji·) *n.* study of man, including all aspects of his evolution, physical and social. **anthropological** *a.* **anthropologically** *adv.* **anthropologist** *n.* [Gk. *anthropos*, man; *logos*, discourse].

an·thro·pom·e·try (an·thrạ·pám′·e·tri·) *n.* the scientific measurement of the human body [Gk. *anthropos*, man; *metron*, a measure].

an·thro·po·mor·phism (an·thrạ·mawr′·fizm) *n.* the conception of God as a human being with human attributes. **anthropomorphist** *n.* **anthropomorphize** *v.t.* to invest with human qualities. **anthropomorphic** *a.* [Gk. *anthropos*, man; *morphe*, form].

an·thro·po·mor·pho·sis (an·thrạ·pạ·mawr′·fō·sis) *n.* transformation into human shape [Gk. *anthropos*, man; *morphe*, form].

an·ti- (an′·ti) *prefix* fr. Gk. *anti*, meaning *against, opposite, instead of*, combining to form derivatives; contracted to **ant-** before a vowel. **anti-aircraft** *a.* used against aircraft.

an·ti·bi·ot·ic (an·ti·bi·át′·ik) *n.* substance which acts as an antibacterial agent [Gk. *anti*, against; *bios*, life].

an·ti·bod·y (an′·ti·bád·i·) *n.* a substance in blood which counteracts growth and harmful action of bacteria; an anti-toxin.

an·tic (an′·tik) *a.* odd; fanciful; fantastic; grotesque; *n.* a buffoon; a comical trick or action [L. *antiquus*, old].

An·ti·christ (an′·ti·krist) *n.* a name given in the New Testament to various incarnations of opposition to Christ.

an·tic·i·pate (an·tis′·ạ·pāt) *v.t.* to be before another; to be beforehand in thought or action; to enjoy prematurely; to forestall. **anticipant** *a.* anticipating; (*Med.*) occurring before the regular time. **anticipation** *n.* the act of anticipating. **anticipative** *a.* full of expectation. **anticipatively, anticipatorily** *adv.* **anticipatory** *a.* happening in advance [L. *ante*, before; *capere*, to take].

an·ti·cli·max (an·ti·klī′·maks) *n.* a sentence or figure of speech in which ideas are arranged in descending order of importance; opp. of *climax*; a sudden drop from the dignified to the trivial.

an·ti·cy·clone (an′·ti·sī′·klōn) *n.* an outward flow of air in a spiral movement (clockwise in N. Hemisphere, anti-clockwise in S. Hemisphere) from an atmospheric area of high pressure, tending to produce steady weather, frosty in winter, hot in summer.

an·ti·dote (an′·ti·dōt) *n.* a remedy which counteracts the effects of a poison; (*Fig.*) anything which counteracts evil. **antidotal** *a.* [Gk. *anti*, against; *doton*, given].

an·ti·freeze (an·ti·frēz′) *n.* a substance added to water in automobile radiators to prevent freezing in very cold weather.

an·ti·gen (an′·ti·jan) *n.* a substance, such as an anti-toxin, which can produce the formation of antibodies in the blood-stream [Gk. *anti*, against; *genesthai*, to be born].

an·ti·his·ta·mine (an·ti·his′·tạ·mēn) *n.* any of several drugs used to treat allergies.

an·ti·knock (an·ti·nạk′) *n.* a substance added to fuel to eliminate or decrease the knocking noise in an internal-combustion engine.

an·ti·log·a·rithm (an·ti·làg′·ạ·rithm) *n.* the complement of a logarithm or of a sine, tangent, or secant; the number corresponding to a logarithm. (*Abbrev.*) **antilog.**

an·til·o·gy (an·til′·ạ·ji·) *n.* a contradiction in terms, or in two separate passages of a book. **antilogous** *a.* [Gk. *logos*, a discourse].

an·ti·ma·cas·sar (an·ti·ma·kas′·ẹr) *n.* an ornamental covering for chair backs, etc. [Gk. *Macassar* oil from Celebes].

an·ti·mo·ny (an′·ti·mōn·i·) *n.* a whitish, brittle chemical element; a bad conductor of heat, it is used as an alloy in medicine and the arts. **antimonial** *a.* **antimoniate** *n.* a salt of antimonic acid. **antimonic, antimonious** *a.* of or containing antimony. **antimonite** *n.* stibnite [L. *antimonium*, antimony].

an·ti·pas·to (àn·ti·pás′·tō) *n.* an appetizer course; hors d'oeuvres [It.].

an·tip·a·thy (an·tip′·ạ·thi·) *n.* opposition; aversion; dislike; enmity; hatred. **antipathetical** *a.* **antipathic** *a.* hostile to; having an opposite nature. **antipathist** *n.* [Gk. *anti*, against; *pathos*, feeling].

an·ti·phon, an·tiph·o·ny (an′·ti·fán) (an·tif′·ạ·ni·) *n.* the chant, or alternate singing, in choirs; an anthem; a response. **-al** *a.; n.* a book of antiphons. **-ally** *adv.* **-ic, -ical** *a.* [doublet of *anthem*].

an·ti·phra·sis (an·tif′·rạ·sis) *n.* (*Rhet.*) use of words in a sense opposite to their proper meaning. **antiphrastic, antiphrastical** *a.* pert. to antiphrasis. **antiphrastically** *adv.* [Gk. *anti*, against; *phrazein*, speak].

an·tip·o·des (an·tip′·ạ·dēz) *n.pl.* those living on opposite side of globe; regions directly opposite any given point on globe; (*Fig.*) anything diametrically opposed to anything else [Gk. *anti*, against; *pous*, a foot].

an·ti·pope (an′·ti·pōp) *n.* one who usurps the papal office; rival to Pope properly elected by Cardinals. **antipapal** *a.*

an·ti·py·ret·ic (an·ti·pī·ret′·ik) *n.* any agent which lowers temperature in fevers; *a.* counteracting fever [Gk. *anti*, against; *puretos*, fever].

an·tique (an·tēk′) *a.* ancient; old-fashioned; obsolete; aged; *n.* relic of bygone times; ancient work of art; the style of ancient art. **antiquarian** *n.* student of antiquity or antiquities; a collector of relics of former times; *a.* pert. to old times or objects; out-of-date; obsolete. **antiquarianism** *n.* study of antiquities. **antiquary** *n.* an antiquarian. **antiquate** *v.t.* to render obsolete. **antiquated** *a.* very old; out of date. **antiquity** *n.* ancient times; former ages; great age; the people of ancient times. **antiquities** *n.pl.* the remains and relics of ancient times; manners and customs of ancient times [Fr. fr. L. *antiquus*, ancient].

an·ti·sem·i·tism (an·ti·sem′·i·tizm) *n.* widespread outburst of hatred against members of the Hebrew race leading to persecution. **antisemite** *n.* one animated with hatred against the Jews. **antisemitic** *a.*

an·ti·sep·sis (an·ti·sep′·sis) *n.* prevention of sepsis; destruction or arresting of growth of living micro-organisms which cause putrefaction. **antiseptic** *n.* a disinfectant; a substance which destroys bacteria; *a.* [Gk. *anti*, against; *sepsis*, putrefaction].

an·ti·so·cial (an·ti·sō′·shạl) *a.* averse to social intercourse; opposed to social order.

an·ti·the·ism (an·ti·thē′·izm) *n.* opposition to the belief in the existence of God. **antitheist** *n.* **antitheistic** *a.*

an·tith·e·sis (an·tith′·ạ·sis) *n.* a direct opposition of words or ideas; a figure in rhetoric in which words or thoughts are set in contrast. *pl.* **antitheses. antithetic, antithetical** *a.*

[Gk. *anti*, opposite; *thesis*, placing].

an·ti·tox·in (an·ti·tạk′·sin) *n.* a toxin which neutralizes another toxin in the blood serum. **antitoxic** *a.* [Gk. *anti*, against; *toxikon*, arrow-poison].

an·ti·trust (an·ti·trust′) *a.* opposed to trusts or monopolies.

ant·ler (ant′·lẹr) *n.* a horn of an animal of the deer family. **-ed** *a.* [L. *ante*, before; *oculus*, the eye].

an·to·nym (an′·tạ·nim) *n.* a word of contrary meaning; the opposite of *synonym* [Gk. *anti*, against; *onoma*, a name].

an·trum (an′·trum) *n.* a cavity, esp. sinus of the upper jaw. *pl.* **antra** [Gk. *antron*].

a·nus (ā′·nus) *n.* the lower orifice of the alimentary canal [L.].

an·vil (an′·vil) *n.* an iron block, usually steel-faced, upon which blacksmith's forgings are hammered and shaped. **-led** *a.* [O.E. *anfilte*].

anx·i·e·ty (ang·zi′·e·ti·) *n.* distress of mind; disquietude; uneasiness; eagerness (to serve, etc.). **anxious** (angk′·shạs) *a.* uneasy; eager. **anxiously** *adv.* [L. *anxius*, anxious].

an·y (en′·i·) *a.* one out of many; some; *adv.* to any extent; at all. **-body** *n.* any person; an ordinary person. **-how** *adv.* at any rate; in a careless manner; in any case. **-one** *pron.* any person. **-thing** *n.* any one thing, no matter what. **-way**, *adv.* in any way or manner; anyhow; carelessly. **-where** *adv.* in any place. **-wise** in any way or respect [O.E. *an*, one]. **A-one** (ā′·wun′) *a.* (*Colloq.*) first class, excellent.

a·or·ta (ā·awr′·tạ) *n.* the great artery leading from the left ventricle of the heart. **aortal, aortic** *a.* [Gk. *aorte*].

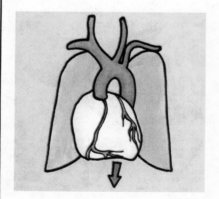

a·pace (ạ·pās′) *adv.* at a quick pace; hastily; swiftly; fast [*a-* and *pace*, at a walk].

A·pach·e (ạ·pa′·chi·) *n.* one of a tribe of American Indians. **apache** (ạ·pàsh′) *n.* a bandit of the Paris underworld, a street hooligan [Amer. Ind. *e patch*, an enemy].

ap·a·nage See **appanage.**

a·part (ạ·pàrt′) *adv.* separately; aside, asunder; at a distance [Fr. *à part*, aside].

a·part·heid (ạ·pàrt′·hād) *n.* racial segregation [S. Afr.].

a·part·ment (ạ·pàrt′·ment) *n.* a room in a house; a suite of rooms; lodgings [Fr. *appartement*, a suite of rooms].

ap·a·thy (ap′·ạth·i·) *n.* want of feeling; indifference. **apathetic** *a.* void of feeling; indifferent; insensible [Gr. *c-*, neg.; *pathos*, feeling].

ape (āp) *n.* a monkey, esp. one without a tail; one of the larger species, e.g. chimpanzee, gorilla, etc.; a mimic; *v.t.* to imitate; to mimic. **-r** *n.* one who apes; a servile imitator. **apery** *n.* mimicry. **apish** *a.* ape-like; inclined to imitate in a foolish manner [O.E. *apa*].

a·per·i·tif (a·pā′·rē·tif) *n.* alcoholic drink taken before meals [L. *aperire*, to open].

ap·er·ture (a′·per·cher) *n.* an opening; a hole [L. *aperire*, to open].

a·pex (ā′·peks) *n.* the top, peak, or summit of anything. *pl.* **apexes** or **apices.**

a·pha·sia (a·fā′·zi·a) *n.* loss of power of expressing ideas in words, often due to brain disease; loss of power of remembering words. **aphasic** *a.* [Gk. *a-*, neg.; *phasis*, speech].

ap·er·ture (a′·per·cher) *n.* an opening; a hole [L. *aperire*, to open].

a·phe·li·on (a·fē′·li·an) *n.* point of planet's orbit most distant from sun [Gk. *apo*, away; *helios*, the sun].

aph·o·rism (af′·er·izm) *n.* a pithy saying; a maxim. **aphoristic** *a.* **aphoristically** *adv.* **aphorize** *v.t.* and *i.* to make or use aphorisms. **aphorist** *n.* [Gk. *aphorismos*, a definition].

a·phra·sia (a·frā′·zi·a) *n.* inability to use connected language; speechlessness [Gk. *a-*, neg.; *phrasis*, speech].

Aph·ro·di·te (af·ra·dī′·tē) *n.* (*Myth.*) the Greek goddess of love and beauty. **aphrodisiac** (af·rō·diz′·i·ak) *a.* exciting sexual desire; *n* anything which so excites.

a·pi·ar·y (ā′·pi·er·i·) *n.* place where bees are kept. **apiarian** (ā·pi·e′·ri·an) *a.* pert. to bees or to bee-keeping. **apiarist** *n.* one who keeps or studies bees. **apiculture** *n.* [L. *apis*, a bee].

a·piece (a·pēs′) *adv.* for each one; to each one [orig. two words].

a·plomb (a·plám′) *n.* perpendicularity; uprightness; (*Fig.*) self-assurance; coolness [L. *ad*, to; *plumbum*, lead].

a·poc·a·lypse (a·pák′·a·lips) *n.* an unveiling of hidden things; revelation; disclosure **Apocalypse** *n.* (*Bib.*) the last book of the New Testament, called the Revelation of St. John. **apocalyptic, -al** pert. to revelation; of style, allegorical; obscure. **apocalyptically** *adv.* [Gk. *apokalupsis*, unveiling].

a·poc·ry·pha (a·pák′·ri·fa) *n.pl.* originally hidden or secret things not suitable to be seen by the uninitiated. **Apocrypha** *n.pl.* (*Bib.*) the collective name for the fourteen books not included in the Old Testament, but incorporated in the Vulgate of the R.C. Church. **apocryphal** *a.* spurious; unauthentic; pert. to the Apocrypha [Gk. *apo*, away; *kruptein*, to hide].

a·pod·o·sis (a·pád′·a·sis) *n.* (*Gram.*) the clause, in a conditional sentence, which expresses result as distinct from the *protasis. pl.* **apodoses** [Gk. *apo*, back; *didonai*, to give].

ap·o·gee (ap′·a·jē) *n.* that point in the orbit of a heavenly body at the greatest distance from the earth (opposed to *perigee*); the culmination; climax; highest point; zenith. **apogeal** (ap·a·jē′·al), **apogean** *a.* [Gk. *apo*, from; *ge*, the earth].

ap·o·logue (ap′·a·lawg) *n.* a parable; a fable [Gk. *apo*, from; *logos*, speech].

a·pol·o·gy (a·pál′·a·ji·) *n.* something spoken in defense; expression of regret at offense; an excuse; a poor substitute (with for). **apologize** *v.i.* to make an apology, or excuse; to express regret. **apologist** *n.* one who makes an apology; a defender of a cause. **apologetic** (a·pál·a·jet′·ik), **apologetical** *a.* **apologetically** *adv.* **apologetics** *n.* the branch of theology charged with the defense of Christianity. **apologia** (ap·a·lō′·ji·a) *n.* a defense in writing of the author's principles, etc. [Gk. *apologia*, a speaking away].

ap·o·thegm (a′·pa·thěm) *n.* a short, pithy saying, a maxim; a proverb. **apothegmatic** (a·pa·theg·mat′·ik), **apothegmatical** *a.* [Gk. *apo*, from; *phthengesthai*, to utter].

ap·o·plex·y (ap′·a·plek·si·) *n.* a sudden loss of consciousness, sensation, and voluntary motion, due generally to rupture of a blood-vessel in the brain. **apoplectic** *a.* [Gk. *apoplexia*].

a·pos·ta·sy (a·pás′·ta·si·) *n.* the act of renouncing one's faith, principles, or party; desertion of a cause. **apostate** *n.* renegade; traitor; deserter; *a.* false; traitorous.

apostatic, -al *a.* **apostatize** *v.i.* to abandon one's faith [Gk. *apo*, apart; *stasis*, a standing].

a pos·te·ri·o·ri (ā·pás·tir′·i·ōr·i) from effect to cause [L. from the subsequent].

a·pos·tle (a·pás′·l) *n.* one sent out to preach or advocate a cause; one of the twelve disciples of Christ sent to preach the Gospel. **apostolate** (a·pás′·ta·lat) *n.* the office or dignity or mission of an apostle. **apostolic, apostolical** *a.* **apostolically** *adv.* **apostolicism** *n.* **Apostles' Creed,** creed supposedly used by apostles, summarizing Christian faith. **Apostolic Church,** church derived from, and incorporating the spirit of, the apostles. **Apostolic see,** the jurisdiction of the Pope. **Apostolic succession,** the derivation of spiritual authority in an unbroken line from the Apostles, through bishops [Gk. *apo*, away; *stellein*, to send].

a·pos·tro·phe (a·pás′·tra·fi) *n.* an address delivered to the absent or the dead, or to an inanimate thing, as if present; a mark (′) indicating possessive case, or omission of one or more letters of a word. **apostrophic** *a.* **apostrophize** *v.t.* and *i.* to address by, or to use, apostrophe [Gk. *apostrophē*, a turning away].

a·poth·e·car·y (a·páth′·a·ker·i·) *n.* one who prepares or sells drugs for medicines [Gk. *apothēkē*, a store house].

a·poth·e·o·sis (a·pá·thi·ō′·sis or a·pá·thē′·a·sis) *n.* the act of raising a mortal to the rank of the gods; deification. **apotheosize** *v.t.* to exalt to the dignity of a god [Gk. *apo*, apart; *theos*, a god].

ap·pall (a·pawl′) *v.t.* to overwhelm with sudden fear; to confound; to scare; to terrify; **-ing** *a.* shocking. [O.Fr. *apalir*, to make pale].

ap·pa·ra·tus (ap·a·rā′·tas or ·rat′·as) *n.* things provided as a means to an end; collection of implements or utensils for effecting an experiment, or given work. *s.* and *pl.* [L. *ad*, to; *parare*, to prepare].

ap·par·el (a·par′·el) *n.* clothing; dress; garments; (*Naut.*) rigging, etc.; *v.t.* to dress; *pr.p.* [O.Fr. *apareiller*, to dress].

ap·par·ent (a·par′·ant) *a.* visible; evident; obvious. **-ly** *adv.* [L. *apparere*, to appear].

ap·pa·ri·tion (ap·a·rish′·an) *n.* appearance (esp. inexplicable); ghost. **-al** *a.* [Fr. fr. L. *apparitio*, appearance].

ap·peal (a·pēl′) *v.i.* to invoke; to call to witness; to solicit aid; (*Law*) to reopen a case before a higher court; to be pleasing to mind or senses. *n.* an urgent call for sympathy or aid; personal attraction. **-able, -ing** *a.* **-ingly** *adv.* **-ingness** *n.* [O.Fr. *apeler*, to call].

ap·pear (a·pēr′) *v.i.* to come in sight; to become visible; to seem; to be obvious or manifest. **-ance** *n.* a coming in sight; semblance; outward look or show; likeness; personal presence. **-er** *n.* [L. *apparere*, to appear].

ap·pease (a·pēz′) *v.t.* to quiet; to calm; to pacify; to satisfy (hunger, etc.); to dispel anger or hatred. **appeasable** *a.* **-ment** *n.* pacifying; policy of making substantial concessions in order to preserve peace. **-r** *n.* [Fr. *apaiser*; O.Fr. *a pais*, at peace].

ap·pel·lant (a·pel′·ant) *n.* (*Law*) one who appeals to a higher court against the verdict of a lower tribunal; one who makes any appeal. **appellancy** *n.* an appeal. **appellate** *a.* (*Law*) pert. to appeals; having power to hear and give decision on appeals. **appellation** *n.* name; title; designation. **appellational** *a.* **appellative** *a.* naming; common to many; pert. to the common noun; *n.* common noun as distinct from *proper* noun. **appellatively** *adv.* **appellee** *n.* (*Law*) the defendant in an appeal [L. *appellare*, to call].

ap·pend (a·pend′) *v.t.* to hang or attach to; to add. **-age** *n.* something added. **-ant** *n.* an adjunct or unessential thing; *a.* hanging to; annexed [L. *appendere*, to hang on].

ap·pen·di·ci·tis (a·pen·di·sī′·tis) *n.* (*Path.*) inflammation of the appendix vermiformis. **appendectomy** (a·pen·dek′·ta·mi·) *n.* surgical removal of appendix [fr. *appendix*].

ap·pen·di·ce (a·pen′·di·kl) *n.* a small appendage. **appendicular** *a.* [L. *appendicula*].

ap·pen·dix (a·pen′·diks) *n.* thing added; an adjunct; supplement at end of book; (*Med.*) the blind tube extending from caecum into pelvis. *pl.* **-es, appendices** [L. *ad*, to; *pendere*, to hang].

ap·per·cep·tion (ap·er·sep′·shan) *n.* (*Philos.*) an act of voluntary consciousness; a mental perception of self as a conscious agent; spontaneous thought [L. *ad*, to; *percipere, perceptum*, to perceive].

ap·per·tain (ap·er·tān′) *v.i.* to belong by nature; to relate. **-ing** *a.* **-ment** *n.* **appertinent** (a·pur′·ta·nant) *a.* belonging to [L. *ad*, to; *pertinere*, to belong].

ap·pe·tite (ap′·a·tit) *n.* desire as for food, drink, rest, etc. **appetitive** *a.* **appetize** *v.t.* to create an appetite. **appetizer** *n.* something taken before a meal to create appetite. **appetizing** *a.* [L. *ad*, to; *petere*, to seek].

ap·plaud (a·plawd′) *v.t.* and *v.* *i.* to praise by clapping; to acclaim; commend; extol. **-er** *n.* **applause** *n.* approval publicly expressed [L. *ad*, to; *plaudere*, to clap].

ap·ple (ap′·l) *n.* fruit of the apple-tree; the apple-tree. **—faced, —cheeked** *a.* of rosy hue. chubby. **— jack** *n.* brandy distilled from hard cider. **—pie order,** perfect order. **— polisher** *n.* (*slang*) flatterer, one who seeks favors by gifts, etc. [O.E. *aeppel*].

ap·pli·ance See under **apply.**

ap·pli·cant (ap′·li·kant) *n.* one who applies; a candidate; a petitioner. **applicability** *n.* the quality of being suitable. **applicable** *a.* suitable; adapted. **applicableness** *n.* **applicably** *adv.* **applicate** *a.* applied or put to some use. **application** *n.* the act of applying; the thing applied; close attention. **applicatory** *a.* [L. *applicare*, to attach to].

ap·plied (a·plid′) *pa.p.* and *pa.t.* of **apply.**

ap·pli·qué (ap·li·kā′) *n.* any ornamentation, sewn or fixed on a material or metal [Fr.].

ap·ply (a·plī′) *v.t.* to place one thing upon another; to employ for a particular purpose; to fix the attention upon; to administer a remedy; *v.i.* to agree with; to be relevant; to have recourse to; to become a candidate. **appliance** *n.* act of applying; thing applied; an instrument or tool [L. *ad*, to; *plicare*, to fold].

ap·point (a·point′) *v.t.* to set apart; to assign; to ordain; to decree; to designate for an office; to fix (a date); to equip. **-ed** *a.* established, furnished. **-ee** *n.* the person appointed. **-ment** *n.* the act of appointing; a new situation; date. **-ments** *n.pl.* equipment; furnishings; fittings [Fr. *à point*, fitly].

ap·por·tion (a·pōr′·shan) *v.t.* to divide and share in just proportion. **-ment** *n.* [L. *ad*, to; *portio*, a share].

ap·po·site (ap′·a·zit) *a.* appropriate; well adapted. **-ly** *adv.* **-ness** *n.* **apposition** (ap·a·zish′·an) *n.* the act of placing beside; (*Gram.*) the relation to a noun (or pronoun) of a noun, adjective, or clause, added by way of explanation. **appositional** *a.* [L. *appositus*, put near].

ap·praise (a·prāz′) *v.t.* to put a price upon; to fix the value of. **appraisal** *n.* the act of appraising; a valuation. **-ment** *n.* **-r** *n.* **appraising** *a.* [L. *ad*, to; *pretium*, price].

ap·pre·ci·ate (a·prē′·shi·āt) *v.t.* to value justly; *v.i.* to rise in value. **appreciation** (a·prē·shi·ā′·shan) *n.* the setting of a value on; a just estimate; rise in value. **appreciative, appreciatory** *a.* **appreciatively** *adv.* **appreciable** *a.* that may be estimated. **appreciably** *adv.* [L. *ad*, to; *pretium*, price].

ap·pre·hend (ap·ri·hend′) *v.t.* to seize; to arrest; to understand; to fear. **apprehensible** *a.* **apprehension** *n.* **apprehensive** *a.* filled with dread; suspicious. **apprehensively** *adv.* [L. *ad*, to; *prehendere*, to grasp].

ap·pren·tice (a·pren′·tis) *n.* one bound to another to learn a trade or art; beginner; *v.t.* to bind as apprentice. **-ship** *n.* [L. *ad*, to; *prehendere*, to grasp].

ap·prise (a·priz′) *v.t.* to inform; to tell; to give notice [Fr. *apprendre*, to inform].

ap·proach (a·prōch′) *v.i.* to come near; *v.t.* to come near to; to enter into negotiations with; to resemble; (*Golf*) to play a shot intended to reach the green; *n.* the act of drawing near; access; a road; approximation; negotiation. **-es** *n.pl.* the works thrown up by besiegers in their advances towards a fortress. **-able** *a.* accessible. **-ability** *n.* [L. *ad*, to; *prope*, near].

ap·pro·ba·tion (ap·ra·bā′·shan) *n.* approval; sanction. **approbate** *v.t.* to approve of. **approbative, approbatory** *a.* approving [L. *ad*, to; *probare*, to test].

ap·pro·pri·ate (a·prō′·pri·āt) *v.t.* to take as one's own; to set apart for a particular purpose; to claim; *a.* suitable; fitting. **-ly** *adv.* **-ness** *n.* **appropriation** *n.* the act of setting apart. **appropriative** *a.* **appropriator** *n.* [L. *ad*, to; *proprius*, one's own].

ap·prove (a·prōōv′) *v.t.* to be pleased with; to commend; to accept; to sanction officially. **approval** *n.* approving [L. *ad*, to; *probare*, to test].

ap·prox·i·mate (a·prák′·si′·māt) *v.t.* to come near to; to bring near; *a.* near to; nearly correct; not quite exact. **-ly** *adv.* **approximation** *n.* a coming near; a close estimate [L. *ad*, to; *proximus*, near].

ap·pur·te·nance (a·pur′·ta·nans) *n.* that which appertains or is annexed to another thing; adjunct; accessory. **appurtenant** *a.* [O.Fr. *apartenance*, a belonging].

a·pri·cot (ā′·pri·kặt) *n.* an oval, orange-yellow fruit [L. *praecox*, early ripe].

A·pril (ā′·pril) *n.* the fourth month of the year [L. *Aprilis*, fr. *aperire*, to open].

à pri·o·ri (ặ·pri·ō′·ri·) from cause to effect [L. from something prior].

a·pron (ā′·pran) *n.* a covering or protection worn in front to protect the clothes; concrete-surfaced area in front of aircraft hangar [O.Fr. *naperon*, a cloth].

a·pro·pos (a·prạ·pō′) *adv.* at the right time; *adj.* apt, relevant [Fr.].

apse (aps) *n.* semi-circular recess at east end of church. **apsidal** *a.* [Gk. *hapsis*, loop].

ap·sis (ap′·sis) *n.* the point at which a planet is nearest to, or farthest from, the sun; *pl.* **apsides** (ap′·si·dēz). **apsidal** *a.* [Gk. *hapsis*, a loop, a vault].

apt (apt) *a.* fit; suitable; prompt; quick-witted. **-ly** *adv.* **aptitude** *n.* natural capacity for; suitableness; faculty for learning; talent. **-ness** *n.* fitness; appropriateness [L. *aptus*, fit].

aq·ua (ak′·wạ, ā′·kwa) *n.* L. = water. **aqua fortis** *n.* nitric acid. **aqua pura**, pure water. **aqua vitae**, any distilled alcoholic liquor.

aq·ua·ma·rine (ak·wạ·ma·rēn) *n.* a semi-precious stone; *a.* of a sea-green color [L. *aqua*, water; *mare*, the sea].

aq·ua·plane (ak′·wạ·plān) *n.* a plank or boat towed by a fast motor-boat [L. *aqua*, water; *planus*, flat].

a·quar·i·um (ạ·kwā′·ri·ạm) *n.* a glass tank in which is kept living specimens of water animals and plants; *pl.* **-s**, or **aquaria** [L. *aqua*, water].

A·quar·i·us (ạ·kwā′·ri·us) *n.* (*Astron.*) the Waterbearer, the 11th sign of the Zodiac.

a·quat·ic (ạ·kwat′·ik) *a.* growing or living in water; practiced on, or in, water [L. *aqua*, water].

aq·ua·tint (ak′·wạ·tint) *n.* an etching process; *v.i.* [L. *aqua*, water, and *tint*].

aq·ue·duct (ak′·we·dukt) *n.* a course, channel, or bridge for conveying water either under or above ground [L. *aqua*, water; *ducere*, to lead].

a·que·ous (ā′·kwi·ạs) *a.* watery; made of, or from, water. **-ly** *adv.* [L. *aqua*, water; *ferre*, to bear].

aq·ui·line (ak′·wi·līn, ·lin) *a.* belonging to the eagle; curving; hooked like the beak of an eagle [L. *aquila*, an eagle].

Ar·ab (ar′·ạb) *n.* native of Arabia; an Arab horse. **street arab**, a homeless urchin of the streets. **Arabian** (ạ·rā′·bi·ạn) *n.* the native of Arabia; *a.* relating to Arabia. **Arabic** (ar′·a·bik) *n.* the language of the Arabians.

Arabian horse

ar·a·besque (ar·ạ·besk′) *n.* an ornament after the Arabian manner, with intricate interlacing of foliage, fruits, etc. **arabesqued** *a.* [It. *Arabesco*, Arabian-like). [L. *arare*, to plough].

ar·a·ble (ar′·ạ·bl) *a.* fit for ploughing or tillage

a·rach·nid (a·rak′·nid) *n.* one of the *Arachnida*, the spiders, scorpions, mites, etc. **arachnoid** *a.* resembling *Arachnida*; cobweb-like. **arachnoidal** *a.* [Gk. *arachne*, a spider].

ar·bi·ter (ár′·bi·tẹr) *n.* (*fem.* **arbitress**) an umpire; a judge in a dispute; one who has supreme control. **arbitrable** *a.* capable of settlement by discussion. **arbitrage** *n.* **arbitral** *a.* pertaining to an arbiter or arbitration. **arbitrary** *a.* guided by will only; high-handed; despotic; absolute. **arbitrarily** *adv.* **arbitrariness** *n.* **arbitrate** *v.t.* and *v.i.* to hear and give an authoritative decision in a dispute. **arbitration** *n.* a method of settling disputes between persons, parties and nations by an agreement on both sides to accept the findings of a third party. **arbitrator** *n.* (*fem.* **arbitratrix**) a referee; an umpire [L. *arbiter*, a judge].

ar·bor (ár′·bẹr) *n.* the Latin word for a *tree*.

ar·bo·ra·ceous *a.* tree-like; wooded; **arboreal** *a.* living in trees. **arboreous** *a.* wooded. **arborescent** *a.* growing like a tree. **arboretum** *n.* botanical garden for special planting and growing of trees; (*pl.* arboreta). **arborous** *a.* formed by trees [L. *arbor*, a tree].

ar·bor (ár′·bẹr) *n.* a garden seat sheltered or enclosed by trees; a bower; a shady retreat. [L. *arbor*, a tree).

ar·bu·tus (ár·bū′·tạs) *n.* evergreen shrub with scarlet berries. [L. *arbutus*, the wild strawberry tree].

arc (árk) *n.* a curved line or any part of a curve forming segment of a circle; the arc-shaped band of light formed by passage of an electric current between two carbon points. **— lamp**, *n.* an electric lamp making use of electric arc, used in spotlights, searchlights, etc. **— welding**, *n.* a method of joining metals by use of electric arc [L. *arcus*, bow].

ar·cade (ár·kād′) *n.* a series of arches, generally supported by pillars; a walk, arched above; a covered street, usually with shops on both sides [L. *arcus*, bow].

Ar·ca·di·a (ár·kā′·di·ạ) *n.* region in the Peloponnesus conceived by poets to be a land of shepherds and shepherdesses. **Arcadian** *a.* Arcady *n.* an ideal rustic place.

ar·ca·num (ár·kā′·num) *n.* a secret; mystery. *pl.* arcana [L. *arcanum*, secret].

arch (árch) *a.* cunning; sly; mischievous; roguish. **-ness** *n.* [Gk. *archein*, to rule].

arch (árch) *prefix* used as *a.* chief; first of a class, as in *arch-bishop*, etc. **-angel** *n.* an angel of supreme order. **-deacon** *n.* a Church dignitary next below bishop. **-duke** *n.* a grand duke. **-duchess** *n.* **-duchy** *n.* the territory of an archduke. **-ducal** *a.* **-enemy** *n.* chief enemy [Gk. *archein*, to rule].

arch (árch) *n.* an arc of a circle; a structure for support; *v.t.* or *v.i.* to form an arch; to bend into an arch. **-ed** *a.* **-way** *n.* arched passage or entrance [L. *arca*, a chest, and *arcus*, a bow].

ar·chae·ol·o·gy, archeology (ár·kē·ál′·ạ·ji·) *n.* the study of human antiquities. **archaeologist** *n.* **archaeological** *a.* [Gk. *archaios*, ancient; *logos*, a discourse].

ar·cha·ic (ár·kā′·ik) *a.* antiquated; ancient; antique; obsolete; primitive. **archaically** *adv.* **archaism** *n.* a word, expression or idiom out of date. **archaist** *n.* an antiquary; one who revives the use of archaisms in his writings. **archaistic** *a.* [Gk. *archaios*, ancient].

ar·che·an (ár·kē′·an) *a.* pert. to the oldest period of geological time [Gk. *archaios*, ancient].

arch·er (árch′·ẹr) *n.* one who shoots with a bow; a bowman. **-y** *n.* art and practice of shooting with bow and arrow [L. *arcus*, a bow].

ar·che·type (ár′·kẹ·tīp) *n.* the original pattern or model from which a thing is made or copied; prototype. **archetypal** *a.* [Gk. *archi-*, chief; *tupos*, a model].

ar·chi·pel·a·go (ár·ki·pel′·ạ·gō) *n.* name originally of Aegean Sea; a group of islands; a stretch of water scattered with isles; *pl.* **archipelagoes**. **archipelagic** (·aj′·ik) *a.* [Gk. *archi-*, chief; *pelagos*, the sea].

ar·chi·tect (ár′·ka·tekt) *n.* one skilled in the art of building; designer or contriver. **architectonics** *n.pl.* the science or art of architecture. **architectural** *a.* **architecturally** *adv.* **architecture** *n.* the art of building; a distinct style of designing buildings [Gk. *archi-*, chief; *tekton*, worker].

ar·chives (ár′·kīvz) *n.pl.* place in which public or historical records, charters and documents are stored and preserved; public records. **archival** *a.* **archivist** *n.* a keeper of archives [Gk. *archeion*, a town-hall].

arc·tic (árk′·tik) *a.* pert. to the regions near the N. Pole; northern; extremely cold; frigid [Gk. *arktos*, a bear].

ar·dent (ár′·dẹnt) *a.* burning; passionate; eager. **-ly** *adv.* **ardency** *n.* warmth of passion; zeal. **ardor** (ár′·dẹr) *n.* heat; warmth of affection; eagerness; zeal [L. *ardere*, to burn].

ar·du·ous (ár′·dū·ạs) *a.* high and lofty; steep; difficult to overcome; laborious; strenuous. **-ly** *adv.* [L. *arduus*, steep].

are (ár) present indicative plural of the verb **to be** [O.E. *aron*].

are (ār) *n.* metric unit of land measure containing 100 square meters, about 119.6 square yards [Fr. fr. L. *area*]

a·re·a (ā′·ri·ạ) *n.* an open space; a tract of

land; a region; scope; total outside surface of a thing; superficial extent [L. *area*, open space].

a·re·na (ạ·rē′·nạ) *n.* oval space of a Roman amphitheater, any place of public contest; a battlefield. **arenaceous** (ar·ạ·nā′·shạs), *a.* like sand; sandy [L. *arena*, sand].

ar·e·om·e·ter (a·re·ám′·e·tẹr) *n.* an instrument for measuring the specific gravity of fluids [Gk. *araios*, rare; *metron*, a measure].

a·rete (a·rāt′) *n.* a sharp mountain ridge; a rocky spur [Fr. = a fish-bone].

ar·gent (ár′·jent) *a.* made of, or like, silver; silvery; *n.* white or silver color in heraldry. **-iferous** *a.* bearing silver. **-ine** *a.* pert. to, or like, silver; sounding like silver; *n.* a variety of carbonate of lime [L. *argentum*, silver].

ar·gil (ár′·jil) *n.* pure clay; potter's earth. [L. *argilla*, white clay].

ar·gon (ár′·gạn) *n.* an inert gas used for filling electric light bulbs [Gk. *argos*, inactive].

ar·go·sy (ár′·gạ·si·) *n.* a large, richly-laden merchant ship [earlier *ragusye*, a ship of *Ragusa*, a Dalmatian port].

ar·got (ár′·gō, ár′·gat) *n.* slang; cant; special vocabulary [Fr.].

ar·gue (ár′·gū) *v.t.* to prove by reasoning; to discuss; to persuade by debate; *v.i.* to prove; to offer reasons; to dispute. **arguable** *a.* capable of being argued. **-r** *n.* one who argues. **argument** *n.* a reason offered in proof for or against a thing; the subject of a speech, etc. **argumentation** *n.* arguing; reasoning. **argumentative** *a.* given to arguing; contentious. **argumentatively** *adv.* **argumentativeness** *n.* [L. *arguere*, to chide].

a·ri·a (á′·ri·ạ, a′·ri·ạ) *n.* (*Mus.*) a melody as distinct from harmony; a solo part in a cantata, opera, oratorio, etc., with musical accompaniment [It. *aria*, an air].

ar·id (ar′·id) *a.* dry; parched; barren; (*Fig.*) uninteresting. **aridity** *n.* absence of moisture; dryness; barrenness [L. *aridus*].

a·right (ạ·rit′) *adv.* rightly [E. *on right*].

a·rise (ạ·riz′) *v.i.* to come up; to stand up; to get up; to come into view; to spring up; to occur; *pr.p.* **arising**. *pap.* **arisen** (ạ·rizn′). *pa.t.* **arose** [O.E. *arisan*].

ar·is·toc·ra·cy (ar·is·ták′·rạ·si·) *n.* originally the rule of the best; later, the rule of an hereditary upper class; privileged class in a state; the nobility; upper classes. **aristocrat** (a·ris′·tạ·krat) *n.* a member of the aristocracy. **aristocratic** *a.* **aristocratically** *adv.* [Gk. *aristos*, best; *kratos*, power].

Ar·is·tot·le (ar·is·tát′·l) *n.* (384-322 B.C.), a great Greek philosopher, pupil and disciple of Plato. **Aristotelian** (ar·is·tạ·tē′·li·ạn) *n.* a follower of Aristotle.

a·rith·me·tic (ạ·rith′·mạ·tik) *n.* the science of numbers; the art of reckoning by figures; a work on this subject. **arithmetical** *a.* **arithmetically** *adv.* **arithmetician** (ạ·rith·mạ-·tish′·an) *n.* one skilled in arithmetic. **arithmetical progression**, a series of numbers which increase or decrease by a common difference, e.g. 2, 4, 6, 8, or 21, 18, 15, 12 [Gk. *arithmos*, number].

ark (árk) *n.* the large floating vessel in which Noah lived during the Flood (Genesis 6-8); vessel of bulrushes in which the infant Moses was placed (Exodus 2). **ark of the Covenant**, the chest containing the two Tables of the Law, a pot of manna, and Aaron's rod (Exodus 25); a chest; a coffer [O.E. *arc*, a box].

arm (árm) *n.* the limb extending from shoulders to hand; anything projecting from main body, as a branch; *v.t.* to give an arm to for support. **-less** *a.* without arms. **-ful** *n.* as much as the arms can hold. **—chair** *n.* a chair with arms. **—pit** *n.* the cavity under the shoulder. **at arm's length**, at a safe distance. **with open arms**, cordially [O.E. *earm*].

arm (árm) *n.* a weapon; a branch of the army, e.g. infantry, artillery, etc.; *pl.* all weapons; exploits; military profession; armor; heraldic bearings; *v.t.* to equip with weapons; *v.i.* to take up arms. **-ed** (ármd, or árm′·ed) *a.* equipped with, or supported by, arms; fortified; strengthened. **armed neutrality**, the condition of holding aloof from a contest, while ready to repel attack. **small arms**, weapons that can be carried by hand, e.g. pistols, revolvers, shotguns, rifles, etc. **under arms**, enlisted for military service; fully equipped for battle. **up in arms**, eager to give battle; roused to anger. **to lay down arms**, to surrender [L. *arma*, weapons].

ar·ma·da (ár·má′·dạ, ár·mä′·dạ) *n.* a fleet of armed ships [Sp. *armar*, to arm].

ar·ma·dil·lo (är·mạ·dil′·ō) *n.* an animal, having the body encased in armor-like covering of small, bony shell plates [Sp. dimin. of *armado*, a man-in-armor].

Ar·ma·ged·don (är·mạ·ged′·ạn) *n.* the scene of the last battle between the powers of good and evil, before Day of Judgment; final decisive battle between great nations. [Or. *Megiddo*, in Palestine].

ar·ma·ment (är′·mạ·mạnt) *n.* land, naval, or air forces equipped for war; munitions; the process of equipping forces in time of war [L. pl. *armamenta*, equipment].

ar·ma·ture (är′·mạ·chẹr) *n.* armor; protective covering (of plants); part of magnet or dynamo which rotates in electrical generator; coil of wire in electric motor which breaks magnetic field [L. *armare*, to arm].

ar·mi·stice (är′·mi·stis) *n.* a temporary or lasting cessation of hostilities; a truce [L. *arma*, weapons; *sistere*, to cause to stop].

arm·let (ärm′·lit) *n.* a small arm, as of sea; band worn round arm. [O.E. *earm*].

ar·mor (är′·mẹr) *n.* defensive covering for the body in battle; orig. chain-mail, etc.; steel plates used to protect ships of war, tanks, cars, etc. **-bearer** *n.* one who carried arms of a superior. **—clad** *a.* **-ed car**, a metal-plated car with machine-gun in revolving turret. **-ed division**, a mobile unit with tanks, armored cars, etc. [L. *armare*, to arm].

ar·mor·y (är′·mẹr·i·) *n.* place where arms are stored; building for headquarters and drill area of National Guard unit; arsenal; (*Arch.*) science of heraldry. [L. *arma*, weapons or arms].

ar·my (är′·mi·) *n.* a body of men trained and equipped for war; a military force commanded by a general; an organized body for some special purpose, e.g. *Salvation Army*; large number of people. **army corps**, a large unit comprising various branches of the service. **standing army**, the regular army in peacetime [L. *arma*, weapons].

a·ro·ma (ạ·rō′·mạ) *n.* fragrance in plants; perfume or flavor; charm; atmosphere. **aromatic** *a.* fragrant; spicy; *n.* a plant, drug with fragrant smell [Gk. *aroma*, spice].

a·round (ạ·round′) *adv.* in a circle; near; *prep.* on all sides of; about [E. *a*, on; *round*].

a·rouse (ạ·rouz′) *v.t.* to excite to action; to awaken; *v.i.* to wake; to become active. **arousal** *n.* [E. *a*, on, and *rouse*].

ar·peg·gi·o (är·pe′·ji·ō) *n.* (*Mus.*) the sounding of notes of a chord in quick succession [It. *arpeggiare*, to play the harp].

ar·que·bus (är′·kwi·bạs) *n.* an ancient form of handgun. Also **harqueous**. **arquebusier** *n.* [O.H.Ger. *Haken*, hook; *Büchse*, a gun].

ar·raign (a·rān′) *v.t.* to call or set a prisoner at the bar; to call to account; to accuse publicly. **-ment** *n.* [L. *ad*, to; *ratio*, account].

ar·range (ạ·rānj′) *v.t.* to put into order; to settle terms; to prepare; to adapt; to adjust; *v.i.* to make agreement; to take steps. **-ment** *n.* act of arranging; the way or manner in which things are placed; needful preparation; (*Mus.*) transcription or adaptation of a piece of music to an instrument other than that for which it was originally composed. **-r** *n.* [Fr. *rang*, rank]. [utter. **-ly** *adv.* (doublet of errant).

ar·rant (ar′·ạnt) *a.* notorious; unmitigated;

ar·ras (ar′·ạs) *n.* tapestry; large tapestries, used as wall hangings [fr. the city of *Arras*, France, where first woven].

ar·ray (ạ·rā′) *v.t.* to set in order; to draw up, as troops for battle; to dress; to equip; *n.* order; equipment; fine apparel [O.Fr. *aréer*].

ar·rear (ạ·rēr′) *n.* the state of being behind. **-s** *n.pl.* moneys still owing; work still to be overtaken. **-age** *n.* [Fr. *arrière*, behind].

ar·rest (ạ·rest′) *v.t.* to stop; to check; to hinder; to seize by authority of law; to engage the attention; *n.* the apprehending of a person by the authority of law; any seizure, physical or moral; stoppage. **arrestation** *n.* act of arresting. **-er**, **-or** *n.* one who, or that which, arrests. **-ing** *a.* impressive; striking. **-ive** *a.* calculated to draw attention. **-ment** *n.* an arrest of a criminal; the seizure of a person's wages, etc. in debt claims [O.Fr. *arester*].

ar·rive (ạ·rīv′) *v.i.* to reach a point; to come to; to attain to any aim or object. **arrival** *n.* act of arriving [Fr. *arriver*, to arrive].

ar·ro·gance (ar′·ạ·gạns) *n.* insolent pride; intolerable presumption; overbearing manner. **arrogant** *a.* presuming on one's rank or pow-

er; haughty; proud. **arrogantly** *adv.* **arrogate** *v.t.* to claim unduly; to take upon one's self without authority; to demand overbearingly; to presume [L. *ad*, for; *rogare*, to ask].

ar·row (ar′·ō) *n.* a barbed missile shot from a bow; a sign ➤ to show direction. **-y** *a.* of, like an arrow. **—grass** *n.* small, erect, grass-like plants **-head** *n.* wedge end of an arrow, the head as separate from the shaft [O. E. *arwe*].

ar·row·root (ar′·ō·ròòt) *n.* a nutritious starch used in puddings, cookies, etc. [So-called because used to counteract the poison of arrows].

ar·roy·o (ạ·roi′·ō) *n.* gulch, small watercourse having steep sides and usually dry [Sp.].

ar·se·nal (är′·sạn·ạl) *n.* factory for military and naval arms and stores; an armory [It. *arsenale*, fr. Ar. *al-sina′ah*, workshop].

ar·se·nic (är′·sạ·nik) *n.* a semi-metallic element; the poisonous, whitish, or steel-grey powder of white oxide of arsenic. **arsenic**, **arsenical** *a.* **arsenous** *a.* [Gk. *arsēn*, male. The alchemists classed metals as male and female].

ar·son (är′·sạn) *n.* the crime of intentionally setting on fire houses, buildings, ships, or other property [L. *ardere*, *arsum*, to burn].

art (ärt) *n.* skill; human skill as opposed to nature; skill applied to music, painting, poetry, etc.; any of the subjects of this skill; a system of rules; a profession or craft; cunning; trick. **arts** *n.pl.* certain branches of learning, languages, history, etc. as distinct from natural science. **-ful** *a.* exhibiting art or skill; crafty; cunning. **-fully** *adv.* **-fulness** *n.* **-less** *a.* free from art; guileless. **-lessly** *adv.* **-lessness** *n.* **-y** *a.* (*Colloq.*) affectedly artistic. **black art**, magic. **fine arts**, painting, sculpture, architecture, music. **useful arts**, those in which the hands, rather than the mind, are used [L. *ars*, *artis*].

ar·ter·y (är′·te·ri·) *n.* a vessel carrying blood from the heart; (*Fig.*) any essential channel of communication. **arterial** (är·tē′·ri·ạl) *a.* pert. to an artery; pert. to a first-class road. **arterialize** *v.t.* to change venous blood into arterial blood by oxygenation. **arterialization** *n.* **arteriole** *n.* a small artery. **arteriosclerosis** *n.* (*Med.*) a hardening of the arteries [Gk. *arteria*, the windpipe, an artery; *logos*, discourse; *skleros*, hard].

ar·te·sian well (är·tē′·zhạn wel) *n.* a well bored deep enough so that water rises to the surface of the ground by internal pressure (the first such well was sunk at *Artois* in the 12th cent.) [Fr. *Artésien*].

ar·thri·tis (är·thrī′·tis) *n.* inflammation of a joint; gout. **arthritic(al)** (är·thrit′·ik) *a.*

ar·thro·pod (är′·thrạ·pàd) *n.* an animal with segmented body and jointed limbs, e.g. a spider, crustacean, etc. **arthropodal** *a.* [Gk. *arthron*, a joint; *pous*, *podos*, a foot].

ar·ti·choke (är′·ti·chōk) *n.* a plant with thistlelike head, which can be cooked and the fleshy base eaten. **Jerusalem artichoke** *n.* an entirely different plant, bearing edible tubers which resemble the potato in appearance [It. *articiocco*, fr. Ar., Jerusalem is corrupt. of It. *girasole*, sun-flower].

ar·ti·cle (är′·ti·kl) *n.* a clause or term in a contract, treaty, etc.; a literary composition in a journal, etc.; a paragraph or section; a point of faith; a rule or condition; an item; a commodity or object; (*Gram.*) one of the words *a*, *an* (the indefinite article) and *the* (the definite article); *v.t.* to apprentice; to accuse specifically [L. *articulus*, a little joint].

ar·tic·u·lar (är·tik′·yoo·lạr) *a.* pert. to the joints [L. *articulus*, a little joint].

ar·tic·u·late (är·tik′·yoo·lāt) *v.t.* to connect by a joint; to utter clearly-defined sounds; *v.i.* to be connected by joints; to speak in distinct syllables or words; *a.* jointed; of speech, clear, distinct. **-ly** *adv.* **-ness** *n.* **articulation** *n.* the act of articulating; a consonant; a joint between two or more bones [L. *articulus*, a little joint, fr. *artus*, a limb].

ar·ti·fact (är′·ti·fakt) *n.* object made by man [L. *ars*, *artis*, art; *facere*, to make].

ar·ti·fice (är′·ti·fis) *n.* an artful or skilful contrivance; a ruse; a trick; cunning. **artificer** *n.* a skilled workman; an inventor. **artificial** (är·ti·fish′·ạl) *a.* made by art; manufactured; affected in manners. **artificially** *adv.* **artificiality** *n.* [L. *artificium*, a trade, fr. *ars*, art; *facere*, to make].

ar·til·ler·y (är·til′·ạ·ri·) *n.* cannon; troops trained in the use of guns; a branch of the armed forces. **artilleryman** *n.* a soldier serving in the artillery [Fr. *artillerie*, fr. O.Fr. *artillier*, to equip].

ar·ti·san (är′·ti·zạn) *n.* a craftsman; a mechanic [Fr. fr. L. *ars*, *artis*, art].

art·ist (är′·tist) *n.* one who practices one of the fine arts, e.g. painting, sculpture, etc.; applicable to any craftsman whose work is of high standard. **-ic(al)** *a.* **-ically** *adv.* **artistry** (ar′·tis·tri·) *n.* artistic ability or effect; beauty of work [L. *ars*, *artis*, art].

ar·tiste (är·tēst′) *n.* an expert in some art, not one of the fine arts; often applied to a member of the theatrical profession [L. *ars*, *artis*, art].

Ar·y·an (ā′·ri·ạn) *n.* the progenitors of the Indo-European group, i.e. Celtic, Teutonic, etc. [Sans. *Arya*, noble].

as (az) *adv.* like; in like manner; similar to; for example; *conj.* since; because; when; while; *pron.* that [form of *also*].

as·bes·tos (as·bes′·tạs) *n.* a fibrous non-inflammable mineral, used in manufacture of fire-proof materials [Gk. *a-*, neg.; *sbestos*, to be quenched].

as·cend (ạ·send′) *v.t.* to climb, to mount; to walk up; *v.i.* to rise; to arise; to soar; to climb; to mount; to go back in time. **-able**, **-ible** *a.* **-ancy**, **-ency** *n.* superior or controlling influence; authority; domination [L. *ad*, to; *scendere*, to climb].

as·cent (ạ·sent′) *n.* the act of rising; the way by which one rises; a slope; a way up [L. *ad*, to; *scandere*, to climb].

as·cer·tain (as·ẹr·tān′) *v.t.* to get to know; to find out for a certainty. **-able** *a.* **-ment** *n.* [L. *ad*, to; *certus*, sure].

as·cet·ic (ạ·set′·ik) *a.* sternly self-denying; austere; strict; *n.* one who practices rigorous self-denial; a hermit; an anchorite. **asceticism** *n.* **-ally** *adv.* [Gk. *askein*, to exercise].

as·cot (as′·kạt) *n.* a kind of scarf or broad tie.

as·cribe (as·krīb′) *v.t.* to attribute; to impute; to assign. **ascribable** *a.* **ascription** *n.* [L. *ascribere*, to add in writing].

a·sep·sis (ạ·sep′·sis) *n.* freedom from putrefaction; freeing from bacteria by use of antiseptics. **aseptic** *a.* not liable to putrefaction; sterilized [Gk. *a-*, neg.; *sepsis*, decay].

a·sex·u·al (ā·sek′·shoo·ạl) *a.* without sex; lacking sexual instinct or reproductive organs. **asexuality** *n.* [L. *a*, away; *sexus*, sex].

ash (ash) *n.* a genus of trees of the olive family having a tough, hard, elastic wood. **-en** *a.* [O.E. *aesce*, the ash-tree].

ash (ash) *n.* the dry white or greyish dust left after a substance has been burned. **-es** *n.pl.* the remains of a human body after cremation; (*Fig.*) a dead body; (*Chem.*) potash. (*Naval Slang*) a depth-charge; a multiple arc lamp used in theaters. **-en** *a.* of the color of ashes; pale. **— tray** *n.* receptacle for cigarette ash. **-y** *a.* **Ash Wednesday**, the first day of Lent [M.E. *asche*, ash].

a·shamed (ạ·shāmd′) *a.* affected by shame; covered with confusion, caused by awareness of guilt [O.E. *ascamian*, to be ashamed].

a·shore (ạ·shōr′) *adv.* on or to shore; on land, opp. to aboard [E. *a*, on; M. E. *shore* fr. O.E. *sciran*, to shear].

A·sian, **A·si·at·ic** (ā′·zhạn, ā·zhi·at′·ik) *a.* pert. to Asia or to the people of Asia [Gk. *Asia*, a part of Lydia].

a·side (ạ·sīd′) *n.* something said in an undertone, esp. on stage by an actor and supposed not to be heard by the other actors; *adv.* on or to one side; apart; dismissed from use [O.E. *a*, on; *sid*, broad].

as·i·nine (as′·in·īn) *a.* pert. to an ass; stupid. **asininity** *n.* [L. *asinus*, an ass].

ask (ask) *v.t.* to seek information; to interrogate; *v.i.* (*for*, *about*) to request; to inquire. **-er** *n.* [O.E. *ascian*, to seek].

a·skance, **a·skant** (ạ·skans′, ạ·skant′) *adv.* towards one corner of the eye; awry; with disdain or suspicion; not straightforward.

a·skew (ạ·skū′) *adv.* askant; aside; awry; obliquely; off the straight [See **skew**].

a·slant (ạ·slant′) *adv.* in a slanting direction.

a·sleep (ạ·slēp′) *adv.* and *a.* in a state of sleep; at rest; benumbed; dormant; dead.

a·slope (ạ·slōp′) *a.* sloping; tilted; oblique. *adv.* with a slope [O.E. *slūpan*, to slip].

a·so·cial (ā·sō′·shạl) *a.* not social, selfish [Gk. *a-*, neg.; social]. [poisonous serpent [Gk. *aspis*].

asp, as·pic (asp, asp'·ik) *n.* a small, hooded,
as·par·a·gus (as·par'·a·gas) *n.* a succulent
vegetable with tender shoots [Gk.].

as·pect (as'·pekt) *n.* look; appearance; position
or situation; view [L. *aspicere*, look at].
as·pen (as'·pin) *n.* a tree known also as the
trembling poplar; *a.* trembling [O.E. *aespe*].

as·per·ate (as·per'·āt) *v.t.* to make harsh or
uneven; to roughen [L.].
as·per·i·ty (as·per'·i·ti·) *n.* roughness of surface, manner, or speech; harshness; crabbed-
ness; sharpness; acrimony [L. *asper*, rough].
as·perse (as·purs') *v.t.* to slander; to defame;
to vilify; to calumniate; to bespatter (with).
-er *n.* **aspersion** *n.* slander. **aspersive, as·**
persory *a.* [L. *ad*, to; *spargere*, to sprinkle].
as·phalt (as'·fawlt), *n.* a black, hard, tar-like
substance, used for paving, roofing, etc. **as·**
phalt *v.t.* to cover with asphalt. **asphaltic** *a.*
bituminous [Gk. *asphaltos*].
as·phyx·i·a, as·phyx·y (as·fik'·si·a, -si·) *n.*
suspended animation due to lack of oxygen in
the blood; it is caused by obstructed breathing, as in drowning, inhalation of gases, etc.
-te *v.t.* to suffocate. **-tion** *n.* [Gk. *asphuxia*,
pulse stoppage].
as·pic (as'·pik) *n.* the asp; (*Bot.*) the great
lavender [L. *spica*, a spike].
as·pic (as'·pik) *n.* savory jelly containing
pieces of fish, fowl, egg, etc. [Fr.].
as·pi·rate (as'·pi·rāt) *v.t.* to pronounce with
a full breathing sound; to prefix the sound *h*
to a word or letter; *n.* a letter marked with a
note of breathing; a breathed sound; *a.* pronounced with a rough breathing. **aspiration**
n. act of breathing; (*Med.*) the removal of
fluids from a cavity in the body by suction [L.
aspiratus, breathed upon].
as·pire (as·pīr') *v.i.* to desire with eagerness;
to strive towards something higher (usually
followed by *to* or *after*). **aspirant** *a.* ambitious; *n.* one who aspires; a candidate. **aspira-**
tion *n.* -**r** *n.* [L. *ad*, to; *spirare*, breathe].
as·pi·rin (as'·pi·rin) *n.* a drug used for relief
of headache, fever, etc.
ass (as) *n.* a quadruped of the horse family; a
donkey; (*Fig.*) a stupid person [L. *asinus*].

as·sail (a·sāl') *v.t.* to leap or fall on; to attack;
to assault; to ply with arguments, reproaches,
etc. **-able** *a.* **-ant** *a.* and *n.* [L. *ad*, to; *salire*,
to leap].
as·sas·sin (a·sas'·in) *n.* one who murders by
secret or treacherous assault. esp. a hired murderer. **-ate** *v.t.* to murder by guile or by
sudden violence. **-ation** *n.* **-ator** *n.* [Moslem
hashish, an intoxicating drug].
as·sault (a·sawlt') *n.* a violent onset or attack;
v.t. to attack violently, both physically and
with words or arguments; to storm. **-able** *a.*
-er *n.* **assault and battery** (*Law*) violent attacking and beating a person [L. *ad*, to; *salire*,
to leap].
as·say (a·sā') *n.* trial; test; examination; analysis of the amount of metal in ores or coins,
or of ingredients in drugs; *v.t.* to test. **-er** *n.*
[Fr. *essayer*, to try].
as·sem·ble (a·sem'·bl) *v.t.* to bring or call
together; to collect; to fit together the parts,
e.g. of a machine; *v.i.* to meet together. **assem-**
blage *n.* a group, gathering. **assembly** *n.*
a meeting; a company gathered; the putting
together of all the different parts to make a
complete machine [L. *ad*, to; *simul*, together].
as·sent (a·sent') *v.i.* to agree; to admit; to
concur; *n.* acquiescence; approval. **assenta-**
tion *n.* servile assent; obsequiousness. **-er, -or**
n. one who assents. **assentient** (a·sen'·shant)
a. giving assent; *n.* one who assents [L. *ad*, to;
sentire, to think].
as·sert (a·surt') *v.t.* to declare strongly; to
maintain or defend by argument. **-er, -or** *n.*
assertion *n.* the act of asserting; affirmation; declaration. **-ive** *a.* positive; self-confident. **-ively** *adv.* **-iveness** *n.* **-ory** *a.* affirmative [L. *asserere*, to claim].
as·sess (a·ses') *v.t.* to fix the amount of a tax
or fine; to tax or fine; to estimate for damage,
taxation, etc.; to rate; to appraise. **-able** *a.*
-ment *n.* assessing; valuation for taxation; a
tax; evaluation of merits. **-or** *n.* [L. *assidere*,
assessum, to sit by a judge].
as·sets (as'·ets) *n.pl.* funds or property available for payment of debts, etc.; the estate of
an insolvent or deceased person; the entire
property of a business company, association,
society, etc.; *n.sing.* an item of such property;
a thing of value [Fr. *assez*, enough].
as·sev·er·ate (a·sev'·er·āt) *v.t.* and *i.* to assert
positively or solemnly; to aver. **asseveration**
n. [L. *asseverare*, fr. *severus*, serious].
as·sid·u·ous (a·sid'·joo·us) *a.* constant in application or attention; diligent; hard-working.
-ly *adv.* **-ness**, **assiduity** (as·i·dū'·i·ti·) *n.*
close application; unremitting attention; devotion [L. *assiduus*, constantly near].
as·sign (a·sīn') *v.t.* to allot; to apportion; to
give out; to fix; to transfer; to ascribe. **-able**
a. **assignation** (a·sig·nā'·shan) *n.* the act
of assigning; an appointment, esp. if made by
lovers; a tryst; (*Law*) an assignment, or the
deed by which it is made. **assignee** (a·si·nē')
n. one to whom something is assigned; a person
appointed to act for another. **-ment** *n.* an
allotting to a particular person or use; a transfer of legal title or interest; a task assigned.
[L. *assignare*, to allot by sign (*signum*)].
as·sim·i·late (a·sim'·i·lāt) *v.t.* to make similar; to change into a like substance; to absorb
into the system; to digest; *v.i.* to become similar; to be absorbed. **assimilation** *n.* the act of
assimilating. (*Fig.*) full comprehension of anything. **assimilative** *a.* capable of assimilating
[L. *assimilare*, to make like].
as·sist (a·sist') *v.t.* to help; to aid; to give
support to; *v.i.* to lend aid; to be present.
-ance *n.* help; aid. **-ant** *a.* helping; acting
under the direction of a superior; *n.* one who
assists; a helper [L. *assistere*, to stand by].
as·size (a·sīz') *v.t.* to fix the rate of; to assess;
n. orig. the regulation of a court fixing selling
price of bread, ale, etc.; edict; a sitting of a
court of justice. **-ment** *n.* inspection of weights
and measures. **-r** *n.* [O.Fr. *assise*, an assembly
of judges].
as·so·ci·ate (a·sō'·shi·āt) *v.t.* to join with as
a friend, colleague, confederate or partner; to
class together; (*reflex.*) to express agreement
with; *v.i.* (foll. by *with*) to keep company; to
combine; *n.* (a·sō'·shi·it) a companion; a coadjutor; a member of a group; a junior member; *a.* affiliated. **associable** *a.* companionable.
associableness, associability, *n.* friendly,
companionable quality; sympathy; **-ship** *n.*
associative *a.* [L. *associare*, fr. *socius*, an
ally].
as·so·nance (as'·a·nans) *n.* a resemblance of
sounds; imperfect rhyme in which vowel sounds
are same, but consonants following are different, e.g *blunder*, *slumber*. **assonant(al)** *a.*
assonate *v.t.* to correspond in sound [L. *ad*,
to; *sonare*, to sound].
as·sort (a·sawrt') *v.t.* to classify; to arrange;
v.i. to suit or agree or match (foll. by *with*).
-ed *a.* classified; varied. **-edness, -ment** *n.*
act of arranging in groups; a miscellaneous
collection [Fr. *assortir*, to match].
as·suage (a·swāj') *v.t.* to soften; to allay; to
mitigate. **-ment** *n.* **-r** *n.* **assuasive** *a.* [L. *ad*,
to; *suavis*, sweet].
as·sume (a·sōóm') *v.t.* to take upon oneself; to
take for granted; to appropriate; to usurp;
v.i. to claim unduly; to be pretentious or arrogant. **assumable** *a.* **assumed** *a.* supposed;
feigned; hypothetical. **assumedly** *adv.* **as-**
suming *a.* arrogant. **assumingly** *adv.* **as-**
sumption *n.* the act of taking to or upon
oneself by force or right; the act of taking for
granted; the thing supposed to be true, or to
have happened. **assumptive** *a.* [L. *ad*, to;
sumere, to take].
as·sure (a·shoor') *v.t.* to make sure or certain;
to affirm; to ensure; to convince. **assurable**
a. **assurance** *n.* the act of assuring; promise;
self-confidence; presumption; *Br.* insurance.
-d *a.* certain, safe; confident. **assuredly** *adv.*
assuredness *n.* certainty. **-r** *n.* **assuringly**
adv. confidently [L. *ad*, to; *securus*, safe].
as·ter (as'·ter) *n.* a genus of plants so called
because the expanded flowers of various hues
are like stars [Gk. *aster*, star].

aster

as·ter·isk (as'·ta·risk) *n.* the mark (*) used in
printing to indicate words for reference or
words omitted. **asterism** *n.* small cluster of
stars; three asterisks (***), indicating point
or passage of special interest [Gk. *asterikos*, a
little star].   [hinder part of ship; behind.
a·stern (a·sturn') *adv.* in, at, or toward the
as·ter·oid (as'·ter·oid) *a.* star-shaped; *n.* one
of the smaller planets; (*Zool.*) star-fish. **aster-**
oidal *a.* [Gk. *aster*, a star; *eidos*, a form].
asth·ma (az'·ma, as'·ma) *n.* a chronic disorder of the respiratory organs, marked by
cough, labored breathing and feeling of suffocation. **asthmatic(al)** *a.* **asthmatically**
adv. [Gk. *asthma*, panting].
a·stig·ma·tism (a·stig'·ma·tizm) *n.* a defect
of eye, attended with dimness of vision, due to
malformation of lens of eye. **astigmatic** *a.*
[Gk. *a-*, neg.; *stigma*, point].   [in motion [E.].
a·stir (a·stur') *adv.* or *a.* on the move; alert;
as·ton·ish (a·stan'·ish) *v.t.* to impress with
sudden surprise, wonder or admiration; to
strike with sudden terror; to amaze; to astound.
-ed *a.* **-ing** *a.* **-ingly** *adv.* **-ment** *n.* [Formerly,
also *astony*, fr. O.Fr. *astoner*].
as·tound (a·stound') *v.t.* to strike dumb with
terror or amazement; to astonish greatly; to
stun. **-ing** *a.* [By-form of *astony*, *astonish*].
as·tra·khan (as'·tra·kan) *n.* the skin of the
young Persian lamb with soft, curling ringlets
of wool; a cheap fabric, made in imitation
[*Astrakhan*, city on the Caspian Sea].
as·tral (as'·tral) *a.* pert. to the stars; star-
shaped [Gk. *astron*, star].
a·stray (a·strā') *adv.* out of the right way; in
the wrong direction.
a·strict (a·strikt') *v.t.* to bind fast; to confine;
to restrict; to contract. **astriction** *n.* restriction; (*Med.*) constipation. **astrictive** *a.* astringent [L. *astrictus*, drawn close].
a·stride (a·strīd') *adv.* straddling; with the
legs apart; *prep.* with one foot on each side of
an object.
as·tringe (a·strinj') *v.t.* to bind together; to
draw together; to astrict; to constipate. **as·**
tringency *n.* the condition of being astringent. **astringent** *a.* binding; strengthening;
constricting; contracting; *n.* a drug which
causes contraction of the muscular fiber-tissues.
-ntly *adv.* [L. *ad*, to; *stringere*, to bind].
as·tro- (as'·trō) *prefix* used in the construction
of compound words having some reference to
stars [Gk. *astron*, star].
as·tro·labe (as'·tra·lāb) *n.* instrument for
finding altitude of stars, etc. [Gk. *astron*, star,
lambnein, to take].
as·trol·o·gy (a·stral'·a·ji·) *n.* science which
professes to interpret the influence of heavenly
bodies on human affairs **astrologer** *n.* **as-**
trologic, -al *a.* [Gk. *astron*, a star; *logos*, a
discourse].
as·trom·e·try (a·stram'·a·tri·) *n.* the determination of the magnitudes of the fixed stars
[Gk. *astron*, a star; *metron*, measure].
as·tro·naut (as'·tra·nawt) *n.* a space traveler;
-ical *a.* **-ics** *n.* science of traveling outside the
earth's atmosphere [Gk. *astron*, a star,
naut(ilos), a sailor].
as·tron·o·my (a·stran'·a·mi·) *n.* the science
which studies the heavenly bodies. **astronomer**
n. one versed in astronomy. **astronomic, -al,**
a. pert. to astronomy; boundless, countless, prodigious. **astronomize** *v.i.* [Gk. *astron*, a star;
nomos, law].
as·tro·phys·ics (as·trō·fiz'·iks) *n.* (*Astron.*)
the study of the physical components of the
stars by means of the spectroscope and other
instruments [Gk. *astron*, a star; *phusis*, nature].
as·tute (a·stōōt') *a.* cunning; shrewd; sagacious; crafty; wily; sly; subtle; keen. **-ly** *adv.*
-ness *n.* [L. *astutus*].
a·sun·der (a·sun'·der) *adv.* apart; into different pieces; in a divided state.
a·sy·lum (a·sī'·lam) *n.* a sanctuary; refuge for
criminals, debtors and others liable to be pursued; any place of refuge; an institution for
the deaf and dumb, the blind, or the insane;
the protection afforded by such places [Gk.
asulon, inviolate].
a·sym·me·try (ā·sim'·a·tri·) *n.* want of symmetry. **asymmetric, -al** *a.*
as·symp·tote (as'·im·tōt) *n.* (*Math.*) a
straight line that continually approaches a
curve, but never meets it within a finite distance [Gk. *a-*, neg.; *sun*, with; *ptosis*, a falling].
a·syn·chro·nism (ā·sin'·kra·nizm) *n.* lack
of synchronism; want of correspondence in
time. **asynchronous** *a.* not simultaneous.
a·syn·de·ton (a·sin'·da·tan) *n.* (*Rhet.*) the
omission of conjunctions. **asyndetic** *a.* [Gk.
asyndetos, unjoined].

at (at) *prep.* denoting rest in a place, presence, or nearness; near to, by, in; engaged on; in the direction of [O.E. *aet*].   [drug.

at·a·brine (at′·ạ·brin) *n.* an anti-malarial

at·a·vism (at′·ạ·vizm) *n.* the recurrence in living organisms of hereditary characteristics, diseases, etc. which have skipped one or more generations; reversion to type. **atavistic** [L. *atavus*, a great-grandfather's grandfather].

a·tax·i·a (ạ·tak′·si·ạ) *n.* (*Med.*) irregularity of bodily functions; irregularity of movement, due to defective muscular control. **ataxic** *a.* [Gk. *a-*, neg.; *taxis*, order].

ate (āt) past tense of the verb *eat*.

at·el·ier (at′·ạl·yā′) *n.* a workshop, esp. of an artist; hence, a studio [Fr. a workshop].

a·the·ism (ā′·thē·izm) *n.* disbelief in the existence of God. **atheist** *n.* one who denies the existence of God. **atheistic, -al** *a.* **athiestically** *adv.* [Gk. *a-*, neg.; *theos*, a god].

A·the·na, A·the·ne (ạ·thē′·na, -nē) *n.* (*Myth.*) Greek goddess of wisdom, art, industries, and prudent warfare. **Athenian** *a.* pert. to Athens. *n.* native of Athens.

a·thirst (ạ·thurst′) *a.* thirsty; eager [fr. *thirst*].

ath·lete (ath′·lēt) *n.* one trained to physical exercises, feats or contests of strength, etc.; a man strong and active by training. **athletic** (ath·let′·ik) *a.* pert. to physical exercises, contests, etc.; strong; vigorous; muscular. **athletics** *n.pl.* athletic sports [Gk. *athlētēs*, a contestant for a prize].

a·thwart (ạ·thwawrt′) *prep.* across; from side to side; *adv.* crosswise in opposition [O.N. *a* and *thvert*, across].

a·tilt (ạ·tilt′) *a.*, *adv.* tilted.

a·tin·gle (ạ·ting′·gal) *a.* tingling.

At·lan·tic (at·lan′·tik) *a.* pert. to the ocean (named after Mt. *Atlas*) separating Europe and Africa from America; *n.* the ocean itself.

At·las (at′·lạs) *n.* (*Myth.*) a Titan, condemned by Zeus to carry the world on his shoulders. **atlas** *n.* a book of maps.

at·mos·phere (at′·mạs·fēr) *n.* the mass of air, clouds, gases, and vapor, surrounding the earth or other heavenly body; any similar mass; atmospheric pressure; the air in any place, esp. if enclosed, e.g. in a theater; (*Fig.*) any surrounding influence. **atmospheric, atmospherical** *a.* pert. to, or depending on, the atmosphere. **atmospherically** *adv.* [Gk. *atmos*, vapor; *sphaira*, a ball].

at·oll (at′·ạl, ạ·tål′) *n.* a ring-shaped coral reef surrounding a lagoon [Native].

at·om (at′·ạm) *n.* the smallest unit. **-ary** constituent of a chemical element; (*Fig.*) anything very small; a tiny unit. **atomic, atomical** *a.* pert. to the atom. **atomicity** *n.* the number of atoms in the molecule of any element; **atomization** *n.* the changing of any liquid into the form of fine spray. **atomize** *v.t.* to reduce to atoms. **atomizer** *n.* an instrument for reducing a liquid to the form of spray. **atomy** *n.* an atom; a tiny being; (*Anat.*) a skeleton. **atom (atomic) bomb**, a bomb of unimaginable destructive power, whose energy is derived from the nuclear disintegration of atoms of elements of high atomic mass, e.g. uranium 235. **atomic energy**, energy derived from the disintegration of the nucleus of an atom. **atomic fission**, the action of disintegrating; the disintegration of the atom. **atomic pile**, apparatus for producing energy by the disintegration of atoms. **atomic weight**, the weight of an atom of an element. [Gk. *a-*, neg.; *tome*, a cutting].

a·ton·al (ā·tōn′·al) *a.* (*Mus.*) without tone; unreferred to any scale or tonic. **atonality** *n.* atonalism (ā·tṓn′·al·izm) *n.* without tone; unaccented; (*Med.*) lacking tone or energy. **atony** (at′·ạ·ni) *n.* lack of tone or accent [Gk. *a-*, neg; *tonos*, tone].

a·tone (ạ·tōn′) *v.t.* to appease; to expiate (*rare*); *v.i.* to make amends or reparation for an offense; to satisfy by giving an equivalent (with *for*). **-ment** *n.* amends; reconciliation,

esp. the reconciliation of God and man [E. (to set) *at one*].   [on top of.

a·top (ạ·tåp′) *a.*, *adv.* on or at the top; *prep.*

a·tri·um (ā′·tri·um) *n.* the principal room of an ancient Roman house; (*Anat.*) an auricle of the heart [L. = a hall].

a·tro·cious (ạ·trṓ′·shạs) *a.* savagely brutal; extremely cruel; very wicked; grievous; (*Colloq.*) of work, etc., of very poor quality. **-ly** *adv.* **-ness** *n.* **atrocity** (ạ·trås′i·ti) *n.* extreme wickedness; a brutal act [L. *atrox*, fierce].

a·tro·phy (at′·ra·fi·) *n.* a wasting away through lack of nutrition or use; emaciation. Also *v.t.* and *i.* to waste away; to cause to waste away. **atrophic, atrophied** *a.* [Gk. *a-*, neg.; *trophē*, nourishment].

at·ro·pin, at·ro·pine (at′·ra·pēn, ·pin) *n.* a poisonous alkaloid obtained from the deadly nightshade, used as a drug to dilate the pupil of the eye [Gk. *Atropos*, one of the *Fates*].

at·tach (ạ·tach′) *v.t.* to bind, fasten, or tie; to take by legal authority; to bind by affection; to assign, e.g. an officer to a regiment; *v.i.* to adhere; to be ascribed to. **-able** *a.* **-ed** *a.* fixed; fond of. **-ment** *n.* [Fr. *attacher*].

at·ta·ché (at·ạ·shā′) *n.* one attached to the staff of an ambassador. **— case,** *n.* small hand-case [Fr. *attacher*].

at·tack (ạ·tak′) *v.t.* to fall on with force; to assail with hostile criticism in words or writing; to set to work on; to begin to affect (of illness); *n.* a violent onset or assault [Fr. *attaquer*].

at·tain (ạ·tān′) *v.t.* to reach by exertion; to obtain by effort; to accomplish; to achieve; *v.i.* to arrive at (generally foll. by *to*). **-able** *a.* **-ability, -ableness** *n.* **-ment** *n.* [L. *attingere*, to reach].

at·taint (ạ·tānt′) *v.t.* to stain or disgrace; to accuse of; to find guilty; to deprive of civil rights for treason; *n.* a taint or disgrace. **attainder** *n.* loss of civil rights after sentence of death or outlawry for treason or felony. **-ment** *n.* [O.Fr. *ataint*, convicted].

at·tar (at′·ẹr) *n.* a fragrant oil obtained from flower-petals [Pers. *atar*, fragrance].

at·tempt (ạ·tempt′) *v.t.* to try; to endeavor to do; to attack; *n.* trial; an effort, esp. unsuccessful; an assault. *a.* [L. *ad*, to; *temptare*, to try].

at·tend (ạ·tend′) *v.t.* to accompany; to be present with or at; to give medical care to; *v.i.* to be present; to pay attention; to take care of; to wait on. **-ance** *n.* the act of attending; persons present. **-ant** *a.* being present; consequent; *n.* one who accompanies as friend or servant; a caretaker. **attention** *n.* careful observation; watching; act of civility; command issued, as in a military sense, to ensure readiness to act. **attentions** *n.pl.* courtship. **attentive** *a.* full of attention. **attentively** *adv.* [L. *ad*, to; *tendere*, to stretch].

at·ten·u·ate (ạ·ten′·ū·āt) *v.t.* to make thin or fine, to make slender; to weaken the potency of; *a.* slender; thin; (*Bot.*) tapering. **attenuant** *a.* tending to make thin, esp. of liquids; diluting. **-d** *a.* **attenuation** *n.* **attenuator** *n.* [L. *ad*, to; *tenuis*, thin].

at·test (ạ·test′) *v.t.* and *v.i.* to bear witness to; to vouch for; to certify; (*Law*) to witness officially (a signature). **-able, -ative** *a.* **-ation** *n.* [L. *attestari*, to bear witness].

At·tic (a′·tik) *a.* pert. to *Attica* or Athens; resembling the refined and elegant style of the Athenian writers. **attic** *n.* a room under the roof of a house where ceiling follows line of the roof (common in Greek archit.); a garret [Gk. *Attikos*, pert. to Attica].

at·tire (ạ·tir′) *v.t.* to dress; to array in splendid garments; *n.* apparel; dress. **-ment, attiring** *n.* [O.Fr. *atirier*, to put in order].

at·ti·tude (at′·ạ·tōōd) *n.* posture of a person; pose (in portrait); (*Fig.*) mental or moral disposition [L. *aptus*, fit].

at·tor·ney (ạ·tur′·ni·) *n.* one put in the *turn* or place of another; one legally authorized by another to transact business; lawyer; solicitor. **attorn** *v.t.* to transfer; *v.i.* to transfer homage; to acknowledge a new landlord. **-ship** *n.* **-dom** *n.* **— general** *n.* chief law officer of a state or nation. **power, letter** or **warrant of attorney,** a legal authorization by which one person may act for another [O.Fr. *atorner*, to direct].

at·tract (ạ·trakt′) *v.t.* and *v.i.* to draw toward; to cause to approach; (*Fig.*) to allure; to provoke notice. **-able** *a.* **-ile** *a.* attractive. **attraction** *n.* the act of drawing to; the force which draws together bodies or particles; the affinity existing between one chemical body and another; (*Fig.*) that which allures, or fascinates. **-ive** *a.* **-ively** *adv.* **-iveness** *n.* [L. *ad*, to; *trahere, tractum*, to draw].

at·tri·bute (ạ·trib′·yoot) *v.t.* to consider as belonging to; to ascribe to. **attribute** (at′·ra·būt) *n.* something inherent in a person or thing; an inseparable property; (*Gram.*) a qualifying word used, not as part of predicate, but adjectivally, as in *red* hair. **attributable** *a.* that may be ascribed to. **attribution** *n.* the act of ascribing to; the quality attributed. **attributive** *a.* [L. *ad*, to; *tribuere*, to bestow].

at·tri·tion (ạ·trish′·ạn) *n.* the act of wearing away by friction; state of being worn; (*Mil.*) deliberate exhaustion of enemy's men and resources before making an attack. **attrite** *a.* worn away by rubbing or friction; (*Theol.*) penitent through fear [L. *attritus*, rubbed away].

at·tune (ạ·tōōn′) *v.t.* to put in tune; to make musical; to make one instrument accord with another; (*Fig.*) to bring into spiritual harmony; to fit for a purpose. *a.* in harmony. **-ment** *n.* [L. *ad*, to; *tune*].

a·typ·i·cal (ā·tip′·ạ·kạl) *a.* not typical; abnormal. **-ly** *adv.* [Gk. *a-*, neg.; typical].

au·burn (aw′·burn) *a.* reddish brown; *n.* rich chestnut color [L.L. *alburnus*, blond].

auc·tion (awk′·shan) *n.* a method of public sale whereby the object for sale is secured by highest bidder; *v.t.* to sell by auction. **-eer** *n.* one licensed to sell by auction; *v.i.* to sell by auction [L. *augere, auctum*, to increase].

auc·tion bridge (awk′·shan brij′) *n.* a card game in which the players bid.

au·da·cious (aw·dā′·shạs) *a.* bold, fearless; impudent; insolent. **-ly** *adv.* **-ness** *n.* **audacity** (aw·da′·si·ti·) *n.* boldness, effrontery, impudence. [L. *audix*, bold].

au·di·ble (aw′·dạ·bl) *a.* capable of being heard. **audibly** *adv.* **audibility** *n.* [L. *audire*, to hear].

au·di·ence (aw′·di·ạns) *n.* the act of hearing; an assembly of hearers or spectators; a ceremonial reception or interview; a judicial hearing. **audient** *a.* listening [L. *audire*, to hear].

au·di·o (aw′·di·ō) *a.* electronic apparatus using audible frequencies (between 15-20,000 cycles) [L. *audire*, hear].

au·dit (aw′·dit) *n.* an examination, by qualified persons, of accounts of a business, public office, or undertaking; *v.t.* to test and vouch for the accuracy of accounts; listen. **audition** *n.* the act, or sense, of hearing; hearing given to a performer as test. **-or** *n.* a hearer; one authorized to investigate the financial condition of a company or society. **auditorium** *n.* the body of a concert hall or theater where the audience are seated; the nave of a church. **-ory** *a.* pert. to the sense of hearing; *n.* a lecture room; an audience [L. *audire*, to hear].

au·ger (aw′·gẹr) *n.* a boring tool for woodwork, like a large gimlet. [*An auger* for *a nauger*, fr. O.E. *nafu*, nave; *gār*, dart].

aught (awt) *n.* anything; any part; zero; *adv.* to any extent [O.E. *awiht*, fr. *a*, ever, and *wiht*, thing].

aug·ment (awg·ment′) *v.t.* to increase; to add to; to make larger; to enlarge; *v.i.* to grow larger. **augment** *n.* an increase; a prefix added to the past tense of verbs to distinguish them from other tenses. **-able** *a.* **-ation** *n.* act of enlarging; an increase. **-ative** *a.* increasing; *n.* a word which expresses with increased force the idea conveyed by the simpler word. **-er** *n.* [L. *augmentum*, an increase].

au·gur (aw′·gẹr) *n.* a soothsayer; a diviner; a member of a college of priests in Rome who claimed to be able to foretell events by observing the flight or other actions of birds; *v.t.* to foretell; to presage; to prognosticate. **-al** *a.* **-ship** *n.* **-y** *n.* divination; omen [L.].

au·gust (aw·gust′) *a.* majestic; imposing; sublime; grand; magnificent; sacred. **-ly** *adv.* **-ness** *n.* [a title first bestowed on the Emperor Octavianus by the Roman Senate, fr. L. *augere*, to increase].

Au·gust (aw′·gạst) *n.* the eighth month of the year [named in honor of the Emperor *Augustus*].

Au·gus·tan (aw·gus′·tạn) *a.* classic; refined; pertaining to the Emperor *Augustus*, 31 B.C.-A.D. 14; *n.* a writer of the Augustan age.

Au·gus·tine (aw·gạs·tēn′) *n.* a member of a monastic order which follows rules framed by St. Augustine (354-430) or deduced from his writings; a Black Friar.

auk (awk) *n.* a marine bird, of the Arctic regions [Icel. *alka*].

aunt (änt, ånt) *n.* a father's or a mother's sister; also applied to an uncle's wife. [L. *amita*, a father's sister].

au·ra (aw'·ra) *n.* a subtle invisible essence or fluid said to emanate from human and animal bodies, and even from things; (*Fig.*) the atmosphere surrounding a person; character; personality; (*Path.*) a premonitory symptom of epilepsy and hysteria, as of cold air rising to the head. **-l** *a.* pert. to the air, or to an aura [L. *aura*, a breeze].

au·ral (aw'·ral) *a.* pert. to the ear, or sense of hearing. **-ly** *adv.* [L. *auris*, the ear].

au·re·ole, au·re·ola (aw'·ri·ōl, aw·rē'·a·la) *n.* a radiance around a sacred figure, in art; a halo; a nimbus [L. *aureus*, golden].

au·re·o·my·cin (aw'·ri·ō·mī'·sin) *n.* an antibiotic [L. *aureus*, Gk. *mukes*, mushroom].

au·ric (aw'·rik) *a.* pert. to gold; (*Chem.*) applied to compounds in which gold is trivalent. **aureate** *a.* golden [L. *aurum*, gold].

au·ri·cle (aw'·ri·kl) *n.* the external ear; each of the two upper cavities of the heart. **auricula** (aw·rik'·yoo·la) *n.* a part like an ear. **auricular** *a.* pert. to ear, or to hearing; told in the ear (of confession). **auriculate, auriform** *a.* ear-shaped [L. *auris*, the ear].

au·rif·er·ous (aw·rif'·a·ras) *a.* yielding gold [L. *aurum*, gold; *ferre*, to bear].

Au·ro·ra (aw·raw'·ra) *n.* (*Myth.*) the Roman goddess of the dawn. **aurora** *n.* the dawn; the rosy tint in the sky before the sun rises; an orange-red color. **aurora borealis** (bō·ri·a'·lis), a luminous phenomenon, supposed to be of electrical origin, seen at night in the northern sky. Also called 'northern lights.'

aus·cul·ta·tion (aws·kul·tā'·shan) *n.* (*Med.*) listening to the movement of heart and lungs either directly with the ear, or with a stethoscope. **ausculate** *v.t.* and *i.* to examine thus [L. *auscultare*, to listen to].

aus·pice (aw'·spis) *n.* favoring influence; an omen based on observing birds; augury; divination; *n.pl.* **auspices**, protection; patronage esp. **under the auspices of. auspicate** *v.t.* to predict; to inaugurate in favorable conditions. **auspicious** (aw·spi'·shus) *a.* giving promise of success; favorable; propitious. **auspiciously** *adv.* **auspiciousness** *n.* [L. *auspicium*, fr. *avis*, a bird; *specere*, to behold].

aus·tere (aw·stēr') *a.* harsh; severe; strict; simple and without luxury. **-ly** *adv.* **-ness, austerity** *n.* severity; extreme simplicity; asceticism [Gk. *austeros*, harsh].   [south wind].

aus·tral (aws'·tral) *a.* southern [L. *auster*, the

au·tar·chy (aw'·tár·ki·) *n.* absolute power; despotism; dictatorship. **autarchic** *a.* [Gk. *autos*, self; *archein*, to rule].

au·then·tic (aw·then'·tik) *a.* genuine; real; not of doubtful origin; trustworthy; of attested authority. Also **-al. -ally** *adv.* **-ate** *vt.* to prove to be genuine; to confirm. **-ation** *n.* **authenticity** *n.* (aw·then·tis'·a·ti·) the quality of genuineness [Gk. *authentikos*, warranted, fr. *authentein*, to have full power].

au·thor (aw'·ther) *n.* (*fem.* **-ess**) the beginner or originator of anything; the writer of a book, article, etc. **-ial** *a.* pert. to an author. **-ship** *n.* the quality or function of being an author; source; origin [L. *auctor*].

au·thor·i·ty (aw·thár'·i·ti·) *n.* legal power or right; accepted source of information; a writing by an expert on a particular subject; the writer himself; justification; influence; permission; a body or group of persons in control (often *pl.*). **authoritarian** *a.* advocating obedience to authority as opposed to individual liberty; *n.* an advocate of authority. **authoritative** *a.* having the weight of authority; justified. **authoritatively** *adv.* [L. *auctoritas*].

au·thor·ize (aw'·tha·riz) *v.t.* to clothe with authority; to empower; to sanction; to make legal; to justify. **authorization** *n.* [L. *auctorari*].

au·to- (aw'·tō) a combining form fr. Gk. *autos*, self, used in many derivatives and meaning *self, oneself, by oneself,* etc.

au·to (aw'·tō) *n.* (*Colloq.*) abbrev. for automobile. **-ist** *n.* a motorist. **-mobile** (aw·ta·-mä'·běl) *n.* a road vehicle driven by mechanical power. **-motive** *a.* pertaining to automobiles; self-propelling [Gk. *autos*, self; L. *mobilis*, mobile].

au·to·bahn (aw'·ta·bán) in Germany, a highway specially constructed for motor traffic [Ger. *Bahn*, a road].

au·to·bi·og·raphy (aw·ta·bī·ág'·ra·fi·) *n.* the story of a person's life, written by himself. **autobiographer** *n.* **autobiographic** *a.* [Gk. *autos*, self; *bios*, life; *graphein*, to write].

au·to·crat (aw'·ta·krat) *n.* monarch who rules by his own absolute right; despot. **-ic -ically** *adv.* **autocracy** (aw·tok'·ra·si·) *n.* uncontrolled power; a state ruled thusly [Gk. *autos*, self; *kratein*, to rule].

au·to·gi·ro (aw·ta·jī·rō) *n.* airplane using horizontal revolving wings for vertical ascent and descent [Gk. *autos*, self; *guros*, a ring].

au·to·graph (aw'·ta·graf) *n.* a person's own handwriting or signature; an original manuscript; *a.* written in one's own handwriting; *v.t.* to write with one's own hand; to write one's signature [Gk. *autos*, self; *graphein*, to write].

au·to·mat·ic (aw·ta·mat'·ik) *a.* self-acting; mechanical; not voluntary; done unconsciously;

n. an automatic pistol. **automat** *n.* a restaurant which serves food using automatic devices. **-ally** *adv.* mechanically. **automate** *v.t.* **automation** (aw·ta·mā'·shan) *n.* the automatic control of production processes by electronic apparatus. **automatism** *n.* involuntary action; power of self-movement without external stimulus. **automaton** (aw·tám'·a·tan) *n.* [Gk. *automatso*, self-acting].

au·to·mo·bile. See **auto.**

au·ton·o·my (aw·tán'·a·mi·) *n.* the right of self-government; independence; **autonomous, autonomic** *a.* [Gk. *autos*, self; *nomos*, a law].

au·top·sy (aw'·táp·si·) *n.* the dissection and examination of a dead body; a post-mortem examination; personal observation. **autoptic, (al)** *a.* self-observed. **autoptically** *adv.* [Gk. *autos*, self; *opsis*, sight].

au·to·sug·ges·tion (aw·tō·sag·jes'·chan) *n.* a mental process similar to hypnotism but applied by the subject to himself.

au·tumn (aw'·tam) *n.* the third season of the year, generally applied to September, October, and November; fall; the season of decay; the time of declining powers. **-al** *a.* [L. *autumnus*].

aux·il·ia·ry (awg·zil'·ya·ri·) *a.* helping; assisting; subsidiary; *n.* a helper; (*Gram.*) a verb which helps to form moods, tenses, or voice of another verb, e.g. *be, have, shall, will, may* [L. *auxilium*, help].

a·vail (a·vāl') *v.i.* to profit by; to take advantage of; *v.t.* to benefit; to profit; *n.* advantage; profit; benefit; utility. **-able** *a.* capable of being used to advantage; procurable. **-ability -ability** *n.* [L. *ad, to*; *valere*, to be strong].

av·a·lanche (av'·a·lansh) *n.* mass of snow and ice moving down from a height and gathering momentum in its descent; (*Fig.*) tremendous downpour [O.Fr. *a val,* into the valley].

av·a·rice (av'·a·ris) *n.* excessive love of money; greed; miserliness; cupidity. **avaricious** *a.* covetous; grasping. **avaricious.y** *adv.* **avariciousness** *n.* [L. *avarus,* greedy].

a·vast (a·vast') *interj.* cease! hold! stop! enough! [Dut. *houd vast,* hold fast].

a·ve (á' vi, á'·vä) *interj.* hail! farewell! *n.* an Ave Maria or Hail Mary; angel Gabriel's salutation (Luke 1) [L.].

a·venge (a·venj') *v.t.* and *v.i.* to take satisfaction for an injury to; to punish a wrong-doer; to seek retribution. **-ful** *a.* desiring retribution. **-ment -r.** *n.* (*fem.* **-ress**) one who avenges [O.Fr. *avengier,* to seek retribution].

av·e·nue (av'·e·nōō) *n.* a wide street with houses and row of trees down each side; (*Fig.*) a means towards, as in *avenue to fame* [L. *ad*, to; *venire*, to come].

a·ver (a·vur') *v.t.* to declare positively; to avouch; to assert; to allege. *pr.p.* **-ring**; *pa.p.* **-red. -ment** *n.* the act of averring; a positive assertion; (*Law*) proof of a plea [L. *ad,* to; *verus,* true].

av·er·age (av'·a·rij) *a.* containing a mean proportion; ordinary; normal; *n.* a medial estimate obtained by dividing the sum of a number of quantities by the number of quantities; *v.t.* to reduce to a mean [O.Fr. *average,* cattle or possessions; fr. L. *habere,* to have].

a·verse (a·vurs') *a.* reluctant (to do) or disinclined for; unwilling; set against (foll. by *to*). **-ly** *adv.* with repugnance. **-ness** *n.* **aversion** *n.* a strong dislike; instinctive antipathy; object of dislike [L. *aversus,* turned away].

a·vert (a·vurt') *v.t.* to turn away from or aside; to ward off. **-ed** *a.* **-edly** *adv.* **-ible** *a.* capable of being avoided [L. *a,* from; *vertere,* to turn].

a·vi·an (ā'·vi·an) *a.* pert. to birds. **aviary** *n.* an enclosed space for breeding, rearing and keeping of birds [L. *avis,* a bird].

a·vi·a·tion (ā·vi·ā'·shan) *n.* the art of flying aircraft. **aviate** *v.i.* to fly. **aviator** *n.* (*fem.* **aviatress, axiatrix**) [L. *avis,* a bird].

av·id (av'·id) *a.* eager; greedy; desirous (foll. by *of* or *for*). **avidity** *n.* greediness; eagerness; hunger; (*Fig.*) zest [L. *avidus,* greedy].

a·vo·ca·do (av·a·ká'·dō) *n.* the alligator pear; juicy eible fruit [Mex.].

a·vo·ca·tion (av·a·kā'·shan) *n.* a distraction; a minor plausable occupation; a hobby; a side interest; **avocative** *a.* calling off; *n.* a dissuasion [L. *a,* away; *vocare,* to call].

a·void (a·void') *v.t.* to shun; to elude; to keep clear of; to eschew; to abstain from; to escape; (*Law*) to invalidate; to annul. **-able** *a.* **-ance** *n.* the act of shunning [L. *ex,* out; and *void*].

av·oir·du·pois (av·er·da·poiz') *n.* a common system of weights; (*Colloq.*) heaviness [corrupt. of O.Fr. *avoir de pois,* goods by weight i.e. not by numbers].

a·vouch (a·vouch') *v.t.* to declare positively; to guarantee [L. *ad,* to; *vocare,* to call].

a·vow (a·vou') *v.t.* to declare openly; to own; to confess freely; to acknowledge. **-able** *a.* **-al** *n.* an open declaration or admission. **-ance,** evidence; testimony. **-edly** *adv.* [Fr. *avouer*].

aw (aw) *interj.* sound of protest; dislike.

a·wait (a·wāt') *v.t.* to wait for; be in store for; attend; be ready for.

a·wake (a·wāk') *v.t.* to rouse from sleep; to stir up; *v.i.* to cease from sleep; to bestir oneself; *pa.t.* **awoke**; *pa.p.* **awoke, awaked**; *a.* not asleep; alert; vigilant; alive. **awaken** *v.t.* and *v.i.* to rouse from sleep; to awake; to excite. **awak(en)ing** *n.* a revival of interest or conscience [O.E. *awacian*].

a·ward (a·wawrd') *v.t.* to adjudge; to determine (a point submitted); to decide authoritatively; to assign judicially; *n.* judgment; the recorded decision of an arbitrator in a court of law; thing awarded; prize [fr. O. Fr. *eswarder*].

a·ware (a·wār') *a.* watchful; mindful; conscious of; possessing knowledge of; sensible. **-ness** *n.* [O.E. *gewaer,* conscious].

a·wash (a·wásh') *adv.* (*Naut.*) level with the surface of the water; washed by the waves.

a·way (a·wā') *adv.* absent; at a distance; on the way; apart; be gone! [O.E. *onweg,* on the way].

awe (aw) *n.* wonder mingled with veneration and dread; *v.t.* to inspire with awe. **-some** *a.* **-struck, -stricken** *a.* **awful** *a.* full of awe; filling with fear and admiration; impressive; venerable; majestic, dreadful; terrible; horrible; ugly; unsightly. **awfulness** *n.* **awfully,** *adv.* (*Colloq.*) very, extremely [O.E. *ege,* awe].

a·weigh (a·wā') *adv.* (*Naut.*) when a ship's anchor is just broken out of the ground by the initial strain on the cable; atrip.

aw·ful. See under **awe.**

a·while (a·whil') *adv.* for a while.

awk·ward (awk'·werd) *a.* unskilful; ungainly; clumsy; difficult to manage; inconvenient; embarrassing. **-ly** *adv.* **-ness** *n.* **awkward age,** adolescence [M.E. *awk,* wrong; and *ward*].

awl (awl) *n.* a small pointed instrument for boring holes in leather [O.E. *awel*].

awn·ing (aw'·ning) *n.* a covering of canvas, etc. to shelter from the sun's rays.

a·woke. See **awake.**

a·wry (a·rī') *adv.* and *a.* twisted to one side; crooked [See **wry**]. [earlier, *on wry*].

ax, axe (aks) *n.* for cutting, chopping or hewing. **an axe to grind,** a private end or purpose to serve [O.E. *aez*].

ax·es (ak'·ses) plural form of **axe** and **axis.**

ax·i·om (ak'·si·am) *n.* a necessary and self-evident proposition, requiring no proof. **-atic, -atical** *a.* self-evident. **-atically** *adv.* [Gk. *axioma* fr. *axioein,* to require].

ax·is (ak'·sis) *n.* the imaginary line round which a solid body rotates or a geometrical figure is symmetrically disposed. *pl.* **axes** (ak'·sēs). **axial** *a.* forming the axis. **axially** (*adv.* [L. *axis,* an axle].

ax·le, ax·le·tree (ak′·sl·trē) *n.* a bar of wood or iron rod on which a wheel, or a system of wheels, turns [O.N. *oxul-tre*].

ay, aye (ī) *adv.* yes; yea. **ayes** (īz) *n.pl.* affirmative votes or voters [*yea*].
aye, ay (ā) *adv.* always; ever [O.N. *ei*].
a·za·le·a (ạ·zā′·li·ạ) *n.* a genus of plants allied to the rhododendron [Gk. *azaleos*, dry].

axle

a·zo·ic (ạ·zō′·ik) *a.* pert. to that part of geologic time before animal life existed [Gk. *a-*, neg.; *zoe*, life].
Az·tec (az′·tek) *n.* a member of a people dominant in Mexican Empire at the time of the Sp. conquest; their language; *a.* pert to the race or its language.
az·ure (azh′·ẹr) *n.* sky blue; the sky; *a.* sky-blue [Fr. *azur*, from Ar.].

B

Ba·al (bā′·ạl) *n.* a false deity. *pl.* **Baalim. Baalist** *n.* a worshipper of Baal. [Heb.].
bab·ble (ba′·bl) *v.t.* and *i.* to chatter senselessly; to prate; to reveal secrets; *n.* prattling; idle talk; murmuring of running water. **-r** *n.* **babbling** *n.* [Onomat].
babe (bāb) *n.* an infant; a young child [earlier *baban*, imit. of baby speech].
ba·bel (bā′·bạl) *n.* a confusion of unintelligible sounds; noisy babble of many people talking at the one time; uproar, at a public meeting. **-dom** *n.* uproar. [Heb. = confusion].
ba·boon (ba·bóon′) *n.* a species of monkey with large body, big canine teeth and capacious cheek-pouches [Fr. *babouin*].

ba·by (bā′·bi·) *n.* an infant; a young child; *a.* pert. to a baby; small, as in **— grand** (piano), etc. **-hood** *n.* the period of infancy. **-ish** *a.* infantile; behaving like a young child. [earlier *baban*, imit of baby speech].
bac·ca·lau·re·ate (bak·ạ·law′·ri·ạt) *n.* the university degree of bachelor; an address to a graduating class [fr. L. *baccalarius*].
Bac·chus (bak·′ạs) *n.* (*Myth.*) the god of wine. **bacchanal** *n.* a worshipper of Bacchus; a drunken reveller; an orgy in honor of Bacchus; *a.* pert. to Bacchus; riotous; drunken. **bacchanalia** *n.pl.* feasts in honor of Bacchus; drunken revels. **bacchanalian** *n.* and *a.* **bacchic** *a.* relating to Bacchus; jovial due to intoxication [L.].
bach·e·lor (bach′·ạ·lẹr) *n.* an unmarried man; a celibate; one who has taken the first degree at a university; a monk who performed menial duties. **-hood, -ism, -ship** *n.* [M.L. *baccalarius*, a small farmer].
ba·cil·lus (bạ·sil′·ạs) *n.* microscopic, rod-like organisms capable of causing certain diseases. *pl.* **bacilli, bacillar, bacillary** *a.* **bacilliform** *a.* of a rod-like shape [L. *baculus*, a rod].

back (bak) *n.* the upper or hinder part of the trunk of an animal; the hinder part of an object; a football player whose position is behind the line of scrimmage; *a.* of the back; at the rear of; not current (as a magazine); reversed; remote; *adv.* to or toward a former

place, state, condition, or time; away from the front; in return; *v.t.* to get, or ride, upon the back of; to provide with a back; to force backward; to place a bet on; to support; to endorse (a check, etc.); *v.i.* to move or go back; of the wind, to change direction counter-clockwise. **-bite** *v.t.* to speak evil of someone in his absence. **backbiter** *n.* **-bone** *n.* the spine or vertebral column; firmness; courage. **backboned** *a.* **-er** *n.* supporter; **-field** *n.* the backs as in football who play behind the line. **-fire** *n.* in internal combustion engines, premature ignition of fuel; *v.i.* to do this; to go awry; **-ground** *n.* part behind foreground of a picture or stage setting; knowledge gained by experience. **—hand** *n.* writing sloped from left to right; a stroke in tennis with the hand turned backwards. **-handed** *a.* with the back of the hand; deceitful; indirect; sarcastic; doubtful. **-ing** *n.* support; sympathy; providing anything with a support. **-lash** *n.* the jarring reaction of a machine due to the degree of play; **-log** *n.* an accumulation, a reserve amount. **— number** *n.* a copy of an out-of-date publication; one behind the times or unprogressive. **-side** *n.* back or hinder part; the rear side; the buttocks; the rump. **-sight** *n.* the rear sight of a rifle. **-slide** *v.i.* to slide backwards; to lapse from a high moral standard. **-stage** *adv.* behind the stage, in the wings, etc. **-stays** *n.pl.* ropes supporting the upper mast. **— talk** *n.* insolent reply; impertinence. **-track** *v.i.* to retreat; to return over the same route. **-ward** *adv.* with the back in advance; towards, or on, the back; to a worse state; in a reverse direction; *a.* directed to the back or rear; dull; behind in one's education; unwilling; late. **-wash** *n.* backward current; (*Slang*) the dire consequences. **-water** *n.* water held back by a dam; water thrown back by a paddle-wheel; a by-way in a river or creek. **-woods** *n.pl.* outlying forest districts or remote undeveloped country. **-woodsman** *n.* [O.E. *bacc*].
back·gam·mon (bak·gam′·ạn) *n.* a game played by two with 15 pieces each on a special board [E. fr. *back* and M.E. *gamen*, play].
ba·con (bā′·kn) *n.* back and sides of hogs after being salted and smoked [O.Fr.].
bac·te·ri·um (bak·ti′·ri·ạm) *n.* group of nonspore forming bacteria. *pl.* **bacteria. bacterial** *a.* **bactericide** *n.* any agent capable of destroying bacteria. **bactericidal** *a.* **bacteriology** *n.* the study of bacteria [Gk. *bakterion*, a little stick].
bad (bad) *a.* ill or evil; wicked. **-dish** *a.* rather bad. **-ly** *adv.* **-ness** *n.* **bad blood**, ill feeling. **bad lands** *n.pl.*, badly eroded, barren land esp. in the Dakotas. **to go bad**, to rot or decay [M.E. *badde*].
bade (bad) past tense of the verb **bid.**
badge (baj) *n.* an emblem, usually symbolic, worn to distinguish members of societies, regiments, etc.; token; mark; symbol [M.E. *bage*].
badg·er (baj′·ẹr) *n.* a greyish-brown hibernating animal; *v.t.* to follow hotly as dogs do the badger; to tease, by persistent questioning; to pester or annoy [from the white stripe or *badge* on the animal's forehead].

bad·i·nage (bad·ạ·nij′) *n.* playful or sportive talk; banter [Fr. *badin*, frivolous].
bad·min·ton (bad′·min·tạn) *n.* a game similar to tennis with the substitution of shuttlecocks for tennis balls [fr. *Badminton* House in Gloucestershire where the game was invented].
baf·fle (baf′·l) *v.t.* to frustrate; to confuse; to check or turn, as wind baffles a ship. **-r** *n.* **baffling** *a.* disconcerting; confusing.
baf·fle (baf′·l) *n.* a plate for regulating the flow of a liquid or gas; a metal plate used between the cylinders of an air-cooled motor engine to break up a stream of heated gases; a baffle-plate; a rigid mounting usually of wood, holding the reproducing diaphragm of a radio receiver.
bag (bag) *n.* a sack or pouch; content of a sack; results of one's fishing or hunting; an udder; *v.t.* to put into a bag; to seize; *v.i.* to hang loosely; to bulge or swell out. *pr.p.* **-ging.** *pa.p.* **-ged. -gage,** *n.* tents and stores of an army; luggage; a dissolute woman. **bag and baggage,** with all one's belongings. **-ging** *n.* cloth or material for bags. **-giness** *n.* the state of being baggy (as trousers). **-gy** *a.* hanging loosely; puffy. **in the bag,** certain, assured. **to let the cat out of the bag,** to reveal a secret unwittingly [O.N. *baggi*].
bag·a·telle (bag·ạ·tel′) *n.* a trifle; a thing of little worth or importance; a game played with balls and a cue on a board; a short piece of music in light style [Fr.].
ba·gel (bā·′gl) *n.* a doughnut-shaped roll.
bag·pipe (bag′·pīp) *n.* musical reed instrument, common to Scotland. **-r** *n.* [M.E. *baggepipe*].

bail (bāl) *n.* (*Law*) security taken by the court that a person charged will attend at a future date to answer to the charge; one who furnishes this security; *v.t.* to obtain the release of a person from prison by giving security against his reappearance. **-able** *a.* **— bond** *n.* a bond given by a person who is being bailed and his surety. **-ee** *n.* the holder of goods in trust who must obey the direction with which the delivery to him is made. **bail out** *v.i.* to jump from an aircraft and descend by parachute [O.Fr. *bailler*].
bail (bāl) *n.* a scoop; a shallow vessel for clearing water out of a boat; *v.t.* to empty of water with some kind of water scoop. **-er** *n.* [F. *baille*, bucket].
bail·iff (bā′·lif) *n.* an under-officer of a sheriff; a minor officer of a court; (*Br.*) land-owner's agent [O.Fr. *baillir*].
bail·i·wick (bāl′·a·wik) *n.* bailiff's jurisdiction; (*Fig.*) one's special domain, or area of skill, work, etc. [O.Fr., *baillif*, a justice; O.E. *wice*, office].
bairn (bern) *n.* (*Scot.*) a child [O.E. *bearn*].
bait (bāt) *n.* food set to entice fish or an animal; a lure; snare; *v.t.* to put food on a hook or in a trap as a lure; to set dogs on an animal; to harass; to tease. **-er** *n.* **-ing** *a.* and *n.* [Icel. *beita*, to cause to bite].

baize (bāz) *n.* a woolen or cotton cloth with long nap [O.Fr.].

bake (bāk) *v.t.* to harden by heat; to cook in an oven or over a fire; *v.i.* to work at baking; to be baked. **-house** *n.* a bakehouse.**baking** *n.* a batch of bread, etc. **a baker's dozen,** thirteen [O.E. *basan*].

Ba·ke·lite (bāk'·ạ·līt) *n.* a hard, strong synthetic resin used as a substitute for wood, bone, celluloid, etc., a trade name [L. H. *Baekeland*, the inventor].

bal·a·lai·ka (bal·a·lī'·kạ) *n.* an old Slavic stringed instrument [Russ.].

bal·ance (bal'·ans) *n.* an apparatus for determining the weight, or comparing the masses, of bodies; a poised beam with two opposite scales; any condition of equilibrium; part of a watch or clock which regulates the beats; a sense of proportion and discretion; poise; payment still due, or cash in hand; *v.t.* to weigh, as in a balance; to render equal in proportion, etc.; to adjust, as an account; *v.i.* to be of the same weight; to be in equipoise. — **sheet** *a.* statement of the assets and liabilities of a company [L. *bis*, twice; *lanx*, a plate].

bal·co·ny (bal'·kạ·ni) *n.* a platform or gallery projecting from a building; a gallery in a theater or concert hall [It. *balcone*].

bald (bawld) *a.* destitute of hair or feathers on the crown of the head; bare; unadorned; undisguised; without literary style; monotonous. **-head, -pate** *n.* one destitute of hair. **-ly** *adv.* **-ness** *n.* [M.E. *balled*].

bal·der·dash (bawl'·dẹr·dash) *n.* a jargon of meaningless words jumbled together; nonsense.

bale (bāl) *n.* that which causes sorrow or ruin; evil; misery; mischief; injury; woe. **-ful** *a.* **-fully** *adv.* [O.E. *bealu*, evil].

bale (bāl) *n.* a package, compactly compressed, and wrapped in a protecting cover; *v.t.* to pack in bales. **-r** *n.* one employed in baling goods [N.E. *balle*].   [whale].

ba·leen (bạ·lēn') *n.* whalebone [L. *balaena*, a

balk (bawk) *n.* a crossbeam or rafter, of squared timber, stretching from wall to wall; an unploughed ridge of land; a barrier or check; a disappointment; a part of a billiard table; in *baseball*, an uncompleted pitch, entitling base runners to advance one base; *v.t.* to frustrate; to bar the way; *v.i.* to stop abruptly; refuse to move. **-y** *a.* [O.E. *balca*, a ridge].

ball (bawl) *n.* any round body; a sphere; a globe; the earth; bullet or shot; a delivery outside the strike zone by a pitcher; the heavy piece of a pendulum; *v.t.* and *i.* to form into a ball. — **bearings** *n.* hardened steel balls interposed in channels or 'races' between the rotating and stationary surfaces of a bearing to lessen friction. — **point pen** *n.* fountain pen with a tiny ball point leaving a fine trace of ink on the paper. **—race** *n.* the grooves in which the balls of a ball-bearing run. **ball and socket,** a joint formed by a ball partly enclosed in a cup and so adjusted that it can move freely in all directions. [Scand. origin].

ball (bawl) *n.* a social gathering for the purpose of dancing; an assembly. **-room** *n.* [L.L. *ballare*, to dance].

bal·lad (bal'·ạd) *n.* a story in verse, of popular origin, generally patriotic and sung orig. to the harp; a concert-room melody, usually sentimental. **-ist** *n.* a composer or singer of ballads. **-ry** *n.* collected ballads; folk songs. **-eer** *n.* [L.L. *ballare*, to dance].

bal·lade (bạ·lād') *n.* a short poem of one to three triplet stanzas of eight lines, each with the same rhymes and refrain, and an envoy of four or five lines [Fr.].

bal·last (bal'·ạst) *n.* heavy material taken on board ship to increase the vessel's draft and steadiness; sandy material dredged from river beds used for concrete; that which renders anything steady; *v.t.* to load with ballast; to steady [obs. *last*, burden].

bal·le·ri·na (bal·ạ·rē'·nạ) *n.* a female ballet dancer [It.].

bal·let (bal'·ā) *n.* a representation, consisting of dancing and miming, aiming to express an idea or tell a story, to the accompaniment of music. **balletomane** (bal·ạt·ạ·mān') *n.* an enthusiast for ballet [Fr.].

bal·lis·ta, balista (bạ·lis'·tạ) *n.* an ancient military contrivance for hurling huge stones. **ballistic** *a.* pert. to a projectile and its flight. **ballistics** *n.pl.* scientific study of motion of projectiles [Gk. *ballein*, to throw].

bal·loon (bạ·lôòn') *n.* bag designed to float in the air and unequipped for mechanical propulsion; anything inflated. **-ing** *n.* **ist** *n.* [Fr. *ballon*].

bal·lot (bal'·ạt) *n.* secret voting; slip of paper used in secret voting; *v.t.* to vote on by ballot; to draw lots [Fr. *ballotte*, little ball].

bal·ly·hoo (bal'·i·hôò)*n.* (*Slang*) advertising; bombast.

balm (bäm) *n.* a fragrant plant; any fragrant or healing ointment; anything which soothes pain. **-iness** *n.* **-y** *a.* fragrant; bearing balm [Fr. *balsamum*].

ba·lo·ney, boloney (bạl·ō'·ni·) *n.* (*Slang*) misleading talk; nonsense; (*Colloq.*) bologna sausage [etym. unknown].

bal·sa, (bawl'·sạ) *n.* the extremely light wood of a W. Indian tree [Sp.].

balloons

bal·sam (bawl'·sạm) *n.* a name applied to many aromatic resins and oils with stimulant and tonic properties; a soothing ointment; a healing agent. **-ic** *n.* soothing, oily. **-ous** *a.* soothing. **-y** *a.* [Gk. *balsamon*].

bal·us·ter (bal'·ạs·tẹr) *n.* a stone or wooden shaft turned and molded, used to support a handrail. **-ed** *a.* provided with balusters. **bal·ustrade** *n.* a row of balusters supporting a railing [Gk. *balaustion*, the pomegranate, whose flowers it resembles].

bam·bi·no (bam·bē'·nō) *n.* a child or baby [It.].

bam·boo (bam·bôò') *n.* a genus of immense grasses in the tropics [Malay].

bam·boo·zle (bam·bôò'·zl) *v.t.* (*Slang*) to mystify; to trick; hoax; cheat; swindle. **-r** *n.*

ban (ban) *n.* proclamation; a sentence of outlawry; excommunication; a curse; a prohibition; *v.t.* to prohibit; to curse; *pr.p.* **-ning.** *pa.t.* and *pa.p.* **-ned** [O.E. *bannan*, to summon, curse].

ba·nal (bān'·ạl, bạn·ál', ban'·ạl) *a.* trite, trivial, petty, vulgar, commonplace. **-ity** *n.*

ba·nan·a (bạ·na'·nạ) *n.* the edible fruit of a tropical plant [Sp.].

band (band) *n.* a cord, tie, or fillet; part of a clerical, legal, or university vestment consisting of two pieces of cambric or linen joined together and worn under the chin; an ornamental strip separating moldings on a building or dividing a wall space; an endless belt used for driving wheels or rollers. **-box** *n.* a light cardboard box for millinery. [O.E. *bindan*, to bind].

band (band) *n.* players of musical instruments in combined performance; a company united for common purpose; a number of armed men; *v.t.* to bind together; *v.i.* to associate, join together. **-master** *n.* director of a military or brass band. **bandsman** *n.* a member of a brass band. **-stand** *n.* an open-air structure suitable for musical performances. **to climb aboard the band wagon,** to participate in a movement when its success is assured. [Fr.].

band·age (band'·ij) *n.* a strip of cloth, used for binding up wounds, etc. *v.t.* to bind with a bandage [Fr. *bande*].

ban·dan·na, ban·dan·a (ban·dan'·ạ)*n.* a large patterned silk or cotton handkerchief [Hind.].

ban·deau (ban'·dō) *n.* a narrow band worn by women to bind the hair; narrow brassiere; *pl.* **bandeaux** [Fr.].

ban·dit (ban'·dit) *n.* robber; brigand; outlaw; highwayman; *pl.* **-s, -ti, -ry** *n.* [It. *bandito*, fr. *bandire*, to outlaw].

ban·do·leer, ban·do·lier (ban·dạ·lēr') *n.* a broad belt worn over the shoulder and fitted with pockets to hold cartridges [It. *bandoliera*].

ban·dy (ban'·di·) *a.* crooked; bent; bandied; bandy-legged; *v.t.* to beat to and fro; to toss from one to another, as 'to bandy words.' **ban·died** *a.* **-legged** *a.* having crooked legs, bending outwards [Fr. *bander*, to bend].

bane (bān) *n.* any cause of ruin; destruction; mischief; noxious substance; poison. **-ful** *a.* **-fulness** *n.* [O.E. *bana*, a murderer].

bang (bang) *v.t.* to beat, as with a club; to handle roughly; to make a loud noise; *n.* a blow with a club or a fist; a loud noise; an explosion. **-ing** *n.* [Scand. *banga*, to hammer].

bang (bang) *v.t.* to cut the front hair square across; *n.* a straight fringe over the forehead or at the end of a horse's tail [nasal variant of *bag*-(cut)].

ban·gle (bang'·gl) *n.* an ornamental ring worn round arm or ankle; bracelet [Urdu, *bangri*, a bracelet].

ban·ish (ban'·ish) *v.t.* to condemn to exile; to drive away; to expel; to cast from the mind. **-ment** *n.* exile [fr. *ban*].

ban·is·ter (ban'·is·tẹr) *n.* Same as **baluster.**

ban·jo (ban'·jō) *n.* a stringed musical instrument [Gk. *pandoura*, a musical instrument].

bank (bangk) *n.* a ridge of earth; a shoal; a sandbank; the edge of a stream or lake; the raised edge of a road, etc.; a mass of heavy clouds or fog; *v.t.* to raise a mound; to dike; to cover a fire with small coal to procure slow combustion; to tilt about the longitudinal axis when turning. **to bank on** *v.t.* to depend on [O.E. *banc*, a bench].

bank (bangk) *n.* a bench on which rowers sit; a tier of oars; a row of objects [Fr. *banc*].

bank (bangk) *n.* an establishment where money is received for custody and repaid on demand; money-box; the money at stake in games of chance; a pool; *v.t.* to deposit money in a bank. **-book** *n.* a pass-book in which a customer's dealings with a bank are recorded. **-er** *n.* one employed in banking; in games of chance the proprietor against whom the other players stake. **-note** *n.* a promissory note on bank of issue promising to pay its face value to bearer on demand. — **rate** *n.* the rate of discount, fixed by a bank or banks [Fr. *banque*].

bank·rupt (bangk'·rupt) *n.* insolvent person compelled to place his affairs in the hands of creditors; *v.t.* to cause to go bankrupt; *a.* insolvent, unable to pay debts; lacking in (ideas, etc.). **-cy** *n.* [E. *bank*; *ruptus*, broken].

ban·ner (ban'·ẹr) *n.* a flag or ensign. **-ed** *a.* [Fr. *bannière*].

ban·nock (ban'·ạk) *n.* (*Scot.*) a flat, thick, cake of oatmeal or barley [Gael. *bonnach*].

banns (banz) *n.pl.* proclamation of intended marriage [fr. *ban*].

ban·quet (bang'·kwet) *n.* a feast; a rich repast; something specially delicious; *v.t.* to entertain at a banquet. **-ing** *n.* [Fr. dim. of *banc*, bench].

ban·shee (ban'·shē) *n.* in Ireland and W. Highlands of Scotland, a fairy-elf who, by shrieks and wailing, foretells the approaching death of a member of a family [Ir. *bean sidhe*, woman of the fairies].

ban·tam (ban'·tạm) *n.* a variety of the small common domestic fowl; *a.* of very light weight; plucky. **-weight,** a boxer weighing less than 118 lbs. [fr. *Bantam*, a village in Java].

ban·ter (ban'·tẹr) *v.i.* to make good-natured fun of someone; to joke, jest; to rally; *n.* wit at expense of another; chaff; pleasantry. **-er** *n.*

Ban·tu (ban'·tôò) *n.* an African language.

ban·yan (ban'·yạn) *n.* the Indian fig; a tree whose branches, bending to the ground, take root and form new stocks, till they become a forest. Hence—**to flourish like the banyantree** [Port.].

bap·tize (bap'·tīz) *v.t.* to administer the sacrament of baptism to; to christen; give a name to. **baptism** *n.* sacrament by which a person is initiated into the membership of the Christian Church. **baptismal** *a.* **Baptist** *n.* one who baptizes; one who insists that the rite of initiation is duly administered only by immersion upon personal profession of faith. **baptistery, baptistry** *n.* an ancient circular building in which baptisms took place [Gk. *baptizein*, to immerse].

bar (bár) *n.* a long piece of any solid material, used as barrier; the bolt of a door; a sand-bank; part of a tavern with a counter for the sale of liquor; a public-house; the rail before the judge's seat where prisoners appear; members of the legal profession allowed to plead in court; (*Her.*) a band crossing the shield; (*Mus.*) a perpendicular line drawn across the stave immediately before the primary accent; *v.t.* to fasten or mark with a bar; to obstruct; to prevent; to exclude; *prep.* except. **-maid, -man, -tender** *n.* a bar attendant. **-ring** *prep.* excepting; *n.* exclusion of any kind. *pr.p.* **-ring.** *pa.p.* **-red.** [Fr. *barre*].

barb (bárb) *n.* a hooked hair; the spike of an arrow, fish-hook, etc.; a horse of great speed and endurance, originally from Barbary; *v.t.* to furnish with barbs or prongs, as an arrow; to trim the beard. **-ed** *a.* bearded; furnished with a barb or barbs. **-ed wire** *n.* a wire armed with sharp points used for defensive purposes [L. *barba*, beard].

bar·bar·i·an (bár·be'·ri·ạn) *n.* orig. one who could not speak Greek, now an uncivilized being without culture; a cruel, brutal man; *a.* savage; rude. **barbaric** *a.* uncivilized; rude; nobly savage. **barbarize** *v.t.* to render barbarous. **barbarism** *n.* incorrect use of idiom or word; want of civilization. **barbarity** *n.* cruelty; savagery. **barbarous** *a.* uncivilized or savage [Gk. *barbaros*, foreign].

bar·be·cue (bár'·bi·kū) *n.* a grid-iron on which meat is roasted over an open fire; an animal so roasted; a lavish open-air feast [Haitian].

bar·ber (bár'·bẹr) *n.* one who shaves or trims and dresses the hair; a hair-dresser [L. *barba*, beard].

bar·ber·ry (bár'·bẹr·i·) *n.* (*Bot.*) a shrub with clusters of red berries [M.L. *berberis*].

bar·bi·tu·rates (bár·bit'·ū·rātz) *n.* (*Med.*) derivatives of barbituric acid, non-habit forming, hypnotic and sedative drugs.

bar·ca·role, bar·ca·rolle, (bár′·ka̤·rōl) *n.* a musical composition written in imitation of the gondoliers' songs of Venice. [It. *barca*, a boat].

bard (bárd) *n.* a Celtic minstrel who celebrated in song the great deeds of heroes; a poet. **-ic** *a.* pert. to bards or their poetry [Celt.].

bare (bār) *a.* without covering; naked; empty; open to view; paltry; *v.t.* to strip off or uncover. **-ly** *adv.* openly; poorly; scarcely. **-ness** *n.* **-facedness** *n.* sheer impudence. [O.E. *baer*].

bar·gain (bár′·gin) *n.* an agreement between parties in buying and selling; a profitable transaction; something purchased cheaply. *v.i.* to make a contract; to chaffer. **-er** *n.* one who haggles over the price. **into the bargain,** over and above what is agreed upon [O.Fr. *bargaigner*].

barge (bárj) *n.* flat-bottomed boat; a ship's boat; *v.i.* to push forward roughly. **-man** *n.* [L. *barca,* a boat].

bar·i·tone (bár′·a̤·tōn) *n.* the male human voice between tenor and bass [Gk. *barys,* heavy; *tonos,* tone].

bar·i·um (bár′·i·a̤m) *n.* metallic element (symbol *Ba*). **baric** *a.* [fr. Gk. *barys,* heavy].

bark (bárk) *n.* the outer covering of a tree; rind; waste tan used in manufacturing white-lead; *v.t.* to strip off bark; to graze the skin. [Scand.].

bark (bárk) *v.t.* to utter a cry like a dog; to yelp; *(Slang)* to advertise by shouting; to speak sharply; **-er,** *n.* **to bark up the wrong tree,** to be on the wrong trail [O.E. *beorcan*].

bark, barque (bárk) *n.* a three masted vessel; a small sailing-ship; *(Poet.)* a ship [Fr. *barque*].

bar·ley (bár′·li·) *n.* a cereal, the grain being used for malt-making, bread, and food for cattle. **-corn** *n.* a grain of barley; the third part of an inch. **John Barleycorn** *(Fig.)* whisky. **— flour** *n.* flour made by grinding barley. **— sugar** *n.* a confection made from sugar boiled till brittle in barley water. [O.E. *bere,* barley].

barm (bárm) *n.* the froth on fermenting malt liquors, used in making bread; yeast. **-y** *a.* pert. to barm; light-headed, flighty, or giddy [O.E. *beorma,* yeast].

barn (bárn) *n.* a covered farm-building for storing grain, hay, etc. and for stabling live stock; *v.t.* to store in a barn. **— dance** *n.* a lively dance in 4-4 time, resembling the schottische. **-yard** *n.* a pert. to domestic fowls. open enclosure attached to barn [O.E. *bere,* barley; *ern,* a place].

bar·na·cle (bár′·na̤·kl) *n.* a shell-fish which attaches itself to the bottoms of ships and to rocks. **-d** *a.* [O.Fr. *bernac*].

ba·rom·e·ter (ba̤·rám′·a̤·ter) *n.* an instrument for recording the weight or pressure of the atmosphere which indicates impending weather changes. **barometric, barometrical** *a.* [Gk. *baros,* weight; *metron,* measure].

bar·on (bar′·a̤n) *n.* a title of nobility, the lowest of the British peerage to sit in the House of Lords; a commercial magnate. *(fem.* **baroness)** [L.L. *baro,* a man].

bar·o·net (bar′·a̤·net) *n.* hereditary title ranking below a baron and above a knight but without privilege of peerage. **baronetcy** *n.* the rank of a baronet [dim. of *baron*].

ba·roque (ba̤·rōk′) *n.* orig. a jeweller's trade term for ill-shaped pearls; *(Art.)* a florid style of the late Renaissance; *a.* over-lavish; extravagantly ornamented [Port. *barrocco*].

bar·o·scope (bar′·a̤·skōp) *n.* an instrument giving rough indications of variations in the atmospheric pressure [Gk. *baros,* weight; *skopein,* to see].

bar·rack (bar′·ak) *n.* a building for the accommodation of soldiers (generally used in the plural) [Sp. *barraca,* a tent].

bar·ra·cu·da (bar·a̤·kōō′·da) *n.* a large edible pike-like fish, found in the Atlantic [Sp.].

bar·rage (ba̤·razh′) *n.* an artificial bar erected across a stream to regulate its flow; a screen of continuous military fire produced to protect the advance of troops or to stop hostile attacks; heavy prolonged attack.

bar·ra·try (bar′·a̤·tri·) *n.* fraudulent breach of duty by the master of a ship entailing loss by the owners or insurers of ship or cargo; habitually inciting riot or stirring up suits and quarrels [O.Fr. *barat,* fraud].

bar·rel (bar′·a̤l) *n.* a cylindrical wooden container consisting of staves bound by hoops; a measure of capacity; anything cylindrical, as a gun-barrel; *v.t.* to stow in barrels. **— organ** *n.* street-organ played by rotating a wooden barrel [Fr. *baril*].

bar·ren (bar′·a̤n) *a.* incapable of producing offspring or fruit; empty, lacking. **-ly** *adv.* **-ness** *n.* sterility [O.Fr.].

bar·rette (ba̤·ret′) *n.* small bar or clasp worn to hold hair in place [Fr. *barre*].

bar·ri·cade (bar′·i·kād) *n.* a make-shift fortification, built as an obstruction; an obstruction which hinders free passage; *v.t.* to build this; formerly **barricado** [Fr. *barrica,* a cask].

bar·ri·er (bar′·i·er) *n.* a chain of military posts to protect frontiers; a railing, fence, or wall; any obstruction; a line of separation [O.Fr. *barrière*].

barrel

bar·ris·ter (bar′·is·ter) *n. (Br.)* a member of the highest branch of the legal profession, with exclusive right of practicing in the superior courts of England [fr. *bar*].

bar·row (bar′·ō) *n.* a small kind of light frame provided with two shafts, for carrying loads [O.E. *beran,* to bear].

bar·row (bar′·ō) *n.* an artificial mound of stone, wood, or earth, piled up in prehistoric times over the remains of the dead; a hillock [O.E. *beorg,* a mound].

bar·ter (bár′·ter) *v.t.* to exchange or give in exchange; *v.i.* to traffic by exchange of one kind of goods for another; *n.* direct exchange of commodities [O.Fr. *barater,* to haggle].

bas·al See **base** *n.*

ba·salt (ba̤·sawlt′) *n.* an igneous rock of a greenish-black color. **-ic** *a.* [L. *basaltes,* black basalt].

bas·cule (bas′·kūl) *n.* a balancing lever. **bascule-bridge** *n.* a counterpoise bridge [Fr. *bas,* down; *cul,* the posterior].

base (bās) *a.* of humble birth or of low degree; morally low. **-ly** *adv.* **-born** *a.* illegitimate [Fr. *bas,* low].

base (bās) *n.* bottom; part of a thing on which it rests; foundation; support; starting-place; fixed point; supply point of an army; station at baseball; main ingredient; *(Chem.)* a substance capable of combining with an acid to form a salt; *v.t.* to put on a base; to found. **basal** *a.* situated at the base. **-less** *a.* having no foundation. **-lessness** *n.* **-ly** *adv.* **-ment** *n.* the lowest story of a building. **basic** *a.* **-board** *n.* a skirting board covering the lower part of a wall [Gk. *basis*].

base (bās) *(Mus.).* See **bass.**

base·ball (bās′·bawl) *n.* ball game, played by two teams of nine players in which a player after batting must make the complete circuit of four bases to score a run; the ball used.

bash (bash) *v.t. (Colloq.)* to smash in; to beat in; to knock out of shape; to beat; a severe blow; a dent. **-ing** *n.* a thrashing [blend of *bat* and *mash*].

bash·ful (bash′·ful) *a.* shy; not desiring to attract notice. **-ly** *adv.* **-ness** *n.* [fr. *abashfull*].

ba·sic (bā′·sik) *a.* relating to or serving as a base; primary; containing a small amount of silica. **English,** simplification of English. **— slag** *n.* a by-product in the manufacture of steel, used as a manure [Gk. *basis,* a base].

bas·il (baz′·il) *n.* aromatic culinary plant; sweet basil [Gk. *basilikos,* royal].

ba·sil·i·ca (ba̤·sil′·i·ka̤) *n.* a public building or hall of the Romans, often converted into a church by early Christians; a spacious church built on the model of the original basilicas. **basilican** *a.* [Gk. *basilikos,* royal].

bas·i·lisk (bas′·a̤·lisk) *n.* a fabulous creature; a cockatrice; *(Zool.)* a harmless tree-dwelling American lizard; [Gk. *basilikos,* royal].

ba·sin (bā′·sn) *n.* a wide, hollow, bowl-shaped container; a sink; a land-locked bay with a good anchorage; the whole tract of country drained by a river [Fr. *bassin*].

ba·sis (bā′·sis) *n.* that on which a thing rests; foundation. *pl.* **bases** [Gk.].

bask (bask) *v.i.* to sun oneself; to lie in warmth or sunshine [Scand.].

bas·ket (bas′·kit) *n.* a container made of willow, cane, rushes, or other flexible materials, interwoven. **-ball** *n.* a game where a ball has to be thrown through a basket. **-ful** *n.* **-ry, -work** *n.* wickerwork.

Basque (bask) *n.* a native or the language of the Basque country (Western Pyrenees); part of a lady's dress, resembling a jacket with a short skirt; *a.* relating to the Basques [Fr.].

bas-re·lief, bass-re·lief (bá or bás·ra̤·lēf′) *n.* or *a.* low relief, sculpture in which figures or objects are raised slightly upon a flat surface, like embossed work [Fr.].

bass (bas) *n.* name applied to any perch-like fish [M.E. *barse, bace*].

bass (bas) *n.* the basswood or linden tree or its inner bark; fiber; matting [O.E. *baest*].

bass, base (bās) *n. (Mus.)* the lowest part of harmony, whether vocal or instrumental; the deepest quality of the human voice or a stringed instrument; *a.* low. **— clef** *n.* the sign on the fourth line of the bass stave. **double-bass** *n.* the largest of the stringed instruments [It. *basso,* low].

bas·set (bas′·it) *n.* a hound formerly used in badger hunting; *(Geol.)* emergence of strata at the surface; out-crop. **— horn** *n.* a rich-toned wind instrument [Fr. *bas,* low].

bas·si·net, bas·si·nette (bas·a̤·net′) *n.* a baby's basket with a hood [Fr. dim. of *bassin*].

bas·so (bas′·ō) *n.* a bass singer; the bass part of a harmony [It. — low].

bas·soon (ba̤·sŏŏn′) *n.* a wood-wind musical instrument with a double reed mouthpiece; organ reed stop of that name. **double —,** one which sounds an octave lower.**-ist** *n.* [It. *basso,* low].

bast (bast) *n.* inner bark of a tree, used for binding purposes; raffia, matting, cordage, etc., made of the bark [O.E. *baest*].

bas·tard (bas′·terd) *n.* a child born out of wedlock; an impure, coarse brown refuse product of sugar-refining, used to color beer; *a.* illegitimate; false; counterfeit; **-y** *n.* act of begetting a bastard; being a bastard. **-ize** *v.t.* to render illegitimate [O.Fr. *bastard,* from *fils de bast,* son of a pack-saddle].

baste (bāst) *v.t.* to sew loosely with long stitches; to moisten (meat) with butter, drippings, etc. while cooking [O.Fr. *bastir,* to stitch loosely].

bas·tille (bas·tēl′) *n.* originally a tower or bastion; a state prison. **The Bastille,** the famous state prison of Paris [Fr. *bastille,* a building].

bas·ti·na·do (bas·ti·nā′·dō) *n.* an oriental form of punishment by beating the soles of the feet [Sp. *baston,* a stick]. [fense [Fr.].

bas·tion (bast′·chan) *n.* a stronghold of de-**bat** (bat) *n.* a club or stick; a shaped club used in cricket or baseball; a piece of a brick; wad of clay; *v.i.* to strike or hit with a bat; *pr.p.* **-ting;** *pa.p.* **-ted, -ter, -man** *n.* [O.E. *batt,* club].

bat (bat) *n.* nocturnal, flying mammal. **-ity** *a. (Slang)* crazy. Also **bats, to have bats in the belfry,** to be crazy or eccentric [Scand. *bakke*].

bat (bat) *v.t. (Colloq.)* to wink. **never batted an eyelid,** showed no emotion whatever; never slept. [var. of *late,* flutter].

batch (bach) *n.* the quantity of bread baked at one time; a number of articles received or dispatched at one time; a set of similar articles [M.E. *batche,* fr. *bake*].

[*abate*].

bate (bāt) *v.t.* to lessen; to abate [form of **bath** (bath) *n.* a vessel or place to bathe in; the water in which to bathe; a solution in which photographic plates are immersed; *v.t.* to wash oneself. **-s** *n.pl.* hot or mineral springs resorted to by invalids. **-house** *n.* **-room** *n.* **blood—** *n.* a massacre. **Turkish bath,** steam bath followed by massage. **sitz bath,** a shallow bath, for bathing hips and buttocks [O.E. *baeth*].

bathe (bāTH) *v.t.* to wash by immersion; *v.i.* to be immersed; to swim; *pr.p.* **bathing.** **-r** *n.* **bathing** *n.* **bathing-pool** *n.* [O.E. *bathian*].

ba·thet·ic See under **bathos.**

bath·i·nette (bath·i·net′) *n.* portable folding bathtub for babies.

ba·thom·e·ter (ba·thŏm′·ȧ·tẽr) n. a spring balance for determining the depth of water [Gk. *bathos*, depth; *metron*, measure].

ba·thos (bā′·thós) n. a term which indicates a ludicrous descent from the sublime to the ridiculous in speech or writing; anti-climax. **bathetic** a. [Gk. *bathos*, depth].

bath·y (bath′·i·) *prefix* from Gk. *bathus*, deep, used in the construction of compound terms relating to sea-depths. **bathysphere** n. a form of deep-sea diving-bell [Gk. *bathus*, deep; *metron*, to measure; s, ˈaira, a ball].

ba·tiste (ba·tēst′) n. a fine kind of linen cloth from Flanders, a variety of cambric [Fr.].

ba·ton (ba·tán′) n. a short staff or club; a truncheon, symbolic of authority or used as an offensive weapon; in music, wand used by conductor in beating time; a marshal's staff. v.t. to strike with a baton [Fr. *baton*].

batt, bat·ting (bat, bat′·ing) n. fiber wadded into sheets [O.E. *batt*].

bat·tal·ion (ba·tal′·yan) n. a military tactical and administrative unit of command consisting of three or more companies or similar units. **-s** n.pl. great numbers, swarms [Fr. *bataillon*, cf. **battle**].

bat·ten (bat′·n) v.t. to fatten; v.i. to grow fat in luxury [Icel. *batna*, to grow better].

bat·ten (bat′·n) n. a piece of wood nailed on a surface to give it strength; board used on ships to fasten down the hatch-covers in stormy weather; v.t. to fasten or form with battens [a form of *baton*].

bat·ter (bat′·ẽr) v.t. to strike or beat continuously; to assault; to wear by hard use; n. a mixture moistened to a paste and briskly beaten up. **-ing ram** n. a suspended beam used to breach walls [Fr. *battre*, to beat].

bat·ter·y (bat′·ẽr·i) n. act of battering; a place where cannon are mounted; a division of artillery; electric cells which store electric current; the pitcher and catcher in baseball [Fr. *battre*, to beat].

bat·tle (bat′·l) n. an encounter between enemies; struggle of any kind; v.i. to fight on a large scale. **—axe** n. primitive weapon; (Slang) cantankerous woman. **— cry** n. a war-shout; a slogan. **-field, -ground** n. scene of battle. **-r** n. one who take part in a battle. **— royal** n. a regular melée where fists are freely used. **-ship** n. the largest and most heavily armed of fast warships [Fr. *bataille*].

bat·tle·ment (bat′·l·mant) n. a protective parapet on a wall [M.E. *batilment*].

bau·ble (baw′·bl) n, a trifling piece of finery; a gew-gaw; a stick with a fool's head on the end, carried by jesters of former times; a. trifling [O.Fr. *baubel*, a toy].

baulk (bawk) See **balk**.

baux·ite (bák′·sit, bō′·zit) n. a hydrated oxide of aluminum and ferric oxide; the principal source of aluminum [fr. *Baux*, near Arles, S. France].

bawd (bawd) n. a procurer or procuress of women for immoral purposes. **-ily** adv. **-iness** n. **-ry** n. **-y** a. obscene; filthy; unchaste. **—house**, n. a brothel (O.Fr. *baud*, gay].

bawl (bawl) v.t. to shout, to proclaim; v.i. to shout out with a loud voice; n. a loud, prolonged cry. **bawl out** (Colloq.) reprimand [M.L. *laulare*, to bark].

bay (bā) a. reddish-brown; n. a chestnut horse. **-ard** n. a bay horse; a spirited horse; one foolishly self-confident; a knight of good fame [L. *badius*, chestnut-colored].

bay (bā) n. an inlet of the sea [Fr. *baie*].

bay (bā) n. the subdivision longitudinally of a building by piers, arches, girders, etc. **— window** n. a window projecting beyond the wall. **sick —**, ship's hospital [Fr. *baie*].

bay (bā) n. the laurel tree. **-s** n.pl. the victor's garland or crown. **— rum** n. an aromatic liquid used as a perfume and cosmetic for the hair [Fr. *baie*, berry].

bay (bā) n. barking, esp. of hounds in pursuit of prey; v.t. to bark at. **at bay**, said of a hunted animal, when all escape is cut off [O.Fr. *baier*, to bark].

bay·ber·ry (bā′·ber·i·) n. evergreen shrub, used for making bay rum; one variety used in candle making [bay and berry].

bay·o·net (bā′·a·net) n. a short spear-like weapon attached to the muzzle of a rifle; v.t. to stab with a bayonet. [fr. *Bayonne*, the town where first made].

ba·zaar, bazar (ba·zär′) n. an Oriental market-place; a sale where articles are sold for charity; shop selling miscellaneous goods [Pers.].

ba·zoo·ka (ba·zoo′·ka) n. a portable light rocket-gun.

B.C. before Christ.

be (bē) v.i. and aux. (pres. indic. **am**; past indic. **was**; past part. **been**), to exist; to live; to have a state, existence, or quality; to remain; to happen; to belong [O.E. *beon*].

be- *prefix* used in the construction of compound words, as *becalm*, etc.

beach (bēch) n. the shore of the sea or of a lake, esp. where sandy or pebbly; the shore; v.t. to run or haul a boat up on to a beach. **-comber** n. a long, rolling wave; a lounger who frequents beaches or seaports; scrounger. **-head** n. a footing gained on hostile shores by an army.

bea·con (bē′·kn) n. a fire lit on a high eminence, usually as a warning; a warning light; a floating buoy; traffic sign indicating a pedestrian crossing; v.t. to mark a channel by beacons [O.E. *beacn*].

bead (bēd) n. a little ball pierced for stringing; any small spherical object such as a front sight on a gun; v.t. to furnish with beads; v.i. to string beads. **-s** n.pl. a rosary, a necklace; flange of a tire; **-ed** a. in bead form. **-ing** n. a small rounded molding imitating beads. **-y** a. bead-like. **to draw a bead on**, to aim a gun at. [O.E. *gebed*, a prayer].

bea·gle (bē′·gl) n. the smallest hound used in hunting; (Fig.) a spy or informer.

beak (bēk) n. the horny bill of a bird, turtle, etc.; anything shaped like a beak (Slang) a beak-shaped nose [Fr. *bec*.].

beak·er (bē′·kẽr) n. a large drinking-cup or vessel; a tumbler-shaped vessel of thin glass used by chemists [Scand. *bikarr*].

beam (bēm) n. a strong, horizontal piece of timber or reinforced concrete for spanning and supporting weights; the part of a balance from which the scales hang; the cross-timber of a ship; the extreme width, measured athwartships, of a ship; wooden cylinder on which the warp is wound in a loom; the pole of a carriage; the shaft of an anchor; a sharply defined ray of light; the sparkle in a person's eyes manifesting extreme pleasure or interest; v.t. to emit beams of light; v.i. to send forth rays of light; to shine; to smile benignly. **-ing** a. radiantly happy; shining; n. rays of light; manifestation of pleasure by smiling. **-less** a. [O.E. *beam*, a tree].

bean (bēn) n. the flat, kidney-shaped seed of various plants, chiefly of the genus *Phaseolus*; (Slang) head. **-bag** n. a toy, a small cloth bag partly filled with beans. **full of beans**, in good fettle; energetic. [O.E. *bean*].

bear (bār) v.t. to support or to carry; to endure; to suffer; to behave; to give birth to; v.i. to produce (as fruit); to endure; to press; pa.t. **bore**; pa.p. **borne** or **born**. **-able** a. able to be borne; tolerable. **-ably** adv. **-er** n. carrier or messenger; a person who helps to carry a coffin; a presenter of a check. **-ing** n. the manner in which a person acts or behaves; the direction in which one thing lies from another; relation to or connection with; **-ings** n.pl. machine surfaces carrying a moving part and bearing friction. **to bear out**, to corroborate. **to bear with**, to endure patiently. **to bring to bear**, to apply pressure. **to lose one's bearings**, to lose all sense of direction [O.E. *beran*].

bear (bār) n. a carnivorous mammal of the Ursidae genus; a rough, boorish person; one who sells stocks before he has bought them, in the hope of a fall in price before settlement; (Astron.) one of two constellations in the northern hemisphere, called respectively the **Great Bear** and the **Lesser Bear**. **— baiting** n. a form of sport where dogs were employed to worry the animal. **-like** a. **skin** n. [O.E. *bera*].

beard (bērd) n. the hair that grows on the chin and cheeks; the awns or prickles of an ear of corn; the gills of oysters; the barb of an arrow; v.t. to pluck the beard of; to confront or defy someone. **-ed** a. **-less** a. [O.E.].

beast (bēst) n. any inferior animal as opposed to man; a four-footed animal especially if wild; cattle; person of brutal nature or of dirty habits. **-ly** a. like a beast in form or nature; filthy; displeasing. **-liness** n. [L. *bestia*].

beat (bēt) v.t. to strike or hit repeatedly; to pommel; to crush; to defeat; to be too difficult for; to spread flat and thin with a tool, as gold leaf; to drive game out of cover; to mark time in music; v.i. to throb; to dash against as waves, wind, etc. pa.t. **beat**; pa.p. **-en**; n. a recurrent stroke; a pulse throb; (Mus.) the divisions in a bar, the movement of a conductor's baton; zig-zag sailing of a ship working up against the wind; the round or course followed repeatedly by someone, e.g. a policeman, a postman; a. (Colloq.) exhausted. **-en** a. hammered into shape by a tool; worn by continual use. **-er** n. **-ing** n. act of giving blows; a thrashing; throbbing; driving out game. **-nik** n. (Colloq.)

one who rebels against the conventions of society. **to beat about the bush**, to approach a subject in a round about way. **to beat a tatoo**, to sound the drums at roll-call. **dead beat** n. (Colloq.) one with a reputation for not paying his bills; (Slang) a loafer; sponger [O.E. *beatan*].

be·at·i·fy (bē·at′·a·fī) v.t. to render supremely blessed or happy; to bless with celestial enjoyment (preliminary to canonization in R.C. Church). **beatific(al)** a. having power of making happy or blessed. **beatifically** adv. **beatification** n. [L. *betaus*, happy].

be·at·i·tude (bē·at′·a·tūd) n. highest form of heavenly happiness; supreme blessedness. **the beatitudes** (Bib.) blessings spoken in regard to particular virtues (Matt. 5) [L. *beatus*, happy].

beau (bō) n. a fop; dandy; sweetheart; suitor. pl. **beaux** (bōz). **— monde** n. the fashionable world and its people [Fr.].

beau·ty (bū′·ti·) n. the inherent quality in an object of pleasing the eye, ear, or mind; a particular grace or excellence; a beautiful woman; a fine specimen. **beauteous** a. full of beauty; very handsome. **beauteously** adv. **beauteousness** n. **beautician** n. expert in use of cosmetics. **beautifier** n. a cosmetic, a decorator. **beautiful** a. highly pleasing to eye, ear, or mind; handsome; lovely; fine; excellent. **beautifully** adv. **beautifulness** n. **beautify** v.t. to make beautiful. **beautiless** a. lacking beauty. **— spot** n. a place noted for its attractive surroundings; a patch placed on the face to heighten beauty [Fr. *beauté*].

bea·ver (bē′·vẽr) n. an amphibious, four-footed rodent valued for its fur and for castoreum, an extract from its glands used in medicine; the fur of the beaver; a beaver hat; a. made of beaver fur [O.E. *beofor*].

be·bop (bē′·bäp) n. (Slang) jazz music characterized by improvisation. **[-ed** a.

be·calm (bi·käm′) v.t. to make calm or quiet.

be·came (bi·kām′) past tense of **become**.

be·cause (bi·kawz′) adv. and conj. for the reason that; since [E. *by*, and *cause*].

beck (bek) n. sign or gesture of the head or hand; a nod; v.i. to make such a gesture; v.t. to call by a nod or a sign; to beckon. **at one's beck and call**, entirely at someone's disposal [fr. *beckon*].

beck·on (bek′·n) v.t. and v.i. to make a sign with the hand or head; to summon with hand or finger [O.E. *becnan*].

be·come (bi·kum′) v.t. to pass from one state to another; to suit or be suitable to; pa.t. **became**; pa.p. **become**. **becoming** a. appropriate or fit [O.E. *becuman*].

bed (bed) n. a couch on which to sleep or take rest; a plot of ground in which plants are cultivated; channel of a stream; the bearing surface of anything; a thin layer of mortar between two surfaces; a layer of rock; stratum; v.t. to place in bed; to plant out; to arrange in layers; pr.p. **-ding**; pa.p. **-ded**. **-bug** n. bloodsucking insect. **-clothes** n.pl. bed coverings, clothes worn to bed. **-ding** n. materials of a bed. **-fast** a. confined to bed; bed-ridden. **-fellow** n. one who sleeps in the same bed with another. **-pan** n. a pan for warming a bed; pan used as toilet. **-plate** n. the foundation plate of an engine lathe, etc. **-post** n. one of the upright supports of a bed. **-rid, -ridden** a. permanently confined to bed by age or infirmity. **-rock** n. the solid rock beneath loose material as sand, etc.; fundamentals. **-room** n. a room for sleeping. **-sore** n. ulcer caused by constant pressure on a part of the body of a bed-ridden patient. **-spread** n. a covering of fine material for a bed. **-stead** n. the framework, of iron or wood, of a bed. **-ticking** n. the cloth case for holding the feathers, hair, etc. of a mattress. **bed and board**, food and lodging [O.E. *bedd*].

be·daub (bi·dawb′) v.t. to smear.

be·daz·zle (bi·daz′·l) v.t. to overpower by employing too strong a light or by a magnificent show.

be·deck (bē·dek′) v.t. to deck, adorn, ornament.

be·dev·il (bi·dev′·l) v.t. to beat with devilish malignity; to torment; to throw into confusion; to confound; to bewitch.

be·dew (bi·dū′) v.t. to moisten with dew.

be·dight (bi·dīt′) a. decked out with ornaments; adorned; arrayed (Poet.).

be·dim (bi·dim′) v.t. to make dim; to darken. pr.p. **-ming**; pa.t. **-med. bedimmed** a.

be·diz·en (bi·diz′·n, bi·dī′·zn) v.t. to dress gaudily or with false taste. **-ed** a.

bed·lam (bed′·lam) n. a mad-house; a lunatic asylum; a mental institution; a scene of uproar; pandemonium. **-ite** n. a lunatic [corrupt. of *Bethlehem*, an asylum].

Bed·ou·in (bed′·oo·in) n. Arab; nomad [Ar. *bādawin*, dwellers in the desert].

be·drag·gle (bi·drag′·l) v.t. to soil by trailing in the wet or mud. **-d** a.

bee (bē) n. highest form of insect belonging to the order Hymenoptera; the honey-bee; a social gathering for common or mutual help, e.g. a spelling-bee; a busy person. **-culture** n. the rearing of bees, apiculture. **-hive** n. a case or box where the bees are housed; a. shaped like a bee-hive. **-keeper** n. **-line** n. the shortest route from one place to another. **-swax** n. the wax secreted by bees; a floor-polish; v.t. to polish with beeswax [O.E. *bēo*].

beech (bēch) *n.* a tree of the temperate and sub-frigid zones, greatly valued for its wood. **-coal** *n.* charcoal made from beechwood. **-en** *a.* made of beech. **beechnut** *n.* the triangular, edible nut of the beech [O.E. *béce*].

beef (bēf) *n.* the flesh of an ox, bull, or cow; flesh and muscle; muscular strength; vigor; *a.* consisting of beef; *v.i.* (*Slang*) to make complaints. **beeves** (bēvz) *n.pl.* oxen. **-eater** *n.* one of the Yeomen of the Guard; a Warder of the Tower of London; a tendency to put on flesh. **-steak** *n.* a thick slice of beef. **-y** *a.* stolid; fat [Fr. *boeuf*, ox].

been (bin) *pa.p.* of the verb *be*.

beer (bēr) *n.* an alcoholic beverage made by brewing and fermentation of cereals. **-y** *a.* pert. to the taste or smell of beer; discolored with beer slops [O.E. *beor*].

beest·ings, biest·ings (bēs´·tingz) *n.* the first milk taken from a cow after calving, thicker than ordinary milk [O.E. *bysting*].

beet (bēt) *n.* a garden or field plant having a succulent tap root, the red variety being used as a vegetable, the white yielding sugar. — **sugar** *n.* crystallized sugar extracted from beetroot [O.E. *béte*, fr. L. *bēta*].

bee·tle (bē´·tl) *n.* heavy wooden mallet for beating down paving-stones or driving in piles; wooden utensil for beating linen, mashing potatoes or stirring porridge, etc. [O.E. *betel*, a mallet].

bee·tle (bē´·tl) *n.* name of a large order of insects, Coleoptera [O.E. *bitula*, a biter].

bee·tle (bē´·tl) *v.i.* to be prominent; to jut out; to overhang. **beetling** *a.* overhanging. **—browed** *a.* with overhanging brows; scowling. **-head** *n.* a dull, stupid person [O.E. *bitel*].

beeves (bēvz) *n.pl.* cattle, oxen [See *beef*].

be·fall (bi·fawl´) *v.t.* to happen to; *v.i.* to come to pass; to happen; *pr.p.* **-ing**; *pat.* **befell**; *pa.p.* **-en** [O.E. *befeallan*].

be·fit (bi·fit´) *v.t.* to fit or be suitable to; to become; be right for; *pr.p.* **-ting**; *pat.*, *pa.p.* **-ted.** **-ting** *a.* **-tingly** *adv.*

be·fog (bi·fawg´) *v.t.* to envelop in a fog; perplex. *pr.p.* **-ging.** *pat.* **-ged.**

be·fore (bi·fōr´) *prep.* in front of; preceding; in the presence of; prior to; previous to; superior to; *adv.* in front of; in advance; a short time ago; already. *conj.* sooner than; rather than. **-hand** *adv.* previously. **-time** *adv.* of old; formerly [O.E. *beforan*].

be·foul (bi·foul´) *v.t.* to foul, soil, dirty.

be·friend (bi·frend´) *v.t.* to act as a friend to; to favor; to help a stranger.

be·fud·dle (bi·fu·dl) *v.t.* to confuse.

beg (beg) *v.t.* to ask earnestly and humbly; to ask for alms; to practice begging; to beseech; *pr.p.* **-ging**; *pat.* and *pa.p.* **-ged.** **-gar** *n.* one who solicits alms; a mendicant; *v.t.* to reduce to beggary; to ruin financially. **-garliness** *n.* **-garly** *a.* like a beggar; poor; mean; squalid; worthless; meagre; trifling; *adv.* meanly. **-gary** *n.* extreme poverty. **-ging** *n.* soliciting alms; *a.* pert. to begging; imploring; soliciting. **to beg the question**, to assume truth of thing to be proved [M.E. *beggen*].

be·gan (bi·gan´) *pat.* of *begin*.

be·get (bi·get´) *v.t.* to generate; to procreate; to produce or to cause; to get; give rise to. *pr.p.* **-ting**; *pat.* **begot, begat**; *pa.p.* **begot, begotten** [O.E. *begitan*, fr. *get*].

be·gin (bi·gin´) *v.t.* to enter on; to start, to commence; *v.i.* to take the first step; to set about. *pr.p.* **-ning**; *pat.* **began**; *pa.p.* **begun.** **-ner** *n.* one who begins; novice. **-ning** *n.* source; first part [O.E. *beginnan*].

be·gird (bi·gurd´) *v.t.* to gird or bind with a girdle or band; *pat.* **begirt** or **-ed.**

be·gone (bi·gawn´) *interj.* go away! depart! **woebegone** *a.* gloomy and miserable.

be·go·ni·a (bi·gōn´·ya) *n.* a genus of tropical plants [Michel *Bégon*, Fr. botanist].

be·got (bi·gåt´) **begotten** *pa.p.* of *beget*.

be·grime (bi·grīm´) *v.t.* to soil with grime.

be·grudge (bi·gruj´) *v.t.* to grudge; to allow reluctantly. **begrudgingly** *adv.*

be·guile (bi·gīl´) *v.t.* to cheat or deceive by trickery; to ensnare; to delude; to while away (time); to amuse or divert. **-ment** *n.* **-r** *n.* **beguilingly** *adv.*

be·gum (bi·gun´) *n.* the Hindustani name given to a Moslem princess.

be·gun (bi·gun´) *pa.p.* of *begin*.

be·half (bi·haf´) *n.* favor; advantage; benefit; support; vindication; defense [O.E. *be healfe*, by the side].

be·have (bi·hāv´) *v.t.* and *v.i.* to conduct oneself; to act. **behavior** *n.* bearing or conduct; deportment. **behaviorism** *n.* theory that man's actions are automatic responses to stimuli and not dictated by consciousness.

be·head (bi·hed´) *v.t.* to sever the head from the body. **-al, -ing** *n.*

be·held (bi·held´) *pa.p.* of *behold*.

be·hest (bi·hest´) *n.* that which is willed or ordered [O.E. *behaes*].

be·hind (bi·hīnd´) *prep.* at the back of; in the rear (of); after; late; farther back than; in an inferior position; *n.* rump; buttocks; posterior. **-hand** *adv.* and *a.* late; backward; in arrears [O.E. *behindan*].

be·hold (bi·hōld´) *v.t.* to look at; to fix the eyes upon; to observe carefully; *v.i.* to look; fix the attention. *pat.* and *pa.p.* **beheld.** **-en** *a.* obliged (to); owing a debt of gratitude (to). **-er** *n.* an on-looker; spectator [O.E. *behealdan*].

be·hoof (bi·hōōf´) *n.* advantage; benefit; profit; use. **behoove, behove** *v.t.* to be necessary, convenient for; to befit [O.E. *behōf*].

beige (bāzh) *n.* very light brown color of unbleached wool [Fr.].   [an animal [fr. *to be*].

be·ing (bē´·ing) *n.* existence; that which exists.

be·la·bor (bi·lā´·ber) *v.t.* to beat soundly; to cudgel; to exert much labor upon; to assail verbally.   [tard. **-d** *a.* **-dness** *n.*]

be·late (bi·lāt´) *v.t.* to cause to be late; to retard.

be·lay (bi·lā´) *v.t.* to make fast a rope, by winding it round a fixed pin or cleat; *n.* in mountaineering, a rock to which a climber anchors himself by a rope. **-ing-pin** *n.* a pin or cleat, to which running rigging may be belayed [Dut. *beleggen*].

belch (belch) *v.t.* to emit wind from the stomach by way of the mouth; to cast forth; *n.* eructation [O.E. *bealcan*].

bel·dam (bel´·dam) *n.* a grandmother; an ugly, old woman; a hag; an irate woman. Also **beldame** [orig. *grandmother*, Fr. *belle dame*].

be·lea·guer (bi·lē´·ger) *v.t.* to surround with an army so as to preclude escape. **-ment** *n.* [Dut. *belegeren*, to besiege].

bel·fry (bel´·fri·) *n.* a bell-tower, or a part of a steeple, where bells are hung. Orig. a watchtower, a bell being the signal [Fr. *beffroi*].

Ba·li·al (bēl´·yal) *n.* Satan; the devil [Heb. = that which is without profit or worth].

be·lie (bi·lī´) *v.t.* to give the lie to; to falsify; to speak falsely of; to misrepresent; *pr.p.* **belying** [O.E. *beleogan*, to deceive].

be·lieve (bi·lēv´) *v.t.* to regard as true; to trust; *v.i.* to have faith (in); to think; to suppose. **belief** *n.* that which is believed; full acceptance of a thing as true; faith; a firm persuasion of the truth of a body of religious tenets. **believable** *a.* credible. **-r** *n.* **to make believe**, to pretend; to fancy [M.E. *beleven*].

be·lit·tle (bi·lit´·l) *v.t.* to make small; to think lightly of; to disparage. **-ment** *n.*

bell (bel) *n.* a hollow, cup-shaped metal vessel which gives forth a clear, musical note when struck; anything shaped like a bell; *v.t.* to provide with a bell. **bells** *n.pl.* (*Naut.*) half hours of a watch at sea, struck on a ship's bell. **-boy** *n.* page-boy in hotel. **-buoy** *n.* a buoy which by its swaying rings a bell attached.

bell (bel) *n.* the cry of an animal; the bellow of the stag in rutting time. Also **-ing**; *v.i.* to bellow; to roar [O.E. *bellan*, to roar].

bel·la·don·na (bel·a·dån´·a) *n.* deadly nightshade from which drugs, hyoscine and atropine, are obtained [It. = fair lady].

belle (bel) *n.* a particularly beautiful woman [Fr. *belle*, fair].

belles-let·tres (bel·let´·r) *n.pl.* polite literature, i.e. literature which includes poetry, the drama, criticism, aesthetics, etc. [Fr.].

bel·li·cose (bel´·a·kōs) *a.* pugnacious; contentious; war-like; quarrelsome. **-ly** *adv.* **bellicosity** *n.* [L. *bellum*, war].

bel·lig·er·ence (be·lij´·er·ans) *n.* the state of being at war; warlike attitude. **belligerency** *n.* a state of war. **belligerent** *n.* a nation, party, or person taking part in war; a contending party; *a.* waging war; pugnacious; bellicose [L. *bellum*, war; *gerere*, to carry on].

bel·low (bel´·ō) *v.i.* to roar like a bull; to shout loudly; to make an outcry; to roar, as of cannon; *n.* a loud hollow roar, as of a bull, cannon, etc.; any deep cry [O.E. *bellan*, to bellow].

bel·lows (bel´·ōz, bel´·az) *n.pl.* an instrument for producing a strong blast of air (to stimulate a fire, to work an organ, etc.) [fr. O.E. *bielg*, belly; the full O.E. name was *blaestbelg*, blast-bag].

bel·ly (bel´·i·) *n.* part of the body which contains bowels; abdomen; stomach; part of anything bulging like a paunch; *a.* ventral; abdominal; *v.i.* to swell out; to bulge. **-ache** *n.* abdominal pains. **-band** *n.* a band under the belly of a horse to secure saddle. **-ful** *n.* sufficiency of food, etc. [O.E. *belg*].

be·long (bi·lawng´) *v.i.* to pertain to; be connected with; to be property or attribute of; to be resident or native of. **-ings** *n.pl.* what belongs to one; possessions [M.E. *belongen*].

be·loved (bi·luv´·ad, bi·luvd´) *a.* greatly loved; *n.* one very dear to others.

be·low (bi·lō´) *prep.* under; beneath; of inferior rank or status; on a lower level than; unworthy of; *adv.* in a lower place; beneath; on earth or hell, as opposed to heaven [*by*, and *low*].

belt (belt) *n.* a band, girdle, or zone, used for encircling; a zone given over to the raising of one plant, e.g. wheat—*v.t.* to encircle, as with a belt; to thrash with a belt. **-ed** *a.* wearing a belt, esp. as a mark of honor, as in 'a belted knight'; thrashed with a belt. **conveyor** — *n.* an endless belt used for conveying material from one place to another. **-ing** *n.* material for skirt or bodice bands; a thrashing [E.].

be·moan (bi·mōn´) *v.t.* to express deep grief for, by moaning; to lament; to mourn for.

be·muse (bi·mūz´) *v.t.* to put into a state of confusion; to stupefy; to daze. **-d** *a.*

ben (ben) *n.* a geographical term, a mountain peak, as Ben Lomond [Gael]; son of [Heb.].

bench (bensh) *n.* a long seat; a table on which woodwork is done; the seat in court of a judge or magistrate; collective name for the body of judges sitting in judgment; *v.t.* to furnish with benches; to place, for exhibit, on a bench [M.E. *benche* fr. O.E. *benc*].

bend (bend) *v.t.* to curve; to arch; to turn out of direct course; to incline; to sway; to subdue or make submissive; to tie, make fast—of ropes and sails; *v.i.* to be moved out of a straight line; to stoop; to lean, to incline; to bow; to yield; *pat.* **bent**, *pa.p.* **bent** or **-ed**; *n.* a curve; crook; curvature; turn. **-er** *n.* an instrument for bending; a hard drinker; a drinking spree. **the bends**, aeroembolism. **to be bent upon**, to be determined upon [O.E. *bendan*].

be·neath (bi·nēth´) *prep.* under; below; lower than; unworthy of; below the level of; *adv.* below [O.E. *beneothan*].

ben·e·dict (ben´·a·dikt) *n.* a man newly married, esp. if considered a confirmed bachelor.

Ben·e·dict (ben´·a·dikt) *n.* the founder of Western monasticism. **Benedictine** *a.* pert. to St. Benedict or his monastic order; *n.* a Black Friar; a cordial or liqueur originally distilled by the Benedictine monks.

ben·e·dic·tion (ben·a·dik´·shan) *n.* a blessing of a formal character; the blessing at the end of a religious service. **benedictory** *a.* imparting a blessing [L. *bene*, well; *dicere*, to speak].

ben·e·fac·tion (ben·a·fak´·shan) *n.* act of doing good; a benefit conferred; donation. **benefactor** *n.* (*fem.* **benefactress**) one who helps others; a donor; a patron. **benefactory** *a* [L. *bene*, well; *facere, factum*, to do].

ben·e·fice (ben′·a·fis) *n.* an ecclesiastical living. **-d** *a.* in enjoyment of a benefice [L. *beneficium*].

be·nef·i·cence (ba·nef′·i·sens) *n.* habitual practice of doing good; charity. **beneficent** *a.* kindly disposed; generous; doing good. **beneficently** *adv.* [L. *beneficium*].

ben·e·fi·cial (ben·a·fish′·al) *a.* conferring benefits; advantageous; helpful. **-ly** *adv.* **-ness** *n.* **beneficiary** *n.* one who benefits from the act of another; a holder of an ecclesiastical benefice [L.L. *beneficialis*].

ben·e·fit (ben′·a·fit) *n.* an act of kindness; a favor conferred; an advantage; profit; interest; a theatrical or other exhibition, the proceeds of which go to charity or an individual; a payment or allowance such as given by an insurance company or public agency; *v.t.* to do good to; to be useful to; to profit; *v.i.* to gain advantage (from). **fringe benefits,** such things as health insurance paid in addition to regular salary [L. *bene*, well; *facere*, to do].

Ben·e·lux (ben′·a·luks) *n.* the economic bloc of the three countries *Belgium*, the *Netherlands*, and *Luxemburg.*

be·nev·o·lence (ba·nev′·a·lans) *n.* disposition to do good; love of mankind; an act of kindness; generosity. **benevolent** *a.* of a kindly nature [L. *bene*, well; *velle*, to wish].

be·night·ed (bi·nit′·ad) *a.* overtaken by night; enveloped in moral or mental darkness; ignorant; unenlightened; lost.

be·nign (bi·nin′) *a.* of a kindly disposition; mild, not malignant (of disease); propitious (of climate). **-ancy** (bi·nig′·nan·si·) *n.* benignant quality. **-ant** *a.* kind; gracious; favorable; beneficial. **-antly** *adv.* **-ity** *n.* **-ly** *adv.* in benign fashion [L. *benignus*, kind].

ben·i·son (ben′·i·zn) *n.* benediction; blessing [L. *benedictio.* Doublet of *benediction*].

Ben·ja·min (ben′·ja·mjn) *n.* (*Bib.*) a youngest son; a favorite child [Heb. = son of the right hand].

ben·ja·min (ben′·ja·mjn) *n.* benzoin, a kind or resin or gum used as a medicine [corrupt. of *benzoin*].

bent (bent) *pa.t.* and *pa.p.* of **bend.**

bent (bent) *n.* (of mind), leaning, bias, or inclination for; a tendency [fr. *bend*].

bent (bent) *n.* bent grass; any stiff, wiry, coarse grass. **-y** *a.* overrun with bent [O.E. *beonet*].

be·numb (bi·num′) *v.t.* to make numb, through cold or fear; to deprive of all sensation; to deaden. **-ed** *a.* [O.E. *beniman*, to deprive].

Ben·ze·drine (ben′·za·dren) *n.* amphetamine, a synthetic drug [Trade Name].

be·queath (bi·kwēTH′) *v.t.* to leave by will, said of personal property; to leave to those who follow on, as a problem, trouble, etc. **bequest** *n.* that which is left by will; legacy [O.E. *becwethan*].

be·rate (bi·rāt′) *v.t.* to scold vigorously.

be·reave (bi·rēv′) *v.t.* to make destitute; to deprive of; *pa.p.* **-d** or **bereft. -d** *a.* robbed by death, esp. of a relative. **-ment** *n.* loss, esp. by death [E. pref. *be*; O.E. *rēafian*, to spoil].

be·ret (ber′·ā, ber′·it) *n.* a soft, round tightfitting cap without any peak [Fr. fr. L.L. *birretum*, a cap].

berg (burg) *n.* a large mass or mountain of ice; an iceberg [Ger. = a mountain].

ber·i·ber·i (ber′·i·ber′·i·) *n.* a nervous disease due to deficiency of vitamin B [Singh.].

ber·lin (bur′·lin) *n.* a four-wheeled closed carriage with two seats [fr. *Berlin*, Germany].

ber·ry (ber′·i·) *n.* a small, pulpy, juicy fruit; strictly a simple fruit with succulent pericarp. **-ing** *n.* **berried** *a.* [O.E. *berie*].

ber·serk, ber·serk·er (ber′·surk, ·ker) *n.* a battle-frenzied Norse warrior; *a.* frenzied. **to go berserk,** to go mad with fury [Scand. = poss. bare of sark or shirt of mail].

berth (burth) *n.* the place where a ship is anchored or moored; a sleeping-place on a ship, etc.; a situation or job. *v.t.* to bring to anchorage. **-age** *n.* dock or harbor dues. **to give a wide berth to,** to steer clear of; to shun; to avoid [Doublet of *birth*].

ber·yl (ber′·il) *n.* a group of green or bluish-green precious stones of exceptional hardness. **-lium** *n.* a rare metal of the magnesium group [Gk. *bērullos*].

be·seech (bi·sēch′) *v.t.* to ask or entreat earnestly; to solicit; beg; implore; *pa.t.* and *pa.p.* **besought. -er** *n.* [M.E. *sechen*, to seek]

be·seem (bi·sēm′) *v.t.* to be fit for; to befit; to suit, to become. **beseeming** *a.*

be·set (bi·set′) *v.t.* to place on, in, or around; to hem in on all sides; to surround; to enclose; to assail; *pr.p.* **-ting.** *pa.t.* and *pa.p.* **beset, -ment** *n.* **-ter** *n.* **-ting** *a.* customary; habitual, as in 'besetting sin' [O.E. *besettan*].

be·shrew (bi′·shrōō′) *v.t.* (*Arch.*) to wish some slight evil to befall one; to curse; to rate.

be·side (bi·sid′) *prep.* and *adv.* at the side of; over and above; in addition to; apart from; distinct from. **-s** *adv.* moreover; *prep.* over and above. — **oneself,** out of one's wits [O.E. *bi sidan*].

be·siege (bi·sēj′) *v.t.* to lay siege to; to surround with armed forces; to pay court to; to beleaguer. **-ment** *n.* **-r** *n.* **besieging** *a.* **besiegingly** *adv.* [M. E. *asege*, fr. Fr. *assiéger*].

be·smear (bi·smir′) *v.t.* to smear over; to soil; to bedaub [O.E. *besmerian*].

be·smirch (bi·smurch′) *v.t.* to soil; to sully; to tarnish one's reputation, etc.

be·sot (bi·sat′) *v.t.* to make sottish by drink; to make stupid. **-ted** *a.* [O.E.]

be·sought (bi·sawt′) *pa.t.* and *pa.p.* of **beseech.**

be·spat·ter (bi·spat′·er) *v.t.* to sprinkle or splash with mud, ink, etc.; to defame.

be·speak (bi·spēk′) *v.t.* to order, speak for, or engage beforehand; to foretell; to indicate; *pa.t.* **bespoke.** *pa.p.* **bespoke** and **bespoken. bespoke, bespoken** *a.* ordered beforehand; of goods [O.E. *besprecan*].

be·speck·le (bi·spek′·l) *v.t.* to mark with speckles or spots; to variegate. **-d** *a.*

Bes·se·mer (bes′·am·er) *a.* applied to steel prepared by the Bessemer process of forcing atmospheric air into molten cast iron [Sir H. *Bessemer*, (1813-98), the inventor].

best (best) *a. superl.* good in the highest degree; excellent beyond all others; most suitable, advantageous, advisable, or appropriate; *adv.* in the most excellent manner; *n.* utmost; highest endeavor; perfection. — **man,** chief attendant to the groom at a wedding. — **seller,** a current popular book with an enormous sale. **to make the best of,** to resign oneself to conditions, etc. [O.E. *bet(e)st*].

bes·tial (bes′·tyal) *a.* pert. to a beast; having the instincts of a beast; like a repulsive beast. **-ity** *n.* beastly depravity [Fr. fr. L. *bestialis*].

be·stir (bi·stur′) *v.t.* to rouse into vigorous action; to exert (oneself); to stimulate. *pr.p.* **-ring.** *pa.t.* **-red** [O.E. *bestyrian*].

be·stow (bi′·stō′) *v.t.* to lay up in store; to expend, as energy; to give ceremoniously; to confer; to award; grant; present; impart. **-al** *n.* **-er** *n.* **-ment** *n.* bestowing; what is bestowed [M.E. *bestowen*, to place].

be·strew (bi·strōō′) *v.t.* to scatter over; to besprinkle. *pa.p.* **-ed, -n.**

be·stride (bi·strid′) *v.t.* to stride over; to stand or sit with the legs extended across. *pr.p.* **bestriding;** *pa.t.* **bestrode, bestrid;** *pa.p.* **bestrid, bestridden.** [O.E. *bestridan*].

bet (bet) *n.* a stake or wager on some problematical event; *v.t.* to stake money upon some contingency; *pr.p.* **-ting;** *pa.t.* and *pa.p.* **bet** or **-ted. -ter, -tor** *n.* [fr. *abet*].

be·ta (bā′·ta, bē′·ta) *n.* the second letter of the Greek alphabet, printed thus, β. — **particles,** fast electrons emitted when certain atoms undergo radioactive breakdown. — **rays,** streams of beta particles emanated by radioactive substances.

be·take (bi·tāk′) *v.t.* to have recourse to; (with reflexive) to go, to repair to; to make one's way; *pr.p.* **betaking;** *pa.t.* **betook;** *pa.p.* **-en** [M.E. *betaken*].

be·tel (bē′·tl) *n.* a species of pepper. — **nut** *n.* the nut of the areca palm [Port. *betle*].

be·think (bi·thingk′) *v.t.* to call to mind; to remind oneself; to cogitate. *pa.t.* **bethought.**

be·tide (bi·tid′) *v.t.* to happen to; *v.i.* to occur; happen [M.E. *betiden*, to happen].

be·times (bi·timz′) *adv.* in good time; seasonably; soon; early; forward [M.E.].

be·to·ken (bi·tō′·kn) *v.t.* to show by some visible sign; to foreshow [M.E. *betacnien*].

be·took (bi·tòòk′) *pa.t.* of **betake.**

be·tray (bi·trā′) *v.t.* to give up treacherously; to be disloyal to; to disclose (a secret); to seduce; to show signs of; deceive. **-al** *n.* **-er** *n.* a traitor; a seducer [L. *tradere*, to give up].

be·troth (bi·trōTH′, ·trawTH′) *v.t.* to promise to give or take in marriage; to affiance. **-al** *n.* an agreement with a view to marriage. **-ed** *n.* a person engaged to be married; fiancé, (*fem.*) fiancée. **-ment** *n.* the state of being betrothed [M.E. *bitreuthien*].

bet·ter (bet′·er) *a.* (compar. of *good*), showing a greater degree of excellence; improved in health; *adv.* (compar. of *well*), in a more excellent or superior manner; more fully; *v.t.* and *i.* to make better; to amend; to raise one's worldly position. **-ment** *n.* improvement; enhanced value of property due to local improvements. **-s** *n.pl.* one's superiors in rank or wealth. — **half,** a jocular term for spouse. — **off,** in more prosperous circumstances. **to get the better of,** to gain an advntage over. **to think better of,** to reconsider [O.E. *betera*].

be·tween (bi·twēn′) *prep.* in the middle of two (of space, time, etc.); in the middle or intermediate space; shared by two; *adv.* midway. **go-between** *n.* an intermediary [O.E. *betweonum*, by twain].

be·twixt (bi·twikst′) *prep.* between; midway.

bev·el (bev′·l) *n.* an angle, not being a right angle, formed by two surfaces; an adjustable instrument used in building, etc. for testing angles; *a.* having the form of a bevel; slanting; *v.t.* to cut to a bevel angle. **-led** *a.* **-ing, -ment** *n.* [Fr. *biveau*, carpenter's rule].

bev·er·age (bev′·a·rij) *n.* a refreshing liquid suitable for drinking [O.Fr. *bevrage*].

bev·y (bev′·i·) *n.* a flock of birds; an assembly; a collection or group.

be·wail (bi·wāl′) *v.t.* to express grief for; to lament; deplore; mourn over.

be·ware (bi·wār′) *v.i.* to be wary of; to be on one's guard; to be alive to impending danger; to take care (lest).

be·wil·der (bi·wil′·der) *v.t.* to lead astray or into confusion; to confound; perplex; puzzle. **-ed** *a.* **-ing** *a.* confusing. **-ment** *n.* [fr. obs. *wildern*, wilderness].

be·witch (bi·wich′) *v.t.* to gain power over, by sorcery; to charm; captivate; entrance. **-er** *n.* **-ery, -ment** *n.* power to bewitch; enchantment. **-ing** *a.* [M.E. *bewicchen*].

be·wray (bi·rā′) *v.t.* to divulge; to disclose; to reveal without intent [O.E. *wregan*, to accuse].

be·yond (bi·yänd′) *prep.* on the farther side of; out of reach of; above; past in time; later than; superior to; *adv.* farther off; at a distance; *n.* the future life [O.E. *geond*, across].

bez·el (bez′·al) *n.* the piece of metal under the setting holding the jewel of a ring; the groove in which the glass of a watch is set; the sloped cutting edge of a tool; the sloping facets of a cut gem. Also **basil** or **bezil** [O.Fr. *bisel*].

bi-, (bi) *prefix* used in the construction of compound nouns, indicating two, twice, or double [L. *bis*, twice].

bi·an·nu·al (bi·an′·yoo·al) *a.* happening twice a year. **-ly** *adv.*

bi·as (bi′·as) *n.* prejudice; prepossession that sways the mind; a diagonal line of direction; *v.t.* to influence; to prejudice; to prepossess (often unduly; *pa.t.* and *pa.p.* **-sed** or **-ed** [Fr. *biais*, oblique].

bib (bib) *n.* piece of cloth worn mainly by children over the breast when eating; part of a workman's overalls to protect chest; *v.t.* and *v.i.* to sip; tipple; drink frequently. *pr.p.* **-bing;** *pa.t.* and *pa.p.* **-bed. -acious** *a.* addicted to tippling. **-ber** *n.* a person given to frequent and excessive imbibing of liquor or wines; a tippler [L. *bibere*, to drink].

Bi·ble (bi′·bl) *n.* the volume which contains the Scriptures of the Old and/or New Testament; an authoritative book on a specific subject. **biblical** *a.* scriptural [Gk. *biblia*, books].

bib·li·o- (bib′·li·ō) *prefix* from Gk. *biblion*, a book, used in the formation of compound words referring to books. **-graphy** *n.* expert knowledge of history of books; a list of books on a specific subject. **-grapher** *n.* one who compiles lists of books for further study of a subject; one interested in various editions of certain books. **-graphic(al)** *a.* **-logy** *n.* knowledge of the production and distribution of books. **-mania** *n.* mania for possessing rare books. **-maniac** *n.* **-phile** *n.* a lover of books. **-pole, -polist** *n.* a dealer in books, esp. rare books. **-poly** *n.* **-theca** *n.* a library. **-thecary** *n.* a librarian [Gk. *biblion*, a book].

bib·u·lous (bib′·ū·las) *a.* given to excessive or frequent drinking; absorbent; spongy. **-ly** *adv.* [L. *bibere*, to drink].

bi·cam·er·al (bi·kam′·a·ral) *a.* pert. to or containing two legislative or other chambers [L. *bis*, twice; *camera*, chamber].

bi·car·bon·ate (bi·kár′·ba·nāt) *n.* a salt or compound containing two equivalents of carbonic acid to one of a base—usually applied loosely for 'bicarbonate of soda.'

bice (bīs) *n.* a blue or green pigment [Fr. *bis*].

bi·ceps (bī′·seps) *n.* two-headed muscle of arm or leg; a flexor muscle. **bicipitial** *a.* [L. *bis*, twice; *caput*, head].

bick·er (bik′·ẹr) *v.i.* to bandy words; to wrangle; to move quickly and lightly. **-ing** *n.* **-ment** *n.* [M.E. *biker(en)*].

bi·cus·pid (bī·kus′·pid) *n.* a tooth with two fangs; *a.* having two cusps or fangs. Also **-ate** [L. *bis*, twice; *cuspis*, a point].

bi·cy·cle (bī′·si·kl) *n.* a vehicle with two wheels, one in front of the other, propelled by pedals; *v.i.* to cycle. **bicyclist** *n.* one who rides a bicycle. **bike** *n.* (*Colloq.*) [L. *bis*, twice; Gk. *kuklos*, a wheel].

bid (bid) *v.t.* to ask; to invite; to order or direct; to offer a price; to give, as good-bye; *pr.p.* **bidding**; *pa.t.* **bid** or **bade**; *pa.p.* **bid**, **-den**; *n.* an offer of a price, esp. at auctions; an attempt. **-dable** *a.* compliant; docile; obedient; submissive; willing; (*Cards*) that may be bid without undue risk. **-der** *n.* **-ding** *n.* invitation; command; offer at an auction; series of bids at cards [confusion of O.E. *beodam*, offer, and *biddan*, request].

bid·dy (bid′·i·) *n.* chicken; hen [orig. uncert.].

bide (bīd) *v.i.* to dwell permanently; abide; remain; continue; tarry; sojourn; reside. *v.t.* to endure; put up with; suffer; tolerate; bear [O.E. *bidan*, to remain].

bi·en·ni·al (bī·en′·i·al) *a.* happening once in two years; lasting for only two years; *n.* a plant which requires two seasons to bloom. **-ly** *adv.* [L. *bis*, twice; *annus*, a year].

bier (bēr) *n.* a frame or carriage for conveying the dead to the grave; a coffin; grave; tomb [O.E. *baer*].   [faces or opposite surfaces.

bi·fa·cial (bī·fā′·shal) *a.* having two like

bi·fo·cal (bī·fō′·kal) *a.* having two foci; *n.pl.* spectacles with a small lens for reading, set into a larger lens for distant vision [L. *bis*, twice; E. *focal*].

bi·fo·li·ate (bī·fō′·li·āt) *a.* (*Bot.*) having two leaflets springing from the same point L. *bis*, twice; *folium*, leaf].

bi·fur·cate (bī′·fur·kāt) *v.t.* to divide into two; *v.i.* to fork. **bifurcate, -d** *a.* **bifurcation** *n.* **bifurcous** *a.* [L. *bis*, twice; *furca*, a fork].

big (big) *a.* bulky; massive; huge; great; pregnant; generous; magnanimous; important. **—hearted** *a.* **-ness** *n.* size; bulk; largeness; importance. **— shot** *n.* (*Colloq.*) **-wig** *n.* (*Colloq.*) a person of great importance or influence.

big·a·my (big′·a·mi·) *n.* the crime of having two wives or husbands at one time. **bigamist** *n.* **bigamous** *a.* **bigamously** *adv.* [L. *bis*, twice; Gk. *gamos*, marriage].

big·horn (big′·hawrn) *n.* a Rocky Mountain wild sheep.

bight (bīt) *n.* a curve; a loop of a rope when folded; a bend in the sea-coast; an open bay [O.E. *byht*].

big·ot (big′·at) *n.* one obstinately and unreasably wedded to a particular belief or creed; dogmatist. **-ed** *a.* **-ry** *n.* the blind zeal of a bigot [Fr. of unknown origin].

bike (bīk) *n.* (*Colloq.*) a bicycle.

bi·ki·ni (bi·kē′·ni·) *n.* a scanty two-piece bathing suit [*Bikini*, Pacific Island].

bi·lat·er·al (bī·lat′·a·ral) *a.* having two sides; affecting two parties. **-ly** *adv.* [L. *bis*, twice; *latus, lateris*, side].

bil·bo (bil′·bō) *n.* formerly a rapier or sword. **bilboes** *n.pl.* shackles for the feet, formerly used for prisoners on ships [fr. *Bilbao*, Spain].

bile (bīl) *n.* a greenish, viscous, bitter fluid secreted by the liver; gall; general disorder of health due to faulty secretion of bile; bad temper. **biliary** (bil′·yẹr·i·) *a.* pert. to the bile. **bilious** *a.* pert. to the bile; affected by bile; choleric; peevish; crabbed; ill-humored. **biliousness** *n.* a disturbance of the digestive system associated with an excess of bile [L. *bilis*].

bilge (bilj) *n.* the swelling part of a cask; the broadest part of a ship's bottom nearest the keel, acting as a sump; (*Colloq.*) nonsense; *v.i.* to spring a leak. **— water** *n.* evil-smelling water which gathers in a ship's bottom.

bi·lin·gual (bī·ling′·gwal) *a.* speaking, or written in, two languages. Also **bilinguar**. **bilinguist** *n.* a person who can speak fluently in two languages [L. *bis*, twice; *lingua*, tongue].

bilk (bilk) *v.t.* to defraud; to swindle. **-er** *n.*

---

bill (bil) *n.* a kind of axle with two sharp pointed spikes mounted on a long staff; a hook-shaped pruning instrument. **-hook** *n.* a small bill with a hooked end for lopping branches [O.E. *bil*].

bill (bil) *n.* printed notice for public display; an account of money owed; a written engagement to pay money under the hand of the granter; a declaration of certain facts in legal proceedings; the draft of a proposed law; *v.t.* to announce by posters; to cover with posters; to placard; to send a statement of money owed. **-board** *n.* a signboard for advertising. **-fold** *n.* a wallet. **-ing** *n.* advertising; invoicing [L.L. *billa* = *bulla*, a seal].

bil·let (bil′·it) *n.* a short note; an order requisitioning accommodation for soldiers; the quarters occupied by soldiers in private houses, etc.; *v.t.* to quarter or lodge troops. **billet-doux** (bil·i·dòò′) *n.* a love letter; *pl.* **billets-doux** [Fr. = a note].

bil·liard (bil′·yẹrd) *a.* pert. to billiards. **billiards**, *n.* a table game played with three balls which are hit by a cue [Fr. *bille*, log].

bil·lion (bil′·yan) *n.* a thousand millions (10^9). **-aire** *n.* a fabulously wealthy person. **-th** *a.* [L. *bis*, twice; *million*].

bil·low (bil′·ō) *n.* a great, swelling wave of the sea; a surge of flame, smoke, cloud, etc.; a breaker; *v.i.* to swell or roll, as waves. **-ed, -y** *a.* [O.N. *bylgja*].

bil·ly (bil′·i·) *n.* (*Colloq.*) a policeman's stick. **bil·ly-goat** (bil′·i·gōt) *n.* a he-goat; a tufted beard [*billy = Willie*].

bi·met·al·lism (bī·met′·al·izm) *n.* in currency, the use of both gold and silver coins at a fixed relative value.

bi·month·ly (bī·munth′·li·) *a.* once in two months or twice in a month; *n.* a periodical which appears once in two months or twice a month.

bin (bin) *n.* a box or enclosed place with a lid, for corn, bread, etc.; a receptacle for bottles of wine; *v.t.* to store in a bin. *pr.p.* **-ning**. *pa.t.* **-ned** [O.E. *binn*, crib].

bi·na·ry (bī′·na·ri·) *a.* composed of two; twofold; double; dual; *n.* a double star. **binate** *a.* growing in pairs [L. *bini*, two by two].

bind (bīnd) *v.t.* to tie together as with a band, cord, etc.; to constrain by moral influence; to secure together and enclose in a cover; to place under legal obligation; to be obligatory; to apprentice; to constipate; *pa.t.* and *pa.p.* **bound. -er** *n.* a person who binds; a machine for binding, as sheaves, books, etc.; cover in filing and loose-leaf systems. **-ery** *n.* a bookbinding establishment. **-ing** *a.* obligatory; constipating; *n.* act of fastening; anything which birds; partial locking of a sliding part of a machine due to faulty lubrication [O.E. *bindan*].

binge (binj) *n.* concerted eating and especially drinking, to celebrate an occasion; a spree [slang].

bin·na·cle (bin′·a·kl) *n.* the box containing the compass of a ship [earlier *bittacle*, fr. L. *habitaculum*, little dwelling].

bin·o·cle (bin′·a·kl) *n.* a telescope fitted with two tubes. **binocular** (bi·nok′·ya·lẹr) *a.* adapted for the use of both eyes; *n.* a binocular telescope. **binoculars** *n.pl.* field-glasses. **binoculate** *a.* having two eyes; adapted for the use of two eyes [L. *bini*, two by two; *oculus*, eye]

binoculars

bi·no·mi·al (bī·nō′·mi·al) *n.* an algebraic expression involving two terms connected by the sign plus (+) or minus (—), e.g. a + b, or c — d; *a.* pert. to binomials. [L. *bis*, twice; *nomen*, name].

bi·nom·i·nal (bī·nám′·i·nal) *a.* (*Bot.*) having two names, the first indicating the genus, the second indicating the species.

bi·o- (bī′·ō) a *prefix* used in the construction of compound terms, to express having organic life [Gk. *bios*, life].

bi·o·chem·is·try (bī·ō·kem′·is·tri·) *n.* physiology considered from the chemical point of view; the chemistry of living things.

bi·o·dy·nam·ics (bī·ō·dī·nam′·iks) *n.pl.* the science which investigates the vital forces; the energy of living functions.

---

bi·o·gen (bī′·a·jen) *n.* a hypothetical protein molecule assumed to be the primary source of all living matter. **biogenesis** *n.* the theory that life develops only from living organisms [Gk. *bios*, life; *genesis*, beginning].

bi·o·graph, bi·o·scope (bī′·ō·graf, -skōp′) *n.* early motion picture projector [Gk. *bios*, life; *graphein*, to write; *skopein*, to see].

bi·og·ra·phy (bī·ág′·ra·fi·) *n.* the detailed story of a person's life and achievements; the section of literature devoted to the writing of the life-stories of individuals. **biographic, -al** [Gk. *bios*, life; *graphein*, to write].

bi·ol·o·gy (bī·al′·a·ji·) *n.* the science of life, whether animal or vegetable. **biologic, biological** *a.* **biologically** *adv.* **biologist** *n.* **biological warfare**, a method of fighting in which disease bacteria would be used [Gk. *bios*, life; *logos*, a discourse].

bi·o·nom·ics (bī·a·nám′·iks) *n.* study of influence of environment on organisms; ecology [Gk. *bios*, life; *nomos*, law].

bi·o·phys·ics (bī·ō·fiz′·iks) *n.* physics of living organisms.   [of living tissue for diagnosis.

bi·op·sy (bī′·áp·si·) *n.* the excision of a piece

bi·o·scope See **biograph.**

bi·ot·ic (bī·ät′·ik) *a.* (*Biol.*) relating to life; vital. **biotics** *n.* the functions, properties, and activities of living things [Gk. *bios*, life].

bi·o·tin (bī′·a·tin) *n.* a constituent of the vitamin B_2 complex essential to many forms of life [Gk. *bios*, life].

bi·par·ti·san (bī·pár′·ti·zan) *a.* pert. to, representing, or composed of, members of two parties [L. *bis*, twice; *partire*, to divide].

bi·par·tite (bī·pár′·tit) *a.* consisting of two corresponding parts; shared by the two parties concerned. **bipartition** *n.* [L. *bis*, twice; *partire*, to divide].

bi·ped (bī′·ped) *n.* a two-footed animal. **biped, bipedal** *a.* [L. *bis*, twice; *pse*, a foot].

bi·plane (bī′·plān) *n.* an airplane or glider having two main wings.

bi·pod [bī′·pád] *n.* a two-legged stand.—cf. **tripod.**

bi·po·lar (bī·pōl′·ẹr) *a.* having two poles [L.].

bi·quad·rate (bī·kwád′·rāt, ·rit) *n.* (*Math.*) the value of the fourth power of a number. **biquadratic** *a.*; *n.* the fourth power [L. *bis*, twice; *quadratus*, squared].

birch (burch) *n.* a tree with slim branches and silvery bark-scales; the hard, close-grained wood of the birch; *v.t.* flog with a birch-rod. **birch, -en** *a.* of birch. **-rod** *n.* a rod of birch twigs for inflicting punishment [O.E. *birce*].

bird (burd) *n.* a feathered animal with wings. **— cage** *n.* a cage made of wire and wood for keeping birds. **-call** *n.* the sounds made by a bird; instrument used to allure birds by imitating their notes [O.E. *brid*, a bird].

bird·ie (burd′·i·) *n.* (*Golf*) holing a ball in one stroke under par.

bi·ret·ta (bi·ret′·a) *n.* a flat, square, stiff cap worn by Catholic clergy [It. *berretta*].

birr (bur) *n.* a whirring noise like that of a revolving wheel; an energetic push; a pronounced accent; strongly trilling the consonant r. Also **burr** [Scand. *burr*].

birth (burth) *n.* act of coming into life or of being born; the delivery of a newly born child alive; descent; origin. **— control** *n.* restriction of conception. **-day** *n.* the day on which one is born; the anniversary of that day. **-mark** *n.* peculiar mark on the body at birth. **-place** *n.* the place where a person is born. **— rate** *n.* the ration of births to the total population. **-right** *n.* anything to which one is entitled by birth [M.E. *birthe*, perh. fr. Scand.].

bis (bis) *adv.* twice; (*Mus.*) to show that the bar or passage is to be performed twice.

bis·cuit (bis′·kit) *n.* a quick bread in small soft cakes; stoneware, earthenware, porcelain, etc. after firing but before being glazed [L. *bis*, twice; *coctus*, cooked].

bi·sect (bī·sekt′) *v.t.* to divide into two equal parts. **bisection** *n.* one of two equal parts. **-or** *n.* a bisecting line. **bisegment** *n.* one of two segments of a bisected line [L. *bis*, twice; *secare*, to cut].

bi·sex·u·al (bī·sek′·shoo·al) *a.* having the organs of both sexes [L. *bis*, twice].

bish·op (bish′·ap) *n.* a clergyman of high rank, chess man moving diagonally. **-ric** *n.* diocese, jurisdiction, or office of a bishop. **-'s lawn,** a fine kind of linen [fr. Gk. *episkopos*, overseer].

bis·muth (biz′·math) *n.* a reddish-white metal the salts of which are used in medicine.

bi·son (bī'.san) *n.* the large buffalo of Western N. Am. [L.].

bisque (bisk) *n.* a smooth, creamy soup; a thick soup made with shellfish or game; unglazed porcelain [Fr.].

bis·tro (bis'·trō) *n.* a small tavern or café [Fr.]

bi·sul·phate (bī·sul'·fāt) *n.* a salt of sulphuric acid in which one-half of the hydrogen in the acid is replaced by a metal.

bit (bit) *pa.t.* of **bite.**

bit (bit) *n.* a mouthful; a morsel; small piece of anything; a fragment; a boring tool generally for use in brace; part of bridle which is placed in a horse's mouth; *v.t.* to put the bit in the mouth of a horse.

bitch (bich) *n.* the female of the dog, wolf, or fox; (*Colloq.*) an opprobrious term for a woman; *v.* (*Slang*) to complain [O.E. *bicce*].

bite (bīt) *v.t.* to cut, crush, seize, or wound with the teeth; to pinch with cold; to eat into, as acid; to corrode; to gnaw; to champ; to nip; to defraud; to cheat; *v.i.* to be given to biting; to be pungent; *pr.p.* **biting;** *pa.t.* **bit;** *pa.p.* **bit** or **bitten** *n.* act of biting; a portion bitten off; food; morsel; sharp, pungent taste; the nibble of a fish at a hook; the grip of an edged tool on metal. **-r** *n.* **biting** *a.* sharp; severe; sarcastic; caustic; pungent; chilling [O.E. *bitan*].

bitt (bit) *n.* a post for securing cables, etc. usually *pl.*; *v.t.* to put around a bitt [Scand.].

bit·ter (bit'·er) *a.* biting or acrid to the taste; causing pain or smart to the feelings; *n.* bitter beer. **-ly** *adv.* **-ness** *n.* the quality of being bitter to the taste; animosity. **-s** *n.* alcoholic liquor containing bitter flavorings. **-sweet** *n.* the woody nightshade whose root, when chewed, tastes first bitter then sweet [O.E. *biter*].

bit·tern (bit'·ern) *n.* a wading marsh-bird of the heron family [O.Fr. *butor*].

bi·tu·men (bi·tū'·men) *n.* an inflammable, mineral pitch, as asphalt, petroleum, etc. **bi·tuminize** *v.t.* to prepare or treat with bitumen. **bituminous** *a.* [L.].

bi·valve (bī'·valv) *a.* having two valves; *n.* an animal with a shell of two parts opening like a hinge; a seed case of this kind. **bivalvous** *a.*

biv·ou·ac (biv'·ōō·ak) *n.* an encampment in the open air, without any cover; *v.i.* to encamp without covering. **bivouacking;** *pa.t.* and *pa.p.* **bivouacked** [Fr.].

bi·week·ly (bī·wēk'·li·) *a.* occurring once in every two weeks; occurring twice in each week; *n.* a periodical issued twice a week or once in two weeks [L. *bis*, twice]. [Fr.].

bi·zarre (bi·zär') *a.* odd; eccentric; strange

blab (blab) *v.t.* to reveal imprudently secrets entrusted to one; *v.i.* to tell tales; *pr.p.* **-bing;** *pa.t.* and *pa.p.* **-bed.** *n.* a chatterer; a gossip; a tell-tale. Also **-ber** [Scand. *blabbre*, to babble].

black (blak) *a.* of the darkest color; dark; night-like; destitute of light; funereal; ominous; *n.* the darkest color; negro; mourning; *v.t.* to make black. **-en** *v.t.* to make black; to polish with blacking; to defame; *v.i.* to grow or turn black. **-ly** *adv.* **-ness** *n.* **-amoor** *n.* a Negro or Moor. **— art** *n.* magic; necromancy. **-ball** *v.t.* to reject a candidate for admission to a club by putting a black ball in the ballot box. **-berry** *n.* a fruit-bearing shrub, the bramble. **-bird** *n.* any of a number of birds which have predominantly black plumage. **-board** *n.* a board painted black, a slate, or any dark surface to write on with chalk. **-bread** *n.* dark bread. **— diamonds** (*Colloq.*) coal. **— eye** *n.* discoloration due to a blow. **-face** *n.* (*Theat.*) entertainer made up as a Negro, usually for a minstrel show. **-flag** *n.* flag popularly associated with pirates. **— friar** *n.* a Dominican friar, from his black mantle. **— frost** *n.* severe frost. **-guard** (blag'·erd) *n.* orig. a menial of the scullery; a low scoundrel; *a.* low; vile; *v.t.* to treat as a blackguard; to revile; *v.i.* to act in a vile manner. **-guardism** *n.* **-guardly** *a.* **-head** *n.* a small black-topped mass which plugs the mouths of the follicles of the skin. **-ing** *n.* an old form of boot polish. **-jack** *n.* a short, leather-covered club with a heavy head on an elastic shaft; the flag of a pirate; a miner's name for zinc-blende. **— lead** *n.* graphite, a form of nearly pure carbon obtained from plumbago, and used in the manufacture of stove-polish and lead pencils. **-list** *n.* any list of undesirable persons; *v.t.* to place on such a list. **-mail** *n.* extortion of money by threats of exposure or denunciation; hush-money; orig. moneys paid over to robbers to obviate constant pillaging. **— mark** *n.* a mark of censure or failure. **-market** *n.* a clandestine market for the sale of goods whose distribution is regulated, and

which are not on free sale. **—out** *n.* temporary loss of vision or memory; a total cutting off of all lights. **— sheep** *n.* a loose, dissolute member of a respectable family [O.E. *blaec*].

blad·der (blad'·er) *n.* a thin musculo-membranous bag, in the pelvis, serving as a reservoir for urine; the windbag of a bagpipe; any membranous sac. **-ed** *a.* swollen like a bladder. **-wort** *n.* water-plant with floating leaves. **-y** *a.* thin and inflated; blistered [O.E. *blaedre*, a blister].

blade (blād) *n.* the leaf, or flat part of the leaf, of a plant; the cutting part of a knife, or tool; the broad part of an oar; a sword; (*Colloq.*) a dashing fellow. **-bone** *n.* the upper bone in shoulder. scapula. **-d** *a.* [O.E. *blaed*].

blame (blām) *v.t.* to express disapprobation of; to censure; *n.* fault. **-less** *a.* **-lessness** *n.* [O.Fr. *blasmer*, to speak evil of].

blanch (blanch) *v.t.* to whiten; to bleach; to strip (the husk); *v.i.* to become white; to turn pale; to gloss over. **-ing** *n.* [Fr. *blanc*, white].

blanc-mange (bla·mánzh') *n.* a pudding [Fr. *blanc*, white; *manger*, to eat].

bland (bland) *a.* mild; gentle; affable. **-ly** *adv.* **-ness** *n.* [L. *blandus*, flattering].

blan·dish (blan'·dish) *v.t.* to flatter and coax; to wheedle. **-ment** *n.* [L. *blandus*].

blank (blangk) *a.* without writing or any marks; empty; confused; *n.* an empty space; a lottery ticket not drawing a prize; the white disc of a target. **-ly** *adv.* **— verse,** unrhymed heroic [Fr. *blanc*, white].

blan·ket (blang'·kit) *n.* a loosely woven woollen bedcover; a covering; a thick canopy of cloud; *v.t.* to cover with a blanket; to toss in a blanket. **-ing** *n.* thick material for blankets; tossing in a blanket. **a wet blanket,** one who depresses others; kill-joy [Fr. *blanc*, white].

blare (blār) *v.t.* and *v.i.* to sound loudly; to trumpet; *n.* a long, prolonged noise [O.E. *blaesan*, to blow].

blar·ney (blár'·ni·) *n.* coaxing, cajoling talk; outrageous flattery; blandishing [fr. *Blarney-stone*, near Cork, Ireland].

bla·sé (blá'·sā) *a.* surfeited with everything; absolutely bored; sophisticated [Fr.].

blas·pheme (blas·fēm') *v.t.* to speak irreverently of God; to desecrate by impious talk; *v.i.* to take God's name in vain; to curse and swear. **-r** *n.* **blaspheming** *n.* impious talk. **blasphemous** *a.* **blasphemously** *adv.* **blasphemy** *n.* irreverence in speaking of sacred matters; profane talk [Gk. *blasphēmein*].

blast (blast) *n.* a gust or puff of air; a forced stream of air; the blowing of a wind instrument; an explosion of gunpowder in rending rocks; a blight affecting plants or cattle. *v.t.* to injure, as by a noxious wind; to blight; to split, as by gunpowder; to abuse vehemently. **-ed** *a.* blighted; accursed; (*Colloq.*) confounded; infernal. **-er** *n.* **— furnace** *n.* a smelting-furnace in which hot air is furnished by bellows or other apparatus. **-ing** *n.* a blast; explosion [O.E. *blaest*].

bla·tant (blā'·tant) *a.* offensively noisy; loud-(voiced); brawling; obtrusive. **blatancy** *n.* **-ly** *adv.* [coined by Spenser].

blath·er, blether (bla'·THer) *n.* one who talks nonsense; *v.i.* to talk nonsense. **-s** nonsensical, foolish talk. **-ing** *n.* **-skite** *n.* one who talks sheer nonsense [Scand. *blathra*, to talk nonsense].

blaze (blāz) *n.* bright flame; a big conflagration; outburst of activity or zeal; display; *v.i.* to burn brightly; to glow with anger. **-r** *n.* sports jacket of bright color. **-s** *pl.* hell, as in 'Go to blazes' [O.E. *blaese*, a flame].

blaze (blāz) *n.* white mark upon a horse's forehead; a mark on a tree made by pathfinders; *v.t.* to mark a trail [L.G. *blase*, white mark on head of horse].

blaze (blāz) *v.t.* to proclaim; spread abroad [O.E. *blaesan*, to blow].

bla·zon (blā'·zn) *v.t.* to make known to everybody; to display armorial bearings in their proper colors; to embellish; *n.* art of drawing or explaining coats of arms. **-er** *n.* **-ment** *n.* **-ry** *n.* art of describing or explaining coats of arms in heraldic terms [Fr. *blason*, shield].

blazon

bleach (blēch) *v.t.* to whiten by exposure to sunlight and air, or by chemical action; *v.i.* to become whiter or paler; *n.* a decolorizing, chemical agent. **-er** *n.* one who, or that which, bleaches. **bleachers** *n.pl.* outdoor, uncovered seat for a spectator in a stadium [O.E. *blaecan*, fr. *blaec*, pale].

bleak (blēk) *a.* without color; pale; desolate and exposed. **-ly** *adv.* **-ness** *n.* [O.E. *blaec*, pale].

blear (blēr) *a.* dim or watery, due to inflammation of the eye or tears; *v.i.* to dim or blur. **-y** *a.* dim [M.E. *bleren*, to have sore eyes].

bleat (blēt) *v.i.* to cry as a sheep; to talk in a complaining, whining fashion; *n.* the sound made by a sheep [O.E. *blaetan*].

bleed (blēd) *v.t.* to draw blood surgically; to extort money from someone; *v.i.* to lose blood; to die in battle; *pa.t.* and *pa.p.* **bled.** **-er** *n.* a person who is afflicted by haemophilia, excessive bleeding. **-ing** *n.* [O.E. *bledan*].

blem·ish (blem'·ish) *n.* any deformity, physical or moral; flaw; disfigurement; unaware of; *v.t.* to mark with a flaw; to mar or disfigure [Fr. *blêmir*].

blench (blensh) *v.i.* to start back from lack of courage; to flinch [O.E. *blencan*, to deceive].

blend (blend) *v.t.* to mix allied articles together smoothly and inseparably; *v.i.* to intermix; to mingle well; *pa.p.* **-ed** or **blent;** *n.* a mixture. **-er** *n.* **-ing** *n.* [Scand. *blanda*, to mix].

blende (blend) *n.* an ore of zinc, consisting of zinc and sulphur; name given to certain lustrous minerals [Ger. *blenden*].

bless (bles) *v.t.* to consecrate; glorify; sanctify; praise; to give thanks to; invoke happiness on; magnify. *pa.p.* **-ed** or **blest. blessed** (bles'·id), **blest** *a.* happy; favored with blessings; hallowed. **-edness** *n.* happiness; heavenly joy; felicity. **-ing** *n.* a source of happiness or gratitude; benefaction; boon; benediction; prayer [O.E. *bletsian*, to consecrate (with blood)].

blew (blōō) *pa.t.* of **blow.**

blight (blīt) *n.* disease of plants caused by certain fungi or parasitic bacteria; anything which has an adverse effect, injures, or destroys; *v.t.* to affect with blight.

blimp (blimp) *n.* a small non-rigid airship.

blind (blīnd) *a.* destitute of sight; ignorant; undiscerning; reckless; unaware of; heedless; at random; invisible; concealed; closed at one end; (*Slang*) drunk; *v.t.* to deprive of sight; to dazzle; to darken or obscure; to hide; to deceive; *n.* a window-covering or screen; something intended to mislead. **— date** *n.* a date arranged with someone not previously known; the person involved. **-ed** *a.* rendered sightless; dazzled; oblivious to all other factors. **-ers** *n.pl.* a horse's blinkers. **-fold** *a.;* *v.t.* to cover the eyes with something; to mislead. **-ing** *a.* **— landing** *n.* grounding an aircraft by depending on radio signals. **-ly** *adv.* **-ness** *n.* lacking power of sight; ignorance; obstinacy [O.E. *blind*].

blink (blingk) *v.i.* to wink; to look with the eyes half-shut; to glimmer, as a candle; *v.t.* to shut out of sight, as a fact or question; to ignore; *n.* a glimpse; a glance. **-ard** *n.* one who blinks; a stupid person. **-ers** *n.pl.* pieces of leather preventing a horse from seeing to either side [M.E. *blenken*].

bliss (blis) *n.* the acme of happiness; perfect felicity; heavenly rapture. **-ful** *a.* supremely happy; enjoyable. **-fully** *adv.* **-fulness** *n.* **-less** *a.* [O.E. *bliths*, fr. *blithe*].

blis·ter (blis′·tẹr) n. a vesicle of the skin filled with a clear or blood-stained serum; a pustule; any like swelling as on plants, paint or steel; a plaster applied to skin to raise a blister; v.t. to raise blisters upon; to wither up with scorn and sarcasm; v.i. to rise in blisters. -y a. [O.Fr. blestre].

blithe (bliTH) a. gay; happy; gladsome; jolly; merry; sprightly. -ly adv. -ness n. -some a. merry; cheerful [O.E. blithe, joyous].

blitz (blits) n. a heavy, sudden attack by enemy bombers; v.t. to bomb from the air. -ed a. also **blitz-krieg** [Ger. Blitz, lightning; krieg, war]. [Ger. bletz, lightening].

bliz·zard (bliz′·ẹrd) n. a blinding snowstorm

bloat (blōt) v.t. to cause to have an unhealthy swollen appearance; to swell or puff out; to cure fish by salting and smoking. -ed a. swollen. -edness n. **bloater** n. a herring—salted, smoked, and dried [fr. Scand. blautr, soft].

blob (blåb) n. anything small and globular; small, round mass [var. of bleb, blister (?)].

bloc (blåk) n. a combination of two or more countries or political parties [Fr.].

block (blåk) n. a solid mass of matter; a roughly squared piece of wood, stone, etc.; the large piece of wood on which persons were beheaded; the wheel of a pulley with its case of wood; a number of buildings forming one compact mass; an obstruction, esp. on roads; mounted plate for printing; v.t. to shut in, to enclose; to obstruct; to shape (a hat); to sketch out roughly. -buster n. a heavy explosive bomb. -ing n. the process of stamping bookcovers with a decorative pattern. -head n. a dullard. -house n. an improvised fort made of logs; a fortified place. — letters n. a form of script where the letters are printed instead of in the usual cursive style. **block and tackle**, a pulley enclosed in a block used for lifting weights [Fr. bloc].

block·ade (blå·kād′) n. prevention of imports into countries usually during a war; v.t. to shut up hostile troops in a town by surrounding it; to prevent trade with a hostile country. — **runner** n. a vessel employed to slip through to a blockaded country [fr. block].

blond (blånd) n. (fem. **blonde**) a person of fair complexion and generally, light blue eyes; a. fair; light golden-brown [Fr.].

blood (blud) n. the red, viscid fluid which circulates in the body of men and animals; relationship, consanguinity, kindred; honorable birth; descent; a rake, man about town; v.t. (Med.) to let blood, to bleed. — **bank** n. a store of blood for use in a transfusion. — **count** n. the number of red and white cells in a specific quantity of blood. -**curdling** a. terrifying. -**hound** n. a hound, with keen sense and perseverance. -**ily** adv. -**less** a. without blood; anemic; spiritless. -**lessness** n. -**letting** n. the withdrawal of blood to allay fever; phlebotomy. -**mobile** n. a mobile unit for collecting blood for blood banks. -**money** n. money paid for betraying another; wages earned at a sweated rate of labor. — **plasma**, the fluid part of blood. — **poisoning** n. a condition due to circulation of bacteria in blood stream. —**pressure** n. the pressure exerted by the blood on the walls of the arteries. —**red** a. crimson. — **serum** n. the fluid part of the blood after the fibrin and the corpuscles have been eliminated. -**shed** n. the shedding of blood; slaughter. -**shot** a. of the eyes, red or congested with blood. -**stain** n. the dried and darkened stain left on clothing, floors, etc. after contact with blood. -**stone** n. a semiprecious stone, a variety of crystalline silica, dark green in color with red spots. Also called heliotrope. -**sucker** n. an animal which sucks blood, esp. the leech; an extortioner. — **test** n. an examination of the blood often to determine to which of the four groups it belongs. -**thirsty** a. eager to shed blood. —**transfusion** n. the transference of blood from one person to another. — **vessel** n. an artery or vein through which blood flows. -**y** a. pert. to blood; stained with or containing blood; ruthless in shedding blood; (Br.) used vulgarly as an expletive to add an intensive force; v.t. to make bloody [O.E. blod].

bloom (blōóm) n. a flower; a blossom; state of freshness and vigor; flush of youth; powdery coating on freshly picked fruit; v.i. to blossom; to glow with youthful vigor; to flourish; v.t. to cause to blossom or flourish.

bloom·ers (blōó′·mẹrz) n.pl. women's loose trousers gathered at the knee, worn for sports; an undergarment of the same design [Mrs. Bloomer, of New York, 1849.]

blos·som (blås′·am) n. the flower of a plant, esp. a tree; v.i. to put forth blossoms; to flourish. -ed a. -y a. rich in blossoms [O.E. blostm].

blot (blåt) v.t. to spot or bespatter esp. with ink; to stain with infamy; to obliterate; to dry with blotting-paper; pr.p. -ting; pa.p. -ted; n. a spot or stain, as of ink; blemish; disgrace. -ter n. a blotting-pad. -ting-paper n. a kind of unsized paper for drying ink [Scand.].

blotch (blåch) n. an irregular, colored spot; an eruption upon the skin; pimple; v.t. to mark with blotches; to make spotted. -y a. [O.Fr. bloche].

blot·to (blåt′·ō) a. (Slang) very drunk.

blouse (blous, blouz) n. a light, loose upper garment; v.i. and v.t. to drape loosely [Fr.].

blow (blō) n. a mass or bed of flowers; v.i. to blossom [O.E. blowan, to blossom].

blow (blō) n. a stroke; a knock; a thump; a smack; a rap; sudden calamity.

blow (blō) v.i. to produce a current of air; to move, as air; to breathe hard or quickly; to puff; to pant; (Slang) to brag; (Slang) to squander; to spout (of whales); v.t. to direct a current of air on; to sound a wind instrument; to put out of breath; pa.t. **blew**; pa.p. -**n**; n. a high wind. -**fly** n. insect, e.g., blue-bottle which blows eggs in meat. -**lamp** n. a portable lamp for applying intense local heat. -**n** a. swelled; tired; out of breath; tainted. -**out** n. (Slang) a feast or big meal; a burst tire. —**pipe** n. an instrument for concentrating the heat of a flame on some point, by blowing; a blowgun. -**y** a. windy [O.E. blawan].

blub·ber (blub′·ẹr) n. the fat of whales and other marine animals; v.i. to weep unrestrainedly. -**ed** a. swollen by weeping. -**ing** n. [imit. formation, with first meaning of bubble].

bludg·eon (bluj′·an) n. a short cudgel with one end loaded; v.t. to knock out with a club [probably Celt., fr. plug].

blue (blōó) n. the color of the clear sky; one of the seven primary colors; a dye or pigment; indigo powder used in laundering; the sea; n.pl. (Slang) a fit of depression; a very slow jazz dance of Negro origin. **blue** a. of the color blue; azure; livid; melancholy; glum; v.t. to make or dye blue. **bluish** a. slightly blue. -**bell** n. the wild hyacinth. -**berry** n. a shrub with edible small berries. -**bird** n. a migratory bird of N. Am. belonging to the thrush family. — **blood** n. an aristocrat. -**bonnet** n. Scottish trooper, from the blue woolen cap at one time in general use. — **book** n. a directory of socially prominent people; a college examination book. -**bottle** n. the cornflower; a large fly whose larvae are often parasites of domestic animals. **Blue Cross**, a system of nonprofit health insurance. -**grass** n. meadow grass of Kentucky which forms thick turf. -**heat**, about 550° F. -**jacket** n. a sailor. -**jay** n. a crested bird of the eastern U.S. and Canada. — **laws** n. laws restricting activities on Sunday. — **pencil** v.t. to edit, to alter. -**print** n. a simple photographic reproduction of technical drawings leaving white lines of plan on a blue background; (Fig.) any projected plan with its details. — **ribbon**, first prize; an emblem of temperance [Fr. bleu].

bluff (bluf) a. steep and broad; rough and ready; frank and hearty in manner; n. a high bank or cliff presenting a steep front; a headland; a cluster of trees on the prairie. -**ness** n. steepness; a frank, blunt manner of speech.

bluff (bluf) n. an attempt to mislead in regard to one's real purpose; v.t. to mislead one by giving a wrong impression. -**er** n. -**ing** n., a.

blun·der (blun′·dẹr) v.i. to make a gross mistake; to err through thoughtlessness; to flounder about; n. a gross mistake. -**er** n. -**head** n. one continually blundering. -**ing** n. and a. continually making mistakes; bungling; clumsy; fumbling. -**ingly** adv. [M.E. blondren, to confuse].

blun·der·buss (blun′·dẹr·bus) n. an obsolete short gun with a bell-shaped muzzle and a wide bore [Dut. donderbus, thunder-box].

blunt (blunt) a. having a dull edge or point; dull; brusque in speech; v.t. to render less sharp; to weaken appetite or desire. -**ly** adv. -**ness** [origin unknown].

blur (blur) n. a spot; stain; smudge; whatever dims without effacing; v.t. to smear; to make indistinct. pr.p. -**ring**; pa.t. and pa.p. -**red**.

blurb (blurb) n. an advertisement, esp. extravagant in praise [word invented by Gelett Burgess].

blurt (blurt) n. a sudden outburst. **to blurt out** v.t. to give information suddenly, indiscreetly, or tactlessly [imit.].

blush (blush) v.i. to redden in the face, from shame, modesty, or confusion; n. a rosy tint; a red color suffusing the face; first glance or view. -**ing** n. a rosy glow on the face; a. modest; coy; bashful. -**ingly** adv. [O.E. blyscan, to shine].

blus·ter (blus′·tẹr) v.i. to blow in boisterous gusts, of wind; to talk with violence and noise; to bully or swagger; n. fitful noise and violence. -**er** n. -**ous**. -**y** a. stormy.

bo·a (bō′·a) n. a genus of constricting, nonvenomous serpents; a long round coil of fur or feathers for the neck. -**constrictor** n. a serpent which crushes its victims [L.].

boar (bōr) n. the male of the swine. —**hound** n. a large dog used in hunting boars [O.E. bar].

board (bōrd) n. a long, narrow strip of timber; a table, hence food or diet; council-table; council itself; a thick paper made by pasting together several layers (card-board, paste-board, etc.); v.t. to cover with boards; to supply with meals and lodging for payment; to embark on a ship, airplane, etc.; v.i. to be a lodger. -**s** n.pl. the stage in a theater; the covers of a book. -**er** n. one who boards a vehicle; one receiving food and lodging. -**ing** n. a wooden fence, floor, etc.; entering a vehicle; obtaining food and lodging. -**ing-house** n. a house in which boarders are accommodated. -**ing-school** n. a school in which the students are

in residence [O.E. bord].

boast (bōst) v.t. to speak with vanity of; to be unduly proud of; v.i. to brag; to vaunt; to praise oneself extravagantly; n. a statement, expressive of pride or vain glory; that which is boasted of. -**er** n. -**ful** a. -**fully** adv. -**fulness**, -**ing** n. indulging in boasting. -**ingly** adv. [M.E. bost].

boat (bōt) n. a small vessel, generally undecked, moved by oars or sails or small motor; a ship; anything resembling a boat, e.g. a sauce-boat; v.t. to carry in a boat; v.i. to row or sail about in a boat. **boatswain** (bō′·sun) n. a ship's officer [O.E. bat].

bob (båb) n. a short, jerking motion; anything which swings when suspended; a jerk; a pendant; the weight of a pendulum; hair cut short and square across; a docked tail; v.t. to move with a jerk; to cut hair semi-short; v.i. to dangle; to move up and down or in and out; pr.p. -**bing**; pa.p. -**bed**.

bob·bin (båb′·in) n. a cylinder or spool on which thread is wound [Fr. bobine].

bob·o·link (båb′·a·lingk) n. a common North American songbird.

bob·by·sox (båb′·i·såks) n. (Colloq.) ankle socks, usually worn by girls in their teens. -**er** n. a girl in her teens.

bob·sled, bob·sleigh (båb′·sled, ·slā) n. two small sleds coupled together; a long toboggan; v.i. to use a bobsled.

bock (båk) n. dark beer [Ger. fr. Eimbeck where first brewed].

bode (bōd) v.t. and v.i. to portend; to presage; to foretell; to foreshadow; to be an omen of. -**ful** a. -**ment** n. an omen; portent; presentiment. **boding** a. ominous; an omen; a presentiment [O.E. bodian, to announce].

bod·ice (båd′·is) n. that part of a woman's dress above the waist, with or without sleeves, and close-fitting [orig. pl. bodies].

bod·kin (båd′·kin) n. (Obs.) a short, sharp dagger or stiletto; an instrument for piercing holes in material; a large blunt needle; a pin for dressing hair [M.E. boidekin].

bod·y (båd′·i·) n. the frame of a human being or of an animal; the main part of anything; coachwork, seating and upholstery of a car; an assemblage of things or persons; a solid substance; strength or consistency of a liquid; v.t. to produce in definite shape; pa.t. and pa.p. **bodied. bodied** a. used in compounds, e.g. able-bodied. **bodiless** a. possessing no body. **bodily** a. pert. to the body; adv. physically, in the body, in the flesh; altogether; completely; in the mass. -**guard** n. life-guard of an important individual; an escort [O.E. bodig].

Boe·o·tian (bē·ō′·shan) a. pert. to Boeotia in ancient Greece; boorish, dull, stupid, as the inhabitants were so considered.

Boer (bōr) n. a S. African of Dutch descent [Dut. cf. boor].

bo·gey (bō′·gi·) n. (Golf) one over par for hole. See bogle [fr. imaginary partner, Colonel Bogey].

bog·gle (båg′·l) v.i. to stop or shrink back through fear; to hesitate; to equivocate; to bungle.

bo·gle (bō′·gl) n. a ghost or demon; a fearsome apparition, imp, or hobgoblin associated with the nursery. **bogey, bogy** *n.* the devil; a bugbear; a goblin. **bogeyman, boggard** *n.* [fr. *bug*].

bo·gus (bō′·gus) *a.* sham; counterfeit; spurious; false [etym. unknown].

Bo·he·mi·an (bō·hē′·mi·an) *a.* pert. to Bohemia or its inhabitants; pert. to the gypsies; unconventional; *n.* a native of Bohemia; a gypsy; one who leads a loose and unsettled life [Fr. *bohémien, gypsy*].

boil (boil) *v.t.* to bring to a seething condition, by heating; to cook, by boiling; *v.i.* to be agitated by the action of heat; to seethe; to reach boiling-point. **-er** *n.* one who boils; a vessel for boiling. **-ing point,** the temperature at which a liquid boils; of water 212° Fahr. [Fr. *bouillir,* to boil].

boil (boil) *n.* local inflammation of the skin round a hair follicle [O.E. *bule,* sore].

bois·ter·ous (bois′·ter·as) *a.* wild; noisy; hearty; turbulent; stormy; windy. **-ly** *adv.* **-ness** *n.* [M.E. *boistous*].

bo·la, bo·las (bō′·a) *n.* a missile used by S. American cowboys, consisting of two or three stone balls attached to the ends of a rope, to entangle the feet of cattle [Sp.].

bold (bōld) *a.* daring; ready to meet danger; courageous; brave; intrepid; valorous; fearless; cheeky. **—faced** *a.* impudent; forward; brazen; of letters, printed with heavy thick strokes. **-ly** *adv.* **-ness** *n.* [O.E. *bald*].

bole (bōl) *n.* the trunk of a tree. **bolling** *n.* a tree with the top and branches cut off; a pollard [Scand. *bolr*].

bo·le·ro (bō·le′·rō) *n.* a national Spanish dance, in triple time; the music for this dance; a short jacket, usually without sleeves, worn over a blouse [Sp.].

boll (bōl) *n.* a seed capsule of cotton, flax, etc. **-weevil, -worm,** larvae of various moths destructive of cotton crops [O.E. *bolla*].

bol·lard (bál′·erd) *n.* a strong post on a wharf, etc., for making fast hawsers [fr. *bole*].

bo·lo·gna (ba·lō′·ni, ·na) *n.* a large smoked, seasoned type of sausage.

bo·lo·ney See **baloney.**

Bol·she·vik (bál′·sha·vik, also bōl·) *n.* a member of the Communist Party; a violent revolutionary. **bolshevism** *n.* theory and practice of Russian or other communism. **bolshevist** *n.* and *a.* **bolshevistic** *a.* **bolshevize** *v.t.* [Russ. *bolshe,* comp. of *veliki,* great].

bol·ster (bōl′·ster) *n.* a long round bed-pillow; anything designated as a support; *v.t.* to sustain; to support; to prop. **-er n. to bolster up,** to support a weak case or person [O.E.].

bolt (bōlt) *n.* a bar for fastening a door, window, etc.; part of a lock which engages with the keeper; a metal pin with a head at one end and screw threads at the other to receive a nut; a roll of cloth; a thunderbolt; an arrow; a sudden rush; *v.t.* to fasten with a bolt; to swallow food hurriedly; to expel suddenly; *v.i.* to rush away; to start suddenly forward [E.].

bomb (bám) *n.* a cast-iron container filled with high explosives, gas, incendiary contents, or smoke-producing substances exploding by percussion or by a timing mechanism. **-er** *n.* an airplane for bombs. **-proof** *a.* secure against small bomb splinters. **-shell** *n.* a bomb; something devastating and quite unexpected. **atom(ic) bomb,** a bomb depending on the release of atomic energy. **bomb sight,** instrument for aiming bombs [Gk. *bombos,* a booming sound].

bom·bard (bám′·bárd) *n.* an early mortar with a wide bore, using stone-shot. **bombard** (bam·bárd′) *v.t.* to batter with heavy artillery fire; to ply with many questions. **-ier** *n.* a gunner in the artillery. **-ment** *n.* a sustained attack with guns, bombs, etc. [O.Fr. *bombarde*].

bom·bast (bám′·bast) *n.* inflated, high-sounding language. **-ic** *a.* **-ically** *adv.* [O.Fr. *bombace,* cotton-wool].

bom·ba·zine, bom·ba·sine (bám·ba·zēn′) *n.* a twilled fabric of silk and worsted or cotton [Fr. *bombasin*].

bombe (bômb) *n.* a melon-shaped or round mold of ice cream [Fr.].

bo·nan·za (bō′·nan′·za) *n.* an exceptionally rich and persistent vein of ore; a profitable enterprise [Sp.].

bon bon (bán′·bán) *n.* a fondant candy. **-nere** (nyár) *n.* candy dish [Fr. *bon,* good].

bond (bánd) *n.* that which binds, a band, a link, a tie; an oath or promise; obligation; duty; the arrangement of bricks or stones in a wall so that successive courses interlock and give stability. **-s** *n.pl.* fetters; chains; captivity. **-age** *n.* a state of being bound; slavery; political subjection [O.E. *bindan,* to bind].

bond (bánd) *n.* a legal engagement in writing to fulfill certain conditions; a certificate of ownership of capital lent to a government, municipality, etc.; a mortgage on a house, etc.; *v.t.* to put dutiable articles on or under bond. **-ed** *a.* placed in bond; mortgaged. **-ed warehouse,** a warehouse for holding goods in bond [O.E. *bindan,* to bind].

bone (bōn) *n.* the hard tissue which forms the skeleton of mammals, birds, reptiles and fishes. **-r** *n.* (*Slang*) a mistake. *v.t.* to remove the bones; to filet (fish); to stiffen corsets with whale-bone, etc. **-s** *n.pl.* human remains; corpse; dice; castanets. **ash** *n.* calcined bones. **-black** *n.* finely ground animal charcoal.

— china *n.* china in which bone ash is used. **-dry** *a.* absolutely dry. **—head** *n.* (*Slang*) a stupid person. **— meal** *n.* a fertilizer for dry soils, made from ground bones. **boniness** *n.* **bony** *a.* full of bones [O.E. *ban*].

bones

bon·fire (bán′·fir) *n.* orig. a fire for burning bones; a large fire specially built and lit to express public joy [fr. *bone* and *fire*].

bon·ho·mie (bon′·a·mē) *n.* frank and simple good nature; geniality [Fr.].

bo·ni·to (ba·nē′·tō) *n.* a fish of the striped tunny kind [Sp.].

bon·net (bán′·et) *n.* a woman's head-gear, often tied under the chin. **-ed** *a.*

bon·ny (bán′·i·) *a.* pretty [Fr. *bon, bonne*].

bo·nus (bō′·nas) *n.* something over and above that which is due [L. *bonus,* good].

boo (bōō) *interj.* an exclamation of disapproval or contempt, often used to startle. **-es** *n.pl.* *v.t.* and *v.i.* to hoot; to show disapproval; *pr.t.* (he) **booes;** *pa.t.* **-ed** [imit.].

book (book) *n.* a number of sheets of paper, etc. bound together; a literary composition or treatise, written or printed; a record of betting transactions; the words of a play, the libretto; *v.t.* to put into a book; to obtain, or give, a business order, ticket (theater, etc.). **-s** *n.pl.* record of business transactions, especially financial; ledgers. **-binder** *n.* one who binds books. **-binding** *n.* **-case** *n.* a case with shelving for books. **— club** *n.* a club to distribute specially chosen books to subscribers. **— ends** *n. pl.* weighted props to keep books upright on a shelf. **-ie** *n.* (*Slang*) a bet taker. **-ing** *n.* entering in to a book a business transaction; recording field observations in surveying; an engagement to perform. **-ing-clerk** *n.* a clerk who issues railway, etc., tickets or registers orders. **-ish** *a.* fond of books and study. **-ishness** *n.* **— jacket** *n.* an attractively printed outer paper wrapper of a book. **-keeper** *n.* **-keeping** *n.* the art of keeping a systematic account of financial transactions. **— learning, -lore** *n.* knowledge acquired by extensive reading. **-let** *n.* a small book; a pamphlet. **-maker** *n.* one who compiles a book from various sources; a professional bettingman who accepts bets. **-mark** *n.* something placed in a book to mark a particular page. **the Book of Books,** the Holy Bible. **-plate** *n.* a label, often illustrated, pasted on the front end-papers of a book to denote ownership. **-seller** *n.* one who sells books. **-selling** *n.* **-shelf** *n.* a shelf for displaying books. **-shop, -stall, -stand** *n.* a place for exhibiting books and periodicals for sale. **-worm** *n.* one who reads intensively; larvae of insects which bore holes through the pages and bindings [O.E. *boc,* a book, the beech].

boom (bōōm) *n.* light spar for stretching bottom of a sail [*Dut.*].

boom (bōōm) *v.i.* to make a deep hollow sound; to be extremely popular and successful; to flourish; *n.* a hollow roar; the cry of the bittern; a sudden advance in popular favor; a sudden demand for an article; economic prosperity. **-er** *n.* **-ing.** *a.* [M.E. *bommen*].

boom·er·ang (bōō′·ma·rang) *n.* a curved wooden missile used by the natives of Australia

boon (bōōn) *n.* some good thing given or asked for; a benefit [Fr. *bon,* good].

boon (bōōn) *a.* gay; merry; jolly [Fr. *bon*].

boor (boor) *n.* a peasant; a rustic; a churl; lout; clown, bumpkin. **-ish** *a.* **-ishly** *adv.* **-ishness** *n.* [Dut. *boer,* peasant].

boost (bōōst) *v.t.* to raise by pushing from beneath; to give a lift to; to help forward; to advertise on a big scale; to increase the output or power of a machine; *n.* a push up. **-er** *n.*

boot (bōōt) *n.* a covering for the foot and leg; a kick; an instrument of judicial torture in which the leg was crushed; *v.t.* to put on boots; to kick. **-black** *n.* one who polishes the shoes of passers-by. **-ee** *n.* a knitted boot. **-leg** *v.t.* to sell illicitly alcoholic liquor; to smuggle. **-legger** *n.* **-legging** *n.* **-licker** *n.* (*Colloq.*) a hanger-on; a flatterer; a sycophant. **-licking** *n.* [Fr. *botte*].

booth (bōōth) *n.* a temporary structure of boards or other materials; a covered stall at a market or fair; a small restaurant compartment [O.N. *buth,* a dwelling].

boo·ty (bōō′·ti·) *n.* spoils of war [Fr. *butin*].

booze (bōōz) *n.* (*Colloq.*) alcoholic liquor; *v.i.* to drink excessively. **-r.** *n.* one who drinks to excess. **-y** *a.* a little intoxicated [Dut.].

bo·rax (bō′·raks) *n.* hydrated sodium borate, used in the manufacture of enamels and glazes, as a softener for hard water, an antiseptic, a soldering fix, etc. **boracic** *a.* **boracic acid,** white powder used as an antiseptic or for checking excessive perspiration. **borate** *n.* a salt of boracic acid [Ar. *búraq*].

bor·deaux (bawr·dō′) *n.* red or white wines of *Bordeaux,* France [Fr.].

bor·der (bawrd′·er) *n.* the outer part or edge of anything; the exterior limit of a place; a frontier; an ornamental design around the outside edge of anything; a flower-bed; *v.t.* to adorn with a border; to adjoin; *v.i.* to touch at the edge; to come near. **-ing** *n.* material for a border. **-land** *n.* land contiguous to a frontier; an indeterminate state or condition. **-line** *a.* on the verge of [Fr. *bordure*].

bore (bōr) *v.t.* to make a hole in; to pierce; to drill; to weary by uninteresting talk; to fatigue; *n.* the hole made by boring; the inside diameter measurement of a cylinder; the hollow interior part of a gun barrel; a thing or person that wearies one. **-dom** *n.* the state of being bored; ennui. **-r** *n.* tool for drilling; insect [O.E. *borian,* to pierce].

bore (bōr) *pa.t.* of **bear.**

Bo·re·as (bō′·ri·as) *n.* (*Myth.*) the god of the North wind. **boreal** *a.* northern [Gk.].

bo·ric (bōr′·ik) *a.* pert. to boron [shortened form of *boracic*].

born (bawrn) *pa.p.* of **bear,** to bring forth; *a.* natural; innate; perfect.

borne (bōrn) *pa.p.* of **bear,** to carry.

bo·ron (bō′·rán) *n.* a non-metallic element whose compounds are useful in the arts and medicine [fr. *borax*].

bor·ough (bur′·ō) *n.* an incorporated town [O.E. *burg, burh,* a fort, a manor-house].

bor·row (bár′·ō) *v.t.* to obtain on loan or trust; to adopt from abroad. **-ed** *a.* **-er** *n.* **-ing** *n.* [O.E. *borgian,* fr. *borg,* a pledge].

bor·zoi (bawr′·zoi) *n.* the Russian wolf-hound, remarkable for grace and swiftness [Russ.].

bosh (básh) *n.* empty talk; nonsense [Turk.].

bosk (bosk) *n.* (*Arch.*) a thicket or small wood. **-y** *a.* bushy; covered with underbrush. **-iness** *n.*

bos·om (boo′·zum) *n.* the breast of a human being; part of the dress over the breast; the heart; embrace; enclosure; a shirtfront; *v.t.* to press to the bosom; *a.* intimate; cherished [O.E. *bosm*].

boss (baws) *n.* a prominent circular projection on any article; a knob; a round, slightly raised ornament; *v.t.* to emboss; to provide with bosses. **-ed** *a.* embossed. **-y** *a.* containing, or ornamented with, bosses [Fr. *bosse,* a hump].

boss (baws) *n.* master; employer; one in charge; *v.t.* to manage; to supervise; (*Colloq.*) to browbeat. **-iness** *n.* **-y** *a.* fussy and masterful. **-ism** *n.* [Dut. *baas,* master].

bo·s'un See **boatswain** (under **boat**).

bot, bott (bát) *n.* usually *pl.* **bots, botts,** larvae of species of gad-fly found in intestines of horses, etc., causing tumor-like swellings [Gael. *botus,* belly-worm].

bot·a·ny (bát′·a·ni·) *n.* that branch of biology which is concerned with the structure and growth of plants. **botanic, botanical** *a.* pert. to botany. **botanically** *adv.* **botanic garden,** a garden where plants are scientifically studied. **botanist** *n.;* **botanize** *v.i.* to study plants; to search for and collect plants for further study [Gk. *botanē,* herb].

botch (bách) *n.* a clumsy patch of a garment; bungled work; *v.t.* to bungle; to patch clumsily; to blunder; spoil. **-er** *n.* a bungler. **-ery, -work** *n.* **-ily** *adv.* **-y** *a.* [M.E. *bocchen,* to patch].

both (bōth) *a.* and *pron.* the one and the other; *conj.* (foll. by *and*) as well [O.E. *bā*].

both·er (báTH′·er) *v.t.* to annoy; worry; trouble; vex; perplex; flurry; tease; plague; *v.i.* to fuss; to be troublesome; *n.* trouble; annoyance; fuss; worry; *interj.* an excalmation of annoyance. **-ation** *n.* trouble and worry; a mild imprecation. **-some** *a.* troublesome.

bot·tle (bát′·l) *n.* a vessel with a narrow neck for holding liquids; its contents; hard drinking; a thermionic valve; *v.t.* to put into bottles; to restrain; to curb. **-d** *a.* enclosed in bottles; of a bottle shape. **-d-up** *a.* confined; not allowed to speak. **— green** *a.* of a dark-green color. **bottling** *n.* and *a.* **-neck** *n.* a narrow section which impedes the smooth flow of traffic or production of goods. **-nose** *n.* a whale with a beaked snout. **— party** *n.* one where the guests provide the liquid refreshments. **-r** *n.* [O.Fr. *botel,* fr. *botte,* a truss].

bot·tom (bŏt'·ăm) *n.* the lowest part of anything; the posterior of human body; the base; bed or channel of a river or lake; foundation or groundwork; origin; *v.t.* to put a bottom on an article; to lay a foundation for a road, etc. **-less** *a.* **-less pit,** hell [O.E. *botm*].

bot·u·lism (băch'·a·lizm) *n.* a rare and dangerous form of food poisoning caused by spoiled foods [L. *botulus*, a sausage].

bou·clé (bōō·klā') *n.* a woven material with raised pile; *a.* pert. to such material [Fr.].

bou·doir (bōō'·dwăr) *n.* a lady's private room.

bouf·fant (bōō·fănt') *a.* puffed out, full, as in draperies, skirts, hair [Fr.].

bou·gain·vil·le·a (bōō'·gan·vil'·i·a) *n.* a S. American plant with great masses of red or lilac bracts [Louis *Bougainville* (1729-1814)].

bough (bou) *n.* an arm or large branch of a tree [O.E. *bog, boh*].

bought (bawt) *pa.t.* and *pa.p.* of **buy.**

bouil·lon (bōōl'·yăn) *n.* broth; stock. **bouillabaisse** (bōō·ya·bes') *n.* a Provençal fish soup or stew [Fr. *bouillir*, to boil].

boul·der (bōl'·der) *n.* a rock torn from its bed, and rounded by water. **—clay** *n.* a stiff clay of the glacial or ice-drift age [M.E. *bulderston*].

boul·e·vard (bōōl'·a·vărd) *n.* a street or promenade planted with trees. **-ier** *n.* one who haunts the boulevards; a man-about-town [Fr. fr. Ger. *Bollwerk*].

bounce (bouns) *v.i.* to move with a bound and rebound; to leap or spring suddenly; *v.t.* to cause to rebound, as a ball; to eject; *n.* a sudden spring or leap; rebound; **-r** *n.* (*Slang*) one who expels disorderly persons. **bouncing** *a.* vigorous; big [Dut. *bonzen*, to strike].

bound (bound) *pa.t.* and *pa.p.* of **bind.**

bound (bound) *v.i.* to leap; jump; spring; skip; frisk; *n.* a leap; jump [Fr. *bondir*, to leap].

bound (bound) *a.* tending to go or on the way, as in *homeward bound* [Scand.].

bound (bound) *n.* usually in *pl.* limit or boundary; confines; precincts; *v.t.* to restrain; to form the boundary of; to set bounds to. **-ed** *a.* restricted; bordered; cramped. **-less** *a.* without limits; wide and spacious; vast; infinite. **-lessness** *n.* [O.E. *bindan*, to bind].

bound·a·ry (bound'·ăr·i·) *n.* a border or limit; a dividing line; barrier.

boun·ty (boun'·ti·) *n.* liberality; generosity; munificence; a payment formerly made to men enlisting voluntarily in the army or navy; a premium offered by a government. **bounteous, bountiful** *a.* generous; liberal; ample; plentiful. **bounteously, bountifully** *adv.*; **bounteousness, bountifulness** *n.* [Fr. *bonté*, goodness].

bou·quet (bō'·kā, bōō'·kā) *n.* a nosegay; a bunch of flowers; a perfume; the aromatic flavor and aroma of wine; (*fig.*) a compliment [Fr.].

bour·bon (bur'·băn) *n.* a whisky distilled from corn and rye [*Bourbon*, Kentucky].

bour·geois (boor·zhwá') *n.* a member of middle-class society; *a.* of commercial or non-manual classes; middle-class; conventional; humdrum; stodgy. **bourgeoisie** (boor'·zhwá·zē) *n.* [Fr.].

bourgeon See **burgeon.**

bourn (bōrn) *n.* a stream; a burn [O.E. *burna*].

bourn, bourne (bōrn, boorn) *n.* a boundary; a limit; a realm; a domain; goal. **last bourne,** the grave [Fr. *borne,* limit].

bourse (boors) *n.* the stock exchange, esp. in Paris [Fr.]. [See **purse.**]

bout (bout) *n.* a turn; a conflict; contest; continuous drinking [Doublet of *bight*].

bou·ton·nier (bōō'·tan·yēr') *n.* a flower or flowers worn in a buttonhole or on a lapel [Fr.].

bo·vine (bō'·vin) *a.* pert. to cattle; ox-like; dull; stupid; stolid; obtuse [L. *bovinus*].

bow (bou) *v.i.* to bend body in respect, assent, etc.; to submit; *v.t.* to bend downwards; to cause to stoop; to subdue; *n.* an inclination of head or body; the rounded forward part of a ship; the stem or prow. **-line** (bō'·lin) *n.* a rope used to keep the weather edge of the sail tight forward; knot used for tying a rope to a post. **-man** *n.* the one who rows the foremost oar in a boat. **-sprit** (bō'·sprit) *n.* a large spar projecting over the stem of a vessel [O.E. *bugan*, to bend].

bow (bō) *n.* anything bent or curved; weapon from which an arrow is discharged; any curved instrument, as a fiddle-stick; a lace or ribbon tied in a slip-knot; a rainbow; *v.t.* to manipulate the bow of a violin, etc. **-ed** *a.* bent like a bow; crooked. **-er** *n.* **-legged** *a.* having crooked legs. **-man** *n.* an archer. **— tie** *n.* a small bow-shaped tie [O.E. *boga*].

bow

bowd·ler·ize (boud'·ler·iz) *v.t.* to leave out indelicate words or passages in a book in the alleged interest of moral purity. **bowdlerism** *n.* [fr. T. *Bowdler's* expurgated edition of Shakespeare, 1818].

bow·el (bou'·al) *n.* an entrail; the entrails; the inside of everything; (*Fig.*) the seat of pity, tenderness, etc. **-s** *n.pl.* the intestines [O.Fr. *boel*].

bow·er (bou'·er) *n.* a shady recess; an arbor; (*Poetic*) a small country dwelling; a boudoir. **-y** *a.* shady [O.E. *bur*, dwelling].

bow·ie-knife (bō'·i·nif) *n.* a long hunting-knife, the point double-edged, the blade straight and single-edged at the hilt [invented by Col. James *Bowie*].

bowl (bōl) *n.* a round vessel; a deep basin; a drinking-cup; the hollow part of anything, as a pipe for smoking; a stadium [O.E. *bolle*].

bowl (bōl) *n.* anything rounded by art; a ball rolled in certain games; a ball with bias; *pl.* a game played on a bowling-green with bowls; *v.t.* to roll, as a bowl; *v.i.* to play with bowls; to move rapidly and smoothly; to deliver a ball. **-er** *n.* one who bowls. **-ing** *n.* [O.Fr. *boule*].

bow·ler (bōl'·er) *n.* (*Br.*) a derby [fr. name of original maker].

bow·sprit (bō'·sprit) *n.* See **bow.**

box (băks) *n.* a small case or chest, generally with a lid; its contents; a compartment. **— kite** *n.* a kite consisting of a square frame **— like** *a.* **— office** *n.* ticket office at a theater. **— pleat** *n.* a double fold with material turned under on both sides with knife edges [O.E.].

box (băks) *n.* a small evergreen shrub. **—berry** *n.* the wintergreen. **-en** *a.* made of or like boxwood. **-wood** *n.* a tree [L. *buxus*].

box (băks) *n.* a blow on the head or the ears; *v.t.* to buffet; *v.i.* to fight with the fists. **-er** *n.* a pugilist. **-ing** *n.* the sport of fighting with fists.

boy (boi) *n.* a male child; a lad. **-hood** *n.* **-ish** *a.* boy-like; puerile. **-ishly** *adv.* **-ishness** *n.* the natural actions of a boy [M.E. *boi, boy*].

boy·cott (boi'·kăt) *n.* a method of coercion by refusing to deal with; *v.t.* to act as above; to ostracize. **-er** *n.* **-ing** *n.* [fr. Capt. *Boycott*].

bra (brá) See **brassiere.**

brace (brās) *n.* a rod or bar crossing a space diagonally to connect two structural parts; a pair; a support; a fastener; a carpenter's tool for boring; a printer's mark ({) used in bracketing words; *v.t.* to furnish with braces; to support; to tighten; to nerve or strengthen. **-s** *n.pl.* suspenders; an arm guard; wires for straightening teeth. **and bit,** small interchangeable boring tool fitted into the socket of a brace. **-r** *n.* a wrist-guard of leather or metal, used esp. by archers; (*Colloq.*) stimulating drink. **bracing** *a.* strengthening; invigorating; refreshing [Fr. *bras*, arm].

brace·let (brās'·let) *n.* an encircling ornament for the wrist. **-s** *n. pl.* (*Colloq.*) handcuffs.

bra·chi·al (brā'·ki·al, brak'·i·al) *a.* belonging to the arm; of the nature of an arm; resembling an arm [L. *brachium*, arm].

brack·en (brak'·an) *n.* a large coarse species of fern [M.E. *braken*].

brack·et (brak'·it) *n.* a projecting support fastened to a wall; one of two hooks, [ ], { }, or ( ), used to enclose explanatory words; *v.t.* to place within brackets; to couple names together as of equal merit, etc. [Fr. *braguette*, fr. L. *bracae*, breeches].

brack·ish (brak'·ish) *a.* somewhat salty; distasteful. **-ness** *n.* [Dut. *brak*, briny].

bract (brakt) *n.* a leaf in the axil of which a flower or inflorescence arises. **-eal** *a.* of the nature of a bract. **-eate** *a.* having bracts; bracteal [L. *bractea*, a thin plate].

brad (brad) *n.* a cut nail tapering in width with a small head projecting at one end. **-awl** *n.* a small hand-boring tool [Scand.].

brag (brag) *v.i.* to boast; to praise oneself or one's belongings; *pr.p.* **-ging**; *pa.t.* and *pa.p.* **-ged**; *n.* boasting; bragging. **-gadocio** (brag·-a·dō'·shi·ō) *n.* a boasting fellow. **-gart** *n.* a boaster. **-ging** *a.*, *n.* **-gingly** *adv.*

Brah·ma (brá'·ma) *n.* the 1st aspect of the Trimurti, or Hindu Trinity, the Creator. **brahman** (Also **brahmin**) *n.* a person of the highest or priestly caste among the Hindus.

braid (brād) *v.t.* to plait, entwine, or interweave; to bind with braid; *n.* a narrow ribbon or tape used as a dress-trimming or in upholstery; a tress of hair. **-ed** *a.* **-ing** *n.* [O.E. *bregdan*].

braille (brāl) *n.* a system of printing books in relief to be read by the blind; also the letters used, consisting of raised dots in combination [Louis *Braille*, inventor].

brain (brān) *n.* the whitish, soft mass in the skull in which are the nerve centers; intellect; mental capacity; understanding; intelligence; *v.t.* to dash out the brains of. **-ed** *a.* having the brains beaten out; used in compound terms as *feather-brained*, etc. **-less** *a.* witless; stupid. **—storm** *n.* (*Colloq.*) a sudden idea, inspiration. **brain trust,** body of experts engaged in research or planning. **-wash** *v.t.* (*Colloq.*) to effect a radical change in beliefs by intensive indoctrination. **— wave** *n.* (*Colloq.*) a spontaneous bright idea. **-y** *a.* highly intellectual; clever [O.E. *braegen*].

braise (brāz) *v.t.* to cook meat by browning in fat and simmering in a covered dish with a small amount of liquid [Fr.].

brake (brāk) *n.* a place overgrown with ferns, etc.; a thicket; brushwood [Scand.].

brake (brāk) *n.* instrument for breaking flax or hemp; a harrow; any device for checking speed; any restraining influence or curb; *v.t.* to pound or crush flax, hemp, etc., by beating; to check by applying a brake. **braking** *n.* **— shoe** *n.* the surface of a block brake.

bram·ble (bram'·bl) *n.* a prickly hedge-plant; the wild blackberry [O.E. *brembel*].

bran (bran) *n.* the ground husk of wheat and other grain, separated in milling from the flour [O.Fr.].

branch (branch) *n.* a limb of a tree or shrub; a bough; a department of a business, etc.; a line of family descent; an off-shoot; ramification; section; part; sub-division; *a.* pert. to a subsidiary section of any business; *v.t.* to divide, as into branches; *v.i.* to spread, in branches; to diverge; **-ed** *a.* **-ing** *a.* shooting out; starting from. **-y** *a.* [Fr. *branche*].

bran·chi·ae (brang'·ki·ē) *n.pl.* the breathing organs of fishes, the gills. **branchial** *a.* pert. to gills. **branchiate** *a.* furnished with gills [Gk. *branchia*, gills].

brand (brand) *n.* a burning, or partly burnt, piece of wood; an iron used for burning marks on; a mark made by a hot iron; a trade-mark; a grade; a sword; a mark of infamy; stigma; *v.t.* to burn a mark on; to fix a stamp on; to designate a commodity by a special name or trade-mark; to stigmatize; to reproach. **-ed** *a.* **-er** *n.* **-ing-iron** *n.* [O.E.].

bran·dish (bran'·dish) *v.t.* to flourish or wave, as a weapon [Fr. *brand*, sword].

bran·dy (bran'·di·) *n.* a spirit distilled from wine [Dut. *brandewijn*, burnt wine].

brant (brant) *n.* small dark wild goose.

brash (brash) *a.* hasty; insolent. **-ness** *n.*

brass (bras) *n.* a yellow alloy of two parts of copper to one of zinc; (*Colloq.*) money; effrontery; impudence; obstinacy; a brazen; made of brass. **-es** *n.pl.* the brass instruments of an orchestra. **— band** *n.* musicians who perform on brass instruments; (*Colloq.*) a military band. **— hat** *n.* (*Colloq.*) staff-officer (from gold braid on hat). **-iness** *n.* bold; impudent. **-y** *a.* pert. sole. **— knuckles** *n.pl.* metal pieces fitted across the knuckles, used in fighting. **to get down to brass tacks** (*Colloq.*) to return to essentials, fundamentals [O.E. *braes*].

bras·sard (bras'·ărd) *n.* a band worn around arm to signify special duty; armor for upper arm [Fr. *bras*, arm].

bras·si·ere (bra·zēr') *n.* a woman's undergarment supporting the breasts; short form **bra** [Fr.]. [offspring [O.E. *bratt*, a pinafore].

brat (brat) *n.* a child (used contemptuously).

bra·va·do (bra·vá'·dō) *n.* showy bravery [Sp.].

brave (brāv) *a.* courageous; noble; fearless; *n.* an Indian warrior; *v.t.* to encounter with courage. **-ly** *adv.* **-ry** *n.* courage; heroism [Fr.].

bra·vo (brä′·vō) *interj.* an expression of applause, well done!; *pl.* **-es** [It.].

brawl (brawl) *v.i.* to flow noisily, as water; to squabble noisily; *n.* a noisy quarrel. **-er** *n.* [Fr. fr. Scand.].

brawn (brawn) *n.* muscular strength. esp. of the arms and legs; muscles; the flesh of a boar; a preparation of meat made from pigs' head. **-er** *n.* a boar fattened for the table. **-iness** *n.* **-y** *a.* muscular; sinewy; athletic; robust; stout [O.Fr. *braon*, fleshy part].

bray (brā) *n.* the harsh noise of a donkey; any harsh, strident noise; continual complaining; *v.i.* to utter a harsh noise, like a donkey [Fr. *braire*].

bray (brā) *v.t.* to pound; to powder; to pulverize; to grind small [O.Fr. *breier*].

braze (brāz) *v.t.* to solder metals with a hard alloy; to make or ornament with brass.**brazing** *n.* [Fr. *braser*, to solder].

bra·zen (brā′·zn) *a.* pert. to, or made of, brass; impudent; shameless; sounding like a brass instrument; *v.t.* to face a situation in a bold, impudent manner. **-ly** *adv.* [M.E. *brasen*].

bra·zier (brāzh′·yẹr) *n.* a portable iron container to hold burning coals; a worker in brass [Fr. *brasier*].

Bra·zil·i·an (bra·zil′·yạn) *n.* a native of Brazil, in S. America; *a.* pert. to Brazil.

breach (brēch) *n.* a break or opening, esp. in a wall; a hole or gap; non-fulfillment of a contract, promise, etc.; an infringement of a rule, duty, etc.; a quarrel; *v.t.* to make a breach or gap in something. **— of promise**, the non-fulfillment of a promise, esp. of marriage [Fr. *brèche*].

bread (bred) *n.* form of food prepared by baking dough made from a cereal; food in general. **— winner** *n.* one who earns a living for his dependents [O.E.].

breadth (bredth) *n.* distance from side to side; width; freedom from narrowness of mind [O.E. *braedu*].

break (brāk) *v.t.* to shatter by force; to mitigate (a blow, a fall); to tame (a horse, etc.); to wean from (a habit); to bankrupt; to weaken or impair (health); to subdue (a person's temper); to violate (promises, etc.); to interrupt (friendship, silence, monotony, etc.); *v.i.* to divide into several parts; to open (as an abscess); curl over (as waves); to burst forth (as a storm); to dawn (as an idea, day, etc.); to crack or falter (as the voice); to make the first stroke at billiards; to change (as a horse); *pa.t.* **broke** *pa.p.* **broken** [O.E. *brecan*].

break (brāk) *n.* the act or state of being broken; a fracture; a gap; an opening; dawn; separation; interruption; a breathing space; (*Slang*) a chance, good luck; a sudden fall in price; a scoring sequence at billiards. **-able** *a.* fragile. **-age** *n.* act of breaking; an allowance for articles broken. **-down** *n.* loss of health; an accident to machinery; suspension of negotiations; *v.t.* to divide into small categories. **-er** *n.* one who breaks; a long wave or crest as it breaks into foam. **-fast** (brek·fast) *n.* the first meal of the day. **-neck** *a.* dangerous to life and limb. **-up** *n.* disintegration; collapse; separation. **-water** *n.* a strong structure to break the force of a wave [O.E. *brecan*, to break].

breast (brest) *n.* the external part of the thorax or chest between neck and abdomen; bosom; seat of the affections and passions; *v.t.* to bear the breast against; to oppose, face, or meet boldly (a wave); to mount (a hill, etc.). **-s** *n.pl.* the milk or mammary glands of women and female animals. **-bone** *n.* the sternum, the flat narrow bone to which the first seven ribs are attached. **-plate** *n.* a metal plate or piece of armor for protecting the chest. **— stroke** *n.* a long-distance stroke in swimming [O.E. *breost*].

breath (breth) *n.* air respired by the lungs; the act of breathing freely; life; respite; a single respiration, or the time of making it; a very slight breeze; whisper; fragrance. **-less** *a.* out of breath; panting; dead; eager and excited; expectant. **-lessness** *n.* **under one's breath**, in a low voice or whisper. **with bated breath**, breath held from fear or excitement [O.E. *braeth*, exhalation].

breathe (brēTH) *v.t.* to draw in and give out air from the lungs; to infuse or inspire, as life, courage, etc.; *v.i.* to inhale and emit air—hence to live; to take breath. **breathable** *a.* **-d** (brēTHd) *a.* (*Phon.*) uttered with breath only. **-r** *n.* a short spell of rest. **breathing** *n.* respiration; a mark (') placed over a vowel in Greek grammar giving it the sound of *h*.

breathing-space, breathing-time, *n.* a pause; relaxation; a short respite [fr. *breath*].

bred *pa.t.* and *pa.p.* of **breed**.

breech (brēch) *n.* the buttocks; the hinder part, esp. of a gun-barrel; *v.t.* to put (a young child for the first time) into breeches; to whip; to flog. **-es** *n.pl.* trousers, esp. those which fit tightly around knees. **-es-buoy** *n.* an apparatus consisting of a canvas bag slung along a rope, used for saving persons from a wreck. **-ing** *n.* that part of the harness which passes round a horse's haunches [O.E. *brec*].

breed (brēd) *v.t.* to beget; to engender; to generate; to propagate; to hatch; to train or bring up; *v.i.* to be produced; to be with young; to increase in number; *pa.t.* and *pa.p.* **bred**; *n.* a race of animals from the same stock; kind; sort. **-er** *n.* one who breeds cattle or other live stock. **-ing** *n.* producing; the rearing of live stock; manners; deportment; courtesy [O.E. *bredan*, to nourish].

breeze (brēz) *n.* a wind of moderate strength. **breezy** *a.* windy; gusty; of a person, animated and brisk [Fr. *brise*].

br'er (brur, brer) *n.* brother; used in the animal stories of Uncle Remus [S. Dial.].

breth·ren (breTH′·rin) *n.pl.* members of the same society or profession [See **brother**].

Bre·ton (bret′·an) *n.* pert. to Brittany; *a.* one of the Celtic dialects, spoken in Brittany; a native of Brittany; a hat with turned-up brim [O.Fr.].

breve (brēv) *n.* the longest note now used in music; a mark distinguishing short vowels; a writ issued by a court [It. fr. L. *brevis*, short].

bre·vet (brev′·et) *a.* a commission, which entitles an officer to an honorary rank in the army above his actual rank. **-cy** *n.* brevet rank [Fr. fr. L. *brevis*, short].

bre·vi·a·ry (brēv′·i·e·ri·) *n.* a book containing the daily service of the R.C. Church [L. *brevis*, short].

brev·i·ty (brev′·a·ti·) *n.* shortness; conciseness; briefness; terseness [L. *brevis*, short].

brew (brōo) *v.t.* to prepare a fermented liquor, from malt, hops, etc.; to infuse (tea); to plot; concoct; mix; *v.i.* to perform the operations of brewing; to be impending; *n.* something brewed; a particular brand or quality of beer. **-er** *n.* **-ery** *n.* a place where brewing is carried on [O.E. *breowan*].

bri·ar See **brier**.

bribe (brīb) *n.* anything bestowed, with a view to influence judgment and conduct; *v.t.* to influence by gifts; *v.i.* to practice bribery. **bribable** *a.* **bribery** *n.* [Fr. *bribe*, fragment].

bric-à-brac (brik′·a·brak) *n.* curios; ornamental articles; knickknacks [Fr.].

brick (brik) *n.* a building material made from a special clay molded into a rectangular block and hardened by drying in the sun or firing in a kiln; (*Colloq.*) a sterling friend; *v.t.* to lay, or pave, with bricks. **-bat** *n.* a fragment of a brick. **-bats** *n.pl.* uncomplimentary comments. **-kiln** *n.* a kiln in which bricks are baked or burnt. **-layer** *n.* one who is skilled in building with bricks. **-laying** *n.* **— red** *a.* of a dull scarlet color like brick [Fr. *brique*].

bride (brīd) *n.* a woman about to be, or just, married. **bridal** *n.* wedding; *a.* pert. to a bride or a wedding; nuptial; connubial; conjugal. **bridal-suite** *n.* apartments set aside for a honeymoon couple. **-groom** *n.* a man newly-married, or about to be married. **-s maid** *n.* an unmarried woman who acts as attendant on a bride [O.E. *bryd*].

bridge (brij) *n.* a structure spanning a river or a valley, etc., in order to afford passage; a support for the strings of a violin; the hurricane deck or bridge deck of a vessel; the bone of the nose, etc.; mounting for false teeth; (*Mus.*) connecting passage; *v.t.* to build a bridge or bridges over. **-head** *n.* a work protecting the end of a bridge nearest the enemy; a footing gained by an attacking force on the far bank of a river. [O.E. *brycg*].

bridge (brij) *n.* a card game for four players.

bri·dle (brī′·dl) *n.* the headgear of a beast of burden, of a horse; a curb; constraint; *v.t.* to put a bridle upon; to check; subdue; curb; control. **— path** *n.* a narrow track used by riders on horseback [O.E. *bridel*].

brief (brēf) *a.* short in duration; using few words; *n.* an abridged statement of a case; an outline of an argument; a writ, summoning one to answer in an action; *v.t.* to instruct or retain counsel by giving him a brief; to inform personnel of the details of an impending action. **— case** *n.* a small flat case for carrying papers, cash, etc. **-ly** *adv.* **-ness** *n.* **-s** *n.pl.* undershorts [Fr. *bref*, fr. L. *brevis*, short].

bridle

bri·er, bri·ar (brī′·ẹr) *n.* the heath of S. France; a pipe made from the root of this brier [Fr. *bruyère*, heather].

bri·er (brī′·ẹr) *n.* any prickly bush; a tangled mass of them; a smoking pipe [O.E.].

brig (brig) *n.* a sailing-ship with two masts, both square-rigged; (*Slang*) guardhouse [shortened **brigatine**, q.v. but not to be confused with it].

bri·gade (bri·gād′) *n.* a sub-division of an army under the command of a general officer; a group of people organized for a specific purpose, such as a *fire brigade*. **brigadier-general** *n.* [It. *brigata*, a troop].

brig·and (brig′·and) *n.* a lawless fellow who lives by plunder; bandit; highwayman. **-age** *n.* [O.Fr. *brigand*, a foot-soldier].

bright (brīt) *a.* shining; full of light or splendor; cheerful; vivacious; sparkling; luminous; radiant; clear; clever; intelligent. **-en** *v.t.* to make bright; *v.i.* to grow bright. **-ly** *adv.* **-ness** *n.* [O.E. *beorht*].

bril·liant (bril′·yạnt) *a.* glittering; sparkling; radiant; shining; illustrious; distinguished; splendid; very clever; *n.* a polished diamond cut to a definite pattern. **-ly** *adv.* **-ness** *n.* **brilliance** *n.* **brilliancy** *a.* [Fr. *brillant*].

brim (brim) *n.* rim or border; the rim of a hat; *v.i.* to be full to the brim. **-ful** *a.* **-med** *a.* **-ming** *a.* [M.E. *brimme*].

brim·stone (brim′·stōn) *n.* sulphur; hellfire; *a.* lemon-colored [M.E. *brenston* = burning-stone].

brin·dle, brindled (brin′·dl, ·dld) *a.* streaked with dark stripes, or spots, on a gray or tan ground [Scand.].

brine (brīn) *n.* water containing an admixture of salt; sea-water; the sea. **brinish** *a.* salty, like brine. **briny** *a.* [O.E. *bryne*].

bring (bring) *v.t.* to carry; to fetch; to convey from one person or place to another; to transfer; to transport; to draw; to lead; to prevail on; *pa.t.* and *pa.p.* **brought** (brawt) [O.E. *bringan*].

brink (bringk) *n.* edge, margin of a steep slope; verge [M.E. *brenk*].

bri·o (brē′·ō) *n.* (*Mus.*) liveliness; vivacity [It.].

bri·quette (bri·ket′) *n.* a brick of compressed coal dust. Also **briquet** [Fr.].

brisk (brisk) *a.* full of activity; *v.t.* and *i.* to enliven; to cheer up. **-ly** *adv.* **-ness** *n.* [Celt.].

bris·ket (bris′·kit) *a.* part of animal's breast which lies next to ribs [O.Fr.].

bris·tle (bris′·l) *n.* a very stiff, erect, coarse hair, as of swine; a quill; *v.t.* to erect the bristles of; *v.i.* to stand up erect, like bristles; to show anger; to be surrounded with. **-d** (bris′·ld) *a.* provided with bristles [O.E. *bryst*].

Bri·tan·ni·a (bri·tan′·ya) *n.* Great Britain personified; a female figure forming an emblem of Great Britain. **Britannic** *a.* pert. to Great Britain [L.].

Brit·ish (brit′·ish) *a.* of or pertaining to Britain; *n.* the inhabitants of Britain. **-er** *n.* a British subject [fr. *Briton*].

Brit·on (brit′·an) *n.* a native of Britain [L. *Brito*].

brit·tle (brit′·l) *a.* easily broken; apt to break; frail; fragile [fr. O.E. *breotan*, to break].

broach (brōch) *n.* a roasting-spit; a tapered, hardened-steel bit for enlarging holes in metal; *v.t.* to pierce; to tap, as a cask; to open; to approach a subject [Fr. *broche*, a roasting-spit].

broad (brawd) *a.* wide, ample, open; outspoken, unrestrained; coarse, indelicate, gross; tolerant, liberal-minded; with a marked local dialect; plain, unmistakable (hint); full (daylight); *n.* (*Slang*) coarse for a woman. **broad, -ly** *adv.* **-brim** *n.* a wide-brimmed hat, much affected by Quakers, and so a Quaker. **-cast** *v.t.* to scatter seed; *n.* a casting of seed from the hand in sowing [See **broadcast**]. **-cloth** *n.* a finely woven woollen, cotton, or rayon cloth for clothing. **-en** *vt.* and *v.i.* to make or grow broad. **— jump** *n.* (*Sports*) a horizontal jump from rest or from a run. **-loom** *n.* woven on a wide loom, of carpets and rugs. **—minded** *a.* tolerant. **-ness** *n.* **-side** *n.* a sheet of paper printed on one side of the paper only; the whole side of a ship above water-line; a volley from the gun on one side of a naval craft; violent abuse [O.E. *brad*].

broad·cast (brawd′·kast) *n.* a transmission by radio of lectures, music, etc.; a program; *a.*; *v.t.* to disseminate by radio-telephone transmitter, news, plays, music, etc., for reception by receiving apparatus. **-er** *n.* a person or organization broadcasting [O.E. *brad*, and Dan. *kaste*].

bro·cade (brō·kād′) n. a fabric woven with elaborate design; v.t. to make brocade; to ornament a fabric with raised designs. -d a. [Sp. brocado].

broc·co·li (brŏk′·ạ·li·) n. a variety of the cauliflower [It. pl. dim. fr. brocco, a shoot].

bro·chette (brō·shet′) n. skewer.

bro·chure (brō·shoor′) n. a printed work of a few sheets of paper; a booklet; a pamphlet [Fr. brocher, to stitch].

brogue (brōg) n. a stout, comfortable, ordinary shoe. Also **brogan** [Ir. brog].

brogue (brōg) n. a mode of pronunciation peculiar to Irish speakers [Ir. brog, shoe].

broi·der (broi′·dẹr) v.t. to adorn with figured needlework; to embroider [Fr. broder].

broil (broil) n. a noisy quarrel; contention; altercation [Fr. brouiller, to trouble].

broil (broil) v.t. to cook on a gridiron over coals, or directly under gas or electric heat in a stove; to grill; v.i. to suffer discomfort through heat; to be overheated [Fr. brûler, to burn].

broke (brōk) pa.t. and old pa.p. of **break**; a. (Colloq.) penniless; ruined; degraded. **-n** pa.p. of **break**; a. shattered; fractured; severed; separated; parted; abrupt; rough; impaired; exhausted; spent. **-n English**, imperfect English, as spoken by a non-native. **-n hearted** a. crushed with grief; inconsolable. **-nly** adv. intermittently. **-nness** n. [break].

brok·er (brōk′·ẹr) n. a person employed in the negotiation of commercial transactions between other parties in the interests of one of the principals; a pawn-broker; a dealer in second-hand goods; an agent. **-age, brokage,** n. the business of a broker; the commission charged by a broker [M.E. brocour].

bro·mide (brō′·mid) n. a compound of bromine with some other element; a sedative drug, employed to induce sleep [See **bromine**].

bro·mine (brō′·mēn, -min) n. one of the elements, related to chlorine, iodine, and fluorine. **bromic** a. [Gk. fr. bromos, stench].

bron·chi, bron·chi·a (brang′·kī, ·ki·ạ) n.pl. the two tubes forming the lower end of the trachea. **-al** a. pert. to the bronchi. **bronchitis,** n. inflammation of the bronchial tubes. [Gr. bronchia].

bron·chus (brang′·kus) n. one of the bifurcations of the windpipe; pl. see **bronchi** [Gk. bronchos, windpipe].

bron·co (brang′·kō) n. an unbroken, or partly broken horse. **— buster** n. [Sp. rough].

bronze (bränz) n. an alloy of copper, tin, and zinc; a work of art cast in bronze; the color of bronze; a. made of or colored like bronze; v.t. to give the appearance of bronze to; to sunburn; to harden. **Bronze Age,** pre-historic period between the Stone and Iron Ages. **bronzy** a. [It. bronzo].

brooch (brōch, brōōch) n. an ornamental clasp with a pin for attaching it to a garment [Fr. broche, a spike, a brooch].

brood (brōōd) v.t. to sit upon, as a hen on eggs; to ponder; v.i. to sit upon to hatch; to meditate moodily; n. off-spring; a family of young, esp. of birds; a tribe; a race. **-er** n. an appliance for rearing incubator-hatched chickens by artificial heat. **— mare** n. a mare kept for breeding. **-y** a. wishing to sit, as a hen; moody; sullen [O.E. brod]. [streamlet [O.E. broc].

brook (brook) n. a small stream. **-let** n. a

brook (brook) v.t. to bear; to endure; to support [O.E. brucan, use, enjoy].

broom (brōōm, broom) n. a wild evergreen shrub producing yellow flowers and pods; an implement for sweeping [O.E. brom].

broth (brawth) n. water in which meat has been boiled with vegetables [O.E. brodh].

broth·el (brath′·ạl) n. house of prostitution [O.E. brothen, degenerate].

broth·er (bruTH′·ẹr) n. a male born of the same parents; one closely resembling another in manner or character; an associate or fellow-member of a corporate body; pl. **-s, brethren. -hood** n. the state of being a brother; an association of men of the same religious order, profession, or society; the mutual regard resulting from this association. **-in-law** n. the brother of one's husband or wife; a sister's husband. **-like, -ly** a. like a brother, affectionate. **-liness** n. [O.E. brothor].

brough·am (brōōm, brō′·ạm) n. a closed horse-carriage with two or four wheels, with an elevated seat for the driver [fr. Lord Brougham].

brought (brawt) pa.t. and pa.p. of **bring**.

brow (brou) n. the ridge over the eyes; the eye-brow; the forehead; the rounded top of a hill. **-beat** v.t. to bully or over-rule a person by over-bearing speakers. **-beater** n. [O.E. bru].

brown (broun) n. a dark color inclining to red or yellow; a mixture of black, red, and-yellow; a. of a brown color; swarthy; sunburnt; v.t. to make or give a brown color to; to sunbathe; to grill or roast brown. **— betty** n. a spiced, bread and apple pudding. **— shirt** n. a member of the German Nazi party. **-stone** n. a reddish-brown sandstone used in building. **— study,** serious reverie. **— sugar,** unrefined or partly refined sugar [O.E. brun].

brown·ie (broun′·i·) n. a good-natured household elf; a member of the junior section of the Girl scouts; a chocolate cookie.

browse (brouz) v.t. and i. to nibble; to graze; to glance through a book shop, etc. **browsing** n. [O.Fr. broust, a shoot].

bruise (brōōz) v.t. to injure by striking or crushing; to contuse; to pound or pulverize; n. a contusion. **-r** n. a prize-fighter; (Colloq.) a tough bully [O.E. brysan, to break].

bruit (brōōt) v.t. to report; to rumor [Fr.].

bru·mal (brōō′·mạl) a. relating to winter [L. bruma, winter].   [a. foggy [Fr. brume, fog].

brume (brōōm) n. mist, fog, vapor. **brumous**

brunch (brunch) n. (Colloq.) breakfast and lunch combined [Portmanteau word].

bru·nette (brōō·net′) n. a woman with dark brown hair or brown complexion; a. [Fr.].

brunt (brunt) n. the main shock of onset; the force of a blow [E., conn. with burn].

brush (brush) n. an implement made of bristles, twigs, feathers, etc., bound together and used for removing dust, dressing the hair, applying paint, and the like; the smaller trees of a forest, brushwood; a sharp skirmish; the bushy tail of a fox or squirrel; in electricity, the stationary contact pieces which collect current from the commutator of a dynamo; v.t. to remove dust, etc., with a brush; to touch lightly in passing; v.i. to touch with light contact. **-off** n. (Slang) an abrupt refusal. **-wood** n. small branches broken or cut from trees; thicket of small trees and shrubs. **-y** a. rough, shaggy [O.Fr. brosse, brushwood].

brusque (brusk) a. blunt; abrupt in speech. **-ness** n. [Fr.].

brute (brōōt) a. irrational; ferocious; brutal; n. a beast; one of lower animals; a low-bred, unfeeling person. **brutal** a. savage; inhuman. **brutalism** n. brutality. **brutality** n. inhumanity; savagery; **brutalize** v.t. to make brutal, cruel, or coarse; to treat with brutality; v.i. to become brutal. **brutally** adv. **brutish** a. [L. brutus, dull; stupid].

bry·ol·o·gy (brī·àl′·ạ·ji·) n. the science of mosses [Gk. bruon, moss; logos, discourse].

Bry·thon·ic (brith·án′·ik) a. term embracing the Welsh, Cornish and Breton group of Celtic languages [W. Brython, a Briton].

bub·ble (bub′·l) n. a hollow globe of water or other liquid blown out with air or gas; a globule of air or gas in liquid or solid substances; a small bladder-like excrescence on surface of paint, metals, etc.; v.i. to rise in bubbles; to effervesce; to make a noise like bubbles; to gurgle; v.t. to cause to bubble. **bubbly** a. [earlier burble, of imit. origin].

bu·bo (bū′·bō) n. lymphatic swelling of the glands in the groin or armpit. **bubonic** a.; pl. **buboes. bubonic plague,** the Black Death of the 14th cent [Gk. boubon, the groin].

buc·ca·neer (buk·ạ·nir′) n. a pirate; v.i. to play the buccaneer [Fr. boucanier, a grill].

bu·cen·taur (bū·sen′·tawr) n. a fabulous monster, half bull, half man [Gk. bous, ox; centaur].

buck (buk) n. the male of the rabbit, hare, sheep, goat, and deer; a gay, spirited young dandy; (Colloq.) a male Indian or Negro; v.i. to attempt to unseat a rider by jumping vertically with arched back and head down; to foil all attempts at improvement. **-shot** n. large leaden shot for killing big game. **-skin** n. a soft leather made of deerskin or sheepskin. **-tooth** n. a tooth which protrudes. **buck up!** (Colloq.) hurry up! cheer up! [M.E. bukke, a he-goat].

buck·board (buk·bōrd) n. a four-wheeled vehicle in which a long elastic board takes the place of steel springs.

buck·et (buk′·it) n. a vessel for carrying water; v.t. to handle anything in a bucket. **-ful** n. the quantity held by a bucket. **— seat** n. a small round-backed seat for one [O.E. buc, pitcher].

buck·le (buk′·l) n. a metal clasp with a rim and tongue, for fastening straps, bands, etc.; a bend, bulge, or kink; v.t. and v.i. to fasten or

clasp with a buckle; to twist out of shape; to bend; to gird with a shield and sword [M.E. bokel].

buckle

buck·ram (buk′·rạm) n. a coarse linen or cotton cloth stiffened with glue and sizing; a. made of buckram [O.Fr. boucaran, goat's skin].

buck·wheat (buk′·hwēt) n. an herb, the seeds of which are ground into flour or fed to animals [O.E. boc, beech tree].

bu·col·ic (bū·kàl′·ik) a. rustic; countrified; n. a pastoral poem [Gk. boukolos, cowherd].

bud (bud) n. the shoot or sprout on a plant containing an unexpanded leaf, branch, or flower; v.i. to put forth buds; to begin to grow; v.t. to graft by budding. **-ding** n. the act of inserting the bud of one tree under the bark of another, for propagation. **-let** n. a little bud. **to nip in the bud,** to destroy at the beginning. pr.p. **-ding.** pa.t. **-ded** [M.E. budde].

Bud·dhism (boo′·dizm) n. the chief religion of E. Asia. **Buddhist** n. a worshipper of Buddha [Sans. buddha, wise].

bud·dy (bud′·i·) n. a person; a bosom friend; a comrade [fr. body].   [bouger, to move].

budge (buj) v.t. and i. to move; to stir [Fr.

budg·et (buj′·it) n. a plan for systematic spending; v.t. to plan one's expenditures of money, time, etc. **-ary** a. [Fr. bougette].

buff (buf) n. a soft, yellow leather prepared from the skin of the buffalo, elk, and other animals; a revolving wooden disc covered with layers of leather or cloth used with an abrasive for polishing; a buff-wheel; a polishing pad or stick; a light yellow-tan color; (Colloq.) a fan or devotee; a. made of, or colored like, buff leather; v.t. to polish with a buff. **-y** a. of a buff color [Fr. buffle, buffalo].

buf·fa·lo (buf′·ạ·lō) n. a ruminating horned animal, resembling an ox, but larger and more powerful [Port. bufalo].

buf·fer (buf′·ẹr) n. a resilient cushion or apparatus to deaden the concussion between a moving body and one on which it strikes; a polisher. **— state,** a country lying between two powerful and rival nations [O.Fr. bouffe, a slap].

buf·fet (buf′·ā) n. a cupboard for displaying fine china, plate, etc.; a freshment bar; a. (a meal) spread on tables or a counter from which guests serve themselves [Fr.].

buf·fet (buf′·it) n. a blow with the fist; a slap; a cuff or the ears; v.t. to strike with the fist; to contend against. **-s** n.pl. hardships [O.Fr. buffet, a slap].

buf·foon (bu·fōōn′) n. a person who acts the clown by his clumsy attempts at humor; a fool. **-ery** n. the silly, vulgar antics or practical jokes of a buffoon. **-ish** a. [Fr. bouffon].

bug (bug) n. name applied to various insects; a difficulty or a defect in a mechanism; a concealed microphone; (Slang) an enthusiast. **-aboo** n. a terrifying object; an imaginary fear. **-bear** n. anything that frightens or annoys. **-gy** a. crazy; swarming with bugs [corrupt. of O.E. budda, bettle]. [types of carriages.

bug·gy (bug′·i·) n. a word applied to various

bu·gle (bū′·gl) n. a wind instrument used because of its penetrating note for conveying orders by certain calls; long glass bead; v.i. to sound a call. **-r** n. [for bugle-horn fr. L. buculus, dim. of box, ox].

build (bild) v.t. to erect a structure; to construct a public work, as a railway, etc.; to fabricate; to establish (a reputation, etc.); to raise (hopes); v.i. to exercise the art or work of building; to depend with on, upon; pa.t. and pa.p. **built;** n. form; construction; physique; style of construction. **-er** n. **-ing** n. [O.E. byldan].

bulb (bulb) *n.* a modified leaf-bud emitting roots from its base and formed of fleshy leaf scales containing a reserve supply of food; any globular form, shaped like a bulb; a dilated glass tube containing filament for electric lighting; *v.i.* to form bulbs; to bulge. **-aceous, -ar, -ed, -ose, -ar** *a.* pert. to bulbs. **-iform** *a.* shaped like a bulb. **-osity** *n.* the state of being bulbous. **-ous** *a.* having the appearance of a bulb; growing from bulbs [L. *bulbus*].

bulge (bulj) *n.* anything rounded which juts out; the part of a cask which swells out; an outer protective hull, below the water-line; *v.i.* to swell out. **bulgy** *a.* [O.Fr. *boulge*].

bulk (bulk) *n.* size; the main body; the majority; the largest portion; unpackaged goods; *v.i.* to pile up; *v.i.* to be of some importance; to swell. **-age** *n.* roughage. **-iness** *n.* **-y** *a.* voluminous and clumsy in shape, so difficult to handle. **in bulk**, unpackaged; in large quantity [O.N. *bulki*, heap, cargo].

bulk·head (bulk'·hed) *n.* a partition in a ship made with boards, etc., to form separate compartments; a horizontal or sloping cover to outside step leading to the cellar of a building.

bull (bool) *n.* the male of any bovine; the male of numerous animals as elephant, whale, seal, moose, elk, deer; a sign of the zodiac, the constellation Taurus; a speculator who buys stocks or shares to make a profit by selling at a higher rate before time of settlement arrives; *v.t.* to attempt to bring about a rise in the price of stocks and shares; *a.* to denote a male animal. **-baiting** *n.* an ancient sport of setting ferocious dogs on a bull tied to a stake. **-dog** *n.* a breed of dog formerly used for bull-baiting; a person who displays obstinate courage; **-dozer** *n.* a tractor with an attached horizontal blade in front. **-fight** *n.* the national sport of certain Latin races, esp. in Spain and consisting of a combat between men and specially bred bulls. **-finch** *n.* a bird of the thrush family with a thicker head and neck. **-frog** *n.* a large, dusky-brown frog. **-headed** *a.* obstinate, headstrong. **— pen**, fenced enclosure; (*Sports*) where baseball pitchers practice. **— ring** *n.* the arena in which a bull-fight is held. **bull's-eye** *n.* the central spot of a target; a shot that hits the center of the target; a small circular window. **— session** (*Colloq.*) informal discussion. **— terrier** *n.* a cross between bulldog and terrier. **to take the bull by the horns**, to face a difficulty resolutely [M.E. *bole*].

bull (bool) *n.* the seal appended to the edicts of the pope; papal edict. **-ary** *n.* a collection of papal bulls [L. *bulla*, a bubble, a seal].

bul·let (bool'·it) *n.* a small projectile to be discharged from a gun. **—headed** *a.* round-headed; stubborn [L. *bulla*, a bubble, a knob].

bul·le·tin (bool'·ə·tin) *n.* a periodical report or publication; a brief statement of facts issued by authority. **-board** *n.* [Fr.].

bul·lion (bool'·yən) *n.* uncoined, refined gold or silver, generally in ingots; the precious metals, including coined metal, when exported or imported [etym. uncertain].

bul·ly (bool'·i·) *n.* noisy, over-bearing person who tyrannizes the weak; *v.t.* to domineer; intimidate; ill-treat; *v.i.* to bluster.

bul·ly (bool'·i·) *n.* canned or corned meat. Also **beef** [Fr. *bouilli*, boiled].

bul·rush (bool'·rush) *n.* name applied to several species of marsh plants [O.E. *bulrysche*].

bul·wark (bool'·wərk) *n.* an outwork for defense; sea defense wall; *pl.* a railing round the deck of a ship; any defense of a ship; *v.t.* to fortify with a rampart [Ger. *Bollwerk*].

bum (bum) *n.* an idle, dissolute person; *a.* worthless, bad; *v.i.* to loaf; to sponge on others; cadge [Ger. *bummeln*, to loaf].

bum·ble-bee (bum'·bəl·be) *n.* a large, hairy, social bee [E. *bumble* = keep bumming].

bum·bling (bum'·bling) *a.* noisy and blundering [See **bumble-bee**].

bump (bump) *n.* a dull, heavy blow; a thump; a swelling resulting from a bump or blow; one of the protuberances on the skull, said by phrenologists to give an indication of mental qualities, character, etc.; *v.t.* to strike against; *v.i.* to collide. **-y** *a.* covered with bumps [imit.].

bump·er (bum'·pər) *n.* a cup or glass filled to the brim, esp. when toasting a guest; (*Auto.*) a horizontal bar in front and rear of car; a buffer; *a.* very large; excellent [fr. *bump*].

bump·kin (bump'·kin) *n.* an awkward, stupid person; a country lout; yokel [E. = *bumkin*, a thick log, fr. Dut.].

bump·tious (bump'·shəs) *a.* rudely self-assertive; self-important. **-ness** *n.* [fr. *bump*].

bun (bun) *n.* a kind of bread roll, light in texture and slightly sweetened; hair twisted into a knot at the back of a woman's head [O.Fr. *bugne*].

bunch (bunch) *n.* a cluster of similar things, tied or growing together; a tuft or knot; a bouquet of flowers; a lump or protuberance; (*Slang*) a group, gang, or party; *v.t.* to tie up or gather together; to crowd; *v.i.* to swell out like a bunch. **bunched** *a.* crowded together. **-y** *a.* growing in bunches [Dan. *bunke*, a heap].

bun·dle (bun'·dl) *n.* a number of things bound together; a package; a definite number of things; *v.t.* to make up into a bundle or roll; *v.i.* to dress warmly [O.E. *byndel*].

bung (bung) *n.* the stopper for an opening in a cask; a large cork; *v.t.* to close or stop up; (*Slang*) to bruise.

bun·ga·low (bung'·gə·lō) *n.* a house in India of a single floor; small detached one-storied house [Hind. *bangla*, fr. *Banga*, Bengalese].

bun·gle (bung'·gl) *v.t.* to make or mend clumsily; to manage clumsily; to botch; *v.i.* to act awkwardly; *n.* a blundering performance. **-r** *n.* **bungling** *a.* [etym. uncertain].

bun·ion (bun'·yən) *n.* an inflamed swelling occurring on the foot.

bunk (bungk) *n.* a box-like structure used as a seat by day and a bed at night; a sleeping-berth on board ship; in a camp, etc.; *v.i.* to sleep in a bunk [Scand.]. [fr. *bunkum*].

bunk (bungk) *n.* (*Colloq.*) humbug; nonsense;

bunk·er (bung'·kər) *n.* a large hopper or bin for holding coal, etc.; storage room on board ship for coal or oil fuel; an underground fortification; a sand-pit placed as an obstacle on a golf course [Scand.].

bun·ny (bun'·i·) *n.* a pet name for a rabbit. **-hug** *n.* a kind of jazz dance [etym. unknown].

Bun·sen burn·er (bun'·sən bur'·nər) *n.* a gas burner in which a strong current of air produces a weakly luminous, but very hot, flame [fr. the inventor, Prof. Bunsen].

bunt (bunt) *n.* the middle or furled part of a sail. **-line** *n.* a rope fastened to the bottom of a sail used to haul it up [Scand.].

bunt (bunt) *v.t.* to butt with horns or head; (baseball) to bounce ball a short distance off the bat.

bun·ting (bun'·ting) *n.* a group of birds of the finch family, including the indigo-, reed-, and snow-buntings; coarse woolen fabric of which flags are made; flags in general.

buoy (boi) *n.* any floating body of wood or iron employed to point out the particular situation of a ship's anchor, a shoal, a navigable channel, etc.; a life-buoy; *v.t.* to fix buoys. **to buoy up**, to keep afloat; to sustain (hopes, etc.). **-age** *n.* a series of buoys in position; the providing of buoys. **-ancy** *n.* capacity for floating in water or air; cheerfulness. **-ant** *a.* floating lightly; lighthearted; hopeful; of stocks and shares, tending to increase in price [Dut. *boei*].

bur (bur) *n.* the rough, sticky seed-case of certain plants with hooked spines to help in its distribution; a burr. See **burr**.

bur·ble (bur'·bl) *v.i.* to bubble up; to gurgle, as of running water; (*Colloq.*) to talk idly.

bur·den (bur'·dn) *n.* that which is borne or carried; anything difficult to bear, as care, sorrow, etc.; *v.t.* to load; to oppress; to encumber. Also (*Arch.*) **burthen. -ous, -some** *a.* heavy, onerous; felt as a burden [O.E. *burthen*].

bur·den (bur'·dn) *n.* the refrain of a song; a chorus [Fr. *bourdon*, deep murmur].

bur·dock (bur'·dåk) *n.* a coarse reed with wide leaves and prickly burs [Dan. *borre*, a bur].

bu·reau (bū'·rō) *n.* a small chest of drawers; an office, esp. for public business; a government department [Fr.].

bu·reau·c·ra·cy (bū·rå'·krə·si·) *n.* administration by bureaus, often excessively numerous and powerful; the officials engaged in such an administration; identified with officialdom and 'red tape.' **bureaucrat** *n.* one who advocates or takes part in such a system of government. **bureaucratic** *a.* [Fr. *bureau*; Gk. *kratein*, to govern].

bu·rette (bū·ret') *n.* a graduated glass tube provided with a stop-cock at the lower end, used for delivering accurately measured quantities of liquid [Fr.].

burg (burg) *n.* (*Colloq.*) a town or village; a common ending of the names of cities in Holland or Germany [O.E. *burh*].

bur·geon (bur'·jan) *v.i.* to sprout; to bud; to put forth branches [Fr.].

bur·glar (burg'·lər) *n.* one who is guilty of house-breaking. **-y** *n.* breaking and entering into a dwelling-house originally between 9 p.m. and 6 a.m. with intent to commit a felony but extended by statute to include daytime.

Bur·gun·dy (bur'·gan·di·) *n.* name given to various wines, red or white [*Burgundy*, Fr.].

bur·i·al (ber'·i·al) *n.* the act of burying; interment; entombment. **— ground**, a cemetery [O.E. *byrgels*, tomb]. — [See **bury**].

burke (burk) *v.t.* to murder, esp. by smothering; to put an end to quietly [fr. *Burke*].

burl (burl) *n.* a knot in wood, thread or yarn. **-ed** *a.* [L. *burra*, coarse].

bur·lap (bur'·lap) *n.* gunny sacking; a coarsely woven canvas of flax, hemp, or jute, used for packing and as a wall covering, etc.

bur·lesque (bur·lesk') *n.* distorting, exaggerating, and ridiculing a work of art; travesty; parody; theatrical performance featuring vulgar comedy and dancing; *a.* comical; ludicrous; risqué; *v.t.* to turn into burlesque [It. *burlesco*].

bur·ly (bur'·li·) *a.* of stout build; big and sturdy. **burliness** *n.* [M.E. *borlich*, massive].

burn (burn) *v.t.* to consume with fire; to subject to the action of fire; to char; to scorch; *v.i.* to be on fire; to flame; flare; blaze; glow; be excited or inflamed with passion; *pa.t.* and *pa.p.* **-ed** or **-t**; *n.* injury or damage caused by burning. **-er** *n.* part of a lamp or gas jet from which the flame issues. **-ing** *n.* act of consuming by fire; inflammation; *a.* flaming; scorching; parching; ardent; excessive. **-ing-glass** *n.* a convex lens which causes intense heat by bending the rays of the sun and concentrating them upon a single point. **burning question**, a topic of universal discussion. **burnt-offering** *n.* a sacrifice of a living person or animal by burning. **burnt sienna**, a fine, reddish-brown pigment from calcined Sienna earth. **burnt umber**, a brown pigment obtained from calcined umber [O.E. *baernan*].

bur·nish (bur'·nish) *v.t.* to polish by continual rubbing; *n.* polish; gloss; luster [O.Fr. *burnisant*, polishing].

bur·noose (bur·nöös') *n.* a hooded cloak worn by Arabs. Also **burnous** [Ar.].

burnt *pa.t.* and *pa.p.* of **burn**.

burr (bur) *n.* a tool for cutting or drilling; a rough edge left on metal by a cutting tool. Also **bur** [Dan. *borre*].

burr (bur) *n.* the trilled guttural sound of *r*, as heard in Northumberland and Scotland; *v.t.* and *i.* to roll the 'r' sound [imit.].

bur·ro (bur'·ō) *n.* a donkey [Sp.].

bur·row (bur'·ō) *n.* a hole dug in the ground by certain small animals to serve as an abode or for concealment; *v.i.* to tunnel through earth; to search assiduously; to live in a burrow [var. of *borough*].

bur·sar (bur'·sər) *n.* a treasurer of a college. **bursary** *n.* (in Scotland) a scholarship [L.L. *bursa*, Fr. *bourse*, a purse].

bur·sa (bur'·sa) *n.* a sac or cavity, especially between joints; **-l** *a.*; **bursitis** *n.* [L.L. = a *purse*, bag].

burst (burst) *v.t.* to fly asunder; to break into pieces; to break open violently; to break suddenly into some expression of feeling; to split; *v.i.* to shatter; to break violently; *pa.t.* and *pa.p.* **burst**; *n.* a bursting; an explosion; an outbreak; spurt [O.E. *berstan*].

bur·y (ber'·i·) *v.t.* to inter in a grave; to put underground; to hide or conceal by covering; *pa.p.* **buried. -ing** *n.* burial; interment. **to bury the hatchet**, to cease from strife; to restore friendly relations [O.E. *byrigan*].

bus, 'bus (bus) *n.* a contraction for *omnibus*; a vehicle for public conveyance of passengers; *pl.* **-es**. [L. *omnibus*, for all and sundry].

bush (boosh) *n.* a shrub; a low woody plant with numerous branches near ground-level; a thicket of small trees and shrubs; the interior of a country; the backwoods; *v.i.* to grow thick or bushy; *v.t.* to plant bushes about. — **fighting** *n.* guerilla warfare where advantage is taken of trees and bushes. **-iness** *n.* the quality of being bushy. **-man** *n.* a member of a negroid race of S. Africa; a settler in the backwoods; a woodsman. **-master** *n.* a large venomous snake. **-whacker** *n.* one skilled in travelling through brush or woods; a guerilla. **-y** *a.* full of bushes; thick and spreading [M.E. *busch*].

bush (boosh) *n.* the internal lining of a bearing, to form a plain bearing surface for a pin or shaft. **-ing** *n.* a removable lining to reduce friction [Dut. *bus*, a box].

bush·el (boosh′·al) *n.* a dry measure of 4 pecks, for corn, fruit, etc. [O.Fr. *boissel*, a little box].

busi·ness (biz′·nis) *n.* employment; profession; vocation; any occupation for a livelihood; trade; firm; concern; action on the stage, apart from dialogue. **-like** *a.* practical; systematic; methodical. **-man** *n.* [fr. *busy*].

bus·kin (busk′·in) *n.* a kind of half-boot worn by ancient Greeks and Roman tragic actors.

buss (bus) *n.* a hearty kiss; *v.t.* to kiss, esp. boisterously [Fr. *baiser*, to kiss].

bust (bust) *n.* sculptured representation of a person from the waist upwards; the upper part of the human body; a woman's bosom. **-ed** *a.* breasted [Fr. *buste*].

bust (bust) *v.i.* and *v.t.* (*Slang*) to burst; to break; *n.* a drinking bout.

bus·tle (bus′·l) *v.i.* to busy oneself with much stir and movement; *n.* great stir. **-r** *n.* [O.E. *bysig*, busy].

bus·tle (bus′·l) *n.* a stuffed pad worn by ladies to support and elevate the back of the skirt just below the waist [Fr. *buste*].

bus·y (biz′·i·) *a.* having plenty to do; active and earnest in work; diligent; industrious; officious; meddling; *v.t.* to make or keep busy; to occupy (oneself). **busily** *adv.* **-body** *n.* a person who meddles in other people's business. **-ness** *n.* state of being busy [O.E. *bysig*].

but (but) *conj.* yet; unless; that not; nevertheless; notwithstanding; *prep.* except; without; *adv.* only. **all but**, nearly [O.E. *butan*, outside].

bu·tane (bū′·tān) *n.* a natural gas used in refrigeration and as a fuel [L. *butyrum*, butter].

butch·er (booch′·er) *n.* one who slaughters animals for food or retails the meat; one who recklessly destroys human life; *v.t.* to slaughter animals for food; to murder in cold blood; to spoil work. **-ing**, *n.* killing for food or lust of blood. **-y** *n.* wanton slaughter [O.Fr. *bochier*, one who kills goats].

but·ler (but′·ler) *n.* a male servant who has charge of the liquors, plate, etc. **-y** *n.* a butler's pantry [O.Fr. *bouteillier*, a bottler].

butt (but) *n.* the lower end of a tree-trunk providing the strongest timber; the end of anything; one continually subject to ridicule; (*Slang*) a cigarette; *v.t.* to strike by thrusting the head downwards; to abut on; to protrude. **-s** *n.pl.* a mound with targets where shooting is practiced. **-er** *n.* an animal, e.g. the goat, which butts. **to butt in** (*Colloq.*) to intervene without permission [Fr. *but*, end].

butt (but) *n.* a large cake. **-ery** *n.* [Fr. *bote*].

butte (būt) *n.* a steep hill standing alone [Fr.].

but·ter (but′·er) *n.* the fatty ingredients of milk, emulsified by churning; gross flattery; *v.t.* to spread with butter; to flatter. **-cup** *n.* plant with cup-shaped, glossy, yellow flowers. **-fingers** *n.* (*Colloq.*) one who has failed to hold a catch or who drops things easily. **-milk** *n.* the fluid residue after butter has been churned from cream. **-scotch** *n.* a kind of taffy with butter as an ingredient. **-y** *a.* [O.E. *butere*].

but·ter·fly (but′·er·flī) *n.* the common name of all diurnal, lepidopterous insects; a gay, flighty woman [O.E. *buter-fleage*].

but·tock (but′·ak) *n.* the rump; rounded lower posterior part of the body; hip; haunch (usually in *pl.*) [prob. dim. of *butt*, thick end].

but·ton (but′·n) *n.* a knob or stud for fastening clothing; a bud; the safety knob at the end of a fencing foil; a small round protuberance, e.g. that of an electric bell; an emblem of membership; *v.t.* to fasten with buttons; *v.i.* to be fastened by a button. **-hole** *n.* the hole or loop in which a button is fastened; *v.t.* to detain a person in talk again his will. **-hook** *n.* a hook for pulling a button through a buttonhole [Fr. *bouton*, bud].

but·tress (but′·ris) *n.* a projecting support to a wall; any prop or support; *v.t.* to support [O.Fr. *bouter*, to thrust].

bu·tyl (bū′·til) *n.* an alcohol radical; a highly elastic synthetic rubber, made from butane, a natural gas [L. *butyrum*, butter].

bux·om (buk′·sam) *a.* full of health; lively; cheery, plump; gay [O.E. *bugan*, to bend].

buy (bī) *v.t.* to obtain by payment; to purchase; to pay a price for; to bribe; *pa.t.* and *pa.p.* **bought. -er** *n.* a purchaser [O.E. *bycgan*].

buzz (buz) *v.i.* to make a humming or hissing sound; *v.t.* to spread news abroad secretly; to tap out signals by means of a buzzer. **-er** *n.* one who buzzes; an apparatus used for telephonic signaling. **-ingly** *adv.* [imit. word].

buz·zard (bus′·erd) *n.* a genus of birds of the hawk family (O.Fr. *busard*].

by (bī) *prep.* near; beside; in the neighborhood of; past; through the agency of; according to; *adv.* near; in the neighborhood; close; out of the way; beyond. **by and by,** soon; in the near future. **-name** *n.* a nick-name. **-pass** *n.* a road for the diversion of traffic from crowded centers; *v.t.* to avoid a place by going round it. **-path** *n.* a side path. **-play** *n.* action carried on apart from the main part of a play; diversion. **-product** *n.* secondary product obtained during manufacture of principal commodity. **-road** *n.* a less frequented side road. **-stander** *n.* an onlooker. **-way** *n.* a secluded path or road. **-word** *n.* a common saying; a proverb [O.E. *bi*].

bye (bī) *n.* anything subordinate; having no opponent in a round of competition. **-bye** (*Colloq.*) good-bye [var. of *by*].

by·law, bye-law (bī′·law) *n.* a local law made by an association [M.E. *bilaw*, fr. *bi*, a borough].

Byz·an·tine (biz·an′·tin, biz′·an·tin, -tin) relating to *Byzantium*, the original name for Constantinople; pert. to Asiatic architecture with Grecian characteristics.

C

cab (kab) *n.* a taxicab; the covered part of a locomotive; driver's accomodation on a truck. **-by** *n.* a taxi driver [short for Fr. *cabriolet*, a light carriage].

ca·bal (ka·bal′) *n.* a secret scheming faction in a state. **-istic** *a.* [Heb. *gabbalah*].

cab·a·la, cabbala (kab′·a·la) *n.* occultism. **cabalism** *n.* **cabalist, cabalistic(al)** *a.* mysterious; occult [Heb. *gabbalah*, mystical interpretation].

cab·a·ret (kab′·ba·rā, -ret) *n.* restaurant providing entertainment and space for dancing [Fr. *cabaret*, a tavern].

cab·bage (kab′·ij) *n.* a garden vegetable of Brassica family [L. *caput*, the head].

cab·in (kab′·in) *n.* a small house; a hut; an apartment in a ship; the space in an airplane for the pilot and passengers; *v.t.* to confine in a cabin; *v.i.* to live in a cabin; to lodge. **boy,** a boy who waits on the officers of a ship [Fr. *cabine*, a cabin; *cabane*, a hut].

cab·i·net (kab′·a·net) *n.* a private room; a council of ministers who advise the chief executive; a chest or case for holding or displaying objects; **-maker** *n.* a maker of cabinets and other furniture [Fr. *cabinet*, fr. *cabine*].

ca·ble (kā′·bl) *n.* a large, strong rope or chain; a stranded insulated conductor of electricity; a submarine telegraph line; a message sent by such line; *v.t.* to fasten with a cable; to send a message by cable. **car** *n.* a car pulled by a moving cable. **-gram** *n.* a telegram sent by cable; a cable [Fr. L.L. *capulum*, a halter].

ca·boo·dle (ka·boo′·dl) *n.* (*Slang*) collection.

ca·boose (ka·boos′) *n.* a car attached to a freight train for the crew [Dut. *kombuis*].

cab·ri·o·let (kab·ri·a·lā′) *n.* a light one-horse carriage with a hood [Fr. fr. L. *caper*, a goat].

ca·ca·o (ka·kā′·ō, ka·kå′·ō) *n.* a tropical tree from the seeds of which cocoa and chocolate are prepared [Mex.].

cache (kash) *n.* orig. a hole in the ground for storing or hiding provisions, etc.; any hiding-place; articles so hidden; *v.t.* to put in a cache; to conceal [Fr. *cacher*, to hide].

ca·chet (ka′·shā) *n.* a seal, as on a letter; distinctive mark [Fr. *cacher*, to hide].

cach·in·na·tion (kak·i·nā′·shan) *n.* loud, immoderate, or hysterical laughter. **cachinnate** *v.i.* [L. *cachinnare*, to laugh loudly].

ca·chou (ka·shōō′) *n.* a tablet or pellet, used to perfume the breath [Fr.].

cack·le (kak′·l) *v.i.* to make a noise like a hen or goose; to gossip noisily; *n.* [imit.].

cac·o- (kak′·a) a combining form fr. Gk. *kakos*, bad, used in derivatives.

ca·cog·ra·phy (ka·kåg′·ra·fi·) *n.* bad writing or spelling [Gk. *kakos*, bad; *graphia*, writing].

ca·coph·o·ny (ka·kåf′·a·ni·) *n.* a harsh or disagreeable sound; a discord; a use of ill-sounding words. **cacophonous** *a.* [Gk. *kakos*, bad; *phōnē*, sound].

cac·tus (kak′·tas) *n.* an American desert plant with thick, fleshy, prickly stems, generally no leaves but frequently producing showy flowers. *pl.* **-es**, or **cacti**. [Gk. *kaktos*, a cardoon].

cad (kad) *n.* a low, mean, vulgar fellow. **-dish** *a.* ill-bred, mean [short for Fr. *cadet*, junior].

ca·dav·er (ka·da′·ver) *n.* (*Med.*) a corpse. **-ous** *a.* corpse-like; gaunt; sickly-looking [L.].

cad·die, cad·dy (kad′·i·) *n.* an attendant who carries a golfer's clubs; *v.i.* fr. *cadet*].

cad·dis, cad·dice (kad′·is) *n.* worm-like aquatic larva of caddis-fly [etym. unknown].

cad·dy (kad′·i·) *n.* a small box for holding tea [Malay, *kati*, a weight, 1⅓ lbs. (for tea)].

cactus

ca·dence (kā′·dens) *n.* a fall of the voice in reading or speaking; a modulation; the beat of any rhythmical action; (*Mus.*) the subsiding of a melody towards a close. **-d** *a.* rhythmical. **cadency** *n.* [L. *cadere*, to fall].

ca·den·za (ka·den′·za) *n.* (*Mus.*) an ornamental passage for a voice or solo instrument in an aria or concerto [It.].

ca·det (ka·det′) *n.* a youth in training for commissioned ranks in the army or air force; **-ship** *n.* [Fr. *cadet*, younger].

cadge (kaj) *v.t.* and *i.* to peddle goods; to beg. **-r** *n.* a peddlar; a beggar; a sponger.

cad·mi·um (kad′·mi·am) *n.* (*Chem.*) a soft, bluish-white metal of zinc group. **cadmia** *n.* an oxide of zinc [Gk. *kadmeia*].

ca·dre (kå′·dri·) *n.* the framework of a military unit [Fr. = a frame].

ca·du·ce·us (ka·dū′·si·as) *n.* the staff carried by Mercury, messenger of the gods; the emblem of the medical profession.

cae·cum (sē′·kam) *n.* (*Med.*) the first part of the large intestine, opening into the colon; *pl.* **caeca. caecal** *a.* [L. *caecus*, blind].

Cae·sar (sē′·zer) *n.* one who acts like Julius Caesar (100-44 B.C.), Roman emperor and dictator; hence, autocrat; dictator. **Caesarean, Caesarian** *a.* pert. to Julius Caesar. **Caesarian section** (*Med.*) delivery of child through an opening cut in abdominal wall (Julius Caesar is said to have been born thus).

cae·si·um See cesium.

cae·su·ra, cesura (sē·zū′·ra) *n.* a break or division in a line of poetry; in English prosody, the natural pause of the voice. **-l** *a.* [L. *caedere, caesum,* to cut].

ca·fé (ka·fā′) *n.* a coffee-house; a restaurant, usually licensed for the sale of light refreshments only [Fr. *café,* coffee].

caf·e·te·ri·a (kaf·i·tir′·i·a) *n.* a restaurant where the customers help themselves [Amer.-Sp. = a coffee-shop].

caf·feine (kaf·ēn′) *n.* the stimulating alkaloid in coffee and tea (Fr. *café,* coffee].

cage (kāj) *n.* a place of confinement; a box-like enclosure, with bars of iron or wire, for keeping animals or birds; *v.t.* to confine in a cage; to imprison. **-ling** *n.* a bird kept in a cage. **-work,** *n.* open frame-work. **-y** *a.* cautious, wary [L. *cavea,* hollow].

ca·hoot (ka·hóōt′) *n.* (*Slang*) league or partnership. *usu. pl.* **in cahoots.**

cai·man See cayman.

cairn (kern) *n.* a rounded or conical pile of stones [Gael. *carn,* a heap].

cais·son (kā′·san) *n.* an ammunition chest or wagon; (*Engineering*) a water-tight chamber of sheet-iron or wood, used for workmen in laying the foundations of piers or bridges, quay-walls, etc.; an apparatus for raising sunken vessels [Fr. *caisse,* a case].

ca·jole (ka·jōl′) *v.t.* to persuade by flattery; to coax; to wheedle. **-r** *n.* **-ry** *n.* the act of cajoling [Fr. *cajoler*].

cake (kāk) *n.* a piece of dough baked; fancy bread; a flattish mass of matter, esp. soap, tobacco, etc.; *v.t.* to make into a cake; *v.i.* to become a flat, doughy mass. **caky** *a.* **-walk** *n.* an American negro dance [O.N. *kaka*].

cal·a·bash (kal′·a·bash) *n.* the bottle-gourd tree; the fruit of this tree; a vessel made from the gourd, or the gourd itself; a species of pear [Ar.].

cal·a·boose (kal′·a·bòos) *n.* (*Slang*) a prison; a jail [Sp.].

cal·a·mine (kal′·a·mīn) *n.* a silicate of zinc, used as a pigment in painting pottery and in skin ointments [Gk. *kadmeia*].

ca·lam·i·ty (ka·lam′·a·ti·) *n.* any great misfortune; disaster; affliction; mischance. **calamitous** *a.* producing distress and misery. **calamitously** *adv.* [Fr. *calamité*].

cal·a·mus (kal′·a·mas) *n.* a reed used in ancient times as a pen, or made into a musical instrument [L. fr. Gk.].

ca·lash (ka·lash′) *n.* a light carriage with low wheels, and a top or hood that can be raised or lowered; a silk hood [Fr. *calèche*].

cal·car·e·ous (kal·ke′·ri·as) *a.* chalky [L. *calx, calcis,* lime].

cal·cif·er·ol (kal′·si·a·ràl) *n.* crystalline vitamine D. used in fortifying margarine. **calciferous** *a.* containing carbonate of lime [L. *calx, calcis,* lime; *ferre,* to bear].

cal·ci·fy (kal′·si·fi) *v.t.* and *i.* to turn into lime; to harden or petrify, by a deposit of lime. **calcification** *n.* [L. *calx,* lime; *facere,* to make].

cal·ci·mine (kal′·si·mīn) *n.* a white or tinted wash for ceiling and walls.

cal·cine (kal′·sin, -sin) *v.t.* to reduce to powder by heat; to expel water and other volatile substances by heat; *v.i.* to be turned into powder. **calcinable** *a.* **calcination** *n.* **calcinatory** *n.* a vessel used in calcination [Fr. *calciner*].

cal·ci·um (kal′·si·am) *n.* the metallic base of lime. **calcic** *a.* containing calcium. **calcite** *n.* native carbonate of lime [L. *calx, calcis,* lime].

cal·cu·late (kal′·kya·lāt) *v.t.* to count; to estimate; to compute; to plan; to expect; *v.i.* to make a calculation. **calculable** *a.* **-d** *a.* adapted to a purpose; intended to produce a certain effect. **calculating** *a.* capable of performing calculations; shrewd in matters of self-interest; scheming. **calculation** *n.* **calculative** *a.* tending to calculate. **calculator** *n.* one who computes; a machine which does automatic computations [L. *calculare,* to count].

cal·cu·lus (kal′·kya·las) *n.* a branch of higher mathematics concerned with the properties of continuously varying quantities; *n.* a hard concretion which forms, esp. in kidney, bladder, etc. usually called stone or gravel; *pl.* **calculi. calculose, calculous** *a.* hard, like stone; gritty [L. *calculus,* a pebble].

cal·dron, cauldron (kawl′·dran) *n.* a large metal kettle or boiler [L. *caldera,* warm pot].

cal·a·fac·tion (kal·a·fak′·shan) *n.* the act of heating, the state of being heated. **calefacient** (kal·a·fā′·shi·ant) *a.* making warm; *n.* a heat-giving remedy. **calefactor** *n.* that which gives heat. **calefactory** *a.* [L. *calere,* to be

warm; *facere,* to make].

caldron

cal·en·dar (kal′·an·der) *n.* a table of days, months or seasons; an almanac; a list of criminal cases; a list of saints; *v.t.* to enter in a list [L. *Calendae,* the calends].

cal·en·der (kal′·an·der) *n.* a hot press with rollers, used to make cloth, etc. smooth and glossy [Fr. *calandre,* a cylinder].

cal·ends (kal′·endz) *n.pl.* the first day of each month, among the Romans. **at the Greek calends,** never (because the Greeks had no calends). Also **kalends** [L. *Calendae*].

calf (kaf) *n.* the young of the cow, and of some other mammals, such as elephant, whale, etc.; a mass of ice detached from a glacier, iceberg, or floe; *pl.* **calves** (kavz). **——love,** a youthful, transitory attachment to one of the opposite sex. **——skin** *n.* a fine, light-colored leather made from the skin of a calf. **calve** (kav) *v.i.* to bring forth a calf [O.E. *cealf*].

calf (kaf) *n.* the thick, fleshy part of the leg below the knee; *pl.* **calves** [O.N. *kalfi*].

cal·i·ber (kal′·a·ber) *n.* the diameter of the bore of a cannon, gun, etc.; the internal diameter of a tube or cylinder; (*Fig.*) capacity; quality of mind; character. **calibrate** *v.t.* to determine the caliber of a firearm tube or other cylindrical object. **calibration** *n.* [Fr. *calibre*].

cal·i·co (kal′·a·kō) *n.* white cotton cloth, first made in *Calicut* in India; printed cotton cloth; *a.* made of calico.

cal·i·pers, callipers (kal′·i·perz) *n.* a two-legged instrument for measuring diameters [Fr. *calibre*].

ca·liph, calif (kal′·if, kā′·lif) *n.* a title given to the successors of Mohammed [Ar. *khalifah,* a successor].

ca·lix See calyx.

calk, caulk (kawk) *v. t.* to press tarred oakum into the seams between the planks of a boat to prevent leaks; to fill or close joints or crevices to make air- or water-tight. **-er** *n.* **-ing** *n.* [L.L. *calicare,* to stop up with lime, *calx*].

calk (kawk) *n.* a pointed stud on a horse-shoe to prevent slipping; *v.t.* [L. *calcar,* a spur].

call (kawl) *v.t.* to announce; to name; to summon; to name, as for office; to utter in a loud voice; *v.i.* to speak in a loud voice; to cry out; to make a brief visit; *n.* a shout; a summons or invitation; a short visit; a public claim; a requisition; authorized command; an invitation, as to be minister of a church; a note blown on a horn, bugle, etc.; the characteristic cry of a bird or animal. **-er** *n.* one who calls. **-ing** *n.* a person's usual occupation. **at call,** on demand. **on call,** of a person, ready if summoned. **-boy,** *n.* a boy who calls actors to go on the stage; a bellboy. **to call down,** to rebuke. **to call up** (*Mil.*) to summon to military service; to telephone [O.E. *ceallian*].

cal·ligra·phy (ka·lig′·ra·fi·) *n.* the art of beautiful writing; penmanship. **calligrapher, calligraphist** *n.* **calligraphic** *a.* [Gk. *kallos,* beauty; *graphein,* to write].

cal·li·o·pe (ka·li′·a·pē) *n.* musical instrument with steam whistles, played like an organ.

cal·lis·then·ics (kal·is·then′·iks) *n.pl.* light gymnastic exercises to promote beauty and grace of movement. **callisthenic** *a.* [Gk. *kallos,* beauty; *sthenos,* strength].

cal·lous (kal′·us) *a.* hardened; hardened in mind; unfeeling; having a callus; **-ly** *adv.* **-ness** *n.* **callosity** *n.* a horny hardness of the skin [L. *callus,* hard skin].

cal·low (kal′·ō) *a.* pert. to the condition of a young bird; unfledged; (*Fig.*) inexperienced; raw. **-ness** *n.* [L. *calvus,* bald].

cal·lus (kal′·as) *n.* a hardened or thickened part of the skin [L. = hard skin].

calm (kám) *a.* still; quiet; at rest; *n.* the state of being calm; *v.t.* to make calm. **-ly** *adv.* **-ness** *n.* [Fr. *calme*].

cal·o·mel (kal′·a·mel) *n.* (*Med.*) sub-chloride of mercury, used as a purgative [Gk. *kalos,* fair; *melas,* black].

ca·lor·ic (ka·lawr′·ik) *n.* heat; *a.* pert. to heat; heat-producing. **caloricity** *n.* the power of animals to develop heat. **calorifacient** *a.* heat-producing. **calorific** *a.* pert. to heat; heat-producing. **calorification** *n.* the production of heat [L. *calor,* heat].

cal·o·rie, calory (kal′·er·i·) *n.* (*Phys.*) the unit of heat; the unit of heat or energy produced by any food substance. **calorimeter** *n.*

a scientific instrument for determining the amount of heat produced by any substance [L. *calor,* heat].

cal·u·met (kal′·yoo·met) *n.* the 'pipe of peace' of the N. Amer. Indians [L. *calamus,* a reed].

ca·lum·ni·ate (ka·lum′·ni·āt) *v.t.* to accuse falsely; to slander; *v.i.* to utter slanders. **calumniation** *n.* false and slanderous representations. **calumniator** *n.* **calumniatory, calumnious** *a.* slanderous. **calumniously** *adv.* **calumny** *n.* a false accusation; malicious slander; libel [L. *calumnia*].

calve (kav) See calf.

Cal·vin·ism (kal′·vin·izm) *n.* the doctrines of John *Calvin,* which lay special stress on the sovereignty of God in the conferring of grace. **Calvinist** *n.* **Calvinistic** *a.*

calx (kalks) *n.* the crumbly substance that remains after the calcination of a metal or mineral; *pl.* **calxes, calces** (kalk′·siz, kal′·sēz) [L. = lime].

ca·lyp·so (ka·lip′·sō) *n.* an improvised song in native rhythm from the West Indies.

ca·lyx, ca·lix (kā′·liks) *n.* a cup-shaped cavity; the outer covering or leaf-like envelope of a flower [Gk. *kalux,* a husk, a cup].

cam (kam) *n.* a projecting part of a wheel used to give an alternating or variable motion to another wheel or piece. **-shaft** *n.* the shaft on which cams are formed for opening the valves [Dut. *kam,* a comb].

camshaft

ca·ma·ra·de·rie (kám·a·rád′·a·rē) *n.* good-fellowship [Fr. *comarade,* a companion].

cam·ber (kam′·ber) *n.* a slight convexity of an upper surface, as of a ship's deck, a bridge, a road surface [Fr. *cambrer,* to arch].

Cam·bri·an (kam′·bri·an) *a.* Welsh; pert. to Cambria or Wales; *n.* a Welshman. [L. fr. *Cymru,* Wales].

cam·bric (kām′·brik) *n.* a fine white linen fabric first made at *Cambrai,* in N. France.

came (kām) *pa.t.* of the verb **come.**

cam·el (kam′·al) *n.* a large ruminant animal of Asia and Africa, with one or two humps, used as a beast of burden. **-eer** *n.* a camel driver [Gk. *kamēlos*].

ca·mel·lia (ka·mēl′·ya) *a.* a species of Asiatic shrub with showy flowers and elegant dark-green, laurel-like leaves [fr. *Kamel,* botanist].

Cam·em·bert (ka′·mam·ber) *n.* a small, soft, rich cheese [fr. a village in Normandy].

cam·e·o (kam′·i·ō) *n.* a gem stone of two layers cut in ornamental relief [etym. unknown].

cam·e·ra (kam′·a·ra) *n.* device for taking photographs. **-man** *n.* a professional motion picture or press photographer [L. *camera,* a vault]

cam·e·ra (kam′·a·ra) *n.* a judge's private room; hence (*Law*) 'to hear a case' **in camera** [L. *camera,* a room].

cam·i·sole (kam′·a·sōl) *n.* a lady's under-bodice; light dressing-jacket [Fr.].

cam·o·mile, chamomile (kam′·a·mil) *n.* an aromatic creeping plant whose flowers are used medicinally [Gk. *chamaimēlon,* the earth-apple].

cam·ou·flage (kam′·a·flazh) *n.* (*Mil.*) a method of visual deception of the enemy by disguising; any form of disguise; *v.t.* to cover with camouflage material; to disguise [Fr.].

camp (kamp) *n.* the area of ground where soldiers or other groups of people are lodged in huts or tents; permanent barracks near a suitable exercise ground; group in agreement; *v.t.* and *i.* to pitch tents. **-er** *n.* one who lives in a camp in open country, esp. living in a tent. **-ing** *n.* the act of living in camp. **—— chair** *n.* a light, portable chair with folding legs.

— **follower** n. a non-combatant who follows the troops, *i.e.*, a prostitute, washer woman, etc. — **meeting** n. a religious meeting in the open air. — **out** v. to live without conveniences [L. *campus*, a field].

cam·paign (kam·pān′) n. a series of operations in a particular theater of war; hence, in politics, business, etc. an organized series of operations (meetings, canvassing, etc.); v.i. to serve in a war; to conduct, or assist in political, etc. operations. **-er** n. [L. *campus*, a plain].

cam·pa·ni·le (kam·pạ·nē′·li·, kam′·pạ·nīl) n. a bell-tower constructed beside a church, but not necessarily attached to it. **campanology** n. the art of bell-ringing, or of bell-founding; bell-lore. [It. *campana*, a bell].

cam·phor (kam′·fẹr) n. a whitish substance with an aromatic taste and smell, obtained from the camphor laurel-tree. **-aceous** (kam.-fẹr·ā′·shạs) a. resembling camphor. **-ate** v.t. to impregnate with camphor. **-ate, -ic** a. pert. to camphor [Malay, *kapur*, chalk].

cam·pus (kam′·pạs) n. the grounds of a college or school [L. *campus*, a plain].

can (kan) *pres. indic.* of a defective, intransitive verb meaning, to be able, to have the power, to be allowed. *pa.p., pa.t.* **could** (kood) [O.E. *cunnan*, to know].

can (kan) n. a metal vessel or container for holding liquids, etc.; v.t. to put into a can for the purpose of preserving; *pr.p.* **-ning.** *pa.p.* and *pa.t.* **-ned. -nery** n. a factory where foods are preserved by canning [O.E. *canne*].

Ca·na·di·an (kạ·nā′·di·ạn) n. an inhabitant of Canada; a. pert. to Canada.

ca·naille (kạ·nāl′) n. the dregs of society; the mob; rabble [Fr. fr. I. *canis*, a dog].

ca·nal (kạ·nal′) n. an artificial watercourse for transport, drainage or irrigation purposes; a duct in the body; a groove. **canalize** v.t. to make a canal through; to convert into a canal [L. *canalis*].

can·a·pé (ka′·nạ·pi·) n. a small piece of toast or bread, with anchovies, etc. on it served as an appetizer [Fr. *canapé*, a sofa].

ca·nard (kạ·nárd′) n. a false rumor; an absurd or extravagant piece of news [Fr.].

ca·nar·y (kạ·nā′·ri·) n. a yellow singing bird, a species of finch; a pale-yellow color; a light wine made in the Canary Islands [Fr. *canari*].

ca·nas·ta (kạ·nas′·tạ) n. a card game played with two packs.

can·can (kan′·kan) n. a kind of dance, once popular in music-halls in France [Fr.].

can·cel (kan′·sạl) v.t. to cross out; to blot out; to annul; to suppress; (*Math.*) to strike out common factors; to balance; to offset. **-lation** n. the act of canceling [L. *cancellatus*, latticed].

can·cer (kan′·sẹr) n. (*Med.*) a malignant growth or tumor. **-ate** v.i. to grow into a cancer. **-ation** n. **-ous** a. pert. to or resembling cancer [L. *cancer*, a crab].

can·de·la·brum (kan·dẹ·lá′·brạm) n. a branched and highly ornamented candle-stick; a chandelier. **candelabra** *n.sing.* and *pl.* [L. fr. *candela*, a candle].

can·did (kan′·did) a. fair; open; frank. **-ly** adv. **-ness** n. frankness; ingenuousness [L. *candidus*, white].

can·di·date (kan′·dạ·dāt) n. one who seeks an appointment, office, honor, etc. **candidature, candidacy** n. the position of being a candidate [L. *candidus*, white (one wearing a white toga)].

can·dle (kan′·dl) n. a stick of tallow, wax, etc. with a wick inside, used for light. **power**, the unit of luminosity. **-stick** n. an instrument for holding a candle [L. *candela*].

Can·dle·mas (kan′·dl·mạs) n. a religious festival to commemorate the Purification of the Virgin and the presentation of Jesus in the temple [*candle* and *mass*].

can·dor (kan′·dẹr) n. candidness; sincerity; frankness [L. *candor*, whiteness].

can·dy (kan′·di·) n. a kind of sweetmeat made of sugar; v.t. to preserve in sugar; to form into crystals, as sugar; v.i. to become candied. **candied** (kan′·did) a. [Ar. *qand*, sugar].

can·dy·tuft (kan′·di·tuft) n. a large genus of herbs or shrubs [fr. *Candia*].

cane (kān) n. the stem of a small palm or long, strong reed; the bamboo, etc.; the sugar-cane; a walking-stick; v.t. to beat with a cane; to fix a cane bottom to, e.g. a chair. **-brake** n. a dense growth of canes. **— sugar** n. sugar from the sugar-cane [Gk. *kanna*, a reed].

ca·nine (kā′·nīn) a. of, or pert. to a dog. **teeth**, the two pointed teeth in each jaw,

one on each side, between the incisors and the molars [L. *canis*, a dog].

can·is·ter (kan′·is·tẹr) n. a small case or box for holding tea, coffee, etc. **— shot** n. a number of small iron balls enclosed in a case of a size to fit the gun-barrel (an early form of shrapnel) [L. *canistrum*, a wicker basket].

can·ker (kang′·kẹr) n. ulceration of the mouth; a disease of trees; a disease affecting horses' feet; (*Fig.*) anything that eats away, corrupts, etc.; v.t. to consume; to gnaw at; to corrupt; v.i. to decay, to become cankered. **-ed** a. corrupted; malignant. **-ous** a. corrupting like a canker. **-y** a. cankered. **-worm** n. a destructive caterpillar [L. *cancer*, a crab].

can·nel-coal (kan′·el·kōl) n. a kind of coal, burning with a clear, smokeless flame, used in the manufacture of gas. Also **candle-coal**.

can·ni·bal (kan′·ạ·bạl) n. one who eats human flesh; a. relating to this practice. **-istic** a. **cannibalize** v.t. to dismantle in the hope of getting spare parts to be used for re-conditioning. [Sp. *canibal* = *Caribal*, a Carib].

can·non (kan′·ạn) n. a large gun; v.i. to cannonade. **-ade** n. an attack with cannon; the firing of cannon; v.t. to bombard. **-eer, -ier** (kan·ạn·ir′) n. one who loads or fires cannon; an artilleryman. **— ball** n. an iron ball to be discharged by cannon. **— shot** n. a cannonball; the range of a cannon [L. *canna*, a tube].

can·not (kan′·át) combination of *can* and *not*, therefore, = not to be able.

can·ny (kan′·i·) a. (*Scot.*) cautious; thrifty.

ca·noe (kạ·nóó′) n. a light, narrow boat propelled by a hand paddle. **-ist** n. [Haiti, *canoa*].

can·on (kan′·ạn) n. a law or rule, esp. of the church; the books of the Scriptures accepted by the Church as of divine authority; rules of faith; a standard; the list of saints; a church dignitary, esp. one connected with a cathedral; (*Mus.*) a form of composition in which the melody is repeated at set intervals by the other parts. **-ess** n. a member of a religious association of women. **canonic, canonical** a. **canonicals** *n.pl.* official dress worn by a clergyman. **canonically** adv. **-ization** n. **-ize** v.t. to place in the list of saints. **-ist** n. one skilled in canon law. **-ry** n. the office of canon. [Gk. *kanōn*, a rule].

can·o·py (kan′·ạ·pi·) n. a covering fixed above a bed, or a dais, or carried on poles above the head; any overhanging shelter [Gk. *kōnōpion*, a couch with mosquito curtains].

cant (kant) n. an inclination from the level; a tilted position; v.t. to tilt; to jerk; to toss; v.i. to have, or take a leaning position [O.Fr.].

cant (kant) n. an insincere or conventional mode of speaking; an expression peculiar to a group [L. *cantare*, to sing].

can't (kant) v. contr. of **cannot**.

can·ta·bi·le (kán·tá′·bi·lā) adv. (*Mus.*) in a flowing, graceful, style, like singing [It.].

can·ta·loupe, can·ta·loup (kan′·tạ·lōp) n. a variety of muskmelon, having a furrowed rind [*Cantalupo*, a town in Italy].

can·tan·ker·ous (kan·tang′·kẹr·ạs) a. perverse; ill-natured; quarrelsome. **-ly** adv.

can·ta·ta (kan·tä′·tạ) n. a short musical composition in oratorio or lyric drama form. **cantatrice, cantatrici** (kan′·tạ·trēs, kan·tä·trē′·chā) a professional female singer [It.].

can·teen (kan·tēn′) n. a small container for carrying water; a store and refreshment-room in camps and barracks for soldiers, sailors, etc.; a similar place in a social or institutional club [It. *cantina*, a cellar].

can·ter (kan′·tẹr) v.i. to move at an easy gallop; n. an easy gallop or gait [fr. *Canterbury gallop*, easy pace of the pilgrims].

can·ti·cle (kan′·ti·kl) n. a little song; a nonmetrical hymn. **Canticles** (*Bib.*) the Song of Songs [L. *canticulum*, a little song].

can·ti·lev·er (kan′·ti·lēv·ẹr) n. a bracket for supporting a cornice or balcony. **cantilever bridge**, a bridge built on the same principle [fr. *cant*, an angle; Fr. *lever*, to raise].

can·to (kan′·tō) n. a division or part of a poem. **-r** n. a precentor; the leader of the singing, esp. in a synagogue [It. fr. L. *canere*, to sing].

can·ton (kan′·tạn) n. a small district (in Switzerland, administered by a separate government); a section of something; v.t. to divide into districts, as territory. **-al** a. **-ment** n. quarters for troops [Fr.].

can·vas (kan′·vạs) n. a coarse cloth made of hemp, for sails, tents, etc.; the sails of a vessel; a special prepared material for painting on; painting [O.Fr. *canevas*; L. *cannabis*, hemp].

can·vass (kan′·vạs) v.t. to sift; to examine thoroughly; to solicit support, or votes, or contributions; v.i. to solicit votes; n. a close examination (by discussion); a scrutiny; solicitation; a seeking to obtain votes. **-er** n. [fr. *canvas* = to sift, as through canvas].

can·yon (kan′·yạn) n. a ravine; a deep gorge. Also **cañon** [Sp.].

cap (kap) n. a brimless covering, for the head; the top or highest point; a small lid used as a cover; v.t. to cover the top or end of; to surpass; (*University, etc.*) to confer a degree on; *pr.p.* **-ping.** *pa.p.* and *pa.t.* **-ped** [O.E. *cappe*, a hood].

ca·pa·ble (kā′·pạ·bl) a. competent; gifted; skillful. **capably** adv. **-ness** n. **capability** n. power [L. *capere*, to hold].

ca·pa·cious (kạ·pā′·shạs) a. roomy; spacious; **-ly** adv. **-ness** n. [L. *capere*, to hold].

ca·pac·i·ty (kạ·pas′·i·ti·) n. power of holding or grasping; room; volume; power of mind; character; ability; cubic content. **capacitate** v.t. to render capable [L. *capacitas*].

cap·à·pie (kap·ạ·pē′) adv. from head to foot [O.Fr. fr. L. *caput*, the head; *pes*, the foot].

ca·par·i·son (kạ·par′·ạ·sạn) n. a covering laid over a horse; trappings; harness; v.t. to cover with a decorated cloth; to adorn with rich dress [O.Fr. *caparasson*, preparation].

cape (kāp) n. a covering for the shoulders [L.L. *cappa*].

cape (kāp) n. a point of land running out into the sea; a headland [L. *caput*, the head].

ca·per (kā′·pẹr) v.i. to leap about like a goat, in a sprightly manner; to skip; to dance; to frolic; n. a frolicsome skip [L. *caper*, a goat].

ca·per (kā′·pẹr) n. a herb or shrub whose flower-buds when pickled in vinegar are used in sauces [Gk. *kapparis*].

cap·il·lar·y (kap′·ạ·ler·i·) a. resembling a hair; as fine as a hair; descriptive of the very fine bore of a tube or similar passage; n. one of the microscopic blood-vessels connecting the arteries and veins. **capillarity** n. **capilliform** a. hair-shaped [L. *capillus*, hair].

cap·i·tal (kap′·ạ·tạl) a. pert. to the head; involving the forfeiture of life; first in importance; chief; principal; excellent; n. (*Archit.*) the head of a column, pilaster, etc.; the city or town which is the seat of government in a state or nation; the estimated total value of a business, property, stock, etc.; ready money; **— punishment** n. the death penalty; **-ize** n. to take advantage of. **-ization** n. to provide with capital letters; to supply with capital [L. *caput*, the head].

cap·i·tal·ism (kap′·ạ·tal·izm) n. form of economic, industrial, and social organization of society involving ownership, control, and direction of production by privately owned business organizations. **capitalist** n.

cap·i·ta·tion (kap·ạ·tā′·shạn) n. a census; a tax or grant per head [L. *capitatio*, a poll-tax].

Cap·i·tol (kap′·ạ·tạl) n. the temple of Jupiter in Rome; the building used by the U.S. Congress for its sessions; a state legislature building [L. *Capitolium*].

ca·pit·u·late (kạ·pit′·ū·lāt) v.i. to surrender; to draw up terms of an agreement. **capitulation** n. **capitulator** n. [L.L. *capitulare*, to draw up a treaty].

ca·pon (kā′·pạn) n. a young castrated cock fed for the table. **caponize** v.t. [O.E. *capun*].

ca·price (kạ·prēs′) n. illogical change of feeling or opinion; a whim; a fancy. **capricious** (kạ·pri′·shạs) a. [L. *caper*, a goat].

cap·si·cum (kap′·sạ·kạm) n. a genus of tropical plants, whose fruits when dried and ground give Cayenne pepper [L. *capsa*, a box].

cap·size (kap·sīz′) v.t. and i. to overturn.

cap·stan (kap′·stạn) n. a heavy cable-holder revolving on an upright spindle [L. *capistrum*, a halter].

cap·stone (kap′·stōn) n. a finishing stone.

cap·sule (kap′·sūl) n. the seed-vessel of a plant; a small gelatinous case containing medicine; a metal cap placed over the mouth of a corked bottle; a. condensed [L. *capsa*, a box].

cap·tain (kap′·tin) *n.* in the army, an officer commanding a company of infantry; in the navy, an officer in command of a man-of-war; the master of a merchant ship or other vessel; in sport, the leader of a team; *v.t.* to command; to lead. **-cy** *n.* the rank or commission of a captain [L. *caput*, the head].

cap·tion (kap′·shan) *n.* the heading of a newspaper, chapter, page, etc.; the title of an illustration [fr. L. *capere*, to take].

cap·tious (kap′·shas) *a.* apt to find fault; difficult to please. **-ly** *adv.* **-ness** *n.* fault-finding [L. *captiosus*, deceiving].

cap·ti·vate (kap′·ta·vāt) *v.t.* to capture the fancy of. **captivating** *a.* winning, charming. **captivation** *n.* [L. *captivus*, captive].

cap·tive (kap′·tiv) *n.* a prisoner; one held in captivity; *a.* made prisoner. **captivity** *n.* imprisonment; bondage; servitude. **captor** *n.* one who takes a prisoner or a prize. **capture** *n.* the act of seizing by force or stratagem; arrest; the thing seized; the prize; *v.t.* to take captive; to take possession of [L. *capere*, to take].

Cap·u·chin (kap′·yoo·chin) *n.* a Franciscan monk (from the hood he wears); a hooded cloak for women; a hooded pigeon; a long-tailed S. American monkey. **capuche** (ka·pŏŏsh′) *n.* a hood; a cowl [It. *cappucino*, a cow].

car (kár) *n.* any kind of vehicle on wheels; abbrev. for motor-car; automobile; the part of a balloon in which the aeronauts sit [L. *carrus*].

car·a·cole (kar′·a·kōl) *v.i.* to wheel [Sp.].

ca·rafe (ka·rȧf′) *n.* a glass water-bottle or decanter [Fr.].

car·a·mel (kar′·a·mel) *n.* burnt sugar, used for coloring and in cooking; a kind of candy [Sp. *caramelo*].

car·at (kar′·at) *n.* a measure of weight for gold and precious stones, the standard carat being 3.16 grains troy [Gk. *keration*, a carob-tree seed].

car·a·van (kar′·a·van, kar·a·van′) *n.* parties of merchants, pilgrims, or others traveling together for greater security, esp. across deserts. **-eer** *n.* the leader of a caravan. **-sary**, **-serai** *n.* a large Eastern inn, with a court in the middle; a large inn [Pers. *karwan*].

car·a·vel (kar′·a·vel) *n.* a light sailing-ship. Also **carvel** [L. *carabus*, a wicker boat].

car·a·way (kar′·a·wā) *n.* a biennial aromatic plant; its seed, used as a flavoring for bread, cakes, etc. [Gk. *karon*].

car·bide (kár′·bid) *n.* a compound of carbon with certain elements, including calcium, manganese, iron, etc. [L. *carbo*, coal].

car·bine, **carabine** (kár′·(a)·bin) *n.* a short rifle. **carbineer**, **carabineer** *n.* a soldier armed with a carbine [etym. uncertain].

car·bo·hy·drate (kár·bō·hí′·drāt) *n.* a substance, such as sugar, starch, cellulose, etc. composed of carbon, hydrogen, and oxygen [L. *carbo*, coal; Gk. *hudō*, water].

car·bol·ic (kár·bál′·ik) *a.* derived from carbon; *n.* carbolic acid. **carbolated** *a.* treated with or containing, carbolic acid. **carbolic acid,** a poisonous acid distilled from coal tar [L. *carbo*, coal].

car·bon (kár′·ban) *n.* a non-metallic element existing pure in nature as diamond, graphite, charcoal, etc. and as a compound of animal and vegetable substances; a thin rod of hard carbon used in an electric arc-lamp; a copy made by using carbon paper. **-aceous** (kár·ban·ā′·shus) *a.* pert. to, or composed of, coal. **-ize** *v.t.* to make into carbon; to coat with carbon. **-ization** *n.* — **paper,** type of paper used for duplicating written work [L. *carbo*, coal]. **carbon dioxide. -d** *a.* **carbonation** *n.*

car·bo·run·dum (kár·ba·run′·dam) *n.* silicon carbide, a black, crystalline substance, of exceptional hardness.

car·boy (kár′·boi) *n.* a large, globular glass bottle, encased in basket-work [Pers. *garabah*].

car·bun·cle (kár′·bung·kl) *n.* a variety of garnet; an inflamed bunion or boil. **carbuncular** *a.* [L. *carbunculus*, a small coal].

car·bu·ret·or (kár′·bu·ret·er) *n.* an apparatus in an internal-combustion engine to convert liquid gasoline into vaporized form. **carburation** *n.* **carburize** *v.t.*, cause to unite with carbon [L. *carbo*, coal].

carburetor

car·cass, carcase (kár′·kas) *n.* the dead body of man or animal, esp. of the latter; the framework or shell of anything [It. *carcassa*, the framework of a ship, etc.].

car·ci·no·ma (kár·si·nō′·ma) *n.* a cancer.

card (kárd) *n.* pasteboard; a small piece of pasteboard often with figures, pictures, etc. on it for playing games; a piece of pasteboard having on it a person's name and address; an ornamented piece of paper or cardboard with a greeting, such as a birthday card; (*Slang*) a humorous fellow. **-board** *n.* finely finished pasteboard. **-sharp** *n.* one who cheats at cards [L. *charta*, paper].

card (kárd) *n.* a toothed instrument for combing wool, flax, etc.; *v.t.* to comb, as wool, flax, etc. **-er** *n.* one who cards [L. *carduus*, a thistle].

car·di·ac See **cardio-**

car·di·gan (kár′·di·gan) *n.* a knitted jacket or jacketlike sweater [fr. an Earl of *Cardigan*].

car·di·nal (kár′·di·nal) *a.* chief; main; of great importance; fundamental; (*Color*) deep scarlet. **-ly** *adv.* — **numbers,** 1, 2, 3, 4, 5, etc. [L. *cardo*, a hinge].

car·di·nal (kár′·di·nal) *n.* the highest rank next to the Pope, in the Catholic Church. **-ate, -ship** *n.* the office of a cardinal [L. *cardo*, a hinge].

car·di·o- (kár′·di·a) *prefix* from Gk. *kardia,* the heart, combining to form derivatives. **cardiac** *a.* pert. to the heart; *n.* a heart stimulant. **-gram** *n.* the graphic tracing of the movements of the heart as recorded by an instrument called the **cardiograph. cardiology** *n.* (*Med.*) the branch of medicine which deals with the functions and diseases of the heart.

care (ker, kár) *n.* concern or anxiety; an object of anxiety; pains or need; caution; charge or oversight; trouble; grief (formerly); *v.i.* to be anxious, concerned; to be affected with solicitude; to have a fondness (with *for*). **-ful** *a.* full of care or solicitude; cautious or watchful; painstaking. **-fully** *adv.* **-fulness** *n.* **-less** *a.* heedless; thoughtless; regardless. **-lessly** *adv.* **-lessness** *n.* **-worn** *a.* showing the wearing effects of care. **-taker** *n.* one who takes over the care of anything or anyone [O.E. *caru*].

ca·reen (ka·rēn′) *v.t.* to turn a ship over on one side; *v.i.* to lean over [L. *caring*, a keel].

ca·reer (ka·rēr′) *n.* rapid motion; a course of action; profession; conduct in life, or progress through life; *v.i.* to speed along; to rush wildly. **-ist** *n.* one who makes his personal advancement his one aim in life [Fr. *carrière*, orig. a chariot course].

ca·ress (ka·res′) *v.t.* to treat with affection; to fondle; to kiss; *n.* a loving touch; an embrace. **-ing** *a.* [L. *carus*, dear].

car·et (kar′·at, kā′·rat) *n.* a mark (∧) which shows where something should be inserted [L. *caret*, is wanting].

car·go (kár′·gō) *n.* the freight of a ship; the goods or merchandise carried [Sp. fr. *cargar*, to load].

car·i·bou (kar′·i·bŏŏ) *n.* the N. American reindeer [Canadian Fr.].

car·i·ca·ture (kar′·i·ka·cher) *n.* a ludicrous exaggeration (usually in picture form) of peculiar personal characteristics; *v.t.* to exaggerate or distort, in words or in pictorial form. **caricaturist** *n.* [It. *caricare*, to load].

car·ies (kar′·ēz) *n.* decay of bone, teeth, etc. **carious** *a.* [L.].

car·il·lon (kar′·i·lán, ka·ril′·yan) *n.* a set or peal of bells of different tones; a melody played on such bells [Fr.].

car·i·ole (kar′·i·ōl) *n.* a small, open, two-wheeled carriage or light cart. Also **carriole** [L. *carrus*].

Car·mel·ite (kár′·mel·īt) *n.* a begging friar of the order of Our Lady of Mount Carmel, established in the 12th cent. [fr. Mount *Carmel*].

car·mine (kár′·min, mīn) *n.* a brilliant crimson, prepared from cochineal. Also *a.* [Fr. or Sp. *carmin*].

car·nage (kár′·nij) *n.* slaughter; massacre; bloodshed [L. *caro, carnis*, flesh].

car·nal (kár′·nal) *a.* pert. to the flesh; sensual; animal; worldly; material, as opposed to spirit-ual. **-ize** *v.t.* to make carnal. **carnality** *n.* fleshly lust. **-ly** *adv.* **-knowledge,** sexual intercouse [L. *caro, carnis*, flesh].

car·na·tion (kár·nā′·shan) *n.* a flesh-color; a variety of the clove-pink, noted for its beauty and sweet scent [L. *carnatio*, fleshiness].

car·nel·ian (kár·nēl′·yan) *n.* a variety of light-red chalcedony, used for jewelry. Also **cornelian** [L. *cornu*, horn].

car·ni·val (kár′·na·val) *n.* a traveling show with amusements such as merry-go-rounds, etc. [L. *carnem levare*, to take away flesh].

car·niv·o·ra (kár·niv′·a·ra) *n.pl.* animals that feed on flesh. **carnivore** (kár′·ni·vōr) *n.* a flesh-eating animal. **carnivorous** *a.* **carnivorously** *adv.* **carnivorousness** *n.* [L. *caro, carnis*, flesh; *vorare*, to devour].

car·ol (kar′·al) *n.* a song of joy, esp. a Christmas hymn; *v.i.* to sing a carol [O.Fr. *carole*].

ca·rot·id (ka·rát′·id) *n.* each of the two main arteries in the neck conveying blood to the head; *a.* pert. to these [Gk. *karōtides*].

ca·rouse (ka·rouz′) *v.i.* to revel; to drink deeply; to hold a drinking-party. **carousal** *n.* a noisy drinking-party. **-r** *n.* [O.Fr. *carous,* fr. Ger. *gar aus* (drink) right to the bottom (of the glass)].

car·ou·sel See **carrousel.**

carp (kárp) *v.i.* to catch at small faults or errors; to find fault petulantly and without reason [O.N. *karpa*, to chatter].

carp (kárp) *n.* a fresh-water fish [Fr. *carpe*].

car·pel (kár′·pal) *n.* (*Bot.*) the seed-bearing part of a plant; part of a compound ovary. **-lary** *a.* [Gk. *karpos*, fruit].

car·pen·ter (kár′·pan·ter) *n.* a worker in lumber as used in building of houses, ships, etc. **carpentry** *n.* [L.L. *carpentarius*, a cartwright].

car·pet (kár′·pit) *n.* a woven or felted covering for floors; **-ing** *n.* a covering similar to a carpet. **-bag** *n.* a 19th cent. traveling bag made of carpet. **-bagger** *n.* a political adventurer. [L.L. *carpita*, patchwork].

car·ra·way See **caraway.**

car·riage (kar′·ij) *n.* the act of carrying passengers or goods; the cost of carrying; a vehicle for passengers; a wheeled or moving support or conveyor; one's posture or bearing; conduct. **-able** (kar′·ij·a·bl) *a.* carriable; passable for carriages [O.Fr. *cariage*, luggage].

car·ri·er (kar′·i·er) *n.* one who carries; one who carries goods for hire, often called a 'common carrier'; a receptacle for carrying objects; a pigeon used for carrying messages; (*Med.*) one who, without showing symptoms of disease, can convey infection to others [O.Fr. *carier,* to loa].

car·ri·ole See **cariole.**

car·ri·on (kar′·i·an) *n.* dead, rotting flesh; anything putrid [L. *caro*, flesh].

car·rot (kar′·at) *n.* a plant cultivated for its edible root. **-y** *a.* reddish-yellow; red-haired [L. *carota*].

car·rou·sel, car·ou·sel (kar·a·sel′) *n.* a merry-go-round; military ornament [Fr.].

car·ry (kar′·i·) *v.t.* to convey; to transport; to impel; to transfer; to obtain possession of by force; to behave; *v.i.* to reach, of a projectile; *n.* range. [O.Fr. *carier* fr. *car*, a vehicle].

cart (kárt) *n.* a two-wheeled vehicle used for the transport of heavy goods; a small four-wheeled vehicle pulled by hand; *v.t.* to convey in a cart. **-age** *n.* carting; the price paid for carting. **-er** *n.* **-wright** *n.* builder or maker of carts [O.N. *kartr*, a cart].

carte blanche (kárt·blánsh) *n.* full authority.

car·tel (kár′·tel) *n.* an international industrial combination for regulating volume and price of output; a trust; an agreement between states at war for exchange of prisoners; a challenge [Fr. fr. L. *cartello*].

car·ti·lage (kár′·ti·lij) *n.* (*Anat.*) gristle; a strong, transparent tissue in the body, very elastic and softer than bone. **cartilaginous** (kár·ti·la′·ji·nas) *a.* [L. *cartilago*, gristle].

car·tog·ra·phy (kár·tág′·ra·fi·) *n.* the art of making charts or maps. **cartographer** *n.* [L. *charta*, chart; Gr. *graphein*, to draw].

car·ton (kár′·tan) *n.* a pasteboard box [Fr. *carton*, pasteboard].

car·toon (kár·tŏŏn′) *n.* a design drawn on strong paper for transference to mosaics, tapestries, frescoes, etc.; an illustration treating current affairs in an amusing fashion; a pictorial caricature; a comic strip; movie comics. **-ist** *n.* [Fr. *carton*, pasteboard].

car·tridge (kár′·trij) *n.* a case made of metal, cardboard, etc. to contain the charge for a gun. [Fr. *cartouche,* fr. L. *charta*, paper].

cartridges

carve (kárv) *v.t.* and *i.* to fashion artistically by cutting; to hew out, as a path, a career, etc.; to cut in pieces or slices, as meat, etc.; to divide. **-r** *n.* one who carves; a large knife for carving. **carving** *n.* [O.E. *ceorfan*].

car·y·at·id (kar·i·at′·id) *n.* (*Archit.*) a draped, female figure used in place of a column. **caryatides** (kar·i·at′·i·dēz) [Gk. *Karuatis,* a woman of *Caryae* in Laconia].

cas·cade (kas·kàd′) *n.* a waterfall; anything resembling this; a wavy fall of lace; *v.i.* to fall in cascades [L. *cadere,* to fall].

cas·car·a (kas-ke′·ra) *n.* **cascara sagrada,** a fluid extracted from dried California buckthorn bark and used as a laxative [Sp. *cascara,* bark; *sagrada,* sacred].

case (kās) *n.* a receptacle; a covering; a sheath; anything which encloses or contains; a box and its contents; a set; (*Print.*) a frame for holding type; *v.t.* to put in a case. **casing** *n.* a case or covering. **-room** *n.* (*Print.*) the room in which type is set. **— shot** *n.* canister shot; small projectiles put in cases or canisters, to be shot from cannon. **-harden** *v.t.* to heat soft steel in contact with carbonaceous material, so that carbon is absorbed, and a surface of harder steel produced. **lower case** (*Print.*) denoting small letters. **upper case** (*Print.*) denoting capital letters [O.Fr. *casse*].

case (kās) *n.* an event, occurrence, or circumstance; a state or condition of things or persons; a question of facts or principles requiring investigation or solution; (*Med.*) a patient under treatment; (*Gram.*) an inflection or terminal change in nouns, pronouns, etc. **casal** *a.* (*Gram.*) pert. to case [L. *cadere,* to fall].

ca·se·in (kā′·si·in) *n.* the curd or cheesy part of milk, a protein [L. *caseus,* cheese].

case·ment (kās′·ment) *n.* a window-frame; a window, or part of a window, opening on hinges [fr. *encase*].

cash (kash) *n.* money, esp. ready money; coin; also, paper-money, bank-note, etc.; *v.t.* to turn into, or exchange for, money. **-register** *n.* an automatic money-till which registers and indicates the amount paid for goods sold [O.Fr. *casse,* a box].

cash·ew (ka′·shòò) *n.* a tropical American tree whose fruit, the cashew-nut, is eaten raw or roasted [Fr. *acajou*].

cash·ier (kash·ir′) *n.* one who has charge of the cash [O.Fr. *casse,* a box].

cash·ier (kash·ir′) *v.t.* to dismiss from office in disgrace; to discard [Fr. *casser,* to annul, to dismiss].

cash·mere (kash′·mir) *n.* a shawl made from the hair of the Kashmir (Cashmere) goat; the material; *a.* [fr. *Cashmere,* in India].

ca·si·no (ka·sē′·nō) *n.* a public assembly-room or building for dancing, gambling, etc. [It. *casino,* a little house].

cask (kask) *n.* a large wooden vessel for holding liquor; a barrel; *v.t.* to put in a cask [Sp. *casco,* a potsherd, a cask].

cas·ket (kas′·kit) *n.* a coffin; a small cask or case; a small box.. [*casco,* a helmet].

casque (kask) *n.* a sort of military helmet [Sp.

cas·se·role (kas′·se·rōl) *n.* a covered baking dish in which food is both cooked and served; a food mixture cooked in such a dish [Fr.].

cas·sia (kash′·a) *n.* a genus of plants, including senna, whose pods are used medicinally as a laxative; a cheap kind of cinnamon [L. *casia*].

cas·si·mere (kas′·a·mir) *n.* a thin twilled, woolen cloth [form of *cashmere*].

cas·sock (kas′·ak) *n.* a long, close-fitting black gown worn by clergymen [Fr. *casaque*].

cast (kast) *v.t.* to fling; to hurl; to direct or bestow, as a glance; to project, as a shadow; to shed, as a skin; to reckon or compute (with *up*); to shape in a mold (as metal); to distribute the parts of a play among the actors; to throw a line in angling; to forecast (to cast a horoscope); to let down (an anchor); to give (a vote); to give birth prematurely; *n.* the act of casting; a throw; the distance a thing is thrown; a mold or form; a change of direction; that which is shed or ejected; a reckoning; a forecast; the actors appearing in a play; expression (of the face); (of the eye). **—down** *a.* depressed. **-ing** *n.* an article cast in a mold; the act of forming and molding. **-ing-vote** *n.* the vote of a chairman, which decides a question when votes are equally divided. **—iron** *a.* made of cast iron; rigid; indefatigable; unshakable; (*Slang*) irrefutable [O.N. *kasta*].

cas·ta·nets (kas′·ta·nets) *n.pl.* two small concave shells of ivory or hard wood, fastened to the thumb and clicked in time to dances and music of a Spanish type [L. *castanea,* a chestnut-tree].

cast·a·way (kast′·a·wā) *n.* a shipwrecked person; an outcast [fr. to *cast away*].

caste (kast) *n.* an exclusive social order [L. *castus,* pure].

cas·tel·lat·ed (kas′·ta·lā·tad) *a.* adorned with turrets and battlements like a castle [L. *castellatus*].

cast·er, castor (kas′·ter) *n.* a small bottle with perforated top for sugar, pepper, etc.; a stand for a set of such bottles; a small swivelled wheel on the foot of a chair-leg, etc. [fr. *cast*].

cas·ti·gate (kas′·ta·gāt) *v.t.* to correct; to rebuke severely; to chastise; to punish. **castigation** *n.* severe chastisement; discipline. **castigator** *n.* [L. *castigare,* to punish].

castle (kas′·l) *n.* a fortified residence; a stronghold, esp. of nobleman; any imposing mansion; a piece (also called rook) in chess. **-d** *a.* having a castle; built like a castle [L. *castellum*].

cas·tor (kas′·ter) *n.* the beaver; a hat made of beaver fur. See **caster** [Gk. *kastor*].

cas·tor-oil (kas′·ter·oil) *n.* an oil used as a cathartic.

cas·trate (kas′·trāt) *v.t.* to deprive of the testicles; to emasculate; to render incapable of generation; to render imperfect. **castration** *n.* [L. *castrare*].

cas·u·al (kazh′·òò·al) *a.* accidental; incidental; occasional; offhand or careless; *n.* a casual or occasional worker; *pl.* troops, etc. **-ly** *adv.* **-ness** *n.* **-ty** *n.* an accident, mishap. **-ties** *n.pl.* (*Mil.*) losses caused by death, wounds, capture, etc. [L. *casuc,* accident, chance].

cas·u·ist (kazh′·òò·ist) *n.* one versed in casuistry. **-ry** *n.* the science of dealing with problems of right or wrong conduct by applying principles drawn from the Scriptures, etc.; the use of specious reasoning and fallacious argument, esp. on matters of morals. **casuistic, casuistical** *a.* **casuistically** *adv.* [Fr. *casuiste*].

cat (kat) *n.* a small domestic quadruped, of the family of felines; the undomesticated cat, usually called wild-cat; related carnivores such as the lion, tiger, leopard, lynx, etc.; a spiteful woman; strong tackle used to hoist an anchor; *v.t.* and *i.* to hoist an anchor. **-ty, -tish** *a.* spiteful. **-bird** *n.* a gray N. Am. songbird having a cry similar to a cat's mew. **— burglary,** a burglar who makes his entry by climbing to windows, roofs, etc. **-call** *n.* a cat-like cry, used by audiences to express disapproval. **—eyed** *a.* able to see in the dark. **— nap** *n.* a very short, light sleep. **-'s-eye** *n.* a gem with reflections like those from a cat's eye. **cat's-paw,** a dupe of another; (*Naut.*) a light breeze. **cat-o-nine-tails** *n.* a whip with nine thongs or lashes. **tabby cat,** a female cat; a striped cat. **tom cat,** a male cat [O.E. *catt*].

cat·a- (kat′·a) a combining form fr. Gk. *kata,* meaning down, away, against, fully, used to form derivatives.

cat·a·chre·sis (kat·a·krē′·sis) (*Rhet.*) a figure by which one word is wrongly used for another [Gk. *katachresis,* misuse].

cat·a·clysm (kat′·a·klizm) *n.* a social or political upheaval; a catastrophe; a sudden and violent alteration in earth's surface. **-al** *a.* **-ic** *a.* [Gk. *kata,* down; *kluzein,* to wash over].

cat·a·combs (kat′·a·kōmz) *n.pl.* underground passageways with niches for tombs [Gr. *kata,* down; *kumbē,* a cavity].

cat·a·falque (kat′·a·falk) *n.* a structure on which a coffin is placed for a lying-in-state [It.].

cat·a·lec·tic (kat·a·lek′·tik) *a.* lacking a syllable at the end of a verse; applied to an incomplete foot in prosody [Gk. *kata,* down; *legein,* to stop].

cat·a·lep·sy (kat′·a·lep·si·) *n.* (*Med.*) suspension of senses and bodily powers, with muscular rigidity; a trance. **cataleptic** *a.* [Gk. *kata,* down; *lepsis,* a seizure].

cat·a·logue (kat′·a·lawg) *n.* a list, usually alphabetical, of names, books, goods, etc.; a descriptive price-list; also **catalog.** *v.t.* to make such a list. **-r** *n.* [Gk. *kata,* throughout; *legein,* to choose].

ca·tal·y·sis (ka·tal′·a·sis) *n.* (*Chem.*) the chemical change effected in one substance by the aid of another which itself undergoes no change. **catalyst** *n.* a substance producing such a change. **catalytic** *a.* [Gk. *kata,* down; *lusis,* a loosening].

cat·a·ma·ran (kat·a·ma·ran′) *n.* a raft consisting of pieces of wood lashed together; a craft with twin parallel hulls; (*Colloq.*) a quarrelsome person [Tamil = a tied tree].

cat·a·pult (kat′·a·pult) *n.* a siege engine for hurling stones, arrows, etc.; a device for launching airplanes from the deck of a ship; *v.t.* [Gk. *kata,* against; *pallein,* to hurl].

cat·a·ract (kat′·a·rakt) *n.* a waterfall; the flow of a large body of water over a precipice; a torrent; (*Med.*) a disease of the eye, characterized by an opaque condition in the lens [Gk. *katarrhaktēs*].

ca·tarrh (ka·tàr′) *n.* (*Med.*) inflammation of the mucous membranes of the body. **-al** *a.* [Gk. *katarrhein,* to flow down].

ca·tas·ta·sis (ka·tas′·ta·sis) *n.* part of drama where action has reached its height [Gk.].

ca·tas·tro·phe (ka·tas′·tra·fe) *n.* a disaster; a calamity; a decisive event in drama; the denouement; the culmination. **catastrophic** *a.* *katastrophe,* an overturning].

catch (kach) *v.t.* to take hold of; to seize; to grasp; to arrest; to trap; to get a disease by infection or contagion; to detect; to understand; to come upon unexpectedly; *v.i.* to seize, and keep hold; to grasp at; *pa.t.* and *pa.p.* **caught** (kawt) *n.* a seizure; anything that holds, stops, etc.; that which is caught; a sudden advantage; gain; the total amount of fish taken by a fisherman; a form of musical composition (a round). **-able** *a.* able to be caught. **-er** *n.* **-ing** *a.* **-y** *a.* containing a hidden difficulty; (*Mus.*) (usually of light music) captivating; attractive. **-all** *n.* a receptacle for miscellaneous objects [L. *capere,* to take].

catch·fly (kach′·flī) *n.* the name of certain plants to whose stems insects adhere.

catch·ment (kach′·ment) *n.* drainage area [fr. *catch*].

catch·pen·ny (kach′·pen·i·) *n.* something of little value and usually showy, made to sell quickly; *a.* cheap and showy.

catch·up, catsup, ketchup (kach′·ap, kat′·sap, kech′·ap) *n.* a bottled sauce made from tomatoes, vinegar, sugar and spices [E. Ind.].

catch·word (kach′·wurd) *n.* a word or short phrase that takes the popular fancy; a slogan; (*Theat.*) an actor's cue; the first word in the column of a dictionary, etc., repeated above the column as a reference.

cat·e·chize (kat′·e·kiz) *v.t.* to instruct by question and answer, esp. in Christian doctrine; to question; to examine orally. **catechism** (kat′·e·kizm) *n.* a set form of question and answer to teach the tenets of religion; a book containing this system. **catechist** *n.* one who catechizes. **catechetical** *a.* consisting of question and answer. **catechetically** *adv.* **catechesis** (kat′·a·kē′·sis) *n.* oral instruction as given to catechumens [Gk. *katēchizein,* to teach by word of mouth].

cat·e·chu·men (kat·a·kū′·man) *n.* one being instructed in the fundamentals of a subject, esp. religion [See **catechize**].

cat·e·go·ry (kat′·a·gōr·i·) *n.* a class, group, or division; in logic, any fundamental conception. **categorical** *a.* pert. to a category; admitting no conditions; absolute; precise. **categorically** *adv.* **categorize** *v.t.* to place in a category [Gk. *katēgoria,* an assertion].

ca·te·na (ka·tē′·na) *n.* a chain; a series of connected things. **catenate** *v.t.* to connect in a series of links. **catenary** (ka′·ta·ne·ri·) *n.* the curve of a chain, wire, etc., hanging freely between two supports. **catenation** *n.* [L. = a chain].

ca·ter (kā′·ter) *v.i.* to buy or procure food; to provide food, entertainment, etc. **-er** *n.* [O.Fr. *acat,* a purchase].

cat·er-cor·nered (kat′·a·kawrn′·erd) *a.* diagonal [F. *quatre,* four, cornered].

cat·er·pil·lar (kat′·er·pil·er) *n.* the grub or larva of butterflies and moths [O.Fr. *chatepelose,* lit. a hairy cat].

cat·er·waul (kat′·ẹr·wawl) *v.i.* to cry like cats in heat [E. *cat*, and imit. sound].

ca·thar·tic (kạ·thár′·tik) *a.* (*Med.*) purgative; cleansing the bowels; *n.* a purging medicine. **catharize** *v.t.* to cleanse; to purify. **cathar·sis** *n.* purgation, also of the emotions, through art [Gk. *katharos*, pure].

Ca·thay (kạ·thā′) *n.* an old name for China or Chinese Tartary.

ca·the·dral (kạ·thē′·drạl) *n.* the principal church in a diocese, which contains the bishop's throne; *a.* pert. to a cathedral [Gk. *kata*, down; *hedra*, a seat].

cath·ode (kath′·ōd) *n.* the negative pole of an electric cell; the conductor by which an electric current leaves an electrolyte, and passes over to the negative pole; opp. of *anode*. — **rays**, negative ions or electrons [Gk. *kathodos*, descent].

cath·o·lic (kath′·ạ·lik) *a.* universal; embracing all Christians; pert. to Roman Catholics; liberal or comprehensive in understanding and sympathies; *n.* a member of the Church Universal, or of the R.C. Church. **catholicism** (kạ·thál′·ạ·sizm) *n.* the faith and practice of Catholic Church, or of R.C. Church; breadth of view; liberality of opinion; catholicity. **catholicity** (·lis·ạ·ti·) *n.* [Gk. *katholikos*, general].

cat·nip (kat′·nip) *n.* an aromatic plant with blue flowers, attractive to cats [*cat* and *mint*].

cat·sup See **catchup**.

cat·tle (kat′·tl) *n.pl.* domestic livestock, esp. cows and bulls [L.L. *capitale*, stock.].

Cau·ca·sian (kaw·kā′·zhạn) *a.* belonging to *Caucasia*; Indo-European, i.e. pert. to the white race. *n.* [fr. the *Caucasus*, mountains near the Black Sea].

cau·cus (kaw′·kạs) *n.* a meeting of leaders of a political party to decide policies, etc.

cau·dal (kaw′·dal) *a.* pert. to a tail. **caudate** *a.* having a tail [L. *cauda*].

cau·dle (kaw′·dl) *n.* a warm drink for invalids [L. *calidus*, hot].

caught (kawt) *pa.p.* and *pa.t.* of **catch**.

caul (kawl) *n.* a net, etc. worn on the head; the membrane covering the head of some babies at birth [etym. unknown].

caul·dron See **caldron**.

cau·li·flow·er (kaw′·lạ·flou·ẹr) *n.* a variety of cabbage [L. *caulis*, a stalk, and *flower*].

caulk See **calk**.

cau·sal (kaw′·zạl) *a.* relating to a cause or causes. **causality** *n.* the manner in which a cause works; the relation of cause and effect. **causation** *n.* agency by which an effect is produced. **causative** *a.* [L. *causa*, cause].

cause (kawz) *n.* that which produces a result or effect; the origin or motive of an action; an action or lawsuit in court; principle supported by a person or party; *v.t.* to produce; to be the occasion of; to induce. **-r** *n.* **-less** *a.* without reason or motive [L. *causa*].

cau·se·rie (kō′·zạ·rē) *n.* a chat; an informal article or essay [Fr. = a talk].

cause·way (kawz′·wā) *n.* a raised paved road [L.L. *calciata*, trodden, fr. *calx*, a heel].

caus·tic (kaws′·tik) *a.* burning; (*Fig.*) biting, bitter, satirical; *n.* a substance that corrodes and destroys animal tissue. **-ally** *adv.* **causticity** *n.* [Gk. *kaustos*, burned].

cau·ter (kaw′·tẹr) *n.* a hot, searing iron. **-ize** *v.t.* to burn or sear animal tissue in order to destroy diseased tissue, or promote healing. **-ization** *n.* **-y** *n.* the act of cauterizing; a hot iron for searing [Gk. *kautērion*, a branding-iron].

cau·tion (kaw′·shạn) *n.* carefulness; prudence; wariness; a warning; (*Colloq.*) an odd or droll person; *v.t.* to advise to take care; to warn or admonish. **cautious** *a.* wary; prudent; discreet. **cautiously** *adv.* **-ary** *a.* containing a warning. **-er** *n.* [L. *cavere, cautum*, to beware].

cav·al·cade (kav′·ạl·kād) *n.* procession on horseback [L.L. *caballus*, a horse].

cav·a·lier (kav·ạ·lir′) *n.* a horseman; a knight; a gallant; an attendant escort to a lady; *a.* gay and offhand; supercilious; haughty and discourteous. **-ly** *adv.* [L.L. *caballus*, a horse].

cav·al·ry (kav′·ạl·ri·) *n.* horse-soldiery [L.L. *caballus*, a horse].

cave (kāv) *n.* a small chamber hollowed out of the earth horizontally, either by nature or by man; a den. — **man** *n.* a very masculine male of primitive ways. **to cave in** (of ground) to fall in, to subside; (*Fig.*) to yield; to admit defeat [L. *cavus*, hollow].

ca·ve·at (kā′·vi·at) *n.* a warning; a legal notice to stop proceedings [L. = let him beware, fr. *cavere*, to beware].

cav·en·dish (kav′·ạn·dish) *n.* tobacco, softened and pressed into plugs [fr. *Cavendish*, the first maker].

cav·ern (kav′·ẹrn) *n.* a deep, hollow place under the earth; a large dark cave. **-ed** *a.* full of caverns. **-ous** *a.* hollow; deep-set [L. *caverna*].

cav·i·ar, caviare (kav′·i·ár) *n.* a delicacy made from the roes of the sturgeon [Turk.].

cav·il (kav′·il) *v.i.* (with 'at') to raise frivolous objections; to find fault unreasonably. *n.* a frivolous objection. **-er** *n.* [L. *cavilla*, raillery].

cav·i·ty (kav′·i·ti·) *n.* a hole; a hollow place of any size [L. *cavus*, hollow].

ca·vort (kạ·vawrt′) *v.i.* (*Colloq.*) to prance; to frisk about [etym. uncertain].

caw (kaw) *v.i.* to cry like a crow or raven; *n.* the sound made by the crow, rook, or raven.

cay·enne (kā·yen′) *n.* a pungent red pepper [fr. *Cayenne*, in S. America].

cease (sēs) *v.t.* to put a stop to; *v.i.* to stop; to discontinue. **-less** *a.* without stopping. **-lessly** *adv.* [L. *cessare*, to cease].

ce·dar (sē′·dẹr) *n.* species of coniferous, ever-green trees yielding durable, fragrant wood. **-n, cedrine** *a.* [Gk. *kedros*].

cede (sēd) *v.t.* to yield; to surrender; to give up, esp. of territory [L. *cedere*].

ce·dil·la (sạ·dil′·ạ) *n.* a small sign (ç), used, principally in French, as a pronunciation mark. It is placed under 'c', when followed by a, o, or u, to indicate that the 's' sound is to be used [Gk. *zēta*, z].

ceil·ing (sē′·ling) *n.* the interior part of the roof of a room; the maximum height to which a particular airplane can ascend; (*Fig.*) the upper limit of production, wages, prices, etc. [Fr. *ciel*, the sky].

cel·e·brate (sel′·ạ·brāt) *v.t.* to make famous; to mark by ceremony, as an event or festival; to observe with solemn rites. **-d** *a.* renowned; famous. **celebration** *n.* the act of celebrating. **celebrant** *n.* one who celebrates. **celebrity** (sẹ·leb′·rạ·ti·) *n.* renown; fame; a person of distinction [L. *celebrare*].

ce·ler·i·ty (sạ·ler′·ạ·ti·) *n.* rapidity of motion; speed; swiftness [L. *celer*, swift].

cel·er·y (sel′·ẹr·i·) *n.* an edible plant cultivated for eating with salads or as a cooked vegetable [Fr. *céléri*, fr. Gk. *selinon*, parsley].

ce·les·ta (sạ·les′·tạ) *n.* (*Mus.*) a small piano-like instrument [Fr.].

ce·les·tial (sạ·les′·chạl) *a.* heavenly; divine; blessed; *n.* an inhabitant of heaven. **-ly** *adv.* [L. *caelum*, heaven].

cel·i·ba·cy (sel′·ạ·bạ·si·) *n.* single life; the unmarried state. **celibate** *n.* one unmarried; *a.* unmarried [L. *caelebs*, unmarried].

cell (sel) *n.* a small room, as in a prison or monastery; a small cavity; the simplest unit in the structure of living matter; a small group of members of a political party; a division of a voltaic or galvanic battery. **-ed** (seld) *a.* furnished with, or containing, cells; contained in cells. **-ular** *a.* consisting of, or containing, cells, as cellular tissue. **-ulated** *a.* having a cellular structure [L. *cella*, a small room].

cel·lar (sel′·ẹr) *n.* an underground room, the lowest story under a building; a storeroom, esp. for wines, liquors. [L. *cellarium*, a pantry].

cel·lo, 'cel·lo (chel′·ō) *n.* (*Mus.*) a contraction for violoncello, a stringed musical instrument. **cellist, 'cellist** *n.* a player on the violoncello.

cel·lo·phane (sel′·ạ·fān) *n.* a tough, transparent, waterproof material used as wrapping tissue, etc. [Trade Name].

cel·lu·loid (sel′·yạ·loid) *n.* name for a hard compound used in the manufacture of imitation ivory, coral, amber, etc. [L. *cellula*, a little cell].

cel·lu·lose (sel′·yạ·lōs) *n.* a chemical substance, one of the carbohydrates, forming the chief constituent of the walls of plant cells; an essential part of wood, paper, linen, cotton, etc. [L. *cellula*, a little cell].

Celt, Kelt (selt, kelt) *n.* one of a race, including the Highlanders of Scotland, the Irish, Welsh, Bretons, Manx, and Cornish. **Celtic, Keltic** *n.* the language spoken by the Celts. *a.* pert. to the Celts [L. *Celticus*].

ce·ment (sạ·ment′) *n.* a plastic mixture that can unite two bodies; mortar; a material used in making concrete for building or paving; a bond or union; *v.t.* to unite by using cement; to join closely. **-ation** *n.* the act of cementing; the conversion of iron into steel [L. *caementum*, stone for building].

cem·e·ter·y (sem′·ạ·ter·i·) *n.* a graveyard; a burying ground [Gk. *koimētērion*, a sleeping-room].

ce·no·bite, coenobite (sē′·nạ·bīt) *n.* member of a religious order, dwelling in community [Gk. *koinos*, common; *bios*, life].

cen·o·taph (sen′·ạ·taf) *n.* a monument erected to one buried elsewhere; an empty sepulcher [Gk. *kenos*, empty; *taphos*, a tomb].

Cen·o·zo·ic (sēn·ạ·zō′·ik) *a.* (*Geol.*) belonging to the third or Tertiary period; the present period of geologic time. Also **Cainozoic** [Gk. *kainos*, recent; *zoē*, life].

cen·ser (sen′·sẹr) *n.* a metal vessel in which incense is burned. **cense** *v.t.* to perfume with incense [L. *incendere*, to burn].

cen·sor (sen′·sẹr) *n.* a Roman official who looked after property, taxes, and the people's morals; one appointed to examine books, plays, newspaper articles, etc. before publication, and ban them if containing anything objectionable; also, in time of war or crisis, to examine letters, etc., and erase anything calculated to convey information to the enemy; one who blames or finds fault; *v.t.* to blame or reprove; to subject to examination by the censor. **-ial** *a.* pert. to correction of morals; pert. to a censor. **-ious** *a.* apt to find fault. **-iously** *adv.* **-iousness** *n.* **-ship** *n.* the office of a censor; the act of censoring [L. *censere*, to estimate].

cen·sure (sen′·sher) *n.* the act of finding fault; disapproval; *v.t.* to reprove; to express disapproval of; to criticize adversely. **censurable** *a.* [L. *censura*, opinion].

cen·sus (sen′·sạs) *n.* an official numbering of the inhabitants of a country. **censual** *a.* [L. *census*, register].

cent (sent) *n.* a hundredth, as 10 per *cent*; a U.S. coin worth the hundredth part of a dollar [L. *centum*].

cen·taur (sen′·tawr) *n.* (*fem.* **centauress**) (*Myth.*) a fabulous being, half man and half horse [Gk. *kentaurion*].

cen·te·nar·y (sen′·te·ner·i·, sen·ten·ạr·i·) *n.* a period of a hundred years; a century; the commemoration of a hundredth anniversary; a centennial. **centenarian** (sen·tạ·ne′·ri·ạn) *n.* a person a hundred years old [L. *centum*, a hundred].

cen·ten·ni·al (sen·ten′·i·ạl) *a.* pert. to a period of 100 years; happening once in a hundred years; *n.* a hundredth anniversary [L. *centum; annus*, a year].

cen·ter (sen′·tẹr) *n.* the mid-point of anything; pivot; axis; a point to which things move or are drawn; a point of concentration; *v.t.* and *i.* to place in the center; to be fixed. **-piece** *n.* an ornament or cloth covering for the center of a table. **centric(al)** *a.* placed in center or middle. **centrically** *adv.* **centricity** (sen·tris′·i·ti·) *n.* the state of being centric. **center of gravity**, the point in a body about which it will balance [L. *centrum*].

cen·ti- (sen′·ti) *prefix* fr. L. *centum*, a hundred, combining to form derivatives. **-grade** *a.* divided into 100 degrees, as the centigrade thermometer on which freezing-point is marked 0°, and boiling-point 100°. **-meter** (sen′·ti-mē·tẹr) *n.* 100th part of a meter = .394 inch.

cen·ti·pede (sen′·ti·pēd) *n.* an insect, of flat and elongated shape, with a segmented body [L. *centum*, a hundred; *pes, pedis*, a foot].

cen·tral (sen′·trạl) *a.* relating to, or placed in, the center; chief; important. **-ly** *adv.* **-ize** *v.t.* to draw to a central point; to concentrate; to put under one control. **-ization** *n.* **-ism** *n.* centralization, esp. of government. **centrality** *n.* the state of being central. — **heating**, heating of a building or group of buildings from one central furnace [L. *centralis*, fr. L. *centrum*].

cen·tri·fu·gal (sen·trif′·yoo·gạl) *a.* tending to move away from the center of a revolving body [L. *centrum*, the center; *fugere*, to flee].

cen·trip·e·tal (sen·trip′·ạ·tạl) *a.* tending to move towards the center [L. *centrum*, the center; *petere*, to seek].

cen·tu·ple (sen′·too·pl) *a.* hundredfold. [L. *centum*, a hundred; *plicare*, to fold].

cen·tu·ry (sen′·chạ·ri·) *n.* a period of a hundred years; a set of a hundred; a company of a Roman legion numbering a hundred soldiers under the command of a **centurion** [L. *centuria*].

ce·phal·ic (sạ·fal′·ik) *a.* pert. to the head; *n.* a medicine for headaches [Gk. *kephalē*, the head].

ce·ram·ic (sẹr·am′·ik) *a.* pert. to pottery. **ceramics** *n.pl.* the art of molding, modelling, and baking clay; the study of pottery as an art [Gk. *keramos*, pottery].

cere (sir) *v.t.* (*Obs.*) to cover with wax; *n.* the wax-like membrane at base of bill in some birds. **ceraceous** (si·rā′·shạs) *a.* waxy. **cerate** *n.* an ointment of wax, oil, etc. **-cloth** *n.* a cloth smeared with melted wax in which dead bodies used to be wrapped. **-ment** *n.* (usually *pl.*) graveclothes [L. *cera*, wax].

ce·re·al (si′·ri·ạl) *a.* pert. to edible grain; *n.* any edible grain (wheat, barley, oats, etc.); a breakfast food made of such grains. [L. *Ceres*, Roman goddess of corn].

ce·re·brum (ser′·ạ·brạm) *n.* the upper and larger division of the brain. **cerebellum** *n.* the part of the brain behind and below the cerebrum. **cerebral** *a.* pert. to the brain. **cerebral hemorrhage**, rupture of an artery of the brain with a consequent escape of blood. **cerebral palsy** *n.* paralysis from cerebral lesion, chiefly characterized by spasms. **cerebrate** *v.i.* to have the brain in action. **cerebration** *n.* cerebrospinal *a.* pert. to both brain and spinal cord [L. *cerebrum*, the brain].

cer·e·mo·ny (ser′·ạ·mō·ni·) *n.* a sacred rite; formal observance; formality; usage of courtesy; prescribed rule; a public or private function. **ceremonial** *a.* pert. to ceremony; formal; *n.* an outward observance; usage followed in performing rites. **ceremonially** *adv.* **ceremonious** *a.* full of ceremony; particular in observing forms. **ceremoniously** *adv.* **ceremoniousness** *n.* **master of ceremonies** *n.* at public functions, etc. one whose business it is to see that all forms, rules, and courtesies are observed [L. *caerimonia*, a rite].

ce·rise (sạr·ēs′) *n.* and *a.* light clear red; cherry-colored [Fr. = cherry].

cer·tain (sur′·tin) *a.* sure; settled; undoubted; inevitable; one; constant; of moderate quantity, degree, etc. **-ly** *adv.* **-ty** *n.* the quality of being certain. **certitude** *n.* freedom from doubt; certainty. **certes** (sur′·tēz) *adv.* (*Arch.*) certainly; in truth [L. *certus*].

cer·ti·fi·cate (sẹr·tif′·ạ·kạt) *n.* a written testimony to the truth of a fact; a testimonial or written statement of qualifications or of accomplishment; *v.i.* (sẹr·ti·fạ·kāt) to attest by a certificate; to furnish with a certificate. **certify** (sur′·ti·fī) *v.t.* to testify to in writing; to vouch for the truth of. **certifiable** *a.* able to be vouched for. **certification** *n.* the act of certifying. **certified** *a.* [L. *certus*, certain; *facere*, to make].

ce·ru·le·an (sạ·ròo′·li·ạn) *a.* sky-blue; deep blue. **ceruleous** *a.* sky-blue [L. *caeruleus*].

ce·ruse (si′·ròos) *n.* white lead. **cerussite** *n.* a carbonate of lead [L. *cerussa*, white lead].

cer·vi·cal (ser′·vi·kạl) *a.* pert. to the neck or neck of the uterus [L. *cervix*, the neck].

ce·si·um, caesium (sē′·zi·ạm) *n.* a silver-white alkaline metal belonging to the sodium and potassium family [L. *caesius*, bluish-gray].

ces·sa·tion (se·sā′·shạn) *n.* stoppage; discontinuance [L. *cessare*, to cease].

ces·sion (se′·shạn) *n.* act of surrendering, as by treated; something yielded, ceded [L. *cessio*].

cess·pool (ses′·pòol) *n.* a pit or hollow for collection of drainage water or sewage.

chafe (chāf) *v.t.* to warm by rubbing; to wear away by rubbing; to irritate; to vex; *v.i.* to be worn by rubbing or friction; to rage or fret; *n.* friction; injury caused by rubbing. **-r** *n.* one who chafes. **chafing dish** *n.* a dish and heating apparatus for cooking or keeping food warm on the table [Fr. *chauffer*, to warm].

chaff (chaf) *n.* the husk of grains; straw cut small for cattle-feeding; worthless matter; refuse. **-y** *a.* [O.E. *ceaf*].

chaff (chaf) *n.* banter; jesting talk; *v.t.* to tease; to make fun of (without spite) [form of *chafe*, to irritate].

cha·grin (shạ·grin′) *n.* ill-humor; vexation; mortification; *v.t.* to vex deeply [Fr.].

chain (chān) *n.* a series of metal rings or links connected and forming a flexible cable; a fetter; a succession of things or events; a mountain range; a measure such as used by engineers or surveyors; *v.t.* to fasten or connect with a chain; to fetter; to restrain. **— bridge** *n.* a suspension bridge. **-drive** *n.* the transmitting of driving-power by means of chain-gear. **— gang** *n.* a number of convicts chained together. **— reaction** *n.* in nuclear physics, a self-sustaining process in which some neutrons from one splitting atom are able to split more atoms, setting free still more neutrons which carry on the reaction indefinitely [L. *catena*, a chain.

chain

chair (chār) *n.* a seat with a back, legs, and sometimes arms, usually for one person; a portable covered vehicle for carrying one person, e.g. a sedan; an official seat occupied by the president of a meeting, a university professor, a bishop, etc.; *v.t.* to install in a chair or office; to provide with chairs. **to take the chair**, to act as chairman of a meeting; to preside. **-man** *n.* the presiding officer of a meeting, board, committee, etc. **-manship** *n.* **-woman** *n.* [Fr. *chaire*, a pulpit, fr. Gk. *kathedra*].

chaise (shāz) *n.* a light, one-horse carriage; a posting-carriage. **— longue** (lawng) *n.* an elongated seat with backrest at one end and support for legs [Fr. *chaise*, a chair, a seat].

chal·ced·o·ny (kal′·se·dō·ni·) *n.* a whitish or bluish-white variety of quartz. **chalcedonic** *a.* [fr. *Chalcedon*, a town in Asia Minor].

cha·let (shạ·lā′) *n.* a timber-built house in the Alps; a country residence like a Swiss mountain cottage [Fr.]. [communion-cup; L. *calix*].

chal·ice (chal′·is) *n.* a wine-cup; a goblet; a

chalk (chawk) *n.* a soft, white, carbonate of lime; a chalk-like material used for marking; *v.t.* to rub or mark with chalk. **-y** *a.* containing or like chalk. **-iness** *n.* **— up** *v.t.* to score; to earn. **French chalk**, tailor's chalk [L. *calx*, limestone].

chal·lenge (chal′·inj) *n.* an invitation to a contest, esp. to a duel; defiance; the warning call of a sentry; exception taken to a juror; *v.t.* to call upon a person to settle a dispute by fighting; to defy; to summon to answer; to call in question. **-able** *a.* **-r** *n.* [L. *calumnia*. Doublet of E. *calumny*]. [fabric.

chal·lis, challie (sha′·li·) *n.* a lightweight

cham·ber (chām′·bẹr) *n.* a room, esp. one used for lodging, privacy, or study; a place where an assembly, such as a legislature meets, and the assembly itself; a cavity; the cavity at the rear end of the bore of a gun; a vessel for urine; *v.t.* to shut up or confine, as in a chamber; *v.i.* to occupy as a chamber. **-ed** *a.* **-s** *n.pl.* a room or rooms where a judge hears cases not requiring action in court. **-maid** *n.* a woman servant who has the care of bedrooms, esp. in hotels, etc. **— music** *n.* music suitable for performance in a house or small hall [L. *camera*, a room].

cham·ber·lain (chām′·bẹr·lin) *n.* court official. **-ship** *n.* [fr. *chamber*].

cham·bray (sham′·brā) *n.* a fine cotton material, a variety of gingham [fr. *Cambrai*, Fr.].

cha·me·le·on (kạ·mēl′·yạn) *n.* a small lizard, which changes color with its surroundings; (*Fig.*) an inconstant person [Gk. *chamai*, on the ground; *leōn*, a lion].

cham·fer (cham′·fẹr) *v.t.* to cut a groove in; to bevel; *n.* a groove; a bevel. **-ed** *a.* [O.Fr. *chanfraindre*, to make angular].

cham·ois (sham′·i·) *n.* a goat-like species of antelope; a kind of soft leather [L.L. *camox*].

champ (champ) *v.t.* and *i.* to bite, chew, or munch noisily. **to champ at the bit** (*Fig.*) to be impatient; *n.* (*Slang*) champion.

cham·pagne (sham·pān′) *n.* a light effervescent, white wine, made in the province of *Champagne* in N.E. France, or elsewhere.

cham·pi·on (cham′·pi·ạn) *n.* one who fought in single combat to defend the honor of another; a defender of any cause; one capable of defeating his competitors in any form of sport; *a.* first-class; *v.t.* to defend; to maintain or support. **-ship** *n.* the position of a champion; defense; advocacy [L.L. *campio*, a fighter in the arena].

chance (chans) *n.* an unforeseen occurrence; risk; likelihood; opportunity; possibility; *a.* accidental; *v.t.* to risk; *v.i.* to happen. **by —**, accidentally [O.Fr. *cheance*, fall of dice].

chan·cel (chan′·sạl) *n.* the east part of a church, where the altar is placed, orig. shut off from the nave [L. *cancelli*, lattice-work].

chan·cel·lor (chan′·sạ·ler) *n.* the title of various high officials in the state, and in the law; the head of a university; the chief secretary of an embassy. **-ship** *n.* the office of chancellor. **chancellery** *n.* the premises of a chancellor. [Fr. *chancelier*, orig. keeper of a barrier].

chan·cer·y (chan′·sẹr·i·) *n.* the office of a chancellor; a chancellery; a court of equity [orig. *chancellory*].

chan·de·lier (chan·dạ·lir′) *n.* a branched framework for holding lights, esp. one hanging from the ceiling; orig. for holding candles [L. *candela*, a candle].

chand·ler (chand′·lẹr) *n.* orig. a candle-maker; now a grocer or dealer in small wares [L. *candela*, a candle].

change (chānj) *v.t.* to alter or make different; to put one thing for another; to shift; to quit one state for another; to exchange, as money; to convert; *v.i.* to become different; to change one's clothes; *n.* the act of changing; alteration; that which makes for variety; money of small denomination given in exchange for money of larger; balance of money returned after payment; fresh clothing; an exchange. **-able** *a.* variable; fickle; unsteady. **-ful** *a.* **-fully** *adv.* **-fulness** *n.* **-less** *a.* unchanging; constant. **-ling** *n.* a child left in place of another taken by the fairies [L. *cambire*, to barter].

chan·nel (chan′·ạl) *n.* a waterway; the deeper part of a river, harbor, etc.; a strait; a groove or furrow; means of access; *a.* frequency band for transmission of radio, television, etc.; *v.t.* to form a channel; to groove or furrow; to direct in a particular course [L. *canalis*].

chant (chant) *v.t.* and *i.* to sing; to celebrate in song; to intone; *n.* a song; melody; sacred words recited in a singing manner. **-er** *n.* (*fem.* **-euse** or **-ress**). **-y** (shan′·ti·) *n.* a sailor's song [L. *cantare*, to sing].

chant·i·cleer (chant′·i·klir) *n.* a cock, rooster [O.Fr. *chanté-cler*, sing-clear].

cha·os (kā′·ás) *n.* complete confusion; state of the universe before creation. **chaotic** *a.* [Gk.].

chap (chap) *v.t.* to cleave; to split; to crack; *v.i.* to become cracked, red, and rough (as the skin in cold weather); *pr.t.* **-ping**. *pa.t.* **-ped**. *n.* a chink; a crack in the skin [related to *chip*, *chop*]. [dler O.E. *caep*, a bargain].

chap (chap) *n.* (*Colloq.*) a fellow; (*Br.*) a ped-

chap·el (chap′·ạl) *n.* a private church; a subordinate place of worship; a division of a church with its own altar [L.L. *cappella*, a sanctuary for relics].

chap·e·ron (shap′·ạ·rōn) *n.* a kind of hood; a mature person who escorts an unmarried lady in public or is in attendance at social gatherings of young people; *v.t.* to escort, accompany. **-age** *n.* [Fr. = a hood].

chap·lain (chap′·lin) *n.* a clergyman. **-cy** *n.* [Fr. *chapelain*].

chap·let (chap′·lit) *n.* a garland or wreath for the head; a string of beads; a division of the rosary [O.Fr. *chapelet*].

chaps (shaps) *n.pl.* leather over-trousers worn by a cowboy [fr. Sp. *chaparejos*].

chap·ter (chap′·tẹr) *n.* a divison of a book or treatise; a bishop's council in a diocese; an organized branch of a society, fraternity, or military order; *v.t.* to divide into chapters [L. *caput*, the head].

char (chär) *n.* a species of trout [Celt.].

char (chär) *v.t.* to reduce to charcoal; to burn to a black cinder; *pr.p.* **-ring**. *pa.p.* and *pa.t.* **-red**. **-coal** *n.* the residue of partially burnt animal or vegetable matter, esp. wood.

char, chare (chār) *n.* a job; work done by the day; *v.i.* to work by the day; to do small jobs. **-woman** *n.* [O.E. *cerr*].

char·ac·ter (kar′·ik·tẹr) *n.* a mark, letter, figure, sign, stamp; any distinctive mark; an essential feature; nature; the total of qualities making up an individuality; moral excellence;

(*Colloq.*) a person noted for eccentricity; a personage in a play or novel; *v.t.* to characterize; to portray; to represent. **-ize** *v.t.* to depict the peculiar qualities of; to distinguish; to give character to. **-istic** *a.* serving to mark the character of; peculiar; distinctive; *n.* that which distinguishes a person or thing from another; **-istically** *adv.* **-ization** *n.* the act or characterizing literary or dramatic portrayal of character [Gk. *charactēr*, an engraved mark].

cha·rade (shạ·rād´) *n.* a game, consisting of the interpretation (usually dramatic) of a word for others to guess [Fr.].

chard (chárd) *n.* leafy vegetable.

charge (chárj) *n.* a load or burden; price or cost; care or trust; an earnest exhortation, as of a judge or bishop; accusation or allegation; a clergyman's parish or the people of that parish; the amount of powder, etc., that a gun is fitted to hold; an impetuous onset or attack, or the signal for it; custody; electrical contents of accumulator or battery; *v.t.* to lay a task, command, trust upon; to ask as payment; to accuse; to load, as a gun; *v.i.* to make an onset. **-able** *a.* **-r** *n.* a large, flat dish; a warhorse [L.L. *carricare*, to load a cart].

char·gé d'af·fairs (shár·zhā´·dạ·fer´) *n.* a minor diplomatic emissary; a deputy ambassador [Fr. = charged with business].

char·i·ot (char´·i·ạt) *n.* in ancient times, a two-wheeled cart used in warfare; a four-wheeled state carriage. **-eer** *n.* [Fr. dim. of *char*, a car, cart].

char·i·ty (char´·i·ti·) *n.* (*Bib.*) love and goodwill to men; liberality to the poor; leniency in judging others; any act of kindness; alms; a charitable cause or institution. **charitable** *a.* pert. to charity; liberal to the poor; generous. **charitably** *adv.* [L. *caritas*, affection].

cha·riv·a·ri (shạ·ri·vá´·ri·) *n.* a mock serenade. Also **shivaree** (shi´·vạ·ri·) [Fr.].

char·la·tan (shár´·lạ·tạn) *n.* a quack or imposter [It. *ciarlare*, to prate, chatter].

char·lotte (shár´·lạt) *n.* (*Cookery*) a kind of pudding made by lining a mold with bread or cake and filling it [Fr.].

charm (chárm) *n.* a magic spell; anything supposed to possess magic power; a talisman; a trinket worn on a bracelet; attractiveness; *v.t.* to subjugate by magic; to attract irresistibly; *v.i.* to please greatly; to be fascinating. **-er** *n.* **-ing** *a.* attractive; alluring; delightful [Fr. *charme*, fr. L. *carmen*, a song].

char·nel (chár´·nel) *a.* containing dead bodies. **— house** *n.* a place where the bodies or bones of the dead are deposited; a sepulcher [L. *caro*, *carnis*, flesh].

chart (chárt) *n.* a map of part of the sea, showing currents, depths, islands, coasts, etc.; a diagram giving information in tabular form; a graph; *v.t.* to represent on a chart; to map; to delineate. **-er** *n.* [L. *charta*, a paper].

char·ter (chár´·ter) *n.* a formal document confirming privileges, titles, or rights; an act of incorporation; the hiring of a vessel; *v.t.* to establish by charter; to hire, as a ship. **-ed** *a.* **— member** *n.* one of the original members [L. *charta*, a paper].

char·treuse (shár·trẹz´) *n.* a liqueur; a light yellowish-green color [Fr.].

char·y (chár´·i·) *a.* careful; sparing. **charily** *adv.* [O.E. *cearig*, full of care].

chase (chās) *v.t.* to pursue; to run after; to hunt; to drive away; *v.i.* to hasten; to hurry; *n.* pursuit; hunting of enemy, game, etc.; what is pursued or hunted. **-r** *n.* one who chases; a mild beverage taken after liquor [L. *captare*, to seize].

chase (chās) *v.t.* to enchase; to engrave metal. **-r** *n.* [abbrev. of *enchase*].

chase (chās) *n.* (*Print.*) an iron frame to hold type when set up; a wide groove [L. *capsa*, a box. Doublet of *case*].

chasm (kazm) *n.* a deep opening in the earth; a cleft [Gk. *chasma*].

chas·sé (sha·sā´) *n.* in dancing, a rapid gliding step to the right or left [Fr.].

chas·sis (sha´·si·) *n.* the framework and undercarriage of an automobile, including the engine; the framework on which a gun is moved; landing gear of an airplane [Fr. *chassis*, a frame].

chaste (chāst) *a.* pure; virtuous; undefiled; pure and simple in taste and style. **-ly** *adv.* **-ness** *n.* **chastity** *n.* purity; virginity [L. *castus*, pure].

chas·ten (chās´·tn) *v.t.* to correct by punishment; to subdue [L. *castigare*, to punish].

chas·tise (chas´·tiz) *v.t.* to inflict pain in order to reform; to punish. **-ment** *n.* [L. *castigare*, to punish].

chas·u·ble (chaz´·yoo·bl) *n.* a sleeveless vestment worn over the alb by the priest during Mass [L.L. *casula*, a mantle].

chat (chat) *v.i.* to talk idly or familiarly; *n.* light, informal talk; *pr.p.* **-ting**; *pa.p.* and *pa.t.* **-ted. -ter** *v.i.* to talk idly or rapidly; to rattle together, of the teeth. **-terbox** *n.* one who chatters excessively. **-terer** *n.* one who chatters. **-tiness** *n.* **-ty** *a.* talkative; gossipy.

cha·teau (sha·tō´) *n.* a castle; a country-seat, esp. in France; a mansion; *pl.* **chateaux** (sha·-tōz´). **chatelain** (sha´·tạ·len) *n.* the mistress of a castle or other fashionable household; a chain fastened around a lady's waist, with keys, seals, etc. attached [O.Fr. *chastel*. Doublet of *castle*].

chat·tel (chat´·l) *n.*, usually in *pl.* **chattels**, any kind of property, except land and buildings. **— mortgage** *n.* a mortgage on personal property [O.Fr. *chatel*, a castle].

chat·ter See **chat**.

chauf·feur (shō·fur´·, shō´·fẹr) *n.* the paid driver of private automobile; *v.t.* to drive [Fr. = a stoker].

chau·vin·ism (shō´·vin·izm) *n.* absurdly exaggerated patriotism; blind enthusiasm for a cause. **chauvinist** *n.* **chauvinistic** *a.* [fr. Nicolas *Chauvin*].

chaw (chaw) *n.* (*Dial.*) See **chew**.

cheap (chēp) *a.* low in price; of low cost, as compared with the value, or the usual cost; contemptible, inferior, vulgar. **-ly** *adv.* **-ness** *n.* **-en** *v.t.* to bring down the price; to lessen the value; to belittle [O.E. *ceap*, a bargain].

cheat (chēt) *v.t.* to deceive; to defraud; to trick; *v.i.* to practice trickery; *n.* a fraud; one who cheats; an impostor. **-er** *n.* [short for *escheat*].

check (chek) *n.* a stop; a restraint; an interruption in progress; an obstacle, obstruction; control or supervision, or one employed to carry out such; a mark placed against items in a list; an order to a bank to pay money; a term in chess to indicate that opponent's king must be moved or guarded; a pattern of squares in cloth, etc.; *v.t.* to restrain; to hinder; to chide or reprove; to verify; to put a mark against, in a list; to leave articles in the custody of another; in chess, to put in check; *v.i.* to come to a sudden stop; to pause. **-ers** *n.pl.* a board game for 2. **-book** *n.* book of blank checks or orders on a bank. **-mate** *n.* the final movement in chess, when the king can be neither moved or protected; complete defeat. **-room** *n.* a place where articles may be left under the temporary protection of others. **-up** *n.* a medical examination [fr. Pers. *shah*, king].

check·er (chek´·ẹr) *v.t.* to variegate with cross lines; to diversify; *v.i.* to produce a checkered effect, esp. of alternate light and shade; *n.* a square; a pattern like a chess-board; a piece in the game of checkers. **-ed** *a.* [Fr. *échiquier*].

Ched·dar (ched´·ar) *n.* a kind of hard, smooth cheese [fr. *Cheddar*, in Somerset].

cheek (chēk) *n.* the fleshy wall or side of the mouth; each side of the face below the eyes; (*Colloq.*) insolence or impudence. **-bone** *n.* the bone below the outer corner of the eye. **-y** *a.* [O.E. *ceace*, the cheek, jaw].

cheep (chēp) *v.i.* to chirp, as a small bird; *n.* a small shrill sound [imit. origin].

cheer (chēr) *n.* good spirits; disposition; state of mind; gaiety; expression of approval, or encouragement, by shouting; rich food; *v.t.* to render cheerful; to comfort; to hearten or encourage; to salute with cheers; *v.i.* to shout hurrah. **-er** *n.* **-ful** *a.* having good spirits. **-fully** *adv.* **-fulness** *n.* **-ily** *adv.* with cheerfulness. **-iness** *n.* **-io!** *interj.* an informal salutation at parting. **-less** *a.* gloomy; comfortless. **-lessness** *n.* **-y** *a.* in good spirits; promoting cheerfulness [O.Fr. *chiere*, countenance; L.L. *cara*, the face].

cheese (chēz) *n.* a curd of milk, separated from the whey, and prepared in several ways as food; a solid mass or cake of this food. **-cloth** *n.* a thin loosely woven cotton cloth, orig. used for wrapping cheese. **cheese it** (*Slang*) Look out! Run! [O.E. *cese*, *cyse*, curdled milk].

chee·tah (chē´·tạ) *n.* the hunting leopard of India and Africa [Hind.].

chef (shef) *n.* a head cook. **chef-d'oeuvre** (shā·devr´) *n.* a masterpiece, esp. in art or literature [Fr.].

chei·ro- See **chiro.**.

chem·i·cal (kem´·ạ·kạl) *a.* pert. to, or made by, chemistry; *n.* a substance used in chemistry, or produced by chemical processes. **-ly** *adv.* according to chemical principles [fr. *Alchemy*].

che·mise (shạm·ēz´) *n.* a woman's undershirt [Fr. *chemise*, a shirt].

chem·ist (kem´·ist) *n.* a person versed in chemistry or professionally engaged in it. **-ry** *n.* the study of the various substances which compose the universe, their combinations, and the processes by which they act one upon another [shortened form of *alchemist*].

chem·o·ther·a·peu·tics (kem´·ō·ther·a·pū´·tiks) *n.* (*Med.*) the use of chemical compounds in the treatment of disease. **chemotherapy** *n.* [E. *chemical*; Gk. *therapeuein*, to heal].

chem·ur·gy (kem´·ẹr·ji·) *n.* applied chemistry directed to developing industrial uses for agricultural produce.

che·nille (shạ·nēl´) *n.* a soft plush-like cord of silk, wool, worsted, etc. used for ornamental trimmings, fringes, etc.; a soft, velvety fabric [Fr. = a caterpillar].

cher·ish (cher´·ish) *v.t.* to hold dear; to treat tenderly; to foster [L. *carus*, dear].

che·root (shạ·rōōt´) *n.* a kind of cigar, open at both ends [Hind.].

cher·ry (cher´·i·) *n.* the bright red fruit of a tree akin to the plum; a cherry tree; *a.* pert. to a cherry; red [Gk. *kerasos*].

cher·ub (cher´·ạb) *n.* a winged creature with a human face; an angel; a celestial spirit; a beautiful child; *pl.* **cherubim** (cher´·ạ·bim) or **-s. cherubic** (chạ·rōō´·bik) *a.* [Heb. *kerub*].

chess (ches) *n.* a game of Eastern origin played by two persons on a board containing sixty-four squares, with two differently colored sets of sixteen pieces or 'men.' **-man** *n.* a piece used in the game [Pers. *shah*, a king].

chest (chest) *n.* a large box; a coffer; a trunk; part of the body enclosed by ribs and breast-bone; *v.t.* to place in a chest. **chest of drawers**, a piece of furniture fitted with drawers. **-y** *a.* having a large chest; conceited [O.E.].

ches·ter·field (ches´·ter·fēld) *n.* a long overcoat, a heavily padded sofa [after Earl of *Chesterfield*].

chest·nut (ches´·nut) *n.* the nut of a forest tree; the tree itself, or its timber; a reddish-brown color; (*Colloq.*) a stale joke or story; *a.* reddish-brown [L. *castanea*].

che·val (shạ·val´) *n.* a support or frame. **— glass** *n.* a large mirror within a supporting frame. **chevalier** (shev·ạ·lir´) *n.* orig. a horseman; a cavalier [Fr. *cheval*, a horse].

Chev·i·ot (chev´·i·ạt) *n.* a famous breed of sheep; cloth made from or like their wool [fr. *Cheviot* Hills, Eng. & Scot.].

chev·ron (shev´·rạn) *n.* a V-shaped bar worn on the sleeve to designate rank [Fr. *chevron*, a rafter].

chew (chōō) *v.t.* to bite and crush with the teeth; to masticate; to ruminate; to champ; *n.* action of chewing; a quid of tobacco. **-ing gum** *n.* a sweet and flavored substance for chewing prepared from *chicle*, the gum of a Mexican rubber-tree [O.E. *ceowan*].

Chi·an·ti (kē·an´·ti·) *n.* an Italian red or white wine [fr. *Chianti* hills in Italy].

chi·a·ro·scu·ro (ki·ár·ạ·skyoo´·rō) *n.* the reproduction in art of the effects of light and shade in nature [It. = bright, dark].

chic (shēk) *n.* style and elegance; effectiveness; *a.* stylish; modish [Fr.].

chi·cane (shi·kān´) *n.* trick or artifice; sharp practice, esp. in legal proceedings; (*Cards*) a bridge hand with no trumps in it; *v.i.* to use trickery. **-ry** *n.* trickery. **-r** *n.* [Fr.].

chick, chicken (chik, chik´·ạn) *n.* the young of fowls, esp. of hen. **-en-hearted** *a.* cowardly; timid. **-en-pox** *n.* a mild, contagious, eruptive disease. **-weed** *n.* weed with small white blossoms [O.E. *cicen*].

chic·le (chik´·l) *n.* a gum-like, milky juice obtained from several Central American trees [Sp. Amer.].

chic·o·ry (chik´·ạ·ri·) *n.* a plant whose tap-root when roasted and ground is used to mix with coffee and whose greens are used for salad [Fr. *chicorée*].

chicory

chide (chīd) *v.t.* to scold; to rebuke; *v.i.* to find fault; *pr.p.* **chiding.** *pa.p.* **chided** or **chid.** *pa.t.* **chid** [O.E. *cidan*].

chief (chēf) *a.* foremost in importance; principal; main; at the head; most influential; *n.* a head or leader; a principal person or thing. **-ly** *adv.* principally; for the most part. **-tain** *n.* (*fem.* **-tainess**) the head of a clan or tribe; a commander [Fr. *chef.* fr. L. *caput*, the head].

chif·fon (shi·fän') *n.* a thin, soft, gauzy material. **chiffonier** (shif-an·ēr') *n.* a high narrow chest of drawers [Fr. *chiffon*, a rag].

chig·ger (chig'·ẽr) *n.* a flea.

chi·gnon (shēn'·yäng) *n.* a rolled-up pad or bun of hair at the back of a woman's head or on the nape of the neck [Fr.].

chil·blain (chil'·blān) *n.* an inflammatory swelling caused by cold and bad circulation [fr. *chill* and *blain*].

child (chīld) *n.* a very young person of either sex; offspring; descendant; *pl.* **children** (chil'·drin) offspring, descendants. **-birth** *n.* the act of bearing a child. **-bearing** *n.* producing children. **-bed** *n.* childbirth. **-hood** *n.* the state of being a child; the time during which one is a child. **-ish** *a.* pert. to a child; silly; trifling. **-ishly** *adv.* **-ishness** *n.* **-less** *a.* **-lessness** *n.* **-like** *a.* like a child; innocent; trustful. **with child**, pregnant [O.E. *cild*].

chil·i, chilli (chil'·i·) *n.* the red pepper, or fruit of the capsicum, called Cayenne pepper when dried and ground [Mex.].

chill (chil) *a.* cold; tending to cause shivering; cool in manner or feeling; discouraging; *n.* a feeling of coldness, attended with shivering; illness caused by cold; discouragement; *v.t.* to cool; to cause to shiver; to benumb; to dispirit; to keep cold; *v.i.* to grow cold. **-y,** cold; creating cold; depressing; ungenial. **-iness** *n.* [O.E. *cele, ciele*, coldness].

chime (chīm) *n.* the musical sound of bells; a set of bells tuned to the musical scale (generally used in the plural); *v.t.* and *i.* to sound harmoniously; to be in harmony; to agree with [M.E. *chimbe*, orig. = *cymbal*].

chi·me·ra, chimaera (ki·mi'·ra) *n.* a fabulous, fire-breathing monster; a creature of the imagination. **chimeric(al)** *a.* [Gk. *chimaira*].

chim·ney (chim'·ni·) *n.* the passage through which the smoke of a fireplace, etc., is carried off; a glass tube around the flame of a lamp. **— sweep** *n.* one who removes the soot from chimneys [Gk. *kaminos*, a furnace].

chim·pan·zee (chim·pan'·zē) *n.* a large African anthropoid ape [W. Africa].

chin (chin) *n.* the part of the face below the mouth; *v.t.* to chat; to raise oneself on a horizontal bar so that the chin is level with the bar. *pr.t.* **-ning.** *pa.t.* **-ned** [O.E. *cin*].

Chi·na (chī'·na) *n.* a vast country in E. Asia; (*l.c.*) a translucent, vitreous ceramic ware; porcelain. **-man** *n.* a native of China. **Chinese** (chī·nēz') *n.* a native, the natives, or the language of China; *a.* **-ware** *n.* dishes of china.

chin·chil·la (chin·chil'·a) *n.* a small animal, with very fine, soft fur; the fur itself; a heavy woolen material used esp. for coats [Sp.].

chine (chīn) *n.* the backbone or spine of an animal; a piece of the backbone, with the flesh, cut for cooking [Fr. *échine*, the spine].

chink (chingk) *n.* a small cleft, rent, or fissure; a gap or crack; *v.t.* to open; *v.i.* to crack [O.E. *cinu*, a fissure].

chink (chingk) *n.* the sound of a piece of metal when struck; the ring of coin; *v.i.* to ring.

Chi·nook (chi·nook') *n.* a tribe of N.W. American Indians; (*l.c.*) a wind; a kind of Salmon.

chintz (chintz) *n.* a printed cotton cloth, glazed or unglazed [Hind. *chint*].

chip (chip) *v.t.* to chop off into small pieces; to break little pieces from; to shape by cutting off pieces, *v.i.* to break or fly off in small pieces; *pr.p.* **-ping.** and *pa.t.* **-ped** *n.* a piece of wood, etc. separated from a larger body by an axe, etc.; a fragment; a counter, instead of money, used in gambling. **-s** *n.pl.*

fried slices of potato; (*Naut.*) a ship's carpenter. **-per** *a.* (*Colloq.*) cheerful; lively. **— shot** *n.* (*Golf*) a short, lofted shot onto the green. **— in,** *v.t.* to contribute [fr. E. *chop*].

chip·munk (chip'·mungk) *n.* a burrowing ground-squirrel or striped gopher [Native].

chip·pen·dale (chip'·pan·dāl) *n.* a style of furniture [fr. cabinet-maker *Chippendale*].

chi·ro- (kī'·rō) prefix fr. Gk. *cheir*, the hand, combining to form derivatives.

chi·ro·man·cy (kī'·rō·man·si·) *n.* divination by inspection of the hand; palmistry [Gk. *cheir*, the hand; *manteia*, divination].

chi·rop·o·dist (ki·ráp'·ạ·dist) *n.* one skilled in the treatment of diseases of the feet. **chiropody** *n.* [Gk. *cheir*, hand; *podos*, foot].

chi·ro·prac·tic (kī·rạ·prak'·tik) *n.* a method of healing which relies upon the removal of nerve interference by manual adjustment of the spine. **chiropractor** *n.* [Gk. *cheir*, hand; *prassein*, to do].

chirp, chir·rup (churp, chir'·ạp) *n.* a short, sharp note, as of a bird or cricket; *v.i.* to make such a sound; to twitter; to talk gaily.

chis·el (chiz'·al) *n.* a tool sharpened to a cutting edge at the end, used in carpentry, sculpture, etc.; *v.i.* to cut or carve with this tool; (*Slang*) to cheat [O.Fr. *cisel*].

chit (chit) *n.* an informal note; a voucher; a permit or pass [Hind. *chitthi*].

chit-chat (chit'·chat) *n.* prattle; trivial talk.

chi·tin (kī'·tin) *n.* a white, horny substance, forming the outer covering of insects, crustacea, etc. *a.* [Gk. *chiton*, a tunic].

chit·ter·lings (chit'·er·lingz) *n.pl.* the smaller intestines of swine, etc., used as food.

chiv·al·ry (shiv'·al·ri·) *n.* the system of knighthood in medieval times; the qualities of a knight, viz. dignity, courtesy, bravery, generosity, gallantry. **chivalric, chivalrous** *a.* pert. to chivalry. **chivalrously** *adv.* [Fr. *chevalerie*, fr. *cheval*, a horse].

chive (chīv) *n.* a small herb of the onion kind [L. *cepa*, an onion].

chlor-, chlo·ro- (klōr) combining forms fr. Gk. *chloros*, green; also denoting chlorine.

chlo·rine (klō'·rēn) *n.* a heavy gas of yellowish-green color used in disinfecting, bleaching, and poison-gas warfare. **chloral** *n.* a sleep-producing drug. **chlorate** *n.* a salt of chloric acid. **chloric** *a.* pert. to chlorine. **chloride** *n.* a compound of chlorine with another element. **chlorinate** *v.t.* disinfect, bleach, or combine with chlorine. **chlorination** *n.* **chlorite** *n.* a mineral of a green color, soft and friable. **chloroform** *n.* a colorless, volatile liquid used as an anesthetic; *v.t.* to make insensible by using chloroform [Gk. *chloros*, pale-green].

chlo·ro·phyll (klō'·rạ·fil) *n.* (*Bot.*) the green coloring matter of plants [Gk. *chloros*, palegreen; *phullon*, a leaf].

chock (chàk) *n.* a wedge to steady a wheel or a cask lying on its side; *v.t.* to make fast, with a block or wedge. **-ful** *a.* packed [fr. *choke*].

choc·o·late (chàk'·ạ·lit) *a.* a paste or hard cake made from the powdered seeds of the cacao plant, mixed with sugar, etc.; a beverage made by pouring boiling water or milk over this; candy; *a.* dark brown [Mex. Sp.].

choice (chois) *n.* the act of choosing; the power or opportunity of choosing; selection; the thing chosen; alternative; *a.* worthy of being chosen; rare; superior [Fr. *choisir*, to choose].

choir (kwīr) *n.* a company of singers, esp. belonging to a church; that part of the church set apart for them [L. *chorus*].

choke (chōk) *v.t.* to stop the breath as by compression of the windpipe; to stifle or smother; *v.i.* to have the wind-pipe stopped; to be suffocated; *n.* the act of choking; an obstructing piece in mechanism; a valve regulating the proportion of gas to air in a motor. **-r.** *n.* one who chokes; something worn closely about the neck, as beads, etc. [M.E. *choken*].

chol·er (kàl'·ẽr) *n.* bile; anger; wrath. **choleric** *a.* passionate; easily angered. **cholera** *n.* deadly, epidemic, bilious disease, marked by purgings, vomiting and gripping pains. [Fr. *colère*, anger, fr. Gk. *cholē*, bile].

cho·les·ter·ol (kạ·les'·ta·rōl) *n.* a fatlike substance found in bile, gallstones, blood, and the brain, also in egg yolks, etc. [Gk. *cholē*, bile; *stereos*, solid].

cho·lic (kol'·ik) *a.* pert. to, or obtained from, bile [Gk. *cholē*, bile].

choose (chooz) *v.t.* to pick out; to select; to take one thing in preference to another; *v.i.* to decide; to think fit. *pa.p.* **chosen;** *pa.t.* **chose. choosey** *a.* (*Slang*) fastidious, difficult to please [O.E. *ceosan*].

chop (chàp) *n.* (usually *pl.*) the jaw of an animal; the jaw of a vise [etym. uncertain].

chop (chàp) *v.t.* to cut into pieces; to mince, by striking repeatedly with a sharp instrument; to sever by blows; *v.i.* to make a quick stroke or repeated strokes with a sharp instrument, as an axe; *n.* the act of chopping; a piece chopped off; a thick slice of meat attached to a rib or other bone; a cutlet. *pr.p.* **-ping.** *pa.p.* and *pa.t.* **-ped. -per** *n.* one who chops; a large heavy knife; cleaver. **-py** *a.* full of fissures; of the sea, having short, broken waves.

chop sticks (chàp stiks) *n.* one of two small sticks of wood, ivory, etc. used by the Chinese in taking food.

chop su·ey (chàp sóò'·i·) also **chop sooey.** A Chinese-American dish of meat, bean sprouts, etc. [fr. Chin.].

cho·ral (kō'·ral) *a.* pert. or belonging to a choir or chorus. **-ly** *adv.* **choric** *a.* pert. to a chorus, esp. Greek dramatic chorus. [Gk. *choros*, a band of dancers and singers].

cho·rale (kō·rȧl') *n.* a simple, dignified melody sung to religious words [Gk. *choros*].

chord (kawrd) *n.* the string of a musical instrument; (*Mus.*) a series of tones having a harmonic relation to each other, when, and sounded simultaneously; (*Geom.*) a straight line between two points in the circumference of a circle [Gk. *chordē*, a string].

chore (chōr) *n.* any odd job, or occasional piece of housework; (*pl.*) routine work [O.E. *cerr*, work].

cho·re·a (kō·rē'·ạ) *n.* (*Med.*) uncontrollable spasms of limbs, body and facial muscles; St. Vitus's dance [Gk. *choreia*, a dancing].

cho·re·og·ra·phy (kō·ri·á'·gra·fi·) *n.* ballet dancing; the art of creating dance compositions for ballet. **choreographer** *n.* **choreographic** *a.* [Gk. *choros*, dance; *graphein*, to write].

chor·is·ter (kawr'·is·ẽr) *n.* a choir member.

cho·rog·ra·phy (kō·rág'·ra·fi·) *n.* the art of making a map, or writing a description, of a region or country. **chorology** *n.* the study of the geographical distribution of plants and animals [Gk. *chora*, land; *graphein*, to write].

chor·tle (chawr'·tl) *v.i.* to chuckle gleefully. **chortling** *n.* [invented by Lewis Carroll from *chuckle* and *snort*].

cho·rus (kō'·rạs) *n.* orig. a band of singers and dancers; a combination of voices singing together; what is sung or spoken by the chorus; in a Greek play, certain performers who witness the action, and at intervals express their feelings regarding it; the refrain; *v.t.* to join in the refrain; to call out or sing together. **choric** *a.* pert. to a chorus [Gk. *choros*, a band of dancers and singers].

chose (chōz) *pa.t.* of **choose.**

chosen (chō'·zn)*pa.p.* of **choose.**

chow·der (chou'·der) *n.* a stew made of fish, pork, onions, etc. [Fr. *chaudièr*, a pot].

Christ (krist) *n.* The Anointed — a name given to Jesus of Nazareth. **-like, -ly** *a.* resembling Christ [Gk. = anointed].

chris·ten (kris'·n) *v.t.* to baptize in the name of Christ; to give a name to. **Christendom** *n.* all Christian countries; the whole body of Christians. **-ing** *n.* baptism [Gk.].

Chris·tian (kris'·chạn) *n.* a follower or disciple of Christ; a professed adherent of the Church of Christ; *a.* pert. to Christ or his religion. **-ize** *v.t.* to make Christian; to convert to Christianity. **Christianity** *n.* the religion of the followers of Christ. **— era,** the era counting from the birth of Christ. **— name,** the name given at baptism; individual name, as opposed to surname or family name.

— Science, a religious doctrine of faithhealing founded in America by Mrs. Mary Eddy [Gk. *Christos*, anointed].

Christ·mas (kris'·mạs) the annual celebration of the birth of Christ, observed on Dec. 25 [E. *Christ* and *Mass*].

chrom- (krōm) combining form fr. Gk. *chroma*, color; word element referring to chromium.

chro·mat·ic (krō·mat'·ik) *a.* pert. to color; (*Mus.*) proceeding by semitones. **-s** *n.* the science of colors; (*Mus.*) chromatic notes. **-ally** *adv.* [Gk. *chroma*, color].

chrome, chro·mi·um (krōm, krō'·mi·um) *n.* a metal, very resistant to corrosion, used generally for plating other metals. **chromic** *a.* pert. to, or obtained from, chrome or chromium. **chromate** *n.* a salt of chromic acid. **chromite** *n.* a mineral, the chief source of chromium [Gk. *chroma*, color].

chro·mo·some (krō'·mạ·sōm) *n.* (*Biol.*) one of the gene-carrying bodies in the tissue of a cell, regarded as the transmitter of hereditary factors from parent to child [Gk. *chroma*, color; *soma*, a body].

chromosome

chron·ic (krän'·ik) a. continuing for a long time; of disease, deep-seated and lasting; confirmed; inveterate. **-ally** [Gk. *chronos*, time].

chron·i·cle (krän'·i·kl) n. a register of events in order of time; a history or account; v.t. to record in order of time. **-r** n. [Gk. *chronika*, annals, fr. *chronos*, time].

chro·no- (krän'·a) a combining form fr. Gk. *chronos*, time. **-graph** n. an instrument for measuring and recording time very exactly. **chronology** (kra·nä'·la·ji·) n. the science that treats of historical dates and arranges them in order; a table of events and dates. **chronologer, chronologist** n. one who records historical events, etc. **chronological** a. arranged in order of time. **chronologically** alv. **chronometer** n. a very accurate watch or time-keeper. **-metric, -metrical** a. **chronometry** n. the process of measuring time by instruments.

chrys·a·lis (kris'·a·lis) n. the case in which a caterpillar encloses itself before it becomes a butterfly or moth; pl.**chrysalides** (kris·al'·i·dēz) **chrysalid** a. [Gk. *chrusos*, gold].

chrys·an·the·mum (kris·an'·tha·mam) n. a mop-headed garden flower [Gk. *chrusos*, gold; *anthemon*, a flower].

chry·so- (kris'·a) a combining form fr. Gk. *chrusos*, gold. **chrysocracy** (kris·ak'·ra·si·) n. the rule of wealth. **chrysolite** n. a yellowish-green precious stone. **chrysoprase** (kris'·a·prāz) used as a gem.

chub (chub) n. a fish of the carp family, small and fat. **-by** a. round and plump. **-biness** n. [M.E. *chubbe*].

chuck (chuk) v.t. (Colloq.) to throw; to toss; to tap under the chin; n. a toss; a pat under the chin.

chuck (chuk) n. in machinery, part of a lathe for holding an object while it is being operated on; a cut of beef from the neck to the shoulder blade [etym. uncertain].

chuck·le (chuk'·l) v.i. to laugh in a suppressed manner; n. a short, quiet laugh [imit. origin].

chuck·le·head (chuk'·l·hed) n. a dolt, a lout [E. *chock*, a block].

chug (chug) n. an explosive sound made by an engine exhaust; v.i. to make an explosive sound. pa p., pa.t. **-ged**. pr.p. **-ging**.

chum (chum) n. an intimate friend; a pal; a roommate; v.i. to be friendly (with); to share a room with. pr.p. **-ming**. pa.p. and pa.t. **med.** **-my** a. friendly; sociable.

chump (chump) n. a lump of wood; the thick end of anything; (Slang) a blockhead.

chunk (chungk) n. a short, thick piece of wood, etc. **-y** a. [etym. uncertain].

church (church) n. building for Christian worship; collective body of Christians; a denomination or sect of the Christian religion; the clergy; the church service; v.t. to bring to church. **-goer** n. one who attends church regularly. **-ly** a. **-man** n. an ecclesiastic; a member of a church. **-warden** n. an officer entrusted with the interests of the church or parish. **-yard** n. the ground adjoining a church [O.E. *circe*, belonging to the Lord].

churl (churl) n. a countryman. **-ish** a. **-ishly** adv. **-ishness** n. [O.E. *ceorl*, a man].

churn (churn) n. a vessel in which cream is violently stirred to produce butter; v.t. to agitate cream so as to produce butter; to stir up violently; v.i. to produce butter [O.E. *cyrin*].

chute (shōot) n. a rapid descent in a river; a rapid; a sloping contrivance for transferring coal, rubbish, etc. to a lower level [Fr. *chute*, a fall].

chut·ney, chutnee (chut'·ni·) n. an E. Indian condiment, generally made with mangoes, peppers and spices [Hind. *chatni*].

ci·ca·da, cicala (si·kä'·da, si·kä'·la) n. an insect, the male of which emits a shrill, chirping sound [L. *cicada*, a cricket].

cic·a·trix, cicatrice (sik'·a·triks) n. a scar left after a healed wound; pl. **cicatrices** (sik·a·trī'·sēz) **cicatrize** (sik'·a·trīz) v.t. to heal and induce the formation of new tissue [L.].

cic·e·ro·ne (sis·a·rō'·ni·) n. one who shows strangers over a place, as a cathedral, etc.; a guide [It. fr. L. *Cicero*].

ci·der (sī'·der) n. a drink made from the juice of apples [Heb. *shakar*, to be intoxicated].

ci·gar (si·gär') n. tobacco leaf made up in a roll for smoking. **-ette** n. finely cut tobacco rolled in thin paper [Fr. *cigarillo*].

cil·i·a (sil'·i·a) n.pl. the eyelashes; (Anat.) hair-like, vibratile processes. **ciliary, ciliate, ciliated, ciliferous, ciliform** a. [L.].

cinch (sinch) n. a saddle-girth; (Slang) a certainty; v.t. to fasten a cinch around; to tighten (girth) [L. *cingula*, a girth].

cin·cho·na (sin·kō'·na) n. a genus of trees from which quinine is extracted; the bark. **-ceous** (sin·ka·nā'·shas) a. [Sp. fr. Countess of Chinchon, who was cured by it in 1638].

cinc·ture (singk'·cher) n. a belt; a girdle; a zone; v.t. to encircle. **-d** a. [L. *cinctura*, a girdle].

cin·der (sin'·der) n. the remains of burned coal; any partially burned combustible substance [O.E. *sinder*].

cin·e·ma (sin'·a·ma) n. a hall or theater where moving pictures are shown; a motion picture; **-scope** n. a wide, panoramic motion picture screen. **-tography** n. **-tographer** n. [Gk. *kinema*, movement].

cin·er·ar·y (sin'·a·re·ri·) a. pert. to ashes; made to hold ashes. **cinerarium** n. (pl. -raria) n. a place for ashes after cremation. **cineration** n. a reducing to ashes; incineration [L. *cinerarius*, ashy].

cin·na·bar (sin'·a·bår) n. red sulphide of mercury used as a pigment; vermilion; a. vermilion colored [Gk. *kinnabari*, vermilion].

cin·na·mon (sin'·a·man) n. the inner bark of a laurel tree of Ceylon; an aromatic substance obtained from the bark, used as a spice; n. and a. a light-brown color [Heb. *qinnamon*].

ci·pher, cy·pher (sī'·fer) n. the arithmetical symbol 0; any figure; a person of no account; a secret writing; a code; the key to a code; v.i. to write in cipher; to work at arithmetic [Fr. *chiffre*, a figure].

cir·ca (sur'·ka) prep. about; around; approximately; (abbrev.) **ca.** or **c.** [L. *circa, circiter*].

cir·cle (sur'·kl) n. a plane figure bounded by a single curved line called its circumference, every point of which is equally distant from a point within called the center; the curved line that bounds such a figure, a circumference; a round body; a sphere; an orb; a ring; the company associated with a person; a society group; club or group, esp. literary; a never-ending series; v.t. to move or revolve round; to encompass, as by a circle; to surround; v.i. to move in a circle [L. *circulus*].

cir·cuit (sur'·kit) n. the act of moving round; the space enclosed within a fixed limit; area; (Law) the round made by judges holding court; the district thus visited; the path of an electric current. **-eer** (sur·ki·tir') one who moves in a circuit. **circuitous** (sur·kū'·i·tas) a. indirect [L. *circuitus*, a going round].

cir·cu·lar (sur'·kya·lar) a. in the form of a circle; round; moving in a circle; roundabout; addressed to a circle of people; n. a notice sent out in quantities. **-ly** adv. **circularity** n. **-ize** v.t. to send circulars to [L. *circularis*].

cir·cu·late (sur'·kya·lāt) v.t. to cause to pass round as in a circle; to spread abroad; v.i. to move around and return to the same point; to be spread abroad. **circulation** n. the act of moving around; the flow of blood from, and back to, the heart; the extent of sale of a newspaper, etc.; the money circulating in a country; currency. **circulative, circulatory** a. circulating. **circulator** n. [L. *circulare*].

cir·cum- (sur·kam) prefix fr. Latin meaning round, about, combining to form many derivatives as in **-ambient** a. surrounding; enclosing. **-ambiency** n. environment. **-ambulate** v.t. and i. to walk around or about [L. *ambire*, to go round; *ambulare*, to walk].

cir·cum·cise (sur'·kam·sīz) v.t. to cut off the foreskin. **circumcision** n. [L. *circum; caedere*, to cut].

cir·cum·fer·ence (ser·kum'·fer·ans) n. the line that bounds a circle; the distance around; area. **circumferential** a. [L. *circum; ferre*, to carry].

cir·cum·flex (sur'·kam·fleks) n. an accent mark placed over a vowel to denote length, contraction, etc. [L. *circum; flectere*, to bend].

cir·cum·flu·ent (sur·kam'·flōō·ant) a. flowing round. **circumfluence** n. [L. *circum; fluere*, to flow].

cir·cum·ja·cent (sur·kam·jā'·sant) a. bordering on every side [L. *circum; facere*, to lie].

cir·cum·lo·cu·tion (sur·kam·lō·kū'·shan) n. a roundabout manner of speaking. **circumlocutory** a. [L. *circum; locutos*, to speak].

cir·cum·nav·i·gate (sur·kam·nav'·i·gāt) v.t. to sail around. **circumnavigable** a. capable of being sailed round. **circumnavigation** n. **circumnavigator** n. one who sails around, esp. the world [L. *circum; navigare*, to sail].

cir·cum·scribe (sur'·kam·skrīb) v.t. to draw a circle around; to enclose within limits; to confine; to define. **circumscription** n. limitation. **circumscriptive** a. confined or limited in space [L. *circum; scribere*, to write].

cir·cum·spect (sur'·kam·spekt) a. watchful on all sides; prudent; discreet. **-ly** adv. **circumspection** n. caution; prudence; discretion; tact. **-ive** a. [L. *circum; spicere*, to look].

cir·cum·stance (sur'·kam·stans) n. a particular fact, event, or case; anything attending on, relative to, or affecting, a fact or event; accident; incident; particular; act; to place in a particular situation. **-s** n.pl. worldly estate; condition as to pecuniary resources; situation; position; details. **circumstantial** a. accidental; not essential; full of details; minute. **circumstantially** adv. **circumstantiality** n. minuteness of detail. **circumstantiate** v.t. to detail exactly [L. *circum; stare*, to stand].

cir·cum·vent (sur·kam·vent') v.t. to get around by stratagem; to outwit; to go around. **-ion** n. **-ive** a. [L. *circum; venire*, to come].

cir·cus (sur'·kas) n. a travelling company of performers, animals, etc.; a circular enclosure for performances; the performance itself [L.].

cir·rho·sis (si·rō'·sis) n. (Med.) hardening and enlargement of the liver. **cirrhotic** a. [Gk. *kirrhos*, tawny].

cir·rus (sir'·as) n. a tendril; a curled filament; a lofty, fleecy cloud; pl. **cirri** (sir'·ī) (L. *cirrus*, a curl of hair).

cis·tern (sis'·tern) n. a large tank for holding water; a reservoir [L. *cisterna*].

cit·a·del (sit'·a·del) n. a fortress or castle in or near a city [It. *cittadella*].

cite (sīt) v.t. to summon; to quote; to name; to bring forward as proof. **citation** n. an official notice to appear; the act of quoting; the passage or words quoted; the mention of gallantry in military orders. **citator** n. **citatory** a. [L. *citare*].

cith·a·ra (sith'·a·ra) n. the ancient Greek lyre. **cithern, cittern** n. a kind of flat-backed guitar [Gk. *kithara*].

cit·i·zen (sit'·i·zn) n. an inhabitant of a city; a member of a state; a. having the character of a citizen. **-ry** n. citizens collectively. **-ship** n. the state of being a citizen; the rights and duties of a citizen [O.Fr. *citeain*].

cit·ron (sit'·ran) n. the fruit of the citron tree, resembling a lemon; the tree itself; the preserved rind of the fruit; a yellow color. **citrate** n. a salt of citric acid. **citric** a. extracted from the citron lemon, etc. **citrus fruits**, citrons, lemons, oranges, etc. [L. *citrus*, a citron-tree].

cit·ron·el·la (sit·ra·nel'·a) n. a sharp smelling oil to keep insects away [See citron].

cit·tern, cithern See cithara.

cit·y (sit'·i·) n. a large town; a corporate town; the business or shopping center of a town; a. pert. to a city [L. *civitas*, a city].

civ·et (siv'·it) n. a perfume, with a strong musk-like smell; the animal from which this perfume is obtained. Also, **— cat**. [Ar. *zabad*].

civ·ic (siv'·ik) a. pert. to a city or a citizen. **-s** n.pl. the study of civic affairs, municipal or national [L. *civis*, a citizen].

civ·il (siv'·il) a. pert. to city, state, or citizen; lay, as opposed to military, etc.; polite. **-ly** adv. **civilian** (sa·vil'·yan) n. one whose employment is non-military; a. pert. to civilian life (e.g. civilian dress). **civility** n. courtesy; politeness; pl. acts of politeness. **civil defense**, an organization to deal with civilians during air raids, etc. **civil engineer**, one who plans bridges, roads, dams, canals, etc. **civil service**, the government positions obtained by examination. **civil war**, war between citizens of the same country [L. *civis*, a citizen].

civ·i·lize (siv'·il·īz) v.t. to reclaim from a savage state; to refine; to enlighten. **-d** a. **civilization** n. the act of civilizing, or state of being civilized [L. *civilis*].

clack (klak) *v.i.* to make a sudden, sharp noise, as by striking; to talk rapidly and continually; to chatter; *n.* a sharp, repeated, rattling sound; continual talk [imit. origin].

clad (klad) *pa.p.* and *pa.t.* of **clothe**; *a.* clothed.

claim (klām) *v.t.* to demand as a right, or as due; to call for; to assert as true; *n.* the demand of a right or supposed right; a title; the thing claimed. **-ant** *n.* one who claims. **—jumper** *n.* one who seizes a piece of land marked out by a settler or miner [L. *clamare*, to shout].

clair·voy·ance (kler·voi'·ạns) *n.* the power of seeing things not normally perceptible to the senses; second sight. **clairvoyant** *n.* one who claims the power of clairvoyance. Also *a.* [Fr.].

clam (klam) *n.* an edible bivalve shell-fish; (*Colloq.*) a reticent person [O.E. *clam*, a bond].

cla·mant (klā'·mạnt) *a.* crying out; clamorous. **clamancy** *n.* [L. *clamare*, to cry out].

clam·ber (klam'·bẹr) *v.i.* to climb with difficulty, holding on with the hands [cf. Ger. *klammern*, to cling to].

clam·my (kla'·mi·) *a.* sticky and moist; cold and damp. **clamminess** *n.* [O.E. *claeman*, to anoint].

clam·or (klam'·ẹr) *n.* loud shouting; tumult; outcry; uproar; *v.i.* to shout loudly; to utter loud complaints or demands. **-ous** *a.* [L. *clamare*, to cry out].

clamp (klamp) *n.* any appliance with parts brought together by a screw for holding anything; a brace; *v.t.* to make firm [Dut. *klamp*].

clan (klan) *n.* a tribe bearing the same surname, united under a chieftain; a set or clique of persons having a common interest. **-nish** *a.* disposed to associate only with members of the same sect or clique. **-nishly** *adv.* **-nishness** *n.* [Gael. *clann*, children].

clan·des·tine (klan·des'·tin) *a.* secret, and contrary to law, morals, etc. **-ly** *adv.* **-ness** *n.* [L. *clandestinus*, fr. *clam*, secretly].

clang (klang) *v.t.* to strike with a ringing, metallic sound; *v.i.* to give forth a ringing, metallic sound; *n.* a sharp, ringing sound. **-ing** *n.* a clang [L. *clangere*].

clan·gor (klang'·ẹr) *n.* a loud harsh, ringing sound. **-ous** *a.* **-ously** *adv.* [L. *clangere*].

clank (klangk) *n.* a brief, hard, metallic sound; *v.t.* and *i.* to produce such a sound [imit.].

clap (klap) *v.t.* to bring together with a sharp sound; to strike the hands together in approval; to slap; *v.i.* to strike the hands together in applause; *n.* a sudden, sharp noise caused by impact; applause; a slap or pat; *pr.p.* **-ping.** *pa.p.* and *pa.t.* **-ped. -per** *n.* one who claps; the tongue of a bell. **-board** *n.* thin board used to cover wooden houses. **-trap** *n.* in speech-making, tricks to win applause; *a.* cheap and showy [M.E. *clap*].

clar·et (klar'·it) *n.* any red Bordeaux wine; *a.* a purplish-red. [Fr. *clairet*, fr. *clair*, clear].

clar·i·fy (klar'·i·fī) *v.t.* to make clear or pure; to explain or clear up; to remove possibility of error; *v.i.* to become clear. **clarification** *n.* **clarity** *n.* clearness; lucidity of mind [L. *clarus*, clear; *facere*, to make].

clar·i·on (klar'·i·ạn) *n.* trumpet with shrill piercing note; its sound. **clarinet, clarionet** *n.* a wood wind instrument. **clarinettist** *n.* [Fr. *clairon*].

clash (klash) *v.t.* to strike noisily together; *v.i.* to dash noisily together; to collide; to conflict; to disagree; *n.* a loud noise; a conflict [imit.].

clasp (klasp) *v.t.* to shut or fasten together with a catch or hook; to embrace; to grasp; to surround and cling to; *n.* a catch or hook for fastening; a close embrace; a grasping of the hands [M.E. *clapse*, fr. *clyppan*, to embrace].

class (klas) *n.* an order or division or grouping of persons or things possessing the same characteristics or status; a group of pupils or students taught together; a grouping of plants or animals; rank or standing in society. *v.t.* to arrange in classes; to rank together; *v.i.* to rank. **-able, -ible** *a.* **-y** *a.* (*Colloq.*) high-class [L. *classis*].

clas·sic (klas'·ik) *n.* a work, writer of recognized worth; an ancient Latin or Greek writer or book; *a.* of model excellence in literature or art; conforming to standards of Greek and Roman art. **-s** *n.pl.* ancient Latin or Greek literature. **-al** *a.* **-ally** *adv.* **ality, -alness** *n.* the quality of being classical. **classicism** (klas'·i·sizm) *n.* classic principles in art and literature; classic style; a classical idiom. **classicist** *n.* [L. *classicus*, of the first rank].

clas·si·fy (klas'·i·fī) *v.t.* to arrange in classes; to put into a class. **classifiable** *a.* **classification** *n.* the act of classifying [L. *classis*, a class; *facere*, to make].

clat·ter (klat'·ẹr) *v.t.* to strike and so make a rattling noise; *v.i.* to make rattling sounds; to prattle; to talk rapidly and idly; *n.* a repeated rattling noise; noisy and idle talk [fr. *clack*].

clause (klawz) *n.* (*Gram.*) a subordinate part of a sentence; (*Law*) an article or distinct portion of a document, contract, etc.; a paragraph; a subdivision [L. *claudere*, to shut].

claus·tral (klaws'·trạl) *a.* pert. to a cloister; cloister-like; secluded. **claustration** *n.* the state of being confined in a cloister [L. *claustrum*, a bar or bolt].

claus·tro·pho·bi·a (klaws·trạ·fō'·ạ) *n.* (*Med.*) a morbid dread of confined spaces [L. *claustrum*, bolt; Gk. *phobia*, fear].

clav·i·chord (kla'·vi·kawrd) *n.* a medieval musical instrument like a spinet [L. *clavis*, a key; *chorda*, a string].

clav·i·cle (klav'·i·kl) *n.* the collarbone. **clavicular** *a.* [L. *clavicula*, dim. fr. *clavis*, a key].

cla·vi·er (kla'·vyẹr) *n.* (*Mus.*) a stringed musical instrument with a keyboard [L. *clavis*, a key].

claw (klaw) *n.* a sharp, hooked nail, as of a beast or bird; anything like this; *v.t.* to pull, tear, or scratch with claws or nails; to grasp [O.E. *clawu*].

clay (klā) *n.* soft earth, consisting of alumina and silica, with water used in making pottery, bricks, etc.; earth in general; the human body. **-ey** *a.* consisting of clay; like clay [O.E. *claeg*].

clean (klēn) *a.* free from dirt, stain, or any defilement; pure; guiltless; *v.t.* to free from dirt; to purify; *adv.* so as to leave no dirt; quite; entirely. **-er** *n.* one who, or that which, cleans. **-liness** (klen'·li·nes) *n.* freedom from dirt; purity. **-ly** (klen'·li) *a.* habitually clean in persons and habits; pure. **-ly** (klēn'·li·) *adv.* in a clean manner; neatly. **-ness** (klēn'·nes) *n.* **—cut** *a.* well-shaped; definite. [O.E. *claene*].

clear (klēr) *a.* bright; free from cloud; undimmed; pure; free from obstruction; plain; distinct; manifest; without defect or drawback; transparent; *adv.* clearly; wholly; *v.t.* to make bright or clear; to make evident; to free from accusation; to acquit; to pass over or through; to cleanse; to empty; to make as profit; to free from difficulty, obstruction, suspicion, etc.; *v.i.* to become clear, bright, transparent, free; (*Naut.*) to leave a port. **-age** *n.* clearance. **-ance** *n.* the act of clearing; a certificate that a ship has been cleared at the custom house; in machinery, distance by which one part is clear of another. **-ing** *n.* a tract of land cleared of wood. **-ing-house** *n.* an office maintained by several banks for balancing accounts, exchanging checks, etc. **-ly** *adv.* **-ness** *n.* **—cut** *a.* sharply defined. **—eyed, —seeing, —sighted** *a.* having acuteness of sight or intellect [L. *clarus*, clear].

clear-sto·ry See clerestory.

cleat (klēt) *n.* a wedge; (*Naut.*) a piece of wood or iron with two projecting ends, round which ropes are fastened; a piece of metal fastened to a shoe [O.E. *cleat*].

cleave (klēv) *v.t.* to split asunder; to cut in two; *v.i.* to fall apart; to split; to open; to crack asunder; *pa.p.* **cloven** or **cleft. cleavage** *n.* of rocks, the quality of splitting naturally; (*Fig.*) separation due to a difference of opinions, etc.; a rupture. **-r** *n.* one who, or that which, cleaves; a butcher's chopper [O.E. *cleofan*].

cleave (klēv) *v.i.* to adhere closely; to stick; to agree; to be faithful to [O.E. *clifian*].

clef (klef) *n.* (*Mus.*) a sign used to indicate the pitch [Fr., fr. L. *clavis*, a key].

cleft (kleft) *pa.p.* and *pa.t.* of the verb **cleave**; *n.* a fissure or split; a chasm; a chink [O. E. *cleofan*].

clem·a·tis (klem'·ạ·tis) *n.* a woody vine [Gk. *klēmatis*, fr. *klēima*, a twig].

clem·en·cy (klem'·en·si·) *n.* leniency; mildness; gentleness; mercy. **clement** *a.* mild; compassionate [L. *clemens*].

clench, clinch (klensh, klinsh) *v.t.* to grasp firmly; to close together tightly (the hands, the teeth); to confirm (a bargain); *n.* a firm closing; decisive proof; a firm grip. **-er** *n.* an unanswerable argument [O.E. *clencean*].

clere·sto·ry (klēr'·stō·ri·) *n.* the upper part of the central nave of churches, which rises clear of the other buildings and has its own row of windows [fr. *clear* and *story*].

cler·gy (klur'·ji·) *n.* the body of men ordained for religious service. **-man** *n.* a minister [Fr. *clergé* fr. L. *clericus*].

cler·ic (kler'·ik) *n.* a clerk or clergyman; *a.* clerical. **clerical** *a.* belonging to the clergy; pert. to a clerk or copyist [L. *clericus*].

clerk (klurk) *n.* one who is employed to do correspondence, keep accounts, etc. in an office; salesman or saleswoman; *v.i.* to act as a clerk or secretary. **-ship** *n.* [O.E. *clerc*, a priest].

clev·er (klev'·ẹr) *a.* able; skillful; ingenious; intelligent. **-ly** *adv.* **-ness** *n.*

clew, clue (klōō) *n.* a ball of thread or cord; (*Myth.*) a ball of thread used as a guide through a maze; hence, anything that serves to guide one in an involved affair or helps to solve a mystery; (*Naut.*) the lower corner of a sail [O.E. *cliven*].

cli·ché (klē·shā') *n.* (*Print.*) an electrotype or stereotype plate; a stereotyped or hackneyed phrase [Fr.].

click (klik) *n.* a slight, short sound, as of a latch in a door; *v.i.* to make such a sound; (*Slang*) to be successful [imit. origin].

cli·ent (klī'·ạnt) *n.* one who employs another (esp. a lawyer) professionally as his agent; a customer. **clientele** (klī·en·tel) *n.* clients or customers collectively [L. *cliens*, a follower].

cliff (klif) *n.* a high rock-face; the sheer side of a mountain [O.E. *clif*].

cli·mac·ter·ic (klī·mak'·tạ·rik) *n.* a period in human life in which a change takes place in the constitution; the menopause; any critical period; *a.* pert. to a climacteric; critical. **-al** *a.* [Gk. *klimaktēr*, rung of a ladder].

cli·mate (klī'·mit) *n.* the general atmospherical conditions (temperature, moisture, etc.) of a country or region. **climatic** *a.* **climatical** *a.* [Gk. *klima, klimatos*, slope].

cli·max (klī'·maks) *n.* an arrangement of words, phrases, etc. such that they rise in rhetorical force and impressiveness; acme; the point of greatest excitement or tension in a play, story, etc. **climactic** *a.* [Gk. = a ladder].

climb (klīm) *v.t.* and *i.* to go up, ascend (as a hill, tree, etc.); to grow upward as a plant by tendrils; to rise in the social scale; to slope upward; *n.* an ascent. **-er** *n.* [O.E. *climban*].

clime (klīm) *n.* a region or country; (*Poet.*) climate [Gk. *klima*, fr. *klinein*, to slope].

clinch (klinsh) *v.t.* and *i.* to grapple or struggle at close quarters in wrestling or boxing; to fasten with a rivet; (*Fig.*) to settle or conclude, as an agreement; *n.* a close holding in wrestling or boxing; a rivet. **-er** *n.* [fr. *clench*].

cling (kling) *v.i.* to adhere or stick close to; to be attached firmly to; *pa.p.* and *pa.t.* **clung** [O.E. *clingan*].

clin·ic (klin'·ik) *n.* the teaching of medical subjects at the bedside; an institution where non-resident patients attend for treatment. **-al** *a.* [Gk. *klinē*, a bed].

clink (klingk) *n.* a slight, sharp, tinkling sound; (*Slang*) prison [imit. origin].

clink·er (kling'·kẹr) *n.* a mass of slag or cinders from furnaces; a kind of brick [Dut.].

clink·er-built (kling'·kẹr·bilt) *a.* (*Naut.*) built with overlapping boards or plates (opp. of *carvel-built*) [fr. *clench*].

clip (klip) *v.t.* to grip tightly. *pr.p.* **-ping.** *pa.t., pa.p.* **-ped.** *n.* any device for grasping or holding a thing firmly [O.E. *clyppan*, to embrace].

clip (klip) *v.t.* to cut with scissors or shears; to prune or cut short; to shear sheep; to pare the edge of a coin; to shorten or slur words; *v.i.* to move quickly; *n.* act of clipping; a season's shearing of wool; a sharp blow; (*Colloq.*) a sharp blow. *pr.p.* **-ping.** *pa.p.* and *pa.t.* **-ped. -per** *n.* one who clips; a fast sailing-vessel, with a long sharp bow; fast, long distance airliner. **-pers** *n.* a two-bladed instrument for cutting hair, shearing sheep, etc. **-ping** *n.* an item cut from a newspaper, etc. [Scand.].

clique (klik) *n.* a narrow circle of persons with common interests; a coterie. **cliquish** *a.* **cliquishness** *n.* [Fr.].

cloak (klōk) *n.* a long, loose, outer garment;

something that conceals; a pretext; *v.t.* to cover with a cloak; to hide; to mask or dissemble. **-room** *n.* a room where coats, hats, etc. may be temporarily left [O.Fr. *cloque*].

clob·ber (klǎb'·ẹr) *v.t.* (*Slang*) to beat decisively.

cloche (klōsh) *n.* glass covering used for intensive cultivation of vegetables, etc.; a close-fitting bell-shaped hat [Fr. = a bell].

clock (klǎk) *n.* a device which measures time. **-wise** *adv.* in the direction of the hands of a clock. **counterclockwise** *adv.* circling in the opposite direction. **-work** *n.* the movements or machinery of a clock; regular movement as of clock; *a.* mechanically regular. **o'clock**, by the clock [Fr. *cloche*, a bell].

clock (klǎk) *n.* an ornament worked on a stocking on each side of the ankle.

clod (klǎd) *n.* a lump of earth clay, or turf; the earth; a dull, stupid fellow. **-hopper** *n.* a rustic; a boor; a clumsy, heavy shoe [O.E. fr. *clot*].

clog (klǎg) *n.* a strong, clumsy shoe with a thick wooden sole; an impediment; an obstruction; *v.t.* to hinder; to encumber; to choke up; *v.i.* to become choked, encumbered. *pr.p.* **-ging** *pa.p. pa.t.* **-ged** [M.E. *clogge*, a block of wood].

clois·ter (klois'·tẹr) *n.* covered arcade running along one or more walls of the inner court of a monastery or college; a monastery or nunnery; a secluded spot; *v.t.* to confine. **-al, cloistral** *a.* **-ed** *a.* [L. *claustrum*, enclosed place].

close (klōz) *v.t.* to shut; to stop up; to finish; to conclude; to complete (a wireless circuit); *v.i.* to come together; to unite; to end. **closing** *a.* ending; *n.* the act of shutting. **closure** (klō'·zhẹr) *n.* the act of shutting; a closing; the close of a debate. [L. *claudere*, to shut].

close (klōs) *a.* shut up; confined; tight; stifling; near at hand; secret; niggardly; familiar; intimate; compact; crowded; searching; *adv.* in a close manner or state; nearly; tightly; *n.* an enclosed place; the precinct of a cathedral; (*Mus.*) a cadence. **-ly** *adv.* **-ness** *n.* — **by,** near. — **call,** a very narrow escape. — **fisted** or — **handed** *a.* miserly, penurious. — **mouthed** *a.* uncommunicative. — **quarters** *n.pl.* a crowded space. **a close shave,** a very narrow escape. —**up** *n.* a close view of anything [L. *claudere*, to shut].

clos·et (klǎz'·it) *n.* a small room or recess for storing things; a small private room; a lavatory; a water closet; *v.t.* to take into a private room for consultation [L. *claudere*, to shut].

clot (klǎt) *n.* a mass or lump, esp. of a soft, slimy character; (*Med.*) a coagulated mass of blood; *v.t.* to form into clots; *v.i.* to coagulate. *pr. p.* **-ting** *pa.p. pa.t.* **-ted** [O.E. *clod*].

cloth (klawth) *n.* any woven fabric of wool, hair, silk, cotton, flax, or other fibers; a cover for a table. *pl.* **cloths** (klawTHz). **the Cloth** (*Fig.*) clergymen [O.E. *clath*].

clothe (klōTH) *v.t.* to put garments on; to cover as with a garment; to furnish raiment; (*Fig.*) to surround with; to wrap up in. *pr.p.* **clothing.** *pa.p.* and *pa.t.* **-d** or **clad. -s** *n. pl.* garments; wearing apparel; short for bedclothes, i.e. sheets, blankets, etc. **clothier** (klōTH'·yẹr) *n.* one who makes, or sells, clothes; a tailor; an outfitter. **clothing** *n.* garments in general; dress; wearing-apparel; raiment. **clothes-horse** *n.* a frame for hanging clothes; one who likes clothes [O.E. *clath*].

clo·ture (klō'·chẹr) *n.* closure, applied to parliamentary debate [L. *clasura*, closure].

cloud (kloud) *n.* a body of visible vapor floating in the atmosphere; a mass of smoke, flying dust, etc.; that which has a dark, threatening aspect; a state of obscurity or impending trouble; a great multitude; *v.t.* to overspread with clouds; to darken; to sadden; to defame; *v.i.* to grow cloudy; to be blurred. **-y** *a.* darkened with clouds; overcast; hazy; dim; blurred; indistinct; gloomy. **-ily** *adv.* **-iness** *n.* **-burst** *n.* a violent downpour of rain; a deluge [O.E. *clud*].

clout (klout) *n.* the center of the target at which archers shoot; (*Colloq.*) a slap or blow; a piece of old cloth used for cleaning, scouring, etc.; *v.t.* (*Colloq.*) to strike with the open hand [O.E. *clut*].

clove (klōv) *n.* the flower-bud of the clove-tree, used as a spice; also yields oil [Fr. *clou*, a nail, fr. L. *clavus*].

clove (klōv) *pa.t.* of **cleave.**

clove hitch (klōv'·hich) *n.* (*Naut.*) a hitch used to secure a rope around a spar.

clo·ven (klōv'·n) *pa.p.* of **cleave.** Also *a.* split; divided into two parts [fr. *cleave*].

clo·ver (klō'·vẹr) *n.* a common field plant of the trefoil family, used for fodder. **-leaf** *n.* a highway intersection in the shape of a four-leaf clover [O.E. *clafre*].

clown (kloun) *n.* the fool or buffoon in a play or circus; a peasant or rustic; an ill-bred man; a boor; *v.i.* to play the fool; to behave like a fool. **-ishly** *adv.* **-ishness** *n.*

cloy (kloi) *v.t.* to induce a sensation of loathing by overmuch of anything, esp. of sweetness, sentimentality, or flattery; to satiate. **-ing** *a.* satiating; disgusting [Fr. *clouer*, to nail].

club (klub) *n.* a heavy stick, thickening towards one end, used as a weapon; a cudgel; a stick used in the game of golf; an association of people united in pursuance of a common interest; the premises in which such an association meets; *v.t.* to beat with a club; to gather into a club; *v.i.* to form a club; to unite for a common end; to pay shares in a common expense. *pr.p.* **-bing.** *pa.p.* and *pa.t.* **-bed. -foot** *n.* a congenitally deformed or crooked foot; talipes [O.N. *klubba*].

clump (klump) *n.* a shapeless mass of any substance; a cluster of trees or shrubs; a heavy extra sole on a shoe; a tramping sound; *v.t.* to put in a clump or group; *v.i.* to tramp heavily [Dut. *klomp*].

clum·sy (klum'·zi·) *a.* ill-made; awkward; ungainly. **clumsily** *adv.* **clumsiness** *n.* [M.E. *clumsen*, to benumb].

clung (klung) *pa.p.* and *pa.t.* of **cling.**

clus·ter (klus'·tẹr) *n.* a bunch; a number of things growing together, as grapes; a collection; *v.t.* to collect into a bunch; *v.i.* to grow, or be, in clusters [O.E. *clyster*].

clutch (kluch) *v.t.* and *i.* to seize or grip with the hand; to grasp; *n.* a grasp; a tight grip; a set of eggs hatched at one time; a brood of chicks; the coupling of two working parts, used in motor vehicles to connect or disconnect engine and transmission gear. **-es** *n.pl.* the claws; the hands; power [O.E. *clyccan*].

clut·ter (klut'·ẹr) *n.* crowded confusion; disorder; noise; *v.t.* to crowd together in disorder; to make untidy [origin uncertain].

co- (kō) *prefix* meaning together, joint, etc. [fr. L. *cum*, with].

coach (kōch) *n.* a railroad passenger car; a tutor who prepares students for examination; a trainer in athletics; *v.i.* to travel in a coach; *v.t.* to tutor or train [Fr. *coche*, a coach].

co·ac·tion (kō·ak'·shạn) *n.* compulsion [L. *cogere, coactum,* to compel].

co·ad·ju·tant (kō·aj'·oo·tạnt) *a.* assisting; *n.* an assistant. **coadjutor** (·tẹr) *n.* an assistant; an associate and destined successor [L. *co-*, together; *adjuvare*, to help].

co·ag·u·late (kō·ag'·yạ·lāt) *v.t.* to cause to curdle or congeal; to solidify; *v.i.* to curdle; to clot. **coagulant** *n.* a substance that causes coagulation. **coagulation** *n.* **coagulative** *a.* [L. *co-*, together; *agere*, to drive].

coal (kōl) *n.* a black substance used for fuel, composed of mineralized vegetable matter; a piece of this substance; *v.t.* to supply with coal; *v.i.* to take in coal. **-s** *n.pl.* glowing embers. — **bin** *n.* a recess for storing coal. — **field** *n.* a district where coal abounds. — **gas** *n.* gases produced from the distillation of coal or from burning coal. — **mine,** — **pit** *n.* the excavation from which coal is dug. — **oil** *n.* kerosene. — **tar** *n.* a thick, sticky substance, produced during the distilling of coal [O.E. *col*].

co·a·lesce (kō·ạ·les') *v.t.* to grow together; to unite into one body or mass; to fuse. **coalescent** *a.* coalescing. **coalescence** *n.* [L. *co-*, together; *alescere*, to grow up].

co·a·li·tion (kō·ạ·lish'·ạn) *n.* a union or combination of persons, parties, or states into one body; a league. **-ist** *n.* [L. *co-*, together; *alescere*, to grow up].

coarse (kōrs) *a.* rough, rude; not refined; without grace or elegance; ill-mannered; vulgar; inferior. **-ly** *adv.* **-n** *v.t.* and *i.* to make or become coarse. **-ness** *n.* [M.E. *cors*; Fr. *gros*].

coast (kōst) *n.* land bordering the sea; the seashore; the country near the shore; *v.t.* and *i.* to sail near or along the coast; to run shut off, or on a bicycle without pedaling; to toboggan. **-al** *a.* pert. to the coast. **-er** *n.* a vessel trading between towns along the coast; a small tray placed under glasses to protect a table. **-guard** *n.* a service organized orig. to prevent smuggling; since 1925, largely a life-saving service; a member of this service. **-line** *n.* the outline of a coast. **-wards** *adv.* toward the coast. **-wise** *adv.* along the coast [L. *costa*, a rib].

coat (kōt) *n.* an outer garment; a jacket; an overcoat; the fur or skin of an animal; a covering; a layer spread over another, as paint; *v.t.* to cover with a coat; to clothe. **-ed** *a.* **-ing** *n.* any covering; a layer; cloth for making coats [Fr. *cotte*, an overall].

coax (kōks) *v.t.* to win over by fond pleading or flattery. **-ingly** *adv.* [etym. uncertain].

co·ax·i·al (kō·ak'·si·ạl) *a.* having a common axis [fr. *axis*].

cob (kob) *n.* a corn-cob; a male swan.

co·balt (kō'·bawlt) *n.* a metallic element classified with iron and nickel, and used as an ingredient of many alloys. **-blue** *n.* a pigment containing an oxide of cobalt. **-ic** *a.* [Ger. *Kobalt*].

co·balt bomb *n.* a type of atomic bomb equal in power to the hydrogen bomb and with more lethal and lasting effects.

cob·ble (kab'·l) *v.t.* to mend or patch coarsely; to mend boots or shoes. **-r** *n.* a mender of shoes; a deep-dish fruit pie with a biscuit crust.

cob·ble (kab'·l) *n.* a stone rounded by the action of water; *v.t.* to pave with cobbles. **-stone** *n.* a rounded stone used in paving.

co·bra (kō'·bra) *n.* the venomous 'hooded' snake of Africa and India. **cobric** *a.* [L. *colubra*, a snake].

cob·web (kab'·web) *n.* a spider's web; anything flimsy, transparent, and fragile; a trap or entanglement [O.E. *coppe*, a spider].

co·ca (kō'·kạ) *n.* a Peruvian plant or its dried leaf, which is a nerve stimulant. **cocaine** (kō·kān') *n.* a drug made from coca leaves, used as a local anesthetic [Native].

coc·cyx (kak'·siks) *n.* the triangular bone ending spinal column. *pl.* **coccyges** (kak'·si·jēz). **coccygeal** *a.* [Gk. *kokkux*, cuckoo].

coch·i·neal (kak'·i·nēl) *n.* a scarlet dye-stuff, made from the dried bodies of insects [L. *coccineus*, scarlet].

coch·le·a (kak'·li·a) *n.* a spiral passage of the inner ear [Gk. *kochlias*, a snail from the shape of its shell].

cock (kak) *n.* the male of birds, esp. of the domestic fowl; a weather-cock; a tap to regulate the flow of fluids; the hammer of a firearm; the cocked position of a hammer (of a firearm); a chief or leader; *v.t.* to draw back the hammer of a gun; to set up, set erect, set at an angle, as a hat; *v.i.* (*Dial.*) to swagger. **-crow** *n.* early morning. **-erel** *n.* a young cock; a swaggering youth. **-eyed** *a.* squinting; (*Slang*) on a slant; foolish. **-scomb** *n.* the comb of a cock; a flowering plant. **-sure** *a.* quite sure. **-tail** *n.* a horse not of pure breed; a drink concocted of liquor, bitters, sugar, etc; a mixture of fruit, or of seafood, served as an appetizer. **-y** *a.* vain and confident; full of self-assurance. **-ily** *adv.* **-iness** *n.* [O.E. *coc*].

cock (kak) *n.* a pile of hay [O.E. *coc*].

cock·ade (ka·kād') *n.* a knot of ribbons, a rosette or badge, often worn on the hat [Fr. *cocarde*, fr. *coq*, a cock].

cock·a·too (kak·ạ·tōō') *n.* a kind of parrot with a crested head [Malay].

cock·a·trice (kak'·ạ·tris) *n.* a fabulous animal represented as a cock with a dragon's tail; a fabulous serpent imagined to possess the powers of the basilisk, whose glance deals death [O.Fr. *cocatrice*].

cock·er (kak'·ẹr) *n.* a cocker spaniel, a small variety of spaniel, used for retrieving game.

cock·le (kak'·l) *n.* a weed that grows among corn; the corn rose [O.E. *coccel*].

cock·le (kak'·l) *n.* a bivalve shell-fish, with a thick ribbed shell; *v.t.* to cause to pucker; to wrinkle. **-shell** *n.* the shell of a cockle; a shallow boat [Fr. *coquille*].

Cock·ney (kak'·ni·) *n.* a native of London. **-dom** *n.* the home of cockneys. **-fied** *a.* like a cockney.

cock·pit (kak'·pit) *n.* in aircraft, a compartment in the fuselage for the pilot and controls; the pit or ring in which game cocks fought, hence any arena of frequent strife.

cock·roach (kak'·rōch) *n.* a black or brown beetle infesting houses [Sp. *cucaracha*].

cock·swain See **coxswain.**

co·co, co·coa (kō'·kō) *n.* a palm tree producing the coconut. **-nut,** the fruit of the coco palm [Sp. and Port. *coco*, a bugbear].

co·coa (kō'·kō) *n.* a powder made from the kernels of the cacao or chocolate plant; a beverage from this [corrupt. fr. *cacao*].

co·coon (kạ·kōōn') *n.* the silky envelope which

the silkworm and other larvae spin for themselves before passing into the pupa stage [O.Fr. *coque*, a shell].

cod, cod·fish (kǎd, kǎd′·fish) *n.* a large fish from northern seas, much used as food.

co·da (kō′·dą) *n.* (*Mus.*) a short passage added at the end of a composition to round it off [It. fr. L. *cauda*, a tail].

cod·dle (kǎd′·l) *v.t.* to boil gently; to pamper or spoil [etym. uncertain].

code (kōd) *n.* an orderly collection of laws; a system of words, symbols, or numbers adopted for secrecy or economy; a cipher; *v.t.* to put into the form of a code. **codify** (kǎ′·di·fī) *v.t.* to collect laws, etc. into a digest. **codification** *n.* act of collecting laws. [L. *codex*, a book].

co·dex (kō′·deks) *n.* an ancient manuscript of a book, esp. of the Bible; a collection of manuscripts; *pl.* **codices** [L. *codex*, a book].

codg·er (kǎj′·ẹr) *n.* (*Colloq.*) an eccentric.

cod·i·cil (kǎd′·ą·sil) *n.* a supplement or appendix to a will [L. *codicillus*, dim. of *codex*, a book].

co·ed·u·ca·tion (kō·ed·ū·kā′·shạn) *n.* the education of boys and girls together in mixed classes. **-al** *a.* **co·ed** *n.* (*Colloq.*) a female student at a coeducational college or university.

co·ef·fi·cient (kō·ą·fish′·ạnt) *a.* cooperating; combining; *n.* that which unites with something else to produce a result; (*Math.*) a number or other factor placed before another as a multiplier; (*Phys.*) a constant number or factor measuring some specified property of a substance. **coefficiency** *n.*

co·e·qual (kō·ē′·kwal) *a.* equal; of the same rank or power as another; *n.* a person having equality with another.

co·erce (kō·urs′) *v.t.* to compel by force; to constrain; to restrain. **coercible** *a.* **coercive** *a.* having power to compel. **coercively** *adv.* **coercion** (kō·ur′·shạn) *n.* coercing; state of being coerced; compulsory force; restraint [L. *coercere*].

co·e·val (kō·ē′·val) *a.* of same age; *n.* contemporary [L. *co-*, together; *aevum*, age].

co·ex·ist (kō·ig·zist′) *v.i.* to exist at the same time or together. **-ence** *n.* **-ent** *a.*

cof·fee (kawf′·i·) *n.* an evergreen shrub, valuable for its berries; the seeds of the berries, esp. when ground and roasted; a drink from this. **-bean** *n.* the seed of the berry. **-house** *n.* a restaurant where coffee and other refreshments are supplied [Ar. *qahwah*].

cof·fer (kawf′·ẹr, kǎf′·ẹr) *n.* a chest for valuables; a large money-box; an ornamental panel in a ceiling or archway; *v.t.* to put in a coffer; to hoard (money, etc.). **-dam** *n.* in engineering, a watertight, box-like, iron structure, used in the construction of the underwater foundations of bridgₑs, etc. [Fr. *coffre*, a box].

cof·fin (kawf′·in) *n.* a box or casket in which the dead are enclosed before burial; *v.t.* to place in a coffin [Gk. *kophinos*, a basket].

cog (kǎg) *n.* one of a series of teeth on a wheel; *v.t.* to fit a wheel with cogs. *pr.p.* **-ging.** *pa.p.* and *pa.t.* **-ged** [M.E. *cogge*].

co·gent (kō′·jạnt) *a.* having great force; powerful; convincing. **-ly** *adv.* **cogence, cogency** *n.* force; convincing power [L. *cogere*, to force].

cog·i·tate (kǎj′·i·tāt) *v.i.* to reflect deeply; to meditate. **cogitation** *n.* contemplation. **cogitative** *a.* [L. *cogitare*].

co·gnac (kōn′·yak) *n.* a French brandy, so called from the town of *Cognac* in S.W. France; brandy in general.

cog·nate (kǎg′·nāt) *a.* allied by blood or birth; of the same stock; from the same origin, formation, etc.; *n.* a relative by birth; anything of the same origin, kind, nature, or effect [L. *cognatus*, born together].

cog·ni·zance (kǎg·nạ·zạns) *n.* knowledge; perception. **cognizable** *a.* capable of being perceived or known. **cognizably** *adv.* **cognizant** *a.* having cognizance or knowledge of; competent to take judicial notice [L. *cognoscere*, to know].

cog·ni·tion (kǎg·ni·shạn) *n.* awareness; state of being able to perceive objects or to remember ideas. **cognitive** *a.* [L. *cogniscere*, to know].

cog·no·men (kǎg·nō′·men) *n.* a surname; a nickname [L. *nomen*, a name].

co·hab·it (kō·hab′·it) *v.i.* to live together as husband and wife (usually of unmarried persons). **-ation, -ant** *n.*

co·here (kō·hir′) *v.i.* to stick together; to be connected; to follow regularly in natural order; to be consistent; to coalesce; to adhere. **-nce, -ncy** *n.* **-nt** *a.* sticking together; connected; consistent. **-ntly** *adv.* **cohesible** *a.* capable

of cohesion. **cohesion** *n.* the act of sticking together. **cohesive** *a.* having the power of cohering. **cohesiveness, cohesibility** *n.* [L. *cohaerere*, to stick together].

co·hort (kō′·hawrt) *n.* a division of a Roman legion, from 300 to 600 soldiers; a company of persons; an associate [L. *cohors*].

coif (koif) *n.* a headdress in the form of a close-fitting cap, worn by nuns. **-feur** (kwä·fur′) (*fem.* **coiffeuse**) *n.* a hairdresser. **coiffure** (kwä·fyoor′) *n.* a headdress; a style of dressing the hair [Fr. *coiffe*].

coign (koin) *n.* a corner, a corner-stone; a wedge [same as *coin*, fr. L. *cuneus*, a wedge].

coil (koil) *v.t.* to wind in rings, as a rope; to twist into a spiral shape; *v.i.* to take on a spiral shape; *n.* the spiral of rings into which anything is wound; one of the rings of the spiral [L. *colligere*, to gather].

coil (koil) *n.* turmoil; tumult; fuss.

coin (koin) *n.* a piece of stamped metal issued by government authority to be used as money; **money**; a wedge or cornerstone; *v.t.* to make **into money**; to mint; or invent or fabricate, as a word or phrase. **-age** *n.* the act of coining; money coined; currency. **-er** *n.* one who makes coins; an inventor [L. *cuneus*, a wedge].

co·in·cide (kō·in·sīd′) *v.i.* to correspond in detail; to happen at the same time; to agree (in opinion). **coincidence** (kō·in′·si·dẹns) *n.* correspondence in nature, circumstances, etc. **coincident, coincidental** *a.* occupying the same space; agreeing; simultaneous. **coincidently** *adv.* [L. *co-*, together; *incidere*, to happen].

coir (koir) *n.* the fiber from the husk of the coconut, used for cordage, matting, etc. [Malay, *kayar*, cord].

co·i·tion (kō′·i·shạn) *n.* sexual intercourse; copulation. Also **coitus** (kō·i·tạs) [L. *co-*, together; *ire*, *itum*, to go].

coke (kōk) *n.* coal half burnt, and used as fuel; *v.t.* to turn into coke [origin uncertain].

col·an·der (kǎl′·an·dẹr) *n.* a vessel with a perforated bottom, used for draining off liquids in cookery; a sieve. Also **cullender** [L. *colare*, to strain].

cold (kōld) *a.* wanting in heat; chill; deficient in the emotions; spiritless; *n.* absence of warmth; chilliness; cold weather; a disorder of the nose, throat and chest, often caused by cold, and characterized by running at the nose, hoarseness and coughing; catarrh. **-ly** *adv.* **-ish** *a.* somewhat cold. **-ness** *n.* **—blooded** *a.* having cold blood, like fish; susceptible to cold; callous or heartless. Also **—hearted** (härt′·ẹd). **— war**, campaign carried on by means of economic pressure, press, radio, etc. [O.E. *ceald*].

cole (kōl) *n.* a name for plants of the cabbage family. **—slaw** *n.* a salad of finely sliced or chopped cabbage. **-wort** *n.* any kind of cabbage whose leaves do not form a compact head [L. *caulis*, a stalk, esp. a cabbage stalk].

Co·le·op·ter·a (kōl·i·áp′·tẹr·ą) *n.pl.* the order of insects, such as beetles, whose outer wings form a horny sheath or covering for the true wings [Gk. *koleos*, a sheath; *pteron*, a wing].

col·ic (kǎl′·ik) *n.* severe paroxysmal pain in the abdomen [Gk. *kolon*, the lower intestine].

co·li·se·um (kǎl·ą·sē′·ạm) *n.* a stadium, amphitheater, or large auditorium [M.L. *colosseum*].

col·lab·o·rate (kạ·lab′·ą·rāt) *v.i.* to work or labor together; to act jointly, esp. in works of literature, art, science. **collaboration** *n.* joint labor; (*World War 2*) willing cooperation with the enemy given by an inhabitant of an occupied country. **collaborator** *n.* [L. *co-*, *laborare*, to work].

col·lapse (kạ·laps′) *v.i.* to fall in; to break down; to fall suddenly; to lose strength; to give way under physical or mental strain; *v.t.* to cause to collapse (as of a lung); *n.* a falling in or down; a sudden and complete failure; a breakdown. **collapsable, collapsible** *a.* [L. *collabi*, *collapsus*, to fall to pieces].

col·lar (kǎl′·ẹr) *n.* something worn around the neck; the part of a garment that fits around the neck; *v.t.* to seize by the collar; to arrest; to capture; to grab; to put a collar on. **-bone** *n.* the bone from the shoulders to the breast-bone; the clavicle [L. *collum*, the neck].

col·late (kạ·lāt′) *v.t.* to compare critically; to arrange in order, as the sheets of a book for binding; to appoint to a benefice. **collation** *n.* the act of collating; a lunch or repast. **collative** *a.* **collator** *n.* [L. *conferre*, *collatum*, to bring together].

col·lat·e·ral (kạl·at′·ą·rạl) *a.* side by side; running parallel; subordinately connected; descended from the same ancestor but through a different line; additional (of a security); *n.* a collateral relative; a kinsman; additional security. **-ly** *adv.* **-ness** [L. *con*; *latus*, the side].

col·league (kǎl′·ēg) *n.* as associate or companion [L. *collega*, an associate].

col·lect (kạ·lekt′) *v.t.* to bring together; to gather; to assemble; to receive payment of; *v.i.* to be assembled; to come together. **collect** (kǎl′·ekt) *n.* a very short prayer. **-able, -ible** *a.* **-ed** *a.* not disconcerted; cool; self-possessed. **-edly** *adv.* **-edness** *n.* **collection** *n.* the act of collecting; a contribution or sum of money gather at a meeting for a religious, charitable, etc. object; assemblage. **-ive** *a.* formed by gathering; gathered into a mass, sum, or body;

expressing a collection or aggregate. **-ively** *adv.* **-ivism** *n.* a term embracing all systems on the Socialistic doctrine of the state, municipal, cooperative, etc. control of the economic life of the country. **-ivist** *n.* **-or** *n.* one who collects; an officer appointed to receive taxes, customs, duties, tolls, etc. [L. *colligere*, *collectum*, to gather together].

col·leen (kǎl′·ēn) *n.* a girl [Ir. *cailin*].

col·lege (kǎl′·ij) *n.* an institution for higher education; the buildings, etc. of such an institution; an association of professional men, e.g. of physicians; an assembly, as of electors or cardinals. **collegial** *a.* pert. to a college. **collegian** (kạ·lē′·ji·ạn) *n.* a member of a college; a student. **collegiate** *a.* pert. to, or instituted like, a college; corporate [L. *collegium*, a society].

col·let (kǎl′·it) *n.* a collar; a neckband; the rim in which the stone of a ring is set [Fr. fr. L. *collum*, the neck].

col·lide (kạ·līd′) *v.i.* to strike or dash together; to clash; to come into conflict. **collision** *n.* (kạ·lizh′·ạn) *n.* the act of striking together; a violent impact; a clash; conflict [L. *collidere*, to dash together].

col·lie (kǎl′·i·) *n.* a breed of sheep dog.

col·lier·y (kǎl′·yą·ri·) *n.* a coal mine [fr. coal]

col·lin·e·ar (kạ·lin′·i·ẹr) *a.* in the same straight line; aligned [L. *collineare*].

col·lo·cate (kǎl′·ō·kāt) *v.t.* to set or place together; to arrange. **collocation** *n.* [L. *collocare*, to place together].

col·lo·di·on (kạ·lō′·di·ạn) *n.* a solution of guncotton in ether, used in preparing photographic plates and in surgery [Gk. *kolla*, glue; *eidos*, form].

col·loid (kǎl′·oid) *a.* like glue; gelatinous; *n.* a glue-like, non-crystalline substance unable to pass through animal membranes. **-al** *a.* like a colloid [Gk. *kolla*, glue; *eidos*, form].

col·lo·quy (kǎl′·ą·kwi·) *n.* conversation; dialogue; discussion; a conference, esp. political; a debate. **colloquial** (kạ·lō′·kwi·ạl) *a.* pert. to, or used in, ordinary conversation. **colloquially** *adv.* **colloquialism** *n.* an expression used in cordinary conversation, but not regarded as slang [L. *colloqui*, to speak together].

col·lu·sion (kạ·lōō′·zhạn) *n.* a secret agreement between two or more persons for a fraudulent purpose, usually in connection with legal proceedings. **collusive** *a.* [L. *colludere*, *collusum*, to play together].

co·logne (kạ·lōn′) *n.* a perfumed toilet water.

co·lon (kō′·lạn) *n.* a punctuation mark (:), separating parts of a sentence that are almost independent and complete in themselves; (*Anat.*) that part of the large intestine extending from the caecum to the rectum. **colonic** *a.* [Gk. *kolon*, a limb or member].

colo·nel (kur′·nạl) *n.* the officer ranking between lieutenant colonel and a brigadier general, usually commanding a regiment. **-cy, -ship** *n.* the rank or quality of colonel [L. *columna*, a column. The pronunciation is due to a Sp. form *coronel*, one also used].

col·on·nade (kǎl·ą·nād′) *n.* a series of columns arranged symmetrically [L. *columna*, a column].

col·o·ny (kǎl′·ạn·i·) *n.* a body of people who settle in a new country but remain subject to the parent state; the country thus occupied; a group of people living in a community for a common purpose; a group of animals or plants living and growing together. **colonial**

a. pert. to a colony; *n.* a colonist. **colonize** *v.t.* to plant or establish a colony; *v.i.* to settle. **colonist** *n.* **colonization** *n.* [L. *colonia*].

col·o·phon (kál'·a·fán) *n.* individual device or inscription used by publishers and printers on the title pages of books, etc. [Gk. *colophon*, the finish].

col·or (kul'·ẹr) *n.* any hue or tint as distinguished from white; paint; complexion; a flush; outward appearance; kind or general character; vividness in writing; in music, variety of timbre; *v.t.* to paint or tinge with color; *v.i.* to blush. **colors** *n.pl.* a flag or standard; a colored badge, device, rosette, etc. used as a distinguishing mark. **-able** *a.* capable of being colored; specious; plausible. **-ably** *adv.* **-ed** *a.* having color; biased; belonging to some other race than white, esp. Negro. **-ful** *a.* having plenty of color. **——blind** *a.* unable to distinguish colors. **——** line, discrimination in status between white and colored races [L. *color*, color].

col·or·a·tion (kul·a·rā'·shan) *n.* coloring; arrangement or dispostion of colors in art. [L. *color*, color].

col·or·a·tu·ra (kál·ar·a·tū'·ra) *n.* (*Mus.*) ornamental runs and trills in vocal music [It.].

co·los·sus (ka·lás'·us) *n.* a gigantic statue, esp. that of Apollo at Rhodes; hence (*Fig.*) any person of great stature or enormous strength. **colossal** *a.* of enormous size [Gk. *kolossos*].

colt (kōlt) *n.* young horse, esp. a male. [O.E.].

Colt (kōlt) *n.* a repeating rifle; also a revolver invented by Samuel Colt.

col·ter (kōl'·tẹr) *n.* the sharp blade of iron placed at the front end of a plow to act as a cutter. Also **coulter** [O.E. *culter*].

col·um·bine (kál'·am·bín) *a.* of, or like, a dove; dove-colored; *n.* a small bell-shaped flower, with five spurred petals [L. *columba*, a dove].

col·umn (kál'·am) *n.* a round pillar; a support; a body of troops drawn up in deep files; a division of a page; a perpendicular line of figures. **-ar** (ka·lum'·nẹr) *a.* formed in columns; having the form of columns. **-ated, -ed** *a.* furnished with, or supported on, columns. **-ist** *n.* a writer who contributes articles to a newspaper, **fifth column**, group of people residing in a country who are in sympathy with and assist its enemies [L. *columna*].

co·ma (kō'·ma) *n.* (*Med.*) a deep sleep or stupor generally resulting from injury to the brain, alcoholic or narcotic poisoning; (*Fig.*) lethargy; drowsiness. **-tose** *a.* lethargic; drowsy [Gk. *koma*].

comb (kōm) *n.* a toothed instrument for separating, cleansing, adjusting, or fastening hair, dressing wool, etc.; also a decoration for a lady's hair; a cock's crest; the crest of a wave; the cell structure in which bees store their honey; *v.t.* to separate, cleanse, dress, etc. with a comb; *v.i.* to roll over or break with a white foam (said of waves). **-er** *n.* one who, or that which, combs; a long, curling wave. **-ing** *n.* **-ings** *n.pl.* hair, wool, etc. removed by combing [O.E. *camb*].

com·bat (kám'·bat') *v.t.* to fight against; to oppose by force; to contend with; *v.i.* to struggle; to contend. **combat** (kám'·bat) *n.* a fight; a struggle; a contest. **-ant** *a.* contending; disposed to contend; *n.* one engaged in a fight. **-ive** *a.* disposed to combat; quarrelsome [Fr. *combattre*, to fight].

com·bine (kam·bīn') *v.t.* to join together; to unite; to connect; *v.i.* to form a union; to co-operate; (*Chem.*) to unite and form a new compound. **combine** (kám'·bīn) *n.* an association formed to further political or commercial interests; a trust; a syndicate; a harvester; an agricultural machines that reaps, threshes and bags the grain in one operation. **combinable** *a.* capable of combining. **combinative, combinatory** *a.* tending to com-

bine. **combination** (kám·ba·nā'·shan) *n.* union or connection; association of persons; alliance; chemical union; series of letters or numbers for operating a lock; an undergarment combining vest and pants. [L.L. *combinare*].

com·bus·tion (kam·bus'·chan) *n.* the act of fire on inflammable substances; the act of burning; chemical action accompanied by heat and light. **combustible** *a.* liable to take fire; inflammable; *n.* a substance that burns readily [L. *comburere*, to burn up].

come (kum) *v.i.* to approach; to arrive; to arrive at some state or condition; to move towards; to reach; to happen (to); to originate (from); to occur; to turn out to be; to appear. *pr.p.* **coming**. *pa.p.* **come**. *pa.t.* **came**. **-back** *n.* a return to a former activity; (*Slang*) a retort [O.E. *cuman*].

com·e·dy (kám'·a·di·) *n.* a play dealing with the lighter side of life; the humorous element in literature, life, or an incident.

co·me·di·an (ka·mē'·di·an) *n.* an actor in comedy; an entertainer whose songs or stories are light and humorous; (*Colloq.*) a funny person; a comic. **comedienne** (kam·ē·di·en') *n. fem.* [Gk. *komoidia*, fr. *komos*, revel; *odē*, song].

come·ly (kum'·li·) *a.* good-looking; graceful. **comeliness** *n.* [O.E. *cyme*, fair].

come·sti·ble (ka·mes'·ti·bl) *a.* fit for eating. [L. *comedere*, to eat up].

com·et (kám'·it) *n.* a heavenly body consisting of a diffuse, nebulous head, a nucleus, and a tail [Gk. *komētes*, long-haired].

come·up·pance (kum·up'·ans) *n.* (*Slang*) deserved punishment.

com·fort (kum'·fẹrt) *v.t.* to allay grief or trouble; to console, cheer, gladden; *n.* solace or consolation; ease of body or mind, or whatever causes it. **-s** *n.pl.* appurtenances or circumstances which give greater ease to life. **-able** *a.* promoting or enjoying comfort. **-ably** *adv.* **-er** *n.* one who comforts; a quilted bedcover. **-less** *a.* **Job's comforter**, one who, in seeking to comfort, achieves the opposite [L. *confortare*, to strengthen].

com·ic (kám'·ik) *a.* pert. to comedy; mirth-provoking; funny; *n.* that which induces amusement or laughter; (*Colloq.*) a comedian; (*Colloq.*) (*pl.*) a comic magazine or newspaper strip. **-al** *a.* droll; ludicrous. **-ally** *adv.* **-ality** *n.* [Gk. *komos*, revel].

com·in·form (kám'·in·fawrm) *n.* Communist Information Bureau.

Com·in·tern (kám'·in·turn) *n.* Communist International, the international association of Communist parties.

com·i·ty (kám'·a·ti·) *n.* courtesy; civility; suavity of manners [L. *comitas*].

com·ma (kám'·a) *n.* a punctuation mark (,), used to mark the shortest pauses in the division of a sentence [Gk. fr. *komma*, short clause].

com·mand (ka·mand') *v.t.* to order or demand with authority; to govern or control; to have at one's disposal; to overlook or have a view over; *v.i.* to be at the head; *n.* an order; the body of troops under an officer; a district or region under a commander; a word of command; mastery or facility. **-ing** *a.* fitted to control; impressive or imperious. **-ant** *n.* officer in charge of a military station or a body of troops. **-eer** (ká·man·dēr') *v.t.* to seize for military purposes; to take forcible possession of. **-er** (ka·man'·dẹr) *n.* a leader; a commanding officer; in the navy, an officer ranking between a lieutenant commander and a captain. **-ment** *n.* a command; precept. **-er-in-chief**, the officer in supreme command of the forces of a state [L. *commendare*, to entrust].

com·man·do (ka·man'·dō) *n.* (*Mil.*) a selected body of men, who undergo special training for particularly dangerous enterprises against the enemy; a member of this body [Sp.].

com·mem·o·rate (ka·mem'·a·rāt) *v.t.* to call to remembrance; to celebrate the memory of someone or something by a solemn act of devotion. **commemoration** *n.* **commemorative, commemoratory** *a.* [L. *commemorare*].

com·mence (ka·mens') *v.t.* to begin, to start, to originate; *v.i.* to originate (in) to take rise; to begin. **-ment** *n.* beginning; the ceremony of conferring degrees in colleges and universities [Fr. *commencer*].

com·mend (ka·mend') *v.t.* to praise; to speak favorably of; to present as worthy; to entrust to. **-able** *a.* **-ably** *adv.* **-ableness** *n.* **-ation** *n.* the act of commending; praise; approval. **-atory** *a.* [L. *commendare*, to entrust].

com·men·su·rate (ka·men'·sha·rit) *a.* equal in extent; proportionate; adequate. **-ly** *adv.* **-ness** *n.* **commensuration** *n.* **commensurable** *a.* having a common measure; suitably proportioned. **commensurably** *adv.* **commensurability** *n.* [L. *con*-; *mensura*, a measure].

com·ment (ká'·ment) *v.t.* and *i.* to make remarks, notes, criticisms; *n.* a note; a collection of notes; an explanation; a critical remark; an observation. **-ary** (ká·man·te'·ri) *n.* a series of notes; an exposition of a book; an historical narrative. **running commentary**, the description of an event while in actual progress, broadcast by an eye-witness. **-ate** *v.t.* to annotate; to interpret the meaning of. **-ator** *n.* an annotator; an expositor; one who speaks a commentary, either on events for broadcasting, or with a film [L. *comminisci, commentus*, to contrive].

com·merce (kám'·urs) *n.* buying and selling; trade; social or personal intercourse. **commercial** (ka·mur'·shal) *a.* pert. to commerce; (*Radio*) broadcast program paid for by an advertiser. **commercialism** *n.* business principles, methods, or viewpoint. **commercialize** *v.t.* **commercially** *adv.* [L. *con*-; *merx*, merchandise].   [gle together.

com·min·gle (ka·ming'·gl) *v.t.* and *i.* to mingle together.

com·mis·er·ate (ka·miz'·a·rāt) *v.t.* and *i.* to have compassion for; to condole with; to pity; to sympathize. **commiseration** *n.* [L. *commiserari*, to bewail with].

com·mis·sar (kám'·i·sár) *n.* one of the heads of a Soviet government department or commissariat [L. *committere*, to entrust].

com·mis·sar·i·at (kám·i·sa'·ri·at) *n.* the army department which supplies food, stores, equipment, transport; any of the governmental divisions of the U.S.S.R. [L. *committere*, to entrust].

com·mis·sa·ry (kám'·i·ser·i·) *n.* one to whom duty is assigned; a deputy; a commissioner; (*Mil.*) a store which supplies food and equipment. **commissarial** *a.* [L. *committere*, to entrust].

com·mis·sion (ka·mish'·an) *n.* the act of committing; something entrusted to be done; payment by a percentage for doing something; a group of people authorized to deal with specified matters; a legal warrant to execute some office, trust, or duty; the power under such warrant; the document that contains it; the thing to be done as agent for another; (*Mil., Naval, etc.*) a warrant of appointment, by the head of a state, to the rank of officer in the army, navy, etc.; *v.t.* to give power to; to authorize; to give an order for; to appoint to the rank of officer. **-ed** *a.* **-er** *n.* one holding a commission to act; the head of a governmental department [L. *committere*, to entrust].

com·mit (ka·mit') *v.t.* to entrust; to give in charge; to perform; to be guilty of; to pledge or bind; to send for trial or confinement; *pr.p.* **-ting**, *pa.p.* and *pa.t.* **-ted. -tal. -ment** *n.* [L. *committere*].

com·mit·tee (ka·mit'·i·) *n.* a number of persons appointed to attend any particular business by a legislative body, court, society, etc. [L. *committere*, to entrust].

com·mode (ka·mōd') *n.* a chest of drawers; a small piece of furniture containing a chamber pot [L. *commodus*, suitable].

com·mo·di·ous (ka·mō'·di·as) *a.* convenient; roomy; spacious. **-ly** *adv.* **-ness** *n.* **commodity** *n.* any useful thing; an article of trade. **commodities** *n.pl.* goods [L. *commodus*, suitable].

com·mo·dore (kám'·a·dōr) *n.* (*Naval*) the rank just below rear admiral; captain of a convoy of ships [etym. uncertain].

com·mon (kám'·an) *a.* shared by or belonging to all, or to several; public; general; ordinary; usual; frequent; vulgar; inferior; of little value; of low social status; *n.* a tract of land belonging to a community for public use. **commons** *n.pl.* the lower House of Parliament, called the **House of Commons**; (*l.c.*) a dining room at a university. **-alty** *n.* the general body of the people with reference to rank, position, etc. **-er** *n.* one of the common people, i.e. not a member of the nobility. **-ly** *adv.* in a common manner; usually; jointly; meanly. **-ness** *n.* **-place** *a.* ordinary; trite; hackneyed; *n.* a common topic; a trite remark. **—— sense** *n.* sound and practical understanding; well-balanced judgment. **—— law**, (*Eng.*) law based on usage and custom, and confirmed by judicial decision; the unwritten law as distinguished from statute law. **the common good**, the welfare of the community as a whole [L. *communis*].

com·mon·weal (kám'·an·wēl) *n.* the public welfare; the common good. **commonwealth** (welth) *n.* the whole body of people; a republican or democratic state. **Commonwealth** *n.* since 1947 the comprehensive term for all territories within the British Empire, including the Dominions [*common* and *weal*].

com·mo·tion (kạ·mō'·shạn) *n.* violent motion; agitation; tumult; public disorder [L. *conmorere, motum*, to move].

com·mune (kạ·mūn') *v.i.* to converse together intimately; to have spiritual intercourse (*with*); (*Eccl.*) to receive the communion. **communion** (kạ·ūn'·yạn) *n.* the act of communing; (*Christianity*) the celebration of the Lord's Supper [L. *communish*, common].

com·mune (kắm'·ūn) *n.* a small administrative district (esp. in France) governed by a mayor. **communal** *a.* pert. to a commune or community; for common use. **communalize** *v.t.* to make over for common use. **communalism** *n.* a system by which small local governments have large powers. **communism** *n.* the theory of a social system in which everything is held in common, private property being abolished. **communist** *n.* **communistic** *a.* [L. *communis*, common].

com·mu·ni·cate (kạ·mū'·nạ·kāt) *v.t.* to impart information; to reveal; to convey; *v.i.* to have connection with; to have dealings, correspondence with. **communicable** *a.* **communicably** *adv.* **communication** *n.* the act of making known; intercourse by speech, correspondence, messages, etc.; information; means of passing from one place to another; a connecting passage. **communicant** *n.* one who imparts information; one who receives communion. **communicative** *a.* ready to converse or to impart information; talkative. [L. *communicare*] [announcement [Fr.]

com·mu·ni·qué (kạ·mū'·ni·kā) *n.* an official

com·mu·ni·ty (kạ·mū'·nạ·ti·) *n.* a locality where people reside; people having common interests; the public, or people in general; common possession or enjoyment [L. *communis*].

com·mute (kạ·mūt') *v.t.* to exchange; to substitute; to mitigate a sentence; travel regularly between home and work. **commutable** *a.* exchangeable. **commutability** *n.* **commutation** *n.* **commutator** *n.* (*Elect.*) a device for reversing the direction of an electric current. **-r** *n.* [L. *con.; mutare*, to change].

com·pact (kạm·pakt') *a.* firm; solid; closely packed; condensed; terse; *v.t.* to press closely together; to make firm. **compact** (kắm'·pakt) *n.* a pocket vanity-case. **-ly** *adv.* **-ness** *n.* **-ed** *a.* firmly united [L. *con.; pangere, pactum*, to fix].

com·pact (kạm'·pakt) *n.* an agreement or contract; a mutual bargain; a league or covenant [L. *con.; pactus*, to make an agreement].

com·pan·ion (kạm·pan'·yạn) *n.* one who is in another's company, habitually or for the moment; comrade; an associate or partner; a match or mate. **-able** *a.* fitted to be a companion; sociable. **-ably** *adv.* **-ability**, **-ableness** *n.* **-ship** *n.* [L. *companium*, fellowship, fr. *con., panis*, bread].

com·pan·ion (kạm·pan'·yạn) *n.* (*Naut.*) a skylight on upper deck, to let light into cabin below. **-way**, cabin staircase [O.Fr. *compagne*].

com·pa·ny (kum'·pạ·ni·) *n.* a gathering of persons; an assembly; a group; an association of persons in business, etc.; visitors; a division of a regiment; a ship's crew [L. *con.; panis*, bread].

com·pare (kạm·pār') *v.t.* to notice or point out the likeness and differences of two or more things; to liken or contrast; (*Gram.*) to state the comparative and superlative of an adjective or adverb; *v.i.* to be like; to compete with. **comparable** (kắm'·par·ạ·bl) *a.* capable of being compared; of equal regard or value. **comparably** *adv.* **comparative** (kạm·par'·ạ·tiv) *a.* estimated by comparison; not absolute; relative; partial; (*Gram.*) expressing 'more'. **comparatively** *adv.* **comparison** *n.* the act of comparing [L. *comparare*, to match].

com·part·ment (kạm·pärt'·mạnt) *n.* a part divided off; a section; a division of a railway car [L. *compartiri*, to divide].

com·pass (kum'·pạs) *n.* an instrument for showing directions (north, east, etc.); (*Mus.*) the range of a voice in the musical scale; circuit; a circumference; measurement around; space; area; scope; reach; *v.t.* to go round; to surround; to contrive; to attain; to accomplish. **-es** *n.pl.* a mathematical instrument for drawing circles, measuring, etc. [L. *con.; passus*, a step].

com·pas·sion (kạm·pash'·ạn) *n.* sympathy with the distress or suffering of another; pity. **-ate** *a.* full of sympathy; showing pity; merciful; *v.t.* to pity. **-ately** *adv.* **-ateness** *n.* [L. *con.; pati, passus*, to suffer].

com·pat·i·ble (kạm·pat'·ạ·bl) *a.* consistent; agreeing with; capable of harmonious union. **compatibly** *adv.* **compatibility** *n.* [L. *con.; pati*, to suffer].

com·pa·tri·ot (kạm·pā'·tri·ạt) *n.* one of the same country; a fellow countryman [L. *con.; and patriot*].

com·peer (kạm·pir') *n.* an equal; a companion; an associate [L. *con.; par*, equal].

com·pel (kạm·pel') *v.t.* to force; to overpower; to bring about by force; *pr.p.* **-ling**. *pa.p.* and *pa.t.* **-led**. **-lable** *a.* [L. *compellere*, to drive together].

com·pen·di·um (kạm·pen'·di·ạm) *n.* an abridgement or summary; an abstract. Also **compend.** *pl.* **-s**, or **compendia**. **compendious** *a.* abridged. **compendiously** *adv.* [L.].

com·pen·sate (kắm'·pạn·sāt) *v.t.* to recompense suitably; to reward; to pay; *v.i.* to make amends; to make up for. **compensation** *n.* recompense; payment for some loss, injury, etc. **compensative**, **compensatory** *a.* [L. *compensare*, to weigh together].

com·pete (kạm·pēt') *v.i.* to strive against others to win something; to vie with. **competition** (kắm·pạ·tish'·ạn) *n.* the act of competing; a contest. **competitive** *a.* **competitively** *adv.* **competitor** *n.* one who competes. **competitory** *a.* [L. *competere*, to seek with].

com·pe·tent (kắm'·pạ·tạnt) *a.* able; properly qualified; proper; suitable; skillful. **-ly** *adv.* **competence**, **competency** *n.* the state of being fit or capable; sufficiency, esp. of means of subsistence [L. *competere*, to seek together].

com·pile (kạm·pīl') *v.t.* to put together literary materials into one book or works; to collect or amass. **-r** *n.* **compilation** *n.* [L. *compilare*, to plunder].

com·pla·cent (kạm·plā'·sạnt) *a.* self-satisfied; pleased or gratified. **-ly** *adv.* **complacence**, **complacency** *n.* self-satisfaction [L. *complacere*, to please greatly].

com·plain (kạm·plān') *v.i.* to express distress, grief, dissatisfaction; to lament; to grumble; to be ailing. **-ant** *n.* a complainer; (*Law*) a plaintiff; one who brings an action against another. **complaint** *n.* the expression of distress, dissatisfaction, etc.; a malady or ailment [L. *con.; plangere*, to bewail].

com·plai·sant (kạm·plā'·zạnt) *a.* desirous to please; affable; obliging; gracious. **-ly** *adv.* **complaisance** *n.* [L. *complacere*, to please greatly].

com·ple·ment (kắm'·plạ·mạnt) *n.* that which supplies a deficiency; something completing a whole; the full quantity or number; *v.t.* to complete; to supply a deficiency. **-al**, **-ary** *a.* completing [L. *complere*, to fill up].

com·plete (kạm·plēt') *a.* entire; finished; perfect, with no part lacking; *v.t.* to bring to a state of entirety; to make perfect; to fulfill; to accomplish. **-ly** *adv.* **-ness** *n.* **completion** (kạm·plē'·shạn) *n.* the act of completing; fulfilment; conclusion [L. *complere*, to fill up].

com·plex (kắm'·pleks) *a.* consisting of two or more parts; not simple; involved or intricate; *n.* a complicated whole; (*Psych.*) a group of repressed emotional ideas responsible for abnormal mental condition; (*Colloq.*) an obsession. **-ly** *adv.* **-ness**, **-ity** *n.* [L. *complectere*, to interweave].

com·plex·ion (kạm·plek'·shạn) *n.* color of the skin, esp. of the face; aspect or appearance; quality or texture; character [L. *complexio*].

com·pli·ance (kạm·plī'·ạns) *n.* submission; a yielding; acquiescence. **compliant** *a.* yielding; obedient; civil. **compliantly** *adv.* **compliable** *a.* inclined to comply [fr. *comply*].

com·pli·cate (kắm'·plạ·kāt) *v.t.* to fold or twist together; to entangle; to make intricate. **-d** *a.* tangled; involved. **complication** *n.* [L. *con.; plicare*, to fold].

com·plic·i·ty (kạm·plis'·ạ·ti·) *n.* the state of being an accomplice, of having a share in the guilt [Fr. *complice*, an accomplice].

com·pli·ment (kắm'·plạ·mạnt) *n.* an expression of regard or admiration; flattering speech; a formal greeting (usually *pl.*); *v.t.* to express approbation; to congratulate; to express respect for. **-ary** *a.* expressing praise, admiration; free. a *complimentary* ticket [L. *complete*, to fill up].

com·ply (kạm·plī') *v.i.* to yield to; to agree; to consent; to conform; to adapt oneself to. **complier** *n.* [L. *complere*, to fill up].

com·po·nent (kạm·pō'·nạnt) *a.* constituting; composing; making up; helping to form a compound; *n.* a part helping to make a whole [L. *componere*, to put together].

com·port (kạm·pōrt') *v.t.* to behave; to conduct oneself; *v.i.* to agree; to accord; to suit [L. *comportare*, to carry together].

com·pose (kạm·pōz') *v.t.* to form by uniting parts; to arrange; to put in order; to write; to invent; to adjust; to calm; to soothe; to set up the types in proper order for printing; *v.i.* to practice composition. **-d** *a.* sedate; quiet; calm. **-dly** *adv.* **-dness** *n.* **-r** *n.* one who composes; an author. **composite** (kạm·pắz'·it) *a.* made up of distinct parts or elements. **composition** (kắm·pạ·zish'·ạn) *n.* the act of composing; the thing formed by composing; a pupil's essay; a literary, musical, artistic, etc. work; the organization of the parts of a work of art. **compositor** (kạm·pắz'·ạ·tẹr) *n.* a typesetter. **composure** (kạm·pō'·zhẹr) *n.* calmness [Fr.

composer].

com·post (kắm'·pōst) *n.* a fertilizing mixture; a composition for plaster work, etc. [L. *componere*, to put together].

com·pote (kắm'·pōt) *n.* fruit stewed or preserved in syrup; a stemmed candy dish [Fr.].

com·pound (kạm·pound') *v.t.* to put together, as elements or parts, to form a whole; to combine; to compromise; to make a settlement of debt by partial payment. **to compound a felony** (*Law*) to refrain, for some consideration, from prosecuting [L. *componere*, to put together].

com·pound (kắm'·pound) *a.* composed of elements, ingredients, or parts; not simple; composite; *n.* a mixture; a joining; a substance to which something has been added; a word, etc. made up of parts; (*Chem.*) a substance composed of two or more elements, which are always present in the same fixed proportions. **— fracture**, a fracture of a bone where a portion pierces the skin, making a surface wound. **— interest**, interest paid on capital plus accumulated interest [L. *componere*, to put together].

com·pound (kắm'·pound) *n.* in the Orient, an enclosure about a house; in S. Africa, an enclosed area in which native laborers reside [Malay, *kampong*, an enclosure].

com·pre·hend (kắm·pri·hend') *v.t.* to understand; to grasp with the mind; to take in; to include; to comprise. **comprehensible** (kắm·pri·hen'·sa·bl) *a.* understandable; conceivable. **comprehensibly** *adv.* **comprehensibility**, **comprehensibleness** *n.* **comprehension** *n.* the act of comprehending; the capacity of the mind to perceive and understand. **comprehensive** *a.* including much within narrow limits; extensive; large; capacious; inclusive [L. *comprehendere*, to grasp].

com·press (kạm·pres') *v.t.* to press together; to reduce the volume by pressure; to condense. **-ed** *a.* **-ible** *a.* **-ibility** *n.* **-ion** (kạm·presh'·ạn) *n.* the act or effect of compressing. **-ive** *a.* tending to compress. **-or** *n.* [L. *compressus*, pressed together].

com·press (kắm'·pres) *n.* (*Med.*) a pad to make pressure on a wound; a wet pad to reduce inflammation.

com·prise (kạm·prīz') *v.t.* to include; to be composed of; to consist of [Fr. *comprendre*, to include].

com·pro·mise (kắm'·prạ·mīz) *n.* a settling of matters by mutual adjustment, each side making some concessions; a middle course; *v.t.* and *i.* to settle by making mutual concessions; to commit oneself; to expose to the risk of scandal or disgrace [L. *con.; promittere*, to promise].

comp·tom·e·ter (kắm(p)·tắm'·ạ·tẹr) *n.* a calculating machine [Trade Name].

comp·trol·ler (kạn·trōl'·ẹr) *n.* a form of controller [L.].

com·pul·sion (kạm·pul'·shạn) *n.* the act or effect of compelling; force; constraint; violence; (*Psych.*) an irresistible impulse. **compulsive** *a.* exercising compulsion. **compulsory** *a.* compelling; constraining; obligatory; enforced [L. *compulsus*, driven together].

com·punc·tion (kạm·pungk'·shạn) *n.* remorse of conscience; scruple. **compunctious** *a.* conscience-stricken; regretful; remorseful [L. *con.; pungere*, to prick].

com·pute (kạm·pūt') *v.t.* to count; to calculate; to estimate. **computable** *a.* **computation** *n.* calculation; reckoning [L. *con.; putare*, to reckon].

com·rade (kắm'·rad) *n.* a close friend or companion; a mate; an associate. **-ship** *n.* close friendship; fellowship; affectionate association [Sp. *camarada*, a room-mate].

con (kǎn) *v.t.* to study; to pore over; to learn by heart. *pr.p.* **-ning**. *pa.t.* **-ned** [O.E. *cunnan*, to know].

con (kǎn) (*Naut.*) *v.t.* and *i.* to superintend the steering of a vessel [L. *conducere*, to guide].

con (kǎn) *adv.* (abbrev. of *contra*), against, e.g. in the phrase **pro and con**, for and against. **the pro and con** *n.* Also *pl.* **the pros and cons**, the advantages and disadvantages [L.].

con (kǎn) *a.* (*Slang*) confidence; *v.t.* to swindle. *pr.p.* **-ning**. *pa.t.* **-ned**.

con- prefix fr. L. *cum*, with, together.

con·cat·e·nate (kạn·kat'·ạ·nāt) *v.i.* to link together; to unite in a series. **concatenation** *n.* a series of things depending on each other;

a connected chain, as of circumstances [L. *con-*; *catena*, a chain].

con·cave (kán'·kāv) *a.* hollow and curved inwards, as the inner surface of a vault. **concavity** (kán·kav'·i·ti.) *n.* hollowness [L. *con-*; *cavus*, hollow].

con·ceal (kạn·sēl') *v.t.* to hide or secrete; to mask or disguise; to withhold from knowledge. **-ment** *n.* [L. *con-*; *celare*, to hide].

con·cede (kạn·sēd') *v.t.* to yield; to admit to be true; to grant; to surrender; *v.i.* to admit [L. *concedere*, to yield].

con·ceit (kạn·sēt') *n.* over-estimation of self; vanity; opinion; fanciful thought. **-ed** *a.* vain. **-edly** *adv.* [fr. *conceive*].

con·ceive (kạn·sēv') *v.t.* to form an idea in the mind; to think; to imagine; to understand; *v.i.* to become pregnant; to have a notion. **conceivable** *a.* that may be believed, imagined, or understood. **conceivably** *adv.* [L. *con-*; *capere*, to take, seize].

con·cen·trate (kán'·sen·trāt) *v.i.* to bring to a common center; to reduce to small space; to increase in strength; to condense; *v.i.* to come together; to devote all attention. **concentration** *n.* the act of concentrating; increased strength; the fixation of the mind on something. **concentration camp**, a place of detention. [L. *con-*; *centrum*, the center].

con·cen·tric (kạn·sen'·trik) *a.* having the center. **-al** *a.* **-ally** *adv.* **concentricity** (kán·san·tris'·a·ti·) *n.*

con·cept (kán'·sept) *n.* an abstract notion; a mental impression of an object. **conception** (kạn·sep'·shạn) *n.* the act of conceiving; the thing conceived; a mental picture; an idea; a notion; (*Med.*) the beginning of pregnancy. **conceptive** *a.* pert. to conception; capable of conceiving. **conceptual** *a.* pert. to conception or to a concept [L. *concipere*, to conceive].

con·cern (kạn·surn') *v.t.* to relate or belong to; to be of importance to; to be the business of; to make uneasy; *n.* that which relates or belongs to one; interest in, or care for, any person or thing; worry; a business establishment. **-ed** *a.* interested; worried; anxious; troubled; involved. **-ing** *prep.* regarding; with respect to. **-ment** *n.* [L. *con-*; *cernere*, to distinguish].

con·cert (kạn·surt') *v.t.* to plan together; to arrange; to design. **-ed** *a.* mutually planned; (*Mus.*) arranged in parts. **concert** (kán'·sert) *n.* agreement in a plan; harmony; a musical entertainment. **concertina** (·tē'·na) *n.* a small hexagonal accordion. **concerto** (kạn·cher'·tō) *n.* a musical composition arranged for a solo instrument with orchestral accompaniment [Fr. *concerter*].

concertina

con·ces·sion (kạn·sesh'·ạn) *n.* the act of conceding; a special privilege; a grant; an admission. **-aire** *n.* one who holds a concession. **-ary** *a.* [L. *con-*; *cedere*, to yield].

conch (kánk, kánch) *n.* a seashell; the spiral shell used as a trumpet by the Tritons [L. *concha*, a shell].

con·chol·o·gy (káng·kál'·ạ·ji·) *n.* the scientific study of shells and shellfish. **conchologist** *n.* [Gk. *konchē*, a shell; *logos*, discourse].

con·cil·i·ate (kạn·sil'·i·āt) *v.t.* to win over to goodwill; to appease; to make peace; to pacify. **conciliation** *n.* **conciliative** *a.* conciliatory. **conciliatory** *a.* tending to pacify [L. *conciliare*, to bring together].

con·cise (kạn·sis') *a.* brief; condensed; comprehensive. **-ly** *adv.* in few words; tersely. **-ness** *n.* [L. *concisus*, fr. *caedere*, to cut].

con·clave (kán'·klāv) *n.* a private meeting of cardinals for the election of a pope; where they meet; any secret meeting [L. *conclave*, a room; fr. *clavis*, a key].

con·clude (kạn·klōōd') *v.t.* to bring to an end; to close; to finish; to complete; to make a final judgment of; to infer; *v.i.* to come to an end [L. *concludere*].

con·clu·sion (kạn·klōō'·zhạn) *n.* the end; the last part of anything; the final judgment; inference; result from experiment. **conclusive** *a.* final; convincing [L. *concludere*, to end].

con·coct (kạn·kákt') *v.t.* to make a mixture; to make up, esp. a story. **concoction** *n.* [L. *concoctus*, cooked].

con·com·i·tant (kạn·kám'·ạ·tant) *a.* accompanying; attending; going along with; *n.* an accompanying circumstance. **concomitance, concomitancy** *n.* the state of being concomitant; coexistence [L. *concomitari*, to go with as companion].

con·cord (kán'·kawrd) *n.* agreement; union between persons, as in opinions, etc.; harmony; unison; consonance; *v.i.* to agree. **concordance** *n.* agreement; an index to the words of a book (esp. of the Bible) with references to the places of their occurrence. **concordant** *a.* harmonious [L. *con-*; *cor, cordis*, the heart].

con·cor·dat (kán·kawr'·dat) *n.* an agreement between the Pope and a sovereign or government on religious questions; a pact; a treaty [L. *con-*; *cor, cordis*, the heart].

con·course (kán'·kōrs) *n.* a gathering together; an assembly; a crowd; a promenade or roadway in a park; a large space in a railroad station [L. *concursus*, running together].

con·cres·cence (kán·kres'·ạns) *n.* a growing together [L. *con-*; *crescere*, to grow].

con·crete (kán'·krēt) *a.* made of concrete; consisting of matter, facts, etc.; solid; not abstract; specific; *n.* a mixture of sand, cement, etc., used in building; anything real or specific; *v.t.* to form into a solid mass; *v.i.* to unite into a mass; to harden. **-ly** *adv.* **-ness** *n.* **concretion** *n.* the state of being concrete; a mass formed of parts pressed together [L. *concrescere*, to grow together].

con·cu·bine (káng'·kū·bīn) *n.* a woman who lives with a man without being his lawful wife. **concubinage** (kán·kū'·bạ·nij) *n.* the living together of a man and a woman not legally married [L. *con-*; *cubare*, to lie].

con·cu·pis·cence (kán·kū'·pạs·ạns) *n.* violent sexual desire; lust. **concupiscent, concupiscible** *a.* lustful [L. *con-*; *cupere*, to desire].

con·cur (kạn·kur') *v.i.* to agree; to express agreement; to meet in the same point; to coincide. *pr.p.* **-ring** *pa.p.* and *pa.t.* **-red.** **-rence** *n.* **-rent** *a.* acting in conjunction; agreeing; taking place at the same time; accompanying; *n.* a joint or contributory cause. **-rently** *adv.* [L. *concurrere*, to run together].

con·cus·sion (kạn·kush'·ạn) *n.* act of shaking by sudden striking; shock; (*Med.*) a violent disturbance of the brain caused by a blow or fall [L. *concussio*, a shaking together].

con·demn (kạn·dem') *v.t.* to blame; to censure; to pronounce guilty; to sentence; to reprove; to declare unfit for use. **-ation** *n.* **-atory** *a.* [L. *condemnare*].

con·dense (kạn·dens') *v.t.* to make more dense, close, or compact; to make more solid; to concentrate; to change a vapor or gas into liquid or solid; to pack into few words; *v.i.* to become more dense or compact; to pass from vapor to liquid or solid. **condensation** *n.* the act of condensing; the state of being condensed; conciseness; in psycho-analysis, the symbolization of two or more ideas by one symbol. **-d** *a.* compressed; concise; (of milk) evaporated and preserved in cans.**-r** *n.* one who, or that which, condenses; an apparatus for changing vapor or gas into liquid or solid; (*Elect.*) a device for accumulating and holding an electric charge [L. *condensare*, fr. *densus, dense*].

con·de·scend (kán·dạ·send') *v.i.* to come down from one's position, rank, or dignity; to stoop; to deign; to be gracious or affable to inferiors; to patronize. **-ing** *a.* **condescension** *n.* [L. *condescendere*, to come down].

con·dign (kạn·din') *a.* deserved; adequate. **-ly** *adv.* [L. *dignus*, worthy].

con·di·ment (kán'·dạ·mạnt) *n.* a relish; seasoning for food [L. *condire*, to pickle].

con·di·tion (kạn·dish'·ạn) *n.* a thing on which a statement, happening, or existing depends; state or circumstances of anything; position as to worldly circumstances; rank; disposition; a prerequisite; a stipulation; *v.t.* to stipulate; to impose conditions on; to render fit and in good health; *v.i.* to make terms. **-al** *a.* depending on conditions; not absolute. **-ally** *adv.* **-ed** *a.* **conditioned reflex**, in psychology, an automatic response [L.].

con·dole (kạn·dōl') *v.i.* to grieve with; to offer sympathy. **condolence, -ment** *n.* an expression of sympathy [L. *condolere*, to suffer with].

con·do·min·i·um (kán·dạ·min'·i·ạm) *n.* joint rule of a state by two or more states [L. *con-*; and *dominium*, dominion].

con·done (kạn·dōn') *v.t.* to pardon; to forgive; to overlook [L. *condonare* to, remit].

con·duce (kạn·dūs') *v.i.* to lead to some end or result; to help; to promote. **conducive** *a.* having a tendency to promote, help, or forward. **conduciveness** *n.* [L. *conducere*, to bring together, to lead].

con·duct (kán'·dukt) *n.* the act of guiding; guidance; management; behavior. **conduct** (kạn·dukt') *v.t.* to guide; to lead; to direct; to manage; to behave. **-ance** *n.* (*Elect.*) the property of a body for conducting electricity. **conductible** *a.* **conduction** *n.* the act of conducting; the transmission or flow of heat from one body to another. **conductive** *a.* able to transmit heat, electricity, etc. **conductivity** *n.* the quality of being conductive. **conductor** *n.* a guide; the leader of a choir or orchestra; one in charge of a bus, train, etc. who collects fares; a substance capable of transmitting heat, electricity, etc. [L. *conducere*, to lead].

con·duit (kán'·dit, ·doo·it) *n.* a pipe or channel for conveying fluids [Fr. fr. *conduire*, to lead].

cone (kōn) *n.* a solid body tapering to a point from a circular base; anything of this shape; the fruit of the pine, fir, etc. **conic, conical** (kán'·i·kạl) *a.* having the form of, or pert. to, a cone. **conically** *adv.* **conics** *n.* (*Geom.*) the branch dealing with conic sections. [Gk. *kōnos*].

con·el·rad (kán'·l·rad) *n.* a system used by radio in time of war to prevent the enemy from locating cities by radio beams.

con·fab (kán'·fab) *n.* (*Colloq.*) a chat.

con·fab·u·late (kạn·fab'·yạ·lāt) *v.i.* to chat. **confabulation** *n.* [L. *confabulari*].

con·fec·tion (kạn·fek'·shạn) *n.* the act of compounding different substances into one compound; candy, ice cream, etc. **-ary** *a.* **-er** *n.* one who makes or sells confections. **-er's sugar** *n.* finely powdered sugar. **-ery** *n.* candies, etc.; a shop where these are sold [L. *conficere*, to make up].

con·fed·er·ate (kạn·fed'·ẹr·it) *a.* united in a league; bound by treaty; allied; *n.* an ally; an accomplice; *v.t.* and *i.* (kạn·fed'·ẹr·āt) to unite in a league. **confederacy** *n.* a union; an alliance. **confederation** *n.* the act of forming a confederacy; an alliance [L. *con-*; *foedus*, a league].

con·fer (kạn·fur') *v.t.* to bestow upon; to grant; to award; *v.i.* to consult together; to take advice; to discuss. *pr.p.* **-ring.** *pa.p.* and *pa.t.* **-red. -ee** *n.* one who takes part in a conference; a recipient of an award. **conference** *n.* a meeting; a consultation [L. *conferre*, to bring together].

con·fess (kạn·fes') *v.t.* to admit; to own; to acknowledge; to grant; to declare one's sins orally to a priest; (of a priest) to hear the sins of; to make confession; plead guilty. **-edly** *adv.* admittedly. **confession** (kạn·fesh'·ạn) *n.* admission; avowal of sins; declaring one's sins to priest. **confessional** *n.* the stall where a priest sits to hear confessions; *a.* pert. to confession. **-or** *n.* a priest who hears confessions. **confession of faith**, a statement of religious beliefs [L. *confiteri, confessus*, to acknowledge].

con·fet·ti (kạn·fet'·i·) *n.pl.* small bits of colored paper, for throwing at weddings, carnivals, etc. [It.].

con·fide (kạn·fīd') *v.t.* to hand over to the charge of; to entrust to; to tell a secret to; *v.i.* to put faith in; to rely on. **confidant** *n.* (*fem.* **confidante**) a person in whom one can confide [L. *con-*; *fidere*, to trust].

con·fi·dence (kän′·fa·dans) *n.* that in which faith is put; belief; trust; feeling of security; self-reliance; presumption; intimacy; a secret. **confident** *a.* having assurance; bold. **confidently** *adv.* **confidential** (kan·fa·den′·shal) *a.* treated with confidence; private; secret. **confidentially** *adv.* [L. *con-; fidere*, to trust].

con·fig·u·ra·tion (kan·fig·ya·rā′·shan) *n.* outward shape, form, or figure; grouping; outline; aspect [L. *con-; figurare*, to fashion].

con·fine (kan·fīn′) *v.t.* to keep within bounds; to limit; to enclose; to imprison; *v.i.* to have a common boundary; **confine** (kän′·fīn) *n.* usually in *pl.* **confines**, boundary; limit. **-ment** *n.* imprisonment; restraint; detention; childbirth [L. *confinis*, having a common frontier].

con·firm (kan·furm′) *v.t.* to make strong; to settle; to make valid by formal assent; to ratify; to make certain; to verify. **confirmation** *n.* the act of making strong, valid, certain, etc.; proof; a religious rite. **-ative** *a.* **-atory** *a.* **-ed** *a.* [L. *confirmare*].

con·fis·cate (kän′·fis·kāt) *v.t.* to seize by authority; to take possession of without compensation; *a.* forfeited. **confiscation** *n.* **confiscator** *n.* **confiscatory** *a.* [L. *confiscare*].

con·fla·gra·tion (kän·fla·grā′·shan) *n.* a destructive fire [L. *con-; flagrare*, to blaze].

con·flict (kan·flikt′) *v.i.* to dash together; to clash; to be at odds with; to be inconsistent with; to differ. **conflict** (kän′·flikt) *n.* a prolonged struggle; a trial of strength; strong disagreement. **-ing** *a.* differing; contradictory [L. *confligere, conflictum*, to strike against].

con·flu·ence (kän′·flōō·ans) *n.* a flowing together; the meeting of two or more rivers, streams, etc.; a large assemblage; a crowd. **confluent** *a.* Also **conflux** [L. *confluere*, to flow together].

con·form (kan·fawrm′) *v.t.* to make like; to bring into agreement; *v.i.* to comply; to agree; *a.* in accord. **-able** *a.* corresponding in form; similar; submissive. **-ably** *adv.* **-ation** *n.* the manner in which a body is formed or shaped; structure. **-ist** *n.* one who complies with usage or custom. **-ity** *n.* [L. *conformare*, to give the same shape].

con·found (kan·found′) *v.t.* to mix up; to bring to confusion; to bewilder. **-ed** *a.* confused; baffled; perplexed; (*Colloq.*) odious [L. *confundere*, to pour together].

con·front (kan·frunt′) *v.t.* to face boldly; to oppose; to bring face to face; to compare. **confrontation** *n.* [Fr. *confronter*, fr. *front*, the brow].

Con·fu·cius (kan·fū′·shas) *n.* Chinese philosopher.

con·fuse (kan·fūz′) *v.t.* to mix up; to jumble together; to muddle; to perplex; hence, to mistake one thing for another. **-d** *a.* mixed up; perplexed. **confusedly** *adv.* **confusion** *n.* the state of being confused; disorder; bewilderment [L. *confundere*, to pour together].

con·fute (kan·fūt′) *v.t.* to prove to be wrong; to disprove. **confutable** *a.* **confutation** *n.* [L. *confutare*].

con·geal (kan·jēl′) *v.t.* and *i.* to freeze, as a fluid; to stiffen; to solidify; to curdle; to coagulate; *v.i.* to become stiff or solidified, from cold. **-able** *a.* **-ment** *a.* a thing congealed; a clot. **congelation** *n.* [L. *con-; gelare*, to freeze].

con·gen·ial (kan·jēn′·yal) *a.* allied in disposition and tastes; kindred; agreeable. **-ly** *adv.* **congeniality** *n.* [L. *con-; genius*, spirit].

con·gen·i·tal (kan·jen′·a·tal) *a.* existing at the time of birth [L. *con-; genitus*, born].

con·gest (kan·jest′) *v.t.* to collect into a mass; to produce a hampering accumulation; to overcrowd. **-ed** *a.* overcrowded. **congestion** *n.* [L. *con-; gerere, gestum*, to bring, to carry].

con·glom·er·ate (kan·gläm′·er·it) *a.* gathered into a mass; clustered; *v.t.* (·rāt′) to bring together into a united mass; *n.* (*Geol.*) rock composed of fragments of rock cemented together. **conglomeration** *n.* a mixed collection; a cluster [L. *con-; glomus*, a mass].

con·grat·u·late (kan·gra′·cha·lāt) *v.t.* to wish joy to; to compliment; to felicitate. **congratulation** *n.* an expression of pleasure at the good fortune of someone; felicitation. **congratulatory** *a.* [L. *congratulari*].

con·gre·gate (kang′·gra·gāt) *v.t.* to gather into a crowd or assembly; *v.i.* to meet together; in a body; (·git) *a.* assembled; collective. **congregation** *n.* the act of assembling; an assemblage; a gathering of persons for worship; a religious body. **congregational** *a.* **Congrega-**

conglomerate rock

-tionalism *n.* a system of church government that gives independence to each local church [L. *con-; grex*, a flock].

con·gress (käng′·gras) *n.* a meeting together of persons; a formal assembly, e.g. of envoys or representatives of governments. **Congress** *n.* the legislative body of the United States. **-man** *n.* a member of the U.S. House of Representatives. **-woman** *n.* **congressional** *a.* [L. *congredi, congressus*, to meet].

con·gru·ent (käng′·groo·ant) *a.* agreeing together; corresponding. **congruence, congruency** *n.* suitableness. **congruity** *n.* **congruous** *a.* accordant; suitable [L. *congruere*, to run together].

con·ic See **cone**.

co·nif·e·rae (kō·nif′·a·rē) *n.pl.* an order of trees bearing a cone-shaped fruit. **coniferous** *a.* [L. *conus*, a cone; *ferre*, to bear].

con·jec·ture (kan·jek′·cher) *n.* a guess; an opinion founded on insufficient proof; surmise; inference; *v.t.* to guess; to surmise; to infer on insufficient grounds. **conjecturable** *a.* **conjectural** *a.* [L. *con-; jacere*, to throw].

con·join (kan·join′) *v.t.* to join together; *a.* united; concerted; associated [L. *conjungere*, join together].

con·ju·gal (kän′·joo·gal) *a.* pert. to marriage; connubial; matrimonial. **-ly** *adv.* **conjugality** (kän′·ja·gal′·i·ti·) *n.* the married state [L. *conjux, conjugis*, a spouse].

con·ju·gate (kän′·joog·āt) *v.t.* (*Gram.*) to recite or write all the different parts of a verb. **conjugation** *n.* the act of uniting; (*Gram.*) a class of verbs inflected in the same manner; (*Biol.*) the fusion of cells or individuals for reproduction [L. *con-; jugum*, a yoke].

con·junct (kan·jungkt′) *a.* joined together; united; associated. **-ly** *adv.* **conjunction** *n.* union; concurrence of events; (*Gram.*) a word used to join clauses, etc. **conjunctive** *a.* closely connected; serving to connect [L. *con-; jungere*, to join].

con·junc·ti·vi·tis (kan·jungk·ta·vī′·tas) *n.* inflammation of the mucous membrane lining the eyelid [L. *con-; jungere*, to join].

con·jure (kan·joor′) *v.t.* to call on by a sacred name; solemnly to implore. **conjure** (kun′·jer) *v.i.* to practice magic; to practice the arts of a conjurer; (*Fig.*) to imagine. **conjuration** *n.* the act of calling upon or summoning by a sacred name. **conjurer, conjuror** *n.* a magician; a juggler [L. *con-; jurare*, to swear].

conk (känk) (*Slang*) a blow; — **out**, fail suddenly.

con·nect (ka·nekt′) *v.t.* to fasten together; to associate; to relate; to attach; to join; *v.i.* to unite; to have a close relation. **-ed** *a.* joined; coherent. **-edly** *adv.* **connection** *n.* a link; the act of uniting, or state of being united; that which connects; a kinsman. **-ive** *a.* binding; *n.* a connecting word. **-or** *n.* **well connected**, of good family [L. *con-; nectere*, to bind].

con·nive (ka·nīv′) *v.i.* to wink at; to pretend not to see; to co-operate secretly (with 'at'). **connivance** *n.* consent in wrong-doing. **-r** *n.* [L. *connivere*, to shut the eyes].

con·nois·seur (kän·a·sur′) *n.* an expert, esp. in fine arts [Fr. *connaître*, to know].

con·note (ka·nōt′) *v.t.* to mean; to imply; to signify; to have a meaning in addition to the primary meaning. **connotate** *v.t.* to connote. **connotation** *n.* a secondary implied meaning. **connotative** *a.* [L. *con-; notare*, to mark].

con·nu·bi·al (ka·nū′·bi·al) *a.* pert. to marriage. **connubiality** *n.* [L. *con-; nubere*, to marry].

co·noid (kō′·noid) *n.* any object shaped like a cone [Gk. *konos*, a cone; *eidos*, form].

con·quer (käng′·ker) *v.t.* to reduce by force, as of arms; to overcome; to subjugate or subdue; to vanquish; to surmount; *v.i.* to be victorious; to prevail. **-able** *a.* **-or** *n.* **conquest** (käng′·kwest) *n.* the act of conquering; that which is conquered [L. *con-; quaerere*, to seek].

con·quis·ta·dor (kän·kwis′·ta·dawr) *n.* a conqueror, applied to the Spanish conquerors of Mexico and Peru in the 16th cent. [Sp.].

con·san·guin·e·ous (kän·sang·gwin′·i·as) *a.* of the same blood; related by birth. **consanguinity** *n.* [L. *con-; sanguis*, blood].

con·science (kän′·shans) *n.* the faculty by which we know right from wrong. **conscientious** (kän·shi·en′·shas) *a.* governed by dictates of conscience. **conscientiously** *adv.* **conscientiousness** *n.* **conscionable** (kän′·shan·a·bl) *a.* governed by conscience. **—stricken** *a.* seized with scruples. **conscien-**

-tious objector, a man who refuses to serve in the armed forces, on moral or religious grounds [L. *conscire*, to be well aware].

con·scious (kän′·shas) *a.* having inward knowledge (of); aware (of); having the use of one's faculties. **-ly** *adv.* **-ness** *n.* the state of being mentally awake to one's surroundings [L. *conscire*, to be aware].

con·script (kan·skript′) *v.t.* to enroll compulsorily for service in the armed forces. **conscript** (kän′·skript) *n.* one compelled to serve as a soldier, sailor, or airman, etc. **conscription** *n.* [L. *con-; scribere*, to write].

con·se·crate (kän′·sa·krāt) *v.t.* to set apart for sacred uses; to dedicate. **consecration** *n.* [L. *con-; sacrare*, to hallow].

con·sec·u·tive (kan·sek′·ya·tiv) *a.* following one another in unbroken order; successive; resulting; (*Gram.*) expressing consequence. **-ly** *adv.* **-ness** *n.* [L. *con-; sequi*, to follow].

con·sen·sus (kan·sen′·sas) *n.* a general agreement; unanimity [L.].

con·sent (kan·sent′) *n.* agreement; assent; permission; *v.i.* to agree. **consentient** (kan·sen′·shant) *a.* united in opinion. **consentience** *n.* [L. *con-; sentire*, to feel].

con·se·quent (kän′·sa·kwent) *a.* following as a result; *n.* effect. **-ly** *adv.* therefore; as a result; by logical sequence. **consequence** *n.* that which naturally follows; result; importance; value. **consequential** (kän·sa·kwen′·shal) *a.* [L. *con-; sequi*, to follow].

con·serve (kan·surv′) *v.t.* to keep safe; to preserve, to maintain; *n.* anything conserved; fruit, etc. prepared with sugar. **conservation** *n.* preservation; safe-guarding; protection; the official safe-guarding of forests, rivers, ports, etc.; the area so protected. **conservative** *a.* tending to conserve; disposed to maintain existing institutions; hostile to change; *n.* one opposed to hasty changes or innovations. *n.* a greenhouse for plants; a school of music. **conservatory** [L. *con-; servare*, to keep].

con·sid·er (kan·sid′·er) *v.t.* to reflect upon carefully; to examine carefully; to be of opinion; to regard as; *v.i.* to deliberate seriously. **-able** *a.* worthy of attention; moderately large. **-ably** *adv.* **-ate** *a.* thoughful for others; circumspect. **-ately** *adv.* **-ateness** *n.* **-ation** *n.* the act of considering; deliberation; fee or recompense; thoughtful regard for others. **-ed** *a.* carefully thought out. **-ing** *prep.* in view of; taking into account [L. *considerare*, observe].

con·sign (kan·sīn′) *v.t.* to give, transfer, or deliver in a formal manner; to entrust (goods) to a carrier for transport by rail, ship, etc.; *v.i.* to agree. **consignee** (cán·si·nē′) *n.* the person to whom goods are consigned. **-er, -or** *n.* the person who consigns goods. **-ment** *n.* [L. *consignare*, to seal].

con·sist (kan·sist′) *v.i.* to be composed of; to be in a fixed or permanent state; to be compatible with. **-ence, -ency** *n.* a condition of being fixed; a degree of firmness or density; agreement or harmony. **consistent** *a.* compatible; constant in adhering to principles, etc. [L. *con-; sistere*, to stand].

con·sis·to·ry (kan·sis′·tar·i·) *a.* pert. to an ecclesiastical court; *n.* any solemn assembly or council [L. *consistorium*, a council].

con·sole (kan·sōl′) *v.t.* to comfort in distress; to solace; to encourage. **consolable** *a.* able to be consoled. **consolation** *n.* the act of comforting; that which comforts; solace; encouragement. **consolatory** *a.* [L. *consolari*].

con·sol·i·date (kan·säl′·a·dāt) *v.t.* and *i.* to make solid; to make firm; to combine into a connected whole; to strengthen. **consolidation** *n.* the act of making or becoming compact and firm [L. *con-; solidus*, solid].

con·som·mé (kän·sa·mā′) *n.* a clear meat soup [Fr.].

con·so·nant (kän′·sa·nant) *a.* agreeing with; in accord; *n.* a sound (or letter) making a syllable only with a vowel; a non-vowel. **-ly** *adv.* **consonance, consonancy** *n.* agreement; harmony [L. *consonare*, to sound with].

con·sort (kän′·sawrt) *n.* a companion or partner; a wife or husband. **consort** (kan·sawrt′) *v.t.* to join; *v.i.* to keep company; to associate; to agree [L. *consors*, fr. *sors*, fate].

con·sor·ti·um (kan·sawr′·shi·am) *n.* an association for a common end; an agreement between countries for mutual assistance and joint action [L.].

con·spec·tus (kan·spek′·tas) *n.* a general sketch or outline of a subject; a synopsis [L. fr. *conspicere*, to look at].

con·spic·u·ous (kan·spik′·yoo·as) *a.* easy to be seen; very noticeable. **-ly** *adv.* **-ness, conspicuity** *n.* [L. *conspicere*, to catch sight of].

con·spire (kan·spīr′) *v.i.* to unite for an evil purpose; to plot together. **conspiracy** (kan·spir′·a·si·) *n.* a combination of persons for an evil purpose; a plot. **conspirator** *n.* (*fem.* **conspiratress**). **conspiratorial** *a.* [L. *conspirare*, lit. to breathe together].

con·sta·ble (kän′·sta·bl, kun·sta′·bl) *n.* a peace officer; a high officer in the Middle Ages. **constabulary** (kan·stab′·ya·ler·i·) *a.* pert. to constables; *n.* [L.L. *comes stabuli*, count of the stable, marshal].

con·stant (kän′·stant) *a.* fixed; steadfast; invariable, permanent, *n.* that which is not subject to change. **-ly** *adv.* **constancy** *n.* steadfastness; resolution; fidelity [L. *constare*, to

con·stel·la·tion (kǎn·stẹ·lā'·shạn) n. a group of fixed stars; an assemblage of notable persons or things [L. con-; stella, a star].

con·ster·na·tion (kǎn·stẹr'·nā'·shạn) n. amazement or terror that throws the mind into confusion. **consternate** v.t. to fill with alarm or dismay [L. con-; sternere, to strew].

con·sti·pate (kǎn'·sta·pāt) v.t. to clog or make sluggish. **constipation** n. insufficient; irregular evacuation of the bowels [L. con-; stipare, to pack].

con·sti·tute (kǎn'·sti·tōōt) v.t. to appoint to an office or function; to establish; to set up; to form; to compose. **constitution** n. the act of constituting; the natural state of body or mind; composition; the system or body of laws under which a state exists. **constitutional** a. pert. to the constitution; due to a person's physical or mental composition; n. a walk for the benefit of health.**constitutionally** adv. **constitutionalist** n. one who upholds constitutional government. **constitutionality** n. **constitutive** (kǎn'·sti·tū·tiv) a. having powers to enact or establish. **constituent** (kǎn·stich'·ōo·ạnt) a. serving to compose or make up; an element [L. constituere, to place together].

con·strain (kǎn·strān') v.t. to force or compel; to confine; to restrain; to limit. **-t** n. compelling force; restraining force; unnaturalness or embarrassment of manner [L. con-; stingere, to press].

con·strict (kǎn·strikt') v.t. to draw together; to cramp; to cause to shrink or contract; to squeeze. **constriction** n. **-ive** a. that which constricts; the boa-constrictor [L. con-; stringere, to bind].

con·struct (kǎn·strukt') v.t. to build; to fabricate; to devise or invent; to compile. **construction** n. the act of building; erection; structure; interpretation or meaning. **-ive** a. **-iveness** n. **-or** n. [L. construere, to build].

con·strue (kǎn·strōō') v.t. to interpret; to put a construction upon; to deduce; to explain the structure of a sentence and the connection of the words in it; to translate. **construable** a. **-r** n. [L. construere, to build].

con·sub·stan·ti·ate (kǎn·sạb·stan'·shi·āt) v.t. and i. to unite in one substance or nature. **consubstantial** a. **consubstantiation** n. (Theol.) the doctrine of the substantial union of Christ's body and blood with the elements of the sacrament [L. consubstantialis, of like nature].

con·sul (kǎn'·sạl) n. an officer appointed by a government to represent it in a foreign country. **-ar** a. **-ate** n. the offices of a consul. **-ship** n. [L.].

con·sult (kǎn·sult') v.t.to ask advice of; to seek the opinion of; to look to for information; to refer to; v.i. to confer. **-ant** n. one who consults; one who gives expert advice. **-ing** a. **-ation** n. the act of consulting; a council or conference. **-ative** a. advisory [L. consulere].

con·sume (kǎn·sōōm') v.t. to waste; to destroy; to use up; to eat or drink up; v.i. to waste away. **consumable** a. **-r** n. [L. consumere, to use up].

con·sum·mate (kǎn'·sạm·āt) v.t. to complete; to finish; to perfect; (Law) to complete marriage by sexual intercourse. **consummate** (kǎn·sum'·it) a. complete; perfect. **-ly** adv. **consummation** n. [L. consummare].

con·sump·tion (kǎn·sump'·shạn) n. the act of consuming; the amount consumed; (Med.) a wasting disease of the lungs; pulmonary tuberculosis. **consumptive** a. destructive; wasteful; wasting; affected with, or inclined to, pulmonary tuberculosis; n. (Med.) a person suffering from consumption [L. consumere, consumptum, to use up].

con·tact (kǎn'·takt) n. a touching; (Colloq.) a meeting; v.t. to get in touch with a person. **-ual** (kǎn·tak'·choo·al) a. implying contact. — **lens**, an invisible eye-glass fitting over the eyeball [L. tangere, tactum, to touch].

con·ta·gion (kǎn·tā'·jạn) n. the transmission of a disease from one person to another; physical or moral pestilence. **contagious** a. communicable [L. contagio, fr. tangere, to touch].

con·tain (kǎn·tān') v.t. to hold; to have room for; to comprise; to include; to restrain. **-able** a. **-er** n. [L. con-; tenere, to hold].

con·tam·i·nate (kǎn·tam'·a·nāt) v.t. to soil; to taint; to corrupt; to infect. **contaminable** a. **contamination** n. pollution; taint; (War) the result of coming into contact with liquid gases or radioactive particles [L. contamen, contagion].

con·temn (kǎn·tem') v.t. to despise; to scorn. **-er** n. [L. contemnere].

con·tem·plate (kǎn'·tem·plāt) v.t. to look at with attention; to meditate on; to have in view; to intend; v.i. to think studiously; to reflect. **contemplation** n. **contemplative** a. **contemplatively** adv. [L. contemplari, to observe].

con·tem·po·ra·ne·ous (kǎn·tem·pạ·rā'·ni··as) a. having or happening at the same time. **-ly** adv. **-ness** n. **contemporary** a. living or happening at the same time; contemporaneous; present-day; n. one who was at the same time as another; a person approximately of one's own age [L. con-; tempus, temporis, time].

con·tempt (kǎn·tempt') n. scorn; disgrace; disregard; open disrespect to court orders or rule. **-ible** a. worthy of contempt; despicable. **-ibleness** n. **-ibly** adv. **-uous** a. expressing contempt or disdain; scornful. **-uously** adv. **-uousness** n. [L. contemnere, contemptum, to despise].

con·tend (kǎn·tend') v.i. to fight or struggle with; to strive for; to dispute; to assert strongly. **-er** n. [L. con-; tendere, to stretch].

con·tent (kǎn·tent') a. satisfied; pleased; willing; v.t. to satisfy the mind of; to please; to appease; n. satisfaction; freedom from anxiety. **-edly** adv. **-edness** n. **-ment** n. satisfaction; pleasure; ease of mind [L. contentus].

con·tent (kǎn·tent') n. that which is contained; extent or area; volume. **-s** n.pl. an index of the topics treated in a book [L. continere, contentum, to contain].

con·ten·tion (kǎn·ten'·shạn) n. strife; debate; subject matter of argument or discussion. **contentious** a. quarrelsome [L. con-; tendere, tentum, to stretch].

con·ter·mi·nous (kǎn·tur'·mạn·ạs) a. having the same boundary; bordering; touching. Also **conterminable, conterminal**.

con·test (kǎn·test') v.t. to strive for; to question or resist, as a claim; to dispute; to oppose; v.i. to contend or vie (with). **contest** (kǎn'·test) n. struggle; conflict; competition; dispute; strike. **-able** a. **-ant** n. a disputant; a competitor [L. contestari, to call to witness].

con·text (kǎn'·tekst) n. that which comes immediately before or after a passage or word quoted, and therefore helps to explain it; the setting of a text. **-ual** a. pert. to the context. **contexture** n. the weaving of parts into one body; structure; style of composition in writing [L. con-; texere, to weave].

con·ti·gu·i·ty (kǎn·ti·gū'·a·ti·) n. the state of being contiguous. **contiguous** a. touching; near; adjacent [L. contiguus, touching].

con·ti·nent (kǎn'·tin·ạnt) n. one of the large divisions of unbroken land. **-al** a. pert. to a continent [L. con-; tenere, to hold].

con·ti·nent (kǎn'·tin·ạnt) a. chaste; temperate; moderate. **continence, continency** n. [L. con-; tenere, hold].

con·tin·gent (kǎn·tin'·jạnt) a. liable to happen, but not sure to do so; possible; dependent; n. contingency; a quota, esp. of troops. **-ly** adv. **contingence, contingency** n. [L. contingere, to happen].

con·tin·ue (kǎn·tin'·ū) v.t. to prolong or extend in duration; to go on with; to persist in; to resume; v.i. to remain in a state or place; to persevere; to last. **continual** a. lasting; without interruption; often repeated; unceasing. **continually** adv. **continuance** n. a remaining in existence; duration; uninterrupted succession. **continuant** a. **continuate** a. uninterrupted. **continuation** n. the act of continuing. **continuity** (kǎn·ti·nōō'·i·ti·) n. the state of being continuous; uninterrupted succession; close union. **continuous** a. united without break; uninterrupted; constant. **continuously** adv. [L. continuare].

con·tort (kǎn·tawrt') v.t. to twist violently; to writhe; to bend out of shape. **contortion** n. a twisting; writhing. **contortionist** n. one who practices contortion. **contortive** a. [L. con-; torquere, tortum, to twist].

con·tour (kǎn'·toor) n. a bounding line; outline; v.t. to draw the contour of [L. con-; tornare, to round off].

con·tra- Latin prefix meaning against, contrary, in opposition to, used to form many compounds.

con·tra·band (kǎn'·trạ·band) a. prohibited by law or treaty; n. goods, the exportation or importation of which is forbidden; smuggled goods. **contraband of war**, goods not to be supplied by a neutral to a belligerent [L. contra; L.L. bandum, a ban].

con·tra·bass (kǎn'·trạ·bās) n. (Mus.) the double-bass. Also **contrabasso**.

con·tra·cep·tion (kǎn·trạ·sep'·shạn) n. the prevention of conception; by artificial means; birth control. **contraceptive** a. and n. a drug or appliance for preventing conception [L. contra; and conception].

con·tract (kǎn·trakt') v.t. to draw together; to shorten; to reduce to a less volume; to incur or bring on; v.i. to become smaller; to become shorter; to agree upon; to become involved in. **contract** (kǎn'·trakt) n. a bargain; an agreement. **-ed** a. drawn together; narrow; mean. **-ible** a. **-ile** a. tending to contract; producing contraction. **-ility** n. **-ion** n. the act of contracting; the shortening of a word by the omission of a letter or syllable. **-or** n. one who undertakes to execute work for a fixed sum. **-ual** a. implying, or connected with, a contract [L. contractus, drawn together].

con·tra·dict (kǎn·trạ·dikt') v.t. to assert the contrary of; to deny. **contradiction** n. denial; direct opposition; discrepancy of statements. **contradictious** a. inclined to contradict. **-ive** a. containing contradiction. **-ory** a. implying a denial; diametrically opposed; inconsistent [L. contradicere, to speak against].

con·tra·dis·tinc·tion (kǎn·trạ·dis·tingk'··shạn) n. direct contrast. **contradistinctive** a. **contradistinguish** v.t. to note the difference between two things by contrasting their different qualities.

con·tral·to (kǎn·tral'·tō) n. the lowest of the three female voices; a singer of that voice [It. contra; alto].

con·trap·tion (kǎn·trap'·shạn) n. (Colloq.) a device; a gadget [perh. fr. contrivance].

con·tra·pun·tal (kǎn·trạ·pun'·tal) a. pert. to counterpoint [See counterpoint].

con·tra·ry (kǎn'·tre·ri·) a. opposed; opposing; different; adverse; self-willed; n. something the exact opposite of. **contrariety** (kǎn·trạ·rī'·ạ·ti) n. something contrary. **contrarily** adv. **contrariness** n. **contrariwise** adv. on the contrary [L. contrarius, fr. contra, against].

con·trast (kǎn·trast') v.t. to bring out differences; to set in opposition for the purpose of comparing; v.i. to be or stand in opposition. **contrast** (kǎn'·trast) n. a striking difference; a comparison to show their relative excellence [L. contra; stare, to stand].

con·tra·vene (kǎn·trạ·vēn') v.t. to oppose; to break or infringe, as a law. **contravention** n. [L. contravenire, to come against].

con·tri·bute (kǎn·trib'·yoot) v.t. to give or pay to a common fund; to help to a common result; to write for a newspaper, magazine, etc.; v.i. to lend assistance. **contributable** a. **contribution** (kǎn·tri·bū'·shạn) n. that which is contributed. **contributive** a. **contributory** a. [L. contribuere].

con·trite (kǎn'·trit) a. penitent; remorseful. **-ly** adv. **-ness** n. **contrition** (kạn·trish'·ạn) n. remorse [L. con-; terere, to grind].

con·trive (kǎn·triv') v.t. and i. to plan; to effect or bring about; to invent. **contrivance** n. the act of planning; the thing contrived; artifice or device; mechanical invention. **-r** n. [L. con-; O.Fr. trover, to find].

con·trol (kǎn·trōl') v.t. to have under command; to regulate; to check; to restrain; to direct; n. authority or power; government; restraint; in spiritualism, the spirit supposed to control the medium; the control system of levers, switches, etc. in aircraft, motor vehicles, etc. pr.p **-ling**. pa.p. and pa.t. **-led**. **-lable** a. **-ler** n. one who controls. **-lership** n. **-ment** n. [L. contra, against; rotulus, a roll].

con·tro·vert (kǎn'·trạ·vurt) v.t. to oppose or dispute by argument; to deny or refute. **-ible** adv. **controversy** n. disputation; argument, esp. by published writings; debate. **controversial** a. consisting of controversy; leading to controversy; likely to provoke argument.

con·tro·ver·sial·ly *adv.* **controversialist** *n.* [L. *contra; vertere*, to turn].

con·tu·ma·cy (kón'·tyoo·ma·si·) *n.* contempt of orders or authority; stubborn disobedience. **contumacious** *a.* rebellious. **-ly** *adv.* **-ness** *n.* [L. *contumacia*].

con·tu·me·ly (kón'·tyoo·ma·li·) *n.* insult; affront; indignity; disdainful insolence. **contumelious** (kán·tū·mē'·li·us) *a.* insolent; haughtily disdainful [L. *contumelia*].

con·tuse (kan·tūz') *v.t.* to bruise or injure without breaking the skin. **contusion** *n.* a bruise [L. *con-; tundere, tusum*, to beat].

co·nun·drum (ka·nun'·dram) *n.* a riddle; anything that puzzles [etym. unknown].

con·va·lesce (kán·va·les') *v.i.* to recover from illness. **convalescent** *a.* **convalescence** *n.* [L. *convalescere*].

con·vec·tion (kan·vek'·shan) *n.* the act or process of transmission, esp. of heat by means of currents in liquids or gases [L. *con-; vehere, vectum*, to carry].

con·vene (kan·vēn') *v.t.* to call together; *v.i.* to come together or assemble. **-r** *n.* **convenable** *a.* [L. *con-; venire*, to come].

con·ven·ient (kan·vēn'·yant) *a.* fit; suitable; affording saving of trouble; handy or easy of access. **-ly** *adv.* **convenience** *n.* that which is convenient; any appliance which makes for comfort [L. *con-; venire*, to come].

con·vent (kán'·vent) *n.* a community, esp. of nuns, devoted to a religious life; a nunnery. **conventual** *a.* [L. *con-; venire*, to come].

con·ven·ti·cle (kan·ven'·ta·kl) *n.* secret gathering, esp. for worship [L. *con-; venire*, to come].

con·ven·tion (kan·ven'·shan) *n.* the act of coming together; a formal assembly of representatives; a provisional treaty; accepted usage, custom, or rule. **-al** *a.* formed by agreement or compact; sanctioned by usage; customary. **-ally** *adv.* **-alism** *n.* that which is established by usage. **-ality** *n.* [L. *con-; venire*, to come].

con·verge (kan·vurj') *v.i.* to tend to one point; to tend to meet; to approach. **convergent** *a.* **convergence, convergency** *n.* coming together [L. *con-; vergere*, to incline].

con·verse (kan·vurs') *v.i.* to talk with. **conversable** *a.* disposed to talk; affable. **conversably** *adv.* **conversance, conversancy** *n* the state of being acquainted with. **conversant** *a.* familiar or acquainted with by use or study. **conversation** *n.* talk. **conversational** *a.* **conversation(al)ist** *n.* one who excels in conversation [L. *conversari*, to dwell with].

con·verse (kán·vurs') *a.* opposite; turned around; reversed in order or relation; *n.* (kán'·vurs) the opposite; the contrary **-ly** *adv.* [L. *conversus*, turned about].

con·vert (kan·vurt') *v.t.* to apply to another purpose; to change; to cause to adopt a religion, an opinion, etc.; *v.i.* to be turned or changed. **convert** (kán'·vurt) *n.* a converted person; one who has turned from sin to holiness. **conversion** *n.* a change from one state to another. **-er** *n.* one who, or that which, converts; (*Elect.*) a machine for changing alternating current into direct current, or altering the pressure of direct current; an iron retort. **-ible** *a.* capable of change; transformable; transmutable; *n.* (*Colloq.*) an automobile with a folding top [L. *convertere*, to turn about].

con·vex (kán·veks') *a.* curving outwards; the opposite of concave; bulging. **-ity, -ness** *n.* [L. *convexus*, arched].

con·vey (kan·vā') *v.t.* to carry; to transport; to transfer; to make over by deed; to impart; to communicate. **-able** *a.* **-ance** *n.* the act of conveying; a means of transit; a vehicle; the transference of property; the legal document by which property, titles, etc., are transferred. **-ancing** *n.* **-er, -or** *n.* [L. *con-; via*, a way].

con·vict (kan·vikt') *v.t.* to prove guilty; to pronounce guilty. **convict** (kán'·vict) *n.* a person serving a sentence. **-ion** *n.* the act of convicting; a verdict of guilty; the state of being convinced; a firm belief [L. *convincere, convictum*, to prove guilty].

con·vince (kan·vins') *v.t.* to bring to a belief; to persuade by argument; to satisfy by proof. **convincible** *a.* **convincing** *a.* **convincingly** *adv.* [L. *convincere*, to prove].

con·viv·i·al (kan·viv'·i·al) *a.* festive; jovial; social; merry. **-ly** *adv.* **conviviality** *n.* [L. *convivium*, a feast].

con·voke (kan·vōk') *v.t.* to call together; to convene; to assemble. **convocation** *n.* the act of calling together; an assembly [L. *convocare*, to call together].

con·volve (kan·válv') *v.t.* and *i.* to roll or wind together; to twist; to coil. **convolute** (kán'·va·lōōt), **convoluted** *a.* rolled together; involved; spiral. **convolution** *n.* the act of rolling together; the state of being coiled; a turn of a coil: a fold of the brain [L. *convolvere*, to roll together].

con·voy (kan·voi') *v.t.* to accompany or escort for protection, by land, sea, or air. **convoy** (kán'·voi) *n.* the act of convoying; escort; escorting protection [L. *con-; via*, a way].

con·vulse (kan·vuls') *v.t.* to shake violently; to affect with violent and irregular spasms; to cause violent disturbance. **convulsion** *n.* any violent agitation; *pl.* (*Med.*) violent and involuntary contractions of the muscles;

spasms; fits of laughter. **convulsive** *a.* characterized by convulsion; spasmodic; jerky [L. *con-; vellere, velsum*, to pluck].

convoy

coo (koo) *v.i.* to make a low, melodius sound like the note of a dove; to act in a loving manner [imit.].

cook (kook) *v.t.* to prepare food by boiling, roasting, baking, etc.; (*Colloq.*) to concoct; to falsify; *v.i.* to prepare food by the action of heat; to undergo cooking; *n.* one whose occupation is to cook food. **-ery** *n.* the art or process of cooking. **-er** *n.* **-out** *n.* meal cooked and eaten outdoors [O.E. *coc*].

cook·y, cook·ie (kook'·i·) *n.* a small sweet cake made of stiff dough which is rolled, dropped, or sliced, and baked [Dut. *koek*, cake].

cool (kool) *a.* slightly cold; self-possessed; dispassionate; chilly or frigid in manner; impudent; *n.* a moderate state of cold; *v.t.* to cause to cool; to moderate or calm; *v.i.* to become cool; to lose one's ardor or affection. **-er** *n.* a container for cooling; (*Slang*) jail. **-ish** *a.* fairly cool. **-ly** *adv.* **-ness** *n.* **-headed** *a.* calm; self-possessed. **— one's heels**, to wait a long time [O.E. *col*].

coo·lie (kool'·li·) *n.* an Asiatic laborer. Also **cooly** [prob. *Kuli*, name of tribe].

coon (koon) *n.* a raccoon [abbrev. of raccoon].

coop (koop) *n.* pen for poultry; (*Slang*) jail; *v.t.* to put up in a coop; confine [M.E. *cupe*, a basket].

coop·er (koop'·er) *n.* a maker of casks or barrels [L. *cupa*, a cask].

shop [L. *cupa*, a cask].

co·op·er·ate (kō·áp'·a·rāt) *v.i.* to act jointly with other; to unite for a common effort. **cooperation** *n.* **co-operative** *a.* **co-operator** *n.* **co-operative store**, the shop of a co-operative society, where members make their purchases and share the profits. Also **co-op** *n.* short form [L. *co-; operari*, to work].

co·opt (kō·ápt') *v.t.* to choose or elect into a body or committee by the votes of its own members. **-ion, -ation** *n.* [L. *co-; optare*, to choose].

co·or·di·nate (kō·awr'·di·nāt) *a.* equal in degree, rank, importance, etc.; *v.t.* to make equal in degree, etc.; to bring into order as parts of a whole; to adjust; *n.* a person or thing of the same rank, importance, etc. as another. **-ly** *adv.* in the same order. **-ness** *n.* **coordination** *n.* **coordinative** *a.* [L. *co-; ordo*, rank, order].

coot (koot) *n.* a small water-fowl of the rail family [M.E. *cote*].

cop (káp) *v.t.* (*Slang*) to catch or arrest. *pr.p.* **-ping.** *pat.* **-ped.** *n.* (*Slang*) a policeman..

co·part·ner (kō·párt'·ner) *n.* a partner; an associate. **-ship** *n.*

cope (kōp) *n.* cloak or mantle; a long, sleeveless vestment worn by ecclesiastics during divine service; *v.t.* to dress with a cope. **coping** *n.* the highest course of masonry in a wall [form of *cape*].

cope (kōp) *v.i.* to contend, esp. on equal terms or with success; to deal successfully (with) [L. *colaphus*, a blow with the fist].

Co·per·ni·can (kō·pur'·ni·kan) *a.* pert. to *Copernicus* the founder of modern astronomy.

cop·i·er (káp'·i·er) *n.* See **copy.**

co·pi·ous (kō'·pi·as) *a.* abundant; plentiful; of style, not concise. **-ly** *adv.* **-ness** *n.* [L. *copia*, plenty].

cop·per (káp'·er) *n.* a red-colored metal; a copper coin; *a.* copper-colored; made of copper; *v.t.* to cover with copper. **-y** *a.* made of copper; like copper. **-head** *n.* a poisonous N. American snake [L. *Cyprium aes*, bronze from the island of Cyprus].

cop·pice (káp'·is) *n.* a wood of small trees. Also **copsewood** *n.* [O.Fr. *coper*, to cut].

co·pra (káp'·ra) *n.* the dried kernel of the coconut palm [Malay.].

cop·u·la (káp'·ya·la) *n.* a connecting link; a bond; (*Gram.*) the word uniting the subject and predicate. **copulate** *v.i.* to unite sexually.

copulation *n.* **-tive** *a.* pert. to copulation; serving to unite [L. = a bond].

cop·y (káp'·i·) *n.* an imitation of an original; a writing like another writing; an exact reproduction; a transcript; a single specimen; anything to be imitated; the manuscript, etc. placed in the compositor's hands; the basic matter for a journalistic article; *v.t.* to write, print, etc. in imitation of an original; to imitate. **-ist** *n.* **copier** *n.* one who copies; an imitator. **-book** *n.* a book in which copies are written for learners to imitate. **-writer** *n.* a writer of advertisements. **-right** *n.* the legal exclusive right which an author, musician, or artist has to print, publish, and sell his own works, during a certain period of time; *a.* protected by the law of copyright [L. *copia*, abundance].

co·quet (kō·ket') *v.i.* to attempt to attract the notice, admiration, or love of; to flirt with. *pr.p.* **-ting.** *pa.p.* and *pa.t.* **-ted. coquetry** (kō'·ket·ri·) *n.* affectation of amorous advances; trifling in love; airy graces to attract admirers. **coquette** *n.* a flirt. **-tish** *a.* [Fr. *coquet*, dim. of *coq*, a cock].

cor·al (kár'·, kawr'·al) *n.* a hard reddish yellow, white, etc. substance growing on the bottom of tropical seas, and composed of the skeletons of zoophytes; *a.* coral-colored; made of coral [Gk. *korallion*].

cord (kawrd) *n.* a thick string or a thin rope of several strands; anything like a cord (e.g. spinal cord, vocal cord); a cubic measure esp. for fuel wood; *v.t.* to bind with a cord or rope. **-age** *n.* an assemblage of ropes and cords, esp. the rigging of a ship. **-ed** *a.* **-ing** *n.* ribbed surface [Gk. *chordē*].

cor·dial (kawr'·jal) *a.* expressing warmth of heart; sincere; stimulating; *n.* anything that invigorates or strengthens; a refreshing drink or medicine. **-ly** *adv.* **-ity** *n.* [L. *cor, cordis*, the heart].

cord·ite (kawrd'·īt) *n.* a smokeless explosive [fr. *cord*].

cor·don (kawr'·dan) *n.* a line of military posts enclosing an area to prevent passage; hence, a circle of persons round any place or thing to prevent access; a tasseled cord or ribbon worn as a badge of honor. **— bleu,** a person of great distinction in his field [Fr.].

cor·do·van (kawr'·da·van) *n.* Spanish leather; goatskin tanned and dressed [fr. *Cordoba*, in Spain].

cor·du·roy (kawr'·da·roi') *n.* a thick cotton fabric, corded or ribbed on the surface. *n.pl.* trousers made of this fabric [Fr. *corde du roi*, king's cord].

core (kōr) *n.* the heart or inner part, esp. of fruit; *v.t.* to take out the core [L. *cor*, the heart].

co·res·pon·dent (kō·ri·spán'·dant) *n.* in a divorce suit the man or woman charged along with the respondent as guilty of adultery.

cork (kawrk) *n.* the outer bark of the cork-tree; a stopper for a bottle, cask, etc.; *a.* made of cork; *v.t.* to stop up with a cork; to stop up generally; to give wine, beer, etc. a corky taste. **-er** *n.* (*Slang*) anything first-class. **-ing** *a.* (*Slang*) excellent. **-screw** *n.* a tool for drawing corks from bottles; *a.* shaped like a corkscrew; with a spiral twist. [L. *cortex*, bark].

cor·mo·rant (kawr'·ma·rant) *n.* a voracious seabird; gluttonous person [Fr. *cormoran*].

corn (kawrn) *n.* a single seed of oats, wheat, rye, barley, maize, etc.; an inclusive term for grain of all kinds; *v.t.* to preserve meat by salting. **-cob** *n.* the head or seed-pod in which are encased the grains of the maize plant; a tobacco pipe with the bowl made from a corn-cob. **-flour** *n.* a foodstuff consisting of the finely ground starch granules of Indian corn (maize). **-flower** *n.* an annual weed growing in cornfields and bearing blue flowers. **-husk** *n.* the outer leaves enclosing an ear of corn. **-starch** *n.* a starch used for thickening puddings, sauces, etc. **-y** *a.* (*Slang*) trite, old-fashioned, unsophisticated [O.E. *corn*].

corn (kawrn) *n.* a horny growth of the skin, usually on toes and feet. **-y** *a.* pert to a corn [L. *cornu*, a horn].

cor·ne·a (kawr'·ni·a)*n.* the transparent membrane which forms part of the outer coat of the eyeball [L. *corneus*, horny].

cor·ner (kawr'·ner) *n.* the point where two lines meet; the part of a room where two sides meet; an angle; a nook; an embarrassing position; *v.t.* to drive into a corner; to put into a position of difficulty, leaving no escape; to establish a monopoly. **-stone** n. the stone which lies at the corner of two walls, and unites them; in an important edifice a corner foundation stone laid with ceremony; something of fundamental importance; **-wise** adv. diagonally; with the corner in front. **to corner the market,** to obtain a monopoly [L. *cornu*, a horn].

cor·net (kawr'·net) n. a kind of trumpet with valves; a cone of paper [L. *cornu*, a horn].

cor·nice (kawr'·nis) n. an ornamental molding around the top of the walls of a room [Fr. *corniche*, a ledge].

cor·nu·co·pi·a (kawr·na·kō'·pi·a) n. the horn of plenty, an emblem of abundance [L. *cornu*, a horn; *copia*, plenty].

cor·ol·lar·y (kár'·, kawr'·a·ler·i·) n. an inference from a preceding statement; a deduction; a consequence [L. *corolla*, a garland].

co·ro·na (ka·rō'·na) n. the flat projecting part of a cornice; a top or crown; a halo around a heavenly body; a make of cigar (Trade Name). **-l** (kawr'·a·nal) a. pert. to a corona; n. a crown; a wreath. **coronary** a. resembling a crown or circlet; (Anat.) encircling, as of a vessel or nerve; pertaining to the arteries which supply the heart tissues. **coronary thrombosis** (Med.) a heart condition caused by a blood clot in a coronary artery. **coronate** v.t. to crown. **coronation** n. the crowning of a sovereign. **coronet** n. a small crown worn by the nobility [L. *corona*, a crown].

cor·o·ner (kár'·, kawr'·a·ner) n. a legal officer appointed to hold an inquest in cases of death [L. *corona*, a crown].

cor·po·ral (kawr'·pa·ral) n. non-commissioned officer of a company or troop, next below a sergeant [L. *caput*, the head].

cor·po·ral (kawr'·pa·ral) a. belonging or relating to the body; bodily; n. a communion ti·) n. the state of having a body; bodily subcloth. **-ly** adv. **corporality** (kawr·pa·ral'·a·stance. **corporate** (kawr'·pa·rit) a. united legally in a body; pertaining to a corporation. **corporately** adv. **corporateness** n. **corporation** (kawr·pa·rā'·shan) n. united body; a legal, municipal, mercantile, or professional association. **corporative** a. **corporeal** (kawr·paw'·ri·al) a. pert. to the body; having a body; bodily; physical. **corporeally** adv. **corporal punishment,** punishment inflicted on the body [L. *corpus*, body].

corps (kawr) n. a division of an army forming a unit; any organized body of persons. pl. **corps** (kawrz) [Fr. fr. L. *corpus*, a body].

corpse (kawrps) n. a dead body, esp. of a human being [L. *corpus*, the body].

cor·pu·lence (kawr'·pya·lans) n. excessive fatness; fleshiness; stoutness. Also **corpulency** n. **corpulent** a. [L. *corpus*, the body].

cor·pus (kawr'·pas) n. a body; the main substance of anything. pl. **corpora** [L. = a body].

cor·pus·cle (kawr'·pus·l) n. a little body; a minute particle, (Anat.) an organic cell, either moving freely, as in the blood, or intimately connected with others, as bone-corpuscles [L. *corpusculum*, dim. of *corpus*, a body].

cor·ral (ka·ral') n. an enclosure for cattle, or for defense; v.t. to drive into a corral [Sp. fr. *corro*, a circle].

cor·rect (ka·rekt') a. right; free from faults; accurate; v.t. to make right; to indicate the errors in; to bring to the standard of truth; to punish; to counteract. **-ly** adv. **-tion** n. amendment; a change to remedy a fault; punishment. **itude** n. **-ional** a. **-ive** a. having power to correct; n. that which corrects or counteracts. **-ness** n. **-or** n. [L. *corrigere*, to make right].

cor·re·late (kár'·, kawr'·a·lāt) v.i. to be mutually related, as father and son; v.t. to place in reciprocal relations; n. a correlative; either of two things or words necessarily implying the other. **correlation** n. reciprocal relation. **correlative** a. reciprocally related; n. one who, or that which, is correspondingly related to an-

other person of thing. **correlativity** n.

cor·re·spond (kár'·, kawr·a·spánd') v.i. to exchange letters; to answer or agree with in some respect; to be congruous. **-ence** n. exchange of letters; the letters themselves; mutual adaptation of one thing to another; suitability. **-ent** a. suitable; conformable; congruous; n. one with whom intercouse is maintained by exchange of letters. **-ing** a. **-ingly** adv. [L. *correspondere*, answer with].

cor·ri·dor (kár'·, kawr'·a·der) n. a gallery or passage in a building [L. *currere*, to run].

cor·ri·gen·dum (kawr·a·jen'·dam) n. something to be corrected, esp. a misprint in a book; pl. **corrigenda** [L. = to be corrected].

cor·ri·gi·ble (kár'·, kawr'·a·jabl) a. capable of being corrected [L. *corrigere*, to correct].

cor·rob·o·rate (ka·ráb'·a·rāt) v.t. to add strength to; to confirm; to support a statement, etc. **corroborant** a. giving strength. **corroboration** n. **corroborative** a. confirming; strengthening [L. *con-*; *robur*, *roboris*, strength].

cor·rode (ka·rōd') v.t. to eat away by degrees (by chemical action, disease, etc.); to rust. **corrodent** a. corrosive; n. a substance which eats away. **corrodible, corrosible** a. capable of being corroded. **corrosion** n. **corrosive** a. having the power of corroding; fretting or vexing; n. any corrosive substance [L. *con-*; *rodere*, to gnaw].

cor·ru·gate (kár'·, kawr'·a·gāt) v.t. to form into folds or alternate furrows and ridges. **corrugation** n. **-iron,** sheet-iron, corrugated to increase its rigidity [L. *con-*; *ruga*, a wrinkle].

cor·rupt (ka·rupt') v.t. and i. to make rotten; to rot; to defile; to contaminate; to make evil; to bribe; a. putrid; depraved; tainted with vice or sin; influenced by bribery; spoiled, by mistakes, or altered from the normal (of words, literary passages, etc.). **-er** n. **-ible** a. capable of being corrupted .**corruption** n. **-ive** a. **-ly** adv. **-ness** n. [L. *corrumpere*, corruptum].

cor·sage (kawr'·sáj) n. a small bouquet worn by a lady; the bodice of a lady's dress [L. *corpus*, the body].

cor·sair (kawr'·sār) n. a pirate; a pirate's vessel [Fr. *corraire*].

cor·set (kawr'·sit) n. undergarment; girdle. **corselet** (kawr'·sa·let), **corselette** (kawrs'·lit) n. a corset. **corslet, corselet** n. a piece of armor to cover the trunk of the body [Fr. *corselet*, double dim. of O.Fr. *cors*, the body, fr. L. *corpus*, the body].

cor·tège (kawr·tezh') n. a train of attendants or procession; a funeral procession [Fr.].

cor·tex (kawr'·teks) n. bark; sheath or skin of a plant. (Anat.) the outer covering of an organ, esp. the outer layer of gray matter of the brain; pl. **cortices** (kawr'·ti·sēz). **cortical** a. **corticate, corticated** a. [L. = the bark of tree].

cor·ti·sone (kawr'·ti·zōn) n. a substance produced in the adrenal glands [fr. *cortex*].

co·run·dum (ka·run'·dam) n. common mineral noted for hardness [Hind. *kurand*].

cor·us·cate (kár'·, kawr'·as·kāt) v.i. to flash; to sparkle, to glitter; to gleam. **coruscation** n. [L. *coruscare*, to glitter, vibrate].

cor·y·bant·ic (kawr'·a·bant·ik) a. rural estate; a. frenzied and delirious [Myth. goddess Cybele].

co·se·cant (kō·sē'·kant) n. (Trig.) the secant of the complement of an angle. (Abbrev.) **cosec** [L. *co-*; *secare*, to cut].

co·sig·na·to·ry (kō·sig'·na·tōr·i·) a. signing jointly; n. a joint signer of a document.

co·sine (kō'·sin) n. (Trig.) the sine of the complement of an angle. (Abbrev.) **cos.**

cos·met·ic (káz·met'·ik) a. making for beauty, esp. of the skin; n. any substance helping to improve or enhance the appearance [Gk. *kosmein*, to arrange, adorn].

cos·mic (káz'·mik) a. See **cosmos.**

cos·mo- (koz'·mō) a combining form from Gk. *kosmos*, the universe.

cos·mog·o·ny (kás·mág'·a·ni·) n. a theory of the creation of the universe and its inhabitants. [Gk. *kosmos*, the universe; *gignesthai*, to be born].

cos·mol·o·gy (kás·mál'·a·ji·) n. the science of the laws which control the universe. **cosmological** a. **cosmologist** n. [Gk. *kosmos*, the universe; *logos*, discourse].

cos·mo·naut (káz'·ma·nát) n. a space traveler.

cos·mo·pol·i·tan (kás·ma·pál'·i·tan) a. relating to all parts of the world; free from national prejudice; n. a cosmopolitan person; a citizen of the world. Also **cosmopolite** n. [Gk. *kosmos*, the universe; *politēs*, a citizen].

cos·mos (káz'·mas) n. the ordered universe; order (as opposed to 'chaos'); a genus of flower-

ing plant. **cosmic, cosmical** a. pert. to the universe, or to the earth as a part of the universe; orderly. **cosmically** adv. **cosmic rays,** radiations of great penetrating power, coming to the earth from outer space [Gk. *kosmos*, order].

Cos·sack (kás'·k) n. member of S. Russ. tribe [Turk. *quazzaq*, an adventurer].

cost (kawst) v.i. to entail the payment, loss, or sacrifice of; to cause to bear or suffer; n. price; the amount paid, or to be paid, for anything; expenditure of time, labor, etc.; suffering undergone for any end. **-liness** n. great cost or expense; expensiveness. **-ly** a. very expensive. **— price,** the wholesale, as opposed to the retail, price [L. *constare*, fr. *stare*, to stand].

cos·tal (kás'·tal) a. pert. to the ribs or to the side of the body [L. *costa*, a rib].

cos·tive (kás'·tiv) a. having sluggish motion; constipated. **-ness** n. [L. *con-*; *stipare*, to press together].

cos·tume (kás'·tūm) n. dress peculiar or appropriate, as to country, period, class, or character; a person's dress or attire. **-r** n. one who makes or deals in costumes. Also **costumier** (kás·tūm'·i·er) n. [It. *costume*, custom, fashion].

co·sy See **cozy.**

cot (kát) n. a cottage [O.E. *cot*].

cot (kát) n. a light, portable bed; (Naut.) a swinging bed on board ship [Hind. *khat*].

co·tan·gent (kō·tan'·jant) n. (Trig.) the tangent of the complement of an angle; (Abbrev.) **cot.**

cote (kōt) n. a shelter or enclosure for animals or birds; a sheep-fold [O.E. *cote*].

co·te·rie (kō'·ti·ri·) n. a set or circle of persons usually with common interests [Fr.].

co·til·lion, cotillon (kō·til'·yan) n. a lively dance, of French origin; a complex dance of elaborate figures; music for the dance [Fr. *cotillon*, a petticoat].

cot·tage (kát'·ij) n. a small dwelling house, esp. in the country or at a resort. **-r** n. one who inhabits a cottage. **— cheese** n. a soft, white cheese [O.E. *cot*].

cot·ter (kát'·er) n. a pin or wedge used for tightening or fastening; a split pin.

cot·ton (kát'·n) n. a soft, downy, substance, resembling wool; cloth or thread made of cotton; a. made of cotton; v.i. (Colloq.) to become friendly; to take to. **— gin** n. a machine for separating the seeds from cotton. **-mouth** n. the water moccasin. **-tail** n. American rabbit. **-wood** n. a type of American poplar tree. **-y** a. [Ar. *qutum*].

cot·y·le·don (kát·a·lē'·dan) n. (Bot.) seed-lobe or primary leaf of the embryo plant [Gk. *kotulēdōn*, a cup-shaped cavity].

couch (kouch) v.t. to cause to lie down, esp. on a bed; to phrase; to express; to lower a lance, spear, etc. for action; v.i. to lie down; to crouch; n. a sofa; davenport. **couchant** (kouch'·ant) a. lying down [Fr. *coucher*, fr. L. *collocare*, to place together].

cou·gar (kōō'·ger) n. the puma or American panther [Native S. Amer.)].

cough (kawf) n. noisy, violent, explosive effort to expel irritating matter from the lungs. v.i. to make such an effort; v.t. to expel from the lungs by a cough. **— up** (Slang) hand over [M.E. *coughen*].

could (kood) p.at. of the verb **can.**

cou·lomb (kōō·lám') n. the quantity transferred by a current of one ampere in one second [Charles de *Coulomb*, a French physicist].

coul·ter See **colter.**

coun·cil (koun'·sal) n. an assembly summoned for consultation or advice; a municipal body; the deliberation carried on in such an assembly. **-man** n. **-lor** n. [L. *concilium*].

coun·sel (koun'·sal) n. advice; opinion; deliberation together; one who gives advice, esp. legal; a lawyer; an advocate; v.t. to advise; admonish; recommend. **-or** n. an adviser; a trial lawyer. **-orship** n. [L. *consulere*, to consult].

count (kount) n. (fem. **countess**) a title of nobility [L. *comes*, *comitis*, companion].

count (kount) v.t. to number; to reckon; to sum up; to consider or esteem; to include; to recite the numerals in regular succession; v.i. to depend or rely (with 'on'); n. the act of reckoning; the number ascertained by counting; (Law) a charge in an indictment. **-able** a. **— down** n. the last check before a missile is launched. **-less** a. not capable of being counted; innumerable. **-er** n. one who counts; a token or disc of metal, wood, etc. is used in reckoning; a table on which money is counted, goods displayed, or business transacted [L. *computare*].

coun·te·nance (koun'·tạ·nans) *n.* the face; the features; aspect; look; appearance; encouragement; support; *v.i.* to favor; to support; to encourage; to approve. **to keep one's countenance,** to preserve one's composure [L. *continentia,* manner of holding oneself].

count·er (koun'·tẹr) *a.* contrary; opposite; opposed; adverse; reciprocal; *adv.* in opposition; the opposite way; *n.* that which is opposite; a return blow or parry; *v.t.* and *i.* to parry; to oppose; to hinder; to do any act which opposes another; to make a counter-move. **-attack** *n.* an attack launched to recapture a position or to stop and drive back an enemy attack. **-attraction** *n.* rival attraction. **-claim** *n.* (*Law*) a claim set up by the defendant in a suit to counter that of the plaintiff. **-clockwise** *adv.* revolving in a direction opposite to the movement of the hands of a clock. **-espionage** *n.* spying directed against the enemy's system of espionage. **-irritant** *n.* a substance, the application of which, by inducing superficial irritation, relieves a more deep-seated irritation. **-tenor** *n.* a high tenor; a man's voice singing alto [L. *contra,* against].

coun·ter·act (koun·tẹr·akt') *v.t.* to act in opposition to; to hinder; to defeat.

coun·ter·bal·ance (koun'·tẹr·bal·ạns) *v.t.* to act against with equal power or effect; to neutralize; *n.* equal opposing weight, power, or agency; a weight balancing another.

coun·ter·charge (koun'·tẹr·chärj) *n.* a charge brought in opposition to another.

coun·ter·check (koun·tẹr·chek') *v.t.* to check by an opposing check; to reprimand.

coun·ter·feit (koun'·tẹr·fit) *v.t.* to copy without authority; to imitate with intent to deceive; to forge; to feign; *a.* sham; forged; false; *n.* an imitation; a forgery; an impostor.**-er** *n.*

coun·ter·mand (koun·tẹr·mand') *v.t.* to cancel an order; *n.* a contrary order [L. *contra; mandare,* to command].

coun·ter·march (koun'·tẹr·märch) *v.i.* to march back; *n.* a marching back.

coun·ter·mine (koun'·tẹr·min) *n.* (*Mil.*) to destroy enemy mines; any scheme to frustrate the designs of an opponent.

coun·ter·pane (koun'·tẹr·pān) *n.* a coverlet; a quilt [L. *culcita puncta,* a stitched quilt].

coun·ter·part (koun'·tẹr·pärt) *n.* a duplicate; something complementary or correlative.

coun·ter·point (koun'·tẹr·point) *n.* (*Mus.*) the art of combining melodies; the addition of a subsidiary melody to another so as to form a perfect melody.

coun·ter·poise (koun'·tẹr·poiz) *v.t.* to act against with equal weight or power; *n.* a weight sufficient to balance another.

coun·ter·sign (koun'·tẹr·sin) *v.t.* to sign a document already signed by another; to ratify; to attest authenticity; *n.* a password.

coun·try (kun'·tri·) *n.* a region; a district; a tract of land; the territory of a nation; the nation itself; land of birth, residence, etc.; rural districts as opposed to town; *a.* rural; rustic; pert. to territory distant from a city. **countrified** *a.* **countrify** *v.t.* to make rural. **— club** *n.* a club with grounds, a house, and facilities for outdoor sports. **-man** *n.* one who lives in the country; a rustic; one born in the same country; a compatriot. **-side** *n.* any rural district [L.L. *contrata*].

coun·ty (koun'·ti·) *n.* a division of a country or state for administrative purposes; the inhabitants of a county. **— seat,** the chief town or capital of a county [Fr. *comté,* fr. *comte,* a count].

coup (kōō) *n.* lit. a stroke or blow; then, a successful stroke or move *pl.* (kōōz) [Fr.].

coup de grâce (kōō·dạ·grâs) *n.* blow, shot, etc. that brings death to a sufferer [Fr.].

coup d'é·tat (kōō·dā·tä') *n.* lit. a stroke of state; a sudden and revolutionary change of government achieved by force [Fr.].

coupe (kōōp) *n.* a two-seat automobile with enclosed body [Fr. *couper,* to cut].

cou·ple (kup'·l) *n.* two things of the same kind taken together; two; a pair; a brace; husband and wife; a leash for two hounds; that which joins two things together; *v.t.* to join together; (*Colloq.*) to marry; *v.i.* to connect. **couplet** *n.* a pair of lines of verse. **coupling** *n.* a connection; that which couples, esp. the device joining railroad cars [L. *copula,* a bond].

cou·pon (kōō'·pän) *n.* an interest certificate attached to a bond; a dividend warrant; a negotiable ticket or voucher; a pass [Fr. *couper,* to cut off].

cour·age (kur'·ảj) *n.* bravery; fearlessness; daring. **courageous** (kạ·rā'·jạs) *a.* full of courage. **courageously** *adv.* **courageousness** *n.* [O.Fr. *corage,* fr. L. *çor,* the heart].

cour·i·er (koo'·ri·ẹr) *n.* a runner or messenger; a state messenger; a tourist guide who accompanies travelers [L. *currere,* to run].

course (kōrs) *n.* the act of passing from one point to another; progress or movement, both in space and in time; the ground traversed; way or direction; line of conduct; the track or ground on which a race is run; career; a series (of lessons, lectures, etc.); each of the succes-

sive divisions of a meal; a continuous line of masonry at one level in a building; *v.t.* to hunt; to pursue; to chase; *v.i.* to run swiftly; to gallop. **-r** *n.* one who courses or hunts; a swift horse [L. *cursus,* running].

court (kōrt) *n.* an uncovered area enclosed by buildings, or by buildings and railings; a yard; the residence of a sovereign; the retinue of a sovereign; the homage or attention paid to a sovereign; a legal tribunal; the judge or judges, as distinguished from the counsel; the hall where justice is administered; (*Sport*) a space, usually rectangular, laid out for certain sports, as tennis, etc. **courteous** (kurt'·i·ạs) *a.* polite; well-bred; of courtlike manners. **courteously** *adv.* **courteousness** *n.* **courtier** (kōrt'·yẹr) one who frequents the courts of princes; one with the manners of a frequenter of courts. **-ly** *a.* elegant; flattering; with the manners of a courtier. **-liness** *n.* **—martial** *n.* a court of military or naval officers for the trial of persons in the army or navy; *pl.* **-s-martial.** [L. *cohors,* an enclosure].

court (kōrt) *v.t.* to seek the favor of; to try to gain the affections of; to seek in marriage; *v.i.* to woo; to play the lover. **-ship** *n.* [L. *cohors,* an enclosure].

cour·te·san (kōr'·tạ·zạn) *n.* a prostitute [It. *cortigiana,* an enclosure].

cour·te·sy (kur'·tạ·si·) *n.* politeness of manners; urbanity [O.Fr. *cortoisie*].

cous·in (kuz'·n) *n.* formerly any kinsman; now, the son or daughter of an uncle or aunt [Fr. fr. L. *consobrinus*].

cou·tu·rier (koo·tu·rya') *n.* a man dressmaker. **-rière** (·ryär) *n. fem.*

cove (kōv) *n.* a small bay [O.E. *cofa,* a chamber].

cov·e·nant (kuv'·ạ·nạnt) *n.* a mutual and solemn agreement; a contract; a compact; a written agreement; *v.t.* to agree to by covenant; *v.i.* to enter into an agreement. **-er** *n.* one who makes a covenant or agreement. **Covenanters** later [L. *venire,* to come].

cov·er (kuv'·ẹr) *v.t.* to be over the whole top of; to overspread; to enclose; to include; to protect; to put hat on; to point a revolver, gun, etc. at; to wager an equal sum of money; *n.* anything that covers; a lid; a wrapper; an envelope; a binding; a cloak; disguise; concealment; shelter; defense. **-ing** *n.* **-let** *n.* a bedcover. **covert** *a.* covered over; concealed; sheltered; secret; veiled; *n.* a thicket; a place sheltering game. **covertly** *adv.* secretly; in private. **coverture** (kuv'·ẹr·chẹr) *n.* covering; shelter; defense. [Fr. *couvrir,* to cover].

cov·et (kuv'·it) *v.t.* to long to possess, esp. what belongs to another; to desire unreasonably or unlawfully; *v.i.* to have strong desire. **-able** *a.* that may be coveted. **-ous** *a.* very desirous; excessively eager; avaricious for gain. **-ously** *adv.* **-ousness** *n.* [L. *cupiditas,* desire].

cov·ey (kuv'·i·) *n.* a brood of partridges or quail; (*Fig.*) a company; a set [Fr. *couveé,* fr. *couver,* to brood].

cow (kou) *n.* the female of a bovine animal; the female elephant, whale, etc. **-ish** *a.* **-boy** *n.* a boy who herds cows; on the western plains, a herdsman employed on a ranch to look after cattle. **-catcher** *n.* a frame in front of a locomotive to remove obstructions. **-herd** *n.* one who herds cows. **-hide** *n.* the hide of a cow; leather made from the hide of a cow. **-lick** *n.* a tuft of hair not easily flattened [O.E. *cu*].

cowcatcher

cow (kou) *v.t.* to frighten into submission; to overawe [O.N. *kuga,* to oppress].

cow·ard (kou'·ẹrd) *n.* one given to fear; one who lacks courage. **-ly** *a.* lacking in courage; afraid. **-ice** (·dis) *n.* want of courage; fear. [Fr. *couard,* fr. L. *cauda,* a tail].

cow·er (kou'·ẹr) *v.i.* to crouch down through fear, shame, cold [etym. uncertain].

cowl (koul) *n.* a monk's hooded cloak; the hood itself; a hooded top for a chimney. **-ed** *a.* [L. *cucullus,* the hood of a cloak].

cow·slip (kou'·slip) *n.* the marsh marigold [OE. *cu-slyppe,* cow dung].

cox·comb (käks'·kōm) *n.* one given to showing off; a fool; a fop. **-ry** *n.*

cox·swain (kák'·sn), **cox** (käks) *n.* the steersman of a boat. **to cox** *vt.* and *i.* to act as coxswain [fr. *cock*-boat and *swain*].

coy (koi) *a.* shy; modest; pretending to be shy. **-ly** *adv.* **-ness** *n.* [Fr. *coi,* fr. L. *quietus*].

coy·o·te (ki'·ōt) *n.* the Amer. prairie wolf [Mex.].

coz·en (kuz'·n) *v.t.* to flatter in order to cheat; to defraud [Fr. *cousiner,* to play the part of *cousin,* in order to sponge on people].

co·zy (kō'·zi·) *a.* snug; comfortable; *n.* a covering to keep a teapot hot (*tea cozy*). Also **cosy. cozily** *adv.* **coziness** *n.*

crab (krab) *n.* an edible crustacean; a disagreeable person; *v.t.* to fish for crabs; (*Slang*) to complain. *pr.p.* **-bing.** *pa.t.* **-bed. -biness** *n.* **-by** *a.* **— grass** *n.* rapid growing coarse grass [O.E. *crabbd,* snatcher].

crab·bed (krab'·ạd) *a.* harsh; austere; faultfinding; perverse; bad-tempered; of writing, hard to read. **-ly** *adv.* **-ness** *n.*

crack (krak) *v.t.* to break with a sharp noise, either wholly or partially; to split or break; to produce a sudden sharp sound; to snap; *v.i.* to break partially; to burst open in chinks; to give forth a sudden, sharp sound; *n.* a partial break; fissure; a sharp noise; a flaw; a break in the voice; a mental flaw; (*Colloq.*) *a.* superior; special; expert. **-ed** *a.* **-er** *n.* one who cracks, that which cracks; a fire-cracker; a thin crisp biscuit.**-er-jack** (*Slang*) *n.* a person or thing of exceptional quality. **— up** *n.* a collision; a defeat; a breakdown [O.E. *cracian*].

crack·le (krak'·l) *v.i.* to produce slight but repeated cracking sounds; *n.* a noise composed of frequent, slight cracking sounds; over-all fine cracks in porcelain glaze. **crackling** *n.* a succession of small sharp reports; rind of roasted pork [O.E. *cracian,* to crack].

cra·dle (krā'·dl) *n.* a bed for infants that can be rocked; infancy; the place of origin of anyone or anything; a framework used as a support; *v.t.* to place or rock in a cradle; to tend or train in infancy; to support on a cradle (as a vessel) [O.E. *cradol*].

craft (kraft) *n.* skill or dexterity; a skilled trade; cunning, artifice, or guile; a vessel; vessels collectively. **-y** *a.* cunning; artful. **-ily** *adv.* **-iness** *n.* **-sman** *n.* one engaged in a craft or trade. **-smanship** *n.* [O.E. *craeft*].

crag (krag) *n.* a steep, rugged rock or peak. **-ged** (krag'·ạd) *a.* **-gy** *a.* full of crags; rough; rugged. **-giness** *n.* [W. *craig,* a rock].

cram (kram) *v.t.* and *i.* to stuff; to pack tightly; (*Colloq.*) to prepare hastily for an examination. *pr.p.* **-ming.** *pa.t.* **-med.** *n.* (*Colloq.*) a crush or crowd of people [O.E. *crammian*].

cramp (kramp) *n.* a painful contraction of muscles of the body; that which restrains; a clamp for holding masonry, timbers, etc. together; *v.t.* to affect with cramp; to restrict or hamper; to hold with a cramp; *a.* narrow; cramped; restricted [O.Fr. *crampe*].

cran·ber·ry (kran'·ber·i·) *n.* a red, sour, berry [prob. orig. *crane-berry*].

crane (krān) *n.* a tall wading-bird with long legs, neck, and bill; a machine for lifting and lowering heavy weights; *v.t.* to stretch out the neck to look at something [O.E. *cran*].

cra·ni·um (krā'·ni·ạm) *n.* the skull. *pl.* **crania. cranial** *a.* pert. to the skull. **craniology** *n.* the study of skulls. **craniological** *a.* [Gk. *kranion,* the skull].

crank (krangk) *n.* a handle attached to a shaft for turning it; the bent portion of an axis, used to change horizontal or vertical into rotatory motion, etc.; (*Colloq.*) a faddist; an eccentric or crotchety person; *v.t.* to provide with a crank; to shape like a crank; to operate by a crank; *v.i.* to turn the crank as in starting an automobile engine (usually with 'up'). **-case** *n.* the housing for a crankshaft. **-shaft** *n.* (*Mach.*) a shaft driven by or driving a crank. **-y** *a.* shaky or in bad condition, of machinery; (*Fig.*) irritable or crotchety; bad-tempered. **-iness** *n.* [O.E. *cranc*].

cran·ny (kran'·i·) *n.* an open crack; a small opening; a crevice; a chink [Fr. *cran,* a notch].

crap, craps (krap, -s) *n.* gambling game played with dice.

crash (krash) *n.* a violent fall or impact accompanied by loud noise; a burst of mixed, loud sound, e.g. of thunder, breaking crockery, etc.; bankruptcy; a sudden collapse or downfall; *v.i.* to make a crash; to fall, come with, strike with, a crash; to collapse; *v.t.* to break into pieces. —**helmet** *n.* a padded helmet worn by aviators and racing motorists [imit. of the sound].

crash (krash) *n.* a coarse linen cloth.

cra·sis (krā'·sis) *n.* (*Gram.*) union of two vowels into one long vowel or diphthong [Gk.].

crass (kras) *a.* thick; gross; dense; stupid. **-ly** *adv.* **-ness** *n.* [L. *crassus*, coarse].

crate (krāt) *n.* a wicker hamper, or open-work packing-case [L. *cratis*, a hurdle].

cra·ter (krā'·ter) *n.* the cup-shaped mouth of a volcano; the cavity resulting from the explosion of a large shell, bomb, mine, etc. [Gk. *krater*, a mixing-bowl].

cra·vat (kra·vat') *n.* a man's necktie or scarf [Fr. *cravate*, Croation (scarf)].

crave (krāv) *v.t.* and *i.* to have a very strong desire for; to long for; to ask with earnestness, submission, or humility; to beg. **-r.** *n.* **craving** *n.* an inordinate desire [O.E. *crafian*, to crave].

cra·ven (krāv'·n) *a.* cowardly; spiritless; chicken-hearted; *n.* a spiritless fellow; a coward [O.Fr. *cravanter*, to overthrow].

craw (kraw) *n.* crop or first stomach of fowls; stomach of any animal [M.E. *crawe*].

craw·fish, crayfish (kraw'·, krā'·fish) *n.* a fresh-water crustacean, resembling the lobster but smaller [Fr. *écrevisse*].

crawl (krawl) *v.i.* to move along the ground on the belly or on the hands and knees; to move very slowly; to move abjectly; to swim with an overarm stroke; *n.* a crawling motion; swimming stroke [O.N. *krafla*, to claw].

cray·on (krā'·an) *n.* a coloring pencil; a drawing made with crayons; *v.t.* to draw with crayons [Fr. *crayon*, a pencil; *craie*, chalk].

craze (krāz) *n.* a strong, habitual desire or passion; a general or individual mania; a very common fashion; to drive crazy; (*Pottery*) to crackle. **-d** *a.* weak in mind. **craziness** *n.* **crazy** *a.* insane; extremely foolish; madly eager (for); falling to pieces. **crazily** *adv.* [Fr. *écraser*, to break].

creak (krēk) *n.* a harsh, grating sound; *v.i.* to make a sharp, harsh, grating sound. **-y** *a.* [imit. sound].

cream (krēm) *n.* the fatty substance that rises to the surface of milk; the best part of anything; anything resembling cream; *v.t.* to take off the cream; to add cream to; *v.i.* to become covered with cream; to froth. **-y** *a.* full of cream; resembling cream. **-ery** *n.* a butter and cheese factory; a center to which milk is sent for distribution. **-iness** *n.* — **cheese** *n.* a soft, smooth, white cheese. — **of tartar**, acid potassium tartrate, a component of baking powder [Gk. *chrisma*, unguent].

crease (krēs) *n.* a line or mark made by folding anything; *v.t.* to make a crease or mark on; *v.i.* to become creased [etym. uncertain].

cre·ate (krē·āt') *v.t.* to bring into existence out of nothing; to originate; to make. **creation** (krē·ā'·shan) *n.* the act of creating, esp. of bringing the world into being; the world; anything created; any original production of the human mind. **creative** *a.* capable of creation; original. **creator** *n.* one who creates; a maker. **Creator** *n.* God. **creature** (krē'·cher) *n.* anything created; any living being [L. *craere*].

cre·dence (krē'·dans) *n.* trust; belief; (*Eccles.*) a small altar table. **credentials** (kri·den'·shalz) *n.pl.* testimonials showing that a person is entitled to belief or credit. **credible** (kred'·a·bl) *a.* worthy of belief. **credibility** *n.* [L. *credere*, to believe].

cre·den·za (kra·den'·za) *n.* a sideboard [fr. *credence*].

cred·it (kred'·it) *n.* belief; trust; trustworthiness; honor or reputation; anything that procures esteem or honor; the amount at a person's disposal in a bank; in commerce, the general system of buying, borrowing and lending based on good faith and confidence; *v.t.* to believe;

to put trust in. **-able** *a.* reliable; meriting credit. **-ably** *adv.* **-ableness** *n.* **-or** *n.* one to whom money is due [L. *credere*, to believe].

cred·u·lous (kre'·ja·las) *a.* too prone to believe. **-ly** *adv.* **-ness** *n.* **credulity** (kra·dū'·la·ti) *n.* gullibility [L. *credulus*, believing].

creed (krēd) *n.* a statement of religious belief; any statement of principles. **credo** (krē'·dō) *n.* a creed [L. *credere* to believe].

creek (krēk) *n.* a small inlet; a branch or small tributary of a river [O.N. *kriki*].

creel (krēl) *n.* an angler's basket [Celt.].

creep (krēp) *v.i.* to move along with the body close to the ground, like a worm or reptile; to spread, like certain plants, by clinging. *pa.t.*, *pa.p.* **crept. -er** *n.* a creeping plant; a genus of small birds. **-y** *a.* causing a creeping sensation on the skin [O.E. *creopan*].

cre·mate (krē'·māt) *v.t.* to consume by burning, esp. the dead; to reduce to ashes. **cremation** (krē·mā'·shan) *n.* the act of cremating the dead. **cremator** *n.* **crematorium** *n.* an establishment for the cremation of bodies. **crematory** *a.* or *n.* [L. *cremare*, to burn].

cre·nate (krē'·nāt) *a.* with the edge notched. **-d** *a.* [L. *crena*, a notch].

Cre·ole (krē'·ōl) *n.* a native of Spanish America or the W. Indies, of European parentage; a white person descended from the French or Spanish settlers of Louisiana; a native of mixed parentage [Fr. fr. Sp. *criollo*].

cre·o·sote (krē'·a·sōt) *n.* an oily liquid obtained from the distillation of coal tar, extensively used to preserve wood from decay [Gk. *sōter*, preserver].

crepe (krāp) *n.* a thin crinkled fabric or paper; mourning cloth; a kind of rough-surfaced rubber used for the soles of shoes, etc. [Fr.].

crept (krept) *pa.p.* and *pa.t.* of **creep.**

cre·pus·cu·lar (kri·pus'·ku·ler) *a.* pert. to twilight; dim. [L. *crepusculum*, twilight].

cre·scen·do (kra·shen'·dō) *n.* (*Mus.*) a gradual increase in loudness; *adv.* with increase in loudness. (*Abbrev.*) **cresc.** [It.].

cres·cent (kres'·ant) *a.* like the young moon in shape; increasing; *n.* the moon in first quarter; a crescent-shaped object [L. *crescere*, to grow].

cress (kres) *n.* various salad greens [O.E. *cerse*, *cresse*, creeper].

cres·set (kres'·it) *n.* an iron basket or cage-like container, filled with inflammable material used as a torch [O.Fr. *craisse*, grease].

crest (krest) *n.* the comb or tuft on a bird's head; the plume or top of a helmet; the top of a mountain, ridge, etc.; the highest part of a wave; a badge above the shield of a coat of arms; *v.t.* to reach the top of. **-fallen** *a.* dispirited; dejected [L. *crista*].

cre·tin·ism (krēt'·in·izm) *n.* condition caused by thyroid deficiency; a form of idiocy. **cretin** *n.* one suffering from cretinism. **cretinous** *a.* [Swiss *crestin*, a Christian].

cre·tonne (kri·tán') *n.* a strong, unglazed printed cotton cloth [*Creton*, in France].

cre·vasse (kra·vas') *n.* a deep open chasm in a glacier; a fissure; a cleft [Fr.].

crev·ice (krev'·is) *n.* a cleft; a narrow fissure; a crack [Fr. *crever*, to burst].

crew (krōo) *n.* a group of workmen; a ship's or boat's company [earlier *crue*, *accrue*, a reinforcement].

crew·el (krōo'·al) *n.* embroidery yarn. **-work** *n.*

crib (krib) *n.* a manger; a stall for cattle; a child's bed with barred sides; a hut or small dwelling; a key or translation (used by students); an enclosure for storing grain [O.E. *cribb*, an oxstall].

crib·bage (krib'·ij) *n.* (*Cards*) a game played by two or four players.

crick (krik) *n.* neck or back spasm or cramp.

crick·et (krik'·it) *n.* a small, brown, chirping insect [Fr. *criquer*, to creak].

crick·et (krik'·it) *n.* a game played with bats, ball, and wickets; (*Colloq.*) fair play.

cri·er (krī'·er) *n.* See **cry.**

crime (krīm) *n.* a violation of the law (usually of a serious nature); an offense. **criminal** (krim'·a·nal) *a.* guilty of, or pert. to, crime; wicked; *n.* one guilty of a crime. **criminality** *n.* guiltiness. **criminally** *adv.* **criminate** *v.t.* to charge with a crime. **crimination** *n.* **criminative, criminatory** *a.* accusing. **criminologist** *n.* **criminology** *n.* science dealing with the cause and treatment of crime and criminals [L. *crimen*, a charge].

crimp (krimp) *v.t.* to form into curls or pleats; to wrinkle; to decoy or press into military or naval service; *n.* an agent who procures men for service as soldiers or sailors; a small waves, as in hair [O.E. *crimpan*, to curl].

crim·son (krim'·zn) *n.* of a rich deep red color; *n.* the color itself [O.Sp. *cremesin*, fr. Arab. *qirmiz*, the cochineal insect].

cringe (krinj) *v.t.* to shrink; to cower; to behave obsequiously [M.E. *crengen*].

crin·kle (kring'·kl) *v.t.* to wrinkle; to make a series of bends or twists in a line or surface; to rustle. **crinkly** *adv.* [O.E. *crincan*].

crin·o·line (krin'·a·lin) *n.* a hoop skirt; a stiff, coarse fabric petticoat [L. *crinis*, hair; *linum*, flax].

crip·ple (krip'·l) *n.* a person without the use of a limb or limbs; a lame person; *a.* lame; *v.t.* to lame [O.E. *crypel*].

cri·sis (krī'·sis) *n.* the decisive moment; the turning point, as in an illness; emergency; a time of difficulty or danger; *pl.* **crises** (krī'·sēz) [Gk. *krisis*, decision].

crisp (krisp) *a.* brittle; breaking with a short snap; of hair, curly; sharp; *v.t.* to make crisp; **-ly** *adv.* **-ness** *n.* [L. *crispus*, curled].

criss·cross (kris'·kraws) *a.* crossing; arranged in crossing lines; *adv.* crossing one another in different directions; *v.t.* and *i.* to mark or be marked with cross lines [corrupt. of *Christ's-cross*].

cri·te·ri·on (krī·tir'·i·an) *n.* a standard of judging; a rule or test by which opinions may be judged. *pl.* **criteria** [Gk.].

crit·ic (krit'·ik) *n.* one who expressed a reasoned judgment on any matter, esp. on art or literature; one whose profession it is to write reviews; one given to expressing adverse judgment or finding fault. **-al** *a.* pert. to criticism or critics; captious or fault-finding; pert. to a crisis; crucial; decisive. **-ally** *adv.* **criticism** *n.* the art of making a reasoned judgment, a critical appreciation. **criticize** *v.t.* and *i.* to pass judgment; to censure. **critique** (kri·tēk') *n.* criticism; review [Gk. *krinein*, to judge].

croak (krōk) *v.t.* and *i.* to make a low, hoarse noise in the throat; (*Slang*) to die; *n.* the hoarse, harsh sound made by a frog or a crow. **-y** *a.* [imit.].

cro·chet (krō·shā') *n.* a kind of needlework consisting of loops; *v.t.* and *i.* to work in crochet [Fr. *crochet*, a small hook].

crock (krák) *n.* an earthenware pot or pitcher; a piece of broken earthenware. **-ery** *n.* vessels and dishes of all kinds, generally made of earthenware [Gael. *crog*, a pitcher].

croc·o·dile (krák'·a·dil) *n.* a large, amphibious reptile of the lizard kind. — **tears**, hypocritical tears; sham grief [Gk. *krokodilos*, a lizard].

cro·cus (krō'·kas) *n.* a bulbous plant; saffron [Gk. *krokos*, crocus, saffron].

crone (krōn) *n.* a wizened old woman.

cro·ny (krō'·ni·) *n.* an intimate friend; a chum [earlier *chrony*, a contemporary, fr. Gk.].

crook (krook) *n.* any hook, bend, or sharp turn; a shepherd's or a bishop's staff; a thief; a swindler; *v.t.* to bend into a crook; to curve; to pervert; *v.i.* to be bent or curved. **-ed** *a.* bent; twisted; (*Fig.*) not straightforward. **-edly** *adv.* **-edness** *n.* **by hook or by crook**, by some means or other; by fair or foul [O.N. *krokr*].

croon (krōon) *v.t.* and *i.* to sing or hum softly; to sing in a sentimental manner. **-er** *n.* **-ing** *n.* [imit.].

crop (kráp) *n.* the cultivated produce of any plant or plants, in a farm, field, country, etc.; a harvest; the best ore; a pouch in a bird's gullet; the craw; a hunting-whip; a closely-cut head of hair; *v.t.* to reap the produce of a field. *pr.p.* **-ping.** *pa.p.* and *pa.t.* **-ped. —eared** *a.* with clipped ears; with hair cut close to head. **-per** *n.* one who, or that which, crops; (*Colloq.*) a heavy fall. **to crop up**, to appear unexpectedly [O.E. *cropp*, the head of a plant, ear of corn, etc.].

cro·quet (krō'·kā) *n.* an outdoor game played with balls, mallets and hoops.

cro·quette (krō·ket') *n.* (*Cookery*) a ball of finely minced meat, fish, etc. seasoned and fried [Fr. *croquer*, to mince].

cro·sier, cro·zier (krō'·zher) *n.* the pastoral staff of a bishop [O.Fr. *crosse*, a crook].

cross (kraws) *n.* a stake used for crucifixion, consisting of two pieces of timber placed upon one another in the shape † or ✗; in particular, **the Cross**, the one on which Christ was crucified; a model or picture of this; anything in the shape of a cross; (*Fig.*) (the Cross being the symbol of suffering) affliction; tribulation; a misfortune; *v.t.* to mark with a cross; to make the sign of the cross. **-let** *n.* a small cross.

-wise *adv.* in the form of a cross [L. *crux*, a cross].

cross (kraws) *a.* transverse; intersecting; interchanged; contrary, adverse; out of temper; dishonest; *n.* an intermixture of breeds or stocks, esp. in cattle-breeding; *v.t.* to place so as to intersect; to pass from one side to the other of; to pass over; to thwart; to oppose; to clash; to modify the breed of animals, plants, etc. by intermixture; *v.i.* to intersect; to move or pass from one side to the other; *adv.* across. **-ing** *n.* the act of passing across; an intersection; a place of crossing; the intermixture of breeds. **-ly** *adv.* **—action** *n.* (*Law*) an action brought by a defendant against a plaintiff on points pert. to the same case. **-bones** *n. pl.* two thigh bones crossed and surmounted by a skull, used as symbol of death, a sign of deadly danger, or the flag of a pirate ship. **-breed** *n.* parents of different breeds; a hybrid. **—examination** *n.* the examination of a witness by counsel on the other side. **-eyed** *a.* with eyes turned in toward the nose. **—grained** *a.* of wood, having the grain running across, or irregularly; of a person, ill-natured. **-hatching** *n.* in drawing, etching, etc. the art of shading by parallel intersecting lines. **— reference** *n.* in a book, e.g. a dictonary, the directing of the reader to another part for related information [L. *crux*, a cross].

cross-bill (kraws'-bil) *n.* a bird of the Finch family, whose mandibles cross.

cross-bow (kraws'-bō) *n.* a medieval weapon. **-man** *n.*

crotch (krách) *n.* a fork or bifurcation; the angle where the legs branch off from the human body. **-ed** *a.* [etym. uncertain].

crotch-et (krách'-at) *n.* a small hook. **-y** *a.* full of whims, or fads [Fr. *crochet*, dim. of *croc.* a hook].

crouch (krouch) *v.i.* to huddle down close to the ground; to stoop low; to cringe or fawn servilely [prob. Fr. *croc*, a hook, crook].

croup (kroop) *n.* the rump or hindquarters of a horse [Fr. *croupe*].

croup (kroop) *n.* (*Med.*) acute inflammation of the windpipe, accompanied by a hoarse cough. **-y** *a.* [O.E. *kropan*, to cry].

crou-pi-er (kroo'-pi-er) *n.* one who assists the chairman at a public banquet; an official in charge of a gaming table [Fr.].

crou-ton (kroo'-tán) *n.* a small cube of toasted bread used in soups, etc. [Fr. *croûte*].

crow (krō) *n.* a large bird, usually wholly black, of the genus Corvus; the cry of the cock; the name of a tribe of American Indians; a crowbar; *v.i.* to give the shrill cry of the cock; to utter a sound of pleasure. **crow's-foot** *n.* a wrinkle about the outer corners of the eyes in adults. **crow's-nest** *n.* a box or perch for the lookout man near the top of the mast [O.E. *crawan*].

crowd (kroud) *v.t.* to press or drive together; to fill or occupy by crushing together; *v.i.* to be numerous; to gather in numbers; *n.* a number of things or persons collected into a close body; a dense multitude or throng; (*Colloq.*) a set or clique [O.E. *crudan*].

crown (kroun) *n.* the diadem or state headdress worn by a sovereign; the sovereign; royalty; anything resembling a crown; something achieved or consummated; the topmost part of the head; the upper part of a hat; the summit; (*Br.*) a five-shilling piece (stamped with a crown); *v.t.* to invest with a crown or with royal dignity; to bestow upon as a mark of honor; to top or surmount; to complete. **— prince** *n.* the heir apparent to the throne. **— wheel** *n.* a wheel with cogs at right angles to its plane [L. *corona*, a crown].

cro-zier See **crosier.**

cru-cial (krōō'-shal) *a.* decisive; critical; cross-shaped [L. *crux*, a cross].

cru-ci-ble (krōō'-si-bl) *n.* vessel capable of withstanding great heat, used for melting metals, etc. (*Fig.*) a severe test [L.L. *crucibulum*].

cru-ci-fy (krōō'-sa-fi) *v.t.* to put to death by nailing to a cross; to torture; to mortify. **crucifier** *n.* **crucifix** *n.* an image of Christ on the Cross. **crucifixion** (krōō-sa-fik'-shan) *n.* **cruciform** *a.* cross-shaped [L. *crux*, a cross; *figere*, to fix].

crude (krōōd) *a.* in the natural or raw state; unripe; rough; unfinished. **-ly** *adv.* **-ness** *n.* **crudity** *n.* [L. *crudis*, raw].

cru-el (krōō'-el) *a.* hard-hearted. **-ly** *adv.* **-ty** *n.* the quality of being cruel [See **crude**].

cru-et (krōō'-it) *n.* a small stoppered bottle for holding vinegar, oil, etc.; a stand for holding such bottles [O.Fr. *cruie*, a pot].

cruise (krōōz) *v.i.* to sail about without precise destination; in motoring and aviation, to go at a normal operating speed; *n.* an organized pleasure-sail. **-r** *n.* [L. *crux*, a cross].

crumb (krum) *n.* a small particle; a bit, esp. of bread; *v.t.* to reduce to crumbs; to cover with crumbs. **-y** *a.* **crummy** *a.* (*Slang*) inferior [O.E. *cruma*].

crum-ble (krum'-bl) *v.t.* to break into crumbs or fragments; *v.i.* to fall into crumbs. **crumbly** *a.* [O.E. *cruma*].

crum-pet (krum'-pit) *n.* (*Br.*) a flat, soft pancake [origin uncertain].

crum-ple (krum'-pl) *v.t.* to wrinkle; to crease; to rumple; *v.i.* to become wrinkled or creased; to shrink irregularly; to collapse.

crunch (krunch) *n.* the sound made by chewing crisp food, treading on gravel, hard snow, etc.; *v.t.* and *i.* to chew, tread, etc. with this sound [imit. origin].

cru-sade (krōō-sād') *n.* a medieval Christian war to recover the Holy Land from the Saracens; a campaign against any evil or vice; *v.i.* to join in a crusade. **-r** *n.* [Fr. *croisade*, fr. L. *crux*, a cross].

cruse (krōōz) *n.* a small earthen pot for holding water, oil, etc. [O.N. *krus*].

crush (krush) *v.t.* to press between two hard bodies so as to break, bruise, or crumple; to break into fragments; to squeeze out by pressure; to defeat utterly; *v.i.* to be broken or compressed by weight or force; *n.* violent pressure; a closely packed crowd of people [O.Fr. *cruissir*].

crust (krust) *n.* the hard outer coat or covering of anything; the outer part of baked bread; pastry, etc. forming the covering of a pie; a deposit from wine collected on the interior of bottles; *v.t.* to cover with a crust; *v.i.* to gather into a crust; to form a crust. **-ated** *a.* covered with a crust; incrusted. **-ation** *n.* **-ily** *adv.* in a crusty manner; peevishly; morosely. **-iness** *n.* **-y** *a.* having a crust; like a crust; hard; peevish; surly [L. *crusta*].

Crus-ta-ce-a (krus-tā'-shi-a) *n.pl.* (*Zool.*) a class of mainly aquatic animals including lobsters, crabs, shrimps, prawns, etc. **-n** *a.* and *n.* pert. to, or one of, the crustacea. **crustaceous** *a.* having a hard shell [L. *crusta*, a rind].

crutch (kruch) *n.* a staff with a cross-piece to go under the armpit for the use of cripples; a support; *v.t.* to support; to aid [O.E. *cryce*].

crux (kruks) *n.* a perplexing problem; a knotty point; the real issue [L. *crux*, a cross].

cry (krī) *v.t.* to call out; to shout; to proclaim; *v.i.* to call loudly; to exclaim vehemently; to weep; *n.* a loud utterance; the shedding of tears; the sound of a pack of hounds on the scent. **crier** *n.* one who cries; a public announcer. **-ing** *a.* **a far cry**, a great distance. **to cry wolf**, to give a false alarm [L. *quiritare*, to wail].

cry-o-lite (krī'-a-līt) *n.* a mineral used in making aluminum [Gk. *kruos*, frost; *lithos*, stone].

crypt (kript) *n.* a cell or chapel under a church, or underground, used for burial. **cryptic(al)** *a.* hidden; secret; mysterious. **cryptically** *adv.* [Gk. *kruptein*, to conceal].

cryp-to- a prefix fr. Gk. *kruptos*, hidden, secret, combining to form many compounds.

cryp-to-gram (krip'-ta-gram) *n.* a writing in secret characters. Also **cryptograph** *n.* **cryptology** *n.* a secret language. **cryptonym** (krip'-ta-nim) *n.* a secret name [Gk. *kruptos*, hidden; *graphein*, to write].

crys-tal (kris'-tal) *n.* a transparent, colorless quartz; an ornament made from it; a ball cut from it for crystal gazing; a superior sort of glass; a table article made from such glass with ornamental cutting; (*Chem.*) a mineral body which has assumed a regular geometrical form; *a.* consisting of, or like, crystal; clear; transparent. **-line** *a.* **-lize** *v.t.* to cause to form crystals; (*Fig.*) to cause to assume a definite shape; *v.i.* to be formed into crystals; (*Fig.*) to become definite in shape. **-lizable** *a.* **-lization** *n.* [Gk. *krustallos*, fr. *kruos*, frost].

cub (kub) *n.* the young of the bear, fox, wolf, etc.; a junior Boy Scout; *v.t.* to bring forth young (of animals) [etym. unknown].

cub-by hole (kub'-i-hōl) *n.* a small place for storing things, or for hiding in [dial. E. *cub*, a pen or shed].

cube (kūb) *n.* (*Geom.*) a solid body with six

---

equal square sides; (*Math.*) the product of a number multiplied twice by itself, as $4 \times 4 \times 4 = 64$, the cube of 4, or 4, to the third power; *v.t.* to raise to the third power. **cubic(al)** *a.* having the form of a cube; of three dimensions, e.g. **cubic foot. cuboid** *a.* resembling a cube in shape. **— root** *n.* the number which gives the stated number if raised to the third power, or cubed, e.g. 4 is the cube root of 64 [Gk. *kubos*].

cu-bi-cle (kū'-bi-kl) *n.* a small partitioned compartment [L. *cubiculum*, a bedroom].

cub-ism (kū'-bizm) *n.* (*Art*) a phase of modern art based on geometrical forms. **cubist** *n.*

cu-bit (kū'-bit) *n.* a measure of length, about 18 inches. **-al** *a.* [L. *cubitum*, the elbow].

cuck-old (kuk'-ald) *n.* a man whose wife is unfaithful to him; *v.t.* to be unfaithful to a husband [O.Fr. *cucu*, a cuckoo].

cuck-oo (koo'-kōō) *n.* a migratory bird named from its call; the call of the bird; a fool; *a.* (*Slang*) crazy; foolish [imit. origin].

cu-cum-ber (kū'-kum-ber) *n.* plant of the gourd family and its fruit [L. *cucumis*].

cud (kud) *n.* food brought up by ruminating animals, from their first stomach, and chewed a second time. **to chew the cud** (*Fig.*) to meditate [O.E. *cudu*].

cud-dle (kud'-l) *v.t.* to caress; to hug; to fondle; *v.i.* to lie close or snug; to nestle; *n.* a close embrace. **-some** *a.* [etym. uncertain].

cudg-el (kuj-al) *n.* a short thick stick; *v.t.* to beat with a cudgel [O.E. *cycgel*, club].

cue (kū) *n.* the last words of an actor's speech as a signal to the next actor to speak; a hint [earlier 'q,' standing for L. *quando*, when (i.e. to come on)].

cue (kū) *n.* a long tapering rod used in pool, billiards, etc. [Fr. *queue*, pigtail].

cuff (kuf) *n.* a blow with the open hand; *v.t.* to strike with the open hand [etym. uncertain].

cuff (kuf) *n.* the ending of a sleeve; the turned-up end of a trouser leg; the wrist-band of a sleeve [M.E. *cuffe*].

cui-rass (kwi-ras') *n.* metal or leather armor, consisting of a breastplate and backplate [Fr. *cuir*, leather].

cui-sine (kwi-zēn') *n.* literally a kitchen; style of cooking [Fr. fr. *cuire*, to cook].

cul-de-sac (kool'-da-sak') *n.* a blind alley [Fr. *cul*, bottom; *sac*, a bag].

cu-li-nar-y (kū'-li-ner-i) *a.* pert. to the kitchen or cookery [L. *culina*, a kitchen].

culinary implement

cull (kul) *v.t.* to select, or pick out; to gather [Fr. *cueillir*, to gather].

cul-mi-nate (kul'-ma-nāt) *v.i.* to reach the highest point (with 'in'); to reach a climax. **culmination** *n.* the attainment of the highest point; climax [L. *culmen*, summit].

cu-lottes (koo-lots') *n.pl.* knee length trousers resembling a skirt [Fr.].

cul-pa-ble (kul'-pa-bl) *a.* deserving blame or censure. **culpably** *adv.* **culpability, -ness** *n.* [L. *culpa*, fault].

cul-prit (kul'-prit) *n.* one accused of a crime; a criminal; an offender [L. *culpa*, a fault].

cult (kult) *n.* a system of religious worship, or rites and ceremonies [L. *cultus*, worship].

cul-ti-vate (kul'-ta-vāt) *v.t.* to prepare for the raising of crops; to till; to produce by tillage, labor, or care; to train; to foster. **-d** *a.* [L. *colere, cultum*, to till].

cul-ture (kul'-cher) *n.* tillage or cultivation; mental training and development; refinement; civilization; the propagation of bacteria and other micro-organisms in artificial media; *v.t.* to cultivate. **cultural** *a.* pert. to culture. **-d** *a.* educated and refined [L. *colere*, to cultivate].

cul-vert (kul'-vert) *n.* an arched drain or conduit for the passage of water under a road, railway, or canal [Fr. *couler*, to flow].

cum-ber (kum'-ber) *v.t.* to burden or hinder with a useless load. **-some** *a.* burdensome; clumsy and unmanageable. **cumbrous** *a.* [O.Fr. *combrer*, to hinder].

cum·mer·bund (kum'·ẹr·bund) *n.* a broad sash worn as a belt [Pers. *kamarband*, a loin band].

cu·mu·late (kū'·mẏạ·lāt) *v.t.* to heap together; *a.* heaped up. **cumulation** *n.* **cumulative** *a.* becoming greater by successive additions; gaining force or effect by additions. **cumulatively** *adv.* [L. *cumulus*, a heap].

cu·mu·lus (kū'·mẏạ·lạs) *n.* a heap; a piled-up cloud mass with rounded outlines. *pl.* **cumuli** [L. *cumulus*, a heap].

cu·ne·i·form, cuniform (kū'·ni·ạ·fawrm) *a.* wedge-shaped [L. *cuneus*, a wedge].

cun·ning (kun'·ing) *a.* wily; sly; artful; *n.* craft or skill; deceit. **-ly** *adv.* [O.E. *cunnan*,to know].

cup (kup) *n.* a drinking vessel; the contents of a cup; anything resembling a teacup in shape; an ornamental vessel given as a prize for sport, etc.; *v.t.* to let blood; to hold, as in a cup; to form into a cup shape. *pr.p.* **-ping.** *pa.t.* **-ped. -ful** *n.* the quantity that a cup holds, 8 fluid oz. **cupboard** (kub'·ẹrd) *n.* a small closet with shelves for cups, plates, etc. **loving cup** *n.* a large cup; trophy, given as a prize [L. *cupa*, a tub].

cu·pid·i·ty (kū·pid'·ạ·ti·) *n.* an eager desire for possession; greed [L. *cupidus*, desirous].

cu·po·la (kū'·pạ·lạ) *n.* a spherical vault or small domed tower on the top of a building [It. *cupola*, fr. L. *cupa*, a tub].

cu·pre·ous (kū'·pri·ạs) *a.* of, pert. to, or containing copper [L. *cuprum*, copper].

cur (kur) *n.* a dog of mixed breed; a mongrel; [O.N. *kurra*, to grumble].

cu·rate (kjoo'·rit) *n.* (*chiefly Br.*) an assistant to a vicar or rector. **curacy** *n.* [L. *cura*, care].

cu·ra·tor (kyoo·rā'·tẹr) *n.* a superintendent, as of a museum, library, etc.; a guardian. **-ship** *n.* [L. fr. *curare*, to care].

curb (kurb) *n.* a chain or strap attached to the bit of a bridle to give control with the reins; any check or means of restraint; an edging to a pavement or sidewalk; *v.t.* to apply a curb to (a horse); to restrain; to confine. **-ing** *n.* [Fr. *courber*, fr. L. *curvare*, to bend].

curd (kurd) *n.* the cheesy part of milk; coagulated milk; the coagulated part of any liquid. **-le** *v.t.* and *i.* to turn into curd; to coagulate [O.E. *crudan*, to press].

cure (kūr) *v.t.* to heal; to restore to health; to remedy; to preserve fish, skins, etc. by salting, drying, etc.; *n.* the act of healing; that which heals; a remedy. **curable** *a.* **curative** *a.* **cure-all** *n.* a remedy for all ills; a panacea [L. *cura*, care].

cu·rette (kū·ret') *n.* instrument for scraping body tissue. **-ment** *n.* [Fr. *curer*, to cleanse].

cur·few (kur'·fū) *n.* the time after which persons may not be out of doors [Fr. *couvre-feu* = cover fire].

cur·ie (kyoo'·ri) *n.* (*Chem.*) the standard unit of emanation from one gram of radium. **curium** (kyoo'·ri·ạm) *n.* a radioactive, inert, gaseous element [fr. M. and Mme. *Curie*, discoverers of radium].

cu·ri·o (kyoo'·ri·ō) *n.* a rare or curious object; a curiosity [abbrev. of *curiosity*].

cu·ri·ous (kyoo'·ri·ạs) *a.* eager to know; inquisitive; (*Colloq.*) puzzling; strange. **-ly** *adv.* **curiosity** *n.* eagerness to know; inquisitiveness; a strange or rare object; a novelty [L. *curiosus*, inquisitive].

curl (kurl) *v.t.* to twist into ringlets; to coil; to bend into spiral or curved shape; *v.i.* to take a spiral or curved shape or path; to turn into ringlets; to ripple; to play at the game of curling; *n.* a ringlet of hair; anything of a similar shape. **-y** *a.* having curls; tending to curl; full of ripples. **-icue** *n.* a lock of hair; a fancy curve in writing. **-iness** *n.* **-ing** *n.* a game like bowls played on ice with large, rounded stones. **-er** *n.* a pin used as a fastener to retain a curl or wave in position [M.E. *crul*, curly].

cur·lew (kur'·lōō) *n.* a long-billed wading bird [Fr. *courlieu*, imit. of its cry].

cur·mudg·eon (kẹr·muj'·ạn) *n.* a grasping ill-natured fellow; a churl [origin unknown].

cur·rant (kur'·ant) *n.* the fruit of various plants allied to the gooseberry.

cur·rent (kur'·ant) *a.* belonging to the present time; in circulation or general use; *n.* a flowing body of water or air in motion; the flow of a river, etc.; tendency; drift; transmission of electricity through a conductor. **-ly** *adv.* in a current manner; commonly. **currency** *n.* money in use or circulation [L. *currere*, to run].

curlew

cur·ric·u·lum (ku·rik'·yạ·lạm) *n.* a specified course of study at a school, college, university, etc.; *pl.* **curricula** [L. *curriculum*, a running, a race-course].

cur·ry (kur'·i·) *n.* (*Cookery*) a highly-flavored and pungent condiment much used in the East. **— powder** *n.* [Tamil].

cur·ry (kur'·i·) *v.t.* to dress leather; to comb, rub down, and clean a horse; to beat or thrash. **currier** *n.* one who dresses tanned leather. **to curry favor**, to try to win favor by flattery. [O.Fr. *correer*, to prepare].

curse (kurs) *v.t.* to utter a wish of evil against; to invoke evil upon; to swear at; to torment; *v.i.* to utter blasphemous words; to swear; *n.* the invocation of evil or injury upon a person; profane words or oaths. **cursed** (kurs'·ạd, kurst) *a.* hateful. **cursedly** *adv.* [O.E. *cursian*].

cur·sive (kur'·siv) *a.* written with a running hand, i.e. with all the letters joined; flowing. **-ly** *adv.* **cursory** *a.* characterized by haste; careless; superficial [L. *currere*, to run].

curt (kurt) *a.* short; concise to the point of rudeness; abrupt; terse. *n.* [L. *curtus*, shortened].

cur·tail (kur·tāl') *v.t.* to cut short; to abridge; to diminish. **-ment** *n.* [L. *curtus*, shortened].

cur·tain (kur'·tin) *n.* a drapery; a screen in front of stage of a theater; anything that shuts off or conceals; *v.t.* to enclose or furnish with curtains. **— raiser** *n.* a short play preceding the main piece in a theater. **iron curtain** (*Fig.*) any hindrance to obtaining information about conditions in a country [L.L. *cortina*].

curt·sy, curtsey (kurt'·si·) *n.* a gesture of civility or respect made by women or girls; *v.i.* to make a curtsy [form of *courtesy*].

curve (kurv) *n.* a bending without angles; that which is bent; an arch; *a.* bent; *v.t.* and *i.* to bend. **curvate** *a.* curved. **curvature** *n.* [L. *curvus*, crooked].

cush·ion (koosh'·ạn) *n.* any stuffed or padded surface used as a rest or protector; *v.t.* to seat on a cushion; to provide or protect with a cushion [Fr. *coussin*, a cushion, fr. L. *coxa*, the hip].

cusp (kusp) *n.* a point or horn of a crescent, as of the moon; a prominence on a molar tooth; the point at which the two branches of a curve have a common tangent. **-id** *n.* a canine tooth. **-idal** *n.* ending in a point [L. *cuspis*, a point].

cus·pi·dor (kus'·pạ·dawr) *n.* a spittoon [Port.].

cuss (kus) *n.* (*Slang*) a fellow; a curse. **-ed** *a.* corrupt. of cursed [fr. *curse*].

cus·tard (kus'·tẹrd) *n.* a sweet dish made with milk and eggs [M.E. *crystade*, a pie with a crust].

cus·to·dy (kus'·tạ·di·) *n.* a keeping or guarding; care; guardianship; imprisonment. **custodial** (kus·tō'·di·ạl) *a.* **custodian, custodier** *n.* a keeper; a caretaker [L. *custodia*, fr. *custos*, a keeper].

cus·tom (kus'·tạm) *n.* fashion; usage; habit; business patronage; toll, tax, or tribute; **-s** *n.pl.* duties levied on imports. **-able** *a.* liable to duty. **-ary** *a.* according to custom; established by common usage; usual; habitual. **-arily** *adv.* **-er** *n.* one who enters a shop to buy. **-house** *n.* office where customs are paid. [O.Fr. *coustume* fr. L. *consuetudo*].

cut (kut) *v.t.* to sever, penetrate, or wound with an edged instrument; to divide; to separate; to intersect; to cross; to mow; to hew; to carve; to trim; to shape; to reduce; to abridge; intentionally to ignore a person; (*Sports*) to hit the ball obliquely in order to impart spin to it. *pr.p.* **-ting.** *pa.p.* and *pa.t.* **cut** *n.* an act of cutting; opening made with an edged instrument; a gash; a wound; a piece cut off, as e.g. a joint of meat; a notch; a reduction, esp. in salary or wages. **-ter** *n.* he who, or that which, cuts; a warship's rowing and sailing boat. **-ting** *n.* an incision; a small branch, slip, etc. cut from a plant, bush, etc. *a.* sarcastic. **— glass** *n.* glass ornamented with

cut designs. **-off** *n.* a road that is a short cut; a device to shut off. **—rate** *a.* below usual price. **-throat** *n.* a murderer; *a.* merciless. **to cut a caper**, to frisk about; to gambol.

cu·ta·ne·ous (kū·tā'·ni·ạs) *a.* belonging to, or affecting, the skin [L. *cutis*, the skin].

cute (kūt) *a.* (*Colloq.*) attractive [short for *acute*].

cu·ti·cle (kū'·ti·kl) *n.* the epidermis, esp. around the fingernails and toenails [L. *cutis*, skin].

cut·las (kut'·lạs) *n.* a short, broad-bladed, curving sword [O.Fr. *coutel*, a knife fr. L. *culter*, a ploughshare].

cut·ler (kut'·lẹr) *n.* one who makes, repairs, or deals in knives and cutting implements. **-y** *n.* business of a cutler; cutting instruments, esp. tableware [Fr. *coutelier*; *couteau*, a knife].

cut·let (kut'·lit) *n.* a piece of meat or chop from the rib bones [Fr. *cotelette*, fr. *côte*, a rib].

cy·a·nide (sī'·ạ·nīd) *n.* a poisonous compound.

cy·an·o·gen (sī·an'·ạ·jen) *n.* (*Chem.*) a colorless, poisonous gas. **cyanic** *a.* blue [Gk. *kuanos*, blue, and root *gen*].

cy·ber·net·ics (sī·bẹr·net'·iks) *n.* the study of the self-organizing machine or mechanical brain [Gk. *kubornasis*, a pilot].

cyc·la·men (sik'·lạ·man) *n.* a tuberous plant of the Primrose family [Gk. *kuklaminos*].

cy·cle (sī'·kl) *n.* a regularly recurring succession of events or phenomena, or the period of time occupied by such a succession; a body of myths or legends, relating to some period, person, or event; a series of songs dealing with various phases of the same subject, and meant to be sung one after the other; a bicycle or tricycle; *v.i.* to pass through a cycle of changes; to ride a bicycle or tricycle. **cyclist** *n.* one who rides a bicycle or tricycle. **cycloid** *n.* (*Geom.*) a curve traced by a point in a circle when the circle revolves along a straight line [Gk. *kuklos*, a circle].

cy·clone (sī'·klōn) *n.* a violent storm characterized by strong winds. **cyclonic** [Gk. *kuklos*, a circle].

cy·clo·pe·di·a See **encyclopedia.**

cy·clo·ram·a (sī·klạ·rá'·mạ) *n.* circular panorama [Gk. *kuklos*, a circle; *orama*, a view].

cy·clo·tron (sī'·klạ·trạn) *n.* a radio oscillator developed to disintegrate atoms, in order to study their internal structure [Gk. *kuklos*, a circle].

cyg·net (sig'·nit) *n.* a young swan [Fr. *cygne*, a swan].

cyl·in·der (sil'·in·dẹr) *n.* a roller-like body with straight sides, the ends being equal, parallel circles; any object of similar shape. **cylindric, cylindrical** *a.* **cylindriform** *a.* [Gk. *kulindros*, a roller].

cym·bal (sim'·bạl) *n.* musical percussion instrument [Gk. *kumbalon*].

cyn·ic (sin'·ik) *n.* one of a set of Greek philosophers who regarded virtue as the supreme good and despised all comfort or refinement; one who believes man's conduct is based on self-interest. **cynic(al)** *a.* sneering; distrustful of people's motives. **cynically** *adv.* **cynicalness** *n.* **cynicism** (sin'·i·sizm) *n.* principles of a cynic; disbelief in goodness; misanthropy [Gk. *kunikos*, doglike, fr. *kuon*, a dog].

cy·no·sure (sī'·nō-, sin'·ō·shoor) *n.* (*Astron.*) the constellation of the Lesser Bear, containing the Pole-star; hence, something to which all eyes are turned; a guiding star [Gk. *kuon*, a dog; *oura*, a tail].

cy·press (sī'·prạs) *n.* a slender coniferous tree with evergreen foliage [L. *cypressus*].

cyst (sist) *n.* (*Med.*) a bladder or membranous sac containing liquid secretion or morbid matter; *a.* pert. to cysts [Gk. *kustis*, a bladder].

Czar (zår) *n.* a title used by various Slavonic rulers, esp. by the Emperors of Russia. **Czarina** (zå·rē'·nạ) *n.* the wife of a Czar. (Other forms are **Tsar, Tzar, Tsarina, Tzarina**, etc.) [fr. L. *Caesar*].

Czech (chek) *n.* a member of the Slavonic race of people inhabiting the western region of Czechoslovakia; the language spoken by them; *a.* pert. to the people or their language. **Czechoslovak** (chek·ạ·slō'·vak, chek·ạ·slō·vak'), **Czechoslovakian** *a.* pert. to the country, the people, or the language of Czechoslovakia; *n.* a native of the country; the language.

D

dab (dab) *n.* Eur. flatfish.
dab (dab) *v.t.* to pat gently and intermittently, **-bing.** *pa.p.* and *pa.t.* **-bed.** *n.* a gentle blow with a soft substance; a small lump of anything soft, as butter [M.E. *dabban*, to strike].
dab·ble (dab'·l) *v.t.* to wet by little dips; to moisten; *v.i.* to play in water; to pursue a subject superficially [M.E. *dabban*, to strike].
dace (dās) *n.* a small fresh-water river fish. Also **dart, dare** [O.Fr. *dars*, dart].
dach·shund (daks'·hoont) *n.* dog with long body, short legs, and drooping ears [Ger. *Dachs*, a badger; *Hund*, a dog].
dac·tyl (dak'·til) *n.* a metrical foot in poetry, consisting of one accented syllable followed by two unaccented syllables (— u u). **-ic** *a.* pert. to or consisting of a dactyl. **-iography** *n.* the history of gem engraving. **-ogram** *n.* a finger print. **-ography** *n.* the science of finger prints. **-ology** *n.* the finger language of the deaf and dumb [Gk. *daktulos*, a finger].
dad, dada, daddy (dad, da'·da, dad'·i·) *n.* father, a word used by little children [W. *tad*, a father].
da·da·ism (dä'·dạ·izm) *n.* a school of art and literature which aims at suppressing all relation between thought and expression.
dad·dy-long-legs (dad'·i·lawng'·legz) *n.* a flying insect; a harvestman [fr. *dad*].
da·do (dā'·dō) *n.* (*Archit.*) the part of a pedestal between the base and cornice; the lower part or wide skirting of the walls of a room [It. *dado*, a pedestal].
dae·mon (dē'·mạn) *n.* an inspiring influence; a divinity; genius. **-ic** *a.* more than human; supernatural [Gk. *daimon*, spirit].
daf·fo·dil (daf'·ạ·dil) *n.* a spring plant of the genus Narcissus; the yellow color of the daffodil [Gk. *asphodelos*, a lily flower].
daft (daft) *a.* insane; foolish. **-ness** *n.* [M.E. *daft*, mild].
dag·ger (dag'·ẹr) *n.* a short, two-edged sword used in close combat; a mark of reference in typography (†) or (‡) [M.F. *daggen*, to slit].

dag·gle (dag'·l) *v.t.* to trail through mud; to bedraggle [Scand. *dagg*, dew].
da·guerre·o·type (dạ·ger'·ạ·tīp) *n.* in photography, an early method of taking pictures on plates of silver or silvered copper [fr. Louis *Daguerre* of Paris, the 19th cent. inventor].
dahl·ia (dal'·yạ) *n.* a genus of plants with large, brightly colored flowers [fr. *Dahl*, a Swedish botanist].
dai·ly (dā'·li·) *a.* or *adv.* happening each day; *n.* a newspaper published each day or each weekday [O.E. *daeg*, day].
dain·ty (dān'·ti·) *a.* pleasing to the taste; refined; pretty and delicate; scrupulous; *n.* a delicacy. **daintily** *adv.* [L. *dignus*, worthy].
dair·y (dā'·ri·) *n.* the place where milk and cream are kept cool, butter is churned, and cheese is made; the shop where milk and its products are sold; a dairy farm. **-ing** *n.* the business of conducting a dairy. **-maid, -man** *n.* [Icel. *deigja*, a dairymaid].
da·is (dā'·is) *n.* the raised platform at the end of a room, esp. of dining hall [O.Fr. *deis*, fr. L.L. *discus*, a table].

dai·sy (dā'·zi·) *n.* a common wild flower; (*Slang*) a person or thing unusually pleasing. **daisied** *a.* [O.E. *daeg*, a day; *eage*, an eye].
dale (dāl) *n.* a low place between hills; a valley or vale; a glen [O.E. *dael*, a valley].

dal·ly (dal'·i·) *v.i.* to waste time; to trifle; to fondle or interchange caresses. **dalliance** *n.* the act of trifling and wasting time; flirtation [M.E. *dalien*, to play].
Dal·ma·tian (dal·mā'·shạn) *n.* a breed of large white dogs with black or liver-colored spots [fr. *Dalmatia*].

dam (dam) *n.* a female parent—used of animals [form of *dame*].
dam (dam) *n.* a barrier of earth, stones, etc. to obstruct the flow of water; the water confined by a dam; *v.t.* to confine water by a dam; to block up [M.E. *dam*, an obstruction].
dam·age (dam'·ij) *n.* any injury or harm to person, property, or reputation; *v.t.* to harm; to hurt. **-s** *n.pl.* legal compensation paid to injured party. **-able** *a.* [L. *damnum*, loss].
dam·ask (dam'·ạsk) *n.* a figured silk or linen fabric, orig. made at Damascus; steel ornamented with wavy pattern; a rose-pink color, like that of damask rose; *a.* woven with figured pattern like damask [fr. *Damascus*, in Syria].
dame (dām) *n.* (*Arch.*) a noble lady; (*Slang*) a woman. **Dame** *n.* (*Br.*) title of the wife of a knight or baronet [Fr. *dame*, a lady].
damn (dam) *v.t.* to consign to everlasting punishment; (*Colloq.*) to condemn irritably (used as interjection); to destroy the reputation of; *n.* an oath; a curse; (*Colloq.*) a trifle. **-able** *a.* **-ably** *adv.* **-ation** *n.* **-ed** *a.* odious [L. *damnare*, to condemn].
dam·o·sel, damozel (dam'·ō·zel) *n.* archaic and poetic var. of *damsel* [O.Fr. *damoisele*, a maiden].
damp (damp) *n.* moist air; humidity; fog; vapor; noxious gases in coal mines, wells, etc. (as fire-damp, choke-damp); *a.* slightly moist; *v.t.* to moisten slightly; to retard combustion (to *damp* down a fire). **-en** *v.t.* to moisten; (*Fig.*) to depress. **-er** *n.* one who or that which damps; a contrivance in a flue to regulate the draft; a device to minimize vibration. **-ish** *a.* [Ger. *Dampf*, steam].
dam·sel (dam'·sạl) *n.* a young unmarried woman [M.E. *damizel*, Fr. *demoiselle*, a maiden].
dam·son (dam'·zạn) *n.* a small dark plum [O.Fr. *damascene*, of Damascus].
dance (dans) *v.t.* and *v.i.* to move with measured steps; to move rhythmically; to caper; *n.* a lively and rhythmical movement with certain steps and gestures; a social gathering for the purpose of dancing. **-r** *n.* one who dances. **danseuse** *n.* a female dancer, esp. in ballet. **to lead someone a dance**, to lead someone in vain pursuit. **St. Vitus's dance** (*Med.*)

nervous disorder accompanied by twitching of muscles [Fr. *danser*, to dance].
dan·de·li·on (dan·dạ·lī'·ạn) *n.* a plant with large yellow flowers, and tooth-edged leaves [Fr. *dent de lion*, lion-toothed].
dan·der (dan'·dẹr) *n.* (*Colloq.*) anger; passion; temper [fr. *dandriff*].
dan·dle (dan'·dl) *v.t.* to move up and down in affectionate play, as an infant; to pet; to caress [It. *dondolare*, to swing].
dan·druff, dandriff (dan'·drạf, ·drif) *n.* a disease affecting the scalp and producing scurf or small scales of skin under the hair.
dan·dy (dan'·di·) *n.* one who affects special finery in dress; a fop; *a.* (*Colloq.*) fine; first-rate. **dandify** *v.t.* to make like a dandy. **dandified** *a.* foppish [etym. poss. Scots corrupt. of St. Andrew].
Dane (dān) *n.* a native of Denmark; a breed of dog, large and smooth coated, usually *great Dane*. **Danish** *a.* pert. to Denmark or the Danes; *n.* the language of the Danes [O.E. *Dene*, a Dane].
dan·ger (dān'·jẹr) *n.* exposure to injury or evil; peril; hazard; jeopardy. **-ous** *a.* **-ously** *adv.* **dangerousness** *n.* [M.E. *danger*, power].
dan·gle (dang'·l) *v.t.* to swing loosely or carelessly; (*Fig.*) to use as a bait; *v.i.* to hang loosely [Scand. *dangle*, to swing].
dank (dangk) *a.* unpleasantly damp or moist. **-ness** *n.* [Scand. *danka*, moist].
dap·per (dap'·ẹr) *a.* neat; trim; smart; little and active [Dut. *dapper*, brave].
dap·ple (dap'·l) *n.* a spot; *a.* spotted, applied to horses and deer. **-d** *a.* spotted, esp. of pattern made by sunlight through trees.
dare (dār) *v.t.* to have courage for; to venture (to); to be audacious enough; *v.i.* to defy; to challenge. **daring** *n.* audacity; a bold action; *a.* bold; courageous; audacious. **daringly** *adv.* **—devil** *n.* a foolhardy, reckless fellow. **I dare say**, I presume [M.E. *durran*, to dare].
dark (dårk) *a.* lacking light; black; somber; evil; unenlightened; *n.* absence of light; gloom; obscurity; evil. **-en** *v.t.* to obstruct light; to render dim; to cloud; (*Fig.*) to sully; *v.i.* to grow dark. **-ish** *a.* rather dark. **-le** *v.i.* to grow dark; to lie hid. **-ling** *adv.* in the dark. **darkly** *adv.* **-ness** *n.* **-y, -ey** *n.* a Negro. — **horse** *n.* (*Fig.*) one unexpectedly nominated for an office. **to darken a door**, to enter a door [O.E. *deorc*, dark.
dar·ling (dår'·ling) *n.* a beloved or lovable one; *a.* cherished [dim. of O.E. *deore*, dear].
darn (dårn) *v.t.* to mend; to repair a hole by weaving threads at right angles to one another; *n.* the place darned. **-ing-needle** *n.* [prob. O.E. *dernan*, to hide].
dart (dårt) *n.* a pointed arrow-like weapon; anything similar which pierces or wounds; a small seam or intake in garment to make it fit more closely; a sharp, forward movement; *v.t.* to send forward quickly; to throw suddenly; *v.i.* to run forward swiftly; to move like a dart. **-s** *n.pl.* a popular game using darts and dartboard [M.E. *dart*, a javelin].

Dar·win·i·an (dår·win'·i·ạn) *a.* pert. to Charles *Darwin* or to his Theory of Evolution; *n.* one who accepts the theories of Darwin.
dash (dash) *v.t.* to throw violently; to cast down; to shatter; *v.i.* to rush forward or move violently; to strike violently against; *n.* a violent clashing of two bodies; a rapid movement; a mark of punctuation (—) to denote parenthesis; a small amount, as a *dash of soda*. **-ing** *a.* daring; spirited; showy. **-y** *a.* showy [M.E. *daschen*, to strike down].
das·tard (das'·tẹrd) *n.* mean or cowardly fellow; *a.* cowardly. **-ly** *a.* **-liness** *n.* [M.E. *dastard*, a stupid or mean person].
da·ta (dā'·ta) *n.pl.* (sing. **datum**) things known and from which inferences may be deduced [L. *data*, things given].

date (dāt) *n.* period of time of an event; epoch; duration; (*Slang*) appointment or engagement; *v.t.* to note or fix the time of; to refer to as a starting point; *v.i.* to reckon back to a given time (foll. by *from* or *back* to). —**line** *n.* approximately the 180° parallel of longitude on each side of which the date of the day differs [L. *datum*, a thing given].

date (dāt) *n.* the stone fruit of the Eastern date palm. — **palm** *n.* tree bearing date fruit [Gk. *dakulos*].

da·tive (dā'·tiv) *n.* the case of a noun which is the indirect object of a verb, or which is preceded by certain prepositions [L. *dare*, to give].

da·tum (dā'·tum) *n.* a fact given; *pl.* **data** [L. *dare*, to give].

daub (dawb) *v.t.* to smear with mud or plaster; to soil; to paint crudely; *n.* a crude painting; a smudge. -**er** *n.* one who daubs; a daub; rough cast for exterior of houses [O.Fr. *dauber*, to plaster].

daugh·ter (daw'·ter) *n.* a female child; *a.* like a daughter. —**in-law** *n.* the wife of one's son [O.E. *dohtor*].

daunt (dawnt, dånt) *v.t.* to subdue the courage of; to dismay; to dishearten; to disconcert. -**less** *a.* fearless; intrepid [O.Fr. fr. L. *domare*, to tame].

dau·phin (daw'·fin) *n.* (*fem.* **dauphiness**) the French Crown prince [O.Fr. *daulphin*].

da·ven·port (dav'·ạn·pōrt) *n.* a sofa [fr. the name of the maker].

dav·its (da'·vits) *n.* uprights fitted with tackle for lowering life-boats over side of ship [Fr. *davire*, forceps].

Da·vy Jones (dā'·vi·jōnz') *n.* a sailor's name for the Devil.

daw (daw) *n.* a bird of the crow family; a jackdaw [imit.].

daw·dle (daw'·dl) *v.i.* to loiter; to move very slowly [prob. conn. with *dandle*].

dawn (dawn) *v.i.* to grow towards daylight; to begin to be visible; (*Fig.*) to come to the mind; *n.* daybreak; morning half-light; beginning [O.E. *daeg*, a day].

day (dā) *n.* the period from sunrise to sunset; the period of the sun's revolution on its axis; 24 hrs.; time of life; epoch. —**bed** *n.* a divan. -**book** *n.* a book kept to record daily transactions. —**break** *n.* dawn. —**dream** *n.* a reverie; *v.i.* to indulge in reveries [O.E. *daeg*, a day].

daze (dāz) *v.t.* to confuse; to stupefy; to bewilder; to stun; *n.* the state of being bewildered; stupefaction. **dazzle** *v.t.* to daze with sudden light; to make temporarily blind; to confuse mentally; *n.* brilliancy. **dazzling** *a.* [M.E. *dāsen*, to stupefy].

dazzle

dea·con (dē'·kạn) *n.* an assistant to a priest or minister; a layman elected to certain duties in the church. -**ess** *n.* -**hood** *n.* the office of deacon. -**ry** *n.* the body of deacons. -**ship** *n.* office of deacon [Gk. *diākonos*, a servant].

dead (ded) *a.* without life; *adv.* wholly; *n.* the most death-like time. -**en** *v.t.* to benumb. -**ness** *n.* —**beat** *a.* without oscillation, applied to measuring instruments in which the pointer comes to rest. —**end** *n.* a street with only one entrance. -**fall** *n.* a trap, esp. for large animals. — **heat** *n.* a race where two or more competitors reach the winning post at exactly the same time. — **language**, a language no longer spoken. — **letter** *n.* an undelivered or persons must not pass; last available date. -**liness** *n.* -**lock** *n.* a state of affairs which renders further progress impossible; an impasse. -**ly** *a.* causing death; virulent; lethal; *adv.* completely. — **pan** (*Slang*) *n.* an immobile face. — **reckoning** *n.* (*Naut.*) the steering of a vessel by compass and not by the stars. — **weight** *n.* the unrelieved weight of inert objects [O.E. *dead*, dead].

deaf (def) *a.* lacking partially or wholly the sense of hearing; heedless; unwilling to listen. -**en** *v.t.* to make deaf; to stun with sound. -**ening** *a.* very loud; thunderous, as applause. -**ly** *adv.* —**mute** *n.* one who is deaf and dumb. —**mutism** *n.* -**ness** *n.* [O.E. *deaf*, deaf].

deal (dēl) *v.t.* to divide; to dole out; to distribute, as in card games; *v.i.* to traffic; to act; to give one's business to; to behave towards; *n.* a part or portion; distribution of playing cards; a business transaction; a bargain. *pa.p.* **dealt** (delt). -**er** *n.* -**ing** *n.* buying and selling; traffic; treatment; *pl.* intercourse or relations with others. **a raw deal**, iniquitously unfair treatment. **a square deal**, fair treatment [O.E. *daelan*, to divide].

dean (dēn) *n.* a dignitary in cathedral or collegiate churches; (in universities) the head of a faculty; an official of a college with disciplinary authority [O.Fr. *deien*, fr. L. *decanus*, an official].

dear (dēr) *a.* precious; much loved; highly esteemed or valued; costly; expensive; scarce; *interj.* expressing sorrow, pity or wonder, as in '*Oh, dear!*' -**ly** *adv.* [O.E. *deore*, precious].

dearth (durth) *n.* scarcity; lack [M.E. *derthe*].

death (deth) *n.* extinction of life; manner of dying; state of being dead; decease; dissolution; (*Fig.*) termination. — **blow** *n.* a fatal stroke. -**less** *a.* immortal. -**lessness** *n.* -**like** *a.* -**ly** *adv.*; *a.* like death. — **mask** *n.* a plaster cast of a person's face taken immediately after death. — **rate** *n.* the mortality rate per thousand of the population at a given time. —**throes** *n.pl.* last struggle before death. — **warrant** *n.* an official document authorizing execution of a criminal. -**watch** *n.* a vigil [O.E. *death*, death].

de·ba·cle (dā·bák'·al) *n.* a sudden collapse; a rout; the breaking up of ice in a river [Fr.].

de·bar (di·bár)' *v.t.* to cut off from entrance; to hinder; to prohibit; to exclude; *pr.p.* -**ring**. *pa.t.*, *pa.p.* -**red.** -**ment** *n.* [L. *de*; and *bar*].

de·bark (di·bárk') *v.t.* and *v.i.* to disembark, oppos. of *embark*. -**ation**, -**ment** *n.* [Fr. *débarquer*, to disembark].

debarkment

de·base (di·bās') *v.t.* to reduce to a lower state; to disagree; to degrade; to adulterate. -**ment** *n.* **debasing** *a.* corrupting, esp. in moral sense.

de·bate (di·bāt') *n.* controversy; wrangle; argument; dispute; *v.t.* to discuss; to dispute; to contend; to argue in detail; *v.i.* to take part in a discussion; to reflect. **debatable** *a.* -**r** *n.* [L. *de*, from; *batuere*, to strike or beat].

de·bauch (di·bawch') *v.t.* to corrupt; to make depraved; to seduce; to pervert; *n.* excess in eating and drinking. -**ed** *a.* -**ee** *n.* a dissipated person. -**ery** *n.* moral corruption. -**ment** *n.* [O.Fr. *debaucher*, to corrupt].

de·ben·ture (di·ben'·char) *n.* a certificate acknowledging a debt and guaranteeing repayment of loan with interest [L. *debentur mihi*, first words of certificate meaning 'these sums are owing to me.'].

de·bil·i·tate (di·bil'·ạ·tāt) *v.t.* to weaken; to make infirm; to enervate. **debilitation, debility** *n.* [L. *debilitare*, to weaken].

deb·it (deb'·it) *n.* an item entered on debtor side of an account (oppos. of *credit*); *v.t.* to charge with debt [L. *debere, debitum*, to owe].

de·bo·nair (deb'·a·nār') *a.* bearing oneself cheerfully and well; sprightly; spruce [Fr. *de bon air*, of amiable disposition].

de·bris, dé·bris (da·brē', dā'·brē) *n.* fragments (taken collectively); rubble; ruins [Fr. *briser*, to break].

debt (det) *n.* something owed to another; a liability; an obligation. -**or** *n.* one who owes a debt [L. *debere, debitum*, to owe].

de·bunk (dạ·bungk') *v.t.* (*Slang*) to remove false sentiment from.

de·but, dé·but (di·bū', dā·bū') *n.* a first appearance in public, socially or as an artist. **debutante** *n.* one, esp. a girl, making her first appearance in society; abbrev. **deb.** [Fr. *début*, a first stroke, aim, or goal].

dec·a- *prefix* fr. Gk. *deka*, ten.

dec·ade (dek'·ād) *n.* a group of ten things; a period of ten years [Gk. *deka*, ten].

de·ca·dence (dek'·ạ·dans, di·kā'·dans) **decadency** *n.* deterioration; degeneration; decay; a falling off in moral or aesthetic standards. **decadent** *a.* deteriorating [L. *decadentia*, a falling away].

dec·a·gon (dek'·ạ·gán) *n.* a plane figure of ten sides and ten angles [Gk. *gonia*, an angle].

dec·a·gram(me) (dek'·ạ·gram) *n.* in the metric system, a weight of 10 grams, i.e. 0.353 oz. [Gk. *deka*, ten; *gramma*, a weight].

dec·a·he·dron (dek·ạ·hē'·drạn) *n.* a solid figure of a body having ten sides. **decahedral** *a.* [Gk. *deka*, ten; *hedra*, face of a solid].

de·cal·ci·fy (dē·cal'·si·fī) *v.t.* to deprive bones (esp. teeth) of lime.

de·cal·i·ter (dek'·ạ·lē·tẹr) *n.* a measure of capacity equal to 10 liters—about 2.64 imperial gallons [Gk. *deka*, ten; Fr. *litre*].

Dec·a·logue (dek'·ạ·lawg) *n.* the Ten Commandments [Gk. *deka*, ten; *logos*, a word of discourse].

dec·a·me·ter (dek'·ạ·mē·tẹr) *n.* in the metric system a measure of ten meters, or 32.8 ft. [Gk. *deka*, ten; *metron*, measure].

de·camp (dē·kamp') *v.i.* to move away from a camping ground; to move off suddenly or secretly [Fr. *décamper*, to break camp].

de·cant (di·kant') *v.t.* to pour off liquid without disturbing sediment, esp. used of wines. -**er** *n.* a slender necked glass bottle into which wine is decanted [L. *de*, from; *canthus*, rim of a cup].

de·cap·i·tate (di·kap'·i·tāt) *v.t.* to cut off the head; to behead. **decapitation** *n.* [L. *de*, from; *caput*, head].

dec·a·pod (dek'·ạ·pád) *n.* a shellfish of the crab family having five pairs of legs; a ten-footed crustacean; *a.* having ten legs. -**al**, -**ous** *a.* [Gk. *deka*, ten; *pous*, a foot].

de·car·bon·ize (dē·kár'·bạ·niz) *v.t.* to deprive of carbon; to remove a deposit of carbon, as from a motor cylinder. Also **decarbonate, decarburize. decarbonization, decarburization** *n.*

dec·a·syl·lab·ic (dek·ạ·si·lab'·ik) *a.* having ten syllables. **decasyllable** *n.* [Gk. *deka*, ten; *syllable*].

de·cath·lon (di·kath'·lán) *n.* a group of ten different contests at Olympic games [Gk. *deka*, ten; *athlon*, a contest].

de·cay (di·kā') *v.i.* to rot away; to become decomposed; to waste away; to deteriorate; *v.t.* to impair; *n.* gradual decline or corruption; deterioration. -**ed** *a.* rotting. [L. *de*, down; *cadere*, to fall].

de·cease (di·sēs') *n.* death; *v.i.* to die. -**d** *a.* dead; *n.* a dead person [L. *decessus*, a departure].

de·ceit (di·sēt') *n.* fraud; duplicity; wile. -**ful** *a.* crafty; fraudulent. -**fulness** *n.* **deceive** *v.t.* to delude; to cheat. **deceivable** *a.* **deceivably** *adv.* **deceiver** *n.* [L. *decipere, deceptum*, to beguile].

de·cel·er·ate (dē·sel'·ẹr·āt) *v.t.* and *v.i.* to reduce speed [L. *de*, from; *celer*, swift].

De·cem·ber (di·sem'·bẹr) *n.* orig. the tenth month of the Roman calendar; the twelfth month of the year [L. *decem*, ten].

de·cen·ni·al (di·sen'·i·ạl) *a.* lasting for ten years or happening every ten years. **decennary** *n.* [L. *decem*, ten; *annus*, a year].

de·cent (dē'·sent) *a.* fitting or becoming; modest; suitable; comely; sufficient. **decency** *n.* the state or quality of being decent. -**ly** *adv.* [L. *decere*, to be fitting].

de·cen·tral·ize (dē·sen'·tral·iz) *v.t.* to remove from the center or point of concentration and distribute among small areas; esp. to enlarge powers of local government at expense of central authority. **decentralization** *n.*

de·cep·tion (di·sep'·shạn) *n.* the act of deceiving; fraud; illusion. **deceptible** *a.* **deceptibility** *n.* **deceptive** *a.* causing a false impression. **deceptively** *adv.* [L. *deceptus*, deceived].

dec·i·bel (des'·ạ·bel) *n.* one transmission unit; one tenth of a bel; the smallest variation in sound that the human ear can detect [L. *decem*, ten; *bel*, a coined word].

de·cide (di·sīd') *v.t.* to determine the result of; to make up one's mind about; to settle an issue; *v.t.* to give a decision; to come to a conclusion. -**d** *a.* clear; not ambiguous; determined. **decidedly** *adv.* **decision** (di·sizh'·ạn) *n.* the act of settling; determination; settlement; judgment. **decisive** *a.* conclusive; resolute. **decisively** *adv.* **decisiveness** *n.* [L. *decidere*, to cut off].

de·cid·u·ous (di·sid'·yoo·ạs) *a.* (of trees) shedding leaves in autumn, oppos. of coniferous or evergreen; not lasting; liable to fall; (used also of a deer's horns) [L. *decidere*, to fall down].

dec·i·mal (des'·ạ·mạl) *a.* pert. to tens; numbered or proceeding by tens; *n.* some power of 10. -**ization** *n.* -**ize** *v.t.* to reduce to the decimal system. — **fraction**, a fraction the (unexpressed) denominator of which is 10 or a power of 10 [L. *decimal*, tenth].

dec·i·mate (des'·ạ·māt) *v.t.* to kill (as in Ancient Rome) every tenth man, chosen by lot, as punishment; to reduce the numbers of, very considerably. **decimation** *n.* [L. *decimus*, tenth].

de·ci·pher (di·sī'·fẹr) *v.t.* to read a cipher; to make out what is illegible, unintelligible or written in strange symbols.

de·ci·sion See **decide**.

deck (dek) *v.t.* to adorn; to cover; to dress up; to cover with a deck (of a ship); *n.* a covering; the horizontal platform extending from one side of ship to the other; a pack of cards, or part of pack remaining after dealing. **—chair** *n.* a light-weight, collapsible chair, made partly of canvas. **— hand** *n.* a person employed on deck of ship. **-ing** *n.* adornment. **hurricane-deck** *n.* a half-deck. **main-deck** *n.* deck below the upper deck. **quarter-deck** *n.* part of the deck abaft the main mast. **double-decker** *n.* a vehicle, as bus, or ferry, with upper and lower passenger-decks [Dut. *dekkan*, to cover].

deck·le (dek'·l) *n.* the gauge on a paper-making machine. **—edge** *n.* untrimmed edge of paper. **—edged** *a.* [Ger. *deckel*, cover].

de·claim (di·klām') *v.t.* to recite in a rhetorical manner; *v.i.* to make a formal speech. **declamation** *n.* a set speech; a rhetorical and dramatic address. **declamatory** (di·klam'·a·tōr·i·) *a.* pert. to a declamation; ostentatiously rhetorical [L. *declamare*, to shout out].

de·clare (di·klēr') *v.t.* to proclaim; to make clear; to state publicly; to state in the presence of a witness; *v.i.* to make a declaration; (at Customs) to admit possession of dutiable goods. **declarable** *a.* **declaration** *n.* the act of declaring; a solemn statement. **declaratory** *a.* making clear or manifest; explanatory [L. *declarare*, to make clear].

de·clen·sion (di·klen'·shan) *n.* the act of falling away; (*Fig.*) deterioration; (*Gram.*) the inflection of nouns, pronouns, adjectives; a class of nouns, etc. so inflected. **-al** *a.* [L. *declinare*, to fall away].

de·cline (di·klīn') *v.t.* to bend downward; to refuse; to avoid; (*Gram.*) to give inflections of a word in oblique cases; *v.i.* to slope; to hang down; to fall in value or quantity; to pine away; to languish; *n.* a downward slope; a falling off. **declinable** *a.* able to be inflected. **declination** (de·kli·nā'·shan) *n.* a sloping away [L. *declinare*, to fall away].

de·cliv·i·ty (di·kliv'·a·ti·) *n.* a downward slope; a gradual descent. **declivitous, declivous** *a.* [L. *declivis*, sloping down].

de·code (dē·kōd') *v.t.* to translate a message in code into ordinary language.

de·col·le·tage (dā·kal·tazh') *n.* the line of a woman's low cut evening dress; the neck and shoulders of a person wearing such a dress. **décolleté** *a.* low-necked [Fr.].

de·com·pose (dē·kam·pōz') *v.t.* to break up into elements; to separate the constituent parts of; *v.i.* to decay; to rot. **decomposition** *n.* act of decomposing; decay; putrefaction.

de·con·tam·i·nate (dē·kan·tam'·a·nāt) *v.t.* to cleanse from effects of poison gas, etc. **decontamination** *n.*

de·con·trol (dē·kan·trōl') *v.t.* to release from government or state control.

de·cor (dā·kawr') *n.* the decoration, or setting of a theater, stage, or room [Fr.].

dec·o·rate (dek'·a·rāt) *v.t.* to beautify; to embellish; to honor a person by giving a medal or badge of honor. **-d** *a.* **decoration** *n.* an ornament; a badge of honor; insignia. **decorative** *a.* **decorativeness** *n.* **decorator** *n.* [L. *decus*, an ornament].

dec·o·rous (dek'·a·ras) *a.* seemly; decent; staid. **-ly** *adv.* **-ness** *n.* **decorum** (di·kōr'·am) *n.* behavior, etc. in keeping with social conventions [L. *decus*, an ornament].

de·coy (di·koi') *v.t.* to lead into a snare; (*Fig.*) to allure; to entice by specially tempting means; (dē'·koi) *n.* a device for leading wild birds into a snare; an enticement [Dut. *kooi*, a cage].

de·crease (dē·krēs') *v.t.* to lessen; to make smaller; to reduce gradually; *v.i.* to become less; to wane; to abate; (dē·crēs') *n.* gradual diminution; a lessening [L. *de*, from; *crescere*, to grow].

de·cree (di·krē') *n.* an order made by a competent authority; an edict; decision in a law court; an established law; (*Theol.*) divine purpose; *v.t.* to determine judicially; to order; *v.i.* to decide authoritatively. **decretal** *a.* pert. to a decree; *n.* an order given by a high authority, esp. the Pope. **decretive** *a.* [L. *decretum*, decreed].

de·cre·ment (dek'·ra·mant) *n.* the act or state of decreasing; the quantity lost by decrease [L. *decrementum*, a decrease].

de·crep·it (di·krep'·it) *a.* worn out or enfeebled by old age; infirm; broken down; (of things) ramshackle. **-ude, -ness** *n.* [L. *decrepitus*, very old].

de·cres·cent (di·kres'·ant) *a.* becoming gradually less; waning.

de·cre·tal See **decree**.

de·cry (di·krī') *v.t.* to bring into disrepute; to abuse. **decrial** *n.* act of decrying [L. *de*, from; Fr. *crier*, to cry].

ded·i·cate (ded'·i·kāt) *v.t.* to set apart and consecrate to a holy purpose; to give oneself wholly to a worthy purpose; to inscribe a book or other object to someone as mark of appreciation or admiration. **-d** *a.* devoted. **dedication** *n.* **dedicatory** *a.* containing a dedication; complimentary [L. *dedicare*, to announce].

de·duce (di·dūs') *v.t.* to draw from; to reach a conclusion by deductive reasoning; to infer; to trace down. **deducible** *a.* inferred. **deduct** *v.t.* to remove; to subtract. **deductible** *a.* **deduction** *n.* the act or process of deducting; the amount subtracted; the inference or conclusion arrived at. **deductive** *a.* capable of being deduced. **deductively** *adv.* [L. *deducere*, to lead down].

deed (dēd) *n.* that which is done; an act; exploit; achievement; a legal document or contract; *v.t.* to convey by deed [O.E. *daed; don*, to do].

deem (dēm) *v.t.* to believe on consideration; to judge [O.E. *dēman*, to judge].

deep (dēp) *a.* extending far below the surface; low in situation; dark; intense; abstruse; low in pitch; sagacious; *adv.* to a great depth; *n.* that which is deep; the sea. **-en** *v.t.* to make deep; *v.i.* to become deeper. **-most** *a.* deepest. **-ness** *n.* depth. **-rooted** *a.* firmly established. **—seated** *a.* not superficial. **depth** *n.* the quality of being deep [O.E. *deop*, deep].

deer (dir) *n.* any of the ruminant quadrupeds, such as stag, roebuck, fallow deer, etc. [O.E. *dēor*, an animal].

de·face (di·fās') *v.t.* to destroy or mar the external appearance of; to disfigure. **-able** *a.* **-ment** *n.* [Fr. *défacer*, to mar].

de·fal·cate (di·fal'·kāt) *v.t.* to misappropriate money; to embezzle. **defalcation** *n.* **defalcator** *n.* [L. *de*, from; *falx*, a sickle].

de·fame (di·fām') *v.t.* to harm or destroy the good name or reputation of; to slander. **defamation** *n.* **defamatory** *a.* [L. *diffamare*, to spread an evil report].

de·fault (di·fawlt') *n.* fault; neglect; defect; failure to appear in a law court when summoned; failure to account for money held in trust; *v.i.* to fail to meet an obligation. **-er** *n.* [O.Fr. *defaillir*, to fail].

de·fea·sance (di·fē'·zans) *n.* defeat; a rendering null and void. **defeasible** *a.* capable of being annulled [O.Fr. *desfaire*, to undo].

de·feat (di·fēt') *v.t.* to overcome; to subdue; to conquer; *n.* act of defeating; overthrow; conquest. **-ism** *n.* the attitude of mind of those who accept defeat as inevitable. **-ist** *n.; a.* pert. to defeatism [O.Fr. *desfait*, undone].

def·e·cate (def'·a·kāt) *v.t.* to clear or strain impurities from, as lees, dregs, etc.; *v.i.* to void excrement from the bowels. **defecation** *n.* [L. *de*, from; *faex*, dregs].

de·fect (dē·fekt', di·fekt') *n.* a want; an imperfection; absence of something necessary for completeness. **defection** *n.* a failure in duty; the act of abandoning allegiance to a cause. **-ive** *a.* incomplete; imperfect; faulty; (*Gram.*) not having all the parts to make the complete conjugation of a verb. **-ively** *adv.* **-iveness** *n.*

de·fend (dē·fend') *v.t.* to protect; to ward off attack; to maintain; to justify; to vindicate; (*Law*) to state the case of an accused person (by counsel). **-able** *a.* **-ant** *a.* one who defends; the accused in a criminal case; the one prosecuted in a civil case. **-er** *n.* [L. *defendere*, to protect].

de·fense (di·fens') *n.* the act of defending; that which shields or protects; vindication; justification; (*Law*) a plea or reply to a charge. **-less** *a.* open to attack. **-lessly** *adv.* **-lessness** *n.* **Civil Defense**, an organization in World War 2 and since, for protection of civilians. **defensible** *a.* **defensibility** *n.* **defensive** *a.* serving to defend; resisting attack; *n.* the position of defending against attack. **defensively** *adv.* [L. *defendere*, to protect].

de·fer (di·fur') *v.i.* to submit; to yield or bow to the opinion of another. **deference** (def'·er·ans) *n.* the act of deferring. **deferential** *a.* showing deference [L. *deferre*, to bring before].

de·fer (di·fur') *v.t.* to put off; to postpone; *v.i.* to delay. *pr.p.* **-ring**; *pa.p.* **-red. -able, -rable** *a.* **-ment** *n.* delay; postponement [L. *deferre*, to postpone].

de·fi·ance (di·fī'·ans) *n.* the act of defying; a challenge to combat; contempt; opposition. **defiant** *a.* aggressively hostile; insolent. **defiantly** *adv.* [Fr. *défier*, to challenge].

de·fi·cient (di·fish'·ant) *a.* wanting; failing; lacking a full supply; incomplete. **deficiency, deficience** *n.* shortcoming, shortage; defect. **-ly** *adv.* **deficit** (def'·a·sit) *n.* shortage or deficiency of revenue; excess of expenditure over income [L. *deficere*, to be wanting].

de·file (di·fīl') *n.* a narrow pass; *v.i.* to march by files [Fr. *défiler*, to thread].

de·file (di·fīl') *v.t.* to make unclean; soil; to dirty; to desecrate. **-ment** *n.* the act of defiling [L. *de*; O.E. *fylan*, to pollute].

de·fine (di·fīn') *v.t.* to determine the boundaries of; to state the exact meaning of; to circumscribe; to designate; to specify. **definable** *a.* **definite** (def'·a·nit) *a.* fixed or defined; exact; precise; specific; restricted. **definitely** *adv.* **definiteness** *n.* **definition** *n.* description of a thing by its properties; explanation of the exact meaning of a word or term; distinctness. **definitive** *a.* limiting; determining; final; positive [L. *de*, down; *finis*, end].

de·flate (di·flāt') *v.t.* to empty of air or gas; to reduce inflated currency. **deflation** *n.* [L. *de*, down, *flare*, to blow].

de·flect (di·flekt') *v.t.* to turn aside; to divert from the right direction; *v.i.* to swerve; to deviate. **-ed** *a.* **deflection** *n.* **-or** *n.* [L. *de*, from; *flectere*, to bend].

de·flow·er (di·flour') *v.t.* to deprive of flowers; to ravish [O.Fr. *defleurer*, to strip of flowers].

de·fo·li·a·tion (di·fō·li·ā'·shan) *n.* the shedding of leaves. **defoliate** *v.t.* to deprive of leaves. **defoliate, defoliated** *a.* [L. *de, folium*, leaf].

de·for·est (dē·fawr'·ast) *v.t.* to deprive of forests. **-ation** *n.*

de·form (di·fawrm') *v.t.* to mar or alter the form of; to make misshapen; to disfigure. **-ed** *a.* **-ation** *n.* **-ity** *n.* the state of being disfigured; a malformation [L. *deformare*, disfigure].

de·fraud (di·frawd') *v.t.* to deprive of, by fraud; cheat [L. *defraudare*].

de·fray (di·frā') *v.t.* to bear the cost of; to provide the money for, as in to *defray the expenses*. **-al** *n.* [O.Fr. *desfrayer*, to pay the cost].

de·frock (dē·frok') *v.t.* to unfrock, as of a priest deprived of ecclesiastical status.

deft (deft) *a.* dexterous; adroit; handy. **-ly** *adv.* **-ness** *n.* [O.E. *gedaeftan*, to make smooth].

de·funct (di·fungkt') *a.* dead; deceased; (of things) obsolete; *n.* a dead person [L. *defunctus*, finished].

de·fy (di·fī') *v.t.* to challenge; to dare; to resist authority [L. *dis*, away; *fidere*, to trust].

de·gen·er·ate (di·jen'·er·āt) *v.i.* to decline from a noble to a lower state of development to become worse physically and morally; *n.* a person of low moral standards; a having become less than one's kind. **degeneracy** *n.* **-ly** *adv.* **-ness** *n.* **degeneration** *n.* **degenerative** *a.* [L. *degenere*, unlike one's race].

de·grade (di·grād') *v.t.* to reduce in status; to lower the moral reputation of; to disgrace. **degradation** (deg·ra·dā'·shan) *n.* the act of degrading; the state or process of being degraded; abasement [L. *de*, down; *gradus*, a step].

de·gree (di·grē') *n.* a step upward or downward; station or status; extent, as in *degree of proficiency*; rank to which one is admitted by a university; the 360th part of a revolution; a measured space on a thermometer, protractor, etc. (*Gram.*) modification of adjectives and adverbs by adding of suffix —*er* (comparative), and —*est* (superlative) to indicate intensifying of meaning. **third degree** (*U.S.*) a long, searching cross-examination by police of a suspect [L. *de*, down; *gradus*, a step].

de·gres·sion (di·gresh'·an) *n.* a going down; a lowering of rate of taxation on certain wage levels [L. *degredi*, to go down].

de·hy·drate (dē·hī'·drāt) *v.t.* to remove water from; *v.i.* to lose water; **dehydration** *n.* the process of reducing bulk and weight of food by removing water from products (e.g. dried eggs, milk, potatoes, etc.) [L. *de*, from; Gk. *hydor*, water].

de·i·cide (dē'·a·sīd) *n.* the killing of a god [L. *deus*, god; *caedere*, to kill].

de·i·fy (dē'·a·fī) *v.t.* to make a god of; to exalt to the rank of divinity; to worship. **deific, -al** *a.* making godlike. **deification** *n.* **deiform** *a.* of godlike form [L. *deus*, a god; *facere*, to make].

deign (dān) *v.i.* to condescend; to stoop; *v.t.* to condescend to do; to grant [L. *dignari*, to deem worthy].

de·ism (dē'·izm) *n.* belief, on purely rational grounds, in the existence of God without accepting the revelation implied in religious dogma. **deist** *n.* **deistic, -al** *a.* **deity** *n.* God, the Supreme Being; a pagan god or goddess [L. *deus*, god].

de·ject (di·jekt') *v.t.* to cast down; to dishearten; to depress; to dispirit. **-ed** *a.* downcast; moody; in low spirits. **-edly** *adv.* **-edness** *n.* **-ion** *n.* lowness of spirits; (*Med.*) evacuation of the bowels [L. *de*, down; *jacere*, to throw].

de·lay (di·lā′) *v.t.* to put off; to postpone; to stop temporarily; *v.i.* to linger; to dawdle; to procrastinate; *n.* a stoppage; tardiness. **-er** *n.* [O.Fr. *delaier*, to prolong].

de·lec·ta·ble (di·lek′·ta·bl) *a.* highly pleasing; delightful; enjoyable. **-ness** *n.* delectably *adv.* **delectation** *n.* pleasure; delight [L. *delectare*, to delight].

del·e·gate (del′·a·gāt) *v.t.* to entrust authority to a deputy. *n.* also (del′·a·git) a deputy; a representative. **delegation** *n.* act of delegating; body of delegates. **delegacy** *n.* [L. *de*, from; *legare*, to send].

de·lete (di·lēt′) *v.t.* to erase; to strike out (word or passage). **delenda** *n.pl.* things to be blotted out. **deletion** *n.* [L. *delere*, to blot out].

del·e·te·ri·ous (del·a·tē′·ri·as) *a.* capable of harming or destroying health; pernicious. **-ly** *adv.* **-ness** *n.* [Gk. *dēleisthai*, to harm].

delft (delft) *n.* glazed earthenware, orig. made at *Delft* in Holland. Also **delf, delft-ware.**

de·lib·er·ate (di·lib′·a·rāt) *v.t.* to weigh in the mind; to discuss; *v.i.* to consider carefully; to take counsel; to hesitate; *a.* (di·lib′·a·rit) carefully considered; slow. **-ly** *adv.* **-ness** *n.* **deliberation** *n.* the act of carefully considering; slowness of action or speech. **deliberative** *a.* [L. *deliberare*, to ponder].

del·i·cate (del′·a·kat) *a.* dainty; frail; exquisitely wrought; nicely adjusted; highly sensitive or perceptive. **delicacy** *n.* fineness of shape, color, texture, or feeling; something which pleases the palate; a dainty; tact. **-ly** *adv.* **-ness** *n.* [L. *delicatus*, delightful].

del·i·ca·tes·sen (del·a·ka·tes′·an) *n.pl.* a shop selling cold cooked meats and other foods requiring little or no preparation [Ger.].

de·li·cious (di·lish′·as) *a.* extremely pleasing to the taste or sense of smell; delightful. **-ly** *adv.* [L. *deliciae*, delight].

de·light (di·līt′) *v.t.* to give great pleasure to; to charm; *v.i.* to take delight; n. the source of pleasure; great satisfaction; joy. **-ed** *a.* **-edly** *adv.* **-ful** *a.* [L. *delectare*, to delight].

de·lim·it (di·lim′·it) *v.t.* to fix the limit or boundaries of. **-ation** *n.*

de·lin·e·ate (di·lin′·i·āt) *v.t.* to draw an outline; to sketch; to portray; (*Fig.*) to describe clearly in words. **delineation** *n.* the act of delineating; a portrayal in line or words; a sketch. **delineator** *n.* [L. *de*, from; *linea*, a line].

de·lin·quent (di·ling′·kwant) *n.* one who fails in duty; an offender or criminal, esp. of a young person; *a.* failing in duty. **delinquency** *n.* [L. *de*, from; *linquere*, to leave].

del·i·quesce (del·a·kwes′) *v.i.* to liquefy by absorbing moisture from the air. **deliquescence** *n.* **deliquescent** *a.* [L. *deliquescere*, to melt away].

de·lir·i·ous (di·lir′·i·as) *a.* wandering in the mind; light-headed; raving; incoherent. **deliration** *n.* madness. **-ly** *adv.* **-ness** *n.* **delirium** *n.* mental disturbance caused by grave physical illness or nervous shock; strong excitement. **delirium tremens** (*abbrev.* D.T.) violent delirium resulting from excessive alcoholism [L. *delirus*, crazy].

de·liv·er (di·liv′·er) *v.t.* to liberate from danger, captivity, restraint; to save; to distribute or hand over; to pronounce (as a speech); to execute (as an attack); to give birth to a child (used passively). **-able** *a.* **-ance** *n.* liberation; state of being delivered; the formal statement of an opinion. **-er** *n.* **-y** *n.* the act of delivering; the style of utterance of a public speech or sermon; (*Med.*) the act of giving birth [L. *de*, from; *liberare*, to set free].

dell (del) *n.* a small, deep valley; a hollow [M.E. *delle*, a dell].

Del·phic, Del·phian (del′·fik, del′·fi·an) *a.* pert. to the town of *Delphia* in Ancient Greece, to the oracle of Apollo in that town; oracular.

del·phin·i·um (del·fin′·i·am) *n.* a genus of flowering plants [Gk. *delphinion*, larkspur].

del·ta (del′·ta) *n.* the fourth letter of the Greek alphabet, Δ (small letter = δ); (*Geog.*) a triangular tract of alluvium at the mouth of a large river. **delta rays**, rays from radioactive metals much less powerful and penetrating than the *alpha* rays [Gk.].

de·lude (di·lood′) *v.t.* to lead into error; to mislead; to deceive. **deludable** *a.* **-r** *n.* **delusion** *n.* the act of deluding; that which deludes; a

mistaken belief. **delusive** *a.* **delusory** *a.* [L. *de*; *ludere*, to play].

delphinium

de·luge (del′·ūj) *n.* a great flow of water; torrential rain; a flood; *v.t.* to flood; to inundate [L. *diluvium*, a washing away]. [quality [Fr.].

de luxe (di looks′) *a.* sumptuous; of superlative

delve (delv) *v.t.* and *v.i.* to carry on intensive research [O.E. *delfan*, to dig].

dem·a·gogue (dem′·a·gâg) *n.* an unprincipled agitator. **demagogic, -al** (dem·a·gâj′(g)·ik·-al) *n.* **demagogy** (dem′·a·gâj(g)·i·) *n.* the beliefs and actions of a demogague. Also **demagoguery** [Gk. *dēmos*, the people; *agein*, to lead].

de·mand (di·mand′) *v.t.* to ask authoritatively or peremptorily; to question; to require; *n.* the act of demanding; urgent claim; earnest inquiry; (*Econ.*) the requirement of purchaser or consumer, oppos. of *supply*. **-ant** *n.* a plaintiff [L. *demandare*, to entrust].

de·mar·ca·tion, demarkation (dē·mår·kā′·-shun) *n.* the act of marking a line or boundary; a boundary. **demarcate** *v.t.* [Fr.].

de·mean (di·mēn′) *v.t.* to conduct or comport oneself. **demeanor** *n.* behavior; conduct [O.Fr. *demener*, to conduct].

de·mean (di·mēn′) *v.t.* to make mean; to debase; to degrade (used reflexively).

de·ment·ed (di·men′·tad) *a.* insane; crazy; suffering from dementia. **dement** *v.t.* to drive mad. **dementia** (di·men′·shi·a) *n.* incipient loss of reason; insanity marked by complete mental deterioration. **dementia praecox**, insanity in adolescence [L. *de*, from; *mens*, the mind].

de·mer·it (dē·mer′·it) *n.* a fault; a mark against one's record [L. *de*, from; *merere*, to deserve].

de·mesne (di·mān′, di·mēn′) *n.* a manor house and the estate adjacent to it; private ownership of land. Also **domain** [Fr.].

dem·i- *prefix* signifying *half* [L. *dimidium*, half; Fr. *demi*].

demi·god (dem′·i·gad) *n.* a classical hero half human, half divine.

dem·i·john (dem′·a·ján) *n.* a glass bottle with large body, slender neck, and enclosed in wicker work [prob. fr. Fr. *dame-Jeanne*].

dem·i·monde (dem′·i·mand) *n.* a class of women of doubtful reputation; prostitutes. [Fr. *demi*, half; *monde*, world].

de·mise (di·miz′) *n.* death; transmission by will to a successor; the conveyance of property; *v.t.* to bequeath; to transmit to a successor [L. *demittere*, to send down].

dem·i·tasse (de·ma·tás′) *n.* a small-sized cup, esp. for after-dinner coffee [Fr.].

de·mo·bi·lize (dē·mō′·ba·līz) *v.t.* to dismiss (troops); to disband. **demobilization** *n.*

de·moc·ra·cy (da·mák′·ra·si·) *n.* a form of government for the people by the will of the majority of the people (based on conception of the equality of man); a state having this form of government. **democrat** (dem′·a·krat) *n.* one who adheres to democracy; member of Democratic party (opp. of Republican party). **democratic, democratical** *a.* [Gk. *dēmos*, the people; *kratein*, to rule].

de·mog·ra·phy (di·mág′·ra·fi·) *n.* science of vital and social statistics [Gk. *dēmos*, people; *graphein*, to write].

de·mol·ish (di·mál′·ish) *v.t.* to destroy; to pull down (of a building); to ruin. **-er** *n.* **demolition** (dem·a·li′·shan) *n.* the act or process of pulling down; destruction [L. *de*, down; *moles*, a heap].

de·mon (dē′·man) *n.* a spirit (esp. evil); a devil; sometimes like *daemon*, a friendly spirit. **demoniac** *a.* pert. to a demon; possessed of an evil spirit; devilish—also **demoniacal**; *n.* a human being possessed of an evil spirit. **-olatry, -ism** *n.* the worship of evil spirits. **-olater** *n.* [Gk. *daimon*, a spirit].

de·mon·e·ti·za·tion (dē·mán·a·tī·zā′·shan) *n.* the act of demonetizing. **demonetize** *v.t.* to diminish or deprive of monetary value [L. *de*, down; *moneta*, money].

dem·on·strate (dem′·an·strāt) *v.t.* to prove by pointing out; to exhibit; to explain by specimens or experiment. **demonstrable** *a.* capable of being demonstrated. **demonstrably** *adv.* **demonstration** *n.* the act of making clear, esp. by practical exposition; proof beyond doubt; a display of emotion. **demonstra-**

-tive *a.* proving by evidence; exhibiting with clearness; inclined to show one's feelings openly;; (*Gram.*) of an adjective or pronoun which points out, as *this* or *that*. **demonstrator** *n.* [L. *demonstrare*, to show].

de·mor·al·ize (di·mawr′·al·iz) *v.t.* to injure the morale of; to corrupt; to throw into confusion.

de·mos (dē′·mas) *n.* the people [Gk.].

de·mur (di·mur′) *v.i.* to object. *pr.p.* **-ring**; *pa.p.* **-red**; *n.* statement of objections. **-rable** *a.* **-rage** *n.* undue detention of a ship, railroad car, etc.; compensation paid for such detention. **-rer** *n.* one who demurs; (*Law*) a plea that a case has insufficient evidence to justify its being pursued further [L. *de*; *morari*, to delay].

de·mure (di·mūr′) *a.* grave; staid; shy; seemingly modest. **-ly** *adv.* **-ness** *n.* [O.Fr. *de murs*, of good manners].

den (den) *n.* a cave or hollow place; lair or cage of a wild beast; disreputable haunt; a private sanctum, study or workshop [O.E. *denn*, a cave].

de·nar·i·us (di·nar′·i·as) *n.* a Roman silver coin; the 'penny' of the N.T. *pl.* **denarii.** **denary** *a.* containing ten [L.].

de·na·ture (dē·nā′·cher) *v.t.* to make unfit for eating or drinking by adulteration. **denaturant** *n.* that which changes the nature of a thing. **denaturation** *n.*

den·dri-, dendro- *prefix* from Gk. *dendron*, a tree, as in **-form** (den′·dri·fawrm) *a.* having the shape or appearance of a tree. **-tic, -tical** *a.* tree-like; arborescent. **dendroid, dendroidal** *a.* having the shape of a tree.

de·ni·al (di·nī′·al) *n.* the act of denying; a flat contradiction; a refusal [L. *de*; *negare*, to deny].

den·i·gra·tion (den·a·grā′·shan) *n.* a blackening of; defamation of a person's character. **denigrate** *v.t.* [L. *de*; *nigrare*, to blacken].

den·im (den′·im) *n.* a stout cotton twill cloth [Fr. serge *de Nimes*].

den·i·zen (den′·a·zn) *n.* a dweller (human or animal); anything successfully naturalized; *v.t.* to make a denizen of [L. *de intus*, from within].

de·nom·i·nate (di·nám′·a·nāt) *v.t.* to give a name to; to designate; to style. **denominable** *a.* **denomination** *n.* the act of naming; a title; a class; a religious sect; (*Arith.*) unit of measure (money, length, etc.). **denominational** *a.* **denominative** *a.* conferring or having a distinctive name; (*Gram.*) a verb made from a noun or adjective. **denominatively** *adv.* **denominator** *n.* the one who, or that which, designates a class; the divisor; the number below the line in a fraction [L. *de*; *nominare*, to name].

de·note (di·nōt′) *v.t.* to signify or imply; to express by a sign; to mean; to be the symbol of; (*Logic*) to indicate the objects to which a term refers. **denotable** *a.* **denotation** *n.* [L. *denotare*, to mark].

dé·noue·ment (dā·nóo′·mang) *n.* the unraveling of the complication of a dramatic plot; the issue or outcome of a situation [Fr. fr. L. *de*, from; *nodare*, to tie with knots].

de·nounce (di·nouns′) *v.t.* to inform against; to accuse in public; to repudiate, as a treaty. **-ment** *n.* **-er** *n.* [L. *de*; *nuntiare*, to announce].

dense (dens) *a.* compact; thick, crowded; (of vegetation) impenetrable, luxuriant; (*Fig.*) stupid. **-ly** *adv.* **-ness** *n.* **density** *n.* the quality of being dense; (*Chem.*) the mass per unit volume of a substance [L. *densus*, thick].

dent (dent) *n.* a small depression made (by a blow) in a surface; *v.t.* to mark by a blow or pressure [O.E. *dynt*, a stroke].

den·tal (den′·tal) *a.* pert. to the teeth or to dentistry; *n.* and *a.* a consonant sound (e.g. *d* or *t*) made by tip of tongue behind the upper front teeth. **dentate** *a.* toothed; sharply notched (e.g. leaf). **dentiform** *a.* having the shape of a tooth. **dentifrice** *n.* powder, paste, or liquid used to clean and whiten teeth. **dentist** *n.* a medically trained specialist in the care of the teeth (also *dental surgeon*). **dentistry** *n.* **dentition** *n.* arrangement of teeth. **dentoid** *a.* tooth-like. **denture** *n.* set or part set of teeth, esp. artificial teeth [L. *dens*, a tooth].

den·ti·cle (den′·ta·kl) *n.* a small tooth or projection. **denticular, denticulate, denticulated** *a.* having notches or sharp projections [L. *dens*, tooth].

de·nude (di·nūd′) *v.t.* to lay bare; to strip. **denudation** *n.* [L. *denudare*, to make bare].

de·nun·ci·ate (di·nun′·si·āt) *v.t.* Same as **denounce. denunciation** *n.* **denunciator** *n.* [L. *de*; *nuntiare*, to announce].

de·ny (di·nī′) *v.t.* to declare to be untrue; to gainsay; to refuse a request; to disavow; to disown; to withhold; (*reflex.*) to abstain from [L. *de*; *negare*, to deny].

de·o·dor·ize (dē·ō′·da·rīz) *v.t.* to deprive of odor. **deodorant, deodorizer** *n.* something which destroys an odor [L. *de*, from; *odor*, smell].

de·ox·i·dize (dē·áks′·a·dīz) *v.t.* to remove oxygen from; to reduce from the state of an oxide.

de·part (di·part′) *v.i.* to go away; to leave; to die; to deviate (as from a policy); *v.t.* to leave (e.g. to *depart this life*). **-ed** *n.* (*sing.* and *pl.*) the dead. **-ment** *n.* a section of a business or administration; a special branch of the arts or science; an administrative district of a country, as in France. **-mental** *a.* pert. to a department.; affecting only a section of a business, etc. **-ure** *n.* the act of going away; divergence from rule [L. *de*, from; *partiri*, to part].

de·pend (di·pend′) *v.i.* to rely on; to be sustained by; to be contingent on; to hang; (*Law*) to be awaiting final judgment. **-able** *a.* trustworthy. **-ably** *adv.* **-ant, -ent** *n.* one who is supported, esp. financially by another; a retainer; a subordinate; *a.* hanging down; relying on for support or favor; varying according to; (spellings -ant, -ent are interchangeable in noun and adjective, but *-ant* is more common in noun, and *-ent* in adjective). **-ence** *n.* **-ency** *n.* **-ently, -antly** *adv.* [L. *dependere*, to hang down].

de·pict (di·pikt′) *v.t.* to present a visual image of; to describe in words. **-tion** *n.* **-ive** *a.* [L. *de*; *pingere*, *pictum*, to paint].

dep·i·late (dep′·ạ·lāt) *v.t.* to remove hair from. **depilation** *n.* **depilatory** *n.* agent for removing superfluous hair from body; *a.* able to remove hair [L. *de*, from; *pilus*, a hair].

de·plete (di·plēt′) *v.t.* to empty; to diminish; to reduce. **depletion** *n.* **depletive, depletory** *a.* [L. *de*, from; *plere*, to fill].

de·plore (di·plōr′) *v.t.* to suffer remorse for; to regret; to express disapproval of. **deplorable** *a.* **deplorably** *adv.* [L. *de*; *plorare*, to weep].

de·ploy (di·ploi′) *v.t.* to spread out; to extend troops in line; *v.i.* to extend from column into line. **-ment** *n.* [Fr. *déployer*, to spread out].

de·po·lar·ize (dē·pō′·lạ·rīz) *v.t.* to deprive of polarity [Gk. *poloz*, pivot].

de·pone (di·pōn′) *v.t.* to give evidence under oath, in a law court. **deponent** *n.* [L. *de*, down; *ponere*, to lay].

de·port (di·pōrt′) *v.t.* to carry away; to expel; to banish into exile (of undesirable aliens); (reflex.) to behave; to bear oneself. **-ation** *n.* the compulsory removal of people from one country to another. **-ment** *n.* conduct of a person [L. *de*, from; *portare*, to carry].

de·pose (di·pōz′) *v.t.* to remove from a throne; to oust from a high position; to degrade; (*Law*) to state upon oath. **deposable** *a.* **deposal** *n.* **deposition** (de·pạ·zi′·shạn) *n.* removal of someone from a high position; (*Law*) act of deponing; a written declaration by a witness [L. *de*, down; *ponere*, to place].

de·pos·it (di·páz′·it) *v.t.* to lay down; to entrust; to let fall (as a sediment); to lodge (in a bank); to store; *n.* that which is deposited or laid down; sediment falling to the bottom of a fluid; money placed in safe-keeping of a bank (usually with interest); a security; partial payment. **-ary** *n.* one with whom anything is left in trust. **-or** *n.* **-ory** *n.* [L. *de*, down; *ponere*, to place].

de·pot (dē′·pō) *n.* a railway station; (*Mil.*) (de′·pō) a storage center for supplies and materials; (formerly) training center for recruits [Fr. *dépôt*].

de·prave (di·prāv′) *v.t.* to make bad or worse; to corrupt; to pervert. **depravation** *n.* **-d** *a.* immoral; vicious. **depravity** *n.* [L. *de*; *pravus*, vicious].

dep·re·cate (dep′·rạ·kāt) *v.t.* to express disapproval of. **deprecatingly** *adv.* **deprecation** *n.* **deprecative, deprecatory** *a.* **deprecator** *n.* [L. *de*, from; *precari*, to pray].

de·pre·ci·ate (di·prē′·shi·āt) *v.t.* to lower in value; (*Fig.*) to disparage; to underrate; *v.i.* to lose quality; to diminish in market value. **depreciation** *n.* decline in value. **depreciative, depreciatory** *a.* **depreciator** *n.* [L. *de*, down; *pretium*, price].

dep·re·date (dep′·ri·dāt) *v.t.* to plunder; to lay waste. **depredation** *n.* the act of laying waste; pillaging [L. *de*, from; *praeda*, plunder].

de·press (di·pres′) *v.t.* to deject or cast a gloom over; to press down; to lower; to diminish the vigor of. **-ed** *a.* dejected; pressed down. **-ible** *a.* **depression** *n.* a hollow; a dip; a sinking; dejection; despondency; a slump (in trade); in meteorology, an area of low barometric pressure. **-or** *n.* [L. *depressus*, pressed down].

de·prive (di·prīv′) *v.t.* to take away; to dispossess; to debar a person from **deprivation** *n.* the act of depriving; the state of being deprived or dispossessed. **deprivable** *a.* **depriver** *n.* [L. *de*, from; *privare*, to deprive].

depth (depth) *n.* deepness; distance measured downwards from surface; distance from front to back, as of a shelf, etc.; profundity or penetration, as of mind [O.E. *deop*, deep].

de·pute (di·pūt′) *v.t.* to send with commission to act for another; to delegate duties to another. **deputation** *n.* the act of deputing; persons authorized to transact business for others; **deputize** *v.i.* to appoint as deputy. **deputy** *n.* (dep′·yoo·ti·) one who is appointed to act for another [L. *deputare*, to esteem, to allot].

de·range (di·rānj′) *v.t.* to put out of order or place; to upset; to make insane. **-d** *a.* mentally unstable; insane. **-ment** *n.* [Fr. *déranger*, to disturb].

der·by (dur′·bi·) *n.* a man's felt hat, with stiff rounded crown and narrow brim.

der·e·lict (der′·ạ·likt) *a.* forsaken; abandoned and disclaimed by owner, esp. used of ships; *n.* a ship abandoned by captain and crew; a person abandoned by society. **dereliction** *n.* [L. *de*, from; *relinquere*, to leave].

de·ride (di·rīd′) *v.t.* to ridicule; to mock; to laugh at with scorn. **-r** *n.* **deridingly** *adv.* **derision** (di·rizh′·ạn) *n.* mockery; ridicule.

depth

derelict

derisive *a.* **derisively** *adv.* **derisiveness** *n.* **derisory** *a.* [L. *de*, down; *ridere*, to laugh].

de·rive (dạ·rīv′) *v.t.* to obtain or draw from a source; to trace the etymology (of a word); to trace the descent or origin (of a person); *v.i.* to have as an origin; to proceed (foll. by *from*). **derivable** *a.* **derivation** (der·ạ·vā′·shạn) *n.* act of deriving or process of being derived; tracing a word back to its roots; etymology. **derivative** *n.* that which is derived or traceable back to something else; a word derived from another; *a.* obtained by derivation; secondary [L. *de*, down; *rivus*, a stream].

der·ma, der·mis (dur′·mạ, dur′·mis) *n.* the true skin below epidermis. **dermal** *a.* **dermatic** *a.* consisting of skin. **-titis** *n.* inflammation of the skin. **-tology** *n.* branch of medical science concerned with the skin and skin diseases. **-tologist** *n.* skin specialist [Gk. *derma*, a skin].

der·o·gate (der′·ạ·gāt) *v.i.* to lessen (as reputation). **derogation** *n.* **derogatory** *a.* tending to impair the value of; detracting. **derogatorily** *adv.* [L. *de*, from; *rogare*, to ask].

der·rick (der′·ik) *n.* an apparatus like a crane for hoisting heavy weights [fr. *Derrick*, a Tyburn hangman of 17th cent.].

der·rin·ger (der′·in·jẹr) *n.* a short-barrelled pistol with a large bore [U.S. inventor].

der·vish (dur′·vish) *n.* a member of one of the mendicant orders among the Mohammedans [Pers. *darvish*, a poor man].

des·cant (des′·kant) *n.* a melody harmonizing with and sung or played as accompaniment to a musical theme; a discourse on a theme; *v.i.* to discourse fully; to sing. **-er** *n.* [L. *dis*, apart; *cantus*, song].

de·scend (di·send′) *v.t.* to go down; to traverse downwards; to flow down; *v.i.* to sink; to lower oneself or stoop to something; to fall (upon an enemy); to be derived by birth. **-ant** *n.* one descended from an ancestor; offspring. **-ent** *a.* descending. **descending** *a.* **descent** *n.* act of coming down; a slope or declivity; lineage [L. *de*, down; *scandere*, to climb].

de·scribe (di·skrīb′) *v.t.* to represent the features of; to portray in speech or writing.

describable *a.* **description** (de·skrip′·shạn) *n.* act of describing; a representation, in words, of the qualities of a person or thing; sort; kind. **descriptive** *a.* **descriptively** *adv.* [L. *de*, down; *scribere*, to write].

de·scry (di·skrī′) *v.t.* to discover by the eye; to perceive from a distance; to make out. **descrier** *n.* [L. *de*, down; *scribere*, to write].

des·e·crate (des′·ạ·krāt) *v.t.* to violate the sanctity of; to profane. **-r, -or** *n.* **desecration** *n.* [L. *de*, away, *sacer*, holy].

de·sert (di·zụrt′) *n.* that which is deserved; reward (for merit); punishment (for demerit) [L. *deszvire*, to serve zealously].

des·ert (dez′·ẹrt) *n.* a wide, sandy waste region; *a.* uncultivated; solitary [L. *deserere*, to abandon].

de·sert (di·zụrt′) *v.t.* to abandon; to leave; *v.i.* to quit the armed forces without authorization. **-ed** *a.* abandoned. **-er** *n.* **desertion** *n.* [L. *deserere*, to abandon].

de·serve (di·sụrv′) *v.t.* to earn by service; to merit; to be entitled to; to warrant; *v.i.* to be worthy of reward. **deservedly** *adv.* justly. **deserving** *a.* worthy; meritorious [L. *deservire*, to serve zealously].

des·ic·cate (des′·ạ·kāt) *v.t.* to extract all moisture from; to dry up; to dehydrate. **desiccant** *a.* drying; *n.* (*Chem.*) substance capable of absorbing moisture. **desiccation** *n.* [L. *desiccare*, to dry up].

de·sign (di·zīn′) *v.t.* to draw the outline of; to plan; *v.i.* to purpose; *n.* sketch in outline (esp. in architecture); a pattern (as in wallpaper, printed cloth, etc.); scheme or plan; purpose. **-able** *a.* **designate** (dez′·ig·nāt) *v.t.* to mark out and make known; to nominate or appoint. **designation** *n.* distinctive title. **designative** *a.* **-edly** *adv.* intentionally. **-er** *n.* one who designs or makes plans or patterns; a schemer or plotter. **-ful** *a.* **-ing** *a.* artful; selfishly interested [L. *de*, down; *signare*, to mark].

de·sire (di·zīr′) *v.t.* to yearn for the possession of; to request; to entreat; *n.* anything desired; a longing; object of longing; lust. **desirable** *a.* worth possessing. **desirably** *adv.* **desirableness, desirability** *n.* the state or quality of being desired. **desirous** *a.* full of desire; covetous [O.Fr. *desirer*, to want].

de·sist (di·zist′) *v.t.* to cease; to discontinue. **-ance, -ence** *n.* [L. *de*, from *sistere*, to stand].

desk (desk) *n.* a table for reading or writing; a lectern [L.L. *desca*, a table].

des·o·late (des′·ạ·lāt) *v.t.* to devastate; to depopulate; to make lonely or forlorn; *a.* (des′·ạ·lit) waste; deserted; unfrequented; dismal. **-ly** *adv.* **ness** *n.* **-r** *n.* **desolation** *n.* the act of laying waste; loneliness; misery. **desolatory** *a.* [L. *desolare*, to forsake].

de·spair (di·sper′) *v.i.* to be without hope; to lose heart; *n.* despondency; hopelessness. **-ing** *a.* full of despair. **-ingly** *adv.* [L. *desparare*, to despair].

des·patch See **dispatch**.

des·pi·ca·ble (des′·pik·ạ·bl) *a.* contemptible; vile; deserving to be despised. **despicably** *adv.* **despicability** *n.* [L. *despicere*, to despise].

de·spise (di·spīz′) *v.t.* to look down upon; to hold in contempt; to disdain; to scorn. **de-**

spisable *a.* [L. *despicere*, to look down on].
de·spite (di·spīt′) *n.* contemptuous treatment; *prep.* in spite of, notwithstanding. **-ful** *a.* **-fully** *adv.* [L. *despicere*, to look down on].
de·spoil (di·spoil′) *v.t.* to take away by force; to rob; to strip. **-er** *n.* a plunderer. **-ment**, **despoliation** *n.* [L. *de*, from; *spolium*, spoil].
de·spond (di·spând′) *v.i.* to be cast down in spirit. **-ence**, **-ency** *n.* dejection of mind; depression. **-ent** *a.* depressed. **-ently** *adv.* **-ingly** *adv.* [L. *de*, from; *spondere*, to promise].
des·pot (des′·pat) *n.* one who rules with absolute power; a tyrant; one who enforces his will on others. **-ic** *a.* **-ically** *adv.* **-ism** *n.* the absolute power of one man unlimited by constitution [Gk. *despotēs*, a master].
des·sert (di·zurt′) *n.* a course served at end of a dinner [O.Fr. *desservir*, to clear the table].
des·tine (des′·tin) *v.t.* to predetermine (usu. passive). **destination** *n.* the purpose for which anything is destined; the place to which one is traveling. **destiny** *n.* state appointed; foreordained lot; fate [L. *destinare*, to establish].
des·ti·tute (des′·ta·tūt) *a.* in want; needy; deprived of means of sustenance. **destitution** *n.* [L. *de*, from; *statuere*, to place].
de·stroy (di·stroi′) *v.t.* to pull down; to turn to rubble; to put an end to; to annihilate. *pa.p.* **-ed. -able** *a.* **-er** *n.* a type of fast warship armed with guns and torpedoes [L. *destruere*].
de·struc·tion (di·struk′·shan) *n.* the act of destroying; state of being destroyed; ruin; death. **destructible** *a.* capable of being destroyed. **destructibleness, destructibility** *n.* **destructive** *a.* [L. *destruere*, to destroy].
des·ue·tude (des′·wi·tūd) *n.* discontinuance of a custom or practice [L. *desuetudo*].
de·sul·to·ry (des′·al·tōr·i·) *a.* leaping from one thing to another; unmethodical; aimless; rambling. **desultorily** *adv.* **desultoriness** *n.* [L. *desultor*, a circus rider].
de·tach (di·tach′) *v.t.* to separate; to disunite; to withdraw; to detail for special service (as troops). **-able** *a.* **-ed** *a.* standing alone (e.g. of a house); impersonal; disinterested; unprejudiced. **-edly** *adv.* **-edness, -ment** *n.* process or state of being detached; that which is detached (as troops) [Fr. *détacher*, to unfasten].
de·tail (di·tāl′) *v.t.* to relate minutely; to record every item; to appoint for a special duty (e.g. troops). **detail** (dē′·tāl or di·tāl′) *n.* a minute part; item; (*Mil.*) special duty. **-ed** *a.* giving every particular fact [Fr. *tailler*, to cut].
de·tain (di·tān′) *v.t.* to keep back or from; to prevent someone proceeding; to maintain possession of; to keep in custody. **-er** *n.* one who detains; (*Law*) illegal detention of another's possessions; a writ to keep in custody. **-ment** *n.* detention *n.* [L. *detinere*, to keep back].
de·tect (di·tekt′) *v.t.* to uncover; to discover; to expose; to bring to light (esp. a crime); to perceive. **-able, -ible** *a.* **-or** *n.* one who or that which detects. **-ion** *n.* **-ive** *a.* employed in detecting; *n.* a member of the police force, not in uniform, who apprehends criminals and investigates cases [L. *detergere*, to uncover].
de·ter (di·ter′) *v.t.* to frighten from; to discourage; to restrain. *pr.p.* **-ring.** *pa.p.* **-red. -ment** *n.* hindrance. **-rent** *a.* having the power to deter; *n.* that which deters. **deterrence** *n.* [L. *deterrere*, to frighten off].
de·terge (di·turj′) *v.t.* to cleanse (wound); to wipe off; to purge. **detergence, detergency** *n.* **detergent** *a.* a cleansing *n.* cleansing substance [L. *detergere*, to wipe off].
de·te·ri·o·rate (di·tir′·i·a·rāt) *v.t.* to make worse; to cause to depreciate; *v.i.* to become worse; to degenerate. **deterioration** *n.* [L. *deterior*, worse].
de·ter·mine (di·tur′·min) *v.t.* to fix the limits of; to define; to regulate the form, scope, or character of; to decide; to ascertain with precision; *v.i.* to make a decision or resolution; (*Law*) to terminate. **determinable** *a.* **determinant** *a.* serving to determine, fix, or limit; *n.* that which determines or causes determination. **determinate** *a.* having fixed limits; decisive; established. **determinately** *adv.* **determination** *n.* the act or process of determining fixed purpose; resolution; adherence to a definite line of action. **-d** *a.* resolute: unwavering; firm; purposeful. **-d** *adv.* **determinism** *n.* the doctrine that man is not a free agent, and that his actions and mental activity are governed by causes or motives outside his own will [L. *determinare*, to limit].
de·test (di·test′) *v.t.* to dislike intensely; to hate; to abhor. **-able** *a.* **-ableness, -ability** *n.* **-ation** *n.* [L. *detestari*, to execrate].
de·throne (dē·thrōn′) *v.t.* to remove from a throne; to depose. **-ment** *n.*
de·to·nate (det′·a·nāt) *v.t.* to cause to explode; *v.i.* to explode with a loud report. **detonation** *n.* a sudden and violent explosion. **detonator** *n.* a detonating substance; device to make another substance explode [L. *detonare*, to thunder].
de·tour (dē′·toor) *n.* a roundabout way, a circuitous route; a digression [Fr. *détour*].
de·tract (di·trakt′) *v.t.* to take away a part from; to defame; *v.i.* (with from) to diminish. **-or** *n.* **-ingly** *adv.* **detraction** *n.* disparagement; depreciation; slander [L. *detrahere*, to draw away].

de·tri·ment (det′·ra·mant) *n.* injury; harm; loss. **-al** *a.* [L. *detrimentum*, a rubbing off].
de·trun·cate (di·trung′·kāt) *v.t.* to lop off from the trunk; to shorten. **detruncation** *n.*
deuce (dūs) *n.* a card or die with two spots; (*Tennis*) score of 40 all [L. *duo*, two].
deuce (dūs) *n.* the devil (in mild imprecations); bad luck [prob. *deus*, a god].
deu·te·ri·um (dū·tir′·i·am) *n.* a form of hydrogen twice as heavy as the normal gas [Gk. *deuteros*, second place].
deu·ter·on·o·my (dū·ter·án′·a·mi·) *n.* the fifth book of the Pentateuch [Gk. *deuteros*, second; *nomos*, law].
de·val·u·ate, devalue (dē·val′·yoo·āt) *v.t.* to reduce the value of (esp. the currency). **devaluation** *n.* [L. *de*, down; *valere*, to be worth].
dev·as·tate (dev′·as·tāt) *v.t.* to lay waste. **devastation** *n.* act of laying waste; the state of being devastated; destruction; havoc [L. *devastare*, to lay waste].
de·vel·op (di·vel′·ap) *v.t.* to cause to grow; to unfold gradually; to increase the resources of; (*Photog.*) to produce image on photographic plate or film by chemical application; *v.i.* to evolve by natural processes; to expand; to open out; to assume definite character. **-er** *n.* one who or that which develops; (*Photog.*) a chemical for producing image on plate or film. **-ment** *n.* a gradual unfolding or growth; expansion; evolution; unraveling of a plot; the result of previous causes [Fr. *développer*, to grow gradually].
de·vi·ate (dē′·vi·āt) *v.i.* to diverge; to turn away from the direct line; to swerve; *v.t.* to cause to swerve. **deviation** *n.* [L. *de*, from; *via*, a way].
de·vice (di·vīs′) *n.* that which is planned out or designed; contrivance; stratagem; (*Her.*) emblem on a shield [M.E. *devisen*, to contrive].
dev·il (dev′·l) *n.* the spirit of evil; in Scripture, tempter; Satan; fiend; any very wicked person; (*Colloq.*) a fellow; *v.t.* (*Colloq.*) to torment; (*cookery*) to prepare with hot or savory seasoning. **-ish** *a.* **-ishly** *adv.* **—may-care** *a.* reckless; happy-go-lucky. **-ment** *n.* mischief; prank. **-ry, -try** *n.* devilish conduct. **-'s advocate**, one appointed by papal court to oppose a proposed canonization; (*Colloq.*) one who maintains an argument with which he really disagrees. **give the devil his due**, give even the worst person credit for something [O.E. *deofol*, the devil; fr. Gk. *diabolos*, slandered].
de·vi·ous (dē′·vi·as) *a.* not direct; circuitous; erring. **-ly, -ness** *n.* [L. *de*, from; *via*, a way].
de·vise (di·vīz′) *v.t.* to invent; to contrive; to scheme; to plan; (*Law*) to leave as a legacy; *v.i.* to consider; *n.* (*Law*) the act of bequeathing real estate by will; clause in will to this effect. **devisable** *a.* **devisal,** *n.* **-r** *n.* one who schemes or contrives. **devisor** *n.* one who bequeaths by will [M.E. *devisen*, to divide].
de·vi·tal·ize (dē·vī′·ta·līz) *v.t.* to deprive of life or vitality. **devitalization** *n.*
de·void (di·void′) *a.* empty; free from; without [L. *de*, from; *viduus*, deprived].
dev·o·lu·tion (dev·a·lōō′·shan) *n.* delegation of powers to subsidiary or local bodies; gradual retrogression (oppos. of evolution) [L. *devolutus*, rolled down]. [See **devolve**].
de·volve (di·válv′) *v.t.* to transmit; to transfer; to delegate; *v.i.* (foll. by *upon*) to fall to the lot of; (*Law*) to pass, by inheritance, from one to another [L. *devolvere*, to roll down].
de·vote (di·vōt′) *v.t.* to give oneself wholly to; to dedicate; to consecrate. **-d** *a.* **-dly** *adv.* **devotedness** *n.* **devotee** (de·va·tē′) *n.* one who is devoted to a cause; a zealous supporter. **devotion** *n.* **devotions** *n.pl.* worship and prayer. **devotional** *a.* pert. to devotions; religious [L. *devovere*, to dedicate by vow].
de·vour (di·vour′) *v.t.* to swallow ravenously; to consume completely and wantonly; to destroy; (*Fig.*) to read avidly. **-ing** *a.* [L. *devorare*, to swallow up].
de·vout (di·vout′) *a.* pious; passionately religious; sincere. **-ly** *adv.* [L. *devovere*, to vow].
dew (dū) *n.* moisture in the atmosphere or in the soil deposited, condensed on exposed surfaces, esp. at night; *v.t.* to moisten; to bedew. **-fall** *n.* the falling of dew, or the time when it falls. **-iness** *n.* **-y** *a.* [O.E. *deaw*, dew].
dex·ter (deks′·ter) *a.* pert. to the right hand; on the right hand side. **dexterity** *n.* manual skill; mental adroitness; cleverness; right-handedness. **-ous, dextrous** *a.* **-ously** *adv.* **-ousness** *n.* **dextral** *a.* right as opposed to left. **dextrality** *n.* right-handedness. **dextrally** *adv.* [L. *dexter*, on the right hand].
dex·trin, dextrine (deks′·trin) *n.* a soluble gummy substance used for stiffening fabrics, sizing paper, mucilage, etc. [L. *dexter*, on the right].
di·a·be·tes (dī·a·bē′·tis, ·ēz) *n.* a disease marked by excessive flow of sugar-urine due to failure of pancreas to produce insulin [Gk. *diabetes*, fr. *dia*, through; *bainein*, to go].
di·a·bol·ic, diabolical (di·a·bál′·ik, ·i·kal) *a.* devilish; fiendish; pert. to the devil. **-ally** *adv.* [Gk. *diabolos*, the devil].
di·a·co·nal (dī·ak′·a·nal) *a.* pert. to a deacon.
di·a·dem (dī′·a·dem) *n.* a fillet or head band worn as the symbol of royal power; a headdress or crown significant of royalty; (*Fig.*) sovereignty. **-ed** *a.* wearing a crown [Gk. *diadēma*, fr. *diadein*, to bind round].

di·a·glyph (dī′·a·glif) *n.* an intaglio [Gk. *dia*, through; *gluphein*, to carve].
di·ag·no·sis (dī·ag·nō′·sis) *n.* a scientific discrimination of any kind; (*Med.*) the identification of a disease from its signs and symptoms; *pl.* **diagnoses. diagnose** *v.t.* (*Med.*) to ascertain from signs and symptoms the nature of a disease; to identify the root-cause of any social or other problems. **diagnostic** *a.* distinguishing; symptomatic; *n.* a symptom distinguishing one disease from another; a clue. **diagnostician** *n.* [Gk. *dia*, through; *gnosis*, an inquiry].
di·ag·o·nal (di·ag′·a·nal) *n.* (*Geom.*) a straight line joining two opposite angles in a rectilineal figure; a line, plane, part, etc. having an oblique direction or position; *a.* from corner to opposite corner; oblique. **-ly** *adv.* [Gk. *dia*, through; *gonia*, a corner].
di·a·gram (dī′·a·gram) *n.* a figure drawn to demonstrate a theorem; a drawing or plan in outline. **-matically** *adv.* [Gk. *dia*, through; *graphein*; to write].
di·al (dī′·al) *n.* an instrument for showing the time of day from the sun's shadow; the face of a sundial, clock, watch, etc.; any plate or face on which a pointer moves, as on a weighing machine; *v.t.* to measure on a dial; to call a number on automatic telephone; *pr.p.* **-ling.** *pa.p.* **-led.**

di·a·lect (dī′·a·lekt) *n.* a group variation of language; a mode of speech peculiar to a district or social group; vernacular [Gk. *dialektos*, manner of speech].
di·a·lec·tic, -al (di·a·lek′·tik, ·al) *a.* pert. to dialectics; *n.* (usually *pl.*) the art of discussion, disputation, or debate; the science of reasoning. **-ally** *adv.* **dialectician** *n.* one skilled in debate; one who studies dialects [Gk. *dialektikē*, the art of debate].
di·a·logue (dī′·a·lawg) *n.* a conversation between two (or more) persons. **dialogistic** *a.* pert. to dialogue. **dialogize** *v.i.* to speak in dialogue [Gk. *dialogos*, a conversation].
di·al·y·sis (dī·al′·a·sis) *n.* (*Chem.*) separation of colloid (non-crystalline) from crystalline substances in solution, by filtration through a membrane; *pl.* **dialyses. dialytic** *a.* [Gk. *dia*, through; *luein*, to loosen].
di·am·e·ter (di·am′·a·ter) *n.* (*Geom.*) a line passing through the center of a circle or other curvilinear figure, and terminated by the circumference; transverse measurement; unit of magnifying power of a lens. **diametric (-al)** *a.* pert. to the diameter; directly opposite [Gk. *dia*, through; *metron*, a measure].

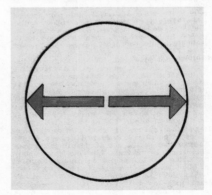

di·a·mond (dī′·a·mand) *n.* one of the crystalline forms of carbon and the hardest substance known; a popular gem stone; a four-sided figure with two acute and two obtuse angles; a rhombus; one of the four suits of playing-cards; one of the smallest types of English printing (4½ point); playing field for baseball. *a.* resembling, set with, consisting of, shaped like diamonds. **— wedding**, the sixtieth anniversary of a marriage. **black diamonds** (*Colloq.*) coal. **rough diamond**, (*Colloq.*) a worthy but uncultured person [Fr. *diamant*, diamond].

diamond

di·a·pa·son (dī·a·pā′·zạn) *n.* correct pitch; harmony; the entire compass of a voice or instrument; the two foundation stops of an organ (open and stopped diapason) [Gk. *dia pason* = through all (the notes)].

di·a·per (dī′·a·per) *n.* a linen or cotton cloth with diamond pattern; a baby's breechcloth; *v.t.* to change a baby's diaper; to ornament with a diaper pattern [O.Fr. *diapre*].

di·aph·a·nous (dī·af′·a·nạs) *a.* having the power to transmit light; transparent; translucent [Gk. *dia*, through; *phainein*, to show].

di·a·pho·ret·ic (dī·a·fa·ret′·ik) *n.* (Med.) a medicine which induces perspiration; *a.* promoting perspiration [Gk. *dia*, through; *phorein*, to carry].

di·a·phragm (dī′·a·fram) *n.* (Anat.) a dividing membrane; a dome-shaped muscular partition between chest and abdomen; vibrating disc in telephone or microphone; a disc with a circular hole used in telescope or camera to cut off part of a ray of light. **-atic**, **-al** *a.* [Gk. *diaphragma*, a barrier].

di·ar·chy (dī′·ar·ki·) *n.* a system of government in which power is held jointly by two authorities [Gk. *dis*, twice; *archein*, to rule].

di·ar·rhe·a, diarrhoea (dī·a·rē′·a) *n.* an excessive and frequent looseness of the bowels. **diarrhetic** *a.* [Gk. *dia*, through; *rhein*, to flow].

di·a·ry (dī′·a·ri·) *n.* a daily record; a book in which a personal record of thoughts, action, etc. is kept. **diarist** *n.* [L. *dies*, a day].

di·a·stase (dī′·a·stās) *n.* an enzyme capable of converting starch into sugar. **diastasic** *a.* [Gk. *diastasis*, separation].

di·as·to·le (dī·as′·ta·lē) *n.* (Med.) a rhythmical dilatation of the heart and arteries alternating with *systole* (contraction); the lengthening of a syllable usually short, before a pause [Gk. = a putting apart].

di·a·ther·mal (dī·a·thurm′·al) *a.* permeable by heat. **diathermanous, diathermous, diathermic** *a.* having the property of transmitting radiant heat. **diathermy** *n.* [Gk. *dia*, through; *thermē*, heat].

di·a·tom (dī′·a·tạm) *n.* one of an order of microscopic unicellular marine or vegetable organisms [Gk. *dia*, through; *tomē*, a cutting].

di·a·tom·ic (dī·a·tám′·ik) *a.* (Chem.) consisting of two atoms.

di·a·ton·ic (dī·a·tán′·ik) *a.* (Mus.) pert. to major or minor scales; proceeding by the tones, intervals, and harmonies of the natural scale [Gk. *dia*, through; *tonos*, tone].

di·a·tribe (dī′·a·trīb) *n.* a vituperative harangue; a wordy denunciation. **diatribist** *n.* [Gk. *diatribē*, a means of passing the time].

dib·ble (dib′·l) *n.* a pointed instrument used in gardening for making holes. Also **dibber**. *v.t.* to plant with a dibble; *v.i.* to make holes. **-r** *n.* [form of *dab*].

dice (dīs) *n.pl.* small cubes on each of the six faces of which are spots representing numbers 1-6; used from Egyptian times in games of chance; *Sing.* form **die**; *v.t.* to cut into small squares; *v.i.* to play with dice. **dicer** *n.* a gambler [O.Fr. *dez*, fr. L. *datus*, given, thrown].

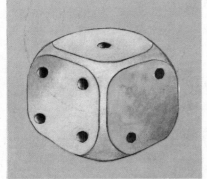

di·ceph·a·lous (dī·sef′·a·lạs) *a.* having two heads [Gk. *dis*, twice; *kephalē*, the head].

di·chot·o·my (dī·kát′·am·i·) *n.* a cutting in two; (Logic) division of ideas into two classes. **dichotomize** *v.t.* and *v.i.* **dichotomous** *a.*

[Gk. *dicha*, apart; *temnein*, to cut].

dick·er (dik′·er) *v.t.* and *v.i.* to barter; to haggle; to quibble; *n.* a bargain; a deal [L. *decuria*, a group of ten (esp. hides)].

dick·ey, dicky (dik′·i·) *n.* a waist front for women; detachable shirt front; seat for servants at back of old-fashioned carriage.

Dic·ta·phone (dik′·ta·fōn) *n.* a machine into which letters, etc. can be dictated and which re-dictates to the typist [Trade Name].

dic·tate (dik·tāt′) *v.t.* to read aloud a passage for another to transcribe; to give orders; *v.i.* to speak with authority; to prescribe; to deliver commands; *n.* an order; command; direction that must be obeyed (usually *pl.*). **dictation** *n.* art or practice of dictating; that which is read aloud for another to write down. **dictator** *n.* one who holds absolute power. **dictatorial** *a.* pert. to or like a dictator; tending to force one's opinions on another. **dictatorially** *adv.* **dictatorship** *n.* [L. *dicere*, to say].

dic·tion (dik′·shan) *n.* choice of words in speaking and writing; verbal style; enunciation [L. *dicere*, to say].

dic·tion·ar·y (dik′·shan·er·i·) *n.* a book containing, alphabetically arranged, the words of a language, their meanings and etymology; a lexicon [L. *dicere*, to say].

dic·to·graph (dik′·ta·graf) *n.* sound-recording telephonic instrument [Trade Name].

dic·tum (dik′·tạm) *n.* a positive assertion; an authoritative statement or opinion; a maxim; *pl.* **dicta** [L. = a thing said].

did (did) *pa.t.* of verb **do** [O.E. *dyde*].

di·dac·tic (dī·dak′·tik) *a.* designed to instruct; containing precepts or doctrines; (of people) opinionated. **-ally** *adv.* **-s** *n.* the science of teaching [Gk. *didaskein*, to teach].

did·y·mous (did′·a·mạs) *a.* twin [Gk. *didumos*].

die (dī) *n.* a small cube of wood, bone, or ivory used in games of chance; *pl.* **dice** (dīs). **the die is cast**, one's fate is irrevocably settled [O.Fr. *det*, fr. L. *datus*, given, thrown].

die (dī) *v.i.* to cease to live; to become extinct or extinguished; to wither; to decline. *pr.p.* **dying**. *pa.p.* **-d**. **dying** *a.* pert. to a person at the point of death; fading; languishing. **to die for** (Colloq.) to want desperately. **to die hard**, to resist stubbornly; to be long in dying [M.E. *deyan*, to die].

die (dī) *n.* a device for cutting in a press; an engraved metal block used for stamping a design as on a coin; the cubical part of a pedestal; a steel block used for cutting screws; *pl.* **dies**. **-casting** *n.* method of making castings in permanent molds [L. *dare*, to give].

di·e·lec·tric (dī·a·lek′·trik) *a.* non-conducting; *n.* name for a substance through or across which electric induction takes place [Gk. *dia*, through; *elektron*, amber].

di·er·e·sis, diaeresis (dī·er′·a·sis) *n.* a mark (··) placed over the second of two consecutive vowels to indicate that each is to be pronounced separately, as in coöperate. *pl.* **diereses, diaereses** (-ēz) [Gk. *diairesis*, division].

Die·sel en·gine (dē′·zl en′·jạn) *n.* an internal combustion engine [fr. R. *Diesel*, the inventor].

di·e·sis (dī′·a·sis) *n.* (Print.) a mark of reference, the double dagger (‡); *pl.* **dieses** [Gk. *diesis*, a quarter tone].

di·et (dī′·at) *n.* a system of food; what one habitually eats and drinks; food specially prescribed by a doctor; a regulated allowance of provisions; *v.i.* to prescribe a special course of foods; *v.i.* (Colloq.) to slim. **-ary** *n.* special course of feeding; daily allowance of food; *a.* pert. to diet. **-etic** *a.* pert. to diet. **-etics** *n.* the science and study of food values, and their effect on health. **-ician, -itian** *n.* [L. *diaeta*, a mode of living].

di·et (dī′·at) *n.* a legislative assembly in certain countries; an international conference [L. *dies*, a day].

dif·fer (dif′·er) *v.i.* to be unlike; to have distinctive characteristics; to disagree (foll. by *from* or *with*); to be at variance. **-ence** *n.* unlikeness; dissimilarity; distinguishing characteristic; disagreement; contention; the amount by which one thing exceeds another in weight or number. **-ent** *a.* unlike; distinct; not the same (used with *from*). **-entia** *n.* (Logic) the essential quality or characteristic distinguishing any one species from another in a genus (e.g. rational power in man); *pl.* **-entiae**. **-ential** *a.* characteristic; special; discriminating; (Math.) pert. to infinitely small quantitative differences; proceeding by increments infinitely small. **-entially** *adv.* **-entiate** *v.t.* to make different; to distinguish; to classify as different; *v.i.* to acquire different characteristics. **-entiation** *n.* **-ently** *adv.* **-ential gear**, a mechanism by which two sets of wheels are made to rotate at different speeds, as wheels of a car [L. *dis-*, apart; *ferre*, to bear].

dif·fi·cult (dif′·a·kult) *a.* hard to do or understand; not easy; laborious; (of persons) hard to please; not amenable. **-ly** *adv.* **-y** *n.* laboriousness; a trouble; objection; demur; that which is not easy to do or understand. **-ies** *n.pl.* financial embarrassment [L. *dis-*, not; *facilis*, easy].

dif·fi·dent (dif′·a·dant) *a.* wanting confidence; timid; shy. **diffidence** *n.* lack of confidence; modesty. **-ly** *adv.* [L. *dis-*, not; *fidere*, to trust].

---

dif·fract (di·frakt′) *v.t.* to break or separate into parts, esp. of rays of light and sound waves. **diffraction** *n.* breaking up of wave motion (light, sound, etc); the phenomenon caused by light passing through a narrow slit [L. *dis*, apart; *frangere*, to break].

dif·fuse (dif·ūz′) *v.t.* to pour out in every direction; to spread; to scatter; to cause gases to mix by diffusion; *v.i.* to mix; to spread, as a liquid. **diffuse** (dif·ūs′) *a.* widely spread; wordy. **diffusely** (di·fūs′·li·) *adv.* **-ness** *n.* **diffusible** *a.* **diffusion** *n.* act or process of scattering abroad; (Chem.) term applied to the intermixture of two gases or fluids without chemical combination. **diffusive** *a.* spreading; expanding; prolix. **diffusively** *adv.* **diffusiveness** *n.* [L. *dis*, away; *fundere*, to pour].

dig (dig) *v.t.* to break and turn up earth, as with a spade; to excavate; to delve; (Colloq.) to poke or nudge someone; *v.i.* to till the soil; to use a spade, etc. *pr.p.* **-ging**. *pa.p., pa.t.* **dug**. *n.* a thrust; poke; jibe or taunt. **-ger** *n.* **-gings** *n.pl.* areas where mining or other digging is carried on [prob. O.Fr. *diguer*, to hollow out].

di·gest (da·jest′) *v.t.* to convert, as food in the stomach, into a substance which can be readily absorbed into the blood; to assimilate in the mind; to think over; *v.i.* to undergo digestion. **digest** (dī′·jest) *n.* a concise summary or *the Digest*, an abridged version of the Roman laws compiled by order of Emperor Justinian; a magazine containing condensed version of articles already published elsewhere. **-er** *n.* **-ible** *a.* capable of being digested; easily assimilated. **-ibility** *n.* **digestion** *n.* the act of digesting. **digestive** *a.* promoting, or pert. to digestion; *n.* any medicine that aids digestion [L. *digerere*, to arrange].

dig·it (dij′·it) *n.* a finger; a finger's breadth, or three-quarters of an inch; (Arith.) integer under 10, so-called from counting on the fingers. **-al** *a.* pert. to the fingers; *n.* one of the keys of piano or organ. **-alin** *n.* the drug obtained from leaves of digitalis. **-alis** *n.* a genus of hardy plants including the foxglove; a strong drug obtained from foxglove, used used medicinally as sedative, narcotic and as cardiac stimulant. **-ate, -ated** *a.* having divisions like fingers. **-igrade** *n.* an animal which walks on its toes (e.g. dog); *a.* walking on the toes [L. *digitus*, a finger or toe].

di·glot (dī′·glát) *a.* speaking two languages [Gk. *dis*, twice; *glotta*, tongue].

dig·ni·fy (dig′·na·fi) *v.t.* to invest with dignity or honor; to exalt; to ennoble. **dignified** *a.* [L. *dignus*, worthy; *facere*, to make].

dig·ni·ty (dig′·na·ti·) *n.* state of being dignified in mind, character, or bearing; loftiness; high office or rank. **dignitary** *n.* one who holds a high position [L. *dignus*, worthy].

di·graph (dī′·graf) *n.* two vowels or two consonants combined to express one sound as *ea* in head [Gk. *dis*, twice; *graphein*, to write].

di·gress (da·gres′, dī·gres′) *v.i.* to wander from the main theme, topic, or argument; to be diffuse. **digression** *n.* **digressional, -ive** *a.* [L. *dis-*, aside; *gradus*, a step].

di·he·dral (dī·hē′·dral) *a.* having two plane faces. **dihedron** *n.* a figure with two plane surfaces [Gk. *dis*, twice; *hedra*, base].

dike, dyke (dīk) *n.* an artificial embankment to prevent inundation of low lying ground, as in Holland; (Geol.) igneous rock, once molten, which has filled up fissures of stratified rocks [O.E. *dic*, a ditch].

di·lap·i·date (da·lap′·a·dāt) *v.t.* (Lit.) to pull stone from stone; to suffer to fall into ruin; to despoil; *v.i.* to be in a condition of disrepair. **-d** *a.* in ruins; decayed; tumbled down; (of persons) shabby; unkempt. **dilapidation** *n.* [L. *dis-*, asunder; *lapis*, a stone].

di·late (dī·lāt′) *v.t.* to swell out; to expand in all directions; to distend; *v.i.* to widen; (Fig.) to expatiate; to speak at length. **dilatable** *a.* capable of dilation; elastic. **dilatancy, dilatation, dilation** *n.* expansion; a spreading or extending in all directions. **dilatant** *a.* **dilator, -r** *n.* [L. *di-*, apart; *latus*, borne].

dil·a·tory (dil′·a·tōr·i·) *a.* tardy; inclined to procrastinate; loitering. **dilatorily** *adv.* **dilatoriness** *n.* [L. *dilatus*, postponed].

di·lem·ma (di·lem′·a) *n.* choice between alternatives equally undesirable; a predicament; (Logic) an argument which presents an antagonist with alternatives equally conclusive against him, whichever he chooses. **on the horns of a dilemma**, confronted with a perplexity [Gk. *dis*, twice; *lēmma*, an assumption].

dil·et·tante (dil·a·tan′·te·) *n.* a lover of the fine arts, esp. in a superficial way; a dabbler. *pl.* **dilettantes, -ti**. **dilettantish** *a.* **dilettantism, dilettanteism** *n.* [It.].

dil·i·gent (dil′·a·jant) *a.* steady and constant in application; industrious; assiduous. **diligence** *n.* **-ly** *adv.* [L. *diligere*, to choose].

dill (dil) *n.* a perennial yellow-flowered herb used in medicines and flavoring [O.E. *dile*].

dil·ly-dal·ly (dil′·i·-dal′·i·) *v.i.* (Colloq.) to loiter; to delay [reduplication of *dally*].

di·lute (di·lūt′) *v.t.* to make thinner or more liquid by admixture; to reduce the strength of by addition of something, esp. water; to weaken the force of; *v.i.* to become thin; *a.* reduced in strength; attenuated; thinned down; **diluent** *a.* diluting; making weaker; *n.* that which thins or weakens the strength, color, etc. **-ness** *n.* **dilution** *n.* [L. *diluere*, dissolve].

di·lu·vi·um (di·lōō'·vi·ạm) *n.* a surface deposit of sand, gravel, etc. regarded as glacial drift. **diluvial, diluvian** *a.* pert. to or produced by a flood, esp. the deluge in Noah's time [L. *diluvium*, flood].

dim (dim) *a.* not bright or distinct; faint; partially obscure; shadowy; (*Fig.*) dull of apprehension; vague; *v.t.* to cloud; to cause to grow dim; *v.i.* to become dull or indistinct. *pr.p.* **-ming.** *pa.p., pa.t.* **-med. -ly** *adv.* **-mer** *n.* in motoring, a device to diminish power of headlights. **-ness** *n.* [O.E. *dim*].

dime (dīm) *n.* U.S. silver coin equal to 10 cents [L. *decima*, a tenth].

di·men·sion (di·men'·shan) *n.* a measurement of extent in a single direction (length, breadth, height, or thickness); usually *pl.* measurement in three directions (e.g. of a room); extent; capacity; (*Fig.*) importance. **-al** *a.* capable of being measured; pert. to a dimension [L. *dimensio*, a measuring].

dim·e·ter (dim'·ạ·tẹr) *n.* a verse with two measures or accents [Gk. *dis*, twice; *metron*, a measure].

di·min·ish (di·min'·ish) *v.t.* to cause to grow less; to weaken; to reduce; (*Mus.*) to lower a note by a semi-tone; *v.i.* to become smaller. **-ed** *a.* lessened; lowered; (*Mus.*) lowered by a semi-tone [L. *diminuere*, to break in small pieces].

di·min·u·en·do (di·min·yoo·en'·dō) *n.* (*Mus.*) a gradual decrease in volume of sound and marked >, the opposite of *crescendo* [It.].

dim·i·nu·tion (dim·ạ·nū'·shan) *n.* the act or process of diminishing; state of being reduced in size, quality, or amount. **diminutive** *a.* of small size; minute; (*Gram.*) applied to a suffix expressing smallness, e.g. *-let, -ock*; *n.* a word formed from another by addition of such a suffix, as *hamlet, hillock* [L. *diminuere*, to break in small pieces].

dim·i·ty (dim'·i·ti·) *n.* a thin cotton cloth ribbed or figured [prob. Gk. *dimitos*, of double thread].

di·morph·ic (di·mawr'·fik) *a.* existing in two forms; (*Chem.*) capable of crystallizing in two forms under different degrees of temperature. **dimorphism** *n.* **dimorphous** *a.* [Gk. *dis*, twice; *morphē*, shape].

dim·ple (dim'·pl) *n.* a slight natural depression or hollow on cheek, chin, arm, etc.; a slight indentation in any surface; *v.t.* to mark with dimples; *v.i.* to become dimpled [prob. dimin. of *dip*].

din (din) *n.* a loud, continuous noise; racket; clamor; *v.t.* to strike, stun with noise; to harass with insistent repetition. *pr.p.* **-ning.** *pa.p., pa.t.* **-ned** [O.E. *dyn*, noise].

dine (dīn) *v.t.* to entertain at dinner; to give facilities or accommodation for dining; *v.i.* to take dinner. **-r** *n.* one who dines; a compartment on a railway train for serving meals to passengers. Also **dining car. dinette** (dī·net') *n.* a small dining room. **dinner** (din'·er) *n.* the principal meal of the day. **dinner jacket,** a black coat (without tails) worn as informal evening dress [Fr. *dîner*, to dine].

ding (ding) *v.t.* to ring, as a bell. **—dong** *n.* the sound of bells continuously rung; *a.* monotonous; strenuously contested as in *ding-dong* struggle [Scand.].

din·ghy, dingy, dingey (ding'·gi·) *n.* a small boat [Hind. *dengi*, a boat].

din·gy (din'·ji·) *a.* soiled; sullied; of a darkish color. **dinginess** *n.* [prob. conn. with *dung*].

di·no·saur (dī'·nạ·sawr) *n.* a gigantic extinct four-footed reptile of the Mesozoic age [Gk. *deinos*, terrible; *sauros*, a lizard].

dint (dint) *n.* a mark or depression made by a blow; force or energy exerted; *v.t.* to make a mark or dent by a blow. **by dint of,** by means of [O.E. *dynl*, a blow].

di·o·cese (dī'·ạ·sēs) *n.* the district in which a bishop exercises ecclesiastical jurisdiction. **diocesan** (dī·ás'·es·ạn or dī'·ạ·sē·zạn) *a.* pert. to a diocese; *n.* a bishop or holder of a diocese [Gk. *dioikēsis*, administration].

di·oe·cious, diecious (dī·ē'·shus) *a.* (*Bot.*) having the stamens (male) and pistils (female) borne by separate plants of the same species; (*Zool.*) having the male and female reproductive organs separate [Gk. *dis*, twice; *oikos*, a dwelling].

di·op·ter, dioptre (dī·áp'·ter) *n.* the unit for measuring power of a lens [Gk. *dioptron*, instrument for measuring angles].

di·o·ram·a (dī·ạ·ra'·mạ) *n.* a miniature, three-dimensional scene; a painting viewed through an opening, varied effects of reality being realized by manipulation of lights [Gk. *dia*, through; *horama*, a sight].

di·ox·ide (dī·ák'·sīd) *n.* a substance the molecules of which comprise one part metal, two parts oxygen [Gk. *dis*, twice; *oxus*, acid].

dip (dip) *v.t.* to immerse momentarily in a liquid; to dye; to lower and raise again, as a flag; to wash as a sheep; to baptize by immersion; *v.i.* to sink below at a certain level; to glance cursorily at; (*Geol.*) to incline downwards. *pr.p.* **-ping.** *pa.p., pa.t.* **-ped.** *n.* a liquid into which something is dipped; immersion; (*Geol.*) inclination downward of rock strata; a candle made by dipping wick in melted tallow. **-per** *n.* something used for dipping; a semi-aquatic diving bird; (*Astron.*) the Great Bear; the Little Bear. **-py** *a.* (*Slang*) crazy [O.E. *dyppan*, to plunge].

diph·the·ri·a (dif·thēr'·i·ạ) *n.* epidemic disease affecting mainly throat and air passages. **-l, diphtheric, diphtheritic,** *a.*

diph·thong (dif'·thawng) *n.* a union of two vowel sounds pronounced as one, as in *poise, mouth*. **-al** *a.* **-ally** *adv.* **-ize** *v.t.* to develop a diphthong from a single vowel. **diphthongization** *n.* [Gk. *dis*, twice; *phthongos*, sound].

di·plex (dī'·pleks) *a.* (*Radio*) pert. to the reception or transmission of two messages simultaneously.

dip·lo·car·di·ac (dip'·lō·kár'·di·ak) *a.* (*Biol.*) having, as some birds, a double or divided heart [Gk. *diplous*, double; *kardia*, the heart].

di·plo·ma (di·plō'·mạ) *n.* a document or certificate conferring some honor, privilege, or degree, as that granted to graduates of a university; *v.t.* to furnish with a diploma [Gk. *diploma*, a folded letter].

di·plo·ma·cy (di·plō'·mạ·si·) *n.* the art of conducting international negotiations; political dexterity; tact in dealing with people. **diplomat, diplomatist** *n.* one skilled in the art of handling difficult international or personal relations; one engaged in administering international law. **diplomatic, -al** *a.* pert. to diplomacy. **diplomatically** *adv.* **diplomatic corps,** the body of accredited foreign diplomatists resident in any capital [Gk. *diploma*, a folded letter].

di·po·lar (dī·pō'·ler) *a.* having two poles, as a magnet. **dipolarize** *v.t.* to magnetize.

dip·so·ma·ni·a (dip·sạ·mā'·ni·ạ) *n.* an uncontrollable craving for alcoholic stimulants. **dipsomaniac** *n.* **dipsomaniacal** *a.* [Gk. *dipsa*, thirst; *mania*, madness].

Dip·ter·a (dip'·ter·ạ) *n.* an order of insects, including common housefly, gnat, mosquito, which have only two wings. **dipteral** *a.* **dipteran** *n.* a dipterous insect. **dipterous** *a.* of the order *Diptera* [Gk. *dis*, twice; *pteron*, a wing].

dip·tych (dip'·tik) *n.* an ancient writing tablet hinged in the middle and folding together like a book; a pair of carvings or pictures similarly hinged [Gk. *diptuchos*, folded double].

dire (dīr) *a.* dreadful; calamitous; disastrous. Also **-ful. -ly, -fully** *adv.* [L. *dirus*, terrible].

di·rect (di·rect', dī'·rect) *a.* straight; straightforward; immediate; in line of descent; sincere; unambiguous; *v.t.* to aim at; to guide; to point out the way; to manage (a business); to prescribe a course or line of procedure; to write the name and address on a missive, etc.; *v.i.* to give direction; to act as a guide; *adv.* in a straight line. **direction** *n.* act of directing; instruction; guidance; management; order; superscription; prescription; address (on a letter); line taken by a moving body. **directional, -ing, -ive** *a.* tending to guide or to advise. **-ive** *n.* orders from a supreme authority. **-ly** *adv.* in a straight line; straightway; immediately after. **-ness** *n.* the quality of being direct, frank, or unimpeded by extraneous details. **-or** *n.* (*fem.* **-ress**) one who directs; a member of a board of managers in a large commercial firm, hospital, etc.; that which regulates a machine; in gunnery, an optical instrument for calculating line of firing. **-orate** *n.* a board of directors. **-orial** *a.* **-ory** *a.* containing directions; guiding; *n.* a book containing the alphabetically arranged names and addresses of the residents of a town or district; a collection of rules. **— current** (*abbrev.* D.C.) (*Elect.*) a current flowing in one direction (contrasting with *alternating current* (A.C.)). **direction finder** (*Radio*) an aerial which determines direction of incoming radio signals (*abbrev.* D/F) [L. *dirigere, directum*, to make straight].

dirge (durj) *n.* a funeral chant; a lament. **-ful** *a.* funereal [fr. L. *dirige* (lead thou), the opening word of Latin burial anthem].

dir·i·gi·ble (dir'·ạ·jạ·bl) *a.* capable of being directed or steered; *n.* a navigable balloon elongated in shape and propelled by engine-driven propellers [L. *dirigere*, to direct].

dirk (durk) *n.* a short dagger; *v.t.* to stab with a dirk.

dirn·dl (durn'·dl) *n.* a type of skirt [Ger. *Dirne*, a girl].

dirt (durt) *n.* any filthy substance, as mud, dust, excrement; loose soil; rubbish; squalor; obscenity. **—cheap** *a.* (*Colloq.*) uncommonly cheap. **-ily** *adv.* in a dirty manner; meanly. **-iness** *n.* **-y** *a.* foul; unclean; muddy; base; (of weather) stormy; rainy; *v.t.* to befoul [M.E. *drit*, excrement].

dis- *pref.* implying *separation*, as in *dis*miss; *negation*, as in *dis*band; *deprivation*, as in *dis*animate; *thoroughness*, as in *dis*annul.

dis·a·ble (dis·ā'·bl) *v.t.* to make incapable or physically unfit; to disqualify. **-ment** *n.* disability. **disability** *n.* the state of being disabled; incapacity.

dis·a·buse (dis·ạ·būz') *v.t.* to free from misapprehension or error; to undeceive.

dis·ad·van·tage (dis·ad·van'·tij) *n.* want of advantage; a drawback; a hindrance; a handicap; detriment; hurt. **disadvantageous** (dis·-ad·van·tā'·jạs) *a.* **disadvantageously** *adv.*

dis·af·fect (dis·ạ·fekt') *v.t.* to alienate the affection of; to estrange; to fill with discontent. **-ed** *a.* discontented; disloyal (esp. to government). **-edly** *adv.* **-edness, disaffection** *n.*

dis·af·firm (dis·ạ·furm') *v.t.* to annul; to invalidate; to reverse a decision. **disaffirmation** *n.*

dis·a·gree (dis'·ạ·grē) *v.i.* to be at variance; to differ in opinion; to be incompatible; to be detrimental to health (of food, climate, etc.). **-able** *a.* **-ably** *adv.* **-ment** *n.* difference of opinion; discord; discrepancy.

dis·al·low (dis·ạ·lou') *v.t.* to refuse to allow; to reject as untrue or invalid. **-able** *a.* **-ance** *n.*

dis·ap·pear (dis·ạ·pir') *v.i.* to vanish; to become invisible; to cease to exist. **disappearance** *n.*

dis·ap·point (dis·ạ·point') *v.t.* to fail to realize the hopes of; to frustrate; to foil. **-ed** *a.* **-ing** *a.* causing disappointment. **-ment** *n.* state of being disappointed; the frustration of one's hopes; miscarriage which disappoints.

dis·ap·pro·ba·tion (dis·ap·rạ·bā'·shan) *n.* act of disapproving; censure; mental condemnation of what is considered wrong.

dis·ap·prove (dis·ạ·prōōv') *v.t.* to form an unfavorable judgment of; to censure; to refuse to sanction; to dislike; *v.i.* (foll. by *of*). **disapproval** *n.* **disapprovingly** *adv.*

dis·arm (dis·árm') *v.t.* to deprive of arms; to render unable to attack; (*Fig.*) to conciliate; to allay; *v.i.* to lay down arms, esp. national armaments. **-ament** *n.* the act of reducing, in peacetime, the output of military and naval weapons as prevention of war; the state of being disarmed. **-ing** *a.* ingenuous.

dis·ar·range (dis·ạ·rānj') *v.t.* to disturb the order or arrangement of; to throw into confusion. **-ment** *n.*

dis·ar·ray (dis·ạ·rā') *v.t.* to break the array of; to throw into disorder; to undress; *n.* disorder; confusion; state of undress.

dis·as·so·ci·ate (dis·ạ·sō'·shi·āt) *v.t.* to disunite; to dissociate.

dis·as·ter (diz·as'·ter) *n.* an adverse happening; sudden misfortune; catastrophe. **disastrous** *a.* [L. *dis; astrum*, a star].

dis·a·vow (dis·ạ·vou') *v.t.* to refuse to acknowledge; to repudiate. **-al, -ment** *n.*

dis·band (dis·band') *v.t.* to disperse (troops); to break up an organization; to dismiss; *v.i.* to break up; to disperse. **-ment** *n.*

dis·bar (dis·bár') *v.t.* (*Law*) to expel a lawyer from the bar or from the legal profession.

pr.p. **-ring.** *pa.p., pat.* **-red. -ment** *n.*
dis·be·lieve (dis·bạ·lēv′) *v.t.* to maintain to be untrue; to refuse to believe; *v.i.* to place no reliance or belief (foll. by *on* or *in*). **disbelief** *n.* **disbeliever** *n.*

dis·burse (dis·burs′) *v.t.* to pay out money; to expend. **-ment** *n.* expenditure. **-r** *n.* [L. *dis,* apart; Fr. *bourse,* purse.]

disc See **disk.**

dis·card (dis·kárd′) *v.t.* and *v.i.* to put aside; to cast off; *n.* (dis′·kárd) the act of discarding; anything thrown out as useless.

dis·car·nate (dis·kár′·nit) *a.* bereft of flesh; having no physical body.

dis·cern (di·surn′) *v.t.* to distinguish clearly esp. by the sight; to perceive by the mind; to behold as separate. **-er** *n.* **-ible** *a.* **-ing** *a.* discriminating; judging with insight. **-ment** *n.* power or faculty of judging [L. *dis,* apart; *cernere,* to sift.]

dis·charge (dis·chárj′) *v.t.* to free from a load or weight; to unload a cargo; to fire off the charge with which gun is loaded; to emit, as smoke; to perform, as a duty; to pay, as an account or a debt; to demobilize, as soldiers, etc.; to dismiss, as for failure in service or duty; *n.* act of discharging; performance; matter which exudes, as from an abscess; that which is discharged; the rate of flow of a liquid or waste matter through a pipe [Fr. *décharger,* to unload.]

dis·ci·ple (di·sī′·pl) *n.* one who receives instruction from another; one who adheres to a particular school of philosophy, religious thought, or art; a follower, esp. one of the twelve apostles of Christ. **-ship** *n.* [L. *discipulus,* a pupil.]

dis·ci·pline (dis′·ạ·plin) *n.* instruction; training of the mind or body, or the moral faculties; subjection to authority; self-control; *v.t.* to train; to improve behavior by judicious penal methods. **disciplinarian** *n.* one who enforces rigid discipline; a martinet. **disciplinary** *a.* **-r** *n.* [L. *disciplina,* training].

dis·claim (dis·klām′) *v.t.* to renounce claim to, or responsibility for; to disown; to repudiate; *v.i.* to give up all claim (foll. by *to*).

-ant *n.* **-er** *n.* denial; disavowal; repudiation.
dis·close (dis·klōz′) *v.t.* to unclose; to reveal; to divulge; to bring to light. **-r** *n.* **disclosure** *n.*

dis·col·or (dis·kul′·er) *v.t.* to spoil the color of; to stain; *v..i* to become discolored or stained. **-ation, -ment** *n.* **-ed** *a.* stained.

dis·com·fit (dis·kum′·fit) *v.t.* to defeat; to disconcert; to foil; to baffle. **-ure** *n.* [O.Fr. *desconfit,* defeated].

dis·com·fort (dis·kum′·fẹrt) *n.* want of comfort; uneasiness; pain; *v.t.* to impair the comfort of; to make uneasy.

dis·com·mode (dis·kạ·mōd′) *v.t.* to put to inconvenience; to incommode; to disturb.

dis·com·pose (dis·kạm·pōz′) *v.t.* to upset the self-possession of; to disturb; to disarrange. **discomposure** *n.*

dis·con·cert (dis·kạn·surt′) *v.t.* to discompose; to embarrass. **-ment** *n.* state of disagreement.

dis·con·nect (dis·kạn·ekt′) *v.t.* to separate; to sever; to disjoint. **-ed** *a.* separated; incoherent.

dis·con·so·late (dis·kán′·sạ·lit) *a.* destitute of comfort or consolation; forlorn; utterly dejected. **-ly** *adv.* **-ness, disconsolation** *n.*

dis·con·tent (dis·kạn·tent′) *a.* not content; dissatisfied; *n.* want of contentment; dissatisfaction; state of being aggrieved; *v.t.* to cause to be ill-pleased; to dissatisfy. **-ed** *a.* **-edly** *adv.* **-edness, -ment** *n.*

dis·con·tin·ue (dis·kạn·tin′·ū) *v.t.* to interrupt; to break off; to stop; *v.i.* to cease. **discontinuance, discontinuation** *n.* interruption; cessation. **discontinuity** *n.* want of continuity. **discontinuous** *a.* intermittent.

dis·cord (dis′·kawrd) *n.* want of concord or agreement; lack of harmony; strife; (*Mus.*) a combination of inharmonious sounds. **discord** (dis·kawrd′) *v.i.* to disagree; to be out of tune. **discordance, discordancy** *n.* lack of spiritual (or musical) harmony. **discordant** *a.* out of harmony; jarring; dissonant. **discordantly** *adv.* [L. *discordia,* variance].

dis·count (dis·kount′) *v.t.* to pay in advance (a bill of exchange not yet due); to deduct a sum or rate per cent from; to disregard; *v.i.* to lend money with discount. **discount** (dis′·-kount) *n.* a sum of money refunded on prompt payment of a bill; the allowance made on the retail price by a wholesaler to a retailer; a deduction [O.Fr. *descompter,* to count off].

dis·coun·te·nance (dis·koun′·tạn·ạns) *v.t.* to refuse to countenance or give approval to.

dis·cour·age (dis·kur′·ij) *v.t.* to deprive of courage; to dishearten; to deter. **-ment** *n.* act of discouraging; state of being discouraged; dissuasion; dejection. **discouraging** *a.*

dis·course (dis′·kōrs) *n.* a formal speech; a sermon; a dissertation; reasoning from premises; conversation. **discourse** (dis·kōrs′) *v.t.* to utter; *v.i.* to lecture; to converse; to hold forth (foll. usually by *upon*) [L. *discursus,* running to and fro].

dis·cour·te·ous (dis·kur′·ti·ạs) *a.* lacking in courtesy; rude. **-ly** *adv.* **discourtesy** *n.*

dis·cov·er (dis·kuv′·er) *v.t.* to find out (esp. something hitherto unknown); to bring to light. **-able** *a.* **-er** *n.* **-y** *n.* the act of finding out; that which is discovered [Fr. *découvrir,* to

reveal].

dis·cred·it (dis·kred′·it) *v.t.* to bring into disrepute; to disbelieve; *n.* loss of credit or of reputation. **-able** *a.* damaging; injurious to reputation.

dis·creet (dis·krēt′) *a.* prudent; circumspect; judicious; cautious (in action or speech). **-ly** *adv.* [L. *discretus,* separated, prudent].

dis·crep·an·cy (dis·krep′·ạn·si·) *n.* inconsistency; variance; difference. **discrepant** *a.* not tallying; inconsistent [L. *discrepare,* to jar].

dis·crete (dis·krēt′) *a.* separate; distinct. **-ly** *adv.* **-ness** *n.* [L. *discretus,* separated].

dis·cre·tion (dis·kresh′·ạn) *n.* the quality of being discreet; prudence; discernment; liberty to act according to one's judgment. **-al, -ary** *a.* **ally** *adv.* [L. *discretus,* separated, prudent].

dis·crim·i·nate (dis·krim′·ạ·nāt) *v.t.* to detect as different; to distinguish; to select; *v.i.* to make a distinction in. **-ly** *adv.* **discriminating** *a.* able to observe subtle differences; distinctive. **discriminatingly** *adv.* **discrimination** *n.* faculty of drawing nice distinctions; perception; a difference in treatment between persons, things, etc. **discriminative** *a.* marking a difference; characteristic [L. *discriminare,* to divide].

dis·cur·sive (dis·kur′·siv) *a.* passing from one topic to another; rambling; digressive; arguing from premises to conclusion. **-ly** *adv.* **-ness** *n.* **discursory** *a.* [L. *discursus*].

dis·cus (dis′·kạs) *n.* a circular plate of stone or metal, used in athletic contests [Gk. *diskos,* quoit].

dis·cuss (dis·kus′) *v.t.* to examine critically; to exchange ideas on; (*Colloq.*) to consume, as wine. **-able** (or **-ible**) *a.* **discussion** *n.* debate; act of exchanging opinions [L. *discutere,* to agitate].

dis·dain (dis·dān′) *v.t.* to look down upon, as unworthy or despicable; to scorn; *n.* scorn; arrogance; contempt. **-ful** *a.* **-fully** *adv.* **-fulness** *n.* [O.Fr. *desdeigner,* to scorn].

dis·ease (di·zēz′) *n.* an unhealthy condition of mind or body; malady; **-d** *a.* [O.Fr. *desaise,* discomfort].

dis·em·bark (dis·em·bárk′) *v.t.* to put on shore; to land passengers, goods, etc.; *v.i.* to land. **-ation, -ment** *n.*

dis·em·bod·y (dis·im·bạd′·i·) *v.t.* to free from the body or flesh. **disembodiment** *n.*

dis·em·bowel (dis·im·bou′·ạl) *v.t.* to take out the bowels; to gut; to eviscerate.

dis·en·chant (dis·in·chant′) *v.t.* to free from enchantment or glamor; to disillusion.

dis·en·fran·chise (dis·in·fran′·chīz) *v.t.* to deprive of the right to vote. **-ment** *n.*

dis·en·gage (dis·in·gāj′) *v.t.* to unfasten; to separate from an attachment; to release. **-d** *a.* unattached; available; at leisure. **-ment** *n.*

dis·en·tan·gle (dis·in·tang′·gl) *v.t.* to unravel; to untwist; to set free.

dis·es·tab·lish (dis·ạs·tab′·lish) *v.t.* to deprive of established position; to deprive (a church) of state aid and recognition. **-ment** *n.*

dis·fa·vor (dis·fā′·ver) *n.* disapproval; dislike; state of being out of favor; *v.t.* to regard unfavorably.

dis·fig·ure (dis·fig′·yẹr) *v.t.* to mar the appearance of; to deface; to deform. **-ment** *n.* a defect; a blemish.

dis·fran·chise See **disenfranchise.**

dis·frock (dis·frák′) *v.t.* to unfrock; to deprive of the right to wear clerical garb.

dis·gorge (dis·gawrj′) *v.t.* to eject from the throat; to pour out (as a river into the sea); to hand over. **-ment** *n.*

dis·grace (dis·grās′) *n.* dishonor; discredit; shameful conduct; *v.t.* to bring dishonor to; to degrade. **-ful** *a.* shameful; discreditable.

dis·grun·tled (dis·grun′·tld) *a.* vexed; sulky.

dis·guise (dis·gīz′) *v.t.* to change the outward appearance of; to misrepresent; *n.* dress, manner, voice, etc. assumed to hide a person's real identity [O.Fr. *desguiser,* to change costume].

dis·gust (dis·gust′) *n.* loathing; nausea; aversion; repugnance; *v.t.* to provoke disgust in. **-edly** *adv.* **-ing** *a.* [L. *dis; gustus,* taste].

dish (dish) *n.* a plate or shallow concave vessel for serving food; the food in such a vessel; any concave object, like a dish; *v.t.* to put in a dish; [O.E. *disc,* a plate].

dis·ha·bille (dis·ạ·bēl′) *n.* partial undress; careless toilet for indoors. Also **deshabille** [Fr.]. [harmony; discord.

dis·har·mo·ny (dis·har′·mạ·ni·) *n.* lack of

dis·heart·en (dis·hár′·tn) *v.t.* to deprive of courage, confidence, or hope; to depress.

dis·hev·el (di·shev′·ạl) *v.t.* to ruffle the hair; to cause the hair or clothes to be untidy or unkempt; *v.i.* to spread in disorder. **-ment** *n.* [L. *dis,* in different directions: *capillus,* hair].

dis·hon·est (dis·án′·ist) *a.* lacking in honesty; inclined to cheat; unprincipled. **-ly** *adv.* **-ty** *n.*

dis·hon·or (dis·án′·er) *n.* loss of honor; disgrace; shame; indignity; *v.t.* to disgrace; to seduce; to refuse payment of. **-able** *a.* shameful; lacking integrity. **-ableness** *n.* **-ably** *adv.*

dis·il·lu·sion (dis·i·lōō′·zhan) *v.t.* to free from illusion; to make the truth apparent; *n.* state of being disillusioned. **-ment** *n.*

dis·in·cline (dis·in·klīn′) *v.t.* to make unwilling; to excite dislike or aversion. **disinclination** *n.* unwillingness; reluctance; dislike.

dis·in·fect (dis·in·fekt′) *v.t.* to free from infection; to destroy disease germs. **-ant** *n.* a germicide. **disinfection** *n.* **-or** *n.*

dis·in·her·it (dis·in·her′·it) *v.t.* to deprive of rights and privileges of an heir. **-ance** *n.*

dis·in·te·grate (dis·in′·tạ·grāt) *v.t.* to break up; *v.i.* to crumble to pieces; to be resolved into elements. **disintegration** *n.* a gradual breaking up.

dis·in·ter (dis·in·tur′) *v.t.* to disentomb; to exhume; to unearth.

dis·in·ter·est·ed (dis·in′·ta·res·tad) *a.* free from self-interest; unprejudiced; (*Colloq.*) indifferent. **-ness** *n.*

dis·join (dis·join′) *v.t.* to sever; to disunite. **-t** *v.t.* to separate at the joints; to make incoherent; *v.i.* to fall to pieces. **-ted** *a.* unconnected; (of speech) rambling; incoherent.

dis·junct (dis·jungkt′) *a.* disjoined. **disjunction** *n.* disunion; severance; disconnection; (*Logic*) a statement of alternative possibilities. **-ive** *a.* [L. *dis: jugere, junctum,* to join].

disk, disc (disk) *n.* a circular plate or surface; the face of sun or moon. **-al** *a.* — **jockey** *n.* (*Colloq.*) announcer of a radio program of recorded music [Gk. *diskos,* a round plate].

dis·like (dis·līk′) *v.t.* to have an aversion to; *n.* distaste; antipathy.

dis·lo·cate (dis·lō′·kāt) *v.t.* to put out of place or out of joint; to upset the normal working of. **dislocatedly** *adv.* **dislocation** *n.* (*Med.*) the displacement of a bone.

dis·lodge (dis·láj′) *v.t.* to remove from a position of rest, hiding, or defense; *v.i.* to depart. **dislodg(e)ment** *n.*

dis·loy·al (dis·loi′·ạl) *a.* failing in duty or allegiance; faithless; treacherous. **-ly** *adv.* **-ty** *n.*

dis·mal (diz′·mal) *a.* gloomy; dreary; depressing; bleak. **-ly** *adv.* **-ness, -ity** *n.* [L. *dies mali,* ill-omened days].

dis·man·tle (dis·man′·tl) *v.t.* to strip of furnishings; to take apart [O.Fr. *desmanteler,* to strip].

dis·may (dis·mā′) *v.t.* to alarm; to deprive of courage; to fill with apprehension; *n.* consternation; loss of courage [L. *dis,* neg.; O.H. Ger. *magan,* to be strong].

dis·mem·ber (dis·mem′·ber) *v.t.* to tear limb from limb; to mutilate. **-ment** *n.*

dis·miss (dis·mis′) *v.t.* to send away; to disperse; to allow to go; to discharge from employment; to banish (from the mind). **-al** *n.*

dis·mount (dis·mount′) *v.i.* to alight from a horse, bicycle, etc.; *v.t.* to bring down from a place of elevation.

dis·o·bey (dis·ạ·bā′) *v.t.* to disregard orders or instructions; to refuse to do what is commanded. **disobedient** *a.* refusing to obey. **disobediently** *adv.* **disobedience** *n.*

dis·o·blige (dis·ạ·blīj′) *v.t.* to offend by an act of incivility; to refuse to grant a request to. **disobliging** *a.* ungracious; unwilling to accede to another's wishes.

dis·or·der (dis·awr′·dẹr) *n.* want of order; muddle; confusion; discomposure; ailment of body or mind; *v.t.* to throw out of order; to upset. **-ed** *a.* out of order; deranged. **-ly** *a.*

dis·or·gan·ize (dis·awr′·gạ·nīz) *v.t.* to upset the structure or regular system of; to throw into disorder. **disorganic** *a.* **disorganization**

dismount

dis·own (dis·ōn′) *v.t.* to repudiate ownership; to renounce.

dis·par·age (dis·par′·ij) *v.t.* to belittle; to lower in rank or reputation; to depreciate. **-ment** *n.* unjust comparison; act of undervaluing [O.Fr. *desparagier*, to marry unequally].

dis·pa·rate (dis′·pa·rit) *a.* essentially different; dissimilar. **-ness** *n.* [L. *dis*, neg.; *par*, equal].

dis·par·i·ty (dis·par′·i·ti·) *n.* difference in form, character, or degree; incongruity.

dis·pas·sion (dis·pash′·an) *n.* lack of feeling; serenity. **-ate** *a.* free from passion; impartial.

dis·patch, despatch (des·pach′) *v.t.* to send away, esp. in haste; to execute promptly (as an order); to dispose of; to kill; *n.* something which is dispatched; speed; official message or document sent by special messenger; the sending out of mails, etc. **-er** *n.* [Fr. *dépêcher*, to expedite].

dis·pel (dis·pel′) *v.t.* to drive away; to scatter; to cause to disappear. *pr.p.* **-ling.** *pa.p., pa.t.* **-led** [L. *dis*, apart; *pellere*, to drive].

dis·pense (dis·pens′) *v.t.* to divide out in parts; to administer, as laws; to make up and distribute medicines; *v.i.* to excuse from; **dispensable** *a.* **dispensary** *n.* a place where medicines are made up and distributed. **dispensation** *n.* the act of distributing; the mode of God's dispensing mercies (e.g. *Mosaic, Christian*); a license to do what is normally prohibited. **-r** *n.* **to dispense with,** to do without [L. *dispensare*, to distribute by weight].

dis·perse (dis·purs′) *v.t.* to scatter here and there; to spread; to distribute; to place at intervals (as troops); *v.i.* to separate; to vanish; to be dispelled. **dispersal** *n.* **dispersedly** *adv.* **dispersedness** *n.* **dispersion** *n.* the act of dispersing; the state of being dispersed; (*Opt.*) the separation of light into its constituent rays by refraction through a prism. **dispersive** *a.* [L. *di-*, asunder; *spargere, sparsum*, to scatter].

dis·pir·it (dis·pir′·it) *v.t.* to deject; to depress; to discourage. **-ed** *a.*

dis·place (dis·plās′) *v.t.* to put out of position; to oust from situation or office. **-able** *a.* **Displaced Persons,** homeless war victims (*abbrev.* **D.P.**). **-ment** *n.* the act of putting out of place or removing from office; the weight of water, measured in tons, displaced by a floating ship.

dis·play (dis·plā′) *v.t.* to unfold; to exhibit; to set out conspicuously; *n.* exhibition; ostentation; exaggerated expression of feeling [L. *displicare*, to unfold].

dis·please (dis·plēs′) *v.t.* and *v.i.* to offend; to cause dissatisfaction to. **displeasure** (dis·plezh′·er) *n.* slight anger or irritation; dislike.

dis·pose (dis·pōs′) *v.t.* to arrange; to regulate; to adjust; to bestow for an object or purpose; to induce a tendency or inclination; *v.i.* to settle; to determine. **disposable** *a.* liable, free, to be disposed of or employed. **disposal** *n.* the the act of disposing or disposing of; control; regulation; management; transference (of property by a will). **disposed** *a.* inclined; minded; arranged. **disposedly** *adv.* **disposition** *n.* the act of disposing; arrangement; guidance; temperament. **to dispose of,** to get rid of; to refute (an argument); to finish (a task) [L. *dis*, apart; *ponere*, to place].

dis·pos·sess (dis·pa·zes′) *v.t.* to put out of possession; to deprive of property; to eject. **-ion** *n.* **-or** *n.*

dis·proof (dis·prōōf′) *n.* the act of disproving; refutation; a proving to be erroneous.

dis·pro·por·tion (dis·pra·pōr′·shan) *n.* want of proportion, symmetry, proper quantity; *v.t.* to make unsuitable; to mismatch. **-able, -al, -ate, -ed** *a.*

dis·prove (dis·prōōv′) *v.t.* to prove to be false; to refute; to prove the opposite of.

dis·pute (dis·pūt′) *v.t.* to consider for and against; to debate; to question the validity of; to argue; to discuss; to contend; *n.* an argument; a debate; a quarrel. **disputable** *a.* **disputably** *adv.* **disputability** *n.* the quality of being disputable. **disputant** *n.* one who takes part in a dispute; a controversialist. **disputation** *n.* a controversy in words; an academic discussion or argument. **disputatious, disputative** *a.* [L. *dis*, apart; *putare*, to think].

dis·qual·ify (dis·kwål′·a·fī) *v.t.* to make unfit for some special purpose; to incapacitate, to make ineligible; to deprive of legal power or right. **disqualification** *n.*

dis·qui·et (dis·kwī′·at) *v.t.* to render uneasy in mind; to disturb; to make restless; *n.* apprehensiveness; uneasiness **-ment, -ude** *n.* uneasiness; want of tranquility.

dis·qui·si·tion (dis·kwa·zish′·an) *n.* a formal enquiry into a subject by argument or discussion; a systematic treatise. **-al, -ary** *a.* [L. *disquirere*, to investigate].

dis·re·gard (dis·ri·gård′) *v.t.* to take no notice of; to ignore; *n.* indifference; lack of attention.

dis·re·pair (dis·ri·per′) *n.* state of being out of repair; delapidation.

dis·re·pute (dis·ri·pūt′) *n.* discredit; state of being unpopular. **disreputable** *a.* degraded; discreditable. **disreputableness** *n.*

dis·re·spect (dis·ri·spekt′) *n.* want of respect or deference; rudeness. **-ful** *a.* **-fully** *adv.*

dis·robe (dis·rōb′) *v.t.* to undress; to discard official dress.

dis·rupt (dis·rupt′) *v.t.* to break or burst asunder; to create a schism. **disruption** *n.* the act or process of disrupting; rent; breach. **disruptive** *a.* a disrupture *n.* a bursting asunder [L. *dis*, apart; *rumpere*, to break].

dis·sat·is·fy (dis·sat′·is·fī) *v.t.* to fail to satisfy; to make discontented. **dissatisfaction** *n.*

dis·sect (dis·sekt′) *v.t.* to cut up; to divide a plant or a dead body of man or animal for minute examination of its parts; (*Fig.*) to criticize in detail. **dissection** *n.* the act or science of dissecting; the part dissected. **-or** *n.* [L. *dis*, apart; *secare*, cut].

dis·sem·ble (dis·sem′·bl) *v.t.* to hide under a false semblance; to disguise; to ignore; *v.i.* to give an erroneous impression; to assume a false appearance; to be hypocritical. **-r** *n.* [L. *dissimulare*, to conceal a fact].

dis·sem·i·nate (dis·sem′·a·nāt) *v.t.* to sow, as seed; to scatter abroad; (*Fig.*) to broadcast; to circulate. **dissemination** *n.* scattering; circulation. **disseminative** *a.* **disseminator** *n.* [L. *dis*, asunder; *seminare*, to sow].

dis·sent (dis·sent′) *v.i.* to differ in opinion; to disagree; to hold views differing from those of the established church; *n.* disagreement; difference of opinion; nonconformity. **dissension** *n.* open disagreement; quarrelling; discord. **-er** *n.* [L. *dis*, apart; *sentire*, to feel].

dis·ser·tate (dis′·er·tāt) *v.i.* to discourse. **dissertation** *n.* a formal treatise or discourse, esp. a written thesis by a candidate for the Doctor's degree [L. *disserere*, to discuss].

dis·serve (dis·surv′) *v.i.* to serve badly another's interests. **disservice** *n.* injury; harm; a bad turn.

dis·sev·er (dis·sev′·er) *v.t.* to separate; to disunite. **-ance, -ation, -ment** *n.*

dis·si·dent (dis′·a·dant) *a.* differing; disagreeing; *n.* a dissenter; a non-conformist. **dissidence** *n.* dissent [L. *dissidere*, to disagree].

dis·sim·i·lar (dis·sim′·a·ler) *a.* unlike; not similar. **dissimilarity, dissimilitude** *n.* unlikeness; difference. **-ly** *adv.*

dis·sim·u·late (dis·sim′·ya·lāt) *v.t.* to dissemble; to feign; *v.i.* to conceal one's true feelings; to be hypocritical. **dissimulation** *n.* the act of pretending [L. *dissimulare*].

dis·si·pate (dis′·a·pāt) *v.t.* to scatter; to squander; to dispel; *v.i.* to disappear; to waste away; to lead a dissolute life. **-d** *a.* dissolute; debauched. **dissipation** *n.* **dissipative** *a.* [L. *dissipare*, to scatter].

dis·so·ci·ate (dis·sō′·shi·āt) *v.t.* to separate; to disunite; (*reflex.*) to disclaim connection with. **dissociability** *n.* **dissociable** *a.* capable of being dissociated; incongruous. **dissocial** *a.* anti-social. **dissociation** *n.* the act of dissociating or state of being dissociated; separation; (*Psych.*) term used to describe disunion of the mind, or split personality. **dissociative** *a.* [L. *dis*, asunder; *sociare*, to unite].

dis·sol·u·ble (di·sål′·ya·bl) *a.* capable of being dissolved, liquefied, melted, or decomposed. **dis·so·lute** (dis′·a·lōōt) *a.* lax in morals; dissipated. **-ly** *adv.* **-ness** *n.* **dissolution** *n.* act of dissolving or passing into solution; disintegration, esp. of body at death; dismissal of an assembly; termination of marriage, partnership, etc.) [L. *dis*, asunder; *solvere*, to loosen].

dis·solve (di·zålv′) *v.t.* to break up, esp. a solid by the action of a liquid; to terminate (as a parliament); to annul (as a marriage); *v.i.* to melt; to waste away; to fade out; to be dismissed. **dissolvability, dissolvableness** *n.* **dissolvable** *a.* **dissolvent** *a.* having the power of dissolving substances [L. *dis*, asunder; *solvere*, to loosen].

dis·so·nant (dis′·a·nant) *a.* discordant; harsh; unharmonious. **dissonance** *n.* Also **dissonancy** [L. *dissonare*, to fail to harmonize].

dis·suade (di·swād′) *v.t.* to persuade not to; to advise against. **-r** *n.* **dissuasion** *n.* **dissuasive** *a.* [L. *dis*, apart; *suadere*, to advise].

dis·syl·la·ble. See **disyllable.**

dis·taff (dis′·taf) *n.* a cleft stick for holding the fiber (wool, flax, etc.) from which thread is made in the process of hand spinning. **the distaff side,** the female line [O.E. *distaef*, the staff holding flax for spinning].

dis·tance (dis′·tans) *n.* the space between two objects; the interval between two events; remoteness; aloofness; reserve; *v.t.* to place at a distance; to outstrip; to surpass. **distant** *a.* far off; remote in time, place, or blood-relationship; aloof; reserved; faint. **distantly** *adv.* [L. *distantia*, remoteness].

dis·taste (dis·tāst′) *n.* dislike, esp. of food; aversion. **-ful** *a.* unpleasant.

dis·tem·per (dis·tem′·per) *n.* a method of painting (also called *tempera*) with pigments, in powder form, mixed with any glutinous substance soluble in water; paint of this kind; *v.t.* to paint in distemper. [O.Fr. *destremper*, to moisten with water].

dis·tem·per (dis·tem′·per) *n.* a disordered state of mind or body; disease, esp. a highly infectious inflammatory disease in young dogs [L. *dis*, apart; *temperare*, to mix].

dis·tend (dis·tend′) *v.t.* to stretch out; to swell; to inflate. *v.i.* to become swollen or puffed out. **distensible** *a.* **distention, distension** *n.* [L. *dis*, apart; *tendere*, to stretch].

dis·til (dis·til′) *v.t.* to vaporize and recondense a liquid; to cause to fall in drops; to cause to trickle; (*Fig.*) to extract the essential quality of (as wisdom); *v.i.* to undergo distillation; to drop; to trickle; to ooze. **-ate** *n.* the essence produced by distilling. **-ation** *n.* act of distilling. **-atory** *a.* used in distilling. **-er** *n.* **-ery** *n.* a place where distilling is carried on, esp. of alcohol [L. *de*, down; *stillare*, to drip].

dis·tinct (dis·tingkt′) *a.* of marked difference; separate; clear; well-defined; obvious; precise. **distinction** *n.* separation; that which indicates individuality; eminence; repute; mark of honor bestowed for merit. **-ive** *a.* marking distinction or difference. **-ively** *adv.* **-iveness** *n.* **-ness** *n.* clarity [L. *distinctus*, separate].

dis·tin·guish (dis·ting′·gwish) *v.t.* to observe the difference between; to keep apart; to give individuality to; to discern; *v.i.* to make distinctions. **-ed** *a.* eminent; dignified. **-ing** *a.* peculiar; characteristic [L. *distinguere*, to separate].

dis·tort (dis·tawrt′) *v.t.* to twist out of shape; to misrepresent; to pervert. **-ed** *a.* **-edly** *adv.* **distortion** *n.* a twisting awry; misrepresentation; (*Radio*) any deviation from the original wave-form of speech or sound during transmission [L. *dis*, asunder; *tortum*, to twist].

dis·tract (dis·trakt′) *v.t.* to draw away (the mind); to divert; to bewilder; to disturb mentally. **-ed** *a.* **-edly** *adv.* **-edness** *n.* **distraction** *n.* **-ive** *a.* **distraught** (dis·trawt′) *a.* perplexed; bewildered; frantic [L. *distractus*, drawn aside].

dis·train (dis·trān′) *v.t.* to seize goods, esp. to enforce payment of debt. **-ment, -t** *n.* seizure of goods. **-or, -er** *n.* [L. *dis*, asunder; *stringere*, to draw tight].

dis·tress (dis·tres′) *n.* extreme pain, mental or physical; misfortune; extreme poverty; *v.t.* to cause pain or anguish to; to harass; (*Law*) to distrain. **-ful** *a.* causing suffering. **-fully** *adv.* **distressed area,** a part of the country where unemployment is rife [L. *distringere*, to pull asunder].

dis·tri·bute (dis·trib′·ūt) *v.t.* to divide among several; to allot or hand out; to spread out; to classify. **distributable** *a.* **distribution** *n.* act of distributing; arrangement. **distributive** *a.* **distributor(-er)** *n.* [L. *dis*, asunder; *tribuere*, to allot].

dis·trict (dis′·trikt) *n.* a defined tract of land; an administrative division of a country; a region; a local; regional; *v.t.* to divide into specified areas [L. *distringere*, tighten].

dis·trust (dis·trust′) *v.t.* to have no faith in; to suspect; to doubt; *n.* want of trust; doubt.

dis·turb (dis·turb′) *v.t.* to upset the normal condition of; to disquiet; to agitate; to ruffle. **-ance** *n.* uproar; confusion; derangement [L. *dis*, asunder; *turbare*, to agitate].

dis·un·ion (dis·ūn′·yan) *n.* separation; discord; dissension. **disunite** *v.t.* to cause separation; to cause a breach between. **disunity** *n.*

dis·use (dis·ūs′) *n.* cessation of use or practice. **disuse** (dis·ūz′) *v.t.* to cease to use.

di·syl·la·ble (di·sil′·a·bl) *n.* a word of two syllables. Also **dissyllable** [Gk. *disyllabos*].

ditch (dich) *n.* a trench dug esp. for drainage or defense; a natural waterway; *v.t.* to cut a ditch in; (*Colloq.*) to get rid of; *v.i.* to make a forced 'landing' on the sea [O.E. *dic*, a ditch].

dith·er (diTH′·er) *n.* (*Colloq.*) a state of nervous agitation or confusion [etym. uncertain]. **dit·to** (dit′·ō) *n.* that which has been said; the same; — **symbol:** ″, placed below thing to be repeated; *adv.* as aforesaid; *v.t.* to copy [L. *dictus*, said].

dit·ty (dit'·i·) *n.* a song; a short poem to be sung [L. *dictare*, to dictate or compose].
dit·ty bag (dit'·i·bag) *n.* a small bag used by soldiers and sailors for holding needles, thread, etc. **ditty box** *n.* a box for the same purpose.
di·u·ret·ic (dī·yoo·ret'·ik) *a.* exciting the discharge of urine; *n.* a medicine which tends to increase the flow of urine. **diuresis** *n.* excessive urinary excretion [Gk. *dia*, through; *ourein*, to make water].
di·ur·nal (dī·ur'·nl̩) *a.* belonging to the day (opp. of *nocturnal*); daily; *n.* a book containing the canonical hours of the R.C. breviary. **-ly** *adv.* [L. *dies*, a day].
di·va (dē'·va) *n.* a popular female singer; a prima donna [L. *diva*, fem. of *divus*, divine].
di·va·lent (dī·vā'·lent or dīv'·a·lent) *a.* (*Chem.*) capable of combining with two radicals; bivalent [Gk. *dis*, twice; L. *valere*, to be strong].
di·van (di·van') *n.* a long cushioned seat; a Turkish council of state; a council room; a smoking room [Pers. *divan*, a long seat].

dive (dīv) *v.i.* to plunge into water head first; to remain under water, as a diver; to penetrate deeply into; to plunge the hand into; *n.* a plunge head-first; (*Slang*) a cheap restaurant of ill-repute. **diving bell** *n.* an apparatus by which deep-sea divers can work under water [O.E. *dufan*, to plunge].
di·verge (di·vurj') *v.i.* to turn in different directions; to deviate from a course; to differ. **-ment, -nce, -ncy** *n.* deviation from a common center. **-nt** *a.* branching off; deviating. **-ntly** *adv.* [L. *dis*, asunder; *vergere*, to incline].
di·vers (dī'·verz) *a.* several; sundry. **diverse** *a.* (modern var. of *divers*) of different kinds. **diversely** *adv.* **diversity** *n.* state of being unlike; variety [L. *diversus*, different].
di·ver·si·fy (di·vur'·sa·fi) *v.t.* to make diverse or various; to give variety to [L. *diversus*, varied; *facere*, to make].
di·vert (di·vurt') *v.t.* to turn aside; to alter the direction of; to draw off; to amuse or entertain. **diversion** *n.* **-ing** *a.* **divertissement** (dē·ver·tēs'·mong) *n.* a diversion; a short ballet or interlude between the acts of a play [L. *dis*, aside; *vertere*, to turn].
di·vest (da·vest') *v.t.* to strip, as of clothes, equipment, etc.; to dispossess **-iture, -ment** *n.* [L. *dis*; *vestire*, to clothe].
di·vide (da·vīd') *v.t.* to separate into parts; to share; to keep apart; to antagonize; (*Math.*) to find how many times one number is contained in another; *v.i.* to be separated; to part; *n.* act of dividing; a watershed. **-rs** *n.pl.* compasses for measuring or dividing lines. **the Great Divide**, death [L. *dividere*, to divide].
div·i·dend (div'·a·dend) *n.* (*Arith.*) the sum to be divided by the divisor to obtain the quotient; interest payable on loans, invested money, etc.; the share of profits paid to holders of stocks, insurance, etc. [L. *dividere*, to share out].
di·vine (da·vīn') *a.* belonging to or having the nature of God, or a god; devoted to the worship of God; holy; sacred; heavenly; superhuman; *n.* a priest; a clergyman; a theologian; *v.t.* and *v.i.* to forecast by supernatural means; to practice divination. **divination** *n.* the art or act of foretelling the future by non-rational methods; intuitive prevision; augury. **divinator, diviner** *n.* one who divines. **-ly** *adv.* **-ness** *n.* **divining rod**, a forked twig, usually of hazel, used to locate underground water. **divinity** *n.* state of being divine; God; a pagan deity; the study of theology [L. *divinus*, divine].
di·vi·sion (da·vizh'·an) *n.* the act of dividing; part of a whole; a section; a partition; difference in opinion; (*Mil.*) an army unit, the normal command of a *major-general*. **divisibility** *n.* **divisible** *a.* capable of being divided. **-al, divisionary** *a.* pert. to or belonging to a division; indicating a separation. **divisor** (da·vī'·zer) *n.* (*Math.*) the number by which another is divided [L. *divisus*, divided].
di·vorce (da·vōrs') *n.* the legal dissolution of a marriage contract; separation; *v.t.* to obtain legal dissolution of a marriage; to separate; to sever; to disunite. **divorcee** *n.* a divorced person. **-ment** *n.* [L. *divortium*].
div·ot (div'·at) *n.* (*Golf*) a piece of turf cut out accidentally by golfer [etym. unknown].

diving bell

di·vulge (da·vulj') *v.t.* to disclose something secret or unknown; **divulgate** *v.t.* to publish. **-ment, -nce** *n.* [L. *dis*, asunder; *vulgus*, the common people].
Dixie (diks'·i·) *n.* the Southern States of the U.S.; a song [etym. unknown].
diz·zy (diz'·i·) *a.* giddy; light-headed; causing giddiness; (*Colloq.*) stupid; *v.t.* to make dizzy. **dizzily** *adv.* **dizziness** *n.* giddiness; vertigo [O.E. *dysig*, foolish].
do (dō) *n.* (*Mus.*) the first tone of the major diatonic scale. Also **doh.**
do (doō) *v.t.* to perform; to execute; to affect; to finish; to prepare; to confer; (*Colloq.*) to swindle; *v.i.* to act; to be; as *auxil.* verb, used to give emphasis to principal verb as in *I do think you should go*; to avoid repetition of another verb, and in negative, emphatic and interrogative sentences. *pr.p.* **-ing.** *pa.t.* **did.** *pa.p.* **done.** *n.* **to do away with,** to destroy. **-er** *n.* an agent. **to do in,** to murder. **-ings** *n.pl.* things done; activities. **done-out** *a.* exhausted. [O.E. *don*, to do].
dob·bin (dob'·in) *n.* a name for patient, quiet workhorse [nickname for *Robin*].
do·cent (dō'·sant) *n.* a teacher in a university below professorial rank [L. *docere*, to teach].
doc·ile (dás'·il) *a.* easily instructed or managed; tractable. **-ly** *adv.* [L. *docere*, to teach].
dock (dák) *v.t.* to cut short; to deduct; to clip (as an animal's tail); *n.* the part of tail left after clipping [M.E. *dok*, a tail].
dock (dák) *n.* wharf, or row of piers with buildings, etc. where ships are berthed, loaded, etc.; enclosed space in a law court where accused stands. **-age** *n.* space available in docks for ships; charge made for use of docks. **-er** *n.* one who works at the docks, esp. loading and unloading cargoes. **-yard,** *n.* an enclosed dock area where ships are built or repaired. **dry dock,** *n.* a dock from which water can be pumped out [O.Dut. *dokke*].
dock·et (dák'·it) *n.* (*Law*) a list of cases for trial; a summary of a written document; a memorandum; a bill or label affixed to goods giving instructions; *v.t.* to summarize; to mark the contents of papers on the back or outside sheet [prob. dim. of *dock*, to curtail].
doc·tor (dák'·ter) *n.* one who holds the highest degree granted by any faculty of a university; a medical practitioner; *v.t.* to treat medically; (*Colloq.*) to adulterate; to falsify; to repair temporarily; *v.i.* to practice medicine; to take medicine. **-ate** *n.* the degree or status of a university doctor. **-ship** *n.* **-ial** *a.* [L. = a teacher, fr. *docere*, to teach].
doc·trine (dák'·trin) *n.* principle of belief; instruction; that which is taught. **doctrinal** *a.* pert. to doctrine, esp. Christian Church. **doctrinally** *adv.* **doctrinaire** (dák·tri·ner') *n.* a theorist who tends to urge the application of a doctrine beyond all practical considerations; *a.* impracticable [Fr. fr. L. *doctrina*, teaching].
doc·u·ment (dák'·ya·mant) *n.* an official paper containing information, giving instructions, or establishing facts; *v.t.* to furnish with written evidence of. **-al, documentary** *a.* pert. to, derived from, or in the form of a document. **-ation** *n.* the use of documentary evidence; the furnishing of such evidence. **-ed** *a.* [L. *documentum*, example].
dod·der (dád'·er) *v.t.* or *v.i.* to totter or tremble, as with age. **-ing** *a.* [prob. dialect word].
do·dec·a·gon (dō·dek'·a·gán) *n.* a plane figure with twelve sides and twelve angles. **-al** *a.* [Gk. *dodeka*, twelve; *gonia*, an angle].

dodge (dáj) *v.t.* to evade or escape by a sudden turning; to prevaricate; *v.i.* to twist aside (physically or morally); *n.* a quick, evasive movement; a trick; (*Colloq.*) **-r** *n.*
do·do (dō'·dō) *n.* an extinct flightless bird. *pl.* **-(e)s** [Port. *doudo*, silly].
doe (dō) *n.* the female of the fallow deer; also female of antelope, rabbit, hare, goat, rat, mouse, ferret. **-skin** *n.* the skin of a doe; a fine close-woven cloth [O.E. *da*, a doe].
does (duz) 3rd pers. sing. pr. ind. of verb **do.**
doff (dáf) *v.t.* to take off, esp. the hat; to rid oneself of [contr. of *do off*].
dog (dawg) *n.* a common, carnivorous quadruped of the same genus as the wolf, mainly domesticated; a worthless fellow; (*Colloq.*) a young man-about-town; one of the two constellations of stars (*Canis Major, Canis Minor*); a metal bar for holding logs of wood or supporting fire-irons; *a.* male, as in *dog-wolf*; *v.t.* to follow closely, as a dog does; to keep at the heels of; to pursue relentlessly. *pr.p.* **-ging.** *pa.p.* **-ged.** **-collar. — days** *n.pl.* the hottest period of the northern summer, generally considered from July 3rd-August 11th. **—eared** *a.* (of a book) having the corners of the pages turned down. **-ged** *a.* stubborn; persistent. **-gedly** *adv.* **-gedness** *n.* **-gish** *a.* surly. **-gy** *a.* pert. to dogs; fond of dogs (*Colloq.*) fashionable. **-house** *n.* a small hut for dogs. **dog Latin**, incorrect barbarous Latin. **-like** *a.* faithful. **— star** *n.* alternative name for Sirius, the principal star in the constellation *Canis Major*, and the brightest star in the heavens. **—tired,** *a.* dead-beat; completely exhausted. **-tooth,** *n.* a canine tooth; the eye-tooth (of a human being). **-watch** *n.* one of the two-hour watches on board ship from 4-6 or 6-8 p.m. **a dog in the manger,** a spoil-sport; one who refuses to let another enjoy what he himself has no use for. **a hot dog,** a hot sausage inside a roll. **in the doghouse,** in disfavor. **to go to the dogs,** to be ruined. **to let sleeping dogs lie,** not to stir up trouble unnecessarily [O.E. *docga*, a dog].
dog·ger·el (dog'·er·el) *n.* irregular, unpoetical burlesque verse; *a.* [etym. unknown].
dog·ma (dáwg'·ma) *n.* a philosophical tenet; theological doctrine authoritatively asserted; a principle or belief. **dogmatic, -al,** *a.* pert. to a dogma; opinionated; authoritative. **dogmatically** *adv.* **dogmatics** *n.* the science of systematized Christian doctrines; doctrinal theology. **-tize** *v.t.* to formulate a dogma; to express an opinion positively or arrogantly. **-tism** *n.* positive assertion; laying down the law. **-tist** *n.* [Gk. *dogma*, an opinion].
doi·ly (doi'·li·) *n.* a small table mat placed under dishes; a small, round, linen or paper mat put on plate holding cakes, etc. [fr. *Doily*, a haberdasher].
dol·ce (dōl'·chā) *a.* (*Mus.*) sweet; soft. [It. *dolce*, sweet].
dol·drums (dál'·dramz) *n.pl.* a belt of calms at the Equator; (*Colloq.*) a state of depression.
dole (dōl) *v.t.* to distribute in small portions; *n.* something given or paid out; alms; a small portion [O.E. *dal*, a part].
dole·ful (dōl'·fal) *a.* grievous; melancholic; dismal. **-ly** *adv.* **-ness** *n.* [O.Fr. *doel*, mourning].
doll (dál) *n.* a puppet; a toy baby as a child's plaything; (*Colloq.*) a pretty, rather brainless girl. **to doll up** (*Colloq.*) to dress up smartly [prob. fr. *Dolly*, abbrev. of Dorothy].

dol·lar (dál'·er) *n.* a silver coin or paper note, the monetary unit of U.S.A. and Canada [Ger. *Taler*, short for *Joachimstaler*, the coin being first made at the silver mines of *Joachimstal*, Bohemia].
dol·lop (dál'·ap) *n.* a lump, a shapeless mass [prob. Scand. *dolp*, a lump].
doll·y (dál'·i·) *n.* a wooden shaft attached to a disc with projecting arms, used in mining, pile-driving, etc.; a mobile platform; a small locomotive used in quarries, etc. **dollied** *a.* [prob. fr. *Dolly*].
dol·man (dál'·man) *n.* a long, loose Turkish garment; Hussar's coat worn like a cape; similar garment worn by women in Victorian days [Turk. *dolaman*, a cloak].
dol·men (dál'·men) *n.* a prehistoric tomb formed by a large unhewn stone resting on two or more unhewn uprights [Breton, *tol*, table; *men*, stone].
dol·or·ous (dō'·ler·as) *a.* full of, expressing, or causing grief. **-ly** *adv.* [L. *dolere*, to grieve].

dol·phin (dȯl´·fin) *n.* a sea mammal; a mooring buoy [Gk. *delphis*, a dolphin].

dolt (dōlt) *n.* a dull, stupid fellow; a blockhead. **-ish** *a.* **-ishly** *adv.* [M.E. *dold*, dulled].

do·main (dō·mān´) *n.* that which one has dominion over; property; (*Fig.*) the scope or sphere of any branch of human knowledge. **-al, dominial** *a.* [L. *dominus*, a lord].

dome (dōm) *n.* a hemispherical vault reared above the roof of a building; a large cupola. **-d, domical** *a.* possessing a dome [L. *domus*, a house].

Domes·day, Doomsday-book. See **doom.**

do·mes·tic (da·mes´·tik) *a.* pert. to a house or home; devoted to home and household affairs; tame (of animals); not foreign (of a country's policy); *n.* a household servant. **-ally** *adv.* **-ate** *v.t.* to make fond of domestic life; to tame animals. **domesticity** *n.* life in a household. **— science,** science of home management, etc. [L. *domus,* a house].

dom·i·cile (dȧm´·a·sil) *n.* an abode; a dwelling-house; (*Law*) a person's permanent residence; *v.t.* to establish in a fixed residence. **domiciliary** *a.* [L. *domicilium,* a dwelling].

dom·i·nant (dȧm´·a·nant) *a.* ruling; prevailing; (*Mus.*) having harmonic importance; *n.* (*Mus.*) the fifth note of the diatonic scale. **dominance** *n.* authority; ascendancy. **dominancy** *n.* **-ly** *adv.* **dominate** *v.t.* and *v.i.* to rule; to influence strongly; to sway; to tower over. **domination** *n.* authority. **dominative** *a.* ruling. **dominator** *n.* **domineer** *v.i.* to rule with arbitrary sway; to be overbearing. **domineering** *a.* arrogant. **dominion** *n.* lordship; sovereignty; territory under one government; a self-governing British colony [L. *dominari,* to be master].

do·min·i·cal (da·min´·i·kal) *a.* belonging to Jesus as Lord, or the Lord's Day [L. *dominicus,* belonging to a lord].

Do·min·i·can (da·min´·i·kan) *a.* belonging to *St. Dominic,* or to the order of preaching friars, founded by him (called also the *Black Friars*); *n.* a member of St. Dominic's order.

dom·i·no (dȧm´·a·nō) *n.* a long cloak of black silk with a hood, worn at masquerades; the person wearing such a cloak; a mask; one of the 28 oblong pieces marked each with a certain number of spots used in the game of *dominoes* [L. *dominus,* a master].

Don (dȧn) *n.* (*fem.* **Doña** (dawn´·yȧ); **Donna** (Italian spelling) *n.* a Spanish title, the equivalent of the English *Sir* (formerly applied only to noblemen); a Spaniard. **don,** *n.* a fellow or tutor of Oxford or Cambridge University; a master at Winchester [Sp. fr. L. *dominus,* a master].

don (dȧn) *v.t.* to put on; to assume. *pr.p.* **-ning** *pa.p., pat.* **-ned** [short fr. *do on*].

do·na·tion (dō·nā´·shan) *n.* act of giving; a gift; a contribution. **donate** *v.t.* to present a gift. **donative** *n.* **donor** *n.* one who gives a donation; a benefactor [L. *donare,* to give].

done (dun) *pa.p.* of the verb **do. done!** agreed.

don·key (dȧng´·ki·) *n.* an ass; (*Colloq.*) a foolish person. **— engine** *n.* a small auxiliary steam engine.

don't (dōnt) *contr.* of **do not.**

doo·dle (dōō´·dl) *v.i.* to scribble aimlessly [prob. form of *dawdle*].

doom (dōōm) *n.* fate; evil destiny; judgment; legal decree; ruin; *v.t.* to destine; to pass sentence on; to condemn. **-ed** *a.* under sentence. **-ful** *a.* **-sday** *n.* the Day of Judgment. **Doomsday or Domesday Book,** the census compiled by order of William the Conqueror, for purposes of taxation [O.E. *dom,* a judgment].

door (dōr) *n.* the wooden or metal structure, hinged or sliding, giving access to house, room, passage, or cupboard; the frame by which an entrance is closed; (*Fig.*) a means of approach. **dead as a door nail** (*Colloq.*) quite dead. **-post** *n.* the jamb. **-step** *n.* the step outside a door. **-way** *n.* the entrance to a house, room, etc. **to darken one's door,** to enter one's house [O.E. *duru,* a door].

dope (dōp) *n.* any thick liquid, or semi-liquid lubricant; a varnish; a preparation for coating the fabric surfaces of aircraft; a drug (orig. given to a horse before a race); any narcotic; (*Slang*) a stupid person; inside information (esp. about racehorses); *v.t.* to apply dope or varnish to; to administer dope to; (*Fig.*) to hoodwink. **dopey** *a.* stupefied with drugs; slow-witted [Dut. *doop,* a dipping].

Do·ri·an (dōr´·i·an) *a.* pert. to *Doris,* in ancient Greece, or to its inhabitants. **Doric,** *a.* pert. to Doris, the Dorians, or the simple style of architecture of the Dorians; (of dialect) unpolished; *n.* a mode of Greek music; the Doric dialect characterized by broad vowel sounds.

door

dor·mant (dȯr´·mant) *a.* sleeping; hibernating; quiescent; not in action; unclaimed (as a title). **dormancy** *n.* state of being quiescent. **dormer-window** *n.* a small vertical window projecting from a roof slope. **dormitory** *n.* a building primarily containing sleeping rooms; a large sleeping apartment. **dormouse** *n.* a small, hibernating rodent [L. *dormire,* to sleep].

dor·sal (dȯr´·sal) *a.* pert. to, near, or belonging to, the back [L. *dorsum,* the back].

do·ry (dō´·ri·) *n.* a flat-bottomed boat.

dose (dōs) *n.* the prescribed quantity of medicine to be taken at one time; a portion; anything disagreeable that must be taken or done; *v.t.* to administer or order in doses; (*Colloq.*) to adulterate. **dosage** *n.* the practice of dosing; the amount of a dose. **dosimeter** *n.* an instrument for measuring minute doses accurately; (*Atomic Warfare*) a small instrument for recording the total dose of radioactivity accumulated up to the moment [Gk. *dosis,* a giving].

dos·si·er (dȧs´·i·ā) *n.* a set of documents [Fr.].

dot (dȧt) *n.* a small point or spot made with a pen, pencil, or sharp instrument; a speck; (*Mus.*) a point placed after a note or rest to lengthen the sound or pause by one-half; *v.t.* to mark with dots; to diversify as with small objects; *v.i.* to make dots. *pr.p.* **-ting.** *pa.p.* **-ted. -ty** *a.* marked with or consisting of dots. **dot and dash,** in Morse code, the short and long symbols [O.E. *dott,* a speck].

dot (dȧt) *n.* a dowry. **dotal** *a.* [Fr.].

dote (dōt) *v.i.* to be in one's dotage; to be foolishly sentimental; to be over-fond of. **dotage** *n.* childishness of old people; senility; excessive fondness. **dotard** *n.* one whose intellect is impaired by old age [O.Dut. *doten,* to be silly].

dou·ble (dub´·l) *a.* denoting two things of the same kind; existing in pairs; twice as much (quantity); twice as good (quality); serving for two; acting two parts; deceitful; ambiguous; *adv.* twice; two-fold; *v.t.* to multiply by two; to make twice as great; to fold in two; *v.i.* to increase to twice as much; to return upon one's track; to run (after marching); *n.* twice as much; that which is doubled over; a fold; a duplicate; an actor's substitute or understudy; a game with two on each side; two faults in succession; a running pace, twice as quick as marching. **— bass** *n.* the largest and lowest pitched of the stringed instruments, played with a bow. **—breasted** *a.* (of a coat) able to fasten over on either side. **—cross** *v.t.* (*Slang*) to cheat a swindler. **—dealing** *n.* duplicity. **—decker** *n.* a ship or bus with two decks. **—edged** *a.* having two edges; (*Fig.*) cutting both ways; effective for and against. **— entry** *n.* in bookkeeping, a system by which every entry is made both on debit and credit side of an account. **—faced** *a.* hypocritical. **-r** *n.* **doublet** *n.* one of a pair; a close-fitting garment for the upper part of body as worn by Elizabethan men; one of two words derived orig. from the same root but varying in spelling and meaning. **— time** *n.* the fastest marching pace next to a run. [L. *duo,* two].

doubt (dout) *v.t.* to disbelieve; to hold questionable; *v.i.* to be in a state of uncertainty; to hesitate; *n.* uncertainty of mind; misgiving; distrust of others. **-able** *a.* **-er** *n.* **-ful** *a.* dubious; uncertain in opinion. **-fully** *adv.* **-fulness** *n.* **-ing** *a.* undecided; hesitant. **-ingly** *adv.* **-less** *adv.* without doubt; probably. **-lessly** *adv.* [L. *dubitare,* to be uncertain].

douche (dōōsh) *n.* a jet of water directed upon or into the body; an apparatus for douching [It. *doccia,* a water-pipe].

dough (dō) *n.* a mass of flour moistened and kneaded, to be baked afterwards; (*Slang*) money. **-boy** *n.* (*Colloq.*) an infantryman. **-nuts** *n.* sweetened dough in shape of balls or rings, fried in fat and finally dipped in sugar. **-y** *a.* [O.E. *dah*].

dough·ty (dou´·ti·) *a.* (*Arch.*) brave; valiant. **doughtily** *adv.* [O.E. *dyhtig,* valiant].

dour (dour) *a.* sullen; gloomy; obstinate; forbidding in manner. **-ly** *adv.* [L. *durus,* hard].

douse, dowse (dous) *v.t.* to dip or plunge into water; (*Naut.*) to lower a sail; to put out.

dove (duv) *n.* a pigeon; a symbol of peace or of the Holy Ghost. **—colored** *a.* soft pinkish grey. **-cot(e)** *n.* nesting box of pigeons, usually on top of a pole. **-tail** *n.* a joint made by fitting one piece toothed with wedge like projections (tenons) (shaped like a dove's tail) into cavities of corresponding shape (mortises)

in another piece of timber; *v.t.* to join together by this method; (*Fig.*) to link together [O.E. *dufe-doppa,* cf. Ger. *Taube*].

dove

dow·a·ger (dou´·a·jer) *n.* (*Law*) widow with property or title left by her husband; (*Colloq.*) a dignified elderly lady [O.Fr. *douage,* a dower].

dow·dy (dou´·di·) *a.* untidy; lacking style; *n.* a dowdy woman. **dowdily** *adv.* **dowdiness** *n.*

dow·el (dou´·al) *n.* a wooden or iron pin for joining two adjacent boards or stones [cf. Ger. *dobel,* a plug].

dow·er (dou´·er) *n.* a widow's share of her husband's property; portion a woman brings in marriage; gift; talent. **-ed** *a.* **-less** *a.* **dowry** *n.* goods given to the husband by the bride or her family at marriage; a natural gift [L. *dotare,* to endow].

down (doun) *n.* the fine, soft feathers of birds. **-y** *a.* resembling or covered with down [Scand. *dunn*].

down (doun) *n.* a hillock of sand by the sea (same as *dune*); treeless land [O.E. *dun,* a hill].

down (doun) *prep.* along a descent; towards a lower place, situation, etc.; towards the mouth of a river; in the same direction as, as in *down wind;* passing from the past to less remote times, as *down* the ages; *adv.* in a downward direction; on the ground; to the bottom; below the horizon. *v.t.* to knock down; used also as an interjection with verb *get, kneel,* etc. understood; *n.* a reversal of fortune (as in the *ups and downs* of life). **-cast** *a.* depressed; (of eyes) lowered; *n.* (in mining) a shaft for ventilation. **-fall** *n.* ruin; a heavy fall of rain, snow. **-fallen** *a.* **-hearted** *a.* despondent. **-hill** *a.* sloping; *adv.* on a slope. **-pour** *n.* a heavy fall of water, esp. rain. **-right** *adv.* completely; in plain terms; *a.* straightforward; unqualified. **-stairs** *adv.* in or to a lower floor of a house; *a.* pert. to the ground floor; *n.* the ground floor. **-stream** *adv.* with the current. **-trodden** *a.* trampled underfoot; oppressed. **-ward** *a.* **-wards** *adv.* **—town,** towards the center of the town [O.E. *of dune,* from the hill].

dowse (douz) *v.t.* and *v.i.* to find subterranean water supply by means of a divining rod. **-r** *n.*

dox·ol·o·gy (dȧks·al´·a·ji·) *n.* a short hymn of praise to God. [Gk. *daxa,* glory; *legein,* speak].

doze (dōz) *v.i.* to sleep lightly; to be half asleep; *n* a nap [Scand. *dose*].

doz·en (duz´·n) *n.* a group of twelve things of the same kind; *a.* twelve. **baker's dozen, devil's dozen,** thirteen [Fr. *douzaine,* twelve].

drab (drab) *n.* a dingy brownish-grey color; *a.* (*Fig.*) dull; monotonous [Fr. *drap,* cloth].

drach·ma (drak´·ma) *n.* a Greek coin; an ancient Greek weight [Gk. *drachmē,* a handful].

draft (draft) *n.* a sketch or rough copy; a current of air; a selection of men for military service; an order directing payment of money by a bank; a drink; drawing of liquid from a cask. *v.t.* to draw the outline of; to compose and write; to take for military service. **-sman** *n.* one who draws plans for buildings, etc. **-smanship** *n.* **-y** *a.* **-iness** *n.* [var. of *draught*].

drag (drag) *v.t.* to draw with something; to trail slowly; to trawl with a drag or net; to harrow (the fields); *v.i.* to move heavily or slowly; to pass tediously. *pr.p.* **-ging.** *pa.p.* **-ged.** *n.* a net or hook to bring up submerged things; a heavy harrow; (*Slang*) a puff; a device acting as a brake on a wheel; anything that slows progress. **-ger** *n.* **-net** *n.* a fishing net for dragging along the sea floor [O.E. *dragan,* to draw].

drag·gle (drag´·l) *v.t.* and *v.i.* to make or become wet and dirty by trailing on the ground.

dra·gon (drag´·an) *n.* a fabulous winged reptile represented as breathing out fire and smoke; (*Fig.*) an over-vigilant chaperon. **-et** *n.* a little dragon; a fish of the *Pegasus* genus. **-fly** *n.* an insect of brilliant coloring, with long slender body and two pairs of large, transparent wings. **-'s blood,** a carmine fruit resin used for coloring varnishes and lacquers; [Gk. *drakon,* a large serpent].

dra·goon (dra·gōōn´) *n.* a cavalryman; *v.t.* to oppress; to enforce harsh disciplinary measures [Fr. *dragon,* a fire-spitting carbine].

drain (drān) *v.t.* to filter; to draw off by degrees; to make dry; to swallow down; to exhaust; to impoverish; *v.i.* to flow off or drip away gradually; *n.* a watercourse; a pipe, sewer or ditch; a gradual exhaustion of means, health, etc. **-able** *a.* **-age** *n.* act of draining; system of carrying away surplus water from an area by rivers, canals. **-er** *n.* a kitchen utensil like a rack, on which plates, etc. are placed to dry; a colander or sieve [O.E. *dragan,* to draw].

drake (drāk) *n.* the male of the duck.
dram (dram) *n.* (contr. of *drachma*) a unit of weight; (*apothecary*) ⅛ of an ounce [Gk. *drachmē*, a weight: orig. a handful].
dra·ma (drä′·ma) *n.* a composition to be acted on the stage; the branch of literature dealing with plays; a series of real emotional events. **dramatic** *a.* pert. to the drama; striking; tense. **dramatically** *adv.* **dramatization** *n.* **dramatize** *v.t.* to adapt a novel, etc. for acting. **dramatist** *n.* a writer of plays. **-turge** *n.* **-turgy** *n.* the art of writing or producing plays. **dramatis personae** (dram′·a·tis per·sòn′·ā) characters of a drama [Gk. *draein*, to do].
drank (drangk) *pa.t.* of **drink**.
drape (drāp) *v.t.* to hang something loosely in folds; to adorn with drapery. **drapery** *n.* cloth; hangings [Fr. *drap*, cloth].
dras·tic (dras′·tik) *a.* very powerful; harsh; thorough [Gk. *drastikos*, active].
drat (drat) *interj.* a mild expletive expressing annoyance [corrupt. of *God rot*].
draught (draft) *n.* **-s** *n.pl.* the game of checkers; *a.* drawn from a barrel, as beer. **-(s)man** *n.* checker. See **draft** [O.E. *dragan*, to draw].
draw (draw) *v.t.* to pull along; to haul towards oneself; to entice; to extract (as a tooth); to elicit an opinion from another; to deduce; to receive (as money, salary, etc.); to inhale; to sketch; to describe; to cast lots; to bring game, such as fox, out of hiding; to take out the entrails; *v.i.* to pull; to attract; to move towards; to pull out a weapon for action; to be equal in a match; to sketch; to cast lots; to have a free passage of air (as a chimney). *pr.p.* **-ing.** *pa.t.* **drew.** *pa.p.* **-n.** *n.* the act of drawing; a game ending with same score for both sides; an attraction. **-able** *a.* **-back** *n.* a disadvantage. **-bridge** *n.* a bridge that can be raised or let down. **-er** *n.* one who or that which draws; one who draws an order, draft, etc.; a lidless, sliding box in a table, chest, etc. **-ers** *n.pl.* close fitting undergarment for lower limbs. **-ing** *n.* the art of pulling; a lottery; the art of representing objects by line or color on paper, canvas, etc. **-ing-room** *n.* orig. a withdrawing room; a room in which guests are entertained; a private compartment on a train. **to draw a blank,** to fail to find what one is seeking. **to draw the line,** to stop. **drawn and quartered** quartered and disemboweled [O.E. *dragan*, to draw].
drawl (drawl) *v.i.* to speak with slow and lengthened tone; *v.t.* to utter (words) in this way; *n.* a manner of speech, slow and drawn out [Scand. *dralla*, to loiter].
dray (drā) *n.* a low cart for heavy goods. [O.E. *dragan*, to draw].

dread (dred) *n.* overwhelming apprehension; awe; terror; *a.* dreadful; awful; *v.t.* to regard with fear; *v.i.* to have fear of the future. **-ed** *a.* feared. **-ful** *a.* terrifying; terrible. **-fully** *adv.* **-fulness** *n.* **-nought** *n.* a large-sized battleship mounting heavy guns; a thick woolen overcoat [O.E. *ondraeden*, to fear].
dream (drēm) *n.* a series of images or thoughts in the mind of a person asleep; an idle fancy; a vision; an aspiration; *v.i.* to imagine things during sleep; to have yearnings *v.t.* to see in a dream; *pa.t.* and *p.p.* **-ed** or **-t** (drēmd or dremt). **-er** *n.* **-ily** *adv.* **-iness** *n.* **-land** *n.* an imaginary land seen in dreams. **-less** *a.* **-like** *a.* visionary; unreal. **-y** *a.* [O.E. *dream*].
drear·y (drir′·i·) *a.* dismal; gloomy; bleak. **drearily** *adv.* **dreariness** *n.* (*Poetic*) **drear** *a.* [O.E. *dreorig*, mournful].
dredge (drej) *v.t.* to sprinkle. **-r** *n.* a flour can with perforated lid [O.Fr. *dragie*, a sweetmeat].
dredge (drej) *n.* a machine like a large scoop for taking up mud from a river bed, harbor, etc.; a dragnet for oysters or zoological specimens. Also **-r.** *v.t.* to scoop up or deepen with a dredge [conn. with *drag*].
dregs (dregz) *n.pl.* sediment in a liquid that falls to the bottom; lees; grounds; (*Fig.*) the most worthless class [Scand. *dreggjar*, dregs].
drench (drench) *v.t.* to wet thoroughly; to soak [O.E. *drencan*, to give to drink].
dress (dres) *v.t.* to put clothes on; to provide with clothes; to adorn; to treat (a sore); *v.i.* to put on one's clothes; *n.* clothes; a frock; adornment. **— circle** *n.* the lowest gallery in a theater, orig. for people in evening-dress. **-er** *n.* one who dresses; a dressing table or bureau. **-ing** *n.* clothes; a sterile substance for a wound; manure; substance used to stiffen fabrics; a sauce (as salad-dressing); stuffing for a fowl. **-ing-down** *n.* (*Colloq.*) a scolding. **-ing gown** *n.* a robe worn while dressing. **-ing table** *n.* a table with mirror used while dressing.

-maker *n.* a person who makes women's dresses, etc. **-making** *n.* **-y** *a.* fond of dress; fashionable [O.Fr. *dresser*, to prepare].
drew (dróó) *pa.t.* of **draw**.
drib·ble (drib′·l) *v.i.* to trickle down, esp. of saliva of babies and idiots; (*Basketball*) to bounce the ball repeatedly; (*Other Sports*) to kick the ball forward by short kicks. **driblet** *n.* a small drop [dim. of *drip*].
dried (drid) *pa.t.* and *pa.p.* of verb **dry**.
drift (drift) *n.* the state or process of being driven; that which is driven; the accumulation of substance driven by the wind, as snow; a slow surface current in the sea caused usually by the prevailing wind; deviation or tendency; *v.t.* to drive into heaps; to cause to float in a certain direction; *v.i.* to be floated along; to be piled in heaps; (*Fig.*) to follow unconsciously some trend in policy, thought or behavior. **-age** *n.* that which has drifted, as snow, seaweed, etc.; deviation of a ship from its course. **— anchor** *n.* an anchor for keeping a ship's head to the wind during a storm. **-er** *n.* an aimless wanderer. **-wood** *n.* wood cast on shore by tide [O.E. *drifan*, to drive].
drill (dril) *v.t.* to pierce; to bore a hole through; to sow, as seeds, in a row; to train in military tactics; to instruct thoroughly (in mental or physical exercises); *n.* revolving tool for boring holes in metal, stone, etc.; an implement for making holes for seed; a row of seeds or root crops; physical exercise or military training; instruction. **drilling** *n.* the process of making drills [prob. Dut. *drillen*, to bore].
drink (dringk) *v.t.* to swallow, as a liquid; to empty, as a glass; to breathe in, as air; *v.i.* to swallow a liquid; to consume intoxicating liquor. *pa.t.*, *pa.p.* **drunk.** *n.* liquid for drinking; intoxicating liquor. **-able** *a.* **-er** *n.* a tippler. **to drink in,** to absorb through the senses [O.E. *drincan*, to drink].
drip (drip) *v.t.* to let fall, drop by drop; *v.i.* to ooze; to trickle. *pr.p.* **-ping.** *pa.t.*, *pa.p.* **-ped.** *n.* a drop; the sound made by water dripping; the projecting edge of a roof; (*Slang*) an insipid person. **-ping** *a.* thoroughly wet; *n.* that which falls in drops; *pl.* fat, from meat while roasting. **-stone** *n.* a projecting molding over doors to deflect rain water [O.E. *dryppan*, to fall in drops].
drive (driv) *v.t.* to urge on; to keep in motion; to guide the course of; to cause (a machine) to work; to strike in, as a nail; to compel; to hurry; to conclude, as a bargain; to hit a ball with force, as in golf, tennis; to chase game towards sportsmen; *v.i.* to be forced along; to ride in a vehicle. *pr.p.* **driving.** *pa.t.* **drove.** *pa.p.* **driven.** *n.* an excursion in a vehicle; a private roadway; driving game towards sportsmen; the capacity for getting things done. **-r** *n.* one who or that which drives; a golf club for hitting ball from the tee; a drover. **to drive at,** to hint at [O.E. *drifan*, to drive].
driv·el (driv′·l) *v.i.* to dribble like a child; to talk nonsense; to be weak or foolish; *n.* nonsense. **-er** *n.* [O.E. *dreflian*, to slobber; conn. with *dribble*].
driz·zle (driz′·l) *v.t.* and *v.i.* to rain gently; *n.* fine rain [O.E. *dreosan*, to fall].
droit (drwä, droit) *n.* legal right [Fr. *droit*].
droll (drōl) *a.* laughable; funny; queer; *n.* a buffoon; a jester; an odd character. **-ery** *n.* [Fr. *drôle*, an amusing rascal].
drom·e·dar·y (dråm′·e·der·i·) *n.* a one-humped Arabian camel [Gk. *dromas*, running].

drone (drōn) *n.* the male of the honey-bee; an idler who lives on the work of others; a deep, humming sound; the largest pipe of the bagpipes; its sound; *v.t.* and *v.i.* to hum; to speak or sing in a monotone [O.E. *dran*, a drone].

drool (dróól) *v.i.* to slaver; to drivel; to speak foolishly [See **drivel**].
droop (dróóp) *v.i.* to hang down; to grow weak; to pine; to sag; to wilt (as flowers); *v.t.* to lower [Scand. *drupa*, to sink].
drop (dráp) *n.* a globular particle of fluid that falls or is allowed to fall; a minute quantity of fluid in medical dose; anything hanging like a drop, or resembling a drop in size (as a jewel in a pendant, ear-ring, etc.); a fall; the trap door of a gallows; *v.t.* to let fall drop by drop; to let fall; to dismiss or break off (as an acquaintance); to set down from a vehicle; to write a letter or pass a remark, in a casual manner; (of animals) to give birth to prematurely; *v.i.* to fall in drops; to fall down suddenly; to sink to a lower level (as prices); to come to an end. *pr.p.* **-ping.** *pa.t.* and *pa.p.* **-ped.** **— curtain** *n.* a painted curtain lowered in front of theater stage between scenes in a play. **-kick** *n.* (*Football*) a kick effected by letting the ball fall from the hands to the ground to be kicked immediately on the rebound. **-let** *n.* a tiny drop of liquid. **-per** *n.* a small glass tube from which liquid is measured out in drops. **-pings** *n.pl.* dung. **to drop in,** to make an informal visit. **a drop in the bucket,** a small amount [O.E. *dropa*, a drop].
drop·sy (dráp′·si·) *n.* a morbid collection of fluid in any part of body. **dropsical** *a.* [Gk. *hudrops*, fr. *hudor*, water].
dross (drás) *n.* the scum of metals thrown off in smelting; refuse [O.E. *dros*, dregs].
drought, drouth (drout, drouth) *n.* dryness; absence of rain over a prolonged period. **-iness** *n.* **-y** *a.* [O.E. *drugath*, dryness].
drove (drōv) *n.* a herd or flock, esp. on the move. **-r** *n.* one who drives cattle or sheep, esp. to market [O.E. *drifan*, to drive].
drown (droun) *v.t.* to suffocate by submerging in water; to deluge; to render inaudible; to overpower; *v.i.* to be suffocated in water [O.E. *druncnian*, to be drunk, to get drowned].
drowse (drouz) *v.t.* to make sleepy; *v.i.* to sleep; be heavy with sleep; *n.* a half-sleep; a doze. **drowsy** *a.* **drowsily** *adv.* **drowsiness** *n.* [O.E. *drusian*, to be sluggish].
drub (drub) *v.t.* to beat; to cudgel; *v.i.* to defeat. *pr.p.* **-bing.** *pa.p.*, *pa.t.* **-bed.** **-bing** *n.* a thrashing [prob. Scand. *drabba*, to hit].
drudge (druj) *v.i.* to toil hard; to labor at menial tasks; *n.* one who must do menial work. **drudgery** *n.* hard, monotonous, toil. **drudgingly** *adv.* [O.E. *dreogan*, to perform].
drug (drug) *n.* any substance used in the composition of a medicine; a narcotic; (*Fig.*) a commodity unsaleable because of over-production; *v.t.* to mix with drugs; to administer a drug to someone; *v.i.* to take drugs habitually and in excess. *pr.p.* **-ging.** *pr.p.* **-ged. -gist** *n.* dealer in drugs; a pharmaceutical chemist.
Dru·id (dróó′·id) *n.* a priest of the ancient Celtic peoples of Britain, Gaul, etc. who worshipped the oak tree. **-ism** *n.* [Celt.].
drum (drum) *n.* (*Mus.*) a percussion instrument comprising a hollow, parchment-covered cylinder beaten with a drumstick; anything drum-shaped; (*Anat.*) the middle portion of ear; *v.t.* to play on a drum; to teach by constant repetition; *v.i.* to beat on drum; to beat rhythmically. *pr.p.* **-ming.** *pa.p.*, *pa.t.* **-med.** **— major** *n.* the leader of a marching drum corps or band. **-mer** *n.* one who plays a drum; a commercial traveler. **-stick** *n.* a padded stick for beating a drum; lower part of leg of cooked fowl [prob. imit. word].

drunk (drungk) *pa.p.* of **drink**; *a.* overcome by strong drink; intoxicated; *n.* a drunk person. **-ard** *n.* one who habitually drinks to excess. **-en** *a.* given to excessive drinking. **-enness** *n.* [O.E. *drincan*, to drink].
drupe (dróóp) *n.* a fleshy fruit, such as plum, cherry, or peach, with a stone or kernel containing the seed [L. *drupa*, an over-ripe olive].

dry (drī) *a.* free from moisture, rain, or mist; sear; not giving milk, as a cow; thirsty; unsweetened, as wines; uninteresting; sarcastic; plain, as facts; pert. to a district subject to prohibition laws; *v.t.* to free from moisture or wetness; to drain; *v.i.* to grow dry; to evaporate; (*Fig.*) to become void of ideas. **drier** *n.* — **battery** *n.* a battery composed of *dry cells* sealed in a container to prevent leakage. **to dry clean,** to clean garments with chemicals. —**fly** *n.* an artificial fly (in dry-fly fishing) played over surface of water. — **goods** *n.pl.* textile fabrics. **-ly, drily** *adv.* — **measure,** a measure of bulk, used for grain, etc. **-ness** *n.* — **rot** *n.* a decay caused by fungous disease. —**shod** *a.* with dry feet; without wetting one's feet [O.E. *dryge,* dry].

dry·ad (drī'·ad) *n.* in Greek mythology a spirit of the trees; a wood-nymph [Gk. *drus,* an oak tree].

du·al (dū'·al) *a.* consisting of two; twofold; (*Gram.*) of noun, etc. denoting two persons or things; *n.* (*Gram.*) the dual number. **duad** *n.* pair of things regarded as one. **-ism** *n.* a twofold division; the belief that two separate elements co-exist in the universe, namely spirit and matter; the belief in the existence of good and evil as separate entities. **-ist** *n.* **-ity** *n.* state of being double [L. *duo,* two].

dub (dub) *v.t.* to knight; to give a nickname to; to make smooth; to dress a fly for fishing; (*Film*) to provide a film with a sound track not in the original language. *pr.p.* **-bing.** *pa.p.* and *pa.t.* **-bed** [M.E. *dubben,* to adorn].

du·bi·ous (dū'·bi·as) *a.* doubtful; liable to turn out well or ill; (of a character) shady. **-ly** *adv.* **-ness** *n.* **dubiety** (dū·bī'·a·ti·) *n.* hesitancy; uncertainty. **dubitable** *a.* doubtful. **dubitancy, dubitation** *n.* [L. *dubius,* doubtful].

du·cal (dū'·kal) *a.* pert. to a duke. **-ly** *adv.* in a ducal manner. **ducat** (duk'·at) *n.* a coin. **duce** (dôô'·chā) *n.* leader, esp. *'Il Duce,'.* **duchess** (duch'·is) *n.* the wife or widow of a duke; a woman who holds a duchy in her own right. **duchy** *n.* dominions of dukes [L. *dux*].

duch·ess (duch'·es) *n.* See **ducal.**

duck (duk) *n.* a coarse cloth or light canvas used for small sails and clothing. **-s** *n.pl.* trousers made of this [Dut. *doeck,* linen cloth].

duck (duk) *n.* any broad-beaked, web-footed, short-legged water bird; female duck as distinct from male **drake;** (*Colloq.*) a darling; a sudden dip; a sudden lowering of head; (*World War 2*) an amphibious truck; *v.i.* to dip suddenly in water; to bend (head) suddenly; to cringe; *v.i.* to plunge into water; to dodge. **-bill** *n.* an Australian burrowing, egg-laying mammal. Also called **-billed platypus.** **-board** *n.* planking to cross swampy areas. **duckling** *n.* a young duck. **-pins,** small bowling pins. **-weed** *n.* minute, floating, green plants growing on all standing waters. [O.E. *ducan,* to dive].

duct (dukt) *n.* a canal or tube for conveying fluids, esp. in animal bodies, plants, etc. **-less glands** (*Anat.*) endocrine glands which discharge their secretions directly into the blood (e.g. thyroid, pituitary) [L. *ducere,* to lead].

duc·tile (duk'·tal) *a.* (of metals) capable of being drawn out in fine threads or hammered thin; (*Fig.*) tractable; easily influenced. **ductility** *n.* [L. *ducere,* to lead].

dud (dud) *n.* anything defective or worthless; *n.pl.* clothes, esp. old and sloppy.

dude (dūd, dôôd) *n.* (*Slang*) a fop; a brainless dandy; an Easterner (a tenderfoot) who vacations on a ranch.

dudg·eon (duj'·an) *n.* anger; resentment, as in phrase *in high dudgeon* [etym. doubtful].

due (dū) *a.* owing; fitting to be paid or done to another; adequate; appointed to arrive (as a train); attributable; *adv.* exactly; duly; directly; *n.* that which is owed; right; (*pl.*) fee; tax. **duly** *adv.* properly; at the right time [O.Fr. *deu,* fr. L. *debere,* to owe].

du·el (dū'·al) *n.* a combat between two persons, generally an affair of honor; any two-sided contest; *v.i.* to fight a duel. **-ist** *n.* [It. from L. *duellum,* a fight between two].

du·en·na (dū·en'·a) *n.* a chaperon [Sp.].

du·et (dū·et') *n.* a musical composition for two performers, vocal or instrumental. **-ist** *n.* [It. *duetto,* fr. L. *duo,* two].

duff (duf) *v.t.* to make old things look like new; to fake; (*Golf*) to make a bad stroke. **-er** *n.* (*Slang*) a poor player, an incompetent person [etym. doubtful, prob. Scand. *dowf,* stupid].

duf·fel, duffle (duf'·l) *n.* a coarse woolen cloth with a thick nap; camping kit. — **bag** *n.* a canvas bag used for carrying clothes, etc. [fr. *Duffel* in Belgium].

dug (dug) *n.* a teat, esp. of an animal [Scand. *daegge,* to suckle].

dug (dug) *p.a.t.* and *pa.p.* of **dig.** **-out** *n.* a canoe hollowed out of a tree trunk; a hole in the ground roughly roofed over to protect in trench warfare; (*Baseball*) covered shelter for players not on field [fr. *dig*].

duke (dūk) *n.* (*fem.* **duchess**) the highest order of nobility in the British peerage. **-dom** *n.*

---

the status or possessions of a duke. See **ducal.**

dul·cet (dul'·sit) *a.* sweet to the ear; melodious [L. *dulcis,* sweet].

dul·ci·mer (dul'·sa·mer) *n.* an old musical instrument probably like a small harp; a modern instrument related to the guitar [L. *dulcis,* sweet; Gk. *melos,* a song].

dull (dull) *a.* stupid; slow of hearing or seeing; tedious; uninspired; sleepy; dim or cloudy; obtuse; blunt; heavy; *v.t.* to stupefy; to blunt; to mitigate; *v.i.* to become dull. **-ard** *n.* a slow-witted person. **-ness** *n.* [O.E. *dol,* dull-witted].

dulse (duls) *n.* an edible reddish-brown seaweed [Gael. *duileasg*].

duly See **due.**

dumb (dum) *a.* lacking permanently the power of speech; mute; temporarily silent; inarticulate; (*Slang*) stupid; unresponsive; *v.t.* to silence. **-bell** *n.* two heavy iron balls connected by a bar for a handle, used in gymnastic exercises; (*Slang*) a nitwit, moron. **-ly** *adv.* mutely; in silence. **-ness** *n.* — **show,** pantomime. —**waiter** *n.* a hand-operated elevator.

dum(b)found *v.t.* to strike dumb; to nonplus; to amaze; **-ed** *a.* **dummy** *a.* dumb; sham; *n.* a dumb person; a tailor's mannequin; a sham package in a shop window; (*Cards*) the exposed hand in bridge or whist [O.E. *dumb,* mute].

dum-dum (dum'·dum) *n.* a soft nosed bullet [Bengal].

dump (dump) *v.t.* to throw down heavily; to deposit; to unload; to sell off surplus goods at a low price; *n.* refuse or scrap heap; a temporary store for munitions, etc.; (*Slang*) a poorly kept up place. **-ling** *n.* a ball of dough boiled in water, stock, etc.; a pudding, boiled or baked containing fruit. **-y** *a.* short; thick; squat. **-iness** *n.* — **truck** *n.* a truck whose body tilts and end opens for unloading.

dun (dun) *a.* greyish-brown color; dark; *n.* this color [O.E. *dunn,* dark brown].

dun (dun) *v.t.* to importune for payment of a debt. *pr.p.* **-ning.** *pa.p.* **-ned** [allied to *din*].

dunce (duns) *n.* one who is slow at learning; a dullard [fr. *Duns Scotus,* 13th cent.].

dun·der·head (dun'·der·hed) *n.* a stupid person; a dunce. **-ed** *a.*

dune (dūn) *n.* a low hill of sand in desert areas or on the seacoast [O.Dut. *duna,* a hill].

dung (dung) *n.* the excrement of animals; manure; *v.t.* to treat with manure; *v.i.* to drop excrement. **-hill** *n.* a mound of dung; (*Fig.*) any mean condition [O.E. *dung,* muck].

dun·ga·ree (dung'·ga·rē) *n.* a coarse hard-wearing cotton cloth. **-s** *n.pl.* trousers or overalls of this material [Hind.].

dun·geon (dun'·jan) *n.* orig. the principal tower or 'keep' of a castle; a damp subterranean prison cell; *v.t.* to confine in a dungeon [Fr. *donjon,* fr. L. *dominus,* a master].

dunk (dungk) *v.t.* to dip (bread) into tea, coffee, soup, etc. [Ger. *Tunker,* a dipper].

du·o (dū'·ō) *n.* a duet; a pair of stage artistes.

du·o·de·cen·ni·al (dū·a·da·sen'·i·al) *a.* occurring every twelve years. **duodenary** *a.* pert. to 12 [L. *duodecim,* twelve; *annus,* a year].

du·o·dec·i·mo (dū·a·des'·a·mō) *n.* formed of sheets folded into twelve leaves (*abbrev.* 12 mo.); a 12 mo. book. **duodecimal** *a.* proceeding by twelves; *n.* a twelfth part. **duodecimals** *n.pl.* a method of computation by denominations of 12 instead of 10. **duodecimally** *adv.* [L. *duodecim,* twelve].

du·o·de·num (dū·a·dē'·nam) *n.* upper part of intestines so called as it is about 12 fingerbreadths long; *pl.* **duodena. duodenal** *a.* pert. to duodenum [L. *duodeni,* twelve each].

dupe (dūp) *n.* one who is easily cheated; *v.t.* to cheat; to mislead. **-ry** *n.* the art of cheating.

du·plex (dū'·pleks) *a.* twofold; double; *n.* a house consisting of two family units. **duple** *a.* double [L. *duplex,* double].

du·pli·cate (dū'·pli·kit) *a.* double; exactly resembling another; *n.* an exact copy; a replica, facsimile; *v.t.* (dū'·pli·kāte) to double; to make a copy. **duplication** *n.* **duplicator** *n.* a machine for making copies of written matter. **duplicity** *n.* double-dealing; deception [L. *duplicatus,* to double].

du·ra·ble (dyoor'·a·bl) *a.* lasting; able to resist wear and tear; not perishable; abiding.

-ness, durability *n.* **durably** *adv.* **durance** *n.* confinement. **duration** *n.* continuance in time; period anything lasts [L. *durare,* to last].

du·ress (dyoo·res') *n.* compulsion; imprisonment; coercion [O.Fr. *duresce,* hardship].

dur·ing (dyoor'·ing) *prep.* in the time of; in course of [*pr.p.* of obsolete *dure*].

dusk (dusk) *a.* tending to darkness; darkish; *n.* twilight; gloaming. **-y** *a.* partially dark; dim; dark-skinned [O.E. *dosc,* dark-colored].

dust (dust) *n.* very fine particles of matter deposited on the ground or suspended in the air; minute particles of gold in a river bed; powder; the ashes of the dead; *v.t.* to remove dust from; to sprinkle with powder. — **jacket** *n.* a book cover. **-er** *n.* one who dusts; a cloth for dusting; a tin with perforated lid for sprinkling flour, sugar, etc.; a light garment used as a robe. **-ily** *adv.* **-iness** *n.* **-ing** *n.* the act or process of removing dust from furniture, etc.; a sprinkling [O.E. *dust,* dust].

Dutch (duch) *a.* pert. to Holland, to its inhabitants, or to their language; *n.* the language, the people of Holland. **-man** *n.* — **treat,** an entertainment for which each person pays his own share. **like a Dutch uncle,** with frankness [M.Dut. *dutsch,* pert. to the Netherlands].

du·ty (dū'·ti·) *n.* that which is due; that which is demanded by law, morality, social conscience, etc.; military service; one's proper employment; a period of work set down for each person on a roster; customs or excise dues. **duteous** *a.* dutiful; obedient. **duteously** *adv.* **dutiable** *a.* subject to customs duties. Also **dutied. dutiful** *a.* attentive to duty; submissive; proceeding from a sense of duty. **dutifully** *adv.* **dutifulness** *n.* —**free** *a.* exempt from customs duty [O.Fr. *dueté,* what is owed].

dwarf (dwawrf) *n.* an animal, plant, or man abnormally small in size; *v.t.* to hinder the growth of; to make diminutive by comparison. **dwarf, -ish** *a.* undersized [O.E. *dweorg*].

dwell (dwel) *v.i.* to abide; to be domiciled; to deal with in detail, as in a speech. **-er** *n.* **-ing** *n.* habitation; abode [O.E. *dwellan,* to tarry].

dwin·dle (dwin'·dl) *v.i.* to grow less; to shrink; *v.t.* to lessen [O.E. *dwinan,* to fade].

dye (dī) *v.t.* to give a new color to; to stain; *v.i.* to undergo change of color. *pr.p.* **-ing.** *pa.p.* **-d** *n.* a coloring matter. **-r** *n.* one who is employed in dyeing. **-stuff** *n.* substance used for dyeing [O.E. *deagian,* to dye].

dying (dī'·ing) *pr.p.* of **die.**

dyke (dik) *n.* See **dike.**

dy·nam·ic (dī·nam'·ik) *a.* pert. to force in motion; pert. to dynamics; (*Med.*) functional; (*Fig.*) possessing energy and forcefulness (of character). Also **-al. -s** *n.* branch of mechanics which deals with *force in motion.* **dynamism** *n.* a school of scientific thought which explains phenomena of universe as resulting from action of natural forces. **dynamist** *n.* **dynamite** *n.* a powerful high explosive, with great disruptive force; *v.t.* to blow up with dynamite. **dynamiter** *n.* one who uses dynamite, esp. for criminal purposes. **dynamo** *n.* a generator for transforming mechanical energy into electrical energy (short for *dynamo-electric machine*); *pl.* **dynamos. dynamograph** *n.* the recording registered on a dynamometer. **dynamometer** *n.* an instrument for measuring force [Gk. *dunamis,* power].

dynamite

dy·nas·ty (dī'·nas·ti·) *n.* a line of kings of the same family; the period of a family's rule. **dynast** *n.* a ruler. **dynastic** *a.* [Gk. *dunastēs,* a lord].

dyne (dīn') *n.* a centimeter-gram-second unit of force, or system [Gk. *dunamis,* force].

dys- (dis) *prefix* fr. Gk. meaning bad, ill, difficult.

dys·en·ter·y (dis'·an·ter·i·) *n.* inflammation of the mucous membrane of the large intestine, accompanied by excessive discharge of the bowels, pain and fever. **dysenteric, -al** *a.* [*dus-,* ill; *entera,* the entrails].

dys·pep·si·a (dis·pep'·si·a) *n.* indigestion. **dyspeptic** *a.* suffering from indigestion; morbid; *n.* one who suffers from dyspepsia [Gk. *dys-,* bad; *peptein,* to digest].

dys·pro·si·um (dis·prō'·zi·um) *n.* one of the rare earths, and the most magnetic metal known [Gk. *dusprositos,* hard to get at].

E

each (ēch) *a.* and *pron.* denoting every one of a number, separately considered. Abbrev. **ea.** [O.E. *aelc*].

ea·ger (ē'·gėr) *a.* inflamed by desire; ardent; yearning; earnest. **-ly** *adv.* **-ness** *n.* [Fr. *aigre*, sour, keen].

ea·gle (ē'·gl) *n.* large bird of prey; a gold 10 dollar piece of the U.S.; a military standard; (*Golf*) a hole played in two under par. **—eyed** *a.* sharp-sighted. **eaglet** *n.* a young eagle.

ear (ēr) *n.* the fruiting spike of a cereal plant; *v.i.* to form ears [O.E. *ear*].

ear (ēr) *n.* the organ of hearing, esp. external part of it; sensitiveness to musical sounds; attention; ear-shaped projection. **-ache** *n.* acute pain in ear. **-drum** *n.* the middle ear or tympanum. **-ed** *a.* **-lobe** *n.* **-mark** *v.t.* to mark the ears for identification; to reserve for a particular purpose. **-shot** *n.* distance at which sounds can be heard. **-splitting** *a.* exceedingly loud and piercing. **-wax** *n.* cerumen, a waxy secretion of glands of ear. **-wig** *n.* an insect with a body terminating in a pair of horny forceps [O.E. *eare*].

earl (url) *n.* a nobleman ranking between a marquis and a viscount. **-dom** *n.* territory or dignity of an earl [O.E. *eorl*].

ear·ly (ur'·li·) *a.* and *adv.* in the beginning of a period of time; belonging far back in time; in the near future. **earliness** *n.* [O.E. *aerlice*].

earn (urn) *v.t.* to gain money by labor; to merit by service; to get. **-ings** *n.pl.* wages; savings [O.E. *earnian*].

ear·nest (ur'·nist) *a.* serious in intention; sincere; zealous; *n.* seriousness. **-ly** *adv.* **-ness** *n.* [O.E. *eornest*, zeal].

ear·nest (ur'·nist) *n.* a pledge; sum paid as binding [M.E. *ernes*].

earth (urth) *n.* the planet on which we live; the soil, dry land, on the surface of the earth; world matters, as opposed to spiritual. **-s** *n.pl.* term in chemistry for certain metallic oxides. **—bound** *a.* fixed firmly in the earth; worldly; **-en** *a.* made of earth. **-enware** *n.* crockery made of earth. **-iness** *n.* **-ling** *n.* a dweller on the earth. **-ly** *a.* belonging to the earth; terrestial; worldly. **-nut** *n.* a name of certain plants whose tubers are edible. **-quake** *n.* disturbance of the earth's surface due to contraction of a section of the crust of the earth. **-work** *n.* embankments. **-worm** *n.* the common worm. **-y** *a.* like or pertaining to earth; gross [O.E. *erothe*].

ease (ēz) *n.* leisure; quiet; freedom from anxiety, bodily effort, or pain; facility; natural grace of manner; *v.t.* to free from pain, disquiet, or oppression. **-ful** *a.* **-ment** *n.* something that comforts; (*Law*) a right in another's

land, e.g. right of way. **easily** *adv.* **easiness** *n.* **easing** *n.* the act of alleviating or slackening. **easy** *a.* at ease; free from pain, care, anxiety; moderate; comfortable. **stand at ease!** military term to relax. **easy-chair** *n.* an armchair **easy-going** *a.* taking matters in an easy way [Fr. *aise*].

ea·sel (ē'·zl) *n.* a wooden frame to support pictures, etc. [Ger. *Esel*, an ass].

east (ēst) *n.* one of the four cardinal points; the part of the horizon where the sun rises; regions towards that; *a.* on, in, or near the east; *adv.* from or to the east. **-ern** *a.* toward, in, or from the east; oriental. **-ing** *n.* distance eastward from a given meridian. **-ward** *adv.* or *a.* toward the east. **-wards** *adv.* **Far East**, China, Japan, etc. **Middle East**, Iran, Iraq, etc. **Near East**, Turkey, Syria, Palestine, etc. [O.E. *east*].

East·er (ēs'·tėr) *n.* a festival commemorating Christ's resurrection, falling on the Sunday after Good Friday [O.E. *Eastre*, spring festival of goddess of dawn].

eas·y See under **ease.**

eat (ēt) *v.t.* to chew and swallow, as food; to consume gradually; to destroy; gnaw; corrode; wear away; *v.i.* to take food. *pa.t.* **ate** (āt). *pa.p.* **-en.** **-able** *a.* or *n.* anything that may be eaten. **-s** *n.pl.* (*Slang*) food ready for consumption [O.E. *etan*].

eau (ō) *n.* French for water; *pl.* **eaux. eau de Cologne,** a perfume obtained by distillation.

eaves (ēvz)*n.pl.* the lower edges of a sloping roof overhanging the walls of a building. **-drop** *v.i.* to listen furtively to a conversation. **-dropper** *n.* [O.E. *efes*, an edge].

ebb (eb) *n.* the reflux of tide-water to the sea; a decline; growing less; diminution; *v.i.* to flow back; to sink; to decline. **— tide** *n.* the ebbing or retiring tide [O.E. *ebba*].

eb·on (eb'·ạn) *a.* black as ebony. **-y,** a cabinet wood which is jet black. **-ite** *n.* hard rubber or form of a vulcanite [L. *ebenus*].

e·bul·lient (i·bul'·yạnt) *a.* boiling over; overflowing; exuberant; enthusiastic. **ebullience** *n.* **ebullition** *n.* act of boiling; outburst of feeling; agitation [L. *bullire*, to boil].

ec·cen·tric (ik·sen'·trik) *a.* departing from the center; not placed, or not having the axis placed, centrally; not circular (in orbit); irregular; odd; of a whimsical temperament; *n.* a disc mounted off center upon a shaft to change the rotary movement of a shaft into an up and down motion; a whimsical person; one who defies the social conventions. **-ally** *adv.* **eccentricity** *n.* the distance of a focus from the center of an ellipse; the deviation of two or more circles from a common center; departure from normal way of conducting oneself [Gk. *ek*, from; *kentron*, center].

ec·cle·si·a (i·klē'·zi·ạ) *n.* the general assembly of the freemen of Athens in classical times; a church; a religious assembly. **ecclesiastic** *n.* a clergyman; a priest; *a.* **ecclesiastical** *a.* **ecclesiasticism** *n.* adherence to ecclesiastical principles. **ecclesiology** *n.* the science and study of church architecture and decoration. **ecclesiologist** *n.* [Gk. *ekklēsia*, church].

ech·e·lon (esh'·ạ·lán) *n.* a level of command; an arrangement of troops in parallel lines, each a little to left or right of another; (*Flying*) formation of airplanes in which each plane flies slightly above and to the right or left of the one in front [Fr. *échelle*, a ladder].

e·chi·nus (e·kī'·nạs) *n.* a sea-urchin; a rounded molding as that below the abacus of a Doric capital [Gk. *echinos*, a hedgehog].

ech·o (ek'·ō) *n.* repetition of sound produced by sound waves reflected from an obstructing object; close imitation of another's remarks or ideas; reverberation; repetition; answer. *pl.* **-es.** *v.t.* to send back the sound of; to repeat with approval; to imitate closely; *v.i.* **-ism** *n.* forming words to imitate natural sounds. [Gk.].

é·clair (ā·kler') *n.* a pastry filled with cream and frosted chocolate [Fr.].

é·clat (ā·klä') *n.* splendor; approbation of success; renown; acclamation [Fr.].

ec·lec·tic (ik·lek'·tik) *a.* selecting at will; *n.* a thinker who selects and reconciles principles,

opinions, belonging to different schools of thought. **-ally** *adv.* [Gk. *eklegein*, to pick out].

e·clipse (i·klips') *n.* an interception of the light of one heavenly body by another; temporary effacement; *v.t.* to obscure or hide; to surpass [Gk. *ek*, out; *leipen*, to leave].

e·clip·tic (i·klip'·tik) *n.* the great circle on ι. celestial sphere which lies in the plane of the sun's apparent orbit round the Earth; *a.* Also **-al** *a.* [Gk. *ek*, out; *leipein*, to leave].

ec·logue (ek'·lawg) *n.* a short poem of a pastoral nature [Gk. *eklogē*, a selection].

e·col·o·gy (e·kál'·ạ·ji·) *n.* a study of relations between animals, plants, people and their environment [Gk. *aikos*, a house; *logos*, discourse].

e·con·o·my (e·kán'·ạ·mi·) *n.* wise expenditure of money; careful use of materials; management of the resources of a community; a saving harmonious organization. **economic, (al)** *a.* **economically** *adv.* **economics** *n.pl.* **political economy**, the science which deals with the production, distribution, and consumption of the world's resources and the management of state income and expenditure in terms of money. **economize** *v.i.* to expend with care and prudence; *v.t.* **economist** *n.* a student of economics; an economizer [Gk. *oikos*, a house; *nomos*, law].

éc·ru (ek'·rōō) *n.* beige [Fr. *écru*, unbleached].

ec·sta·sy (ek'·stạ·si·) *n.* abnormal emotional excitement when the mind is ruled by one idea, object, or emotion; a sense of uplift and joyfulness and increased well-being; excessive joy. **ecstatic** *a.* to be in a state of rapture; overjoyed. **ecstatically** *adv.* [Gk. *ekstasis*].

ec·to-, ect-, a prefix implying *outside, without* [Gk. *ektos*].

ec·to·plasm (ek'·tạ·plazm) *n.* (*Zool.*) exterior protoplasm of a cell; in spiritualism, an ethereal substance in which psychic phenomena may manifest themselves. **ectoplasmic** *a.* [Gk. *ektos*, outside; *plasma*, anything formed].

ec·u·men·ic, ecumenical (ek·yoo·men'·ik, ·i·kạl) *a.* universal; representative of the Church, universal or catholic. Also **oecumenic, -al** [Gk. *oikoumenē*, the inhabited world].

ec·ze·ma (ek'·sạ·mạ, eg·zē'·mạ) *n.* disease of the skin, characterized by itchiness and inflammatory eruption [Gk. *ekzema*].

ed·dy (ed'·i·) *n.* a current of air, smoke, or water, swirling back contrary to the main current; a vortex; *v.i.* to move in a circle [O.E. *ed* = black].

e·del·weiss (ā'·dl·vīs) *n.* a small white flowering plant found in the Swiss Alps [Ger. *edel*, noble; *weiss*, white].

E·den (ē'·dạn) *n.* the garden where Adam and Eve lived; a place of delight; a paradise.

e·den·tate (ē·din'·tāt) *a.* without front teeth; lacking teeth; *n.* an edentate animal [L. *e*, out of; *dens*, tooth].

edge (ej) *n.* the thin cutting side of the blade of an instrument; the part adjacent to the line of division; rim; keenness; *v.t.* to put an edge on; to sharpen; to fringe; to move almost imperceptibly; *v.i.* to move sideways. **-d** *a.* sharp; bordered. **-less** *a.* **-ways, -wise** *adv.* in the direction of the edge; sideways. **edging** *n.* border or fringe; narrow lace. **edgy** *a.* having an edge; irritable. **to be on edge,** to be irritable [O.E. *ecg*].

ed·i·ble (ed'·ạ·bl) *a.* fit for eating; *n.* an eatable. **edibility** *n.* [L. *edere*, to eat].

e·dict (ē'·dikt) *n.* a law or decree; order proclaimed by a government or king [L. *e; dicere*, to say].

e·di·fy (ed'·ạ·fi) *v.t.* to build up, esp. in character or faith; to instruct in moral and relig.ous knowledge. *pa.t.* and *pa.p.* **edified. edification** *n.* improvement of the mind or morals. **edifice** *n.* a fine building. **edifier** *n.* **edifying** *a.* [L. *aedificare*, to build].

ed·it (ed'·it) *v.t.* to prepare for publication; to compile; to direct a newspaper or periodical; to revise and alter or omit. **edition** *n.* the form in which a book is published; the number of copies of a book, newspaper, etc. printed at one time; an issue; copy or prototype. **-or** *n.* one who edits; **editorial** *n.* an article in a newspaper presenting the newspaper's point of view; *a.* pert. to or written by an editor [L. *edere*, to give out].

ed·u·cate (ej'·oo·kāt) *v.t.* to cultivate and discipline the mind and other faculties by teaching; send to school. **educable** *a.* able to absorb education. **educability** *n.* **education** *n.* process of training; knowledge. **educational** *a.* **educationally** *adv.* **educative** *a.* tending to educate. **educator** *n.* one who educates [L. *e, out; ducere*, to lead].

e·duce (i·dōōs') *v.t.* to draw or bring out that which is latent; to elicit; to extract; to develop. **educible** *a.* **educt** *n.* that which is educed. **eduction** *n.* [L. *educere*, to lead out].

eel (ēl) *n.* a group of fishes with elongated bodies [O.E. *ael*].

e'en, e'er (ēn, er) *contr.* for *even, ever*.

ee·rie, eery (ē'·ri·) *a.* weird, superstitiously timid; frightening. **eerily** *adv.* **eeriness** *n.* [O.E. *earg*, timid].

ef·face (i·fās') *v.t.* to erase or scratch out. **-ment** *n.* the act of effacing [Fr. *effacer*].

ef·fect (ạ·fekt') *n.* that which is produced by an agent or cause; result; consequence; *v.t.* to bring about. **-s** *n.pl.* property. **-ive** *a.* in a condition to produce desired result; efficient; powerful. **-ively** *adv.* **-iveness** *n.* **-ual** *a.* producing the intended result; efficacious; successful. **-uality** *n.* **-ually** *adv.* **-uate** *v.t.* to bring to pass; to achieve; to effect. **in effect**, really; for practical purposes. **to take effect**, to become operative [L. *efficere*, to bring about].

ef·fem·i·nate (i·fem'·ạ·nit) *a.* unmanly; womanish [L. *effeminatus*, made womanish].

ef·fer·ent (ef'·er·ạnt) *a.* conveying outward, or away from the center [L. *ex*, out; *ferre*, to carry].

ef·fer·vesce (ef·er·ves') *v.i.* to bubble, to seethe, as a liquid giving off gas; to be in a state of excitement; to froth up. **-nce** *n.* **-ent** *a.* bubbling; lively; sparkling [L. *effervescere*].

ef·fete (e·fēt') *a.* no longer capable of bearing young; sterile; unfruitful; worn-out; spent [L. *effetus*, exhausted by breeding].

ef·fi·ca·cious (ef·ạ·kā'·shạs) *a.* productive of effects; producing the desired effect. **-ly** *adv.* **-ness, efficacity, efficacy** *n.* power to produce effects [L. *efficere*, to effect].

ef·fi·cient (ạ·fish'·ạnt) *a.* causing effects; producing results; capable; able; effective. **efficiency** *n.* power to produce the result required; competency. **-ly** *adv.* [L. *efficere*, to effect].

ef·fi·gy (ef'·ạ·ji·) *n.* an image or representation of a person. **hang in effigy**, to hang an image of a person as a public expression of hatred [L. *effigies*, fr. *fingere*, to form].

ef·flo·resce (ef·lō·res') *v.i.* to burst into bloom; to blossom; (*Chem.*) to lose water of crystallization on exposure to air, so that crystals fall into powder. **-nce, -ncy** *n.* blooming; the time of flowering. **-ent** *a.* [L. *efflorescere*].

ef·flu·ent (ef'·loo·ạnt) *a.* flowing out; *n.* a stream which flows out from another river or lake. **effluence** *n.* a flowing out; issue; emanation [L. *effluens*].

ef·flu·vi·um (e·flōō'·vi·ạm) *n.* an exhalation with a disagreeable smell. *pl.* **effluvia. effluvial** *a.* [L. fr. *effluere*].

ef·flux (ef'·luks) *n.* the act of flowing out; that which flows out [L. *effluere*, flow out].

ef·fort (ef'·ẹrt) *n.* putting forth an exertion of strength or power, bodily or mental; attempt; achievement. **-less** *a.* [L. *ex*, out; *fortis*, strong]

ef·fron·ter·y (i·frun'·ter·i·) *n.* brazen impudence; audacity [Fr. *effronté* = without brow (for blushing)].

ef·fulge (e·fulj') *v.i.* to shine brightly. **-nce** *n.* **-nt** *a.* diffusing a flood of light; radiant [L. *ex*, out, *fulgere*, to shine].

ef·fuse (e·fūz') *v.t.* to pour out or forth; *a.* (*Bot.*) spread out; (of shells) slightly separated. **effusion** *n.* act of pouring out; that which is poured out. **effusive** *a.* gushing; demonstrative [L. *ex*, out; *fundere, fusum*, to pour].

e·gad (i·gad') *interj.* a mild imprecation = by God.

egg (eg) *v.t.* to urge on; to encourage one to take action [O.N. *eggja*, fr. *egg*, edge].

egg (eg) *n.* an oval body laid by birds and a few animals in which the embryo continues development apart from parent body; matured female germ cell or ovum; anything egg-shaped. **— cell** *n.* the ovum, as distinct from any other cells associated with it. **-nog** *n.* a drink made of egg, milk, sugar, and wine. **-shell** *n.* **-plant**

n. an edible plant with somewhat egg-shaped purple fruit [O.N. *egg*].

eggs

e·gis See **aegis**.

eg·lan·tine (eg'·lạn·tīn) *n.* the sweet brier; the honeysuckle [Fr. *églantine*].

e·go (ē'·gō, eg'·ō) *n.* I; the whole person; self; the personal identity. **-centric** *a.* self-centered. **-centricism, -centricity** *n.* **-ism** *n.* systematic selfishness; theory that bases morality on self-interest. **-ist** *n.* **-istic, -istical** *a.* **-mania,** *n.* abnormal self-esteem. **-tism** *n.* the habit of talking or writing incessantly of oneself; selfishness. **-tist** *n.* **-tistic, -tistical** *a.* **-tistically** *adv.* [L. *ego*, I].

e·gre·gious (i·grē'·jạs) *a.* remarkably flagrant. **-ly** *adv.* [L. *e*, out; *grex*, a flock].

e·gress (ē'·gres) *n.* act of leaving an enclosed place; exit; the right of departure. **egression** *n.* [L. *egressus*].

e·gret (ē'·grit) *n.* several species of heron [Fr. *aigrette*].

E·gypt (ē·jipt) *n.* African country **-ian** *n.* a native of Egypt. **Egyptology** *n.* study of Egyptian history, antiques, and inscriptions. **Egyptologist** *n.*

ei·der (ī'·dẹr) *n.* **the eider duck,** a species of sea ducks. **— down** *n.* the breast down of the *eider duck;* a quilt stuffed with this down [O.N. *aethr*].

eight (āt) *n.* and *a.* one more than seven, written as 8 or VIII. **-een** *n.* and *a.* eight more than ten, written 18 or XVIII. **-eenth** *n.* and *a.* the eighth after the tenth, written 18th. **-fold** *a.* eight times any quantity. **eighth** *n.* and *a.* the first after the seventh; *n.* one of eight equal parts; 8th; (*Mus.*) the interval of an octave; the eighth note of the diatonic scale. **-ieth** *a.* ordinal corresponding to eighty, coming after the seventy-ninth; written 80th; *n.* one of eighty equal parts of a whole, written ⅟₈₀. **-y** *n.* and *a.* eight times ten; four-score [O.E. *eahla*].

ei·ther (ē'·, ī'·THẹr) *a.* or *pron.* one or the other; one of two; each; *adv.* or *conj.* bringing in the first of alternatives or strengthening an added negation [O.E. *aegther*].

e·jac·u·late (i·jak'·yạ·lāt) *v.t.* to utter suddenly and briefly; to eject; to utter ejaculations. **ejaculation** *n.* a short, sudden exclamation; a sudden emission. **ejaculatory** *a.* [L. *e*, out; *jacere*, to throw].

e·ject (i·jekt') *v.t.* to throw out; to cast forth; to turn out; to dispossess of a house or estate. **-a** *n.* waste matter. **ejection** *n.* the act of casting out. **-ment** *n.* expulsion; dispossession; (*Law*) the forcible removal of a defaulting tenant by legal process from land or house. **-or** *n.* [L. *e*, out; *jacere*, to throw].

eke (ēk) *v.t.* to add or augment. **— out,** to supplement; to use makeshifts [O.E. *ecan*].

e·lab·o·rate (i·lab'·ạ·rāt) *v.t.* to put much work and skill on; to work out in detail; to take pains with; *v.i.* to give fuller treatment; *a.* (i·lab'·ạ·rit) worked out in details; highly finished; complicated. **-ly** *adv.* **-ness, elaboration** *n.* act of elaborating; progressive improvement [L. *e*, out; *labor, labor*].

é·lan (ā·làng') *n.* dash; impetuosity [Fr.].

e·land (ē'·lạnd) *n.* the largest of the antelopes, found in Africa [Dut.].

e·lapse (i·laps') *v.i.* of time, to pass by; to slip away [L. *e; labi, lapsus*, slide].

e·las·tic (i·las'·tik) *a.* possessing the property of recovering the original form when a distorting or constraining force has been removed; flexible; resilient; springy; *n.* a fabric whose threads are interwoven with strands of rubber; a rubber band. **elasticity** *n.* [Gk. *elaunein*, to drive].

e·late (i·lāt') *v.t.* to raise or exalt the spirit of; make proud. **-d** *a.* **elation** *n.* exultation [L. *elatus*, lifted up].

el·bow (el'·bō) *n.* the joint between the arm and forearm; right angle bend for joining two pipes; any sharp bend or turn; *v.t.* and *v.i.* to push with the elbows; to jostle. **— grease** *n.* (*Colloq.*) hard work, as in rubbing vigorously. **— room** *n.* ample room for free movement [O.E. *elnboga*].

el·der (el'·dẹr) *a.* older; senior; prior; *n.* one who is older; a senior; an office bearer in certain Protestant churches. **-liness** *n.* **-ly** *a.* somewhat old; up in years. **eldest** *a.* the oldest of a family [O.E. *eldo*].

el·der (el'·dẹr) *n.* a flowering shrub which yields berries [O.E. *ellern*].

El Do·ra·do, Eldorado (el·dạ·rá'·dō) *n.* a fabulous city abounding in gold and precious stones; any similar place [Sp.=the gilded one].

e·lect (i·lekt') *v.t.* to choose; to choose by vote; to appoint to office; to select; *v.i.* to determine on a course of action; *a.* chosen; selected from a number; (after a noun) appointed but not yet in office; *n.* those predestined to eternal life. **election** *n.* the act of electing or choosing; public voting for office. **electioneer** *v.i.* to work for the election of a candidate. **-ive** *a.* appointed by; dependent on choice. **-ively** *adv.* **-or** *n.* one with right to vote at election. **-oral** *a.* pertaining to electors or to elections. **-oral college** *n.* a body of electors chosen by voters in the states to elect the president and vice-president of the U.S. **-orate** *n.* the whole body of electors [L. *eligere*].

e·lec·tric (i·lek'·trik) *a.* pertaining to, charged with, worked by, producing electricity; thrilling. **— chair,** used for electrocuting criminals. **— eel,** a fresh water fish of S. America which is capable of inflicting powerful shocks. **-al** *a.,* **-ally** *adv.* **-ity** (tris'·ạ·ti·). *n.* a form of energy generated by friction, induction, or chemical change, and having magnetic and radiant effects; state of strong tension. **— unit,** of pressure = *volt;* of current = *ampere;* of power = *watt;* of resistance = *ohm* [Gk. *ēlektron*, amber].

e·lec·tri·cian (i·lek·trish'·ạn) *n.* a mechanic who makes or repairs electrical apparatus.

e·lec·tri·fy (i·lek'·trạ·fi) *v.t.* to charge with electricity; to thrill, startle, excite by an unexpected statement or action.

e·lec·tro- (i·lek'·trō) *prefix*, used in the construction of compound words referring to some phase of electricity. **-analysis** *n.* chemical analysis by electrolysis. **-cardiogram** *n.* a tracing of electrical changes of contractions of heart. **-cardiograph** *n.* machine which makes the tracing.

electrocardiogram

e·lec·tro·cute (i·lek'·trạ·kūt) *v.t.* to cause death by electric shock. **electrocution** *n.*

e·lec·trode (i·lek'·trōd) *n.* a metallic conductor of an open electric circuit in contact with some other kind of conductor [Gk. *ēlektron*, amber; *hodos*, way].

e·lec·tro·dy·nam·ics (i·lek·trō·dī·nam'·iks) *n.* a branch of the science of electricity which treats of the laws of electricity in motion or of electric currents and their effects.

e·lec·tro·ki·net·ics (i·lek'·trō·ki·net·iks) *n.* Same as **electrodynamics.**

e·lec·trol·y·sis (i·lek·trạl'·ạ·sis) *n.* the resolution of dissolved or fused chemical compounds into elements by passing a current of electricity through them; (*Surg.*) destruction of hair roots, tumors, by an electric current. **electrolyze** *v.t.* to subject to electrolysis. **electrolyte** *n.* the liquid which carries the electric current between two electrodes [Gk. *ēlektron*, amber; *luein*, to loosen].

e·lec·tro·mag·net (i·lek·trō·mag'·nit) *n.* a mass of soft iron temporarily magnetized by being placed within a coil of insulated copper wire through which a current of electricity is passing. **-ic** *a.* **-ism** *n.* branch of electrical science which deals with the relation of magnetism and electricity.

e·lec·trom·e·ter (i·lek·trám'·e·tẹr) *n.* an instrument for measuring electricity.

e·lec·tro·mo·tion (i·lek·trạ·mō'·shạn) *n.* the flow of an electric current in a voltaic circuit.

electromotive *a.* producing motion by means of electricity.

e·lec·tron (i·lek'·trȧn) *n.* the lightest known particle, a constituent of all atoms around whose nuclei they revolve in orbits. **electronics** *n.* the branch of physics which deals with the behavior of free electrons. **— microscope,** an instrument of immense magnifying power in which controlled rays of electrons are used instead of light rays.

e·lec·tro·neg·a·tive (i·lek·trȧ·neg'·ȧ·tiv) *a.* carrying a negative charge of electricity.

e·lec·trop·a·thy (i·lek·tráp'·ȧ·thi·) *n.* treatment of disease by means of electricity. Also **electrotherapy. electrotherapeutics** *n.*

e·lec·tro·plate (i·lek'·trȧ·plāt) *v.t.* to cover with a coating of metal by means of electrolysis; *n.* an article so covered.

e·lec·tro·pos·i·tive (i·lek·trȧ·pás'·ȧ·tiv) *a.* carrying a positive charge of electricity.

e·lec·tro·stat·ics (i·lek·trȧ·stat'·iks) *n.* the branch of electrical science which treats of the behavior of electricity in equilibrium or at rest.

e·lec·tro·type (i·lek'·trȧ·tip) *n.* a facsimile printing plate of type or illustrations.

e·lec·trum (i·lek'·trȧm) *n.* an alloy of gold and silver [Gk. *ēlektron*].

el·ee·mos·y·nar·y (el·ȧ·mos'·ȧ·ner·i·) *a.* by way of charity; given in charity [Gk. *eleēmosunē*, alms].

el·e·gant (el'·ȧ·gȧnt) *a.* graceful; tasteful; refined; luxurious. **-ly** *adv.* **elegance** *n.* grace; beauty; propriety; gentility; delicate taste [L. *elegans*].

el·e·gy (el'·ȧ·ji·) *n.* a poem of mourning; a funeral song. **elegiac** *a.* pertaining to elegy; written in elegiacs. **elegiacs** *n.pl.* elegiac verse or couplets, each made up of a hexameter and a pentameter. **elegiacal** *a.* **elegiast, elegist** *n.* a writer of elegies [Gk. *elegos*, a lament].

e·lek·tron (i·lek'·trȧn) *n.* a magnesium alloy of unusual lightness. See **elektrum** [Gk. = amber].

el·e·ment (el'·ȧ·mȧnt) *n.* the first principle or rule; a component part; ingredient; constituent; essential point; the habitation most suited to a person or animal; (*Chem.*) a substance which cannot be separated into two or more substances. **-s** *n.pl.* the bread and wine used in the Lord's Supper; fire, air, water and earth, supposed to be foundation of all things; the physical forces of nature which determine the state of the weather. **-al** *a.* of the powers of nature; not compounded; basic; fundamental. **-ary** *a.* pertaining to the elements or first principles of anything; rudimentary; simple [L. *elementum*].

el·e·phant (el'·ȧ·fȧnt) *n.* the largest four-footed animal, having a long flexible trunk, two ivory tusks, and exceedingly thick skin. **-ine** *a.* huge; unwieldy; ungainly. **-oid** *a.* like an elephant [Gk. *elephas*].

el·e·phan·ti·a·sis (el·ȧ·fȧn·tī'·ȧ·sis) *n.* disease in which there is gross enlargement of the affected parts [Gk. *elephas*, an elephant].

el·e·vate (el'·ȧ·vāt) *v.t.* to lift up; to raise to a higher rank or station; to elate. **elevated** *a.* raised; dignified; exhilarated; *n.* a railroad on elevated tracks. **elevation** *n.* the act of elevating or the state of being raised; elevated place, a hill, a height; (*Archit.*) geometrical projection, drawn to scale, of the vertical face of any part of a building or object. **elevator** *n.* the person or thing which lifts up; a lift or hoist; a silo where grain is stored; the rudder-like airfoil hinged to the tail of an aircraft. **elevatory** *a.* tending or having power to elevate [L. *levis*, light].

e·lev·en (i·lev'·n) *n.* and *a.* one more than ten, written as 11 or XI; a full team at football or hockey. **-th** *a.* the ordinal number corresponding to eleven, the next after tenth; *n.* one of 11 equal parts of a whole [O.E. *endlufan*].

elf (elf) *n.* a supernatural, diminutive being of folk-lore with mischievous traits; a hobgoblin; a dwarf; *pl.* **elves** (elvz). **-in** *n.* a little elf; **elfish** *a.* elf-like; roguish [O.E. *aelf*].

e·lic·it (i·lis'·it) *v.t.* to draw out; to extract; to bring to light facts by questioning or reasoning [L. *elicere*].

e·lide (i·līd') *v.t.* to cut off or suppress a vowel or syllable. **elision** *n.* the suppression of a vowel or syllable [L. *elidere*, to strike out].

el·i·gi·ble (el'·i·jȧ·bl) *a.* legally qualified; fit and worthy to be chosen; desirable. **eligibility** *n.* [L. *eligere*, to choose].

e·lim·i·nate (i·lim'·ȧ·nāt) *v.t.* to remove; get rid of; set aside; separate; leave out of consideration; excrete; expel; obliterate. **elimination** *n.* **eliminator** *n.* [L. *eliminare*, to put out of doors].

e·li·sion See **elide**.

e·lite (i·lēt') *n.* a choice or select body; the best part of society [Fr.].

e·lix·ir (i·lik'·ser) *n.* a cure-all; a medicine; the essence, vainly sought by the alchemists, which would have the power to transmute base metals into gold [Ar. *al-iksir*].

E·liz·a·be·than (i·liz·ȧ·bē'·thȧn) *a.* pert. to Queen Elizabeth I or her times; *n.* a writer or distinguished person of her reign.

elk (elk) *n.* the largest member of the deer family in the N. of Europe; in America, the wapiti; a leather used for shoes, etc. [O.E. *eolh*].

ell (el) *n.* an addition to a building, usually at right angles [from letter L].

el·lipse (i·lips') *n.* a regular oval, formed by the line traced out by a point moving so that the sum of its distance from two fixed points always remains the same; the plane section across a cone not taken at right angles to the axis. **ellipsoid** *n.* a closed solid figure of which every plane section is an ellipse. **elliptic(al)** *a.* oval; pertaining to an ellipse [See **ellipsis**]. [Gk. *elleipsis*, a defect].

el·lip·sis (i·lip'·sis) *n.* in English syntax a term denoting the omission of a word or words from a sentence whereby the complete meaning is obtained by inference. **elliptic(al)** *a.* [Gk.].

elm (elm) a genus of trees [O.E.].

el·o·cu·tion (el·ȧ·kū'·shȧn) *n.* art of effective public speaking from the point of view of enunciation, voice-production, delivery. **-ary** *a.* **-ist** *n.* [L. *e*, out; *loqui*, to speak].

e·lon·gate (i'·lawng·gāt) *v.t.* to make longer; to lengthen; to extend; to draw out; *a.* (*Bot.*) tapering. **elongation** *n.* the act of stretching out; the part extended [L. *longus*, long].

e·lope (i·lōp') *v.i.* to run away with a lover; to marry secretly; to bolt unexpectedly. **-ment** *n.* [O.Fr. *alouper*].

el·o·quence (el'·ȧ·kwȧns) *n.* the art or power of expressing thought in fluent, impressive and graceful language; oratory; rhetoric; fluency. **eloquent** *a.* **eloquently** *adv.* [L. *e*, out; *loqui*, to speak].

else (els) *adv.* besides; other; otherwise; instead. **-where** *adv.* in or to some other place [O.E. *elles*].

e·lu·ci·date (i·lòò'·sȧ·dāt) *v.t.* to make clear or manifest; to throw light upon; to explain; illustrate. **elucidation** *n.* act of throwing light upon or explaining. **elucidative, elucidatory** *a.* **elucidator** *n.* [L. *e*; *lux*, light; *dare*, to give].

e·lude (i·lòòd') *v.t.* to keep out of sight; to escape by stratagem, artifice, or dexterity; to evade; to baffle. **elusion** *n.* act of eluding; evasion. **elusive** *a.* **elusory** *a.* [L. *e*, out; *ludere*, to play].

el·van, elves, elvish See **elf**.

E·ly·si·um (e·lizh'·i·ȧm) *n.* (*Myth.*) according to the Greeks, the abode of the virtuous dead where the inhabitants lived a life of passive blessedness; any place of perfect happiness. **Elysian** *a.* like a paradise; blissful.

em- *prefix* in or with; or adding a transitive or causal sense in the composition of verbs.

em (em) *n.* (*Print.*) Typographical unit of width, known as a pica or 12 pt. em (approx. ⅙th of an in.) used for measuring the length of a line of type.

e·ma·ci·ate (i·mā'·shi·āt) *v.t.* to make lean; to reduce one to flesh and bones; *v.i.* to waste away; to become extremely thin. **-d** *a.* **emaciation** *n.* [L. *emaciare*, fr. *macies*, leanness].

em·a·nate (em'·ȧ·nāt) *v.i.* to issue from; to originate; to proceed from; to arise (of intangible things). **emanant** *a.* flowing from. **emanation** *n.* a flowing out from; that which issues from a source; radioactive, chemically inert gas given off by radium, thorium and actinium. **emanative, emanatory** *a.* [L. *emanare*, to flow out].

e·man·ci·pate (i·man'·sȧ·pāt) *v.t.* to set free from slavery or servitude; to set free from any restraint or restriction. **emancipation** *n.* **emancipator** *n.* [L. *emancipare*].

e·mas·cu·late (i·mas'·kȧ·lāt) *v.t.* to castrate; to deprive of masculine qualities; to render effeminate. **emasculation** *n.* **emasculatory** *a.* [L. *e*; *masculus*, masculine].

em·balm (im·bám') *v.t.* to preserve a corpse from decay by means of antiseptic agents, balm, aromatic oils and spices; to perfume; to cherish tenderly some memory of. **-er** *n.* **-ing, -ment** *n.* [Fr. *embaumer*].

em·bank (im·bangk') *v.t.* to enclose or defend with a bank, mound, or earthwork. **-ment** *n.* the act of embarking; an earthwork built to prevent flooding or hold up a road, etc.

em·bar·go (im·bár'·gō) *n.* in international law, an order by which a government prevents a foreign ship from entering or leaving port; an order forbidding the despatch of a certain class of goods, usually munitions, to another country; a general prohibition. *pl.* **embargoes.** *v.t.* to lay an embargo upon [Sp. *embargar*, to impede].

em·bark (im·bárk') *v.t.* to put on board a ship; to enter on some business or enterprise; *v.i.* to

go on board a ship. **-ation** *n.* [Fr. *embarquer*].

embankment

em·bar·rass (im·bar'·ȧs) *v.t.* to disconcert; to perplex; to abash; to impede; to involve one in difficulties, esp. regarding money matters. **-ed** *a.* **-ing** *a.* disconcerting. **-ment** *n.* [Fr. *embarrasser*].

em·bas·sy (em'·bȧ·si·) *n.* the person sent abroad as an ambassador along with his staff; the residence of an ambassador [O.Fr. *ambasée*].

em·bat·tle (em·bat'·l) *v.t.* to furnish with battlements. **-ment** *n.*

em·bat·tle (em·bat'·l) *v.t.* to draw up in order of battle. **-d** *a.* [O.F. *embatailler*].

em·bed (im·bed') *v.t.* to lay as in a bed; to bed in soil. Also **imbed**.

em·bel·lish (im·bel'·ish) *v.t.* to make beautiful or elegant with ornaments; to add fanciful details to a report or story. **-er** *n.* **-ingly** *adv.* **-ment** *n.* [Fr. *embellir*, to beautify].

em·ber (em'·ber) *n.* a live piece of coal or wood; *pl.* red-hot ashes [O.E. *aemerge*].

em·bez·zle (im·bez'·l) *v.t.* to misappropriate fraudulently. **-ment** *n.* **-r** *n.* [O.Fr. *enbesiler*, to damage, steal].

em·bit·ter (im·bit'·er) *v.t.* to make bitter. **-ed** *a.*

em·bla·zon (em·blā'·zan) *v.t.* to adorn with heraldic figures; to deck in blazing colors; to proclaim. **-ment** *n.* **-ry** *n.* emblazoning.

em·blem (em'·blȧm) *n.* an object, or a representation of an object, symbolizing and suggesting to the mind something different from itself; sign; badge; symbol; device. **-atic, -al** *a.* **-atically** *adv.* **-atize** *v.t.* to represent by an emblem; to be an emblem of [Gk. *emblema*, a thing put in].

em·bod·y, imbody (im·bod'·i·) *v.t.* to form into a body; to incorporate; to give concrete expression to; to represent. **embodiment** *n.* an act of embodying; bodily representation.

em·bold·en (im·bōl'·d'n) *v.t.* to give boldness or courage to; to encourage.

em·bo·lism (em'·bȧ·lizm) *n.* the insertion of days between other days to adjust the reckoning of time; (*Med.*) the result of the presence in the blood stream of a solid foreign substance; as a clot. **embolismal** *a.* [Gk. *embolē*, an insertion].

em·bos·om, imbosom (em·, im·booz'·ȧm) *v.t.* to clasp or receive into the bosom; to enclose; to shelter; to foster.

em·boss (im·baws') *v.t.* to raise or form a design above the surrounding surface. **-ed** *a.* **-ment** *n.* a boss or protuberance [O.Fr. *bosc*].

em·bow·el (em·bou'·ȧl) *v.t.* to disembowel.

em·bow·er (em·bou'·er) *v.t.* to lodge, or set in a bower; to surround (with flowers).

em·brace (em·brās') *v.t.* to clasp in the arms; to press to the bosom; to avail oneself of; to accept; to encircle; *n.* a clasping in the arms; a hug [Fr. *embrasser*, fr. *bras*, arm].

em·bra·sure (em·brā'·zher) *n.* the splay or bevel of a door or window where the sides slant on the inside; opening in a parapet of a fort to allow cannon-fire [Fr.].

em·bro·cate (em'·brŏ·kāt) v.t. to moisten and rub with lotion, etc. **embrocation** n. [Gk. embrochē, lotion].

em·broi·der (im·broi'·der) v.t. to ornament fabrics with threads of silk, linen, etc. to form a design; to embellish, exaggerate a story. **-er** n. **-y** n. ornamental needlework [O.Fr. broder].

em·broil (em·broil') v.t. to involve in a quarrel or strife; to entangle; to confound. **-ment** n. [Fr. embrouiller, to entangle].

em·bry·o (em'·bri·ŏ), **embryon** (em'·bri·án) n. foetus during first months of gestation before quickening; a plant in rudimentary stage of development within seed; initial or rudimentary stage of anything; a. rudimentary; in the early stage. **-logic, -logical** a. pert. to embryology. **-logist** n. **-logy** n. science which deals with the growth and structure of the embryo. **-nic** a. rudimentary; at an early stage of development [Gk. embruon].

e·mend (i·mend') v.t. to remove faults or blemishes from; to amend, esp. of correcting a literary text; to alter for the better. **emendate** v.t. **emendation** n. correction of errors or blemishes. **emendator** n. **-atory** a.

em·er·ald (em'·er·ald) n. precious stone of beryl species, transparent and bright green in color. **Emerald Isle**, Ireland [Fr. émeraude].

e·merge (i·merj') v.i. to rise out of a fluid; to come forth; to come into view; to come to notice. **-nce** n. coming into view; an outgrowth from a plant. **-ncy** n. state of pressing necessity; difficult situation; urgent need. **-nt** a. emerging; rising into view [L. e, out; mergere, to plunge].

e·mer·i·tus (i·mer'·a·tas) n. and a. one who has honorably resigned or retired from a position of trust or responsibility but is retained on the rolls [L. = a veteran, fr. e, out; merere, to earn].

e·mer·sion (ē·mur'·shan) n. an emerging.

em·er·y (em'·er·i·) n. a naturally occurring mixture of corundum and iron oxide, used as an abrasive for polishing; v.t. to rub with emery [Gk. smuris].

e·met·ic (i·met'·ik) a. inducing vomiting; n. any agent which causes vomiting [Gk. emetikos, provoking sickness].

em·i·grate (em'·a·grāt) v.i. to leave one's country to settle in another. **emigrant** a. pert. to emigration; n. one who emigrates. **emigration** n. [L. e, out; migrare, to remove].

em·i·nent (em'·a·nant) a. exalted in rank, office, or public estimation; prominent. **eminence** n. elevation; rising ground; height; rank; official dignity; fame [L. eminere, to stand out].

e·mir (a·mēr') n. a title bestowed on Moslem chiefs [Ar. amir].

em·is·sar·y (em'·a·ser·i·) n. agent charged with a secret mission; one sent on a mission [L. e, out; mittere, missum, to send].

e·mit (i·mit') v.t. to send forth; to utter (a declaration). pr.p. **-ting**. pa.p., pa.t. **-ted**. **emission** n. **emissive** a. [L. e, out; mittere, to send].

e·mol·lient (i·mál'·i·ant) a. softening; relaxing; assuaging; a soothing agent or medicine [L. mollis, soft].

e·mol·u·ment (i·mál'·yoo·mant) n. profit arising from office or employment; gain; pay; salary; fee [L. moliri, to toil].

e·mo·tion (i·mō'·shan) n. strong, generalized feeling; excitement or agitation. **-al** a. easily excited or upset. **-alism** n. tendency to emotional excitement. **-ally** adv. **-less** a. **emotive** a. causing emotion [L. emotio, fr. emovere, to stir].

em·pa·thy (em'·pa·thi·) n. intellectual identification of oneself with another [Gk. en, in; pathos, feeling].

em·per·or (em'·per·er) n. the title assumed by the ruler of an empire [L. imperare].

em·pha·sis (em'·fa·sis) n. stress on anything such as force of voice given to words or syllables. pl. **emphases, emphasize** v.t. to stress. **emphatic, emphatical** a. [Gk.].

em·pire (em'·pir) n. imperial power; dominion; a country with its satellite states under the rule of an emperor or some other supreme control [L. imperium, command].

em·pir·ic, em·pir·i·cal (em·pir'·ik, -al) a. based on the results of experiment, observation, or experience, and not from mathematical or scientific reasoning; having reference to actual

facts. **empiric** n. a quack; one who depends for his knowledge entirely on experience. **-ally** adv. **empiricism** n. the philosophical doctrine that sensory experience is the only source of knowledge; the formulation of scientific laws by the process of observation and experiment. **empiricist** n. [Gk. en, in; peira, trial].

em·place·ment (em·plās'·mant) n. the place or site of a building; a fortified position for a gun; placing in position.

em·ploy (em·ploi') v.t. to give occupation to; to make use of; to hire or engage; to busy; to engross; to exercise; to occupy; (em'·ploi) n. paid service. **-able** a. **-ee** n. one who is employed at a wage or salary. **-er** n. **-ment** n. [Fr. employer].

em·po·ri·um (em·pō'·ri·am) n. a place of extensive commerce or trade; a mart; a big shop. pls. **emporia** [Gk. emporos, trader].

em·pow·er (im·pou'·er) v.t. to give legal or moral power or authority to; to authorize.

em·press (em'·pris) n. the wife of an emperor; a female who exercises similar supreme power to that of an emperor.

emp·ty (emp'·ti·) a. containing nothing; wanting force or meaning; void; vacant; unoccupied; destitute; hollow; unreal; senseless; (Colloq.) hungry; v.t. to make empty; to pour out; to drain; v.i. to become empty; to discharge; **emptiness** n. [O.E. aemtig].

em·py·e·ma (em·pī·ē'·ma) n. (Med.) a collection of pus in body cavity, esp. in pleura [Gk. en; puon, pus].

em·pyr·e·al (em·pir'·i·al) a. of pure fire or light; pert. to highest and purest regions of heaven. **empyrean** a. empyreal; n. highest heaven, or region of pure elemental fire; the firmament [Gk. en, in; pur, fire].

e·mu, emeu (ē'·mū) n. a large flightless bird, native of Australia [Port.].

em·u·late (em'·yoo·lāt) v.t. to strive to equal or surpass; to rival; to imitate. **emulation** n. act of attempting to equal or excel. **emulative** a. **emulator** n. **emulous** a. anxious to emulate or outdo another [L. aemulari, to rival].

e·mul·sion (i·mul'·shan) n. a liquid mixture in which a fatty or oily substance is suspended in water and by aid of a mucilaginous medium forms a smooth milky white fluid; the coating of silver salts on a photographic film or plate. **emulsic** a. **emulsification** n. **emulsify** v.t. **emulsive** a. yielding a milk-like substance [L. e, out; mulgere, to milk].

en (en) n. a printer's unit of measurement equal to half an em [See **em**].

en- prefix in; with; or adding transitive or causal force in verb composition.

en·a·ble (in·ā'·bl) v.t. to make able; to authorize to empower; to fit; to qualify.

en·act (in·akt') v.t. to make into a law; to act the part of. **-ing** a. **-ive** a. **-ment** n. the passing of a bill into law; a decree; a law.

e·nam·el (i·nam'·l) n. a vitreous compound fused into surface of metal, pottery, or glass for utility and ornament; the hard, glossy surface of teeth; paint with glossy finish; v.t. to enamel [Fr. émail, enamel].

en·am·or (in·am'·er) v.t. to inflame with love; to captivate; to charm; to fascinate.

en·camp (in·kamp') v.t. to form into a camp; v.i. to settle in or pitch a camp; to settle down temporarily. **-ment** n. an encamping; camp site.

en·case See **incase**.

en·caus·tic (en·kaws'·tik) a. pertaining to the fixing of colors by burning; n. an ancient style of decorative art, consisting in painting on heated wax [Gk. en, in; kaustikos, burnt].

en·ceinte (en·sānt') a. pregnant; with child; n. the precincts within the walls of a fort [Fr.]

en·ceph·a·lon (en·sef'·a·lán) n. the brain. **encephalic** a. cerebral; relating to the brain. **encephalitis** n. inflammation of the brain. [Gk. en, in; kephalē, the head].

en·chain (en·chān') v.t. to fasten with a chain; to hold fast. **-ment** n.

en·chant (in·chant') v.t. to charm by sorcery; to hold, as by a spell. **-ed** a. delighted; held by a spell. **-er** n. (fem. **-ress**) one who enchants; a sorcerer. **-ingly** adv. **-ment** n. act of enchanting; incantation; magic; delight; fascination [Fr. enchanter].

en·chase (en·chās') v.t. to adorn with chased work; to set with jewels. **-d** a.

en·cir·cle (in·sur'·kl) v.t. to enclose in a circle; to surround. **-ment** n.

en·clave (en'·klāv) n. a country, e.g. Switzerland, or an outlying province of a country, entirely surrounded by territories of another power; anything entirely enclosed into something else [L. in; clavis, a key].

en·clit·ic (en·klit'·ik) n. a word or particle united, for pronunciation, to another word so as to seem a part of it, e.g. thee in prithee [Gk. en, in; klinein, to lean].

en·close, inclose (in·klōz') v.t. to shut in; to surround; to envelop; to contain. **enclosure** n.

en·co·mi·um (en·kō'·mi·am) n. high commendation; formal praise. pl. **-s, encomia. encomiast** n. eulogist. **encomiastic(al)** a. **encomiastically** adv. [Gk.].

en·com·pass (in·kum'·pas) v.t. to include; to contain; to encircle. **-ment** n.

en·core (ang'·kōr) interj. again! once more! n. a recall awarded by an audience to a performer, artist, etc.; the item repeated; v.t. to applaud with encore [Fr. = again].

en·coun·ter (in·koun'·ter) v.t. to meet face to face; to meet unexpectedly; to meet in a hostile manner; to contend against; to confront; n. an unexpected meeting; a fight or combat [Fr. encontrer].

en·cour·age (in·kur'·ij) v.t. to give courage to; to inspire with hope; to embolden. **-ment** n. that which gives courage; act of encouraging. **encouraging** a. [Fr. encourager].

en·croach (in·krōch') v.i. to invade the rights or possessions of another; to intrude on other's property. **-er** n. **-ingly** adv. **-ment** n. [Fr. accrocher, to hook on].

en·crust, encrustation See **incrust**.

en·cum·ber (in·kum'·ber) v.t. to load; to impede; to burden; to saddle with debts. **encumbrance** n. a burden; a dependent person; a legal claim on an estate [Fr. encombrer].

en·cyc·li·cal (en·sik'·li·kl) a. intended to circulate among many people and in many places; n. an encyclical letter, a letter addressed by the Pope to the bishops of the R.C. Church. Also **encyclic** [Gk. en, in; kuklos, a circle).

en·cy·clo·pe·di·a, encyclopaedia (en·sī··kla·pē'·di·a) n. works which give detailed account, in alphabetical order, of whole field of human knowledge, or of some particular section in it. **encyclopedian** a. embracing all forms of knowledge. **encyclopedic** a. having universal knowledge; full of information. **encyclopedist** n. a compiler of an encyclopedia [Gk. enkuklios paideia, all around education].

en·cyst (en·sist') v.t. or v.i. to enclose or become enclosed in a sac or cyst.

end (end) n. the extreme point of a line; the last part in general; termination; conclusion; limit; extremity; final condition; issue; consequence; result; object; purpose; aim; death; a fragment; v.t. to bring to an end or conclusion; to destroy; to put to death; v.i. to come to the ultimate point; to finish; to be finished; to cease. **-ed** a. **-ing** n. termination; conclusion; the terminating syllable or letter of a word; suffix. **-less** a. **-lessly** adv. **-lessness** n. **at loose ends**, bored. **at one's wits' end,** perplexed; unable to proceed. **to make both ends meet,** to keep out of debt; to balance income and expenditure [O.E. ende].

en·dan·ger (in·dān'·jer) v.t. to place in jeopardy; to expose to loss or injury.

en·dear (in·dēr') v.t. to render dear or more beloved. **-ed** a. **-ing** a. **-ingly** adv. **-ment** n. the state of being, or act of, endearing; tender affection; loving word; a caress.

en·deav·or (in·dev'·er) v.i. to exert all strength for accomplishment of object; to attempt; to strive; n. attempt; effort; struggle [Fr. devoir, duty].

en·dem·ic, endemical (en·dem'·ik, -al) a. terms applied to recurring diseases confined to certain people or localities and which arise from local causes. **endemic** n. an endemic disease [Gk. en, in demos, a people].

en·dive (en'·dīv, án·dēv') n. an annual plant of the family Compositae, used for salads [Fr.].

en·do- (en'·dō) prefix indicating within [Gk. endon].

en·do·car·di·tis (en·dō·kár·dī'·tis) n. (Med.) inflammation of the lining membrane of the heart [Gk. endon, within; kardia, heart].

en·do·car·di·um (en·da·kár'·di·am) n. the lining membrane of the heart. **endocardiac** a. **endocardial** a.

en·do·crine (en'·da·krin) a. (Zool.) describing the tissues and organs giving rise to an internal secretion; n. any such secretion. **endocrinology** n. study of internal secretions of ductless glands [Gk. endon, within; krinein, to separate].

en·do·ga·my (en·dá'·ga·mi·) n. the custom of compulsory marriage within the limits of a tribe or clan or between members of the same race. **endogamous** a. [Gk. endon, within; gamos, marriage].

en·do·plasm (en'·da·plazm) n. inner portion of cytoplasm of a cell [Gk. endon, within; plasma, a formation].

en·dorse, indorse (in·dors') v.t. to write (esp. to sign one's name) on back of, as a check; to back (a bill, etc.); to sanction; to confirm; to vouch for; to ratify; **endorsable** a. **endorsee** n. the person to whom a bill of exchange, etc. is assigned by endorsement. **-ment** n. act of endorsing. **-r** n. [Fr. endosser, fr. dos, back; L. dorsum].

en·do·scope (en'·da·skōp) n. (Med.) an instrument for inspecting the cavities of internal parts of the body [Gk. endon, within; skopein, to see].

en·do·sperm (en'·dō·spurm) n. (Bot.) the nutritive starchy tissue which surrounds the embryo in many seeds. **-ic** a. [Gk. endon, within; sperma, seed].

en·dow (in·dou') v.t. to settle, by deed or will, a permanent income on; to enrich or furnish. **-er** n. **-ment** n. the act of settling a fund or permanent provision for an institution or individual; grant; bequest; natural capacity [O.Fr. endouer].

en·dure (in·door') v.t. to remain firm under; to bear with patience; to put up with; to sustain; to suffer; to tolerate; v.i. to continue; to last. **endurable** a. can be endured, borne, or suffered. **endurableness** n. **endurably** adv. **endurance** n. power of enduring; act of bearing pain or distress; continuance; patience; fortitude; stamina. **-r** *n.* **enduring** *a.* and *n.* **enduringly** *adv.* [L. *indurare*; fr. *durus*, hard].

endosperm

en·e·ma (en'·ạ·mạ) *n.* a liquid solution injected into intestine through rectum; device for this [Gk. fr. *en*, in; *hienai*, to send].
en·e·my (en'·ạ·mi·) *n.* one actuated by hostile feelings; an armed foe; opposing state; something harmful; *a.* of an enemy; due to an enemy [Fr. *ennemi*, fr. L. *inimicus*].
en·er·gy (en'·ẹr·ji·) *n.* vigor; force; activity; (*Mech.*) the power of doing mechanical work; **energetic(al)** *a.* exerting force; vigorous; active; forcible. **energetically** *adv.* **energize** *v.t.* to give energy to; *v.i.* to act energetically [Gk. *energeia*, activity].
en·er·vate (en'·ẹr·vāt) *v.t.* to deprive of nerve, strength, or courage; *a.* spiritless. **enervating**, **enervative** *a.* **enervation** *n.* [L. *enervare*, to deprive of sinew].
en·fee·ble (in·fē'·bl) *v.t.* to render feeble.
en·fi·lade (en·fạ·lād') *n.* a line or straight passage; narrow line, as of troops in marching; fire from either flank along a line; *v.t.* to direct enfilading fire [Fr. *enfiler*, to string on a thread].
en·fold See **infold**.
en·force (in·fōrs') *v.t.* to give strength to; to put in force; to impress on mind; to compel; to impose (action) upon; to urge on; to execute. **-able** *a.* **enforcedly** *adv.* under threat or compulsion. **-ment** *n.* [O.Fr. *enforcer*].
en·fran·chise (en·fran'·chiz) *v.t.* to set free from slavery; to extend political rights to; to grant the privilege of voting. **-ment** *n.*
en·gage (en·gāj') *v.t.* to bind by contract, pledge, or promise; to hire; to order; to employ; to undertake; to occupy; to busy; to attract; to bring into conflict; to interlock; *v.i.* to begin to fight; to employ oneself (in); to promise. **-d** *a.* **-ment** *n.* act of engaging; state of being engaged; obligation by contract or agreement; pledge; betrothal; occupation; affair of business or pleasure; battle; encounter. **engaging** *a.* attractive; pleasing [Fr. *engager*].
en·gen·der (in·jen'·dẹr) *v.t.* to beget; to cause to exist; to sow the seeds of; to breed; to occasion or cause (strife) [Fr. *engendrer*].
en·gine (en'·jạn) *n.* any mechanical contrivance for producing and conveying motive power; a machine; *a.* **engineer** *n.* one who constructs, designs, or is in charge of engines, military works, or works of public utility (roads, docks, etc.); *v.t.* to direct or design work as a skilled engineer; to contrive; to bring about; to arrange. **engineering** *n.* the art of constructing and using machines or engines; the profession of an engineer [Fr. *engin*, fr. L. *ingenium*, skill].
Eng·lish (ing'·glish) *a.* belonging to England or its inhabitants; *n.* the people or the language of England; *v.t.* to anglicize. **-man** *n.* **Old English**, language to about 1150 A.D. **Middle English**, 1150-1500. **Modern English**, from 1500. **Basic English**, a skeleton form of the English language of less than a thousand words [O.E. *Englisc*, fr. *Engle*, Angle].
en·gorge (en·gawrj') *v.t.* to swallow greedily and in large quantities; *v.i.* to feed with voracity; to devour. **-ment** *n.* [Fr. *engorger*, fr. *gorge*, the throat].
en·graft, ingraft (en·graft') *v.t.* to graft on; to incorporate; to add to. **-ation** *n.* **-ment** *n.*
en·grain See **ingrain**.
en·grave (en·grāv') *v.t.* to draw on a metal plate a design or picture by means of an incised line or on wood by leaving a raised surface; to imprint; to make a deep impression; *v.i.* to practice the art of engraving. **-r** *n.* **engraving** *n.* the art of cutting designs, etc. on wood, metal, or stone; an impression on art paper taken from an engraved block or plate; a print [See **grave**].
en·gross (en·grōs') *v.t.* to occupy wholly; to absorb; to copy in a large fair hand or in legal form; to buy wholesale with a view to cornering the market; to monopolize. **-er** *n.* **-ing** *v.t.* **-ment** *n.* [Fr. *en gros*, in a large hand].
en·gulf, ingulf (in·gulf') *v.t.* to swallow up or absorb as in a gulf; to encompass wholly.
en·hance (in·hans') *v.t.* to intensify; to increase in value or worth; to add to the effect. **-ment** *n.* [Fr. *hausser*, to raise].

engraving

en·har·mon·ic, enharmonical (en·hár-mán'·ik, -al) *a.* (*Mus.*) having the same pitch but written in different notation, as G♯ and A♭; pert. to one of the three ancient Greek scales, the others being diatonic and chromatic [Gk, *en*, in; *harmonia*, harmony].
e·nig·ma (i·nig'·ma) *n.* an obscure question or saying difficult of explanation; anything or anybody puzzling; a riddle. **-tic(al)** *a.* **-tically** *adv.* [Gk. *ainigma*].
en·jamb·ment (in·jam'·mant) *n.* in verse, continuation of a sentence from one line into the next [Fr. *en*, in; *jambe*, leg].
en·join (in·join') *v.t.* to direct with authority; to order; to impose; to prescribe; (*Law*) to prohibit by judicial order; to put an injunction on. **-ment** *n.* [Fr. *enjoindre*].
en·joy (in·joi') *v.t.* to delight in; to take pleasure in; to have the use or benefit of. **-able** *a.* pleasurable. **-ably** *adv.* **-ment** *n.* [Fr. *joie*].
en·large (in·lärj') *v.t.* and *v.i.* to make or become larger; to broaden. **-d** *a.* **-ment** *n.* act of enlarging; expansion; an enlarged reproduction.
en·light·en (in·lit'·n) *v.t.* to give information to; to instruct; to make clear; to free from superstition, etc. **-ment** *n.* act of enlightening; state of being enlightened; intellectual revival in Europe during 18th cent.
en·list (in·list') *v.t.* to enter on a list; to enroll; to secure support of; *v.i.* to engage in public service, as soldiers; to enter heartily into a cause. **-ment** *n.*
en·liv·en (in·liv'·ạn) *v.t.* to give life, action, or motion to; to quicken; to make gay. **-er** *n.*
en masse (in mas', àn màs') in a group [Fr.].
en·mesh, immesh, inmesh (en·mesh') *v.t.* to catch in a mesh or net; to entangle; to trap.
en·mi·ty (en'·mạ·ti·) *n.* the quality of being an enemy; hostile or unfriendly disposition; hatred; rancour; hostility [Fr. *inimitié*].
en·no·ble (en·nō'·bl) *v.t.* to make noble; to raise to the peerage; to exalt; to dignify **-ment** *n.*
en·nui (àn'·wē) *n.* boredom; listlessness due to satiety or lack of interest.
e·nor·mous (i·nawr'·mạs) *a.* huge; vast; prodigious; immense; atrocious. **enormity** *n.* quality of being enormous; great wickedness; atrocity. **-ly** *adv.* **-ness** *n.* [L. *enormis*, abnormal].
e·nough (i·nuf') *a.* as much or as many as need be; sufficient; adequate. *n.* a sufficiency; as much as satisfies conditions; *adv.* sufficiently; fully [O.E. *genog*].
e·nounce (ē·nouns') *v.t.* to state; to declare; to pronounce; to proclaim. **-ment** *n.* [L. *enuntiare*, to declare].
en·quire, enquiry See **inquire, inquiry.**
en·rage (in·rāj') *v.t.* to fill with rage; to provoke to frenzy or madness; to anger immoderately. **-d** *a.*
en·rapture (in·rap'·chẹr) *v.t.* to transport with pleasure; to delight excessively; to charm. **-d, enrapt** *a.*
en·rich (in·rich') *v.t.* to make rich; to add to; to enhance; to embellish. **-ment** *n.*
en·robe (en·rōb') *v.t.* to dress; to clothe.
en·roll (in·rōl') *v.t.* to enter a name in a roll or register; to enlist; to record. *pa.t.* **-ment** *n.* the act of enrolling; number of persons enrolled [Fr. *enrôler*].
en·sconce (en·skáns') *v.t.* to shelter; to hide securely; to settle snugly [L. *in*; *condere*, to hide].
en·sem·ble (àn·sám'bl) *n.* all the parts taken together; general effect; an entire costume; (*Mus.*) concerted playing by a number of musicians; the group of players [Fr. = together].
en·shrine (in·shrin') *v.t.* to enclose in a shrine; to treasure with affection. **-ment** *n.*
en·shroud (en·shroud') *v.t.* to shroud; to hide from view.
en·sign (en'·sin) *n.* a badge of rank or insignia of office; a flag or banner; an emblem; (*U.S. Navy*) the lowest commissioned officer. **-cy, -ship** *n.* rank of an ensign [Fr. *enseigne*.]
en·sil·age (en'·sil·ij) *n.* a process of storing crops such as hay, etc. while green, to serve as winter food for cattle; fodder so stored [Fr.].
en·slave (en·slāv') *v.t.* to reduce to slavery or bondage. **-ed** *a.* **-ment** *n.*

ensign

en·snare, insnare (en·snār') *v.t.* to catch in a snare; to entrap; to entangle.
en·sue (en·sōō') *v.i.* to follow; to happen after; to be the consequence of. **ensuing** *a.* [Fr. *ensuivre*, fr. L. *insequi*, to follow up].
en·sure (in·shoor') *v.t.* to make sure, safe, or certain; to bring about.
en·tail (in·tāl') *n.* law restricting inheritance of land to a particular heir or line of heirs; a predetermined order of succession; an estate; *v.t.* to settle land on persons in succession, none of whom can then dispose of it; to involve as a result; to bring about or cause. **-ment** *n.* [Fr. *entailler*, to cut into].
en·tan·gle (in·tang'·gl) *v.t.* to twist or interweave so as not to be easily separated; to perplex; to ensnare. **-ment** *n.*
en·tente (àn·tánt') *n.* cordial agreement or understanding; the nations or parties involved [Fr.].
en·ter (en'·tẹr) *v.t.* to go or come into; to pass within; to pierce; to penetrate; to invade; to join (a society, etc.); to put down one's name; *v.i.* to go or come in; to make a beginning; to take a part or interest in. **to enter on, upon,** to begin [Fr. *entrer*].
en·ter- (en'·tẹr) Gk. *prefix* used in the construction of compound words relating to the intestine. **-a** *n.pl.* of or pertaining to the intestine; **-itis** *n.* inflammation of the intestines [Gk. *enteron*, intestine].
en·ter·prise (en'·tẹr·priz) *n.* that which is undertaken or attempted; force of character in launching out; daring spirit; a bold attempt; **enterprising** *a.* adventurous; energetic. **enterprisingly** *adv.* [Fr.].
en·ter·tain (en·tẹr·tān') *v.t.* to receive a guest; to show hospitality to; to lodge; to amuse; to divert; to consider favorably; to cherish; to hold in the mind. **-er** *n.* **-ing** *a.* **-ment** *n.* [Fr. *entretenir*].
en·thrall (en·thrawl') *v.t.* to thrill; to captivate; to hold spellbound; to reduce to slavery.
en·throne (in·thrōn') *v.t.* to place on a throne; to raise to sovereignty; to exalt. **-ment** *n.*
en·thu·si·asm (in·thū'·zi·azm) *n.* passionate zeal for a person, object or pursuit; keen interest. **enthusiast** *n.* one who is carried away by enthusiasm. **enthusiastic(al)** *a.* **enthusiastically** *adv.* [Gk. *enthousiasmos*, inspiration].
en·tice (in·tis') *v.t.* to draw on by exciting hope or desire; to lead astray. **-able** *a.* **-ment** *n.* act of enticing; that which incites to evil; allurement. **enticing** *a.* **enticingly** *adv.* [O.Fr. *enticier*, to provoke].
en·tire (in·tir') *a.* complete in all parts; whole; unimpaired; not castrated. **-ly** *adv.* **-ness, -ty** *n.* completeness [Fr. *entier*, fr. L. *integer*].
en·ti·tle (in·ti'·tl) *v.t.* to give a title to; to name; to qualify; to fit for; to give claim to; O.Fr. *entiteler*].
en·ti·ty (en'·tạ·ti·) *n.* a real being; reality; existence; a material substance [L.L. *entitas*, fr. *esse*, to be].
en·tomb (in·tōōm') *v.t.* to deposit in a tomb; to inter; to bury. **-ment** *n.*
en·to·mol·o·gy (en·tạ·mál'·ạ·ji·) *n.* scientific study, classification, and collection of insects. **entomological** *a.* **entomologically** *adv.* **entomologize** *v.t.* to pursue the study of insects. **entomologist** *n.* [Gk. *entomon*, insect; *logos*, a discourse].
en·tou·rage (àn·tōō·rázh') *n.* surroundings; one's habitual associates; retinue [Fr.].
en·tr'acte (àn·trakt') *n.* the interval or musical interlude between two acts of a play [Fr.].
en·trails (en'·tralz) *n.pl.* the bowels; the intestines; the internal parts of anything [Fr.].
en·train (in·trān') *v.t.* to enter or put into a railway train.
en·trance (en'·trans) *n.* the act of entering; right of access; a door, gateway, or passage to enter by; the beginning. **entrant** *n.* one who enters; a competitor.
en·trance (in·trans') *v.t.* to put into a trance; to ravish with delight and wonder. **-ment** *n.* **entrancing** *a.*
en·trap (in·trap') *v.t.* to catch, as in a trap; to ensnare. **-ment** *n.*
en·treat (in·trēt') *v.t.* to ask earnestly; to implore; *v.i.* to make an earnest request. **-y** *n.* act of entreating; supplication [O.Fr. *entraiter*].
en·tree (àn'·trā) *n.* right of access; a dish served before the main course, as a main course,

or between main courses (used mostly now as a term for the main course); right of access [Fr.].

en·trench, intrench (in·trench') v.t. to dig a trench; to surround, fortify as with a trench; v.i. to encroach. **-ment** n. a ditch or trench; any fortification or defense.

en·tre·pre·neur (än·trạ·prạ·nur') n. a contractor; an organizer of business, trade, or entertainment [Fr. *entreprendre*, to undertake].

en·trust, intrust (in·trust') v.t. to charge with a responsibility; to confide to the care of.

en·try (en'·tri·) n. the act of entering; a place to enter by; an item noted down in a ledger, catalogue, or notebook; one entered in a contest [Fr. *entrer*].

en·twine, intwine (in·twīn') v.t. to twist together; to plait; to encircle.

e·nu·mer·ate (i·nōō'·mạ·rāt) v.t. to count, one by one; to give in detail; to count. **enumeration** n. **enumerator** n. [L. *enumerare*, to number off].

e·nun·ci·ate (i·nun'·si·āt) v.t. to state clearly; to proclaim; to announce; to pronounce each syllable distinctly. **enunciable** a. **enunciation** n. the act of enunciating; articulation or pronunciation; a declaration or announcement. **enunciator** n. [L. *e*, out; *nuntiare*, to announce].

en·ure See **inure**.

en·vel·op (in·vel'·ạp) v.t. to cover by folding or wrapping; to surround. **envelope** (en'·vạ·lōp) n. a cover or wrapper, esp. the cover of a letter. **-ment** n. [Fr. *envelopper*].

en·ven·om (en·ven'·ạm) v.t. to impregnate with venom; to poison; to embitter.

en·vi·a·ble, envious See **envy**.

en·vi·ron (in·vī'·rạn) v.t. to surround; to encompass; to encircle; to envelop. **-ment** n. that which environs; external conditions which determine modifications in the development of organic life. **-s** n.pl. adjacent districts; neighborhood; suburbs [Fr. = about].

en·vis·age (en·viz'·ij) v.t. to look in the face of; to face; to imagine; to visualize [Fr. *envisager*].

en·voy (en'·voi) n. a diplomatic agent of a country below the rank of ambassador; messenger [Fr. *envoyer*, to send].

en·voy, envoi (en'·voi) n. an author's postscript, esp. in an additional stanza of a poem.

en·vy (en'·vi·) v.t. to grudge another person's good fortune; to feel jealous of; pr.p. **-ing**; pa.p. **envied.** n. pain or vexation excited by the sight of another's superiority or success; jealousy. **enviable** a. **envious** a. full of envy. **enviously** adv. [Fr. *envie*].

en·wrap, inwrap (en·rap') v.t. to wrap up; to envelop; to engross.

en·wreathe, inwreathe (en·rēTH') v.t. to encircle, as with a wreath.

en·zyme, enzym (en'·zīm) n. a complex organic substance which in solution produces fermentation and chemical change in other substances apparently without undergoing any change itself; a form of catalyst; digestive ferment. **enzymetic** a. [Gk. *en*, in; *zumē*, leaven].

E·o·li·an, Eolic See **Aeolian, Aeolic**.

e·o·lith (ē'·ạ·lith) n. the oldest known stone implement used by pre-historic men **-ic** a. pertaining to the earliest stage of human culture [Gk. *eos*, dawn; *lithos*, stone].

eon See **aeon**.

e·pact (ē'·pakt) n. the excess of a solar over a lunar month or year in number of days [Gk. *epagein*, to intercalate].

ep·au·let, epaulette (ep'·ạ·let) n. an ornamental shoulder-piece or badge of rank [Fr. *épaule*, shoulder].

é·pée (ā·pā') n. a dueling sword with a sharp point but no cutting edge, used in fencing [Fr.].

e·pergne (i·purn') n. an ornamental piece for center of table [Fr.].

ep·ex·a·ge·sis (ep·eks·ạ·jē'·sis) n. a further explanation of a previous statement. **epexegetic, epexegetical** a. [Gk. *epi*, further; and *exegesis*].

e·phed·rine (ef'·ạ·drēn) n. an alkaloid drug, derived from plants of the genus *Ephedra* [Gk. *ephedra*].

e·phem·er·a (i·fem'·ẹr·ạ) n. anything of temporary interest and value; a genus of insects, better known as May flies, which as adults, live only for one day; pl. **ephemerae. -l** a. lasting only a very short period of time; transitory. [Gk. *epi*, for; *hēmera*, a day].

e·phem·er·is (i·fem'·ẹr·is) n. (*Astron.*) a table or calendar giving for successive days the positions of heavenly bodies; pl. **ephemerides** [Gk. *epi*, for; *hēmera*, a day].

epi- Gk. *prefix* meaning upon, at, in addition to, etc., used in the construction of compound terms.

ep·ic (ep'·ik) n. a long narrative poem in the grand style, usually dealing with the adventures of great soldiers or heroes whose deeds are part of the history of a nation; a worthy subject for such a poem; a. in the grand style; lofty in conception; memorable; heroic [Gk. *epos*, a word].

ep·i·car·di·um (ep·i·kar'·di·ạm) n. (*Med.*) the serous membrane of the pericardium, the sac which envelops the heart. **epicardial** a. [Gk. *epi*, upon; *kardia*, the heart].

ep·i·cene (ep'·ạ·sēn) a. common to both sexes; (*Gram.*) of common gender, of nouns with but one form for both genders, e.g. sheep; n. a person having characteristics of both sexes; a hermaphrodite.

ep·i·cen·ter (ep'·ạ·sen·tẹr) n. the point on the upper crust of the earth below which an earthquake has originated.

ep·i·crit·ic (ep·ạ·krit'·ik) a. pert. to fine sensitivity, e.g. to the slightest sensation of heat or touch.

Ep·i·cu·rus (ep'·i·kyoor·ạs) n. a Greek philosopher (342–270 B.C.), the founder of the Epicurean school. **epicure** n. one with a refined taste in food and dring; one who applies himself to gross sensualism, the delights of the table. **epicurean** a. n. a follower of Epicurus; a sensualist. **epicureanism** n. the doctrine that the chief end of man was physical and mental happiness.

ep·i·cy·cle (ep'·ạ·sī·kl) n. a circle whose center moves round in the circumference of a greater circle [Gk. *epi*, upon; *kuklos*, a wheel].

ep·i·dem·ic, epidemical (ep·ạ·dem'·ik, ·ạl) a. common to, or affecting a whole people or community; prevalent; general; prevailing for a time. **epidemic** n. the temporary appearance of infectious disease attacking whole communities [Gk. *epi*, among; *dēmos*, the people].

ep·i·der·mis (ep·ạ·dur'·mis) n. (*Anat.*) the outer protective layer of skin, otherwise the scarf skin, which covers the dermis or true skin underneath; (*Bot.*) a sheath, usually one cell in thickness, which forms a layer over surface of leaves. **epidermatoid, epidermic, epidermal, epidermidal** a. [Gk. *epi*, upon; *derma*, the skin].

ep·i·glot·tis (ep·ạ·glåt'·is) n. a covering of elastic, cartilaginous tissue, which closes the opening leading into the larynx during the act of swallowing. **epiglottic** a. [Gk. *epi*, upon; *glotta*, the tongue].

ep·i·gram (ep'·ạ·gram) n. a neat, witty, pointed saying; originally an epitaph couched in verse form, and developed by the Latin epigrammatists into a short poem designed to display their wit. **-matic, -matical** a. **matically** adv. **-matize** v.t. **-matist** n. [Gk. *epi*, on; *gramma*, a writing].

ep·i·graph (ep'·ạ·graf) n. an inscription, esp. on a building, statue, etc.; an appropriate motto or saying at the beginning of a book or chapter [Gk. *epi*, upon; *graphein*, to write].

ep·i·lep·sy (ep'·ạ·lep·si·) n. a nervous disease characterized by sudden convulsions and unconsciousness, followed by temporary stoppage of breath and rigidity of the body. **epileptic** n. one subject to epilepsy [Gk. *epilēpsis*, seizure].

ep·i·logue (ep'·ạ·lawg) n. a short speech or poem recited at the end of a play; conclusion of

a literary work [Gk. *epi*, upon; *logos*, speech].

E·piph·an·y (i·pif'·an·i·) n. a Church festival held on the twelfth day after Christmas; the manifestation of a god [Gk. *epi*, to; *phainein*, to show].

ep·i·phyte (ep'·i·fīt) n. a plant which grows on but does not draw nourishment from another plant [Gk. *epi*, upon; *phuton*, a plant].

e·pis·co·pa·cy (i·pis'·kạ·pas·i·) n. the government of the church by bishops; the office of a bishop; prelacy; the body of bishops. **episcopal** a. belonging to or vested in bishops; governed by bishops. **episcopalian** a. of an episcopal system or church; n. a member or adherent of an episcopal church. **episcopalianism** n. the system of church government by bishops. **episcopally** adv. **episcopate** n. a bishopric; the office or order of bishop [Gk. *episkopos*, overseer].

ep·i·sode (ep'·ạ·sōd) n. an incident; an incidental narrative or series of events; a digression, only remotely relevant to the plot of a play or novel; (*Mus.*) an intermediate passage between various parts of a fugue. **episodal, episodic, episodical** a. **episodically** adv. [Gk. *epeisodion*, the part of a play between choral songs].

ep·is·tle (i·pis'·l) n. a letter, usually of the less spontaneous type, written for effect or for instruction, as the epistles of the New Testament. **epistolary** a. [Gk. *epistolē*].

ep·i·taph (ep'·ạ·taf) n. an inscription placed on a tombstone or cenotaph in commemoration of the dead [Gk. *epi*, upon; *taphos*, tomb].

ep·i·tha·la·mi·um (ep·i·thạ·lā'·mi·ạm) n. a nuptial song.

ep·i·the·li·um (ep·i·thē'·li·ạm) n. cellular tissue covering cutaneous, mucous, and serous surfaces [Gk. *epi*, upon; *thēlē*, a nipple].

ep·i·thet (ep'·ạ·thet) n. phrase or word used adjectively to express some quality or attribute of its object; appellation; title; appellation. **epithetic, -al** a. [Gk. *epithetos*, added].

e·pit·o·me (i·pit'·ạ·mē) n. a brief summary; an abridgement of a book; abstract; synopsis; digest. **epitomize** v.t. to make or be a short abstract of [Gk. fr. *epitemnein*, to cut into].

e·poch (ep'·ạk) n. a fixed point or duration of time from which succeeding years are reckoned, as being specially marked by notable events; era; date; period; age. **-al** a. [Gk. *epochē*, a stop].

e·qua·ble (ek'·wạ·bl) a. uniform in action or intensity; not variable; of unruffled temperament. **equability, -ness** n. **equably** adv. [L. *aequabilis*].

e·qual (ē'·kwạl) a. having the same magnitude, dimensions, value, degree, or the like; identical; equable; tantamount (to); not lop-sided; n. a person of the same rank, age, etc.; v.t. to be or make equal. **-ization** n. **-ize** v.t. to make or become equal. **-itarian** n. one who holds that all men are equal in status. **-ity** n. the state of being equal. **-ly** adv. [L. *aequus*, equal].

e·qua·nim·i·ty (ē·kwạ·nim'·ạ·ti·) n. evenness of mind or temper; composure; calmness [L. *aequus*, even; *animus*, mind].

e·quate (i·kwāt') v.t. to make or treat as equal; to state or assume the equality of. **equation** n. the act of making equal; allowance for any inaccuracies; (*Math.*) an expression of the equality of two like algebraic magnitudes or functions by using the sign of equality (=) as **equational** a. **equationally** adv. [L. *aequus*, equal].

e·qua·tor (i·kwā'·tẹr) n. a great circle supposed to be drawn round the earth 90° from each pole and dividing the globe into the N. & S. hemispheres; (*Astron.*) the celestial equator, another name for the equinoctial. **equatorial** a. of or pertaining to the equator; n. an astronomical telescope, so mounted that it automatically follows the diurnal course taken by the heavenly body under observation. **equatorially** adv. [L. *aequus*, equal].

e·quer·ry (ek'·wẹr·i·) n. one charged with the care of horses; an officer whose duty it is to accompany the sovereign or royal prince when riding in state [Fr. *écurie*, stable].

e·ques·tri·an (i·kwes'·tri·ạn) a. pertaining to horses or horsemanship; mounted on a horse; n. (*fem.* **equestrienne**) a rider or circus-performer on a horse. **-ism** n. [L. *equus*, a horse].

e·qui- prefix fr. L. *aequus*, equal, used in the construction of compound words.

e·qui·an·gu·lar (ē·kwi·ang'·gyạ·lẹr) a. having equal angles.

e·qui·dis·tance (ē·kwạ·dis'·tạns) n. an equal distance from some point. **equidistant** a.

e·qui·lat·er·al (ē·kwǎ·lat′·ẹr·ǎl) *a.* having all the sides equal.

e·qui·li·brate (ē·kwǎ·lī′·brāt) *v.t.* to balance exactly; to equipoise. **equilibrant** *n.* (*Phys.*) the single force which will balance any system of forces or produce equilibrium when used in conjunction with these forces. **equilibration** *n.* **equilibrator** *n.* in aviation the stabilizing fin which controls the balance of an airplane [L. *aequus*, equal; *libra*, a balance].

e·qui·lib·ri·um (ē·kwǎ·lib′·ri·ụm) *n.* (*Mech.*) the state of rest of a body produced by action and reaction of a system of forces; equipoise; a state of balance [L. *aequus*, equal; *libra*, a balance].

e·quine, equinal (e′·kwīn, ·ǎl) *a.* pert. to a horse; *n.* a horse [L. *equis*, a horse].

e·qui·noc·tial (ē·kwǎ·nǎk′·shǎl) *a.* pert. to the equinoxes; *n.* (*Astron.*) a great circle in the heavens corresponding to the plane of the equator when extended (cf. **equinox**).

e·qui·nox (e′·kwǎ·noks) *n.* the time at which the sun crosses the plane of the equator, approx. March 21 and Sept. 22, and day and night are equal; *pl.* [L. *aequus*, equal; *nox*, night].

e·quip (i·kwip′) *v.t.* to fit out; to supply with all requisites for service; to furnish; to array; to dress; *pr.p.* **-ping.** *pa.p., pa.t.* **-ped. equipage** (ek′·wi·pij) *n.* furniture, especially the furniture and supplies of a vessel or army; a carriage, horses and attendants; accoutrements. **-ment** *n.* act of equipping; the state of being equipped; outfit, especially a soldier's; apparatus [Fr. *équiper*].

e·qui·poise (e′·kwǎ·poiz) *n.* the state of equality of weight or force; even balance.

eq·ui·ta·ble (ek′·wit·ǎ·bl) *a.* giving, or disposed to give, each his due; just. **-ness** *n.* **equitably** *adv.* fairly; justly [L. *aequus*, equal].

eq·ui·ta·tion (ek·wi·tā′·shǎn) *n.* skill in horsemanship; a ride on horseback [Fr. fr. L. *equus*, a horse].

eq·ui·ty (ek′·wǎ·ti·) *n.* fairness; equal adjustment or distribution; giving to each his due according to the sense of natural right [L. *aequitas*].

e·quiv·a·lent (i·kwiv′·ǎ·lẹnt) *a.* and *n.* equal in value, power, import, etc.; (*Chem.*) of equal valency. **equivalence** *n.* identical value; state or condition of being equivalent. **equivalency** *n.* [L. *aequus*, equal; *valere*, to be worth].

e·quiv·o·cal (i·kwiv′·ǎ·kǎl) *a.* of double or doubtful meaning; questionable; ambiguous; doubtful; dubious. **-ly** *adv.* **-ness** *n.* **equivocate** *v.i.* to use words of doubtful signification to mislead; to prevaricate. **equivocation** *n.* **equivocator** *n.* [L. *aequus*, equal; *vox, vocis*, a voice].

e·ra (ēr′·a) *n.* a fixed point of time from which a series of years is reckoned; epoch; time; age; a memorable date or period [L. *aera*, counters, used in computation].

e·rad·i·cate (i·rad′·i·kāt) *v.t.* to pull up by the roots; to extirpate; to destroy. **eradicable** *a.* **eradication** *n.* [L. *e*, out; *radix*, a root].

e·rase (i·rās′) *v.t.* to rub or scrape out; to efface. **erasable** *a.* **-d** *a.* **-r** one who or that which erases. **-ment** *n.* **erasure** *n.* [L. *e*, out; *radere*, rasum, to scrape].

ere (ār) *adv.* before; sooner; *prep.* before; *conj.* sooner than [O.E. *aer*].

e·rect (i·rekt′) *v.t.* to set upright; to raise, as a building, etc.; to elevate; to construct; *a.* upright; pointing upwards. **-ion** *n.* **-or** *n.* [L. *erectus*, set upright].

erg (urg) *n.* the absolute unit of measurement of work and energy in the metric system; the work done by a force which produces a velocity of a centimeter per second in a mass of one gram [Gk. *ergon*, work].

er·go (ur′·gō) *adv.* therefore; consequently [L.].

er·got (ur′·gǎt) *n.* a dried fungus used as a drug to stop bleeding and contract muscles [Fr. = bird's spur].

Er·in (ār′·in) *n.* Ireland.

er·mine (ur′·min) *n.* a member of weasel family the white winter coat of which is highly prized as a fur; the robe of a judge in England and so used as a synonym for *judge* [O.Fr.].

e·rode (i·rōd′) *v.t.* to eat into; to wear away; to corrode. **erodent** *n.* a caustic drug. **erose** *a.* appearing as if gnawed or worn irregularly. **erosion** *n.* act or operation of eating away; corrosion; denudation. **erosive** *a.* [L. *erodere*].

E·ros (ēr′·os, er′·os) *n.* (*Myth.*) the Greek god of love. **erotic** (i·rát·ik) *a.* pertaining to love;

amatory; *n.* a love poem; **erotics** *n.pl.* science and art of love. **erotica** *n.* literature dealing with sexual love. **eroticism, erotism** *n.* in psycho-analysis, love in all its manifestations [Gk. *eros*, love].

err (ur) *v.i.* to commit a mistake; to be mistaken; to deviate; to go astray; to sin. **-atic(al)** (i·rat′·ik) *a.* roving; wandering; eccentric; changeable; capricious; not dependable. **-atic** *n.* a wanderer; a boulder transported by a glacier or other natural force. **-atically** *adv.* **-atum** *n.* an error in writing or printing. *pl.* **-ata** [L. *errare*, to wander].

er·rand (er′·ǎnd) *n.* commission; message [O.E. *aerende*, a message].

er·rant (er′·ǎnt) *a.* wandering; roving; wild; abandoned; *n.* a knight-errant. **-ly** *adv.* **-ry** *n.* a state of wandering about, esp. of a knighterrant in search of adventures [L. *errare*, to wander].

erratic, erratum etc. See **err.**

er·ror (er′·ẹr) *n.* a deviation from right or truth; a mistake; blunder; sin. **erroneous** *a.* wrong; incorrect; inaccurate; false. **erroneously** *adv.* **erroneousness** *n.* [L. *errare*, to wander].

er·satz (er′·zȧts′) *a.* substituted for articles in everyday use; artificial; makeshift [Ger.].

erst (urst) *adv.* (*Arch.*) formerly; of old; hitherto. **-while** *adv.* former [O.E. *aerest*].

e·ruct, e·ruc·tate (i·rukt′, ·tāt) *v.t.* to belch. **eructation** *n.* belching [L. *e*, out; *ructare*, to belch].

er·u·dite (er′·yoo·dīt) *a.* learned; deeply read; scholarly. **-ly** *adv.* **erudition** *n.* learning; scholarship [L. *eruditus*].

e·rupt (i·rupt′) *v.i.* to throw out; to break through; to break out in eruptions. **eruption** *n.* act of bursting forth; outburst of lava, ashes, gas, etc. from the crater of a volcano; a rash on the skin. **eruptive** *a.* breaking forth or out [L. *e*, out; *rumpere*, to burst].

er·y·sip·e·las (er·a·sip′·a·lǎs) *n.* contagious disease causing acute inflammation of the skin [Gk. fr. *eruthos*, red; *pella*, skin].

es·ca·lade (es·kǎ·lād′) *n.* mounting the walls of a fortress by means of ladders; *v.t.* to scale [Fr. fr. L. *scala*, a ladder].

es·ca·la·tor (es′·kǎ·lā·tẹr) *n.* continuous, moving stairway [L. *scala*, a ladder].

es·cape (e·skāp′) *v.t.* to gain freedom; to evade; to elude; to pass unnoticed; *v.i.* to hasten away; to avoid capture; to become free from danger; *n.* flight from danger; evasion; leakage (of gas, etc.); an outlet for purposes of safety; a gardenplant growing wild and thriving; a conscious effort to forget mental troubles by taking up some other powerful interest. **escapable** *a.* **escapade** *n.* a wild prank or exploit. **-ment** *n.* the act or means of escaping; the contrivance in a time-piece which connects the wheelwork with the pendulum, allowing a tooth to escape at each vibration. **escapism** *n.* morbid desire to escape from the realities of life by concentrating on some other interest. **escapist** *n.* [Fr. *échapper*].

es·carp (es·kȧrp′) *v.t.* to make into a steep slope; *n.* **-ment** *n.* a steep, sloping bank [Fr. *escarper*].

es·cha·tol·o·gy (es·kǎ·tȧl′·ǎ·ji·) *n.* the department of theology which treats of the last things, such as death, the return of Christ, the resurrection, the end of the world, etc. [Gk. *eschatos*, last; *logos*, discourse].

es·cheat (es·chēt′) *n.* the legal process of property reverting to the crown or government on the tenant's death without heirs; an estate so lapsing; *v.t.* to forfeit; to confiscate; *v.i.* to revert to the crown or lord of the manor [O.Fr. *escheoir*, to fall due].

es·chew (es·chōō′) *v.t.* to shun; to avoid; to abstain from [O.Fr. *eschuer*].

es·cort (es′·kawrt) *n.* an armed guard for a traveller, etc.; a person or persons accompany-

ing another on a journey for protection or as an act of courtesy. **escort** (i·skawrt′) *v.t.* to accompany; to convoy [Fr. *escorte*].

es·cri·toire (es·kri·twȧr′) *n.* a writing-desk provided with drawers [O.Fr. *escriptoire*].

Es·cu·la·pi·an (es·kū·lā′·pi·ạn) *a.* pertaining to the art of healing [*Aesculapius*, in classic mythology, the god of medicine].

es·cu·lent (es′·kyǎ·lǎnt) *a.* suitable as a food for man; edible; *n.* something which is eatable [L. *esculentus*].

es·cutch·eon (is·kuch′·ạn) *n.* in heraldry, a shield bearing armorial bearings; that part of a vessel's stern on which her name is inscribed; an ornamental plate or shield placed round a keyhole opening. **-ed** *a.* [L. *scutum*, a shield].

Es·ki·mo, Esquimau (es′·kǎ·mō) *n.* and *a.* one of an aboriginal people thinly scattered along the northern seaboard of America and Asia and in many of the Arctic islands; *pl.* **Eskimos, Esquimaux** [etym. doubtful].

e·soph·a·gus (ē·sáf′·ạ·gạs) *n.* the gullet [L. *oesophagus*].

es·o·ter·ic (es·ạ·ter′·ik) *a.* term applied to doctrines intended only for the inner circle of initiates; secret; profound [Gk. *esoterikos*, fr. *eso*, within].

es·pe·cial (ạs·pesh′·ạl) *a.* distinguished; preeminent; more than ordinary; particular. **-ly** *adv.* [O.Fr. *especiel*, fr. L. *species*].

Es·pe·ran·to (es·pạ·rǎn′·tō) *n.* a universal auxiliary language [coined word].

es·pi·o·nage (es′·pi·ȧ·nij or ·nȧzh) *n.* the practice of employing secret agents; spying [Fr. *espion*, a spy].

es·pla·nade (es·plạ·nād) *n.* a level space, esp. for a promenade as along the seafront of a town [Fr.].

es·pouse (ȧs·pouz′) *v.t.* to marry; to support, attach oneself to (a cause, etc.). **espousal** *n.* act of espousing. **espousals** *n.pl.* nuptials. **-r** *n.* [O.Fr. *espouser*].

es·prit (es·prē′) *n.* spirit; wit; liveliness. **esprit de corps** (es·prē·da·kȯr′) loyalty and attachment to the group of which one is a member [Fr.].

es·py (ạs·pi′) *v.t.* to catch sight of [Fr. *espier*, to spy out].

-esque (esk) *suffix* in the manner or style of.

es·quire (es′·kwīr) *n.* originally, a squire or shield-bearer, one of two attendants on a knight; now a courtesy title [O.Fr. *escuyer*, fr. L. *scutarius*, a shield-bearer].

es·say (es′·ā) *n.* a literary composition, shorter than a treatise; a trial; an attempt. **essay** *v.t.* to try; to make experiment or trial of; to attempt. **-ist** *n.* a writer of essays [Fr. *essayer*, to try].

es·sence (es′·ạns) *n.* the very being or power of a thing; the formal cause of being; peculiar nature or quality; a being; essential part; a concentration of the active ingredients of a substance in a smaller mass; (*Med.*) a solution of essential oils in rectified alcohol; a perfume. **essential** *a.* belonging to the essence; necessary to the existence of a thing; inherent; n. something indispensable; a chief point; a leading principle. **essentiality** *n.* **essentially** *adv.* **essentialness** *n.* [Fr. from L. *esse*, to be].

es·tab·lish (ạs·tab′·lish) *v.t.* to make stable or firm; to set up; to found; to enact or decree by authority; to confirm; to prove; to verify; to substantiate; to set up and endow, as a state church by law. **-ed** *a.* fixed; settled; on the permanent staff; supported by the State. **-er** *n.* **-ment** *n.* act of establishing; that which is established; an institution; settlement; place of business, residence, etc.; the church established by the state. **-mentarian** *a.* and *n.* supporting church establishment [L. *stabilire*, fr. *stare*, to stand].

es·tate (ạs·tāt′) *n.* a piece of landed property; condition of life; rank; position; quality; property, real or personal; the total assets and liabilities of a bankrupt or of a deceased person. **the Three Estates,** in France, nobles, clergy, and middle class. **the Fourth Estate,** a satirical term for the press. **real estate,** property in land [O.Fr. *estat*].

es·teem (ạs·tēm′) *v.t.* to regard with respect or affection; to set a value on; to rate highly; *n.* high regard; favorable opinion [L. *aestimare*, to estimate].

es·thet·ic See **aesthetic.**

es·ti·ma·ble (es′·tạ·mạ·bl) *a.* able to be estimated or esteemed; worthy of regard. **estimably** *adv.* [L. *aestimare*].

es·ti·mate (es′·tạ·māt) *v.t.* to judge and form an opinion of the value, size, weight, etc. of; to compute; to calculate; *v.i.* to offer to complete certain work at a stated cost; *n.* appraisement; conjecture. **estimator** *n.* one who appraises. [L. *aestimare*].

es·ti·va·tion, aestivation (es·tạ·vā′·shạn) *n.* a state of torpor, affecting some insects, during the dry summer months. **estival** *a.* pertaining to or continuing throughout the summer aestival. **estivate** *v.i.* (cf. *hibernate*) [L. *aestus*, summer].

Es·to·ni·an, Esthonian (es·t(h)ō′·ni·ạn) *a.* pert. to *Est(h)onia*, a country on the Baltic; the Finnish-Ugrian language.

es·top (es·tȧp′) *v.t.* (*Law*) to impede; to bar by one's own act [Fr. *étouper*, to stop up].

es·trange (ạs·trānj′) *v.t.* to alienate, as the affections; to divert from its original use, purpose, or possessor. **-d** *a.* **-ment** *n.* [O.Fr. *estrangier*, to make strange].

es·tu·ar·y (es′·choo·er·i·) *n.* a narrow arm of the sea at the mouth of a river, up which the tides penetrate twice daily. **estuarine** *a.* pert. to an estuary [L. *aestus*, tide].

e·su·ri·ent (ī·soor′·i·ạnt) *a.* hungry; voracious; gluttonous [L. *esuriens*, being hungry].

et cet·er·a (et set′·ẹr·ạ) phrase meaning "and the others"; and so on; (*abbrev*) **etc.** [L.].

etch (ech) *v.t.* to make an engraving by eating away the surface of a metal plate with acid; *v.i.* to practice this art. **-er** *n.* one who etches. **-ing** *n.* the act or art of etching; the printed impression taken from an etched plate [Ger. *ätzen*, to eat into].

e·ter·nal (i·tur′·nạl) *a.* without beginning or end in relation to time; everlasting; timeless; ceaseless; immortal; imperishable. **eternalize, eternize** *v.t.* to make eternal or immortal; to perpetuate. **-ly** *adv.* **eternity** *n.* the infinity of time; the future state after death [L. *aeternus*].

eth·ane (eth′·ān) *n.* a colorless, odorless, inflammable gas [fr. *ether*].

e·ther (ē′·thẹr) *n.* the hypothetical non-material, imponderable medium supposed by physicists to permeate the whole of space and to transmit the waves of light, radiant heat, and electromagnetic radiation; the higher regions beyond the earth. **ethereal** *a.* pertaining to the ether; celestial; airy; delicate. **etherealization** *n.* **etheralize** *v.t.* to render ethereal or spiritual. **ethereality** *n.* the quality or state of being ethereal. **ethereally** *adv.* [Gk. *aithēr*, the upper air].

e·ther (ē′·thẹr) *n.* a volatile liquid, prepared by the action of sulfuric acid on alcohol, used as a solvent and as an anesthetic.

eth·ic, eth·i·cal (eth′·ik, ·ạl) *a.* relating to morals or moral principles. **-ally** *adv.* **-s** *n.pl.* philosophy which treats of human character and conduct, of distinction between right and wrong, and moral duty and obligations to the community [Gk. *tehos*, character].

E·thi·o·pi·a (ē·thi·ō′·pi·ạ) *n.* a kingdom in E. Africa; Abyssinia. **-n** *n.* a native of Ethiopia; a Negro; *a.* pertaining to Ethiopia [Gk. *aithein*, to burn; *ops*, the countenance].

eth·nic, eth·ni·cal (eth′·nik, ·ạl) *a.* pert. to races or peoples, esp. speech groups; ethnological; heathen; pagan. **ethnography** *n.* detailed study of the physical characteristics and social customs of racial groups. **ethnographer** *n.* **ethnographic** *a.* **ethnology** *n.* the science which traces the origin and distribution of races, their peculiarities and differences. **ethnological** *a.* **ethnologist** *n.* [Gk. *ethnos*, a people].

e·thos (ē′·thȧs) *n.* the character, customs, and habits which distinguish a people or community from another; in art, the inherent quality which conveys nobility, universality, etc. [Gk. *ethos*, custom].

eth·yl (eth′·ạl) *n.* (*Chem.*) the univalent radical C_2H_5; an antiknock fluid. — **alcohol** common alcohol [fr. *ether*, and Gk. *hulē*, material].

e·ti·o·late (ē′·ti·ạ·lāt) *v.t.* to render pale or unhealthy by denying light and fresh air; *v.i.* to become pale by being deprived of light, etc. **etiolation** *n.* [Fr. *étioler*, to become pale].

e·ti·ol·o·gy (ē·ti·ȧl′·ạ·ji·) *n.* the study of the causes of diseases. Also **aetiology** [Gk. *aitia*, cause; *logos*, discourse].

et·i·quette (et′·i·ket) *n.* the conventional code of good manners which governs behavior in society and in professional and business life decorum [Fr.].

E·ton·i·an (ē·tōn′·i·ạn) *n.* one educated at Eton College. **Eton collar**, white starched collar worn outside the jacket. **Eton jacket**, a boy's very short and tailless jacket.

E·tru·ri·an (i·troor′·i·ạn) *a.* of Etruria, the ancient Roman name of part of N.W. Italy. **Etruscan** *n.* a native of ancient Etruria; *a.* pert. to Etruria, its language, people and especially art and architecture.

e·tude (ā·tōōd′) *n.* (*Mus.*) a study; a short musical composition [Fr.].

et·y·mol·o·gy (et·ạ·mȧl′·ạ·ji·) *n.* the investigation of the origins and meanings of words

and word-forms. **etymological** *a.* **etymologically** *adv.* **etymologist** *n.* one versed in etymology [Gk. *etumon*, true meaning; *logos*, a discourse].

eu·caine (ū·kān′) *n.* a synthetic drug, resembling cocaine, used as a local anesthetic [Gk. *eu*, well; (*co*)*caine*].

eu·ca·lypt (ū′·kạ·lipt) *n.* any member of the genus Eucalyptus. **eucalyptus** *n.* the gum tree of Australia with tough and durable wood. **eucalyptol** *n.* eucalyptus oil, a colorless, aromatic, oily liquid distilled from the leaves of the eucalyptus [Gk. *eu*, well; *kaluptos*, covered].

Eu·cha·rist (ū·kạ·rist) *n.* Holy Communion; the consecrated elements at the sacrament of the Lord's Supper. **-ic, -ical** *a.* [Gk. *eucharistia*, thanksgiving].

eu·chre (ū′·kẹr) *v.t.* (*Colloq.*) to outwit; to get the best of [game of *euchre*].

Eu·clid·e·an (ū·klid′·ạ·ạn) *a.* pert. to Euclid of Alexandria who founded a school of mathematics about 300 B.C.; geometric; three dimensional.

eu·de·mon·ism, eudaemonism (ū·dē′·mạn··izm) *n.* the doctrine that the attainment of personal happiness, power and honor is the chief end and good of man. **eudemonist** *n.* [Gk. *eu*, well; *daimon*, a spirit].

eu·gen·ic (ū·jen′·ik) *a.* pertaining to eugenics; relating to, or tending towards, the production of fine offspring. **-s** *n.pl.* the scientific application of the findings of the study of heredity to human beings with the object of perpetuating those inherent and hereditary qualities which aid in the development of the human race. **eugenist** *n.* [Gk. *eu*, well; *genes*, producing].

eu·gen·ol (ū′·jạ·nȯl) *n.* an aromatic acid, obtained from the oil of cloves [Prince *Eugène* of Savoy, a patron of botany].

eu·lo·gy, eu·lo·gi·um (ū′·lạ·ji·, ū·lō′·ji·ạm) *n.* a speech or writing in praise, especially a speech praising a dead person. **eulogic, -al** *a.* commendatory; laudatory. **eulogize** *v.t.* to speak in flattering terms. **eulogist** *n.* **eulogistic** *a.* commendatory; laudatory. **eulogistically** *adv.* [Gk. *eulogia*, praise].

eu·nuch (ū′·nạk) *n.* a castrated male, especially in the Near East, in charge of the women of the harem [Gk. *eunē*, a bed; *echein*, to keep].

eu·pep·sia (ū·pep′·sha) *n.* healthy normal digestion—opposed to *dyspepsia*. **eupeptic** *a.* [Gk. *eu*, well; *peptein*, to digest].

eu·phe·mism (ū·fạ·mizm) *n.* a figure of speech where a less disagreeable word or phrase is substituted for a more accurate but more offensive one. **euphemize** *v.t.* or *v.i.* to soften down an expression. **euphemistic** *a.* [Gk. *euphēmizein*, to use words of good omen].

eu·pho·ny (ū′·fạ·ni·) *n.* pleasantness or smoothness of sound; assonance; assimilation of the sounds of syllables to facilitate pronunciation and to please the ear. **euphonic, euphonious** *a.* **euphoniously** *adv.* [Gk. *eu*, well; *phonē*, sound].

eu·pho·ri·a (yoo·fōr′·i·ạ) *n.* a sense of health and well-being which may, however, be misleading; state of irrational happiness. **euphoric** *a.* [Gk.].

eu·phu·ism (ū′·fyoo·izm) *n.* an affected, elaborate, bombastic prose style of language, so called from *Euphues*, a work by John Lyly (1553-1606), in that style; a stilted expression. **euphuist** *n.* **euphuistic** *a.*

Eu·ra·sian (yoor·ā′·zhạn) *n.* offspring of mixed European and Asiatic parentage; *a.* pert. to Europe and Asia considered as one landmass or continent [fr. *Europe* and *Asia*].

eu·rhyth·mics (yoo·riTH′·miks) *n.pl.* an art of rhythmical free movement to music [Gk. *eu*, well; *rhuthmos*, rhythm].

Eu·rope (yoor′·ạp) *n.* the continent which extends from the Atlantic Ocean to Asia. **European** *a.* belonging to Europe; *n.* a native or inhabitant of Europe.

Eu·sta·chi·an (ū·stā′·ki·ạn, ·shạn) *a.* derived from Bartolommeo *Eustachio* (c. 1500-1574), an Italian anatomist. **Eustachian tube**, open duct extending from throat near tonsils to middle ear.

Europe

eu·tec·tic (yoo·tek′·tik) *a.* easily melted or fused; *n.* in metallurgy, a particular mixture or alloy of metals whose melting point is lower than other mixtures of the same ingredients [Gk. *eu*, well; *tēktos*, molten].

eu·tha·na·sia (ū·thạ·nā′·zhạ) *n.* an easy, painless death; the putting of a person to death painlessly, esp. one in a hopeless condition. Also **euthanasy** [Gk. *eu*, well; *thanatos*, death].

e·vac·u·ate (i·vak′·yoo·āt) *v.t.* to make empty; to withdraw from; to excrete; *v.i.* to quit. **evacuant** *n.* a purgative. **evacuation** *n.* the act of evacuating, emptying out, withdrawing from; system by which noncombatants, in time of war, are sent to safe areas; (*Med.*) the discharge of fecal matter from the rectum. **evacuative** *a.* **evacuator** *n.* **evacuee** *n.* a person temporarily removed from dangerous area [L. *e*, out; *vacuus*, empty].

e·vade (i·vād′) *v.t.* to avoid by dexterity, artifice, or stratagem; to elude; to escape; to avoid; to shun; to frustrate; to baffle. **evadable** *a.* [L. *e*, out; *vadere*, to go].

e·val·u·ate (i·val′·yoo·āt) *v.t.* to appraise or determine the value of. **evaluation** *n.* estimation of worth [Fr. *évaluer*].

ev·a·nesce (ev·ạ·nes′) *v.i.* to vanish; to fade or melt away. **-nce** *n.* **-nt** *a.* vanishing; fleeting; transitory; scarcely perceptible. **-ntly** *adv.* [L. *evanescere*, to vanish].

e·van·gel (i·van′·jạl) *n.* good tidings; the Gospel; one of the first four books of the New Testament. **evangelic, evangelical** *a.* consonant with the Gospel; applied to those forms of Christianity which regard the atonement of Christ as the ground and central principle of the Christian faith; orthodox. **evangelical** *n.* one who holds the views of the evangelical school. **evangelically** *adv.* **evangelicalness, evangelicism, evangelicalism, evangelism** *n.* a religious movement to spread actively the tenets of the Gospel. **-ization** *n.* the preaching of the Gospel; conversion. **-ize** *v.t.* and *v.i.* to convert, by preaching the Gospel. **-ist** *n.* **-istic** *a.* [Gk. *eu*, well; *angelia*, tidings].

e·va·po·rate (i·vap′·ạ·rāt) *v.t.* and *v.i.* to pass off in vapor, as a fluid; to disperse; to disappear; to vaporize. **evaporable, evaporative** *a.* **evaporation** *n.* [L. *e*, out; *vapor*].

e·va·sion (i·vā′·zhạn) *n.* the act of evading or eluding; subterfuge to escape the force of an accusation, interrogation, or argument; excuse; dodge. **evasible** *a.* may be evaded. **evasive** *a.* tending to evade; marked by evasion; not straightforward. **evasively** *adv.*

eve (ēv) *n.* evening; the evening before some particular day; the period immediately preceding an event or important occasion. **even** *n.* evening (poetical). **even-song** *n.* evening prayer. **even-tide** *n.* evening [O.E. *aefen*].

e·ven (ēv′·n) *a.* level; equal in surface; uniform in rate of motion or mode of action; flat; smooth; uniform in quality; equal in amount; balanced; horizontal; equable; calm; unruffled; impartial; exactly divisible by two; *v.t.* to make even; to smooth; to equalize; *adv.* evenly; just; still; fully. **-handed** *a.* fair, impartial (of justice); just. **-ly** *adv.* **-ness** *n.* **—tempered** *a.* not irascible [O.E. *efen*].

eve·ning (ēv′·ning) *n.* the close of day; the decline or end of life. **evening dress**, formal dress worn at evening functions [O.E. *aefnung*].

e·vent (i·vent′) *n.* that which happens; a notable occurrence; affair; result; effect; item at a sports meeting. **-ful** *a.* full of exciting events; momentous. **-ual** *a.* happening as a consequence; resulting in the end; ultimate. **-uality** *n.* contingency; force of circumstances. **-ually** *adv.* **-uate** *v.i.* to happen [L. *evenire*, to come out].

ev·er (ev′·ẹr) *adv.* at any time; at all times; perpetually; constantly; unceasingly. **-glade** *n.* a swampy, grassy tract. **-green** *a.* always green; *n.* nondeciduous tree or shrub which remains green throughout the year. **-more** *adv.* unceasingly; eternally. **ever so** (*Colloq.*) extremely. **for ever and a day**, always.

ev·er·last·ing (ev·ẹr·last′·ing) *a.* enduring for ever; eternal; *n.* eternity; a flower which does not lose shape or color when dried.

e·vert (ē·vurt′) *v.t.* to turn inside out. **eversible** *a.* capable of being turned inside out. **eversion** *n.* [L. *e*, out; *vertere*, to turn].

ev·er·y (ev′·ri·) *a.* each of all; all possible. **-body** *n.* every person. **-day** *a.* ordinary. **-where** *adv.* in every place; universally. **-other**, every second; alternately [O.E. *aefre*, *yle*, ever each].

e·vict (i·vikt′) *v.t.* to dispossess by a judicial process; to expel; to eject; to turn out. **eviction** *n.* ejectment. **-or** *n.* [L. *evincere*, to conquer, to recover property by law].

ev·i·dent (ev′·a·dant) *a.* visible; clear to the vision; obvious. **evidence** *n.* that which makes evident; information in a law case; a witness; sign; indication; ground for belief; testimony; proof; attestation; corroboration; *v.t.* to render evident; to manifest. **evidential, evidentiary** *a.* furnishing evidence; proving conclusively. **-ly** *adv.* apparently; plainly. **to turn State's evidence**, to give evidence, on the part of one accused, against an accomplice [L. *e*, out; *videre*, to see].

e·vil (ē′·vl) *a.* having bad natural qualities; bad; harmful; disagreeable; vicious; corrupt; wicked; calamitous; unfortunate; *n.* harm; misfortune; wickedness; depravity; sinfulness; wrong; *adv.* in an evil manner. **— eye** *n.* the power of bewitching others by the glance of the eyes. **-ly** *adv.* **-ness** *n.* [O.E. *yfel*].

e·vince (i·vins′) *v.t.* to prove beyond any reasonable doubt; to show clearly; to make evident. **evincible** *a.* **evincibly** *adv.* **evincive** *a.* tending to prove [L. *evincere*, to prove].

e·vis·cer·ate (i·vis′·er·āt) *v.t.* to disembowel; to take out the entrails or viscera. **evisceration** *n.* [L. *e*, out; *viscera*, bowels].

e·voke (i·vōk′) *v.t.* to call up; to summon forth; to draw out; to bring to pass. **evocation** *n.* [L. *evocare*, to call out].

ev·o·lu·tion (ev·a·lōō′·shan) *n.* gradual unfolding or growth; development; evolving; the scientific theory according to which the higher forms of life have gradually developed from simple and rudimentary forms; a movement to change position, order, and direction carried out by a body of troops. **-al, -ary** *a.* **-ism** *n.* **-ist** *n.* a biologist who accepts the scientific theory of evolution [L. *evolvere*, *evolutum*, to roll out].

e·volve (i·vȯlv′) *v.t.* to develop gradually; to give off, as odors; to unfold; *v.i.* to develop, esp. by natural process; to open out [L. *evolvere*, to roll out].

ewe (ū) *n.* a female sheep [O.E. *eowy*].

ew·er (yoo′·er) *n.* a large water jug with a wide spout [O.Fr. *euwier*, fr. *eau*, water].

ex- *prefix* fr. L. *ex*, out of, used in the construction of compound terms, signifying *out of*, *from*, *former* (as ex-M. P.)

ex·ac·er·bate (igz-, iks·as′·er·bāt) *v.t.* to render more bitter; to increase the violence of; to exasperate; to irritate; to aggravate. **exacerbation** *n.* [L. *ex*, out of; *acerbus*, bitter].

ex·act (ig·zakt′) *a.* accurate; correct; precise; strict; *v.t.* to demand; to extort; to enforce; to insist upon. **-ing** *a.* making severe demands on; demanding extreme care or accuracy. **exaction** *n.* **-itude** *n.* extreme accuracy; correctness. **-ly** *adv.* precisely [L. *ex*, out; *agere*, *actum*, to drive].

ex·ag·ger·ate (ig·zaj′·a·rāt) *v.t.* to represent as greater than truth or justice will warrant; to magnify in the telling, describing, etc. **exaggeratedly** *adv.* **exaggeration** *n.* a statement going beyond the facts. **exaggerative** *a.* **exaggerator** *n.* **exaggeratory** *a.* [L. *exaggerare*, to heap up].

ex·alt (ig·zawlt′) *v.t.* to elevate as in rank; to praise; to elate with joy. **-ation** . **-ed** *a.* [L. *ex*, out; *altus*, high].

ex·am·ine (ig·zam′·in) *v.t.* to inquire into and determine; to try and assay by the appropriate tests; to inspect; to scrutinize; to explore; to investigate; to interrogate. **exam** *n.* (Colloq.) examination. **examinee** *n.* one who undergoes an examination test. **examination** *n.* the act of examining; interrogation; a scholastic test of knowledge, written or oral; judicial inquiry. **-r** *n.* [L. *examinare*, to weigh accurately].

ex·am·ple (ig·zam′·pl) *n.* a pattern; a thing illustrating a general rule; a specimen; sample [L. *exemplum*, a sample].

ex·as·per·ate (ig·zas′·per·āt) *v.t.* to irritate in a high degree; to rouse angry feelings; to provoke beyond endurance. **exasperating** *a.*

extremely trying; provoking. **exasperation** *n.* **-r** *n.* [L. *ex*, out; *asper*, rough].

ex·ca·vate (eks′·ka·vāt) *v.t.* to hollow out; to form a cavity or hole in; to dig out. **excavation** *n.* **excavator** *n.* [L.].

ex·ceed (ik·sēd′) *v.t.* to pass or go beyond the limit of; *v.i.* to be greater; to surpass; to excel. **-ing** *a.* surpassing; excessive. **-ingly** *adv.* very; to a very high degree [L. *ex*, out; *cedere*, to go].

ex·cel (ik·sel′) *v.t.* to surpass, especially in good qualities; to be better than; to exceed; to outstrip; to outdo; *v.i.* to be very good; to be pre-eminent. *pr.p.* **-ling** *pa.t.* and *pa.p.* **-led**. **-lence, -lency** *n.* complimentary title borne by ambassadors, etc. **-lent** *a.* worthy; choice; remarkably good. **-lently** *adv.* [L. *excellere*, to rise above].

ex·cept (ek·sept′) *it.* to leave out; to exclude; *v.i.* to take exception to; to object; *prep.* with exclusion of; leaving out; excepting; all but; save; *conj.* with the exception (that). **-ing** *prep.* excluding. **exception** *n.* an excepting; that which is not included in a rule; objection. **exceptionable** *a.* objectionable. **exceptionably** *adv.* **exceptional** *a.* outstanding; superior. **exceptionally** *adv.* [L. *exceptus*, taken out].

ex·cerpt (ek·surpt′) *v.t.* to extract, to quote (a passage from a book, etc.). **excerpt** (ek′·surpt) *n.* a passage, quoted or culled from a book, speech, etc. [L, *excerpere*, to pluck out].

ex·cess (ek·ses′) *n.* that which surpasses or goes beyond a definite limit; extravagance; intemperance; surplus; *a.* immoderate; more than usual. **-ive** *a.* more than enough. **-ively** *adv.* **-iveness** *n.*

ex·cheq·uer (eks·chek′·er) *n.* the public treasury [O.Fr. *eschequier*].

ex·change (eks·chānj′) *v.t.* to give or take in return for; to barter; *n.* the act of giving or taking one thing in return for another; the transfer of goods between countries; a place for buying and selling stocks, securities, etc., or where other business of a special nature is carried on; the conversion of the currency of one country to that of another; the settling of debts by the transfer of credits or the interchange of drafts, etc. **-able** *a.*

ex·cheq·uer (eks·chek′·er) *n.* the public treasury; (Brit.) the department in charge of public revenues; (Colloq.) funds [O.Fr. *eschequier*].

ex·cise (ek·sīz′) *n.* a tax or duty upon certain articles of home production and consumption; also includes licenses on certain employments, sports, etc.; *v.t.* to impose an excise duty on. **excisable** *a.* liable to excise duty [Dut. *accijns*, excise].

ex·cise (ek·sīz′) *v.t.* to cut out; to cut off; to expunge. **excision** (ek·sizh′·an) *n.* act of cutting; surgical operation [L. *ex*, out; *caedere*, to cut].

ex·cite (ek·sīt′) *v.t.* to rouse; to call into action; to stir up; to set in motion; to move to strong emotion; to stimulate. **excitability** *n.* **excitable** *a.* capable of being easily excited. **excitant** (ek·sī·tant) *a.* a stimulant. **excitation** *n.* the act of exciting; the excitement produced; the action of a stimulant on an organ of the body or of a plant. **excitative** *a.* **excitatory** *a.* tending to excite. **excited** *a.* **excitedly** *adv.* **-ment** *n.* abnormal activity; agitation; perturbation; commotion. **exciting** *a.* rousing to action; thrilling. **excitingly** *adv.* [L. *excitare*].

ex·claim (eks·klām′) *v.i.* and *v.t.* to utter loudly and vehemently; to declare suddenly. **exclamation** (eks·kla·mā′·shan) *n.* loud remark or cry, expressing joy, surprise, etc.; vehement utterance. **exclamation mark**, the mark (!) used to suggest sudden emotion. **exclamatory** *a.* [L. *ex*, out; *clamare*, to call].

ex·clude (eks·klōōd′) *v.t.* to thrust out; to shut out; to debar from; to eject. **exclusion** *n.* the act of excluding or debarring. **exclusive** *a.* excluding; debarring; limited to a special favored few. **exclusively** *adv.* **exclusiveness** *n.* [L. *ex*, out; *claudere*, to shut].

ex·cog·i·tate (eks·kaj′·a·tāt) *v.t.* to find out by thinking; to think out. **excogitation** *n.* [L. *ex*, out; *cogitare*, to think].

ex·com·mu·ni·cate (eks·kam·mūn′·a·kāt) *v.t.* to expel from the communion and membership of the church by an ecclesiastical sentence; to deprive of spiritual privileges. **excommunication** *n.* [L. *excommunicare*, to expel from a community].

ex·co·ri·ate (eks·kō′·ri·āt) *v.t.* to strip, wear, or rub the skin off; to flay. **excoriation** *n.* [L. *ex*, out; *corium*, the skin].

ex·cre·ment (eks′·ka·mant) *n.* matter excreted; feces. **-al** *a.* **-itious** *a.* resembling feces [L. *excrementum*].

ex·cres·cence (eks·kres′·ans) *n.* an abnormal protuberance which grows out of anything, as a wart or tumor; a normal outgrow, such as hair. **excrescent** *a.* growing out unnaturally; superfluous [L. *ex*, out; *crescere*, to grow].

ex·crete (eks·krēt′) *v.t.* to eject waste matter from the body; to expel. **excreta** *n.pl.* the normal discharges from the animal body as urine, feces, and sweat. **excretion** *n.* **excretive** *a.* **excretory** *a.* [L. *excernere*, to sift out].

ex·cru·ci·ate (iks·krōō′·shi·āt) *v.t.* to inflict the severest pain on; to torture, in body or mind. **excruciating** *a.* [L. *ex*, out; *cruciare*, to torture].

ex·cul·pate (eks′·kul·pāt) *v.t.* to clear from

charge or imputation of fault or guilt. **exculpation** *n.* vindication. **exculpatory** *a.* [L. *ex*, out; *culpa*, fault].

ex·cur·sion (eks·kur′·zhan) *n.* a short trip for a special purpose; deviation; digression. **-ist** *n.* one who makes a journey for pleasure. **excursive** *a.* prone to wander; rambling; digressive; diffusive. **excursus** *n.* a dissertation appended to a book and containing a fuller exposition of some relevant point [L. *ex*, out; *currere*, to run].

ex·cuse (eks·kūz′) *v.t.* to free from fault or blame; to free from obligation or duty; to pardon; to justify; to apologize; to exempt; to let off. **excuse** (eks·kūs′) *n.* a plea offered in extenuation of a fault; a pretext; an apology. **excusable** *a.* [L. *ex*, out; *causa*, a cause, accusation].

ex·e·crate (eks′·i·krāt) *v.t.* to feel or express hatred for; to curse; to abominate; to loathe; to detest utterly. **execrable** *a.* **execrably** *adv.* **execration** *n.* act of execrating; the object execrated; a curse; imprecation [L. *exsecrari*, to curse].

ex·e·cute (eks′·i·kūt) *v.t.* to carry out a task to the end, to accomplish; to give effect to; to perform; to complete; to enforce a judgment of a court of law; to sign a deed; to put to death by sentence of a court. **executable** *a.* **executant** *n.* a performer, esp. of music. **execution** *n.* the act of executing or performing; death penalty inflicted by law; performance; accomplishment; mode of performance; workmanship. **executioner** *n.* one who executes; a hangman. **executive** *a.* capable of executing or performing; administrative; *n.* a body appointed to administer the affairs of a corporation, a company, etc.; a high official of such a body; the administrative branch of a government. **executively** *adv.* **executor** *n.* (*fem.* **executrix, executress**) one who executes or performs; a person appointed under a will to fulfill its terms and administer the estate. **executorial** *a.* [L. *exsequi*, to follow out].

ex·e·ge·sis (eks·a·jē′·sis) *n.* literary commentary; interpretation and elucidation of Scripture. **exegete, exegetist** *n.* one versed in interpreting the text of the Scriptures. **exegetic, exegetical** *a.* [Gk. *ex*, out; *hēgeesthai*, to lead].

ex·em·plar (ig·zem′·pler) *n.* a person or thing to be imitated; an original or pattern; model. **-ily** in a manner to be imitated; by way of warning or example. **-iness** *n.* **-y** *a.* serving as a pattern or model; commendable [L. *exemplum*, sample].

ex·em·pli·fy (ig·zem′·pli·fī) *v.t.* to show by example; to illustrate; to make an attested copy of. *pr.p.* **-ing**. *pa.t.*, *pa.p.* **exemplified**. **exemplification** *n.* [L. *exemplum*, an example; *facere*, to make].

ex·empt (ig·zempt′) *v.t.* to free from; to grant immunity from; *a.* not included; not liable for some duty; freed from; not affected by. **-ible** *a.* **exemption** *n.* act of exempting; state of being exempt; immunity [L. *exemptum*, taken out].

ex·er·cise (eks′·er·sīz) *n.* the act of exercising; use (of limbs, faculty, etc.); use of limbs for health; practice for the sake of training; *pl.* military drill; a ceremony; *v.t.* to put in motion; to use or employ; to exert; to apply; to engage; to practice; *v.i.* to take exercise [L. *exercere*, to keep at work].

ex·ert (ig·zurt′) *v.t.* to put forth, as strength, force, or ability; to exercise; to strive; to labor. **exertion** *n.* **-ive** *a.* [L. *exserere*, to put forth].

ex·hale (eks·hāl′) *v.t.* to breathe out; to give off as vapor or odor; to discharge; *v.i.* to rise or be given off as vapor. **exhalable** *a.* **exhalant** *a.* having the property of exhalation. **exhalation** *n.* [L. *ex*, out; *halare*, to breathe].

ex·haust (ig·zawst′) *v.t.* to draw out or drain off completely; to empty; to weaken; to tire; to use up; to squander; to discuss thoroughly; *n.* conduit through which steam, waste gases and the like, after performing work, pass from the cylinders to the outer air; the steam or gases themselves. **-ed** *a.* tired out; fatigued; emptied; drawn out; consumed. **-ible** *a.* **exhaustion** *n.* act of exhausting or consuming; state of being completely deprived of strength or vitality. **-ive** *a.* tending to exhaust; comprehensive; thorough. **-ively** *adv.* [L. *ex*, out; *haurire*, *haustum*, to draw].

exhibit 78 exquisite

exhaust

ex·hib·it (ig·zi′·bit) *v.t.* to hold forth or to expose to view; to present; to show; to display; to manifest; to express; *n.* anything displayed at an exhibition. **-er, -or** *n.* one who sends articles to an exhibition for display. **exhibition** (ek·sa·bi′·shan) *n.* the act of exhibiting; show; display; a public show (of works of art, etc.). **exhibitionism** *n.* a tendency to show off before people. **exhibitionist** *n.* **exhibitory** *a.* [L. *exhibere*, to hold forth].

ex·hil·a·rate (ig·zil′·a·rāt) *v.t.* to make cheerful; to animate. **exhilarant** *a.* exhilarating; exciting joy, mirth, or pleasure; *n.* anything which exhilarates. **exhilarating** *a.* **exhilaration** *n.* [L. *exhilarare*, fr. *hilaris*, happy].

ex·hort (ig·zawrt′) *v.t.* to incite by words of advice; to advise strongly; to admonish earnestly. **-ation** *n.* **-ative, -atory** *a.* tending to exhort [L. *ex; hortari*, to encourage].

ex·hume (iks·hūm′) *v.t.* to dig up, as from a grave; to unearth; to disinter. **exhumation** *n.* **-r** *n.* [L. *ex*, out; *humus*, the ground].

ex·i·gent (ek′·sa·jant) *a.* calling for immediate action or aid; pressing; urgent. **exigence, exigency** *n.* urgent want; emergency. **exigible** *a.*

ex·i·gu·i·ty (ek·sa·gū′·i·ti·) *n.* smallness; slenderness. **exiguous** *a.* [L. *exiguus*].

ex·ile (eg′·zīl, ek′·sīl) *n.* separation or enforced banishment; a banished person; one living away from his native country; *v.t.* to banish or expel [L. *exsilium*, banishment].

ex·ist (eg·zist′) *v.t.* to be; to have a being, whether material or spiritual; to continue in being; to live; to subsist; to occur. **-ence** *n.* the condition of objectivity; being; state of being actual; entity; life. **-ential** *a.* consisting in existence; ontological. **-entialism** *n.* (*Philos.*) a school which describes, analyzes and classifies the experiences of an individual mind considered as *existences*. **-ibility** *n.* [L. *existere*, to come forth].

ex·it (eg′·zit, ek′·sit) *n.* a departure; a way out of a place; stage direction to indicate when an actor is to leave the stage. **exeunt**, stage direction [L. = he goes out].

ex·o- *prefix* fr. Gk. *exo*, outside, without.

ex·o·dus (ek′·sa·das) *n.* a departure, esp. of a crowd. **Exodus** *n.* (*Bib.*) the second book of the Old Testament [Gk. *exodos*, way out].

ex·og·a·my (eks·ág′·a·mi·) *n.* a custom compelling a man to marry outside his tribe or clan. **exogamous** *a.* [Gk. *exo*, outside; *gamos*, marriage].

ex·on·er·ate (eg·zán′·er·āt) *v.i.* to declare free from blame or responsibility; to relieve of a charge or obligation. **exoneration** *n.* **exonerator** *n.* [L. *exonerare*, to unburden].

ex·o·ra·ble (ek′·ser·a·bl) *a.* capable of being moved by entreaty [L. *exorare*, to persuade by entreaty].

ex·or·bi·tant (ig·zawr′·ba·tant) *a.* very excessive; extravagant. **exorbitance, exorbitancy** *n.* **-ly** *adv.* [L. *ex*, out; *orbis*, a circle].

ex·or·cise (ek′·sawr·sīz) *v.t.* to cast out (evil spirits) by invocation; to free a person of evil spirits. **exorcism** *n.* [Gk. *exorkizein*].

ex·or·di·um (ig·zawr′·di·am) *n.* a beginning; the introduction part of a discourse or treatise. **exordial** *a.* [L. fr. *ex*, out; *ordiri*, to begin].

ex·o·skel·e·ton (ek·sō·skel′·a·tan) *n.* (*Zool.*) external hard supporting structure such as scales, nails, feathers. **exoskeletal** *a.* [Gk. *exo*, outside].

---

exoskeleton

ex·o·ter·ic, extrical (ek·sa·ter′·ik, ·al) *a.* capable of being understood by, or suited for, the many; not secret; the opposite to *esoteric* [Gk. *exoterikos*, external].

ex·ot·ic (eg·zát′·ik) *a.* introduced from a foreign country; not indigenous; unusual or colorful. **-ism** (ig·zát′·i·cizm) *n.* [Gk. *exotikos*].

ex·pand (ik·spand′) *v.t.* to spread out; to enlarge; to increase in volume or bulk; to extend; to stretch; to develop. **expanse** *n.* a wide extent of surface. **-able, expansible** *a.* **expansibly** *adv.* **expansion** *n.* act of expanding; condition of being expanded; increase in one or more of the dimension of a body; spreading; distension; enlargement. **expansive** *a.* widely extended; effusive; communicative; diffusive. **expansively** *adv.* **expansiveness** *n.* [L. *ex*, out; *pandere*, to stretch].

ex·pa·ti·ate (ik·spā′·shi·āt) *v.i.* to speak or write at great length (on); **expatiation** *n.* **expatiative** *a.* [L. *exspatiari*, to wander].

ex·pa·tri·ate (eks·pā′·tri·āt) *v.t.* to banish from one's native land; to exile; (·it) *n.* **expatriation** *n.* [L. *ex*, out; *patria*, fatherland].

ex·pect (ek·spekt′) *v.t.* to look forward to; to look on as likely to happen; to look for as one's due; to anticipate; (*Colloq.*) to suppose. **-ance, -ancy** *n.* the act or state of expecting; that which is expected. **-ant** *a.* waiting; hopeful. **-antly** *adv.* **-ation** *n.* act or state of looking forward to an event. **-ations** *n.pl.* prospects in life; probable gain [L. *exspectare*, to look out for].

ex·pec·to·rate (ek·spek′·ta·rāt) *v.t.* or *v.i.* to spit; to cough up. **expectorant** *a.* aiding expectoration; *n.* a drug or agent which promotes expectoration. **expectoration** *n.* the act of expectorating; sputum; spittle [L. *ex*, out; *pectus*, breast].

ex·pe·di·ent (ik·spē′·di·ant) *a.* suitable; fitting; advisable; politic; desirable; convenient; useful; *n.* suitable means to accomplish an end; means devised or employed in an exigency; shift; contrivance. **expediency** *n.* **-ly** *adv.* [L. *expedire*, to be fitting].

ex·pe·dite (ek′·spi·dīt) *v.t.* to free from hindrance or obstacle; to hurry forward; *a.* quick; ready; unencumbered. **-ly** *adv.* **expedition** *n.* a journey for a specific purpose; the persons and equipment involved; efficient promptness; speed; **expeditionary** *a.* **expeditious** *a.* prompt; speedy [L. *ex*, out; *pes, pedis*, a foot].

ex·pel (ek·spel′) *v.t.* to drive or force out; to cast out; to eject; to exclude; *pr.p.* **-ling.** *pa.t.* and *pa.p.* **-led** [L. *ex*, out; *pellere*, to drive].

ex·pend (ek·spend′) *v.t.* to consume by use; to spend; to use up; to exhaust. **-able.** **-iture** *n.* act of expending; that which is expended; expense; cost. **expense** *n.* big outlay; cost; expenditure. **expensive** *a.* costly; dear [L. *expendere*, to weigh out].

ex·pe·ri·ence (ek·spir′·i·ans) *n.* practical knowledge gained by trial or practice; personal proof or trial; continuous practice; evidence; an event in one's life; *v.t.* to undergo; to feel; to endure; to encounter. **-d** *a.* skilled; expert; wise; capable; thoroughly conversant with. **experiential** *a.* relating to or having experience; empirical [L. *experiri*, to try].

ex·per·i·ment (ek·sper′·a·mant) *n.* the action of trying anything; putting to the proof or test; practical test; a trial to find out what happens; *v.i.* to make an experiment. **-al** *a.* founded on or known by experiment; pertaining to experiment. **-alist** *n.* **-ally** *adv.* **-ation** *n.* **-tative** *a.* **-er, -ist** *n.* [L. *experiri*, to try].

ex·pert (ek·spurt′) *a.* taught by use, practice, or experience; adroit; dexterous; skillful. (ex′·purt) *n.* an authority; a specialist. **-ly** *adv.* **-ness** *n.* [L. *expertus*, having tried].

ex·pi·ate (eks′·pi·āt) *v.t.* to make satisfaction or reparation for; to atone for; to make amends for. **expiable** *a.* **expiation** *n.* [L. *expiare*, to make amends for].

ex·pire (ek·spir′) *v.t.* to breathe out; to emit; to exhale; *v.i.* to die; to die away; to come to an end. **expirant** *a.* one who is dying. **expiration** *n.* the exhalation of air from the lungs; end of a period of time; close; termination. **expiratory** *a.* **expiring** *a.* **expiry** *n.* conclusion [L. *ex*, out; *spirare*, to breathe].

ex·plain (eks·plān′) *v.t.* to make plain, manifest, or intelligible; to account for; to elucidate; to define. **-able** *a.* **explanation** *n.* act or method of explaining, expounding, or interpreting; the meaning of or reason given for anything. **explanative, explanatory** *a.* serving to explain [L. *explanare*, to make smooth].

ex·ple·tive (eks′·pli·tiv) *a.* serving only to fill out a sentence, etc.; added for ornamentation only; *n.* a word inserted to fill up or to add force to a phrase; an exclamation; an oath [L. *expletivus*, filling out].

---

ex·pli·cate (eks′·pli·kāt) *v.t.* to unfold the meaning of; to explain; to interpret; to elucidate. **explicable** *a.* **explication** *n.* **explicative, explicatory** *a.* [L. *explicare*, to unfold].

ex·plic·it (iks·plis′·it) *a.* stated in detail; stated, not merely implied; unambiguous; clear; unequivocal. **-ly** *adv.* **-ness** *n.* [L. *explicitus*].

ex·plode (ik·splōd′) *v.t.* to cause to blow up; to discredit; to expose (a theory, etc.); *v.i.* to burst with a loud report; to become furious with rage; to burst into unrestrained laughter. **-d** *a.* rejected; debunked. **explosion** *n.* the act of exploding; sudden release of gases, accompanied by noise and violence; a manifestation of rage. **explosive** *a.* liable to explode; *n.* a chemical intended to explode [L. *ex*, out; *plaudere*, to clap with the hands].

explosion

ex·ploit (eks·ploit′) *n.* a brilliant feat; a heroic deed; remarkable action, often in a bad sense; *v.t.* to make the most of; to utilize for personal gain. **-able** *a.* **-age, -ation** *n.* **-er** *n.* [Fr.].

ex·plore (ik·splōr′) *v.t.* to search through with the view of making discovery; to leave the beaten tracks; to investigate; to examine. **exploration** *n.* **exploratory** *a.* **-r** *n.* [L. *explorare*, to search out].

ex·plo·sive See **explode**.

ex·po·nent (ek·spō′·nant) *n.* one who expounds, demonstrates, or explains; a symbol; in algebra, index number or quantity, written to the right of and above another to show how often the latter is to be multiplied by itself, e.g. $a^3 = a \times a \times a$. [L. *ex*, out; *ponere*, to place].

ex·port (eks·pōrt′) *v.t.* to send goods or produce out of a country. (ex′·port) *n.* act of exporting; that which is exported. **-able** *a.* **-ation** *n.* **-er** *n.* [L. *ex*, out; *portare*, to carry].

ex·pose (ik·spōz′) *v.t.* to lay open; to leave unprotected; to exhibit; to disclose; to submit a photographic plate or film to the light. **exposé** (eks·pō·zā′) *n.* an exposure or disclosure of discreditable facts. **exposition** *n.* act of exhibiting or expounding; exhibition; display; explanation. **expositor** *n.* **expository** *a.* **exposure** *n.* the act of exposing, laying bare, or disclosing shady or doubtful transactions; the state of being laid bare; aspect of a building relative to the cardinal points of the compass [L. *ex*, out, *ponere*, to place].

ex·pos·tu·late (ik·spás′·cha·lāt) *v.i.* to remonstrate with; to reason earnestly. **expostulation** *n.* **expostulative, expostulatory** *a.* [L. *expostulare*, to demand urgently].

ex·pound (ek·spound′) *v.t.* to explain; to set forth; to interpret; [L. *exponere*].

ex·press (ik·spres′) *v.t.* to make known one's opinions or feelings; to put into words; to represent by pictorial art; to designate; to press or squeeze out; to send by express; *a.* definitely stated; closely resembling; specially designed; explicit; clear; plain; speedy; *adv.* post-haste; by express messenger or train; specially; on purpose; *n.* a messenger sent on a special errand; a fast train making few stops en route; a message. **-ible** *a.* **-ion** *n.* act of expressing; lively or vivid representation of meaning, sentiment, or feeling; the reflection of character or mood in the countenance; utterance; declaration; phrase; term; remark; aspect; look; (*Math.*) a quantity denoted by algebraic symbols. **-ionism** *n.* an antirealistic art theory that all art depends on the expression of the artist's creative self. **-ionist** *n.* **-ionless** *a.* **-ive** *a.* full of expression. **-ively** *adv.* **-iveness** *n.* **-ly** *adv.* plainly; explicitly; specially [L. *expressus*, squeezed out, clearly stated].

ex·pro·pri·ate (eks·prō′·pri·āt) *v.t.* to dispossess; to take out of the owner's hand. **expropriation** *n.* [L. *ex*, out; *proprius*, one's own].

ex·pul·sion (ik·spul′·shan) *n.* the act of expelling or casting out; ejection; banishment. **expulsive** *a.* [L. *expulsus*, driven out].

ex·punge (ik·spunj′) *v.t.* to strike out; to erase; to obliterate; to cancel [L. *expungere*, to strike out].

ex·pur·gate (ek′·sper·gāt) *v.t.* to remove objectionable parts (from a book, etc.); to cleanse; to purify; to purge. **expurgation** *n.* **expurgator** *n.* [L. *expurgare*, to purge].

ex·qui·site (eks′·kwi·zit) *a.* of extreme beauty or delicacy; of surpassing excellence; extreme, as pleasure or pain. **-ly** [L. *exquisitus*, sought out].

ex·ser·vice (eks'·sur·vis) *a.* of or pertaining to one who has served in the armed forces.

ex·sic·cate (ek'·si·kāt) *v.t.* to dry up; to evaporate. **exsiccation** *n.* [L. *ex*, out; *siccus*, dry].

ex·tant (ik·stant', ek'·stant) *a.* still existing [L. *ex*, out; *stare*, to stand].

ex·tem·po·re (ik·stem'·pa·ri·) *a.* or *adv.* without previous study or meditation; offhand; on the spur of the moment. **extemporal, ex-temporaneous, extemporary** *a.* impromptu. **extemporization** *n.* act of speaking extempore. **extemporize** *v.i.* to speak extempore; to create music on the inspiration of the moment [L. *ex*, out of; *tempus, temporis*, time].

ex·tend (ik·stend') *v.t.* to prolong in a single direction, as a line; to stretch out; to prolong in duration; to offer; to expand; to enlarge; *v.i.* to be continued in length or breadth; to stretch. **-ible, extensible, extensile** *a.* capable of being stretched, expanded, or enlarged. **extensibility** *n.* **extension** *n.* **extensional** *a.* **extensive** *a.* having wide extent; large; comprehensive; spacious. **extensively** *adv.* **extensiveness** *n.* **extensor** *n.* a muscle which straightens or extends a limb. **extent** *n.* space or degree to which a thing is extended; size; scope, a space; area; degree; volume; length; expanse [L. *extendere*, to stretch out].

ex·ten·u·ate (ek·sten'·yoo·āt) *v.t.* to palliate, as a crime; to mitigate; to make less blameworthy. **extenuating** *a.* **extenuation** *n.* [L. *ex*, out; *tenuare*, to make thin].

ex·te·ri·or (ek·stir'·i·ęr) *a.* outer; outward; external; coming from without; *n.* the outside; outer surface; outward appearance.

ex·ter·mi·nate (ek·stur'·ma·nāt) *v.t.* to root out; to destroy utterly. **extermination** *n.* **exterminator** *n.* [L. *ex*, out; *terminus*, boundary].

ex·ter·nal (ik·stur'·nal) *a.* not inherent or essential; outward; exterior; superficial; extrinsic; apparent; **-s** *n.pl.* outward appearances; **-ly** *adv.* [L. *externus*, outside].

ex·tinct (eks·tingkt') *a.* extinguished; put out; no longer existing; dead. **-ion** *n.* [L. *extinctus*].

ex·tin·guish (ek·sting'·gwish) *v.t.* to put out; to put an end to; to quench; to destroy; to obscure by superior splendor. **-able** *a.* **-er** *n.* [L. *extinguere*, to quench].

extinguisher

ex·tir·pate (ek'·ster·pāt) *v.t.* to pull or pluck up by the roots; to destroy utterly. **extirpable** *a.* **extirpation** *n.* **extirpator** *n.* [L. *exstirpare* fr. *stirps*, stem].

ex·tol (ek·stōl') *v.t.* to praise highly. *pr.p.* **-ling.** *pa.t.* and *pa.p.* **-led** [L. *extollere*, to lift up].

ex·tort (ek·stawrt') *v.t.* to obtain by force or threats; to extract. **extorsive** *a.* serving or tending to extort. **-ion** *n.* act of extorting; illegal compulsion; unjust exaction. **-ionary, -ionate** *a.* **-ioner, -ionist** *n.* [L. *ex*, out; *torquere*, to wrench].

ex·tra- *prefix* fr. L. meaning *beyond, on the other side of, on the outside of*; used in many compound words denoting *beyond, without, more than, further than*, or generally, *excess*. (eks'·tra) *a.* extraordinary; additional; *adv.* unusually; especially; *n.* something extra; over and above the usual charges; additional item; special edition of a news paper; a person employed casually by film producers to play a minor role in a production. **-curricular** *a.* pert. to the studies or activities which are not included in the curriculum. **-judicial** *a.* out of the proper court or the ordinary legal procedure. **-mural** *a.* beyond the walls, as outside a university. **-ive** *a.* **-or** *n.* **-sensory** (eks·tra·sen'·ser·i·) *a.* beyond the senses. **-sensory perception**, (*abbrev. E.S.P.*) an awareness of events not presented to the physical senses. **-territorial** *a.* outside the limits of a country or its jurisdiction [L.].

ex·tract (ik·strakt') *v.t.* to take out, esp. by force; to obtain against a person's will; to get by pressure, distillation, etc.; to copy out; to quote; to elicit; (*Math.*) to calculate. **extract** (eks'·trakt) *n.* matter obtained by distillation; concentrated drug, solution, syrup, etc.; a passage from a book, speech, etc. **-able, -ible** *a.* **extraction** *n.* act of extracting; that which is extracted; chemical operation of removing one or more substances from others by means of a solvent; parentage; ancestry; lineage; descent; arithmetical process of finding the root of a number. **-ive** *a.* **-or** *n.* [L. *ex*, out; *trahere*, *tractum*, to draw].

ex·tra·dite (eks'·tra·dīt) *v.t.* to deliver up a fugitive to another nation or authority. **extradition** *n.* [L. *ex*, out of; *tradere*, to deliver].

ex·tra·ne·ous (ek·strā'·ni·as) *a.* not naturally belonging to or dependent on a thing; not essential; foreign. **-ly** *adv.* [L. *extraneus*].

ex·tra·or·di·na·ry (eks·trawr'·da·ner·i·) *a.* beyond or out of the common order or method; exceeding the common degree or measure; employed on a special errand or duty. **extraordinarily** *adv.* **extraordinariness** *n.* [L. *extra*, beyond; *ordo, ordinis*, order].

ex·trav·a·gant (eks·trav'·a·gant) *a.* profuse in expense; excessive; prodigal; wasteful; unrestrained. **extravagance** *n.* **extravagate** *v.i.* to wander beyond proper limits [L. *extra*, beyond, *vagari*, to wander].

ex·trav·a·gan·za (eks·trav'·a·gan'·za) *n.* an extravagant, farcical, or fantastic composition, literary or musical [It.].

ex·tra·va·sate (eks·trav'·a·sāt) *v.t.* to let out of the proper vessels, as blood; *a.* let out of its proper vessel [L. *extra*, beyond; *vas*, a vessel].

ex·tra·vert See **extrovert.**

ex·treme (ek·strēm') *a.* at the utmost point, edge, or border; outermost; of a high or highest degree; severe; excessive; last; most urgent; *n.* the utmost point or degree; a thing at one end or the other; the first and last of a series; great necessity. **-ly** *adv.* **extremism** *n.* holding extreme views or doctrines. **extremist** *n.* **extremity** *n.* the most distant point or side. **extremities** *n.pl.* hands and feet; arms and legs; extreme measures [L. *extremus*].

ex·tri·cate (eks'·tra·kāt) *v.t.* to free from difficulties or perplexities. **extricable** *a.* **extrication** *n.* [L. *extricare*].

ex·trin·sic, extrinsical (eks·trin'·sik, ·al) *a.* developing or having its origin from outside the body; not essential; not inherent [L. *extrinsecus*, on the outside].

ex·tro·vert (eks'·trō·vert) *n.* in psychology, a person whose emotions express themselves readily in external actions and events, as opposed to an *introvert*. **extroversion** *n.* [L. *extra*, outside of; *vertere*, to turn].

ex·trude (eks·trōōd') *v.t.* to thrust out; to press out; to expel. **extrusion** *n.* [L. *ex*, out; *trudere*, to thrust].

ex·u·ber·ant (ek·zoō'·ber·ant) *a.* effusive; vivacious; over abundant; prolific; **exuberance, exuberancy** *n.* state of being exuberant. **-ly** *adv.* [L. *ex:uber*, fertile].

ex·ude (eg·zoōd') *v.t.* to discharge through the pores, as sweat; to discharge sap by incision, as a tree; *v.i.* to ooze out; to escape slowly, as a liquid [L. *ex*, out; *sudare*, to sweat].

ex·ult (eg·zult') *v.i.* to rejoice exceedingly; to triumph; **-ance, -ancy** *n.* **-ant** *a.* **-tation** *n.* [L. *exultare*, to leap for joy].

ex·u·vi·ae (eg·zoō'·vi·ē) *n.pl.* (*Zool.*) cast off skin, teeth, shells, etc. of animals. **exuvial** *a.* **exuviate** *v.i.* [L. *exuere*, to strip off].

eye (i) *n.* the organ of sight or vision; the power of seeing; sight; perforation; eyelet; bud; shoot; view; observation; judgment; keen sense of value; vigilance; anything resembling an eye; a small staple or ring to receive a door hook; an aperture for observing; *v.t.* to observe closely or fixedly; to look at; to view; *pr.p.* **eying** or **-ing.** *pa.t.* and *pa.p.* **-d** (id). **-ball** *n.* the globe of the eye. **-brow** *n.* the arch of hairs. **-d** *a.* having eyes; spotted as if with eyes. **-glass** *n.* a glass to assist the sight; a monocle; the eye-piece of an optical instrument. *pl.* spectacles. **-lash** *n.* one of the hairs which edge the eyelid. **-let** *n.* a small eye or hole for a lace or cord, as in garments, sails, etc.; *v.i.* to make eyelets. **-lid** *n.* folds of skin which may be drawn at will over the eye. **— opener** *n.* surprising news; revealing statement. **-piece** *n.* lens in an optical instrument by means of which the observer views the image of the object formed in the focus of the other lenses. **-sight** *n.* power of vision; view; observation. **-sore** *n.* an object offensive to the eye. **-tooth** *n.* either of the two canine teeth of the upper jaw. **-wash** *n.* eye lotion. **-witness** *n.* one who gives testimony as to what he actually saw. **the green eye,** jealousy. **to see eye to eye,** to agree; to think alike [O.E. *eage*].

ey·rie (ār'·i·) *n.* the nest of a bird of prey.

F

fa·ble (fā′bl) *n.* a short tale or prolonged personification, often with animal characters, intended to convey a moral truth; a myth; a fiction; a falsehood; *v.t.* and *v.i.* to tell fables; to lie. *a.* mythical; legendary. **fabular fabulize** *v.i.* to compose fables. **fabulist** *n.* **fabulous** *a.* feigned or fabled; amazing; exaggerated [L. *fabula*, a story].

fab·ric (fab′.rik) *n.* structure; framework; woven, knitted or felted cloth; texture. **fabricate** *v.t.* to frame; to construct mechanically; to build according to standard specifications; to assemble from standardized components; to fake; to concoct. **-ation** *n.* **-ator** *n.* [L. *fabrica*, a workshop].

fa·cade (fa·sad′) *n.* the front view or elevation of a building [Fr. fr. It. *facciata*, the front of a building].

face (fās) *n.* the front of the head including forehead, eyes, nose, mouth, cheeks and chin; the outer appearance; cast of countenance; the outer or upper surface of any thing; the dial of a clock, etc.; the front; prestige; *v.t.* to confront; to stand opposite to; to admit the existence of (as facts); to oppose with courage; to put a layer of different material on to, or to trim an outer surface; *v.i.* to turn. — **card** *n.* a playing card, as king, queen and jack; — **cloth** *n.* a square of Turkish towelling for washing the face. — **lifting** *n.* an operation performed to remove wrinkles from the face. — **piece** *n.* the front part of a respirator. — **value** *n.* apparent worth. **facial** *a.* pert. to the face; *n.* (*Colloq.*) a beauty treatment for the face. **facies** (fā′·shi.ēz) *n.* the general appearance of anything. **facing** *n.* a covering in front for ornament or defense; material applied to the edge of a garment. [L. *facies*, a face].

facet (fas′.it) *n.* a small surface, as of a crystal or precious stone; aspect; *a.* having facets [Fr. *facette*, dim. of *face*].

fa·ce·tious (fa·sē′.shas) *a.* witty; jocular. **facetiae** (fa·sē′·shi.ē) *n.pl.* witty or humorous writings or sayings. *adv.* **-ness** *n.* [L. *facetus*, elegant].

fac·ile (fas′.l) *a.* easy; fluent; easily done; courteous; glib. **-ly** *adv.* **-ness** *n.* **facilitate** *v.t.* to make easy; to expedite. **facilitation** *n.* **facility** *n.* ease; deftness; aptitude; easiness of access [L. *facilis*, easy].

fac·sim·i·le (fak·sim′.a.li.) *n.* an exact copy; identical; *v.t.* to make a facsimile. **facsimilist** *n.* **in facsimile**, accurately [L. *fac*, make (imper.); *simile*, like].

fact (fakt) *n.* anything done; anything actually true; that which has happened. **matter-of-fact** *a.* pert. to facts; actual. **matter-of-fact** *a.* prosaic; unimaginative [L. *factum*, thing done].

fac·tion (fak′.shan) *n.* a group of people working together, esp. for subversive purposes; dissension; party clique. **factious** *a.* **factiously** *adv.* [L. *factio*, a doing].

fac·ti·tious (fak·tish′.as) *a.* made or imitated by art, oppos. of *natural*; artificial; manufactured [L. *factitare*, to do frequently].

fac·tor (fak′.ter) *n.* (*Math.*) one of numbers which, multiplied together, give a given number; a contributory element or determining cause; *v.t.* (*Math.*) to express as a product of two or more quantities. **-ial** *a.* pert. to a factor. *v.t.* (*Math.*) to find the factors of a given number. **-ship** *n.* **-y** *n.* a building where things are manufactured [L. *facere*, to do].

fac·to·tum (fak·tō′.tam) *n.* one who manages all kinds of work for an employer [L. *fac*, do (imper.); *totum*, all].

fac·ul·ty (fa′.kal.ti.) *n.* ability or power to act; mental aptitude; talent; natural physical function; a university department; the teaching body; the members of a profession, esp. medical; authorization. **facultative** *a.* optional [L. *facultas*, power].

fad (fad) *n.* a pet whim; a fancy or notion. **-dish** *a.* **-dy** *a.* **-dist** *n.* [etym. unknown].

fade (fād) *v.i.* to lose freshness, brightness, or strength gradually; to disappear slowly.

-less *a.* not liable to fade; fast (of dye) [O.Fr. *fade*, dull].

fa·er·ie, faery (fē′.ri.) *n.* fairyland; *a.* pert. to fairyland; fairy-like [var. of *fairy*].

fag (fag) *n.* toil; a tedious task; (Br. *Slang*) a cigarette; *v.t.* to exhaust; **-end** *n.* the tail end of anything; a remnant [etym. doubtful].

fag·ot, fag·got (fag′.at) *n.* a bundle of sticks for fuel; a bundle of steel rods cut for welding; *v.t.* to tie together; to embroider with a fagot stitch. **-ing, faggoting,** *n.* a kind of embroidery [Fr. *fagot*, a bundle of sticks].

Fahr·en·heit (far′.an.hīt) *n.* the term applied to a type of thermometer graduated so that freezing point of water is fixed at 32°, and boiling point at 212°. [German physicist, *Fahrenheit* (1686-1736)].

fail (fāl) *v.i.* to be lacking; to diminish; to deteriorate; to miss; to be unsuccessful in; to go bankrupt; *v.t.* to disappoint or desert; to omit; (*Colloq.*) to refuse to pass a candidate under examination. *pr.p.* **-ing.** *pa.p.* **-ed. -ing** *n.* a fault; a weakness; a shortcoming; just; in default of. **-ure** *n.* bankruptcy; lack of success [O.Fr. *faillir*, to deceive].

fain (fān) *adv.* (*Poetic*) gladly. [O.E. *faegen*, joyful].

faint (fānt) *a.* lacking strength; indistinct; giddy; timorous; *v.i.* to become weak; to grow discouraged; to swoon; *n.* a swoon. **-heart** *n.* and *a.* **-hearted** *a.* cowardly; timorous. *adv.* indistinctly [O.Fr. *feint*, *pa.p.* of *feindre*, to feign].

fair (fer) *a.* clear; free from fault or stain; light-colored; blond; beautiful; not cloudy; hopeful; just; plausible; middling; *adv.* in a fair or courteous manner; according to what is just. — **copy** *n.* a rewritten, corrected copy. — **game**, open to banter. **-ish** *a.* rather fair. **-ly** *adv.* justly; tolerably; wholly. **-ness** *n.* — **play** *n.* straightforward justice. — **spoken** *a.* polite; plausible. **-way** *n.* a navigable channel on a river; (*Golf*) the stretch of ground between the tee and the green, which is freed from rough grass. **fair and square**, honest; honestly [O.E. *faeger*, pleasant].

fair (fer) *n.* periodic competitive exhibition for showing produce of a district; a sale of fancy articles to raise money for charitable purposes [O.Fr. *feire*, L. *feria*, a holiday].

fair·y (fer′.i.) *n.* an imaginary creature in the form of a diminutive human being, supposed to meddle, for good or for ill, with the affairs of men; *a.* fairy-like; dainty. **-land** *n.* land of the fairies; wonderland. — **tale** *n.* a story about fairies and magic; (*Colloq.*) improbable tale [O.Fr. *faerie*, enchantment].

faith (fāth) *n.* belief, esp. in a revealed religion; trust or reliance; a system of religious doctrines believed in; loyalty; pledged word. **-ful** *a.* loyal; reliable; honorable; exact. **-fully** *adv.* **-fulness** *n.* [O.Fr. *fei*, faith].

fake (fāk) *v.t.* to conceal the defects of, by artifice; to copy, as an antique, and pass it off as genuine; *v.i.* to pretend; *n.* a fraud; a deception; a forgery; a faker. **-r** *n.* [prob.

Dut. *feague*, to touch up].

fa·kir (fa.kir′, fā′.ker) *n.* a member of a sect of religious mendicants in India [Ar. *faqir*, a poor man].

Fa·lan·gists (fa.lanj′.ists) *n.pl.* Spanish military Fascists, who co-operated with Franco during Spanish Civil War (1936-39).

fal·cate (fal′.kāt) *a.* (*Bot.* and *Zool.*) sickle shaped; crescent [L. *falx*. a sickle].

fal·con (faw′.kn, fàl′.kan) *n.* a sub-family of birds of prey, allied to the hawk, with strong curved beak and long sickle-shaped claws; one of these birds, trained to hunt game; **-er** *n.* one who breeds and trains falcons or hawks for hunting wild-fowl. **-ry** *n.* the sport of flying hawks in pursuit of game [O.Fr. *faucon*, a falcon].

fal·de·ral (fal·der·al′) *n.* the refrain to a song; anything trifling; a gew-gaw. Also

fald·stool (fawld′.stool) *n.* a portable, folding stool; stool before which kings kneel at their coronation; a litany-desk [O.H. Ger. *faldstuol*, a folding stool].

fall (fawl) *v.i.* to descend from a higher to a lower position; to drop; to collapse; to abate; to decline in value; to become degraded; to happen; to be captured. *pr.p.* **-ing.** *pa.t.* **fell.** *pa.p.* **-en.** *n.* the act of falling; a drop; capitulation; the amount (of rain, snow, etc.) deposited in a specified time; a cascade; a wrestling bout; a moral lapse, esp. that of Adam and Eve; diminution in value, amount, or volume; the autumn. **-en** *a.* prostrate; degraded; of loose morals. **-ing-star** *n.* a meteor. **-out** *n.* radioactive particles which descend to earth after a nuclear explosion. [O.E. *feallan*, to fall].

fal·la·cy (fal′.a.si.) *n.* deceptive appearance; a delusion; an apparently forcible argument which is really illogical; sophistry. **fallacious** *a.* misleading; illogical. **fallaciously** *adv.* [L. *fallax*, deceitful].

fal·li·ble (fal′.a.bl) *a.* liable to error; not reliable. **fallibility** *n.* the quality of being fallible. **fallibly** *adv.* [L. *fallere*, to fail].

fal·low (fal′.ō) *a.* left untilled for a season; (*Fig.*) untrained (of the mind); *n.* land which has lain untilled and unsown for a year or more; *v.t.* to plough without sowing [etym. doubtful, prob. O.E. *fealh*, a harrow].

fallow (fal′.ō) *a.* a pale yellow or light brown color. [O.E. *fealwes*, of a brown color].

false (fawls) *a.* untrue; inaccurate; dishonest; deceptive; artificial. — **face** *n.* a mask. **-hood** *n.* an untruth; a lie. **-ly** *adv.* **-ness** *n.* **falsifiable** *a.* capable of being falsified. **falsification** *n.* **falsifier** *n.* one who falsifies. **falsify** *v.t.* to distort the truth; to forge; to tamper with; to prove to be untrue. **falsity** *n.* an untrue statement; deception [L. *falsus*, mistaken].

fal·set·to (fawl·set′.ō) *n.* forced high notes esp. of a male voice [It. dim. of *falso*, false].

fal·ter (fawl′.ter) *v.i* to stumble; to hesitate; to lack resolution; to stammer.

fame (fām) *n.* public report or rumor, esp. good repute. **-d** *a.* celebrated. **famous** *a.* celebrated; noted; (*colloq.*) excellent. **famously** *adv.* [L. *fama*, a report].

fa·mil·iar (fa.mil′.yer) *a.* intimate; informal; free; unconstrained; well-known; current; conversant with; *n.* a close acquaintance. **-ize** *v.t.* to make familiar; (*Reflex.*) to get to know thoroughly (foll. by *with*). **familiarity** *n.* intimacy; forwardness. **-ly** *adv.* [L. *familiaris*, pert. to a household].

fam·i·ly (fam′.a.li.) *n.* parents and their children; the children of the same parents; descendants of one common ancestor; (*Biol.*) group of individuals within an order or subdivision of an order; a group of languages derived from a common parent tongue. — **tree**, a diagram representing the genealogy of a family. — **way**, pregnancy [L. *familia*].

fam·ine (fam′.in) *n.* large-scale scarcity of food; extreme shortage; starvation. **famish** *v.t.* to starve; *v.i.* to feel acute hunger, famished *a.* [L. *fames*, hunger].

fan (fan) *n.* an instrument to produce currents of air or assist ventilation; a decorative folding object, made of paper, silk, etc. used to cool face; a winnowing-implement; a small sail on a windmill to keep large sails to the wind; *v.t.* to cool with a fan; to ventilate; to winnow; to cause to flame (as a fire); to excite; to spread out like a fan. *pr.p.* **-ning.** *pa.p.* **-ned. -light** *n.* a window, usually semicircular, over a doorway. **-ner** *n.* [O.E. *fann*, a winnowing-fan].

fan (fan) *n.* (*Slang*) a devoted admirer [*abbrev. of fanatic*].

fa·nat·ic (fa·nat'·ik) *n.* a person inspired with excessive and bigoted enthusiasm, esp. a religious zealot; devotee; *a.* over-enthusiastic; immoderately zealous. **-al** *a.* **-ally** *adv.* **fanaticism** *n.* violent enthusiasm [L. *fanum*, a temple].

fan·cy (fan'·si·) *n.* the faculty of creating within the mind images of outward things; an image thus conceived; a whim; a notion; partiality; *a.* pleasing to the taste; guided by whim; elaborate; *v.t.* to imagine; to have a liking for; to desire; to breed (as dogs). **fancier** *n.* one who has a specialized knowledge, esp. of the breeding of animals. **fanciful** *a.* capricious; unreal; fantastic; **fancifully** *adv.* **fancifulness** *n.* **— ball** *n.* a ball at which the dancers wear costumes. **-free** *a.* heart-free [contr. fr. *fantasy*].

fan·fare (fan'·fār) *n.* a flourish of trumpets; a showy display. [Fr. *fanfarer*, to blow trumpets].

fang (fang) *n.* the canine tooth of a carnivorous animal; the long perforated tooth of a poisonous serpent [O.E. = a seizing].

fan·gled (fang'·gld) *a.* orig. meant fashionable, now exists only in the epithet *new-fangled*, new fashioned, hence unfamiliar.

fan·tan (fan'·tan) *n.* a Chinese gambling game [Chin.].

fan·ta·sy (fan'·ta·si) *n.* fancy; mental image; caprice; hallucination. Also **phantasy. fantasia** (fan·tā'·zha) *n.* (*Mus.*) a composition not conforming to the usual rules of music. **fantasied** *a.* fanciful. **fantasm** *n.* same as **phantasm. fantastic, -al** *a.* fanciful; wild; irregular; capricious. **fantastically** *adv.* [Gk. *phantasia*, appearance].

far (fär) *a.* distant; remote; more distant of two; *adv.* to a great extent or distance; to a great height; considerably; very much; *n.* a distant place. **-ther** *a.* (*comp.*) **-thest** *a.* (*superl.*) *adv.* — **East**, that part of Asia including India, China, Japan. **-fetched** *a.* (*Fig.*) incredible; strained. **-seeing**, or **-sighted** *a.* seeing to a great distance; (*Fig.*) taking a long view; prudent [O.E. *feor*, far].

far·ad (far'·ad) *n.* the unit of electrostatic capacity—the capacity of a condenser which requires one coulomb to raise its potential by one volt. **faraday**, *n.* the quantity of electricity required to liberate 1 gram-equivalent of an ion. **faradaic, faradic** *a.* pert. to induced electrical currents [fr. M. *Faraday*, scientist].

farce (färs) *n.* orig. a dramatic interlude; a style of comedy marked by boisterous humor and extravagant gesture; absurd or empty show; a pretense. **farceur** (far·sur') *n.* a joker; a wag. **farcical** *a.* pert. to a farce; absurdly ludicrous; sham. **farcically** *adv.* [O.Fr. *farce*, stuffing].

fare (fer) *v.i.* to be in any state, bad or good; to get on; to happen; to be entertained at table; *n.* the sum paid by a passenger on a vehicle; a passenger; food and drink at table. **-well** *interj.* (*Lit.*) may it go well with you; good-bye; *n.* a parting wish for someone's welfare; the act of taking leave; *a.* parting; last [O.E. *faran*, to go].

fa·ri·na (fa·rē'·na, fa·rī'·na) *n.* flour or meal of cereal grains, used for cereal and puddings; starch [L. *farina*, ground corn].

farm (färm) *n.* a tract of land set apart for cultivation or for other industries, as dairy farm, etc.; the buildings on this land; *v.t.* cultivate land for agricultural purposes; to collect (taxes, etc.) on condition of receiving a percentage of what is yielded; *v.i.* and *t.* to cultivate; to operate a farm. **-er** *n.* **-ing** *n.* the occupation of cultivating the soil. **-stead** *n.* a farm with all the outbuildings attached to it. **-yard** *n.* enclosure surrounded by farm buildings [M.E. *ferme*, payment].

far·o (fer'·ō) *n.* a gambling game of cards [fr. *Pharaoh*, one of the cards].

far·ra·go (far·ā'·gō, far·ā'·gō) *n.* a medley; a miscellaneous collection. **farraginous** *a.* confusedly mixed [L. *farrago*, mixed fodder].

far·ri·er (far'·i·er) *n.* a blacksmith; (*Br.*) a veterinarian. **-y** *n.* [L. *ferrum*, iron].

far·row (far'·ō) *n.* a litter of pigs; *v.t.* to give birth to (pigs); *v.i.* to bring forth pigs [O.E. *fearh*, a pig].

far·ther (fär'·THer) *a.* more far; more remote; *adv.* to a greater distance. **-most** *a.*

far·thing (fär'·THing) *n.* (*Brit.*) the fourth of a penny [O.E. *feorthing*, a fourth part].

fas·ci·a (fash'·i·a) *n.* a band, fillet, or bandage; (*Archit.*) a strip of flat stone between two moldings; [L. *fascia*, a band].

fas·ci·cle (fas'·i·kl) *n.* (*Bot.*) a close cluster of leaves or flowers as in the sweet william; a small bundle of nerve fibers; a serial division of a book. **fascicular, fasciculate** *a.* [L. *fasciculus*, a small bundle].

fas·ci·nate (fas'·a·nāt) *v.t.* to enchant; to deprive of the power of movement, by a look. **fascinating** *a.* **fascination** *n.* the act of fascinating; enchantment; irresistible attraction. **fascinator** *n.* [L. *fascinare*].

fas·cism (fash'·ism) *n.* a centralized autocratic national regime with extremely nationalistic policies with an economic system based on state-controlled capitalism. **Fascist** *n.* [It. *fascio*, a bundle].

fash·ion (fash'·an) *n.* the style in which a thing is made or done; pattern; the mode or cut, esp. of a dress; custom; appearance; *v.t.* to form; to shape. **-able** *a.* **-ably** *adv.* [O.Fr. *facon*, a manner].

fast (fast) *v.i.* to abstain from food; to deny oneself certain foods as a form of religious discipline; *n.* abstinence from food; a day of fasting [O.E. *faestan*, to fast].

fast (fast) *a.* rapid; securely fixed; firm; tight shut; profound; immovable; permanent, as a dye; stable; in advance of the correct time, as a clock; loyal, as friends; dissipated, as *a fast life*; *adv.* firmly; soundly; securely; dissipatedly; rapidly. **-ness** *n.* security; a stronghold [O.E. *faest*, firm].

fas·ten (fas'·n) *v.t.* to fix firmly; to hold together; *v.i.* to fix itself; to catch (of a lock). **-er** *n.* a contrivance for fixing things firmly together. **-ing** *n.* that by which anything fastens, as a lock, bolt, nut, screw [O.E. *faest*, firm].

fas·tid·i·ous (fas·tid'·i·as) *a.* difficult to please; discriminating. **-ly** *adv.* **-ness** *n.* [L. *fastidium*, loathing].

fat (fat) *a.* (*comp.*) **-ter** (*superl.*) **-test.** fleshy; plump; oily; yielding a rich supply; productive; profitable; *n.* an oily substance found in animal bodies; solid animal or vegetable oil; the best or richest part of anything; *v.t.* to make fat; *v.i.* to grow fat. *pr.p.* **-ting.** *pa.p.* **-ted. -head** *n.* (*Slang*) a stupid person. **-headed** *a.* **-ling** *n.* a young fattened animal. **-ness** *n.* the quality or state of being fat; corpulence; fertility. **-ted** *a.* fattened. **-ten** *v.t.* to make fat; to make fertile; *v.i.* to grow fat. **-tener** *n.* **-tiness** *n.* **-ty** *a.* resembling or containing fat; greasy [O.E. *faet*, fat].

fate (fāt) *n.* an inevitable and irresistible power supposedly controlling human destiny; appointed lot; death; doom. **the Fates,** the three goddesses supposed to preside over the course of human life. **fatal** *a.* causing death; appointed by fate; calamitous. **fatalism** *n.* the doctrine that all events are predetermined and unavoidable. **fatalist** *n.* **fatalistic** *a.* **fatality** *n.* accident causing death; the state of being fatal; inevitable necessity. **-d** *a.* destined; pre-ordained; doomed. **-ful** *a.* momentous; irrevocable. **-fully** *adv.* **-fulness** *n.* [L. *fatum*].

fa·ther (fä'·THer) *n.* a male parent; a male ancestor more remote than a parent; a title of respect paid to one of seniority or rank, esp. to church dignitaries, priests, etc.; the first person of the Trinity; oldest member of a community; a producer, author or contriver; *v.t.* to make oneself the father of; to adopt; to assume or admit responsibility for. **-hood** *n.* the state of being a father; paternity. **—in-law** *n.* (*pl.* **-s-in-law**) the father of one's wife or husband. **-land** *n.* the land of one's fathers. **-less** *a.* without a father living. **-liness** *n.* *a.* and *adv.* like a father in affection and care; paternal; benevolent. **-ship** *n.* [O.E. *faeder*, a father].

fath·om (faTH'·am) *n.* a nautical measure of depth, 6 ft. *v.t.* to ascertain the depth of; to sound; (*Fig.*) to get to the bottom of; to understand. **-able** *a.* **-less** *a.* incapable of being fathomed; unplumbed. **-lessly** *adv.* [O.E. *faethm*, the outstretched arms].

fa·tigue (fa·tēg') *n.* weariness from bodily or mental exertion; toil; non-military routine work of soldiers; *v.t.* to weary by toil; to exhaust the strength of; to tire out. *pr.p.* **-ing.** *pa.p.* **-d** [Fr. *fatiguer*, to weary].

fat·u·ous (fa'·choo·as) *a.* silly. **fatuity** *n.* unconsciously foolish; inanity; foolishness. **-ness** *n.* [L. *fatuus*, silly].

fau·cet (faw'·sit) *n.* a fixture for controlling the flow of liquid from a pipe, etc.; a tap [O.Fr. *fausset*].

OPEN

CLOSED

faugh (faw) *interj.* an exclamation of contempt or disgust [imit.].

fault (fawlt) *n.* a failing; blunder; mistake; defect; flaw; responsibility for error; (*Geol.*) a dislocation of rock strata; in hunting, the loss of the scent trail; (*Elect.*) a defect in electrical apparatus. **-ed** *a.* (*Geol.*) broken by one or more faults. **-ily** *adv.* **-iness** *n.* **-less** *a.* without flaws; perfect. **-lessly** *adv.* **-lessness** *n.* perfection. **-y** *a.* imperfect. [O. Fr. *faute*, error].

fau·na (fawn'·a) *n.* a collective term for the animals of any given geographical region or geological epoch [L. *Fauna*, sister of *Faunus*, a god of agriculture].

fa·ve·o·late (fav·ē'·ō·lāt) *a.* pitted; cellular; resembling a honeycomb. [L. *faveolus*, a little honeycomb].

fa·vor (fā'·ver) *n.* a gracious act; kind regard; goodwill; partiality; token of generosity or esteem; a gift; *v.t.* to regard with kindness; to show bias towards; to tend to promote; (*Colloq.*) to resemble in feature. **-able** *a.* friendly; propitious; advantageous; suitable; satisfactory. **-ableness** *n.* **-ably** *adv.* **-ed** *a.* fortunate; lucky featured, as in *ill-favored*. **-ite** *n.* a person or thing regarded with special favor; the likely winner; *a.* regarded with particular affection; most esteemed. **-itism** *n.* undue partiality [L. *favor*, partiality].

fawn (fawn) *n.* a young deer; its color; *a.* delicate yellowish-brown; *v.i.* to give birth to a fawn [O.Fr. *faon*, fr. L. *fetus*, offspring].

fawn (fawn) *v.i.* to flatter unctuously; to curry favor. **-er** *n.* **-ing** *n.* servile flattery; *a.* over-demonstrative. **-ingly** *adv.* **-ingness** *n.* [M.E. *faunen*, to rejoice].

fay (fā) *n.* a fairy; an elf [O.Fr. *fae*].

fe·al·ty (fē'·al·ti) *n.* fidelity; obligations binding a vassal to his lord [O.Fr. *fealte*, fidelity].

fear (fir) *n.* alarm; dread; solicitude; anxiety; reverence towards God; *v.t.* to regard with dread or apprehension; to anticipate (as a disaster); to hold in awe; *v.i.* to be afraid;

to be anxious. **-ful** *adv.* **-fulness** *n.* **-less** *a.* without fear; intrepid; dauntless. **-lessly** *adv.* **lessness** *n.* courage; intrepidity. **-some** *a.* causing fear; terrifying [O.E. *faer,* danger].

fea·si·ble (fē'·zạ·bl) *a.* capable of being done; suitable. **-ness, feasibility** *n.* **feasibly** *adv.* [Fr. *faisible,* that can be done].

feast (fēst) *n.* a day of joyful or solemn commemoration; a banquet; something very enjoyable; *v.t.* to feed sumptuously; to regale; *v.i.* to eat sumptuously; to be highly gratified or delighted. **-er** *n.* [L. *festum,* a holiday].

feat (fēt) *n.* an exploit or action of extraordinary strength, courage, skill, or endurance [Fr. *fait,* fr. L. *factum,* a deed].

feath·er (feTH'·ẹr) *n.* one of the epidermal growths forming the body-covering of a bird; a plume; the feathered end or an arrow; feathers, as a cap or arrow. **-bed** *n.* a mattress stuffed with feathers; *v.t.* (*Colloq.*) to pamper; to keep supernumeraries on a job. **-brained, -headed, -pated** *a.* weak-minded; inane. **-stitch** *n.* an embroidery stitch resembling a feather. **-weight,** the lightest weight that may be carried by a racehorse; a boxer weighing not more than 126 lbs.; any very light or insignificant person or thing. **-y** *a.* pert. to, covered with, or resembling feathers [O.E. *fether,* feather].

fea·ture (fē'·cher) *n.* any part of the face; distinctive characteristic; main attraction; *pl.* the face; *v.t.* to portray; to outline; to present as the leading attraction. **-less** *a.* void of striking features. [O.Fr. *faiture,* something made].

feb·ri·fuge (feb'·rạ·fūj) *n.* a drug taken to allay fever. **febrifugal** *a.* **febrile** (fē'·bril, feb'·ril) *a.* feverish; accompanied by fever. **febrility** *n.* [L. *febris,* fever].

Feb·ru·ar·y (feb'·rōò·e·ri.) *n.* the second month of the year [L. *Februarius,* fr. *Februa,* the Roman festival of purification].

fe·ces, faeces (fē'·sēz) *n.pl.* dregs; the solid waste matter from the bowels. **fecal** (·kạl) *a.* [L. *faeces,* grounds].

fe·cund (fē'·kạnd) *a.* fruitful; fertile. **-ate** (fē'·kun'·dāt, fek'·un·dāt) *v.t.* to make fruitful; to impregnate. **-ation** *n.* **-ity** *n.* the quality or power of reproduction; fertility; productiveness [L. *fecundus,* fruitful].

fed (fed) *pa.t.* and *pa.p.* of the verb **feed.**

fed·er·al (fed'·er·al) *a.* pert. to a league or treaty, esp. between states; of an association of states which, autonomous in home affairs, combine for matters of wider national and international policy; pert. to such a central government; pert. to the Union in the Civil War. **federacy** *n.* **-ize** *v.t.* to form a union under a federal government. **-ism** *n.* **-ist** *n.* a supporter of such a union. **federate** *v.t.* to unite states into a federation. *a.* united; allied. **federation** *n.* a federal union. **federative** *a.* [L. *foedus,* a compact].

fee (fē) *n.* orig. land held from a lord on condition of certain feudal services; remuneration for professional services; payment for special privilege; *v.t.* to pay a fee to. **fee-simple,** unrestricted ownership or inheritance [O.E. *feoh,* cattle or property].

fee·ble (fē'·bl) *a.* weak; deficient in strength; frail; faint. **-minded** *a.* mentally subnormal. **-ness** *n.* **feebly** *adv.* [Fr. *faible,* weak].

feed (fēd) *v.t.* to give food to; to supply with nourishment; to supply with material (as a machine); *v.i.* to eat; to subsist. *pa.p.* and *pa.t.* **fed.** *n.* that which is consumed, esp. by animals; the material supplied to a machine or the channel by which it is fed. **-er** *n.* one who feeds; a device for supplying a machine with material; a channel taking water to a reservoir; a branch railway-line. **-ing** *n.* act of eating; that which is consumed; grazing. [O.E. *fedan,* to feed].

feel (fēl) *v.t.* to perceive by the touch; to handle; to be sensitive to; to experience emotionally; to have an intuitive awareness of; *v.i.* to know by the touch; to be conscious of being; to give rise to a definite sensation; to be moved emotionally. *pa.p. pa.t.* **felt** *n.* the sensation of touch; the quality of anything touched. **-er** *n.* (*Zool.*) one of the tactile organs (antennae, tentacles, etc.) of certain insects and animals; a tentative remark, proposal, etc. to sound the opinions or attitude of others. **-ing** *n.* sense of touch; awareness by touch; intuition; sensibility; sympathy. **-ings** *n.pl.* emotions; *a.* kindly; responsive; possessing great sensibility. **-ingly** *adv.* [O.E. *felan,* to feel].

feet (fēt) *n.pl.* of **foot.**

feign (fān) *v.t.* to invent; to pretend; to counterfeit. **-ed** *a.* pretended; disguised. **-edly** *adv.* **-edness** *n.* **-ing** *n.* pretense; invention. **feint** *n.* an assumed appearance; a misleading move in boxing, military operations, etc. *v.i.* to make a deceptive move [Fr. *feindre,* to feign].

feld·spar (feld'·spár) *n.* a constituent of granite and other igneous rocks; a crystalline mineral comprising silicates of aluminium with varying proportions of potassium, calcium and sodium. *a.* [Ger. *Feld,* field; *Spath,* a spar].

fe·lic·i·ty (fi.lis'·a.ti.) *n.* happiness; bliss; skill. **felicitate** *v.t.* to express joy or pleasure to; to congratulate. **felicitation** *n.* congratulation; the act of expressing good wishes. **felicitous** *a.* happy; appropriate; aptly expressed [L. *felix,* happy].

fe·line (fē'·lin) *a.* pert. to cats; cat-like; (*Fig.*) treacherous [L. *feles,* a cat].

fell (fel) *a.* cruel; ruthless; deadly [O.Fr. *fel.* cruel].

fell (fel) *n.* an animal's skin or hide [O.E. *fel,* a skin].

fell (fel) *pa.t.* of the verb **fall.**

fell (fel) *v.t.* to cause to fall; to cut down; to sew an overlapping flax seam. **-er** *n.* [O.E. *fellan,* to cause to fall].

fell (fel) *n.* a tract of high moorland, as in the English Lake District [Scand. *fiall,* rock].

fel·low (fel'·ō) *n.* a man; boy; (*Colloq.*) suitor; an associate; an equal; a person; a worthless person; a graduate student on a grant for special study; member of a literary or scientific society. **— traveller** *n.* sympathizer with the Communist Party, but not a member of it. **-ship** *n.* the state of being a fellow; companionship; community of feeling, interest, etc.; a foundation for the maintenance of a resident university graduate; the grant made by such a foundation [M.E. *felawe,* a partner].

fel·on (fel'·ạn) *n.* one who has committed felony; (*Med.*) inflammation of top joint of the finger; a whitlow; *a.* fierce; traitorous. **-ious** *a.* **-iously** *adv.* **-iousness** *n.* **-y** *n.* (*Law*) a crime more serious than a *misdemeanor* (as murder, manslaughter, etc.) [O.Fr. *felon,* a traitor].

felt (felt) *pa.t.* and *pa.p.* of **feel.**

felt (felt) *n.* a closely matted fabric of wool, hair, etc.; *v.t.* to make into felt; to cover with felt; *v.i.* to become matted like felt. **-ing** *n.* the art or process of making felt; the felt itself [O.E. *felt,* something compact]

fe·male (fē'·māl) *n.* one of the sex that bears young; (*Bot.*) a plant which produces fruit; *a.* pert. to the child-bearing sex; feminine. **femineity** (fe·ma·nē'·a·ti.) *n.* the quality of being a woman. **feminine** *a.* pert. to or associated with women; womanly; tender; (of males) effeminate. **femininely** *adv.* **feminineness, femininity** *n.* the nature of the female sex; womanliness. **feminism** *n.* the doctrine that maintains the equality of the sexes; advocacy of women's rights. **feminist** *n.* [L. *femina*].

fe·mur (fē'·mer) *n.* the thigh-bone. **femoral** *a.* [L. *femur,* the thigh].

fen (fen) *n.* (*Brit.*) low-lying marshy land [O.E. *fenn,* a bog].

fence (fens) *n.* a wall or hedge for enclosing; the art of fencing; a receiver of stolen goods; *v.t.* to enclose with a fence; to guard; *v.i.* to practise the art of sword-play; to evade a direct answer to an opponent's challenge; to equivocate. **-r** *n.* one who is skilled in fencing. **fencing** *n.* the art or practice of self-defense with the sword, foil, etc.; the act of enclosing by a fence; the materials of which a fence is made [abbrev. of *defence*].

fend (fend) *v.t.* to ward off; *v.i.* to resist; to parry; (*Colloq.*) to provide. **-er** *n.* that which acts as a protection; the metal part over wheels of an automobile; a metal guard to prevent coals falling beyond hearth; a device, usually a bundle of rope, to break the impact of a ship drawing alongside a wharf or other vessel [abbrev. of *defend*].

fe·nes·tra (fi.nes'·tra) *n.* a hole; an opening. Also **fenester, fenestra. fenestrate, fenestrated** *a.* (*Bot.*) having transparent spots; (*Archit.*) having windows. **fenestration** *n.* the state of being perforated; arrangement of windows in a building [L. *fenestra,* a window].

fen·nel (fen'·el) *n.* a perennial umbelliferous plant with yellow flowers [O.E. *finul,* fr. L. *faenum,* hay].

fe·ral (fi'·ral) *a.* wild; not domesticated; run wild (of plants). **ferine** *a.* [L. *ferus,* wild].

fer·ment (fur'·ment) *n.* a substance which causes fermentation, as yeast; ferment; (*Fig.*) tumult; agitation. (fer·ment') *v.t.* to induce fermentation in; to arouse a commotion; *v.i.* to undergo fermentation; to work (of wine); to become excited; to be in a state of agitation. **-ability** *n.* **-able** *a.* **-ation** *n.* the decomposition of organic substances produced by the action of a living organism, or of certain chemical agents. **-ative** *a.* [L. *fermentum,* leaven].

fern (furn) *n.* plant characterized by fibrous roots, and leaves called fronds. **-y** *a.* [O.E.].

fe·roc·i·ty (fa·ràs'·a·ti.) *n.* cruelty; savage fierceness of disposition. **ferocious** *a.* fierce; violent; wild. **ferociously** *adv.* **ferociousness** *n.* [L. *ferox,* wild].

fer·ret (fer'·it) *n.* a small, partially domesticated variety of polecat; *v.t.* to hunt out to search out [O.Fr. *furet,* a ferret].

fer·ric (fer'·ik) *a.* pert. to or extracted from iron; applied to compounds of trivalent iron. **— acid,** an acid containing iron and oxygen. [L. *ferrum,* iron].

fer·ro- (fer'·ō) prefix fr. L. *ferrum,* containing or made of iron, occurring in compound words **-concrete** *n.* reinforced concrete; concrete with inner skeleton of iron or steel. **-magnetic** *a.* reacting like iron in a magnetic field. **ferrous** *a.* pert. to iron.

ferroconcrete

fer·rule (fer'·al, fer'·ōól) *n.* a metal tip or ring on a cane, etc. to prevent splitting. Also **ferule** [O.Fr. *virelle,* a bracelet].

fer·ry (fer'·i.) *v.t.* to transport over stretch of water by boat. *n.* a place where one is conveyed across a river, etc. by boat; the ferryboat; the right of transporting passengers and goods by this means. **ferriage** *n.* transport by ferry; the fare paid for such transport [O.E. *faran,* to go].

fer·tile (fur'·til) *a.* producing or bearing abundantly; prolific; fruitful; (*Fig.*) inventive. **-ly** *adv.* **-ness, fertilization** *n.* the act of fertilizing; enrichment of soil, by natural or artificial means; (*Biol.*) union of the female and male cells. **fertilize** *v.t.* to make fruitful; (*Biol.*) to fecundate; (*Bot.*) to pollinate. **fertilizer** *n.* one who, or that which, fertilizes; material (e.g. manure, nitrates) to enrich soil. **fertility** *n.* [L. *fertilis,* fruitful].

fer·ule (fer·al, fer'·ōól) *n.* a rod or ruler for punishing children [L. *ferula,* rod].

fer·vent (fur'·vant) *a.* glowing; ardent; zealous; enthusiastic. **fervency** *n.* ardor; intensity of devotion. **-ly** *adv.* **fervid** *a.* burning; vehement; intense. **fervidity** *n.* **fervidly** *adv.* **fervidness** *n.* zeal; enthusiasm. **fervor** *n.* heat; ardor; passion [L. *fervere,* to boil].

fes·cue (fes'·kū) *n.* a kind of tough grass; a teacher's small pointer [M.E. *festu,* a bit of straw].

fes·tal (fes'·tạl) *a.* pert. to feast or festival; joyous; gay. **-ly** *adv.* [O.Fr. *feste,* a feast].

fes·ter (fes'·ter) *v.t.* to cause to putrefy; *v.i.* to become inflamed; to suppurate; to rot; to become embittered; *n.* an ulcer; a sore [O.Fr. *festre,* an ulcer].

fes·tive (fes'·tiv) *a.* festal; joyous; convivial. **festival** *n.* a feast or celebration; an annual competition or periodic gathering of musical or dramatic societies. **-ly** *adv.* **festivity** *n.* merriment; merrymaking; festival [L. *festivus,* festive].

fes·toon (fes·tōon') *n.* garland hanging in a curve; *v.t.* [Fr. fr. L.L. *festo,* a garland].

fetch (fech) *v.t.* to go for and bring; to summon; to bring or yield (a price); *v.i.* to go and bring things; the act of bringing; a trick or artifice; an apparition; a person's double. **-ing** *a.* attractive; alluring [O.E. *feccan,* to bring].

fete (fāt) *n.* a festival; a holiday; *v.t.* to honor with celebrations. **feted** *a.* honored [L. *festum*, a feast].

fet·id (fet'·id) *a* having a strong, offensive smell. Also **foetid** [L. *fetidus*, stinking].

fe·tish, fetich, fetiche (fet'·ish) *n.* an object or image superstitiously invested with divine or demoniac power, and, as such, reverenced devoutly; anything regarded with exaggerated reverence. **-ism,** *n.* fetish worship. **-istic,** *a.* [Port. *feitico*, magic].

fet·lock (fet'·lòk) *n.* the tuft of hair on a horse's leg.

fet·ter (fet'·er) *n.* a chain or shackle for the feet (usually *pl.*); an impediment or restriction; *v.t.* to shackle; to restrain [O.E. *fetor*, fr. *fet*, the feet]. [girdle].

fet·tle (fet'·l) *n.* condition [O.E. *fetel*].

fe·tus, foetus (fē'·tas) *n.* the young of vertebrate animals between the embryonic and independent states. **fetal, foetal** *a.* **fetation, foetation** *n.* pregnancy. **feticide, foeticide** *n.* destroying of the fetus; abortion [L. *fetus*, a bringing forth].

feud (fūd) *n.* a lasting, hereditary strife between families or clans; deadly hatred [M.E. *fede*, enmity].

feud (fūd) *n.* an estate or land held on condition of service; a fief. **-al** *a.* pert. to feuds or to feudalism. **-alism** *n.* a system which prevailed in Europe in the Middle Ages, by which vassals held land from the King and the tenants-in-chief in return for military service. Also **feudal system. -ary, -atory** *a.* holding land by feudal tenure; *n.* a vassal holding land in fee [L. L. *feudum*, a fief].

fe·ver (fē'·ver) *n.* bodily disease marked by unusual rise of temperature and usually a quickening of pulse; violent mental or emotional excitement; *v.t.* to put into a fever. *v.i.* to become fevered. **-ed** *a.* affected with fever; frenzied. **ish** *a.* slightly fevered; agitated. **-ishly** *adv.* [O.E. *fefor*, forever].

few (fū) *a.* not many; *n.* and *pron.* a small number. **-ness** *n.* [O.E. *feawe*, few].

fez (fez) *n.* a red, brimless felt hat with tassel worn in Egypt, Turkey, etc. [prob. fr. *Fez* in Morocco].

fi·a·cre (fi·à'·kr) *n.* a hackney coach [fr. *Hotel St. Fiacre* [Paris].

fi·an·ce (fē·an·sā') *n.* (*fem.* **fiancee**) a betrothed man [Fr. *fiancer*, to betroth].

fi·as·co (fē·as'·kō) *n.* any spectacular failure [It. *fiasco*, a bottle].

fi·at (fi'·at) *n.* a formal command; an authoritative order [L. *fiat*, let it be done].

fib (fib) *n.* a falsehood; a mild lie; *v.i.* to tell a petty lie *pr.p.* **-bing.** *pa.p.; pa.t.* **-bed.**

fi·ber (fi'·ber) *n.* one of the bundles of thread-like tissue constituting muscles, etc.; any thread-like substance used for weaving fabric; character, as in *moral fiber.* **-ed** *a.* **-less** *a.* **fibriform** *a.* **fibril** *n.* a very small fiber. **fibrillose** *a.* (*Bot.*) covered with fibers. **fibrillous** *a.* composed of small fibers. **fibrin** *n.* a protein formed in coagulation of blood. **fibroid** *a.* of a fibrous nature; *n.* a fibrous tumor. **fibrous** *a.* composed of fibers. **fibrousness** *n.* [L. *fibra*, a fiber].

fib·u·la (fib'·ya·la) *n.* (*Archeal.*); (*Med.*) the slender outer bone of the leg between knee and ankle. **-r** *a.* [L.*fibula*, a clasp].

fich·u (fi'·shōō) *n.* a triangular cape worn over the shoulders and tying in front; a ruffle of lace, etc. worn at the neck [Fr.].

fick·le (fik'·l) *a.* inconstant; capricious; unreliable. **-ness** *n.* [O.E. *ficol*, cunning].

fic·tile (fik'·til) *a.* capable of being molded; plastic; used of all objects shaped in clay by a potter [L. *fictilis*].

fic·tion (fik'·shan) *n.* literature dealing with imaginary characters and situations; something invented, or imagined. **-al** *a.* **fictitious** *a.* imaginary; feigned; false; **fictitiously** *adv.* [L. *fictus*, invented].

fid·dle (fid'·l) *n.* a stringed musical instrument; a violin; wooden framework around dining-tables on board a ship; *v.t.* and *v.i.* to play on a fiddle; to trifle. — **bow** *n.* the bow used in playing a violin. —**dee-dee** *n.* nonsense. —**faddle** *v.i.* to trifle; to dawdle; *n.* triviality; rubbish' —**sticks** (*interj.*) nonsense. **fiddling** *a.* trifling [O.E. *fithele*].

fi·del·i·ty (fi·del'·a·ti·) *n.* faithfulness; loyalty; devotion to duty; adherence to marriage vows; accuracy [L. *fidelis*, faithful].

fidg·et (fij'·it) *v.i.* to move restlessly; to be uneasy; *n.* uneasiness. **-s** *n.pl.* nervous restlessness. **-y** *a.* [fr. Scand. *fikja*].

fiddle

fi·du·ci·ar·y (fi·dōō'·shi·er·i·) *a.* holding or held in trust; (of paper currency) depending for its value on public confidence; *n.* a trustee. **fiducial** *a.* having faith or confidence [L. *fiducia*, confidence].

field (fēld) *n.* cleared land; a division of farm land; scene of a battle; the battle itself; any wide expanse; areas of observation; locality of operations, as in surveying; sphere of influence within which magnetic, electrostatic, or gravitational forces are perceptible; the surface of an escutcheon; the background of a flag, coin, etc. on which a design is drawn; the people following a hunt; (sports) area of ground used for sports; (*Cricket*) the side which is not batting; a collective term for all the competitors in an athletic contest or all the horses in a race; an area rich in some natural product (e.g. coal-field, oil-field); *v.t.* (*Baseball*) to catch the ball; *v.i.* to act as fielder. — **artillery** *n.* light guns for active operations. — **battery** *n.* battery of field guns. — **book** *n.* book used for notes by land surveyor or naturalist. — **day** *n.* a day for athletic contests; a gala day. **-er** *n.* one who fields at cricket, baseball, etc. — **glass** *n.* a binocular telescope. — **gun** *n.* a small cannon on a carriage. — **marshal** *n.* the highest rank in the British and several other armies. — **officer** *n.* a commissioned officer in rank between a captain and a general. **-piece** *n.* a fieldgun. —**sports** *n.pl.* out-of-door sports as hunting, racing, etc. [O.E. *feld*, a field].

field gun

fiend (fēnd) *n.* a demon; the devil; a malicious foe; (*Colloq.*) one who is crazy about something, as, *a fresh-air fiend.* **-ish** *a.* [O.E. *feond*, an enemy].

fierce (fērs) *a.* ferocious; violent; savage; intense. **-ly** *adv.* **-ness** *n.* ferocity; rage [O.Fr. *fers*, bold].

fi·er·y (fi'·er·i·) *a.* flaming; hot; (*Fig.*) ardent; fierce; vehement; irritable. **fierily** *adv.* **fieriness** *n.* [fr. *fire*].

fife (fif) *n.* a high-pitched flute. **-r** *n.* one who plays the fife [O.Fr. *fifre*, a fife].

fif·teen (fif'·tēn) *a.* and *n.* five and ten; the symbol, 15 or XV. *a.* the fifth after the tenth; making one of fifteen equal parts. [O.E. *fif*, five; *tene*, ten].

fifth (fifth) *a.* next after the fourth; *n.* one of five equal parts of a whole. — **column,** any organization within a country deliberately assisting the enemy by acts of sabotage, etc. — **columnist** *n.* **-ly** *adv.*

fif·ty (fif'·ti·) *a.* and *n.* five times ten; the symbol 50 or L. **fiftieth** *a.* next in a series of forty-nine others; making one of fifty equal parts of a whole; *n.* a fiftieth part. **to go fifty-fifty** (*Colloq.*) share and share alike [O.E. *fiftig*, fifty].

fig (fig) *n.* a Mediterranean tree or its fruit (*Colloq.*) something insignificant [Fr. *figue*].

fight (fit) *v.t.* to wage war against; to contend against; to oppose; *v.i.* to take part in single combat or battle; to resist. *pa.p.* **fought** (fawt). *n.* a combat; a battle; a struggle; pugnacity. **-er** *n.* one who fights; an aircraft designed for fighting. **-ing** *a.* able to, or inclined to, fight; pert. to a fight [O.E. *feohtan*].

fig·ment (fig'·mant) *n.* an invention, fiction, or fabrication [L. *figmentum*, an image].

fig·ure (fig'·yer) *n.* outward form of anything; the form of a person; a diagram, drawing, etc.; a design; an appearance; steps in a dance; the sign of a numeral, as 1, 2, 3; *v.t.* to cover with patterns; to note by numeral characters; to calculate; to symbolize; to image in the mind; *v.i.* to make a figure. **-d** *a.* esp. adorned with patterns, as *figured muslin.* **figurative** *a.* representing by a figure; not literal; abounding in figures of speech. **figuratively** *adv.* **figurativeness** *n.* **-head** *n.* the nominal head of an organization, without real authority; ornamental figure under the bowsprit of a ship. **figurine** *n.* a statuette. **figure of speech,** an unusual use of words to produce a desired effect, such as metaphor, simile, etc. [L. *figura*, fr. *fingere*, to form].

fil·a·ment (fil'·a·ment) *n.* a slender thread; a fiber. (*Bot.*) the stalk of a stamen; (*Elect.*) a fine wire, usually of tungsten, which glows to incandescence by the passage of an electric current. *a.* like a filament. **-ous** *a.* thread-like [L. *filum*, thread].

fil·bert (fil'·bert) *n.* the nut of the hazel-tree

filch (filch) *v.t.* to steal; to pilfer. **-er** *n.*

file (fil) *n.* an orderly line; a cabinet, wire, or portfolio for keeping papers in order; the papers or cards thus kept; *v.t.* to set in order in a public record office; *v.i.* to march in a file; to make application. **Indian** or **single file,** a single line of men marching one behind the other. **rank and file,** non-commissioned soldiers; the general mass of people as distinct from well-known figures [L. *filum*, a thread].

file (fil) *n.* a steel instrument for smoothing rough surfaces or cutting through metal. *v.t.* to cut or abrade with a file. *pr.p.* **filing.** *pa.p.* **-d. filing** *n.* a particle of metal rubbed off by a file; the action of abrading stone or cutting metal [O.E. *feol*, a file].

fil·i·al (fil'·i·al) *a.* pert. to or befitting a son or daughter. **-ly** *adv.* **filiation** *n.* being a child of a certain parent; derivation [L. *filius*, a son].

fil·i·bus·ter (fil'·a·bus·ter) *n.* one who deliberately obstructs legislation, esp. by making long speeches; a lawless adventurer; a buccaneer. *v.i.* to act as a filibuster [Fr. *filibustier*, a freebooter].

fil·i·form (fil'·a·form) *a.* thread-like [L. *filum*, a thread].

fil·i·gree (fil'·i·grē) *n.* ornamental openwork of gold or silver wire; anything highly ornamental but fragile. **-d** *a.* [L. *filum*, thread; *granum*, grain].

Fil·i·pi·no (fil·a·pēn'·ō) *n.* a native of the Philippine Islands.

fill (fil) *v.t.* to make full; to replenish; to occupy as a position; to supply as a vacant office; to pervade; to stop up (a tooth); *v.i.* to become full; *n.* a full supply. **-er** *n.* one who, or that which, fills; a funnel-shaped vessel for filling bottles; **-ing** *n.* that which fills up a space, as gold, etc. used by dentists; a mixture put into sandwiches, cakes, etc.; *a.* satisfying; ample. **filling station,** a roadside depot for supplying gasoline, oil etc., to motorists [O.E. *fyllan*, to make full].

fil·let (fil'·it) *n.* a narrow band, esp. round the head; (fi·lā') piece of meat cut from the thigh; a piece of meat boned and rolled; fish after bones are removed; *v.t.* to bind with a fillet; to bone (meat or fish, etc.); [Fr. *filet*, a thread].

fil·lip (fil'·ap) *v.t.* to strike with the nail of the finger, first placed against the ball of the thumb then released with a sudden jerk; to incite; to spur on; a jerk of the finger; an incentive; a stimulus [form of *flip*].

fil·ly (fil'·i·) *n.* a young mare; a lively or wanton young woman [dim. of *foal*].

film (film) *n.* a thin coating or membrane; a delicate filament; dimness over the eyes; (*Photog.*) a roll of flexible, sensitized material used for photography; pictures taken on this roll; *pl.* (*Colloq.*) a movie show; *v.t.* to cover with a film; to take a moving picture of; to reproduce on a film. **-iness** *n.* **-y** *a.* composed of or covered with film; membranous; sheer [O.E. *filmen*, membrane].

fi·lose (fi'·lōs) *a.* having a thread-like ending [L. *filum*, thread].

fil·ter (fil'·ter) *n.* a device for separating liquids from solids, or for straining impurities from liquids; any porous material such as filter paper, charcoal, etc.; a device for removing dust from the air; (*Photog.*) a piece of colored glass placed in front of the lens, passing certain rays only; *v.t.* to purify by passing through a filter; to filtrate; *v.i.* to pass through a filter; **filtrate** *v.t.* to filter; *n.* the liquid which has been strained through a filter. **filtration** *n.* **-bed** *n.* a layer of sand or gravel at bottom of a reservoir for purifying the water. [O.Fr. *filtre*, a strainer].

filth (filth) *n.* foul matter; dirt; pollution; (*Fig.*) immorality; obscenity. **-ily** *adv.* **-iness** *n.* **-y** *a.* [O.E. *fylth*, foulness].

fim·bri·a (fim'·bri·a) *n.* (*Zool.*) a fringe or fringe-like structure. **fimbriate, fimbriated** *a.* fringed [L. *fimbria*, thread].

fin (fin) *n.* a paddle-like organ of fishes and other aquatic forms serving to balance and propel; (*Aero.*) a vertical surface, fixed usually on the tail of an aircraft to aid lateral and directional stability. [O.E. *finn*, a fin].

fi·nal (fī'·nal) *a.* pert. to the end; last; decisive; conclusive; ultimate; *n.* the last stage of anything; *pl.* the last examination or contest in a series. **-ist** *n.* a competitor who reaches the finals of a contest. **-ity** *n.* the state of being final; conclusiveness. **-ize** *v.t.* to give a final form to. **-ly** *adv.* [L. *finis*, the end].

fi·na·le (fi·nä'·li·) *n.* the end; (*Mus.*) the last movement of a musical composition; final scene; a conclusion [It. *finale*, the end].

fi·nance (fa·nans' or fī'·nans) *n.* the science of controlling public revenue and expenditure; the management of money affairs; *pl.* the income of a state or person; resources; funds; *v.t.* to provide funds for; to supply capital. **financial** *a.* pert. to. **fiscal. financially** *adv.* **financier** (fin·an·sēr') *n.* one who deals in large-scale money transactions [Fr. fr. L.L. *finare*, to pay a fine].

finch (finch) *n.* the name applied to various species of small, seed-eating birds including the *chaffinch, bullfinch* [O.E. *finc*, finch].

find (find) *v.t.* to come to by searching; to meet with; to discover; to perceive; to experience; (*Law*) to give a verdict; *pa.t., pa.p.* **found.** *n.* a discovery, esp. of unexpected value. **-er** *n.* **-ing** *n.* the act of one who finds; a legal decision arrived at by a jury after deliberation; a discovery [O.E. *findan*, to find].

fine (fin) *a.* excellent; thin; slender; minute; delicate; noble; polished; showy; striking; refined (as *fine gold*); keen; appealing aesthetically (as the *Fine Arts*); perceptive; *v.t.* to make fine; to refine or purify; *v.i.* to become fine, pure, or slender; *adv.* **—drawn** *a.* invisibly mended (of cloth); delicately thin (of wire); subtly conceived (of an argument); **-ly** *adv.* **-ness** *n.* the state of being fine; the amount of gold in an alloy. **-r** *n.* refiner. **-ry** *n.* ornament; gay clothes; a furnace for making wrought iron. **—spun,** *a.* drawn out to a gossamer thread; (*Fig.*) subtle; ingenious. **finesse** (fa·nes') *n.* subtlety of contrivance to gain a point; stratagem; (*Whist, Bridge, etc.*) the attempt to take a trick with a low card while holding a higher card; *v.i.* and *v.t.* to use artifice; to try to take a trick by finesse [Fr. *fin*, exact].

fine (fin) *n.* a sum of money imposed as a penalty for an offense; conclusion, as in phrase *in fine*; *v.t.* to impose a fine on [L.L. *finis*, a payment].

fi·nesse See *fine.*

fin·ger (fing'·ger) *n.* a digit; any one of the extremities of the hand, excluding thumb; the width or length of a finger; something like a finger; *v.t.* to touch with fingers; to handle; to perform with fingers; to purloin; to meddle with; *v.i.* to use the fingers. **— alphabet** *n.* the finger-language of the deaf and dumb. **— board** *n.* that part of a violin, etc. on which fingers are placed; the keyboard of a piano. **— bowl** *n.* a small bowl of water to cleanse fingers at dinner. **-ing** *n.* the act of touching or handling lightly with fingers; the manner of manipulating the fingers in playing an instrument. [O.E. *finger*, a finger].

fin·i·al (fin'·i·al) *a.* ornamental topping of lamp, gable, etc. [L. *finire*, to finish].

fin·i·cal (fin'·i·kal) *a.* affectedly fine; over-fastidious. **-ly** *adv.* **finicking, finicky,** *a.* over-particular [prob. fr. *fine*].

fi·nis (fi'·nis) *n.* an end; conclusion [L.].

fin·ish (fin'·ish) *v.t.* to bring to an end; to terminate; to destroy; to complete; *v.i.* to

conclude; *n.* that which finishes, or perfects; last stage; the final coat of paint, etc. **-ed** *a.* terminated; perfect; polished; talented; **-er** *n.* one who or that which finishes or gives the final touches. **-ing school,** a school for completing the education of young women [Fr. *finir*, to finish].

fi·nite (fi'·nit) *a.* limited in quantity, degree, or capacity; bounded; countable; measurable (*Gram.*) used of a *predicating* verb (limited by number and person), oppos. of *infinitive* of verb. **-ly** *adv.* **-ness,** **finitude** *n.* [L. *finire*, to finish].

Finn (fin) *n.* a native of Finland. **Finnic, Finnish** *a.* **Finlander** *n.* a Finn.

fin·nan-had·dock (fin'·an·ha'·dak) *n.* smoked haddock, esp. that cured at Findon, Scotland. Also **finnan haddie.**

fir (fur) *n.* cone-bearing, evergreen tree, yielding valuable timber. **—cone** *n.* fruit of the fir. [O.E. *furh-* (*wudu*), fir-(wood)].

fire (fir) *n.* heat and light caused by combustion; burning; conflagration; ignited fuel; flame; discharge of firearms; ardor; spiritual or mental energy; impassioned eloquence; *v.t.* to set on fire; to kindle; to supply with fuel; to discharge (firearms, etc.); to inflame; to incite; (*Colloq.*) to dismiss; *v.i.* to be ignited; to be stimulated; to discharge firearms. **— alarm** *n.* an alarm giving warning of an discharges by fire exploding gunpowder. outbreak of fire. **-arm** *n.* a weapon which discharges by fire exploding gunpowder. **-ball** *n.* a meteor; (*Mil.*) a ball filled with combustibles. **—bomb** an incendiary bomb. **-box** *n.* the fire chamber of a locomotive. **-brand** *n.* a piece of flaming wood; a torch; (*Fig.*) one who incites others to strife. **— brigade** *n.* men specially trained to deal with fire. **-bug** *n.* an incendiary; (*Colloq.*) one guilty of arson. **-damp** *n.* gas generated in coal mines, which mixed with air, explodes violently in contact with a naked light. **-dog** *n.* (Same as andirons). **— escape** *n.* iron stair used as emergency exist from burning building. **-fly** *n.* a type of beetle which has light-producing organs. **-man** *n.* a member of a fire-fighting unit; a man who tends a furnace; a stoker. **-place** *n.* hearth or grate. **-plug** *n.* a hydrant for drawing water by hose to extinguish a fire. **-proof** *a.* **-r** *n.* **— screen** *n.* a movable protective screen in front of a fire. **-side** *n.* the hearth; (*Fig.*) home. **-water** *n.* term used by Am. Indians for whisky, brandy, etc. **-wood** *n.* wood for fuel; kindling. **-work** *n.* a preparation containing gunpowder, sulfur, etc. for making spectacular explosions. **firing line** *n.* the area of a battle zone within firing range of the enemy. **firing party** or **squad,** soldiers detailed to fire the final salute at a military funeral, or to shoot a condemned person [O.E. *fyr*, a fire].

fir·kin (fur'·kin) *n.* a small cask [O.Dut. *vierde*, four; and dim. suffix kin].

firm (furm) *a.* fixed; solid; compact; rigid; steady; unwavering; stern; inflexible. **-ly** *adv.* **-ness** *n.* [L. *firmus*, steadfast].

firm (furm) *n.* the name, title, or style under which a company transacts business [It. *firma*, a signature].

fir·ma·ment (fur'·ma·mant) *n.* the expanse of the sky; the heavens [L. *firmamentum*, a support, the sky].

first (furst) *a.* preceding all others in a series or in kind; foremost (in place); earliest (in time); most eminent; most excellent; highest; chief; *adv.* before anything else in time, place, degree, or preference; *n.* beginning; a first-class honors degree at a university. **— aid** *n.* preliminary treatment given to injured person before the arrival of a doctor. **—born** *n.* eldest child. **—class** *a.* first-rate; of highest worth; of superior accommodation; *adv.* in the first-class (of a train, boat, etc.). **—fruits** *n.pl.* earliest gathered fruits, orig. dedicated to God; (*Fig.*) earliest results or profits. **—hand** *a.* obtained direct from the source. **-ly** *adv.* **—rate** *a.* of highest excellence [O.E. *fyrst*, first].

firth (furth) *n.* (*Scot.*) a long narrow inlet of the sea or estuary of a river [O.N. *fjord*].

fisc (fisk) *n.* the State treasury; public revenue. **fiscal** *a.* pert. to the public treasury or revenue; pert. to financial matters generally.

fish (fish) *n.* a cold-blooded, aquatic vertebrate animal, with limbs represented by fins,

and breathing through its gills; the flesh of fish; *pl.* **fish, fishes.** *v.t.* to catch by fishing; *v.i.* to follow the occupation of a fisherman, for business or pleasure; to extract information, etc. by indirect, subtle questions (foll. by *for*). **-er** *n.* one who fishes; a marten. **-erman** *n.* one whose employment is to catch fish; one who fishes for pleasure; an angler. **-ery** *n.* the business of fishing; a fishing-ground; the legal right to fish in a certain area. **-hook** *n.* a barbed hook for catching fish by line. **-ily** *adv.* **-iness** *n.* **-ing** *n.* the act of fishing. **-ing rod** *n.* a long supple rod with line attached, used by anglers. **-ing tackle** *n.* an angler's gear comprising, rod, lines, hooks, etc. **— meal** *n.* dried fish ground into meal. **— story** (*Colloq.*) *n.* an unbelievable story. **-tail** *a.* shaped like the tail of a fish. **-wife** *n.* a woman selling fish in the streets; a shrill, nagging woman. **-y** *a.* abounding in fish; pert. to fish (of smell); expressionless; glazed (of eye); dubious (of a story). [O.E. *fisc*, fish].

fish (fish) *n.* a strip of wood fixed longitudinally to strengthen a mast, or clamp two pieces together; *v.t.* to splice; to join together. **-plate, — joint** *n.* a metal clamp used to join lengths of train rails together [Fr. *fiche*, a pin or peg].

fis·sile (fis'·il) *a.* capable of being split or cleft in the direction of the grain [L. *findere, fissum,* to cleave].

fis·sion (fish'·an) *n.* the process of splitting or breaking up into parts; (*Biol.*) cell-cleavage; in nuclear physics, the splitting of an atomic nucleus into two approx. equal fragments and a number of neutrons, with the liberation of a large amount of energy; *v.t. and i.* to split into two parts. **-able** *a.* [L. *findere, fissum,* to cleave].

fis·sure (fish'·ar) *n.* a cleft, crack, or slit [L. *findere, fissum,* to cleave].

fist (fist) *n.* the hand clenched with fingers doubled into the palm; (*Colloq.*) handwriting. **-ic** *a.* pugilistic. **-icuff** *n.* a blow with the fist; **-icuffs** *n.pl.* boxing; a brawl. **-y** *a.* [O.E. *fust*, the fist].

fis·tu·la (fis'·choo·la) *n.* (*Med.*) a narrow duct; an infected channel in the body leading from an internal abscess to the surface. **-r,** **fistulous** *a.* (*Bot.*) hollowed like a pipe [L. *fistula,* a pipe].

fit (fit) *a.* (*comp.*) **-ter.** (*superl.*) **-test.** adapted to an end or purpose; becoming; suitable; qualified; proper; vigorous (of bodily health); *v.t.* to make suitable; to qualify; to adapt; to adjust; to fashion to the appropriate size; *v.i.* to be proper or becoming; *pr.p.* **-ting.** *pa.p., p.t.* **-ted.** **-ly** *adv.* **-ness** *n.* the state of being fit; appropriateness; sound bodily health. **-ter** *n.* one who or that which makes fit; a tailor or dressmaker who fits clothes on a person; a mechanic who assembles separate parts of a machine. **-ting** *a.* appropriate; suitable; *n.* anything used in fitting up; a trial of a garment to see that it fits. **-tings** *n.pl.* fixtures; equipment. **-tingly** *adv.*

fit (fit) *n.* a sudden and violent attack of a disorder; a paroxysm; a seizure; a spasmodic attack (as of sneezing); a momentary impulse. **-ful** *a.* spasmodic; intermittent. **-fully** *adv.* [O.E. *fitt*, a struggle].

fit (fit) *n.* a song, or division of a poem; a canto [M.E. *fitte*, a stanza].

five (fiv) *n.* four and one; the symbol 5, or V; *a.* one more than four. **-fold** *a.* five times repeated; quintuple. **-r** *n.* (*Colloq.*) a five-dollar bill [O.E. *fif*].

fix (fiks) *v.t.* to make firm; to establish; to secure; to make permanent, as a photograph; to make fast, as a dye; to immobilize; to determine; to gaze at; to repair; to put in order; *v.i.* to settle permanently; to become hard; *n.* (*Colloq.*) dilemma; predicament; determination of the position of a ship or airplane by observations or radio signals. **-ation** *n.* the act of fixing; steadiness; (*Med.*) in psycho-analysis, an emotional arrest of part of the psycho-sexual development. **-ative** *n.* a fixing agent; a chemical which preserves specimens in a life-like condition; *a.* capable of fixing colors or structure of specimens. **-ed** *a.* settled, permanent, not apt to change; steady. **-edly** *adv.* **-edness** *n.* **-er** *n.* one who, or that which, fixes. **-ity** *n.* fixedness; immobility. **-ings** *n.pl.*

(*Colloq.*) apparatus; trimmings. **-ture** *n.* that which is fixed or attached; (house) anything of an accessory nature considered a part of the real property [L. *fixus*, fixed].

fizz (fiz) *v.i.* to make a hissing sound; to splutter; to effervesce; *n.* a hissing sound; any effervescent liquid. **fizzle** *v.i.* to fizz or splutter. *n.* (*Colloq.*) a fiasco. **-y** *a.* [imit.].

fjord See **fiord**.

flab·ber·gast (flab'·er·gast) *v.t.* (*Colloq.*) to overcome with amazement; to confound [prob. conn. with *flabby*].

flab·by (flab'·i·) *a.* soft; yielding to the touch; drooping; weak; lacking in moral fiber. **flabbily** *adv.* **flabbiness** *n.* [fr.*flap*].

flac·cid (flak'·sid) *a.* soft; flabby; limp. **-ly** *adv.* **-ness, -ity** *n.* [L. *flaccidus*, flabby].

flag (flag) *v.i.* to hang loosely; to grow spiritless or dejected; to become languid; to lose vigor, *pr.p.* **-ging**. *pa.p.* **-ged**.

flag (flag) *n.* a flat paving stone; a type of sandstone which splits easily into large slabs. Also **-stone** [Ice. *flaga*, a slab].

flag (flag) *n.* (*Bot.*) a popular name of certain species of plants belonging to the genus *Iris*, with long sword-shaped leaves.

flag (flag) *n.* an ensign or colors; a standard; a banner as a mark of distinction, rank, or nationality; the bushy tail of a setter dog; *v.t.* to decorate with flags or bunting; to convey a message by flag signals. **— officer** *n.* an admiral, entitled to display a flag indicating his rank; the commander of a fleet or squadron. **-ship** *n.* the ship flying the admiral's flag. **white flag**, the symbol of truce or surrender. **yellow flag**, a flag indicating that a ship is in quarantine. **to dip the flag**, to lower, then hoist, flag as a mark of respect.**to fly a flag half-mast**, to hoist flag half-way as token of mourning [etym. doubtful, prob. Scand.].

flag·el·late (flaj'·a·lāt) *v.t.* to whip; to scourge; to flog; *a.* (*Biol.*) having a long thread-like appendage, like a lash. **flagellantism, flagellation** *n.* **flagellant** *n.* an ascetic who voluntarily scourges himself as punishment for sin [L. *flagellare, to scourge*].

flag·eo·let (flaj·a·let') *n.* a small non-reed wind instrument [dim. of O.Fr. *flageol*, a pipe].

fla·gi·tious (fla·jish'·as) *a.* shamefully criminal [L. *flagitiosus* disgraceful].

flag·on (flag'·an) *n.* a vessel for holding liquids, usually with handle, spout and lid [Fr. *flacon*, a flask].

fla·grant (flā'·grant) *a.* glaring; notorious; scandalous. **flagrance, flagrancy** *n.* **-ly** *adv.* [L. *flagrare*, to burn].

flail (flāl) *n.* an implement for threshing grain by hand, consisting of a stout stick attached to a handle [L. *flagellum*, a whip].

flair (fler) *n.* instinctive discernment; a keen scent [Fr. *flairer*, to scent out].

flak (flak) *n.* anti-aircraft fire (*World War 2*) [Ger. (*abbrev.*) *Flugabwehrkanone*, anti-aircraft gun].

flake (flāk) *n.* a scale-like particle; a piece of a thin layer; *v.t.* to form into flakes; to cover with flakes; *v.i.* to scale; to fall in flakes. **flaky** *a.* consisting of flakes [Scand. *flaki*, flake].

flam·beau (flam'·bō) *n.* a flaming torch; an ornamental candlestick; *pl.* **flambeaux** [Fr. fr. L. *flamma*, a flame].

flam·boy·ant (flam·boi'·ant) *a.* (*Archit.*) characterized by flame-like tracery and florid ornamentation of windows, panels, etc.; florid; showy; ornate. **flamboyance, flamboyancy** *n.* [Fr. *flamboyer*, to flame].

flame (flām) *n.* a mass of burning vapor or gas; a blaze of light; fire in general; ardor; vehemence of mind or imagination; (*Slang*) a sweetheart; *v.i.* to blaze; to blush; to become violently excited, fervent, or angry. **—colored** *a.* of the color of a flame; bright red or yellow. **— thrower** *n.* a short range trench weapon throwing ignited fuel into the enemy's lines. **flaming** *a.* blazing; gaudy; fervent. **flamingly** *adv.* **flammability** *n.* **flammable** *a.* [L. *flamma*, a flame].

fla·min·go (fla·ming'·gō) *n.* tropical wading bird [L. *flamma*, a flame].

flan (flan) *n.* a pastry shell or cake filled with fruit filling [O.Fr. *flaon*, a flat cake].

flange (flanj) *n.* a projecting edge, as of a railway-car wheel to keep it on the rails, or

of castings to fasten them together; *v.t.* [O.Fr. *flanche*, fr. *flanc*, a side].

flank (flangk) *n.* the fleshy part of side of animal between ribs and hip; the right or left side of an army; part of a bastion; the side of a building; *v.t.* to stand at the side of; to protect the flank of an army, etc.; to border *v.i.* [O.Fr. *flanc*, the side].

flan·nel (flan'·al) *n.* a soft-textured, loosely woven woolen cloth. **-s** *n.pl.* clothes made of this, esp. sports garments; woolen undergarments; *a.* made of flannel; *v.t.* to cover or rub with flannel. **-ette** *n.* a cotton material like flannel [W. *gwlanen*, fr. *gwlan*, wool].

flap (flap) *n.* the motion or noise of anything broad and hanging loose; a piece of flexible material attached on one side only and usually covering an opening, as of envelope; anything hinged and hanging loose; *v.t.* to cause to sway or flutter; to strike with something broad and flexible, such as a duster; to move rapidly up and down; *v.i.* to flutter; to fall like a flap; to move, as wings. *pr.p.* **-ping**. *pa.p.* **-ped**. **-jack** *n.* a broad, flat pancake. **-per** *n.* one who or that which flaps; (*Slang*) the hand; (*Colloq.*) an adolescent girl; a flighty, young woman [imit.].

flare (fler) *v.i.* to burn with a glaring, unsteady or fitful flame; to burst out with flame, anger, etc.; to curve out; *n.* an unsteady, blazing light; a brilliant, often colored, light used as a signal; a spreading or curving out, as the hull of a ship; a sudden burst of flame, passion, etc. **flared** *a.* (of a skirt) spreading gradually out toward the bottom. **flaring** *a.* [Scand. *flara*, to blaze].

flash (flash) *n.* a sudden brief burst of light; an instant or moment; a fleeting emotional outburst; (*Colloq.*) thieves' language; rush of water; a news story; *a.* showy; tawdry; pert. to thieves; *v.i.* to blaze suddenly and die out; to give out a bright but fitful gleam; to shine out, as a stroke of wit or sudden idea; to pass swiftly; *v.t.* to cause to flash; to transmit instantaneously, as news by radio, telephone, etc. **— back** *n.* momentary turning back to an episode in a story. **— bulb** *n.* (*Photog.*) an electric bulb giving brilliant flash for night picture. **-ily** *adv.* **-iness** *n.* **-light** *n.* a portable light powered by batteries or a small generator. **-y** *a.* showy; tawdry; cheap. [M.E. *flarihe(n)*, rise and dash].

flask (flask) *n.* a narrow-necked, usually flat bottle easily carried in the pocket; a wicker-covered bottle; a powder-horn. **-et** *n.* a small flask; a long, shallow basket [It. *fiasco*].

flat (flat) *a.* (*comp.*) **-ter**. (*superl.*) **-test**. level; even; tasteless; monotonous; dull; unqualified; without point or spirit; uniform; spread out; downright; (*Mus.*) below the true pitch (opp. of *sharp*); *n.* a level surface; low-lying sometimes flooded, tract of land; a shoal; (*Mus.*) a note, a semitone below the natural; the symbol for this; a piece of canvas or board mounted on a frame used as stage scenery. *adv.* prone; exactly. (*Mus.*) in a manner below true pitch. **—finish** *n.* a flat surface in paint work. **—footed** *a.* having fallen arches in the feet. **-iron** *n.* an iron for smoothing linen, etc. **-ly** *adv.* peremptorily. **-ness** *n.* **— rate**, uniform rate. **-ten** *v.t.* to make flat; to lower the true musical pitch of; **-top** *n.* an aircraft carrier. **-ware** *n.* silver knives, forks, etc. [Scand. *flatr*, flat].

flat·ter (flat'·er) *v.t.* to praise unduly and insincerely; to pay fulsome compliments to; to depict as being an improvement on the original. **-er** *n.* **-ing** *a.* **-ingly** *adv.* **-y** *n.* the act of flattering; undue praise [O.Fr. *flater*, to smooth].

flat·u·lent (fla'·cha·lant) *a.* pert. to or affected with wind or gas in stomach and intestines; (*Fig.*) empty; vapid. **flatulence, flatulency** *n.* distension of stomach or intestines by excessive accumulation of wind or gas. **-ly** *adv.* **flatus** *n.* air or gas in stomach, etc. [L. *flare*, to blow].

flaunt (flawnt) *v.t.* to display ostentatiously or impudently; *v.i.* to wave or move in the wind; to parade showily; *n.* a vulgar display.

fla·vor (flā'·ver) *n.* savor; quality affecting taste or smell; distinctive quality of a thing. *v.t.* to season; (*Fig.*) to give zest to. **-ous** *a.* **-ing** *n.* substance to add flavor to a dish, e.g. spice, essence [O.Fr. *flaur*, smell].

flaw (flaw) *n.* a crack; a defect; a weak point as in an argument; *v.t.* to break; to crack; **-less** *a.* perfect [Scand. *flaga*, a slab].

flaw (flaw) *n.* a sudden gust of wind; a squall [Dut. *vlaag*, a gust of wind].

flax (flaks) *n.* the fibers of an annual blue-flowered plant, *Linum*, used for making linen; the plant itself. **-en** *a.* pert. to or resembling flax; loose or flowing; of the color of unbleached flax, hence yellowish or golden (esp. of hair) [O.E. *flaex*, flax].

flay (flā) *v.t.* to skin; (*Fig.*) to criticize bitterly [O.E. *flean*, to strike].

flea (flē) *n.* a small, wingless, very agile insect with irritating bite. **-bitten** *a.* bitten by a flea; (*Fig.*) mean; worthless [O.E. *fleah*, a flea].

fleck (flek) *n.* a spot; a streak; *v.t.* to spot; to dapple [Scand. *flekka*, to spot].

fled (fled) *pa.t.* and *pa.p.* of **flee**.

fledge (flej) *v.t.* to supply with feathers for flight, as an arrow; to rear a young bird; *v.i.* to acquire feathers; to become able to fly (of birds). **-ling** *n.* a young bird just fledged; (*Fig.*) a young untried person [O.E. *flycge*, feathered].

flee (flē) *v.i.* to fly or retreat from danger; *v.t.* to hasten from; *pr.p.* **-ing**. *pa.p., p.t.* **fled** [O.E. *fleon*, to fly].

fleece (flēs) *n.* the coat of wool covering a sheep or shorn from it; anything resembling wool; *v.t.* to shear wool (from sheep); (*Fig.*) to rob; to swindle. **fleecy** *a.* woolly; resembling wool [O.E. *fleos*, fleece].

fleet (flēt) *n.* a group of ships; a force of naval vessels under one command; (*Fig.*) a number of motor vehicles, etc. organized as a unit [O.E. *fleot*, a ship].

fleet (flēt) *n.* a creek, inlet, or small stream [O.E. *fleot*, an inlet].

fleet (flēt) *a.* swift; nimble. *v.i.* to pass swiftly; *v.t.* to make to pass quickly. **-ing** *a.* transient; ephemeral; passing. **-ingly** *adv.* **-ness** *n.* swiftness. **-footed** *a.* swift of foot [O.E. *fleotan*, to swim].

Flem·ing (flem'·ing) *n.* a native of Flanders, **Flemish** *a.* pert. to Flanders [Dut. *Vlaamsch*].

flense (flens) *v.t.* to cut up the blubber of, as a whale [Dan. *flense*].

flesh (flesh) *n.* the body tissue; the muscles, fat, etc. covering the bones of an animal; the body as distinct from the soul; mankind; kindred; sensuality; the pulpy part of fruit; *v.t.* to incite to hunt, as a hound, by feeding it on flesh; to glut; to thrust into flesh, as a sword; to remove flesh from the under side of hides preparatory to tanning process. **-color** *n.* the pale pink color of the human skin (of white races). **-iness** *n.* state of being fleshy; plumpness. **-ings** *n.pl.* flesh-colored tights worn by dancers, acrobats, etc. **-less** *a.* **-liness** *n.* **-ly** *a.* corporeal; worldly; sensual. **-pot** *n.* a vessel in which meat is cooked; (*Fig.*) luxurious living. **— wound** *n.* **-y** *a.* pert. to flesh; corpulent; gross; (*Bot.*) thick and soft. **proud flesh** (*Med.*) a growth of granular tissue over a wound [O.E. *flaesc*, flesh].

fletch (flech) *v.t.* to feather (as an arrow). *n.pl.* feathers on an arrow [Fr. *flèche*, an arrow].

fleur-de-lis (flur·da·lē') *n.* a design based on the shape of an iris; the royal insignia of France [Fr. *fleur-de-lis*, flower of the lily].

flew (flōō) *pa.t.* of verb **fly**.

flex (fleks) *v.t.* and *v.i.* to bend (as the joints of the body). **-ibility** *n.* quality of being pliable; (*Fig.*) adaptability; versatility. **-ible** *a.* **-ibly** *adv.* **-ile** *a.* bendable. **-ion, flection** *n.* a bend; a fold; an inflection. **-or** *n.* a muscle. **-uose, -uous** *a.* bending; tortuous. **-ure** *n.* act of bending; a bend [L. *flexus*, bent].

flick (flik) v.t. to strike lightly, as with whip; n. light, smart stroke.

flick·er (flik'·er) v.i. to flutter; to waver; to quiver; to burn unsteadily. n. act of wavering; quivering [O.E. *flicorian*, to flutter].

flight (flīt) n. the act or power of flying; the distance covered in flying; a journey by airplane; a formation of planes forming a unit; a flock of birds; a soaring, as of the imagination; a discharge of arrows; a volley; a series of steps between successive landings. — **deck**, n. the deck of an aircraft carrier for planes to land or take off. **-y** a. capricious; giddy; volatile [O.E. *flyht*, flight].

flight (flīt) n. the act of fleeing; retreat. **to put to flight**, to rout [O.E. *fleon*, to flee].

flim·sy (flim'·zi·) a. thin; fragile; unsubstantial; n. thin, transfer-paper; (Slang) a banknote. **flimsily** adv. **flimsiness**.

flinch (flinch) v.i. to shrink from pain or difficulty; to wince. **-ing** n. the act of flinching [O.Fr. *flenchir*, to turn aside].

fling (fling) v.t. to throw from the hand; to hurl; to send out; to plunge; v.i. to flounce; to throw oneself violently. pa.t., pa.p. **flung**. n. a cast or throw; a gibe; abandonment to pleasure; lively dance. **-er** n. [Scand. *flanga*, to move violently].

flint (flint) n. quartz, which readily produces fire when struck with steel; anything hard; a prehistoric stone weapon; a. made of flint. **-lock** n. a gunlock with a flint fixed on the hammer for firing the priming. **-y** a. made of, or resembling, flint; (Fig.) hard-hearted; cruel [O.E. *flint*].

flintlock

flip (flip) n. a drink composed of eggs, sugar and liquor [prob. fr. verb *flip*].

flip (flip) v.t. to flick; to jerk. pr.p. **-ping**. pa.t., pa.p. **-ped**, n. a flick; a snap. **-per** n. the limb of an animal which facilitates swimming; (Slang) the human hand [var. of *flap*].

flip·pant (flip'·ant) a. pert. to shallow; smart or pert in speech. **flippancy** n. **-ly** adv.

flirt (flurt) v.t. to jerk, as a bird's tail; to move playfully to and fro, as a fan; v.i. to move about briskly; to play the coquette; to dally; n. a jerk; a philanderer; a flighty girl. **-ation** n. **-atious** a. [etym. doubtful].

flit (flit) v.i. to fly away; to dart along; to flutter. pr.p. **-ting**. pa.t., pa.p. **-ted** [Scand. *flytja*, to cause to float].

flit·ter (flit'·er) v.i. to flutter.

float (flōt) v.i. to rest or drift on the surface of a liquid; to be buoyed up; to be suspended in air; to wander aimlessly; v.t. to cause to stay on the surface of a liquid; to cover a surface with water; to set going, as a business company; to put into circulation; n. anything which is buoyant; a raft; cork or quill on a fishing line, or net; a hollow floating ball of metal indicating depth of liquid in tank or cistern; a plasterer's trowel; (Aero.) a streamlined attachment to a seaplane enabling it to float; theater footlights. **-able** a. **-age** n. See **flotage**. **-ation** n. **flotation. -er** n. **-ing** a. buoyant on surface of the water or in air; movable; fluctuating; in circulation. **-ing dock**, a floating dry dock. **-ingly** adv. **-ing population**, shifting population. **-ing ribs**, lower ribs not connected to breastbone [O.E. *flotian*, to float].

flo·cus (flak'·as) n. a long tuft of wool or hair; pl. **flocci** (flok'·sī) **floccose** (flak'·ōs) **flocculent**, a. woolly; having tufts; flaky [L. *floccus*, flock of wool].

flock (flak) n. a small tuft of wool; refuse of wool in cloth making, used for stuffing cushions, etc.; small wool fibers used in making wall paper [L. *floccus*, flock of wool].

flock (flak) n. a collection of animals; a crowd of people; a Christian congregation; v.i. to come together in crowds [O.E. *flocc*, a band].

floe (flō) n. an extensive field of ice floating in the sea [Scand. *flo*, a layer].

flog (flag) v.t. to beat or strike, as with a rod or whip; to thrash. pr.p. **-ging**. pa.t., pa.p. **-ged** [L. *flagellare*, to whip].

flood (flud) n. an overflow of water; an inundation; a deluge; the flowing in of the tide; (Lit. and Fig.) a torrent. v.t. to overflow; to drench; (Fig.) to overwhelm; v.i. to spill over; to rise (as the tide). **-lighting** n. artificial lighting by lamps fitted with special reflectors.— **tide** n. the rising tide; (Fig.) peak of prosperity [O.E. *flod*, a stream].

floor (flōr) n. the horizontal surface of a room upon which one walks; a story; any level area; inside bottom surface of anything (room, sea, etc.); minimum level, esp. of prices. v.t. to cover with a floor; to strike down; (Colloq.) to perplex; to stump (in argument). **-age** n. floor space. **-cloth** n. a heavy material used for covering floors. **-er** n. a knock-out blow; (Colloq.) a baffling examination question or situation. **-ing** n. materials for floors. — **show** n. a show at a nightclub. — **walker** n. a person employed by a store to supervise one floor [O.E. *flor*].

flop (flop) v.t. to flap; to set down heavily. v.i. to drop down suddenly or clumsily. pr.p. **-ping**. pa.t. pa.p. **-ped**. n. a fall, as of a soft, outspread body; (Slang) a fiasco. **-py** a. slack; (of a hat brim) wide and soft [var. of *flap*].

flo·ra (flō'·ra) n. the plants native to a certain geographical region or geological period; a classified list of such plants. **floral** a. **florally** adv. adorned with flowers. **floriated**, a. **floret** n. a single flower in a cluster of flowers; a small compact flower head. **florist** n. a grower or seller of flowers [L. *Flora*, the goddess of flowers].

flo·res·cence (flō·res'·ans) n. a bursting into flower. **florescent** a. [L. *florescere*, to burst into flower].

flor·id (flawr'·id) a. bright in color; overelaborate; ornate; (of complexion) highly colored; (Archit.) overly decorative. **-ly** adv. **-ity** n. [L. *floridus*, flowery].

floss (flas) n. untwisted threads of very fine silk; the outer fibers of a silkworm's cocoon. **-silk** n. very soft silk thread. **-y** a. [It. *floscio*, soft].

flo·tage (flō'·tij) n. state or act of floating; the floating capacity of anything; (Colloq.) flotsam [O.E. *flotian*, to float].

flo·ta·tion (flō·tā'·shan) n. the act of floating; science of floating bodies; act of launching, esp. a business venture, loan, etc. Also **floatation** [O.E. *flotian*, to float].

flo·til·la (flō·til'·a) n. a fleet of small vessels [Sp. *flotilla*, a little fleet].

flot·sam (flat'·sam) n. goods lost by shipwreck and found floating on the sea [O.Fr. *flotaison*, a floating].

flounce (flouns) v.i. to turn abruptly; to flounder about; n. a sudden, jerky movement [Scand. *flunsa*, to plunge].

flounce (flouns) n. a plaited border or frill on hem of a dress; v.t. to trim with a flounce. **flouncing** n. material used for flounces [M.E. *frounce*, a plait].

floun·der (floun'·der) n. a small, edible flatfish [Scand. *flundra*, a flounder].

floun·der (floun'·der) v.i. to struggle helplessly, as in marshy ground; to tumble about; (Fig.) to stumble hesitatingly, as in a speech.

flour (flour) n. the finely ground meal of wheat, etc.; any finely powdered substance; v.t. to turn into flour; to sprinkle with flour. **-y** a. [Fr. *fleur de farine*, the flower (i.e. the best) of meal].

flour·ish (flur'·ish) v.t. to decorate with flowery ornament or with florid diction; to brandish; v.i. to grow luxuriantly; to prosper; to execute ostentatiously a passage of music; n. ornament; a fanciful stroke of the pen; rhetorical display; (Mus.) florid improvisation either as prelude or addition to a composition; a fanfare; brandishing (of a weapon); **-ing** a. thriving; vigorous [M.E. *florisshen*, to blossom].

flout (flout) v.t. to mock; to disregard with contempt; v.i. to jeer; n. an expression of contempt; a gibe; an insult [prob. fr. M.E. *flouten*, to play the flute].

flow (flō) v.i. to run, as a liquid; to rise, as the tide; to circulate, as the blood; to issue forth; to glide along; to proceed from; to fall in waves, as the hair; v.t. to overflow; n. a stream; a current; the rise of the tide; any easy expression of thought, diction, etc.; copiousness; output. **-ing** a. moving; running; fluent; curving gracefully, as lines; falling in folds, as drapery. **-ingly** adv. [O.E. *flowan*, to flow].

flow·er (flou'·er) n. (Bot.) the reproductive organ in plants; a blossom; the choicest part of anything; the finest type; a figure of speech; an ornament in shape of a flower. **-s** n.pl. a substance in the form of a powder, as *flowers of sulphur*; v.t. to adorn with flowers or flower-like shapes; v.i. to produce flowers; to bloom; to prime condition. **-ed** a. decorated with a flower pattern, as fabric. **-et** n. a small flower; a floret. **-ing** a. having flowers. **-y** a. abounding in, or decorated with flowers; (of style) highly ornate; euphuistic [L. *flos*, a flower].

flown (flōn) pa.p. of **fly**.

flu (flōo) n. (Colloq.) influenza.

fluc·tu·ate (fluk'·choo·āt) v.i. to move up and down, as a wave; to be unstable; to be irresolute. **fluctuant** a. **fluctuation** n. a vacillation [L. *fluctus*, a wave].

flue (flōo) n. a shaft or duct in a chimney; a pipe for conveying air through a boiler; the opening in the pipe of an organ.

flu·ent (flōo'·ant) a. flowing; ready in the use of words; (of lines) gracefully curved. **fluency** n. adv. [L. *fluere*, to flow].

fluff (fluf) n. light, floating down; downy growth of hair on skin; v.t. to give a fluffy surface to; v.i. to become downy; (Slang) to make errors in the speaking of a stage part. **-y** a. [prob. var. of *flue*].

fluid (flōo'·id) n. a substance which flows (liquid, gas, etc.); a non-solid; a. capable of flowing; liquid; gaseous; shifting. **-ify** v.t. to make fluid. **-ity, -ness** n. the state or quality of being a non-solid; (Fig.) the state of being alterable. **-ly** adv. [L. *fluidus*, flowing].

fluke (flōok) n. the flounder; a parasitic worm [O.E. *floc*, a flat-fish].

fluke (flōok) n. the flattened barb at the extremity of either arm of an anchor [O.E. *floc*, a flat-fish].

fluke (flōok) n. (Colloq.) any lucky chance.

flung (flung) pa.t. and pa.p. of **fling**.

flunk (flungk) (Colloq.) v.i. to fail as in an examination or course; v.t. to fail in; to disqualify a student for low achievement; to give a student a failing grade; n. a failure.

flun·ky (flung'·ki·) n. a liveried manservant; a toady; an obsequious person. **-ism** n. [Fr. *flanquer*, to run at the side of].

flu·or (flōo'·er) n. a mineral, fluoride of calcium, usually called *fluorite*; principle source of fluorine. **-esce** v.i. to exhibit fluorescence. **-escence** n. the property of some substances which emit surface reflections of light different in color from the mass of the material upon exposure to external radiation. **-escent** a. **-ide** n. a compound of fluorine with another element. **-ine** n. a pale yellow very active gaseous element. **-escent lighting**, a form of artificial diffused lighting, giving the effect of permanent daylight [L. *fluere*, to flow].

flur·ry (flur'·i·) n. a sudden, brief gust of wind; bustle; commotion; v.t. to agitate; to fluster [prob. imit. flutter and hurry].

flush (flush) v.i. to turn red in the face; to blush; to flow with a rush v.t. to cause to blush or turn red; to animate with high spirits; to cleanse with a rush of water; n. a flow of water; a rush of blood to the face; elation; freshness [origin uncertain].

flush (flush) v.t. to cause to start, as a hunter, a bird; v.i. to fly up quickly and suddenly from concealment; n. the act of starting up; a flock of birds flying up suddenly [M.E. *fluschen*, to fly up].

flush (flush) n. a run of cards of the same suit [L. *fluxus*, a flowing].

flush (flush) v.t. to level up; a. being in the same plane; well-supplied, as with money; full; (Print.) even with margins.

flus·ter (flus'·ter) v.t. to make agitated; to flurry; v.i. to be confused and flurried; n. confusion; nervous agitation. **-ed** a. [Scand. *flaustr*, hurry].

flute (flōot) n. a musical tubular wind-instrument; a stop in the pipe-organ; (Archit.) a vertical groove in the shaft of a column; a similar groove as in a lady's ruffle; v.i. to play the flute; to sing or recite in flute-like tones; v.t. to play (tune) on the flute; to make flutes or grooves in. **fluted** a. ornamented with grooves, channels, etc. **fluting** n. action of playing a flute; the ornamental vertical grooving on a pillar, on glass, or in a lady's ruffle. **flutist** n. one who plays a flute. Also **flautist**. **fluty** a. [L.L. *flauta*].

flut·ter (flut'·er) v.t. to cause to flap; to throw into confusion; to move quickly; v.i. to flap the wings; to move with quick vibrations; (of heart) to palpitate; n. quick and irregular motion; nervous hurry; confusion [O.E. *flotorian*, to float about].

flu·vi·al (flōo'·vi·al) a. pert. to, or produced by, a river. [L. *fluvius*, a river].

flux (fluks) n. the act of flowing; fluidity; (Phys.) the rate of flow; (Med.) morbid discharge of body-fluid, esp. blood; dysentery; (Chem.) a substance added to another to promote fusibility; continuous process of change; v.t. to fuse; to melt; v.i. to flow. **-ion** n. a flow or flux [L. *fluere*, to flow].

fly (flī) *v.t.* to cause to fly; to direct the flight of; to flee from; *v.i.* to move through the air, as a bird or an aircraft; to become airborne; to travel by airplane; to move rapidly; to flee; *pr.p.* **-ing** *pa.t.* **flew** (flōō). *pa.p.* **flown.** *n.* a winged insect, esp. of the order *Diptera*; a housefly; a fishhook in imitation of a fly; a flap on a garment covering a row of buttons or other fastener; (*Sports*) a ball sent high in the air (*pa.t., pa.p.* in baseball, **flied**). **flies** *n.pl.* the space above a theater stage where scenery is moved. **-ing** *n.* moving through the air; air navigation; *a.* capable of flight; streaming; swift. **-ing-boat** *n.* a seaplane. **-ing-buttress** (*Archit.*) an arched prop attached only at one point to the mass of masonry whose outward thrust it is designed to counteract. **-ing-saucer** *n.* name given to a saucer-like object reputedly seen flying at tremendous speeds and high altitudes. **-ing squirrel,** squirrel-like rodent with expanding fold of skin between front and hind legs. **-ing visit,** a hasty, unexpected visit. **-leaf** *n.* the blank page at the beginning or end of a book. **-man** *n.* a scene-shifter in the theater. **-paper** *n.* a paper smeared with sticky substance to trap flies. **-wheel** *n.* a heavy-rimmed wheel attached to the crankshaft of an engine to regulate its speed or accumulate power [O.E. *fleogan*, to fly].

flywheel

foal (fōl) *n.* the young of a mare or she-ass; a colt or a filly; *v.t.* and *v.i.* to bring forth a foal [O.E. *fola*, a young animal].
foam (fōm) *n.* froth; spume; the bubbles of air on surface of effervescent liquid; *v.i.* to froth; to bubble; to gather foam; **-ing** *a.* **-ingly** *adv.* — **rubber** *n.* latex made into a soft, elastic, and porous substance, resembling a sponge. **-y** *a.* frothy [O.E. *fam*, foam].
fob (fŏb) *n.* a small pocket in the waistband for holding a watch; a chain with seals, etc. dangling from the pocket [Dial H. Ger. *fuppe*, a pocket].

fo'c's'le See **forecastle.**
fo·cus (fō'·kus) *n.* the point at which rays of light meet after reflection or refraction; (*Geom.*) one of two points connected linearly to any point on a curve; any point of concentration; *pl.* **-es, foci** (fō'·sī); *v.t.* to bring to a focus; to adjust; to concentrate; *v.i.* to converge. *pr.p.* **-ing.** *pa.p.* **-ed.** **focal** *a.* pert. to a focus. **focalize** *v.t.* to bring into focus; to cause to converge; to concentrate. **focalization** *n.* **in focus,** clearly outlined; well defined. **out of focus,** distorted [L. *focus*, a fireplace].
foe (fō) *n.* an enemy; an adversary; a hostile army [O.E. *fah*, hostile].
foe·tus See **fetus.**
fog (fŏg) *n.* thick mist; watery vapor in the lower atmosphere; a cloud of dust or smoke obscuring visibility; (*Fig.*) mental confusion; *v.t.* to shroud in fog; to perplex the mind. *v.i.* to become cloudy or obscured. — **bank** *n.* a mass of fog. **-bound** *a.* hindered by fog from reaching destination, as a ship, train, etc. **-gily** *adv.* **-giness** *n.* **-gy** *a.* **-horn** *n.* a loud siren used during fog for warnings.
fo·gy, fogey (fō'·gi·) *n.* dull, old fellow; an elderly person whose ideas are behind the times.
foi·ble (foi'·bl) *n.* weakness of character; a failing [O.Fr. *foible*, weak].
foil (foil) *v.t.* to frustrate; to baffle; to put off the scent *n.* a blunt sword, with button on point, for fencing practice [O.Fr. *fuler*, to trample on].
foil (foil) *n.* a thin leaf of metal, as *tinfoil*; a thin leaf of metal placed under gems to increase their brilliancy or color; a thin coating of quicksilver amalgam on the back of a

mirror; (*Archit.*) a leaf-like ornament in windows, niches, etc. (*trefoil, quatrefoil, cinquefoil,* etc.); (*Fig.*) anything serving to set off something else [L. *folium*, a leaf].
foist (foist) *v.t.* to palm off; to insert surreptitiously or unwarrantably. **-er** *n.* [prob. Dut. *vuisten*, to take in the hand].
fold (fōld) *n.* a doubling over of a flexible material; a pleat; a coil (or rope); a crease or a line made by folding; (*Geol.*) a dip in rock strata caused originally by pressure; *v.t.* to double over; to enclose within folds or layers; to embrace; *v.i.* to be pleated or doubled. **-er** *n.* the one who or that which folds; a folded, printed paper; a file for holding papers, etc. [O.E. *fealdan*, to fold].
fold (fōld) *n.* an enclosure for sheep; a flock of sheep; the church; a congregation; *v.t.* to confine in a fold [O.E. *fald*, a stall].
fol·der·al See **falderal.**
fo·li·age (fō'·li·ij) *n.* leaves of a plant in general; leafage. **-d** *a.* having leaves. **foliate** *v.t.* to hammer (metal) into laminae or foil; (*Archit.*) to ornament with leaf design; to number the leaves (not pages) of a book; *a.* resembling a leaf; having leaves. **foliated** *a.* **foliation** *n.* **foliolate** *a.* pert. to leaflets or the separate parts of a compound leaf [L. *folium*, a leaf].
fo·li·o (fō'·li·ō) *n.* a sheet of paper once folded; a book of such folded sheets; the two opposite pages of a ledger used for one account and numbered the same; (*Print*) page number in a book; *a.* pert. to or formed of sheets folded so as to make two leaves; *v.t.* to number the pages of a book on one side only [L. *folium*, a leaf].
folk (fōk) *n.* people in general, or as a specified class. **-s** *n.pl.* (*Colloq.*) one's own family and near relations; *a.* originating among the common people. — **dance** *n.* a traditional country dance. **-lore** *n.* popular superstitions or legends; the study of traditional beliefs [O.E. *folc*, the people].
fol·li·cle (fŏl'·i·kl) *n.* (*Bot.*) a one-celled seed vessel; (*Zool.*) a small sac; (*Anat.*) a gland, as in *hair-follicle.* **follicular** *a.* pert. to a follicle [L. *folliculus*, a little bag].
fol·low (fŏl'·ō) *v.t.* to go after; to move behind; to succeed (in a post); to adhere to (a belief); to practice (as a trade or profession); to comprehend; to watch carefully; to keep in touch with; *v.i.* to come after; to pursue; to occur as a consequence; *n.* the act of following. **-er** *n.* one who comes after; adherents; vocation; *a.* coming next after [O.E. *folgian*, to accompany].
fol·ly (fŏl'·i·) *n.* want of sense; weakness of mind; a foolish action; (*pl.*) a theatrical revue [O.Fr. *fol*, a fool].
fo·ment (fō·ment') *v.t.* to encourage or instigate; to bathe with warm water to relieve pain. **-ation** *n.* instigation, of discord, etc.; the action of applying warm lotions; the lotion applied. **-er** *n.* [L. *fomentum*, a poultice].
fond (fŏnd) *a.* loving; doting; very affectionate. **fond of,** much attached to; **-le** *v.t.* to caress; to stroke tenderly. **-ly** *adv.* **-ness** *n.* [M.E. *fonned*, infatuated].
fon·dant (fŏn'·dant) *n.* a thick, creamy sugar candy [Fr. *fondre*, to melt].
font (fŏnt) *n.* a stone basin for holding baptismal water; a receptable for holy water [L. *fons*, a fountain].

food (fōōd) *n.* matter which one feeds on; solid nourishment as contrasted with liquids; that which, absorbed by any organism, promotes growth; (*Fig.*) mental or spiritual nourishment. **-stuff** *n.* edible commodity with nutritional value [O.E. *foda*, food].
fool (fōōl) *n.* one who behaves stupidly; one devoid of common sense; a simpleton, a clown; a dupe; *v.t.* to make a fool of, to impose on; to trick *v.i.* to behave like a fool; to trifle. **-ery** *n.* silly behavior; foolish act. **-hardily** *adv.* **-hardiness** *n.* **-hardy** *a.* recklessly daring; venturesome. **-ish** *a.* weak in intellect; ill-considered; stupid. **-ishly** *adv.* **-ishness** *n.* **-ing** *n.* foolery. **-proof** *a.* (of machines) so devised that mishandling cannot cause damage to machine or personnel. **-scap** *n.* any of various sizes of writing paper. [L. *folis*, a windbag].

foot (foot) *n.* the extreme end of the lower limbs, below the ankle; a base or support, like a foot; the end of a bed, couch, etc. where the feet would normally lie; footsoldiers; a measure of length = 12 inches; (*Prosody*) a combination of syllables measured according to quantity or stress-accent; the bottom of a page, ladder, etc.; the total of an account; *pl.* **feet.** *v.t.* to traverse by walking; (*Colloq.*) to add (an account); (*Colloq.*) to pay (a bill); to put a new foot on; *v.i.* to dance; to walk. **-age** *n.* the length expressed in feet. **-ball** *n.* a game played by two teams of eleven each trying to carry or pass the ball over the opponents' goal line; the elongated inflated leather ball used in the game; the round ball used in soccer. **-ed** *a.* having feet or a foot (usually in compounds as *two-footed, sure-footed*). **-fall** *n.* a step; sound of a step. **-gear** *n.* boots and shoes; stockings, socks. **-hold** *n.* a support for the foot; space to stand on. **-ing** *n.* ground to stand on; the part of a construction contacting the ground; status (in society) **-lights** *n.pl.* a row of screened lights along the front of the stage; (*Fig.*) the theater; the profession of acting. **—loose** *a.* free to do as one likes. **-man** *n.* liveried man-servant; a trivet. **-note** *n.* a note of reference or explanation at foot of a page. **foot and mouth disease,** a highly contagious disease of sheep, swine, and esp. horned cattle. [O.E. *fot*, foot].
fop (fŏp) *n.* a conceited, effeminate man; a dandy. **-pery** *n.* affection in dress and manners. **-pish** *a.* vain. **-pishly** *adv.* **-pishness** *n.* [M.E. *foppe*, a fool].
for (fawr) *prep.* in place of; instead of; because of; during; as being; considering; in return for; on behalf of; in spite of; in respect to; intended to belong to; suited to; with the purpose of. *conj.* because. **as for,** regarding [O.E. *for*, for].
for- *prefix.* survives in a few words of O.E. origin, with various meanings; utterly, as in *forlorn*; prohibition, as in *forbid*; neglect, as in *forsake*; away, as in *forget*.
for·age (fawr'·ij) *n.* food for horses and cattle; the search for this or any provisions; *v.t.* to supply with provender; to plunder; *v.i.* to rove in search of food; (*Fig.*) to rummage. [O.Fr. *fourage*, forage].
fo·ra·men (fō·rā'·man) *n.* a small aperture, esp. in a bone; *pl.* **foramina** [L. a hole].
for·as·much (fawr·az·much') *conj.* seeing that; because; since.
for·ay (fawr'·ā) *n.* a raid to get plunder; *v.t.* to pillage.
for·bade (fer·bad') *pa.t.* of **forbid.**
for·bear (fawr·bār') *v.t.* to abstain from; to avoid; to bear with; *v.i.* to refrain from; to control one's feelings. *pa.t.* **forbore.** *pa.p.* **forborne. -ing.** *a.* long-suffering [O.E. *forberan*, to suffer, endure].
for·bid (fer·bid') *v.t.* to prohibit; to order to desist; to exclude. *pa.t.* **forbade** (fer·bad') or **forbad.** *pa.p.* **-den. -den** *a.* prohibited. **-ding** *a.* repellent; menacing; sinister. **-dingly** *adv.* [O.E. *forbeodan*, to prohibit].
force (fōrs) *n.* strength; energy; efficacy; coercion; power; operation; body of soldiers, police, etc.; (*Mech.*) that which produces a change in a body's state of rest or motion; (*Law*) unlawful violence to person or property. **Forces** *n.pl.* Army, Navy and Air Force; *v.t.* to compel (physically or morally); to strain; to ravish; to overpower (*Hort.*) to cause plants to bloom, or ripen before normal time. **-d** *a.* achieved by great effort, or under compulsion; lacking spontaneity, as *forced laugh.* **-ful** *a.* full of energy; vigorous. **-fully** *adv.* **-less** *a.* weak; inert. **-r** *n.* **forcible** *a.* having force; compelling; cogent; effective. **forcibly** *adv.* **forcing** *n.* the action of using force or applying pressure; the art of ripening plants, fruits, etc. before their season. [O.E. *force*, strength].
for·ceps (fawr'·seps) *n.* a surgical instrument like tongs. [L.].

ford (fōrd) *n.* a shallow part of a stream, etc. where a crossing can be made on foot; *v.t.* to cross by a ford. **-able** *a.* [O.E. *faran*, to go].
fore (fōr) *a.* in front; forward; prior; *adv.* in front, as opp. to *aft*; *n.* the front. *interj.* (*Golf*) a warning cry to person in the way [O.E. *fore*, before].
fore- *prefix* meaning in front or beforehand.
fore-arm (fōr'·ärm) *n.* the part of the arm between the elbow and the wrist.
fore·arm (fōr·ärm') *v.t.* to take defensive precautions.

ford

fore·bear, for·bear (fōr′·bār) n. an ancestor.
fore·bode (fōr·bōd′) v.t. to predict (esp. something unpleasant); to prognosticate; to presage. **-ment** n. **foreboding** n. an intuitive sense of impending evil or danger.
fore·cast (fōr′·kast) n. a prediction; (Meteor.) a general inference as to the probable weather to come; v.t. and v.i. to conjecture beforehand; to predict.
fore·cas·tle, fo'c'sle (fōk′·sl) n. (Naut.) the upper deck forward of the foremast; forepart under deck, forming crew's quarters.
fore·close (fōr·klōz′) v.t. (Law) to prevent; to exclude; to deprive of the right to redeem a mortgage or property. **foreclosure** n.
fore·date (fōr·dāt′) v.t. to antedate.
fore·doom (fōr·dōōm′) v.t. to judge in advance; to predestine to failure, etc.
fore·fa·ther (fōr′·fà·ŦHer) n. an ancestor.
fore·fin·ger (fōr′·fing·ger) n. the finger next to the thumb; the index finger.
fore·foot (fōr′·foot) n. one of the front feet of a quadruped.   [the center of interest.
fore·front (fōr′·frunt) n. the foremost place;
fore·go (fōr·gō′) v.t. to precede. **-ing** a. preceding; just mentioned. **-ne** a. predetermined or inevitable, as in a foregone conclusion.
fore·ground (fōr′·ground) n. the part of the ground nearest the spectator; the part of a picture which seems nearest the observer.
fore·hand (fōr′·hand) n. the part of a horse in front of the rider; a. done beforehand; (Tennis) used of a stroke played forward on the right or natural side, as opp. to backhand. **-ed** a.
fore·head (fawr′·id, fawr′·hed) n. the upper part of the face above the eyes; the brow.
for·eign (fawr′·in) a. situated outside a place or country; alien; irrelevant; introduced from outside. **-er** n. a native of another country; an alien. **-ism** n. [O.Fr. forain, fr. L. foris, outside].
fore·know (fōr·nō′) v.t. to know or sense beforehand. **foreknowledge** n.
fore·land (fōr′·land) n. a promontory; a cape; shore area round a port.
fore·lock (fōr′·làk) n. a lock of hair on the forehead.
fore·man (fōr′·man) n. the principal member and spokesman of a jury; the overseer of a group of workmen.
fore·mast (fōr′·mast) n. the mast in the forepart of a vessel, nearest the bow.

fore·most (fōr′·mōst) a. first in place or time; first in dignity or rank.   [tioned.
fore·named (fōr′·nāmd) a. already men-
fore·noon (fōr′·nōōn) n. the part of the day before noon; morning.
fo·ren·sic (fà·ren′·sik) a. pert. to the law courts, public discussion, or debate. **-ally** adv. [L. forensis, pert. to the forum].
fore·or·dain (fōr·awr·dān′) v.t. to predetermine; to decree beforehand.
fore·part (fōr′·pàrt) n. the part before the rest; the beginning.
fore·run (fōr·run′) v.t. to run before; to precede; to outrun. **-ner** n. a messenger sent in advance; a harbinger; a precursor.
fore·said (fōr′·sed) a. mentioned before.
fore·sail (fōr′·sàl or fō′sl) n. the lowest square sail on the foremast.
fore·see (fōr·sē′) v.t. to see beforehand; to foreknow. pa.t. **foresaw**, pa.p. **foreseen**.
foresight n. wise forethought; prudence; (Mil.) front sight on gun [O.E. foreseon].
fore·sha·dow (fōr·shad′·ō) v.t. to shadow or indicate beforehand; to suggest in advance.
fore·shore (fōr′·shōr) n. the part of the shore between the level of high tide and low tide.
fore·short·en (fōr·shōr′·ten) v.t. to represent (in art) according to perspective; to depict to the eye, as seen obliquely.

fore·show (fōr·shō′) v.t. to prognosticate.
fore·skin (fōr′·skin) n. the skin covering the glans penis; prepuce.
for·est (fawr′·ist) n. a tract of wooded, uncultivated land; the trees alone; a. sylvan; v.t. to cover with trees. **-er** n. one who practices forestry; one who has forest land, game, etc. under supervision. **-ry** n. the science of growing timber [L. foris, outside].
fore·stall (fōr·stawl′) v.t. to thwart by advance action; to buy up goods before they reach the market, so as to resell at maximum price; to get in ahead of someone else. **-er** n. **-ment** n. [O.E. foresteall intervention].
fore·taste (fōr′·tāst) n. a taste beforehand; anticipation; v.t. to taste before full possession.
fore·tell (fōr·tel′) v.t. to predict; to prophesy. pr.p. **-ing** pa.t., pa.p. **foretold**.
fore·thought (fōr′·thawt) n. anticipation; provident care; a thinking beforehand.
fore·to·ken (fōr′·tō·kan) n. a token or sign received beforehand; a prophetic sign; v.t. to indicate beforehand [O.E. foretacn].
fore·top (fōr′·tàp) n. (Naut.) platform at the head of the foremast; an animal's forelock.
for·ev·er (fer·ev′·er) adv. always; eternally; n. eternity. **-more** adv.   [tion in advance.
fore·warn (fōr·wawrn′) v.t. to warn or cau-
fore·word (fōr′·wurd) n. a preface; an introductory note to a book.
for·feit (fōr′·fit) v.t. to be deprived of, as a punishment; n. that which is forfeited; a fine or penalty. **-able** a. **-ure** n. the act of forfeiting; the state of being deprived of something as a punishment; the thing confiscated [O.Fr. forfaire, to transgress].
for·gather, foregather (fōr·gaŦH′·er) v.i. to meet with friends; to come together socially.
for·gave (fer·gāv′) pa.t. of verb **forgive**.
forge (fōrj) v.t. a furnace for heating iron red hot so that it can be hammered into shape; to fabricate; to counterfeit; v.i. to work with metals; to commit forgery. **-r** n. **forgery** n. the making of an imitation of money, work of art, etc., and representing it as genuine; the act of falsifying a document, or illegally using another's signature; that which is forged [L. fabrica, a workshop].
forge (fōrj) v.i. to move forward steadily.
for·get (fer·get′) v.t. to lose remembrance of; to neglect inadvertently; to disregard. pr.p. **-ting**. pa.t. **forgot**. pa.p. **forgot** or **forgotten**. **-table** a. **-ful** a. apt to forget; heedless; oblivious. **-fully** adv. **-fulness** n. [O.E. forgietan, to forget].
for·give (for·giv′) v.t. to pardon; to cease to bear resentment against; to cancel (as a debt); v.t. to exercise clemency; to grant pardon. pa.t. **forgave**. pa.p. **forgiven**. **for·givable** a. **-ness** n. **forgiving** a. ready to pardon [O.E. forgiefan, to give up].
for·go (fōr·gō′) v.t. pa.t. **forwent**, pa.p. **foregone**. to renounce; to abstain from possession or enjoyment.
fork (fōrk) n. an implement with two or more prongs at the end; a table utensil of silver, etc. usually with four prongs; anything shaped like a fork; a pronged instrument which when struck gives forth a fixed musical note (tuning-fork); the bifurcation of a road, etc.; each part into which anything divides, as a road, river, etc.; v.i. to divide into branches; v.t. to pitch with a fork, as hay; to lift with a fork (as food); to form a fork. **-ed**, **-y** a. shaped like a fork; cleft. [O.E. forca, a fork].
for·lorn (faur·lōrn′) a. deserted; forsaken; adv. **-ness** n. [O.E. forleosan, to lose].
form (fōrm) n. shape or appearance; configuration; the human body; a mold; state of health; model; style; method of arrangement of details; etiquette; an official document or questionnaire with details to be filled in by applicant; v.t. to give shape to; to construct; to devise; to be an element of; to arrange to conceive; to build up (as a sentence); v.i. to assume position; to develop. **-al** a. according to form; regular; methodical; conventional; ceremonious. **-alization** n. **-alize** v.t. and v.i. to give form to; to make formal. **-alism** n. the quality of being formal; undue insistence on conventional forms, esp. in religion or the arts. **-alist** n. **-ality** n. quality of being conventional or pedantically precise; propriety. **-ally** adv. **-ation** n. the act of forming; structure; an arrangement, of troops, aircraft, etc. **-ative** a. giving form; conducive to growth. **-less** a. [L. forma, shape].
-form suff. in the shape of, as cruciform in the shape of a cross.
form·al·de·hyde (fōr·mal′·da·hīd) n. a colorless, pungent gas, soluble in water, used as a disinfectant and preservative.
for·mat (fōr′·mat) n. the general make-up of a book, its size, shape, style of binding, quality of paper, etc. [L. forma, a shape].
for·mer (fōr′·mer) a. preceding in time; long past; first mentioned. **-ly** adv.
for·mic (fōr′·mik) a. pertaining to ants [L. formica, an ant].
for·mi·da·ble (fōr′·mi·da·bl) a. exciting fear or apprehension; overwhelming. **formidability**, **-ness** n. **formidably** adv. [L. formidare, to fear].

for·mu·la (fōr′·mya·la) n. a prescribed form; a conventional phrase; a confession of faith; (Math.) a general rule or principle expressed in algebraic symbols; (Chem.) the series of symbols denoting the component parts of a substance; (Med.) a. prescription; pl. **-s**, **formulae** (·lē). **formularization**, **formulation** n. **formulary** n. a book containing formulas, or prescribed ritual; a. prescribed. **formulate**, **formulize** v.t. to reduce to a formula; to express in definite form [L. dim. of forma, a shape].
for·ni·cate (fōr′·ni·kāt) v.i. to indulge in unlawful sexual intercourse. **fornication** n. sexual intercourse between unmarried persons. **fornicator** n. [L. fornix, a brothel].
for·sake (fer·sāk′) v.t. to abandon; to leave or give up entirely. pr.p. **forsaking**. pa.t. **forsook** pa.p. **forsaken**. **forsaken** a. deserted [O.E. forsacan, to relinquish].
for·sooth (fer·sōōth′) adv. in truth; indeed.
for·swear (fōr·swār′) v.t. to renounce on oath; to deny; v.i. to swear falsely; to commit perjury. pa.t. **forswore**. pa.p. **forsworn** [O.E. forswerian, to renounce].
for·syth·i·a (fer·sith′·i·a) n. a spring-flowering shrub with bright yellow blossoms [Eng. 18th cent. botanist William Forsyth].

fort (fōrt) n. a stronghold; a small fortress; outpost [L. fortis, strong].

forte (fōrt) n. a strong point; that in which one excels [Fr. fort, strong].
forte (fōr′·te) a. and adv. (Mus.) loud; loudly; n. a loud passage. **fortissimo** adv. very loudly [It. fr. L. fortis, strong].
forth (fōrth) adv. forwards, in place or time; out from concealment; into view; away. **-coming** a. ready to come forth or appear; available. **-right** a. straightforward; frank. **-with** adv. immediately [O.E. fore, before].
for·ti·fy (fōr′·ta·fī) v.t. to strengthen, as by forts, batteries, etc.; to invigorate; to corroborate. pr.p. **-ing**. pa.t., pa.p. **fortified**, **fortification** n. the art or act of strengthening; a defensive wall; a fortress [L. forotis, strong; facere, to make].
for·ti·tude (fōr′·ta·tūd) n. power to endure pain or confront danger; resolute endurance; **fortitudinous** a. courageous [L. fortitudo].
fort·night (fōrt′·nīt) n. the space of fourteen days; two weeks. **-ly** a. and adv. at intervals of a fortnight [contr. of O.E. feowertyne niht, fourteen nights].
for·tress (fōr′·tris) n. a fortified place; a stronghold [O.Fr. forteresse, a stronghold].
for·tu·i·tous (fōr·tū′·a·tas) a. happening by chance; accidental. **-ness**, **fortuity** n. [L. fortuitus, casual].
for·tune (fōr′·chan) n. chance; that which befalls one; good luck or ill luck; possessions, esp. money or property. **fortunate** a. lucky; propitious. **fortunately** adv. **fortunateness** n. **-teller** n. one who reveals the future by palmistry, crystal-gazing, etc. [L. fortuna].
for·ty (fōr′·ti·) a. and n. four times ten; a symbol expressing this, as 40, XL. **fortieth** a. fortieth part. [O.E. feowertig, forty].
fo·rum (fō′·ram) n. the market place of ancient Rome where legal as well as commercial business was conducted; a public discussion of questions of common interest; tribunal [L. forum, the market-place].
for·ward (fōr′·werd) adv. towards a place in front; onwards in time; in a progressive or conspicuous way; a. toward or at the forepart, as in a ship; eager; progressive; bold; n. (Sports) a player in the front line; v.t. to promote; to redirect (letter, parcel) to

fos·sil (fǎs'·il) *n.* any portion of an animal or vegetable organism or imprint of such, which has undergone a process of petrifaction and lies embedded in the rock strata; (*Colloq.*) an antiquated person or thing; *a.* pert. to or resembling a fossil. **-iferous** *a.* bearing or containing fossils. **-ize** *v.t.* to turn into a fossil; to petrify; *v.t.* to become a fossil [L. *fodere, fossum*, to dig].

fos·ter (faws'·ter) *v.t.* to rear; to promote; to cherish. — **brother** *n.* a boy fostered with another child of different parents. — **child** *n.* a child reared by one who is not the parent. — **daughter** — **son** *n.* a child brought up as a daughter or son, but not so by birth. — **father**, — **mother**, — **parent** *n.* [O.E. *fostrian*, to nourish].

fought (fawt) *pa.t.* and *pa.p.* of verb **fight.**

foul (foul) *a.* filthy; containing offensive or putrescent matter; obscene; wicked; stormy of weather; contrary (of wind); full of weeds; entangled (of ropes); unfair; *n.* the breaking of a rule (in sports); *v.t.* to make foul; to obstruct deliberately; to clog or jam; *v.i.* to become foul, clogged, or jammed; to come into collision. **-ly** *adv.* **-mouthed** *a.* using language scurrilous, obscene, or profane. — **play**, cheating; (*Law*) criminal violence; murder [O.E. *ful*, filthy].

found (found) *pa.t.* and *pa.p.* of verb **find.** **-ling** *n.* a small child who has been found abandoned.

found (found) *v.t.* to lay the basis or foundation of; to establish; to endow; *v.i.* to rely; to depend. **-ation** *n.* the act of founding; the base or substructure of a building; groundwork; underlying principle; an endowment; an endowed institution. **-er** *n.* [Fr. *fonder*, to establish].

found (found) *v.t.* to melt (metal, or materials for glassmaking) and pour into a mold; to cast. **-er** *n.* **-ing** *n.* metal casting. **-ry** *n.* works for casting metals; the process of metal casting [Fr. *fondre*, to melt].

foun·der (foun'·der) *v.t.* to cause inflammation in the feet (of a horse) so as to lame; to cause to sink (as a ship); *v.i.* to collapse; to fill with water and sink; to fail; to stumble and become lame [O.Fr. *fondrer*, to fall in].

foun·tain (foun'·tan) *n.* a natural spring; an artificial jet of water. **fount** *n.* a spring of water; a source. **-head** *n.* source of a stream; (*Fig.*) the origin. [L. *fons*, a spring].

four (fōr) *a.* one more than three; twice two; *n.* the sum of four units; the symbol representing this sum—4, IV. **-flusher** *n.* (*Slang*) one who bluffs. **-fold** *a.* quadruple; folded or multiplied four times. **—in-hand** *n.* a necktie; a team of four horses drawing a carriage; the carriage itself. **—poster** *n.* a bed with four posts. **—some** *n.* a group of four persons. **—square** *a.* having four equal sides and angles. **-teen** *n.* the sum of four and ten; the symbol representing this—14, XIV; *a.* four and ten. **-teenth** *a.* making one of fourteen equal parts. **-th** *n.* next after third; *n.* one of four equal parts. **-thly** *adv.* [O.E. *feower*, four].

fowl (foul) *n.* barnyard cock or hen; the flesh of a fowl; a similar game bird; *pl.* **-s,** fowl. *v.i.* to catch or kill wild fowl. **-er** *n.* one who traps wild fowl. **-ing-piece** *n.* a light shotgun for shooting wild fowl [O.E. *fugol*, a bird].

fox (fǎks) *n.* (*fem.* **vixen**) an animal of the canine family, genus *Vulpes*, reddish-brown or gray in color, with large, bushy tail and erect ears; a wily person; *v.t.* to trick; to make sour, in fermenting; to mislead. — **brush** *n.* the bushy tail of a fox. **-glove** *n.* a tall plant with white or purple-pink bell-shaped flowers and leaves which yield digitalis used medicinally as heart stimulant. **-hole** *n.* (*Mil.*) a small trench; a dugout for one or more men. — **hunt** *n.* the pursuit of a fox by huntsmen and hounds. **-iness** *n.* the quality of being foxy; discoloration (in paper); the state of being sour (of beer). — **terrier** *n.* a popular breed of dog sometimes trained for unearthing foxes. — **trot** *n.* a social dance. **-y** *a.* pert. to foxes; cunning; reddish-brown in color. **-ily** *adv.* slyly [O.E. *fox*, a fox].

fox

foy·er (foi'·er) *n.* a theater or hotel lobby; an entrance hall [Fr.].

fra·cas (frā'·kas) *n.* a noisy quarrel; a disturbance; a brawl [Fr.].

frac·tion (frak'·shan) *n.* a small portion; a fragment; (*Arith.*) a division of a unit. **decimal fraction,** a fraction expressed with numerator above, and denominator below the line. **-al** *a.* **fractious** *a.* quarrelsome; peevish. **fractiously** *adv.* **fracture** *n.* the act of breaking; a breach or rupture; the breaking of a bone; *v.t.* to break; to crack; *v.i.* to become broken. **compound fracture,** a fracture of a bone, the jagged edge of which protrudes through the skin. **simple fracture,** a fracture where the bone is broken, but surrounding tissues and skin are undamaged [L. *frangere, fractum,* to break].

frag·ile (fraj'·al) *a.* easily broken; frail; brittle. **fragility** *n.* [L. *fragilis*, breakable].

frag·ment (frag'·mant) *n.* a portion broken off; a part; an unfinished portion, as of a literary composition. **-al** *a.* (*Geol.*) composed of fragments of different rocks. **-ary** *a.* broken [L. *frangere*, to break].

fra·grant (frā'·grant) *a.* sweet smelling. **fragrance, fragrancy** *n.* sweet scent; perfume; pleasant odor. **-ly** *adv.* [L. *fragrare*].

frail (frāl) *a.* fragile; easily destroyed; infirm; morally weak. **-ly** *adv.* **-ness, -ty** *n.* quality of being weak [O.Fr. *fraile*, weak].

frame (frām) *v.t.* to construct; to contrive; to provide with a frame; to put together, as a sentence; (*Colloq.*) to bring a false charge against; *v.i.* to take shape; *n.* anything made of parts fitted together; the skeleton of anything; a structure; the case or border around a picture; a mood of the mind; a glazed structure in which plants are protected from frost; a structure upon which anything is stretched. **-work** *n.* the fabric which supports anything. **framing** *n.* [O.E. *framian*, to be helpful].

franc (frangk) *n.* a coin (100 centimes) and monetary unit of France, Belgium and Switzerland [O.Fr. *franc*].

fran·chise (fran'·chiz) *n.* the right to vote; a privilege conferred by a government; permission by a manufacturer to sell his products [O.Fr. *franc*, free].

Fran·cis·can (fran·sis'·kan) *n.* one of the order of friars founded by Francis of Assisi.

Fran·co- (frangk'·ō) *prefix*, French, in combinations. **Francophile** *n.* one who admires France and all things French. **Francophobe** *n.* one who hates things French.

fran·gi·ble (fran'·ji·bl) *a.* breakable; fragile. **frangibility** *n.* [L. *frangere*, to break].

frank (frangk) *a.* open; candid; unreserved; *v.t.* to exempt from charge, esp. postage; *n.* a signature on outside of a letter authorizing its free delivery. **-ly** *adv.* candidly. **-ness** *n.* openness; honesty; candor [Fr. *franc*, free].

Frank (frangk) *n.* a member of one of the Germanic tribes which settled in Gaul giving France its name.

Frank·en·stein (frangk'·an·stīn) *n.* any creation which brings disaster or torment to its author [from Mary Shelley's novel].

frank·furter (frangk'·fer·ter) *n.* a smoked sausage [G. City of Frankfurt].

frank·in·cense (frangk'·in·sens) *n.* a dry, perfumed resin, burned as incense [Fr. *franc*, pure; *encens*, incense].

Frank·lin (frangk'·lin) *n.* a type of open iron stove [fr. Benj. *Franklin*].

fran·tic (fran'·tik) *a.* frenzied; wild. **-ally** *adv.* [O.Fr. *frenetique*, frenetic].

fra·ter·nal (fra·tur'·nal) *a.* pert. to a brother or brethren; brotherly. *adv.* **fraternization** *n.* **fraternize** *v.i.* to associate with others in a friendly way. **fraternizer** *n.* **fraternity** *n.* a student society, designated by letters of the Greek alphabet; brotherhood; a group of men associated for a common purpose [L. *frater*, a brother].

frat·ri·cide (frat'·ri·sid) *n.* the crime of killing a brother; one who commits this crime. **fratricidal** *a.* [L. *frater*, a brother; *caedere*, to kill].

fraud (frawd) *n.* deception deliberately practiced; trickery; (*Colloq.*) a cheat; imposter. **-ulence, -ulency** *n.* trickery; deceitfulness. **-ulent** *a.* pert. to or practicing fraud; dishonest. **-ulently** *adv.* [L. *fraus*, a fraud].

fraught (frawt) *a.* loaded; charged [Dut. *vracht*, a load].

fray (frā) *n.* an affray; a brawl; a contest [contr. of *affray*].

fray (frā) *v.t.* to wear through by friction; to ravel the edge of cloth; (*Fig.*) to irritate, as the nerves, or temper; *v.i.* to become

frayed [Fr. *frayer*, to rub].

fraz·zle (fraz'·l) *v.t.* to fray; to exhaust; *n.* exhaustion [etym. unknown].

freak (frēk) *n.* a sudden whim; a prank; capricious conduct; something or someone abnormal; *a.* odd; unusual. **-ish** *a.* **-ishly** *adv.* **-ishness** *n.* [prob. O.E. *frec*, bold].

freak (frēk) *v.t.* to spot or streak or dapple; *n.* a streak [prob. from *freckle*].

freck·le (frek'·l) *n.* a small brownish spot on the skin; any small spot; *v.t.* to color with freckles; *v.i.* to become covered with freckles. **freckly,** *a.* [M.E. *frakin*, a freckle].

free (frē) *a.* having political liberty; unrestricted; loose; independent; open; liberal; spontaneous; irregular; licentious; exempt from impositions, duties, or fees (as trade, education); *adv.* without hindrance; gratis; *v.t.* to set at liberty; to emancipate; to clear; to disentangle. *pr.p.* **-ing.** *pa.p.* **-d. -booter** *n.* one who wanders about for plunder; a pillager. **-man** *n.* one who has been freed from slavery. **-dom** *n.* liberty; immunity; indecorous familiarity; **-hand,** unrestricted authority; drawn by hand without instruments, etc. **-handed** *a.* generous; liberal. **-hold** *n.* the tenure of property in fee simple, or fee tail, or for life; *a.* held by freehold. **free-holder** *n.* **—lance** *n.* orig. a mercenary soldier who sold his services to any country, esp. said of a journalist, not attached to a particular staff. — **love** *n.* doctrine that sexual relations should be unhampered by marriage, etc. **-ly** *adv.* **-man** *n.* a man who is not a slave; one who enjoys the full privileges of a corporate body. **-mason** *n.* orig. a member of an organization of skilled masons; now, a member of a fraternal association for mutual assistance and social enjoyment. **-masonic** *a.* **-masonry** *n.* **-ness** *n.* **—spoken** *a.* accustomed to speak without reserve. **-stone** *n.* a building-stone easily quarried, cut, and carved; peach, plum, etc. in which the pit does not cling. **-thinker** *n.* one who professes to be independent of all religious authority; a rationalist. **-thinking, — thought** *n.* — **trade,** the policy of unrestricted, international trade. **-trader** *n.* — **verse** *n.* a form of verse unrestricted in length of line, meter, stanza form, and generally without rhyme. — **will** *n.* the power of the human will to choose without restraint; a voluntary [G.E. *freo*, free].

freeze (frēz) *v.t.* to harden into ice; to congeal; to preserve by refrigeration; to paralyze with cold or terror; to render credits unrealizable; become congealed or stiff with cold. *pr.p.* **freezing.** *pa.t.* **froze.** *pa.p.* **frozen** *n.* frost. **freezing point** *n.* the temperature at which a liquid turns solid, esp. that at which water freezes, marked 32° F. or 0° C. [O.E. *freosan*, to freeze].

freight (frāt) *n.* the cargo of a ship, etc.; a load; charge for conveyance of goods; *v.t.* to load a ship, etc. **-age** *n.* charge for transport of goods; freight. **-er** *n.* one who receives and forwards freight; a cargo boat [late form of *fraught*].

French (french) *a.* pert. to France or its inhabitants; *n.* the inhabitants or the language of France. **French chalk,** a variety of talc. — **horn** *n.* a musical wind instrument with mellow note like a hunting horn. **-man** (*fem.* **Frenchwoman**) *n.* a native of France. — **window,** one functioning as door and window.

French horn

fren·zy (fren'·zi·) *n.* violent agitation of the mind; madness; *v.t.* to render frantic. **frenzied** *a.* **frenetic** (also **phrenetic**) *a.* mad; frenzied [Gk. *phrenitis*, inflammation of the brain].

fre·on (frē'·ǎn) *n.* gas used in refrigeration and for air-conditioning [fr. *freeze*].

fre·quent (frē'·kwant) *a.* happening at short intervals; constantly recurring; repeated.

frequent (fri·kwent') *v.t.* to visit often. **frequency** *n.* the state of occurring repeatedly; periodicity; (*Phys.*) number of vibrations per second of a recurring phenomenon. **-ation** *n.* the practice of visiting repeatedly. **-ative** *a.* (*Gram.*) denoting the repetition of an action; *n.* (*Gram.*) a word, usually a verb, expressing frequency of an action. **-er** *n.* **-ly** *adv.* **-ness** *n.* [L. *frequens*].

fres·co (fres'·kō) *n.* a method of mural decoration on walls of fresh, still damp, plaster. *v.t.* to paint in fresco [It. *fresco*, fresh].

fresh (fresh) *a.* vigorous; unimpaired; new; not stale; brisk; original; unsalted; (*Slang*) impudent; *n.* a stream of fresh water; a freshet. **-en** *v.t.* to make fresh; *v.i.* to grow fresh; to become vigorous. **-ener** *n.* **-et** *n.* an inundation caused by rains or melting snows; a fresh-water stream. **-man** *n.* a first-year University or high school student. **-ness** *n.* **—water** *a.* pert. to or living in water which is not salt [M.E. *fresch*, fresh].

fret (fret) *v.t.* to wear away by friction; to eat away; to ruffle; to irritate; *v.i.* to wear away; to be corroded; to be vexed or peevish; *pr.p.* **-ting** *pa.t.*, *pa.p.* **-ted.** *n.* irritation; erosion. **-ful** *a.* querulous, peevish. **-fulness** *n.* [O.E. *fretan*, to devour].

fret (fret) *n.* ornamental work, consisting usually of strips, interlaced at right angles. **-ted, -ty** *a.* ornamented with frets. **-work** *n.* decorative, perforated work on wood or metal [O.Fr. *frete*, interlaced work].

fret (fret) *n.* a small piece of wood or wire fixed on the fingerboard, as of a guitar, under the strings [prob. O.Fr. *frete*, ferrule].

Freud·i·an (froi′·di·an) *a.* pert. to *Sigmund Freud*, (1856-1939) the Austrian psychoanalyst, or to his theories.

fri·a·ble (frī·a·bl) *a.* easily crumbled or reduced to powder. **-ness, friability** *n.* [L. *friabilis*, crumbling].

fri·ar (frī′·er) *n.* a member of one of the orders (*R.C.*) of mendicant monks. **-y** *n.* a monastery [L. *frater*, a brother].

frib·ble (frib′·l) *n.* a frivolous person or thing; *v.i.* to fritter away time.

fri·cas·see (frik·a·sē′) *n.* a dish of fowl, rabbit, etc. stewed with rich gravy sauce; *v.t.* to make a fricassee [Fr.].

fric·tion (frik′·shan) *n.* the act of rubbing one thing against another; (*Phys.*) the resistance which a body encounters in moving across the surface of another with which it is in contact; unpleasantness. **fricative** *a.* produced by friction. **-al** *a.* caused by friction. **-ally** *adv.* [L. *fricare*, to rub].

Fri·day (frī′·di·) *n.* the sixth day of the week [O.E. *Frig*, wife of Odin; *daeg*, a day].

fried (frid) *pa.t.* and *pa.p.* of verb **fry.**

friend (frend) *n.* one attached to another by esteem and affection; an intimate associate; a supporter. **Friend** *n.* a member of the Quakers. **-less** *a.* without friends. **-liness** *n.* **-ly** *a.* having the disposition of a friend; kind; propitious. **-ship** *n.* attachment; comradeship. **Society of Friends,** the Quaker sect [O.E. *freond*, a friend].

frieze (frēz) *n.* a heavy woolen cloth with nap on one side [Fr. *frise*, a curl].

frieze (frēz) *n.* decoration on the upper part of the wall, around a mantel, etc. [Fr. *frise*, a fringe].

fri·gate (frig′·it) *n.* a fast 2-decked sailing ship of war of the 18th and 19th centuries. [It. *fregata*, a frigate].

fright (frīt) *n.* sudden and violent fear; extreme terror; alarm; (*Colloq.*) an ugly or grotesque person or object; *v.t.* to make afraid. **-en** *v.t.* to terrify; to scare. **-ened** *a.* **-ful** *a.* terrible; calamitous; shocking. **-fully** *adv.* terribly; (*Colloq.*) very. **-fulness** *n.* **-some** *a.* frightful [O.E. *fyrhto*, fear].

frig·id (frij′·id) *a.* very cold (esp. of climate); unfeeling; passionless; stiff. **-ity** *n.* coldness. **-ly** *adv.* **-ness** *n.* **-aire** *n.* a refrigerator [L. *frigidus*, cold].

frill (fril) *n.* a gathered cloth or paper edging; a ruffle; (*Fig.*) excessive ornament (as in style); *v.t.* to ornament with a frill; *v.i.* to become crinkled like a frill [etym. doubtful].

fringe (frinj) *n.* loose threads as ornamental edging of cloth; anything suggesting this, as a fringe of hair; the outside edge of anything; *v.t.* to adorn with fringe; to border [O.Fr. *fringe*, a border].

frip·per·y (frip′·er·i·) *n.* tawdry finery; ostentation [Fr. *fripperie*, old clothes].

frisk (frisk) *v.i.* to leap; to gambol; to skip; *v.t.* (*slang*) to feel a person's clothing for concealed weapons; (*Slang*) to steal in this way; *n.* a frolic. **-ily** *adv.* **-iness** *n.* **-y** *a.* lively [O.Fr. *frisque*, lively].

frit·ter (frit′·er) *n.* a slice of fruit or meat dipped in batter and fried to form a cake [O.Fr. *friture*, something fried].

frit·ter (frit′·er) *v.t.* to waste (time, energy, etc.) in a futile way. **-er** *n.* [prob. conn. with L. *frangere*, to break].

friv·ol (friv′·al) *v.t.* and *v.i.* to squander, esp. time or energy; to fritter away. **frivolity** *n.* the act or habit of idly wasting time; lack of seriousness. **-ous** *a.* **-ously** *adv.* **-ousness** *n.* [L. *frivolus*, paltry].

frizz (friz) *v.t.* to curl; to crisp; *n.* a row of small curls. **-zle** *v.t.* to curl; in cooking, to crisp by frying; *n.* curled hair [O.Fr. *friser*].

fro (frō) *adv.* from; back, as in *to* and *fro.*

frock (frak) *n.* a woman's dress; a monk's long, wide sleeved garment. **— coat** *n.* a double-breasted, full skirted coat worn by men [O.Fr. *froc*, a monk's frock].

frog (frag) *n.* an amphibious, tailless animal, (developed from a tadpole); hoarseness caused by mucus in the throat; a V-shaped horny pad on the sole of a horse's foot; a V-shaped section of track where two sets of rails cross; ornamental braiding on uniform, or ornamental fastening of loop and button; *v.t.* to ornament with frogs. **-men** *n.* the nickname given to underwater swimming men [O.E. *frogga*, a frog].

frol·ic (fral′·ik) *n.* a merry-making; gaiety; *a.* full of pranks; merry; *v.i.* to play merry pranks; to have fun. *pr.p.* **-king.** *pa.t.*, *pa.p.* **-ked. -some** *a.* [Dut. *vroolijk*, merry].

from (frum) *prep.* away; forth; out of; on account of; at a distance [O.E. *fram*, from].

frond (frand) *n.* (*Bot.*) an organ of certain flowerless plants, such as ferns, in which leaf and stem are combined and bear reproductive cells [L. *frons*, a leaf].

front (frunt) *n.* the forepart, the forehead; the human countenance; (*Mil.*) firing line; battle zone; (*Colloq.*) outward appearance *a.* pert. to, or at the front of, anything; *adv.* to the front; *v.t.* and *v.i.* to have the face or front towards any point. **-age** *n.* the front part of general exposure of a building; land abutting on street, river, or sea. **-al** *a.* pert. to the forehead or foremost part; (*Mil.*) direct, as an attack, without flanking movement; *n.* a bone of the forehead; an ornamental cloth for altar front [L. *frons*, the forehead].

fron·tier (frun′·tir) *n.* border of a country; the undeveloped areas of a country, knowledge, etc.; *a.* bordering; pioneering. **-sman** *n.* one who settles on a frontier [Fr.].

fron·tis·piece (frun′·tis·pēs) *n.* (*Archit.*) the main face of a building; an engraving or decorated page fronting the title page of a book [L. *frons*, the front; *specere*, to see].

frost (frawst) *n.* condition when water turns to ice, i.e. when temperature falls below 32° F.; severe cold; frozen dew; (*Slang*) a failure; a disappointment; *v.t.* to cover with hoar-frost; to nip (as plants); to ice a cake **-bite** *n.* freezing of the skin and tissues due to exposure to extreme cold. **-bitten** *a.* **-ed** *a.* covered with frost or anything resembling it. **-ily** *adv.* **-iness** *n.* **-y** *a.* accompanied with frost; chilly; white; grey-haired; frigid (in manner or feeling) [O.E. *forst*, fr. *freosan*, to freeze].

froth (frawth) *n.* spume; foam; trivial things or ideas; *v.t.* to cause to froth; *v.i.* to bubble. **-iness** *n.* **-y** *a.* [Scand. *frotha*, froth].

frounce (frouns) *v.t.* to curl the hair [O.Fr. *fronce*, a plait].

fro·ward (frō′·erd) *a.* perverse; refractory. **-ly** *adv.* **-ness** *n.* [O.E. *fra*, away, and *ward*].

frown (froun) *v.i.* to wrinkle the brow; to scowl; *v.t.* to rebuke by a stern look; *n.* a wrinkling of the brow to express disapproval [O.Fr. *froignier*, to look sullen].

frow·zy (frou′·zi·) *a.* musty; unkempt.

fro·zen (frō′·zan) *pa.p.* of the verb **freeze.**

fruc·ti·fy (fruk′·ti·fi) *v.t.* to make fruitful; to fertilize; *v.i.* to bear fruit. **fructiferous** *a.* fruitbearing. **fructose** *n.* fruit sugar; levulose [L. *fructus*, fruit].

fru·gal (froo′·gal) *a.* sparing; thrifty; economical. **-ly** *adv.* **-ity** *n.* [L. *frugalis*, thrifty].

fruit (froot) *n.* the produce of the earth used for man's needs; the edible produce or seed of a plant; offspring; the consequence or outcome; *v.i.* to produce fruit. **-age** *n.* fruit

collectively. **fruitarian** *n.* one who lives almost wholly on fruit. **-er** *n.* fruit grower; fruit-carrying ship. **-ful** *a.* producing fruit; abundant; profitable. **-fully** *adv.* **-fulness** *n.* **-ing** *n.* the process of bearing fruit. **-less** *a.* having no fruit; (*Fig.*) profitless; vain; empty. **-lessly** *adv.* **-lessness** *n.* **— sugar** *n.* glucose; levulose. **-y** *a.* resembling fruit; mellow [O.Fr. *fruit*, fruit].

fru·i·tion (froo·ish′·an) *n.* fulfillment of hopes and desires [L. *fruitio*, enjoyment].

frump (frump) *n.* a dowdy, cross woman.

frus·trate (frus′·trāt) *v.t.* to bring to nothing; to balk; to thwart; to circumvent. **frustration** *n.* disappointment; defeat. **frustrative** *a.* [L. *frustrari*, to deceive].

frus·tum (frus′·tam) *n.* (*Geom.*) the remaining part of a solid figure when the top has been cut off by a plane parallel to the base. *pl.* **-s, frusta** [L. *frustrum*, a piece].

fry (frī) *v.t.* to cook with fat in a pan over the fire; *v.i.* to be cooked in a frying pan; to sizzle. *pr.p.* **-ing** *pa.t.*, *pa.p.* **fried. -er, frier** *n.* [O.Fr. *frire*, to roast].

fry (frī) *n.* young fish just spawned; young children [M.E. *fri*, offspring].

fuch·sia (fū′·sha) *n.* a genus of flowering plants, with drooping bright purplish red flowers [fr. *Fuchs*, German botanist].

fud·dle (fud′·l) *v.t.* to make confused.

fudge (fuj) *interj.* stuff; nonsense; *n.* a soft chocolate candy; space reserved in a newspaper for last minute news.

fu·el (fū′·al) *n.* anything combustible to feed a fire, as wood, coal; *v.t.* to provide with fuel [O.Fr. *fouaille*, fr. L. *focus*, a health].

fu·gi·tive (fū′·ja·tiv) *a.* escaping; fleeing; fleeting; wandering; *n.* a refugee; one who flees from justice. [L. *fugere*, to flee].

fugue (fūg) *n.* (*Mus.*) a musical composition for voices and or instruments based on chief and subsidiary themes [L. *fuga*, flight].

ful·crum (ful′·kram) *n.* (*Mech.*) the pivot of a lever; (*Fig.*) means used to achieve a purpose. *pl.* **-s, fulcra** [L. *fulcrum*, a bedpost].

ful·fill (fool·fil′) *v.t.* to carry into effect; to execute; to discharge; to satisfy (as hopes). **-er** *n.* **-ment** *n.* accomplishment; completion [O.E. *full*, full; *fyllan*, to fill].

ful·gent (ful′·jant) *a.* shining; dazzling. **fulgency** *n.* **-ly** *adv.* [L. *fulgere*, to shine].

fu·lig·i·nous (fū·lij′·an·as) *a.* sooty; dusky [L. *fuligo*, soot].

full (fool) *a.* filled to capacity; replete; crowded; complete; plump; abundant; showing the whole surface (as the moon); ample (of garments, etc.); clear and resonant (of sounds); *n.* the utmost extent; highest degree. *adv.* quite; completely; exactly. **—blooded** *a.* of pure race; vigorous. **—blown** *a.* fully developed, as a flower. **— dress** *n.* dress worn on ceremonial occasions; *a.* formal. **-y** *adv.* completely [O.E. *full*, full].

full (fool) *v.t.* to cleanse, shrink and thicken cloth in a mill; *v.i.* to become thick or felted. **-er** *n.* one who fulls cloth [O.E. *fullian*, to whiten cloth].

ful·mi·nate (ful′·mi·nāt) *v.t.* to flash; to explode; to thunder forth official censure; *n.* a compound of fulminic acid exploding by percussion, friction, or heat, as *fulminate of mercury.* **fulminant** *a.* fulminating. **fulmination** *n.* the act of fulminating; an explosion; a biting denunciation. **fulminatory, fulmineous, fulminous** *a.* pert. to or like thunder and lightening [L. *fulmen*, lightning].

ful·some (fool′·sam) *a.* excessive; insincere. **-ly** *adv.* **-ness** *n.* [O.E. *full*].

ful·vous (ful′·vas) *a.* tawny; dull yellow. [L. *fulvus*, tawny].

fu·ma·role (fū′·ma·rōl) *n.* a small fissure in volcano [Fr. *fumerole*, a smoke-hole].

fum·ble (fum′·bl) *v.i.* to grope blindly or awkwardly; *v.t.* to handle clumsily [Scand. *fumla*, to grope].

fume (fūm) *n.* pungent vapor from combustion or exhalation; (*Fig.*) excitement; rage; *v.i.* to smoke; to be in a rage; *v.t.* to send forth as fumes [L. *fumus*, smoke].

fu·mi·gate (fū′·mi·gāt) *v.t.* to expose to poisonous gas or smoke, esp. for the purpose of destroying germs; to perfume or deodorize. **fumigator** *n.* apparatus or substance used in fumigation [L. *fumigare*, to smoke].

fun (fun) *n.* merriment; hilarity; sport. **-nies** *n.pl.* (*Colloq.*) comic strips. **-nily** *adv.* **-niness** *n.* **-ny** *a.* full of fun [M.E. *fonnen*].

fu·nam·bu·late (fū·nam′·bya·lāt) *v.i.* to balance and walk on a tight-rope. **funambulist** *n.* [L. *funis*, a rope; *ambulare*, to walk].

func·tion (fungk′·shan) *n.* performance; the special work done by an organ or structure; office; ceremony; (*Math.*) a quantity the value of which varies with that of another quantity; a social entertainment; *v.i.* to operate; to fulfil a set task. **-al** *a.* having a special purpose; pert. to a duty or office. **-ally** *adv.* **-ary** *n.* an official [L. *functus*, to perform].

fund (fund) *n.* permanent stock or capital; an invested sum, the income of which is used for a set purpose; a store; ample supply; *pl.* money in hand; *v.t.* to establish a fund for the payment of interest or principal. **-ed** *a.* [L. *fundus*, the bottom].

fun·da·men·tal (fun·dạ·men′·tạl) *a.* pert. to the foundations; basic; essential; original; *n.* a primary principle; (*Mus.*) the bottom note of a chord. **-ism** *n.* belief in literal truth of the Bible. **-ist** *n.* **-ly** *adv.* [L. *fundamentum*, the foundation].

fu·ne·ral (fū′·nạ·ral) *n.* the ceremony of burying the dead; obsequies; *a.* pert. to or used at burial. **funerary, funereal** *a.* gloomy [L. *funus*, burial rites].

fun·gus (fung′·gas) *n.* any of a group of thallophytes (molds, mushrooms, mildews, puffballs, etc.) (*Path.*) a spongy, morbid growth; proud flesh. *pl.* **fungi** (fun′·jī), **-es**, **fungiform** *a.* a fungus or mushroom-shaped. **fungicide** *n.* any preparation which destroys molds or fungoid growths. **fungoid, fungous** *a.* pert. to or caused by fungus [L. *fungus*, a mushroom].

fu·ni·cle (fū′·ni·kl) *n.* (*Bot.*) the stalk of a seed. **funicular** *a.* pert. to, or worked by rope. **funicular railway**, a cable railway [L. *funiculus*, dim. of *funis*, a cord].

funk (fungk) *n.* (*Colloq.*) abject terror; panic; *v.i.* and *v.t.* to be terrified of or by.

fun·nel (fun′·al) *n.* an inverted hollow metal cone with tube, used for filling vessels with narrow inlet; the smokestack of a steamship [L. *fundere*, to pour].

fur (fur) *n.* the short, fine, soft hair of certain animals; animal pelts used for coats, etc.; coating on the tongue; deposit on inside of kettles, etc. *v.t.* to line, face, or cover with fur; to coat with morbid matter. *pr.p.* **-ring.** *pa.p.* **-red. -rier** *n.* a dealer in furs. **-ry** *a.* [M.E. *forre*, fur].

fur·be·low (fur′·bạ·lō) *n.* an ornament; a ruffle [Sp. *falbala*, a flounce].

fur·bish (fur′·bish) *v.t.* to polish; to burnish; to renovate [O.Fr. *fourbir*, to polish].

fur·cate (fur′·kāt) *a.* forked; branched like a fork; *v.i.* to branch out [L. *furca*, a fork].

fu·ri·ous (fyoo′·ri·ạs) *a.* raging; violent; savage. **-ly** *adv.* [L. *furiosus*, raging].

furl (furl) *v.t.* to roll, as a sail [contr. of O.Fr. *fardel*, a bundle].

fur·long (fur′·lawng) *n.* eighth of mile; 220 yards [O.E. *furh*, a furrow; *lang*, long].

fur·lough (fur′·lō) *n.* leave of absence; *v.t.* to grant leave [Dut. *verlof*, permission].

fur·nace (fur′·nạs) *n.* an enclosed structure for the generating of heat required for smelting ores, warming houses, etc.; a place of severe trial [L. *fornus*, an oven].

fur·nish (fur′·nish) *v.t.* to supply; to equip; to fit out. **-er** *n.* **-ings** *n.pl.* fittings, of a house, esp. furniture, curtains, carpets, etc.

fur·ni·ture (fur′·ni·cher) *n.* equipment; that which is put into a house, office, etc. for use or ornament [Fr. *fournir*, to provide].

fu·ror (fū′·rawr) *n.* wild excitement; enthusiasm [L. *furor*, rage].

fur·row (fur′·ō) *n.* a trench made by a plough; channel; groove; deep wrinkle; *v.t.* to plough; to mark with wrinkles. **-y** *a.* [O.E. *furh*, a furrow].

fur·ther (fur′·THẹr) *a.* more remote; additional; *adv.* to a greater distance; moreover. **-more** *adv.* moreover; besides. **-most** *a.* most remote. **furthest** *adv.* and *a.* most remote. (**farther, farthest** are preferred as *comp.* and *superl.* of *far*) [O.E. *furthor*, comp. of *forth*, forwards].

fur·ther (fur′·THẹr) *v.t.* to help forward; to promote. **-ance** *n.* the act of furthering [O.E. *fyrthia*, to promote].

fur·tive (fur′·tiv) *a.* done stealthily; covert; sly. **-ly** *adv.* [L. *fur*, a thief].

fu·ry (fyoo′·ri·) *n.* rage; passion; frenzy [L. *furia*, rage].

fus·cous (fus′·kạs) *a.* of a dark greyish-brown color [L. *fuscus*, dark].

fuse (fūz) *v.t.* to melt (as metal) by heat; to amalgamate; *v.i.* to become liquid; *n.* a tube filled with combustible matter, used in blasting or discharge of bombs, etc.; a device used as a safety measure in electric lighting and heating systems. **fusibility** *n.* **fusible** *a.*

fusion *n.* the act or process of melting; the state of being melted or blended; coalition [L. *fundere, fusum*, to melt].

fu·see (fū·zē′) *n.* the spindle-shaped wheel in a clock or watch, round which the chain is wound; a match; a red signal flare. Also **fuzee** [Fr. *fuseé*, a spindleful].

fu·se·lage (fū′·sa·lij or fū·zạ·lazh′) *n.* the body of an airplane [O.Fr. *fusel*, a spindel].

fu·sil (fū′·sil) *n.* a light flintlock musket. **-lade** *n.* the simultaneous discharge of firearms [O.Fr. *fuisil*, a flintmusket].

fuss (fus) *n.* bustle; unnecessary ado; needless activity; *v.i.* to become nervously agitated; *v.t.* to bother another with excessive attentions. **—budget** *n.* (*Colloq.*) a fussy person. **-ily** *adv.* **-iness** *n.* **-y** *a.*

fus·tian (fust′·chạn) *n.* a coarse cotton twilled fabric, corduroy, velveteen; (*Fig.*) bombast [M.E. *fustyane*, fr. *Fustat* (*Egypt*)].

fus·ti·ga·tion (fus·tạ·gā′·shạn) *n.* a thrashing with a stick. **fustigate** *v.t.* to cudgel [L. *fustigare*, to cudgel].

fu·tile (fū′·til) *a.* ineffectual, unavailing, useless. **-ly** *adv.* **futility** *n.* uselessness; fruitlessness [L. *futilis*, worthless].

fu·ture (fūt′·cher) *a.* about to happen; that is to come hereafter; *n.* time to come. **futurism** *n.* a modern aesthetic movement marked by complete departure from tradition. **futurist** *n.* **futuristic** *a.* **futurity** *n.* time to come [L. *futurus*, about to be].

fuzz (fuz) *n.* fine, light particles; fluff; **-iness** *n.* **-y** *a.*

G

gab (gab) *n.* (*Colloq.*) trifling talk; chatter; *v.i.* to chatter. *pr.p.* **-bing.** *pa.t.* **-bed. -by** *a.* **-ble** *n., v.i.* **the gift of gab,** a talent for talking.

gab·ar·dine (gab′·ẹr·dēn) *n.* a firm, woven twilled fabric of cotton, rayon or wool. Also **gaberdine** [Sp. *gabardina*].

ga·ble (gā′·bl) *n.* the end of a house, esp. the vertical triangular ends of a building from the eaves to the top; a similar construction projecting from a roof [O.N. *gafl*].

gad (gad) *v.i.* to go about idly; to ramble. *pr.p.* **-ding.** *pa.p.* and *pa.t.* **-ded. -about** *v.i.* to wander idly; *n.* a pleasure seeker [O.E. *gaedeling*, a comrade].

gad·fly (gad′·flī) *n.* a cattle biting fly; (*Fig.*) a tormentor [fr. *gad*, a goad].

gadg·et (gaj′·it) *n.* (*Colloq.*) a general term for any small mechanical contrivance or device.

Gael (gāl) *n.* a Scottish Highlander of Celtic origin. **-ic** *a. n.* the language of the Gaels.

gaff (gaf) *n.* a barbed fishing spear; a stick with an iron hook for landing fish; *v.t.* to seize (a fish) with a gaff [Fr. *gaffe*].

gaf·fer (gaf′·ẹr) *n.* (*Brit.*) an old man, esp. a country man [contr. of *grandfather*].

gag (gag) *n.* something thrust into or over the mouth to prevent speech; *v.t.* to apply a gag to; to silence by force; *v.i.* to heave with nausea. *pr.p.* **-ging.** *pa.t., pa.p.* **-ged.** [imit.].

gag (gag) *n.* (*Colloq.*) words inserted by an actor which are not in his part; a joke.

gage (gāj) *n.* a pledge or pawn; a glove, gauntlet, cast down as challenge; a challenge; [O.Fr. *guage*]. [Sir William *Gage*].

gage (gāj) *n.* a kind of plum; a greengage [fr. Sir William *Gage*].

gage (gāj) *v.t.* See **gauge.**

gag·gle (gag′·l) *v.i.* to cackle like geese; *n.* a flock of geese [imit.].

gai·e·ty (gā′·ạ·ti·) *n.* mirth; merriment; glee; jollity. **gaily** *adv.* merrily [Fr. *gai*].

gain (gān) *v.t.* to attain to, or reach; to get by effort; to get profit; to earn; to win; *v.i.* to have advantage or profit; to increase; to improve; to make an advance; *n.* profit; advantage; increase. **-ful** *a.* profitable; lucrative. **-fully** *adv.* **-fulness** *n.* [Fr. *gagner*, to earn].

gain·say (gān·sā′) *v.t.* to contradict; to deny.

pa.p. and *pa.t.* **-said** [O.E. *gean*, against, and *say*].

gait (gāt) *n.* manner of walking or running; pace [var. of *gate*].

gai·ter (gā′·tẹr) *n.* covering for instep and ankle fitting over the shoe; a spat [Fr. *guêtre*].

gal (gal) *n.* (*Slang*) a girl.

ga·la (gā′·lạ) *n.* a show or festivity; *a.* festive [It. *gala*, finery].

gal·ax·y (gal′·ạk·si·) *n.* a band of stars encircling the heavens; a brilliant assembly of persons. (G) the Milky Way. **galactic** *a.* [Gk. *gala, galaktos*, milk].

gale (gāl) *n.* a wind between a stiff breeze and a hurricane; (*Colloq.*) an outburst of noise.

gale (gāl) *n.* a shrub found in marshes, giving off a pleasant fragrance [O.E. *gagel*].

ga·le·na (gạ·lē′·nạ) *n.* sulfide of lead, the principal ore from which lead is extracted [L. *galena*, lead ore].

gall (gawl) *n.* bile secreted in the liver; anything bitter; bitterness; rancor; (*Slang*) effrontery; impudence. **— bladder** *n.* a small sac on the other side of the liver, in which the bile is stored. **-stone** *n.* a concretion formed in the gall bladder [O.E. *gealla*].

gall (gawl) *v.t.* to fret and wear away by rubbing; to vex, irritate, or harass; *n.* a skin wound caused by rubbing. **-ing** *a.* irritating [O.E. *gealla*].

gal·lant (gal′·ạnt) *a.* splendid or magnificent; noble in bearing or spirit; brave; chivalrous; courteous to women; amorous. (gạ·lant′) *n.* a brave, high-spirited man; a courtly or fashionable man; a lover or paramour. **-ly** *adv.* **-ry** *n.* bravery; chivalry [Fr. *galant*].

gal·leon (gal'·i·ạn) *n.* a large, clumsy sailing ship built up high at bow and stern [Sp.].

gal·ler·y (gal'·ẹr·i·) *n.* a long corridor, hall, or room; a room or series of rooms in which works of art are exhibited; a balcony; the uppermost tier of seats, esp. in theater; audience or spectators; a passage in a mine; a tunnel [Fr. *galerie*].

gal·ley (gal'·i·) *n.* a low, one-decked vessel, navigated both with oars and sails; a large rowboat; the kitchen of a ship; (*Print.*) an oblong tray on which type is placed when set up. **— proof** *n.* (*Print.*) a proof taken from the galley on a long strip of paper, before it is made up in pages. **— slave** *n.* one who was condemned for some criminal offence to row in the galleys [L.L. *galea*].

gal·liard (gal'·yẹrd) *n.* a lively dance [Fr.].

Gal·lic (gal'·ik) *a.* pert. to ancient Gaul, or France; French. **gallicize** *v.t.* to make French in opinions, manners [L. *Gallia*, Gaul].

gal·li·mau·fry (gal·ạ·maw'·fri·) *n.* a hash of various meats; a hodgepodge [O.Fr. *galimafree*].

gal·li·na·ceous (gal·ạ·nā'·shạs) *a.* belonging to the order of birds which includes domestic fowls, pheasants, etc. [L. *galling*, a hen].

gal·li·pot (gal'·i·pạt) *n.* a small earthenware pot, for medicines [*galley*, and *pot*].

gal·li·um (gal'·i·ạm) *n.* a soft grey metal of extreme fusibility [L. *gallus*, a cock. *Lecoq* the discoverer].

gal·li·vant (gal·ạ·vant') *v.i.* to gad about.

gal·lon (gal'·ạn) *n.* a measure of capacity both for liquid and dry commodities, containing four quarts [O.Fr. *jalon*].

gal·lop (gal'·ạp) *n.* fastest gait of horse, when it lifts forefeet together, and hind feet together; a ride at a gallop; *v.i.* to ride at a gallop; to go at full speed; *v.t.* to cause to gallop. **-ing** *a.* speedy; swift [Fr. *galoper*].

gal·lows (gal'·ōz) *n.* a frame from which criminals are hanged [O.E. *galga*].

gal·lus·es (gal'·ạs·iz) *n.pl.* suspenders [fr. *gallows*].

ga·loot (ga·lōōt') *n.* (*Colloq.*) an uncouth or awkward fellow.

gal·op (gal'·ạp) *n.* a lively dance [Fr.].

ga·lore (ga·lōr') *adv.* abundantly; in plenty [Gael. *gu leor*, enough].

ga·losh, golosh (ga·lash') *n.* (usually pl.) a rubber overshoe [Fr. *galoche*].

gal·va·nism (gal'·vạ·nizm) *n.* the branch of science which treats of the production of electricity by chemical action. **galvanic** *a.* **galvanize** *v.t.* to apply galvanic action to; to stimulate by an electric current; (*Fig.*) to stimulate by words or deeds; to coat metal with zinc. **galvanization** *n.* **galvanizing** *n.* coating with zinc (by galvanic action). **galvanometer** *n.* an instrument for detecting and measuring the strength and direction of electric currents. **galvanoscope** *n.* an instrument for detecting the existence and direction of an electric current. **galvanic battery**, an apparatus for generating electricity by chemical action on a series of zinc or copper plates. **galvanized iron**, iron coated with zinc to prevent rust [fr. Luigi *Galvani*, inventor].

gamb (gam) *n.* an animal's leg. **gam** *n.* (Slang) a woman's leg [L. *gamba*, leg].

gam·bit (gam'·bit) *n.* in chess, opening move involving sacrifice of pawn [It. *gambetto*, wrestler's trip, fr. *gamba*, leg].

gam·ble (gam'·bl) *v.i.* to play for money; to risk esp. by financial speculation; *v.t.* to lose or squander in speculative ventures; a risky undertaking; a reckless speculation. **-r** *n.* [O.E. *gamen*, a game].

gam·bol (gam'·bạl) *v.i.* to leap about playfully; to skip and dance about. *n.* a dancing or skipping about; a frolic [Fr. *gambade*].

game (gām) *n.* any sport; a pastime; a contest for amusement; a trial of strength, skill, or chance; an exercise or play for stakes; victory in a game; frolic; mockery; hence, an object of ridicule; animals and birds protected by law and hunted by sportsmen; *a.* pert. to animals hunted as game; brave; plucky; *v.i.* to gamble. *n.pl.* athletic contests. **-ly** *adv.* **-ness** *n.* **-ster** *n.* a gambler. **gaming** *a.* playing cards, dice, etc. for money; gambling. **gamy** *a.* having the flavor of dead game which has been kept uncooked for a long time. **— cock** *n.* breed of cock trained for cockfighting. **— preserve,** land stocked with game for hunting or shooting. **— warden** *n.* an official who enforces game laws. **big game,** all large animals hunted for sport. **fair game** (*Fig.*) a person considered easy subject for jest. **to play the game,** to act in a sportsmanlike way [O.E. *gamen*].

game (gām) *a.* (*Colloq.*) of an arm or leg, lame; injured [O.Fr. *gambi*, bent].

gam·ete (gam·ēt') *n.* a protoplasmic body, ovum, or sperm, which unites with one of opposite sex for conception [Gk. *gamos*, marriage].

gam·in (gam'·in) *n.* a street-urchin [Fr.].

gam·ma (gam'·ạ) *n.* the third letter of the Greek alphabet. **— rays,** electro-magnetic radiations, of great penetrative powers, given off by radioactive substances, e.g. radium.

gam·mon (gam'·ạn) *n.* the thigh of a pig, smoked or cured [Fr. *jambon*, ham].

gam·ut (gam'·ạt) *n.* the whole series of musi-

cal notes; a scale; the compass of a voice; the entire range [L. *gamma*, and *ut*, names of notes].

gan·der (gan'·dẹr) *n.* a male goose; (Slang) a look [O.E. *gandra*].

gang (gang) *n.* people banded together for some purpose, usually bad; body of laborers working together. *v.i.* (*Colloq.*) to act as a gang (followed by *up*) **-ster** *n.* one of a gang of criminals [O.E. *gangan*, to go].

gan·gling (gang'·gling) *a.* lanky and loosely knit in build [O.E. *gangan*, to go].

gan·gli·on (gang'·gli·ạn) *n.* a globular, hard tumor, situated on a tendon. *pl.* **-s, ganglia.** **gangliate** *a.* furnished with ganglia. **-ic** *a.* [Gk. *ganglion*, an encysted tumor].

gang plank (gang' plangk') *n.* a moveable plank bridge between a ship and the shore.

gan·grene (gang'·grēn) *n.* the first stage of mortification or death of tissue in the body; *v.t.* and *v.i.* to affect with, or be affected with, gangrene. **gangrenous** *a.* mortified; putrefying [Gk. *gangraina*].

gang·way (gang'·wā) *n.* a passageway; a platform and ladder slung over the side of a ship; *interj.* make way, please! [O.E. *gangweg*].

gan·net (gan'·it) *n.* the solan goose, a seafowl of the pelican tribe [O.E. *ganot*].

gant·let (gant'·lit) *n.* a former military or naval punishment in which the offender was made to run between files of men who struck him as he passed. **to run the gantlet** (erroneously, **gauntlet**), to undergo this ordeal; to face any unpleasant ordeal [Scand.].

gan·try (gan'·tri·) *n.* a structure to support a crane, railway-signal, etc.

gaol (jāl) *n.* (*Brit.*) a jail. **-er** *n.* [form of *jail*].

gap (gap) *n.* an opening; a breach; a mountain pass [O.N. = chasm].

gape (gāp) *v.i.* to open wide, esp. the mouth; to stare with open mouth; to yawn. *n.* a wide opening; the act of gaping. **the gapes,** a fit of yawning; a disease of poultry and other birds, characterized by gaping [O.N. *gapa*].

gar (gár) *n.* a fish of the pike family. Also **garfish** [O.E. *gar*, a dart, spear].

ga·rage (gạ·razh', gạ·raj') *n.* a covered enclosure for motor vehicles; a fuel and repair station for motor vehicles; *v.t.* to place in a garage [Fr. *garer*, a station].

garb (gárb) *n.* clothing; mode or style of dress; *v.t.* to dress [O.Fr. *garbe*, dress].

gar·bage (gár'·bij) *n.* kitchen refuse; anything worthless.

gar·ble (gár'·bl) *v.t.* to pervert or mutilate, as a story, a quotation, an account, etc. by picking out only certain parts [Ar. *ghirbal*, a sieve].

gar·den (gár'·dn) *n.* ground for cultivation of flowers, vegetables, etc. generally attached to a house; pleasure grounds; *v.i.* to cultivate, or work in, a garden. **-er** *n.* **-ing** *n.* the act of tending a garden [Fr. *jardin*].

gar·de·nia (gár·dē'·ni·ạ) *n.* a genus of tropical trees and shrubs with sweet-scented, beautiful white flowers [fr. A. *Garden*, Amer. botanist].

gar·gan·tu·an (gár·gan'·choo·ạn) *a.* immense, enormous, esp. of appetite [fr. *Gargantua*, hero of Rabelais' book].

gar·gle (gár'·gl) *v.t.* to rinse (mouth or throat), preventing water from going down throat by expulsion of air from lungs; *v.i.* to make a sound of gargling; to use a gargle; *n.* a throat wash [O.Fr. *gargouille*, throat].

gar·goyle (gár'·goil) *n.* a projecting spout, often in the form of a grotesque carving, found on old buildings and intended to carry off the water [O.Fr. *gargouille*, the throat].

gar·ish (gár'·ish) *a.* gaudy; showy; glaring; dazzling. **-ly** *adv.* [M.E. *gauren*, to stare].

gar·land (gár'·lạnd) *n.* a wreath of flowers, branches, feathers, etc.; an anthology; *v.t.* to ornament with a garland [O.Gr. *garlande*].

gar·lic (gár'·lik) *n.* a plant having a bulbous root, a strong smell like onion, and a pungent taste. **-ky** *a.* [O.E. *garleac*].

gar·ment (gár'·mạnt) *n.* any article of clothing [Fr. *garnement*, equipment].

gar·ner (gár'·nẹr) *n.* a granary; *v.t.* to store in a granary; to gather up [L. *granarium*].

gar·net (gár'·nit) *n.* a semi-precious stone, usually of a dark-red color and resembling a ruby; a dark-red color [Fr. *grenat*].

gar·nish (gár'·nish) *v.t.* to adorn; to embellish; to ornament; (*Cookery*) to make food attractive or appetizing; *n.* ornament; decoration; **-ment** *n.* **garniture** *n.* that which garnishes [Fr. *garnir*, to furnish].

garlic

ga·rotte See **garrote.**

gar·ret (gar'·it) *n.* upper floor of a house immediately under roof; an attic [O.Fr. *garite*, a place of safety].

gar·ri·son (gar'·ạ·sn) *n.* a body of troops stationed in a fort, town, etc.; the fort or town itself; *v.t.* to occupy with a garrison [O.Fr. *garison*, fr. *garir*, to protect].

gar·rote (gạ·rát', ·rōt') *n.* a Spanish mode of execution by strangling, with an iron collar affixed to a post and tightened by a screw; apparatus for this punishment; *v.t.* to execute by strangulation; to seize by the throat, in order to throttle and rob. [Sp. *garrote*, a cudgel].

gar·ru·lous (gar'·ạ·lạs) *a.* talkative; loquacious. **-ly** *adv.* **-ness** *n.* **garrulity** *n.* [L. *garrire*, to chatter].

gar·ter (gár'·tẹr) *n.* a string or band worn near the knee to keep a stocking up; the badge of the highest order of knighthood in Great Britain; *v.t.* to support with a garter [O.Fr. *gartier*, fr. *garet*, the bend of the knee].

gas (gas) *n.* an elastic fluid such as air, esp. one not liquid or solid at ordinary temperatures; mixture of gases, used for heating or lighting; an anesthetic; (*Warfare*) a chemical substance used to poison or incapacitate the enemy; (Slang) empty talk; (*Colloq.*) gasoline; *v.t.* to poison with gas; *v.i.* (Slang) to talk emptily; to talk unceasingly. *pr.p.* **-sing.** *pa.p.* and *pa.t.* **-sed.** **-eous** *a.* like, or in the form of gas. **-ification** *n.* **-ify** *v.t.* to convert into gas, as by the action of heat, or by chemical processes. **-sy** *a.* full of gas. **-bag** *n.* (Slang) a very talkative person. **— burner** *n.* a gas jet or stove. **— jet** *n.* a nozzle or burner of a gas burner; the burner itself. **— mask** *n.* a respirator worn to protect against poisonous gases. **— meter** *n.* a metal box used to measure the amount of gas consumed. **-ometer** *n.* an apparatus for measuring or storing gas. **— range** *n.* a gas cooking stove[coined by D. chemist, Van Helmont fr. Gr. *chaos*, chaos].

Gas·con (gas'·kạn) *n.* a native of *Gascony*, in S.W. France; (*l.c.*) a boaster.

gash (gash) *v.t.* to make a long, deep cut in; *n.* a deep cut [O.Fr. *garser*, to slash].

gas·ket (gas'·kit) *n.* (*Naut.*) a flat, plaited cord, used to furl the sail or tie it to the yard; a washer between parts such as the cylinder head and cylinder block [Fr. *garcette*].

gas·o·line, gasolene (gas'·ạ·lēn) *n.* a volatile, inflammable, liquid mixture produced by the distillation of petroleum, used as a fuel, solvent, etc. [*gas*; L. *oleum*, oil; *-ine*].

gasp (gasp) *v.i.* to struggle for breath with open mouth; to pant; *v.t.* to utter with gasps; *n.* the act of gasping; a painful catching of the breath [O.N. *geispa*, to yawn].

gas·tric (gas'·trik) *a.* pert. to the stomach. **gastritis** (gas·trī'·tis) *n.* inflammation of the stomach. **gastro-enteritis** *n.* inflammation of the stomach and intestines. **gastrology** *n.* [Gk. *gastēr*].

gas·tron·o·my (gas·trán'·ạ·mi·) *n.* the art of good eating; epicurism. **gastronome, gastronomer** *n.* one fond of good living. Also **gastronomist, gastronomic, gastronomical** *a.* [Gk. *gaster*, the stomach; *nemein*, regulate].

gas·tro·pod (gas'·trạ·pád) *n.* a class of molluscs, e.g. snails and whelks, having a fleshy, ventral disk, which takes the place of feet. [Gk. *gaster*, the stomach; *pous, podos*, the foot].

gat (gat) *n.* (Slang) a pistol. Abbrev. of **gatling-gun.**

gate (gāt) *n.* an opening into an enclosure, through a fence, wall, etc.; a mountain pass or defile; an entrance; a device for stopping passage of water through a dam or lock; the number of people paying to watch a game; also the money taken; **—crasher** *n.* one attending a social function uninvited. **-way** *n.* an entrance [O.E. *geat*, a way].

gath·er (gaTH'·ẹr) *v.t.* to bring together; to collect; to pick; in sewing, to draw into puckers; to infer or deduce; to harvest; *v.i.* to come together; to congregate; to increase; to wrinkle, as the brow; to swell up and become full of pus (of a sore or boil); *n.* a pucker or fold in cloth. **-ing** *n.* an assemblage; a crowd; an abscess [O.E. *gaderian*, fr. *gador*, together].

Gat·ling-gun (gat'·ling-gun) *n.* machine gun invented by R. J. Gatling.

gauche (gōsh) *a.* awkward; clumsy; tactless. **gaucherie** (gō'·shạ·rē) *n.* [Fr.].

gau·cho (gou'·chō) *n.* a cowboy of the S. American pampas [Sp.].

gaud (gawd) *n.* a piece of worthless finery; a trinket. **-ily** *adv.* **-y** *a.* [L. *gaudium*, joy].

gauge (gāj) *v.t.* to ascertain the capacity of; to measure the ability of; to estimate; *n.* an instrument for determining dimensions or capacity; a standard of measure; test; criterion; the distance between the rails of a railway. **-r** *n.* one who gauges, esp. an exciseman who measures the contents of casks [O.Fr. *gauge*].

Gaul (gawl) *n.* an old name for France; a Frenchman [L. *Gallia*].

gaunt (gawnt) *a.* lean and haggard; pinched and grim; desolate. **-ly** *adv.* **-ness** *n.*

gaunt·let (gawnt'·lit) *n.* a glove with metal plates on the back, worn formerly as armor; a glove with a long cuff. **to run the gauntlet,** see **gantlet. to throw down, to take up, the gauntlet,** to give, accept, a challenge [Fr. *gant*, a glove].

gauss (gous) *n.* (*Elect.*) the unit of density of a magnetic field [fr. Karl F. *Gauss*, a German scientist, 1777-1855].

gauze (gawz) *n.* a thin, transparent fabric. **gauziness** *n.* **gauzy** *a.* [Fr. *gaze*].

gave (gāv) *p.at.* of **give**.

gav·el (gav'·al) *n.* a mallet; a small wooden hammer used by a chairman or auctioneer.

ga·votte (ga·vát') *n.* an old dance after the style of the minuet but not so stately; the music for it [Fr. *gavotte*].

gawk (gawk) *n.* an awkward person; a simpleton; a booby; *v.i.* to stare stupidly. **-y** *a.*

gay (gā) *a.* lively; merry; light-hearted; showy; dissipated. **-ly, gaily** *adv.* **-ety, gaiety** *n.* [Fr. *gai*].

gaze (gāz) *v.i.* to look fixedly; to stare; *n.* a fixed, earnest look; a long, intent look. **-r** *n.* one who gazes.

ga·ze·bo (ga·zē'·bō) *n.* a summerhouse commanding a wide view; a belvedere.

ga·zelle (ga·zel') *n.* a small, swift, graceful antelope [Ar. *ghazal*].

ga·zette (ga·zet') *n.* a newspaper (now used in newspaper titles). **gazetteer** (gaz·r·tēr') *n.* formerly a writer for a gazette; now, a geographical dictionary [It. *gazetta*].

gear (gir) *n.* apparatus; equipment; tackle; a set of tools; harness; rigging; clothing; goods; utensils; a set of toothed wheels working together, esp. by engaging cogs, to transmit power or to change timing; *v.t.* to provide with gear; to put in gear; *v.i.* to be in gear. **-ing** *n.* the series of toothed wheels for transmitting power, changing speed, etc. **—wheel** *n.* a wheel having teeth or cogs [M.E. *gere*].

gee (jē) *interj.* a command to a horse to turn to the right; exclamation of surprise.

geese (gēs) *n.* plural of **goose.**

gee·zer (gē'·zer) *n.* (*Slang*) an old fellow; a queer old chap [corrupt. of *guiser*].

Gei·ger counter (gī'·ger) *n.* a hypersensitive instrument for detecting radio-activity, cosmic radiation, etc. [H. *Geiger*, Ger. physicist].

gei·sha (gā'·sha) *n.* a Japanese dancing girl.

gel (jel) *n.* (*Chem.*) a colloidal solution which has set into a jelly; *v.i.* to become a gel. **-ling.** *pa.t., pa.p.* **-led. -ation** *n.* a solidifying by means of cold [L. *gelare*, tc freeze].

gel·a·tin, gelatine (jel'·a·tin) *n.* a glutinous substance gotten by boiling parts of animals (bones, hoofs, etc.) which is soluble in hot water and sets into a tremulous jelly. **-ous** (ja·lat'·i·nas) *a.* of the nature or consistency of gelatin; like jelly. **-ate, -ize** *v.t.* to convert into gelatine. **-ation** *n.* [It. *gelata*, jelly].

geld (geld) *v.t.* to castrate. **-ing** *n.* a castrated animal, esp. a horse [O.N. *geldr*, barren].

gel·id (jel'·id) *a.* cold as ice. **-ly** *adv.* **-ness, gelidity** *n.* [L. *gelidus*, fr. *gelu*, frost].

gem (jem) *n.* a precious stone of any kind; a jewel; anything of great value; *v.t.* to adorn with gems. *pr.p.* **-ming.** *pa.p., pa.t.* **-med** [L. *gemma*].

gem·i·nate (jem'·a·nāt) *a.* doubled; existing in pairs; *v.i.* and *t.* to make or become paired or doubled. **gemination** *n.* [L. *geminare*, to double].

Gem·i·ni (jem'·a·nī) *n.pl.* the third sign of the Zodiac; a constellation containing the two bright stars Castor and Pollux, twin heroes of Greek legend [L. *geminus*, twin-born].

gem·ma (jem'·a) *n.* (*Bot.*) a bud; (*Zool.*) a bud-like outgrowth which becomes a separate individual. *pl.* **gemmae. gemmate** *a.* having buds; *v.i.* to propagate by buds, as coral. **gemmation** *n.* budding; (*Zool.*) reproduction by gemmae. **gemmiparous** *a.* producing buds; (*Zool.*) propagating by buds [L. *gemma*, a bud].

gen·darme (zhàn·dàrm') *n.* an armed military policeman in France. **gendarmeria** (zhàn·dàrm'·rē) *n.* the corps of armed police [Fr. fr. *gens d'armes*, men-at-arms].

gen·der (jen'·der) *n.* (*Colloq.*) sex, male or female; (*Gram.*) the classification of nouns according to sex (actual or attributed) or animateness [L. *genus, generis*, a kind].

gene (jēn) *n.* the hereditary factor which is transmitted by each parent to offspring and which determines hereditary characteristics [Gk. *genos*, origin].

ge·ne·al·o·gy (jēn·i·ál'·a·ji·) *n.* a record of the descent of a person or family from an ancestor; the pedigree of a person or family; lineage. **genealogist** *n.* one who traces the descent of persons or families. **genealogical** *a.* [Gk. *genea*, birth; *logos*, discourse].

gen·er·a (jen'·a·ra) *n.* See **genus.**

gen·er·al (jen'·a·ral) *a.* relating to a genus or kind; pert. to a whole class or order; not precise, particular, or detailed; usual, ordinary, or prevalent; embracing the whole, not local or partial; *n.* (*U.S. Army*) brigadier general, lieutenant general, major general, general, general of the Army, or general of the Armies. **-ly** *adv.* as a whole; for the most part; commonly; extensively. **generality** *n.* indefiniteness; vagueness; a vague statement; the main body. **-ship** *n.* military skill in a commander; leadership. **-issimo** *n.* the chief commander of all the country's forces in China and the U.S.S.R. **in general,** in most respects. **general practitioner,** a doctor whose work embraces all types of cases [L. *generalis*].

gen·er·al·ize (jen'·er·al·īz) *v.t.* to reduce to general laws; to make universal in application; *v.i.* to draw general conclusions from particular instances; to speak vaguely. **generalization** *n.* a general conclusion from particular instances [fr. *general*].

gen·er·ate (jen'·e·rāt) *v.t.* to bring into being; to produce; (*Math.*) to trace out. **generation** *n.* a bringing into being; the act of begetting; the act of producing; that which is generated; a step in a pedigree; all persons born about the same time; the average time in which children are ready to replace their parents (about 30 years); family. **generative** (jen'·e·rā·tiv) *a.* having the power of generating or producing; prolific. **generator** *n.* one who, or that which, generates; a begetter; an apparatus for producing steam, etc.; a machine for converting mechanical into electrical energy [L. *generare*, to procreate].

ge·ner·ic (ja·ner'·ik) *a.* pert. to a genus; of a general nature in regard to all members of a genus. **-ally** *adv.* [L. *generus*, kind].

gen·er·ous (jen'·er·as) *a.* liberal, free in giving; abundant; copious; of wine, rich. **-ly** *adv.* **generosity** *n.* magnanimity; liberality in giving [L. *generosus*, of noble birth].

gen·e·sis (jen'·a·sis) *n.* origin; creation; production; birth. *pl.* **geneses** (jen'·e·sēs). **Genesis** *n.* (*Bib.*) the first book of the Old Testament [Gk.].

gen·et·ic (ja·net'·ik) *a.* pert. to origin, creation, or reproduction. **-s** *n.* the scientific study of the heredity of individuals, esp. of inherited characteristics. **geneticist** *n.* [Gk. *gignesthai*, to be born].

Ge·ne·van (ja·nē'·van) *a.* pert. to Geneva, in Switzerland. **Geneva Conventions,** international agreements, signed at Geneva in 1864, 1868, 1906 and 1949, to lessen sufferings of the wounded in war by providing for the neutrality of hospitals, ambulances, etc.

gen·ial (jēn'·yal) *a.* kindly; sympathetic; cordial; sociable; of a climate, mild and conducive to growth. **geniality** (jē·ni·al'·i·ti·) *n.* the quality of being genial; friendliness; sympathetic cheerfulness. **-ly** *adv.* [L. *genialis*].

ge·ni·e (jē'·ni·) *n.* a jinni. *pl.* **genii** (jē'·ni·ī) [corrupt. of Arab. *jinnee*].

gen·i·tal (jen'·a·tal) *a.* pert. to generation, or the organs of generation. **-s** *n.pl.* the external sexual organs. Also **genitalia** (jen·a·tā'·li·a) [L. *genitalis*, fr. *gignere*, to beget].

gen·i·tive (jen'·a·tiv) *a.* pert. to, or indicating, source, origin, possession, etc.; *n.* (*Gram.*) the case used to indicate source, origin, possesion and the like [L. *genitivus*].

gen·ius (jēn'·yas) *n.* one's mental endowment or individual talent; the animating spirit of a people, generation or locality; uncommon intellectual powers; a person endowed with the highest mental gifts [L.].

gen·o·cide (jen'·a·sīd) *n.* race murder. **genocidal** *a.* [Gk. *genos*, race; L. *caedere*, to kill].

gen·re (zhàn'·ra) *n.* a kind; sort; style. — **painting**, painting which portrays scenes in everyday life [Fr. = style, kind].

gent (jent) *n.* (*Colloq.*) a gentleman; a would-be gentleman [abbrev. fr. *gentleman*].

gen·teel (jen·tēl') *a.* possessing the qualities belonging to high birth and breeding; well-bred; stylish; refined. **-y** *adv.* **-ness** *n.* **gentility** (jen·til'·i·ti·) *n.* [Fr. *gentil*].

gen·tian (jen'·shan) *n.* the common name of Gentiana, plants whose root is used medicinally as a tonic and stomachic; its flower is usually of a deep, bright blue [L. *gentiana*].

gen·tile (jen'·til) *n.* one who is not a Jew; *a.* formerly (among Christians), heathen [L. *gens*, a nation].

gen·tle (jen'·tl) *a.* kind and amiable; mild and refined in manner; quiet and sensitive of disposition; meek; moderate; gradual; of good family; *v.t.* to tame; to make docile. **gently** *adv.* **-folk** *n.pl.* persons of good breeding and family. **-ness** *n.* **gentry** (jen'·tri·) *n.* people of birth and good breeding; the class of people between the nobility and the middle class [L. *gentilis*].

gen·tle·man (jen'·tl·man) *n.* a man of good breeding and refined manners; a man of good family; a polite term for a man. *pl.* **gentlemen. -ly** *adv.* **-like** *a.* **gentlewoman** *n.* a woman of good family or of good breeding; a woman who waits upon a person of high rank. **-'s gentleman,** a valet. **-'s agreement,** one binding in honor but not legally [L. *gentilis*].

gen·u·flect (jen'·yoo·flekt) *v.i.* to bend the knee, esp. in worship. **genuflection, genuflexion** *n.* **-or** *n.* **-ory** *a.* [L. *genu*, the knee; *flectere*, to bend].

gen·u·ine (jen'·yoo·in) *a.* real; true; pure; authentic; sincere. **-ly** *adv.* [L. *genuinus*].

ge·nus (jē'·nas) *n.* a class; an order; a kind; (*Nat. Hist.*) a subdivision ranking next above species, and containing a number of species having like characteristics. *pl.* **genera** (jen'·a·ra) [L. *genus, generis*, a kind].

ge·o-, ge- combining forms fr. Gk. *gē*, meaning earth, ground, soil. **geocentric** *a.* (*Astron.*) having reference to the earth as center [Gk. *kentron*, the center].

ge·ode (jē'·ōd) *n.* in mineralogy, a rounded nodule of stone, containing a cavity, usually lined with crystals [Gk. *geodēs*, earth-like].

ge·od·e·sy (jē·àd'·a·si·) *n.* the mathematical survey and measurement of the earth's surface, involving allowance for curvature. **geodetic, geodetical** *a.* [Gk. *gē*; *daiein*, to divide].

ge·og·ra·phy (jē·àg'·ra·fi·) *n.* the science of the earth's form, its physical divisions into seas, rivers, mountains, plains, etc.; a book on this. **geographer** *n.* one versed in geography. **geographic, geographical** *a.* pert. to geography. **geographically** *adv.* [Gk. *gē*, the earth; *graphein*, to write].

ge·ol·o·gy (jē·àl'·a·ji·) *n.* the science of the earth's crust, the rocks, their strata, etc. **geological** *a.* **geologically** *adv.* **geologist** *n.* [Gk. *gē*, the earth; *logos*, discourse].

ge·om·e·try (jē·àm'·a·tri·) *n.* the mathematical study of the properties of lines, angles, surfaces, and solids. **geometric(al)** *a.* pert. to geometry. **geometrically** *adv.* **geometrician** *n.* one skilled in geometry. **geometric progression** (*Math.*) a series of quantities in which each quantity is obtained by multiplying the preceding term by a constant factor, e.g. 2, 6, 18, 54, etc. (3 being the constant factor) [Gk. *gē*, the earth; *metron*, a measure].

ge·oph·a·gy (jē·àf'·a·ji·) *n.* the practice of eating earth, dirt, clay, etc. Also **geophagism** *n.* [Gk. *gē*, earth; *phagein*, to eat].

ge·o·pol·i·tics (jē·ō·pàl'·a·tiks) *n.pl.* the study of the influence of geographical situation upon the politics of a nation. **geopolitical** *a.* [Gk. *gē*, the earth; *politēs*, a citizen].

geor·gette (jawr·jet') *n.* a fine semi-transparent silk fabric [fr. *Georgette*, Fr. modiste].

geor·gic (jawr'·jik) *n.* a pastoral poem [Gk. *gē*, the earth; *ergon*, a work].

ge·ot·ro·pism (jē·àt'·ra·pizm) *n.* (*Bot.*) the tendency of a growing plant to direct its roots downwards. **geotropic** *a.* [Gk. *gē*, the earth; *tropos*, a turning].

ge·ra·ni·um (ja·rā′·ni·am) *n.* plant having showy flowers [Gk. *geranos*, a crane].

ger·i·at·rics (jer·i·at′·riks) *n.* science of the diseases and care of the old [Gk. *geras*, old age].
germ (jurm) *n.* the rudimentary form of a living thing, whether animal or plant; a microscopic organism; a microbe; a bud; that from which anything springs. **-icide** *n.* a substance for destroying disease-germs. **germicidal** *a.* — **warfare** waged with bacteria for weapons [L. *germen*, a bud].
ger·man (jur′·man) *a.* closely related. **germane** (jer·mān′) *a.* appropriate; relevant; allied; akin [L. *germanus*, fully akin].
Ger·man (jur′·man) *a.* belonging to *Germany*; *n.* a native of Germany; the German language. **Germanic** *a.* pert. to Germany; Teutonic. **Germanize** *v.t.* to make German. **German measles**, a disease like measles, but less severe [L. *Germanus*].
ger·man·der (jer·man′·der) *a.* genus of herblike plants having medicinal properties [Gk. *chamai*, on the ground; *drus*, a tree].
ger·ma·ni·um (jur·mā′·ni·am) *n.* a rare metallic element [L. *Germanus*, German].
ger·mi·nal (jur′·ma·nal) *a.* pert. to a germ or seed-bud [L. *germen*, bud].
ger·mi·nate (jur′·ma·nāt) *v.i.* to sprout; to bud; to shoot; to begin to grow; *v.t.* to cause to grow. **germinative** *a.* pert. to germination. **germination** *n.* [L. *germen*, a bud].
ger·on·tol·o·gy (jer·an·tál′·a·ji·) *n.* the science that studies the decline of life, esp. of man [Gk. *geron*, an old man].
ger·ry·man·der (ger·, jer·i·man′·der) *v.t.* to arrange or redistribute electoral districts to private advantage [fr. Gov. *Gerry* of Mass.].
ger·und (jer′·and) *n.* part of the Latin verb used as a verbal noun: the dative of the O.E. or modern English infinitive, used to express purpose. **gerundial** *a.* of the nature of a gerund. **gerundive** *n.* the future passive participle of a Latin verb expressing the action of having to be done [L. *gerere*, to do].
ge·stalt (ge·shtawlt′) *n.* pattern; a whole which is more than the sum of its parts [Ger.].
Ge·sta·po (ga·stáp′·ō) *n.* the secret police of the German Nazi party [contr. of *Geheime Staatspolizei* = secret state-police].
ges·ta·tion (jes·tā′·shan) *n.* carrying young in womb; pregnancy [L. *gestare*, to bear].
ges·tic·u·late (jes·tik′·ya·lāt) *v.i.* to make violent gestures or motions, esp. with hands and arms, when speaking. **gesticulation** *n.* a gesture [L. *gestus*, gesture].
ges·ture (jes′·cher) *n.* a motion of the hand, hands, etc. as a mode of expression; an act indicating attitude of mind; *v.i.* to make gestures [L. *gerere*, to do].
get (get) *v.t.* to procure; to obtain; to gain possession of; to come by; to win, by almost any means; to receive; to earn; to induce or persuade; (*Colloq.*) to understand; (*Arch.*) to beget; *v.i.* to become; to reach or attain; to bring one's self into a condition. *pr.p.* **-ting**. *pa.t.* **got**. *pa.p.* **got, gotten. -away** (get′·a·wā) *n.* (*Colloq.*) escape. **get-up** *n.* (*Colloq.*) equipment; dress; energy [O.E. *gitan*].
gew·gaw (gū′·gaw) *n.* a showy trifle; a bauble [O.E. *gifu*, a gift].
gey·ser (gī′·zer) *n.* a hot spring which spouts water intermittently [O.N. *geysa*, to gush].

ghast·ly (gast′·li·) *a.* horrible; shocking. Also *adv.* **ghastliness** *n.* [O.E. *gaestlic*, terrible].
gher·kin (gur′·kin) *n.* a small species of cucumber used for pickling [Dut. *agurkje*].
ghet·to (get′·ō) *n.* a section to which Jews were restricted; a section of a city in which members of a national or racial group live or are restricted [It.].

ghost (gōst) *n.* the apparition of a dead person; a specter; a disembodied spirit; semblance or shadow; (*Colloq.*) a person who does literary or artistic work for another, who takes the credit for it. **-ly** *a.* **-liness** *n.* **-like** *a.* **Holy Ghost**, the Holy Spirit; the third element in the Trinity [O.E. *gast*].
ghoul (gōōl) *n.* imaginary evil being. **-ish** *a.* [Ar. *ghul*].
gi·ant (ji′·ant) *n.* (*fem.* **giantess**) a man of extraordinary bulk and stature; a person of unusual powers, bodily or intellectual; *a.* like a giant. **-ism** *n.* (*Med.*) abnormal development [Fr. *géant*].
gib·ber (jib′·er) *v.i.* and *t.* to speak rapidly and inarticulately; to chatter. **-ish** *n.* meaningless speech; nonsense [i.mit. origin].
gib·bet (jib′·it) *n.* a gallows; *v.t.* to hang on a gallows [O.Fr. *gibet*, a stick].
gib·bon (gib′·an) *n.* a tailless, long-armed ape of S.E. Asia [Fr.].
gib·bous (gib′·as) *a.* rounded and bulging [L. *gibbus*, a hump].
gibe, jibe (jīb) *v.i.* to taunt; to sneer at; to scoff at; *n.* an expression of contempt; a taunt. **gib·lets** (jib′·lits) *n. pl.* the internal edible parts of poultry, e.g. heart, liver, gizzard, etc. [O.Fr. *gibelet*].
gid·dy (gid′·i·) *a.* dizzy; feeling a swimming sensation in the head; liable to cause this sensation; whirling; flighty; frivolous. **giddily** *adv.* **giddiness** *n.* [O.E. *gydig*, insane].
gift (gift) *n.* a present; a thing given; a donation; natural talent; faculty; power; *v.t.* to endow; to present with; to bestow. **-ed** *a.* possessing natural talent. **-edness** *n.* [fr. *give*].
gig (gig) *n.* a light carriage with one pair of wheels, drawn by a horse; a ship's boat.
gi·gan·tic (ji·gan′·tik) *a.* like a giant; of extraordinary size; huge. **-ally** *adv.* [Gk. *gigas*].
gig·gle (gig′·l) *v.i.* to laugh in a silly way, with half-suppressed catches of the breath; *n.* such a laugh. **-er** *n.* **giggling** *n.* [imit. origin].
gig·o·lo (jig′·a·lō) *n.* a professional male dancing-partner [Sp.].
gild (gild) *v.t.* to overlay with gold-leaf or gold-dust; to make gold in color; to brighten; to give a fair appearance to; to embellish [O.E. *gyldan*].
gill (jil) *n.* a measure of capacity containing one fourth of a pint [O.Fr. *gelle*].
gill (gil) *n.* the organ of respiration in fishes and other water animals (usually *pl.*) [Scand.].

gill (gil) *n.* a ravine or narrow valley, with a stream running through it. Also **ghyll** [O.N. *gil*, a fissure].
gilt (gilt) *n.* a thin layer of gold, or something resembling gold; *a.* yellow like gold; gilded. **-edged** *a.* having the edges gilded; of the best quality [O.E. *fyldan*].
gim·bals (jim′·balz, gim′·balz) *n.pl.* a contrivance of rings and pivots for keeping a ship's compass, etc. always in a horizontal position [L. *gemelli*, twins].
gim·crack (jim′·krak) *n.* a showy or fanciful trifle; *a.* showy but worthless [E. *jim*, neat; *crack*, a lad, a boaster].
gim·let (gim′·lit) *n.* a small implement with a screw point and a cross handle, for boring holes in woods; *v.t.* [O.Fr. *guimbelet*].

gim·mick (gim′·ik) *n.* (*Slang*) any device by which a magician works a trick; a gadget.
gimp (gimp) *n.* a narrow fabric or braid used as an edging or trimming [Fr. *guimpe*].
gin (jin) *n.* a distilled alcoholic beverage, flavored with juniper berries, orange peel, etc. [Fr. *genièvre* fr. L. *juniperus*, juniper].
gin (jin) *n.* a snare or trap; a machine for separating the seeds from cotton; *v.t.* to clear cotton of seeds by a gin; to catch in a snare. *pr.p.* **-ning**. *pa.p.* and *pa.t.* **-ned** [fr. *engine*].
gin·ger (jin′·jer) *n.* a plant of the Indies with a hot-tasting spicy root; (*Slang*) spirit; a light reddish-yellow color; *v.t.* to flavor with ginger.

— **ale** *n.* an effervescent beverage. **-bread** *n.* a cake, flavored with ginger and molasses; showy ornamentation. **-y** *a.* hot and spicy [L. *zingiber*].
gin·ger·ly (jin′·jer·li·) *adv.* cautiously; carefully.
ging·ham (ging′·am) *n.* a kind of cotton cloth, usually checked or striped [Jav. *ginggang*, striped].
gin·gi·vi·tis (jin·ji·vī′·tis) *n.* inflammation of the gums [L. *gingiva*, the gum; *-itis*, inflammation].
gin rum·my (jin·rum′·i·) *n.* a card game for two or more players.
gin·seng (jin′·seng) *n.* a plant, the root valued as medicine [Chin. *jin-tsan*].
gip·sy See **Gypsy**.
gi·raffe (ja·raf′) *n.* an African animal with spotted coat and very long neck and legs [Fr. fr. Ar. *zaraf*].

gird (gurd) *v.t.* to encircle with any flexible band; to put a belt around; to equip with, or belt on, a sword. *pa.p.* and *pa.t.* **-ed** or **girt. -er** *n.* an iron or steel beam used as a support in constructional engineering [O.E. *gyrdan*].
gir·dle (gur′·dl) *n.* that which girds or encircles, esp. the waist; a tight-fitting undergarment worn for support of the lower part of the body; *v.t.* [O.E. *gyrdel*.]
girl (gurl) *n.* a female child; a young unmarried woman. **-hood** *n.* the state, or time, of being a girl. **-ish** *a.* like a girl. **-ishly** *adv.* **-ishness** *n.* [M.E. *gurle*].
girt (gurt) alternate *pa.p.* and *pa.t.* of **gird**.
girth (gurth) *n.* band to hold a saddle, blanket, etc. in place on a horse; a girdle; the measurement around a thing [fr. *gird*].
gist (jist) *n.* the main point of a question; the substance or essential point of any matter [O.Fr. *gist*, it lies].
give (giv) *v.t.* to bestow; to make a present of; to grant; to deliver; to impart; to assign; to yield; to supply; to make over; to cause to have; to pronounce, as an opinion, etc.; to pledge, as one's word; *v.i.* to yield; to give away; to move; *n.* elasticity; a yielding to pressure. *pr.p.* **giving**. *pa.p.* **given**. *pa.t.* **gave. -n** *a.* granted; admitted; supposed; certain; particular; addicted to; inclined to. **-r** *n.* **to give away**, to bestow; (*Colloq.*) to betray [O.E. *giefan*].
giz·zard (giz′·erd) *n.* a bird's strong muscular second stomach [O.Fr. *gezier*].

gla·cé (gla·sā′) *a.* of a cake, iced; of a kind of leather, polished or glossy; of fruits, candied [Fr. *glace*, ice].
gla·cier (glā′·sher) *n.* a mass of ice, formed by accumulated snow in high cold regions, which moves very slowly down a mountain. **glacial** (glā′·shal) pert. to ice or its action; pert. to glaciers; icy; frozen; crystallized. **glaciate** *v.t.* to cover with ice; to turn to ice. **glaciology** *n.* the scientific study of the formation and action of glaciers [Fr. *glace*, ice].
glad (glad) *a.* pleased; happy; joyous; giving joy. **-den** *v.t.* to make glad; to cheer; to please. **-ly** *adv.* with pleasure; joyfully; cheerfully. **-ness** *n.* **-some** *a.* giving joy; cheerful; gay. **glad rags** (*Slang*) dressy clothes [O.E. *glaed*].
glade (glād) *n.* a grassy open space in a wood
glad·i·a·tor (glad′·i·ā·ter) *n.* literally, a swordsman; a combatant who fought in the arena; one involved in a fight [L. *gladius*, a sword].
glad·i·o·lus (glad·i·ō′·las) *n.* a plant of the iris family, with long sword-shaped leaves [L. *gladius*, a sword].
Glad·stone (glad′·stōn) *n.* a leather traveling-bag hinged along the bottom to open out flat [fr. Brit. statesman, W. E. *Gladstone*].

glair (glēr) *n.* white of egg; size or gloss made from it; any substance resembling it; *v.t.* to smear with glair. **-eous, -y** *a.* [Fr. *glaire*].

glam·our (glam'·ẽr) *n.* deceptive or alluring charm; witchery. **-ous** *a.* Also **glamor** [corrupt. of *gramarye*, magic].

glance (glans) *n.* a quick look; a glimpse; a flash or sudden gleam of light; an allusion or hint; an oblique hint; *v.t.* to cast a glance; *v.i.* to give a swift, cursory look; to allude; to fly off in an oblique direction; to flash or gleam. **glancing** *a.* [Ger. *Glanz*, luster].

gland (gland) *n.* an organ or collection of cells secreting and abstracting certain substances from the blood and transforming them into new compounds. **-ers** *n.* a disease of horses. **-ular, -ulous** *a.* consisting of or pert. to glands [L. *glans*, an acorn].

glare (glār) *n.* a strong, dazzling light; an overwhelming glitter; showiness; a fierce, hostile look or stare; *v.i.* to shine with a strong dazzling light; to be too showy; to stare in a fierce and hostile manner. **glaring, glary** *a.* brilliant; open and bold [O.E. *glaer*, amber].

glass (glas) *n.* a hard, brittle, generally transparent substance formed by fusing silica with fixed alkalis; articles made of glass, e.g. a drinking-glass or tumbler, a looking-glass or mirror, a telescope, a weather glass or barometer; the quantity contained in a drinking glass; *a.* made of glass; *v.t.* to cover with glass; to glaze. **-es** *n.pl.* spectacles. **-y** *a.* made of glass; vitreous; like glass; dull or lifeless. **-ily** *adv.* **-iness** *n.* **-ful** *n.* the contents of a glass. **— blowing** *n.* the art of shaping and fashioning glass by inflating it through a tube, after heating. **— blower** *n.* **-ware** *n.* articles made of glass [O.E. *glaes*].

glau·co·ma (glaw·kō'·ma) *n.* (*Med.*) a serious eye disease causing tension and hardening of the eyeball with progressive loss of vision [Gk.].

glau·cous (glaw'·kas) *a.* sea-green; covered with a fine bloom, as a plum [Gk. *glaukos*, blue-gray].

glaze (glāz) *n.* the vitreous, transparent coating of pottery or porcelain; any glossy coating; *v.t.* to furnish with glass, as a window; to overlay with a thin, transparent surface, as earthenware; to make glossy. **-r** *n.* a workman who glazes pottery, cloth, etc. **glazier** (glā'·zhẽr) *n.* one who sets glass in windows, etc. [O.E. *glaes*, glass].

gleam (glēm) *n.* a faint or transient ray of light; brightness; glow; *v.i.* to shoot or dart, as rays of light; to flash; to shine faintly [O.E.].

glean (glēn) *v.t.* to gather after a reaper, as grain; to collect with patient labor; to cull the fairest portion of; to pick up (information); *v.i.* to gather. **-er** *n.* **-ings** *n.pl.* what is collected by gleaning [O.Fr. *glener*].

glebe (glēb) *n.* soil; ground; land belonging to a parish church [L. *gleba*, a clod].

glede (glēd) *n.* a bird of prey [O.E. *glida*].

glee (glē) *n.* mirth; merriment; joy; a part song for three or more voices. **-ful** *a.* **-fully** *adv.* **-fulness** *n.* — **club** *n.* a group of singers [O.E. *gleo*, mirth].

gleet (glēt) *n.* thin watery discharge from a sore [O.Fr. *glete*, a flux].

glen (glen) *n.* a valley, usually wooded and with a stream [Gael. *gleann*].

glen·gar·ry (glen·gar'·i·) *n.* a Highlander's cap, boat-shaped, with two ribbons hanging down behind [fr. *Glengarry*, Scotland].

glib (glib) *a.* smooth; fluent. **-ly** *adv.* **-ness** *n.*

glide (glīd) *v.i.* to move gently or smoothly; to go stealthily or gradually; of an airplane, to move, or descend, usually with engines shut off; *n.* a sliding movement. **-r** *n.* one who or that which, glides; a plane capable of flight without motive power, by utilizing air currents [O.E. *glidan*].

glim·mer (glim'·ẽr) *v.i.* to shine faintly and unsteadily; to flicker; *n.* a faint, unsteady light; a faint glimpse; an inkling. Also **-ing** *n.* and *a.* [M.E. *glimeren*].

glimpse (glimps) *n.* a momentary view; a passing appearance; a faint notion; *v.t.* to catch a glimpse of; *v.i.* to look briefly [M.E. *glimsen*, to shine faintly].

glint (glint) *n.* glitter; a faint gleam; a flash; *v.i.* to glitter [M.E. *glent*].

glis·sade (gli·säd', ·sād') *n.* the act of sliding down a slope of ice or snow; in dancing, a gliding step sideways; *v.i.* to perform a glissade [Fr. *glisser*, to slide].

glis·ten (glis'·n) *v.i.* to glitter; to sparkle; to shine; *n.* [O.E. *glisnian*].

glit·ter (glit'·ẽr) *v.i.* to shine with a bright, quivering light; to sparkle; to be showy and attractive; *n.* a bright, sparkling light; brilliance [O.N. *glitra*].

gloam·ing (glō'·ming) *n.* twilight; dusk [O.E.].

gloat (glōt) *v.i.* to gaze with adulation; to think about with evil satisfaction. **-ing** *a.*

globe (glōb) *n.* a round body; a sphere; a heavenly sphere, esp. the earth; a sphere with a map of the earth or the stars; anything approximately of this shape, e.g. a fish bowl, a lamp shade, etc. **global** *a.* taking in the whole world. **globate, globated** *a.* spherical. **globoid** *a.* globe-shaped. **globose, globous** *a.* round, spherical (or nearly so). **globosity**

n. **globular** *a.* globe-shaped (or nearly so). **globularity** *n.* **globularly** *adv.* **globule** (glåb'·yool) *n.* a small particle of matter of a spherical form; a tiny pill. **globulous** *a.* **-trotter** *n.* traveler; tourist [L. *globus*, a round mass].

glob·u·lin (glåb'·ya·lin) *n.* one of the proteins of the blood [fr. *globule*].

glock·en·spiel (glåk'·an·spēl) *n.* a musical instrument consisting of a row of bells suspended from a rod, or of a series of flat bars, which when struck with a mallet give forth a bell-like sound; a carillon [Ger. *Glocke*, a bell; *Spiel*, play].

glom·er·ate (glåm'·a·rit) *a.* gathered into a cluster. **glomeration** *n.* [L. *glomus*, a ball].

gloom (glōōm) *n.* thick shade; partial or almost total darkness; melancholy; *v.i.* to become dark or threatening; to be dejected. **-y** *a.* dark and dreary; melancholy. **-ily** *adv.* **-iness** *n.* [O.E. *glom*].

glo·ry (glō'·ri·) *n.* renown; whatever brings honor; praise and adoration; divine happiness; height of excellence or prosperity; splendor or brilliance; a halo; *v.i.* to be proud; boast; to exult triumphantly. **gloriole** (glō'·ri·ōl) *n.* a halo. **glorious** *a.* illustrious; conferring renown; splendid; noble. **gloriously** *adv.* **gloriousness** *n.* **glorify** *v.t.* to exalt; to praise esp. in worship; to make eternally blessed; to shed radiance on; to magnify. **glorifier** *n.* **glorification** *n.* [L. *gloria*].

gloss (glaws) *n.* luster from a smooth surface; polish; a deceptively fine exterior; *v.t.* to make smooth and shining; to render plausible; (with *over*) to mitigate or excuse something harsh or unpleasant. **-y** *a.* smooth and shining [O.N. *glossi*, a blaze].

gloss (glaws) *n.* an explanatory note upon some word or passage in a text, written in the margin or between the lines; *v.t.* and *i.* to annotate [Gk. *glossa*, the tongue].

glos·sal (glás·al) *a.* (*Anat.*) pert. to the tongue [Gk. *glossa*, the tongue].

glos·sa·ry (glás'·a·ri·) *n.* a vocabulary of obscure or technical words; vocabulary to a book. **glossarial** *a.* **glossarist** *n.* a compiler of a glossary [Gk. *glossa*, the tongue].

glot·tis (glåt'·is) *n.* (*Anat.*) the narrow opening at the top of the larynx or windpipe, between the vocal chords. **glottal** *a.* [Gk. fr. *glossa, glotta*, the tongue].

glove (gluv) *n.* a cover for the hand and wrist with a sheath for each finger; *v.t.* to cover with a glove. **-r** *n.* one who makes or sells gloves [O.E. *glof*].

glow (glō) *v.i.* to shine with an intense heat; to be bright or red; to feel hot, as the skin; to burn; to rage; *n.* incandescence; warmth or redness; sensation of warmth; ardor. **-ing** *a.* bright; warm; excited; enthusiastic. **-ingly** *adv.* [O.E. *glowan*].

glow·er (glou'·ẽr) *v.i.* to stare sullenly or with anger; a scowl.

gloze (glōz) *v.t.* to smooth over; to explain away; to flatter [M.E. *glosen*].

glu·cose (glōō'·kōs) *n.* a white crystalline sugar obtained from fruits and honey [Gk. *glukus*, sweet].

glue (glōō) *n.* an adhesive, gelatinous substance made by boiling skins, hoofs, etc. of animals; *v.t.* to join with glue; to cause to stick as with glue. **-y** *a.* [O.Fr. *glu*].

glum (glum) *a.* sullen; moody; morose. **-ness** *n.* **-ly** *adv.* [M.E. *glommen*, to frown].

glut (glut) *v.t.* overindulge; to fill to excess. *pr.p.* **-ting.** *pa.p., pa.t.* **-ted** *n.* an oversupply [L. *gluttire*, to swallow].

glu·ten (glōō'·tẹn) *n.* the protein of wheat and other cereals. **-ous** *a.* [L.].

glut·ton (glut'·n) *n.* one who eats too much; (*Fig.*) one eager for anything in excess, e.g. work, books, etc.; carnivore of weasel family, wolverine. **-ize** *v.i.* to eat to excess. **-ous** *a.* **-ously** *adv.* **-y** *n.* [Fr. *glouton*].

glyc·er·ine (glis'·ẽr·in) *n.* a sweet, colorless, odorless, syrupy liquid. Also **glycerol** [Gk. *glukeros*, sweet].

gly·co·gen (glī'·ka·jin) *n.* the form in which the body stores carbohydrates (starch); animal starch [Gk. *glukus*, sweet].

gly·col (glī'·kōl) *n.* an artificial compound linking glycerine and alcohol used as an antifreeze.

glyph (glif) *n.* a shallow vertical channel or carved fluting [Gk. *gluphein*, to carve].

glyp·tic (glip'·tik) *a.* pert. to carving, esp. on gems. **-s** *n.pl.* the art of engraving on precious stones. **glyptograph** *n.* the engraving. **glyptography** *n.* [Gk. *gluptos*, carved].

gnar (när) *v.i.* to growl; to snarl.

gnarl (närl) *n.* a knot in wood or on the trunk of a tree. **-ed** (närld), **-y** *a.* knotty; knobby [M.E. *knurre*].

gnash (nash) *v.t.* to grind the teeth together, as in anger or pain; *n.* a grinding of the teeth. **-ing** *n.* [imit. origin].

gnat (nat) *n.* a kind of small biting insect [O.E.].

gnaw (naw) *v.t.* to wear away by scraping with the teeth; to bite steadily, as a dog a bone; to fret; to corrode; *v.i.* to use the teeth in biting; to cause steady pain. **-er** *n.* **-ing** *a., n.* [O.E. *gnagan*].

gneiss (nīs) *n.* a metamorphic rock similar to granite [Ger.].

gneiss

gnome (nōm) *n.* a fabled being resembling a misshapen dwarf, the guardian of precious metals hidden in the earth; a goblin [Gk. *gnōmē*, intelligence].

gnome (nōm) *n.* a wise saying; a maxim. **gnomic, gnomical** *a.* [Gk. *gnōmē*, thought].

gno·mon (nō'·mán) *n.* the pin, rod, or plate which casts the shadow on a sundial; an indicator; (*Geom.*) the part of a rectangular figure which remains when a similar rectangle is taken from one corner of it. **-ic, -ical** *a.* [Gk. *gnōmōn*, pin of a sundial.]

gno·sis (nō'·sis) *n.* mystical knowledge. **gnostic** (nás'·tik) *a.* pert. to knowledge; having special knowledge [Gk. *gignoskein*, to know].

gnu (nōō) *n.* antelope, resembling an ox; the wildebeest [Kaffir, *ngu*].

go (gō) *v.i.* to pass from one place or condition to another; to move along; to be in motion; to proceed; to depart; to elapse; to be kept; to put; to be able to be put: to result; to contribute to a result; to tend to; to pass away; to become; to fare. *pr.p.* **-ing** *pa.p.* **gone** (gawn). *pa.t.* **went.** *n.* a going; (*Colloq.*) vigor; (*Colloq.*) an attempt; (*Colloq.*) a success. **-er** *n.* **-ing** *n.* the state of the ground or roads; working conditions. *a.* moving; successful. **-ings on** (*Colloq.*) usually in a bad sense, behavior; conduct. **gone** *a.* lost; beyond recovery; weak and faint. **-between** *n.* an intermediary. **-cart** *n.* wooden framework on casters, for teaching infants to walk. **to go in for**, to indulge in. **to go off**, to depart; to explode; to disappear; to become less efficient, popular, fashionable, etc. [O.E. *gan*].

goad (gōd) *n.* a sharp, pointed stick for driving cattle; anything that urges to action; *v.t.* to drive with a goad; to urge on; to irritate [O.E. *gad*].

goal (gōl) *n.* an object of effort; an end or aim; in a race, the winning post; in football, hockey, etc., the space marked by two upright posts and a cross-bar; the act of kicking or driving the ball between these posts [Fr. *gaule*, a pole].

goat (gōt) *n.* a long-haired, ruminant quadruped with cloven hoofs and curving horns; the 10th sign of the Zodiac, Capricorn; (*Slang*) one who must take the blame for another. **-ee** (gō·tē') *n.* a small tuft of beard on the chin. **—herd** *n.* one who tends goats. **-ish** *a.* like a goat; lecherous. **to get one's goat** (*Colloq.*) to annoy or irritate one [[O.E. *gat*].

gob (gäb) *n.* a lump or mass. **gobbet** *n.* a small mass; a mouthful [O.Fr. *gobe*, a mouthful].

gob (gäb) *n.* (*Slang*) a nickname for U.S. sailor.

gob·ble (gäb'·l) *v.t.* to eat hurriedly or greedily. **-r** *n.* a greedy eater [O.Fr. *gober*, to devour].

gob·ble (gäb'·l) *n.* the throaty, gurgling cry of the turkey cock; *v.i.* to make such a noise. **-r** *n.* a turkey [imit.].

gob·ble·dy·gook (gäb'·l·di·gook) *n.* (*Slang*) pompous, wordy talk or writing [fr. *gobble*].

Gob·e·lin (gäb'·a·lin) *n.* rich French tapestry [fr. *Gobelin*, tapestry makers in Paris].

gob·let (gäb'·lit) *n.* a drinking glass with a stem and foot [O.Fr. *gobelet*].

gob·lin (gäb'·lin) *n.* an evil or mischievous sprite or elf; a gnome [Gk. *kobalos*, a mischievous spirit].

god (gäd) *n.* a being of more than human powers; a divinity; an idol; any person honored unduly; any object esteemed as the chief good; *n.pl.* false deities; (G) the Supreme Being; Jehovah. **-dess** *n.* a female god or idol. **godly** *a.* reverencing God; pious; devout. **godliness** *n.* holiness; righteousness. **-less** *a.* wicked; impious; acknowledging no God. **godsend** *n.* an unexpected piece of good fortune. **-speed** *n.* a prosperous journey; a wish for success given at parting. **-forsaken** *a.* dreary; dismal [O.E. *god*, cf. Ger. *Gott*].

god·child (gäd'·child) *n.* one for whom a person becomes sponsor, guaranteeing his religious education. Also. **-daughter, -son, -parent, -mother, -father**, the sponsor.

god·wit (gåd'·wit) *n.* a long-billed wading bird [O.E. *god*, good; *wiht*, a creature].

gog·gle (gåg'·l) *v.i.* to roll the eyes; to stare; *n.* a rolling of the eyes; *a.* rolling; bulging; protruding (of the eyes). **-s** *n.pl.* spectacles to protect the eyes [Gael. *gog*, a nod].

goi·ter (goi'·ter) *n.* a swelling on the front of the neck, the enlargement of the thyroid gland. **goitrous** *a.* [L. *guttur*, the throat].

gold (gōld) *n.* a precious metal of a bright yellow color; money; riches; a bright yellow color; *a.* made of gold; of color of gold. **-en** *a.* made of gold; having the color of gold; precious. **-finch** *n.* a beautiful bird, so named from its color. **-fish** *n.* a small fish of the carp family named from its color. **-smith** *n.* one who manufactures vessels and ornaments of gold. **-beater** *n.* one who beats gold into gold leaf. **-digger** *n.* one who digs or mines gold; (*Slang*) an unscrupulous flirt, expert at obtaining money from male friends. **-dust** *n.* gold in very fine particles. **-leaf** *n.* gold beaten into an extremely thin leaf or foil, used for gilding. **-mine** *n.* a mine from which gold is due; a source of wealth. **-plate** *n.* vessels or utensils made of gold (collectively). **-rush** *n.* the mad scramble to reach a new goldfield. **— standard,** a currency system under which banknotes are exchanged for gold at any time. **-en age,** the most flourishing period in the history of a nation. **-enrod,** a plant with branching clusters of small yellow flowers. **-en rule,** the rule of doing as you would be done by. **-en wedding,** the fiftieth wedding anniversary [O.E.].

golf (gålf) *n.* out door game played with set of clubs and a ball, in which the ball is driven with the fewest possible strokes, into a succession of holes. *v.i.* to play this game. **-er** *n.* **— course, — links** tract of land for playing golf [Dut. *kolf*, a club].

gol·ly (gål'·i·) *interj.* to express joy, sorrow, surprise, etc. [fr. *God*].

go·losh See **galosh**.

gon·ad (gòn'·ad) *n.* (*Biol.*) a gland that produces reproductive cells; ovary or testis. **-al** *a.* [Gk. *gonos*, seed].

gon·do·la (gån'·da·la) *n.* a long, narrow, flat-bottomed boat, used in the canals of Venice. **gondolier** (gon·da·lēr') *n.* the boatman [It.].

gone (gawn) *pa.p.* of the verb **go**. **-r** *n.* (*Slang*) one who is in a hopeless state; *a.* beyond recovery [O.E. *gan*].

gong (gång) *n.* a circular metal plate which gives out a deep note when struck with a soft mallet; anything used in this way; as a call to meals [Malay].

gon·o·coc·cus (gån·a·kåk'·as) *n.* (*Med.*) microbe of gonorrhea. **gonorrhea** (gån·a·rē'·a) *n.* [Gk. *gonos*, seed; *kokkos*, a berry; *rhoia*, a flowing].

good (good) *a.* commendable; right; proper; suitable; excellent; virtuous; honest; just; kind; affectionate; safe; sound; valid; solvent; adequate; full, as weight, measure, etc.; skillful. *comp.* **better.** *superl.* **best.** *n.* that which is good; welfare; well-being; profit; advantage; *n.pl.* property; wares; commodities; merchandise; (*Colloq.*) evidence of guilt; textiles; *interj.* well! right! so be it! **-ish** *a.* (of quality) pretty good; (of quantity) fairly plentiful. **-ly** *a.* handsome; pleasant; of considerable size. **-liness** *n.* **-ness** *n.* the quality of being good; *interj.* used for emphasis; *pl.* **-ies** candy; sweets. **—by** *interj.* contraction of God be with you!; farewell! *n.* a farewell. **— day** *interj.* greeting at meeting or parting. **—for-nothing** *a.* worthless; shiftless; *n.* a shiftless person; a loafer. **— humor** *n.* a happy or cheerful state of mind. **—humored** *a.* **— nature** *n.* natural kindness of disposition; **—natured** *a.* **—naturedly** *adv.* **— turn,** a kindly action. **— will** *n.* benevolence; kindly disposition; (*Commerce*) the right, on transfer or sale of a business, to the reputation, trade, and custom of that business. **to be to the good,** to show a profit [O.E. *god*].

goof (goof) *n.* (*Slang*) a silly person; a mistake. *v.*

goose (goos) *n.* a web-footed bird like a duck but larger; the flesh of the bird; a simpleton; a tailor's smoothing iron; *pl.* **geese** (gēs). **gosling** (gåz'·ling) *n.* a young goose. **— flesh** *n.* a bristling state of the skin due to cold or fright. **— step** *n.* (*Mil.*) a marching step with legs kept stiff and lifted high at each step; *v.i.* to use the goose step [O.E. *gos*].

goose·ber·ry (goos'·ber·i·) *n.* a thorny shrub cultivated for its fruit; fruit of the shrub.

go·pher (gō'·fer) *n.* in N. America, the ground-squirrel; a kind of rat with pouched cheeks [Fr. *gaufre*, a honeycomb].

gore (gōr) *n.* thick or clotted blood; blood. **gory** *a.* bloody [O.E. *gor*, dirt].

gore (gōr) *v.t.* to pierce with a spear, horns, or tusks [O.E. *gar*, a spear].

gore (gōr) *n.* a tapering piece of material inserted in a garment or a sail, to widen it; *v.t.* to cut into a wedge shape; to supply with a gore [O.E. *gara*, a pointed piece of land].

gorge (gawrj) *n.* a narrow pass between mountains; a full meal; *v.t.* to swallow with greediness; *v.i.* to feed greedily and to excess [L. *gurges*, a whirlpool].

gor·geous (gawr'·jis) *a.* splendid; showy; magnificent; richly colored. **-ly** *adv.* [O.Fr. *gorgias*].

Gor·gon (gawr'·gan) *n.* (*Myth.*) one of three sisters of terrifying aspect. (*l.c.*) any one, esp. a woman, who is terrifying or repulsive looking. **-esque** *a.* repulsive [Gk. *gorgos*].

Gor·gon·zo·la (gawr·gan·zō'·la) *n.* a milk cheese made in Italy [fr. *Gorgonzola*, Italy].

go·ril·la (ga·ril'·a) *n.* an ape inhabiting W. Africa, of great size and strength [Afr.].

gor·mand See **gourmand**.

gorse (gawrs) *n.* (*Brit.*) a prickly shrub, bearing yellow flowers [O.E. *gorst*].

gosh (gåsh) *interj.* (*Colloq.*) a minced and very mild oath [corrupt. of *God*].

gor·y See **gore**.

gosh (gåsh) *interj.* (*Colloq.*) a minced and very mild oath [corrupt. of *God*].

gos·hawk (gås'·hawk) *n.* a large powerful hawk [O.E. *gos*, a goose; *hafoc*, a hawk].

gos·ling See **goose**.

gos·pel (gås'·pal) *n.* glad tidings; the revelation of the Christian faith; story of Christ's life as found in first four books of New Testament; doctrine; belief accepted as infallibly true; *a.* pert. to, or in accordance with, the gospel [O.E. *god*, good; *spell*, a story].

gos·sa·mer (gås'·a·mer) *n.* a filmy substance, like cobwebs; thin, gauzy material; *a.* light, thin and filmy [M.E. *gossomer*].

gos·sip (gås'·ap) *n.* idle talk about others, regardless of fact; idle talk or writing; one who talks thus; *v.i.* to talk gossip; to chat [M.E *god*, God; *sib*, related].

got (gåt) *pa.p.* and *pa.t.* of **get**.

Goth (gåth) *n.* a member of ancient Teutonic tribe; a barbarian. **-ic** *a.* pert. to Goths; barbarous; pert. to pointed-arch style of architecture; *n.* the language of Goths; (*l.c.*) a printing type Gothic [L. *Gothicus*].

got·ten *pa.p.* of **get**.

gouache (gwäsh) *n.* water-color painting with opaque colors mixed with water and gum; a picture painted thus [It. *guazzo*, a wash].

Gou·da (gou'·da) *n.* a well-known Dutch cheese [fr. *Gouda*, Holland].

gouge (gouj) *n.* a chisel with a curved cutting edge, for cutting grooves or holes; *v.t.* to cut or scoop out with a gouge; to hollow out; to force out, as the eye of a person, with the thumb or finger [Fr.].

gou·lash (goo'·låsh) *n.* a Hungarian stew.

gourd (gawrd) *n.* trailing or climbing plant; pumpkin, squash, etc.; large, fleshy fruit of this plant; its dried rind used as bottle, drinking vessel, etc.; a small-necked bottle or flask [L. *cucurbita*, a gourd].

gour·mand (goor'·mand) *n.* one fond of eating; a judge of fine foods. Also **gormand, gourmet** (goor'·mā) [Fr.].

gout (gout) *n.* a disease characterized by acute inflammation and swelling of the smaller joints. **-iness** *n.* **-y** *a.* [Fr. *goutte*, a drop].

gov·ern (guv'·ern) *v.t.* to rule; to direct; to guide; to control; to regulate by authority; to keep in subjection; (*Gram.*) to be followed by a case, etc.; *v.i.* to exercise authority; to administer the laws. **-able** *a.* **-ance** *n.* directions; control; management. **-ess** *n.* woman with authority to control and direct; a lady, usually resident in a family, in charge of children's education. **-ment** *n.* act of governing; exercise of authority; the system of governing in a state or community; the ruling power in a state; territory over which rule is exercised; the administrative council or body; the executive power; control; rule. **-mental** *a.* **-or** *n.* the executive head of a state; a ruler; regulating mechanical device for velocity, pressure, etc. [L. *gubernare*, to steer].

gown (goun) *n.* a loose, flowing garment; outer dress of a woman; official robe of professional men and scholars, as in a university; *v.t.* to dress in a gown; *v.i.* to put on a gown [O.Fr. *gonne*, loose robe].

grab (grab) *v.t.* to grasp suddenly; to snatch; to clutch; to seize. *pr.p.* **-bing.** *pa.p.* and *pa.t.* **-bed.** *n.* a sudden clutch; unscrupulous seizure.

grace (grās) *n.* charm; attractiveness; easy and refined motion, manners, etc.; favor; divine favor; a short prayer of thanksgiving before or after a meal; a period of delay granted as a favor; the ceremonious title used when addressing a duke, or archbishop; *v.t.* to adorn; to honor; to add grace to. **-ful** *a.* displaying grace or charm in form or action; elegant; easy. **-fully** *adv.* **-fulness** *n.* **-less** *a.* lacking grace. **gracious** (grā'·shas) *a.* favorable; kind; friendly; merciful; pleasing; proceeding from divine grace; **graciously** *adv.* **graciousness** *n.* **— note** *n.* (*Mus.*) a note that is an embellishment, not essential to the melody [L. *gratia*, favor].

grac·ile (gras'·il) *a.* slender; gracefully slight. **gracility** *n.* [L. *gracilis*, slender].

gra·da·tion (gra·dā'·shan) *n.* successive stage in progress; degree; a step, or series of steps; the state of being graded or arranged in ranks. **gradate** (grā'·dāt) *v.t.* to cause to change by imperceptible degrees, as from one color to another [L. *gradatio*].

grade (grād) *n.* a step or degree in rank, merit, quality, etc.; a class or category; a mark or rating of a student's work; degree of rise of a slope; a gradient; *v.t.* to arrange in order, degree, or class; to gradate [L. *gradus*, a step].

gra·di·ent (grā'·di·ant) *a.* moving by steps; rising or descending by regular degrees; *n.* the degree of slope of a road or railway; an incline [L. *gradiens*, going, stepping].

grad·u·al (gra'·joo·al) *a.* proceeding by steps or degrees; progressive; changing imperceptibly; *n.* (*Eccl.*) book of music sung by the choir. **-ly** *adv.* [L. *gradus*, a step].

grad·u·ate (graj'·oo·āt) *v.t.* to grant a diploma or university degree; to mark with degrees; to divide into regular steps; *v.i.* to receive a diploma or university degree; (graj'·oo·it) *n.* one who has received a diploma or degree upon completing a course of study. **graduator** *n.* an instrument for dividing a line into regular intervals. **graduation** *n.* [L. *gradus*, a step].

graft, graff (graft, graf) *v.t.* to insert a bud or small branch of a tree into another; to transplant living tissue, e.g. skin, bone, etc. from one part of the body to another; *n.* a bud, etc. so inserted, or a piece of tissue so transplanted [Fr. fr. Gk. *grapheion*, a pencil].

graft (graft) *v.i.* to exercise political privilege; to use influence unfairly for self-advancement or profit; *n.* self-advancement or profit by unfair means. **-er** *n.*

gra·ham (grā'·am) *a.* made of whole-wheat flour [S. *Graham*, Amer. physician].

grail (grāl) *n.* a cup. **The Holy Grail,** in medieval legend, the cup or vessel used by Jesus at the Last Supper [O.Fr. *graal*, a flat dish].

grain (grān) *n.* a kernel, esp. of corn, wheat, etc.; fruit of certain kindred plants, viz. corn, wheat, rye, barley, oats, etc. (used collectively); any small, hard particle; slightest amount; the smallest unit of weight; that arrangement of the particles of any body which determines its roughness, markings or texture; (*Fig.*) natural temperament or disposition; *v.t.* to paint in imitation of the grain of wood; to form into grains, as sugar, powder, etc. **-ed** (grānd) *a.* **against the grain,** *i.e.* against the fiber of the wood; hence (*Fig.*) against a natural inclination [L. *granum*, seed].

gram (gram) *n.* unit of weight in metric system = 15.432 grains. Also **gramme** [Fr. fr. Gk. *gramma*, small weight].

gram·mar (gram'·er) *n.* the science of language; a system of general principles for speaking and writing according to the forms and usage of a language; a textbook for teaching the elements of language. **-ian** (gra·me'·ri·an) *n.* a philologist; **grammatical** (gra·mat'·i·kal) *a.* pert. to grammar; according to the rules of grammar [Gk. *gramma*, a letter].

gramme See **gram**.

gram·o·phone (gram'·a·fōn) *n.* a phonograph [Gk. *gramma*, a letter; *phone*, sound].

gram·pus (gram'·pas) *n.* a blowing and spouting sea creature of the dolphin family [L. *crassus piscis*, a fat fish].

gran·a·ry (gran'·a·ri·) *n.* a storehouse for threshed grain; a barn [L. *granum*, grain].

grand (grand) *a.* great; high in power and dignity; illustrious; eminent; distinguished; imposing; superior; splendid; lofty; noble; sublime; dignified; majestic; chief; final; indicating family relationship of the second degree; *n.* (*Mus.*) a grand piano; (*Slang*) a thousand dollars. **-child** *n.* a son's or daughter's child. **-daughter, -son** *n.* a son's or daughter's daughter. **-ee** (gran·dē') n. a Spanish or Portuguese nobleman; a great personage. **-eur** (gran'·jẽr) n. nobility of action; majesty; splendor; magnificence. **-father (-mother)** n. a father's or mother's father (mother). **-father('s)-clock**, n. a tall, old-fashioned clock, standing on the floor. **-iloquence** (gran·dil'·ạ·kwens) n. lofty words or phrases; pomposity of speech. **-iloquent** a. **-iose** (gran'·di·os) a. imposing; striking; bombastic. **-iosely** adv. **-iosity** n. **-ly** adv. in a grand manner, splendidly. **-ma** n. grandmother. **-mother-clock** n. similar to a grandfather-clock but smaller. **-ness** n. greatness; magnificence. **-pa** n. a grandfather. **-parent** n. grandfather or grandmother. — **piano**, a large harp-shaped piano, with a horizontal frame. — **slam** (Cards) the winning of all the tricks at Bridge. **-stand** n. main seating structure for spectators at a sporting event [L. grandis, great].

grandfather-clock

grange (grānj) n. a farm; (Cap.) an association of farmers [L. granum, grain].
gran·ite (gran'·it) n. a hard igneous rock, consisting of quartz, feldspar, and mica; gray or pink in color [It. granito, grained].
gran·ny (gran'·i·) n. (Colloq.) grandmother; an old woman [abbrev. of grandmother].
grant (grant) v.t. to allow; to yield; to concede; to bestow; to confer; to admit as true; n. a bestowing; a gift; an allowance. **-er, -or** n. (Law) the person who transfers property [O.Fr. garanter, to promise].
gran·ule (gran'·yool) n. a little grain; a small particle. **granular** a. consisting of grains or granules. **granulate** v.t. to form into grains; to make rough on the surface; v.i. to be formed into grains. **granulated** a. **granulation** n. the process of forming into grains; (Med.) the development of new tissue in a wound, characterized by the formation of grain-like cells [L. granulum, dim. of granum, a grain].
grape (grāp) n. the fruit of the vine. **-ry** n. a place for the cultivation of grapes. — **fruit** n. a large round citrus fruit with yellow rind. — **sugar** n. a simple sugar, found abundantly in grapes; dextrose. **-vine** n. the grape-bearing vine plant; (Colloq.) a person-to-person means of secret communication. **sour grapes** (Fig.) things falsely despised merely because unattainable [Fr. grappe, a bunch of grapes].
graph (graf) n. a diagram or curve representing the variation in value of some phenomenon or relationship of two or more things, according to stated conditions; v.t. to show variation by means of a diagram. **-ic(al)** a. pert. to writing or delineating; truly descriptive; vivid. **-ically** adv. **-ic arts**, drawing, engraving, and painting. **-ics** n. the art of drawing, esp. mechanical drawing. **-ite** n. a natural form of carbon used in the making of the 'lead' of pencils; plumbago; blacklead. **-ology** n. the study of handwriting as an index of character [Gk. graphein, to write].
grap·nel (grap'·nạl) n. an iron instrument with hooks or claws for clutching an object; a small anchor with several claws [O.Fr. grape, a hook].

grap·ple (grap'·l) v.t. to seize firmly; to seize with a grapnel; v.i. to come to grips; to contend; n. a grapnel; a grip; a contest at close quarters. **grappling-iron** n. a large grapnel [O.Fr. grape, a hook].
grasp (grasp) v.t. to seize firmly; to clutch; to take possession of; to understand. v.i. to en-

deavor to seize; to catch at; n. a firm grip of the hand; the power of seizing and holding; reach of the arms; mental power or capacity. **-ing** a. seizing; greedy of gain [O.E. graspen].
grass (gras) n. herbage; pasture for cattle; ground covered with grass; v.t. to cover with grass; to feed with grass. **-y** a. **-hopper** n. a jumping, chirping insect, allied to the locust family. **-land** n. permanent pasture-land. **-roots** a. close to, or from, the people. — **widow** n. a woman separated or divorced from her husband [O.E. gaers].

grasshopper

grate (grāt) n. a frame of bars for holding fuel while burning; a framework of crossed bars. **grating** n. a partition of parallel or cross bars [L. cratis, a hurdle].
grate (grāt) v.t. to rub or scrape into small bits; to rub together with a harsh sound; v.i. sound harshly; to irritate. **-r** n. an instrument with a rough surface for rubbing off small particles [Fr. gratter, to scratch].
grate·ful (grāt'·fạl) a. thankful; pleasant; [L. gratus, pleasing].
gra·ti·fy (grat'·ạ·fi) v.t. to give pleasure to; to satisfy. **-ing** a. **gratifier** n. one who gratifies. **gratification** n. the act of pleasing; satisfaction [L. gratus, pleasing].
grat·in (grā'·tạn) n. (Cookery) a dish prepared with a covering of bread crumbs or cheese. **au gratin** (ō grā'·tạn) a. food so cooked [Fr. gratin, fr. gratin, fr. gratter, to grate].
gra·tis (grā'·tis) adv. free; for nothing [L. gratia, a favor].
grat·i·tude (grat'·ạ·tūd) n. thankfulness [L. gratus, pleasing, thankful].
gra·tu·i·ty (grạ·tū'·ạ·ti·) n. a gift of money for services rendered; a tip; something given freely. **gratuitous** a. free; voluntary; granted without obligation; asserted without cause or proof. **gratuitously** adv. [L. gratuitus, done without profit].
gra·va·men (grạ·vā'·mạn) n. stress laid on a part; substantial ground or reason for a charge; a grievance [L. gravis, heavy].
grave (grāv) n. a hole dug for a dead body; a place of burial; (Fig.) death. **-stone** n. a memorial stone set at a grave. **-yard** n. a burial ground [O.E. braef].
grave (grāv) a. solemn; serious; weighty; important. **grave** (grāv) n. the 'grave' accent in French or its sign ('). **-ly** adv. [L. gravis, heavy].
grave (grāv) v.t. to engrave; to impress deeply. **-n image**, an idol [O.E. grafan, to dig].
grave (grāv) v.t. to clean a ship's bottom [Fr. grève, a beach].
grav·el (grav'·al) n. small stones; coarse sand; small pebbles; (Med.) an aggregation of minute crystals in the urine; v.t. to cover with gravel; to puzzle. (Colloq.) to irritate. **-ly** a. [O.Fr. grave, the beach].
grav·id (grav'·id) a. pregnant [L. gravis, heavy].
grav·i·tate (grav'·ạ·tāt) v.i. to obey the law of gravitation; to tend towards a center of attraction; to be naturally attracted to. **gravitation** n. the act of gravitating; the tendency of all bodies to attract each other. **gravitational, gravitative** a. [L. gravis, heavy].
grav·i·ty (grav'·ạ·ti·) n. weight; heaviness; seriousness; the force of attraction of one body for another, esp. of objects to the earth. **specific gravity**, the relative weight of any substance as compared with the weight of an equal volume of water [L. gravitas, fr. gravis, heavy].
gra·vy (grā'·vi·) n. the juices from meat in cooking; sauce made with this. (Slang) easy profit. — **boat** n. a dish for holding gravy.
gray, grey (grā) a. between black and white in color, as ashes or lead; clouded; turning white; hoary; aged; n. a gray color; a gray horse; v.t. to cause to become gray; v.i. to become gray. **-ish** a. somewhat gray. — **matter** the gray nerve tissue of the brain and spinal cord; (Colloq.) brains, intellect. **-ness** n. **-lag** n. wild goose [O.E. graeg].
graze (grāz) v.t. to touch lightly in passing; to abrade the skin thus; n. a light touch in passing; a grazing.
graze (grāz) v.t. to feed, as cattle, with grass; v.i. to eat grass or herbage [O.E. grasian].
grease (grēs) n. soft melted fat of animals; thick oil as a lubricant; (grēz, grēs) v.t. to apply grease to; (Slang) to bribe. **greasy** a. like grease; oily; fat; (Fig.) slippery. — **monkey** (Slang) a mechanic. — **paint** actors' make-up. **-r** n. **greasiness** n. [Fr. graisse, fr. gras, fat].
great (grāt) a. large in size or number; long in time or duration; admirable; eminent; uncommonly gifted; of high rank; mighty; pregnant; denoting relationship, either in the ascending

or descending line; (Slang) splendid. **-ly** adv. **-ness** n. **-coat** n. an overcoat. **great-grandchild** n. the child of a grandchild. **Great Britain** England, Wales and Scotland. **Great Dane**, a large dog with short, smooth hair [O.E.].
greaves (grēvz) n.pl. the dregs of melted tallow [O.N.].
Gre·cian (grē'·shạn) a. Greek; pert. to Greece; n. a native of Greece; a Greek scholar [L. Graecus].
greed (grēd) n. an eager and selfish desire; covetousness; avarice. **-y** a. having a keen desire for food, drink, wealth, etc.; ravenous. **-ily** adv. **-iness** n. [O.E. graedig, hungry].
Greek (grēk) a. pert. to Greece; Grecian; n. a native of Greece; the language of Greece [L. Graecus].
green (grēn) a. of color between blue and yellow; grass-colored; emerald-colored; containing its natural sap; unripe; inexperienced; easily deceived; sickly; wan. n. the color; a communal piece of grass-covered land; (Golf) the putting-green. n.pl. fresh leaves or branches; wreaths; green leafy vegetables. **-ery** n. a place where plants are cultivated; vegetation. **-ish** a. somewhat green. **-ness** n. the quality of being green; freshness. **-eyed** a. having green eyes; (Fig.) jealous. —**eyed monster**, jealousy. **-gage** n. a small, green plum. **-heart** n. a very hard wood. **-horn** n. an inexperienced person. **-house** n. a glass building for keeping or growing plants. — **light** traffic signal to go; (Colloq.) authorization. — **thumb** apparent skill in growing plants. **-sward** n. turf [O.E.].

greenhouse

Greenwich time, (grin'·ij, gren·ich) the basis for calculating standard time everywhere.
greet (grēt) v.t. to salute; to welcome; to accost; to receive. **-ing** n. a salutation; expression of good wishes [O.E. gretan].
gre·gar·i·ous (gri·gar'·i·ạs) a. living in flocks or herds; fond of company. **-ly** adv. **-ness** n. [L. gregarius, fr. grex, a flock].
Gre·go·ri·an (gre·gō'·ri·ạn) a. pert. to the Popes Gregory I through XIII. — **calendar**, the present day calendar, introduced in 1582. — **chants**, unaccompanied music used in R.C. worship.
grem·lin (grem'·lin) n. (World War 2) a mischievous pixy haunting aircraft and causing engine trouble [Fr. dial. grimelin, brat].
gre·nade (gri·nād') n. an explosive shell or bomb, thrown by hand or shot from a rifle; a glass projectile containing chemicals. **grenadier** (gren·ạ·dir') n. formerly, a soldier trained to throw grenades; a soldier in the Grenadier Guards of Brit. Army [Fr. grenade, a pomegranate].
gren·a·dine (gren'·ạ·dēn) n. a syrup for flavoring drinks [Fr. fr. grenade].
grew pa.t. of **grow**.
grey See **gray**.
grey·hound (grā'·hound) n. a swift, slender dog, used in racing [O.E. grighund].

grid (grid) n. a frame of bars; a grating; a grid-iron; (Elect.) a lead or zinc plate in a storage battery; (Electronics) an electrode of wire mesh in an electron tube [O.Fr. gredil].
grid·dle (grid'·l) n. flat utensil for cooking over direct heat; v.t. to cook on a griddle. [O.Fr. gredil, fr. L. cratis, hurdle].
grid·i·ron (grid'·i·ẽrn) n. a framework of metal bars, for broiling meats, fish, etc.; a football field [O.Fr. gredire, gredil, a griddle].
grief (grēf) n. deep sorrow; pain; the cause of sorrow or distress [Fr. fr. L. gravis, heavy].
grieve (grēv) v.t. to cause grief; to afflict; to vex; to offend; v.i. to feel grief; to be distressed;

to lament. **grievance** *n.* a real or imaginary complaint; a cause of grief or uneasiness. **-r** *n.*
grievous *a.* causing sadness; atrocious. **grievously** *adv.* [O.Fr. *grever*, to afflict].
grill (gril) *v.t.* to broil on a gridiron; to question relentlessly; *n.* a cooking utensil for broiling meat, fish, etc.; the food cooked on one [Fr. *gril*, a gridiron].
grille (gril) *n.* a metal grating screening a window, doorway, etc. **grillwork** *n.* [O.Fr. *gredil*, a griddle].
grim (grim) *a.* stern; severe; of forbidding aspect; fierce; surly. **-ly** *adv.* **-ness** *n.* [O.E. *grimm*, fierce].
gri·mace (gri·mās′) *n.* a distortion of the face to express contempt, dislike, etc.; a wry face; *v.i.* to make a grimace [Fr.].
gri·mal·kin (gri·mawl′·kin) *n.* an old cat, esp. a she-cat; a spiteful old woman.
grime (grim) *n.* ingrained dirt; soot; *v.t.* to soil deeply; to dirty. **grimy** *a.* dirty.
grin (grin) *v.i.* to show the teeth as in laughter derision, or pain. *pr.p.* **-ning.** *pa.t.,* *pa.p.* **-ned.** *n.* a wide smile [O.E. *grennian*].
grind (grind) *v.t.* to crush to powder between hard surfaces; to sharpen by friction; to rub harshly; to turn a crank to operate; to grate; *v.i.* to grind; (*Colloq.*) to work hard. *pa.p.* and *pa.t.* **ground.** *n.* the action of grinding; (*Colloq.*) a laborious task; (*Colloq.*) a hardworking student. **-ers** *n.pl.* (*Colloq.*) the teeth [O.E. *grindan*].
grin·go (gring′·gō) *n.* in Spanish-speaking America, a contemptuous name for a foreigner.
grip (grip) *n.* a firm hold; a grasp or pressure of the hand; a clutch; mastery of a subject, etc·a handle; a suitcase; *v.t.* to grasp or hold tightly; (*Fig.*) to hold the attention of. *pr.p.* **-ping.** *pa.p.,* *pa.t.* **-ped. -per** *n.* [O.E. *gripa*].
gripe (grip) *v.t.* to grip; to oppress; to afflict with sharp pains; *v.i.* to grasp at gain; to suffer griping pains; (*Colloq.*) to complain constantly; *n.* grasp; clutch; severe intestinal pain. **griping** *a.* [O.E. *gripan*].
grippe (grip) *n.* influenza [Fr.].
gris·ly (griz′·li·) *a.* grim; horrible. **grisliness** *n.* [O.E. *grislic*, terrible].
grist (grist) *n.* a supply of grain to be ground; the meal ground; (*Fig.*) profit; gain [O.E.].
gris·tle (gris′·l) *n.* a smooth, solid, elastic substance in animal bodies; cartilage [O.E.].
grit (grit) *n.* the coarse part of meal; particles of sand; coarse sandstone; (*Fig.*) courage; spirit; resolution; *pl.* grain coarsely ground; *v.t.* to grind (the teeth); to grate; *v.i.* to cover with grit. *pr.p.* **-ting.** *pa.t.,* *pa.p.* **-ted. -ty** *a.* [O.E. *greot*, sand].
griz·zle (griz′·l) *n.* gray hair. **-d** *a.* gray; grayhaired. **grizzly** *a.* gray; *n.* a grizzly bear, a large ferocious bear of N. Amer. [Fr. *gris,* gray].
groan (grōn) *v.i.* to make a low deep sound of grief or pain; to be overburdened; *n.* the sound. **-er** *n.* **-ing** *n.* [O.E. *granian,* to weep].
groats (grōts) *n.pl.* hulled grain, esp. oats [O.E. *greot,* a particle].
gro·cer (grō′·ser) *n.* storekeeper. **-y.** *n.* a store. **groceries** *n.pl.* goods sold by a grocer [O.Fr. *grossier,* wholesale].
grog (grág) *n.* a mixture of spirits, esp. **rum** and cold water. **-gy** *a.* drunk; unsteady; shaky [fr. Admiral Vernon (*Brit.*) who wore *grogram* breeches].
grog·ram (grág′·ram) *n.* a coarse material of silk and mohair [O.Fr. *grosgrain*].
groin (groin) *n.* the depression where the abdomen joins the thigh.
grom·met (gràm′·it) *n.* a metal eyelet used for fastening [Fr. *gourmette,* a curb-chain].
groom (grōom) *n.* a servant in charge of horses; a bridegroom; an officer in the English royal household; *v.t.* to dress with neatness and care; to tend a horse.
groove (grōov) *n.* a channel or hollow, esp. one cut by a tool; a rut; a routine; *v.t.* to cut a groove in [Dut. *groefe,* a trench].
grope (grōp) *v.t.* to feel about; to search blindly as if in the dark [O.E. *grapian*].
gros·beak (grōs′·bĕk) *n.* a bird of the Finch family [Fr. *gros,* big; *bec,* beak].
gros·grain (grō′·grān) *n.* corded ribbon or cloth [Fr. *gros grain,* large grain].
gross (grōs) *a.* coarse; indecent; crude; thick; rank; glaring; total, not net; *n.* twelve dozen; mass; bulk; *v.t.* to earn a total of. **-ly** *adv.* **-ness** *n.* [Fr. *gos,* big].
gro·tesque (grō·tesk′) *a.* wildly formed; irregular in design or form; a whimsical figure; a caricature. **-ness** [Fr. fr. It. *grotta,* a grotto].
grot·to (grát′·ō) *n.* a natural cave; an artificial structure in gardens, etc. in imitation of such a cave. [It. *grotta*].
grouch (grouch) *n.* (*Colloq.*) a complaint; a grumbler; *v.i.* to grumble. **-y** *a.* **-iness** *n.* [fr. *grudge*].
ground (ground) *pa.p.* and *pa.t.* of **grind.**
ground (ground) *n.* the surface of the earth; dry land; territory; a special area of land; soil; the sea bottom; reason; motive; basis; (*Elect.*) a conducting line between electrical equipment and the ground; (*Art*) the surface or coating to work on; *v.t.* to establish; to instruct in elementary principles; to place on the ground; (*Naut.*) to run ashore; *v.i.* to come to the ground. **-s** *n.pl.* dregs; sediment; lands around

a house. **-less** *a.* without reason. **-ed** *a.* (*Aviat.*) of aircraft, unable to fly because of weather conditions. **-ing** *n.* the background; thorough knowledge of the essentials of a subject. **-work** *n.* foundation; basis; the essential part; first principles. — **rent** *n.* rent paid to a landlord for the privilege of building on his ground. — **swell** *n.* a broad, deep swell of the ocean felt some distance from a storm [O.E. *grund*].
group (grōop) *n.* a number of persons or things near, placed, or classified together; a class; a cluster, crowd, or throng; a military unit; (*Art*) two or more figures forming one artistic design; *v.t.* to arrange in groups; *v.i.* to fall into groups [Fr. *groupe*].
grouse (grous) *n.* a round, plump game-bird.
grouse (grous) *v.i.* (*Colloq.*) to grumble; to complain; *n.* a complaint.
grout (grout) *n.* coarse meal; thin mortar to fill cracks; plaster; *v.t.* to fill with grout [O.E. *gaut,* coarse meal].
grove (grōv) *n.* a group of trees [O.E. *graf*].
grov·el (gráv′·l, gruv′·l) *v.i.* to lie face downward, from fear or humility; to crawl thus; to abase oneself. **-er** *n.* **-ing** *a.* servile [O.N. *a grufa,* face downwards].
grow (grō) *v.t.* to produce by cultivation; to raise; *v.i.* to develop naturally; to increase in size, height, etc.; to become by degrees. *pa.p.* **-n.** *pa.t.* **grew** (grōō). **-er** *n.* **-th** (grōth) *n.* the process of growing; something already grown; (*Med.*) a morbid formation; a tumor. **grown-up** *n.* an adult [O.E. *growan*].
growl (groul) *v.i.* to make a low guttural sound, of anger or menacing like an animal; to grumble; *n.* such a sound. **-er** *n.* [imit. origin].
grub (grub) *v.t.* to dig superficially; to root up; *v.i.* to dig; to rummage; (*Fig.*) to plod; *n.* the larva of a beetle; that which is dug up for food; (*Slang*) food. *pr.p.* **-bing.** *pa.p.,* *pa.t.* **-bed. -ber** *n.* **-biness** *n.* the state of being grubby. **-by** *a.* unclean; dirty, grimy [M.E. *grobben,* to dig].
grudge (gruj) *v.t.* to be reluctant to give or allow; to envy; *n.* a feeling of ill will; resentment. **grudging** *a.* [O.Fr. *groucer*].
gru·el (grōō′·al) *n.* a food made by boiling oatmeal in water; a thin porridge; *v.t.* to subject to great strain. **-ing** *a.* exhausting [O.E. = crushed meal].
grue·some (grōō′·sam) *a.* causing horror, fear or loathing [M.E. *grue,* to shudder].
grum·ble (grum′·bl) *v.i.* to murmur with discontent; to complain; to make growling sounds; *n.* grumbling; a complaint [imit. origin].
grump·y (grum′·pi·) *a.* surly; irritable; gruff. **grumpily** *adv.* **grumpiness** *n.* [imit. origin].
grunt (grunt) *v.i.* of a pig, to make its characteristic sound; to utter a sound like this; *n.* a deep, guttural sound; a pig's sound. **-er** *n.* **-ing** *a.* [O.E. *grunnettan*].
Gru·yère (grōō·yer′) *n.* a whole-milk cheese [fr. *Gruyère,* Switzerland].
guar·an·tee (gar·an·tē′) *n.* formal assurance given by way of security; an assurance of the truth, genuineness, permanence, etc. of something; the person who gives such promise or assurance; guaranty; security; an assurance; *v.t.* to promise; to answer for. **guaranty** (gar′·an·ti·) *n.* a pledge of commitment; security; basis of security. **guarantor** *n.* [Fr. *garantir,* to protect].
guard (gárd) *v.t.* to protect from danger; to accompany for protection; to watch by way of caution or defense; *v.i.* to keep watch; to take precautions; *n.* he who, or that which, guards; a sentry; a watch, as over prisoners; a protective device. **-ed** *a.* cautious; wary. **-edly** *adv.* **-house** *n.* a place for the detention of military prisoners. **-ian** *n.* a keeper; a protector; (*Law*) one who has custody of a minor. **-ianship** *n.* [Fr. *garde*].
gua·va (gwä′·va) *n.* a genus of tropical American trees and shrubs, bearing pear-shaped fruit used for jelly [Sp. *guayaba*].
gu·ber·na·to·ri·al (gōō·ber·na·tōr′·i·al) *a.* pert. to a governor [L. *gubernare,* to govern].
gudg·eon (guj′·un) *n.* a metal pin at the end of an axle on which the wheel turns; the socket of a hinge into which the pin fits [O.Fr. *goujon,* pivot].
guer·don (gur′·dan) *n.* (*Poetic*) a reward [O.Fr. *gueredon*].
Guern·sey (gurn′·zi) *n.* breed of dairy cattle. **guernsey** *n.* knitted woolen shirt.

guer·ril·la guerilla (ga·ril′·a) *n.* a member of a band of irregular troops taking part in a war independently of the principal combatants; *a.* pert. to this kind of warfare [Sp. *guerrilla,* dim. of *guerra,* war].
guess (ges) *v.t.* and *i.* to estimate without calculation or measurement; to judge at random; to conjecture; to suppose; *n.* a rough estimate; a random judgment [M.E. *gessen*].
guest (gest) *n.* a visitor received or entertained; one living in a hotel, boarding-house, etc. [O.E. *gest*].
guf·faw (guf·aw′) *n.* a burst of boisterous laughter; *v.i.* to laugh boisterously [imit.].
guide (gid) *n.* one who shows the way; an adviser; an official accompanying tourists; a sign, mark, or device to indicate direction; a book of instruction or information; *v.t.* to lead; to direct; to influence; to act as a guide to. **guidance** *n.* direction. **-book** *n.* a descriptive handbook for tourists, travelers, etc. **guided missile,** powered rocket or other projectile which can be directed by remote control. **-post** *n.* a sign-post [O.Fr. *guider,* to guide].
guild (gild) *n.* a society for mutual help, or with a common object [O.E. *gild,* money].
guile (gil) *n.* craft; cunning. **-ful** *a.* **-less** *a.* honest; innocent; sincere [O.Fr. *guile,* deceit].
guil·lo·tine (gil′·a·tēn) *n.* a machine for beheading by the descending stroke of a heavy blade; a paper cutting machine; *v.t.* to use a guillotine upon [fr. Joseph *Guillotin*].

guilt (gilt) *n.* the fact or state of having offended; criminality and consequent liability to punishment. **-y** *a.* judged to have committed a crime. **-ily** *adv.* **-iness** *n.* **-less** *a.* innocent [O.E. *gylt,* crime, fr. *gildan,* to pay].
guimpe (gimp) *n.* a short-sleeved blouse [Fr.].
guin·ea (gin′·i·) *n.* a former Brit. gold coin. — **fowl** *n.* a fowl allied to the pheasant. — **pig** *n.* (corrupt. of *Guiana* pig) a small rodent, used frequently in scientific experiments; (*Fig.*) a person used as a subject for experimentation [fr. *Guinea,* in W. Africa].
guise (giz) *n.* external appearance, semblance; pretense [Fr. *guise,* manner].
gui·tar (gi·tár′) *n.* a six-stringed musical instrument resembling the lute. **-ist** *n.* a player of the guitar [Fr. *guitare*].

gulch (gulch) *n.* a ravine; a deep-walled valley.
gulf (gulf) *n.* a large bay; a sea extending into the land; a deep chasm; any wide separation; *v.t.* to swallow up [Gk. *kolpos,* a bay].
gull (gul) *n.* a long-winged, web-footed seabird [Bret. *gwelan,* to weep].
gull (gul) *n.* a dupe; a fool; *v.t.* to deceive; to trick; to defraud. **-ible** *a.* easily imposed on; credulous. **-ibility** *n* [fr. *gull,* the sea-bird considered to be stupid].
gul·let (gul′·it) *n.* the tube from mouth to stomach; the throat [L. *gula,* the throat].
gul·ly (gul′·i·) *n.* a channel or ravine worn by water; a ravine; a ditch [fr. *gullet*].
gulp (gulp) *v.t.* to swallow eagerly; to swallow in large amounts; *v.t.* to gasp; to choke; *n.* an act of gulping; an effort to swallow; a large mouthful [imit.].
gum (gum) *n.* the firm flesh in which the teeth are set [O.E. *goma,* the jaws].
gum (gum) *n.* a sticky substance issuing from certain trees; this substance used for stiffening or adhesive purposes; resin; an adhesive; chewing gum; *v.t.* to coat with gum; *v.i.* to exude gum; to become clogged. *pr.p.* **-ming.** *pa.p.,* *pa.t.* **-med. -miness** *n.* **-my** *a.* consisting of gum; sticky. — **elastic** *n.* rubber. **-drop** *n.* small jelly-like candy. — **tree** *n.* any species of gum yielding tree: the eucalyptus, sour gum, sweet gum, etc. **chewing gum** *n.* a sticky preparation for chewing [Fr. *gomme*].
gum·bo (gum′·bō) *n.* okra; soup thickened with this.
gump·tion (gump′·shan) *n.* (*Colloq.*) resourcefulness; courage; common sense; courage.

gun (gun) *n.* a weapon consisting of a metal tube from which missiles are thrown by explosion; a firearm, cannon, rifle, pistol, etc.; a gun-like device; *v.i.* to shoot with a gun. *pr.p.* **-ning** *pa.p., pa.t.* **-ned. -ner** *n.* one who works a gun. **-nery** *n.* the firing of guns; the science of artillery. **-ning** *n.* the shooting of game. **-boat** *n.* a small armed patrol ship. **— metal** *n.* dark gray. **-powder** *n.* an explosive. **-runner** *n.* a gun smuggler. **-shot** *n.* the range of a gun; a shot fired from a gun. **-smith** *n.* one who makes, repairs, deals in guns. **a son of a gun** (*Colloq.*) a rascal [M.E. *gunne*].

gun·ny (gun′·i·) *n.* strong, coarse sacking made from jute [Hind.].

gun·nel See **gunwale**.

gun·wale (gun′·l) *n.* upper edge of the side of a boat or ship. Also **gunnel** [fr. *Gunhilda*, a medieval war engine].

gup·py (gup′·i·) *n.* tiny fresh-water fish [fr. R. T. L. *Guppy* of Trinidad].

gur·gi·ta·tion (gur·jạ·tā′·shạn) *n.* a surging rise and fall [L. *gurgitare*, to flood].

gur·gle (gur′·gl) *n.* a bubbling noise; *v.i.* to make a gurgle [imit.].

gush (gush) *v.i.* to flow out suddenly and copiously; (*Colloq.*) to display exaggerated and effusive affection; *n.* a sudden copious flow; (*Colloq.*) effusive talk. **-er** *n.* a gushing person; an oil-well with a natural flow. **-iness** *n.* **-ing, -y** *a.* effusive.

gus·set (gus′·it) *n.* a triangular piece of material inserted in a garment to strengthen or enlarge it [Fr. *gousset*, the arm-pit].

gust (gust) *n.* a sudden blast of wind; a burst of rain, etc.; an outburst of passion. **-y** *a.* [O.N. *gustr*].

gus·to (gus′·tō) *n.* keen enjoyment; zest; artistic style [L. *gustus*, taste].

gut (gut) *n.* a material made from animal intestines, as violin strings, etc.; tennis rackets; a narrow passage; a strait; *n.pl.* entrails; intestines; (*Colloq.*) courage; pluck; determina-

tion; *v.t.* to remove the entrails from; to destroy the interior as by fire.*pr.p.* **-ting.** *pa.p.* and *pa.t.* **-ted** [O.E. *guttas*, (pl.)].

gut·ter (gut′·er) *n.* a passage for water; a trough or pipe for conveying rain from the eaves of a building; a channel at the side of a road for carrying water; *v.t.* to make channels in; *v.i.* to flow in streams; of a candle to melt away so that wax runs off in channels. **-snipe** *n.* the common snipe; a child homeless or living in the streets [L. *gutta*, a drop].

gut·tur·al (gut′·er·ạl) *a.* pert. to or produced in the throat; *n.* a guttural sound [L. *guttur*, throat].

guy (gī) *n.* a rope or chain to steady a thing; *v.t.* to guide with a guy. Also **-rope** [O.Fr. *guier*, to guide].

guy (gī) *n.* (*Slang*) a fellow; *v.t.* (*Slang*) to ridicule; to make fun of [fr. *Guy* Fawkes].

guz·zle (guz′·l) *v.t.* and *i.* to drink greedily. **-r** *n.* [Fr. *gosier*, the gullet].

gybe See **jib, jibe**.

gym·kha·na (jim·kà′·nạ) *n.* a place for athletic games; a sports meet [Urdu *gend-khana*, a racket court, *lit.* a ball house].

gym·na·sium (jim·nā′·zi·ạm) *n.* a building or room equipped for physical training or sports; (gim·nà′·zi·ạm) in Germany, a High School. *pl.* **gymnasia** or **-s. gymnast** (jim′·nàst) *n.* an expert in gymnastics. **gymnastic** *a.* **gymnastics** *n.pl.* muscular and bodily exercises. **gym** *n.* a gymnasium; a school athletic course [Gk. *gymnasion* fr. *gumnos*, naked].

gy·ne·col·o·gy (jī· (or jĭ)·nạ·kàl′·ạ·ji·) *n.* (*Med.*) the science which deals with the diseases and disorders of women, esp. the organs of generation. **gynecologist** *n.* Also **gynaecology**, etc. [Gk. *gunē*, a woman; *logos*, discourse].

gyp (jip) (*Slang*) *v.t.* to swindle, to steal; *n.* a cheat; a swindle.

gyp·sum (jip′·sạm) *n.* a mineral, consisting mostly of sulfate of lime, used for making

plaster of Paris [Gk. *gupsos*, chalk].

Gyp·sy (jip′·si·) *n.* one of a nomadic tribe of Indian origin· (*l.c.*) a person who resembles or lives like a Gypsy; *a.* of or like a Gypsy [corrupt. fr. *Egyptian*].

gy·rate (jī′·rāt) *v.i.* to revolve around a central point; to move in a circle; to move spirally. **gyratory** *a.* **gyration** *n.* a circular or spiral motion [L. *gyrare*, to turn, whirl].

gy·ro·man·cy (jī′·rō·man·si·) *n.* divination performed by drawing a circle, and walking in it till dizziness causes a fall [Gk. *guros*, a circle; *manteia*, divination].

gy·ro·scope (jī′·rạ·skōp) *n.* a wheel so mounted that its axis can turn freely in any direction when set rotating and left undisturbed, it will maintain the same direction in space, independently of its relation to the earth Gk. *guros*, a circle; *skopein*, to view].

H

ha (hä) *interj.* denoting surprise, joy, or grief [imit. origin].

ha·be·as cor·pus (hā′·bi·ạs kawr′·pạs) *n.* writ requiring that a prisoner be brought to court to determine legality of confinement [L. = that you have the body].

ha·ber·dash·er (hab′·er·dash·er) *n.* a dealer in men's furnishings. **-y** *n.* [etym. uncertain].

ha·bil·i·ment (hạ·bil′·ạ·mạnt) *n.* (usually in *pl.*) dress [Fr. *habiller*, to clothe].

hab·it (hab′·it) *n.* custom; usage; tendency to repeat an action in the same way; mental condition acquired by practice; dress, esp. a *riding-habit*; *v.t.* to dress; to clothe. **-ual** *a.* formed by habit. **-ually** *adv.* **habituate** *v.t.* to accustom to a practice or usage; to familiarize; (*Colloq.*) to frequent. **-nation** *n.* **-ude** *n.* customary manner of action; repetition of an act, thought, or feeling; confirmed practice. **-ué** (hạ·bich′·ạ·wā) *n.* a frequenter (of a place) [L. *habitus*, attire, state, fr. *habere*, to have].

hab·it·a·ble (hab′·it·ạ·bl) *a.* fit to live in. **-ness, habitability** *n.* **habitably** *adv.* **habitant** *n.* an inhabitant. **habitat** *n.* the natural home of an animal or plant; place of residence. **habitation** *n.* the act of inhabiting; a place of abode [L. *habitare*, to dwell].

ha·chure (hash′·oor) *n.* shading on a map to show mountains; *v.t.* to mark with this [Fr.].

ha·cien·da (hà·si·en′·dạ) *n.* a ranch; an estate in S. America [Sp.].

hack (hak) *v.t.* to cut irregularly; to notch; *v.i.* to make cuts or notches; to give harsh dry coughs; *n.* a cut; a notch; an ax, a pick; a short cough [O.E. *haccian*].

hack (hak) *n.* a horse for ordinary riding; a horse worn out by over work; a drudge, esp. literary; a hackneyed; hired; a hired carriage; (*Colloq.*) a taxi; *v.t.* to let out for hire; to hackney; *v.i.* (*Colloq.*) to drive a taxi [short for *hackney*].

hack·ney (hak′·ni·) *n.* a horse for riding or driving; a horse (and carriage) kept for hire; *a.* to let out for hire; *v.i.* to use often; to make trite or commonplace. **-ed** *a.* commonplace [Fr. *haquenée*, a pacing horse].

had (had) *pa.p.* and *pa.t.* of **have**.

had·dock (had′·ạk) *n.* a fish of the cod family.

Ha·des (hā′·dēz) (*Myth.*) the underworld; (*l.c.*) (*Colloq.*) hell [Gk. = the unseen].

haft (haft) *n.* a handle, esp. of a knife; a hilt; *v.t.* to set in a handle [O.E. *haeft*].

hag (hag) *n.* an ugly old woman; a witch. **-gish** *a.* like a hag. **-gishly** *adv.* **-ridden** *a.* troubled with nightmares [O.E. *haegtesse*, a witch].

hag·gard (hag′·erd) *a.* wild-looking; lean and gaunt; *n.* untrained hawk. **-ly** *adv.* [O.Fr. *hagard*].

hag·gle (hag′·l) *v.t.* to hack; to mangle; *v.i.* to dispute terms; to be difficult in bargaining; *n.* act of haggling. **-r** *n.* [O.N. *hoggva*, to chop]

Hag·i·og·ra·pha (hag·i·., hā·ji·àg′·rạ·fạ) *n.pl.* the last of the three divisions of the Old Testament [Gk. *haigos*, holy; *graphein*, to write].

hag·i·ol·o·gy (hag·i·., hā·ji·àl′·ạ·ji·) *n.* a history of the lives of saints. **hagiologist** *n.* **hagiography** *n.* the branch of literature which treats of the lives of saints [Gk. *hagios*, holy; *logos*, discourse; *graphein*, to write].

ha·ha (hà·hà′) *n.* a sunken fence [Fr.].

hail (hāl) *n.* frozen rain falling in pellets; *v.i.* to rain hail; *v.t.* to pour down like hail. **-stone** *n.* frozen raindrops [O.E. *hagol*].

hail (hāl) *v.t.* to greet, salute or call; *n.* an exclamation of respectful salutation. **— fellow** *n.* (often **hail-fellow well met**) an intimate

companion; *a.* on intimate terms. **to hail from**, to come from [O.N. *heill*, healthy].

hair (hār) *n.* a filament growing from the skin of an animal; such filaments collectively, esp. covering the head; bristles; anything small or fine. **-ed** *a.* having hair. **-iness** *n.* **-y** *a.* covered with, made of, resembling hair. **-breadth** (hār′·bredth). **-s-breadth** *n.* the breadth of a hair; a very small distance; a. very narrow. **-brush** *n.* a brush for the hair. **-cloth** *n.* cloth made wholly or partly of hair. **-dresser** *n.* one who dresses or cuts hair; (*Brit.*) a barber. **-pin** *n.* a special two-legged pin for controlling hair. **-pin bend**, a bend of the road in the form of a U. **—raising** *a.* terrifying; alarming. **— shirt** *n.* a shirt made of haircloth, worn by penitents, ascetics, etc. **-splitting** *n.* and *n.* minute distinctions in reasoning. **-spring** *n.* a fine spring in a watch. **— trigger** *n.* a secondary trigger releasing the main one by very slight pressure [O.E. *haer*].

hal·cy·on (hal′·si·ạn) *n.* the kingfisher; *a.* calm. **— days**, peaceful, tranquil days; calm weather just before and after the winter solstice [Gk. *halkuon*, kingfisher, associated with calm sea].

hale (hāl) *a.* robust; sound; healthy, esp. in old age. **-ness** *n.* [O.E. *hal*, whole].

hale (hāl) *v.t.* to haul [O.Fr. *haler*, to pull].

half (haf) *n.* either of two equal parts of a thing. *pl.* **halves** (havz); (*Golf*) a hole neither won nor lost; *a.* forming a half; *adv.* to the extent of half. **-and-half** *n.* a mixture of two things in equal proportions; *adv.* in two equal portions. **-back** *n.* (*Football*) a player, or position, behind the forward line. **-baked** *a.* underdone; immature; silly. **-breed** *n.* one whose parents are of different races. **— brother** *n.* a brother by one parent only. **-caste** *n.* a half-breed. **— dozen** *n.* six. **— hearted** *a.* lukewarm. **— mast** *n.* the position of a flag lowered halfway down the staff, as a signal of distress, or as a sign of mourning. **— measure** *n.* inadequate means to achieve an end. **— moon** *n.* the moon when half its disk appears illuminated; a semicircle. **— nelson** *n.*

a hold in wrestling. — **title** n. the name of a book, or subdivision of a book, occupying a full page. —**tone** n. an illustration printed from a relief plate, showing light and shade by minute dots, made by photographing the subject through a closely ruled screen. —**wit** n. an imbecile; a blockhead. —**witted** a. halve (hav) v.t. to divide into two equal portions; to reduce to half the previous amount [O.E. *haelf*].

hal·i·but (hal′·ạ·bạt) n. a large, flat sea fish [M.E. *haly*, holy; *butt*, a flatfish].

hal·i·to·sis (hal·ạ·tō′·sis) n. foul or offensive breath [L. *halitus*, breath].

hall (hawl) n. a corridor in a building; a place of public assembly; a room at the entrance of a house; a building belonging to a collegiate institution, guild, etc.; **-mark** n. the mark used to indicate the standard of tested gold and silver; any mark of quality [O.E. *heal*].

Hal·le·lu·jah, Halleluiah (hal·ẹ·lōō′·ya) n. and *interj.* used in songs of praise to God [Heb. *hallelu*, praise ye; *Jah*, Jehovah].

hal·liard See **halyard**.

hal·loo (hạ·lōō′) n. a hunting cry; a shout or call to draw attention; v.t. to encourage with shouts, esp dogs in hunting [imit.].

hal·low (hal′·ō) v.t. to make holy; to consecrate; to treat as sacred; to reverence. **-ed** a. **Hallowe'en** n. the evening before All Hallows' or All Saints' day (Oct. 31st).

hal·lu·ci·nate (hạ·lōō′·sạ·nāt) v.t. to produce illusion in the mind of. **hallucination** n. illusion; seeing something that is not present; delusion. **hallucinative, hallucinatory** a. [L. *hallucinari*, to wander in mind].

ha·lo (hā′·lō) n. a circle of light around the moon, sun, etc.; a ring of light around a saint's head in a picture. *pl.* **-s, -es** [Gk. *halos*, a threshing-floor; a disk].

hal·o·gen (hal′·ạ·jẹn) n. (*Chem.*) one of the elements chlorine, bromine, iodine, and fluorine [Gk. *hals*, salt; root *gen-*, producing].

halt (hawlt) n. a stoppage on a march or journey; v.t. to cause to stop; v.i. to make a stop [Ger. *Halt*, stoppage].

halt (hawlt) v.i. to falter in speech or walk; to hesitate; n. cripple. **-ing** a. [O.E. *healt*].

hal·ter (hawl′·tẹr) n. a rope or strap with headstall to fasten or lead horses or cattle; a noose for hanging a person; v.t. to fasten with a rope or strap [O.E. *haelftre*].

halve (hav) v.t. to divide into two equal parts.

hal·yard, halliard (hal′·yẹrd) n. (*Naut.*) a rope for hoisting or lowering yards or sails [corrupt. of *halier*, fr. *hale* = to haul].

ham (ham) n. the thigh of any animal, esp. a hog's thigh cured by salting and smoking; the region behind the knee; (*Slang*) an actor who overacts; an amateur transmitter and receiver of radio messages. **-string** n. a tendon at the back of the knee; v.t. to cripple by cutting this [O.E. *hamm*].

ham·burg·er (ham′·bur·gẹr) n. ground beef, seasoned and formed into cakes, frequently served in a bun [Ger. *Hamburg*].

ham·let (ham′·lit) n. a small village [O.E. *ham*, a dwelling].

ham·mer (ham′·ẹr) n. a tool, usually with a heavy head at the end of a handle, for beating metal, driving nails, etc.; a contrivance for exploding the charge of a gun; v.t. and i. to beat with, or as with, a hammer; to work hard at. **-head** n. a rapacious kind of shark. **-headed** a. having a head shaped like a hammer. **to hammer out** (*Fig.*) to find a solution by full investigation of all difficulties. **to come under the hammer**, to be sold by auction. [O.E. *hamor*].

ham·mock (ham′·ạk) n. a kind of hanging bed, consisting of a piece of canvas, and suspended by cords from hooks [Sp. *hamaca*].

ham·per (ham′·pẹr) n. a large covered basket for conveying goods [O.Fr. *hanapier*, a case for *hanaps*, goblets].

ham·per (ham′·pẹr) n. (*Naut.*) cumbrous equipment; v.t. to impede; to obstruct the movements of [etym. uncertain].

ham·shack·le (ham′·shak·l) v.t. to fasten the head of an animal to one of the forelegs [fr. *hamper* and *shackle*].

ham·ster (ham′·stẹr) n. a species of rodent, remarkable for having cheek pouches [Gk.].

ham·string See **ham**.

hand (hand) n. the extremity of the arm beyond the wrist; a pointer on a dial, e.g. on a watch; a measure of the hand's breadth, four inches; a style of handwriting; cards dealt to a player; a manual worker; a sailor; side; direction; agency; service; aid; skill; a. belonging to, worn on, carried in, the hand; made or operated by hand; v.t. to give with the hand; to deliver; to pass; to hold out. **-y** a. convenient; close at hand; clever with the hands. **-y man** n. one hired for odd jobs. **-ily** adv. **-iness** n. **-bag** n. a bag for carrying in the hand. **-bill** n. printed sheet for circulation by hand. **-book** n. a short treatise; a manual. **-breath** n. the breadth of a hand (about four inches). **-cart** n. a small cart drawn or pushed by hand. **-cuff** n. shackle around wrist connected by a chain with one on other wrist; a manacle; v.t. to manacle. **-ful** n. as much as the hand will grasp or contain. **-maid(en)** n. a female servant. **— out** (*Slang*) food or money given to a beggar. **-rail** n. the rail of a staircase. **— to hand** a. in personal encounter; at close quarters. **— to mouth** a. precarious; without thought of the future. **-writing** n. the way a person writes. **at first hand**, direct from the original source. **in hand**, under control. **off-hand** adv. without attentive consideration; immediately. **on hand**, ready for distribution; available for disposal. **with a heavy hand**, sternly; severely. **with a high hand**, arrogantly. **an old hand**, a person with experience; a veteran. **second hand**, not new; having already been used. **to change hands**, to become the property of another. **to show one's hand**, to reveal one's intentions. [O.E. *hand*].

hand·i·cap (han′·di·kap) n. a race or contest in which competitors' chances are equalized by starts given, weights carried, etc.; a condition so imposed; (*Fig.*) a disability; v.t. to hinder or impede [fr. *hand in cap*; orig. a lottery game].

hand·i·craft (han′·di·kraft) n. manual occupation or skill; work performed by the hand [O.E. *handcraeft*].

hand·ker·chief (hang′·kẹr·chif) n. a small square of fabric carried in the pocket for wiping the nose, etc.; a kerchief for head or neck.

han·dle (hand′·d'l) v.t. to touch or feel with the hand; to manage; to wield; to deal with; to deal in; n. the part of a thing by which it is held; (*Fig.*) a fact that may be taken advantage of [O.E. *handlian*].

hand·some (han′·sạm) a. of fine appearance; generous. **-ly** adv. **-ness** n. [orig. = pleasant to handle].

hang (hang) v.t. to suspend; to put to death by suspending from gallows; to cover with, as wallpaper, curtains, pictures, etc.; to fix on hinges, as a door; to display; v.i. to be suspended; to incline; to be in suspense; to linger; to cling to. *pa.p.* and *p.t.* **-ed** or **hung**. n. the way in which a thing hangs; (*Colloq.*) meaning; manner of doing. **-dog** n. a degraded fellow; a. having a sneaking look. **-er** n. that by which a thing is suspended, e.g. a *coat-hanger*. **-ing** n. death by suspension; that which is hung, as curtains, etc. for a room (used chiefly in *pl.*); a. punishable by death; suspended. **-man** n. one who hangs another; a public executioner. **-nail** n. piece of skin hanging from root of fingernail. **-over** n. depressing after-effects of drinking. **to hang in the balance**, to be in doubt or suspense. **hang! hang it! hang it all!** mild oaths [O.E. *hangian*].

han·gar (hang′·ẹr) n. a shed for aircraft [Fr. = a shed].

hank (hangk) n. a coil, esp. as a measure of yarn (of cotton = 840 yards; of worsted = 560 yards); (*Naut.*) a ring at the corner of a sail [O.N. *hanki*].

han·ker (hang′·kẹr) v.i. to long for; to crave. **-ering** n. an uneasy longing for; a craving.

han·som (han′·sạm) n. a light two-wheeled cab with the driver's seat at the back [fr. the inventor, Joseph A. *Hansom*, 1803-1882].

hap·haz·ard (hap·haz′·ẹrd) n. chance; accident; a. random; without design. **-ly** adv. **-ness** n. [O.N *happ*, luck]. [*happ*, luck].

hap·less (hap′·lis) a. unlucky. **-ly** adv. [O.N.

hap·pen (hap′·in) v.i. to come by chance; to occur; to take place. **-ing** n. occurrence; event [O.N. *happ*, luck].

hap·py (hap′·i) a. glad; content; lucky; fortunate; apt; fitting. **happily** adv. **happiness** n. [O.N. *happ*, luck].

ha·ra·ki·ri (hä·rạ·kēr′·i·) n. a method of suicide by disembowelment, practiced by the Japanese. Also **hari-kari** [Jap. *hara*, the belly; *kiri*, to cut].

ha·rangue (hạ·rang′) n. a loud, passionate speech; v.i. to deliver a harangue; v.t. to speak vehemently to. **-r** n. [O.H. Ger. = a ring of hearers].

har·ass (har′·ạs, hạ·ras′) v.t. to attack repeatedly; to worry; to trouble. **-ed** a. **-er** n. **-ing** a. **-ment** n. [Fr. *harasser*].

har·bin·ger (här′·bin·jẹr) n. one who announces another's approach; a forerunner [M.E. *herbergeour*, one sent on to provide lodgings].

har·bor (här′·bẹr) n. shelter for ships; a port; any shelter; v.t. to give shelter to; to protect v.i. to take shelter [M.E. *herberwe*].

hard (härd) a. firm; solid; resisting pressure; difficult; harsh; unfeeling; difficult to bear; strenuous; bitter, as winter; keen, as frost; of water, not making lather well with soap; strong; said of alcoholic liquors; adv. vigorously; intently; solidly. **-en** v.t. to make hard or more hard; to strengthen; to confirm in wickedness or obstinacy; to make less sympathetic; v.i. to become hard. **-ly** adv. with difficulty; not quite; scarcely; severely. **-ness** n. severe toil or suffering; ill-luck; privation; suffering. **hard and fast**, strict; rigid. **-bitten** a. tough; stubborn. **—boiled** a. boiled till hard, e.g. of an egg; (*Slang*) tough; unfeeling. **— by**, near; close at hand. **— cash**, gold and silver coins, as opposed to paper money. **-headed** a. shrewd; intelligent; practical. **-hearted** a. cruel; merciless; unsympathetic. **-tack**, a large coarse unsalted biscuit. (*Colloq.*) **— up**, very short of money; poor. **-ware** n. articles made of metal, e.g. tools, locks, fixtures, etc. **to die hard**, to die after a fierce struggle. **a die-hard** (*Fig.*) one who clings desperately to long-held opinions [O.E. *heard*].

har·dy (här′·di·) a. robust; vigorous; bold; brave; daring; able to bear exposure. **-ily** adv. **-ihood** n. extreme boldness. **-iness** n. vigor; robustness [Fr. *hardi*, bold].

hare (hār) n. a rodent with long hind legs, long ears, short tail, and divided upper lip, noted for its speed. **-brained** a. wild; heedless. **-lip** n. (*Med.*) a congenital fissure in the upper lip. **-lipped** a. [O.E. *hara*].

har·em (hār′·ạm) n. apartment for females in a Mohammedan household; the occupants [Ar. *haram*, forbidden].

ha·ri·ka·ri, form of **hara-kari**.

hark (härk) v.i. to listen; *interj.* listen! hear! **to hark back** (*Fig.*) to return to some previous point in an argument [M.E. *herkien*; cf. E. *hearken*].

har·lot (här′·lạt) n. a prostitute. **-ry** n. prostitution [O.Fr. = a vagabond].

harm (härm) n. injury; hurt; damage; misfortune; v.t. to hurt; to injure. **-ful** a. hurtful; injurious. **-fully** adv. **-fulness** n. **-less** a. **-lessly** adv. **-lessness** n. [O.E. *hearm*].

har·mo·ny (här′·mạ·ni·) n. agreement; concord; friendliness; peace; a melodious sound; a combination of musical notes to make chords; the science that treats of musical sounds in their combination and progression. **harmonic** (här·mán′·ik), **harmonical** a. **harmonically** adv. **harmonica** n. a mouth organ. **harmonicon** n. a mouth organ; an orchestration. **harmonics** n. the science of harmony, of musical sounds. **harmonious** (här·mō′·ni·ạs) a. vocally or musically concordant; symmetrical; living in peace and friendship. **harmoniously** adv. **harmoniousness** n. **harmonize** v.t. to bring into harmony; to cause to agree; to reconcile; (*Mus.*) to arrange into parts for the voice, or with instrumental accompaniments; v.i. to be in harmony; to agree; (*Colloq.*) to sing in harmony. **harmonizer** n. **harmonist** n. a harmonizer; a musical composer. **harmonium** n. a small reed organ. **harmonic progression**, a series of numbers whose reciprocals are in arithmetical progression, e.g. $\frac{1}{2}$, $\frac{1}{3}$, $\frac{1}{4}$, etc. or 10, 12, 15 [Gk. *harmonia*, fr. *harmozein*, to fit together].

har·ness (här′·nis) n. the working gear, straps, bands, etc. of a draft animal, esp. a horse; v.t. to put harness on [Fr. *harneis*].

harp (härp) n. a stringed musical instrument played by hand; v.i. to play on the harp; to dwell persistently upon a particular subject. **-ist** n. a player on the harp. **-sichord** (härp′·si·kawrd) n. an old-fashioned musical instrument, a forerunner of the piano [O.E. *hearpa*].

har·poon (här·pōōn′) n. a barbed spear with a rope attached for catching whales, etc.; v.t. to strike with a harpoon. **-er** n. [Fr. *harpon*].

Har·py (här′·pi·) n. (*Myth.*) ravenous monster, with head and breast of woman and wings and claws of vulture; (*l.c.*) a rapacious woman [Gk. *harpazein*, to seize].

har·ri·dan (har′·i·dạn) n. a haggard old woman; a shrew [corrupt. of Fr. *haridelle*, a worn-out horse].

har·row (har′·ō) n. a toothed agricultural implement to level, break clods, or cover seed when sown; v.t. to draw harrow over; (*Fig.*) to distress greatly. **-er** n. **-ing** a. [M.E. *harwe*].

har·ry (har′·i·) v.t. to ravage; to pillage; to torment [O.E. *hergian*, to make war].

harsh (hàrsh) a. rough; unpleasing to the touch or taste; severe; unfeeling. **-ly** adv. **-ness** n. [M.E. *harsk*].

hart (hàrt) n. a male deer or stag, esp. over five years old [O.E. *heort*].

harte·beest (hàrt′·bēst) n. a large S. African antelope [Dut.].

har·um-scar·um (hār′·ạm-skār′·ạm) a. reckless; wild; n. a rash person [perh. *hare*, and *scare*].

har·vest (hàr′·vist) n. (season for) gathering crops; the crop itself; v.t. to gather in. **-er** n. one who harvests; a reaping-machine. **— moon** n. the full moon nearest the autumn equinox [O.E. *haerfest*, autumn].

has (haz) 3rd sing. pres. indic. of the verb **have. —been** n. (*Colloq.*) a person long past his best.

hash (hash) v.t. to chop into small pieces; to mince; n. that which is hashed; a dish of hashed meat and potatoes; (*Slang*) a mess [Fr. *hacher*, to chop].

hasp (hasp) n. a clasp passing over a staple for fastening a door, etc.; v.t. to fasten with a hasp [O.E. *haepse*].

has·sock (has′·ạk) n. a padded cushion for kneeling or for a footstool; a tuft of grass [O.E. *hassuc*, coarse grass].

haste (hāst) n. speed; quickness; hurry; v.i. (*Poetic*) to hasten. **hasten** (hās′·n) v.t. to urge forward; to accelerate; v.i. to hurry. **hastener** n. **hasty** a. speedy; quick; over-eager; rash; passionate. **hastily** adv. [O.Fr. *haste*].

hat (hat) n. covering for head, usually with brim; red hat of cardinal, hence, dignity of a ·cardinal. **-ter** n. one who makes, or sells hats. **top hat,** a silk hat with a high crown. **to pass (round) the hat,** to make a collection, esp. to pay expenses [O.E. *haett*].

hatch (hach) v.t. to bring forth young birds from the shell; to incubate; to plot; v.i. to come forth from the shelf; n. the act of hatching; the brood hatched. **-er** n. **-ery** n. a place for hatching eggs, esp. of fish [M.E. *hacchen*].

hatch (hach) n. the lower half of a divided door; an opening in a floor or roof; the boards, etc. covering a hatchway; the hatchway itself. **-way** n. a square opening in a ship's deck through which cargo, etc. is lowered [O.E. *haec*, a gate].   [*hacher*, to chop].

hatch (hach) v.t. to shade with lines [Fr.

hatch·et (hach′·at) n. a small ax with a short handle. **— faced** a. having a face with sharp features **to bury the hatchet,** to make peace [Fr. *hache*, an axe].

hate (hāt) v.t. to dislike strongly; to bear malice to; to detest; n. strong dislike; aversion; hatred. **-ful** a. detestable. **-fully** adv. **-fulness** n. **-r** n. **hatred** n. aversion; active ill-will; enmity [O.E. *hatian*, to hate; *hete*, hatred].

haugh·ty (haw′·ti·) a. proud. **haughtily** adv. **haughtiness** n. [Fr. *haut*, high, fr. L. *altus*].

haul (hawl) v.t. to pull with force; to drag; to steer a ship closer to the wind; v.i. to pull; (of wind) to shift, to veer; n. a hauling; a catch; good profit, gain, or acquisition. **-age** n. the act of pulling; the charge for hauling; the carrying of goods, material, etc. by road. **-er** n. one who hauls. **close-hauled** a. (*Naut.*) of a ship, with the sails trimmed tọ keep her close to the wind [Fr. *haler*].

haunch (hawnch) n. the part of the body between the ribs and thighs; the hip; a leg and loin of venison, etc. [Fr. *hanche*].

haunt (hawnt) v.t. to frequent; of ghosts, to visit regularly; v.i. to loiter about a place; n. a place of frequent resort. **-ed** a. frequently visited by ghosts [Fr. *hanter*, to frequent].

haut·boy (hō′·boi) n. an older form of the oboe [Fr. *haut*, high; *bois*, wood].

hau·teur (hō·tur′) n. haughtiness; haughty manner or spirit; arrogance [Fr.].

Ha·van·a (ha·van′·ạ) n. a fine brand of cigar [named from *Havana*, the capital of Cuba].

have (hav) v.t. to hold or possess; to be possessed or affected with; to seize; to bring forth; to enjoy; to be obliged (to do); (as an auxiliary verb, forms the perfect and other tenses); pr.p. **having.** pa.p. and pa.t. **had** [O.E. *habban*].

ha·ven (hā′·vn) n. a bay or inlet giving shelter for ships; any place of shelter [O.E. *haefen*].

hav·er·sack (hav′·ẹr·sak) n. a soldier's canvas ration-bag; a similar bag for travelers [Ger. *Habersack*, an oat sack].

hav·oc (hav′·ạk) n. pillage; devastation; ruin [orig. to 'cry havoc,' to give the signal for pillage; O.Fr. *havot*, plunder].

haw (haw) n. a hesitation in speech; v.i. to speak hesitatingly [imit.].

haw (haw) interj. a command to horses, usually to turn left; v.t. and v.i. to turn left [O.E. *havian*].

hawk (hawk) n. a bird of prey of the falcon family; v.t. and i. to hunt with hawks, as in falconry. **hawker** n. a falconer. **-ing** n. falconry [O.E. *hafoc*].

hawk (hawk) v.i. to clear the throat noisily; n. an audible clearing of the throat.

hawk (hawk) v.i. to carry about wares for sale; to peddle. **-er** n. an itinerant dealer; a peddler [Dut. *heuker*, a huckster].   [plaster.

hawk (hawk) n. a plasterer's tool for holding

hawse (hawz) n. the part of a ship's bows with holes for cables [O.E. *heals*, the prow].

haw·ser (haw′·zẹr) n. a large rope or small cable [O.Fr. *haucier*, to raise].

hay (hā) n. grass mown and dried for fodder. **— fever** n. irritation of the mucous membrane of the nose (generally by pollen from grasses). **-maker** n. one who cuts and dries grass for hay. **-rick** n. **-stack** n. a large pile of hay with ridged or pointed top. **-seed** n. grass seed; (*Colloq.*) a rustic; a country bumpkin [O.E. *hieg*].

haz·ard (haz′·ẹrd) n. chance; a chance; risk; danger; (*Golf*) an inclusive term for all obstacles on the golf course; a game played with dice; v.t. to expose to risk; to run the risk of. **-ous** a. dangerous; risky [Fr. *hasard*].

haze (hāz) n. a misty appearance in the air; mental obscurity. **hazy** a. **hazily** adv.

haze (hāz) v.t. to torment or punish by the imposition of disagreeable task; to play tricks on [O.Fr. *haser*, to annoy].

ha·zel (hā′·zl) n. a nut-bearing bush or small tree; the reddish-brown color of the nuts; a. of this color. **-nut** n. the nut of the hazel tree [O.E. *haesel*].

he (hē) pron. the 3rd pers. sing. masc. pronoun. **—man** n. (*Colloq.*) a very virile man [O.E.].

head (hed) n. the upper part of a man's or animal's body; the brain; intellectual capacity; upper part of anything; the top; the chief part, a chief; something the shape of a head; progress; a section of a chapter; the source of a stream; a cape or headland; a crisis; freedom to go on; a. chief; principal; of wind, contrary; v.t. to lead; to be at the head of; to direct; to go in front, so as to hinder; v.i. to originate; to form a head; to make for. **-y** a. impetuous; apt to intoxicate. **-ily** adv. **-iness** n. **-ache** (hed′·āk) n. a nerve-pain in the head. **-achy** a. **-er** n. (*Colloq.*) a plunge, head foremost into water; in building, a brick laid so that its end forms part of the surface of the wall. **-gear** n. a hat; the harness about an animal's head. **—hunting** n. raiding to procure human heads as trophies. **-ing** n. the act of providing

with a head; a title. **-land** n. a cape; a promontory. **-light** n. a strong light carried on the front of a locomotive, motor vehicle, etc. **—line** n. a summary of news in large print in a newspaper; a caption. **-long** adv. with the head foremost; rashly; a. steep; rash; reckless. **-man** n. the chief, esp. of a tribe. **-master, -mistress** n. the person in charge of a school; the principal. **-most** a. most advanced; foremost. **—on** a. meeting head to head; head first. **-phone** n. a telephone-receiver to clip on head (usually in *pl.*). **-piece** n. a helmet; the head; brain-power; ornamental engraving at beginning of book or chapter. **-quarters** n.pl. (*Mil.*) a center of operations. **-sail,** any sail forward of the mast. **-sman** n. an executioner. **-stall** n. the part of the bridle that fits round the head. **-stone** n. a memorial stone placed at the head of a grave. **-strong** a. obstinate; stubborn; self-willed. **-way** n. progress. **head over heels,** completely; deeply. **to keep one's head,** to keep calm [O.E. *heafod*].

heal (hēl) v.t. to make whole; to restore to health; to make well; v.i. to become sound. **-er** n. **-ing** a. tending to cure [O.E. *haelan*, fr. *hal*, whole].

health (helth) n. soundness of body; general condition of the body; a toast drunk in a person's honor. **-y** a. having, or tending to give, health; sound; vigorous; wholesome. **-ily** adv. **-iness** n. **-ful** a. [O.E. *haelth*, fr. *hal*, whole].

heap (hēp) n. a number of things lying one on another; a pile; a mass; (*Colloq.*) a great quantity; v.t. to throw or lay in a heap; to amass [O.E. *heap*].

hear (hēr) v.t. to perceive with the ear; to listen to; to heed; (*Law*) to try (a case); v.i. to perceive sound; to learn by report. pr.p. **-ing.** pa.p. and pa.t. **heard** (hurd). **-er** n. **-ing** n. the act of perceiving sound; the sense by which sound is perceived; audience; earshot. **-say** n. rumor: common talk. **hear! hear!** interj. indicating approval of a speaker's words or opinions [O.E. *hieran*].

hearse (hurs) n. a vehicle to carry a coffin to the place of burial [Fr. *herce*, a harrow].

heart (hàrt) n. the hollow, muscular organ which makes the blood circulate; the seat or source of life; the seat of emotions and affections; the inner part of anything; courage; warmth or affection; a playing-card marked with a figure of a heart. **-y** a. cordial; friendly; vigorous; in good health; of a meal, satisfying the appetite. **-ily** adv. **-iness** n. **-less** a. without heart; unfeeling. **-en** v.t. to encourage; to stimulate. **-ache** n. sorrow; anguish. **-blood** n. life; essence. **-break** n. overpowering sorrow. **-broken** a. overwhelmed with grief. **-burn** n. a form of dyspepsia. **-strings** n.pl. (*Fig.*) affections; emotions. **at heart,** at bottom, inwardly. **by heart,** by rote; by memory. **to wear one's heart on one's sleeve,** to show one's feelings openly [O.E. *heorte*].

hearth (hàrth) n. the fireside; the house itself; home [O.E. *heorth*].

heat (hēt) n. hotness; a sensation of this; hot weather or climate; warmth of feeling; anger; excitement; sexual excitement in animals, esp. female; (*Sport*) a race to decide the persons to compete in a deciding one; v.t. to make hot; to excite; v.i. to become hot. **-ed** a. (*Fig.*) of argument, etc. passionate; intense. **-edly** adv. **-er** n. **— wave** n. a spell of abnormally hot weather [O.E. *haetu*].

heath (hēth) n. waste land; moor; shrub of genus Erica. **-y** a. [O.E. *haeth*].

hea·then (hē′·THạn) n. one who is not an adherent of a religious system; an infidel; a pagan; an irreligious person; a. pagan; **-ish** a. **-ism** n. pagan worship; the condition of being heathen [O.E. *haethen*].

heath·er (heTH′·ẹr) n. a small plant of the genus Erica, bearing purple, and sometimes white, bell-shaped flowers; heath [fr. *heath*].

heave (hēv) v.t. to lift with effort; to throw (something heavy); to utter (a sigh); to pull on a rope, etc.; to haul; (*Geol.*) tc displace; v.i. to rise and fall in alternate motions, e.g. of heavy breathing, of waves, etc.; to try to vomit; n. a heaving; an effort to lift something; a rise and fall; an attempt to vomit; pr.p. **heaving.** pa.p. and pa.t. **heaved** or **hove. to heave to,** to bring a ship to a standstill [O.E. *hebban*].

heav·en (hev′·n) n. the sky; the upper air; the abode of God; God Himself; a place of bliss; supreme happiness. **-ly** a. pert. to, or like, heaven; pure; divine; adv. in a heavenly manner. **-liness** n. **-ward, -wards** adv. toward heaven. **in seventh heaven,** in a state of supreme bliss [O.E. *heofon*].

Heav·i·side lay·er (hev′·i·sīd lā′·ẹr) n. the upper part of the atmosphere, which reflects radio waves [fr. Oliver *Heaviside*, English physicist, 1850-1925].

heav·y (hev′·i·) a. weighty; striking or falling with force; large in amount, as a debt; rough, as the sea; abundant, as rain; clayey, as soil; sad; hard to bear; difficult; dull; sluggish; serious; over compact; indigestible. **heavily** adv. **heaviness** n. **—handed** a. awkward; severe; oppressive. **— headed** a. drowsy. **—hearted** a. sad. **—weight** n. (*Boxing*) a boxer exceeding 175 lbs. in weight [O.E. *hefig*, fr. *hebban*, to heave].

heb·do·mad (heb'·da·mad') *n.* a group of seven things; a week [Gk. *hebdomas*, seventh].

He·brew (hē'·brōō) *n.* one of the ancient inhabitants of Palestine; an Israelite; a Jew; language. **Hebraic** (hē·brā'·ik) *a.* pert. to the Hebrews, or to their language [Heb. *'ibhri*,' one from across the river Euphrates].

hec·a·tomb (hek'·a·tōm) *n.* any large number of victims [Gk. *hekaton*, a hundred; *bous*, an ox].

heck·le (hek'·l) *n.* a comb for cleaning flax; *v.t.* to comb flax; to ask awkward questions of a speaker at a public meeting.

hec·tic (hek'·tik) *a.* exciting; wild; feverish; affected with persistent fever [Gk. *hektikos*, habitual].

hec·to- *prefix* combining to form derivatives used in the metric system. **-gram, -gramme** hek'·ta·gram) *n.* a weight of 100 grammes = 3.527 ounces. **-liter** (hek'·ta·lēt·er) *n.* a unit of capacity, containing 100 liters = 26.418 U.S. gallons. **-meter** (hek·ta·mē·ter) *n.* a unit of length = 100 meters = 109.363 yards [fr. Gk. *hekaton*, one hundred].

hec·to·graph (hek'·ta·graf) *n.* an apparatus for multiplying copies of writings [Gk. *hekaton*, a hundred; *graphein*, to write].

Hec·tor (hek'·ter) *n.* the chief hero of Troy in war with Greeks. (*l.c.*) *n.* a bully; a brawler; a blusterer; *v.t.* and *i.* to bully; to bluster.

hedge (hej) *n.* a fence of bushes; a protecting barrier; *v.t.* to enclose with a hedge; to fence, as fields; to obstruct; to hem in; *v.i.* to bet on both sides so as to guard against loss; to shift; to shuffle; to skulk. **hedging** *n.* **hedgy** *a.* **-hog** *n.* a small quadruped, covered on the upper part of its body with prickles or spines. **-hopping** *n.* in aviation, flying very low. **-row** *n.* a row of bushes forming a hedge [O.E. *hecg*].

hedgehog

he·don·ism (hē'·d'n·izm) *n.* the doctrine that pleasure is the chief good. **hedonist** *n.* [Gk. *hēdonē*, pleasure].

heed (hēd) *v.t.* to take notice of; to care for; to mind; to observe; *n.* attention; notice; care; caution. **-ful** *a.* watchful; attentive. **-fully** *adv.* **-fulness** *n.* **-less** *a.* [O.E. *hedan*].

hee-haw (hē'·haw) *v.i.* to bray, as of an ass [imit. origin].

heel (hēl) *n.* back part of foot, shoe, boot, or stocking; back part of anything; (*Slang*) an undesirable person; *v.t.* to add a heel to, as in knitting; to touch ground, or a ball, with the heel. **— of Achilles** (*Fig.*) a vulnerable part. **down at the heels**, slovenly; seedy; ill-shod [O.E. *hela*].

heel (hēl) *v.i.* of a ship; to lean to one side; to incline; *v.t.* to cause to do this [O.E. *hieldan*, to incline].

heft (heft) *v.t.* to try the weight by lifting; (*Colloq.*) to heave up or lift; *n.* weight. **-y** *a.* heavy; vigorous [fr. *heave*].

he·gem·o·ny (hi·jem'·a·nē, hej'·a·mōn·i·) *n.* leadership; predominance. **hegemonic** *a.* [Gk. *hēgemōn*, a leader].

He·gi·ra, hejira (hi·jī'·ra) *n.* Mohammed's flight from Mecca to Medina, A.D. 622 [Ar. *hijrah*, flight].

heif·er (hef'·er) *n.* a young cow that has not had a calf [O.E. *heahfore*].

height (hīt) *n.* measurement from base to top; quality of being high; a high position; a hill; eminence. **-en** *v.t.* to make high or higher; to intensify [O.E. *hiehthu*].

hei·nous (hā'·nas) *a.* extremely wicked; atrocious; odious [Fr. *haineux*, hateful].

heir (ār) *n.* (*fem.* **-ess**) a person legally entitled to succeed to property or rank. **— apparent** *n.* the person who is first in the line of succession to an estate, crown, etc. **-loom** *n.* article of personal property which descends to heir along with inheritance; a thing that has been in a family for generations [L. *heres*].

he·ji·ra See **hegira**.

held (held) *pa.p.* and *pa.t.* of **hold**.

hel·i·cal (hel'·i·kal) *a.* pert. to a helix; spiral.

helicopter *n.* an airplane which can rise or descend vertically; an autogiro [Gk. *helix*, spiral; *pteron*, a wing].

he·li·o·gram (hē'·li·a·gram) *n.* a message transmitted by heliograph [Gk. *hēlios*, the sun; *gramma*, a writing].

he·li·o·graph (hē'·li·a·graf) *n.* signaling apparatus employing a mirror to reflect the sun's rays; an instrument for photographing the sun; *v.t.* to signal by means of a heliograph. **-ic** *a.* **heliography** *n.* [Gk. *hēlios*, the sun; *graphein*, to write].

he·li·o·trope (hē'·li·a·trōp) *n.* a plant with fragrant purple flowers; the color of the flowers, or their scent; a bloodstone. **heliotropism** *n.* (*Bot.*) the tendency of plants to direct their

growth towards light [Gk. *hēlios*, the sun; *tropos*, a turn].

helicopter

he·li·um (hē'·li·am) *n.* (*Chem.*) an inert non-inflammable,light gas [Gk. *hēlios*, the sun].

he·lix (hē'·liks) *n.* a spiral, e.g. wire in a coil, or a corkscrew; (*Zool.*) a genus including the snail; (*Anat.*) the outer rim of the ear. **helical** *a.* spiral [Gk. *helix*, a spiral].

hell (hel) *n.* the abode of the damned; the lower regions; a place or state of vice, misery, or torture. **-ish** *a.* infernal. **-ishly** *adv.* **-ishness** *n.* **-ion** *n.* troublemaker [O.E. *hel*].

Hel·lene (hel'·ēn) *n.* an ancient Greek; a subject of modern Greece. **Hellenic** *a.* **Hellen·ism** *n.* Grecian culture; a Greek idiom. **Hellenist** *n.* a Greek scholar. **Hellenistic** *a.* [Gk. *Hellēn*].

hel·lo (ha·lō', he·lō') *interj.* a greeting or call to attract attention.

helm (helm) *n.* (*Naut.*) a tiller or wheel for turning the rudder of a ship; (*Fig.*) control; guidance; *v.t.* to steer; to control [O.E. *helma*].

helm (helm) *n.* (*Arch.*) a helmet. **helmet** *n.* a defensive covering for the head; anything similar in shape or position [O.E. *helm*].

hel·minth (hel'·minth) *n.* an intestinal worm. [Gk. *helmins*, a worm].

hel·ot (hēl'·at, hē'·lat) *n.* a serf in ancient Sparta; a slave; serfdom [Gk. *Heilōtēs*].

help (help) *v.t.* to aid; to assist; to support; to succor; to relieve; to prevent; *v.i.* to lend aid; to be useful; *n.* the act of helping; one who, or that which, helps; aid; assistance; support; a domestic servant. **-er** *n.* **-ful** *a.* **-fulness** *n.* **-ing** *n.* a portion of food. **-less** *a.* not able to take care of oneself; weak; dependent. **-lessly** *adv.* **-lessness** *n.* an assistant; a partner; a wife or husband. Also **-meet** [O.E. *helpma*]. [order: in hurry and confusion.

hel·ter-skel·ter (hel'·ter·skel'·ter) *adv.* in dis-

Hel·ve·tia (hel·vē'·sha) *n.* the Latin, and political, name for Switzerland.

hem (hem) *n.* border, esp. one made by sewing; *v.t.* to fold over and sew down; to edge; to enclose (followed by *in*). *pr.p.* **-ming**. *pa.p.* and *pa.t.* **-med** [O.E.].

hem (hem) *interj.* and *n.* a kind of suppressed cough, calling attention or expressing doubt; *v.i.* to make the sound.

he·ma-, hemo- (hē'·ma) a word element meaning "blood" [Gk. *haima*].

he·mal, haemal (hē'·mal) *a.* of the blood; on same side of body as the heart and great blood-vessels [Gk. *haima*, blood].

hem·a·tin, haematin (hem'·a·tin, hē'·ma·tin) *n.* the constituent of hemoglobin containing iron [Gk. *haima*, blood].

hem·i-, *prefix* from Greek *hēmi*, half, combining to form derivatives.

hem·i·sphere (hem'·a·sfēr) *n.* a half sphere; half of the celestial sphere; half of the earth **hemispheric, hemispherical** *a.*

hem·i·stich (hem'·a·stik) *n.* half a line of verse.

hem·lock (hem'·lak) *n.* a poisonous umbelliferous plant; a coniferous spruce [O.E. *hemlic*].

he·mo·glo·bin, haemoglobin (hē·ma·glō'·bin) *n.* the coloring matter of the red blood corpuscles [Gk. *haima*, blood; L. *globus*, a ball].

he·mo·phil·i·a, haemophilia (hē·ma·fil'·i·a) *n.* (*Med.*) tendency to excessive bleeding due to a deficiency in clotting power of blood; *n.* a bleeder [Gk. *haima*, blood; *philein*, to love].

hem·or·rhage, haemorrhage (hem'·a·rij) *n.* (*Med.*) a flow of blood; a discharge of blood from the blood vessels; bleeding. **hemorrhagic** *a.* [Gk. *haima*, blood; *rhēgnunai*, to burst].

hem·or·rhoids, haemorrhoids (hem'·a·-

roidz) *n.pl.* dilated veins around anus; piles. [Gk. *haima*, blood; *rhein*, to flood].

hemlock

he·mo·stat·ic, haemostatic (hē·ma·stat'·ik) *n.* an agent which stops bleeding; a styptic. Also *a.* [Gk. *haima*, blood; *stasis*, a standing].

hemp (hemp) *n.* a plant whose fiber is used in the manufacture of coarse cloth, ropes, cables, etc. **-en** *a.* [O.E. *henep*].

hen (hen) *n.* the female of any bird, esp. the domestic fowl; (*Colloq.*) the female of certain crustaceans, e.g. the lobster, crab, etc. **-coop** *n.* a large cage for poultry. **-party** *n.* (*Slang*) a social gathering of women only. **-peck** *v.t.* to domineer over a husband [O.E. *henn*].

hence (hens) *adv.* from this point; for this reason; *interj.* go away! begone! **-forth, -forward** *adv.* from now [M.E. *hennes*].

hench·man (hench'·man) *n.* a servant; a loyal supporter [M.E. *henxi-man*, a groom].

hen·dec·a·gon (hen·dek'·a·gán) *n.* a plane figure having eleven sides [Gk. *hendeka*, eleven; *gōnia*, an angle; *sullabē*, a syllable].

hen·na (hen'·a) *n.* a shrub or small tree of the Near East; a dye made from it [Ar. *hinna*].

hep (hep) *a.* (*Slang*) informed; smart.

he·pat·ic (hi·pat'·ik) *a.* pert. to the liver. **hepatitis** *n.* [Gk. *hēpar*, the liver].

hep·ta- (hep'·ta) *prefix* from Greek, *hepta*, seven, combining to form derivatives. **-l** *n.* a group of seven. **-gon** *n.* a plane figure with seven sides. **-gonal** *a.* **-meter** *n.* a line of verse of seven feet.

hep·tar·chy (hep'·tár·ki·) *n.* government by seven persons; the country governed by them; a group of seven kingdoms [Gk. *hepta*, seven; *archein*, to rule].

her (hur) *pron.* the objective case of the pronoun **she**; also, the possessive case used adjectivally. **hers** *pron.* the absolute possessive case. **herself** *pron.* emphatic and reflexive form [O.E. fr. *hire*, gen. and dat. of *heo*, she].

her·ald (her'·ald) *n.* an officer who makes royal proclamations, arranges ceremonies, keeps records of those entitled to armorial bearings, etc.; a messenger; an envoy; a forerunner. **heraldic** (he·ral'·dik) *a.* **-ry** *n.* the art or office of a herald; the science of recording genealogies and blazoning armorial bearings [O.Fr. *herault*].

herb (urb, hurb) *n.* a plant with a soft stem which dies down after flowering; a plant of which parts are used for medicine, food, or scent. **-aceous** (hur·bā'·shas) *a.* pert. to herbs. **-age** *n.* herbs; nonwoody vegetation; (*Brit.*) green food for cattle. **-al** *a.* pert. to herbs; *n.* a book on herbs. **-alist** *n.* dealer in herbs [L. *herba*, grass].

Her·cu·les (hur'·kya·lēz) *n.* (*Myth.*) Latin name of Greek hero Heracles distinguished for his prodigious strength; hence any person of extraordinary strength and size. **Herculean** *a.*

herd (hurd) *n.* a number of animals feeding or traveling together; a drove of cattle; a large number of people; *v.i.* to go in a herd; *v.t.* to tend (a herd); to drive together. **-er** *n.* **-sman** *n.* one who tends cattle [O.E. *hirde*].

here (hēr) *adv.* in this place; at or to this point (opposed to *there*). **-about, -abouts** *adv.* about this place. **-after** *adv.* after this; *n.* a future existence. **-by** *adv.* by means of this; by this. **-in** *adv.* in this. **-on** *adv.* hereupon. **-to** *adv.* to this. **-tofore** *adv.* up to the present; formerly. **-with** *adv.* with this [O.E. *her*].

he·red·i·ty (ha·red'·a·ti·) *n.* the transmission of characteristic traits and qualities from parents to offspring. **hereditable** *a.* heritable **hereditament** *n.* (*Law*) property that may be inherited. **hereditary** *a.* descending by inheritance [L. *heres*, an heir].

her·e·sy (her'·a·si·) *n.* opinion contrary to orthodox opinion, teaching, or belief. **heresiarch** (ha·rē'·zi·árk) *n.* the originator or leader of a heresy. **heretic** *n.* one holding opinions contrary to orthodox faith. **heretical** *a.* [Gk. *hairesis*, a choice, a school of thought].

her·it·a·ble (her'·a·ta·bl) *a.* that can be inherited; attached to the property or house, as opposed to movable. **heritage** *n.* that which may be or is inherited. **heritor** *n.* one who inherits [L. *heres*, an heir].

her·maph·ro·dite (hur·maf'·ra·dīt) *n.* and *a.* animal or flower with the characteristics of both sexes; having normally both sexual organs. **hermaphroditic, hermaphroditical** *a.* **hermaphrodism, hermaphroditism** *n.* [Gk. *Hermaphroditos*, the son of *Hermes* and *Aphrodite* who became joined in one body with a nymph called Salmacis].

her·met·ic (hur·met′·ik) a. pert. to alchemy; magical; sealed. — **sealing**, the airtight closing of a vessel by fusion [Gk. *Hermes*].

her·mit (hur′·mit) n. a person living in seclusion, esp. from religious motives; a recluse. **-age** n. the abode of a hermit [Gk. *erēmitēs*, fr. *erēmos*, solitary].

her·ni·a (hur′·ni·a) n. (Med.) the external protrusion of any internal part through the enclosing membrane; rupture [L.].

he·ro (hē′·rō) n. (fem. **heroine** (her′·ō·in)) one greatly regarded for his achievements or qualities; the chief man in a poem, play, or story; an illustrious warrior. pl. **-es. heroic** a. pert. to a hero; bold; courageous; illustrious; narrating the exploits of heroes, as a poem; denoting the verse or measure in such poems. **heroical** a. **heroically** adv. **heroics** n.pl. high-flown language; bombastic talk. **heroism** (her′·ō·izm) n. courage; valor; bravery [Gk. *hērōs*, a demigod, a hero].

her·o·in (her′·ō·in) n. (Med.) habit-forming drug used as a sedative [Ger. trade name].

her·on (her′·an) n. a long-legged wading bird. [O.Fr. *hairon*; Fr. *héron*].

her·pes (hur′·pēz) n. a skin disease. **herpetic** a. [Gk. fr. *herpein*, to creep].

her·pe·tol·o·gy (her·pa·tàl′·a·ji·) n. the study of reptiles [Gk. *herpein*, to creep].

Herr (her) n. the German equivalent of Mr. pl. **Herren** [Ger. *Herrenvolk*, master race].

her·ring (her′·ing) n. a familiar sea-fish, moving in shoals, much used as a food. **-bone** n. a zig-zag pattern. **red herring**, herring cured and dried by a special process; (Fig.) subject deliberately introduced into a discussion to divert criticism from main issue [O.E. *haering*].

hers See **her**.

hes·i·tate (hez′·a·tāt) v.i. to feel or show indecision; to hold back; to stammer. **hesitant** a. pausing; slow to decide. **hesitance, hesitancy** n. **hesitation** n. doubt; indecision. **hesitantly, hesitatingly** adv. [L. *haesitare*, fr. *haerere*, to stick fast].

Hes·per·us (hes′·per·as) n. the planet Venus as the evening star. **Hesperian** (hes·pē′·ri·an) a. western [Gk. *hesperos*, evening].

Hes·sian (he′·shan) a. pert. to Hesse, in Germany; n. a native of Hesse. — **boots**, high, tasseled boots first worn by Hessian troops.

het·er·o·dox (het′·a·ra·dàks) a. contrary to accepted opinion, esp. in theology; not orthodox; heretical. **-y** n. [Gk. *heteros*, different; *doxa*, an opinion].

het·er·o·ge·ne·ous (het·er·a·jē′·ni·as) a. composed of diverse elements; differing in kind; dissimilar. **heterogeneity, -ness** n. [Gk. *heteros*, different; *genos*, kind].

het·er·o·gen·e·sis (het·er·ō·jen′·a·sis) n. (Biol.) spontaneous generation. **heterogenetic** a. [Gk. *heteros*, different; *genesis*, generation].

het·er·o·sex·u·al (het·er·ō·sek′·shoo·al) a. directed towards the opposite sex [Gk. *heteros*, different; L. *sexus*].

hew (hū) v.t. to chop or cut with an ax or sword; to cut in pieces; to shape or form. pa.p. **-ed** or **-n. -er** n. [O.E. *heawan*].

hex (hex) n. a witch; (Colloq.) a jinx.

hex·a- prefix from Gk. *hex*, six, combining to form derivatives, e.g. **-gon** n. a plane figure having six sides and six angles. **-gonal** a. **-hedron** n. solid figures having six faces, e.g. a cube. [Gk. *gōnia*, an angle; *hedra*, a base; L. *angulus*, a corner].

hexagon

hex·ad (hek′·sad) n. a group of six [Gk. *hex*, six].

hex·am·e·ter (hek·sam′·a·ter) n. a verse of six feet [Gk. *hex*, six; *metron*, a measure].

hex·a·pod (hek′·sa·pàd) n. a six-footed insect [Gk. *hex*, six; *pous*, a foot].

hey (hā) interj. used to call attention, or to express joy, wonder, or interrogation. **-day** n. the time of fullest strength and greatest vigor.

hi·a·tus (hi·ā′·tas) n. a gap in a series: an opening; a lacuna; the pronunciation without elision of two adjacent vowels in successive syllables [L. fr. *hiare*, to gape].

hi·ber·nate (hi′·ber·nāt) v.i. to winter; to pass the winter, esp. in a torpid state. **hibernation** n. [L. *hibernare*, fr. *hiems*, winter].

Hi·ber·ni·a (hi·bur′·ni·a) the Latin name for Ireland. **Hibernian** a., n.

hi·bis·cus (hi·bis′·kas) n. (Bot.) a genus of shrubs or tree with large flowers [Gk. *hibiskos*].

hic·cup (hik′·up) n. a spasm of the breathing organs with an abrupt cough-like sound; the sound itself; v.i. to have this. pr.p. **-ping**. pa.p. and pa.t. **-ped** [of imit. origin].

hick (hik) n. (Slang) a farmer.

hick·o·ry (hik′·a·ri·) n. a nut-bearing tree; its tough wood [*pohickery*, native name].

hi·dal·go (hi·dal′·gō) n. a Spanish nobleman [Sp. *hijo de algo* = son of something].

hide (hid) v.t. to put or keep out of sight; to keep secret; v.i. to lie concealed. pa.p. **hidden, hid. pa.t. hid. hidden** a. concealed; secret; unknown. **hiddenly** adv. **hiding** n. concealment; a place of concealment [O.E. *hydan*].

hide (hid) n. skin of an animal; the dressed skin of an animal; (Slang) human skin; v.t. (Colloq.) to flog. **-bound** a. of animals, having the skin too close to the flesh; bigoted; narrow-minded. **hiding** n. (Colloq.) a flogging [O.E. *hyd*].

hid·e·ous (hid′·ē·as) a. repulsive; revolting; horrible; frightful. **-ly** adv. [Fr. *hideux*].

hie (hi) v.i. and refl. to go quickly; to hurry on; to urge on [O.E. *higian*, to strive].

hi·er·arch (hi′·er·àrk) n. one who has authority in sacred things; a chief priest. **-al, -ical** a. **-ically** adv. **-y** n. a graded system of people or things; government by priests; the organization of the priesthood according to different grades; each of the three orders of angels. [Gk. *hieros*, holy; *archein*, to rule].

hi·er·at·ic (hi·er·at′·ik) a. priestly; pert. to a cursive style of ancient Egyptian writing, used by the priests [Gk. *hieratikos*, priestly].

hi·er·o- prefix from Gk. *hieros*, holy, combining to form derivatives, e.g. **hierograph** n. a sacred inscription. **hierology** n. the science or study of sacred things, esp. of the writings of the ancient Egyptians.

hi·er·o·glyph·ic (hi·er·a·glif′·ik) (usually pl.) n. ancient Egyptian characters or symbols used in place of letters; picture-writing. Also **hieroglyph. hieroglyphic, hieroglyphical** a. [Gk. *hieros*, holy; *gluphein*, to carve].

hig·gle (hig′·l) v.i. to dispute about terms, esp. in bargaining [fr. E. *haggle*].

high (hi) a. elevated; tall; towering; far up; elevated in rank, etc.; chief; eminent; proud; loud; angry, as words; strongly marked, as color; dear; costly; extreme; sharp, as tone or voice; tainted, as meat; remote from equator, as latitude; (Colloq.) drunk; adv. far up; strongly; to a great extent. **-ly** adv. **-ball** n. mixed whisky and soda. —**born** a. of noble birth. **-bred** a. of superior breeding, thoroughbred. **-brow** a. and n. (Colloq.) intellectual, esp. in a snobbish manner. —**falutin', -fa·luting** a. pretentious. —**frequency** n. (Radio) any frequency above the audible range. —**flown** a. elevated; extravagant. **-flyer, -flier** n. (Fig.) an ambitious person. **-lands** n.pl. a mountainous region. **Highlander** n. an inhabitant of a mountainous region, esp. highlands of Scotland. **-lights** n.pl (Art.) the brightest parts of a painting; (Fig.) moments of crisis; persons of importance. **-ness** n. the quality of being high; a title of honor to princes and princesses. **-pitched** a. of a shrill sound. **-road** n. a main road. — **school**, a school (grades 9 through 12), following grammar school; a school (grades 10 through 12), following junior high school (grades 7 through 9); — **seas**, the sea or ocean beyond the three-mile belt of coastal waters. **-spirited** a. bold; daring. —**strung** a. in a state of tension. — **treason**, any breach of allegiance due from a citizen to the government. — **water** n. a high tide at which the tide reaches its highest elevation. **-way** n. a main road; a public road; an ordinary route. **-wayman** n. a robber on a public road, esp. a mounted one [O.E. *heah*].

hi·jack·er (hi′·jak·er) n. (Slang) one who robs; a smuggler or a bootlegger.

hike (hik) v.i. to walk; to tramp; v.t. to hoist or carry on one's back; n. a journey on foot. **-r** n.

hi·lar·i·ous (hi·la′·ri·as) a. mirthful; joyous.

-ly adv. **hilarity** n. merriment; boisterous joy [Gk. *hilaros*, cheerful].

hill (hil) n. a natural elevation of land; a small mountain; a mound; v.t. to heap up. **-y** a. full of hills. **-iness** n. **-ock** n. a small hill [O.E. *hyll*].

hilt (hilt) n. the handle of a sword, dagger, etc. [O.E. *hilt*].

him (him) pron. the objective case of the pronoun **he. -self** pron. emphatic and reflexive form of **he** and **him** [O.E.].

hind (hind) n. the female of the deer.

hind, hind·er (hind, hind′·er) a. at the back; placed at the back; a combining form in such words as **-leg. -most** a. the furtherest behind; the last [O.E. *hinder*].

hin·der (hin′·der) v.t. to prevent from progressing; to stop. **-er** n. **hindrance** n. the act of impeding progress; obstruction; obstacle [O.E. *hindrian*, to keep back].

Hin·du·stan (hind′·doo·stan) n. (Geog.) the name applied to the country of the upper valley of the R. Ganges, India. **Hindi, Hindes** (hin′·dē) n. an Indo-Germanic language spoken in N. India. **Hindoo** (hin′·dòò) n. a native of Hindustan. **Hindustani, Hindoostanee** n. chief language of Hindu India; also known as 'Urdu' [Urdu, *Hind*, India].

hinge (hinj) n. a movable joint, as that on which a door, lid, etc. hangs; point on which thing depends; v.t. to attach with, or as with a hinge; v.i. to turn on; to depend on [M.E. *heng*].

hint (hint) n. a slight allusion; an indirect suggestion; an indication; v.t. and i. to allude to indirectly [O.E. *hentan*, to seize].

hin·ter·land (hint′·er·land) n. the district inland from the coast or a river [Ger.].

hip (hip) n. the upper part of the thigh; the haunch; the angle of 2 sloping sides of a roof; interj. a cheer [O.E. *hype*].

hip (hip) n. the fruit of the rose, esp. of the wild-rose [O.E. *heope*].

hip·ped (hipt) a. (Slang) obsessed (with on) [corrupt. of *hypochondria*].

Hip·poc·ra·tes (hi·pák′·ra·tēz) n. a Greek physician, the 'Father of Medicine,' born about 460 B.C. **Hippocratic** a. pert. to him.

hip·po·drome (hip′·a·drōm) n. in ancient Greece and Rome, a stadium for horse and chariot races; an arena [Gk. *hippos*, a horse; *dromos*, a course].

hip·po·pot·a·mus (hip·a·pát′·a·mas) n. a very large pachydermatous African quadruped frequenting rivers. pl. **-es** or **hippopotami** (hip·a·pát′·a·mi) [Gk. *hippos*, a horse; *potamos*, a river].

hir·cine (hur′·sin) a. pert. to a goat; strong-smelling (like a goat) [L. *hircus*, a goat].

hire (hir) n. payment for the use of a thing; wages; a hiring or being hired; v.t. to pay for the use of a thing; to contract with for wages; to take care of or give on hire. **-r** n. **-ling** n. one who serves for wages (generally used in contempt) [O.E. *hur*, wages].

hir·sute (hur′·sòòt) a. hairy; (Bot.) set with bristles [L. *hirsutus*, hairy].

his (hiz) pron. and a. the possessive case of the pronoun **he**, belonging to him [O.E.].

his·pid (his′·pid) a. (Bot.) bristly; having rough hairs [L. *hispidus*, rough].

hiss (his) v.i. to make a sound like that of *ss* as in 'ass,' esp. to express strong dislike or disapproval; n. the sound. **-ing** n. [imit.].

hist (hist) interj. a word used to command attention or silence.

his·ta·mine (his′·ta·mēn) n. substance released by the tissues in allergic reactions [*histidine* + *amine*].

his·to- prefix from Gk. *histos*, a web or tissue, combining to form derivatives, e.g. —**histology** (his·tál′·a·ji·) n. the science that treats of the minute structure of the tissues of animals, plants, etc. [Gk. *histos*, tissue; *logos*, a discourse]

his·to·ry (his′·tạ·ri·) *n.* the study of past events; a record of events in the life of a nation, state, institution, epoch, etc.; a description of animals, plants, minerals, etc. existing on the earth, called **natural history. historian** (his·tō′·ri·ạn) *n.* a writer of history. **historic** *a.* pert. to, or noted in, history. **historical** *a.* of, or based on, history; belonging to the past. **historically** *adv.* **historicity** *n.* the historical character of an event; the genuineness of it [Gk. *historia*, an inquiry].

his·tri·on·ic (his·trē·án′·ik) *a.* theatrical; affected. **-al** *a.* **-ally** *adv.* **-s** *n.pl.* theatrical representation [L. *histrio*, an actor].

hit (hit) *v.t.* to strike with a blow or missile; to affect severely; to find; *v.i.* to strike; to light (upon). *pr.p.* **-ting.** *pa.p.* and *pa.t.* **hit.** *n.* a blow; a stroke; a success [O.E. *hyttan*].

hitch (hich) *v.t.* to raise or move with a jerk; to fasten with a loop; etc.; to hobble; to be caught or fastened; *n.* a jerk; a fastening, loop, or knot; a difficulty; (*Slang*) to marry. **-er** *n.* **to -hike**, to travel by begging rides from motorists, etc. [etym. uncertain].

hith·er (hiTH′·ẹr) *adv.* to or toward this place; *a.* situated on this side. **-most** *a.* nearest in this direction. **-to** *adv.* up to now [O.E. *hider*].

hive (hiv) *n.* a place where bees live; place of great activity; *v.t.* to gather or place bees in a hive; *v.i.* to enter a hive; to take shelter together; to live in company [O.E. *hyf*].

hives (hivz) *n.* an eruptive skin disease.

hoar (hōr) *a.* gray with age; grayish-white. **-y** *a.* white or gray with age; venerable; of great antiquity. **-frost** *n.* white frost; frozen dew [O.E. *har*].

hoard (hōrd) *n.* a stock or store, esp. if hidden away; a treasure; *v.t.* to store secretly; *v.i.* to lay up a store. **-er** *n.* [O.E. *hord*, treasure].

hoarse (hōrs) *a.* rough and harsh sounding; husky; having a hoarse voice. **-ly** *adv.* **-ness** *n.* [O.E. *has*].

hoax (hōks) *v.t.* to deceive by an amusing or mischievous story; to play a trick upon for sport; *n.* a practical joke. **-er** *n.* [contr. fr. *hocus*].

hob (hắb) *n.* the flat-topped casing of a fireplace where things are placed to be kept warm. **-nail** *n.* a large-headed nail for boot soles.

hob (hắb) *n.* an elf; (*Colloq.*) mischief. **-goblin** *n.* a mischievous elf; a bogy [corrupt. of *Robin* or *Robert*].

hob·ble (hắb′·l) *v.i.* to walk lamely; to limp; *v.t.* to tie the legs together of a horse, etc.; to impede; *n.* a limping gait; a fetter; a rope for hobbling [etym. uncertain].

hob·ble·de·hoy (hắb′·l·di·hoi) *n.* a clumsy youth [etym. uncertain, perh. fr. *hobble*].

hob·by (hắb′·i·) *n.* formerly a small horse; a favorite pursuit or pastime. **-horse** *n.* a stick with a horse's head, or a rocking horse used as a child's toy; at fairs, etc. a wooden horse on a merry-go-round [*Hob*, for *Robert*].

hob·nail See **hob.**

hob·nob (hắb′·nắb) *v.i.* to drink together; to be very friendly with [etym. uncertain].

ho·bo (hō′·bō) *n.* a vagrant; a tramp.

hock (hắk) *n.* the joint of a quadruped's hind leg between the knee and the fetlock [O.E. *hoh*, the heel].

hock (hắk) *v.t., n.* pawn [D. *hok*, debt].

hock·ey (hắk′·i·) *n.* a game played with a ball or disk and curved sticks [perh. fr. O.Fr. *hoquet*, a crook].

ho·cus (hō′·kạs) *v.t.* to hoax; to stupefy with drugs. **hocus-pocus** *n.* an incantation; a juggler's trick; trickery [a sham L. formula used by jugglers].

hod (hắd) *n.* a small trough on a staff used by builders for carrying mortar, bricks, etc. [Fr. *hotte*, a basket].

hodge-podge (hắj′·pắj) *n.* a medley or mixture. Also **hotchpotch** [fr. *hocher*, to shake; *pot*, a pot].

hoe (hō) *n.* a tool for breaking ground, scraping out weeds, etc.; *v.t.* to break up or weed with a hoe. **-r** *n.* [O.Fr. *houe*].

hoe-down (hō′·doun) *n.* lively square dance.

hog (hawg, hắg) *n.* a swine; a pig, esp. if reared for fattening; (*Colloq.*) a greedy or dirty fellow; *v.t.* (*Slang*) to take more than one's share of; to cut (horse's mane short); *v.i.* to arch the back. **-gish** *a.* like a hog. **-back, -s-back** *n.* a crested hill-ridge. **-tie** *v.*

(*Colloq.*) to make incapable as if by tying up. **-wash** *n.* kitchen swill etc. used for feeding pigs; anything worthless [O.E. *hogg*].

hogs-head (hawgz′·, hågz′·hed; hawgz′·ạd) *n.* a large cask; a liquid measure [etym uncertain].

hoi pol·loi (hoi′·pạ·loi′) *n.pl.* the masses [Obs.].

hoist (hoist) *v.t.* to raise aloft, esp. of flags; to raise with tackle, etc.; *n.* a hoisting; an elevator; a lift [Dut. *hijschen*, to hoist].

hold (hōld) *v.t.* to keep fast; to grasp; to support in or with the hands, etc.; to own; to occupy; to detain; to celebrate; to believe; to contain; *v.i.* to cling; not to give way; to abide (by); to keep (to); to proceed; to be in force. *pa.p.* and *pa.t.* **held.** *n.* a grasp; grip; handle; binding power and influence; a prison. **-er** *n.* **-ing** *n.* land, farm, etc. rented from another; stocks held. **to hold up**, to support; to cause delay; to obstruct; to commit robbery with threats of violence [O.E. *healdan*].

hold (hōld) *n.* the space below the deck of a ship, for cargo [earlier *hole*].

hole (hōl) *n.* a hollow; cavity; pit; den; lair; burrow; opening; a perforation; mean habitation; (*Colloq.*) awkward situation; *v.t.* to make a hole in; to perforate; to put into a hole; *v.i.* to go into a hole [O.E. *hol*, a hollow].

hol·i·day (hắl′·ạ·dā) *n.* a day of rest from work esp. in memory of an event or a person [fr. *holy day*].

Hol·land·er (hắl′·ạn·dẹr) *n.* a native of Holland, the Netherlands.

hol·ler (hắl′·ẹr) *v.* (*Dial.*) shout; yell.

hol·low (hắl′·ō) *n.* a cavity; a hole; a depression; a valley; *a.* having a cavity; not solid; empty; *v.t.* to make a hollow in. **-eyed** *a.* with sunken eyes. **-toned** *a.* deep toned. **-ware** *n.* silver serving dishes [O.E. *holh*].

hol·ly (hắl′·i·) *n.* an evergreen shrub with prickly leaves and red berries [O.E. *holegn*].

hol·ly·hock (hắl′·ē·hắk) *n.* a tall garden plant [A.S. = *holy hock*, O.E. *hoc*, mallow].

hol·o- a combining form, fr. Gk. *holos*, whole, used in many derivatives. **-caust** (hắl′·ạ·kawst) *n.* a burnt offering; destruction, or slaughter. **-graph** *n.* and *a.* any writing, as a letter, deed, will, etc. wholly in the handwriting of the signer of it. **-graphic** *a.* [Gk. *kaustos*, burnt; *graphein*, to write]. [tol. **-ed** *a.* [Dut.].

hol·ster (hōl′·stẹr) *n.* a leather case for a pis-

ho·ly (hō′·li·) *a.* belonging to, or devoted to, God; morally perfect; divine; sacred; pious; religious. **holily** *adv.* **holiness** *n.* the quality of being holy. **-day** *n.* a religious festival. **Holy Ghost, Holy Spirit**, the third person of the Godhead or Trinity. **Holy Land**, Palestine. **-orders** *n.* the office of a clergyman; the Christian ministry [O.E. *halig*].

hom·age (hắm′·ij, ắm′·ij) *n.* in feudal times, service due by a vassal to his over-lord; tribute; respect paid; reverence; deference [Fr. *hommage*, fr. *homme*, a man].

hom·burg (hắm′·burg) *n.* a type of men's soft, felt hat [fr. *Homburg*, in Germany].

home (hōm) *n.* one's fixed residence; a dwellingplace; a native place or country; an institution for the infirm, sick, poor, etc.; *a.* pert. to, or connected with, home; not foreign; domestic; *adv.* to or at one's home; to the point aimed at; close. **-economics** *n.pl.*, theory and practice of homemaking. **-lessness** *n.* the state of being without a home. **-ly** *a.* belonging to home; plain; ugly. **-liness** *n.* **-grown** *a.* grown in one's own garden, locality, etc. **-land** *n.* one's native land. **-made** *a.* made at home. **-rule** *n.* self-government. **-run** *n.* (*Baseball*) a safe hit that allows a batter to touch all bases to score a run. **-sick** *a.* depressed in spirits through absence from home. **-sickness** *n.* **-spun** *a.* spun or made at home; anything plain or homely. **-stead** *n.* a house with

land and buildings. **-stretch** *n.* on a racecourse, the part between the last curve and the finish line; the final stage. **-work** *n.* schoolwork to be done outside of class. [O.E. *ham*].

home (hōm) *v.i.* of a pigeon, to fly home; *v.t.* in naval warfare, to guide (another ship or aircraft) by radio to the attack of a target.

ho·me·op·a·thy (hō·mē·áp′·ạ·thi·) *n.* the treatment of disease by the administration of very small doses of drugs which would produce in a healthy person effects similar to the symptoms of the disease. Also **homeotherapy. homeopath, homeopathist** *n.* **homeopathic** *a.* [Gk. *homoios*, like; *pathos*, feeling].

hom·i·cide (hắm′·ạ·sīd) *n.* manslaughter; the one who kills. **homicidal** *a.* [L. *homo*, a man; *caedere*, to kill].

hom·i·ly (hắm′·ạ·li·) *n.* a discourse on a religious or moral subject; a sermon. **homilist** *n.* [Gk. *homilia*, converse].

hom·i·ny (hắm′·ạ·ni·) *n.* maize porridge [Amer.-Ind.].

ho·mo- a combining form fr. Gk. *homos*, the same, used in derivatives. **-centric** *a.* having the same center.

ho·moe·o·path. See **homeopathy.**

ho·mog·e·ne·ous (hō·mạ·jē′·ni·ạs) *a.* of the same kind or nature; similar; uniform. **-ness, homogeneity** (hō·mạ·jạ·nē′·ạ·ti·) *n.* sameness; uniformity. **homogenize** *v.* to make uniform [Gk. *homo*, the same; *genos*, a kind].

hom·o·graph (hắm′·ạ·graf) *n.* a word having the same spelling as another, but different meaning and origin [Gk. *homos*, the same; *graphein*, to write].

ho·mol·o·gate (hō·mắl′·ạ·gāt) *v.t.* to approve; to confirm. **homologous** *a.* having the same relative value, position, etc. **homologation** *n.* [Gk. *homos*, the same; *legein*, to say].

hom·o·nym (hắm′·ạ·nim) *n.* a word having the same pronunciation as another but a different meaning, e.g. *air* and *heir*. Also **homophone** [Gk. *homos*, the same; *onoma*, a name].

ho·mo sa·pi·ens (hō′·mō·sā′·pi·ạns) scientific term for human being, man.

ho·mo·sex·u·al·i·ty (hō·mạ·sek·shoo·al′·ạ·ti·) *n.* attraction between individuals of the same sex. **homosexual** *n.* a person thus perverted [Gk. *homos*, the same; and *sex*].

hone (hōn) *n.* a stone for sharpening knives, etc. *v.t.* to sharpen on one [O.E. *han*, a stone].

hon·est (án′·ist) *a.* upright; dealing fairly; just; faithful; free from fraud; unadulterated. **-ly** *adv.* **-y** *n.* upright conduct or disposition; (*Bot.*) a small flowering plant with semi-transparent, silvery pods [L. *homestus*, honorable].

hon·ey (hun′·i·) *n.* the sweet, thick fluid collected by bees from flowers; anything very sweet; sweetness; (*Colloq.*) sweetheart; darling; *a.* sweet; luscious; *v.t.* to sweeten. *pa.p.* and *a.* **-ed** (hun′·id). Also **honied** *a.* sweet; (*Fig.*) flattering. **-bee** *n.* the common hive-bee. **-comb** *n.* the structure of wax in hexagonal cells in which bees place honey, eggs, etc.; anything resembling this; *v.t.* to fill with cells or perforations. **-combed** *a.* **-dew** (hun′·i·dū) *n.* a sweet sticky substance found on plants; a melon. **-moon** *n.* the holiday taken by a newlywed couple. Also, *v.i.* **-suckle** *n.* a climbing plant with yellow flowers [O.E. *hunig*].

honk (hawngk) *n.* the cry of the wild goose; any sound resembling this [imit.].

honk·y-tonk (háng′·ki·tángk) *n.* (*Slang*) a cheap saloon [echoic].

hon·or (án′·ẹr) *n.* high respect; renown; glory; reputation; sense of what is right or due; a source or cause of honor; high rank or position; a title of respect given to a judge, etc.; chastity; *v.t.* to respect highly; to confer a mark of distinction on; to accept or pay (a bill, etc.) when due. **-s** *n.pl.* public marks of respect or distinction; distinction given a student for outstanding work. **-able** *a.* worthy of honor; upright; a title of distinction or respect. **-ably** *adv.* **-ableness** *n.* **an affair of honor**, a duel. **maid of honor**, a lady in the service of a queen or princess; chief attendant of a bride. [Fr. *honneur*, fr. L. *honor*].

hon·or·ar·y (án′·ạ·rer·i·) *a.* conferred for the sake of honor only; holding a position without pay or usual requirements. **honorarium** (án·ạ·re′·ri·ạm) *n.* a sum of money granted voluntarily to a person for services rendered. **honorific** *a.* conferring honor; *n.* term of respect [L. *honorarius*].

hooch (hōōch) *n.* (*Slang*) alcoholic liquor [fr. Amer.-Ind. *hoochinoo*, spirit].

hood (hood) *n.* a covering for the head and neck, often part of a cloak or gown; an appendage to a graduate's gown designating his university and degree; the cover of an automobile engine; *v.t.* to cover with a hood. **-wink** *v.t.* to blindfold; to deceive [O.E. *hod*].

hood·lum (hōōd′·lạm) *n.* a hooligan.

hoo·doo (hōō′·dōō) (*Colloq.*) *n.* uncanny, bad luck; a cause of such luck [same as voodoo].

hoo·ey (hōō′·i·) *interj., n.* (*Slang*) nonsense.

hoof (hoof, hōōf) *n.* the horny casing of the foot of a horse, ox, sheep, etc.; *pl.* **-s, hooves** [O.E.]

hook (hook) *n.* a bent piece of metal, etc. for catching hold, hanging up, etc.; a bent piece of barbed steel for catching fish; anything curved or bent like a hook; *v.t.* and *i.* to fasten, draw, catch, etc. with a hook; to catch a fish with a hook; (*Golf*) to drive a ball in a curve to the left; (*Boxing*) to deliver a blow with bent elbow. **hooks and eyes**, bent metallic clips and catches used for fastening. **-up** *n.* the interconnection of broadcasting stations for relaying program; a connection [O.E. *hoc*].

hook·ah, hoo·ka (hoo'·ka) *n.* a tobacco pipe in which the smoke is drawn through water and a long tube [Ar. *huqqah*, a vessel].

hook·worm (hook'·wurm) *n.* (*Med.*) a parasitic worm, infesting the intestines.

hoo·li·gan (hoo'·i·gan) *n.* one of a gang of street roughs; a rowdy [name of a person].

hoop (hoop, hoop) *n.* a band for holding together the staves of casks, etc.; a circle of wood or metal for rolling as a toy; a stiff circular band to hold out a woman's skirt; *v.t.* to bind with a hoop. [O.E. *hop*].

hoot (hoot) *n.* the cry of an owl; a cry of disapproval; *v.t.* to assail with hoots; *v.i.* to cry as an owl; to cry out in disapproval. **-er** *n.* [imit.].

hooves (hoovz, hoovz) *pl.* of **hoof**.

hop (hap) *v.i.* of persons, to spring on one foot; of animals or birds, to leap or skip on all feet at once. *pr.p.* **-ping.** *pa.p.* and *pa.t.* **-ped.** *n.* an act or the action of hopping; (*Slang*) a dance; (*Aviation*) one stage in a flight. **-per** *n.* one who hops; a device for feeding material into a mill or machine; a railroad car with dumping device for coal, sand, etc. **hop·o·my·thumb** *n.* a dwarf [O.E. *hoppian*].

hop (hap) *n.* a climbing plant with bitter cones used to flavor beer, etc.; *v.t.* to flavor with hops. **-s** *n.pl.* the cones of the hop plant [Dut.].

hope (hop) *n.* a desire combined with expectation gives grounds for hoping; thing desired; *v.t.* to desire, with belief in possibility of obtaining; *v.i.* to feel hope. **-ful** *a.* **-fully** *adv.* **-fulness** *n.* **-less** *a.* **-lessly** *adv.* [O.E. *hopian*].

hop·scotch (hap'·skach) *n.* a child's game, played on an arrangement of squares [E. *hop*; *scotch*, a slight cut or score].

ho·ral (ho'·ral) *a.* of or pert. to an hour; hourly [L. *hora*, an hour].

horde (hord) *n.* a great multitude; a troop of nomads or tent-dwellers [Turk. *ordu*, a camp].

hore·hound (hor'·hound) *n.* a plant with bitter juice, used for coughs or as a tonic; a candy flavored with the herb. Also **hoarhound** [O.E. *harehune*].

ho·ri·zon (ha·ri'·zan) *n.* the boundary of the part of the earth seen from any given point; the line where earth (or sea) and sky seem to meet. **horizontal** (har·a·zan'·tal) *a.* parallel to the horizon; level. **horizontally** *adv.* [Gk. *horizein*, to bound].

hor·mone (hawr'·mon) *n.* a substance secreted by certain glands which passes into the blood and stimulates the action of various organs [Gk. *hormaein*, to set moving].

horn (hawrn) *n.* a hard projecting organ growing from heads of cows, deer, etc.; substance forming this organ; tentacle of a snail, etc.; a wind instrument of music; a drinking cup; a utensil for holding gunpowder; a sounding contrivance on motors as warning; either of the extremities of the crescent moon; *v.t.* to furnish with horns; to gore. **-y** *a.* of, or made of, horn; hard or callous. **-beam** *n.* a small tree or shrub. **-book** *n.* a primer for children, formerly covered with horn to protect it. **-pipe** *n.* an old musical instrument; a vigorous dance; the lively tune for such a dance. **horn of plenty**, or cornucopia; a representation of a horn, filled with flowers, fruit and grain [O.E.].

hor·net (hawr'·nat) *n.* a large insect of the wasp family [O.E. *hyrnet*, dim. of *horn*].

ho·ro- from Gk. *hora*, time; used as a combining form, e.g.—**horologe** (hawr'·a·loj) *n.* an instrument of any kind for telling the time. **horologer, horologist** *n.* **horology** *n.* the

science of measuring time; the art of making timepieces [Gk. *hora*, time; *legein*, to tell; *metron*, a measure].

hor·o·scope (hawr'·a·skop) *n.* a chart of of the heavens which predicts the character and potential abilities of the individual as well as future events. **horoscopic** *a.* [Gk. *hora*, time; *skopein*, to observe].

hor·rent (hawr'·ant) *a.* (*Poet.*) standing erect, as bristles; bristling [L. *horrere*, to bristle].

hor·ri·ble (hawr'·a·bl) *a.* tending to excite horror, fear, dread. **horribly** *adv.* **-ness** *n.* **horrid** *a.* frightful; shocking; abominable. **horrify** *v.t.* to strike with horror, dread, repulsion; to shock. **horrific** (ha, haw·rif'·ik) *a.* causing horror [L. *horrere*, to bristle].

hor·ror (ha', haw'·rer) *n.* a painful emotion of fear, dread and repulsion; that which excites dread and abhorrence [L. from *horrere*, to bristle].

horse (hawrs) *n.* a large hoofed quadruped used for riding, drawing vehicles, etc.; the male of the horse species, as distinct from the female (the mare); mounted soldiers; in gymnastics, a vaulting-block; a frame for drying clothes; *v.t.* to provide with a horse, or horses; to carry or support on the back; *v.i.* to mount on a horse. **horsy** *a.* pert. to horses; fond of, or interested in, horses. **horsiness** *n.* **-back** *n.* the back of a horse. **-fly** *n.* a stinging fly troublesome to horses. **-hair** *n.* hair from the tail or mane of a horse; haircloth. **-laugh** *n.* a loud boisterous laugh. **-man** *n.* a man on horseback; a skilled rider. **-manship** *n.* the art of riding or of training horses. — **opera** (*Film Slang*) a thriller film with a Wild West setting. **-pistol** *n.* an old kind of large pistol. **-play** *n.* rough and boisterous play. **-power** *n.* (abbrev. **h.p.**), the power a horse is capable of exerting; estimated (in *Mechanics*) to be the power of lifting 33,000 lb. one foot high in one minute. **-radish** *n.* a cultivated plant used for sauces, salads, etc. **-sense** *n.* (*Colloq.*) common sense. **-shoe** *n.* a curved, narrow band of iron for nailing to the underpart of the hoof [O.E. *hors*].

hor·ta·tive, hor·ta·tory (hawr'·ta·tiv, hawr'·ta·to·ri·) *a.* tending or serving to exhort; advisory [L. *hortari*, to exhort].

hor·ti·cul·ture (hawr'·ti·kul·cher) *n.* gardening; the art of cultivating a garden [L. *hortus*, garden; *colere*, to cultivate].

ho·san·na (ho·zan'·a) *n.* a cry of praise to God; an exclamation of adoration [Gk.].

hose (hoz) *n.* stockings; socks; a covering for the legs and feet; tight-fitting breeches or pants; a flexible tube or pipe for conveying water; *v.t.* to water with a hose. **hosier** (ho'·zher) *n.* dealer in hosiery. **hosiery** *n.* a collective word for stockings and similar garments [O.E. *hosa*].

hos·pice (has'·pis) *n.* a traveler's house of rest kept by a religious order [L. *hospitium*, fr. *hospes*, a guest].

hos·pi·ta·ble (has'·pi·ta·bl) *a.* receiving and entertaining guests in a friendly and liberal fashion. **hospitality** *n.* generous reception of strangers and guests [L. *hospes*, a guest].

hos·pi·tal (has'·pi·tal) *n.* an institution for the care of the sick. **-ization** *n.* being in the hospital. **-ize** *v.t.* [L. *hospes*, a guest].

host (host) *n.* one who lodges or entertains another; an innkeeper; an animal or plant which has parasites living on it. **-ess** *n.* a woman who entertains guests. **hostel** (has'·tal) *n.* a lodging place for young people who are hiking or traveling by bicycle; (*Arch.*) an inn. **hostelry** *n.* (*Arch.*) an inn [L. *hospes*, a host or guest].

host (host) *n.* a large number; a multitude; a crowd; (*Arch.*) an army. **the heavenly host**, the angels and archangels; the stars and planets [L. *hostis*, an enemy].

Host (host) *n.* the bread consecrated in the Eucharist [L. *hostia*, a sacrificial victim].

hos·tage (has'·tij) *n.* one handed over to the enemy as security [O.Fr. *hostage*, fr. L. *hospes*, a guest].

hos·tel See **host**.

hos·tile (has'·tal) *a.* of, or pert. to, an enemy; unfriendly; opposed. **-ly** *adv.* **hostility** *n.* opposition; *pl.* state or acts of warfare [L. *hostis*, an enemy].

hos·tler, ostler (has'·ler, as'·ler) *n.* (*Arch.*) a groom at an inn [O.Fr. *hostel*].

hot (hat) *a.* of high temperature; very warm; of quick temper; ardent or passionate; (of dance music) florid and intricate. **-ly** *adv.* **-ness** *n.* **-bed** *n.* in gardening, a glass-covered bed for bringing on plants quickly; hence (*Fig.*) any place conducive to quick growth (e.g. of scandal, vice, etc.). —**blooded** *a.* high-spirited; quick to anger. **-dog** *n.* (*Colloq.*) a sandwich roll with hot sausage inside. **-foot** *adv.* swiftly; in great haste. **-head** *n.* an impetuous person. **-house** *n.* heated house, usually of glass for rearing of plants [O.E. *hat*].

ho·tel (ho·tel') *n.* a large and superior kind of inn. **-keeper** *n.* [Fr. *hotel*].

Hot·ten·tot (hat'·n·tat) *n.* a member of a native race of S. Africa [Dut. imit.].

hound (hound) *n.* a dog used in hunting, esp. in hunting by scent; (*Slang*) despicable man; (*Slang*) an addict or fan; *v.t.* to chase with, or as with, hounds; (with 'on') to urge or incite;

to pursue, to nag [O.E. *hund*].

hour (our) *n.* the twenty-fourth part of a day, or 60 minutes; the time of day; an appointed time or occasion; *pl.* the fixed times of work, prayers, etc. **-glass** *n.* a sand-glass running for an hour. — **hand** *n.* the index which shows the hour on the face of a watch, clock, or chronometer. **-ly** *adv.* happening every hour; frequently [L. *hora*].

hou·ri (hoo'·ri; hou'·ri·) *n.* a nymph of the Mohammedan paradise [Pers. *huri*].

house (hous) *n.* a dwelling-place; a legislative or other assembly; a family; a business firm; audience at theater, etc.; dynasty; a school residence hall. *pl.* **houses** (houz'·ez). **house** (houz) *v.t.* to shelter; to receive; to store; *v.i* to dwell. **housing** (hou'·zing) *n.* shelter; the providing of houses; a support for part of a machine, etc. **-ful** *a.* **-less** *a.* **-hold** *n.* the inmates of a house; *a.* domestic. **-keeper** *n.* the woman who attends to the care of the household. **-wife** *n.* the mistress of a family; a little case or bag for materials used in sewing. **-wifery** (hous'·wif·ri·) *n.* housekeeping. **-boat** *n.* a flat-bottomed barge, with a house-like superstructure. **—fly** *n.* the common fly or *musca domestica*. — **physician, — surgeon** *n.* the resident medical officer of a hospital, etc. **-warming** *n.* a merrymaking to celebrate entry into a new house. **the House**, the House of Representatives [O.E. *hus*].

hous·ing (hou'·zing) *n.* a saddle-cloth; *pl.* the trappings of a horse [Fr. *housse*].

hove (hov) *pa.p.* and *pa.t.* of **heave**.

hov·el (huv'·al, hav'·al) *n.* a small, mean house; *v.t.* to put in a hovel [dim. of O.E. *hof*, a dwelling].

hov·er (huv'·er, hav'·er) *v.i.* to hang fluttering in the air, or on the wing; to loiter; to waver.

how (hou) *adv.* in what manner; by what means; to what degree or extent; in what condition. **-beit** (hou·be'·it) *adv.* nevertheless. **-ever** (hou·ev'·er) *adv.* in whatever manner or degree; *conj.* in spite of how. **-soever** *adv.* however [O.E. *hu*].

how·itz·er (hou'·it·ser) *n.* a form of gun, with a high trajectory [Bohemian *houfnice*, an engine for hurling stones].

howl (houl) *v.i.* to utter a prolonged, wailing cry such as that of a wolf or dog; to cry; (*Colloq.*) to laugh heartily; *v.i.* to utter with howling; *n.* a wail or cry. **-er** *n.* one who howls; (*Colloq.*) a ridiculous blunder [imit. origin].

hoy·den, hoiden (hoi'·dn) *n.* a rude, bold girl; a tomboy. **-ish** *a.* romping; bold; boisterous.

hub (hub) *n.* the central part, or nave, of a wheel; center of activity [var. of *hob*].

hub·bub (hub'·ub) *n.* a commotion [imit.].

hub·by (hub'·i·) *n.* (*Colloq.*) husband.

huck·a·back (huk'·a·bak) *n.* a kind of coarse linen with an uneven surface, much used for towels. Also **huck** [L. Ger. *hukkebak*].

huck·le·ber·ry (huk'·l·ber·i·) *n.* an American shrub which bears small black or dark blue berries [O.E. *heorot-berge*].

huck·le·bone (huk'·l·bon) *n.* the hipbone; the anklebone [dim. of *huck*, hook].

huck·ster (huk'·ster) *n.* retailer of small articles; a street peddler; a mean, mercenary fellow; (*Colloq.*) an advertising man; *v.i.* to peddle [O.Dut. *hoekster*].

hud·dle (hud'·l) *v.t.* to crowd together; to heap together confusedly; *v.i.* to press together. **to go into a huddle with** (*Slang*) to meet in conference with [etym. uncertain].

hue (hu) *n.* color; tint. **-d** *a.* having a color (generally in compounds) [O.Fr. *hiw*].

hue (hu) *n.* an outcry; now only used in **hue and cry**, a loud outcry [Fr. *huer*, to hoot].

huff (huf) *n.* a fit of petulance or anger; *v.t.* to bully; *v.i.* to take offense. **-y** *a.*

hug (hug) *v.t.* to clasp tightly in the arms; to embrace; to cling to. *pr.p.* **-ging**. *pa.t.*, *pa.p.* **-ged.** *n.* a close embrace [etym. uncertain].

huge (huj) *a.* very large; immense; enormous. **-ly** *adv.* **-ness** *n.* [O.Fr. *ahuge*].

Hu·gue·not (hu'·ga·nat) *n.* a 16th cent. French Protestant [etym. uncertain].

huh (hu) *interj.* expressing contempt, surprise or to ask a question.

hu·la (hoo'·la) *n.* native Hawaiian dance.

hulk (hulk) *n.* the body of a ship, esp. dismantled ship; anything big and unwieldy; *v.i.* to be bulky; (*Dial.*) to slouch. **-ing, -y** *a.* unwieldy; clumsy [O.E. *hulc*, ship].

hull (hul) *n.* husk of any fruit, seed, or grain; frame or body of a vessel; *v.t.* to remove shell or husk; to pierce hull of, as of a ship [O.E. *hulu*, husk].

hul·la·ba·loo (hul'·ạ·bạ·lòò) *n.* uproar; outcry [imit. origin].

hul·lo, hul·loa (hạ·lō') *niterj.* hello.

hum (hum) *v.t.* to sing with the lips closed; *v.i.* to make droning sound, as bee. *n.* the noise of bees or the like; a low droning; (*Colloq.*) to be very busy. *pr.p.* **-ming.** *pa.p.* and *pa.t.* **-med** [imit. origin].

hu·man (hū'·mạn) *a.* belonging to, or having the qualities of, man or mankind. **-ly** *adv.* **-ness** *n.* **humane** (hū·mān') *a.* having the moral qualities of; man; kind; benevolent. **-ness** *n.* **-ism** *n.* a philosophic mode of thought devoted to human interests; literary culture. **-ist** *n.* one who pursues the study of human nature or the humanities. **-istic** *a.* pert. to humanity; pert. to humanism or humanists. **-ize** *v.t.* to render human or humane. **humanity** *n.* the quality of being human; human nature; the human race; kindness or benevolence. **humanities** *n.pl.* language, literature, art, philosophy, etc. **humanitarian** *n.* one who denies the divinity of Jesus; a philanthropist. **-kind** *n.* the whole race of man [L. *humanus*].

hum·ble (hum'·bl) *a.* lowly; meek; not proud, arrogant, or assuming; modest; *v.t.* to bring low; to make meek. **humbly** *adv.* **-ness** *n.* [L. *humilis*, fr. *humus*, the ground].

hum·bug (hum'·bug) *n.* a hoax; sham; nonsense; an impostor; *v.t.* to hoax; to deceive.

hum·drum (hum'·drum) *a.* commonplace; dull [redupl. of *hum*, imit. of monotony].

hu·mer·al (hū'·mẹr·ạl) *a.* belonging to the shoulder. **humerus** *n.* the long bone of the upper arm [L. *humerus*, the shoulder].

hu·mid (hū'·mid) *a.* damp; moist. **-ly** *adv.* **humidify** *v.t.* to make humid. **humidity**, **-ness** *n.* dampness; moisture. **humidor** *n.* a device for keeping the air moist in a jar, case, etc., such a case. [L. *humidus*, moist].

hu·mil·i·ate (hū·mil'·i·āt) *v.t.* to humble; to lower the dignity of. **humiliating** *a.* painfully humbling. **humiliation** *n.* **humility** *n.* the state of being humble and free from pride [L. *humiliare*, fr. *humilis*, low].

hum·mock (hum'·ạk) *n.* a hillock; a ridge on an ice field [dim. of *hump*].

hu·mor (hū'·, ū'·mẹr) *n.* quality of imagination quick to perceive the ludicrous or to express itself in an amusing way; fun; caprice; disposition; mood; state of mind; the fluids of animal bodies; *v.t.* to indulge; to comply with mood or whim of. **-esque** (hū·mẹr·esk') *n.* musical composition of fanciful character. **-ist** *n.* one who shows humor in speaking or writing. **-ous** *a.* full of humor. **-ously** *adv.* [L. *humor*, moisture].

hump (hump) *n.* the protuberance or hunch formed by a crooked back; a hillock; *v.t.* to bend into a hump shape. **-back** *n.* a person with a crooked back. **—backed** *a.* [etym. uncertain].

hu·mus (hū'·mạs) *n.* a brown or black constituent of the soil, composed of decayed vegetable or animal matter [L. *humus*, the ground].

Hun (hun) *n.* a barbarian.

hunch (hunch) *n.* a hump; (*Slang*) an intuition or presentiment; *v.t.* to bend or arch into a hump; *v.i.* to move forward in jerks.

hun·dred (hun'·drạd) *n.* a cardinal number, the product of ten times ten; the symbol 100 or C; *a.* ten times ten. **-fold** *a.* a hundred times as much. **-th** *a.* last, or one, of a hundred; *n.* one of a hundred equal parts. **-weight** *n.* an avoirdupois weight of 100 lb. written *cwt.* [O.E. *hund*, hundred, with *raed*, reckoning].

hung (hung) *pa.p.* and *pa.t.* of **hang.**

hun·ger (hung'·gẹr) *n.* discomfort or exhaustion caused by lack of food; a craving for food; any strong desire; *v.i.* to feel hunger; to long for; *v.t.* to starve. **hungry** *a.* feeling hunger. **hungrily** *adv.* **— strike** *n.* refusal of all food as a protest [O.E. *hungor*].

hunk (hungk) *n.* a lump [Prov. E.].

hunt (hunt) *v.t.* to pursue and prey on (as animals on other animals); to pursue animals or game for food or sport; to search diligently after; to drive away; to use in hunting (as a pack of hounds); *v.i.* to go out in pursuit of game; to search; *n.* the act of hunting; chase; search; an association of huntsmen. **-er** *n.* one who hunts; a horse or dog used in hunting [O.E. *huntian*].

hur·dle (hur'·dl) *n.* a barrier in a race course; an obstacle; *v.t.* to enclose with hurdles; to jump over; to master a problem, etc. [O.E. *hyrdle*].

hur·dy-gur·dy (hur'·di·gur'·di·) *n.* an old-fashioned musical instrument played by turn-

ing a handle; a street-organ [imit. origin].

hurdle

hurl (hurl) *v.t.* to send whirling; to throw with violence; *n.* a violent throw [etym. uncertain].

hur·ly-bur·ly (hur'·li·bur'·li·) *n.* tumult; bustle; confusion [etym. uncertain].

hur·rah, hurra (hạ·rá') *interj.* used as a shout of joy. Also **hurray** [Ger.].

hur·ri·cane (hur'·i·kān) *n.* a wind of 60 m.p.h. or over; a violent cyclonic storm of wind and rain. **— deck** *n.* the upper deck of steamboats. **— lamp** *n.* a candlestick or lamp with a chimney [Sp. *huracán*].

hur·ry (hur'·i·) *v.t.* to hasten; to impel to greater speed; to urge on; *v.i.* to move or act with haste; *n.* the act of pressing forward in haste; quick motion. **hurried** *a.* done in haste; working at speed. **hurriedly** *adv.*

hurt (hurt) *v.t.* to cause pain; to wound or bruise; to impair or damage; to wound feelings; *v.i.* to give pain; *n.* wound, injury, or harm. **-ful** *a.* [Fr. *heurter*, to run against].

hur·tle (hur'·tl) *v.t.* to fling, to dash against; *v.i.* to move rapidly; to rush violently; to dash (against) [See *hurt*].

hus·band (huz'·bạnd) *n.* a married man; *v.t.* to manage with economy; (*Obs.*) to till the soil. **-man** *n.* a farmer. **-ry** *n.* farming; thrift [O.E. *husbonda*, the master of the house].

hush (hush) *interj.* or *imper.* be quiet! silence! *n.* silence or stillness; *v.t.* to make quiet; (with *up*) to keep secret; *v.i.* to be silent [imit].

husk (husk) *n.* the dry, external covering of certain seeds and fruits; the chaff of grain; *pl.* waste matter; refuse; *v.t.* to remove the outer covering. **-y** *a.* full of husks; dry, esp. of the throat, hence, rough in tone; hoarse; (*Colloq.*) big and strong. **-ily** *adv.* **-iness** *n.*

husk·y (hus'·ki·) *n.* an Eskimo sled-dog.

hus·sar (hu·zàr') *n.* one of the light cavalry of European armies [Hung. *huszar*, a freebooter].

hus·sy (hus'·, huz'·i·) *n.* an ill-behaved woman; a saucy girl [contr. fr. *housewife*].

hus·tings (hus'·tingz) *n.* any platform from which political campaign speeches are made; election proceedings [O.E. *hus*, a house; thing, an assembly].

hus·tle (hus'·l) *v.t.* to push about; to jostle; *v.i.* to hurry; to bustle; *n.* speed; jostling. **-r** *n.* [Dut. *hutselen*, to shake up].

hut (hut) *n.* a small house or cabin [Fr. *hutte*].

hutch (huch) *n.* a chest or box; a grain-bin; a pen for rabbits, etc. [Fr. *huche*, a coffer].

huz·za, huzzah (hu·zà') *n.* a shout of joy or approval [Ger.].

hy·a·cinth (hi'·ạ·sinth) *n.* a bulbous plant; a purplish-blue color; a red variety of zircon. [Gk. *huakinthos*, doublet of *jacinth*].

hy·a·line (hi'·ạ·lin) *a.* glassy; transparent; crystalline [Gk. *hualos*, glass].

hy·brid (hi'·brid) *n.* the offspring of two animals or plants of different species; a mongrel; a word compounded from different languages; *a.* cross-bred [L. *hibrida*].

hy·dra (hi'·drạ) *n.* (*Myth.*) a monstrous water-serpent with many heads, slain by Hercules; (*Zool.*) a small fresh-water polyp [Gk. *hudra*, a water-snake].

hy·dran·gea (hi·drān'·ja) *n.* a genus of shrubs producing large flower clusters [Gk. *hudor*, water; *angeion*, a vessel].

hy·drant (hi'·drạnt) *n.* a water-pipe with a nozzle to which a hose can be attached; a fire-plug [Gk. *hudor*, water].

hy·drate (hi'·drāt) *n.* (*Chem.*) a compound of water with another compound or an element; *v.t.* to combine with water. **hydrated** *a.* **hydration** *n.* [Gk. *hudor*, water].

hy·drau·lic (hi·draw'·lik) *a.* pert. to hydraulics; relating to the conveyance of water; worked by water power [Gk. *hudor*, water; *aulos*, a pipe].

hy·dro- *prefix* fr. Gk. *hudor*, water, combining to form derivatives; in many compounds used to indicate hydrogen. **-carbon** *n.* a compound of hydrogen and carbon. **-cephalus** (hi·drŏ·sef'·ạ·las) *n.* (*Med.*) an excess of cerebrospinal fluid in the brain; water on the brain. **-cephalic, -cephalous** *a.* **-chloric** *a.* containing hydrogen and chlorine. **-chloric acid,**

a strong acid [Gk. *kelē*, a tumor; *kephalē*, the head; *chloros*, green].

hydrant

hy·dro·dy·nam·ics (hi·drŏ·dī·nam'·iks) *n.pl.* the branch of physics which deals with the flow of fluids, whether liquid or gases [Gk. *hudor*, water; *dunamis*, power; *kinein*, to move].

hy·dro·e·lec·tric (hi·drŏ·i·lek'·trik) *a.* pert. to the generation of electricity by utilizing water power [Gk. *hudor*, water].

hy·dro·gen (hi'·drạ·jạn) *n.* an inflammable, colorless, and odorless gas, the lightest of all known substances. **hydrogenous** (hi·drâ'·je·nạs) *a.* **— bomb** *n.* atom bomb of enormous power [Gk. *hudor*, water; *gennaein*, to produce].

hy·drol·o·gy (hi·dral'·ạ·ji·) *n.* the science of the properties, laws, etc. of water. **hydrolysis** (hi·drál'·ạ·sis) *n.* a chemical process by which the oxygen or hydrogen in water combines with an element, or some element of a compound, to form a new compound. **hydrolytic** *a.* [Gk. *hudor*, water; *logos*, a discourse; *luein*, to loosen].

hy·drom·e·ter (hi·dràm'·ạ·tẹr) *n.* a graduated instrument for finding the specific gravity, and thence the strength of liquids [Gk. *hudor*, water; *metron*, a measure].

hy·drop·a·thy (hi·dráp'·ạ·thi·) *n.* the treatment of diseases with water, including the use of cold or warm baths. Also **hydrotherapy.** [Gk. *hudor*, water; *pathos*, suffering].

hy·dro·pho·bi·a (hi·drạ·fō'·bi·ạ) *n.* an acute infectious disease in man caused by the bite of a mad dog; rabies; an extreme dread of water, esp. as a supposed symptom of the disease [Gk. *hudor*, water; *phobos*, fear].

hy·dro·plane (hi'·drạ·plān) *n.* an airplane designed to land on and take off from water; a kind of flat-bottomed boat designed to skim over the surface of the water [Gk. *hudor*, water; *sphaira*, a sphere].

hy·drous (hi'·drạs) *a.* containing water; containing hydrogen [Gk. *hudor*, water].

hy·e·na (hi·ē'·nạ) *n.* a carnivorous mammal of Asia and Africa, allied to the dog. **laughing hyena**, the striped hyena [Gk. *huaina*, sow-like].

hy·giene (hi·jēn) *n.* medical science which deals with the preservation of health. **hygienic** (hi·gē·en'·ik, hi·jen'·ik) *a.* pert. to hygiene; sanitary. **hygienist** *n.* [Gk. *hugiēs*, healthy].

hy·gro- *prefix* fr. Gk. *hugros*, moist, combining to form derivatives.

hy·gro·scope (hi'·grạ·skŏp) *n.* an instrument which indicates variations of humidity in the atmosphere, without showing its exact amount [Gk. *hugros*, moist; *skopein*, to view].

Hy·men (hi'·mạn) *n.* (*Myth.*) the god of marriage; (*l.c.*) membrane fold at entrance to female sex organs. **hymeneal** (hi·mạ·nē'·ạl) *a.* pert. to marriage [Gk. *humēn*].

hy·me·nop·ter·ous (hi·mạ·náp'·tẹr·as) *a.* belonging or pert. to an order of insects (Hymenoptera) as the bee, the wasp, etc. [Gk. *humēn*, membrane; *pteron*, a wing].

hymn (him) *n.* an ode or song of praise, esp. a religious one; a sacred lyric; *v.t.* to praise in song; *v.i.* to sing in worship. **-al** (him'·nạl) *n.* a hymn book [Gk. *humnos*, a festive song].

hy·per·bo·la (hi·pur'·bạ·la) *n.* (*Geom.*) a curve formed by a section of a cone when the cutting plane makes a greater angle with the base than the side of the cone makes. **hyperbolic** *a.* [Gk. *huper*, over; *bolē*, a throw].

hy·per·bo·le (hi·pur'·bạ·lē) *n.* (*Gram.*) a figure of speech which expresses much more or much less than the truth, for the sake of effect; exaggeration. **hyperbolic, hyperbolical** *a.* **hyperbolically** *adv.* **hyperbolize** *v.t.* and *i.* to state with hyperbole [Gk. *huper*, beyond; *bolē*, a throw].

hy·per·crit·ic (hi·pẹr·krit'·ik) *n.* one who is critical beyond measure or reason. **-al -ally** *adv.* [Gk. *huper*, over; *kritikos*, critical].

hy·per·phys·i·cal (hi·pẹr·fiz'·i·kal) *a.* supernatural [Gk. *huper*, beyond; *phusis*, nature].

hy·per·sen·si·tive (hi·pẹr·sen'·sạ·tiv) *a.* abnormally sensitive. **-ness, hypersensitivity** *n.* [Gk. *huper*, beyond; L. *sentire*, to feel].

hy·per·tro·phy (hi·pur'·trạ·fi·) *n.* (*Med.*) abnormal enlargement of organ or part of body [Gk. *huper*, over; *trophē*, nourishment].

hy·phen (hī′·fạn) *n.* a mark (-) used to connect syllables or compound words; *v.t.* to connect with a hyphen. **-ated** *a.* [Gk. *hupo*, under; *hen*, one].

hyp·no·sis (hip·nō′·sạs) *n.* the state of being hypnotized; abnormal sleep. **hypnotic** *a.* tending to produce sleep; pert. to hypnotism; *n.* a drug that induces sleep; a hypnotized person. **hypnotize** *v.t.* to produce a mental state resembling sleep. **hypnotism** *n.* an abnormal mental state resembling sleep. **hypnotist** *n.* [Gk. *hupnos*, sleep].   [beneath, below.

hy·po- (hī′·pŏ) *prefix* fr. Gk. meaning under,

hy·po·chon·dri·a (hip·ạ·kán′·dri·ạ) *n.* a mental disorder, in which one is tormented by melancholy and gloomy views, especially about one's own health. **hypochondriac** *a.* affected by hypochondria; *n.* a person so affected [Gk. *hupo*, under; *chondros*, a cartilage].

hy·poc·ri·sy (hi·pák′·ra·si·) *n.* simulation or pretense of goodness; feigning to be what one is not; insincerity. **hypocrite** (hip′·ạ·krit) *n.* one who dissembles his real nature; a

pretender to virtue or piety; a deceiver. **hypocritical** *a.* [Gk. *hupowritēs*, an actor].

hy·po·der·mic (hī·pạ·dur′·mik) *a.* pert. to parts underlying the skin; *n.* the injection of a drug beneath the skin by means of a needle and small syringe. **-ally** *adv.* [Gk. *hupo*, under; *derma*, the skin].

hy·pos·ta·sis (hī·pás′·tạ·sạs) *n.* essential nature of anything; the substance of each of the three divisions of the Godhead; (*Med.*) a deposit of blood in an organ; *pl.* **hypostases** [Gk. *hupo*, under; *stasis*, state].

hy·pot·e·nuse (hī·pát′·e·nōós) *n.* (*Geom.*) the side of a right-angled triangle which is opposite the right angle [Gk. *hupoteinousa*, extending under].

hy·poth·e·cate (hī·pá′·thạ·kāt) *v.t.* to give in security; to mortgage [Gk. *hupothēkē*, a pledge].

hy·poth·e·sis (hī·páth′·ạ·sis) *n. pl.* **hypotheses**, a supposition used as a basis from which to draw conclusions; a theory. **hypothesize** *v.i.* and *v.t.* to form and to assume by a hypothesis. **hypothetic, hypothetical** *a.* [Gk. *hupothesis*, a proposal].

hypotenuse

hys·te·ri·a, hysterics (his·ti′·ri·ạ, his·ter′·iks) *n.* an affection of the nervous system, characterized by excitability and lack of emotional control. **hysteric, hysterical.** *a.* **hysterically** *adv.* [Gk. *hustera*, womb].

I

I (ī) *pron.* the pronoun of the first person singular, the word by which a speaker or writer denotes himself [O.E. *ic*; cf. Ger. *ich*; L. *ego*; Gk. *egō*].

i·am·bus (ī·am′·bạs) *n.* a metrical foot of two syllables, the first short or unaccented, and the second long or accented. **iamb** *n.* shorter form of *iambus*, **iambic** *a.* [Gk.].

i·at·ric, iatrical (ī·at′·rik, ·al) *a.* pert. to physicians, medicine [Gk. *iatros*, physician].

I·ber·i·an (ī·bī′·ri·an) *a.* pert. to Iberia, viz. Spain and Portugal; *n.* early inhabitant of ancient Iberia [L. *Iberia*, Spain].

i·bex (ī′·beks) *n.* variety of wild goat [L.].

i·bis, *n.* a stork-like wading bird, allied to the spoonbills [Gk.].

I·car·i·an (ī·ker′·i·an) *a.* adventurous in flight; rash [fr. *Icarus*].

ice (īs) *n.* frozen water; a frozen dessert made with fruit juices and water; (*Slang*) diamonds; *v.t.* to cover with ice; to freeze; to chill with ice; to frost a cake; *pr.p.* **icing.** **— age** (*Geol.*) Pleistocene period, the series of glacial epochs. **—belt** *n.* the belt of ice fringing land in Arctic and Antarctic regions. **-berg** *n.* a detached portion of a glacier floating in the sea. **-blink** *n.* a whitish light due to reflection from a field of ice. **-boat** *n.* a boat adapted for being pulled over ice. **-bound** *a.* surrounded by or jammed in ice. **-breaker** *n.* a vessel designed to open passage through ice-bound waters; social start. **-cap** *n.* a glacier formed by the accumulation of snow and ice on a plateau and moving out from the center in every direction. **— cream** *n.* a frozen food made esp. of cream or milk sweetened and flavored. **—fall** *n.* a glacier as it flows over a precipice. **— field** *n.* a vast expanse of sea either frozen or covered with floating masses of ice. **— floe** *n.* a large mass of floating ice. **— hockey** *n.* game played by skaters on ice with a hard rubber disk (the puck). **— pack** *n.* drifting field of ice, closely packed together. **— pick** *n.* an implement for cutting ice. **— skate** *n.* a shoe fitted with a metal runner for skating on ice. **— sheet** *n.* an enormous glacier covering a huge area, valleys and hills alike. **icily** *adv.* coldly. **iciness** *n.* **icing** *n.* a covering of sugar on cakes, etc.; formation of ice on part of an airplane. **icy** *a.* pert. to ice; ice-like; frigid [O.E. *is*; Ger. *Eis*].

Ice·land·er (īs′·lan·dẹr) *n.* a native of Iceland. **Icelandic** *a.*

ich·nol·o·gy (ik·nál′·ạ·ji·), *n.* the classification of fossil footprints [Gk. *ichnos*, track; *logos*, a discourse].

i·chor (ī′·kawr, ·kẹr) *n.* (*Gk. Myth*) the fluid which flowed in the veins of the Gods; the colorless, watery discharge from ulcers. **-ous** *a.* [Gk. *ichor*].

ich·thy·ol·o·gy (ik·thi·ál′·ạ·ji·) *n.* the branch of zoology which treats of fishes. **ichthyological** *a.* **ichthyologist** *n.* **ichthyic** *a.* pert. to fish. **ichthyoid** *a.* fish-like [Gk. *ichthus*, fish; *logos*, discourse].

icebreaker

i·ci·cle (ī′·si·kl) *n.* a hanging conical mass of ice, slowly built up by freezing of drops of water [O.E. *isgicel*].

i·con (ī′·kán) *n.* any sign which resembles the thing it represents; a venerated representation of Christ, an angel, or a saint, found in Greek and Orthodox Eastern Churches. **-ic, -ical** *a.* pert. to icons. **-oclasm** *n.* act of breaking images; an attack on the cherished beliefs or enthusiasms of others. **-oclast** *n.* a breaker of images; one who exposes or destroys shams of any kind. **-ography** *n.* the making of an icon; the subject matter, or the analysis of an icon. **-olater** *n.* an image worshipper. **-olatry** *n.* image worship [Gk. *eikōn*, an image].

ic·ter·us (ik′·tạ·ras) *n.* jaundice. **icteric, icterical** *a.* [Gk. *ikteros*, jaundice].

id (id) *n.* in psycho-analysis, the primary source in individuals of instinctive energy and impulses [L. = it].

i·de·a (ī·dē′·ạ) *n.* a product of intellectual action; way of thinking; a thought; belief; plan; aim; principle at the back of one's mind. **ideal** *a.* existing in fancy only; perfect; satisfying desires; *n.* an imaginary type or norm of perfection to be aimed at. **idealization** *n.* **idealize** *v.t.* to represent or look upon as ideal; to make or render ideal; to refine. **idealizer** *n.* an idealist.

idealism *n.* tendency to seek the highest spiritual perfection; imaginative treatment in comparative disregard of the real; the doctrine that appearances are purely the perceptions, the ideas, of subjects, that the world is to be regarded as consisting of mind; **-list** *n.* **-listic** *a.* pert. to idealism or idealists; perfect; consummate. **-lity** *n.* ideal state or quality; capacity to form ideals of beauty and perfection; condition of being mental. **-lly** *adv.* **-tion** *n.* the process of forming an idea. **-tional** *a.* [Gk. *idea*, fr. *idein*, to see].

i·den·ti·cal (ī·den′·ti·kal) *a.* the very same; not different. **-ly** *adv.* **-ness** *n.* exact sameness [L. *idem*, the same].

i·den·ti·fy (ī·den′·tạ·fī) *v.t.* to establish the identity of; to ascertain or prove to be the same; to recognize; to associate (oneself) in interest, purpose, use, etc. **identifiable** *a.* **identification** *n.*

i·den·ti·ty (ī·den′·tạ·ti·) *n.* state of having the same nature or character with; absolute sameness, as opposed to mere similarity; individuality [L. *idem*, the same].

id·e·o·graph (id′·ē·ạ·graf) *n.* a picture, symbol, diagram, etc., suggesting an idea or object without specifically naming it; a character in Chinese and kindred languages. **ideogram** *n.* an ideograph. **-ic, -ical** *a.* **ideography** *n.* [Gk. *idea*, an idea; *graphein*, to write].

i·de·ol·o·gy (ī·dē·ál′·a·ji·) *n.* the body of beliefs of any group; (*Philos.*) science of origin of ideas; visionary theorizing. **ideologic, ideological** *a.* **ideologist** *n.* a theorist. [Gk. *idea*; *logos*, discourse].

ides (īdz) *n.pl.* in the Roman calendar, the 15th day of March, May, July, and October, and the 13th day of the other months [Fr. fr. L. *Idus*].

id·i·o·cy *n.* See **idiot.**

id·i·om (id′·i·ạm) *n.* a peculiar mode of expression; the genius or peculiar cast of a language; colloquial speech; dialect. **-atic, -atical** *a.* **-atically** *adv.* [Gk. *idios*, one's own].

id·i·o·syn·cra·sy (id·i·a·sin′·kra·si·) *n.* a peculiarity in a person; fad; peculiar view. **idiosyncratic, idiosyncratical** *a.* [Gk. *idios*, peculiar; *sunkrasis*, mixing together].

id·i·ot (id′·i·at) *n.* one mentally deficient; a born fool. **idiocy** *n.* state of being an idiot; extreme and permanent mental deficiency. **-ic, -ical** *a.* utterly senseless or stupid. **-ically** *adv.* **-ism** *n.* natural imbecility [Gk. *idiōtes*, a private person].

i·dle (ī′·dl) *a.* doing nothing; inactive; lazy; unused; frivolous; *v.t.* to spend in idleness; *v.i.* to be idle or unoccupied. **-ness** *n.* **-r** *n.* **idly** *adv.* [O.E. *idel*].

i·dol (ī′·dạl) *n.* an image of a diety as an object of worship; an object of excessive devotion. **-ater** *n.* (*fem.* **idolatress**) a worshipper of idols. **-atrize** *v.t.* to worship as an idol. **-atrous** *a.* **-atrously** *adv.* **-atry** *n.* worship of idols or false gods; excessive and devoted admiration. **-ization** *n.* **-ize** *v.t.*

to make an idol of; to love or venerate to excess. **-izer** *n.* [Gk. *eidolon*, image].

i·dyl, idyll (i′·dal) *n.* a short pastoral poem; a picture of simple perfection and loveliness. **-lic** *a.* pert. to idyls; of a perfect setting; blissful [Gk. *eidullion*, dim. of *eidos*, a picture].

if (if) *conj.* on the condition or supposition that; whether; in case that [O.E. *gif*].

ig·loo (ig′·lōō) *n.* a dome-shaped house built of blocks of hard snow by Eskimos [Eskimo].

ig·ne·ous (ig′·ni·as) *a.* resembling fire; (*Geol.*) resulting from the action of intense heat [L. *ignis*, fire].

ig·nite (ig·nit′) *v.t.* to set on fire; to kindle; *v.i.* to catch fire; to begin to burn. **ignitible** *a.* **ignition** *n.* act of kindling or setting on fire; (internal-combustion engine) the process or device which ignites the fuel [L. *ignis*, fire].

ig·no·ble (ig·nō′·bl) *a.* of humble birth or family; mean; base; inferior. **ignobility, -ness** *n.* **ignobly** *adv.* [L. *in*, not; *nobilis*, noble].

ig·no·min·y (ig′·na·min·i) *n.* public disgrace or dishonor; infamous conduct. **ignominious** *a.* humiliating; dishonorable. **ignominiously** *adv.* **ignominiousness** *n.* [L. *ignominia*].

ig·no·ra·mus (ig·na·ra′·mas) *n.* an ignorant person [L. = we are ignorant].

ig·no·rant (ig′·na·rant) *a.* uninstructed; uninformed; unlearned. **ignorance** *n.* **-ly** *adv.* [L. *ignorare*, not to know].

ig·nore (ig·nōr′) *v.t.* to refuse to take notice of; not to recognize [L. *ignorare*, not to know].

i·gua·na (i·gwa′·na) *n.* a family of lizards, found in tropical America [Sp.].

i·lex (i′·leks) *n.* the common holly of Europe; a genus of evergreen trees and shrubs, including the holm oak [L.].

ilk (ilk) *a.* the same. **of that ilk,** family or kind [O.E. *ilc*].

ill (il) *a.* bad or evil in any respect; sick; unwell; wicked; faulty; ugly; disastrous; unfavorable; *n.* evil of any kind; misfortune; misery; pain; *adv.* not well; faultily; unfavorably; not rightly (*compar.* **worse**; *superl.* **worst**). **-ness** *n.* sickness [O.N. *illr*].

ill- *prefix*, used in the construction of compound words, implying badness in some form or other. **—advised** *a.* badly advised. **—disposed** *a.* not friendly; hostile; maliciously inclined. **—fated** *a.* destined to bring misfortune. **—favored** *a.* ugly. **—gotten** *a.* not honestly obtained. **—humor** *n.* bad temper. **—natured** *a.* surly; cross; peevish. **—omened** *a.* inauspicious; attended by evil omens. **—starred** *a.* born under the influence of an unlucky star; unlucky. **—tempered** *a.* quarrelsome. **—will** *n.* malevolence; bad feeling; enmity [O.N. *illr*].

il·le·gal (i·lē′·gal) *a.* contrary to law; unlawful. **-ize** *v.t.* to render unlawful. **-ity** *n.* unlawful act. **-ly** *adv.* [L.*il* + *legalis*, law].

il·leg·i·ble (i·lej′·a·bl) *a.* incapable of being read or deciphered; unreadable; indistinct. **-ness, illegibility** *n.* **illegibly** *adv.*

il·le·git·i·mate (i·li·jit′·a·mit) *a.* unlawful; not authorized by good usage; born out of wedlock. **illegitimacy** *n.* bastardly; illegality. **-ly** *adv.* [L. *in*, not; *legitimate*].

il·lib·er·al (i·lib′·er·al) *a.* not liberal; not free or generous; niggardly; narrow-minded; intolerant. **illiberality** *n.*

il·lic·it (i·lis′·it) *a.* not permitted; unlawful; unlicensed. **-ly** *adv.* **-ness** *n.*

il·lim·it·a·ble (i·lim′·it·a·bl) *a.* incapable of

being limited or bounded; immeasurable; infinite.

il·lit·er·ate (i·lit′·er·it) *a.* unable to read or write; unlettered; *n.* a person unable to read or write. *adv.* **-ness, illiteracy** *n.*

il·log·i·cal (i·làj′·i·kal) *a.* not according to the rules of logic; unsound; fallacious. **-ly** *adv.* **-ness, illogicality** *n.*

il·lu·mi·nate (i·lōō′·ma·nāt) *v.t.* to enlighten, literally and figuratively; to light up; to throw light upon; to embellish, as a book or manuscript with gold and colors. **illuminable** *a.* **illuminant** *a.* and *n.* a source of light. **illumination** *n.* act of giving light; that which supplies light; instruction; enlightenment; decoration on manuscripts and books. **illuminative** *a.* giving light; instructive; explanatory. **illuminator** *n.* **illumine** *v.t.* and *v.i.* [L. *illuminare*, to light].

il·lu·sion (i·lōō′·zhan) *n.* an erroneous interpretation or unreal image presented to the bodily or mental vision; a false perception; deceptive appearance, esp. as a conjuring trick; fallacy. **illusionist** *n.* a professional entertainer who produces illusions. **illusive, illusory** *a.* deceiving by false appearances. **illusively** *adv.* **illusiveness** *n.* [L. *illusio*, mocking].

il·lus·trate (il′·as·trāt, il·us′·trāt) *v.t.* to make clear or bright; to exemplify, esp. by means of figures, diagrams, etc.; to adorn with pictures. **illustration** *n.* act of making clear or bright; explanation; a pictorial representation accompanying a printed description. **illustrative, illustratory** *a.* serving to illustrate. **illustratively** *adv.* **illustrator**, *n.* [L. *illustrare*, to light up].

il·lus·tri·ous (i·lus′·tri·as) *a.* conferring honor; possessing honor or dignity. **-ness** *n.* [L. *illustris*, clear].

im·age (im′·ij) *n.* a mental picture of any object; a representation of a person or object; a copy; a symbol; idol; figure of speech; (*Optics*) the representation of an object formed at the focus of a lens or mirror by rays of light refracted or reflected to it from all parts of the object; *v.t.* to form an image of; to reflect; to imagine. *n.* images regarded collectively; figures of speech; imagination. **imagism** *n.* clear-cut presentation of a subject. **imagist** *n.* one of a modern poetical group who concentrates on extreme clarity by the use of precise images. [L. *imago*, an image].

im·ag·ine (i·maj′·in) *v.t.* to form in the mind an idea or image; to conjecture; to picture; to believe; to suppose; *v.i.* to form an image of; to picture in the mind. **imaginable** *a.* **imaginableness** *n.* **imaginably** *adv.* **imaginary** *a.* existing only in imagination or fancy; fanciful; unreal. **imaginative** *a.* proceeding from the imagination; gifted with the creative faculty; fanciful. **imagination** *n.* the mental faculty which apprehends and forms ideas of external objects; the poetical faculty. **imaginatively** *adv.* **imaginativeness** *n.* [L. *imago*, an image].

i·mam, imaum (i·mám′, i·mawm′) *n.* a Moslem priest [Ar. *imam*, a chief].

im·be·cile (im′·ba·sil) *a.* mentally feeble; silly; idiotic; *n.* one of feeble mentality. **imbecility** *n.* [L. *imbecillus*, weak in mind or body].

im·bed (im·bed′) *v.t.* See **embed.**

im·bibe (im·bib′) *v.t.* to drink in; to absorb; to receive into the mind; *v.t.* to drink. **imbiber** *n.* [L. *in*; *bibere*, to drink].

im·brue (im·brōō′) *v.t.* to wet; to drench as in blood [O.Fr. *embuer*, to drink in].

im·bro·glio (im·brōl′·yō) *n.* an intricate, complicated plot; confusion [It.].

im·bue (im·bū′) *v.t.* to inspire; to tinge deeply; to saturate [L. *imbuere*, to wet].

im·i·tate (im′·a·tāt) *v.t.* to follow, as a pattern, model, or example; to copy. **imitable** *a.* capable or worthy of being copied. **imitation** *n.* a servile reproduction of an original; a copy; mimicry. **imitative** *a.* inclined to imitate; not original. **imitatively** *adv.* **imitativeness** *n.* **imitator** *n.* [L. *imitari*].

im·mac·u·late (i·mak′·yoo·lat) *a.* without blemish; spotless; unsullied; pure; undefiled. **-ly** *adv.* **-ness** *n.* **Immaculate Conception,** the dogma that the Blessed Virgin Mary was conceived and born without taint of sin.

im·ma·nent (im′·a·nant) *a.* abiding in; inherent; intrinsic; innate. **immanence, immanency** *n.* [L. *in*; *manere*, to dwell].

im·ma·te·ri·al (im·a·ti′·ri·al) *a.* not consisting of matter; incorporeal; of no essential consequence; unimportant. **-ize** *v.t.* to separate from matter. **-ism** *n.* doctrine that matter only exists as a process of the mind; pure idealism. **-ist** *n.*

im·ma·ture (im·a·toor′) *a.* not mature or ripe; raw; unformed; undeveloped; untimely. **-ness, immaturity** *n.*

im·meas·ur·a·ble (i·mezh′·er·a·bl) *a.* incapable of being measured; illimitable; infinite; boundless. **immeasurably** *adv.*

im·me·di·ate (i·mē′·di·at) *a.* occurring at once; without delay; present; not separated by others. **immediacy** *n.* immediateness. **-ly** *adv.* **-ness** *n.* [L.L. *immediatus*].

im·me·mo·ri·al (i·ma·mōr′·i·al) *a.* beyond the range of memory; of great antiquity.

im·mem·or·a·ble *a.* **-ly** *adv.*

im·mense (i·mens′) *a.* unlimited; immeasurable; very great; vast; huge; prodigious; enormous. **-ly** *adv.* **-ness, immensity** *n.* vastness; boundlessness [L. *immensus*, unmeasured].

im·merge (i·murj′) *v.t.* to plunge into [L. *in*; *mergere*, to plunge].

im·merse (i·murs′) *v.t.* to plunge into anything, esp. a fluid; to dip; to baptize by dipping the whole body; to absorb. **immersable, immersible** *a.* **-d** *a.* doused; submerged; engrossed. **immersion** *n.* [L. *in*; *mergere, mersum*, to plunge].

im·mi·grate (im′·a·grāt) *v.i.* to migrate into a country. **immigrant** *n.* **immigration** *n.* [L. *in*: *migrare*, to remove].

im·mi·nent (im′·a·nant) *a.* threatening immediately to fall or occur. **imminence** *n.* **-ly** *adv.* [L. *imminere*, to overhang].

im·mis·ci·ble (i·mis′·i·bl) *a.* not capable of being mixed. **immiscibility** *n.*

im·mit·i·ga·ble (i·mit′·i·ga·bl) *a.* incapable of being mitigated or appeased; relentless.

im·mo·bile (i·mō′·bal) *a.* incapable of being moved; fixed; immovable. **immobilize** *v.t.* to render immobile.

im·mod·er·ate (i·mad′·er·at) *a.* exceeding just bounds; excessive. **-ness** *n.* extravagance. **-ly** *adv.* **immoderation** *n.*

im·mod·est (i·mad′·ist) *a.* wanting in modesty or delicacy; indecent; shameless; impudent. **-ly** *adv.* **-y** *n.* shamelessness.

im·mo·late (im′·a·lāt) *v.t.* to sacrifice; to offer as a sacrifice; to kill as a religious rite. **immolation** *n.* **immolator** *n.* [L. *immolare*, to sprinkle with sacrificial meal].

im·mor·al (i·mar′·, i·mawr′·al) *a.* uninfluenced by moral principle; wicked. **-ity** *n.* vice; profligacy; injustice. **-ly** *adv.*

im·mor·tal (i·mawr′·tal) *a.* not mortal; having an eternal existence; undying; deathless; *n.* one exempt from death or decay; a divine being. **immortalize** *v.t.* to make famous for all time; to save from oblivion. **immortality** *n.* perpetual life. **flower** [Fr.].

im·mov·a·ble (i·mōōv′·a·bl) *a.* incapable of being moved; firmly fixed; fast; resolute. **-ness, immovability** *n.* **immovably** *adv.*

im·mune (i·mūn′) *a.* exempt; free from infection; protected against any particular infection; *n.* one who is so protected. **immunization** *n.* the process of rendering a person or animal immune. **immunize** *v.t.* **immunity** *n.* [L. *in-*, not; *munis*, serving].

im·mure (i·myoor′) *v.t.* to enclose within walls; to imprison [L. *in*; *murus*, a wall].

im·mu·ta·ble (i·mū′·ta·bl) *a.* not susceptible to any alteration; invariable; unalterable. **immutability, immutableness** *n.*

imp (imp) *n.* a little demon; a mischievous child. **-ish** *a.* like an imp; mischievous [O.E. *impa*, fr. Gk. *emphytos*, grafted on].

im·pact (im·pakt′) *v.t.* to press or drive forcibly together. **impact** (im′·pact) *n.* impulse communicated by one object striking another; collision [L. *in*, into; *pingere*, to strike].

im·pair (im·per′) *v.t.* to diminish in quantity, value, excellence, or strength; to injure; to weaken [Fr. *empirer*, to grow worse].

im·pale (im·pāl′) *v.t.* to fix on a sharpened stake; inclose with stakes; to put to death by fixing on an upright, sharp stake. **-ment**

n. [L. *in*. into; *palus*, a stake].

im·pal·pa·ble (im·pal'·pa·bl) *a.* not capable of being felt or perceived by the senses, esp. by touch; exceedingly fine in texture; not readily understood or grasped. **impalpability** *n.* **impalpably** *adv.*

im·pan·el (im·pan'·al) *v.t.* to place a name on a panel or list; to enter the names of a jury on a panel; to form a jury by roll-call. **-ment** *n.*

im·part (im·párt') *v.t.* to bestow a share or portion of; to grant; to divulge; to disclose.

im·par·tial (im·pár'·shal) *a.* not partial; without prejudice; not taking sides; unbiased. **impartiality, impartialness** *n.*

im·part·i·ble (im·párt'·i·bl) *a.* not divisible (of landed property).

im·pas·sa·ble (im·pas'·a·bl) *a.* incapable of being passed; impervious; impenetrable; pathless. **impassability, impassableness** *n.*

im·passe (im·pas', im'·pas) *n.* deadlock; dilemma; fix [Fr.].

im·pas·sion (im·pash'·an) *v.t.* to move or affect strongly with passion. **-ed** *a.*

im·pas·sive (im·pas'·iv) *a.* not susceptible of pain or suffering; insensible; showing no emotion; calm. **-ly** *adv.* **-ness, impassivity** *n.*

im·pa·tient (im·pā'·shant) *a.* uneasy or fretful under trial or suffering; averse to waiting; restless. **impatience** *n.* **-ly** *adv.*

im·pav·id (im·pav'·id) *a.* fearless [L. *in* + *pavidus*, fearing].

im·peach (im·pēch') *v.t.* to charge with a crime or misdemeanor; to call to account; to denounce; to challenge. **-able -er** *n.* **-ment** *n.* the trial of a public official, by the upper house of the legislature, the lower house having made the charge [orig. to hinder, Fr. *empêcher*, to prevent].

im·pec·ca·ble (im·pek'·a·bl) *a.* not liable to sin or error; perfect. **impeccability, impeccancy** *n.* [L. *in-*, not; *peccare*, to sin].

im·pe·cu·ni·ous (im·pi·kū'·ni·as) *a.* having no money; poor; hard up. **impecuniosity** *n.* dire poverty [L. *in-*, not; *pecunia*, money].

im·pede (im·pēd') *v.t.* to stop the progress of; to hinder; to obstruct. **impedance** *n.* hindrance; (*Elect.*) opposition offered to an alternating current by resistance, inductance, or capacity, or by combined effect of all three. **impedible** *a.* **impediment** *n.* that which hinders; stammer. **impedimenta** *n.pl.* baggage, esp. military; encumbrances. **impedimental** *a.* [L. *impedire*, to shackle].

im·pel (im·pel') *v.t.* to drive or urge forward; to induce; to incite. *pr.p.* **-ling.** *pa.t.* and *pa.p.* **-led. -lent** *a.* impelling; *n.* a force which impels. **-ler** *n.* [L. *in*, into; *pellere*, to drive].

im·pend (im·pend') *v.i.* to hang over; to threaten; to be imminent. **-ence, -ency** *n.* **-ent** *a.* impending; threatening [L. *impendere*, to hang over].

im·pen·e·tra·ble (im·pen'·a·tra·bl) *a.* incapable of being penetrated or pierced; obscure. **impenetrability** *n.* quality of being impenetrable; that property of matter by which it excludes all other matter from the space it occupies.

im·pen·i·tent (im·pen'·a·tant) *a.* not repenting of sin; not contrite; obdurate.

im·per·a·tive (im·per'·a·tiv) *a.* expressive of command; authoritative; obligatory; absolutely necessary; peremptory. **-ly** *adv.* [L. *imperare*, to command].

im·per·cep·ti·ble (im·per·sep'·ta·bl) *a.* not discernible by the senses; minute. **-ness, imperceptibility** *n.* **imperceptibly** *adv.* **imperceptive** *a.* not having power to perceive.

im·per·fect (im·pur'·fikt) *a.* wanting some part or parts; defective; faulty; *n.* (*Gram.*) tense denoting an action in the past but incomplete, or continuous action in the past. **-ly** *adv.* **imperfection** *n.*

im·per·fo·rate, imperforated (im·pur'·fa·rāt) *a.* not perforated or pierced.

im·pe·ri·al (im·pi'·ri·al) *a.* pertaining to an empire or to an emperor; royal; sovereign; majestic. **-ism** *n.* the system of government in an empire; policy of national territorial expansion. **-ist** *a.* **-istic** *a.* [L. *imperium*].

im·per·il (im·per'·il) *v.t.* to bring into peril; to endanger; to hazard; to risk.

im·pe·ri·ous (im·pi'·ri·as) *a.* commanding; domineering; dictatorial. **-ly** *adv.* **-ness** *n.* [L. *imperiosus*, full of command].

im·per·ish·a·ble (im·per'·ish·a·bl) *a.* not liable to decay or oblivion; indestructible. **-ness** *n.* **imperishability** *n.*

im·per·ma·nence (im·pur'·ma·nans) *n.* want of permanence or stability.

im·per·me·a·ble (im·pur'·mē·a·bl) *a.* not permitting passage, as of fluid or gas, through its substance; impervious. **impermeability** *n.* **-ness** *n.* **impermeably** *adv.*

im·per·son·al (im·pur'·san·al) *a.* having no personal reference; objective; (*Gram.*) form of verb used only in 3rd person singular with nominative *it*. e.g. *it* hails. **-ly** *adv.*

im·per·son·ate (im·pur'·san·āt) *v.t.* to invest with a real form, body or character; to represent in character or form; to act a part on the stage; to imitate. **impersonation** *n.* **impersonator** *n.*

im·per·ti·nent (im·pur'·ta·nant) *a.* having

---

no bearing on the subject; irrelevant; impudent; saucy. **impertinence** *n.*

im·per·turb·a·ble (im·per·tur'·ba·bl) *a.* incapable of being disturbed or agitated; unmoved; composed. **imperturbability** *n.* **imperturbably** *adv.* **imperturbation** *n.*

im·per·vi·ous, im·per·vi·ous (im·pur'·vi·abl, ·vi·us) *a.* not admitting of entrance or passage through; impenetrable; impassable; not to be moved by argument or importunity. **-ness, imperviability** *n.* **imperviously** *adv.*

im·pe·ti·go (im·pa·tī'·gō) *n.* (*Med.*) a pustulous skin disease [L. *impetere*, to rush upon].

im·pet·u·ous (im·pech'·choo·as) *a.* rushing with a body moves; vehement; hasty. **-ly** *adv.* **-ness, impetuosity** *n.* precipitancy; fury [L. *impetus*, attack].

im·pe·tus (im'·pa·tas) *n.* the force with which a body moves; momentum; boost [L.].

im·pi·e·ty (im·pī'·a·ti·) *n.* lack of reverence.

im·pinge (im·pinj') *v.i.* (foll. by *on, upon, against*) to fall or dash against; to touch on; to infringe [L. *impingere*, to strike].

im·pi·ous (im'·pi·as) *a.* not pious; proceeding from or manifesting a want of reverence. **-ly** *adv.* **-ness, impiety** *n.*

im·pla·ca·ble (im·plak'-, im·plāk'·a·bl) *a.* inexorable; not to be appeased; unrelenting. **-ness, implacability** *n.*

im·plant (im·plant') *v.i.* to set in; to insert; to sow (seed); to plant (shoots); to instill, or settle in the mind or heart.

im·plead (im·plēd') *v.t.* to sue at law.

im·ple·ment (im'·pla·mant) *n.* a weapon, tool, or instrument; a utensil; *v.t.* (im'·pla·ment) to fulfill an obligation or contract which has been entered into; to give effect to; to carry out; to supplement. **-al** *a.* **-ation** *n.* [L *implere*, to fill up].

im·pli·cate (im'·pli·kāt) *v.t.* to involve; to include; to entangle; to imply. **implication** *n.* the implied meaning; a logical deduction; entanglement. **implicative** *a.* tending to implicate. **implicatively** *adv.* **implicit** *a.* implied; without questioning. **implicitly** *adv.* [L. *implicare* to entangle].

im·plore (im·plōr') *v.t.* to entreat earnestly; to beseech. **imploration** *n.* **-r** *n.* **imploringly** *adv.* [L. *in*, in; *plorare*, to weep].

im·ply (im·plī') *v.t.* to contain by implication; to involve as necessary; to signify; to insinuate; to suggest [L. *implicare*, to entangle].

im·po·lite (im·pa·līt') *a.* uncivil; rude; discourteous. **-ly** *adv.* **-ness** *n.*

im·pol·i·tic (im·pál'·a·tik) *a.* ill-advised; not in the best interests of; inexpedient. **impolicy** *n.* injudicious action. **-ly** *adv.*

im·pon·der·a·ble (im·pan'·der·a·bl) *a.* without perceptible weight; not able to be weighed; *n.pl.* natural phenomena such as heat, electricity, etc., which do not alter the weight of substances; the unknown factors which may influence human activities. **-ness, imponderability** *n.*

im·port (im·pōrt') *v.t.* to bring in from abroad; to convey a meaning; to be of consequence. **-ance** *n.* consequence; moment. *a.* **-antly** *adv.* **-ation** *n.* act of bringing from another country [L. *in*, into; *portare*, to carry].

im·por·tune (im·per·tūn') *v.t.* to request with urgency; to pester with requests; to entreat; to solicit. **importunacy, importunateness** *n.* **importunate** *a.* earnestly solicitous; persistent in urging a claim; troublesome. **importunately** *adv.* [L. *importunus*, troublesome].

im·pose (im·pōz') *v.t.* to lay on; to levy; to lay, as a charge or tax; to force oneself upon others; to lay on hands in ordination; *v.i.* (with *upon*) to deceive; to take undue advantage of a person's good-nature; to impress. **imposable** *a.* **imposing** *a.* adapted to impress considerably; commanding; grand. **imposition** *n.* act of imposing, laying on, enjoining, indicting, etc.; that which is imposed; a tax; a burden [Fr. *imposer*].

im·pos·si·ble (im·pás'·a·bl) *a.* that which cannot be done; incapable of existing in conception or in fact; unfeasible; unattainable. *interj.* absurd! **impossibility** *n.*

---

im·post (im'·pōst) *n.* tax duty [Fr. *impôt*].

im·pos·tor (im·pás'·ter) *n.* one who assumes a false character; one who deceives others; a cheat. **imposture** *n.* deception [L. *imponere*, to place upon].

im·po·tent (im'·pa·tant) *a.* powerless; wanting natural strength; without sexual power (of a male). **impotence, impotency** *n.*

im·pound (im·pound') *v.t.* to confine cattle in a pound or pen; to restrain within limits; (*Law*) to retain documents in a civil case with a view to criminal proceedings.

im·pov·er·ish (im·pav'·er·ish) *v.t.* to reduce to poverty; to exhaust the strength, richness, or fertility of land. **-ed** *a.* **-ment** *n.* [O. Fr. *empovrir*].

im·prac·ti·ca·ble (im·prak'·ti·ka·bl) *a.* not able to be accomplished; unfeasible. **impracticability, impracticableness** *n.* **impractical** *a.* not practical.

im·pre·cate (im'·pri·kāt) *v.t.* to invoke by prayer (evil) upon; to curse. **imprecation** *n.* **imprecatory** *a.* [L. *imprecari*, to invoke by prayer].

im·preg·na·ble (im·preg'·na·bl) *a.* not to be stormed or taken by assault; not to be moved, impressed, or shaken. **impregnability** *n.* **impregnably** *adv.* [Fr. *imprenable*, fr. L. *in-*, not; *prehendere*, to take].

im·preg·nate (im·preg'·nāt) *v.t.* to make pregnant; to render fertile; to saturate; to imbue. **impregnable** *a.* **impregnation** *n.* [L. *impregnare*].

im·pre·sa·ri·o (im·pra·sà'·ri·ō) *n.* an organizer of public entertainments, a teacher or manager of concert artists [It].

im·press (im·pres') *v.t.* to take forcibly, persons or goods, for public service; to commandeer. **-ment** *n.* [L. *in*, in, into; *praestare*, to furnish].

im·press (im·pres') *v.t.* to press in or upon; to make a mark or figure upon; to fix deeply in the mind; to stamp. (im'·pres) *n.* a mark made by pressure; stamp; impression wrought on the mind. **-ibility** *n.* susceptibility. **-ible** *a.* capable of being impressed. **-ibly** *adv.* **impression** *n.* act of impressing; a mark or stamp made by pressure; psychological effect or influence on the mind; opinion; idea. **impressionable** *a.* susceptible to external influences. **-ive** *a.* making or fitted to make a deep impression on the mind. **-ively** *adv.* **-iveness** *n.* [L. *imprimere*, fr. *premere*, to press].

im·pres·sion·ism (im·presh'·an·izm) *n.* a revolutionary modern movement, originating in France, in art, literature and music, aiming at reproducing the *impression* which eye and mind gather, rather than representing actual fact. **impressionist** *n.*

im·pri·ma·tur (im·pra·mā'·ter) *n.* a license to print a book; official approval [L. = 'let it be printed'].

im·print (im·print') *v.t.* to mark by pressure; to fix indelibly, as on the mind; to print. (im'·print) *n.* an impression; name of printer or publisher on title page or at the end of a book.

im·prob·a·ble (im·prab'·a·bl) *a.* unlikely. **improbability** *n.* **improbably** *adv.*

im·pro·bi·ty (im·prō'·bi·ti·) *n.* want of integrity or rectitude; dishonesty.

im·promp·tu (im·pramp'·tóo) *adv.* or *a.* offhand [Fr. fr. L. *promptus*, ready].

im·prop·er (im·prap'·er) *a.* unsuitable to the end or design; unfit; indecent; inaccurate. **-ly** *adv.* **impropriety** *n.* offense against rules of conduct; the use of a word in its wrong sense.

im·prove (im·próov') *v.t.* to make better; to employ to good purpose; to make progress; *v.i.* to grow better; to become more prosperous. **improvability, improvableness** *n.* **improvable** *a.* **improvably** *adv.* **-ment** *n.* the act of improving; state of being improved; progress. **improvingly** *adv.*

im·prov·i·dent (im·prav'·a·dant) *a.* not prudent or foreseeing; neglecting to provide for the future. **improvidence** *n.*

im·pro·vise (im·pre·viz') *v.t.* to extemporize; to make the best of materials at hand; to compose, speak or perform without preparation. **improvisation** (im·prav·i·zā'·shan) *n.* **-r** *n.* [L. *in-*, not; *provisus*, foreseen].

im·pru·dent (im·próo'·dant) *a.* lacking in discretion. **imprudence** *n.* **-ly** *adv.*

im·pu·dent (im'·pya·dant) *a.* brazen; boldfaced; rude. **impudence** *n.* **-ly** *adv.* [L. *impudens*, shameless].

im·pugn (im·pūn') *v.t.* to call in question; to contradict; to challenge the accuracy of a statement. **-able** *a.* **-er** *n.* **-ment** *n.* [L. *impugnare*, to assail].

im·pulse (im'·puls) *n.* the motion or effect produced by a sudden action or applied force; push; thrust; momentum; sudden thought. **impulsion** *n.* impelling force; incitement. **impulsive** *a.* having the power of impelling; acting momentarily without due thought. **impulsively** *adv.* **impulsiveness** *n.* [L. *impellere, impulsion*, to urge on. Cf. *impel*].

im·pu·ni·ty (im·pūn'·a·ti·) *n.* exemption from punishment, injury, or loss [L. *impunitas*, without punishment].

im·pure (im·pyoor') *a.* not pure; mixed; adulterated; foul; unchaste. **-ly** *adv.* **im·**

purity, impureness *n.*

im·pute (im-pūt') *v.t.* to ascribe to (in a bad sense); to attribute to. **imputable** *a.* **imputableness, imputability** *n.* **imputation** *n.* act of imputing; suggestion of evil. **imputative** *a.* **imputatively** *adv.* [L. *in; putare,* to reckon, to think].

in (in) *prep.* within; inside of; indicating a present relation to time, space, or condition; *adv.* inside; closely; with privilege or possession; immediately. **in so far as,** to the extent that. **inasmuch as,** considering that [O.E.].

in·a·bil·i·ty (in-a-bil'-a-ti-) *n.* want of strength, means, or power; impotence.

in·ac·cu·rate (in-ak'-yar-at) *a.* not correct; not according to truth or reality; erroneous. **inaccuracy** *n.* **-ly** *adv.*

in·ac·tive (in-ak'-tiv) *a.* not disposed to action or effort; idle; inert; lazy; (*Chem.*) showing no tendency to combine with other elements. **inaction** *n.* **inactivate** *v.t.* to make inactive. **inactivation** *n.* **-ly** *adv.* **inactivity** *n.* want of action or energy.

in·ad·e·quate (in-ad'-a-kwat) *a.* insufficient; too cramped; incapable. **inadequacy** *n.* **-ly** *adv.* **-ness** *n.*

in·ad·mis·si·ble (in-ad-mis'-a-bl) *a.* not allowable; improper. **inadmissibly** *adv.*

in·ad·vert·ent (in-ad-vur'-tant) *a.* not turning the mind to a matter; inattentive; thoughtless; careless. **inadvertence, inadvertency** *n.* **-ly** *adv.*

in·ad·vis·a·ble (in-ad-vī'-za-bal) *a.* not recommended; inexpedient. **inadvisability** *n.* **inadvisably** *adv.*

in·al·ien·a·ble (in-āl'-yan-a-bl) *a.* incapable of being separated or transferred.

in·ane (in-ān') *a.* empty; void; foolish; silly. **inanition** *n.* state of being empty; exhaustion; starvation. **inanity** *n.* vacuity; silly remark [L. *inanis*].

in·an·i·mate (in-an'-a-mat) *a.* destitute of life or spirit. **inanimation** *n.* **-ness** *n.*

in·ap·pli·ca·ble (in-ap'-lik-a-bl) *a.* not applicable; unsuitable; irrelevant; inappropriate.

in·ap·pre·ci·a·ble (in-a-prē'-shi-a-bl) *a.* not worth reckoning; not able to be valued.

in·ap·pro·pri·ate (in-a-prō'-pri-at) *a.* unsuitable; at the wrong time. **-ly** *adv.* **-ness** *n.*

in·apt (in-apt') *a.* inappropriate; unsuitable; awkward; clumsy. **-itude** *n.* unfitness; awkwardness. **-ly** *adv.*

in·ar·tic·u·late (in-ar-tik'-ya-lat) *a.* unable to put one's ideas in words; not uttered distinctly; not jointed. **-ly** *adv.* **-ness** *n.* **inarticulation** *n.*

in·as·much *adv.* See **in.**

in·au·di·ble (in-aw'-di-bl) *a.* not able to be heard; noiseless; silent. **inaudibility, inaudibleness** *n.* **inaudibly** *adv.*

in·au·gu·rate (in-aw'-gya-rāt) *v.t.* to induct into an office in a formal manner; to install; to set in motion or action; to begin. **inaugural, inauguratory** *a.* **inauguration** *n.* opening ceremony. **inaugurator** *n.* [L. *inaugurare,* to take auguries before action].

in·aus·pi·cious (in-aw-spish'-as) *a.* not auspicious; ill-omened. **-ly** *adv.* **-ness** *n.*

in·born (in'-bawrn) *a.* born in or with; innate; natural; inherent.

in·bred (in'-bred) *a.* bred within; innate; inherent. **inbreed** *v.t.* to mate animals of the same blood stock; to marry within the family or tribe. **inbreeding** *n.*

in·cal·cu·la·ble (in-kal'-kya-la-bl) *a.* countless; beyond calculation; uncertain. **incalculability, -ness** *n.*

in·can·des·cent (in-kan-des'-ant) *a.* glowing with white heat and providing light. **incandescence** *n.* white heat [L. *in,* in; *candescere,* to begin to glow].

in·can·ta·tion (in-kan-tā'-shan) *n.* a formula or charm-words used to produce magical or supernatural effect. **incantatory** *a.* [L. *incantare,* to sing spells. Cf. *enchant*].

in·ca·pa·ble (in-kā'-pa-bl) *a.* wanting ability or capacity; not admitting of; not susceptible of. **incapability** *n.*

in·ca·pa·ci·tate (in-ka-pas'-a-tāt) *v.t.* to render incapable. **incapacitation** *n.* act of disqualifying. **incapacity** *n.* want of capacity; lack of normal intellectual power; inability; incapability; legal disqualification.

in·car·cer·ate (in-kar'-ser-āt) *v.t.* to confine; to imprison. **incarcerator, incarceration,** *n.* [L. *in; carcer,* prison].

in·car·na·dine (in-kár'-na-dīn) *a.* flesh-colored; of a carnation color; crimson; *v.t.* to dye crimson [Fr. fr. L. *caro,* flesh].

in·car·nate (in-kár'-nāt) *v.t.* to put into concrete form; to embody in flesh, esp. in human form; *a.* (in-kár'-nat) embodied in flesh; typified. **incarnation** *n.* embodiment; that which embodies and typifies an abstraction [L. *in; caro, carnis,* flesh].

in·cen·di·ar·y (in-sen'-di-er-i-) *n.* one who maliciously sets fire to property; an agitator who inflames passions; a fire bomb; *a.* pert. to malicious burning of property; tending to inflame dissension. **incendiarism** *n.* arson [L. *incendere,* to set on fire].

in·cense (in-sens') *v.t.* to inflame to violent anger [L. *incendere,* to set on fire].

in·cense (in'-sens) *n.* a mixture of aromatic gums and spices which, when burned, produces a sweet-smelling smoke, used for religious purposes; flattery; adulation; *v.t.* to perfume with incense [L. *incendere,* to burn].

in·cen·tive (in-sen'-tiv) *a.* inciting; provoking; *n.* motive; spur; stimulus; encouragement [L. *incentivus,* setting the tune].

in·cep·tion (in-sep'-shan) *n.* beginning; start; origin. **inceptive** *a.* **inceptively** *adv.* [L. *incipere, inceptum,* to begin].

in·ces·sant (in-ses'-ant) *a.* continuing or following without interruption. **incessancy** *n.* **-ly** *adv.* [L. *in-,* not; *cessare,* to cease].

in·cest (in'-sest) *n.* sexual intercourse of kindred within the forbidden degrees. **-uous** *a.* [L. *in-,* not; *castus,* chaste].

inch (inch) *n.* twelfth part of a linear foot; a small degree or quantity; *v.i.* to push forward by slow degrees; to edge forward [L. *uncia,* twelfth part of anything].

in·cho·ate (in'-kō-at) *a.* just begun; rudimentary; incipient. **-ly** *adv.* **inchoation** *n.* early stage or state. **inchoative** *a.* [L. *in, choare,* to begin].

in·ci·dent (in'-sa-dant) *a.* liable to happen; subordinate to; falling upon, as a ray of light upon a reflecting surface; naturally attaching to; *n.* that which takes place; event; occurrence; episode; subordinate action. **incidence** *n.* range of influence; the manner of falling upon. **-al** *a.* and *n.* **-ally** *adv.* **-alness** *n.* [L. *incidere,* to fall in].

in·cin·er·ate (in-sin'-er-āt) *v.t.* to consume by fire; to burn to ashes. **incineration** *n.* **incinerator** *n.* furnace for consuming refuse [L. *incinerare,* to reduce to ashes].

incinerator

in·cip·i·ent (in-sip'-i-ant) *a.* beginning; originating. **incipience, incipiency** *n.* [L. *incipere,* to begin].

in·cise (in-sīz') *v.t.* to cut into; to carve; to engrave. **incision** (in-sizh'-an) *n.* the act of cutting with a sharp instrument; a cut; gash. **incisive** *a.* having the quality of cutting or penetrating; sharp; biting; trenchant; **incisively** *adv.* **incisiveness** *n.* **incisor** *n.* one of the eight front cutting teeth[L. *incidere,* to cut into].

in·cite (in-sīt') *v.t.* to move the mind to action; to spur on. **incitant** *n.* a stimulant; *a.* exciting. **incitation** (in-sī-tā'-shun) *n.* **-ment** *n.* act of inciting; motive; incentive. *n.* [L. *incitare,* to rouse].

in·clem·ent (in-klem'-ant) *a.* not clement; severe; harsh; stormy. **inclemency** *n.*

in·cline (in-klīn') *v.t.* to cause to deviate from a line or direction; to give a tendency to, as to the will or affections; to bend; to turn from the vertical. *v.i.* to deviate from the vertical; to be disposed. (in'-klin) *n.* an ascent or descent; a slope. **inclination** *n.* act of inclining; bent of the mind or will; leaning; tendency towards; favor for one thing more than another. **-d** *a.* [L. *in; clinare,* to lean].

in·clude (in-klóod') *v.t.* to confine within; to comprise. **inclusion** *n.* act of including; state of being included or confined. **inclusive** *a.* taking in the stated limit, number, or extremes; enclosing; embracing. **inclusively** *adv.* [L. *includere,* to shut in].

in·cog·ni·to (in-kåg'-ni-tō) *a.* and *adv.* in a disguise; in an assumed character and under an assumed name; *n.* (*fem.* **incognita**) the state of being unknown; a person who conceals his identity under a false name [L. *incognitus,* unknown].

in·co·her·ent (in-kō-hir'-ant) *a.* not connected or clear; confused. **incoherence** *n.* **-ly** *adv.* **incoherency** *n.*

in·com·bus·ti·ble (in-kam-bust'-a-bl) *a.* not capable of being burned. **incombustibility, incombustibleness** *n.* **incombustibly** *adv.*

in·come (in'-kum) *n.* the gain or reward from one's labors or investments; annual receipts; rent; profit; interest. **-r** *n.* a newcomer. **incoming** *n.* a coming in; revenue; *a.* coming in; entering; **— tax,** tax levied on income.

in·com·men·su·ra·ble (in-ka-men'-sa-ra-bl) *a.* having no common measure or standard of comparison. **-ness** *n.* **incommensurably** *adv.* **incommensurate** *a.* not admitting of a common measure; unequal; out of proportion. **incommensurately** *adv.*

in·com·mode (in-ka-mōd') *v.t.* to put to inconvenience or discomfort; to hinder. **incommodious** *a.* inconvenient; too small. **incommodiously** *adv.* **incommodity** *n.* [L. *in-,* not; *commodus,* convenient].

in·com·mu·ni·ca·ble (in-ka-mū'-ni-ka-bl) *a.* incapable of being communicated or shared. **incommunicability** *n.* **-ness** *n.* **incommunicably** *adv.* **incommunicative** *a.* reserved; not ready to impart information.

in·com·mu·ni·ca·do (in-ka-mū-ni-kā'-dō) *a.* of a prisoner, deprived of communication with other people [Sp.].

in·com·pa·ra·ble (in'-kåm'-per-a-bl) *a.* not admitting any degree of comparison; unequaled; unrivaled. **incomparability** *n.* **-ness** *n.* **incomparably** *adv.*

in·com·pat·i·ble (in-kam-pat'-a-bl) *a.* incapable of existing side by side; unable to live together in harmony. **incompatibility, incompatibleness** *n.* **incompatibly** *adv.*

in·com·pe·tent (in-kåm'-pa-tant) *a.* not efficient in the performance of function; inadequate; incapable. **incompetence** *n.* **incom-**

in·com·plete (in-kam-plēt') *a.* defective; unfinished; imperfect. **-ly** *adv.*

in·com·pre·hen·si·ble (in-kåm-pri-hen'-sa-bl) *a.* incapable of being comprehended or understood. **-ness, incomprehensibility, incomprehension** *n.* difficulty of understanding; quality or state of being incomprehensible. **incomprehensibly** *adv.* **incomprehensive** *a.* limited; not extensive.

in·com·pres·si·ble (in-kam-pres'-a-bl) *a.* cannot be compressed or reduced in bulk.

in·con·ceiv·a·ble (in-kan-sēv'-a-bl) *a.* not capable of being conceived in the mind; unthinkable. **inconceivability, inconceivableness** *n.* **inconceivably** *adv.*

in·con·clu·sive (in-kan-klóo'-siv) *a.* not decisive or conclusive; not settling a point in debate or a doubtful question. **-ly** *adv.*

in·con·gru·ous (in-káng'-groo-as) *a.* inappropriate; not reciprocally agreeing; (*Math.*) not coinciding. **incongruent** *a.* **incongruity, incongruousness** *n.*

in·con·se·quent (in-kån'-sa-kwent) *a.* not following from the premises; illogical; irrelevant. **inconsequence** *n.* **inconsequential** *a.* not to the point; illogical; of no import; trivial. **inconsequentially** *adv.*

in·con·sid·er·a·ble (in-kan-sid'-er-a-bl) *a.* unworthy of consideration; unimportant.

in·con·sid·er·ate (in-kan-sid'-er-at) *a.* thoughtless; careless of others' feelings.

in·con·sis·tent (in-kan-sis'-tant) *a.* liable to sudden and unexpected change; changeable; not agreeing. **inconsistency** *n.* **-ly** *adv.*

in·con·spic·u·ous (in-kan-spik'-yoo-as) *a.* scarcely noticeable; hardly discernible.

in·con·stant (in-kán'-stant) *a.* not constant or consistent; subject to change. **inconstancy** *n.* **-ly** *adv.*

in·con·ti·nent (in-kán'-ta-nant) *a.* morally incapable of restraint. **incontinence, incontinency** *n.* **-ly** *adv.*

in·con·tro·vert·i·ble (in-kán-tra-vur'-ta-bl) *a.* too clear or certain to admit of dispute; unquestionable. **incontrovertibly** *adv.*

in·con·ven·ient (in-kan-vēn'-yant) *a.* awkward; unsuitable. **inconvenience** *v.t.* to put to trouble or annoyance. **inconvenience, inconveniency** *n.* **-ly** *adv.*

in·con·vert·i·ble (in-kan-vur'-ta-bl) *a.* cannot be changed or exchanged; of paper money, notes which cannot be converted into gold on demand. **inconvertibility** *n.*

in·co·or·di·nate (in-kō-awr'-da-nat) *a.* not in orderly relation with one another.

in·cor·po·rate (in-kawr'-pa-rāt) *v.t.* and *v.i.* to combine, as different ingredients, into one body or mass; to give a material form to; to constitute into a corporation; *a.* formed into an incorporation. **incorporation** *n.* act of incorporating; state of being incorporated; the formation or embodying of an association or society. **incorporative** a. **incorporeal** a. not possessed of a body; immaterial; unsubstantial; spiritual. **incorporeality** n.

in·cor·rect (in·ka·rekt′) a. not in accordance with the truth; improper.**-ly** adv. **-ness** n.

in·cor·ri·gi·ble (in·kawr′·i·ja·bl) a. beyond any hope of reform or improvement in conduct; n. such a person.

in·cor·rupt (in·kar·upt′) a. morally pure; not open to bribery; free from decay. **-ible** a. **-ibility** n. **-ly** adv. **-ness** n.

in·crease (in·krēs′) v.t. to make greater; to extend; to lengthen; v.i. to become greater; to multiply by the production of young. (in′·krēs) n. growth; produce; profit; interest; progeny; offspring; enlargement; addition. **increasable** a. **increasingly** adv. [L. in; crescere, fr. crescere, to grow].

in·cred·i·ble (in·kred′·a·bl) a. impossible to be believed; surpassing belief; amazing. **incredibility**, **-ness** n. **incredibly** adv.

in·cred·u·lous (in·krej′·a·las) a. not disposed to believe; showing unbelief. **incredulity** n. disbelief. **-ness** n. **-ly** adv.

in·cre·ment (in′·kra·mant) n. increase; matter added; growth; annual augmentation of a fixed amount to a salary. **-al** a. [L. incrementum, fr. increscere, to increase].

in·crim·i·nate (in·krim′·i·nāt) v.t. to charge with a crime; to involve one in a criminal action. **incriminatory** a. [L. in; crimen, a charge].

in·crust, encrust (in·, en·krust′) v.t. to cover with a crust; v.i. to form a hard covering or crust on the surface. **-ation** n.

in·cu·bate (in′·kya·bāt) v.i. to sit, as on eggs, for hatching; to brood; of disease germs, to pass through the stage between infection and appearance of symptoms; v.t. to hatch; to ponder over. **incubation** n. **incubative, incubatory** a. **incubator** n. a cabinet, in which the heat is automatically regulated, used to hatch eggs; similar devices for premature infants or bacterial cultures. [L. in; cubare, to lie].

incubator

in·cu·bus (ing′·, in′·kya·bas) n. a nightmare; any burdensome or depressing influence [L. in, upon; cubare, to lie].

in·cul·cate (in·kul′·kāt) v.t. (foll. by in or on) to urge forcibly and repeatedly; to impress by admonition. **inculcation** n. **inculcator** n. [L. inculcare, to stamp in].

in·cum·bent (in·kum′·bant) a. lying or resting upon; resting on, as duty; n. holder of an office. **incumbency** n. [L. incumbere, to lie upon].

in·cur (in·kur′) v.t. to become liable to; to bring upon oneself. pr.p. **-ring**. pa.t. and pa.p. **-red** [L. in, into; currere, to run].

in·cur·a·ble (in·kyoor′·a·bl) a. not able to be cured; n. one beyond cure. **incurability** n.

in·cu·ri·ous (in·kyoo′·ri·as) a. not inquisitive or curious; indifferent. **in·cur·sion** (in·kur′·zhan) n. a raid into a territory with hostile intention. **incursive** a. [L. in, into; currere, to run].

in·curve (in·kurv′) v.t. to bend into a curve; v.i. to bend inward. **incurvate** v.t. to bend inward or upward; a. curved in.

in·debt·ed (in·det′·ad) a. placed under an obligation; owing; beholden. **-ness** n.

in·de·cent (in·dē′·sant) a. unbecoming; immodest; obscene. **indecency** n. lack of decency. **-ly** adv.

in·de·ci·pher·a·ble (in·di·sī′·fer·a·bl) a. incapable of being deciphered; illegible.

in·de·ci·sion (in·di·sizh′·an) n. want of decision; irresoluteness; shilly-shallying. **indecisive** a. inconclusive; doubtful; wavering. **indecisively** adv. **indecisiveness** n.

in·de·clin·a·ble (in·di·klīn′·a·bl) a. (Gram.) having no inflections or cases.

in·dec·o·rous (in·dek′·a·ras, in·di·kōr′·as) a. contrary to good manners. **-ly** adv. **-ness**, **indecorum** n. impropriety.

in·deed (in·dēd′) adv. in reality; in truth; in fact; certainly. interj. denotes surprise.

in·de·fat·i·ga·ble (in·di·fat′·i·ga·bl) a. incapable of being fatigued; unwearied; untiring. **-ness, indefatigability** n. **indefatigably** adv. [L. in; defatigare, to tire].

in·de·fea·si·ble (in·di·fēz′·a·bl) a. not to be defeated; incapable of being made void; irrevocable. **indefeasibility** n. **indefeasibly** adv. [O.Fr. defaire, to undo].

in·de·fen·si·ble (in·di·fen′·sa·bl) a. incapa-

ble of being maintained, vindicated, or justified; untenable; unjustifiable; unexcusable.

in·de·fin·a·ble (in·di·fīn′·a·bl) a. not able to be defined. **indefinably** adv.

in·def·i·nite (in·def′·a·nit) a. having no known limits; (Gram.) not pointing out with precision the person, thing, or time to which a part of speech refers. **-ly** adv. **-ness, indefinitude** n. want of precision. **— article**, a, an.

in·del·i·ble (in·del′·a·bl) a. not to be blotted out or erased; ineffaceable; ingrained. **indelibility, -ness** n. **indelibly** adv. [L. in-, not; delere, to destroy, blot out].

in·del·i·cate (in·del′·a·kat) a. offensive to good manners or to purity of mind; indecorous. **indelicacy** n. **-ly** adv.

in·dem·ni·fy (in·dem′·na·fī) v.t. to reimburse; to give security against; to free one from the consequences of a technically illegal act. **indemnification** n. **indemnitor** n. **indemnity** n. an agreement to render a person immune from a contingent liability; compensation [L. indemnis, unharmed].

in·de·mon·stra·ble (in·de·man′·stra·bl) a. cannot be demonstrated or proved.

in·dent (in·dent′) v.t. to cut into points or inequalities; to make notches or holes in; to make an order (upon some one for); to indenture; (Print.) to begin the first line of a paragraph farther away from the margin than the remaining lines; v.i. to wind back and forth; to make an agreement; to make out an order in duplicate. (in′·dent) n. a cut or notch; a dent; a mark, as of a tooth; an order for goods. **-ation** n. a notch; a depression. **-ure** n. a contract of apprenticeship; [L. in, in; dens, a tooth].

indentation

in·de·pen·dent (in·di·pen′·dant) a. not dependent; not subject to the control of others; unrelated; free; self-supporting. **independence, independency** n. **-ly** adv.

in·de·scrib·a·ble (in·di·skrīb′·a·bl) a. incapable of being described.

in·de·struct·i·ble (in·di·struk′·ta·bl) a. not able to be destroyed; imperishable. **indestructibility** n. **indestructibly** adv.

in·de·ter·mi·na·ble (in·di·tur′·min·a·bl) a. cannot be determined, classified, or fixed. **-ness** n. **indeterminably** adv. **indeterminate** a. not settled or fixed in detail; indefinite. **indeterminately** adv. **indeterminateness, indetermination** n. an unsettled or wavering state of the mind.

in·dex (in′·deks) n. any table for facilitating reference in a book; a directing sign; that which points out, shows, indicates, or manifests; a pointer or hand which directs to anything; the forefinger or pointing finger; the ratio between the measurement of a given substance and that of a fixed standard; (Math.) the figure or letter showing the power of a quantity; the exponent of a power. pl. **-es, indices**. v.t. to provide with an index or table references; to place in alphabetical order in an index. **-er** n. one who compiles an index [L. = an indicator].

In·di·a (in′·di·a) n. a country in Asia, named from river Indus. **— ink**, ink composed of lamp-black mixed into a paste with gum. **— paper**, a very thin tough and opaque paper made from fibers. **— rubber** n. natural rubber obtained from latex [Sans. sindhu, a river].

In·di·an (in′·di·an) a. pert. to India in Asia, to the East Indies, or to the aborigines of America; n. a native of India in Asia, of the East Indies, or one of the aboriginal inhabitants of America. **— club**, bottle-shaped

wooden club, used in physical exercise. **— corn**, maize. **— file**, single file. **— giver** n. (Colloq.) one who takes back a gift. **— red** an earthy pigment with a purple-russet color, due to the presence of peroxide of iron. **— summer** mild, warm, hazy weather of autumn [Cans. sindhu, a river].

Indian clubs

in·di·cate (in′·da·kāt) v.t. to point out; to be a sign of; to denote; to show; to signify. **indication** n. act of indicating; mark; token; sign. **indicative** a. pointing out; denoting; (Gram.) applied to that mood of the verb which affirms or denies; n. the direct mood of a verb. **indicatively** adv. **indicator** n. one who indicates; a pointer; an instrument used to gauge and record varying conditions. **indicatory** a. [L. indicare, to show].

in·dict (in·dīt′) v.t. to charge with a crime; to accuse; to arraign. **-able** a. **-ment** n. the act of indicting; a formal charge of crime. [L. in; dicere, to declare].

in·dif·fer·ent (in·dif′·er·ant) a. uninterested; without concern; not making a difference; having no influence or weight; of no account; neither good nor bad. **indifference** n. **-ly** adv.

in·di·gene (in′·da·jēn) n. an aborigine; a native animal or plant. Also **indigen**. **indigenous** a. born or originating in a country; native. **indigenously** adv. [L. indigena, a native].

in·di·gent (in′·da·jent) a. destitute of property or means of subsistence; needy; poor. **indigence** n. [L. indigere, to lack].

in·di·gest·ed (in·da·jest′·ad) a. not digested; lacking order or system. **indigestibility** n. **indigestible** a. incapable of being digested. **indigestibly** adv. **indigestion** n. inability to digest food or difficulty and discomfort in doing so; dyspepsia. **indigestive** a.

in·dig·nant (in·dig′·nant) a. moved by a feeling of wrath, mingled with scorn or contempt; roused. **-ly** adv. **indignation** n. righteous wrath. **indignity** n. affront; contemptuous treatment [L. in-, not; dignari, to deem worthy].

in·di·go (in′·di·gō) n. a blue dye-stuff derived from many leguminous plants; a. of a deep-blue color [L. indicum, fr. Indicus, of India].

in·di·rect (in·da·rekt′) a. not direct or straight; crooked; dishonest. **-ion** n. roundabout way; deliberate attempt to mislead; trickery. **-ly** adv. **-ness** n.

in·dis·creet (in·dis·krēt′) a. not discreet; imprudent; injudicious; reckless. **-ly** adv. **indiscretion** (in·dis·kresh′·an) n. an indiscreet act; the quality of being indiscreet.

in·dis·crim·i·nate (in·dis·krim′·a·nat) a. wanting discrimination; not making any distinction. **-ly** adv. **indiscriminating, indiscriminative** a. **indiscrimination** n.

in·dis·pen·sa·ble (in·dis·pen′·sa·bl) a. absolutely necessary; not to be set aside. **indispensability, -ness** n. **indispensably** adv.

in·dis·pose (in·di·spōz′) v.t. to render unfit or unsuited; to make somewhat ill; to render averse or disinclined (toward). **-d** a. averse; ill. **indisposition** n.

in·dis·put·a·ble (in·dis·pū′·ta·bl, in·dis′·pyoo·ta·bl) a. too obvious to be disputed.

in·dis·sol·u·ble (in·dis·al′·ya·bl) a. not capable of being dissolved; perpetually binding or obligatory; inviolable. **-ness, indissolubility** n. **indissolubly** adv.

in·dis·tinct (in·dis·tingkt′) a. not distinct or distinguishable; not clearly defined or uttered; obscure; dim. **-ive** a. not capable of making distinctions; not distinctive. **-ly** adv.

in·dis·tin·guish·a·ble (in·dis·ting′·gwish·a·bl) a. may not be distinguished. **-ness** n. **indistinguishably** adv.

in·dite (in·dīt′) v.t. to compose; to write. **-ment** n. [O. Fr. enditer].

in·di·vid·u·al (in·da·vij′·òò·al) a. not divided; single; peculiar to single person or thing; distinctive; n. a single being, or thing. **-ization** n. **-ize, individuate** v.t. to distinguish individually; to particularize. **-ism** n. quality of being individual; a political or economic theory which asserts the rights of the individual as against those of the community. **-ist** n. **-istic** a. **-ity** n. separate or distinct existence; personality. **-ly** adv. [L. individuus, undivided].

in·di·vis·i·ble (in·da·viz′·a·bl) a. not divisible; not separate. **indivisibility, -ness** n. **indivisibly** adv.

in·doc·tri·nate (in·dàk′·tri·nāt) v.t. to instruct; to imbue with political or religious principles and dogmas. **indoctrination** n.

in·do·lent (in′·da·lant) a. habitually idle or

lazy; indisposed to exertion. **indolence, indolency** *n.* **-ly** *adv.* [L. *in-*, not; *dolere*, to feel pain].

in·dom·i·ta·ble (in·dâm'·ạt·ạ·bl) *a.* not to be subdued; that cannot be overcome. **indomitably** *adv.* [L. *in-*, not; *domitare*, to tame].

In·do·ne·sia (in·dạ·nē'·zhạ) *n.* Republic of S.E. Asia (since 1945). **-n** *a.* [*Indo*, and Gk. *nēsos*, an island].

in·door (in'·dōr) *a.* being within doors; under cover. **indoors** *adv.*

in·dorse, in·dorse·ment See **en·dorse.**

in·du·bi·ta·ble (in·dū'·bit·ạ·bl) *a.* too obvious to admit of doubt; unquestionable; quite certain. **indubitably** *adv.*

in·duce (in·dūs') *v.t.* to overcome by persuasion or argument; to persuade; to produce or cause (as electricity) **-ment** *n.* that which induces or persuades to action. **-r** *n.* **inducible** *a.* [L. *inducere*, to lead in].

in·duct (in·dukt') *v.t.* to bring in or introduce; to install or put formally into office; to bring into military service. **-ile** *a.* of a metal not capable of being drawn out into wires or threads. **-ility** *n.* **-ion** *n.* installation of a person in an office; an introduction to a poem or play; (*Elect.*) the transfer of a magnetic or electric state from an electrified to a non-electrified body, by proximity; (*Logic*) a process of finding explanations. **-ional** *a.* **-ive** *a.* **-ively** *adv.* **-or** *n.* [L. *in*, into; *ducere*, to lead].

in·dulge (in·dulj') *v.t.* to give freedom or scope to; to allow one his own way; to gratify; *v.i.* (usu. followed by *in*) to give oneself to the habit or practice of. **-nce** *n.* **-nt** *a.* yielding; compliant; very forbearing. **-ntly** *adv.* [L. *indulgere*, to be indulgent].

in·du·rate (in'·dyạ·rāt) *v.t.* to make hard; to deprive of sensibility; *v.i.* grow hard; to harden. [L. *in*, in; *durus*, hard].

in·dus·try (in'·dạs·tri·) *n.* habitual diligence in any employment, bodily or mental; steady application to work; a particular branch of trade or manufacture. **industrial** *a.* pert. to industry or manufacture. **industrialism** *n.* system of industry or manufacture on a large scale. **industrially** *adv.* **industrious** *a.* diligent in business or study. **industriously** *adv.* **industriousness** *n.* [L. *industria*].

in·e·bri·ate (in·ē'·bri·āt) *v.t.* to make drunk; to intoxicate; to exhilarate; *a.* intoxicated; *n.* a habitual drunkard. **inebriation, inebriety** *n.* drunkenness. **inebrious** *a.* stupidly drunk [L. *in*; *ebrius*, drunk].

in·ed·i·ble (in·ed'·ạ·bl) *a.* not eatable; unfit for food. **inedibility** *n.*

in·ef·fa·ble (in·ef'·ạ·bl) *a.* incapable of being expressed in words; indescribable; unutterable. **-ness**, **ineffability** *n.* **ineffably** *adv.* [L. *in-*, not; *effabilis*, speakable].

in·ef·face·a·ble (in·ạ·fās'·ạ·bl) *a.* incapable of being rubbed out. **ineffaceably** *adv.*

in·ef·fec·tive (in·ạ·fek'·tiv) *a.* incapable of producing any effect or the effect intended; useless; inefficient. **-ly** *adv.* **ineffectual** *a.* not producing the proper effect; vain; fruitless; futile. **ineffectuality, ineffectualness** *n.* **ineffectually** *adv.*

in·ef·fi·ca·cy (in·ef'·ạ·kạ·si·) *n.* want of power to produce the proper effect. **inefficacious** *a.* **inefficaciously** *adv.*

in·ef·fi·ci·ent (in·ạ·fish'·ạnt) *a.* not fitted to perform the work in a capable, economical way. **inefficiency** *n.* **-ly** *adv.*

in·e·las·tic (in·i·las'·tik) *a.* not elastic; rigid; unyielding. **inelasticity** *n.*

in·el·e·gant (in·el'·ạ·gant) *a.* lacking in form or beauty; wanting grace or ornament. **inelegance, inelegancy** *n.* **-ly** *adv.*

in·el·i·gi·ble (in·el'·i·jạ·bl) *a.* unsuitable; legally disqualified. **ineligibility** *n.*

in·e·luc·ta·ble (in·i·luk'·tạ·bl) *a.* inevitable. **ineluctability** *n.* [L. *in-*; *eluctari*, to struggle out].

in·ept (in·ept') *a.* not apt or fit; inexpert; unsuitable; foolish. **-itude, -ness** *n.* **-ly** *adv.* [L. *in*, not; *aptus*, fit].

in·e·qual·i·ty (in·i·kwal'·ạ·ti·) *n.* want of equality; disparity; inadequacy; unevenness.

in·eq·ui·ta·ble (in·ek'·wi·tạ·bl) *a.* not fair or just; not according to equity.

in·e·rad·i·ca·ble (in·i·rad'·i·kạ·bl) *a.* incapable of being rooted out; deep-seated.

in·ert (in·urt') *a.* without the power of action or resistance; sluggish; without active chemical properties. **inertia** (in·ur'·shạ) *n.* inactivity; that property of matter by which it tends when at rest to remain so, and when in motion to continue moving in a straight line. **-ly** *adv.* **-ness** *n.* [L. *iners*, sluggish].

in·es·cap·a·ble (in·ạ·skāp'·ạ·bl) *a.* inevitable; incapable of escape or of being evaded.

in·es·sen·tial (in·ạ·sen'·shạl) *a.* not necessary; immaterial; of little consequence.

in·es·ti·ma·ble (in·es'·ti·mạ·bl) *a.* not possible to be estimated; of untold value; incalculable. **inestimably** *adv.*

in·ev·i·ta·ble (in·ev'·i·tạ·bl) *a.* unavoidable; certain to take place or appear. **-ness, inevitability** *n.* **inevitably** *adv.* [L. *in-*; *evitare*, to avoid].

in·ex·act (in·ig·zakt') *a.* not exact; not strictly true. **-itude, -ness** *n.*

in·ex·cus·a·ble (in·ik·skūz') *a.* not admitting excuse or justification; unpardonable.

in·ex·haus·ti·ble (in·ig·zaws'·tạ·bl) *a.* incapable of being exhausted, emptied, or spent; unfailing. **inexhaustibility** *n.* **inexhaustibly** *adv.* **inexhaustive** *a.*

in·ex·o·ra·ble (in·ek'·ser·ạ·bl, in·egz'·er·ạ·bl) *a.* not to be persuaded or moved by entreaty; unyielding. **-ness, inexorability** *n.* **inexorably** *adv.* [L. *in-*; *exorare*, to entreat].

in·ex·pe·di·ent (in·ik·spē'·di·ạnt) *a.* not advisable; impolitic; undesirable at the moment. **inexpedience, inexpediency** *n.*

in·ex·pen·sive (in·ik·spen'·siv) *a.* cheap.

in·ex·pe·ri·ence (in·ik·spēr'·i·ạns) *n.* absence or want of experience. **-d** *a.*

in·ex·pert (in·ek'·spurt) *a.* unskilled; clumsy; awkward. **-ness** *n.*

in·ex·pi·a·ble (in·ek'·spi·ẹ·bl) *a.* admitting of no atonement; implacable; inexorable.

in·ex·pli·ca·ble (in·eks'·pli·kạ·bl) *a.* incapable of being explained. **inexplicability,** *n.* **inexplicably** *adv.*

in·ex·plic·it (in·iks·plis'·it) *a.* not explicit; not clearly stated; ambiguous; equivocal.

in·ex·press·i·ble (in·iks·pres'·ạ·bl) *a.* cannot be expressed; indescribable. **inexpressibly** *adv.*

in·ex·pres·sive (in·iks·pres'·iv) *a.* not expressive; lacking emphasis; insignificant.

in·ex·ten·si·ble (in·ik·sten'·sạ·bl) *a.* not capable of extension. **inextensibility** *n.*

in·ex·tin·guish·a·ble (in·ik·sting'·gwish·ạ·bl) *a.* cannot be extinguished; unquenchable.

in·ex·tri·ca·ble (in·eks'·tri·kạ·bl, in·iks·tri'·kạ·bl) *a.* not to be extricated or disentangled, as a knot or coil; incapable of being cleared up or explained. **inextricably** *adv.*

in·fal·li·ble (in·fal'·ạ·bl) *a.* incapable of error; certain; unerring; sure. **infallibilism, infallibility** *n.* **infallibly** *adv.*

in·fa·my (in'·fạ·mi·) *n.* total loss of reputation; public disgrace; ill-fame. **infamous** *a.* (in'·fạ·mạs) of evil fame or reputation. **infamously** *adv.* [L. *in-*; *fama*, report].

in·fant (in'·fạnt) *n.* a young baby; (*Law*) a person under 21; *a.* pert. to infants or infancy. **infancy** *n.* the early stage of life preceding childhood; (*Law*) life to the age of twenty-one; the first stage of anything. **infanticide** (in·fan'·tạ·sid) *n.* the killing of a newly-born child. **-ile** *a.* pert. to infants; extremely childish. **infantilism** *n.* arrested development, carrying childish characteristics into adult life. **infantile paralysis,** an infectious disease, poliomyelitis, which leads to paralysis [L. *infans*, unable to speak].

in·fan·try (in'·fạn·tri·) *n.* foot-soldiers [It. *infanteria*].

in·fat·u·ate (in·fach'·ōō·wāt) *v.t.* to render foolish; to inspire with a foolish passion. **-d** *a.* greatly enamored. **infatuation** *n.* excessive and foolish love [L. *in*; *fatuus*, foolish].

in·fea·si·ble (in·fē'·zạ·bl) *a.* not capable of being done or accomplished; impracticable.

in·fect (in·fekt') *v.t.* to affect (with disease); to make noxious; to corrupt; to influence the mood or emotions of people. **-ion** *n.* **-ious**, **-ive** *a.* causing infection; catching. **-iously** *adv.* [L. *inficere*, to dip into].

in·fe·lic·i·ty (in·fạ·lis'·ạ·ti·) *n.* unhappiness; anything not appropriate. **infelicitous** *a.*

in·fer (in·fur') *v.t.* to draw as a conclusion; to deduce; to conclude; to imply. *pr.p.* **-ring.** *pa.t.* and *pa.p.* **-red. -able** *a.* **-ence** *n.* deduction. **-ential** *a.* deduced or deducible by inference. **-entially** *adv.* [L. *inferre*, to bring in].

in·fe·ri·or (in·fi'·ri·ẹr) *a.* lower in rank, order, place, or excellence; of less value; poorer in quality; *n.* a person of a lower rank or station. **-ity** *n.* a lower state of condition. **-ly** *adv.* **-ity complex,** subconscious sense of inferiority [L. comp. of *inferus*, low].

in·fer·nal (in·fur'·nạl) *a.* pert. to the lower regions; hellish. **-ity** *n.* **-ly** *adv.* **inferno** *n.* hell; any place resembling hell; furnace. [L. *infernus*, fr. *inferus*, low].

in·fest (in·fest') *v.t.* to inhabit; to swarm in such numbers as to be a source of annoyance. **-ed** *a.* covered with body parasites as lice, etc.; plagued **-ation** *n.* [L. *infestare*, fr. *infestus*, unsafe].

in·fi·del (in'·fạ·dạl) *a.* unbelieving; skeptical; *n.* one who is without religious faith; unbeliever; **-ity** *n.* unfaithfulness to the marriage contract; treachery; lack of religious faith [L. *infidelis*, unfaithful].

in·field (in'·fēld) *n.* (*Baseball*) the three basemen and the short stop, or the diamond; a field in close proximity to a farmhouse. **-er** *n.*

in·fil·trate (in·fil'·trāt) *v.t.* to filter into; to enter gradually; to pass through enemy's lines, one by one; *v.i.* to pass in or through by filtering, or as by filtering. *n.* that which infiltrates. **infiltration** *n.*

in·fi·nite (in'·fạ·nit) *a.* unlimited in time or space; without end, limits, or bounds; (*Math.*) greater than any assignable quantity; numberless; immeasurable; *n.* the boundlessness and immeasurableness of the universe; the Almighty, the Infinite Being. **-ly** *adv.* exceedingly. **-ness** *n.* **infinitesimal** *a.* infinitely small. **infinitesimality** *n.* **infinitesimally** *adv.* **infinitude** *n.* boundlessness (of space and time). **infinity** *n.* unlimited and endless extent. [L. *infinitus*, unbounded].

infield

in·fin·i·tive (in·fin'·ạ·tiv) *n.* the simple form of the verb which can be preceded by *to* (*to be*); *a.* not defined or limited. [L. *infinitus*, unbounded].

in·firm (in·furm') *a.* not strong; feeble; weak; sickly; irresolute. **-ary** *n.* a hospital for the weak and infirm. **-ity** *n.* disease; failing. **-ly** *adv.* [L. *in-*; *firmus*, strong].

in·flame (in·flām') *v.t.* to set on fire; to arouse, as desire; to provoke; to be affected with inflammation. **inflammable** *a.* combustible; easily aroused. **inflammability, inflammableness** *n.* **inflammably** *adv.* **inflammation** *n.* inflaming; diseased condition of a part of the body characterized by heat, redness and pain. **inflammatory** *a.* tending to arouse passions; pert. to inflammation [L. *inflammare*, to set on fire].

in·flate (in·flāt') *v.t.* to swell with air or gas; to raise (price) artificially; to increase (currency) abnormally. **-d** *a.* swollen; bloated; bombastic; pumped up. **inflatable** *a.* **inflation** *n.* swelling; increase in the amount of fiduciary (paper or token) money issued, beyond what is justified by the country's tangible resources; a rise in prices. **inflationary** *a.* [L. *in*; *flare*, to bowl].

in·flect (in·flekt') *v.t.* to bend; to modulate the voice; to modify (words) to show grammatical relationships. **-ion**, *n.* a bending inwards or deviation; a variation in the tone of the voice; variation in the terminations of words to express grammatical relations. **-ional** *a.* **-ive** *a.* subject to inflection. **inflexibility** *n.* **inflexible** *a.* incapable of being bent; unyielding to influence or entreaty; unbending. **inflexibly** *adv.* [L. *in*, in; *flectere*, to bend].

in·flict (in·flikt') *v.t.* to lay on; to impose (a penalty, etc.); to afflict with something painful. **-ion** *n.* pain; burden. **-ive** *a.* [L. *in*, in; *fligere*, to strike].

in·flu·ence (in'·flōō·ạns) *n.* power over men or things; effect on the mind; (*Electrostatics*) induction of a charge by a charged conductor; *v.t.* to act on the mind; to sway; to bias; to induce. **influential** *a.* exerting influence or power; possessing great authority. **influentially** *adv.* [L. *in*, in; *fluere*, to flow].

in·flu·en·za (in·flōō·en'·za) *n.* (*Med.*) an acute, infectious epidemic catarrhal fever [It. = influence].

in·flux (in'·fluks) *n.* act of flowing in; the mouth of a stream; the place where one stream flows into another.

in·fold, enfold (in-, en·fōld') *v.t.* to wrap up; to enclose; to encircle.

in·form (in·fawrm') *v.t.* to tell; to accumulate knowledge; to inspire; *v.i.* to give information.

in·form (in·fawrm') *a.* without form. **-al** *a.* without formality; unceremonious. **-ality** *n.* **-ant** *n.* one who imparts news. **-ation** *n.* knowledge; intelligence; news. **-ative, -atory** *a.* educational. **-ed** *a.* educated. **-er** *n.* one who gives information about a violation of the law [L. *informare*, to give form to].

in·frac·tion (in·frak′·shan) *n.* breach; violation.

in·fran·gi·ble (in·fran′·ja·bl) *a.* not capable of being broken; not to be violated. **infrangibility** *n.* [L. *in-*, not; *frangere*, to break].

in·fra·red (in·fra·red′) *a.* of the longer invisible heat rays below the red end of the visible spectrum.

in·fre·quent (in·frē′·kwant) *a.* seldom happening; rare; uncommon. **infrequence, infrequency** *n.* **-ly** *adv.*

in·fringe (in·frinj′) *v.t.* to violate; to transgress. **-ment** *n.* breach; breaking (of a law) [L. *in; frangere*, to break].

in·fu·ri·ate (in·fyoor′·i·āt) *v.t.* to make furious, to enrage; to madden. **infuriation** *n.* [L. *in; furia*, rage].

in·fuse (in·fūz′) *v.t.* to pour into; to instill; to inspire; to steep in order to extract soluble properties. **infusible** *a.* capable of being infused; not capable of fusion. **infusibility** *n.* **infusion** *n.* act of infusing, instilling, or inspiring; aqueous solution containing the soluble parts of a substance, made by pouring boiling water over it, cooling and straining [L. *in*, in; *fundere, fusum*, to pour].

in·gen·ious (in·jēn′·yas) *a.* skilled in inventing or thinking out new ideas; curious or clever in design; skillfully contrived. **-ly** *adv.* **-ness, ingenuity** (in·ja·nōō′·i·ti·) *n.* [L. *ingenium*, natural ability].

in·ge·nue (an·zha·nōō′) *n.* an artless, naive, girl; an actress who plays such a part [Fr.].

in·gen·u·ous (in·jen′·yoo·as) *a.* frank; artless; innocent. **-ly** *adv.* **-ness** *n.* [L. *ingenuus* free-born, frank].

in·got (ing′·gat) *n.* a metal casting, esp. of unwrought silver or gold [O.E. *in; geotan*, to pour].

in·grain, engrain (in-, en·grān′) *v.t.* to fix firmly in the mind. (in′·grain) *a.* firmly fixed; dyed, before manufacture into articles. **-ed** *a.*

in·grate (in′·grāt) *n.* an ungrateful person. **ingratitude** *n.* want of gratitude; unthankfulness.

in·gra·ti·ate (in·grā′·shi·āt) *v.t.* to work oneself into favor with another **ingratiation** *n.* [L. *in; gratia*, favor].

in·gre·di·ent (in·grē′·di·ant) *n.* a component part of any mixture; one part or element of a compound [L. *ingredi*, to go in].

in·gress (in′·gres) *n.* entrance; power, right, or means of entrance [L. *ingredi, ingressum*, to go in].

in·grow·ing (in′·grō·ing) *a.* growing inwards, esp. of a toenail. **ingrowth** *n.* **ingrown** *a.*

in·gur·gi·tate (in·gur′·ja·tāt) *v.t.* to swallow up greedily or hastily; to engulf. **ingurgitation** *n.* [L. *in*, in; *gurges*, a whirlpool].

in·hab·it (in·hab′·it) *v.t.* to live or dwell in; to occupy. **-able** *a.* possible to be dwelt in. **-ant** *n.* one who inhabits; a resident. **-ation** *n.* [L. *in*, in; *habitare*, to dwell].

in·hale (in·hāl′) *v.t.* to breathe in, as air, tobacco smoke, etc.; to draw in the breath. **inhalant** *n.* a volatile medicinal remedy to be inhaled. *a.* **inhalation** *n.* act of drawing air into the lungs. **inhalator** *n.* apparatus to help one inhale [L. *in*, in; *halare*, to breathe].

in·here (in·hir′) *v.i.* (usu. followed by in) to exist in; to belong naturally to; to be a quality of; to be vested in, as legal rights. **-nce, -ncy** *n.* **-nt** *a.* existing in something so as to be inseparable. **-ntly** *adv.* [L. *in*, in; *haerere*, to stick].

in·her·it (in·her′·at) *v.t.* to receive by descent, or by will; to fall heir to; to derive (traits, etc.) from parents; *v.i.* to succeed as heir. **-able** *a.* **-ance** *n.* what is inherited. **-or** *n.* (*fem.* **-ress, -rix**) [L. *in*, in; *heres*, an heir].

in·hib·it (in·hib′·it) *v.t.* to hold back; to forbid; to restrain. **inhibition** (in·i·bi′·shan) *n.* a subconscious repressed emotion which controls or colors a person's attitude or behavior. **-ory** *a.* prohibiting; forbidding; restraining [L. *inhibere*, to hold in].

in·hos·pi·ta·ble (in·hàs′·pi·ta·bl) *a.* averse to showing kindness to strangers or guests; discourteous. **-ness, inhospitality** *n.* **inhospitably** *adv.* [L. *hospes*, a guest].

in·hu·man (in·hū′·man) *a.* not human or humane; without feeling or pity. **inhumane** (in·hū·mān′) *a.* cruel. **-ity** *n.*

in·hume (in·hūm′) *v.t.* to put into the ground; to bury. **inhumation** *n.* [L. *humus*, ground].

in·im·i·cal (in·im′·i·kal) *a.* like an enemy; unfriendly. **-ly** *adv.* [L. *inimicus*, an enemy].

in·im·i·ta·ble (in·im′·i·ta·bl) *a.* defying imitation; incomparable. **inimitably** *adv.*

in·iq·ui·ty (in·ik′·wa·ti·) *n.* gross injustice; want of moral principle; wickedness; a crime. **iniquitous** *a.* **iniquitously** *adv.* [L. *iniquitas* fr. *in-*, not; *aequus*, fair, even].

in·i·tial (i·nish′·al) *a.* occurring at the beginning; commencing; early; *v.t.* to put one's initials to, in the way of acknowledgment. *n.* the first letter of a word, esp. a name. **initiate**, *v.t.* to begin; to start (a movement, etc.); to instruct in the rudiments of; to admit into a society, etc., with formal rites; *n.* one who is initiated. **initiation** *n.* **initiative** *a.* serving to initiate; *n.* the first step; the quality of being able to set things going for the first time. **initiator** *n.* **initiatory** *a.* introductory [L. *initialis*, fr. *initium*, a beginning].

in·ject (in·jekt′) *v.t.* to throw in; to force in; to introduce (a fluid) under the skin by means of a hollow needle. **-ion** *n.* the act of injecting or throwing into; fluid so injected. **-or** *n.* [L. *injicere*, fr. *jacere*, to throw].

in·ju·di·cious (in·jōō·dish′·as) *a.* ill-advised; imprudent; lacking in judgment **injudicial** *a.* not according to the form of law. **-ly** *adv.*

in·junc·tion (in·jungk′·shan) *n.* an order or command; an exhortation; a precept [L. *in*, in; *jungere, junctum*, to join].

in·jure (in′·jer) *v.t.* to do wrong, injury, damage, or injustice to. **injurious** *a.* causing injury or damage. **injuriously** *adv.* **injury** *n.* wrong; damage; harm [L. *injuria*, fr. *jus*, law].

in·jus·tice (in·jus′·tis) *n.* an unjust act; want of justice; wrong.

ink (ingk) *n.* a fluid, black or colored, used for writing, printing and sketching; *v.t.* to cover or smear with ink. **-well** *n.* container for ink. **-iness** *n.* **-y** *a.* resembling ink [O.Fr. *enque = Fr. encre*].

ink·ling (ingk′·ling) *n.* a hint or whisper; slight knowledge [etym. doubtful].

in·land (in′·land) *a.* remote from the sea; interior; carried on within a country; *n.* (in·land′) the interior part of a country. **-er** *n.*

in·laws (in′·lawz) *n.pl.* (*Colloq.*) one's relations by marriage.

in·lay (in·lā′) *v.t.* to ornament, by cutting out part of a surface and inserting pieces of pearl, ivory, wood, etc., to form a pattern. *pa.p.* **inlaid.** *n.* inlaid pattern.

in·let (in′·let) *n.* an entrance; a small bay or creek; an insertion.

in·mate (in′·māt) *n.* a dweller in a house or institution; a fellow-lodger.

inn (in) *n.* a house which provides lodging accommodation for travelers; a hotel; restaurant or tavern. **-keeper** *n.* one who keeps an inn. [O.E.].

in·nate (i·nāt′) *a.* inborn; native; natural; inherent; congenital. **-ly** *adv.* [L. *innatus*].

in·ner (in′·er) *a.* farther in; interior; private; not obvious. **-most, inmost.** *a.* farthest in. [O.E. *innera*, comp. fr. *inne*, within].

in·ner·vate (in′·er·vāt). Also **innerve**, *v.t.* to give nervous strength to; to stimulate. **innervation** *n.* [L. *in; nervus*, sinew].

in·ning (in′·ing) *n.* in games, a side's turn of batting; the ingathering of grain; reclaiming of land [O.E. *inn*, in, within].

in·no·cent (in′·a·sant) *a.* free from guilt; blameless; harmless, sinless; simple; *n.* an innocent person, esp. a child; a guileless, unsuspecting person. **innocence, innocency** *n.* **-ly** *adv.* [L. *in-*, not; *nocere*, to harm].

in·noc·u·ous (in·àk′·yoo·as) *a.* producing no ill effects; harmless. **-ly** *adv.* **-ness** [L. *in-*, not; *nocere*, to harm].

in·no·vate (in′·a·vāt) *v.t.* to make changes by introducing something new. **innovation** *n.* a new idea [L. *innovare*, fr. *novus*, new].

in·nox·ious (in·àk′·shas) *a.* innocuous; harmless in effects [L. *innoxius*].

in·nu·en·do (in·ū·en′·dō) *n.* an allusive remark (usually deprecatory); an indirect hint [L. = by nodding to, fr. *nuere*, to nod].

in·nu·mer·a·ble (i·nū′·mer·a·bl) *a.* not able to be numbered; countless; very numerous. **innumerability** *n.* **innumerably** *adv.*

in·nu·tri·tion (in·nōō·trish′·an) *n.* want of nutrition. **innutritious** *a.*

in·ob·serv·ant (in·ab·zer′·vant) *a.* not observant; heedless. **inobservance** *n.* failure to observe (the law, church-going, etc.).

in·oc·u·late (in·àk′·ya·lāt) *v.t.* (*Med.*) to introduce into the body pathogenic bacteria (e.g. typhoid inoculation) or living virus (e.g. smallpox vaccination) to secure immunity; to imbue strongly with opinions. **inoculation** *n.* [L. *inoculare*, fr. *oculus*, eye, bud].

in·op·er·a·ble (in·àp′·er·a·bl) *a.* (*Surgery*) not in a condition for operating on. **inoperative** *a.* not operating; without effect.

in·op·por·tune (in·àp·er·tūn′) *a.* unseasonable in time; not convenient; untimely. **-ly** *adv.* **inopportunity** *n.*

in·or·di·nate (in·awr′·da·nat) *a.* not limited; disordered. **-ness** *n.* **-ly** *adv.* excessively.

in·or·gan·ic (in·awr·gan′·ik) *a.* devoid of an organized structure; not derived from animal or vegetable life. **-ally** *adv.*

in·os·cu·late (in·às′·kya·lāt) *v.t.* and *v.i.* to join by openings (arteries, etc.).

in·pa·tient (in′·pā·shant) *n.* a patient who is lodged and fed while receiving medical attention in a hospital.

in·put (in′·poot) *n.* (*Elect.*) the power supplied to battery, condenser, etc.

in·quest (in′·kwest) *n.* a judicial inquiry, esp. one presided over by a coroner, with or without a jury, into the cause of a person's death.

in·qui·e·tude (in·kwī′·a·tūd) *n.* uneasiness either of body or of mind; restlessness.

in·quire, enquire (in-, en·kwīr′) *v.i.* to ask questions; to make investigation; to seek information; *v.t.* to ask about. **-r** *n.* **inquiring** *a.* given to inquiring; prying. **inquiringly** *adv.* **inquiry** *n.* investigation; a question [L. *inquirere*, fr. *quaerere*, to seek].

in·qui·si·tion (in·kwa·zish′·an) *n.* a strict investigation; official inquiry; an ecclesiastical tribunal, 'the Holy Office,' established by the R.C. Church in the Middle Ages for the trial and punishment of heretics. **-al** *a.* **inquisitive** *a.* apt to ask questions; prying; curious to know. **inquisitively** *adv.* **inquisitiveness** *n.* **inquisitor** *n.* one whose official duty it is to make inquiries; a member of the Court of Inquisition. **inquisitorial** *a.* **inquisitorially** *adv.* [L. *inquisitio*, fr. *inquirere*, to search out].

in·re (in·rē′, ·rā′) *prep.* in the matter of; concerning (often abbreviated to **re**) [L.]

in·road (in′·rōd) *n.* a sudden incursion into enemy territory; a sudden invasion; raid.

in·sane (in·sān′) *a.* unsound in mind; mentally diseased; lunatic. **-ly** *adv.* **-ness, insanity** *n.* lunacy; madness.

in·sa·tia·ble (in·sā′·sha·bl) *a.* incapable of being satisfied; voracious; rapacious. **-ness, insatiability** *n.* **insatiably** *adv.*

in·sa·ti·ate (in·sā′·shi·at) *a.* not to be satisfied. **-ly** *adv.* **-ness** *n.*

in·scribe (in·skrīb′) *v.t.* to write upon; to engrave; to address or dedicate; to draw a geometrical figure inside another so as to touch but not intersect. **inscribable** *a.* **-r** *n.* **inscription** *n.* act of inscribing; words inscribed on a monument, coin, etc.; dedication of a book, etc.; **inscriptional, inscriptive** *a.* [L. *in; scribere*, to write].

in·scru·ta·ble (in·skrōō′·ta·bl) *a.* incapable of being searched into and understood by inquiry or study; mysterious. **inscrutability, -ness** *n.* **inscrutably** *adv.* [L. *in-*, not; *scrutari*, to search].

in·sect (in′·sekt) *n.* one of a class of invertebrate animals called the *Insecta.* *a.* pert. to insects; small; insignificant. **insecta** *n.* the insect or hexapod (six-legged) class of arthropods. **insecticide** *n.* killing insect pests; chemical preparation for the destruction of noxious insects. **-ivorous** *a.* living on insects [L. *in*, in; *secare*, to cut].

in·se·cure (in·si·kyoor′) *a.* not securely fixed; dangerous to life or limb; unsafe; unguarded; having doubts and fears. **insecurity** *n.*

in·sem·i·nate (in·sem′·a·nāt) *v.t.* to sow; to impregnate. **insemination** *n.* conception [L. *in*, into; *semen*, seed].

in·sen·sate (in·sen'·sāt) *a.* destitute of sense; without power of feeling. **-ly** *adv.*

in·sen·si·ble (in·sen'·sa·bl) *a.* without bodily sensation; not perceived by the senses; unconscious; callous; imperceptible **-ness** *n.* **insensibility, insensibly** *adv.*

in·sen·si·tive (in·sen'·sa·tiv) *a.* not sensitive; callous. **-ness, insensitivity** *n.*

in·sen·ti·ent (in·sen'·shi·ant) *a.* not having perception; inanimate.

in·sep·a·ra·ble (in·sep'·a·ra·bl) *a.* not divisible or separable; always in close association; *n.pl.* persons or things that are seldom seen apart. **inseparably** *adv.*

in·sert (in·surt') *vt.* to put in; to place among; to introduce. (in'·surt) *n.* anything inserted. **-ion** *n.* the act of inserting; that which is inserted [L. *in.* in; *serere*, to join].

in·side (in'·sīd) *prep.* or *adv.* within the sides of; in the interior; *a.* internal; interior; *n.* the part within; *pl.* (*Colloq.*) inward parts; guts. **-r** *n.* (*Colloq.*) one who is within a certain group or has special advantages.

in·sid·i·ous (in·sid'·i·as) *a.* lying in wait; treacherous; advancing imperceptibly. **-ly** *adv.* **-ness** *n.* [L. *insidiosus*, fr. *insidere*, to lie in wait.].

in·sight (in'·sīt) *n.* view of the interior of anything; mental penetration; clear understanding; power of discernment.

in·sig·ni·a (in·sig'·ni·a) *n.pl.* symbols of authority, dignity, or office; badges; emblems [L. fr. *signum*, sign].

in·sig·ni·fi·cant (in·sig·nif'·a·kant) *a.* signifying very little; having little importance, use, or value; trifling. **insignificance, insignificancy** *n.* **-ly** *adv.*

in·sin·cere (in·sin·sir') *a.* not sincere; dissembling; hypocritical; not to be trusted. -ly *adv.* **insincerity** *n.* hypocrisy.

in·sin·u·ate (in·sin'·ya·wāt) *v.t.* to introduce gently and adroitly; to suggest by remote allusion; to work oneself into favor; *v.i.* to ingratiate oneself. **insinuating** *a.* **insinuatingly** *adv.* **insinuation** *n.* act of gaining favor by artful means; hint; suggestion. **insinuative** *a.* **insinuator** *n.* **insinuatory** *a.* [L. *insinuare*, to introduce tortuously].

in·sip·id (in·sip'·id) *a.* destitute of taste; deficient in spirit, life, or animation. **-ly** *adv.* **-ness, -ity** *n.* [L. *insipidus*, tasty].

in·sip·i·ent (in·sip'·i·ant) *a.* not wise; foolish. **insipience** *n.* [L. *insipiens*].

in·sist (in·sist') *v.i.* to dwell upon as a matter of special moment; to be urgent or pressing; (foll. by *on* or *upon*) to hold firmly to. **-ence** *n.* persistent demand or refusal to give way. **-ency** *n.* pertinacity. **-ent** *a.* [L. *insistere*, fr. *sistere*, to stand].

in·so·bri·e·ty (in·sa·brī'·a·ti·) *n.* drunkenness.

in·so·lent (in'·sa·lant) *a.* proud and haughty; overbearing. **insolence** *n.* contemptuous rudeness or arrogance. **-ly** *adv.* [L. *in-*, not; *solere*, to be accustomed].

in·sol·u·ble (in·sál'·ya·bl) *a.* incapable of being dissolved; inexplicable; not to be explained. **insolubility, -ness** *n.* **insolvable** *a.*

in·sol·vent (in·sál'·vant) *a.* not able to pay one's debts; bankrupt; *n.* one who is bankrupt. **insolvency** *n.*

in·som·ni·a (in·sam'·ni·a) *n.* chronic sleeplessness from any cause [L.].

in·so·much (in·sa·much') *adv.* so that; to such a degree; in such wise that.

in·sou·ci·ance (in·sōō'·si·ans) *n.* carelessness of feeling or manner; an air of indifference. **insouciant** *a.* carefree; indifferent [Fr.].

in·spect (in·spekt') *v.t.* to view narrowly and critically; to examine officially as troops, arms, or goods offered for sale, etc. **-ingly** *adv.* **inspection** *n.* careful survey; official examination. **inspectional, -ive** *a.* **-or** *n.* official examiner; a police officer ranking below a superintendent; anyone who inspects. **-orate** *n.* a district under an inspector; a body of inspectors generally. **-orial** *a.* [L. *inspicere*, to look into].

in·spire (in·spīr') *v.t.* to breathe in; to infuse thought or feeling into; to affect as with a supernatural influence; to arouse; *v.i.* to give

inspiration; to inhale. **inspirable** *a.* **inspiration** *n.* act of drawing in the breath; communication of ideas from a supernatural source; a bright idea. **inspirational, inspiratory** *a.* tending to inspire; encouraging. **inspired** *a.* inhaled; actuated by Divine influence [L. *in; spirare*, to breathe].

in·sta·bil·i·ty (in·sta·bil'·a·ti·) *n.* want of stability or firmness.

in·stall (in·stawl') *v.t.* to place in position; to have something put in; to induct, with ceremony, a person into an office. **installation** *n.* complete equipment of a building for heating, lighting, etc.; generally, placing in position for use. **-ment** *n.* act of installing; a periodical payment of the part cost of something; a portion.

in·stance (in'·stans) *n.* case in point; example; *v.t.* to mention as an example; to cite. **instant** *a.* urgent; pressing; immediate; current (usu. abbreviated to inst.); *n.* a particular point of time; moment. **instantaneity** *n.* **instantaneous** *a.* done in an instant; happening in a moment. **instantaneously** *adv.* **instantaneousness** *n.* **instantly** *adv.* at once [L. *in; stare*, to stand].

in·stead (in·sted') *adv.* in the stead, place, or room; in one's stead [*stead*].

in·step (in'·step) *n.* the arched upper part of the human foot, near the ankle, which gives spring to the step; that part of a shoe, etc., which covers the instep; the hind-leg of a horse from the hock to the pastern joint.

in·sti·gate (in'·sta·gāt) *v.t.* to goad or urge forward; to incite, esp. to evil; to bring about. **instigation** *n.* **instigator** *n.* [L. *instigare*, to incite].

in·still (in·stil') *v.t.* to put in by drops; to infuse slowly; to introduce by degrees (into the mind). **-ed. -ation, -ment** *n.* [L. *in; stillare*, to drip].

in·stinct (in'·stingkt) *n.* intuition (in *neurology*) compound reflex action; (in *psychology*) an innate train of reflexes; inborn impulse or propensity; unconscious skill; intuition. (in·stingkt') *a.* charged; full; urged from within; animated. **instinctively, instinctly** *adv.* **instinctivity** *n.* [L. *instinctus*, fr. *instinguere*, to urge].

in·sti·tute (in'·sta·tūt) *v.t.* to establish; to found; to appoint; to set going; to originate; to lay down as a law; *n.* a society or organization established for promoting some particular work, scientific, educational, etc. **institutes** *n.pl.* a book of precepts, principles or rules; a text-book on legal principles. **institution** *n.* the act of instituting or establishing; an established law, custom, or public occasion; an institute; (*sociol.*) an organized pattern of group behavior established and generally accepted as a fundamental part of a culture, such as slavery. **institutional** *a.* **institutionally** *adv.* **institutive** *a.* tending or intended to instigate or establish; endowed with the power to ordain; **institutively** *adv.* **institutor, -r** *n.* [L. *instituere*, to set up].

in·struct (in·strukt') *v.t. to* teach; to inform; to prepare someone for (e.g., an examination); to order or command; to give directions to. **-ible** *a.* **-ion** *n.* the act of instructing or teaching; education; order. **-ional, -ive** *a.* fitted to instruct; containing edifying matter; conveying knowledge or information. **-ively** *adv.* **-iveness** *n.* **-or** *n.* [L. *instructus*].

in·stru·ment (in'·stra·mant) *n.* a tool or implement; a person or thing made use of; a means of producing musical sounds; (*Law*) a formal or written document. **-al** (in·stra·ment'·al) *a.* serving as an instrument or means; helpful; pert. to musical, surgical, or other instruments; performed with or composed for a musical instrument or instruments; (*Gram.*) in some inflected languages, denoting a case, having as chief function the indication of means or agency. **-alist** *n.* one skilled in playing upon a musical instrument. **-ality** *n.* the quality of being instrumental, of serving some purpose; agency or means; good offices. **-ally** *adv.* **-ation** *n.* the art of writing and arranging musical compositions for the individual instruments of a band or orchestra; orchestration. [L. *instruere*, to build].

in·sub·or·di·nate (in·sa·bawr'·da·nit) *a.* disobedient; unruly. **insubordination** *n.*

in·suf·fer·a·ble (in·suf'·er·a·bl) *a.* not able to be endured; intolerable. **insufferably** *adv.*

in·suf·fi·cient (in·sa·fish'·ant) *a.* not enough; deficient. **insufficiency** *n.* **-ly** *adv.*

in·su·lar (in'·syoo·ler) *a.* pert. to or like an island; isolated; narrow-minded or prejudiced. **-ism, -ity** *n.* **-ly** *adv.* [L. *insula*, an island].

in·su·late (in'·sa·lāt) *r.t.* to keep rigidly apart from contact with other people; to bar the passage of electricity, heat, sound, light, dampness, or vibration by the use of non-conducting materials. **insulation** *n.* [L. *insula*, an island].

in·su·lin (in'·sa·lin) *n.* a hormone secreted in the pancreas; organic drug for the treatment of diabetes [L. *insula*, island].

in·sult (in·sult') *r.t.* to treat with insolence or contempt by words or action; to abuse; to affront. (in'·sult) *n.* gross abuse offered to another [L. *insultare*, to leap upon].

in·su·per·a·ble (in·sōō'·per·a·bl) *a.* not able to be overcome or surmounted; invincible. **insuperability, n. insuperably** *adv.*

in·sup·port·a·ble (in·sa·pōr'·ta·bl) *a.* incapable of being borne or endured. **-ness** *n.* **insupportably** *adv.*

in·sure (in·shoor') *r.t.* to make sure or certain; to make safe (against); to ensure; to secure the payment of a sum in event of loss, death, etc., by a contract and payment of sums called premiums. **insurable** *a.* **insurance** *n.* contract between two parties whereby the insurer agrees to indemnify the insured upon the occurrence of a stipulated contingency [L. *in; securus*, secure].

in·sur·gent (in·sur'·jant) *a.* rising in opposition to lawful authority; rebellious; *n.* one in revolt; a rebel. **insurgency** *n.* incipient stage of revolt. Also **insurgence**.

in·sur·mount·a·ble (in·ser·moun'·ta·bl) *a.* not able to be surmounted or overcome. **insurmountability** *n.* **insurmountably** *adv.*

in·sur·rec·tion (in·sa·rek'·shan) *n.* a rising against civil or political authority. **-al, -ary** *a.* **-ist** *n.* [L. *insurgere*, to rise upon].

in·sus·cep·ti·ble (in·sa·sep'·ta·bl) *a.* not susceptible; not to be moved, affected, or impressed. **insusceptibility** *n.*

in·take (in'·tāk) *n.* that which is taken in; quantity taken in; inlet of a tube or cylinder; a point of narrowing or contraction.

in·tan·gi·ble (in·tan'·ja·bl) *a.* not perceptible to the touch; not clear to the mind. **-ness, intangibility** *n.* **intangibly** *adv.*

in·te·ger (in'·ta·jer) *n.* the whole of anything; whole number (as opposed to a fraction or a mixed number). **integral** (in'·ta·gral) *a.* denoting a whole number or quantity; constituting an essential part of a whole; *n.* a whole number; (*Math.*) a sum of differentials. **integrally** *adv.* **integrate** *v.t.* to make entire; to give the sum or total. **integration** *n.* act of making a whole out of parts. **integrator** *n.* **integrity** *n.* the state of being entire; wholeness; probity; honesty; uprightness [L. *integer*, entire].

in·teg·u·ment (in·teg'·ya·mant) *n.* the outer protective layer of tissue which covers a plant or animal; the skin. **integumentary** *a.* [L. *integumentum*, fr. *integere*, to cover].

in·tel·lect (in'·ta·lekt) *n.* the faculty of reasoning and thinking; mental power; mind; understanding; *pl.* the senses. **-ive** *a.* pert. to intellect as distinguished from the senses.

in·tel·lect·u·al (in·ta·lek'·choo·al) *a.* of high mental capacity; having the power of understanding; *n.* one well endowed with intellect. **-ism** *n.* the doctrine that knowledge is derived from pure reason; emphasis on the value of the rational faculties. **-ity** *n.* intellectual powers. **-ly** *adv.* [L. *intelligere*, to understand].

in·tel·li·gent (in·tel'·a·jant) *a.* having or showing good intellect; quick at understanding. **intelligence** *n.* inborn quickness of understanding and adaptability to relatively new situations; information. **-ly** *adv.* **-sia** *n.* the intellectual or cultured classes. **intelligible** *a.* that can be readily understood; rational. **intelligibleness, intelligibility** *n.* **intelligibly** *adv.* **intelligence quotient** (abbrev. I.Q.) the numerical rating of general intelligence by use of psychological tests [L. *intelligere*, to understand].

in·tem·per·ate (in·tem'·per·at) *a.* immoderate; indulging to excess any appetite or passion; addicted to an excessive use of liquor; extreme in climate. **intemperance** *n.* excess of any kind. **-ly** *adv.* [L. *intemperatus*].

in·tend (in·tend') *v.t.* and *v.i.* to design; to purpose; to mean; to have in mind. **-ant** *n.* one who has the charge of some public business. **-ancy** *n.* the office of an intendant. **-ed** *a.* and *n.* (*Colloq.*) betrothed [L. *intendere*, to bend the mind on].

in·tense (in·tens') *a.* to an extreme degree; very strong or acute; emotional. **-ly** *adv.* **-ness, intensity** *n.* severity; ardor; earnestness; the strength of an electric current. **intensification** *n.* **intensify** *v.t.* to render more intense; to increase or augment; *v.i.* to become more intense. *pa.t.* and *pa.p.* **intensified. intensive** *a.* giving emphasis; unrelaxed; increasing in force. **intensively** *adv.* [L. *intendere, intensum*, to stretch].

in·tent (in·tent') *a.* having the mind bent on an object; eager in pursuit of; firmly resolved; preoccupied; absorbed; *n.* intention; aim; purpose; view; object. **-ion** *n.* design; aim; purpose. **-ional, -ioned** *a.* done purposely. **-ionally** *adv.* **-ly** *adv.* **-ness** *n.* [L. *intendere*, to turn the mind to].

in·ter- (in'·ter) *prefix* fr. L. *inter*, between, among, with, amid.

in·ter (in·tur') *v.t.* to bury. *pr.p.* **-ring.** *pat.* and *pa.p.* **-red.** **-ment** *n.* burial [Fr. *enterrer*, fr. L. *in; terra*, earth].

in·ter·act (in·ter·akt') *v.i.* to act mutually on each other. **-ion** *n.*

in·ter·cede (in·ter·sēd') *v.i.* to act as peacemaker; to plead in favor of one; to mediate. **-r** *n.* **intercession** *n.* the act of interceding. **intercessor** *n.* a mediator; a pleader. **intercessorial, intercessory** *a.* [L. *inter*, between; *cedere*, to go].

in·ter·cept (in·ter·sept') *v.t.* to stop or obstruct passage; to seize in transit; (*Math.*) to cut off a part of a line at two points; *n.* the part of a line between any two points. **-er, -or** *n.* **-ion** *n.* **-ive** *a.* [L. *inter*, between; *capere, captum*, to seize].

in·ter·ces·sion, intercessor See **intercede.**

in·ter·change (in·ter·chānj') *v.t.* to exchange; to reciprocate; *v.i.* to exchange alternately; to exchange places; *n.* (in'·ter·chānj) access to a freeway; a mutual exchange. **-able** *a.* **-ability, -ableness** *n.*

in·ter·com (in'·ter·kám) (*Slang*) *n.* internal telephonic system. **-municate** (in·ter·ka·mū'·ni·kāt) *v.t.* to exchange conversations or messages. **-munication** *a.,n.* **-municative** *a.*

in·ter·con·nect (in·ter·ka·nekt') *v.t.* and *v.i.* to connect mutually and intimately.

in·ter·cos·tal (in·ter·kás'·tal) *a.*(*Anat.*) between the rigs [L. *inter*, between; *costa*, a rib].

in·ter·course (in'·ter·kōrs) *n.* communication between individuals; exchange of goods; correspondence by letter; coition [O.Fr. *entre·cours*, fr. L. *inter*, between; *currere*, to run].

in·ter·cur·rent (in·ter·kur'·ant) *a.* running between or among; occurring during the course of another (disease); intervening.

in·ter·de·pend (in·ter·di·pend') *v.i.* to depend mutually. **-ence** *n.* **-ent** *a.* **-ently** *adv.*

in·ter·dict (in·ter·dikt') *v.t.* to forbid; to prohibit; to restrain; to debar from communion with a church; to lay under an interdict. (in'·ter·dikt) *n.* prohibition; (*Law*) a prohibitory act or decree; a papal ordinance by which certain persons are debarred from participating in the sacraments, church offices or ecclesiastical burial. **-ion** *n.* **-ive, -ory** *a.* [L. *interdicere*, to prohibit].

in·ter·est (in'·ter·ast, in'·trist) *v.t.* to engage and keep the attention of; to arouse the curiosity of; to cause to feel interest; *n.* special attention; concern; regard to personal profit or advantage; curiosity; the profit per cent derived from money lent. **-ed** *a.* having a share in; feeling an interest in. **-edly** *adv.* **-edness** *n.* **-ing** *a.* appealing to or exciting one's interest or curiosity. **-ingly** *adv.* **compound** —, interest on the principal and also on the added interest as it falls due. **simple interest,** interest only on the principal during the time of loan. [L. *interesse*, to be of concern to].

in·ter·fere (in·ter·fīr') *v.i.* to be in or come into, opposition; to enter into or take part in the concerns of others; to intervene. **-nce** *n.* meddling with other people's business; uncalled-for intervention; (*Radio*) anything generally which prevents the proper reception of radio waves. **-r** *n.* **interferingly** *adv.* [L. *inter*, between; *ferire*, to strike].

in·ter·im (in'·ter·im) *n.* the time between; the meantime; *a.* for the time being; temporary; provisional [L.].

in·te·ri·or (in·tī'·ri·ęr) *a.* inner; internal; inland, away from coast or frontiers; *n.* the inside part or portion; the inland part of a country. **-ly** *adv.* [L. compar. of *interus*, fr L. *intra*, within].

in·ter·ject (in·ter·jekt') *v.t.* to throw between; to insert; to exclaim abruptly. **-ion** *n.* act of throwing between; a word which expresses strong emotion or passion when suddenly uttered. **-ional, -ionary, -ory** *a.* **-ionally** *adv.* [L. *inter*, between; *jacere, jactum*, to throw].

in·ter·lace (in·ter·lās') *v.t.* to lace together; to entwine; to unite; to interweave.

in·ter·lard (in·ter·lárd') *v.t.* to diversify by mixture (of words, etc.).

in·ter·line (in·ter·līn') *v.t.* to write or mark between the lines of a book, document, etc.; to put an inner lining in a garment between the outer material and the regular lining. **-al, -ar** *a.* between lines. **-ate** *v.t.* to mark between the lines. **interlining** *n.* inner lining of a garment; interlineation [L. *interlineare*].

in·ter·lock (in·ter·lak') *v.t.* to unite by locking together; to fasten together so that one part cannot move without the other; *v.i.* to be locked or jammed together.

in·ter·lo·cu·tion (in·ter·lō·kū'·shan) *n.* dialogue; a conference; speaking in turn. (in·ter·lák'·ya·ter) *n.* one who speaks in his turn; one who questions another [L. *interloqui*, to speak between].

in·ter·lope (in·ter·lōp') *v.i.* to traffic without a proper license; to intrude into other people's affairs. **-r** *n.* [L. *inter*, between; Dut. *loopen*, to run].

in·ter·lude (in'·ter·lōōd) *n.* a dramatic or musical performance given between parts of an independent play; an interval; an incident during a pause in the proceedings [L. *inter*, between; *ludus*, play].

in·ter·mar·ry (in·ter·mar'·i·) *v.i.* to connect families or races by a marriage between two of their members; to marry within close relationship. **intermarriage** *n.*

in·ter·me·di·ate (in·ter·mē'·di·at) *a.* lying or being between two extremes; in a middle position; intervening; *n.* anything in between; *v.i.* to mediate; to intervene. **intermediacy** *n.* state of being intermediate; mediation. **intermediary** *a.* acting between; interposed; intermediate; *n.* one who acts as a go-between or mediator. **intermedium** *n.* intervening person or instrument. **intermediation** *n.* [L. *inter*, between; *medius*, middle].

in·ter·ment See **inter.**

in·ter·mez·zo (in·ter·met'·sō, med'·zō) *n.* a light dramatic entertainment between the acts of a tragedy, grand opera, etc.; an interlude; (*Mus.*) a short movement connecting more important ones in a symphony, sonata, opera, etc. [It. = in between].

in·ter·mi·na·ble (in·tur'·mi·na·bl) *a.* endless; unlimited. **-ness** *n.* **interminably** *adv.*

in·ter·min·gle (in·ter·ming'·gl) *v.t.* to mingle or mix together.

in·ter·mit (in·ter·mit') *v.t.* to give up or forbear for a time; to interrupt; *v.i.* to cease for a time. *pr.p.* **-ting.** *pa.t., pa.p.* **-ted.** **intermission** *n.* intervening period of time; suspension; interval. **intermissive.** *a.* coming after temporary cessations. **-tence, -tency** *n.* **-tent** *a.* occurring at intervals; ceasing at intervals; coming and going. **-tently** *adv.* [L. *inter*, between; *mittere, missum*, to send].

in·ter·mix (in·ter·miks') *v.t.* and *v.i.* to mix together. **-ture** *n.*

in·tern (in·turn') *v.t.* to confine (in a place), esp. aliens or suspects in time of war; (in'·turn) *n.* a resident doctor in a hospital. Also **interne. internee** *n.* one who is confined to a certain place. **-ment** *n.* **-ship** *n.* [L. *internus*, internal].

in·ter·nal (in·tur'·nal) *a.* interior; inner; inward; domestic, as opposed to foreign. **-ly** *adv.* — **combustion**, the process occurring by exploding in one or more piston-fitted cylinders a mixture of air and fuel [L. *internus*, inward].

in·ter·na·tion·al (in·ter·nash'·an·al) *a.* pert. to the relations between nations; *n.* a game or match between teams representing their respective countries; a player who participates in such. **-ism** *n.* a political theory which aims at breaking down the artificial barriers which separate nations. **-ist** *n.* **-ly** *adv.*

in·ter·ne·cine (in·ter·nē'·sin) *a.* mutually destructive; deadly [L. *inter*; *necare*, to kill].

in·ter·nee See **intern.**

in·ter·nist *n.* (in·tur'·nist) a specialist in internal medicine.

in·ter·nun·ci·o (in·ter·nun'·shi·ō) *n.* the pope's representative; an envoy. **internuncial** *a.* [L. *internuntius*, a messenger].

internal combustion

in·ter·pel·late (in·ter·pel'·āt) *v.t.* to interrupt a speaker in a legislative assembly by demanding an explanation. **interpellation** *n.* **interpellator** *n.* [L. *inter; pellere*, to drive].

in·ter·pen·e·trate (in·ter·pen'·a·trāt) *v.t.* to grow through one another; to penetrate thoroughly. **interpenetration** *n.*

in·ter·plan·e·tar·y (in·ter·plan'·a·ter·i·) *a.* situated between the planets.

in·ter·play (in'·ter·plā) *n.* reciprocal action of two things; interchange of action and reaction; give and take.

in·ter·po·late (in·tur'·pa·lāt) *v.t.* to insert new (esp. misleading) matter into a text; to interpose with some remark; (*Math.*) to infer the missing terms in a known series of numbers. **interpolation** *n.* **interpolator** *n.* [L. *interpolare*, to furbish up].

in·ter·pose (in·ter·pōz') *v.t.* and *i.* to place or come between; to thrust in the way; to offer, as aid or service; to interrupt. **interposal** *n.* **-r** *n.* **interposition** *n.* [L. *inter; ponere*, to place].

in·ter·pret (in·tur'·prat) *v.t.* to explain the meaning of; to put a construction on; to translate orally for the benefit of others. **-able** *a.* **-ation** *n.* act of interpreting; translation; meaning; artist's version of a dramatic part or musical composition. **-ative** *a.* explanatory. **-er** *n.* [L. *interpres*, an interpreter].

in·ter·reg·num (in·ter·reg'·nam) *a.* the time a throne is vacant between the death or abdication of a king and the accession of his successor; any interruption in continuity. [L. *inter; regnum*, rule].

in·ter·re·la·tion (in·ter·ri·lā'·shan) *n.* reciprocal or mutual relation. **-ship** *n.*

in·ter·ro·gate (in·ter'·a·gāt) *v.t.* to question; to examine by questioning, esp. officially. **interrogation** *n.* close questioning; a question. **interrogation mark,** the mark (?) placed after a question. **interrogative** *a.* **interrogatory** *a.* [L. *inter; rogare*, to ask].

in·ter·rupt (in·ta·rupt') *v.t.* to break in upon; to stop course of; to break continuity of. **-edly** *adv.* **-er** *n.* **-ion** *n.* intervention; suspension; hindrance. **-ive** *a.* [L. *interruptus*, broken apart].

in·ter·sect (in·ter·sekt') *v.t.* to cut into or between; to divide into parts; to cross one another. **-ion** *n.* an intersecting; the point where lines, roads, etc., cut or cross one another. **-ional** *a.* [L. *intersectus*, cut off].

intersection

in·ter·sperse (in·ter·spurs') *v.t.* to scatter or place here and there, in no fixed order; to mingle. **interspersion** *n.* [L. *inter*, among; *spargere, sparsum*, to scatter].

in·ter·stel·lar (in·ter·stel'·er) *a.* passing between, or situated among, the stars. Also **-y.**

in·ter·stice (in·tur'·stis) *n.* a small gap or chink in the body of an object or between two things; a crevice. **interstitial** (in·ter·stish'·al) *a.* [L. *interstitium*].

in·ter·twine (in·ter·twīn') *v.t.* to twine or twist together.

in·ter·val (in'·ter·val) *n.* time or distance between; a pause; a break; (*Mus.*) difference in pitch between any two tones [L. *intervallum*, fr. *inter; vallum*, a wall].

in·ter·vene (in·ter·vēn') *v.i.* to come or be between; to happen in the meantime; to interfere; to interrupt; to interpose. **-r** *n.* **intervention** *n.* **interventionist** *n.* or *a.* [L. *inter; venire*, to come].

in·ter·view (in'·ter·vū) *n.* a meeting or conference; a meeting of a journalist and a person whose views he wishes to publish; *v.t.* to have an interview with. **-er** *n.* [Fr. *entrevue*].

intertwine

in·tes·tate (in·tes′·tāt) *a.* not having made a valid will; not disposed of by will; *n.* a person who dies intestate. **intestacy** *n.* [L. *in-*, not; *testari*, to make a will].

in·tes·tine (in·tes′·tin) *a.* internal; domestic; civil (of war, etc.); *n.pl.* the bowels; the entrails. **intestinal** *a.* [L. *intestinus*].

in·ti·mate (in′·ta·mat) *a.* innermost; familiar; closely-related; close; *n.* an intimate friend; *v.t.* **intimate** (in′·ta·māt) to hint; to imply. **intimacy** *n.* the state of being intimate; sexual relations. **-ly** *adv.* **intimation** *n.* a notice; a hint [L. *intimus*, inmost].

in·tim·i·date (in·tim′·a·dāt) *v.t.* to force or deter by threats; to inspire with fear; to frighten into action; to cow. **intimidation** *n.* **intimidator** *n.* [L. *in*; *timidus*, fearful].

in·to (in′·too) *prep.* expresses motion to a point within, or a change from one state to another.

in·tol·er·a·ble (in·tål′·a·ra·bl) *a.* insufferable; unbearable. **-ness** *n.* **intolerably** *adv.* **intolerance** *n.* **intolerant** *a.* **intolerantly** *adv.*

in·tone (in·tōn′) *v.t.* to utter or recite with a long drawn out musical note or tone; to chant; *v.i.* to modulate the voice; to give forth a deep protracted sound. **intonate** *v.t.* to intone. **intonation** *n.*

in·tox·i·cate (in·tåk′·sa·kāt) *v.t.* to make drunk; to excite beyond self-control. **intoxicating** *a.* producing intoxication; heady. **intoxicant** *n.* an intoxicating liquor. **intoxication** *n.* [Gk. *toxikon*, poison].

in·tra- (in′·tra) *prefix* fr. L. *intra*, within, inside of, used in the construction of many compound terms. **-cellular** *a.* within a cell. **-muscular** *a.* inside a muscle. **-venous** *a.* within a vein.

in·trac·ta·ble (in·trak′·ta·bl) *a.* not to be managed or governed; unmanageable; stubborn. **intractability, intractably** *adv.*

in·tra·mu·ral (in·tra·myoo′·ral) *a.* pert. to a single college or its students; within the walls or limits.

in·tran·si·gent (in·tran′·sa·jant) *a.* refusing in any way to compromise or to make a settlement (esp. in political matters); irreconcilable; *n.* one who adopts this attitude. **intransigence**, *n.* **-ly** *adv.* [Fr. *intransigeant*].

in·tran·si·tive (in·tran′·sa·tiv) *a.* (*Gram.*) denoting such verbs as express an action or state which is limited to the agent, or which does not pass over to, or operate upon, an object.

in·trep·id (in·trep′·id) *a.* free from fear or trepidation; undaunted courage. **-ity** *n.* **-ly** *adv.* [L. *in-*, not; *trepidus*, alarmed].

in·tri·cate (in′·tri·kat) *a.* involved; entangled; complicated; difficult. **intricacy, -ness** *n.* **-ly** *adv.* [L. *intricare*, to entangle].

in·trigue (in′·trig) *n.* a plot to effect some purpose by secret artifices; illicit love; (in·trēg′) *v.i.* to scheme secretly; to plot; to carry on illicit love; *v.t.* to fascinate; to arouse interest in; to puzzle. *pr.p.* **intriguing. intrigant, -r** *n.* **intriguing** *a.* **intriguingly** *adv.* [Fr. fr. L. *intricare*, to entangle].

in·trin·sic (in·trin′·sik) *a.* from within; having internal value; inherent. **-ality** *adv.* **-ally** *adv.* [L. *intrinsecus*, inwardly].

in·tro- (in′·trō) *prefix*, a variation of intra, inwards, used in compound terms.

in·tro·duce (in·tra·dūs′) *v.t.* to lead or bring in; to bring forward; to insert; to make known formally (one person to another); to import; to begin. **introduction** (in·tra·duk′·shan) *n.* act of introducing or bringing into notice; the act of making persons formally acquainted with one another; the preliminary section of a speech or discourse; prologue; the preface to a book; an elementary treatise on some branch of knowledge. **introductory, introductive** *a.* **introductively, inductorily** *adv.* [L. *introducere*, to lead in].

in·tro·spect (in·tra·spekt′) *v.t.* to look within; to inspect; *v.i.* to pre-occupy oneself with one's own thoughts, emotions and feelings. **-ion** *n.* close (often morbid) examination of one's thoughts and feelings. **-ive** *a.* **-ively** *adv.* [L. *intro*, within; *specere*, to look].

in·tro·vert (in·tra·vurt′) *v.t.* to turn inward; (in′·tra·vurt) *n.* a self-centered, introspective individual. Cf. *extrovert.* **introversion** *n.* **introversive, -ive** *a.* [L. *intro*, within; *vertere*, to turn].

in·trude (in·trood′) *v.i.* to thrust oneself in; to enter unwelcome or uninvited into company; to trespass; *v.t.* to force in. **-r** *n.* **intrusion** *n.* **intrusive** *a.* **intrusively** *adv.* **intrusiveness** *n.* [L. *in*; *trudere*, to thrust].

in·trust See **entrust.**

in·tu·i·tion (in·too·ish′·an) *n.* immediate and instinctive perception of a truth; direct understanding without reasoning. **intuit** *v.t.* and *v.i.* to know intuitively. **-al** *a.* **-alism, -ism** *n.* the doctrine that the perception of good and evil is by intuition. **-alist** *n.* **intuitive** *a.* having instinctively immediate knowledge or perception of something. **intuitively** *adv.* [L. *intueri*, to look upon].

in·tu·mesce (in·too·mes′) *v.i.* to swell; to enlarge or expand, owing to heat. **-nce** *n.*

in·twine See **entwine.**

in·un·date (in′·an·dāt, in·un′·dāt) *v.t.* to overflow; to flood; to overwhelm. **inundation** *n.* [L. *inundare*, to flood, fr. *unda*, a wave].

in·ure (in·yoor′) *v.t.* to accustom (to); to habituate by use; to harden (the body) by toil. etc. **-ment** *n.* [*in*, into + obs. *ure*, to work, fr. Fr. *œuvre*, work].

in·vade (in·vād′) *v.t.* to attack; to enter with hostile intentions; to violate; to encroach upon. **-r** *n.* **invasion** *n.* **invasive** *a.* [L. *invadere*, to go in].

in·val·id (in·val′·id) *a.* not valid; void; of no legal force; weak. **-ate** *v.t.* to render invalid. **-ate** *v.* **-ation** *n.* **-ity, -ness** *n.*

in·va·lid (in′·va·lid) *n.* a person enfeebled by sickness or injury; ill; sickly; weak; *a.* **-ity** and *v.i.* to make invalid; to send away as an invalid. [L. *invalidus*, infirm].

in·val·u·a·ble (in·val′·ya·bl) *a.* incapable of being valued; priceless; of very great value.

in·var·i·a·ble (in·ve′·ri·a·bl) *a.* not displaying change; always uniform; (*Math.*) constant. **-ness, invariability** *n.* **invariably** *adv.* **invariant** *n.* a constant quantity.

in·va·sion (in·vā′·zhan) *n.* See **invade.**

in·vec·tive (in·vek′·tiv) *n.* violent outburst of censure; abuse; vituperation. *a.* abusive [L. *invectio*, fr. *invehere*, to bring against].

in·veigh (in·vā′) *v.i.* to exclaim or rail against. **-er** *n.* [L. *invehere*, to bring against].

in·vei·gle (in·vā′·gl) *v.t.* to entice by deception or flattery; to allure; to mislead into something evil; to seduce. **-ment** *n.* **-r** *n.* [Fr. *aveugler*, to blind].

in·vent (in·vent′) *v.t.* to devise something new or an improvement; to contrive; to originate; to think out something untrue. **-ion** *n.* act of producing something new; an original contrivance; a deceit, fiction, or forgery. **-ive** *a.* able to invent; of an ingenious turn of mind; resourceful. **-ively** *adv.* **-or** *n.* [L. *invenire*, to come upon, to discover].

in·ven·to·ry (in′·van·tōr·i·) *n.* a detailed list of articles comprising the effects of a house, etc.; a catalog of moveables; *v.t.* to make a list or enter on a list [L. *inventarium*, a list of things found].

in·verse (in′·vurs) *a.* inverted; opposite in order or relation. **-ly** *adv.* **inversion** *n.* the act of inverting; the state of being inverted; change of order or time; (*Gram.*) a change of the natural arrangement of words. **inversive** *a.* [L. *in*, *vertere*, *versum*, to turn].

in·vert (in·vurt′) *v.t.* to turn over; to put upside down; to place in a contrary order. **-edly** *adv.* [L. *in*; *vertere*, to turn].

in·ver·te·brate (in·vur′·ta·brat, -brāt) *a.* not having a vertebral column or backbone; spineless, weak-willed; *n.* animal, such as an insect, snail, etc., with no spinal column.

in·vest (in·vest′) *v.t.* to lay out capital with a view to profit; to clothe, as with office or authority; to dress; to lay siege to; *v.t.* to make a purchase or an investment. **-iture** *n.* ceremony of installing anyone in office. **-ment** *n.* the act of investing; the capital invested to produce interest or profit; blockade. **-or** *n.* [L. *investire*, to clothe].

in·ves·ti·gate (in·ves′·ta·gāt) *v.t.* to inquire into; to examine thoroughly. **investigable** *a.* **investigation** *n.* **investigator** *n.* **investigatory** *a.* [L. *restigare*, to track].

in·vet·er·ate (in·vet′·er·it) *a.* firmly established by long continuance; obstinate; deep-rooted. **-ly** *adv.* **-ness, inveteracy,** *n.* [L. *inveterare*, to grow old].

in·vid·i·ous (in·vid′·i·as) *a.* likely to provoke envy, ill-will or hatred; offensive. **-ly** *adv.* **-ness** *n.* [L. *invidia*, envy].

in·vig·o·rate (in·vig′·er·āt) *v.t.* to give vigor to; to animate with life and energy; to strengthen. **invigoration** *n.* **-d** *a.* [L. *in*; *rigor*, force].

in·vin·ci·ble (in·vin′·sa·bl) *a.* unconquerable; insuperable. **-ness, invincibility** *n.* **invin-**

cibly [L. *in-*, not; *vincere*, to conquer].

in·vi·o·la·ble (in·vī′·al·a·bl) *n.* not to be violated; sacred. **inviolably** *adv.* **inviolate** *a.* unprofaned; uninjured. **inviolately** *adv.* **inviolateness** *n.* [L. *in*; *violare*, to violate].

in·vis·i·ble (in·viz′·a·bl) *a.* incapable of being seen; unseen; indiscernible, **invisibility, -ness** *n.* **invisibly** *adv.*

in·vite (in·vīt′) *v.t.* to ask by invitation; to attract. **invitation** (in·vi·tā′·shan) *n.* act of inviting; the spoken or written form with which a request for a person's company is extended. **-r** *n.* **inviting** *a.* alluring, attractive. **invitingly** *adv.* [L. *invitare*].

in·vo·ca·tion (in·va·kā′·shan) *n.* act of addressing in prayer; a petition for divine help and guidance. **invocatory** *a.* [See **invoke**.]

in·voice (in′·vois) *n.* a detailed list of goods, with prices, sold or consigned to a purchaser; *v.t.* to make such a list. [pl. of obs. **invoy**, fr. Fr. *envoi*, a sending].

in·voke (in·vōk′) *v.t.* to address (esp. God) earnestly or solemnly in prayer; to beg for protection or assistance; to implore; to summon [L. *in*; *vocare*, to call].

in·vol·un·ta·ry (in·väl′·an·te·ri·) *a.* outside the control of the will; not proceeding from choice; unintentional; instinctive. **involuntarily** *adv.* **involuntariness** *n.*

in·vo·lute (in′·va·lōōt) *a.* (*Bot.*) rolled inwardly or spirally; *n.* the locus of the far end of a perfectly flexible thread unwound from a circle and kept constantly taut. **involution** *n.* that in which anything is involved; the process of raising a quantity to any power; entanglement; complication. [See **involve**].

in·volve (in·valv′) *v.t.* to envelop; to wrap up; to include; to comprise; to embrace; to implicate (a person); to complicate (a thing); to entail; to include; to twine; to interlace; to overwhelm; to multiply a number any number of times by itself. **-ment** *n.* [L. *in*; *volvere*, *volutum*, to roll].

in·vul·ner·a·ble (in·vul′·ner·a·bl) *a.* incapable of being wounded or injured. **invulnerability**, *n.* **invulnerably** *adv.*

in·ward (in′·werd) *a.* placed within; towards the inside; interior; internal; seated in the mind or soul; *n.* that which is within. esp. in *pl.*, the viscera; *adv.* toward the inside; into the mind. Also **inwards; -ly** *adv.* in the parts within, secretly; in the mind or soul [O.E. *inneweard*].

i·o·dine (ī′·a·dīn, dēn) *n.* a non-metallic chemical element belonging to the halogen group. **iodiferous** *a.* yielding iodine. **iodize** *v.t.* to treat with compounds of iodine, e.g. common salt. **iodoform** *n.* a powdered crystalline compound of iodine [Gk. *ioeidēs*, violet-like, from the color of its fumes].

i·on (ī′·an, ·än) *n.* electrically charged atom or radical which has gained, or lost, one or more electrons and which facilitates the transport of electricity through an electrolyte or the gas in a gas-discharge tube. **ionic** *a.* pert. to ions. **-ization** *n.* splitting up of a liquid during electrolysis or of a gas during a glow discharge, into ions. **-ize** *v.t.* **ionosphere** *n.* the layer of ionized molecules in the upper atmosphere beyond the stratosphere [Gr. *ion*].

I·on·ic (i·än′·ik) *a.* pert. to section of Greece; (*Archit.*) denoting type of column with fluted molding and ram's horn design.

i·on·o·sphere (i·än′·a·sfir) *n.* See **ion.**

i·o·ta (ī·ō′·ta) *n.* a very small quantity or degree; a jot [Gk. the name of the smallest letter of the Greek alphabet = I. i].

ir- (ir) *prefix* for *in*; not, before 'r.'

i·ras·ci·ble (i·ras′·a·bl) *a.* easily provoked; hot-tempered, **irascibility** *n.* **irascibly** *adv.* [L. *irasci*, to be angry].

i·rate (ī·rāt′) *a.* angry; incensed; enraged [L. *iratus*, fr. *irasci*, to be angry].

ire (īr) *n.* anger; wrath. **-ful** *a.* **-fully** *adv.* **-fulness** *n.* [L. *ira*, anger].

irid-, irido-, *prefix* fr. Gk. *iris*, rainbow, used in the construction of compound terms, pertaining to the iris of the eye or to the genus of plants, as **iridescence** (i·ra·des′·ans) *n.* rainbow-like display of colors. **iridescent** *a.*

i·ris (ī′·ris) *n.* (*Anat.*) the thin contractile, colored membrane between the cornea and the lens of the eye, perforated in the center by an opening called the pupil; (*Bot.*) a genus of flowering plants of the natural order *Iridaceae*, the rainbow; an appearance resembling the rainbow [Gk. *iris*, rainbow].

I·rish (ī′·rish) *a.* pert. to Ireland; *n.* the early language spoken in Ireland—now known as *Erse.* **-ism** *n.* a mode of speaking, phrase, or idiom of Ireland. **-man, -woman** *n.* — **moss,** carageen, a form of edible seaweed.

irk (urk) *v.t.* to weary; to trouble; to distress (used impersonally as, **it irks me**). **-some** *a.* wearisome; annoying. **-somely** *adv.* [M.E.]

i·ron (ī′·ẹrn) *n.* the most common and useful of the metallic elements; something hard and unyielding; an instrument or utensil made of iron; an instrument used, when heated, to press and smooth cloth; in golf, an iron-headed club. **-s** *n.pl.* fetters; manacles; *a.* made of iron; resembling some aspect of iron; robust; inflexible; unyielding; *v.t.* to smooth with a heated flat iron; *v.i.* to furnish or arm with iron; to fetter. **-clad** *a.* covered or protected with sheets of iron; *n.* a vessel prepared for naval warfare by having the parts above water plated with iron. **-er** *n.* — **gray** *a.* of a dark color. — **horse** *n.* a locomotive. — **lung** *n.* an apparatus which maintains artificial respiration continuously. — **ore** *n.* a rock containing iron-rich compounds from which commercial iron is obtained. **-smith** *n.* a worker in iron. **-stone** *n.* any ore of iron mixed with clay, etc. **-y** *a.* made of or resembling iron. **cast iron, pig iron** *n.* the iron obtained by smelting iron ore with charcoal, coke, or raw coal in a blast furnace. **corrugated iron,** plate of galvanized iron, corrugated to give it stiffness, used for temporary roofing, fencing, etc. **galvanized iron,** sheet iron coated with zinc to minimize the effects of rusting. — **age,** period following Bronze age, when iron was substituted for bronze in the making of tools, weapons, and ornaments. — **Curtain,** the ban placed by the U.S.S.R. on free exchange of information, news, etc., between Eastern and Western Europe. **to have too many irons in the fire,** to attempt to do too many things at the same time [O.E. *iren*].

i·ro·ny (ī′·rạ·ni·) *n.* a mode of speech in which the meaning is the opposite of that actually expressed; sarcasm; satire. **ironic, ironical** (i·ràn′·ik, ·al) *a.* **ironically** *adv.* [Gk. *eirōneia,* dissimulation in speech].

ir·ra·di·ate (i·rā′·di·āt) *v.t.* to shine upon, throw light upon; to illuminate; *v.i.* to emit rays; to give forth light; *a.* illumined with beams of light. **irradiance, irradiancy** *n.* effulgence; emission of rays of light; splendor. **irradiant** *a.* **irradiation** *n.* exposure to X-rays, ultra-violet rays, solar rays, etc.; illumination; brightness; enlightenment. **irradiative** *a.* **irradiator** *n.*

ir·ra·tion·al (i·rash′·an·al) *a.* incompatible with or contrary to reason. **-ity** *n.* **-ly** *adv.*

ir·re·claim·a·ble (ir·i·klā′·ma·bl) *a.* incapable of being reclaimed. **irreclaimably** *adv.*

ir·rec·on·cil·a·ble (i·rek·a·sīl′·a·bl) *a.* incapable of being reconciled; inconsistent. **-ness, irreconcilability** *n.* **irreconcilably** *adv.*

ir·re·cov·er·a·ble (ir·i·kuv′·ẹr·a·bl) *a.* cannot be recovered; irreparable; irretrievable. **-ness** *n.* **irrecoverably** *adv.*

ir·re·deem·a·ble (ir·i·dēm′·a·bl) *a.* not redeemable; incorrigible; hopelessly lost; not convertible (as paper money into specie). **-ness, irredeemability** *n.* **irredeemably** *adv.*

ir·re·duc·i·ble (ir·i·dūs′·a·bl) *a.* that which cannot be reduced or lessened. **-ness, irreducibility** *n.* **irreducibly** *adv.*

ir·ref·u·ta·ble (i·ri·fū′·ta·bl, ir·ref′·ya·ta·bl) *a.* that cannot be refuted. **irrefutability** *n.* **irrefutably** *adv.*

ir·reg·u·lar (i·reg′·ya·ler) *a.* not regular; not according to rule; deviating from the moral standard; (*Gram.*) not inflected according to normal rules; *n.* a member of an armed force outside government control. **-ity** *n.* **-ly** *adv.*

ir·rel·a·tive (i·rel′·a·tiv) *a.* not relative; unconnected. **-ly** *adv.*

ir·rel·e·vant (i·rel′·a·vant) *a.* not logically pertinent. **irrelevancy** *n.*

ir·re·li·gion (ir·i·lij′·an) *n.* state of indifference or opposition to religious beliefs. **irreligious** *a.* **irreligiously** *adv.* profanely; impiously. **irreligiousness** *n.* ungodliness.

ir·re·me·di·a·ble (ir·i·mē′·di·a·bl) *a.* not to be remedied or redressed. **-ness** *n.* **irremediably** *adv.*

ir·re·mis·si·ble (ir·i·mis′·i·bl) *a.* that cannot be passed by or forgiven; unpardonable.

ir·rep·a·ra·ble (i·rep′·ar·a·bl) *a.* that cannot be repaired or rectified. **-ness** *n.* **irreparability** *n.* **irreparably** *adv.*

ir·re·place·a·ble (ir·i·plā′·sa·bl) *a.* that cannot be replaced; indispensable; unique.

ir·re·press·i·ble (ir·i·pres′·a·bl) *a.* not able to be kept under control. **irrepressibility** *n.* **-ness** *n.* **irrepressibly** *adv.*

ir·re·proach·a·ble (ir·i·prōch′·a·bl) *a.* free from blame; faultless. **irreproachably** *adv.*

ir·re·sist·i·ble (ir·i·zis′·a·bl) *a.* incapable of being resisted; too strong, fascinating, charming, etc., to be resisted. **-ness, irresistibility** *n.* **irresistibly** *adv.*

ir·res·o·lute (i·rez′·a·lōōt) *a.* infirm or inconstant in purpose; vacillating. **-ly** *adv.* **-ness, irresolution** *n.*

ir·re·spec·tive (ir·i·spek′·tiv) *a.* and *adv.* without regard to; apart from. **-ly** *adv.*

ir·re·spon·si·ble (ir·i·spàn′·sa·bl) *a.* not liable to answer (for consequences); carefree; without a due sense of responsibility. **irresponsibility** *n.* **irresponsibly** *adv.*

ir·re·spon·sive (ir·i·spàn′·siv) *a.* not responsive (to); unanswering; taciturn. **-ness** *n.*

ir·re·triev·a·ble (ir·i·trē′·va·bl) *a.* incapable of recovery or repair. **-ness** *n.* **irretrievability** *n.* **irretrievably** *adv.*

ir·rev·er·ent (i·rev′·a·rant) *a.* not reverent; disrespectful. **irreverence** *n.* **-ly** *adv.*

ir·re·vers·i·ble (ir·i·vur′·sa·bl) *a.* that cannot be reversed, turned back, recalled, or annulled. **irreversibly** *adv.*

ir·rev·o·ca·ble (i·rev′·a·ka·bl) *a.* incapable of being recalled or revoked. **-ness, irrevocability** *n.* **irrevocably** *adv.*

ir·ri·gate (ir′·a·gāt) *v.t.* to water (by artificial channels). **irrigable, irrigative** *a.* **irrigation** *n.* the artificial application of water to the land for the purpose of increasing its fertility; (*Med.*) the washing out of a wound, etc. to keep it moist. **irrigator** *n.* [L. *irrigare,* fr. *rigare,* to water].

ir·ri·tate (ir′·a·tāt) *v.t.* to excite to anger; to annoy; to excite heat and redness in the skin by friction. **irritability** *n.* **irritable** *a.* easily provoked or annoyed; fretful; able to be acted upon by stimuli. **irritableness** *n.* **irritably** *adv.* **irritant** *a.* irritating; *n.* that which irritates or causes irritation. **irritation** *n.* exasperation; anger; the act of exciting heat, redness, or action in the skin or flesh by external stimulus. **irritative** *a.* tending to irritate [L. *irritare*].

ir·rup·tion (i·rup′·shan) *n.* a sudden invasion; a violent incursion into a place; a breaking or bursting in. **irruptive** *a.* **irruptively** *adv.* [L. *irruptio*].

is (iz) *v.* the *third pers. sing. pres. indic.* of the verb **to be** [O.E.].

is·land (ī′·land) *n.* a piece of land surrounded by water; anything resembling this, e.g. a street-refuge. **-er** *n.* an inhabitant of an island [earlier *iland,* O.E. *iegland*].

isle (īl) *n.* an island. **islet** (ī′·let) *n.* a tiny island [O.Fr. *isle.* L. *insula*].

-ism (izm) *n.* a jocular reference to any distinctive doctrine, theory, or practice [English suffix, *-ism*].

i·so- (ī′·so) *prefix fr.* Gk. *isos,* equal, used in the construction of compound terms.

i·so·bar (ī′·sa·bár) *n.* a line on a map joining up all those points where the mean height of the barometer is the same; *pl.* species of atoms having the same atomic weight but different atomic numbers. **-ic** *a.* consisting of isobars. **-ometric** *a.* showing equal barometric pressure (Gk. *isos,* equal; *baros,* weight].

i·so·dy·nam·ic (ī·sa·dī·nam′·ik) *a.* having equal force or power.

i·so·gon (ī′·sa·gàn) *n.* a plane figure having equal angles. **isogonal** (i·sàg′·a·nal) *a.* **-ic** *a.* [Gk. *isos,* equal; *gonia,* angle].

i·so·late (ī′·sa·lāt) *v.t.* to place in a detached position; to place apart or alone; to insulate; (*Chem.*) to obtain a substance in a pure state. **isolation** *n.* state of being isolated. **isolation hospital,** a hospital for infectious diseases. **isolationist** *n.* one who advocates non-participation in world-politics [It. *isolato,* detached, fr. L. *insula,* an island].

i·so·met·ric (ī·sa·met′·rik) *a.* of equal measurement.

i·so·mor·phism (ī·sa·mawr′·fizm) *n.* similarity of structure, esp. between the crystals of different chemical substances. **isomorphic** *a.* **isomorphous** *a.* [Gk. *isos,* equal; *morphē,* shape].

i·sos·ce·les (ī·sàs′·a·lēz) *a.* having two sides which are equal (said of a triangle) [Gk. *isos,* equal; *skelos,* a leg].

i·so·topes (ī′·sa·tōps) *n.pl.* (*physics*) of most of the elements, atoms with nuclei of slightly different weights [Gk. *isos,* equal; *topos,* place].

Is·ra·el (iz′·ri·al) *n.* since 1948, the name of the Jewish State in Palestine; (*Bib.*) the Jewish people **Israeli** (iz·rāl′·i·) *n.* an inhabitant of Israel. **-ite** *n.* (*Bib.*) a descendant of Israel or Jacob; a Jew. **-itic, -itish,** *a.* [Heb. *Israel,* he who striveth with God].

is·sue (ish′·ōō) *n.* act of passing or flowing out; the act of sending out; that which is issued; a topic of discussion or controversy; a morbid discharge from the body; outlet; edition; consequence; result; progeny; offspring; (*Law*) the specific point in a suit between two parties requiring to be determined; *v.t.* to send out (a book, etc.); to put into circulation; to proclaim or set forth with authority; to supply with equipment, etc.; *v.i.* to pass or flow out; to come out; to proceed; to be born or spring from. **-less** *a.* **-er** *n.* **at issue** (point) to be debated or settled. **to join issue,** to take opposite views on a point in debate [O.Fr. *issir,* to go out].

isth·mus (is′·mas) *n.* a narrow neck of land connecting two larger portions. **isthmian** *a.* [Gk. *isthmos*].

it (it) *pron.* the neuter pronoun of the third person; *n.* (*Colloq.*) sexual attractiveness; sex appeal; perfection [O.E. *hit*].

I·tal·ian (i·tal′·yan) *a.* pert. to Italy, its inhabitants or their language.

i·tal·ics (i·tal′·iks) *n.pl.* a printing type having the type sloping from the right downwards. *as these letters.* **italicization** *n.* **italicize** *v.t.* to print thus.

itch (ich) *n.* an irritation in the skin; scabies; an irrepressible desire; *v.i.* to feel uneasiness or irritation in the skin; to be inordinately anxious or desirous to; to be hankering after. **-iness** *n.* **-y** *a.* **an itching palm,** a grasping disposition; greed [O.E. *giccan,* to itch].

i·tem (ī′·tam) *n.* a piece of news, as in a newspaper; an entry in an account or list; a detail. **itemize** *v.t.* to list by items; to give particulars [L.].

it·er·ate (it′·a·rāt) *v.t.* to repeat; to do again. **iteration** *n.* **iterative, iterant** *a.* repeating [L. *iterare,* fr. *iterum,* again].

i·tin·er·ant (i·tin′·a·rant) *a.* traveling from place to place; traveling on circuit; of no settled abode. *n.* one who goes from place to place, esp. on business. **itineracy, itinerancy** *n.* **-ly** *adv.* **itinerary** *n.* a record of travel; a route, line of travel; a guide-book for travelers. **itinerate** *v.i.* to travel up and down a country, esp. in a regular circuit. **itineration** *n.* [L. *iter, itineris,* a journey].

its (its) the *possessive case* of *pron.* it. **itself** *pron.* the neuter reciprocal pronoun applied to things; the reflexive form of it.

i·vo·ry (ī′·va·ri·) *n.* the hard, white, opaque, dentine constituting tusks of elephant, walrus, etc.; as carving of ivory; creamy white color. *n.pl.* (*Colloq.*) keys of a piano; the teeth. *a.* made of or like ivory [Fr. *ivoire,* fr. L. *ebur,* ivory].

i·vy (ī′·vi·) *n.* a climbing evergreen plant. **ivied** *a.* covered with ivy [O.E. *ifig*].

J

jab (jab) *v.t.* to poke sharply; to stab; *pr.p.* **-bing.** *pa.t., pa.p.* **-bed.** *n.* a sharp poke, stab, or thrust [prob. imit.].
jab·ber (jab'·ẹr) *v.i.* to chatter; to speak quickly and indistinctly; *v.t.* to utter indistinctly; *n.* rapid, incoherent talk. **-er** *n.* **-ingly** *adv.* [prob. imit.].
ja·bot (zha·bō') *n.* a frill or fall of lace on a woman's dress; orig. a ruffle on a man's shirt.
ja·cinth (jā'·sinth) *n.* the hyacinth [contr. of L. *hyacinthus,* a precious stone].
Jack (jak) *n.* a popular nickname and diminutive of *John;* (*l.c.*) a fellow; a laborer, as *steeple-jack;* a sailor; the knave in a pack of cards; a device to facilitate removal of boots, as a *boot-jack;* a mechanical device for turning a roasting-spit; a portable apparatus for raising heavy weights, esp. for raising a motor vehicle to change a tire; a flag or ensign; the male of certain animals, as *jackass; v.t.* to raise with a jack. Also **jack up. -boot** *n.* a long boot reaching above the knee formerly worn by cavalry. **—in-the-box** *n.* a child's toy comprising a small figure which springs out of a box when the lid is lifted. **-knife** *n.* a strong clasp knife. **— o' lantern,** a lantern made from hollowed-out pumpkin, with holes cut to make a face. **—of-all-trades** *n.* one who can turn his hand to anything. **-pot** *n.* a pool, in poker, which cannot be opened except by player holding two jacks or better; (*Slang*) the pay-off. **-rabbit** *n.* a hare with very long ears. **-tar,** a sailor. **Union Jack,** the national flag of Gt. Britain. **yellowjack** *n.* yellow fever [fr. *John,* infl. by *Jacques*].
jack·al (jak'·al, ·awl) *n.* a bushy-tailed carnivorous animal of Asia and Africa; wild dog; (*Fig.*) a servile creature [Pers. *shaghal*].

jack·ass (jak'·as) *n.* a male ass; a stupid fellow; a blockhead [*Jack,* the male; and *ass*].
jack·daw (jak'·daw) *n.* a glossy, black bird of the crow family [fr. *Jack; daw*].
jack·et (jak'·it) *n.* a short, sleeved coat; outer covering or skin (as of potatoes); an outer casing, as for a boiler to keep in heat; a loose dust-cover for a book. *v.t.* to cover with a jacket [O.Fr. *jaquet,* dim. of *jaque,* a coat of mail].
Jac·o·be·an (jak·a·bē'·an) *a.* pert. to reign of James I; used mainly of architecture, indoor decoration, and furniture (dark oak) of Stuart period; *n.* person of this period [L. *Jacobus,* James].
Jac·o·bin (jak'·a·bin) *n.* a French Dominican friar, so called from monastery of *St. Jacques,* Paris; a member of society of French Revolutionists [Fr. fr. L. *Jacobus,* James].
Ja·cob's lad·der (jā'·kabz·lad'·ẹr) *n.* (*Naut.*) a rope ladder with wooden rungs [Heb. *ya'aqob,* Jacob].
jac·quard (ja·kārd') *n.* a pattern woven into fabrics [fr. Fr. inventor of loom, *Jacquard*].
jade (jād) *n.* an over-worked, worn-out horse; a mean woman; a saucy wench; *v.t.* to tire; to wear out. *pr.p.* **jading.** *pa.p.* **jaded.** **jaded** *a.* tired; weary; sated [Scand. *jalda,* a mare].
jade (jād) *n.* a very hard, compact silicate of lime and magnesia, of various colors, carved for ornaments [Span. (*piedra de*) *ijada,* a stone for curing a pain in the side].
jag (jag) *n.* a notch; a ragged protuberance; (*Bot.*) cleft or division; *v.t.* to notch; to slash; *pr.p.* **-ging.** *pa.p.* **-ged, -ged, -gy** *a.* notched;

rough-edged; sharp. **-gedness** *n.* (*Slang*) a spree, as **a talking jag** [etym. doubtful].
jag·uar (jag'·wàr) *n.* a large spotted yellowish beast of prey [Braz.].

jail (jāl) *n.* a prison; *v.t.* to take into custody. (*Br.*) **goal. — bird** *n.* a prisoner; a criminal. **-er, -or** *n.* one who has charge of prisoners in the cells [O.Fr. *gaole,* a prison].
jal·ap (jal'·ap) *n.* a drug used as a purgative esp. in dropsy [fr. *Xalapa,* in Mexico]. |car.
ja·lop·y (ja·làp'·i·) *n.* (*Slang*) an old, decrepit |car.
jal·ou·sie (jal'·a·sē) *n.* a blind or shutter with slats at an angle. **-d** *a.* [Fr. *jalousie,* suspicion]
jam (jam) *n.* preserve made from fruit, boiled with sugar. **-my** *a.* [etym. doubtful].
jam (jam) *v.t.* to squeeze tight; to wedge in; to block up; to stall (a machine); *v.i.* to cease to function because of obstruction. *pr.p.* **-ming.** *pa.p.* **-med.** *n.* a crush; a hold-up (as of traffic); (*Colloq.*) a tight corner. **-ming** *n.* (*Radio*) to interfere with signals by sending out others of like frequency [prob. var. of *champ*].
jamb (jam) *n.* the side piece of a door, fireplace, etc. [Fr. *jambe,* a leg].
jam·bo·ree (jam·ba·rē') *n.* a large, usually international, rally of Boy Scouts; (*Slang*) a noisy gathering [etym. unknown].
jan·gle (jang'·gl) *v.t.* to ring with a discordant sound; *v.i.* to sound out of tune; to wrangle; *n.* a discordant sound; a dispute. **jangling** *n.* [imit. O.Fr. *jangler*].
jan·i·tor (jan'·i·tẹr) *n.* (*fem.* **janitress**) a caretaker of a building; a doorkeeper; a porter [L. *janitor*].
Jan·i·zar·y (jan'·a·zar·i·) *n.* a soldier of the Turkish Sultan [Turk. *yenitsheri,* the new soldiers].
Jan·u·ar·y (jan'·ya·wer·i·) *n.* the first month, dedicated by Romans to *Janus,* the god with two faces. **janus-faced** *a.* untrustworthy [L. *Janus,* a Roman deity].
Ja·pan (ja·pan') *n.* a N.E. Asiatic insular country. **-ese** (ja·pa·nēz') *n.* a native of Japan; *a.* pert. to Japan, the people or language. **japan** *v.t.* to make black and glossy; to lacquer with black varnish. *pr.p.* **-ning.** *pa.p.* **-ned.** *n.* the black laquer japanned [Jap.].
jape (jāp) *n.* a jest [O.Fr. *japer,* to jest].
jar (jàr) *n.* vessel narrower at top than at base, with or without handles [Fr. *jarre*].
jar (jàr) *v.i.* to give forth a discordant sound; to vibrate discordantly; to affect the nerves, feelings, etc. unpleasantly; to conflict; *v.t.* to cause to vibrate by sudden impact; to shake physically or mentally. *pr.p.* **-ring.** *pa.p.* **-red.** *n.* a harsh, grating sound; a jolting movement; conflict. **-ringly** *adv.* [prob. imit.].
jar·gon (jàr'·gan) *n.* confused speech; gibberish; slang; technical phraseology.
jas·mine (jas'·min) *n.* a shrub with fragrant white, yellow or pink flowers. Also **jessamine** [Pers. *yasmin,* jasmine].
jas·per (jas'·pẹr) *n.* an opaque form of quartz, often highly colored [Gk. *iaspis,* chalcedony].
ja·to (jā'·tō) *n.* kind of rocket to assist the take-off of heavily loaded aircraft [*Jet Assisted Take Off*].
jaun·dice (jawn'·dis, jàn'·dis) *n.* a disease, characterized by yellowness of skin and eyes; *v.t.* to affect with jaundice. **-d** *a.* affected with jaundice; (*Fig.*) jealous; prejudiced [Fr.

jaune, yellow].
jaunt (jawnt, jànt) *v.i.* to make an excursion; *n.* an outing; a ramble. **-ing** *a.* rambling.
jaun·ty (jawn'·ti·, jàn'·ti·) *a.* sprightly; airy; trim. **jauntily** *adv.* [Fr. gentil, genteel].
jave·lin (jav'·lin) *n.* a light hand-thrown spear [Fr.].
jaw (jaw) *n.* one of the two bones forming framework of mouth and containing the teeth; the mouth; part of any device which grips or crushes object held by it, as a vice; (*Slang*) loquacity; *pl.* narrow entrance to a gorge; (*Slang*) to scold; (*Slang*) to gossip. **-bone** *n.* bone of the mouth in which teeth are set. **-breaker** (*Colloq.*) a word hard to pronounce; (*Colloq.*) a large piece of hard candy.
jay (jā) *n.* a chattering, perching bird with gay plumage; (*Fig.*) a foolish person. **-walker** *n.* (*Colloq.*) a careless or absent-minded pedestrian who disregards traffic rules [etym. doubtful].
jazz (jaz) *n.* syncopated, noisy music played as accompaniment to dancing; *a.* like or pert. to jazz; *v.t.* and *v.i.* to dance to or play jazz music; (*Slang*) to put vigor and liveliness into. **-y** *a.* [Negro word].
jeal·ous (jel'·as) *a.* envious; suspicious; apprehensively watchful; solicitous; zealously careful. **-y** *n.* [O.Fr. fr. Gk. *zelos,* emulation].
jean (jēn) *n.* a strong, twilled cotton cloth; *n.pl.* overalls; trousers [prob. fr. L. *Genua,* Genoa].
jeep (jēp) *n.* light motor utility truck designed in *World War 2* [G.P., of general purposes].

jeer (jir) *v.i.* to mock; to deride; *v.t.* to treat scoffingly; *n.* a gibe; a railing remark. **-er** *n.*
Je·ho·vah (ji·hō'·va) *n.* (*Bib.*) Hebrew name of the supreme God [Heb. *Yahweh*].
je·june (ji·jōōn') *a.* empty; barren; uninteresting; dry. **-ly** *adv.* [L. *jejunus,* hungry].
jel·ly (jel'·i·) *n.* any gelatinous substance; the juice of fruit boiled with sugar. **jell** *v.i.* to stiffen. **jellied** *a.* of the consistency of jelly. **jellify** *v.t.* to make into jelly; *v.i.* to become set like a jelly. **-fish** *n.* popular name given certain marine animals of soft gelatinous structure [Fr. *gelée,* frost].
jen·ny (jen'·i·) *n.* a spinning machine; a female ass; a female bird, the wren (usually *jenny-wren*) [dim. of *Jane*].
jeop·ar·dy (jep'·ẹr·di·) *n.* danger; risk. **jeopardize** *v.t.* to endanger; to imperil [Fr. *jeu parti,* a divided game].
Jer·e·mi·ah (jer·a·mi'·a) *n.* (*Bib.*) a Hebrew prophet and author of the Book of Lamentations; any doleful prophet. **jeremiad** *n.* a tale of grief or complaint.
jerk (jurk) *v.t.* to throw with a quick motion; to twitch; to give a sudden pull, twist, or push; *n.* a short, sudden thrust, pull, start, etc.; a spasmodic twitching. **-er** *n.* **-ily** *adv.* **-iness** *n.* **-water** *a.* (*Colloq.*) insignificant. **-y** *a.* fitful; spasmodic; lacking rhythm [imit. word].
jerk (jurk) *v.t.* to cure (meat) by cutting in long slices and drying in the sun. **-ed** *a.* [Peruv. *charqui,* dried beef].
jer·kin (jur'·kin) *n.* a close-fitting jacket or waistcoat [prob *Dut.* jurk, a frock].
jer·o·bo·am (jer·a·bō'·am) *n.* a large bowl; a huge bottle, in capacity eight times the ordinary size [1 Kings, 11].
Jer·ry (jer'·i·) *n.* (*Slang*) a German soldier [shortening of German].

Jer·sey (jur'·zi·) *n.* the largest of the Channel Islands; a cow of Jersey breed; *a.* pert. to State of New Jersey. **jersey** *n.* a close-fitting, knitted, woolen jacket, vest, or pullover; a knitted cloth [fr. *Jersey*].

jess (jes) *n.* a strap of leather or silk tied round the legs of a hawk; *v.t.* to put jesses on [O.Fr. *ges*, a throw].

jest (jest) *n.* a joke; a quip; banter; an object of ridicule; *v.i.* to joke; to scoff. **-er** *n.* one who jests; a professional fool, originally attached to the court or lord's manor. **-ful** *a.* **-ingly** *adv.* [M.E. *jeste*, an exploit].

Jes·u·it (jezh'·ū·it) *n.* one of a religious order founded by Ignatius Loyola in 1534 under the title of The Society of Jesus; (commonly) a crafty person; a prevaricator [fr. *Jesus*].

jet (jet) *n.* a variety of very hard, black lignite, capable of a brilliant polish and much used for ornaments; *a.* made of, or having the glossy blackness of jet. — **black** *a.* black like jet. **-tiness** *n.* **-ty** *a.* [O.Fr. *jet*].

jet (jet) *n.* a sudden rush, as of water or flame, from a pipe; the spout or nozzle emitting water, gas, etc.; a jet airplane; *v.t.* to spout; *v.i.* to shoot forth. **jet propulsion**, propulsion of a machine by the force of a jet of fluid or of heated gases, expelled backwards from the machine. *pr.p.* **-ting.** *pa.t.* **-ted** [Fr. *jeter*, to throw].

jet·sam (jet'·sam) *n.* goods thrown overboard to lighten a ship in distress; goods washed ashore from a wrecked ship. **jettison** *n.* act of throwing overboard; jetsam; *v.t.* to throw overboard, as cargo; (*Fig.*) to abandon, as a scheme [O.Fr. *jetée*, thrown out].

jet·ty (jet'·i·) *n.* a structure of piles, stones, etc. built to protect a harbor; a landing pier [O.Fr. *jetée*, thrown out].

Jew (jōō) *n.* (*fem.* **-ess**) a Hebrew or an Israelite. **—baiting**, persecution of the Jews. **-ish** *a.* of or belonging to Jews. **-ishness** *n.* **-ry** *n.* the Jewish people; a ghetto. **jew's harp**, a small, lyre-shaped musical instrument [Heb. *Yehudah*, Judah].

jew·el (jōō'·al) *n.* a precious stone; an ornament set with gem(s); a highly valued person or thing; *v.t.* to adorn with jewels; to fit (as a watch) with a jewel for pivot-bearings. **-er** *n.* one who makes or deals in jewels. **-ery** *n.* jewels collectively [O.Fr. *joel*, jewel].

Jez·e·bel (jez'·a·bel) *n.* a wicked, wanton woman [*Jezebel*, wife of Ahab].

jib (jib) *n.* (*Naut.*) a triangular stay-sail in front of forward mast; the projecting beam of a crane or derrick; *v.t.*, *v.i.* jibe (var. of *gybe*). (*Colloq.*) to agree; *n.* a jeer [var. of *gibe*].

jibe (jib) *v.t.* to swing (the sail) from one side of the ship to the other; *v.i.* to swing round (of the sail) when running before the wind; to alter the course so that the sail shifts; (*Colloq.*) to agree; *n.* a jeer [var. of *gibe*].

jif·fy (jif'·i·) *n.* (*Colloq.*) a moment; an instant.

jig (jig) *n.* a lively dance; music for this; (*Slang*) a trick; a tool or fixture used to guide cutting tools in the making of duplicate parts; *v.t.* to jerk up and down; *v.i.* to dance; to bob up and down. *pr.p.* **-ging.** *pa.p.* **-ged. -saw** *n.* a narrow saw in a frame for cutting curves, etc. **-saw puzzle**, a picture cut into irregular pieces for putting together again.

jig·ger (jig'·er) *n.* one who or that which jigs; any mechanical device which operates with jerky movement esp. an apparatus for washing and separating ores by shaking in sieves under water; an iron-headed golf club for approach shots; a bridge for a billiard cue; (*Naut.*) light tackle; (*Naut.*) a sail nearest the stern; (*Colloq.*) any gadget; a 1½ oz. measure for liquor.

jig·ger (jig'·er) *n.* Also **chigger**. a flea, the female of which burrows under the human flesh to lay its eggs [var. of *chigoe*].

jig·gle (jig'·l) *v.i.* and *v.t.* to move with repeated short, quick jerks; *n.* a short, quick movement [etym. uncertain].

ji·had (ji·had') *n.* a holy war to the death proclaimed by Mohammedans against the foes of Islam; (*Fig.*) a campaign launched against any doctrine. Also **jehad** [Ar.].

jilt (jilt) *n.* one, esp. a woman, who capriciously disappoints a lover; *v.t.* to deceive or disappoint in love; to break an engagement to marry [prob. fr. *jillet*, dim. of *Jill*].

Jim Crow (jim-krō) *a.* discriminating against or segregating Negroes [*Jim* and *crow*].

jim·my (jim·i·) *n.* a small crowbar, as used by burglars; *v.t.* to force open [var. of *James*].

jin·gle (jing'·gl) *v.t.* to cause to give a sharp, tinkling sound; *v.i.* to tinkle; to give this effect in poetry; *n.* a tinkling sound, as of bells; correspondence of sounds, rhymes, etc., in verse to catch the ear [imit.].

jin·go (jing'·gō) *n.* a mild oath, as in *By Jingo*; one who expresses vehement patriotism (from the popular songs of the late 1870's, 'We don't want to fight, but *by Jingo* if we do...'). **jingo, -ish** *a.* **-ism** *n.*

jinks (jingks) *n.pl.* lively pranks [Scot.].

jinn (jin) *n.pl.* (*sing.* **jinnee, jinni, genie**) spirits of Mohammedan mythology, supposedly able to assume the forms of men and animals [Ar. *jinni*].

jin·rik·i·sha (jin·rik'·sha) *n.* a small, two-wheeled hooded carriage pulled by one or more men, commonly used in Japan (*abbrev.* **rickshaw**) [Jap. *jin*, a man; *riki*, power; *sha*, a carriage].

jinx (jingks) *n.* a person or thing of ill-omen; *v.* to bring bad luck.

jit·ney (jit'·ni·) *n.* public bus or car traveling a regular route.

jit·ters (jit'·ers) *n.pl.* (*Slang*) a state of nervous agitation. **jitterbug** *n.* a jazzdancer. **jittery** *a.* [prob. imit.].

jiu-jit·su See jujutsu.

jive (jiv) *n.* and *v.i.* (*Slang*) exuberant variation on modern swing-time dance steps.

job (jäb) *n.* a piece of work; labor undertaken at a stated price or paid for by the hour; position; habitual employment or profession; *a.* lumped together (of miscellaneous articles); *v.i.* to do odd jobs; to act as a jobber; to use influence unscrupulously; *v.t.* to buy and sell as a jobber; to let out work in portions. *pr.p.* **-bing.** *pa.p.* **-bed. -ber** *n.* a wholesale dealer who sells to retailers; one who transacts public business to his own advantage; one who does odd jobs. **-bery** *n.* underhand means to gain private profit at the expense of public money; fraudulent dealings. **-bing** *a.* — **lot**, a large amount of goods as handled by a jobber; a lot of inferior quality. **printing, — work**, the printing of handbills, circulars, etc.

Job (jōb) *n.* (*Bib.*) a Hebrew patriarch of the Old Testament regarded as a monument of patience; any person accepting continued disaster with infinite patience. **a Job's comforter**, one who aggravates the distress of another while pretending to console him.

jock·ey (jäk'·i·) *n.* a professional rider in horse-races; *v.t.* to ride as a jockey; to maneuver for one's own advantage; to trick; *v.i.* to cheat. **-ism, -ship** *n.* [dim. of *Jock*].

jo·cose (jō·kōs') *a.* given to jesting; waggish. **-ly** *adv.* **-ness**, **jocosity** (jō·käs'·a·ti·) *n.* the quality or state of being jocose. **jocular** (jäk'·ya·lar) *a.* given to jesting; facetious. [L. *jocus*, a jest].

joc·und (jäk'·and) *a.* merry; gay; genial. **-ity, -ness** *n.* **-ly** *adv.* [L. *jucundus*, gay].

jodh·purs (jäd'·poorz) *n.pl.* long riding breeches, close-fitting from knee to ankle [fr. *Jodhpur*, a native Indian State].

jog (jäg) *v.t.* to push with the elbow or hand; to nudge; to stimulate (as the memory); *v.i.* to move on at a slow jolting pace; to plod on. *pr.p.* **-ging.** *pa.p.* **-ged;** *n.* a nudge; a reminder; a slow walk, trot, etc.

jog (jäg) *n.* a projecting part [var. of *jag*].

jog·gle (jäg'·l) *v.t.* to shake slightly; to join by notches to prevent sliding apart; *v.i.* to shake; to totter; *n.* a jolt; a joint of two bodies so constructed by means of notches, that sliding apart is prevented; a metal pin joining two pieces of stone [dim. of *jog*].

John (jän) *n.* a proper name; a familiar appellation. — **Barleycorn**, whisky. — **Bull**, the typical Englishman. — **Doe**, fictitious plaintiff in a law-case. — **Hancock** (*Colloq.*) one's signature. **johnny cake** corn bread; *i.e.* (*Slang*) a toilet [L. *Johannes*, John].

John·so·ni·an (jän·sō'·ni·an) *a.* pert. to *Dr. Samuel Johnson* (1709-84), or to his literary style.

join (join) *v.t.* to bring together; to fasten; to unite; to act in concert with; to become a member of; to return to (as one's ship); to unite in marriage; *v.i.* to meet; to become united in marriage, partnership, league, etc.; to be in contact; *n.* a junction; a fastening. **joinder** *n.* (*Law*) a union. **-er** *n.* one who or that which joins; a carpenter. **-ery** *n.* the trade of a joiner. **to join battle**, to begin fighting. **to join issue**, to take different sides on a point in debate [Fr. *joindre*, to join].

joint (joint) *n.* the place where two things are joined; the articulation of two or more bones in the body; a hinge; (*Bot.*) the point where a leaf joins the stem; a cut of meat with bone prepared by butcher for the table; (*Slang*) a low-class public house; *v.t.* to unite; to provide with joints; to cut at a joint, as meat; *v.i.* to fit like joints; *a.* jointed; held in common. **-ed** *a.* having joints. **-ly** *adv.* together; co-operatively. **—stock company**, a mercantile, banking, or co-operative association with capital made up of transferable shares. **-ure** *n.* property settled on a woman at marriage to be hers on the decease of her husband. **out of joint**, dislocated; (*Fig.*) disordered [Fr. *joindre*, to join].

joist (joist) *n.* a beam to which the boards of a floor or the laths of a ceiling are nailed [O.Fr. *giste*, fr. *gésir*, to lie].

joke (jōk) *n.* something said or done to provoke laughter; a witticism; a prank; *v.t.* to make merry with; to banter; *v.i.* to make sport; to be merry. **-r** *n.* one who makes jokes or plays pranks; (*Slang*) a fellow; (*Cards*) an extra card in the pack, used in some games, such as poker; a hidden clause which changes the original intent of a bill, document, etc. **jokingly** *adv.* [L. *jocus*, a joke].

jol·ly (jäl'·i·) *a.* jovial; gay; enjoyable; *v.t.* (*Colloq.*) to humor a person with pleasant talk; (*Colloq.*) to tease. **jollification** *n.* a celebration; a noisy party. **jolliness, jollity** *n.* mirth; boisterous fun [O.Fr. *joli*, gay].

jol·ly-boat (jäl'·i·bōt) *n.* a ship's small boat [prob. Dut. *jolle*, a boat].

jolt (jōlt) *v.t.* to shake with a sudden jerk; *v.i.* to shake, as a vehicle on rough ground; *n.* a sudden jerk [etym. unknown].

Jo·nah (jō'·na) *n.* (*Bib.*) a Hebrew prophet; (*Colloq.*) a person who brings bad luck.

Jon·a·than (jän'·a·than) *n.* a variety of eating apple. [Fr. fr. L. *juncus*, a rush].

jon·quil (jän'·kwil) *n.* a variety of narcissus

jo·rum (jō'·ram) *n.* a large drinking vessel; a large quantity of liquid. [to banter.

josh (jäsh) *v.t.* and *v.i.* to make fun of, to tease,

joss (jäs) *n.* a Chinese idol [corrupt of Port. *deos*, a god].

jos·tle (jäs'·l) *v.t.* to push against, esp. with the elbow; *v.i.* to push; to strive for position; *n.* a pushing against [fr. *joust*].

jot (jät) *n.* an iota; something negligible; *v.t.* to scribble down; to make a memorandum of. *pr.p.* **-ting.** *pa.p.* **-ted. -ter** *n.* **not to care a jot**, not to care at all [Gk. *iota*, the letter i].

joule (jōōl, joul) *n.* (*Elect.*) a unit of work; the energy expended in 1 sec. by 1 ampere flowing through a resistance of 1 ohm [fr. *J. P. Joule*, English physicist, 1818-89].

jour·nal (jur'·nal) *n.* a diary; a book recording daily transactions of a business firm; a daily newspaper; a periodical. **-ese** *n.* a term of contempt for the second-rate literary style of journalists. **-ize** *v.i.* to write for a journal; to keep a daily record of events. **-ism** *n.* **-ist** *n.* one who writes professionally for a newspaper or periodical. **-istic** *a.* [Fr. fr. L. *diurnalis*, daily].

jour·ney (jur'·ni·) *n.* travel from one place to another; distance covered in a specified time; *v.i.* to travel. *pr.p.* **-ing.** *pa.p.* **-ed. -man** *n.* orig. one hired to work by the day; a skilled mechanic or artisan who has completed his apprenticeship [O.Fr. *journée*, a day].

joust (joust, just) *n.* a mock encounter on horseback; a tournament; *v.i.* to tilt [O.Fr. *juster*, to approach].

Jove (jōv) *n.* Jupiter. **jovial** *a.* orig. born under the influence of the planet Jupiter; gay; convivial. **joviality, jovialness** *n.* **jovially** *adv.* [L. *jovialis*, of Jupiter].

jowl (joul) *n.* the jaw; the cheek; the dewlap, of cattle [O.E. *ceafl*, a jaw].

joy (joi) *n.* gladness; exhilaration of spirits; *v.i.* to rejoice; to exult. *pr.p.* **-ing.** *pa.p.* **-ed. -ful** *a.* **-fully** *adv.* **-fulness** *n.* **-less** *a.* dismal. **-lessly** *adv.* **-lessness** *n.* **-ous** *a.* full of joy. **-ously** *adv.* **-ousness** *n.* **-ride** *n.* (*Slang*) a pleasure ride or stolen ride. **-stick** *n.* (*Colloq.*) the control stick of an aircraft [O.Fr. *joie*, joy].

ju·bi·lant (jōō'·ba·lant) *a.* exulting; rejoicing. **-ly** *adv.* **jubilate** *v.i.* to rejoice; to exult. **jubilate** (jōō·ba·lā'·tē) *n.* the hundredth psalm as a canticle in the Anglican church service. **jubilation** *n.* rejoicing; exultation [L. *jubilare*, to shout for joy].

ju·bi·lee (jōō'·bi·lē) *n.* the fiftieth anniversary of any outstanding event; a festival or time of rejoicing. **silver jubilee**, the twenty-fifth anniversary. **diamond jubilee**, the sixtieth anniversary [Heb. *yobel*, a ram, or ram's horn trumpet].

Ju·da·ism (jōō'·dē·izm) *n.* the religious doctrines and rites of the Jewish people. **Judaic, -al** *a.* pert. to the Jews. **Judaically** *adv.* [L. *Judacus*, a Jew].

Ju·das (jōō'·das) *n.* (*Bib.*) the disciple of Christ who betrayed him; a traitor. **—kiss** *n.* a treacherous act disguised as kindness.

judge (juj) *n.* one who judges; an officer authorized to hear and determine civil or criminal cases, and to administer justice; an arbitrator; *pl.* a book of the Old Testament; *v.t.* to decide; to hear and try a case in a court of law; to give a final opinion or decision (as in a performance); to criticize; *v.i.* to act as a judge; to form an opinion; to come to a conclusion. **-ship** n. the office of a judge. **judgment** n. the act of judging; a legal decision arrived at by a judge in a court of law; discernment; an opinion. **Judgment Day,** doomsday [L. *judex,* a judge].

ju·di·ca·ture (jōōd'·i·ka·cher) n. the power of of justice; a judge's period of office. **judicable** a. capable of being tried or judged. **judicative** a. having the power to judge. **judicatory** a. dispensing justice. **judicial** a. pert. to a court of justice or to a judge; impartial. **judicially** adv. **judiciary** n. judicial branch of government; the judicial system; judges collectively; a. pert. to the courts of law; passing judgment or sentence. **judicious** a. wise; prudent; showing discrimination [L. *judicare,* to judge].

ju·do (jōō'·dō) n. a form of jujitsu [Jap.].

jug (jug) n. a vessel of earthenware, glass, etc., with handle and narrow neck; other vessels for holding liquids; (*Slang*) jail; v.t. to put in a jug; (*Slang*) to put in jail. pr.p. **-ging.** pa.p. **-ged** [etym. uncertain].

jug·ger·naut (jug'·er·nawt) n. any fanatical idea for which people are prepared to sacrifice their lives; any irresistible, tyrannical force which crushes all that obstructs its path [Hind. *Jagannath,* the lord of the universe].

jug·gle (jug'·l) v.t. to toss up and keep in motion a number of balls, plates, etc.; to defraud; v.i. to perform tricks with the hands; to use trickery; n. a trick by sleight of hand; verbal trickery. **juggler** n. one who juggles; a twister; a cheat. **jugglery** n. [O.Fr. *jogler,* to jest].

jug·u·lar (jug'·ya·ler) a. pert. to the neck or throat; n. one of the large veins of the neck [L. *jugulum,* the throat].

juice (jōōs) n. sap; the liquid constituent of fruits or vegetables; (*Slang*) gasoline or electricity. **juiciness** n. **juicy** a. [L. *jus,* broth].

ju·jit·su (jōō·jit'·sōō) n. a form of wrestling, originating in Japan. Also **jujutsu** [Jap.].

juke box (jōōk'·bàks) n. (*Colloq.*) a coin operated phonograph.

ju·lep (jōō'·lap) n. a sweet drink, esp. one in which medicine is taken. **mint julep** [Pers. *gul,* rose; *ab,* water].

Ju·li·an (jōōl'·yan) a. pert. to Julius Caesar. **Julian Calendar,** the calendar as adjusted by Julius Caesar in 46 B.C. in which the year was made to consist of 365 days, 6 hours.

ju·li·enne (jōō·li·en') n. a clear soup containing vegetables finely shredded; a. of vegetables in thin strips [Fr.].

Ju·ly (jōō·lī') n. the seventh month of the year [fr. *mensis Julius,* month of Julius Caesar].

jum·ble (jum'·bl) v.t. to mix in a confused mass; v.i. to be in a muddle; n. a miscellaneous collection; a chaotic muddle [prob. from *jump* and *tumble*].

jum·ble (jum'·bl) n. a thin, sweet, sticky cake.

jum·bo (jum'·bō) n. a huge person, animal, or thing, esp. the famous elephant in the 1880's.

jump (jump) v.t. to spring over; to spring off; to skip (as page of a book); v.i. to lift feet from ground and alight again; to spring; n. a leap; a bound; a sudden, nervous start; pl. (*Colloq.*) nervousness. **-er** n. **-iness** n. nervous twitching. **-y** a. **-ing-bean** n. the seed of a Mexican plant containing larva which make it appear to jump [prob. imit.].

jum·per (jump'·er) n. a one-piece sleeveless dress [prob. fr. Fr. *jupe,* a petticoat].

junc·tion (jungk'·shan) n. the act of joining; the place or point of joining; a connection. **juncture** n. a joint; an exigency; a particular moment in the trend of affairs [L. *jungere,* to join].

June (jōōn) n. the sixth month of the year [L. *Junius,* the month of Juno].

jun·gle (jung'·gl) n. land covered with forest trees, tangled undergrowth, esp. the dense forests of equatorial latitudes. **— fever** n. a severe form of malaria [Hind. *jungal,* forest].

jun·ior (jōōn'·yer) a. younger, esp. of a son with the same name as his father: of lower status; n. a young person; the younger of two; a minor; one in a subordinate position; a student in the next to last year of study [L. compar. of *juvneis,* young].

ju·ni·per (jōō'·na·per) n. a genus of evergreen coniferous shrub [L. *juniperus*].

junk (jungk) n. a flat-bottomed Chinese vessel [Port. *junco,* a boat].

junk (jungk) n. useless, discarded articles; pieces of old cordage used for oakum; (*Naut.*) hard, dry salted meat; v.t. to turn into junk. **—dealer, -man** n. one who buys and sells junk [L. *juncus,* a rush].

Jun·ker (yoong'·ker) n. a young German noble; a member of that reactionary political party in Prussia which stood for the landed interests of the aristocracy. **-ism** n. [Ger. *Junker,* a young noble].

jun·ket (jung'·kit) n. a dessert of milk curded with flavored rennet; a pleasure excursion; v.i. to feast; to picnic; to go on a pleasure trip; v.t. to entertain [L. *juncus,* a rush].

jun·ta (hoon'·ta, jun'·ta) n. a meeting; a council of state in Spain or Italy [Sp. *junta,* a committee]. [cabal [Sp. *junta,* a committee].

jun·to (jun'·tō) n. a group of conspirators; a

Ju·pi·ter (jōō'·pa·ter) n. in Roman mythology, the supreme god and ruler of heaven. Also **Jove,** the largest and brightest of the outer planets [L. fr. *Jovis, pater,* father Jove].

ju·rid·i·cal (joo·rid'·ik·al) a. pert. to law, or the administration of justice. **-ly** adv. [L. *juridicus,* judicial].

ju·ris·dic·tion (joor·is·dik'·shan) n. the administration of justice; legal authority; the limit or extent within which this authority may be exercised. **-al, jurisdictive** a. [L. *jus,* law; *dicere,* to say].

ju·ris·pru·dence (joor·is·prōō'·dans) n. the science of law; the study of the fundamental principles underlying any legal system; a body of laws. **medical jurisprudence,** forensic medicine, study of medicine as it concerns criminal law [L. *jus,* law; *prudentia,* knowledge].

ju·rist (joor'·ist) n. one versed in the law [L. *jus,* law].

ju·ry (joor'·i·) n. a body of citizens selected and sworn to give a verdict from the evidence produced in court; a committee chosen to decide the winners in a competition. **juror** n. one who serves on a jury. **-man, -woman** [O.Fr. *jurée,* an oath].

jus·sive (jus'·iv) a. (*Gram.*) expressing a command; n. a grammatical form expressing a command [L. *jubere,* to command].

just (just) a. equitable; true; founded on fact; proper; fair; well-deserved; adv. exactly; closely; scarcely. **-ly** adv. in a just manner; deservedly; uprightly. **-ness** n. equity; fairness [L. *justus,* upright].

jus·tice (jus'·tis) n. the quality of being just; equity; merited reward or punishment; the administration of the law; a judge; a magistrate. **-ship** n. the office of a judge. **justiciary** a. pert. to the administration of the law. **Justice of the Peace** (J.P.), a local officer authorized to try minor cases, administer oaths, perform marriages, etc. [L. *justitia,* justice].

jus·ti·fy (jus'·ta·fi) v.t. to prove the justice of; to vindicate; to excuse; to adjust. pr.p. **justifying.** pa.p. **justified. justifiable** a. defensible; excusable. **justifiableness** n. **justifiably** adv. **justification** n. vindication; (*Theol.*) absolution [L. *justificare,* to justify].

jut (jut) v.i. to project. pr.p. **-ting.** pa.t., pa.p. **-ted** [a form of *jet*].

jute (jōōt) n. fiber of an Indian plant [Bengali fr. Sans. *juta,* a tress of hair].

Jutes (jōōts) n.pl. a Teutonic tribe [O.E. *Jote*].

ju·ve·nes·cent (jōō·van·es'·ant) a. becoming young. **juvenescence** n. [L. *juvenis,* young].

ju·ve·nile (jōō'·va·nil, -nal) a. young; youthful; puerile; n. a young person; a book written for children. **-ness, juvenility** n. **juvenilia** n.pl. works of author produced in childhood and early youth [L. *juvenilis,* youthful].

jux·ta·pose (juks·ta·pōs') v.t. to place side by side. **juxtaposition** n. the act of placing side by side; contiguity [L. *juxta,* near; *ponere,* to place].

jugular

K

ka·i·nite (kā'·nīt) n. hydrated compound of the chlorides and sulphates of magnesium and potassium [Gk. *kainos,* new].

Kai·ser (kī'·zer) n. the name derived from the Latin *Caesar,* given to the emperors of the Old Holy Roman Empire, and of the rulers of the German Empire. **-ship** n. [Ger.].

kale (kāl) n. colewort; a hardy member of the mustard family with curled leaves; [O.E. *cawel,* fr. L. *caulis,* a stalk].

ka·lei·do·scope (ka·lī'·da·skōp) n. an optical instrument, varying symmetrical, colorful patterns being displayed on rotation. **kaleidoscopic** a. ever-changing in beauty and form; variegated [Gk. *kalos,* beautiful; *eidos,* form; *skopein,* to view].

kame (kāme) n. a high narrow ridge of gravel and sand left by a glacier.

ka·mi·ka·ze (ka·ma·ka'·zi·) n. a suicide attack by Jap. pilot [Jap.].

kam·pong (kam·pawng') n. a native Hawaiian; a native of any South Sea island [Hawaiian = a man].

kan·ga·roo (kang·ga·rōō') n. a ruminating marsupial found in Australia.

Kant·i·an (kan'·ti·an) a. pert. to the German philosopher, Immanuel Kant, or his school of philosophy.

ka·o·lin (kā'·a·lin) n. China clay; fine porcelain clay chiefly produced from feldspar in China, U.S.A. and Cornwall by weathering [Chin. *kaoling,* high hill].

ka·pok (kā·pak') n. a silky white vegetable fiber used for stuffing and for sound insulation; W. Indian evergreen tree [Malay].

ka·put (ka·poot') a. (*Slang*) finished; no good; all over; done for [Ger.].

kar·at (kar'·at) n. in fineness of gold, a twenty-fourth part (pure gold being 24 karats fine) [Gk. *Keras,* horn].

kath·ode See **cathode.**

kat·i·on, cation (kat'·i·an) n. an electro-positive ion which, in electrolysis, travels towards the cathode; a neutral atom which in consequence of losing an electron, has a positive charge [Gk. *kata,* down; *ienai,* to go].

ka·ty·did (kā'·ti·did) n. a green insect of the grasshopper family [Imit.].

ka·va (kā'·va) n. an intoxicating Polynesian beverage [Hawaiian].

kay·ak (kī'·ak) n. the Eskimo seal-skin canoe,

long, narrow and covered over.
keck (kek) *v.i.* to retch, as if about to vomit; to show disgust [imit. of the sound].
keck·le (kek′·l) *v.t.* to protect a cable or hawser from damage by fraying, by wrapping old rope, etc., round the length likely to be affected [etym. doubtful].
kedge (kej) *n.* a small anchor *v.t.* to warp, as a ship; to move a ship by means of small anchors and hawsers [Fr.].
keel (kēl) *n.* the length-wise beam of a ship on which the frames of the ship rest; hence, a ship; a similar part on some other structure; *v.i.* to turn up the keel; to provide with a keel **-haul** *v.t.* to haul under the keel of a ship by ropes attached to the yard-arms **to keel over**, (*Colloq.*) to fall over; to capsize [O.E. *ceol*, a ship].
keen (kēn) *a.* having a fine cutting edge; sharp; penetrating; piercing (of wind); eager; intense; acrimonious; caustic (tongue); shrewd; discerning. **-ly** *adv.* [O.E. *cene*].
keen (kēn) *n.* Irish dirge; *v.i.* to wail over the dead before burial [Ir. *caoine*].
keep (kēp) *v.t.* to retain possession of; to detain; to observe; to carry out; to have the care of; to maintain; to cause to continue; to reserve; to manage; to commemorate; *v.i.* to remain (in good condition); to continue; *pa.p.*, *pa.t.* **kept** *n.* guardianship; maintenance; the chief tower or dungeon (donjon) of a castle; a stronghold. **-er** *n.* one who keeps or guards; an attendant; a gamekeeper; a finger-ring to prevent another from slipping off. **-ing** *n.* care; custody; support; harmony. **-sake** *n.* anything given to recall the memory of the giver [O.E. *cepan*].
keg (keg) *n.* a small barrel [O.N. *kaggi*, cask].
kelp (kelp) *n.* the calcined ash of certain sea-weeds, used as a source of iodine; a general name for large sea-weeds [etym. unknown].
Kelt, Keltic Same as **Celt, Celtic.**
kelt (kelt) *n.* a salmon which has just spawned.
kemps (kemps) *n.pl.* coarse rough hairs in wool.
ken (ken) *n.* view; range of sight or knowledge [O.E. *cennan*, to know].
ken·nel (ken′·al) *n.* a house or shelter for dogs; an establishment where dogs are bred or lodged; the hole of a fox or other animal; a small hovel of a house; *v.t.* to confine in a kennel; *v.i.* to live in a kennel. *pr.p.* **-ling**. *pa.p.* **-led** [Fr. *chenil.* fr. L. *canis.* a dog].

ken·ning (ken′·ing) *n.* a descriptive, poetical name used in place of the usual name of a thing or person [Ice.].
kent·ledge (kent′·lij) *n.* pig iron placed in a ship's hold for permanent ballast.
kep·i (kep′·i.) *n.* a light military cap, flat-topped with a straight peak [Fr.].
kept (kept) *pa.t.* and *pa.p.* of **keep.**
ker·a·sine (ker′·a·sin) *n.* horny; [Gk. *keros*, a horn].
ker·at′(o)-, ker·at(a)) *prefix,* fr. Gk. *keras*, a horn, used in the formation of compound terms. **keratin** (ker′·a·tin) *n.* an essential constituent of horny tissue. **keratoid** *a.* horny. **keratosis** *n.* (*Med.*) a skin disease characterized by abnormal thickening.
ker·chief (ker′·chif) *n.* any cloth used in dress, esp. on the head or around the neck. **-ed.** *a.* [Fr. *couvre-chef*, cover-head].
ker·mis, kermess (kur′·mis) *n.* a festival or fair in the Low Countries; (*U.S.*) a similar affair, usually for charitable purposes; originally a dedication service at the opening of a new church [Dut. *kerk*, church; *mis*, mass].
kern (kurn) *n.* (*Print.*) a part of the face of a type projecting beyond the body, as an italic *f* [L. *cardo*, hinge].
ker·nel (kur′·nal) *n.* the inner portion, the seed, of the stony endocarp of a drupe; the edible part of a nut; a seed; the central or essential part; the nucleus [O.E. *cyrnel*, dim. of *corn*].
ker·o·sene (ker′·a·sēn) *n.* an illuminating or burning oil [Gk. *kēros*, wax].
ker·sey (kur′·zi·) *n.* coarse woolen cloth, usually ribbed [*Kersey*, England].
ketch (ketch) *n.* a small two-masted vessel.
ketch·up, catch·up, cat·sup (kech′·ap) *n.* a sauce made from mushrooms, tomatoes or walnuts [Malay *kechap*].
ket·tle (ket′·l) *n.* a metal vessel, with spout and handle, used for heating and boiling water or other liquids; a cooking pot. **-drum** *n.* a musical percussion instrument made of a hemispherical copper shell covered with vellum. **-drummer** *n.* **a pretty kettle**

kettle

of fish, an awkward affair [O.N. *ketilla*].

key (kē) *n.* a low-lying island or reef near the coast, used esp. of Spain's former possessions off the coast of Florida [Sp. *cayo*, a reef].
key (kē) *n.* an instrument which shuts or opens a lock; an instrument by which anything is turned or opened; a spanner; the highest central stone of an arch; a lever in a musical instrument, depressed by the fingers in playing; a lever on a typewriter for actuating the mechanism; in engineering, a hand tool for valve control; a switch adapted for making and breaking contact in an electric circuit; in carpentry, a small piece of hardwood inserted in joints to prevent sliding; (*Mus.*) the keynote of a scale, or tonality; the pitch of a voice; solution or explanation; a translation of a book, esp. the classics, or solutions to questions set. *a.* critical; of vital importance; controlling. **-board** *n.* the whole range of keys on a keyed instrument. **-hole** *n.* a hole in a door or lock for receiving a key. **— industry,** an industry on which vital interests of the country or other industries depend. **— man** *n.* an indispensable employee. **-note** *n.* (*Mus.*) the first tone of the scale in which a passage is written; the essential spirit of speech, thought, etc.; the policy to be followed by a political party, etc., as set forth in an initial address. **— ring** *n.* a ring for keeping a number of keys together. **— signature** *n.* (*Mus.*) the essential sharps and flats placed at the beginning of a piece after the clef to indicate the tonality. **-stone** *n.* the wedge-shaped central stone at the crown of an arch; something on which other things depend. **all keyed up,** agog with excitement and expectation [O.E. *caeg*].

khak·i (ka′·ki·) *a.* dust-colored or buff; *n.* a cloth of this color, used for the uniforms of soldiers [Urdu = *dusty*].
khan (kän) *n.* a title of respect in various Mohammedan countries among Mongol races, a king, prince, or chief. **-ate** *n.* the dominion of a Khan [Pers. = a lord or prince].
khe·dive (ka·dēv′) *n.* the title of the Turkish ruler of Egypt [Fr. Fr. Pers. = prince].
kib·itz (kib′·its) *v.i.* (*Colloq.*) to act as a kibitzer. **-er** *n.* (*Colloq.*) a spectator of a game, esp. cards, who looks at a player's hand over his shoulder; someone who gives unwanted advice [G. *kiebitz*].
kib·lah, keb·lah (kib′·la, keb′·la) *n.* the point towards which Mohammedans turn their faces in prayer [Ar. *qiblah*].
ki·bosh (kī′·bash, ki·bäsh′) *n.* (*Colloq.*) nonsense; rubbish. **to put the kibosh on,** to silence; to defeat; to make impossible.
kick (kik) *v.t.* to strike or hit with the foot; *v.i.* to strike out with the foot; (*Colloq.*) to resist; to recoil violently (of a rifle, etc.); *n.* a blow with the foot; the recoil of a gun; (*slang*) stimulation; (*Colloq.*) thrill (*Colloq.*) complaint. **-er** *n.* **-back** *n.* (*Colloq.*) a vigorous response; a portion of a worker's wages taken out by his supervisor. **-off** *n.* the commencement of a game of football. **to kick over the traces,** to throw off all restraint; to rebel openly. **to kick the bucket** (*Slang*) to die. **drop kick** *n.* (football) a kick made as the ball, just dropped from the hand, rebounds from the ground. **place kick** *n.* kicking a football placed or held on the ground [M.E. *kiken*, of unknown origin].
kid (kid) *n.* a young goat; leather made from the skin of a goat; (*Slang*) a child; *pl.* gloves of smooth kid leather; *a.* made of kid leather [O.N. *kith*].
kid (kid) *vt.* and *i.* (*Slang*) to tease; to fool. *pr.p.* **-ding.** *pap.,* *pat.* **-ded.** *n.* teasing. **-der** *n.*
kid·nap (kid′·nap) *v.t.* to carry off, abduct, or forcibly secrete a person (esp. a child). **-er** *n.* **-ing** *n.* [E.*kid,* a child; *nap,* to nab].
kid·ney (kid′·ni·) *n.* one of two glandular organs in the lumbar region of the abdominal cavity which excrete urine; animal kidney

used as food; kind; temperament. **— bean,** the kidney-shaped seed of a bean plant.
kill (kil) *v.t.* to deprive of life; to slay; to put to death; to destroy; to neutralize; to weaken or dilute; to render inactive; to pass (time); *n.* the act or time of killing; the animal killed. **-er** *n.* **-er whale** *n.* the grampus, a whale capable of swallowing seals, porpoises, etc., whole. **-ing** *a.* depriving of life; very exhausting; fascinating; (*Colloq.*) exceedingly funny. *n.* the act of destroying life; game killed on a hunt; (*Colloq.*) a profitable business deal. **-ingly** *adv.*
kiln (kil, kiln) *n.* furnace or oven for burning, baking or drying something. **—dry** *v.t.* to dry in a kiln [L. *culina*, an oven].
ki·lo- *prefix* fr. Gk. *chilioi*, one thousand, in the metric system denoting a thousand. **-cycle** *n.* the unit for measuring vibrations, the frequency of electromagnetic waves, 1000 complete cycles or oscillations per second. **-gram** *n.* 1000 grams, equal to 2.2046 lbs. avoirdupois. **-liter** *n.* 1000 liters. **-meter** *n.* 1000 meters, 3280.899 feet or nearly ⅝ of a mile. **-watt** *n.* an electric unit of power equal to 1000 watts. **-watt-hour,** one kilowatt expended for one hour, approximately 1.34 hp.
kilt (kilt) *n.* a short skirt usually of tartan cloth, deeply pleated, reaching from waist to knees [Dan. *kilte*, to tuck up].
kim·bo (kim′·bō) *a.* crooked; bent; **akimbo.**
ki·mo·no (ka·mō′·na) *n.* a striped or flowered overgarment with short wide sleeves, worn in Japan by both men and women; a dressing-gown in imitation of this style [Jap.].
kin (kin) *n.* family relations; relationship; affinity; of the same nature or kind; kindred; akin. **next of kin,** the person or persons closest in relationship to a deceased person [O.E. *cynn*].
-kin (kin) *noun suffix,* used as a diminutive, e.g. *lambkin,* a little lamb.
kind (kīnd) *n.* genus; sort; variety; class; particular nature; *a.* having a sympathetic nature; considerate; good; benevolent; obliging. **-hearted** *a.* **-heartedness** *n.* **-liness** *n.* benevolence. **-ly** *a.* and *adv.* **-ness** *n.* kind feeling or action. [O.E. *gecynde,* nature].
kin·der·gar·ten (kin′·der·gar′·tn) *n.* a school for young children where they are taught by the organizing of their natural tendency to play [Ger. = children's garden].
kin·dle (kin′·dl) *v.t.* to set on fire; to light; to excite (the passions); to inflame; *v.i.* to catch fire; to become bright or glowing; to grow warm or animated. **kindling** *n.* the act of starting a fire; the material for starting a fire [O.N. *kynda*].
kin·dred (kin′·drad) *n.* relation by birth; affinity; relatives by blood or marriage; *a.* related; cognate; of like nature; congenial; similar [M.E. *kinrede*].
kine (kīn) *n.pl.* a plural form of **cows.**
kin·e·mat·ic, kin·e·mat·i·cal (kin·a·mat′·ik, ·i·kal) *a.* relating to pure motion. **-s** *n.pl.* the branch of mechanics dealing with problems of motion [Gk. *kinēma*, movement].
kin·es·the·si·a (kin·as·thē′·zha) *n.* muscle sense; the perception of muscular effort. **kinesthetic** *a.* Also **kinaesthesia, kinesthesis** [Gk. *kinein*, to move; *aisthēsia*, perception].
ki·net·ic, kinetical (ka·net′·ik, ·i·kal) *a.* relating to motion; imparting or growing out of motion. **-s** *n.* the science which treats of changes in movements of matter produced by forces [Gk. *kinein,* to move].
king (king) *n.* (*fem.* **queen**) supreme ruler of a country; a sovereign; a monarch; one who is distinguished above all others of his compeers; a playing card in each suit with a picture of a king; the chief piece in the game of chess; in checkers, a man which is crowned. **-craft** *n.* **-dom** *n.* realm; sphere; domain; one of the great divisions (animal, vegetable, and mineral) of Natural History. **-fisher** *n.* a stout-billed bird, with brilliant plumage. **-hood** *n.* kingship. **-let** *n.* a petty king; small bird **-like, -ly** *a.* **-pin** *n.* (*Fig.*) in bowling, the pin at the front apex when the pins are set up (*Fig.*) the most important person in a group. **-'s English,** correct English usage. [O.E. *cyning*].
kink (kingk) *n.* a short twist, accidentally formed, in a rope, wire, chain, etc.; in the neck, a cramp or crick; a mental twist; a whim; *v.i.* and *v.t.* to twist spontaneously; to form a kink (in).
kins·folk (kinz′·fōk) *n.* blood relations; kin; members of the same family; also **kinfolk. kinship** *n.* state or condition of being related by birth. **kinsman, kinswoman** *n.* [kin].
ki·osk (kē·ásk′) *n.* an open pavilion or summerhouse, supported by pillars; an erection, resembling a sentry box, for the sale of periodicals, candy, tobacco, etc.; a bandstand [Turk. *kioshk*].
kip (kip) *n.* the untanned hide of young cattle; a bundle of a definite number of hides.
kip·per (kip′·er) *n.* herring, salmon, etc. split, then smoked; *v.t.* to cure fish by splitting, salting, smoking, or drying.
kirk (kurk) *n.* (*Scot.*) a church building; the (Established) Church of Scotland [Scand.].
kis·met (kis′·met) *n.* fate or destiny [Ar.].
kiss (kis) *v.t.* and *v.i.* to touch with the lips, in affection or reverence; to touch gently; *n.*

a salute by touching with lips. **-able** *a*. **-er** *n*. one who kisses; (*Slang*) the mouth. [O.E. *cyssan*].

kit (kit) *n*. a soldier's outfit, excluding his uniform; a set of tools or implements; personal effects; a wooden tub.

kitch·en (kich'·an) *n*. a room in which food is prepared and cooked. **-ette** *n*. a small kitchen. — **garden** *n*. a garden for raising vegetables for the table. — **police** (abbrev. **K.P.**) soldiers on kitchen duty. **-ware** *n*. cooking utensils [L. *coquina*, a kitchen].

kite (kit) *n*. bird of prey of Falcon family; a sheet of paper, silk, etc., stretched over a light frame and flown by means of a cord attached and held from ground [O.E. *cyta*].

kith (kith) *n*. in phrase **kith and kin**, friends and acquaintances [O.E. *cuththu*].

kit·ten (kit'·n) *n*. a young cat; *v.i.* to bring forth young cats. **-ish** *a*. like a kitten; playful. **kitty** *n*. a pet name for a cat [dim. of *cat*].

kit·ty (kit'·i·) *n*. the pool in card games; cards left over after a deal to be used as part of the game.

ki·wi (kē'·wē) *n*. a New Zealand flightless bird; the apteryx [imit. fr. its cry].

klang (klang) *n*. the sound of metal striking metal; a complex musical tone, consisting of a fundamental with its harmonics [Ger.].

klax·on (klak'·san) *n*. electric horn on motor cars. [Trade Name].

klep·to·ma·ni·a (klep·ta·mā'·ni·a) *n*. an uncontrollable impulse to steal or secrete things. **-c** *n*. [Gk. *kleptein*, to steal; *mania*, madness].

klick See **click**.

klieg eyes (klēg īz) *n.pl.* eye strain due to the excessive brilliancy of incandescent floodlighting lamps. **klieg light** *n*. a powerful incandescent lamp used in film studios for floodlighting [proper name].

knack (nak) *n*. inborn dexterity; adroitness; mannerism; habit [origin. uncertain].

knag (nag) *n*. a knot in wood; *a*. knotty; rough [M.E. *knagge*, a knot in wood].

knap·sack (nap'·sak) *n*. a bag for food and clothing, borne on the back; a rucksack [Dut. *knapzak*].

knar (när) *n*. a knot in a tree or in timber. [Dut. *knorf*. knot].

knave (nāv) *n*. a dishonest person; a rascal; (*Cards*) a jack. **-ry** *n*. roguery; trickery; sharp practice. **knavish** *a*. fraudulent; mischievous; roguish. **knavishly** *adv*. [O.E. *cnafa*, a boy. Cf. Ger. *Knabe*, a boy].

knead (nēd) *v.t.* to work dough by pressing with the heel of the hands, and folding over; to work or shape anything by pressure; to massage. **-er** *n*. [O.E. *cnedan*].

knee (nē) *n*. the joint formed by the articulation of the femur and the tibia, the two principal bones of the leg; a similar joint or region in other vertebrates; part of a garment covering the knee; *v.t.* to touch with the knees. **-breeches** *n.pl.* breeches reaching and fastened just below the knee. **-cap** *n*. the patella, a flattened bone in front of knee joint; a covering to protect the knees, esp. of horses. [O.E. *cneow*].

kneel (nēl) *v.i.* to bend a knee to the floor; to fall on the knees; to rest on the knees as in prayer. *pa.t.* and *pa.p.* **-ed** or **knelt. -ing** *n*. [fr. *knee*].

knell (nel) *n*. the stroke of a bell rung at a funeral or death; a death signal; a portent of doom; *v.i.* to toll; *v.t.* to summon by tolling bell [E. *cnyll*].

knew (nū) *pa.t.* of **know**.

knick·er·bock·ers (nik'·er·bak'·erz) *n.pl.* loose breeches gathered in at the knees. Also **knickers** [fr. the pseudonym of Washington Irving].

knick-knack (nik'·nak) *n*. a trifle, toy, or trinket. **-ery** *n*. knick-knacks collectively [reduplication of *knack*].

knife (nīf) *n.pl.* **knives** (nīvz) a cutting instrument; *v.t.* to stab with a knife. — **edge** *n*. the sharp edge of a knife; anything with a thin, sharp edge [O.E. *cnif*].

knight (nīt) *n*. orig. in feudal times, a young man admitted to the privilege of bearing arms; a minor piece in chess bearing a horse's head; *v.t.* to dub or create a knight. **—errant** *n*. a knight who wandered about in search of adventures. **—errantry** *n*. **-hood** *n*. the dignity or order of knights. **-liness** *n*. **-ly** *a*. and *adv*. [O.E. *cniht*, youth].

knit (nit) *v.t.* to form fabric by the interlooping of yarn or thread by means of needles or a machine; to cause to grow together, as a fractured bone; to contract (the brows); to unite closely; *v.i.* to be united closely. *pr.p.* **-ting.** *pa.t.* and *pa.p.* **-ted. -ter** *n*. **-ting** *n*. **-wear** *n*. knitted garments [O.E. *cnyttan*].

knives (nīvz) pl. of **knife**.

knob (nab) *n*. a rounded lump; a hard protuberance or swelling; a boss or stud; small round handle of a door, etc.; a rounded hill. **-bed** *a*. set with or containing knobs. **-biness** *n*. **-by** *a*. full of knobs; lumpy. [M.E. *knop*].

knock (nak) *v.t.* and *v.i.* to strike or beat with something hard or heavy; to strike against; to rap; to make a periodic noise, due to a faulty bearing in a reciprocating engine or to pinking in a gasoline engine; (*Colloq.*) to disparage, to criticize adversely; *n*. a stroke with something heavy; a rap on a door; a blow; the noise of a faulty engine. **-er** *n*. one who knocks; an ornamental metal attachment on a door. **—kneed** *a*. having the knees bent inward. **-out** *n*. (*Slang*) something or someone overwhelmingly attractive; a blow in a boxing match which knocks out an adversary [O.E. *cnocian*].

knoll (nōl) *n*. a small rounded hill; the top of a hill; a hillock; a mound [O.E. *cnoll*].

knoll Same as **knell**.

knot (nät) *n*. a complication of threads, cords, or ropes, formed by tying or entangling; in cordage, a method of fastening a rope to an object or to another rope; an epaulet; ribbon folded in different ways; a bond of union; a small group (of people or things); a difficulty; a hard lump, esp. of wood where a branch has sprung from the stem; (*Bot.*) a node in a grass stem; (*Naut.*) a measure of speed of ships, equal to one nautical mile (6,080 ft.) per hour; *v.t.* to form a knot in; *v.i.* to form knots. *pr.p.* **-ting.** *pa.t. pa.p.* **-ted. -hole** *n* a hole in a board where a piece of a knot has fallen out. **-tiness** *n*. **-ty** *a*. full of knots; difficult; puzzling [O.E. *cnotta*].

knout (nout) *n*. a whip consisting of leather, thongs, [Russ. *knut*, a whip].

know (nō) *v.t.* to be aware of; to have information about; to have fixed in the mind; to be acquainted with; to recognize; to have experience; to understand; to have sexual intercourse with; *v.i.* to have information or understanding. *pa.t.* **knew** (nū). *pa.p.* **-n. -ing** *a*. professing to know; shrewd; deliberate; clever. **-ingly** *adv*. **to know the ropes**, to know from experience what to do [O.F. *cnawan*].

know·ledge (nàl'·ij) *n*. direct perception; understanding; acquaintance with; practical skill; information; learning. **-able** *a*. well informed [E. *know*].

knuck·le (nuk'·l) *n*. the joint of a finger; the knee-joint of a calf or pig; *v.t.* to strike with the knuckles; *v.i.* to hold the knuckles close to the ground in the game of marbles. **brass knuckle** *n.pl.* iron or brass rings fitting across the knuckles, used to deliver

murderous blows. **to knuckle down**, to tackle a job vigorously. **to knuckle down** or **under**, to yield or submit [M.E. *knokel*].

knurl (nurl) *n*. a series of ridges or rough indentations on the edge of a thumbscrew, coin, etc.; *v.t.* to roughen edges of a circular object; to mill; to indent. **-ed.** *a*.

ko·a·la (kō·à'·la) *n*. a small marsupial ot arboreal habit, native to Australia [Aborig].

ko·dak (kō'·dak) *n*. any of several small hand cameras [trademark].

kohl (kōl) *n*. powdered antimony or lead sulfide used in the East for darkening eyebrows and eyelashes [Ar.].

kohl·ra·bi (kōl'·rà·bi·) *n*. a variety of cabbage with an edible turnip-shaped stem [Ger.].

ko·la (kō'·la) *n*. an African tree whose seeds or nuts contain a large quantity of caffeine and are used as a stimulant [Native].

ko·lin·sky (ka·lin'·ski·) *n*. Siberian polecat or mink; its fur [*Kola Peninsula*].

kood·doo (kóò'·dòò) *n*. the striped antelope of Africa. Also **kudu** [S. Afr.].

kook·a·bur·ra (kook'·a·ber'·a) *n*. the great kingfisher with a laugh-like cry [Austral.].

Ko·ran (ka·rän', kō'·ran) *n*. sacred book of Islam, containing revelations received by Mohammed. [Ar. *quaran*, reading].

ko·sher (kō'·sher) *a*. (of food) pure, clean, esp. meat, made ceremonially clean according to Jewish ordinances [Heb. *kasher*, proper].

kow·tow, kotow (kou'·tou) *v.i.* to perform the Chinese ceremony of prostration; to abase oneself; to fawn on someone [Chin.].

kraal (kräl) *n*. a Hottentot or Kaffir village consisting of a group of huts encircled by a stockade [Dut. fr. Port. *curral*, a cattlepen].

kra·sis (krā'·sis) *n*. mixture of wine and water used for the Eucharist [Gk.].

krem·lin (krem'·lin) *n*. the citadel of a Russian town or city; (*cap.*) the citadel of Moscow, the seat of Soviet government [Russ.].

kreut·zer (kroit'·zer) *n*. an old German coin; a modern Austrian monetary unit [Ger. *Kreuz*, a cross, stamped on coin].

Krish·na (krish'·na) *n*. in Hinduism the last incarnation of Vishnu [Sans.].

kro·ne (krōn'·e) *n*. a silver coin of Denmark and Norway; *pl.* **kroner**. Also an old coin of Austria and Germany. *pl.* **kronen**.

kryp·ton (krip'·tan) *n*. a non-metallic chemical element belonging to the group of rare-gases, present in the proportion of about one part in twenty millions in the atmosphere [Gk. *kruptein*, to conceal].

ku·dos (kū'·dàs) *n*. fame; glory; credit [Gk.].

ku·du Same as **koodoo**.

Ku Klux Klan (kū'·kluks·klan) *n*. a lawless secret society, founded c. 1865, to oppose granting of privileges to the freed Negroes [Gk. *kuklos*, a circle].

ku·lak (kòò'·làk) *n*. a prosperous land holder in Russia who resisted the efforts of the Soviet to nationalize agriculture [Russ. = a fist, a forestaller].

kum·mel (kim'·al) *n*. a liqueur flavored with cumin and caraway seeds [Ger. = caraway].

kum·quat (kum'·kwàt) *n*. a shrub, native to China and Japan, producing a small orange-like fruit [Chinese = a golden orange].

Kuo·min·tang (kwō'·min·tàng) *n*. political party in China, founded by Sun Yat Sen.

ky·pho·sis (ki·fō'·sis) *n*. humpback, angular deformity of the spine [Gk.].

kyr·i·e (kir'·i·ē) *n*. the words and music of part of the service in the R.C. Church; the response in the Anglican communion service after each of the Ten Commandments [Gk.].

L

la (lä) *n.* (*Mus.*) syllable for sixth tone of scale in tonic sol-fa notation.

lab·da·num (lab·dạ·nạm) *n.* a fragrant resin used in perfumes, etc. [Also **ladanum** [Gk. *ladanon*].

la·bel (lā′·bẹl) *n.* paper, card, etc., affixed to anything, denoting its contents, nature, ownership, destination, etc.; (*Fig.*) a classifying phrase or word applied to persons, etc.; (*Archit.*) a dripstone; *v.t.* to affix a label to; to identify by a label [O.Fr. *label*, a strip].

la·bel·lum (lạ·bel′·ạm) *n.* the posterior petal of a flower of the orchid type [L. *labellum*, a small lip].

la·bi·al (lā′·bi·ạl) *a.* pert. to the lips; formed by the lips, as certain speech sounds such as *p, b, w, o*; *n.* a sound formed by the lips. **-ize** *v.t.* to give a labial character to a sound. **labiate, -d** *n.* (*Bot.*) with calyx or corolla formed in two parts, resembling lips [L. *labium*, lip].

la·bi·o·den·tal (lā′·bi·ō·den′·tạl) *a.* pert. to the lips and teeth; a sound made with the lips and teeth, as *f* and *v.* **labium** *n.* a lip or lip-like structure. *pl.* **labia** [L. *labium*, a lip].

la·bor (lā′·bẹr) *n.* exertion of body or mind; toil; work demanding patience and endurance; manual workers collectively or politically; (*Med.*) the pains of childbirth; *v.i.* to work strenuously; to take pains; to move with difficulty; (*Med.*) to suffer the pains of childbirth; (*Naut.*) to pitch and roll. **-ious** *a.* toilsome; industrious. **-iously** *adv.* **-iousness** *n.* **-ed** *a.* **-er** *n.* — **union** *n.* an organization of workers for mutual aid and protection and for collective bargaining [L. *labor*, work].

lab·o·ra·to·ry (lab′·rạ·tōr·i·) *n.* a placed used for experiments or research in science, pharmacy, etc., or for manufacture of chemicals in industry (*Colloq.* abbrev. **lab.**) [L. *laborare*, to work].

la·bret (lā′·bret) *n.* an ornament inserted into a hole pierced in the lip, worn by some primitive tribes. **labral** *a.* **labrose** *a.* having thick lips. **labrum** *n.* a liplike structure. *pl.* **labra** [L. *labrum*, a lip].

la·bur·num (lạ·bur′·nạm) *n.* a small, hardy deciduous tree [L.].

lab·y·rinth (lab′·ạ·rinth) *n.* a system of intricate winding passages: a maze: (*Med.*) the intricate passages of the internal ear. **-ian**, **-ine** *a.* [Gk. *laburinthos*, a maze].

lac, lakh (lak) *n.* one hundred thousand, as a *lac of rupees* [Hind. *lakh*, 100,000].

lac (lak) *n.* a deep-red resinous substance, the excretion of an insect, found specially on trees in southern Asia, and used as a dye, in varnishes, sealing wax, etc. **seed-lac** *n.* the resinous substance cleared from twigs, etc. **shellac, shellac** *n.* the resin melted and cleared of impurities [Hind. *lakh*, 100,000].

lace (lās) *n.* a string or cord used for fastening dress, shoes, etc.; a net-like fabric of linen, cotton or silk with ornamental design interwoven by hand or machine; a tissue of silver or gold threads used as trimming; *v.t.* to fasten with a lace; to ornament with lace; to mix, as coffee, with a dash of brandy; *v.i.* to be fastened with a lace. **lacing** *n.* a fastening formed by a lace threaded through eyeholes; a trimming of lace; (*Colloq.*) a thrashing. **lacy** *a.* [O.Fr. *las*, a noose].

lac·er·ate (las′·ẹ·rāt) *v.t.* to tear; to rend; to injure; to afflict sorely. **-d** *a.* torn; mangled. **laceration** *n.* [L. *lacerare*, to tear].

lach·ry·mal (lak′·rạ·mạl) *a.* pert. to or producing tears, as *lachrymal* duct, the tear duct; *n.* one of the tear glands; a small vessel, in ancient graves, supposed to contain tears of the bereaved [L. *lacrima*, a tear].

lack (lak) *v.t.* and *v.i.* to be destitute of; to want; *n.* deficiency; shortage; need; want. **-luster** *a.* dim; wanting in brightness; *n.* dimness [M.Dut. *lak*, deficiency].

lack·a·dai·si·cal (lak·ạ·dā′·zi·kạl) *a.* affectedly pensive or languid [abbrev. of *Alack-a-day*].

lack·ey (lak′·i·) *n.* a liveried manservant; a footman; a follower; *v.t.* or *v.i.* to attend or serve as a lackey. Also **lacquey** [O.Fr. *laquais*].

la·con·ic (lạ·kán′·ik) *a.* brief; concise; expressing maximum meaning in the minimum of words. Also **-al. ally** *adv.* **laconism** *n.* a brief, pithy style of speech; terse, sententious saying [Gk. *lakōn*, Spartan].

---

lac·quer, lacker (lak′·ẹr) *n.* a varnish consisting of a solution of shellac in alcohol; *v.t.* to cover with a film of lacquer; to varnish [Fr. *lacre*, a kind of sealing-wax].

la·crosse (lạ·kraws′) *n.* an outdoor ball game played with a *crosse* or stick which has a net at the end [Fr. *la crosse*, the crook].

lac·te·al (lak·ti·ạl) *a.* pert. to milk; milky; resembling chyle; *n.* an absorbent vessel conveying chyle from the intestines to the thoracic duct. **lactate** *n.* (*Chem.*) a salt of lactic acid; *v.i.* to produce milk. **lactation** *n.* the act of giving or secreting milk; the period during which a mother suckles her child. **lacteous** *a.* resembling milk. **lactic** *a.* pert. to milk; procured from milk or whey, as *lactic acid.* **lactose** *n.* milk-sugar [L. *lacteus*, milky].

la·cu·na (lạ·kū′·nạ) *n.* a hollow; a hiatus; an omission. *pl.* **lacunae** [L. *lacuna*, a pit].

lad (lad) *n.* (*fem.* **lass**) a young man; a boy [M.E. *ladde*, a serving-man].

lad·der (lad′·ẹr) *n.* a frame of wood, steel, ropes, etc., consisting of two sides connected by rungs for climbing; anything resembling a ladder; a means of ascent [O.E. *hlaeder*].

lade (lād) *v.t.* to load; to burden; to draw (fluid) by means of a ladle. *pa.t.* **-d.** *pa.p.* **-n. lading** *n.* the act of loading; freight [O.E. *hladan*, to load].

la·dle (lā′·dl) *n.* a long-handled spoon; *v.t.* to draw off with a ladle [O.E. *hladan*, to lade].

la·dy (lā′·di·) *n.* a well-bred woman; orig. a woman having authority over a household or estate; a woman of social distinction, position; a polite term for any woman. *pl.* **ladies. Lady** *n.* (*Brit.*) the title given to the wife of any nobleman ranking below a duke; the title of the daughter of a duke, marquis, or earl; the courtesy title of the wife of a knight or baronet. **-bird** *n.* a small spotted beetle. **-finger** *n.* a finger-shaped cake. — **in waiting** *n.* a lady appointed to attend a queen or princess. **-ish** *a.* affecting the airs of a lady. —**killer** *n.* (*Slang*) a man who imagines he has a fascination to women. **-like** *a.* **-love** *n.* a sweetheart. **-ship** *n.* the title of a lady [O.E. *hlaefdige*, a kneader of bread].

lag (lag) *v.t.* to bind round, as pipes, boiler, etc., with non-conducting material to prevent loss of heat; *n.* piece of lagging material [Scand. *lög*, a barrel stave].

lag (lag) *n.* time lapse; retardation; *v.i.* to move slowly; to fall behind. *pr.p.* **-ging.** *pa.p.* **-ged. -gard** *n.* a listless person. **-ger** *n.* **-ging** *a.* loitering. **-gingly** *adv.* [Celt].

lag (lag) *n.* (*Colloq.*) a convict [etym. unknown]

la·ger-beer (lä′·gẹr-bēr) *n.* a light German beer [Ger. *lager*, a store; *Bier*, beer].

la·goon (lạ·goon′) *n.* a shallow pond or lake; a lake in a coral atoll [It. *laguna*].

la·ic (lā′·ik) *a.* lay; secular; *n.* a layman. **-ally** *adv.* **-ize** (lā·ạ·siz) *v.t.* to secularize; to render lay or laic [Gk. *laos*, the people].

laid (lād) *pa.t.* and *pa.p.* of the verb **lay;** *a.* put down; (of paper) having a slightly ribbed surface showing the marks of the close parallel wires on which pulp was laid. — **up**, indisposed; (*Naut.*) dismantled, temporarily out of service, for repairs [Fr. verb *lay*].

lain (lān) *pa.p.* of verb **lie.**

lair (lār) *n.* a den or bed of a wild animal; a place to rest. *v.t.* and *v.i.* to place or lie in a lair [O.E. *leger*, a bed].

lais·sez-faire (les′·ā·fār′) *n.* a policy of non-interference. Also **laisser-faire** [Fr. *laissez-faire*, 'let do.']. [from the clergy [See *lay*].

la·i·ty (lā′·ạ·ti·) *n.* the people, as distinct

lake (lāk) *n.* a large sheet of water within land. [O.E. *lac*, a lake].

lake (lāk) *n.* a deep-red coloring matter [Fr. *laque*]. [See *lac*].

lakh Same as *lac.* [100,000].

lam (lam) *v.t.* (*Slang*) to beat; to flog [Scand. *lama*, to beat].

lam (lam) *n.* (*Slang*) hasty escape; *v.i.* to run

---

off quickly.

lake

la·ma (lä′·mạ) *n.* a Buddhist priest in Tibet. **Lamaism** *n.* form of Buddhist religion practiced in Tibet. **Dalai-Lama** *n.* or **Grand Lama**, the chief of the lamas [Tib. *blama*, a spiritual teacher].

lamb (lam) *n.* the young of a sheep; the flesh of lamb as food; a young and innocent person; *v.i.* to bring forth lambs. **-kin** *n.* a little lamb. **-like** *a.* gentle. **-skin** *n.* [O.E. *lamb*, a lamb].

lam·baste (lam·bāst′) *v.t.* (*Slang*) to beat or scold severely.

lam·bent (lam′·bạnt) *a.* playing on the surface; gleaming; flickering; playing lightly and gracefully over a subject; said of wit. **lambency** *n.* [L. *lambere*, to lick].

lame (lām) *a.* crippled in a limb; hobbling; (*Fig.*) unsatisfactory, as an excuse; imperfect; *v.t.* to cripple. **-duck** *n.* (*Colloq.*) formerly, a Congressman serving at the last session of his term; temporarily disabled. **-ly** *adv.* **-ness** *n.* **-ish** *a.* rather lame [O.E. *lama*].

lamé (la·mā′) *n.* a textile containing metal threads giving a gold or silver effect [Fr.].

la·mel·la (lạ·mel′·ạ) *n.* a thin plate-like structure or scale. *pl.* **lamellae. lamellar, lamellate** *a.* composed of thin plates or scales. [L. *lamella*, a thin plate].

la·ment (lạ·ment′) *v.i.* to utter cries of sorrow; to bemoan; to mourn for; *v.t.* to deplore; *n.* a heartfelt expression of sorrow; an elegy or dirge. **lamentable** (lam′·ạn·tạ·bl) *a.* grievous; sad. **lamentably** *adv.* **-ation** *n.* the act of lamenting; audible expression of grief. **Book of Lamentations** (*Bib.*) one of the poetical books of the Old Testament. **-ed** *a.* mourned. **-ing** *a.* grieving. **-ingly** *adv.* [L. *lamentari*, to wail].

lam·i·na (lam′·ạ·nạ) *n.* a thin plate or scale lying over another; (*Bot.*) the blade of a leaf. *pl.* **laminae. laminar, laminary** *a.* consisting of, or resembling, thin plates. **laminate** *v.t.* to cause to split into thin plates; to make into thin layers (as metal); to cover with one layer or build up with many layers; *v.i.* to split into layers. **laminate, -d** *a.* formed of thin plates; stratified. **lamination** *n.* [L. *lamina*, a thin plate].

lamp (lamp) *n.* a vessel containing combustible oil to be burned by a wick, or inflammable gas from a jet; any light-giving contrivance. **-black** *n.* a fine soot formed by the smoke of burning gas, oil, etc.; the pigment from this soot [Gk. *lampas*, a torch].

lam·poon (lam·pòòn′) *n.* a bitter personal satire, usually in verse; abusive or scurrilous publication; *v.t.* to abuse in written satire. **-er** *n.* **-ry** *n.* [O.Fr. *lampon*, a drinking song].

la·nate (lā′·nāt) *a.* wooly; (*Bot.*) covered with fine hairs resembling wool [L. *lama*, wool].

lance (lans) *n.* a former war weapon consisting of a spearhead on a long wooden shaft; the soldier armed with a lance; a lancet; *v.t.* to pierce with a lance; to open with a lancet. **-r** *n.* a cavalry soldier armed with a lance; *pl.* a square dance, like quadrilles. **lancet** *n.* a small two-edged surgical knife. **lancet arch** *n.* narrow, pointed arch. **a free lance**, one who

---

acts on his own initiative; a journalist not attached to the staff of any particular newspaper [O.Fr. *lance*, a light spear].

lance

lan·ci·nate (lan′·sạ·nāt) *v.t.* to tear; to lacerate [L. *lancinare*, to tear].

land (land) *n.* earth; the solid matter of surface of globe; any area of the earth; ground; soil; the inhabitants of a country; real estate; *v.t.* to set on land; to bring to land; (*Colloq.*) to gain; to catch; *v.i.* to go on shore; to disembark; (*Aero.*) to bring an aircraft to rest on land or water. — **breeze** *n.* an off-shore current or air. **-ed** *a.* pert. to, or possessing, real estate. **-fall** *n.* sighting of land by a ship at sea. — **grant** *n.* a grant of land from the government esp. for colleges, railroads, etc. —**grant college** *n.* a college supported with the aid of such grants according to the Morrill Acts (1862, 1890). **-holder** *n.* a proprietor of land. **-ing** *n.* the act of coming to land; disembarkation; the level part of a staircase between two flights of steps; the place where passengers land. **-ing gear** *n.* the wheeled under-carriage of an airplane on which it rests when landing or taking off. **-ing net** *n.* a net used by anglers for landing a fish already caught by rod. **-lady** *n.* the owner of property who leases land, buildings, etc. to tenants; one who lets rooms in a house; the proprietress of an inn. **-locked** *a.* enclosed by land. **-lord** *n.* the owner of houses rented to tenants; the proprietor of an inn, etc. **-lubber** *n.* a landsman (term used by sailors); one who knows little or nothing about boats. **-mark** *n.* a mark to indicate a boundary; any outstanding or elevated object indicating general direction or distinguishing a particular locality. — **mine** *n.* military high-explosive bomb. — **office** *n.* a government office for business concerning public lands. **-scape** *n.* that portion of land which the eye can comprehend in a single view; a pictorial representation of an actual or imagined inland scene. **-scape architecture** *n.* art of aesthetically arranging or changing features of the landscape. **-scape gardener,** one who is employed professionally to lay out gardens, etc. **-scapist** *n.* a painter of landscape. **-slide** *n.* a fall of rock from a hillside or cliff; (*Fig.*) a sudden overwhelming victory [O.E. *land*, land].

landing gear

landing net

lan·dau (lan′·daw) *n.* a carriage, the top of which may be opened and thrown back. **landaulet, landaulette** *n.* an automobile with folding hood [fr. *Landau* (in Germany)].

land-grave (land′·grāv) *n.* a German nobleman [Ger. *Land*, land; *Graf*, a count].

lane (lān) *n.* a narrow track between hedges or across fields; a narrow street or road; a specified route followed by ships or airplanes; part of a street or highway for one line of traffic [O.E. *lane*, an alley].

lan·guage (lang′·gwij) *n.* speech; expression of ideas by words or written symbols; mode of speech peculiar to a nation, a class, profession, etc.; communication of animals, etc. or by any means. **dead language,** a language not spoken now, as opposed to *living language* [Fr. *langue*, language].

lan·guid (lang′·gwid) *a.* indifferent; listless; flagging from exhaustion. **-ly** *adv.* **-ness** *n.* **languish** *v.i.* to become languid; to droop with weariness; to pine or suffer; to become wistful. **-ing** *a.* drooping; sentimental. **-ingly** *adv.* **-ment** *n.* **languor** *n.* lassitude; sentimental softness [L. *languere*, to be weary].

lan·gur (lung′·gŏor) *n.* a long-tailed Indian monkey [Hind.].

lank (langk) *a.* drooping; gaunt and thin; long and straight, as hair. **-y** *a.* tall and slender. **-ly** *adv.* **-ness, -iness** *n.* [O.E. *hlanc*, lean].

lan·o·lin, lanoline (lan′·a·lin) *n.* an oily substance obtained from wool [L. *lana*, wool; *oleum*, oil].

lan·tern (lan′·tern) *n.* something portable or fixed, enclosing a light and protecting it from wind, rain, etc.; a little dome over a roof to give light; a square turret placed over the junction of the cross in a cathedral, with windows in each side of it; the light chamber of a lighthouse. — **jaws** *n.* hollow cheeks. **Chinese lantern,** a colored, collapsible paper lantern. **magic lantern,** an instrument by means of which magnified images of small objects or pictures are thrown on a screen in a dark room [Fr. *lanterne*, a lamp].

lan·yard, laniard (lan′·yerd) *n.* a short rope or line for fastening; a cord, with knife attached, worn round the neck [Fr. *lanière*, a rope].

La·o·di·ce·an (lā·ạ·dạ·sē′·an) *a.* like the Christians of *Laodicea*; lukewarm in religion; lacking strong feeling on any subject; (Rev. 3) [fr. *Laodicea*].

lap (lap) *n.* that part of the clothing between waist and knees of a person who is sitting; the part of the body thus covered; an overlying part of any substance or fixture; a course or circuit, as in bicycle-racing, etc.; that in which anything rests or is fostered as the *lap* of *luxury*; *v.t.* to lay over or on; *v.i.* to be spread or laid on or partly over; to be turned over or on; to lie upon and extend beyond. **-el** *n.* that part of a coat or dress which laps over the facing. **-ped** *a.* **-ful** *n.* that which fills a lap. **-pet** *n.* a part of a garment which hangs loose; a fold of flesh. **-peted** *a.* [O.E. *laeppa*, loosely].

lap (lap) *v.i.* to take up food or drink by licking; to make a sound like an animal lapping its food; *v.t.* to lick up; to wash or flow against. *pr.p.* **-ping.** *pa.p.* **-ped.** *n.* the act or sound of lapping; something lapped up [O.E. *lapian*, to drink].

la·pel See lap.

lap·i·dar·y (lap′·a·der·i·) *a.* pert. to stones or to the art of cutting stones; pert. to inscriptions and monuments; *n.* one who is skilled in the cutting, polishing and engraving of precious stones. **lapidate** *v.t.* to stone (to death). **lapillus** *n.* a small rounded fragment of lava. *pl.* **lapilli, lapis lazuli** *n.* an opaque mineral, sapphire-blue in color, much used in jewelry, ornaments, mosaics, etc. [L. *lapis*, a stone].

Lapp (lap) *n.* a native of Lapland. Also **Laplander. Laplandish, Lappish** *a.*

lapse (laps) *v.i.* to slip or fall; to fail to maintain a standard of conduct; to pass from one proprietor to another because of negligence; to pass slowly or by degrees; *n.* a slip or fall; a gliding; a passing of time; an error of omission; failure to do one's duty; (*Law*) termination of legal possession through negligence. **lapsable, -d** *a.* no longer valid or operative; [L. *lapsus*, a fall].

lar·ce·ny (lår′·san·i·) *n.* theft. **larcenist** *n.* a thief. **larcenous** *a.* thieving; pilfering [O.Fr. *larrecin*, theft].

larch (lårch) *n.* a genus of cone-bearing deciduous tree [L. *larix*].

lard (lård) *n.* the clarified fat of swine; *v.t.* to smear with fat; to stuff, as meat or fowl, with bacon or pork; (*Fig.*) to embellish, as to *lard one's speech with metaphors.* **-aceous** *a.* fatty. **-y** *a.* [L. *lardum*, the fat of bacon].

lard·er (lår′·der) *n.* a pantry where meat and food stuffs are kept; supply of provisions [O.Fr. *lardier*, a bacon tub].

large (lårj) *a.* of great size; spacious; extensive; liberal; numerous; extravagant; *adv.* in a large way. **-hearted** *a.* generous; liberal. **-ly** *adv.* **-ness** *n.* bigness [L. *largus*, abundant].

lar·gess (lår′·jes) *n.* a generous gift; a donation. Also **largesse** [L. *largiri*, to give freely].

lar·ghet·to (lår·get′·ō) *a.* (*Mus.*) rather slow; less slow than *largo* (*Mus.*) *a.* and *adv.* slow and stately [It. *largo*, slow].

lar·i·at (lar′·i·at) *n.* a lasso; a rope or thong of leather, with a noose for catching wild horses, etc. [Sp. *la reata*, the rope].

lark (lårk) *n.* a frolic; a prank; *v.i.* to play practical jokes [O.E. *lac*, play].

lark (lårk) *n.* a small songbird. **-spur** *n.* the delphinium [M.E. *laverock*, a lark].

lar·rup (lar′·ap) *v.t.* (*Colloq.*) to thrash. **-er** *n.* [Dut. *larpen*, to beat].

lar·va (lår′·va) *n.* an insect in the caterpillar, grub, or maggot stage. *pl.* **larvae. -l** *a.* [L. *larva*, a ghost].

lar·ynx (lar′·ingks) *n.* the upper part of the trachea or windpipe; a cartilaginous cavity containing the vocal cords. *pl.* **-es, larynges**

lark

(·in·jēz). **laryngeal, laryngal** *a.* pert. to the larynx. **laryngitis** *n.* inflammation of the larynx. **laryngoscope** *n.* a special mirror for examining the larynx [Gk. *larunx*, the throat].

las·civ·i·ous (lạ·siv′·i·as) *a.* loose; lustful; wanton. **-ly** *adv.* **-ness** *n.* [L. *lascivus*, wanton].

lash (lash) *n.* the thong of a whip; a cord; a stroke with a whip; a satirical or sarcastic reproof; an eyelash; *v.t.* to strike with a lash; to dash against, as waves; to bind with a rope; to scourge with bitter criticism; *v.i.* to ply the whip. **-ing** *n.* the act of whipping; the ropes fastening anything securely [etym. doubtful].

lass (las) *n.* a young woman; a girl; a sweetheart. **lassie** *n.* a little girl [prob. Scand.].

las·si·tude (las′·a·tūd) *n.* exhaustion of body or mind; languor [L. *lassus*, faint].

las·so (las′·ō) *n.* a long rope with a noose, used for catching wild horses; a lariat. *pl.* **-s, es** *v.t.* to catch with the lasso [Sp. fr. L. *laqueus*, a noose].

last (last) *a.* following all the rest; most recent; most unlikely; final; supreme; *adv.* finally; immediately before in time; in conclusion; *n.* the end. **-ly** *adv.* **the Last Supper,** the memorial supper celebrated by Jesus on the eve of his betrayal. **at last,** finally [contr. of *latest.*]

last (last) *n.* a model of the human foot in wood on which shoes are made or repaired; *v.t.* to fit with a last [O.E. *last*, a trace or track].

last (last) *v.i.* to continue in time; to endure; to remain unimpaired in strength or quality; to suffice. **-ing** *a.* durable; permanent [O.E. *laestan*, to continue on a track].

las·tex (las′·teks) *n.* a fine rubber thread wound with cotton, rayon, or silk and woven into cloth or knitted into fabrics [coined word].

lat·a·ki·a (lat·ạ·kē′·ạ) *n.* a superior quality of Turkish tobacco from *Latakia* in Syria.

latch (lach) *n.* a small piece of iron or wood used to fasten a door; a catch; *v.t.* to fasten with a latch. **-key** *n.* a key used for raising the latch of a door; a pass-key [O.E. *laeccan*, to catch].

late (lāt) *a.* behindhand; coming after; delayed; earlier than the present time; occurring at the close of a period of time; no longer in office; deceased; *adv.* after the usual time; not long ago; far into the night, day, week, etc. **-ly** *adv.* **-ness** *n.* tardiness [O.E. comp. of *late*] subsequent; posterior. **-st** *a.* (superl. of *late*) longest after the usual time; most recent or up-to-date, as news. **latter** (lat′·er) *a.* (var. of *later*) later or more recent; the second of two just mentioned; modern. **latterly** *adv.* **of late,** recently [O.E. *laet*, slow].

la·tent (lā′·tant) *a.* not visible or apparent; dormant; hid; concealed. **latency** *n.* **-ly** *adv.* — **heat,** heat which is absorbed in changing a body from solid to liquid, or liquid to gas, without increasing its temperature [L. *latere*, to lie hid].

lat·er·al (lat′·er·al) *a.* relating to the side. **-ly** *adv.* — **pass** (*Football*) a short pass parallel to the goal line [L. *latus, lateris*, side].

Lat·er·an (lat′·er·an) *n.* the Pope's cathedral Church in Rome; *a.* pert. to church councils [fr. *Lateranus*, orig. owner of land].

la·tex (lā′·teks) *n.* the milky sap of trees, plants, the milky juice of the rubber tree. *pl.* **latices** [L. *Latex*, a liquid].

lath (lath) *n.* a thin, narrow slip of wood to support plaster, slates, etc. *pl.* **laths** (laTHz); *v.t.* to line with laths. **-er** *n.* **-ing** *n.* the process of constructing with laths; the work done [O.E. *laettu*, a thin strip].

lathe (lāTH) *n.* a machine-tool for turning articles of wood, metal, etc.; *v.t.* to shape on a lathe [Scand.].

lath·er (laTH′·er) *n.* foam or froth made with

soap and water; froth from sweat; v.t. to spread over with lather; v.i. to form a lather [O.E. *leathor*, lather].

Lat·in (lat'·in) a. pert. to *Latium*, a part of ancient Italy with Rome as its chief center, or its inhabitants; written or spoken in Latin; pert. to the Roman Catholic Church (as distinct from the Greek Church); n. language or person descended linguistically from the ancient Latins. **-ize** v.t. to give a Latin form to; to translate into Latin; v.i. to use Latin words. **-ism** n. a Latin idiom. **-ist** n. a Latin scholar or expert. **-ity** n. the Latin language and its idiom. — **America**, parts of Central and South America where Romance languages are spoken. — **Church**, the Roman Catholic Church using Latin as its official language. — **languages**, those languages derived mainly from Latin as French, Italian, Spanish, Rumanian.

lat·i·tude (lat'·a·tūd) n. distance, measured in degrees, north or south of the equator; any region defined according to latitude; the angular distance of a heavenly body from the ecliptic; (Fig.) breadth of signification; deviation from a standard, esp. religious or ethical; scope; range. **latitudinal** a. pert. to latitude. **latitudinarian** a. broad; liberal, esp. in religious principles; n. one who departs from, or is indifferent to, strictly orthodox religious principles. **latitudinal** a. [L. *latitudo*, breadth].

la·trine (la·trēn') n. a toilet, esp. in barracks, hospitals, etc. [L. *latrina*, bath].

lat·ten (lat'·an) n. a metallic alloy of copper and zinc, with appearance of brass; metal in thin sheets [Ger. *Latte*, a thin plate].

lat·ter See late.

lat·tice (lat'·is) n. framework of wood, metal, etc., formed by strips, laths, or bars crossing each other; a gate, trellis, or window thus formed; v.t. to furnish with a lattice. **-work** n. a trellis, etc. [Fr. *latte*, a lath].

Lat·vi·an (lat'·vi·an) a. pert. to the Baltic state of Latvia; Lettish.

laud (lawd) v.t. to praise in words or singing; to extol; n. a eulogy; praise; pl. in R.C. services, the prayers immediately after matins. **-ability** n. praiseworthiness. **-able** a. commendable. **-ableness** n. **-ably** adv. **-ation** n. praise; eulogy; the act of praising highly. **-atory** a. expressing praise [L. *laudare*, to praise].

laugh (laf) v.i. to express mirth spontaneously; to make an involuntary explosive sound of amusement; to be merry or gay; n. mirth peculiar to human species; laughter. **-able** a. droll; ludicrous; comical. **-ableness** n. **-ably** adv. **-er** n. **-ing** a. happy; merry. **-ing gas** n. nitrous oxide gas used as anesthetic in dental operations. **-ing hyena** n. the spotted hyena with a peculiar cry like a human laugh. **-ing jackass** n. the great kingfisher of Australia. **-ingly** adv. **-ing stock** n. object of ridicule. **-ter** n. merriment; audible expression of amusement. **to laugh up one's sleeve**, to laugh inwardly [O.E. *hlihan*, to laugh].

launch, **lanch** (lawnch, lanch) v.t. to throw as a lance; to let fly; to cause to slide into the water for the first time, as a ship; to initiate, as an attack; to start a new activity; v.i. to go into the water; to push out to sea; to go forth; to expatiate, as in talk; to embark upon; n. the sliding of a ship into the water for the first time. — **vehicle** n. a rocket used to place a satellite or space vehicle in orbit. **-ing pad** n. platform from which a missile is fired by remote control [M.E. *lanchen*, to drop].

launch (lawnch, lánch) n. the largest boat carried on a warship; an open boat driven by steam, gasoline, or electricity [Sp. *lancha*, a pinnace].

laun·dry (lawn'·dri·, lán'·dri·) n. a place where clothes are washed, dried, and ironed; the process of washing clothes, etc.; clothes thus washed, etc. **launder** v.t. to wash clothes; n. (Mining) a long hollow trough for conveying powdered ore from the box where it is bruised. **launderer** n. **laundress** n. a woman who washes and irons clothes. **-man** n. a man who collects and delivers laundry or who works in a laundry [L. *lavandus*, to be washed].

lau·rel (law'·ral) n. evergreen shrub, much used formerly to make wreaths symbolic of honor; pl. (Fig.) honors; a. consisting of laurel. **laureate** a. crowned with laurel; n. esp. in *Poet Laureate*. **laureateship** n. **-ed** a. [L. *laurus*, a bay-tree].

la·va (lá'·va) n. the molten rock, ejected by a volcano, hardening as it cools [It. fr. L. *lavare*, to wash].

la·va·bo (la·vā'·bō) n. ceremonial washing of

a celebrant's hands after the offertory and before the eucharist, esp. in R.C. service; the towel or basin used in this ceremony [L.].

lave (lāv) v.t. (Poetic) to wash; to bathe; v.i. to bathe; to wash oneself. **lavatory** n. a place for washing [L. *lavare*, to wash].

lav·en·der (lac'·an·dẽr) n. an aromatic plant of mint family, yielding an essential oil; pale-lilac color of lavender flowers; dried flowers used as a sachet; v.t. to sprinkle or perfume with lavender [Fr. *lavande*, fr. L. *lavare*, to wash].

lav·ish (lav'·ish) a. over-generous; extravagant; ample; v.t. to expend or bestow extravagantly. **-ly** adv. n. [O. E. *lafian*, to pour out].

law (law) n. a rule established by authority; a body of rules the practice of which is authorized by a community or state; legal science; established usage; a rule, principle, or maxim of science, art, etc.; the legal profession; legal procedure; (Theol.) the Jewish or Mosaic code, as distinct from the Gospel. **-abiding** a. well-behaved; conforming to the law. — **court** n. a court in which lawcases are heard and judged. **-ful** a. allowed by law; legitimate. **-fully** adv. **-fulness** n. **-giver** n. a legislator. **-less** a. not conforming to the law; violent. **-lessly** adv. **-lessness** n. — **officer** n. a policeman. **-suit** n. a process in law for recovery of a supposed right. **-yer** n. a practitioner of law. **common law**, body of laws established more by custom than by definite legislation. **written law**, statute law, codified and written down, as distinct from *Common law* [O.E. *lagu*, a thing laid down].

lawn (lawn) n. a stretch of closely-cut, carefully-tended grass. — **mower** n. a machine for cutting grass [O.Fr. *launde*, a plain].

lawn mower

lawn (lawn) n. a fine linen or cambric; a. made of lawn [fr. *Laon*, a town in France].

lax (laks) a. slack; flabby; loose, esp. in moral sense; careless; not constipated. **-ative** a. having purgative effect; n. an aperient. **-ity**, **-ness** n. slackness; looseness of moral standards; want of exactness [L. *laxus*, loose].

lay (lā) v.t. to place or put down; to apply; to beat down, as corn; to cause to subside; to exorcise, as an evil spirit; to spread on a surface; to wager; to produce; to prepare; to station, as an ambush; to form, as a plot; to set out dishes, etc. (on a table); to charge, as with a responsibility; v.i. to produce eggs. pr.p. **-ing**. pa.t., pa.p. **laid**. n. a situation; disposition. **-er** n. a person who or that which lays, as a bricklayer, hen, etc.; a thickness or coating laid down; a stratum of rock or vegetation; the shoot of a plant partly covered with earth, thus laid to encourage propagation. **-erage** n. the artificial propagation of plants by layers. — **off** n. a slack time in industry. — **out** n. that which is laid out; the design or plans, as of a garden. — **over** n. stop, or break, in a trip. [O.E. *lecgan*, to lay].

lay (lā) past tense of **lie** (to recline).

lay (lā) n. a song; a narrative poem such as was recited by minstrels [O.Fr. *lai*, a song].

lay (lā) a. pert. to the laity, as distinct from the clergy; unprofessional. **laicize** v.t. to deprive of clerical character. **laity** n. — **brother** n. a servant in a monastery. **-figure** n. a jointed figure used by artists in imitation of the human form; a person of rather negative character. **-man** n. one of the laity, or people; one who is not an expert in a branch of knowledge. — **sister** n. a woman who serves the nuns in a convent [Gk. *laos*, the people].

lay·ette (lā·et') n. a complete outfit for a new-born baby [Fr.].

laz·ar (laz'·ẽr) n. a person afflicted with a loathsome disease, like *Lazarus*, the beggar [fr. *Lazarus*, the beggar, Luke 16].

laze (lāz) v.i. (Colloq.) to be lazy; to lounge [fr. *lazy*].

la·zy (lā'·zi·) a. disinclined to exertion; slothful; v.i. to be lazy. **lazily** adv. **laziness** n. **-bones** n. (Colloq.) a lazy fellow; an idler [O.Fr. *lasche*, weak].

lea (lē) n. (Poetic) a meadow; land left untilled; pasturage [O.E. *leah*, a field].

leach (lēch) v.t. to wash by causing water to pass through; (Bot.) to remove salts from soil by percolation; v.i. to pass through by percolation; n. act of leaching; material leached; a vessel used for leaching. Also **letch**. **-y** a. porous [O.E. *leccan*, to moisten].

lead (led) n. a well-known malleable bluish-grey metal, ductile and heavy, used for roofing, pipes, etc.; a plummet for sounding ocean depths; a thin strip of type metal to separate lines of print; graphite for pencils; bullets;

pl. sheets of lead for roof coverings; a. made of, or containing lead. **-ed** a. fitted with lead; set in lead, as panes of glass. **-en** a. made of lead; heavy; dull. **-ing** n. frame or cover of lead. — **pencil** n. a pencil containing graphite. — **poisoning** n. a form of poisoning called plumbism caused by lead being absorbed into the blood and tissues. **-y** a. [O.E. *lead*, lead].

lead (lēd) v.t. to show the way; to guide; to direct; to persuade; to precede; (Cards) to play the first card of a round; v.i. to go in front and show the way; to outstrip; to conduct; to tend to; n. front position; precedence; guidance; direction; priority; principal part in a play or film; an electric wire or cable; the first card played in a card-game; a dog's chain or leash. **-er** n. a guide; a conductor; a commander; (chiefly Brit.) the leading editorial in a newspaper; the foremost horse in a team; (Mus.) a performer who leads an orchestra or choir; (Print.) a series of dots (...) to guide the eye across the page. **-ership** n. the state or function of a leader. **-ing** n. direction; the act of guiding. **-ing-article** n. a leader or editorial in a newspaper. **-ing-lady**, **-man** n. the actress (or actor) playing the principal role. **-ing-question** n. (Law) a question so phrased as to suggest the answer expected. **to lead astray**, to tempt from virtue [O.E. *laedan*, to lead].

leaf (lēf) n. thin deciduous shoot from the stem or branch of a plant; anything resembling a leaf in shape or thinness; a sheet of paper, esp. as part of a book, with a page on each side; side of a double door or a shutter; one of the sections of a dropleaf or extension table; a hinged flap; a very thinly beaten plate, as of gold. pl. **leaves**. v.i. to shoot out leaves. **-age** n. leaves collectively; foliage. **-iness** n. **-less** a. devoid of leaves. **-let** n. a tiny leaf; a printed sheet advertisement, notice of meeting, etc. — **mold** n. leaves decayed and reduced to mold, used as manure. **-y** a. full of leaves. **to turn over a new leaf**, to reform [O.E. *leaf*, leaf].

league (lēg) n. an old nautical measure equal to three geographical miles [O.Fr. *legue*, fr. (L.L.) *leuca*, a Gallic mile of 1500 paces].

league (lēg) n. a compact made between nations or individuals for mutual aid and the promoting of common interests; an association, as of football clubs, for match games to be played during a season; v.i. to combine in an association [Fr. *ligue*, a conspiracy].

lea·guer (lē'·gẽr) n. a military camp, esp. a siege camp [Dut. *leger*, a camp].

leak (lēk) n. a crack, crevice, fissure, or hole in a vessel; the oozing of liquid from such; (Elect.) an escape of electrical current from a faulty conductor; v.i. to let fluid into, or out of, a defective vessel. **-age** n. an oozing or quantity of liquid which passes through a defect in a vessel; (Fig.) the giving away of secrets, news, etc., through unauthorized channels. **-iness** n. **-y** a. having leaks. **to spring a leak**, to develop a crack or flaw [Scand. *leka*, a drip].

lean (lēn) v.t. to incline; to cause to rest against; v.i. to deviate from the perpendicular; to incline. pa.t. and pa.p. **leaned** or **leant** (lent). n. a slope; a rest against. **-ing** n. inclination (of body or mind). — **to** n. a shed built against a wall or side of a house or supported at one end by posts or trees [O.E. *hlaenan*, to cause to incline].

lean (lēn) a. thin; wanting in flesh or fat; (Fig.) empty; impoverished; n. that part of meat consisting of flesh without fat. **-ly** adv. **-ness** n. [O.E. *hlaene*, thin].

leap (lēp) v.i. to spring; to jump up or forward; to vault; v.t. to pass over by leaping. pr.p. **-ing** pa.t. and pa.p. **-ed** or **leapt** (lept). n. jumping up or forward; a sudden rise (as of book-sales). **-frog** n. a game, in which one stoops down, and another vaults over his head. — **year** n. a year of 366 days [O.E. *hleapan*, to leap].

learn (lurn) v.t. to acquire knowledge; to get to know; to gain skill by practice; v.i. to gain knowledge; to take example from. pa.t. and pa.p. **-ed** (lurnd) or **-t. -ed** (lurn'·ad) a. having knowledge; erudite. **-edly** adv. **-edness** n. **-er** n. **-ing** n. that which is learned; letters; science; literature; erudition [O.E. *leornian*].

lease (lēs) n. a contract renting lands, houses, farms, etc., for a specified time; time covered by lease; any tenure; v.t. to grant possession of lands, etc., to another for rent; to hold a lease. — **hold** a. held on lease [O.Fr. *laissier*, to transmit].

leash (lēsh) n. a line by which a hawk, dog, or

other animal is held; a set of three hounds, or hares or foxes held in leash; *v.t.* to hold by a leash; to bind [O.Fr. *lesse*, a thong].

least (lēst) *a.* (superl. of **little**) smallest; faintest; most minute; *adv.* in the smallest degree; *n.* the smallest amount. **-ways, -wise** (*Colloq.*) *adv.* at least; however. **at least**, at any rate [O.E. *laest*, smallest].

leath·er (leTH'·ẹr) *n.* the skin of an animal dressed and prepared for use; anything made of leather; *v.t.* to apply leather to; (*Colloq.*) to thrash with a strap. **— back** *n.* a large sea turtle. **— bound** *a.* (of a book) bound in calf, morocco, or other leather. **-ing** *n.* (*Colloq.*) a thrashing. **-n** *a.* made of leather. **-neck** *n.* (*Slang*) a U.S. marine. **-y** *a.* like leather; tough. **patent leather**, leather with shiny, varnished surface [O.E. *lether*, leather].

leave (lēv) *n.* liberty granted; formal good-bye; furlough; permission to be temporarily absent from duty. **French leave**, absence without permission [O.E. *leaf*, permission].

leave (lēv) *v.t.* to quit; to forsake; to omit; to remove; to allow to remain unaltered; to bequeath; to permit; to entrust; to refer; *v.i.* to depart from; to withdraw. *pr.p.* **leaving.** *pa.p.* **left. leavings** *n.pl.* things left; relics; refuse [O.E. *laefan*, to bequeath].

leav·en (lev'·n) *n.* a substance due to fermentation which causes bread dough to rise; (*Fig.*) anything which causes a general change in the mass; *v.t.* to raise with leaven; to create a spiritual change [L. *levare*, to raise].

lech·er (lech'·ẹr) *n.* a man given to lewdness; a fornicator. **-ous** *a.* lascivious; lustful. **-ously** *adv.* **-ousness, -y** *n.* [O.Fr. *lechier*, to lick].

lec·tern (lek'·tẹrn) *n.* a reading desk in a church [L.L. *lectrum*, a reading-desk].

lec·tion (lek'·shạn) *n.* a variation in copies of a manuscript; a portion of scripture read during a church service. **-ary** *n.* a book containing portions of the Scripture to be read on particular days. **lector** *n.* a reader; a minor ecclesiastic in the early church; a lecturer in a college or university [L. *legere*, to read].

lec·ture (lek'·chẹr) *n.* a discourse on any subject; a formal reproof; *v.t.* to instruct by discourses; to reprove; *v.i.* to deliver a formal discourse. **-r** *n.* one who lectures; an assistant to a professor in a university department. **-ship** *n.* [L. *legere, lectum*, to read].

led (led) *pa.t.* and *pa.p.* of verb **lead.**

ledge (lej) *n.* a projection, as from a wall or cliff; a shelf; a ridge of rock near the surface of the sea [M.E. *legge*, a bar].

ledg·er (lej'·ẹr) *n.* a book in which a business firm enters all debit and credit items in summary form; a cash book; a flat stone lying horizontally as on a grave; one of the pieces of timber used in a scaffolding; *a.* stationary (only in compound words). **— line** *n.* a line with hook and sinker to keep it stationary; (*Mus.*) an additional line above or below the staff for notes outside the normal range. Also **leger** [prob. M.E. *leggan*, to lie].

lee (lē) *n.* a place protected from the wind; shelter; *a.* pert. to the part or side farthest from the wind. **-board** *n.* a plank lowered on the side of a boat to diminish its drifting to leeward. **-gage** *n.* the sheltered side. **— shore** *n.* the shore on the lee-side of a vessel. **-side** *n.* the side of a vessel opposite to the direction from which the wind is blowing. **— tide** *n.* a current running in the direction the wind is blowing. **-ward** (lē'·wẹrd, lōō'·wẹrd) *a.* pert. to, or in, the direction towards which the wind is blowing. **-way** *n.* the side movement of a vessel to the leeward of her course; loss of progress; (*Colloq.*) extra time, space, etc. [O.E. *hleo*, a shelter].

leech (lēch) *n.* a blood-sucking worm used for bloodletting; (*Archaic*) physician; *v.t.* to bleed by application of leeches [O.E. *laece*, one who heals].

leek (lēk) *n.* a biennial bulbous plant allied to the onion; also, the national emblem of Wales [O.E. *leac*, leek].

leer (lēr) *n.* a sly or furtive look expressive of malignity, lasciviousness, or triumph; *v.i.* to look with a leer [O.E. *hleor*, cheek].

leer·y (lēr'·i·) *a.* wary; suspicious.

lees (lēz) *n.pl.* the sediment which settles at the bottom of a wine-cask; dregs [Fr. *lie*].

left (left) *a.* on the side of the body which is westward when one is facing north. Also **left-hand.** *n.* the side opposite to the right; in some legislative assemblies, the left side of the speaker's chair where the opposition members sit, hence an extreme or radical party; *adv.* on or on the left. **—hand** *n.* the left side; *a.* situated on the left side; executed with the left hand. **—handed** *a.* using the left hand more easily than the right; awkward. **—handedness** *n.* **— wing** *n.* a political group with extremist views [M.E. *lift*, weak].

leek

left (left) *pa.t.* and *pa.p.* of the verb **leave.**

leg (leg) *n.* the limb of an animal used in supporting the body and in walking, esp. that part of the limb between the knee and the foot; any support, as leg of a table; one of the two divisions of a forked object, as compasses; part of a garment covering the leg; (*Naut.*) a ship's course covered on one tack; *v.i.* (*Colloq.*) to walk briskly; to run. *pr.p.* **-ging.** *pa.t.* and *pa.p.* **-ged. -ged** *a.* having legs, as **three-legged stool. -ging** *n.* a garment to cover the legs. **-gy** *a.* having disproportionately long legs, as a very young animal. **-less** *a.* without legs. **-of-mutton** *a.* shaped like a leg of mutton, as of a sleeve; triangular, as a sail [Scand. *legar*, a leg].

leg·a·cy (leg'·ạ·si·) *n.* a bequest; a gift of personal property by will. **legatee** *n.* one who receives a legacy [L. *legare*, to bequeath].

le·gal (lē'·gạl) *a.* pert. to, or according to, the law; defined by law; statutory; binding; constitutional. **-ization** *n.* **-ize** *v.t.* to make lawful; to sanction. **-ity** *n.* conformity to law. **-ly** *adv.* **— tender**, the form of money, coin, or notes, which may be lawfully used in paying a debt [L. *lex, legis*, a law].

leg·ate (leg'·at) *n.* Pope's highest diplomatic envoy; a diplomatic minister below ambassadorial rank. **-ship** *n.* **legatine** *a.* of a legate. **legation** (li·gā'·shạn) *n.* a minister and his staff; the official residence or offices of a diplomatic minister [L. *legatus*, an envoy].

le·ga·to (li·gà'·tō) *adv.* (*Mus.*) in a smooth, gliding manner [L. *ligare*, to tie].

leg·end (lej'·ạnd) *n.* orig. a chronicle of the lives of the saints; any traditional story of ancient times; an inscription on a coin, medal, etc. **-ary** *n.* book of, relater of, legends; *a.* comprising legends; fabulous; strange. **-ry** *n.* legends collectively [L. *legendus*, to be read].

le·ger·de·main (lej·ẹr·dạ·mān') *n.* a sleight of hand; trickery [Fr. *léger de main*, light of hand].

leg·er·line (lej'·ẹr·lin) *n.* See **ledger.**

Leg·horn (leg'·hawrn) *n.* a plaited straw, from Leghorn in Italy; (*l.c.*) a hat made of this straw; a breed of domestic fowl.

leg·i·ble (lej'·ạ·bl) *a.* capable of being read. **legibly** *adv.* **-ness, legibility** *n.* [L. *legere*, to read].

le·gion (lē'·jạn) *n.* in ancient Rome, a body of infantry of from three to six thousand; a military force; a great number. **-ary** *a.* relating to, or consisting of, a legion or legions; containing a great number; *n.* a soldier of a legion. **-naire** *n.* a legionary; (*Cap.*) member of the American Legion [L. *legio, legionis*].

leg·is·late (lej'·is·lāt) *v.i.* to make or enact laws. **legislation** *n.* act of legislating; laws made. **legislative** *a.* having power to make laws; constitutional. **legislatively** *adv.* **legislator** *n.* one who enacts laws; a member of the legislature. **legislature** *n.* the body empowered to make and repeal laws [L. *lex*, a law; *ferre, latum*, to carry].

le·git·i·mate (li·jit'·ạ·mit) *a.* lawful; in accordance with the law; born in lawful wedlock; justifiable; reasonable; genuine; *v.t.* (li·jit'·ạ·māt) to make lawful; to render legitimate; to pronounce lawful or proper. **legitimacy** *n.* the state of being legitimate. **-ly** *adv.* **-ness** *n.* **legitimation** *n.* the act of investing with the rights and privileges of lawful birth. **legitimize** *v.t.* to legitimate. **legitimism** *n.* **legitimist** *n.* one who upholds legitimate authority, esp. hereditary monarchical government [L. *legitimus*, lawful].

leg·ume (leg'·ūm) *n.* a seed pod with two valves and having the seeds attached at one suture, as the pea; a plant bearing seed-pods. Also **legumen.** *pl.* **legumens, legumina. leguminous** *a.* [Fr. *légume*, a vegetable].

lei (lā) *n.* a garland of flowers worn around the neck [Haw.].

lei·sure (lē'·zhẹr) *n.* freedom from occupation; spare time; a. unoccupied. **leisurable** *a.* **-d** *a.* free from business duties. **-ly** *a.* unhurried; slow; *adv.* slowly [O.Fr. *leisir*, to be lawful].

leit·mo·tif (lit'·mō·tēf) *n.* (*Mus.*) a theme associated with a person or idea, constantly recurring in a composition [Ger. *leit*, leading; Fr. *motif*, motive].

lem·ma (lem'·ạ) *n.* (*Math.*) a subsidiary proposition; (*Logic*) a premise taken for granted;

a theme; a heading of an entry [Gk. *lemma*, something taken for granted].

legume

lem·on (lem'·ạn) *n.* an oval-shaped fruit with rind pale yellow in color and containing very acid pulp and juice; the tree which provides this fruit; (*Colloq.*) an inferior product; *a.* of the color of lemon rind. **-ade** *n.* a cooling drink made of lemon juice, sugar, and water [Fr. *limon*, the lemon fruit].

le·mur (lē'·mẹr) *n.* one of a family of nocturnal monkey-like mammals found in Madagascar [L. *lemur*, a ghost].

lend (lend) *v.t.* to grant the temporary use of; to give in general; to let out money at interest; to serve for; *v.i.* to make a loan. *pr.p.* **-ing.** *pa.p.* **lent. -er** *n.* [O.E. *laen*, a loan].

lend-lease, the pooling of material resources of Allied nations in the struggle against Germany and Japan (W.W. II); *v.t.* to grant (material aid) to a foreign country in accordance with the Lend-Lease Act of March 11, 1941.

length (length) *n.* the measurement of anything from end to end; extension; duration of time; extent; intervening distance, as in a race; the quantity of a syllable or vowel in prosody. **-en** *v.t.* to extend in length; to protract; *v.i.* to grow longer. **-ily** *adv.* **-iness** *n.* **-wise** *a.* in the direction of the length. **-y** *a.* [O.E. *lang*, long].

le·ni·ent (lē'·ni·ẹnt) *a.* clement; acting without severity. **lenience, leniency** *n.* the quality of being lenient; clemency. **-ly** *adv.* **lenitive** *n.* a medicine which eases pain; *a.* soothing; emollient. **lenity** *n.* [L. *lenis*, soft].

lens (lenz) *n.* (*Optics*) a piece of glass or other transparent substance ground with one or both sides curved so as to refract rays of light, and thereby modify vision; the crystalline biconvex tissue between the cornea and retina of the eye. *pl.* **lenses** [L. *lens*, a lentil].

Lent (lent) *n.* the season of 40 days from Ash Wednesday until Easter Day. **-en** *a.* pert. to Lent [O.E. *lencten*, spring].

len·tic·u·lar (len·tik'·yoo·lẹr) *a.* shaped like a lens or lentil; resembling a double-convex lens. Also **lentiform. lentoid** *a.* lens-shaped [L. *lenticula*, a small lentil].

len·til (len'·til) *n.* a Mediterranean plant allied to the bean [L. *lens*, a lentil].

len·to (len'·tō) *adv.* (*Mus.*) slowly [It.].

l'en·voi (len·voi' or lawng'·vwä) *n.* a kind of postscript to a poem; a short, final stanza [O.Fr. *l'envoi*, the sending].

Le·o (lē'·ō) *n.* the lion, the fifth sign of the Zodiac which the sun enters about July 22nd. **leonine** *a.* of or like a lion [L. *leo*, a lion].

leo·pard (lep'·ẹrd) *n.* a large carnivorous member of the cat family, of a yellow or fawn color with black spots [Gk. *leōn*, lion; *pardos*, pard].

le·o·tard (lē'·ạ·tárd) *n.* a one-piece tight-fitting garment worn by dancers [after *Léotard*, 19th cent. Fr. aerial performer].

lep·er (lep'·ẹr) *n.* a person afflicted with leprosy; (*Fig.*) an outcast. **leprosy** *n.* a chronic contagious disease affecting skin, tissues and nerves. **leprous** a. [Gk. *lepros*, scaly].

Leo

Lep·i·dop·ter·a (lep.ạ.dắp'.tẹr.ạ) *n.pl.* an order of insects having four wings covered with gossamer scales, as moths, butterflies, etc. **-l, lepidopterous** a. [Gk. *lepis*, a scale; *pteron*, a wing].

lep·re·chaun (lep'.rạ.kawn) *n.* a sprite; a brownie commonly referred to in Irish folk-stories [Ir.].

lep·ro·sy (lep'.rạ.si.) *n.* See **leper**.

Les·bi·an (lez'.bi.ạn) *a.* pert. to the island of *Lesbos* (Mytilene) in the Aegean Sea, or to the ancient school of lyric poets there; amatory; *n.* a woman who is sexually attracted to another woman; a homosexual woman [Gk. *lesbrōs*].

lese maj·es·ty (lēz'.maj.is.ti.) *n.* (*Law*) a crime committed against the sovereign, or sovereign power of a state; high treason [Fr. fr. L. *laesa majesta*, injured majesty].

le·sion (lē'.zhạn) *n.*(*Med.*) any morbid change in the structure or functioning of the living tissues of the body; injury; (*Law*) loss or injury [L. *laedere*, *laesum*, to hurt].

less (les) *a.* smaller in size; not equal to in number; lower; inferior; *adv.* in a smaller or lower degree; *n.* a smaller portion; the inferior. **-en** *v.t.* to make less; to diminish; *v.i.* to contract; to decrease. **-er** *a.* smaller; inferior [O.E. *laes*, less].

les·see (les.ē') *n.* one to whom a lease is granted [fr. *lease*].

les·son (les'.n) *n.* a reading; a piece of instruction; something to be learned by pupils; a Scripture passage read aloud as part of church service; instruction gained by experience; reproof; *v.t.* to teach [Fr. fr. L. *legere*, to read].

lest (lest) *conj.* for fear that [O.E.].

let (let) *v.t.* to allow; to give permission; to cause to do (foll. by *infin.* without *to*); to grant the temporary use of, for hire; *v.i.* to be rented; (*Colloq.*) to be dismissed (foll. by *out*). *pr.p.* **-ting**. *pa.t.* and *pa.p.* **let**. [O.E. *laeten*, to permit].

le·thal (lē'.thạl) *a.* deadly; mortal. **lethiferous** a. deadly [L. *letum*, death].

leth·ar·gy (leth'.ẹr.ji.) *n.* unnaturally heavy drowsiness; overpowering lassitude; inertia. **lethargic, lethargical** a. drowsy; apathetic. **lethargically** adv. [Gk. *lēthargos*, forgetful].

le·the (lē'.thē) *n.* oblivion. **-an** [Gk. *lēthē*, a forgetting].

let·ter (let'.ẹr) *n.* a mark or symbol used to represent an articulate, elementary sound; a written or printed communication; an epistle; the literal statement; printing-type; *pl.* learning; erudition; *v.t.* to impress or form letters on. **— box** *n.* a box for receiving letters, as on inside of house door. **— carrier** *n.* a postman. **-ed** a. literate; educated; versed in literature, science, etc.; inscribed with lettering. **-er** *n.* **— file** *n.* a device for holding letters for reference. **-head** *n.* printed heading on business stationery. **-ing** *n.* the act of impressing letters; the letters impressed. **-press** *n.* printed matter as distinct from illustrations, diagrams, etc.; print. **letter of credit**, a letter authorizing money to be paid by a bank to the bearer. **letters patent**, a document under seal of the state, granting some property privileges or authority, or conferring the exclusive right to use an invention or design [L. *littera*, a letter].

Let·tic (let'.ik) *a.* pert. to the Letts or to their language; *n.* the language of the Letts. Also **Lettish. Letts** *n.pl.* the inhabitants of Lithuania and Latvia.

let·tuce (let'.is) *n.* a common garden plant, used in salads [L. *lactuca*, lettuce].

leu·co·cyte (lōō'.kạ.sīt) *n.* one of the white corpuscles of the blood, destroying bacteria [Gk. *leukos*, white; *kutos*, a cell].

leu·ke·mi·a, leukaemia (lōō.kē'.mē.ạ) *n.* a disease characterized by an excessive number of white corpuscles in the blood [Gk. *leukos*, white].

Le·vant (lạ.vant') *n.* Eastern Mediterranean countries; (*l.c.*) a superior grade of morocco leather. **-er** *n.* wind blowing from E. Spain towards Levant. **-ine** a. pert. to Levant; *n.* native of the Levant [L. *levare*, to raise].

le·va·tor (lạ.vā'.tẹr) *n.* a muscle in the body which raises any part, as the eyelid, lips, etc. [L. *levare*, to raise].

lev·ee (lev'.ē, lạ.vē') *n.* a reception; orig. a reception held by royal personage on rising from bed [Fr. *lever*, to rise].

lev·ee (lev'.ē) *n.* a river embankment to prevent flooding; a quay [Fr. *levée*, raised].

lev·el (lev'.ạl) *n.* a line or plane which is everywhere parallel to the horizon; the horizontal plane on which a thing rests; a state of equality; an instrument for finding or drawing a true horizontal line; *a.* not having one part higher than another; even; horizontal; equal in rank or degree; *v.t.* to make horizontal; to reduce to the same height with something else; to raze; to make equal in rank, etc.; to point a gun or arrow at the mark. **—headed** a. balanced; prudent. **-er** *n.* **-ing** *n.* the act of making a surface even with another; the process of ascertaining the difference of elevation between two points, by the use of a *leveling* instrument. **-ing rod** *n.* a graduated rod used in surveying [L. *libella*, a water-level].

lev·er (lev'.ẹr, lē'.vẹr) *n.* a bar used to exert pressure or sustain a weight at one point of its length by receiving a force or power at a second, and turning at a third on a fixed point called a fulcrum; a crowbar for forcing open; *v.t.* to raise up; to force open. **-age** *n.* the action of a lever; mechanical advantage gained by use of the lever [L. *levare*, to raise].

le·vi·a·than (lạ.vī'.ạ.thạn) *n.* a huge aquatic animal; a whale; a sea-monster; anything of colossal size [Heb. *livyathan*, a sea-monster].

lev·i·ta·tion (lev.ạ.tā'.shạn) *n.* the act of making buoyant or light; the phenomenon of heavy bodies being made to float in air by spiritual agencies. **levitate** *v.t.* [L. *levis*, light].

Le·vite (lē'.vīt) *n.* one of the tribe of Levi; lesser priest in ancient Jewish synagogue. **Levitic, -al** (le.vit'.ik, .al) a. **Leviticus** *n.* (*Bib.*) third book of Old Testament [fr. *Levi*].

lev·i·ty (lev'.ạ.ti.) *n.* lightness; buoyancy; lack of seriousness [L. *levis*, light].

le·vo·ro·ta·tion (lē.vạ.rō.tā'.shạn) *n.* counterclockwise or left-hand rotation. **levorotatory** a. [L. *laevus*, left].

lev·u·lose (lev'.yoo.lōs) *n.* fruit sugar found in honey and certain fruits [L. *laevus*, left].

lev·y (lev'.i.) *v.t.* to raise by assessment, as taxes; to enlist or collect, as troops; to impose, as a fine; *v.i.* to make a levy; *n.* collection of assessment by authority or compulsion, for public services; the money or troops thus collected [L. *levare*, to raise].

lewd (lōōd) *a.* obscene; indecent; given to unlawful indulgence. **-ly** adv. **-ness** n. [O.E. *laewede*, lay].

lew·is (lōō'.is) *n.* an iron clamp dove-tailed into a stone block to raise it [etym. unknown].

lex·i·con (lek'.si.kạn) *n.* a dictionary, esp. of Greek, Latin, or Hebrew; a vocabulary list relating to a particular subject, class, etc. **lexical** a. pert. to a lexicon. **lexicographer** n. one who compiles a dictionary. **lexicographic, -al** a. **lexicologist** n. an expert in lexicology. **lexicography** n. the art or process of compiling a dictionary. **lexicology** n. the science which deals with the exact significance and use of vocabulary [Gk. *lexis*, speech; *graphein*, to write; *logos*, a discourse].

li·a·ble (lī'.ạ.bl) *a.* obliged in law or equity; subject; answerable: responsible. **liability** n. the state of being liable; responsibility; obligation; *pl.* debts [Fr. *lier*, to bind].

li·ai·son (lē.ā.zán') *n.* a union; connection; illicit intimacy between a man and a woman; (*Mil.*) contact maintained between one unit or command and another; the sounding, as in French, of the final consonant of a word before the initial vowel or mute *h* of the next word [Fr. fr. L. *ligare*, to bind].

li·a·na (li.ản'.ạ) *n.* a climbing tropical plant [Fr. *liane*].

li·ar (lī'.ẹr) *n.* one who tells lies [fr. *lie*].

li·ba·tion (lī.bā'.shạn) *n.* the ceremonial pouring of wine in honor of some deity; the liquid itself; (*Colloq.*) a drink [L. *libare*, to pour].

li·bel (lī'.bạl) *n.* a defamatory writing or printed picture; (*Law*) a written statement by the plaintiff of his allegations in a law case; (*Colloq.*) a statement injurious to a person's character; *v.t.* to defame by a writing, picture, etc.; to proceed against, by filing a libel. **-er** *n.* **-ous, -lous** a. defamatory; containing a libel. **-ously** adv. [L. *libellus*, a little book].

lib·er·al (lib'.ẹr.ạl) *a.* open-minded; generous; catholic; unbiased; (in politics) favoring democratic or progressive ideals, and freedom of religion; *n.* one who favors greater political and religious freedom from tradition; supporter of a liberal political party. **-ization** n. the process of gaining greater freedom. **-ize** *v.t.* to cause to be freer or more enlightened. **-ism** n. liberal principles. **-ist** n. **liberality** n. generosity; munificence; catholicity of mind. **-ly** adv. **liberate** v.t. to set free. **liberation** n. the act of setting free; the state of being free from bondage. **liberator** n. one who sets others free, esp. from tyranny [L. *liberalis*, befitting a freeman].

lib·er·ty (lib'.ẹr.ti.) *n.* freedom from bondage or restraint; power to act according to one's natural rights as an individual; privilege; undue freedom of act or speech; *pl.* rights, privileges, etc., conferred by grant or prescription. **libertarian** n. one who upholds the doctrine of freewill. **libertarianism** n. **libertine** (lib'.ẹr.tēn) n. one who leads a dissolute life; a. dissolute [L. *libertas*, liberty].

li·bi·do (li.bē'.dō, li.bī'.dō) *n.* in psychology, the emotional craving behind all human impulse; esp. used by Freud to denote the sexurge. **libidinous** (li.bid'.ạ.nạs) a. lewd; obscene; lustful. **libidinously** adv. [L. *libido*, desire].

Li·bra (lī'.brạ) *n.* the balance, the 7th sign of the Zodiac [L. *libra*, a balance].

li·brar·y (lī'.bre.ri.) *n.* a collection of books; the room or building which contains it. **librarian** n. the person in charge of a library; one trained and engaged in library work. **librarianship** n. **— science** n. the knowledge and skills required for library service [L. *liber*, a book].

li·brate (lī'.brāt) *v.i* to be poised; to oscillate. **libration** n. balancing; a quivering motion. **libratory** a. [L. *libra*, a balance].

li·bret·to (li.bret'.ō) *n.* the words of an opera or oratorio. **librettist** n. the writer of librettos [It. fr. L. *libro*, a little book].

Lib·y·an (lib'.i.ạn) *a.* pert. to *Libya* in N. Africa or to the language of the district.

lice (līs) *pl.* of **louse**.

li·cense (lī'.sạns) *n.* authority granted to do any act; a legal permit; excess of liberty; *v.t.* to permit by grant of authority. **licensable** a. **-d** a. privileged; holding a license. **licensee** n. one who is given a license. **-r** n. one legally entitled to grant a license. **licentiate** n. one who has a license to practice a profession. **licentious** a. using excessive license; absence of moral or legal restraints. **licentiously** adv. **licentiousness** n. [L. *licentia*, freedom].

li·chen (lī'.kạn) *n.* one of an order of cellular flowerless plants; (*Med.*) a skin eruption [L. fr. Gk. *leichēn*, moss].

lic·it (lis'.it) *a.* lawful; allowable. **-ly** adv. [L. *licitus*, lawful].

lick (lik) *v.t.* to pass or draw the tongue over; to lap; to take in by the tongue; to touch lightly (as flames); (*Colloq.*) to thrash; to be superior over; *n.* a lap with the tongue; a small portion; (*Colloq.*) a brief attempt; *pl.* a beating. **-er** n. **-ing** n. a lapping with tongue; a flogging; a beating (in a competition) [O.E. *liccian*].

lic·o·rice, liquorice (lik'.ạ.ris) *n.* a Mediterranean plant, the root of which contains a sweet juice; the brittle, black substance extracted from the roots of this plant, and used medicinally and in candy [Gk. *glukus*, sweet; *rhiza*, a root].

lic·tor (lik'.tẹr) *n.* an officer who attended a Roman magistrate, bearing the fasces [L. fr. *ligare*, to bind].

lid (lid) *n.* a cover of a vessel or box; the covering of the eye [O.E. *hlid*, a cover].

lie (lī) *v.i.* to utter untruth; to misrepresent; to deceive; to make false statement. *pr.p.* **lying**. *pa.t.* and *pa.p.* **-d**. *n.* a deliberate falsehood. **liar** n. one who utters a falsehood. **lying** a. addicted to telling lies [O.E. *leogan*, to lie].

lie (lī) *v.i.* to be recumbent; to be in a horizontal position or nearly so; to be situated; to lean; to be at rest; to press upon; (*Law*) to be admissible. *pr.p.* **lying**. *pa.t.* **lay**. *pa.p.* **lain**. *n.* manner of lying [O.E. *licgan*, to lie].

lie·der (lē'.dẹr) *n.pl.* German lyrics set to music; *sing.* **lied** [Ger. *Lied*, a song].

lief (lēf) *adv.* gladly; willingly [O.E. *leof*, loved].

liege (lēj) *a.* bound by feudal tenure; (of a lord) entitled to receive homage; *n.* a vassal; a feudal lord to whom allegiance is owed [O.Fr. *liege*, an overlord].

li·en (lēn, lī'.ạn) *n.* (*Law*) a legal claim upon real or personal property for the satisfaction of some debt or duty [Fr. fr. L. *ligare*, to bind].

lieu (lōō) *n.* place; stead, as in phrase 'in lieu of' [Fr.].

lieu·ten·ant (lōō.ten'.ạnt) *n.* a deputy; an officer who takes the place of a superior in his absence; rank below a captain (*Army*) or below a lieutenant commander (*Navy*). **— colonel** n. the rank below a colonel. **— commander** n. (*Navy*) the rank intermediate between that of lieutenant and commander corresponding to that of major (*Army*). **— general** n. military rank intermediate between that of major general and general. **— governor** n. state official ranking below a governor [Fr. *lieu*, place; *tenant*, holding].

life (līf) *n.* existence; vitality; condition of plants, animals, etc. in which they exercise functional powers; the span between birth and death; mode of living; narrative of a person's history; animation; *pl.* **lives**. **— and death** a. desperate. **— assurance** or **insurance** n. insurance of a person's life. **— belt** n. a belt either inflated, or made buoyant with cork, for keeping person afloat in case of shipwreck. **-boat** n. a special type of boat, designed for stability in stormy seas, for saving of human lives. **— expectancy** n. probable life span. **-guard** n. someone employed at a swimming pool, etc. to prevent accidents. **— history** n. the cycle of life of a person, organism, etc. **— interest** n. interest in an estate or business which continues during one's life, but which cannot be bequeathed by will. **—jacket** n. a life belt. **-less** a. inanimate; dead; inert. **-lessly** adv. **-lessness** n. **-like** a. like a living creature; resembling closely. **-line** n. a line attached to a lifebuoy or lifeboat; a line fired by rocket from the shore to a ship in distress; the line which lowers and raises a deep-sea diver; (*Fig.*) that which keeps a nation alive. **-long** a. lasting a lifetime. **— preserver** n. any apparatus (as life belt, -buoy, -line) for preserving or rescuing life. **-r** n. (*Colloq.*) a criminal who has received a life sentence. **-sav-er** n. someone who rescues a person, esp. from drowning; (*Slang*) a person or thing which spares one embarrassment, difficulty, etc. **-size** *a.* resembling in proportions the living model. **-time** *n.* the duration of person's life. **-work** *n.* any task, usually creative, demanding a lifetime's work [O.E. *lif*, life].

life belt

lift (lift) *v.t.* to raise; to take up and remove; to elevate socially; to exalt spiritually; (*Colloq.*) to steal; to take passengers on a bus, etc.; *v.i.* to rise; to be dispersed; *n.* the act of lifting; assistance; the helping of a person on his way by offering conveyance in one's car; (chiefly Brit.) an elevator; a rise in the ground; (*Aero.*) an air force acting at right angles on aircraft's wing, thereby lifting it [Scand. *lypta*, to raise].

lig·a·ment (lig′·a·mant) *n.* anything which binds one thing to another; (*Anat.*) strong fibrous tissue bands connecting the bones of the body; a bond. **-al, -ary, -ous** *a.* **ligate** (li·gāt) *v.t.* to bind; to bandage. **ligation** *n.* the act of binding; the state of being bound with a ligature. **ligature** *n.* anything which binds; a bandage; (*Mus.*) a line connecting two notes; (*Print.*) type consisting of two or more letters joined [L. *ligare*, to bind].

light (līt) *v.i.* to come to by chance; to alight; to settle. *pr.p.* **-ing.** *pa.p.* **-ed** or **lit** [O.E. *lihtan*, to dismount].

light (līt) *a.* having little weight; not heavy; easy; active; nimble; loose or sandy, as soil; moderate, as wind; spongy, as cake; not heavily armed, as a cruiser; unsettled; volatile; trivial; wanton; easily disturbed, as sleep. **-en** *v.t.* to make less heavy; to jettison; to enliven; *v.i.* to become less heavy or gloomy. **light, -ly** *adv.* **-er** *n.* a barge used in loading and unloading ships anchored out from the dock. **-erage** *n.* the price paid for loading and unloading ships. **-erman** *n.* **-fingered** *a.* dexterous, esp. in picking pockets. **-footed** *a.* agile. **-handed** *a.* delicate of touch; empty-handed. **-headed** *a.* delirious; frivolous. **-hearted** *a.* carefree; gay. **-minded** *a.* frivolous. **-s** *n.pl.* the lungs of a slaughtered animal. **-some** *a.* lively; cheerful. **-weight** *a.* (of a boxer) weighing less than 135 lbs.; *n.* (*Colloq.*) a person of little importance; **-ness** *n.* quality of being light [O.E. *leoht*, light].

light (līt) *n.* that form of radiant energy which stimulates visual perception; anything which has luminosity; day; illumination; a source of illumination; the illuminated part of a scene or picture; point of view; aspect; spiritual or mental enlightenment; any opening admitting light into a building; *a.* bright; not dark; whitish; pale (of color); *v.t.* to give light or fire to; *v.i.* to begin to burn; to become bright; to express joy (as in the face). *pr.p.* **-ing.** *pa.t.* and *pa.p.* **-ed** or **lit** *v.t.* to illuminate. **-er** *n.* a mechanical device for producing a flame, as a cigarette-lighter; one who lights street lamps, etc. **-house** *n.* a tower-like structure built at danger points on seacoast and provided with very powerful light to serve as warning to ships. **-ing** *n.* illumination; the arrangement of lights in a building; the effect of light, esp. in a picture. **-ish** *a.* rather light or pale in color. **-ness** *n.* **-ship** *n.* a floating lighthouse. **-year** *n.* (*Astron.*) the distance in a year (calculated at 5,878,000,000,000 miles) light travels. **to see the light,** to be born; to comprehend. **footlights** *n.pl.* the row of electric lights along the edge of the stage in a theater. **Northern Lights,** aurora borealis. **lit** (*Slang*) drunk [O.E. *leoht*, light].

lighthouse

light·ning (līt′·ning) *n.* a flash produced by an electrical discharge between two clouds, or

between cloud and ground. **— bug** *n.* a firefly. **— rod** *n.* a rod serving, by a connected wire called a **lightning-conductor,** to carry electric current into the earth or water, thereby preventing building from being struck by lightning [M.E. *lihtnen*, to flash].

lightning

lig·ne·ous (lig′·ni·as) *a.* woody; resembling wood. **lignify** *v.t.* to convert into wood. **lignin** *n.* an organic substance formed in the woody tissues of plants. **lignite** *n.* coal of recent origin still showing ligneous texture; brown coal [L. *lignum*, wood].

lig·ure (lig′·yoor) *n.* a precious stone [fr. *Liguria*, a district of Italy].

like (līk) *a.* equal; similar; *n.* an equal; a person or thing resembling another; an exact resemblance; *prep.* similarly to; *conj.* (*Colloq.*) as; as if. **-lihood** *n.* probability. **-ly** *a.* probable; credible; of excellent qualities; *adv.* probably. **liken** *v.t.* to represent as similar; to compare. **-ness** *n.* resemblance; an image, picture, or statue. **-wise** *adv.* in like manner; also; moreover [O.E. *gelic*, similar].

like (līk) *v.t.* to be pleased with or attracted by; to enjoy; to approve; *v.i.* to be pleased; *n.* a liking, as in phrase, '*likes and dislikes.*' **lik(e)able** *a.* pleasing; congenial; attractive. **lik(e)ableness** *n.* **-ly** *a.* pleasing. **liking** *n.* [O.E. *lician*, to please].

li·lac (lī′·lak) *n.* a shrub, with delicately perfumed flower clusters, purple, pale mauve, or white in color; *a.* pale mauve color; *a.* of lilac color [Pers. *lilak*, the indigo flower].

li·li·pu·tian (lil·i·pū′·shan) *n.* an inhabitant of *Lilliput* described by Jonathan Swift in his *Gulliver's Travels*; a person of diminutive size; *a.* diminutive; dwarfed.   [*v.i.* to sing.

lilt (lilt) *n.* a light or rhythmic tune; *v.t.* and

li·ly (lil′·i·) *n.* a bulbous plant, with fragrant and showy bell-shaped flowers; *a.* resembling a lily; pure; pale; delicate. **liliaceous** *a.* pert. to lilies. **-livered** *a.* cowardly. **-white** *a.* pure white; unsullied [L. *lilie*, a lily].

limb (lim) *n.* an extremity of the human body, as an arm or leg; a branch of a tree [O.E.].

limb (lim) *n.* an edge or border; (*Astron.*) the rim of a heavenly body; (*Bot.*) the expanded part of a petal [L. *limbus*, a hem].

lim·ber (lim′·ber) *n.* the detachable front part of a gun-carriage; *v.t.* to attach to a gun-carriage [Fr. *limonière*, a cart with shafts].

lim·ber (lim′·ber) *a.* easily bent; pliant; supple.

lim·bo (lim′·bō) *n.* a region intermediate between heaven and hell in which the souls of unbaptized children etc., are confined after death; a region of forgotten things; neglect; oblivion; jail [L. *limbus*, the edge].

lime (līm) *n.* the linden tree; *a.* pert. to the linden tree [corrupt. of O.E. *lind*, the linden tree].

lime (līm) *n.* a tree which produces a small sour kind of lemon; the fruit of this tree [Fr. fr. Span. *lima*].

lime (līm) *n.* birdlime; oxide of calcium; white, caustic substance obtained from limestone, shells, marble, etc.; a calcium compound to enrich soil; *v.t.* to smear with lime; to ensnare; to cement; to manure with lime. **-kiln** *n.* a furnace in which limestone is heated to produce lime. **-light** *n.* a powerful light, as on a stage; the public view. **-stone** *n.* a rock consisting chiefly of carbonate of lime. **limy** *a.* covered with or impregnated with lime; sticky; resembling lime [O.E. *lim*, cement].

li·men (lī′·man) *n.* the threshold of consciousness. **liminal** *a.* [L. *limen*, threshold].

lim·er·ick (lim′·er·ik) *n.* a five-lined nonsense verse [said to be from a song introducing the place name *Limerick*].   [esp. a sailor.

lim·ey (li·mi·) *n.* (*Slang*) a British person,

lim·it (lim′·it) *n.* boundary; edge; utmost extent; (*Slang*) an outrageous or intolerable person or thing; *v.t.* to confine within certain bounds; to curb; to restrict the signification of. **-able** *a.* that may be bounded or restricted. **-ary** *a.* of, pert. to, or serving as a limit; restricted. **limitation** *n.* **-ative**, **-ed** *a.* circumscribed; narrow. **-edly** *adv.* **-edness** *n.* **-less** *a.* boundless; immeasurable; infinite. **limited liability**, said of a joint stock company in which liability of the shareholder is in proportion to the amount of his stock [L. *limes*, a boundary].

limn (lim) *v.t.* to draw or paint; to illuminate a manuscript. **limner** *n.* painter; one who

decorates books with pictures [M.E. *limnen*, to decorate].

lim·ou·sine (lim′·a·zēn) *a.* pert. to a type of closed automobile with roof over the driver's head; *n.* a closed car [fr. *Limousin*, a French province].   [O.E. *lemp-healt*, lame].

limp (limp) *v.i.* to walk lamely; *n.* lameness

limp (limp) *a.* wanting in stiffness, as covers of a book; flaccid; flexible; (*Fig.*) lethargic; exhausted [Scand. *limpa*, weakness].

lim·pet (lim′·pat) *n.* a small, univalve conical shaped shellfish which clings firmly to rocks. **—mine** *n.* (*World War 2*) a small suction mine attached by hand to the hull of a ship [O.E. *lempedu*, a lamprey].

lim·pid (lim′·pad) *a.* clear; translucent; crystal. **-ness, -ity** *n.* **-ly** *adv.* [L. *limpidus*, clear].

linch·pin (linch′·pin) *n.* a pin used to prevent a wheel from sliding off the axle tree [O.E. *lynis*, axletree; and *pin*].

lin·den (lin′·dan) *n.* a tree with yellowish flowers and heart-shaped leaves [O.E. *lind*, the lime-tree].

line (līn) *n.* a rope, wire or string; a slender cord; a thread-like mark; an extended stroke; (*Math.*) that which has one dimension, length, but no breadth or thickness; a curve connecting points which have a common significance (as the Equator, isotherms, isobars, contours, etc.); a boundary; a row or continued series; progeny; a verse; a short letter or note; a course of conduct, thought, or policy; a trend; a department; a trade, business or profession; a system of buses, trains, or passenger aircraft under one management; a railway track; a formation of naval vessels; the regular infantry of an army; harmony; graceful cut (as of a costume, dress); a path; a thin crease; parts of a play memorized by an actor or actress; military fieldworks; *v.t.* to mark out with lines; to form in a line; to border. **linage** *n.* number of lines on a page; payment according to the number of lines. **lineage** *n.* descendants in a line from common progenitor; pedigree. **lineal** *a.* composed of lines; pert. to, or in the direction of, a line; directly descended from a common ancestor. **lineality** *n.* **lineally** *adv.* **lineament** *n.* feature; form; characteristic; outline of a body or figure. **linear** *a.* pert. to, or consisting of, a line; drawn in lines. **linearly** *adv.* **lineate(d)** *a.* marked by lines. **lineation** *n.* the act of marking with lines; the lines marked or engraved. **-d** *a.* marked with lines; ruled. **— engraving** *n.* a process of engraving lines on a copper plate. **-r** *n.* a steamship or passenger aircraft belonging to a regular transport line. **linesman** *n.* one who installs and repairs telephone and electric lines, etc.; an official (at football or tennis match) who determines whether ball has crossed the outside line or not. **—up** *n.* a marshaling of forces, or resources. **the line,** the Equator [L. *linea*, a string of flax].

line (līn) *v.t.* to cover on the inside, as a garment, pan, etc. **lining** *n.* the material used; contents [M.E. *linen*, to cover].

lin·en (lin′·an) *n.* thread or cloth made from flax; underclothing; napery; *a.* made of flax or linen [O.E. *lin*, flax].

lin·ger (ling′·ger) *v.i.* to delay; to dally; to loiter. **-er** *n.* **-ing** *a.* protracted [O.E. *lengan*, to protract].

lin·ge·rie (lan′·ja·rā, lan′·zha·rē) *n.* orig. linen goods; women's underclothing [Fr. *linge*, linen].

lin·go (ling′·gō) *n.* language; a dialect; jargon corrupt. of L. *lingua*, language].

lin·gual (ling′·gwal) *a.* pert. to the tongue; *n.* a sound or letter made by the tongue, as *d*, *l*, *n.* **-ly** *adv.* **linguiform** *a.* shaped like a tongue. **linguist** *n.* fluent speaker of several languages; an expert in linguistics. **linguistic** *a.* **linguistically** *adv.* **linguistics** *n.* study of human speech including its sounds, history, nature, structure, etc.; comparative philology. **lingulate, lingular** *a.* (*Bot.*) shaped like a tongue [L. *lingua*, a tongue].

lin·i·ment (lin′·a·mant) *n.* a lotion or soft ointment [L. *linere*, to besmear].

link (lingk) *n.* a single ring of a chain; anything doubled and closed like a link; a connection; the $\frac{1}{100}$ part of a chain (7.92 inches). *v.t.* to connect by a link; (*Fig.*) to combine for a common purpose; *v.i.* to be coupled. **-age** *n.* a system of connections. **missing link,** a connection without which a chain of argument is incomplete; (*Zool.*) that form of animal life the scientific knowledge of which is required to complete the chain of evolution of man from the ape [O.E. *hlence*, a ring].   [ridge].

links (lingks) *n.pl.* a golf course [O.E. *hlinc*, a

lin·net (lin′·at) *n.* a small song bird of the finch family [O.Fr. *linette*, fr. L. *linum*, flax].

li·no·le·um (li·nō′·li·am) *n.* a hard floor covering of burlap impregnated with a cement of linseed oil, cork, etc. [L. *linum*, flax; *oleum*, oil].

lin·o·type (lin′·a·tip) *n.* a type-setting machine in which the matter is cast in solid lines of type [L. *linea*, line, and *type*].

lin·seed (lin′·sēd) *n.* flaxseed. **— cake,** compressed mass of husks of linseed, after oil has been pressed out, much used for cattle feeding. **— oil,** the oil pressed out of linseed [O.E. *linsaed*, flaxseed].

lin·sey-wool·sey (lin′·zi--wool′·zi·) *a.* made of wool and linen mixed; (*Fig.*) shoddy; *n.* inferior stuff [O.Fr. *linsel*, and *wool*].

linnet

lint (lint) n. a linen material, one side with a soft, wooly surface formerly used for dressing wounds; scraps of thread; fluff from cloth [L. *linteum*, a linen cloth].
lin·tel (lin'·tǝl) n. a horizontal beam or stone over a doorway or window [L.L. *lintellus*].

li·on (lī'·ǝn) n. (fem. **-ess**) the largest of the cat tribe, tawny-colored, with powerful, tufted tail, the male having a shaggy mane; (Fig.) a person of fierce courage; a celebrity; (Astron.) a sign of the Zodiac (Leo). **—hearted** a. courageous. **-ize** v.t. to treat as a celebrity [L. *leo*, a lion].

lip (lip) n. one of the two fleshy, outer edges of the mouth; a liplike part; the edge of anything; brim; (Slang) impertinent talk; pl. the organs of speech as represented by the lips; v.t. to touch with the lips; to speak; a. pert. to or made by the lips. **-ped** a. having a lip or lips. **— reading** n. the art of 'hearing' by reading the motions of a speaker's lips; this system as taught to the deaf. **— service** n. superficial devotion to a person or cause. **-stick**, a salve, in the form of a small stick, used by women to redden the lips [O.E. *lippa*].
li·quate (lī'·kwāt) v.t. to melt; to separate or purify solids or gases by liquefying. **liquation** n. [L. *liquare*, to be fluid].
liq·ue·fy (lik'·wǝ·fī) v.t. to transform a liquid; to melt; v.i. to become liquid. **liquefaction** n. the act of liquefying; the state of being liquefied. **liquefiable** a. [L. *liquefacere*, to melt].
li·queur (li·kur') n. a preparation of distilled liquors flavored with fruits or aromatic substances [Fr.].
liq·uid (lik'·wid) a. fluid; in a state intermediate between a solid and a gas; flowing smoothly; (of sounds) pleasing to the ear; n. a substance intermediate between a solid and a gas which assumes the shape of the vessel which contains it; the name popularly applied to a consonant which has a smooth flowing sound (l, r). **-ate** v.t. to settle a debt; to wind up the affairs of business, etc.; to convert into cash; to destroy; v.i. (of business) to be wound up. **-ation** n. **-ator** n. **-ity** n. [L. *liquidus*, fluid].
liq·uor (lik'·ǝr) n. any liquid or fluid, esp. alcoholic [Fr. fr. L. *liquere*, to be fluid].
li·ra (lī'·ra, lē'·ra) n. the monetary unit and a silver coin of Italy; a monetary unit and gold coin of Turkey [It.].
lisle (līl) n. a fine hard-twisted cotton or linen thread [formerly made at *Lille*, France].
lisp (lisp) v.i. to speak imperfectly, esp. to substitute the sound *th* for *s*; v.t. to pronounce with a lisp; n. the habit of lisping. **-ing** n. [O.E. *wlisp*, stammering].
lis·some (lis'·ǝm) a. supple; flexible; lithe. **-ness** n. [fr. *lithesome*].
list (list) n. the outer edge or selvage of woven cloth; a row or stripe; a roll; a catalogue; a register; a boundary line enclosing a field of combat at a tournament, esp. in pl. **lists**; the field thus enclosed; v.t. to sew together strips of cloth; to enter in a catalogue or inventory; v.i. to enlist [O.E. *liste*, a border].

list (list) v.i. (Naut.) to lean or incline (of a ship); v.t. to cause to lean; n. an inclination to one side [O.E. *lystan*, to desire].
lis·ten (lis'·n) v.i. to attend closely; to yield to advice. **list** v.t. and v.i. to listen (Poet). **-er** n. **to listen in**, to listen without taking part; to eavesdrop [O.E. *hlyst*, hearing].
list·less (list'·lǝs) a. indifferent; languid; apathetic. **-ly** adv. **-ness** n. [O.E. *lust*, pleasure].
lit (lit) pa.t. and pa.p. of verb **light**.
lit·a·ny (lit'·a·ni·) n. an earnest prayer of supplication [Gk. *litaneia*, supplication].
li·ter (lē'·tǝr) n. a unit of volume in the metric system, equal to 1.0567 quarts. Also **litre** [Gr. *litra*, pound].
lit·er·al (lit'·a·rǝl) a. according to the letter; real; not figurative; word for word, as a translation. **-ism** n. keeping to the literal sense; exact representation in art or literature. **-ist** n. **-istic** a. **-ize** v.t. **-ly** adv. [L. *litera*, a letter].
lit·er·ar·y (lit'·ǝr·er·i·) a. pert. to letters or literature; versed in literature. **literacy** n. state of being literate, opp. of *illiteracy*. **literate** a. versed in learning and science; educated; n. one who is able to read and write. **literati** n.pl. men of letters; educated people. [L. *litera*, a letter].
lit·er·a·ture (lit'·a·ra·choor, ·chǝr) n. the body of writings of a language, period, subject, etc.; (Colloq.) any printed matter, as advertisements, brochures [L. *litteratura*, learning].
lithe (lith) a. capable of being easily bent; supple; pliant. **-ly** adv. **-ness** n. **-some** a. [O.E. *lithe*, gentle].
li·thog·e·nous (li·thaj'·a·nǝs) a. rock-producing, as certain corals [Gk. *lithos*, a stone; *genesthai*, to be born].
lith·o·glyph (lith'·ō·glif) n. an engraving on a precious stone [Gk. *lithos*; *gluphein*, to carve].
lith·o·graph (lith'·a·graf) v.t. to trace on stone, zinc, or aluminum, and transfer to paper by special printing process; n. a print from stone, etc. **lithographer** (li·thag'·ra·fǝr) n. **lithographic, -al** a. **lithographically** adv. **lithography** n. the art of tracing designs on stone or other media, and taking impressions of these designs [Gk. *lithos*, a stone; *graphein*, to write].
lith·oid, -al (lith'·oid, ·al) a. resembling a stone [Gk. *lithos*, a stone].
li·thol·o·gy (li·thál'·a·ji·) n. the science which treats of the characteristics of rocks; (Med.) the study of calculi in the body [Gk. *lithos*, a stone; *logos*, a discourse].
lith·o·tint (lith'·a·tint) n. the lithographic production of a tinted picture; the picture itself [Gk. *lithos*, a stone; and *tint*].
lith·o·tome (lith'·a·tōm) n. a stone resembling an artificially cut gem; (Surg.) an instrument for performing a lithotomy. **lithotomic** a. **lithotomist** n. **lithotomy** (li·thát'·a·mi·) n. (Surg.) the operation by which stones are removed from the bladder [Gk. *lithos*, a stone; *tomē*, a cutting].
lith·o·type (lith'·a·tīp) n. a stereotype plate; print from this plate. **lithotypy** n. [Gk. *lithos*, a stone; *tupos*, type].
Lith·u·a·ni·an (lith·oo·ā'·ni·ǝn) n. a native of Lithuania; the language. Also **Lett**.
lit·i·gate (lit'·a·gāt) v.t. to contest in law; v.i. to carry on a lawsuit. **litigable** a. **litigant** n. a person engaged in a lawsuit; a. engaged in a lawsuit. **litigation** n. judicial proceedings. **litigator** n. one who litigates. **litigiosity** (la·tij·i·ás'·a·ti·) n. **litigious** a. given to engaging in lawsuits [L. *litigare*, to dispute].
lit·mus (lit'·mǝs) n. a bluish purple vegetable dye (obtained from lichens) which turns red with an acid, and blue with an alkali. **— paper**, used to test solutions.
li·to·tes (lī'·ta·tēz) n. a figure of speech which expresses a strong affirmative, by using the negative of its contrary, as in phrase, *not a few* [Gk. *litos*, simple].
lit·ter (lit'·er) n. a heap of straw as bedding for animals; a vehicle containing bed carried on men's shoulders; a stretcher; odds and ends left lying about; state of disorder; a family of young pigs, puppies, etc., brought forth at one birth; v.t. to bring forth young; to scatter indiscriminately about; to make untidy with odds and ends [Fr. *litière*, a bed].
lit·tle (lit'·l) a. small in size, extent, or quantity; brief; slight; mean; n. a small quantity or space; adv. in a small quantity or degree (comp. **less**; superl. **least**). **-ness** n. [O.E. *lytel*].
lit·to·ral (lit'·ǝr·ǝl) a. pert. to a lake or seashore [L. *litoralis*, pert. to the seashore].
lit·ur·gy (lit'·ǝr·ji·) n. the established ritual for public worship in a church, esp. the Mass. **liturge** n. a leader in public worship. **liturgic, -al** a. **liturgically** adv. **liturgics** n. the study of church worship and its ritual. **liturgist** n. [Gk. *leitourgia*, a public service].
live (liv) v.i. to have life; to subsist; to be conscious; to dwell; to enjoy life; to keep oneself (as on one's income); v.t. to spend; to pass. **livable** a. habitable [O.E. *lifian*, to live].
live (līv) a. having life; quick; active; vital; unexploded, as a mine; burning, as coal; full of zest; dynamite. **lived** (līvd) a. used in compounds as *long-lived*, *short-lived*. **—circuit** a. a circuit through which an electric current is passing. **liven** (līv'·n) v.t. to enliven. **-stock** n. the general term for horses, cattle, pigs, etc., on a farm. **— wire** n. a wire carrying an electric

current; an energetic person [O.E. *lif*, life].
live·li·hood (līv'·li·hood) n. a means of living; sustenance [O.E. *lif*, life; *lad*, a way].
live·long (liv'·lawng) a. the entire [O.E. *leof*, dear].
live·ly (līv'·li·) a. animated; active; gay; exciting; light; adv. briskly. **livelily** adv. **liveliness** n. [O.E. *liflic*, life-like].
liv·er (liv'·er) n. (Anat.) glandular organ in body secreting bile; the flesh of this organ in animals or fowls used as food. **-ish** a. off-color because of a disordered liver. **-wort** n. a moss-like plant with liver-shaped leaves. **-wurst** n. a sausage with a large amount of liver. **lily-livered** a. cowardly [O.E. *lifer*, liver].
liv·er·y (liv'·ǝr·i·) n. orig. the special dress or food *delivered* by a lord to his household retinue; a dress peculiar to a certain group, as members of a medieval guild or trade; any characteristic uniform of an employee, as of a chauffeur; a livery stable; the body of liverymen. **liveried** a. clothed in a livery. **-man** n. one who works in a livery stable. **— stable** n. a stable where horses and vehicles are kept for hire [O.Fr. *livrée*, an allowance].
liv·id (liv'·id) a. black and blue; discolored, as flesh, by bruising. **-ness**, **lividity** n. [L. *lividus*, bluish].
liv·ing (liv'·ing) a. having life; active; flowing (of water); resembling closely; contemporary; n. livelihood; maintenance; mode of life. **— language**, a language still in use. **— room** n. a sitting-room [O.E. *lif*, life].
liz·ard (liz'·ǝrd) n. an order of four-footed scale-clad reptiles [L. *lacerta*].

lla·ma (lä'·ma) n. a S. America two-toed ruminant, used as a beast of burden [Peruv.].
lo (lō) interj. look! behold! [O.E. *lā*, (imit.)].
loach (lōch) a small river fish [Fr. *loche*].
load (lōd) n. a burden; the amount normally carried at one time; any heavy weight; a cargo; (Elect.) amount of electrical energy drawn from a source; (Fig.) burden of anxiety; pl. (Colloq.) plenty; heaps; v.t. to burden; to put on, for conveyance; to freight; to overweight; to overwhelm (with gifts, adulation, etc); to charge (a gun); to weight (as dice); to insert a spool into (as a camera); v.i. to take on a load or cargo; to charge a firearm; to become loaded. **-ed** a. weighted; (Slang) drunk. **-ing** n. the act of loading; freight. **— line** n. a line painted on the side of a vessel to indicate maximum immersion when loaded. **-stone** n. a metal which attracts other metals [O.E. *lad*].
loaf (lōf) n. shaped portion of dough baked in the oven; a lump of sugar. pl. **loaves**. **meat·loaf** n. meat cooked in a loaf tin or shaped in a mass [O.E. *hlaf*, a loaf].
loaf (lōf) v.i. to spend (time) idly; to lounge. **-er** n. one who loafs; a moccasin style of shoe.
loam (lōm) n. a rich, fertile soil of clay, sand, oxide of iron, and carbonate of lime; a mixture of clay, sand, and chopped straw used in making molds for founding [O.E. *lam*, clay].
loan (lōn) n. the act of lending; that which is lent, esp. money for interest; v.t. to lend; to lend at interest. **-ee**, **-er** n. **— office** n. a pawnbroker's shop [O.N. *lan*, loan].
loath, loth (lōth) a. unwilling; reluctant; disinclined [O.E. *lath*, hateful].
loathe (lōTH) v.t. to detest; to abominate; to be nauseated by. **loathing** n. disgust; repulsion. **loathly** a. **loathsome** a. detestable; repugnant. **loathsomely** adv. **loathsomeness** n. [O.E. *lath*, hateful].
lob (láb) n. (Tennis) a ball rising high in air over opponent's head; v.t. to bowl underhand; to hit (tennis ball, shuttle-cock) high into air; v.i. to deliver a lob. pr.p. **-bing**. pa.p. **-bed**. [Scand. *lobbe*, a lump of fat].
lob·by (láb'·i·) n. a passage, or hall, forming the entrance to a public building or private dwelling; a waiting-room; a pressure group seeking to influence members of a legislature; v.i. to solicit votes of members of a legislature; v.t. to secure the passage of a bill, to influence a legislator by lobbying. **-ing** n. **-ism** n. **-ist** n. [L.L. *lobia*, a portico].
lobe (lōb) n. a rounded division of an organ; the lower, fleshy, rounded part of human ear; a division of the lung; (Bot.) rounded division of a leaf. **lobar** a. **lobate, lobed, lobose** a. having a lobe or lobes [Gk. *lobos*].
lo·bel·ia (lō·bē'·li·a) n. a genus of herbaceous plants (including the blue dwarf variety) [fr. *Lobel*, botanist to James I].
lob·lol·ly (láb'·lál·i·) n. a pine tree of the southern U.S.
lob·ster (láb'·stǝr) n. an edible, marine, long-tailed crustacean, with pincer-claws. **— pot**, a trap in which lobsters are caught [corrupt. of L. *locusta*, a lobster].
lo·cal (lō'·kǝl) a. pert. to a particular place; confined to a definite spot, district, or part; circumscribed; n. some person or thing belonging to a district; a suburban train. **locale** n.

the scene of an occurrence; the scene of a film-shot. **localization** *n.* the act of localizing. **localize** *v.t.* to assign to a definite place; to decentralize. **locality** *n.* position of a thing; site; neighborhood. **-ly** *adv.* **locate** *v.t.* to set in a particular place; to find the exact position of. **location** *n.* act of locating; situation; geographical position; the out-of-doors site of a film production. **locative** (lăk'·a·tiv) *n.* (*Gram.*) the case form denoting the 'place where.' [L. *locus*, a place].

loch (lắk) *n.* a lake, esp. in Scotland; an arm of the sea (as Loch Fyne) [Gael.].

lock (lăk) *n.* a strand or tress of hair; *pl.* hair of the head [O.E. *locc*, a tress].

lock (lăk) *n.* a device for fastening a door, box, case, etc.; a mechanism on a gun to keep it from firing; an appliance to check the revolution of a wheel; an accidental stoppage of any mechanism; an enclosure in a canal with gate at each end for allowing vessels to pass from one level to another; the grappling hold, in wrestling; *v.t.* to fasten with a lock and key; to furnish with locks, as a canal; to hold tightly; *v.i.* to become fastened; to jam. **-er** *n.* a drawer, small chest, etc. where valuables may be locked. **-et** *n.* a small case containing portrait, lock of hair, worn on a chain. **-jaw** *n.* a contraction of the muscles of the jaw; tetanus. **-nut** *n.* a second nut screwed on top of the first nut to prevent loosening. **-out** *n.* a refusal by an employer to admit employees until a dispute has been amicably settled. **-smith** *n.* one who makes and repairs locks. **-up** *n.* a prison [O.E. *loc*, a fastening].

locket

lo·co·mo·tion (lō·ka·mō'·shan) *n.* the act or process of moving from place to place. **loco-motive** *a.* capable of moving from one place to another; *n.* an engine which moves by its own power, as a railway engine. **locomotivity** *n.* **locomotor** *n.* person or thing with power to move; *a.* pert. to locomotion [L. *locus*, a place; *movere, motum,* to move].

lo·cus (lō'·kas) *n.* the exact position of anything; (*Math.*) the path traced out by a point moving in accordance with some mathematical law; *pl.* **loci** (lō'·sī) [L. *locus,* a place].

lo·cust (lō'·kast) *n.* a winged insect, allied to the grasshopper and found in N. Africa, Asia, and the U.S.; a thorny-branched N. American tree with very durable wood [L. *locusta*].

lo·cu·tion (lō·kū'·shan) *n.* speech; mode or style of speaking [L. *loqui,* to speak].

lode (lōd) *n.* a metallic vein; a body of ore. **-star, loadstar** *n.* a star by which one steers, esp. the Pole-star. **lodestone** see **loadstone** [O.E. *lad,* a course].

lodge (lăj) *n.* a small country-house; a cottage at the entrance to an estate; a branch of a society, as of Freemasons, or the building where such a society meets; *v.i.* to dwell in temporarily; to reside; to become embedded in; *v.t.* to deposit for preservation; to infix; to rent out rooms; to lay flat; to harbor; to put (as money) in a bank; to allege, as an accusation. **lodg(e)ment** *n.* lodgings; accumulation of something deposited; (*Mil.*) occupation of a position by a besieging party. **-r** *n.* one who occupies rooms for rent. **lodging(s)** *n.* room(s) let temporarily [O.Fr. *loge,* an apartment].

loft (lawft) *n.* an upper room; an attic in space between top story and roof; the gallery in a church, as the *organ-loft*; (*Golf*) to strike a ball high. **-ily** *adv.* **-iness** *n.* **-y** *a.* elevated; towering; haughty [Scand. *lopt,* air].

log (lawg, lăg) *n.* an unhewn piece of timber; an apparatus to measure the speed of a ship and distance covered; the tabulated record of a ship's voyage; a logbook; *a.* made of logs; *v.t.* to fell and trim trees; to clear woodland; to keep records of. *pr.p.* **-ging.** *pa.t., pa.p.* **-ged. -book** *n.* a daily record of events on a ship's voyage. **— cabin** *n.* a hut made of lopped tree trunks. **-ger** *n.* a lumberjack. **-ging** *n.* the process of cutting trees and getting the logs to a sawmill to be cut for lumber. **-rolling** *n.* act of clearing logs, esp. from a neighbor's land, hence mutual help esp. in politics [M.E. *logge*].

lo·gan·ber·ry (lō'·gan·ber·i·) *n.* a shrub, a

cross between raspberry and blackberry [hybridized by *Logan*, 1881].

log·a·rithm (lawg'·, lăg'·a·riTHm) *n.* the index of the power to which a fixed number or base must be raised to produce the number; a method of reducing arithmetical calculations to a minimum by substituting addition and subtraction for multiplication and division. [Gk. *logos*, ratio; *arithmos,* a number].

log·ger·head (lawg'·, lăg'·er·hed) *n.* a blockhead; a dunce; a kind of turtle. **at logger-heads,** quarrelling; at cross-purposes [fr. *log* and *head*].

log·gia (lăj'·i·a, law'·jä) *n.* a kind of open elevated gallery with pillars, common in Italian buildings [Cf. **lodge**].

log·ic (lăj'·ik) *n.* the science of reasoning; the science of pure and formal thought; (*Colloq.*) commonsense. **-al** *a.* pert. to formal thought; skilled in logic; reasonable. **logicality, -alness** *n.* **-ally** *adv.* **logician** *n.* one skilled in logic [Gk. *logos,* speech].

lo·gis·tic, -al (laj·is'·tik, -al) *a.* pert. to calculating. **-s** *n.pl.* (used as *sing.*); (*Mil.*) branch of military science which deals with the moving of and providing for troops [Gk. *logizesthai,* to compute].

log·o·gram (lawg'·, lăg'·a·gram) *n.* a symbol representing a whole word or phrase [Gk. *logos,* a word; *gramma,* a letter].

lo·go·gra·pher (lō·găg'·ra·fer) *n.* a speech-writer in ancient Greek times. **logography** *n.* a method of printing in which words cast in a single type are used instead of single letters [Gk. *logos,* a word; *graphein,* to write].

loin (loin) *n.* part of animal or man above hips and on either side of spinal column; a cut of meat from this part of an animal. **-cloth** *n.* [L. *lumbus,* loin].

loi·ter (loi'·ter) *v.i.* to linger; to be slow in moving; to spend time idly. **-er** *n.* **-ingly** *adv.* [Dut. *leuteren,* to delay].

loll (lăl) *v.i.* to lounge about lazily; to hang out, as the tongue; *v.t.* to permit to hang out [Scand. *lolla,* to be lazy].

lol·li·pop lollipop (lăl'·i·pàp) *n.* a piece of flavored toffee or hard candy on a stick [etym. doubtful].

lone (lōn) *a.* solitary; standing by itself. **-liness, -ness** *n.* **-ly** *a.* alone; unfrequented. **-some** *a.* solitary. **-somely** *adv.* **-someness** *n.* [abbrev. fr. *alone*].

long (lawng) *a.* extended in distance or time; drawn out in a line; protracted; slow in coming; continued at great length; *adv.* to a great extent; at a point of duration far distant; *v.i.* to be filled with a yearning to desire. **-ago** *adv.* in the remote past. **-boat** *n.* the largest boat carried by a sailing ship. **-bow** *n.* a bow drawn by hand, and usually 5½-6 feet long—so called to distinguish it from the *Cross-bow.* **-drawn** *a.* protracted. **longeron** (lăn'·jer·àn) *n.* (*Aero.*) a main longitudinal strength member of a fuselage. **longevity** (lawng·jev'·a·ti·) *n.* length of life; uncommonly prolonged duration of life. **longevous** *a.* long-lived. **-hand** *n.* ordinary handwriting (opp. *shorthand*). **-headed** *a.* far-seeing; prudent. **-horn** *n.* a kind of cattle of Mexico and U.S. **— house** *n.* a long communal dwelling of the Iroquois Indians. **— hundred** *n.* Br. hundredweight, 112 pounds. **-ing** *n.* a yearning; a craving. **-ingly** *adv.* **-ish** *a.* rather long. **longitude** (lăn'·ja·tūd) *n.* angular distance east or west of a given meridian, measured in degrees; (*Astron.*) angular distance from vernal equinox on the ecliptic. **longitudinal** *a.* pert. to length or longitude; lengthwise; *n.* a girder running lengthwise in a ship or airship. **longitudinally** *adv.* **— measure** *n.* linear measure. **-range** *a.* having the power to fire a great distance, as a gun; able to fly or sail great distances without refueling, as aircraft, submarine, etc. **-shore** *a.* existing or employed on the shore. **-shoreman** *n.* a dock laborer. **-sightedness** *n.* (*Med.*) hypermetropia, an abnormal eye condition whereby the rays of light are focused *beyond* and not on the retina. **-standing** *a.* having existed for some time. **-suffering** *a.* patiently enduring. **-winded** *a.* able to run a great distance without becoming short of breath; tedious; loquacious. **-wise, -ways** *a.* lengthwise. **before long,** soon [O.E. *lang,* long].

long house

loo (lōō) *n.* a card-game; *v.t.* to win in a game of loo [abbrev. fr. *lanterloo*].

look (look) *v.i.* to turn one's eyes upon; to seem to be; to consider; to seem; to face, as a dwelling; *v.i* to express by a look; *n.* the act of directing one's gaze upon; facial expression generally; aspect; view. **-er** *n.* one who looks.

-er-on *n.* a spectator. **-ing** *n.* a search. **-ing glass** *n.* a mirror. **-out** *n.* a watch; a place from which a careful watch is kept; person stationed to keep watch [O.E. *locian,* to look].

loom (lōōm) *n.* a machine for weaving cloth from thread by interlacing threads called the *woof* through threads called the *warp;* part of the shaft of an oar inside the rowlock [O.E. *geloma,* a tool].

loom (lōōm) *v.i.* to emerge indistinctly and larger than the real dimensions; to appear over the horizon; (*Fig.*) to assume great importance.

loom (lōōm) *n.* a kind of guillemot; a puffin; a loon [Scand. *lomr,* a sea bird].

loon (lōōn) *n.* a large fish-eating diving bird of the northern regions [same as **loom**].

loon·y (lōōn'·i·) *n.* (*Colloq.*) a crazy person; *a.* (*Slang*) very foolish [fr. *lunatic*].

loop (lōōp) *n.* a doubling of string or rope, through which another string may run; anything with a similar shape; (*Aero.*) an aerial maneuver in which plane describes a complete circle; *v.t.* to fasten by a loop; to form into a loop. **-ed** *a.* [prob. Ir. *lub,* a bend].

loop·hole (lōōp'·hōl) *n.* a narrow slit or opening as in the walls of a fortification; (*Fig.*) a way out of a difficult situation.

loose (lōōs) *v.t.* to free from constraint; to untie; to disconnect; to relax; to discharge; *v.i.* to set sail; to let go; *a.* free; slack; unsewed; unbound; flowing; diffuse; incoherent; careless; inaccurate; lax; inclined to diarrhea. **-jointed** *a.* loosely built. **-leaf** *a.* having sheets of paper which can be removed and rearranged. **-ly** *adv.* **loosen** *v.t.* to make loose; to unfasten; *v.i.* to become loose; to become relaxed. **loosener** *n.* **-ness** *n.* **-tongued** *a.* prating; indiscreet [O.E. *leas,* loose].

loot (lōōt) *n.* plunder; the act of plundering; *v.t.* and *v.i.* to plunder; to appropriate illegally [Sans. *lut,* booty].

lop (lăp) *v.t.* to cut off, esp. top of anything; to cut away superfluous parts. *pr.p.* **-ping.** *pa.t., pa.p.* **-ped.** *n.* twig from tree; act of lopping. **-per** *n.* **-ping** *n.* [Dut. *lubben,* to cut].

lop (lăp) *v.i.* to hang down loosely. *pr.p.* **-ping.** *pa.t., pa.p.* **-ped. —eared** *a.* having drooping ears. **-sided** *a.* heavier on one side than the other; askew [prob. imit.].

lope (lōp) *v.i.* to run with a long, leisurely gait; *n.* an easy gait [O.N. *hlaupa,* to leap].

lo·qua·cious (lō·kwā'·shas) *a.* talkative; babbling; garrulous. **-ly** *adv.* **-ness, loquacity** *n.* talkativeness [L. *loquax,* talkative].

lo·quat (lō'·kwàt) *n.* a low-growing Japanese plum tree; the fruit itself [Chinese].

lo·ran (lō'·ran) *n.* (*Flying*) a navigational device which locates the position of an airplane [From *long + range + navigation*].

lord (lawrd) *n.* a master; a ruler; a king; (*Brit.*) a proprietor of a manor; any peer of the realm; courtesy title; the holder of certain high government offices; (*Cap.*) the Supreme Being; Jehovah; God; Christ; *v.i.* to play the lord; to domineer. **-liness** *n.* **-ling** *n.* a petty or unimportant lord. **-ly** *a.* pert. to, or like, a lord; imperious; proud; magnificent. **-ship** *n.* the state of being a lord; authority; estate owned by a lord; (*Brit.*) (with *his, your*) a formal mode of address in speaking to a lord, bishop [O.E. *hlaford,* the keeper of the bread].

lore (lōr) *n.* learning; erudition; traditional knowledge [O.E. *lar,* lore].

lor·gnette (lawr·nyet') *n.* a pair of eyeglasses attached to a long handle; an opera glass [Fr. *lorgner,* to stare at].

lo·ri·ca (la·rī'·ka) *n.* a cuirass; (*Zool.*) a protective covering of bony plates, scales, etc., like a cuirass. **loricate** *v.t.* to clothe in mail; to cover with a coating; *a.* (*Zool.*) having protective covering of bony plates, as crocodiles [L. *lorica,* a breastplate].

lorn (lawrn) *a.* (*Arch.*) lost; forsaken; desolate [O.E. *loren, pa.p.* of *leosan,* to lose].

lor·ry (lawr'·i·) *n.* (esp. *Brit.*) a wagon for transporting heavy loads; a car on rails, used in factories, mines, etc.; (*Brit.*) a truck.

lose (looz) *v.t.* to be deprived of; to mislay; to forfeit; to fail to win; to miss; to waste, as time; to destroy; *v.i.* to fail; to suffer loss; to become bewildered. *pr.p.* **losing**. *pa.t.* and *pa.p.* **lost. losable** *a.* **-r** *n.* **losing** *a.* producing loss. **loss** *n.* the act of losing; that which is lost; defeat; diminution; bereavement; harm; waste by escape or leakage; number of casualties suffered in war. **lost** *a.* mislaid; bewildered; bereft [O.E. *leosan*, to lose].

lot (lắt) *n.* what happens by chance; destiny; object used to determine something by chance; the choice thus determined; a separate part; a large number of articles such as at an auction sale; (*Motion Pictures*) the area covered by film studio and its subsidiary buildings; (*Colloq.*) a great many; *v.t.* to allot; to separate into lots. **-tery** *n.* a scheme by which prizes are given to people, not on merit, but by drawing lots. **a job-lot**, a miscellaneous collection of articles, sold as one item [O.E. *hlot*, a share].

loth (lŏth) *a.* Same as **loath**.

Lo-thar-i-o (lŏ-thar'·i·ŏ) *n.* libertine, rake [fr. *Lothario*, in Rowe's *The Fair Penitent*].

lo-tion (lŏ'·shạn) *n.* a fluid with healing, antiseptic properties esp. for the skin [L. *lavare*, *lotum*, to wash].

lot-to (lăt'·ŏ) *n.* a game of chance [fr. *lot*].

lo-tus (lŏ'·tạs) *n.* the Egyptian water lily; a decorative representation, as in Egyptian and Hindu art; a genus of plants including the British bird's-foot trefoil; a N. African shrub, the fruit of which was reputed, in Greek legend, to induce in those who consumed it an overpowering lethargy. Also **lotos. -eater** *n.* (*Fig.*) one who gives up an active life for one of slothful ease [Gk. *lōtus*].

loud (loud) *a.* making a great sound; noisy; flashy; obtrusive; vulgar. **loud**, **-ly** *adv.* **-ness** *n.* **-speaker** *n.* a device which makes speech, music, etc. audible at a distance [O.E. *hlud*].

lou-is (lŏŏ'·i·) *n.* an obsolete French gold coin worth 20 francs. Also — **d'or.** — **quatorze**, — **quinze**, — **seize**, applied to architecture, furniture, style of interior decoration characteristic of the reigns of the French Kings Louis XIV, VX, XVI [Fr.].

lounge (lounj) *v.i.* to recline at ease; to loll; to spend time idly; *n.* the act of lounging; a room in which people may relax; a kind of sofa.

louse (lous) *n.* a small wingless parasitic insect infesting hair and skin of human beings; a sucking parasite found on mammals or plants. *pl.* **lice. lousily** (louz'·ạ·i·) *adv.* **lousiness** *n.* **lousy** *a.* infested with lice; (*Slang*) mean; despicable [O.E. *lus*, a louse].

lout (lout) *n.* a clumsy fellow; a bumpkin; *v.i.* to bend. **-ish** *a.* **-ishly** *adv.* [etym. uncertain].

lou-ver (lŏŏ'·vẹr) *n.* an opening in the roof of ancient buildings for the escape of smoke or for ventilation; a slot for ventilation [O.Fr. *louvert* for *l'ouvert*, the open space].

love (luv) *n.* affection; strong liking; goodwill; benevolence; charity; devoted attachment to one of the opposite sex; passion; the object of affection; the personification of love: Cupid; (*Tennis*) no score; *v.t.* to show affection for; to be delighted with; to admire passionately; *v.i.* to be in love; to delight. **lovable** *a.* worthy of affection; engaging. **lovableness** *n.* — **affair** *n.* a passionate attachment between two members of the opposite sex. — **apple** *n.* the tomato. — **bird** *n.* a small parrot with bright-colored plumage. **-charm** *n.* a philter. — **child** *n.* an illegitimate child. — **feast** *n.* a religious festival among the early Christians during which collections were made for the poor. — **in-a-mist** *n.* fennel. — **in-idleness** *n.* the pansy. — **knot** *n.* a bow of ribbon tied in a special way, as a token of love. **-less** *a.* lacking love; not founded on love. — **letter** *n.* a letter written to a sweetheart. **-lies-bleeding** *n.* a garden flower with reddish-purple spike flowers. **-liness** *n.* — **lock** *n.* a curl worn on the forehead or over the temple. **-lorn** *a.* forsaken. **-ly** *a.* very beautiful; **-making** *n.* courtship. — **match** *n.* a marriage founded on true love. — **philter** *or* — **potion** *n.* a drink supposed to induce the emotion of love towards a chosen person. **-r** *n.* one who loves, esp. one of the opposite sex; an admirer, as of the arts. **loverlike** *a.* **loverly** *adv.* — **seat** *n.* a seat for two. **-sick** *a.* pining because of love. **-song** *n.* lyric inspired by love. **-token** *n.* an object, as a ring, given as a symbol of love. **loving** *a.* affectionate; loyal. **loving-cup** *n.* large drinking-vessel with two handles, given as a prize or trophy. **lovingly** *adv.* **lovingness** *n.* [O.E. *lufu*, love].

low (lō) *a.* not high; lying near the ground; depressed below the adjacent surface; near the horizon; shallow; not loud, as a voice; moderate, as prices; dejected; lewd; weak; cold, as a temperature; humble; (of dress) décolleté; *adv.* not high; in a low voice; cheaply. **-born** *a.* of humble birth. **-boy** *n.* a chest about three feet high usu. with two tiers of drawers and on slender legs. **-brow** *n.* a non-intellectual. **Low Countries**, the Netherlands, Belgium, and Luxemburg. **-down** *a.* mean; underhand; *n.* (*Slang*) full information. **-er** *v.t.* to cause to descend; to take down; to humble; to diminish resistance; to make cheap; to reduce pitch; *a.* (*compar.* of *low*) less exalted. **-er case** *n.* abbrev. *l.c.*) small letters as opposed to capitals. **-land** *n.* country which is relatively flat in comparison with surrounding hilly district. **-lander** *n.* an inhabitant of flat land, esp. in Scotland. **-liness** *n.* **-ly** *a.* humble; meek; **-pressure**, having only a small expansive force (less than 50 lbs. to the square inch) said of steam and steam engines [O.N. *lagr*].

low (lō) *v.i.* to bellow as an ox or cow; *n.* the noise made [O.E. *hlowan*, to low].

low-er (lou'·ẹr) *v.i.* to frown; to look gloomy or threatening, as the sky; *n.* a scowl; sullenness. **-ing** *a.* **-ingly** *adv.* Also **lour** [M.E. *louren*, to frown].

lox (lắks) *n.* liquid oxygen [from *liquid oxygen*]. *n.* salty smoked salmon [Yid. *lachs*, salmon].

loy-al (loi'·ạl) *a.* faithful to the lawful government, the sovereign, a cause, or a friend. **-ist** *n.* a faithful follower of a cause. **-ly** *adv.* **-ty** *n.* fidelity [Fr. fr. L. *lex*, a law].

loz-enge (lăz'·inj) *n.* a figure with two acute and two obtuse angles; small (often medicated) confection orig. lozenge-shaped.

lub-ber (lub'·ẹr) *n.* a heavy, clumsy fellow.

lu-bri-cate (lŏŏ'·bri·kāt) *v.t.* to make smooth or slippery; to smear with oil, grease, etc., to reduce friction. **lubricant** *n.* any oily substance used to reduce friction; *a.* having the property of reducing friction. **lubrication** *n.* **lubricative** *a.* **lubricator** *n.* **lubricity** *n.* slipperiness [L. *lubricare*, to make slippery].

luce (lŏŏs) *n.* a fresh-water fish, the pike when full grown [O.Fr. *lus*, a pike].

lu-cent (lŏŏ'·sạnt) *a.* shining; bright. **lucency** *n.* **lucernal** *a.* pert. to a lamp [L. *lucere*].

lu-cid (lŏŏ'·sid) *a.* shining; clear; easily understood, as of style; normally sane. **-ness**, **-ity** *n.* **-ly** *adv.* [L. *lux*, light].

Lu-ci-fer (lŏŏ'·sạ·fẹr) *n.* the planet Venus, when appearing as the morning star; Satan. [L. *lucifer*, light-bearing].

lu-cite (lŏŏ'·sit) *n.* a very clear plastic compound [Trade Name].

luck (luk) *n.* accidental fortune, good or bad; fate; chance. **-ily** *adv.* **-iness** *n.* **-less** *n.* unfortunate. **-lessly** *adv.* **-lessness** *n.* **-y** *a.* fortunate; fortuitous [Dut. *luk*, fate].

lu-cre (lŏŏ'·kẹr) *n.* material gain; profit, esp. ill-gotten. **lucrative** *a.* profitable. **lucratively** *adv.* **filthy lucre** (*Slang*) money [L. *lucrum*].

lu-cu-brate (lŏŏ'·kyạ·brāt) *v.i.* to study by lamp or candlelight, or at night. **lucubration** *n.* nocturnal study; the product of such study. **lucubrator** *n.* **lucubratory** *a.* [L. *lucubrare*, to work by candlelight].

lu-cu-lent (lŏŏ'·kyạ·lạnt) *a.* clear; self-evident. **-ly** *adv.* [L. *lux*, light].

lu-di-crous (lŏŏ'·di·krạs) *a.* provoking laughter; ridiculous; droll. **-ly** *adv.* **-ness** *n.* [L. *ludus*, sport].

luff (luf) *v.t.* to turn the head of a ship towards the wind; to sail nearer the wind; *n.* the windward side of a ship [M.E. *lof*, a paddle].

Luft-waf-fe (lŏŏft'·vå·fạ) *n.* the German Air Force [Ger. *Luft*, the air; *Waffe*, a weapon].

lug (lug) *v.t.* to pull with force; to tug; to haul; to drag. *pr.p.* **-ging**. *pa.t.* and *pa.p.* **-ged**. **-gage** *n.* a traveler's trunks, baggage, etc. [Scand. *lugga*, to pull the hair].

lug (lug) *n.* a projecting piece by which an object may be grasped, supported, etc. [Scand. *lugga*, a forelock].

lu-gu-bri-ous (lŏŏ·gū'·bri·ạs) *a.* mournful; woeful; dismal. **-ly** *adv.* [L. *lugere*, to mourn].

lug-worm (lug'·wurm) *n.* a large earthworm.

luke-warm (lŏŏk'·wawrm) *a.* moderately warm; tepid; indifferent. **-ly** *adv.* **-ness** *n.* [M.E. *leuk*, tepid; *warm*].

lull (lul) *v.t.* to soothe to sleep; to quiet; *v.i.* to become quiet gradually; *n.* a period of quiet in storm or noise. **-aby** (·ạ·bi) *n.* a song sung to a child to soothe it to sleep [Scand. *lulla*].

lum-ba-go (lum·bā'·gō) *n.* a painful rheumatic affection of the lumbar muscles. **lumbaginous, lumbar, lumbral** *a.* pert. to the lower part of the back [L. *lumbus*, the loin].

lum-ber (lum'·bẹr) *n.* anything useless and cumbersome; odds and ends hoarded; timber cut and split for market; *v.i.* to prepare timber for market; *v.t.* to heap in disorder. **-er, -jack, -man,** *n.* **-ing** *n.* **-yard** *n.* [fr. *Lombard*, a pawnbroker's shop].

lum-ber (lum'·bẹr) *v.i.* to move heavily. **-er** *n.* **-ing** *a.* [Scand. *lomra*, to resound].

lu-mi-nar-y (lŏŏ'·mạ·ner·i·) *n.* any body which gives light, esp. one of the heavenly bodies; (*Fig.*) a person of outstanding qualities. **luminant** *n.* giving out light. **lumination** *n.* **luminescence** *n.* the quality of being luminescent; phosphorescence. **luminescent** *a.* **lumeniferous** *a.* yielding light. **luminous**

a. shining; brilliant; glowing; brilliant in mind; lucid; comprehensible. **luminously** *adv.* [L. *lumen*, a light].

lump (lump) *n.* a small mass of matter of indefinite shape; a swelling; the gross; (*Colloq.*) a stupid, clumsy person; *a.* in a mass; *v.t.* to throw into a mass; to take in the gross. **lumpy** *a.* full of lumps; uneven. **in the lump**, taken as an aggregate [Scand. *lump*, a block].

lu-nar (lŏŏ'·nẹr) *a.* pert. to the moon; measured by revolutions of the moon. Also **lunary**. **lunacy** *n.* madness, formerly supposed to be influenced by changes of moon. **lunatic** *a.* insane; *n.* a mad person. **lunation** *n.* the period from one new moon to the next. **lunar month**, period of the moon's revolution, about 29½ days. **lunar year**, period of twelve synodic lunar months (354⅓ days). **lunate** *a.* crescent-shaped [L. *luna*, the moon].

lunch (lunch) *n.* a light meal taken between breakfast and dinner. Also **-eon**. *v.i.* to take lunch. **-eonette** *n.* [dial. *lunsh*, a lump].

lune (lŏŏn) *n.* anything in the shape of a half-moon. **lunette** *n.* a crescent-shaped opening in a vault to let in light [L. *luna*, the moon].

lung (lung) *n.* one of the two main organs of respiration in a breathing animal. **-ed** *a.* [O.E. *lungen*, lungs].

lunge (lunj) *n.* in fencing, a sudden thrust; *v.i.* to thrust [Fr. *allonger*, to stretch].

lu-pine (lŏŏ'·pin) *a.* wolflike [L. *lupus*, a wolf].

lu-pine (lŏŏ'·pạn) *n.* a genus of leguminous plants, some cultivated for their flowers, others for cattle fodder [L. *lupinus*, pert. to a wolf].

lu-pus (lŏŏ'·pạs) *n.* a spreading tubercular condition affecting the skin [L. *lupus*, a wolf].

lurch (lurch) *n.* a sudden roll of a ship to one side; a staggering movement; *v.i.* to stagger.

lurch (lurch) *n.* a critical move in the game of cribbage. **to leave in the lurch**, to desert in a moment of need [Fr. *lourche*, a game].

lure (loor) *n.* a decoy used by the falconer to recall the hawk; an artificial bait; *v.t.* to entice; to decoy [Fr. *leurre*, a bait].

lu-rid (lŏŏ'·rid) *a.* extravagantly colored; (*Fig.*) startling; ghastly pale. **-ly** *adv.* [L. *luridus*, pale yellow].

lurk (lurk) *v.i.* to lie hidden; to lie in wait. **-er** *n.* [Scand. *lurka*, to go slowly].

lus-cious (lush'·ạs) *a.* excessively sweet; cloying. **-ly** *adv.* **-ness** *n.* [etym. doubtful].

lush (lush) *a.* luxuriant; juicy [*luscious*].

lush (lush) *n.* (*Slang*) a habitually drunken person.

lust (lust) *n.* longing desire; sexual appetite; craving; *v.i.* to desire passionately; to have sexual appetites; sensual. **-ful** *a.* having inordinate carnal desires; sensual. **-fully** *adv.* **-fulness** *n.* **-iness** *n.* **-ily** *adv.* **lusty** *a.* vigorous; robust [O.E. *lust*, pleasure].

lus-ter (lus'·tẹr) *n.* clearness; glitter; gloss; renown; radiance; chandelier with drops or pendants of cut glass; a cotton dress fabric with glossy, silky surface; a pottery glaze. **lustrous** *a.* gleaming; bright. **lustrously** *adv.* [L. *lustrare*, to make bright]. [Fr.].

lus-trine (lus'·trin) *n.* a glossy silk fabric.

lus-trum (lus'·trạm) *n.* a period of five years; purification, (Rom. times) every five years. **lustral** *a.* pert. to, or used in, purification. **lustration** *n.* the act of purifying; the sacrifice or ceremony by which cities, fields, armies, or people were purified [L. *lustrare*, to purify].

lute (lŏŏt) *n.* a stringed instrument with a pear-shaped body. **lutanist, luter, lutist** *n.* a lute-player. **-string** *n.* [O.Fr. *lut*].

Lu-ther-an (lŏŏ'·thẹr·ạn) *a.* pert. to *Luther* the German reformer, or to his doctrines; *n.* a follower of Martin Luther; a member of the Lutheran Church. **-ism** *n.* **Lutherism**.

lu-thern (lŏŏ'·thẹrn) *n.* a dormer-window.

lux-ate (luk'·sāt) *v.t.* to put out of joint; to dislocate. **luxation** *n.* [L. *luxare*, to dislocate].

luxe See **de luxe**.

lux-u-ry (luk'·shạ·ri·) *n.* indulgence in the pleasures which wealth can procure; that which is not a necessity of life. **luxuriance, luxuriancy, luxuriety** *n.* **luxuriant** *a.* in great abundance; dense or prolific, as vegetation. **luxuriantly** *adv.* **luxuriate** *v.i.* to grow luxuriantly; to live luxuriously. **luxurious** *a.* self-indulgent in appetite, etc.; sumptuous. **luxuriously** *adv.* **luxuriousness** *n.* [L. *luxus*, excess].

Ly-ce-um (li·sē'·ạm) *n.* orig. a place in Athens where Aristotle taught his pupils; (*l.c.*) a lecture hall [Gk. *Lukeion*].

lyd-dite (lid'·it) *n.* picric acid; a powerful explosive used in shells [fr. *Ludd* in Kent].

lye (li) *n.* alkaline solution of wood ashes and water; used in soap making [O.E. *leah*].

ly·ing (lī′·ing) *a.* recumbent. **lying-in** *n.* the confinement of a pregnant woman [fr. *lie*].
ly·ing (lī′·ing) *a.* untruthful; *n.* habit of being untruthful. **-ly** *adv.* [fr. *lie*].
lymph (limf) *n.* an alkaline fluid, watery in appearance, contained in the tissues and organs of the body. **-atic** *a.* pert. to lymph; sluggish. **-atics** *n.pl.* small vessels in the body containing lymph. **-oid** *a.* like, composed of, lymph [L. *lympha*, water].
lynch (linch) *v.t.* to inflict capital punishment (on an accused) illegally [fr. *Charles Lynch*, Virginia planter (18th cent.)].
lynx (lingks) *n.* an animal of the cat tribe with abnormally keen sight [Gk. *lunx*].
ly·on·naise (lī′·a̠·nāz) *a.* prepared with onions [Fr.].
lyre (līr) *n.* a stringed, musical instrument in use among ancient Greeks, esp. to accompany minstrels. **lyrate** *a.* shaped like a lyre. **-bird** *n.* an Australian bird with tail feathers which

curve upward in the shape of a lyre. **lyric.** *n.* orig. a poem sung to music; a short, subjective poem expressing emotions of poet. **lyric, -al**

lynx

lyre

a. pert. to the lyre; suitable to be sung to a musical accompaniment; used of poetry expressing emotion. **lyricism** *n.* lyrical quality of a poem; emotional expression. **lyrist** *n.* **lyricist** *n.* [Gk. *lura*, a lyre].

M

ma′am (mam) *n.* contr. of **madam.**
ma·ca·bre (ma̠·kä′·ber) *a.* gruesome; ghastly; grim. **macaberesque** *a.* [O.Fr. *macabre*].
mac·a·dam (ma̠·kad′·am) *n.* a road-surface material of crushed stones. **-ize** *v.t.* [fr. J. L. *MacAdam*, the inventor (d. 1836)].
ma·caque (ma̠·käk′·) *n.* a genus of Asian monkeys. **macaco** *n.* Braz. monkey [Port. *macaco*, a monkey].
mac·a·ro·ni (mak·a̠·rō′·ni·) *n.* a paste of wheat flour made in long slender tubes; a dandy of the 18th cent. **macaronic** *a.* affected; burlesque verse in modern words with Latinized endings [It.].
mac·a·roon (mak′·a̠·ròòn) *n.* a small cooky made of white of egg, ground almonds and sugar [Fr. *macaroon*].
ma·caw (ma̠·kaw′) *n.* a long-tailed S. Amer. parrot [Brazil. *macao*].
mace (mās) *n.* a heavy club of metal; a staff carried as an emblem of authority; a billiard cue [O. Fr. *mace*, a mallet].

mace (mās) *n.* a spice made from nutmeg.
mac·er·ate (mas′·a̠·rāt) *v.t.* to soften by soaking; to cause to grow thin; *v.i.* to become soft; to waste away. **maceration** *n.* [L. *macerare*, to steep].
ma·che·te (ma̠·che′·ti·) *n.* a heavy knife or cleaver used to cut down sugar canes, and as a weapon [Sp.].
Mach·i·a·vel·lian (mak·i·a·vel′·i·a̠n) *a.* pert. to Machiavelli; unscrupulous; crafty; *n.* an unprincipled ruthless ruler. **-ism** *n.* [fr. *Machiavelli*, Florentine statesman].
mach·i·nate (mak′·a̠·nāt) *v.t.* to contrive, usually with evil or ulterior motive; *v.i.* to conspire. **machination** *n.* the act of contriving or plotting, with evil intent; an intrigue. **machinator** *n.* one who plots [L. *machinari*, to plot].
ma·chine (ma̠·shēn′) *n.* (*Mech.*) any contrivance for the conversion and direction of motion; an apparatus for doing some kind of work; an engine; a vehicle; a person who acts like an automaton; a politically controlled organization; a contrivance in the ancient Greek theater to indicate a change of scene; *v.t.* to use a machine. **— gun** *n.* an automatic small-arms weapon capable of continuous firing. **machinery** *n.* machines collectively; the parts of a machine; any combination of means to an end. **— tool** *n.* a tool for cutting, shaping and turning operated by machinery. **machinist** *n.* one who makes machinery; one who works at a machine [L. *machina*, a machine].
mack·er·el (mak′·er·a̠l) *n.* an edible sea fish with blue and black stripes above and silver color below [O.Fr. *mackerel*].
mack·i·naw (mak′·a̠·naw) *n.* a short woolen coat, usually plaid [Ojibwa Indian, turtle].
mack·in·tosh (mak′·in·täsh) *n.* a waterproof coat [fr. *Charles MacIntosh*, the inventor].
mac·ra·mé (mak′·ra̠·mā) *n.* a coarse fringe.
mac·ro·bi·ot·ic (mak·rō·bī·át′·ik) *a.* long

lived. **macrobiosis** *n.* long life. **macrobiotics** *n.* study of longevity [Gk. *makros*, long; *bios* life].
mac·ro·cosm (mak′·ra̠·käzm) *n.* the great universe. **-ic** *a.* [Gk. *makros*, long; *cosmos*, the world].
ma·cron (mā′·krän) *n.* short line put over vowel to show it is long in quantity or quality, as *fāte* [Gk. *makros*, long].
mac·ro·scop·ic (mak·ra̠·skäp′·ik) *a.* visible to the naked eye; opp. of *microscopic*. **-ally** *adv.* [Gk. *makros*, long; *skopein*, to see].
mac·u·la (mak′·ya̠·la) *n.* a spot. *pl.* **maculae.** **maculate** *v.t.* to spot. **maculation** *n.* the act of spotting; a spot. **maculose** *a.* spotted [L.].
mad (mad) *a.* (*comp.* **-der**; *superl.* **-dest**) deranged in mind; insane; crazy; frenzied; angry; infatuated; irrational, as a scheme. **-cap** *n.* a rash person; *a.* uncontrolled. **-den** *v.t.* to enrage; to drive mad; to annoy; *v.i.* to behave as a madman. **-dening** *a.* **-ly** *adv.* **-house** *n.* an asylum for patients with mental disorders; a place of confusion. **-man** *n.* a lunatic. **-ness** *n.* insanity; anger [O.E. *gemaed*, foolish].
mad·am (mad′·a̠m) *n.* a formal mode of address in speaking to a married or elderly woman. **madame** (ma̠·dam′) *n.* French form. *pl.* **mesdames** (mā·dam′) [O.Fr. *ma dame*, my lady].
Ma·dei·ra (ma̠·dir′·a) *n.* a rich amber-colored wine from *Madeira*, Port.
ma·de·moi·selle (mad·a̠·ma·zel′) *n.* French mode of addressing unmarried lady [Fr.].
Ma·don·na (ma̠·dän′·a) *n.* the Virgin Mary; a statue of the Virgin [It. *mia*, my; *donna*, a lady].
mad·ras (mad′·ra̠s) *n.* a fine cotton cloth,usu. striped or plaid [fr. *Madras*, India].
mad·re·pore (mad′·ra̠·pōr) *n.* white perforate coral [It. *madre*, a mother; L. *porus*, a pore].
mad·ri·gal (mad′·ri·ga̠l) *n.* a short love poem; an unaccompanied part-song, usually syncopated in rhythm, popular in 16th and 17th cents.
mael·strom (māl′·stra̠m) *n.* a whirlpool; (*Fig.*) menacing state of affairs [fr. *Maelström* = a whirlpool].
ma·es·to·so (mī·stō′·sō) *a.* and *adv.* (*Mus.*) with dignity [It.].
maes·tro (mīs′·trō) *n.* master, esp. an eminent composer, conductor, or teacher of music [It.].
Mae West (mā·west) *n.* an inflatable life-jacket [fr. *Mae West*, film star].
ma·fi·a (mä′·fi·a) *n.* a criminal Sicilian secret society; hostility to the law. Also **maffia** [It.].
mag·a·zine (mag′·a̠·zēn) *n* a military store-house; part of a ship where ammunition is stored; compartment in a rifle holding the cartridges; a periodical containing miscellaneous articles [Fr. *magasin*, a warehouse].
ma·gen·ta (ma̠·jen′·ta) *n.* a purplish dye from coal tar [discovery in *Magenta*, It.].
mag·got (mag′·at) *n.* a grub; larva of a house-fly; (*Fig.*) a whim [M.E. *maddok*, a flesh worm].
Ma·gi (mā′·jī) *n.pl.* a class of priests among the ancient Persians; in the N.T. the Wise Men who came to visit the infant Jesus [Gk. *magos*, a magician].
mag·ic (maj′·ik) *n.* the feigned art of influencing nature or future events by occult means; sorcery; charm. **-al** **-ally** *adv.* **-ian** (ma̠·jish′·a̠n) *n.* one skilled in magic; a conjurer. **— lantern**, early form of projector using slides. **black magic**, magic by aid of evil

spirits [Gk. *magikos*].
mag·is·te·ri·al (maj·as·tir′·i·a̠l) *a.* pert. to or conducted by a magistrate; authoritative; judicial; overbearing. **-ly** *adv.* [L. *magister*].
mag·is·trate (maj′·as·trāt) *n.* a person vested with public judicial authority; a justice of the peace. **magistracy** *n.* the position of a magistrate; the body of magistrates [L. *magistratus*].
mag·ma (mag′·ma) *n.* a paste of mineral or organic matter; (*Geol.*) the molten rock beneath the earth's crust; (*Pharm.*) a salve [Gk. to knead].
Mag·na Car·ta (**Charta**) (mag′·na kär′·ta) *n.* Great Charter of English public and private liberties signed by King John, 1215 (L.).
mag·na·nim·i·ty (mag·na·nim′·a·ti·) *n.* greatness of mind; generosity of heart esp. in forgiveness. **magnanimous** *a.* **magnanimously** *adv.* [L. *magnus*, great; *animus*, the mind].
mag·nate (mag′·nāt, -net) *n.* an eminent person, esp. a wealthy business man [L. *magnus*, great].
mag·ne·si·um (mag·nē′·zē·am, -zham) *n.* the silvery-white metallic base of magnesia, burning with an intensely brilliant white light and used for fireworks, flash bulbs, etc. [Gk. *Magnesia* (lithos), magnesian stone].
mag·net (mag′·nat) *n.* the loadstone; a bar of iron having property of attracting iron or steel and, when suspended, of pointing N. and S.; a person or thing with powers of attraction. **-ic** *a.* pert. to a magnet; attractive. **-ically** *adv.* **-ist** *n.* an expert in magnetism. **-izable** *a.* **-ization** *n.* **-ize** *v.t.* to give magnetic properties to; to attract; *v.i.* to become magnetic. **-ism** *n.* the natural cause of magnetic force; the science of the phenomena of magnetic force; attraction. **magneto** *n.* a magnetoelectric machine, esp. used to generate ignition spark in internal-combustion engine. **magnetic field**, the sphere of influence of magnetic forces. **magnetic needle**, a small magnetized pivoted steel bar of a compass which always points approximately north. **magnetic north**, the north as indicated by the pivoted bar of the mariner's compass. **magnetic poles**, two nearly opposite points on the earth's surface [Gk. *magnētis* (lithos), a magnet].
mag·ni·fy (mag′·na̠·fī) *v.t.* to make greater; to cause to appear greater. **Magnificat** *n.* the song of the Virgin Mary. **magnification** *n.* the act of magnifying. **magnificent** *a.* splendid; brilliant;. **magnificence** *n.* **magnificently** *adv.* **magnifico** *n.* a Venetian nobleman; person of importance. **magnified** *n.* one who or the instrument which magnifies [L. *magnus*, great; *facere*, to make].

mag·nil·o·quent (mag·nil′·ạ·kwạnt) a. speaking pompously; boastful. **magniloquence** n. [L. magnus, great; loqui, to speak].

mag·ni·tude (mag′·nạ·tūd) n. greatness; size; importance [L. magnitudo, greatness].

mag·no·li·a (mag·nō′·li·ạ) n. a species of tree bearing large perfumed flowers [fr. Magnol, French botanist].

mag·num (mag′·nạm) n. a wine-bottle holding two quarts. —**opus** n. one's best artistic or literary work [L. magnus, great].

mag·pie (mag′·pi) n. a bird of the crow family, with a harsh chattering cry; an idle chatterer [contr. of Margaret and pie].

Mag·yar (mag′·yár) n. dominant people of Hungary; the language of Hungary.

ma·ha·ra·jah (má·ha·rá′·jạ) n. (fem. **maharani** or **maharanee**) the title of an Indian prince [Sans. maha, great; raja, a prince].

ma·hat·ma (ma·hát′·mạ) n. a man of saintly life with supernatural powers derived from purity of soul [Sans. mahatma, high-souled].

mah·jong (má·jáng′) n. old Chinese game for four played with small tiles [Chin.].

ma·hog·a·ny (ma·hág′·a·ni·) n. a tree of hard, reddish wood used for furniture; the red-brown color of mahogany [W. Ind.].

maid (mād) n. a girl or unmarried woman; a female domestic servant. **old maid**, a spinster; a game of cards. **-en**, n. a maid; a. pert. to a maid; unmarried; unused; first. **-enhair** n. a kind of fern with delicate fronds. **-enhood**, n. virginity; purity. **-enliness** n. **-enly** a. gentle; modest. **-en name**, surname of a woman before marriage [O.E. maegden, a maid].

mail (māl) n. defensive armor composed of steel rings or plates; v.t. to clothe in armor [O.Fr. maille, mail].

mail (māl) n. letters, packages, etc., carried by post; the person or means of conveyance for transit of letters, parcels, etc.; v.t. to post; to send by mail. **-bag** n. the sack in which letters are put for transit. **-boat, -car, -plane, -train, -man** n. means of conveyance of letters [O.Fr. male, a trunk or mail].

maim (mām) v.t. to deprive of the use of a limb; to disable; to disfigure. **-er** n. [O.Fr. mahaing, a bruise].

main (mān) a. principal; first in size, importance, etc.; sheer; n. the chief part; strength, as in might and main; (Poet.) the open sea or ocean or the mainland; the principal pipe or line in water, gas, or electricity system. **-land** n. a continent as distinct from islands. **-ly** adv. **-spring** n. the principal spring in a watch or other mechanism; motive power. **-stay** n. the chief support [O.E. maegen, main].

main·tain (mān·tān′) v.t. and v.i. to hold or keep in any state; to sustain; to preserve; to defend, as an argument; to support. **-able** a. **-er** n. **maintenance** n. the act of maintaining; means of support [Fr. maintenir, to hold].

maize (māz) n. Indian corn, a cereal; yellow [Sp. maiz].

maj·es·ty (maj′·ạs·ti·) n. grandeur; exalted dignity; royal state; the title of a sovereign. **majestic, -al** a. [L. majestas, dignity].

ma·jol·i·ca (mạ·jạl′·i·kạ) n. a decorative, enameled pottery [fr. Majorca].

ma·jor (mā′·jẹr) a. greater in number, quality, quantity, or extent; (Mus.) greater by a semitone; pert. to a field of study; n. a person who has reached the age of 21; an officer in the army ranking below a lieutenant-colonel; a

principal field of study. v.i. to specialize. —**domo** n. a steward; (Colloq.) an organizer. — **general** n. an army officer in rank below a lieutenant-general. **majority** n. the greater part; more than half; full legal age (21) [L. major, greater].

make (māk) v.t. to cause to be or do; to create; to constitute; to compel; to appoint; to secure; to arrive at; to reckon; to perform; v.i. to go; to start; p.a.t. and pa.p. **made**. —**believe** n. pretense; v.i. to pretend. **-r** n. **Maker** n. God. **-shift** n. a temporary expedient. **-up** n. arrangement or layout of a printed page, magazine, etc.; cosmetics; nature; a making up for [O.E. macian, to make].

mal·a·chite (mal′·ạ·kīt) n. a green carbonate of copper, used for inlaid work [Gk. malachē, mallow].

mal·ad·just·ment (mal·ạ·just′·mạnt) n. faulty adjustment; inability to adjust to one's environment.

mal·ad·min·is·tra·tion (mal·ạd·min·ạ·strā′·shạn) n. faulty administration, esp. of public affairs. [ward. **-ness** n.

mal·a·droit (mal·ạ·droit′) a. clumsy; awkward.

mal·a·dy (mal′·ạ·di·) n. a disease; ailment. **mal de mer**, seasickness [Fr. malade, sick].

Mal·a·gas·y (mal·ạ·gas′·i·) n. a native of, or the language of, Madagascar; a. [Fr.].

ma·laise (ma·lāz′) n. a physical discomfort

mal·a·prop(ism) (mal′·ạ·prạp·(izm) n. the ludicrous misuse of a word [Fr. mal à propos, ill-suited].

ma·lar·i·a (mạ·lar′·i·ạ) n. a febrile disease transmitted by the bite of mosquito; **malarious** a. [It. malaria, bad air].

Ma·lay (mā′·lā) n. a native of the Malay Peninsula; a. Also **Malayan**.

mal·con·tent (mal′·kạn·tent) a. discontented; rebellious. **-ed** a. **-edly** adv. **-edness** n.

male (māl) a. pert. to the sex which begets young; masculine; (Bot.) having stamens; n. a male animal [L. masculus, male].

mal·e·dic·tion (mal·ạ·dik′·shạn) n. evil-speaking; a curse. **maledictory** a. slander [L. male, badly; dicere, to speak].

mal·e·fac·tor (mal′·ạ·fakter) n. an evil-doer; a criminal. **malefaction** n. a crime [L. male, badly; facere, to do].

ma·lev·o·lent (ma·lev′·ạ·lạnt) a. evilly disposed; malicious. **malevolence** n. ill will; malice. **-ly** adv. [L. male, badly; velle, to wish].

mal·fea·sance (mal·fē′·zans) n. misconduct, esp. in public affairs [Fr.].

mal·for·ma·tion (mal·fawr·mā′·shạn) n. irregular formation. **malformed** a. deformed.

mal·func·tion (mal·fungk′·shạn) v.i. to fail to operate correctly or normally [L. male, badly; L. functio]. [apple].

mal·ic (mā′·lik) a. from the apple [L. malum,

mal·ice (mal′·is) n. ill will; spite; desire to injure others; (Law) criminal intention. **malicious** a. spiteful; showing malice. **maliciously** adv. **maliciousness** n. **with malice aforethought** (Law) with deliberate criminal intention [L. malitia, ill-will].

ma·lign (mạ·līn′) a. malicious; evil; spiteful; v.t. to slander; to vilify. **malignance, malignancy** n. **malignant** a. being evilly disposed; harmful; (of disease) virulent; likely to prove fatal. **malignantly** adv. **-er** n. **malignity** n. [L. malignus, ill-disposed].

ma·lin·ger (ma·ling′·gẹr) v.i. to feign illness in order to avoid duty. **-er** n. a shirker [Fr. malingre, ailing].

mall (mawl) n. a level, shaded walk; a heavy mallet used in game of pall-mall (var. of maul) L. malleus, a hammer].

mal·lard (mal′·ẹrd) n. a wild drake or duck.

mal·le·a·ble (mal′·i·ạ·bl) a. capable of being hammered or extended by beating; amenable; tractable. **malleability** n. **malleate** v.t. to hammer; to draw into a plate or leaf by beating. **malleation** n. [L. malleus, a hammer].

mal·let (mal′·ạt) n. any of various types of wooden hammer [Fr. maillet, a small hammer].

mal·low (mal′·ō) n. plant with downy leaves, and having emolient properties [L. malva].

mal·nu·tri·tion (mal·nū·tri′·shạn) n. the state of being undernourished.

mal·o·dor·ous (mal·ō′·dẹr·ạs) a. having an offensive odor. **malodor** n.

mal·prac·tice (mal·prak′·tis) n. professional impropriety or negligence.

malt (mawlt) n. barley or other grain steeped in water till it germinates, then dried in a kiln for use in brewing; v.t. to make into malt; v.i. to become malt. **-ed milk** n. a powder of malted grains and dried milk; a drink made by mixing this with milk and ice cream. — **extract** n. a medicinal body-building food. — **liquor**, a liquor made from malt by fermentation and not by distillation, as beer, stout, ale. **-ose** n. a sugar produced by the action of malt on starch [O.E.]. [dialect and people.

Mal·tese (mawl′·tēz) n. a native of Malta; its

mal·treat (mal·trēt′) v.t. to ill-treat; to abuse; to handle roughly. **-ment** n.

mal·ver·sa·tion (mal·vẹr·sā′·shạn) n. corruption in office; fraudulent handling of public funds [L. male, ill; versari, to be engaged in].

mam·bo (mám′·bō) n. rhythmic music and dance of Sp. Amer. origin. [Africa [Kaffir].

mam·ba (mám′·bạ) n. a poisonous snake of

mam·ma (mam′·ạ) n. child's name for mother [imit.].

mam·ma (mam′·ạ) n. milk-secreting gland in females. pl. **mammae**. **mammary** a. [L. the breast].

Mam·ma·li·a (ma·mā′·li·ạ) n.pl. (Zool.) the class of mammals or animals which suckle their young. **mammal** n. one of the Mammalia. **-n** a. [L. mamma, the breast].

mam·mon (mam′·ạn) n. wealth personified and worshiped [Syrian mamon, wealth].

mam·moth (mam′·ạth) n. a huge extinct elephant; a. colossal [Russ. mammant].

mam·my (mam′·i·) n. a Negro woman who took care of white children in the South; Mother: a child's word [Dial.].

man (man) n. a human being; an adult male; a manly person; a male servant; a husband; the human race; a piece used in such games as chess, checkers, etc. pl. **men**. v.t. to furnish with men; to fortify; pr.p. **-ning**. pa.t. and pa.p. **-ned**. —**eater**, a cannibal; a tiger, etc.; a shark. **-ful** a. vigorous; sturdy. **-fully** adv. **-fulness** n. **-hole** n. an opening large enough to admit a man leading to a drain, sewer, etc. **-hood** n. the state of being a man; courage. —**hour** n. work performed by one man in one hour. **-kind** n. human beings. **-liness** n. **-ly** a. bold; resolute; dignified; not effeminate; masculine. **-nish** a. like a man. **-nishly** adv. **-nishness** n. —**of-war**, a warship. —**power** n. a unit of power equal to one-eighth of a horse-power; the total number of people in industry, the armed forces, etc. **-servant** n. a male servant. **-slaughter** n. culpable homicide without malice aforethought. **man in the street**, average man [O.E. mann].

man·a·cle (man′·ạ·kl) n. a handcuff; v.t. to fetter with handcuffs [O.Fr. manicle].

man·age (man′·ij) v.t. to direct; to control; to carry on; to cope with; v.i. to direct affairs; to succeed. **-ability** n. **-able** a. capable of being managed. **-ment** n. the act of managing; administration; body of directors controlling a business. **-r** n. one who manages; one in charge. **managerial** a. [L. manus, the hand].

Man·chu (man′·chōō) n. one of the original inhabitants of Manchuria; a. of Manchuria [Chin.].

man·ci·ple (man′·si·pl) n. a steward; a caterer [L. manceps, a purchaser].

man·da·mus (man·dā′·mus) n. a written order [L., we command].

man·da·rin (man′·dạ·rin) n. a European name for a Chinese provincial governor; the language used in Chinese official circles; a small orange; a long brocade coat with loose sleeves [Port. mandarin].

man·date (man′·dāt) n. an official order; a precept; a prescript of the Pope; a commission to act as representative of a body of people. **mandatary**, one to whom a mandate is given by a mandator. **-d** a. committed to a mandate, as mandated territories. **mandatory** a. containing a mandate; obligatory [L. mandatum, an order].

man·di·ble (man′·di·bl) n. a jaw; in vertebrates, the lower jaw; in birds, the upper or lower beak. **mandibular** a. [L. mandibula].

man·do·lin (man′·dạ·lin) n. a musical instrument with a rounded pear-shaped body [It. mandola, a lute].

man·drake (man′·drāk) n. a narcotic plant, the root thought to resemble human form [M.E. mandragge].

man·drel (man′·drel) n. a shaft on which objects may be fixed for turning, milling, etc.; the spindle of a lathe. Also **mandril**.

man·drill (man′·dril) n. a large African baboon [Fr.].

mane (mān) n. long hair on the neck of an animal [O.E. manu, neck].

ma·nège (ma·nezh′) n. the art of horsemanship; a riding-school [Fr.].

ma·neu·ver (ma·nōō′·ver) n. a controlled strategic movement; scheme; artifice. pl. peacetime exercises of troops; v.t. to direct skillfully; **-able** a. **-ability** n. **-er** n. [Fr. fr. L. to work by hand].

man·ga·nese (mang′·gạ·nēz) n. a greyish, hard, brittle metal which oxidizes rapidly in humid atmosphere [O.Fr. manganese].

mange (mānj) n. a parasitic disease affecting the skin of animals causing hair to fall out. **manginess** n. **mangy** a. [O.Fr. manjue, itch].

man·ger (mān′·jẹr) n. a trough for holding

fodder for cattle [Fr. *manger*, to eat].

man·gle (mang'·gl) *n.* a machine for pressing linen between rollers; *v.t.* to smooth with a mangle. **-r** *n.* [Dut. *mangel*].

man·gle (mang'·gl) *v.t.* to hack; to mutilate; to spoil the beauty of [prob. O.Fr. *mahaigner*, to maim].

man·go (mang'·gō) *n.* a tropical tree, the unripe fruit used in making chutney [Malay, *mangga*].

man·grove (man'·grōv) *n.* a tropical tree the bark of which is used in tanning [Malay, *man-gri* + *grove*].

man·han·dle (man'·han·dl) *v.* to handle roughly.

man·hat·tan (man·hat'·n) *n.* a cocktail containing whisky, vermouth, bitters [Amer].

ma·ni·a (mā'·ni·a) *n.* madness; a violent excitement; extravagant enthusiasm; obsession. **maniac** *n.* a madman; *a.* raving; frenzied. **maniacal** *a.* [Gk.].

man·i·cure (man'·a·kyoor) *n.* the care of the hands and nails. **manicurist** *n.* one who gives this treatment; *v.t.* to file, and polish the nails [L. *manus*, the hand; *cura*, care].

man·i·fest (man'·a·fest) *a.* clearly visible; apparent to the mind or senses; *v.t.* to make clear; to reveal; *n.* a detailed list of goods transported. **-able, -ible** *a.* capable of being clearly revealed. **-ation** *n.* the act of revealing; the state of being revealed; display; disclosure. **-ly** *adv.* obviously. **manifesto** *n.* a public declaration of the principles or policy of a leader or party; *pl.* **manifestoes** [L. *manifestus*, clear].

man·i·fold (man'·a·fōld) *a.* many and varied; numerous; *v.t.* to make many copies of, as letters, by a machine, such as a duplicator; *n.* something with many parts; (*Mech.*) a pipe fitted with several lateral outlets [fr. *many* and *fold*].

man·i·kin (man'·a·kin) *n.* a little man; a dwarf; a model of the human body used in medical schools; a mannequin. Also **manakin** [Dut. *mannekin*, a double dim. of **man**].

ma·nil·a (ma·nil'·a) *n.* a cigar made in Manila, capital of the Philippine Islands. **— hemp**, a fiber used for making ropes, twine, sails, etc. **— paper**, a stout buff-coolred paper.

man·i·ple (man'·a·pl) *n.* part of a Roman legion; a scarf worn by celebrant at mass. **manipular** *a.* [L. *manipulus*, a handful].

ma·nip·u·late (ma·nip'·yoo·lāt) *v.t.* to operate with the hands; to manage (a person) in a skillful, esp. unscrupulous way; to falsify; *v.i.* to use the hands. **manipulation** *n.* **manipular, manipulative, manipulatory** *a.* **manipulator** *n.* [L. *manipulus*, a handful].

man·na (man'·a) *n.* the food supplied miraculously to the Israelites in the wilderness; sweetish juice of the ash; spiritual nourishment; [Heb. *man*, a gift].

man·ne·quin (man'·a·kin) *n.* one employed to model new fashions; figure for a similar purpose. Also **mannequin, manikin** [Fr. *manne-quin*, a puppet].

man·ner (man'·er) *n.* way of doing anything; custom; style; a person's habitual bearing; *pl.* social behavior; customs. **-ed** *a.* having manners (in compound *well-mannered*). **-ism** *n.* personal peculiarity of bearing, speech, or style of expression; affection. **-liness** *n.* politeness; decorum. **-ly** *a.* having good manners; courteous; civil; respectful; *adv.* civilly; respectfully. **to the manner born**, having natural talent for special work or position [Fr. *manière*, manner].

man·or (man'·er) *n.* (*Brit.*) the land belonging to a lord; a unit of land in feudal times over which the owner had full jurisdiction [O.Fr. *manoir*, a dwelling].

man·sard roof (man'·sárd róof) *n.* roof in which lower slope is nearly vertical and upper much inclined (fr. F. *Mansard*, Fr. arcritect).

manse (mans) *n.* a minister's residence [L.L. *mansa*, a dwelling].

man·sion (man'·shan) *n.* a large, imposing house; a manor house [L. *manere*, to remain].

man·sue·tude (man'·swa·tōōd) *n.* gentleness; tameness [L. *manus*, a hand; *suescere*, to accustom].

man·tel (man'·tl) *n.* the shelf above a fireplace; the framework around a fireplace. **-piece** *n.* the shelf [form of *mantle*].

man·til·la (man·til'·a) *n.* a veil covering head and shoulders, worn by Spanish women; a short cape [dim. of Sp. *mante*, a cloak].

man·tis (man'·tis) *n.* a genus of insects holding the forelegs folded as if praying [Gk. *man-tis*, a prophet].

---

mantel

man·tis·sa (man·tis'·a) *n.* the decimal part of a logarithm [L. *mantissa*, a makeweight].

man·tle (man'·tl) *n.* a loose outer garment; a cloak; a covering; *v.t.* to cover; to hide; *v.i.* to form a covering; to suffuse; to flush. **mantlet** *n.* (*Mil.*) a bullet-proof shelter [L. *mantellum*, a cloak].

man·tu·a (man'·choo·a) *n.* a woman's loose gown [Fr. *manteau*].

man·u·al (man'·yoo·al) *a.* pert. to, made by or done with the hand; *n.* a handbook or small textbook; a keyboard of a pipe-organ. **-ly** *adv.* [L. *manus*, the hand].

man·u·fac·ture (man·ya·fak'·cher) *n.* making goods either by hand or by machine (esp. mass-production; anything produced from raw materials; *v.t.* to make from raw materials; to fabricate; *v.i.* to be engaged in manufacture. **manufactory** *n.* a factory. **-r** *n.* [L. *manus*, the hand; *facere*, to make].

man·u·mit (man·ya·mit') *v.t.* to give freedom to a slave; to emancipate. *pr.p.* **-ting**. *pa.p.*, *pa.t.* **-ted**. **manumission** *n.* [L. *manumit-tere*, to send from one's hand].

ma·nure (ma·noor') *v.t.* to enrich soil with fertilizer; *n.* animal excrement used as fertilizer [contr. of Fr. *manoeuvrer*, to work with the hands].

man·u·script (man'·ya·skript) *a.* written, or typed, by hand; *n.* a book written by hand; an author's script or typewritten copy for perusal by publisher [L. *manus*, hand; *scribere*, *scrip-tum*, to write].

man·y (men'·i·) *a.* comprising a great number (*comp.* **more**; *superl.* **most**); *n. pro.* a number of people or things. **-sided** *a.* talented [O.E. *manig*, many].

map (map) *n.* a representation, esp. on a plane surface, of the features of the earth, or of part of it; a chart of the heavens; a plan or delineation; *v.t.* to draw a map of; to fill in details in a blank map; to plan; *pr.p.* **-ping**. *pa.t.* and *pa.p.* **-ped** [L. *mappa*, a napkin].

ma·ple (mā'·pl) *n.* a deciduous tree, valuable for its timber and the sap from which sugar is extracted [O.E. *mapultreow*, the maple tree].

mar (már) *v.t.* to injure; to impair; to disfigure. *pr.p.* **-ring**. *pa.p.* **-red** [O.E. *merran*, to hinder].

mar·a·bou (mar'·a·bòò) *n.* a kind of stork; the feathers of this bird used as trimming.

ma·ra·ca (ma·rá'·ka) *n.* gourd shaped rattle [Braz.].

mar·a·schi·no (mar·a·skē'·nō) *n.* a sweet liqueur distilled from cherries [It. *amarasca*, a sour cherry].

mar·a·thon (mar'·a·thán) *n.* a foot race (approx. 26 miles); endurance contest [Gk. Myth. runner, *Marathon* to *Athens*)].

ma·raud (ma·rawd') *v.i.* to rove in quest of plunder; to loot. **-er** *n.* **-ing** *n.* and *a.* [O.Fr. *marauder*, to play the rogue].

mar·ble (már'·bl) *n.* hard limestone which takes on a brilliant polish and is used for ornaments, statuary, etc.; a little ball of marble, glass, etc., used in games; *a.* made of marble; cold; insensible; *v.t.* to color like streaked marble. **-ed** *a.* veined like marble. **marbly** *a.* **-ize**, *v.t.* make like marble [Gk. *marmairein*, to sparkle].

mar·ca·site (már'·ka·sīt) *n.* white iron pyrite used in jewelry because of its brilliance [Fr.].

mar·cel (már·sel') *n.* an artificial hair wave. **-led** *a.* [fr. *Marcel*, the inventor].

March (márch) *n.* third month of year, named after Mars, Roman god of war.

march (márch) *n.* a border; a frontier; *pl.* [O.E. *mearc*, mark].

march (márch) *v.i.* to move in order, as soldiers; to proceed at a steady pace; *v.t.* to cause to move in military array; *n.* distance marched; a musical composition to accompany a march; steady advance, as the *march of time*. **-er** *n.* [Fr. *marcher*, to walk].

mar·chion·ess (már'·shan·is) *n.* the wife of a marquis; lady, holding in her own right, the rank of marquis [L.L. *marchionissa*, fem. of *marchio*, ruler of the march].

march·pane See **marzipan**.

mare (mer) *n.* the female of the horse, mule, donkey, etc. [O.E. *mere*, fem. of *mearh*, a horse].

mar·ga·rine (már'·ja·ran) *n.* pearly wax-like substance obtained from animal fat; a fatty extract of certain vegetable oils; a butter substitute made from vegetable oils or animal fats [Gk. *margaron*, a pearl].

mar·gin (már'·jan) *n.* a border; a blank space

---

at top, bottom and sides, of a written or printed page; allowance made for contingencies; *v.t.* to provide with margin; to enter in the margin. **-al** *a.* pert. to a margin; entered in the margin. **-alia** *n.pl.* notes jotted in the margin. **-al** *a.* **-ally** *adv.* **-ate, -d** *a.* [L. *margo*, the edge].

mar·gue·rite (már'·ga·rēt) *n.* a large ox-eye daisy [L. *margarita*, a pearl].

mar·i·gold (mar'·a·gōld) *n.* name applied to a plant bearing yellow or orange flowers [prob. fr. Virgin *Mary* and *gold*].

ma·ri·jua·na (mar·a·hwá'·na) *n.* a type of hemp dried and used as tobacco, having a narcotic effect [Sp.].

ma·rim·ba (ma·rim'·ba) *n.* a jazz-band instrument resembling the xylophone [Afr.].

ma·ri·na (ma·rē'·na) *n.* a small harbor or boat basin [L. *marinus*, the sea].

mar·i·nade (mar·a·nād') *n.* a seasoned vinegar or wine used for steeping meat, fish, vegetables. *v.t.* to marinate. **marinate** *v.t.* to let food stand in a marinade [Fr. *mariner*, pickle in brine].

ma·rine (ma·rēn') *a.* pert. to the sea; found in, or near, the sea; pert. to shipping or overseas trade. **-r** (mar'·i·ner) *n.* a sailor or seaman [L. *mare*, the sea].

mar·i·o·nette (mar·i·a·net') *n.* a puppet worked by strings [Fr. dim. of *Marion*].

mar·i·tal (mar'·a·tal) *a.* pert. to a husband or to marriage [L. *maritus*, married].

mar·i·time (mar'·a·tim) *a.* pert. to the sea; bordering on the sea; living near the sea; pert. to overseas trade or navigation [L. *maritimus*, fr. *mare*, the sea].

mar·jo·ram (már'·ja·ram) *n.* an aromatic plant of the mint family used in cookery.

mark (márk) *n.* a visible sign; a cross; a character made by one who cannot write; a stamp; a proof; a target; a point; an attainable standard; a numerical assessment of proficiency, as in an examination; a flaw or disfigurement; a peculiarity or distinguishing feature; (*Running*) starting post; indication of position, depth, etc. *v.t.* to make a sign upon; to stamp or engrave; to notice; to assess, as an examination paper; *v.i.* to observe particularly. **-ed** *a.* outstanding; notorious. **-edly** *adv.* noticeably. **-er** *n.* **-ing** *n.* design of marks. **-sman** *n.* one who is expert at hitting a target. **-smanship** *n.* shooting skill. **-up** *n.* the amount added to the cost of an article in determining the selling price. **trade mark**, a special symbol marked on commodities to indicate the maker [O.E. *mearc*, a boundary].

mark (márk) *n.* unit of exchange of various countries [O.E. *marc*].

mar·ket (már'·kit) *n.* a public meeting place for the purchase and sale of commodities; a trading-center; demand; country or geographical area regarded as a buyer of goods; price or value at a stated time; *v.i.* to buy or sell; *v.t.* to produce for sale in a market. **-able** *a.* suitable for selling. **-ably** *adv.* **-place** *n.* **— price** *n.* the current price of a commodity [L. *mercatus*, trade].

marl (márl) *n.* a crumbly soil used for fertilizer and in brick making; to manure with marl. **-y** *a.* [O.Fr. *marle*, marl].

mar·lin (már'·lin) *n.* a large slender deep-sea fish [fr. *marlin*, spike (snout)].

mar·line (már'·ljn) *n.* a small rope used to secure a splicing. **-spike** *n.* a pointed tool used to separate strands of a rope in splicing [Dut. *marren*, to bind; *lijn*, a line].

mar·ma·lade (már'·ma·lād) *n.* a preserve made of the pulp and peel of fruit [Port. *marmelo*, a quince].

mar·mo·set (már'·ma·set, ·zet) *n.* a small monkey of S. America [Fr. *marmouset*, a small grotesque figure (on fountains)].

mar·mot (már'·mat) *n.* a bushy-tailed rodent; the prairie dog [Fr. *marmot*, a mountain rat].

ma·roon (ma·roon') *n.* orig. a fugitive slave of the W. Indies; a marooned person; *v.t.* to put ashore on a desolate island; to isolate, cut off; *v.i.* to live as if marooned [Sp. (*ci*)*marron*, a runaway slave].

ma·roon (ma·roon') *a.* brownish-crimson; *n.* [Fr. *marron*, a chestnut].

marque (márk) *n.* seizure by way of retaliation. usually **letter of marque** [Fr. fr. Prov. *mar-car*, to seize as a pledge].

mar·quee (már·kē') *n.* a roof-like structure or awning outside a public building [orig. *mar-quees*, fr. Fr. *marquise*, the tent of a marquis].

mar·que·try (már'·ka·tri) *n.* decorative, inlaid wood; the process of inlaying wood with designs. Also **marqueterie** [Fr. *marqueter*, to variegate].

mar·quis (már'·kwis, ·kē) *n.* noble ranking next below a duke. Also **marquess** (*fem.* **marchioness**). **marquise** (már·kēz') *n.* in France, the wife of a marquis; pointed oval diamond [O.Fr. *marchis*, ruler of the marches].

mar·que·sette (már·kwi·zet', ·ki·zet') *n.* thin, lightweight fabric.

mar·riage See **marry**.

mar·row (mar'·ō) *n.* the soft substance in the cavities of bones; the essence of anything. **-bone** *n.* a bone containing marrow; *pl.* the knees [O.E. *meary*, marrow].

mar·ry (mar'·i·) *v.t.* to unite, take, or give in wedlock; *v.i.* to enter into matrimony. **marriage** (mar'·ij) *n.* the legal union of husband

and wife; the ceremony, civil or religious, by which two people of opposite sex become husband and wife. **-able** a. [L. *maritare*, to marry].

Mars (márz) n. the Roman god of war; the planet nearest to the earth. **Martian** n. an imaginary inhabitant of Mars [L.].

Mar·seil·laise (már·sǎ·yez′ or már·sǎ·lāz′) n. the French national anthem.

marsh (mársh) n. a tract of low, swampy land; a. pert. to swampy areas. **-fever** n. malaria. **-gas** n. a gaseous product of decomposing organic matter. **-mallow** n. a red flowered plant growing in marshes; a confection made from the root of this, or from gelatin. **-y** a. boggy; swampy [O.E. *merisc*, full of meres].

mar·shal (már′·shạl) n. a civil officer of a district with powers of a sheriff; a person in charge of arrangements for ceremonies, etc.; military rank in Fr. and Brit. armed forces. *v.t.* to dispose in order, as troops; (*Fig.*) to arrange, as ideas [O.Fr. *mareschal*, a horse servant].

mar·su·pi·al (már·sòò′·pi·ạl) a. having an external pouch, as of certain animals; n. a marsupial or pouched animal (opossum, kangaroo) [L. *marsupium*, a pouch].

mart (márt) n. a market [contr. of *market*].

mar·ten (már′·tạn) n. a kind of weasel, valued for its fur [O.Fr. *martre*].

mar·tial (már′·shạl) a. pert. to war or to the armed services; warlike; military. (*Cap.*) a. pertaining to Mars. **-ly** adv. — **law**, law enforced by military authorities and superseding civil law [L. *Mars*, the god of war].

mar·tin (már′·tin) n. a bird of the swallow family [fr. *Martin*].

mar·ti·net (már′·tạ·net) n. a strict disciplinarian [fr. Fr. officer, *Martinet*].

mar·tin·gale (már′·tin·gāl) n. a strap fastened to a horse's girth to keep its head down; (*Naut.*) a stay for a jib boom. Also **martingal**.

mar·ti·ni (már·tē′·ni·) n. a cocktail of vermouth, gin and bitters.

mar·tyr (már′·tẹr) n. one who suffers punishment or the sacrifice of his life for adherence to principles or beliefs; a constant sufferer; *v.t.* to put to death for refusal to abandon principles. **-dom** n. the suffering and sacrifice of a martyr. **-ology** n. a history of martyrs [L. Gk. *martus*, a witness].

mar·vel (már′·vạl) n. anything wonderful; *v.i.* to wonder exceedingly. **-ous** a. wonderful; astonishing. **-ously** adv. **-ousness** n. [O.Fr. *merveille*, a wonder].

Marx·ism (márk′·sizm) n. the doctrines of *Karl Marx*, which profoundly influenced Socialists and communists of Europe in later part of 19th cent. **Marxian, Marxist** a. **Marxist** n.

mar·zi·pan (már′·zạ·pan) n. a paste of ground almonds, sugar and egg white made into confections. Also **marchpane**.

mas·car·a (mas·ka′·rạ) n. a cosmetic preparation for eyelashes.

mas·cot (mas′·kǎt) n. a person or thing reputed to bring good luck.

mas·cu·line (mas′·kyạ·lin) a. male; strong; virile; (of a woman) mannish; (*Gram.*) of male gender. **-ness**, **masculinity** n. [L. *masculus*, male].

mash (mash) *v.t.* to beat to a pulp or soft mass; to mix malt with hot water; n. a thick mixture of malt and hot water for brewing; a mixture of bran meal, etc. given to horses and cattle; a pulpy mass [O.E. *masc*, mash].

mash (mash) *v.t.* (*Slang*) to pay court to; to flirt. **-er** n. a lady-killer.

mash·ie (mash′·i·) n. a golf club with short iron head [prob. corrupt. of Fr. *massue*, a club].

mask (mask) n. a covering for the face; an impression of a human face, as a *deathmask*; a respirator to be worn as protection against poison gas; a false face, as worn by children at Hallowe'en; a disguise; a masquerade; (*Fig.*) a pretext; *v.t.* to hide, as with a mask; *v.i.* to assume a disguise [Fr. *masque*].

mas·och·ism (mas′·ạ·kizm) n. a form of sex gratification by endurance of physical or mental pain. **masochist** n. [fr. *von Sascher-Masoch*, Austrian novelist].

ma·son (mā′·sn) n. a builder in stone, brick, etc.; a Freemason. **-ic** a. pert. to freemasonry. **-ry** n. the work of a mason; stonework; free-

masonry [Fr. *maçon*, a mason].

ma·son·ite (mā′·sạn·īt) n. a fiberboard made from pressed wood fibers used in building [fr. W. H. *Mason*, Amer. engineer].

mas·quer·ade (mas·kạ·rād′) n. an assembly of masked persons; disguise; *v.i.* to take part in a masquerade; to disguise [Fr. *mascarade*].

mass (mas) n. the quantity of matter in a body; a shapeless lump; magnitude; crowd; chief portion; *v.t.* to collect in a mass; *v.i.* to assemble in large numbers. **-ive** a. forming a mass; bulky; weighty. **-ively** adv. **-iveness** n. **— meeting** n. a large public meeting or demonstration. **— production** n. cheap production in great quantities. **the masses,** the common people [L. *massa*, a lump].

Mass (mas) n. the communion service in the R.C. Church; the music to accompany High Mass. **High Mass**, Mass celebrated with music. **Low Mass**, a simple celebration of Mass without music. Also **mass** [O.E. *maesse*, fr. L. *missa*, mass].

mas·sa·cre (mas′·ạ·kẹr) n. general, ruthless slaughter; carnage; *v.t.* to slaughter indiscriminately [O.Fr. *maçacre*, slaughter].

mas·sage (mạ·sàzh′) n. a treatment of physical disorders by kneading, rubbing, carried out by specialists; *v.t.* to treat by massage. **massagist, masseur** n. (*fem.* **masseuse**) a specialist in massage [Fr. fr. Gk. *massein*, to knead].

mas·sive See **mass**.

mast (mast) n. upright pole supporting rigging and sails of a ship; *v.t.* to furnish with mast or masts. **-ed** a. **-head** n. top portion of a ship's mast; newspaper or magazine trademark or business information [O.E. *maest*, the stem of a tree].

mast (mast) n. fruit of oak, beech, esp. as food for swine [O.E. *maest*, fodder].

mas·ter (mas′·tẹr) n. one who directs and controls; an employer of labor; male head of a household; a ship captain; a graduate degree in arts, or science (*abbrevs.* M.A., M.Sc.); courtesy title given the sons of a family, esp. by servants; an expert; a famous artist, esp. an *old master;* one who organizes and leads a fox hunt, as *master of foxhounds;* a. chief; dominant; skilled; *v.t.* to become the master of; to become expert at; to overcome. **-ful** a. compelling; domineering. **-fully** adv. **-fulness** n. **— key** n. a key which opens several locks. **-ly** a. highly competent; supremely proficient; adv. with the skill of an expert. **-mind** n. a first-class mind; chief controlling power behind a scheme. **— of ceremonies** n. one who presides over entertainment. **-piece** n. a brilliantly executed work. **-stroke** n. a masterly action. **— switch** n. an electric switch which must be turned on before other switches will function. **-y** n. supremacy; action of mastering; consummate skill; victory [L. *magister*, a master].

mas·ti·cate (mas′·tạ·kāt) *v.t.* to chew; to reduce to a pulp. **masticable** a. capable of being chewed. **mastication** n. the process of chewing. **masticator** n. crushing machine [L. *masticare*, to chew].

mas·tiff (mas′·tif) n. a powerful breed of dog [O.Fr. *mastin* confused with *mestif*, mongrel].

mas·ti·tis (mas·tī′·tis) n. (*Med.*) inflammation of the breast [Gk. *mastos*, the breast].

mas·to·don (mas′·tạ·dàn) n. an extinct mammal resembling an elephant. **mastodontic** a. [Gk. *mastos*, the breast; *odous*, the tooth].

mas·toid (mas′·toid) a. nipple-shaped; n. the prominence on the temporal bone behind the human ear. **-itis** n. inflammation of the mastoid area [Gk. *mastos*, the breast].

mas·tur·bate (mas′·tẹr·bāt) *v.i.* to practice self-excitation; auto-eroticism. **masturbation** n. **masturbator** n. [L. *masturbari*].

mat (mat) n. a coarse fabric of twin, rope, or rushes for wiping the shoes on; a rug; a heat-resisting covering of cork, plastic, etc., for protecting surface of a table; a border or frame for a picture; a tangled mass of hair; *v.t.* to lay or cover with mats; *v.i.* to become a tangled mass. *pr.p.* **-ting**. *pa.t.* and *pa.p.* **-ted** [L. *matta*, a mat].

mat, matte (mat) a. having a dull finish; not shiny [Fr. *mate*].

mat·a·dor, matadore (mat′·ạ·dawr) n. the man who kills the bull in a Sp. bullfight [Sp. fr. L. *mactare*, to kill].

match (mach) n. splint of wood or taper tipped with a substance capable of ignition by friction with a rough surface; a piece of rope for firing a gun; a fuse [Fr. *mèche*, a wick].

matches

match (mach) n. a person or thing equal to or resembling another; a sporting contest; a marriage; a mate; *v.i.* to correspond in quality, quantity, color, etc.; *v.t.* to compete with; to unite in marriage; to be the same as. **-less** a. having no match; peerless; unique. **-maker** n. one who schemes to bring about a marriage [O.E. *gemaecca*, a mate].

mate (māt) n. a companion; a spouse; one of a pair; an assistant; *v.t.* to match; to mar; *v.i.* to pair [O. Dut. *maet*, a companion].

mate (māt) *v.t.* to checkmate (chess); n. checkmate [abbrev. of *checkmate*].

ma·té, mate (má′·tā) n. an evergreen tree of Brazil and Paraguay, the leaves of which are dried and used as tea [Native *mati*, the vessel for infusing tea].

ma·te·ri·al (ma·ti′·ri·ạl) a. consisting of matter corporeal; (of persons) not spiritually minded; essential; appreciable; worthy of consideration; n. the substance out of which something is fashioned; fabric; the accumulated data out of which a writer creates a work of literary, historical, or scientific value; materials collective. **-ization** n. **ize** *v.t.* to render material; to give bodily form to; *v.i.* to become fact. **-ism** n. the theory that matter, and matter only, exists in the universe; an attitude which ignores spiritual values. **-istic, -al** a. **-ly** adv. appreciably [L. *materia*, matter].

ma·té·ri·el (ma·tir·i·el′) n. weapons, equipment, tools, supplies necessary [Fr. = material].

ma·te·ri·a med·i·ca (mạt·tir′·i·ạ med′·i·kạ) n. (*Med.*) the substances used in the making of medicines, drugs, etc.; the science relating to medicines and their curative properties [L.].

ma·ter·nal (mạ·tur′·nạl) a. pert. to a mother; motherly; related on the mother's side. **-ly** adv. **maternity** n. motherhood; childbirth [L. *mater*, a mother].

math·e·mat·ics (math·ạ·mat′·iks) n. the science of quantity and space, including arithmetic, algebra, trigonometry, geometry. **mathematical** a. pert. to mathematics; accurate. **mathematician** n. [Gk. *mathēma*, learning].

mat·in (mat′·in) n. a morning song; a morning service [Fr. *matin*, morning].

ma·tri·arch (mā′·tri·árk) n. a woman in a position analogous to that of a patriarch. **-al** a. **-alism** n. government exercised by a mother [L. *mater*, a mother; Gk. *archein*, to rule].

ma·tri·cide (mat′·rạ·sīd) n. the murder of a mother; one who kill his own mother [L. *mater*, a mother; *caedere*, to kill].

ma·tric·u·late (mạ·trik′·yạ·lāt) *v.t.* and *v.i.* to enroll as a student, esp. of a college; to enter, by matriculation. **matriculation** n. [L. *matricula*, a register].

mat·ri·mo·ny (mat′·rạ·mō·ni·) n. marriage; wedlock. **matrimonial** a. [L. *matrimonium*].

ma·trix (mā′·triks or mat′·riks) n. the womb; the cavity where anything is formed; a mold, esp. for casting printer's type; rock where minerals are embedded. *pl.* **matrices, -es** [L. *matrix*, the womb].

ma·tron (mā′·trạn) n. a married woman; a woman in charge of domestic affairs of an institution. **-like, -ly** adv. like a matron; mature; staid [L. *matrona*, a married lady].

matte See **mat.**

mat·ter (mat′·ẹr) n. that which occupies space and is the object of the senses; substance; cause of a difficulty; subject of a book, speech, sermon; occasion; (*Med.*) pus; *v.i.* to be of importance; to signify; (*Med.*) to discharge pus. **-of-fact** a. prosaic; unimaginative [L. *materia*, matter].

mat·ting (mat′·ing) n. mat work; coarse material used as floor covering [fr. *mat*].

mat·tock (mat′·ạk) n. a kind of pickaxe with only one end pointed, used for loosening soil [O.E. *mattuc*].

mat·tress (mat′·rạs) n. a casing of strong fabric filled with hair, foam rubber, cotton, etc. used on or as a bed [O.E. fr. Ar. *natrah*, a place where anything is thrown].

mat·u·rate (mach′·ạ·rāt) *v.i.* to mature. **maturation** n. [L. *maturus*, ripe].

ma·ture (ma·toor') *a.* ripe; fully developed; (*Med.*) come to suppuration; resulting from adult experience; due for payment, as a bill; *v.t.* to ripen; to perfect; *v.i.* to become ripe; to become due, as a bill. **maturable** *a.* **-ly** *adv.* **-ness, maturity** *n.* ripeness; the state or quality of being fully developed [L. *maturus*, ripe].

ma·tu·ti·nal (ma·too'·te·nal) *a.* morning; early. **-ly** *adv.* [L. *matutinus*, of the morning].

maud·lin (mawd'·lin) *a.* over-sentimental; tearful [contr. of O.Fr. *Maudeleine*, Mary Magdalen, painted as weeping].

maul (mawl) *n.* a heavy wooden hammer; *v.t.* to maltreat; to handle roughly. **-er** *n.* [L. *malleus*, a hammer].

Mau Mau (mou'·mou') *n.* a secret, terrorist society in Kenya.

maun·der (mawn'·der) *v.i.* to mutter; to talk or to wander aimlessly.

mau·so·le·um (maw·sa·lē'·am) *n.* a large imposing tomb. **mausolean** *a.* [orig. the tomb of *Mausolus*, King of Caria, 350 B.C.].

mauve (mōv, mawv) *n.* a delicate purple color; *a.* of this color [Fr. fr. L. *malva*, the mallow].

mav·er·ick (mav'·er·ik) *n.* an unbranded calf; an independent [fr. S. *Maverick*, Texas rancher].

maw (maw) *n.* the stomach of an animal; in birds, the craw [O.E. *maga*, maw].

mawk·ish (mawk'·ish) *a.* loathsome; sickly sweet; maudlin. **-ly** *adv.* [M.E. *mathek*, a maggot].

max·il·lar·y (mak'·sa·ler·i·) *a.* pert. to the upper jawbone or jaw; *n.* a jawbone. **maxilla** *n.* the upper jaw; *pl.* **maxillae** [L. *maxilla*, a jawbone].

max·im (mak'·sim) *n.* an accepted principle; an axiom; a proverb or precept [L. *maximus*].

max·i·mum (mak'·sa·mam) *a.* greatest; *n.* the greatest number, quantity or degree; the highest point; peak; opp. *minimum.* **maximal** *a.* of the greatest value [L. superl. of *magnus*, great].

may (mā) *v.i.* expressing possibility, permission, contingency; uncertainty; hope. *pa.t.* **might** (mit). **maybe, (mayhap,** *Arch.*) *adv.* perhaps; possibly [O.E. *maeg*, may].

May (mā) *n.* the fifth month of the year; (*Fig.*) youthful prime. **-day** *n.* the first day of May. (*l.c.*)**-flower** *n.* trailing arbutus; any flower blooming in May. **-flower** *n.* the ship in which the Pilgrims sailed to Plymouth, Mass. in 1620. **-fly** *n.* an ephemeral insect; an artificial fly for fishing. **-pole** *n.* a pole with streamers, around which people danced on May Day [L. *Maius*, the month of May].

may·hem (mā'·hem) *n.* (*Law*) the offense of maiming by violence [O.Fr. *mahaigne*, injury].

may·on·naise (mā·a·nāz') *n.* a sauce or dressing for salads [Fr.].

may·or (mā'·er) *n.* the chief official of a city or town. **-al** *a.* **-alty, -ship** *n.* the office of mayor [Fr. *.naire*, mayor].

maze (māz) *n.* a network of intricate paths; a labyrinth; confused condition; mental perplexity [M.E. *masen*, to confuse].

ma·zur·ka, ma·zour·ka (ma·zur'·ka) *n.* a Polish dance; the music for this [Pol.].

me (mē) *pron.* the objective case of first pers. pronoun, 'I'.

mead (mēd) *n.* a fermented drink made of honey, yeast and water [O.E. *meodu*].

mead·ow (med'·ō) *n.* a low, level tract of grassland; pasture. **— lark** *n.* a yellow-breasted Amer. songbird. **-y** *a.* [O.E. *mawan*, to mow].

mea·ger (mē'·ger) *a.* scanty; having little flesh; gaunt. **-ly** *adv.* **-ness** *n.* [Fr. *maigre*, thin].

meal (mēl) *n.* the food served at one time; a repast [O.E. *mael*, time].

meal (mēl) *n.* edible grain coarsely ground. **-iness** *n.* **— worm** *n.* an insect found in meal. **-y** *a.* like meal; powdery; spotty. **-y-mouthed** *a.* apt to mince words; not blunt [O.E. *melo*, meal].

mean (mēn) *a.* humble in rank or birth; sordid; lacking dignity; stingy; malicious; (*Colloq.*) disagreeable; selfish; (*Slang*) skillful. **-ly** *adv.* **-ness** *n.* [O.E. *gemaene*, common].

mean (mēn) *a.* in a middle position; average; *n.* the middlepoint of quantity, rate, position, or degree; *pl.* resources; wealth; agency. **-time,** the interval between two given times. **-time, -while** *adv.* in the intervening time [L. *medius*, the middle].

mean (mēn) *v.t.* to have in view; to intend; to signify; *v.i.* to form in the mind; to be disposed. *pa.t.* and *pa.p.* **meant** (ment). **-ing** *n.* that which is meant; sense; signification; *a.* expressive. **-ingful** *a.* **-ingless** *a.* [O.E. *maenan*, to signify].

me·an·der (mē·an'·der) *v.i.* to flow with a winding course; to saunter aimlessly; *n.* a circuitous stroll; the winding course of a river (usu. *pl.*). **-ing** *a.* winding. **meandrous** *a.* [Gk. *Maiandros*, a winding river of Asia Minor].

mea·sles (mē'·zalz) *n.* (*Med.*) a highly contagious disease, characterized by rash of bright red spots; a disease affecting cattle and pigs caused by tapeworms. **measly** *a.* having measles; (*Fig.*) worthless; skimpy. **German measles,** a disease resembling measles but less severe [Dut. *mazelen*, measles].

meas·ure (mezh'·er) *n.* dimension reckoned by some standard; an instrument for measuring; a vessel of predetermined capacity; a course of action; an act of legislation; means to an end; (*Mus.*) tempo; the notes between two bars in staff notation; *pl.* (*Geol.*) layers of rock; strata; *v.t.* to ascertain the quantity or dimensions of; to assess; to distribute by measure; *v.i.* to have an ascertained value or extent; to compare favorably with. **measurable** *a.* capable of being measured. **measurably** *adv.* **-d** *a.* of specified measure; uniform; calculated. **-less** *a.* boundless; infinite. **-ment** *n.* dimension, quantity, etc., ascertained by measuring with fixed unit. **-r** *n.* [L. *mensura*, a measure].

meat (mēt) *n.* flesh used as food; food of any kind. **-iness** *n.* **-y** *a.* full of meat; (*Fig.*) pithy; compact with ideas [O.E. *mete*, food].

Mec·ca (mek'·a) *n.* the reputed birthplace of Mohammed; a holy city; (*l.c.*) the focal point for people drawn by common interest.

me·chan·i·cal (ma·kan'·i·kal) *a.* pert. to machines, mechanism, or mechanics; produced or operated by machinery; automatic. **mechanic** *n.* one who works with or repairs machines or instruments. **-ly** *adv.* **mechanician** *n.* a machine-maker or repairer. **mechanics** *n.* that branch of applied mathematics which deals with force and motion; the science of machines. **mechanization** *n.* the change to mechanical power. **mechanize** *v.t.* to make mechanical; to equip with machines. **mechanized** *a.* **mechanism** *n.* the structure of a machine; machinery; a piece of machinery; (*Fig.*) technique; the philosophical doctrine that all phenomena of life admit of physio-chemical proof. **mechanist** *n.* **mechanistic** *a.* [Gk. *mēchanē*, a contrivance].

Mech·lin (mek'·lin) *n.* and *a.* a kind of lace, made in *Mechlin* (Malines) in Belgium.

med·al (med'·l) *n.* a piece of metal, struck like a coin, as a memento or reward; *v.t.* to decorate with a medal. **-ic** (ma·dal'·ik) *a.* pert. to medals. **medallion** *n.* a large medal; a metal disk, usually round, with portrait in bas-relief. **-ist** *n.* a maker of medals; one who has been awarded a medal [Fr. *médaille*, a metal disc].

med·dle (med'·l) *v.i.* to interfere officiously; to tamper with. **-r** *n.* **-some** *a.* interfering [L. *miscere*, to mix].

me·di·a See **medium.**

me·di·al (mē'·di·al) *a.* in, or through, the middle; pert. to a mean or average. **median** *a.* situated in the middle; *n.* (*Geom.*) a line drawn from vertex of a triangle to the middle point of the opposite side [L. *medius*, the middle].

me·di·ate (mē'·di·at) *a.* being between two extremes; intervening; depending on an intermediary; not direct; (mē'·di·āte) *v.i.* to interpose between contending parties to effect a reconciliation; *v.t.* to settle by mediation. **mediacy** *n.* **-ly** *adv.* **mediation** *n.* the act of mediating; the steps taken to effect a reconciliation. **mediatize** *v.t.* to annex a small state, still leaving the ruler his title. **mediator** *n.* [L. *medius*, the middle].

med·ic (med'·ik) *n.* a leguminous plant with leaves like clover, used as fodder; (*Colloq.*) a doctor [Gk. *mēdikē* (*poa*), 'Median' grass].

med·i·cal (med'·i·kal) *a.* pert. to medicine or the art of healing; medicinal. **medicable** *a.* capable of being cured. **-ly** *adv.* **medicament** *n.* any healing remedy. **medicate** *v.t.* to treat with medicine. **medicated** *a.* **medication** *n.* **medicative** *a.* [L. *medicus*, a physician].

med·i·cine (med'·i·sn) *n.* any substance used in the treatment of disease; the science of healing and prevention of disease; magic (as practiced in primitive tribes); (*Fig.*) salutary lesson; *v.t.* to administer medicine to. **medicinal** *a.* pert. to medicine; remedial. **medicinally** *adv.* **— man,** a magician with supposed powers of healing; a witch doctor. **medico** *n.* (*Colloq.*) a doctor or medical student [L. *medicus*, a physician].

me·di·e·val, mediaeval (med·i·ē'·val) *a.* pert. to or characteristic of the Middle Ages. **medi(a)evalist** *n.* one who makes a special study of the Middle Ages [L. *medius*, middle; *aevum*, an age].

me·di·o·cre (mē'·di·ō·ker) *a.* middling; neither good nor bad; second-rate. **mediocrity** *n.* [L. *mediocris*].

med·i·tate (med'·a·tāt) *v.t.* to consider thoughtfully; to intend; *v.i.* to ponder, esp. on religious matters. **-d** *a.* planned. **meditation** *n.* the act of meditating; deep thought. **meditative** *a.* given to reflection. **meditatively** *adv.* [L. *meditari*, to consider].

med·i·ter·ran·e·an (med·a·ter·rā'·ni·an) *a.* (of water) encircled by land. **Mediterranean** *a.* pert. to the almost landlocked water between S. Europe and N. Africa, so called because it was regarded as being in the *middle* of the Old World. **Mediterranean climate,** a climate of warm wet winters, hot dry summers [L. *medius*, the middle; *terra*, the earth].

me·di·um (mē'·di·am) *n.* that which is in the middle; a means; an agency; in spiritualism, an intermediary professing to give messages from the dead; in bacteriology, a substance used for cultivation of bacteria. *pl.* **-s** or **media.** *a.* middle; average; middling [L. *medius*, the middle].

med·ley (med'·li·) *n.* a miscellaneous collection of things; a miscellany [O.Fr. *medler*, to mix].

me·dul·la (ma·dul'·a) *n.* marrow in a bone; inner tissue of a gland; pith of hair or plants. *pl.* **-e.** *a.* comprising or resembling marrow, covered with medullary substance, etc. **medullate(d)** *a.* **medullose** *a.* like pith [L. *medulla*, marrow].

me·du·sa (me·dōō'·sa) *n.* a kind of jellyfish, with tentacles [Gk. *Medousa*].

meed (mēd) *n.* reward; recompense [O.E. *med*].

meek (mēk) *a.* submissive; humble; mild. **-ly** *adv.* **-ness** *n.* [O.E. *meoc*, meek].

meer·schaum (mir'·sham, ·shawm) *n.* a fine, white clay used for the bowl of tobacco pipes; a pipe of this [Ger. *Meer*, the sea; *Schaum*, foam].

meet (mēt) *a.* fit; suitable. **-ly** *adv.* **-ness** *n.* [O.E. (*ge*)*maele*, suitable].

meet (mēt) *v.t.* to encounter; to join; to find; to satisfy; to pay, as a debt; to await arrival, as of a train; *v.i.* to converge at a specified point; to combine; to assemble in company. *pa.t.* and *pa.p.* **met.** *n.* an assembly of people, as at a fox-hunt. **-ing** *n.* a coming together, as of roads, rivers; encounter; people gathered together for worship, entertainment, discussion, sport, etc. [O.E. *metan*, to meet].

me·ga- Gr. *prefix* meaning great, mighty.

meg·a·cycle (meg'·a·si·kl) *n.* (*Elect.*) one million cycles [Gk. *megas*, great; *kuklos*, a circle].

meg·a·lith (meg'·a·lith) *n.* a huge stone. **-ic** *a.* pert. to huge ancient stone monuments or circles [Gk. *megas*, great; *lithos*, a stone].

meg·a·lo·ma·ni·a (meg·a·lạ·mā'·ni·ạ) *n.* a form of insanity in which the patient has grandiose ideas of his own importance; lust for power. **-c** *n.* [Gk. *megas*, great; *mania*, madness].

meg·a·phone (meg'·a·fōn) *n.* a large funnel-shaped device to increase the volume of sounds [Gk. *megas*, great; *phōnē*, a sound].

meg·a·ton (meg'·a·tán) *n.* a unit for measuring the power of thermonuclear weapons.

meg·ohm (meg'·ōm) *n.* one million ohms [Gk. *megas*, great; and *ohm*].

me·grim (mē'·grim) *n.* a severe headache usu. on one side; *pl.* depression [Gk. *hemi-*, half; *kranion*, the skull].

mei·o·sis (mi·ō'·sis) *n.* (*Rhet.*) a figure of speech which makes a deliberate understatement to achieve emphasis; a form of litotes [Gk. *meiosis*, lessening].

mel·an·chol·y (mel'·an·kál·i·) *n.* depression of spirits; morbidity; *a.* gloomy; depressed; pensive. **melancholia** *n.* morbid state of depression; abnormal introspectiveness bordering on insanity [Gk. *melas*, black; *cholē*, bile].

Mel·a·ne·sian (mel·a·nē'·shan) *a.* pert to *Melanesia,* a S. Pacific dark-skinned island group; *n.* a native; the language of Melanesia [Gk. *melas*, black; *nēsos*, island].

mé·lange (mā·lánzh') *n.* a mixture; a medley [Fr. *mêler*, to mix].

mel·a·nin (mel'·a·nin) *n.* a black pigment found in the eye, hair and skin. **melanic** *a.* black. **melanism** *n.* an excess of coloring matter in the skin [Gk. *melas*, black].

Mel·ba toast (mel'·ba tōst') *n.* thin slice of toast.

meld (meld) *v.t.* and *i.* to blend; merge; a combination of cards melded [fr. *melt, weld*].

mê·lée (mā'·lā) *n.* a confused, hand-to-hand

fight [Fr. *mêler*, to mix].

mel·io·rate (mēl′·yạ·rāt) *v.t.* to improve; *v.i.* to become better. **melioration** *n.* **meliorator** *n.* **meliorism** *n.* the doctrine that the world is capable of improvement [L. *melior*, better].

mel·lif·er·ous (ma·lif′·ẹr·ạs) *a.* producing honey. **mellifluence** *n.* a flowing sweetly or smoothly. **mellifluent, mellifluous** *a.* **mellifluently, mellifluously** *adv.* [L. *mel*, honey; *ferre*, to bear].

mel·low (mel′·ō) *a.* soft and ripe; well-matured; genial; jovial; resonant, as a voice; (*Slang*) somewhat intoxicated; *v.t.* to soften; to ripen; *v.i.* to become soft or ripe; to become maturely wise. **-ly** *adv.* **-ness** *n.* [O.E. *meary*, soft].

me·lo·de·on (mạ′·lō·di·ạn) *n.* a small hand keyboard organ; a kind of accordion [Gk.].

mel·od·ic See **melody**.

mel·o·dra·ma (mel·ạ·drám′·a) *n.* a dramatic entertainment, sensational and emotional; a play of romantic sentiment and situation. **-tic** *a.* [Gk. *melos*, a song; *drama*, a play].

mel·o·dy (mel′·ạ·di·) *n.* a rhythmical succession of single sounds forming an agreeable musical air; a tune. **melodic** *a.* pert. to melody; melodious. **melodious** *a.* tuneful; pleasing to the ear. **melodiously** *adv.* **melodiousness** *n.* **melodist** *n.* a musical composer or singer [Gk. *melōdia*, a song].

mel·on (mel′·ạn) *n.* a kind of gourd with a sweet, juicy pulp, and a center full of seeds [Gk. *mēlon*, an apple].

melt (melt) *v.t.* to reduce to a liquid state; to dissolve; to soften; to make tender; *v.i.* to become liquid or molten; to blend; to vanish; to become tender. **-ing** *n.* making liquid; *a.* softening; languishing, as looks; tender. **-ingly** *adv.* [O.E. *meltan*, to melt].

mem·ber (mem′·bẹr) *n.* a limb, esp. of an animal body; a constituent part of a complex whole; one of a society, group, etc. **-ed** *a.* having limbs. **-ship** *n.* the state of being a member, or one of a group; members collectively [L. *membrum*, a limb].

mem·brane (mem′·brān) *n.* (*Anat.*) a thin, flexible tissue forming or lining an organ of the body; a sheet of parchment. **membranous** *a.* [L. *membrana*, parchment].

me·men·to (mi·men′·tō) *n.* anything which serves as a reminder of a person or event; a souvenir [L. *meminisse*, to remember].

mem·o (mem′·ō) *n.* (*Colloq.*) memorandum.

mem·oir (mem′·wăr) *n.* a short, biographical sketch; a scientific record of personal investigations on a subject; *pl.* reminiscences. **-ist** *n.* [L. *memoria*, memory].

mem·o·ry (mem′·ạ·ri·) *n.* the faculty of retaining and recalling knowledge; recollection; remembrance. **memorabilia** *n.pl.* things worthy of note. **memorable** *a.* noteworthy; remarkable. **memorably** *adv.* **memorandum** *n.* a note or reminder; (*Law*) a summary of a transaction; in diplomacy, an outline of the state of a question. *pl.* **-s** or **memoranda**. **memorial** *a.* serving as a reminder; contained in the memory; *n.* anything intended to commemorate a person or an event; a written statement of facts in the form of a petition presented to a governing body. **memorialize** *v.t.* to commemorate; to present a memorial. **memorize** *v.t.* to commit to memory. **memorization** *n.* [L. *memoria*, memory].

men (men) *n.pl.* of **man**.

men·ace (men′·as) *n.* a threat or threatening; potential danger; *v.t.* to threaten. **menacing** *a.* **menacingly** *adv.* [L. *minari*, to threaten].

mé·nage (mạ·nǎzh′) *n.* a household; housekeeping [Fr. L. *mansio*, a dwelling].

me·nag·er·ie (mạ·naj′·ẹr·i·) *n.* a collection of caged wild animals for exhibition [Fr. *ménage*, a household].

mend (mend) *v.t.* to repair; to set right; to improve. *v.i.* to improve; to a mended place; improvement. **-er** *n.* **-ing** *n.* the act of repairing [fr. *amend*].

men·da·cious (men·dā′·shạs) *a.* given to telling lies; untruthful. **-ly** *adv.* **mendacity** *n.* prevarication; a tendency to lying [L. *mendax*].

men·di·cant (men′·di·kạnt) *a.* begging; living as a beggar; *n.* a beggar. **mendicancy, mendicity** *n.* the practice of living by alms [L. *mendicare*, to beg].

me·ni·al (mē′·ni·ạl) *a.* pert. to domestic service; servile; *n.* a servant; a servile person. **-ly** *adv.* [O.Fr. *mesnee*, a household].

me·nin·ges (mạ·nin′·jēz) *n.pl.* the three membranes enveloping the brain and spinal cord.

sing. **meninx, meningitis** (·ji′·tis) *n.* (*Med.*) inflammation of these membranes [Gk. *mēninx*, a membrane].

me·nis·cus (mạ·nis′·kạs) *n.* a lens convex on one side and concave on the other; the curved surface of a liquid in a vessel; (*Math.*) a crescent. **meniscal, meniscate** *a.* **menisciform** *a.* crescent-shaped [Gk. *mēniskos*, a crescent].

Men·non·ite (men′·ạn·īt) *n.* a member of or pert. to a Prot. sect favoring plain dress and plain living [fr. *Menno* Simons, leader].

men·o·pause (men′·ạ·pawz) *n.* female change of life [Gk. *mēn*, a month; *pausis*, cessation].

men·sal (men′·sạl) *a.* monthly [L. *mensis*].

men·ses (men′·sēz) *n.pl.* the monthly discharge from the uterus of the female. **menstrual** *a.* monthly; pert. to the menses. **menstruate** *v.i.* to discharge the menses. **menstruation** *n.* **menstruous** *a.* [*pl.* of L. *mensis*, a month].

men·stru·um (men′·stroo·ạm) *n.* a solvent [L. *menstrua*, the menses].

men·sur·a·ble (men′·sher·a·bl) *a.* capable of being measured. **mensurability** *n.* **mensural** *a.* pert. to measure. **mensuration** *n.* the act, process, or art of measuring; (*Math.*) the determination of length, area, and volume. **mensurative** [L. *mensura*, measure].

men·tal (men′·tạl) *a.* pert. to, or of, the mind; performed in the mind; (*Colloq.*) mentally ill. **-ity** (men·tal′·ạ·ti·) *n.* intellectual power; mental attitude. **-ly** *adv.* — **deficiency** subnormal intelligence [L. *mens*, the mind].

men·thol (men′·thawl) *n.* a camphor obtained from oil of peppermint. **-ated** *a.* treated or flavored with menthol [L. *mentha*, mint].

men·tion (men′·shạn) *n.* a brief notice; a casual comment; *v.t.* to notice; to name. **-able** *a.* fit to be remarked on [L. *mentio*].

men·tor (men′·tẹr) *n.* an experienced and prudent adviser. **-ial** *a.* [Gk. *Mentōr*, the adviser of Telemachus].

men·u (men′·ū) *n.* a bill of fare; the food served [Fr. *menu*, a list].

Meph·i·stoph·e·les (mef·is·tǎf′·ạ·lēz) *n.* (*Myth.*) the devil. **Mephistophelean** *a.* sinister.

me·phi·tis (me·fī′·tis) *n.* noxious exhalation, esp. from the ground or from decaying matter. **mephitic** *a.* [L.].

mer·can·tile (mur′·kạn·til, ·til) *a.* pert. to commerce. **mercantilism** *n.* the mercantile system. **mercantilist** *n.* — **system**, the economic theory that money alone is wealth and that a nation's exports should far exceed its imports [L. *mercari*, to traffic].

mer·ce·nar·y (mur′·se·ner·i·) *a.* working merely for money or gain; hired; greedy.*n.* a hired soldier. **mercenarily** *adv.* **mercenariness** *n.* [L. *merces*, wages].

mer·cer·ize (mur′·sạ·rīz) *v.t.* to treat cotton fabrics with caustic lye to impart a silky finish. **-d** *a.* [fr. J. *Mercer*, inventor of the process].

mer·chant (mur′·chant) *n.* one who engages in trade; a storekeeper. *a.* pert. to trade or merchandise. **merchandise** *n.* commodities bought and sold. **-man** *n.* a ship carrying goods. — **marine**, the ships and men engaged in commerce [L. *mercari*, to traffic].

Mer·cu·ry (mur′·kyạ·ri·) *n.* the planet of the solar system nearest to the sun. (**m**) *n.* a metallic chemical element, silvery white in color, with very low melting point (also called *quicksilver*), used in barometers, thermometers, etc. **mercurial** *a.* pert to, or consisting of, mercury; sprightly; agile; erratic. **mercurialize** *v.t.* to make mercurial; to treat with mercury. **mercurous, mercuric** *a.* (*Chem.*) pert. to compounds of mercury [L. *Mercurius*, prob. fr. *merx*, goods; also Gk. *Myth*].

mercury

mer·cy (mur′·si·) *n.* forbearance; clemency; leniency shown to a guilty person; compassion. **merciful** *a.* full of mercy; compassionate. **mercifully** *adv.* **mercifulness** *n.* **merciless** *a.* void of pity; callous; cruel. **mercilessly** *adv.* **mercilessness** *n.* [L. *merces*, reward].

mere (mēr) *n.* (*Poetic*) a pool or lake [O.E. *mere*, a stretch of water].

mere (mēr) *a.* nothing but; simple. **-ly** *adv.* simply; solely [L. *merus*, undiluted].

mer·e·tri·cious (mer·ạ·trish′·ạs) *a.* tawdry; cheap (as of style). **-ly** *adv.* **-ness** *n.* [L. *meretrix*, a harlot].

mer·gan·ser (mẹr·gan′·sẹr) *n.* a diving fish-eating bird [L. *mergus*, a diving bird; *anser*, a goose].

merge (murj) *v.t.* to cause to be swallowed up; to plunge or sink; *v.i.* to lose identity by being absorbed in something else; to be swallowed up or lost. **-r** *n.* a combine of commercial or industrial firms [L. *mergere*, to dip].

me·rid·i·an (mạ·rid′·i·ạn) *n.* an imaginary line passing through the poles at right angles to the equator; (*Astron.*) a circle passing through the poles of the heavens and the zenith of the observer; the highest attitude of sun or star; midday; *a.* pert. to midday; supreme.

meridional *a.* pert. to the meridian; southerly. **meridionally** *n.* [L. *meridianus*, pert. to noon].

me·ringue (mạ·rang′) *n.* a mixture of sugar and white of egg whipped till stiff, and baked in a cool oven; a small cake or pie topping of this [Fr.].

me·ri·no (mạ·rē′·nō) *n.* a breed of sheep with very fine, thick fleece, orig. from Spain; a dress fabric of this wool; *a.* pert. to the merino [Sp. *merino*, an inspector of sheepwalks].

mer·it (mer′·it) *n.* quality of deserving reward; excellence; worth; *pl.* the rights and wrongs, as of a law case; *v.t.* to earn; to deserve. **-orious** *a.* deserving reward. **-oriously** *adv.* [L. *meritum*, desert].

mer·lin (mur′·lin) *n.* a species of falcon [O.Fr. *esmerillon*, a falcon].

mer·lon (mur′·lạn) *n.* solid part of a parapet between two openings [Fr. fr. L. *murus*, a wall].

mer·maid (mur′·mād) *n.* an imaginary sea-creature with the upper body and head of a woman, and the tail of a fish. **merman** *n.* the male equivalent [O.E. *mere*, a lake; and *maid*].

mer·ry (mer′·i·) *a.* gay; hilarious; lively. **merrily** *adv.* **merriment, merriness** *n.* gaiety with noise and laughter; hilarity. **-go-round** *n.* a revolving platform with horses, cars, etc. **-making** *n.* festivity [O.E. *myrge*, pleasant].

mer·thi·o·late (mẹr·thī′·ạ·lāt) *n.* an antiseptic and germicide [fr. *mercuri-thiosalicylate*].

me·sa (mā′·sạ) *n.* a high plateau [Sp. = table].

mes·dames (mā·dạm′) *n.pl.* of madam, Mrs. [Fr.].

mes·en·te·ry (mes′·ạn·ter·i·) *n.* a fold of abdominal tissue keeping the intestines in place. **mesenteric** *a.* [Gk. *mesos*, middle; *enteron*, intestine].

mesh (mesh) *n.* the space between the threads of a net; network; *v.t.* to net; to ensnare; *v.i.* to become interlocked, as gears of a machine [O.E. *max*, net].

mes·mer·ism (mez′·mẹr·izm) *n.* exercising an influence over will and actions of another; hypnotism. **mesmeric, -al** *a.* of or pert. to mesmerism. **mesmerization** *n.* **mesmerize** *v.t.* to hypnotize. **mesmerizer, mesmerist** *n.* [fr. F. A. *Mesmer*, a Ger. physician].

mesne (mēn) *a.* middle; (*Law*) intermediate [O.Fr. *mesne*, middle].

mes·o·lith·ic (mez·ạ·lith′·ic) *a.* of period between paleolithic and neolithic ages [Gk. *mesos*, middle; *lithos*, a stone].

me·son (mez′·ạn) *n.* a particle equal in charge to, but having greater mass than, an electron or positron, and less mass than a neutron or proton [Gk. *meson*, neut. of *mesos*, middle].

Mes·o·po·ta·mi·a (mes·ạ·pạ·tā′·mi·ạ) *n.* the land between Euphrates and Tigris; now Iraq [Gk. *mesos*, middle; *potamos*, a river].

Mes·o·zo·ic (mes·ạ·zō′·ik) *a.* pert. to the second geological period [Gk. *mesos*, middle; *zōē*, life].

mess (mes) *n.* unpleasant mixture; disorder; a muddle; *v.t.* to dirty; to muddle. **-y** *a.* dirty; untidy; chaotic [form of *mash*].

mess (mes) *n.* a dish of food served at one time; the meal; a number of people who eat together, esp. in army, navy, etc.; *v.t.* to supply meals to; *v.i.* to eat in company. **-kit** *n.* a soldier's portable eating equipment [O.Fr. *mes*, a dish].

mes·sage (mes′·ij) *n.* a communication, verbal or written, sent by one person to another; an inspired utterance. **messenger** *n.* one who delivers a communication; one employed to deliver goods [L. *mittere*, to send].

mes·si·ah (mạ·sī′·ạ) *n.* an expected savior or liberator. **messianic** *a.* [Heb. *mashiah*, anointed].

mes·suage (mes′·wij) *n.* (*Law*) a dwelling-house with lands and outbuildings [O.Fr. *mesuage*, a holding of land].

mes·ti·zo (mes·tē′·zō) *n.* a half-caste, esp. the offspring of a Spaniard and an Amer. Indian [Sp. fr. L. *miscere*, to mix].

met (met) *pa.t.* and *pa.p.* of the verb **meet**.

me·ta·bo·lism (mạ·tab′·ạl·izm) *n.* the name given to the chemical changes continually going on in the cells of living matter. **metabolic** *a.* **metabolize** *v.t.* [Gk. *metabolē*, change].

me·ta·car·pus (met·ạ·kär′·pạs) *n.* the hand between the wrist and fingers; the bones of this part. **metacarpal** *a.* [Gk. *meta*, after; *karpos*, the wrist].

met·age (mĕt′·ij) n. official weighing, as of coal; the price paid for this [fr. *mete*].

met·al (met′·ąl) n. a mineral substance, opaque, fusible and malleable, capable of conducting heat and electricity; molten glass; (*Fig.*) courage; mettle; v.t. to furnish or cover with metal. **-lic** (mą·tal′·ik) a. pert. to, like, or consisting of, metal. **-lically** adv. **-ize** v.t. to make metallic. **-loid** n. an element with both metallic and non-metallic properties, as arsenic; a. pert. to a metal. **base metals**, copper, lead, zinc, tin as distinct from precious metals, gold and silver [Gk. *metallon*, a mine].

met·al·lur·gy (met′·al·ur·ji·) n. the art of working metals or of obtaining metals from ores. **metallurgic** a. **metallurgist** n. [Gk. *metallon*, a metal; *ergon*, a work].

met·a·mor·pho·sis (met·ą·mawr′·fą·sis) n. a change of form or structure; evolution; pl. **metamorphoses. metamorphic** a. subject to change of form. **metamorphism** n. the state of being metamorphic. **metamorphose** v.t. to transform in form or nature [Gk. *meta*, over; *morphē*, shape].

met·a·phor (met′·ą·fawr, fẹr) n. a figure of speech which makes an *implied* comparison between things which are not *literally* alike. **-ically** adv. **-ist** n. **mixed metaphor**, a combination of metaphors drawn from different sources [Gk. *metapherein*, to transfer].

met·a·phrase (met′·ą·frāz) n. literal, word for word translation from foreign language (opp. of *paraphrase*); v.t. to translate literally. **metaphrast** n. one who makes a literal translation. **metaphrastic** a. literal [Gk. *meta*, over; *phrasis*, a saying].

met·a·phys·ics (met·ą·fiz′·iks) n. the science which investigates first causes of all existence and knowledge; speculative philosophy. **metaphysical** a. **metaphysically** adv. **metaphysician** n. [Gk. *meta*, after; *phusis*, nature].

me·tas·ta·sis (mą·tas′·tą·sis) n. change of position, state, or form; shift of malignant cells from one part of the body to another. pl. **metastases. metasticize** v.i. [Gk. removal].

met·a·tar·sus (met·ą·tár′·sąs) n. the front part of the foot excluding the toes. **metatarsal** a. [Gk. *meta*, beyond; *tarsos*, the flat of the foot].

me·tath·e·sis (mą·tath′·ą·sis) n. the transposition of a letter or letters in a word, as in *curl*, orig. *crul*. **metathetic** a. [Gk. *meta*, over; *thesis*, a placing].

met·a·zo·a (met·ą·zō′·ą) n.pl. multi-cellular organisms. **metazoan** n. sing. and a. **metazoic** a. [Gk. *meta*, after; *zōon*, an animal].

mete (mēt) v.t. to distribute by measure; to allot, as punishment [O.E. *metan*, to measure].

me·te·or (mē′·ti·ẹr) n. any rapidly passing, luminous body seen in the atmosphere; a shooting star. **-ic** a. pert. to a meteor; influenced by atmospheric conditions; swift; dazzling. **-ite** n. a mass of stone or metal from outer space which lands on earth. **-ograph** n. an instrument for automatically recording weather conditions. **-ography** n. **-oid** n. a body in space which becomes a meteor on passing through the atmosphere of the earth. **-ological** a. **-ologist** n. **-ology** n. the science which treats of atmospheric phenomena, esp. in relation to weather forecasts [Gk. *meteōros*, lofty].

me·ter (mē′·tẹr) n. a unit of length in the metric system, 39.37 U.S. inches. **metric** a. **metric system,** a decimal system based on the French meter. **metrology** n. the science of weights and measures [Gk. *metron*, a measure].

me·ter (mē′·tẹr) n. an instrument for recording the consumption of gas, electricity, water, etc. [Gk. *metron*, a measure].

me·ter (mē′·tr) n. in poetry, the rhythmical arrangement of syllables, these groups being termed *feet*; verse; stanza-form; (*Music*) rhythmical structure indicated by measures; time or beat. **metrical** a. pert. to meter or measurement. **metrically** adv. **metronome** n. (*Mus.*) an instrument like an inverted pendulum for beating out time in music [Gk. *metron*].

metronome

meth·ane (meth′·ān) n. an inflammable, hydrocarbon gas. **methanol** n. methyl or wood alcohol [fr. *methyl*].

meth·od (meth′·ąd) n. manner of proceeding esp. in scientific research; orderliness; system; technique. **-ic, -ical** a. arranged systematically; orderly. **-ically** adv. **-ology** n. [Gk. *meta*, after; *hodos*, a way].

Meth·o·dist (meth′·ą·dist) n. a member of Protestant sect founded in 18th cent. by Charles and John Wesley [fr. *method*].

meth·yl (meth′·ąl) n. the chemical basis of wood [Gk. *methu*, wine; *hulē*, wood].

me·tic·u·lous (mą·tik′·yą·ląs) a. orig. afraid to make a mistake; over-scrupulous as to detail; over-exact. **-ly** adv. **-ness** n. [L. *metus*, fear].

mé·tier (māt′·yā) n. one's profession or vocation; the occupation for which one is best suited [Fr.].

me·ton·y·my (me·tàn′·ą·mi·) n. (*Rhet.*) a figure of speech in which the name of one thing is put for another associated with it. **metonym** n. **metonymic, -al** a. **metonymically** adv. [Gk. *meta*, expressing change; *onoma*, a name].

me·tro·nym·ic (mē·trą·nim′·ik) a. a name derived from a female ancestor.

me·trop·o·lis (mą·tráp′·ą·lis) n. the chief city of an area; a large city; a diocese. **metropolitan** a. pert. to a metropolis; pert. to the see of a metropolitan bishop; n. one who lives in a metropolis or has the manners, etc. of one who does [Gk. *mētēr*, a mother; *polis*, a city].

met·tle (met′·l) n. spirit; courage. **-some** a. **to be on one's mettle,** to be roused to do one's best [fr. *metal*].

mew (mū) n. a seagull [O.E. *maew*, a gull].

mew (mū) v.t. to shed or cast; to confine, as in a cage; v.i. to molt; n. a cage for hawks; a den. n.pl. stables around a court or alley [O.Fr. *muer*, to change; *mew*, a cage].

mewl (mūl) v.i. to whimper or whine [fr. *mew*].

Mex·i·can (mek′·są·kąn) n. a native or inhabitant of Mexico; a.

mez·za·nine (mez′·ą·nēn) n. (*Archit.*) a low story between two main ones; in a theater usu. the first few rows in the balcony [It. *mezzo*, middle].

mez·zo (met′·sō) a. middle; moderately. **—soprano** n. voice between soprano and contralto. **-tint** n. a method of copperplate engraving in which a roughened surface is scraped according to degrees of light and shade required. [It. *mezzo*, half].

mi·as·ma (mī·az′·mą) n. noxious exhalations from decomposing matter. **-l, -tic, miasmic** a. [Gk. *miasma*, a stain].

mi·ca (mī′·ką) n. a group of mineral silicates capable of cleavage into very thin, flexible, and often transparent laminae. a. [L. *mica*, a crumb].

mice (mīs) pl. of **mouse.**

Mich·ael·mas (mik′·l·mąs) n. the feast of the archangel Michael, Sept. 29.

mi·crobe (mī′·krōb) n. a minute organism; a bacterium or disease germ. **microbial, microbian, microbic** a. **microbiology** n. the science of microbes. **microbiological** a. [Gk. *mikros*, small; *bios*, life].

mi·cro·ceph·a·lous (mī·krō·sef′·ą·ląs) a. (*Med.*) having a very small head [Gk. *mikros*, small; *kephalā*, the head].

mi·cro·coc·cus (mī·krō·kák′·ąs) n. a spherical or oval organism or bacterium [Gk. *mikros*, small; *kokkos*, a berry].

mi·cro·cosm (mī′·krą·kázm) n. miniature universe; man, regarded as the epitome of the universe; a community symbolical of humanity as a whole. **microcosmic,** a. [Gk. *mikros*, small; *kosmos*, the universe].

mi·cro·film (mī′·krą·film) n. film used to make reduced photographic copies of books, etc. [Gk. *mikros*, small; and *film*].

mi·cro·graph (mī′·krą·graf) n. an instrument for producing microscopic engraving; a microphotograph. **micrographer** n. **micrography** n. the study of microscopic objects; the art of writing or engraving on a minute scale [Gk. *mikros*, small; *graphein*, to write].

mi·crol·o·gy (mī·kráľ·ą·ji·) n. the science which deals with microscopic objects; (*Fig.*) overscrupulous attention to small details [Gk. *mikros*, small; *logos*, a discourse].

mi·crom·e·ter (mī·kràm′·ą·tẹr) n. an instrument for measuring very small distances or angles. **micrometric, -al** a. [Gk. *mikros*, small; *metron*, a measure].

mi·cron (mī′·krán) n. the millionth part of a meter [Gk. *mikros*, small].

mi·cro·or·gan·ism (mī·krō·awr′·gąn·izm) n. a microscopic organism [Gk. *mikros*, small; *organon*, an instrument].

mi·cro·phone (mī′·krą·fōn) n. an instrument for turning sound waves into electrical waves so enabling them to be transmitted; mouthpiece for broadcasting (*Colloq.* abbrev. **mike**); an instrument for making faint sounds louder. [Gk. *mikros*, small; *phōne*, a sound].

mi·cro·pho·tog·ra·phy (mī·krą·fą·tág′·rą·fi·) n. the art of producing minute photographs. **microphotograph** n. [Gk. *mikros*, small; *phos*, light; *graphein*, to write].

mi·cro·scope (mī′·krą·skōp) n. an optical instrument for magnifying minute objects. **microscopic, -al** a. visible only with a microscope; very minute. **microscopically** adv. **mi-**

croscopy n. [Gk. *mikros*, small; *skopein*, to see].

microphone

microscope

mi·cro·zo·a (mī·krą·zō′·ą) n.pl. microscopic animals. **-n** a. and n. sing. [Gk. *mikros*, small; *zōon*, an animal; *zumē*, leaven].

mic·tu·ri·tion (mik·chą·rish′·ąn) n. (*Med.*) the passing of urine. **micturate** v.i. [L. *micturire*, to pass urine].

mid (mid) a. situated between extremes; middle, as in *mid-air, mid-Atlantic.* **-day** n. and a. noon; pert. to noon. **-night** n. twelve o'clock at night. **-shipman** n. rank in U.S. Navy and Coast Guard held by young men attending service academies; **-ships** adv. amidships. **-summer** n. the middle of summer. **-way** adv. halfway. **-winter** n. middle of the winter [O.E.].

mid (mid) prep. amidst (in poetry).

mid·dle (mid′·l) a. equidistant from the extremes; intermediate; n. middle point. **-aged** a. pert. to the period of life between 40 and 60. **-man** n. an agent acting between producer and consumer; a go-between. **-weight** n. (*Boxing*) a boxer of a weight not more than 160 lbs. **middling** a. of medium size, quality; adv. moderately. **Middle Ages,** the period of European history from the Fall of the Roman Empire (about A.D. 476) to the Fall of Constantinople (1453). **— class,** that section of the community between the very wealthy higher social classes and the laboring classes; the bourgeoisie. **Middle East,** that part of the world between the *Near East* and the *Far East*; Egypt, Syria, Palestine, Arabia, Iraq and Iran. **Middle English,** the English language as written and spoken between 1150-1500 (approx.) [O.E. *middel*].

mid·dy (mid′·i·) n. (*Colloq.*) a midshipman; a loose blouse with a sailor collar.

midge (mij) n. a gnat; a very small person. **midget** n. a dwarf; a. miniature [O.E. *mycge*, a gnat].

mid·riff (mid′·rif) n. the diaphragm; body part between chest and abdomen [O.E. *mid*, middle; *hrif*, the belly].

midst (midst) n. the middle; prep. amidst [M.E.].

mid·wife (mid′·wīf) n. a woman who assists another at childbirth. pl. **midwives** [O.E. *mid*, with; *wif*, a woman]. [pearance.

mien (mēn) n. manner; bearing; general appearance.

miff (mif) v.t. and i. to offend or take offense [Ger. *muffen*, to sulk].

might (mīt) pa.t. of verb **may.**

might (mīt) n. power; strength; energy. **-iness** n. the state of being powerful; greatness. **-y** a. having great strength or power; exalted [O.E. *meaht*, might].

mi·gnon·ette (min′·yą·net) n. a sweet-scented, greenish-gray flowered plant [dim. Fr. *mignon*, a darling].

mi·graine (mī′·grān) n. severe headache often accompanied by nausea. cf. **megrim.**

mi·grate (mī′·grāt) v.i. to remove one's residence from one place to another; (of birds) to fly to another place in search of warmer climate. **migrant** n. a person or creature who migrates. **migration** n. the act of migrating; a mass removal. **migratory** a. [L. *migrare*, to go].

Mi·ka·do (mą·kả′·dō) n. the Emperor of Japan [Jap. *mi*, august; *kado*, the door].

mike (mīk) n. (*Colloq.* abbrev.) a microphone.

mil (mil) n. .001 in., a unit of measurement in calculating the diameter of wire [L. *mille*, a thousand].

milch (milch) a. giving milk [M.E. *milch*, milk].

mild (mīld) a. gentle; kind; placid; calm, or temperate, as weather. **-ly** adv. **-ness** [O.E. *milde*, gentle].

mil·dew (mil′·dòò) n. whitish coating of minute fungi on plants; a mold on paper, cloth, leather caused by dampness; *v.t.* and *v.i.* to taint or be tainted with mildew. **-y** *a.* [O.E. *mele*, honey; *deaw*, dew].

mile (mil) *n.* a measure of length equal to 5280 ft. **geographical** or **nautical mile**, 1/60 of 1 degree of the earth's equator, 6,080.2 ft. **-age** *n.* distance in miles; rate of travel calculated on the number of miles traveled. **-r** *n.* a man or horse trained to run a mile. **-stone** *n.* roadside marker; a stage or crisis in one's life [O.E. *mil*, fr. L. *mille passus*, 1000 paces].

mil·i·ar·y (mil′·i·er·i·) *a.* like millet seeds. **miliaria**, *n.* (*Med.*) a fever, accompanied by a rash resembling millet seeds (heat rash) [L. *milium*, millet].   [dle].

mi·lieu (mēl′yoo′) *n.* environment [Fr. = mid-**mil·i·tant** (mil′·i·tant) *a.* aggressive; serving as a soldier. **militancy** *n.* war-like, fighting spirit. **-ly** *adv.* **militarism** *n.* military spirit; excessive emphasis on military power; opp. of *pacifism.* **militarist** *n.* one who upholds the doctrine of militarism; a student of military science. **military** *a.* pert. to soldiers, arms, or war; warlike; *n.* the army. **military police**, soldiers performing duties of police in the army. **militate** *v.i.* to be combative; to work against (or for); to have an adverse effect on [L. *miles*, a soldier].

mi·li·tia (ma·lish′·a) *n.* a citizen army, liable to be called out in an emergency [L. *miles*, a soldier].

milk (milk) *n.* a white fluid secreted by female mammals for nourishment of their young and in some cases used for humans; the juice of certain plants; *v.t.* to draw milk from; *v.i.* to give milk. **— and water** *a.* insipid. **—bar** *n.* a counter where milk drinks, etc. are sold. **-er** *n.* a milking-machine; a cow which yields milk. **— fever**, a fever sometimes contracted after childbirth **-iness** *n.* **-ing** *n.* the quantity of milk yielded at one time; the drawing of milk. **-like** *a.* **-maid** *n.* a dairymaid or woman who milks cows. **-man** *n.* a man who milks cows; a man who delivers milk. **-sop** *n.* a weak, effeminate man. **-tooth** *n.* one of the temporary baby teeth. **-weed** *n.* wild plant with milky sap. **-wood** *n.* kind of tropical trees yielding latex. **-y** *a.* like, full of, or yielding milk. **Milky Way**, the Galaxy, an irregular, luminous belt in the heavens, from the light of innumerable stars. **condensed milk**, milk with sugar added and evaporated to the consistency of syrup. **evaporated milk**, unsweetened condensed milk [O.E. *meolc*, milk].

mill (mil) *n.* a building equipped with machinery to grind grain into flour; an apparatus for grinding, as *coffee-mill*; a factory or machinery used in manufacture, as *cotton-mill, paper-mill*; (*Slang*) a boxing match. *v.t.* to grind; to cut fine grooves on the edges of (coins); to full (cloth); to dress or purify (ore); (*Slang*) to box; *v.i.* to go round in circles, as cattle, or crowds of people. **-board** *n.* stout pasteboard used in bookbinding. **-dam** *n.* a dam built to provide water for turning a mill wheel. **-ed** *a.* having the edges raised and grooved, as coins; rolled into sheets, as metal. **-er** *n.* **-ing** *n.* grinding in a mill; fulling cloth, or grooving raised edges of a coin, or pressing crude rubber under rollers; *a.* (*Slang*) confused; without direction, as *milling crowds*. **-pond** *n.* milldam. **-race** *n.* the current of water which turns millwheel. **-stone** *n.* one of the flat stones used in grinding grain; a burden. **— wheel** *n.* a water wheel for driving mill machinery. **-wright** *n.* one who sets up machinery in a mill [O.E. *myln*, to grind].

mill (mil) *n.* one thousandth of a dollar; one tenth of a cent [L. *mille*, thousand].

mil·len·ni·um (mil·en′·i·am) *n.* a thousand years; a future time or perfect peace on earth. **millennarian** *n.* one who believes in the millennium. **millennary** *a.* comprising a thousand; *n.* a period of a thousand years. **millennial** *a.* [L. *mille*, a thousand; *annus*, a year].

mil·li·pede (mil′·i·pēd) *n.* an insect with many legs [L. *mille*, thousand; *pes*, a foot].

mil·li- *prefix* one thousandth of. **-gram** *n.* one thousandth of a gram. **-meter** *n.* one thousandth of a meter [L. *mille*, a thousand].

mil·liard (mil′·yerd) *n.* a thousand millions; a billion [Fr.].

mil·li·ner (mil′·an·er) *n.* one who makes or sells ladies' hats. **-y** *n.* [fr. *Milan*].

mil·lion (mil′·yan) *n.* a thousand thousands (1,000,000). **-aire** *n.* one whose wealth amounts to a million (or more) dollars. **-fold** *a.* **-th** *n. a.* one of a million parts; **the millions**, the masses [Fr.].

milque·toast (milk·tōst) *n.* a timid shrinking person [fr. H. T. Webster's comic strip character].

milt (milt) *n.* the spleen; the reproductive glands or secretion of the male fish; *v.t.* to impregnate the female roe. **-er** *n.* [O.E. *milte*].

mime (mīm) *n.* a farce in which scenes of real life are expressed by gesture only; an actor in such a farce; *v.i.* to act in a mime; to express by gesture. **mimetic(al)** *a.* imitative. **mimic** (mi′·mik) *v.t.* to imitate; to burlesque; to ridicule by imitating another. *pr.p.* **-king** *pa.p., pa.t.* **-ked**. *n.* one who mimics or caricatures; *a.* mock, as in *mimic battle*; feigned. **mimicry** *n.*

the art or act of mimicking [Gk. *mimos*, an actor].

mim·e·o·graph (mim′·i·a·graf) *n.* a form of duplicating-machine [Gk. *mimeisthai*, to imitate; *graphein*, to write].

Mi·mo·sa (mi·mō′·sa) *n.* a genus of leguminous plants, shrubs, or trees, with small, fluffy flowers [Gk. *mimos*, an imitator].

min·a·ret (min·a·ret′) *n.* a turret on a Mohammedan mosque [Ar. *manarat*, a lighthouse].

min·a·to·ry (min′·a·tōr·i·) *a.* threatening; menacing. **minacious** *a.* **minacity** *n.* [L. *minari*, to threaten].

mince (mins) *v.t.* to cut or chop into very small pieces; (*Fig.*) to tone down; *v.i.* to speak or walk with affected elegance. **-meat** *n.* currants, raisins, spices, apple, suet and sugar, chopped and mixed together, used as pie filling (*Fig.*) anything chopped up. **mincing** *a.* speaking or walking with affected elegance. **mincingly** *adv.* [O.E. *minsian*, to make small].

mind (mind) *n.* the intellectual faculty; the understanding; memory; opinion; inclination; purpose; a person regarded as an intellect; *v.t.* to obey; to attend to; to heed; to object to; to take care of; *v.i.* to be careful; to care. **-ed** *a.* disposed; inclined. **-edness** *n.* **-ful** *a.* attentive; observant; aware. **-fully** *adv.* **-fulness** *n.* **-less** *a.* stupid; careless. **— reader** *n.* one who can sense another's thoughts. **absent minded**, forgetful [O.E. *gemynd*, the mind].

mine (min) *n.* a pit in the earth from which minerals are excavated; a hidden explosive to blow up a wall, vessel, etc.; a profitable source; *pl.* the mining industry; *v.i.* and *v.t.* to place mines; to dig a mine or in a mine; to burrow; to undermine; to sap. **— field** *n.* an area of land or stretch of the sea where mines have been placed. **— layer** *n.* a vessel which places submarine or floating mines. **— sweeper** *n.* a vessel with nets for clearing a mine field [Fr. *miner*, to mine].

mine (min) *poss. pron.* belonging to me; [O.E. *min*].

min·er·al (min′·er·al) *n.* any substance, generally inorganic, taken from the earth by mining; a chemical element or compound occurring in nature; *a.* pert. to or containing minerals; inorganic. **-ization** *n.* **-ize** *v.t.* to convert into or impregnate with minerals. **-ogy** (min·er·al′·a·ji·) *n.* the science of minerals and their classification. **mineralogist** *n.* **— water**, water, impregnated with mineral substance, used medicinally [Fr. *miner*, to mine].

mi·ne·stro·ne (min·a·strō′·ni·) *n.* thick vegetable soup [It.].

min·gle (ming′·gl) *v.t.* to mix; to blend; to join in; *v.i.* to become mixed. **-r** *n.* **mingling** *n.* blend [O.E. *mengan*, to mix].

min·i·a·ture (min′·i·a·cher) *n.* a small-sized painting done on ivory, vellum, etc.; anything on a small scale; *a.* minute. **miniaturize** *v.t.* to make on a small scale [L. *miniare*, to paint red].

min·i·fy (min′·i·fi) *v.t.* to lessen; to minimize [L. *minor*, less; *facere*, to make].

min·im (min′·im) *n.* anything very minute; (*Med.*) 1/60 of a fluid dram; a drop; (*Mus.*) a half note. **minimal** *a.* smallest possible. **minimize** *v.t.* to reduce; to depreciate. **minimization** *n.* **minimum** *n.* the least to which anything may be reduced [L. *minimus*, least].

min·ion (min′·yan) *n.* a favorite; a servile

flatterer; (*Print.*) a small type [Fr. *mignon*, a darling].

min·is·ter (min′·is·ter) *n.* an agent or instrument; a clergyman; (*Brit.*) one entrusted with a govt. department; to serve; *v.i.* to supply things needed. **-ial** *a.* executive; pert. to the work of a minister. **-ially** *adv.* **-ing** *a.* serving. **ministrant** *n.* one who ministers; a helper. **ministration** *n.* the act of performing a service. **ministrative** *a.* **ministry** *n.* the act of ministering; the office or functions of a minister; the clergy [L. *minister*, a servant].

min·i·ver (min′·a·ver) *n.* fine white fur [O.Fr. *menu*, small; *vair*, fur].

mink (mingk) *n.* a semiaquatic animal of the weasel tribe; its fur [Scand.].

min·now (min′·ō) *n.* a small freshwater fish [O.E. *myne*, a small fish].

mi·nor (mi′·ner) *a.* lesser; inferior in bulk, degree, importance, etc.; subordinate; (*Mus.*) lower by a semi-tone; *n.* a person under 21. **-ity** (mi·nàr′·i·ti·) *n.* the state of being under age; the lesser number, oppos. of *majority*. **— key** (*Mus.*) a key characterized by a minor third, sixth, or seventh [L. *minor*, less].

Mi·nor·ca (min·awr′·ka) *n.* a breed of fowl [Sp. fr. *Minorca* island].

min·ster (min′·ster) *n.* church cathedral [O.E. *mynster*, a monastery].

min·strel (min′·strel) *n.* a medieval poet or wandering singer; an entertainer in a minstrel show (a comic variety show with performers in blackface) [O.Fr. *menestrel*, a jester].

mint (mint) *n.* the place where money is coined; a great amount of money; *a.* as issued (before use); *v.t.* to make by stamping, as coins; to invent. **-age** *n.* process of minting money [O.E. *mynet*, money].

mint (mint) *n.* an aromatic plant used for medicinal and culinary purposes; a candy flavored with it. **— julep**, an iced drink of whiskey and sugar flavored with mint [L.E. *minte*].

min·u·end (min′·ū·end) *n.* the number from which another is to be subtracted [L. *minuendus*, to be made less].

min·u·et (min·ū·et′) *n.* a slow, stately dance; music, to which the minuet is danced [Fr. *menuet*, minu, small].

mi·nus (mi′·nas) *prep.* less by; *a.* showing subtraction; negative *n.* the sign (—) of subtraction; an amount less than nothing. **-cule** (mi·nus′·kūl) *a.* small; *n.* a lower-case letter, oppos. of *majuscule* [L. *minor*, less].

mi·nute (mi·nōot′) *a.* very small; slight; particular; exact. **-ly** *adv.* **-ness** *n.* **minutiae** (min·ū′·shi·ē) *n.pl.* minute details [L. *minuere*, *minutum*, to lessen].

min·ute (min′·it) *n.* the 60th part of an hour or degree; a moment. *pl*, the official record of a meeting; *v.t.* to make a note of. **— hand** *n.* longer of two hands on clock or watch indicating minutes. **-ly** *adv.* occurring every minute [L. *minuere minutum*, to lessen].

minx (mingks) *n.* a pert, saucy girl [Ger. *mensch*].

mir·a·cle (mir′·a·kl) *n.* a wonder; a supernatural happening; a prodigy. **— play**, a popular medieval form of drama based on the lives of the saints, or on Biblical history. **miraculous** *a.* supernatural; extraordinary. **miraculously** *adv.* [L. *miraculum*, wonder].

mi·rage (mi·räzh′) *n.* an optical illusion; a delusion [L. *mirare*, to wonder at].

mire (mir) *n.* slimy soil; mud; defilement; *v.t.* to plunge into or cover with mud; *v.i.* to sink in mud. **miriness** *n.* **miry** *a.* [O.N. *myrr*, marsh].

mir·ror (mir′·er) *n.* a looking glass; a brilliantly polished reflecting surface; a pattern or model; a reflection, as a *mirror of the times*. *v.t.* to reflect [L. *mirare*, to look at].

mirth (murth) *n.* gaiety; merriment; joyousness; laughter. **-ful** *a.* **-fulness** *n.* **-less** *a.* grim. **-lessly** *adv.* [O.E. *myrgth*, merry].

mis- (mis) *prefix.* wrong; ill. prefixed to words of O.E. or O.Fr. origin.

mis·ad·ven·ture (mis·ad·ven′·cher) *n.* an unlucky adventure; a mishap.

mis·ad·vise (mis·ad·viz′) *v.t.* to advise wrongly. **-d** *a.* ill-advised.

mis·al·li·ance (mis·a·li′·ans) *n.* an unfortunate alliance, esp. in marriage.

mis·an·thrope (mis′·an·thrōp) *n.* a hater of

mankind; one who has no faith in his fellow men. **misanthropically** *adv.* **misanthropy** *n.* hatred of mankind [Gk. *miseein*, to hate; *anthrōpos*, a man].

mis·ap·ply (mis·a·plī') *v.t.* to apply wrongly or dishonestly. **misapplication** *n.*

mis·ap·pre·hend (mis·ap·ri·hend') *v.t.* to apprehend wrongly; to misconceive. **misapprehension** *n.* **misapprehensive** *a.*

mis·ap·pro·pri·ate (mis·a·prō'·pri·āt) *v.t.* to use wrongly, esp. to embezzle money. **misappropriation** *n.*

mis·be·got·ten (mis·bi·gát'·n) *a.* unlawfully conceived; illegitimate.

mis·be·have (mis·bi·hāv') *v.i.* to behave badly, improperly or dishonestly. **misbehavior** *n.*

mis·be·lieve (mis·bi·lēv') *v.t.* to believe wrongly. **misbelief** *n.* belief in false ideas.

mis·cal·cu·late (mis·kal'·kya·lāt) *v.t.* to calculate wrongly. **miscalculation** *n.*

mis·car·riage (mis·kar'·ij) *n.* failure; premature birth. **miscarry** *v.i.* to fail to fulfill the intended effect; to give birth prematurely.

mis·ce·ge·na·tion (mis·i·ja·nā'·shan) *n.* a mixture of races by interbreeding [L. *miscere*, to mix; *genus*, a race].

mis·cel·la·ne·ous (mis·al·ā'·ni·as) *a.* mixed; heterogeneous. **-ly** *adv.* **miscellanist** *n.* a writer of miscellanies. **miscellany** *n.* a medley, esp. a collection. **miscellanea** *n.pl.* odds and ends [L. *miscellaneus*, fr. *miscere*, to mix].

mis·chance (mis·chans') *n.* a mishap; ill-luck.

mis·chief (mis'·chif) *n.* harm; damage; conduct intended to annoy; the cause of such trouble. **-maker** *n.* one who stirs up trouble. **mischievous** *a.* tending to stir up trouble; playfully annoying. **mischievously** *adv.* **mischievousness** *n.* [O.Fr. *meschever*, to come to grief].

mis·ci·ble (mis'·i·bl) *a.* capable of being mixed. **miscibility** *n.* [L. *miscere*, to mix].

mis·con·ceive (mis·kan·sēv') *v.t.* to misunderstand. **misconception** *n.*

mis·con·duct (mis·kán'·dukt) *n.* bad management; dishonest conduct. **misconduct** (mis··kan·dukt') *v.t.* to mismanage.

mis·con·strue (mis·kan·strōō') *v.i.* to interpret wrongly; misunderstand. **misconstruction** *n.*

mis·count (mis·kount') *v.t.* to count wrongly; to miscalculate; (mis'·kount) *n.* a wrong count.

mis·cre·ant (mis'·krē·ant) *n.* unprincipled person [O.Fr. *mescreant*, disbelieving].

mis·cue (mis·kū') *n.* (*Billiards*) a stroke spoiled by the cue slipping; a mistake; *v.t.*

mis·date (mis·dāt') *v.t.* to put a wrong date on; *n.* a wrong date.

mis·deal (mis·dēl') *v.t.* and *i.* to deal cards wrong. *pa.t.* **misdealt** *n.* wrong deal.

mis·deed (mis·dēd') *n.* an evil deed, a crime.

mis·de·mean·or (mis·da·mēn'·er) *n.* dishonest conduct; (*Law*) a crime less than felony. **misdemean** *v.i.* to misbehave.

mis·di·rect (mis·da·rekt') *v.t.* to direct or advise wrongly. **-tion** *n.*

mi·ser (mī'·zer) *n.* one who hoards money and lives in wretched surroundings. **-ly** *a.* greedy; stingy. **-liness** *n.* [L. = wretched].

mis·er·a·ble (miz'·er·a·bl) *a.* unhappy; causing misery; worthless; deplorable. **miserably** *adv.* [L. *miser*, wretched].

mis·e·re·re (miz·a·re'·ri·) *n.* Psalm 51, a cry for mercy [L. = take pity].

mis·er·y (miz'·e·ri·) *n.* great unhappiness; extreme pain of body or mind [L. *miser*].

mis·fea·sance (mis·fē'·zans) *n.* (*Law*) wrongdoing; a misuse of lawful authority [O.Fr. *mesfaire*, to do wrong].

mis·fire (mis·fīr') *n.* (of internal combustion engine, gun, etc.) failure to start or go off; *v.i.* to fail to start or fire.

mis·fit (mis'·fit) *n.* a bad fit; *v.t.* and *i.*

mis·for·tune (mis·fawr'·chan) *n.* ill luck; a calamity.

mis·give (mis·giv') *v.t.* to fill with doubt; to cause to hesitate; *v.i.* to fail *pa.t.* **misgave**. *pa.p.* **misgiven**. **misgiving** *n.* distrust; suspicion. [ly. **-ment** *n.*

mis·gov·ern (mis·guv'·ern) *v.t.* to govern badly.

mis·guide (mis·gīd') *v.t.* to lead astray; to advise wrongly. **misguidance** *n.*

mis·han·dle (mis·hand'·dl) *v.t.* to maltreat; to bungle.

mis·hap (mis'·hap) *n.* accident.

mish·mash (mish'·mash) *n.* a jumble [fr. *mash*].

mis·in·form (mis·in·fawrm') *v.t.* to give wrong information to. **-ant, -ation** *n.*

mis·in·ter·pret (mis·in·tur'·prit) *v.t.* to interpret or explain wrongly. **-ation** *n.* **-er** *n.*

mis·join·der (mis·join'·der) *n.* (*Law*) introduction into court of parties or causes not belonging.

mis·judge (mis·juj') *v.t.* to judge wrongly; to miscalculate. **-ment** *n.*

mis·lay (mis·lā') *v.t.* to lay down something in a place which cannot later be recollected. *pa.t.*, *pa.p.* **mislaid**.

mis·lead (mis·lēd') *v.t.* to lead astray; to delude. *pa.p.* **misled**. **-ing** *a.*

mis·man·age (mis·man'·ij) *v.t.* to manage incompetently. **-ment** *n.*

mis·name (mis·nām') *v.t.* to call by the wrong name.

mis·no·mer (mis·nō'·mer) *n.* a wrong name;

incorrect designation [O.Fr. *mesnommer*, to name wrongly].

mi·so·ga·my (mi·ság'·a·mi·) *n.* hatred of marriage. **misogamist** *n.* [Gk. *miseein*, to hate; *gamos*, marriage].

mi·sog·y·ny (mi·sáj'·a·ni·) *n.* hatred of women. **misogynist** *n.* **misogynous** *a.* [Gk. *miseein*, to hate; *gunē*, a woman].

mis·place (mis·plās') *v.t.* to place wrongly; to mislay.

mis·print (mis·print') *v.t.* to make an error in printing; (mis'·print) *n.* a printing error.

mis·pro·nounce (mis·pra·nouns') *v.t.* to pronounce incorrectly. **mispronunciation** *n.*

mis·quote (mis·kwōt') *v.t.* to quote incorrectly.

mis·reck·on (mis·rek'·n) *v.t.* to estimate or reckon incorrectly. **-ing** *n.*

mis·rep·re·sent (mis·rep·ri·zent') *v.i.* to represent falsely; to report inaccurately. **-ation** *n.*

mis·rule (mis·rōōl') *n.* disorder; misgovernment.

Miss (mis) *n.* title of unmarried women; girl [contr. of *mistress*]..

miss (mis) *v.t.* to fail to hit, reach, find, catch, notice; to be without; to feel the want of; to avoid; to omit; *v.i.* to fail to hit; to fall short of one's objective; *n.* failure to hit, reach, find, etc.; escape, as in *a lucky miss*. **-ing** *a.* lost; failing [O.F. *missan*, to fail].

mis·sal (mis'·al) *n.* a book containing the R.C. service of the mass for a year [L. *missa*, mass].

mis·sel (mis'·l) *n.* the large European thrush, supposed to eat *mistletoe berries* [O.E. *mistel*, mistletoe].

mis·shape (mis·shāp') *v.t.* to shape badly; to deform. **-en** *a.*

mis·sile (mis'·l) *n.* that which is thrown or shot. **guided missile** *n.* a projected unmanned object which travels above the earth and performs some specific function, such as communication; *a.* capable of being thrown or shot [L. *mittere. missum*, to send].

mis·sion (mish'·an) *n.* the act of sending; the duty on which one is sent; a group of people sent to a foreign country for religious work; a delegation sent to a foreign country; vocation. **-ary** *a.* pert. to missions or missionaries; *n.* one sent to preach religion, esp. in a foreign country; one who does social service among the poor. [L. *mittere, missum*, to send].

mis·sive (mis'·iv) *n.* a letter or message [L. *missum*, to send].

mis·spell (mis·spel') *v.t.* to spell incorrectly. **-ing** *n.* an error in spelling.

mis·spend (mis·spend') *v.t.* to spend foolishly; to squander. *pa.t.* and *pa.p.* **misspent**.

mist (mist) *n.* visible vapor in the lower atmosphere; droplets of rain; a cloudiness or film; *v.t.* or *v.i.* to dim or be dimmed, as by a mist. **-y** *a.* dim; obscured. **-ily** *adv.* **-iness** *n.* [O.E. *mist*, darkness].

mis·take (mis·tāk') *v.t.* to misunderstand; to take one person for another; *v.i.* to err; *n.* an error. *pa.t.* **mistook**. *pa.p.* **mistaken**. **mistakable** *a.* **mistaken** *a.* wrong; misunderstood. **mistakenly** *adv.* [M.E. *mistaken*, to take wrongly].

mis·ter (mis'·ter) *n.* sir; title of courtesy to a man (*abbrev.* **Mr.**) [form of *master*].

mis·time (mis·tīm') *v.t.* to time wrongly. **-d** *a.*

mis·tle·toe (mis'·l·tō) *n.* a parasitic, evergreen plant with white berries [O.E. *mistel*, mistletoe; *tan*, a twig].

mis·tral (mis'·tral) *n.* a cold, often violent, N.W. wind which blows over S. France [Fr. *mistral*, a master (wind)].

mis·tress (mis'·tris) *n.* (*fem.* of **master**) a woman in authority (as over a household, animal, institution); a kept woman; formerly, a title of address [O.Fr. *maistresse*, fem.].

mis·tri·al (mis·trī'·al) *n.* a trial made invalid by an error in proceedings.

mis·trust (mis·trust') *n.* lack of confidence; *v.t.* to suspect; to lack faith in. **-ful** *a.*

mis·un·der·stand (mis·un·der·stand') *v.t.* to interpret incorrectly; to form a wrong judgment. **-ing** *n.* a misconception; a slight quarrel.

mis·use (mis·ūz') *v.t.* to use improperly; to maltreat. (mis·ūs') *n.* improper use. **misusage** *n.* abuse.

mite (mīt) *n.* any very small thing or person; a kind of arachnid, as *cheese-mite*; a very small coin [O.Dut. *mijt*, a small coin].

mi·ter (mī'·ter) *n.* a bishop's headdress, a tall cap; in carpentry, a joint made by two pieces of wood fitting into each other at an angle of 45°; to confer an angle. **mitral, mitriform** *a.* shaped like a miter; (*Bot.*) conical. — **block, — board,** or — **box** *n.* a piece of wood acting as a guide in sawing a *miter-joint*. **-d** *a.* wearing a miter; cut like a miter [Gk. *mitra*, a headband].

mit·i·gate (mit'·a·gāt) *v.t.* to relieve; to alleviate; to temper. **mitigable** *a.* capable of being lessened. **mitigation** *n.* alleviation. **mitigative, mitigatory** *a.* **mitigator** *n.* [L. *mitigare*, to lessen].

mi·to·sis (mi·tō'·sis) *n.* (*Biol.*) method of cell division in which chromatin divides into chromosomes [Gk. *mitos*, thread; *osis*, action].

mitt (mit) *n.* a covering for wrist and hand leaving fingers exposed; a baseball glove, with palm heavily padded; (usu. *pl.*) padded mitten worn by boxers. **-ten** *n.* a glove with thumb, but palm and fingers all in one [L. *medius*, middle].

mix (miks) *v.t.* to unite into a mass; to blend; to combine a mixture; to associate; *v.i.* to become mingled; to associate; *n.* a muddle; a mixture. **-able** *a.* **-ed** *a.* mingled; blended; **-er** *n.* one who or that which mixes; one who is sociable, as a *good mixer*. (*Slang*) a social gathering. **-ture** *n.* the act of mixing; that which is mixed; (*Chem.*) a combination of substances which retain their individual properties, as contrasted with a *compound*. **-up** *n.* (*Colloq.*) confusion. **-ed marriage,** a marriage between two people of different religions [L. *miscere*].

miz·zen, mizen (miz'·n) *n.* fore-and-aft sail of a vessel. **-mast** *n.* the mast bearing the mizzen [Fr. *misaine*, a fore-sail].

mne·mon·ic, -al (ni·mán'·ik, -al) *a.* assisting the memory. **-s** *n.pl.* the art of assisting the memory; artificial aids to memory [Gk. *mnēmōn*, mindful].

mo·a (mō'·a) *n.* an extinct N. Z. flightless bird of very large size [Maori].

moan (mōn) *n.* a low cry of grief or pain; *v.i.* to utter a low, wailing cry; *v.t.* to lament [O.E. *maenan*, to lament].

moat (mōt) *n.* a deep trench around a castle, usu. filled with water [O.Fr. *mote*, a trench].

mob (máb) *n.* a disorderly crowd of people; a rabble; the populace; *v.t.* to attack in a disorderly crowd; to jostle. *pr.p.* **-bing**. *pa.p.*, *pa.t.* **-bed**. **-ocracy** *n.* the rule of the mob. **-ocrat** mob leader. **-ster** *n.* (*Slang*) gangster [L. *mobile vulgus*, the fickle masses].

mob·cap (máb'·kap) *n.* a frilled cap, tied under the chin, worn by women in the 18th cent. [Dut. *mop*, a coif].

mo·bile (mō'·bl) *a.* easily moved; changing; facile; (of troops) mechanized; capable of moving rapidly from place to place; *n.* (mō'·bēl) an artistic arrangement of wires, etc., easily set in motion. **mobilization** *n.* the wartime act of calling up men and women for active service. **mobilize** *v.t.* to gather together available resources. **mobility** *n.* the state of being mobile [L. *mobilis*, movable].

moc·ca·sin (mák'·a·sin) *n.* a shoe of soft leather worn by N. American Indians, trappers, etc.; a bedroom slipper of similar shape; a poisonous water snake [N. Amer. Ind.].

mo·cha (mō'·ka) *n.* a coffee orig. from *Mocha* in Yemen; *a.* flavored with coffee.

mock (mák) *v.t.* to laugh at; to ridicule; to make a fool of; to defy; to mimic; substitute. **-er** *n.* **-ery, -ing** *n.* the act of mocking; derision; travesty; false show. **-heroic** *a.* burlesquing the serious or heroic style. **-ing** *a.* scornful; derisive. **-ing bird,** a N. American bird which imitates other birds. — **orange,** shrub with fragrant white flowers. — **turtle,** a soup made of calf's head and spices to imitate turtle soup [Fr. *moquer*].

mode (mōd) *n.* manner, form, or method; custom; fashion; (*Mus.*) one of the two classes of keys (major or minor); (*Gram.*) the *mood* of the verb. **modal** *a.* relating to mode or form. **modality** *n.* **modish** *a.* fashionable. **modishly** *adv.* **modishness** *n.* **modiste** (mōd·ēst') *n.* a dealer in fashion [L. *modus*, maner].

mod·el (mád'·l) *n.* an exact, three-dimensional representation of an object, in miniature; a pattern or standard to copy; one who poses for an artist; a mannequin; *a.* serving as a model or criterion; to make in model; to copy from a pattern or standard to shape, as clay, wax, etc.; *v.i.* to practice modeling. **-er** *n.* **-ing** *n.* the art of working in plastic materials or of making models; shaping [O.Fr. *modelle*, a pattern].

mod·er·ate (mád'·er·it) *a.* restrained; temperate; average; not extreme; (mȧd'.ẹr.āt) v.t. to restrain; to control; to decrease the intensity or pressure of; v.i. to become less violent or intense; to act as moderator; n. a person of moderate opinions in politics, etc. **-ly** adv. **-ness** n. **moderation** n. moderating; freedom from excess. **moderatism** n. non-extremist views. **moderator** n. arbitrator [L. moderare, to limit].

mod·ern (mȧd'.ẹrn) a. pert. to present or recent time; up-to-date; n. a person living in modern times; one up-to-date in outlook and ideas. **-ization** n. **-ize** v.t. to bring up-to-date. **-ism** n. sympathy with modern ideas. **-ist** n. one who upholds modern ideas. **modernity** n. the state or quality of being modern [L. modernus, fr. modo, just now].

mod·est (mȧd'.ist) a. unassuming; restrained; decent; retiring in manner; not excessive, as modest means. **-ly** adv. **-ty** n. the quality of being modest [L. modestus, moderate].

mod·i·cum (mȧd'.i.kạm) n. a small amount [L. modicus, moderate].

mod·i·fy (mȧd'.ȧ.fī) v.t. to moderate; to alter the form or intensity of; (Philol.) to change the sound of a vowel by the influence of a following vowel; (Gram.) to qualify the meaning of, as of a verb by an adverb. **modifiable** a. **modification** n. the act of modifying; the state of being modified; a change of form, manner, or intensity. **modifier** n. [L. modificare].

mod·u·late (mȧj'.oo.lāt) v.t. to regulate, esp. the pitch of the voice; to adapt; (Mus.) to change the key of; v.i. (Mus.) to pass from one key to another. **modular** a. of a mode, modulation, or module. **modulation** n. the act of modulating; the changing of the pitch or key; (Elect.) the variation of the amplitude or frequency of continuous waves, usu. by a lower frequency. **modulator** n. one who, or that which modulates. **module** n. a unit of measurement; (Arch.) the radius of a shaft at its base. **modulus** n. (Math.) a constant number, co-efficient, or quantity which measures a force, function, or effect. (pl. **moduli**) [L. modulari, to measure].

mo·gul (mō'.gul) n. a powerful or important person [Pers. Mughul, Mongolian conqueror].

mo·hair (mō'.hār) n. the silky hair of the Angora goat; fabric from this or similar hair. a. [Ar. mukhayyar, hair-cloth].

Mo·ham·me·dan (mo.ham'.ȧ.dạn) a. of Mohammed or the Moslem religion; n. a Moslem. **-ism** n. Moslem religion; Islam [fr. Mohammed, Ar. prophet, 570?-632].

Mo·ha·ve (mō.hȧ'.vi.) n. a tribe of Amer. Indians. Also **Mojave** [Amer. Ind.].

Mo·hawk (mō'.hawk) n. the name of a N. Amer. Indian tribe [Amer. Ind.].

Mo·hi·can (mō.hē'.kạn) n. a N. Amer. Indian tribe of Algonquin stock. Also **Mahican, Mohegan** [Amer. Ind.].

moi·e·ty (moi'.ȧ.ti.) n. half [Fr. moitié, half].

moire (mwȧ.rā') n. watered fabric; a. having a wavy pattern [var. of mohair].

moist (moist) a. damp; humid; rather wet. **-en** (mois'.n) v.t. to make moist; to dampen. **moistness, moisture** (mois'.chẹr) n. that which causes dampness; condensed vapor. **-ureless** [O.Fr. moiste, fresh].

mo·lar (mō'.lẹr) a. grinding or able to grind, as back teeth; n. a back double-tooth [L. molere, to grind].

mo·las·ses (mȧ.las'.ạz) n. sing. a dark-colored syrup obtained from sugar; treacle [L. mellaceus, honey-like].

mold (mōld) n. a pattern, form or matrix for giving shape to something in a plastic or molten state; a shape to form a model; character; v.t. to shape; to influence. **-er** n. one who molds or makes molds. **-ing** n. anything molded, esp. anything molded, esp. ornamentation of wood. Also **mould** [L. modulus, a small measure].

mold (mōld) n. fine, soft soil; the upper layer of the earth. **-er** v.i. to decay; to crumble away; to turn to dust. Also **mould** [O.E. molde].

mold (mōld) n. a downy fungus which grows on leather, cheese, bread, etc. if exposed to dampness; mildew. **-iness** n. **-y** a. affected by mold; musty; (Fig.) antiquated. Also **mould.**

mole (mōl) n. a slightly raised, dark spot on the skin [O.E. mal, a spot].

mole (mōl) n. a small burrowing animal; v.i. to burrow. **-hill** n. a small mound of earth. **-skin** n. the fur of a mole; a fabric with soft surface [M.E. molle, a mole].

mole (mōl) n. a breakwater [L. moles, a mass].

mol·e·cule (mȧl'.ȧ.kūl) n. the smallest portion

of a substance which can retain the characteristics of that substance. **molecular** a. **molecular weight**, the weight of a molecule of a substance in relation to the weight of a hydrogen atom [dim. fr. L. moles, a mass].

mo·lest (mȧ.lest') v.t. to trouble; to accost with sinister intention. **-ation** n. [L. molestus, troublesome].

mol·li·fy (mȧl'.ȧ.fī) v.t. to appease; to placate; to soften. **mollifiable** a. **mollification** n. **mollifier** n. [L. mollificare, to make soft].

mol·lusk, mol·lusc (mȧl'.ȧsk) n. an invertebrate animal with soft, pulpy body and a hard outer shell (oyster, snail, etc.) **molluscan** a. **molluscoid, -cous** a. like a mollusk [L. mollusca, a soft nut].

mol·ly·cod·dle (mȧl'.i.kȧd.l) n. a milksop; v.t. or v.i. to coddle or be coddled or pampered [dim. of Mary; coddle].

molt (mōlt) v.t. and i. to shed feathers, as of birds, or skins, as of snakes; n. the act of shedding. Also **moult** [L. mutare, to change].

mol·ten (mōl'.tạn) a. melted; of metals, liquified [Arch. pa.p. of melt].

mo·lyb·de·num (mạl.ib'.dạ.nạm) n. a rare metal, used in alloys [Gk. molubdos, lead].

mom (mȧm) n. (Colloq.) mother. Also **mommy.**

mo·ment (mō'.mạnt) n. a short space of time; interval; importance; the measure of a force by its effect in causing rotation. **-arily** adv. **-ariness** n. **-ary** a. very brief. **-ous** (mō.men'.tas) very important. **-tum** (mō.men'.-tạm) n. the impetus in a body; increasing force [L. momentum, movement].

mon·a·chism (mȧn'.ȧ.kizm) n. monasticism. **monachal** a. of monks [L. monachus, a monk].

mon·ad (mȧn'.ad) n. (Biol.) a single-celled organism; (Chem.) an atom with the valence of one; (Philos.) an individual thought of as a microcosm. **-ism, -ology** n. the theory of monads [Gk. monas, alone].

mon·arch (mȧn'.ẹrk) n. a hereditary sovereign; the supreme ruler of a state; a. supreme. **-ial, -ic, -al** a. pert. to a monarch or a monarchy. **-ically** adv. **-ism** n. the principles of monarchy; devotion to a royalist cause. **-ist** n. advocate of monarchy; a royalist. **-y** n. government by a single ruler; a kingdom or empire [Gk. monos, alone; archein, to rule].

mon·as·ter·y (mȧn'.ȧs.ter.i.) n. a settlement of monks. **monasterial, monastic** a. pert. to monasteries, monks or nuns. **monastic** n. a monk. **monasticism** (mạn.as'.ti.sizm) n. the monastic way of life [Gk. monasterion].

mon·au·ral (mȧn.aw'.rạl) a. of sound reproduction from one source only.

Mon·day (mun'.di.) n. the second day of the week [O.E. mona, the moon].

mon·e·tary (mȧn'.ȧ.ter.i) a. concerning money or coinage [L. moneta, a mint].

mon·ey (mun'.i.) n. any form of token, as coin, banknote, used as medium of exchange, and stamped by state authority; currency; wealth. pl. **monies.** — **bags** n.pl. a wealthy person. **-ed** a. wealthy. — **lender** n. one who lends money and charges interest. **—making** a. profitable. — **order,** an order for money, issued at one post office and payable at another [L. moneta, a mint].

mon·ger (mung'.gẹr) n. (Brit.) a dealer, usu. in compound words, as fishmonger, ironmonger, rumormonger [O.E. mangere, a merchant].

Mon·gol (mȧng'.gạl) n. a native of Mongolia (Asia); a. Mongolian. **-ism** n. arrest of physical and mental development with Asiatic features. **-oid** a. resembling the Mongols.

mon·goose (mȧn'.gò̀ọs) n. a small weasel-like animal, a snake-killer. pl. **mongooses** [Tamil].

mon·grel (mȧng'.grạl) n. a. impure; hybrid of mixed breed [O.E. mang, a mixture].

mon·ism (mōn'.izm) n. the philosophical doctrine which seeks to explain varied phenomena by a single principle. **monist** n. **monistic** a. [Gk. manos, single].

mo·ni·tion (mō.nish'.ạn) n. cautionary advice; admonition; notice; (Law) a summons. **monitive** a. expressing warning [L. monitio, warning].

mon·i·tor (mȧn'.i.tẹr) n. one who cautions; one appointed to help keep order; a large lizard; (Arch.) armed warship for coastal service; v.t. to watch or check on a person or thing, radio or TV. **-ial** (mȧn.i.tōr'.i.ạl) a. **-ially** adv. **-y** a. warning [L. monere, monitum, to warn].

monk (mungk) n. a hermit; a member of a religious community living in a monastery. **-hood** n. **-ish** a. monastic. **-hood** n. a herbaceous poisonous plant [Gk. monachos].

mon·key (mung'.ki.) n. a long-tailed mammal of the order of Primates resembling man in organization; mischievous child; the weighted head of a pile driver; a hammer for driving home bolts; v.i. to imitate as a monkey; (Colloq.) to meddle with, as to monkey with. **-shine** (Slang) n. a prank. — **wrench** n. wrench with movable jaw.

mo·no- prefix meaning sole, single [Gk. monos, alone, single].

mon·o·bloc (mȧn'.ȧ.blȧk) n. the cylinders of the internal-combustion engine in one casting [Gk. monos, single; and block].

mon·o·car·pous (mȧn.ȧ.kȧrp'.ạs) a. bearing fruit only once. **monocarp** n. [Gk. monos, single; karpos, fruit].

mon·o·chord (mȧn'.ȧ.kawrd) n. a one-stringed instrument; a one-stringed device for

measuring musical intervals.

monkey wrench

mon·o·chrome (mȧn'.ȧ.krōm) n. a painting in different tones of the same color. **monochromatic, monochromic** a. **monochromatism** n. color-blindness [Gk. monos, single; chrōma, color].

mon·o·cle (mȧn'.ȧ.kl) n. a single eyeglass [Gk. monos, single; L. oculus, the eye].

mon·o·cot·y·le·don (mȧn.ȧ.kȧt·ȧ.lē'.dạn) n. a plant with only one seed lobe. **-ous** a. [Gk. monos, single; kotulē, a cup].

mo·noc·ra·cy (mȧ.nȧk'.rȧ.si.) n. government by a single person. **monocrat** n. [Gk. monos, single; kratein, to rule].

mon·o·dy (mȧn'.ȧ.di.) n. an elegy expressive of mourning; a monotonous tone. **monodic, -al** a. **monodist** n. [Gk. monos, single; ōdē, song].

mo·nog·a·my (mȧ.nȧg'.ȧ.mi.) n. the state of being married to one person at a time. **monogamist** n. **monogamous** a. [Gk. monos, single; gamos, marriage].

mon·o·gen·e·sis (mȧn·ȧ.jen'.ȧ.sis) n. the descent of an organism or all living things, from a single cell. **monogenetic** a. **monogenism** n. the theory of the descent of all human beings from an original single pair. Also **monogeny** [Gk. mnoos, single; gignesthai, to be born].

mon·o·gram (mȧn'.ȧ.gram) n. two or more letters, as initials of a person's name, interwoven. **monogrammatic** a. [Gk. manos, alone; gramma, a letter].

mon·o·graph (mȧn'.ȧ.graf) n. a specialized treatise on a single subject or branch of a subject. **-er** n. (mȧ.nȧg'.rȧ.fẹr) **-ist** n. **monographic, -al** a. [Gk. monos, single; graphein, to write].

mo·nog·y·nous (mȧ.nȧj'.ȧ.nus) a. (Bot.) having single pistil; (Zool.) mating with a single female. **monogyny** n. the custom of having only one female mate [Gk. monos, single; gunē, a female].

mon·o·lith (mȧn'.ȧ.lith) n. a monument or column fashioned from a single block of stone. **-al, -ic** a. [Gk. monos, alone; lithos, a stone].

mon·o·logue (mȧn'.ȧ.lawg) n. a dramatic scene in which an actor soliloquizes; a dramatic entertainment by a solo performer. **-ist** n. Also **monolog. monologist** n. [Gk. monos, single; logos, a speech].

mon·o·ma·ni·a (mȧn.ȧ.mā'.ni.ȧ) n. a form of mental derangement in which sufferer is irrational on one subject only, or is obsessed by one idea. **monomaniac** n. **monomaniacal** a. [Gk. monos, single; mania, madness].

mo·no·mi·al (mȧn.ō'.mi.ȧl) a. (Math.) comprising a single term or expression; n. an algebraic expression containing a single term [Gk. monos, single; onoma, a name].

mon·o·nym (mȧn'.ȧ.nim) n. a name comprising a single term. **mononymic** a. [Gk. monos, single; onoma, a name].

mon·o·pho·bi·a (mȧn.ȧ.fō'.bi.ȧ) n. (Path.) a morbid fear of being alone [Gk. monos, single; phobos, fear].

mon·o·plane (mȧn'.ȧ.plān) n. an aircraft with only one set of wings.

mo·nop·o·ly (mȧ.nȧp'.ȧ.li.) n. the sole right to trade in certain commodities; exclusive possession or control; a commodity so controlled; a controlling company. **monopolize** v.t. to have a monopoly; to take possession to exclusion of others. **monopolizer, monopolist** n. **monopolistic** a. [Gk. manos, single; pōlein, to sell].

mon·o·syl·la·ble (mȧn.ȧ.sil'.ȧ.bl) n. a word of one syllable. **monosyllabic** a. having one syllable; speaking in words of one syllable. **monosyllabism** n.

mon·o·the·ism (mŏn′·a·thē·izm) *n.* the doctrine which admits of one God only. **monotheist** *n.* **monotheistic** *a.*

mon·o·tint (mŏn′·a·tint) *n.* a sketch or painting in one tint.

mon·o·tone (mŏn′·a·tōn) *n.* a single, unvaried tone or sound; a series of sounds of uniform pitch; sameness of any kind. **monotonic, monotonous** (ma·nät′·a·nas) uttered or recited in one tone; dull; unvaried. **monotony** (ma·nät′·a·ni·) *n.* tedious uniformity of tone; lack of variety or variation; sameness [Gk. *monos*, single; *tonos*, a tone].

mon·o·type (mŏn′·a·tip) *n.* (*Biol.*) a genus with one species; (*Print.*) a two-part machine for setting and casting type in individual letters, as distinct from *linotype*. **monotypic** *a.* [Gk. *monos*, single; and *type*].

mon·o·va·lent (mŏn·a·vā′·lant) *a.* (*Chem.*) having a valency of one; univalent. **monovalence, monovalency** *n.*

mon·ox·ide (ma·nak′·sid) *n.* oxide containing one oxygen atom in a molecule.

Mon·sei·gneur (mawn·se′·nyer) *n.* my lord; a title (*abbrev.* **Mgr.**) given in France to princes, bishops, etc. *pl.* **Messeigneurs** (me·sen·yurz′) **Monsignor** (mán·sēn′·yer) (*abbrev.* **Mgr.** or **Monsig.**), an Italian title given to prelates. Also **monsignore.** *pl.* **monsignori** [L. *meus*, my; *senior*, older].

mon·soon (mán·sōōn′) *n.* a seasonal wind of S. Asia which blows *on-shore* from the S.W. in summer, and *off-shore* from the N.E. in winter; the very heavy rainfall season in summer, esp. in India. **-al** *a.* [Ar. *mausin*, a season].

mon·ster (mŏn′·ster) *n.* a creature of unnatural shape; a person of abnormal callousness, cruelty, or wickedness. **monstrosity** *n.* an unnatural production; an abnormal creature; a freak. **monstrous** *a.* abnormal; enormous; horrible; shocking. **monstrously** *adv.* [L. *monstrum*, a marvel].

mon·strance (mŏn′·strans) *n.* a shrine for the consecrated host in R.C. services [L. *monstrare*, to show].

mon·tage (mŏn·tázh′) *n.* (*Motion pictures*) assembling various shots of a film into one well-arranged series; a picture made by superimposing various elements from several sources [Fr. *monter*, to mount].

Mon·tes·so·ri Sys·tem (mŏn·ta·sō′·ri sis′·tam) *n.* educational system to give free scope to child's individuality and creative powers [fr. Maria *Montessori*].

month (munth) *n.* one of the twelve divisions of the year—a **calendar month**, 31, 30 or 28 (29) days; the period of the complete revolution of the moon—a **lunar month**, about 29 days; a period of 28 days, or four complete weeks. **-ly** *a.* lasting, performed in, a month; *n.* a publication produced once each month; *pl.* the menses; *adv.* once a month [O.E. *monath*, a month].

mon·u·ment (mŏn′·ya·mant) *n.* any structure, as a tombstone, building tablet, erected to the memory of person, or event; an ancient record; an achievement of lasting value. **-al** *a.* like, or worthy of a monument; massive; colossal. **-ally** *adv.* [L. *monumentum*, fr. *monere*, to remind].

moo (mōō) *v.i.* to make the noise of a cow; to low; *n.* the lowing of a cow [imit.].

mooch (mōōch) *v.t.* and *v.i.* (*Colloq.*) to loiter; to sponge from another [O.Fr. *muchier*, to hang about].

mood (mōōd) *n.* (*Gram.*) the inflection of a verb expressing its function, as *indicative, imperative, subjunctive, infinitive*; (*Logic*) a form of syllogism; (*Mus.*) mode; the arrangement of intervals in the scale, as *major, minor* [var. of *mode*].

mood (mōōd) *n.* disposition; frame of mind; temper. **-ily** *adv.* **-iness** *n.* temporary depression of spirits; captiousness. **-y** *a.* peevish; sulky; depressed; angry [O.E. *mod*, mind].

moon (mōōn) *n.* the satellite which revolves around the earth in the period of a lunar month; any secondary planet; a month; anything crescent-shaped or shining like the moon; *v.i.* to gaze or wander about aimlessly. **-beam** *n.* a ray of moonlight. **-calf** *n.* a fool. **-faced** *a.* having a round, expressionless face. **-shine** *n.* light of the moon; nonsense; (*Colloq.*) smuggled liquor. **-stone** *n.* an almost pellucid form

of feldspar. **-struck** *a.* dazed [O.E. *mona*].

Moor (moor) *n.* a native of the Barbary States; one of the conquerors of Spain in the 8th cent. **-ish** *a.* [L. *Maurus, Mauretania*].

moor (moor) *n.* (*Brit.*) marshy wasteland. **-ish, -y** *a.* a heath [O.E. *mor*, marshland].

moor (moor) *v.t.* to secure by cables and anchors, as a vessel. **-age** *n.* place where vessel or airship is moored; charge for mooring. **-ing** *n.* the act of securing a ship; the place where a ship is moored [prob. Dut. *marren*, to tie].

moose (mōōs) *n.* largest species of deer; elk [Amer. Ind.].

moot (mōōt) *v.t.* to debate; to discuss; *a.* debatable; *n.* a discussion; in olden times, a council. **— court** *n.* a mock court [O.E. *gemot*, an assembly].

mop (måp) *n.* a bunch of soft cotton yarn or rags attached to handle for washing or polishing; a bushy head of hair; *v.t.* to wipe or polish. *pr.p.* **-ping.** *pa.p.* **-ped** [L. *mappa*, a napkin].

mope (mōp) *v.i.* to be dull or depressed; to sulk. **moping** *a.* listless; gloomy. **mopishly** *adv.* dispiritedly [Dut. *moppen*, to sulk].

mop·pet (måp′·at) *n.* (*Colloq.*) a doll; a child [fr. *mop*].

mo·raine (ma·rān′) *n.* rock debris which accumulates along the sides or at the end of a glacier [Fr.].

mor·al (mår′·al, mawr′·al) *a.* pert. to right conduct or duties of man; ethical; virtuous; chaste; discriminating between right and wrong; didactic; verified by reason or probability; *n.* the underlying meaning implied in a fable, allegory, etc. *pl.* ethics; conduct, esp. concerning sex-relations; habits. **-ization** *n.* **-ize** *v.t.* to explain in a moral sense; to draw a moral from; *v.i.* to reflect on ethical values of. **-izer** *n.* **-ist** *n.* one who moralizes; one who studies or teaches ethics; one who accepts ethics instead of religion as an adequate guide to good living. **-istic** *a.* **-ity** (ma·ral′·i·ti·) *n.* the practice of moral duties; virtue; ethics; an early form of drama, in which the characters were the virtues and vices of men personified. **-ly** *adv.* **— victory**, a defeat, which in a deeper sense, is a victory [L. *moralis*, of manners or customs].

mo·rale (ma·ral′) *n.* the disposition or mental state which causes a man or body of people to face an emergency with spirit, fortitude and unflagging zeal [Fr.].

mo·rass (ma·ras′) *n.* marshy ground; difficult state of affairs [Dut. *moeras*, a marsh].

mor·a·to·ri·um (mawr·a·tō′·ri·am) *n.* a law to delay payment of debts for a given period of time; the period of suspension of payments; **moratory** *a.* delaying [L. *mora*, delay].

mo·ray (mawr′·rā) *n.* a sharp-toothed marine eel [Gk. *muraina*].

mor·bid (mawr′·bid) *a.* diseased; unhealthy; (of the mind) excessively gloomy. **-ity** *n.* **-ly** *adv.* **-ness** *n.* **morbific** *a.* causing unhealthiness of body or mind [L. *morbus*, disease].

mor·dant (mawr′·dant) *n.* any substance, metallic or vegetable, which fixes dyes; a corrosive acid used in etching; *a.* biting; corrosive; sarcastic. **mordacious** *a.* acrid; sarcastic. **mordaciously** *adv.* **mordacity** *n.* **-ly** *adv.* [L. *mordere*, to bite].

mor·dent (mŏr′·dant) *n.* (*Mus.*) a trill [L. *mordere*, to bite].

more (mōr) *a.* greater in amount, degree, quality, etc.; in greater number; additional; *adv.* in a greater quantity, extent, etc.; besides; *n.* something additional. (*comp.* of **much, many**; *superl.* **most**) [O.E. *mara*].

mor·el (ma·rel′) *n.* an edible mushroom [Fr. *morille*].

mo·rel (ma·rel′) *n.* the common and deadly nightshade [O.Fr. *morel*, black].

mo·rel·lo (ma·rel′·ō) *n.* a variety of dark red cherry used in manufacture of brandy. Also **morel** [It. *morello*, dark-skinned].

more·o·ver (mōr·ō′·ver) *adv.* besides; also; further [fr. *more*].

mor·ga·nat·ic (mawr·ga·nat′·ik) *a.* applied to a marriage between a man of high, esp. royal rank, and a woman of lower station, the issue having no claim to his rank or property. **-ally** *adv.* [Ger. *Morgengabe*, a morning gift].

mo·res (maw′·rāz) *n.pl.* customs [L.].

morgue (mawrg) *n.* a place where bodies of people killed in accidents, etc., are taken to await identification; a library of clippings, etc. kept by a newspaper or publication [Fr.].

mor·i·bund (mawr′·i·bund) *a.* at the point of death [L. *moribundus*, dying].

Mor·mon (mawr′·man) *n.* alleged 4th cent. prophet & author, writings published 1830 by Joseph Smith, founder of the Church of Jesus Christ of Latter-Day Saints; member of The Church professing Theocracy &, formerly, polygamy. **-ism** *n.*

morn (mawrn) *n.* (*Poetic*) the early part of the day [O.E. *morgen*, morning].

morn·ing (mawr′·ning) *n.* the first part of the day between dawn and midday; (*Fig.*) the first part of anything; *a.* pert. to or happening at this time. **—glory** *n.* a twining vine with flowers. **—coat** *n.* a tail-coat with cutaway front. **— star** *n.* a planet visible before sunrise [M.E. *morwening*, the coming of the day].

mo·ron (mōr′·ån) *n.* an adult with the mental development of an 8-12 yr. old child. **moronic** *a.* [Gk. *moros*, stupid].

mo·rose (ma·rōs′) *a.* sullen; gloomy; soured in nature. **-ly** *adv.* **-ness** *n.* [L. *morosus*, fretful].

mor·pheme (mawr′·fēm) *n.* (*Gram.*) the smallest meaningful linguistic unit; *free form* as **boy**, or *bound form* as *ish* in *boyish.*

mor·phine (mawr′·fēn) *n.* an alkaloid of opium; a drug used to induce sleep and to deaden pain. [fr. *Morpheus*, Gk. god of sleep].

mor·ph-, morphic, morphous word elements meaning form or shape [Gk.].

mor·row (mawr′·ō) *n.* next day; (*Poet.*) morning [O.E. *morgen*, the morning].

Morse (mawrs) *n.* a system of telegraphic signals in which the alphabet is represented by combinations of dots and dashes [fr. Amer. inventor S. F. B. *Morse*].

mor·sel (mawr′·sal) *n.* a mouthful; a small piece [O.Fr. dim fr. L. *morsus*, a bite].

mor·tal (mawr′·tal) *a.* subject to death; fatal; meriting damnation, as sin; implacable, as a foe; *n.* a human being. **-ity** (mawr·tal′·i·ti·) *n.* death; death-rate; the human race. **-ly** *adv.* [L. *mortalis*, fr. *mors*, death].

mor·tar (mawr′·ter) *n.* a thick bowl of porcelain, glass, etc., in which substances are pounded with a pestle; a mill for pulverizing ores; (*Mil.*) a short-barreled cannon for short-distance firing of heavy shells; a cement made of lime, sand and water, used in building; *v.t.* to pound in a mortar; to cement, with mortar. **-board** *n.* a square board used when mixing mortar; an academic cap [L. *mortarium*].

mort·gage (mawr′·gij) *n.* (*Law*) a conveyance of property in security of a loan; the deed effecting this; *v.t.* to pledge as security. **mortgagee** *n.* one to whom a mortgage is given. **mortgagor** *n.* one who gives a mortgage to a mortgagee [O.Fr. *mort*, dead; *gage*, a pledge].

mor·ti·cian (mawr·tish′·an) *n.* an undertaker [L. *mors*, death].

mor·ti·fy (mawr′·ta·fi) *v.t.* to discipline the flesh; to humiliate; to vex; *v.i.* (*Med.*) to become gangrenous. **mortification** *n.* the act of mortifying or the state of being mortified; humiliation; (*Med.*) gangrene; the death of one part of a living body [L. *mors*, death; *facere*, to make].

mor·tise (mawr′·tis) *n.* a hole in a piece of wood to receive the projection or tenon of another piece, made to fit it. Also **mortice.** *v.t.* to cut or make a mortise in; to join with a mortise.

mort·main (mawrt′·mān) *n.* an inalienable bequest; the holding of land by a corporation, which cannot be transferred [O.Fr. *mortmain*, dead hand].

mor·tu·ar·y (mawr′·choo·er·i·) *n.* a place for the temporary reception of dead bodies; *a.* pert. to burial [L. *mortus*, dead].

mo·sa·ic (mō·zā′·ik) *a.* pert. to or made of mosaic; *n.* inlaid work of colored glass or marble [Gk. *mousa*, a muse].

Mo·sa·ic (mō·zā′·ik) *a.* (*Bib.*) pert. to *Moses*, or to the laws and writing attributed to him.

Mo·selle (mō·zel′) *n.* a light wine (fr. *Moselle*, Fr.).

Mos·lem (måz′·lam) *n.* a Mohammedan; *a.* pert. to the Mohammedans or their religion. Also **Muslim** [Ar. *salama*, submit to God].

mosque (måsk) *n.* a Mohammedan temple [Ar. *masjid*, temple].

mos·qui·to (ma·skē′·tō) *n.* an insect which draws blood, leaving a raised, itchy spot. **-net**, a net covering to ward off mosquitos [L. *musca*, a fly].

moss (maws) *n.* a small, thickly growing plant which thrives on moist surfaces; lichen. **— agate** *n.* an agate with moss-like markings. **-back** *n.* (*Colloq.*) an extreme conservative. **-iness** *n.* **-y** *a.* covered with moss [O.E. *mos*, bog-land].

most (mōst) *a.* (*superl.* of **much, many**; *comp.* is **more**) the greatest number or quantity; greatest; *adv.* in the greatest degree; *n.* the greatest quantity, number, etc. **-ly** *adv.* for the most part [O.E. *maest*, most].

mot (mō) *n.* pithy, witty saying [Fr. = word].

mote (mōt) *n.* a small particle; a speck of dust [O.E. *mot*, a particle].

mo·tel (mō′·tel) *n.* lodging for travelers [motor + hotel].

mo·tet (mō·tet′) *n.* a musical composition for (unaccompanied) voices, to words from Scripture [Fr. dim. of *mot*, a word].

moth (mawth) *n.* a nocturnal winged insect; larva of this insect which feeds on cloth, esp. woolens. —**balls** *n.pl.* balls of moth repellent. —**eaten** *a.* eaten into holes by moth larva; decrepit [O.E. *moththe*].

moth·er (muTH'·er) *n.* a female parent; the head of a convent; the origin of anything; *a.* characteristic of a mother; native; original; *v.t.* to be the mother or author of; to adopt as one's own; to cherish, as a mother her child. —**hood** *n.* the state of being a mother. —**in-law** *n.* the mother of one's wife or husband. —**liness** *n.* -**ly** *a.* having attributes of a mother. — **of pearl** *n.* the iridescent lining of several kinds of shells. **Mother Superior,** the head of a convent. — **tongue** *n.* one's native language [O.E. *modor*, a mother].

mo·tif (mō·tēf') *n.* the dominant theme in a literary or musical composition [Fr.].

mo·tion (mō'·shan) *n.* the act of moving; movement; a gesture; a proposal made in an assembly; *v.t.* to guide by gesture; *v.i.* to gesture. —**less** *a.* still; immobile. — **picture** *n.* a series of photographs projected on a screen rapidly, as to approximate lifelike movement [L. *movere, motum,* to move].

mo·tive (mō'·tiv) *n.* that which incites to action; inner impulse; motif; *a.* causing movement or motion; *v.t.* to impel; to motivate. **motivate** *v.t.* to incite. **motivation** *n.* -**less** *a.* without purpose or direction. **motivity** *n.* capacity to produce motion [L. *movere, motum,* to move].

mot·ley (mát'·li·) *a.* vari-colored; diversified; *n.* a jester's dress; a diversified mixture.

mo·tor (mō'·ter) *n.* that which imparts motion; a machine which imparts motive power, esp. the internal-combustion engine; *a.* causing motion; (*Anat.*) producing muscular activity, as *motor nerves; v.t.* and *v.i.* to travel by, or convey in, a motor driven vehicle. -**cade** *n.* procession of automobiles. -**ize** *v.t.* to mechanize (the transport of the army). -**ist** *n.* one who drives or travels in an automobile. -**man** *n.* one who drives a streetcar [L. *motor,* a mover].

mot·tle (mát'·l) *v.t.* to mark with spots of different colors; to dapple. -**d** *a.* variegated [prob. fr. *motley*].

mot·to (mát'·ō) *n.* a maxim or principle of behavior [L. *muttum,* a murmur].

moue (mōō) *n.* a pout [Fr.].

mou·lage (mōō'·lázh) *n.* the making of molds [Fr.].

mound (mound) *n.* an artificial elevation of earth; a knoll; an earthwork for defensive purposes; a heap; (*Baseball*) point from which pitcher delivers the ball; *v.t.* to fortify with a mound; to heap [O.E. *mund,* a defense].

mount (mount) *n.* (*poet.,* except in proper names) a mountain or hill; that on which anything is mounted for exhibition; a horse for riding; *v.t.* to raise up; to ascend; to get on a horse or bicycle; to frame (a picture); to set (gem-stones) ; to put on a slide for microscope examination; to stage a play with costumes, scenery, etc.; to raise guns into position; *v.i.* to rise up; to get up; to increase. -**ed** *a.* -**ing** *n.* **to mount guard,** to be on sentry duty; to keep watch over [L. *mons,* a mountain].

moun·tain (mount'·n) *n.* a high hill; *a.* pert. to a mountain; growing or living on a mountain. — **ash** *n.* any of a variety of small trees. — **dew** *n.* (*Scot.*) whisky. -**eer** *n.* one who lives on or climbs high mountains. — **goat** *n.* the Rocky Mountain goat. — **laurel** *n.* American laurel. -**ous** *a.* very steep; full of mountains; colossal. — **range** *n.* a series or system

of mountains [L. *mons,* a mountain].

moun·te·bank (moun'·ta·bangk) *n.* a quack doctor; a charlatan [It. *montambanco,* mount on bench or platform].

Mount·ie (moun'·ti·) *n.* a member of the Canadian N.W. Mounted Police.

mourn (mōrn, mawrn) *v.t.* to grieve over; to lament; *v.i.* to express grief; to wear mourning. -**er** *n.* -**ful** *a.* sad; dismal. -**fully** *adv.* -**fulness** *n.* -**ing** *n.* the act of grieving; lamentation; wearing of black as a sign of grief; the period during which such clothes are worn [O.E. *murnan,* to grieve].

mouse (mous) *n.* a small rodent found in fields, or houses; a timid person. *pl.* **mice. mouse** (mouz) *v.t.* and *v.i.* to catch mice; to search for patiently or slyly; to prowl. —**color** *a.* dark greyish brown. -**r** *n.* an animal which catches mice. —**trap** *n.* **mousy** *a.* resembling a mouse in color; timid; quiet drab [O.E. *mus,* a mouse].

mousse (mōōs) *n.* a light-frozen dessert [Fr. *mousse,* froth].

mouth (mouth) *n.* an opening between lips of men and animals through which food is taken; lips, as a feature; the cavity behind the lips containing teeth, tongue, palate, and vocal organs; an opening as of a bottle, cave, etc.; the estuary of a river; a wry face. *pl.* **mouths** (mouTHz); *v.t.* (mouTH) to speak, with noticeable use of the mouth; to put or take into the mouth; to mumble; *v.i.* to make grimaces. -**ful** *n.* as much as the mouth conveniently holds; a small amount. — **organ** *n.* harmonica. -**piece** *n.* the part of a musical instrument, pipe, etc., held in mouth; (*Fig.*) a spokesman; a newspaper (as expressing public opinion) [O.E. *muth,* the mouth].

move (mōōv) *v.t.* to set in motion; to stir emotions of; to prevail on; to incite; to propose for consideration; *v.i.* to change one's position, posture, residence, etc.; to march; to make a proposal or recommendation; *n.* the act of moving; a change of residence; a movement, as in game of checkers. **movable, moveable** *a.*; *n.pl.* (*Law*) the furnishings of a house which are not permanent fixtures. -**ment** *n.* the act of moving; the part of a machine which moves; organized activity of a society; a division of a musical composition; evacuation of the bowels. -**r** *n.* **movies** *n.pl.* (*Colloq.*) motion pictures. **moving** *a.* causing motion; affecting the emotions; pathetic. **moving picture** *n.* motion picture. **moving staircase,** an escalator [L. *movere,* to move].

mow (mō) *v.t.* to cut down with a scythe or machine; to cut down in great numbers, as enemy. -**er** *n.* one who or that which mows [O.E. *mawan,* to mow].

mow (mou) *n.* a heap of hay, or corn, in a barn; *v.t.* to put into a mow as a *haymow* [O.E. *muga,* a heap].

much (much) *a.* (*comp.* **more;** *superl.* **most**) great in quantity or amount; abundant; *n.* a great quantity; *adv.* to a great degree or extent; almost. -**ness** *n.* greatness. -**ly** *adv.* (*Colloq.*) much. **to make much of,** to treat as of great importance [M.E. *muchel*].

mu·cid (mū'·sid) *a.* moldy, musty. Also -**ous.** -**ness** *n.* [L. *mucidus,* moldy].

mu·ci·lage (mū'·sa·lij) *n.* a gummy substance extracted from plants and animals; an adhesive. **mucilaginous** *a.* slimy; sticky [L. *mucus, mucus*].

muck (muk) *n.* moist manure; anything vile or filthy; *v.t.* to manure; to make filthy. -**iness** *n.* -**y** *a.* filthy [O.N. *myki,* dung].

muck·rake (muk'·rāk) *n.* one esp. a reporter, who searches for corruption, scandal [fr. a *muck raker,* coined by T. Roosevelt].

mu·cus (mū'·kas) *n.* a viscid fluid secreted by the mucous membranes; slimy. **mucoid** *a.* like mucus. **mucous** *a.* of mucus; slimy [L.].

mud (mud) *n.* soft, wet dirt; aspersions, as in *to throw mud at a person* -**dily** *adv.* -**diness** *n.* -**dy** *a.* consisting of mire or mud; dull; cloudy, as liquid; *v.t.* to soil with mud; to confuse. *pr.p.* -**ding.** *pa.p.,* *pa.t.* -**ded.** -**flat** *n.* a stretch of mud below high-water. -**guard** *n.* a shield to protect from mud splashes [O.L. Ger. *mudde,* mud].

mud·dle (mud'·l) *v.t.* to make muddy; to confuse; to bewilder; to mix up; *v.i.* to be confused; *n.* confusion; jumble [fr.mud].

muff (muf) *n.* a warm covering for both hands, usu. of fur, shaped like a cylinder and open at both ends; (*Baseball*) failure to hold a ball one has caught; *v.t.* to bungle [fr. Dut. *mof,* mitten].

muf·fin (muf'·in) *n.* a small cup-shaped bread, usu. eaten hot.

muf·fle (muf'·l) *v.t.* to wrap up for warmth or to hide something; to deaden (sound of); *n.* something used to deaden sound or provide warmth. -**d** *a.* -**r** *n.* a scarf; a silencer [O.Fr. *moufle,* a thick glove].

muf·ti (muf'·ti·) *n.* a Mohammedan advisor in regard to religious law; civilian dress worn by soldiers when off duty [Ar.].

mug (mug) *n.* a straight-sided earthenware or metal cup with or without a handle; the contents of this; (*Slang*) the face or mouth, a grimace, a rough person; *v.t.* (*Slang*) to attack from behind, by strangling, with intent to rob. *v.i.* (*Slang*) to grimace or overact. *pr.p.* -**ging.** *pa.p.,* *pa.t.* -**ged.** -**ger** *n.*

mug·gins (mug'·inz) *n.* (*Brit.*) a simpleton; a game of dominoes.

mug·gy (mug'·i·) *a.* warm and humid, as

weather; close; enervating. **mugginess** *n.* [O.N. *mugga,* a mist].

mug·wump (mug'·wump) *n.* one who holds independent political views [N. Amer. Ind. *mugquomp,* big chief].

mu·lat·to (ma·lat'·ō) *n.* offspring of white person and Negro. *pl.* -**es** [Port. *mulato,* of mixed breed].

mul·ber·ry (mul'·ber·i·) *n.* a deciduous tree on the leaves of which the silkworm feeds; the fruit of this tree; a purplish-brown color [L. *morum;* A.S. *herie*].

mulch (mulch) *n.* a protective covering of straw, manure, etc., for plants; *v.t.* to treat with mulch [M.E. *molsh,* soft].

mulct (mulkt) *n.* a fine imposed as a penalty; *v.t.* to punish with a fine; to deprive of [L. *mulcia,* a fine].

mule (mūl) *n.* the hybrid offspring of a donkey or horse; a small tractor for hauling, in mines, along canals, etc.; a heelless bedroom slipper; an obstinate person. -**teer** *n.* a mule driver. **mulish** *a.* obstinate; pig-headed. **mulishly** *adv.* **mulishness** *n.* [O.E. *mul,* a he-ass].

mull (mul) *v.t.* to heat, sweeten and spice (wine, ale, etc.). -**ed** *a.*

mull (mul) *v.i.* to muse upon; to cogitate.

mul·let (mul'·at) *n.* an edible fish [L. *mullus*].

mul·li·gan (mul'·i·gan) *n.* a stew made from left-over meat and vegetables.

mul·li·ga·taw·ny (mul·i·ga·taw'·ni·) *n.* a rich soup flavored with curry, thickened with rice [Tamil].

mul·lion (mul'·yan) *n.* a dividing upright between the lights of windows, panels, etc. *v.t.* to divide by mullions. -**ed** *a.* [L. *mancus,* maimed].

mul·ti- *prefix,* fr. L. *multus,* many.

mul·ti·col·or (mul'·ti·kul·er) *a.* having many colors. -**ed** *a.*

mul·ti·far·i·ous (mul·ta·far'·i·as) *a.* manifold; made up of many parts [L. *manifold*].

mul·ti·form (mul'·ti·fawrm) *a.* having many forms. -**ity** *n.*

mul·ti·lat·er·al (mul·ti·lat'·er·al) *a.* having many sides. -**ly** *adv.* [L. *multus,* many; *latus,* a side].

mul·ti·mil·lion·aire (mul'·ti·mil'·yan·er) *n.* a person who is worth several million dollars.

mul·ti·par·tite (mul·ti·pàr'·tit) *a.* having many parts; (*Govt.*) pert. to an agreement among three or more states; multilateral.

mul·ti·ped (mul'·ti·ped) *n.* and *a.* (animal) with many feet. Also **multipede.**

mul·ti·ple (mul'·ta·pl) *a.* manifold; of many parts; repeated many times; *n.* (*Math.*) a quantity containing another an exact number of times. — **fission** *n.* repeated division [L. *multiplex,* manifold].

mul·ti·ply (mul'·ta·pli) *v.t.* to increase in number; to add a number to itself a given number of times; *v.i.* to increase; to grow in number. **multiplex** *a.* multiple; (of telegraph) capable of transmitting numerous messages over the same wire. **multipliable, multiplicable** *a.* **multiplicand** *n.* the number to be multiplied. **multiplication** *n.* the act of multiplying; a rule or operation by which any given number may be added to itself any specified number of times (the symbol $\times$). **multiplicative** *a.* **multiplicator** *n.* a multiplier. **multiplicity** *n.* the state of being multiplied; great number. **multiplier** *n.* a number by which another, the **multiplicand,** is multiplied [L. *multus,* many; *plicare,* to fold].

mul·ti·tude (mul'·ta·tūd) *n.* a great number; numerousness; a crowd; an assemblage. **multitudinous** *a.* made up of a great number [L. *multitudo*].

mul·ti·va·lent (mul·ta·vā'·lant) *a.* (*Chem.*) having a valency of more than two. **multivalence, multivalency** *n.*

mul·ti·valve (mul'·ti·valv) *a.* having many valves; *n.* a mollusk with a shell of many valves.

mum (mum) *a.* silent; *n.* silence. **mum's the word,** keep it a secret [imit.].

mum (mum) *v.t.* to perform in dumb show; to act in a mask. -**mer** *n.* one who performs. -**mery** *n.* exaggerated ceremony. *pr.p.* -**ming.** *pa.p.,* *pa.t.* -**med** [Dut. *mommen,* to mask].

mum·ble (mum'·bl) *v.t.,* *i.* to utter, speak indistinctly; *n.* an indistinct utterance [fr. *mum*].

mum·bo jum·bo (mum'·bō jum'·bō) *n.* meaningless ritual [fr. Afr. idol worship].

mum·my (mum'·i·) *n.* a dead body preserved by embalming. **mummified** *a.* **mummification** *n.* **mummify** *v.t.* to embalm and dry as a mummy; *v.i.* to become dried up like a mummy [Pers. *mum,* wax].

mumps (mumps) *n.* a highly infectious disease causing painful swelling of face and neck glands (form of *mum*).

munch (munch) *v.t.* and *v.i.* to chew noisily and steadily [M.E. imit.].

mun·dane (mun'·dān) *a.* pert. to this world; worldly [L. *mundus,* the world].

mu·nic·i·pal (mū·nis'·a·pal) *a.* pert. to local government or to internal affairs (not international). -**ity** (mū·nis·a·pal'·i·ti·) *a* town or district with its own local self-government. -**ly** *adv.* [L. *municipium,* a free town].

mu·nif·i·cence (mū·nif'·a·sans) *n.* liberality; generosity. **munificent** *a.* very generous. **munificently** *adv.* [L. *munus,* a gift; *facere,* to make].

mu·ni·ment (mū'·na·mant) *n.* means of protection. *pl.* title deeds; charter [L. *munire,* to fortify].

mu·ni·tion (mū·nish′·ạn) *v.t.* to equip with the weapons of war; *n.* (usually *pl.*) military stores or weapons [L. *munifus*, fortified].

mu·ral (mūr′·ạl) *a.* pert. to a wall; on a wall; *n.* a wall painting [L. *muralis*].

mur·der (mur′·der) *n.* homicide with premeditated and malicious intent; *v.t.* to commit a murder; to kill; to mar by incompetence. **-er** *n.* (*fem.* **-ess**) **-ous** *a.* bloody; homicidal. **-ously** *adv.* [O.E. *morthor*, murder].

mu·ri·ate (myoo′·ri·āt) *n.* a chloride. **muriated** briny. **muriatic acid**, hydrochloric acid [L. *muria*, brine].

murk (murk) *a.* dark; *n.* darkness; gloom. **-y** *a.* dark; misty. **-ily** *adv.* **-iness** *n.* [O.E. *mirce*, dark].

mur·mur (mur′·mẹr) *n.* a low, unbroken sound, as of wind, water, etc.; a complaint expressed in subdued tones; softly uttered speech; *v.i.* to make a low sound; to speak in subdued tones; to complain. **-er** *n.* [L. *murmur*, a low sound].

mur·rain (mur′·in) *n.* a disease affecting cattle, foot-and-mouth disease [O.Fr. *morine*, a plague].

mus·cat (mus′·kat) *n.* a sweet grape; **-el** (mus·ka·tel′) *n.* a wine made from this grape [It. *moscato*, musk-flavored].

mus·cle (mus′·l) *n.* a band of contractile fibrous tissue which produces movement in an animal body; strength. **—bound** *a.* with muscles enlarged and stiffened from too much exercise. **-d** *a.* having muscle; muscular. **muscular** *a.* pert. to muscle; brawny; strong. **muscularity** *n.* **muscularly** *adv.* **to muscle in** (*Slang*) to break in by force [L. *musculus*, a muscle].

mus·coid (mus′·koid) *a.* (*Bot.*) like moss. **muscology** *n.* the study of mosses [L. *muscus*, moss].

Mus·co·vite (mus′·kạ·vīt) *n.* a native or inhabitant of Moscow or of Russia. **muscovite** *n.* white mica; *a.* pert. to Moscow or to Russia.

Muse (mūz) *n.* (*Gk. myth.*) one of the nine daughters of Zeus and Mnemosyne, who each presided over one of the liberal arts. *n.* inspiration. **the muse**, poetry [Gk. *Mousa*].

muse (mūs) *v.i.* to think over dreamily; to ponder; to consider meditatively; *n.* reverie; contemplation. **musingly** *adv.* reflectively [O.Fr. *muser*, to loiter].

mu·sette (mū·zet′) *n.* a small bagpipe; a melody for this instrument; a reed stop on an organ; a country dance [O.Fr. a small bagpipe].

mu·se·um (mū·zē′·ạm) *n.* a building or room housing a collection of works of art, antiques, objects of natural history, the sciences, etc. [Gk. *Mouseion*, a temple of the Muses].

mush (mush) *n.* a pulp; (*U.S.*) porridge of corn meal; a soft mass; (*Slang*) sentimentality. **-y** *a.* **-iness** *n.* [form of *mash*].

mush (mush) *v.i.* to journey on foot with dogs over snowy wastes; *interj.* command to dogs to start or speed up.

mush·room (mush′·room) *n.* an edible fungus of very quick growth; (*Fig.*) an upstart; *a.* of rapid growth; shaped like a mushroom; *v.i.* to gather mushrooms; to grow quickly [prob. fr. Fr. *mousse*, moss].

mu·sic (mū′·zik) *n.* the art of combining sounds or sequences of notes into harmonious patterns pleasing to the ear and satisfying to the emotions; melody; musical composition or score. **-al** *a.* *pert.* to music; set to music; appreciative of music; trained or skilled in the art of music. **-ally** *adv.* **— box** *n.* a box which when wound up plays a tune. **-al comedy**, a form of light entertainment in which songs, dialogue, dancing, humor are combined with a not too serious plot. **-ale** (mū·zi·kal′) *n.* a private party with music. **— hall** *n.* a hall for musical programs. **-ian** (mū·zi′·shạn) *n.* a

composer or skilled performer of musical compositions. **-ology** *n.* the scientific study of music [Gk. *mousikos*, pert. to the Muses].

mushroom

musk (musk) *n.* a fragrant substance obtained from a gland of the musk deer; the perfume of this; any plant with a musky perfume. **-cat** *n.* civet. **— deer** *n.* a small, hornless deer. Also **Muscovy-duck.** **-melon** *n.* common melon. **— ox** *n.* a sheep-like ox with brown, long-haired shaggy coat. **-rat** *n.* a large N. Amer. water rat with musk-gland, valued for its fur. **— rose** *n.* a climbing rose with white blossoms faintly perfumed with musk. **-y** *a.* having the smell of musk [L. *muscus*, musk].

mus·ket (mus′·kit) *n.* (formerly) a hand gun or matchlock. **-eer** *n.* a soldier armed with a musket [O.Fr. *mousquet*, a sparrow hawk].

Mus·lim (muz′·lạm) *n.* See **Moslem.**

mus·lin (muz′·lin) *n.* a thin cotton cloth of open weave; *a.* made of muslin [fr. *Mosul*, in Iraq].

mus·quash (mus′·kwash) *n.* the muskrat, or its fur [Amer. Ind.].

muss (mus) *v.t.* (*Colloq.*) to disorganize; to make messy. **-y** *a.*

mus·sel (mus′·l) *n.* a class of marine bivalve shellfish [L. *musculus*, mussel].

must (must) *v.i.* to be obliged, by physical or moral necessity; *v.aux.* to express compulsion, obligation, probability, certainty, dependent on verb used with it; *n.* a necessity [O.E. *moste*, pret. of verb, *not*, may].

must (must) *n.* wine newly pressed from grapes but not fermented [L. *mustus*, new].

mus·tache (mạs·tash′) *n.* the hair on the upper lip [Fr. *moustache*].

mus·tang (mus′·tang) *n.* a wild horse of the Amer. prairies; a bronco [Sp. *mestengo*, belonging to graziers].

mus·tard (mus′·terd) *n.* a plant with yellow flowers and pungent seeds; a powder or paste made from the seeds, used as a condiment. **— gas**, dichlorodiethyl sulphide, an oily liquid, irritant war-gas [O.Fr. *moustarde*].

mus·ter (mus′·ter) *v.t.* to assemble, as troops for a parade; to gather together, as one's resources; *v.i.* to be assembled together; *n.* an assembling of troops, etc. **to pass muster**, to be up to standard [O.Fr. *mostre*, show].

mus·ty (mus′·ti) *a.* moldy; stale. **mustily** *adv.* **-iness** *n.* [L. *mustum*, new wine].

mu·ta·ble (mū′·tạ·bl) *a.* subject to change; inconstant. **-ness, mutability,** *n.* **mutably** *adv.* **mutate** *v.t.* to change, as a vowel by the influence of another in a subsequent syllable. **mutation** *n.* change; the process of vowel change; (*Biol.*) a complete divergence from racial type which may ultimately give rise to a new species. **mutative, mutatory** *a.* [L. *mutare*, to change].

mute (mūt) *a.* dumb; silent; unexpressed in

words; not sounded, as *e* of *cave*; *n.* a person who cannot speak; (*Mus.*) a device to soften or muffle tone; *v.t.* to muffle the sound of. **-ly** *adv.* **-ness** *n.* [L. *mutus*, dumb].

mu·ti·late (mū′·tạ·lāt) *v.t.* to maim; to cut off; to impair by removing an essential part. **mutilation** *n.* **mutilator** *n.* [L. *mutilus*, maimed].

mu·ti·ny (mū′·ti·ni·) *n.* insurrection against lawful authority, esp. military or naval; *v.i.* to rise in mutiny. **mutineer** *n.* **mutinous** *a.* rebellious; seditious [Fr. *mutin*, mutinous].

mutt (mut) *n.* (*Slang*) a fool; a dog, a mongrel.

mut·ter (mut′·er) *v.t.* to speak indistinctly or in a low voice; to grumble. **-er** *n.* **-ing** *n.*

mut·ton (mut′·n) *n.* the flesh of sheep, esp. mature sheep, as food. **—chop whiskers,** side whiskers [Fr. *mouton*, a sheep].

mu·tu·al (mū′·choo·ạl) *a.* reciprocally acting or related; interchanged; done by each to the other; common to several, as a *mutual friend.* **-ity** *n.* the quality of being reciprocal. **-ly** *adv.* [L. *mutuus*, borrowed].

mu·zhik (mŏŏ·zhēk′) *n.* a Russian peasant.

muz·zle (muz′·l) *v.t.* the snout; the mouth and nose of an animal; a cage-like fastening for the mouth to prevent biting; the open end of a gun; *v.t.* to put a muzzle on; to gag; to enforce silence [L. *musus*, a snout].

muz·zy (muz′·i·) *a.* (*Colloq.*) dazed; bewildered.

my (mī) *poss. a.* belonging to **me** [contr. of *mine*; O.E. *min*, of me].

my·col·o·gy (mī·kál′·ạ·ji·) *n.* the science of fungi. **mycologist** *n.* **mycophagy** *n.* the eating of fungi [Gk. *mukēs*, a mushroom].

my·e·lin (mī′·ạ·lạn) *n.* (*Zool.*) the fatty substance forming the sheath of nerve fibers. **myelitis** *n.* inflammation of the spinal cord or bone marrow [Gk. *muelos*, marrow].

my·na(h) (mī′·nạ) *n.* a tropical starling, one variety mimics human speech [Hind.].

my·o- *prefix* from Gk. **mys, myos** meaning muscle.

my·o·car·di·tis (mī·ạ·kár·dīt′·ạs) *n.* (*Med.*) inflammation of the heart muscle.

my·o·ma (mī·ō′·mạ) *n.* tumor of muscle tissue.

my·o·pi·a (mī·ō′·pi·ạ) *n.* near-sightedness. **myopic** *a.* [Gk. *muein*, to close; *ōps*, the eye].

my·o·sis (mī·ō′·sis) *n.* prolonged contraction of the pupil of the eye [Gk. *myein*, to close; *-osis*].

my·o·so·tis (mī·ạ·sō′·tis) *n.* a genus of herbs including the forget-me-not [Gk. = mouse-ear].

myr·i·ad (mir′·i·ạd) *n.* an indefinitely large number; *a.* countless [Gk. *murias*, ten thousand].

myr·i·a·pod (mir′·i·ạ·pảd) *n.* (*Zool.*) an animal with great number of legs, as centipede [Gk. *murias*, ten thousand; *pous*, a foot].

myr·me·col·o·gy (mur·mạ·kál′·ạ·ji·) *n.* the scientific study of ants and ant life [Gk. *murmēx*, an ant].

myrrh (mur) *n.* a transparent yellow-brown aromatic gum resin formerly used as incense, now used in antiseptics [Gk. *murrha*, myrrh].

myr·tle (mur′·tl) *n.* an evergreen plant with fragrant flowers and glossy leaves; (*U.S.*) the periwinkle [O.Fr. *myrtille*, the myrtle-berry].

my·self (mī·self′) *pron.* I or me, used emphatically, or reflexively.

mys·ter·y (mis′·ter·i·) *n.* anything strange and inexplicable; a puzzle; a religious truth beyond human understanding; secrecy; a medieval drama based on Scripture; *pl.* rites known to and practiced by initiated only. **mysterious** *a.* strange; occult; incomprehensible. **mysteriously** *adv.* [Gk. *mystēria*, secret religious rites].

mys·tic (mis′·tik) *a.* pert. to a mystery, to secret religious rites, or to mysticism; symbolical of spiritual truth; strange; *n.* one who believes in mysticism; one who seeks to have direct contact with the Divine by way of spiritual ecstasy and contemplation. **-al** *a.* **-ally** *adv.* **-ism** (mis′·ti·zịm) *n.* the doctrine of the mystics; study of spiritual experience; obscurity of doctrine. **mystification** *n.* **mystify** *v.t.* to perplex: to puzzle [Gk. *mustikos*, pert. to one initiated in the mysteries].

myth (mith) *n.* a fable; a legend embodying primitive faith in the supernatural; an invented story; an imaginary person or thing. **-ic, -ical** *a.* pert. to myths; fabulous; non-existent. **-ically** *adv.* **-ologic, (-al)** *a.* pert. to mythology; legendary. **-ologically** *adv.* **-ologist** *n.* one who has studied myths of various countries; a writer of fables. **-ology** *n.* a collection of myths; the science of myths; a treatise on myths [Gk. *muthos*, a story].

myx·e·de·ma (mik·sạ·dē′·mạ) *n.* (*Med.*) a disease caused by deficiency of secretion from thyroid gland [Gk. *muxa*, mucus; *oidēma*, swelling].

N

nab (nab) *v.t.* to catch hold of; to seize suddenly. *pr.p.* **-bing**. *pa.t.*, *pa.p.* **-bed** [Dan. *nappe*, to catch].

na·bob (nā'·bŏb) *n.* a Mohammedan chief in India; any man of great wealth [Hind. *nawwab*].

na·celle (nạ·sĕl') *n.* the part fixed to the wing of any aircraft serving to enclose engine, crew, passengers, and goods [Fr. fr. L. *navicella*, a little ship].

na·cre (nā'·kẹr) *n.* mother-of-pearl. **nacreous** *a.* [Fr. fr. Sp. *nacar*].

na·dir (nā'·dẹr) *n.* point of the heavens directly opposite the zenith; the lowest or most depressed stage [Ar. *nazir*, opposite].

nag (nag) *n.* a small horse; an old horse; (*Colloq.*) any horse [etym. uncertain].

nag (nag) *v.t.* and *v.i.* to worry by constant faultfinding; to scold. *pr.p.* **-ging**. *pa.t.* and *pa.p.* **-ged**. **-ger** *n.* [Sw. *nagga*, to peck].

nai·ad (nā'·ad, or nī'·ad) *n.* (*Class. Myth.*) a nymph of the streams. [Gk. *naias*].

nail (nāl) *n.* the horny shield covering the ends of the fingers or toes; a claw; a strip of pointed metal provided with a head, for fastening wood, etc.; *v.t.* to fasten with a nail; to fix or secure; to confirm or pin down; (*Colloq.*) to seize hold of. — **brush** *n.* a small brush for cleaning the fingernails. **-er** *n.* a factory where nails are made. [O.E. *naegel*].

na·ïve (nạ·ēv') *a.* having native or unaffected simplicity; childishly frank; artless. **-ly** *adv.* **naiveté** (nạ·ēv·tā') *n.* childlike ingenuousness. Also **naivety** [Fr.].

na·ked (nā'·kid) *a.* having no clothes; exposed; bare; nude; uncovered; unarmed; manifest; evident; undisguised; simple; sheer. **-ly** *adv.* **-ness** *n.* [O.E. *nacod*].

nam·by-pam·by (nam'·bi·pam'·bi·) *a.* insipid, lacking strength of character; weakly sentimental [a nickname for *Ambrose Philips*, a poet who wrote childishly affected verse].

name (nām) *n.* the term by which any person or thing is known; appellation; designation; title; fame; reputation; family; *v.t.* to give a name to; to call or mention by name; to nominate; to specify; to christen; **-less** *a.* without a name; dishonored; obscure; unspeakable. **-lessly** *adv.* **-ly** *adv.* by name; that is to say. **-sake** *n.* a person who bears the same name as another [O.E. *nama*].

nan·keen (nan·kēn') *n.* a cotton fabric dyed buff [*Nanking*, China, where first woven].

nan·ny (nan'·i·) *n.* (*Brit.*) a child's nurse. — **goat** *n.* a she-goat.

nap (nap) *n.* a short sleep; a doze; *v.i.* to indulge in a short sleep; to be unprepared. *pr.p.* **-ping** *pa.t.*, *pa.p.* **-ped** [O.E. *knappian*].

nap (nap) *n.* fine hairy surface of cloth; the pile of velvet [Dut. *nop*].

na·palm (nā'·pám) *n.* jellied gasoline used in flame throwers.

nape (nāp) *n.* the back part of the neck [O.E. *hnaepp*, bowl].

na·per·y (nā'·per·i·) *n.* household linen, esp. for the table [O.Fr. *naperie*].

naph·tha (nap'·tha, naf'·tha) *n.* a clear, volatile, inflammable liquid distilled from petroleum, wood, etc. **-lene** *n.* a white, solid crystalline hydrocarbon distilled from coal tar and familiar in the form of moth balls [Gk.].

nap·kin (nap'·kin) *n.* a cloth used for wiping the hands or lips at table [Fr. *nappe*, cloth].

---

na·po·le·on (nạ·pōl'·yạn) *n.* a pastry of several cream-filled layers; a French gold coin; a card game. **-ic** *a.* pert. to Napoleon I or III.

Nar·cis·sus (nár·sis'·ạs) *n.* bulbous plant genus including the daffodil, jonquil, narcissus; **narcissism** *n.* in psychoanalysis, an abnormal love and admiration for oneself. **narcissist** *n.* [fr. *Gk. Myth.*].

nar·cot·ic (nár·kát'·ik) *a.* producing stupor or inducing sleep; *n.* a substance which relieves pain and induces sleep, and in large doses, insensibility and stupor; one addicted to the habitual use of narcotics. **narcosis** *n.* a state of unconsciousness or stupor with deadening of sensibility to pain, produced by narcotics [Gk. *narkōtikos*, benumbed].

nard (nárd) *n.* the spikenard, a plant which yields an odorous unguent. **-ine** *a.* [Pers.].

nar·rate (nạ·rāt', nar'·āt) *v.t.* to relate; to tell (story) in detail; to give an account of; to describe. **narration** *n.* an account. **narrative** *n.* a tale; a detailed account of events; *a.* pert. to, containing, narration, **narratively** *adv.* **narrator** *n.* [L. *narrare*].

nar·row (nar'·ō) *a.* of little breadth; not wide or broad; limited; bigoted; illiberal; *v.t.* to make narrow; *v.i.* to become narrow; *n.pl.* straits. **-ly** *adv.* **-minded** *a.* bigoted; illiberal; prejudiced [O.E. *nearu*].

nar·whal (nar'·whạl) *n.* a cetaceous mammal, closely related to the white whale, with one large protruding tusk. [Dan. *narhval*].

na·sal (nā'·zạl) *a.* pert. to the nose; *n.* a nasal sound or letter, such as *m* or *n.* **-ize** *v.i.* to render (a sound) nasally. **-ity** *n.* the quality of being nasal. **-ly** *adv.* [L. *nasus*, the nose].

nas·cent (nas'·, nās'·ạnt) *a.* at the moment of being born; just beginning to exist **nascence, nascency** *n.* [L. *nasci*, to be born].

na·stur·tium (nạ·stur'·sham) *n.* (*Bot.*) a common trailing garden plant of the genus Tropaeolum [L. = twisting the nose].

nas·ty (nas'·ti·) *a.* very dirty; filthy; disgusting; offensive; repulsive; unpropitious (of the weather, etc.); ill-natured; indecent. **nastily** *adv.* **nastiness** *n.* [etym. uncertain].

na·tal (nā'·tạl) *a.* pert. to one's place of birth or date of birth; **-ity** *n.* birth-rate. — **day**, birthday [L. *natus*, born].

na·tant (nā'·tạnt) *a.* (*Bot.*) floating on the surface. **natation** *n.* swimming. **natatorial** *a.* natatory. **natatorium** *n.* a swimming pool. **natatory** *a.* used or adapted for swimming [L. *nature*, to swim].

na·tion (nā'·shạn) *n.* a people inhabiting a country under the same government; an ag-

---

gregation of persons of the same origin and language [L. *natio*, a tribe].

na·tion·al (nash'·an·al) *a.* belonging to or pertaining to a nation; public; general; *n.* member of a nation. **-ization** *n.* **-ize** *v.t.* to make national; to acquire and manage by the state; to make a nation of. **-ism** *n.* devotion to the interests of one's nation, often to the detriment of common interests of all nations. **-ist** *n.* one who advocates a policy of national independence. **-ity** *n.* the quality of being a nation or belonging to a nation; one's nation; patriotism. **-ly** *adv.* — **anthem**, a hymn or song expressive of patriotism, praise, or thanksgiving, commonly sung by people of a nation at public gatherings. — **debt**, the debt due from a nation to individual creditors. **National Guard**, State military force which can be called to active duty [L. *natio*].

na·tive (nā'·tiv) *a.* pert. to one's birth; belonging by birth; innate; indigenous; natural; of metals, occurring in a natural state; pert. to natives; *n.* a person born in a place; **-ly** *adv.* **nativity** *n.* the time or circumstances of birth; in astrology, the position of the stars at a person's birth [L. *nativus*, inborn].

nat·ty (nat'·i·) *a.* neat; trim; tidy; spruce. **nattily** *adv.* [etym. unknown].

nat·u·ral (nach'·ạ·ral) *a.* in accordance with, belonging to, or derived from, nature; inborn; unconstrained; normal; in a state of nature; unaffected; unassuming; true to life; illegitimate; (*Mus.*) not modified by a flat or sharp; *n.* an idiot; (*Colloq.*) a person or thing naturally suitable; (*Mus.*) a character used to remove the effect of an accidental sharp or flat which has preceded it. **-ization** *n.* **-ize** *v.t.* to give to an alien the rights of a native subject; to adopt a foreign word etc., as native; to accustom, as to a climate. **-ism**, *n.* natural condition or quality; the system of those who deny miracles, prophecies, etc.; theory of art, etc. which holds that any artistic creation must be a reproduction of nature or reality. **-ist** *n.* one versed or interested in natural history. **-istic** *a.* in accordance with nature. **-istically** *adv.* **-ly** *adv.* **-ness** *n.* — **gas**, an inflammable product, usually methane, occurring in association with mineral oil deposits. — **history**, the science which deals with the earth's crust and its productions, but applies more especially to biology or zoology. — **philosophy**, the science of nature and of the physical properties of bodies; physics. — **religion**, religion which is derived from nature and reason without resource to revelation. — **science**, the science of nature as distinguished from mental and moral science and mathematics. [fr. *nature*].

na·ture (nā'·chẹr) *n.* the world, the universe, known and unknown; the power underlying all phenomena in the material world; the innate or essential qualities of a thing; the environment of man; the sum total of inheritance; natural disposition; innate character; of a material, the average excellence of its qualities when unaffected by deteriorating influences; **good-, bad-natured** *a.* showing one's innate disposition. [L. *natura*].

naught (nawt) *n.* (*Arch.*) nothing; figure 0; zero; Also **nought.** **-y** *a.* wayward; not behaving well; mischievous; bad. **-ily** *adv.* **naughtiness** *n.* [O.E. *nawiht*, no whit].

nau·se·a (naw'·zē·a, naw'·s(h)ē·a, naw'·zha) *n.* any sickness of the stomach accompanied with a propensity to vomit; a feeling of disgust; sea-sickness. **-te** *v.i.* to feel nausea; *v.t.* to loathe; to fill with disgust; to affect with nausea. **nauseous** *a.* loathsome; disgusting; producing nausea. **nauseously** *adv.* [Gk. = seasickness, fr. *naus*, a ship].

nau·ti·cal (naw'·ti·kal) *a.* pert. to ships, seamen, or to navigation. **-ly** *adv.* — **mile**, 6,080.2 ft. [Gk. *nautēs*, a sailor].

nau·ti·lus (naw'·ta·lạs) *n.* a genus of cephalopod mollusc with many-chambered spiral shells. **nautiloid** *a.* [Gk. *nautilos*, a sailor].

na·val (nā'·val) *a.* pert. to ships, esp. warships; belonging to or serving with the navy [L. *navis*, a ship].

nave (nāv) *n.* the middle or body, of a church [L. *narvis*, a ship].

na·vel (nā'·vl) *n.* the umbilicus, place of attachment of the umbilical cord to the body of the embryo, marked by a rounded depression in the center of the lower part of the abdomen; the central part [O.E. *nafela*].

na·vic·u·lar (na·vik′·ya·ler) *a.* shaped like a boat; relating to small ships or boats; *n.* one of the bones of the wrist and ankle [L. *navicularis*; fr. *navis*, a ship].

nav·i·gate (nav′·i·gāt) *v.t.* and *v.i.* to steer or manage a ship or aircraft; to sail upon or through; **navigable** *a.* may be sailed over or upon; seaworthy; steerable (of balloons). **navigability, navigableness** *n.* **navigably** *adv.* **navigation** *n.* the science of directing course of seagoing vessel and of ascertaining its position at any given time; the control and direction of aircraft in flight; **navigator** *n.* [L. *navigare*, to sail].

na·vy (nā′·vi·) *n.* a fleet; the warships of a country with their crews and organization. — **blue** *n.* and *a.* dark blue [L. *navis*, a ship].

nay (nā) *adv.* no; not only this, but; *n.* denial; refusal [O.N. *nei*, never].

Naz·a·rene (naz′·a·rēn) *n.* a native of *Nazareth*; name given to Jesus; *pl.* an early Christian sect.

Na·zi (nät′·zi·) *n.* and *a.* a member of the National Socialist Party of Germany (1922-1945). **-sm, -ism** *n.* [Ger. *nazional*, national].

Ne·an·der·thal (nē·an′·der·täl) *a.* denoting a man of the earliest long-headed race in Europe which became extinct at least 20,000 years ago [fr. a cave in *Neanderthal*, Ger.].

neap (nēp) *a.* low; *n.* neap tide. — **tide** *n.* the tide whose rise and fall is least marked [O.E. *nep*.].

Ne·a·pol·i·tan (nē·a·päl′·a·tan) *a.* and *n.* pert. to Naples or its inhabitants [Gk. *Neapolis*, fr. *neos*, news; *polis*, a city].

near (nir) *adv.* at or to a short distance; *prep.* close to; *a.* close; closely related; stingy; *v.t.* and *v.i.* to approach. **-by** *a.* in close proximity; adjacent. — **East**, part of Asia nearest Europe, from Asia Minor to Persia. **-ly** *adv.* closely; intimately; almost. **-ness** *n.* **-side** *n.* of horses, vehicles, etc., the left side. **-sighted** *a.* myopic; short-sighted. **-sighted-ness** *n.* [O.E. *near*, nigher].

neat (nēt) *a.* orderly; clean; trim; well-fitting; undiluted; clever; in good taste; dexterous; precise; net. **-ly** *adv.* **-ness** *n.* [Fr. *net*, clean, pure].

neb (neb) *n.* the bill or beak of a bird; the nose [O.E. *nebb*, the face].

neb·u·la (neb′·ya·la) *n.* a slight greyish speck on the cornea of the eye; a cloudlike celestial phenomenon consisting of vastly diffused gas or of tenuous material throughout which fine dust in an incandescent state is distributed. *pl.* **-e.** **-r** *a.* **nebulosity** *n.* cloudiness; vagueness. **nebulous** *a.* cloudy, hazy, indistinct; vague; formless; pert. to nebula. **nebulousness** *n.* [L. = mist].

nec·es·sar·y (nes′·a·ser·i·) *a.* needful; requisite indispensable; that must be done; *n.* a needful thing; essential need. **necessarily** *adv.* [L. *necessarius*].

ne·ces·si·ty (na·ses′·a·ti·) *n.* pressing need; indispensability; compulsion; needfulness; urgency; poverty; a requisite; an essential. **necessitate** *v.t.* to make necessary or indispensable; to force; to oblige. **necessitous** *a.* needy; destitute [L. *necessitas*].

neck (nek) *n.* the part of the body joining the head to the trunk; the narrower part of a bottle, etc.; a narrow piece of anything between wider parts; *v.t.* (Slang) to hug; to cuddle. **-erchief** *n.* a band of cloth or kerchief worn round the neck. **-lace** *n.* a string of beads or precious stones worn round neck. **-piece** *n.* a scarf, usually of fur, **-tie** *n.* a tie for the neck. **neck and neck**, just even [O.E. *hnecca*, nape of neck].

ne·cro- *prefix*, fr. Gk. *nekros*, a dead body, used in the construction of compound terms, signifying death in some form. **-logy** *n.* a register of deaths; a collection of obituary notices. **-mancy** *n.* the art of predicting future events by conjuring up the spirits of the dead: black magic; enchantment. **-mancer** *n.* a sorcerer; a magician. **-mantic** *a.* pert. to magic. **-polis** *n.* a cemetery. **-psy, -scopy** *n.* a postmortem; autopsy. **-sis** *n.* gangrene, mortification. **-tic** *a.*

nec·tar (nek′·ter) *n.* the fabled drink of the gods; any delicious beverage; honey-like secretion of the nectary gland of flowers. **-eal, -ean,- -eous, -ous** *a.* sweet as nectar; resembling nectar; delicious. **-ed** *a.* flavored with nectar; very sweet. **-ine** *a.* sweet as nectar; *n.* a smooth-skinned variety of peach. [Gk. *nektar*].

need (nēd) *n.* a constitutional or acquired craving or want, appeased by recurrent satisfactions; want; necessity; requirement; poverty; destitution; extremity; urgency; *v.t.* to be in want of; to require; *v.i.* to be under

---

a necessity. **-ful** *a.* necessary; requisite **-fully** *adv.* **-fulness** *n.* **-ily** *adv.* **-iness** *n.* condition of need. **-less** *a.* unnecessary; not needed. **-lessly** *adv.* **-lessness** *n.* **-y** *a.* in need; indigent [O.E. *nied*].

nee·dle (nēd′·l) *n.* a slender pointed instrument with an eye, for passing thread through cloth, etc.; a slender rod for knitting; anything like a needle, as the magnet of a compass, a hypodermic syringe, an etcher's burin, an obelisk, a sharp-pointed rock, leaf of the pine, etc.; the reproducing needle of a phonograph. **-point** *n.* a hand-made lace; canvas with a design worked in yarn. **-work** *n.* **-ly** *a.* thorny [O.E. *naedl*].

ne·er (ner) *adv.* poetical form of never. **-do-well** *a.* and *n.* good-for-nothing; worthless.

ne·far·i·ous (ni·fa′·ri·as) *a.* wicked in the extreme; iniquitous [L.].

ne·gate (ni·gāt′) *v.t.* to deny; to prove the contrary. **negation** *n.* the act of denying; negative statement; disavowal; contradiction [L. *negare*, to deny].

neg·a·tive (neg′·a·tiv) *a.* expressing denial, prohibition, or refusal; lacking positive qualities; not positive; stopping or withholding; (*Elect.*) at a lower electric potential; (*Algebra*) minus; *n.* a proposition in which something is denied; a negative word; a photographic plate in which lights and shades are reversed; *v.t.* to refuse to sanction; to reject. **-ly** *adv.* **-ness** *n.* [L. *negare*, to deny].

neg·lect (ni·glekt′) *v.t.* to disregard; to take no care of; to fail to do; to omit through carelessness; to slight; *n.* omission; disregard; careless treatment; slight. **-edness** *n.* **-er** *n.* **-ful** *a.* careless; inclined to be heedless. **-fully** *adv.* [L. *negligere*, to neglect].

neg·li·gee (neg·la·zhā′) *n.* a woman's loose dressing gown [Fr.].

neg·li·gence (neg′·la·jans) *n.* want of due care; carelessness; habitual neglect. **negligent** *a.* careless; inattentive; untidy. **negligently** *adv.* **negligible** *a.* hardly worth noticing [L. *negligere*, to neglect].

ne·go·ti·ate (ni·gō′·shi·āt) *v.t.* to settle by bargaining; to arrange; to transfer (a bill, etc.); (*Colloq.*) to surmount; *v.i.* to discuss with a view to finding terms of agreement; to bargain. **negotiable** *a.* capable of being negotiated; transferable. **negotiability** *n.* **negotiation** *n.* **negotiant, negotiator** *n.* [L. *negotiari*, fr. *negotium*, business].

Ne·gro (nē′·grō) *n.* member of one main ethnological group of human race, with dark skin. *a.* pert. to black African race. **Negress** *n.* Negro woman. **-id** *a.* resembling or related to the Negroes [Sp. fr. L. *niger*, black].

neigh (nā) *v.i.* to whinny, like horse; *n.* cry of horse [O.E. *hnaegan*].

neigh·bor (nā′·ber) *n.* a person who lives, works, near another; *a.* neighboring; *v.t.* to adjoin; to be near. **-hood** *n.* adjoining district and its people; proximity; vicinity. **-ing** *a.* close by. **-ly** *a.* friendly; sociable; helpful. **-liness** *n.* [O.E. *neahgebur*].

nei·ther (nē′·THer, ni′·THer) *a.* and *pron.* not the one or the other; *adv.* not on the one hand; not either; *conj.* nor yet; not either [O.E. *nahwaether*, not whether].

nem·a·tode, nematoid (nem′·a·tōd, ·toid) *a.* thread-like. **nematoidea** *n.pl.* roundworms, threadworms [Gk. *nēma*, thread; *eidos*, form].

nem·e·sis (nem′·a·sis) *n.* inevitable retributive justice [Gk. *nemein*, to distribute, deal out].

ne·o- (nē′·ō) *prefix* used in the construction of compound terms, signifying *new, recent* [Gk.].

ne·o·dym·i·um (nē·ō·dim′·i·am) *n.* a metallic element belonging to the group of rare earth metals [Gk. *neos*, new; and *didymium* (a once supposed element)].

ne·o·lith·ic (nē·ō·lith′·ik) *a.* (*Geol.*) pert. to the late Stone Age.

ne·ol·o·gy (nē·äl′·a·ji·) *n.* the introduction of new words into a language; new doctrines, esp. rationalistic, in theology. **neologian, neologist** *n.* one who coins new words or holds novel doctrines in religion. **neologic, neological** *a.* **neologize** *v.i.* to coin new words. **neologism** *n.* a newly-coined word or phrase; a new doctrine [Gk. *neos*, new; *logos*, word].

ne·on (nē′·an) *n.* a non-metallic chemical element belonging to the group of the rare gases. — **light,** — **sign,** or — **tube**, one containing neon gas and glowing with a characteristic reddish-orange light [Gk. *neos*, new].

ne·o·pho·bi·a (nē·ō·fō′·bi·a) *n.* a dread of the unknown [Gk. *neos*, new; *phobos*, fear].

ne·o·phyte (nē′·a·fīt) *n.* a novice; a convert [Gk. *neos*, new; *phutos*, grown].

ne·pen·the, nepenthes (ni·pen′·thē, ·thēz) *n.* in Greek mythology, a drug with power of banishing grief; any narcotic drug to relieve pain; genus of Asiatic plants [Gk. *nē-*, not; *phenthos*, grief].

neph·ew (nef′·ū) *n.* a brother's or sister's son; son of one's husband's or wife's brother or sister [Fr. *neveu*, fr. L. *nepos*, a nephew].

nephr- (or nephro-) *prefix* used in the construction of compound terms, from Greek *nephros*, a kidney. **-algia, -algy** *n.* pain in the kidney. **-ic** *a.* pert. to the kidneys. **-itic(al)** *a.* pert. to (diseases of) the kidneys. **-itis** *n.* Bright's disease, non-infective inflammation of the kidney.

---

nep·o·tism (nep′·a·tizm) *n.* undue favoritism in awarding public appointments to one's relations [L. *nepos*, a nephew].

Nep·tune (nep′·tūn) *n.* (*Myth.*) the Roman god of the sea; second most remote planet of solar system [L.].

nerve (nurv) *n.* one of the bundles of fibers which convey impulses either *from* brain (motor nerves) to muscles, etc., producing motion, or *to* brain (sensory nerves) from skin eyes, nose, etc., producing sensation; mid-rib or vein of a leaf; sinew; tendon; fortitude; courage; cool assurance; (*Slang*) impudence. *pl.* irritability; unusual sensitivity to fear, annoyance, etc.; *v.t.* to give courage or strength to. **-d** *a.* **-less** *a.* lacking in strength or will; incapable of effort. **-lessness** *n.* **nervine** *a.* acting on the nerves; *n.* a nervetonic. **nervy** *a.* (*Slang*) bold; showing courage [L. *nervus*, sinew].

nerv·ous (nurv′·as) *a.* pert. to, containing, or affecting nerves; uneasy; apprehensive. **-ly** *adv.* **-ness** *n.* — **breakdown** *n.* a condition of mental depression [L. *nervus*, a sinew].

nes·cience (nesh′·ans) *n.* the condition of complete ignorance; lack of knowledge; agnosticism. **nescient** *a.* ignorant; agnostic [L. *nescier*, not to know].

nest (nest) *n.* the place in which a bird or other animal lays and hatches its eggs; any snug retreat; a set of boxes, tables, etc., which fit into one another; *v.t.* to form to place in a nest; *v.i.* to occupy or build a nest. **-ling** *n.* a bird too young to leave the nest. — **egg** *n.* an egg left in a nest to induce a bird to lay; a small sum of money put aside for some later purpose [O.E.].

nes·tle (nes′·l) *v.i.* to settle comfortably and close to one another; to lie snugly, as in a nest; (of a house) to be situated in a sheltered spot [O.E. *nestlian*].

net (net) *n.* an open-work fabric of meshes of cord, etc.; sections of this used to catch fish, protect fruit, etc.; lace formed by netting; a snare. *a.* made of netting; reticulate; caught in a net; *v.t.* to cover with, or catch in, a net; to veil; *v.t.* to make net or network. *pr.p.* **-ting** *pa.t.* and *pa.p.* **-ted. -ted** *a.* **-ting** *n.* the act or process of forming network; netlike fabric; snaring by means of a net. **-work** *n.* anything made like, or resembling, a net; (*Radio*) a group of transmitting stations producing programs carried by long-distance telephone wires to affiliated stations for broadcasting [O.E. *nett.*].

net (net) *a.* left after all deductions; free from deduction; *v.t.* to gain or produce as clear profit; *pr.p.* **-ting.** *pa.p.* **-ted.** — **price**, net price without discount [Fr. = clean].

neth·er (neTH′·er) *a.* lower; low-lying; lying below; belonging to the lower regions. **-most** *a.* lowest. **-ward(s)** *adv.* in a downward direction [O.E. *neothera*].

net·tle (net′·l) *n.* a common weed covered with fine stinging hairs; *v.t.* to irritate; to provoke; to make angry; to rouse to action. — **rash** *n.* an irritating eruption in the skin [O.E. *netele*].

neur-, neuro- *prefix* from Gk. *neuron*, a nerve.

neu·ral (nyoo′·ral) *a.* pert. to the nerves or nervous system [Gk. *neuron*, a nerve].

neu·ral·gia (nyoo·ral′·ja) *n.* a spasmodic or continuous pain occurring along the course of one or more distinct nerves. **neuralgic** *a.* [Gk. *neuron*, a nerve; *algos*, pain].

neu·ras·the·ni·a (nyoor·as·thē′·ni·a) *n.* a condition of nervous debility characterized by lack of energy, restlessness, headache and insomnia. **neurasthenic** *a.* [Gk. *neuron*, a nerve; *astheneia*, weakness].

neu·rax·is (nyoo·rak′·sis) *n.* the cerebrospinal axis, or central nervous system, including the brain and spinal cord.

neu·ri·tis (nyoo·rī′·tis) *n.* an inflammatory condition of a nerve [Gk. *neuron*, a nerve].

neu·rol·o·gy (nyoo·räl′·a·ji·) *n.* the study of the structure, function and diseases of the nervous system. **neurological** *a.* **neurolo-**

gist n. [Gk. *neuron*; *logos*, discourse].
neu·ron (nyoor′·ån) n. a nerve cell and all its processes [Gk. = nerve].

nettle

neu·ro·path (nyoo′·rạ·path) n. a person subject to a nervous disorder. **-ic, -ical** a. pert. to nervous diseases. **-ist** (nyoo·răp′·ạ·thist) n. an abnormal or diseased condition of the nervous system [Gk. *neuron*, nerve; *pathos*, suffering].
neu·ro·sis (nyoo·rō′·sis) n. a psychic or mental disorder resulting in partial personality disorganization. pl. **neuroses. neurotic** (nyoo·rát′·ik) a. pert. to the nerves; n. a highly strung person [Gk. *neuron*, a nerve].
neu·ter (nū′·ter) a. neither masculine nor feminine; (Bot.) possessing neither stamens nor carpels; n. the neuter gender; an imperfectly developed female, as the worker-bee [L. = neither].
neu·tral (nū′·trạl) a. taking neither side in a war, dispute, etc.; indifferent; without bias; grey; intermediate (shade of color); neither acid nor alkaline; asexual; n. nation, person, not taking sides in a dispute; the position in a gear-mechanism when no power is transmitted. **-ize** v.t. to render neutral; to make ineffective; to counterbalance. **-izer** n. nonintervention by a state or third-party in a dispute; the state of being neutral. **-ly** adv. **-ity** n. [L. *neuter*, neither].
neu·tron (nū′·trån) n. one of the minute particles composing the nucleus of an atom [L. *neuter*, neither].
nev·er (nev′·er) adv. at no time; not ever; in no degree; (Colloq.) surely not. **-more** adv. **-theless** conj. none the less; in spite of that; notwithstanding [O.E. *naefre*].
new (nū) a. not existing before; lately discovered or invented; not ancient; adv. (usually **new-**), recently; freshly; **-ly** adv. **-ish** a. somewhat new. **-ness** n. **-born** a. recently born; born anew. **-comer** n. one who has just settled down in a strange place or taken up a new post. **-fangled** a. lately devised; novel (in a deprecatory sense). **-fashioned** a. just come into fashion; the latest in style. **New Style** n. a term to denote dates reckoned by the Gregorian calendar. **New Deal**, a campaign initiated in 1933 by President Franklin Roosevelt involving social reforms. **New Englander**, a native or resident of any of the six N. E. states of the U.S.A. **New Learning**, the Renaissance. **— moon**, the period when the first faint crescent of the moon becomes visible. **New Testament**, later of the two main divisions of Bible. **New World**, N. and S. America [O.E. *niwe*].
new·el (nū′·ạl) n. the post supporting the balustrade to a flight of stairs [L. *nodus*, a knot].

news (nooz) n.sing. report of recent happenings; fresh information; tidings; intelligence. **-boy** n. a boy who sells or distributes newspapers. **— bulletin** n. the latest news, esp. as disseminated by radio or television. **-monger** n. busy-body; gossip. **-paper** n. a regular publication giving latest news. **-print** n. cheap paper for newspapers. **-reel** n. a short film depicting items of news and topical features. **-stand** n. a stand where newspapers,

and sometimes magazines, are sold. **-y** a. gossipy; full of news.
newt (nūt) n. a salamander; an eft [a newt for an ewt, fr. O.E. *efeta*. an eft].
next (nekst) a. nearest; immediately following in place or time; adv. nearest or immediately after; on the first future occasion; prep. nearest to. **-ly** adv. in the next place. **— of kin**, n. nearest blood relative **-door** a. [O.E. *niehst*, superl. of *neah*, nigh].
nex·us (nek′·sạs) n. a tie, connection, or bond [L. *nectere*, to bind].
nib (nib) n. something small and pointed; beak of a bird; point of a pen; **-bed** a. having a nib [form of *neb*].

nib·ble (nib′·l) v.t. to bite a little at a time; v.i. to catch at (as a fish); to bite gently; to dally with; n. a tiny bite [L.G. *nubbelen*].
nib·lick (nib′·lik) n. a golf-club with an iron-head, well laid back, designed for lofting.
nice (nīs) a. agreeable; attractive; kind; exact; discriminating; delicate; dainty. **-ly** adv. **-ness** n. **-ty** (nī′·sạ·ti.) n. precision; delicacy; exactness; refinement [O.Fr. *nice*, foolish].
niche (nich) n. a recess in a wall for a statue, bust, etc.; one's ordained position in life or public estimation; v.t. to place in a niche. **-d** a. [Fr. fr. It. *nicchia*].

nick (nik) v.t. to make a notch in; to indent; to catch exactly; n. a notch; a slit; the opportune moment as *in the nick of time*.
nick·el (nik′·ạl) n. a silver white metallic element, malleable and ductile, and much used in alloys and plating; a five-cent piece; v.t. to plate with nickel. **— plating** n. plating of metals with nickel to provide a bright surface and to keep down rust. **— silver** n. an alloy of copper, nickel and zinc; German silver [Sw. abbrev. fr. Ger. *Kupfernickel*, copper nickel (ore)].
nick·el·o·de·on (nik·al·ō′·di·an) n. a player phonograph operated by the insertion of a nickel [Fr.].
nick·nack See **knickknack**.
nick·name (nik′·nām) n. a name given in contempt, derision, or familiarity to some person, nation, or object [orig. *an eke name*, an added name, fr. *eke*, to increase].
nic·o·tine (nik′·ạ·tēn) n. a colorless, highly poisonous alkaloid present in the tobacco plant; [Jean *Nicot*, who introduced the plant into Fr.].
nid·i·fi·ca·tion (nid·ạ·fạ·kā′·shn) n. the act of building a nest. **nidify** v.i. to build a nest. **nidus** (ī) n. a nest; (Med.) a nucleus of infection [L. *nidus*, a nest; *facere*, to make].
nidus See **nidification**.
niece (nēs) n. the daughter of a brother or sister or of one's husband's or wife's brother or sister [Fr. *nièce*, fr. L. *neptis*].
nif·ty (nif′·ti·) a. (Colloq.) fine; smart.
nig·gard (nig′·erd) n. a very miserly person; a. stingy. Also **-ly. -liness** n. meanness.
nig·ger (nig′·er) n. (offensive) a Negro [Fr. *nègre*].
nig·gle (nig′·l) v.i. to trifle; to be too particular about details. **-r** n. **niggling, niggly** a. and n. [etym. uncertain].
nigh (nī) a. near; direct. adv. near [O.E. *neah*].
night (nīt) n. the time of darkness from sunset to sunrise; end of daylight; intellectual or spiritual darkness; ignorance; death. **-ly** a. happening or done every night; of the night; adv. every night; by night. **-cap** n. a cap worn in bed; (Colloq.) an alcoholic drink at bedtime. **— club** n. establishment for dancing around a person or thing; in representation

and entertainment remaining open until early morning. **-dress, -gown** n. a loose gown worn in bed. **-fall** n. the close of day. **-hawk** n. a nocturnal bird; (Colloq.) one who is up late habitually. **-light** n. bulb of low wattage kept burning all night. **-long** a. persisting all night. **-mare** n. a terrifying feeling of oppression or suffocation arising during sleep; a frightening dream. **— owl** n. (Colloq.) one who habitually keeps late hours. **— school** n. a school for the continuation of studies after working hours. **— shift** n. employees who work regularly during night; duration of this work. **-shirt** n. a loose shirt used for sleeping in. **-time** n. period of night; **-ward** a. towards night. **— watchman** n. [O.E. *niht*].
night·in·gale (nīt′·ạn·gāl) n. a bird of the thrush family, the male being renowned for its beautiful song at night [O.E. *niht*, night; *galan*, to sing].
ni·hil, nil (nī′·hil, nil) n. nothing; zero.
nihilism n. the rejection of all religious and moral principles as the only means of obtaining social progress; the denial of all reality in phenomena; in 19th cent. the opposition in Russia to all constituted authority or government. **nihilist** n. **nihilistic** a. [L.].
Ni·ke (nī′·kē) n. a U.S. Army supersonic guided missile [fr. Gk. *Myth* goddess of victory].
nim·ble (nim′·bl) a. light and quick in motion. **-ness** n. **-witted** a. quick-witted. **nimbly** adv. [O.E. *niman*, to take].
nim·bus (nim′·bas) n. a cloud or atmosphere of saints, angels, etc., the circle of light surrounding the head; a halo; an aureole. pl. **-es** or **nimbi** [L. = cloud].
nin·com·poop (nin′·kạm·pōōp) n. a foolish person; a simpleton [origin uncertain].
nine (nīn) a. and n. one more than eight; the symbol 9 or IX; a baseball team; **-fold** a. nine times repeated. **-teen** a. and n. nine and ten. **-teenth** a. the tenth after the eighteenth. **-ty** a. and n. ninth a. the first after the eighth; n. **ninthly** adv. **-pins** n. a game in which nine erect wooden pegs are to be knocked down by a ball. **the Nine**, the Muses [O.E. *nigon*].
nin·ny (nin′·i·) n. a fool; a dolt [It. *ninno*, a child].
ni·non (nē′·nån) n. a glossy lightweight dress fabric of silk [Fr. proper name].
nip (nip) v.t. to pinch sharply; to detach by pinching; to check growth (as by frost); to smart. pr.p. **-ping**. pa.t. and pa.p. **-ped**. n. a pinch; sharp touch of frost; a sip. **-per** n. one who or that which nips; the great claw (as of a crab); pl. small pincers. **-piness** n. **-pingly** adv. **-py** a. sharp in taste; curt; smarting [etym. uncertain, cf. Dut. *nijpen*].
nip·ple (nip′·l) n. the protuberance in the center of a breast by which milk is obtained from the female during breast-feeding; a teat; the mouthpiece of a nursing bottle; a small metal projection pierced so that oil or grease may be forced into a bearing surface by means of a grease gun [etym. uncertain, cf. *nib*].
Nip·pon (nip′·ån) n. Japan. **-ese** n., a. [Jap. = rising of the sun].
Nir·va·na (nir·vá′·nạ) n. in Buddhism, that state of blissful repose or absolute existence reached by one in whom all craving is extinguished [Sans].
ni·sei (nē′·sā′) n. Am. citizen born of Japanese parents.
ni·si (nī′·si) conj. unless. **decree nisi** (Law) a decree to take effect after a certain period of time has elapsed unless some valid objection arises [L.].
nit (nit) n. the egg of an insect parasite, esp. of a louse [O.E. *hnitu*].
ni·ter (nī′·ter) n. potassium nitrate; saltpeter, a white crystalline solid used in the manufacture of gunpowder, acids, etc. **nitrate** n. a salt of nitric acid; a fertilizer. **nitrated** a. combined with nitric acid. **nitration** n. the conversion of nitrites into nitrates by the action of bacteria; the introduction of a nitro-group (NO_2) into an organic substance. **nitric** a. containing nitrogen. **nitric acid**, a powerful, corrosive acid. **nitride** n. a compound of a metal with nitrogen. **nitrify** v.t. to treat a metal with nitric acid; to oxidize to nitrates or nitrites, esp. by action of bacteria. **nitrite** n. a salt of nitrous acid. **nitrous oxide**, laughing gas, used as an anaesthetic in dentistry [Gk. *nitron*].
ni·tro- (nī·trạ) prefix used in the formation of compound terms, signifying, formed by, or containing, *niter*. **-glycerine** n. a powerful oily liquid explosive [Gk. *nitron*, native soda].
ni·tro·gen (nī′·trạ·jạn) n. a non-metallic gaseous chemical element, colorless, odorless and tasteless, forming nearly four-fifths of the atmosphere. **nitrogenous** a.
nit·wit (nit′·wit) n. (Colloq.) a fool. **-ted** a. [Dut. *niets*, nothing; O.E. *witan*, to know].
nix (niks) n. (Slang) nothing [Dut. *niets*].
no (nō) a. not any; adv. expresses a negative reply to a question or request; not at all; n. a refusal; a denial; a negative vote. **-es** n.pl. term used in parliamentary proceedings, *the noes have it*. **no man's land**, the terrain between the front lines of opposing forces [O.E. *na*].

nob (nåb) n. (*Slang*) the head [fr. *knob*].

No·bel Prize (nō'·bel' prīz) n. one of a series of five prizes awarded annually to persons who have distinguished themselves in physics, chemistry, medicine, literature, or the promotion of peace [Alfred *Nobel*, Swedish inventor (1833-96)].

no·bil·i·ty (nō·bil'·a·ti·) n. the class holding special rank, usually hereditary, in a state; the quality of being noble; grandeur; loftiness and sincerity of mind or character [L. *nobilis*, noble].

no·ble (nō'·bl) a. distinguished by deeds, character, rank, or birth; of lofty character; titled; n. a nobleman; a peer; an old English gold coin. **-man** n. (*fem.* **-woman**). **-ness** n. **nobly** adv. **the noble art**, boxing [L. *nobilis*].

no·bod·y (nō'·bàd·i·) n. no one; a person of no importance.

nock (nåk) n. notch, esp. of bow or arrow; upper end of fore-and-aft sail [*notch*].

noc·turn (nåk'·turn) n. a service held during the night. **nocturne** n. a painting of a night scene; a musical composition of a gentle and simple character. **-al** a. pertaining to night; happening or active by night; n. a primitive instrument for determining latitude at night. **-ally** adv. [L. *nocturnus*, of the night].

noc·u·ous (nåk'·yoo·as) a. hurtful; noxious. **-ly** adv. [L. *nocere*, to hurt].

nod (nåd) v.t. and v.i. to incline the head forward by a quick motion, signifying assent or drowsiness; to droop the head; to be sleepy; to sway; to bow by way of recognition. *pr.p.* **-ding.** *pa.t.* and *pa.p.* **-ded.** n. an act of nodding. **-der** n. [etym. uncertain].

nod·al See **node**.

nod·dle (nåd'·l) n. (*Colloq.*) the head; v.i. to nod repeatedly.

nod·dy (nåd'·i·) n. a simpleton; a fool; a sea-bird [fr. *nod*].

node (nōd) n. a knot or knob; (*Geom.*) a point at which a curve crosses itself to form a loop; (*Elect.*) a point in a circuit carrying alternating currents at which the amplitude of current or voltage is a minimum; (*Astron.*) one of two points at which the orbit of a planet intersects the plane of the ecliptic; (*Phys.*) a point of permanent rest in a vibrating body; (*Med.*) a small protuberance or hard swelling; (*Bot.*) the part of a stem to which a leaf is attached; an articulation. **nodal, nodical** a. pert. to nodes. **nodated** a. knotted. **nodation** n. the knots. **nodular** a. like a nodule. **nodulated** a. having nodules. **nodule** n. a small node or act of making knots. **nodiferous** a. (*Bot.*) having nodes. **nodose, nodous** a. full of swelling [L. *nodus*, a knot].

No·ël (nō'·el) n. Christmas; a carol. Also **Nowel** [Fr. fr. L. *natalis*, birthday].

nog (någ) n. a wooden peg or block [Scand.].

nog (någ) n. a beverage made with eggs and usually liquor; eggnog; a kind of strong ale. **-gin** n. a small mug; a very small drink; (*Slang*) the head [Ir. *noigin*].

no·how (nō'·hou) adv. (*substandard*) in no way; not at all.

noise (noiz) n. sound; din; loud outcry; v.t. to spread by rumor; v.i. to sound loud. **-less** a. making no noise; silent. **-lessly** adv. **-lessness** n. **noisy** a. making much noise; clamorous. **noisily** adv. **noisiness** n. [Fr.].

noi·some (noi'·sam) a. injurious to health; noxious; offensive; disgusting; evil smelling. **-ly** adv. **-ness** n. [obs. *noy*, for *annoy*].

no·mad (nō'·mad) a. roaming from pasture to pasture; n. a wanderer; a member of a wandering tribe. **nomadic** a. pert. to nomads; having no fixed dwelling place. **nomadically** adv. **-ism** n. [Gk. *nomas*, pasturing].

nom·de·plume (nám'·da·plóom) a pen name [Fr.].

no·men·cla·tor (nō'·man·klā·ter) n. one who gives names to things. **nomenclatural** a. **nomenclature** (nō'·man·klā·cher) n. a system of naming; the vocabulary of a science, etc. [L. *nomen*, a name; *calare*, to call].

nom·i·nal (nåm'·a·nal) a. pert. to a name; existing only in name, ostensible; titular; (*Gram.*) pert. to a noun. **-ism** n. the doctrine that the universal, or general, has no objective existence or validity, being merely a name expressing the qualities of various objects resembling one another in certain respects. **-ist** n. one who holds these views, the opposite of a realist. **-istic** a. **-ly** adv. in name only; not really [L. *nominalis*, fr. *nomen*, a name].

nom·i·nate (nåm'·a·nāt) v.t. to put forward the name of, as a candidate; to propose; to designate. **nomination** n. act of nominating; power or privilege of nominating. **nominative** a. (*Gram.*) denoting the subject; n. a noun or pronoun which is the subject of a verb. **nominator** n. one who nominates. **nominee** n. one who is nominated [L. *nominare*, to name].

non- *prefix* from L. *non* = not, used in the formation of compound terms signifying absence or omission. **-combatant** n. a member of the armed forces whose duties do not entail an active part in military operations, e.g., chaplain, surgeon, etc.; an unarmed civilian. **-commissioned** a. of ranks between a private and warrant officer; (*abbrev.* **noncom**) **-commital** a. deliberately avoiding any direct statement as to one's opinions

or course of future action. **-conductor** n. a substance which will not conduct electricity, heat, or sound; insulator. **-ferrous** a. of an alloy or metal containing no, or only the merest trace of, iron. **-intervention** n. not intervening or interfering in the affairs or policies of another, esp. in international affairs. **-stop** a. not stopping.

non·age (nån'·ij) n. minority (under 21 years of age); a period of immaturity [L. *non*, not; and *age*].

non·age·nar·i·an (nån·a·ja·ner'·i·an) n. one who is ninety years old or upwards; a. relating to ninety [L. *nonaginta*, ninety].

nonce (nåns) n. **for the nonce**, for the occasion only; for the present [earlier *the*(n) -anes, the once].

non·cha·lance (nån'·sha·làns) n. unconcern; coolness; indifference; **nonchalant** a. **nonchalantly** adv. [Fr. *non*, not; *chaleur*, heat].

non·con·form·ist (nån·kan·fawr'·mist) n. one who refuses to comply with the usages and rites of an established church, etc. **nonconforming** a. **nonconformity** n.

non·de·script (nån'·da·skript) a. lacking in distinction; hard to classify; n. [*nom*, not; *descriptus*, described].

none (nun) a. and *pron.* no one; not anything. **-such, nonsuch** n. a person or thing without a rival or equal. **nonetheless**, nevertheless; all the same [O.E. *nan*].

nones (nōnz) n. *pl.* one of the canonical hours of the R.C. Breviary, the *ninth* hour after sunrise at the equinox, viz. 3 p.m., or the appropriate mass celebrated at this time [L. *nonus*, ninth].

non·en·ti·ty (nån·en'·ta·ti·) n. a thing not existing; nonexistence; a person of no importance; a mere nobody [L. *non*, not; *ens, entis*, a being].

non·ju·ror (nån·joor'·er) n. one who refuses to swear allegiance or take an oath. **nonjuring** a.

non·pa·reil (nån·pa·rel') n. a person or thing without an equal; a printing type, between ruby and emerald, counting 6 points; a. unrivalled; peerless; matchless [Fr. *non*, not; *pareil*, equal].

non·plus (nån'·plus) n. perplexity; puzzle; inability to say or do more; quandary; v.t. to confound or bewilder completely [L. *non*, not; *plus*, more].

non·sense (nån'·sens) n. lack of sense; language without meaning; absurdity; silly conduct. **nonsensical** a. **nonsensically** adv. [L. *non*, not].

non·such See **none**.

noo·dle (nóó'·dl) n. a simpleton; (*Slang*) the head [conn. with *noddy*].

noo·dle (nóó'·dl) n. a strip of dough, made of flour and eggs, baked and served in soups [Ger. *nudel*].

nook (nook) n. a corner; a recess; a secluded retreat [ME. *nok*].

noon (nóón) n. midday; twelve o'clock by day; the exact instant when, at any given place, the sun crosses the meridian. **-day, -tide** n. and a. midday [L. *nona* (*hora*), ninth hour; See **nones**.

noose (nóós) n. a running loop with a slip knot which binds closer the more it is drawn; snare; tight knot; v.t. to tie, catch in noose [L. *nodus*, knot].

nor (nawr) a particle introducing the second clause of a negative proposition; and not [M.E. *nother*].

Nor·dic (nawr'·dik) a. of or pert. to peoples of Germanic, esp. Scandinavian, stock.

norm (nawrm) n. a rule or authoritative standard; a unit for comparison; a standard type or pattern; a model; a class-average test score. **-a** n. a rule, pattern, or standard; a pattern or templet; a mason's square for testing. **-al** a. conforming to type or natural law; (*Math.*) perpendicular; n. (*Math.*) a perpendicular to a line, surface, or tangent at point of contact; the standard; the average. **-alcy** (nawr'·mal·si·) n. normality. **normality** n. normal state or quality. **-ly** adv. **-ative** a. setting up a norm; regulative. **-al school**, a training college for teachers [L. *norma*, a rule].

Nor·man (nawr'·man) n. a native of Normandy; a. pert. to Normandy or the Normans. **— architecture**, a style of medieval architecture characterized by rounded arch and massive simplicity. [O.Fr. *Normant*, fr. Scand. = Northmen].

Norse (nawrs) a. pert. to ancient Scandinavia, esp. Norway, its language, or its people; n. Norwegians or ancient Scandinavians; the old Scandinavian language [Scand. *norsk*, north].

Norman architecture

north (nawrth) n. the region or cardinal point in the plane of the meridian to the left of a person facing the rising sun; the part of the world, of a country, etc., towards this point; adv. towards or in the north; a. to, from, or in the north. **northerly** (nawr'·THer·li·) a. towards the north; of winds, coming from the north. **northern** a. pert. to the north; in or of the north. **northerner** n. an inhabitant of the northern parts of a country. **northernly** adv. in a northerly direction. **northernmost** a. situated at the most northerly point. **-ward, -wardly** a. situated towards the north; adv. in a northerly direction. **-wards** adv. **-east (-west)** n. the point between the north and the east (west); a. pert. to, or from, the northeast (-west). **-easter (-wester)** n. a wind from the northeast (-west). **-easterly (-westerly)** a. towards or coming from the northeast (-west). **-eastern (-western)** a. belonging to the northeast (-west). **-eastward (-westward)** a. towards the northeast (-west). **northern lights**, aurora borealis. **North Pole**, northern extremity of earth's axis. **North Star** n. polar star.

North Pole

Nor·we·gian (nawr·wē'·jan) a. pert. to Norway; n. a native or language of Norway.

nose (nōz) n. the organ for breathing and smelling; power of smelling or detecting; any projection resembling a nose, as prow of a ship; v.t. to detect by smell; to nuzzle; to sniff; to move forward; v.i. to smell; to pry; to push forward. **— bag** n. a bag containing provender fastened to a horse's head. **— dive** n. in aviation, a sudden steep plunge directly towards an objective, usually from a great height; v.i. to perform this evolution. **-gay** n. a bunch of sweet-smelling flowers; a bouquet. **nosing** n. the molded projecting edge of the tread of a step. **nosy** a. (*Colloq.*) inquisitive [O.E. *nosu*].

nose- *prefix* fr. Greek, *nosos*, disease, used in formation of compound words. **nosology** (nō·sàl'·a·ji·) n. branch of medicine treating generally of diseases; systematic classification of phases of disease. **nosological** a. **nosologist** n.

nos·tal·gia (nås·tal'·ja) n. homesickness; a phase of melancholia due to the unsatisfied desire to return home. **nostalgic** a. [Gk. *nostos*, return; *algos*, pain].

nos·tril (nås'·tril) n. one of the external openings of the nose [O.E. *nosy*, nose; *thyrel*, opening].

nos·trum (nås'·tram) n. a quack remedy; a patent medicine of doubtful efficacy; a pet scheme, pushed by some visionary [L. = our].

not (nåt) adv. a word expressing denial, negation, or refusal [*nought*].

no·ta·ble (nō'·ta·bl) a. worthy of notice; remarkable; n. a person of distinction. **notabilia** n.pl. things worth noting; famous remarks. **notability** n. an eminent person. **-ness** n. **notably** adv. [L. *nota*, note].

no·ta·ry (nō'·ta·ri·) n. a *notary-public*, a person authorized to record statements, to certify deeds, to take affidavits, etc., on oath [L. *notarius*, a secretary].

no·ta·tion (nō·tā'·shan) n. any system of figures, signs and symbols which conveys information; the act or process of noting; a note [L. *nota*, a mark].

notch (nǎch) *n.* a V-shaped cut or indentation; nick; a groove formed in a piece of timber to receive another piece; (*U.S.*) a pass between mountains; *v.t.* to make notches in; to indent; to secure by a notch; to score (a run) [O.F. *osche*, a notch].

note (nōt) *n.* a mark; a brief comment; *pl.* a record of a lecture, speech, etc.; a memorandum; a short letter; a diplomatic paper; a written or printed promise of payment; a musical tone; a character to indicate a musical tone; notice; distinction; fame; *v.t.* to observe; to set down in writing; to attend to; to heed. **-book** *n.* a book for jotting down notes, memoranda, etc. **-d** *a.* well-known by reputation or report; celebrated; **-dly** *adv.* **-dness** *n.* — **paper** *n.* a small size of writing paper. **-worthy** *a.* worthy of notice; remarkable. — **of hand**, a promissory note [L. *notare*, to mark].

noth·ing (nuth'·ing) *n.* not anything of account, value, note, or the like; non-existence; nonentity; nought; zero; trifle; *adv.* in no degree; not at all. **-ness** *n.* [Fr. no thing].

no·tice (nō'·tis) *n.* act of noting; remarking, or observing; cognizance; regard; note; heed; consideration; news; a review; a notification; *v.t.* to observe; to remark upon; to treat with regard. **-able** *a.* **-ably** *adv.* **to give notice**, to warn beforehand. **to receive one's notice**, to be informed that one's services are about to be terminated [L. *notus*, known].

no·ti·fy (nō'·ta·fi) *v.t.* to report; to give notice of or to; to announce; to inform. **notifiable** *n.* **notification** *n.* act of making known or giving notice; official notice or announcement [L. *notus*, known; *facere*, make].

no·tion (nō'·shan) *n.* apprehension; idea; conception; opinion; belief; sentiment; fancy; inclination; *pl.* small articles such as sewing supplies, etc. [L. *notio*].

no·to·ri·e·ty (nō·ta·rī'·at·i·) *n.* the state of being generally known, esp. in a disreputable way; discreditable publicity. **notorious** *a.* generally known (usually in a bad sense); infamous. **notoriously** *adv.* **notoriousness** *n.* [L. *notus*, known].

not·with·stand·ing (not·with·stand'·ing) *adv.* nevertheless; however; yet; *prep.* in spite of; despite; *conj.* although.

nou·gat (noo'·gat) *n.* a confection of almonds, pistachio-nuts, or other nuts, in a sugar and honey paste [Fr.].

nought See **naught.**

noun (noun) *n.* (*Gram.*) a word used as a name of a person, quality, or thing; a substantive [L. *nomen*, a name].

nour·ish (nur'·ish) *v.t.* to supply with food; to feed and cause to grow; to nurture; to encourage. **-ing** *a.* nutritious. **-ment** *n.* food; nutriment; the act or state of nourishing [Fr. *nourrir*, fr. L. *nutrire*, to feed].

no·va (nō'·va) *n.* a new star. *pl.* **novae** [L. = new].

nov·el (náv'·al) *a.* of recent origin or introduction; new; unusual; *n.* a fictitious prose tale dealing with the adventures or feelings of imaginary persons so as to portray, by the description of action and thought, the varieties of human life and character. **-ette** *n.* a shorter form of novel. **-ist** *n.* a writer of novels. **-ty** *n.* newness; something new or unusual [L. *novus*, new].

No·vem·ber (nō·vem·ber) *n.* the eleventh month of the year [L. *novem*, nine].

no·ve·na (nō·vē'·na) *n.* (*R.C.*) devotions on nine consecutive days; lasting nine days [L. *novem*, nine].

nov·ice (náv'·is) *n.* a candidate for admission to a religious order; one new to anything; an inexperienced person; a beginner. **novicate, novitiate** *n.* the state or time or being a novice; a novice [L. *novus*, new].

no·vo·caine (nō'·va·kān) *n.* a nonirritant drug which has replaced cocaine as a local anesthetic [L. *novus*, new; and *cocaine*].

now (nou) *adv.* at the present time; *conj.* this being the case; *n.* the present time. **-adays** *adv.* in these days. **now! now!** a form of admonition. **now and then**, occasionally [O.E. *nu*].

no·where (nō'·hwer) *adv.* not in any place. **nowise** *adv.* not in any manner or degree.

nox·a (nák'·sa) *n.* (*Med.*) anything harmful to the body; *pl.* **-e**. **noxal** *a.* **noxious** *a.* hurtful; pernicious; unwholesome. **noxiously** *adv.* **noxiousness** *n.* [L. *noxa*, injury].

noz·zle (náz'·l) *n.* a projecting spout or vent; the outlet end of a pipe, hose, etc.; (*Colloq.*) the nose [dim. of *nose*].

nozzle

nu·ance (noo·áns') *n.* a shade or subtle variation in color, tone of voice, etc.; (*Mus.*) a delicate gradation of tone and expression in performance on an instrument [Fr. = a shade].

nub (nub) *n.* a knob; lump; protuberance; (*Colloq.*) point; gist.

nu·cle·us (nū'·kli·as) *n.* a central part of anything; the starting point of some project or idea; (*Astron.*) the dark center of a sunspot; the denser core or head of a comet; (*Biol.*) the inner essential part of a living cell; (*Physics*) the core of the atom, composed of protons and neutrons. *pl.* **nuclei** (nū'·kli·i). **nuclear** *a.* **nuclear energy**, a more exact term for atomic energy; energy freed or absorbed during reactions taking place in atomic nuclei. **nuclear fission**, a process of disintegration which breaks up into chemically different atoms. **nucleate** *v.t.* to gather into or round a nucleus. **nucleolus** *n.* a minute body of condensed chromatin inside a nucleus [L. = kernel].

nude (nūd) *a.* bare; naked; undraped; uncovered; *n.* a picture or piece of sculpture in the nude. **-ly** *adv.* **-ness, nudity,** *n.* nakedness. **nudism** *n.* cult emphasizing practice of nudity for health. **nudist** *n.* [L. *nudus*, naked].

nudge (nuj) *v.t.* to touch slightly with the elbow; *n.* a gentle push [etym. uncertain].

nug·get (nug'·it) *n.* rough lump or mass, esp. of native gold [etym. uncertain].

nui·sance (nū'·sans) *n.* something harmful, offensive, or annoying; a troublesome person; a pest; an inconvenience [Fr. *nuisant*, harming; fr. L. *nocere*, to harm].

null (nul) *a.* of no legal validity; void; nonexistent; of no importance; *v.t.* to annul; to render void. **-ify** *v.t.* to make null; to render useless; to invalidate; **-fication** *n.* **ifier** *n.* **-ity** *n.* state of being null and void [L. *nullus*, none].

numb (num) *a.* insensible; insensitive; chilled; *v.t.* to benumb; to paralyze. **-ness** *n.* [O.E. *numen*, taken].

num·ber (num'·ber) *n.* a word used to indicate how great any quantity is when compared with the unit quantity, one; a sum or aggregate of quantities; a collection of things; an assembly; a single issue of a publication; a piece of music; (*Gram.*) classification of words as to singular or plural; *pl.* metrical feet or verse; rhythm; *v.t.* to give a number to; to count; to reckon; to estimate; *v.i.* to amount to. **-s** *n.pl.* (*Bib.*) fourth book of Pentateuch. **-er** *n.* **-less** *a.* innumerable. **numerability, numerableness** *n.* **numerable** *a.* may be numbered or counted [Fr. *nombre*, fr. L. *numerus*].

nu·mer·al (nū'·mer·al) *a.* designating a number; *n.* a sign or word denoting a number. **numerable** *a.* able to be counted. **numerably** *adv.* **-ly** *adv.* according to number. **numerary** *a.* belonging to, or an integral part of, a certain number, as opposed to *supernumerary*. **numerate** *v.t.* to count; to read figures according to their notation. **numeration** *n.* **numerator** *n.* top part of a fraction, figure showing how many of the fractional units are taken. **numeric(al)** *a.* of, or in respect of, numbers. **numerically** *adv.* **numerous** *a.* many. **numerously** *adv.* **numerousness** *n.* [L. *numerus*, a number].

nu·mis·mat·ic (nū·mis·mat'·ik) *a.* pert. to coins and medals, esp. as an aid to study of archaeology. **numismatist** *n.* **numismatography, numismatology** *n.* science of coins and medals in relation to archaeology and history. **numismatologist** *n.* [L. *numisma*, current coin].

num·skull (num'·skul) *n.* (*Colloq.*) dolt; dunce; a stupid person [*numb, skull*].

nun (nun) *n.* a female member of a religious order, vowed to celibacy, and dedicated to active or contemplative life. **-nery** *n.* convent of nuns [L.L. *nonna*].

nun·ci·o (nun'·shi·ō) *n.* a diplomatic representative of the Pope abroad. **nunciature** *n.* [It. fr. L. *nuntius*, a messenger].

nun·cu·pate (nung'·kyoo·pāt) *v.t.* and *v.i.* to vow publicly; to dedicate; to declare orally, as a will. **nuncupation** *n.* **nuncupative** *a.* oral; not written. **nuncupator** *n.* **nuncupatory** *a.*

oral; verbal [L. *nuncupare*, to name].

nup·tial (nup'·shal, ·chal) *a.* pert. to or constituting ceremony of marriage; *pl.* wedding ceremony; marriage [L. *nuptiae*, wedding].

nurse (nurs) *n.* a person trained for the care of the sick or injured; a woman tending another's child; *v.t.* to tend, as a nurse; to suckle; to foster; to husband; to harbor (a grievance); to manage skillfully (the early stages of some project). **-maid, nursery-maid** *n.* a girl in charge of young children. **-r** *n.* **nursery** *n.* a room set aside for children; a place for the rearing of plants. **nurseryman** *n.* one who raises plants for sale. **nursery rhymes**, jingling rhymes written to amuse young children. **nursery school**, a school for children of 2-5 years of age. **nursling** *n.* an infant; anything which is carefully tended at inception. **wet-nurse** *n.* woman who suckles infant of another [Fr. *nourrice*, fr. L. *nutrix*, a nurse].

nur·ture (nur'·cher) *n.* nurturing; education; rearing; breeding; nourishment; (*Biol.*) the various environmental forces, which combined, act on an organism and further its existence; *v.t.* to nourish; to cherish; to tend; to train; to rear; to bring up. **-r** *n.* [Fr. *nourriture*, nourishment].

nut (nut) *n.* a fruit consisting of a hard shell enclosing a kernel; a hollow metal collar, the internal surface of which carries a groove or thread into which the thread of a screw fits; (*Slang*) the head; blockhead; *v.i.* to gather nuts; *pr.p.* **-ting.** *pa.t.* and *pa.p.* **-ted.** **-brown** *a.* of the color of a nut. — **butter**, a butter substitute made from nut oil. **-cracker** *n.* an instrument for cracking nuts; bird of crow family. **-hatch** *n.* a climbing bird, allied to titmice. **-shell** *n.* the hard shell enclosing the kernel of a nut. **-ter** *n.* one who gathers nuts. **-tiness** *n.* taste of nuts. **-ting** *n.* **-ty** *a.* abounding in nuts; having a nut-flavor; (*Slang*) silly; imbecile. **a hard nut to crack**, a difficult problem to solve; a person difficult to deal with [O.E. *hnutu*].

nu·tant (nū'·tant) *a.* (*Bot.*) hanging with the apex of the flower downwards; nodding. **nutation** *n.* nodding; (*Astron.*) slight periodic wobbling of direction of Earth's axis [L. *nutare*, to nod].

nuthatch

nut·meg (nut'·meg) *n.* an aromatic flavoring spice [E. *nut*; O.Fr. *mugue*, musk].

nu·tri·ent (nū'·tri·ant) *a.* nourishing; *n.* something nutritious. **nutriment** *n.* that which nourishes; food; sustenance. **nutrition** *n.* the act of nourishing. **nutritional, nutritious, nutritive, nutritory** *a.* nourishing; promoting growth [L. *nutrire*, to nourish].

nuz·zle (nuz'·l) *v.t.* and *v.i.* to rub with the nose; to nestle; to burrow or press with the nose [*nose*].

nyc·ta·lo·pi·a (nik·ta·lō'·pi·a) *n.* night blindness [Gk. *nux*, night; *alaos*, blind; *ēps*, eye].

ny·lon (nī'·lan) *n.* an artificial fabric the yarn of which is produced synthetically; *n.pl.* stockings made of nylon yarn [fr. *N* (ew) *Y* (ork), *Lon*(don)].

nymph (nimf) *n.* a lesser goddess inhabiting a mountain, grove, fountain, river, etc.; a girl distinguished by her grace and charm. **-al, -ean, -ic, -ical** *a.* **-like** *a.* **-omania** *n.* a morbid and uncontrollable sexual desire in women. **-omaniac** *n.* [Gk. *nymphē*, a bride].

nymph (nimf) *n.* the pupa or chrysalis of an insect [Gk. *nymphē*, a nymph].

nys·tag·mus (nis·tag'·mas) *n.* eye disease with involuntary twitching oscillation of eyes [Gk. *nustazein*, to nod].

O

O, oh (ō) *interj.* an exclamation of address, surprise, sorrow, wonder, entreaty [O.E. *ea*].

oaf (ōf) *n.* a changeling; dolt; lout; simpleton. *pl.* **oafs** or **oaves. -ish** *a.* loutish; awkward [O.N. *alfr*, an elf].

oak (ōk) *n.* a familiar forest tree yielding a hard, durable timber and acorns as fruit. **-en** *a.* made of oak. — **apple** *n.* a gall or swelling on oak leaves caused by the gallfly [O.E. *ac*].

oar (ōr) *n.* a wooden lever with a broad blade worked by the hands to propel a boat; an oarsman; *v.t.* and *v.i.* to row. **-ed** *a.* having oars. **-man** *n.* a rower. **-manship** *n.* art of rowing. **to put in one's oar** (*Slang*) to meddle; to interfere [O.E. *ar*].

o·a·sis (ō·ā′·sis) *n.* a fertile spot in the desert. *pl.* **oases** (ō·ā′·sēz) [Gk.].

oat (ōt) *n.* but usually in *pl.* **oats**, the grain of a common cereal plant, used as food; the plant; (*Poet.*) a shepherd's musical pipe; a pastoral song. **-en** *a.* made of oat-straw or oatmeal. **-cake** *n.* a thin cake of oatmeal. **-meal** *n.* meal made from oats. **to sow wild oats**, to indulge in youthful follies before settling down [O.E. *ate*].

oath (ōth) *n.* confirmation of the truth by naming something sacred, esp. God; a statement or promise confirmed by an appeal to God; a blasphemous use of the name of God; any imprecation. *pl.* **oaths** (ōTHz) [O.E. *ath*].

ob·li·ga·to (ȧb·li·gȧ′·tō) *n.* (*Mus.*) a part in a musical composition for a particular instrument, of such importance that it is indispensable to the proper rendering of the piece; —also *a.* Also **obligato** [It.].

ob·du·rate (ȧb′·dyoo·rat) *a.* hard-hearted; stubborn; unyielding. **-ly** *adv.* **obduracy** *n.* [L. *obduratus*, hardened].

o·be·di·ent (ō·bē′·di·ȧnt) *a.* subject to authority; willing to obey. **-ly** *adv.* **obedience** *n.* submission to authority; doing what one is told [L. *obedire*].

o·bei·sance (ō·bā′·sȧns) *n.* a bow, curtsy or gesture of deference [Fr. *obéissance*, obedience].

ob·e·lisk (ȧb′·ȧ·lisk) *n.* a tall, four-sided, tapering pillar, ending in a small pyramid; in printing, a reference mark (†) also called 'dagger'; an **obelus** (*pl.* **obeli**), the marks — or ÷ [Gk. *obeliskos*].

o·bese (ō·bēs′) *a.* fat; fleshy. **obesity** *n.* excessive fatness [L. *obesus*].

o·bey (ō·bā′) *v.i.* to be obedient; *v.t.* to comply with the orders of; to yield submission to; to be ruled by [L. *obedire*].

ob·fus·cate (ȧb·fus′·kāt) *v.t.* to darken; to confuse or bewilder. **obfuscation** *n.* obscurity; confusion [L. *obfuscare*, to darken].

o·bit (ō′·bit) *n.* (*Slang*) abbrev. of **obituary. obituary** *a.* pert. to death of person; *n.* a notice, often with a biographical sketch, of the death of a person [L. *obitus*, approach, fr. *obire*, to go to meet].

ob·ject (ȧb′·jekt) *n.* anything presented to the mind or senses; a material thing; an end or aim; (*Gram.*) a noun, pronoun, or clause governed by, and dependent on, a transitive verb or a preposition. **-less** *a.* having no aim or purpose [L. *objetus*, thrown in the way].

ob·ject (ȧb·jekt′) *v.t.* to offer in opposition; to put forward as reason against; *v.i.* to make verbal opposition; to protest against; to feel dislike or reluctance. **objection** (ȧb·jek′·shȧn) *n.* act of objecting; adverse reason; difficulty or drawback; argument against. **objectionable** *a.* **objectionably. -or** *n.* [L. *ob*, in the way of; *jacere*, to throw].

ob·jec·tive (ȧb·jek′·tiv) *a.* pert. to the object; relating to that which is external to the mind; unbiased; (*Gram.*) denoting the case of the object. **-ly** *adv.* **objectivity** *n.* the quality of being objective [Fr. *objectif*].

ob·jur·gate (ȧb′·jer·gāt) *v.t.* to reprove; to blame; to berate. **objurgation** *n.* **objurgatory** *a.* [L. *objurgare*, to blame].

ob·late (ȧb·lāt′) *a.* (*Geom.*) flattened at the poles (said of a spheroid, like the earth). **-ness** *n.* [L. *oblatus*, brought forward].

ob·late (ȧb′·lāt) *n.* a person dedicated to religious work, esp. the monastic service. **oblation** *n.* something offered to God, or a god; a gift to the church [L. *oblatus*, brought forward, offered].

ob·li·gate (ȧb′·li·gāt) *v.t.* to bind, esp. by legal contract; to put under obligation. **obligation** *n.* the binding power of a promise or contract; indebtedness for a favor of kindness; a duty; a legal bond. **obligatory** (ȧ·blig′·ȧ·tōr·i·) *a.* binding legally or morally; compulsory. **obligatorily** *adv.* [L. *obligare*, fr. *ligare*, to bind].

o·blige (ȧ·blīj′) *v.t.* to constrain by physical, moral, or legal force; to lay under an obligation; to do a favor to; to compel. **-d** *a.* grateful; indebted. **-ment** *n.* a favor. **obliging** *a.* helpful; courteous. **obligingly** *adv.* **obligingness** *n.* [L. *obligare*, fr. *ligare*, to bind].

ob·lique (ō·blēk′) *a.* slanting; inclined; indirect; obscure; not straightforward; underhand. **-ly** *adv.* **-ness, obliquity** (ȧ·blik′·wi·ti·) *n.* slant or inclination; deviation from moral uprightness; dishonesty [L. *obliquus*.].

ob·lit·er·ate (ȧ·blit′·a·rāt) *v.t.* to blot out; to efface or destroy. **obliteration** *n.* the act of blotting out; destruction; extinction. **obliterative** *a.* [L. *obliterare*, fr. *litera*, a letter].

ob·liv·i·on (ȧ·bliv′·i·ȧn) *n.* a forgetting, or being forgotten; forgetfulness; heedlessness. **oblivious** *a.* forgetful; causing to forget; heedless. **obliviously** *adv.* **obliviousness** *n.* [L. *oblivisci*, to forget].

ob·long (ȧb′·lawng) *a.* longer than broad; *n.* (*Geom.*) a rectangular figure with adjacent sides unequal [L. *oblongus*].

ob·lo·quy (ȧb′·lȧ·kwi·) *n.* abusive speech; disgrace [L. *obloquium*, a speaking against].

ob·nox·ious (ȧb·nȧk′·shȧs) *a.* offensive; objectionable. **-ly** *adv.* **-ness** *n.* [L. *obnoxius*, exposed to harm].

o·boe (ō′·bō) *n.* (*Mus.*) a woodwind instrument, long and slender, with tone produced by a double reed; an organ reed stop. **oboist** *n.* [Fr. *hautbois*, high, wood].

ob·scene (ȧb·sēn′) *a.* offensive to modesty; indecent; filthy. **-ly** *adv.* **-ness** *n.* **obscenity** (ȯb·sen′.i.ti·) *n.* lewdness; indecency [L.].

ob·scure (ȧb·skūr′) *a.* dark; hidden; dim; uncertain; humble; *v.t.* to dim; to conceal; to make less intelligible; to make doubtful. **-ly** *adv.* **-ness** *n.* **obscurity** *n.* absence of light; a state of retirement; lack of clear expression or meaning [L. *obscurus*, covered over].

ob·se·quy (ȧb′·sa·kwi·) *n.* funeral rite; a funeral. **obsequial** *a.* [L.L. *obsequiae*].

ob·se·qui·ous (ȧb·sē′·kwi·ȧs) *a.* servile; fawning. **-ly** *adv.* **-ness** *n.* [L. *obsequi*, to comply with].

ob·serve (ȧb·zurv′) *v.t.* to watch; to note systematically; to perform or keep religiously; to remark; *v.i.* to take notice; to make a remark; to comment. **observable** *a.* **observance** *n.* the act of observing; a paying attention; the keeping of a law, custom, religious rite; a religious rite; a rule or practice. **observant** *a.* quick to notice; alert; carefully attentive; obedient to. **observantly** *adv.* **observation** *n.* the action or habit of observing; the result of watching, examining, and noting; attentive watchfulness; a comment; a remark. **observatory** *n.* a building for the observation and study of astronomical, meteorological, etc., phenomena. **-r** *n.* [L. *observare*, to watch].

ob·sess (ȧb·ses′) *v.t.* to haunt; to fill the mind completely; to preoccupy. **-ion** *n.* complete domination of the mind by one idea; a fixed idea [L. *obsidere, obsessum*, to besiege].

ob·sid·i·an (ȧb·sid′·i·an) *n.* vitreous lava or glassy volcanic rock [fr. *Obsius*, the discoverer].

ob·so·lete (ȧb·sa·lēt) *a.* no longer in use; out of date. **-ly** *adv.* **-ness** *n.* **obsolescent** *a.* becoming obsolete; going out of use. **obsolescence** *n.* [L. *obsolescere*, to grow out of use].

ob·sta·cle (ȧb′·sta·kl) *n.* anything that stands in the way; an obstruction; a hindrance [L. *ob*, in the way of; *stare*, to stand].

ob·stet·rics (ȧb·stet′·riks) *n.* (*Med.*) the science dealing with the care of pregnant women; midwifery. **obstetric, obstetrical** *a.* **obstetrician** *n.* [L. *obstetrix*, a midwife].

ob·sti·nate (ȧb′·sta·nat) *a.* stubborn; not easily moved by argument; unyielding. **-ly** *adv.* **-ness** *n.* **obstinacy** *n.* unreasonable firmness; stubbornness [L. *obstinatus*].

ob·strep·er·ous (ab·strep′·a·ras) *a.* noisy; clamorous; vociferous; unruly; *adv.* **-ness** *n.* [L. *ob*, against; *strepere*, to make a noise].

ob·struct (ȧb·strukt′) *v.t.* to block up; to impede; to hinder the passage of; to retard; to oppose; to block out. **-er, -or** *n.* **-ion** *n.* the act of obstructing; that which obstructs or hinders. **-ive, -ively** *adv.* [L. *ob*, against; *struere*, to build up].

ob·tain (ȧb·tān′) *v.t.* to gain; to acquire; to procure; *v.i.* to be customary or prevalent; to hold good. **-able** *a.* procurable. **-ment** *n.* Also **obtention** [L. *obtinere*].

ob·trude (ȧb·trōōd′) *v.t.* to thrust forward unsolicited; to push out; *v.i.* to intrude. **-r** *n.* **obtrusion** *n.* the act of obtruding. **obtrusive** *a.* **obtrusively** *adv.* [L. *ob; trudere*, to thrust].

ob·tuse (ȧb·tōōs′) *a.* blunt; dull of perception; stupid; (*Geom.*) greater than a right angle, but less than 180°. **-ly** *adv.* **-ness** *n.* [L. *obtundere, obtusum*, to blunt].

ob·verse (ȧb′·vurs, ȧb·vurs′) *a.* having the base narrower than the apex; being a counterpart; facing the observer; of a coin, bearing the head; *n.* face of a coin, medal, etc. (opp. of 'reverse'); the front or principal aspect. **-ly** *adv.* [L. *ob*, toward; *versum*, to turn].

ob·vi·ate (ȧb′·vi·āt) *v.t.* to intercept and remove (as difficulties); to make unnecessary [L. *ob; viare*, to go].

ob·vi·ous (ȧb′·vi·ȧs) *a.* easily seen or understood; evident; apparent. **-ly** *adv.* **-ness** *n.* [L. *obvius*, in the way].

oc·a·ri·na (ȧk·a·rē′·na) *n.* a small musical wind-instrument with finger holes [It. *oca*, a goose, from its shape].

oc·ca·sion (a·kā′·zhan) *n.* opportunity; a juncture favorable for something; reason or justification; a time of important occurrence; *v.t.* to cause; to bring about. **-al** *a.* occurring now and then; incidental; meant for a special occasion. **-ally** *adv.* from time to time [L. *occasio*, fr. *cadere*, to fall].

oc·ci·dent (ȧk′·sa·dant) *n.* part of the horizon where the sun sets, the west. **occidental** *a.* western; *n.* (*Cap.*) native of Europe or America [L. *occidere*, to go down].

oc·ci·put (ȧk′·si·put) *n.* the back part of the head. **occipital** (ȧk·sip′·i·tal) *a.* [L. *ob*, over against; *caput*, the head].

oc·clude (a·klōōd′) *v.t.* to shut in or out; (*Chem.*) to absorb gas. **occlusion** *n.* **occlusive** *a.* [L. *ob; claudere, clausum*, to shut].

oc·cult (a·kult′) *a.* secret; mysterious; magical; supernatural; *v.t.* to conceal; to hide from view; to eclipse. **-ly** *adv.* **occultation** *n.* the eclipse of a heavenly body by another.

-ism *n.* the doctrine or study of the supernatural, magical, etc. [L. *occulere*, to hide].

oc·cu·py (ăk'·yą·pī) *v.t.* to take possession of; to inhabit; to fill; to employ. **occupancy** *n.* the act of having or holding possession; tenure. **occupant** *n.* one who occupies or is in possession. **occupation** *n.* occupancy; possession; temporary possession of enemy country by the victor; employment; trade; calling; business, profession. **occupational** *a.* **occupier** *n.* [L. *occupare*, to take possession of].

oc·cur (ą·kur') *v.i.* to come to the mind; to happen; to be met with. *pr.p.* **-ring.** *pa.p.* and *pa.t.* **-red. -rence** *n.* a happening; an event. [L. *occurrere*, to run against].

o·cean (ō'·shạn) *n.* great body of salt water surrounding land of globe; one of the large divisions of this; the sea; (*fig.*) to the great sea. **oceanic** (ō·shi·an'·ik) *a.* pert. to, found, or formed in the ocean. **-ography** *n.* the scientific description of ocean phenomena. **-ographer** *n.* **-ographic, -ographical** *a.* **-ology** *n.* science which relates to the ocean [Gk. *ōkeanos*, a stream encircling the world].

o·ce·lot (ō'·są·lät) *n.* a S. Amer. quadruped of the leopard family [Mex. *ocelotl*].

o·cher (ō'·ker) *n.* various natural earths used as yellow, brown, or red pigments. **-ous, -y** *a.* [Gk. *ōchra*, yellow ocher].

o'clock (ą·klȯk') *adv.* by the clock.

oct-, octa-, octo- *prefix* fr. Gk. *oktō*, eight, combining to form derivatives. **-agon** (ăk'·tą·gạn) *n.* a plane figure with 8 sides and 8 angles. **-agonal** *a.* **-ahedron** *n.* a solid figure with 8 plane faces. **-ahedral** *a.* **-ane** *n.* (*Chem.*) a hydrocarbon of the paraffin series, obtained from petroleum and used as a fuel, esp. for airplanes. **-angular** *a.* having 8 angles. **-ant** *n.* the eighth part of a circle; an instrument for measuring angles, having an arc of 45°.

octagon

oc·tave (ȯk'·tāv) *n.* the week following the celebration of a principal Church festival; the day falling a week after a festival; a stanza of 8 lines; (*Mus.*) an interval of 8 diatonic notes comprising a complete scale; a note 8 tones above or below another note; a group of 8 [L. *octavus*, eighth].

oc·ten·ni·al (ȯk·ten'·i·ạl) *a.* happening every eighth year; lasting for 8 years [L. *octo*, eight; *annus*, a year].

oc·tet (ȯk·tet') *n.* (*Mus.*) a group of 8 musicians or singers; a composition for such a group; a group of 8 lines, esp. the first 8 lines of a sonnet. Also **octette** [L. *octo*, eight].

Oc·to·ber (ȯk·tō'·ber) *n.* tenth month [eighth month of ancient Roman year].

oc·to·ge·nar·i·an (ȯk·tą·ją·ne'·ri·ạn) *a.* and *n.* (one) between 80 and 90 years of age [L. *octogenarius*, of eighty].

oc·to·pus (ȯk'·tą·pạs) *n.* a mollusk with 8 arms or tentacles covered with suckers [Gk. *oktō*, eight; *pous*, a foot].

oc·u·lar (ȯk'·yą·ler) *a.* pert. to the eye, or to sight; visual; *n.* the eyepiece of an optical in-

---

strument. **oculist** *n.* a specialist in the defects and diseases of the eye [L. *oculus*, the eye].

o·da·lisque (ō'·dą·lisk) *n.* a female slave or concubine in a Turkish harem. Also **odalisk** [Fr. fr. Turk.].

odd (ȧd) *a.* not even; not divisible by two; left over after a round number has been taken; extra; surplus; casual or outside the reckoning; occasional; out-of-the-way; queer or eccentric; strange. **-ity** *n.* quality of being odd; peculiarity; queer person or thing. **-ly** *adv.* **-ness** *n.* **odds** *n.pl.* the difference in favor of one as against another; advantage or superiority; the ratio by which one person's bet exceeds another's; likelihood or probability. [O.N. *odda- (tala)*, odd-point].

ode (ōd) *n.* a lyric poem of exalted tone [Gk. *ōdē*, a song].

o·di·um (ō'·di·ạm) *n.* hatred; the state of being hated; general abhorrence incurred by a person or action; stigma. **odious** *a.* **odiously** *adv.* **odiousness** *n.* [L. = hatred].

o·dont- (ō·dȧnt') *prefix* from the Gk. *odous, odontos,* a tooth. **odontalgia** (ō·dȧn·tȧl'·ji·ą) *n.* toothache. **odontology** *n.* the science of the teeth [Gk. *algos*, pain; *logos*, discourse].

o·dor (ō'·der) *n.* smell; fragrance; perfume; repute or estimation. **-iferous** (ō·dą·rif'·ą·ras) a sweet-scented; having a strong smell. **-iferously** *adv.* **-iferousness** *n.* **-less** *a.* **-ous** *a.* fragrant; scented. [L. *odor*].

O·dys·seus (ō·dis'·ūs, ō·dis'·ē·ạs) *n.* (*Myth.*) (L. Ulysses) hero of Homer's **Odyssey** (ȯd'·i·si·) *n.* a Greek epic poem glorifying the adventures and wanderings of Odysseus; hence, any long, adventurous journey.

Oed·i·pus (ē·dą·pạs) *n.* (*Myth.*) a king of Thebes who unwittingly slew his father and married Jocasta, his mother. **Oedipus complex,** in psychoanalysis, a complex involving an abnormal love by a person for the parent of opposite sex.

o'er (ȯr) *prep.* (*Poet.*) a contr. for **over.**

oe·soph·a·gus See **esophagus.**

of (ȧv, uv) *prep.* belonging to; from; proceeding from; relating to; concerning [O.E.].

off (awf) *adv.* away; in general, denotes removal or separation, also completion, as in *to finish off; prep.* not on; away from; *a.* distant; on the farther side; less than satisfactory; discontinued; free; *interj.* begone! depart! **-ing** *n.* the more distant part of the sea visible to an observer; **-ish,** *a.* inclined to stand aloof; **-ishly** *adv.* **-ishness** *n.* in the offing, not very distant. **—chance** *n.* a slight chance. **—color** *a.* poor in color; of doubtful propriety. **—hand** *a.* without preparation; free and easy; curt; *adv.* without hesitation; impromptu. **-set** *n.* a shoot or side-branch; a sum set off against another as an equivalent; compensation; (*Print.*) the smudging of a clean sheet; a process in lithography; *v.t.* to counterbalance or compensate. **-shoot** *n.* that which shoots off or separates from a main branch or channel; a descendant. **— side** *a.* (*Football, etc.*) of a player, being illegally ahead of the ball, etc. **-spring** *n.* children; progeny; issue. **off and on,** intermittently [form of *of*].

of·fal (awf'·ạl) *n.* waste meat; entrails of animals; refuse [fr. *off* and *fall*].

of·fend (ą·fend') *v.t.* to displease; to make angry; to wound the feelings of; *v.i.* to cause displeasure; to do wrong; to sin. **-er** *n.* [L. *offendere*, to strike against].

of·fense (ą·fens') *n.* transgression; sin; insult; wrong; resentment; displeasure; a cause of displeasure. **offensive** *a.* causing or giving offense; used in attack; insulting; unpleasant; *n.* attack; onset; aggressive action. **offensively** *adv.* **offensiveness** *n.* [L. *offendere*, to strike against].

of·fer (awf'·er) *v.t.* to present for acceptance or refusal; to tender; to bid, as a price; to propose; to attempt; to express readiness to do; *v.i.* to present itself or to occur; *n.* an act of offering; a presentation; a price bid; a proposal, esp. of marriage. **-ing** *n.* that which is offered, as a contribution through the church; a sacrifice; a gift. **-er** *n.* [L. *offerre*].

of·fer·to·ry (awf'·er·tor·i·) *n.* (*R.C.*) a part of the mass during which the elements are offered up; the collection of money during the church service; the part of the service, or the music, when offerings are made [L. *offertorium*].

of·fice (awf'·is) *n.* a place for doing business; a duty; a service; a function; an official position; a form of worship; a religious service; **-s** *n.pl.* acts of kindness; help. **-r** *n.* a person who holds an official position; one who holds commissioned rank in the navy, army, air force, etc. [L. *officium*, duty].

of·fi·cial (ą·fish'·ạl) *a.* pert. to an office; vouched for by one holding office; authorized; *n.* one holding an office, esp. in a public body. **-ly** *adv.* **-dom** *n.* officials collectively; their work, usually in contemptuous sense [L. *officium*, a duty].

of·fi·ci·ate (ą·fish'·i·āt) *v.i.* to perform the duties of an officer; to perform a divine service [L. *officium*, duty].

of·fi·cious (ą·fish'·ạs) *a.* given to exaggerate the duties of an office; importunate in offering service; meddlesome. **-ly** *adv.* **-ness** *n.* [L. *officium*, a duty].

---

of·ten (awf'·n) *adv.* frequently; many times. **oft, -times, ofttimes,** *adv.* archaic forms of 'often' [O.E. *oft.*].

o·gle (ō'·gl, á'·gl) *v.i.* to make eyes: *v.t.* to make eyes at; to cast amorous glances at; *n.* an amorous glance. **-r** *n.* [L.Ger. *oegeln*, fr. *oegen*, to eye].

o·gre (ō·ger) *n.* (*fem.* **ogress**) a fabulous man-eating giant. **-ish, ogrish** *a.* [Fr.]

oh (ō) *interj.* an exclamation of surprise, sorrow, pain, etc. Also **oho!**

ohm (ōm) *n.* the standard unit of electrical resistance. **-meter** *n.* an instrument for measuring electrical current and resistance [fr. George S. *Ohm* (1787-1854)].

oil (oil) *n.* one of several kinds of light viscous liquids, obtained from various plants, animal substances, and minerals, used as lubricants, illuminants, fuel, medicines, etc.; *v.t.* to apply oil to; *v.i.* to take oil aboard as fuel. **-er** *n.* one who, or that which, oils; an oilcan. **-y** *a.* consisting of, or resembling, oil; greasy; fawning; subservient. **-ily** *adv.* **-iness** *n.* **-s** *n.pl.* (*Paint.*) short for 'oil-colors' **-cloth** *n.* coarse canvas cloth coated with oil and pigment to make waterproof, used for table coverings, etc. **— colors** *n.pl.* (*Paint.*) colors made by grinding pigments in oil. **— field** *n.* a region rich in mineral oil. **— painting** *n.* one done in oil colors. **-skin** *n.* cloth made waterproof with oil; *pl.* rain clothes of this material. **— well** *n.* boring made in district yielding petroleum [L. *oleum*].

oint·ment (oint'·mạnt) *n.* an unguent; [O.Fr. *oignement*].

o·kay (ō·kā') *a.* and *adv.* abbrev. to **O.K.,** an expression signifying approval.

old (ōld) *a.* advanced in age; having lived or existed long; belonging to an earlier period; not new or fresh; stale; out of date. **-en** *a.* old; ancient; pert. to the past. **-ish** *a.* somewhat old. **-ness** *n.* **—fashioned** *a.* out of date; not modern. **Old Harry,** the devil; Satan. **— maid,** a spinster; (*Cards*) a round game. **— master,** a painting by a famous artist, esp. of 15th and 16th cents. **Old Nick,** the devil. **— school.** *a.* old-fashioned. **Old Testament,** the first division of Bible. **Old World,** the Eastern hemisphere [O.E. *eald*].

o·le·ag·i·nous (ō·lē·aj'·ą·nạs) *a.* oily; greasy; (*Fig.*) fawning; unctuous [L. *oleum*, oil].

o·le·an·der (ō·lē·an'·der) *n.* a beautiful, evergreen shrub with red and white flowers [Fr.].

o·le·as·ter (ō·lē·as'·ter) *n.* the wild olive [L. fr. *olea*, an olive].

o·le·o (ō'·lē·ō) *prefix* fr. L. *oleum,* oil. **-graph** *n.* a lithograph in oil colors [Gk. *graphein,* to write].

o·le·o·mar·ga·rine (ō·lē·ō·márj'·ą·rạn) *n.* a butter substitute. *Abbrev.* oleo.

ol·fac·tion (ȧl·fak'·shạn) *n.* smelling; sense of smell. **olfactory** *a.* pert. to smelling [L. *olere,* to smell; *facere,* to make].

ol·i·gar·chy (ȧl'·i·gȧr·ki·) *n.* government in which supreme power rests with a few; those who constitute the ruling few. **oligarch** *n.* a member of an oligarchy. **oligarchal** *a.* Also **oligarchic(al)** [Gk. *oligos,* few; *archein,* to rule].

ol·i·go·cene (ȧl'·i·gō·sēn) *a.* (*Geol.*) pert. to a geological period between the eocene and miocene [Gk. *oligos,* little; *kainos,* recent].

o·li·o (ō'·li·ō) *n.* a highly-spiced stew of meat and vegetables; a medley [Sp. *olla,* fr. L. *olla,* a pot].

ol·ive (ȧl'·iv) *n.* an evergreen tree, long cultivated in the Mediterranean countries for its fruit; its oval, oil-yielding fruit; a color, of a greyish, ashy green; *a.* of the color of an unripe olive, or of the foliage. **-branch** *n.* an emblem or offer of peace. **— oil** *n.* oil expressed from olives [L. *oliva*].

O·lym·pi·a (ō·lim'·pi·ą) (*Class. Hist.*) a plain in ancient Greece, the scene of the Olympic Games. **Olympiad** *n.* the name given to period of four years between each celebration of Olympic Games. **Olympic** *a.* pert. to Olympia, or to the games. **Olympics** *n.pl.* the OlympicGames. **-n** pert. to Mount *Olympus.*

o·me·ga (ō·meg'·ą) *n.* the last letter of the Greek alphabet; hence, the end. **the alpha and omega,** the beginning and the end [Gk.].

om·e·let, omelette (ȧm'·let) *n.* (*Cookery*) a dish of eggs beaten with milk and seasonings and cooked in a frying pan [Fr.].

o·men (ō'·mạn) *n.* a sign of future events; a foreboding; *v.t.* to foreshadow by means of signs; to augur [L.].

om·i·nous (ȧm'·ą·nạs) *a.* foreboding evil; threatening; inauspicious. **-ly** *adv.* **-ness** *n.* [L. *ominosus,* fr. *omen*].

o·mit (ō·mit') *v.t.* to leave out; to neglect; to fail to perform. *pr.p.* **-ting** *pa.p.*, *pa.t.* **-ted.**

omission *n.* the act of omitting; neglect; failure to do; that which is omitted or left undone. **omissible** *a.* that may be omitted. **omissive** *a.* [L. *omittere*].

om·ni- (ăm′·nĭ·) *prefix fr.* L. *omnis,* all.

om·ni·bus (ăm′·nạ·bus) *n.* a bus; a used in the sense of 'several in one,' *e.g.* — **volume,** a book containing reprints of several works originally published separately; an anthology [L. *omnibus* = for all].

om·ni·far·i·ous (ăm′·nĭ·fār′·ĭ·ạs) *a.* consisting of all varieties [L.].

om·ni·po·tent (ăm·nĭp′·ạ·tạnt) *a.* all-powerful, esp. of God; almighty. **-ly** *adv.* **omnipotence** *n.* unlimited power.

om·ni·pres·ent (ăm·nĭ·prez′·ạnt) *a.* present in all places at the same time. **omnipresence** *n.* [L. *omnis,* all; and *present*].

om·nis·cience (ăm·nĭsh′·ạns) *n.* infinite knowledge. **omniscient** *a.* all-knowing.

om·niv·o·rous (ăm·nĭv′·ạ·rạs) *a.* all-devouring; eating every kind of food. **-ly** *adv.* [L. *omnis,* all; and *vorare,* to devour].

on (awn, ăn) *prep.* above and touching; in addition to; following from; referring to; at; near; towards, etc.; adv. so as to be on; forwards; continuously [O.E.].

once (wuns) *adv.* at one time; on one occasion; formerly; ever; *n.* one time. **at once,** immediately [fr. *one*].

on·com·ing (awn′·, ăn′·kum·ing) *a.* approaching; *n.* approach [fr. *on* and *coming*].

one (wun) *a.* single; undivided; only; without others; identical; *n.* the number or figure 1, I; the lowest cardinal number; unity; a single specimen; any person. *pron.* a particular but not stated person; any person. **-ness** *n.* unity; uniformity; singleness. **-self** *pron.* one's own self or person. **-horse** *a.* drawn by one horse; *(Colloq.)* of no importance; insignificant; paltry. **-sided** *a.* esp. of a contest, game, etc., limited to one side; considering one side only; partial; unfair. **-way** *a.* denoting a system of traffic circulation in one direction only [O.E. *an*].

on·er·ous (ŏn′·ẹr·ạs) *a.* burdensome; oppressive. **-ly** *adv.* **-ness** *n.* [L. *oneris,* a load].

on·go·ing (awn′·, ăn′·gō·ing) *n.* a going on; advance; procedure; *a.* continuing.

on·ion (un′·yạn) *n.* an edible, bulbous plant with pungent odor. — **skin** *n.* thin, glazed paper [L. *unio*].

on·look·er (awn′·, ăn′·look·ẹr) *n.* a spectator; an observer [fr. *on* and *look*].

on·ly (ōn′·lĭ·) *a.* being the one specimen; single; sole; *adv.* solely; singly; merely; exclusively; *conj.* but then; except that; with this reservation [O.E. *anlic,* one like].

on·o·mat·o·poe·ia (ăn·ạ·mat·ạ·pē′·yạ) *n.* the formation of a word by using sounds that resemble or suggest the object to be named; *e.g.* hiss, ping-pong. **onomatopoeic, onomatopoetic** *a.* [Gk. *onoma,* a name; *poiein,* to make].

on·set (awn′·, ăn·set) *n.* a violent attack; an assault [fr. *on* and *set*].

on·shore (awn′·, ăn′·shōr) *a.* towards the land, esp. of a wind [fr. *on* and *shore*].

on·slaught (awn′·, ăn′·slawt) *n.* attack; an onset; an assault [Dut. *aanslag*].

on·to (awn′·, ăn′·tòò) *prep.* upon; on the top; to.

on·tol·o·gy (ăn·tăl′·ạ·jĭ·) *n.* the science that treats of reality of being; metaphysics. **ontological** *a.* **ontologist** *n.* [Gk. *ōn, ontos,* being; *logos,* discourse].

o·nus (ō′·nạs) *n.* burden; responsibility [L.].

on·ward (awn′·, ăn·wẹrd) *a.* and *adv.* advancing; going on; forward. **-s** *adv.* in a forward direction; ahead [E. *on;* O.E. *weard,* in the direction of].

on·yx (ăn′·ĭks) *n.* a variety of quartz [Gk. *onux,* a fingernail].

oo·dles (ōō′ dlz) *n.pl. (Slang)* superabundance.

ooze (ōōz) *n.* soft mud or slime; a gentle flow; a kind of deposit on the bottom of the sea; *v.i.* to flow gently as if through pores; to leak or percolate; *v.t.* to exude or give out slowly. **oozy** *a.* [M.E. *wose,* fr. O.E. *wase,* mud].

o·pad·i·ty See **opaque.**

o·pal (ō′·pạl) *n.* a mineral much used as a gem owing to its beautiful and varying hues of green, yellow and red. **-escent** (ō·pạl·es′·ạnt) *a.* of changing iridescent color, like an opal. **-escence** *n.* **-ine** (ō′·pạl·in) *a.* like opal [L. *opalus*].

o·paque (ō·pāk′) *a.* not transparent; impenetrable to light; not lucid; dull-witted. **-ly** *adv.* **-ness** *n.* **opacity** *n.* [L. *opacus*].

ope (ōp) *v.t.* and *i. (Poet.)* to open.

o·pen (ō′·pn) *a.* not shut or blocked up; allowing passage in or out; not covered (with trees); not fenced; without restrictions; available; exposed; frank and sincere; *n.* clear, unobstructed space; *v.t.* to set open; to uncover; to give access to; to begin; to cut or break into; *v.i.* to become open; to begin; *(Theater)* to have a first performance. **-er** *n.* one who or that which opens. **-ing** *a.* first in order; initial; *n.* a hole or gap; an open or cleared space; an opportunity; a beginning. **-ly** *adv.* publicly; frankly. **-ness** *n.* **-cast** *a. (Mining)* excavated from the surface, instead of from underground. **-handed** *a.* generous; liberal. **-hearted** *a.* frank. **-minded** *a.* free from prejudices [O.E.].

op·er·a (ăp′·ạ·rạ) *n.* a musical drama; *(Colloq.)* the theater where opera is performed. **operatic** *a.* pert. to opera. **operetta** *n.* a short light opera. **grand opera,** opera in which no spoken dialoge is permitted. — **bouffe** (bōōf) a farcical play set to music. — **glass** (or **glasses**) *n.* a small binocular used in theaters. — **hat** *n.* a man's collapsible tall hat [It. fr. L. *opera,* work].

op·er·ate (ăp′·ạ·rāt) *v.t.* to cause to function; to effect; *v.i.* to work; to produce an effect; to exert power; to perform an act of surgery; to deal in stocks and shares, esp. speculatively. **operation** *n.* the act of operating; a method or mode of action; treatment involving surgical skill; movement of an army or fleet (usu. in *pl.*). **operational** *a.* **operative** *a.* having the power of acting; exerting force; producing the desired effect; efficacious; *n.* artisan or workman; factory hand. **operator** *n.* [L. *operari,* to work].

op·er·cu·lum (ō·pur′·kyạ·lạm) *n.* a lid or cover, in plants; a lid-like structure in mollusks [L. fr. *operire,* to cover].

op·er·ose (ăp′·ạ·rōs) *a.* laborious; industrious. **-ly** *adv.* **-ness** *n.* [L. *opus,* work].

oph·i·(o)- *prefix fr.* Gk. *ophis,* a snake. **ophidian** (ō·fĭd′·ĭ·ạn) *n.* a snake; *a.* snakelike.

oph·thal·mi·a (ăf·thal′·mĭ·ạ) *n. (Med.)* inflammation of the eye. **ophthalmic** *a.* of the eye. **ophthalmologist** *n.* a physician skilled in the study and treatment of the eye. **ophthalmology** *n.* the science dealing with the structure, functions, and diseases of the eye. **ophthalmoscope** *n.* an instrument for viewing the interior of the eye [Gk. *ophthalmos,* the eye; *logos,* discourse; *skopein,* to view].

o·pi·ate (ō′·pĭ·ạt) *n.* any preparation of opium; a narcotic; anything that dulls or stupefies; *a.* containing opium; inducing sleep. **opiatic** *a.* [fr. *opium*].

o·pine (ō·pīn′) *v.t.* and *i.* to think or suppose; to hold or express an opinion [L. *opinari*].

o·pin·ion (ạ·pĭn′·yạn) *n.* judgment or belief; estimation; formal statement by an expert. **-ated** *a.* dogmatic [L. *opinio*].

o·pi·um (ō′·pĭ·ạm) *n.* narcotic used to induce sleep or allay pain [Gk. *opion,* poppy-juice].

o·pos·sum (ạ·păs′·ạm) *n.* a small marsupial animal. Also **possum** [N. Amer. Ind.].

op·po·nent (ạ·pō′·nạnt) *a.* opposite; opposing; antagonistic; *n.* one who opposes [L. *opponere,* to place against].

op·por·tune (ăp·ẹr·tūn′) *a.* well-timed; convenient. **-ly** *adv.* **-ness** *n.* **opportunism** *n.* the policy of doing what is expedient at the time regardless of principle. **opportunist** *n.* **opportunity** *n.* a fit or convenient time; a good chance [L. *opportunus*].

op·pose (ạ·pōz′) *v.t.* to set against; to resist; to compete with. **opposable** *a.* **-r** *n.* [L. *opponere,* to place against].

op·po·site (ăp′·ạ·zit) *a.* contrary facing; contrary; diametrically different; *n.* the contrary; *prep.* and *adv.* in front of; on the other side; across from; **-ly** *adv.* facing each other. **-ness** *n.* **opposition** (ăp·ạ·zish′·ạn) *n.* the state of being opposite; resistance; contradiction; an obstacle; a party opposed to that in power [L. *opponere, oppositum,* to place against].

op·press (ạ·pres′) *v.t.* to govern with tyranny; to treat severely; to lie heavily on. **-ion** (ạ·presh′·ạn) *n.* harshness; tyranny; dejection. **-ive** *a.* unreasonably burdensome; hard to bear. **-ively** *adv.* **-iveness** *n.* **-or** *n.* [L. *opprimere, oppressum,* to press down].

op·pro·bri·um (ạ·prō′·brĭ·ạm) *n.* reproach; disgrace; infamy. **opprobrious** *a.* reproachful and contemptuous; shameful. [L.].

op·pugn (ạ·pūn′) *v.t.* to dispute; to oppose. **-er** *n.* **oppugnant** (ạ·pug′·nạnt) *a.* opposing. **-ancy** *n.* opposition [L. *oppugnare,* to fight against].

opt (ăpt) *v.i.* to make a choice; to choose. **-ative** (ăp′·tạ·tiv) *a.* expressing wish or desire; *n. (Gram.)* a mood of the verb expressing wish. [L. *optare,* to wish].

op·tic (ăp′·tic) *a.* pert. to the eye or to sight; pert. to optics; *n.* the eye. **-s** *n.* the science which deals with light and its relation to sight. **-al** *a.* pert. to vision; visual. **-ally** *adv.*

optician (ăp·tish′·ạn) *n.* a maker of, or dealer in, optical instruments, esp. spectacles [Gk. *optikos*].

op·ti·mism (ăp′·tạ·mizm) *n.* belief that everything is ordered for the best; disposition to

look on bright side. **optimist** *n.* believer in optimism; one who takes hopeful view. **optimistical** *a.* [L. *optimus,* best].

op·tion (ăp′·shạn) *n.* the power or right of choosing; choice. *a.* left to one's free choice. **-ally** *adv.* [L. *optare,* to choose].

op·u·lent (ăp′·yạ·lạnt) *a.* wealthy; abundantly rich. **-ly** *adv.* **opulence, opulency** *n.* wealth; riches [L. *opulentus*].

o·pus (ō′·pạs) *n.* a work; a musical composition; *pl.* **opera** (ăp′·ạ·rạ). **magnum opus,** a writer's most important work [L. *opusculum* dim. of *opus,* work].

or (awr) *conj.* introducing an alternative; if not; *(Arch.)* before [M.E. *other*].

or·a·cle (awr′·ạ·kl) *n.* shrine where ancient Greeks consulted deity; response given, often obscure; a person of outstanding wisdom. **o·rac·u·lar** (aw·rak′·yạ·lẹr) *a.* **oracularly** *adv.* [L. *oraculum*].

o·ral (ō′·rạl) *a.* spoken; pert. to the mouth. **-ly** *adv.* [L. *os, oris,* the mouth].

or·ange (awr′·inj) *n.* a juicy, gold-colored citrus fruit; tree bearing it; reddish yellow color like an orange; *a.* reddish yellow in color. **-ade** (or·anj·ād′) *n.* drink of orange juice, sugar, and water [Arab. *naranj*].

o·rang·u·tan, o·rang·ou·tang (ō·rang′·ōō·tang) *n.* a large long-armed ape [Malayan = man of the woods].

o·rate (ō·rāt′) *v.i.* to talk loftily; to harangue. **oration** (ō·rā′·shạn) *n.* a formal and dignified public speech. **orator** *n.* one who delivers an oration; one distinguished for gift of public speaking. **oratorical** *a.* pert. to orator(y); rhetorical. **oratorically** *adv.* **oratorio** (or·ạ·tō′·ri·ō) *n.* a religious musical composition for voices and orchestra. **oratory** *n.* the art or exercise of speaking in public; eloquence; a chapel or small room for private devotions [L. *orare,* to speak].

orb (awrb) *n.* a sphere or globe; *(Poet.)* a heavenly body; the globe surmounted by a cross, which forms part of the regalia in England; *(Poet.)* the eye. **-it** *n. (Astron.)* path traced by one heavenly body in its revolution round another; range of influence or action; the eye socket. **-ital** *a.* [L. *orbis,* a circle].

or·chard (awr′·cherd) *n.* a garden or enclosure containing fruit trees [O.E. *ortgeard*].

or·ches·tra (awr′·kis·trạ) *n.* the space in a theater occupied by musicians; the main floor of a theater; a group of performers on various musical instruments. **orchestral** *a.* **orchestrate** *v.t.* to arrange music for performance by an orchestra. **-tion** *n.* [Gk. *orcheisthai,* to dance].

or·chid, orchis (awr′·kid, awr′·kis) *n.* a genus of plants with fantastically-shaped flowers of varied and brilliant colors. **-aceous** *a.* pert. to the orchid [Gk. *orchis,* a testicle].

or·dain (awr·dān′) *v.t.* to decree; to destine; to appoint; to admit to the Christian ministry; to confer holy orders upon. **-ment** *n.* (rare). **ordination** *n.* the act of ordaining admission to the ministry [L. *ordo,* order].

or·deal (awr′·dēl, awr′·dē·ạl) *n.* an ancient method of trial by requiring the accused to undergo a dangerous physical test; a trying experience; a test of endurance [O.E. *ordal,* a judicial test].

or·der (awr′·dẹr) *n.* rank; class; group; regular arrangement; sequence; succession; method; regulation; a command or direction; mode of procedure; an instruction; a monastic society; one of the five styles of architecture (Doric, Ionic, Corinthian, Tuscan, and Composite); a subdivision of a class of plants or animals, made up of genera; an honor conferred for distinguished civil or military services; in trade, detailed instructions, by a customer, of goods to be supplied. *v.t.* to arrange; to command; to require; to regulate; to systematize; to give an order for. **-ly** *a.* methodical; tidy; well regulated; peaceable; *n.* a soldier following an officer to carry orders; in a hospital, an attendant; *adv.* in right order. **-liness** *n.* **holy orders**, generally, ordination to the Christian ministry. **to take orders**, to accept instructions; (*Church*) to be ordained. **by order**, by command. **in order to**, for the purpose of [L. *ordo*, order].

or·di·nal (awr'·di·nal) *a.* and *n.* showing order or position in a series, e.g. *first, second*, etc.; pert. to an order, of plants, animals, etc. a church service book for use at ordinations [L. *ordo*, order].

or·di·nance (awr'·di·nans) *n.* an established rule, religious rite, or ceremony; a decree [O. Fr. *ordenance*].

or·di·nar·y (awr'·di·ner·i·) *a.* usual; regular; habitual; normal, commonplace; plain; *n.* something customary; a church service book. **ordinarily** *adv.* [L. *ordo*, order].

or·di·na·tion See **ordain**.

ord·nance (awrd'·nans) *n.* collective term for heavy mounted guns; military weapons of all kinds, ammunition, etc. [var. of *ordinance*].

or·dure (awr'·jer) *n.* dung; filth [O.Fr. *ord*. vile].

ore (ōr) *n.* a native mineral from which metal is extracted [O.E. *ora*].

or·gan (awr'·gan) *n.* a musical instrument of pipes worked by bellows and played by keys; a member of an animal or plant exercising a special function; a medium of information. **organic** *a.* pert. to or affecting bodily organs; having either animal or vegetable life; derived from living organisms; systematic; organized. **organically** *adv.* **-ism** *n.* an organized body or system; a living body. **-ist** *n.* a player on the organ. **— grinder** *n.* a player of a barrel organ. **— loft** *n.* gallery for an organ. **— stop** *n.* a series of pipes of uniform tone or quality; one of a series of knobs for manipulating and controlling them. **organic chemistry**, the branch of chemistry dealing with the compounds of carbon [Gk. *organon*, an instrument].

or·gan·dy (awr'·gan·di·) *n.* a muslin of great transparency and lightness. Also **organdie** [Fr. *organdi*].

or·gan·ize (awr'·ga·nīz) *v.t.* to give a definite structure; to prepare for transaction of business; to get up, arrange, or put into working order; to unite in a society. **organizable** *a.* **organization** *n.* act of organizing; the manner in which the branches of a service, etc., are arranged; individuals systematically united for some work; a society. **-r** *n.* [Gk. *organon*, an instrument].

or·gasm (awr'·gazm) *n.* immoderate action or excitement, esp. sexual. **orgastic** *a.* [Gk. *orgaein*, to be lustful].

or·gy (awr'·ji·) *n.* a drunken or licentious revel; a debauch. **orgiastic** *a.* [Gk. *orgia* (*pl.*) Bacchic rites].

o·ri·el (ō'·ri·al) *n.* a projecting window; the recess in a room formed by such a window [O.Fr. *oriol*, a porch].

o·ri·ent (ō'·ri·ant) *a.* rising, as the sun; lustrous (applied to pearls); *n.* the east; Eastern countries; *v.t.* to place so as to face the east; to determine the position of, with respect to the east; to take one's bearings. **oriental** *a.* eastern; pert. to, coming from, of, the east; *n.* (*Cap.*) an Asiatic. **orientate** *v.t.* and *i.* to orient; to bring into clearly understood relations. **orientation** *n.* the act of turning to, or determining, the east; sense of direction; determining one's position [L. *oriens*, rising, fr. *oriri*, to rise].

or·i·fice (awr'·a·fis) *n.* a mouth or opening; perforation; vent [L. *orificium*, fr. *os*, the mouth; *facere*, to make].

or·i·gin (awr'·a·jin) *n.* beginning; starting point; a source; parentage; birth; nationality. **original** (a·rij'·a·nal) *a.* earliest; first; new, not copied or derived; thinking or acting for oneself; *n.* origin; model; a pattern. **originally** *adv.* **originality** *n.* the quality of being original; initiative. **originate** *v.t.* to bring into being; to initiate; *v.i.* to begin; to arise. **originative** *a.* **origination** *n.* **originator** *n.* [L. *origo*, fr. *oriri*, to rise].

o·ri·ole (ō'·ri·ōl) *n.* bird of the thrush family [O.Fr. *oriol*, fr. L. *aurum*, gold.]

or·i·son (awr'·i·zan) *n.* a prayer [L.*orare*, to pray].

or·mo·lu (awr'·ma·lóō) *n.* an alloy of copper, zinc and tin [Fr. *or*, gold; *moulu* ground, fr. *moudre*, to grind].

or·na·ment (awr'·na·mant) *n.* decoration; any object to adorn or decorate; *v.t.* to adorn; to beautify; to embellish. **ornamental** *a.* serving to decorate. **ornamentally** *adv.* **ornamentation** *n.* decoration. **ornate** *a.* richly decorated. **ornately** *adv.* **ornateness** *n.* [L. *ornamentum*].

or·ni·tho- *prefix* fr. Gk. *ornis, ornithos*, a bird, used in derivatives. **ornothology** (awr·na·thál'·a·ji·) the scientific study of birds. **ornithological** *a.* **ornithologist** *n.* [Gk. *logos*, discourse; *rhunchos*, the beak].

o·ro·tund (ō'·ra·tund) *a.* of voice or speech, full, clear, and musical; of style, pompous [L. *os, oris*, the mouth; *rotundus*, round].

or·phan (awr'·fan) *n.* and *a.* a child bereft of one or both parents; *v.t.* to make an orphan. **-age** *n.* a home or institution for orphans. **-hood, -ism** *n.* [Gk. *orphanos*, bereaved].

or·pi·ment (awr'·pi·mant) *n.* a yellow mineral of the arsenic group, used as a dye [L. *aurum*, gold; *pigmentum*, a pigment].

or·rer·y (awr'·a·ri·) *n.* a mechanical model of the solar system, showing the revolutions of the planets, etc. [fr. the Earl of *Orrery*, for whom one was made in 1715].

or·ris (awr'·is) *n.* a kind of iris. **-root** *n.* the dried root, used as a powder in perfumery and medicine [form of *iris*].

or·tho·dox (awr'·tha·daks) *a.* having the correct faith; sound in opinions or doctrine; conventional. **-ly** *adv.* **-y** *n.* soundness of faith, esp. in religion. **-ness** *n.* [Gk. *orthos*, right; *doxa*, opinion].

or·thog·ra·phy (awr·thág'·ra·fi·) *n.* correct spelling. **orthographer** *n.* **orthographic, orthographical** *a.* **orthographically** *adv.* [Gk. *orthos*, correct; *graphein*, to write].

or·tho·pe·dics, orthopaedics (awr·tha·pēd'·iks) *n.* treatment and cure of bodily deformities, esp. in children. Also **orthop(a)edia, orthop(a)edy. orthopedic** *a.* **orthopedist** *n.* [Gk. *orthos*, straight; *pais, paidos*, a child].

os·cil·late (ás'·a·lāt) *v.i.* to swing to and fro; to vibrate; to vary between extremes; (*Radio*) to set up wave motion in a receiving set. **oscillation** *n.* a pendulum-like motion; variation between extremes. **oscillator** *n.* **oscillatory** *n.* [L. *oscillare*, to swing].

os·cu·late (ás'·kya·lāt) *v.t.* and *i.* to kiss; (*Math.*) to touch, as curves; *a.* of species sharing characteristics. **osculant, osculation** *n.* kissing; contact. **osculatory** *a.* [L. *osculum*, a kiss].

os·mi·um (áz'·mi·am) *n.* (*Chem.*) a hard, bluish-white metal [fr. Gk. *osmē*, smell].

os·mo·sis (ás·mō'·sis) *n.* (*Chem.*) the tendency of fluid substances, if separated by a porous membrane, to filter through it and become equally diffused. **osmotic** (ás·mát'·ik) *a.* [Gk. *ōsmos*, fr. *ōthein*, to push].

os·prey (ás'·prē, ·prā) *n.* the fish hawk or sea eagle; erroneously applied to an egret plume used in millinery [corrupt. of *ossifrage*, the sea eagle].

oss- (ás·) *prefix* fr. L. *os, ossis*, bone, used in many derivatives. **-eous** (ás'·ē·as) *a.* pert. to or resembling bone; bony. **-icle** *n.* a small bone, esp. of the middle ear. **-iferous** *a.* containing, or yielding, bones. **-ification** *n.* hardening into bone. **-ify** *v.t.* to harden into bone; *v.i.* to become bone, of cartilage, etc. **-uary** (ás'·ū·er·i·) *n.* a memorial place for holding the bones of the dead.

os·si·frage (ás'·a·frij) *n.* the osprey [L. *ossifraga*, the bonebreaker].

os·te·al (ás'·ti·al) *a.* (*Med.*) pert. to, or like, bone. **osteitis** *n.* inflammation of the bone [Gk. *osteon*, bone].

os·ten·si·ble (ás·ten'·sa·bl) *a.* professed; used as a blind; apparent. **ostensibly** *adv.* **ostensibility** *n.* [L.*ostendere*, to show].

os·ten·ta·tion (ás·tan·tā'·shan) *n.* vainglorious display; showing off. **ostentatious** *a.* fond of display; characterized by display **ostentatiously** *adv.* **ostentatiousness** *n.* [L. *ostendere*, to show].

os·te·o- (ás'·ti·ō) *prefix* fr. Gk. *osteon*, bone, used in derivatives mainly medical. **-arthritis** (ár·thrī'·tis) *n.* chronic inflammation of a joint. **osteoid** *a.* resembling bone. **osteology** *n.* that branch of anatomy dealing with bones, their structure, etc. **osteologist** *n.*

os·te·op·a·thy (ás·ti·á'·path·i·) *n.* a system of healing, based on the belief that the human body can effect its own cure with the aid of manipulative treatment of the spinal column, joints, etc.; manipulative surgery. **osteopath** *n.* a practitioner of this system. **osteopathic** *a.* [Gk. *osteon*, bone; *pathos*, feeling].

os·tra·cise (ás'·tra·sīz) *v.t.* to exclude from society; to exile; to boycott. **ostracism** *n.* exclusion from society; social boycotting [Gk. *ostrakon*, a shell].

os·trich (ás'·trich) *n.* a large flightless bird, native of Africa [Gk. *strouthos*].

oth·er (uTH'·er) *a.* not this; not the same; different; opposite; additional; *adv.* otherwise. **-wise** *adv.* differently; in another way; *conj.* else; if not. **every other**, every second (one); each alternate. **-worldly** *a.*

spiritual [O.E. *other*].

ostrich

o·ti·ose (ō'·shi·ōs, ō'·ti·ōs) *a.* at ease; at leisure; superfluous; futile [L. *otium*, easel].

o·ti·tis (ō·tī'·tis) *n.* (*Med.*) inflammation of the ear. **otology** *n.* [Gk. *ous, ōtos*, the ear].

ot·ta·va ri·ma (a·tá·va·rē'·ma) *n.* a stanza of eight lines [It. *ottava*, octave + *rhyme*].

ot·ter (át'·er) *n.* an aquatic, fish-eating animal of the weasel family [O.E.*otor*].

Ot·to·man (át'·a·man) *a.* pert. to the Turks; *n.* a cushioned seat without back or arms [fr. Turkish Sultan *Othman*, or *Osman*].

ought (awt) *auxil. v.* to be bound by moral obligation or duty [O.E. *ahte*, owed].

ought (awt) *n.* a form of 'nought'; nothing.

oui·ja (wē'·ja, ·jē) *n.* board with letters, used at seances to answer questions [Trademark, coined fr. Fr. *oui*, yes; Ger. *ja*, yes].

ounce (ouns) *n.* a unit of weight, abbrev. oz.; in avoirdupois weight $= \frac{1}{16}$ of a pound; in troy weight $\frac{1}{12}$ of a pound; a fluid measurement [L. *uncia*, a twelfth part].

ounce (ouns) *n.* snow leopard [O.Fr. *once*].

our (our) *n.* belonging to us. **-s** *poss. pron.* used with a noun. **-self** *pron.* myself (in regal or formal style). **-selves** *pron. pl.* we, i.e. not others [O.E. *ure*].

oust (oust) *v.t.* to put out; to expel; to dispossess, esp. by unfair means [O.Fr. *oster*; Fr. *ôter*, to remove].

out (out) *adv.* on, at, or to, the outside; from within; from among; away; not in the usual or right place; not at home; in bloom; disclosed; exhausted; destitute; in error; at a loss; on strike; unemployed; *a.* outlying; remote; *prep.* outside; out of; *interj.* away! begone! *v.t.* to put out; to knock out; **-er** *a.* being on the outside; away from the inside. **-ermost, -most** *a.* [O.E. *ut*].

out·bal·ance (out·bal'·ans) *v.t.* to exceed in weight; to be heavier than.

out·bid (out·bid') *v.t.* to bid more than; to offer a higher price.

out·board (out'·bōrd) *a.* projecting beyond and outside the hull of a ship, e.g. of a ladder; also, of a detachable motor.

out·break (out'·brāk) *n.* a sudden breaking out; a burst, esp. of anger; the beginning, esp. of an epidemic of disease, of war, etc.

out·build·ing (out'·bild·ing) *n.* an outhouse; a building detached from the main building.

out·burst (out'·burst) *n.* a bursting out, esp. of anger, laughter, cheering, etc.

out·cast (out'·kast) *a.* cast out as useless; *n.* one rejected by society.

out·class (out·klas') *v.t.* to exceed in skill or quality; to surpass.

out·come (out'·kum) *n.* issue; result.

out·crop (out'·kráp) *n.* the coming out of a stratum of rock, coal, etc.

out·cry (out'·krī) *n.* a loud cry; a cry of distress, complaint, disapproval, etc.

out·dis·tance (out·dis'·tans) *v.t.* to surpass in speed; to get ahead of.

out·do (out·dóō') *v.t.* to excel; surpass.

out·door (out'·dōr) *a.* out of doors; in the open air. **-s** *adv.* outside.

out·field (out′·fēld) *n.* the field or fields farthest from the farm buildings; (*Baseball*) the part of the field beyond the diamond or infield; the players there.

out·fit (out′·fit) *n.* a supply of things, esp. clothes, tools, etc., required for any purpose; equipment; kit; (*Slang*) a company of people; a crowd; *v.t.* to supply with equipment, etc. **-ter** *n.* one who supplies equipment.

out·flank (out·flangk′) *v.t.* (*Mil.*) to succeed in getting beyond the flank of the enemy.

out·go (out·gō′) *v.t.* to go beyond; *n.* (out′·gō) expenditure; outlay. **-ing** *a.* sociable; departing; going out.

out·grow (out·grō′) *v.t.* to surpass in growth; to become too large or old for; to grow out of. **-th** *n.* what growth out of anything.

out·house (out′·hous) *n.* a building, separate from main building; a privy.

out·ing (out′·ing) *n.* a going out; an excursion; a trip; an airing.

out·land·ish (out·lan′·dish) *a.* remote; barbarous; not according to custom; queer.

out·law (out′·law) *n.* one placed beyond the protection of the law; a bandit; *v.t.* to declare to be an outlaw. **-ry** *n.* defiance of the law.

out·lay (out′·lā) *n.* expenditure; expenses.

out·let (out′·let) *n.* a passage or way out; an exit; a vent; an opening.

out·line (out′·līn) *n.* the lines that bound a figure; a boundary; a sketch without details; a rough draft; a general plan; *v.t.* to draw in outline; to give a general plan of.

out·live (out·liv′) *v.t.* to live longer than.

out·look (out′·look) *n.* a looking out; a prospect; a person's point of view; prospects.

out·ly·ing (out′·lī·ing) *a.* lying at a distance; remote; isolated; detached.

out·mod·ed (out·mō′·dəd) *a.* out of fashion.

out·num·ber (out·num′·ber) *v.t.* to exceed in number.

out·pa·tient (out′·pā′·shənt) *n.* a patient who comes to a hospital, infirmary, etc., for treatment but is non-resident.

out·post (out′·pōst) *n.* (*Mil.*) a small detachment posted some distance from the main body.

out·pour (out·pōr′) *v.t.* to pour out; to flow over. **-pour, -ing** *n.* an overflow.

out·put (out′·poot) *n.* production; the amount of goods produced in a given time.

out·rage (out′·rāj) *n.* excessive violence; violation of others' rights; gross insult or indignity; *v.t.* to do grievous wrong or violence to; to insult grossly. **outrageous** (out·rā′·jas) *a.* violent; atrocious. **outrageously** *adv.*

out·ride (out·rīd′) *v.t.* to ride faster than; to ride farther than; (*Naut.*) of a ship, to live through a storm. **-r** *n.* a servant on horseback who rides beside a carriage.

out·rig·ger (out′·rig·er) *n.* (*Naut.*) a projecting spar for extending sails, ropes, etc.; a frame on the side of a rowing-boat with a rowlock at the outer edge; projecting framework, with a float attached to it, to prevent a canoe from upsetting [earlier *outligger*; Dut. *uitlegger*, outlyer].

out·run (out·run′) *v.t.* to exceed in speed; to run farther or faster than; to leave behind.

out·set (out′·set) *n.* a setting out; commencement; beginning; start.

out·side (out·sīd′) *n.* the outer surface; the exterior; the farthest limit; *a.* pert. to the outer part; exterior; external; outdoor; *adv.* not inside; out of doors; in the open air; *prep.* on the outer part of. **-r** *n.* one not belonging to a particular party, set, circle, etc.

out·size (out′·sīz) *a.* and *n.* larger than the normal size, esp. of garments.

out·skirt (out′·skurt) *n.* generally in *pl.* the border; the suburbs of a town.

out·spo·ken (out·spō′·kn) *a.* not afraid to speak aloud one's opinions; bold of speech.

out·stand·ing (out·stand′·ing) *a.* standing out; prominent; conspicuous; of debts, unpaid; of work, etc., still to be done.

out·strip (out·strip′) *v.t.* to surpass; to outrun; to leave behind.

out·vote (out·vōt′) *v.t.* to defeat by a greater number of votes.

out·ward (out′·werd) *a.* pert. to the ouside; external; exterior; *a.* towards the outside. **-s** *adv.* outward; toward the outside. **-ly** *adv.*

out·weigh (out·wā′) *v.t.* to exceed in weight, value, influence, etc.

out·wit (out·wit′) *v.t.* to defeat by cunning, stratagem, etc.; to get the better of.

o·va (ō′·va) *n.pl.* eggs; the female germ cells; *sing.* **ovum** (ō′·vum) **ovary** *n.* one of two reproductive organs in female animal in which the ova are formed and developed; (*Bot.*) the part of the pistil containing the seed. **ovarial, ovarian** (ō·ver′·i·al, -an) *a.* pert. to the ovary [L. *ovum*, an egg].

o·val (ō′·val) *a.* egg-shaped; elliptical; *n.* an oval figure. **-ly** *adv.* [L. *ovum*, and egg].

o·va·tion (ō·vā′·shən) *n.* an enthusiastic burst of applause; a triumphant reception [L. *ovatio*, to celebrate a triumph].

ov·en (uv′·n) *n.* an enclosed chamber in a stove, for baking or heating [O.E. *ofen*].

o·ver (ō′·ver) *prep.* above; on; upon; more than; in excess of; across; from side to side of; throughout; etc.; *adv.* above; above and beyond; going beyond; in excess; too much; past; finished; across; *a.* upper; outer; covering; *n.* **-all** *a.* inclusive [O.E. *afer*].

oval

oven

o·ver·act (ō·ver·akt′) *v.t.* and *i.* to play a part (in a play) in an exaggerated manner.

o·ver·all (ō′·ver·awl) *n.* loose trousers worn over the ordinary clothing as a protection against dirt, etc. Also *n.pl.*

o·ver·arm (ō′·ver·arm) *a.* and *adv.* in swimming, ball, etc., with the hand and arm raised.

o·ver·awe (ō·ver·aw′) *v.t.* to restain by awe.

o·ver·bal·ance (ō·ver·bal′·ans) *v.t.* to exceed in weight, value, etc.; *v.i.* to lose balance.

o·ver·bear (ō·ver·ber′) *v.t.* to bear down; to repress; to overpower. **-ing** *a.* domineering.

o·ver·board (ō′·ver·bōrd) *adv.* over the side of a ship; out of a ship into the water.

o·ver·cast (ō·ver·kast′) *v.t.* to cast over; to cloud; to darken; to stitch over roughly. **overcast** *a.* cloudy; dull.

o·ver·charge (ō·ver·charj′) *v.t.* and *i.* to load too heavily; to charge too high a price.

o·ver·coat (ō′·ver·kōt) *n.* an outdoor garment for men worn over ordinary clothing.

o·ver·come (ō·ver·kum′) *v.t.* and *i.* to conquer; to overpower; to get the better of.

o·ver·do (ō·ver·dōō′) *v.t.* to do too much; to fatigue; to exaggerate. *pa.t.* **overdid.** *pa.p.* **overdone** *a.* exaggerated; over-acted; overcooked.

o·ver·dose (ō·ver·dōs′) *v.t.* to give an excessive dose; *n.* to take too great a dose.

o·ver·draw (ō·ver·draw′) *v.t.* and *i.* to exaggerate; to draw money in excess of one's credit. **overdraft** *n.* act of overdrawing; amount drawn from bank in excess of credit.

o·ver·dress (ō·ver·dres′) *v.t.* and *i.* to dress too showily for good taste.

o·ver·due (ō·ver·dū′) *a.* unpaid at right time; not having arrived at right time.

o·ver·es·ti·mate (ō·ver·es′·ta·māt) *v.t.* to estimate too highly.

o·ver·flow (ō·ver·flō′) *v.t.* to flow over; to flood; to fill too full; *v.i.* to flow over the edge, bank, etc.; to abound. *n.* what flows over; flood; excess; superabundance; surplus.

o·ver·grow (ō·ver·grō′) *v.t.* to grow beyond; to cover with growth; *v.i.* to grow beyond normal size. **overgrown** *a.* covered with grass, weeds, etc. **overgrowth** *n.*

o·ver·hand (ō′·ver·hand) *a.* and *adv.* (*Ball, Swimming, etc.*) with the hand raised.

o·ver·hang (ō·ver·hang′) *v.t.* and *i.* to hang over; to jut over; to threaten.

o·ver·haul (ō·ver·hawl′) *v.t.* to examine thoroughly and set in order; to overtake in pursuit. **overhaul** *n.* a thorough examination, esp. for repairs; repair.

o·ver·head (ō′·ver·hed) *a.* and *adv.* over the head; above; aloft; in the sky; the permanent expenses of running a business.

o·ver·hear (ō·ver·hir′) *v.t.* to hear by accident. *pa.p.* and *pa.t.* **overheard.**

o·ver·joy (ō·ver·joi′) *v.t.* to fill with great joy.

o·ver·land (ō′·ver·land) *a.* and *adv.* wholly by land, esp. of a journey.

o·ver·lap (ō·ver·lap′) *v.t.* and *i.* to lap over; to rest upon and extend beyond.

o·ver·lay (ō·ver·lā′) *v.t.* to spread over, to cover completely; to span. *n.* a covering, as a transparent sheet, superimposed on another.

o·ver·lie (ō·ver·lī′) *v.t.* to lie on the top of; to smother a baby by lying on it in bed.

o·ver·load (ō·ver·lōd′) *v.t.* to place too heavy a load on. *n.* an excessive load.

o·ver·look (ō·ver·look′) *v.t.* to look over; to inspect; to superintend; to fail to notice by carelessness; to excuse; to pardon.

o·ver·lord (ō′·ver·lawrd) *n.* one who is lord over another; a feudal superior.

o·ver·much (ō·ver·much′) *a.* and *adv.* too much.

o·ver·night (ō·ver·nīt′) *adv.* through and during the night; on the previous evening.

o·ver·pow·er (ō·ver·pou′·er) *v.t.* to conquer by superior strength; to subdue; to crush.

o·ver·rate (ō·ver·rāt′) *v.t.* to put too high a value on; to assess too highly.

o·ver·reach (ō·ver·rēch′) *v.t.* to reach beyond; to cheat.

o·ver·ride (ō·ver·rīd′) *v.t.* to ride over; to ride too much; to set aside; to cancel. *n.* a gear; larger than usual payment.

o·ver·rule (ō·ver·rōōl′) *v.t.* to rule against or over; to set aside by superior authority.

o·ver·run (ō·ver·run′) *v.t.* to run over; to grow over, e.g. as weeds; to take possession by spreading over, e.g. as an invading army.

o·ver·seas (ō′·ver·sēz) *a.* and *adv.* from or to a country of place over the sea; foreign.

o·ver·see (ō·ver·sē′) *v.t.* to superintend; to supervise. **overseer** *n.* a supervisor.

o·ver·shad·ow (ō·ver·shad′·ō) *v.t.* to cast a shadow over; to outshine (a person).

o·ver·shoe (ō′·ver·shōō) *n.* a shoe made of rubber, felt, etc., worn over the ordinary shoe.

o·ver·shoot (ō·ver·shōōt′) *v.t.* to shoot beyond or over; to send too far; to go too far.

o·ver·sight (ō·ver·sīt) *n.* failure to notice; unintentional neglect; management.

o·ver·state (ō·ver·stāt′) *v.t.* to exaggerate, **-ment** *n.* exaggeration.

o·ver·strain (ō·ver·strān′) *v.t.* and *i.* to strain too much; (*Fig.*) to work too hard; *n.* overwork. **-ed** *a.*

o·ver·strung (ō·ver·strung′) *a.* too highly strung; in a state of nervous tension.

o·vert (ō′·vurt) *a.* open to view. **-ly** *adv.* [Fr. *ouvert*, open].

o·ver·take (ō·ver·tāk′) *v.t.* to come up with; to catch; to take by surprise.

o·ver·throw (ō·ver·thrō′) *v.t.* to throw over or down; to upset; to defeat. *pa.t.* **overthrew;** *pa.p.* **overthrown. overthrow** *n.* the act of throwing over; defeat; ruin; fall.

o·ver·time (ō′·ver·tīm) *n.* time at work beyond the regular hours; the extra wages paid for such work.

o·ver·ture (ō·ver·cher) *n.* an opening of negotiations; a proposal; an offer; (*Mus.*) an orchestral introduction [Fr. *ouvrir*, to open].

o·ver·turn (ō·ver·turn′) *v.t.* and *i.* to throw down or over; to upset; to turn over.

o·ver·ween·ing (ō·ver·wē′·ning) *a.* conceited; arrogant [O.E. *oferwenian*, to become insolent].

o·ver·weight (ō·ver·wāt′) *n.* excess weight; extra weight beyond the just weight.

o·ver·whelm (ō·ver·hwelm′) *v.t.* to crush; to submerge; to overpower. **-ing** *a.* decisive; irresistible. **-ingly** *adv.* [M.E. *whelmen*, to overturn].

o·ver·work (ō·ver·wurk′) *v.t.* and *i.* to work too hard. **overwork** *n.* **overwrought** (ō·ver·rawt′) *a.* tired out; highly excited.

o·vi- (ō′·vi) *prefix* fr. L. *ovum*, an egg, used in derivatives. **oviduct** *n.* a passage for the egg, from the ovary. **oviferous** *a.* egg-bearing. **oviform** *a.* egg-shaped. **oviparous** *a.* producing eggs.

o·vine (ō′·vin) *a.* pert. to sheep; like a sheep [L. *ovis*, a sheep].

o·vo- *prefix* fr. L. *ovum*, an egg, used in derivatives. **ovoid** (ō′·void) *a.* egg-shaped; oval.

o·vum *see* **ova.**

owe (ō) *v.t.* to be bound to repay; to be indebted for. **owing** (ō′·ing) *a.* requiring to be paid [O.E. *agan*].

owl (oul) *n.* a night bird of prey; a solemn person. **-et** *n.* a young owl; a small owl. **-ish** *a.* owllike in appearance [O.E.*ule*].

own (ōn) *a.* is used to emphasize possession, e.g. my *own* money; *v.t.* to possess; to acknowledge; to admit; *v.i.* to confess. **-er** *n.* the rightful possessor. **-ership** *n.* right of possession [O.E. *agen* (*a.*), *agnian* (*v.*)].

ox (åks) *n.* a large cloven-footed and usually horned farm animal; a male cow. *pl.* **-en. -eye** *n.* daisylike plant. **-bow** *n.* U-shaped part of ox yoke [O.E. *oxa*].

ox·al·ic ac·id (åk·sal′·ik as′·ạd) *n.* a poisonous acid found as an acid salt in wood sorrel. [Gk. *oxus*, sharp bitter].

ox·blood (åks′·blud) *n.* deep red color.

ox·ford (åks′·ferd) *n.* a low shoe laced over the instep [Oxford (England)].

ox·ide (åk′·sīd) *n.* a compound of oxygen and one other element. **oxidize, oxidate** *v.t.* and *i.* to combine with oxygen to form an oxide;

of metals, to rust, to become rusty. **oxidization** *n.* [Gk. *oxus*, acid].

ox·y- *prefix* fr. Gk. *oxus* sharp, used in derivatives. **-acetylene** (åk′·si·ạ·set′·ạ·lēn) *a.* denoting a very hot blowpipe flame, produced by a mixture of oxygen and acetylene, and used in cutting steel plates, etc.

ox·y·gen (åk′·si·jạn) *n.* a colorless, odorless, and tasteless gas, forming about ⅕ by volume of the atmosphere, and essential to life, combustion, etc. **-ate, -ize** *v.t.* to combine or treat with oxygen. **-ation** *n.* **-ous** (åk·sij′·ạ·nạs) *a.* pert. to or obtained from, oxygen [Gk.

oxas, acid; *gignesthai*, to be born].

ox·y·mo·ron (åk·si·mō′·rån) *n.* a figure of speech in which two words or phrases of opposite meaning are set together for emphasis or effect, e.g. 'falsely true' [Gk. *oxus*, sharp; *moros*, dull, stupid].

oys·ter (ois′·ter) *n.* an edible, bivalve shellfish; something from which one may get an advantage [Gk. *ostreon*].

o·zone (ō′·zōn) *n.* a condensed and very active form of oxygen with a peculiar, pungent odor; (*Colloq.*) invigorating air. **ozonic** *a.* [Gk. *ozein*, to smell.]

P

pab·u·lum (pab′·ya·lam) *n.* food; nourishment (for body and mind). **pabular** *a.* [L.].

pace (pās) *n.* a step; the length of a step in walking (about 30 inches); gait; rate of movement; *v.t.* to measure by steps; to set the speed for; *v.t.* to walk with measured fashion. **-d** *a.* having a certain gait. **-r** *n.* one who sets the pace for another [L. *passus*, a step].

pach·y (pak′·i·) *prefix* from Gk. *pachus*, thick, **-derm** (pak′·i·durm) *n.* a thick-skinned, nonruminant quadruped, e.g. the elephant. **-dermatous** *a.* thick-skinned; insensitive.

pac·i·fy (pas′·ạ·fī) *v.t.* to appease; to tranquilize. **pacifism** *n.* a doctrine which advocates abolition of war; antimilitarism. **pacifist** *n.* **pacific** *a.* peaceful; calm or tranquil; peaceable; not warlike. **pacification.** *n.* **pacificatory** *a.* tending to make peace; conciliatory. **pacifier** *n.* [L. *pacificus*, peace-making, fr. *pax*, peace].

pack (pak) *n.* bundle for carrying, esp. on back; a lot or set; a band (of animals); a set of playing cards; mass of floating ice; treatment of a fevered patient by enveloping in moist wrapping; army rucksack; *v.t.* to arrange closely in a bundle, box or bag; to stow away within; to fill, press together; to carry; to load; (with *off*) to dismiss summarily; *v.i.* to collect in packs, bales, or bundles. **-age** *n.* a bundle or parcel. **-er** *n.* **-et** *n.* a small package; a packet boat or mail boat. **-et boat** *n.* a ship that sails regularly for the conveyance of mail and passengers. **— horse** *n.* a horse for carrying burdens, in panniers or in packs. **-ing** *n.* any material used to pack, fill up, or make close. **-ing case** *n.* a box in which to pack goods. **-man** *n.* a pedlar. **-saddle** *n.* a saddle for supporting loads on animal's back [Fr. *paquet*].

pact (pakt) *n.* an agreement; a compact [L. *pactum*, a thing covenanted].

pad (pad) *n.* anything stuffed with soft material, to fill out or protect; a cushion; sheets of paper fastened together in a block; the foot or sole of certain animals; *v.t.* to furnish with a pad; to stuff; to expand. *pr.p.* **-ding.** *pa.p.* and *pa.t.* **-ded. -ding** *n.* the material used in stuffing; unnecessary matter inserted in a book, speech, etc., to expand it [etym. uncertain].

pad (pad) *n.* an easy-paced horse; a highway robber; *v.i.* to trudge along; to travel on foot [Dut. *pad*, a path].

pad·dle (pad′·l) *n.* a short oar with a broad blade at one or each end; a balance or float of a paddle wheel, a flipper; *v.t.* and *i.* to propel by paddles [etym. uncertain].

pad·dle (pad′·l) *v.i.* to walk with bare feet in shallow water; to dabble [etym. uncertain].

pad·dock (pad′·ak) *n.* a small grass field or enclosure where horses are saddled before race [earlier *parrock*, fr. O.E. *pearroc*, a park].

pad·dy (pad′·i·) *n.* rice in the husk; rice in general [Malay *padi*].

pad·lock (pad′·låk) *n.* a detachable lock with a hinged hoop to go through a staple or ring; *v.t.* to fasten with a padlock [etym. uncertain].

pa·dre (pā′·drā, drē) *n.* priest; chaplain [It. and Sp. = father, fr. L. *pater*].

pae·an (pē′·ạn) *n.* orig. a joyful song in honor of Apollo; any shout, song, or hymn of triumph or praise [Gk. *Paian*, the physician of the Gods, epithet of Apollo].

pa·gan (pā′·gan) *n.* a heathen; *a.* heathenish; idolatrous, **-ish** *a.* **-ize** *v.t.* to render pagan. **-ism** *n.* [L. *paganus*, a peasant].

page (pāj) *n.* one side of a leaf of a book or manuscript; *v.t.* to number the pages of. [Fr. *page*, fr. L. *pagina*, a leaf].

padlock

page (pāj) *n.* formerly a boy in service of a person of rank; a uniformed boy attendant esp. in a hotel; *v.t.* to summon by sending a page to call [Fr. *page*].

pag·eant (paj′·ạnt) *n.* a show of persons in costume in procession, dramatic scenes, etc. a spectacle. **-ry** *n.* a brilliant display; pomp [L. *pagina*, a stage].

pa·go·da (pạ·gō′·dạ) *n.* a temple or sacred tower in India, Burma, etc. [Port. *pagode*].

paid (pād) *pa.p.* and *pa.t.* of the verb **pay.**

pail (pāl) *n.* a round, open vessel of wood, tin, etc., for carrying liquids; a bucket.

pain (pān) *n.* bodily or mental suffering; distress; *pl.* trouble; exertion; *v.t.* to inflict bodily or mental suffering upon. **-ful** *a.* full of pain; causing pain; difficult; **-fully** *adv.* **-fulnes** *n.* **-less** *a.* **-lessly** *adv.* **-lessness** *n.* **-staking** *a.* carefully laborious [L.*poema*, punishment].

paint (pānt) *n.* coloring matter for putting on surface with brush, etc.; *v.t.* to cover or besmear with paint; to make a picture with paint; to adorn with, or as with, paint; *v.i.* to practice the art of painting. **-er** *n.* **-ing** *n.* laying on colors; the art of representing natural objects in colors; a picture in paint [L. *pingere*, to paint].

paint·er (pān′·ter) *n.* a rope at the bow of a boat used to fasten it to any other object [Gk. *panthera*, hunting net].

pair (par) *n.* two things of a kind; a single article composed of two similar pieces, e.g. a pair of scissors; a courting, engaged, or married couple; a mated couple of animals or birds; *v.t.* to unite in couples; *v.i.* to be joined in couples; to mate [L. *par*, equal].

pa·ja·mas (pạ·já′·maz) *n.pl.* loose trousers, worn by Mohammedans; a sleeping suit. Also **pyjamas** [Pers. *pāejāmas*, a leg garment].

pal (pal) *n.* (*Colloq.*) a close friend [Gipsy].

pal·ace (pal′·is, ås) *n.* the house in which a great personage, resides; any magnificent house. **palatial** (pạ·lā′·shạl) *a.* [L. *palatium*].

pal·a·din (pal′·ạ·din) *n.* a knight-errant; one of the twelve peers of Charlemagne [L. *palatinus*, an officer of the palace].

pal·an·quin, palankeen (pal·ạn·kēn′) *n.* a light, covered litter suspended from poles and borne on the shoulders of men—used in India

and the East. [Hind. = a bed].

pal·ate (pal′·ạt) *n.* the roof of the mouth; sense of taste; relish; liking. **palatable** *a.* agreeable to the taste or mind; savory. **palatably** *adv.* **palatal** *a.* pert. to palate; of a sound, produced by placing tongue against palate [L. *palatum*].

pa·la·tial See **palace.**

pal·a·tine (pal′·ạ·tīn) *a.* pert. to a palace; having royal privileges; *n.* one who possesses royal privileges; a count palatine. **palatinate** *n.* the office or dignity of a palatine; the territory under his jurisdiction [L. *Mons Palatinus*, the Palatine hill].

pa·lav·er (pạ·lā′·ver) *n.* idle talk; empty conversation [Port. *palavra*, a word].

pale-, palae-, paleo-, palaeo- *prefix* from Gk. *palaios*, ancient. **-ography** (pāl·ē·åg′·rạ·fi·) *n.* ancient writings; act of deciphering ancient writings. **-ographic** *a.* **-ographer** *n.* **-olith** (pāl′·ē·ạ·lith) *n.* an unpolished stone implement of the earlier stone age. **-olithic** *a.* **-ology** (pāl·ē·àl′·ạ·ji·) *n.* study of antiquities; archaeology. **-ologist** *n.* **-ontology** (pāl·ē·an·tàl·ạ·ji·) *n.* study of fossils. **-ontologist** *n.* **-ontological** *a.* **-ozoic** (pāl·ē·ạ·zō′·ik) *a.* denoting the lowest fossiliferous strata and the earliest forms of life.

pale (pāl) *a.* faint in color; not ruddy or fresh; whitish; dim; wan; *v.i.* to make pale; *v.i.* to become pale. **-ly** *adv.* **-ness** *n.* **palish** *a.* somewhat pale. **-face** *n.* name given to a white person by Red Indians [Fr. *pâle*, fr. L. *pallidus*, pale].

pale (pāl) *n.* a pointed wooden stake; a narrow board used for making a fence; a boundary; *v.t.* to enclose with stakes; to encompass. [fr. L. *palus*, a stake].

pal·ette (pal′·it) *n.* a thin oval board on which a painter mixes his colors [L. *pala*, a spade].

pal·frey (pawl′·fri·) *n.* a small saddle horse, esp. for a lady [O. Fr. *palefrei*, fr. L. *paraveredus*, an extra post horse].

Pa·li (pā′·lē) *n.* the sacred language of the Buddhists [Sans. *pāli*, canon].

pal·in·drome (pal′·in·drōm) *n.* a word or sentence that is the same when read backward or forward, e.g. *level* [Gk. *palin*, back; *dromos*, running].

pal·i·sade (pal·ạ·sād′) *n.* fence of pales or stakes; (*pl.*) an expanse of high cliffs; *v.t.* to enclose with palisades [L. *palus*, stake].

pall (pawl) *n.* a large, usually black cloth laid over the coffin at a funeral; an ecclesiastical mantle; something that spreads gloom [L. *pallium*, a cloak].

pall (pawl) *v.t.* to make tedious or insipid; *v.i.* to become tedious or insipid [prob. shortened fr. *appal*].

Pal·la·di·an (pạ·lā′·di·ạn) *a.* denoting a classical style of architecture [fr. Andria *Palladio*, a 16th cent. Italian architect].

pal·la·di·um (pạ·lā′·di·ạm) *n.* a rare metal of the platinum group [fr. Gk. *Pallas*].

pal·la·di·um (pạ·lā′·di·ạm) *n.* a safeguard; *pl.* **paladia.** [Gk. *Palladion*].

pal·let (pal′·it) n. a palette; a tool with a flat blade used by potters, etc. [form of *palette*].

pal·li·ate (pal′·i·āt) v.t. to lessen or abate without curing; to excuse or extenuate. **palliation** n. **palliative** (pal′·i·ā·tiv) a. serving to extenuate, to mitigate. n. that which mitigates, alleviates [L. *palliatus*, dressed in a cloak].

pal·lid (pal′·id) a. deficient in color; pale; wan. **-ly** adv. **-ness** n. **pallor** n. paleness [L. *pallidus*, pale].

palm (pàm) n. the inner, slightly concave surface of hand, between wrist and fingers; lineal measure, reckoned as 3 or 4 inches; flat, expanding end of any arm-like projection, esp. blade of oar; that part of glove that covers palm; v.t. to conceal in the palm; to impose by fraud (with 'off'). **palmar** (pàl′·mer) a. pert. to the palm. **palmate** a. having shape of hand; (*Zool.*) web-footed. **-ist** n. one who claims to tell fortunes by the lines on the palm of the hand. **-istry** n. [L. *palma*, the palm].

palm (pàm) n. a branchless, tropical tree; a branch or leaf of this tree used as a symbol of victory; prize or honor. **-er** (pà′·mer) n. in the Middle Ages, one who visited the Holy Land, who bore a branch of palm in token thereof; an itinerant monk. **-etto** n. a species of palm tree. **-y** a. bearing palms; (*Fig.*) prosperous; flourishing. (*Cap.*) — **Sunday,** Sunday before Easter [L. *palma*, a palm].

pal·my·ra (pal·mī′·ra) n. a tall E. Indian palm [Port. *palmeira*].

pal·pa·ble (pal′·pa·bl) a. capable of being touched or felt; certain; obvious. **palpably** adv. **-ness** n. **palpate** v.t. (*Med.*) to examine with the hand. **palpation** n. [L. *palpare*, to feel].

pal·pi·tate (pal′·pa·tāt) v.i. to beat rapidly, as heart; to throb; to pulsate. **palpitation** n. [L. *palpitare*, fr. *palpare*, to feel].

pal·sy (pawl′·zi) n. paralysis; v.t. to paralyze. **palsied** a. [fr. *paralysis*].

pal·ter (pawl′·ter) v.i. to trifle with; to deal evasively; to use trickery; to dodge. **-er** n. **paltry** a. mean; worthless. **paltriness** n.

pam·pas (pam′·paz) n.pl. vast grassy, treeless plains in S. America [Sp. *pampas*, fr. Peruv. *bamba*, a plain].

pam·per (pam′·per) v.t. to gratify unduly; to over-indulge; to coddle. **-er** n. [perh. L. Ger. *pampen*, to cram].

pam·phlet (pam′·flit) n. a thin, paper-covered, unbound book; a short treatise or essay on a current topic. **-eer** n. a writer of pamphlets [O.Fr. *Pamphilus*, the title of a medieval poem].

pan (pan) n. a broad, shallow metal vessel for house hold use; anything resembling this; of an old type of gun, part of the flintlock that held the priming; abbrev. of brainpan; the upper part of the skull; v.t. and i. to wash gold-bearing soil in a pan in order to separate earth and gold; (*Colloq.*) to criticize; to turn out (fr. *panorama*) [O.E. *panne*].

pan- (pan) prefix fr. Gk. *pas, pantos,* all, used in such words as **Pan-American** a. pert. to movement of the American republics to foster collaboration between N. and S. America.

pan·a·ce·a (pan·a·sē′·a) n. a cure for all diseases; a universal remedy [Gk. *panakeia,* universal remedy].

pan·ache (pa·nash′) n. plume of feathers used as an ornament on a cap, etc. [Fr.].

Pan·a·ma (pan·a·má′) n. a hat made of fine, pliant strawlike material [made in S. America, but not in *Panama*].

pan·cake (pan′·kāk) n. a thin cake of batter fried in a pan; v.i. to land an airplane almost vertically and in a level position.

pan·chro·mat·ic (pan·krō·mat′·ik) a. (*Phot.*) pert. to plates or films which, although reproduced in monochrome, give to all colors their proper values [Gk. *pan,* all; *chrōma,* color].

pan·cre·as (pan′·krē·as) n. (*Anat.*) digestive gland behind stomach; in animals, the sweetbread. **pancreatic** a. [Gk. *pan,* all; *kreas,* flesh].

pan·da (pan′·da) n. a raccoon-like animal; the bearcat [Native word].

pan·dect (pan′·dekt) n. usually a treatise that contains the whole of any science; pl. any code of laws [Gk. *pandektēs,* all receiving, comprehensive].

pan·dem·ic (pan·dem′·ik) a. of a disease, universal; widely distributed; affecting a nation [Gk. *pan,* all; *dēmos,* people].

pan·de·mo·ni·um (pan·da·mō′·ni·am) n. the abode of evil spirits; any disorderly, noisy place or gathering; a riotous uproar [Gk. *pan,* all; *daimōn,* a demon].

pan·der (pan′·der) n. a go-between in base love intrigues; v.i. to act as a pander; to help to satisfy any unworthy desires [fr. *Pandarus,* in Chaucer's *Troilus and Cressida*].

pane (pān) n. a sheet of glass in a window; a square in a pattern. **-d** (pānd) a. [Fr. *pan,* a flat section].

pan·e·gyr·ic (pan·a·jir′·ik) n. a speech or writing of praise; a eulogy. **-al** a. **panegyrist** n. one who writes or pronounces a eulogy. **panegyrize** v.t. to praise highly [Gk. *pan,* all; *agora,* an assembly].

pan·el (pan′·al) n. a rectangular piece of cloth, parchment, or wood; a sunken portion of a door, etc.; a list of jurors; a jury; a group of speakers, etc. v.t. to divide into, or decorate with panels. **-ing** n. paneled work. **-ist** n. member of a panel [O.Fr. = a small panel].

pang (pang) n. a sudden pain, physical or mental [etym. doubtful].

pan·ic (pan′·ik) n. sudden terror, often unreasoning; infectious fear; a. extreme and illogical (of fear); v.i. to be seized with sudden, uncontrollable fright. pr.p. **panicking.** pa.p. and pa.t. **panicked. panicky** a. affected by panic. — **stricken,** — **struck** a. seized with paralyzing fear [Gk. = fear excited by *Pan*].

pan·ier (pan′·yer) n. one of a pair of baskets carried on each side of a pack animal; a puffing-out round hips of a lady's skirt; framework to achieve this [L. *panarium,* a breadbasket].

pan·o·ply (pan′·a·pli·) n. a complete suit of armor; anything that covers or envelops completely. **panoplied** a. fully armed [Gk. *pan,* all; *hopla,* arms].

pan·o·ram·a (pan·a·rá′·ma) n. a complete view in every direction; a picture exhibited by being unrolled and made to pass continuously before the spectator. **panoramic** a. [Gk. *pan.* all; *horama,* a view].

pan·sy (pan′·zi·) n. a cultivated species of violet with richly colored flowers; (*Slang*) an effeminate man [Fr. *pensée,* thought].

pant (pant) v.i. to breathe quickly and in a labored manner; to gasp for breath; to yearn (with 'for' or 'after'); v.t. to utter gaspingly; n. a gasp [O.Fr.].

pan·ta·loon (pan·ta·lòòn′) n.(pl.) tight trousers [It. *pantalone,* buffoon].

pan·the·ism (pan′·thē·izm) n. the doctrine that identifies God with the universe, everything being considered as part of or a manifestation of Him. **pantheist** n. **pantheistic (al)** a. **pantheology** n. a system which embraces all religions and all gods [Gk. *pan,* all; *theos,* god].

pan·ther (pan′·ther) n. (*fem.* **-ess**) a variety of leopard [Gk. *panthēr*].

pan·to- (pan′·ta) prefix fr. Gk. *pas, pantos,* all, used in derivatives. **-graph** (pant′·a·graf) n. an instrument for copying drawings, maps, etc., on an enlarged, a reduced, or the same scale [Gk. *graphein,* to write].

pan·to·mime (pant′·a·mīm) n. a dramatic entertainment in dumb show; a gesture without speech; v.t. and i. to act or express by gestures only. **pantomimic** a. **pantomimist** n. [Gk. *pas, pantos,* all; *mimos,* mimic].

pan·try (pan′·tri·) n. a small room for storing food or kitchen utensils [L. *panis,* bread].

pants (pants) n.pl. (*Colloq.*) trousers [abbrev. of *pantaloons*].

pap (pap) n. soft food for infants, etc. [fr. baby language].

pap (pap) n. a nipple; a teat; something resembling a nipple [M.E. *pappe*].

pa·pa·cy (pā′·pa·si·) n. the office and dignity of the Pope; Popes collectively. **papal** (pā′·pál) a. [It. *papa,* father].

pa·pav·er·ous (pa·pav′·er·as) a. pert. to or resembling the poppy. Also **papaveraceous** a. [L. *papaver,* the poppy].

pa·paw, pawpaw (pa·paw′) n. a N. American tree with purple flowers and edible yellow fruit [Sp. *papayo*].

pa·per (pā′·per) n. a material made by pressing pulp of rags, straw, wood, etc., into thin flat sheets; a sheet of paper written or printed on; a newspaper; an article or essay; a document; wall covering; a set of examination questions; n.pl. document(s) establishing one's identity; ship's official documents; a. consisting of paper; v.t. to cover with paper. **-y** a. resembling paper. — **clip** n. a device for holding together sheets of paper. — **hanger** n. one who hangs paper on walls. — **knife** n. a knife with a blunt blade for opening envelopes, etc. — **money** n. official pieces of paper issued by a government or bank for circulation. **-weight** n. small, heavy object to prevent loose sheets of paper from being displaced [O.F. *papier,* fr. L. *papyrus,* paper].

pa·pier-mâ·ché (pā·per·ma·shā′) n. paper pulp, mixed with glue, etc., shaped or molded into articles [Fr. *papier,* paper; *mâché,* chewed].

pa·pil·la (pa·pil′·a) n. a small nipple-shaped protuberance in a part of the body, e.g. on surface of tongue [L. *papilla,* the nipple].

pa·pist (pā′·pist) n. a supporter of the papal system; a Roman Catholic. **papistic(al)** a. **-ry** n. [Fr. *papiste,* fr. *pape,* the Pope].

pa·poose (pa·pòòs′) n. a N. Amer. Indian baby.

pap·pus (pap′·as) n. down, as on the seeds of the thistle, dandelion, etc. **pappose** (pap·ōs′) a. downy [Gk. *pappos,* down].

pap·ule (pap′·ūl) n. a pimple [L.].

pa·py·rus (pa·pī′·ras) n. a species of reed, the pith of which was used by the ancients for making paper; a manuscript on papyrus. pl. **papyri** [Gk. *papyros,* an Egyptian rush].

par (pár) n. equality of value or circumstances; face value (of stocks and shares); (*Golf*) the number of strokes for hole or course in perfect play [L. *par,* equal].

par·a·ble (par′·a·bl) n. story or allegory with a moral. **parabolical a. parabolically** adv. [Gk. *parabolē,* a comparison].

pa·rab·o·la (pa·rab′·a·la) n. (*Geom.*) a conic section made by a plane parallel to side of cone. **parabolic** a. **paraboloid** n. solid formed when parabola is revolved round its axis [Gk. *para,* beside; *bolē,* a throw].

par·a·chute (par′·a·shòòt) n. a collapsible umbrellalike device used to retard the descent of a falling body. **parachutist** n. — **troops** n.pl. See paratroops [Fr. *parer,* to make ready; *chute,* a fall].

par·a·clete (par′·a·klēt) n. (*Bib.*) the name given to the Holy Spirit; one called to aid or support; an advocate [Gk. *paraklētos,* called to help].

pa·rade (pa·rād′) n. a public procession; a muster of troops for drill or inspection; the ground on which such a muster takes place; display; show; v.t. to make a display or spectacle of; to marshal in military order; v.i. to march in military array; to march in procession with display [L. *parare,* to prepare].

par·a·digm (par′·a·dim) n. an example; a model; (*Gram.*) a word, esp. a noun, verb, etc., given as an example of grammatical inflexions. **-atic** (par·a·dig·mat′·ik) a. **-atically** adv. [Gk. *paradeigma,* a model].

par·a·dise (par′·a·dis) n. the garden of Eden; Heaven; a state of bliss. **paradisaic** (par·a·di·sā′·ik), **paradisaical** a. pert. to or like paradise [Gk. *paradeisos,* a pleasure-ground].

par·a·dox (par′·a·dáks) n. a statement seemingly absurd or self-contradictory, but really founded on truth. **-ical -ically** adv. [Gk. *para,* against; *doxa,* an opinion].

par·af·fin (par′·a·fin) n. a white wax-like substance obtained from crude petroleum, shale, coal tar, wood, etc. [L. *parum,* little; *affinis,* related].

par·a·gon (par′·a·gan) n. a pattern of excellence [It. *paragone*].

par·a·graph (par′·a·graf) n. a distinct part of a writing; a section or subdivision of a passage, indicated by the sign ¶, or begun on a new line; v.t. to arrange in paragraphs. **-ic** a. [Gk. *paragraphos,* a marginal stroke].

par·a·keet (par′·a·kēt) n. a small long-tailed parrot. Also **parrakeet, paroquet** [Fr. *perroquet,* a parrot].

par·al·de·hyde (pa·ral′·da·hīd) n. a powerful hypnotic [Gk. *para* and *aldehyde*].

par·al·lel (par′·a·lel) a. continuously at equal distance apart; precisely corresponding; similar; n. a line equidistant from another at all points; a thing exactly like another; a comparison; a line of latitude; v.t. to make parallel; to represent as similar; to compare. **-ism** n. the state of being parallel; comparison, resemblance. — **bars,** horizontal bars for gymnastic exercises [Gk. *parallēlos,* beside one another].

par·al·lel·o·gram (par·a·lel′·a·gram) n. a four-sided plane figure with both pairs of opposite sides parallel [Gk. *parallēlos,* beside one another; *gramma,* a line].

pa·ral·y·sis (pa·ral′·a·sis) n. (*Med.*) loss of

power of movement or sensation. **paralyze** (pàr'.ạ.liz) v.t. to affect with paralysis; to make useless; to cripple. **paralytic** a. pert. to, affected with, paralysis; n. one affected with paralysis. **infantile paralysis,** inflammation of grey matter in spinal cord, usually in children; poliomyelitis [L., fr. Gr. *paralysis*, to loosen at the side].

par.a.mount (pàr'.ạ.mount) a. superior; of highest importance; chief. **-cy** n. **-ly** adv. [Fr. *par amont*, upwards].

par.a.mour (pàr'.ạ.moor) n. a partner in an illicit love intrigue [Fr. *par amour*, through love].

par.a.noi.a, paranoea (par.ạ.noi'.ạ, .ně'.ạ) n. (*Med.*) a form of chronic insanity, often characterized by delusions of grandeur, persecution, etc. **paranoiac** a. and n. [Gk. *para*, beside; *noein*, to think].

par.a.pet (pàr'.ạ.pet) n. a low wall or railing at the edge of a bridge, quay, balcony, etc.; a breastwork to protect soldiers [It. *parare*, to ward off; *petto*, the breast].

par.a.pher.na.li.a (par.ạ.fẹ(r).nā'.li.ạ, .nāl'.ya) n.pl. personal belongings; furnishings or accessories; (*Law*) goods of wife beyond dowry [Gk. *para*, beyond; *pherné*, a dower].

par.a.phrase (pàr'.ạ.frāz) n. a restatement of a passage; a free translation into the same or another language; an interpretation; v.t. to express in other words; to interpret freely. [Gk. *para*; *phrazein*, to speak].

par.a.site (pàr'.ạ.sit) n. formerly, one who habitually ate at the table of another, repaying with flattery; a hanger-on; a plant or animal that lives on another. **parasitic** a. **parasitically** adv. **parasitology** n. the study of parasites, esp. as causes of disease. **parasitological** a. **parasitologist** n. [Gk. *parasitos*; fr. *para*, beside; *sitos*, food].

par.a.sol (pàr'.ạ.sawl) n. a small, light sun umbrella [It. *parare*, to ward offi; *sole*, the sun].

par.a.troops (pàr'.ạ.tróóps) n.pl. (*World War* 2) troops organized to descend by parachute with their equipment from airplanes and gliders. **paratrooper** n.

par.boil (pàr'.boil) v.t. to boil partially; to precook [L. *per*, thoroughly, confused with 'part'; *boil*].

par.cel (pàr'.sạl) n. (*Arch.*) a part or portion, a bundle or package (wrapped in paper); a number of things forming a group or lot; a piece of land; v.t. to divide into portions; to distribute; to wrap up. [Fr. *parcelle*, a little part].

parch (pàrch) v.t. to scorch; to shrivel with heat; to dry to an extreme degree; v.i. to be dry from heat [M.E. *parchen*].

parch.ment (pàrch'.mạnt) n. the skin of a sheep or goat, etc., prepared for writing on; a document written on this [fr. *Pergamum* in Asia Minor, here first used].

par.don (pàr'.dạn) v.t. to forgive; to free from punishment; to excuse; n. forgiveness; remission of a penalty. **-able** a. excusable. [Fr. *pardonner*].

pare (par) v.t. to cut or shave off; to remove the outer skin; to peel. **-er** n. **paring** n. the action of peeling; that which is pared off [Fr. *parer*, to make ready].

par.e.gor.ic (par.ạ.gawr'.ik) a. soothing; assuaging pain; n. a soothing medicine [Gk. *parēgorikos*, comforting].

par.ent (par'.ạnt) n. a father or mother; one who, or that which, brings forth or produces. **-age** n. descent from parents; birth; extraction. **parental** (pạ.ren'.tạl) a. pert. to, or becoming, parents; tender; affectionate. **parentally** adv. [L. *parere*, to bring forth].

pa.ren.the.sis (pạ.ren'.thạ.sis) n. a word or sentence inserted in a passage independently of the grammatical sequence and usually marked off by brackets, dashes, or commas; **parentheses** (-sēz) n.pl. round brackets ( ), used for this. **parenthetic, parenthetical** a. expressed as a parenthesis; interposed. [Gk. *para*, beside; *en*, in; *thesis*, a placing].

pa.ri.ah (pạ.rī'.ạ) n. in S. India, one deprived of all religious or social rights; a member of the lowest or no caste; an outcast from society [Tamil, *paraiyar*, a drummer].

pa.ri.e.tal (pạ.rī'.ạ.tạl) a. pert. to a wall; pert. to the wall of the body or its cavities [L. *paries* a wall].

par.ish (par'.ish) n. an ecclesiastical district under a priest or clergyman; a local church and its area of activity; a. pert. to a parish.

parishioner (pạ.rish'.ạn.ẹr) n. an inhabitant of a parish; a member of a parish church [Gk. *para*, beside; *oikos*, a dwelling].

par.i.ty (par'.ạ.ti.) n. equality; analogy; close correspondence [L. *par*, *paris*, equal].

park (pàrk) n. a large piece of ground, usually with grass and trees for public use and ... ...ea- tion; a sports' ground; grounds around a country house; v.t. to enclose in a park; to leave an automobile in a certain place [O.E. *pearroc*; Fr. *parc*].

par.ka (pàr'.kạ) n. an Eskimo garment of undressed skin; a hooded outer garment [Aleutian].

par.lance (pàr'.lạns) n. a way of speaking; **parley** (pàr'.li.) n. a meeting between leaders of opposing forces to discuss terms; v.i. to hold a discussion about terms [Fr. *parler*, to speak].

par.lia.ment (pàr'.lạ.mạnt) n. (*usually cap.*) the supreme legislature of the United Kingdom, composed of the House of Lords and House of Commons; any similar assembly. **-ary** a. pert. to, enacted by, or according to, the established rules of parliament; of language, admissible in parliamentary debate, hence, decorous and non-abusive. **-arian** n. a skilled debater in parliament [Fr. *parlement*, fr. *parler*, to speak].

par.lor, parlour (pàr'.lẹr) n. living room; a semi-private room in an inn [Fr. *parloir*, fr. *parler*, to speak].

par.lous (pàr'.lạs) a. (*Arch.*) perilous; critical [fr. *perilous*].

Par.nas.sus (pàr.nas'.ạs) n. a mountain in ancient Greece, sacred to Apollo and the Muses; (*Fig.*) poetry; an anthology of poetry.

pa.ro.chi.al (pạ.rō'.ki.ạl) a. pert. to a parish; provincial; narrow-minded **-ly** adv. **-ism** n. [L. *parochia*, a parish, fr. Gk. *paroikein* to dwell near].

par.o.dy (par'.ạ.di.) n. an imitation of a poem, song, etc., where the style is the same but the theme ludicrously different; a feeble imitation; v.t. to write a parody of; to burlesque in verse. **parodist** n. [Gk. *para*, beside (i.e. imitating); *ōdē*, a song].

pa.role (pạ.rōl') n. release of a prisoner on condition of good behavior; word of honor, esp. a promise given by a prisoner of war not to attempt to escape [Fr. *parole*, a word].

par.o.no.ma.si.a (par.ạ.nō.mā'.zhi.ạ, .zi.ạ) n. a play on words; a pun. **paronym** n. a word similar to another in having the same derivation or root. **paronymous** a. [Gk. *para*, beside; *anoma*, a name].

pa.rot.id (pạ.rát'.id) a. near the ear; n. a large salivary gland, in front of and below the ear [Gk. *para*, beside; *ous*, *ōtos*, the ear].

par.ox.ysm (par'.ạk.sizm) n. sudden, violent attack of pain, rage, laughter; fit; convulsion [Gk. *para*, beyond; *oxus*, sharp].

par.quet (pàr'.kā, -ket) n. flooring of wooden blocks; v.t. to lay such a floor. **-ry** n. [Fr. *flooring*].

parr (pàr) n. a young salmon.

par.ri.cide (par'.ạ.sid) n. one who murders his parent, a near relative, or a person who is venerated; the crime itself [L. *pater*, a father; *caedere*, to kill].

par.rot (par'.ạt) n. tropical bird; one who repeats words, actions, ideas, etc. of another [Fr. *perroquet*, a parrot].

par.ry (par'.i.) v.t. to ward off; to turn aside; to avoid [L. *parare*, to prepare].

parse (pàrs) v.t. to classify a word or analyze a sentence in terms of grammar. **parsing** n. [L. *pars*, part, *pars orationis*, part of speech].

Par.see, parsi (pàr'.sē) n. a follower of the disciples of Zoroaster; a fire worshipper. **-ism** n. [Pers. *Parsi*, a Persian].

par.si.mo.ny (pàr'.sạ.mō.ni.) n. stinginess; undue economy. **parsimonious** a. **parsimoniously** adv. **parsimoniousness** n. [L. *parcere*, to spare].

pars.ley (pàrs'.li.) n. a garden herb, used as a flavoring or garnish in cookery [Gk. *petroselinon*, rock parsley].

pars.nip (pàrs'.nip) n. a root vegetable, carrot-like in shape [L. fr. *pastinare*, to dig up].

par.son (pàr'.sn) n. a clergyman; the incumbent of a parish. **-age** n. the residence of a parson. (*Colloq.*) **-'s nose**, the rump of a fowl [*person*].

part (pàrt) n. a portion, fragment, or section of a whole; a share or lot; a division; an actor's role; duty; interest; a melody in a harmonic piece; pl. accomplishments or talents; region; v.t. to divide; to separate; to share; v.i. to separate; to take leave; to part

with or give up. **-ing** n. the act of separating; leave-taking; division; dividing line; a. given on taking leave. **-ly** adv. in part; in some measure or degree. **-ible** a. divisible. **-ibility** n. [L. *pars*, a part].

par.take (pàr.tāk') v.t. and i. to have or take a share in; to take food or drink. pr.p. **partaking**. p.p. **-n**. p.a.t. **partook**. **-r** n. [fr. *part* and *take*].

par.terre (pàr.ter') n. an ornamental arrangement of flower beds; the rear section of the main floor of a theater [Fr. *par terre*, on the earth].

par.the.no.gen.e.sis (pàr.thạ.nō.jen'.ạ.sis) n. reproduction without sexual union [Gk. *parthenos*, virgin; *genesis*, birth].

Par.the.non (pàr'.thạ.nàn) n. famous Doric temple of Athena [Gr. *parthenos*, virgin].

par.tial (pàr'.shạl) a. affecting only a part; not total; inclined to favor unreasonably. **-ly** adv. **partiality** n. quality of being partial; favoritism; fondness for [L. *pars*, part].

par.tic.i.pate (pàr.tis'.ạ.pāt) v.t. and i. to share in; to partake (foll. by 'in'). **participant** n. a partaker; a. sharing. **participator** n. **participation** (pàr.tis.ạ.pā'.shạn) n. [L. *pars*, part; *capere*, to take].

par.ti.ci.ple (pàr'.tạ.si.pl) n. (*Gram.*) an adjective formed by inflection from a verb. **participial** a. [L. *particeps*, sharing].

par.ti.cle (pàr'.tạ.kl) n. a minute portion of matter; (*Gram.*) a part of speech which is uninflected and of subordinate importance [L. *particula*, a little part].

par.ti-col.ored, party-colored (pàr'.ti.kul.erd) a. having different colors; variegated.

par.tic.u.lar (pàr.tik'.yạ.lẹr) a. relating to a single person or thing, not general; considered apart from others; minute in details; fastidious in taste; n. a single point or circumstance; a detail or item. **-ly** adv. especially; in a high degree; with great attention. **particularity** n. quality or state of being particular; individual characteristic. **-ize** v.t. and i. to mention one by one; to give in detail; to specify. **-ization** n. [L. *particularis*].

par.ti.san, partizan (pàr'.tạ.zạn) n. adherent, often prejudiced, of a party or cause; a member of irregular troops engaged in risky enterprises; a. adhering to a faction. **-ship** n. [Fr.].

par.ti.san (pàr'.tạ.zạn) n. a long-handled pike [O.Fr. *pertuisane*].

par.ti.tion (pàr.tish'.ạn) n. division or separation; any of the parts into which a thing is divided; that which divides or separates, as a wall, etc.; v.t. to divide into shares; to divide by walls. **partitive** n. a word expressing partition; a distributive; a. denoting a part. **partitively** adv. [L. *partitio*].

part.ner (pàrt'.nẹr) n. a partaker; a sharer; an associate, esp. in business; a husband or wife; one who dances with another; in golf, tennis, etc., one who plays with another; v.t. in games, to play with another against opponents. **-ship** n. the state of being a partner; the association of two or more persons for business [L. *pars*, a part].

par.tridge (pàr'.trij) n. a small game bird of the grouse family [Gk. *perdix*].

par.tu.ri.ent (pàr.tyoo'.ri.ạnt) a. bringing forth or about to bring forth young. **parturition** n. the act of bringing forth young [L. *parturire*, to be in labor].

par.ty (pàr'.ti.) n. a number of persons united in opinion; a political group; a social assembly; a participator; an accessory; a litigant; a. pert. to a party or faction. **——colored** a. parti-colored [O.Fr. *partir*, to divide].

par.ve.nu (pàr'.vạ.nū) n. an upstart; one who has risen socially, esp. by the influence of money [Fr. fr. *parvenir*, to arrive at].

Pasch (pask) n. Passover; Easter. **-al** a. **— lamb**, lamb eaten at Passover; (P-L, in *Christ.*) Christ [Heb. *pesach*, to pass over].

pas.quin (pas'.kwin) n. a writer of lampoons or satires; a lampoon or satire; v.t. and i. to lampoon. **-ade** n. a lampoon [fr. It. *Pasquino*, Roman statue on which political lampoons were posted].

pass (pas) v.t. to go by, beyond, through etc.; to spend; to exceed; to approve; to disregard; to circulate; to send through; to move; v.i. to go; to elapse; to undergo examination successfully; to happen; to die; to circulate. pa.p. **-ed**, **past**. pa.t. **-ed**. n. a passage or way, esp. a narrow and difficult one; a passport; a permit; success in an examination, test, etc.; in football, hockey, etc., the passing of the ball from one player to another. **-able** a. that may be passed or crossed; fairly good; admissible; current. **-ably** adv. **-book** n. a bankbook. **-key** n. a latchkey; a masterkey. **-port** n. an official document, issued by a State Department, granting permission to travel abroad. **-word** n. (*Mil.*) a selected word given to sentries, soldiers, etc. used to distinguish friend from enemy. **to pass the buck** (*Slang*) to shift responsibility to another [L. *passus*, a step].

pas.sage (pas'.ij) n. the act, time, or right of passing; movement from one place to another; a voyage across the sea; fare for a voyage; an entrance or exit; part of a book, etc.; the passing of a law. **passage of arms,**

a feat of arms. **bird of passage**, a migratory bird [Fr. fr. L. *passus*, a step, a pace].

pas·sé (pa·sā′) *a.* past one's best; faded; rather out of date; antiquated [Fr.].

pas·sen·ger (pas′·ạn·jẹr) *n.* a traveller, esp. by some conveyance; *a.* adapted for carrying passengers [O.Fr. *passager*].

Pas·ser·i·for·mes (pas′·ẹr·i·fawr·mēz) *n.* the largest order of birds [L. *passer*, a sparrow].

pas·sim (pas′·im) *a.* here and there [L.].

pas·sion (pash′·ạn) *n.* intense emotion, as of grief, rage, love; eager desire; (*Cap.*) the story of Christ's suffering and last agony. **-ate** *a.* easily moved to anger; moved by strong emotions; vehement. **-ately** *adv.* **-ateness** *n.* **-less** *a.* **— play** *n.* a theatrical representation of Christ's passion. **— week** *n.* the week immediately preceding Easter [L. *passio*, fr. *pati*, to suffer].

pas·sive (pas′·iv) *a.* inactive; submissive; acted upon, not acting; *n.* (*Gram.*) (or passive voice) the form of the verb which expresses that the subject is acted upon. **-ly** *adv.* **-ness** *n.* [L. *pati*, *passus*, to suffer].

Pass·o·ver (pas′·ō·vẹr) *n.* a feast of the Jews to commemorate the time when God, smiting the first-born of the Egyptians, passed over the houses of Israelites [pass and over].

past *pa.p.* of **pass**.

past (past) *a.* pert. to former time; gone by; elapsed; ended; *n.* former state; bygone times; one's earlier life; *prep.* beyond; after; exceeding; beyond the scope of; *adv.* by; beyond. **— master**, a former master of a guild, freemasons, etc.; one adept or proficient [fr. *pass*].

paste (pāst) *n.* a soft composition, as of flour and water; dough prepared for pies, etc.; any soft plastic mixture or adhesive; a fine glass for making artificial gems; *v.t.* to fasten with paste; (*Slang*) to strike. **pasty** *a.* (pās′·ti·) like paste. **pastry** (pās′·tri·) *n.* the crust of pies and tarts; articles of food made of paste or dough. **pastry-cook** *n.* who makes and sells pastry. **-board** *n.* a stiff, thick paper; *a.* made of pasteboard; flimsy or unsubstantial [O.Fr.].

pas·tel (pas′·tel) *n.* a colored chalky crayon; a drawing made with such crayons. **— shades**, delicate and subdued colors [F., fr. It. *pastello*, dim. fr. L. *pasta*, paste].

pas·tern (pas′·tern) *n.* part of horse's leg between fetlock and hoof [O.Fr. *pasturon*, shackle of horse at pasture].

Pas·teur (pas·tur′) *n.* a French chemist and biologist. **pasteurization** *n.* the sterilization of milk, etc. by heating to 140° F. or over and then cooling. **pasteurize** *v.t.*

pas·tic·cio, pastiche (pas·tēch′·ō, pas·tēsh′) *n.* a medley made up from various sources; a picture or literary composition in the style of a recognized author or artist [It.].

pas·tille, pastil (pas·tēl′, pas′·til) *n.* an aromatic substance burned for cleansing or scenting a room; a small lozenge, aromatic or medicated [Fr. fr. L. *pastillus*, a little loaf].

pas·time (pås′·tīm) *n.* that which amuses and makes time pass agreeably; recreation; diversion [fr. *pass* and *time*].

pas·tor (pas′·tẹr) *n.* a minister of the gospel. **-al** *a.* pert. to shepherds or rural life; relating to a pastor and his duties. *n.* a poem describing rural life; an idyll. **-ally** *adv.* **-ate** *n.* the office or jurisdiction of a spiritual pastor. **-ship** *n.* [L. *pastor*, a herdsman].

pas·ture (pas′·chẹr) *n.* grass for food of cattle; ground on which cattle graze; *v.t.* to feed on grass; *v.i.* to graze. **pasturable** *a.* **pasturage** *n.* pasture land; the business of grazing cattle [L. *pascere*, to feed].

pas·ty See **paste**.

pat (pat) *n.* a light, quick blow, esp. with hand or fingers; a small lump, esp. of butter; *v.t.* to strike gently. *pr.p.* **-ting**. *pa.p.* and *pa.t.* **-ted** [imit. origin].

pat (pat) *a.* ready; apt; at right moment; *adv.* opportunely; exactly. **-ness** *n.* [fr. *pat*].

patch (pach) *n.* a piece of material used to mend a hole, rent, etc.; a covering for a wound; small spot of black silk formerly worn on cheek by ladies; *v.t.* to mend with a patch; to repair clumsily. **-y** *a.* full of patches; unequal. **-work** *n.* work made by sewing together pieces of cloth of different material and color [O.Fr. *pieche*, a piece].

pate (pāt) *n.* the top of the head; the head.

pâ·té de foie gras (påt·ā′ dạ fwå·grå) a paste of goose liver [Fr.].

pa·tel·la (pạ·tel′·ạ) *n.* the kneecap [L. = small pan].

pat·en (pat′·ạn) *n.* the plate on which the bread of the Eucharist is placed [L. *patina*, a plate].

pat·ent (pā′·tạnt, pat′·ạnt) *a.* open; evident; protected by a patent; *n.* short for *letters patent*, an official document granting a right or privilege, or securing the exclusive right to invention; the invention itself. *v.t.* to secure or protect by a patent. **-ly** *adv.* openly; evidently. **-ee** (pat·ạn·tē′) *n.* one who has secured a patent. **— leather**, leather with a varnished or lacquered surface [L. *patens*, open].

pa·ter·nal (pạ·tur′·nạl) *a.* pert. to a father; fatherly; hereditary. **-ly** *adv.* **paternity** *n.* the relation of a father to his offspring; authorship [L. *pater*, a father].

pa·ter·nos·ter (pat·ẹr·nås′·tẹr) *n.* the Lord's Prayer [L. *pater*, father; *noster*, our].

path (path) *n.* a way, course, or track of action, conduct, or procedure. **-finder** *n.* a pioneer. **-way** *n.* a narrow footway [O.E. *paeth*].

pa·thet·ic (pạ·thet′·ik) *a.* affecting or moving the tender emotions; causing pity; touching. Also **-al. -ally** *adv.*

path·o- *prefix* fr. Gk. *pathos*, suffering, feeling, used in derivatives. **-genesis, pathogeny** (path·ạ·jen′·ạ·sis, pạ·thaj′·ạ·ni·) *n.* the origin and development of disease. **-genetic, -genic** *a.* causing disease. **-logy** *n.* the science and study of diseases, their causes, nature, cures, etc. **-logic, -logical** *a.* **-logically** *adv.* **-logist** *n.* [Gk. *genesis*, birth; *logos*, discourse].

pa·thos (pā′·thås) *n.* the power of exciting tender emotions; deep feeling [Gk. *pathos* fr. *paschein*, to suffer].

pa·tient (pā′·shạnt) *a.* bearing trials without murmuring; not easily made angry; calm; not hasty; *n.* a person under medical treatment. **-ly** *adv.* **patience** *n.* the quality of enduring with calmness; quiet perseverance [L. *pati*, to suffer].

pa·ti·o (på′·ti·ō) *n.* the inner court of a Spanish house [Sp.].

pat·ois (pat′·wä) *n.* a dialect; illiterate or provincial form of speech; jargon [Fr.].

pa·tri·arch (pā′·tri·ärk) *n.* the father and ruler of a family, esp. in Biblical history; the highest dignitary in the Eastern church; a venerable old man. **-al** *a.* dignity or jurisdiction of a patriarch. **-y** *n.* government by the head or father of a tribe [Gk. *pater*, father; *archein*, to rule].

pa·tri·cian (pạ·trish′·ạn) *a.* pert. to the senators of ancient Rome and their descendants; of high birth; noble or aristocratic; *n.* [L. *patricius*, fr. *pater*, father, senator].

pat·ri·cide (pat′·rạ·sid) *n.* murder of one's father [L. *pater*, father; *caedere*, to kill].

pat·ri·mo·ny (pat′·rạ·mō′·ni·) *n.* a right or estate inherited from one's father or ancestors; heritage; a church estate or revenue. **patrimonial** *a.* **patrimonially** *adv.* [L. *patrimonium* fr. *pater*, father].

pa·tri·ot (pā′·tri·ạt) *n.* one who loves his country and upholds its interests. **-ic** *a.* filled with patriotism. **-ically** *adv.* **-ism** *n.* love for, and loyalty to, one's country [L. *patria*, fatherland].

pa·trol (pạ·trōl′) *v.t.* and *i.* to go or walk around a camp, garrison, etc. in order to protect it. *pr.p.* **-ling**. *pa.p.* and *pa.t.* **-led**. *n.* a going of the rounds by a guard; the man or men who go to the rounds [O.Fr. *patrouiller*].

pa·tron (pā′·trạn) *n.* (*fem.* **-ness**) a man who protects or supports a person, cause, entertainment, artistic production, etc.; a guardian saint; (*Eccles.*) one who has the right of appointment to a benefice; a regular customer. **-age** *n.* countenance, support, or encouragement given to a person or cause; condescending manner; in trade, regular customer. **-ize** *v.t.* to act as a patron to; to assume the air of a superior towards; to frequent, as a customer. **patronizing** *a.* **patronizingly** *adv.* **— saint**, a saint who is regarded as the spe-

cial protector of a person, city, trade, etc. [L. *patronus*, fr. *pater*, father].

pat·ro·nym·ic (pat·rạ·nim′·ik) *n.* a name derived from parent or ancestor; a surname [Gk. *pater*, father; *onoma*, a name].

pat·ten (pat′·ạn) *n.* a wooden sandal worn in wet weather [Fr. *patin*].

pat·ter (pat′·ẹr) *v.i.* to make a quick succession of small taps or sounds, like those of rain falling [frequentative of *pat*].

pat·ter (pat′·ẹr) *v.t.* to speak rapidly and indistinctly; to mutter; *v.i.* to talk glibly or mechanically; to say prayers; *n.* chatter; prattle; lingo of a profession or class; jargon [fr. *paternoster*].

pat·tern (pat′·ẹrn) *n.* a model, example, or guide; a decorative design; *v.t.* to design from a pattern; to imitate [M.E. *patron*, a model].

pat·ty (pat′·i·) *n.* a little pie [Fr. *pâté*].

pau·ci·ty (paw′·sa·ti·) *n.* fewness; scarcity; smallness of quantity [L. *paucus*, few].

paunch (pawnch, pänch) *n.* the belly **-iness** *n.* **-y** *a.* [L. *pantex*].

pau·per (paw′·pẹr) *n.* (*fem.* **-ess**) a very poor person, esp. one supported by the public. **-ize** *v.t.* to reduce to pauperism [L., poor].

pause (pawsz) *n.* a temporary stop or rest; cessation; hesitation; a break in speaking, reading, or writing; in music, a sign ⌒ or · placed under or over a note to indicate the prolongation of a note or rest; *v.i.* to make a short stop; to cease for a time [Gk. *pausis*].

pave (pāv) *v.t.* to form a level surface with stone, brick, etc.; to make smooth and even; (*Fig.*) to prepare. **-ment** *n.* a paved floor, road, or sidewalk; material used [L. *pavire*, to ram down].

pav·id (pav′·id) *a.* timid; shy [L. *pavidus*].

pa·vil·ion (pạ·vil′·yạn) *n.* orig. a tent; hence, anything like a tent, e.g. a garden summerhouse [Fr. fr. L. *papilio*, a butterfly, a tent].

paw (paw) *n.* the foot of an animal having claws; (*Slang*) the hand; *v.t.* and *i.* to scrape with the paws; (*Colloq.*) to stroke or fondle with hands clumsily, rudely [O.Fr. *poe*].

pawn (pawn) *n.* something deposited as security for money borrowed; a pledge; the state of being pledged; *v.t.* to deposit as security for a loan; to pledge. **-broker** *n.* one who lends money on something deposited with him. [L. *pannus*, cloth].

pawn (pawn) *n.* a piece of the lowest rank in the game of chess; (*Fig.*) a person who is a mere tool in the hands of another [L.L. *pedo*, a foot soldier].

pay (pā) *v.t.* to discharge one's obligations to; to give money, etc., for goods received or services rendered; *v.i.* to recompense; to be remunerative; to be worth the trouble. *pa.p.* and *pa.t.* **paid** (pād). *n.* reward; compensation; wages; salary. **-able** *a.* justly due; profitable. **-ee** (pā·ē′) *n.* one to whom money is paid. **-er** *n.* one who pays. **-ment** *n.* the act of paying; discharge of a debt; recompense [L. *pacare*, to appease].

pay (pā) *v.t.* (*Naut.*) to cover with pitch; to make waterproof [L. *picare*, to pitch].

pea (pē) *n.* the fruit, growing in pods, of a leguminous plant; the plant itself. **-nut** *n.* the earth nut. **— soup** *n.* soup made of dried peas. **sweet pea**, a climbing garden annual, bearing sweet-scented flowers [Gk. *pisos*].

peace (pēs) *n.* calm; repose; freedom from disturbance, war, or hostilities. **-able** *a.* in a state of peace; disposed to peace; not quarrelsome. **-ably** *adv.* **-ableness** *n.* **-ful** *a.* free from war, tumult, or commotion; mild; undisturbed. **-fully** *adv.* **-fulness** *n.* **-maker** *n.* one who makes peace [L. *pax*, *pacis*].

peach (pēch) *n.* a juicy fruit with light orange flesh, and a velvety skin; the tree which bears this fruit; a pale orange-pink color. **-y** *a.* peach-like; (*Slang*) excellent [Fr. *pêche*].

peach (pēch) *v.i.* (*Slang*) to inform against; to tell tales [abbrev. fr. *impeach*].

pea·cock (pē′·kåk) *n.* (*fem.* **peahen**) a bird remarkable for the beauty of its plumage, and for its large tail; a person vain of his appearance. **peafowl** *n.* the peacock or peahen. **— blue**, lustrous greenish blue [L. *pavo*, a peacock; and *cock*].

peak (pēk) *v.i.* to waste or pine away. **-y** *a.* thin, sickly. **-ed** *a.* [etym. unknown].

peak (pēk) *n.* the sharp top of a hill; the pointed top of anything; the projecting part of a cap brim; the maximum point of a curve or record. [Fr. *pic*; conn. with *pike*].

peal (pēl) *n.* a loud sound, or succession of loud sounds, as of thunder, bells, laughter, etc.; a set of bells attuned to each other; *v.t.* and *i.* to sound loudly [abbrev. fr. *appeal*].

peach

pear (pår, per) *n.* a sweet, juicy fruit of oval shape; tree on which it grows [L. *pirum*].

pearl (purl) *n.* a hard, smooth, lustrous substance, found in several mollusks, particularly pearl oyster, and used as a gem; something very precious; a small size of printing type, a creamy grey; *a.* made of pearls; pert. to pearls; *v.t.* to adorn with pearls; to take a round form like pearls. **-y** *a.* of the color of pearls; like pearls; abounding in pearls; clear; pure. **-iness** *n.* [Fr. *perle*].

peas·ant (pez'·ant) *n.* a rural laborer; a rustic; *a.* rural. **-ry** *n.* peasants collectively [Fr. *paysan*].

peat (pēt) *n.* a brown, fibrous turf, formed of decayed vegetable matter, which is used as fuel. **-y** *a.* like peat, in texture or color. **—bog, —moss** *n.* [etym. uncertain].

peb·ble (peb'·l) *n.* a small, roundish stone; transparent and colorless rock crystal. *v.t.* to hit or pave with pebbles; to grain paper with a rough surface pebbles [O.E. *papol*].

pe·can (pi·kăn', ·kan') *n.* a smooth-shelled for spectacle lenses. **-d, pebbly** *a.* full of oval nut with edible kernel; the tree on which it grows [Amer. Indian].

pec·ca·ble (pek'·a·bl) *a.* liable to sin. **peccability** *n.* liability to sin. **peccant** *a.* sinful; offensive; causing trouble; (*Med.*) morbid. **peccancy** *n.* [L. *peccare*, to sin].

pec·ca·dil·lo (pek·a·dil'·ō) *n.* a trifling offense; an indiscreet action. [Sp. *pecadillo*, fr. *pecado*, a sin; L. *peccare*, to sin].

peck (pek) *n.* a measure of capacity for dry goods = 2 gallons, or the fourth part of a bushel; a great deal [O.Fr. *pek*].

peck (pek) *v.t.* and *i.* to strike with the beak; to pick up with the beak; to dab; to eat little quantities at a time; *n.* (*Colloq.*) a kiss. **-er** *n.* [form of *pick*].

pec·tin (pek'·tin) *n.* a carbohydrate from fruits which yields a gel [Gr. *pektos*, congealed].

pec·to·ral (pek'·ter·al) *a.* pert. to the breast or chest [L. *pectus*, the breast].

pec·u·late (pek'·ya·lāt) *v.t.* and *i.* to embezzle. **peculation** *n.* **peculator** *n.* [L. *peculari*].

pe·cu·liar (pi·kūl'·yer) *a.* belonging solely to; appropriate; particular; singular; strange. **-ly** *adv.* **peculiarity** (pi·kū·li·ar'·a·ti·) *n.* something that belongs to only one person, thing, class, people; a distinguishing feature; characteristic [L. *peculium*, property].

pe·cu·ni·ar·y (pe·kū'·ni·e·ri·) *a.* pert. to, or consisting of, money. **pecunniarily** *adv.* [L. *pecunia*, money, fr. *pecus*, cattle].

ped·a·gogue (ped'·a·gòg) *n.* a schoolteacher; a pedantic person. **pedagogic** (ped·a·gáj'·ik), **pedagogical** *a.* **pedagogy** (ped'·a·gō·ji·), **pedagogics** *n.* science of teaching [Gk. *pais*, a boy; *agogos*, leading].

pe·dal (ped'·al) *a.* pert. to the foot; *n.* a mechanical contrivance to transmit power by using foot as a lever, e.g. on bicycle, sewing-machine. *v.t.* and *i.* to use the pedals of an organ, piano, etc.; to propel a bicycle by pedaling. [L. *pes, pedis*, the foot].

ped·ant (ped'·ant) *n.* one who insists unnecessarily on petty details of book learning, grammatical rules, etc.; one who shows off his learning. **-ic, -ical** *a.* **pedantically** *adv.* **-ry** *n.* [perh. conn. with *pedagogue*].

ped·dle (ped'·l) *v.t.* to travel from place to place selling small articles; *v.t.* to sell or hawk goods thus. **-r** *n.* **pedlar** *n.* one who peddles goods; [O.E. *ped*, a basket].

ped·es·tal (ped'·is·tal) *n.* anything that serves as a support or foundation; the base of a column, statue, etc. [Fr. *piédestal*].

pe·des·tri·an (pa·des'·tri·an) *a.* going on, performed on, foot; of walking; commonplace; *n.* a walker; one who journeys on foot

[L. *pedester*, fr. *pes*, a foot].

pe·di·at·rics (pēd·i·at'·riks) *n.* (*Med.*) the branch dealing with the diseases and disorders of children. **pediatric** *a.* **pediatrician** *n.* [Gk. *paidos*, a child; *iatrikos*, healing].

pe·dic·u·lar (pi·dik'·ya·ler) *pert.* to lice [L. *pediculus*, a louse].

ped·i·cure (ped'·i·kūr) *n.* treatment of the feet [L. *pes, pedis*, the foot; *cura, care*].

ped·i·gree (ped'·a·grē) *n.* a line of ancestors; genealogy; *a.* having a line of ancestors [M.E. *pedegru* fr. Fr. *pied de grue*, crane's foot].

ped·i·ment (ped'·a·ment) *n.* (*Archit.*) the triangular ornamental facing of a portico door, or window, etc. **pedimental** *a.* [earlier *periment*, perh. fr. *pyramid*].

pe·dom·e·ter (pi·dåm'·a·ter) *n.* an instrument which measures the distance walked by recording the number of steps [L. *pes, pedis*, the foot; Gk. *metron*, a measure].

pe·dun·cle (pi·dung'·kl) *n.* a flower stalk; (*Zool.*) a stalk or stalklike process in an animal body. **peduncular** *a.* [dim. of L. *pes, pedis*, a foot].

peek (pēk) *v.i.* to peep; to peer; *n.* a glance [etym. uncertain].

peel (pēl) *v.t.* to strip off the skin, bark, or rind; to free from a covering; *v.i.* to come off, as the skin or rind; *n.* the outside skin of a fruit; rind or bark [L. *pilare*, to deprive of hair].

peel (pēl) *n.* wooden shovel used by bakers [L. *pala*, a spade].

peep (pēp) *v.i.* to look through a crevice; to look furtively or slyly; to emerge slowly; *n.* a furtive or sly glance. **— show** *n.* a small exhibit, viewed through an aperture containing a magnifying glass [etym. uncertain].

peep (pēp) *v.i.* to cry, as a chick [imit.].

peer (pir) *n.* (*fem.* **-ess**) an equal in any respect; a nobleman; a member of the House of Lords; an associate. **-age** *n.* the rank of a peer; the body of peers. **-less** *a.* having no equal. **-lessly** *adv.* **-lessness** *n.* [L. *par*, equal].

peer (pir) *v.i.* to look closely and intently; to peer; to appear [etym. doubtful].

pee·vish (pē'·vish) *a.* fretful; irritable; hard to please; childish. **-ly** *adv.* **-ness** *n.* **peeve** *v.t.* to annoy.

peg (peg) *n.* a nail or pin of wood or other material; (*Colloq.*) a step or degree; *v.t.* to fix or mark with a peg; *v.i.* to persevere. *pr.p.* **-ging** *pa.t., pa.p.* **-ged** [etym. uncertain].

Pe·king·ese' (Pē·kan·ēz') *n.* a breed of Chinese lap-dog. *abbrev.* **peke.**

pe·koe (pē'·kō) *n.* a black tea of superior quality [Chin. *pek*, white; *ho*, down (i.e. with 'down' on the leaves)].

pel·i·can (pel'·i·kan) *n.* a large water fowl [Gk. *pelekan*].

pe·lisse (pa·lēs') *n.* formerly, a robe of silk or other material, worn by ladies; a fur-lined coat [L. *pellis*, skin].

pel·let (pel'·it) *n.* a little ball; a pill; small shot [Fr. *pelote*, a ball].

pell-mell (pel-mel') *adv.* in utter confusion; helter-skelter [Fr. *mêler*, to mix; *pêle*, being a rhyme with *mêle*].

pel·lu·cid (pa·lòò'·sid) *a.* perfectly clear; translucent. **-ly** *adv.* **-ness** *n.* [L. *per*, very; *lucidus*, clear].

pelt (pelt) *n.* raw hide; undressed skin of fur-bearing animal [L. *pellis*, skin].

pelt (pelt) *v.t.* to strike with missiles; *v.i.* of rain, etc. to fall heavily; to throw missiles; to run fast [etym. uncertain].

pel·vis (pel'·vis) *n.* (*Anat.*) the bony basin-shaped cavity at the base of the human trunk. **pelvic** *a.* [L. = a basin].

pen (pen) *n.* an instrument for writing with ink; a large wing feather (a quill) used for writing; *v.t.* to write; to compose and set down. *pr.p.* **-ning** *pa.p.* and *pa.t.* **-ned**. **-knife** *n.* a pocketknife. **-man** *n.* one who writes a good hand; an author. **-manship** *n.* **— name** *n.* an assumed name of author. [L. *penna*, a feather].

penknife

pen (pen) *n.* a small enclosure, as for sheep; a coop. *v.t.* to confine in a pen; to shut in. *pr.p.* **-ning** *pa.p., pa.t.* **-ned** [O.E. *penn*].

pe·nal (pē'·nal) *a.* pert. to, prescribing, incurring, inflicting, punishment. **-ize** *v.t.* to make penal; to impose a penalty upon; to handicap. **-ly** *adv.* **penalty** (pen'·al·ti·) *n.* punishment for a crime or offense; in games, a handicap imposed for infringement of rule, etc.; **penology** *n.* study and arrangement of prisons and prisoners [L. *poena*, punishment].

pen·ance (pen'·ans) *n.* suffering submitted to in penitence; act of atonement [L. *penitentia*].

pence (pens) *n.pl.* See **penny**.

pen·chant (pen'·chant) *n.* a strong mental inclination [Fr. *pencher*, to lean].

pen·cil (pen'·sil) *n.* a stick of graphite encased in wood, used for writing or drawing; (*Math.*) a system of rays which converge to, or diverge from, a point; *v.t.* to draw, write with pencil. **-ed** *a.* marked, as with pencil; having pencils or rays. **-ing** *n.* the work of a pencil [L. *penicillum*, a little tail].

pend·ant (pen'·dant) *n.* a hanging ornament, esp. a locket or earring; a lamp or chandelier hanging from the ceiling; a complement or parallel. **pendent** *a.* suspended; hanging; projecting. **pendently** *adv.* **pending** *a.* awaiting settlement; in suspense; undecided; *prep.* during; until [L. *pendere*, to hang].

pen·du·lous (pen'·ja·las) *a.* hanging loosely; swinging. **-ly** *adv.* **-ness** *n.* **pendulum** *n.* a body suspended from a fixed point, and swinging freely; the swinging rod with weighted end which regulates movements of a clock, etc. [L. *pendulus*, hanging].

pen·e·trate (pen'·a·trāt) *v.t.* to enter into; to pierce; to pervade or spread through; to touch with feeling; to arrive at the meaning of; *v.i.* to make a way to, or through. **penetrating** *a.* **penetrable** *a.* capable of being entered or pierced; susceptible. **penetrably** *adv.* **penetrability** *n.* **penetration** *n.* [L. *penetrare*].

pen·guin (pen'·gwin) *n.* a flightless sea bird inhabiting the S. temperate and Antarctic regions [W. *pen*, head; *gwyn*, white].

pen·i·cil·lin (pen·i·sil'·in) *n.* an antibacterial agent produced from the fungus *penicillium*.

pen·in·su·la (pa·nin'·sa·la) *n.* a portion of land nearly surrounded by water, and connected with the mainland by an isthmus **-r** *a.* [L. *paene*, almost; *insula*, an island].

pe·nis (pē'·nis) *n.* the male organ of generation. **penial** *a.* [L.].

pen·i·tent (pen'·a·tant) *a.* deeply affected by sense of guilt; contrite; repentant; *n.* one who repents of sin. **-ly** *adv.* **penitence** *n.* sorrow for having sinned; repentance. **penitential** (pen·a·ten'·shal) *a.* pert. to or expressing penitence; *n.* among R.Cs, a book containing rules of penance. **penitentially** *adv.* **penitentiary** (pen·a·ten'·sha·ri·) *a.* pert. to punish by confinement; *n.* a prison; (*R.C.*) an officer who prescribes penance; [L. *paenitere*, to repent].

pen·nant (pen'·ant) *n.* a very long, narrow flag tapering to a point. Also **pennon** [Fr. *pennon*, fr. L. *penna*, a feather].

pen·nate (pen'·āt) *a.* winged; feathered. Also **pennated. penniform** *a.* feather-shaped [L. *penna*, a feather].

pen·ny (pen'·i·) *n.* the U.S. and Canadian cent; an English coin (about 2 U.S. cents); a small sum. *pl.* **pennies. penniless** *a.* without money; poor. **-weight** (pen'·i·wāt) *n.* a troy weight of 24 grains (*abbrev.* **pwt.**).

pen·sile (pen'·sl) *a.* hanging; suspended; pendulous [L. *pensilis*].

pen·sion (pen'·shan) *n.* an annual grant of money for past services; an annuity paid to retired officers, soldiers, etc.; *v.t.* to grant a pension to. **-er** *n.* one who receives a pension [L. *pensio*, payment].

pen·sive (pen'·siv) *a.* thoughtful; deep in thought; somewhat melancholy **-ly** *adv.* **-ness** *n.* [Fr. *pensif*, fr. *penser*, to think].

pent (pent) *a.* closely confined; shut up [fr. *pen* = an enclosure].

pen·ta- (pen'·ta) *prefix* fr. Gk. *pente*, five, used in derivatives. **-gon, -gram** *n.* (*Geom.*) a plane figure having five angles and five sides. **-gonal** *a.* **-cle** *n.* a five-pointed star, formerly a magic symbol. **-meter** *n.* verse of five feet.

pen·tane (pen'·tān) *n.* a paraffin hydrocarbon, a very inflammable liquid [Gk. *pente*, five].

Pen·ta·teuch (pen'·ta·tūk) *n.* the first five books of the Old Testament [Gk. *pente*, five; *teuchos*, a book].

Pen·te·cost (pen'·te·kawst) *n.* a Jewish festival, celebrated on the 50th day after the Passover; a Christian festival (Whitsunday) commemorating the descent of the Holy Ghost on the Apostles.**Pentecostal** *a.* [Gk. *pentō-kostos*, fiftieth].

pent·house (pent'·hous) *n.* an apartment, or structure, on the roof of a building; a shed attached to a main building, its roof sloping down from the wall [Fr. *appentis*, fr. L. *pendere*, to hang].

pen·to·thal (pen'·ta·thawl) *n.* sometimes called the 'truth' drug; an anesthetic [Trade Name].

pe·nult (pē·nult') *n.* the next to last syllable of a word. **penultimate** (pi·nul'·ti·mat) *a.* next to last [L. *paene*, almost; *ultimus*, last].

pe·num·bra (pin·um'·bra) *n.* in an eclipse, the partially shadowed region which surrounds the full shadow [L. *paene*, almost; *umbra*, shade].

pen·u·ry (pen'·ya·ri·) *n.* extreme poverty; want or indigence; scarcity. **penurious** (pa·noo'·ri·as) *a.* miserly. **penuriously** *adv.* **penuriousness** *n.* [L. *penuria*].

pe·on (pē'·an, ·an) *n.* in Mexico, a day laborer or serf; in India, a foot soldier, or messenger. **-age** *n.* [Sp., L. *pes*, a foot].

pe·o·ny (pē'·a·ni·) *n.* plant having beautiful, showy flowers [Gk. *paiōnia*, healing, fr. *Paiōn*, the physican of the gods].

peo·ple (pē'·pl) *n.* the body of persons that compose a community, tribe, nation, or race; the populace as distinct from rulers; *v.t.* to populate [L. *populus*].

pep (pep) *n.* (*Slang*) vigor; energy. **-py** *a.* **-piness** *n.* [short for *pepper*].

pep·per (pep'·er) *n.* a pungent, spicy condiment obtained from an E. Indian plant; *v.t.* to sprinkle with pepper; to pelt with missiles. **-y** *a.* having the qualities of pepper; pungent; irritable. **-iness** *n.* **-corn** *n.* the berry or fruit of the pepper-plant; something of insignificant value. **-mint** *n.* a pungent plant which yields a volatile oil; essence gotten from this oil; a lozenge flavored with this essence [Gk. *peperi*].

peppermint

pep·sin, pepsine (pep'·sin) *n.* a ferment formed in gastric juice of man and animals, and serving as an aid to digestion. **peptic** *a.* pert. to pepsin and to digestion; *n.pl.* medicines that promote digestion. **peptone** (pep'·tōn) *n.* one of the soluble compounds due to the action of pepsin, etc. on proteins. **peptonize** *v.t.* to convert food into peptones [Gk. *pepsis*, digestion].

per·ad·ven·ture (pur·ad·ven'·cher) *adv.* by chance; perhaps; possibly; *n.* doubt; question [O.Fr. *par aventure*].

per·am·bu·late (per·am'·bya·lāt) *v.t.* to walk through or over; formerly to survey the boundaries of; *v.i.* to walk about; to stroll. **perambulation** *n.* **perambulator** *n.* one who perambulates; a small carriage for a child. **perambulatory** *a.* [L. *per*; *ambulare*, to walk].

per·an·num (per·an'·nam) L. by the year; annually.

per·cale (per·kal') *n.* closely woven cotton cloth [Fr. *pargal*].

per cap·i·ta (per·kap'·a·ta) L. for each person.

per·ceive (per·sēv') *v.t.* to obtain knowledge of through the senses; to see, hear, or feel; to understand. **perceivable** *a.* **perceivably** *adv.* **-r** *n.* **perceptible** (per·sep'·ti·bl) *a.* capable of being perceived; discernible. **perceptibly** *adv.* **perceptibility** *n.* **perception** (per·sep'·shan) *n.* the faculty of perceiving; intuitive judgment. **perceptive** *a.* having perception; used in perception. **perceptual** *a.* involving perception [L. *percipere*].

per·cent·age (per·sen'·tij) *n.* proportion or rate per hundred. **per centum** (abbrev. **per cent**) by, in, or for, each hundred; portion -[L. *per*, through; *centum*, a hundred].

perch (purch) *n.* an edible fresh-water fish [Gk. *perkē*].

perch (purch) *n.* roosting bar for birds; high place; lineal measure (also 'pole' or 'rod') = 5½ yards; a measure of area = 30¼ square yards; *v.t.* to place on a perch; *v.i.* to alight or settle on a perch [L. *pertica*, a pole].

per·chance (per·chans') *adv.* perhaps; by chance [L. *per*, through; and *chance*].

per·cip·i·ent (per·sip'·i·ant) *a.* having the faculty of perception; perceiving; *n.* one who

has the power of perceiving. **percipience, percipiency** *n.* [L. *percipere*, to perceive].

per·co·late (per'·ka·lāt) *v.t.* and *i.* to pass slowly through small openings, as a liquid; to filter. **percolation** *n.* **percolator** *n.* a coffee pot fitted with a filter [L. *per*, through; *colare*, to strain].

percolator

per·cuss (per·kus') *v.t.* to strike sharply. **percussion** (per·kush'·an) *n.* a collision; an impact; (*Med.*) tapping the body to determine condition of internal organ. **-ive** *a.* [L. *percutere*, to strike].

per·di·em (per·di'·am) L. daily.

per·di·tion (per·dish'·an) *n.* utter loss; ruin; damnation [L. *perdere*, to lose].

per·e·gri·nate (per'·a·gri·nāt) *v.i.* to travel from place to place; to journey. **peregrination** *n.* a wandering about. **peregrinator** *n.* [L. *peregrinus*, foreign].

per·emp·to·ry (pa·remp'·ta·ri·) *a.* authoritative; dictatorial; non-debatable; decisive; absolute. **peremptorily** *adv.* **peremptoriness** *n.* [L. *perimere, peremptum*, to destroy].

per·en·ni·al (pa·ren'·i·al) *a.* lasting through the year; lasting; everlasting; lasting more than two years; *n.* a plant lasting for such a time.**-ly** *adv.* [L. *per*, through; *annus*, a year].

per·fect (pur'·fikt) *a.* complete; faultless; correct; excellent; of the highest quality; (*Gram.*) a tense denoting completed action; complete; to make perfect; to improve; to make skillful. **perfect** (pur'·fekt or per·fekt') *v.t.* to finish or complete; to make perfect; to improve; to make skillful. **-ly** *adv.* **perfectible** *a.* capable of becoming perfect. **perfectibility** *n.* **perfection** *n.* state of being perfect. **perfectionist** *n.* one who believes that moral perfection is attainable, or that he has attained it [L. *perfectus*, done thoroughly].

per·fer·vid (per·fur'·vid) *a.* very eager [L.].

per·fi·dy (pur'·fa·di·) *n.* treachery; breach of faith; violation of trust. **perfidious** *a.* treacherous. **perfidiously** *adv.* **perfidiousness** *n.* [L. *perfidia*, faithlessness].

per·fo·rate (pur'·fa·rāt) *v.t.* to pierce; to make a hole or holes in. **perforation** *n.* act of perforating; a hole, or series of holes [L. *per*, through; *forare*, to bore].

per·force (per·fōrs') *adv.* by force; of necessity [L. *per*; and *force*].

per·form (per·fawrm') *v.t.* to do; to accomplish; to fulfill; to represent on the stage; *v.i.* to do; to play, as on a musical instrument. **-ing** *a.* trained to act a part or do tricks. **-er** *n.* **-ance** *n.* act of performing; execution or carrying out; the thing done [L. *per*, thoroughly; Fr. *fournir*, to furnish or complete].

per·fume (pur'·fūm) *n.* a sweet scent or fragrance; a substance which emits an agreeable scent. (per·fūm') *v.t.* to fill or imbue with an agreeable odor; to scent. **-r** *n.* a maker or seller of perfumes. **perfumery** *n.* perfumes in general; the art of making perfumes [L. *per*, through; *fumare*, to smoke].

per·func·to·ry (per·fungk'·ta·ri·) *a.* done as a duty, carelessly and without interest; indifferent; superficial. **perfunctorily** *adv.* [L. *perfungi*, to perform].

per·go·la (pur'·ga·la) *n.* an arbor or covered walk formed of growing plants trained over trelliswork. [It.].

per·haps (per·haps') *adv.* it may be; possibly; perchance [L. *per*, through; E. *hap*, chance].

per·i·car·di·um (per·i·kàr'·di·am) *n.* (Anat.) the double membranous sac which encloses the heart. **pericardiac, pericardial** *a.* [Gk. *peri*, round; *kardia*, the heart].

per·i·gee (per'·a·jē) *n.* that point in the moon's orbit nearest to the earth. opp. to *apogee* [Gk. *peri*, round; *gē*, the earth].

per·il (per'·al) *n.* danger; hazard; exposure to injury or loss; *v.t.* to expose to dangers, etc. **-ous** *a.* full of peril. **-ously** *adv.* **-ousness** *n.* [L. *periculum*, danger].

per·im·e·ter (pa·rim'·a·ter) *n.* (Geom.) the outer boundary of a plane figure; the sum of all its sides; circumference. **perimetrical** *a.* [Gk. *peri*, around; *metron*, a measure].

pe·ri·od (pē'·ri·ad) *n.* a particular portion of time; the time in which a heavenly body makes a revolution; a series of years; a cycle; conclusion; a punctuation mark (.), at the end of a sentence; menstruation; *a.* of furniture, dress, a play, etc., belonging to a particular period in history. **periodic** *a.* recurring at regular intervals. **periodical** *a.* periodic; pert. to a periodical; *n.* a publication, esp. a magazine issued at regular intervals. [Gk. *peri*, around; *hodos*, a way].

per·i·pa·tet·ic (per·a·pa·tet'·ik) *a.* walking

about; pert. to the philosophy of Aristotle. **-ism** *n.* [Gk. *peri*, around, about; *patein*, to walk].

pe·riph·er·y (pa·rif'·a·ri·) *n.* circumference; perimeter; the outside. **peripheral** *a.* [Gk. *peri*, around; *pherein*, to bear].

pe·riph·ra·sis (pa·rif'·ra·sis) *n.* a roundaway of speaking or writing; circumlocution. *pl.* **periphrases. periphrastic** *a.* circumlocutory. **periphrastically** *adv.* [Gk. *peri*, around; *phrasis*, speaking].

per·i·scope (per'·a·skōp) *n.* an optical instrument which enables an observer to view surrounding objects from a lower level [Gk. *peri*, around; *skopein*, to see].

per·ish (per'·ish *v.t.* and *i.* to die; to waste away; to decay; to be destroyed. **-able** *a.* liable to perish, decay, etc., e.g. fish, fruit, etc. [L. *perire*; *per*, completely; *ire*, to go].

per·i·to·ne·um (per·a·ta·nē'·am) *n.* membrane which lines abdominal cavity, and surrounds intestines, etc. **peritonitis** *n.* inflammation of peritoneum [Gk. *peritonaion*, stretch over].

per·i·wig (per'·i·wig) *n.* a wig; a peruke. **-ged** *a.* [Fr. *perruque*, a wig].

per·i·win·kle (per'·i·wing·kl) *n.* an edible shellfish [O.E. *pinewincle*, a whelk].

per·i·win·kle (per'·i·wing·kl) *n.* a trailing shrub with blue flowers; myrtle [L. *pervinca*].

per·jure (pur'·jer) *v.t.* to violate one's oath (used reflex.). **-d** *a.* guilty of perjury. **perjury** *n.* false testimony; the crime of violating one's oath. **-r** *n.* [L. *per*; *jurare* to swear].

perk (purk) *v.t.* to make spruce or trim; *v.i.* to become brisk and lively again (with 'up'). **-y** *a.* jaunty; pert; trim [Celt.].

per·ma·nent (pur'·ma·nant) *a.* remaining unaltered; lasting. *n.* a wave put into the hair to last several months. **-ly** *adv.* **permanence** *n.* [L. *per*, through; *manere*, to remain].

per·man·ga·nate (pur·mang'·ga·nāt) *n.* a salt of an acid of manganese, which, dissolved in water, forms a disinfectant and antiseptic.

per·me·ate (pur'·mi·āt) *v.t.* to penetrate and pass through; to diffuse itself through; to saturate. **permeable** *a.* admitting of passage of fluids. **permeably** *adv.* **permeability** (pur·mē·a·bil'·a·ti·) *a.* capable of permeating [L. *per*, through; *meare*, to pass].

per·mit (per·mit') *v.t.* to allow; to give leave or liberty to; *v.t.* to give leave. **permit** (pur'·mit) *n.* written permission. *pr.p.* **-ting.** *pa.p.* and *pa.t.* **-ted. permission** *n.* authorization; leave or license granted. **permissible** *a.* allowable. **permissibly** *adv.* **permissive** *a.* allowing. **permissively** *adv.* [L. *permittere*].

per·mute (per·mūt') *v.t.* to change the order of. **permutable** *a.* **permutably** *adv.* **permutableness, permutability** *n.* **permutation** *n.* (Math.) the arrangement of a number of quantities in every possible order [L. *per*, thoroughly; *mutare*, to change].

per·ni·cious (per·nish'·as) *a.* having the quality of destroying or injuring; wicked. **-ly** *adv.* **-ness** *n.* [L. *per* thoroughly; *nex*, death by violence].

per·nick·et·y (per·nik'·a·ti·) *a.* (Colloq.) unduly fastidious about trifles [Scot.].

per·o·ra·tion (per·a·rā'·shan) *n.* the concluding part of an oration. **perorate** *v.i.* to deliver a speech [L. *perorare*, to speak to the end].

per·ox·ide (pa·ràk'·sīd) *n.* (Chem.) oxide containing more oxygen than the normal oxide of an element; *v.t.* (Colloq.) to bleach the hair with peroxide of hydrogen.

per·pen·dic·u·lar (pur·pan·dik'·ya·ler) *a.* exactly upright or vertical; at right angles to the plane of the horizon; at right angles to a given line or surface; *n.* a line at right angles to the plane of the horizon or to any line or plane; the latest of the styles of English Gothic architecture, marked by stiff, straight lines; upright position. **-ly** *adv.* [L. *perpendiculum*, a plumb-line].

per·pe·trate (pur'·pa·trāt) *v.t.* to commit (something bad, esp. a crime). **perpetration** *n.* **perpetrator** *n.* [L. *perpetrare*, to accomplish].

per·pet·u·al (per·petch'·oo·wal) *a.* continuing indefinitely; everlasting. **-ly** *adv.* **perpetuate** *v.t.* to make perpetual; not to allow to be forgotten. **perpetuation** *n.* **perpetuity** (pur·pa·tū'·a·ti·) *n.* the state or quality of being perpetual [L. *perpetualis*].

per·plex (per·pleks') *v.t.* to make intricate, or difficult; to puzzle; to bewilder. **-ed** *a.*

puzzled; bewildered. **-ing** a. **-ity** n. bewilderment; a confused state of mind [L. *per*, thoroughly; *plectere*, to weave].

per·qui·site (pur'·kwạ·zit) n. a casual payment in addition to salary, etc.; a tip [L. *perquisitum*, a thing eagerly sought].

per·se·cute (pur'·si·kūt) v.t. to oppress unjustly for the holding of an opinion; to subject to persistent ill-treatment; to harass. **persecution** n. **persecutor** n. [L. *persequi*, to pursue].

per·se·vere (pur·sạ·vēr) v.i. to persist; to maintain an effort; not to give in. **persevering** a. **perseveringly** adv. **perseverance** n. [L. *per*, thoroughly; *severus*, strict].

per·sian (pur'·zhạn) a. pert. to Persia (now Iran) its people, or the language. — **cat**, a breed of cat with long, silky fur.

per·si·flage (pur'·si·flázh) n. idle banter [Fr. fr. L. *per*, through; *sifilare*, *sibilare*, to hiss].

per·sim·mon (per·sim'·ạn) n. an American tree with plumlike fruit [Amer.-Ind.].

per·sist (per·sist') v.i. to continue firmly in a state or action in spite of obstacles or objections. **-ent** a. persisting; steady; persevering; lasting. **-ently** adv. **-ence**, **-ency** a. [L. *persistere*, fr. *sistere*, to stand].

per·son (pur'·sạn) n. a human being; an individual; the body of a human being; a character in a play; (*Gram.*) one of the three classes of personal pronouns (first, second, or third) showing the relation of the subject to a verb, as speaking, spoken to, or spoken of. **-able** a. attractive in appearance. **-age** n. a person, esp. of rank or social position. **-al** a. pert. to, peculiar to, or done by, a person; pert. to bodily appearance; directed against a person; (*Gram.*) denoting the pronouns, I, you, he, she, it, we, you, and they. **-ally** adv. in person; individually. **-ality** n. individuality; distinctive personal qualities. **personalty** (pur'·sạn·ạl·ti·) n. (*Law*) personal effects; movable possessions. **-ate** v.t. to assume character of; to pretend to be. **-ator** n. **-ation** n. [L. *persona*].

per·son·i·fy (per·sán'·ạ·fi) v.t. to endow inanimate objects or abstract ideas with human attributes; to be an outstanding example of. **personification** n. [L. *persona*, a person; *facere*, to make].

per·son·nel (pur·sạn·el') n. the persons employed in a public service, business, office, etc.; staff [Fr. fr. L. *persona*, person].

per·spec·tive (per·spek'·tiv) n. the art of drawing objects on a plane surface to give impression of the relative distance of objects, indicated by the convergence of their receding lines; relation of parts of a problem, etc. in the mind [L. *per*, through; *specere*, to look].

per·spi·ca·cious (pur·spi·kā'·shạs) a. of acute discernment; of keen understanding. **-ly** adv. **perspicacity** (pur·spi·kas'·ạ·ti·) n. quick mental insight or discernment. **perspicuous** (per·spik'·ū·ạs) a. clear to the understanding; lucid. **perspicuously** adv. **perspicuousness** n. **perspicuity** (pur·spi·kū'·ạ·ti·) n. clearness [L. *perspicax*, keen of sight].

per·spire (per·spīr') v.t. to emit through the pores of the skin; v.i. to evacuate the moisture of the body through the pores of the skin; to sweat. **perspiration** n. the process of perspiring; the moisture emitted [L. *per*, through; *spirare*, to breathe].

per·suade (per·swād') v.t. to influence by argument, entreaty, etc.; to win over. **persuasive** (per·swā'·siv) a. having the power of persuading. **persuasively** adv. **persuasiveness** n. **persuasion** (per·swā'·zhạn) n. the act of persuading; the quality of persuading; conviction; belief; sect. **persuasible** a. [L. *per*, thoroughly; *suadere*, to advise].

pert (purt) a. bold; forward; saucy. **-ly** adv. **-ness** n. [O.Fr. *apert*].

per·tain (per·tān') v.i. to belong; to concern [L. *pertinere*, to belong].

per·ti·na·cious (pur·tạ·nā'·shạs) a. adhering to an opinion, etc. with obstinacy; persevering; resolute. **-ly** adv. **-ness** n. **pertinacity** (per·ti·nas'·ạ·ti·) n. [L. *pertinax*, tenacious].

per·ti·nent (pur'·tạ·nạnt) a. related to the subject or matter in hand. **-ly** adv. **pertinence**, **pertinency** n. [L. *pertinere*, to belong].

per·turb (per·turb') v.t. to disturb; to trouble greatly. **-ation** (pur·ter·bā'·shạn) n. mental uneasiness or disquiet; disorder [L. *per*, thoroughly; *turbare*, to disturb].

Pe·ru (pạ·röö') n. a republic on the west coast of S. America. **-vian** n. a native of Peru; a. pert. to Peru.

pe·ruse (pạ·rööz') v.t. to read through, esp. with care. **perusal** n. the act of perusing [*per*, thoroughly; and *use*].

per·vade (per·vād') v.t. to spread through the whole of; to be diffused through all parts of. **pervasion** (per·vā'·zhun) n. **pervasive** a. [L. *per*, through; *vadere*, to go].

per·verse (per·vurs') a. obstinately or unreasonably wrong; refusing to do the right, or to admit error; self-willed. **-ness**, **perversity** n. [L. *per*, thoroughly; *vertere*, to turn].

per·ver·sion (per·vur'·zhan) n. a turning from the true purpose, use, or meaning; corruption; unnatural manifestation of sexual

desire. **perversive** a. tending to pervert [L. *per*, thoroughly; *vertere*, to turn].

Peru

per·vert (per·vurt') v.t. to turn from its proper purpose; to misinterpret; to lead astray; to corrupt. **pervert** (pur'·vẹrt) n. one who has deviated from the normal, esp. from right to wrong [L. *per*, thoroughly; *vertere*, to turn].

per·vi·ous (pur'·vi·ạs) a. giving passage to; penetrable. **-ness** n. [L. *per*, through; *via*, way].

pes·si·mism (pes'·ạ·mizm) n. the doctrine that the world is fundamentally evil; the tendency to look on the dark side of things (opp. of *optimism*); melancholy. **pessimist** n. **pessimistic** a. **pessimistically** adv. [L. *pessimus*, worst].

pest (pest) n. a plague or pestilence; a troublesome or harmful thing or person; nuisance. **-iferous** a. pestilential; carrying disease; (*Colloq.*) annoying [L. *pestis*, a plaque].

pes·ter (pes'·ter) v.t. to trouble or vex persistently; to annoy [O.Fr. *empestrer*, fr. L.L. *pastorium*, a foot shackle].

pest·i·cide (pes'·tạ·sīd) n. a pest killer.

pes·ti·lence (pes'·i·lẹns) n. any infectious or contagious, deadly disease. **pestilent** a. producing disease; noxious; harmful to morals. **pestilential** (pes·tạ·len'·shal) a. pert. to, or producing, pestilence; destructive; wicked [L. *pestis*, plague].

pes·tle (pes'·l, pes'·tl) n. an instrument for pounding substances in a mortar [L. *pistillum*, fr. *pinsere*, to pound].

pet (pet) n. an animal or person kept or regarded with affection; a favorite; a. favorite; v.t. to make a pet of; to indulge. pr.p. **-ting**. pa.p. and pa.t. **-ted** [etym. uncertain].

pet (pet) n. a sudden fit of peevishness [etym. uncertain].

pet·al (pet'·ạl) n. a colored flower-leaf.**-ed**, **-led** a. having petals. **-ine** a. pert. to, resembling, a petal [Gk. *petalon*, a thin plate].

pe·ter (pē'·ter) v.i. (*Colloq.*) to become exhausted, gradually smaller, weaker, etc. (with *out*) [fr. name *Peter*].

pet·it (pet'·i·, pe·tē') (*Law*) small; minor. *fem.* **petite** (pạ·tēt') small, dainty, trim of figure. — **point** a. slanting stitch used in embroidery and tapestry [Fr.].

pe·ti·tion (pạ·tish'·ạn) n. a formal request or earnest prayer; v.t. and v.i. to present a petition to; to entreat. **-ary** a. **-er** n. [L. *petere*, to ask].

pet·ri·fy (pet'·rạ·fī) v.t. to turn into stone; to make hard like stone; to make motionless with fear; v.i. to become like stone. pr.p. **petrified**, **pertifactive** a. [L. and Gk. *petra*, rock, stone; *facere*, to make].

pe·tro prefix fr. L. and Gk. *petra*, rock, stone, used in derivatives. **petrography** (pạ·trág'·rạ·fi·) n. the science of describing and classifying rocks. **petrographic(al)** a. **petrology** n. a branch of geology dealing with the composition, structure, and classification of rocks, their origin and sequence of formation. **petrologic(al)** a. **petrous** (pe'·trạs) a. pert. to, or like, rock; rocky; hard [Gk. *graphein*, to write; *logos*, discourse].

pe·tro·le·um (pạ·trō'·li·ạm) n. a mineral oil drawn from the earth by means of wells. **petrol** n. (*Brit.*) gasoline. **petrolic** a. [L. *petra*, rock; *oleum*, oil].

pet·ti·coat (pet'·i·kōt) n. a woman's underskirt; (*Colloq.*) a woman; a. feminine [orig.

petty coat, a small coat].

pet·ti·fog·ger (pet'·i·fág·ẹr) n. a low class person given to mean dealing in small matters. **pettifog** a. **-y** n. low trickery. **pettifogging** a. [etym. uncertain].

pet·tish (pet'·ish) a. petulant; easily annoyed. **-ly** adv. **-ness** n. [fr. *pet*, a fit of temper].

pet·ty (pet'·i·) a. small; unimportant; trivial; small-minded; of lower rank. **pettily** adv. **pettiness** n. — **cash**, small items of expenditure, esp. in an office. — **officer**, a noncommissioned officer in the Navy [Fr. *petit*, small].

pet·u·lant (pech'·ạ·lạnt) a. given to small fits of temper; irritable. **-ly** adv. **petulance**, **petulancy** n. peevishness; crossness; fretfulness [L. *petulans*, wanton].

pe·tu·ni·a (pạ·tū'·ni·ạ) n. a common garden plant with showy flowers [Braz. *petun*, tobacco].

pew (pū) n. a long, fixed bench in a church [O.Fr. *puie*, a platform].

pe·wee (pē'·wē) n. a small bird, the phoebe. Also **pewit** [imit. of its note].

pew·ter (pū'·tẹr) n. an alloy of tin and lead or some other metal, esp. copper; ware made of this; a. made of pewter [O.Fr. *peutre*].

phae·ton (fā'·tạn) n. a light, four-wheeled, open carriage.

phal·ange See **phalanx**.

pha·lan·ger (fạ·lan'·jẹr) n. genus of furry marsupial, some winged; flying squirrel [Gk. *phalangion*, a spider's web].

pha·lanx (fā'·langks) n. in ancient Greece, a company of soldiers in close array; hence, any compact body of people; (*Anat.*) a small bone of a toe or finger. pl. **-es**, **phalanges** [Gk.].

phal·lus (fal'·ạs) n. sexual organs. pl. **phalli**. **phallic** a. [Gk. *phallos*].

phan·tasm (fan'·tazm) n. an imaginary vision; a phantom; a specter. **-al**, **-ic** a. **phantasmagoria** (fan·taz·mạ·gō'·ri·ạ) n. an exhibition of optical illusions; a shifting scene of dim or unreal figures. **phantasmagoric** a. **phantasy** n. See **fantasy**. **phantom** (fan'·tam) n. an apparition; a specter; a ghost; a. spectral [Gk. *phainein*, to show].

Phar·aoh (fā'·rō) n. 'The Great House' a title of the kings of ancient Egypt.

Phar·i·see (far'·i·sē) n. (*Bib.*) one of a Jewish sect noted for their strict observance of the forms of the Law. **Pharisaic** (far·ạ·sā'·ik), **Pharisaical** a. **Pharisaically** adv. **-ism**, **Pharisaism**, n. [Heb. *parash*, to separate].

phar·ma·ceu·ti·cal (fár·mạ·sū'·tik·ạl) a. pert. to pharmacy. **pharmaceutics** n.pl. the science of pharmacy. **pharmaceutist** n. [Gk. *pharmakon*, a drug].

phar·ma·cy (fár'·mạ·si·) n. the science of preparing, compounding, and dispensing drugs and medicines; a drugstore. **pharmacist** n. one skilled in pharmacy. **pharmacology** n. the study of drugs and their action. **pharmacologist** n. one skilled in pharmacy. **pharmacopoeia** (fár·mạ·kạ·pē'·yạ) n. an authoritative book containing information on medicinal drugs [Gk. *pharmakon*, a drug].

phar·ynx (far'·ingks) n. the cavity at back of mouth, opening into the gullet. pl. **pharynges**. **pharyngeal** (fạ·rin'·jạl) a. Also **pharyngal**. **pharyngitis** (far·in·jī'·tis) n. (*Med.*) inflammation of pharynx. **pharyngoscope** n. instrument for examining throat [Gk. *pharunx*, the pharynx].

phase (fāz) n. (*Astron.*) an aspect of moon or a planet; a stage in development; an aspect of a subject or question. **phasic** a. [Gk. *phasis*, an appearance].

pheas·ant (fez'·ạnt) n. a gamebird with brilliant plumage [Gk. *Phasis*, a river in Colchis, whence the bird first came].

phe·nom·e·non (fạ·nám'·ạ·nán) n. anything appearing or observed, esp. if having scientific interest; a remarkable person or thing; (*Philos.*) sense appearance as opposed to real existence. pl. **phenomena**. **phenomenal** a. pert. to a phenomenon; remarkable; extraordinary. **phenomenally** adv. [Gk. *phainomenon*, a thing appearing].

phew (fū) interj. expressing disgust, impatience, relief, etc.

phi·al (fī'·ạl) n. a small glass bottle; a vial [Gk. *phialē*, a flat vessel].

phi·lan·der (fạ·lan'·der) v.i. to flirt. **-er** n. [Gk. *philos*, loving; *anēr*, a man].

phi·lan·thro·py (fi·lan'·thrạ·pi·) n. love of mankind, esp. as shown in acts of charity; an act of charity. **philanthropic** (fil·an·throp'·ik), **philanthropical** a. **philanthropically** adv. **philanthropist** n. one who loves and seeks to do good to his fellowmen. Also **philanthrope** [Gk. *philos*, loving; *anthrōpos*, man].

phi·lat·e·ly (fạ·lat'·ạ·li·) n. stamp collecting. **philatelic** a. **philatelist** n. [Gk. *philos*, loving; *ateles*, franked].

phil·har·mon·ic (fil·ẹr·mán'·ik   fil·har·mán'·ik) a. loving harmony or music; musical [Gk. *philos*, loving; *harmonia*, harmony].

Phi·lis·tine (fil'·ạs·tīn, ·tin) n. one with no love of music, painting, etc.; an uncultured person [Bib. Phillistine].

phi·lol·o·gy (fi·lál'·ạ·ji·) n. scientific study of origin, development, etc. of languages. **philological** a. **philologian** (fi·lạ·lō'·ji·an)

philologist *n.* one versed in philology [Gk. *philos*, loving; *logos*, word, speech].

phi·los·o·phy (fạ·lǒs'·ạ·fi·) *n.* originally, any branch of investigation of natural phenomena; now, the study of beliefs regarding God, existence, conduct, etc. and of man's relation with the universe; a calmness of mind; composure. **philosopher** *n.* a student of philosophy. **philosophic** (fil·ạ·sǎf'·ik) **philosophical** *a.* pert. to philosophy; wise; calm. **philosophically** *adv.* **philosophize** *v.i.* to reason like a philosopher; to theorize; to moralize. **philosophism** *n.* a pretended system of philosophy; sophism [Gk. *philos*, loving; *sophia*, wisdom].

phil·ter (fil'·tẹr) *n.* a drink supposed to excite love; any magic potion. Also **philtre** [Gk. *philtron*, fr. *philos*, loving].

phle·bi·tis (flạ·bī'·tis) *n.* (*Med.*) inflammation of a vein. **phlebitic** *a.* **phlebotomy** *n.* (*Surg.*) blood-letting [Gk. *phleps*, a vein].

phlegm (flem) *n.* a secretion of thick mucous substance discharged from throat by expectoration; calmness; apathy; sluggishness. **phlegmatic** (fleg·mat'·ik) *a.* cool and collected; unemotional. [Gk. *phlegma*].

phlox (flǎks) *n.* a genus of garden plants [Gk. = a flame].

phoe·be (fē·bǐ·) *n.* a small American flycatcher [imit.]

pho·bi·a (fō'·bi·ạ) *n.* a morbid dread of anything; used esp. as a suffix, e.g. claustrophobia, hydrophobia, etc. [Gk. *phobos*, fear].

Phoe·nix, Phenix (fē'·niks) *n.* (*Myth.*) a fabulous Arabian bird, symbol of immortality; a paragon [Gk. *phoinix*].

phone (fōn) *n., v.t.* and *i.* (*Colloq.*) abbrev. of **telephone** [Gk. *phōnē*, sound].

phone (fōn) *n.* a sound made in speaking. **phonic** *a.* pert. to sound, esp. to speech sounds. **phonics** *n.* method of teaching reading, etc. on basis of speech sounds [Gk. *phone*].

pho·neme (fō'·nēm) *n.* a member of the set of smallest units of speech sounds that serve to distinguish utterances. **phonemic** *a.* **phonemically** *adv.* **phonemics** *n.* branch of linguistics which deals with phonemes. [F.]

pho·net·ic (fō·net'·ik) *a.* pert. to the voice; pert. to, or representing, vocal sounds. Also **-al** *a.* **-ally** *adv.* **-s** *n.* the branch of the study of language which deals with speech sounds, and their production. **-ize** *v.t.* to represent phonetically. **— spelling**, a simplified system of spelling in which same letter or symbol is always used for same sound, e.g. cat = kat [Gk. *phōnē*, sound].

pho·no- (fō'·nō) *prefix* fr. Gk. *phōnē*, sound, used in many derivatives. **-gram** *n.* a character or symbol, esp. in shorthand, used to represent a speech sound. **-graph** *n.* an instrument for reproducing sounds from records. **phonography** *n.* a system of shorthand. **phonology** (fō·nǎl'·ạ·ji·) *n.* study of speech sounds; phonetics. **-logic(al)** *a.*

pho·ny, phoney (fō'·ni·) *a.* (*Slang*) sham; counterfeit.

phos·phate (fǎs'·fāt) *n.* a salt of phosphoric acid. **phosphatic** *a.* **— of lime**, commercially, bone-ash. **phosphide** *n.* a compound of phosphorus with another element, e.g. copper [fr. *phosphorus*].

phos·pho·rus (fǎs'·fẹr·ạs) *n.* a non-metallic element, a yellowish waxlike substance giving out a pale light in the dark. **phosphorous** *a.* pert. to phosphorus. **phosphorescence** (fǎs·fẹr·es'·ạns) *n.* the giving out of light without heat, as phosphorus, the glow-worm, decaying fish, etc. **phosphorescent** *a.* **phosphoric** *a.* pert. to, or obtained from, phosphorus; phosphorous. **phosphureted** *a.* combined with phosphorus [Gk. *phōs*, light; *phoros*, bearing].

pho·to (fō'·tō) *n.* (*Colloq.*) abbrev. of photograph; *v.t.* to photograph.

pho·to (fō'·tō) *prefix* fr. Gk. *phōs*, *phōtos*, light, used in derivatives. **-chemistry** (fō·tō·kem'·is·tri·) *n.* the branch of chemistry which treats of the chemical action of light. **-electron** *n.* an electron liberated from a metallic surface by the action of a beam of ultraviolet light. **— finish**, in racing, a photo taken at the finish to show correct placing of contestants. **-genic** *a.* producing light; of a person, having features, etc. that photograph well.

pho·tog·ra·phy (fạ·tǒg'·rạ·fi·) *n.* the art of producing pictures by the chemical action of light on a sensitive plate or film. **photograph** *n.* a picture so made; *v.t.* to make a photograph of. **photographer** *n.* **photographic(al)** *a.* pert. to, resembling, or produced by, photography. **photographically** *adv.* [Gk. *phōs*, light; *graphein*, to write; Fr. *gravure*, an engraving; Gk. *lithos*, a stone].

pho·tol·o·gy (fō·tǒl'·ạ·ji·) *n.* the science of light. **photometer** *n.* an instrument for measuring the intensity of light [Gk. *phōs*, light; *logos*, discourse; *metron*, a measure].

pho·ton (fō'·tǎn) *n.* the unit of measurement of light intensity [Gk. *phōs*, *phōtos*, light].

pho·to·stat (fō'·tō·stat) *n.* a photographic apparatus for making copies of documents, etc. directly on paper; *v.t.* to copy thus. **photostatic** *a.* [Trade Name].

pho·to·syn·the·sis (fō·tō·sin'·thạ·sis) *n.* the process by which a plant, under the influence of sunlight, can build up, in its chlorophyll-containing cells, carbohydrates from the carbon dioxide of the atmosphere and from the hydrogen of the water in the soil [Gk. *phōs*, *phōtos*, light; *sun*, together; *thesis*, a placing].

phrase (frāz) *n.* a small group of words forming part of a sentence; a short pithy expression; a characteristic mode of expression; (*Mus.*) a short, distinct part of a longer passage; *v.t.* to express suitably in words. **phraseogram** (frā'·zi·ạ·gram) *n.* in shorthand, a symbol used to represent a phrase. **-ology** *n.* a mode of expression; the choice of words used in speaking or writing [Gk. *phrazein*, to speak].

phre·net·ic (fri·net'·ik) *a.* having the mind disordered; frenzied; frantic [Gk. *phrēn*, the diaphragm, the mind].

phre·nol·o·gy (fri·nal'·ạ·ji·) *n.* character reading from the shape of the head. **phrenologic(al)** *a.* **phrenologically** *adv.* **phrenologist** *n.* [Gk. *phrēn*, mind; *logos*, discourse].

phthi·sis (thī'·sis) *n.* (*Med.*) a wasting away of the lungs; consumption. **phthisic** (tiz'·ik), **phthisical** (tiz'·ik·ạl) *a.* [Gk. fr. *phthiein*, to waste away].

phy·lac·ter·y (fạ·lak'·tạ·ri·) *n.* a charm or amulet; a small leather case containing strips of vellum, inscribed with certain verses of the Law and worn on the forehead or left arm by male Jews during morning prayer [Gk. *phylassein*, to guard].

phy·log·e·ny (fī·lǎj'·ạ·ni·) *n.* (*Bot.*) the evolution of an animal or plant type. **phylum** (fī'·lạm) *n.* one of the primary divisions of the animal or plant kingdoms. *pl.* **phyla** [Gk. *phylon*, a race; *genesis*, origin].

phys·ic (fiz'·ik) *n.* (*Arch.*) a cathartic; medicine; *v.t.* to give a dose of physic to. *pr.p.* **physicking.** *pa.p.* and *pa.t.* **physicked. physician** (fạ·zish'·ạn) *n.* one skilled in the art of healing; a medical doctor [Gk. *physis*, nature].

phys·i·cal (fiz'·ik·ạl) *a.* pert. to physics; pert. to nature; bodily, as opposed to mental or moral; material. **-ly** *adv.* [Gk. *physis*, nature].

phys·ics (fiz'·iks) *n.* sciences (excluding chemistry and biology) which deal with natural phenomena, e.g. motion, force, light, sound, electricity, etc. **physicist** (fiz'·i·sist) *n.* [Gk. *physis*, nature].

phys·i·og·no·my (fiz·i·ǎg'·nạ·mi·, fiz·i·ǒn'·ạ·mi·) *n.* art of judging character from contours of face; face itself; expression of the face. **physiognomic, physiognomical** *a.* **physiognomist** *n.* [Gk. *physis*, nature; *gnōmōn*, a judge].

phys·i·og·ra·phy (fiz·i·ǎg'·rạ·fi·) *n.* the study and description of natural phenomena; physical geography. **physiographer** *n.* [Gk. *physis*, nature; *graphein*, to write].

phys·i·ol·o·gy (fiz·i·ǎl'·ạ·ji·) *n.* science which deals with functions and life processes of plants, animals, and human beings. **physiological** *a.* **physiologist** *n.* [Gk. *physis*, nature; *logos*, discourse].

phys·i·o·ther·a·py (fiz·i·ō·ther'·a·pi·) *n.* the application of massage, manipulation, light, heat, electricity, etc., for treatment of certain disabilities [Gk. *physis*, nature; *therapeuein*, to cure].

phy·sique (fi·zēk') *n.* bodily structure and development [Fr. fr. Gk. *physis*, nature].

phy·to (fī'·tō) *prefix* fr. Gk. *phyton*, a plant. **phytogenesis** (fī·tō·jen'·ạ·sis), **phytogeny** (fī·tǎj'·ạ·ni·) *n.* the evolution of plants.

pi (pī) *n.* the Greek letter π, esp. as a mathematical symbol for the ratio of the circumference of a circle to its diameter, approx. $3\frac{1}{7}$, or 3.14159.

pi·a·no (pē·à'·nō) *adv.* (*Mus.*) softly. **pianissimo** *adv.* very softly [It.].

pi·a·no (pē·à'·nō) *n.* abbrev. of **pianoforte** (pē·à·nō·fôr'·te) *n.* a musical instrument having wires of graduated tension, struck by hammers moved by notes on a keyboard. **pianist** (pē'·ạ·nist, pē·an'·ist) *n.* one who plays the piano [It. *piano e forte* = soft and strong].

pi·as·ter (pi·as'·tẹr) *n.* a monetary unit of several Eastern countries [It. *piastra*].

piano

pi·az·za (pē·az'·ạ, pē·at'·sạ) *n.* a porch of a house; a public square [It.].

pi·ca (pī'·ka) *n.* (*Print.*) a size of type, having 6 lines to the inch [L. *pica*, a magpie].

pic·a·dor (pik·ạ·dawr') *n.* a mounted bullfighter armed with a lance to prod the bull [Sp. *pica*, a pike].

pic·a·roon (pik'·ạ·róon) *n.* an adventurer; a pirate. **picaresque** (pik·ạ·resk') *a.* of a novel, dealing with the lives and adventures of rogues [Sp. *picaro*, a rogue].

pic·ca·lil·li (pik·ạ·lil'·i·) *n.* a pickle of vegetables [etym. uncertain].

pic·co·lo (pik'·ạ·lō) *n.* (*Mus.*) a small flute, sounding an octave higher than the ordinary flute [It.].

pick (pik) *v.t.* to peck at, like birds with their bills; to pierce with a pointed instrument; to open with a pointed instrument, as a lock; to pluck, or cull, as flowers, etc.; to raise or lift (with 'up'); to choose or select; to rob; to pluck the strings of a musical instrument; (*Colloq.*) to eat; *v.i.* to eat daintily or without appetite; *n.* a sharp-pointed tool; the choicest or the best of anything. **-ax** *n.* an instrument for digging. **-ing** *n.* the act of one who picks; stealing; *pl.* gleanings; perquisites, often obtained by slightly underhand methods. **— on** (*Colloq.*) to nag; to find fault. **— pocket** *n.* one who steals from pockets. **-me-up** *n.* a drink that acts as a stimulant or restorative [M.E.].

pick·a·nin·ny (pik'·ạ·nin·i·) *a* small child; a Negro baby [Sp. *pequeño*, small].

pick·er·el (pik'·ạ·rạl) *n.* a young pike; a kind of pike [dim. fr. *pike*].

pick·et (pik'·it) *n.* a sharpened stake (used in fortifications, etc.); a peg or pale; a guard posted in front of an army; a party sent out by trade unions to dissuade men from working during a strike; *v.t.* to fence with pickets [Fr. *piquet*, fr. *pic*, a pike].

pick·le (pik'·l) *n.* brine or vinegar in which fish, meat, or vegetables are preserved; any food preserved in brine or vinegar; (*Colloq.*) a difficult situation; *v.t.* to preserve with salt or vinegar. **-d** *a.* (*Slang*) drunk. **-s** *n.pl.* vegetables in vinegar and spices [M.E. *pykyl, pikille*].

pic·nic (pik'·nik) *n.* pleasure excursion with meal out of doors; agreeable situation; *v.i.* to go on a picnic. *pr.p.* **-king.** *pa.p.* and *pa.t.* **-ked** [Fr. *pique-nique*, etym. uncertain].

pi·cot (pē'·kō) *n.* a small projecting loop of thread forming part of an ornamental edging to ribbon, lace, etc. [Fr.].

pic·ric (pik'·rik) *a.* pert. to **— acid**, a poisonous, crystalline substance used in solution as a dressing for burns, for dyes, explosives, etc. [Gk. *pikros*, bitter].

pic·to·graph (pik'·tạ·graf) *n.* a picture representing an idea [L. *pingere, pictum*, to paint; Gk. *graphein*, to write].

pic·to·ri·al (pik·tō'·ri·ạl) *a.* pert. to pictures; expressed by pictures; illustrated. **-ly** *adv.* [L. *pictor*, a painter, fr. *pingere*, to paint].

pic·ture (pik'·chẹr) *n.* a representation of objects or scenes on paper, canvas, etc. by drawing, painting, photography, etc.; a mental image; a likeness or copy; an illustration; picturesque object; a graphic or vivid description in words; *v.t.* to draw or paint an image or representation of; to describe graphically; to recall vividly. **picturesque** (pik·chẹr·esk') *a.* making effective pictures; vivid in description. **-squely** *adv.* **-squeness** *n.* **— gallery** *n.* a hall containing a collection of pictures for exhibition. [L. *pingere, pictum*, to paint].

pid·dle (pid′·l) *v.i.* to trifle. **piddling** *a.* trifling [etym. uncertain].

pidg·in (pij′·in) *n.* Chinese corruption of English word *business*. **pidgin** or **pigeon English**, a jargon used in China between foreigners and natives.

pie (pī) *n.* (*Cookery*) a dish of meat or fruit covered with upper or lower pastry crust or both; (*Print.*) a confused mass of type [etym. uncertain].

pie (pī) *n.* a magpie. **-bald** (pī′·bawld) *a.* irregularly marked; streaked with any two colors. **-d** *a.* piebald; variegated [L. *pica*, a magpie: *bald* = *balled*, streaked].

piece (pēs) *n.* a part of anything; a bit; a portion; a single object; a separate example; a coin; a counter in chess, checkers, etc.; a literary work; a musical composition; a gun; a plot of land; *v.t.* to mend; to put together. **— goods** *n.pl.* textile fabrics sold by measured lengths of the material. **— meal** *adv.* little by little; gradually. **— work** *n.* work paid for by the amount done, and not by the hour, day, etc. **— of eight**, an old Spanish dollar = eight reals [Fr. *pièce*].

pier (pir) *n.* a piece of solid, upright masonry, as a support or pillar for an arch, bridge, or beam; a structure built out over the water as a landing. **— glass** *n.* a tall mirror, esp. a wall mirror between two windows [Fr. *pierre*, stone, fr. L. *Petra*].

pierce (pirs) *v.t.* to thrust into, esp. with a pointed instrument; to make a hole in; to penetrate; *v.i.* to enter; to penetrate. **piercing** *a.* penetrating; sharp; keen. **piercingly** *adv.* [Fr. *percer*].

pi·e·ty (pī′·a·ti·) *n.* the quality of being pious; devotion to religion; affectionate respect for one's parents. **pietist** *n.* an ultrapious person; a sanctimonious person. **pietistic** *a.* **pietism** *n.* [L. *pietas*, fr. *pius*, pious].

pig (pig) *n.* a hoofed domestic animal, reared for its flesh; oblong mass of smelted metal, as pig iron; *v.i.* to bring forth pigs. **-gish** *a.* pert. to, or like, pigs; dirty; greedy; stubborn. **-tail** *n.* the tail of a pig; a braid of hair hanging from the back of the head; a roll of twisted tobacco. **—eyed** *a.* having small, sly eyes. **-headed** *a.* obstinate; stupidly perverse. **— iron**, **— lead**, iron, lead, cast in rough oblong bars. **-nut** *n.* the nut of the brown hickory. **-skin** *n.* strong leather made from the pig's skin, and used for saddles, etc. (*Colloq.*) a football. **-sticking** *n.* hunting wild boar with a spear, popular in India. **-sty** *n.* a covered enclosure for keeping pigs; a dirty house or room [M.E. *pigge*].

pi·geon (pij′·an) *n.* any bird of the dove family, both wild and domesticated; a simpleton or dupe. **— English** *n.* See **pidgin English**. **-hearted** *a.* timid. **-hole** *n.* a little division in a desk or case, for holding papers, etc.; *v.t.* to place in the pigeonhole of a desk, etc.; to shelve for future reference; to classify. **—toed** *a.* having turned-in toes [Fr. fr. L. *pipio, pipionis*, a young piping bird].

pig·ment (pig′·mant) *n.* paint; coloring matter; coloring matter in animal tissues and cells. **-ation** *n.* (*Biol.*) coloring matter [L. *pigmentum*].

pigmy. See **pygmy**.

pike (pīk) *n.* a sharp point; an old weapon consisting of a long, wooden shaft with a flat-pointed steel head; a voracious freshwater fish; a turnpike or tollgate. **-staff** *n.* a staff with a sharp metal spike [O.E. *pic*, a point].

pi·las·ter (pī′·las·ter, pī·las′·ter) *n.* a square column, usually set in a wall [It. *pilastro*, fr. L. *pila*, a pillar].

pil·chard (pil′·cherd) *n.* a sea fish resembling the herring, but smaller [etym. uncertain].

pile (pīl) *n.* a mass or collection of things; a heap; a large building or mass of buildings; in atomic energy research, the nuclear energy furnace, made by accumulation of uranium and graphite. (*Colloq.*) a large fortune; *v.t.*

to throw into a pile or heap; to accumulate [L. *pila*, a pillar].

pile (pīl) *n.* a beam driven vertically into the ground to support a building, a bridge etc.; *v.t.* to drive piles into; to support with piles. **-driver** *n.* a machine for driving in piles [O.E. *pil*, a dart].

pile (pīl) *n.* fur or hair; nap of a fabric, esp. if thick and close-set, as in velvet [L. *pilus*, hair].

piles (pīlz) *n.pl.* a disease of the rectum; hemorrhoids [L. *pila*, a ball].

pil·fer (pil′·fer) *v.t.* and *i.* to steal in small quantities [O.Fr. *pelfrer*].

pil·grim (pil′·grim) *n.* a traveler, esp. one who journeys to visit a holy place. **-age** *n.* journey to a holy place; any long journey [O.Fr. *pelegrin*, fr. L. *peregrinus*, a stranger].

pill (pil) *n.* a small ball of medicine, to be swallowed whole; anything disagreeable that has to be endured; (*Slang*) an unpopular person. **-box** *n.* (*Mil.*) a small concrete fort [L. *pilula*, dim. fr. *pila*, a ball].

pil·lage (pil′·ij) *n.* the act of plundering; plunder or spoil; *v.t.* to plunder [Fr. *piller*, fr. L. *pilare*, to plunder].

pil·lar (pil′·er) *n.* a slender upright structure of stone, iron, etc.; a column; a support. **-ed** *a.* [L. *pila*, a column].

pil·lion (pil′·yan) *n.* a cushioned pad put behind the saddle on a horse as a seat for a second person [Gael. *pillean*, a pack-saddle].

pil·lo·ry (pil′·a·ri·) *n.* an old instrument used to punish offenders, consisting of a frame with holes for head and hands in which the person was confined and exposed to pelting and ridicule; *v.t.* to punish by putting into a pillory; to expose to ridicule and abuse. [Fr. *pilori*]

pil·low (pil′·ō) *n.* a cushion, esp. for the head of a person in bed; *v.t.* to place on a pillow. **-case**, **-slip** *n.* a removable covering for a pillow [O.E. *pyle*].

pi·lose (pī′·lōs) *a.* hairy; covered with hair. Also **pilous pilosity** *n.* [L. *pilosus*, hair].

pi·lot (pī′·lat) *n.* a person qualified to take charge of a ship entering or leaving a harbor, or where knowledge of local waters is needed; one qualified to operate an aircraft; a steersman; a guide; a small jet of gas kept burning in order to light a stove, etc.; *v.t.* to direct the course of; to guide through dangers or difficulties. **— engine** *n.* a locomotive sent on ahead to clear the way for a train [Fr. *pilote*].

pi·men·to (pi·men′·tō) *n.* allspice; a reddish pepper [Sp. fr. L. *pigmentum*, spice].

pimp (pimp) *n.* a procurer; a pander; *v.i.* to pander [Fr. *pimper*, to dress up].

pim·per·nel (pim′·per·nel) *n.* an annual plant of the primrose family [Fr. *pimprenelle*].

pim·ple (pim·′pl) *n.* a small, red, pustular spot on the skin. **-d**, **pimply** *a.*

pin (pin) *n.* a short, thin piece of stiff wire with a point and head for fastening soft materials together; a wooden or metal peg or rivet; an ornament that fastens on cloth; (*Golf*) a thin metal or wooden stick (with a flag) to mark the position of the hole; a rolling pin; a clothespin; a trifle; *pl.* (*Slang*) the legs; *v.t.* to fasten with pins; to seize and hold fast. *pr.p.* **-ning.** *pa.p.* and *pa.t.* **-ned. -cushion** *n.* a small pad in which pins are stuck. **— money** *n.* an allowance for incidental or personal expenses. **-point** *v.t.* to locate (a target) with great accuracy. **-up girl** (*Colloq.*) one whose photograph is pinned up on the wall; hence, any good-looking girl [O.E. *pinn*, a peg].

pin·a·fore (pin′·a·fōr) *n.* an apron for a child or young girl [E. *pin* and *afore*].

pince-nez (pans′·nā) *n.* a pair of eyeglasses fixed to the nose by a spring clip [Fr. *pincer*, to pinch; *nez*, the nose].

pin·cers (pin′·serz) *n.pl.* a tool for gripping, composed of two limbs crossed and pivoted; nippers; pliers; the claw of a lobster, crab, etc. [Fr. *pincer*, to pinch)].

pinch (pinch) *v.t.* to nip or squeeze, e.g. between the thumb and finger; to stint; to make thin, e.g. by hunger; (*Slang*) to steal; to arrest; *v.i.* to press hard; to be miserly; *n.* as much as can be taken up between the thumb and finger; an emergency. **-ed** *a.* (*Fig.*) thin and hungry looking [Fr. *pincer*].

Pin·dar (pin′·der) *n.* great lyric poet of ancient Greece (522-443 B.C.). **Pindaric** (pin·dar′·ik) *a.* pert. to the poet or his poetry; *n.* an imitation of one of his odes.

pine (pīn) *n.* a coniferous tree with evergreen, needlelike leaves; wood of this tree; (*Colloq.*) a pineapple. **-y, piny** *a.* **-apple** *n.* tropical plant and its fruit resembling a pine cone; the ananas; (*Mil. Slang*) a hand grenade. **— cone** *n.* fruit of the pine [L. *pinus*].

pine (pīn) *v.t.* to waste away from grief, anxiety, want, etc.; to languish; to wither; to desire eagerly [O.E. *pinian*, fr. *pin*, pain].

pin·fold (pin′·fōld) *n.* a pound; enclosure for stray cattle [for *pindfold* = pound-fold].

ping (ping) *n.* the sound that a bullet makes **—pong** *n.* table tennis [imit.].

pin·ion (pin′·yan) *n.* the outermost joint of a bird's wing; wing; feather; a small wheel with teeth working into the teeth of a larger wheel; *v.t.* to cut off the pinion; to restrain by binding arms to body; to shackle [O.Fr. *pignon*].

pineapple

pink (pingk) *n.* a carnation, a garden flower of various colors; a light crimson color; that which is supremely excellent; *a.* of a pale crimson color [etym. uncertain].

pink (pingk) *v.t.* to pierce with small holes; to pierce with a sword, etc.; to ornament the edge with notches, etc. [M.E. *pinken*, to prick].

pink (pingk) *v.t.* of a motor engine, to make a metallic, knocking sound [imit.].

pin·na (pin′·a) *n.* a feather; the fin of a fish. **-te**, **-ted** *a.* feather-shaped; having wings or fins [L.*pinna*, for *penna*, a feather].

pin·na·cle (pin′·a·kl) *n.* a slender turret elevated above the main building; a rocky mountain peak; a summit; (*Fig.*) the climax [L. *pinna*, a feather, a battlement].

pint (pīnt) *n.* a liquid and a dry measure equal to ½ quart [Fr. *pinte*].

pin·to (pin′·tō) *n.* a piebald horse [Sp.].

pi·o·neer (pī·a·nēr′) *n.* one who originates anything or prepares the way for others; *v.i.* to open a way or originate; an explorer; (*Mil.*) one of an advance body clearing or repairing a road for troops [Fr. *pionnier*, fr. *pion*, a foot-soldier].

pi·ous (pī′·as) *a.* having reverence and love for God; marked by pretended or mistaken devotion; **-ly** *adv.* [L. *pius*].

pip (pip) *n.* the seed of an apple, orange, etc. **-less** *a.* [abbrev. fr. *pippin*].

pip (pip) *n.* a disease in the mouth of fowls [L.L. *pipita*, fr. *pituita*, phlegm].

pip (pip) *n.* a rootstock of a plant; (*Radio*) each of the six shrill notes broadcast as a time signal.

pipe (pīp) *n.* a tubular instrument of music; any long tube; a tube of clay, wood, etc. with a bowl for smoking; a bird's note; a pipeful of tobacco; a pipe-like vein of ore; *pl.* bagpipes; *v.t.* to perform on a pipe; to utter in a shrill tone; to convey by means of pipes; to ornament with a piping or fancy edging; *v.i.* to play on a pipe, esp. the bagpipes; to whistle. **piped** (pīpt) *a.* furnished with a pipe; tubular; conveyed by pipes. **piping** *a.* giving forth a shrill sound; *n.* the act of playing on a pipe; a system of pipes (for gas, water, etc.); a kind of cord trimming for ladies' dresses; ornamentation made on cakes **— clay** *n.* a fine, whitish clay used in the manufacture of tobacco pipes; *v.t.* to whiten with pipe clay. **— line** *n.* a long line of piping for conveying water, oil, etc. [O.E. *pipe*, fr. L. *pipa*].

pi·pette (pi·pet′) *n.* a thin, glass tube used for withdrawing small quantities of a liquid from a vessel [Fr. dim. of *pipe*].

pip·it (pīp′·it) *n.* small bird resembling the lark [imit.].

pip·pin (pip′·in) *a.* one of several kinds of apple [O.Fr. *pepin*, a seed].

pi·quant (pē′·kant) *a.* agreeably pungent to the taste; arousing interest. **-ly** *adv.* **piquancy** (pē′·kan·si·) *n.* [Fr. *piquer*, to prick].

pique (pēk) *v.t.* to irritate; to hurt the pride of; to displease; to stimulate; to pride oneself. *pr.p.* **piquing.** *pa.p.* and *pa.t.* **piqued** (pēkt); *n.* annoyance from a slight; vexation [Fr. *piquer*, to prick].

pi·qué (pi·kā′) *n.* a ribbed cotton fabric [Fr.].

pi·rate (pī′·rat) *n.* a sea robber; a vessel manned by sea robbers; a publisher, etc. who infringes copyright; *v.t.* and *v.i.* to act as a pirate; to plunder; to publish or reproduce regardless of copyright. **piratical** *a.* **pirati-**

cal·ly adv. **piracy** n. [Gk. peirates, fr. peira-ein, to attempt].

pir·ou·ette (pir·óó·et′) n. a spinning round on the toes of one foot; v.i. to do this [Fr.].

pis·ca·tol·o·gy (pis·ka·tăl′·a·ji·) n. the study of fishing. **piscator** (pis·kā′·tor) n. an angler; a fisherman. **piscatorial, piscatory** a. pert. to fishermen or fishing. [L. piscis, a fish].

Pis·ces (pis′·ēz) n.pl. (Astron.) the Fishes, the twelfth sign of the zodiac [L. piscis, a fish].

pis·ci·na (pis·ī·na) n. a stone basin near the altar. -l a. [L. piscis, a fish].

pis·cine (pis′·īn) a. pert. to fishes [L.].

pis·ta·chi·o (pis·ta′(tă′)·shi·ō) n. the nut of an Asiatic tree, whose kernel is used for flavoring [Sp. fr. Gk. pistakion].

pis·til (pis′·tl) n. the seed-bearing organ of a flower, consisting of the stigma, style, and ovary. **-late** a. having a pistil but sometimes no stamen [L. pistillum, a pestle].

pis·tol (pis′·tl) n. a small handgun; v.t. to shoot with a pistol [Fr. pistole].

pis·ton (pis′·tan) n. a closely fitting metal disk moving to and fro in a hollow cylinder, e.g. as in a steam engine, automobile, etc. — **rod** n. a rod which connects the piston with another part of the machinery [It. pistone, fr. L. pinsere, pistum, to pound].

pit (pit) n. a deep hole in the ground, esp. one from which coal etc. is dug or quarried; the abyss of hell; a hollow or depression; an area for cock-fighting, etc.; in the theater, the section for musicians in front of stage; in motor racing, the base where cars are refilled, etc.; v.t. to mark with little hollows, as by pustules; to place in a pit; to put forward as an antagonist in a contest. pr.p. **-ting**. pa.p. and pa.t. **-ted**; a. marked with small hollows. **-fall** n. a pit lightly covered, intended to entrap animals; any hidden danger [O.E. pytt, fr. L. puteus, a well].

pit·a·pat (pit′·a·pat) adv. in a flutter; with palpitation; n. a light, quick step; v.i. to go pitapat. pr.p. **-ting**. pa.p., pa.t. **-ted** [reduplication of pat].

pitch (pich) n. a thick, black, sticky substance obtained by boiling down tar; v.t. to cover over, smear with pitch. **-iness** n. —**black, —dark** a. very dark [L. pix].

pitch (pich) v.t. to throw, toss, fling; to set up (a tent, camp, wickets, etc.); (Music) to set the keynote of; v.i. to alight; to fix one's choice on (with 'on'); to plunge or fall forward; to slope down; of a ship, to plunge. n. the act of tossing or throwing; a throw or toss; steepness of a roof; downward slope; the highest point; the plunging motion of a vessel lengthwise; degree of acuteness of musical note; the distance between consecutive threads of a screw, or between successive teeth of a gear. **-ed** (picht) a. **-er** n. **-fork** n. a fork for tossing hay, etc.; v.t. to lift with a pitchfork [form of pick].

pitch·er (pich′·er) n. a jug; a vessel for pouring liquids, usually with a handle and a lip or spout [L.L. picarium, a goblet].

pith (pith) n. the soft, spongy substance in the center of plant stems; the essential substance; force or vigor. **-y** a. consisting of pith; terse and forceful; energetic. **-ily** adv. **-iness** n. **-less** a. [O.E. pitha].

pit·tance (pit′·ans) n. an allowance for living expenses; a very small income [Fr. pitance, allowance of food in a monastery].

pi·tu·i·tar·y (pi·tū′·a·ter·i) a. pert. to the pituitary gland. — **gland**, a ductless gland at base of the brain, secreting an endocrine influencing growth [L. pituita, mucus].

pit·y (pit′·i·) n. sympathy or sorrow for others' suffering; a cause of grief or regret; v.t. to feel grief or sympathy for. **-ing** a. expressing pity. **-ingly** adv. **pitiable** a. deserving pity. **pitiably** adv. **pitiful** a. full of pity; tender; woeful; exciting pity. **pitifully** adv. **pitifulness** n. **pitiless** a. feeling no pity; hardhearted. **pitilessly** adv. **pitilessness** n. **piteous** (pit′·i·as) a. fitted to excite pity; sad or sorrowful [L. pietas, piety].

piv·ot (piv′·at) n. a pin or shaft on which a

wheel or other body turns; that on which important results depend; v.t. to turn as on a pivot. **-al** a. **-ally** adv. [Fr.].

pix·y, pixie (pik′·si·) n. a fairy or elf. **pix-ilated** a. amusingly eccentric [etym uncert.].

piz·zi·ca·to (pit·si·kà′·tō) a. (Mus.) a direction for stringed instruments denoting that the strings be plucked with the fingers [It.].

pla·ca·ble (plak′·a·bl, plā′·ka·bl) a. readily appeased or pacified; willing to forgive. **-ness, placability** n. **placate** (plak′·āt) v.t. to appease, conciliate. **placatory** a. [L. placare, to appease].

plac·ard (plak′·erd) n. a written or printed paper posted in a public place. **placard** (pla-kard′) v.t. to post placards [Fr.].

place (plās) n. a particular part of space; a spot; a locality; a building; rank; position; priority of position; stead; duty; office or employment; (Sport) a position among the first three competitors to finish; v.t. to put in a particular spot; to find a position for; to appoint; to fix; to put; to identify. **-d** a. in a race, etc., to be first, second, or third at the finish. — **kick** n. (Football) one made by kicking the ball after it has been placed on the ground for the purpose. **to give place**, to make room for [L. platea, a broad street; fr. Gk. platus, broad].

pla·cen·ta (pla·sen′·ta) n. (Med.) the soft, spongy substance (expelled from the womb after birth) through which the mother's blood nourishes the fetus; (Bot.) the part of the plant to which the seeds are attached. **-l** a. [L. = a flat cake].

plac·id (plas′·id) a. calm; peaceful. **-ly** adv. **-ity** n. mildness; sweetness; serenity [L. placidus, fr. placere, to please].

plack·et (plak′·it) n. a slit at the top of a woman's skirt [Fr. plaquet].

pla·gia·rize (plā′·ji·a·riz) v.t. to steal the words, ideas, etc. of another and use them as one's own. **plagiarism** n. the act of plagiarizing; literary theft. **plagiarist** n. **plagiary** n. [L. plagiarius, a kidnapper].

plague (plāg) n. a deadly, epidemic, and infectious disease; a pestilence; a nuisance; v.t. to vex; to trouble or annoy. pr.p. **plaguing**. pa.p. and pa.t. **-d**. **plaguy** (plā′·gi·) a. [L. plaga, a blow].

plaid (plad) n. a long, woolen garment, usually with a tartan pattern, worn as a wrap by Scottish Highlanders; a. marked with stripes. **-ed** a. [Gael. plaide].

plain (plān) a. evident; clear; unobstructed; not intricate; simple; ordinary; without decoration; not beautiful; level; flat; even; adv. clearly; n. a tract of level country. **-ly** adv. **-ness** n. — **sailing** n. an unobstructed course of action. — **song** n. the traditional chants of the Christian church, sung in unison [L. planus, smooth].

plaint (plānt) n. (Poet.) a lamentation; (Law) a statement in writing of the complaint, accusation, etc. **-iff** n. the one who sues in a court of law. **-ive** a. expressing grief; sad; mournful. **-ively** adv. [L. plungere, planctum, to lament].

plait (plāt, plat) n. a fold; a braid of hair, straw, etc., v.t. to interweave strands of hair, straw, etc. Also **pleat** (plēt) [L. plicatus, folded].

plan (plan) n. a drawing representing a thing's horizontal section; a diagram; a map; a project; a design; a scheme; v.t. to make a plan of; to arrange beforehand. pr.p. **-ning**. pa.p. and pa.t. **-ned** [L. planus, flat].

plane (plān) n. a flat, level surface; (Geom.) a surface such that, if any two points on it be joined by a straight line, that line will lie wholly on the surface; a. perfectly level; pert. to, or lying in, a plane. — **geometry**, branch of geometry which deals with plane, not solid, figures [L. planus, level].

plane (plān) n. abbrev. of 'airplane'; the wing of an airplane or glider; v.i. to glide [Fr. planer, to hover].

plan·et (plan′·at) n. a celestial body revolving round the sun (e.g. Venus, Mars, etc.) as distinct from the fixed stars. **-arium** (plan·a-te′·ri·am) n. a working model of the planetary system; a projected representation of the heavens on a dome. **-ary** a. pert. to planets; of the nature of a planet; erratic; wandering; (Astrol.) under the influence of a planet. **-oid** n. a minor planet [Gk. planētēs, wanderer].

plan·gent (plan′·jant) a. of sound, vibrating; resounding. **plangency** n. [L. plangere, to beat].

plan·ish (plan′·ish) v.t. to make smooth or flat by light hammering; to flatten between rollers. **-er** n. [L. planus, level].

plank (plangk) n. a thick, heavy board; an article of policy in a political program; v.t. to lay with planks. **-ing** n. planks collectively [L. planca].

plank·ton (plangk′·tan) n. (Biol.) the minute animal and vegetable organisms floating in the ocean [Gk. planktos, wandering].

plant (plant) n. a living organism belonging to the vegetable kingdom, generally excluding trees and shrubs; a slip or cutting; machinery, tools, etc., used in an industrial undertaking; (Slang) a swindle, hoax, trick; v.t. to set in ground for growth; to implant (ideas, etc.). **-ation** (plan·tā′·shan) n. large estate for growing a certain crop. **-er** n. one who plants; the owner of a plantation [O.E.].

plaque (plak) n. a thin, flat, ornamental tablet hung on a wall or inserted into a wall or furniture [Fr.].

plash (plash) n. a puddle; a splashing sound; v.i. to dabble in water. **-y** a. [Dut. plassen, to splash].

plas·ma (plaz′·ma) n. (Biol.) protoplasm; the fluid part of the blood, as opposed to the corpuscles. Also **plasm**. **-tic, plasmic** a. [Gk. plasma, fr. plassein, to form or mold].

plas·ter (pas′·ter) n. a composition of lime, water, and sand, for coating walls; gypsum, for making ornaments, molds, etc.; (Med.) an adhesive, curative application; (Surg.) a composition used to hold a limb, etc. rigid; v.t. to cover with plaster; to smooth over or conceal. **-er** n. [Gk. plassein, to mold].

plas·tic (plas′·tik) a. capable of molding or of being molded; pliable; capable of change; n. a substance capable of being molded; a group of synthetic products derived from casein, cellulose, etc. which may be molded into any form. **plasticity** (plas·tis′·a·ti·) n. quality of being plastic. — **art**, the art of representing figures in sculpture or by modeling in clay. — **surgery**, the art of restoring lost or damaged parts of the body by grafting on sound tissue [Gk. plassein, to mold].

Plas·ti·cine (plas′·ti·sēn) n. modeling material easily manipulated [Trade Name].

plat (plat) n. map [fr. plot].

plate (plāt) n. a shallow, round dish from which food is eaten; a plateful; a flat, thin sheet of metal, glass, etc.; (Dentistry) a thin sheet of vulcanic, or metal, to hold artificial teeth; (Photog.) short for 'photographic plate'; a separate page of illustrations in a book; v.t. to cover with a thin coating of gold, silver, or other metal; to protect with steel plates, e.g. as a ship. **-r** n. — **armor** n. very heavy, protective armor for warships. — **glass** n. thick glass, rolled in sheets and used for windows, mirrors, etc. [Gk. platus, broad].

pla·teau (pla·tō′) n. a tract of level, high ground. pl. **plateaus, plateaux** (pla·tōz′) [Fr. fr. Gk. platus, flat].

plat·en (plat′·an) n. (Print.) the plate which presses the paper against the type; the roller of a typewriter [O.Fr. platine, a flat piece].

plat·form (plat′·fawrm) n. a wooden structure raised above the level of the floor, as a stand for speakers; a landing area at a railway-station; (Mil.) a stage on which a gun is mounted; policy of a political party [Fr. plate-forme = flat form].

plat·i·num (plat′·a·nam) n. a hard, silvery-white, malleable metal. **platinic, platinous** a. **platinoid** n. a metal found associated with platinum, e.g. iridium; an alloy of copper, zinc, nickel, and tungsten [Sp. platina, fr. plata, silver].

plat·i·tude (plat′·a·tūd) n. a commonplace remark; dullness of writing or speaking. **platitudinous** a. [Fr. fr. Gk. platus, flat].

Pla·to (plā′·tō) n. a famous Greek philosopher (427–347 B.C.). **Platonic** (pla·tàn′·ik) **-nical** a. pert. to Plato or to his philosophy. **-nism** n. the doctrines of Plato. **-nist** n. **Platonic love**, spiritual affection between man and woman without sexual desire.

pla·toon (pla·tóón′) n. (Mil.) a small body of soldiers employed as a unit [Fr. peloton, a knot, a ball].

plat·ter (plat′·er) n. a large, shallow plate or dish [Fr. plat, a dish].

plat·y·pus (plat′·a·pas) n. a small, aquatic, furred animal of Australia; the duckbill [Gk. platus, flat; pous, a foot].

plau·dit (plaw′·dit) n. enthusiastic applause. **-ory** a. expressing approval [L. plaudere, to clap the hands].

plau·si·ble (plaw′·za·bl) a. having the appearance of being true; apparently right; fair-spoken. **plausibly** adv. **plausibility** n. [L. plaudere, to praise].

play (plā) v.t. and i. to move with light or irregular motion; to frolic; to flutter; to amuse oneself; to take part in a game; to gamble; to act a part on the stage; to perform on a musical instrument; to operate; to trifle with; n. a brisk or free movement; activity; action; amusement; fun; frolic; sport gambling; a dramatic piece or performance. **-er** n. **-able** a. **-ful** a. fond of play or fun; lively. **-fully** adv. **-bill** n. a bill or poster to advertise a play. **-boy** n. a habitual pleasure-seeker. **-fellow** n. a playmate. **-ground** n. an open space or courtyard for recreation. **-house** n. a theater. **-mate** n. a companion in play. **-pen** n. a portable enclosure for small children to play in. **-thing** n. a toy. **playwright** (plā′·rīt) n. a writer of plays; a dramatist. **-ing card**, one of a set of cards, usually 52 in number, used in card games [O.E. plegan, to play].

plea (plē) n. (Law) the defendant's answer to the plaintiff's declaration; an excuse; entreaty [Fr. plaider, to plead].

plead (plēd) v.t. to allege in proof or vindication; (Law) to argue at the bar; v.i. to carry on a lawsuit; to present an answer to the declaration of a plaintiff; to urge reasons in support of or against; to beg or implore. pa.p. and pa.t. **-ed**. Also (Colloq.) **pled**. **-er** n. **-ing** a. entreating; n. the art of conducting a cause as an advocate; entreaty; supplication [Fr. plaider].

pleas·ance (plez′·ạns) *n.* a pleasure garden [L. *placere*, to please].

please (plēz) *v.t.* to excite agreeable sensations or emotions in; to gratify; to delight; to satisfy; *v.i.* to give pleasure; used as *abbrev.* of 'if you please,' in a polite request. **pleasant** (plez′·ạnt) *a.* fitted to please; cheerful; lively; merry; agreeable. **pleasantly** *adv.* **pleasantness** *n.* **pleasantry** (plez′·ạnt·ri·) *n.* playfulness in conversation; a joke; a humorous act; *pl.* **pleasantries**. **pleasing** (plē′·zing) *a.* agreeable; gratifying. **pleasingly** *adv.* **pleasingness** *n.* **pleasure** (plezh′·ẹr) *n.* agreeable sensation or emotion; gratification of the senses or mind; amusement, diversion, or self-indulgence; choice; a source of gratification. **pleasurable** *a.* **pleasurably** *adv.* [L. *placere*, to please].

pleat (plēt) *n.* a flattened fold fastened in position; *v.t.* to make pleats [var. of *plait*].

ple·be·ian (pli·bē′·an) *a.* pert. to or belonging to the common people; vulgar; uncultured; *n.* a common person [L. *plebs*, common people].

pleb·i·scite (pleb′·i·sīt, pleb′·i·sit) *n.* a vote of the whole community or nation [L. *plebis citum*, a decree of the plebs].

plec·trum (plek′·trạm) *n.* a small device used for plucking the strings of a mandalin, etc. Gk. *plēktron*, fr. *plēssein*, to strike].

pledge (plej) *n.* something deposited as a security; a sign or token of anything; a drinking to the health of; a solemn promise; *v.t.* to deposit in pawn; to leave as security; to engage for, by promise or declaration; to drink the health of [O.Fr. *plege*].

ple·na·ry (plē′·nạ·ri·, ple′·nạ·ri·) *a.* full, entire, complete; unqualified; (for an assembly) fully attended. **plenarily** *adv.* **plenariness** *n.* **plenipotentiary** (plen·ạ·pạ·ten′·shạ·ri·) *n.* an ambassador with full powers; *a.* possessing full powers. **plenitude** (plen′·ạ·tūd) *n.* fullness; abundance [L. *plenus*, full; *potens*, potent].

plen·ty (plen′·ti·) *n.* a full supply; abundance; quite enough; sufficiency. **plenteous** (plen′·ti·as) *a.* copious; abundant; rich. **plenteously** *adv.* **plentiful** *a.* abundant; ample. **plentifully** *adv.* [L. *plenus*, full].

ple·num (plē′·nạm) *n.* space as considered to be full of matter (opposed to *vacuum*); a condition of fullness [L. *plenus*, full].

pleth·o·ra (pleth′·ạ·ra) *n.* an excess of red corpuscles in the blood; superabundance. **plethoric** *a.* [Gk. *plethōra*, fullness].

pleu·ra (ploo′·ra) *n.* (*Med.*) the membrane lining the chest and covering the lungs. *pl.* **-e.** **-l** *a.* **pleurisy** *n.* (*Med.*) inflammation of the pleura [Gk. *pleura*, the side].

plex·us (pleks′·ạs) *n.* a network, esp. of nerves, blood vessels, fibers, etc. **plexal** *a.* [L. = a twining].

pli·a·ble (plī′·ạ·bl) *a.* easily bent; easily influenced. Also **pliant** (plī′·ạnt). **pliably** *adv.* **pliantly** *adv.* **pliability, pliancy** *n.* [L. *plicare*, to fold].

pli·ca (plī′·kạ) *n.* a fold. **-te, -ted** *a.* (*Bot.*) folded; pleated [L. *plicare*, to fold].

pli·ers (plī′·ẹrz) *n.pl.* small pincers with a flat grip [fr. *ply*, to bend].

plight (plīt) *n.* a state or condition of a distressing kind; predicament [L. *plicare*, to fold; O.E. *plit*, a fold or plait].

plight (plīt) *v.t.* to pledge, as one's word of honor; to betroth [O.E. *pliht*, risk].

plinth (plinth) *n.* a square slab, forming the base of a column; the projecting band running along the foot of a wall [Gk. *plinthos*, a brick].

plod (plåd) *v.t.* to tread with a heavy step; *v.i.* to walk or work laboriously; to toil or drudge *pr.p.* **-ding** *pa.t.*, *pa.p.* **-ded** [imit.].

plot (plåt) *n.* a small patch of ground; a plan of a field, farm, etc. drawn to scale; the plan of a play, novel, etc.; a secret scheme; a conspiracy. *v.t.* to draw a graph or plan of; to plan or scheme. *v.i.* to conspire. *pr.p.* **-ting** *pa.t.*, *pa.p.* **-ted** [O.Fr. *pelote* clod; *Fr. complot*].

---

plov·er (pluv′·ẹr) *n.* one of various kinds of wading birds [L. *pluvia*, rain].

plow (plou) *n.* an implement with a heavy cutting blade for turning up the soil; *v.t.* to turn up with the plow; to furrow; to advance laboriously; *v.i.* to till the soil with a plow. **-share** *n.* the heavy iron blade of a plow [O.E. *ploh*].

pluck (pluk) *v.t.* to pull off; to pick, as flowers; to strip off feathers, as a fowl; to snatch, or pull with sudden force; *n.* a pull or jerk; the act of plucking; courage or spirit. **-y** *a.* brave; spirited. **-iness** *n.* [O.E. *pluccian*].

plug (plug) *n.* anything used to stop a hole; a cake of compressed tobacco; (*Elect.*) a device for connecting and disconnecting of a circuit; *abbrev.* for spark plug; *v.t.* to stop with a plug; to insert a plug in; (*Slang*) to shoot; (*Slang*) to advertise a song or tune by having it played constantly; *v.i.* (*Colloq.*) to keep doggedly at work (with 'at'). *pr.p.* **-ging.** *pa.p.* and *pa.t.* **-ged** [Dut.].

plum (plum) *n.* a round or oval fruit; the tree that bears it; a particularly good appointment or position; a dark purplish color [O.E. *plume*].

plum·age (ploo′·mij) *n.* a bird's feathers, collectively [Fr. fr. L. *pluma*, a feather].

plumb (plum) *n.* a weight of lead attached to a line, and used to determine perpendicularity; the perpendicular position; *a.* perpendicular; *adv.* perpendicularly; (*Colloq.*) utterly, absolutely; *v.t.* to adjust by a plumb line; to sound or take the depth of water with a plummet. **-er** (plum′·ẹr) *n.* one who installs or repairs water and sewage systems. **-ic** *a.* (*Chem.*) containing lead. **-ing** (plum′·ing) *n.* the trade of a plumber; the system of water and sewage pipes in a building. **— line** *n.* a weighted string for testing the perpendicular. **— bob** *n.* the weight at the end of this line [L. *plumbum*, lead].

plum·ba·go (plum·bā′·gō) *n.* black lead; graphite [L. *plumbum*, lead].

plume (ploom) *n.* a feather or tuft of feathers; a crest on a helmet; a token of honor; *v.t.* to furnish with plumes; (*Fig.*) to boast of [L. *pluma*, a feather].

plum·met (plum′·it) *n.* a plumb bob; a weight; *v.i.* to fall like a dead weight [L. *plumbum*, lead].

plump (plump) *a.* of rounded form; moderately fat. **-ness** *n.* [Dut. *plomp*, blunt].

plump (plump) *v.i.* to fall or sit down heavily and suddenly; to vote for one candidate; *v.t.* to drop or throw abruptly; *a.* direct; abrupt; downright; *adv.* heavily; abruptly; bluntly; *n.* a sudden fall [perh. imit. origin].

plu·mule (ploo′·mūl) *n.* a small, downy feather; [L. *pluma*, a feather].

plun·der (plun′·dẹr) *v.t.* to rob systematically; to take by force; *n.* the act of robbing by force; property so obtained. [Ger. *plündern*].

plunge (plunj) *v.t.* to thrust forcibly into; to immerse suddenly in a liquid; *v.i.* to throw oneself headlong into; (*Colloq.*) to gamble recklessly; *n.* the act of plunging; a dive; a sudden rush. **-r** *n.* one who plunges; a solid, cylindrical rod used as a piston in pumps [Fr. *plonger*, fr. L. *plumbum*, lead].

plu·per·fect (ploo′·pur·fikt) *a.* (*Gram.*) of a tense, expressing action completed before another action in the past [L. *plus quam perfectum*, more than perfect].

plu·ral (ploo′·ral) *a.* more than one; (*Gram.*) denoting more than one person or thing; *n.* (*Gram.*) a word in its plural form. **-ly** *adv.* **-ism** *n.* (*Philos.*) doctrine that existence has more than one ultimate principle. **-ist** *n.* **-istic** *a.* **-ity** *n.* large number; a majority of votes; state of being plural [L. *plus*, more].

---

plus (plus) *n.* symbol of addition (+); positive quantity; extra quantity; *a.* to be added; (*Math.*, *Elect.*, etc.) positive; *prep.* with the addition of. **— fours** *n.pl.* wide knickers worn by golfers [L. *plus*, more].

plush (plush) *n.* a fabric with a long, velvet-like nap [Fr. *peluche*, fr. L. *pilus*, hair].

Plu·to (ploo′·tō) *n.* (*Myth.*) god of the lower world; the planet farthest from the sun. **-nic rocks** (*Geol.*) name given to igneous rocks formed by action of intense subterranean heat. **-nium** *n.* a metal of high atomic weight made by bombarding atoms of uranium with neutrons.

plu·toc·ra·cy (ploo·tåk′·rạ·si·) *n.* government by the wealthy class. **plutocrat** *n.* a wealthy person. **plutocratic** *a.* [Gk. *ploutos*; *kratein*, to rule].

plu·vi·al (ploo′·vi·ạl) *a.* pert. to rain; rainy. Also **pluvious** [L. *pluvia*, rain].

ply (plī) *v.t.* to wield; to work at steadily; to use or practice with diligence; to urge; *v.i.* to work steadily; of a boat, etc. to run regularly between fixed places [fr. *apply*].

ply (plī) *n.* a fold; a strand of yarn; thickness. *pl.* **plies.** **-wood** *n.* board made of two or more thin layers of wood cemented together [Fr. *plier*, to fold, fr. L. *plicare*].

pneu·mat·ic (nū·mat′·ik) *a.* pert. to air or gas; inflated with wind or air; operated by compressed wind or air. **-s** *n.pl.* the branch of physics dealing with the mechanical properties of gases [Gk. *pneuma*, breath].

pneu·ma·tol·o·gy (nū·mạ·tál′·a·ji·) *n.* the doctrine of spiritual existences [Gk. *pneuma*, spirit; *logos*, a discourse].

pneu·mo·nia (nū·mō′·ni·ạ) *n.* acute inflammation of a lung [Gk. *pneuma*, breath].

poach (pōch) *v.t.* to cook eggs, by breaking them into a pan of boiling water [Fr. *pocher*].

poach (pōch) *v.t.* and *i.* (*chiefly Brit.*) to take game or fish from another's property without permission. **-er** *n.* [Fr. *poche*, a pocket].

pock (påk) *n.* pustule on skin, as in smallpox. **— mark** *n.* pit left in skin by pock [O.E. *poc*, a pustule].

pock·et (påk′·it) *n.* a small pouch or bag inserted into a garment; a cavity or hollow; (*Mil.*) isolated area held by the enemy; *v.t.* to put in the pocket; to take surreptitiously, esp. money; to accept without resentment, as an insult. **— battleship** *n.* a heavily armored, high-powered, German battleship, of not more than 10,000 tons. **-book** *n.* a small bag or case for holding money or papers. **— money** *n.* money for small, personal expenses, e.g. allowance to child. **in pocket**, having funds [Fr. *pochette*, dim. of *poche*, pouch].

pod (påd) *n.* a seed vessel of a plant, esp. a legume, as peas, beans, etc.

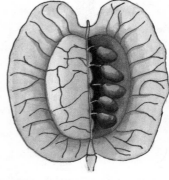

po·em (pō′·ạm) *n.* a composition in verse; any composition written in elevated and imginative language; opp. to 'prose.' **poesy** *n.* poetry. **poetically** *adv.* **poetics** *n.* principles of art of poetry; criticism of poetry. **poetry** (pō′·it·ri·) *n.* language of imagination expressed in verse; metrical composition. **poetaster** (pō′·it·as·tẹr) *n.* a would-be poet; a petty rhymster. **poeticize, poetize** *v.t.* and *i.* to treat poetically; to write poetry. **poetic justice**, ideal justice, in which crime is punished and virtue rewarded. **poetic license**, latitude in grammar or facts, allowed to poets. **poet laureate**, official poet [Gk. *poiēma*, fr. *poiein*, to make].

poign·ant (poin′·ạnt, poin′·yạnt) *a.* acutely painful; strongly appealing; pungent. **-ly** *adv.* **poignancy** *n.* [L. *pungere*, to prick].

point (point) *n.* sharp or tapering end of anything; dot or mark; dot in decimal system; punctuation mark; full stop; (*Geom.*) that which has position but no magnitude; item or detail; gist of argument; striking or effective part of a speech, story, etc.; moment of time; purpose; physical quality in animals, esp. for judging purposes; (*Geog.*) headland; one of the 32 direction marks of a compass; unit of scoring in certain games; (*Print.*) unit of measurement of size of type (72 points = 1 inch); a fine lace made with a needle; *v.t.* to sharpen; to give value, force, etc. to words, etc.; to aim or direct; to fill up joints with mortar; to punctuate: *v.i.* to show direction or position by extending a finger, stick, etc.; of a dog, to indicate the position of game by standing facing it. **-ed** *a.* having a sharp point; direct; telling; aimed; (*Archit.*) pert. to the style having pointed arches, i.e. Gothic. **-edly** *adv.* **-edness** *n.* **-less** *a.* having no point; blunt; irrelevant; insipid.**-er** *n.* **-ing** *n.* punctuation; filling the crevices of walls with mortar.—**blank** *a.* aimed horizontally; straightforward; *adv.* at short range [L. *punctum*, fr. *pungere*, to prick].

poise (poiz) *v.t.* to place or hold in a balanced or steady position; *v.i.* to be so held; to hover; to balance; *n.* equilibrium; carriage of the head, body, etc.; self-possession [L. *pendere*, to weigh].

poi·son (poi'·zn) *n.* any substance which kills or injures when introduced into a living organism; that which has an evil influence on health or moral purity; to give poison to; to infect; to corrupt. **-er** *n.* **-ous** *a.* having a deadly or injurious quality; corrupting. **-ously** *adv.* — **ivy** *n.* a vine which, if touched, causes a skin rash. **-pen** *n.* writer of malicious, anonymous letters [L. *potio*, *potion*].

poke (pōk) *v.t.* to push or thrust against with a pointed object, e.g. with a finger, stick, etc.; to thrust in; to tease; *v.i.* to make thrusts; to pry; to dawdle; a thrust or push; a woman's bonnet with a projecting brim.**-r** *n.* a metal rod for stirring the fire. **poky** *a.* small; slow [M.E. *poken*].

poke (pōk) *n.* (*Dial.*) a sack; a small bag [Fr. *poche*, a pocket].

pok·er (pō'·ker) *n.* a card game in which the players bet on the value of their hands. —**faced** *a.* having an expressionless face.

po·lar (pō'·ler) *a.* pert. to, or situated near, the North or South Poles; pert. to the magnetic poles (points on the earth's surface where a magnetic needle dips vertically); pert. to either pole of a magnet; directly opposed; having polarity. **-ity** (pō·lar'·a·ti·) *n.* the state of being polar; the condition of having opposite poles; the power of being attracted to one pole, and repelled from the other. — **bear**, a large, white bear, found in the Arctic regions [Gk. *polos*, a pivot].

polar bear

po·lar·ize (pō'·la·rīz) *v.t.* to give polarity to; (*Elect.*) to reduce the electromotive force (E.M.F.) of a primary cell by the accumulation of certain electrolytic products on the plates; (*Chem.*) to separate the positive and negative charges on a molecule; (*Light*) to confine the vibrations of light waves to certain directions, e.g. to a plane. **polarization** *n.* **polaroid** *n.* [fr. *polar*].

pole (pōl) *n.* a long, rounded piece of wood or metal; a measure of length = 5½ yards; a measure of area = 30¼ square yards; *v.t.* to propel with a pole. — **jump** *n.* in athletics, a jump over a high bar with the help of a long pole [L. *palus*, a stake].

pole (pōl) *n.* either of the ends of the axis of a sphere, esp. of the earth (in the latter case called the North Pole and South Pole); either of the opposite ends or terminals of a magnet, electric battery, etc. **-star** *n.* the North Star; a guide; an indicator [Gk. *polos*, a pivot].

Pole (pōl) *n.* a native of Poland. **Polish** *a.* pert. to Poland or the Poles.

pole·axe (pōl'·aks) *n.* a battle axe with a long handle. [E. *poll*, the head, and *axe*].

pole·cat (pōl'·kat) *n.* a small, carnivorous animal, resembling the weasel; a skunk [O.Fr. *pole*, a hen (fr. its preying on poultry)].

po·lem·ic (pō·lem'·ik) *a.* controversial; disputatious; *n.* controversy; controversialist. **-s** *n.pl.* art of controversy; controversial writings or discussions, esp. religious. Also **polemical** *a.* **polemically** *adv.* [Gk. *polemos*, war].

po·lice (pa·lēs') *n.* the civil force which maintains public order; the members of the force; *v.t.* to control with police; to keep in order. —**man**, — **officer** *n.* (*fem.* **-woman**) member

of a police force. — **court** *n.* a court for the trial of minor offenses. — **station** *n.* the headquarters of the police [Gk. *polis*, a city].

pol·i·cy (pál'·a·si·) *n.* a course of action adopted, esp. in state affairs; prudent procedure [Gk. *polis*, a city].

pol·i·cy (pál'·a·si·) *n.* a document containing a contract of insurance [Gk. *apodeixis*, proof].

pol·i·o·my·e·li·tis (pōl·i·ō·mī·a·lī'·tis) *n.* (*Med.*) inflammation of the grey matter of the spinal cord; infantile paralysis; *abbrev.* **polio** [Gk. *polios*, grey; *muelos*, marrow].

pol·ish (pál'·ish) *v.t.* to make smooth and glossy; to make polite and cultured; *v.i.* to become polished; *n.* the act of polishing; a smooth, glassy surface; a substance used in polishing; refinement; elegance of manners. **-er** *n.* [Fr. *polir*, fr. L. *polire*].

Pol·ish See Pole.

po·lite (pa·līt') *a.* elegant in manners; well-bred; courteous; refined. **-ly** *adv.* **-ness** *n.* [L. *politus*, polished].

pol·i·tic (pál'·a·tik) *a.* prudent; wise; shrewd; cunning; advisable. **-s** *n.pl.* the art of government; political affairs, life, or principles. **-ly** *adv.* **-al** *a.* pert. to the state or its affairs; pert. to politics. **-ally** *adv.* **politician** (pál·a·tish'·an) *n.* a holder of a political position; a statesman; a member of a political party. **polity** *n.* civil government; the form or constitution of government. **political economy**, the science dealing with the nature, production, distribution, and consumption of wealth [Fr. *politique*, fr. Gk. *polis*, a city].

pol·ka (pōl'·ka) *n.* a lively dance of Bohemian origin; music for it [fr. *Polish*].

poll (pōl) *n.* (top of the) head; a register of persons; a list of persons entitled to vote; (the place) of voting; number of votes recorded; *v.t.* to cut off the top of, e.g. tree; to cut short horns of cattle; to canvass; to receive (votes); to cast a vote; *v.i.* to vote. — **tax** *n.* a tax on each person who votes. [Low Ger. *polle*, the head].

pol·lack (pál·ak) *n.* fresh water fish.

pol·lard (pál'·erd) *n.* a tree on which a close head of young branches has been made by polling; a hornless animal of a normally horned varietye. See **poll**.

pol·len (pál'·an) *n.* the fertilizing dust of a flower. **pollinate** *v.t.* to fertilize a flower by conveying pollen to the pistil [L. = fine flour].

pol·lute (pa·lóōt') *v.t.* to make foul or unclean; to defile; to desecrate. **pollution** *n.* [L. *polluere*].

po·lo (pō'·lō) *n.* a game like hockey played on *horseback*; also **water polo**.

pol·o·naise (pál·a·nāz') *n.* a slow stately dance, of Polish origin; the music for it [Fr. = Polish].

po·lo·ni·um (pa·lō'·ni·am) *n.* a metallic, radio active chemical [fr. *Poland*].

pol·ter·geist (pōl'·ter·gist) *n.* a mysterious spirit believed to create noise and disturbance [Ger. *Polter*, uproar; *Geist*, a ghost].

pol·troon (pál·tróōn') *n.* a coward. **-ery** *n.* [Fr. *poltron*, fr. It. *poltro*, lazy].

pol·y- prefix fr. Gk. *polus*, many words used in derivatives. **polyandry** (pál'·i·an·dri·) *n.* a custom by which a wife has more than one husband. **-androus** *a.* (*Bot.*) having more than 20 stamens. **-chrome** *n.* a picture, statue, etc. in several colors. **-chromatic**, **-chromic**, **-chromous** *a.* many-colored.

po·lyg·a·my (pa·lig'·a·mi·) *n.* the practice of having more than one wife at the same time. **polygamous** *a.* **polygamist** *n.* [Gk. *polus*, many; *gamos*, marriage].

pol·y·glot (pál'·i·glát) *a.* pert. to, or speaking, several languages; *n.* a person who speaks several languages; a book, esp. the Bible, in which the text is printed side by side in different languages [Gk. *polus*, many; *glotta*, tongue].

pol·y·gon (pál'·i·gán) *n.* a plane figure with more than four sides or angles. **polygonal** *a.* [Gk. *polus*, many; *gōnia*, an angle].

po·lyg·y·ny (pa·lij'·a·ny) *n.* practice of polygamy [See *polygamy*].

pol·y·he·dron (pál·i·hē'·dran) *n.* (*Geom.*) a solid figure with many faces, usually more than six [Gk. *polus*, many; *hedra*, a base].

pol·y·mor·phous (pál·i·mawr'·fas) *a.* assuming many forms. Also **polymorphic**. **polymorphism** *n.* [Gk. *polus*, many; *morphē*, form].

Pol·y·ne·sia (pál·a·nē'·zha) *n.* (*Geog.*) a group of islands in the S. Pacific, east of Australia; *n.* a. [Gk. *polus*, many; *nēsos*, an island].

pol·y·no·mi·al (pál·i·nō'·mi·al) *n.* (*Alg.*) a quantity having many terms [Gk. *polus*, many; L. *nomen*, a name].

pol·y·phon·ic (pal·i·fan'·ik) *a.* pert. to polyphony. **polyphony** (pal·if'·an·i·) *n.* (*Mus.*) a kind of composition in which melodic

strains are simultaneously developed without being subordinate to each other [Gk. *polus*, many; *phonē*, a voice].

pol·y·syl·la·ble (pál·i·sil'·a·bl) *n.* a word of three or more syllables. **polysyllabic** *a.* [Gk. *polus*, many, and *syllable*].

pol·y·tech·nic (pál·i·tek'·nik) *a.* pert. to many arts and sciences; *n.* a school or college of applied arts and sciences [Gk. *polus*, many; *technē*, art].

pol·y·the·ism (pál·i·thē·izm) *n.* belief in the existence of many gods, or in more than one. **polytheist** *n.* **polytheistic** *a.* [Gk. *polus*, many; *theos*, a god].

po·made (pō·mād') *n.* scented ointment for the hair. Also **pomatum**. **pomander** *n.* ball of case for mixture of perfumes [L. Fr. *pommade*].

pome (pōm) *n.* any fruit having a fleshy body, core, etc. like the apple, pear, pomegranate, etc. [L. *pomum*, an apple].

pome·gran·ate (pám'·gra·nit) *n.* a large fruit containing many seeds in a red pulp [L. *pomum*, an apple, *granatum*, having seeds].

pom·er·a·ni·an (pám·a·rā'·ni·an) *n.* a small breed of dog with bushy tail, sharp pointed muzzle, pointed ears and long silky hair [fr. *Pomerania*, in Germany].

pom·mel (pum'·al) *n.* the knob of a sword hilt; the front part of a saddle; *v.t.* to strike repeatedly, as with the fists [O. Fr. *pomel*, a little apple].

pomp (pámp) *n.* splendid display or ceremony; magnificence. **-ous** *n.* showy with grandeur; of a person, self-important; of language, inflated. **-ously** *adv.* **-ousness** *n.* **-osity** *n.* [Gk. *pompē*, a solemn procession].

pom·pa·dour (pám'·pa·dōr) *n.* woman's high swept hairstyle; man's hair style with hair brushed up from forehead [Fr. *Marquese de Pompadour*].

pom·pa·no (pám'·pa·nō) *n.* food fish [Sp.].

pom·pon (pám'·pán) *n.* the ball of colored wool worn in front of the shako, etc.; small, compact chrysanthemum [Fr.].

pond (pánd) *n.* a pool of water, either naturally or artificially enclosed [same as *pound*].

pon·der (pán'·der) *v.t.* to weigh in the mind; to consider attentively; *v.i.* to meditate. **-er** *n.* **-ing** *a.* [L. *pondus*, weight].

pon·der·ous (pán'·der·as) *a.* very heavy; weighty; massive; unwieldy; dull or lacking in spirit. **-ly** *adv.* **-ness** *n.* **ponderosity** *n.*

pon·iard (pán'·yerd) *n.* a slender dagger [Fr. *poignard*, fr. *poing*, the fist].

pon·tiff (pán'·tif) *n.* the Pope; a bishop; a high priest. **pontifical** *a.* belonging to a high priest; popish; pompous and dogmatic; *n.pl.* the garb of a priest, bishop, or pope. **pontifically** *adv.* **pontificate** *n.* the state, dignity, or term of office of a priest, bishop, or pope. [L. *pontifex*, a high priest].

pon·toon (pán·tóōn') *n.* a low, flat-bottomed boat; a support in building a temporary bridge [Fr. fr. L. *pons*, a bridge].

po·ny (pō'·ni·) *n.* a small breed of horse; [O.Fr. *poulenet*, fr. *poulain*, a colt].

poo·dle (póō'·dl) *n.* one of a breed of dogs with thick, curly hair, often clipped into ornamental tufts [Ger. *Pudel*].

pooh (póō) *interj.* an exclamation of scorn or contempt. **pooh-pooh** *v.t.* to express contempt.

pool (póōl) *n.* a small body of still water; a deep place in a river [O.E. *pol*].

pool (póōl) *n.* the collective stakes in various games; the place where the stakes are put; a variety of billiards; a combination of capitalists to fix prices and divide into a common fund; *v.i.* to form a pool [Fr. *poule*, a hen].

poop (póōp) *n.* the stern of a ship; raised deck at the stern [L. *puppis*, the stern].

poor (poor) *a.* having little or no money; without means; needy; miserable; wretched; unfortunate; feeble; deserving of pity; unproductive; of inferior quality. **-ly** *adv.* inadequately; with little or no success; without spirit; *a.* (*Colloq.*) somewhat ill; out of sorts. **-ness** *n.* —**spirited** *a.* cowardly; mean. **-house** *n.* an institution for lodging the poor at public expense [L. *pauper*, poor].

pop (páp) *n.* an abrupt, small explosive sound; a shot; an effervescing drink; *v.i.* to make a sharp, quick sound; to go or come unexpectedly or suddenly; to dart; *v.t.* to put or place suddenly; *adv.* suddenly. *pr.p.* **-ping** *pa.p.* and *pa.t.* **-ped. -corn** *n.* Indian corn exposed to heat causing it to burst open. **-gun** *n.* a child's toy gun for shooting pellets, etc. by the expansion of compressed air [imit. origin].

Pope (pōp) *n.* the Bishop of Rome and head of the R.C. Church. **popish** (pō′-pish) *a.* pert. to the Pope or the papacy. **-dom** *n.* the office, dignity, or jurisdiction of the Pope. [L. *papa*, father].

pop-in-jay (pắp′-in-jã) *n.* a vain, conceited fellow [O.Fr. *papegai*, a parrot].

pop-lar (pắp′-ler) *n.* a tree noted for its slender tallness [L. *populus*].

pop-lin (pắp′-lin) *n.* a corded fabric of silk, cotton, or worsted [etym. uncertain].

pop-py (pắp′-i) *n.* a bright flowered plant, one species of which yields opium [L. *papaver*, a poppy].

pop-py-cock (pắp′-i-kắk) *n.* nonsense.

pop-u-lace (pắp′-ya-lis) *n.* the common people; the masses. **populate** *v.t.* to people. **population** *n.* the total number of people in a country, town, etc. **populous** *a.* thickly inhabited [L. *populus*, the people].

pop-u-lar (pắp′-ya-ler) *a.* pert. to the common people; liked by the people; finding general favor; easily understood. **-ly** *adv.* **-ize** *v.t.* to make popular; to make familiar, plain, easy, etc. to all. **-ization** *n.* **-ity** *n.* public favor [L. *populus*, the people].

por-ce-lain (pōrs′-lin, pōr′-sa-lin) *n.* the finest kind of earthenware—white, glazed and semi-transparent; china; *a.* made of porcelain [It. *porcellana*, a delicate shellfish].

porch (pōrch) *n.* a covered entrance to a doorway; a veranda [L. *porticus*, a colonnade].

por-cine (pawr′-sin) *a.* pert. to, or like, swine; swinish [L. *porcus*, a pig].

por-cu-pine (pawr′-kya-pin) *n.* a large quadruped of the rodent family, covered with spines [L. *porcus*, a pig; *spina*, a spine].

pore (pōr) *n.* a minute opening in the skin for the passage of perspiration. **porous** *a.* full of pores [Gk. *poros*, a passage].

pore (pōr) *v.i.* to look at with steady attention, esp. in reading or studying (with 'over').

pork (pōrk) *n.* the flesh of swine used for food. **-y** *a.* like pork; fat; greasy. **-er** *n.* a hog, fattened for eating. [L. *porcus*, a pig].

por-nog-ra-phy (pawr-nắg′-ra-fi-) *n.* obscene literature or pictures. **pornographer** *n.* **pornographic** *a.* [Gk. *pornē*, a harlot; *graphein*, to write].

por-poise (par′-pas) *n.* a blunt-nosed cetacean mammal 5 to 8 feet long, frequenting the northern seas; a dolphin [L. *porcus*, a hog; *piscis*, a fish].

por-ridge (pawr′-ij) *n.* (*Brit.*) a soft breakfast food [form of *pottage*].

por-rin-ger (pawr′-in-jer) *n.* a small bowl for porridge [Fr. *potager*, a soup-basin].

port (pōrt) *n.* a harbor; a town with a harbor; a haven; a refuge [L. *portus*].

port (pōrt) *n.* the way in which a person carries himself; *v.t.* (*Mil.*) to carry (a rifle) slanting upwards in front of the body. **-ly** *a.* dignified in appearance; corpulent [L. *portare*, to carry].

port (pōrt) *n.* a strong, sweet, dark-red wine [fr. *Oporto*, Portugal].

port (pōrt) *n.* the left side of a ship, looking towards the bow.

port-a-ble (pōr′-ta-bl) *a.* capable of being easily carried. **portability** *n.* [L. *portare*, to carry].

por-tage (pōr′-tij) *n.* the act of carrying or transporting goods; the charge for transport; [L. *portare*, to carry].

por-tal (pōrt′-al) *n.* a gate or entrance. [Fr. *portail*, fr. L. *porta*, a gate].

por-tend (pōr-tend′) *v.t.* to foretell; to give warning in advance; to be an omen of. **portent** *n.* an omen, esp. of evil. **portentous** *a.* serving to portend; ominous [L. *portendere*, to foretell].

por-ter (pōr′-ter) *n.* a door- or gatekeeper; railway sleeping-car attendant [L. *porta*, gate].

por-ter (pōr′-ter) *n.* one employed to carry baggage, esp. at stations or hotels. **-age** *n.* fee for hire of a porter.

por-ter-house (pōr′-ter-house) *n.* place where beer (porter) was served. **— steak** choice cut of beef next to the sirloin [L. *portare*, to carry].

port-fo-li-o (pōrt-fō′-li-ō) *n.* case for holding loose documents, drawings, etc.; office of a minister of state [L. *portare*, to carry; *folium*, a leaf].

port-hole (pōrt′-hōl) *n.* window in side of

---

ship [L. *porta*, gate].

por-ti-co (pōr′-ti-kō) *n.* (*Archit.*) a row of columns in front of the entrance to a building; a covered walk [L. *porticus*].

por-tion (pōr′-shan) *n.* a piece; a part; a share; a helping of food; destiny; lot; a dowry; *v.t.* to divide into shares; to give a dowry to. **-less** *a.* [L. *portio*].

por-tray (pōr-trã′) *v.t.* to represent by drawing, painting, acting, or imitating; to describe vividly in words. **-al** *n.* the act of portraying; the representation. **-er** *n.* **portrait** (pōr′-trãt) *n.* picture of a person, esp. of the face; a graphic description of a person in words. **portraiture** *n.* the art of portrait painting [L. *protrahere*, to draw forth].

Por-tu-guese (pōr′-cha-gēz′) *a.* pert. to Portugal, its inhabitants, or language.

pose (pōz) *n.* attitude or posture of a person, natural or assumed; a mental attitude or affectation; *v.t.* to place in a position for the sake of effect; to lay down or assert; *v.i.* to assume an attitude; to affect or pretend to be of a certain character [Fr. *poser*, to place].

pose (pōz) *v.t.* to puzzle; to embarrass by a difficult question. **-r** *n.* [short fr. *oppose*].

pos-it (pắz′-it) *v.t.* to place or set in position; to lay down as a fact or principle [L. *ponere*, *positum*, to place].

po-si-tion (pa-zish′-an) *n.* place; situation; the manner in which anything is arranged; posture; social rank or standing; employment [L. *ponere positum*, to place].

pos-i-tive (pắz′-a-tiv) *a.* formally laid down; clearly stated; absolute; dogmatic; of real value; confident; not negative; plus; (*Math.*) pert. to a quantity greater than zero; (*Gram.*) denoting the simplest value of an adjective or adverb; (*Colloq.*) utter; downright; *n.* the positive degree of an adjective or adverb, i.e. without comparison; in photography, a print in which the lights and shadows are not reversed (as in the negative). **-ly** *adv.* **-ness** *n.* **positivism** *n.* the philosophical system which recognizes only matters of fact and experience. **positivist** *n.* a believer in this doctrine. **— pole**, of a magnet, the north-seeking-pole. **— sign**, the sign (+ read *plus*) of addition [L. *ponere*, *positum*, to place].

pos-i-tron (pắz′-a-trān) *n.* particle differing from an electron in that it has positive electrical charge; a positive electron.

pos-se (pắs′-i-) *n.* a company or force, usually with legal authority; men under orders of the sheriff, maintaining law and order [L. *posse*, to be able].

pos-sess (pa-zes′) *v.t.* to own or hold as property; to have as an attribute; to enter into and influence, as an evil spirit or passions. **-ed** *a.* influenced, as by an evil spirit; demented. **-ion** *n.* the act of possessing; ownership; actual occupancy; the state of being possessed; the thing possessed. **-ive** *a.* denoting possession; *n.* (*Gram.*) the possessive case or pronoun. **-ively** *adv.* **-or** *n.* [L. *possidere*, *possessum*, to possess].

pos-si-ble (pắs′-a-bl) *a.* capable of being or of coming into, being; feasible. **possibly** *adv.* **possibility** *n.* [L. *possibilis*].

pos-sum (pắs′-am) *n.* (*Colloq.*) an opossum. **to play possum**, to feign; to pretend; to deceive [fr. *opossum*].

post (pōst) *n.* a piece of timber or metal, set upright as a support; a prop or pillar; *v.t.* to attach to a post or wall, as a notice or advertisement. **-er** *n.* one who posts bills; a large placard for posting [L. *postis*].

post (pōst) *n.* a fixed place; a military station or the soldiers occupying it; an office or position of trust, service, or emolument; a trading settlement; formerly, a stage on the road for riders carrying mail; *v.t.* to station or place; *v.i.* to inform; to travel with speed. **-age** *n.* the cost of conveyance by mail. **-al** *a.* pert. to the post office or mail service. **-man** *n.* one who delivers mail. **-mark** *n.* a post office mark which cancels the postage stamp and gives place and time of mailing. **-master** *n.* the manager of a post office. **-master general** *n.* the chief of the post office department of a government. **— card** *n.* a stamped card on which a message may be sent through the mail. **-haste** *adv.* with great speed. **— office** *n.* an office where letters and parcels are received for distribution; the government postal department. **-age stamp** *n.* an adhesive stamp, affixed to mail to indicate payment [L. *ponere*, *positum*, to place].

post- (pōst) *adv.* and *prefix* fr. L. *post*, after, behind, used in many compound words. **-date** *v.t.* to put on a document, letter, etc., a date later than the actual one. **-diluvian** *a.* living or happening after the Flood. **-graduate** *n.* of academic study, research, etc., undertaken after taking a university degree. **-impressionism** *n.* a movement in painting, sculpture, etc. which aims at artistic self-expression, or subjective as opposed to objective representation of things. **-mortem** *a.* after death; *n.* the dissection of a body after death; an autopsy. **-natal** *a.* after birth. **-primary** *a.* of education, beyond the elementary school. **pos-te-ri-or** (pắs-tī′-ri-er) *a.* coming after; situated behind; later; hinder; *n.* the rump. **-ly** *adv.* **-ity** *n.* the state of being later or subsequent. **posterity** (pắs-ter′-at-i-) *n.*

---

future generations [L. *posterus*, behind].

pos-tern (pōs′-tern) *n.* a back door or gate; *a.* rear; private [L. *posterus*, behind].

post-hu-mous (pắs′-cha-mas) *a.* born after the death of the father; published after the death of the author; occurring after death. **-ly** *adv.* [L. *postumus*, last, but confused with L. *humus*, the ground].

pos-til-lion, postillion (pōs-til′-yan) *n.* the rider mounted on the near horse of a team drawing a carriage [Fr. *postillon*].

post-pone (pōst-pōn′) *v.t.* to put off till a future time; to defer; to delay. **-ment** *n.* **-r** *n.* [L. *post*, after; *ponere*, to place].

post-pran-di-al (pōst-pran′-di-al) *a.* after-dinner [L. *post*, after; *prandium*, repast].

post-script (pōst′-skript) *n.* something added to a letter after the signature; *abbrev.* **P.S.** [L. *post*, after; *scribere*, *scriptum*, to write].

pos-tu-late (pắs′-cha-lãt) *v.t.* to assume without proof; to lay down as self-evident; to stipulate; *n.* a prerequisite; a proposition assumed without proof. **postulant** *n.* one who makes a request or petition; a candidate, esp. for admission to a religious order. **postulation** *n.* [L. *postulare*, to demand].

pos-ture (pắs′-cher) *n.* the position of a body, figure, etc. or of its several members; attitude; *v.i.* to assume an artificial or affected attitude. **postural** *a.* [L. *ponere*, *positum*, to place].

po-sy (pō′-zi-) *n.* a bouquet; a flower [poesy].

pot (pắt) *n.* a rounded vessel of metal, earthenware, etc., used for cooking, holding fluids, plants, etc.; the contents of a pot; (*Slang*) a large sum of money; *v.t.* to plant in pots; to preserve (as jam, chutney, etc.). *pr.p.* **-ting**. *p.p.* and *pa.t.* **-ted. -bellied** *a.* corpulent. **-hole** *n.* cavity formed in rock by action of stones in the eddy of a stream; a hole in the roadway. **-luck** *n.* whatever may happen to have been provided for a meal. **-shot** *n.* a shot at random [O.E. *pott*].

po-ta-ble (pō′-ta-bl) *a.* drinkable. **potation** *n.* a drinking; a draft [L.*potare*, to drink].

pot-ash (pắt′-ash) *n.* a powerful alkali obtained from wood ashes. **potassium** *n.* metallic base of potash [pot and ash].

po-ta-to (pa-tã′-tō) *n.* an edible tuber widely grown for food. *pl.* **-es** [Sp. *patata*].

po-tent (pō′-tnt) *a.* having great authority or influence; powerful; mighty; procreative. **-ly** *adv.* **potency** *n.* moral or physical power; influence; energy; efficacy. **-ate** *n.* one who possesses power; a monarch. **-ial** (pa-ten′-shal) *a.* latent; existing in possibility but not in actuality; *n.* inherent capability of doing anything; (*Elect.*) the level of electric pressure. **-ially** *adv.* **-iality** (pa-ten-shi-al′-a-ti-) *n.* possibility as distinct from actuality. **-ial difference** (*Elect.*) the difference of pressure between two points; voltage [L. *potens*, powerful, fr. *posse*, to be able].

poth-er (pắTH′-er) *n.* disturbance; fuss; *v.i.* and *v.t.* to harass; to worry [etym. uncertain].

po-tion (pō′-shan) *n.* a dose, esp. of liquid, medicine, or poison [fr. L. *potare*, to drink].

pot-pour-ri (pō-poo-rē′) *n.* a mixture of dried rose petals, spices, etc.; a musical or literary medley [Fr. *pot*, a pot; *pourri*, rotten].

pot-tage (pắt′-ij) *n.* soup or stew; (*Bib.*) a dish of lentils [Fr. *potage*, soup].

pot-ter (pắt′-er) *n.* a maker of earthenware vessels. **-y** *n.* pots, vessels, etc. made of earthenware; the place where it is made; the art of making it [fr. *pot*].

pouch (pouch) *n.* a small bag or sack; a bag-like receptacle in which certain animals, e.g. the kangaroo, carry their young; *v.t.* to pocket; to cause to hang like a pouch [Fr. *poche*, a pocket].

poult (pōlt) *n.* a young fowl. **poultry** (pōl'tri·) *n.* domestic fowls. **-erer** *n.* a dealer in poultry [Fr. *opulet*, a chicken].

poul·tice (pōl'·tis) *n.* a hot, moist mixture applied to a sore, etc.; *v.t.* to apply a poultice to [L. *puls*, porridge].

pounce (pouns) *v.i.* to spring upon suddenly; to swoop; *n.* a swoop or sudden descent.

pounce (pouns) *n.* a fine powder used to prevent ink from spreading on unsized paper; a powder used for dusting over perforations in order to trace a pattern; *v.t.* to sprinkle with pounce [L. *pumex*, pumice].

pound (pound) *n.* a measure of weight (abbrev. **lb.**), 16 ounces avoirdupois, or 12 ounces troy; a unit of British money (abbrev. **£**), **-age** *n.* charge of so much per pound. **-al** *n.* a unit of force [L. *pondus*, weight].

pound (pound) *v.t.* and *i.* to beat or strike; to crush to pieces or to powder; to walk, run, etc., heavily [O.E. *punian*].

pound (pound) *n.* an enclosure for animals; *v.t.* to shut up in one [O.E. *pund*].

pour (pōr) *v.i.* to come out in a stream, crowd, etc.; to flow freely; to rain heavily; *v.t.* to cause to flow, as a liquid from a vessel; to shed; to utter [etym. unknown].

pout (pout) *v.i.* to thrust out the lips, as in displeasure, etc.; to look sullen or sulky; *n.* the act of pouting; a protrusion of the lips. **-er** *n.* one who pouts; a pigeon with the power of inflating its crop [etym. uncertain].

pov·er·ty (pav'·er·ti·) *n.* the state of being poor; poorness; lack of means [L. *pauperlas*, fr. *pauper*, poor].

pow·der (pou'·der) *n.* dust; a solid matter in fine dry particles; a medicine in this form; short for gunpowder, face powder, etc.; *v.t.* to reduce to powder; to pulverize; to sprinkle with powder; *v.i.* to fall into powder; to crumble. **-y** *a.* like powder. **— magazine** *n.* a place where ammunition is stored. [Fr. *poudre*, fr. L. *pulvis*, dust].

pow·er (pou'·er) *n.* a capacity for action, physical, mental, or moral; energy; might; agency or motive force; authority; one in authority; influence or ascendancy; a nation; mechanical energy; (*Math.*) the product arising from the continued multiplication of a number by itself. **-ful** *a.* having great power; capable of producing great effect. **-fully** *adv.* **-fulness** *n.* **-less** *a.* **-lessly** *adv.* **-lessness** *n.* **-house, — station** *n.* a building where electric power is generated [O.Fr. *poer*].

pow·wow (pou'·wou) *n.* orig. a feast, dance, or conference among N. American Indians; hence, any conference [N. Amer. Ind.].

pox (päks) *n.* a disease attended with pustules on the skin, as smallpox, chickenpox, etc.; syphilis [orig. pl. of *pock*].

prac·tice (prak'·tis) *n.* performance or execution, as opposed to theory; custom or habit; systematic exercise for instruction; training; exercise of a profession. **practice** or **practise** *v.t.* to put into action; to do frequently or habitually; to exercise a profession; to exercise in; to train; *v.i.* to perform certain acts customarily; to exercise a profession. **practicable** (prak'·ti·ka·bl) *a.* capable of being accomplished or put into practice; capable of being used, e.g. a weapon, a road, etc. **practically** *adv.* **practicableness** *n.* **practicability** *n.* **practical** *a.* pert. to practice or action; capable of being turned to account; useful; virtual. **practically** *adv.* **practicalness** *n.* **practicality** *n.* **practitioner** (prak·tish'·an·er) *n.* one engaged in a profession, esp. law or medicine [Gk. *praktikos*, pert. to business].

prag·mat·ic, pragmatical (prag·mat'·ik, ·i·kal) *a.* pert. to state affairs; concerned with practical consequences; matter-of-fact; officious or meddlesome. **-ally** *adv.* **-alness** *n.* **pragmatize** *v.t.* to represent an imaginary thing as real. **pragmatism** *n.* a philosophy based on the conception that the truth of a doctrine is to be judged by its practical consequences. **pragmatist** *n.* [Gk. *pragmatikos*, pert. to business].

prai·rie (prer'·ri·) *n.* a large tract of grassland, destitute of trees. **— chicken** *n.* grouse. **— dog** *n.* a small burrowing rodent. **— schooner** *n.* a covered wagon. **— wolf** *n.* the coyote [Fr. fr. L. *pratum*, a meadow].

praise (prās) *v.t.* to express approval or admiration; to glorify; *n.* approval of merit; commendation; worship. **—worthy** *a.* deserving of praise [O.Fr. *preiser*].

pra·line (prā'·lēn) *n.* a candy made by roasting almonds in boiling sugar [Fr. fr. *Duplessis-Praslin*, who first made it].

prance (prans) *v.i.* to spring or bound like a high-spirited horse; to swagger; to caper, esp. of children; to a prancing movement. *n.*

pran·di·al (pran'·di·al) *a.* pert. to dinner [L. *prandium*, lunch].

prank (prangk) *n.* a mischievous trick; a practical joke.

prate (prāt) *v.t.* and *i.* to talk idly; to utter foolishly; *n.* chatter. **prattle** *n.* [M.E. *praten*].

prawn (prawn) *n.* an edible crustacean of the shrimp family [etym. unknown].

prairie wolf

prawn

prax·is (prak'·sis) *n.* practice; a set of examples for practice [Gk. fr. *prassein*, to do].

pray (prā) *v.i.* to ask earnestly; to entreat; to petition; *v.i.* to make a request or confession, esp. to God; to commune with God. **-er** *n.* one who prays; the act of praying; an earnest entreaty; the words used; the thing asked for; a petition **-erful** *a.* devout [L. *precari*].

pre- *prefix* fr. L. *prae*, before, beforehand, used with many nouns and verbs.

preach (prēch) *v.i.* and *t.* to deliver a sermon; to speak publicly on a religious subject, esp. as a clergyman; to advocate. **-er** *n.* **-ment** *n.* a sermon, esp. one of exaggerated solemnity [L. *praedicare*, to proclaim].

pre·am·ble (prē'·am·bl) *n.* the introductory part of a discourse, story, document, etc.; a preface [L. *praeambulus*, walking before].

pre·ar·range (prē·a·rānj') *v.t.* to arrange beforehand. **-ment** *n.*

pre·car·i·ous (pri·ka'·ri·as) *a.* depending on the will or pleasure of another; depending on circumstances; uncertain; dangerous; perilous. **-ly** *adv.* **-ness** *n.* [L. *precarius*, obtained by entreaty].

pre·cau·tion (pri·kaw'·shan) *n.* care taken beforehand; *v.t.* to forewarn. **-ary** *a.* characterized by precaution.

pre·cede (prē·sed') *v.t.* to go before in place, time, rank, or importance. **-nt** *a.* preceding; **-nt** (pref'·sa·dant) *n.* something done, or said, that may serve as an example in similar cases. **-ntly** *adv.* **-nce** (prē·sē'·dans) *n.* the act of preceding; priority in position, rank, or time. **preceding** *a.* [L. *prae*, before; *cedere*, to go].

pre·cen·tor (prē·sen'·ter) *n.* one who leads a church choir [L. *prae*, before; *cantor*, a singer].

pre·cept (prē'·sept) *n.* an instruction intended as a rule of conduct, esp. moral conduct; a maxim; a commandment or exhortation; (*Law*) a written warrant or mandate given to an administrative officer. **-ive** *a.* [L. *praecipere*, *praeceptum*, to order].

pre·ces·sion (prē·sesh'·an) *n.* a going before. **-al** *a.* [L. *praecedere*, to go before].

pre·cinct (prē'·singt) *n.* a division of a city for police protection, voting, etc.; a boundary or limit; a minor territorial division. [L. *prae*, before; *cigere*, to gird].

pre·cious (presh'·as) *a.* of great value or price; costly; highly esteemed; over-refined; fastidious; *adv.* (*Colloq.*) extremely. **-ly** *adv.* [Fr. *précieux*, fr. L. *pretium*, price].

prec·i·pice (pres'·a·pis) *n.* a very steep or perpendicular place, as a cliff-face. **precipitous** *a.* very steep. **precipitously** *adv.* **precipitousness** *n.* [L. *praeceps*, headlong].

pre·cip·i·tate (pri·sip'·a·tāt) *v.i.* to throw headlong; to urge on eagerly; to hasten the occurrence of; (*Chem.*) to cause to separate and fall to the bottom, as a substance in solution; of vapor, to condense; *v.i.* (*Chem.*) to fall to the bottom of a vessel, as a sediment; *n.* (*Chem.*) that which is precipitated in a liquid; sediment; *a.* headlong; rash or over-hasty. **-ly** *adv.* **precipitable** *a.* **precipitance, precipitancy** *n.* headlong hurry; rash haste. **precipitant** *a.* falling headlong; too hasty; unexpectedly hastened; *n.* (*Chem.*) a substance which, added to a liquid, decomposes it and precipitates a sediment. **precipitantly** *aav.* **precipitation** (pre·sip·i·tā'·shun) *n.* the act of precipitating; rash haste; a falling headlong; condensation of vapor, rain, snow, etc. [L. *praeceps*, headlong].

pré·cis (prā·sē') *n.* a concise statement; an abstract or summary [Fr.].

pre·cise (pri·sis') *a.* exact; definite; distinct; prim. **-ly** *adv.* **-ness** *n.* **precision** (pre·sizh'·un) *n.* accuracy; definiteness; *a.* done with,

great accuracy [Fr. *précis*, exact].

pre·clude (pri·klōōd') *v.t.* to shut out; to hinder; to prevent from happening **preclusion** *n.* **preclusive** *a.* [L. *prae*, before; *claudere*, to shut].

pre·co·cious (pri·kō'·shas) *a.* (*Bot.*) ripe or developed too soon; having the mental powers or bodily growth developed at an early age; premature; forward. **-ly** *adv.* **-ness, precocity** *n.* [L. *praecox*; early ripe].

pre·con·ceive (prē·kan·sēv') *v.t.* to form an opinion or idea of beforehand. **preconception** *n.* a prejudice.

pre·con·cert (prē·kan·surt') *v.t.* to settle beforehand.

pre·cur·sor (pri·kur'·ser) *n.* a person or thing going before; a forerunner; a harbinger. **-y, precursive** *a.* [L. *prae*, before; *currere*, to run].

pre·da·cious (pri·dā'·shus)*a.* living on prey; predatory. **predatory** (pred'·a·tor·i·) *a.* living by preying on others; plundering; pillaging. Also **predaceous** [L. *praeda*, booty].

pre·date (prē·dāt') *v.t.* to date earlier than the true date; to antedate [*pre* and *date*].

pred·e·ces·sor (pre·da·ses'·er) *n.* one who has preceded another in an office, position, etc. [L. *prae*, before; *decedere*, to withdraw].

pre·des·tine (prē·des'·tin) *v.t.* to destine beforehand; to foreordain. **predestinate** *v.t.* to determine beforehand; to foreordain. **predestination** *n.* (*Theol.*) the doctrine that the salvation or damnation of individuals has been foreordained by God; the determination beforehand of future events; destiny; fate. **predestinarian** *n.* a believer in this doctrine.

pre·de·ter·mine (prē·di·tur'·min) *v.t.* to determine beforehand. **predeterminate** *a.* determined beforehand. **predetermination** *n.*

pred·i·ca·ble (pred'·i·ka·bl) *a.* able to be predicated or affirmed; *n.* anything that can be affirmed of something. **predicability** *n.* [L. *praedicare*, to proclaim].

pre·dic·a·ment (pri·dik'·a·mant) *n.* an awkward plight; a trying situation [L. *praedicare*, to proclaim].

pred·i·cate (pred'·i·kāt) *v.t.* to assert; to declare; (pred'·i·kat) *n.* that which is predicated; (*Gram.*) a statement made about the subject of the sentence. **predication** *n.* **predicative** *a.* **predicatively** *adv.* [L. *praedicare*, to proclaim].

pre·dict (prē·dikt') *v.t.* to tell beforehand; to foretell; to prophesy. **-able** *a.* **-ion** *n.* the act of foretelling; prophecy. **-ive** *a.* **-or** *n.* [L. *praedicere*, to say before].

pre·di·gest (prē·di·jest') *v.t.* to subject food to artificial digestion before eating.

pre·di·lec·tion (prē·di·lek'·shan) *n.* a prepossession of mind in favor of something; partiality [L. *prae*, before; *dilectus*, chosen].

pre·dis·pose (prē·dis·pōz') *v.t.* to incline beforehand; to give a tendency or bias to; to render susceptible to. **predisposition** *n.*

pre·dom·i·nate (pri·dám'·a·nāt) *v.i.* to surpass in strength, influence, or authority; to rule; to have ascendancy; to prevail. **predominance, predominancy** *n.* ascendancy; superiority. **predominant** *a.* superior in influence, authority, etc.; having ascendancy. **predominantly** *adv.* [*pre* and *dominate*].

pre·em·i·nent (prē·em'·a·nant) *a.* distinguished above others; outstanding. **-ly** *adv.* **preeminence** *n.*

pre·emp·tion (prē·em(p)'·shan) *n.* the act or right of purchasing before others. **pre·empt** (prē·em(p)t') *v.t.* to appropriate beforehand. [L. *prae*, before; *emptio*, a buying].

preen (prēn) *v.t.* to trim or dress with the beak, as birds do their feathers; to primp [form of *prune*].

pre·ex·ist (prē·ig·zist') *v.i.* to exist beforehand; or before something else. **-ence** *n.* **-ent** *a.*

pre·fab (prē·fab') *n.* a prefabricated house.

pre·fab·ri·cate (prē·fab'·ri·kāt) *v.t.* to build houses and ships in standardized units in factories for rapid assembly. **prefabrication** *n.*

pref·ace (pref'·as) *n.* introductory remarks at beginning of book, or spoken before a discourse; foreword; *v.t.* to furnish with a preface. **prefatory** (pref'·a·tō·ri·) *a.* introductory [L. *prae*, before; *fari*, to speak].

pre·fect (prē'·fekt) *n.* an ancient Roman magistrate; head of a department. **-orial** *a.* **-ship** *n.* [L. *praefectus*, set before].

pre·fer (pri·fur') *v.t.* to like better; to choose rather; to promote to an office or dignity. **-able** (pref'·er·a·bl) *a.* worthy of preference; more desirable. **-ably** *adv.* **-ence** *n.* what is preferred; choice. **-ential** (pref·a·ren'·shal) *a.* giving or receiving a preference. **-ment** *n.* advancement or promotion; a position of honor [L. *prae*, before; *ferre*, to bear].

pre·fix (prē'·fiks) *n.* a letter, syllable, or word put at the beginning of another word to modify its meaning, e.g. predigest, underground. **prefix** (prē·fiks') *v.t.*

preg·na·ble (preg'·na·bl) *a.* able to be taken by assault or force [L. *prehendere*, to take].

preg·nant (preg'·nant) *a.* being with child; fruitful; full of meaning. **-ly** *adv.* **pregnancy** *n.* [L. *praegnans*].

pre·hen·sile (prē·hen'·sil) *a.* (*Zool.*) capable of grasping [L. *prehendere*, to seize].

pre·his·to·ry (prē·hist'·er·i·) *n.* the period before written records were kept; the study of this period. **prehistoric** *a.*

prej·u·dice (prej'·oo·dis) *n.* an opinion, favorable or unfavorable (more often the latter), formed without fair examination of facts; bias; *v.t.* to bias; to influence; to injure.

prejudicial (prej·oo·dish'·al) *a.* injurious. [L. *prae*, before; *judicium*, judgment].

prel·ate (prel'·at) *n.* a bishop, or other church dignitary of equal or higher rank. **prelatic, prelatical** *a.* pert. to or of the office or dignity of a prelate; government by prelates; episcopacy; bishops collectively. [L. *praelatus*, put before].

pre·lect (prē·lekt'·) *v.i.* to deliver a lecture or discourse in public. **prelection** *n.* a lecture. [L. *prae*, before; *legere, lectum*, to read].

pre·lim·i·nary (pri·lim'·a·ner·i·) *a.* introductory; preparatory; *n.* an introduction; a preparatory measure; (often used in *pl.*) [L. *prae*, before; *limen*, a threshold].

prel·ude (prel'·ūd) *n.* an introductory performance or event; a musical introduction; a preliminary; *v.t.* to serve as a prelude or forerunner to. **prelusive, prelusory** *a.* introductory [L. *prae*, before; *ludere*, to play].

pre·ma·ture (prē'·ma·tūr) *a.* ripe before the natural or proper time; untimely; overhasty. **-ly** *adv.* **-ness, prematurity** *n.*

pre·med·i·tate (prē·med'·a·tāt) *v.t.* to consider, or revolve in the mind beforehand.

pre·mier (prē'·myer) *a.* first; chief or principal; most ancient; *n.* (*Great Britain, France*) the prime minister. **-ship** *n.* [Fr. fr. *primarius*, of the first rank].

pre·miere (pri·myir') *n.* a first public performance of a play, etc. [Fr. = first].

prem·ise (pri·mīz') *v.t.* to set forth beforehand, or as introductory to the main subject; to lay down general propositions on which the subsequent reasonings rest. **premise** (prem'·is) *n.* Also **premiss**, a proposition previously supposed or proved; a proposition from which an inference or conclusion is drawn. *n.pl.* a building with its adjuncts [L. *prae*, before; *mittere, missum*, to send].

pre·mi·um (prē'·mi·am) *n.* a prize; a fee paid to learn a trade or profession; money paid for insurance; the amount exceeding the par value of shares of stock. **at a premium**, in great demand [L. *praemium*, reward].

pre·mo·ni·tion (prē·ma·nish'·an) *n.* previous warning; an instinctive foreboding; presentiment. **premonitory** *a.* **premonitorily** *adv.* [L. *prae*, before; *monere*, to warn].

pre·na·tal (prē·nā'·tal) *a.* previous to birth.

pre·oc·cu·py (prē·ák'·ya·pī) *v.t.* to take possession of before another; to engage the attention of. **preoccupied** *a.* occupied previously; engrossed in thought; absorbed in mediation. **preoccupancy** *n.* **preoccupation** *n.*

pre·or·dain (prē·awr·dān') *v.t.* to ordain beforehand; to foreordain. **preordination** *n.*

prep (prep) *n.* (*Colloq.*) preparatory school.

pre·paid (prē·pād') *a.* paid in advance.

pre·pare (pri·par') *v.t.* to make ready for use; to fit for a particular purpose; to provide; to fit out; *v.i.* to make things ready; to make oneself ready. **preparation** (prep·a·rā'·shan) *n.* the act of making ready for use; readiness; a substance, esp. medicine or food, made up for use. **preparative** *a.* tending to prepare for; *n.* anything which serves to prepare. **preparatively** *adv.* **preparatory** *a.* preparing the way; preliminary; introductory. **preparedness** (pra·par'·ad·nas) *n.* [L. *prae*, before; *parare*, to make ready].

pre·pay (prē·pā') *v.t.* to pay beforehand [*pre* and *pay*].

pre·pon·der·ate (pri·pán'·der·āt) *v.i.* to exceed in power, influence, numbers, etc.; to outweigh. **preponderance** *n.* superiority of power, numbers, etc. **preponderant** *a.* **preponderantly** *adv.* [L. *prae*, before; *pondus, ponderis*, a weight].

prep·o·si·tion (prep·a·zish'·an) *n.* (*Gram.*) a word, e.g. *with, by, for*, etc., used before a noun or pronoun to show the relation to some other word in the sentence. **-al** *a.* [L. *prae*, before; *ponere, positum*, to place].

pre·pos·sess (prē·pa·zes') *v.t.* to possess beforehand; to influence a person's mind, heart, etc. beforehand; to prejudice favorably. **-ing** *a.* tending to win a favorable opinion; attractive. **-ingly** *adv.* **prepossession** *n.*

pre·pos·ter·ous (pri·pás'·ter·as) *a.* contrary to nature, truth, reason, or common sense; utterly absurd. **-ly** *adv.* **-ness** *n.* [L. = before, behind, fr. *prae*, before; *posterus*, after].

pre·rog·a·tive (pri·rág'·a·tiv) *n.* an exclusive right or privilege by reason of rank, position, etc. [L. *prae*, before; *rogare*, to ask].

pres·age (pres'·ij) *n.* an indication of what is going to happen; an omen. **presage** (pri·sāj') *v.t.* to foretell; to forebode; to have a presentiment of. **-ful** *a.* warning [L. *prae*, before; *sagire*, to perceive acutely].

pres·by·o·pi·a (prez·bi·ō'·pi·a) *n.* far-sightedness (occurring in advancing age) [Gk. *presbūtēs*, an old man; *ops*, an eye].

pres·by·ter (prez'·bi·ter) *n.* a priest or elder in the early Christian Church; in Episcopal churches, one ordained to the second order in the ministry; a member of a presbytery. **Pres·by·te·ri·an** (prez·bi·tir'·i·an) *n.* one belonging to Presbyterian Church. **-ism** *n.*

presbytery *n.* a body of elders; court of pas-

---

tors [Gk. *presbuteros*, elder, fr. *presbuteros*, elder, fr. *presbus*, old].

pre·sci·ence (prē'·shi·ans) *n.* knowledge of events before they take place. **prescient** *a.* [O.Fr. fr. L. *praescientia*, foreknowledge].

pre·scribe (pri·skrīb') *v.t.* to lay down authoritatively for direction; to set out rules for; (*Med.*) to order or advise the use of. **-r** *n.* **prescript** *n.* direction; ordinance. **prescription** (pri·skrip'·shan) *n.* the act of prescribing or directing; a doctor's direction for use of medicine. **prescriptive** *a.* [L. *praescribere*, to write before].

pres·ent (prez'·ant) *a.* being in a certain place; here or at hand; now existing; (*Gram.*) pert. to time that now is; *n.* present time; (*Gram.*) the present tense. **presence** *n.* the state of being present; nearness or proximity; the person of a superior; mien or appearance; apparition. **-ly** *adv.* at once; soon; by and by [L. *praesens*, being present].

pre·sent (pri·zent') *v.t.* to introduce into the presence of; to exhibit or offer to the notice; to offer as a gift; to bestow; to aim, as a weapon; *n.* (prez'·ant) a gift. **-able** *a.* fit to be presented. **-ation** (prez·an·tā'·shan) *n.* the act of presenting; the state of being presented; that which is presented. **-ment** *n.* the act or state of presenting; representation; the laying of a formal statement [L. *praesentare*, to place before].

pre·sen·ti·ment (pri·zen'·ta·mant) *n.* a previous notion or opinion; anticipation of evil; foreboding.

pre·serve (pri·zurv') *v.t.* to keep from injury or destruction; to keep in a sound state; *n.* that which is preserved, as fruit, etc.; any medium used in preserving; a place for the preservation of game, fish, etc. **-r** *n.* **preservable** *a.* **preservation** (prez·er·vā'·shan) *n.* the act of preserving or keeping safe; the state of being preserved; safety. **preservative** *n.* that which preserves; *a.* having the power of preserving. **preservatory** *a.* [L. *prae*, before; *servare*, to protect].

pre·side (pri·zīd') *v.i.* to be chairman of a meeting; to direct; to control; to superintend. **president** (prez'·a·dant) *n.* the head of a society, company, association, etc.; the elected head of a republic. **presidency** *n.* the office, or term of office, of a president. **presidential** *a.* pert. to a president, his office, dignity, etc. [L. *prae*, before; *sedere*, to sit].

press (pres) *v.t.* to push or squeeze; to crush; to hug; to embrace closely; to drive with violence; to hurry; to urge steadily; to force; to solicit with importunity; to constrain; to smooth by pressure; *v.i.* to exert pressure; to strive eagerly; to crowd; to throng; to hasten; *n.* an instrument or machine for squeezing, compressing, etc.; a printing machine; printing and publishing; newspapers collectively; a crowd; a throng; urgent demands; stress; a cupboard for clothes, etc. **-ing** *a.* urgent; persistent. **— agent** *n.* one employed to advertise and secure publicity for any person or organization. **to go to press**, of a newspaper, to start printing [L. *pressare*, fr. *premere*, to squeeze].

---

press (pres) *v.t.* to force to serve in the navy or army [L. *praestare*, to furnish].

pres·sure (presh'·er) *n.* the act of pressing; state of being pressed; influence; urgency.

pres·su·ri·za·tion (presh·er·a·zā'·shan) *n.* maintenance of pressure inside aircraft at great altitudes. **pressurize** (presh'·er·īz) *v.t.*

pres·ti·dig·i·ta·tion (pres·ta·dij·a·tā·shan) *n.* conjuring; sleight of hand. **prestidigitator** *n.* a conjurer (conjuror); a magician [L. *praesto*, ready; *digitus*, a finger].

pres·tige (pres·tēzh', pres'·tēj) *n.* influence resulting from past achievement, character, reputation, etc. [Fr. = marvel].

pres·to (pres'·tō) *adv.* (*Mus.*) quickly [It. fr. L. *praesto*, ready].

pre·sume (pri·zōōm') *v.t.* to take for granted; to suppose to be true without proof; to venture; *v.i.* to act in a forward manner; to take liberties. **presumable** *a.* probable. **presumably** *adv.* **presumption** (pri·zum(p)'·shan) *n.* the act of, or grounds for, presuming; strong probability; that which is taken for granted; arrogance of opinion or conduct; boldness. **presumptive** (pri·zum(p)'·tiv) *a.* presuming; based on probability; that may be assumed as true or valid until the contrary is proved. **presumptively** *adv.* **presumptuous** *a.* forward; taking liberties. *n.* [L. *prae*, before; *sumere*, to take].

pre·sup·pose (prē·sa·pōz') *v.t.* to assume or take for granted beforehand.

pre·tend (pri·tend') *v.t.* to assert falsely; to counterfeit; to make believe; *v.i.* to lay claim (to); to make pretense; to aspire (to) **-er** *n.* one who simulates or feigns; a claimant, esp. to the throne. **pretense** *n.* simulation; the act of laying claim; assumption; pretext. **pretentious** (pri·ten'·shas) *a.* given to outward show; presumptuous and arrogant. **pretentiously** *adv.* **pretentiousness** *n.* [L. *prae*, before; *tendere*, to stretch].

pre·ter- prefix fr. L. *praeter*, meaning beyond, above, more than, etc., used in combining forms. **-natural** (prē·ter·nach'·er·al) *a.* beyond or different from what is natural.

pret·er·it, preterite (pret'·er·it) *a.* (*Gram.*) past (applied to the tense that expresses past action or state); *n.* (*Gram.*) the preterit or past definite tense [L. *praeter*, beyond; *ire, itum*, to go].

pre·text (prē'·tekst) *n.* ostensible reason or motive which cloaks the real reason; pretense [L. *prae*, before; *texere*, to weave].

pret·ty (prit'·i·) *a.* of a beauty that is charming and attractive, but not striking or imposing; neat and tasteful; pleasing; fine or excellent in an ironical sense; *adv.* in some degree; moderately; fairly; rather. **prettily** *adv.* **prettiness** *n.* [O.E. *praettig*, crafty].

pre·vail (pri·vāl') *v.i.* to gain the upper hand or mastery; to succeed; to be current; to be in force; to persuade or induce (with 'on' or 'upon'). **-ing** *a.* **prevalent** (prev'·a·lant) *a.* most generally; extensively existing; rife. **prevalently** *adv.* **prevalence** *n.* [I. *prae*, before; *valere*, to be strong].

pre·var·i·cate (pri·var'·a·kāt) *v.i.* to evade the truth. **prevarication** *n.* **prevaricator** *n.* [L. *prae*, before; *varus*, crooked].

pre·vent (pri·vent') *v.t.* to keep from happening; to stop. **-able** *a.* **-ion** *n.* obstruction; hinderance; preventive. **-ive** *a.* tending to prevent or ward off; *n.* that which prevents; antidote to keep off disease [L. *prae*, before; *venire, ventum*, to come].

pre·view (prē'·vū) *n.* a private showing of works of art, films, etc. before being exhibited in public [*pre* and *view*].

pre·vi·ous (prē'·vi·as) *a.* preceding; happening before; (*Slang*) hasty. **-ly** *adv.* **-ness** *n.* [L. *prae*, before; *via*, a way].

pre·vise (pri·vīz') *v.t.* to foresee; to forewarn. **prevision** *n.* foresight; foreknowledge [L. *prae*, before; *videre, visum*, to see].

prey (prā) *n.* any animal hunted and killed for food by another animal; a victim; *v.i.* (with 'on' or 'upon') to seize and devour; to weigh heavily; to pillage [Fr. *proie*, fr. L. *praeda*].

price (prīs) *n.* the amount at which a thing is valued, or sold; value; cost; *v.t.* to fix the price of; to ask the cost of. **-less** *a.* beyond any price. [L. *pretium*, price].

prick (prik) *n.* a sharp-pointed instrument; a puncture made by a sharp point; the act of pricking; a sharp, stinging pain; hence, (*Fig.*) remorse; a spur; *v.t.* to pierce slightly with a sharp point; to incite; to affect with sharp pain; to sting; to erect (the ears). **-er** *n.* [O.E. *prica*, a point].

prick·le (prik'·l) *n.* a small sharp point; a thorn; a spike; a bristle; (*Colloq.*) a pricking feeling; *v.t.* to prick slightly; *v.i.* to feel a tingling sensation. **prickly** *a.* full of prickles; stinging; tingling [O.E. *prica*, a point].

pride (prīd) *n.* the state or quality of being proud; too high an opinion of oneself; worthy self-esteem. **-ful** *a.* **to pride oneself on** (**upon**), to be proud of; to take credit for [O.E. *pryte*, fr. *prut*, proud].

priest (prēst) *n.* (*fem.* **-ess**) a clergyman; in R.C. and Episcopal churches; in pagan times, one who officiated at the altar, or performed the rites of sacrifice. **-like, -ly** *a.* **-liness** *n.* **-hood** *n.* [O.E. *preost*, fr. Gk. *presbuteros*, elder].

prig (prig) *n.* a conceited person who pro-prickle

fesses superiority. **-gish** a.

prim (prim) a. formal and precise; affectedly nice; prudish. **-ly** adv. **-ness** n. [O.Fr. fr. L. primus, first].

pri·ma (prē'·ma) a. first. — **donna**, the principal female singer in an opera. — **facie** (fā'·shi·) at first view. — **facie case**, a case based on sufficient evidence to go to a jury [It. prima, first; donna, a woman; L. facies, appearance].

pri·ma·cy See **primate**.

pri·mal (prī'·mal) a. first, original; chief. **primary** a. first in order of time, development, importance; preparatory; elementary; n. that which stands highest in rank or importance; a preliminary election (often pl.); **primarily** adv. in the first place. **primary colors**, red, yellow and blue from which other colors may be made [L. primus, first].

pri·mate (prī'·māt) n. (Brit.) the chief dignitary in a church; an archbishop. **primacy** (prī'·ma·si·) n. the chief dignity in a national church; the office or dignity of an archbishop [L.L. primas, a chief, fr. primus, first].

prime (prīm) a. first in time; original; first in degree or importance; foremost; of highest quality; (Math.) that cannot be separated into factors; n. the earliest stage or beginning; spring; youth; full health or strength; the best portion; v.t. to prepare a firearm by charging with powder; to prepare wood with a protective coating before painting it; to fill with water, etc., as a pump, to make it start working; to instruct beforehand. **-r** n. one who, or that which, primes, esp. a percussion cap, etc. used to ignite the powder of cartridges, etc.; (prim'·er) a small elementary book used in teaching. **-ly** adv. **-ness** n. **priming** n. the powder, etc. used to fire the charge in firearms. — **minister**, the first minister of state in some countries. — **number**, a number divisible without remainder only by itself or one [L. primus, first].

pri·me·val (prī·mē'·val) a. original; primitive; **-ly** adv. [L. primus, first; aevum, age].

prim·i·tive (prim'·a·tiv) a. pert. to the beginning or origin; being the earliest of its kind; old-fashioned; plain and rude; (Biol.) rudimentary; undeveloped; **-ly** adv. **-ness** n. [L. primitivus, fr. primus, first].

pri·mo·gen·i·ture (prī·ma·jen'·a·cher) n. the state of being the first-born child; the right of the eldest son to inherit his parents' property. **primogenital, primogenitary** a. **primogenitor** n. the earliest ancestor [L. primus, first; genitor, a father, fr. gignere, to beget].

pri·mor·di·al (prī·mawr'·di·al) a. existing from the beginning; first in order; primeval [L. primus, first; ordiri, to begin].

prim·rose (prim'·rōz) n. a plant bearing pale-yellow and other colored flowers in spring [M.E. primerole, fr. L. primus, first].

prince (prins) n. (fem. **princess**) a ruler or chief; the son of a king or emperor; a title of nobility. **-dom** n. the jurisdiction, rank, or estate of a prince. **-ly** a. stately; august; dignified. **-liness** n. **Prince Consort**, the husband of a reigning queen [L. princeps, a prince].

prin·ci·pal (prin'·sa·pal) a. chief in importance; first in rank, character, etc.; n. the chief person in authority; a leader; the head of certain institutions, esp. a school; the chief actor in a crime; a chief debtor; a person for whom another is agent; a sum of money lent and yielding interest. **-ly** adv. **-ship** n. the office or dignity of a principal. **principality** n. the territory or dignity of a prince; sovereignty [L. principalis].

prin·cip·i·a (prin·sip'·i·a, pring·kip'·i·a) n.pl. first principles; beginnings [L. principium, a beginning].

prin·ci·ple (prin'·sa·pl) n. a fundamental truth or law; a moral rule or settled reason of action; uprightness; honesty; an element. **-d** a. guided by certain rules of conduct [L. principium, a beginning].

print (print) v.t. to impress; to reproduce words, pictures, etc. by pressing inked types on paper, etc.; to produce in this way; to write in imitation of this; to publish; n. an impression or mark left on a surface by something pressed against it; printed fabric; printed lettering; an engraving; a photograph. **-er** n. one engaged in the setting of type for, and the printing of books, newspapers, etc. **-ing press** n. a machine for reproducing on paper, etc. impressions made by inked type [L. premere, to press].

pri·or (prī'·er) a. previous; former; earlier; preceding in time; n. (fem. **-ess**) the superior of a priory; one next in dignity to an abbot. **-ity** (prī·awr'·a·ti·) n. the state of being antecedent in time; precedence; preference in regard to privilege. **-y** n. a religious house [L. prior, former].

prism (prizm) n. (Geom.) a solid whose bases or ends are any similar, equal, and parallel plane figures, and whose sides are parallelograms; (Optics) a transparent figure of this nature, usually with triangular ends. **-atic(al)** a. **-atically** adv. **prismatic colors**, the seven colors, red, orange, yellow, green, blue indigo, violet, into which a ray of light is separated by a prism [Gk. prisma; eidos, form].

pris·on (priz'·n) n. building for confinement of criminals; jail; any place of confinement or restraint. **-er** (priz'·ner) n. one confined in prison; one captured in war [L. prensio, fr. prehendere, to seize].

pris·tine (pris'·tēn) a. belonging to the earliest time; original; pure [L. pristinus, fr. priscus, of old].

pri·vate (prī'·vat) a. not public; belonging to or concerning an individual; peculiar to oneself; personal; secluded; secret; of a soldier, not holding any rank; n. a common soldier. **-ly** adv. **-ness** n. **privacy** (prī'·va·si·) n. the state of being in retirement from company; solitude; seclusion; secrecy [L. privatus, fr. privus, single].

pri·va·teer (prī·va·tir') n. an armed private vessel commissioned by a government to attack enemy ships.

pri·va·tion (prī·vā'·shan) n. the state of being deprived, esp. of something required; destitution; want. **privative** (priv'·a·tiv) a. causing privation; consisting in the absence of something; denoting negation.

priv·et (priv'·it) n. an evergreen shrub.

priv·i·lege (priv'·i·lij) n. a special right or advantage; v.t. to grant some special favor to. **-d** a. enjoying a special right or immunity [L. privilegium, private law, fr. lex, a law].

priv·y (priv'·i·) a. private; admitted to knowledge of a secret; n. a person having an interest in a law suit; a latrine. **privily** adv. **privity** n. private knowledge; connivance. — **to**, secretly informed of. **Privy Council**, (Brit.) the council which advises the sovereign on matters of government [Fr. privé, fr. L. privatus, private].

prize (prīz) n. a reward given for success in competition; a reward given for merit; a thing striven for; a thing won by chance, e.g. in a lottery. v.t. to value highly; to esteem. — **fight** n. a professional boxing match. — **fighter** n. [O.Fr. pris].

prize (prīz) n. an enemy ship or property captured in naval warfare. — **court** n. court to adjudicate on prizes captured in naval warfare [Fr. prise, a seizing].

pro- (prō) prefix fr. L. or Gk. meaning for; instead of; on behalf of; in front of; before; forward; according to.

prob·a·ble (práb'·a·bl) a. likely; to be expected; having more evidence for than against. **probably** adv. **probability** n. likelihood; anything that has appearance of truth [L. probare, to prove].

pro·bate (prō'·bāt) n. the process by which a last will and testament is legally authenticated after the testator's death; an official copy of a will; v.t. to establish the validity of a will [L. probare, to prove].

pro·ba·tion (prō·bā'·shan) n. a trial or test of a person's character, conduct, ability, etc.; the testing of a candidate before admission

to full membership of a body, esp. a religious sect or order; a system of releasing offenders, esp. juveniles, and placing them under supervision of. **-al** a. **-ary** a. **-er** n. a person undergoing probation. **probative** (prō'·ba·tiv) a. pert. to, serving for, or offering, trial or proof [L. probare, to prove].

probe (prōb) n. (Med.) instrument for examining a wound, ulcer, cavity, etc.; an investigation; v.t. to explore a wound, etc. with a probe; to examine thoroughly [L. probare, to prove].

pro·bi·ty (prō'·ba·ti·) n. integrity; rectitude; honesty [L. probus, good].

prob·lem (práb'·lem) n. a matter proposed for solution; a question difficult of solution; a puzzle. **-atical** a. questionable; uncertain; disputable; doubtful. **-atically** adv. [Gk. problēma, a thing thrown before].

pro·bos·cis (prō·bás'·is) n. an elephant's trunk; the snout of other animals [Gk. fr. pro, before; boskein, to feed].

pro·ceed (prō·sēd') v.i. to move onward; to advance; to renew progress; to pass from one point or topic to another; to come forth; to carry on a series of acts; to take legal proceedings. **-ing** n. going forward; movement or process; pl. (Law) the several steps of prosecuting a charge, claim, etc.; a record of business done by a society. **proceeds** (prō'·sēdz) n.pl. yield; sum realized by a sale. **procedure** (pra·sē'·jer) n. act, method of proceeding [L. procedere, to go forward].

pro·cess (prá'·ses) n. continued forward movement; lapse of time; a series of actions or measures; a method of operation; (Anat.) a projecting part or growth; (Law) procedure; v.t. to subject to some process, as food or material. **procession** (pra·, prō·sesh'·an) n. a moving line of people, cars, animals, etc.; regular progress. **-ional** a. pert. to a procession; n. a hymn sung during a church procession — **server** n. one who serves notices to appear in court [L. processus].

pro·claim (prō·klām') v.t. to make known by public announcement; to declare, **-ant, -er** n. one who proclaims. **proclamation** (prak·la·mā'·shan) n. the act of announcing publicly; an official public announcement [L. pro, before; clamare, to cry out].

pro·cliv·i·ty (prō·kliv'·a·ti·) n. inclination; propensity; proneness; aptitude [L. pro, forward; clivus, a slope].

pro·cras·ti·nate (prō·kras'·ta·nāt) v.i. to put off till some future time. **procrastination** n. **procrastinator** n. [L. procrastinare, fr. cras, tomorrow].

pro·cre·ate (prō'·krē·āt) v.t. to bring into being; to beget; to generate. **procreation** n. **procreative** a. having the power to beget; productive. **procreativeness** n. **procreator** n. [L. pro, forth; creare, to produce].

proc·tor (prák'·ter) n. (Law) one who manages the affairs of another in a court; one who supervises students in an examination; v.t. to supervise in an examination. **-ial** a. **-ship** n. [abbrev. of procurator].

pro·cum·bent (prō·kum'·bant) a. lying face down; (Bot.) growing along the ground [L. pro, forward; cumbere, to lie down].

proc·u·ra·tion (prák·ya·rā'·shan) n. management of another's affairs; power of attorney. [L. pro, for; curare, to care for].

pro·cure (prō·kyoor')v.t. to acquire; to obtain; to get; to bring about; v.i. to act as a procurer. **procurable** a. obtainable. **-ment** n. **-r** n. (fem. **procuress**) one who procures; one who supplies women for immoral purposes [L. pro, for; curare, to see to].

prod (prád) v.t. to poke with something pointed; to goad; n. a pointed instrument; a poke, pr.p. **-ding**. pa.p. and pa.t. **-ded**.

prod·i·gal (prád'·i·gal) a. wasteful; spending recklessly; n. one who spends recklessly; a spendthrift. **-ly** adv. **-ity** n. reckless extravagance [L. prodigere, to squander].

prod·i·gy (prád'·i·ji·) n. a person or thing causing wonder; a marvel; a very gifted person; a monster; a portent. **prodigious** (pra·dij'·as) a. like a prodigy; marvelous; enormous; extraordinary. **prodigiously** adv. [L. prodigium, a portent or sign].

pro·duce (pra·dōōs') v.t. to bring forth; to exhibit; to give birth to; to yield; to make; to cause; of a play, to present it on the stage. **produce** (prád'·ōōs) n. that which is produced; product; agricultural products; crops. **-r** n. [L. pro, forward; ducere, to lead].

prod·uct (prád'·akt) n. that which is produced; (Arith.) a number resulting from the multiplying of two or more numbers. **production** (pra·duk'·shan) n. the act of producing; the things produced. **-ive** a. having the power to produce; creative; fertile; efficient. **-ively** adv. **-iveness, -ivity** n. [L. pro, forward; ducere, to lead].

pro·em (prō'·em) n. a preface; an introduction. **-ial** a. [Gk. pro, before; oimos, a path].

pro·fane (prō·fān') a. not sacred; irreverent; blasphemous; vulgar; v.t. to treat with irreverence; to put to a wrong or unworthy use; to desecrate. **-ly** adv. **-ness** n. **-r** n. **profanation** (práf·a·nā'·shan) n. the act of violating sacred things. **profanity** (prō·fan'·i·ti·) n. profaneness; irreverence; the use of bad language [L. pro, before; fanum, a temple].

pro·fess (pra·fes') v.t. to make open declaration of; to confess publicly; to affirm belief

in; to pretend to knowledge or skill in. **-ed** a. openly acknowledged. **-ion** (prō·fesh'·an) n. the act of professing; that which one professes; occupation or calling, esp. one requiring learning. **-ional** a. pert. to a profession or calling; engaged in for money, as opposed to *amateur*; n. one who makes a livelihood in sport or games (*abbrev.* **pro**). **-ionally** adv. [L. *profiteri, professus*, to acknowledge].
pro·fes·sor (prō·fes'·er) n. one who makes profession; a teacher of the highest rank in a university. **professorial** (prō·fa·sō'·ri·al) a. **-ially** adv. **professoriate** (prō·fa·sō'·ri·it) n. the office of a professor; his period of office; body of professors. **-ship** n. [L. *profiteri, professus*, to acknowledge].
prof·fer (práf'·er) v.t. to offer for acceptance; **-er** n. [L. *proferre*, to bring forward].
pro·fi·cient (pra·fish'·ant) a. thoroughly versed or qualified in any art or occupation; skilled; n. an expert. **-ly** adv. **proficience, proficiency** n. [L. *proficere*, to be useful].
pro·file (prō'·fil) n. an outline or contour; a portrait in a side view; the side face; short biographical sketch; v.t. to draw the outline of [L. *pro*, before; *filum*, thread].

prof·it (práf'·it) n. advantage or benefit; the excess of returns over expenditure; pecuniary gain in any transaction or occupation; v.t. to be of service to; v.i. to gain advantage; to grow richer. **-able** a. yielding profit or gain; advantageous; helpful. **-ably** adv. **-ableness** n. **profiteer** (práf·a·tēr')n. one who makes excessive profits; v.i. to make such profits [L. *profectus*, fr. *proficere*, to make progress].
prof·li·gate (práf'·la·gat, ·gāt) a. abandoned to vice; dissolute; extravagant; n. a depraved person. **-ly** adv. **-ness** n. **profligacy** (práf'·li·ga·si·) n. a vicious and dissolute manner of living [L. *profligatus*, ruined].
pro·found (pra·found') a. deep; intellectually deep; learned; deeply felt. **-ly** adv. **profundity** n. depth of place, knowledge, skill, feeling [L. *profundus*, deep].
pro·fuse (pra·fūs') a. giving or given generously; lavish; extravagant. **-ly** adv. **-ness, profusion** (pra·fū'·zhan) n. great abundance [L. *pro*, forth; *fusum*, to pour].
prog·e·ny (práj'·a·ni·) n. descendants; offspring; children. **progenitive** a. pert. to the production of offspring. **progenitor** (prō·jen'·i·ter) n. ancestor; forefather [L. *pro*, before; *gignere*, to beget].
prog·no·sis (prág·nō'·sis) n. a forecast; (*Med.*) foretelling the course of a disease. *pl.* **prognoses. prognostic** (prág·nás'·tik) a. foretelling; forecasting; predicting; n. a forecast; a prediction. **prognosticate** v.t. to foretell; to predict; to prophesy. **prognostication** n. **prognosticator** n. [Gk. *pro*, before; *gnōsis*, knowledge].
pro·gram, programme (prō'·gram) n. a plan or detailed notes of intended proceedings at a public entertainment, ceremony, etc.; a party policy at election time [Gk. *pro*, before; *gramma*, a writing].
prog·ress (prág'·res) n. a moving forward; advancement; development. **progress** (pra·gres') v.i. to move forward; to advance; to develop; to improve. **-ion** (pra·gresh'·an) n. the act of moving forward; onward movement; progress. **-ional** a. **-ive** a. moving forward gradually; advancing; improving; favoring progress or reform. **-ively** adv. **-iveness** n. **arithmetical progression**, a series of numbers increasing or decreasing by the same amount, e.g. 3, 6, 9, 12, 15, etc. **geometrical progression**, a series of numbers increasing or decreasing by a common ratio, e.g. 3, 9, 27, 81, etc. [L. *progredi, progressus*, to go forward].
pro·hib·it (prō·hib'·it) v.t. to forbid; to prevent; to hinder. **-er, -or** n. **-ion** (prō·(h)a·bish'·an) n. the act of forbidding; interdict; the forbidding by law of manufacture, importation, sale, or purchase of alcoholic liquors. **-ionist** n. one in favor of prohibition. **-ive, -ory** a. tending to forbid, prevent, or exclude; exclusive. **-ively** adv. [L. *prohibere*].
pro·ject (pra·jekt') v.t. to throw or cast forward; to plan; to contrive; to throw a photographic image on a screen; v.i. to jut out; to

protrude. **project** (práj'·ekt) n. a plan; a scheme; a task. **-ile** (pra·jek'·til) a. capable of being thrown; n. a heavy missile, esp. a shell or cannon ball. **-ion** n. the act of projecting; something that juts out; a plan; delineation; the representation on a plane of a curved surface or sphere; in psychology, mistaking for reality something which is only an image in the mind. **-ive** a. **-or** n. an apparatus for throwing photographic images, esp. films, on a screen [L. *projicere, propectum*, to throw forward].

projector

pro·lapse (prō'·laps) n. (*Med.*) the falling down of a part of the body from its normal position, esp. womb or rectum [L. *prolapsus*, fr. *prolabi*, to fall or slide forward].
pro·lep·sis (prō·lep'·sis) n. a figure of speech by which objections are anticipated and answered; an error in chronology, consisting in antedating an event; *pl.* **prolepses. proleptical** a. [Gk. *pro*, before; *lēpsis*, a taking].
pro·le·tar·i·an (prō·la·te'·ri·an) a. pert. to the proletariat; belonging to the working class; n. one of the proletariat. **proletariat** (prō·la·te'·ri·at) n. propertyless wage-earners who live by sale of their labor [L. *proles*, offspring].
pro·lif·er·ous (prō·lif'·er·as) a. (*Biol.*) reproducing freely by cell division; developing anthers. **-ly** adv. **proliferate** v.t. to bear; v.i. to reproduce by repeated cell division. **proliferation** n. increase [L. *proles*, offspring; *ferre*, to bear].
pro·lif·ic (pra·lif'·ik) a. bringing forth offspring; fruitful, abundantly productive; bringing about results. **-ally** adv. [L. *proles*, offspring; *facere*, to make].
pro·lix (prō'·liks) a. long drawn out; diffuse; wordy. **-ly** adv. **-ity** n. [L. *prolixus*].
pro·lo·cu·tor (prō·lák'·ya·ter) n. a chairman of an assembly [L. *pro; locutus*, to speak].
pro·logue (prō'·lawg) n. the preface or introduction to a discourse, poem, book, or performance, esp. the address spoken before a dramatic performance; v.t. to preface [Gk. *pro*, before; *logos*, discourse].
pro·long (prō·lawng') v.t. to lengthen out; to extend the duration of. **-ation** n. the act of lengthening out; a part prolonged; extension [L. *pro; longus*, long].
prom (prám) n. (*Colloq.*) a formal ball [*Abbrev. of* promenade].
prom·e·nade (prám·a·nād', nád) n. a leisurely walk, generally in a public place; a place adapted for such a walk; a march of dancers, as at the opening of a ball or in a square dance; v.i. to walk for pleasure, display, or exercise. **-r** n. [Fr.].
prom·i·nent (prám'·a·nant) a. sticking out; projecting; conspicuous; distinguished. **-ly** adv. **prominence, prominency** n. [L. *prominere*, to jut out].
pro·mis·cu·ous (pra·mis'·kyoo·as) a. mixed without order or distinction; indiscriminate. **-ly** adv. **-ness, promiscuity** (prám·is·kū'·a·ti·) n. [L. *promiscuus*, fr. *miscere*, to mix].
prom·ise (prám'·is) n. an undertaking to do or not to do something; cause or grounds for hope; v.t. to give one's word to do or not to do something; to give cause for expectation; to agree to give; v.i. to assure by a promise; to give grounds for hope. **-r** n. **promisor** n. (*Law*) the person by whom a promise is made. **promising** a. likely to turn out well or to succeed; hopeful [L. *promittere, promissum*, to promise].
prom·is·so·ry (prám'·a·sōr·i·) a. containing a promise. **-note**, written agreement to pay sum to named person at specified date [L. *promittere*, to promise].
prom·on·to·ry (prám'·an·tōr·i·) n. a point of high land jutting out into the sea [L. *promontorium*, fr. *mons*, a mountain].
pro·mote (pra·mōt') v.t. to move forward; to move up to a higher rank or position; to encourage the growth or development of; to help organize a new business venture or company. **-r** n. a supporter; an initiator, esp. of a new business venture, etc. **promotion** n. advancement; preferment; a higher rank, station, or position. **promotive** a. [L. *promovere, promotum*, to move forward].
prompt (prámpt) a. ready and quick to act; done at once; punctual; v.t. to excite to action; to suggest; to help out (actor or speaker) by reading, suggesting next words.

-ly adv. **-er** n. one who reminds or helps out an actor, speaker, etc. **-itude, -ness** n. readiness; quickness of decision and action. [L. *promptus*, fr. *promere*, to put forth].
pro·mul·gate (prám'·al·gāt) v.t. to proclaim; to publish; to make known officially. **promulgation** n. [L. *promulgare*].
prone (prōn) a. lying face downward; sloping; inclined; naturally disposed. **-ly** adv. **-ness** n. inclination; tendency [L. *pronus*].
prong (práng) n. one of the pointed ends of a fork; a spike [etym. uncertain].

pro·noun (prō'·noun) n. (*Gram.*) a word used instead of a noun [*pro* and *noun*].
pro·nounce (pra·nouns') v.t. to speak with the correct sound and accent; to speak distinctly; to utter formally or officially; to declare or affirm. **-d** a. strongly marked; very definite or decided. **-able** a. **-ment** n. a formal declaration. **-r** n. **pronouncing** a. teaching or indicating pronounciation. **pronunciation** (pra·nun·si·ā'·shan) n. the act of uttering with the proper sound and accent; [L. *pronuntiare*, to proclaim].
pron·to (prán'·tō) adv. (*Colloq.*) promptly; quickly [Sp.].
proof (proof) n. something which proves; a test or trial; any process to ascertain correctness, truth, or facts; demonstration; evidence that convinces the mind and produces belief; argument; standard strength of alcoholic spirits; (*Print.*) a trial impression from type, on which corrections may be made; a. firm in resisting; serving as proof or designating a certain standard or quality; v.t. to render proof against. **-reader** n. one who corrects printer's proofs [L. *probare*, to prove].
prop (práp) v.t. to support by placing something under or against; to sustain. *pr.p.* **-ping.** *pa.t.* *pa.p.* **-ped.** n. that which supports; a stay [M.E. *proppe*].

prop·a·gan·da (práp·a·gan'·da) n. the propagating of doctrines or principles; the opinions or beliefs thus spread; (*R.C.*) a society in Rome charged with the management of missions. **propagandize** v.t. and i. to spread propaganda. **propagandist** n. [fr. L. *de propaganda fide*, concerning the spreading of the faith].
prop·a·gate (práp'·a·gāt) v.t. to cause to multiply or reproduce by generation; to breed; to spread the knowledge of; to transmit or carry forward; v.i. to have young; to breed. **propagation** n. propagation [L. *propagare*, to propagate plants by slips].
pro·pel (pra·pel') v.t. to drive forward; to press onward by force; to push. *pr.p.* **-ling.** *pa.p.* **-led. -ler** n. one who, or that which, propels; a revolving shaft with blades for driving a ship or airplane [L. *pro*, forward; *pellere*, to drive].

propeller

pro·pen·si·ty (pra·pen'·sa·ti·) n. bent of mind; leaning or inclination [L. *pro*, forward; *pendere, pensum*, to hang].
prop·er (práp'·er) a. fit; suitable; correct or according to usage. **-ly** adv. **— fraction**

(Arith.) one in which the numerator is less than the denominator [L. *proprius*, own].

prop·er·ty (prŏp′·er·ti·) *n.* an inherent or essential quality or peculiarity; ownership; the thing owned; possessions; land; *pl.* theatrical requisites, as scenery, costumes, etc. [L. *proprietas*, fr. *proprius*, own].

proph·e·cy (prŏf′·a·si·) *n.* the foretelling of future events; prediction; revelation of God's will. **prophesy** (prŏf′·a·sī) *v.t.* to foretell; to predict; to utter by divine inspiration; *v.i.* to utter predictions. **prophet** (prŏf′·it) *n.* (*fem.* **prophetess**) one who foretells future events; an inspired teacher or revealer of the Divine Will. **prophetic(al)** *a.* [Gk. *prophētēs*, aforespeaker].

pro·phy·lac·tic (prō·fa·lak′·tik) *a.* (*Med.*) tending to prevent disease, preventive; *n.* medicine or treatment tending to prevent disease. **prophylaxis** *n.* preventive treatment of disease [Gk. *phulassein*, to guard].

pro·pin·qui·ty (prō·ping′·kwa·ti·) *n.* nearness in time or place; nearness in blood relationship [L. *propinquitas*, fr. *prope*, near].

pro·pi·ti·ate (pra·pish′·i·āt) *v.t.* to appease; to conciliate; to gain the favor of. **propitiation** *n.* appeasement; conciliation; atonement. **propitiator** *n.* **propitiatory** *a.* serving, or intended, to propitiate. **propitious** (pra·pish′·as) *a.* favorable; favorably inclined. **propitiously** *adv.* [L. *propitiare*].

pro·po·nent (pra·pō′·nant) *n.* one who supports or makes a proposal [see **propound**].

pro·por·tion (pra·pōr′·shan) *n.* relative size, number, or degree; comparison; relation; relation between connected things or parts; symmetrical arrangement, distribution, or adjustment; (*Arith.*) equality of ratios; the rule of three; *n.pl.* dimensions; *v.t.* to arrange the proportions of. **-al** *a.* a number of quantity in arithmetical or mathematical proportion. **-ally** *adv.* **-ality** *n.* **-ate** *a.* **-ed** *a.* **-ment** *n.* [L. *proportio*, fr. *portio*, a share].

pro·pose (pra·pōz′) *v.t.* to offer for consideration; to suggest; to nominate; *v.i.* to form a plan; to intend; to offer oneself in marriage. **proposal** *n.* the act of proposing; what is offered for consideration; an offer, esp. of marriage. **-r** *n.* **proposition** (prăp·a·zish′·an) *n.* a proposal; a statement or assertion. **propositional** *a.* [L. *proponere*, to put forward].

pro·pound (pra·pound′) *v.i.* to offer for consideration; to propose; to set (a problem) [L. *pro*, forth; *ponere*, to place].

pro·pri·e·tor (pra·prī′·a·ter) *n.* (*fem.* **proprietress, proprietrix**) one who is the owner of property, a business, restaurant, etc. **proprietary** *a.* pert. to an owner; made and sold by an individual or firm having the exclusive rights of manufacture and sale. **-ship** *n.* [L. *proprius*, one's own].

pro·pri·e·ty (pra·prī′·a·ti·) *n.* properness; correct conduct [L. *proprius*, one's own].

pro·pul·sion (pra·pul′·shan) *n.* the act of driving forward. **propulsive, propulsory** *a.* tending, or having power, to propel [L. *pro*, forward; *pellere, pulsum*, to drive].

pro·rate (prō′·rāt) *v.t.* and *i.* to divide or distribute proportionally. **proratable** *a.* **pro rata** in proportion [fr. L.].

pro·sa·ic (prō·zā′·ik) *a.* dull and unimaginative; commonplace. Also **-al, -ally** *adv.* [L. *prosus*, straight-forward].

pro·sce·ni·um (prō·sē′·ni·am) *n.* the part of the stage in front of the curtain [Gk. *pro*, before; *skēnē*, the stage].

pro·scribe (prō·skrīb′) *v.t.* to put outside the protection of the law; to outlaw; to prohibit. **-r** *n.* **proscription** *n.* **proscriptive** *a.* [L. *proscribere*, to publish].

prose (prōz) *n.* ordinary language in speech and writing; language not in verse; *a.* pert. to prose; not poetical; *v.i.* to write prose; to speak or write in a dull, tedious manner. **prosy** *a.* dull and tedious. **prosily** *adv.* [L. *prosa* (*oratio*), direct (speech)].

pros·e·cute (prăs′·i·kūt) *v.t.* to follow or pursue with a view to reaching or accomplishing something; (*Law*) to proceed against judicially; *v.i.* to carry on a legal suit. **prosecution** *n.* (*Law*) the institution and carrying on of a suit in a court of law; the party by which legal proceedings are instituted, as opposed to the *defense*. **prosecutor** *n.* (*fem.* **prosecutrix**) [L. *prosequi*, to follow].

pros·e·lyte (prăs′·e·līt) *n.* a convert to some party or religion; *v.t.* to convert. **proselytize** *v.t.* to make converts. **proselytism** *n.* [Gk. *prosēlutos*, a newcomer].

pros·o·dy (prăs′·a·di·) *n.* the science of versification. **prosodic** (pra·sŏd′·ik) *a.* **prosodist** *n.* one skilled in prosody [Gk. *pros*, to, *ōdē*, a song].

pros·pect (prăs′·pekt) *n.* a wide view; anticipation; reasonable hope; promise of future good. *v.t.* and *i.* to search or explore (a region), esp. for precious metals, oil, etc. **-ive** *a.* looking forward; relating to the future. **-ively** *adv.* **-or** *n.* **-us** *n.* a preliminary statement of an enterprise [L. *prospicere*, to look forward].

pros·per (prăs′·per) *v.t.* to cause to succeed; *v.i.* to succeed; to do well. **-ity** *n.* **-ous** *a.* **-ously** *adv.* [L. *prosper*, fortunate].

pros·tate (prăs′·tāt) *n.* a small gland at the neck of the bladder in males. Also — **gland**

[Gk. *pro*, before; *statos*, placed].

pros·ti·tute (prăs′·ta·tūt) *n.* a harlot; *v.t.* to make a prostitute of; to put to base, infamous, or unworthy use. **prostitution** *n.* [L. *prostituere*, to offer for sale].

pros·trate (prăs′·trāt) *a.* lying on the ground, esp. face downwards; mentally or physically exhausted; *v.t.* to lay flat, as on the ground; to bow down in adoration; to overcome. **prostration** *n.* [L. *pro*, forward; *sternere, stratum*, to lay flat].

pro·tag·o·nist (prō·tag′·an·ist) *n.* the principal actor in a drama; a leading character [Gk. *prōtos*, first; *agōnistēs*, an actor].

pro·tect (pra·tekt′) *v.t.* to defend; to guard; to put a tariff on imports to encourage home industry. **-ion** *n.* defending from injury or harm; state of being defended; that which defends. **-ionism** *n.* the doctrine of protecting industries by taxing competing imports. **-ive** *a.* affording protection; sheltering. **-ively** *adv.* **-or** *n.* one who or that which, defends, **-orate** *n.* (period of) office of a protector of a state; political administration of a state or territory by another country [L. *pro*, in front of; *tegere*, to cover].

pro·té·gé (prō′·ta·zhā) *n.* (*fem.* **protégée**) one under the care, protection, or patronage of another (Fr. *protéger*, to protect).

pro·te·in (prō′·tēn) *n.* a nitrogenous compound required for all animal life processes. Also **proteid** [Gk. *prōtos*, first].

pro·test (pra·test′) *v.i.* to assert formally; to make a declaration against; *v.t.* to affirm solemnly; to object to. **protest** (prō′·test) *n.* a declaration of objection. **-ant** (pra·tes′·tant) *n.* one who holds an opposite opinion. **Protestant** (prăt′·as·tant) *a.* pert. to or belonging to any branch of the Western Church outside the Roman communion; *n.* a member of such a church. **Protestantism** *n.* **protestation** *n.* a solemn declaration, esp. of dissent [L. *pro*, before; *testari*, to witness].

pro·tha·la·mi·on (prō·tha·lā′·mi·an) *n.* a song written in honor of a marriage. Also **prothalamium** [Gk. *pro*, before; *thalamos*, the bridal chamber].

pro·to- (prō′·tō) *prefix* fr. Gk. *prōtos*, first; hence, original; primitive. **-plasm** *n.* a semifluid substance forming the basis of the primitive tissue of animal and vegetable life; living matter. **-plasmatic, -plasmic** *a.* **-type** (prō′·ta·tip) *n.* original or model from which anything is copied; a pattern, **-typal, -typic(al)** *a.* **Protozoa** (prō·ta·zō′·a) *n.pl.* first or lowest division of animal kingdom, consisting of microscopic, unicellular organisms. **-zoon** (prō·ta·zō′·an) *n.* a member of this division. **-zoal, -zoan, -zoic** *a.*

pro·to·col (prō′·ta·kŏl) *n.* an original copy; a rough draft, esp. a draft of terms signed by negotiating parties as the basis of a formal treaty or agreement; rules of diplomatic etiquette [Gk. *prōtokollon*, a flyleaf glued on to a book].

pro·ton (prō′·tŏn) *n.* in physics, the unit of positive electricity, found in the nuclei of all atoms [Gk. *prōtos*, first].

pro·tract (prō·trakt′) *v.t.* to lengthen; to draw out; to prolong; to draw to scale. **-ed** *a.* prolonged; long drawn out; tedious. **-ion** *n.* **-ive** *a.* **-or** *n.* a mathematical instrument for measuring angles; a muscle which draws forward or extends a limb [L. *pro*, forward; *trahere, tractum*, to draw].

protractor

pro·trude (prō·troŏd′) *v.t.* and *i.* to stick out; to project; to thrust forward. **protrusion** *n.* the act of thrusting forward; the state of being protruded or thrust forward; that which protrudes. **protrusive** *a.* [L. *pro*, forward; *trudere, trusum*, to thrust].

pro·tu·ber·ant (prō·tū′·ber·ant) *a.* bulging; swelling out; prominent. **-ly** *adv.* **protuberance** *n.* [L. *protuberare*, to swell].

proud (proud) *a.* haughty; self-respecting. **-ly** *adv.* — **flesh**, excessive granulation in tissue of healing wound [O.E. *prut*, proud].

prove (proōv) *v.t.* to try by experiment; to ascertain as fact, by evidence; to demonstrate; to show; to establish the validity of (a will, etc.) *v.i.* to turn out (to be, etc.); to be found by trial. *pr.p.* **proving.** *pa.p.* **-d** or **-n.** *pa.t.* **provable** *a.* able to be proved. [L. *probare*, to test].

prov·e·nance (prŏv′·a·nans) *n.* source or place of origin. Also **provenience** (prō·vē′·ni·ans) [L. *pro*, forth; *venire*, to come].

prov·en·der (prŏv′·an·der) *n.* a dry food for beasts; fodder; hence provisions; food [O.Fr. *provendre*].

prov·erb (prŏv′·erb) *n.* a short pithy saying to express a truth or point a moral; an adage.

Proverbs *n.pl.* (*Bib.*) book of Old Testament. **-ial** *a.* pert. to or resembling a proverb; well-known. **-ially** *adv.* [L. *proverbium*, fr. *verbum*, a word].

pro·vide (pra·vīd′) *v.t.* to supply; to furnish; to get or make ready for future use; *v.i.* to make preparation; to furnish support (for). **providence** (prŏv′·i·dens) *n.* prudence; wise economy; God's care; an event regarded as an act of God. **Providence** *n.* God Himself. **provident** *a.* prudent; thrifty. **providently** *adv.* **providential** (prŏv·a·den′·shal) *a.* effected by divine foresight; fortunate; lucky. **-r** *n.* [L. *pro*, before; *videre*, to see].

prov·ince (prŏv′·ins) *n.* a division of a country or empire; an administrative district; a district under the jurisdiction of an archbishop; a sphere of action; a department of knowledge; one's special duty. **provincial** (pra·vin′·shal) *a.* pert. to a province or the provinces; countrified; narrow; *n.* an inhabitant of a province. **provincially** *adv.* [L. *provincia*].

pro·vi·sion (pra·vizh′·an) *n.* the act of providing; measures taken beforehand; store esp. of food (generally in *pl.*); a condition or proviso; *v.t.* to supply with provisions. **-al** *a.* temporary; adopted for the time being. **-ally** *adv.* [L. *pro*, before; *videre, visum*, to see].

pro·vi·so (pra·vī′·zō) *n.* a condition or stipulation in a deed or contract. *pl.* **-s** or **-es.** **-ry** *a.* containing a proviso or condition; temporary [L. *proviso quod*, it being provided that].

pro·voke (pra·vōk′) *v.t.* to excite or stimulate to action, esp. to arouse to anger or passion; to bring about or call forth. **provoking** *a.* **provocation** (prŏv·a·kā′·shan) *n.* the act of provoking; that which provokes. **provocative** (pra·vŏk′·a·tiv) *a.* serving or tending to provoke. **provocatively** *adv.* **provocativeness** *n.* [L. *provocare*, to call forth].

prov·ost (prŏv′·ast) *n.* in certain colleges an administrative assistant to the president. — **marshal** (prō′·vō·mar′·shal) *n.* an officer in charge of the military police (army), or of prisoners (navy) [L. *praepositus*, placed before].

prow (prou) *n.* the forepart or bow of a ship; (*Poetic*) a ship [L. *prora*].

prow·ess (prou′·is) *n.* bravery, esp. in war; valor; achievement [Fr. *prouesse*].

prowl (proul) *v.i.* to roam about stealthily; *n.* the act of prowling [M.E. *prollen*].

prox·i·mate (prăk′·si·mit) *a.* next or nearest; closest; immediately following or preceding. **-ly** *adv.* **proximity** *n.* being next in time, place, etc.; immediate nearness. **proximo** *adv.* in or of the coming month [L. *proximus*, nearest].

prox·y (prăk′·si·) *n.* an authorized agent or substitute; one deputed to act for another; a writing empowering one person to vote for another [short fr. *procuracy*].

prude (proōd) *n.* a woman of affected or over-sensitive modesty or reserve. **prudish** *a.* **-ry** *n.* affected modesty; primness; stiffness [O.Fr. *prode*, discreet].

pru·dent (proō·dant) *a.* cautious and judicious; careful; not extravagant. **-ly** *adv.* **prudence** *n.* **prudential** (proō·den′·shal) *a.* **ially** *adv.* [L. *prudens*, foreseeing].

prune (proōn) *n.* a dried plum [Fr. fr. L. *prunum*, a plum].

prune (proōn) *v.t.* to cut off dead parts, excessive branches, etc.; to remove anything superfluous. [O.Fr. *proignier*].

pru·ri·ent (proōr′·i·ant) *a.* given to, or springing from, unclean or lewd thoughts. **-ly** *adv.* **prurience, pruriency** *n.* [L. *prurire*, to itch].

Prus·sia (prush′·a) *n.* (*Geog.*) formerly the leading state of Germany, and the recognized home of German militarism. **-n** *n./a.* **-n blue**, a deep blue salt of potassium and iron, used as a pigment. **prussic acid**, hydrocyanic acid.

pry (prī) *v.i.* to look curiously; to peer; to nose about. *pr.p.* **-ing.** *pa.p.* and *pa.t.* **pried** (prīd). **prier, -er** *n.* [M.E. *prien*, to peer].

psalm (säm) *n.* a sacred song or hymn. **the Psalms** (*Bib.*) a book of the Old Testament. **psalmist** (säm′·ist, sal′·mist) *n.* a writer of psalms. **psalmody** (sa′·ma·di·, sal′·ma·di·) *n.* the art or practice of singing sacred music; psalms collectively. **-odist** *n.* a singer of psalms. **Psalter** (sawl′·ter) *n.* the Book of Psalms. **psaltery** *n.* an obsolete stringed instrument like the zither [Gk. *psalmos*, a twanging of strings].

pseu·d(o)- (sū′·dō) *prefix* fr. Gk. *pseudes*, false, used in many derivatives to signify, false; pretended; sham; not real; wrongly held to be, etc. **-nym** (sū′·da·nim) *n.* a fictitious name; a pen name. **pseudonymous** *a.*

pshaw (shaw) *interj.* expressing contempt, impatience, etc. [imit.].

psit·ta·co·sis (sit·a·kō′·sis) *n.* (*Med.*) a fatal disease found in parrots and communicable to man [L. *psittacus*, a parrot].

pso·ri·a·sis (sa·rī·a·sis) *n.* (*Med.*) chronic skin disease.

psy·che (sī·kē) *n.* the soul personified; the principle of life [Gk. *psychē*, soul, mind].

psy·chi·a·try (sī·kī′·a·tri·) *n.* study and treatment of mental disorders. **psychiater**,

psychiatrist n. a specialist in mental disorders. **psychiatric(al)** a. [Gk. *psychē*, mind; *iatros*, a physician].

psy·chic(al) (sī'·kik, ·ki'·kal) a. pert. to soul, spirit, or mind; spiritualistic. **-ally** adv. **psychic** n. one sensitive to spiritualistic forces; medium. **-ist** n. [Gk. *psychē*, soul, mind].

psy·cho·an·a·ly·sis (sī'·kō·an·al'·a·sis) n. process of studying the unconscious mind; **psychoanalyze** v.t. **psychoanalyst** n. **psychoanalytic(al)**.

psy·chol·o·gy (sī·kál'·a·ji·) n. the scientific study of the mind, its activities, and human and animal behavior. **psychological** a. **psychologically** adv. **psychologist** n. [Gk. *psychē*, the mind; *logos*, a discourse].

psy·cho·pa·thol·o·gy (sī·kō·pa·thál'·a·ji·) n. the science or study of mental diseases. **psychopathy** n. mental affliction. **psychopath** n. one so afflicted. **psychopathic** a.

psy·cho·sis (sī·kō'·sis) n. a general term for any disorder of the mind. pl. **psychoses** [Gk. *psychē*, the mind].

psy·cho·so·mat·ic (sī·kō·sa·mat'·ik) a. of mind and body as a unit; treatment of physical diseases as having a mental origin [Gk. *soma*, body].

psy·cho·ther·a·py (sī·kō·ther'·a·pi·) n. the treatment of disease through the mind, e.g. by hypnotism, auto-suggestion, etc. **psychotherapeutic (-al)** a.

ptar·mi·gan (tar'·ma·gan) n. a bird of the grouse family [Gael. *tarmachan*].

pter·o- (ter'·ō) prefix fr. Gk. *pteron*, a wing. **-dactyl** (ter·a·dak'·til) n. extinct flying reptile with bat-like wings [Gk. *dactylos*, a finger].

pto·maine (tō'·mān, tō·mān') n. substance, usually poisonous, found in putrefying organic matter [Gk. *ptōma*, a corpse].

pu·ber·ty (pū'·ber·ti·) n. the earliest age at which an individual is capable of reproduction. **pubescence** (pū·bes'·ans) n. the period of sexual development; puberty. **pubescent** a. [L. *pubertas*, fr. *pubes*, adult].

pub·lic (pub'·lik) a. of, or pert. to, the people; not private or secret; open to general use; accessible to all; serving the people; n. community or its members; a section of community. **-ly** adv. **-ation** n. making known to the public; proclamation; printing a book, etc. for sale or distribution; a book, periodical, magazine, etc. **publicize** v.t. to make widely known; to advertize. **publicist** n. one versed in, or who writes on, international law, or matters of political or economic interest. **publicity** (pub·lis'·a·ti·) n. the state of being generally known; notoriety; advertisement. **— prosecutor**, the legal officer appointed to prosecute criminals in serious cases on behalf of the state. **— school**, one of a system of schools maintained at public expense [L. *publicus*, fr. *populus*, the people].

pub·lish (pub'·lish) v.t. to make generally known; to proclaim; to print and issue for sale (books, music, etc.); to put into circulation. **-er** n. [L. *publicus*].

puce (pūs) a. a brownish purple; n. the color [Fr. = a flea].

puck (puk) n. a rubber disk used in ice hockey; a mischievous sprite.

puck·er (puk·er) v.t. and i. to gather into small folds or wrinkles; to wrinkle; n. a wrinkle; a fold; **-y** a. [fr. *poke*, a bag].

pud·ding (pood'·ing) n. name of various forms of cooked foods, usually in a soft mass, served as a dessert.

pud·dle (pud'·l) n. a small pool of dirty water; a mixture of clay and water used as rough cement; v.t. to make muddy; to line embankments, etc. with puddle; to stir molten pig iron; v.i. to make muddy. **puddling** n. **-r** n. [O.E. *pudd*, a ditch].

pu·er·ile (pū'·er·il) a. childish; foolish; trivial. **-ly** adv. **puerility** n. childishness; triviality [L. *puer*, a boy].

pu·er·per·al (pū·ur'·per·al) a. pert. to, or caused by childbirth. **— fever** (Med.) a fever developing after childbirth [L. *puer*, a child; *parere*, to bear].

puff (puf) n. a short blast of breath or wind; its sound; a small quantity of smoke, etc.; a swelling; a light pastry; a soft pad for applying powder; exaggerated praise, esp. in a newspaper; a quilt; v.i. to send out smoke, etc. in puffs; to breathe hard; to pant; to swell up; v.t. to send out in a puff; to blow

out; to smoke hard; to cause to swell; to praise unduly. **-er** n. **-ing** n. **-ingly** adv. **-y** a. inflated; swollen; breathing hard. **-iness** n. **— paste** n. a short, flaky paste for making light pastry [imit. origin].

puf·fin (puf'·in) n. a sea bird of the auk family with a parrot-like beak [M.E. *pofin*].

pug (pug) n. a small, snub-nosed dog; a. **— nose** n. a turned-up nose.

pug (pug) v.t. to make clay plastic by grinding with water; to fill in spaces with mortar in order to deaden sound [etym. uncertain].

pu·gil·ism (pū'·ja·lizm) n. the art of fighting with the fists; boxing. **pugilist** n. a boxer. **pugilistic** a. [L. *pugil*, a boxer, fr. *pugnus*, the fist].

pug·na·cious (pug·nā'·shas) a. given to fighting; quarrelsome. **-ly** adv. **pugnacity** (pug·nas'·a·ti·) n. [L. *pugnare*, to fight].

pu·is·sant (pū'·i·sant, pwis'·ant) a. powerful; mighty. **-ly** adv. **puissance** n. power [Fr. fr. L. *potens*, powerful].

puke (pūk) v.t. and i. to vomit.

pul·chri·tude (pul'·kri·tūd) n. beauty; comeliness [L. *pulcher*, beautiful].

pule (pūl) v.i. to chirp; to cry weakly; to whimper; to whine [imit. origin].

pull (pool) v.t. to draw towards one; to drag; to haul; to tug at; to pluck; to row a boat; v.i. to draw with force; to tug; n. act of pulling; force exerted by it; a tug; a means of pulling; effort; (Slang) influence, unfair advantage; (Print.) a rough proof; (Golf) a curving shot to the left. **-er** n. **—over** n. sweater put on by pulling over head [O.E. *pullian*].

pul·let (pool'·it) n. a young hen [Fr. *poulet*].

pul·ley (pool'·i·) n. a small wheel with a grooved rim on which runs a rope, used for hauling or lifting weights [Fr. *poulie*].

Pull·man·car (pool'·man·kàr) n. a railway car. Also **Pullman** [fr. G. M. *Pullman* (1831-97), the inventor].

pul·mo- (pul'·ma) prefix from L. *pulmo*, the lung. **-nary** (pul'·ma·ner·i·) a. pert. to or affecting the lungs. **-nic** a. pert. to, or affecting, the lungs.

pulp (pulp) n. a soft, moist, cohering mass of animal or vegetable matter; the soft, succulent part of fruit; the material of which paper is made; v.t. to reduce to pulp; to remove the pulp from. **-y** a. like pulp. **-iness** n. [L. *pulpa*, flesh, pith].

pul·pit (pool'·pit) n. elevated place in a church for preacher [L. *pulpitum*, a stage].

pul·sate (pul'·sāt) v.t. to beat or throb, as the heart; to vibrate; to quiver. **pulsation** n. **pulsatile** a. producing sounds by being struck, as a drum. **pulsative**, **pulsatory** a. capable of pulsating; throbbing [L. *pulsare*, to throb].

pulse (puls) n. the beating or throbbing of the heart or blood vessels, esp. of the arteries; the place, esp. on the wrist, where this rhythmical beat is felt; any measured or regular beat. v.i. to throb or pulsate [L. *pulsus*, beating].

pulse (puls) n. leguminous plants or their seeds, as beans, peas, etc. [L. *puls*, porridge].

pul·ver·ize (pul'·ver·īz) v.t. to reduce to a fine powder; to smash or demolish; v.i. to fall

down into dust. **pulverization** n. **-r** n. [L. *pulvis*, dust].

pu·ma (pū'·ma) n. a large American carnivorous animal of the cat family; cougar [Peruv.].

pum·ice (pum'·is) n. Also **— stone**, a light, porous variety of lava, used for cleaning, polishing, etc. [L. *pumex*].

pum·mel See **pommel**.

pump (pump) n. an appliance used for raising water, putting in or taking out air or liquid, etc.; v.t. to raise with a pump, as water; to free from water by means of a pump; to extract information by artful questioning; v.i. to work a pump; to raise water with a pump [Fr. *pompe*].

pump (pump) n. a low, thin-soled shoe [Dut.].

pump·kin (pump'·kin) n. a plant of the gourd family; its fruit, used as food [O.Fr. *pompon* fr. Gk. *pepon*, ripe].

pun (pun) n. a play on words similar in sound but different in sense; v.i. to use puns. pr.p. **-ning**. pa.p. and pa.t. **-ned**. **-ster** n. one who makes puns.

punch (punch) n. a drink made of fruit juices, sugar, and water, sometimes carbonated or with liquor [Hind. *panch*, five (ingredients)].

punch (punch) n. a tool used for making holes or dents; a machine for perforating or stamping; v.t. to perforate, dent, or stamp with a punch [Fr. *poinçon*, an awl, fr. L. *pungere*, to pierce].

punch (punch) v.t. to strike with the fist; to beat; to bruise; of cattle, to drive; n. a blow with the fist; (Slang) energy [fr. *punish*].

punc·tate (pungk'·tāt) a. having many points; having dots scattered over the surface. Also **punctated** [L. *pungere*, to pierce].

punc·til·i·o (pungk·til'·i·ō) n. a fine point of etiquette; formality. a. attentive to punctilio; strict in the observance of rules of conduct, etc.; scrupulously correct. **-usly** adv. **-usness** n. [L. *punctum*, a point].

punc·tu·al (pungk'·choo·al) a. arriving at the proper or fixed time; prompt; not late; (Geom.) pert. to a point. **-ly** adv. **-ity** n. [L. *punctum*, a point].

punc·tu·ate (pungk'·choo·āt) v.t. to separate into sentences, clauses, etc. by periods, commas, colons, etc.; to emphasize in some significant manner; to interrupt at intervals. **punctuation** n. the act or system separating by the use of **punctuation marks** (the period, comma, colon, semi-colon, etc.) [L. *punctum*, a point].

punc·ture (pungk'·cher) n. an act of pricking; a small hole made by a sharp point; a perforation; v.t. to make a hole with a sharp point [L. *pungere*, to prick].

pun·dit (pun'·dit) n. a title given to a Hindu scholar; any learned person [Hind. *pandit*].

pun·gent (pun'·jant) a. sharply affecting the taste or smell; stinging; sarcastic; caustic. **-ly** adv. **pungency** n. [L. *pungere*, to prick].

pun·ish (pun'·ish) v.t. to inflict a penalty for an offense; to chastise. **-able** a. **-ment** n. **punitive** (pū'·ni·tiv) a. pert. to or inflicting punishment [L. *punire*, to punish].

punk (pungk) n. crumbly, decayed wood; a. (Slang) worthless [etym. uncertain].

punt (punt) v.t. and i. to kick a football, when dropped from the hands, before it touches the ground; n. such a kick.

pu·ny (pū'·ni·) a. small and feeble; petty. **puniness** n. [O.Fr. *puisne*].

pup (pup) n. a puppy or young dog; a young seal; v.i. to bring forth puppies or whelps. pr.p. **-ping**. pa.p., pa.t. **-ped** [short fr. *puppy*, fr. Fr. *poupée*, a doll or puppet].

pu·pa (pū'·pa) n. the third stage in the metamorphosis of an insect, when it is in a co-

coon; a chrysalis. *pl.* **pupae** (pū′·pē). **-1** *a.*
-te *v.i.* to become a pupa [L. *pupa*, a girl].
pu·pil (pū′·pil) *n.* a student; a boy or girl
under the care of a guardian; the small circular opening in the center of the iris of the eye.
-age *n.* the state of being a pupil; the period
of time during which one is a pupil. **-lary**
a. pert. to a pupil or ward; pert to the pupil
of the eye [L. *pupillus*, an orphan boy].
pup·pet (pup′·it) *n.* a marionette; a person
whose actions are completely controlled by
another. **-ry** *n.* a puppet show [Fr. *popuée*,
a doll; L. *puppa*].
pup·py See **pup.**
pur·blind (pur′·blīnd) *a.* almost blind; dull in
understanding. **-ly** *adv.* **-ness** *n.* [fr. *pure*
and *blind*].
pur·chase (pur′·chas) *v.t.* to buy; to obtain
by any outlay of labor, time, sacrifice, etc.;
(*Law*) to obtain by any means other than
inheritance; *n.* acquisition of anything for a
price or equivalent; a thing bought; **pur-
chasable** *a.* **-r** *n.* [Fr. *pourchasser*, to obtain
by pursuit].
pure (pyoor) *a.* free from all extraneous matter; untainted; spotless; blameless; unsullied;
chaste; innocent; absolute; theoretical, not
applied. **-ly** *adv.* entirely; solely. **-ness** *n.*
purity *n.* freedom from all extraneous matter; freedom from sin or evil [L. *purus*].
pu·rée (pyoo·rā′) *n.* a thick soup [Fr.].
purge (purj) *v.t.* to purify; to cleanse; to
clear out; to clear from guilt, accusation, or
the charge of a crime, etc.; to remove from
an organization, political party, army, etc.
undesirable or suspect members; to cleanse
the bowels by taking a cathartic medicine;
n. a cleansing, esp. of the bowels; a purgative. **purgation** (pur·gā′·shan) *n.* act of
cleansing or purifying; act of freeing from
imputation of guilt; purging. **Purgative**
(pur′·ga·tiv) *a.* having the power of purging; *n.* any medicine which will cause evacuation of bowels. **purgatory** (pur′·ga·tōr·i·)
a. tending to cleanse; purifying; expiatory;
n. in R.C. faith, place where souls of dead
are purified by suffering; (*Fig.*) a place or
state of torment. **purgatorial** *a.* [L. *purgare*,
fr. *purus*, pure].
pu·ri·fy (pyoor′·a·fī) *v.t.* to make pure, clear,
or clean; to free from impurities; to free
from guilt or defilement; *v.i.* to become pure.
purification (pyoor·a·fa·kā′·shan) *n.* **puri-
ficative** *a.* **purifier** *n.* [L. *purus*, pure;
facere, to make].
pur·ist (pyoor′·ist) *n.* an advocate of extreme
care or precision in choice of words, etc.; a
stickler for correctness [L. *purus*, pure].
Pu·ri·tan (pyoor′·a·tan) *n.* a member of the
extreme Protestant party, who desired further
purification of the Church after the Elizabethan
reformation; (*l.c.*) a person of extreme strictness in morals or religion; *a.* pert. to Puritans or to puritan. **-ic(al)** *a.* pert. to Puritans, their doctrine and practice; over-scrupulous. **-ically** *adv.* **-ism** *n.* doctrine and
practice of Puritans; narrow-mindedness [L.
puritas, purity, fr. *purus*].
purl (purl) *n.* an embroidered border; a
knitting stitch that is reverse of plain stitch;
v.t. to ornament with purls; *v.i.* to knit in
purl. Also **pearl** [fr. *purfle*].
purl (purl) *v.i.* to flow with a burbling sound
or gentle murmur [imit. origin].
pur·lieu (pur′·loo) *n.* ground bordering on
something; *pl.* outlying districts; outskirts
[O. Fr. *puralleé*, a survey].
pur·loin (pur·loin′) *v.i.* to steal; to pilfer
[O.Fr. *purloigner*, to put far away].
pur·ple (pur′·pl) *n.* a color between crimson
and violet; robe of this color, formerly reserved for royalty; royal dignity; *a.* purple-
colored; dark red; *v.i.* to make or dye a purple color; *v.i.* to become purple. **born to the
purple,** of princely rank [Gk. *porphura*,
shellfish that gave Tyrian purple].
pur·port (pur′·pōrt) *n.* meaning; apparent
meaning; import; aim. **purport** (per·pōrt′)
v.t. to mean; to be intended to seem [O. Fr.
porporter, to embody].
pur·pose (pur′·pas) *n.* object in view; aim;
end; plan; intention; effect; purport; *v.t.* to
intend; to mean to. **-ly** *adv.* intentionally;
expressly. **-ful** *a.* determined resolute. **-fully**
adv. **-less** *a.* aimless. **-lessly** *adv.* **purposive**
a. done with a purpose [O.Fr. *porpos*, fr. *por-
poser*, to propose].
pur·pu·ra (pur′·pya·ra) *n.* (*Med.*) the appearance of purple patches under the skin,

caused by hemorrhage; shellfish, yielding
purplish fluid. **purpureal** (per·pū′·rē·al) *a.*
purple. **purpuric** *a.* pert. to purpura [Gk.
porphura]. See **purple.**
purr (pur) *n.* a low, murmuring sound made
by a cat; *v.i.* to utter such a sound.
purse (purs) *n.* a small bag or pouch to carry
money in; money offered as a prize, or collected as a present; money; *v.t.* to wrinkle
up; to pucker. **-r** *n.* (*Naut.*) officer in charge
of accounts, etc. on board a ship. **-ful** *a.*
enough to fill a purse. — **strings** *n.pl.* power
to control expenditure [Fr. *bourse*, a purse,
fr. Gk. *bursa*, a hide].
pur·sue (per·sū′) *v.t.* to follow with the aim
of overtaking; to run after; to chase; to aim
at; to seek; to continue; *v.i.* to go on; to proceed; **-r** *n.* **pursuance** *n.* the act of pursuing.
pursuant *a.* done in consequence, or performance, of anything. **pursuit** (per·sūt′) *n.* the
act of pursuing; a running after; chase; profession; occupation. **pursuivant** (pur′·swi-
vant) *n.* an attendant [Fr. *poursuivre*, fr. L.
prosequi, to follow].
pu·ru·lent (pyoor′·a·lant) *a.* pert. to, containing, or discharging pus, or matter; septic;
suppurating. **purulence, purulency** *n.* [L.
pus, puris, matter].
pur·vey (per·vā′) *v.t.* (*Brit.*) to furnish or
provide; to supply, esp. provisions. **-ance** *n.*
act of purveying; supplies; former royal prerogative of requisitioning supplies, or enforcing personal service. **-or** *n.* [L. *providere*, to
provide].
pur·view (pur′·vū) *n.* the enacting clauses of
a statute; scope; range. [Fr. *pourvu*, pro-
vided].
pus (pus) *n.* the yellowish-white matter produced by suppuration [L. *pus*, matter].
push (poosh) *v.t.* to move or try to move away
by pressure; to drive or impel; to press hard;
to press or urge forward; to shove; *v.i.* to
make a thrust; to press hard in order to move;
n. a thrust; any pressure or force applied;
emergency; enterprise; (*Mil.*) an advance or
attack on a large scale. **-er** *n.* **-ing** *a.* given
to pushing oneself or one's claims; self-
assertive. **-ingly** *adv.* [Fr. *pousser*, fr. L.
pellere, to drive].
pu·sil·lan·i·mous (pū·sa·lan′·a·mas) *a.* cowardly; faint-hearted; mean-spirited. **-ly** *adv.*
pusillanimity *n.* [L. *pusillus*, very small;
animus, spirit].
puss (poos) *n.* a cat; *slang* face. **-y** *n.*
pus·tule (pus′·chool) *n.* a small swelling or
pimple containing pus. **pustular, pustulous**
a. [L. *pustula*, a blister].
put (poot) *v.t.* to place; to set; to lay; to
apply; to state; to propose; to throw; *v.i.* to
go. *pr.p.* **-ting.** *pa.p.* and *pa.t.* **put.** *n.* a
throw, esp. of a heavy weight. **to put about**
(*Naut.*) to alter a ship's course [Late O.E.
putian].
pu·ta·tive (pū′·ta·tiv) *a.* commonly thought;
supposed; reputed. **-ly** *adv.* **putation** *n.* [L.
putare, to think].
pu·tre·fy (pū′·tra·fī) *v.t.* and *i.* to make or
become rotten; to decompose; to rot. **putrefaction** *n.* the rotting of animal or vegetable
matter; rottenness; decomposition. **putrefac-
tive** *a.* **putrescence** *n.* tendency to decay;
rottenness. **putrescent** *a.* **putrid** (pū′·trid)
a. in a state of decay; (*Colloq.*) very bad.
putridity, putridness *n.* [L. *putere*, to rot;
facere, to make].
putt (put) *v.t.* and *i.* (*Golf*) to hit a ball in
the direction of the hole; (*Scot.*) to throw (a
weight or iron ball) from the shoulder; *n.* the
stroke so made in golf; the throw of the
weight. **-er** *n.* one who putts; a short golf
club [var. of *put*].

putter

put·ter (put′·er) *v.i.* to work or act in a
feeble, unsystematic way; to dawdle. Also
potter. [var. of *potter*, O.E. *potian*, to poke].
put·ty (put′·i·) *n.* a kind of paste or cement,
used by plasterers; *v.t.* to fix, fill up, etc. with
putty. **puttier** *n.* [Fr. *potée*, the contents of
a pot].
puz·zle (puz′·l) *n.* a bewildering or perplexing
question; a problem, etc. requiring clever
thinking to solve it; a conundrum; *v.t.* to
perplex; to bewilder; (with 'out') to solve
after hard thinking; (with 'over') to think

hard over; *v.i.* to be bewildered. **-r** *n.* **puzzling** *a.* bewildering, perplexing [fr. M.E.
opposal, a question, interrogation].
py·e·mi·a, pyaemia (pī·ē′·mi·a) *n.* (*Med.*)
blood-poisoning [Gk. *pyon*, pus; *haima*, blood].
Pyg·my, Pigmy (pig′·mi·) *n.* one of a race
of dwarf Negroes of C. Africa. (*l.c.*) a very
small person or thing; a dwarf; *a.* diminutive
[Gk. *pygmē*, a measure of length from elbow
to knuckles].
py·lon (pī′·lan) *n.* a post or tower marking
an entrance, a course for air races, etc.; the
gateway of an ancient support; power-trans-
mission cables [Gk. *pylōn*, a gateway].

py·or·rhe·a (pī·a·rē′·a) *n.* (*Med.*) a dental
discharge of pus from the gums. Also **pyor-
rhoea** [Gk. *pyon*, pus; *rhoia*, a flowing].
pyr·a·mid (pir′·a·mid) *n.* a solid figure on a
triangular, square, or polygonal base, and with
sloping sides meeting at an apex; a structure
of this shape. **-al** *a.* pert. to, or having the
form of a pyramid. **-ally** *adv.* [Gk. *pyramis*].

pyre (pīr) *n.* a pile of wood for burning a dead
body; funeral pile [Gk. *pyra*, fire].
py·ret·ic (pī·ret′·ik) *a.* (*Med.*) pert. to, producing, or relieving, fever; feverish. **pyrexia**
n. fever [Gk. *pyretos*, fever, fr. *pur*, fire].
py·rite (pī′·rīt) *n.* a yellow mineral formed
of sulphur and iron; iron pyrites. **pyrites**
(pī·rī′·tēz, pī′·rīt) *n.pl.* a name for many
compounds of metals with sulphur, esp. iron
pyrites, or copper pyrites. **pyritic, pyritif-
erous, pyritous** *a.* pert. to, or yielding,
pyrites [Gk. *pyra*, fire].
py·ro- (pī′·ra) *prefix* fr. Gk. *pur*, fire, used in
many derivatives. — **electricity** *n.* the property possessed by some crystals, of becoming
electrically polar when they are heated.
py·ro·ma·ni·a (pī·ra·mā′·ni·a) *n.* a mania
for setting things on fire. **pyromaniac** *n.*
[Gk. *pyr*, fire; and *mania*].
py·ro·tech·nics (pī·ra·tek′·niks) *n.pl.* the
art of making fireworks; the art of displaying
them. Also **pyrotechny. pyrotechnic, pyro-
technical** *a.* [Gk. *pyr*, fire; *technē*, art].
Py·thag·o·ras (pi·thag′·a·ras) *n.* a Greek
philosopher and mathematician (582-507 B.C.).
py·thon (pī′·than) *n.* a large, non-poisonous
snake that kills its prey by crushing it; a
spirit; [Gk. *Pythōn*, the serpent slain by
Apollo near Delphi].
pyx (piks) *n.* the vessel in which the consecrated bread or Host is kept; a box at a Brit.
mint in which specimen coins are kept for
trial and assay; *v.t.* to test by assay. **-is** *n.* a
small pyx; a casket [Gk. *pyxis*, fr. *pyxos*,
a box tree].

Q

quack (kwak) *v.i.* to cry like a duck; to act as a quack; *n.* cry of duck or like sound; one who pretends to skill in an art, esp. in medicine; a charlatan; *a.* pert. to quackery. **-ery** *n.* **-salver** *n.* a quack doctor [imit.].
Quad·ra·ges·i·ma (kwod·ra·jes′·i·ma) *n.* (*Church*) the first Sunday of Lent. **-l** *a.* pert. to Lent [L. *quadragesimus*, fortieth].
quad·ran·gle (kwȧd′·rang·gl) *n.* in geometry, a plane figure having four sides and angles; a square or court surrounded by buildings (*abbrev.* **quad**) **quadrangular** *a.* [L. *quattuor*, four and *angle*].
quad·rant (kwȧd′·rant) *n.* the fourth part of the area of a circle; an arc of 90°; an instrument for taking altitude of heavenly bodies; in gunnery, an instrument to mark the degrees of a gun's elevation [L. *quadrans*, a fourth part].

quad·rate (kwȧd′·rāt) *a.* having four sides and four right angles; square; divisible by four (used chiefly in anatomical names); *n.* ɑ square; **quadrate** *v.i.* to agree; to suit.
quadratic (kwȧd·rat′·ik) *a.* pert. to, or resembling, a square; square; (*Alg.*) involving the second but no higher power of the unknown quantity, esp. in **quadratic equation**.
quadrature (kwȧd′·ra·cher) *n.* the act of squaring or reducing to a square; the position of one heavenly body with respect to another 90° away [L. *quadratus*, squared].
quad·ri- (kwod′·ri·) *comb. form*, four [L. *quattuor*, four].
quad·ri·cen·ten·ni·al (kwȧd·ra·sen·ten′·i·al) *a.* pert. to a period of four hundred years; *n.* the four hundredth anniversary [L. *quattuor*, four; *centum*, hundred; *annus*, a year].
quad·ri·lat·er·al (kwȧd·re·lat′·er·al) *a.* having four sides; *n.* (*Geom.*) a plane figure having four sides [L. *quattuor*, four; *latus*, side].
qua·drille (kwa·dril′, ka·dril′) *n.* an 18th cent. card game; a square dance; also, the music played to such a dance [L. *quadrus*, square].
quad·ril·lion (kwȧd·ril′·yon) *n.* a number represented in the Fr. and U.S. notation by one with 15 ciphers annexed; in Great Britain and Ger. by one followed by 24 ciphers [L. *quattuor*, four and *million*].
quad·ri·no·mi·al (kwȧd·ra·nō′·mi·al) *a.* (*Alg.*) consisting of four terms.
quad·ri·par·tite (kwȧd·ra·pȧr′·tīt) *a.* divided into four parts.
quad·roon (kwȧd·róon·) *n.* offspring of mulatto and white; one who is one-fourth Negro [Sp. *cuarteró*, fr. L. *quartus*, fourth].
quad·ru·mane (kwȧd′·roo·mān) *n.* an animal which has all four feet formed like hands. **quadrumanous** *a.* four-handed [L.*quatiuor*, four; *manus*, the hand].
quad·ru·ped (kwȧd′·roo·ped) *n.* an animal having four feet; *a.* having four feet [L. *quattuor*, four; *pes*, *pedis*, a foot].
quad·ru·ple (kwȧd′·róō·pl) *a.* fourfold; *n.* a four fold amount; a sum four times as great as another; *v.t.* to multiply by four; *v.i.* to be multiplied by four. **-t** one of four children born at a birth. **quadruplicate** *v.t.* to multiply by four; *n.* one of four things corresponding exactly; *a.* fourfold. **quadruplication** *n.* [L. *quadru-plus*, fourfold].
quaff (kwȧf) *v.t.* and *i.* to swallow in large drafts; *n.* a drink.

quag·mire (kwag′·mīr) *n.* soft, wet land, yielding under the feet; a bog; (*Fig.*) a difficult position. **quaggy** *a.* spongy; boggy; like quagmire. [fr. *quake*].
quail (kwāl) *v.i.* to lose spirit; to shrink or cower; to flinch [Fr. *cailler*, to curdle].
quail (kwāl) *n.* a game bird [Fr. *caille*].
quaint (kwānt) *a.* interestingly old-fashioned or odd; curious and fanciful; whimsical. **-ly** *adv.* **-ness** *n.* [O.Fr. *cointe*, prudent].
quake (kwāk) *v.i.* to tremble or shake with fear, cold, or emotion; to quiver or vibrate; *n.* a shaking or trembling; *abbrev.* of 'earthquake' [O.E. *cwacian*].
Quak·er (kwāk′·er) *n.* (*fem.* **-ess**) a member of the Society of Friends, a religious sect founded in the 17th cent. by George Fox. **-ism** *n.*
qual·i·fy (kwȧl′·a·fī) *v.t.* to ascribe a quality to; to describe (as); to fit for active service or office; to prepare by requisite training for special duty; to furnish with the legal title to; to limit; to diminish; *v.i.* to make oneself competent; to show oneself fit for. **qualifier** *n.* **qualifiable** *a.* **qualification** *n.* the act of qualifying or condition of being qualified; any endowment or acquirement that fits a person for an office or employment; modification; restriction [L. *qualis*, of what kind; *facere*, to make].
qual·i·ty (kwȧl′·a·ti·) *n.* a particular property inherent in a body or substance; an essential attribute, distinguishing feature, or characteristic; character or nature; degree of excellence; excellence or superiority of sound, tonal color. **qualitative** *a.* relating to quality; concerned with quality. [L. *qualitas*, of what kind].
qualm (kwȧm) *n.* a sudden attack of illness, faintness, nausea, distress; a scruple of conscience [Ger. *qualm*, vapor].
quan·da·ry (kwȧn′·dri·, da·ri·) *n.* a state of perplexity; a predicament; a dilemma.
quan·ti·fy (kwȧn′·ta·fī) *v.t.* to fix or express the quantity of; to measure. **quantification** *n.* [L. *quantus*, how much; *facere*, to make].
quan·ti·ty (kwȧn·ta·ti·) *n.* property of things ascertained by measuring; amount; bulk; a certain part; a considerable amount; number; (*Pros.*) the length or shortness of vowels, sounds, or syllables; *pl.* abundance; profusion. **quantitative** (kwȧn′·ta·tā·tiv) *a.* relating to quantity [L. *quantus*, how much].
quan·tum (kwȧn′·tam) *n.* quantity or amount; a specified, desired, or required amount. *pl.* **quanta**. [L. *quantus*, how much].
quar·an·tine (kwawr′·an·tēn) *n.* isolation of infected persons to prevent spread of serious disease; the period during which a ship, with infectious disease aboard, is isolated; *v.t.* to put under quarantine [Fr. *quarantaine*, forty days].
quar·rel (kwawr′·al) *n.* rupture of friendly relations; an angry altercation; a dispute; *v.i.* to dispute; to wrangle; to disagree; *pr.p.* **-er** *n.* **-some** *a.* apt to quarrel; irascible; contentious [L. *queri*, to complain].
quar·ry (kwawr′·i·) *n.* an excavation whence stone is dug for building; any source from which material may be extracted; *v.t.* to dig from a quarry. *pa.p.* and *pa.t.* **quarried** [L. *quadrare*, to square, hew (stones)].
quar·ry (kwawr′·i·) *n.* prey; victim [O.Fr. *cuiree*, fr. L. *corium*, skin].
quart (kwawrt) *n.* the fourth part of a gallon; one eighth of a peck [L. *quartus*, fourth].
quar·ter (kwawr′·ter) *n.* fourth part; (*U.S. and Canada*) one fourth of a dollar, or the coin valued at this amount; one of the four cardinal points of the compass; one limb of a quadruped with the adjacent parts; a term in a school, etc.; part of a ship's side aft of mainmast; a region; a territory; a division of a town, or county; clemency; *pl.* assigned position; lodgings, esp. for soldiers; shelter; *v.t.* to divide into four equal parts; to divide up a traitor's body; to furnish with shelter; *v.i.* to have temporary residence. **-ing** *n.* an assignment of quarters for soldiers. **-ly** *a.* consisting of a fourth part; occurring every quarter of a year; *n.* a review or magazine published four times a year; *adv.* by quarters; once in a quarter of a year. **—deck** *n.* a part of deck of a ship which extends from stern to mainmast. **-master** *n.* (*Mil.*) an officer in

charge of quarters, clothing, stores, etc.; (*Naut.*) a petty officer who attends to steering, signals, stowage, etc. **-master-sergeant** *n.* the N.C.O. assistant to the quartermaster. [L. *quartarius*, fr. *quartus*, fourth].
quar·tet, quartette (kwawr·tet′) *n.* (*Mus.*) a composition of four parts, each performed by a single voice or instrument; set of four who perform this; a group of four [Fr.].
quar·to (kwawr′·tō) *a.* denoting the size of a book in which the paper is folded to give four leaves to the sheet (*abbrev.* **4to**); *n.* a book of the size of the fourth of a sheet [L. *in quarto*, in a fourth part].
quartz (kwawrts) *n.* kinds of mineral, consisting of pure silica or silicon dioxide [Ger. *quarz*].
quash (kwȧsh) *v.t.* to crush; to quell; (*Law*) to annul, overthrow, or make void [L. *quassare*, to shake].
qua·si (kwā′·sī, kwȧ′·sē) as if; as it were; in a certain sense or degree; seeming; apparently; it is used as adj. or adv. and as prefix to noun, adj., or adv. [L.].
quat·rain (kwȧt′·rān) *n.* (*Pros.*) a stanza of four lines [L. *quattoor*, four].
qua·ver (kwā′·ver) *v.i.* to shake, tremble, or vibrate; to sing or play with tremulous modulations; *v.t.* to utter or sing with quavers or trills; *n.* a trembling, esp. of the voice.
quay (kē, kwā) *n.* a landing place used for the loading and unloading of ships; a wharf. **-age** *n.* payment for use of a quay; space occupied by quays [Fr. *quai*].
quea·sy (kwē′·zi·) *a.* affected with nausea; squeamish; fastidious. **queasily** *adv.* **queasiness** *n.* [etym. uncertain].
queen (kwēn) *n.* the consort of a king; a woman who is the sovereign of a kingdom; the sovereign of a swarm of bees, ants, etc.; any woman who is pre-eminent; one of the chief pieces in a game of chess. *v.i.* to act the part of a queen (usu. 'to queen it'). **-ly** *a.* like, appropriate to a queen; majestic. **-liness** *n.* **-hood** *n.* state or position of a queen. **— consort** *n.* the wife of a king. **— dowager** *n.* the widow of a king. **— mother** *n.* a queen dowager who is also mother of reigning monarch. **— regent** *n.* a queen reigning in her own right. [O.E. *cwen*, a woman].
queer (kwir) *a.* odd; singular; quaint; (*Colloq.*) of a questionable character; faint or out of sorts; *v.t.* (*Slang*) to spoil. **-ly** *adv.* **-ish** *a.* somewhat queer. **-ness** *n.* [Ger. *quer*, oblique, crosswise].
quell (kwel) *v.t.* to subdue; to put down; to suppress forcibly. **-er** *n.* [O.E. *cwellan*, to kill].
quench (kwench) *v.t.* to extinguish; to put out, as fire or light; to cool or allay; to stifle; to slake (thirst). **-able** *a.* **-less** *a.* **-er** *n.* [O.E. *cwencan*].
quer·u·lous (kwer′·a·las) *a.* peevish; fretful. **-ly** *adv.* **-ness** *n.* [L. *queri*, to complain].
que·ry (kwir′·i·) *n.* a question; an inquiry; a mark of interrogation; *v.t.* to inquire into; to call in question; to mark as of doubtful accuracy [L. *quaerere* to seek or inquire].
quest (kwest) *n.* search; the act of seeking; the thing sought; *v.i.* to search; to seek [L. *quaerere*, *quaestum*, to seek].
ques·tion (kwes′·chan) *n.* interrogation; inquiry; that which is asked; subject of inquiry or debate; (subject of) dispute; a matter of doubt or difficulty; a problem; *v.t.* to inquire of by asking questions; to be uncertain of; to challenge; to take objection to; to interrogate; **-able** *a.* doubtful; suspicious. **-ably** *adv.* **-ableness** *n.* or *n.* **— mark** *n.* a mark of interrogation (?). **out of the question**, not to be thought of. **to beg the question**, to assume as fact something which is to be proved [L. *quaestio*, fr. *quaerere* to seek, ask].
ques·tion·naire (kwes·cha·ner′) *n.* a list of questions [Fr.].
queue (kū) *n.* a pigtail [Fr. fr. L. *cauda*, a tail].
quib·ble (kwib′·l) *n.* an evasion of the point in question by a play upon words, or by stressing unimportant aspect of it; equivocation; *v.i.* to use quibbles. **-r** *n.* [dim. of obs. *quib*].
quick (kwik) *a.* animated; sprightly; ready or prompt; sensitive; rapid; hasty; impatient;

fresh and invigorating; pregnant; *n.* living persons; sensitive flesh under nails; (*Fig.*) one's tenderest susceptibilities; *adv.* also **-ly**, rapidly; promptly. **-ness** *n.* **-en** *v.t.* to make alive; to make active or sprightly; to hasten; to sharpen or stimulate; *v.i.* to become alive; to move with greater rapidity. **-ener** *n.* **-ening** *n.* a making or becoming quick; first movement of fetus in womb. **-sand** *n.* sand, readily yielding to pressure, esp. if loose and mixed with water. **-silver** *n.* mercury. **-step** *n.* a march; a lively dance step [O.E. *cwic,* alive].

quid (kwid) *n.* a portion suitable for chewing, esp. of tobacco; a cud [form of *cud*].

quid (kwid) *n.* (*Brit. Slang*) a pound sterling.

quid-di-ty (kwid'·a·ti·) *n.* a trifling nicety; a quibble; the essence of anything [L. *quidditas* fr. *quid,* what?].

qui-es-cent (kwi·es'·ant) *a.* still; inert; motionless; at rest. **-ly** *adv.* **quiescence, quiescency** *n.* [L. *quiescere,* to rest].

qui-et (kwi'·at) *a.* still; peaceful; not agitated; placid; of gentle disposition; not showy; *n.* calm; peace; tranquillity; *v.t.* to reduce to a state of rest; to calm; to allay or appease; to silence; *v.i.* to become quiet. **-en** (*Dial.*) *v.t.* and *i* to quiet. **-ly** *adv.* **-ness** *n.* **-ude** *n.* freedom from noise, disturbance, alarm; tranquillity; repose. **quietus** (kwi·ē'·tas) *n.* final acquittance, of debt, etc.; (*Fig.*) extinction [L. *quietus*].

quill (kwil) *n.* a large, strong, hollow feather used as a pen; a spine or prickle, as of a porcupine; a piece of small reed on which weavers wind thread; an implement for striking the strings of certain instruments; *v.t.* to plait or form into small ridges [M.E. *quil*].

quilt (kwilt) *n.* any thick, warm coverlet; *v.t.* to stitch together, like a quilt, with a soft filling; to pad. **-ed** *a.* [L. *culcita,* a cushion].

qui-na-ry (kwi'·na·ri·) *a.* consisting of, or arranged in, fives [L. *quinque,* five].

quince (kwins) *n.* a hard, yellow, acid fruit, somewhat like an apple [Fr. *coing;* L. *cydonium;* fr. *Cydonia,* a city in Crete].

qui-nine (kwi·nin) *n.* a bitter alkaloid obtained from various species of cinchona bark;

it is used as a tonic and febrifuge. **quinic** *a.* [Peruv. *kina,* bark].

quin-qu(e)- (kwin'·kw(a)), *prefix* fr. L. *quinque,* five.

Quin-qua-ges-i-ma (kwing·kwa·jes'·a·ma) *n.* the Sunday before Ash Wednesday, so called because fifty days before Easter [L. *quinquagesimus,* fiftieth].

quin-sy (kwin'·zi·) *n.* a severe inflammation of the throat and tonsils [Gk. *kunanchē,* fr. *kuōn,* a dog; *anchein,* to choke].

quin-tes-sence (kwin·tes'·ans) *n.* the pure essence of anything; the perfect embodiment of a thing. **quintessential** *a.* [L. *quinta essentia,* fifth essence].

quin-tet, quintette (kwin·tet') *n.* (*Mus.*) a composition for five voices or instruments; a company of five singers or players; a set of five [L. *quintus,* fifth].

quin-til-lion (kwin·til'·yan) *n.* (*U.S. and France*) a number represented by one with 18 ciphers following; (*Great Britain and Germany*) one with 30 ciphers following [fr. L. *quintus,* fifth, and million].

quin-tu-ple (kwin'·tóò·pl) *a.* multiplied by five; fivefold; *v.t.* to make fivefold; to multiply by five. **-ts** *n.pl.* five children at a birth (*Colloq.* **quints**) [fr. L. *quintus,* fifth, by imit. of quadruple].

quip (kwip) *n.* a smart, sarcastic turn of phrase; a gibe; a witty saying. **-ster** *n.* [L. *quippe,* indeed (ironical)].

quire (kwir) *n.* 24 sheets of paper of the same size, the twentieth part of a ream [O.Fr. *quaier,* fr. L. *quattuor,* four].

quirk (kwurk) *n.* sudden turn or twist; a quibble; a peculiarity. **-y** *a.* [etym. uncertain].

quit (kwit) *v.t.* to depart from; to leave; to cease from; to give up; to let go; *v.i.* to depart; to stop doing a thing; *a.* released from obligation; free. *pr.p.* **-ting** *pa.p., pa.t.,* **quit** or **-ted. -tance** *n.* discharge from a debt of obligation; receipt. **-ter** *n.* (*Colloq.*) a person easily discouraged. **to be quits,** to be equal with another person by repayment (of money, of good, or evil) [O.Fr. *quiter,* fr. L. *quietare,* to calm].

quite (kwit) *adv.* completely; wholly; entirely; positively [M.E. *quite,* free].

quiv-er (kwiv'·er) *n.* a case or sheath for holding arrows [O.Fr. *cuivre,* fr. Ger.].

quiv-er (kwiv'·er) *v.i.* to shake with a tremulous motion; to tremble; to shiver; *n.* the act of quivering; a tremor [O.E. *cwifer,* to risk].

Qui-xo-te (kē·hōt'·i·, kwik'·sát) *n.* the hero of the great romance of Miguel Cervantes. **quixotic** (kwik·sát'·ik) *a.* like Don Quixote; ideally and extravagantly romantic. **quixotically** *adv.* **quixotism. quixotry** *n.*

quiz (kwiz) *n.* a test or examination; a hoax or jest. *v.t.* to question. *pr.p.* **-zing** *pa.p. pa.t.* **zed, -zer** *n.* **-zical** *a.* odd; amusing; teasing [etym. unknown].

quoin (koin) *n.* (*Archit.*) the external angle, esp. of a building; a cornerstone; (*Gun.*) a metalic wedge inserted under the breech of a gun to raise it; (*Print.*) a small wooden wedge used to lock the types in the galley etc. [Fr. *coin,* a corner].

quoit (kwoit) *n.* a flat, iron ring to be pitched at a fixed object in play; *v.i.* the game of throwing these on to a peg; *v.i.* to play at quoits.

quon-dam (kwán'·dam) *a.* former; that was once; sometime [L. = formerly].

quo-rum (kwō'·ram) *n.* the number of members that must be present at a meeting to make its transactions valid [L.]

quo-ta (kwō'·ta) *n.* a proportional part or share [L. *quot,* how many?].

quote (kwōt) *v.t.* to copy or repeat a passage from; to cite; to state a price for; *n.* a quotation; *pl.* quotation marks. **quotation** (kwō·tā'·shan) *n.* — **marks** *n.pl.* marks ("—") used to indicate beginning and end of a quotation [Late L. *quotare,* to distinguish by numbers, fr. L. *quot,* how many?].

quoth (kwōth) *v.t.* (*Arch.*) said; spoke (used only in the 1st and 3rd persons) [O.E. *cwethan,* to say].

quo-tid-i-an (kwō·tid'·i·an) *a.* daily; *n.* thing returning daily, esp. fever [L. *quotidie,* daily].

quo-tient (kwō'·shant) *n.* number resulting from division of one number by another [L. *quotiens,* how many times?].

R

rab-bet (rab'·it) *n.* a groove made so as to form, with a corresponding edge, a close joint; *v.t.* to cut such an edge [O.Fr. *raboter,* to plane].

rab-bi (rab'·l), **rab-bin** (rab'·in) *n.* a Jewish teacher of the Law. **-nic(al)** [Heb. = my master].

rab-bit (rab'·it) *n.* a small, burrowing rodent mammal, like the hare, but smaller. — **hutch** *n.* an enclosure for rearing tame rabbits. **-ry,** — **warren** *n.* the breeding place of wild rabbits [etym. uncertain].

rab-ble (rab'·l) *n.* a noisy, disorderly crowd; the common herd; *v.t.* to mob.

rab-id (rab'·id) *a.* furious; fanatical; affected with rabies. **-ly** *adv.* **-ness, -ity** *n.* [L. *rabidus*].

ra-bies (rā'·bēz) *n.* canine madness; hydrophobia [L. fr. *rabere,* to be mad].

rac-coon, racoon (ra·kòòn') *n.* one of a genus of plantigrade carnivorous mammals of N. America [Algonquin].

race (rās) *n.* the descendants of a common ancestor; distinct variety of human species; a peculiar breed, as of horses, etc.; lineage; descent. **racial** *a.* pert. to race or lineage. **racially** *adv.* **racialism, racism** *n.* animosity shown to peoples of different race [It. *razza*].

race (rās) *n.* swift progress; rapid motion; a contest involving speed; a strong current of water; the steel rings of an antifriction ball bearing; *v.t.* to cause to run rapidly; *v.i.* to

run swiftly; of an engine, pedal, etc., to move rapidly without control. **-r** *n.* one who races; a racehorse, yacht, car, etc., used for racing. — **horse** *n.* a horse bred to run for a stake or prize. — **track** *n.* a track used for horse racing, etc. **racing** *n.* [O.E. *ras,* a swift course].

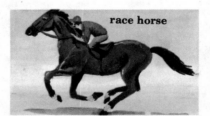

race horse

ra-chis (rā'·kis) *n.* an axial structure, such as vertebral column in animals, the stem of a plant, a quill, etc. *pl.* **rachides. rachitic** *a.* having rickets. **rachitis** (ra·kī'·tis) *n.* rickets [Gk. *rhachis,* the spine].

rack (rak) *n.* an instrument for stretching; an instrument of torture by which the limbs were racked to point of dislocating; hence, torture; an open framework for displaying books, bottles, hats, baggage, etc.; a framework in which hay is placed; a straight cogged bar to gear with a toothed wheel to produce linear motion from rotary motion, or vice-versa; *v.t.* to stretch almost to breaking point; to overstrain; to torture; to place in a rack. **-ed** *a.* **-ing** *a.* agonizing (pain). — **and ruin** destruction [Dut. *rak,* fr. *rekken,* to stretch].

rack-et racquet (rak'·it) *n.* bat used in tennis, etc.; *pl.* a ball game played in a paved court with walls; a snowshoe [Fr. *raquette*].

rack-et (rak'·it) *n.* a confused, clattering noise' din; (*Slang*) an occupation by which much money is made illegally; *v.i.* to make noise or clatter. **-eer** *n.* a gangster.

racket

rac-on-teur (rak·an·tur') *n.* one skilled in telling anecdotes [Fr. *raconter,* to recount].

rac-y (rā'·si·) *a.* lively; having a strong flavor; spicy; pungent. **racily** *adv.* **raciness** *n.*

ra-dar (rā'·dar) *n.* radiolocation or apparatus used in it (fr. initial letters of *radio, detection, and ranging*).

ra-di-al (rā'·di·al) *a.* pert. to a ray, radius, or radium; branching out like spokes of a wheel [L. *radius,* a ray].

ra-di-an (rā'·di·an) *n.* (*Math.*) the angle subtended by an arc of a circle equal in length to the radius of a circle.

ra-di-ant (rā'·di·ant) *a.* emitting rays; beaming; radiating; *n.* (*Astron.*) point in sky from which a shower of meteors appears to come; (*Opt.*) luminous point from which rays of light emanate. **radiance, radiancy** *n.* radiant intensity; brilliancy; splendor. **-ly** *adv.* [L. *radius,* a ray].

ra-di-ate (rā'·di·āt) *v.i.* to branch out like the spokes of a wheel; to emit rays; to shine; *v.t.* to emit rays, as heat, etc. *a.* with rays diverging from a center. **radiation** *n.* emission and diffusion of rays from central point. **radiator** *n.* any device which radiates or emits rays of heat or light; apparatus for heating rooms; in motoring, apparatus to split up and cool circulating water in water-cooling system [L. *radius,* a ray].

rad-i-cal (rad'·i·kal) *a.* pert. to the root; original; basic; complete; thorough; of extreme or advanced liberal views; *n.* (*Gram.*) a root; a primitive word; a politician who advocates thorough reforms; (*Chem.*) a basal atomic group of elements which passes unchanged through a series of reactions of the compound of which it is a part; (Bot.) a radicle; a root-let; (Math.) a quantity expressed as the root of another. **-ism** n. root and branch political reform. **-ly** adv. **-ness** n. [L. radix, a root].

radiator

rad·i·cle (rad′·i·kəl) n. (Med.) the initial fibril of a nerve; (Bot.) the primary root of an embryo plant; any rootlet [L. radix, a root].

ra·di·o- (rā′·di·ō) prefix used in forming compound terms with the meaning 'of rays,' 'of radiation,' 'of radium,' as in — **active** (rād·ē·ō·ak′·tiv) a. emitting from an atomic nucleus invisible rays which penetrate matter. **-activity** n. **-element** n. metallic chemical element having radioactive properties. **-graph** n. an instrument for measuring and recording the intensity of the heat given off by the sun; a photograph taken by means of X-ray or other rays. **-grapher** n. **-graphy** n. **-logy** n. the science of radioactivity in medicine. **-logist** n. **-scopy** n. examination by X-rays. **-therapy**, **-therapeutics** n. treatment of disease by radium or X-rays [L. radius, a ray].

ra·di·o (rā′·di·ō) n. wireless telephony or telegraphy; apparatus for reception of broadcast; a radio telegram. **-gram** n. a telegram transmitted by radio. [L. radius, a ray].

rad·ish (rad′·ish) n. an annual herb with pungent edible root [L. radix, a root].

ra·di·um (rā′·di·əm) n. a metallic, radioactive element [L. radius, a ray].

ra·di·us (rā′·di·əs) n. a straight line from center of circle to circumference; the spoke of a wheel; distance from any one place; the bone on the thumb side of forearm; movable arm of a sextant. pl. **-es, radii** [L. = a ray].

ra·dix (rā′·diks) n. a root; source; origin; a radical; (Anat.) the point of origin of a structure, as the root of a tooth; (Math.) fundamental base of system of logarithms or numbers. pl. **-es, radices** [L. = root].

ra·don (rā′·dån) n. a gaseous, radioactive element; radium emanation.

raff (raf) n. the mob; a worthless fellow. **-ish** a. cf. **riff-raff** [O. Fr. raffer, to snatch].

raf·fi·a (raf′·i·a) n. the fiber from a cultivated palm used for mats, baskets, etc. [Native].

raf·fle (raf′·l) n. a lottery; cloth to sell by raffle. **-r** n. [orig. a dicing game, Fr. rafle].

raft (raft) n. an improvised float of planks fastened together; a mass of logs chained together for easy transportation down a river; v.i. to proceed by raft [O.N. raptr].

raft (raft) n. (Colloq.) a great quantity.

raft·er (raf′·ter) n. a sloping beam, from the ridge to the eaves, to which the roof covering is attached; v.t. to provide with rafters [O.E. raefter].

rag (rag) n. a fragment of cloth; a remnant; a scrap; (Slang) a newspaper; pl. mean or tattered attire; a. made of rags. **-amuffin** n. a ragged, dirty and disreputable person. **-man**, **-picker** n. one who collects rags. **-tag** n. the rabble; riffraff. **-time** n. popular dance music, of Negro origin, marked by strong syncopation. **-weed** n. a widespread weed, common cause of hay fever [O.E. ragg].

rag (rag) v.t. to tease; to nag; pr.p. **-ging** pa.t. and pa.p. **-ged** [etym. uncertain].

rage (rāj) n. violent excitement; extreme anger; craze; fashion; v.i. to be furious with anger; to rave; to proceed violently and without check (as a storm; battle, etc.]. **raging** a. **ragingly** adv. [Fr. fr. L rabies, madness].

rag·ged (rag′·əd) a. worn to tatters; dressed in rags; jagged; slip-shod; imperfectly performed; not rhythmical. **-ly** adv. **-ness** n.

rag·lan (rag′·lən) n. an overcoat with wide sleeves running up to the neck, not to the shoulders [fr. Lord Raglan, 1788-1855].

ra·gout (ra·gōō′) n. fragments of meat, stewed and highly seasoned; a hash [Fr.].

raid (rād) n. a hostile incursion depending on surprise and rapidity; surprise visit by police to suspected premises; an attack on a town by hostile aircraft; v.t. to make a sudden attack upon. **-er** n. [var. of road].

rail (rāl) n. a piece of timber or metal extending from one post to another, as of a fence or balustrade; bars of steel on which the flanged wheels of vehicles run; a track for locomo-tives; a railway; a horizontal bar for support; top of ship's bulwarks; v.t. to enclose with rails; to send by railway. **-ing** n. material for rails; a construction of rails. **-road** n. a road on which steel rails are laid for wheels to run on; a system of such rails and all equipment; the company that runs it. **-way** n. a line of tracks, for wheeled vehicles [O.Fr. reille, fr. L. regula, a rule].

rail (rāl) n. wading birds [Fr. râle].

rail (rāl) v.i. to use insolent and reproachful language; to utter abuse. **-er** n. **-lery** n. good-humored banter; ridicule [Fr. railler].

rai·ment (rā′·mənt) n. (Poetic) clothing dress; apparel [for arraiment, fr. array].

rain (rān) n. condensed moisture, falling in drops from clouds; a shower; v.t. and v.i. to fall as rain; to pour down like rain. **-bow** n. arch showing seven prismatic colors and formed by refraction and reflection of sun's rays in falling rain. — **check** n. a ticket for a future performance, game, etc. when one is stopped by rain. **-coat** n. a light, rainproof overcoat. **-fall** n. a fall of rain; the amount of rain, in inches, which falls in a particular place in a given time. **-iness** n. **-less** a. **-proof** a. impervious to rain. **-y** a. [O.E. regn].

raise (rāz) v.t. to cause to rise; to elevate; to promote; to build up; to collect; to produce by cultivation; to rear; to increase; to enliven; to give up (seige); to heighten (voice); a. **-d** a. elevated. **raising** n. [O.N. reisa].

rai·sin (rā′·zn) n. a dried grape [O.Fr. raizin fr. L. racemus, a bunch of grapes].

raj (rāj) n. sovereignty; rule; dominion. **raja**, **rajah** n. king, prince, or noble of the Hindus [Hind. raja].

rake (rāk) n. a long-handled garden implement; an agricultural machine used in hay-making; v.t. and v.i. to scrape with a toothed implement; to draw together, as mown hay; to sweep or search over; to ransack; to scour; to fire shot lengthwise into a ship, etc. a **rake-off** (Slang) a monetary commission esp. if illegal [O.E. raca].

rake (rāk) n. a dissolute man of fashion; a libertine **rakish** a. **rakishly** adv. [M.E. rakel; corrupt, of rake-hell].

rake (rāk) n. an angle of inclination; the inclination of masts from the perpendicular; the projection of the upper parts of the stem and stern beyond the keel of a ship; v.i. to incline from perpendicular. **rakish** a. having a backward inclination of the masts; speedy-looking. **rakishly** adv. [Scand. raka, to reach].

ral·ly (ral′·i·) v.t. and v.i. to reassemble; to collect and restore order, as troops in confusion; to recover (strength; health); to return a ball (in tennis). n. act of rallying; assembly; outdoor demonstration; lively exchange of strokes in tennis [Fr. rallier].

ram (ram) n. male sheep; a swinging beam with a metal head for battering; a hydraulic engine; a beak projecting from bow of warship; (Astron.) Aries, one of the signs of zodiac; v.t. to consolidate loose material with a rammer; to drive against with violence; to butt; to cram; pr.p. **-ming** pa.t. and pa.p. **-med, -er** n. [O.E. ram].

ram·ble (ram′·bl) v.i. to walk without definite route; to talk or write incoherently; n. a short stroll or walk. **-r** n. one who rambles; a climbing rose. **rambling** a. wandering.

ram·bunc·tious (ram·bung(k)′·shəs) a. boisterous; noisy (Slang).

ram·e·kin (ram′·a·kin) n. a cheese preparation or other food mixture baked in a small dish; the dish itself [F. ramequin].

ram·i·fy (ram′·a·fī) v.t. and v.i. to branch out in various directions. **ramification** n. a branch; any subdivision proceeding from a main structure [L. ramus, a branch; facere, to make].

ramp (ramp) v.i. to rear up on hind legs; n. a gradual slope; [Fr. ramper, to climb].

ram·page (ram′·pāj) n. a state of excitement or passion, as **on the rampage;** v.i. (ram-pāj′) to rush about, in a rage; to act violently. **-ous** a. [fr. ramp].

ramp·ant (ramp′·ant) a. rearing; violent; in full sway; rank. **rampancy** n. [Fr. ramper, to climb].

ram·part (ram′·pårt) n. mound of earth around fortified place; that which provides security; v.t. to strengthen with ramparts [Fr. rempart].

ram·rod (ram′·råd) n. rod used in ramming down charge of a gun; a rod for cleaning barrel of a rifle, etc. [fr. ram.].

ram·shack·le (ram′·shak·l) a. tumble-down; rickety; beyond repair [fr. shake].

ran (ran) pa.t. of run.

ranch (ranch) n. prairie land for sheep and cattle rearing; a farm; v.i. to keep a ranch. **-er** n. man who owns or works on a ranch [Sp. Amer. rancho, a grazing farm].

ran·cid (ran′·sid) a. having a rank smell; smelling or tasting like stale fat. **-ly** adv. **-ness, -ity** n. [L. rancidus].

ran·cor (rang′·ker) n. bitter and inveterate ill-feeling. **-ous** a. evincing intense and bitter hatred; malignant. **-ously** adv. [L. rancor].

rand (rand) n. thin inner sole of shoe; high land above river valley [O.E. rand, a border].

ran·dom (ran′·dəm) a. done haphazardly; aimless; fortuitous; n. in phrase, **at random,** haphazard [O.Fr. random, headlong rush].

ra·nee, rani (rán′·ē) n. in India, a queen or wife of a prince.

rang (rang) pa.t. of ring.

range (rānj) v.t. to set in a row; to rank; to rove over; v.i. to extend; to roam; to be in line with; to pass from one point to another; to fluctuate between, as prices, etc.; n. limits, or distance within which something is possible; a row; a large kitchen stove; line of mountains; compass or register of voice or instrument; distance to a target; place for practice shooting; pasture land. **-er** n. keeper of park or forest. **rangy** a. roaming; long-limbed; slender [Fr. ranger, fr. rang, a rank].

rank (rangk) n. row or line; soldiers standing side by side; grade in armed services; status; a class; social position; eminence; relative position; pl. enlisted soldiers; v.t. to arrange in class, order, or division; to place in line or abreast; to take rank over; v.i. to be placed in a rank or class; to possess social or official distinction. **-er** n. **-ing** n. arrangement; disposition [Fr. rang].

rank (rangk) a. growing too thickly; exuberant; offensively strong of smell; rancid; gross; vile; excessive. **-le** v.i. to be inflamed; to become more violent; to remain a sore point with. **-ly** adv. **-ness** n. [O.E. ranc, strong, proud].

ran·sack (ran′·sak) v.t. to search thoroughly; to plunder [O.N. rannsaka].

ran·som (ran′·səm) n. a price paid for release of prisoner; immense sum of money; v.t. to redeem from captivity [O.Fr. fr. L. redemptio, buying back].

rant (rant) v.i. to rave; to talk wildly and noisily; n. noisy and meaningless declamation; boisterous talk. **-er** n. [O.Dut. ranten, to rave].

rap (rap) n. a smart, light blow; a knock on door, etc.; a tap; v.t. and v.i. to deliver a smart blow; to knock; pr.p. **-ping** pa.t. and pa.p. **-ped** [prob. imit.].

ra·pa·cious (ra·pā′·shas) a. subsisting on prey; greedy; grasping. **-ly** adv. **-ness, rapacity** n. [L. rapere, to seize].

rape (rāp) n. carnal knowledge of a female against her will; the act of snatching or carrying off by force; v.t. to ravish or violate [L. rapere, to seize].

rape (rāp) n. an annual of the cabbage family, the seeds of which yield vegetable oils [L. rapum, turnip].

rap·id (rap′·id) a. very quick; fast; speedy; hurried; descending steeply. **-s** n.pl. part of a river where current rushes over rocks. **-ity** n. **-ly** adv. **-ness** n. [L. rapidus].

ra·pi·er (rā′·pi·ẹr) n. a light, slender, pointed sword, for thrusting only [Fr. rapière].

rap·ine (rap′·in) n. act of plundering; pillage; plunder [L. rapina, fr. rapere, to snatch].

rap·port (ra·pōr′) n. harmony; agreement. **en rapport,** in relation to; in harmony with [Fr.].

rap·proche·ment (ra·prōsh·màng′) n. reconciliation; restoration of friendly relations [Fr.].

rap·scal·lion (rap·skal′·yạn) n. a scamp; a rascal. See **rascal.**

rapt (rapt) a. intent; transported; in a state of rapture. **-ure** n. extreme joy; ecstasy; bliss; exultation. **-urous** a. ecstatic; exulting. **-urously** adv. [L. rapere, raptum, to snatch away].

rare (rer) a. underdone (of meat) [O.E. hrere, boiled gently].

rare (rer) a. uncommon, few and far between; thin, not dense, as air; extremely valuable; of the highest excellence. **-faction** n. act of rarefying; decrease of quantity of a gas in fixed volume. **rarefy** (rer′·a·fī) v.t. to make rare or less dense; v.i. to become less dense. **-ly** adv. **-ness** n. **rarity** n. state of being rare; thinness; something rare or seldom seen [L. rarus].

rare·bit (rer′·bit) n. (Cookery) Welsh rabbit; cheese sauce on toast, etc. [corrupt. of rabbit].

ras·cal (ras′·kal) n. a rogue; a scoundrel; a scamp; a. dishonest; low. **-ity** n. knavery; base villainy. **-ly** a. [O.Fr. rascaille, the rabble].

rash (rash) a. without reflection; precipitate. **-ly** adv. **-ness** n. [Dut. rasch, quick].

rash (rash) n. a temporary, superficial eruption of the skin [O.Fr. *rasche*, itch].

rash·er (rash'·ẹr) *n.* a thin slice of bacon [Fr. *arracher*, to tear up].

rasp (rasp) *v.t.* to rub or file; to scrape (skin) roughly; to speak in grating manner; to irritate; *n.* a form of file with one side flat and the other rounded; a rough, grating sound. **-ing** *a.* emitting a harsh, grating sound; irritating. **-ingly** *adv.* [O.Fr. *rasper*].

rasp·ber·ry (raz'·ber·i·) *n.* a plant, cultivated for its fruit; a small drupe, the fruit of the plant; (*Slang*) derisory applause [E. *rasp*, rough, like a file].

rat (rat) *n.* large rodent; (*Slang*) one who deserts his party; (*Colloq.*) padding to puff out women's hair; *v.i.* to hunt rats; to abandon party or associates in times of difficulty. *pr.p.* **-ting** *pat.* and *pa.p.* **-ted. -ter** *n.* a rat-catcher; a terrier which kills rats. **-ting** *n.* [O.E. *raet*].

rat·a·fi·a (rat·a·fē'·a) *n.* a liqueur, such as curaçoa; a cordial [Fr.].

ratch·et (rach'·it) *n.* a bar or piece of mechanism turning at one end upon a pivot, while the other end falls into teeth of wheel, allowing the latter to move in one direction only [Fr. *rochet*, ratchet of a clock].

rate (rāt) *n.* established measure; degree; standard; proportion; ratio; value; price; movement, as fast or slow; *v.t.* to estimate value; to settle relative scale, rank, price or position of; *v.i.* to be set in a class; to have rank. **-able, ratable** *a.* **ratability** *n.* **rating** *n.* assessment; (*Naut.*) classification of a ship; amount set as a rate [O.Fr. fr. L. *rata* (*pars*), fixed portion].

rate (rāt) *v.i.* to take to task; to chide.

rather (raTH'·ẹr) *adv.* preferably; on the other hand; somewhat [O.E. *hrathe*, quickly].

rat·i·fy (rat'·a·fī) *v.t.* to confirm or sanction officially; to make valid. **ratification** *n.* [L. *ratus*, fixed; *facere*, to make].

rat·ing See **rate**.

ra·tio (rā'·shō) *n.* relation one quantity has to another, as expressed by number of times one can be divided by the other; proportion [L.].

ra·ti·oc·i·nate (rash·i·as'·a·nāt) *v.i.* to reason logically. **ratiocination** *n.* deductive reasoning. **ratiocinative** *a.* [L.*ratiocinari*, to reckon].

ra·tion (ra'·shan, rā'·shan) *n.* fixed allotted portion; daily allowance of food, drink, etc., to armed forces; *pl.* provisions; *v.t.* to limit to fixed amount [Fr. fr. L. *ratio*].

ra·tion·al (rash'·an·al) *a.* sane; sensible; reasonable; (*Math.*) a quantity expressed in finite terms or whose root is a whole number. **-e** (rash·a·nal') *n.* logical basis; exposition of principles. **-ization** *n.* in psychology, the attempt to square one's conscience by inventing reasons for one's own conduct; **-ize** *v.t.* **-ism** *n.* philosophy which makes reason the sole guide; system opposed to supernatural or divine revelation. **-ist** *a.* **istic(al)** *a.* **-istically** *adv.* **-ity** *n.* the power or faculty of reasoning; soundness of mind. **-ly** *adv.* [L. *rationalis*, fr. *ratio*, reason].

rats·bane (ratz'·bān) *n.* rat poison.

rat·tan, ratan (ra·tan') *n.* a species of palm found in India and the Malay Peninsula, the stems used for wickerwork, etc.; a walking-stick made from a rattan cane [Malay, *rotan*].

rat·tle (rat'·l) *v.i.* to clatter; to speak (on) eagerly and noisily; *v.t.* to move along, quickly and noisily; (*Colloq.*) to disconcert, or ruffle; *n.* a rapid succession of clattering sounds; a toy for making a noise; rings at the end of a rattlesnake's tail. **-brained, -headed, -pated** *a.* empty-headed; giddy; lacking stability. **-snake** *n.* an American poisonous snake. **rattling** *n.* clattering; *a.* brisk; lively; first-rate; *adv.* extremely; very [M.E. *ratelen*].

rat·ty (rat'·i·) *a.* full of rats; (*Slang*) shabby.

rau·cous (raw'·kas) *a.* hoarse; harsh; rough. **-ly** *adv.* [L.*raucus*].

rav·age (rav'·ij) *v.t.* to lay waste; to despoil; to plunder; *n.* ruin; destruction [Fr.].

rave (rāv) *v.i.* to talk in delirium or with great enthusiasm. **-r** *n.* **raving** *n.* delirium; incoherent or wild talk; *a.* delirious; (*Colloq.*) exceptional. **ravingly** *adv.* [O.Fr. *raver*].

rav·el (rav'·al) *v.t.* to entangle; to make intricate; to fray out; *v.i.* to become twisted and involved; to fall into confusion. *n.* complication; unraveled thread [Dut. *ravelen*].

ra·ven (rā'·van) *n.* crow with glossy black plumage, predatory in habit; *a.* glossy black,

---

esp. of hair [O.F. *hraefn*].

rav·en, ravin (rav'·n) *v.t.* and *v.i.* to devour; to prowl for prey; to be ravenous; *n.* rapine; plunder; spoil. **-er** *n.* a plunderer. **-ous** *a.* famished; voracious; eager for prey. **-ously** *adv.* [Fr. *ravir*, fr. L. *rapere*, to seize].

ra·vine (ra·vēn') *n.* a deep, narrow gorge; a gully [O.Fr. fr. L. *rapere*, to carry off].

rav·ish (rav'·ish) *v.t.* to seize and carry away by violence; to rape; to enrapture; to charm eye or ear. **-er** *n.* **-ing** *a.* entrancing; captivating. **-ingly** *adv.* **-ment** *n.* [Fr. *ravir*, fr. L. *rapere*, to carry off].

raw (raw) *a.* not cooked; not covered with skin; chilly and damp; untrained; not manufactured. *n.* a sore; naked state. **-boned** *a.* having little flesh; gaunt. **-hide** *n.* compressed untanned leather; a riding whip of untanned leather. **-ly** *adv.* **-ness** *n.* — **deal**, unfair and undeserved treatment [O.E. *hreaw*].

ray (rā) *n.* a narrow beam of light; the path along which light and electro-magnetic waves travel in space; a heat radiation; one of a number of lines diverging from a common point or center; a gleam or suggestion (of hope, truth, etc.); *v.t.* and *v.i.* to radiate; to send forth rays. **-ed** *a.* having rays [O.Fr. *raye*, fr. L. *radus*, a beam].

ray (rā) *n.* a flat fish allied to skate, shark, and dogfish [O.Fr. *raye*].

ray·on (rā'·an) *n.* a synthetic fibrous material in imitation of silk [Fr.].

raze, rase (rāz) *v.t.* to level to the ground; to destroy completely; to demolish [Fr. *raser*, fr. L. *radere, rasum*, to scrape].

ra·zor (rā'·zẹr) *n.* a keen-edged cutting appliance for shaving. **-back** *n.* kind of hog; rorqual or finbacked whale [Fr. *rasoir*, fr. L. *radere, rasum*, to scrape].

razz (raz) *v.t.* to ridicule [fr. *raspberry*].

re-, *prefix* used in the formation of compound words, usually to signify *back* or *again* [L.]

re (rē) *prep.* in reference to; concerning. **in re**, in the case (of) [L. *res*, thing].

reach (rēch) *v.t.* to extend; to stretch; to touch by extending hand; to attain to or arrive at; to come to; to obtain; to gain; *v.i.* to stretch out the hand; to strain after; to be extended; to arrive; *n.* reaching; easy distance; mental range; scope; grasp; straight stretch of water, etc. **-able** *a.* [O.E. *raecan*, to stretch out].

re·act (rē·akt') *v.i.* to respond to stimulus; to exercise a reciprocal effect on each other; to resist the action of another body by an opposite effect; (*Chem.*) to cause or undergo a chemical or physical change when brought in

---

contact with another substance or exposed to light, heat, etc. **-ance** *n.* (*Elect.*) resistance in a coil to an alternating current due to capacity or inductance in the circuit. **-ion** *n.* action in opposite direction to another; the response to stimulus, influence, events, etc. **-ionary** *a.* tendency to reaction. *n.* one opposed to progressive ideas in politics, religion, thought, etc. **-ionist** *n.* **-ivation** *n.* restoration to an activated state. **-ive** *a.*

re·act (rē'·akt) *v.t.* to act again; to repeat.

re·ac·tor (rē·act'·ẹr) *n.* apparatus for generating heat by nuclear fission.

read (rēd) *v.t.* to peruse and understand written or printed matter; to interpret mentally; to read and utter; to understand any indicating instrument (as a gas meter); *v.i.* to perform the act of reading; to find mentioned in writing or print; to surmise. *pat.* and *pa.p.* **read** (red). **read** (red). *a.* versed in books; learned. **-able** (rēd) *a.* well written; informative; interesting; legible. **-ably** (rēd) *adv.* **-er** (rēd) *n.* one who reads; one whose office is to read prayers; one who determines suitability for publication of manuscripts offered to publisher; corrector of printer's proofs; a reading book. **-ing** (rēd) *a.* pert. to reading; *n.* act of reading; a public recital of passages from books; interpretation of a passage from a book [O.E. *raedan*, to make out].

read·i·ly, readiness See **ready**.

re·ad·just (rē·a·just') *v.t.* to adjust or put in order again. **-ment** *n.*

read·y (red'·i·) *a.* prepared; fitted for use; handy; prompt; quick; willing; apt; *v.t.* to prepare. *n.* position of a fighting unit or their weapons, as *at the ready*. **readily** *adv.* **readiness** *n.* **-made** *a.* not made to measure. — **money**, cash in hand [O.E. *raede*].

re·a·gent (rē·ā·'jant) *n.* any substance employed to bring about a characteristic reaction in chemical analysis. **reagency** *n.*

re·al (rē'·al) *a.* actual; not sham; not fictitious or imaginary; not assumed; unaffected; (*Law*) heritable; denoting property not movable or personal, as lands and tenements. **reality** (ri·al'·a·ti·) *n.* actuality; fact; truth. **-ly** *adv.* actually; indeed; *interj.* is that so? **-ty** *n.* real estate. — **estate**, — **property**, immovable property [L.L. *realis*, fr. L. *res*, a thing].

re·al (rē'·al) *n.* an obsolete Spanish coin [Sp. fr. L. *regalis*, royal].

re·al·ize (rē'·al·īz) *v.t.* to make real; to yield (profit); to convert into money; to apprehend or grasp the significance of. **realization** *n.* **realism** *n.* interest in things as they are; practical outlook on life; representation in art or letters of real life, even if sordid and repellent; (*Philos.*) doctrine that matter has a separate existence apart from conceptions of it in the mind; doctrine that general terms and ideas have objective existence and are not mere names. **realist** *n.* **realistic** *a.* pert. to realism; factual; practical; true to life. **realistically** *adv.* [Fr. *réaliser*].

reality, realtor, realty See **real** (1).

realm (relm) *n.* kingdom; province; region [O.Fr. *realme*, fr. L. *regalis*, royal].

ream (rēm) *n.* a paper measure containing from 472 to 516 sheets, usually 500 sheets (20 quires) [Ar. *rizmah*, bundle].

ream (rēm) *v.t.* to enlarge or make a tapered or conical hole with a reamer. **-er** *n.* a machine tool for enlarging a hole [O.E. *rum*, room].

reap (rēp) *v.t.* to cut down ripe grain for harvesting; to harvest; to receive as fruits of one's labor. **-er** *n.* a harvester; a reaping machine [O.E. *ripan*].

reaper

rear (rir) *n.* back of hindmost part; part of army or fleet behind the others. **-most** *a.* last of all; at the very back [L. *retro*, behind].

rear (rir) *v.t.* to raise; to bring to maturity, as young; to erect or build; *v.i.* to rise up on the hindlegs, as a horse [O.E. *raeran*].

re·arm (rē·ārm') *v.t.* to equip the fighting services with new weapons. **-ament** *n.*

re·ar·range (rē·a·rānj') *v.t.* to arrange anew; to set in a different order. **-ment** *n.*

rea·son (rē'·zn) *n.* a faculty of thinking; power of understanding; intelligence; the logical premise of an argument; cause; motive; purpose; excuse; *v.i.* to use rational faculty; to deduce from facts or premises; to argue with; *v.t.* to discuss by arguments.

-able a. rational; just; fair. **-ableness** n. **-ably** adv. **-er** n. **-ing** n. [Fr. raison, fr. L. ratio, reason].

re-as-sure (rē.a.shoor′) v.t. to free from fear; to allay anxiety; to restore confidence, or spirit to **reassurance** n. **reassuring** a.

re-bate (rē′.bāt) v.t. to allow as discount; n. deduction [Fr. rabattre, to beat down].

re-bate. See **rabbet.**

reb-el (reb′.al) n. one who resists the lawful authority of a government; revolter; revolutionist; one who is defiant; a. rebellious. **rebel** (ri.bel′) v.i. to take up arms against state or government; to revolt. pr.p. **-ling.** pa.t. and pa.p. **-led. -lion** n. organized resistance to authority; insurrection; mutiny. **-lious** a. [L. rebellare, fr. bellum, war].

re-birth (rē.burth′) n. state of being born again, spiritually; renaissance, as in the Rebirth of Learning.

re-bound (rē.bound′) v.i. to leap back; to recoil; to bound repeatedly; v.t. to cause to fly back; (rē′.bound) n. rebounding; recoil..

re-buff (ri.buf′) n. a blunt, contemptuous refusal; a snub; a repulse; v.t. to beat back; to check; to snub [It. rebuffo, reproof].

re-buke (ri.būk′) v.t. to censure; to reprove; to reprimand; n. reprimand; reproof [O.Fr. revuchier, repulse].

re-bus (rē′.bas) n. an enigmatical representation of a name, word, or phrase by pictures suggesting syllables [L. = by things].

re-but (ri.but′) v.t. to refute, to disprove; pr.p. **-ting.** pa.t. and pa.p. **-ted. -table** a. **-tal** n. refutation of an argument [Fr. revoutier, to repulse].

re-cal-ci-trate (ri.kal′.si.trāt) v.i. to kick back; to be refractory. **recalcitrant** n. one who defies authority; a. refractory; willfully disobedient. **recalcitrance, recalcitration** n. [L. recalcitrare, to kick back].

re-call (ri.kawl′) v.t. to call back; to take back (a gift, etc.); to annul or revoke; to call to mind; to remember; n. (rē′.kawl) act of recalling; a summons to return.

re-cant (ri.kant′) v.t. to take back, words or opinions; to retract; v.i. to unsay. **-ation** n. [L. recantare, fr. re-, back; cantare, to sing].

re-ca-pit-u-late (rē.ka.pich′.a.lāt) v.t. to relate in brief the matter or substance of a previous discourse; v.i. to sum up what has been previously said. **recapitulation** n. [L. capitulum, a small head].

re-cap-ture (rē.kap′.cher) v.t. to capture back; to regain; n. act of retaking.

re-cast (rē.kast′) v.t. to cast or mold again; to remodel; to throw back; to add up figures in a column a second time.

re-cede (ri.sēd′) v.i. to move or fall back; to retreat; to withdraw; to ebb. **receding** a.

re-ceipt (ri.sēt′) n. the act of receiving; a written acknowledgment of money received; a recipe in cookery; pl. money received; v.t. to give a receipt for [L. recipere, receptum, to receive].

re-ceive (ri.sēv′) v.t. to take; to accept; to get (an offer, etc.); to acquire; to welcome or entertain; to hold; to take or buy stolen goods. **receivable** a. **-r** n. one who receives; receptacle, place of storage, etc.; one who receives goods knowing them to have been stolen; appointed by court to receive profits of business being wound up by that court; (Chem.) a vessel into which spirits are emitted in distillation; a radio receiving set; earpiece of a telephone. **receiving** n. [O.Fr. fr. L. recipere, receptum, to receive].

re-cent (rē′.sant) a. that has lately happened; new; **-ly** adv. **-ness** n. [L. recens].

re-cep-ta-cle (ri.sep′.ta.kal) n. a vessel—that which receives, or into which anything is received and held [L. recipere, receptum, to receive].

re-cep-tion (ri.sep′.shan) n. receiving; welcome; ceremonial occasion when guests are personally announced; the quality of signals received in broadcasting. **receptible** a. receivable. **-ist** n. person in hotel, office, etc., who receives guests or clients. **receptive** a. able to grasp ideas or impressions quickly. **receptiveness, receptivity** n. [L. recipere, receptum, to receive].

re-cess (rē′.ses) n. a withdrawing from usual activity; suspension of business; vacation, as of legislative body or school; a secluded place; a niche or cavity in a wall; (Zool.) a small cleft or indentation in an organ; v.t. to make, or place in, a recess; v.i. to go on a recess. **-ed** a. fitted with recess. **-ion** n. act of receding or withdrawing; a period of reduced trade or business; a procession at the close of a service. **-ional** a. pert. to recession; n. hymn sung as clergyman leaves chancel. **-ive** a. **-iveness** n. [L. recessus, fr. recedere to recede].

re-cher-che (re.shur′.shā) a. of studied elegance; choice; exquisite; exclusion [Fr.].

rec-i-pe (res′.a.pē) n. a prescription; a cookery receipt [L. imper. recipere, take].

re-cip-i-ent (ri.sip′.i.ant) a. receptive; n. one who receives [L. recipere, to receive].

re-cip-ro-cal (ri.sip′.ra.kal) a. moving backwards and forwards; alternating; mutual;

complementary; (Gram.) reflexive; n. idea or term alternating with, or corresponding to, another by contrast or opposition; quantity arising from dividing unity by any quantity; pl. two numbers which multiplied give unity, e.g. ⅝ × ⅞ = 1. **-ly** adv. **-ness** n. **reciprocate** v.t. to make return for; to interchange; v.i. to move backwards and forwards; to act interchangeably; to alternate. **reciprocating, reciprocatory** a. **reciprocation** n. mutual giving and receiving. **reciprocative** a. **reciprocity** (res.a.präs′.a.ti.) n. action and reaction; the discharge of mutual duties or obligations; in international trade, equal facilities or advantages gained by abolition of prohibitory or protective duties, or by equalizing rates [L. reciprocus, turning back].

re-ci-sion (ri.sizh′.an) n. the act of cutting, annulling [L. rescindere, rescissus, to cut off].

re-cite (ri.sīt′) v.t. and v.i. to repeat aloud esp. before an audience. **recital** n. act of reciting; what is recited; detailed narration; a musical or dramatic performance by one person or by one composer or author. **recitation** n. reciting; repetition of something from memory. **recitative** (res.a.ta.tēv′) n. declamation to musical accompaniment, as in opera; a. in the style of recitative. **-r** n. [L. recitare, to read aloud].

reck (rek) v.t. and v.i. (Arch.) to heed. **-less** a. rashly negligent. **-lessly** adv. **-lessness** n. [O.E. reccan, to care for].

reck-on (rek′.n) v.t. and v.i. to count; to calculate; to estimate; to value; (Colloq.) to think; to be of opinion. **-er** n. one who reckons; table of calculations. **-ing** n. computing; calculation; a bill [Ger. rechnen, to count].

re-claim (ri.klām′) v.t. to bring into a state of productiveness, as waste land, etc.; to win back from error or sin. **-able** a. able to be reclaimed or reformed. **reclamation** (rek.la.mā′.shan) n.

re-claim (rē.klām′) v.t. to demand the return of.

re-cline (ri.klīn′) v.t. to lean back; v.i. to assume a recumbent position; to rest. **-r** n. [L. reclinare].

re-cluse (rek′.lōōs) a. secluded from the world; solitary; n. a hermit. [L. reclusus, shut away].

rec-og-nize (rek′.ag.nīz) v.t. to know again; to identify; to acknowledge; to treat as valid; to realize; to salute. **recognizable** a. **recognizably** adv. **recognizance** n. acknowledgment of a person or thing; an obligation, under penalty, entered into before some court or magistrate to do, or to refrain from doing, some particular act; sum pledged as surety. **recognition** n. recognizing; acknowledgment. **recognitive, recognitory** a. [L. recognoscere].

re-coil (ri.koil′) v.i. to start, roll, bound, fall back; to draw back; to rebound; n. return motion; a starting or falling back [Fr, reculer, to spring back].

re-col-lect (rek.a.lekt′) v.t. to recall; to remember. **recollection** n. power of recalling ideas to the mind; remembrance; things remembered. [L. recolligere, to collect again].

rec-om-mend (rek.a.mend′) v.t. to speak well of; to commend; to advise. **-able** a. worthy of recommendation. **-ation** n. recommending; a statement that one is worthy of favor or trial.

rec-om-pense (rek′.am.pens) v.t. to repay; to reward, to make an equivalent return for service, loss, etc.; to make up for; n. repayment; requital [Fr. récompenser].

rec-on-cile (rek′.an.sīl) v.t. to conciliate; to restore to friendship; to make agree; to become resigned (to); to adjust or compose. **reconcilable** a. **-ment, reconciliation** n. renewal of friendship; harmonizing of apparently opposed ideas, etc.; (Bib.) expiation; **reconciliatory** a. [L. reconciliare].

rec-on-dite (rek′.an.dīt) a. hidden from view or mental perception; obscure; little known. **-ness** n. [L. reconditus, hidden away].

re-con-di-tion (rē.kan.dish′.an) v.t. to restore to sound condition, either person or thing; to renovate; to repair.

re-con-nais-sance (ri.kan′.a.sans) n. an examination or survey, by land or air, for engineering or military operations [Fr.].

re-con-noi-ter (rē.ka.noi′.ter) v.t. to make a preliminary survey of, esp. with a view to military operations; v.i. to make reconnaissance; to scout; n. a preliminary survey [Fr. reconnoître, reconnaître, to recognize].

re-con-sid-er (rē.kan.sid′.er)v.t. to consider again; to take up for renewed discussion.

re-con-sti-tute (rē.kán′.sta.tōōt) v.t. to constitute anew; to reconstruct; to restore a dehydrated substance to original form.

re-con-struct (rē.kan.strukt′) v.t. to rebuild; to enact (crime) on actual spot, in course of judicial proceedings. **reconstruction** n.

re-cord (ri.kawrd′) v.t. to commit to writing; to make a note of; to register (a vote); to inscribe; to make a sound record; v.i. to speak, sing, etc. for reproduction on a record. **record** (rek′.erd) n. register; authentic copy of any writing; personal history; list; finest performance or highest amount ever known; a disk, cylinder, roll, etc. for mechanical reproduction of sound; pl. public documents. **-er** n.

one who registers writings or transactions; apparatus for registering data, by some form of symbol or line; instrument which transforms sounds into disk impressions; an instrument which registers sounds on wire tape; an ancient, flute-like musical instrument. **-ing** n. the making, or reproduction of, sound by mechanical means. **off the record**, unofficial [L. recordari, to remember].

recorder

re-count (rē.kount′, ri.kount′) v.t. to count again; to relate; to recite; to enumerate; n. a second enumeration [O.Fr. reconter].

re-coup (ri.kōōp′) v.t. to recover equivalent for what has been lost or damaged; to compensate [Fr. recouper, to cut again].

re-course (rē′.kōrs) n. application made to another in difficulty or distress; person or thing resorted to [L. recurrere, to run back].

re-cov-er (ri.kuv′.er) v.t. to get back; to revive; to reclaim; to rescue; (Law) to obtain (damages) as compensation for loss, etc.; v.i. to regain health or a former state; **-able** a. **-y** n. regaining, retaking, or obtaining possession; restoration to health; amends for a bad start in business, sport, etc. [O.Fr. recuvrer. L. recuperare].

re-cov-er (rē.kuv′.er) v.t. to put a fresh cover on; to cover again.

rec-re-ant (rek′.ri.ant) a. cowardly; craven; false; n. a craven; an apostate. **recreancy** n. [O.Fr. recroire, to take back one's pledge].

re-cre-ate (rek′.ri.āt) v.t. to give fresh life to; to restore; to reanimate; to refresh from weariness. **recreation** n. recreating; any pleasurable interest; amusement. **recreational** a. [L. recreare, to make again].

re-crim-i-nate (ri.krim′.a.nāt) v.t. and v.i. to charge an accuser with a similar crime. **recrimination** n. a counter-charge brought by the accused against the accuser; mutual abuse and blame. **recriminative, recriminatory** a. [L. re-, back; crimen, charge].

re-cru-desce (rē.krōō.des′) v.i. to break out again; to revive; **-nce, -ncy** n. **-nt** a. [L. recrudescere, to become raw again].

re-cruit (ri.krōōt′) v.t. to enlist persons for army, navy, etc.; to repair by fresh supplies; to renew in strength; v.i. to obtain new adherents; to gain health, spirits, etc.; n. a newly enlisted soldier; a fresh adherent. **-al, -ing, -ment** n. [O.Fr. recruter, fr. L. recrescere, to grow again].

rec-tan-gle (rek′.tang.gl) n. a four-sided figure with four right angles. **rectangular** a. [L. rectus, right, straight; angulus, an angle].

rec-ti-fy (rek′.ta.fī) v.t. to set right; to correct; to purify; to convert an alternating current of electricity into a direct current; **rectifiable** a. **rectification** n. **rectifier** n. one who corrects; a device which rectifies; a transformer; one who refines spirits by repeated distillations [L. rectus, straight; facere, to make].

rec-ti-lin-e-al, rectilinear (rek.ta.lin′.i.al, -ar) a. consisting of, or bounded by straight lines [L. rectus, straight; linea, a line].

rec-ti-tude (rek′.ta.tūd) n. moral uprightness; honesty of purpose [L. fr. rectus, right].

rec-to (rek′.tō) n. the right-hand page of an open book—opp. to verso [L. = on the right].

rec-tor (rek′.ter) n. clergyman of Episcopal Church who has charge of a parish; (R.C.) head of a religious house, college. **-y** n. house of a rector [L. fr. regere, rectum, to rule].

rec-tum (rek′.tam) n. lower end of the large intestine. pl. **recta. rectal** a. [L. rectus, straight].

re-cum-bent (ri.kum′.bant) a. reclining; lying on back [L. recumbere, to lie down].

re-cu-per-ate (ri.kū′.per.āt) v.i. to win back health and strength; to recover from financial loss. **recuperation** n. convalescence. **recuperative** a. [L. recuperare, to recover].

re-cur (ri.kur′) v.i. to happen again; to return periodically; pr.p. **-ring.** pa.t. and pa.p. **-red. -rence, -rency** n. **-rent** a. returning periodically [L. re-, again; currere, to run].

re-curve (ri.kurv′) v.t. to bend backwards.

rec-u-sant (rek′.ū.zant) a. obstinate in refusal; n. dissenter or nonconformist who refuses to conform to authority, esp. in religious matters. [L. recusare, to refuse].

red (red) a. (comp. **-der**; superl. **-dest**) of the color of aterial blood, rubies, glowing fire, etc.; of color, including shades, as scarlet, crimson, vermilion, orange-red and the like; of or connected with bloodshed, revolution, left-wing politics, etc.; n. color of blood; a socialist; communist; bolshevist; a Russian soldier; a danger signal. **-den** v.t. to make red; v.i. to become red; to blush. **-ness** n. state or quality of being red. **-blooded** a. vigorous; manly. **-breast** n. the robin. **-cap** n. a porter at a transportation terminal. **-coat** n. a British soldier, because of the bright scarlet tunic. — **corpuscle**, a colored blood corpuscle, containing hemoglobin and carrying oxygen. **Red Cross**, international emblem of organization for relief of sick and wounded in war time and for helping distressed persons in emergencies, as floods. **—handed** *a.* having red hands—hence, in the very act, orig. of a murderer. **— hat,** a cardinal's hat. **— heat** *n.* temperature of a body emitting red rays, about 700°-800° C. **— herring,** the common herring, cured by drying, smoking and salting; (*Colloq.*) any topic introduced to divert attention from main issue. **—hot** *a.* heated to redness; eager; enthusiastic. **Red Indian** *n.* a copper-colored aboriginal native of N. America. **—letter** *a.* applied to principal holy days, —hence, any memorable (day). **— pepper,** seasoning, such as cayenne. **-skin** *n.* a N. American Indian. **— tape,** slavish adherence to official regulations, fr. red tape used for tying up government documents. **-wing** *n.* a blackbird with a red patch on wings. **-wood** *n.* any wood yielding a red dye; the sequoia tree of California, a gigantic evergreen coniferous tree. **to paint the town red,** to have a noisy good time. **to see red,** to become infuriated [O.E. *read*].

Red Cross

re·dact (ri·dakt′) *v.t.* to digest or reduce to order, literary, or scientific materials. **-ion** *n.* **-or** *n.* an editor [L. *redactum,* to drive back].
re·deem (ri·dēm′) *v.t.* to purchase back; to regain, as mortaged property, by paying principal, interest and costs of mortgage; to take out of pawn; to ransom; to deliver from sin; to make good; to recover. **-able** *a.* **-ableness** *n.* **-er** *n.* [L. *redimere,* to buy back].
re·demp·tion (ri·demp′·shan) *n.* redeeming or buying back; deliverance from sin; salvation. **-er** *n.* one who has redeemed himself. **redemptive** *a.* redeeming. **redemptory** *a.* [L. *redimmere, redemptum,* to buy back].
red·in·te·grate (ri·din′·ta·grāt) *v.t.* to make whole again; to renew. **redintegration** *n.* [L. *redintegrare,* to make whole again].
re·di·rect (rē·di·rekt′) *v.t.* to direct again; to readdress a communication. **-ion** *n.*
re·dis·trib·ute (rē·dis·trib′·ūt) *v.t.* to deal out or apportion again. **redistribution** *n.*
red·o·lent (red′·a·lant) *a.* diffusing a strong or fragrant odor; scented; reminiscent (of). **redolence** *n.* [L. *redolere,* to smell strongly].
re·doubt (ri·dout′) *n.* a central part within fortifications for a final stand by the defenders [Fr. *reduote,* fr. L. *re-,* back; *ducere,* to lead].
re·doubt·able (ri·dou′·ta·bl) *a.* dreaded; formidable; valiant. [O.Fr. *redouter,* to fear].
re·dound (ri·dound′) *v.i.* to contribute or turn to; to conduce (to); to recoil; to react (upon) [L. *re-,* back; *undare,* to surge].
re·draft (rē·draft′) *v.t.* to draft or draw up a second time; *n.* a second copy; a new bill of exchange.
re·dress (ri·dres′) *v.t.* to make amends for; to set right; to compensate; to adjust; (rē·dress) *n.* reparation; amendment; relief; remedy. **-er** *n.* **-ible** *a.* [Fr. *redresser*].
re·duce (ri·dūs′) *v.t.* to diminish in number, length, quantity, value, price, etc.; to lower; to degrade; (*Chem.*) to remove oxygen or add hydrogen; to decrease valency number; to separate metal from its ore by heat and chemical affinities; to add electrons to an ion; (*Arith.*) to change, as numbers, from one denomination into another without altering value; to slim; to impoverish; to subdue; to capture (as a fort). **-d** *a.* **reducible** *a.* **reduction** *n.* reducing; subjugation; diminution; curtailment; amount by which something is reduced. **reductive** *a.* having the power of reducing. **reductively** *adv.* **reducing agent,** a reagent for abstracting oxygen or adding hydrogen [L. *re-; ducere,* to lead].
re·dun·dant (ri·dun′·dant) *a.* superfluous; serving no useful purpose; using more words than necessary for complete meaning **redundance, redundancy** *n.* **-ly** *adv.* [L. *redundare,* to overflow].
re·ech·o (rē·ek′·ō) *v.t.* to echo back.
reed (rēd) *n.* a tall hollow-stemmed grass growing in water or marshes; in certain wind-instruments, a thin strip of cane or metal which vibrates and produces a musical sound; a musical instrument made of the hollow joint of some plant; a pastoral pipe; thatching straw; an arrow; *pl.* a molding *v.t.* to thatch; to fit with a reed. **-ed** *a.* covered with reeds; molded like reeds. **-er** *n.* a thatcher. **-iness** *n.* **—instrument** *n.* (*Mus.*) a wind-instrument played by means of a reed, as the oboe, English horn, bassoon, clarinet, saxophone, etc. **— pipe** *n.* organ pipe whose tone is produced by vibration of metal tongue. **— stop** *n.* organ stop owing its tone to vibration of little metal

tongues. **-y** *a.* [O.E. *hreod*].
reef (rēf) *n.* a portion of a square sail which can be rolled up and made fast to the yard or boom; *v.t.* to reduce the area of sail by taking in a reef. **-er** *n.* one who reefs; a sailor's close-fitting jacket. **— knot** *n.* (*Naut.*) a square knot [O.N. *rif,* reef, rib].
reef (rēf) *n.* a ridge of rock near the surface of the sea; a lode of auriferous rock [O.N. *rif*].

reek (rēk) *n.* smoke; vapor; fume; *v.i.* to emit smoke; to steam; to smell strongly unpleasant. **-ing** *a.* **-y** *a.* [O.E. *rec*].
reel (rēl) *n.* frame or bobbin on which yarn or cloth is wound; cylinder turning on an axis on which seamen wind the log lines, and anglers their fishing line; in motion pictures, a flanged spool on which film is wound; a portion of film, usually 1000 feet; *v.t.* to wind upon a reel; to draw (in) by means of a reel. **to reel off,** to recite rapidly [O.E. *hreol*].

reel (rēl) *v.i.* to stagger; to sway from side to side; to whirl; to be dizzy [O.E. *hreol*].
reel (rēl) *n.* a sprightly dance tune; a Scottish dance for two or more couples [Gael. *righil*].
reeve (rēv) *v.t.* to pass line through any hole in a block, cleat, ring, etc., for pulling a larger rope after it [Dut. *reef,* a reef].
reeve (rēv) *n.* official in early English times as shire reeve (sheriff) [O.E. *gerefa*].
re·fec·tion (ri·fek′·shan) *n.* refreshment; a simple repast; a lunch. **refectory** *n.* a hall in a monastery, convent, school, or college where meals are served [L. *reficere, refectum,* to remake].
re·fer (ri·fur′) *v.t.* to direct to; to assign to; *v.i.* to have reference or relation to; to offer, as testimony in evidence of character, qualification, etc.; to allude (to). *pr.p.* **-ring.** *pa.t.* and *pa.p.* **-red. referable, referrable** *a.* may be referred to or assigned to. **referee** *n.* an arbitrator; an umpire; a neutral judge in various sports. **reference** *n.* appeal to the judgment of another; relation; one of whom inquiries can be made; one named by a candidate for a post as willing to give testimony of character, etc.; a passage in a book to which reader is referred; a quotation; a testimonial. **referendum** *n.* a popular vote for ascertaining the public will on a single definite issue. **referential** *a.* containing a reference; used for reference [L. *re-,* back; *ferre,* to carry].
re·fine (ri·fīn′) *v.t.* to purify; to reduce crude metals to a finer state; to clarify; to polish or improve; to free from coarseness, vulgarity, etc.; *v.i.* to become pure; to improve in accuracy, excellence, or good taste. **-d** *a.* purified or clarified; polished; well-bred. **-dly** *adv.* **-ment** *n.* **-ry** *n.* place where process of refining sugar, oil, metals, etc. is effected [Fr. *raffiner*].
re·flect (ri·flekt′) *v.t.* to throw back, esp. rays of light, heat, or sound, from surfaces; to mirror; *v.i.* to throw back light, heat, etc.; to meditate; to consider attentively; to cast discredit on; to disparage. **-ed** *a.* **-ing** *a.* thoughtful; throwing back rays of light, etc. **ingly** *adv.* **-ion** *n.* reflecting; return of rays of heat or light, or waves of sound, from a surface; image given back from mirror or other reflecting surface; meditation; contemplation. **-ive** *a.* reflecting; meditative; (*Gram.*) reflective; reciprocal. **-ively** *adv.* **-iveness** *n.* **-or** *n.* a reflecting surface [L. *reflectere,* to bend back].
re·flex (rē′·fleks) *a.* turned, bent, or directed backwards; reflected; (*Mech.*) produced by reaction; (*Anat.*) denoting the involuntary action of the motor nerves under a stimulus from the sensory nerves; involuntary; automatic; *n.* reflection; a reflected image; a re-

flex action; *v.t.* (ri·fleks′) to bend back; to reflect. **-ible** *a.* **-ibility** *n.* **-ive** *a.* bending or turned backwards; reflective; of certain verbs, whose subject and object are the same person or thing; of pronouns which serve as objects to reflexive verbs; as *myself,* etc. **-ively** *adv.* **-ly** *adv.* **conditioned reflex,** reflex action due to power of association and suggestion [L. *re-,* back; *flectere,* to bend].
re·flux (rē′·fluks) *n.* a flowing back; ebbing.
re·form (ri·fawrm′) *v.t.* to restore; to reclaim; to amend; to improve; to eliminate (abuse, malpractice); *v.i.* to amend one's ways; to improve; *n.* amendment; improvement; rectification; correction. **-able** *a.* **reformation** (ref′·er·mā·shan) *n.* reforming; change for the better; religious movement of 16th cent. in which a large section of the church broke away from Rome. **-ative** *a.* aiming at reform. **-atory** *a.* tending to reform; *n.* institution for reforming young law-breakers. **-ed** *a.* amended; reclaimed **-er** *n.* one who reforms; an advocate of reform.
re·fract (ri·frakt′) *v.t.* to bend sharply; to cause to deviate from a direct course, as rays of light on passing from one medium to another. **-able** *a.* **-ed** *a.* **-ing** *a.* serving to refract; refractive. **-ion** *n.* **-tive** *a.* **-or** *n.* [L. *re-,* back; *frangere, fractum,* to break].
re·frac·to·ry (ri·frak′·ta·ri·) *a.* sullen or perverse in opposition or disobedience; suitable for lining furnaces because of resistance to fusion at very high temperatures; (*Med.*) resistant to treatment. **refractorily** *adv.* [L. *re-,* back; *frangere,* to break].
re·frain (ri·frān′) *v.i.* to abstain. **-ment** *n.* [L. *refrenare,* to bridle].
re·frain (ri·frān′) *n.* chorus recurring at end of each verse of song; constant theme [Fr. fr. L. *refringere,* to break off].
re·fran·gi·ble (ri·fran′·ja·bl) *a.* able to be refracted [L. *re-,* back; *frangere,* to break].
re·fresh (ri·fresh′) *v.t.* to make fresh again; to revive; to renew; to enliven; to provide with refreshment; to freshen up. **-er** *n.* one who, or that which, refreshes; (*Slang*) a refreshing drink. **-ing** *a.* invigorating; reviving. **-ment** *n.* restoration of strength; that which adds fresh vigor, as rest, drink, or food— hence, *pl.* food and drink [O.Fr. *refrescher*].
re·frig·er·ate (ri·frij′·er·āt) *v.t.* to make cold or frozen; to preserve food, etc., by cooling; *v.i.* to become cold. **refrigerant** *a.* **refrigeration,** *n.* **refrigerative, refrigeratory** *a.* cooling. **refrigerator** *n.* apparatus and plant for the manufacture of ice; chamber for preserving food by mechanical production of low temperatures [L. *re-,* again; *frigus,* cold].

refrigerator

ref·uge (ref′·ūj) *n.* shelter; asylum; retreat; harbor. **refugee** *n.* one who flees to a place of safety [L. *re,* back; *fugere,* to flee].
re·ful·gent (ri·ful′·jant) *a.* shining; splendid. **refulgence** *n.* splendor. Also **refulgency** [L. *re-,* again; *fulgere,* to shine].
re·fund (ri·fund′) *v.t.* to return in payment or compensation for; to repay. **refund** (rē′·fund) *n.* repayment [L. *re-,* back; *fundere,* to pour].
re·fur·bish (rē·fur′·bish) *v.t.* to furbish up again; to retouch; to renovate; to polish up.
re·fuse (rē·fūz′) *v.t.* to deny or reject; to decline; *v.i.* to decline something offered; not to comply. **refusal** *n.* act of refusing; the first chance of accepting or declining an offer; an option [Fr. *refuser,* fr. L. *recusare,* to refuse].
ref·use (ref′·ūs) *a.* rejected; worthless; *n.* waste matter; trash [Fr. *refuser,* to refuse].
re·fuse (rē·fūz′) *v.t.* of metals, to fuse or melt again. **refusion** *n.*
re·fute (ri·fūt′) *v.t.* to overthrow by argument; to prove to be false. **refutable** *a.* capable of being refuted. **refutably** *adv.* **refutation** *n.* [L. *refutare,* to repel].
re·gain (ri·gān′) *v.t.* to recover; to retrieve; to get back; to reach again.
re·gal (rē′·gal) *a.* pert. to a king; kingly; royal. **regalia** (re·gā′·li·a) *n.pl.* insignia of royalty, as crown, scepters, orbs, etc. **regality** *n.* royalty; sovereignty; an ensign of royalty. **-ly** *adv.* [L. *regalis,* royal].
re·gale (ri·gāl′) *v.t.* to entertain in sumptuous manner; *v.i.* to feast [Fr. *régaler*].
re·gard (ri·gàrd′) *v.t.* to observe; to gaze; to consider; to pay respect to; *n.* aspect; esteem;

refuse

account; gaze; heed; concern; *pl.* compliments; good wishes. **-able** *a.* **-ful** *a.* heedful. **-fully** *adv.* **-ing** *prep.* concerning—also **in, with, regard to, as regards. -less** *a.* without regard; careless; neglectful. **-lessly** *adv.* [Fr. *regarder*].

re·gat·ta (ri·gat′·a) *n.* boat races [*It.* orig. a gondola race in Venice].

re·gen·cy See **regent.**

re·gen·er·ate (ri·jen′·ēr·āt) *v.t.* and *v.i.* to give fresh life or vigor to; to reorganize; to recreate the moral nature; to cause to be born again; *a.* born anew; changed from a natural to a spiritual state; regenerated. **regeneracy, regeneration** *n.* **regenerative** *a.*

re·gent (rē′·jant) *a.* holding the office of regent; exercising vicarious authority; *n.* one who governs a kingdom during the minority, absence, or disability of sovereign. **regency** *n.* office and jurisdiction of a regent [L. *regere*, to rule].

reg·i·cide (rej′·a·sīd) *n.* one who kills, or the killing of, a king. **regicidal** *a.* [L. *rex, regis,* a king; *caedere,* to slay].

re·gime (rā·zhēm′) *n.* style or tenure of rule or management; administration; an ordered mode of dieting [Fr.].

reg·i·men (rej′·a·man) *n.* orderly government; systematic method of dieting, exercising, etc. [L. = rule, government].

reg·i·ment (rej′·a·mant) *n.* a body of soldiers commanded by a senior officer and consisting of companies, batteries, battalions, or squadrons, according to branch of service; *v.t.* to form into a regiment; to systematize. **-al** *a.* **-ation** *n.* thorough systemization and control [L. *regimentum,* government].

re·gion (rē′·jan) *n.* territory of indefinite extent; district; part of body; sphere or realm. **-al** *a.* **-ally** *adv.* [L. *regio,* a district].

reg·is·ter (rej′·is·ter) *n.* a written account; an official record; a list; the book in which a record is kept; an alphabetical index; an archive; a catalog; a registration; a metal damper to close a heating duct; any mechanical contrivance which registers or records; (*Mus.*) row of organ pipes with same tone color; organ stop; compass of a voice or instrument; *v.t.* to record; to enroll; to indicate, by cash register, scales, etc., by facial expression. **registrable** *a.* **-ed** *a.* **registrant** *n.* one who registers. **registrar** *n.* an official who keeps a register or record. **registration** *n.* entry or record; total entries registered. **registry** *n.* office for registering births, deaths and marriages. **-ed mail,** a method of postal delivery by which mail is insured against loss or damage in transit [O.Fr. *registre*].

reg·nal (reg′·nal) *a.* pert. to reign of monarch. **regnancy** *n.* rule; reign [L. *regnare,* to reign].

re·gress (rē′·gres) *n.* passage back; the power of passing back; re-entry. *v.i.* (ri·gres′) to go or fall back; to return to a former state; (*Astron.*) to move from east to west. **-ion** *n.* returning; retrogression; (*Psych.*) diversion of psychic energy, owing to obstacles encountered, into channels of fantasy instead of reality. **-ive** *a.* [L. *regressus,* fr. *regredi,* to go back].

re·gret (ri·gret′) *v.t.* to grieve over; to lament; to deplore; *pr.p.* **-ting.** *pa.t.* and *pa.p.* **-ted.** *n.* grief; sorrow; remorse. **-ful** *a.* **-fully** *adv.* **-table** *a.* deserving regret; lamentable. **-tably** *adv.* **-ter** *n.* [Fr. *regretter*].

reg·u·lar (reg′·ya·ler) *a.* conforming to, governed by rule; periodical; symmetrical; orderly; strict; habitual; straight; level; natural; standing (army); (*Colloq.*) out and out; belonging to a monastic order (opp. to *secular*); *n.* a member of any religious order who professes to follow a certain rule (*regula*) of life; a soldier belonging to a permanent, standing army. **-ization** *n.* **-ity** *n.* conformity to rule; uniformity. **-ly** *adv.* [L. *regula,* a rule].

reg·u·late (reg′·ya·lāt) *v.t.* to adjust by rule, method, etc.; to arrange; to control. **regulation** *n.* regulating or controlling; state of being reduced to order; a law; an order. **regulator** *n.* [L. *regula,* a rule].

re·gur·gi·tate (rē·gur′·ja·tāt) *v.t.* to throw, flow, or pour back in great quantity; *v.i.* to be thrown or poured back. **regurgitation** *n.* [L. *re-,* back; *gurges,* a gulf].

re·ha·bil·i·tate (rē·(h)a·bil′·a·tāt) *v.t.* to restore to reputation or former position; to re-

condition. **rehabilitation** *n.* [L. *re-,* again; *habitare,* to make *fit*].

re·hash (rē·hash′) *v.t.* to mix together and use or serve up a second time.

re·hearse (ri·hers′) *v.t.* and *v.i.* to repeat aloud; to practice (play, etc.); to recite; to recapitulate; to narrate. **rehearsal** *n.* trial performance of a play, opera, etc. [O.Fr. *rehercer,* to repeat (lit. rake over again)].

Reich (rīk) *n.* German Confederation of States. **-stag** *n.* the German parliament. [Ger.].

re·i·fy (rē′·i·fī) *v.t.* to make concrete or real. **reification** *n.* [L. *res,* a thing; *facere,* to make].

reign (rān) *n.* royal authority; the period during which a sovereign occupies throne; influence; *v.i.* to possess sovereign power [O.Fr. *regne,* fr. L. *regnare,* to rule].

re·im·burse (rē·im·burs′) *v.t.* to refund; to pay back; to give the equivalent of. **-ment** *n.* **-r** *n.* [Fr. *rembourser,* fr. *bourse,* a purse].

rein (rān) *n.* strap of bridle to govern a horse, etc.; means of controlling, curbing; restraint; *pl.* power, or means of exercising power [O.Fr. *reine,* fr. L. *retinere,* to hold back].

re·in·car·nate (rē·in·kár′·nāt) *v.t.* to embody again in the flesh. **reincarnation** *n.*

rein·deer (rān′·dir) *n.* large deer of colder regions. **— moss** *n.* lichen, the winter food of reindeer [O.N. *hreinndýri*].

re·in·force (rē·in·fōrs′) *v.t.* to strengthen with new force, esp. of troops or ships; to increase. **-ment** *n.* **reinforced concrete** *n.* concrete strengthened by the inclusion in it of steel nets, rods, girders, etc. [Fr. *renforcer*].

re·in·state (rē·in·stāt′) *v.t.* to restore to former position. **-ment** *n.*

re·is·sue (rē·ish′·oo) *v.t.* to issue again; to republish; *n.* a new issue; a reprint.

re·it·er·ate (rē·it′·er·āt) *v.t.* to repeat again and again. **reiterant** *a.* **reiteration** *n.*

re·ject (ri·jekt′) *v.t.* to cast from one; to throw away; to refuse; to put aside; (rē′jekt) *n.* a person or thing rejected as not up to standard. **-ion** *n.* [L. *re-,* back; *jacere,* to throw].

re·joice (ri·jois′) *v.t.* to give joy to; to cheer; to gladden; *v.i.* to exult; to triumph. **rejoicing** *n.* act of expressing joy; *pl.* public expression of joy; festivities. [Fr. *réjouir*].

re·join (rē·join′) *v.t.* to unite again; to meet again; to enter again, as society, etc.; *v.i.* to become united again; to reply. **-der** *n.* an answer to a reply [Fr. *rejoindre*].

re·ju·ve·nate (ri·jōō′·va·nāt) *v.t.* to make young again. **rejuvenation** *n.* **rejuvenator** *n.* **rejuvenesce** *v.i.* to grow young again. **rejuvenescence** *n.* **rejuvenescent** *a.* [L. *re-,* again; *juvenis,* young].

re·lapse (ri·laps′) *v.i.* to slide back, esp. into state of ill health, error, evil ways; *n.* a falling back [L. *relapsus,* to slip back].

re·late (ri·lāt′) *v.t.* to tell; to establish relation between; *v.i.* to have relation (to); to refer (to). **-d** *a.* connected by blood or marriage; allied; akin. **relation** *n.* telling; *pl.* dealings between persons or nations; connection between things; kindred; connection by consanguinity or affinity; a relative. **relational** *a.* indicating some relation. **relationship** *n.* [L. *referre, relatum,* to bring back].

rel·a·tive (rel′·a·tiv) *a.* dependent on relation to something else, not absolute; comparative; respecting; connected; related; (*Gram.*) noting a relation or reference to antecedent word or sentence; *n.* a person connected by blood or affinity; a word relating to an antecedent word, clause, or sentence. **-ly** *adv.* comparatively. **-ness** *n.* relativity *n.* being relative; doctrine that measurement is conditioned by the choice of co-ordinate axes e.g., all observable motion, and time, are relative [fr. *relate*].

re·lax (ri·laks′) *v.t.* to make less severe or stern; to loosen; *v.i.* to become loosened or feeble; to unbend; to become less severe; to ease up. **-ation** *n.* act of relaxing; recreation; mitigation. **-ing** *a.* [L. *re-,* again; *laxus,* loose].

re·lay (rē·lā′, ri·lā′) *n.* supplies conveniently stored at successive stages of a route; a gang of men, a fresh set of horses, etc., ready to relieve others; a device for making or breaking a local electrical circuit; an electro-magnetic device for allowing a weak signal from a distance to control a more powerful local electrical circuit; a low-powered broadcasting station which broadcasts programs originating in another station; *v.t.* to pass on, as a message, broadcast, etc. **— race,** a race between teams of which each runner does a part of the distance [Fr. *relais,* a rest].

re·lease (ri·lēs′) *v.t.* to set free; to allow to quit; to exempt from obligation; (*Law*) to remit a claim; *n.* liberation; exemption; discharge; acquittance; a catch for controlling mechanical parts of a machine; (*Law*) a surrender of a right or claim. **releasable** *a.* [O.Fr. *relaissier*].

rel·e·gate (rel′·a·gāt) *v.t.* to send away; to banish; to consign; to demote. **relegation** *n.* [L. *re-* back; *legare,* to send].

re·lent (ri·lent′) *v.i.* to give up harsh intention; to yield. **-less** *a.* showing no pity or sympathy. **-lessly** *adv.* **-lessness** *n.* [Fr. *ralentir,* to slacken].

rel·e·vant (rel′·a·vant) *a.* bearing upon the

case in hand; pertinent. **relevance, relevancy** *n.* **-ly** *adv.* [L. *relevare,* to raise up].

re·li·a·ble (ri·lī·a·bl) *a.* trustworthy; honest; creditable. **-ness, reliability** *n.* **reliably** *adv.* **reliance** *n.* trust; confidence; dependence. **reliant** *a.* [fr. *rely*].

rel·ic (rel′·ik) *n.* something surviving from the past [L. *reliquus,* remaining].

re·lief (ri·lēf′) *n.* removal or alleviation of pain, distress, or other evil; help; remedy; one who relieves another at his post; prominence; a sculptured figure standing out from a plane surface. **— map** *n.* a map showing the elevations and depressions of a country in relief [L. *re-,* again; *levare,* to raise].

re·lieve (ri·lēv′) *v.t.* to alleviate; to free from trial, evil, or distress; to release from a post by substitution of another; to remedy; to lighten (gloom, etc.). **relieving** *a.* serving to relieve. [L. *re-,* again; *levare,* to raise].

re·li·gion (ri·lij′·an) *n.* belief in supernatural power which governs universe; recognition of God as object of worship; practical piety; any system of faith and worship. **-ist** *n.* **-ary, -er** *n.* one who makes inordinate professions of religion. **religiosity** *n.* sense of, or tendency towards, religiousness. **religious** *a.* pert. to religion; pious; teaching religion; conscientious. **religiously** *adv.* [L. *religio*].

re·lin·quish (ri·ling′·kwish) *v.t.* to give up; to yield. **-er** *n.* **-ment** *n.* [L. *relinquere*].

rel·i·quar·y (rel′·a·kwer·i) *n.* a depository or casket in which relics of saints or martyrs are preserved; a shrine [Fr. *reliquaire*].

rel·ish (rel′·ish) *v.t.* to taste with pleasure; to like immensely; *v.t.* to have a pleasing taste; to savor; *n.* savor; flavor; what is used to make food more palatable, as sauce, seasoning, etc.; liking [O.Fr. *reles,* aftertaste].

re·luc·tant (ri·luk′·tant) *a.* unwilling; disinclined. **reluctance** *n.* **reluctancy** *n.* **-ly** *adv.* [L. *reluctari,* to struggle against].

re·ly (ri·lī′) *v.i.* to trust; to depend; **relier** *n.* [L. *religare,* to bind fast].

re·main (ri·mān′) *v.i.* to stay; to continue or endure; to be left; *n.pl.* a corpse; unpublished literary works of deceased. **-der** *n.* what remains; remnant; in real property law, an interest in an estate which only operates after the termination of a prior interest [L. *re-,* back; *manere,* to stay].

re·mand (ri·mand′) *v.t.* to send back, as an accused person sent back to prison while further inquiries are made; *n.* such a recommittal [*re-,* back; *mandare,* to commit].

re·mark (ri·márk′) *v.t.* to take notice of; to express in words or writing; to comment; notice; heed; regard. **-able** *a.* extraordinary. **-ableness** *n.* **-ably** *adv.* [Fr. *remarquer*].

rem·e·dy (rem′·a·di·) *n.* a means of curing or relieving a disease, trouble, fault, etc.; legal means to recover a right, or to obtain redress; cure; antidote; *v.t.* to restore to health; to heal; to cure; to put right. *a.* curable. **remedial** *a.* affording a remedy [L. *remedium*].

re·mem·ber (ri·mem′·ber) *v.t.* to retain in the memory; to recollect; to reward for services rendered; *v.i.* to have in mind. **-able** *a.* **remembrance** *n.* act or power of remembering; state of being remembered; recollection; memory; token; memento; keepsake [L. *re-; memor,* mindful].

re·mind (ri·mīnd′) *v.t.* to cause to remember. **-er** *n.* one who, or that which reminds.

rem·i·nis·cence (rem·a·nis′·ans) *n.* state of calling to mind; a recollection of past events; a remembrance; *pl.* memoirs. **reminiscent** *a.* [L. *reminisci,* to remember].

re·mise (ri·mīz′) *v.t.* to send back or remit, esp. in law; to resign or surrender (property, etc.) by deed; *n.* (*Law*) a surrender [O.Fr.].

re·miss (ri·mis′) *a.* not prompt or exact in duty; careless. **-ful** **-ible** *a.* able to be pardoned or remitted. **-ion** *n.* act of remitting; abatement; diminution; period of moderation of intensity of a fever or other disease; pardon; forgiveness of sin. **-ive** *a.* **-ly** *adv.* **-ness** *n.* [L. *remissus,* sent back].

re·mit (ri·mit′) *v.t.* to send back; to transfer; to send accused for trial back to a lower court; to transmit to a distance, as money bills; to return; to restore; to slacken (efforts); to forgive; to refrain from exacting debt, etc.); *v.i.* to abate in force; to slacken off. *pa.p.* **-ting.** *pa.t.* and *pa.p.* **-ted.** *n.* **re·mittal** *n.* act of remitting to another court. **remittance** *n.* transmitting money bills, or the like to a distant place; the money sent **remittent** *a.* increasing and decreasing at periodic intervals [L. *remittere,* to send back].

rem·nant (rem′·nant) *n.* fragment of cloth; scrap; residue; remainder [O.Fr. *remanant*].

re·mon·strate (ri·mán′·strāt) *v.t.* to make evident by strong protestations *v.i.* to present strong reasons against; to speak strongly against. **remonstrance** *n.* expostulation; protest. **remonstrant** *n.* one who remonstrates; *a.* expostulatory. **remonstration** *n.* **remonstrative, remonstratory** *a.* [L. *re-,* again; *monstrare,* to point out].

re·morse (ri·mawrs′) *n.* self-reproach excited by sense of guilt; repentance. **-ful** *a.* penitent; repentant. **-fully** *adv.* **-less** *a.* relentless; pitiless [L. *remordere,* to bite back].

re·mote (ri·mōt′) *a.* far back in time or space; not near; slight; **-ly** *adv.* **-ness** *n.* **— control,** control of apparatus from a distance [L. re-, back; movere, motum, to move].

**remote
control**

re·move (ri·mòòv') v.t. to take or put away; to dislodge; to transfer; to withdraw; to extract; to banish; to dismiss from a post; v.i. to change place or residence; n. removal; change of place; a step in any scale of gradation. **removable** a. not permanently fixed. **removal** n. removing; transferring to another house; dismissal from a post. **-d** a. denoting distance of relationship. **-r** n. [L. re-, back; movere, to move].

re·mu·ner·ate (ri·mū'·na·rāt) v.t. to reward for services; to recompense; to compensate. **remunerable** a. that may, or should be, remunerated. **remuneration** n. reward; recompense; salary **remunerative** a. [L. re-, again; munerare, to give].

ren·ais·sance (ren·a·sàn(t)s', ·zàn(t)'s) (Cap.) n. a rebirth; a period of intellectual revival, esp. of learning in fourteenth to sixteenth, cents.; a. pert. to renaissance. Also **renascence** [Fr.].

re·nal (rē'·nal) a. pert. to kidneys [L. renes].

re·nas·cent (ri·nas'·ant) a. springing into being again; regaining lost vigor. **renascence** n. See **renaissance** [L. re-, again; nasci, to be born].

rend (rend) v.t. to tear asunder; to pull to pieces; to split; to lacerate. pat. and pa.p. **rent** [O.E. rendan, to cut].

ren·der (ren'·der) v.t. to give in return; to deliver up; to supply; to present; to make or cause to be; to translate from one language into another; to interpret music; to portray; to extract animal fats by heating. **-able** a. **-er** n. **-ing** n. **rendition** n. rendering [Fr. rendre].

ren·dez·vous (ràn'·da·vòò) n. an appointed place for meeting; v.i. to assemble at a prearranged place [Fr. = betake yourselves].

ren·di·tion See **render**.

ren·e·gade (ren'·a·gād) n. one faithless to principle or party; a deserter; a. apostate; false. **renege** (ri·nig') v.t. and v.i. to deny; to desert; to break a promise; to revoke at cards [L. re-, again; negare, to deny].

re·new (ri·nū') v.t. and v.i. to restore; to renovate; to revive; to begin again; to recommence. **-able** a. **-al** n. revival; restoration; regeneration.

ren·net (ren'·it) n. any preparation used for curdling milk and in preparation of cheese; junket, etc. [M.E. rennen, to run, congeal].

re·nounce (ri·nouns') v.t. to disavow; to give up; to reject; v.i. to fail in following suit when a card of the suit is in the player's hand. **-ment** n. renunciation [L. renuntiare, to protest against].

ren·o·vate (ren'·a·vāt) v.t. to make as good as new; to overhaul and repair. **renovation** n. [L. renovare, fr. novus, new].

re·nown (ri·noun') n. great reputation; fame. **-ed** a. famous; noted; eminent [O.Fr. renoun, fr. renomer, to make famous].

rent (rent) pa.t. and pa.p. of **rend**; n. an opening made by rending; a tear; a fissure; a split; a breach; a rupture; a rift.

rent (rent) n. a periodical payment at an

agreed rate for use and enjoyment of something, esp. land, houses; rental; hiring charge; v.t. to lease; to hold by lease; to hire; v.i. to be leased or let for rent. **-able** a. **-al** n. the amount of rent; a rent roll; a. pert. to rent. **-er** n. one who rents [Fr. rente, income].

renovate

re·nun·ci·a·tion (ri·nun·si·ā'·shan) n. a surrender of claim or interest; rejection; repudiation. Also **renunciance. renunciative, renunciatory** a. See **renounce**.

re·or·gan·ize (rē·awr'·ga·niz) v.t. to organize anew.   [cotton, or silk fabric.

rep, repp (rep) n. a thick corded worsted,

re·pair (ri·per') v.t. to restore to a sound or good state after injury; to mend; to redress; n. restoration; mending. **-able** a. **-er** n. [O. Fr. reparer].

re·pair (ri·pār') v.i. to go; to betake oneself [L. repatriare, to return to one's country].

rep·a·ra·ble (rep'·a·ra·bl) a. that can be made good. **reparably** adv. **reparation** n. repairing or making amends; redress; compensation. **reparative** a. [O.Fr. reparer].

rep·ar·tee (rep·er·tē') n. apt, witty reply; gift of making such replies [Fr. repartie, orig. answering thrust in fencing].

re·past (ri·past') n. a meal [Fr. repas, a meal].

re·pa·tri·ate (rē·pā'·tri·āt) v.t. to restore to one's own country; to bring back prisoners of war and refugees from abroad. **repatriation** n. [L.L. repatriare].

re·pay (rē·pā') v.t. to pay back; to make return or requital for; to require. pat. and pa.p. **repaid. -able** a. **-ment** n.

re·peal (ri·pēl') v.t. to revoke, rescind, annul, as a deed, will, law, or statute; to abrogate; to cancel; n. revocation; abrogation. **-able** a. [O.Fr. rapeler, fr. appeler, to appeal].

re·peat (ri·pēt') v.t. to say or do again; to reiterate; to echo; to tell; n. repetition; encore; (Mus.) sign that a movement is to be performed twice, indicated by inclusion within dots of part to be repeated. **-able** a. **-ed** a. frequent; recurring. **-edly** adv. **-er** n. one who, or that which, repeats; firearm which may be discharged many times in quick succession: a person who repeats a course of study. **-ing** n. **-ing decimal** (Arith.) a decimal in which same figure(s) repeat ad infinitum. [L. repetere, to try or seek again].

re·pel (ri·pel') v.t. to drive back; to repulse; to oppose; to excite revulsion in; v.i. to have power to drive away; to cause repugnance. pr.p. **-ling**. pa.t. and pa.p. **-led. -lence, -lency** n. **-lent** a. driving back; tending to repel; n. that which repels. **-ler** n. [L. re-, back; pellere, to drive].

re·pent (ri·pent') v.t. and v.i. to feel regret for a deed or omission; to desire to change one's life as a result of sorrow for one's sins. **-ance** n. sorrow for a deed or regret; contrition; penitence **-ant** a. [Fr. se repentir].

re·per·cus·sion (rē·per·kush'·an) n. act of driving back; reverberation; rebound; recoil; echo; indirect effect. [Fr. percussion].

rep·er·toire (rep·er·twàr') n. list of plays, operas, musical works, dramatic rôles, within sphere of operations of a company or of an individual. **repertory** n. a repertoire; a place in which things are disposed in an orderly manner; a. pert. to the stock plays of a resident company [Fr. fr. L. repertorium].

rep·e·ti·tion (rep·a·tish'·an) n. act of repeating; the thing repeated; a copy. **repetitious** a. full of repetitions. **repetitive** a. involving much repetition [fr. repeat].

re·pine (ri·pin') v.i. to fret. **repining** n.

re·place (ri·plās') v.t. to put back into place; to supply an equivalent for; to substitute for. **-able** a. **-ment** n. restoration; substitution.

re·plen·ish (ri·plen'·ish) v.t. to fill up again; to restock; to refill; to furnish; to supply. **-ment** n. [L. re-, again; plenus, full].

re·plete (ri·plēt') a. full; completely filled; surfeited. **-ness, repletion** n. satiety; surfeit; (Med.) fullness of blood; plethora [L. re-, again; plere, pletum, to fill].

rep·li·ca (rep'·li·ka) n. exact copy of work of art by the artist of the original; facsimile. **-te** v.t. to fold or bend back; to duplicate. **-tion** n. an answer; reply; (Law) reply of a plaintiff to defendant's plea; a copy [L. replicare, to fold back].

re·ply (ri·pli') v.t. and v.i. to return an answer; to respond; to rejoin. n. answer; response [O.Fr. replier, fr. L. replicare, to fold back].

re·port (ri·pōrt') v.t. to relate; to take down in writing; to give an account of; to name as an offender; to narrate; v.i. to make official statement; to furnish in writing an account of a speech, or the proceedings of a public assembly; to present oneself as to superior officer; n. an official statement of facts; rumor; reverberation, as of gun; account of proceedings, debates, etc. of public bodies; repute; reputation. **-er** n. one who reports, esp. for newspapers. [L. reportare, to bring back].

re·pose (ri·pōz') v.t. to rely on; to put trust (in). **reposit** v.t. to lay up, to lodge, in a place of safety. **repository** n. place where valuables are deposited for safety; a burial vault; a storehouse [Fr. reposer, fr. L. reponere, to place back].

re·pose (ri·pōz') v.i. to rest; to sleep; to recline; to depend on; v.t. to lay at rest; n. sleep; relaxation. **-al** n. **-ful** a. **-fully** adv. [L. repausare, to pause again].

re·pous·sé (ra·poo·sā') a. embossed; hammered into relief from reverse side; n. a style of raised ornamentation in metal [Fr.].

rep·re·hend (rep·ri·hend') v.t. to find fault with; to blame; to rebuke. **reprehensible** a. blameworthy. **reprehensibly** adv. **reprehension** n. act of reprehending; reproof. [L. reprehendere, lit. to take hold again].

rep·re·sent (rep·ri·zent') v.t. to be or express the counterpart or image of; to recall by description or portrait; to pretend to be; to be the agent for; to act or play the part of; to personate; to be the member (of the House of Representatives, etc.) for. **-able** a. **-ation** n. describing, or showing; that which represents, as a picture; description; account; a dramatic performance; the act of representing (in parliament, etc.). **-ational** a. **-ative** a. typical; representing; exhibiting a likeness; n. an agent, deputy, delegate, or substitute; local member of a legislative body. [Fr. représenter].

re·press (ri·pres') v.t. to keep under control; to put down; to reduce to subjection; to quell; to check. **-er, -or** n. **-ible** a. **-ibly** adv. **-ion** n. check; restraint; in psychoanalysis, the rejection from consciousness of anything unpleasant. **-ive** a. [L. reprimere, repressum, to repress].

re·prieve (ri·prēv') v.t. to remit or commute a sentence; to grant temporary relief; n. temporary suspension of execution of sentence; rest or relief [Fr. Fr. reprendre, to take back].

rep·ri·mand (rep'·ra·mand) v.t. to reprove severely; to chide. n. a sharp rebuke; a severe admonition [Fr. réprimande].

re·print (rē·print') v.t. to print again. (rē'·print) n. a second or a new impression or edition of any printed work.

re·pris·al (ri·pri'·zal) n. an act of retaliation or retribution [Fr. représaille].

re·proach (ri·prōch') v.t. to censure; to upbraid; to rebuke; n. reproof; rebuke; discredit; an object of scorn. **-ful** a. expressing censure. **-fully** adv. **-fulness** n. [Fr. reprocher].

rep·ro·bate (rep'·ra·bāt) v.t. to disapprove with signs of extreme dislike; to exclude from hopes of salvation; a. depraved; cast off by God; n. profligate; hardened sinner; scoundrel. **reprobation** n. condemnation; censure; rejection [L. reprobare, to reprove].

re·pro·duce (rē·pra·dūs') v.t. to produce over again; to produce likeness or copy of; to imitate; v.i. to propagate; to generate. **reproducible** a. **reproduction** n. a repeat; a facsimile, as of a painting, photograph, etc.; process of multiplication of living individuals or units whereby the species is perpetuated, either sexual or asexual. **reproductive** a. pert. to reproduction; yielding a return or profits.

re·proof (ri·prōōf') n. reprimand; rebuke; censure; admonition. **reprove** v.t. to charge with a fault; to rebuke. **reprovable** a. deserving or calling for censure. **reproval** n. [O.Fr. reprover, fr. L. reprobare, to reprove].

rep·tile (rep'·til) n. animal of class **Reptilia**, cold-blooded, air-breathing vertebrates which move on their bellies or by means of small, short legs; a groveling or contemptible person [L. reptilis, creeping].

re·pub·lic (ri·pub'·lik) n. a state, without a hereditary head, in which supremacy of the people or its elected representatives is formally acknowledged; commonwealth. **-an** a. pert. to republic; (Cap.) one of the two traditional political parties of the U.S.A. **-anism** n. [L.

res publica, common weal].

re·pu·di·ate (ri·pū'·di·āt) *v.t.* to cast off; to reject; to disclaim; to disown. **repudiation** *n.* [L. *re-*, away; *pudere*, to be ashamed].

re·pug·nance (ri·pug'·nans) *n.* state or condition of being repugnant. **repugnancy** *n.* a settled or habitual feeling of aversion. **repugnant** *a.* contrary; distasteful in a high degree; offensive; adverse [L. *repugnare*, to fight back].

re·pulse (ri·puls') *v.t.* to beat or drive back; to repel decisively; to reject; *n.* state of being repulsed; act of driving off; rebuff; rejection. **repulsion** *n.* act of driving back; state of being repelled; feeling of aversion; repugnance. **repulsive** *a.* loathsome. **repulsively** *adv.* [L. *repulsum*, to drive back].

re·pute (ri·pūt') *v.t.* to account or consider; to reckon; *n.* good character; reputation; credit; esteem. **reputation** (rep·ya·tā'·shan) *n.* estimation in which a person is held; repute; known or reported character; general credit; good name; fame; renown. **reputable** *a.* held in esteem; respectable; creditable. **reputably** *adv.* **reputedly** *adv.* generally understood or believed [L. *reputare*, to reckon].

re·quest (ri·kwest') *v.t.* to ask for earnestly; to petition; to beg; *n.* expression of desire for; petition; suit; demand **-er** *n.* [L. *requestae*].

Re·qui·em (rek'·wi·am) *n.* (*R.C.*) celebration of the mass for soul of a dead person; dirge; music for such a mass [L.].

re·quire (ri·kwīr') *v.t.* to claim as by right; to make necessary; to demand; to need. **-ment** *n.* act of requiring; what is required; need; an essential condition [L. *requirere*, to seek].

req·ui·site (rek'·wa·zit) *a.* necessary; needful; indispensable; essential; *n.* something necessary or indispensable. **requisition** *n.* a demand made on a community by a military force; formal demand made by one state to another; a written order for materials or supplies; a formal demand; *v.t.* to demand certain supplies or materials, esp. for troops; to request formally; to seize. **requisitionist** *n.* one who makes a requisition [L. *requirere*, *requisitum*, to seek].

re·quite (ri·kwīt') *v.t.* to return an equivalent in good or evil; to repay; to make retaliation. **requital** *n.* that which requires or repays; compensation [*re-*, and *quit*].

re·scind (ri·sind') *v.t.* to annul; to cancel; to revoke; to repeal; to reverse; to abrogate. **-able** *a.* **recission** *n.* act of rescinding. **rescissory** *a.* [L. *rescindere*, to cut off].

re·script (rē'·skript) an edict or decree [L. *rescriptum*, written back].

res·cue (res'·kū) *v.t.* to free from danger, evil, or restraint; to set at liberty; to deliver. *n.* rescuing; deliverance. **-r** *n.* [O.Fr. *rescourre*].

re·search (ri·surch', rē'·surch) *n.* diligent search or inquiry; scientific investigation and study to discover facts; *a.* pert. to research; *v.i* to make research; to examine with care. **-er** *n.*

re·seat (rē·sēt') *v.t.* to provide with a new seat or set of seats; to patch (trousers, etc.).

re·sem·ble (ri·zem'·bl) *v.t.* to be like or similar to; **resemblance** *n.* likeness; similarity. **resembling** *a.* [Fr. *ressembler*].

re·sent (ri·zent') *v.t.* to consider as an injury or affront; to take ill; to be angry at. **-er** *n.* **-ful** *a.* full of, or readily given to, resentment. **-fully** *adv.* **-ment** *n.* deep sense of affront; indignation [L. *re-*, again; *sentire*, to feel].

re·serve (ri·zurv') *v.t.* to hold back; to set apart; to keep for future use; to retain; to keep for some person; *a.* acting as a reserve; *n.* keeping back; what is reserved; supply of stores for future use; troops, etc., held back from line of battle to assist when necessary; body of men discharged from armed forces but liable to be recalled in an emergency; funds set aside for possible contingencies; reticence; an area of land for a particular purpose. **reservation** *n.* reserving or keeping back; what is kept back; booking of a hotel room, etc.; a proviso or condition; a tract of land reserved for some public use. **-d** *a.* kept back; retained or booked; self-restrained; uncommunicative. **-dly** *adv.* **-dness** *n.* **reservist**, a member of the armed forces belonging to reserves. [L. *reservare*, to keep back].

res·er·voir (rez'·er·vwár) *n.* area for storage and filtering of water; a large supply [Fr.].

reservoir

re·set (rē·set') *v.t.* to set again. *pr.p.* **-ting.** *pa.p.* and *pa.t.* **reset.**

re·side (ri·zīd') *v.i.* to dwell permanently; to abide; to live; to be vested in; to be inherent in. **-nce** *n.* act, or time, of dwelling in a place; place where one resides; house. **-ncy** *n.* a residence. **-nt** *a.* dwelling; residing; *n.* one who resides in a place. **-ntial** *a.* pert. to a residence; pert. to a part of a town consisting mainly of dwelling houses. **-ntiary** *a.* having residence; *n.* a resident, esp. clergyman required to reside for a certain time within precincts of cathedral [L. *residere*, fr. *sedere*, to sit].

res·i·due (rez'·a·dū) *n.* balance or remainder. **residual** *a.* remaining after a part is taken away. **residuary** *a.* pert. to residue or part remaining. **residuum** *n.* what is left after any process of separation or purification; balance or remainder [L. *residuum*].

re·sign (ri·zīn')*v.t.* and *v.i.* to relinquish formally (office, etc.); to yield to; to give up; to submit to. **resignation** (rez·ig·nā'·shan) *n.* giving up, as a claim, possession, office, or place; relinquishment; patience and endurance. **-ed** *a.* relinquished; surrendered; acquiescent; submissive; patient. **-edly** *adv.* [L. *resignare*, to unseal].

re·sile (ri·zīl') *v.i.* to draw back from a previous offer, decision, etc.; to retreat; to recoil; to rebound. **resilience** (ri·zil'·yans), **resiliency** *n.* springing back or rebounding; elasticity, esp. of mind. **resilient** *a.* springing back; rebounding; elastic; buoyant; possessing power of quick recovery [L. *resilire*, to jump back].

res·in (rez'·in) *n.* general term for brittle, glassy, thickened juices exuded by certain plants; a resinous substance left after distillation of crude turpentine; fossilized remains, as amber, copal, kauri gum, etc.; *v.t.* to dress or coat with resin. **-ous** *a.* [L. *resina*].

re·sist (ri·zist') *v.t.* and *v.i.* to oppose; to withstand; to strive against. **-ance** *n.* opposition; hindrance; (*Elect.*) opposition offered by a circuit to passage of a current through it; power possessed by an individual to resist disease; in physics, forces tending to arrest movements. **-ant** *n.* one who, or that which, resists. *a.* offering or making resistance. **-er** *n.* **-ibility, -ibleness** *n.* the quality or state of being resistible. **-ible** *a.* **-ibly, -ingly** *adv.* **-less** *a.* irresistible; unable to resist. **-lessly** *adv.* **-lessness** *n.* **-or** *n.* a resistance coil or similar apparatus possessing resistance to electrical current. **-ance coil,** a coil of insulated wire whose resistance has been adjusted to a stated value. **-ance movement,** the organized, underground movement [L. *resistere*, to oppose].

res·o·lute (rez'·a·lūt) *a.* having a decided purpose; determined; *n.* a determined person; **-ly** *adv.* **-ness** *n.* determination. **resolution** *n.* act, purpose, or process of resolving; intention; firmness; solution; decision of court or vote of assembly; motion or declaration [L. *resolvere*, *resolutum*, to unite].

re·solve (ri·zalv') *v.t.* to separate the component parts of; to solve and reduce to a different form; to make clear; to unravel; (*Math.*) to solve; (*Med.*) to clear of inflammation; *v.i.* to determine; to decide; to purpose; to melt; to dissolve; to determine unanimously or by vote; *n.* act of resolving; that which is resolved on; firm determination. **resolvable** *a.* **-d** *a.* determined; resolute. **-dly** *adv.* **-dness** *n.* [L. *resolvere*, to untie].

res·o·nant (rez'·a·nant) *a.* resounding; echoing; sonorous; ringing. **resonance** *n.* [L. *re-*, again; *sonare*, to sound].

re·sort (ri·zawrt') *v.i.* to go; to have recourse; to frequent; *n.* a frequented place; vacation spot; recourse; aid. **last resort,** the last resource [Fr. *ressortir*, to rebound, to go back].

re·sound (ri·zound') *v.i.* to sound back; to send back sound; *v.i.* to echo; to reverberate.

re·source (ri·sōrs', rē·sōrs') *n.* that to which one resorts, or on which one depends, for supply or support; skill in improvising; means; contrivance; *pl.* pecuniary means; funds; wealth. **-ful** *a.* clever in devising fresh expedients. **-fully** *adv.* **-fulness** *n.* [Fr. *ressource*].

re·spect (ri·spekt') *v.t.* to esteem; to honor; to refer to; to relate to; *n.* consideration; deference; *pl.* expression of esteem; good

wishes. **-able** *a.* worthy of respect; reputable; decent; moderate. **-ability, -ableness** *n.* **-ably** *adv.* **-ful** *a.* deferential; polite. **-fully** *adv.* **-fulness** *n.* **-ing** *prep.* regarding; concerning. **-ive** *a.* relative; not absolute. **-ively** *adv.* each [L.*respicere*, to look back].

re·spire (ri·spīr') *v.t.* and *v.i.* to breathe. **respirable** *a.* fit to be breathed. **respiration** *n.* process of breathing. **respirational** *a.* respiratory. **respirator** *n.* a device to produce artificial respiration. **respiratory** (res'. or res·pī') *a.* serving for, pert. to, respiration [L. *respirare*].

res·pite (res'·pit) *n.* a temporary intermission; suspension of execution of a capital sentence;*v.t.* to grant a respite to; to reprieve; to relieve by interval of rest [O.Fr. *rrspit*].

re·splend·ent (ri·splen'·dant) *a.* shining with brilliant luster; very bright; dazzling. **resplendence, resplendency** *n.* **-ly** *adv.* [L. *resplendere*, to shine].

re·spond (ri·spånd') *v.i.* to answer; to reply; to correspond to; to react **-ent** *a.* answering; giving response; *n.* (*Law*); defendant; one who refutes in a debate [L. *respondere*, to reply].

re·sponse (ri·spåns') *n.* answer or reply; part of liturgy said or sung by choir and congregation in answer to versicles of priest; in R.C. church, anthem after morning lessons, etc. **responsibility** *n.* state of being responsible; that for which any one is responsible; a duty; a charge; an obligation **responsible** *a.* accountable; trustworthy; rational. **responsibly** *adv.* **responsive** *a.* able, ready, or inclined, to respond. **responsively** *adv.* **responsiveness** *n.* [L. *respondere*, *responsum*, to reply].

rest (rest) *n.* repose; a cessation from motion or labor; that on which anything rests or leans; a place where one may rest; a pause; *v.t.* to lay at rest; *v.i.* to cease from action; to repose; to stand or be fixed (on); to sleep; to be dead; to remain (with), for decision, etc.; to be undisturbed. **-ful** *a.* soothing; peaceful; quiet. **-fully** *adv.* **-fulness** *n.* **-less** *a.* continually on the move; unsettled in mind; uneasy. **-lessly** *adv.* **-lessness** *n.* **to lay to rest,** to bury [O.E.].

rest (rest) *v.i.* to remain; to continue to be; *n.* that which is left over or remainder [L. *restare*, to remain].

res·tau·rant (res'·ta·rånt) *n.* a place where customers are provided with meals on payment. **restaurateur** (res·to'·ra·ter) *n.* proprietor of a restaurant [Fr.].

res·ti·tu·tion (res·ta·tōō'·shan) *n.* the act of restoring, esp. to the rightful owner; reparation; indemnification; compensation. **restitutive** *a.* **restitutor** *n.* [L. *restituere*, *restitutum*, to replace].

res·tive (res'·tiv) *a.* impatient; fidgety; uneasy; obstinate; stubborn. **-ly** *adv.* **-ness** *n.* [O.Fr. *restif*, stubborn].

re·store (ri·stōr') *v.t.* to give back or return; to recover from ruin or decay; to repair; to renew; to replace; to reinstate; to heal; to revive; to cure. **restorable** *a.* **restoration** *n.* replacement; recovery; reconstruction; reestablishment; (*Cap.*) establishment of monarchy by return of Charles II in 1660. **restorative** *a.* having power to renew strength, vigor, etc.; *n.* a remedy for restoring health and vigor [L. *restaurare*, to repair].

re·strain (ri·strān') *v.t.* to hold back; to hinder; to check. **-able** *a.* **-edly** *adv.* with restraint. **-ment** *n.* **-t** *n.* curb; repression; hinderance; imprisonment [O.Fr. *restraindre*, fr. L. *re-*, back; *stringere*, to bind].

re·strict (ri·strikt') *v.t.* to restrain within bounds; to limit **-ed** *a.* limited. **-edly** *adv.* **-ion** *n.* act of restricting; state of being restricted; limitation, confinement; restraint. **-ive** *a.* **-ively** *adv.* [L. *restringere*, to bind fast].

re·sult (ri·zult') *v.i.* to follow, as a consequence; to issue (in); to terminate; *n.* issue; effect; outcome; answer to a calculation. *a.* following as a result [L. *resultare*, to leap back].

re·sume (ri·zūm') *v.t.* to renew; to recommence; to take again. **résumé** (rā·zū·mā') *n.* a summing up; an abstract. **resumable** *a.* **resumption** *n.* act of taking back or taking again; a fresh start. **resumptive** *a.* resuming [L. *re-*, again; *sumere*, to take].

re·surge (ri·surj') *v.i.* to rise again. **-nce** *n.* **-nt** *a.* rising again (from the dead) [L. *re-*, again; *surgere*, to rise].

res·ur·rect (rez'·a·rekt') *v.t.* to restore to life; to use again. **-ion** *n.* rising of the body after death; (*Cap.*) Christ's arising from the grave after Crucifixion; a revival. **-ion, -ionary** *a.* **-ionist** *n.* one who resurrects, revives, etc.; a believer in resurrection; one who stealthily exhumed bodies from the grave to sell for anatomical purposes [L. *re-*, again; *surgere*, to rise].

re·sus·ci·tate (ri·sus'·a·tāt) *v.t.* to restore to life one apparently dead; to revive; *v.i.* to come to life again. **resuscitable** *a.* **resuscitation** *n.* **resuscitative** *a.* tending to revive or reanimate. **resuscitator** *n.* [L. *resuscitare*, to raise up again].

re·tail (rē·tāl') *v.t.* to sell to consumer, esp. in small quantities; to tell. **retail** *a.* denoting sale to consumer, as opposed to wholesale; *n.* sale in small quantities. **-er** *n.* **-ment** *n.* [O.F. *retailler*, to cut up].

re·tain (ri·tān′) *v.t.* to continue to keep in possession; to hold; to reserve; to engage services of. **-able** *a.* **-er** one who retains; adherent or follower; a fee paid to secure services of, esp. lawyer. **-ment** *n.* [L. *retinere*, to hold back].

re·tal·i·ate (ri·tal′·i·āt) *v.t.* and *v.i.* to repay in kind; to return like for like; to requite. **retaliation** *n.* **retaliative, retaliatory** *a.* **retaliator** *n.* [L. *retaliare*, fr. *talis*, like].

re·tard (ri·tard′) *v.t.* to hinder progress; to make slow or late; to impede. **-ation** *n.* delaying; hindrance; diminishing velocity of a moving body; rate of loss of velocity; delayed mental development in children. **-ment** *n.* [L. *retardare*, fr. *tardus*, slow].

retch (rech) *v.i.* to strain at vomiting. **-ing** *n.* [O.E. *hraecan*].

re·ten·tion (ri·ten′·shan) *n.* act or power of retaining; memory. **retentive, retentively** *adv.* **retentiveness** *n.* [fr. *retain*].

ret·i·cent (ret′·a·sant) *a.* reserved; uncommunicative. **reticence** *n.* also **reticency. -ly** *adv.* [L. *reticere*, fr. *tacere*, to be silent].

ret·i·cle (ret′·a·kl) *n.* a group of lines or wires in the focus of an optical instrument. **reticule** *n.* a little bag; a reticle. **reticular, reticulary** *a.* having the form of a net; intricate. **reticulate** *v.t.* to cover with netlike lines; to make like a net; *a.* Also **reticulated. reticulation** *n.* [Fr. *reticule*, fr. L. *rete*, a net].

re·ti·form (rē′·ta·fawrm) *a.* having form of a net; reticulated [L. *rete*, a net; *forma*, form].

ret·i·na (ret′·i·na) *n.* innermost, semi-transparent, sensory layer of the eye from which sense impressions are passed to the brain. **-l** *a.* [L. *rete*, a net].

ret·i·nue (ret′·i·nū) *n.* a body of hired servants or followers; a train of attendants; suite [Fr. *retenir*, to retain].

re·tire (ri·tīr′) *v.t.* to compel one to retire from office; to withdraw from circulation notes or bills; to reserve; to withdraw; to retreat; to give up formally one's work or office; to go to bed. **retiral** *n.* act of retiring; occasion when one retires from office, etc. **-d** *a.* secluded; private; sequestered; withdrawn permanently from one's daily work. **-dly** *adv.* **-ment, -dness** *n.* act of retiring; state of being retired. **retiring** *a.* reserved; modest [Fr. *retirer*, to pull back].

re·tort (ri·tawrt′) *v.t.* to repay in kind; to hurl back as a reply; *v.i.* to make a smart reply; *n.* vigorous reply or repartee; a vessel in which substances are distilled [L. *retorquere, retortum*, to twist back].

re·trace (rē·trās′) *v.t.* to trace back or over again; to go back the same way. **-able** *a.*

re·tract (ri·trakt′) *v.t.* and *v.i.* to draw back; to take back, as a statement; to go back on one's word. **-able** *a.* **-ation** *n.* recalling of a statement or opinion; recantation. **-ile** *a.* (*Zool.*) capable of being drawn back or inwards, as claws, etc. **-ion** *n.* the act of drawing back; disavowal; recantation; retractile power. **-ive** *a.* **-ively** *adv.* [L. *re-*, back; *trahere, tractum*, to draw].

re·tread (rē·tred′) *v.t.* to tread again; to replace a worn tread on the outer cover of a

rubber tire with a new tread.

re·treat (ri·trēt′) *n.* retiring or withdrawing; a military signal for retiring; a military call at sunset, on a bugle; place of seclusion; period of retirement for prayer and meditation; *v.i.* to move back; to betake oneself to a place of security; to retire before an enemy. **-ing** *a.* sloping backward, as forehead or chin [Fr. *retraite*, fr. *retraire*, to draw back].

re·trench (ri·trench′) *v.t.* to cut down (expense, etc.); to curtail; to remove; *v.i.* to economize. **-ment** *n.* diminution of expenditure; economy; (*Fort.*) extra parapet and ditch within a rampart to prolong defense [Fr. *retrancher*, to cut off].

ret·ri·bu·tion (ret·ri·bū′·shan) *n.* just or suitable return; esp. for evil deeds; requital; repayment. **retributive, retributory** *a.* [L. *retributio*].

re·trieve (ri·trēv′) *v.t.* to gain back; to recover; to reestablish (former position, fortune, etc.); to repair; (of a dog) to find and bring back shot game. **retrievable** *a.* **retrievably** *adv.* **-ment, retrieval** *n.* **-r** *n.* dog trained to find and bring back game [Fr. *retrouver*, to find again].

ret·ro- (ret′·rō) *prefix* fr. L. *retro*, back, backward, used in the formation of compound words.

ret·ro·act (ret·rō·akt′) *v.i.* to act backwards; to react **-ion** *n.* **-ive** *a.* acting in regard to past events; retrospective. **-ively** *adv.* [L. *retro*, backward; *agere, actum*, to act].

ret·ro·cede (ret·rō·sēd′) *v.t.* to go or move back. **retrocession** *n.* going back [L. *retro*, backward; *cedere*, to go].

ret·ro·grade (ret′·rō·grād) *v.i.* to move backward; to deteriorate; to decline; *a.* tending to a backward direction; deteriorating; reactionary; retrogressive. **retrogradation** *n.* **retrogress** *v.i.* to move backwards; to deteriorate. **retrogression** *n.* act of going backward; a decline into an inferior state of development. **retrogressive** *a.* moving backward; reactionary; degenerating; assuming baser characteristics. **retrogressively** *adv.* [L. *retro*, backward; *gradi*, to go].

re·trorse (rē·trawrs′) *a.* bending or pointing backwards, as feathers of birds. Also **retroverse. -ly** *adv.* [L. *retro*, backwards; *vertere, versum*, to turn].

ret·ro·spect (ret′·rō·spekt) *n.* a looking back; survey of past events; a review. **-ion** *n.* **-ive** *a.* tending to look back; applicable to past events; of laws, rules, etc., having force as if enacted or authorized at earlier date. **-ively** *adv.* [L. *retro*, backward; *specere*, to look].

ret·ro·verse (ret′·rō·vers) *a.* bent backwards; reverse. **retroversion** *n.* **retrovert** (rē′·ret·′) *v.t.* to turn back [L. *retro*, backward; *vertere, versum*, to turn].

re·turn (ri·turn′) *v.t.* to bring, give, or send back; to restore; to report officially; to elect; to yield (a profit); to reciprocate; *v.i.* to go or come back; to recur; to reply; *n.* coming back to the same place; what is returned, as a payment; profit; an official report, esp. as to numbers; repayment; restitution. **-able** *a.* **— match** *n.* second game played by same opponents. **— ticket** *n.* ticket for journey, there and back [Fr. *retourner*].

re·un·ion (rē·ūn′·yan) *n.* union formed anew after separation; a social gathering. **reunite** *v.t.* and *v.i.* to unite again; to join after separation.

rev (rev) *n.* (*Colloq.*) revolution of an engine; *v.t.* and *v.i.* to run (an engine). *pr.p.* **-ving.** *pa.t.* and *pa.p.* **-ved.**

re·veal (ri·vēl′) *v.t.* to disclose; to show. **-able** *a.* **-er** *n.* **-ment** *n.* disclosure; revelation. **-ed law,** divine law. **-ed religion,** founded on revelation. Opposite of *natural religion* [L. *revelare*, to draw back the veil].

re·veil·le (rev′·a·li·) *n.* the bugle call or roll of drums sounded in military establishments at daybreak to rouse inmates [Fr. *réveillez (-vous)* wake up!].

rev·el (rev′·al) *v.i.* to make merry; to carouse; to delight in. *pr.p., pat., pa.p.* and *n.* festivity; noisy celebration; *pl.* entertainment, with music and dancing. **-er** *n.* **-ment, -ry** *n.* [O.Fr. *reveler*, to make tumult].

rev·e·la·tion (rev·a·lā′·shan) *n.* act of revealing; God's disclosure of himself to man; (*Cap.*) last book of New Testament. **-al, revelatory** *a.* [L. *revelare*, to draw back the veil].

rev·e·nant (rev′·a·nant) *n.* one returned from long absence or apparently from the dead; a specter; a ghostly visitant [Fr.].

re·venge (ri·venj′) *v.t.* to make retaliation for; to return injury for injury; to avenge; *n.* revenging; infliction of injury in return for injury; passion for vengeance. **-ful** *a.* **-fully** *adv.* **-fulness** *n.* [O.Fr. *revenger*, fr. L. *re-*, again; *vindicare*, to claim].

rev·e·nue (rev′·a·nū) *n.* income derived from any source, esp. annual income of a state or institution; proceeds; receipts; profits. [Fr. *revenue*, return, fr. L. *revenire*, to come back].

re·ver·ber·ate (ri·vur′·ber·āt) *v.t.* and *v.i.* to send back, as sound; to reflect, as light or heat; to re-echo; to resound. **reverberant** *a.* resounding; beating back. **reverberation** *n.* **reverberative** *a.* tending to reverberate. **re-**

verberator *n.* **reverberatory** *a.* producing reverberation [L. *reverberare*, to beat back].

re·vere (ri·vir′) *v.t.* to regard with mingled fear, respect and affection; to reverence. **-nce** *n.* awe mingled with respect and esteem; veneration; a bow, curtsy, or genuflection; (*Cap.*) a title applied to a clergyman; *v.t.* to revere; to venerate; a title of respect given to clergy (*abbrev.* **Rev.**) **-nt** *a.* feeling, showing, behaving with, reverence. **-ntial** *a.* respectful. **-ntially, -ntly** *adv.* [O.Fr. *reverer*, fr. L. *vereri*, to feel awe].

rev·er·ie, revery (rev′·er·i·) *n.* state of mind, akin to dreaming; rhapsody; musing [Fr. *rêverie*, fr. *rêver*, to dream].

re·vers (ra·vir′) *n.* part of garment turned for ornamentation, as lapel [O.Fr. = reverse].

re·verse (ri·vurs′) *v.t.* to change completely; to turn in an opposite direction; to give a contrary decision; to annul; to overturn; to transpose; to invert; *v.i.* to change direction; *n.* side which appears when object is turned round; opposite or contrary; crest side of coin or medal, as distinguished from *obverse*; check; defeat; misfortune; gear to drive a car backward; *a.* turned backward; opposite. **reversal** *n.* reversing, changing, overthrowing, annulling. **-d** *a.* turned in opposite direction; inverted; annulled. **-ly** *adv.* **reversibility** *n.* property of being reversible. **reversible** *a.* capable of being used on both sides or in either direction. **reversibly** *adv.* **reversion** *n.* returning or reverting; a deferred annuity; right or hope of future possession; (*Law*) return of estate to grantor or his next-of-kin, after death of grantee or legatee; interest which reverts to a landlord after expiry of lease; (*Biol.*) a tendency to revert to long-concealed characters of previous generations; atavism. **reversional, reversionary** *a.* involving a reversion. **reversive** *a.* [L. *re-*, back; *vertere, versum*, to turn].

re·vert (ri·vurt′) *v.i.* to return to former state or rank; to come back to subject; to turn backwards; (*Law*) to return by reversion to donor; *v.t.* to turn back or reverse. **-ible** *a.* [L. *re-*, again; *vertere*, to turn].

re·view (ri·vū′) *v.t.* to re-examine; to consider critically (book); to inspect troops, etc. *n.* revision; survey; inspection, esp. of massed military forces; a critical notice of a book, etc.; periodical devoted to critical articles, current events, etc. **-er** *n.* one who writes critical reviews; examiner; inspector [Fr. *revoir*, to see again].

re·vile (ri·vīl′) *v.t.* to abuse with opprobrious language; to vilify; to defame. **-ment** *n.* **-r** *n.* [O.Fr. *reviler*].

re·vise (ri·vīz′) *v.t.* to look over and correct; to review, alter and amend; *n.* a revised form; a further printer's proof to ensure all corrections have been made. **revisal** *n.* review; reexamination. **revision** *n.* revisal; revised copy of book or document. **-r** *n.* **revisional, revisionary** *a.* pert. to revision. **revisory** *a.* having power to revise (*Cap.*). **-d Version,** new translation of Bible in 1881 (New Testament) and 1884 (Old Testament) [L. *revisere*].

re·vive (ri·vīv′) *v.i.* to come back to life, vigor, etc.; to awaken; *v.t.* to resuscitate; to re-animate; to renew; to recover from neglect; to refresh (memory). **revivability** *n.* **revivable** *a.* capable of being revived. **revivably** *adv.* **revival** *n.* reviving or being revived; renewed activity, of trade, etc.; a wave of religious enthusiasm worked up by powerful preachers; awakening; reappearance of old, neglected play, etc. **revivalism** *n.* religious fervor of a revival. **revivalist** *n.* one who promotes religious revivals. **-r** *n.* one who, or that which, revives; a stimulant. **revivification** *n.* renewal of life and energy. **revivify** *v.t.* to reanimate; to reinvigorate [L. *re-*, again; *vivere*, to live].

re·voke (ri·vōk′) *v.t.* to annul; to repeal; to reverse (a decision); *v.i.* at cards, to fail to follow suit. *n.* neglect to follow suit at cards. **-r** *n.* **revocable** *a.* able to be revoked. **revocableness, revocability** *n.* **revocably** *adv.* **revocation** *n.* repeal; reversal. **revocatory** *a.* [L. *revocare*, to recall].

re·volt (ri·vōlt′) *v.i.* to renounce allegiance; to rise in rebellion; to feel disgust; *v.t.* to shock;

to repel; *n.* act of revolting; rebellion; mutiny; disgust; loathing. **-er** *n.* **-ing** *a.* disgusting. **-ingly** *adv.* [Fr. *révolter*].

rev·o·lu·tion (rev·a·lū′·shan) *n.* motion of body round its orbit or focus; turning round on axis, time marked by a regular recurrence (as seasons); a radical change in constitution of a country after revolt. **-ary** *a.* pert. to revolution; marked by great and violent changes; *n.* one who participates in a revolution. **-ize** *v.t.* to change completely [L. *revolvere, revolutum,* to turn round].

re·volve (ri·valv′) *v.i.* to turn round on an axis; to rotate; to meditate; *v.t.* to cause to turn; to rotate; to reflect upon. **revolvable** *a.* **-r** *n.* pistol [L. *revolvere,* to turn round].

re·vue (ri·vū′) *n.* theatrical entertainment, partly musical comedy, with little continuity of structure or connected plot [Fr.].

re·vul·sion (ri·vul′·shan) *n.* sudden, violent change of feeling; repugnance or abhorrence; reaction; (*Med.*) counterirritation. **revulsive** *a.* [L. *revellere, revulsum,* to tear away].

re·ward (ri·wawrd′) *v.t.* to give in return for; to recompense; to remunerate; *n.* what is given in return; return for voluntary act; assistance in any form. **-er** *n.* **-ing** *a.* [O.Fr. *rewarder* = Fr. *regarder,* to look upon].

rhab·do- (rab·da) *prefix* used in formation of scientific compound terms, signifying *a rod* or *rod-like.* **rhaboid** *a.* rod-shaped. **-mancy** *n.* divination by rod or wand, to trace presence of ores or water underground [Gk. *rhabdos,* a rod].

rhap·so·dy (rap′·sa·di·) *n.* collection of verses; an intense, rambling composition or discourse; (*Mus.*) an irregular composition in a free style. **rhapsodic(al)** *a.* in extravagant, irregular style. **rhapsodically** *adv.* **rhapsodize** *v.t.* and *v.i.* to sing or recite, as a rhapsody; to be ecstatic over. **rhapsodist** *n.* one who recites or composes a rhapsody [Gk. *rhapsōdía*].

Rhen·ish (ren′·ish) *a.* of or pert. to River Rhine; *n.* wine from grapes grown in Rhineland [L. *Rhenus*].

rhe·o- *prefix* used in the formation of scientific compound terms, signifying *flowing* from Gk. *rhein,* to flow. **rheometer** (rē·ám′·a·ter) *n.* instrument for measuring force of flow of fluids. **-stat** *n.* instrument for controlling and varying within limits value of resistance in electrical circuit. **rheostatic** *a.*

rhe·sus (rē′·sas) *n.* small Indian monkey. **rhesian** *a.* **rhesus factor** (*Med.*) Rh factor; a peculiarity of red cells of blood of most individuals, the so-called **rhesus positive,** rendering transfusion of their blood unsuitable for rhesus negative minority of patients. [L.]

rhet·o·ric (ret′·a·rik) *n.* art of persuasive or effective speech or writing; declamation; artificial eloquence or sophistry; exaggerated oratory. **rhetorical** *a.* concerning style or effect; of the nature of rhetoric. **rhetorical question,** statement in the form of question to which no answer is expected. **rhetorically** *adv.* **rhetorician** *n.* a teacher of or one versed in principles of rhetoric [Gk. *rhetorikos,* fr. *rhētōr,* a public speaker].

rheum (room) *n.* thin, serous fluid secreted by mucous glands and discharged from nostrils or eyes during catarrh or a common cold. **-atic, -atical** *a.* pert. to or suffering from rheumatism. **-atism** *n.* a disease with symptoms of sharp pains and swelling in muscles and larger joints. **-atoid** *a.* resembling rheumatism. **-y** *a.* (*Literary*) full of rheum (esp. eyes); damp. **rheumatoid arthritis,** severe chronic inflammation of joints, esp. knees and fingers [Gk. *rheuma,* flow].

rhi·nal (rī′·nal) *a* pert. to the nose [Gk. *rhis, rhinos,* nose].

rhine·stone (rīn′·stōn) *n.* paste imitation of diamonds [fr. the *Rhine*].

rhi·noc·er·os (rī·nás′·a·ras) *n.* thick-skinned mammal allied to elephant, hippopotamus, etc. with strong horn (sometimes two) on nose [Gk. *rhis, rhinos,* the nose; *keras,* a horn].

rhi·zo- (rī·zō) *prefix* used in construction of compound terms, from Greek, *rhiza,* a root. **rhizome** (rī′·zōm) *n.* subterranean shoot, often bearing scales which are membranous, and usually giving off adventurous roots. **-matous** *a.* of the nature of a rhizome.

rhod-, rhodo- *prefix* used in the formation of compound terms, signifying rose-colored from

---

Greek, *rhodon,* a rose. **-ocyte** *n.* red blood corpuscle. **rhododendron** *n.* evergreen flowering shrub with magnificent red or white blossoms.

rhom·bus (rám′·bas) *n.* (*Geom.*) parallelogram whose sides are all equal but whose angles are not right angles. **rhomb** *n.* a lozenge or diamond-shaped figure; rhombus. **rhombic, rhombiform, rhomboid, rhomboidal** *a.* **rhomboid** *n.* parallelogram like rhombus, but having only opposite sides and angles equal [Gk. *rhombos*].

rhu·barb (róó′·bárb) *n.* two species of cultivated plants, familiar rhubarb of kitchen garden, and an eastern variety whose roots are used as a purgative. (*Slang*) heated discussion [Gk. *rha,* rhubarb; *barbaron,* foreign].

rhumb, rumb (rum, rumb) *n.* any of 32 cardinal points on compass [Gk. *rhombos,* a rhomb].

rhyme (rīm) *n.* identity of sound in word endings of verses; verses in rhyme with each other; word answering in sound to another word; *v.t.* to put into rhyme; *v.i.* to make verses. **-r, rhymster** *n.* one who makes rhymes; a minor poet; a poetaster. **— scheme,** pattern or arrangement of rhymes in stanza [O.E. *rim,* number].

rhythm (rithm) *n.* regular or measured flow of sound, as in music and poetry, or of action, as in dancing; measured, periodic movement, as in heart pulsations; regular recurrence; symmetry. **-ic(al)** *a.* **-ically** *adv.* **-ics** *n.* science of rhythm [Gk. *rhuthmos,* fr. *rhein,* to flow].

ri·ant (rī′·ant) *a.* laughing; merry; genial. **-ly** *adv.* [Fr. *rire,* to laugh].

rib (rib) *n.* one of arched and very elastic bones springing from vertebral column; anything resembling a rib, as a bar of a firegrate, wire support of umbrella. *v.t.* to furnish with ribs. *pr.p.* **-bing.** *pa.t.* and *pa.p.* **-bed. -bing** *n.* an arrangement of ribs [O.E. *ribb*].

rib·ald (rib·ald) *a.* low; vulgar; indecent. **-ry** *n.* vulgar language or conduct; obscenity. **-ish** *a.* [Fr. *ribaud*].

rib·bon (rib′·an) *n.* woven strip of material such as silk or satin, as trimming or fastening for a dress; colored piece of silk as war medal; part of insignia of order of knighthood; anything in strips resembling ribbon; inked tape in a typewriter. **Blue Ribbon,** first prize award [O.Fr. *riban*].

ri·bo·fla·vin (rī·ba·flā′·vin) *n.* chemical substance present in vitamin B2 complex, with marked growth promoting properties [L.L. *ribus,* currant; *flavus,* yellow].

rice (rīs) *n.* annual grass plant, cultivated in Asia, the principal food of one-third of world. **— paper** *n.* very thin and delicate paper used in China and Japan for drawing and painting [Gk. *oruza*].

rich (rich) *a.* wealthy; abounding in possessions; well supplied; fertile; abounding in nutritive qualities; of food, highly seasoned or flavored; mellow and harmonious (voice); *n.* the wealthy classes. **-es** *n.pl.* wealth. **-ly** *adv.* **-ness** *n.* [O.E. *rice,* rich].

rick·ets (rik′·its) *n.* rachitis, infantile disease marked by defective development of bones. **rickety** *a.* affected with rickets; shaky; unstable; insecure [etym. uncertain].

rick·shaw. See **jinrickisha.**

ric·o·chet (rik′·a·shā) *n.* glancing rebound of object after striking flat surface at oblique angle; *v.t.* and *v.i.* to rebound [Fr.].

rid (rid) *v.t.* to free of; to relieve of; to remove by violence; to disencumber. *pr.p.* **-ding.** *pa.t.* and *pa.p.* **rid** or **-ded. -dance** *n.* deliverance; removal. **a good riddance,** a welcome relief [O.E. *hreddan,* to snatch away].

rid·den (rid′·n) *pa.p.* of **ride.**

rid·dle (rid′·l) *n.* large sieve for sifting or screening gravel, etc.; *v.t.* to separate, as grain from chaff, with a riddle; to pierce with holes as in a sieve; to pull (theory, etc.) to pieces. **riddlings** *n.pl.* coarse material left in sieve [O.E. *hridder*].

rid·dle (rid′·l) *n.* enigma; puzzling fact, thing, person; *v.i.* to speak in, make, riddles [O.E. *raedelse.* fr. *raedan,* to read, to guess].

ride (rīd) *v.t.* to be mounted on horse, bicycle, etc.; to traverse or cover distance; *v.i.* to be carried on back of an animal; to be borne along in a vehicle; to lie securely at anchor; to float lightly. *pr.p.* **riding.** *pa.t.* **rode;** *pa.p.* **ridden.** *n.* act of riding; journey on horseback, in a vehicle, etc.; roadway, etc. **-r** *n.* one who rides; addition to a document; supplement to original motion or verdict. **riding** *a.* used for riding on; used by a rider; *n.* act of riding. **riding habit** *n.* outfit worn by ladies on horseback. **to ride over,** to tyrannize. **to ride rough-shod,** to show no consideration for others [O.E. *ridan*].

ridge (rij) *n.* line of meeting of two sloping surfaces; long narrow hill; strip of upturned soil between furrows; highest part of roof; horizontal beam to which tops of rafters are fixed; tongue of high pressure on meteorological map; *v.t.* to form into ridges; *v.i.* to rise in ridges; to wrinkle. **-d** *a.* having ridges on its surface. **— pole** *n.* horizontal beam at peak of roof, tent, etc. [O.E. *hrycg,* the back].

---

rid·i·cule (rid′·a·kūl) *n.* mockery; raillery; derision; *v.t.* to deride; to mock; to make fun of. **-r** *n.* **ridiculous** *a.* exciting ridicule; ludicrous, laughable. [L. *ridere,* to laugh].

rife (rīf) *a.* prevailing; prevalent; abundant; plentiful. **-ly** *adv.* **-ness** *n.* [O.E.].

riff·raff (rif′·raf) *n.* the rabble (*Dial*) trash [M.E. *rif* and *raf*].

ri·fle (rī·fl) *v.t.* to search and rob; to strip; to plunder. **-r** *n.* **rifling** *n.* pillaging [O.Fr. *rifler,* fr. Ice. *hrifa,* to seize].

ri·fle (rī′·fl) *v.t.* to make spiral grooves in (gun barrel, etc.), *n.* a shoulder weapon or artillery piece whose barrel is grooved. **rifling** *n.* the arrangement of grooves in a gun barrel or rifle tube. **-man.** *n.* a man armed with rifle [Dan. *rifle,* to groove].

rift (rift) *n.* cleft; fissure; *v.t.* and *v.i.* to crack [fr. *rive,* to rend].

rig (rig) *v.t.* to provide (ship) with spars, ropes, etc.; to equip; (*Colloq.*) to arrange fraudulently; to clothe. *pr.p.* **-ging.** *pa.t.* and *pa.p.* **-ged** *n.* manner in which masts and sails of vessel are rigged; equipment used in erecting or installing machinery, etc.; (*Colloq.*) dress; a horse and trap. **-ger** *n.* **ging** *n.* system of ropes and tackle, esp. for supporting mast or controlling sails; adjustment of different components of an aircraft [Scand.].

right (rīt) *a.* straight; proper; upright; in accordance with truth and duty; being on same side of person toward the east when facing north; in politics, implying preservation of existing, established order or of restoring former institutions; (*Geom.*) applied to regular figures rising perpendicularly; correct; true; *adv.* in a right manner; according to standard of truth and justice; very; correctly; properly; exactly to the right hand; *n.* that which is correct; uprightness; a just claim; legal title; that which is on right side, or opposite to left; political party inclined towards conservatism and preservation of status quo; *v.t.* to set upright; to do justice to; to make right; to recover proper or natural position; to become upright. **-ful** *a.* legitimate; lawful; true; honest; reasonable; fair. **-fully** *adv.* **-fulness** *n.* **-ly** *adv.* in accordance with justice; correctly. **-ness** *n.* correctness; justice. **-about** *adv.* in or to the opposite direction. **-angled** *a.* having a **right angle,** one of ninety degrees. **—hand** *a.* belonging to the right hand; pert. to most reliable assistant. **— of way** *n.* right of passage [O.E. *riht*].

right·eous (rī′·chas) *a.* doing what is right; just; upright; godly. **-ly** *adv.* **-ness** *n.* [O.E. *riht,* right; *wis,* wise].

rig·id (rij′·id) *a.* stiff; not easily bent; strict; rigorous. **-ness, -ity** *n.* **-ly** *adv.* [L. *rigidus*].

rig·ma·role (rig′·ma·rōl) *n.* a succession of meaningless, rambling statements; foolish talk [corrupt. of *ragman roll,* a list of names].

rig·or (rig′·er) *n.* strictness, severity, stiffness, (*Med.*) a chill with fever; insensitive state of plants or animals. **-ism** *n.* strictness; austerity. **-ist** *n.* a person of strict principles. **-ous** *a.* **-ously** *adv.* **-ousness** *n.* **— mortis,** stiffening of body after death [L.].

rile (rīl) *v.t.* (*Colloq.* or *Dial.*) to anger; to exasperate; to irritate [a form of *roil*].

rill (ril) *n.* a small brook; rivulet; a streamlet. **-et** *n.* a tiny stream [Ger. *Rille,* a furrow].

rim (rim) *n.* margin; brim; border; metal ring forming outer part of a car wheel and carrying the tire; *v.t.* to furnish with a rim; *pr.p.* **-ming.** *pa.t.* and *pa.p.* **-med. -less** *a.* [O.E. *rima*].

rime Same as **rhyme.**

rime (rīm) *n.* white or hoarfrost; frozen dew or vapor. **rimy** *a.* [O.E. *hrim*].

ri·mose (rī′·mōs) *a.* having surface covered with fissures or cracks. Also **rimous** [L. *rimosus*].

rind (rīnd) *n.* the external covering or coating

of trees, fruits, cheese, bacon, etc.; skin; peel, etc. *v.t.* to strip off rind [O.E. *rindle*].

rim

ring (ring) *n.* small circle of gold, etc. esp. on finger; band, coil, rim; circle formed for dance or sports; round enclosure, as in circus, auction mart, etc.; area within roped square for boxing, etc.; a combination of persons to control prices within a trade; *v.t.* to encircle; to put ring through an animal's nose; to cut a ring around trunk of a tree. **-ed** *a.* wearing, marked with, formed of, or surrounded by, a ring or rings. **-ing** *n.* **-leader** *n.* the leader of people associated together for a common object, usually in defiance of law and order. **-less** *a.* **-let** *n.* small ring; long curl of hair. **-mail** *n.* chain armor. **-master** *n.* one who directs performance in circus ring. **-worm** *n.* contagious disease of skin, esp. of scalp, leaving circular bare patches [O.E. *hring*].

ring (ring) *v.t.* to cause to sound, esp. by striking; to produce, by ringing; *v.i.* to give out a clear resonant sound, as a bell; to chime; to resound; to be filled, as with praise, tidings, etc.; to continue sounding, as ears. *pa.t.* **rang**, rarely **rung**. *pa.p.* **rung**. *n.* a resonant note; chime (of church bells); act of ringing; a telephone call. **to ring down**, to cause theater curtain to be lowered. **to ring false**, to sound insincere [O.E. *hringan*].

rink (ringk) *n.* place for skating or curling; members of a side at bowling or curling; floor for roller skating, etc.; broad strip of a bowling-green [etym. doubtful].

rinse (rins) *v.t.* to wash out, by filling with water, etc., and emptying; to wash without the use of soap; **rinsing** *n.* [Fr. *rincer*].

ri·ot (rī'.at) *n.* tumultuous disturbance of peace; wanton behavior; noisy festivity; tumult; uproar; profusion, as of color. *v.i.* to make, or engage in, riot; to revel; to disturb peace. **-er** *n.* **-ing** *n.* **-ous** *a.* engaging in riot; unruly; boisterous. **-ously** *adv.* **-ousness** *n.* **-ry** *n.* riotous conduct. **to read the riot act** (*Colloq.*) to scold and threaten punishment. **to run riot**, to behave wildly, without restraint [O.Fr. *riotte*].

rip (rip) *v.t.* to rend; to slash; to tear off or out; to slit; to saw wood along direction of grain; *v.i.* to tear; to move quickly and freely. *pr.p.* **-ping**. *pa.t.* and *pa.p.* **-ped**. *n.* rent; tear. **-per** *n.* **-ping** *a.* **-cord** *n.* cord to withdraw parachute from pack so that ascending air forces it open. **— roaring** (*Slang*) *a.* hilarious. **-saw** *n.* saw with large teeth for cutting timber in direction of grain [O.N. *rippa*, to scratch].

rip (rip) *n.* a stretch of broken water in sea or river. **— current**, **— tide** [etym. doubtful].

ri·par·i·an (ra.., rī.pār'.i.an) *a.* pert. to, or situated on, banks of a river [L. *ripa*, a river bank].

ripe (rīp) *a.* ready for reaping; mature; fully developed; sound (judgment, etc.); ready (for) **-ly** *adv.* **-n** *v.t.* to hasten process of ripening; to mature; *v.i.* to grow ripe; to come to perfection. **-ness** *n.* [O.E.].

ri·poste (ri.pōst') *n.* quick return thrust in fencing; smart reply; repartee [Fr.].

rip·ple (rip'.l) *n.* fretting or dimpling of surface of water; a little wave; subdued murmur or sound; *v.t.* to cause ripple in; *v.i.* to flow or form into little waves. [var. of *rimple*, for O.E. *hrimpan*, to wrinkle].

rise (rīz) *v.i.* to ascend; to get up; to get out of bed; to appear above horizon; to originate; to swell; to increase in value, price, power; to revolt; to reach a higher rank; to revive. *pr.p.* **rising**. *pa.t.* **rose**. *pa.p.* **-n**. *n.* act of rising; that which rises or seems to rise; increase, as of price, wages, etc.; source; elevation. **-r** *n.* one who, or that which, rises; vertical part of a step. **rising** *n.* getting up; revolt; insurrection; *a.* mounting; advancing. **to get a rise out of,** to tease someone to the point of anger [O.E. *risan*].

ris·i·ble (riz'.a.bl) *a.* very prone to laugh; capable of exciting laughter; mirth provoking. **-ness, risibility** *n.* **risibly** *adv.* [L. *risibilis*, fr. *ridere*, to laugh].

risk (risk) *n.* danger; peril; hazard; amount covered by insurance; person or object insured; *v.t.* to expose to danger or possible loss. **-er** *n.* **-y** *a.* [Fr. *risque*].

ris·qué (ris.kā) *a.* daringly close to impropriety [F. *risquer*].

ri·sot·to (ri.zawt'.tō) *n.* Italian dish of

shredded onions, meat, and rice [It.].

ris·sole (ris'.ōl) *n.* fish or meat minced and fried with bread crumbs and eggs [Fr.].

rite (rit) *n.* formal practice or custom, esp. religious; form; ceremonial. **ritual** *a.* pert. to rites; ceremonial; *n.* manner of performing divine service; prescribed book of rites. **ritualism** *n.* adherence to and fondness for decorous ceremonial customs in public worship. **ritualist** *n.* **ritualistic** *a.* **ritually** *adv.* [L. *ritus*].

ri·val (rī'.val) *n.* competitor; opponent; *a.* having same pretensions or claims; competing; *v.t.* to vie with; to strive to equal or excel. **-ry** *n.* keen competition; emulation [L. *rivalis*].

rive (rīv) *v.t.* to rend asunder; to split; to cleave; *v.i.* to be split or rent asunder. **-d**. *pa.p.* **-d, -n** [O.N. *rifa*].

riv·er (riv'.er) *n.* natural stream of water flowing in a channel; a copious flow; abundance. **-ine** *a.* situated near or on river. **— basin** *n.* area drained by a river and its tributaries. **-bed** *n.* channel of a river. **— horse** *n.* the hippopotamus. **-side** *n.* the bank of a river [Fr. *rivière*].

riv·et (riv'.it) *n.* cylindrical iron or steel pin with strong flat head at one end, used for uniting two overlapping plates, etc. by hammering down the stub end; *v.t.* to fasten with rivets; to clinch; to fasten firmly [Fr.].

riv·u·let (riv'.ya.lit) *n.* a little river.
roach (rōch) *n.* fresh-water fish [O. Fr. *roche*].

roach. See cockroach.

road (rōd) *n.* a track or way prepared for passengers, vehicles, etc., direction; way; route; a place where vessels may ride at anchor. **-block** *n.* an obstruction placed across a road to stop someone. **-house** *n.* a restaurant, hotel, etc., at the roadside. **— show**, traveling company of actors. **-side** *n.* strip of ground along edge of road. **-way** *n.* a road. **to take to the road,** to adopt life of a tramp [O.E. *rad*, riding].

roam (rōm) *v.t.* and *v.i.* to wander; to ramble; to rove; *n.* a ramble; a walk. **-er** *n.*

roan (rōn) *a.* having coat in which the main color is thickly interspersed with another, esp. bay or sorrel or chestnut mixed with white or grey; *n.* a roan horse; smooth-grained sheepskin, dyed and finished [Fr. *rouan*].

roar (rōr) *v.t.* and *v.i.* to shout; to bawl; to make loud, confused sound, as winds, waves, traffic, etc.; to laugh loudly; *n.* sound of roaring, deep cry. **-ing** *n.* act or sound of roaring. **-ingly** *adv.* **-ing trade**, brisk, profitable business [O.E. *rarian*].

roast (rōst) *v.t.* to cook by exposure to open fire or in oven; to expose to heat (as coffee, etc.); (*Slang*) to reprimand; *v.i.* to become over-heated; *n.* what is roasted, as joint of meat; *a.* roasted. **-ing** *n.* **-er** *n.* [O.Fr. *rostir*].

rob (rab) *v.t.* to take by force or stealth; to plunder; to steal. *pr.p.* **-bing**. *pa.t.* and *pa.p.* **-bed. -ber** *n.* **-bery** *n.* forcibly depriving a person of money or of goods [O.Fr. *rober*].

robe (rōb) *n.* a long outer garment, esp. of flowing style; ceremonial dress denoting state, rank, or office; gown; large covering, as lap robe; *v.t.* to invest with a robe; to array; to dress. **robing** *n.* [Fr.].

rob·in (rab'.in) *n.* brown red-breasted bird of thrush family; Also **— redbreast** [O.Fr. *Robin*, for Robert].

ro·bot (rō'.bàt) *n.* automaton; mechanical man; person of machine-like efficiency [fr. play, R.U.R. (Rossum's Universal Robots, by Karel Capek). Pol. *robotnik*, workman].

ro·bust (rō.bust') *a.* strong; muscular, vigorous. **-ly** *adv.* **-ness** *n.* [L. *Robustus*, fr. *robur*, an oak, strength].

Ro·chelle salt (rō.shel'.sawlt) *n.* tartrate of sodium and potassium, used as aperient [*La Rochelle*, a town in France].

roch·et (rach'.it) *n.* garment like a surplice, of white lawn, usually with tight sleeves, worn by bishops [O.Fr.].

rock(rak) *n.* large mass of stone; (*Geol.*) any

natural deposit of sand, earth, or clay when in natural beds; firm foundation. **-ery** *n.* small artificial mound of stones planted with flowers, ferns, etc. **-iness** *n.* **-y** *a.* full of rocks; resembling rocks; unfeeling. **— bottom** *a.* lowest possible; *n.* lowest level. **— crystal** *n.* transparent quartz used in making certain lenses. **— garden** *n.* a garden laid out with rocks and plants. **— salt** *n.* unrefined sodium chloride found in great natural deposits. **the Rock**, Gibraltar. **on the rocks** (*Colloq.*) having no money or resources [Fr. *roche*].

rock (rak) *v.t.* to sway to and fro; to put to sleep by rocking; to lull; to sway, with anger, etc.; *v.i.* to be moved, backward and forward; to reel; to totter. **-er** *n.* curving piece of wood on which cradle or chair rocks; rocking horse or chair; pivoted lever having a rocking motion. **-y** *a.* disposed to rock; shaky. **-ing** *n.* **-ing chair** *n.* chair mounted on rockers. **-ing horse** *n.* wooden horse mounted on rockers; a hobbyhorse. **off one's rocker** (*Slang*) eccentric [O.E. *roccian*].

rock·et (rak'.it) *n.* cylindrical tube filled with a mixture of sulfur, niter, and charcoal, which, on ignition, hurls the tube forward by action of liberated gases; a similar tube which draws a life-line towards ship in distress; firework; *v.i.* to soar up; to increase rapidly in price, etc. [It. *rochetta*, dim. of *rocca*, a dist off].

ro·co·co (rō.kō'.kō) *n.* style of architecture, overlaid with profusion of delicate ornamentation [Fr.].

rod (rad) *n.* slender, straight, round bar, wand, stick, or switch; birch rod for punishment; cane; emblem of authority; fishing-rod; lightning conductor; linear measure equal to $5\frac{1}{2}$ yards or $16\frac{1}{2}$ feet [O.E. *rodd*].

rode (rōd) *pa.t.* of **ride**.

ro·dent (rō'.dant) *a.* gnawing; *n.* gnawing animal, as rabbit, rat [L. *rodere*, to gnaw].

ro·de·o (rō.dī.ō) *n.* roundup of cattle to be branded or marked; exhibition and contest in steer wrestling and bronco busting by cowboys [Sp.].

rod·o·mont (rad'.a.mant) *n.* a braggart; *a.* boasting; bragging. **rodomontade** *n.* vain boasting; bluster; rant; *v.i.* to boast; to brag; to bluster [*Rodomonte*, the blustering opponent of Charlemagne, depicted in Ariosto's *Orlando Furioso*].

roe (rō) *n.* small deer; female hart. **-buck** *n.* male of roe [O.E. *rah*].

roe (rō) *n.* the eggs or spawn of fish [Scand.].

roent·gen (rent'.gen) *n.* (*Nuclear Physics*) measuring unit of radiation dose. **— rays** *n.pl.* X-rays. **-ize** *v.t.* to submit to action of X-rays. Also **Röntgen** [Wilhelm von Roentgen (1845-1923), German physicist].

ro·ga·tion (rō.gā'.shan) *n.* in ancient Rome demand, by consuls or tribunes, of a law to be passed by people; supplication. **Rogation Days**, three days preceding Ascension Day, on which special litanies are sung or recited by R.C. clergy and people in public procession, invoking a blessing on crops. **rogatory** *a.* commissioned to gather information [L. *rogare*, to ask].

rogue (rōg) *n.* vagrant; rascal; knave; mischievous person. **roguery** *n.* knavish tricks; cheating; waggery. **roguishly** *adv.* **roguishness** *n.* **rogues' gallery**, a collection of photographs of convicted criminals [O.Fr. *rogue*, proud].

rogue (rōg) *v.t.* and *v.i.* to remove plant from crop (potatoes, cereals, etc.) when that plant falls short of standard or is of another variety from the crop, in order to keep strain pure; *n.* plant so removed; plant that falls short of a standard or has reverted to original type.

rois·ter (rois.ter) *v.i.* to bluster; to bully; to swagger. **-er** *n.* **-ous** *a.* [O.Fr. *ruster*, a rough, rude fellow, fr. L. *rusticus*, rustic].

role (rōl) *n.* a part played by an actor in a drama—hence, any conspicuous part or task in public life [Fr.].

roll (rōl) *v.t.* to turn over and over; to move by turning on an axis; to form into a spherical body; to drive forward with a swift and easy motion; to level with a roller; to beat with rapid strokes, as a drum; to utter vowels, letter r) with a full, long-drawn sound; *v.i.* to move forward by turning; to revolve upon an axis; to keep falling over and over; to sway; to reel; to rock from side to side, as ship; of aircraft, to turn about the axis, *i.e.* a line from nose to tail, in flight; *n.* rolling; a piece of paper, etc. rolled up; any object thus shaped; bread baked into small oval or rounded shapes; official list of members; register; catalog; continuous sound, as thunder; a full corkscrew revolution of an airplane about its longitudinal fore and aft axis during flight. **-able** *a.* **— call** *n.* calling over list of names to check absentees. **-er** *n.* cylinder of wood, stone, metal, etc. used in husbandry and the arts; a cylinder which distributes ink over type in printing; long, swelling wave; long, broad bandage; small, insectivorous bird which tumbles about in the air. **-er skate** n. skate with wheels or rollers instead of steel runner. **-ing** a. moving on wheels; turning over and over; undulating, as a plain; n. (Naut.) reeling of a ship from side to side. **-ing pin** n. cylindrical device for rolling out dough. **-ing stone**, person incapable of settling down in any one place [Fr. rouler, fr. L. rotula, a little wheel].

roller skates

rol·lick (ràl´·ik) v.i. to move about in a boisterous, careless manner; n. frolicsome gaiety. **-ing** a. jovial; high-spirited [etym. unknown]. **ro·ly-po·ly** (rō´·li-pō´·li.) a. plump and rounded. [redupl. of roll].
Ro·ma·ic (rō·mā´·ik) n. modern Greek [Fr. romaïque, fr. Mod. Gk. Rhōmaikos fr. Rhōmē, Rome].
Ro·man (rō´·man) a. pert. to Rome or Roman people; pert. to R.C. religion; in printing, upright letters as distinguished from Italic characters; expressed in letters, not in figures, as I., IV., i., iv., etc. (as distinguished from Arabic numerals, 1, 4, etc.). **-ic** a. **-ize** v.t. to introduce many words and idioms derived from Latin; to convert to Roman Catholicism; v.i. to use Latin expressions; to conform to R.C. opinions or practices. **-ism** n. tenets of Church of Rome. **-ist** n. relating to Rome or to R.C. church. **Romist** n. Roman Catholic. **— candle**, a firework which throws out differently colored stars. **— Catholic**, a member or adherent of section of Christian Church which acknowledges supremacy of Pope; a. pert. to Church of Rome. **— Catholicism** [L. Romanus, fr. Roma, Rome].
Ro·mance (rō·mans´) n. languages; a. pert. to these languages. **romance** n. narrative of knight-errantry in Middle Ages; ballad of adventures in love and war; any fictitious narrative treating of olden times; historical novel; story depending mainly on love interest; romantic spirit or quality; (Mus.) composition sentimental and expressive in character; v.i. to write or tell romances; embroider one's account or description with extravagances. **-r,** n. **romanesque,** a. pert. to the portrayal of fabulous or fanciful subjects in literature (Cap.) pert. to any form of architecture derived from Roman, as Lombard, Saxon, etc., developed in the 10th to 13th centuries in southern western Europe. **romantic** a. pert. to romance; fictitious; fanciful; sentimental; imaginative. **romantically** adv. **romanticism** n. the reactionary movement in literature and art against formalism and classicism; state of being romantic. **romanticist** n. [O.Fr. romans, It. romanza].
Rom·a·ny, Rommany (räm´·a·ni·) n. a Gypsy; the language of the Gypsies [Gypsy rom, a man].
romp (rämp) v.i. to leap and frisk about in play; to frolic; n. a tomboy; a boisterous form of play. **-ers** n.pl. a child's overall, with leg openings. **-ish** a. [earlier, ramp].
ron·deau (ron´·dō) n. poem, usually of thirteen lines with only two rhymes, the opening words recurring additionally, after eighth and thirteenth lines; (Mus.) rondo. **rondel** n. poem of thirteen or fourteen iambic lines, first two lines of which are repeated in middle and at close. **rondo** n. musical setting of a rondeau; sonata movement in music in which a principle theme is repeated two or three times [Fr.].
Rönt·gen. See roentgen.
rood (rood) n. a length of 5½ to 8 yards; fourth part of acre, equal to 40 square rods or 1,210 square yards; a cross or crucifix, esp. one placed in a church over entrance to choir. **— loft** n. a small gallery over rood screen of church. [O.E. rōd, a rod, a cross].
roof (roof, roof) n. outside structure covering building; framework suppporting this covering; stratum immediately above seam in mine; upper part of any hollow structure or object, as roof of cave, mouth, etc.; ceiling; v.t. to cover with a roof; to shelter. **— garden** n. miniature garden on flat roof. **-tree** n. the ridgepole or roof itself [O.E. hrof].
rook (rook) n. in chess, one of the four pieces placed on corner squares of the board; also known as a castle [Pers. rukh].
rook (rook) n. blueblack,hoarse-voiced bird of crow family; swindler; a card-sharp; v.t. to cheat; to swindle. **-ery** n. colony of rooks and their nests **-ie** n. Army slang for a recruit [O.E. hroc].
room (room, room) n. (enough) space; apart-

ment or chamber; scope; opportunity; occasion; pl. lodgings; v.i. to lodge. **-ful** a. **-ily** adv. **-iness** n. spaciousness. **-y** a. spacious; wide [O.E. rum].

rook

roost (roost) n. pole on which birds rest at night; perch; collection of fowls roosting together; v.i. to settle down to sleep, as birds on a perch; to perch. **-er** n. a cock [O.E. hrost].
root (root, root) n. part of plant which grows down into soil seeking nourishment for whole plant; plant whose root is edible, as beetroot; part of anything which grows like root, as of tooth, cancer, etc.; source; origin; vital part; basis; bottom; primitive word from which other words are derived; (Math.) factor of quantity which, when multiplied by itself the number of times indicated by the index number, will produce that quantity, e.g. 4 is third (or cube) root of 64 (symbol $\sqrt{}$), for $4 \times 4 \times 4 = 64$; v.t. to plant and fix in earth; to impress deeply in mind; to establish firmly; to pull out by roots (followed by out) v.i. to enter earth, as roots; to be firmly fixed or established. **-ed** a. firmly established. **-stock** n. a rhizome. **root and branch**, entirely; completely [O.E. wyrt].

root (root) v.t. and v.i. to turn up with the snout, as swine; to rummage; to uncover (with up) [O.E. wrot, a snout].
root (root) v.i. to cheer [Slang].
rope (rōp) v.t. stout cord of several twisted strands of fiber or metal wire; row of objects strung together, as onions, pearls, etc.; v.t. to fasten with a rope; to mark off a race track, etc., with ropes; to lasso. **-ladder, -bridge,** etc. n. one made of ropes [O.E. rap].
Roque·fort (rōk´·fert) n. a cheese of ewe's milk [Roquefort, in France].
ror·qual (rawr´·kwal) n. a genus of whale [Scand. röd, red; hval, whale].
Ro·sa·ceae (rō·zā´·sē·ī) n.pl. order of plants including rose, strawberry, blackberry, spiraea. **rosaceous** a. roselike; belonging to rose family. **rosarium** n. rose garden [L. rosa, rose].
ro·sa·ry (rō´·za·ri·) n. rose garden; string of prayer beads [L. rosa, a rose].
rose (rōz) pa.t. of rise.
rose (rōz) n. typical genus (Rosa) of plant family of Rosaceae; shade of pink; rosette; perforated nozzle of tube or pipe, as on watering can. **-ate** a. rosy; full of roses; blooming; optimistic. **-bud** n. the bud of the rose; **—colored** a. having color of a rose; unwarrantably optimistic. **— water** n. water tinctured with roses by distillation **— window** n. circular window with a series of mullions diverging from center. **-wood** n. rich, dark red hardwood from S. America, used for furniture making. **rosily** adv. **rosiness** n. **rosy** a. like a rose; blooming; red; blushing; bright; favorable [L. rosa, rose].
rose·mar·y (rōz´·me·ri·) n. a small fragrant evergreen shrub, emblem of fidelity [L. ros, dew; marinus, marine].
ro·sette (rō·zet´) n. something fashioned to resemble a rose, as ribbon; a rose-shaped architectural ornament. [Fr. dim. of rose].

ros·in (räz´·in) n. resin in solid state; v.t. to rub or cover with rosin. **-y** a. [Fr. résine].

ros·ter (räs´·ter) n. a list or plan showing turns of duty; register of names [Dut. rooster, a corrupt. of L. register].
ros·trum (ras´·tram) n. snout or pointed organ; beak of a ship; raised platform; pulpit. **rostral** a. pert. to a rostrum. **rostrate, rostrated** a. beaked [L. = a beak].
ros·y, See rose.
rot (ràt) v.t. and v.i. to decompose naturally; to become morally corrupt; to putrefy; to molder away. pr.p. **-ting.** pa.t. and pa.p. **-ted** n. rotting; decomposition; decay; disease of sheep, as **foot-rot;** form of decay which attacks timber, usually **dry rot** (Slang) nonsense [O.E. rotian].
ro·ta (rō´·ta) n. roster, list, or roll; an ecclesiastical tribunal in the R.C. church which acts as court of appeal [L. = wheel].
ro·ta·ry (rō´·ter·i·) a. turning, as a wheel; rotatory; n. (Cap.) international association of business men's clubs. **Rotarian** n. member of Rotary Club. **— engine** (Aero.) engine in which cylinder and crankcase rotate with propeller [L. rota, a wheel].
ro·tate (rō´·tāt) v.t. to cause to revolve; v.i. to move around pivot; to go in rotation; to revolve; a. (Bot.) wheel-shaped, as a calyx. **rotation** n. turning, as a wheel or solid body on its axis; (Astron.) period of rotation of planet about its imaginary axis; serial change, as **rotation of crops. rotational** a. **rotator** n. **rotatory** a. turning on an axis, as a wheel; going in a circle; following in succession [L. rota, a wheel].
rote (rōt) n. mechanical repetition [O.Fr. rote, track].
ro·tis·ser·ie (rō·tis´·er·i·) n. grill with a turning spit [Fr. rotir, to roast].
ro·tor (rō´·ter) n. revolving portion of dynamo, motor, or turbine [short for rotator].
rot·ten (rät´·n) a. putrefied; decayed; unsound; corrupt; (Slang) bad; worthless. **-ly** adv. **-ness** n. **rotter** n. (Slang) a worthless, unprincipled person [fr. rot].
ro·tund (rō·tund´) a. round; globular; plump. **-a** n. circular building or hall, covered by dome. **-ity, -ness** n. globular form; roundness [L. rotundus, fr. rota, a wheel].
rou·é (roo´·ā) n. a libertine; a profligate; a rake [Fr. = one broken on the wheel].
rouge (roozh) n. fine red powder used by jewelers; cosmetic for tinting cheeks; v.t. and v.i. to tint (face) with rouge [Fr. = red].
rough (ruf) a. not smooth; rugged; uneven; unhewn; shapeless; uncut; unpolished; rude; harsh; boisterous; stormy; approximate; having aspirated sound of h; adv. in rough manner; n. crude, unfashioned state; parts of golf course adjoining fairway and greens; v.t. to make rough; to roughen; to rough-hew; to shape out in rough and ready way. **-age** n. fibrous, unassimilated portions of food which promote intestinal movement. **— diamond,** uncut diamond; a person of ability and worth, but uncouth. **-en** v.t. to make rough; v.i. to become rough. **—hew** v.t. to hew coarsely; to give first form to a thing. **-house** n. rowdy, boisterous play. **-ly** adv. **-neck** n. (Slang) ill-mannered fellow; a tough. **-ness** n. **to rough it,** to put up with hardship and discomfort [O.E.ruh].
rou·lade (roo·låd´) n. (Mus.) embellishment; trill [Fr. rouler, to roll].
rou·leau (roo·lō´) n. little roll; roll of coins in paper; little roll or chain of red corpuscles; pl. **-x, -s** [Fr. dim. of O.Fr. role, a roll].
rou·lette (roo·let´) n. game of chance, played with a revolving disk and a ball [Fr. dim. of O.Fr. roule, wheel].
round (round) a. circular; spherical; curved; whole; total; not fractional, as a number; plump; smooth; flowing, as style or diction; plain; (of vowel) pronounced with rounded lips; n. circle; ring; globe; circuit; cycle; series; a course of action performed by persons in turn; toasts; a certain amount (of applause); walk by guard to visit posts, sentries, etc.; beat of policeman, milkman, etc.; a game (of golf); one of successive stages in competition; 3-minute period in boxing match; step of a ladder; ammunition unit; circular dance; short, vocal piece, in which singers start at regular intervals after each other; adv. on all sides; circularly; back to the starting point; about; v.t. to make circular, spherical, or cylindrical; to go around; to smooth; to finish; v.i. to grow or become round or full in form. **-about** a. indirect; circuitous. **-el** n. round window or panel; kind of dance; rondel; small circular shield. **-elay** n. round or country dance; an air or tune in three parts, in which the first strain is repeated in the others. **-er** n. a tool for rounding off objects; one who makes rounds; habitual drunkard or criminal. **Roundhead** n. a Puritan (so called from practice of cropping hair close); republican in time of Commonwealth. **-house** n. (Naut.) a cabin built on after part of quarterdeck; circular building for locomotives. **-ly** adv. vigorously; fully; open. **-ness** n. **— robin** n. petition, etc. having signatures arranged in a circular form so as to give no clue to order of signing. **-table conference,** one where all participants are on equal footing. **-up,** n. collecting cattle into herds; throwing cordon around area by police or mili-

tary for interrogating all found within; *v.t.* to collect and bring into confined space. **to round off,** to [Fr. *rond*].

roup (roop) *n.* a contagious disease of domestic poultry [O.E. *hropan,* to cry].

rouse (rouz) *v.t.* to wake from sleep; to excite to action; to startle or surprise; *v.i.* to awake from sleep or repose. **-r** *n.* **rousing** *a.*

rout (rout) *n.* tumultuous crowd; rabble; defeat of army or confusion of troops in flight; *v.t.* to defeat and throw into confusion [L. *ruptus,* broken].

rout (rout) *v.i.* to roar; to snore [O.E. *hrutan*].

rout (rout) *v.t.* to turn up with the snout; to cut grooves by scooping or gouging; to turn out of bed; *v.i.* to poke about [fr. *root,* dig.].

route (root) *n.* course or way which is traveled or to be followed. **en route,** on the way [Fr.].

rou·tine (roo·tēn´) *n.* regular course of action adhered to by order or habit; *a.* in ordinary way of business; according to rule [Fr.].

rove (rōv) *v.t.* to wander or ramble over; to plough into ridges; *v.i.* to wander about; to ramble. **-r** *n.* wanderer; pirate ship; roving machine. **roving** *n.* and *a.* [Dut. *roofer,* a robber].

row (rō) *n.* persons or things in straight line; a rank; a file; a line [O.E. *raw*].

row (rō) *v.t.* to impel (a boat) with oars; to transport, by rowing; *v.t.* to labor with oars; *n.* spell of rowing; a trip in a rowboat. **-boat** *n.* boat impelled solely by oars [O.E. *rowan*].

row (rou) *n.* riotous, noisy disturbance; a dispute. **-dy** *a.* noisy and rough; *n.* hooligan. **-dyism, -diness** *n.* [etym. uncertain].

row·an (rō´·an) *n.* mountain ash producing clusters of red berries. [Scand.].

row·el (rou´·al) *n.* wheel of a spur, furnished with sharp points [Fr. *roue,* a wheel].

roy·al (roi´·al) *a.* pert. to the crown; worthy of, befitting, patronized by, a king or queen; kingly; *n.* a size of paper; small sail above topgallant-sail; third shoot of stag's horn. **-ism** *n.* principles of government by king. **-ist** *n.* adherent to sovereign, or one attached to kingly government. **-ly** *adv.* **-ty** *n.* kingship; kingly office; person of king or sovereign; members of royal family; royal prerogative; royal domain; payment to owner of land for right to work minerals, or to inventor for use of his invention, or to author depending on sales of his book [Fr. fr. L. *regalis,* fr. *rex,* a king].

rub (rub) *v.t.* to subject to friction; to abrade; to chafe; to remove by friction; to wipe; to scour; to touch slightly; *v.i.* to come into contact accompanied by friction; to become frayed or worn with friction. *pr.p.* **-bing.** *pa.t.* and *pa.p.* **-bed.** *n.* rubbing; difficulty, impediment; a sore spot from rubbing; **-ber** *n.* **-bing** *n.* impression of coin, lettering on book, etc. obtained by rubbing thin paper placed on object with pencil or similar article; applying friction to a surface. **to rub in,** to emphasize by constant reiteration [etym. obscure].

rub·ber (rub´·er) *n.* coagulated sap of certain tropical trees; caoutchouc; gum elastic; India rubber for erasing pencil marks, etc. a series of an odd number, usually three, of games; the winning game in the series; *pl.* overshoes; galoshes: *a.* made of rubber. **-ized** *a.* impregnated or mixed with rubber, as rubberized fabrics. **-neck** *n.* (*Slang*) a tourist eager to see every important building, sight, or spectacle [fr. *rub*].

rub·bish (rub´·ish) *n.* waste or rejected matter; anything worthless: refuse; nonsense [etym. uncertain].

rub·ble (rub´·l) *n.* upper fragmentary decomposed mass of stone overlying a solid stratum of rock; masonry built of rough stone, of all sizes and shapes; rough stones used to fill up spaces between walls, etc. **-rubbly** *a.* [O.Fr. *robel,* dim. of *robe, robbe,* trash].

rube (roob) *n.* (*Slang*) a farmer; a rustic [abbrev. fr. *Reuben*].

Ru·bi·con (roo´·bi·kan) *n.* stream in Italy, between Roman Italy and Cisalpine Gaul. **to cross the Rubicon,** to take a decisive, irrevocable step.

ru·bi·cund (roo´·ba·kund) *a.* ruddy; florid; reddish. **-ity** *n.* [L. *rubicundus,* fr. *ruber,* red].

ru·bid·i·um (roo·bid´·i·am) *n.* rare silvery metallic element, one of the alkali metals [L. *rubidus,* red].

ru·ble (roo´·ble) *n.* Russian monetary unit. Also **rouble** [Russ. *rubl*].

ru·bric (roo´·brik) *n.* medieval manuscript or printed book in which initial letter was illumined in red; heading or portion of such a work, printed in red—hence, the title of a chapter, statute, etc. originally in red; an ecclesiastical injunction or rule; *v.t.* to illumine with or print in red. **-al** *a.* colored in red; to formulate as a rubric. **-ian** *n.* one versed in the rubrics. **rubricist** *n.* a strict

adherent to rubrics; a formalist [L. *rubrica,* red earth, fr. *ruber,* red].

ru·by (roo´·bi·) *n.* a red variety of corundum valued as a gem; purple-tinged red color; *a.* having the dark-red color of a ruby [L. *ruber,* red].

ruche (roosh) *n.* pleated trimming for dresses, sewn down the middle and not at top, as in box pleatings. **ruching** *n.* material for ruches; ruches collectively [Fr.].

ruck (ruk) *v.t.* to wrinkle; to crease; *v.i.* to be drawn into folds; *n.* fold; crease; wrinkle [O.N. *hrukka*].

ruck (ruk) *n.* rank and file; common herd [etym. doubtful].

ruck·sack (ruk´·sak) *n.* pack carried on back by climbers, etc. [Ger. = 'back-pack'].

ruc·tion (ruk´·shan) *n.* (*Colloq.*) disturbance; row; rumpus [perh. fr. *eruption*].

rudd (rud) *n.* British fresh-water fish allied to the roach [O.E. *rudu,* redness].

rud·der (rud´·er) *n.* flat frame fastened vertically to stern of ship, which controls direction; in plane, flat plane surface hinged to tail unit and used to provide directional control and stability; anything which guides, as a bird's tail-feathers [O.E. *rothor*].

rud·dle (rud´·l) red ocher, used for marking sheep; *v.t.* to mark (sheep) with ruddle [O.E. *rudu,* redness].

rud·dock (rud´·ok) *n.* European robin [O.E. *rudig,* reddish].

rud·dy (rud´·i·) *a.* of a red color; of healthy flesh color; rosy; **ruddiness** *n.* [O.E. *rudig,* reddish].

rude (rood) *a.* uncivil; primitive; roughly made. **-ly** *adv.* **-ness** *n.* [L. *rudis,* rough].

ru·di·ment (roo´·da·mant) *n.* beginning; germ; vestige; (*Biol.*) imperfectly developed or formed organ; *pl.* elements, first principles, beginning (of knowledge, etc.) **-al, -ary** *a.* **-arily** *adv.* [L. *rudimentum,* fr. *rudis,* rude].

rue (roo) *v.t.* and *v.i.* to grieve for; to regret; to repent of. *pr.p.* **-ing. -ful** *a.* woeful; mournful; sorrowful. **-fully** *adv.* [O.E. *hreowan,* to be sorry for].

rue (roo) *n.* aromatic, bushy, evergreen shrub; any bitter infusion [L. *ruta*].

ruff (ruf) *n.* broad, circular collar, plaited, crimped, or fluted; something similar; light-brown mottled bird, the male being ringed with ruff or frill of long, black, red-barred feathers during breeding season; (*fem.*) **reeve;** neck fringe of long hair or feathers on animal or bird. **-ed** *a.* [etym. uncertain].

ruff (ruf) *n.* trumping at cards when one cannot follow suit; *v.t.* to trump instead of following suit [O.Fr. *roffle*].

ruf·fi·an (ruf´·i·an) *n.* a rough, lawless fellow; desperado; *a.* brutal. **-ism** *n.* conduct of a ruffian. **-ly** [O.Fr. fr. It. *ruffiano*].

ruf·fle (ruf´·l) *v.t.* to make into a ruff; to draw into wrinkles, open plaits, or folds; to furnish with ruffles; to roughen surface of; to annoy; to put out (of temper); *v.i.* to flutter; to jar; to be at variance; to grow rough; *n.* a strip of gathered cloth, attached to a garment, a frill; agitation; commotion [Dut. *ruifelen,* to rumple].

ru·fous (roo´·fas) *a.* (*Bot.*) brownish red [L. *rufus,* red].

rug (rug) *n.* piece of carpeting [Scand.].

rug·by (rug´·bi·) *n.* English form of football, played with teams of 15 players each [fr. *Rugby,* public school].

rug·ged (rug´·id) *a.* rough; uneven; jagged; wrinkled; harsh; inharmonious; homely; unpolished; sturdy, vigorous. **-ly** *adv.* **-ness** *n.* [rug].

ru·gose (roo´·gōs) *a.* wrinkled; ridged. **-ly** *adv.* **rugosity** *n.* [L. *ruga,* a wrinkle].

ru·in (roo´·in) *n.* downfall; remains of demolished or decayed city, fortress, castle, work of art, etc.; state of being decayed; *v.t.* to bring to ruin; to injure; to spoil; to mar; to cause loss of fortune or livelihood, etc. **-s** *n.pl.* ruined buildings, etc. **-ation** *n.* state of being ruined; act or cause of ruining. **-er** *n.* **-ous** *a.* fallen to ruin; dilapidated; injurious; destructive. **-ously** *adv.* [L. *ruina,* fr. *ruere,* to rush down].

rule (rool) *n.* act, power, or mode of directing; government; sway; control; authority; precept; prescribed law; established principle or mode of action; regulation; habitual practice; standard; an instrument to draw straight lines; (*Print.*) thin strip of brass or type metal, type high, to print a line or lines; *v.t.* to govern; to control; to determine; to decide authoritatively; to mark with straight lines, using ruler; *v.i.* to have command; to order by rule; to prevail. **-r** *n.* one who rules; sovereign; instrument with straight edges for drawing lines. **ruling** *a.* governing; managing; predominant; *n.* an authoritative decision; a point of law settled by a court of law [L. *regula,* fr. *regere,* to govern].

rum (rum) *n.* spirit distilled from sugar-cane skimmings or molasses. **-runner** *n.* smuggler. **-my** *n.* (*Slang*) a drunkard [etym. uncertain].

rum·ba (rum´·ba) *n.* Cuban dance [Sp.].

rum·ble (rum´·bl) *v.i.* to make a low, vibrant, continuous sound; to reverberate; *v.t.* to cause to roll along or utter with a low heavy sound; to polish in a tumbling box *n.* dull, vibrant, confused noise, as of thunder; seat for footmen at back of carriage; a tumbling box; (*Slang*) fight. **-r** *n.* [imit.].

ru·mi·nant (roo´·ma·nant) *n.* animal which chews cud, as sheep, cow; *a.* chewing cud. **ruminate** *v.t.* to chew over again; to ponder over; to muse on; *v.i.* to chew cud; to meditate. **ruminatingly** *adv.* **rumination** *n.* **ruminative** *a.* **ruminator** *n.* [L. *ruminare,* to chew cud].

rum·mage (rum´·ij) *v.t.* to search thoroughly into or through; to ransack; *v.i.* to make a search; *n.* careful search; odds and ends. **-r** *n.* [orig. stowage of casks, O.Fr. *arrumage*].

rum·my (rum´·i·) *n.* a simple card game for any number of players.

ru·mor (roo´·mer) *n.* current but unproved report; common talk; *v.t.* to spread as a rumor [L. *rumor,* noise].

rump (rump) *n.* end of backbone of animal with the parts adjacent; buttocks; hinder part; remnant of anything [Scand.].

rum·ple (rum´·pl) *v.t.* to muss; to crease; to crumple; *n.* an irregular fold [O.E. *hrimpan,* to wrinkle].

rum·pus (rum´·pas) *n.* (*Colloq.*) an uproar; a noisy disturbance [etym. doubtful].

run (run) *v.i.* to move rapidly on legs; to hurry; to contend in a race; to stand as candidate for; to travel or sail regularly; to extend; to retreat; to flee; to flow; to continue in operation; to continue without falling due, as a promissory note or bill; to have legal force; to fuse; to melt; to average; to turn or rotate; to be worded; *v.t.* to cause to run; to drive, push, or thrust; to manage; to maintain regularly, as bus service; to operate; to evade (a blockade); to smuggle; to incur (risk). *pr.p.* **-ning.** *pa.t.* **ran.** *pa.p.* **run.** *n.* flow; channel; act of running; course run; regular, scheduled journey; pleasure trip by car, cycle, etc.; unconstrained liberty; range of ground for grazing cattle, feeding poultry, etc.; trend; kind or variety; vogue; point gained in cricket or baseball; a great demand; period play holds the stage; (*Mus.*) rapid scale passage, roulade. **-about** *n.* motorboat or a small open car; a gadabout. **-away** *n.* fugitive; horse which has bolted. **-ner** *n.* one taking part in a race; messenger; a long, slender prostrate stem which runs along the ground; one of curved pieces on which sleigh, skate, etc slides; device for facilitating movement of sliding doors, etc.; narrow strip of carpet; smuggler. **-ner-up** *n.* one who gains second place. **-ning** *a.* flowing; entered for a race, as a horse; successive (numbers); continuous (as an order, account); discharging (pus); cursive; easy in style; effortless; *n.* moving or flowing quickly; chance of winning; operation of machine, business, etc. **-ning board** *n.* narrow, horizontal platform running along locomotive, carriage, car, etc., to provide step for entering or leaving. **-ning commentary,** broadcast description of event by eye-witness. **-ning knot,** knot made so as to tighten when rope is pulled. **-way** *n.* prepared track on airfields for landing and taking off. **also ran,** an unsuccessful competitor. **in the long run,** in the end; ultimately. **to run amok,** to go mad. **to run riot,** to give way to excess. **to run to earth,** to capture after a long pursuit [O.E. *rinnan*].

running board

run·dle (run′·dl) *n.* a rung or step of a ladder; something which rotates like a wheel [fr. *round*].

rune (róom) *n.* letter or character of old Teutonic and Scandinavian alphabets; magic; mystery. **runic** *a.* [O.N. *run*, a mystery].

rung (rung) *pa.p.* of **ring.**

rung (rung) *n.* rounded step of a ladder; crossbar or spoke [O.E. *hrung*, a beam].

run·nel (run′·al) *n.* small brook or rivulet; a gutter [O.E. *rinnelle*, a brook].

runt (runt) *n.* small, weak specimen of any animal, person or thing [etym. doubtful].

ru·pee (róo·pē′) *n.* standard Indian monetary unit, silver coin [Urdu, *rupiyah*].

rup·ture (rup′·cher) *n.* breaking or bursting; state of being violently parted; breach of concord between individuals or nations; hernia; forcible bursting, breaking, or tearing of a bodily organ or structure; *v.t.* to part by violence; to burst (a blood-vessel, etc.) [L. *ruptura*, fr. *rumpere*, to break].

ru·ral (roo′·ral) *a.* pert. to the country; pert. to farming or agriculture; rustic; pastoral. **-ize** *v.t.* to make rural; *v.i.* to live in the country; to become rural. **-ism** *n.* **-ly** *adv.* [L. *ruralis*, fr. *rus*, the country].

ruse (róoz) *n.* artifice; trick; strategem [Fr.].

rush (rush) *v.t.* to carry along violently and rapidly; to take by sudden assault; to hasten forward; *v.i.* to move violently or rapidly; to speed; *n.* heavy current of water, air, etc.; haste; eager demand (for an article); **-er** *n.* [M.E. *ruschen*].

rush (rush) *n.* name of plants of genus Juncus, found in marshy places; stem as a material for baskets, etc.; thing of little worth; taper; straw. **—bottomed** *a.* of chair with seat made of rushes. **-y** *a.* [O.E. *rysc*].

rusk (rusk) *n.* biscuit or light, hard bread [Sp. *rosca*, roll of bread].

rus·set (rus′·it) *a.* of reddish-brown color; *n.* homespun cloth dyed this color; apple of russet color [Fr. *roux*, red].

Rus·sian (rush′·an) *a.* pert. to Russia; *n.* general name for Slav races in Russia; native or inhabitant of Russia; Russian language. **Russo-** *prefix* Russian. **— dressing** *n.* mayonnaise mixed with catchup or chili sauce.

rust (rust) *n.* coating formed on iron or various other metals by corrosion; reddish fungus disease on plants; *v.t.* to corrode with rust; to impair by inactivity; *v.i.* to become rusty; to dissipate one's potential powers by inaction. **-ily** *adv.* **-iness** *n.* **— proof** *a.* not liable to rust. **-y** *a.* [O.E.].

rus·tic (rus′·tik) *a.* pert. to the country; rural; awkward; *n.* a simple country person. **-ally** *adv.* **-ate** *v.t.* to compel to reside in country; to make rustic; *v.i.* to live in the country. **-ation** *n.* **-ity** *n.* [L. *rusticus*, fr. *rus*, the country].

rus·tle (rus′·l) *v.i.* to make soft, swishing sounds, like rubbing of silk cloth or dry leaves; (*Slang*) to be active and on the move; *v.t.* (*U.S.*) to steal, esp. cattle; *n.* a soft whispering sound. **-r** *n.* one who, or that which, rustles; (*Slang*) hustler; cattle thief. **rustling** *n.* [imit. origin].

rut (rut) *n.* furrow made by wheel; settled habit or way of living; groove; *v.t.* to form ruts in; *pr.p.* **-ting.** *pa.t.* and *pa.p.* **-ted** [Fr. *route*, a way, track, etc.].

rut (rut) *n.* time of sexual excitement and urge among animals, esp. of deer; *v.i.* to be in heat [O.Fr. fr. L. *rugire*, to roar].

ruth·less (rooth′·las) *a.* pitiless; cruel. **-ly** *adv.* **-ness** *n.* [*rue*].

rye (rī) *n.* a kind of grass allied to wheat, whiskey made from rye [O.E. *ryge*].

S

Sab·bath (sab′·ath) *n.* seventh day of week; Sunday; Lord's Day. **Sabbatarian** *n.* member of certain Christian sects, e.g. Seventh-day Adventists, who observe seventh day Saturday, as the Sabbath; strict observer of Sabbath. **Sabbatarianism** *n.* **Sabbatic, -al** *a.* pert. to Sabbath; (*l.c.*) rest-bringing. *n.* (*l.c.*) a period of leave from a job. **Sabbatical year,** in the Jewish ritual, every seventh, in which the lands were left untilled, etc.; (*l.c.*) a year periodically interrupting one's normal course of work, wholly devoted to further intensive study or one's special subject [Heb. *shabbath*].

saber (sā′·ber) *n.* sword with broad and heavy blade, slightly curved toward the point; cavalry sword; *v.t.* to wound or cut down with saber. Also **sabre** [Fr.]

Sa·bine (sā′·bīn) *n.* one of an ancient tribe of Italy who became merged with the Romans; *a.* pert. to the Sabines.

sa·ble (sā′·bl) *n.* small carnivorous mammal of weasel tribe; sable fur; (*Her.*) tincture or color black; *pl.* mourning garments; *a.* black; made of sable [O.Fr.].

sab·ot (sab′·ō) *n.* a wooden shoe worn by the peasantry of France and Belgium [Fr.].

sab·o·tage (sa·ba·tazh′) *n.* willful damage or destruction of property perpetrated for political or economic reasons. **saboteur** *n.* one who commits sabotage [Fr. *sabot*].

sac (sak) *n.* pouch-like structure or receptacle in animal or plant; cyst-like cavity [Fr. = sack].

saccharin, saccharine (sak′·a·rin) *n.* a white crystalline solid substance, with an intensely sweet taste. **saccharine** *a.* pert. to sugar; over-sweet; cloying; sickly sentimental.

saccharify *v.t.* to convert into sugar. **saccharinity** *n.* **saccharize** *v.t.* to convert into sugar. **saccharoid, -al** *a.* having granular texture resembling that of loaf sugar. **saccharose** *n.* cane sugar [Gk. *sakchari*, sugar].

sac·cule (sak′·ūl) *n.* a small sac. **saccular** *a.* like a sac [dim. of L. *saccus*, a bag].

sac·er·do·tal (sas·er·dō′·tal) *a.* pert. to priests, or to the order of priests. **-ism** *n.* the system, spirit, or character of priesthood; **-ist** *n.* **-ly** *adv.* [L. *sacerdos*, a priest].

sa·chem (sā′·cham) *n.* a Red Indian chief; a political boss, esp. a Tammany leader [Amer.-Ind.].

sa·chet (sa·shā′) *n.* a small scent-bag or perfume cushion [Fr.].

sack (sak) *n.* a large bag, usually of coarse material; contents of sack; also **sacque,** loose garment or cloak; any bag; *v.t.* to put into sacks. **-cloth** *n.* coarse fabric of great strength used for making sacks; in Scripture, garment worn in mourning or as penance. **-ful** *n.* quantity which fills sack. **-ing** *n.* coarse cloth or canvas. **— race** *n.* race in which legs of contestants are encased in sacks [Heb. *saq*, a coarse cloth].

sack (sak) *n.* old name for various kinds of dry wines, esp. Spanish sherry [Fr. *sec*, dry].

sack (sak) *v.t.* to plunder or pillage; to lay waste; *n.* pillage of town. **-ing** *n.* [Fr. *sac*, plunder].

sac·ra·ment (sak′·ra·mant) *n.* one of the ceremonial observances in Christian Church. Lord's Supper; solemn oath; materials used in a sacrament. **-al** *n.* any observance, ceremony, or act of the nature of a sacrament instituted by R.C. Church; *a.* belonging to, or of nature of, sacrament; sacred. **-ally** *adv.* **-arian** *n.* one who believes in efficacy of sacraments. **-arianism** *n.* [L. *sacer*, sacred].

sac·ri·fice (sak′·ra·fis, ·fiz) *v.t.* to consecrate ceremonially an offering of some kind as expiation or propitiation to deity; to surrender for sake of obtaining some other advantage; to offer up; to immolate; *v.i.* to make offerings to God of things consumed on the altar; *n.* anything consecrated and offered to divinity; anything given up for sake of others. **-r** *n.* **sacrificial** *a.* relating to, pertaining to sacrifice. **sacrificially** *adv.* [L. *sacrificium*].

sac·ri·lege (sak′·ra·lij) *n.* profanation of sacred place or thing; church robbery. **sacrilegious** *a.* violating sacred things; profane; desecrating. **sacrilegiously** *adv.* **sacrilegiousness** *n.* [L. *sacer*, sacred; *legere*, to gather].

sac·ris·tan (sak′·ris·tan) *n.* officer in church entrusted with care of sacristy or vestry. **sexton. sacristy** *n.* vestry [L. *sacer*, sacred].

sac·ro·sanct (sak′·rō·sangkt) *a.* inviolable and sacred in the highest degree. **-ity** *n.* [L. *sacrosanctus*, consecrated].

sa·crum (sā′·kram) *n.* a composite bone, triangular in shape, at the base of the spinal column. *pl.* **sacra** [L. = the sacred (bone)].

sad (sad) *a.* sorrowful; affected with grief; deplorably bad; somber-colored. **-den** *v.t.* to make sad or sorrowful; *v.i.* to become sorrowful and downcast. **-ly** *adv.* **-ness** *n.* [O.E. *saed*, sated].

sad·dle (sad′·l) *n.* rider's seat to fasten on horse, or form part of a cycle, etc.; part of a shaft; joint of mutton or venison containing part of backbone with ribs on each side; ridge of hill between higher hills; *v.t.* to put a saddle upon; to burden with; to encumber. **-bag** *n.* one of two bags united by strap and hanging on either side of horse. **-bow** *n.* bow or arch in front of saddle. **-cloth** *n.* housing or cloth placed upon saddle. **-girth** *n.* band passing under belly of horse to hold saddle in place. **— horse** *n.* horse for riding, as distinguished from one for driving. **-r** *n.* one who makes saddles and harness for horses. **saddlery** *n.* materials for making saddles and harness; occupation of saddler; room for storing saddles. **—shaped** *a.* **-tree** *n.* frame of saddle [O.E. *sadol*].

sad·ism (sā′·dizm, sad′·izm) *n.* insatiate love of inflicting pain for its own sake. **sadist** *n.* one who practices this; a consistently inhumane person. **sadistic** *a.* [Marquis de Sade (1740-1814) whose writings exemplify it].

sa·fa·ri (sa·fä′·ri·) *n.* hunting expedition

[Swahili, **safar**, a journey].

safe (sāf) *a.* free from harm; unharmed; unhurt; sound; protected; sure; *n.* a fireproof chest for protection of money and valuables; case with wire gauze panels to keep meat, etc. fresh. **—conduct** *n.* passport to pass through a dangerous zone. **— deposit** *a.* pert. to box or vault where valuables are stored and protected. **-guard** *n.* protection; precaution; convoy; escort; passport; *v.t.* to make safe; to protect. **-ly** *adv.* **-ness** *n.* **-ty** *n.* **-ty belt** *n.* belt to keep person afloat in water, to prevent injury in automobile, aircraft, etc. **-ty catch** *n.* contrivance to prevent accidental discharge of gun. **-ty razor** *n.* one in which blade fits into holder with guard to ensure safety for rapid shaving. **-ty valve** *n.* automatic valve fitted to boiler, to permit escape of steam when pressure reaches danger point; outlet for pent-up emotion [Fr. *sauf*, fr. L. *salvus*].

saf-fron (saf'.ran) *n.* plant of iris family, used in medicine and as a flavoring and coloring in cookery; *a.* deep yellow [Fr. *safran*].

sag (sag) *v.i.* to sink in middle; to hang sideways or curve downwards under pressure; to give way; to tire. *pr.p.* **-ging.** *pa.p.* **-ged.** *n.* a droop [M.E. *saggen*].

sa-ga (sa'.ga) *n.* a prose narrative, written in Iceland in the 12th and 13th centuries, concerning legendary and historic people and actions of Norway and Iceland; novels describing life of a family [O.N. = tale].

sa-ga-cious (sa.gā'.shas) *a.* quick of thought; acute; shrewd. **-ly** *adv.* **-ness, sagacity** *n.* shrewdness; discernment; wisdom [L. *sagax*].

sage (sāj) *n.* dwarf shrub of mint family, used for flavoring [Fr. *sauge*, fr. L. *salvia*].

sage (sāj) *a.* wise; discerning; solemn; *n.* wise man. **-ly** *adv.* **-ness** *n.* [Fr. fr. L. *sapere*, to be wise].

sage-brush (sāj'.brush) *n.* a shrub smelling like sage and found chiefly on western plains of U.S.

Sa-git-ta (saj'.it.a) *n.* a constellation north of Aquila—the Arrow. **sagittal, sagittate** *a.* shaped like an arrow or arrowhead. **sagittally** *adv.* **Saggitarius** *n.* the Archer, 9th sign of zodiac; constellation in Milky Way [L. = arrow].

sa-go (sā'.gō) *n.* dry, granulated starch [Malay, *sagu*].

sa-hib (sä'.ib) *n.* (fem. **sahiba** or **mem sahib**) courtesy title in India for European or high-born Indian [Ar. = lord, master].

said (sed) *pa.t.* and *pa.p.* of **say**; the beforementioned; already specified; aforesaid.

sail (sāl) *n.* sheet of canvas to catch wind for propelling ship; sailing vessel; a journey upon the water; arm of windmill; *v.t.* to navigate; to pass in a ship; to fly through; *v.i.* to travel by water; to begin a voyage; to glide in stately fashion. **-able** *a.* navigable. **-boat** *n.* a boat propelled by sails. **-cloth** *n.* canvas used in making sails. **-ing** *n.* art of navigating. **-less** *a.* **-or** *n.* mariner; seaman; tar. **-or-hat** *n.* straw hat. **full sail**, with all sails set. **under sail**, to have sails spread. **to sail close to the wind**, to sail with sails of ship barely full; to run great risks. **to sail under false colors**, to act under false pretenses [O.E. *segel*].

saint (sānt) *n.* outstandingly devout and virtuous person; one of the blessed in heaven; one formally canonized by R.C. Church; *v.t.* to canonize. **-ed** *a.* pious; hallowed; sacred; dead. **-hood** *n.* **-like, -ly** *a.* devout; godly; pious. **-liness** *n.* **-'s day**, day on which falls celebration of particular saint. **All-Saints' Day**, 1st November. **St. Bernard**, dog famous for guiding and rescuing travelers lost in snow. **St. Patrick's Day**, 17th March. **St. Valentine's Day**, 14th February. **St. Vitus's dance**, chorea. **Latter-day Saints**, the Mormons. **patron saint**, saint held to be a protector [Fr. fr. L. *sanctus*, consecrated].

St. Bernard

sake (sāk) *n.* cause; behalf; purpose; account; regard. **for the sake of**, on behalf of [O.E. *sacu*, dispute at law].

sa-ke (sa'.ki) *n.* national beverage of Japan, fermented from rice [Jap.].

sal (sal) *n.* salt (much used in compound words pert. to pharmacy). **— ammoniac** *n.* ammonium chloride, used in composition of electric batteries and in medicine as expectorant and stomachic. **— volatile** *n.* mixture of ammonium carbonate with oil of nutmeg, oil of lemon and alcohol, used as a stimulant, antacid, or expectorant [L.].

sa-laam (sa.läm') *n.* salutation, a low bow, of ceremony or respect in the East; *v.t.* to salute; to greet [Ar. = peace].

sa-la-cious (sa.lā'.shas) *a.* lustful; lewd; lecherous. **-ly** *adv.* **-ness, salacity** *n.* [L. *salax*, fr. *salire*, to leap].

sal-ad (sal'.ad) *n.* green vegetables raw or cooked, meat, fish, fruit, dressed with various seasonings or dressings. **—dressing** *n.* a sauce for salads. **— days**, early years of youthful inexperience [Fr. *salade*, fr. L. *sal*, salt].

sal-a-man-der (sal'.a.man.der) *n.* small, tailed amphibian, allied to newt. **salamandriform, salamandrine** *a.* pert. to or shaped like a salamander; fire-resisting [Gk. *salamandra*].

sa-la-mi (sa.lä'.mi.) *n.* Italian salted sausage.

sal-a-ry (sal'.a.ri.) *n.* fixed remuneration, usually monthly, for services rendered; stipend. **salaried** *a.* [L. *salarium*, saltmoney, soldier's pay].

sale (sāl) *n.* exchange of anything for money; demand (for article); public exposition of goods; a special disposal of stock at reduced prices. **-able, salable** *a.* capable of being sold. **-ableness** *n.* **-ably** *adv.* **— price** *n.* special, low price. **-sman** *n.* man who sells. **-smanship** *n.* art of selling goods. **-swoman** *n.* [O.E. *sala*].

sal-i-cin (sal'.a.sin) *n.* a bitter white crystalline glucocide obtained from bark of aspen and used as drug. **salicylate** *n.* any salt of salicylic acid. **salicylic** *a.* derived from salicin. **salicylic acid**, white crystalline solid obtained from aspen bark or synthetically from phenol [L. *salix*, a willow].

sa-li-ent (sā'.li.ant) *a.* moving by leaps; proangle formed by intersection of adjacent surfaces; projecting angle in line of fortifications, etc. **-ly** *adv.* [L. *salire*, to leap].

sa-lif-er-ous (sa.lif'.er.as) *a.* bearing or producing salt [L. *sal*, salt; *ferre*, to bear].

sal-i-fy (sal'.a.fi) *v.t.* to form a salt by combining an acid with a base; to combine with a salt. **salifiable** *a.*

sa-line (sā'.līn) *a.* of or containing salt; salty; *n.* a saline medicine. **salina** *n.* salt marsh; saltworks. **saliniferous** *a.* producing salt. **salinity** *n.* [L. *salinus*].

sa-li-va (sa.lī'.va) *n.* digestive fluid or spittle, secreted in mouth by salivary glands. **-ry** *a.* pert. to; producing saliva. **-te** *v.t.* to produce abnormal secretion of saliva [L.].

sal-low (sal'.ō) *a.* of sickly yellow color; of pale, unhealthy complexion. **-ish** *a.* **-ness** *n.* [O.E. *salo*].

sal-ly (sal'.i.) *n.* sudden eruption; issuing of troops from besieged place to attack enemy; sortie; witticism; *v.i.* to issue suddenly. [L. *satire*, to leap].

salm-on (sam'.an) *n.* silver-scaled fish with orange-pink flesh. **—pink** *n.* orange pink. **— trout** *n.* sea or white-trout, fish resembling salmon in color but smaller [L. *salmo*].

sa-lon (sa.län') *n.* spacious apartment for reception of company; hall for exhibition of art [Fr.].

sa-loon (sa.lòòn') *n.* public dining room; principal cabin in steamer; a place where liquor is sold and drunk. [Fr. *salon*].

sal-si-fy, salsafy (sal'.sa.fi.) *n.* hardy, biennial, composite herb with edible root; oyster plant [Fr. fr. It. *sassefrica*, goat's beard].

salt (sawlt) *n.* sodium chloride or common salt, substance used for seasoning food and for preservation of meat; etc; compound resulting from reaction between acid and a base; savor; piquancy; wit; (*Colloq.*) an old sailor; *pl.* (*Chem.*) combinations of acids with alkaline or salifiable bases; (*Med.*) saline cathartics, as Epsom, Rochelle, etc.; *a.* containing or tasting of salt; preserved with salt; pungent; *v.t.* to season or treat with salt. **-er** *n.* **-ern** *n.* saltworks. **-ing** *n.* land covered regularly by tide. **-less** *a.* **— lick** *n.* salt for animals to lick. **— marsh** *n.* land with low growth liable to be overflowed by sea. **-ness** *n.* salt taste; state of being salt. **—water** *n.* water impregnated with salt; sea water. **-y** *a.* **salt of the earth**, persons of the highest reputation or worth. **to take with a grain of salt**, to be sceptical of [O.E. *sealt*].

sal-tant (sal'.tant) *a.* leaping; jumping; dancing. **saltation** *n.* [L. *salire*, to leap].

sal-tire, saltier (sal'.tir) *n.* cross in the shape of an X, or St. Andrew's cross [O.Fr. *saulloir*].

salt-pe-ter (sawlt'.pē'.ter) *n.* common name for niter or potassium nitrate, used in manufacture of glass, nitric acid, etc. [L. *sal petrae*, salt of the rock].

sa-lu-bri-ous (sa.lū'.bri.as) *a.* wholesome; healthy. **-ly** *adv.* **-ness** *n.* **salubrity** *n.* [L. *salus*, health].

sal-u-ta-ry (sal'.ya.ter.i.) *a.* wholesome; resulting in good; healthful; beneficial. **salutarily** *adv.* **salutariness** *n.* [L. *salus*, health].

sa-lute (sa.lūt') *v.t.* to address with expressions of kind wishes; to recognize one of superior rank by a sign; to honor by a discharge of cannon or small arms, by striking colors, etc.; to greet; *n.* greeting showing respect.

salutation *n.* saluting; words uttered in welcome; opening words of a letter. **salutatory** *a.* welcoming; *n.* opening address of welcome at commencement exercises of school or college. **salutatorian** *n.* student of graduating class who delivers such an address [L. *salutare*, to wish health to].

salvage See **salve**.

sal-va-tion (sal.vā'.shan) *n.* preservation from destruction; redemption; deliverance. **Salvation Army**, international religious organization for revival of religion among the masses. **Salvationist** *n.* active member of Salvation Army [L. *salvare*, to save].

salve (salv) *v.t.* to save or retrieve property from danger or destruction. **salvability** *n.* **salvable** *a.* capable of being used or reconstructed in spite of damage. **salvage** *n.* compensation allowed to persons who assist in saving ship or cargo, or property in general, from destruction; property, so saved; *v.t.* to save from ruins, shipwreck, etc. **-r, salvor** *n.* [L. *salvare*, to save].

salve (sav) *n.* healing ointment applied to wounds or sores; *v.t.* to anoint with such; to heal; to soothe (conscience) [O.E. *sealf*].

sal-ver (sal'.ver) *n.* a tray for visiting cards [Sp. *salva*, a foretasting, fr. L. *salvare*, to save].

sal-vo (sal'.vō) *n.* guns fired simultaneously, or in succession as salute; sustained applause or welcome from large crowd. *pl.* **salvo(e)s** [It. *salva*, a volley].

sal volatile See **sal**.

Sa-mar-i-tan (sa.mar'.a.tan) *a.* pert. to Samaria in Palestine; *n.* native or inhabitant of Samaria; kind-hearted, charitable person (fr. parable of good Samaritan, Luke 10).

sam-ba (sam'.ba) *n.* a dance of S. American origin; the music for such a dance [Sp.].

sam-bo (sam'.bō) *n.* offspring of black person and mulatto [Sp. *zambo*].

Sam Browne (sam broun) *n.* military belt.

same (sām) *a.* identical; not different; of like kind; unchanged; uniform; aforesaid. **-ly** *adv.* **-ness** *n.* near resemblance; uniformity [O.N. *samr*].

sam-ite (sam'.it) *n.* rich silk material; any lustrous silk stuff [Fr. *samit*, fr. Gk. *hexamitos*, woven with six threads].

sam-o-var (sam'.a.vär) *n.* Russian tea urn.

Sam-o-yed (sam'.a.yed) *n.* Mongolian race inhabiting N. shores of Russia and Siberia; breed of dog, orig. a sledge dog.

sam-pan (sam'.pan) *n.* a Chinese light river vessel. Also **sanpan** [Malay fr. Chin. *san*, three; *pan*, a board].

sam-phire (sam'.fir) *n.* European herb found on rocks and cliffs, St. Peter's wort [corrupt. fr. Fr. *Saint Pierre*].

sam-ple (sam'.pl) *n.* specimen; example; *v.t.* to take or give a sample of; to try; to test; to taste. **-r** *n.* one who samples; beginner's exercise in embroidery [M.E. *essample*; fr. L. *exemplum*, example].

sam-u-rai (sam'.oo.rī) *n.* (*s.* and *pl.*) member of hereditary military caste in Japan from 12th to mid 19th cent. [Jap.].

san-a-tive (san'.a.tiv) *a.* having power to cure or heal. **-ness** *n.* **sanatorium** *n.* (*pl.* **sanatoria**) institution for open-air treatment of tuberculosis; institution for convalescent patients. Also **sanitarium**. See **sanitary**. **sanatory** *a.* healing [L. *sanare*, to heal].

sanc-ti-fy (sangk'.ta.fi) *v.t.* to set apart as sacred or holy; to hallow; to consecrate; to purify. **sanctification** *n.* purification and freedom from sin. **sanctified** *a.* hallowed; sanctimonious. **sanctifiedly** *adv.* **sanctimonious** *a.* hypocritically pious. **sanctimoniously** *adv.* **sanctimoniousness, sanctimony** *n.* affected piety. **sanctitude** *n.* saintliness; holiness. **sanctity** *n.* quality of being sacred; state of being pure and devout; state of being solemnly binding on one; inviolability [L. *sanctus*, holy].

sanc-tion (sangk'.shan) *n.* solemn ratification; express permission; authorization; approval; legal use of force to secure obedience to law; anything which serves to secure obedience to law; anything which serves to move a person to observe or refrain from given mode of conduct; *v.t.* and *v.i.* to confirm; to authorize; to countenance. **sanctions** *n.pl.* measures to enforce fulfillment of international treaty obligations [L. *sanctus*, holy].

sanc·tu·ar·y (sangk'·choo·er·i·) *n.* holy place; shrine; the chancel; a church or other place of protection for fugitives. **sanctum** *n.* sacred place; private room or study. **sanctum sanctorum**, holy of holies in Jewish temple; exclusive private place [L. *sanctus*, holy].

sand (sand) *n.* fine, loose grains of quartz or other mineral matter formed by disintegration of rocks; *n.pl.* sandy beach; desert region; moments of time; *v.t.* to sprinkle or cover with sand; to smooth with sandpaper. **-bag** *n.* bag filled with sand or earth, for repairing breaches in fortification, etc. **-bank** *n.* shoal of sand thrown up by sea. **— bar** *n.* barrier of sand facing entrance of river estuary. **-blast** *n.* jet of sand driven by a blast of air or steam, for roughening, cleaning, cutting. **— dune** *n.* ridge of loose sand. **-ed** *a.* sprinkled with sand. **— glass** *n.* hourglass, instrument for measuring time by running of sand. **-iness** *n.* state of being sandy; a sandy color. **-ing** *n.* cleaning up wood by rubbing with sandpaper. **-paper** *n.* stout paper or cloth coated with glue and then sprinkled over with sand, used as an abrading agent for smoothing wood, etc. *v.t.* to smooth with sandpaper. **-piper** *n.* small wading bird of plover family. **-stone** *n.* rock employed for building and making grindstones. **-storm** *n.* a storm of wind carrying dust. **-y** *a.* like or covered with sand; not firm or stable; yellowish brown [O.E.].

sand glass

san·dal (san'·dal) *n.* a shoe consisting of flat sole, bound to foot by straps or thongs. **-led** *a.* [Gk. *sandalon*].

san·dal·wood (san'·dal·wood) *n.* fragrant heartwood of santalum [Ar. *sandal*].

sand·er·ling (san'·der·ling) *n.* a wading bird of the plover family.

sand·wich (sand'·wich) *n.* two thin pieces of bread with slice of meat, etc., between them (said to have been a favorite dish of Earl of *Sandwich*); *v.t.* to make into sandwich; to form of alternating layers of different nature; to insert or squeeze in between, making a tight fit. **— man** *n.* man carrying two advertising boards, one slung before and one behind him.

sane (sān) *a.* of sound mind; not deranged; rational; reasonable; lucid. **-ly** *adv.* **-ness** *n.* [L. *sanus*, healthy].

sang (sang) *pa.t.* of **sing**.

sang-froid (sán·frwá') *n.* composure of mind; imperturbability [Fr. *sang*, blood; *froid*, cold].

san·guine (sang'·gwin) *a.* hopeful; confident; cheerful; deep red; florid; in a sanguine; blood-red color. **sanguinarily** *adv.* **sanguinariness** *n.* **sanguinary** *a.* bloody; bloodthirsty; murderous. **-ly** *adv.* **-ness** *n.* **-ous** *a.* bloody; blood-red; blood-stained; containing blood. [L. *sanguis*, blood].

San·he·drin (san'·hē·drin) *n.* supreme court of Ancient Jerusalem; any similar Jewish assembly. Also **Sanhedrim**. [Heb. fr. Gk. *sun*, together; *hedra*, seat].

san·i·tar·y (san'·a·te·ri·) *a.* pert. to health; hygienic; clean; free from dirt, germs, etc. **sanitarian** *n.* one interested in the promotion of hygienic reforms. **sanitarily** *adv.* **sanitation** *n.* the measures taken to promote health and to prevent disease; hygiene. **sanitarium**, *n.* private hospital for treatment of special or chronic diseases; health retreat; sanitorium. **sanitary napkin**, pad or absorbent material for use during menstruation [L. *sanitas*, health].

san·i·ty (san'·a·ti·) *n.* state of being sane; soundness of mind [L. *sanus*, sane].

sank (sangk) *pa.t.* of the verb **sink**.

sans-cu·lotte (sanz·kū·lat') *n.* ragged fellow; a name given in the first French Revolution to extreme republican party [Fr. = without knee breeches].

San·skrit, Sanscrit (san'·skrit) *n.* classic literary language of ancient India, member of Indo-European family of languages [Sans. *samskrita*, perfected, finished].

San·ta Claus (san'·ta klawz) *n.* traditional 'Father Christmas' of children [corrupt. of *St. Nicholas*, patron saint of children].

sap (sap) *n.* watery juice of plants, containing mineral salts, proteins and carbohydrates; (*Slang*) a stupid person. **-head** *n.* (*Slang*) dolt. **-less** *a.* **-ling** *n.* young tree; youth. doltishness. **-py** *a.* juicy; (*Slang*) silly.

-wood *n.* alburnum, exterior part of wood of tree next to bark [O.E. *saep*].

sap (sap) *n.* tunnel driven under enemy positions for purpose of attack; *v.t.* and *v.i.* to undermine; to impair insidiously; to exhaust gradually. *pr.p.* **-ping**. *pa.t.* and *pa.p.* **-ped** [It. *zappa*, a spade].

sap·id (sap'·id) *a.* savory; palatable; tasty. **-ity** *n.* [L. *sapere*, to taste].

sa·pi·ent (sā'·pi·ant) *a.* discerning; wise; sage. **sapience** *n.* **-ly** *adv.* [L. *sapiens*, wise].

sap·o·na·ceous (sap·a·nā'·shas) *a.* resembling soap; slippery, as if soaped. **saponify** *v.t.* to convert into soap. **saponin** *n.* glycoside obtained from many plants used for foam baths, fire extinguishers, detergents, etc. due to frothy qualities [L. *sapo*, soap].

sa·por (sā'·per) *n.* taste; savor; flavor. **-oific** *a.* producing taste or flavor. **-osity** *n.* [L. = taste].

Sap·phic (saf'·ik) *a.* pert. to Sappho, lyric poetess of Greece of 7th cent. B.C.; denoting verse in which three lines of five feet each are followed by line of two feet; *n.* Sapphic verse. **sapphism** *n.* unnatural sexual relations between women.

sap·phire (saf'·īr) *n.* translucent precious stone of various shades of blue; *a.* deep, pure blue [Gk. *sapheiros*].

sar·a·band (sar'·a·band) *n.* slow, stately dance, introduced by Moors into Spain in 16th cent.; in England, country dance [Pers. *sarband*, a fillet].

Sar·a·cen (sar'·a·san) *n.* Arab or Mohammedan who invaded Europe and Africa; an infidel. **-ic** *a.* [L. *Saracenus*].

Sar·a·to·ga trunk (sar·a·tō'·ga·trungk) *n.* a large trunk for ladies' dresses.

sar·casm (sár'·kazm) *n.* taunt; scoffing gibe; veiled sneer; irony; use of such expressions. **sarcastic, -al** *a.* bitterly satirical and cutting; taunting. **sarcastically** *adv.* [Gk. *sarkasmos*].

sar·coph·a·gus (sár·kåf'·a·gas) *n.* kind of limestone used by Greeks for coffins and believed to consume flesh of bodies deposited in it; stone coffin; monumental chest or case of stone, erected over graves. *pl.* **sarcophagi** [Gk. *sarx*, flesh; *phagein*, to eat].

sar·dine (sár·dēn') *n.* small fish of herring family in young stage salted and preserved in oil [It. *sardina*, fr. the island of Sardinia].

sar·don·ic (sár·dàn'·ik) *a.* (of laugh, smile) bitter, scornful, derisive, mocking. **-ally** *adv.* [L. *sardonicus*].

sar·do·nyx (sár'·da·niks) *n.* semi-precious stone [Gk. = Sardinian onyx].

sar·gas·sum (sár·gas'·am) *n.* genus of seaweeds. **sargasso** *n.* gulfweed. **Sargasso Sea**, part of Atlantic covered with seaweed [Sp. *sargazo*].

sa·ri (sá'·rē) *n.* long outer garment of Hindu women. Also **saree** [Hind.].

sa·rong (sa·rawng') *n.* garment draped round waist by Malayans [Malay].

sar·sa·pa·ril·la (sárs·(a)·pa·ril'·a) *n.* several plants of genus Smilax, with roots yielding medicinal sarsaparilla, a mild diuretic; a soft drink flavored with the extract [Sp. *zarzaparilla*].

sar·to·ri·al (sár·tō·'·ri·al) *a.* pert. to tailor, tailoring [L. *sartor*, a tailor].

sash (sash) *n.* silken band; belt or band, usually decorative, worn round body [Arab. *shash*].

sash (sash) *n.* frame of window which carries panes of glass [Fr. *chassis*].

sas·sa·fras (sas'·a·fras) *n.* a tree of the laurel family; the dried bark of the root, used for flavoring beverages, etc.

sat (sat) *pa.t.* and *pa.p.* of **sit**.

Sa·tan (sā'·tan) *n.* the devil. **-ic, -al** *a.* devilish; infernal; diabolical. **-ically** *adv.* [Heb. = enemy].

satch·el (sach'·al) *n.* small bag for books, etc. [L. *saccellus*, small sack].

sate (sāt) *v.t.* to satisfy appetite of; to glut [earlier *sade*, to make sad].

sa·teen (sa·tēn') *n.* glossy cloth for linings, made of cotton in imitation of satin [fr. satin].

sat·el·lite (sat'·a·līt) *n.* one constantly in attendance upon important personage; an obsequious follower; (*Astron.*) a secondary body which revolves round planets of solar system; a moon. **satellite (earth)** *n.* an object launched into space by man to orbit the earth for scientific purposes. **satellitic** *a.* [L. *satelles*].

satellite

sa·ti·ate (sā'·shi·āt) *v.t.* to satisfy appetite of; to surfeit; to sate. **satiability** *n.* **satiable** *a.* capable of being satisfied. **satiation** *n.* state of being satiated. **satiety** (sa·tī'·a·ti·) *n.* state of being satiated; feeling of having had too much [L. *satiare*, fr. *satis*, enough].

sat·in (sat'·n) *n.* soft, rich, usually silk fabric with smooth, lustrous surface; *a.* made of satin; smooth; glossy. **-et** *n.* thin kind of satin; glossy cloth of cotton warp and woolen weft, to imitate satin. **-wood** *n.* beautiful hard yellow wood, valued in cabinet work for veneers. **-y** *a.* [Fr. fr. It. *seta*, silk].

sat·ire (sat'·īre) *n.* literary composition holding up to ridicule vice or folly of the times; use of irony, sarcasm, invective, or wit. **satiric, -al** *a.* satirically *adv.* **satiricalness** *n.* **satirize** *v.t.* to make object of satire. **satirist** *n.* [L. *satira*, a literary medley].

sat·is·fy (sat'·is·fi) *v.t.* to gratify fully; to pay, fulfill, supply, recompense, adequately; to convince; to content; to answer; to free from doubt; *v.i.* to give content; to supply to the full; to make payment. **satisfaction** *n.* **satisfactorily** *adv.* **satisfactoriness** *n.* **satisfactory** *a.* affording satisfaction, esp. of food. **-ingly** *adv.* [L. *satisfacere*].

sa·trap (sā'·trap) *n.* governor of province under ancient Persian monarchy; petty, despotic governor. **-al** *a.* **-y** *n.* government, jurisdiction of satrap [Gk. *satrapēs*].

sat·u·rate (sach'·a·rāt) *v.t.* to soak thoroughly; to steep; to drench. **-d** *a.* **saturation** *n.* act of saturating; complete penetration; condition of being saturated; solution of a body in a solvent, until solvent can absorb no more; in magnetism, state when increase of magnetizing force produces no further increase of flux-density in magnet; purity of color, free from white. **saturator** *n.* contrivance for saturating air of factory, etc. with water-vapor [L. *saturare*].

Sat·ur·day (sat'·er·di) *n.* seventh day of week [O.E. *Saeterdaeg*, day of Saturn].

Sat·urn (sat'·ern) *n.* old deity, father of Jupiter; sixth of major planets in order of distance from sun. **Saturnalia** *n.pl.* festival in ancient Rome in honor of Saturn; time of carnival and unrestrained license; orgy. **saturnalian** *a.* **Saturnian** *a.* pert. to epoch of Saturn; golden; distinguished for prosperity and peacefulness. **saturnine** *a.* gloomy, sluggish in temperament [L. *Saturnus*, god of agriculture].

sat·yr (sā'·ter, sat'·er) *n.* woodland deity in Greek mythology, part human and part goat, fond of sensual enjoyment; lecherous person. **satyriasis** *n.* excessive and morbid desire for sexual intercourse exhibited by men. **-omaniac** *n.* **-ical** *a.* pert. to satyrs [Gk. *saturos*].

sauce (saws) *n.* liquid or soft seasoning for food to render it more palatable or to whet appetite; condiment; relish; (*Colloq.*) impudence; cheek; *v.t.* to season with sauce; to give flavor or interest to; (*Colloq.*) to be rude in speech or manner. **-pan** *n.* meal pot with lid and long handle used for cooking. **saucy** *a.* bold; pert; cheeky. **saucily** *adv.* **sauciness** *n.* [Fr. fr. L. *sal.* salt].

sau·cer (saw'·ser) *n.* orig. vessel for sauce; small plate put under cup [Fr. *saucière*].

sauer·kraut (sour'·krout) *n.* cabbage cut fine and allowed to ferment in brine [Ger.].

saun·ter (sawn'·ter) *v.i.* to stroll. *n.* leisurely walk or stroll. **-er** *n.* **-ing** *n.*

sau·ri·an (saw'·ri·an) *n.* lizard-like reptile [Gk. *sauros*, a lizard].

sau·sage (saw'·sij) *n.* meat minced and seasoned and enclosed in thin membranous casing obtained from small entrails of pig or sheep [Fr. *saucisse*].

sau·té (sō·tā) *a.* cooked in little fat [Fr.].

sau·terne (sō·turn′) *n.* a well-known white wine, from *Sauternes*, S. W. France.

sav·age (sav′·ij) *a.* remote from human habitation; wild; uncivilized; primitive; cruel; *n.* man in native state of primitiveness; a barbarian. **-ly** *adv.* **-ry** *n.* ferocity; barbarism [L. *silvaticus*, fr. *silva*, a wood].

sa·vant (sa·vånt′, sav′·ant) *n.* a man of learning [Fr. fr. *savoir*, to know].

save (sāv) *v.t.* to rescue, preserve from danger, evil, etc.; to redeem; to protect; to secure; to maintain (face, etc.); to keep for future; to lay by; to hoard; to obviate need of; to spare; to except; *v.i.* to lay by money; to economize; *prep.* except; *conj.* but. **savable** *a.* capable of being saved; retrievable. **-r** *n.* **saving** *a.* frugal; thrifty; delivering from sin; implying reservation, as *saving clause; prep.* excepting; with apology to; *n.* economy; *pl.* earnings or gains put by for future. **savingly** *adv.* **savings bank** *n.* bank for receipt and accumulation of savings [Fr. *sauver*, fr. L. *salvare*, to save].

sav·ior (sāv′·yer) *n.* one who saves or delivers from destruction or danger; *(Cap.)* the Redeemer, Jesus Christ. Also **saviour** [L. *salvare*, to save].

sa·voir-faire (sav·wår·fer′) *n.* the knack of knowing the right thing to do at the right time; tact [Fr.].

sa·vor (sā′·ver) *n.* taste; flavor; relish; odor; smack; distinctive quality; *v.t.* to like; to taste or smell with pleasure; to relish; *v.i.* to have a particular smell or taste; to resemble; to indicate the presence of. **-ily** *adv.* **-less** *a.* **-y** *a.* having savor; tasty. Also *savour* [L. *sapor*, taste].

sa·vor·y (sā′·ver·i·) *n.* genus of aromatic plants, often grown as pot-herbs, the leaves being used in cooking as flavoring [fr. *savour*].

sav·vy (sav′·i·) *v.t.* (*Slang*) to understand; *n.* intelligence [Sp. *saber*; Fr. *savoir*, to know].

saw (saw) *pa.t.* of the verb **see**.

saw (saw) *n.* old saying; maxim; proverb; aphorism; adage [O.E. *sagu*].

saw (saw) *n.* hand or mechanical tool with thin blade, band, or circular disk with serrated edge, used for cutting; *v.t.* and *v.i.* to cut with a saw; *pa.t.* **sawed.** *pa.p.* **sawed** or **sawn. -·ones** *n.* (*Slang*) surgeon. **-dust** *n.* small particles of wood, etc. made by action of a saw. **-er** *n.* **-mill** *n.* place where logs are sawn by mechanical power. **-toothed** *a.* having serrations like a saw. **-yer** *n.* one who saws timber; wood-boring larva of longicorn beetle [O.E. *saga*].

sax·horn (saks′·hawrn) *n.* brass wind instrument [Adolphe *Sax*, inventor, c. 1842].

sax·i·frage (sak′·sa·frij) *n.* popular name of various plants, most of them true rock plants [L. *saxum*, a stone; *frangere*, to break].

Sax·on (sak′·san) *n.* one of the people who formerly dwelt in N. Germany and who invaded England in the 5th and 6th cents.; a person of English race; native of Saxony; language of Saxons; *a.* pert. to Saxons, their country, their language; Anglo-Saxon [O.E. *Seaxa, Seaxan,* fr. *seax,* a knife].

Sax·o·ny (sak′·sa·ni·) *n.* very fine quality of wool; flannel [*Saxony,* where first produced].

sax·o·phone (sak′·sa·fōn) *n.* brass wind instrument, with a reed and clarinet mouthpiece, fingered like an oboe [A. J. *Sax,* the inventor; Gk. *phōnē,* a sound].

say (sā) *v.t.* to utter with speaking voice; to state; to express; to repeat (lesson, etc.); to recite; to take as near enough. *pa.t.* and *pa.p.* **said** (sed). *n.* something said; what one has to say; share in a decision. **-er** *n.* **-ing** *n.* a verbal utterance; spoken or written expression of thought; proverbial expression; adage [O.E. *secgan*].

scab (skab) *n.* crust forming over open wound or sore; contagious skin disease, resembling mange, which attacks horses, cattle and sheep; disease of apple and pear; non-union worker; (*Slang*) despicable person; *v.i.* to heal over; to form a scab. *pa.t.* and *pa.p.* **-bed.** *pr.p.* **-bing. -bed** *a.* covered with scabs. **-bedness** *n.* **-by** *a.* [O.N. *skabbi*].

scab·bard (skab′·erd) *n.* sheath for sword or dagger; *v.t.* [O.Fr. *escalberc*].

sca·bies (skā′·bēz) *n.* skin disease caused by parasite; the itch; the scab [L.].

scabbard

sca·bi·ous (skā′·bi·as) *a.* consisting of scabs; scabby; itchy [L. *scabies,* the itch].

sca·brous (skā′·bras) *a.* rough; scaly; harsh; full of difficulties; indelicate. **-ly** *adv.* **-ness** *n.* [L. *scaber* rough].

scad (skad) *n.* a species of mackerel; *pl.* (*Slang*) a great quantity [form of *shad*].

scaf·fold (skaf′·ald) *n.* temporary structure for support of workmen, used in erecting, altering, or repairing buildings; framework; stage; platform, esp. for execution of criminal; *v.t.* to furnish with a scaffold; to prop up. **-ing** *n.* scaffold [O.Fr. *eschafault*].

scal·a·wag, scallawag (skal′·a·wag) *n.* (*Colloq.*) scamp; worthless fellow.

scald (skawld) *v.t.* to burn with moist heat or hot liquid; to cleanse by rinsing with boiling water; to heat to point approaching boiling point; *n.* injury by scalding [L. *ex,* out of; *calidus,* hot].

scald See **skald.**

scale (skāl) *n.* dish of a balance; balance itself; machine for weighing, chiefly in *pl.;* Libra, one of signs of zodiac; *v.t.* to weigh, as in scales [O.N. *skal,* bowl].

scale (skāl) *n.* horny or bony plate-like outgrowth from skin of certain mammals, reptiles, and fishes; any thin layer or flake on surface; *v.t.* to remove scales; *v.i.* to come off or peel in thin layers. **-d** *a.* having scales. **-less** *a.* **scaliness** *n.* being scaly. **scaling** *n.* removing of scales. **scaly** *a.* covered with scales; resembling scales [O.Fr. *escale,* husk].

scale (skāl) *n.* series of steps or gradations; comparative rank in society; ratio between dimensions as shown on map, etc. to actual distance, or length; scope; basis for a numerical system, as *binary scale;* instrument for measuring, weighing, etc. (*Mus.*) succession of notes arranged in order of pitch between given note and its octave; gamut; *v.t.* to climb as by a ladder; to clamber up; to measure; *v.i.* to mount [L. *scala,* a ladder].

sca·lene (skā·lēn) *a.* uneven; (*Geom.*) having all three sides unequal; *n.* a scalene triangle [Gk. *skalēnos,* uneven].

scal·lion (skal′·yan) *n.* a variety of shallot [L. (*cepa*) *Ascalonia,* onion of Ascalon].

scal·lop, scollop (skal′·ap) *n.* bivale mollusk with ribbed, fan-shaped shell and beautiful coloring; ornamental edge of rounded projections; dish resembling scallop shell to serve oysters, etc.; *v.t.* to cut edge of material into scallops [O.Fr. *escalope,* a shell].

scalp (skalp) *n.* covering dome of cranium consisting of skin and hair; skin and hair torn off by Indian warriors as token of victory; *v.t.* to deprive of integument of head; to make quick profits in buying and prompt reselling [contr. of *scollop*].

scal·pel (skal′·pel) *n.* small, straight surgical knife with convex edge [L. *scalpere,* to cut].

scamp (skamp) *n.* scoundrel; rascal; rogue; *v.t.* to execute work carelessly [O.Fr. *escamper,* to decamp].

scam·per (skam′·per) *v.i.* to run about; to run away in haste and trepidation; *n.* a hasty, impulsive flight [fr. *scamp*].

scan (skan) *v.t.* to examine closely; to scrutinize; to measure or read (verse) by its metri-

cal feet (*Radar*) to traverse an area with electronic beams. *v.i.* to be metrically correct. *pr.p.* **-ning.** *pa.t.* and *pa.p.* **-ned. -ning** *n.* (*Television*) process of dissecting a picture to be transmitted. **-sion** *n.* act or mode of scanning poetry [L. *scandere,* to climb].

scan·dal (skan′·dal) *n.* malicious gossip; disgraceful action; disgrace; injury to a person's character; **-bearer, -monger** *n.* one who delights in spreading malicious scandal and gossip. **-ize** *v.t.* to shock by disgraceful actions **-ous** *a.* bringing shame; disgraceful. **-ously** *adv.* **-ousness** *n.* [Gk. *skandalon,* a cause of stumbling].

Scan·di·na·vi·a (skan·da·nā′·vi·a) *n.* peninsula of Norway, Sweden, and Finland, but historically and linguistically includes Denmark and Iceland. **-n** *a.* pert. to Scandinavia [L. *Scandinavia* or *Scandia*].

scansion. See **scan.**

scant (skant) *a.* barely sufficient; inadequate; *v.t.* to put on short allowance; to fail to give full measure; **-ily** *adv.* **-iness** *n.* **-ly** *adv.* sparingly; scarcely; barely. **-ness** *n.* scantiness; insufficiency. **-y** *a.* [O.N. *skamt,* short].

scant·ling (skant′·ling) *n.* a small amount; a small piece of timber; a stud [Fr. *échantillon,* a sample].

scape·goat (skāp′·gōt) *n.* in Mosaic ritual, goat upon whose head were symbolically placed sins of people; one who has to shoulder blame due to another. **scapegrace** *n.* graceless, good-for-nothing fellow [fr. *escape*].

scaph·oid (skaf′·oid) *a.* boat-shaped [Gk. *skaphē,* a boat; *eidos,* form].

scap·u·la (skap′·ya·la) *n.* shoulder blade. *pl.* **scapulae. -r** *a.* pert. to scapula; *n.* bandage for shoulder blade; part of habit of certain religious orders in R.C. church; sleeveless monastic garment. Also **-ry** [L. *scapulae,* the shoulder blades].

scar (skár) *n.* permanent mark left on skin after healing of a wound, burn; a cicatrix; any blemish; *v.t.* to mark with scar; *v.i.* to heal with a scar [O.Fr. *escare*].

scar·ab (skar′·ab) *n.* beetle regarded by ancient Egyptians as emblematic of solar power; gem cut in shape of this beetle, as amulet [L. *scarabaeus*].

scarce (skers) *a.* not plentiful; deficient; wanting; rare; infrequent; uncommon; scanty; **-ly** *adv.* hardly; not quite. **-ness, scarcity** *n.* being scarce; lack; deficiency [O.Fr. *escars*].

scare (sker) *v.t.* to terrify suddenly; to alarm; to drive away by frightening; *n.* sudden alarm (esp. causeless); panic; fright. **-crow** *n.* figure set up to frighten away birds from crops; a miserable-looking person in rags. **-monger** *n.* alarmist [O.N. *skirra*].

scarf (skárf) *n.* long, narrow, light article of dress worn loosely over shoulders or about neck; a muffler. *pl.* **-s, scarves** [O.Fr. *escrepe,* a purse hanging from the neck].

scarf (skárf) *v.t.* to unite lengthways to pieces of timber by letting notched end of one into a similar end of the other, then securing them with bolt or strap. *n.* joint for connecting timbers lengthways, the two pieces overlapping [Scand. = *skarf,* a joint].

scar·i·fy (skar′·a·fi) *v.t.* to scratch or slightly cut the skin; to stir the surface soil of; to lacerate; to criticize unmercifully. **scarification** *n.* **scarifier** *n.* [L. *scarificare*].

scar·la·ti·na (skar·la·tē′·na) *n.* scarlet fever [It.].

scar·let (skár′·lit) *n.* bright red color of many shades; cloth of scarlet color; *a.* of this color — **fever** *n.* childhood disease characterized by a scarlet rash. **-hat** *n.* a cardinal's hat. — **pimpernel,** small annual herb with red flowers. — **runner** *n.* bean plant with twining stem and scarlet flowers [O.Fr. *escarlate*].

scarp (skárp) *n.* steep inside slope of ditch in fortifications; *v.t.* to make steep. **-ed** *a.* steeply sloping [It. *scarpa*].

scar·y (sker′·i·) *a.* (*Colloq.*) producing fright or alarm; exceedingly timid [fr. *scare*].

scat (skat) *v.i.* to hurry off; *v.t.* to order off with "scat!"

scathe (skāth) *v.t.* to criticize harshly. **scathing** *a.* damaging; cutting; biting. **scathingly** *adv.* [O.N. *skatha*].

sca·tol·o·gy (ska·tål′·a·ji·) *n.* scientific study of fossilized excrement of animals; interest in obscene literature. **scatological** *a.* [Gk. *skor, skatos,* dung].

scat·ter (skat′·er) *v.t.* to strew about; to sprinkle around; to put to rout; to disperse; *v.i.* to take to flight; to disperse. **-brain** *n.* a giddy, thoughtless person. **-brained** *a.* **-ed** *a.* widely separated or distributed; distracted. **-er** *n.* **-ing** *n.* act of dispersing; effect of irregularly reflected light; (*Radio*) general re-radiation of wave-energy when a ray meets an obstacle in its path; *a.* dispersing; sporadic; diversified. **-ingly** *adv.*

scav·en·ger (skav′·in·jer) *n.* one employed in cleaning streets, removing refuse, etc.; animal which feeds on carrion; *v.i.* to scavenge. **scavenge** *v.t.* to cleanse streets, etc. [orig. *scavager,* inspector of goods for sale, later, of street cleansing, fr. O.E. *sceawian,* to inspect].

sce·nar·i·o (sa·ner′·i·ō) *n.* script or written version of play to be produced by motion picture; plot of a play. **scenarist** *n.* [It.].

scene (sēn) *n.* place, time of action of novel,

play, etc.; a division of a play; spectacle, show, or view; episode; unseemly display of temper; minor disturbance. **-ry** *n.* stage settings; natural features of landscape which please eye. — **shifter** *n.* one who manages the scenery in theatrical representation. **scenic** *a.* pert. to scenery; theatrical; picturesque. **scenographic, -al** *a.* drawn in perspective. **scenographically** *adv.* **scenography** *n.* [L. *scena*].

scent (sent) *v.t.* to discern or track by sense of smell; to give a perfume to; to detect; to become suspicious of; *v.i.* to smell; *n.* odor or perfume; fragrance; aroma; trail left by odor. **-ed** *a.* perfumed. **to put off the scent,** to mislead wilfully [Fr. *sentir*, to smell].

sceptic. See **skeptic.**

scepter (sep'·ter) *n.* ornamental staff or baton, as symbol of royal power; royal or imperial dignity. **-ed** *a.* invested with a scepter, regal. Also **sceptre** [Gk. *skēptron*, a staff].

sched·ule (skej'·ool) *n.* document containing list of details forming part of principal document, deed, etc.; tabulated list; order of events; timetable; *v.t.* to note and enter in a schedule [L. a small scroll].

sche·ma (skē'·ma) *n.* plan or diagram; outline; scheme; *pl.* **-ta. -tic** *a.* **-tically** *adv.* **-tize** *v.t.* to form a scheme [Gk.].

scheme (skēm) *n.* plan; design; system; plot; draft; outline; a syllabus; tabulated statement; diagram; *v.t.* to plan; to contrive; to frame; *v.i.* to intrigue; to plot. *pr.p.* **scheming. -r** *n.* **scheming** *n.* and *a.* planning; plotting. **schemist** *n.* schemer [Gk. *schéma*, form].

scher·zo (sker'·tsō) *n.* (*Mus.*) composition of a lively, playful character [It. = a jest].

schil·ling (shil'·ing) *n.* orig. a German coin, re-introduced into Austrian monetary system in 1925 [Ger.].

schism (sizm) *n.* split of a community into factions; division of a church or religious denomination; crime of promoting this. **schismatic** *a.—n.* one who separates from a church. **-atical** *a.* schismatic. **-atically** *adv.* [Gk. *schisma*, a cleft].

schiz·o- (skiz'·ō) *prefix fr.* Greek, *schizein*, to cleave, used in the construction of compound terms. **schizoid** *a.* exhibiting slight symptoms of schizophrenia. **-phrenia** (skiz·a·frē'·ni.a) *n.* mental disorder known as 'split personality,' characterized by a social behavior, introversion, and loss of touch with one's environment. **-phrenic** *a.*

schnapps, schnaps (shnaps) *n.* kind of Holland gin [Ger.].

schol·ar (skál'·er) *n.* learned person; holder of scholarship. **-ly** *a.* learned. **-ship** *n.* learning; erudition; a grant to aid a student. **scholastic** *a.* pert. to schools, scholars, or education; pert. to schools or scholars of philosophy of Middle Ages; pedantic; *n.* schoolman who expounded medieval philosophy; Jesuit student who has not yet taken Holy Orders. **scholastically** *adv.* **Scholasticism** *n.* system of philosophy during Middle Ages [Gk. *scholē*, a school].

scho·li·ast (skō'·li·ast) *n.* ancient commentator or annotator of classical texts. **scholiastic** *a.* **scholium** *n.—pl.* **scholia,** marginal note or comments [Gk. *scholiastēs*, commentator].

school (skool) *n.* a shoal (of fish, whales, etc.) [Dut. *school*, crowd].

school (skool) *n.* institution for teaching or giving instruction in any subject; pupils of a school; sessions of instruction; group of writers, artists, thinkers, etc. with principles or methods in common; branch of study, in a university; *v.t.* to educate; to discipline; to instruct; to train. **-boy** *n.* boy attending school or of school age. **-mate** *n.* contemporary at school. **-man** *n.* learned doctor of Middle Ages, versed in scholasticism. **-master** *n.* master in charge of school; male teacher in school. **-room** *n.* **-teacher** *n.* **boarding school,** residential school for boys or girls. **preparatory school,** private school which prepares young people for public school. **public school,** *see* **public** [Gk. *scholē*, leisure; place for discussion].

schoon·er (skoo'·ner) *n.* small sharp-built vessel, having two masts, fore-and-aft rigged; (*Colloq.*) extra large glass for holding beer; [orig. *scooner*, fr. Prov. E. *scoon,* to make flat stone skip along surface of water. O.E. *scunian*].

schot·tische, shottish (shát'·ish) *n.* round dance resembling polka; music in 2/4 time for this dance. **Highland schottische,** lively dance to strathspey tunes, Highland fling [Ger. = Scottish].

sci·at·i·ca (si·at'·i·ka) *n.* neuralgia of sciatic nerve, with pains in region of hip. **sciatic, -al** *a.* situated in, or pert. to, hip region. **-lly** *adv.* [Late L. fr. Gk. *ischion,* hip-joint].

sci·ence (sī'·ans) *n.* systematic knowledge of natural or physical phenomena; truth ascertained by observation, experiment, and induction; ordered arrangement of facts known under classes or heads; theoretical knowledge as distinguished from practical; knowledge of principles and rules of invention, construction, mechanism, etc. as distinguished from art. **scientific, -al** *a.* **scientifically** *adv.* **scientism** *n.* outlook and practice of scientist.

scientist *n.* a person versed in science, esp. natural science. **Christian Science,** religious doctrine of faith healing, bodily diseases being due to errors of mortal mind and therefore curable by faith and prayer. **domestic science,** study of good housekeeping. **natural science, physical science,** science which investigates nature and properties of material bodies and natural phenomena. **pure science,** science based on self-evident truths, as mathematics, logic, etc. [L. *scientia*, knowledge].

scim·i·tar (sim'·a·ter) *n.* short saber with curved, sharp-edged blade broadening from handle [Pers. *shimshir*].

scin·til·la (sin·til'·a) *n.* spark; least particle. **-nt** *a.* emitting sparks; sparkling. **-te** *v.i.* to emit sparks; to sparkle; to glisten. **-tion** *n.* [L. = a park].

sci·o·lism (sī'·a·lizm) *n.* superficial knowledge used to impress other. **sciolist** *n.* one possessed of superficial knowledge; charlatan. **sciolistic** *a.* [L. *scire,* to know].

sci·on (sī'·an) *n.* slip for grafting; offshoot; a descendant; heir [Fr.].

scis·sile (sis'·al) *a.* (*Bot.*) capable of being cut, split, or divided. **scission** *n.* act of cutting; division [L. *scindere, scissum,* to cut].

scis·sors (siz'·erz) *n.pl.* instrument of two sharp-edged blades pivoted together for cutting; small shears. **scissor** *v.t.* to cut with scissors [Fr. *ciseaux*].

scle·ro- (sklēr'·a) *prefix fr.* Gk. *sklēros,* hard, used in the construction of compound terms, implying hardness or dryness. **sclera** (sklir'·a) *n.* strong, opaque fibrous membrane forming outer coat of eyeball, the white of the eye. **scleral** *a.* hard, bony. **scleritis** *n.* inflammation of sclera of eye. **scleroderma, sclerodermia** *n.* chronic skin disease characterized by hardness and rigidity. **sclerodermatous** *a.* (*Zool.*) possessing a hard, bony, external structure for protection. **sclerodermatous, sclerodermic, sclerodermous** *a.* pert. to scleroderma; having a hard outer skin. **scleroid** *a.* of hard texture. **scleroma** *n.* hardening of tissues. **sclerosal** *a.* pert. to sclerosis. **sclerosis** *n.* hardening of organ as a result of excessive growth of connective tissue; induration.

scoff (skáf, skawf) *v.i.* to treat with derision; to mock; to jeer; *n.* expression of scorn; an object of derision. **-er** *n.* **-ingly** *adv.* [Scand.].

scold (skōld) *v.t.* and *v.i.* to find fault (with); to chide; to reprove angrily; to rebuke; *n.* one who scolds; a nagging, brawling woman. **-er** *n.* **-ing** *n.* rebuke. **-ingly** *adv.* [Ger. *schelten,* to brawl].

sconce (skáns) *n.* ornamental bracket fixed to wall, for carrying a light; small fort or breastwork; [O.Fr. *esconce,* fr. L. *abscondere,* to hide].

scone (skōn) *n.* a thin, flat cake.

scoop (skoop) *n.* article for ladling; kind of shovel; hollow place; (*Colloq.*) lucrative speculation; (*Slang*) publication of exclusive news in newspaper; *v.t.* to ladle out, shovel, lift, dig or hollow out with scoop; (*Slang*) to publish exclusive news; [prob. fr. Sw. *skopa,* a scoop].

scoot (skoot) *v.i.* to move off quickly; to dart away suddenly; to scamper off. **-er** *n.* a toy consisting of flat board mounted on two wheels, on which one foot rests, propelled by other foot and guided by handle attached to front wheel [fr. *shoot*].

scope (skōp) *n.* range of activity or application; space for action; room; play; outlet; opportunity [It. *scopo,* a target].

scor·bu·tic (skawr·bū'·tik) *a.* affected with, or relating to, scurvy.

scorch (skawrch) *v.t.* to burn the surface of; to parch; to shrivel; to char; to singe; to wither; to blast; *v.i.* to be burnt on surface; to dry up; to parch; (*Colloq.*) to drive at excessive speed. **scorched-earth policy,** destroying everything of value in path of hostile army. **-er** *n.* anything which scorches; a biting, sarcastic remark; (*Colloq.*) one who drives furiously; hot, sultry day. **-ing** *a.* burning superficially; oppressively hot.

score (skōr) *n.* a cut, notch, line, stroke; tally-mark, reckoning, bill, account; number twenty; reason; sake; number of points, runs, goals, etc. made in a game; arrangement of different parts of a musical composition on the page so that each bar may be read in all parts simultaneously; *v.t.* to mark with lines, scratches, furrows; to cut; to write down in proper order; to orchestrate; to enter in account book, to record; to make (points, etc.) in game; *v.i.* to add a point, run, goal, etc. in a game; to make a telling remark; to achieve a success. **-r** *n.* one who keeps official record of points, runs, etc. made in the course of a game; one who makes the point, run, etc. in a game. **scoring** *n.* **-book, -card, -sheet,** *n.* [O.N. *skor,* notch].

sco·ri·a (skō'·ri·a) *n.* dross or slag resulting from smelting of metal ores; rough, angular material sent out by volcano. *pl.* **scoriae. scorify** *v.t.* to reduce to dross or slag [Gk. *skoria,* dross].

scorn (skawrn) *n.* extreme disdain or contempt; object of derision; *v.t.* to contemn; to despise; to spurn. **-ful** *a.* **-fully** *adv.* [O.Fr. *escarnir*].

Scor·pi·o (skawr'·pi·ō) *n.* Scorpion, 8th sign of zodiac; scorpion. **-n** *n.* insect allied to spiders having slender tail which ends in very acute sting; whip armed with points like scorpion's tail; vindicative person with virulent tongue [L.].

scot (skát) *n.* formerly, tax, contribution, fine. **-free** *a.* unhurt; exempt from payment [O.N. *skot,* a tax].

Scot (skát) *n.* native of Scotland [O.E. *Scottas* (*pl.*) Irishmen].

Scotch (skách) *a.* pert. to Scotland or its inhabitants; Scots (adj. form usually preferred in Scotland); Scottish; *n.* Scots; Scots dialect; Scotch whiskey. — **broth,** broth made of pearl barley, various vegetables and beef for seasoning. — **pine,** Northern pine and Baltic fir or pine. **-man** *n.* a Scotsman. — **terrier,** small short-legged, rough-coated dog.

scotch (skách) *v.t.* to support, as a wheel, by placing some object to prevent its rolling; to prevent progress being made; to kill project in its initial stages; *n.* prop., wedge, strut.

scotch (skách) *v.* to wound slightly; to cut; *n.* scratch; mark or score.

Scots (skáts) *n.* dialect of English spoken in lowland Scotland; *a.* pert. to Scotland; Scottish. **-man, -woman** *n.* [O.E. *Scottas*].

Scot·tish (skát'·ish) *a.* pert. to Scotland or its people; Scots; Scotch [O.E. *Scottas*].

scoun·drel (skoun'drel) *n.* rascal; villain. **-ly** *a.* [etym. uncertain].

scour (skour) *v.t.* to clean or polish the surface of, by hard rubbing; to purge violently; to flush out; *v.i.* to clean by rubbing; *n.* act or material used in scouring. **-er** *n.* [O.Fr. *escurer*].

scour (skour) *v.t.* to pass rapidly along or over in search of something; to range; *v.i.* to scamper; to rove over; to scurry along. **-er** *n.* [etym. uncertain].

scourge (skurj) *n.* whip made of leather thongs; lash; punishment; a grievous affluction; one who or that which inflicts pain or devastates country; *v.t.* to flog; to lash; to chastise; to torment [L. *excoriare*].

scout (skout) *n.* one sent out to reconnoiter; lookout; a Boy Scout or Girl Scout; reconnaissance airplane; *v.t.* to reconnoiter; to spy out. **-master** *n.* adult instructor and organizer in the Boy Scouts [O.Fr. *escoute,* fr. *escouter,* to listen].

scout (skout) *v.t.* to reject with contempt; to sneer at [O.N. *skuta,* a taunt].

scow (skou) *n.* large flat-bottomed barge, with square ends; lighter [Dut. *schouw*].

scowl (skoul) *v.i.* to wrinkle brows in displeasure; to frown gloomily or sullenly; to look sullen, or annoyed; *n.* an angry frown [Scand.].

scrab·ble (skrab'·l) *v.t.* to scribble; to scrawl; *v.i.* to scratch with hands; [var. of *scrapple,* frequentative of *scrape*].

scrag (skrag) *n.* anything thin, lean, gaunt, or shrivelled; (*Slang*) long, thin neck; lean end of neck of mutton; (*Slang*) to wring neck of; to hang; to execute. **-ged** *a.* lean; thin. **-gedness, -gily** *n.* **-gily** *adv.* **-gly** *a.* rough and unkempt. **-gy** *a.* lean; jagged [earlier *crag*].

scram (skram) *interj.* (*Slang*) clear out'

scramble (skram'·bl) *v.i.* to move by crawling, climbing, etc. on all fours; to clamber; to struggle with others for; *v.t.* to collect together hurriedly and confusedly; to cook eggs by stirring when broken, in frying pan; *n.* scrambling; disorderly proceeding. **scrambling** *a.*

scrap (skrap) *n.* small detached piece or fragment; material left over which can be used as raw material again; *pl.* odds and ends; *v.t.* to make into scraps; to discard; *pa.t.* and *pa.p.* **-ped.** *pr.p.* **-ping. -book** *n.* a blank book in which to put clippings, pictures, etc. **-heap** *n.* a rubbish heap; pile of old iron, etc. **-py** *a.* consisting of scraps; fragmentary

[O.N. *skrap*].

scrap (skrap) *n.* and *v.i.* (*Slang*) fight; quarrel. **-pily** *adv.* **-piness** *n.* [var. of *scrape*].

scrape (skrāp) *v.t.* to abrade; to grate; to scratch; to remove by rubbing; to clean or smooth thus; *v.i.* to produce grating noise; to live parsimoniously; to bow awkwardly with drawing back of foot; to scratch in earth, as fowls; *n.* act or sound of scraping; scratch; predicament; embarrassing situation. **-r** *n.* one who, or that which, scrapes; tool with thin blade for scraping [O.E. *scrapian*].

scraper

scratch (skrach) *v.t.* to score or mark a narrow surface wound with claws, nails, or anything pointed; to abrade skin; to erase; to scrape; to withdraw name of entrant for race or competition; to write in a hasty, careless manner; to rub an itchy spot; *v.i.* to use claws or nails in tearing, abrading, or shallow digging; to strike out one's name from list of competitors; *n.* slight wound, mark, or sound made by sharp instrument; mark indicating the starting point in a handicap race; one who concedes a start in distance, time, etc. to other competitors; *a.* taken at random, brought together in a hurry, as *a scratch team;* denoting competitor without handicap. **-er** *n.* **-y** *a.* [mixture of earlier *scrat* and *cratch,* both of Teut. origin].

scrawl (skrawl) *v.t.* to write or draw untidily; to scribble; *v.i.* to write unskillfully; *n.* hasty, careless writing; **-er** *n.* [perh. fr. *scrabble*].

scraw·ny (skraw′·ni·) *a.* lean; scraggy; rawboned. **scrawniness** *n.* [var. of *scranny*].

scream (skrēm) *v.t.* and *v.i.* to utter a piercing cry; to shriek; to laugh immoderately; *n.* a shrill, piercing cry; a person who excites much laughter; laughter-provoking incident. **-ing** *a.* [imit. origin].

scree (skrē) *n.* pile of débris at base of cliff or hill; a talus [etym. uncertain].

screech (skrēch) *v.i.* to utter a harsh, shrill cry; *n.* a shrill and sudden, harsh cry. — **owl** *n.* owl with persistent harsh call [earlier *scritch,* of imit. origin].

screed (skrēd) *n.* long letter or passage; long boring speech [O.E. *screade,* a shred].

screen (skrēn) *n.* covered frame to shelter from heat, light, draft, or observation; partition of stone, metal, or wood, cutting off one part of ecclesiastical building from the rest; coarse, rectangular sieve for grading coal, pulverized material, etc.; white surface on which image is projected by optical means; troops thrown out towards enemy to protect main body; *v.t.* to provide with shelter or concealment; to protect from blame or censure; to sift; to film; to project film, lantern slide, etc. on a screen; to subject a person to political scrutiny. **-ing** *n.* employing a metal sheath to screen a magnetic field from the outside surroundings; (*Nuclear Physics*) reduction in intensity of radiations on passing through matter. **the screen,** the movies. **smoke screen** *n.* dense smoke artificially disseminated to conceal movements [O. Fr. *escran*].

screw (skrōō) *n.* in mechanics, a machine consisting of an inclined plane wound round a cylinder; cylinder with a spiral ridge running round it, used as holding agent or as mechanical power; turn of screw; twist to one side; a screw propeller; *v.t.* to fasten with screw; to press or stretch with screw; to work by turning; to twist round; to obtain by pressure; to extort; *v.i.* to assume a spiral motion; to move like a screw. **-driver** *n.* tool for turning screws. **-ed** *a.* **-er** *n.* **-ing** *a.* — **propeller** *n.* revolving shaft carrying two or more symmetrically arranged fan-like blades or flanges to create forward thrust of a ship. — **thread** *n.* spiral ridge, triangular or rectangular in section, on a screw cylinder. **-y** *a.* tortuous, like the thread or motion of a screw; (*Slang*) crazy; daft [O.Fr. *escroue*].

scrib·ble (skrib′·l) *v.t.* and *v.i.* to write carelessly; to draw meaningless lines; to scrawl; *n.* something scribbled. **-r** *n.* bad or careless

writer; a writer of unimportant trifles; **scribbling** *a.* used for scribbling; *n.* careless writing [L. *scribere,* to write].

scribe (skrīb) *n.* a writer; official or public writer; clerk; copyist; official copyist and expounder of Mosaic and traditional Jewish law; *v.t.* to incise wood, metal, etc. with a sharp point as a guide to cutting; **scribal** *a.* pert. to a scribe. **-r** *n.* sharp-pointed instrument used to mark off work [L. *scribere,* to write].

scrim·mage (skrim′·ij) *n.* a confused struggle; a tussle for the ball in football [Cf. *skirmish*].

scrimp (skrimp) *v.t.* to make too short or small; to stint. **-ed** *a.* **-ily** *adv.* **-iness** *n.* **-y** *a.* [O.E. *scrimman,* to shrink].

scrim·shaw (skrim′·shaw) (*Naut.*) *v.t.* and *v.i.* to make decorative article out of bone, whale's tooth, shell, etc.; *n.* such work.

scrip (skrip) *n.* a writing; interim certificate of holding bonds, stock, or shares [var. of *script*].

script (skript) *n.* kind of type, used in printing and typewriting, to imitate handwriting; handwriting; text of words of play, or of scenes and word of film; text of spoken part in broadcast; (*Law*) original or principal document [L. *scribere, scriptum,* to write].

scrip·ture (skrip′·cher) *n.* anything written; sacred writing; passage from Bible. **the Scriptures,** Old and New Testaments. **scriptural, scripture** *a.* according to Scriptures; biblical [L. *scribere, scriptum,* to write].

scriv·en·er (skriv′·an·er) *n.* rotary [L. *scribere,* to write].

scrof·u·la (skrŏf′·ya·la) *n.* a tuberculous condition most common in childhood. **scrofulitic, scrofulous** *a.* [L. = a little sow].

scroll (skrōl) *n.* roll of paper or parchment; a list; flourish at end of signature; ornament consisting of spiral volutes; (*Her.*) motto-bearing ribbon or inscription. **-ed** *a.* formed like, or contained in, a scroll [O.Fr. *escrou*].

scro·tum (skrō′·tam) *n.* external muscular sac which lodges testicles of the male.

scrounge (skrounj) *v.t.* and *v.i.* (*Slang*) to pilfer. **-r** *n.* **scrounging** *n.*

scrub (skrub) *v.t.* to clean with a hard brush, etc. and water; to scour; to rub; *v.i.* to clean by rubbing; to work hard for a living; *pa.t.* and *pa.p.* **-bed.** *pr.p.* **-bing.** *n.* act of scrubbing [D. *schrubben*].

scrub (skrub) *n.* stunted growth of trees and shrubs; an animal of unknown or inferior breeding; *a.* stunted; inferior; (*Sports*) pert. to a substitute team without training. **-by** *a.* mean and small; stunted; covered with scrub; unshaved [var. of *shrub*].

scruff (skruf) *n.* the back of the neck; nape. Also **skruff** (etym. uncertain).

scrump·tious (skrump′·shas) *a.* (*Slang*) delicious; delightful; nice.

scrunch (skrunch) *v.t.* to crush with the teeth; to crunch; to crush [fr. *crunch*].

scru·ple (skrōō′·pl) *n.* very small quantity; feeling of doubt; conscientious objection; qualm; *v.i.* to hesitate from doubt; to have compunction. **scrupulous** *a.* extremely conscientious; attentive to small points. **scrupulously** *adv.* **scrupulousness, scrupulosity** *n.* [L. *scrupulus*].

scru·ti·ny (skrōō′·ta·ni·) *n.* close search; critical examination; searching look or gaze. **scrutator** *n.* one who examines closely. **scrutinate, scrutinize** *v.t.* to examine into critically [L. *scrutari,* to examine closely].

scud (skud) *v.i.* to move quickly; to run before a gale; *pr.p.* **-ding.** *pa.t.* and *pa.p.* **-ded.** *n.* act of moving quickly; ragged cloud drifting rapidly in strong wind [Scand.].

scuff (skuf) *v.t.* to graze against; *v.i.* to shuffle along without raising the feet. *n.* a mark left by scuffing; a flat slipper with covering only over toes [Sw. *skuffa,* to push].

scuf·fle (skuf′·l) *v.i.* to struggle at close quarters; to fight confusedly; to shuffle along; *n.* confused fight, or struggle; a shuffling. **-r** *n.* [Sw. *skuffa,* to push].

scull (skul) *n.* short light oar pulled with the one hand; light racing boat of a long, narrow build; *v.t.* to propel boat by two sculls; to propel boat by means of oar placed over stern and worked alternately, first one way and then the other [O.Fr. *escuelerie,* fr. *escuele,* a dish].

scul·lion (skul′·yan) *n.* (*Arch.*) male under-servant who performed menial work; low,

mean, dirty fellow [O.Fr. *escouillon,* a dish-cloth].

sculp·ture (skulp′·cher) *n.* art of reproducing objects in relief or in the round out of hard material by means of chisel; carved work; art of modeling in clay or other plastic material, figures or objects to be later cast in bronze or other metals; *v.t.* to represent by sculpture. **sculptor** *n.* (*fem.* **sculptress**) one who carves or molds figures. **sculptural** *a.* [L. *sculpere, sculptum,* to carve].

scum (skum) *n.* impurities which rise to surface of liquids; foam or froth of dirty appearance; vile person or thing, riffraff; *v.t.* to take scum off; to skim; *v.i.* to form scum. *pr.p.* **-ming.** *pa.t.* and *pa.p.* **-med, -my** *a.* covered with scum; low-bred [Dan. *skum,* froth].

scup·per (skup′·er) *n.* channel alongside bulwarks of ship to drain away water from deck; [O.Fr. *escopir,* to spit out].

scurf (skurf) *n.* dry scales or flakes formed on skin; anything scaly adhering to surface. **-y** *a.* covered with scurf [O.E. *sceorf*].

scur·ril·ous (skur′·i·las) *a.* indecent; abusive; vile. **-ness, scurrility** *n.* vulgar language; vile abuse. **-ly** *adv.* [L. *scurrilis*].

scur·ry (skur′·i·) *v.i.* to hurry along; to run hastily. **-ing** *n.* [fr. *scour*].

scur·vy (skur′·vi·) *n.* deficiency disease due to lack of vitamin C; (*Med.*) scorbutus; *a.* afflicted with the disease; mean; low; vile. **scurvily** *adv.* in a scurvy manner. **scurviness** *n.* [fr. *scurf*].

scut (skut) *n.* a short tail, as that of a hare [O.N. *skjota,* to jut out].

scu·tate (skū′·tāt) *a.* (*Bot.*) shield-shaped; (*Zool.*) protected by scales or shieldlike processes [L. *scutum,* a shield].

scutch·eon. See **escutcheon.**

scu·tel·lum (skū·tel′·am) *n.* horny plate or scale. **scutellate, -d** *a.* (*Bot.*) rounded and nearly flat, like a saucer. **scutelliform** *a.* scutellate. **scutiform** *a.* (*Bot.*) shield-shaped [L. = a salver].

scut·tle (skut′·l) *n.* wide-mouthed vessel for holding coal [O.E. *scutel*].

scut·tle (skut′·l) *n.* hole with a cover, for light and air, cut in ship's deck or hatchway; hinged cover of glass to close a port-hole; *v.t.* to make holes in ship, esp. to sink it. **-butt** *n.* (*Naut.*) a water cask; (*Slang*) rumor [O.Fr. *escoutille,* a hatchway].

scut·tle (skut′·l) *v.i.* to rush away; to run hurriedly [freq. of *scud*].

scythe (sīTH) *n.* mowing implement; *v.t.* to cut with scythe; to mow [O.E. *sithe*].

sea (sē) *n.* mass of salt water covering greater part of earth's surface; named broad tract of this; certain large expanses of inland water, when salt; billow, or surge; swell of ocean; vast expanse; flood; large quantity. — **anemone** *n.* beautifully colored radiate marine animal, found on rocks on seacoast. **-board** *n.* coastline and its neighborhood; seashore. **-borne** *a.* carried on the sea or on a seagoing vessel. — **breeze** *n.* one which blows from sea toward land. **-coast** *n.* shore or border of land adjacent to sea. — **dog** *n.* dogfish; seal; pirate; old, experienced sailor. **-faring** *a.* **-girt** *a.* encircled by the sea. **-going** *a.* pert. to vessels which make long voyages by sea. — **green** *a.* having color of sea water; being of faint green color, with a slightly bluish tinge. — **gull** *n.* any gull. — **horse** *n.* a small fish, allied to pipedish, with horselike head; the walrus; fabulous animal, part horse, part fish. — **legs** *n.pl.* ability to walk on ship's deck in spite of rough seas. — **level** *n.* level of the sea taken at mean tide. — **lion** *n.* lion-headed, eared type of seal, eared seal. **-man** *n.* a sailor. **-manlike, -manly** *a.* **-manship** *n.* art of managing and navigating properly ship at sea. **-plane** *n.* airplane which can take off from and alight on sea. **-port** *n.* town with harbor. — **power,** command of the seas; nation with powerful fleet. **-scape** *n.* a picture representing maritime scene or view. — **serpent** *n.* enormous marine animal of serpentine form said to inhabit ocean. — **shell** *n.* a marine shell. **-shore** *n.* land adjacent to sea; (*Law*) ground between ordinary high-water mark and low-water mark. **-sick** *a.* suffering from seasickness. **-sickness** *n.* a disturbance of the nervous system with nausea and vomiting, produced by rolling and pitching of vessel at sea. **-side** *n.* and *a.* land adjacent to the sea. — **wall** *n.* embankment to prevent erosion or flooding. **-ward** *a.* and *adv.* towards the sea. **-weed** n. collective name for large group of marine plants (Algae). **-worthy** n. fit for proceeding to sea; able to stand up to buffetings of waves. **-worthiness** n. **at sea**, on the ocean; away from land; bewildered. **high seas**, the open sea [O.E. *sae*].

seal (sēl) n. an aquatic carnivorous animal with flippers as limbs, of which the eared variety furnishes rich fur pelt as well as oil; v.i. to hunt for seals. **-er** n. ship, or person, engaged in seal fishing. **-ery** n. seal-fishing station. **-skin** n. dressed skin or fur of eared seal; a. made of sealskin [O.E. *seolh*].

seal (sēl) n. piece of metal or stone engraved with a device, cipher, or motto for impression on wax, lead, etc.; impression made by this (on letters, documents, etc.); that which closes or secures; symbol, token, or indication; arrangement for making drainpipe joints airtight; v.t. to affix a seal to; to confirm; to ratify; to settle, as doom; v.t. to close up joints, cracks, etc. **-ed** a. having a seal affixed; enclosed; ratified. **-ing wax** n. wax composed of shellac or other resinous substances and turpentine tinted with coloring matter. — **ring** n. a signet ring. [O.Fr. *seel*, fr. L. *sigillum*, a seal].

seam (sēm) n. line of junction of two edges, e.g. of two pieces of cloth, or of two planks; thin layer or stratum, esp. of coal; v.t. to join by sewing together; to mark with furrows or wrinkles; to scar. **-less** a. having no seams; woven in the piece. **-ster** n. (*fem.* **-stress, sempstress**) one who sews by profession. **-y** a. showing seams; sordid [O.E. fr. *siwian*, to sew].

sé·ance (sā′·ans) n. assembly; meeting of spiritualists for consulting spirits and communicating with 'the other world' [Fr.].

sear (sir) v.t. to scorch or brand with a hot iron; to dry up; to wither; to render callous; to brown meat quickly a. (*Poetic.*) dry; withered [O.E. *searian*].

search (surch) v.t. to look over or through in order to find; to probe into; v.i. to look for; to seek; to explore; n. searching; quest; inquiry; investigation. **-ing** a. thorough; penetrating; keen; minute. **-ingly** adv. **-ingness** n. **-light** n. electric arc-light which sends concentrated beam in any desired direction. — **warrant** n. warrant to enable police to search premises of suspected person [Fr. *rechercher*, to look for].

sea·son (sē′·zn) n. one of four divisions of year—spring, summer, autumn, winter; in tropical regions, the wet or dry period of year; busy holiday period; time of the year for certain activities, foods, etc.; convenient time; period; time; v.t. to render suitable; to habituate; to give relish to; to spice; to mature; v.i. to grow fit for use; to become adapted. **-able** a. suitable or appropriate for the season; opportune; timely; fit. **-ableness** n. **-ably** adv. **-al** a. depending on, or varying with, seasons. **-ally** adv. **-ing** n. flavoring. — **ticket** n. one valid for definite period. **open season**, time when something is permitted [L. *satio*, sowing].

seat (sēt) n. thing made or used for sitting; manner of sitting (of riding, etc.); right to sit (e.g. in council, etc.); sitting part of body; part of trousers which covers buttocks; locality of disease, trouble, etc.; country house; place from which a country is governed; v.t. to place on a seat; to cause to sit down; assign a seat to; to fit up with seats; to establish. **-ed** a. fixed; confirmed; settled. [O.N. *saeti*].

se·ba·ceous (si·bā′·shas) a. made of, or pert. to tallow or fat; secreting oily matter [L. *sebum*, tallow].

se·cant (sē′·kant, kant) a. cutting; dividing into two parts; n. any straight line which cuts another line, curve, or figure; a straight line drawn from center of circle through one end of an arc, and terminated by a tangent drawn through other end; in trigonometry, ratio of hypotenuse to another side of a right-angled triangle is secant of angle between these two sides. [L. *secare*, to cut].

se·cede (si·sēd′) v.i. to withdraw formally from federation, alliance, etc. **-er** n. **secession** n. seceding from fellowship, alliance, etc.; withdrawal; departure [L. *secedere*, to go apart].

se·clude (si·klood′) v.t. to shut up apart; to guard from or to remove from sight or resort. **-d** a. shut off; remote; sequestered. **-dly** adv. **seclusion** n. **seclusive** a. tending to seclude; retiring [L. *secludere*, to shut away].

sec·ond (sek′·and) a. next to first; other; another; inferior; subordinate; n. one who, or that which, follows the first; one next and inferior; one assisting, esp. principal in duel

or boxing-match; sixtieth part of a minute; (*Mus.*) interval contained between two notes on adjacent degrees of the staff; moment; n.pl. inferior quality of commodity or article; v.t. to support, esp. a motion before a meeting or council; to back; to encourage.**Second Advent**, belief that Christ will return to earth in visible form. **—best** n. and a. best except one. — **childhood**, dotage, senility. **—class** a. of an inferior order; mediocre. **—hand** a. not new; having been used or worn; indirect. — **lieutenant** n. lowest commissioned rank in Army. **-ly** adv. in the second place. — **nature**, acquired habit. **—rate** a. of inferior quality, value, etc. — **sight** n. prophetic vision. **to play second fiddle**, to play or act subordinate part [L. *secundus*].

sec·ond·ar·y (sek′·an·der·i·) a. succeeding next in order to the first; of second place, origin, rank; second-rate; inferior; unimportant; pert. to education and schools intermediate between elementary schools and university; (*Geol.*) relating to Mesozoic period; n. one who occupies a subordinate place. — **color**, color obtained by combination of primary colors, blue, red, and yellow. **secondarily** adv. in a secondary or subordinate manner; not primarily. [fr. *second*].

se·cret (sē′·krit) a. kept or meant to be kept from general knowledge; concealed; unseen; private; n. something kept secret or concealed; a mystery; governing principle known only to initiated. **secrecy** n. keeping or being kept secret; fidelity in keeping a secret; retirement; privacy; concealment. **-ly** adv. **-ness** n. secrecy. **secretive** (or ·krē′·) a. uncommunicative; reticent; underhand. **-ively** adv. **-iveness** n. [L. *secretus*, separated].

sec·re·tar·y (sek′·ra·ter·i·) n. one employed to deal with papers and correspondence, keep records, prepare business, etc.; confidential clerk; official in charge of a particular department of government; a desk with bookshelves on top. **secretarial** a. pert. to duties of a secretary. **secretariat** n. administrative office or officials controlled by secretary; the secretarial force of an office. **-ship** n. office or post of a secretary [L. *secretum* (something) secret].

se·crete (si·krēt′) v.t. to hide or conceal; of gland, etc. to collect and supply particular substance in body; a. separate; distinct. **secreta** n.pl. products of secretion. **secretion** n. substance elaborated by gland out of blood or body fluids; process of so secreting or elaborating. **secretional** a. **secretive** a. promoting or causing secretion. **secretor** n. a secreting organ or gland. **secretory** a. [L. *secernere*, *secretum*, to set apart].

sect (sekt) n. religious denomination; followers of philosopher or religious leader; faction. **-arian** a. pert. to a sect; n. one of a sect; a bigot; a partisan. **-arianism** n. devotion to the interests of a sect. **-ary** n. one of a sect; a dissenter [L. *secta*, fr. *sequi*, to follow].

sec·tion (sek′·shan) n. cutting or separating by cutting; part separated from the rest; division; portion; a piece; a subdivision of subject matter of book, chapter, statute; printer's reference mark (§) used for footnotes; representation of portion of building or object exposed when cut by imaginary vertical plane so as to show its construction and interior; surveyor's scaled drawing showing variations in surface level of ground along base-line; (*Geom.*) plane figure formed by cutting a solid by another plane; line formed by intersection of two surfaces; distinct part of a city, country, people, etc.; small military unit; (*Bot.* and *Zool.*) thin, translucent slice of organic or inorganic matter mounted on slide for detailed microscopic examination. **-al** a. pert. to, made up of sections; partial; local; (of paper) ruled in small squares. **-alism** n. partial regard for limited interests of one particular class at expense of others. **-ally** adv. **-ize** v.t. to divide out in sections [L. *secare*, *sectum*, to cut].

sec·tor (sek′·ter) n. portion of circle enclosed by two radii and the arc which they intercept; mathematical instrument; (*Mil.*) a subdivision of the combat area. **-al** a. [L. *secare*, *sectum*, to cut].

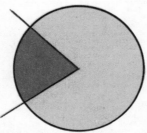

sec·u·lar (sek′·ya·ler) a. worldly; temporal, as opposed to spiritual; lay; pert. to anything not religious; lasting for, occurring once in, a century or age; n. layman; clergyman, not

bound by vow of poverty and not belonging to religious order. **-ization** n. **secularize** v.t. to convert from spiritual to secular use; to make worldly. **secularism** n. ethical doctrine which advocates a moral code independent of all religious considerations or practices. **-ist** n. **-ity** n. worldliness; secularism. **-ly** adv. [L. *saecularis*, fr. *saeculum*, an age, a century].

se·cure (si·kūr′) a. free from care, anxiety, fear; safe; fixed; stable; in close custody; certain; confident; v.t. to make safe, certain, fast; to close, or confine, effectually; to gain possession of; to obtain; to assure. **securable** a. **securance** n. assurance; act of securing. **-ly** adv. **-ness** n. free from anxiety; feeling of security. **-r** n. **security** n. being secure; what secures; protection; assurance; anything given as bond, caution, or pledge. **Security Council** n. branch of United Nations Organization, set up in 1945, to settle international disputes and to prevent aggression. **securities** n.pl. general term for shares, bonds, stocks, debentures, etc.; documents giving to holder right to possess certain property [L. *securus*, fr. *se-*, without; *cura*, care].

se·dan (si·dan′) n. old-time closed conveyance with a chair inside for one, carried on two poles; a sedan chair; a closed automobile with two full seats [orig. made at *Sedan*, France].

se·date (si·dāt′) a. staid; not excitable, composed; calm. **-ly** adv. **-ness** n. **sedative** a. tending to calm; soothing; n. agent, external or internal, which soothes [L. *sedare*, to calm].

sed·en·tar·y (sed′·an·ter·i·) a. sitting much; requiring sitting posture, as certain forms of employment; inactive. **sedentariness** n. [L. *sedere*, to sit].

sedge (sej) n. any marshgrass. **sedgy** a. [O.E. *secg*].

sed·i·ment (sed′·a·mant) n. matter which settles to bottom of liquid; lees; dregs. **-ary** a. composed of sediment, esp. of rock laid down as deposits by water action. **-ation** n. [L. *sedere*, to settle].

se·di·tion (si·dish′·an) n. any act aimed at disturbing peace of realm or producing insurrection. **-ary** n. one who incites sedition. **seditious** a. pert. to, tending to excite sedition. **seditiously** adv. **seditiousness** n. [L. *seditio*, a going apart].

se·duce (si′·dūs′) v.t. to lead astray; to draw aside from path of rectitude and duty; to induce woman to surrender chastity; to allure. **-ment** n. seduction. **-r** n. **seducible** a. liable to be led astray; corruptible. **seduction** n. act of seducing. **seductive** a. **seductively** adv. **seductiveness** n. [L. *seducere*, to lead aside].

sed·u·lous (sej′·a·las) a. diligent; steady; industrious; persevering. **sedulity** n. **-ness** n. **-ly** adv. [L. *sedulus*].

see (sē) n. diocese or jurisdiction of bishop; province of archbishop. **the Holy See**, the papal court [O.Fr. *siet*, fr. L. *sedere*, to sit].

see (sē) v.t. to perceive by eye; to behold; to observe; to form an idea; to understand; to have interview with; to visit; to meet with; v.i. to have the power of sight; to pay regard; to consider; to give heed; to understand; to apprehend. pa.t. **saw.** pa.p. **seen. -r** n. one who sees; one who foresees events, has secondsight; a prophet. **-ing** conj. considering; since; n. act of perceiving; sight [O.E. *seon*].

seed (sēd) n. ovule, which gives origin to new plant; one grain of this; such grains saved or used for sowing; that from which anything springs; origin; source; progeny; offspring; sperm; first principle; v.t. to sow with seed; to remove seeds from; to arrange draw for sports tournament, so that best players, etc. should not be drawn against each other in earlier rounds; v.i. to produce seed; to shed seed. **-ed** a. sown. **-ily** adv. in seedy manner. **-iness** n. being seedy; shabbiness. **-less** a. **-ling** n. young plant or tree, grown from seed. **-y** a. abounding with seeds; run to seed; shabby; worn out; miserable looking. **to run to seed**, to produce flowers and seed at expense of leaves or roots; to go to waste or ruin [O.E. *saed*].

seek (sēk) v.t. to make search or enquiry for; to look for; to ask for; to strive after; v.i. to make search. pa.t. and pa.p. **sought. -er** n. [O.E. *secan*].

seem (sēm) v.i. to appear (to be or to do); to look; to appear to one's judgment. **-ing** a. appearing like; apparent; n. appearance; apparent likeness; **-ingly** adv. **-liness** n. **-ly**

a. fit; becoming; *adv.* in a decent or proper manner [O.N. *sōma*].

seen (sēn) *pa.p.* of **see.**

seep (sēp) *v.i.* to ooze; to trickle; to leak away. **-age** *n.* [O.E. *sipian*, to soak].

se·er (sē'·er) *n.* a prophet [fr. *see*].

seer·suck·er (sir'·suk·er) *n.* a cotton fabric of alternating plain and crinkled stripes [fr. Pers. *shir o shakkar* = milk and sugar].

see·saw (sē'·saw) *n.* game in which two children sit at opposite ends of plank supported in middle and swing up and down; plank for this; up-and-down motion; *a.* moving up and down or to and fro; reciprocal; *v.i.* to move up and down [imit.].

seethe (sēTH) *v.t.* to soak; *v.i.* to be in a state of ebullition; to be violently agitated; [O.E. *seothan*, to boil].

seg·ment (seg'·mant) *n.* part cut off from a figure by a line; part of circle contained between chord and arc of that circle; section; portion; part; *v.t.* and *v.i.* to separate into segments. **-al** *a.* relating to a segment. **-ary**, **-ate** *a.* **-ation** *n.* **-ed** *a.* [L. *segmentum*].

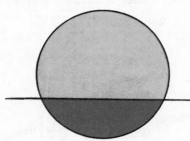

seg·re·gate (seg'·ra·gāt) *v.t.* and *v.i.* to set or go apart from the rest; to isolate; to separate; *a.* set apart; separate from the others. **segregation** *n.* [L. *segregare*, to remove from the flock (*grex*)].

se·gui·dil·la (se·gē·dē'·lya) *n.* graceful, lively Spanish dance; music for it [Sp.].

seign·ior (sēn'·yawr), **sei·gneur** (sēn·yur') *n.* a feudal lord of a manor; title of honor or respectful address. **-age, seignorage** *n.* anything claimed by sovereign or feudal superior as prerogative. **-ality** *n.* authority or domains of a seignior. **-ial, -ial, signorial** *a.* manorial. **grand seignor,** Sultan of Turkey [Fr. fr. L. *senior*, elder].

seine (sān) *n.* open net for sea fishing. *v.t.* to catch fish by dragging a seine through water [Fr. fr. L. *sagena*, a fishing net].

seism (sizm) *n.* earthquake. **-al, -ic** *a.* pert. to or produced by earthquake. **-ogram** *n.* record of earthquake made by seismograph. **-ograph** *n.* instrument which records distance and intensity of slightest earth tremors. **-ologic, -al** *a.* **-ologist** *n.* one versed in seismology. **-ology** *n.* the study of earthquakes and their causes and effects [Gk. *seismos*, an earthquake].

seize (sēz) *v.t.* to grasp; to take hold of; to take possession by force or legal authority; to arrest; to capture; to comprehend; *v.i.* to take hold. **seizable** *a.* **seizure** *n.* act of seizing; thing or property seized; sudden attack, as apoplectic stroke [Fr. *saisir*].

sel·dom (sel'·dam) *adv.* rarely [O.E. *seldum*].

se·lect (sa·lekt') *v.t.* to choose; to cull; to prefer; *a.* of choice quality; of special excellence; chosen; picked; exclusive; *n.* the best people. **-ed** *a.* **-edly** *adv.* **-ion** *n.* selecting; variety of articles from which to select; (*Mus.*) medley; (*Biol.*) process, according to the evolutionary theory, by which certain members of species survive and others, unfit, are gradually eliminated. **-ive** *a.* having power of selection; discriminating. **-ively** *adv.* **-ivity** *n.* **-or** *n.* [L. *legere, selectum*].

sel·e·nite (sel'an·it) *n.* a colorless and translucent crystalline form of gypsum (calcium sulphate) [Gk. *selēnē*, the moon].

self (self) *n.* one's individual person; one's personal interest; ego; subject of individual consciousness; selfishness. *pl.* **selves** (selvz). *pron. affix* used to express emphasis or a reflexive usage; *a.* of same color, uniform, same throughout; of same material, etc.; *prefix* used in innumerable compounds. **—abandonment** *n.* disregard of self. **—abnegation** *n.* self-denial. **—abuse** *n.* masturbation; abuse of one's own powers. **—assurance** *n.* self-confidence. **—centered** *a.* egoistic. **—confidence** *n.* whole-hearted reliance on one's own powers and resources. **—confident** *a.* **—consciousness** *n.* an embarrassed state of mind leading to confusion due to belief that one is object of critical judgment by others present. **—conscious** *a.* **—contained** *a.* of a reserved nature; complete in itself; (of a house) having a separate entrance, detached. **—control** *n.* control over oneself, temper, emotions, and desires. **—defense** *n.* the act of defending one's person or justifying one's actions. **—denial** *n.* refraining from gratifying one's desires or appetites; unselfishness, to the point of deprivation. **—determina-**

tion *n.* free will; right of a people or nation to work out its own problems and destiny, free from interference from without. **—governing** *a.* autonomous; having a legislature elected by, and responsible to, those governed. **—government** *n.* **—indulgence** *n.* undue gratification of one's appetites or desires. **—interest** *n.* selfishness. **-ish** *a.* concerned unduly over personal profit or pleasure; lacking consideration for others; mercenary; greedy. **-less** *a.* unselfish. **—pity** *n.* morbid pleasure in nursing one's own woes. **—possessed** *a.* calm and collected; able to control one's feelings and emotions; composed; undisturbed. **—preservation** *n.* instinctive impulse to avoid injury or death. **—respect** *n.* a proper regard for one's own person, character, or reputation. **—respecting** *a.* **—respectful** *a.* **—righteous** *a.* thinking oneself faultless; esteeming oneself as better than others; pharisaical; sanctimonious. **—sacrifice** *n.* foregoing personal advantage or comfort for the sake of others. **-same** *a.* the very same; identical. **—satisfaction** *n.* personal reassurance; (in a bad sense) smug conceit. **—satisfied** *a.* **—seeker** *n.* one who seeks only his own profit or pleasure. **—seeking** *a.* seeking one's own interest or happiness. **—starter** *n.* an automatic contrivance used for starting internal-combustion engine of automobile. **—styled** *a.* so-called, without any real warrant or authority; self-assumed. **—sufficient** *a.* sufficient in itself; relying on one's own powers. **—supporting** *a.* not dependent on others for a living [O.E.].

sell (sel) *v.i.* to dispose of for an equivalent, usually money; to deal in; to betray for money or a consideration; to delude; (*Slang*) to trick; to have for sale; to promote sale of; *v.t.* to fetch a price; to be in demand; *pa.t.* and *pa.p.* **sold.** *n.* deception; hoax. **-er** *n.* one who sells; vendor [O.E. *sellan*].

Selt·zer (selt'·ser) *n.* a carbonated mineral water; artificial mineral water; aerated with carbon dioxide [corrupt. of *Selters*].

sel·vage, selvedge (sel'·vij) *n.* edge of cloth finished to prevent raveling; strong edging of web [fr. *self-edge*].

selves (selvz) *n.pl.* of **self.**

se·man·tic (sa·man'·tik) *a.* pert. to meaning of words. **-s** *n.pl.* branch of linguistic research concerned with studying meaning and changes in meaning of words [Gk. *sēmainein*, to mean].

sem·a·phore (sem'·a·fōr) *n.* a post with movable arm or arms used for signaling; a system of signaling by human or mechanical arms [Gk. *sēma*, sign; *pherein*, to bear].

se·ma·si·ol·o·gy (sa·mā·si·ál'·a·ji·) *n.* the science of the development of the meanings of words, semantics. **semasiological** *a.* [Gk. *sēmasia*, meaning; *logos* a discourse].

sem·blance (sem'·blan(t)s) *n.* real or seeming likeness; appearance; image; form; figure [Fr. *sembler*, to seem].

se·men (sē'·man) *n.* male secretion containing sperm [L. = seed].

se·mes·ter (sa·mes'·ter) *n.* one of two or three divisions of the school year [Fr. *semestre*, fr. L. *sex*, six; *mensis*, a month].

sem·i- (sem'·i) *prefix* with the meaning of half, partly, imperfectly, etc., used in the construction of compound terms, the meaning being usually obvious. **-annual** *a.* half-yearly. **-breve** *n.* (*Mus.*) a whole note. **-circle** *n.* plane figure bounded by diameter and portion of circumference of a circle which it cuts off. **-circled, -circular** *a.* **-colon** *n.* punctuation mark (;) used to separate clauses of a sentence requiring a more marked separation than is indicated by a comma. **-final** *n.* a match, round, etc. qualifying winner to contest the final. **-tone** *n.* (*Mus.*) half a tone; smallest interval used in music [L. = half].

sem·i·nal (sem'·a·nal) *a.* pert. to seed of plants or semen of animals; reproductive. **semination** *n.* act of sowing or disseminating; seeding. **seminiferous, seminific** *a.* seedbearing [L. *semen*, seed].

sem·i·nar (sem'·a·när) *n.* group of advanced students pursuing research in a specific subject under supervision [L. *semen*, seed].

sem·i·nar·y (sem'·a·ner·i·) *n.* academy; secondary school for girls; a training college for priesthood or ministry; *a.* trained in seminary. **seminarist** *n.* [L. *seminarium*, nursery].

Sem·i·nole (sem'·a·nōl) one of a nomadic tribe of American Indians, formerly living

S.E. of the Mississippi (Florida, etc.).

se·mi·ol·o·gy (sē·mi·al·a·ji·) *n.* (*Med.*) study of signs and symptoms of disease; symptomatology. **semiotics** *n.* science or language of signs. [Gk. *sēmeion*, a mark].

Sem·ite (sem'·it) *n.* member of a speech family comprising Hebrews, Arabs, Assyrians, etc.; descendant of Shem (Genesis x). **Semitic** *a.*

sem·o·li·na (sem·a·lē'·na) *n.* hard grains of wheat used in production of spaghetti, macaroni, etc. Also **semola** [L. *simila*, wheatmeal].

sen (sen) *n.* Japanese copper coin.

sen·ate (sen'·it) *n.* supreme legislative and administrative assembly in ancient Rome; upper house of legislature, e.g. U.S., France, Canada, and others; governing or advisory body in many universities. **senator** *n.* a member of a senate. **senatorial** *a.* [L. *senatus*, council of old men, fr. *senex*, old man].

send (send) *v.t.* to cause to go; to transmit; to forward; to despatch; to throw; *v.i.* to despatch messenger; to transmit message. *pa.t.* and *pa.p.* **sent** [O.E. *sendan*].

se·nes·cence (sa·nes'·ans) *n.* the state of growing old; decay; old age. **senescent** *a.* growing old [L. *senescere*, to grow old].

sen·es·chal (sen'·a·shal) *n.* functionary who superintended household affairs of feudal lord in Middle Ages; steward [O.Fr.].

se·nile (sē'·nil) *a.* pert. to old age; aged; doting. **senility** *n.* degenerative physical or mental conditions accompanying old age; old age [L. *senex*, old man].

sen·ior (sēn'·yer) *a.* older; superior in rank or standing; pert. to highest class of school or college; *n.* a person older, or of higher rank, or of longer service, than another; an aged person; a member of a senior class. **-ity** *n.* state of being older; precedence in rank, or longer in service; priority [L. = older].

sen·na (sen'·a) *n.* a valuable purgative drug [Ar. *sana*].

se·ñor (sān·yawr') *n.* Spanish form of address; sir; gentleman; equivalent to Mr.; **-a** *n.* lady; madam; Mrs. **-ita** *n.* young lady; Miss.

sen·sa·tion (sen·sā'·shan) *n.* what we learn through senses; state of physical consciousness; effect produced on a sense organ by external stimulus; excited feeling or state of excitement; exciting event; strong impression. **sensate** *a.* perceived by the senses. **-al** *a.* pert. to perception by senses; producing great excitement and surprise; melodramatic. **-alist** *n.* **-ally** *adv.* [L. *sensus*, feeling].

sen·sa·tion·al·ism (sen·sā'·shan·a·liz·am) *n.* matter, language or style designed to excite and please vulgar taste; sensualism. (*philos.*) doctrine that all knowledge originates in sense perception [L. *sensus*, feeling].

sense (sens) *n.* any of the bodily faculties of perception or feeling; sensitiveness of any or all of these faculties; ability to perceive; mental alertness; consciousness; significance; meaning; coherence; wisdom; good judgment; prudence. *pl.* wits; faculties. *v.t.* to perceive; to suspect; (*Colloq.*) to understand. **-less** *a.* destitute of sense; insensible; unfeeling; silly; foolish; stupid; absurd. **-lessly** *adv.* **-lessness** *n.* [L. *sentire, sensum*, to feel].

sen·si·ble (sen'·sa·bl) *a.* capable of being perceived by the senses; characterized by good sense; perceptible; aware; conscious; appreciable; reasonable. **sensibility** *n.* power of experiencing sensation; faculty by which mind receives intuitions; capacity of feeling. **sensibly** *adv.* [fr. *sense*].

sen·si·tive (sen'·sa·tiv) *a.* open to, or acutely affected by, external stimuli or impressions; easily affected or altered; responsive to slight changes; easily upset by criticism. **-ly** *adv.* **-ness** *n.* quality or state of being sensitive. **sensitivity** *n.* sensitiveness; keen sensibility; capacity to receive and respond to external stimuli [Fr. *sensitif*, fr. L. *sentire*, to feel].

sen·si·tize (sen'·sa·tiz) *v.t.* to render sensitive; in photography, to render film, paper, etc. sensitive to the chemical action of light. **sensitizer** *n.* [L. *sensus*, feeling].

son·so·ry (sen'·sa·ri·) *a.* pert. to, or serving, senses; conveying sensations, as the nervefibers [L. *sensus*, feeling].

sen·su·al (sen'·shoo'·al) *a.* pert. to the senses; given to pursuit of pleasures of sense; self-indulgent; voluptuous; lewd. **-ization** *n.* **-ize** *v.t.* to make or render sensual. **-ism** *n.* fleshly indulgence. **-ist** *n.* one given to lewd or loose mode of life; **-istic** *a.* **-ity** *n.* **-ly** *adv.* **sensuous** *a.* stimulating, or apprehended by, senses. **sensuously** *adv.* **sensuousness** *n.* [L. *sensus*, feeling].

sent (sent) *pa.t.* and *pa.p.* of **send.**

sen·tence (sen'·tans) *n.* combination of words, which is complete as expressing a thought; opinion; judgment passed on criminal by court or judge; decision; *v.t.* to pass sentence upon; to condemn. **sentENTious** (sen·ten'·chas) *a.* abounding with axioms and maxims; short and energetic; pithy; moralizing [L. *sententia*, an opinion].

sen·tient (sen'·shi·ant) *a.* feeling or capable of feeling; perceiving by senses; sensitive. **sentience, sentiency** *n.* consciousness at a sensory level. **-ly** *adv.* [L. *sentire*, to feel].

sen·ti·ment (sen'·ta·mant) *n.* abstract emotion; tendency to be moved by feeling rather than idea; opinion. **sentimental** (sen·ta·men'·tal) *a.* abounding with sentiment; romantic; emotional; foolishly tender. **-alism, -ality** *n.* affected and distorted expression of sentiment revealing a superficiality of feeling. **-alist** *n.* one given to sentimental talk; one swayed by emotions rather than by reason. [O.Fr. *sentement*, fr. L. *sentire*, to feel].

sen·ti·nel (sen'·ta·nal) *n.* guard; sentry; *a.* acting as sentinel; watching [Fr. *sentinelle*].

sen·try (sen'·tri·) *n.* soldier on guard; sentinel; duty of sentry. — **box** *n.* small shelter used by sentry [fr. *sanctuary*, a place of safety].

sentry box

se·pal (sē'·pal) *n.* (*Bot.*) leaf-like member of outer covering, or calyx, of flower. **-ous** *a.* having sepals [Fr. *sépale*].

sep·a·rate (sep'·a·rāt) *v.t.* to part in any manner; to divide; to disconnect; to detach; to withdraw; to become disunited; *a.* divided; disconnected; apart; distinct; individual. **separability** *n.* **separable** *a.* **-ly** *adv.* **-ness** *n.* **separation** *n.* act of separating; state of being separate. **separationist** *n.* one who supports policy of breaking away from a union of states or countries; a separatist. **separatism** *n.* act or policy of separating or withdrawing from any union, esp. religious or political. **separatist** *n.* [L. *separare*].

se·pi·a (sē'·pi·a) *n.* brown pigment obtained from ink bags of cuttlefish, uased as watercolor [Gk. = cuttlefish].

sep·sis (sep'·sis) *n.* (*Med.*) state of having bodily tissue infected by bacteria. **septic** *a.* [Gk. = putrefaction].

sept (sept) *n.* clan, race, or family, proceeding from common progenitor.

Sep·tem·ber (sep·tem'·ber) *n.* ninth month of year (L. *septem*, seven, as being 7th month of Roman year).

sep·te·nar·y (sep'·ta·ner·i·) *a.* crossing of seven; lasting seven years; occurring once in seven years. [L. *septem*, seven].

sep·tet, septette (sep·tet') *n.* (*Mus.*) composition for seven voices or instruments [L. *septem*, seven].

sep·tic (sep'·tik) *a.* pert. to sepsis; infected. **-emia, -aemia** (sep·ta·sē·mi·a) *n.* blood poisoning. **-ally** *adv.* [Gk.].

sep·tu·a·ge·nar·i·an (sep·t(y)oo·a·ja·ner'·i·an) *n.* person between seventy and eighty years of age. **septuagenary** *a.* consisting of seventy; seventy years old; *n.* a septuagenarian [L. *septuaginta*, seventy].

Sep·tu·a·ges·i·ma (sep·t(y)oo·a·jes'·a·ma) *n.* third Sunday before Lent, seventy days before Easter. [L. *septuagesimus*, seventieth].

Sep·tu·a·gint (sep'·too·a·jint) *n.* the first and only complete version in Greek of the Old Testament. **-al** *a.* [L. *septuaginta*, seventy (compilers)].

sep·tu·ple (sep'·too·pl) *a.* sevenfold; *v.t.* to multiply by seven [L. *septem*, seven].

sep·ul·cher (sep'·al·ker) *n.* tomb; grave; burial vault; *v.t.* to place in a sepulcher.

sepulchral (sa·pul'·kral) *a.* pert. to burial, the grave, or monuments erected to dead; funereal; mournful. **sepulture** *n.* act of burying dead [L. *Sepulcrum*].

se·qua·cious (sa·kwā'·shas) *a.* following; attendant; easily led. **-ness, sequacity** *n.* [L. *sequi*, to follow].

se·quel (sē'·kwal) *n.* that which follows; consequence; issue; end; continuation, complete in itself, of a novel or narrative previously published [L. *sequi*, to follow].

se·quence (sē'·kwans)·*n.* connected series; succession; run of three or more cards of same suit in numerical order; part of scenario of film; (*Mus.*) repetition of musical figure, either melodic or harmonic, on different degrees of sale. **sequent** *a.* following; succeeding; *n.* sequence. **sequential** *a.* in succession. **sequentially** *adv.* [L. *sequi*, to follow].

se·ques·ter (si·kwes'·ter) *v.t.* to put aside; to separate; to seclude; to cause to retire into

se·quin (sē'·kwin) *n.* small, ornamental metal disk on dresses, etc. [It. *zecchino*, fr. *zecca*, mint].

Se·quoi·a (si·kwoi'·a) *n.* genus of gigantic coniferous evergreen trees native to California [fr. *Sequoiah*, a Cherokee Indian chief].

se·rag·lio (si·ral'·yō) *n.* harem or women's quarters in royal household [It. *serraglio*, an enclosure, fr. L. *sera*, a bolt].

ser·aph (ser'·af) *n.* member of the highest order of angels. **-s, -im** *n.pl.* **-ic, -ical** *a.* [Heb.].

Serb, Serbian (surb, sur'·bi·an) *a.* pert. to Serbia; *n.* native or inhabitant of Serbia, the chief constituent state of Yugoslavia.

sere (sir) *a.* dry; withered [fr. *sear*].

ser·e·nade (ser·a·nād') *n.* music of quiet, simple, melodious character sung or played at night below person's window, esp. by lover; *v.t.* to entertain with serenade. **-r** *n.* **serenata** *n.* instrumental work, between suite and symphony [It. *serenata*, fr. *sereno*, the open air].

ser·en·dip·i·ty (ser·an·dip'·a·ti·) *n.* knack of stumbling upon interesting discoveries in a casual manner ['The Three Princes of Serendip' by Horace Walpole].

se·rene (sa·rēn') *a.* clear and calm; unclouded; fair; unruffled; quiet; placid; composed. **-ly** *adv.* **-ness, serenity** *n.* condition or quality of being serene [L. *serenus*, clear].

serf (surf) *n.* under feudalism; a bondman; vassal. **-age, -dom, -hood** *n.* [L. *servus*, a slave].

serge (surj) *n.* hard-wearing worsted fabric [L. *serica*, silk].

sergeant, sergeant (sar'·jant) *n.* noncommissioned officer in army, ranking above corporal; police officer ranking above constable; officer of a law court. **-s, sergeancy** *n.* — **at arms** *n.* officer attendant on legislative body, charged with preservation of order. — **major** *n.* highest noncommissioned officer [Fr. *sergent*, fr. L. *serviens*, serving].

se·ri·al (sir'·i·al) *a.* consisting of a series; appearing in successive parts or installments; *n.* a periodical publication; a tale or writing published or broadcast, etc., in successive numbers or programs. **-ize** *v.t.* to publish as a serial. **-ly, seriately** *adv.* in a regular series or order. **seriatim** (sir·ē·āt'·am) *adv.* point by point; one after another [fr. *series*].

se·ries (sir'·ēz) *n.* s. and *pl.* succession of related objects or matters; sequence; order; related objects or matters; sequence; set; books, bound and printed in same style, usually on kindred subjects; (*Elect.*) end-to-end arrangement of batteries or circuits which are traversed by the same current [L. *series*].

ser·if (ser'·if) *n.* (*Printing*) a fine line at the end of the stems and arms of unconnected Roman type letters, as M, y, etc.

se·ri·ous (sir'·i·as) *a.* grave in manner or disposition; earnest; important; attended with danger; in earnest. **-ly** *adv.* **-ness** *n.* [L. *serius*].

ser·jeant. See **sergeant**.

ser·mon (sur'·man) *n.* discourse for purpose of religious instruction usually based on Scripture; serious and admonitory address. **-ic, -al** *a.* of the nature of a sermon. **-ize** *v.t.* to preach earnestly; to compose a sermon. **-izer** *n.* [L. *sermo*, a discourse].

se·rous (sir'·as) *a.* pert. to, containing, or producing serum; watery; thin. **serosity** *n.* state of being serous [L. *serum*].

ser·pent (sur'·pant) *n.* snake; reptile without feet; treacherous or malicious person; kind of firework; (*Cap.*) constellation in northern hemisphere (*Mus.*) bass wooden wind instrument bent in a serpentine form; *a.* deceitful treacherous. **-ine** *a.* relating to, or like, serpent; winding; spiral; meandering; crafty; treacherous; *n.* skin; *v.i.* to wind in and out like a serpent. **-inely** *adv.* [L. *serpere*, to creep].

ser·rate, serrated (ser'·āt, ·ed) *a.* notched or cut like saw, as a leaf edge. **serration** *n.* formation in shape of saw. **serrature** *n.* series of notches, like that of saw. **serriform** *a.* toothed like a saw. [L. *serra*, a saw].

ser·ried (ser'·id) *a.* in close order; pressed shoulder to shoulder [Fr. *serrer*, to lock].

se·rum (sir'·am) *n.* watery secretion; whey; thin straw-colored fluid, residue of plasma or

liquid part of the blood; such fluid used for inoculation or vaccination [L. = whey].

serpent

serv·ant (sur'·vant) *n.* personal or domestic attendant; one who serves another. **civil servant**, member of the civil service; government employee [L. *servire*, to serve].

serve (surv) *v.t.* to work for; to be a servant to; to minister to; to wait on; to attend; to help; to distribute, as rations, stores, etc.; to promote; to advance; to forward; to satisfy; to deliver formally; *v.i.* to work under another; to carry out duties; to be a member of a military, naval, etc. unit; to be useful, or suitable, or enough; in tennis, to resume play by striking the ball diagonally across court; *n.* in tennis, act of serving a ball. **servable** *a.* capable of being served. **-r** *n.* one who serves; a salver or small tray [L. *servire*, to serve].

serv·ice (sur'·vis) *n.* state of being a servant; work done for and benefit conferred on another; act of kindness; department of public employment; employment of persons engaged in this; military, naval, or air-force duty; advantage; use; form of divine worship; regular supply, as water, bus, electricity, etc.; (*Law*) serving of a process or summons; turn for serving ball at tennis, etc.; a set of dishes, etc.; *v.t.* to perform service for, e.g., automobiles, etc. **-able** *a.* useful; helpful; convenient; in fair working order. — **station** *n.* a place for buying gasoline, oil, etc. and making minor repairs on automobiles. **active service**, military, naval, or air force service against an enemy. **dinner-service, table-service, tea-service**, complete set of the appropriate dishes. **the Services**, the armed forces [L. *servire*, to serve].

serv·ice (sur'·vis) *n.* a small fruit tree; the shadbush [corrupt. of L. *sorbus*].

ser·vi·ette (sur·vi·et') *n.* a table napkin [Fr.].

ser·vile (sur'·val) *a.* pert. to or befitting a servant or slave; submissive; dependent; menial. **-ly** *adv.* **servility** *n.* [L. *servilis*, slavish].

ser·vi·tor (sur'·va·ter) *n.* attendant; follower or adherent. **servitude** *n.* slavery; bondage [L. *servire*, to serve].

ses·a·me (ses'·a·mē) *n.* annual herbaceous plant cultivated in India and Asia Minor for seeds from which oil is extracted. [Gk.].

ses·qui- (ses'·kwi) *prefix* denoting a proportion of 3:2. **-alteral, -alterate, -alterous** *a.* one and a half more. **-centennial** *a.* pert. to a century and a half more; *n.* the 150th anniversary. **-pedalian** *a.* measuring a foot and a half long; applied humorously to any long cumbersome technical word or to one given to using unnecessarily long words. **-pedalianism** *n.* [L. *sesqui*, one half more].

ses·sile (ses'·al) *a.* attached by the base, as a leaf; fixed and stationary [L. *sessilis*, low, fr. *sedere*, *sessum*, to sit].

ses·sion (sesh'·an) *n.* actual sitting of a court, council, etc. for transaction of business; term during which a court, council, and the like, meet for business; a period of time at school or college when a definite course of instruction is given. **-al** *a.* [L. *sessio*, fr. *sedere*, to sit].

ses·tet, seste (ses'·tet) *n.* (*Mus.*) composition for six instruments or voices; last six lines of a sonnet [L. *sextus*, sixth].

set (set) *v.t.* to put; to cause to sit; to seat; to place; to plant; to make ready; to adjust; to arrange (of hair) while wet; to fix, as precious stone in metal; to convert into curd; to extend (sail); to reduce from dislocated or fractured state, as limb; to adapt, as words to music; to compose type; to place a brooding fowl on nest of eggs; to crouch or point, as dog, to game; to clench (teeth); to stake; *v.i.* to pass below horizon; to go down; to strike root; to become fixed or rigid; to congeal or solidify; to put forth an effort; to begin. *pr.p.* **-ting.** *pa.t.* and *pa.p.* **set.** [O.E. *settan*].

set (set) *n.* a number of things or persons associated as being similar or complementary or used together, etc.; the manner in which a thing is set, hangs, or fits, as a dress; permanent change of shape or figure in consequence of pressure or cooling; an attitude or posture; young plant, cutting, or slip for planting out; direction, tendency, drift; figure of square dance; group or clique; setting of sun; equipment to form the ensemble of a scene for stage or film representation; (*Radio*) complete apparatus for reception (or transmission) of radio signals and broadcasts; (*Tennis*) series of games forming unit for match-scoring purposes; (*print.*) width of type character; a wooden or granite block or set; *a.* fixed; firm; prescribed; regular; established;

arranged; appointed; obstinate; determined. **-back** *n.* check to progress [O.Fr. *sette*, sect or O.E. *settan*].
se·ta (sē'·ta) *n.* bristle or bristlelike structure. **setaceous, setose** *a.* bristly [L. = a bristle].
set·tee (se·tē') *n.* couch or sofa [Cf. *settle*].
set·ter (set'·er) *n.* hunting, formerly dog trained to crouch or set when game was perceived [fr. *set*].
set·ting (set'·ing) *n.* fixing, adjusting, or putting in place; descending below horizon, as of sun; bezel which holds a precious stone, etc. in position; mounting of scene in play or film; background or surroundings [fr. *set*].
set·tle (set'·l) *v.t.* to put in place, order, arrangement, etc.; to fix; to establish; to make secure or quiet; to decide upon; to bring (dispute) to an end; to reconcile; to calm; to pay; to liquidate; to secure by legal deed, as a pension, annuity, etc.; to take up residence in; to colonize; *v.i.* to become fixed or stationary; to arrange; to come to rest; to (cause to) sink to bottom; to subside; to take up residence in; to dwell; to become calm; to become clear (of liquid). **-d** *a.* fixed; permanent; deep-rooted; decided; quiet; methodical; adjusted by agreement. **-ment** *n.* act of settling; state of being settled; colonization; a colony; (*Law*) transfer of real or personal property to a person; sum secured to a person. **-r** *n.* one who makes his home in a new country; colonist. **settling** *n.* the act of making a settlement; act of subsiding; adjusting of matters in dispute; *pl.* sediment [O.E. *setl*, a seat].
set·tle (set'·l) *n.* long high-backed bench; settee [O.E. *setl*, a seat].
sev·en (sev'·an) *a.* one more than six; *n.* number greater by one than six, symbol 7 or VII; **-fold** *a.* repeated seven times; increased to seven times the size; *adv.* seven times as much or as often. [O.E. *seofon*].
sev·en·teen (sev'·an·tēn) *a.* one more than sixteen; *n.* sum of ten and seven; symbol 17, or XVII *a.* and *n.* the seventh after the tenth [O.E. *seofontiene*].
sev·enth (sev'·anth) *a.* constituting one of seven equal parts; *n.* one of seven equal parts. **Seventh-day Adventists,** Christian sect observing seventh day as Sabbath. **Seventh heaven,** supreme ecstasy or beatitude. [fr. *seven*].
sev·en·ty (sev'·an·ti·) *a.* seven times ten; *n.* sum of seven times ten; the symbol 70 or LXX. **seventieth** *a.* constituting one of seventy equal parts [O.E. *seofontig*].
sev·er (sev'·er) *v.t.* to part or divide by violence; to sunder; to cut or break off; *v.i.* to divide; to make a separation. **-able** *a.* **-ance** *n.* separation; partition [Fr. fr. L. *separare*].
sev·er·al (sev'·er·al) *a.* more than two; some; separate; distinct; various; different; *pron.* several persons or things. **-ly** *adv.* apart from others [O.Fr. fr. L. *separare*].
se·vere (sa·vir') *a.* serious; rigidly methodical; harsh; not flowery, as style. **-ly** *adv.* **-ness, severity** *n.* sternness; harshness; rigor; austerity; intensity [L. *severus*].
Sè·vres (se'·vr) *n.* and *a.* name of a fine porcelain made at *Sèvres*, France.
sew (sō) *v.t.* to fasten together with needle and thread; to join with stitches; *v.i.* to practice sewing. **-er** *n.* one who sews. **-ing** *n.* and *a.* **-ing-machine** *n.* automatic machine adapted for all kinds of sewing operations [O.E. *seowian*].
sew·age (sōō'·ij) *n.* drainage; organic refuse carried off by a regular system of underground pipes [fr. *sewer*].
sew·er (sōō'·er) *n.* underground drain or conduit to remove waste water and organic refuse. **-age** *n.* underground system of pipes and conduits to carry off surface water and organic refuse [O.Fr. *esseveur*].
sex (seks) *n.* state of being male or female; sum total of characteristics which distinguish male and female organisms; function by which most animal and plant species are perpetuated; males or females collectively. **— appeal,** what makes person sexually desirable or attractive. **-ual** *a.* pert. to sex or sexes; pert. to genital organs. **-ual intercourse,** coition. **-uality** *n.* **-ually** *adv.* [L. *sexus*].
sex-, comb. form, six.
sex·ag·e·nar·y (seks·aj·a·ner·i·) *a.* pert. to the number sixty; proceeding by sixties. **sexagenarian** *n.* person of age of sixty [L. *seraginta*, sixty].
Sex·a·ges·i·ma (seks·a·jas'·a·ma) *n.* second Sunday before Lent, sixty days before Easter **sexagesimal** *a.* *sexagesimus*, sixtieth].
sex·en·ni·al (seks·en'·i·al) *a.* continuing for six years; happening once every six years. Also **sextennial. -ly , sextennially** *adv.* [L. *sex*, six; *annus*, a year].
sex·tant (seks'·tant) *n.* an astronomical instrument used in measuring angular distances [L. *sextus*, sixth].
sex·ten·nial. See **sexennial.**
sex·tet, sex·tette (seks·tet') *n.* musical composition for six voices or instruments; company of six singers or instrumentalists [L. *sex*, six].
sex·ton (seks'·tan) *n.* church lay officer acting as caretaker and may also be grave digger [corrupt. of *sacristan*].

sex·tu·ple (seks'·yoo·pl) *a.* sixfold; six times as many; *v.t.* to multiply by six [L. *sex*, six; *plicare*, to fold].
sfor·zan·do (sfawr·tsàn'·dō) *a.* (*Mus.*) forced or pressed; strongly accented. Usually *abbrev.* to **sf., sfz.,** or denoted by symbols ∧, >. [It.].
shab·by (shab'·i·) *a.* torn or worn to rags; poorly dressed; faded; worn; mean. **shabbily** *adv.* **shabbiness** *n.* [O.E. *sceabb*, scab].
shack (shak) *n.* roughly built wooden hut; shanty [fr. *ramshackle*].
shack·le (shak'·l) *n.* metal loop or staple; U-shaped steel link with a pin closing the free ends; *pl.* fetters; manacles; anything which hampers; restraints; *v.t.* to fetter; to hamper [O.E. *sceacul*, a bond].

shad (shad) *n.* name of several species of herring family [O.E. *sceadd*].
shade (shād) *n.* partial darkness, due to interception of light; place sheltered from light. heat, etc.; screen; darker part of anything; depth of color; tint; hue; a very minute difference; *pl.* invisible world or region of the dead; Hades; *v.t.* to shelter or screen, from light or a source of heat; to darken; to dim; to represent shades in a drawing; to pass almost imperceptibly from one form or color to another. **-d** *a.* **shadily** *adv.* in shady manner. **shadiness** *n.* quality of being shady. **shading** *n.* interception of light; slight variation; light and color values in a painting or drawing. **shady** *a.* providing shade; in shade; (*Colloq.*) disreputable; not respectable; doubtful; suspicious [O.E. *sceadu*].
shad·ow (shad'·ō) *n.* patch of shade; dark figure projected by anything which intercepts rays of light; darker or less illuminated part of picture; inseparable companion; ghost; phantom; gloom; slight trace; *v.t.* to cast a shadow over; to follow and watch closely. **— boxing** *n.* boxing practice, without opponent. **-er** *n.* one who dogs the footsteps of another. **-iness** *n.* gradation of light and color; shading. **-y** *a.* full of shadow; serving to shade; faint; unsubstantial; obscure; unreal [O.E. *sceadu*].

shaft (shaft) *n.* straight rod, stem, or handle; shank; stem of arrow; arrow; anything long and slender, as a tall chimney, the well of an elevator, vertical passage leading down to mine or excavation, etc.; part of column between base and capital; revolving rod for transmitting power; stem of feather; pole of carriage. **-ing** *n.* system of long rods and pulleys used to transmit power to machinery [O.E. *sceaft*].

shag (shag) *n.* coarse, matted wool or hair; long and coarse nap on some types of woolen fabrics; strong mixture of tobacco leaves cut and shredded for smoking; *a.* rough; shaggy. **-gedness, -giness** *n.* **-gy** *a.* covered with rough hair or wool; rough; unkempt [O.E. *sceacga*, a head of hair].
shah (sha) *n.* *abbrev.* of Shah-in-Shah (King of Kings), the title given to the monarchs of Iran, Persia [Pers.].
shake (shāk) *v.t.* to cause to move with quick vibrations; to weaken stability of; to impair resolution of; to trill, as note in music; to agitate; *v.i.* to tremble; to shiver; to totter. *pa.t.* **shook.** *pa.p.* **-n.** *n.* shaking; vibration;

jolt; severe shock to system; friendly grasping of hands by two individuals; (*Mus.*) trill; (*Colloq.*) moment. **-down** *n.* (*Colloq.*) extortion of money. **-n** *a.* weakened; agitated; cracked. **shakily** *adv.* **shakiness** *n.* **shaky** *a.* easily moved; unsteady; weak; tottering; unreliable. **to shake off,** to get rid of [O.E. *sceacan*].
shak·o (shak'·ō) *n.* military peaked headdress, shaped like truncated cone and usually plumed in front [Hung. *csako*].

shale (shāl) *n.* (*Geol.*) clay or mud become hardened and which splits into thin plates, parallel to stratification [O.E. *scealu*, scale].
shall (shall) *v.i.* and *aux.* used to make compound tenses or moods to express futurity, obligation, command, condition or intention [O.E. *sceal*].
shal·low (shal'·ō) *a.* having little depth of water; having little knowledge; superficial; *n.* place where water is of little depth; shoal, flat, or sandbank. **-ly** *adv.* **-ness** *n.*
sham (sham) *n.* any trick, fraud, or device which deludes; pretense; counterfeit; imitation; *a.* counterfeit; false; pretended; *v.t.* to counterfeit; to feign, to pretend; *v.i.* to make false pretenses. *pr.p.* **-ming.** *pa.t.* and *pa.p.* **-med** [etym. uncertain].
sham·ble (sham'·bl) *v.i.* to walk unsteadily with shuffling gait [etym. uncertain].
shame (shām) *n.* emotion caused by consciousness of something wrong or dishonoring in one's conduct or state; cause of disgrace; dishonor; ignominy; *v.t.* to cause to feel shame; to disgrace; to degrade; to force by shame (into). **-faced** *a.* bashful; modest. **-facedly** *adv.* **-facedness** *n.* **-ful** *a.* disgraceful. **-fully** *adv.* **-fulness** *n.* **-less** *a.* destitute of shame; brazen-faced; immodest. **-lessly** *adv.* **-lessness** *n.* [O.E. *sceamu*].
sham·my. See **chamois.**
sham·poo (sham·pōō') *v.t.* to wash (scalp); to massage; *n.* act of shampooing; preparation used. **-er** *n.* [Hind. *champna*, to knead].
sham·rock (sham'·rak) *n.* small trefoil plant; national emblem of Ireland [Ir. *seamrog*, trefoil].
shang·hai (shang·hī') *v.t.* to drug or render a man unconscious by violence so that he may be shipped as member of a crew; to bring by deceit and force; *pa.t.* and *pa.p.* **shanghaied** [*Shanghai*, China].
Shan·gri·la (shang'·gri·la) *n.* a peaceful, untroubled place to which one may escape [From the name of the hidden retreat in James Hilton's *Lost Horizon*].
shank (shangk) *n.* lower part of leg, from knee to ankle; shin-bone; stem of anchor, pipe, etc.; shaft of a column; long connecting part of an appliance. **-'s mare,** one's own legs [O.E. *sceanca*, leg].
shan·tung (shan·tung') *n.* silk cloth with rough, knotted surface made from the wild silkworm [Chinese province].
shan·ty (shant'·i·) *n.* shabby dwelling; crude wooden building [Fr. *chantier*, a workshop].
shan·ty (shant'·i·) *n.* sailor's song. Also **chanty, chantey** [Fr. *chanter*, to sing].
shape (shāp) *v.t.* to mold or make into a particular form; to give shape to; to figure; to devise; *v.i.* to assume a form or definite pattern; *n.* form; figure; appearance; outline; pattern; mold; condition; **-able, shapable** *a.* capable of being shaped; shapely. **-less** *a.* without regular shape or form; deformed; ugly. **-lessness** *n.* **-liness** *n.* beauty of shape or outline. **-ly** *a.* [O.E. *scieppan*].
shard (shàrd) *n.* broken fragment, esp. of earthenware; hard wing-case of beetle. Also **sherd** [O.E. *sceard*, a fragment].
share (sher) *n.* pointed, wedge-shaped, cutting blade of plough [O.E. *scear*].
share (sher) *n.* part allotted; portion; unit of ownership in public company entitling one to share in profits; *v.t.* to give or allot a share; to enjoy with others; to apportion; *v.i.* to take a share; to partake; to participate. **-cropper** *n.* a tenant farmer, esp. in the South. **-r** *n.* [O.E. *scearu*, a cutting or division].
shark (shàrk) *n.* general name applied to certain voracious marine fishes; swindler; rapacious fellow; (*Slang*) an expert. **-skin** *n.* stiff, smooth-finished rayon fabric [etym. unknown].
sharp (shàrp) *a.* having keen, cutting edge or fine point; abrupt; having ready perception; quick; shrewd; acid; acrid; pungent; sarcastic; harsh; painful intense dealing cleverly but unfairly artful; strongly marked, esp. in outline; shrill; (*Mus.*) raised a semi-tone in pitch; *n.* acute sound, esp. note raised semi-tone above its proper pitch; (*Mus.*) sign indicating this; (*Colloq.*) an expert; *v.t.* and *v.i.*

to raise or sound a half tone above a given tone; *adv.* punctually. **-en** *v.t.* to give a keen edge or fine point to; to make more eager or intelligent; to make more tart or acid; (*Mus.*) to raise a semi-tone. **-ener** *n.* one who, or that which, sharpens; instrument for putting fine point on lead-pencil, etc. **-er** *n.* swindler; cheat; **—eyed** *a.* very observant. **-ly** *adv.* **-ness** *n.* **-shooter** *n.* skilled, long-range marksman. **-shooting** *n.* **-sighted** *a.* having acute mind [O.E. *scearp*].

shark

shat·ter (shat′·er) *v.t.* to break into many pieces; to smash; to disorder; *v.i.* to fly in pieces [doublet of *scatter*].
shave (shāv) *v.t.* to pare away; to cut close, esp. hair of face or head with razor; to cut off thin slices; to miss narrowly; to graze; *v.i.* to shave oneself; *pa.p.* **-d** or **-n.** *n.* act of shaving; thin slice or shaving; tool for shaving; narrow escape; close miss. **-r** *n.* one who shaves; (*Colloq.*) a young lad. **shav·ing** *n.* act of shaving; what is shaved off. **close** or **near shave,** very narrow escape from danger [O.E. *sceafan*, to scrape].
Sha·vi·an (shā′·vi·an) *n.* of or pertaining to George Bernard Shaw.
shawl (shawl) *n.* cloth used by women as loose covering for neck and shoulders; *v.t.* to wrap in a shawl [Pers. *shal*].
shay (shā) *n.* an obsolete one-horse carriage [var. of *chaise*].
she (shē) *pron.* this or that female; feminine pronoun of the third person; a female (used humorously as a noun); also, in compound words, as *she-bear* [O.E. *seo*].
sheaf (shēf) *n.* bundle of stalks of wheat, rye, oats, or other grain; any similar bundle; a sheave; *pl.* **sheaves.** *v.t.* to make sheaves; *v.i.* to collect and bind corn, etc. into sheaves [O.E. *sceaf*].

shear (shir) *v.t.* to clip or cut through with shears or scissors; to clip wool (from sheep); to fleece; *v.i.* to divide by action of shears; to reap with a sickle. *pa.t.* **-ed.** *pa.p.* **-ed, shorn** *n.* (*Engineering*) stress in a body in a state of tension due to a force acting parallel with its section; shearing; curve; *pl.* a cutting instrument, consisting of two blades movable on a pin; large pair of scissors. **-er** *n.* **-ing** *n.* operation of clipping or cutting with shears; wool, etc. cut off with shears [O.E. *sceran*].
sheath (shēth) *n.* close-fitting cover, esp. for knife or sword; scabbard; thin protective covering. **-e** *v.t.* to put into a sheath; to envelop; to encase. **-ing** *n.* that which sheathes; metal covering for underwater structures as a protection against sea organisms, etc. [O.E. *scaeth*].
sheave (shēv) *n.* grooved wheel in block, etc. on which a rope works [doublet of *shive*].
sheave (shēv) *v.t.* to bind into sheaves; to sheaf [fr. *sheaf*].
shed (shed) *n.* shelter used for storage or workshop [doublet of *shade*].
shed (shed) *v.t.* to cause to emanate, proceed, or flow out; to spill; to let fall; to cast off, as hair, feathers, shell; to spread; to radiate; *v.i.* to come off. *pr.p.* **-ding.** *pa.t.* and *pa.p.* **shed.** [O.E. *sceadan*, to divide].
sheen (shēn) *n.* gloss; glitter; brightness; light reflected by a bright surface. **-y** *a.* [O.E. *sciene*, beautiful].
sheep (shēp) *n. sing.* and *pl.* ruminant mammal, valued for its flesh and its solf fleecy wool; simple, bashful person; *pl.* pastor's church congregation. **-cote** *n.* enclosure affording shelter for sheep. **-dip** *n.* tank containing insecticide through which sheep are passed to free them from ticks; anti-parasitic solution or sheep-wash so used. **-dog** *n.* any breed of dog trained to tend and round up sheep. **-fold** *n.* sheepcote. **-ish** *a.* like a sheep; bashful; shy and embarrassed; awkwardly timid and diffident. **-ishly** *adv.* **-ishness** *n.* **-'s eyes,** fond, languishing glances. **-shank** *n.* knot or hitch for temporarily shortening

rope, halyard, etc. **-shearer** *n.* one who clips wool from sheep. **-shearing** *n.* **-skin** *n.* skin of sheep; leather, parchment, or rug made from this; (*Colloq.*) diploma; **black sheep,** disreputable member of family; rogue [O.E. *sceap*].

sheepshank

sheer (shir) *a.* pure; unmixed; absolute; downright; perpendicular; of linen or silk, very thin; *adv.* quite; completely [O.E. *scir*, pure, bright].
sheer (shir) *v.i.* to deviate from the right course; to swerve; *n.* longitudinal, upward curvature of ship's deck towards bow or stern; a swerve [Dut. *scheren*].
sheet (shēt) *n.* any broad expanse; a broad piece of cloth spread on bed; broad piece of paper; newspaper; broad expanse of water, or the like; broad, thinly expanded portion of metal or other substance; *v.t.* to cover, as with a sheet. **— metal,** etc. *n.* metal in broad, thin sheets. **-ing** *a.* process of forming into sheets; cloths used for bed coverings; **— lightning** *n.* sudden glow appearing on horizon due to reflection of forked lightning. **-music** *n.* music printed on unbound sheets of paper [O.E. *scete*].
sheik, sheikh (shēk, shāk) *n.* Arab chief; a title of respect to Moslem ecclesiasts [Ar.].
shek·el (shek′·l) *n.* among ancient Hebrews, orig. weight, and later name of a gold or silver coin. *pl.* (*Colloq.*) money; coins; cash [Heb. *sheqel*].
shel·drake (shel′·drāk) *n.* (*fem.* **shelduck**) genus of wild duck [O.E. *sheld, variegated*; and *drake*].
shelf (shelf) *n.* board fixed horizontally on frame, or to wall, for holding things; ledge of rocks; sandbank in sea, rendering water shallow. *pl.* **shelves** (shelvz). *a.* [O.E. *scelf*].
shell (shel) *n.* hard, rigid, outer, protective covering of many animals, particularly mollusks; outer covering of eggs of birds; protective covering of certain seeds; hollow steel container, filled with high explosive, for discharging from mortar or gun; outer part of structure left when interior is removed; frail racing boat or skiff; group of electrons in atom all having same energy. **-back** *n.* old sailor. **-ed** *a.* having shell; stripped of shell; damaged by shellfire. **-fish** *n.* aquatic animal with external covering of shell, as oysters, lobster, crustacean, mollusk. **-proof** *a.* capable of withstanding bombs or high-explosives. **-shock** *n.* war neurosis, disturbance of mind and nervous system due to war conditions [O.E. *sciell*].
shel·lac (sha·lak′) *n.* refined, melted form of seed lac, obtained from resinous deposit secreted by insects on certain Eastern trees, used as varnish. *v.t.* to cover with shellac [*shel(l)* and *lac*].
shel·ter (shel′·ter) *n.* place or structure giving protection; that which covers or defends; a place of refuge; asylum; *v.t.* to give protection to; to screen from wind or rain; *v.i.* to take shelter. **-er** *n.* [etym. uncertain].
shelve (shelv) *v.t.* to furnish with shelves; to place on a shelf; to put aside, as unfit for use; to defer consideration of; *v.i.* to slope gradually; to incline. **shelving** *n.* [fr. *shelf*].
she·nan·i·gan (sha·nan′·a·gan) *n.* (*Slang*) nonsense. *usu. pl.* foolishness.
shep·herd (shep′·erd) *n.* (*fem.* **shepherdess**) one who tends sheep; pastor of church; *v.t.* to tend sheep; to watch over and guide. **-'s-crook** *n.* long staff, with end curved to form large hook. [O.E. *sceaphirde*].
Sher·a·ton (sher′·a·tan) *n.* style of furniture design distinguished for grace and beauty [Thomas *Sheraton* (1751-1806), the designer].
sher·bet (sher′·bat) *n.* a frozen dessert made with fruit juices, milk, egg white or gelatin [Ar. *sharbat*, a drink].
sherd. *See* **shard.**
she·rif, shereef (sha·rēf′) *n.* a descendant of Mohammed [Ar. *sharif*, noble].
sher·iff (sher′·if) *n.* orig. governor of a shire, a 'shire-reeve' in England; chief law enforcement officer [O.E. *scirgerefa*, a shire-reeve].
Sher·pa (sher′·pa) *n.* one of Nepal tribe, employed as porter or guide on Himalayan mountaineering expeditions.
sher·ry (sher′·i·) *n.* Spanish wine of deep amber color [fr. *Jerez*, near Cadiz].
Shet·land (shet′·land) (*Geog.*) group of islands off N. coast of Scotland. **-er** *n.* **— pony** small breed of pony.
shib·bo·leth (shib′·ba·leth) *n.* testword or password; a distinctive custom [Heb.].
shield (shēld) *n.* broad piece of armor carried on arm; buckler; anything which protects or defends; escutcheon or field on which are placed bearings in coats of arms; *v.t.* to protect; to defend; to screen; to ward off; to forfend [O.E. *scield*].

Shetland pony

shield

shift (shift) *v.t.* to change position (of); to transfer from one place to another; to move; to change gears in an automobile; *v.i.* to move; to change place, course; to change in opinion; *n.* change; evasion; expedient; squad or relay of workmen; time of their working. **-er** *n.* **-iness** *n.* trickiness of character or behavior. **-ing** *a.* changing place or position; displacing; fickle; unreliable. **-less** *a.* lacking in resource or character; aimless; not to be depended upon. **-lessness** *n.* **-y** *a.* not to be trusted; unreliable. **make-shift,** to manage or contrive somehow [O.E. *sciftan*, to arrange].
shil·le·lagh, shillelah (sha.lā′.li.) *n.* a club or cudgel. [*Shillelagh*, Co. Wicklow].
shil·ling (shil′·ing) *n.* British silver coin of the value of twelve pence [O.E. *scilling*].
shil·ly-shal·ly (shil′·i·shal′·i·) *n.* vacillation; indecision; *v.i.* to hesitate or trifle; to waver. **shilly-shallier** *n.* [redupl. of *shall* I].
shim·mer (shim′·er) *v.i.* to shine with faint, tremulous light; to glisten; *n.* faint, quivering light or gleam. **-ing** *n.* **-y** *a.* [O.E. *scimian*].
shim·my (shim′·i·) *n.* dance characterized by exaggerated wriggling; wobbling, as in wheel of a car; *v.i.* to wobble [fr. *chemise*].
shin (shin) *n.* forepart of leg, between ankle and knee; shank; *v.i.* to climb (up) with aid of one's arms and legs. Also **-ny. -bone** *n.* tibia, larger of two bones of leg [O.E. *scinu*].
shin·dig (shin′·dig) *n.* (*Colloq.*) social affair [var. of *shindy*].
shin·dy (shin′·di·) *n.* (*Slang*) excessive noise and tumult; uproar [Romany, *chindi*, quarrel].
shine ((shin) *v.i.* to give out or reflect light; to radiate; to sparkle; to perform in brilliant fashion. *pa.t.* and *pa.p.* **shone.** *v.t.* to cause to shine; to polish, shoes, etc. *pa.t.* and *pa.p.* **shined.** *n.* brightness; gloss; (*Colloq.*) liking. **-r** (*Slang*) a black eye. **shining** *a.* glistening; splendid. **shininess** *n.* **shiny** *a.* bright; glossy; unclouded [O.E. *scinan*].
shin·gle (shing′·gl) *n.* rounded water-worn pebbles. **shingly** *a.* [Norw. *singel*].
shin·gle (shing′·gl) *n.* thin, rectangular slat for roofing and house siding; a short haircut; small signboard (esp. of physician, lawyer); *v.t.* to cover with shingles; to crop women's hair close [L. *scindula*].
shin·gles (shing′·glz) *n.pl.* (*Med.*) herpes zoster, viral infection of nerve ganglia, accompanied by severe pain and a vesicular eruption along the nerve course [L. *cingulum*, a belt].
Shin·to (shin′·tō) *n.* native religion of Japan, **-ism** *n.* [Chin. *shin*, god; *tao*, the way].
ship (ship) *n.* a vessel for carriage of passengers and goods by sea; *v.t.* to engage for service on board a ship; to place object in position, as oar; to take in water (over the side); to transport. *pr.p.* **-ping.** *pa.t.* and *pa.p.* **-ped. -board** *n.* deck or side of ship. **-builder** *n.* one who constructs ships; naval architect. **-building** *n.* **-master** *n.* captain **-mate** *n.* fellow sailor. **-ment** *n.* process of shipping; cargo. **-owner** *n.* **-per** *n.* one who forwards commodities. **-ping** *n.* collective body of ships in one place; mercantile vessels generally; tonnage; the business of transporting goods. **-shape** *a.* orderly, trim; *adv.* properly. **-wreck** *n.* loss of ship by accident; total destruction; ruin. **-wright** *n.* one engaged in building or repairing ships. **-yard** *n.* place where ships are built or repaired [O.E. *scip*].
shire (shir) *n.* territorial division in Great Britain; county [O.E. *scir.* district].
shirk (shurk) *v.t.* to evade; to try to avoid (duty, etc.) **-er** *n.* one who seeks to avoid duty.
shirr (shur) *n.* in needlework, row of puckering or gathering; *v.t.* to gather with parallel threads; to bake eggs.
shirt (shurt) *n.* garment for upper part of body. **-sleeve** *a.* simple; plain. **-waist** *n.* woman's blouse. **to keep one's shirt on** (*Slang*) to be patient [O.E. *scyrfe*].
shiv·er (shiv′·er) *v.i.* to quiver or shake from cold or fear; to tremble; to shudder; *v.t.* to

cause to shake; *n.* shaking or shuddering; a vibration. **-y** *a.* inclined to shiver; tremulous.

shiv·er (shiv′.ẹr) *n.* small piece or splinter; *v.t.* and *v.i.* to break into many small pieces or splinters; to shatter [M.E. *scifre*].

shoal (shōl) *n.* large number of fish swimming together; a crowd; *v.i.* to crowd together [O.E. *scolu*, company, fr. L. *schola*, a school].

shoal (shōl) *n.* a sandbank or bar; shallow water; *a.* shallow; *v.i.* to become shallow. **-y** *a.* full of shoals [O.E. *sceald*, shallow].

shoat (shōt) *n.* a young pig [M.E. *schote*].

shock (shàk) *n.* violent impact or concussion when bodies collide; clash; percussion; conflict; emotional disturbance produced by anything unexpected, offensive, or displeasing; sudden depression of the system due to violent injury or strong mental emotion; paralytic stroke; effect of electric discharge through body; *v.t.* to strike against suddenly; to strike with surprise, horror, or disgust. **—absorber** *n.* anything to lighten a blow, shock, or ordeal. **-er** *n.* **-ing** *a.* appalling; terrifying; frightful; repulsive; offensive. **-ingly** *adv.* **—proof** *a.* able to withstand shocks [Fr. *choquer*].

shock (shàk) *n.* disordered mass of hair; *a.* shaggy; bushy. [O.E. *scucca*, a demon].

shock (shàk) *n.* group of sheaves of grain; *v.t.* to make into shocks [Dut. *schocke*].

shod (shàd) *pa.t.* and *pa.p.* of **shoe**.

shod·dy (shàd′.i·) *n.* inferior textile material; *a.* inferior; of poor quality.

shoe (shóò) *n.* covering for foot, but not enclosing ankle; metal rim or curved bar nailed to horse's hoof; various protective plates or under-coverings; apparatus which bears on the live rail in an electric railways in order to collect current to actuate the motor; *v.t.* to furnish with shoes; to put shoes on. **-ing** *pa.t.*, *pa.p.* **-horn** *n.* curved piece of horn, metal, etc. used to help foot into shoe. **lace** *n.* for fastening shoe on foot. **-less** *a.* **-maker** *n.* **-r** *n.* one who makes or repairs shoes. **-string** *n.* a shoelace; (*Colloq.*) small amount of money [O.E. *scoh*].

shone (shōn) *pa.t.* and *pa.p.* of **shine**.

shoo (shóò) *interj.* begone (used esp. in scaring away fowls and other animals); *v.t.* to scare or drive away [imit.].

shook (shook) *pa.t.* of **shake**.

shoot (shóòt) *v.t.* to discharge missile from gun, etc.; to kill or wound with such a missile; to propel quickly; to thrust out; to pass swiftly over (rapids) or through (arch of bridge); to photograph episode or sequence of motion picture; *v.i.* to move swiftly and suddenly; to let off a gun, etc.; to go after game with gun; to just out; to sprout; to bud; to dart through (as severe pain); to advance; to kick towards goal. *pa.t.* and *pa.p.* **shot.** *n.* shooting; young branch or stem. **-er** *n.* **-ing** *n.* act of discharging firearms, etc.; the act of killing game. **-ing-gallery** *n.* long room for practice with rifles. **-ing-star** *n.* incandescent meteor. [O.E. *sceotan*].

shop (shàp) *n.* building where goods are made, or sold; workshop; store *v.i.* to visit shops to purchase articles. *pr.p.* **-ping** *pa.t.* and *pa.p.* **-ped. -keeper** *n.* one who keeps retail shop. **-keeping** *n.* **-lifter** *n.* one who makes petty thefts from shop counters. **-ping** *n.* visiting shops with view to purchasing. **-ping-bag**, or **-basket** *n.* receptacle for holding articles purchased. **-worn** *a.* soiled or tarnished by long exposure in shop. [Fr. *échoppe*, a booth].

shore (shōr, shawr) *n.* land adjoining sea or large lake; *v.t.* to put ashore [Dut. *schor*].

shore (shōr, shawr) *n.* strong beam set obliquely against wall of building or ship to prevent movement during alterations; *v.t.* to support by post or buttress; to prop. **shor·ing** *n.* props for support [etym. uncertain].

shorn (shawrn) *pa.p.* of **shear**; *a.* cut off; having the hair or wool cut off [fr. *shear*].

short (shawrt) *a.* having little length; not long in space; low; not extended in time; limited or lacking in quantity; hasty of temper; crumbling in the mouth; pronounced with less prolonged accent; brief; near; concise; pithy; abrupt; destitute; crisp; *adv.* suddenly; abruptly; without reaching the end; *n.* short film to support feature film; short circuit; *pl.* short trousers reaching down to above knees. **-age** *n.* insufficient supply; deficiency. **-bread** *n.* rich cake or butter cooky. **-cake** *n.* sweetened biscuit or cake filled and topped with fruit and whipped cream. **— circuit** *n.* passage of electric current by a shorter route than that designed for it; *v.t.* to cause short circuit; to by-pass. **-coming** *n.* failing; fault; defect. **-cut** *n.*

quicker but unorthodox way of reaching a place or of accomplishing a task, etc. **-en** *v.t.* to make shorter; to render friable, as shortbread, with butter or lard; to abridge; to lessen; *v.t.* to contract; to lessen. **-ening** *n.* lard, butter, or other fat used when baking pastry, etc. **-hand** *n.* system of rapid reporting by means of signs or symbols. **—handed** *a.* not having the full complement or staffon duty. **-horn** *n.* a breed of English cattle with short horns. **-ly** *adv.* in a brief time; soon; in a few words; curtly. **-ness** *n.* **— shrift**, summary treatment. **-sighted** *a.* not able to see distinctly objects some distance away; lacking in foresight.**—sightedly** *adv.* **-sightedness** *n.* **-tempered** *a.* easily roused to anger. **— waves** (*Radio*) electromagnetic waves whose wave length is, by international definition, between 10 and 50 meters. **—winded** *a.* affected with shortness of breath; easily made out of breath. **in short,** briefly. [O.E. *scort*].

shot (shàt) *pa.t.* and *pa.p.* of **shoot.**

shot (shàt) *a.* pert. to fabrics woven with warp and weft of contrasting tints or colors, so that shade changes according to angle of light [fr. *shoot*].

shot (shàt) *n.* act of shooting; skilled marksman; one of small pellets, contained in cartridge fired from sporting rifle; heavy, solid, round missile; heavy, fired from cannon; range of such missiles; charge of blasting powder; stroke in billiards, tennis, etc.; a photograph; a try to attempt; (*Slang*) injection of a drug; *v.t.* to load or weight with shot. *pr.p.* **-ting.** *pa.t.* and *pa.p.* **-ted. -gun** *n.* smoothbore gun for shooting small game or birds. [O.E. *sceot*].

should (shood) *v.* and *aux.* used in Future-in-the-Past tenses of verbs with pronouns I or we; auxiliary used after words expressing opinion, intention, desire, probability, obligation, etc. (Cf. *shall*).

shoul·der (shōl′.der) *n.* ball and socket joint formed by humerus (bone of the upper arm) with scapula (shoulder-blade); upper joint of foreleg of animal; anything resembling human shoulder, as prominent part of hill; graded strip along edge of road; *v.t.* to push forward with shoulders; to bear (burden, etc.); to accept (responsibility); *v.i.* to push forward through crowd. **— blade** *n.* flat bone of shoulder; scapula. [O.E. *sculdor*].

shout (shout) *n.* loud, piercing cry; call for help; *v.t.* and *v.i.* to utter loud sudden cry.

shove (shuv) *v.t.* to push; to press against; to jostle; *v.i.* to push forward; to push off from shore in a boat, using oar; *n.* act of pushing; push [O.E. *scufan*].

shov·el (shuv′.l) *n.* spade wtih broad blade slightly hollowed; scoop; machine for scooping and lifting; *v.t.* to lift or move with a shovel; *v.i.* to use shovel. **-ler** *n.* [O.E. *scofl*].

show (shō) *v.t.* to present to view; to point out; to display; to exhibit; to disclose; to explain; to demonstrate; to prove; to conduct; to guide; *v.i.* to appear; to be visible; to come into sight. *pa.p.* **-n** or **-ed.** *n.* act of showing; that which is shown; spectacle; exhibition; display; (*Colloq.*) theatrical performance or movie. **-bill** *n.* broad sheet containing advertisement. **-bread** *n.* Same as **shewbread**. **-case** *n.* glass case for display of goods, museum exhibits, etc. **-down** *n.* laying down of cards, face upwards, at poker or other card games; open disclosure of truth, clarification. **-er** *n.* one who shows or exhibits. **-ily** *adv.* **-man** *n.* one who presents a show; one who is skilled at presenting things. **-manship** *n.* **— place** *n.* place of local interest made especially attractive to draw tourists. **-room** *n.* room where goods are laid out for inspection. **-y** *a.* gaudy; attracting attention; ostentatious. **to show off,** to make an ostentatious display. **to show up,** to stand out prominently; to hold up to ridicule; to appear [O.E. *sceawian*, to look at].

show·er (shou′.er) *n.* a brief fall of rain or hail; anything coming down like rain; great number; *v.t.* to wet with rain; to give abundantly; *v.i.* to rain; to pour down. **— bath** *n.* bath equipped with fine-spraying apparatus. **— proof** *a.* impervious to rain. **-y** *a.* raining intermittently [O.E. *scur*].

shrank (shrangk) *pa.t.* of **shrink**.

shrap·nel (shrap′.nạl) *n.* shell timed to explode over, and shower bullets and splinters on, personnel; shell splinters [Gen. *Shrapnel*].

shred (shred) *n.* long, narrow piece cut or torn off; strip; fragment; scrap; *v.t.* to cut or tear to shreds; to tear into strips. *pr.p.* **-ding.** *pa.t.* and *pa.p.* **-ded** [O.E. *screade*].

shrew (shróò) *n.* noisy, quarrelsome woman;

a termagant; diminutive mammal, resembling, but unrelated to, mouse. **-ish** *a.* having manners of a shrew. **-ishly** *adv.* **-ishness** *n.* [O.E. *screawa*, shrew mouse].

shrewd (shróòd) *a.* intelligent; discerning; sagacious; knowing; cunning. **-ly** *adv.* **-ness** *n.* [Fr. *shrew*].

shriek (shrēk) *v.t.* and *v.i.* to scream, from fright, anguish, or bad temper; to screech; *n.* a loud, shrill cry [imit. origin].

shrift (shrift) *n.* confession made to a priest; absolution. **short shrift**, summary treatment [O.E. *scrifan*, to prescribe (penance)].

shrike (shrīk) *n.* bird which preys on birds, frogs, and insects, and impales victims on thorns; butcherbird [imit. of cry O.E. *scric*].

shrill (shril) *a.* uttering an acute sound; piercing; high-pitched; *v.i.* to sound in a shrill tone. **-y** *adv.* piercingly [M.E. *shrille*].

shrimp (shrimp) *n.* small edible crustacean allied to prawns; small person; *v.i.* to catch shrimps with net. **-er** *n.* [M.E. *shrimpe*].

shrine (shrīn) *n.* case in which sacred relics are deposited; tomb of saint; place of worship; any sacred place [L. *scrinium*, chest, box].

shrink (shringk) *v.i.* to contract; to dwindle; to recoil; to draw back; *v.t.* to cause to contract. *pa.t.* **shrank, shrunk.** *pa.p.* **shrunk. -age** *n.* act or amount of shrinking. **shrunken** *a.* narrowed in size [O.E. *scrincan*].

shrive (shrīv) *v.t.* to give absolution to; to confess (used reflexively); *v.i.* to receive or make confession *pa.t.* **-d** or **shrove.** *pa.p.* **shriven** [O.E. *scrifan*, to prescribe].

shriv·el (shriv′.l) *v.t.* and *v.i.* to cause to contract and wrinkle; to wither.

shroud (shroud) *n.* that which clothes or covers; sheet for a corpse; winding sheet; *pl.* strongest of the wire-rope stays which support mast athwartships; *v.t.* to enclose in winding sheet; to cover wtih shroud; to screen; to wrap up; to conceal [O.E. *scrud*, a garment].

shrove (shrōv) *pa.t.* of the verb **shrive. Shrovetide** *n.* period immediately before Lent, ending on Shrove Tuesday [fr. *shrive*].

shrub (shrub) *n.* any hard-wooded plant of smaller and thicker growth than tree; bush; low, dwarf tree. **-bery** *a.* collection of shrubs. **-by** *a.* of nature of shrub; full of shrubs [O.E. *scrybb*].

shrug (shrug) *v.i.* to raise and narrow shoulders in disdain, etc. *v.t.* to move (shoulders) thus. *pr.p.* **-ging.** *pa.t.* and *pa.p.* **-ged.** *n.* drawing up of shoulders [ME *schruggen*].

shrunk, shrunken See **shrink**.

shuck (shuk) *n.* husk or pod; shell of nut; *v.t.* to remove husk, pod, or shell from [Cf. *chuck*, to throw].

shud·der (shud′.er) *v.i.* to tremble violently, esp. with horror or fear; to shiver; to quake; *n.* trembling or shaking. **-ing** *n.* and *a.* trembling; shivering [M.E. Cf. Ger. *schaudern*].

shuf·fle (shuf′.l) *v.t.* to shove one way and the other; to throw into disorder; to mix (cards); to scrape (feet) along ground; *v.i.* to change position of cards in pack; to prevaricate; to move in a slovenly manner; to scrape floor with foot in dancing or walking; *n.* act of throwing into confusion by change of places; artifice or pretext; scraping movement of foot in dancing. **—board** *n.* a game in which disks are shoved into numbered divisions at the end of a long playing area.

shun (shun) *v.t.* to keep clear of; to avoid. *pr.p.* **-ning.** *pa.t.* and *pa.p.* **-ned** [O.E. *scunian*].

shunt (shunt) *v.t.* to move or turn off to one side; to move (train) from one line to another; to divert (electric current); *v.i.* to go aside; to turn off. *n.* act of shunting. **-er** *n.* railway employee who shunts rolling-stock.

shut (shut) *v.t.* to close to hinder ingress or egress; to forbid entrance to; *v.i.* to close itself; to become closed. *pr.p.* **-ting.** *pa.t.* and *pa.p.* **shut.** *a.* closed; made fast. **-down** *n.* stoppage of work or activity. **-ter** *n.* one who, or that which,shuts; movable protective screen for window; automatic device in camera which allows light from lens to act on film or plate for a predetermined period. **to shut down,** to stop working; to close (business, etc.). **to shut up,** to close; to fasten securely; (*Colloq.*) to stop talking [O.E. *scyttan*].

shut·tle (shut′.l) *n.* instrument used in weaving for shooting thread of woof between threads of warp; similar appliance in sewing machine to form a lock stitch; *v.t.* and *v.i.* to move backwards and forwards. **-cock** *n.* cork with fan of feathers for use with battledore or in badminton; game itself. [O.E. *scytel*, a missile].

shy (shī) *a.* sensitively timid; reserved; easily frightened; bashful; cautious; falling short; *v.i.* to start suddenly aside. *pa.t.* and *pa.p.* **shied. -ly** *adv.* **-ness** *n.* **-ster** *n.* unscrupulous lawyer or person. [*eschif*].

shy (shī) *v.t.* to throw; to fling. *pa.t.* and *pa.p.* **shied.** *n.* throw; cast.

Si·a·mese (sī.a.mēz′) *a.* pert. to Siam, the people, or language; *n.* native of Siam; the language. **— twins,** joined twins.

sib (sib) *a.* having kinship; related by blood; akin; *n.* a blood relation [O.E. Cf. Ger. *sippe*].

Si·be·ri·an (sī.bi′.ri.ạn) *a.* pert. to Siberia,

part of the Soviet Union.

shutter

shuttlecock

sib·i·lance (sib′·ạ·lạns) *n*. hissing sound; quality of being sibilant. Also **sibilancy**. **sibilant** *a. n*. letter uttered with hissing of voice, as *s, x*, etc. **sibilate** *v.t.* to pronounce with hissing sound [L. *sibilare*, to whistle].

sib·yl (sib′·il) *n*. a name applied to certain votaresses of Apollo, endowed with visionary, prophetic power; prophetess; witch. **-lic**, **-line** *a*. [Gk. *Sibulla*].

sic (sik) *adv*. abbreviated form of *sic in originail* (Lat. = so it stands in the original) printed in brackets as guarantee that passage has been quoted correctly; so; thus[L.].

sic·ca·tion (si·kā′·shạn) *n*. act or process of drying. **siccative** *a*. drying; causing or tending to dry; *n*. a drier [L. *siccus*, dry].

Si·cil·i·an (si·sil′·yạn) *a*. pert. to island of Sicily; *n*. native of Sicily.

sick (sik) *a*. affected with physical or mental disorder; diseased; ill; ailing; tired of. — **bay** *n*. place set aside on ship for treating the sick. — **benefit** *n*. allowance made to insured person while ill and off duty. **-en** *v.t.* to make sick; to disgust; *v.i.* to become sick; to be filled with abhorrence. **-ening** *a*. causing sickness or disgust; nauseating. **-eningly** *adv*. — **headache** *n*. migraine. **-ly** *a*. somewhat sick; ailing; weak; pale; arising from ill health. **-ness** *n*. state of being sick; illness; disordered state of stomach [O.E. *seoc*].

sick·le (sik′·l) *n*. reaping hook with semi-circular blade and a short handle [L. *secula*, fr. *secare*, to cut].

side (sīd) *n*. one of surfaces of object, esp. upright inner or outer surface; one of the edges of plane figure; margin; border; any part viewed as opposite to another; part of body from hip to shoulder; slope, as of a hill; one of two parties, teams, or sets of opponents; body of partisans; sect or faction; line of descent traced through one parent; *a*. being on the side; lateral; indirect; incidental; *v.i.* (with) to hold or embrace the opinions of another; to give support to one of two or more contending parties. — **arms** *pl*. weapons carried on side of body. **-board** *n*. piece of furniture designed to hold dining utensils, etc. in dining room. **-car** *n*. small box-shaped body attached to motorcycle. — **issue** *n*. subsidiary to main argument or business. — **light** *n*. any source of light situated at side of room, door, etc.;

lantern, showing red or green, on side of a vessel; incidental information or illustration. — **line** *n*. any form of profitable work which is ancillary to one's main business or profession; (*Sports*) line marking the side boundaries of playing field. **—long** *a*. lateral; oblique; not directly forward; *adv*. obliquely; on the side. **-r** *n*. **-saddle**, saddle for woman on horseback, not astride, but with both feet on one side of horse. **-show** *n*. minor entertainment or attraction; subordinate affair. **-slip** *n*. involuntary skid or slide sideways; *v.i.* to skid. **-splitting** *a*. exceedingly ludicrous and laughter-provoking. **—step** *n*. to step to one side; *v.i.* to step to one side. **-stroke** *n*. style of swimming where body is turned on one side. **-swipe** (*U.S.*) *n*. a blow with or on the side; *v.t.* to strike such a blow. **-track** *v.t.* to shunt into siding; to postpone indefinitely; to shelve; *n*. a railway siding. **siding** *n*. short line of rails on which trains are shunted from main line. **sidle** *v.i.* to move sideways; to edge

si·de·re·al (sī·di′·rē·ạl) *a*. relating to constellations and fixed stars; measured or determined by apparent motion of stars [L. *sidus, sideris*, a star].

sid·er·ite (sid′·er·īt) *n*. brown ironstone [Gk. *sidēritis*, the lodestone].

siege (sēj) *n*. the surrounding of a town or fortified place by hostile troops in order to induce it to surrender either by starvation or by attack at suitable juncture; continuous effort to gain (affection, influence, etc.); *v.t.* to besiege [Fr. *siège*, seat, siege].

si·en·na (sē·en′·a) *n*. natural yellow earth which provides pigment. **burnt sienna**, pigment giving ɪeddish-brown tint. **raw sienna**, pigment giving a yellowish-brown tint [fr. *Sienna*, Italy].

si·er·ra (sē·er′·a) *n*. chain of mountains with saw-like ridge [Sp. fr. L. *serra*, a saw].

si·es·ta (sē·es′·tạ) *n*. rest or sleep in afternoon esp. in hot countries; afternoon nap [Sp. = the sixth (hour) i.e. moon].

sieve (siv) *n*. utensil with wire netting or small holes for separating fine part of any pulverized substance from the coarse; *v.t.* to sift [O.E. *sife*].

sift (sift) *v.t.* to separate coarser portion from finer; to sieve; to bolt; to scrutinize; to examine closely [O.E. *sife*, a sieve].

sigh (sī) *v.i.* to make a deep, single respiration, as expression of exhaustion or sorrow; *v.t.* to utter sighs over; *n*. long, deep breath, expression of sorrow, fatigue, regret, or relief [O.E. *sican*].

sight (sīt) *n*. one of the five senses; act of seeing; faculty of seeing; that which is seen; view; glimpse; anything novel or remarkable; exhibition; spectacle; (*Colloq*.) pitiful object; a piece of metal near breech of firearm to assist the eye in correct aiming; any guide for eye to assist direction; *v.t.* to catch sight of; to see; to give proper elevation and direction to instrument by means of a sight; *v.i.* to take aim by means of a sight. **-less** *a*. blind; invisible. **-lessly** *adv*. **-lessness** *n*. **-liness** *n*. comeliness. **-ly** *a*. pleasing to the eye; graceful; handsome. **second-sight** *n*. gift of prophetic vision [O.E. *sihth*, fr. *seon*, to see].

sig·il (sij′·il) *n*. seal; signet; occult sign. **sigillary** *a*. [L. *sigillum*, a seal].

sig·ma (sig′·ma) *n*. the Greek letter (Σ, σ, s) corresponding to letter *s*; symbol indicating, in mathematics, etc., summation; 200; millesecond or $1/1000$ second. **sigmate, sigmoid** *a*. curved like letter S. [Gk.].

sign (sīn) *n*. movement, mark, or indication to convey some meaning; token; symbol; omen; signboard; password; (*Math*.) character indicating relation of quantities, or operation to be performed, as +, ×, ÷, = etc.; (*Mus*.) any character, as flat, sharp, dot, etc.; (*Astron*.) the twelfth part of the ecliptic or zodiac; *v.t.* to represent by sign; to affix signature to; to ratify; *v.i.* to make a signal, sign, or gesture; to append one's signature. **-board** *n*. board displaying, advertising, name of business firm, etc. **-manual** *n*. an autograph signature appended [L. *signum*].

sig·nal (sig′·nạl) *n*. sign to give notice of some occurrence, command, or danger to persons at a distance; that which in the first place impels any action; sign; token; semaphore, esp. on railway; (*Radio*) any communication made by emission of radio waves from a transmitter; *v.t.* to communicate by signals; *v.i.* to make signals. *pr.p.* **-ing.** *pa.t.* and *pa.p.* **-ed.** *a*. pert. to a signal; remarkable; conspicuous. **-ize** *v.t.* to make notable, distinguished, or remarkable; to point out. **-er** *n*. **-ly** *adv*. eminently; remarkably [L. *signum*, a sign].

sig·na·to·ry (sig′·nạ·tō·i·) *a*. and *n*. (one) bound by signature to terms of agreement. [L. *signare*, to sign].

sig·na·ture (sig′·nạ·cher) *n*. a sign, stamp, or mark impressed; a person's name written by himself; act of writing it; letter or number printed at bottom of first page of section of book to facilitate arrangement when binding; (*Mus*.) the flats or sharps after clef which indicate key (**key signature**), followed by appropriate signs giving value of the measures contained in each bar (**time signature**).

[L. *signare*, to sign].

signal

sig·net (sig′·nit) *n*. seal used for authenticating documents. — **ring** *n*. finger ring on which is engraved monogram or seal of owner [L. *signum*, a mark].

sig·ni·fy (sig′·ni·fī) *v.t.* to make known by a sign; to convey notion of; to denote; to indicate; to mean; *v.i.* to express meaning; to be of consequence. *pa.t.* and *pa.p.* **signified. significance** *n*. importance; weight; meaning; import. **significant** *a*. fitted or designed to signify or make known something; important. **significantly** *adv*. **signification** *n*. act of signifying that which is expressed by signs or words; meaning; sense. **significative** *a*. **significatory** *a*. having meaning [L. *significare*, fr. *signum*, a sign; *facere*, to make].

sig·nor (sē′·nyōr) *n*. Italian lord or gentleman; title of respect or address equivalent to *Mr*. **signora** (sē·nyō′·ra) *n. fem*. [It.].

si·lage (sī′·lij) *n*. compressed, acid-fermented fodder, orig. packed green in a silo for preservation [fr. *ensilage*].

si·lence (sī′·lạns) *n*. stillness; quietness; calm; refraining from speed; muteness; secrecy; oblivion; *interj*. be quiet!; *v.t.* to cause to be still; to forbid to speak; to hush; to calm; to refute; to gag; to kill. **-r** *n*. **silent** *a*. **silently** *adv*. **silentness** *n*. [L. *silentium*].

si·lex (sī′·leks) *n*. silica; trade name for coffee maker made of heat-resistant glass [L. = flint].

sil·hou·ette (sil·ȯȯ·et′) *n*. portrait or picture cut from black paper or done in solid black upon a light ground; outline of object seen against the light; *v.t.* to represent in outline; to cause to stand out in dark shadow against a light background [Fr.].

sil·i·ca (sil′·i·ka) *n*. silicon dioxide, main component of most rocks, occurring in nature as sand, flint, quartz, etc. **silicate** *n*. salt of silicic acid. **silicated** *a*. combined or coated with silica. **silicate of soda**, waterglass. **siliceous** (sạl·ish′·ạs) *a*. pert. to silica in a finely divided state. Also **silicious. silicic** (sạl·is′·ik) *a*. derived from or containing silica [L. *silex*].

sil·i·cones (sil′·a·kōnz) *n.pl*. new family of materials—petroleum, brine, ordinary sand [L. *silex*, flint].

silk (silk) *n*. fine, soft, lustrous thread obtained from cocoons made by larvae of certain moths, esp. silkworm; thread or fabric made from this; *a*. made of silk. **-en** *a*. made of, or resembling, silk; soft; smooth; silky. **-iness** *n*. **-screen** *a*. and *n*. (pert. to) the reproduction of a design by means of a pattern made on a screen of nylon or silk. **-worm** *n*. caterpillar of any moth which produces silk, esp. Bombyx mori. **-y** *a*. [O.E. *seolor*].

sill (sil) *n*. base or foundation; horizontal member of stone, brick, or wood at the bottom of window frame, door, or opening [O.E. *syll*].

sil·ly (sil′·i) *a*. weak in intellect; foolish; senseless; stupid; (*Arch*.) simple; *n*. silly person. **sillily** *adv*. **silliness** *n*. foolishness [O.E. *saelig*, happy, fortunate].

si·lo (sī′·lō) *n*. large, airtight tower, elevator, or pit in which green crops are preserved for future use as fodder; *v.t.* to preserve in a silo. Cf. [Sp.].

silt (silt) *n*. fine, alluvial, soil, particles; mud; sediment; *v.t.* to choke or obstruct with silt (generally with up); *v.i.* to become filled up with silt [etym. uncertain].

sil·ver (sil'·ver) *n.* soft, white, metallic element, very malleable and ductile; silverware; silver coins; anything resembling silver; *a.* made of, or resembling, silver; white or gray, as hair; having a pale luster, as moon; soft and melodious, as voice or sound; bright, silvery; *v.t.* to coat or plate with silver; to apply amalgam of tinfoil and quicksilver to back of a mirror; to tinge with white or gray; to render smooth and bright; *v.i.* to become gradually white, as hair. **-ize** *v.t.* to coat or cover thinly with a film of silver. *n.* **— lining,** prospect of better times to come. **-plate** *n.* metallic articles coated with silver. **-plated** *a.* **-plating** *n.* deposition of silver on another metal by electrolysis. **-ware** *n.* articles made of silver. **— wedding,** 25th anniversary of marriage. **-ry** *a.* like silver; lustrous; (of sound) soft and clear [O.E. *siolfor*].

sim·i·an (sim'·i·an) *a.* pert. to or like an ape generally; *n.* a monkey or ape [L. = ape].

sim·i·lar (sim'·a·ler) *a.* like; resembling; exactly corresponding; (*Geom.*) of plane figures, differing in size but having all corresponding angles and side ratios uniform. **-ity** *n.* quality or state of being similar. **-ly** *adv.* [L. *similis*, like].

sim·i·le (sim'·a·lē) *n.* figure of speech using some point of resemblance observed to exist between two things which differ in other respects [L. *similis*, like].

si·mil·i·tude (sa·mil'·a·tūd) *n.* state of being similar or like; resemblance; likeness; parable [L. *similis*, like].

sim·mer (sim'·er) *v.t.* to cause to boil gently; *v.i.* to be just bubbling or just below boiling-point; to be in a state of suppressed anger or laughter; *n.* gentle, gradual heating [imit.].

si·mo·ni·ac (sa·mō'·ni·ak) *n.* one guilty of simony. **-al** *a.* **-ally** *adv.* **simonist** *n.* one who practices simony [Cf. *simony*].

si·mo·ny (sī'·ma·ni·, sim'·a·ni·) *n.* the offense of offering or accepting money or other reward for nomination or appointment to an ecclesiastical office or other benefit [See *Acts* 8].

sim·per (sim'·per) *v.i.* to smile in a silly, affected manner; *n.* smile with air of silliness or affectation. **-er** *n.* [etym. uncertain].

sim·ple (sim'·pl) *a.* single; not complex; entire; mere; plain, sincere; clear; intelligible; simple-minded; (*Chem.*) composed of a single element; *n.* something not compounded. **— interest,** money paid on principal borrowed but not on accrued interest as in compound interest. **-minded** *a.* ingenuous; open; frank; mentally weak. **-ness** *n.* **-ton** *n.* foolish person; person of weak intellect. **simplicity** *n.* artlessness; sincerity; clearness; simpleness. **simplification** *n.* act of making simple or easy; thing simplified. **simplificative** *a.* tending to simplify. **simplify** *v.t.* to make or render simple, plain, or easy. *pa.t.* and *pa.p.* **simplified. simply** *adv.* in a simple manner; plainly; unostentatiously; without affectation [L. *simplus*].

sim·u·la·crum (sim·ya·lā'·kram) *n.* image; representation. *pl.* **simulacra** [L.].

sim·u·lant (sim'·ya·lant) *a.* simulating; having the appearance of; *n.* one simulating something. **simular** *a.* simulated; counterfeit; feigned; *n.* one who pretends to be what he is not; a simulator.

sim·u·late (sim'·ya·lāt) *v.t.* to assume the mere appearance of, without the reality; to feign. **simulation** *n.* **simulator** *n.* [L. *simulare*, to make like].

si·mul·ta·ne·ous (sim·al·tā'·nē·as) *a.* existing or occurring at same time. **-ness, simultaneity** *n.* **-ly** *adv.* [L. *simul*].

sin (sin) *n.* transgression against divine or moral law, esp. when committed consciously; conduct or state of mind of a habitual or unrepentant sinner; iniquity; evil; *v.i.* to depart from path of duty prescribed by God; to violate any rule of duty; to do wrong. *pr.p.* **-ning.** *pa.t.* and *pa.p.* **-ned. -ful** *a.* iniquitous; wicked; unholy. **-fully** *adv.* **-fulness** *n.* **-ner** *n.* [O.E. *synn*].

since (sins) *adv.* from then till now; subsequently; ago; *prep.* at some time subsequent to; after; *conj.* from the time that; seeing that; because; inasmuch as [earlier *sithens*, O.E. *siththan*].

sin·cere (sin·sir') *a.* not assumed or merely professed; straightforward. **-ly** *adv.* **-ness, sincerity** (sin·ser'·a·ti·) *n.* state or quality of being sincere; honesty of mind or intention; truthfulness [L. *sincerus*, pure].

sine (sīn) *n.* (*abbrev.* **sin**) (*Math*) perpendicular drawn from one extremity of an arc to diameter drawn through other extremity; function of one of the two acute angles in a right-angle triangle, ratio of line subtending this angle to hypotenuse [L. *sinus*, a curve].

si·ne·cure (sī'·ni·kūr, sin'·a·kūr) *n.* office, position, etc. with salary but with few duties. **sinecurist** *n.* one who holds, or seeks sinecure [L. *sine cura*, without care].

sin·ew (sin'·ū) *n.* ligament or tendon which joins muscle to bone; strength; source of strength or vigor. **-ed** *a.* having sinews; strong; firm. **-y** *a.* well braced; muscular;

strong [O.E. *sinu*].

sing (sing) *v.t.* to utter with musical modulations of voice; to celebrate in song; to praise in verse; *v.i.* to utter sounds with melodious modulations of voice; to pipe, twitter, chirp, as birds; to hum; to reverberate. *pa.t.* **sang** or **sung.** *pa.p.* **sung. -er** *n.* one who sings; vocalist. **-ing** *n.* art of singing; vocal music; a humming noise (in the ear, on a telephone circuit, etc.) [O.E. *singan*].

singe (sinj) *v.t.* to burn the surface slightly; to burn loose fluff from yarns, etc. *pr.p.* **-ing.** *n.* superficial burn [O.E. *sencgan*, to make hiss].

Sin·gha·lese (sing·ga·lēz') *a.* pert. to Ceylon, its people, or language. *n.* a native of Ceylon [Sans. *Sinhala*].

sin·gle (sing'·gl) *a.* sole; alone; separate; individual; not double; unmarried; sincere; whole-hearted; straightforward; upright; *n.* unit; (*Cricket*) one run; (*Tennis*) game confined to two opponents; *v.t.* (with *out*) to select from a number; to pick; to choose. **—breasted** *a.* of a garment, buttoning on one side only. **— entry** *n.* in bookkeeping, entry of each transaction on one side only of an account. **—handed** *a.* and *adv.* without help; unassisted. **-hearted** *a.* sincere. **—minded** *a.* having but one purpose or aim; sincere. **-ness** *n.* state of being single; honesty of purpose; freedom from deceit or guile; sincerity. **singly** *adv.* one by one; by oneself [L. *singuli*, one at a time].

sin·gle·ton (sing'·gl·tan) *n.* (*Cards*) hand containing only one card of some suit, or the card itself [dim. of *single*].

sing·song (sing'·sawng) *n.* rhythmical, monotonous fashion of uttering. *a.* monotonous; droning [redup. of *sing*].

sin·gu·lar (sing'·gya·ler) *a.* existing by itself; denoting one person or thing; individual; unique; outstanding; *n.* single instance; word in the singular number. **-ize** *v.t.* to make singular or unique. **-ity** *n.* state of being singular; anything unusual or remarkable; oddity. **-ly** *adv.* [L. *singularis*].

Sin·ic (sin'·ik) *a.* Chinese. **Sinicise** (sin'·a·sīz) *v.t.* to give a Chinese character to. **-ism** *n.* mode of thought or customs peculiar to the Chinese [Gk. *Sinai*, the Chinese].

sin·is·ter (sin'·is·ter) *a.* on left hand; evil-looking; unlucky (left being regarded as unlucky side). **sinistral** *a.* to the left; reversed; (*Bot.*) having whorls not turning normally [L. = on the left hand].

sink (singk) *v.t.* to cause to descend; to submerge; to lower out of sight; to dig; to excavate; to ruin; to suppress; to invest; *v.i.* to subside; to descend; to penetrate (into); to decline in value, health, or social status; to be dying; to droop; to decay; to become submerged. *pa.t.* **sank** or **sunk.** *pa.p.* **sunk.** *n.* a receptacle for washing up, with pipe for carrying away waste water; marsh or area in which river water percolates through surface and disappears; place notoriously associated with evildoing. **-er** *n.* weight fixed to anything to make it sink, as on net, fishing-line, etc. **-ing** *n.* operation of excavating; subsidence; settling; abatement; ebb; part sunk below surrounding surface. **-ing fund,** fund set aside at regular intervals to provide replacement of wasting asset or repayment of particular liability [O.E. *sincan*].

Si·no-, in compounds, meaning Chinese [Gk. *Sinai*, Chinese].

Si·nol·o·gy (si·nál'·a·ji·) *n.* that branch of knowledge which deals with the Chinese language, culture, history, religion and art. [Gk. *Sinai*, the Chinese; *logos*, a discourse].

sin·u·ate (sin'·yoo·āt) *v.i.* to bend in and out; to wind; to turn; *a.* (sin'·yoo·it) (*Bot.*) wavy; tortuous; curved on the margin, as a leaf. Also **-d. sinuation** *n.* **sinuose, sinuous** *a.* bending in and out; of serpentine or undulating form; morally crooked; supple. **sinuously** *adv.* [L. *sinus*, a fold].

si·nus (sī'·nas) *n.* (*Anat.*) opening; hollow; cavity; (*Path.*) groove or passage in tissues leading to a deep-seated abscess, usually in nose or ear. **-itis** *n.* inflammation of sinus [L. *sinus*, a curve].

Sioux (soo) *n.* member of great Siouan division of N. American aborigines; their language. *pl.* **Sioux** (soo, sooz).

sip (sip) *v.t.* and *v.i.* to drink or imbibe in very small quantities; to taste. *pr.p.* **-ping.** *pa.t.* and *pa.p.* **-ped.** *n.* a small portion of liquid sipped with the lips [O.E. *sypian*, to soak].

si·phon, syphon (sī'·fan) *n.* a bent tube or pipe by which a liquid can be transferred by atmospheric pressure from one receptacle to another; bottle provided with internal tube and lever top, for holding and delivering aerated water; projecting tube in mantle of shell of bivalve; *v.t.* to draw off by means of a siphon. *n.* action of a siphon [Gk. = tube].

sir (sur) *n.* a title of respect to any man of position; title of knight or baronet [var. of *sire*].

sire (sīr) *n.* title of respect to a king or emperor; male parent of an animal (applied esp. to horses); *pl.* (*Poetic*) ancestors; *v.t.* to beget (of animals) [Fr. fr. L. *senior*, elder].

si·ren (sī'·ran) *n.* (*Myth.*) one of several nymphs said to sing with such sweetness that

sailors were lured to death; seductive alluring woman; form of horn which emits series of loud, piercing notes used as warning signal; steam whistle; the mud-eel; *a.* pert. to, or resembling a siren; alluring; seductive [Gk. *Seirēn*].

siphon

Sir·i·us (sir'·i·as) *n.* (*Astron.*) a star of the first magnitude known as the Dog Star [L.]. **sir·loin** (sur'·loin) *n.* the upper part of a loin of beef [O.Fr. *surloigne*].

si·roc·co (si·rák'·ō) *n.* a hot, southerly, dust-laden wind from Africa, chiefly experienced in Italy, Malta and Sicily [It.].

si·sal (sis'·al, sī'·sal) *n.* fiber plant, native to Florida and Yucatan providing **sisal-grass** (**sisal-hemp**) [*Sisal*, a seaport in *Yucatan*].

sis·sy (sis'·i·) *n.* (*Colloq.*) ineffective effeminate man or boy; *a.* effeminate.

sis·ter (sis'·ter) *n.* female whose parents are same as those of another person; correlative of brother; woman of the same faith; female of the same society, convent, abbey; nun; *a.* standing in relation of sister; related; of a similar nature to, as institute, college, etc. **-hood** *n.* state of being a sister; society of women united in one faith or order. **-in-law** *n.* husband's or wife's sister; brother's wife. *pl.* **-s-in-law, -like, -ly** *a.* [O.N. *systir*].

Sis·tine (sis'·tēn) *a.* pert. to any Pope named Sixtus. **— Chapel,** the Pope's private chapel in the Vatican at Rome.

sit (sit) *v.i.* to rest upon haunches, a seat, etc.; to remain; to rest; to perch, as birds; (of hen) to cover and warm eggs for hatching; to be officially engaged in transacting business, as court, council, etc.; to be in session; to be representative in legislature for constituency; to pose for portrait; to press or weigh (upon); to fit (of clothes); *v.t.* to keep good seat, upon, as on horseback; to place upon seat; *pr.p.* **-ting.** *pa.t.* and *pa.p.* **sat.** *n.* position assumed by an object after being placed. **-ter** *n.* one who sits; one who poses for artist; bird sitting on its eggs; one who stays with children while parents are out. **-ting** *n.* state of resting on a seat, etc.; act of placing oneself on a seat; session; business meeting; time given up to posing for artist; clutch of eggs for incubation; *a.* resting on haunches; perched. **-ting-room** *n.* [O.E. *sittan*].

site (sīt) *n.* situation; plot of ground for, or with, building; locality; place where anything is fixed; *v.t.* to place in position; to locate [L. *situs*, a site].

si·tol·o·gy (sī·tál'·a·ji·) *n.* dietetics [Gk. *sitos*, food; *logos*, a discourse].

sit·u·ate (sich'·oo·āt) *v.t.* to give a site to; to place in a particular state or set of circumstances; to locate; **-d** *a.* located; placed with reference to other affairs, etc. **situation** *n.* location; place or position; site; condition; job; post; plight [L. *situs*, a site].

six (siks) *a.* one more than five; *n.* sum of three and three; symbol 6 or VI. **-fold** *a.* six times as much or as many. **-footer** *n.* person six feet in height. **-pence** *n.* silver coin in British currency of value of six pennies. **-penny** *a.* worth sixpence; paltry; of small value. **-shooter** *n.* a six-chambered revolver. **-teen** *n.* and *a.* six and ten, symbol 16 or XVI. **-teenth** *a.* sixth after the tenth; being one of sixteen equal parts into which anything is divided; *n.* one of sixteen equal parts; a division of the inch; (*Mus.*) semiquaver. **-th** *a.* next in order after the fifth; one of six equal parts; n. (Mus.) an interval comprising six degrees of the staff, as A to F. **-ty** a. six times ten; three score; n. symbol 60 or LX. **-tieth** a. next in order after the fifty-ninth; one of sixty equal parts; n. **at sixes and sevens**, in disorder and confusion [O.E. siex].

size (sīz) n. bulk; bigness; comparative magnitude; dimensions; extent; conventional measure of dimension; r.t. to arrange according to size. **-able, sizable** a. of considerable size or bulk. **to size up**, to estimate possibilities of; to take measure of [contr. of assize].

size (sīz) n. substance of a gelatinous nature, like weak glue; v.t. to treat or cover with size [Fr. assise, a layer (e.g. of paint, etc.)].

siz-zle (siz'-l) v.i. to make hissing or sputtering noise; (Colloq.) to suffer from heat. n. hissing, sputtering noise. **sizzling** n. [imit.].

skald (skåld) n. ancient Scandinavian poet **-ic** a. Also **scald** [O.N. skald].

skate (skāt) n. steel blade attached to boot, used for gliding over ice; v.i. to travel over ice on skates. **-r** n. **skating. skating-rink** n. stretch of ice or flat expanse for skating; ice-rink. **roller skate** n. skate with wheels in place of steel blade [Dut. schaats].

skate (skāt) n. a large, edible, flat fish of the ray family [O.N. skata].

skean (skēn) n. Highland dagger or dirk; long knife [Gael. sgian, knife].

ske-dad-dle (ski-dad'-l) v.i. (Colloq.) to scamper off; n. hasty, disorderly flight.

skeet (skēt) n. trapshooting with clay targets thrown into the air.

skein (skān) n. small hank, of fixed length, of thread, silk, or yarn, doubled and secured by loose knot [O.Fr. escaigne].

skel-e-ton (skel'-a-tan) n. body framework providing support for human or animal body; any framework, as of building, plant, etc.; general outline; a. pert. to skeleton; containing mere outlines. Also **skeletal. — crew, staff,** etc., minimum number of men employed on some essential duty [Gk. skeletos, dried up].

skel-ter. See **helter-skelter.**

skep (skep) n. beehive made of straw; light basket [O.N. skeppa, a basket].

skep-tic (skep'-tik) n. one who doubts, esp. existence of God, or accepted doctrines; rationalist; agnostic; unbeliever; **-al** a. doubtful; doubting; disbelieving. **-ally** adv. **-alness** n. **skepticize** v.i. to doubt everything. **skepticism** n. doubt in absence of conclusive evidence; theory that positive truth is unattainable by human intellect [Gk. skeptesthai, to investigate].

sker-ry (sker'-i.) n. rocky isle; reef [O.N.].

sketch (skech) n. first rough draft or plan of any design; outline; drawing in pen, pencil, or similar medium; descriptive essay or account, in light vein; a short, humorous one-act play; v.t. to draw outline of; to make rough draft of; v.i. to draw; to make sketches. **-er** n. **-ily** adv. **-iness** n. lack of detail. **-y** a. containing outline or rough form; inadequate; incomplete [Dut. schets].

skew (skū) a. awry; oblique; askew; turned aside; n. anything set obliquely or at an angle to some other object; a deviation; v.t. to put askew; to skid. **—bald** a. of horse, bay and white in patches. [O.Fr. escuer].

skew-er (skū'-er) n. pointed rod for fastening meat to a spit, or for keeping it in form while roasting; v.t. to fasten with skewers.

ski (skē, in Norway, shē) n. long wooden runner strapped to foot, for running, sliding and jumping over snow; v.i. to run, slide, or jump on skis. **-er** n. [Norw.].

ski-a-graph (skī'-a-graf) n. an X-ray photograph. Also **skiagram. -er** n. one who takes X-ray photographs. **-ic** a. [Gk. skia, a shadow; graphein, to write].

skid (skid) n. a piece of timber to protect side of vessel from injury; drag placed under wheel to check speed of vehicle descending steep gradient; inclined plane down which logs, etc. slide; low, wooden platform for holding and moving loads; v.i. to slide or slip sideways; v.t. to slide a log down a skid; to place on skids. pr.p. **-ding** pa.p., pa.t. **-ded** [O.N. skidh].

skiff (skif) n. a small rowboat or sailboat [Fr. esquif].

skill (skil) n. practical ability and dexterity; knowledge; expertness; aptitude. **-ful** a. expert; skilled; dexterous. **-fully** adv. **-fulness** n. **-ed** a. [O.N. skil, distinction].

skil-let (skil'-it) n. a frying pan [O.Fr. escuellete].

skim (skim) v.t. to remove from surface of liquid; to glide over lightly and rapidly; to glance over in superficial way; to graze; v.i. to pass lightly over; to glide along; to hasten over superficially. pr.p. **-ming.** pa.t. and pa.p. **-med.** n. skimming; matter skimmed off. **-mer** n. **— milk** n. milk from which cream has been removed [O.Fr. escumer].

skimp (skimp) v.t. to stint; v.i. to be mean or parsimonious; to economize in petty fashion. **-y** a. scant; meager; stingy.

skin (skin) n. external protective covering of animal bodies; epidermis; a hide; a pelt; coat of fruits and plants; husk or bark; thick scum; v.t. to strip off skin or hide of; to flay; to graze; to peel; (Slang) to cheat; to swindle. **—deep** a. superficial. **—flint** n. miser. **— game** n. cheating and swindling. **— grafting** n. transplanting healthy skin to wound to form new skin. **-ner** n. dealer in hides; furrier. **-niness** n. leanness. **-ny** a. of skin; very lean or thin. **— tight** a. fitting close to skin. [O.N. skinn].

skip (skip) v.t. to leap over lightly; to omit without noticing; v.i. to leap lightly, esp. in frolic; to frisk; to pass from one thing to another; to clear repeatedly a rope swung in play under one's feet; (Colloq.) to run away hastily. pr.p. **-ping.** pa.t. and pa.p. **-ped.** n. light leap, spring, or bound; an omission. **-ping** a. characterized by skips.

skip-per (skip'-er) n. captain of ship or team [Dut. schipper].

skirl (skurl) v.i. to sound shrilly. n. shrill, high-pitched sound of bagpipe [var. of shrill].

skir-mish (skur'-mish) n. irregular, minor engagement between two parties of soldiers; v.i. [Fr. escarmouche].

skirt (skurt) n. lower part of coat, gown; outer garment of a woman fitted to and hanging from waist; petticoat; flap; border; margin; edge; rim; v.t. to be on border; to go around. **-ing** n. material for women's skirts; border [O.N. skyrta].

skit (skit) n. satirical gibe; lampoon; short, usually humorous, play; v.i. to leap aside. **-tish** a. frisky; frivolous; fickle; apt to shy, of a horse. **-tishly** adv. **-tishness** n.

skit-tle (skit'-l) n. game of ninepins.

skive (skīv) v.t. in shoe-making, to pare away edges of leather [Ice. skifa, to split].

skiv-vy (skiv'-i.) n. (Slang) undershirt.

skoal (skōl) interj. salutation, hail! in toasting [Dan. skaal, bowl; a toast].

skulk (skulk) v.i. to sneak out of the way; to lurk or keep out of sight in a furtive manner; to act sullenly; n. one who skulks.

skull (skul) n. bony framework which encloses brain; cranium along with bones of face. **— cap** n. brimless cap fitting close to head. **— and crossbones**, a symbol for poison, formerly used on pirate flags [M.E. skulle].

skunk (skungk) n. small N. American burrowing animal, allied to weasel, which defends itself by emitting evil-smelling fluid; (Colloq.) a base, mean person [Amer.-Ind. seganku].

sky (skī) n. the apparent vault of heaven; heavens; firmament; climate. v.t. **—blue** n. and a. azure; cerulean. **-ey** a. (Poetic) like the sky. **—gazer** n. visionary. **—high** a. and adv. at a great elevation; carried away with excitement or anticipation. **-lark** n. bird which sings as it soars; v.i. (Colloq.) to indulge in boisterous byplay. **—larking** n. **-light** n. glazed opening in roof or ceiling. **-line** n. horizon; silhouette of buildings, etc. on horizon. **-scraper** n. lofty building with numerous stories. **-writing** n. writing in air for advertising or propaganda purposes by smoke from an airplane [O.N. sky, a cloud].

Skye (skī) n. or **Skyeterrier**, breed of Scotch terrier, with long hair. [Isle of Skye].

slab (slab) n. thickish, flat, rectangular piece of anything; concrete paving-block; thick slice of cake, etc.

slack (slak) a. not taut; not closely drawn together; not holding fast; remiss about one's duties; easy-going; n. part of a rope which hangs loose; quiet time. **-en** v.t. to loosen; to moderate; to relax; to leave undone; to slake; v.i. to become slack; to lose cohesion; to relax; to dodge work; to languish; to flag. **-er** n. one who shirks work. **-ly** adv. **-ness** n. **-s** n.pl. loose trousers worn by men or women. [O.E. slaec].

slack (slak) n. the finer screenings of coal which pass through a half-inch mesh; coal-dust; dross. **-heap** n. [Ger. Schlacke, dross].

slag (slag) n. silicate formed during smelting of ores; scoria of a volcano; v.i. to form slag [Ger. Schlacke, dross].

slain (slān) pa.p. of the verb **slay.**

slake (slāk) v.t. to quench; to extinguish; to combine quicklime with water; to slacken; v.i. to become mixed with water [O.E. slacian].

slam (slam) v.t. to shut violently and noisily; to bang; to hit; to dash down; to win all, or all but one, of the tricks at cards. pr.p. **-ming.** pa.t. and pa.p. **-med.** n. act of slamming; bang. **slam (grand** or **small)** thirteen or twelve tricks taken in one deal in cards.

slan-der (slan'-der) n. false or malicious statement about person; defamation of character by spoken word; calumny; v.t. to injure by maliciously uttering false report; to defame. **-er** n. **-ous** a. [Fr. esclandre].

slang (slang) n. word or expression in common colloquial use but not regarded as standard English; jargon peculiar to certain sections of public, trades, etc.; argot; a. pert. to slang; v.t. to vituperate; to revile; to scold.

slant (slant) v.t. to turn from a direct line; to give a sloping direction to; v.i. to lie obliquely; to slope; to incline; n. slanting direction or position; slope; point of view or illuminating remark (on); a. sloping; oblique. **-ingly** adv. **-ly, -wise** adv. [Swed. slinta, to slide].

slap (slap) n. blow with open hand or flat instrument; insulting remark; v.t. to strike with open hand or something flat. pr.p. **-ping.** pa.t. and pa.p. **-ped.** adv. with a sudden blow; (Colloq.) instantly; directly. **-stick** n. boisterous farce of pantomine or low comedy. [imit. origin].

slash (slash) v.t. to cut by striking violently and haphazardly; to make gashes in; to slit; v.i. to strike violently and at random with edged weapon; n. long cut; gash; cutting stroke; large slit in garment. **-er** n. [O.Fr. esclachier, to sever].

slat (slat) n. narrow strip of wood, metal, etc. a lath pl. (Slang) ribs. **-ted** a. covered with slats [O.Fr. esclat, fragment].

slate (slāt) n. a form of shale, composed mainly of aluminum silicate, which splits readily into thin leaves; prepared piece of such stone, esp. thin piece for roofing houses, etc.; dark blue-gray color; list of candidates for offices; a. made of slate; bluish-gray; v.t. to cover with slates; to put on a list for nomination, etc. **slating** n. act of covering with slates; roof-covering thus put on. **slaty** n. [O.Fr. esclat, a splinted].

slat-tern (slat'-ern) n. slut; slovenly woman or girl. **-liness** n. **-ly** a. like a slattern; adv. in slovenly manner [Scand. slat, to strike].

slaugh-ter (slaw'-ter) n. act of slaughtering; carnage; massacre; butchery; killing of animals to provide food; v.t. to kill; to slay in battle; to butcher. **-er** n. **-house** n. place where cattle are slaughtered. **-ous** a. bent on slaughter; destructive. **-ously** adv. [O.N. slatr, butcher's meat].

Slav (slâv) n. a member of a group of peoples in E. and S.E. Europe, comprising Russians, Ukrainians, White Russians, Poles, Czechs, Slovaks, Serbians, Croats, Slovenes and Bulgarians; a. relating to the Slavs; Slavic; Slavonic. **-ic** a. **-onic** a. [etym. unknown].

slave (slâv) n. person held legally in bondage to another; bondman; one who has lost all powers of resistance to some pernicious habit or vice; v.i. to work like a slave, to toil unremittingly. **-driver** n. an overseer in charge of slaves at work; exacting taskmaster. **-r** n. person or ship engaged in slave traffic. **-ry** n. condition of slave compelled to perform compulsory work for another; bondage; servitude. **— trade** n. traffic in human beings. **— trader** n. **slavish** a. pert. to slaves; menial; drudging; servile; base; mean; imitative. **slavishly** adv. **slavishness** n. **white slavery**, traffic in women and girls for immoral purposes [Fr. esclave, fr. Slav].

slav-er (slâv'-er) n. saliva running from mouth; sentimental nonsense; v.t. to smear with saliva issuing from mouth; v.i. to slobber; to talk in a weakly sentimental fashion. **-er** n. [O.N. slafra, to slaver].

slaw (slaw) *n.* sliced cabbage served cooked, or uncooked, as a salad [Dut. *sla*, salad].

slay (slā) *v.t.* to kill; to murder; to slaughter. *pa.t.* **slew.** *pa.p.* **slain. -er** *n* [O.E. *slean*, to smite].

sleave (slēv) *n.* knotted or entangled part of silk or thread; a fine wisp of silk made by separating a thread; *v.t.* to separate and divide as into threads [etym. uncertain].

slea·zy (slē'·zi) *a.* thin or poor in texture.

sled, sledge (sled, slej) *n.* a vehicle on runners, for conveying loads over hard snow or ice; a sleigh; a small flat sled for coasting; *v.t.* to convey on a sled; *v.i.* to ride on a sled [Dut. *slede*].

sledge (slej) *n.* large, heavy hammer. [O.E. *slecg*].

sleek (slēk) *a.* having a smooth surface; glossy; not rough; ingratiating; *v.t.* to make smooth; to calm; to soothe; *adv.* **-ly** *adv.* **-ness** *n.* [O.N. *slikr*, smooth].

sleep (slēp) *v.i.* to rest by suspension of exercise of powers of body and mind; to become numb (of limb); to slumber; to doze; to repose; to rest; to be dead. *pa.t.* and *pa.p.* **slept.** *n.* slumber; repose; rest; death. **-er** *n.* one who sleeps; railway sleeping car; **-ily** *adv.* in drowsy manner. **-iness** *n.* **-ing** *a.* resting in sleep; inducing sleep; adapted for sleeping; *n.* state of resting in sleep; state of not being raised or discussed. **-ing-bag** *n.* bag of thick material, waterproofed on outside, for sleeping in the open. **-ing-car** *n.* railway car with berths, compartments, etc. **-ing sickness** *n.* brain infection causing increased drowsiness. **-less** *a.* wakeful; restless; alert; vigilant; unremitting. **-lessly** *adv.* **-lessness** *n.* **-walker** *n.* one who walks in his sleep or in a trance; somnambulist. **-walking** *n.* **-y** *a.* inclined to sleep; drowsy [O.E. *slaepan*].

sleet (slēt) *n.* rain that is partly frozen; *v.i.* to fall as fine pellets of ice. **-iness** *n.* **-y** *a.* [M.E. *slete*].

sleeve (slēv) *n.* part of garment which covers arm; casing surrounding shaft of engine; wind-sock used on airfields as wind-indicator; *v.t.* to furnish with sleeves. [O.E. *sliefe*].

sleigh (slā) *n.* a sled; an open carriage on runners, usually horse-drawn; *v.i.* to drive in a sleigh [Dut. *slee*].

sleight (slīt) *n.* artful trick; skill. **— of hand** *n.* legerdemain; juggling [O.N. *slaegth*].

slen·der (slen'·der) *a.* thin or narrow; weak; feeble; not strong. **-ly** *adv.* **-ness** *n.* [M.E. *slendre*].

slept (slept) *pa.t.* and *pa.p.* of **sleep.**

sleuth (slooth) *n.* bloodhound; a relentless tracker; (*Colloq.*) detective. **-hound** *n.* bloodhound [O.N. *sloth*, a track].

slew (sloo) *pa.t.* of **slay.**

slew, slue (sloo) *v.t.* and *v.i.* to turn about; to swing round [etym. unknown].

slice (slis) *v.t.* and *v.i.* to cut off thin flat pieces; to strike a ball so that its line of flight diverges well to the right; to part like the cut of a knife; *n.* thin, flat piece cut off; broad, flat, thin knife for serving fish; spatula; share or portion; stroke at golf, etc. in which ball curls away to the right. **-r** *n.* [O.Fr. *esclice*].

slick (slik) *a.* smooth; sleek; smooth-tongued; smart; clever; slippery; *adv.* deftly; cleverly; *v.t.* to sleek; to make glossy. *n.* a smooth spot, as one covered with oil. See **sleek.**

slick·er (slik'·er) *n.* waterproof coat.

slid, slidden See **slide.**

slide (slid) *v.i.* to slip smoothly along; to slip, to glide, esp. over ice; to pass imperceptibly; to deteriorate morally; *v.t.* to move something into position by pushing along the surface of another body; to move smoothly and imperceptibly. *pr.p.* **sliding.** *pa.t.* **slid.** *pa.p.* **slid** or **slidden.** *n.* sliding; track on ice made by sliding; sliding part of mechanism; anything which moves freely in or out; photographic film holder for projecting; smooth and easy passage; chute; a narrow piece of glass to carry small object to be examined under microscope; moving part of trombone or trumpet. **-r** *n.* **— rule** *n.* mathematical instrument for rapid calculations. **sliding-scale** *n.* schedule of wages, prices, duties, etc. showing automatic variations [O.E. *slidan*].

slight (slīt) *a.* trifling; inconsiderable; not substantial; slim; slender; *n.* contempt by ignoring another; disdain; insult; *v.t.* to ignore; to disdain; to insult. **-ing** *n.* act or instance of disrespect; a disparaging. **-ingly** *adv.* **-ly** *adv.* to slight extent; not seriously. **-ness** *n.* [O.N. *slettr*].

slim (slim) *a.* of small diameter or thickness; slender; thin; slight; unsubstantial; *comp.* **-mer,** *superl.* **-mest.** *v.t.* and *v.i.* to make or become slim; *pa.t.*, *pa.p.* **-med.** *pr.p.* **-ming. -ly** *adv.* frail [Dut. = crafty].

slime (slim) *n.* soft, sticky, moist earth or clay; greasy, viscous mud; mire; viscous secretion of snails, etc.; **slimily** *adv.* **sliminess** *n.* **slimy** *a.* [O.E. *slim*].

sling (sling) *n.* pocket of leather, etc., with a string attached at each end for hurling a stone; catapult; swinging throw; strap attached to rifle; hanging bandage, for supporting an arm or hand; rope, chain, belt, etc. for hoisting weights; *v.t.* to throw by means of sling or swinging motion of arm; to hoist or lower by means of slings; to suspend. *pa.t.* and *pa.p.* **slung. -er** *n.* [O.N. *slyngra*].

sling (sling) *n.* American iced drink of sweetened gin (or rum) with water, fruit juice [Ger. *schlingen*, to swallow].

slink (slingk) *v.i.* to move in a stealthy, furtive manner. *pa.t.* and *pa.p.* **slunk** [O.E. *slincan*, to creep].

slip (slip) *v.t.* to move an object smoothly, secretly, or furtively into another position; to put on, or off easily; to loosen; to release (dog); to omit; to miss; to overlook; to escape (memory); to escape from; of animals, to give premature birth to; *v.i.* to lose one's foothold; to move smoothly along surface of; to withdraw quietly; to slide; to make a mistake; to lose one's chance; to pass without notice. *pr.p.* **-ping.** *pa.t.* and *pa.p.* **-ped.** *n.* act of slipping; unintentional error; false step; twig for grafting separated from main stock; leash for dog; long, narrow, piece; loose garment worn under woman's dress; covering for a pillow; skid; inclined plane from which ships are launched. **— cover** *n.* a removable covering for upholstered furniture. **-knot** *n.* running knot which slips along rope around which it is made, forming loop. **-per** *n.* light shoe for indoor use; dancing-shoe. **-perily** *adv.* **-periness** *n.* condition of being slippery. *a.* so smooth as to cause slipping or to be difficult to hold or catch; not affording a firm footing; unstable; untrustworthy; changeable; artful; wily. **-shod** *a.* having shoes down at heel; untidy; slovenly; inaccurate. **-up** *n.* (*Colloq.*) a mistake [O.E. *slipan*].

slit (slit) *v.t.* to cut lengthwise; to cut open; to sever; to rend; to split; *v.i.* to be slit. *pr.p.* **-ting.** *pa.t.* and *pa.p.* **slit.** *n.* straight, narrow cut or incision; narrow opening. **-ter** *n.* [O.E. *slitan*].

slith·er (sliTH'·er) *v.i.* to slide and bump (down a slope, etc.); to move in a sliding, snakelike fashion; *n.* act of slithering; rubble [var. of *slidder*].

sliv·er (sliv'·er) *v.t.* to divide into long, thin strips; *v.i.* to split; to become split off; *n.* thin piece cut lengthwise; splinter [O.E. *slifan*, to split].

slob·ber (slab'·er) *v.i.* to let saliva drool from mouth; dribble; *v.t.* to cover with saliva. *n.* saliva coming from mouth; sentimental drivel. Also **slabber. -er** *n.* [var. of *slaver*].

sloe (slō) *n.* blackthorn; small dark fruit of blackthorn. **— gin** *n.* liqueur from gin and sloes [O.E. *sla*].

slog (slag) *v.t.* to hit wildly and vigorously; *v.i.* to work or study with dogged determination; to trudge along; *pr.p.* **-ging.** *pa.t.* and *pa.p.* **-ged, -ger** *n.* [O.E. *slean*, to strike].

slo·gan (slō'·gan) *n.* war cry of Highland clan in Scotland; distinctive phrase used by a political party; catchword for focusing public interest, etc. [Gael. *sluagh-ghairm*].

sloop (sloop) *n.* one-masted sailing vessel [Dut. *sloep*].

slop (slap) *n.* liquid carelessly spilled; puddle; *pl.* water in which anything has been washed; liquid refuse; *v.t.* to spill; to soil by spilling over; *v.i.* to overthrow or be spilled. *pr.p.* **-ping.** *pa.t.* and *pa.p.* **-ped. —basin, —bowl** *n.* basin or bowl for holding dregs from tea-

cups. **-pily** *adv.* **-piness** *n.* **-py** *a.* wet; muddy; slovenly; untidy; (*Colloq.*) mawkishly sentimental [O.E. *sloppe*].

slope (slōp) *n.* upward or downward inclination; slant; side of hill; *v.t.* to form with slope; to place slanting; *v.i.* to assume oblique direction; to be inclined. **sloping** *a.* [O.E. *slupan*, to slip away].

slosh (slash) *n.* soft mud; *v.t.* to stir in liquid; *v.i.* to splash, stir about, in mud, water, etc. [fr. *slush*].

slot (slat) *n.* slit cut out for reception of object or part of machine; slit where coins are inserted into automatic machines; *v.t.* to make a slot in. *pr.p.* **-ting.** *pa.t.* and *pa.p.* **-ted. — machine** *n.* automatic machine worked by insertion of coin [O.Fr. *esclot*].

sloth (slawth) *n.* lethargy; indolence. **-ful** *a.* inactive; sluggish; lazy. **-fully** *adv.* **-fulness** *n.* [O.E. *slaewth*, fr. *slaw*, slow].

sloth (slōth, slawth) *n.* group of edentate mammals of S. America which cling mostly to branches of trees [fr. *slow*].

slouch (slouch) *n.* ungraceful, stooping manner of walking or standing; shambling gait; *v.i.* to shamble; to sit or stand in a drooping position; *v.t.* to depress; to cause to hang down loosely. **— hat** *n.* soft hat with a broad, flexible brim. **-y** *a.* inclined to slouch.

slough (slou) *n.* bog; swamp [O.E. *sloh*].

slough (sluf) *n.* cast-off outer skin, esp. of snake; dead mass of soft tissues which separates from healthy tissues in gangrene or ulcers; *v.t.* to cast off, or shed, as a slough; *v.i.* to separate as dead matter which forms over sore; to drop off [etym. uncertain].

Slo·vak (slō·vak') *n.* member of Slav people in northern Carpathians, closely related to Czechs; language spoken in Slovakia; *a.* pert. to Slovaks. Also **Slovakian.**

slov·en (sluv'·n) *n.* person careless of dress, or negligent of cleanliness. **-liness** *n.* **-ly** *a.* *adv.* in slipshod manner [etym. uncertain].

slow (slō) *a.* not swift; not quick in motion; gradual; indicating time earlier than true time; mentally sluggish; dull; wearisome; *adv.* slowly; to render slow; to retard; to reduce speed of; *v.i.* to slacken speed. **-ly** *adv.* **— match** *n.* fuse made so as to burn slowly, for firing mines, etc. **— motion** *n.* and *a.* in motion pictures, motion shown in exaggeratedly slow time. **-ness** *n.* **-witted** *a.* mentally slow; dull; apathetic. [O.E. *slaw*, sluggish].

sludge (sluj) *n.* mud which settles at bottom of waterways, of vessel containing water, or a shaft when drilling; semi-solid; slimy matter precipitated from sewage in sedimentation tank. **sludgy** *a.* [var. of *slush*].

slug (slug) *n.* one of land snails without a shell, a common pest in gardens. **-gard** *n.* person habitually lazy and idle; *a.* disinclined to exert oneself; habitually indolent; slothful; slow-moving. **-gishly** *adv.* **-ishness** *n.* [Scand.].

slug (slug) *n.* small thick disk of metal; a piece of metal fired from gun; solid line of type cast by linotype process.

slug (slug) (*Colloq.*) *v.i.* to strike heavily; to slog; *n.* heavy blow [O.E. *slean*, to strike].

sluice (sloos) *n.* valve or shutter for regulating flow; a natural channel for drainage; artificial channel along which stream flows; sluicing; *v.t.* to drain through a sluice; to wash out, or pour over with water; *v.i.* to run through a sluice or other stream of water. **— box** *n.* trough used in goldmining [O.Fr. *escluse*].

slum (slum) *n.* squalid street, or quarter of town, characterized by gross over-crowding, dilapidation, poverty, vice and dirt; *v.i.* to visit slums. *pr.p.* **-ming** *pa.t.* and *pa.p.* **-med.**

slum·ber (slum'·ber) *v.i.* to sleep lightly; to be in a state of negligence, sloth, or inactivity; *n.* light sleep; doze. **-er** *n.* **-ous, slumbrous** *a.* inducing slumber; drowsy [O.E. *sluma*].

slump (slump) *n.* act of slumping; sudden, sharp fall in prices or volume of business done; industrial or financial depression; *v.i.* to drop suddenly; to droop; to decline suddenly in value, volume, or esteem; to sink suddenly when crossing snow, ice, boggy ground, etc.

slung (slung) *pa.t.* and *pa.p.* of **sling.**

slunk (slungk) *pa.t.* and *pa.p.* of **slink.**

slur (slur) *v.t.* to pass over lightly; to depreciate; to insult; to pronounce indistinctly; (*Mus.*) to sing or play in a smooth, gliding style; to run one into the other, as notes. *pr.p.* **-ring.** *pa.t.* and *pa.p.* **-red.** *n.* slight blur in print; stigma; reproach; implied insult; (*Mus.*) mark, thus (‿ or ⌢) connecting notes that are to be sung to same syllable, or made in one continued breath; indistinct sound [O. Dut. *slooren*, to trail (in mud)].

slush (slush) *n.* half-melted snow; soft mud; any greasy, pasty mass; overly sentimental talk or writings;*v.t.* to splash or cover with slush; to flush a place with water. **-y** *a.* [var. of *sludge*].

slut (slut) *n.* dirty, untidy woman; slattern. **-tish** *a.* untidy and dirty. [M.E. *slutte*].

sly (slī) *a.* artfully cunning; mischievous. **-ly** *adv.* **-ness** *n.* [O.N. *slaegr*].

smack (smak) *v.t.* to make a loud, quick noise (with lips) as in kissing or after tasting; to slap loudly; to strike; to make sharp, quick noise with lips; *n.* quick, sharp noise, esp. with lips; a loud kiss; a slap [imit.].

smack (smak) *v.i.* to have a taste or flavor; to give a suggestion (of); *n.* a slight taste [O.E. *smaec*, taste].

smack (smak) *n.* small sailing vessel, usually for fishing [Dut. *smak*].

small (smawl) *a.* little in size, number, degree, etc.; not large; unimportant; short; weak; slender; mean; *n.* small or slender part, esp. of back. **-ish** *a.* rather small. **-ness** *n.* **— arms** *n.pl.* hand firearms, e.g. rifles, pistols, etc. **— change**, coins of small value, e.g. pennies, nickels, dimes, etc. **— fry** *n.* young fish; children. **— talk** *n.* gossip; light conversation [O.E. *smael*].

small-pox (smawl′·paks) *n.* infectious disease, characterized into pustules [E. *small*; O.E. *poc*, a pustule].

smart (smárt) *n.* sharp, stinging pain; pang of grief; hurt feelings, etc. *v.i.* to feel such a pain; to be punished (with 'for'); *a.* causing a sharp, stinging pain; clever; active; shrewd; trim; neat; well-dressed; fashionable. **-ly** *adv.* **-ness** *n.* **smarten** (smár′·tn) *v.t.* and *v.i.* to make more spruce [O.E. *smeortan*, to feel pain].

smash (smash) *v.t.* to break into pieces to shatter; to hit hard; to ruin; *v.i.* to break into pieces; to dash violently against; of a business firm, to fail; *n.* crash; heavy blow; accident, wrecking vehicles; utter ruin; of business firm, bankruptcy. **-ing** *a.* [fr. E. *mash*. to mix up].

smat·ter (smat′·er) *v.i.* to talk superficially; **-ing** *n.* slight, superficial knowledge.

smear (smēr) *v.t.* to rub over with a greasy, oily, or sticky substance; to daub; to impute disgrace to; (*U.S. Slang*) to defeat thoroughly; *n.* mark, stain. **-iness** *n.* **-y** *a.* [O.E. *smeru*, fat].

smell (smel) *n.* sense of perceiving odors by nose; act of smelling; (unpleasant) odor; scent; perfume; *v.t.* to perceive by nose; to detect; *v.i.* to use nose; to give out odor. *pr.p.* **-ing.** *pa.p.* and *pa.t.* **-ed** or **smelt. -ing** *n.* **-y** *a.* having unpleasant smell. **-ing salts** *n.pl.* scented ammonium carbonate used to relieve faintness, headache, etc. [M.E. *smel*].

smelt (smelt) *n.* small, silvery fish of salmon family [O.E. *smelt*].

smelt (smelt) *v.t.* to melt or fuse ore in order to extract metal. **-ing** *n.* [Sw. *smalla*, to melt].

smi·lax (smī′·laks) *n.* genus of evergreen climbing shrubs [Gk. = bindweed].

smile (smīl) *v.i.* to express pleasure, approval, amusement, contempt, irony, etc. by curving lips; to look happy; *v.t.* to express by smile; *n.* act of smiling; pleasant facial expression. **smiling** *a.* cheerful; gay joyous. [Sw. *smila*].

smirch (smurch) *v.t.* to dirty; to soil; to stain; to bring disgrace upon; *n.* stain [M.E. *smeren*, to smear].

smirk (smurk) *v.i.* to smile in an affected or conceited manner; *n.* [O.E. *smercian*, to smile].

smite (smīt) *v.t.* to hit hard; to strike with hand, fist, weapon, etc.; to defeat; to afflict; *v.i.* to strike. *pa.p.* **smitten** (smit′·n). *pa.t.* **smote** (smōt). **-r** *n.* [O.E. *smitan*, to smear].

smith (smith) *n.* one who shapes metal, esp. with hammer and anvil; blacksmith. **-y** *n.* smith's workshop; forge [O.E. *smith*].

smith·er·eens (smiTH·er·ēnz′) *n.pl.* (*Colloq.*) small bits. Also **smithers** [fr. *smite*].

smit·ten (smit′·n) *pa.p.* of **smite.**

smock (smák) *n.* a loose garment worn over other clothing as a protection while working. **-ing** *n.* embroidered gathering of dress, blouse, etc. into honeycomb pattern [O.E. *smoc*].

smog (smág, smawg) *n.* mixture of smoke and fog in atmosphere [from *smoke* and *fog*].

smoke (smōk) *n.* cloudy mass of suspended particles that rises from fire or anything burning; spell of tobacco smoking; cigar or cigarette; *v.t.* to consume (tobacco opium, etc.) by smoking; to expose to smoke (esp. in curing fish, etc.); *v.i.* to inhale and expel smoke of burning tobacco; to give off smoke. **-r** *n.* one who smokes tobacco; railroad car or section in which smoking is permitted; social gathering for men at which smoking is allowed. **smoking** *n.* **smokiness** *n.* **smoky** *a.* emitting smoke; filled with smoke; having color, taste of smoke [O.E. *smoca*].

smol·der (smōl′·der) *v.i.* to burn slowly without flame; of feelings, esp. anger, resentment, etc., to exist inwardly [M.E. *smolder*].

smolt (smōlt) *n.* young salmon.

smooth (smóoTH) *a.* not rough; level; polished; gently flowing; calm; steady in motion; pleasant; easy; *v.t.* to make smooth; to polish; to calm; to soothe; to make easy; *adv.* in a smooth manner. **-ly** *adv.* [O.E. *smoth*].

smor·gas·bord (smŏr′·gas·bŏrd) *n.* meal of appetizers served buffet style [Sw.].

smote (smōt) *pa.p.* and *pa.t.* of **smite.**

smoth·er (smuTH′·er) *v.t.* to destroy by depriving of air; to suffocate; to conceal; *v.i.* to be stifled; to be without air; *n.* thick smoke or dust [O.E. *smorian*, to choke].

smudge (smuj) *n.* smear; stain; dirty mark; blot; smoky fire to drive off insects or protect fruit trees from pests; *v.t.* to smear; to make a dirty mark; *v.i.* to become dirty or blurred.

smug (smug) *a.* very neat and prim; self-satisfied; complacent. **-ly** *adv.* **-ness** *n.* [L. Ger. *smuk*, neat].

smug·gle (smug′·l) *v.t.* to import or export goods secretly to evade customs duties. **-r** *n.* **smuggling** *n.* [L. Ger. *smuggeln*].

smut (smut) *n.* black particle of dirt; spot caused by this; fungoid disease of cereals, characterized by blackening of ears of oats, barley, etc.; lewd or obscene talk or writing; *v.t.* to blacken; to smudge. *pr.p.* **-ting.** *pa.p.* and *pa.t.* **-ted. -ty** *a.* soiled with smut; obscene; lewd. **-tily** *adv.* **-tiness** *n.*

smutch (smuch) *v.t.* to blacken, as with soot, etc.; *n.* dirty spot; stain; smudge.

snack (snak) *n.* share; slight, hasty meal. **— bar** *n.* place for service of light, hurried meals [fr. *snatch*].

snaf·fle (snaf′·l) *n.* horse's bridle bit jointed in middle but without curb; *v.t.* to put one on a horse [Dut. *snavel*, nose of animal].

snag (snag) *n.* stump projecting from tree-trunk; stump or tree-trunk sticking up in a river impeding passage of boats; any obstacle, drawback, or catch; *v.t.* to catch on a snag. *pr.p.* **-ging.** *pa.p.*, *pa.t.* [O.T. *snagi*, a point].

snail (snāl) *n.* slow-moving mollusk with spiral shell; slow person [O.E. *snaegel*].

snake (snāk) *n.* long, scaly, limbless reptile; serpent; treacherous person; *v.t.* (*U.S.*) to drag along, e.g. log; *v.i.* to move like a snail. **snaky** *a.* pert. to, or resembling, snake; full of snakes [O.E. *snaca*].

snap (snap) *v.t.* to break abruptly; to crack; to seize suddenly; to snatch; to bite; to shut with click; (*Photog.*) to take snapshot of; *v.i.* to break short; to try to bite; to utter sharp, cross words; to make a quick, sharp sound; to sparkle. *pr.p.* **-ping.** *pa.p.* and *pa.t.* **-ped.** *n.* act of seizing suddenly, esp. with teeth; bite; sudden breaking; quick, sharp sound; small spring catch, as of a bracelet; crisp cooky; short spell of frosty weather; (*Photog.*) short for snapshot; (*Slang*) an easy job; *a.* sudden; unprepared; without warning. **-per** *n.* one who snaps; kind of fresh-water turtle. **-py** *a.* lively; brisk; (*Colloq.*) smartly dressed; quick. **-dragon** *n.* (*Bot.*) a flowering plant. **-shot** *n.* photograph [Dut. *snappen*].

snare (snār) *n.* running noose of cord or wire, used to trap animals or birds; a trap; anything by which one is deceived; *n.pl.* (*Mus.*) catgut strings across lower head of snare drum to produce rattling sound; *v.t.* to catch with snare; to entangle. **— drum** *n.* small drum carried at the side [O.N. *snara*].

snarl (snárl) *v.i.* to growl like an angry dog; to speak in a surly manner; *n.* growling sound; surly tone of voice. **-er** *n.* [imit.].

snarl (snárl) *n.* tangle or knot of hair, wool, etc.; complication; *v.t.* and *v.i.* to entangle or become entangled [fr. *snare*].

snatch (snach) *v.t.* to seize hastily or without permission; to grasp; *v.i.* to make quick grab or bite (at); *n.* quick grab; small bit or fragment [M.E. *snacchen*].

sneak (snēk) *v.i.* to creep or steal away; to slink; *v.t.* (*Slang*) to steal; *n.* furtive, cowardly fellow. **-er** *n.* **-ers** *n.pl.* (*U.S.*) light, soft-soled shoes. **-ing** *a.* mean; contemptible; secret. **-ingly** *adv.* **-iness, -ingness** *n.* quality of being sneaky; slyness. **-y** *a.* sneaking; mean; underhand [O.E. *snican*, to creep].

sneer (snēr) *v.i.* to show contempt by facial expression, as by curling lips; to smile, speak, or write scornfully; *n.* look of contempt or ridicule; scornful utterance. **-er** *n.* **-ing** *a.*

sneeze (snēze) *v.i.* to expel air through nose and mouth with sudden convulsive spasm and noise; *n.* a sneezing [O.E. *fneosan*].

snick (snik) *n.* small cut; notch; nick; *v.t.* to cut; to notch; to clip [Scand. *snikka*, to cut].

snicker (snik′·er) *v.i.* to laugh with small, audible catches of voice; to giggle; *n.* half-suppressed laugh [imit. origin].

sniff (snif) *v.i.* to draw in breath through nose with sharp hiss; to express disapproval, etc. by sniffing; to snuff; *v.t.* to take up through nose; to smell; *n.* act of sniffing; that which is sniffed. **-le** *v.i.* to sniff noisily through nose; to snuffle. **-er** **snifter** (*Slang*) small drink of liquor [imit. origin].

snip (snip) *v.t.* to clip off with scissors; to cut; *n.* a single, quick stroke, as with scissors; a bit cut off; small piece of anything; *pl.* strong hand shears for cutting sheet metal. *pr.p.* **-ping.** *pa.p.* and *pa.t.* **-ped.** **-per** *n.* **-pet** *n.* a fragment [Dut. *snippen*].

snipe (snīp) *n.* long-billed gamebird, frequenting marshy places; a shot; *v.i.* to shoot snipe; (*Mil.*) to shoot from cover; *v.t.* to hit by so shooting. **-r** *n.* [O.N. *snipa*].

sniv·el (sniv′·l) *n.* running at the nose; sham emotion; whining, as a child. *v.i.* to run at the nose; to show sham or real sorrow; to cry or whine, as children [O.E. *snyflan*].

snob (snáb) *n.* one who judges by social rank or wealth rather than merit; one who ignores those whom he considers his social inferiors. **-bery** *n.* **-bish** *a.* **-bishly** *adv.* **-bishness** *n.* [etym. uncertain].

snood (snóod) *n.* ribbon formerly worn to hold back hair; fillet; netlike covering for head or part of hat [O.E. *snod*].

snoop (snóop) *v.i.* (*Colloq.*) to investigate slyly; to pry into; *n.* one who acts thus.

snoot (snóot) *n.* snout; nose; contemptuous; **-ily** *adv.* arrogantly; **-iness** *n.*; **-y,** *a.* (*Colloq.*) snobbish [ME *snute*].

snooze (snóoz) *n.* (*Colloq.*) short sleep; nap; *v.i.* to take a snooze [perh. fr. *snore*].

snore (snōr) *v.i.* to breathe heavily and noisily during sleep; *n.* such noisy breathing. **-r** *n.* [O.E. *snora*, a snore].

snor·kel (snōr′·kal) *n.* device for submarines and divers for air intake [Gr. *Schnorkel*, spiral].

snort (snawrt) *v.i.* to force air with violence through nose, as horses; to express feeling by such a sound; *v.t.* to express by snort; *n.* snorting sound [imit. origin].

snout (snout) *n.* projecting nose and jaws of animal, esp. of pig; any projection like a snout [O.E. *snut*].

snow (snō) *n.* frozen vapor which falls in flakes; snowfall; mass of flakes on the ground; (*Slang*) narcotic drug, in powdered form; *v.t.* to let fall like snow; to cover with snow; *v.i.* to fall as or like snow.**-y** *a.* covered with, full of snow; white. **-ily** *adv.* **-iness** *n.* **-ball** *n.* round mass of snow pressed or rolled together; shrub bearing balllike clusters of white flowers; anything increasing like snowball; *i.t.* to pelt with snowballs; *v.i.* to grow rapidly; like a rolling snowball. **— blindness** *n.* temporary blindness caused by glare of sun from snow. **—bound** *a.* shut in by heavy snowfall. **-drift** *n.* mass of snow driven into a heap by wind. **-drop** *n.* bulbous plant bearing white flowers in early spring. **-fall** *n.* falling of snow; amount of snow falling in given time or place. **-flake** *n.* small, thin, feathery mass of snow. **— line** *n.* line on mountain above which snow never melts. **-plow** *n.* machine for clearing snow from roads, etc. **-shoe** *n.* light, wooden framework with interwoven leather thongs for traveling over deep snow [O.E. *snaw*].

snowplow

snub (snub) *v.t.* to check or rebuke with rudeness or indifference; to repress intentionally; *pr.p.* **-bing.** *pa.p.* and *pa.t.* **-bed.** *n.* intentional slight; rebuff; check; *a.* of nose, short and slightly turned up [O.N. *snubba*, to rebuke].

snowshoes

snuff (snuf) *n.* charred part of wick of candle or lamp; *v.t.* to nip this off; to extinguish. **-ers** *n.pl.* instrument resembling scissors, for snuffing candles [M.E. *snoffe*].

snuff (snuf) *v.t.* to draw up or through nostrils; to sniff; to smell; to inhale; *v.i.* to draw air or snuff into nose; to take snuff; *n.* powdered tobacco for inhaling through nose; sniff. **-er** *n.* **-box** *n.* a small box for snuff [Dut. *snuffen*].

snuf·fle (snuf'·l) *v.i.* to breathe noisily through nose, esp. when obstructed; to sniff continually; to speak through nose; *n.* act of snuffling; a nasal twang. **-r** *n.* [fr. *snuff*].

snug (snug) *a.* cosy; trim; comfortable; sheltered; close fitting. **-ly** *adv.* **-ness** *n.* cosiness. **-gery** *n.* a cosy room. **-gle** *v.i.* to lie close to, for warmth or from affection; to nestle [Scand.].

so (sō) *adv.* in this manner or degree; in such degree; very; to such degree (with *as* or *that* coming after); the case being such; accordingly; *conj.* therefore; in case that; *interj.* well! **— long** (*Colloq.*) good-bye. **so-so** *a.* (*Colloq.*) fair; middling; tolerable; *adv.* fairly; tolerably [O.E. *swa*].

soak (sōk) *v.t.* to steep; to wet thoroughly; to permeate; *v.i.* to lie steeped in water or other fluid; (*Colloq.*) to drink to excess; *n.* a soaking; the act of soaking; heavy rain; (*Colloq.*) a hard drinker. **-er** *n.* **-ing** *n.* wetting thoroughly; drenched; *n.* [O.E. *soca*].

soap (sōp) *n.* compound of oil or fat with alkali, used in washing; *v.t.* and *v.i.* to apply soap to. **-y** *a.* pert. to soap; covered with soap; like soap. **-iness** *n.* **— bubble** *n.* iridescent bubble from soapsuds. **— opera** *n.* (*Colloq.*) highly dramatized radio serial. **-stone** *n.* soft, smooth stone, with soapy feel; talc. **-suds** *n.pl.* foamy mixture of soap and water [O.E. *sape*].

soar (sōr) *v.i.* to fly high; to mount into air; to glide; to rise far above normal or to a great height [L. *ex*, out of; *aura*, the air].

sob (sáb) *v.i.* to catch breath, esp. in weeping; to sigh with convulsive motion. *pr.p.* **-bing.** *pa.p.* and *pa.t.* **-bed.** *n.* convulsive catching of breath, esp. in weeping or sighing [imit.].

so·ber (sō'·ber) *a.* temperate; not intoxicated; exercising cool reason; subdued; *v.t.* and *v.i.* to make or become sober. **-ly** *adv.* **-ness** *n.* **sobriety** (sō·brī'·e·ti·) *n.* habit of being sober; habitual temperance; moderation; seriousness [L. *sobrius*].

so·bri·quet (sō'·bri·kā) *n.* nickname, an assumed name. Also **soubriquet** (sōō-) [Fr.].

soc·cer (sák'·er) *n.* association football [fr. *soc* in association].

so·cia·ble (sō'·sha·bl) *a.* inclined to be friendly; fond of company. **sociably** *adv.* **-ness** *n.* **sociability** *n.* friendliness; geniality [L. *socius*, a companion].

so·cial (sō'·shal) *a.* pert. to society; affecting public interest; pert. to world of fashion, etc.; living in communities, as ants; sociable; companionable; convivial; *n.* social meeting. **sociably** *adv.* **-ite** (sō'·shal·īt) *n.* member of fashionable society [L. *socius*, a companion].

so·cial·ism (sō'·shal·izm) *n.* economic and political system, aiming at public or government ownership of means of production, etc. **socialize** *v.t.* to make social; to transfer industry, etc. from private to public or government ownership. **socialization** *n.* **socialist** *a.* pert. to socialism. **socialistic** *a.* **socialistically** *adv.* [L. *socius*, a companion].

so·ci·e·ty (sa·sī'·a·ti·) *n.* people in general; community; people of culture and good breeding in any community; the wealthy classes; the world of fashion; fellowship; wealthy; a company; an association; a club [L. *socius*, a companion].

so·ci·ol·o·gy (sō·shi·ál'·a·ji·) *n.* science of origin, development, and nature of problems confronting society; social science. **sociological** *a.* **sociologist** *n.* [L. *socius*, a companion; Gk. *logos*, a discourse].

sock (sák) *n.* orig. a low-heeled shoe; a short stocking [L. *soccus*, a light shoe].

sock (sák) *v.t.* (*Slang*) to hit hard; *n.* a blow.

sock·et (sák'·et) *n.* opening or hollow into which anything is fitted; cavity of eye, tooth, etc.; *v.t.* to provide with, or place in, socket.

sock·eye (sák'·ī) *n.* a red salmon.

sod (sád) *n.* flat piece of earth with grass; turf; *v.t.* to cover with turf. *pr.p.* **-ding.** *pa.p.*, *pa.t.* **-ded.**

so·da (sō'·da) *n.* name applied to various compounds of sodium, e.g. *baking soda*, *caustic soda*, *washing soda*. (See **sodium**); (*Colloq.*) soda water. **— fountain** *n.* case for holding soda water; shop selling soft drinks, ices, etc. **— water** *n.* drink made by charging water with carbon dioxide [It. fr. L. *solidus*, firm].

so·dal·i·ty (sō·dal'·a·ti·) *n.* fellowship; an association [L. *sodalis*, a comrade].

sod·den (sád'·n) *a.* soaked; soft with moisture; dull and heavy; stupid.

so·di·um (sō'·di·am) *n.* silvery-white metallic alkaline element, the base of soda (symbol, **Na.** fr. L. *natrium*). **— bicarbonate**, compound of sodium and carbon, used in cooking, medicine, etc.; baking soda. **— carbonate**, washing soda. **— chloride**, common household salt [fr. *soda*].

sod·o·my (sád'·am·i·) *n.* unnatural sexual intercourse, esp. between males or with an animal [fr. *Sodom*, Bib. city].

so·fa (sō'·fa) *n.* an upholstered couch [Ar. *Suffah*, cushion].

soft (sawft) *a.* yielding easily to pressure; not hard; easily shaped or molded; smooth; gentle; melodious; quiet; susceptible; sentimental; weak; weak in intellect; not astringent; containing no alcohol; in phonetics, esp. of consonants 'c' and 'g,' pronounced with a sibilant sound; *adv.* softly; quietly. **-ish** *a.* somewhat soft. **-ly** *adv.* **-ness** *n.* **-headed** *a.* weak in intellect. **-hearted** *a.* kind; gentle; merciful [O.E. *softe*].

soft·ball (sawft'·bawl) *n.* variant of the game of baseball [*soft* and *ball*].

soft·en (sawf'·n) *v.t.* to make soft or softer; to lighten; to mitigate; to tone down; to make less loud; *v.t.* to become soft or softer. **-ing** *n.* act, process, or result of becoming soft or softer. **-ing** *n.* act, process, or result of becoming soft or softer [O.E. *softe*].

sog·gy (sàg'·i·) *a.* soaked with water; sodden [Icel. *soggr*, damp].

soi·gné (swán'·yā) *a.* well finished; exquisitely groomed [Fr.].

soil (soil) *v.t.* to make dirty; to defile; to dirty marks; filth; manure; top layer of earth's surface; earth, as food for plants [O.Fr. *soile*].

soi·rée (swá·rā') *n.* a social evening, a reception [Fr. = evening].

so·journ (sō'·journ) to dwell for a time; (sō'jurn') *n.* short stay [L. *sub*, under; *diurnus*, of a day].

sol·ace (sàl'·as) *n.* comfort in grief; consolation; *v.t.* to console [L. *solari*, to comfort].

so·lan (sō'·lan) *n.* large sea bird like a goose; a gannet. Also **— goose** [O.N. *sula*].

so·lar (sō'·ler) *a.* pert. to, caused by, measured by sun. **-ize** *v.t.* and *v.i.* to expose to sun's rays. **solarium** (sō·lar!·i·um) *n.* a sun room or porch. *pl.* **solaria.** **— plexus** (*Med.*) network of nerve tissue and fibers at back of stomach; (*Colloq.*) the pit of the stomach. **— system**, sun and all the heavenly bodies revolving around it [L. *sol*, the sun].

sold (sōld) *pa.p.* and *pa.t.* of **sell.**

sol·der (sád'·er) *n.* easily melted alloy for joining metals; *v.t.* to join or mend with solder [L. *solidare*, to make solid].

sol·dier (sōl'·jer) *n.* man engaged in military service; an enlisted man as distinguished from commissoined officer. **-y** *n.* soldiers collectively; troops. **— of fortune**, military adventurer [L. *solidus*, a coin].

sole (sōl) *n.* flat of the foot; under part of boot or shoe; lower part of anything, or that on which anything rests; small flatfish, used for food; *v.t.* to supply with a sole [L. *solea*].

sole (sōl) *a.* being, or acting, without another; alone; only. **-ly** *adv.* alone; only [L. *solus*].

sol·e·cism (sàl'·a·sizm) *n.* breach of grammar; a breach of etiquette. **solecist** *n.* one guilty of solecism [Gk. *soloikos*, speaking incorrectly].

sol·emn (sàl'·am) *a.* marked, or performed, with religious ceremony; impressive; grave; inspiring awe or dread. **-ly** *adv.* **-ness** *n.* **-ize** (sàl'·am·nīz) *v.t.* to perform with ceremony or legal form. **-ity** (sol·em'·ni·ti·) *n.* sacred rite or formal celebration; gravity; seriousness [L. *sollemnis*, yearly, solemn].

so·len (sō'·lan) *n.* genus of bivalve molluscs having a long, slender shell; razor-shell.

solenoid *n.* (*Elect.*) cylindrical coil of wire (without fixed iron core) forming electromagnet when carrying current [Gk. *sōlēn*, a channel pipe; *eidos*, form].

sol·fa (sōl·fà!) *v.i.* to sing notes of scale [It. fr. *sol, fa*].

so·lic·it (sa·lis'·it) *v.t.* to ask with earnestness; to petition; to entreat; *v.i.* to try to obtain, as trade, etc.; to accost. **-ant** *n.* one who solicits; petitioner. **-ation** *n.* earnest request; invitation; petition. **-or** *n.* one who solicits; official in charge of legal matters of city, department of government, etc. **-ous** *a.* anxious; eager; earnest. **-ously** *adv.* **-ousness, -ude** *n.* being solicitous; uneasiness; anxiety [L. *sollicitare*, to stir up].

sol·id (sàl'·id) *a.* not in a liquid or gaseous state; hard; compact; firm; not hollow; dependable; sound; unanimous; (*Geom.*) having

length, breadth, and thickness; whole; complete; *n.* a firm, compact body; (*Geom.*) that which has length, breadth and thickness; (*Physics*) substance which is not liquid nor gaseous. **-ly** *adv.* **-arity** *n.* state of being solidly united in support of common interests, rights, etc. **-ity** *n.* state of being solid; compactness; hardness [L. *solidus*, firm].

so·lid·i·fy (sa·lid'·a·fī) *v.t.* to make solid or firm; to harden; *v.i.* to become solid [L. *solidus*, firm; *facere*, to make].

sol·i·dus (sàl'·i·das) *n.* oblique stroke (/) in fractions, dates, etc. *pl.* **solidi** [L.].

so·lil·o·quy (sa·lil'·a·kwi·) *n.* talking to oneself; monologue, esp. by actor alone on stage. **soliloquize** *v.i.* to recite a soliloquy; to talk to oneself [L. *solus*, alone; *logui*, to speak].

sol·i·taire (sàl'·a·ter) *a.* living alone; done or spent alone; lonely; secluded; single; sole; *n.* hermit; recluse; a single gem set by itself. **solitarily** *adv.* **solitariness** *n.* **solitude** *n.* being alone; seclusion; lonely place or life [L. *solus*, alone].

so·lo (sō'·lō) *n.* musical composition played or sung by one person; in aviation, flight by single person; *pl.* (sō'·lōz) or **soli** (sō'·lē) *a.* done or performed by one person; unaccompanied; alone. **soloist** (sō'·lō·ist) *n.* (*Mus.*) performer of solos [It. fr. L. *solus*, alone].

sol·stice (sàl'·stis) *n.* either of two points in sun's path at which sun is farthest N. or S. from equator, about June 21 and December 22 respectively. **solstitial** (sàl·sti'·shal) *a.* [L. *sol*, the sun; *sistere*, to cause to stand].

sol·u·ble (sàl'·ya·bl) *a.* capable of being dissolved in a liquid; able to be solved or explained. **solubility** *n.* [L. *solubilis*, fr. *solvere*, to loosen].

so·lus (sō'·las) *a.* as a stage direction, alone. *fem.* **sola**]L. = alone].

so·lu·tion (sa·lōō'·shan) *n.* process of finding answer to problem; answer itself; dissolving gas, liquid, or solid, esp. in liquid; mixture so obtained; commonly, a mixture of a solid in a liquid; *v.t.* to coat with solution, as a puncture. **solute** *n.* substance dissolved in a solution [L. *solvere*, *solutum*, to loosen].

solve (sálv) *v.t.* to work out; to find the answer to; to explain; to make clear. **solvable** *a.* capable of explanation; able to be worked out. **-r** *n.* **solvent** *a.* having the power to dissolve another substance; able to pay all one's debts; *n.* substance, able to dissolve another substance. **-ncy** *n.* state of being able to pay one's debts [L. *solvere*, to loosen].

so·mat·ic (sō·mat'·ik) *a.* pert. to the body; corporeal; physical. Also **-al** [Gk. *sōma*, a body].

som·ber (sàm'·ber) *a.* dark; gloomy; melancholy. **-ly** *adv.* **-ness** *n.* **sombrous** *a.* (*Poet.*) somber **sombrously** *adv.* [Fr. fr. L. *sub umbra*, under shade].

som·bre·ro (sàm·bre'·rō) *n.* broad-brimmed felt hat [Sp. *sombre*, shade].

some (sum) *a.* denoting an indefinite number, amount, or extent; amount of; one or other; a certain; particular; approximately; (*Colloq.*) remarkable; (*pron.*) portion; particular persons not named; *adv.* approximately. **-body** *n.* person not definitely known; person of importance. **-how** *adv.* in one way or another; by any means. **-one** *pron.* somebody; person not named. **-such** *a.* denoting person or thing of the kind specified. **-thing** *n.* thing not clearly defined; an indefinite quantity or degree; *adv.* in some degree. **-time** *adv.* at a time not definitely stated; at one time or other; at a future time; *a.* former. **-times** *adv.* at times; now and then; occasionally. **-what** *n.* indefinite amount or degree; *adv.* to some extent; rather. **-where** *adv.* in an unnamed or unknown place [O.E. *sum*].

som·er·sault (sum'·er·sawlt) *n.* a movement in which one turns heels over head; *v.i.* [L. *supra*, above; *saltus*, a leap].

som·nam·bu·late (sàm·nam'·bya·lāt) *v.i.* to walk in one's sleep. **somnambulation** *n.* **somnambulism** *n.* habit of walking in one's sleep; sleepwalking. **somnambulist** *n.* a sleepwalker. **somnambulistic** *a.* [L. *somnus*, sleep; *ambulare*, to walk].

som·ni·fa·cient (sàm·ni·fā'·shant) *a.* inducing sleep; *n.* soporific. **somniferous** *a.* inducing sleep. **somnific** *a.* causing sleep [L. *somnus*, sleep; *facere*, to make; *ferre*, to bring].

som·no·lent (sàm'·na·lant) *a.* sleepy; drowsy. **-ly** *adv.* drowsily. **somnolence** *n.* sleepiness; drowsiness. Also **somnolency** *n.* **somnolescent** *a.* half asleep [L. *somnus*].

son (sun) *n.* male child; male descendant.

so·nant (sō′·nant) *a.* pert. to sound; (*Phonetics*) of certain alphabetic sounds, voiced; *n.* a syllabic sound. **sonance** *n.* [L. *sonare*].

however distant; term of affection; native of a place; disciple. **—in-law** *n.* the husband of one's daughter [O.E. *sunu*].

so·na·ta (sạ·nä′·tạ) *n.* a musical composition in three or four movements. **sonatina** (sä·nạ·tē′·nạ) *n.* a short sonata [It. fr. L. *sonare*, to sound].

song (sawng) *n.* singing; poem, or piece of poetry, esp. if set to music; piece of music to be sung; musical sounds made by birds; (*Colloq.*) a mere trifle. **— bird** *n.* a singing bird. **-ster** *n.* (*fem.* **songstress**) one who sings; a song bird [O.E. *sang*, fr. *singan*, to sing].

son·ic (sän′·ik) *a.* pertaining to sound; devoting speed approximate to that of sound.

son·net (sän′·ạt) *n.* poem of fourteen lines of iambic pentameter, with a definite rhyme scheme. **soneteer** *n.* a writer of sonnets [It. *sonetto*, fr. L. *sonus*, a sound].

so·no·rous (sạ·nōr′·as) *a.* giving out a deep, loud sound when struck; resonant; high-sounding. *adv.* **-ness**, **sonority** *n.* [L. *sonorus*, noisy].

soon (sōōn) *adv.* in a short time; shortly; without delay; willingly [O.E. *sona*, at once].

soot (soot) *n.* a black powdery substance formed by burning coal, etc.; *v.t.* to cover with soot. **-y** *a.* pert. to, or like, soot; covered with soot; black; dingy; dirty [O.E. *sot*].

sooth (sōōth) *n.* (*Arch.*) truth; reality. **-sayer** *n.* one who claims to be able to foretell future. **-saying** *n.* [O.E. *soth*, true].

soothe (sōōTH) *v.t.* to please with soft words or kind actions; to calm; to comfort; to allay, as pain. **soothing** *a.* **soothingly** *adv.* [O.E. *sothian*, to show to be true].

sop (säp) *n.* piece of bread, etc., dipped in a liquid; anything given to pacify or quieten; bribe; *v.t.* to steep in liquid. *pr.p.* **-ping**. *pa.p.* and *pa.t.* **-ped.** **-ping** *a.* soaked; wet through. **-py** *a.* soaked; rainy [O.E. *sopp*, fr. *supan*, to sip].

soph·ism (säf′·izm) *n.* specious argument; clever but fallacious reasoning. **sophist** *n.* orig. in ancient Greece, teacher of sound, rhetoric, philosphy; one who uses fallacious or specious arguments. **sophistry** *n.* practice of sophists. **sophistic, sophistical** *a.* **sophistically** *adv.* **sophisticate** *v.t.* to deceive by using sophisms; to make artificial; to make wise in the ways of the world. **sophisticated** *a.* **sophistication** *n.* [Gk. *sophisma*, wise].

soph·o·more (säf′·ạ·mōr) *n.* second-year student of university, college, or high school [Gk. *sophos*, wise].

so·por (sō′·per) *n.* unnaturally deep sleep. **-ific** *a.* causing or inducing sleep; *n.* drug, which induces deep sleep. **-iferous, soporose** *a.* causing sleep; sleepy. [L. *sopor*, deep sleep].

so·pran·o (sạ·pra′·nō) *n.* highest type of female or boy's voice; soprano singer; *pl.* **-s**, **soprani** (sō·prä′·ni) [It. fr. *sopra*, above].

sor·cer·y (sawr′·sạ·ri·) *n.* witchcraft; magic; enchantment. **sorcerer** *n.* a magician. *fem.* **sorceress**, a witch [L. *sortiri*, to cast lots].

sor·did (sawr′·did) *a.* filthy; squalid; meanly avaricious. **-ly** *adv.* **-ness** *n.* [L. *sordidus*].

sore (sōr) *a.* painful when touched; causing pain; tender; distressed; grieved; (*Colloq.*) angry; *n.* diseased, injured, or bruised spot on body; **-ly** *adv.* **-ness** *n.* [O.E. *sar*].

sor·ghum (sawr′·gạm) *n.* cereal grasses of several varieties, used for making molasses, forage, hay, brooms, etc.; the syrup from sweet sorghums [etym. uncertain].

so·ror·i·ty (sạ·rawr′·i·ti·) *n.* a girls' or women's society [L. *soror*, a sister].

so·ro·sis (sạ·rō′·sis) *n.* compound fleshy fruit, e.g. pineapple; women's club [Gk. *sōros*, heap].

sor·rel (sawr′·ạl) *n.* meadow plant with sour taste [O.Fr. *surelle*].

sor·rel (sawr′·ạl) *a.* reddish-brown; *n.* (horse of) reddish-brown color [O.Fr. *sorel*].

sor·row (sär′·ō, sawr′·ō) *n.* pain of mind; grief; sadness; distress; cause of grief, etc.; *v.i.* to feel pain of mind; to grieve. **-er** *n.* **-ful** *a.* causing sorrow; sad; unhappy. **-fully** *adv.* **-fulness** *n.* [O.E. *sorh*].

sor·ry (sär′·i; sawr′·i·) *a.* feeling regret; pained in mind; mean; shabby; wretched; worthless. **sorriness** *n.* [O.E. *sarig*].

sort (sawrt) *n.* kind or class; persons or things having same qualities; quality; character; order or rank; *v.t.* to classify; to put in order. **-er** *n.* [L. *sors*, a share, a lot].

sor·tie (sawr′·tē) *n.* sally by besieged forces to attack besiegers; flight by warplane [Fr. *sortir*, to go out].

S.O.S. (es·ō·es) *n.* international code signal call of distress, esp., by radio telegraph (· · · · — — — · · · ·); any appeal for help.

sot (sät) *n.* confirmed drunkard. **-tish** *a.* stupid through drink [Fr. *sot*, foolish].

sot·to vo·ce (sät′·tō vō′·chä) *adv.* under one's breath [It. *sotto*, under; *voce*, the voice].

sou (sōō) *n.* former French coin of various values [Fr. fr. L. *solidus*, a coin].

soubriquet See **sobriquet**.

souf·flé (sōō·flā′) *n.* a delicate dish made of eggs and baked [Fr. *scuffler*, to blow].

sough (suf, sou) *n.* low murmuring, sighing sound; *v.i.* [O.E. *swogan*, to resound].

---

sought (sawt) *pa.p.* and *pa.t.* of **seek**.

soul (sōl) *n.* spiritual and immortal part of human being; seat of emotion, sentiment, and aspiration; the center of moral powers; spirit; the essence; the moving spirit; a human being. **-ful** *a.* full of soul, emotion, or sentiment. **-fully** *adv.* **-less** *a.* without a soul; not inspired; prosaic [O.E. *sawol*].

sound (sound) *a.* healthy; in good condition; solid; entire; profound; free from error; reliable; solvent, as a business firm; *adv.* soundly; completely. **-ly** *adv.* thoroughly. **-ness** *n.* [O.E. *gesund*, healthy].

sound (sound) *n.* long, narrow stretch of water; channel; strait [O.E. *sund*].

sound (sound) *v.t.* to find depth of water, by means of line and lead; (*Fig.*) to try to discover the opinions of; *v.i.* to find depth of water; of a whale, to dive suddenly. **-ing** *n.* measuring the depth of water, esp. with a weighed line; measurement obtained [Fr. *sonder*].

sound (sound) *n.* that which is heard; auditory effect; the distance within which a sound is heard; noise; *v.t.* to cause to make a sound; to utter; to play on; to signal; to examine with stethoscope; *v.i.* to make a noise; to be conveyed by sound; to appear; to seem. **-ing** *a.* making a sound; resonant. **— barrier** (*Aero.*) colloq. term for phenomena occurring when an aircraft reaches speed in excess of that of sound. **— track** *n.* strip on one side of motion-picture film which records sound vibrations and so produces dialogue. **—waves** *n.pl.* vibrations of the air producing sound. **-board, -ing box** *n.* board or box which reinforces sound from musical instrument; canopy over pulpit for directing voice towards the congregation [L. *sonus*].

soup (sōōp) *n.* liquid food made by boiling meat, vegetables, etc. [Fr. *soupe*, fr. *souper*, to sup].

soup·çon (sōōp·sän′) *n.* suspicion; hence, very small quantity; a taste [Fr.].

sour (sour) *a.* acid; having a sharp taste; pungent; rancid; cross; *v.t.* and *v.i.* to make or become sour. **-ed** *a.* embittered; aggrieved. **-ly** *adv.* **-ness** *n.* [O.E. *sur*].

source (sōrs) *n.* spring; fountain; origin (of stream, information, etc. [L. *surgere*, to rise].

sour·dough (sour′·dō) *n.* fermented batter of flour and water used to leaven fresh dough; prospector; pioneer [*sour* and *dough*].

souse (sous) *v.t.* to steep in brine; to pickle; to plunge into a liquid; to soak; *n.* a pickle made with salt; brine; anything steeped in it; a drenching [form of *sauce*, fr. L. *sal*, salt].

sou·tane (sōō·tän′) *n.* gown worn by R.C. priests; cassock [L. *subtus*, beneath].

south (south) *n.* cardinal point of compass opposite north; region lying to that side; *a.* pert. to, or coming from, the south; *adv.* toward or in the south; *v.i.* to move towards the south. **southerly** *a.* (suTH′·er·li·) *a.* pert. to south. **-ern** *a.* in, from, or towards the south. **-erner** *n.* native of south of a country, etc. **-ernly** *adv.* towards the south. **-ernmost** (also **-ermost, —most**) *a.* lying farthest towards the south. **—ward** *a.* and *adv.* towards south; *n.* southern direction. **—wardly** *a.* and *adv.* **—wards** *adv.* **sou-wester** (or **—wester**) *n.* a strong wind from southwest; waterproof hat [O.E. *suth*].

sou·ve·nir (sōō·vạ·nir′, sōō′·vạ·nir) *n.* a keepsake; a memento [Fr. *souvenir*, to remind].

sov·er·eign (säv′·rạn) *n.* ruler; British gold coin = one pound sterling = 20 shillings; *a.* supreme in power; chief; efficacious in highest degree. **-ty** *n.* supreme power [O.Fr. *sovrain*, fr. L. *supra*, above].

so·vi·et (sō′·vi·et) *n.* council. **Soviet** *n.* political body, consisting of representatives of workers and peasants, elected to local municipalities, regional councils, etc. and sending delegates to higher congresses. *a.* **Soviet Union**, short for the Union of Socialist Soviet Republics,' i.e. Russia; *abbrev.* **U.S.S.R.** [Russ. = a council].

sow (sou) *n.* female pig; in smelting, bar of cast iron [O.E. *su*].

sow (sō) *v.t.* to scatter or deposit (seed); to spread abroad; to disseminate; *v.i.* to scatter seed. *pa.p.* **sown** (sōn) or **sowed** (sēd). *pa.t.* **-ed. -er** *n.* [O.E. *sawan*].

---

soy (soi) *n.* sauce made from soybean **-bean** *n.* seed of leguminous plant of Far East [Jap. *shoyu*].

soybeans

Spa (spa) *n.* inland watering place in Belgium. **spa** *n.* any place with mineral spring.

space (spās) *n.* expanse of universe; area; room; period of time; extent; empty place; *v.t.* to place at intervals. **spacious** (spā′·shas) *a.* roomy; capacious; extensive. **spaciously** *adv.* [Fr. *espace*. fr. L. *spatium*].

spade (spād) *n.* digging tool, with flat blade and long handle; *v.t.* to dig with spade. **-work** *n.* preliminary tasks [O.E. *spadu*].

spade (spād) *n.* (*Cards*) one of two black suits, marked by figure like a pointed spade [Sp. *espada*, a sword].

spa·ghet·ti (spạ·get′·ti·) *n.* foodstuff resembling macaroni but thinner [It. *spago*, cord].

spake (spāk) (*Arch.*) of **speak**.

span (span) *pa.t.* of **spin**.

span (span) *n.* distance between thumb and little finger, when fingers are fully extended; this distance as measure = 9 in; short distance or period of time; distance between supports of arch. roof, etc.; of airplane, distance from wing-tip to wing-tip; pair, of horses or oxen harnessed together; *v.t.* to reach from one side of to the other; to extend across. *pr.p.* **-ning**. *pa.p.* and *pa.t.* **-ned. -ner** *n.* one who spans; tool for tightening screw nuts [O.E. *spann*].

span·drel (span′·drạl) *n.* (*Archit.*) the space between outer curves of arch and square head over it; ornamental design in corner of postage stamp [etym. uncertain].

span·gle (spang′·gl) *n.* a small piece of glittering metal, used to ornament dresses; *v.t.* to adorn with spangles; *v.i.* to glitter [O.E. *spang*, a buckle].

Span·iard (span′·yerd) *n.* native of Spain. **Spanish** *a.* of, or pert. to, Spain; *n.* language of Spain.

span·iel (span′·yạl) *n.* breed of dogs, with long, drooping ears; fawning person [O.Fr. *espagneul*, Sanish].

spank (spangk) *v.i.* to move with vigor or spirit. **-ing** *a.* moving with quick, lively step; dashing. **-er** *n.* fast-going horse, ship, etc.; (*Naut.*) fore-and-aft sail attached to the mast nearest the stern [Dan. *spanke*, to strut].

spank (spangk) *v.t.* to strike with flat of hand, esp. on buttocks as punishment; *n.* slap [imit. origin].

spar (spár) *v.i.* to fight with the fists, in fun or in earnest; to fight with spurs, as in cock fighting; to dispute, bandy words. *pr.p.* **-ring**. *pa.p.* and *pa.t.* **-red** [etym. uncertain].

spar (spár) *n.* pole or beam, esp. as part of ship's rigging [O.N. *sparri*].

spar (spár) *n.* crystalline mineral which has luster [O.E. *spaerstan*, gypsum].

spare (sper) *v.t.* and *v.i.* to use frugally; to do without; to save; to omit; to leave unhurt; to give away; *a.* frugal; scanty; scarce; parsimonious; thin; lean; additional; in reserve; not in use; *n.* that which is held in reserve; a duplicate part. **-ly** *adv.* **-ness** *n.* thinness; leanness. **sparing** *a.* **sparingly** *adv.* [O.E. *sparian*].

spark (spárk) *n.* small glowing or burning particle; flash of light; trace or particle of anything; in internal-combustion engines, electric flash which ignites explosive mixture in cylinder; (Colloq.) gay, dashing young fellow; v.i. to send out sparks. — **plug** n. in internal-combustion engines, device for igniting explosive gases; (Colloq.) one who animates a group [O.E. spearca].

spark plug

spar·kle (spärk′·l) n. small spark; a glitter; a gleam; vivacity; v.i. to emit small flashes of light; to gleam; to glitter; to effervesce. **-r** n. one who, or that which, sparkles; (Slang) a diamond. **sparkling** a. [O.E. spearca].

spar·row (spar′·ō) n. small brown bird of finch family. **—grass** n. (Colloq.) asparagus. [O.E. spearwa].

sparse (spärs) a. thinly scattered; scanty; rare. **-ly** adv. **-ness** n. scantiness [L. spargere, sparsum, to scatter].

Spar·ta (spär′·ta) n. ancient Greek city-state. **Spartan** n. citizen of this town; one who is frugal and faces danger, etc. without flinching; a. pert. to Sparta; dauntless.

spasm (spaz′·am) n. sudden, involuntary contraction of muscle(s); sudden, convulsive movement, effort, emotion, etc.; fitful effort. **spasmodic(al)** a. pert. to spasms; convulsive; fitful. **spasmodically** adv. by fits and starts. **spastic** a. (Med.) pert. to spasms; in a rigid condition, due to spasm; applied to people suffering from cerebral palsy. n. such a person [Gk. spasmos, fr. spaein, to draw].

spat (spat) pa.t. of **spit**.

spat (spat) n. kind of cloth gaiter, reaching a little above ankle. Usually in pl. **spats** [abbrev. of spatterdash].

spat (spat) n. spawn of shellfish or oyster; v.i. to spawn, of oysters [fr. spit].

spate (spāt) n. flood in a river, esp. after heavy rain; inundation [Gael. speid].

spathe (spāTH) n. leaflike sheath enveloping flower cluster. **spathed, spathose** a. [Gk. spathē, a broad blade].

spa·tial (spā′·shal) a. pert. to space. **-ly** adv. [L. spatium].

spat·ter (spat′·er) v.t. to cast drops of water, mud, etc. over; to splash; v.i. to fall in drops; n. the act of spattering; a slight splash [Dut. spatten, to burst].

spat·u·la (spach′·a·la) n. broad-bladed implement for spreading paints, turning foods in frying pan, etc. **spatular, spatulate** a. [Gk. spathē, a broad blade].

spav·in (spav′·in) n. swelling on horse's leg, causing lameness. **-ed** a. [O.Fr. esparvain].

spawn (spawn) n. eggs of fish, frogs; offspring; v.t. and v.i. of fish, frogs, to cast eggs; to produce offspring [O.Fr. espandre, fr. L. expandere, to spread out].

speak (spēk) v.i. to utter words; to tell; to deliver a discourse; v.t. to utter; to pronounce; to express in words; to express silently or by signs; pr.p. **-ing**, pa.p. **spoken**, pa.t. **spoke. -er** n. one who speaks; orator. **the Speaker**, presiding officer of the House of Representatives and of similar legislative bodies. **-ing** n. a. having power to utter words; eloquent; lifelike, e.g. of picture. **-easy** n. (Slang) illegal saloon, esp. during prohibition [O.E. sprecan].

spear (sper) n. long, pointed weapon, used in fighting, hunting, etc.; sharp-pointed instrument for catching fish; lance; pike; v.t. to pierce or kill with spear. **-head** n. iron point, barb, or prong of a spear; leader of an advance; **— side** n. male branch of a family [O.E. spere].

spe·cial (spesh′·al) a. pert. to a species or sort; particular; beyond the usual; distinct; intimate; designed for a particular person or purpose. **-ly** adv. **-ize** v.t. to make special or distinct; to adapt for a particular purpose; v.i. to devote oneself to a particular branch of study. **-ization** n. act of specializing. **-ist** n. one trained and skilled in a special branch. **-istic** a. **-ty** n. a special characteristic of a person or thing; a special product; that in which a person is highly skilled. [L. species, a kind].

spe·cie (spē′·shē) n. coined money [L. species, a kind].

spe·cies (spē′·shēz) n. kind; variety; sort; class; subdivision of a more general class or genus [L. species, a kind].

spe·cif·ic (spi·sif′·ik) a. pert. to, or characteristic of, a species; peculiar to; well defined; precise; n. a specific statement, etc. **-ally** adv. **— gravity**, weight of substance expressed in relation to weight of equal volume of water [L. species, a kind; facere, to make].

spec·i·fi·ca·tion (spes·a·fa·kā′·shan) n. act of specifying; statement of details, requirements, etc. **specify** v.t. to state definitely; to give details of; to indicate precisely. **specifiable** a. [L. species, a kind; facere, to make].

spec·i·men (spes′·a·man) n. part of anything, or one of a number of things, used to show nature and quality of the whole; sample [L. specere, to look].

spe·cious (spē′·shas) a. having a fair appearance; superficially fair or just; apparently acceptable, esp. at first sight. **-ly** adv. **-ness speciosity** n. [L. speciosus, fair to see].

speck (spek) n. small spot; particle; very small thing; v.t. to mark with specks. **-le** n. a small speck or spot; v.t. to mark with small spots. **speckled** a. [O.E. specca].

spec·ta·cle (spek′·ta·kl) n. sight; show; thing exhibited; a pageant. **spectacles** n.pl. eyeglasses. **-ed** a. wearing spectacles. **spectacular** a. showy; making great display. **spectacularly** adv. [L. spectare, to look at].

spec·ta·tor (spek′·tā·ter) n. an onlooker; ghost; apparition. **spectral** a. pert. to a specter; ghostly; pert. to spectrum. **spectrally** adv. **spectrum** n. the colored band into which a ray of light can be separated as in the rainbow; pl. **spectra** [L. spectrum, an image].

spec·tro- (spek′·trō) prefix fr. L. spectrum, an image, used in many derivatives. **-graph** n. scientific instrument for photographing spectra. **-scope** n. instrument for production and examination of spectra. **-scopic, -scopical** a. [Gk. graphein, to write; skopein, to view].

spec·u·late (spek′·ya·lāt) v.i. to make theories or guesses; to meditate; to engage in risky commercial transactions. **speculation** n. act of speculating; theorizing; guess; practice of buying shares, etc. in the hope of selling at a high profit. **speculative** a. given to speculation. **speculatively** adv. **speculator** n. **speculatory** a. [L. speculari, to observe].

spec·u·lum (spek′·ya·lam) n. mirror; reflector of polished metals, esp. as used in reflecting telescopes; (Surg.) instrument for examining interior cavity of body. pl. **specula** [L. fr. specere, to observe].

sped (sped) pa.p. and pa.t. of **speed**.

speech (spēch) n. power of speaking; what is spoken; faculty of expressing thoughts in words; enunciation; remarks; conversation; language; formal address; an oration. **-less** a. without power of speech; dumb; silent. **-lessly** adv. **-lessness** n. **-ify** v.i. to make speech, esp. long and tedious one. **-ifier** n. [O.E. spraec].

speed (spēd) n. swiftness of motion; rate of progress; velocity; v.t. to cause to move faster; to aid; to bid farewell to; v.i. to move quickly or at speed beyond legal limit; to increase speed. pa.p. and pa.t. **sped. -y** a. quick; rapid; prompt. **-ily** adv. **-boat** n. very fast motor boat. **-ometer** n. instrument indicating speed, usually in miles per hour. **-way** n. track for racing [O.E. sped].

speedboat

spell (spel) n word or words supposed to have magical power; magic formula; fascination. **-bind** v.t. to hold as if by spell; to enchant; to fascinate. pa.p., pa.t. **-bound** a. [O.E. spell, a narrative].

spell (spel) n. a turn of work or duty; a brief period of time [O.E. spelian, to act for].

spell (spel) v.t. to read letter by letter; to mean; v.i. to form words with proper letters. pa.p. and pa.t. **-ed** or **spelt** [O.E. spell, a narrative].

spe·lunk·er (spē′·lungk·er) one who explores caves.

spend (spend) v.t. and v.i. to pay out; to disburse; to pass, as time; to employ; to waste; to exhaust. pa.p., pa.t., **spent** a. exhausted; worn out; of a fish, having deposited spawn. **-er** n. **-thrift** n. one who spends money foolishly or extravagantly; a. extravagant [O.E. spenden].

sperm (spurm) n. fertilizing fluid of male animals; the male cell. **—oil** n. oil obtained from sperm whale. **— whale** n. cachalot, large whale, valuable for its oil and for spermaceti. **spermaceti** (spur·ma·sē′·ti·, spur·ma·set′·i·) n. waxlike substance obtained from head of sperm whale. **-atic** a. pert. to sperm [Gk. sperma, seed].

sperm·a·to- prefix fr. Gk. sperma, seed. **spermatoid** a. resembling sperm. **spermatozoon** (spur·ma·ta·zō′·an) n. male generative cell, found in semen. pl. **-zoa, -zoal, -zoan** a.

spew, spue (spū) v.t. and v.i. to eject from the stomach; to vomit [O.E. spiwan].

sphere (sfir) n. round, solid body, ball; globe; celestial body; range of knowledge, influence, etc.; field of action; social status; position; v.t. to put in a sphere; to encircle. **spheral** (sfi′·ral) a. formed like a sphere. **spheric** (sfer′·ik) a. pert. to heavenly bodies. **spherical** a. sphere-shaped. **spherically** adv.

sphe·ric·i·ty n. roundness. **spheroid** (sfi′·roid) n. body almost, but not quite, spherical, e.g. orange, earth, etc. **spheroidal** a. having form of spheroid. Also **spheroidic. spherule** (sfir′·ūl) n. a small sphere. **spherular, spherulate** a. [Gk. sphaira, a globe].

sphinc·ter (sfingk′·ter) n. (Anat.) circular muscle which contracts or expands orifice of an organ, e.g. round anus [Gk. sphingein, to bind tight].

sphinx (sfingks) n. (Myth.) fabulous monster, with winged body of lion and head of woman, which proposed riddles; statue of this; (Fig.) one whose thoughts are difficult to guess; enigmatic person. (Cap.) huge statue of recumbent lion with man's head in Egypt [Gk. sphinx, literally, the strangler].

sphyg·mus (sfig′·mas) n. (Med.) pulse. **sphygmic** a. [Gk. sphugmos, the pulse].

spice (spīs) n. aromatic substance, used for seasoning; spices collectively (Fig.) anything that adds flavor, zest, etc. v.t. to season with spice. **spicery** n. spices collectively. **spicy** a. **spicily** adv. [O.Fr. espice].

spi·der (spī′·der) n. small, eight-legged insectlike animal that spins web to catch flies; a frying pan; a trivet; an evil person. a. like a spider; full of spiders; very thin. **—monkey** n. monkey with long, thin legs and tail [O.E. spinnan, to spin].

spied (spīd) pa.p. and pa.t. of **spy**.

spig·ot (spig′·at) n. peg for stopping hole in cask; a faucet which controls flow [L. spica, an ear of corn].

spike (spīk) n. sharp-pointed piece of metal or wood; large nail; ear of corn, etc.; (Bot.) flower-cluster growing from central stem; v.t. furnished with spikes; pointed (Slang) to add liquor to a drink. **spiky** a. to supply, set, fasten, or pierce with spikes; pointed [O.N. spik, a nail].

spill (spil) v.t. to cause to flow out; to pour out; to shed (blood); to throw off, as from horse, etc.; to upset; v.i. to flow over; to be shed; to be lost or wasted; n. a spilling; fall or tumble, as from vehicle, horse, etc. pa.p. and pa.t. **-ed** or **spilt. -er** n. **-way** n. channel for overflow water from dam [O.E. spillian, to destroy].

spill (spil) n. thin strip of wood or twist of paper, for lighting a fire, pipe, etc.; a peg [Dut. speld, a splinter].

spin (spin) v.t. to twist into threads; to cause to revolve rapidly; to whirl; to twirl; to draw out tediously, as a story; to prolong; v.i. to make thread, as a spider, etc.; to revolve rapidly; to move swiftly; n. rapid whirling motion; short, quick run or drive. pr.p. **-ning**. pa.p. and pa.t. **spun** or (Arch.) **span. -ner** n. **-ning jenny** n. machine for spinning several threads simultaneously. **-ning wheel** n. outdated device for spinning cotton, wool, flax, etc. into thread or yarn [O.E. spinnan].

spin·ach (spin′·ich) n. leafy vegetable used for food. **spinaceous** a. [O.Fr. espinage].

spin·dle (spin′·dl) n. long, slender rod, used in spinning, for twisting and winding the thread; measure of yarn, thread, or silk; shaft; axis; v.i. to grow long and slender. **spindly** a. long and slender. **spindling** a. [O.E. spinel, fr. spinnan, to spin].

spine (spin) n. thorn; quill; backbone; back of book. **spinal** a. pert. to spine or backbone. **-less** a. having no spine; weak of character. **spiny** a. full of spines; like a spine; thorny; prickly; perplexing. **spinule** n. small spine. **spinal column**, the backbone [L. spina, a thorn].

spin·et (spin′·it) n. musical instrument like a harpsichord [O.Fr. espinette, fr. L. spina].

spin·na·ker (spin′·a·ker) n. a large triangular sail [etym. uncertain].

spin·ster (spin′·ster) n. orig. one who spins; unmarried woman. **-hood** n. **spinstress** n. woman who spins [O.E. spinnan, to spin].

spi·ra·cle (spī′·ra·kl, spir′·a·kl) n. breathinghole; blowhole of whale. **spiracular, spiraculate** a. [L. spirare, to breathe].

Spi·rae·a (spi·rē′·a) n. a genus of herbaceous plants, including meadowsweet, bearing white or pink flowers [Gk. speira, a coil].

spi·rant (spī′·rant) n. consonant pronounced with perceptible emission of breath [L. spirare, to breathe].

spire (spir) n. winding line like threads of screw; curl; coil. **spiral** a. winding; coiled; n. spiral curve; coil; whorl; v.i. to follow spiral line; to coil; to curve [Gk. speira, coil].

spire (spīr) *n.* blade of grass; stalk; slender shoot; anything tall and tapering to point; (tapering part of) steeple; peak; *v.i.* to rise high, like spire. **spiral** *a.* like a spire. **spiry** *a.* having spires; tapering [O.E. *spir*, a stalk].

spir·it (spir'·it) *n.* vital force; immortal part of man; soul; specter; ghost; frame of mind; disposition; temper; eager desire; mental vigor; courage; essential character; (*Cap.*) Holy Spirit; liquid got by distillation, esp. alcoholic; *v.t.* to carry away mysteriously; to put energy into. **spirits** *n.pl.* a state of mind; mood; distilled alcoholic liquor. **-ed** *a.* full of spirit and vigor; lively; animated. **-edly** *adv.* **-edness** *n.* **-ism** *n.* See **spiritualism. -less** *a.* without spirit or life; lacking energy; listless. **-essly** *adv.* **-uous** *a.* containing alcohol; distilled [L. *spiritus*, fr *spirare*, to breathe]. **spir·it·u·al** (spir'·it·choo·al) *a.* pert. to spirit or soul; not material; unworldly; pert. to sacred things; holy; *n.* Negro sacred song or hymn. **-ly** *adv.* **-ize** *v.t.* to make spiritual; to make pure in heart. **-ism, spiritism** *n.* belief that spirits of dead can communicate with living people. **-ist** *n.* [L. *spiritus*, breath].

spit (spit) *n.* pointed rod put through meat for roasting; narrow point of land projecting into sea; *v.t.* to thrust spit through; to impale *pr.p.* **-ting.** *pa.p.* *pa.t.* **-ted.** [O.E. *spitu*].

spit (spit) *v.t.* to eject from mouth; to expel; *v.i.* to eject saliva from mouth; to expectorate; to hiss, esp. of cats; *pr.p.* **-ting.**.*pa.p.* *pa.t.* **spat.** *n.* saliva; act of spitting; like fall of fine rain; (*Colloq.*) an exact likeness. **-ter** *n.* **-tle** *n.* saliva ejected from mouth; frothy secretion of certain insects. **-toon** *n.* a vessel for spittle; cuspidor [O.E. *spittan*].

spite (spīt) *n.* malice; ill will; *v.t.* to treat maliciously; to try to injure or thwart; to annoy. **-ful** *a.* **-fully** *adv.* **-fulness** *n.* **in spite of,** in defiance of [fr. *despite*].

spit·fire (spit'·fīr) *n.* hot tempered person [*spit* and *fire*].

spitz (spitz) *n.* a kind of Pomeranian dog [Ger. = pointed].

splash (splash) *v.t.* to spatter water, mud, etc. over; to soil thus; to print in bold headlines; *v.i.* to dash or scatter, of liquids; to dabble in water; to fall in drops; *n.* sound of object falling into liquid, water, mud, etc. dashed about; spot; daub; patch of color. **-y** *a.* full of dirty water; wet and muddy. **-board** *n.* mud guard [imit. origin].

splat·ter (splat'·er) *v.t.* and *v.i.* to splash; to spatter [fr. *spatter*].

splay (splā) *v.t.* to slope; to slant; to spread outwards; *a.* turned outwards; at and broad; *n.* slanting surface of opening, as at window. **-foot** *n.* flat foot [fr. *display*].

spleen (splēn) *n.* ductless organ lying to left of stomach; ill humor; spite; melancholy; irritability [Gk. *splēn*].

splen·did (splen'·did) *a.* magnificent; gorgeous; (*Colloq.*) excellent. **-ly** *adv.* **splendor** (splen·der) *n.* brilliant luster; pomp. **splendorous** *a.* [L. *splendere*, to shine].

sple·net·ic (spli·net'·ik) *a.* pert. to spleen; morose; irritable. *n.* one suffering from disease of spleen; irritable person [Gk. *splēn*].

splice (splīs) *v.t.* to join together; to join, as wood, etc. by overlapping and binding; (*Colloq.*) to marry; *n.* union [Dut. *splissen*].

splint (splint) *n.* rigid piece of material for holding broken limb in position; bony excrescence on inside of horse's leg; *v.t.* to bind with splints. **-er** *n.* thin piece of wood, metal, etc. split off; *v.t.* and *v.i.* to make or break into thin pieces. **-ery** *a.* [Swed. *splint*].

split (split) *v.t.* to cut lengthwise; to cleave; to tear apart; to separate; to divide; *v.i.* to break asunder; to part lengthwise; to dash to pieces; to separate; *n.* crack; fissure; a breach; a share. *pr.p.* **-ting.** *pa.p.* *pa.t.* **split.** **-ing** *n.* cleaving or rending; *a.* severe; distressing. — **infinitive,** insertion of adverb or adverbial phrase between 'to' and verb of infinitive. —**level** *a.* describing a home that has several levels separated by steps. **to split hairs,** to make fine distinctions [Dut. *splitten*].

splut·ter (splut'·er) *v.t.* to utter incoherently with spitting sounds; to emit such sounds; to speak hastily and confusedly; *n.* such sounds or speech; a confused noise. **-er** *n.* [imit. origin].

Spode (spōd) *n.* highly decorated porcelain [Josiah *Spode*, pottery manufacturer].

spoil (spoil) *v.t.* to damage; to injure; to cause to decay; to harm character of by indulgence; *v.i.* to go bad; to decay; *n.* booty; prey; plunder. *pa.p.* and *pa.t.* **-ed** or **-spoilt** *n.* one who takes a delight in interfering with enjoyment of others [L. *spoliare*].

spoke (spōk) *pa.p.* of the verb **speak.** *pa.p.* **spoken** (spōk'·n). **-s-man** *n.* one deputed to speak for others.

spoke (spōk) *n.* one of small bars connecting hub of wheel with rim; rung of ladder. **-shave** *n.* planing tool [O.E. *spaca*].

spo·li·ate (spō'·li·āt) *v.t.* to rob; to plunder; *v.i.* to practice plundering. **spoliative** *a.* **spoliation** *n.* the act of despoiling; robbery; destruction. **spoliator** *n.* [L. *spoliare*].

spon·dee (spän'·dē) *n.* in poetry, a foot of two long syllables, marked (— —). **spondaic** (spän·dā'·ik) *a.* [Gk. *spondē*, drink offering].

spoke

sponge (spunj) *n.* marine animal of cellular structure, outer coating of whose body is perforated to allow entrance of water; skeleton of this animal, used to absorb water; act of cleaning with sponge; (*Colloq.*) parasite; sponger; hanger-on; (*Colloq.*) habitual drinker; *v.t.* to wipe, cleanse, with sponge; *v.i.* to live at expense of others. **-r** *n.* **spongy** (spun'·ji·) *a.* sponge-like; of open texture; full of small holes; absorbent; wet and soft, esp. of ground. **sponginess** *n.* **-cake** *n.* light, sweet cake. **to throw in the sponge,** to acknowledge defeat [Gk., L. *spongia*].

spon·sor (spän'·ser) *n.* one who is responsible for another; surety; godfather or godmother; guarantor; a patron; *v.t.* to support; to act as guarantor or patron of; to pay for a radio or television program including advertisements of one's own goods. **-ial** *a.* **-ship** *n.* [L. *spondere, sponsum,* to promise].

spon·ta·ne·ous (spän·tā'·nē·as) *a.* of one's own free will; voluntary; natural; produced by some internal cause, said of physical effects, as combustion, growth, etc. **-ly** *adv.* **-ness, spontaneity** (spän·ta·nē'·a·ti·) *n.* [L. *sponte,* of one's own free will].

spoof (spōof) *n.* (*Slang, chiefly Brit.*) hoax; swindle; *v.t.* to fool; to hoax.

spook (spōōk) *n.* (*Colloq.*) ghost; apparition. **-ish, -y** *a.* [Dut.].

spool (spōōl) *n.* small cylinder for winding thread, wire, etc.; *v.t.* to wind on spool [O.Fr. *espole*].

spoon (spōōn) *n.* implement, with bowl at end of handle, for carrying food to the mouth. etc.; golf club with wooden head; *v.t.* and *v.i.* to use, hit with spoon; (*Golf*) to scoop ball high in air; (*Colloq.*) to make love. **-ful** *n.* quantity spoon can hold; small quantity; (*Med.*) half an ounce. **-bill** *n.* long-legged wading bird with spoon-shaped bill —**feed** *v.t.* to feed with a spoon; (*Fig.*) to do overmuch for a person, thus weakening his self-reliance pa.p., *pa.t.* **-fed** *a.* [O.E. *spon*].

spoon·er·ism (spōōn'·er·ism) *n.* transposition of letters of spoken words, causing a humorous effect, e.g. a *half-warmed fish* for a 'half-formed wish' [fr. Dr. A. W. *Spooner*].

spoor (spōōr) *n.* track or trail of wild animal [Dut. = a track].

spo·rad·ic (spa·rad'·ik) *a.* occurring singly here and there; occasional. Also **-al. -ally** *adv.* [Gk. *sporadikos,* fr. *speirein,* to sow].

spore (spōr) *n.* in flowerless plants, e.g. in ferns, minute cell with reproductive powers; germ; seed. **sporangium** *n.* spore case. *pl.* **sporangia. sporangial** *a.* **sporoid** *a.* sporelike [Gk. *spora,* seed].

spor·ran (spawr'·an) *n.* large pouch worn in front of the kilt [Gael. *sporan*].

sport (spōrt) *n.* that which amuses; diversion; pastime; merriment; object of jest; mockery; outdoor game or recreation esp. of athletic nature; freak of nature; (*Colloq.*) a dandy; good loser; one willing to take a chance; *v.t.* (*Colloq.*) to display in public; to show off; *v.i.* to play; to take part in out-door recreation. **-s** *n.pl.* games; athletic meetings. **-ing**

a. pert. to sport or sportsmen; (*Colloq.*) willing to take a chance. **-ive** *a.* pert. to sport; playful. **-s-man, -s-woman** *n.* **-s-manship** *n.* practice or skill of a sportsman; fairmindedness. **-s-manlike** *a.* [fr. *disport*].

spot (spät) *n.* speck; blemish, esp. on reputation; place; locality; *v.t.* to cover with spots; to stain; to place billiard ball on marked point; (*Colloq.*) to detect; to recognize; *v.i.* to become marked. *pr.p.* **-ting.** *pa.p.* and *pa.t.* **-ted. -less** *a.* without spot or stain; scrupulously clean; pure; innocent. **-lessly** *adv.* **-lessness** *n.* **-ted, -ty** *a.* marked with spots or stains; irregular. **-tedness, tiness** *n.* **-ter** *n.* — **cash,** immediate payment; ready money. **-light** *n.* apparatus used to throw concentrated beam of light on performer on stage; light thrown; the public eye. **on the spot,** immediately; (*Slang*) in a dangerous or embarrassing position [O.N. *spotti*].

spotlight

spouse (spous) *n.* married person, husband or wife. **spousal** *a.* pert. to spouse, marriage [L. *sponsus,* promise].

spout (spout) *v.t.* to shoot out, as liquid through a pipe; (*Colloq.*) to utter in a pompous manner; to recite; *v.i.* to gush out in jet; (*Colloq.*) to speak volubly; *n.* projecting tube, pipe, etc., for pouring liquid; a pipe or tube for leading off rain from roof. **-er** *n.*

sprag (sprag) *n.* piece of wood or metal used to lock wheel of vehicle; device to prevent vehicle running backwards on hill [Dan.].

sprain (sprān) *v.t.* to wrench or twist muscles or ligaments of a joint; to overstrain; *n.* such an injury.

sprang (sprang) *pa.t.* of the verb **spring.**

sprat (sprat) *n.* small sea fish, allied to herring and pilchard [O.E. *sprot*].

sprawl (sprawl) *v.i.* to sit or lie with legs outstretched or in ungainly position; to move about awkwardly; to spread out irregularly; to write carelessly and irregularly; *n.* act of sprawling [O.E. *spreawlian*].

spray (sprā) *n.* twigs; small, graceful branch with leaves and blossoms; sprig.

spray (sprā) *n.* fine droplets of water driven by wind from tops of waves, etc.; shower of fine droplets of any liquid, e.g. medicine, perfume, etc.; spraying machine; atomizer; *v.t.* to sprinkle. **-er** *n.* [L. Ger. *Sprei*].

spread (spred) *v.t.* to stretch out; to extend; to cover surface with; to scatter; to unfold, as wings; to circulate, as news, etc.; to convey from one to another, as disease; to set and lay food on table; *v.i.* to extend in all directions; to become spread, scattered, circulated, etc.; *n.* extension; expanse; covering for bed, etc.; (*Colloq.*) feast. *pa.p.* and *pa.t.* **spread. -ing** *n.* act of extending. **—eagle** *n.* eagle with wings stretched out; *a.* with arms and legs stretched out; bombastic; *v.t.* to lie with outstretched limbs [O.E. *spraedan*].

spree (sprē) *n.* lively frolic; drinking bout [Ir. *spre,* a spark].

sprig (sprig) *n.* small shoot or twig; ornament in form of spray; scion; youth; small, headless nail; *v.t.* to mark, adorn, with figures of sprigs or sprays. *pr.p.* **-ging.** *pa.p., pa.t.* **-ged** [O.E. *spraec,* a twig].

spright·ly (sprīt'·li·) *a.* lively; airy; vivacious. **sprightliness** *n.* [old form of *sprite*].

spring (spring) *v.i.* to leap; to jump; to shoot up, out, or forth; to appear; to recoil; to result, as from a cause; to issue, as from parent or ancestor; to appear above ground; to grow; to thrive; *v.t.* to cause to spring up; to produce unexpectedly; to start, as game; to cause to explode, as a mine; to develop leak; to bend so as to weaken; to release, as catch of trap; *n.* a leap; a bound; a jump; recoil; a contrivance of coiled or bent metal with much resilience; resilience; flow of water from earth; fountain; any source; origin; a crack; season of year; upward curve of arch. *pa.p.* **sprung.** *pa.t.* **sprang** or **sprung. -er** *n.* one who springs; breed of spaniel. **-y** *a.* elastic; light in tread or gait. **-iness** *n.* **-board** *n.* springy board used in jumping and diving. **-time** *n.* season of spring [O.E. *springan*].

springe (sprinj) *n.* snare with a spring noose; *v.t.* to catch in a springe [fr. *spring*].

sprin·kle (spring'·kl) *v.t.* to scatter small drops of water, sand, etc.; to scatter on; to baptize with drops of water; *v.i.* to scatter (a liquid or any fine substance); *n.* small quantity scattered; occasional drops of rain. **-d** *a.* marked by small spots. **-r** *n.* one who sprinkles.

sprinkling *n.* act of scattering; small quantity falling in drops [O.E. *sprengan*].

sprint (sprint) *v.i./n.* short run at full speed. **-er** *n.* [Cf. *spurt*].

sprit (sprit) *n.* (*Naut.*) small spar set diagonally across fore-and-aft sail to extend it [O.E. *spreot*, a pole].

sprite (sprīt) *n.* elf; a fairy; a goblin [older form = *spright*, fr. L. *spiritus*, spirit].

sprock·et (sprǎk'·it) *n.* toothlike projection on outer rim of wheel, e.g. of bicycle, for engaging links of chain [etym. uncertain].

sprout (sprout) *v.i.* to begin to grow; to put forth shoots; to spring up; *n.* shoot; bud. [O.E. *sprutan*].

spruce (sproos) *a.* neat in dress; smart; dapper; trim; *v.t.* and *v.i.* to dress smartly. **-ly** *adv.* **-ness** *n.* [fr. *Pruce*, Prussia].

spruce (sproos) *n.* common name of some coniferous trees [M.E. *Spruce*, Prussia].

sprung (sprung) *pa.p.* and *pa.t.* of **spring**.

spry (sprī) *a.* nimble; agile [*Scand.*].

spud (spud) *n.* small spadelike implement; (*Colloq.*) potato [etym. uncertain].

spue. See **spew**.

spume (spūm) *n. v.i.* froth; foam; scum. **spumous** *a.* **spumy** *a.* [*L.* spuma].

spun (spun) *pa.p.* and *pa.t.* of verb **spin**.

spunk (spungk) *n.* wood that readily takes fire; (*Colloq.*) spirit. **-y** *a.* (*Colloq.*) plucky [L. *spongia*, a sponge].

spur (spur) *n.* pricking instrument worn on horseman's heels, used as goad; anything that incites to action; projection on the leg of a cock; mountain projecting from range; projection; *v.t.* to apply spurs; to urge to action; *v.i.* to ride hard; to press forward. *pr.p.* **-ring**. *pa.p.* and *pa.t.* also *a.* **-red** spurd), wearing spurs; (*Bot.*) having spur-like shoots; incited [O.E. *spora*].

spurge (spurj) *n.* plant of several species, having milky juice [L. *expurgare*, to purge].

spu·ri·ous (spyoo'·ri·as) *a.* not genuine or authentic; false. **-ly** *adv.* [L. *spurius*].

spurn (spurn) *v.t.* to reject with disdain; to scorn; *n.* disdainful rejection [O.E. *spornan*].

spurt (spurt) *v.t.* to force out suddenly in a stream; to squirt; *v.i.* to gush out with force; to make a short, sudden, and strong effort, esp. in a race; *n.* a sudden, strong flow or effort. Also **spirt** [O.E. *spryttan*].

sput·ter (sput'·er) *v.t.* to throw out in small particles with haste and noise; to utter excitedly and indistinctly; *v.i.* to scatter drops of saliva, as in excited speech; to speak rapidly; to fly off with crackling noise, as sparks from burning wood; *n.* act of sputtering; sound made. **-er** *n.* [fr. *spout*].

spu·tum (spū'·tam) *n.* spittle; saliva. *pl.* **spu·ta** [L. *spuere*, *sputum*, to spit].

spy (spī) *n.* one who enters enemy territory secretly, to gain information; secret agent; one who keeps watch on others. *v.t.* to catch sight of; to notice; to discern; *v.i.* to act as a spy. **-glass** *n.* small telescope [Fr. *espion*, fr. L. *specere*, to look].

squab (skwáb) *a.* fat and short; *n.* nestling pigeon used for food [etym. uncertain].

squab·ble (skwáb'·l) *v.i.* to wrangle; to dispute noisily; *n.* petty, noisy quarrel [*imit.*].

squad (skwád) *n.* (*Mil.*) smallest unit of soldiers, etc.; small party of men at work; gang [Fr. *escouade*].

squad·ron (skwád'·ran) *n.* a military tactical unit; an athletic team [It. *squadra*, a square].

squal·id (skwál'·id) *a.* mean and dirty, esp. through neglect; filthy; foul. *adv.* **-ity, -ness, squalor** *n.* filth; foulness [L.*squalidus*].

squall (skwawl) *v.t.* and *v.i.* to scream or cry out violently; *n.* loud scream; sudden gust of wind. **-y** *a.* [imit. origin].

squa·ma (skwā'·ma) *n.* scale; scalelike part *pl.* **squamae** (skwā'·mē) [L. = a scale].

squan·der (skwán'·der) *v.t.* to waste; to dissipate. **-er** *n.* spendthrift [*Scand.*].

square (skwār) *n.* plane figure with four equal sides and four right angles; anything shaped like this; in town, open space of this shape; carpenter's instrument for testing or drawing right angles; body of soldiers drawn up in form of square; (*Math.*) product of a number or quantity multiplied by itself; *a.* square shaped; rectangular; at right angles; giving equal justice; fair; balanced or settled, as account or bill; *adv.* squarely; directly; *v.t.* to make like a square; to place at right angles; (*Math.*) to multiply by itself; to balance; to settle; to put right; (*Colloq.*) to win over by bribery; *v.i.* to agree exactly; **-ly** *adv.* **-ness** *n.* **squarish** *a.* nearly square. **— dance**, old-fashioned dance for four couples. **— inch, foot, yard**, etc., area equal to surface of square with sides one inch, foot, yard, etc. long. **—rigged** *a.* (*Naut.*) of a ship, fitted

with square sails. **— root**, number or quantity which, when multiplied by itself, produces the number of which it is the square root. **-shooter** *a.* (*Colloq.*) person who is honest [L. *quadrare*, to square, fr. *quattuor*, four].

squash (skwásh) *v.t.* to beat or crush flat; to squeeze to pulp; to suppress; *v.i.* to fall into a soft, flat mass; *n.* anything soft and easily crushed; packed crowd; game played with rackets. **-iness** *n.* **-y** *a.* [L. *ex*, out; *quassus*, to shake].

squash (skwásh) *n.* gourdlike fruit [Amer.-Ind. *asquash*, raw, green].

squat (skwát) *v.i.* to sit on heels; to crouch, as animal; to settle on land without having title to it, or in order to acquire title; *a.* short and thick; sitting close to ground. *pr.p.* **-ting**. *pa.p.* and *pa.t.* **-ted. -ter** *n.* [O.Fr. *esquatir*].

squaw (skwaw) *n.* N. American Indian woman, esp. wife [N. Amer. Ind. *eskaw*].

squeak (skwēk) *n.* short, sharp, shrill sound; sharp, unpleasant, grating sound; (*Colloq.*) a narrow escape; *v.i.* to utter, or make, such sound; (*Slang*) to give away secret. **-y** *a.*

squeal (skwēl) *n.* long, shrill cry; *v.i.* to utter long, shrill cry; (*Slang*) to turn informer. **-er** *n.* [imit. origin].

squeam·ish (skwēm'·ish) *a.* easily made sick; easily shocked; over-scrupulous; fussy. **-ly** *adv.* **-ness** *n.* [O.Fr. *escoymous*].

squee·gee (skwē'·jē) *n.* implement with rubber edge on head, for clearing water from deck of ship, floor, pavement, etc. Also **squil-gee** [fr. *squeeze*].

squeeze (skwēz) *v.t.* to press or crush; to compress; to extract by pressure; to force into; (*Colloq.*) to subject to extortion; *v.i.* to force one's way; to press; *n.* pressure; compression; close hug or embrace; (*Colloq.*) difficult situation. **squeezable** *a.* [O.E. *cwisan*].

squelch (skwelch) *n.* crushing blow; suppression; sound made when withdrawing feet from sodden ground; *v.t.* to crush down; (*Colloq.*) to silence with a crushing remark; *v.i.* to make sound of a squelch [etym. uncertain].

squid (skwid) *n.* a kind of sea mollusc.

squil·gee (skwil·'·jē) *n.* Same as **squeegee**.

squill (skwil) *n.* plant of lily family whose bulb has emetic properties. **-s** *n.pl.* drug from bulb of squill [Gk. *skilla*].

squint (skwint) *a.* looking obliquely; having eyes turned in; *v.t.* to cause to squint; *v.i.* to be cross-eyed; to glance sideways; to look with eyes partly closed; *n.* act, habit of squinting; (*Med.*) strabismus; hasty glance; peep. **-eyed** *a.* squinting; cross-eyed; spiteful.

squire (skwīr) *n.* formerly, knight's attendant; (*Brit.*) rural landowner; lady's escort; *v.t.* to escort [fr. *esquire*].

squirm (skwurm) *v.i.* to move like a snake, eel, worm, etc.; to wriggle. **-iness** *n.* **-y** *a.*

squir·rel (skwur'·al) *n.* small graceful animal with bushy tail, living in trees and feeding on nuts; its fur [O.Fr. *escureul*].

squirt (skwurt) *v.t.* and *v.i.* to eject, or be ejected, in a jet; to spurt; *n.* instrument for squirting; syringe; thin jet of liquid. **-er** *n.*

stab (stab) *v.t.* to pierce or wound with pointed instrument; to hurt feelings of; *v.i.* to strike with pointed weapon; *n.* blow or wound so inflicted; sudden pain. *pr.p.* **-bing**. *pa.p.* and *pa.t.* **-bed. -ber** *n.* [fr. Gael. *stob*, stake].

sta·bi·lize (stā'·ba·līz) *v.t.* to make stable, fixed, etc.; to fix exchange value of currency of a country. **stabilization** *n.* **stabilizer** *n.* that which stabilizes; horizontal tailplane of aircraft. **stability** (sta·bil'·a·ti·) *n.* steadiness [L. *stabilis*, fr. *stare*, to stand].

sta·ble (stā'·bl) *a.* firmly fixed, established; steady; lasting; resolute; **stably** *adv.* Also **stabile**. [L. *stabilis*, fr. *stare*, to stand].

sta·ble (stā'·bl) *n.* building for horses, usually divided into stalls; racehorse trainer's establishment; *v.t.* to put into, or keep in, stable; *v.i.* to be in stable [L. *stabulum*, a stall, fr. *stare*, to stand].

stac·ca·to (sta·kà'·tō) *a.* and *adv.* (*Mus.*) short, sharp, and distinct [It. fr. L. *staccare*, to separate].

stack (stak) *n.* large heap or pile, esp. of hay, straw, or wood; number of chimneys standing together; a chimney; (*Colloq.*) a great number; *pl.* book shelves. *v.t.* to heap or pile up; to arrange cards for cheating [O.N. *stakkr*].

sta·di·um (stā·di·am) *n.* arena for sports events, entertainments, etc., with seats for spectators [L. fr. Gk. *stadion*].

staff (staf) *n. pl.* **-s** or **staves** (stāvz): pole or stick used in walking, climbing, etc. or for support or defense; prop; stick, as emblem of office or authority; flagpole; (*Mus.*) five lines and four spaces on which music is written; (*Arch.*) stanza. (with *pl.* **-s**) body of persons working in office, school, etc.; *v.t.* to provide with staff. [O.E. *staef*].

stag (stag) *n.* male of red or other large deer; man who attends party without a woman. (*Slang*) party for men only [O.E. *stagga*].

stage (stāj) *n.* raised floor or platform esp. of theater, etc.; theatrical profession; dramatic art of literature; scene of action; degree of progress; point of development; distance between two stopping places on a journey; *v.t.* to put (a play) on stage. **staging** *n.* scaffolding. **-coach** *n.* four-wheeled passenger vehicle, horse drawn. **-fright** *n.* extreme nervousness felt when facing audience. **-struck** *a.* smitten with love for stage as career. **-whisper** *n.* loud whisper intended to be heard [O.Fr. *estage*, fr. L. *stare*, to stand].

stag·ger (stag'·er) *v.i.* to walk or stand unsteadily; to reel; to totter; to hestitate; *v.t.* to cause to reel; to cause to hesitate; to shock; to distribute in overlapping periods; to arrange in zigzag fashion; *n.* act of staggering; unsteady movement. **-ing** *a.* amazing; astounding [O.N. *stakra*, to reel].

stag·nate (stag'·nāt) *v.i.* to cease to flow; to be motionless; to be dull. **stagnant** *a.* of water, not flowing; hence, foul; impure; not brisk; dull. **stagnantly** *adv.* **stagnation** *n.* [L. *stagnum*, pool].

staid (stād) *a.* of sober and quiet character; steady; sedate; **-ly** *adv.* **-ness** *n.* [fr. *stay*].

stain (stān) *v.t.* and *v.i.* to discolor; to spot; to blot; to dye; to color, as wood, glass, etc.; to mark with guilt; *n.* discoloration; spot; dye; taint of guilt; disgrace. **-less** *a.* without a stain; not liable to stain or rust, esp. of a kind of steel. **-ed-glass**, glass with colors fused into it [L. *tingere*, to color].

stained-glass

stair (stār) *n.* steps one above the other for connecting different levels. **-s** *n.pl.* flight of steps. **-case** *n.* flight of steps with railings, etc. Also **-way** [M.E. *steire*, climb].

stake (stāk) *n.* sharpened stick or post; post to which one condemned to be burned, was tied; death by burning; money laid down as wager; interest in result of enterprise; *pl.* money in contention; *v.t.* to mark out with stakes; to wager; to risk; to pledge. **at stake**, risked; involved [O.E. *staca*].

sta·lac·tite (sta·lak'·tīt) *n.* deposit of carbonate of lime, hanging like icicle from roof of cave. **stalactic, stalactitic** *a.* **stalactical** *a.* [Gk. *stalaktos*, droppings].

sta·lag (sta'·lág) *n.* (*World War 2*) prisoner-of-war camp [Ger. *Stammlager*].

sta·lag·mite (sta·lag'·mīt) *n.* deposit of carbonate of lime from floor of cave. **stalagmitic(al)** [Gk. *stalagma*, that which drops].

stale (stāl) *a.* not fresh; kept too long, as bread; tasteless; musty; having lost originality; trite; common; *v.t.* to make tasteless; *v.i.* to lose freshness. **-ly** *adv.* **-ness** *n.* [O.Fr. *estale*, spread out].

stale (stāl) *v.i.* of horses, to make water; *n.*

stale·mate (stāl'·māt) *n.* (*Chess*) position, resulting in drawn game; deadlock; standstill; *v.t.* to bring to a standstill [*stale* and *mate*].

stalk (stawk) *n.* stem of plant, leaf, etc., [M.E.].

stalk (stawk) *v.i., t.* to steal up to game cautiously; to walk in stiff and stately manner; *n.* act of stealing up to game; stiff and stately gait. **-er** *n.* **-ing-horse** *n.* horse or figure of one, behind which a sportsman takes cover when stalking game; pretense; feint; pretext

[O.E. *stealcian*, to walk cautiously].

stall (stawl) *n.* compartment for animal in stable; erection for display and sale of goods; a pew or enclosed seat in cathedral or church; protective sheath for injured finger; *v.t.* and *v.i.* to place or keep in stall; to come to a standstill; of engine or automobile, to stop running unintentionally; of aircraft, to lose flying speed and controllability [O.E. *steall*, a standing place, esp. for cattle].

stall (stawl) (*Slang*) pretense, trick; *v.i.* to evade question [O.E. *stelan*, to steal].

stal·lion (stal'·yan) *n.* an uncastrated male horse kept for breeding [fr. *stall*].

stal·wart (stawl'·wert) *a.* sturdy; strong; brave; steadfast; *n.* strong, muscular person; staunch supporter. **-ly** *adv.* [O.E. *staelworthe*].

sta·men (stā'·man) *n.* (*Bot.*) male organ of flowering plant, pollen-bearing part. **stamina·l** *a.* pert. to stamens, or to stamina. L. = fiber, thread].

stam·i·na (stam'·a·na) *n.* power of endurance; staying power; vigor.

stam·mer (stam'·er) *v.i.* to speak with repetition of syllables or hesitatingly; to stutter; *n.* halting enunciation; stutter. **-er** *n.* **-ing** *n.* stammer; stutter [O.E. *stamerian*].

stamp (stamp) *v.i.* to put down a foot with force; *v.t.* to set down (a foot) heavily or with force; to make an official mark on; to affix postage stamp; to distinguish by a mark; to brand; to fix deeply; *n.* act of stamping; instrument for making imprinted mark; mark imprinted; die; piece of gummed paper printed with device, as evidence of postage, etc.; character; form. **-er** *n.* [O.E. *stempan*].

stam·pede (stam·pēd') *n.* sudden, frightened rush, esp. of herd of cattle, crowd, etc.; *v.t.* to put into a state of panic; *v.i.* to take part in a stampede; to rush off in a general panic [Sp. *estampido*, a crash].

stance (stans) *n.* position of feet in certain games, e.g. golf [L. *stare*, to stand].

stanch (stánch) *v.t.* to stop or check flow (of blood); *a.* firm; loyal; trustworthy. **-ly** *adv.* **-ness** *n.* Also **staunch** [O.F. *estancher*].

stan·chion (stan'·chan) *n.* upright support; iron bar, used as prop [O.Fr. *estance*, fr. L. *stare*, to stand].

stand (stand) *v.i.* to remain at rest in upright position; to be situated; to become or remain stationary; to stop; to endure; to adhere to principles; to have a position, order, or rank; to consist; to place oneself; to adhere to; to persist; to insist; to be of certain height; (*Naut.*) to hold course or direction; to continue in force; (*Colloq.*) to treat; *v.t.* to endure; to sustain; to withstand; to set; *pa.p.* and *pa.t.* **stood.** *n.* place where one stands; place for taxicabs; structure for spectators; piece of furniture on which things may be placed; stall for display of goods; position on some question. **-by** *n.* something in reserve. **-in** *n.* (*Film*) actor or actress who stands in the place of principal player until scene is ready to be shot. **-off, -offish** *a.* haughty; reserved; aloof. **-offishness** *n.* **-point** *n.* a point of view. **to stand-down** (*Law*) to leave the witness stand. **to stand out,** to be conspicuous [O.E. *standan*].

stand·ard (stan'·derd) *n.* weight, measure, model, quality, etc. to which others must conform; criterion; pole with a flag; flag esp. ensign of war; royal banner; upright support; *a.* serving as established rule, model, etc.; having fixed value; uniform; standing upright. **-ize** *v.t.* to make of, or bring to, uniform level of weight, measure, quality, etc. **-ization** *n.* [O.Fr. *estendard*, a royal banner].

stand·ing (stan'·ding) *a.* established by law, custom, etc.; settled; permanent; not flowing; erect; *n.* duration; existence; continuance; reputation. **— army,** force maintained in peacetime. **— orders,** permanent rules [O.E. *standan*].

stank (stangk) *pa.t.* of the verb **stink.**

stan·za (stan'·za) *n.* group of lines or verses of poetry having definite pattern; loosely, division of poem. **stanzaic** (stan·zā'·ik) *a.* [It. stanza, fr. L. *stare*, to stand].

sta·ple (stā'·pl) *n.* settled market; chief product of a country or district; unmanufactured material; fiber of wool, cotton, flax, etc.; *a.* established in commerce; settled; regularly produced or made for market; principal; chief; *v.t.* of textiles, to grade according to length and quality of fiber. **-r** *n.* [O.Fr. *estaple*, a general market].

sta·ple (stā'·pl) *n.* U-shaped piece of metal with pointed ends to drive into wood used with hook, as locking device for a door, etc.; piece of wire to hold sheets of paper together **-r** *n.* mechanical device for fastening papers together [O.E. *stapel*, a prop].

star (stár) *n.* shining celestial body, seen as twinkling point of light; five or six-pointed figure asterisk; leading actor or actress; *v.t.* to set or adorn with stars; to cast (in play) as leading actor; *v.i.* to shine, as star; to play principal part. *pr.p.* **-ring;** *pa.p.*, *pa.t.* **-red. -let** *n.* small star; beginning actress. **-light** *n.* light from stars. **-lit** *a.* **-red** *a.* **-ry** *a.* **-riness** *n.* **-fish** *n.* marine animal shaped like a star. **-gazing** *n.* practice of observing stars; astrology [O.E. *steorra*].

star·board (stár'·berd) *n.* right-hand side of

a ship, looking forward; *a.* pert. to, or on this side; *v.t.* to put (the helm) to starboard [O.E. *steorbord*, the steer side].

stapler

starfish

starch (stárch) *n.* substance forming main food element in bread, potatoes, etc. and used, mixed with water, for stiffening linen, etc.; formality; primness; *v.t.* to stiffen with starch. **-y** *a.* pert. to, containing, starch; (*Colloq.*) stiff; formal. **-ily** *adv.* **-iness** *n.* [O.E. *stearce*, rigid].

stare (ster) *v.i.* to look fixedly; to gaze; *v.t.* to abash by staring at; *n.* fixed, steady look. **-r** *n.* **staring** *n. a.* [O.E. *starian*].

stark (stárk) *a.* stiff; rigid; desolate; naked; downright; utter; *adv.* completely. **-ly** *adv.* [O.E. *stearc*, rigid].

star·ling (stár'·ling) *n.* bird, bluish-black and speckled [O.E. *staer*, starling].

start (stárt) *v.i.* to make sudden movement; to spring; to wince; to begin, esp. journey; to become loosened or displaced; *v.t.* to cause to move suddenly; to set going; to begin; to loosen; to displace; *n.* sudden involuntary movement, spring or leap; act of setting out; beginning; in sports, advantage of lead in race. **-er** *n.* [O.E. *sturtan*].

star·tle (stár'·tl) *v.t.* to cause to start; to excite by sudden alarm; to give a fright to; *v.i.* to move abruptly, esp. from fright, apprehension, etc. **startling** *a.* alarming; astonishing; surprising. **startlingly** *adv.* [fr. *start*].

starve (stárv) *v.i.* to suffer from hunger; to die of hunger; to be short of something necessary; *v.t.* to cause to suffer or die from lack of food, etc. **starvation** *n.* the suffering from lack of food, warmth, etc. [O.E. *steorfan*, to die].

state (stāt) *n.* condition of person or thing; place or situation; temporary aspect of affairs; rank; high position; formal dignity; politically organized community; civil powers of such; *a.* pert. to state; governmental; ceremonial; *v.t.* to set forth; to express in words; to specify. **-d** *a.* fixed; regular; settled. **-ly** *a.* dignified; imposing; majestic. **-liness** *n.* **-ment** *n.* act of expressing in words; what is expressed; formal account of indebtedness. **-craft** *n.* political sagacity; statesmanship. **-less** *a.* without nationality. **-room** *n.* a private cabin in a ship, train, etc. **-sman** *n.* one skilled in art of government; able politician. **-sman-like** *a.* **-smanship** *n.* [L. *status*, fr. *stare*, to stand].

stat·ic (stat'·ik) *a.* pert. to bodies at rest, or in equilibrium; motionless; *n.* (*Radio*) crackling noises during reception due to atmospheric electricity. **-al** *a.* static. **-s** *n.pl.* branch of mechanics dealing with bodies at rest [Gk. *statikos*, causing to stand].

sta·tion (stā'·shan) *n.* place where thing or person stands; position; situation; condition of life; rank; regular stopping place for trains, etc.; local or district office for police force, fire-brigade, etc.; *v.t.* to put in a position; to appoint to place of duty. **-ary** *a.* not moving; fixed; regular; stable [L. *stare*, to stand].

sta·tion·er (stā'·shan·er) *n.* one who deals in writing materials. **-ery** *n.* wares sold by stationer [L. *stationaries*, stationary].

sta·tis·tics (sta·tis'·tiks) *n.pl.* numerical data collected systematically, summarized, and tabulated; science of collecting and interpreting such information. **statistic(al)** *a.* **statistically** *adv.* **statistician** (stat·as·tish'·an) *n.* one skilled in statistics. **statist** (stā'·tist) *n.* statistician [Gk. *statizein*, to set up].

sta·tor (stā'·ter) *n.* (*Elect.*) the stationary part of a generator [L. *stare*, to stand].

stat·ue (stach'·óó) *n.* image of person or animal, carved out of solid substance or cast in metal. **statuary** *n.* collection of statutes.

statuesque (stach·oo·esk') *a.* like a statue; imposing. **statuette** (stach·oo·et') *n.* small statute [L. *statua*, a standing image].

stat·ure (stach'·er) *n.* the heights of a person or animal [L. *statura*, fr. *stare*, to stand].

sta·tus (stā'·tas) *n.* position; rank; position of affairs [L. fr. *stare*, to stand].

stat·ute (stach'·óó) *n.* law passed by legislature; established rule or law. **statutory** *a.* enacted, defined, or authorized by statute [L. *statutum*, that which is set up].

staunch. See **stanch.**

stave (stāv) *n.* one of curved strips of wood forming cask; rung of ladder; staff; five lines and spaces on which musical notes are written; verse or stanza; *v.t.* to fit with staves; to break stave(s) of (cask); to knock hole in side of; to ward off; to deter. *pa.p.* and *pa.t.* **-d** or **stove** [fr. *staff*].

staves (stāvz) *n.pl.* See **staff** and **stave.**

stay (stā) *v.t.* to restrain; to check; to stop; to support; to satisfy; to last; *v.i.* to remain; to continue in a place; to dwell; to pause; *n.* remaining or continuing in a place; halt; support; postponement, esp. of a legal proceeding. **-s** *n.pl.* laced corset [O.E. *staeg*].

stay (stā) *n.* (*Naut.*) strong rope or wire to support a mast or spar; *v.t.* to support or incline to one side with stays; to put on the other track; *v.t.* to change tack; to go about [O.E. *staeg*].

stead (sted) *n.* place which another had; place; use; benefit; advantage; service; frame of bed. [O.E. *stede*, position, place].

stead·fast (sted'·fast) *a.* firmly fixed; steady; constant. **-ly** *adv.* **-ness** *n.* [O.E. *stede*, place; *faest*, firm].

stead·y (sted'·i·) *a.* firm; constant; uniform; temperate; industrious; reliable; *v.t.* to make steady; to support; *v.i.* to become steady. **steadily** *adv.* **steadiness** *n.* [O.E. *stede*, position, place].

steak (stāk) *n.* slice of meat, esp. beef; also, slice of fish [O.N. *steik*].

steal (stēl) *v.t.* to take by theft; to get by cunning or surprise; to win gradually by skill, affection, etc.; *v.i.* to take what is not one's own; to move silently, or secretly. *pa.p.* **stolen** (stōlan). *pa.t.* **stole** (stōl). **stealth** (stelth) *n.* secret means used to accomplish anything; concealed act. **stealthy** (stel'·thi·) *a.* done by stealth. **stealthiness** *n.* [O.E. *stelan*].

steam (stēm) *n.* vapor rising from boiling water; water in gaseous state; any exhalation of heated bodies; *a.* worked by steam; *v.t.* to apply steam; to; to cook or treat with steam; *v.i.* to give off steam; to rise in vapor; to move under power of steam. **-y** *a.* pert. to, or like, steam; full of steam; misty. **-iness** *n.* **-er** *n.* steamship; vessel for cooking or washing by steam; something operated by steam. **-roller** *n.* heavy roller, driven by steam, used in road making [O.E. *steam*].

ste·a·rin (stē·a·rin) *n.* solid substance occurring in natural fats; hard, waxy solid used in manufacture of candles. Also **stearine. stearic** *a.* [Gk. *stear*, suet].

steed (stēd) *n.* horse [O.E. *steda*, stallion].

steel (stēl) *n.* hard and malleable metal, made by mixing carbon in iron; tool or weapon of steel; *a.* made of steel; hard; inflexible; unfeeling; *v.t.* to overlay, point, or edge, with steel; to harden; to make obdurate. **-y** *a.* made of, or like, steel; hard; obdurate; relentless. **-iness** *n.* **— engraving** *n.* method of incising on steel; the print [O.E. *style*].

steel·yard (stēl'·yárd) *n.* balance with unequal arms and movable weight [etym. uncertain].

steep (stēp) *a.* having abrupt or decided slope; precipitous; (*Colloq.*) very high or exorbitant, esp. of prices; *n.* steep place; precipice. **-ly** *adv.* **-en** *v.t.* and *v.i.* to make, or become, steep [O.E. *steap*].

steep (stēp) *v.t.* to soak in a liquid; to drench; to saturate; *v.i.* to be soaked; *n.* act or process of steeping; liquid used [O.N. *steypa*, to pour out].

stee·ple (stē·pl) *n.* a church tower with a spire. **-chase** *n.* a cross-country horse race; horse race on a course specially set with artificial obstacles; a cross-country footrace. **-jack** *n.* a skilled workman who climbs steeples, tall chimneys, etc. [O.E. *steap*, lofty].

steer (stir) *n.* a young male ox; a bullock [O.E. *steor*, a bullock].

steer (stir) *v.t.* to guide or direct the course of (a ship, car, etc.) by means of a rudder, wheel, etc.; *v.i.* to guide a ship, automobile, etc.; to direct one's course. **-age** *n.* the part of a ship allotted to passengers paying the lowest fare. **-er, -sman** *n.* the man who steers; the helmsman of a ship. **-ing gear** *n.* the mechanism for steering a vessel, vehicle, etc. [O.E. *stieran*].

stel·lar (stel'·er) *a.* pert. to, or like, stars; starry. **stellate, stellated** *a.* arranged in the form of a star; star-shaped; radiating. **stelliform** *a.* **stellular** *a.* [L. *stella*, a star].

stem (stem) *n.* the principal stalk of a tree or plant; any slender stalk of a plant; any slender shaft resembling a stalk; branch of family; curved or upright piece of timber or metal to which two sides of ship are joined; part of word to which inflectional endings are added; *v.t.* to remove the stem of; *v.i.* to originate. *pr.p.* **-ming** *pa.p.* and *pat.* **-med** [O.E. *stefn*]

stem (stem) *v.t.* to check; to stop; to dam up. *pr.p.* **-ming**. *pa.p.* and *pat.* **-med** [O.N. *stemma*].

stench (stench) *n.* strong, offensive odor [O.E. *stenc*].

sten·cil (sten'·sil) *n.* thin sheet of metal, paper, etc. pierced with pattern or letters, so that when placed on any surface and brushed over with paint, ink, etc., the design is reproduced; design so reproduced; *v.t.* to mark or paint thus. *pr.p.* **-ing.** *pa.p.* and *pat.* **-ed**

ste·nog·ra·phy (ste·nag'·ra·fi·) *n.* shorthand writing. **stenograph** *n.* character used in stenography; the script; stenographic machine; *v.i.* to write in shorthand. **stenographer, stenographist** *n.* **stenotype** *n.* a machine for writing shorthand. **stenographic, stenographical** *a.* [Gk. *stenos*, narrow; *graphein*, to write].

step (step) *v.i.* to move and set down the foot; to walk, esp. short distance; to press with the foot; *v.t.* to set or place, as foot; to measure in paces; (*Naut.*) to set up (mast); *n.* act of stepping; complete movement of foot in walking, dancing, etc.; distance so covered; manner of walking; footprint; footfall; tread of stair; degree of progress; measure; grade; (*Naut.*) socket for mast; *pr.p.* **-ping.** *pa.p.* and *pat.* **-ped. -per** *n.* **-ping stone** *n.* stone for stepping on when crossing stream, etc.; (*Fig.*) aid to success [O.E. *staeppan*].

step- (step) *prefix*, showing relationship acquired by remarriage. **-father** *n.* second, or later, husband of one's mother. Similarly **-mother, -brother, -sister.**

steppe (step) *n.* vast, treeless plain, as in Siberia [Russ. = a heath].

ster·e·o- (ster'·i·ō, stir'·i·ō·) fr. Gk. *stereos*, solid, used in referring to hardness solidity, three-dimensionality. **-phonic** *a.,* of or denoting a system of placing microphone to impart greater realism of sound.

ster·e·o·scope (stir'·i·, ster'·i·a·skōp) *n.* optical instrument in which two pictures taken at different viewpoints are combined into one image, with effect of depth and solidity. **-scopic(al)** *a.* **-scopically** *adv.* **-scopy** *n.* [Gk. *stereos*, solid; *skopein*, to view].

ster·e·o·type (stir'·i·, ster'·i·a·tīp) *n.* in printing, plate made by pouring metal into mold of plaster or papier-maché made from original type; fixed form. *a.* pert. to stereotypes; *v.t.* to make a stereotype from; to print from stereotypes; to fix unalterably; to reduce to empty formula; to make always the same. **-d** *a.* **-r, stereotypist** *n.* [Gk. *stereos*, solid; and *type*].

ster·ile (ster'·il) *a.* barren; not fertile; unable to have offspring; producing no fruit, seed, or crops; (*Med.*) entirely free from germs of all kinds. **sterilize** *v.t.* to make steril; to deprive of power of having offspring; to destroy germs, esp. by heat or antiseptics. **sterilization** *n.* **sterilizer** *n.* **sterility** *n.* barrenness [L. *sterilis*, barren].

ster·ling (stur'·ling) *a.* pert. to standard value, weight, or purity of silver 92½% pure); of solid worth; genuine; pure; denoting British money.

stern (sturn) *a.* severe; strict; rigorous. **-ly** *adv.* **-ness** *n.* [O.E. *styrne*].

stern (sturn) *n.* after part of ship; rump or tail of animal [O.N. *stjorn*, steering].

ster·num (stur'·nam) *n.* breastbone. *pl.* **sterna. sternal** *a.* [Gk. *sternon*, the chest].

ster·nu·ta·tion (ster·nya·tā'·shan) *n.* act of sneezing; sneeze [L. *sternutare*].

ster·tor (stur'·ter) *n.* heavy, sonorous breathing. **-ous** *a.* **-ously** *adv.* [L. *stertere*, to snore].

stet (stet) *v.i.* word used by proofreaders as instruction to printer to cancel previous correction. *pr.p.* **-ting.** *pa.p.,* *pat.* **-ted.** [L. =

---

let it stand]

steth·o·scope (steth'·a·skōp) *n.* instrument for listening to action of lungs or heart. [Gk. *stēthos*, chest; *skopein*, to see].

ste·ve·dore (stēv'·a·dōr) *n.* one who loads and unloads ships [Sp. *estivador*, a wool packer, fr. L. *stipare*, to press together].

stew (stū) *v.t.* to cook slowly in a closed vessel; to simmer; *v.i.* to be cooked slowly; to feel uncomfortably warm; (*Slang*) to fuss or worry; *n.* stewed meat, etc. (*Colloq.*) nervous anxiety; **-ed** *a.* [O.Fr. *estuve*, a stove].

stew·ard (stū'·erd) *n.* one who manages another's property; on ship, attendant on passengers; catering-manager of club. **-ess** *n. fem.* female steward. **-ship** *n.* office of steward; management [O.E. *stigweard,* fr. *stig*, a house; *weard*, a ward].

stib·i·um (stib'·i·am) *n.* antimony **stibial** *a.* [L.].

stich (stik) *n.* verse or line of poetry, of whatever measure or number of feet **-ic** *a.* pert. to stich. **-ometry** *n.* measurement of manuscript by number of lines it contains. **-ometric, ometrical** *a.* [Gk. *stichos*, row].

stick (stik) *n.* small branch cut off tree or shrub; staff; rod; (*Print.*) instrument in which types are arranged in words and lines; set of bombs dropped one after the other; (*Colloq.*) stiff or dull person [O.E. *sticca*].

stick (stik) *v.t.* to stab; to pierce; to jab; to puncture; to fasten; to cause to adhere; to fix; to thrust; (*Colloq.*) to endure; *v.i.* to pierce; to adhere closely; to remain fixed; to hesitate; to be unable to proceed; to be puzzled, e.g. by a problem. *pa.p.* and *pat.* **stuck. -er** *n.* **-y** *a.* adhesive; viscous; tenacious; (*Colloq.*) embarrassing. **-iness** *n.* **-ing plaster** *n.* adhesive bandage for small wounds, cuts, etc. **stuck up**, conceited [O.E. *stician,* to pierce].

stick·le (stik'·l) *v.i.* to hold out stubbornly. **-r** *n.* one who insists on trifles of procedure, etc. [O.E. *stihlan*, to control].

stick·pin (stik'·pin) *n.* necktie pin.

stiff (stif) *a.* not easily bent; not flexible or pliant; moved with difficulty; firm; hard; stubborn; formal in manner; high in price; *n.* (*Slang*) corpse. **-ly** *adv.* **-ness** *n.* **-en** *v.t.* and *v.i.* to make or become stiff or stiffer. **-ener** *n.* one who, or that which, stiffens. **-necked** *a.* stubborn; obstinate [O.E. *stif*].

sti·fle (stī'·fl) *v.t.* and *v.i.* to smother; to suppress; to repress. **stifling** *a.* airless; close.

stig·ma (stig'·ma) *n.* brand; mark of disgrace; stain on character; blemish on skin; (*Bot.*) top of pistil of a flower. *pl.* **-s** or **-ta. stigmata** (stig'·ma·ta) *n.pl.* marks resembling five wounds of Christ, said to have been miraculously impressed on bodies of certain saints. **-tic(al)** *a.* pert. to, or marked with stigma; giving reproach or disgrace; **-tization** *n.* **-tizer** *n.* [Gk. *stigma*, a tattoo mark].

stile (stīl) *n.* arrangement of steps for climbing fence or wall; a turnstile; in paneling or framing, upright sidepiece [O.E. *stigel*].

sti·let·to (sti·let'·ō) *n.* small dagger; pointed instrument used in needlework [It. fr. L. *stilus*, a pointed instrument].

still (stil) *a.* motionless; silent; quiet; peaceful; of wine, not sparkling; *n.* stillness; (*Photog.*) enlargement of one unit of film; *v.t.* to quiet; to silence; to calm; *adv.* to this time; yet; even; *conj.* yet; however. **-ness** *n.* **-birth** *n.* state of being dead at time of birth. **-born** *a.* **— life** (*Art*) inanimated objects as subject of painting [O.E. *stille*].

still (stil) *n.* apparatus for distilling [L. *stillare*, to drip].

stilt (stilt) *n.* pole with foot-rest, for walking raised from ground; *v.i.* to walk on stilts. **-ed** *a.* formal; stiff; pretentious [Dut. *stelt*].

stim·u·lus (stim'·ya·las) *n.* goad; incentive; stimulant; (*Bot.*) sting; prickle. *pl.* **stimuli. stimulate** *v.t.* to rouse to activity; to excite; to increase vital energy of. **stimulater** *n.* **stimulant** *a.* serving to stimulate; *n.* that which spurs on; (*Med.*) any agent or drug which temporarily increases action of any organ of body. **stimulation** *n.* **stimulative** *a., n.* [L. *stimulus*, a goad].

sting (sting) *n.* pointed organ often poisonous, of certain animals, insects, or plants; thrust, wound, or pain of one; any acute physical or mental pain; *v.t.* to thrust sting into; to cause sharp pain to; to hurt feelings; to incite to action; (*Slang*) to overcharge; *v.i.* to use a sting. *pa.p.* and *pat.* **stung. -er** *n.* **-ing** *a.* **-ingly** *adv.* [O.E. *stingan*].

stin·gy (stin'·ji·) *a.* meanly avaricious; miserly. **stinginess** *n.* [fr. *sting*].

stink (stingk) *v.i.* to give out strongly offensive smell; *pa.p.* **stunk** (stungk) *pat.* **stank** (stangk) or **stunk.** *n.* stench. **-er** *n.* one who, or that which, stinks; (*Slang*) objectionable person or thing. **-ing** *a.* [O.E. *stincan*].

stint (stint) *v.t.* to limit; to keep on short allowance; to skimp; *v.i.* to be frugal; *n.* limitation of supply or effort; allotted task. **-ed** *a.* [O.E. *styntan*, to blunt].

sti·pend (stī'·pend) *n.* money paid for a person's services; regular payment. **-iary** *a.* receiving salary; *n.* one who performs services for fixed salary [L. *stipendium*, wages].

stip·ple (stip'·l) *v.t.* and *v.i.* to engrave, draw, or paint by using dots instead of lines; *n.* this process. **-r** *n.* **stippling** *n.* [Dut. *slip*, a point].

---

stip·u·late (stip'·ya·lāt) *v.i.* to arrange; to settle definitely; to insist on in making a bargain or agreement. **stipulation** *n.* specified condition. **stipulator** *n.* [L. *stipulari*].

stir (stur) *v.t.* to set or keep in motion; to move; to mix up ingredients, materials, etc. by circular motion of utensil; to rouse; to incite; *v.i.* to begin to move; to be in motion; to be emotionally moved; *pr.p.* **-ring.** *pa.p.* and *pat.* **-red.** *n.* act of stirring; commotion. **-rer** *n.* **-ring** *a.* active; energetic; exciting; rousing; *n.* act of stirring [O.E. *styrian*].

stir·rup (stur'·ap) *n.* metal loop hung from strap, for foot of rider on horse. [O.E. *stigrap*, mount rope].

stitch (stich) *n.* in sewing, a single pass of needle; loop or turn of thread thus made; in knitting, crocheting, etc., single turn of yarn or thread around needle or hook; bit of clothing; sharp, sudden pain in the side; *v.t.* and *v.i.* to form stitches; to sew. **-er** *n.* **-ing** *n.* work done by sewing [O.E. *stician*, to pierce].

stith·y (stith'·i·) *n.* anvil; forge [O.N. *stethi*, anvil].

stoat (stōt) *n.* ermine or weasel, esp. in its summer fur of reddish-brown color.

stock (stak) *n.* stump or post; stem or trunk of tree or plant; upright block of wood; piece of wood to which the barrel, lock, etc. of firearm are secured; crossbar of anchor; ancestry; family; domestic animals on farm; supply of goods merchant has on hand; government securities; capital of company or corporation; quantity; supply; juices of meat, etc. to form a liquid used as foundation of soup; close-fitting band of cloth worn round neck; garden plant bearing fragrant flowers; gillyflower; *pl.* frame of timber supporting a ship while building; old instrument of punishment in form of wooden frame with holes in it, to confine hands and feet of offenders; *v.t.* to lay in supply for future use; to provide with cattle, etc. *a.* used, or available, for constant supply; commonplace; pert. to stock. **-breeder** *n.* one who raises cattle, horses, etc. **-broker** *n.* one who buys and sells stocks or shares for others. **-broking** *n.* **— exchange**, building in which stockbrokers meet to buy and sell stocks and shares. **-in-trade** *n.* goods merchant, shopkeeper, etc. has on hand for supply to public. **-market**, stock exchange. **-still** *a.* still as stock or post; motionless. **—taking** *n.* act of preparing inventory of goods on hand; sizing up of a situation. **— yard** *n.* large yard with pens for cattle, sheep, pigs, etc., esp. for those to be slaughtered [O.E. *stocc*, a stick].

stock·ade (stä·kād') *n.* enclosure or pen made with posts and stakes; *v.t.* to surround, enclose, or defend by erecting line of stakes [Sp. *estacada*, a stake].

stock·fish (stäk'·fish) *n.* codfish, hake, etc., split and dried in open air [fr. *stock*].

stock·ing (stäk'·ing) *n.* woven or knitted covering for foot and leg [fr. *stock*].

stock·y (stäk'·i·) *a.* short and stout; thickset. **stockily** *adv.* [fr. *stock*].

stodge (stäj) *v.i.* to stuff; to cram. **stodgy** *a.* heavy; lumpy; indigestible; (*Fig.*) dull and uninteresting. **stodginess** *n.*

sto·ic (stō'·ik) *n.* disciple of Greek philosopher Zeno; one who suffers without complaint; person of great self-control; one indifferent to pleasure or pain. **-al** *a.* suffering without complaint; being indifferent to pleasure or pain. **-ally** *adv.* **-ism** *n.* endurance of pain, hardship, etc. without complaint [Gk. *stoa*, porch (where Zeno taught his philosophy)].

stoke (stōk) *v.t.* and *v.i.* to stir up, feed, or tend (fire). **-r** *n.* [Dut. *stoken*, to kindle a fire].

stole (stōl) *pat.* of **steal.**

stole (stōl) *n.* long, narrow scarf worn by bishops, priests, etc. during mass; woman's long, narrow scarf [Gk. *stole*, a robe].

stol·en (stōl'·n) *pa.p.* of **steal.**

stol·id (stäl'·id) *a.* dull or stupid; not easily excited. **-ly** *adv.* **-ness, -ity** *n.* [L. *stolidus*].

stom·ach (stum'·ak) *n.* chief digestive organ in any animal; appetite; desire; *v.t.* to put up with; to endure. **-er** *n.* formerly part of a woman's dress. **-ic** *n.* (*Med.*) any medicine for aiding digestion [Gk. *stomachos,* the gullet, fr. *stoma*, a mouth].

stone (stōn) *n.* hard, earthy matter of which rock is made; piece of rock; (*chiefly Brit.*) a measure of weight equal to 14 lb.; hard center of certain fruits; gem; concretion in kidneys or bladder; *a.* made of stone, stoneware, earthenware; *v.t.* to pelt with stones; to remove stones from, as from fruits. **stony**

a. like stone; full of stones; pitiless. **stonily** *adv.* **stoniness** *n.* **Stone Age,** primitive stage of human development when man used stone for tools and weapons. **-blind** *a.* entirely blind. **-crop** *n.* creeping plant found on old walls, etc. **-deaf** *a.* completely deaf. **-mason** *n.* worker or builder in stone. **-'s throw** *n.* as far as one can throw a stone; hence, not far away [O.E. *stan*].

stomach

stood (stood) *pa.p.* and *pa.t.* of **stand.**
stooge (stōōj) *n.* (*Slang*) one who bears blame for others; (*Colloq.*) actor serving as butt of another's jokes; *v.t.* to act as stooge.
stool (stōōl) *n.* chair with no back; low backless seat for resting feet on; seat for evacuating bowels; discharge from bowels. **-pigeon** *n.* pigeon used to trap other pigeons; (*Slang*) person used as decoy. [O.E. *stol*].
stoop (stōōp) *v.i.* to bend body; to lean forward; to have shoulders bowed forward, as from age; to bow one's head; to condescend; to lean forward; *n.* act of stooping; stooping carriage of head and shoulders [O.E. *stupian*].
stoop (stōōp) *n.* raised entrance landing or porch in front of doorway [D. *stoep*].
stop (stȧp) *v.t.* to fill up opening; to keep from opening; to keep from going forward; to bring to a halt; to obstruct; to check; to impede; to hinder; to suspend; to withhold; to desist from; to bring to an end; *v.i.* to cease; to halt; *pr.p.* **-ping.** *pa.p.* and *pa.t.* **-ped;** *n.* act of stopping; state of being stopped; halt; halting place; pause; delay; hindrance; any device for checking movement, e.g. peg, pin, plug, etc.; (*Mus.*) any device for altering or regulating pitch, e.g. vent hole in wind instrument; set of organ pipes; lever for putting it in action; consonant (p, t, etc.) produced by checking escape of breath from mouth by closure of lips, teeth, etc. **-page** *n.* state of being stopped; act of stopping; obstruction; cessation. **-per** *n.* one who, or that which, stops; plug for closing mouth of bottle, etc.; *v.t.* to close with a stopper. **-cock** *n.* valve for regulating flow of liquid. **-gap** *n.* a temporary substitute. **— watch** *n.* special watch whose hands can be started or stopped instantly [O.E. *stoppian*, to plug].
store (stōr) *n.* great quantity; abundance; reserve supply; stock; shop; *pl.* supplies; *v.t.* to collect; to accumulate; to hoard; to place in a warehouse. **storage** *n.* act of placing goods in a warehouse; space occupied by them; price paid. [L. *instaurare*, to restore].
stork (stawrk) *n.* large wading bird allied to heron and ibis [O.E. *storc*].

storm (stawrm) *n.* violent wind or disturbance of atmosphere with rain, snow, etc.; tempest; gale; assault on fortified place; commotion; outburst of emotion; *v.t.* to take by storm; to assault; *v.i.* to raise tempest; to rage; to fume; to scold violently. **-y** *a.* tempestuous; boisterous; violent; passionate. **-ily** *adv.* **-iness** *n.* **-bound** *a.* delayed by storms. [O.E. *storm*].
sto·ry (stō'·ri·) *n.* history or narrative of facts or events; account; tale; legend; anecdote; plot; rumor; (*Colloq.*) falsehood; a lie.

storied (stō'·rid) *a.* told in a story; having a history. **-teller** *n.* one who tells stories [Gk. *historia*].
story (stō'·ri·) *n.* horizontal division of building; set of rooms on one floor. **storied** *a.*
stoup (stōōp) *n.* holy-water basin [O.N.].
stout (stout) *a.* strong; robust; vigorous; bold; resolute; thickset; bulky; *n.* strong, dark-colored beer; porter. **-ly** *adv.* **-ness** *n.* **-hearted** *a.* brave; courageous; intrepid [O.F. *estout*, proud, fierce].
stove (stōv) *n.* apparatus heated by gas, electricity, etc. for cooking, warming room, etc.; oven of blast furnace; **-pipe** *n.* metal pipe for carrying off smoke from stove [O.E. *stofa*, a heated room].
stove (stōv) *pa.p.* and *pa.t.* of **stave.**
stow (stō) *v.t.* to fill by packing closely; to arrange compactly, as cargo in ship; (*Slang*) to cease; to conceal. **-age** *n.* act of packing closely; space for stowing goods; charge made for stowing goods. **-away** *n.* one who hides on ship to obtain free passage [O.E. *stow*, a place].
strad·dle (strad'·l) *v.i.* to spread legs wide; to stand or walk with legs apart; *v.t.* to bestride something; (*Colloq.*) to seem to favor both sides of an issue; *n.* act of straddling; **astraddle** *adv.* astride [fr.*stride*].
Strad·i·var·i·us (strad·a·va'·ri·as) *n.* a violin, usually of great value, made at Cremona, Italy, by Antonio *Stradivari* (1649-1737).
strafe (strāf) *v.t.* (*Mil. Slang*) to bombard heavily; to attack with machine-gun fire from airplanes [Ger. *strafen*, to punish].
strag·gle (strag'·l) *v.i.* to wander from direct course; to stray; to get dispersed; to lag behind; to stretch beyond proper limits; as branches of plant. **-r** *n.* one who, or that which, straggles. **straggling** *a.*
straight (strāt) *a.* passing from one point to another by nearest course; without a bend; direct; honest; upright; frank; (*U.S.*) of whisky, etc. undiluted; *n.* straightness; straight part, e.g. of racing-track; *adv.* in a direct line or manner; directly; without ambiguity; at once. **-ly** *adv.* **-en** *v.t.* to make straight. **-ener** *n.* **-away** *n.* a straight forward. **-forward** *a.* proceeding in a straight course; honest; frank; simple [O.E. *streht*].
strain (strān) *n.* race; breed; stock; inherited quality [O.E. *streon*].
strain (strān) *v.t.* to stretch tight; to stretch to the full or to excess; to exert to the utmost; to injure by over-exertion, as muscle; to wrench; to force; to stress; to pass through sieve; to filter; *v.i.* to make great effort; to filter; *n.* act of straining; stretching force; violent effort; injury caused by over-exertion; wrench, esp. of muscle; sound; tune; style; manner; tone of speaking or writing. **-ed** *a.* done with effort; forced; unnatural; **-er** *n.* filter; sieve [L. *stringere*, to make tight].
strait (strāt) *n.* narrow channel of water connecting two larger areas; difficulty; financial embarrassment. **-en** *v.t.* to narrow; to put into position of difficulty or distress. **— jacket** *n.* garment for restraint of violently insane. **—laced** *a.* laced tightly in stays; puritanical; austere [L. *stringere, strictum*, to draw tight].
strand (strand) *n.* (*Poetic*) edge of sea or lake; the shore; *v.t.* to cause to run aground; to drive ashore; to leave in helpless position; *v.i.* to run aground. **-ed** *a.* [O.E. *strand*].
strand (strand) *n.* single string or wire of rope; any string. e.g. of hair, pearls, etc.; *v.t.* to make rope by twisting strands together [O.Fr. *estran*, a rope].
strange (strānj) *a.* unaccustomed; not familiar; uncommon; odd; extraordinary. **-ly** *adv.* **-ness** *n.* **-r** *n.* one from another country, town, place, etc.; unknown person; newcomer; one unaccustomed (to) [O.Fr. *estrange*].
stran·gle (strang'·gl) *v.t.* to kill by squeezing throat; to choke; to stifle; to suppress. **-r** *n.* **strangulate** *v.t.* to constrict so that circulation of blood is impeded; to compress; to strangle. **strangulation** *n.* [L. *strangulare*].
strap (strap) *n.* long, narrow strip of leather, cloth, or metal; strop; strip of any material for binding together or keeping in place; *v.t.* to fasten, bind, chastise with strap; to sharpen (a razor). *pr.p.* **-ping.** *pa.p.* and *pa.t.* **-ped.** **-ping** *n.* act of fastening with strap; material used; punishment with strap; *a.* (*Colloq.*) tall; robust [O.E. *strop*].
stra·ta (strā'·ta) *n.pl.* See **stratum.**
strat·a·gem (strat'·a·jam) *n.* artifice in war; scheme for deceiving enemy; ruse [Gk. *stratēgein*, to lead an army].
strat·e·gy (strat'·a·ji·) *n.* art of conducting military or naval operations; generalship; skillful management in getting the better of an adversary. **strategic** (stra·tē'·jik) *a.* pert. to, based on, strategy. **strategics** *n.pl.* strategy. **strategical** *a.* **strategically** *adv.* **strategist** *n.* [Gk. *stratēgein*, to lead army].
strat·i·fy (strat'·a·fi) *v.t.* to form or deposit in strata or layers. **stratification** *n.* [L. *stratum*, a layer].
strat·o·sphere (strat'·a·sfir) *n* upper part of atmosphere, six miles or more above earth [L. *stratum*, layer, and *sphere*].

stra·tum (strā'·tam, strat'·am) *n.* bed of earth, rock, coal, etc. in series of layers; any bed or layer; class in society. *pl.* **strata.**
stratus *n.* cloud form, in low, horizontal layers or bands. *pl.* **strati** [L. *stratum*, fr. *sternere*, to spread out].
straw (straw) *n.* stalk of wheat, rye, etc. after grain has been thrashed out; collection of such dry stalks, used for fodder, etc.; hollow tube for sipping beverage; thing of very little value; *a.* made of straw [O.E. *streaw*].
straw·ber·ry (straw'·be·ri·) *n.* a red berry with delicious taste [O.E. *steaw*, straw; *berige*, a berry].

stray (strā) *v.i.* to wander from path; to digress; *a.* wandering; strayed; lost; occasional; *n.* stray animal; lost child [O.Fr. *estraier*].
streak (strēk) *n.* line, or long band, of different color from the background; stripe; flash of lightning; trait; strain; *v.t.* to mark with streaks. **-ed, -y** *a.* [O.E. *strica*, a stroke].
stream (strēm) *n.* flowing body of water, or other liquid; river, brook, etc.; current; course; steady flow of air or light, or people; *v.i.* to issue in stream; to flow or move freely; to stretch in long line; to float or wave in air; *v.t.* to send out in a stream; to send forth rays of light. **-y** *a.* **-er** *n.* long, narrow flag; pennant; auroral beam of light shooting up from horizon. **-let** *n.* little stream. **-line** *n.* line of current of air; shape of a body (e.g. car, ship, etc.) calculated to offer least resistance to air or water when passing through it; *v.t.* to design body of this shape [O.E.].
street (strēt) *n.* road in town or village, usually with houses or buildings at the side. **-walker** *n.* one who walks the streets; prostitute [L. *strata (via)*, a paved (way)].
strength (strength) *n.* quality of being strong; capacity for exertion; ability to endure; power or vigor; physical, mental, or moral force; potency of liquid, esp. of distilled or malted liquors; intensity; force of expression; vigor of style; support; security; force in numbers, e.g. of army. **-en** *v.t.* to make strong or stronger; to reinforce; *v.i.* to become or grow strong or stronger. **-ener** *n.* [O.E. *strengthu*].
stren·u·ous (stren'·yoo·as) *a.* eagerly pressing; energetic; full of, requiring effort. **-ly** *adv.* **-ness** *n.* **strenuosity** *n.* [L. *strenuus*].
strep·to·coc·cus (strep·ta·kák'·as) *n.* (*Med.*) bacterium of chain formation, the organism responsible for serious infections. *pl.* **streptococci** (·kák'·i) [Gk. *streptos*, bent; *kokkos*, grain].
strep·to·my·cin (strep·tō·mī'·san) *n.* (*Med.*) antibiotic drug related to penicillin [Gk. *streptos*, bent; *mukēs*, fungus].
stress (stres) *n.* force; pressure; strain; emphasis; weight or importance; accent; (*Mech.*) force producing change in shape of body; *v.t.* to lay stress on [O.Fr. *estrecier*]...
stretch (strech) *v.t.* to pull out; to tighten; to reach out; to strain; to exaggerate; *v.i.* to be drawn out; to be extended; to spread; *n.* extension; strain; effort; extent; expanse; long line or surface; unbroken period of time. **-er** *n.* one who, or that which, stretches; a frame or litter for carrying sick or wounded; brick or stone laid lengthwise along line of wall [O.E. *streccan*].

stretcher

strew (strōō) *v.t.* to scatter over surface; to spread loosely. *pa.p.* **-ed** or **-n,** *pa.t.* **-ed** [O.E. *streowian*].
stri·a (strī'·a) *n.* line or small groove. *pl.* **-e** (strī'·ē) thread-like lines, as on surface of shells, rocks, crystals, etc. **-te, -ted** *a.* marked with striae. **-tion** *n.* [L. *stria*, a furrow].
strick·en (strik'·n) *a.* struck; smitten; afflicted; worn out [fr. *strike*].
strict (strikt) *a.* stern; severe; exacting;

rigid; unswerving; without exception; accurate. **-ly** *adv.* **-ness** *n.* **-ure** *n.* severe criticism; (*Med.*) morbid contraction of any passage of body, esp. urethra [L. *stringere, strictum*, to tighten].

stride (strīd) *n.* long step, or its length; *v.t.* to pass over with one long step; *v.i.* to walk, with long steps. *pa.p.* **stridden** (strid'·n). *pa.t.* **strode** [O.E. *stridan*].

stri·dent (strī'·dant) *a.* harsh in tone; grating; jarring.**stridence, stridency** *n.* **-ly** *adv.* [L. *stridere*, to creak].

strife (strīf) *n.* conflict; struggle [O.Fr. *estrif*].

strike (strīk) *v.t.* to hit; to smite; to dash against; to collide; to sound; to cause to sound; to occur to; to impress; to afflict; to stamp; to cause to light, as match; to lower, as flag or sail; to take down, as tent; to ratify; to conclude; to come upon unexpectedly, as gold; to cancel; *v.i.* to hit; to deliver blow; to dash; to clash; to run aground; to stop work for increase of wages, etc.; to take root, of a plant; *n.* a stoppage of work to enforce demand; find, esp. in prospecting for gold; stroke of luck. *pa.p.* **struck**, or **-n** *pa.t.* **struck. striking** *a.* affecting with strong emotions; impressive. **strikingly** *adv.* [O.E. *strican*, to move, to wipe].

string (string) *n.* cord; twine; ribbon; thick thread; cord or thread on which things are arranged, e.g. *string of pearls*; chain; succession; series; stretched cord of gut or wire for musical instrument; vegetable fiber, as *string beans*; all race horses from certain stable; *pl.* stringed musical instruments collectively; *v.t.* to furnish with strings; to put on string, as beads, pearls, etc.; *v.i.* to stretch out into a long line; to form strings; to become fibrous. *pa.p.* and *pa.t.* **strung. -ed** *a.* **-y** *a.* fibrous; of person, long and thin. **-iness** *n.* [O.E. *streng*].

strin·gent (strin'·jant) *a.* binding strongly; strict; rigid; severe. **-ly** *adv.* **-ness, stringency** *n.* [L. *stringere*, to tighten].

strip (strip) *v.t.* to pull or tear off; to peel; to skin; to lay bare; to divest; to rob; *v.i.* to take off one's clothes; *n.* long, narrow piece of anything. *pr.p.* **-ping.** *pa.p.* and *pa.t.* **-ped** (stript). **-ling** *n.* youth [O.S. *strypan*, to plunder].

stripe (strip) *n.* narrow line, band, or mark; strip of material of a different color from the rest; (*Mil.*) V-shaped strip of material worn on sleeve as badge of rank; chevron; stroke made with lash, whip, scourge, etc.; *v.t.* to mark with stripes; to lash. **-d** (stript) *a.* [Dut. *streep*].

strive (strīv) *v.i.* to try hard; to make an effort; to struggle; to contend. *pa.p.* **-n.** *pa.t.* **strove.** *n.* [O.Fr. *estriver*].

strode (strōd) *pa.t.* of **stride.**

stroke (strōk) *n.* blow; paralytic fit; apoplexy; any sudden seizure of illness, misfortune, etc.; sound of bell or clock; mark made by pen, pencil, brush, etc.; completed movement of club, stick, racquet, etc.; in swimming, completed movement of arm; in rowing, sweep of an oar; rower nearest stern who sets the time and pace; entire movement of piston from one end to other of cylinder; single, sudden effort, esp. if successful, in business, diplomacy, etc.; piece of luck; *v.t.* to set time and pace for rowers [O.E. *stracian*, to strike].

stroke (strōk) *v.t.* to pass hand gently over; to caress; to soothe; *n.* act of stroking [O.E. *stracian*, to strike].

stroll (strōl) *v.i.* to walk leisurely from place to place; to saunter; to ramble; *n.* a leisurely walk. **-er** *n.* [etym. uncertain].

strong (strawng) *a.* having physical force; powerful; muscular; able to resist attack; healthy; firm; solid; steadfast; well-established; violent; forcible; intense; determined; not easily broken; positive. **-ly** *adv.* [O.E. *strang*].

stron·ti·um (stran'·shi·am) *n.* (*Chem.*) a yellowish, reactive, metallic element [*Strontian*, Scotland].

strop (strap) *n.* strip of leather for sharpening razor; *v.t.* to sharpen on strop. *pr.p.* **-ping.** *pa.p.* and *pa.t.* **-ped** (stropt) [L. *struppus*].

stro·phe (strō'·fē) *n.* in ancient Greek drama, song sung by chorus while dancing from right to left of orchestra; stanza. **strophic** *a.* [Gk. *strophē*, a turning].

strove (strōv) *pa.t.* of **strive.**

struck (struk) *pa.p.* and *pa.t.* of **strike.**

struc·ture (struk'·cher) *n.* that which is built; building; manner of building; arrangement of parts or elements; organization. **structural** *a.* **structurally** *adv.* [L. *struere, structum*, to build].

stru·del (stroo'·dl) *n.* type of Ger. pastry.

strug·gle (strug'·l) *v.i.* to put forth great efforts, esp. accompanied by violent twistings of body; to contend; to strive; *n.* violent physical effort; any kind of work in face of difficulties; strife. *n.* [etym. uncertain].

strum (strum) *v.t.* and *v.i.* to play badly and noisily on (stringed instrument). *pr.p.* **-ming.** *pa.p.* and *pa.t.* **-med** [imit. origin].

strum·pet (strum'·pit) *n.* prostitute; harlot.

strung (strung) *pa.p.* and *pa.t.* of **string.**

strut (strut) *v.i.* to walk pompously; to walk with affected dignity; *n.* stiff, proud and affected walk; pompous gait. *pa.p.* **-ting.** *pa.p.* and *pa.t.* **-ted** [O.E. *strutian*, to stick out stiffly].

strut (strut) *n.* rigid support, usually set obliquely; support for rafter; *v.t.* to brace.

strych·nine (strik'·nīn) *n.* highly poisonous alkaloid; stimulant. Also **strychnin** [Gk. *nightshade*].

stub (stub) *n.* stump of a tree; short, remaining part of pencil, cigarette, etc.; *v.t.* to clear (ground) by rooting up stumps of trees; to strike toe against fixed object. *pr.p.* **-bing.** *pa.p.* and *pa.t.* **-bed. -bed** *a.* short and blunt like stump; obtuse. **-by** *a.* abounding in stubs; short and thickset. **-biness** *n.* [O.E. *stybb*].

stub·ble (stub'·l) *n.* short ends of cornstalks left after reaping; short growth of beard. **-d** *a.* **stubbly** *a.* [L. *stipula*, fr. *stipes*, stalk].

stub·born (stub'·ern) *a.* fixed in opinion; obstinate. *adv.* **-ness** *n.* [M.E. *stoburn*].

stuc·co (stuk'·ō) *n.* plaster of lime, sand, etc. used on walls, and in decorative work; *v.t.* to make stucco [It.].

stuck (stuk) *pa.p.* and *pa.t.* of **stick. -up** *a.* (*Colloq.*) conceited.

stud (stud) *n.* a movable, double-headed flat-headed nail; boss; upright wooden support, as in wall; *v.t.* to furnish with studs; to set thickly in, or scatter over. *pr.p.* **-ding.** *pa.p.* and *pa.t.* **-ded** [O.E. *studu*, a post].

stud (stud) *n.* collection of horses, kept for breeding, or racing; place where they are kept. **-book** *n.* official book for recording pedigrees of thoroughbred animals [O.E. *stod*].

stu·dent (stū'·d(a)nt) *n.* one who studies; scholar at university or other institutions for higher education. [L. *studere*, to be zealous].

stu·di·o (stū'·di·ō) *n.* workroom of artist, sculptor, or professional photographer; where film plays are produced; a room equipped for broadcasting of radio and television programs [It.].

stu·di·ous (stū'·di·as) *a.* given to, or fond of, study; thoughtful; contemplative; painstaking; careful (of); deliberate. **-ly** *adv.* [L. *studium*, zeal].

stud·y (stud'·i·) *n.* application of the mind to books, etc. to gain knowledge; subject of such application; branch of learning; thoughtful attention; meditation; room for study; preliminary sketch by an artist; *v.t.* to set the mind to; to examine carefully; to scrutinize; to ponder over; *v.i.* to read books closely in order to gain knowledge. **studied** (stud'·id) also *a.* examined closely; carefully considered and planned [L. *studium*, zeal].

stuff (stuf) *n.* essential part; material; (*Brit.*) cloth not yet made into garments; goods; belongings; useless matter; worthless things, trash, esp. in *stuff and nonsense*; *v.t.* to fill by pressing closely; to cram; in cookery, to fill, e.g. chicken with seasoning; to fill skin, e.g. of animal, bird, etc. to preserve it as specimen; *v.i.* to eat greedily. **-ing** *n.* material used to stuff or fill anything [O.Fr. *estoffe*, fr. L. *stupa*, tow].

stuff·y (stuf'·i·) *a.* badly ventilated; airless; dull; conceited **stuffiness** *n.* [Fr. *étouffer*, to choke, stifle].

stul·ti·fy (stul'·ta·fī) *v.t.* to make to look ridiculous; to make ineffectual; to destroy the force of [L. *stultus*, foolish].

stum·ble (stum'·bl) *v.i.* to trip in walking and nearly fall; to walk in unsteady manner; to fall into error; to speak hesitatingly; *v.t.* to cause to trip; to mislead; *n.* act of stumbling; wrong step; error. **stumblingly** *adv.* **stumbling block** *n.* obstacle; hindrance [M.E. akin to *stammer*].

stump (stump) *n.* part of tree left after trunk is cut down; part of limb, tooth, etc. after main part has been removed; remnant; *pl.* (*Colloq.*) legs; *v.t.* to reduce to a stump; to cut off main part; to puzzle or perplex; (*Colloq.*) to tour (district) making political speeches; *v.i.* to walk noisily or heavily. **-y** *a.* full of stumps; short and thick [ME *stumpe*].

stun (stun) *v.t.* to knock senseless; to daze; to stupefy; to amaze. *pr.p.* **-ning.** *pa.p.* and *pa.t.* **-ned** (stund). **-ner** *n.* **-ning** *a.* rendering senseless (*Slang*) striking; excellent [O.Fr. *estoner*].

stump

stung (stung) *pa.p.* and *pa.t.* of **sting.**

stunk (stungk) *pa.p.* and *pa.t.* of **stink.**

stunt (stunt) *v.t.* to check the growth of; to dwarf. **-ed** *a.* [O.E. *stunt*, dull].

stunt (stunt) *n.* (*Colloq.*) any spectacular feat of skill or daring, esp. if for display, or to gain publicity [etym. uncertain].

stu·pe·fy (stū'·pa·fī) *v.t.* to deprive of full consciousness; to dull the senses; to stun; to amaze. **stupefier** *n.* **stupefaction** *n.* act of making stupid; dazed condition; utter amazement. **stupefactive** *a.* **stupefacient** *a.* and *n.* [L. *stupere*, to be amazed; *facere*, to make].

stu·pen·dous (stū·pen'·das) *a.* astonishing, esp. because of size, power, etc.; amazing. **-ly** *adv.* **-ness** *n.* [L. *stupere*, to be amazed].

stu·pid (stū'·pid) *a.* slow-witted; unintelligent; foolish; dull. **-ly** *adv.* **-ness, -ity** *n.* [L.].

stu·por (stū'·per) *n.* complete or partial loss of consciousness; dazed state; lethargy. **-ous** *a.* [L. *stupere*, to be struck senseless].

stur·dy (stur'·di·) *a.* hard; robust; vigorous; strongly built; firm. **sturdily** *adv.* **sturdiness** *n.* [O.Fr. *estourdi*, stunned, amazed].

stur·geon (stur'·jan) *n.* large fish, whose roe is made into caviar [Fr. *esturgeon*].

stut·ter (stut'·er) *v.i.* and *v.t.* to speak with difficulty; to stammer; *n.* the act or habit of stuttering. **-er** *n.* **-ing** *a.* [M.E. *stoten*].

sty (stī) *n.* place to keep pigs; hence, any filthy place [O.E. *stig*].

sty, stye (stī) *n.* small abscess on edge of eyelid [O.E. *stigend*].

styg·i·an (stij'·i·an) *a.* pert. to river *Styx* in Hades; infernal; gloomy; dismal [L. *Stygius*].

style (stīl) *n.* pointed instrument used by the ancients for writing on waxed tablets; engraving-tool; etching-needle; manner of expressing thought in writing, speaking, acting, painting, etc.; in the arts, mode of acting, painting, etc.; in the arts, mode of expression or performance peculiar to individual, group, or period; in games, manner of play and bodily action; mode of dress; fashion; fine appearance; mode of address; title; mode of reckoning time; sort, kind, make, shape, etc. of anything; (*Bot.*) stem-like part of pistil of flower, supporting stigma; pin of a sundial; *v.t.* to give title, official or particular, in addressing or speaking of (person); to term; to name; to call. **-t** *n.* stiletto; probe.**stylize** *v.t.* to make conform to convention. **stylish** *a.* fashionable; elegant. **stylishly** *adv.* **stylishness** *n.* **stylist** *n.* writer, who is attentive to form and style; one who is master of style. **stylistic** *a.* **stylistically** *adv.* **stylus** *n.* style [L. *stilus*].

sty·mie (stī'·mi·) *n.* (*Golf*) position on putting-green resulting from one player's ball coming to rest between hole and opponent's ball; (*Fig.*) to thwart [etym. unknown].

styp·tic (stip'·tik) *a.* contracting; astringent; *n.* (*Med.*) any substance used to arrest bleeding [Gk. *stuphein*, to contract].

sua·sion (swā'·zhạn) *n.* persuasion; advisory influence [L. *suadere*, to advise].

suave (swáv, swāv) *a.* pleasant; agreeable; smoothly polite; bland. **-ly** *adv.* **suavity** *n.* [L. *suavis*, sweet].

sub (sub) *n.* (*Colloq.*) shortened form of subaltern, sub-lieutenant, subscription, substitute, submarine, etc.

sub- (sub) *prefix*, meaning under, below, from below, lower, inferior, nearly, about, somewhat, slightly, moderately, used in many words, e.g. **-acute** *a.* moderately acute or severe [L.].

sub·al·tern (sạ·bawl'·ţẹn) (*Mil.*) *a.* of lower rank [L. *sub*, under; *alternus*, in turn].

sub·a·que·ous (sub·ā'·kwi·ạs) *a.* living, lying, or formed under water. **subaquatic** *a.*

sub·arc·tic (sub·árk'·tik) *a.* pert. to region or climate immediately next to the Arctic.

sub·con·scious (sub·kán'·shạs) *a.* pert. to unconscious activities which go on in mind; partially conscious; *n.* subconscious mind. **-ly** *adv.*

sub·cu·ta·ne·ous (sub·kū·tā'·ni·ạs) *a.* under the skin. **-ly** *adv.*

sub·di·vide (sub·dạ·vīd') *v.t.* to divide a part, or parts of, into other parts; to divide again; *v.i.* to be subdivided. **subdivision** *n.* act of subdividing; result of subdividing.

sub·duc·tion (sub·duk'·shạn) *n.* withdrawal; deduction [L. *subducere*, to withdraw].

sub·due (sub·dū') *v.t.* to bring under one's power; to conquer; to bring under control; to reduce force or strength of; to soften. **-d** *a.* **-r** *n.* **subdual** *n.* act of subduing; state of being subdued [L. *subducere*, to withdraw, to withdraw].

sub·ed·it (sub·ed'·it) *v.t.* to act under an editor; to be assistant editor. **-or** *n.*

sub·head·ing (sub·hed'·ing) *n.* division of main heading.

sub·hu·man (sub·hū'·mạn) *a.* less than human.

sub·ject (sub'·jikt) *a.* under power or control of another; owing allegiance; subordinate; dependent; liable to; prone; exposed; *n.* one under the power or control of another; one owing allegiance to a sovereign, state, government, etc.; a person, animal, etc. as an object of experiment, treatment, operation, etc.; matter under consideration or discussion, written or spoken; topic; theme; (*Mus.*) principal theme or melody of movement; (*Gram.*) a word or words in sentence of which something is affirmed; (*Philos.*) conscious self; thinking mind. **subject** (sub·jekt') *v.t.* to bring under power or control of; to subdue; to cause to undergo; to submit. **-ion** *n.* act of bringing under power or control; state of being under control. **-ive** *a.* pert. to subject; existing in the mind; arising from senses; relating to, or reflecting, thoughts and feelings of person; (*Gram.*) pert. to subject of sentence. **-ively** *adv.* **-iveness** *n.* **-ivity** *n.* [L. *sub*, under; *jacere*, to throw].

sub·join (sub·join') *v.t.* to append; to annex. **-der** *n.* something added at end.

sub·ju·gate (sub'·jŏŏ·gāt) *v.t.* literally, to bring under the yoke; to force to submit; to conquer. **subjugation** *n.* **subjugator** *n.* [L. *sub*, and *jugum*, yoke].

sub·junc·tive (sạb·jungk'·tiv) *a.* denoting subjunctive mood; mood of verb implying condition, doubt, or wish [L. *sub*; *jungere*, to join].

sub·lease (sub'·lēs) *n.* lease granted to another tenant by one who is himself a tenant; (sub·lēs') *v.t.* to grant or hold a sublease.

sub·let (sub·let') *v.t.* to let to another tenant property of which one is a tenant; *pr.p.* **-ting.** *pa.t. pa.p.* **sublet.**

sub·li·mate (sub'·li·māt) *v.t.* (*Chem.*) to convert solid directly into vapor and then allow it to solidify again; to purify thus; to direct repressed impulses, esp. sexual, towards new aims and activities. *n.* (*Chem.*) substance that has been sublimated. **sublimation** *n.* [L. *sublimare*, to lift up].

sub·lime (sạ·blim') *a.* exalted; eminent; inspiring awe, adoration, etc.; majestic; grandiose; *n.* that which is sublime; *v.t.* to sublimate; to purify; to exalt; to ennoble. **-ly** *adv.* **-ness**, **sublimity** (sạ·blim'·a·ti·) *n.* [L. *sublimis*, high].

sub·lim·i·nal (sub·lim'·an·al) *a.* in psychology, below level of consciousness.

sub·ma·chine gun (sub·mạ·shēn'·gun) *n.* (*Mil.*) light, portable machine gun.

sub·ma·rine (sub·mạ·rēn') *a.* situated, living, or able to travel under surface of sea; *n.* submersible boat, esp. one armed with torpedoes.

sub·merge (sạb·murj') *v.t.* to put under water; to cover with water; to flood; (*Fig.*) to overwhelm; *v.i.* to go under water. **-nce** *n.* [L. *sub*; *mergere*, to dip].

sub·merse (sạb·murs') *v.t.* to submerge; to put under water. **submersible** *a.* **submersion** *n.* [L. *submergere*].

sub·mit (sạb·mit') *v.t.* to put forward for consideration; to surrender; *v.i.* to yield oneself to another; to surrender. *pr.p.* **-ting.** *pa.p.* and *pa.t.* **-ted. submission** *n.* act of submitting; humility; meekness. **submissive** *a.* ready to submit; obedient; docile; humble. **submissively** *adv.* **submissiveness** *n.* resignation [L. *sub*; *mittere*, to put].

sub·mul·ti·ple (sub·mul'·tạ·pl) *n.* number or quantity that divides into another exactly.

sub·nor·mal (sub·nawr'·mal) *a.* below normal.

sub·or·di·nate (sạ·bawr'·dạ·nit) *a.* lower in rank, importance, power, etc.; *n.* one of lower rank, importance, etc. than another; one under the orders of another; *v.t.* (sạ·bawr'·dạ·nāt) to make or treat as subordinate; to make subject. **-ly** *adv.* **-ness**, **subordinacy** *n.* **subordination** *n.* [L. *sub*, under; *ordinare*, to set in order].

sub·orn (sạ·bawrn') *v.t.* to induce (person) to commit perjury; to bribe to do evil. **-ation** *n.* **-er** *n.* [L. *sub*, under; *ornare*, to furnish].

sub·poe·na (su(b)·pē'·na) *n.* (*Law*) writ summoning person to appear in court (under penalty for non-appearance); *v.t.* to issue such an order [L. under penalty].

sub·rep·tion (sub·rep'·shạn) *n.* concealment or misrepresentation of truth. **subreptitious** *a.* [L. *sub*, under; *rapere*, to seize].

sub·scribe (sạb·skrīb') *v.t.* to write underneath; to sign at end of paper or document; to give, or promise to give, (money) on behalf of cause; to contribute; *v.i.* to promise in writing to give a sum of money to a cause; (with *to*) to pay in advance for regular supply of issues of newspaper, magazine, etc.; to agree with or support. **-r** *n.* **subscript** *a.* written underneath. **subscription** *n.* act of subscribing; name or signature of subscriber; money subscribed or gifted; receipt of periodical for fee paid.

sub·se·quent (sub'·si·kwant) *a.* following or coming after in time; happening later. **-ly** *adv.* [L. *sub*; *sequi*, to follow].

sub·serve (sạb·surv') *v.t.* to serve in small way; to help forward; to promote. **subservient** *a.* serving to promote some purpose; submissive; servile. **subserviently** *adv.* **subservience, subserviency** *n.* state of being subservient.

sub·side (sạb·sīd') *v.i.* to sink or fall to the bottom; to settle; to sink to lower level; to abate. **subsidence, subsidency** *n.* act of subsiding [L. *sub*, under; *sidere*, to settle].

sub·sid·i·ar·y (sạb·sid'·e·ri·) *a.* pert. to subsidy; aiding, helping, supplementary, secondary; auxiliary; *n.* one who, or that which, helps; auxiliary [L. *subsidium*, a reserve].

sub·si·dy (sub'·si·di·) *n.* financial aid; government grant for various purposes, e.g. to encourage certain industries, to keep cost of living steady, etc.; also in return for help in time of war. **subsidize** *v.t.* to pay subsidy to [L. *subsidium*].

sub·sist (sạb·sist') *v.i.* to continue to be; to exist; to live (on); to support with food; to feed. **-ent** *a.* having real being; existing. **-ence** *n.* act of subsisting; things or means by which one supports life; livelihood [L. *subsistere*, fr. *sistere*, to stand].

sub·soil (sub'·soil) *n.* the layer of earth lying just below the top layer.

sub·son·ic (sub·sán'·ik) *a.* pert. to speeds less than that of sound; below 700–750 m.p.h.

sub·stance (sub'·stans) *n.* essence; material, etc. of which anything is made; matter; essential matter of book, speech, discussion, etc.; real point; property. **substantial** (sạb·stan'·shi·ạt) *v.t.* to make substantial; to give substance to; to bring evidence for; to establish truth of. **substantiation** *n.* **substantive** *a.* having independent existence; real; fixed; (*Gram.*) expressing existence; pert. to noun, or used as noun; *n.* (*Gram.*) noun. **substantively** *adv.* [L. *substart*, to be present].

sub·sti·tute (sub'·sti·tūt) *v.t.* to put in place of another; to exchange. *v.i.* to take place of another; *n.* one who, that which, is put in place of another. **substitution** *n.* **substitutional, substitutionary** *a.* **substitutionally** *adv.* [L. *sub*, under; *statuere*, to appoint].

sub·stra·tum (sub·strā'·tạm) *n.* underlying stratum or layer of soil, rock, etc.; a basic element. *pl.* **substrata. substrative** *a.*

sub·sume (sạb·sōom') *v.t.* to include under a class as belonging to it, e.g. 'all sparrows are birds.' **subsumption** *n.* **subsumptive** *a.*

sub·ten·ant (sub·ten'·ant) *n.* tenant who rents house, farm, etc. from one who is himself a tenant. **subtenancy** *n.*

sub·tend (sạb·tend') *v.t.* (*Geom.*) of line, to extend under or be opposite to, e.g. angle.

sub·ter·fuge (sub'·ter·fūj) *n.* that to which a person resorts in order to escape from a difficult situation; to conceal real motives, to avoid censure, etc.; an underhand trick; evasion [L. *subter*, under; *fugere*, to flee].

sub·ter·ra·ne·an (sub·tạ·rā'·nē·an) *a.* being or lying under surface of earth. Also **subterraneous, subterrene** (sub·tạ·rēn'), **subterrestrial** [L. *sub*, under; *terra*, the earth].

sub·ti·tle (sub'·tī·tl) *n.* additional title of book; half-title; film caption.

sub·tle (sut'·l) *a.* delicate; acute; discerning; clever; ingenious; intricate; making fine distinctions. **subtly** *adv.* **-ness, -ty** (sutl'·ti·) *n.* quality of being subtle; artfulness; a fine distinction [L. *subtilis*, fine woven].

sub·tract (sub·trakt') *v.t.* to take away (part) from rest; to deduct one number from another to find difference. **-ion** *n.* act or operation of subtracting. **-ive** *a.* **subtrahend** *n.* quantity or number to be subtracted from another [L. *sub*; *trahere*, to draw].

sub·trop·i·cal (sub·tráp'·i·kạl) *a.* designating zone just outside region of the tropics.

sub·urb (sub'·urb) *n.* residential district on outskirts of town; *pl.* outskirts. **suburban** *a.* and *n.* **-ia** *n.* suburbs and their inhabitants [L. *sub*, under; *urbs*, city].

sub·ven·tion (sub·ven'·shạn) *n.* act of coming to the help of; government grant; subsidy [L. *sub*, under; *venire*, to come].

sub·vert (sạb·vurt') *v.t.* to overthrow, esp. government; to destroy; to ruin utterly; **-er** *n.* **subversion** *n.* the act of subverting; overthrow; ruin. **subversive** *a.* [L. *sub*, under; *vertere*, to turn].

sub·way (sub'·wā) *n.* underground passage; underground railway.

suc·ceed (sạk·sēd') *v.t.* to come immediately after; to follow in order; to take place of, esp. of one who has left or died; *v.i.* to come next in order; to become heir (to); to achieve one's aim to prosper. **-er** *n.* **success** *n.* favorable accomplishment; prosperity; one who has achieved success. **successful** *a.* **successfully** *adv.* **successfulness** *n.* **succession** (sạk·sesh'·ạn) *n.* act of following in order; sequence; series of persons or things according to some established rule; line of descendants; act or right of entering into possession of property, place, office, title, etc., of another, esp. of one near of kin. **successional** *a.* **successionally** *adv.* **successive** *a.* following in order; consecutive. **successively** *adv.* **successor** *n.* one who succeeds or takes place of another [L. *succedere*].

suc·cinct (sạk·singkt') *a.* closely compressed; expressed in few words; terse; concise. **-ly** *adv.* **-ness** *n.* [L. *succingere*, to gird up].

suc·cor (suk'·er) *v.t.* to help esp. in great difficulty or distress; to relieve; to comfort; *n.* aid; support. **-er** *n.* [L. *succurrere*].

suc·cu·lent (suk'·yạ·lant) *a.* full of juice; juicy. **-ly** *adv.* **succulence** *n.* juiciness [L. *succus*, juice].

suc·cumb (sạ·kum') *v.i.* to yield, to submit; to die [L. *sub*, under; *cumbere*, to lie down].

such (such) *a.* of like kind; of that kind; of same kind; similar; of degree, quality, etc. mentioned; certain or particular; *pron.* used to denote a certain person or thing; these or those. **-like** *a.* similar; *pron.* similar things (but not defined); this or that [O.E. *swylc*].

suck (suk) *v.t.* to draw into mouth (by using lips and tongue); to draw liquid from (by using mouth); to roll (candy) in mouth; to absorb; *v.i.* to draw in with mouth; to drink from mother's breast; *n.* act of drawing with the mouth; milk drawn from mother's breast. **-er** *n.* one who, or that which, sucks; organ by which animal adheres by suction to any object; fresh water fish; shoot of plant from roots or lower part of stem; (*Slang*) person easily deceived. **-ing** *a.* **-le** *v.t.* to give suck to; to feed at mother's breast. **-ling** *n.* young child or animal not yet weaned [O.E. *sucan*].

su·crose (sŏŏ'·krōs) *n.* white, sweet, crystalline substance; cane sugar, beet sugar, etc. [Fr. *sucre*, sugar].

suc·tion (suk'·shạn) *n.* act of sucking or drawing in; act of drawing liquids, gases, dust, etc. into vessel by exhausting air in it; 'force' that causes one object to adhere to another when air between them is exhausted. **— pump** *n.* pump in which water or other liquid is raised by atmospheric pressure [L. *sugere*, to suck].

suction pump

sud·den (sud′·n) *a.* happening without notice or warning; coming unexpectedly; done with haste; abrupt. **-ly** *adv.* **-ness** *n.* [Fr. *soudain*, fr. L. *subitus*, unexpected].

suds (sudz) *n.pl.* water in which soap has been dissolved; froth and bubbles on it [O.E. *seothan*, to seethe].

sue (sōō) *v.t.* (*Law*) to seek justice by taking legal proceedings; to prosecute; *v.i.* to begin legal proceedings; to petition [L. *sequi*, follow].

suède (swād) *n.* soft, undressed kid leather; *a.* made of undressed kid [Fr. *Suède*, Sweden].

su·et (sū′·it) *n.* hard animal fat around kidneys and loins, used in cooking. **-y** *a.* [L. *sebum*, fat].

suf·fer (suf′·er) *v.t.* to endure; to undergo; to allow; to tolerate; *v.i.* to undergo pain, punishment, etc.; to sustain a loss. **-able** *a.* **-ableness** *n.* **-ably** *adv.* **-ance** *n.* the state of suffering; toleration [L. *sub*, under; *ferre*, to bear].

suf·fice (sa·fīs′·) *v.t.* to satisfy; *v.i.* to be enough; to meet the needs of. **sufficient** (sa·fish′·ant) *a.* enough; satisfying the needs of. **sufficiently** *adv.* **sufficiency** *n.* [L. *sufficere*, to satisfy].

suf·fix (suf′·iks) *n.* letter or syllable added to end of word; affix. *v.t.* to add to end of. **-al** *a.* **-ion** *n.* [L. *sub*; *figere*, to fix].

suf·fo·cate (suf′·a·kāt) *v.t.* to kill by choking; to smother; to stifle; *v.i.* to be choked, stifled, or smothered. **suffocating** *a.* **suffocatingly** *adv.* **suffocation** *n.* [L. *suffocare*].

suf·frage (suf′·rij) *n.* vote; right to vote. **-tte** *n.* woman who agitated for women's right to vote [L. *suffragium*, a vote].

suf·fuse (sa·fūz′) *v.t.* to spread over, as fluid; to well up; to cover. **suffusion** *n.* **suffusive** *a.* [L. *sub*, under; *fundere*, to pour].

sug·ar (shoog′·er) *n.* sweet, crystalline substance; any substance like sugar; (*Fig.*) sweet words; flattery; *v.t.* to sweeten with sugar; *v.i.* to turn into sugar. *a.* made of, tasting of, or containing sugar; sweet; flattering. **-iness** *n.* **— cane**, tall grass whose sap yields sugar. **— loaf** *n.* a cone-shaped mass of hard, refined sugar. **— plum** *n.* sweetmeat; bonbon [Fr. *sucre*].

sugar cane

sug·gest (sag·jest′) *v.t.* to bring forward; to propose; to hint; to insinuate. **-er** *n.* **-ion** *n.* proposal; hint; in psychiatry, influence exercised over subconscious mind of a person, resulting in a passive acceptance by him of impulses, beliefs, etc. **-ive** *a.* tending to call up an idea to the mind; hinting at; tending to bring to the mind indecent thoughts; improper. **-ively** *adv.* **-iveness** *n.* [L. *suggerere*, to carry up].

su·i·cide (sōō′·a·sīd) *n.* one who kills himself intentionally; act of doing this. **suicidal** (sōō·a·sī′·dal) *a.* pert. to, tending to suicide; (*Fig.*) disastrous; ruinous. **suicidally** *adv.* [L. *sui*, of oneself; *caedere*, to kill].

suit (sōōt) *n.* act of suing; petition; request; action in court of law; courtship; series or set of things of same kind or material; set of clothes; any of four sets in pack of cards; *v.t.* to fit; to go with; to appropriate; to be adapted to; to meet desires of; *v.i.* to agree; to be convenient. **-able** *a.* proper; appropriate; becoming. **-ably** *adv.* **-ability, -ableness** *n.* **-ing** *n.* material for making suits. **-or** *n.* one who sues; a wooer; a lover. [Fr. *suivre*, to follow, fr. L. *sequi*].

suite (swēt) *n.* train of followers or attendants; retinue; a number of things used together, e.g. set of apartments, furniture; (*Mus.*) series of dances or other pieces [Fr. fr. *suivre*, to follow].

su·ki·ya·ki (sōō·kē·ya′·kē) *n.* Jap. dish of fried meat, vegetables, etc.

sul·cus (sul′·kas) *n.* groove; a furrow. **sulcate, sulcated** *a.* **sulcation** *n.* [L.].

sul·fa (sul′·fa) *n.* abbrev. for *sulfa drugs*, a group of antibacterial compounds used in the treatment of disease, injury, etc.

sul·fate (sul′·fāt) *n.* salt of sulfuric acid. **sulfide** *n.* compound of sulfur with metal or other element. **sulfite** *n.* salt of sulfurous acid [L. *sulphur*].

sul·fur (sul′·fer) *n.* yellow, nonmetallic element, burning with blue flame and giving off suffocating odor. **-ous** *a.* **-y** *a.* **-ic acid**, colorless acid, having strong corrosive action [L. *sulphur*].

sulk (sulk) *v.i.* to be silent owing to ill humor, etc.; to be sullen; to be sullen fit or mood. **-y** *a.* silent and sullen; morose; *n.* light two-wheeled carriage for one person. **-ily** *adv.* **-iness** *n.*

sul·len (sul′·an) *a.* gloomily ill-humored; silently morose. **-ly** *adv.* **-ness** *n.* the state of being sullen [L. *solus*, alone].

sul·ly (sul′·i·) *v.t.* to soil; to stain; to disgrace; *v.i.* to be sullied [Fr. *souiller*, to soil].

sul·tan (sul′·tan) *n.* Mohammedan prince or ruler. **-a** *n.* wife, mother, or daughter of sultan; kind of raisin [Fr. fr. Ar. *sultan*, victorious].

sul·try (sul′·tri·) *a.* hot, close, and oppressive; sweltering. **sultrily** *adv.* **sultriness** *n.* [form of *sweltry*, fr. *swelter*].

sum (sum) *n.* result obtained by adding together two or more things, quantities, etc.; total; aggregate; summary; quantity of money; *v.t.* (generally with *up*) to add up; to find total amount; to make summary of main parts. *pr.p.* **-ming.** *pa.p.* and *pa.t.* **-med. -mation** *n.* act of summing up; total reckoning [L. *summa*, total amount].

sum·ma·ry (sum′·a·ri·) *a.* expressed in few words; concise; done quickly and without formality; *n.* abridgment or statement of chief points of longer document, speech; etc.; epitome. **summarily** *adv.* **summarize** *v.t.* **summarist** *n.* **summarization** *n.* **summarizer** *n.* [Fr. *sommaire*].

sum·mer (sum′·er) *n.* warmest of four seasons of year, season between spring and autumn; commonly, months of June, July, and August; *a.* pert. to period of summer; *v.i.* to pass the summer. *a.* like summer. **-y** *a.* [O.E. *sumor*].

sum·mer·sault *n.* See **somersault**.

sum·mit (sum′·it) *n.* highest point; top, top of mountain [L. *summus*, highest].

sum·mon (sum′·an) *v.t.* to demand appearance of, esp. in court of law; to send for; to gather up (energy, etc.). **-er**, **-s** *n.* (*Law*) document ordering person to appear in court; any authoritative demand; *v.t.* to serve with summons [L. *summonere*, to hint].

sump (sump) *n.* lowest part of excavation, esp. of mine, in which water collects; well in crankcase of motor vehicle for oil [Dut. *somp*].

sump·tu·ar·y (sump′·chōō·er·i·) *a.* pert. to. or regulating, expenditure. **sumptuous** *a.* costly; lavish; magnificent. **sumptuously** *adv.* sumptuousness *n.* [L. *sumptus*, cost].

sun (sun) *n.* luminous body round which earth and other planets revolve; its rays; any other heavenly body forming the center of system of planets; anything resembling sun, esp. in brightness; *v.t.* to expose to sun's rays; to warm (oneself) in sunshine; to bask. *pr.p.* **-ning.** *pa.p.* and *pa.t.* **-ned. -ny** *a.* pert. to, like, sun; exposed to sun; warmed by sun; cheerful. **-niness** *n.* **-bathe** *v.i.* to expose body to sun. **-beam** *n.* ray of sunlight. **-burn** *n.* darkening of skin, accompanied often by burning sensation) due to exposure to sun; *v.t.* and *v.i.* to darken by exposure to sun. **-burned, burnt** *a.* **— dial** *n.* device for showing time by shadow which a raised pin casts on plate marked with hours. **-down** *n.* sunset; **-flower** *n.* tall plant with large, round, yellow-rayed flowers. **-light** *n.* light of sun. **-lit** *a.* lighted by sun. **-rise** *n.* first appearance of sun above horizon in morning; time of its appearance; dawn; east. **-set** *n.* descent of sun below horizon; time of its disappearance; west. **-shade** *n.* parasol. **-shine** *n.* light of sun; cheerfulness. **-shiny** *a.* **-spot** *n.* dark, irregular patche seen periodically on surface of sun. **-stroke** *n.* feverish and sudden prostration caused by undue exposure to very strong sunlight [O.E. *sunne*].

sunflower

sun·dae (sun′·di) *n.* ice-cream served with topping [perh. fr. *Sunday*].

Sun·day (sun′·di) *n.* first day of week; [O.E. *sunnan*, sun; *daeg*, day].

sun·der (sun′·der) *v.t.* to separate; to divide; to sever; *v.i.* to come apart. **sundry** *a.* separate; several; various. **sundries** *n.pl.* sundry things; odd items [O.E. *syndrian*, separate].

sung (sung) *pa.p.* of **sing.**

sunk (sungk) *pa.p.* and alt. *pa.t.* of **sink.**

sunk·en (sungk′·an) alt. *pa.p.* of **sink.**

sup (sup) *v.t.* to take in sips; to sip; to eat with spoon, as soup; *v.i.* to have supper; to sip; *n.* small mouthful; sip.*pr.p.* **-ping.** *pa.p.* and *pat.* **-ped** [O.E. *supan*]

su·per (sōō′·per) *n.* supernumerary (actor); (*Colloq. abbrev.*) superintendent; (*Colloq.*) short for superfine, super-excellent, etc.; hence; first-rate [L. *super*, above].

su·per- (sōō′·per) *prefix* fr. L. *super*, above, over, higher, superior, to extra, etc.

su·per·a·ble (sōō′·per·a·bl) *a.* capable of being overcome [L. *superare*, to overcome].

su·per·a·bound (sōō′·per·a·bound′) *v.i.* to be exceedingly abundant. **superabundant** *a.* much more than enough; excessive. **superabundantly** *adv.* **superabundance** *n.*

su·per·an·nu·ate (sōō·per·an′·yoo·āt) *v.t.* to pension off because of age or infirmity.**superannuation** *n.* pension [L. *super*, above; *annus*, year].

su·perb (soo·purb′) *a.* grand; splendid; magnificent; stately; elegant. **-ly** *adv.* **-ness** *n.* [L. *superbus*, proud].

su·per·car·go (sōō′·per·kár′·gō) *n.* ship's officer who takes charge of cargo.

su·per·charge (sōō′·per·charj) *v.t.* to charge or fill to excess. **-r** *n.* in internal-combustion engine, device for forcing extra supply of gasoline mixture into cylinders.

su·per·cil·i·ar·y (sōō·per·sil′·i·er·i·) *a.* pert. to eyebrow. **supercilious** *a.* lofty with pride; haughty and indifferent. **superciliously** *adv.* [*supercilium*, the eyebrow].

su·per·cool (sōō·per′·kōōl) *v.t.* (*Chem.*) to cool (liquid) below its freezing point without solidifying it. **-ing** *n.*

su·per·e·go (sōō·per·ē′·gō) *n.* in psychoanalysis, that unconscious morality which directs action of censor.

su·per·er·o·ga·tion (sōō·per·er·a·gā′·shan) *n.* doing more than duty or necessity requires. [L. *super*, above; *erogare*, to expend].

su·per·fi·cial (sōō·per·fish′·al) *a.* on surface; not deep; shallow; understanding only what is obvious. **-ly** *adv.* **-ity** (fish·i·al′·a·ti·) [L. *super*, above; *facies*, the face].

su·per·fine (sōō′·per·fīn) *a.* fine above others; of first class quality; very fine.

su·per·flu·ous (soo·pur′·floo·as) *a.* more than is required or desired; useless. **-ly** *adv.* **superfluity** *n.* state of being superfluous; quantity beyond what is required; a superabundance. **-ness** *n.* [L. *super*, over; *fluere*, to flow].

su·per·heat (sōō·per·hēt′) *v.t.* to heat (steam) above boiling point of water, done under a pressure greater than atmospheric; to heat (liquid) above its boiling point.

su·per·het·er·o·dyne (sōō·per·het′·ar·a·dīn) *n.* (*Radio*) receiving set of great power and selectivity. *abbrev.* **superhet.**

su·per·hu·man (sōō·per·hū′·man) *a.* more than human; divine; excessively powerful.

su·per·im·pose (sōō·per·im·pōz′) *v.t.* to lay upon another thing. **superimposition** *n.*

su·per·in·tend (sōō·per·in·tend′) *v.t.* to manage; to supervise; to direct; to control; *v.i.* to supervise. **-ence, -ency** *n.* **-ent** *a.* superintending; *n.* one who superintends [L. *super-intendere*].

su·pe·ri·or (sa·pi′·ri·er) *a.* upper; higher in place, position, rank, quality, etc.; surpassing others; being above, or beyond, power or influence of; too dignified to be affected by; supercilious; snobbish; *n.* one who is above another, esp. in rank or office; head of monastery or other religious house. **superiority** (sa·per·i·ar′·i·ti·) *n.* [L. *superior*, higher].

su·per·la·tive (sa·pur′·la·tiv) *a.* of or in the highest degree; surpassing all others; supreme; (*Gram.*) denoting, as form of adjective or adverb, highest degree of quality; *n.* superlative degree of adjective or adverb. **-ly** *adv.* [fr. L. *super*, above; *ferre*, *latum*, to carry].

su·per·man (sōō′·per·man) *n.* ideal man; one endowed with powers beyond those of the ordinary man.

su·per·nal (sōō·pur′·nal) *a.* pert. to things above; celestial; heavenly; exalted.

su·per·nat·u·ral (sōō·per·nach′·a·ral) *a.* beyond powers or laws of nature; miraculous.

su·per·nu·mer·ar·y (sōō·per·nū′·mer·er·i·) over and above; extra; *n.* person or thing in excess of what is necessary or usual; actor with no speaking part [L. *super*, above; *numerus*, a number].

su·per·scribe (sōō·per·skrīb′) *v.t.* to write or engrave on outside or top of. **superscription** *n.* act of superscribing; words written or engraved on top or outside of anything.

su·per·sede (sōō·per·sēd′) *v.t.* to set aside; to replace by another person or thing; to take the place of. **supersession** *n.* [L. *super*, above; *sedere*, to sit].

su·per·son·ic (sōō·per·sán′·ik) *a.* pert. to soundwaves of too high a frequency to be audible; denoting a speed greater than that of sound, i.e. more than 750 miles per hour.

su·per·sti·tion (sōō·per·stish′·an) *n.* belief in, or fear of, what is unknown, mysterious, or supernatural; religion, opinion, or practice based on belief in divination, magic, omens, etc. **superstitious** *a.* pert. to, believing in, or based on, superstition. **superstitiously** *adv.* [L. *superstitio*, excessive fear of the gods].

su·per·struc·ture (sōō′·per·struk′·cher) *n.* structure built on top of another; the part of

building above foundation. **superstructive,
superstructural** a.

su·per·vene (sŏŏ·per·vēn′) v.i. to happen in
addition, or unexpectedly; to follow closely
upon. **supervenient** a. **supervenience,
supervention** n. act of supervening [L.
super, above; venire, to come].

su·per·vise (sŏŏ·per·vīz′) v.t. to oversee; to
superintend; to inspect; to direct and control.
supervision (vizh′·an) n. act of supervis-
ing; superintendence; inspection. Also **super-
visal** n. **supervisor** (vī′·zer) n. **supervi-
sory** a. [L. super, over; videre, visum, to see].

su·pine (sŏŏ′·pīn) a. lying on one's back; indolent; inactive [L. supinus, fr. sub, under].

sup·per (sup′·per) n. the last meal of the day
[Fr. souper, to sup].

sup·plant (sa·plant′) v.t. to displace (person)
esp. by unfair means; to take the place of.
-er n. [L. supplantare, to trip up, fr. planta,
the sole of the foot].

sup·ple (sup′·l) a. easily bent; flexible; lim-
ber; obsequious; v.t. and v.i. to make or
become supple. **-ly** adv. **-ness** n. [L. supplex,
suppliant].

sup·ple·ment (sup′·la·mant) n. something
added to fill up or supply deficiency; appendix; special number of newspaper; extra
charge; (Geom.) number of degrees which
must be added to angle or arc to make 180° or
two right angles. **supplement** (sup′·la·ment)
v.t. to fill up or supply deficiency; to add to;
to complete. **-al** a. **-ary** a. added to additional
[L. supplementum, fr. supplere, to fill up].

sup·pli·ant (sup′li·ant) a. supplicating; asking humbly and submissively; beseeching; n.
one who supplicates. **-ly** adv. **supplicant** a.
supplicating; n. one who supplicates; suppli-
ant. **supplicate** v.t. and v.i. to ask humbly;
to beg earnestly; to petition. **supplication** n.
[L. supplicare, to kneel down, fr. plicare, to
fold].

sup·ply (sa·plī′) v.t. to provide what is
needed; to furnish; to fill the place of; n. act
of supplying; what is supplied; stock; store;
supplies n.pl. food or money. **supplier** n.
[L.supplere, to fill up].

sup·port (sa·pōrt′) v.t. to keep from falling;
to bear weight of; to sustain; to bear or
tolerate; to encourage; to furnish with means
of living; n. act of sustaining; advocacy;
maintenance or subsistence; one who, or that
which, supports. **-er** n. [L. sub, under; portare, to carry].

sup·pose (sa·pōz′) v.t. to assume as true
without proof; to advance or accept as a possible or probable fact, condition, etc.; to
imagine. **-d** a. imagined; accepted; put forward as authentic. **supposedly** (sa·pōz′·
id·li·) adv. **supposable** a. [Fr. supposer].

sup·po·si·tion (sup·a·zish′·an) n. act of supposing; assumption; that which is supposed;
-ally adv. **supposititious** (sa·páz·a·tish′·
as) [L. sub, under; ponere, positum, to place].

sup·pos·i·to·ry (sa·páz′·a·tōr·i·) n. medicinal substance, cone-shaped, introduced into a
body canal [L. sub, under; ponere, positum,
to place].

sup·press (sa·pres′) v.t. to put down or subdue; to overpower and crush; to quell; to stop.
suppression (sa·presh′·an) n. **-ive** a.
-or n. [L. sub, under; premere, pressum, to
press].

sup·pu·rate (sup′·ya·rāt) v.i. to form pus; to
fester. **suppurative** a. tending to suppurate.
suppuration n. [L. sub, under; pus, matter].

su·prá- (sŏŏ′·pra) L. prefix, meaning above.

su·preme (sa·prēm′) a. holding highest
authority; highest or most exciting; greatest
possible; uttermost. **-ly** adv. **-ness** n. **supremacy** (sa·prem′·a·si·) n. state of being
highest in power and authority; utmost
excellence [L. supremus].

sur- prefix, meaning over, above, upon, in
addition [Fr. fr. L. super, over].

sur·cease (sur·sēs′) v.t. (Arch.) to cause to
cease; v.i. to cease; n. cessation [L. super-
sedere, to refrain from].

sur·charge (sur·chárj′) v.t. to make additional
charge; to overload or overburden. **surcharge**
(sur′·chárj) n. excessive charge, load, or
burden; additional words or marks superimposed on postage stamp.

sur·cin·gle (sur′·sing·gl) n. belt, band, or
girth for holding something on a horse's back
[L. super, over; cingulum, a belt].

sur·coat (sur′·kōt) n. long and flowing cloak
worn by knights over armor [O.Fr. surcote].

surd (surd) a. (Math.) not capable of being
expressed in rational numbers; radical;
(Phon.) uttered with breath alone, not voice,
as f, p, k, etc.; n. (Math.) quantity that cannot be expressed by rational numbers, or
which has no root [L. surdus, deaf].

sure (shoor) a. certain; positive; admitting of
no doubt; firmly established; strong or secure.
-ly adv. certainly; undoubtedly; securely.
-ness n. **-ty** (shoor′·a·ti·) n. certainty; that
which makes sure; security against loss or
damage; one who makes himself responsible
for obligations of another [L. securus, sure].

surf (surf) n. foam or water of sea breaking
on shore or reefs, etc.

sur·face (sur′·fis) n. external layer or outer
face of anything; outside; exterior; a. in-

volving the surface only; v.t. to cover with
special surface; to smooth; v.i. to come to the
surface [L. super, over; facies, the face].

surf

sur·feit (sur′·fit) v.t. to overfeed; to fill to
satiety; n. excess in eating and drinking;
oppression caused by such excess. **-er** n.
-ing n. [Fr. surfaire, to overdo].

surge (surj) n. rolling swell of water, smoke,
people; large wave or billow; v.i. to swell; to
rise high and roll, as waves. **surging** a. [L.
surgere, to rise].

sur·geon (sur′·jan) n. medical man qualified
to perform operations; one who practices
surgery. **surgery** n. branch of medicine dealing with cure of disease or injury by manual
operation; operating room. **surgical** a.
surgically adv. [Fr. chirurgien].

surgery

sur·ly (sur′·li·) a. of unfriendly temper; rude;
uncivil; sullen. **surlily** adv. **surliness** n.

sur·mise (ser·mīz′) v.t. to imagine or infer
something without proper grounds; to make
a guess; to conjecture; n. supposition; a
guess or conjecture [O.Fr. surmise, accusa-
tion].

sur·mount (ser·mount′) v.t. to rise above; to
overtop; to conquer or overcome. **-able** a.
[Fr. sur, over; monter, to mount].

sur·name (sur′·nām) n. family name [Fr.
surnam].

sur·pass (ser·pas′) v.t. to go beyond; to excel;
to outstrip. **-ing** a. excellent; in an eminent
degree; exceeding others [Fr. sur, beyond;
passer, to pass].

sur·plice (sur′·plis) n. white linen vestment
worn over cassock by clergy [L.L. super-
pellicium, overgarment].

sur·plus (sur′·plus) n. excess beyond what is
wanted; excess of income over expenditure;
a. more than enough [L. super, over; plus,
more].

sur·prise (se(r)·prīz′) v.t. to fall or come
upon unawares; to capture by unexpected
attack; to strike with astonishment; n. act of
coming upon unawares; astonishment; unexpected event, piece of news, gift, etc.
surprisal n. act of surprising or state of
being surprised. **surprising** a. **surprisingly**
adv. [L. super, over; prehendere, to catch].

sur·re·al·ism (sa·rē′·al·iz·am) n. 20th cent.
phase in art and literature of expressing subconscious in images without order or coherence, as in dream. **surrealist** n. **surrealistic**
a. [Fr. sur, over; realism].

sur·ren·der (sa·ren′·der) v.t. to yield or hand
over to power of another; to resign; to yield
to emotion, etc.; v.i. to cease resistance; to
give oneself up into power of another; to
capitulate; n. act of surrendering. **-er** n.
[L. super, over; reddere, to restore].

sur·rep·ti·tious (sur·ap·tish′·as) a. done by
stealth; furtive; clandestine. **-ly** adv. [L.
surripere, fr. sub; rapere, to seize].

sur·rey (sur′·i.) n. lightly-built, four-wheeled
carriage [prob. fr. proper name].

sur·ro·gate (sur′·a·gāt) n. deputy or delegate; deputy who acts for bishop or chancellor
of diocese. **-ship** n. [L. sub, under; rogare,
to ask].

sur·round (sa·round′) v.t. to be on all sides
of; to encircle; (Mil.) to cut off from com-

munication or retreat; **-ings** n. that which
surrounds; pl. things which environ; neighborhood [L. superundare, to overflow].

surrey

sur·tax (sur′·taks) n. additional tax; v.t. to
impose extra tax on.

sur·veil·lance (ser·vā′·lans) n. close watch;
supervision [Fr. fr. surveiller, to watch over].

sur·vey (ser·vā′) v.t. to look over; to view as
from high place; to take broad, general view;
to determine shape, extent, position, contour,
etc. of tract of land by measurement. **survey**
(sur′·vā) n. general view, as from high place;
attentive scrutiny; measured plan or chart of
any tract of country. **-or** n. one who surveys
[L. super, over; videre, to see].

sur·vive (ser·vīv′) v.t. to live longer than;
to outlive or outlast; v.i. to remain alive.
survival n. living longer than, or beyond life
of another person, thing, or event; any rite,
habit, belief, etc. remaining in existence after
what justified it has passed away. **survivor**
n. **surviving** a. [L. super, over; vivere, to
live].

sus·cep·ti·ble (sa·sep′·ta·bl) a. capable of;
readily impressed; sensitive **susceptibly** adv.
·-ness n. **susceptibility** n. capacity for
catching disease, for feeling, or emotional
excitement; sensitiveness; pl. sensitive spots
in person's nature. **susceptive** a. receptive
susceptivity, susceptiveness n. [L. sus-
cipere, to take up, receive].

sus·pect (sa·spekt′) v.t. to imagine existence
or presence of; to imagine to be guilty; to
conjecture; to mistrust. **suspect** (sus′·pekt)
n. suspected person; a. inspiring distrust. **-er**
n. [L. suspicere, to look at secretly].

sus·pend (sa·spend′) v.t. to cause to hang; to
bring to a stop temporarily; to debar from an
office or privilege; to defer or keep undecided.
-er n. one who suspends; pl. pair of straps
for holding up trousers, skirt, etc. **suspense**
n. state of being suspended; state of uncertainty or anxiety; indecision. **suspension** n.
act of suspending or state of being suspended;
delay or deferment; temporary withdrawal
from office, function or privilege. **suspensive**
a. **suspensively** adv. **suspensor** n. **suspen-
sory** a. [L. sub, under; pendere, to hang].

sus·pi·cion (sa·spish′·an) n. act of suspect-
ing; imagining of something being wrong, on
little evidence; doubt; mistrust; slight trace
or hint. **suspicious** a. feeling suspicion; mis-
trustful; arousing suspicion. **suspiciously**
adv. [L. suspicere, to look at secretly].

sus·tain (sa·stān′) v.t. to keep from falling or
sinking; to nourish or keep alive; to endure
or undergo; (Law) to allow the validity of.
-able a. **-er** n. **sustenance** (sus′·ta·nans)
n. that which sustains (life); food, nourishment. **sustentation** n. **sustentative** a.
sustention n. [L. sustinere, to support].

sut·ler (sut′·ler) n. formerly person who followed army and sold provisions, liquors, etc.,
to troops [Dut. zoetelaar, a small tradesman].

su·ture (sŏŏ′·cher) n. sewing up of wound;
a stitch; connection or seam, between bones
of skull; v.t. to join by stitching. **sutural** a.
united by sutures [L. suere, sutum, to sew].

su·ze·rain (sŏŏ′·za·ran, ·rān) n. feudal lord;
paramount ruler. **-ty** n. authority or dominion
of **suzerain** [Fr. suzerain, paramount].

svelte (svelt) a. supple; lithe; slender [Fr.].

swab (swáb) n. mop for rubbing over floors,
decks, etc.; bit of cotton on stick for applying
medicine, cleaning parts of body, etc. v.t. to
clean with mop or swab. pr.p. **-bing**. pa.t.
and pa.p. **-bed. -ber** n. [Dut. zwabber, ship's
drudge].

swad·dle (swád′·l) v.t. to bind or wrap as
with bandages; n. the cloth wrapping [O.E.
swathy a bandage].

swag (swag) n. (Colloq.) bundle; stolen goods
or booty; [O.N. swagga, to walk unsteadily].

swage (swāj) n. tool for bending, marking, or
shaping metal. v.t. [L.L. soca, a rope].

swag·ger (swag′·er) v.i. to walk with a conceited or defiant strut; to boast or brag; n.
defiant or conceited bearing; boastfulness.
-er n. **-ing** a. [perh. fr. swag].

Swa·hi·li (swä·hē′·li·) n. people of mixed
Bantu and Arab stock, occupying Zanzibar
and adjoining territory; their language.
(Poetic) **-an** a. [Ar. = coast-man].

swain (swān) n. (Poetic) country lad; rustic
lover; suitor [O.N. sveinn, a boy, a servant].

swal·low (swál′·ō) n. small migratory, pas-
serine, insectivorous bird. **-tail** n. forked tail;
kind of butterfly [O.E. swealwe].

swal·low (swál′·ō) v.t. to receive into stomach
through mouth and throat; to absorb;
(Colloq.) to accept without criticism or
scruple; v.i. to perform act of swallowing; n.
act of swallowing; amount taken down at one

gulp. **-er** *n.* [O.E. *swelgan*].
swam (swam) *pa.t.* of **swim.**
swamp (swámp, swawmp) *n.* tract of wet, spongy, low-lying ground; marsh; *v.t.* to cause to fill with water, as boat; *v.i.* to overwhelm; to sink. **-y** *a.* [Scand.].
swan (swän) *n.* large, web-footed bird of goose family, having very long, gracefully curving neck. **-nery** *n.* place where swans are bred. **-'s-down** *n.* fine, soft feathers on swan, used for powder puffs, etc.; thick cotton or woolen cloth with soft nap on one side.. **-song** song which, according to myth, swan sings before dying; |O.E.].
swank (swangk) *v.i.* (*Slang*) to show off; to swagger; *n.* (*Slang*) style; swagger; *a.* (*Slang*) ostentatious; showy. **-y** *a.*
swap (swáp) *v.t.* and *v.i.* to exchange; to barter; *n.* exchange. *pr.p.* **-ping.** *pa.p.* and *pa.t.* **-ped.** Also **swop** [M.E. *swappe*, strike].
sward (swawrd) *n.* land covered with short green grass; turf; *v.t.* to cover with sward. **-ed** *a.* [O.E. *sweard*, skin of bacon].
swarm (swawrm) *n.* large number of insects esp. in motion; crowd; throng; great multitude or throng; *v.i.* to collect in large numbers [O.E. *swearm*].
swarm (swawrm) *v.i.* to climb with arms and legs [etym. uncertain].
swarth·y (swawr'.THi.) *a.* dark in hue; of dark complexion [O.E. *sweart*].
swash·buck·ler (swásh'.buk.ler) *n.* swaggering bully. **swashbuckling** *a.* [imit.].
swas·ti·ka (swás'.ti.ka) *n.* symbol in form of Greek cross with ends of arms bent at right angles, all in same direction, thus 卐, used as badge of Nazi party [Sans. *svasti*, well being].

swat (swát) *v.t.* (*Colloq.*) to hit smartly; to kill, esp. insects. *pr.p.* **-ting.** *pa.t.*, *pa.p.* **-ted.**
swatch (swách) *n.* piece of cloth, cut as a sample of quality [var. of *swath*].
swath (swáth, swawth) *n.* line of hay or grain cut by scythe or mowing machine; Also **swathe** (swāTH) [O.E. *swaeth*, a track].
swathe (swāTH) *v.t.* to bind with bandage; to envelop in wraps; *n.* bandage; folded or draped band [O.E. *swathian*].
sway (swā) *v.t.* to cause to incline to one side or the other; to influence or direct; *v.i.* to incline or be drawn to one side or the other; to swing unsteadily; to totter; *n.* swaying or swinging movement; control. **-er** *n.* **-back** *a.* having inward curve of the spine [M.E. *sweyen*].
swear (swār) *v.t.* to utter, affirm or declare on oath; *v.i.* to utter solemn declaration with appeal to God for truth of what is affirmed; (*Law*) to give evidence on oath; to use name of God or sacred things profanely; to curse. *pa.p.* **sworn.** *pa.t.* **swore. -er** *n.* **-ing** *n.* **to swear by,** (*Colloq.*) to have great confidence in [O.E. *swerian*].
sweat (swet) *n.* moisture excreted from skin; perspiration; moisture exuding from any substance; state of sweating; (*Colloq.*) state of anxiety; *v.t.* to cause to excrete moisture from skin; to employ at wrongfully low wages; *v.i.* to excrete moisture; (*Colloq.*) to toil or drudge at. **-er** *n.* warm knitted jersey or jacket. **-y** *a.* damp with sweat; causing sweat; like sweat. **-ily** *adv.* **-iness** *n.* [O.E. *swat*].
Swede (swēd) *n.* native of Sweden. **Swedish** *a.* pert. to Sweden; *n.* language of Swedes.
sweep (swēp) *v.t.* to pass brush or broom over to remove loose dirt; to pass rapidly over, with brushing motion; to scan rapidly; *v.i.* to pass with swiftness or violence; to move with dignity; to extend in a curve; to effect cleaning with a broom; *n.* act of sweeping; reach of a stroke; curving or wide-flung gesture, movement, or line; powerful force forward, covering large area; long, heavy oar, used either to steer or to propel. *pa.p.* and *pa.t.* **swept. -er** *n.* **-ing** *a.* moving swiftly; of great scope; comprehensive. **-ingly** *adv.* **— stake(s)** *n.* gambling on race or contest, in which participators' stakes are pooled, and apportioned to drawers of winning horses [O.E. *swapan*].
sweet (swēt) *a.* tasting like sugar; having agreeable taste; fragrant; melodious; pleasing to eye; gentle; affectionate; dear or beloved; likeable; *n.* sweetness; darling; *pl.* confections. **-en** *v.t.* to make sweet, pleasing, or kind. **-ening** *n.* act of making sweet; ingredient which sweetens. **-ly** *adv.* **-ness** *n.* **-bread** *n.* pancreas or thymus of animal, as food. **-heart** *n.* lover or beloved person; darling. **meat** *n.* confection; candy. **-pea** *n.* climbing plant with fragrant flowers. **-potato** *n.* sweet, starchy tuber [O.E. *swete*].

sweetpotato

swell (swel) *v.t.* to increase size, sound, etc.; to dilate; to augment; *v.i.* to grow larger; to expand; to rise in waves; to grow louder; to be filled to bursting point with some emotion. *n.* act of swelling; increase in bulk, intensity, importance, etc.; slight rise in ground level; slow heaving and sinking of sea after storm; *pa.p.* **swollen** or **swelled.** *pa.t.* **-ed. -ing** *n.* act of swelling; state of being swollen; prominence or protuberance; (*Med.*) enlargement [O.E. *swellan*].
swel·ter (swel'.ter) *v.i.* to be oppressive, or oppressed, with heat; to perspire profusely; *n.* heated or sweaty state. **-ing** *a.* **sweltry** *a.* [O.E. *sweltan*, to swoon or perish].
swept (swept) *pa.t.* and *pa.p.* of **sweep.**
swerve (swurv) *v.i.* to depart from straight line; to deviate; *v.t.* to cause to bend or turn aside; *n.* act of swerving [O.E. *sweorfan*, to rub, file].
swift (swift) *a.* quick; rapid; prompt; moving quickly. **-ly** *adv.* **-ness** *n.* speed; a quick-flying migratory bird, resembling swallow; common newt [O.E. *swifan*, to move quickly].
swig (swig) *v.t.* and *v.i.* (*Colloq.*) to gulp down; to drink in long drafts; *n.* long draft. *pr.p.* **-ging.** *pa.p.*, *pa.t.* **-ged** [O.E. *swelgan*, to swallow].
swill (swill) *v.t.* and *v.i.* to drink greedily; *n.* act of swilling; pig food; hogwash slops. **-er** *n.* [O.E. *swilian*, to wash].
swim (swim) *v.i.* to propel oneself in water by means of hands, feet, or fins, etc.; to float on surface; to move with gliding motion, resembling swimming; *v.t.* to cross or pass over by swimming; to cause to swim; *n.* act of swimming; spell of swimming. *pr.p.* **-ming** *pa.p.* **swum.** *pa.t.* **swam. -mer** *n.* **-mingly** *adv.* easily, successfully [O.E. *swimmen*, to be in motion].
swim (swim) *v.i.* to be dizzy or giddy; *n.* dizziness or unconsciousness *pr.p.* **-ming.** *pa.p.* **swum;** *pa.t.* **swam.** [O.E. *swima*, to faint].
swin·dle (swin'.dl) *v.t.* and *v.i.* to cheat or defraud; to obtain by fraud; *n.* act of defrauding [Ger. *schwindeln*, to cheat].
swine (swīn) *n. sing.* and *pl.* thick-skinned domestic animal, fed for its flesh; pig; hog. **—herd** *n.* one who tends swine. **swinish** *a.* like swine; gross, brutal [O.E. *swin*].
swing (swing) *v.i.* to move to and fro, esp. as suspended body; to sway; to turn on pivot; to progress with easy, swaying gait; (*Colloq.*) to be executed by hanging; to wheel around; *v.t.* to attach so as to hang freely; to move to and fro; to cause to wheel about a point; to brandish; *n.* act of swinging or causing to swing; extent, sweep, or power of anything that is swung; motion to and fro; seat suspended by ropes, on which one may swing. *pa.p.* and *pa.t.* **swung. -er** *n.* **-ing** *a.* moving to and fro; moving with vigor and rhythm. **-ingly** *adv.* [O.E. *swingan*, to swing, whirl].
swing (swing) *n.* (*Mus.*) kind of jazz music [O.E. *swingan*].
swipe (swip) *v.t.* and *v.i.* to strike with a wide, sweeping blow, as with a bat, racket, etc.; (*Slang*) to steal; *n.* sweeping stroke [O.E. *swipian*, to beat].
swirl (swurl) *n.* eddy of wind or water; whirling motion; a twist of something; *v.i.* to whirl; *v.t.* to carry along with whirling motion [O.N. *svirla*, to whirl round].
swish (swish) *n.* whistling or hissing sound; *v.i.* to move with hissing or rustling sound.
Swiss (swis) *n. sing.* and *pl.* native of Switzerland; people of Switzerland; *a.* pert. to Switzerland or the Swiss [O. Ger. *Swiz*].
switch (swich) *n.* flexible twig or rod; tress of false hair; on railway, movable rail for transferring train from one set of tracks to another; (*Elect.*) device for making, breaking, or transferring, electric current; act of switching; *v.t.* to strike with switch; to whisk; to shift or shunt (train) to another track; (*Elect*) to turn electric current off or on with switch; to transfer one's thoughts to another subject; to transfer. **-er** *n.* **—like** *a.* **-back** *n.* zigzag ascent of ascending slopes. **-board** *n.* set of switches at telephone exchange [Old Dut. *swick*, a whip].
swiv·el (swiv'.l) *n.* ring turning on pivot, forming connection between two pieces of mechanism and enabling one to rotate independently of the other; *v.i.* to swing on pivot; *v.t.* to turn as on pivot [O.E. *swifan*, to revolve].
swol·len (swōl'.an) *a.* swelled. *pa.p.* of **swell.**
swoon (swoōn) *v.i.* to faint; *n.* fainting fit [O.E. *swogan*, to sigh deeply].
swoop (swoōp) *v.t.* to catch up with sweeping motion (with 'up'); *v.i.* to sweep down swiftly upon prey, as hawk or eagle; *n.* sweeping downward flight [O.E. *swapan*, to rush].
swop. See **swap.**
sword (sōrd, sawrd) *n.* weapon for cutting or

thrusting, having long blade; emblem of judicial punishment or of authority. **-fish** *n.* large fish with sword-like upper jaw. **-play** *n.* fencing. **-sman** *n.* one skillful with sword.

swivel

—smanship *n.* [O.E. *sword*].
swore (swōr) *pa.t.* of **swear.**
sworn *pa.p.* of **swear.**
swum (swum) *pa.p.* of **swim.**
swung (swung) *pa.p.* and *pa.t.* of **swing.**
syb·a·rite (sib'.a.rit) *n.* person devoted to luxury and pleasure. **sybaritic, sybaritical** *a.* [L. *Sybaris*, Greek city].
syc·a·more (sik'.a.mōr) *n.* tree with broad leaves, allied to plane tree and maple; kind of fig tree of Egypt and Asia Minor [Gk. *sukon*, fig; *moron*, black mulberry].

syc·o·phant (sik'.a.fant) *n.* flatterer, or one who fawns on rich or famous; parasite; *a.* servile; obsequious. **sychophancy, -ism** *n.* **-ic, -ical, -ically** *adv.* **-ish** *a.* [Gk. *sukophantēs*, to show].
syl·la·ble (sil'.a.bl) *n.* sound uttered at single effort of voice, and constituting word, or part of word; *v.t.* to utter in syllables; to articulate. **syllabic, syllabical** *a.* pert. to, or consisting of, a syllable(s). **syllabically** *adv.* **syllabicate, syllabify, syllabize,** *v.t.* to divide into syllables [Gk. *sullabē*, that which is held together].
syl·la·bus (sil'.a.bas) *n.* outline or program of main points in a course of lectures, etc. [Gk. *sun*, together; *lambanein*, to take].
syl·lo·gism (sil'.a.jizm) *n.* formal statement of argument, consisting of three parts, major premise, minor premise, and conclusion, conclusion following naturally from premises. **syllogize** *v.t.* and *v.i.* to reason by means of syllogisms. **syllogization** *n.* **syllogizer** *n.* **syllogistic, syllogistical** *a.* [Gk. *sullogismos*, a reckoning together].
sylph (silf) *n.* elemental spirit of the air; fairy or sprite; graceful girl. **-id** *n.* little sylph. **-like** *a.* graceful [Fr. *sylphe*].
syl·van (sil'.van) *a.* forest-like; abounding in forests; pert. to or inhabiting the woods [L. *silva*, a wood].
sym·bi·o·sis (sim·bi·ō'·sis) *n.* (*Biol.*) living together of different organisms for mutual benefit, as in the lichens. **symbiotic** *a.* **symbiont** *n.* organism living in symbiosis [Gk. *sun*, together; *bios*, life].
sym·bol (sim'.bal) *n.* something that represents something else, esp. concrete representation of moral or intellectual quality; emblem; type character or sign used to indicate relation or operation in mathematics; in chemistry, letter or letters standing for atom of element. **-ic, -ical** *a.* **-ically** *adv.* **-ize** *v.t.* to stand for, or represent; to represent by a symbol or symbols. **-ism** *n.* representation by symbols; system of symbols; in art and literature, tendency to represent emotions by means of symbols, and to invest ordinary objects with imaginative meanings. **-ist** *n.* one who uses symbols; adherent of symbolism in art and literature [Gk. *sumbolon*, a token].
sym·me·try (sim'.a.tri·) *n.* due proportion between several parts of object; exact correspondence of opposite sides of an object to each other. **symmetric, symmetrical** *a.* **symmetricalness** *n.* **symmetrize** *v.t.* [Gk. *sun*, together; *metron*, measure].
sym·pa·thy (sim'.pa.thi·) *n.* fellow feeling, esp. feeling for another person in pain or grief; sharing of emotion, interest, desire, etc.; compassion or pity. **sympathetic(al)** *a.* exhibiting or expressing sympathy; compassionate; congenial; (*Med.*) denoting a portion of the nerve system in body. **sympathetically** *adv.* **sympathize** *v.i.* **sympathizer** *n.* [Gk. *sun*, together; *pathos*, feeling].
sym·pho·ny (sim'.fa.ni·) *n.* (*Mus.*) composition for full orchestra, consisting of four contrasted sections or movements. **symphonic** *a.* **symphonist** *n.* composer of symphonies.

[Gk. *sun*, together; *phŏnē*, sound].

sym·po·si·um (sim·pŏ'·zi·am) *n.* gathering, esp. one at which interchange or discussion of ideas takes place; series of short articles by several writers dealing with common topic. *pl.* **symposia** [Gk. *sun*, together; *posis*, a drinking].

symp·tom (simp'·tam) *n.* (*Med.*) perceptible change in body or its functions, which indicates disease; sign of the existence of something. **-atic**, **-atical** *a.* [Gk. *sun*, together; *ptŏma*, a fall].

syn- (sin) *prefix* from Gk. *sun*, meaning with, together, at the same time; becomes *sym-*, before *p*, *b*, and *m*, and *syl-* before *l*.

syn·a·gogue (sin'·a·gŏg) *n.* congregation of Jews met for worship; Jewish place of worship. **synagogical** (sin·a·gǒj'·a·kal) *a.* [Gk. *sun*, together; *agein*, to lead].

syn·chro·nize (sing'·kra·nīz) *v.i.* to agree in time; to be simultaneous; *v.t.* to cause to occur at the same time; to run machines at exactly the same speed. **synchronization** *n.* **synchronism** *n.* concurrence of events in time; simultaneousness. **synchronal** *a.* **synchronous** *a.* [Gk. *sun*, together; *chronos*, time].

syn·chro·tron (sing'·kra·trän) *n.* scientific machine, used in atom research, for accelerating electrons to very high speeds [Gk. *sun*, together; *chronos*, time].

syn·co·pate (sing'·ka·pāt) *v.t.* (*Gram.*) to contract, as a word, by taking one or more sounds or syllables from middle; in music, to alter rhythm by accenting a usually unaccented note, or causing the accent to fall on a rest, or silent beat. **syncopation** *n.* [Gk. *sun*, together; *kopē*, a cutting].

syn·cope (sing'·ka·pē) *n.* the omission of one or more letters from the middle of a word:

(*Med.*) a fainting or swooning. **syncopal**, **syncopic** *a.* [see **syncopate**].

syn·dic (sin'·dik) *n.* magistrate or government official having different duties in different countries; legal representative chosen to act as agent for corporation or company. **-ate** *n.* council of syndics; body of persons associated to carry out enterprise; association of industrialists or financiers formed to carry out industrial project; *v.t.* to acquire monopoly in certain goods; *v.t.* to control by a syndicate; to publish news, etc. simultaneously in several periodicals owned by one syndicate [Gk. *sundikos*, an advocate].

syn·ec·do·che (si·nek'·da·kē) *n.* (*Rhet.*) figure of speech by which the whole is put for the part, or a part for the whole. **synecdochic, synecdochical** *a.* [Gk.].

syn·od (sin'·ad) *n.* an assembly of ecclesiatus; convention or council. **-al**, **-ic**, **-ical**, **-ically** *adv.* [Gk. *sunodos*, assembly].

syn·o·nym (sin'·a·nim) *n.* word which has same meaning as another. **-ous** *a.* **-ously** *adv.* [Gk. *sun*, together; *onoma*, name].

syn·op·sis (si·náp'·sis) *n.* general outlook, view; summary. *pl.* **synopses** (sēz). **synoptic, synoptical** *a.* **synoptically** *adv.* [Gk. *sun*, together; *opsis*, view].

syn·tax (sin'·taks) *n.* rules governing sentence construction. **syntactic, syntactical** *a.* **syntactically** *adv.* [Gk. *sun*, together; *tassein*, to put in order].

syn·the·sis (sin'·tha·sis) *n.* combination or putting together; combining of parts into whole (opp. to *analysis*); (*Chem.*) uniting of elements to form compound; (*Gram.*) building up of words into sentences, and of sentences into one of a more complex nature. *pl.* **syntheses** (·sēz). **synthetic, synthetical** *a.*

pert. to, consisting in synthesis; not derived from nature; artificial; spurious. **synthetically** *adv.* **synthesize, synthetize** *v.t.* **synthesist, synthetist** *n.* [Gk. *sun*, together; *thesis*, a placing].

syph·i·lis (sif'·a·lis) *n.* contagious venereal disease. **syphilitic** *a.* [fr. *Syphilus*, shepherd in Latin poem (1530)].

sy·phon. See **siphon.**

Syr·i·a (sir'·i·a) *n.* country in W. Asia. **-c** *n.* language of Syria. **-n** *n.* native of Syria; *a.* pert. to Syria.

syr·inge (sa·rinj' sir'·inj) *n.* tube and piston serving to draw in and then expel fluid; *v.t.* to inject by means of syringe [Gk. *surinx*, a pipe or reed].

syr·inx (sir'·ingks) *n.* (*Mus.*) Pan-pipe; (*Anat.*) the Eustachian tube; vocal organ of birds. *pl.* **-es**, **syringes** (gēz). **syringeal** (si·rin'·je·al) *a.* [Gk.*surinx*, a reed or pipe].

syr·up, sirup (sir'·ap) *n.* fluid separated from sugar in process of refining. **-y** *a.* [O.Fr. *syrop*, fr. Ar. *sharab*, a beverage].

sys·tem (sis'·tam) *n.* assemblage of objects arranged after some distinct method, usually logical or scientific; whole scheme of created things regarded as forming one complete whole; universe; organization; classification; set of doctrines or principles; the body as functional unity. **-atic**, **-atical** *a.* **-atically** *adv.* **-atize, -ize** *v.t.* to reduce to system; to arrange methodically. **-atization, -ization** *n.* [L.L. *systema*, organized whole].

sys·to·le (sis'·ta·lē) *n.* contraction of heart and arteries for expelling blood and carrying on circulation. opp. to *diastole*; (*Gram.*) shortening of long syllable. **systolic** *a.* contracting [Gk. fr. *sun*, together, *stellein*, to place].

T

tab (tab) *n.* small tag or flap; a label [fr. *tape*].

tab·ard (tab'·erd) *n.* sleeveless tunic worn over armor by knights; tunic emblazoned with royal arms, worn by heralds. Also **taberd.**

tab·by (tab'·i·) *n.* stout kind of watered silk; striped cat, esp. female; old maid; a malicious gossip; *a.* striped; *v.t.* to give watered finish to, as silk [Ar. *attabi*, a watered silk].

tab·er·nac·le (tab'·er·nak.l) *n.* movable shelter esp. for religious worship by Israelites; place for worship; human body [L. *tabernaculum*, a small tent].

tab·la·ture (tab'·la·cher) *n.* painting on ceiling or wall; mental picture [fr. *table*].

ta·ble (tā'·bl) *n.* smooth flat surface of wood, etc. supported by legs, as article of furniture for working at, or serving meals; any flat surface, esp. slab bearing inscription; food served on table; systematic arrangement of figures, facts, etc. as *multiplication table*; index, scheme, or schedule; synopsis; one of the divisions of decalogue; upper, flat surface of gemstone; *a.* pert. to or shaped like a table; *v.t.* to form into a table or catalogue; to lay down, as money in payment of a bill; to postpone for subsequent consideratioon. **-spoon** *n.* a large spoon for serving, measuring, etc., holding ½ fluid ounce. **-tennis** *n.* game of indoor tennis played on a table; ping-pong; **-ware** *n.* utensils (incl. china, glass and silver) for table use [L. *tabula*, a board].

tab·leau (tab'·lō) *n.* vivid representation of scene in history, literature, art, etc. by group of persons appropriately dressed and posed. *pl.* **tableaux** (tab'·lōz). — **vivant** (tab'·lō·vě'·vánt) *n.* living picture; tableau [Fr. *tableau*, a picture].

tab·let (tab'·lit) *n.* anything flat on which to write; pad; slab of stone with inscription; small, compressed solid piece of medication, detergent, etc. [dim. of *table*].

tab·loid (tab'·loid) *n.* illustrated newspaper, giving topical and usually sensational events in compressed form; compressed lozenge.

ta·boo (ta·bóó) *n.* system among natives of the Pacific islands by which certain objects and persons are set aside as sacred or accursed; political, social, or religious prohibition; *a.* prohibited; proscribed; *v.t.* to forbid the use of; to ostracize [Polynesian *tapu*, consecrated].

ta·bor (tā'·ber) *n.* small drum like a tambourine. **-et** *n.* small tabor; embroidery frame; low cushioned stool [O.Fr. *tabour*, a drum].

tab·u·lar (tab'·ya·ler) *a.* pert. to, or resembling, a table in shape; having a broad, flat top; arranged systematically in rows or columns. **-ize** *v.t.* to tabulate. **-ly** *adv.* **tabulate** *v.t.* to put or form into a table, scheme or synopsis [L. *tabula*, a table].

ta·chom·e·ter (ta·kám'·a·ter) *n.* instrument for measurement of speed [Gk. *tachus*, swift; *metron*, a measure].

tac·it (tas'·it) *a.* implied, but not expressed; silent; **-ly** *adv.* **-urn** *a.* silent; reserved of speech. **-urnity** *n.* **-urnly** *adv.* [L. *tacitus*].

tack (tak) *n.* small sharp-pointed nail; long stitch; ship's course in relation to position of her sails; course of action; *v.t.* to fasten with long, loose stitches; to append; to nail with; *v.t.* to change ship's course by moving position of sails; to change policy. **-er** *n.* **-iness** *n.* stickiness. **-y** *a.* sticky; viscous [O.Fr. *tache*, nail].

tack (tak) *n.* food; fore.

tack·le (tak'·l) *n.* mechanism of ropes and pulleys for raising heavy weights; rigging, etc. of ship; equipment or gear; (*Football*) move by player to grasp and stop opponent; *v.t.* to harness; to lay hold of; to undertake; (*Football*) to seize and stop. **tackling** *n.* gear; rigging of a ship. — **block** *n.* pulley [Scand. *taka*, to grasp].

tact (takt) *n.* intuitive understanding of people; awareness of right thing to do or say to avoid giving offense. **-ful** *a.* **-fully** *adv.* **-ile** *a.* pert. to sense of touch; capable of being

touched or felt; tangible. **-less** *a.* wanting in tact. **-ual** *a.* pert. to sense of touch [L. *tangere, tactum*, to touch].

tac·tics (tak'·tiks) *n. sing.* science of disposing of military, naval, and air units to the best advantage; adroit management of situation. **tactic, -al** *a.* **tactically** *adv.* **tactician** *n.* [Gk. *taktika*, tactics].

tad·pole (tad'·pōl) *n.* young of frog in its first state before gills and tail are absorbed [O.E. *tad*, a toad; and *poll*].

taf·fe·ta (taf'·a·ta) *n.* light-weight glossy silk of plain weave. Also **taffety** [Pers. *taftah*, woven].

tag (tag) *n.* metal point at end of a shoelace, etc.; tab on back of boot; tie-on label; appendage; catchword; hackneyed phrase; ragged end; refrain; game in which one player chases and tries to touch another; *v.t.* to fit with tags; to add on; (*Colloq.*) to follow behind. *pr.p.* **-ging.** *pa.t.* and *pa.p.* **ged.** [Scand. *tagg*, a spike].

Ta·hi·tian (ta·hē'·ti·an, tä·hē') *a.* pert. to island of Tahiti or its inhabitants.

Ta·ic (tä'·ik) *a.* pert. to inhabitants of Indo-China or their language; *n.* [Chin.].

tail (tāl) *n.* (*Law*) a limitation of ownership; entail; *a.* being entailed. **-age** *n.* [Fr. *taille*, cutting].

tail (tāl) *n.* flexible prolongation of animal's spine; back, lower, or inferior part of anything; (*Colloq.*) *pl.* reverse side of coin; queue; train of attendants; (*Aero.*) group of stabilizing planes or fins at rear of airplane; *pl.* tail-coat; *v.t.* to furnish with tail; to extend in line; to trail. **-board** *n.* movable board at back of cart. **-coat** *n.* man's evening dress coat with tails. **-ed** *a.* **-less** *a.* **-light** *n.* usu. red rear light of vehicle. **-piece** *n.* ebony strip below bridge of violin to which strings are attached; ornamental design marking close of chapter in book. **-plane** n. (Aero.) stabilizing surface at rear of aircraft [O.E. taegl, a tail].

tailplane

tai·lor (tāl′·er) n. one who makes clothes; v.t. and v.i. to make men's suits, women's costumes, etc. **-ing** n. work of a tailor. **-less** a. **-made** a. made by tailor; plain in style and fitting perfectly [O.Fr. taillier, to cut].

taint (tānt) v.t. to impregnate with something poisonous; to contaminate; v.i. to be infected with incipient putrefaction; n. touch of corruption; (Fig.) moral blemish [L. tingere, tinctum, to dye].

take (tāk) v.t. to grasp; to capture; to receive; to remove; to win; to inhale; to choose; to assume; to suppose; to photograph; v.i. to be effective; to catch; to please; to go; to direct course of; to resort to; pr.p. **taking.** pa.t. **took.** pa.p. **-n.** n. quantity of fish caught at one time; one of several movie shots of same scene; act of taking; receipts n. (Slang) fraud; hoax. **-off** n. (Colloq.) mimicry; caricature; (Aero.) moment when aircraft leaves ground. n. **taking** n. act of taking or gaining possession; agitation; pl. cash receipts of shop, theater, etc.; a. attractive; infectious. **takingly** adv. **takingness** n. quality of being attractive [Scand. taka, to seize].

talc (talk) n. hydrated silica of magnesia; fine, slightly perfumed powder; mineral with soapy feel. **-ose** a. pert. to or composed of talc. **-um** n. powdered talc, as toilet powder [Ar. talq.].

tale (tāl) n. narrative; story; what is told; false report; gossip. **-bearer** n. one who spitefully informs against another [O.E. talu, a reckoning].

tal·ent (tal′·ant) n. ancient weight and denomination of money; faculty; special or outstanding ability. **-ed** a. gifted [Gk. talanton].

tal·is·man (tal′·is·man) n. object endowed with magical power of protecting the wearer from harm; lucky charm. **-ic, -al** a. [Gk. telesma, payment].

talk (tawk) v.t. and v.i. to converse; to speak; to discuss; to persuade; n. conversation; short dissertation; rumor; gossip. **-ative** a. loquacious; chatty. **-atively** adv. **-ativeness** n. **-er** n. **-ie** n. (Colloq.) a sound film. **-ing** a. capable of speaking [M.E. talken, to speak].

tall (tawl) a. high in stature; lofty; (Slang) excessive; exaggerated. **-ness** n.

tal·low (tal′·ō) n. animal fat melted down and used in manufacture of candles, etc.; v.t. to smear with tallow. **-ish** a. pasty; greasy. **-like, -y,** a. [M.E. talgh, tallow].

tal·ly (tal′·i·) n. something on which a score is kept; the score; business account; match; identity label; v.t. to score; to furnish with a label; v.i. to correspond; to agree. pa.t. and pa.p. **tallied. tallier** [L. talea, a slip of wood].

Tal·mud (tal′·mud) n. standard collection of texts and commentaries on Jewish religious law. **-ic(al)** a. **-ist** n. student of the Talmud. **-istic** a. [Aramaic talmud, instruction].

tal·on (tal′·an) n. hooked claw of bird of prey. **-ed** a. having talons [L. talus, the heel].

tam·a·risk (tam′·a·risk) n. evergreen shrub with pink and white flowers [L. tamarix].

tam·bour (tam′·boor) n. small flat drum; circular embroidery-frame; piece of embroidery worked in metal threads on tambour [Fr. = a drum].

tam·bour·ine (tam·ba·rēn′) n. round, shallow, single-sided drum with jingling metal disks, used to accompany Spanish dances [Fr.].

tame (tām) a. domesticated; subdued; insipid; dull; cultivated; v.t. to domesticate; to discipline; to curb; to reclaim. **-ability, tamability, -ableness** n. **-able** a. **-ly** adv. **-ness** n. **-r** n. [O.E. tam, tame].

tam o' shan·ter (tam′·a·shan′·ter) n. round flat cap, abbrev. **tam** [fr. Burns's poem].

tamp (tamp) v.t. to ram down; to plug a shot-hole with clay during blasting operations.

tam·per (tam′·per) v.i. to meddle; to interfere with; to alter or influence with malicious intent. **-er** n. [var. of temper].

tam·pon (tam′·pan) n. (surg.) a plug of cotton, etc. to close a wound, retard bleeding [Fr.].

tan (tan) n. bark of oak, etc. bruised to extract

tannic acid for tanning leather; yellowish brown color; sunburn; v.t. to convert skins into leather by soaking in tannic acid; to make bronze-colored; (Colloq.) to thrash; v.i. to become sunburned. pr.p. **-ning.** pa.t. and pa.p. **-ned. -nate** n. (Chem.) salt of tannic acid. **-ner** n. one who works in tannery. **-nery** n. place where leather is made. **-nic** a. pert. to tannin. **-nin** n. now called **tannic acid. -ning** n. [Fr. tannique fr. tannin, tan].

tan·dem (tan′·dam) adv. one behind the other; n. pair of horses so harnessed; a bicycle for two people [L. tandem, at length].

tang (tang) n. a projection or prong (of a tool) which connects with the handle; a pungent smell or taste; a distinctive flavor; v.t. to furnish (a tool) with a tang. **-ed, -y** a. [Scand. tange, a point].

tan·gent (tan′·jant) n. (Geom.) line which touches curve but, when produced, does not cut it; a. touching but not intersecting. **tangency, tangence** n. state of touching. **tangential** a. pert. to, or in direction of, a tangent; digressing. **tangentially** adv. [L. tangere, to touch].

tan·ge·rine (tan·ja·rēn′) n. small sweet orange originally grown near Tangiers.

tan·gi·ble (tan′·ji·bl) a. perceptible by the touch; palpable; concrete. **tangibility** n. **tangibility** adv. [L. tangere, to touch].

tan·gle (tang′·gl) n. knot of raveled threads, hair, etc.; confusion; v.t. to form into a confused mass; to muddle.

tan·go (tang′·gō) n. S. American dance of Spanish origin in two-four time [Sp.].

tank (tangk) n. large basin, cistern, or reservoir for storing liquids or gas; part of a railway engine, car, etc. where water, gas, etc. is stored; a mechanically propelled bullet-proof heavily armored vehicle with caterpillar treads; v.t. to store or immerse in a tank. **-age** n. storage of water, oil, gas, etc. in a tank; cost of this; liquid capacity of tank; fertilizing agent from refuse. **-er** n. vessel designed to carry liquid cargo [L. stagnum, a pool].

tank·ard (tang′·kerd) n. large drinking vessel, with lid and handle [O.Fr. tancquard, drinking-vessel].

tan·nin See tan.

tan·sy (tan′·si·) n. common perennial plant used in medicine [ML. athanasia, immortality].

tan·ta·lize (tan′·ta·līz) v.t. to torment by keeping just out of reach something ardently desired; to tease. **tantalizing** a. provocative; teasing [fr. Tantalus, Gr. Myth.].

tan·ta·lum (tan′·ta·lam) n. (Chem.) rare metallic element, symbol **Ta,** used for filaments of electric lamps, chemical apparatus, and surgical instruments [fr. Tantalus].

tan·ta·mount (tan′·ta·mount) a. equivalent in value or significance [L. tantus, so much].

tan·trum (tan′·tram) n. fit of bad temper.

Tao·ism (tou′·izm) n. a Chinese philosophical and religious system founded on the doctrines of Lao-tsze. **Taoist** n. **Taoistic** a. [Chin. tao, a way].

tap (tap) v.t. to strike lightly; to fix patch of leather or metal on shoe; v.i to strike gentle blow. pr.p. **-ping.** pa.p. **-ped.** n. a rap; pl. military signal for lights out; leather patch or piece of metal on shoe sole. — **dance** n. a dance step audibly tapped out with the feet. **-dance** v.i. [imit].

tap (tap) n. hole, pipe, or screw device with valve, through which liquid is drawn; liquor of particular brewing in a cask; instrument of hardened steel for cutting internal screwheads; (Elect.) connection made at intermediate point on circuit; v.t. to pierce to let fluid flow out, as from a cask, tree, etc.; to furnish (cask) with tap; (Surg.) to draw off fluid from body, as from lung, abdomen, etc.; to listen in deliberately on telephone conversation; pr.p. **-ping.** pa.p. **-ped. -per** n. one who taps. **-room** n. bar, of inn or hotel, for sale of liquor. **-root** n. the root of a plant which goes straight down into earth without dividing. **on tap,** of liquor, drawn from cask, not bottled; (Fig.) at hand [O.E. taeppa].

tape (tāp) n. narrow piece of woven material used for tying, fastening clothes, etc.; strip of this marking finish line on racetrack; strip of paper used in a printing telegraph instrument, etc., strip of paper or linen marked off in inches used for measuring; v.t. to tie or fasten with tape; to measure. — **measure** n. strip marked in inches. **-worm** n. parasite found in alimentary canal of vertebrates [O.E. taeppe, a band].

ta·per (tā′·per) n. long wick for lighting

candles; a slender candle; v.i. to narrow gradually toward one end; v.t. to cause to narrow. **-ing** a. narrowing gradually [O.E. tapor].

tape measure

tap·es·try (tap′·as·tri·) n. fabric covering for furniture, walls, etc. woven by needles, not in shuttles [Fr. tapis, carpet].

tap·i·o·ca (tap·i·ō·ka) n. starchy granular substance used for desserts, thickening, etc. [Braz. tipi, residue; ok, to press out].

ta·pir (tā′·per) n. ungulate mammal with piglike body and flexible proboscis [Braz.].

tap·is (tap′·ē, tap′·is) n. carpeting; tapestry [Fr. tapis, carpet].

tap·pet (tap′·it) n. small lever [O.Fr. tapper, to rap].

tar (tar) n. (Colloq.) sailor [fr. tarpaulin].

tar (tár) n. dark-brown or black viscid liquid, a by-product in destructive distillation of wood (esp. pine), coal, etc., used for waterproofing, road-laying, and as antiseptic and preservative; v.t. to smear, cover, or treat with tar. pr.p. **-ring.** pa.t. and pa.p. **-red. -ry** a. pert. to, smeared with, or smelling of, tar [O.E. teru, pitch].

tar·an·tel·la (tar′·an·tel′·a) n. Italian dance with rapid, whirling movements; music for it [fr. Taranto, in S. Italy].

ta·ran·tu·la (ta·ranch′·a·la) n. large, hairy, venomous spider [fr. Taranto].

tar·boosh (tár′·bŏŏsh) n. cap resembling a fez, usually red with dark blue tassel [Ar.].

tar·dy (tár′·di·) a. slow; dilatory; late. **tardily** adv. **tardiness** n. [L. tardus].

tare (ter) n. plant grown for fodder; a weed.

tare (ter) n. allowance made for weight of container, such as cask, crate, etc. in reckoning price of goods [Ar. tarhah, to reject].

tar·get (tár′·git) n. mark to aim at in shooting, esp. flat circular board with series of concentric circles; circular railway signal near switches; butt; object of attack [fr. targe].

tar·iff (ta′·rif) n. list of goods (imports and exports) on which duty is payable; the duty imposed. [Ar. ta′rif, giving information].

tarn (tárn) n. (Literary) small lake among mountains [Scand.].

tar·nish (tárnish) v.t. to lessen luster of; to sully, as one's reputation; v.i. to become dull, dim, or sullied [Fr. ternir, to tarnish].

ta·ro (tá′·rō) n. plant of Pacific islands, cultivated for edible leaves and root [Native].

tar·pau·lin (tár·paw′·lin) n. canvas sheet treated with tar to make it waterproof; oilskin coat, hat, etc. [fr. tar and pauling, a covering].

tar·pon (tár′·pan) n. large edible fish of herring family.

tar·ra·gon (tar′·a·gan) n. perennial herb cultivated for its aromatic leaves [Gk. drakon, a dragon].

tar·ry (tar′·i·) v.i. to stay; to linger; to delay; to stay behind [L. tardus, slow].

tar·sus (tár′·sas) n. ankle. pl. **tarsi. tarsal** a. [Gk. tarsos, the sole of the foot].

tart (tárt) a. sour to taste; acid; (Fig.) caustic; severe. **-ish** a. rather sour. **-ly** adv. **-ness** n. [O.E. teart, acid].

tart (tárt) n. small pastry cup containing fruit

or jam; (*Slang*) girl; prostitute [O.Fr. *tarte*].

tar·tan (tár′·tạn) *n.* woolen cloth of colored plaids, each genuine Scottish clan possessing its own pattern; *a.* made of tartan.

Tar·tar (tár′·ter) *n.* native of Tartary. Also **Tatar. tartar** *n.* irritable, quick-tempered person [fr. *Tatar*, a Mongol tribe].

tar·tar (tár′·ter) *n.* crude potassium tartrate; crust deposited in wine cask during fermentation (purified, it is called **cream of tartar;** in crude form, **argol**); acid incrustation on teeth. **-ous** *a.* consisting of tartar; containing tartar. **-ic** *a.* pert. to, or obtained from, tartar. **tartrate** *n.* a salt of tartaric acid. **-ic acid,** organic hydroxy-acid found in many fruits; in powder form used in manufacture of cooling drinks. **cream of tartar,** purified form of tartar used medicinally and as raising agent in baking [Fr. *tartre*].

task (task) *n.* specific amount of work apportioned and imposed by another; set lesson; duty; *v.t.* to impose task on; to exact. **-er** *n.* — **force** *n.* body of soldiers sent to do specific operation. **-master** (*fem.* **-mistress**) *n.* overseer [L. *taxare*, to rate].

Tas·ma·ni·an (taz·mā′·ni·ạn) *a.* pert. to or belonging to Tasmania, island south of Australia; *n.* native of Tasmania. [fr. *Tasman*, discoverer].

Tass (tàs) *n.* official news agency of the U.S.S.R. [Russ. *Telegrafnoje Agentstvo Sovjetskovo Sojuza = Soviet Telegraphic Agency*].

tas·sel (tas′·l) *n.* ornamental fringed knot of silk, wool, etc.; pendent flower of some plants. **-ed** *a.* [L. *taxillus*, a small die].

taste (tāst) *v.t.* to perceive or test by tongue or palate; to appraise flavor of by sipping; to experience; *v.i.* to try food with mouth; to eat or drink very small quantity; to have specific flavor; *n.* act of tasting; one of five senses; flavor; predilection; aesthetic appreciation; judgment; small amount. **-ful** *a.* having or showing good taste. **-fully** *adv.* **-fulness** *n.* **-less** *a.* insipid. **-lessly** *adv.* **-lessness** *n.* **-r** *n.* one whose palate is trained to discern subtle differences in flavor, as *tea-taster.* **tastily** *adv.* with good taste. **tasty** *a.* savory [L. *taxare*, to rate].

tat (tat) *v.i.* to make tatting. *pr.p.* **-ting.** *pa.t.*, *pa.p.* **-ted.** **-ting** *n.* lace-like edging made from fine crochet or sewing thread [prob. Scand. *taeta*, shreds].

tat·ter (tat′·er) *n.* rag; shred of cloth or paper hanging loosely; *v.t.* and *v.i.* to tear or hang in tatters. **-demalion** *n.* ragged fellow. **-ed** *a.* **-y** *a.* [Scand. *toturr*, rag].

tat·tle (tat′·l) *v.i.* to prattle; to gossip; to tell a secret; *n.* chatter. **-r** *n.* [imit.].

tat·too (ta·tōō′) *n.* beat of drum or bugle as signal to return to quarters; a rapping sound; *v.i.* to beat tattoo [Dut. *taptoe*].

tat·too (ta·tōō′) *v.t.* to prick colored designs, initials, etc. into skin with indelible colored inks; *n.* such design.**-er** *n.* [Tahitian *tatau*].

tau (tou, taw) *n.* Greek letter T.

taught (tawt) *pa.t.* and *pa.p.* of verb teach.

taunt (tawnt) *v.t.* to reproach with insulting words; to gibe at; to sneer at; *n.* gibe; sarcastic remark. **-er** *n.* **-ing** *a.* [O.Fr. *tanter*, to provoke].

tau·rus (tawr′·ạs) *n.* Bull, 2nd sign of Zodiac, which sun enters about April 21st. **taurian** *a.* pert. to a bull. **taurine** *a.* bovine. [Gk.].

taut (tawt) *a.* tight; fully stretched; (of a ship) trim. **-en** *v.t.* to make tight or tense. **-ness** *n.* [a form of tight].

tau·tol·o·gy (taw·tál′·a·ji·) *n.* needless repetition of same idea in different words in same sentence. **tautologic, -al** *a.* **tautologically** *adv.* **tautologism** *n.* superfluous use of words [Gk. *tauto*, the same; *logos*, a word].

tav·ern (tav′·ern) *n.* licensed house for sale of liquor; inn [L. *taberna*, booth].

taw (taw) *n.* large marble for children's game; the line from which the marble is shot; a game of marbles [Gk. letter T.].

taw·dry (taw′·dri·) *a.* showy but cheap; gaudy. **tawdrily** *adv.* **tawdriness** *n.* [fr. St. *Audrey*, cheap laces sold at her fair].

taw·ny (taw′·ni·) *a.* of yellow-brown color. **tawniness** *n.* [O.Fr. *tanné*, tanned].

tax (taks) *n.* levy imposed by state on income, property, etc.; burden; severe test; *v.t.* to impose tax on; to subject to severe strain; to challenge or accuse; (*Law*) to assess cost of actions in court. **-able** *a.* **-ness, -ability** *n.* **-ably** *adv.* **-ation** *n.* act of levying taxes; assessing of bill of costs; aggregate of particular taxes. [L. *taxure*, to rate].

tax·i (tak′·si·) *n.* (abbrev. of **taximeter cab**) an automobile for hire, fitted with a taximeter; any car plying for hire; *v.i.* to travel by taxi; of aircraft, to travel on ground (or surface of water) under its own power. *pr.p.* **-ing.** *pa.p.* **-ed, -cab** *n.* automobile for public hire. — **driver,** — **man** *n.* **-meter** *n.* instrument which automatically registers mileage and corresponding fare of journey by taxi.

tax·i·der·my (tak′·sa·dur·mi·) *n.* art of preparing and preserving pelts of animals and stuffing them for exhibition. **taxidermist** *n.* **taxidermal, taxidermic** *a.* [Gk. *taxis*, an arrangement].

tea (tē) *n.* dried and prepared leaf of tea plant, native to China and Japan, and grown in India, Ceylon, etc.; infusion of dry tea in boiling water; any infusion of tea plant leaves,

etc. or of chopped meat; reception at which tea is drunk. — **service** *n.* — **set** *n.* cups, saucers, plates, etc. for use at tea. **-spoon** *n.* small-sized spoon used with the teacup. **-spoonful** *n.* ½ tablespoon. **black tea,** tea allowed to ferment between two processes of rolling and firing. **green tea,** tea left exposed to air for only short time before firing. **Russian tea,** tea served in glasses with slice of lemon and sugar [Chin.].

teach (tēch) *v.t.* to instruct; to educate; to discipline; to impart knowledge of; *v.i.* to follow profession of a teacher. *pa.t.* and *pa.p.* **taught** (tawt). **-ability** *n.* **-able** *a.* capable of being taught; willing to learn. **-ableness** *n.* **-er** *n.* one who instructs [O.E. *taecan*].

teak (tēk) *n.* tree of E. Indies yielding very hard, durable timber [Malay].

team (tēm) *n.* two or more oxen, horses, or other beasts of burden harnessed together; group of people working together for common purpose; side of players in game, as *football team.* **-ster** *n.* one who drives team or a truck, as an occupation. **-work** *n.* co-operation among members of a group [O.E. *team*, offspring].

tear (tir) *n.* small drop of fluid secreted by lachrymal gland, appearing in and flowing from eyes, chiefly due to emotion; any transparent drop; *pl.* grief; sorrow. **drop** *n.* tear. **-ful** *a.* weeping. **-fully** *adv.* **-fulness** *n.* — **gas** *n.* irritant gas causing abnormal watering of eyes and temporary blindness. **-less** *a.* dry-eyed [O.E. *tear*, a tear]

tear (ter) *v.t.* to pull apart forcibly; to rend; *v.i.* to become ripped or ragged; (*Colloq.*) to move violently; to rush; to rage. *pr.p.* **-ing.** *pa.t.* **tore.** *pa.p.* **torn.** *n.* rent; fissure. **-er** *n.* [O.E. *teran*, to tear].

tease (tēz) *v.t.* to comb or card wool, hair, etc.; to raise pile of cloth; to harass; to annoy in fun; to chaff. **-r** *n.* **-teasing** *a.* [O.E. *taesan*, to pluck].

teat (tit) *n.* nipple of female breast; dug of animal; rubber nipple of baby's feeding bottle [O.E. *tit*].

tech·nic·al (tek′·ni·kal) *a.* pert. to any of the arts, esp. to useful or mechanical arts; connected with particular art or science; accurately defined; involving legal point. **-ity** *n.* state of being technical; term peculiar to specific art; point of procedure. **-ly** *adv.* **-ness** *n.* **technician** *n.* expert in particular art or branch of knowledge. **technics** *n.pl.* arts in general; industrial arts. **technique** (tek·nēk′) *n.* skill acquired by thorough mastery of subject; method of handling materials of an art. **technologic, -al** *a.* pert. to technology. **technologically** *adv.* **technologist** *n.* **technology** *n.* science of mechanical and industrial arts, as contrasted with fine arts; technical terminology [Gk. *technē*, art].

Tech·ni·col·or (tek′·ni·kul·er) *n.* trade name for color movie photography.

tec·ton·ic (tek·tán′·ik) *a.* pert. to building; (*Geol.*) pert. to earth's crust [Gk. *tekton*, builder].

te·di·ous (tē′·di·ạs) *a.* wearisome; protracted; irksome. **-ness** *n.* **-ly** *adv.* **tedium** *n.* wearisomeness [L. *taedium*, weariness].

tee (tē) *n.* tiny cone of sand, wooden peg, etc. on which golf ball is placed for first drive of each hole; teeing ground which marks beginning of each hole on golf course. *v.t.* to place (ball) on tee [etym. uncertain].

tee (tē) *n.* the letter T; anything shaped like a T; *a.* having the form of a T.

teem (tēm) *v.i.* to bring forth, as animal; to be prolific; to be stocked to overflowing. **-ing** *a.* prolific [O.E. *team*, offspring].

teens (tēnz) *n.pl.* the years of one's age, thir*teen* through nine*teen.* **teen-ager** *n.* a young person of this age.

tee·ny (tēn′·i·) (*Colloq.*) very small [*tiny*].

tee·ter (tē′·ter) *v.i.* (*Colloq.*) to seesaw; vacillate; *n.* a seesaw or motion of seesaw [fr. *titter*].

teeth. See **tooth.**

teeth·ing (tēTH′·ing) *n.* the process, in babyhood, of cutting the first teeth. **teethe** *v.i.* to cut the first teeth [fr. tooth].

tee·to·tal (tē·tō′·tal) *a.* pert. to teetotalism; abstemious. **-er** *n.* one who abstains from intoxicating liquors. **-ism** *n.* [redupl. of initial letter of *total*].

teg·u·ment (teg′·ya·mạnt) *n.* covering, esp. of living body; skin; integument. **-al, -ary** *a.* [L. *tegere*, to cover].

tel·e·cast (tel′·a·kast) *v.i.* to transmit program by television [Gk. *tēle*, far; and *cast*].

tel·e·gram (tel′·a·gram) *n.* message sent by telegraph. **-mic** *a.*

tel·e·graph (tel′·a·graf) *n.* electrical apparatus for transmitting messages by code to a distance; a message so sent; *v.i.* to send a message by telegraph. **-er** (or ta·leg′·ra.fer) **-ist** (or ta·leg′·) *n.* one who operates telegraph, **-ic(al)** *a.* **-ically** *adv.* **telegraphy** *n.* electrical transmission of messages to a distance. [Gk. *tēle*, far; *graphein*, to write].

tel·e·ol·o·gy (tel·i·ál′·a·ji·) *n.* science or doctrine of final causes. **teleologic, -al** *a.* **teleologically** *adv.* **teleologist** *n.* [Gk. *telos*, end; *logos*, discourse].

te·lep·a·thy (ta·lep′·a·thi·) *n.* occult communication of facts, feelings, impressions

between mind and mind at a distance; thought-transference. **telepathic** *a.* [Gk. *tēle*, far; *pathos*, feeling].

tel·e·phone (tel′·a·fōn) *n.* electrical instrument by which sound is transmitted and reproduced at a distance; *v.t.* and *v.i.* to communicate by telephone. **telephonic** *a.* **telephonically** *adv.* **telephonist** *n.* telephone operator, esp. at switchboard of exchange. **telephony** *n.* art or process of operating telephone [Gk. *tēle*, far; *phonē*, a sound].

tel·e·pho·to (tel·a·fō′·tō) *a.* pert. to a camera lens which makes distant objects appear close.

Tel·e·promp·ter (tel′·a·prámp′·ter) *n.* in television, a device to enable the speaker to refer to his script out of sight of the cameras, thus giving viewers the impression of a talk without script [Trademark].

tel·e·scope (tel′·a·skōp) *n.* optical instrument for magnifying distant objects; *v.t.* to slide or drive together, as parts of telescope; *v.i.* to be impacted violently, as cars in railway collision. **telescopic, -al** *a.* pert. to or like a telescope. [Gk. *tēle*, afar; *skopein*, to see].

tel·e·type (tel′·a·tīp) *n.* automatically printed telegram; the apparatus by which this is done [Gk. *tēle*, far; and *type*; Trademark].

tel·e·vi·sion (tel′·a·vizh′·ạn) *n.* transmission of scenes, persons, etc. at a distance by means of electro-magnetic radio waves. **televise** *v.t.* [Gk. *tēle*, far; and *vision*].

tell (tel) *v.t.* to recount or narrate; to divulge; to inform; to count; *v.i.* to produce marked effect; to betray (as secret); to report. *pa.t.* and *pa.p.* **told. -er** *n.* narrator; bank clerk who pays out money; one who counts votes; enumerator. **-ing** *a.* effective; striking. **-ingly** *adv.* **-tale** *n.* one who betrays confidence; an informer; *a.* warning; tending to betray [O.E. *tellan*, to count].

te·mer·i·ty (ta·mer′·a·ti·) *n.* rashness; audacity [L. *temere*, rashly].

tem·per (tem′·per) *v.t.* to mingle in due proportion; to soften, as clay, by moistening; to bring (metal) to desired degree of hardness and elasticity by heating, cooling, and reheating; to regulate; to moderate; *n.* consistency required and achieved by tempering; attitude of mind; composure; anger; irritation. **-ed** *a.* having a certain consistency, as clay, or degree of toughness, as steel; having a certain disposition, as *good-tempered, bad-tempered.* **-edly** *adv.* **-ing** *n.* **-er** *n.* [L. *temperare*, to combine in due proportion].

tem·per·a (tem′·per·a) *n.* process of painting using pigments mixed with size, casein, or egg instead of oil. also **tempora** [It. = to temper].

tem·per·a·ment (tem′·per(a)mạnt) *n.* natural disposition; physical, moral and mental constitution peculiar to individuals; (*Mus.*) system of adjusting tones of keyboard instrument, such as a piano, so as to adapt the scale for all keys. **-al** *a.* liable to moods; passionate **-ally** *adv.* [L. *temperamentum*, disposition].

tem·per·ance (tem′·per·ạns) *n.* moderation; self-discipline, esp. of natural appetites; total abstinence from, or modification in, consumption of intoxicating liquors; sobriety [L. *temperantia*, moderation].

tem·per·ate (tem′·per·it) *a.* moderate; abstemious; (of climate) equable; not extreme. **-ly** *adv.* **-ness** *n.* **temperative** *a.* **temperature** *n.* degree of heat or cold of atmosphere or of a human or living body; fevered condition. — **zones,** areas of earth between polar circles and tropics. [L. *temperare*, to moderate].

tem·pest (tem′·pist) *n.* wind storm of great violence; any violent commotion. **-uous** *a.* pert. to tempest; violent. **-uously** *adv.* **-uousness** *n.* [L. *tempestas*, weather, storm].

tem·ple (tem′·pl) *n.* place of worship; place dedicated to pagan deity; a building devoted to some public use. [L. *templum*, a sacred place].

tem·ple (tem′·pl) *n.* part of forehead between outer end of eye and hair. **temporal** *a.* [L. *tempora*, the temples].

tem·plet, tem·plate (tem′·plit) *n.* pattern of wood or metal cut to shape required for finished flat object [prob. fr. L. *templum*, small rafter].

tem·po (tem′·po) *n.* (*Mus.*) time; degree of speed or slowness at which passage should be played or sung; the degree of movement, as in the plot of a drama [It.].

tem·po·ral (tem'·pạ·ral) a. pert. to time or to this life; transient; secular; **temporality** n. concept of time; state of being temporal or temporary; pl. material possessions, esp. ecclesiastical revenues. **-ly** adv. **temporariness** n. **temporarily** adv. only for a time. **temporariness** n. **temporary** a. lasting only for a time; fleeting. **temporization** n. **temporize** v.i. to act so as to gain time; to hedge; to compromise. **temporizer** n. **temporizing** n. [L. tempus, time].

tempt (tem(p)t) v.t. to induce to do something; to entice. **-ation** n. act of tempting; that which tempts; inducement to do evil; **-er** n. (fem. **-ress**) one who tempts, esp. Satan. **-ing** a. attractive; seductive. **-ingly** adv. **-ingness** n. [O.Fr. tempter, to entice].

ten (ten) a. twice five; one more than nine; n. the number nine and one; the figure or symbol representing this, as 10, X. **-fold** a. ten times repeated; adv. ten times as much. **-th** a. next after the ninth; being one of ten equal divisions of anything; n. one of ten equal parts; tenth part of anything; tithe. **-thly** adv. [O.E. ten, ten].

ten·a·ble (ten'·ạ·bl) a. capable of being held, defended, or logically maintained. **-ness, tenability** n. [L. tenere, to hold].

te·na·cious (tạ·nā'·shạs) a. holding fast; adhesive; retentive; pertinacious. **-ly** adv. **-ness, tenacity** n. [L. tenax, holding fast].

ten·ant (ten'·ạnt) n. (Law) one who has legal possession of real estate; one who occupies property for which he pays rent; v.i. to hold or occupy as tenant. **tenancy** n. act and period of holding land and property as tenant; property held by tenant. **-able** a. fit for occupation. **-ry** n. tenants or employees collectively on estate [L. tenere, to hold].

tend (tend) v.i. to hold a course; to have a bias or inclination. **-ency** n. inclination; bent. **-entious** a. (of writings) having a biased outlook [L. tendere, to stretch].

tend (tend) v.t. to look after; to minister to. **-er** n. one who tends; small vessel supplying larger one with stores, etc., or landing passengers; car attached to locomotive, carrying water and fuel [contr. of attend].

ten·der (ten'·der) v.t. to offer in payment or for acceptance; n. an offer, esp. contract to undertake specific work, or to supply goods at fixed rate. **legal tender**, currency recognized as legally acceptable in payment of a debt [L. tendere, to stretch out].

ten·der (ten'·der) a. soft; delicate; expressive of gentler passions; considerate; immature; sore; not tough (of meat). **-foot** n. one not yet hardened to ranching or mining life; novice. **-ly** adv. **-ness** n. [L. tener, delicate].

ten·der·loin (ten'·der·loin) choice cut of beef between loin and ribs; (Cap.) district in a city noted for vice and police corruption.

ten·don (ten'·dạn) n. a tough fibrous cord attaching muscle to bone. **tendinous** a. [L. tendere, to stretch].

ten·dril (ten'·dril) n. spiral shoot of climbing plant by which it clings to another body for support; curl, as of hair. **-lar, -ous** a. [Fr. tendrille].

ten·e·brous (ten'·ạ·brạs) a. dark; obscure; **tenebrosity** n. [L. tenebrae, darkness].

ten·e·ment (ten'·ạ·mạnt) n. building divided into separate apartments, usu. of very poor quality, and let to different tenants. **-al, tenementary** a. [L. tenere, to hold].

ten·et (ten'·it) n. any opinion, dogma, or principle which a person holds as true [L. tenere, to hold].

ten·nis (ten'·is) n. game for two or four players, played on a court by striking a ball with rackets, across a net; a version of this played on a grass called lawn tennis. — **court** n. specially marked enclosed court for tennis.

tennis court

ten·on (ten'·ạn) n. end of piece of wood shaped for insertion into cavity (mortise) in another piece to form a joint; v.t. to join with tenons. [L. tenere, to hold].

ten·or (ten'·er) n. general drift, course, or direction, of thought; purport; (Mus.) highest male adult voice; one who sings tenor; a. pert. to tenor voice [L. tenere, to hold].

tense (tens) n. (Gram.) form of verb which indicates time of action, as present, past or future tense [L. tempus, time].

tense (tens) a. stretched; strained almost to breaking point; unrelaxed; (of vowel) made by tongue tensed, as ē. **-ly** adv. **-ness** n. **tensibility, -ness** n. the quality of being **tensile. tensible, tensile** a. capable of being stretched or subjected to stress, as metals; capable of being made taut, as violin

strings. **tension** n. act of stretching; strain; a state of being nervously excited or overwrought; (of metals) pulling stress as opposed to compressive stress; (Elect.) potential. **tensor** n. body muscle which stretches [L. tendere, to stretch].

tent (tent) n. portable canvas shelter stretched and supported by poles and firmly pegged ropes; small plug of compressed absorbent gauze, or lint, which swells when moistened, used to keep open a wound, etc.; v.i. to live in tent; to pitch tent; v.t. to keep open, as wound, with tent. **-ed** a. covered with tents. [L. tendere, to stretch].

ten·ta·cle (ten'·tạ·kl) n. long flexible appendage of head or mouth in many lower animals for exploring, touching, grasping, and sometimes moving; feeler. **tentacular** a. **—like** a. [L. tentare, to feel].

ten·ta·tive (ten'·tạ·tiv) a. experimental; done or suggested as a feeler or trial. **-ly** adv. [L. tentare, to try].

ten·ter (ten'·ter) n. machine for stretching cloth by means of hooks; v.t. to stretch on hooks. **-hook** n. one of the sharp hooks by which cloth is stretched on a tenter. **on tenterhooks,** state of anxiety [L. tendere, to stretch].

ten·u·i·ty (ten·ū'·i·ti·) n. smallness of diameter; thinness. **tenuous** a. slender; gossamerlike; unsubstantial. **tenuously** adv. **tenuousness** n. [L. tenuis, thin].

ten·ure (ten'·yer) n. holding of office, property, etc.; condition of occupancy [L. tenere, to hold].

te·pee (tē'·pē) n. Indian wigwam or conical tent. Also **teepee.**

tep·e·fy (tep'·ạ·fi) v.t. to make moderately warm. **tepefaction** n. [L. tepere, to be warm; facere, to make].

tep·id (tep'·id) a. moderately warm; lukewarm. **-ity, -ness** n. [L. tepidus, warm].

ter·cel (tur'·sạl) n. a young male falcon [dim. of L. tertius, third].

ter·cen·te·nar·y (tur·sen'·tạ·ne·ri· or tur'·sen·ten·ạ·ri·) n. the 300th anniversary of an event; a. pert. to a period of 300 years [L. ter, thrice; centum, a hundred].

ter·cet (tur'·set) n. (Mus.) triplet; (Pros.) group of three lines or verses [L. ter, thrice].

ter·gi·ver·sate (tur'·ji·ver·sāt) v.i. to make use of subterfuges; to be shifty or vacillating; to apostatize. **tergiversation** n. **tergiversator** n. [L. tergum, the back; vertere, to turn].

term (turm) n. limit, esp. of time; period during which law courts are sitting, schools, universities, etc. are open; fixed day when rent is due; word or expression with specific meaning; (Math.) member of compound quantity; pl. stipulation; relationship, as on friendly terms; charge as for accommodation, etc. as hotel terms; v.t. to give name to; to call. **-inological** a. pert. to terminology. **-inologically** adv. **-inologist** n. **-inology** n. technical words; nomenclature [L. terminus, end].

ter·ma·gant (tur'·mạ·gant) n. quarrelsome, shrewish woman; a. scolding; quarrelsome. [Tervagan, Mohammedan diety].

ter·mi·nate (tur'·mạ·nāt) v.t. to set limit to; to end; to conclude; v.i. to come to an end; to finish. **terminable** a. capable of being terminated; liable to cease. **terminal** a. extremity; large railroad station with yards, shops, etc. (Elect.) metal attachment such as screw, block, clamp for connecting end of circuit; a. pert. to end; belonging to terminus or terminal; occurring in, or, at end of, a term; (Bot.) growing at tip. **terminally** adv. **termination** n. act of terminating; finish; conclusion; ending of word. **terminational** a. **terminative** a. **terminatively** adv. **terminus** n. end; farthest limit; railway station, airport, etc., at end of line; pl. **termini, terminuses** [L. terminus, the end].

ter·mite (tur'·mit) n. insect, very destructive to wood [L. termes, a wood worm].

tern (turn) n. sea bird allied to gull [Scand.].

tern (turn) n. that which consists of three; a. threefold. **-al, -ary** a. consisting of three; proceeding by threes; (Chem.) comprising three elements, etc. **-ate** a. arranged in threes; (Bot.)having three leaflets. **-ion** n. group of three [L. terni, three each].

Terp·sich·o·re (turp·sik'·ạ·rē) n. (Myth.) Muse of choral song and dancing. **-an** a. pert. to Terpsichore or to dancing [Gk. Terpsichorē, fond of dancing].

termite

ter·ra (ter'·ạ) n. earth as in various Latin phrases. — **cotta** n. reddish, brick-like earthenware, porous and unglazed. — **firma** n. dry land. — **incognita** n. unexplored territory, **terranean** a. belonging to surface of earth. **-neous** a. growing on land. **terraqueous** (ter·ā'·kwe·ạs) a. comprising both land and water, as the globe [L. terra, the earth].

ter·race (ter'·ạs) n. level shelf of earth, natural or artificial; flat roof used for open-air activities; v.t. to form into terraces [L. terra, the earth].

ter·rain (ter'·ān, tạ·rān') n. tract of land, esp. as considered for suitability for various purposes [L. terra, the earth].

ter·ra·pin (ter'·ạ·pin) n. edible tortoise found in eastern U.S. [Amer.-Ind.].

ter·raz·zo·pav·ing (tạ·rat'·tsō·pāv'·ing) n. kind of mosaic paving in concrete chips [It.].

ter·rene (te·rēn') a. pert. to earth; earthy; terrestrial [L. terra, the earth].

ter·res·tri·al (tạ·res'·tri·al) a. pert. to earth; existing on earth; earthly, as opp. to celestial; n. inhabitant of earth [L. terra, the earth].

ter·ri·ble (ter'·ạ·bl) a. calculated to inspire fear or awe; frightful; dreadful; formidable; (Colloq.) very bad. **-ness** n. **terribly** adv. [L. terrere, to frighten].

ter·ri·er (ter'·i·er) n. breed of small or medium-sized dog, originally trained for hunting foxes, badgers, etc. [M.E. terrere, a burrowing dog].

ter·ri·fy (ter'·ạ·fi) v.t. to frighten greatly; to inspire with terror. p.a.t. **terrific** a. causing terror or alarm; (Colloq.) tremendous. **terrifically** adv. [L. terrere, to terrify; facere, to make].

ter·ri·to·ry (ter'·ạ·tōr·i·) n. large tract of land, esp. under one governmental administration; part of country which has not yet attained political independence. **territorial** a. pert. to territory; limited to certain district. **territoriality** n. [L. terra, the earth].

ter·ror (ter'·er) n. extreme fear; violent dread; one who or that which causes terror. **-ization** n. **-ize** v.t. to fill with terror; to rule by intimidation. **-izer** n. **-ism** n. massorganized ruthlessness. **-ist** n. one who rules by terror [L. terrere, to frighten].

ter·ry cloth (ter'·i·klȯth) n. cotton fabric with pile of uncut loops on both sides.

terse (turs) a. (of speech, writing, etc.) concise; succinct; brief. **-ly** adv. **-ness** n. [L. terpere, tersum, to smooth].

ter·tian (tur'·shạn) a. (Med.) occurring every other day; n. fever, such as malaria, with paroxysms occurring at intervals of forty-eight hours [L. textius, third].

ter·ti·ar·y (tur'·she·ri·) a. of third formation or rank; (Geol.) (Cap.) pert. to era of rock formation following Mezozoic; n. (Geol.) (Cap.) the tertiary era [L. tertius, third].

ter·za·ri·ma (ter'·tsarē'·ma) n. form of stanza arrangement of iambic pentameter lines in groups of three, rhyming aba, bcb, cdc [It. terza, third; rima, rhyme].

tes·sel·late (tes'·ạ·lāt) v.t. to pave with tesserae; to make mosaic paving with square-cut stones. **tessella, tessera** n. (pl. **tessellae, tesserae**) one of the square stones etc. used in tessellated paving. **tessellation** n. [L. tessera, a square block].

test (test) n. critical examination; grounds for admission or exclusion; (Chem.) reagent; substance used to analyze compound into its several constituents; a touchstone; vessel in which metals are refined; v.i. to make critical examination of; to put to proof; (Chem.) to analyze nature and properties of a compound. — **case** n. (Law) case tried for purpose of establishing a precedent. **-er** n. **-ing** n. a. demanding endurance. — **paper** n. examination paper; litmus or other impregnated paper used to test acid or alkaline content of chemical solution. — **pilot** n. experienced pilot engaged in testing flying qualities of new types of aircraft. — **tube** n. glass tube rounded and closed at one end, used in chemical tests [L. testa, earthen pot].

tes·ta·ment (tes'·tạ·mạnt) n. solemn declaration of one's will; one of the two great divisions of the Bible, as the Old Testament, or the New Testament. **testamental, testamentary** a. pert. to testament or will; bestowed by will [L. testari, to witness].

test tube

tes·tate (tes'·tāt) *a.* having left a valid will. **testacy** *n.* state of being testate. **testator** *n.* (*fem.* **testatrix**) one who leaves a will [L.*testari*, to witness].

tes·ter (tes'·ter) *n.* flat canopy, esp. over a bed [O.Fr. *teste*, the head].

tes·ti·cle (tes'·ti·kl) *n.* one of the two male reproductive glands. **testicular** *a.* **testiculate, -d** *a.* having testicles; resembling testicle in shape. **testis** *n.* a testicle. *pl.* **testes** [L. *testis* testicle].

tes·ti·fy (tes'·ta·fī) *v.i.* to bear witness; to affirm or declare solemnly; to give evidence upon oath. *v.t.* to bear witness to; to manifest. **testifier** *n.* [L. *testis*, a witness; *facere*, to make].

tes·ti·mo·ny (tes'·ta·mō·ni·) *n.* solemn declaration or affirmation; proof of some fact; in Scripture, the two tables of the law; divine revelation as a whole. **testimonial** *a.* containing testimony; *n.* written declaration testifying to character and qualities of person, esp. of applicant for a position; a tribute to person's outstanding worth [L. *testimonium*].

tes·ty (tes'·ti·) *a.* fretful; irascible [O.Fr. *teste*, head].

tet·a·nus (tet'·a·nas) *n.* a disease in which a virus causes spasms of violent muscular contraction; lockjaw; spasmodic muscular contraction or rigidity caused by intake of drugs. **tetanic** *a.* [Gk. *tetanos*, stretched].

tetch·y (tech'·i.) *a.* peevish; fretful. **tetchily** *adv.* Also **techy** [Fr. *tache*, blemish].

teth·er (teTH'er) *n.* rope or chain fastened to grazing animal to keep it from straying; *v.t.* to confine with tether; to restrict movements of [Scand.].

te·tre- (tet'·ra) *prefix meaning* four [Gk.].

tet·rad (tet'·rad) *n.* the number four; group of four things [Gk. *tetras*].

tet·ra·gon (tet'·ra·gàn) *n.* a plane figure, having four angles. **tetragonal** *a.*

tet·ra·gram (tet'·ra·gram) *n.* word of four letters; (*Geom.*) figure formed by four right angles.

tet·ra·he·dron (tet·ra·hē'·dran) *n.* solid figure enclosed by four triangles; triangular-based pyramid. **tetrahedral** *a.* [Gk. *tetra-*, four; *hedra*, a base].

te·tral·o·gy (te·tral'·a·ji·)*n.* group of four dramas or operas connected by some central event or character [Gk. *tetra-*, four; *logos*, a discourse]. [four measures.

te·tram·e·ter (te·tram'·a·ter) *n.* verse of

te·trarch (tet'·rärk) *n.* Roman governor of fourth part of a province. **-ate** *v.* *n.* office of tetrarch; province ruled by tetrarch. **-ic, -al** *a.* [Gk. *tetra-*, four; *archos*, ruler].

tet·ter (tet'·er) *n.* skin disease; ringworm; *v.t.* to affect with this. **-ous** *a.* [O.E. *teter*, ringworm].

Teu·ton (tū'·tan) *n.* member of one of Germanic tribes; (*Colloq.*) a German. **Teutonic** (tū·tàn'·ik) *a.* pert. to Teutons or their language. [L. *Teutones*].

text (tekst) *n.* original words of author, orator, etc. as distinct from paraphrase or commentary; verse or passage of Scripture chosen as theme of sermon. **-book** *n.* manual of instruction. **-ual** *a.* pert. to text or subject matter; based on actual text or wording; literal. **-ually** *adv.* [L. *texere*, to weave].

tex·tile (teks'·til, tal) *a.* pert. to weaving; capable of being woven; *n.* fabric made on loom [L.*texere*, to weave].

tex·ture (teks'·cher) *n.* quality of surface of a woven material; disposition of several parts of anything in relation to whole; surface quality; that which is woven [L. *texere*].

Thai·land (ti'·land) *n.* Siam.

tha·las·sic (tha·las'·ik) *a.* pert. to the sea; living in the sea [Gk. *thalassa*, the sea].

thal·lus (thal'·as) *n.* simple plant organism which shows little or no differentiation into leaves, stem, or root as in *fungi, algae*, etc. *pl.* **thalli** [Gk. *thallos*, green shoot].

than (THan) *conj.* introducing adverbial clause of comparison and occurring after comparative form of an adjective or adverb [O.E. *thonne*, than].

thane (thān) *n.* in Anglo-Saxon community, member of class between freemen and nobility. **-dom** *n.* property held by a thane [O.E. *thegn*, soldier].

thank (thangk) *v.t.* to express gratitude to *n.* expression of gratitude (usually in *pl.*). **-fulness** *n.* **-less** *a.* ungrateful; unappreci-ated by others. **-lessly** *adv.* **-lessness** *n.* **-sgiving** *n.* act of rendering thanks; service held as expression of thanks for Divine goodness. **-sgiving Day**, day, fourth Thursday in November set apart for rendering thanks to God for blessings granted to nation [O.E. *thanc*, thanks].

that (THat) *demons. pron.* or *a.* (*pl.* **those**) pointing out a person or thing, or referring to something already mentioned; not this but the other; *rel. pron.* who or which; *conj.* introducing a noun clause, adjective clause, or adverbial clause of purpose, result, degree or reason [O.E. *thaet*].

thatch (thach) *n.* straw, rushes, heather, etc. used to roof cottage, or cover stacks of grain; (*Colloq.*) hair; *v.t.* to roof with thatch. **-er** *n.* **-ing** *n.* [O.E. *thaec*, a roof, thatch].

thaw (thaw) *v.t.* to cause to melt by increasing temperature; to liquefy; *v.i.* to melt, as ice, snow, etc.; to become warmer; (*Fig.*) to become genial; *n.* melting of ice or snow [O.E. *thawian*, to melt].

the (THa, emphatic THē) *a. or definite article*, placed before nouns, and used to specify general conception, or to denote particular person or thing; *adv.* by so much; by that amount, as *the more, the merrier* [O.E.].

the·ar·chy (thē'·är·ki·) *n.* theocracy; government by gods **thearchic** *a.* [Gk. *theos*, a god; *arché*, rule].

the·a·ter (thē'·a·ter) *n.* in Ancient Greece, a large, open-air structure used for public assemblies, staging of dramas, etc.; building for plays or motion pictures; lecture or demonstration room for anatomy studies; field of military, naval, or air operations. **theatric, -al** *a.* **theatrically** *adv.* **theatricals** *n.pl.* dramatic performances, esp. by amateurs [Gk. *theatron*]. [thou.

thee (THē) (*Arch.*) *pron.* objective case of

theft (theft) *n.* act of stealing [O.E. *theof*, a thief].

their (THer) *a.* and *pron.* of them; possessive case of **they. theirs** *poss. pron.* form of *their* used absolutely [Scand. *theira*, their].

the·ism (thē'·izm) *n.* belief in existence of personal God who actively manifests Himself in world. **theist** *n.* **theistic, -al** *a.* [Gk. *theos*, a god].

them (THem) *pron.* objective and dative case of **they** [O.E. *thaem*].

theme (thēm) *n.* subject of writing, discourse, or discussion; brief essay; (*Mus.*) groundwork melody recurring at intervals and with variations. **thema** *n.* subject. **thematic** *a.* **thematically** *adv.* — **song** *n.* recurring melody in play, film [Gk. *thema*, something laid down].

them·selves (THem·selvz') *pron. pl.* of **himself, herself,** and **itself;** emphatic form of **them** or **they;** reflexive form of them.

then (THen) *adv.* at that time (past or future); immediately afterwards; thereupon; that being so; for this reason; in consequence of; *conj.* moreover; therefore; *a.* existing or acting at particular time. **now and then,** occasionally [doublet of *than*].

thence (THens) *adv.* from that place; from that time; for that reason. **-forth** *adv.* from that time on. [M.E. *thennes*].

the·oc·ra·cy (thē·àk'·ra·si·) *n.* government of state professedly in the name, and under direction, of God; government by priests. **theocrat, theocratist** *n.* ruler under this system. **theocratic, -al** *a.* **theocratically** *adv.* [Gk. *theos*, a god; *kratos*, power].

the·od·o·lite (thē·àd'·a·lit) *n.* instrument for measuring angles, used in surveying.

the·ol·o·gy (thē·àl'·a·ji.) *n.* science which treats of facts and phenomena of religion, and relations between God and man. **theologian** *n.* one learned in theology. **theologic, -al** *a.* pert. to theology. **theologically** *adv.* **theologize** *v.t.* to render theological; to theorize upon theological matters. **theologist** *n.* [Gk. *theos, god; logos*, discourse].

the·oph·a·ny (thē·àf'·a·ni·) *n.* manifestation of God to men, in human form. **theophanic** *a.* [Gk. *theos*, a god; *phainesthai*, to appear].

the·o·rem (thē'·a·ram) *n.* established principle; (*Math.*) proposition to be proved by logical reasoning; algebraical formula. **-atic, -al** *a.* [Gk. *theorēma*, speculation].

the·o·ry (thē'·a·ri·) *n.* supposition put forward to explain something; speculation; exposition of general principles as distinct from practice and execution; (*Colloq.*) general idea; notion. **theoretic, -al** *a.* pert. to or based on theory; speculative as opp. to *practical*. **theoretics** *n.pl.* speculative side of science. **theorize** *v.t.* to form a theory; to speculate. **theorizer, theorist** *n.* **theorization** *n.* [Gk. *theoria*, speculation].

ther·a·peu·tic (ther·a·pū'·tik) *a.* pert. to healing. **-ally** *adv.* **-s** *n.* branch of medicine concerned with treatment and cure of diseases. **therapeutist** *n.* [Gk. *therapeuein*, to attend (medically)].

ther·a·py (ther'·a·pi·) *n.* remedial treatment, as *radio-therapy* for cure of disease by radium [Gk. *therapeia*, (medical) attendance].

there (THer) *adv.* in that place; farther off opp. to *here*; as an introductory adverb it adds little to the meaning of the sentence as '*There is someone at the door*'; *interj.* expressing surprise, consolation, etc. **-about, -abouts** *adv.* near that place, number or quantity. **-after** *adv.* after that time. **-by** *adv.* by that means; in consequence. **-fore** *conj.* and *adv.* consequently; accordingly. **-in** *adv.* in that, or this place, time, or thing; in that particular. **-inafter** *adv.* afterwards in same document. **-of** *adv.* of that or this. **-to** *adv.* to that or this. **-upon** *adv.* upon that or this; consequently; immediately. **-with** *adv.* with that or this; straightway. [O.E. *thaer*, there].

therm (thurm) *n.* a unit of heat; the large calorie, also small calorie; unit of 1,000 large calories. **-ae** *n.pl.* hot springs; Roman baths. **-al** *a.* pert. to heat. **-ic** *a.* caused by heat. [Gk. *thermē*, heat].

therm·i·on (thur'·mi·an) *n.* positively or negatively charged particle emitted from incandescent substance. **thermionic** *a.* pert to thermions. **thermionic current** (*radio*) flow of electrons from filament to plate of thermionic valve. **thermionics** *n.* branch of science dealing with thermions [Gk. *thermē*, heat; *ion*, going].

ther·mo·chem·is·try (thur·mō·kem'·is·tri·) *n.* branch of science which deals with heat in relation to chemical processes.

ther·mo·dy·nam·ics (thur·mō·dī·nam'·iks) *n.* branch of science which deals with the conversion of heat into mechanical engery.

ther·mo·e·lec·tric·i·ty (thur·mō·i·lek·tris'·a·ti·) *n.* electricity developed by action of heat alone on two different metals. **thermoelectric, -al** *a.* [Gk. *thermē*, heat; and *electricity*].

ther·mo·gen·e·sis (thur·mō·jen'·a·sis) *n.* production of heat, esp. in body. **thermogenetic, thermogenic** *a.*

ther·mom·e·ter (ther·màm'·a·ter) *n.* instrument for measuring temperature, usually consisting of graduated and sealed glass tube with bulb containing mercury. **thermometric, -al** *a.* **thermometrically** *adv.* **thermometry** *n.* [Gk. *thermē*, heat; *metron*, measure].

ther·mo·mo·tor (thur·ma·mō'·ter) *n.* engine worked by heat or hot air.

ther·mo·pile (thur'·ma·pil) *n.* instrument for measuring minute variations in temperature.

ther·mo·scope (thur'·ma·skōp) *n.* instrument for detecting fluctuations in temperature without actual measurement.

Ther·mos (thur'·mas) *n.* double-walled bottle or the like which substantially retains temperature of liquids by the device of surrounding interior vessel with a vacuum jacket [Trade Name].

ther·mo·stat (thur'·ma·stat) *n.* instrument which controls temperature automatically. **thermostatic** *a.* **thermostatics** *n.* science dealing with equilibrium of heat [Gk. *thermē*, heat; and *static*].

ther·mot·ic (ther·màt'·ik) *a.* pert. to heat. Also **-al** *n.* the science of heat [Gk. *thermotēs*, heat].

the·sau·rus (thi·sawr'·as) *n.* treasury of knowledge, etc.; lexicon; encyclopedia [Gk. *thēsauros*, treasure-house].

thess (THēz) *demons. a.* and *pron. pl.* of this.

the·sis (THē'·sis) *n.* what is laid down as a

proposition; dissertation *pl.* **theses. thetic** *a.* dogmatic [Gk. *thesis*, placing].

thermostat

Thes·pis (thes′·pis) an Athenian of 6th cent. B.C. supposed inventor of trageday. **Thespian** *a.* pert. to drama; *n.* an actor; a tragedian.

the·ur·gy (thē′·ur′·ji.) *n.* art of working so-called miracles by supernatural agency. **theurgic, -al** *a.* **theurgically** *adv.* **theurgist** *n.* [Gk. *theos*, god; *ergon*, a work].

thew (thū) *n.* muscle; sinew; brawn (usually *pl.* [O.E. *theaw*, manner, or strength].

they (THā) *pron. pers. pl.* of **he, she, it**; indefinitely, for a number of persons.

thi·a·mine (thī′·a·mēn, man) *n.* Vitamin B, complex compound, deficiency of which causes beriberi also **thiamin** [Gk. *theion*, sulphur, and *amine*].

thick (thik) *a.* dense; foggy; not thin; abundant; packed; muffled, as *thick voice*; mentally dull; (*Slang*) intimate; *n.* thickest part; *adv.* thickly; to a considerable depth. **-en** *v.t.* to make thick; *v.i.* to become thick. **-ening** *n.* something added to thicken. **-et** *n.* dense growth of shrubs, trees, etc. **-headed** *a.* dull mentally. **-ly** *adv.* **-ness** *n.* quality of being thick; measurement of depth between opposite surfaces; layer. **—set** *a.* closely planted; sturdily built [O.E. *thicce*, thick].

thief (thēf) *n.* (*pl.* **thieves**) one who steals the goods and property of another. **thieve** *v.t.* to take by theft; *v.i.* to steal. **thievery** *n.* **thievish** *a.* addicted to stealing. **thievishness** *n.* [O.E. *theof*].

thigh (thī) *n.* fleshy part of leg between knee and trunk [O.E. *theoh*, thigh].

thim·ble (thim′·bl) *n.* metal or bone cap for tip of middle finger, in sewing; anything shaped like a thimble. **-ful** *n.* the quantity contained in a thimble; very small amount [O.E. *thymel*, thumb].

thin (thin) *a. comp.* **-ner.** *superl.* **-nest.** having little depth or thickness; slim; lean; flimsy; sparse; fine; *adv.* sparsely; not closely packed *v.t.* to make thin; to rarefy; *v.i.* to grow or become thin. *pr.p.* **-ning.** *pa.p., pa.t.* **-ned.** **-ly** *adv.* **-ness** *n.* **-ning** *n.* [O.E. *thynne*, thin].

thine (THīn) *pron. poss.* form of **thou** (*Arch.*) belonging to thee; thy [O.E. *thin*].

thing (thing) *n.* material or inanimate object; entity; specimen; commodity; event; action; person (in pity or contempt); *pl.* belongings; clothes, furniture [O.E. *thing*, an object].

think (thingk) *v.t.* to conceive; to surmise; to believe; to consider; to esteem; *v.i.* to reason; to form judgment; to deliberate; to imagine; to recollect. *pa.t.* and *pa.p.* **thought** (thawt). **-able** *a.* **-ing** *a.* reflective; rational [O.E. *thencan*].

thi·o (thī′·ō) word element used in chemistry to illustrate the replacement by sulfur of part or all of the oxygen atoms in a compound. Also **thi-**.

third (thurd) *a.* next after the second; forming one of three equal divisions; *n.* one of three equal parts; (*Mus.*) interval of three diatonic degrees of the scale. **-class** *a.* pert. to accommodation for passengers not traveling first or second class; inferior. **— estate**, the commons. **-ly** *adv.* **—rate** *a.* of third-class quality; inferior [O.E. *thridda*, third].

thirst (thurst) *n.* desire to drink; suffering endured by too long abstinence from drinking; craving; *v.i.* to crave for something to drink; to wish for earnestly. **-er** *n.* **-ily** *adv.* **-iness** *n.* **-y** *a.* having a desire to drink; dry; parched; eager for [O.E. *thurst*, thirst].

thir·teen (thur′·tēn) *a.* ten and three; *n.* sum

of ten and three; symbol representing thirteen units, as 13, XIII. **-th** *a.* next in order after twelfth; being one of thirteen equal parts; *.n.* one of these parts [O.E. *threo*, three; *tyn*, ten].

thir·ty (thur′·ti.) *a.* three times ten; *n.* sum of three times ten; symbol representing this, as 30, XXX. **thirtieth** *a.* next in order after twenty-ninth; being one of thirty equal parts; *n.* thirtieth part [O.E. *thritig*, thirty].

this (THis) *demons. pron.* and *a.* denoting a person or thing near at hand, just mentioned, or about to be mentioned [O.E.].

this·tle (this′·l) *n.* one of the numerous prickly plants of the genus *Carduus*, with yellow or purple flowers; national emblem of Scotland. **—down** *n.* feathery down of thistle seeds. **thistly** *a.* [O.E. *thistel*, a thistle].

thith·er (thiTH′·er) *adv.* to that place; to that point, end, or result. **-ward** *adv.* toward that place [O.E. *thider*].

thole (thōl) *v.t.* pin in gunwale of boat to keep oar in rowlock. Also **-pin** [O.E. *thol*, a rowlock].

Tho·mism (tō′·mizm) *n.* doctrines expounded in theology of *Thomas Aquinas* (1226-74). **Thomist** *n.* adherent of Thomism.

thong (thawng) *n.* narrow strap of leather used for reins, whiplash, etc.; long narrow strip of leather used in leathercraft [O.E. *thwang*, a thong].

tho·rax (thōr′·aks) *n.* part of body between neck and abdomen; chest cavity containing heart, lungs, etc. **thoracic** *a.* [Gk. *thorax*].

thorn (thawrn) *n.* sharp, woody shoot on stem of tree or shrub; prickle; hawthorn; (*Fig.*) anything which causes trouble or annoyance; name in O.E. of the rune for *th*. **-y** *a.* full of thorns; prickly; beset with difficulties [O.E. *thorn*, a prickle].

thor·ough (thur′·ō) *a.* complete; absolute. **-bred** *a.* (of animals) pure bred from pedigree stock; (of people) aristocratic hence, high-spirited; mettlesome; *n.* animal (esp. horse) of pure breed. **-fare** *n.* passage through; highway. **-ly** *adv.* **-ness** *n.* [form of *through*].

those (THōz) *a.* and *pron. pl.* of **that**.

thou (THou) *pron. pres., 2nd sing.* denoting the person addressed (used now only in solemn address, and by the Quakers).

though (THō) *conj.* granting; admitting; even if; notwithstanding; however [O.E. *theah*].

thought (thwat) *pa.t.* and *pa.p.* of **think**.

thought (thawt) *n.* act of thinking; that which one thinks; reflection; opinion; serious consideration. **-ful** *a.* contemplative; attentive; considerate. **-fully** *adv.* **-fulness** *n.* **-less** *a.* without thought; heedless; impulsive; inconsiderate. **-lessly** *adv.* **-lessness** *n.* [O.E. *gethoht*, thought].

thou·sand (thou′·zand) *a.* consisting of ten hundred; used indefinitely to express large number; *n.* the number ten hundred; symbol for this, 1,000 or M; any large number. **-fold** *a.* multiplied by a thousand. **-th** *a.* constituting one of thousand equal parts; next in order after nine hundred and ninety-nine; *n.* thousandth part [O.E. *thusend*].

thrall (thrawl) *n.* slave; bondsman; servitude. **-dom, thraldom** *n.* bondage [O.N. *thrael*, bondage].

thrash (thrash) *v.t.* to thresh; to flog; to defeat soundly. **-er** *n.* **thrashing** *n.* act of thrashing; corporal punishment; flogging. [var. of *thresh*].

thra·son·i·cal (thrā·san′·i·kal) *a.* boastful; bragging. **-ly** *adv.* [fr. *Thraso*, a braggart].

thread (thred) *n.* very thin twist of wool, cotton, linen, silk, etc.; filament as of gold, silver; prominent spiral part of screw; consecutive train of thought; *v.t.* to pass thread through eye of needle; to string together, as beads; to pick one's way with careful deliberation. **-bare** *a.* worn away with wear; shabby; hackneyed; trite. **-worm** *n.* thread-like parasitic worm often found in intestines of children. **-y** *a.* [O.E. *thrawan*, to twist].

threat (thret) *n.* declaration of determination to harm another; menace. **-en** *v.t.* to menace; to declare intention to do harm to; to portend. **-ener** *n.* **-ening** *a.* menacing; portending something undesirable; (of clouds or sky) lowering [O.E. *threatnian*, to urge].

three (thrē) *a.* two and one; *n.* sum of two and one; symbol of this sum, 3 or iii. **-fold** *a.* triple. **-ply** *a.* having three layers or thicknesses; having three strands twisted together, as wool. **-score** *a.* and *n.* sixty. **-some** *n.* game (as golf) played by three players; group of three people. **the three R's,** reading, riting, rithmetic [O.E. *threo*, three].

thren·o·dy (thren′·a·di·) *n.* song of lamentation; dirge. Also **threnode. threnodial, threnodic** *a.* pert. to threnody; funereal.

[Gk. *thrēnos*, lament; *odē*, song].

thresh *v.t.* to separate grain from chaff by use of flail or machine; to beat. **-er** *n.* [O.E. *therscan*, to beat].

thresh·old (thresh′·ōld) *n.* door sill; point of beginning [O.E. *therscan*, to thresh; *wald*, wood].

threw (thrōò) *pa.t.* of **throw**.

thrice (thrīs) *adv.* three times; repeatedly; much, as in *thrice blessed* [O.E. *thriwa*].

thrift (thrift) *n.* economical management; frugality; plant, the sea pink. **-ily** *adv.* **-iness** *n.* frugality. **-less** *a.* extravagant; wasteful. **-lessly** *adv.* **-y** *a.* [fr. *thrive*].

thrill (thril) *n.* emotional excitement; quivering sensation running through nerves and body; *v.t.* to stir deeply; to arouse tingling emotional response; *v.i.* to feel a glow of excitement, enthusiasm, etc. **-er** *n.* (*Colloq.*) sensational novel, play, or film, etc. **-ing** *a.* **-ingly** *adv.* [O.E. *thyrlian*, to bore a hole].

thrive (thrīv) *v.i.* to prosper; to grow abundantly; to develop healthily. *pa.t.* **throve** and **-d.** *pa.p.* **thriven** (thriv′·n) **-d. thriving** *a.* **thrivingly** *adv.* [O.N. *thrifa*, to grasp].

throat (thrōt) *n.* forepart of neck; passage connecting back of mouth with lungs, stomach, etc.; narrow entrance. **-iness** *n.* quality of having throaty or muffled voice. **-y** *a.* guttural; muffled [O.E. *throte*, the throat].

throb (thrab) *v.i.* to pulsate; to beat, as heart, with more than usual force. *pr.p.* **-bing.** *pa.t.* and *pa.p.* **-bed.** *n.* pulsation; palpitation (of heart, etc.); beat [etym. doubtful].

throe (thrō) *n.* suffering; pain; *pl.* pains of childbirth [O.E. *thrawa*, suffering].

throm·bo·sis (thram·bō′·sis) *n.* formation of blood clot in vein or artery [Gk. *thrombos*].

throne (thrōn) *n.* chair of state; royal seat; bishop's seat in his cathedral; sovereign power and dignity; *v.t.* to place on royal seat; to exalt. *pr.p.* **throning.** *pa.p.* **-d** [Gk. *thronos*, a seat].

throng (thrawng) *n.* multitude; crowd; *v.t.* to mass together; to press in crowds [O.E. *thringan*, to press].

throt·tle (thrat′·l) *n.* windpipe; valve controlling amount of vaporized fuel delivered to cylinders in internal-combustion engine, or pressure of steam in steam engine; *v.i.* to choke by external pressure on windpipe; to obstruct steam in steam engine; (*Fig.*) to suppress; to silence; *v.i.* to pant for breath, as if suffocated [dim. of *throat*].

through (thrōò) *prep.* from end to end of; going in at one side and out the other; by passing between; across; along; by means of; as consequence of; *adv.* from one end or side to the other; from beginning to end. *a.* (of railway train) passing from one main station to another without intermediate stops; unobstructed, as *through-road*. **through and through,** completely. **-ly** (*Arch.*) *adv.* thoroughly. **-out** *adv.* and *prep.* wholly; completely; during entire time of [O.E. *thurh*, through].

throve (thrōv) *pa.t.* of **thrive**.

throw (thrō) *v.t.* to fling, cast, or hurl; to propel; to send; to twist into thread, as silk; to mold on potter's wheel; to unseat, as of a horseman; to shed, as snake's skin; to produce offspring, as animal; to spread carelessly; *v.i.* to cast, to hurl. *pr.p.* **-ing.** *pa.t.* **threw.** *pa.p.* **-n.** *n.* the act of throwing; distance something can be thrown; light blanket. **-er** *n.* **-n** *a.* [O.E.*thrawan*].

thrum (thrum) *n.* fringe of threads left on loom after web is cut off [O.N. *thromr*, edge].

thrum (thrum) *v.t.* to strum on instrument; to play carelessly; to drum with fingers *pr.p.* **-ming.** *pa.p., pa.t.* **-med.** [O.N. *thruma*, rattle].

thrush (thrush) *n.* song bird [O.E. *thrysce*].

thrush (thrush) *n.* (*Med.*) inflammatory disease affecting mouth, tongue and lips, commonly found in young children; a disease affecting the feet of horses, etc. [O.E. *thyrre*, dry].

thrust (thrust) *v.t.* to push or drive with sudden force; to pierce; *v.i.* to make a push; to attack with a pointed weapon; to intrude; to push way through. *pa.t.* and *pa.p.* **thrust.** *n.* push; stab; assault; horizontal outward pressure as of arch against its abutments; stress acting horizontally, as in machinery; (*Geol.*) upward bulge of layer of rock due to lateral pressure. **-er** *n.* [Scand. *thrysia*, to press].

thud (thud) *n.* dull sound made by blow or heavy fall; *v.i.* to make sound of thud; [O.E. *thoden*, noise].

thug (thug) *n.* cutthroat; ruffian; gangster. **-gery** *n.* [Hind. *thag*].

Thule (thū′·lē) *n.* name in ancient times for most northerly part of world. Orkneys, Shetlands, Iceland, etc. [Gk. *Thoulē*].

thumb (thum) *n.* short, thick finger of human hand; part of glove which covers this; *v.t.* to manipulate awkwardly; to soil with thumb marks; (*Slang*) to hold up thumb, to solicit lift in automobile. **-ed** *a.* having thumbs; soiled with thumb marks. **-less** *a.* **-like** *a.* **-nail** *n.* nail on human thumb. **-nail sketch,** miniature; succinct description. **-screw** *n.* old instrument of torture by which thumb was compressed till the joint broke. **by rule of thumb,** by rough estimate [O.E. *thuma,* a thumb].

thumbscrew

thump (thump) *n.* blow of fist; sudden fall of heavy body or weight; thud; *v.t.* to beat with something heavy; *v.i.* to strike or fall with a thud. **-er** *n.* **-ing** *a.* very large; much exaggerated [imit.].

thun·der (thun'·der) *n.* rumbling sound which follows lightning flash; any very loud noise; *v.t.* to declaim or rage with loud voice; *v.i.* to rumble with thunder; to roar. **-bolt** *n.* flash of lightning followed by peal of thunder; anything totally unexpected and unpleasant. **-clap** *n.* a peal of thunder. **the thundered,** the god Jupiter. **-ing** *n.* thunder; booming, as of guns. *a.* making a loud noise; (*Colloq.*) outstanding; excessive. **-ous** *a.* **-ously** *adv.* **-storm** *n.* storm of thunder and lightning with torrential rain **-struck** *a.* speechless with amazement. **-y** *a.* **to steal someone's thunder,** to win applause expected by someone else; to expose or use first someone else's chief point(s) [O.E. *thunian,* to rattle].

thu·ri·ble (thyoo'·ra·bl) *n.* a metal censer. **thurifer** *n.* one who carries and swings a thurible [L. *thus, thuris,* frankincense].

Thurs·day (thurz'·dē) *n.* fifth day of week, after *Thor,* Scandinavian god of thunder.

thus (THus) *adv.* in this or that manner; to this degree or extent; so; in this wise. **thus far,** so far [O.E. *thus,* by this].

thwack (thwak) *v.t.* to beat; to flog; *n.* heavy blow; a hard slap [O.E. *thaccian,* to stroke].

thwart (thwawrt) *a.* lying across; transverse; athwart; *v.t.* to hinder; to frustrate; to stop; *n.* seat across or athwart a row boat; *adv.* and *prep.* across. **-er** *n.* **-ing** *a.* [O.N. *thvert,* across].

thy (THi) *poss. a.* of thee; belonging to thee [contr. fr. *thine*].

thyme (tim) *n.* small flowering shrub cultivated for its aromatic leaves for use as flavoring in cookery [Gk. *thumon*].

thy·mus (thi'·mas) *n.* small ductless gland in upper part of the chest [Gk.].

thy·roid (thi'·roid) *a.* signifying cartilage of larynx or a gland of trachea. **— gland,** ductless gland situated in neck on either side of trachea, secreting hormone which profoundly affects physique and temperament of human beings [Gk. *thureos,* a shield; *eidos,* a form].

thy·self (THi·self') *pron. reflex. or emphatic,* of a person, thou or thee.

ti·ar·a (tī·or'·a, ti·âr'·a) *n.* lofty turban worn by ancient Persian kings and dignitaries; triple, gem-studded crown worn by Pope on ceremonial occasions; gem-studded coronet worn by ladies [Gk. *tiara,* headdress].

tib·i·a (tib'·i·a) *n.* shinbone; inner and usually larger of two bones of leg, between knee and ankle. *pl.* **-s, tibiae. -l** *a.* [L. *tibial*].

tic (tik) *n.* spasmodic twitching of muscle, esp. of face [Fr. *tic,* twitching].

tick (tik) *n.* a parasitic bloodsucking insect [M.E. *teke*].

tick (tik) *n.* cover of mattress, pillow, etc. **-ing** *n.* specially strong material used for mattress covers, etc. [Gk. *thēkē,* a case].

tick (tik) *v.i.* to make small, recurring, clicking sound, as watch; *n.* sound made by watch. **-er** *n.* anything which ticks regularly; machine

which records on tape; (*Colloq.*) watch or clock; the heart [imit.].

tick (tik) *v.t.* to mark or dot lightly; *n.* small mark placed after word, entry, etc., esp. in checking; [M.E. *tek,* a touch].

tick·et (tik'·it) *n.* piece of cardboard or paper entitling admission to anything, to travel by public transport, to participate in function, etc.; price tag; label; (*U.S.*) list of candidates in an election; *v.t.* to mark with ticket. **season ticket,** ticket entitling holder to attend a series of concerts, lectures, etc. or to travel daily between certain specified stations over a certain period of time [O.Fr. *etiquet,* label].

tick·le (tik'·l) *v.t.* to touch skin lightly so as to excite nerves and cause laughter; to titillate; to amuse; *v.i.* to feel sensation of tickling; to be gratified. **-r** *n.* **ticklish** *a.* easily tickled; requiring skillful handling. **ticklishly** *adv.* **ticklishness** *n.* [freq. of *tick.* to touch lightly].

tid·bit (tid'·bit) *n.* choice morsel. Also **titbit** [Scand. *titto,* small bird].

tid·dly·winks (tid'·li·wingks) *n.pl.* game in which players try to snap small disks into cup.

tide (tid) *n.* time; season, as in *eventide, Eastertide;* periodical rise and fall of ocean due to attraction of moon and sun; (*Fig.*) trend. **to tide over,** to manage temporarily; to surmount meantime. **tidal** *a.* pert. to tide. **tidal basin,** harbor which is affected by tides. **tidal wave,** mountainous wave as caused by earthquake, atom bomb explosion, etc. **-less** *a.* having no tides. **ebb,** or **low, tide,** the falling level of the sea. **flood,** or **high, tide,** the rising level of the sea. **neap tide,** minimum tide. **spring tide,** maximum tide [O.E. *tid,* time].

ti·dings (ti'·dingz) *n.pl.* news; information [O.N. *tithindi,* to happen].

ti·dy (ti'·dy·) *a.* neat; orderly; (*Colloq.*) comfortable; of fair size; *n.* chair-back cover; *v.t.* to put in order [M.E. *tidy,* timely].

tie (tī) *v.t.* to fasten by rope, string, etc.; to fashion into knot; to bind together, as rafters, by connecting piece of wood or metal; to hamper; (*Mus.*) to connect two notes with tie; *v.t.* (*Sport*) to make equal score, etc. *pr.p.* **tying.** *pa.t.* and *pa.p.* **tied.** *n.* knot; necktie; fastening; connecting link; equality of score; (*Mus.*) curved line connecting two notes indicating that sound is sustained for length of both notes; traverse supports for railroad tracks. **— beam** *n.* horizontal timber connecting two rafters. **-r** *n.* [O.E. *teah,* a rope].

tier (tir) *n.* row or rank, esp. when two or more rows are arranged behind and above the other [Fr. *tirer,* to draw].

tierce (tirs) *n.* cask containing third of pipe or 42 wine gallons; third of canonical hours, or service at 9 a.m.; in fencing, particular thrust (third position) [Fr. *tiers,* third].

tiff (tif) *n.* slight quarrel; *v.i.* to quarrel [etym. doubtful].

ti·ger (ti'·ger) *n.* (*fem.* **tigress**) fierce carnivorous quadruped of cat tribe, with tawny black-striped coat. **-cat** *n.* wild cat; ocelot or margay. **— lily** *n.* tall Chinese lily with flaming orange flowers spotted with black [Gk. *tigris*].

tight (tit) *a.* firm; compact; compressed; not leaky; fitting close or too close to body; tense; (*Colloq.*) restricted for want of money; (*Slang*) drunk; *adv.* firmly. **-en** *v.t.* to make tight or tighter; to make taut; *v.i.* to become tight or tighter. **-ener** *n.* **-ly** *adv.* **-ness** *n.* **-rope** *n.* a strong, taut rope, or steel wire on which acrobats perform. **-s** *n.pl.* close-fitting woven hose and trunks worn by acrobats, dancers, etc. [O.N. *thettr,* watertight].

til·de (til'·da) *n.* the mark (~) placed over the letter n in Spanish, to indicate a following *y* sound, as in **cañon** (canyon).

tile (til) *n.* a thin piece of slate, baked clay, plastic, asphalt, etc. used for roofs, walls, floors, drains, etc.; (*Slang*) a silk top-hat; *v.t.* to cover with tiles. **-r** *n.* **tiling** *n.* [L. *tegula*].

till (til) *n.* a money box or drawer in a shop counter; a cash register [etym. doubtful].

till (til) *prep.* as late as; until; *conj.* to the time when [M.E. *til,* up to].

till (til) *v.t.* to cultivate; to plow the soil, sow seeds, etc. **-age** *n.* the act of preparing the soil for cultivation; the cultivated land. **-er** *n.* [O.E. *tilian,* to till].

till (til) *n.* boulder clay or glacial drift.

til·ler (til'·er) *n.* a bar used as a lever, esp. for turning a rudder [O.Fr. *tellier,* weaver's beam].

tilt (tilt) *v.t.* to raise one end of; to tip up; to thrust, as a lance; to forge with a tilt hammer; *v.i.* to charge on horseback with a lance, as in a tournament; to slant; *n.* a thrust, as with a lance; a medieval sport in which competitors armed with lances charged each other; inclination. **-er** *n.* **— hammer** *n.* a heavy hammer used in iron works and tilted by a lever [O.E. *tealt,* tottering].

tilt (tilt) *n.* canvas covering of a cart; a small canvas awning; *v.t.* to cover with a tilt [O.E. *teld,* a tent].

tim·bal (tim'·bal) *n.* kettledrum [Sp. *timbal*].   [a kettledrum.

tim·ber (tim'·ber) *n.* trees or wood suitable for building purposes; trees collectively; single unit of wooden framework of house; rib of ship; *v.t.* to furnish with timber. **-ed** *a.* **— line** *n.* tree line, above which altitude trees

will not grow [O.E. *timber,* material for building a house].

tiller

tim·bre (tim'·ber, tán'·br) *n.* special tone quality in sound of human voice or instrument [Fr. *timbre*].   [bourine [O.Fr. *timbre*].

tim·brel (tim'·bral) *n.* kind of drum, or tam-

time (tim) *n.* particular moment; period of duration; conception of past, present, and future, as sequence; epoch; system of measuring duration, as *Greenwich time;* opportunity; occasion; (*Mus.*) rhythmical arrangement of beats within measures or bars; *pl.* period characterized by certain marked tendencies, as *Victorian times;* term indicating multiplication, as *four times four; v.t.* to ascertain time taken, as by racing competitor; to select precise moment for; (*Mus.*) to measure; *v.i.* to keep or beat time. **— bomb** *n.* delayed-action bomb. **—honored** *a.* revered because of age; venerable. **-keeper** *n.* one who keeps a record of men's hours of work; clock or watch. **-less** *a.* eternal; unending. **-lessly** *adv.* **-liness** *n.* **-ly** *a.* opportune. **-piece** *n.* clock. **-r** *n.* a stop watch. **-server** *n.* **-serving** *n.* selfish opportunism. **-table** *n.* booklet containing times of departure and arrival of trains, buses, steamers, etc. **-worn** *a.* aged; decayed. **timing** *n.* control of speed of an action or actions for greatest effect. **Greenwich time,** *British* standard time as settled by passage of sun over meridian at Greenwich [O.E. *tima,* time].

tim·id (tim'·id) *a.* lacking courage or self-confidence; shy. **-ness, -ity** *n.* **-ly** *adv.* **timorous** *a.* frightened; very timid. **timorously** *adv.* **timorousness** *n.* [L. *timidus*].

ti·moc·ra·cy (ti·mák'·ra·si·) *n.* government in which possession of property is necessary qualification for holders of offices [Gk. *timē,* honor; *kratos,* power].

tim·o·thy (tim'·a·thi·) *n.* grass grown for hay, and valued as fodder.

tim·pa·no (tim'·pa·nō) *n.* kettledrum, esp. as part of percussion section of orchestra. *pl.* **timpani. timpanist. tympanist** *n.* [Gk. *tumpanon,* a kettledrum].

tin (tin) *n.* soft, whitish-gray metal, very malleable and ductile, used for plating, as constituent of alloys (e.g. pewter, bronze) and for food containers in canning industry; tin can; (*Slang*) money; *a.* made of tin or plated with tin; *v.t.* to plate with tin. *pr.p.* **-ning.** *pa.p.* and *pat.* **-ned.** **— foil** *n.* wafer-thin sheets of tin; **-ned** *a.* preserved in a tin; plated with tin. **-ner, -man** *n.* a tin miner; one who makes tin plate. **-ning** *n.* **-ny** *a.* like tin; making a sound like tin when struck. **-type** *n.* (*Photog.*) ferrotype; positive on varnished tin plate. **-ware** *n.* utensils, etc. made of tin plate [O.E. *tin,* tin].

Tin Pan Alley (tin'·pan·a'·li·) (*Slang*) the world of the composers of popular music.

tinc·ture (tingk'·cher) *n.* tinge or shade of color; faint trace; (*Pharm.*) solution of a substance in alcohol; *v.t.* to tinge; to imbue; to affect to a small degree [L. *tinctura,* dyeing].

tin·der (tin'·der) *n.* anything inflammable used for kindling fire from a spark [O.E. *tynder,* tinder].

tine (tin) *n.* tooth or prong of fork; spike of harrow; branch of deer's antler. *a.* [O.E. *tind,* point].

ting (ting) *n.* sharp, ringing sound, as of bell; tinkle; *v.t.* and *v.i.* to tinkle. [imit.].

tinge (tinj) *v.t.* to color or flavor slightly; to temper. *n.* a faint touch [L. *tingere*].

tin·gle (ting'·gl) *v.i.* to feel faint thrill or pricking sensation; *n.* pricking sensation [prob. freq. of *ting*].

tink·er (tingk'·er) *n.* mender of pots, kettles, etc., esp. one who travels round countryside; jack of all trades; *v.i.* to do the work of a tinker; to attempt to mend [M.E. *tinker,* one who makes a sharp sound].

tin·kle (tingk'·l) *v.t.* to cause to make small, quick, metallic sounds; *v.i.* to make series of quick, sharp sounds; to jingle; *n.* small, sharp, ringing sound. **tinkling** *n. a.* [M.E. *tinken,* to chink].

tin·sel (tin'·sal) *n.* very thin, glittering, metallic strips for decorations, etc.; (*Fig.*) anything showy or flashy; *a.* gaudy; showy and cheap; *v.t.* to decorate with tinsel; to make gaudy. **—like** *a.* [Fr. *étincelle,* a spark].

tint (tint) *n.* hue or dye; faint tinge; color with admixture of white; *v.t.* to give faint coloring to; to tinge **-er** *n.* [L. *tinctus,* dyed].

tin·tin·nab·u·la·tion (tin·ti·nab·ya·lā'·shan) *n.* tinkling sound of bells pealing. **tintinnab-**

ular, tintinnabulary, tintinnabulous *a.* [L. *tintinnare*, to jingle].

ti·ny (ti′·ni·) *a.* very small; diminutive. Also **teeny.**

tip (tip) *n.* point of anything slender; end; top; *v.t.* to form a point on; to cover tip of. *pr.p.* **-ping.** *pa.p.* **-ped. -toe** *adv.* on tips of toes; *v.t.* to walk on tips of toes; to walk stealthily. [var. of *top*].

tip (tip) *v.t.* to touch lightly; to tap; to tilt; to overturn; to weigh down, as scales; (*Slang*) to give useful hint to, esp. about betting odds; to recompense with small gratuity; *v.i.* to fall to one side; to give gratuity; *n.* light stroke; private information; gratuity; *n.* **-ping** *n.* **-ster** *n.* one who sells tips regarding horse-racing, etc. [M.E. *tipen*, to overthrow].

tip·pet (tip′·it) *n.* scarf or cloth of fur [L. *tapete*, tapestry].

tip·ple (tip′·l) *v.i.* to drink small quantities of intoxicating liquor frequently; *v.t.* to drink excessively. *n.* strong drink. **-r** *n.* [Scand. *tipla*, to drink little and often].

tip·sy (tip′·si·) *a.* intoxicated; staggering. **tipsily** *adv.* **tipsiness** *n.* [fr. *tipple*].

ti·rade (ti·rād′) *n.* long denunciatory speech; volley of abuse [It. *tirata*, a drawing out].

tire (tīr) *v.t.* to weary or fatigue; *v.i.* to become wearied, bored, or impatient. **-d** *a.* wearied; bored. **-dness** *n.* **-less** *a.* **-lessly** *adv.* **-some** *a.* [O.E. *tiorian*, to be tired].

tire (tīr) *n.* hoop of iron, rubber, or rubber tube, etc. placed around a wheel [form of *attire*].

tir·o See **tyro.**

tis·sue (tish′·ōo) *n.* (*Biol.*) any of cellular structures which make up various organs of plant or animal body; unbroken series; web; fine cloth interwoven with gold or silver; *a.* made of tissue. **-d** *a.* made of or resembling tissue. **— paper** *n.* very thin, white or colored semi-transparent paper [Fr. *tissu*, fr. L.*texere*, to weave].   [a little bird.

tit (tit) *n.* small bird, e.g. titmouse [O.N. *tittr*.

tit (tit) *n.* teat [O.E. *tit*, a nipple].

Ti·tan (tī′·tan) *n.* (*Gk. Myth.*) one of sons of Uranus and Gaea (Heaven and Earth); (*l.c.*) person of magnificent physique or of brilliant intellectual capacity; *a.* pert. to Titans; (*l.c.*) colossal; mighty. **Titanic** *a.* pert. to Titans; colossal.

tithe (tīTH) *n.* tenth part; orig. tenth part of produce of land and cattle given to the church, later paid in form of tax; small portion; *v.t.* to levy a tithe; *v.i.* to give a tithe. **-r** *n.* **-less** *a.* [O.E. *teotha*, tenth].

tit·ian (tish′·an) *a.* rich auburn; from color of hair in many portraits by Titian, Italian painter.

tit·il·late (tit′·a·lāt) *v.t.* to tickle, usually in sense of stimulating mind, palate, etc.— **titillation** *n.* process of titillating; any pleasurable sensation. **titillative** *a.* [L. *titillare*, tickle].

tit·i·vate (tit′·i·vāt) *v.t.* and *v.i.* (*Slang*) to put finishing touches to one's general appearance **titivator** *n.* [perh. fr. *tidy*].

ti·tle (tī′·tl) *n.* inscription put over, or under, or at beginning of, anything; designation; appellation denoting rank or office; that which constitutes just claim or right; (*Law*) legal proof of right of possession; title deed. **-d** *a.* having title, esp. aristocratic title. **— deed** *n.* document giving proof of legal ownership of property. **— page** *n.* page of book on which is inscribed name of book, author and publication data. **— role** *n.* part in play from which it takes its name [L. *titulus*, title].

tit·mouse (tit′·mous) *n.* small bird which builds in holes of trees; tit; tomtit. *pl.* **titmice** [M.E. *tit*, small; *mase*, name for several small birds].

ti·trate (tī′·trāt) *v.t.* to determine amount of ingredient in solution by adding quantities of standard solution until required chemical reaction is observed. **titration** *n.* [Fr. *titre*, title].

tit·ter (tit′·er) *v.i.* to give smothered laugh; to giggle; *n.* **-er** *n.* [imit.].

tit·tle (tit′·l) *n.* minute particle; whit; jot [L. *titulus*, superscription, small stroke to indicate contraction].

tit·u·lar (tich′·(y)a·ler) *a.* pert. to or having a title; nominal; ruling in name but not in deed. **titularity** *n.* **-y** *a.* titular; *n.* nominal holder of title [L. *titulus*, a title].

tme·sis (mē′·sis) *n.* separation of two parts of compound word by one or more interpolated words, as 'from *what* direction *soever*' [Gk. fr. *temnein*, to cut].

to (tōō) *prep.* expressing motion towards; as far as; regarding; unto; upon; besides; compared with; as to; expressing purpose, as in gerundial infinitive indicating dative case or indirect object; preceding infinitive mood of the verb; *adv.* forward; into customary position [O.E. *to*, to].

toad (tōd) *n.* amphibian resembling frog, but brownish with dry warty skin and short legs; mean, detestable person. **-stool** *n.* fungus resembling mushroom, but poisonous. **-y** *n.* obsequious flatterer; social parasite; *v.i.* to flatter excessively; to fawn on. *pr.p.* **-ying.** *pa.t.* and *pa.p.* **-ied. -yish** *a.* **-yism** *n.* sycophancy [O.E. *tadige*, a toad].

toast (tōst) *v.t.* to dry or warm by exposure

to fire; to crisp and brown (as bread) before fire, under grill, etc.; to drink to health of, or in honor of; *v.i.* to drink a toast; *n.* slice of bread crisped and browned on both sides by heat; person in whose honor toast is drunk; the drink itself. **-er** *n.* **-master** *n.* one who presides at luncheon or dinner, proposes toasts, introduces speakers, etc. [L. *tostus*, roasted].

toadstool

to·bac·co (ta·bak′·ō) *n.* plant, dried leaves of which are used for chewing, smoking, or as snuff. *pl.* **-s, -es** [Sp. *tabaco*].

to·bog·gan (ta·bàg′·an) *n.* flat-bottomed sled used for coasting down snow-clad hill slopes; *v.i.* to slide down hills on toboggan. **-ing** *n.* [Amer.-Ind.].

to·by (tō′·bi·) *n.* small jug in shape of an old man wearing a three-cornered hat [fr. *Toby*, personal name].

toc·ca·ta (ta·kà′·ta) *n.* (*Mus.*) composition for organ or piano which tests player's technique and touch [It.].   [sound [Fr.

toc·sin (tàk′·sin) *n.* alarm bell or its ringing

to·day, to·day (ta·dā′) *n.* this day; present time; *adv.* on this day; at the present time [O.E. *to-daege*, today].

tod·dle (tàd′·l) *v.i.* to walk with short, hesitating steps. *n.* unsteady gait. **-r** *n.* child just learning to walk [prob. form of *totter*].

tod·dy (tàd′·i·) *n.* fermented juice of certain E. Indian palm trees; drink of whisky, sugar, and hot water [Hind. *tari*, juice of palm tree].

to·do (ta·dōō′) *n.* a commotion; a fuss [fr. *to* and *do*].

toe (tō) *n.* one of five small digits of foot; forepart of hoof; part of boot, shoe, or stocking covering toes; outer end of head of golf club; *v.t.* to touch or reach with toe; *v.i.* to tap with toes. **-d** *a.* having toes [O.E. *ta*, the toe].

tof·fee, tof·fy (tàf′·i·) *n.* hard candy made of sugar, butter, flavoring, etc. boiled together. Also **taffy** [etym. uncertain].

tog (tàg) *n.* (*Slang*) clothes. usu. in *pl. v.i.* to dress *pr.p.* **-ging.** *pa.p., pa.t.* **-get** [prob. fr. L. *toga*, a robe].

to·ga (tō′·ga) *n.* loose outer garment worn by Roman citizens. **-ed, togated** *a.* wearing a toga [L. fr. *tegere*, to cover].

to·geth·er (ta·geTH′·er) *adv* in company; in or into union; simultaneously; in same place [O.E. *to*, to; *geador*, together].

toil (toil) *v.i.* to labor; to move with difficulty; *n.* exhausting labor; drudgery; task. **-er** *n.* **-ful, -some** *a.* laborious. **-somely** *adv.* **-someness** *n.* **-worn** *a.* weary with toil; (of hands) hard and lined with toil [O.Fr. *touiller*, to entangle].

toil (toil) *n.* a net or snare; mesh. usu. *pl.* [Fr. *toile*, cloth].

toi·let (toi′·lit) *n.* process of dressing; mode of dressing; a lavatory. Also **toilette** (twa·let′). **— articles** *n.pl.* objects used in dressing, as comb, brush, mirror, toothbrush, etc. **— paper** *n.* thin paper for lavatory use. **— powder** *n.* talcum powder [Fr. *toilette*, dim. of *toile*, cloth].

to·ken (tō′·kan) *n.* sign; symbol; concrete expression of esteem; coin-like piece of metal for special use, as *bus token, etc.* **— payment** *n.* deposit paid as token of later payment of full debt [O.E. *tacen*, symbol].

told (tōld) *pa.t.* and *pa.p.* of verb **tell.**

tol·er·ate (tàl′·a·rāt) *v.t.* to permit to be done; to put up with. **tolerable** *a.* endurable; supportable; passably good. **tolerability, tolerableness** *n.* **tolerably** *adv.* **tolerance** *n.* forbearance. **tolerant** *a.* forbearing; broad-minded. **tolerantly** *adv.* **toleration** *n.* act of tolerating; practice of allowing people to worship as they please; granting to minorities political liberty. **tolerationist** *n.* **tolerator** *n.* [L. *tolerare*, to bear].

toll (tōl) *n.* tax, esp. for right to use bridge, ferry, public road, etc.; charge for long-distance telephone call. *v.i.* to exact toll. **— bar** *n.* formerly bar which could be swung across road to stop travelers to pay toll. [O.E. *toll*, tax].

toll (tōl) *v.t.* to cause to ring slowly, as bell, esp. to signify death; *v.i.* to peal with slow, sonorous sounds; *n.* [M.E. *tollen*, to pull].

tom (tàm) *n.* used to denote male animal as tomcat. **-boy** *n.* girl of boyish behavior; hoyden, romping, mischievous girl. **-fool** *n.* complete fool. **-foolery** *n.* nonsensical behavior. [fr. *Thomas*].

tom·a·hawk (tàm′·a·hawk) *n.* war hatchet used by N. American Indians; *v.t.* to wound

or kill with tomahawk [Amer.-Ind.].

tomahawk

to·ma·to (ta·mā′·tō) *n. pl.* **-es.** plant with red or yellow fruit much used in salads. [Sp. *tomate*].

tomato

tomb (tōōm) *n.* a grave; underground vault; any structure for a dead body. **-stone** *n.* stone erected over grave [Gk. *tumbos*, a sepulchral mound].

tome (tōm) *n.* a book; a large, heavy volume [Gk. *tomos*, a piece cut off].

to·mor·row (ta·mawr′·ō) *n.* day after today; *adv.* on the following day [O.E. *to*, and *morgen*, morning].

tom·tit (tàm′·tit) *n.* a small bird [fr. *tit* as in *titmouse*].

tom-tom (tàm′·tàm) *n.* small drum used by Indian and African natives. Also **tam-tam** [Hind.]

ton (tun) *n.* weight consisting of 20 cwt. or 2000 lb.; measure of capacity varying according to article being measured; *pl.* (*Colloq.*) great amount or number. **-nage** *n.* cubical content (100 cub. ft.) or burden (40 cub. ft.) of ship in tons; duty on ships estimated per ton; shipping collectively assessed in tons. Also **tonnage** [O.E. *tunne*, vat].

ton (tàn) *n.* fashion; latest mode [Fr.].

tone (tōn) *n.* quality or pitch of musical sound; modulation of speaking or singing voice; color values of picture; (*Mus.*) one of larger intervals of diatonic scale, smaller intervals being called *semitones*; (*Med.*) natural healthy functioning of bodily organs; general character, as of manners, morals, or sentiment; (*Gram.*) pitch on one syllable of word; *v.t.* to give tone or quality to; to modify color or general effect of, as in photograph; to tune (instrument); *v.i.* to blend (with). **tonal** *a.* **tonality** *n.* quality of tone or pitch; system of variation of keys in musical composition; color scheme of picture. **tonally** *adv.* **— deaf** *a.* unable to distinguish musical intervals. *a.* having tone etc. [Gk. *tonos*, tension].

ton·ga (tàng′·ga) *n.* a light, two-wheeled vehicle used in India [Hind.].

tong (tàng, tawng) *n.* (in *U.S.*) an association exclusively for Chinese people [Chin. *t'ang*, meeting-place].

tongs (tàngz, tawngz) *n.pl.* implement consisting of pair of pivoted levers, for grasping e.g. pieces of coal [O.E. *tange*, tongs].

tongue (tung) *n.* flexible muscular organ in mouth used in tasting, swallowing, and for speech; facility of utterance; language; anything shaped like a tongue; clapper of bell; narrow spit of land; slip of wood fitting into groove; *v.t.* to modulate with tongue as notes of flute; to chide; *v.i.* to use tongue as in playing staccato passage on flute; to chatter. **-d** *a.* having a tongue. **—tied** *n.* having tongue defect causing speech impediment; speechless through shyness [O.E. *tunge*].

ton·ic (tàn′·ik) *a.* pert. to tones or sounds; having an invigorating effect bodily or mentally; *n.* a medicine which tones up the system; anything invigorating; (*Mus.*) a key note **-ally** *adv.* **tonicity** (tō·nis′·a·ti·) *n.* **— sol-fa,** a system of musical notation in which sounds are represented by syllables as do, ray, me, fah, etc. [Gk. *tonos*, act of stretching].

to-night, to-night (ta.nīt′) this night; night following this present day; *adv.* on this night [fr. *to* and *night*].

ton-nage *n.* See **ton**.

ton-sil (tán′.sil) *n.* one of two oval-shaped lymphoid organs on either side of pharynx. **-(l)itis** *n.* inflammation of the tonsils [L. *tonsillae,* tonsils].

ton-sure (tán′.sher) *n.* act of shaving part of head as token of religious dedication; shaved crown of priest's head. **tonsor** *n.* barber. **ton-sorial** *a.* pert. to a barber or his work (usu. humorous) [L. *tonsura,* clipping].

ton-tine (tán′.tēn) *n.* shared annuity [fr. *Lorenzo Tonti,* the originator].

too (tōo) *adv.* in addition; more than enough; moreover [stressed form of *to*].

took (took) *pa.t.* of **take**.

tool (tōol) *n.* implement or utensil operated by hand, or by machinery; cutting or shaping part of a machine; means to an end; *v.t.* to cut, shape, or mark with a tool; to indent a design on leather book cover, etc. with pointed tool. **-ing** *n.* [O.E. *tol,* a tool].

toot (tōot) *v.t.* to cause to sound, as an automobile horn or wind instrument; *n.* sound of horn, etc.; hoot. [imit.].

tooth (tōoth) *n.* hard projection in gums of upper and lower jaws of vertebrates, used in mastication; prong as of comb, saw, rake; cog of wheel. *pl.* **teeth.** *v.t.* to provide with teeth; to indent; *v.i.* to interlock. **-ache** *n.* pain in tooth. **-brush** *n.* small brush for cleaning teeth. **-ed** *a.* palatable; pleasant to taste. **-y** *a.* having prominent teeth; toothed [O.E. *toth,* a tooth].

top (táp) *n.* highest part of anything; upper side; highest rank; first in merit; green part of plants above ground; (*Naut.*) platform surrounding head of lower mast. *a.* highest; most eminent; best; *v.t.* to cover on the top; to rise above; to cut off top of; to hit, as golf ball, above center; to surpass; *v.i.* to be outstanding. **-coat** *n.* overcoat. — **hat** *n.* tall silk hat. **-heavy** *a.* unbalanced; having top too heavy for base. **-most** *a.* supreme; highest. **-notch** *a.* describing persons of high ability or anything which is super-excellent. **-per** something placed on the top; (*Slang*) top hat; topcoat. **-ping** *n.* act of lopping off top of something, as highest branches of tree; what is cut off; something put on top of a thing as decoration, to complete it, etc. *a.* **-pingly** *adv.* **-sail** *n.* square sail on top-mast. **-soil** *n.* surface layer of soil [O.E. *top,* summit]. [pointed end.

top hat

top (táp) *n.* child's toy made to spin on its **to-paz** (tō′.paz) *n.* gem stone, translucent and of varied colors [etym. uncertain].

tope (tōp) *v.i.* to drink hard or to excess. **-r** *n.* [Fr. *toper,* to clinch bargain].

to-pee (tō.pē′) *n.* pith helmet worn by Europeans in tropical climates. Also **topi** [Hind. *topi,* hat].

to-pi-a (tō′.pi.a) *n.* mural decoration comprising landscapes, popular in Roman houses. **topiary** *a.* cut into ornamental shapes, as trees, hedges, etc. *n.* topiary work or art; a garden or single shrub so trimmed. **topiarist** *n.* [L. *topia,* ornamental gardening].

top-ic (táp′.ik) *n.* subject of essay, discourse, or conversation; branch of general subject. **-al** *a.* pert. to a place; concerning local matters. **-ally** *adv.* [Gk. *topos,* a place].

to-pog-ra-phy (ta.pág′.ra.fi.) *n.* description of a place; scientific or physical features of region. **topographer** *n.* **topographic, -al** *a.* [Gk. *topos,* a place; *graphein,* to write].

top-ple (táp′.l) *v.t.* to throw down; to overturn; *v.i.* to overbalance [freq. of *top*].

top-sy-tur-vy (táp′.si.tur′.vi.) *adv.* upside down; *a.* turned upside down; *n.* disorder; chaos [prob. O.E. *top,* and *tearflian,* to roll].

toque (tōk) *n.* brimless woman's hat [Fr.].

To-rah (tōr′.a) *n.* the Pentateuch; (l.c.) whole scripture of Judaism [Heb. law].

torch (tawrch) *n.* piece of wood with some substance at the end soaked in inflammable liquid, and used as portable light. **-bearer** *n.* [L. *torquere,* to twist].

tore (tōr) *pa.t.* of **tear**.

tor-e-a-dor (tawr′.i.a.dawr) *n.* bull fighter [Sp. fr. L. *taurus,* a bull].

tor-ment (tawr′.ment) *n.* extreme pain of body; anguish of mind; misery; cause of anguish. **torment** *v.t.* to inflict pain upon; to torture; to vex; to tease. **tormenting** *a.* **tormentingly** *adv.* **tormentor, tormenter** *n.* [L. *tormentum,* instrument of torture].

torn (tōrn) *pa.p.* of **tear**.

tor-na-do (tawr.nā′.dō) *n.* whirling progressive windstorm causing wide-spread devastation. [Sp. *tronada,* thunderstorm].

tor-pe-do (tawr.pē′.dō) *n.* cigar-shaped underwater projectile with high explosive charge; type of explosive mine; electric ray fish which electrocutes its prey. *pl.* **-es.** *v.t.* to attack, hit, or sink with torpedoes. **-ist** *n.* expert in handling and firing torpedoes [L. *torpere,* to be numb].

tor-pid (tawr′.pid) *a.* dormant, as hibernating animal; lethargic; physically or mentally inert. **-ity** *n.* inactivity; lethargy. **-ly** *adv.* **-ness** *n.* **torpor** *n.* sluggishness; inertia. **torporific** *a.* [L. *torpere,* to be numb].

torque (tawrk) *n.* collar of gold wires twisted together, worn by ancient Britons, Gauls, etc. Also **torc** (*Mech.*) rotating power in mechanism. *-d a.* [L. *torquere,* to twist].

tor-re-fy (tawr′.a.fi) *v.t.* to scorch; to parch; to roast, as metals. **torrefaction** *n.* [L. *torrere,* to burn; *facere,* to make].

tor-rent (tawr′.ant) *n.* swift-flowing stream, downpour, as of rain; rapid flow, as of words. **-ial** *a.* pert. to, resembling torrent; overwhelming [L. *torrens,* a boiling stream].

tor-rid (tawr′.id) *a.* extremely hot, dry or burning; passionate. **-ness, torridity** *n.* **-ly** *adv.* — **zone,** broad belt lying between Tropics of Cancer and Capricorn [L. *torrere,* to burn].

tor-sion (tawr′.shan) *n.* act of turning or twisting; (*Mech.*) force with which twisted wire or similar body tends to return to original position. *a.* — **balance,** delicate scientific instrument for measuring minute forces by means of small bar suspended horizontally at end of very fine wire [L. *torquere,* to twist].

tor-so (tawr′.sō) *n.* trunk of human body; statue with head and limbs cut off [It.].

tort (tawrt) *n.* (*Law*) private injury to person or property for which damages may be claimed in court of law. **-ious** *a.* **-iously** *adv.* [L. *torquere,* to twist].

tor-til-la (tawr.tē′.(y)a) *n.* round, thin cake of corn meal [Sp. dim. of *torta,* a tart].

tor-toise (tawr′.tas) *n.* land reptile or turtle; a very low person or thing; **-shell** *n.* horny mottled brown outer shell of tortoise used commercially for combs, etc.; *a.* mottled like tortoise shell [L. *tortus,* twisted].

tor-tu-ous (tawr′.choo.as) *a.* full of twists; crooked; devious; circuitous; deceitful. **-ity** *n.* **-ly** *adv.* **-ness** *n.* [L. *tortuosus*].

tor-ture (tawr′.cher) *n.* act of deliberately inflicting extreme pain as punishment or reprisal; anguish; torment; *v.t.* to put to torture; to inflict agony. **-r** *n.* **torturing** *a.* **torturous** *a.* [L. *tortura,* twisting].

to-ry (tōr′.i.) *a.* supporter of Britain in the American Revolution; (*Brit.*) a member of the Conservative party. **-ism** *n.* [Ir. *toruighe,* a pursuer].

toss (taws) *v.t.* to throw upwards with a jerk; to cause to rise and fall; to agitate violently; *v.i.* to be tossed; to roll and tumble; to be restless; *n.* fling; sudden fall from horseback; distance anything is tossed. **-er** *n.* **-ing** *n.* **-up,** tossing of coin to decide issue; (*Colloq.*) even chance [W. *tosio,* to jerk].

tot (tát) *n.* anything small, esp. a child; [Scand. *tottr,* dwarf].

to-tal (tō.tal) *a.* full; complete; utter; absolute; *n.* the whole; sum; aggregate; *v.t.* to sum; to add; *v.i.* to amount to. **-izator,** *n.* machine which registers totals. **-ity** *n.* whole sum; entirety. **-ly** *adv.* **-ness** *n.* [L. *totus* whole].

to-tal-i-tar-i-an (tō.tal.a.tar′.i.an) *a.* relating to open-party dictorial form of government. **totalitarianism** *n.*

tote (tōt) *v.t.* (*Colloq.*) to carry; to bear; to transport.

to-tem (tō′.tam) *n.* natural object, such as animal or plant, taken by primitive tribe as emblem of hereditary relationship with that object; image of this. **-ic** *a.* **-ism** *n.* **-ist** *n.* member of tribe. **-istic** *a.* — **pole** *n.* pole with totems carved on it, one above the other [Amer.-Ind.].

totem pole

tot-ter (tát′.er) *v.i.* to walk with faltering steps; to sway; to shake; to reel. **-er** *n.* **-ing** *a.* **-ingly** *adv.* **-y** *a.* unsteady [O.E. *tealt,*

unsteady].

tou-can (tōo′.kan, too.kán′) *n.* bird of tropical Am. [Braz.].

touch (tuch) *v.t.* to come in contact with; to finger; to reach; to attain; to treat of, superficially; to move deeply; to equal in merit; to play on; (*Slang*) to borrow from; *v.i.* to be in contact; to take effect on; *n.* contact; sense of feeling; quality of response in handling of instrument or color; individual style of execution; unique quality; trace or tinge; test; mild attack. **-able** *a.* **-ableness** *n.* — **and go,** precarious situation. — **down** (*Football*) scoring by having ball behind goal line. **-ed** *a.* (*Slang*) crazy. **-er** *n.* **-ily** *adv.* **-iness** *n.* **-ing** *a.* emotionally moving; pathetic; *prep.* concerning; referring to. **-ingly** *adv.* **-ingness** *n.* **-stone** *n.* variety of compact, siliceous stone, used for testing purity of gold and silver; criterion; standard of judgment. **-y** *a.* easily offended; hypersensitive. [Fr. *toucher*].

tough (tuf) *a.* flexible but not brittle; not easily broken; firm; difficult to chew; stouthearted; vigorous; hardy; difficult to solve; (*Slang*) vicious; *n.* a bully; a ruffian. **-en** *v.t.* to make tough, or hardy; *v.i.* to become tough. **-ly** *adv.* **-ness** *n.* [O.E. *toh,* tough].

tou-pee (tōo.pā′) *n.* wig or artificial lock of hair [Fr. *toupet,* a tuft of hair].

tour (toor) *n.* journey from place to place in a country; excursion; spell of duty; *v.t.* to travel round; to visit as part of tour. **-ism** *n.* **-ist** *n.* one who makes a tour; sightseer [Fr. *tour,* a turn].

tour-ma-lin(e) (toor′.ma.lin) *n.* crystalline mineral [fr. Singh. *toramalli,* cornelian].

tour-na-ment (tur-, toor′.na.mant) *n.* mock fight, common form of contest and entertainment in medieval times; any sports competition or championship. **tourney** *n.* a tournament [O.Fr. *tournoiement,* a turning].

tour-ni-quet (toor′.ni.ket) *n.* surgical device for arresting hemorrhage by compression of a blood vessel, as a bandage tightened by twisting [Fr. fr. *tourner,* to turn].

tous-le (tou′.zal) *v.t.* to make untidy by pulling, as hair; to dishevel. *n.* untidy [conn. with *tussle*].

tout (tout) *v.i.* and *v.t.* to solicit business, etc.; to give a tip on a race horse; to praise highly *n.* one who pesters people to be customers; hanger-on at racing stables. **-er** *n.* [O.E. *totian,* to peep out].

tow (tō) *v.t.* to drag through water by rope or chain; to pull along; *n.* act of pulling; rope or chain used for towing; coarse fiber of hemp used in rope making. **-age** *n.* act of or charge for towing. **-(ing)-path** *n.* path alongside canal used by horses towing canal barge. **to take in tow,** to pull along; (*Fig.*) to take charge of [O.E. *togian,* to pull].

towpath

to-ward(s) (tōrd(z), tawrd(s)) *prep.* in direction of; near (of time); with respect to; regarding [O.E. *toweard,* future].

tow-el (tou′.al) *n.* cloth or paper for drying skin, or for domestic purposes. **-ing** *n.* soft fabric for making towels. [O.H. Ger. *twahan,* to wash].

tow-er (tou′.er) *n.* lofty, round or square structure; *v.i.* to be lofty or very high; to soar; to excel. **-ed** *a.* having towers. **-ing** *a.* lofty; violent [L. *turris,* tower].

town (toun) *n.* collection of houses etc., larger than village; inhabitants of town; *a.* pert. to town. — **clerk** *n.* official in charge of administrative side of a town's affairs. **-ship** *n.* a division of a county. **-speople** *n.* inhabitants of town [O.E. *tun,* an enclosure].

tox-i-col-o-gy (ták.sa.kál′.a.ji.) *n.* science of poisons, their effects, nature, etc. **toxemia,** *n.* bloodpoisoning. **toxemic** *a.* **toxic, -al** *a.* poisonous. **toxically** *adv.* **toxicant** *n.* poisonous; *n.* poison. **toxicological** *a.* **toxicologist** *n.* **toxin** *n.* poison usually of bacterial origin [Gk. *toxikon,* poison].

tox-o-phi-lite (ták.sáf′.a.līt) *n.* student of, or expert in, archery. **toxophilitic** *a.* [Gk. *toxon,* bow; *philos,* fond of].

toy (toi) *n.* child's plaything; bauble; trifle; *v.i.* to daily; to trifle [Dut. *tuig.* tool].

trace (trās) *n.* mark; footprint; vestige; minute quantity; remains; outline; barely perceptible sign; *v.t.* to copy or draw exactly on a superimposed sheet; to follow track or traces of; to work out step by step; *v.i.* to move. **-able** *a.* capable of being traced or detected; attributable. **-ableness** *n.* **-ably** *adv.* **-er** *n.* **tracing** *n.* traced copy of drawing. **tracing-paper** *n.* specially prepared, transparent paper for tracing design, etc. [L. *trahre,* to draw].

trace (trās) *n.* strap, rope, chain, by which

horse pulls vehicle [L. *trahere*, draw].

tra·che·a (trā′·ki·a, tra·kē′·a) *n.* windpipe between lungs and back of throat. *pl.* **tracheae, -l** *a.* **tracheotomy** *n.* (*Surg.*) operation by which opening is made in windpipe [Gk. *tracheia* (*artēria*), windpipe, and *trachēlos*, neck].

track (trak) *n.* mark left by something; footprint; pathway trodden out by usage; laid-out course for racing; (or railway) metal rails forming a permanent way; (of motor vehicles) distance between wheels on one axle; (of aircraft) actual direction along which airplane is passing over ground; wheelband of tank or tractor; (*Fig.*) evidence; trace; *v.t.* to follow trail or traces of; to make a track of footprints on; *v.i.* to follow a trail; to run in the same track (of wheels); to be in alignment. **-er** *n.* **— meet**, athletic contest in sports held on a track, racing, jumping, etc. [O.Fr. *trac*, track of horse].

tract (trakt) *n.* region of indefinite extent; continuous period of time; short treatise, esp. on practical religion. **-ability** *n.* quality or state of being tractable. **-able** *a.* docile; amenable to reason. **-ableness** *n.* **-ably** *adv.* **-ile** *a.* capable of being drawn out; (of metals) ductile. **-ility** *n.* **traction** (trak′·shan) *n.* act of drawing or pulling; gripping power, as of a wheel on a road.**tractional** *a.* **traction-engine** *n.* locomotive, steam-driven, for haulage. **-ive** *a.* having power to haul heavy loads; pulling. **-or** *n.* motor vehicle for drawing agricultural machinery [L. *trahere, tractum*, to draw].

traction-engine

trade (trād) *n.* the business of buying and selling; commerce; barter; occupation, esp. in industry, shopkeeping, etc.; employees collectively in a particular trade; vocation; *v.t.* to carry on a trade; to engage in commerce; *v.t.* to exchange. **-mark** *n.* registered name or device on maker's goods. **— name** *n.* name given by manufacturer to proprietary article. **-r** *n.* merchant (wholesale or retail); trading vessel. **— union** *n.* legally recognized association of workmen; a labor union. **— unionist** *n.* member of trade union. **— wind** *n.* one of two prevailing winds which blow steadily between the tropics and the Equator. **trading** *n.* [O.E. *tredan*, to tread].

trademark

trade wind

tra·di·tion (tra·dish′·an) *n.* belief, custom, narrative, etc. transmitted by word of mouth from age to age; religious doctrine preserved orally from generation to generation. **-al, -ary** *a.* **-alism** *n.* **-alist** *n.* **-alistic** *a.* [L. *tradere*, to hand over].

tra·duce (tra·dūs′) *v.t.* to defame the character of; to calumniate. **-r** *n.* a slanderer [L. *traducere*, to lead along].

traf·fic (traf′·ik) *n.* commerce; business dealings; illegal buying and selling, as *drug traffic*; movement of people, vehicles, etc. to and fro, in streets; coming and going of ships, trains, aircraft, etc.; people, vehicles, etc. collectively in any given area; *v.i.* to carry on trade; to do business, esp. illegally; *pr.p.* **—king.** *pa.t.* and *pa.p.* **-ked. -ker** *n.* [Fr. *trafiquer*, to traffic].

trag·e·dy (traj′·a·di·) *n.* serious and dignified dramatic composition in prose or verse with unhappy ending; sad or calamitous event. **tragedian** (tra·jēd′·i·an) *n.* actor in or writer of tragedy. **tragedienne** *n. fem.* **trag·ic, -al** *a.* pert. to tragedy; distressing; calamitous. **tragically** *adv.* **tragicalness** *n.* **tragic irony**, use in tragedy of words which convey a deeper meaning to audience than to speaker—form of *dramatic irony.* **tragi-comedy** *n.* drama combining tragedy and comedy [Gk. *tragōidia*, goat-song (reason for name variously explained)].

trail (trāl) *v.t.* to draw along ground or through water; to follow track of; (*Colloq.*) to follow behind; to carry rifle in hand at an angle, with butt close to the ground; to make a track by treading the ground; *v.i.* to dangle loosely, touching ground; to grow to great length as plant; to drag one foot wearily after other; *n.* track followed by hunter; visible trace left by anything; scent of hunted animal; something drawn behind; part of gun-carriage which rests on ground during firing. **-er** *n.* vehicle towed by another. **-less** *a.* [O.Fr. *trailer*, to tow a boat].

train (trān) *v.t.* to discipline; to instruct or educate; to submit person to arduous physical exercise, etc. for athletics; to teach animal to be obedient, to perform tricks, or compete in races; to cause plant to grow in certain way; to aim, as gun, before firing; *v.i.* to exercise body or mind to achieve high standard of efficiency; *n.* retinue; procession of people; line of cars drawn by locomotive on railway track; trailing folds of lady's evening dress; string of pack animals; sequence of events, ideas, etc.; trail of gunpowder to lead fire to explosive charge. **-ed** *a.* **-ee** *n.* one who is training. **-er** *n.* **-ing** *n.* [O.Fr. *trahiner*, to drag].

trail oil (trāl′·oil) *n.* oil extracted from blubber of whales [O.Dut. *traen*, whale oil].

traipse (trāps) *v.i.* (*Colloq.*) to walk aimlessly.

trait (trāt) *n.* distinguishing feature, esp. in character [Fr. *trait*, a feature].

trai·tor (trā′·ter) *n.* (*fem.* **traitress**) one who betrays person, country, or cause. **-ous** *a.* guilty of treachery; pert. to treason or to traitors. **-ously** *adv.* [L. *tradere,*, to hand over].

tra·jec·to·ry (tra·jek′·ta·ri·) *n.* curve of projectile in its flight through space [L. *trans*, across; *facere*, to throw].

tram·mel (tram′·al) *n.* long net for catching birds or fish; shackle for training horse to walk slowly; anything which impedes movement; *v.t.* to impede; to hinder; to confine. **-er,** *n.* [O.Fr. *tramail*, a net].

tramp (tramp) *v.t.* to tread heavily; to hike over or through; *v.i.* to go on a walking tour; to plod; to wander as vagrant; *n.* homeless vagrant; a long walk; cargo boat with no regular route. **-er** *n.* [M.E. *trampen*].

tram·ple (tram′·pl) *v.t.* to tread heavily underfoot; to oppress; to treat with contempt; *v.i.* to tread heavily; *n.* act of trampling. **-r** *n.* [freq. of *tramp*].

tram·po·line (tram′·pa·lēn) *n.* canvas springboard. **trampolinist** *n.* [It. *trampolino*, a springboard].

trance (trans) *n.* state of insensibility; a fit of complete mental absorption; (*Spiritualism*) condition in which medium is supposedly controlled by outside agency; semi-conscious condition [O.Fr. *transe*, a swoon].

tran·quil (trang′·kwil) *a.* calm; serene; undisturbed. **-ly** *adv.* **tranquillity** *n.* **-ness** [L. *tranquillus*].

trans- (tranz, trans) *pref.* meaning across, beyond, on the other side of [L. *trans*, across].

trans·act (tranz·, trans·akt′) *v.t.* to carry through; to negotiate; *v.i.* to do (business). **-or** *n.* **-ion** *n.* act of transacting business; *pl.* records of, or lectures delivered to, a society. **-ional** *a.*

trans·al·pine (tranz·, trans·al′·pīn) *a.* north of Alps (as from Rome).   [the Atlantic.

trans·at·lan·tic (tranz·, trans·at·lan′·tik) *a.* across

tran·scend (tran·send′) *v.t.* to go beyond; to excel; to surpass. **-ence, -ency** *n.* quality of being transcendent; (*Theol.*) supremacy of God above all human limitations. **-ent** *a.* supreme in excellence; surpassing all; beyond all human knowledge. **-ently** *adv.* **-entness** *n.* **-ental** *a.* abstruse; supernatural; intuitive. **-entalism** *n.* **-entalist** *n.* **-entally** *adv.* [L. *trans*, across; *scandere*, to climb].

trans·con·ti·nen·tal (trans·kan·ta·nen′·tal) *a.* crossing a continent.

tran·scribe (tran·skrīb′) *v.t.* to copy out; to write over again; to reproduce in longhand or typescript notes taken in shorthand; (*Mus.*) to rearrange composition for another instrument or voice. **-r** *n.* **transcript** *n.* that which is transcribed; written copy. **transcription** *n.* act of copying; transcript.

tran·sect (tran·sekt′) *v.t.* to cut transversely.

tran·sept (tran′·sept) *n.* transverse portion of church at right angles to nave. **-al, -ally** *adv.* [L. *septum*, enclosure].

trans·fer (trans·fur′) *v.t.* to move from one place to another; to transport; to remove; to pass an impression from one surface to another, as in lithography, photography, etc.; to convey, as property, legally to another. *pr.p.* **-ring.** *pa.t.* and *pa.p.* **-red. transfer** (trans′·fer) *n.* removal from one place to another; ticket allowing change of vehicle during single trip without further charge; design to be, or which has been transferred. **-ability** *n.* **-able** *a.* capable of being transferred; valid for use by another. **-ence** *n.* the act of transferring; in psychoanalysis, redirection of emotion, when under, analytical examination, towards someone else. **thought transference** *n.* telepathy. **-or, -rer** *n.* [L. *trans*, across; *ferre*, to bear].

trans·fig·ure (trans·fig′·yer) *v.t.* to change outward appearance of; to make more beautiful or radiant. **-ment** *n.* **transfiguration** *n.* change of appearance.

trans·fix (trans·fiks′) *v.t.* to pierce through; to impale; to astound; to stun. **-ion** *n.*

trans·form (trans·fawrm′) *v.t.* to change form, nature, character, or disposition of; to transmute; *v.i.* to be changed. **-able** *a.* **-ation** *n.* change of outward appearance or inner nature. **-ative** *a.* **-er** *n.* one who or that which transforms; an electrical device for changing voltage up or down. **-ing** *a.* [L. *transformare*, to change].

trans·fuse (trans·fūz′) *v.t.* to pour, as liquid, from one receptacle into another; (*Med.*) to transfer blood from one person to vein of another. **-r** *n.* **transfusible** *a.* **transfusive** *a.* **transfusion** *n.* [L. *trans*, across; *fundere, fusum*, to pour].

trans·gress (tranz·, trans·gres′) *v.t.* to overstep a limit; to violate law or commandment; *v.i.* to offend by violating a law; to sin. **transgression** *n.* act of violating civil or moral law; offense. **-ive** *a.* **-ively** *adv.* **-or** *n.* [L. *transgressus*, to step across].

tran·sient (tran′·shant) *a.* fleeting; ephemeral; momentary; not permanent. **transience, transiency** *n.* **-ly** *adv.* **-ness** *n.* [L. *trans*, across; *ire*, to go].

tran·sit (tran′·sit, ·zit) *n.* the act of conveying; conveyance; (*Astron.*) apparent passage of celestial body across meridian of a place, or of a smaller planet across disc of larger; a surveyor's instrument for measuring angles. **transition** *n.* passage from one place to another; change from one state or condition to another; (*Mus.*) passing directly from one key to another. **transitional, transitionary** *a.* **transitionally** *adv.* **transitive** *a.* having power of passing across; (*Gram.*) denoting verb, the action of which passes on to direct object, as *he broke his leg.* **-ively** *adv.* **-iveness** *n.* **-orily** *adv.* **-oriness** *n.* state of being transitory. **-ory** *a.* [L. *transitus*, a passing across].

trans·late (tranz·, trans·lāt′) *v.t.* to turn from one language into another; to change from one medium to another; to remove from one place to another; to appoint bishop to different see; to convey to heaven without death; *v.i.* to be capable of translation. **translatable** *a.* **translation** *n.* **translator** *n.* [L. *transferre, translatum*, to carry over].

trans·lit·er·ate (tranz·, trans·lit′·a·rāt) *v.t.* to write words of language in alphabetic symbols of another. **transliteration** *n.* **transliterator** *n.*

trans·lu·cent (tranz·, trans·lōō′·sant) *a.* semitransparent; diffusing light but not revealing definite contours of object, as *frosted* glass. **translucence, translucency** *n.* **-ly** *adv.* **translucid** *a.* translucent [L. *trans*, across; *lucere*, to shine].

trans·mi·grate (tranz·, trans·mī′·grāt) *v.i.* to pass from one country to another as permanent residence; (of soul) to pass at death into another body or state. **transmigration** *n.* **transmigrator** *n.* **transmigratory** *a.*

trans·mit (trans·mit′) *v.t.* to send from one person or place to another; to communicate;

to pass on, as by heredity. *pr.p.* **-ting.** *pa.t.* and *pa.p.* **-ted. transmissibility** *n.* **transmissible, transmittible** *a.* capable of being transmitted. **transmission** *n.* act of transmitting; in motoring, gear by which power is transmitted from engine to axle; (*Radio.*) radiation of electromagnetic waves by transmitting station. **-tal** *n.* transmission. **-tance** *n.* **-ter** *n.* one who or that which transmits; apparatus for transmitting radio waves through space [L. *trans*, across; *mittere*, to send].

trans·mute (tranz·, trans·mūt′) *v.t.* to change from one nature, species, form, or substance into another. **transmutable** *a.* **transmutableness** *n.* **transmutability** *n.* **transmutably** *adv.* **transmutant** *a.* **transmutation** *n.* act or process of transforming; alteration, esp. biological transformation of one species into another; in alchemy, supposed change of baser metals into gold. **transmutative** *a.* **-r** *n.* [L. *trans*, across; *mutare*, to change].

tran·som (tran′·sam) *n.* window over a doorway; lintel separating it from door; horizontal crossbar in window; transverse beam across sternpost of ship [L. *transtrum*, crossbeam].

trans·par·ent (trans·par′·ant) *a.* that may be distinctly seen through; pervious to light; clear; ingenuous; obvious. **transparence, transparency** *n.* **-ly** *adv.* **-ness** *n.* [L. *trans*, across; *parere*, to appear].

tran·spire (tran·spīr′) *v.t.* to emit through pores of skin; *v.i.* to exhale; (*Bot.*) to lose water by evaporation; to come out by degrees; to become known; loosely used as a synonym for *to happen.* **transpiration** *n.* **transpiratory** *a.* [L. *trans*, across; *spirare*, to breathe].

trans·plant (tranz·plant′) *v.t.* to remove and plant elsewhere; (*Surg.*) to graft live tissue from one part of body to another. **-able** *a.* **-ation** *n.* **-er** *n.*

trans·port (trans·pōrt′) *v.t.* to convey from one place to another; to banish, as criminal, to penal colony; to overwhelm emotionally. **transport** *n.* vehicles collectively used in conveyance of passengers; a troopship; passion; ecstasy. **-able** *a.* **-ability** *n.* **-er** *n.* **-ation** *n.* act or means of transporting from place to place; banishment, for felony. **-ted** *a.* [L. *trans*, across; *portare*, to carry].

trans·pose (trans·pōz′) *v.t.* to change respective place or order of two things; to alter order of words; (*Mus.*) to change key of a composition. **transposable** *a.* **transposal** *n.* change of order. **transposition** *n.* **transpositional** *a.* [L. *trans*, across; *ponere*, *positum*, to place].

tran·sub·stan·ti·ate (tran·sab·stan′·shi·āt) *v.t.* to change into another substance. **transubstantiation** *n.* doctrine held by R.C. Church that the 'whole substance' of the bread and wine in the Eucharist is, by reason of its consecration, changed into flesh and blood of Christ, the appearance only of the bread and wine remaining the same [L. *trans*, across; *substantia*, substance].

tran·sude (tran·sūd′) *v.i.* to pass through pores of substance [L. *trans*, across; *sudare*, to sweat].

trans·verse (trans·vurs′) *a.* lying in crosswise direction. **transversal** *a.* line which cuts across, two or more parallel lines. **-ly** *adv.* [L. *trans*, across; *vertere*, *versum*, to turn].

trap (trap) *n.* device, mechanical or otherwise, for catching animals, vermin, etc.; snare; U-shaped bend in pipe which, by being always full of water, prevents foul air or gas from escaping; stratagem; plot to catch person unawares; *v.t.* to catch in a trap, or by stratagem. *pr.p.* **-ping.** *pa.p.*, *pa.t.* **-ped. -door** *n.* hinged door in floor or ceiling. **-per** *n.* [O.E. *traeppe*].

trap (trap) *n.* one of several dark-colored igneous rocks. **-pean, -pose, -py** *a.* [Scand. *trappa*, stairs].

trap (trap) *pl.* (*Colloq.*) one's belongings, luggage, etc.; *v.t.* to adorn. **-ping.** *pa.p.*, *pa.t.* **-ped. -pings** *n.pl.* ornaments, gay coverings [Fr. *drap*, cloth].

tra·pe·zi·um (tra·pē′·zi·am) *n.* quadrilateral with no parallel sides; (*Anat.*) one of wrist bones *pls.* **trapezia. trapeze** *n.* apparatus comprising horizontal crossbar swing for gymnastics, acrobatic exhibitions, etc. **trapezoid** *n.* quadrilateral with only two of its sides parallel. **trapezoidal** *a.* [Gk. *trapezion*, a little table].

trash (trash) *v.t.* to lop off, as branches, leaves, etc.; *n.* worthless refuse; rubbish; loppings of trees, bruised sugar canes, etc. **-ily** *adv.* **-iness** *n.* **-y** *a.* worthless; cheap; shoddy [prob. Scand. *tros*, twigs for fuel].

trass (tras) *n.* volcanic material used in making cement [Dut. *tras*].

trau·ma (traw′·ma) *n.* (*Med.*) bodily injury caused by violence; emotional shock (psychic trauma) with a lasting effect. *pl.* **-ta. -tic** *a.* [Gk. *trauma*, a wound].

trav·ail (trav′·āl) *n.* painful, arduous labor; pains of childbirth; *v.i.* (*Arch.*) to labor with difficulty; to suffer pangs of childbirth [Fr. *travail*, labor].

trave (trāv) *n.* beam; frame in blacksmith's shop to keep horse steady [L. *trabs*, beam].

trav·el (trav′·al) *v.t.* to journey over; to pass;

v.i. to move; to journey on foot or in a vehicle; to tour, esp. abroad. *n.* act of traveling; journey; touring, esp. abroad; (*Mach.*) distance a component is permitted to move; *pl.* prolonged journey, esp. abroad; book describing traveler's experiences and observations. **-ed** *a.* **-er** *n.* **-er's check,** check issued by bank, express company, etc. which may be cashed by anyone in whose presence it is endorsed. **-ing.** *a.* **-ogue** *n.* travel lecture illustrated by slides, film, etc.; geographical film [a form of *travail*].

tra·verse (trav′·ers) *a.* lying across; built crosswise; anything set across; a partition; (*Archit.*) barrier, movable screen, or curtain; gallery across church; zigzag course of a ship; lateral movement; *v.t.* to cross; to thwart; to obstruct; to survey across a plot of ground; to rake with gun fire from end to end; to pivot laterally; to discuss, as topic, from every angle; to deny formally, in pleading at law; *v.i.* to turn, as on pivot; to move sideways. **traversable** *a.* **-r** *n.* [L. *trans*, across; *vertere*, *versum*, to turn].

trav·es·ty (trav′·is·ti·) *n.* burlesque imitation of a work; parody; *v.t.* to make a burlesque of; to caricature [Fr. *travestir*, to disguise].

trawl (trawl) *v.t.* to catch fish with a trawl; *v.i.* to drag with a trawl; *n.* a strong fishing net, shaped like a large bag with one end open. **-er** *n.* who fishes with a trawl; fishing vessel. **-ing** *n.* [O.Fr. *trauler*, to drag].

tray (trā) *n.* flat, shallow, rimmed vessel used for carrying dishes, food, etc. [O.E. *trog*, a trough].

treach·er·y (trech′·er·i·) *n.* violation of allegiance or faith; treason; perfidy. **treacherous** *a.* **treacherously** *adv.* [O.Fr. *trechier*, to deceive].

tread (tred) *v.i.* to walk; to move with stately or measured step; (of fowls) to copulate; to crush; *v.t.* to step or walk one; to crush with foot; to oppress; to operate with foot, as treadle. *pa.t.* **trod.** *pa.p.* **trod** or **trodden.** *n.* act of stepping; pace; that which one steps on, as surface of horizontal step of flight of stairs; sole of boot or shoe; part of a rubber tire in contact with ground. **-ing** *n.* **-le,** *n.* part of machine operated by foot pressure as sewing machine, etc.; pedal; *v.i.* to work treadle. **-ler** *n.* **-mill** *n.* mill worked by persons or animals treading upon steps on periphery of a wheel; drudgery [O.E. *tredan*, to tread].

treadle

trea·son (trē′·zn) *n.* disloyalty to country; act of betrayal. **-able** *a.* treason. **-ableness** *n.* **-ably** *adv.* **-ous** *a.* [O.Fr. *traison*, betrayal].

treas·ure (trezh′·er) *n.* accumulated wealth; hoard of valuables: that which has great worth; *v.t.* to hoard; to value; to cherish, as friendship. **— chest** *n.* box for storing valuables. **-r** *n.* person appointed to take charge of funds of society, church, club, etc. **-ship** *n.* **—trove** *n.* any money, bullion, treasure, etc., of unknown ownership, which one finds. **treasury** *n.* place where treasure, hoarded wealth, or public funds are deposited; storehouse of facts and information; anthology. **Treasury** *n.* government department which controls management of public revenues. **treasury note** *n.* currency note issued by the United States Treasury [Fr. *trésor*, treasure].

treat (trēt) *v.t.* to entertain with food or drink; to pay for another's entertainment or refreshment; to behave towards; to apply a remedy to; to subject, as a substance, to chemical experiment; to consider as a topic for discussion; to discourse on; *v.i.* to discourse; to come to terms of agreement, as between nations; to give entertainment; *n.* entertainment given as a celebration or expression of regard; (*Colloq.*) something that gives special pleasure; one's turn to pay for another's entertainment. **-er** *n.* **-ing** *n.* act of standing treat. **-ise** *n.* dissertation on particular theme. **-ment** *n.* act or mode of treating person, subject, artistic work, etc.; method of counteracting disease or of applying remedy for injury. **-y** *n.* a negotiated agreement between states; a pact [L. *tracture*, to handle].

tre·ble (treb′·l) *a.* threefold; triple; (*Mus.*) playing or singing highest part; *n.* highest part; *n.* highest of four principal parts in music; soprano part or voice; *v.t.* to multiply by three; *v.i.* to become three times as much.

trebly *adv.* [L. *triplus*].

tree (trē) *n.* perennial plant, having trunk, bole, or woody stem with branches; any plant resembling form of tree; (*Arch.*) cross of Christ; *v.t.* to chase up a tree; to corner. **-less** *a.* **-lessness** *n.* **-top** *n.* uppermost branches of tree. **family tree,** genealogical table of ancestry [O.E. *treow*, tree].

tre·foil (trē′·foil) *n.* plant of genus *Trifolium*, with leaves comprising three leaflets; clover; (*Archit.*) ornament of three cusps in circle resembling three-leaved clover [L. *tres*, three; *folium*, leaf].

trek (trek) *v.i.* to migrate; *pr.p.* **-king.** *pa.p.*, *pa.t.* **-ked.** *n.* journey by wagon; mass-migration. **-ker** *n.* [Dut. *trekken*, to draw].

trel·lis (trel′·is) *n.* light-weight lattice structure esp. as frame for climbing plants. **-ed** *a.* **-work** *n.* lattice work [L. *trilix*, three-ply].

trem·ble (trem′·bl) *v.i.* to shake involuntarily to quiver; to quake; *n.* involuntary shaking; quiver; tremor. **-r** *n.* **trembling** *n.* **tremblingly** *adv.* **trembly** *a.* shaky; **tremulant, tremulous** *a.* quivering; quaking; fearful. **tremulously** *adv.* **tremulousness** *n.* [L. *tremere*, to shake].

tre·men·dous (tri·men′·das) *a.* awe-inspiring; formidable; (*Colloq.*) great. **-ly** *adv.* **-ness** *n.* [L. *tremere*, to tremble].

tre·mo·lan·do (trem·a·lan′·dō) *a.* (*Mus.*) tremulous. **tremolo** *n.* quivering of singing voice; device on organ to produce similar sound. [It.].

trem·or (trem′·er) *n.* involuntary quiver; a nervous thrill; shaking, as caused by earthquake. **-less** *a.* steady [L.].

trem·u·lous See **tremble.**

trench (trench) *v.t.* to cut or dig, as a ditch; to turn over soil by digging deeply; to fortify with ditch using earth dug out for rampart; *v.i.* to encroach; *n.* ditch; deep ditch to protect soldiers from enemy fire. **-ancy** *n.* quality of being trenchant. **-ant** *a.* penetrating; keen; clear-cut. **— coat** *n.* waterproof coat. **-ing** *n.* [O.Fr. *trenchier*, to cut].

trench·er (tren′·cher) *n.* (*Arch.*) wooden plate for holding food [O.Fr. *trenchoir*, platter].

trend (trend) *v.i.* to stretch in a certain direction; *n.* inclination; tendency; general direction [O.E. *trendln*, to make round].

tre·pan (tri·pan′) *n.* heavy tool for boring shafts; (*Surg.*) obsolete cylindrical saw (improved version called **trephine** (tri·fin′) *v.t.* to cut disks out of metal plates, etc.; to operate with trepan. *pr.p.* **-ning.** *pa.t.* **-ned. -ation, -ning** *n.* [Gk. *trupanon*, borer].

trep·id (trep′·id) *a.* quaking. **-ation** *n.* involuntary trembling; alarm; fluster [L. *trepidus*].

tres·pass (tres′·pas, pas) *v.i.* to cross boundary line of another's property unlawfully; to intrude; to encroach; to violate moral law; *n.* **-er** *n.* [L. *trans*, across; *passus*, a step].

tress (tres) *n.* long lock, curl, braid or strand of hair; ringlet. **-ed** *a.* [O.Fr. *tresse*].

tres·tle (tres′·l) *n.* frame consisting of two pairs of braced legs fixed underneath horizontal bar, used as support; similar construction supporting a bridge [O.Fr. *trested*, a crossbeam].

tri- (trī) *prefix* meaning three, thrice, threefold [L. *tres*, Gk. *treis*, *tria*, three].

tri·ad (trī′·ad) *n.* union of three; (*Chem.*) trivalent atom; (*Mus.*) the common chord, one of three notes; poem with triple grouping, common in Celtic literature. **-ic** *a.* **-ist** *n.* writer of triads [Gk. *trias*, group of three].

tri·al (trī′al) *n.* act of trying, testing, or proving properties of anything; experimental examination; affliction; judicial examination in law court of accused person [*Fr. try*].

tri·an·gle (trī′·ang·gl) *n.* (*Math.*) figure bounded by three lines and containing three angles; anything shaped like a triangle; (*Mus.*) small percussion instrument consisting of a bar of steel bent in shape of triangle and struck with small steel rod. **-d** *a.* **triangular** *a.* **triangularity** *n.* **triangularly** *adv.*

tri·ar·chy (trī′·ár·ki·) *n.* government by three persons; a state so governed.

tri·a·tom·ic (trī·a·tàm′·ik) *a.* consisting of three atoms; having valency of three.

tribe (trīb) *n.* family, race, or succession of generations descending from same progenitor; nation of barbarian clans each under one leader; group of plants or animals within which members reveal common characteristics; (*Colloq.*) very large family. **tribal** *a.* **tribalism** *n.* tribal feeling; tribal life. **tribally** *adv.* **-sman** *n.* one of a tribe [L.

tribus, one of *three* divisions of Roman people].

triangle

trigger

trib·u·la·tion (trib·yạ·lā′·shạn) *n.* severe affliction; prolonged suffering, esp. of mind [L. *tribulum*, instrument for threshing corn].

trib·une (trib′·ūn) *n.* in ancient Rome, magistrate chosen by the people to defend their rights; champion of the masses; a raised platform or pulpit. **tribunal** *n.* bench on which judge or magistrates sit; court of justice. **tribunate, tribuneship** *n;* office or functions of tribune [L. *tribus*, a tribe].

tri·bute (trib′·ūt) *n.* personal testimony to achievements or qualities of another; prearranged payment made at stated times by one state to another as price of peace and protection; tax. **tributarily** *adv.* **tributary** *a.* paying tribute; subordinate; contributory; (of river) flowing into main river; *n.* one who pays tribute; stream flowing into larger river [L. *tribuere*, to assign].

trice (trīs) *n.* moment; a very short time [O.Dut. *trisen*, to hoist].

tri·ceps (trī′·seps) *a.* three-headed; *n.* three-headed muscle as at back of upper arm [L. *tres*, three; *caput*, the head].

trich·i·no·sis (trik·ạ·nō′·sis) *n.* disease due to the presence of the nematode worm **trichina** in the intestines and muscular tissue [Gk. *trichinos*, hair].

tri·cho- *pref.* fr. Gk. *thrix, trichos*, hair.

tri·chol·o·gy (tri·kȯl′·ạ·ji·) *n.* study of hair and diseases affecting it. [ing the hair.

tri·cho·sis (tri·kō′·sis) *n.* any disease affect-

tri·chot·o·mous (trī·kȧt′·ạ·mạs) *a.* divided into three or threes. **trichotomy** *n.* [Gk. *tricha*, in three; *tomē*, a cutting].

trick (trik) *n.* artifice or stratagem designed to deceive; conjurer's sleight of hand; prank for mischief, or to annoy; mannerism; dexterity; cards played out in one round, and taken by player with winning card; spell at the helm of ship; *v.t.* to deceive; to hoax; to mystify; to dress, trim, or decorate. **-er** *n.* **-ery** *n.* practice of playing tricks; fraud. **-ily** *adv.* **-iness** *n.* **-sy** *a.* tricky; ingenious; neat. **-ster,** *n.* cheat; swindler. **-y** *a.* full of tricks; crafty; requiring great dexterity; intricate [O.Fr. *tricher*, to beguile].

trick·le (trik′·l) *v.i.* to flow gently in a slow, thin stream; to move slowly, one by one; *n.* thin flow of liquid; slow movement of anything.

tri·col·or (trī′·kul·ẹr) *n.* national flag of three colors, esp. French national flag. **-ed** *a.*

tri·corn (trī′·kawrn) *a.* having three horns, or points; *n.* three-cornered hat [L. *tricornis*].

tri·cot (trē′·cot) *n.* fabric of wool; machine-made knitwear fabric. **-tine** *n.* a ribbed, fine woolen fabric, machine-made [Fr. *tricot*, knitting].

tri·cus·pid (trī·kus′·pid) *a.* having three cusps or points, as certain teeth, or a valve of the right ventricle of the heart.

tri·cy·cle (trī′·si·kl) *n.* three-wheeled cycle, esp. for children's use; *v.i.* to ride a tricycle. **tricyclist** *n.* [Gk. *treis*, three; *kuklos*, a circle].

tri·dent (trī′·dạnt) *n.* three-pronged scepter, symbol of Neptune; any three-pronged instrument, such as fish-spear. **-ate,** *a.* having three prongs [L. *tres*, three; *dens*, a tooth].

tried See try.

tri·en·ni·al (trī·en′·i·ạl) *a.* lasting for three years; happening once every three years. **-ly** *adv.* [L. *tres*, three; *annus*, a year].

tri·fle (trī′·fl) *n.* anything of little value or importance; paltry amount; pewter; *v.i.* to speak or act lightly; to be facetious; to toy, or waste time. **-r** *n.* **trifling** *a.* trivial.**trifling,** **-ly** *adv.* [O.Fr. *trufle*, mockery].

tri·form (trī′·fawrn) *a.* having a triple form. Also **-ed.** **-ity** *n.*

tri·fur·cate (trī·fẹr′·kāt) *a.* having three branches. **trifurcation** *n.* [L. *tres*, three; *furca*, a fork]. firm].

trig (trig) *a.* trim; neat; strong [O.N. *tryggr*].

trig·ger (trig′·ẹr) *n.* catch of firearm which, when pulled, releases hammer of lock [Dut. *trkken*, to pull].

tri·glyph (trī′·glif) *n.* grooved rectangular block in Doric frieze, repeated at equal intervals. **-ic, -al** *a.* [Gk. *treis*, three; *gluphein*, to carve].

trig·o·nom·e·try (trig·ạ·nam′·ạt·ri·) *n.* branch of mathematics which deals with relations between sides and angles of triangle. **trigonometer** *n.* instrument for solving plane right-angled triangles by inspection. **trigonometric, -al** *a.* **trigonometrically** *adv.* [Gk. *trigonon,* a triangle; *metron,* a measure].

tri·he·dral (trī·hē′·drạl) *a.* (*Math.*) having three sides or faces. **trihedron** *n.* [Gk. *treis,* three; *hedra,* seat].

tri·lat·er·al (trī·lat′·ẹr·ạl) *a.* having three sides; arranged by three parties, as *trilateral pact.* **-ly** *adv.*

tri·lin·e·ar (trī·lin′·ē·ẹr) *a.* consisting of three lines [L. *tres,* three; *linea,* a line].

tri·lin·gual (trī·ling′·gwạl) *a.* expressed in three languages; speaking three languages.

trill (tril) *v.t.* and *v.i.* to sing or play (instrument) with vibratory quality; to pronounce, as letter 'r'; *n.* shake or vibration of voice, in singing; consonant, such as 'r' pronounced with trill [It. *trillare,* to shake].

tril·lion (tril′·yạn) *n.* million million million (British) i.e. 1 with 18 ciphers; a million million (U.S.) i.e. 1 with 12 ciphers.

tril·o·gy (tril′·ạ·ji·) *n.* group of three plays, novels, etc. with common theme, or common central character [Gk. *treis,* three; *logos,* a speech or discourse].

trim (trim) *a.* (*compar.*) **-mer.** (*superl.*) neat; in good order; to dress; to decorate, as hat; to clip shorter; to supply with oil and adjust wick, as lamp; (*Naut.*) to arrange sails according to wind direction; *v.i.* to balance; to fluctuate between two parties, so as to appear to favor each. *pr.p.* **-ming.** *pa.t.* and *pa.p.* **-med.** *n.* dress; decoration; order; anything trimmed off; **-ly** *adv.* **-mer** *n.* one who trims; instrument for clipping; **-ming** *n.* that which trims, edges, or decorates; a beating; **-ness** *n.* neatness; compactness; readiness for use [O.E. *trymian,* to strengthen].

trim·e·ter (trim′·ạ·tẹr) *n.* verse containing three measures; *a.* **trimetric, -al** *a.*

tri·nal (trī′·nạl) *a.* threefold; of three, as *trinal unity,* three in one. **trinary** *a.* consisting of three parts; ternary. **trine** *a.* threefold; *n.* group of three; aspect of two planets distant from each other 120°, or one-third of the zodiac [L. *trinus*]...

tri·ni·tro·tol·u·ene (trī·nī·trō·tȧl′·yoo·ēn) *n.* (*abbrev.* **T.N.T.**) high explosive.

Trin·i·ty (trin′·ạ·ti·) *n.* union of one Godhead of Father, Son, and Holy Ghost; (*l.c.*) any combination of three people or things as one. **Trinitarian** *a.* pert. to doctrine of the Trinity; *n.* one who believes in this doctrine. **Trinitarianism** *n.* [L. *trinitas,* three].

trin·ket (tring′·kit) *n.* small ornament worn as ring, brooch, etc.; ornament of little value. **-ry** *n.* [prob. fr. M.E. *trenket,* small knife].

tri·no·mi·al (trī·nō′·mi·ạl) *a.* (*Bot. Zool.*) having three names as of *order, species* and *subspecies;* (*Math.*) consisting of three terms connected by sign + or −; *n.* a trinomial quantity [L. *tres,* three; *omen,* a name].

tri·o (trē′·ō) *n.* group of three persons or things; (*Mus.*) composition arranged for three voices, or instruments. [It. fr. L. *tres,* three].

tri·ode (trī′·ōd) *n.* (*Radio*) three-electrode thermionic valve [Gk. *treis,* three; *hodos,* a way].

tri·o·let (trī′·ō·lit) *n.* a short poem of eight lines with rhyme pattern abaaabab [Fr. *triolet,* a little trio].

tri·ox·ide (trī·ȧk′·sīd) *n.* (*Chem.*) compound comprising three atoms of oxygen with some other element [*tri-,* and *oxide*].

trip (trip) *v.t.* to cause to stumble; to frustrate; to loose, as ship's anchor; to start up, as machine, by releasing clutch; *v.i.* to walk or dance lightly; to stumble over an obstacle; to make a false step; (with *up*) to detect an error in another's statement. *pr.p.* **-ping.** *pa.p.* **-ped.** *n.* quick, light step; a journey; false step; indiscretion in speech or conduct. **-per** *n.* one who trips; device to start a mechanism. **-ping** *a.* light-footed. **-pingly** *adv.* [M.E. *trippen,* to tread on].

tri·par·tite (trī·pär′·tīt) *a.* divided into three parts; having three corresponding parts; arranged or agreed to, by three parties or nations, as *tripartite pact.* **tripartition** *n.*

tripe (trīp) *n.* large stomach of ruminating animal, prepared for food; (*Slang*) rubbish.

triph·thong (trif′·thawng) *n.* a syllable containing three vowels together as in *beauty* [Gk. *treis,* three; *phthongos,* a sound].

tri·ple (trip′·l) *a.* consisting of three united; three times repeated; *v.t.* to make three times as much or as many; *v.i.* to become trebled. **-crown** *n.* papal tira. **triplet** *n.* three of a kind; three consecutive verses rhyming together; (*Mus.*) three notes played in the time of two; one of three children born at a birth. **triplex** *a.* threefold; *n.* (*Mus.*) triple time. **triplicate** *a.* threefold; made three times as much; *n.* third copy corresponding exactly to two others; *v.t.* to treble; to make three copies of. **triplication** *n.* [L. *triplex,* threefold].

tri·pod (trī′·pȧd) *n.* stool, vessel, etc. on three-legged support; three-legged, folding stand for for a camera, etc.; *a.* having three legs. **tri·tripodal, tripodic** *a.* [Gk. *treis,* three; *pous,* a foot].

trip·o·li (trip′·ạ·li·) *n.* mineral substance used for polishing metals, stones, etc.; originally brought from *Tripoli.*

trip·tych (trip′·tik) *n.* writing tablet in three parts; altarpiece or picture in three panels, [Gk. *treis,* three; *plux, pluchos,* a fold].

tri·sect (trī·sekt′) *v.t.* to divide into three equal parts, as a line or angle. **-ion** *n.*

triste (trēst) *a.* sad; melancholy [Fr.].

tri·sul·fide (trī·sul′·fid) *n.* (*Chem.*) chemical compound containing three sulfur atoms.

tri·syl·la·ble (trī·sil′·ạ·bl) *n.* word of three syllables. **trisyllabic, -al** *a.* **trisyllabically** *adv.* [Gk. *treis,* three; *sullabē,* syllable].

trite (trīt) *a.* made stale by use; hackneyed; banal. **-ly** *adv.* **-ness** *n.* [L.*tritus,* rubbed away].

Tri·ton (trī′·tạn) *n.* (*Gk. Myth.*) god of the sea. **triton** *n.* (*Zool.*) marine mollusk with spiral shell.

trit·u·rate (trich′·ạ·rāt) *v.t.* to rub or grind to a very fine powder. **triturable** *a.* **trituration** *n.* [L. *triturare,* to pulverize].

tri·umph (trī′·ạmf) *n.* victory; conquest; rejoicing; great achievement; *v.i.* to celebrate victory with great pomp and ceremony; to achieve success; to prevail; to exult. **-al** *a.* pert. to triumph; expressing joy for success. **-antly** *adv.* [L. *triumphus,* a solemn procession].

tri·um·vir (trī·um′·vẹr) *n.* one of three men sharing governing power in ancient Rome. *pl.* **-i, -s. -al** *a.* **-ate** *n.* coalition of three men in office or authority [L. *tres,* three; *vir,* a man].

tri·une (trī′·ūn) *a.* three in one. **triunity** *n.* [L. *tres,* three; *unus,* one].

tri·va·lent (trī′·vā·lạnt) *a.* (*Chem.*) having valency of three; capable of combining with or replacing three atoms of hydrogen. **trivalence** *n.*

triv·et (triv′·it) *n.* three-legged stool or support; iron tripod for standing a pot or kettle over fire; short-legged metal rack to put under a hot platter, etc. [L. *tres,* three; *pes,* foot].

triv·i·al (triv′·i·ạl) *a.* paltry; of little consequence. **-ism** *n.* **triviality** *n.pl.* trifles; insignificant matters. **-ly** *adv.* **-ness** *n.* [L. *trivialis,* pert. to crossroads, hence commonplace].

tro·che (trō′·kē) *n.* medicinal lozenge [Gk. *trochos,* pill].

tro·chee (trō′·kē) *n.* in English prosody, metrical foot of two syllables, first one accented, as *ho′·ly.* **trochaic** *n.* trochaic foot or verse. **trochaic, -al** *a.* [Gk. *trochaios,* running].

trod, trodden *pa.t., pa.p.* of **tread.**

trog·lo·dyte (trȧg′·lạ·dīt) *n.* cave dweller; a hermit. [Gk. *troglē,* a cave; *duein,* to enter].

troi·ka (troi′·kạ) *n.* Russian carriage or sledge drawn by three horses abreast; triunal.

Tro·jan (trō′·jạn) *a.* pert. to ancient Troy; *n.* inhabitant of Troy.

troll (trōl) *n.* (*Scand. Myth.*) a giant; mischievous hump-backed cave-dwelling dwarf.

troll (trōl) *v.t.* and *v.i.* to roll; to sing in a rich, rolling voice; to sing in succession the parts of a round; to fish with baited line trailing behind boat; *n.* a round or catch; act of trolling. **-er** *n.*

trol·ley (trȧl′·i·) *n.* form of truck, body of which can be tilted over; device to connect electric streetcar with wires. — **bus,** passenger bus not operating on rails but drawing powers from overhead wires. — **car** *n.* electric streetcar.

trol·lop (trȧl′·ạp) *n.* a slattern; a prostitute; **-y** *a.* slovenly; tawdry [prob. fr. *troll*].

trom·bone (trȧm′·bōn) *n.* deep-toned brass musical instrument. **trombonist** *n.* [It. *tromba,* a trumpet].

troop (trŏŏp) *n.* large assembly of people; body of cavalry; *pl.* soldiers collectively; an army; *v.i.* to flock; to gather in a crowd. **-er** *n.* mounted policeman; state policeman; horse cavalryman. **-ship** *n.* vessel for transporting soldiers [Fr. *troupe*].

trope (trōp) *n.* word or phrase used metaphorically. **tropical** a. figurative. **tropically** adv. **tropist** n. one who uses figurative language. **tropological, -al** a. containing figures of speech. **tropology** n. figurative language; study of such language; a metaphorical interpretation of the Bible [Gk. *tropos*, a turn].

troph·ic, -al (tráf'.ik, -al) a. pert. to nutrition. **trophi** n.pl. masticating organs of insect. **trophology** n. the scientific study of nutrition [Gk. *trophē*, feeding].

tro·phy (trō'.fi.) n. orig. pile of arms taken from vanquished enemy; memorial of victory; memento; mural decoration, as stag's antlers; prize, esp. for sports, etc. [Gk. *tropaion*].

trop·ic (tráp'.ik) n. one of the two circles of celestial sphere, situated 23½° N. (*Tropic of Cancer*) and 23½° S. (*Tropic of Capricorn*) of equator, and marking the point reached by the sun at its greatest declination north and south; one of the two corresponding parallels of latitude on terrestrial globe. pl. region (*torrid zone*) between tropics of Cancer and Capricorn. **tropic, -al** a. pert. to or within tropics; (of climate) very hot. **-ally** adv. [Gk. *tropos*, a turn].

trop·o·sphere (trpōp'.a.sfir) n. lower layer of atmosphere below stratosphere [Gk. *tropos*, a turn; *sphaira*, sphere].

trop·po (tráp'.ō) adv. (*Mus.*) too much. **non troppo**, moderately [It.].

trot (trát) v.i. (of horse) to move at sharp pace; (of person) to move along fast; v.t. to cause to trot. **-ting**, pa.p., pa.t. **-ted**. n. brisk pace of horse; quick walk. **-ter** n. one who trots; horse which trots; foot of an animal [O.Fr. *troter*].

troth (trawth, tráth, trōth) n. (*Arch.*) truth; fidelity. **to plight one's troth**, to become engaged to be married [O.E. *treowth*, truth].

trou·ba·dour (tróo'.ba.dōr) n. one of school of Provençal poets between 11th and 13th cents., whose poems were devoted to lyrical and amatory subjects [Prov. *trobador*, poet].

trou·ble (trub'.l) v.t. to stir up; to vex; to distress; to bother; v.i. to take pains; to feel anxiety; n. disturbance; agitation of mind; unrest; ailment; inconvenience. **-r** n. **-some** a. difficult; vexatious; irksome. **-somely** adv. **-someness** n. **—shooter** n., expert in discovering and eliminating trouble [L. *turbulare*, to disturb].

trough (trawf) n. long, open vessel for water or fodder for animals; channel; depression, as between waves; part of cyclone where atmospheric pressure is lowest [O.E. *trog*, hollow vessel of wood].

trounce (trouns) v.t. to punish or beat severely; (*Colloq.*) to defeat completely [Fr. *tronce*, a stump].

troupe (tróop) n. company or troop, esp. of actors, acrobats, etc. **-r** n. member of a theatrical troupe [Fr.].

trou·sers (trou'.zerz) n.pl. a man's two-legged outer garment extending from waist to ankles; slacks. **trousered** a. wearing trousers. **trouserless** a. [O.Fr. *trousses*, breeches].

trous·seau (tróo'.sō) n. bride's outfit of clothes, etc. pl. **trousseaux** or **trousseaus** [Fr.]

trout (trout) n. fish resembling salmon [O.E. *truht*, trout].

trow·el (trou'.al) n. mason's tool for spreading and dressing mortar; garden tool for scooping out earth, plants, etc.; v.t. to smooth or lift with trowel [L. *trulla*, a small ladle].

troy weight (troi'.wāt) n. system of weight for precious metals and gems [fr. *Troyes*, in France].

tru·ant (tróo'.ant) n. one who shirks his duty; pupil who absents himself from school; a. wandering from duty; idle; v.i. to play truant. **truancy** n. [O.Fr. *truant*, vagrant].

truce (tróos) n. temporary cessation of hostilities; armistice; lull [O.E. *treow*, faith].

truck (truk) v.t. to exchange; to barter; v.i. to deal with by exchange; n. exchange of commodities; (*Colloq.*) dealings; (*Colloq.*) rubbish; junk; (*U.S.*) garden produce. **-er** n. **— farm** n. a small farm on which vegetables are grown for market [Fr. *troquer*, to truck].

truck (truk) n. horsedrawn or automotive vehicle for hauling, small wooden wheel; porter's barrow for heavy luggage. **-age** n. transport by trucks; cost of such transport. **-le** n. small wheel or castor; truckle bed; v.i. to fawn on. **— bed** n. low bed on castors which may be pushed beneath another [Gk. *trochos*, a wheel].

truc·u·lent (truk'.ya.lant) a. fierce; aggressive; ruthless. **truculence, truculency** n. **-ly** adv. [L. *trux*, fierce].

trudge (truj) v.t. to go on foot; to plod along;

n. wearisome walk.

trudg·en (truj'.an) n. fast racing stroke in swimming. [fr. J. *Trudgen*, English swimmer].

true (tróo) a. conformable with fact; genuine; exact; loyal; trustworthy; v.t. to adjust accurately, as machine; to straighten; adv. truly conforming to type (of plants, etc.). **—blue** a. unchanging; stanch; true. **-ness** n. **truism** n. self-evident truth. **truly** adv. [O.E. *treowe*, true].

truf·fle (truf'.l) n. tuber-shaped edible underground fungus with unique flavor [prob. L. *tuber*, a swelling, truffle].

tru·ism See **true**.

trull (trul) n. a trollop [var. of *troll*].

trump (trump) n. (*Arch.*) trumpet; its sound. **-et** n. wind instrument of brass, consisting of long tube bent twice on itself, ending in wide bell-shaped mouth, and having finger stops; powerful reed stop of pipe organ with full trumpet-like sound; call of the elephant; v.t. to proclaim by trumpet; to bellow; (*Fig.*) to praise loudly; v.i. to play on trumpet; (of elephant) to utter characteristic cry through trunk. **-eter** n. one who plays on trumpet; kind of domestic pigeon; long-necked S. American bird, resembling crane; wild swan of N. America. **-eting** n. [Fr. *trompe*].

trump (trump) n. one of the suit of cards, declared by cutting, dealing, or bidding which takes any card of another suit; (*Colloq.*) excellent fellow; v.t. and v.i. to play trump card; to take a trick with trump. [Fr. *triomphe*, triumph, game of cards].

trump (trump) v.t. to fabricate; to deceive. **-ery** n. anything showy but of little value; rubbish [Fr. *tromper*, to deceive].

trun·cate (trung'.kāt) v.t. to cut off; to lop; to maim. **truncate, -d, truncation** a. appearing as if cut off at tip; blunt [L. *truncare*].

trun·dle (trun'.dl) n. anything round or capable of being rolled; a small wheel or caster; act of rolling; v.t. to roll on little wheels; to roll, as child's hoop, barrel, etc. v.i. to roll. **— bed** n. a truckle bed [O.E. *trendel*, a wheel].

trunk (trungk) n. stem of tree, as distinct from branches and roots; body minus head and limbs; torso; shaft of column; main part of anything; main lines of railway, bus, or telephone system; large box of metal, hide, etc., with hinged lid, for storage or as luggage; proboscis of elephant; pl. short, tight-fitting pants, esp. for swimming.

truss (trus) n. bundle; as hay or straw; tuft of flowers on top of a long stem; framework of beams or girders constructed to bear heavy loads; (*Med.*) appliance to keep hernia in place; (*Naut.*) iron clamp fixing lower yards to masts; v.t. to bind or pack close; to support, as a roof, or bridge span, with truss; to skewer, as fowl, before cooking [Fr. *trousse*].

trust (trust) n. confidence; reliance; implicit faith; moral responsibility; property used for benefit of another; combine of business firms in which shareholders turn over stock to board of trustees; v.t. to rely upon; to have implicit faith in; to give credit; to entrust; to hope; to believe; v.i. to be confident or to confide in; a. held in trust. **-ee** n. person or group which manages the business affairs of another; **-eeship** n. **-er** n. **-ful** a. **-fully** adv. **-fulness** n. **-ily** adv. **-iness** n. quality of being trusty. **-ing** a. confiding. **-ingly** adv. **-worthiness** n. **-worthy** a. **-y** a. reliable; n. reliable prisoner given special privileges [O.N. *traust*, confidence].

truth (tróoth) n. honesty; conformity to fact or reality; veracity; constancy; true statement; undisputed fact. **-ful** a. **-fully** adv. **-fulness** n. **-less** a. [O.E. *treowth*, true].

try (trī) v.t. to test; to attempt; (*Law*) to examine judicially; to purify or refine, as metals; v.i. to endeavor; to make effort. pa.t. and pa.p. **tried**. n. trial; effort; (*Colloq.*) attempt. **tried** a. **trier** n. [O.Fr. *trier*, to pick out].

tryst (trist) n. appointment to meet; place appointed for meeting. **-er** n. [var. of *trust*].

Tsar (tsär) n. same as *Czar*.

tset·se (tset'.sē) n. African fly, its bite causing sleeping sickness [S. Afr.].

T square (tē·skwer) n. ruler with crossbar at one end for drawing parallel lines.

tub (tub) n. vessel to bathe in; open, wooden vessel formed of staves, heading and hoops, as

used for washing clothes, etc.; small cask; (*Colloq.*) slow, cumbersome boat. **-by** a. shaped like a tub; (of persons) squat and portly. [M.E. *tubbe*, a tub].

T square

tu·ba (tū'.ba) n. (*Mus.*) largest brass instrument of orchestra; organ stop. pl. **-s, tubae** [L. *tuba*, trumpet].

tube (tūb) n. long hollow cylinder for conveyance of liquids, gas, etc.; pipe; siphon; abbrev. for tube-railway where rails are laid through immense steel tubes; (*Anat.*) cylindrical-shaped organ; small container with screw cap; stem of plant; inner rubber tire of bicycle or automobile wheel; **tubing** n. **tubular** a. **tubulate, -d, tubulous, tubulose** a. **tubule** n. a small tube [L. *tubus*, a tube].

tub·er (tū'.ber) n. fleshy, rounded underground stem or root, containing buds for new plant; (*Med.*) a swelling. **-ous, -ose** a. [L. *tuber*, a swelling].

tu·ber·cle (tū'.ber.kl) n. small swelling; nodule; (*Med.*) morbid growth, esp. on lung causing *tuberculosis*. a. having tubercles. **tubercular, tuberculate, -d, tuberculose, tuberculous** a. pert. to tubercles; nodular; affected with tuberculosis. **tuberculin** n. liquid extract from tubercle bacillus used as injection in testing for, or in treatment of, tuberculosis. **tuberculosis** n. (*Colloq. abbrev.* **T.B.**) consumption; phthisis, disease caused by infection with the tubercle bacillus. **tuberculum** n. tubercle [L. *tuberculum*, a small tuber].

tuck (tuk) v.t. to make fold(s) in cloth before stitching down; to roll up, as sleeves; to make compact; to enclose snugly in bed clothes; n. flat fold in garment to shorten it, or as ornament; **-er** n. tucked linen or lace front worn by women; v.t. (*slang*) to exhaust [M.E. *tukken*, to pull].

Tu·dor (tū'.der) a. pert. to period of Tudors (1485-1603) or to style of architecture in that period.

Tues·day (tūz'.di.) n. third day of week [O.E. *Tiwesdaeg*, day of *Tiw*, god of war].

tuft (tuft) n. cluster; bunch of something soft, as hair, feathers, threads, etc.; v.t. to adorn with, arrange in tufts. **-ed, -y** a.

tug (tug) v.t. to pull with effort; to haul along; v.i. to pull with great effort; to comb, as hair, with difficulty. pr.p. **-ging**. pa.t. and pa.p. **-ged**. n. strong pull; tussle; tugboat. **-boat** n. a small but powerful boat used for towing larger vessel. **tug of war** n. sports contest, in which two teams pull at either end of rope, until losing team is drawn over center line [O.N. *toga*, to pull].

tu·i·tion (tū.ish'.an) n. the price for instruction; teaching. **-al, -ary** a. [L. *tueri*, to watch].

tu·lip (tū'.lap) n. bulbous plant popular in Holland [Turk. *tulbend*, turban].

tulle (tóol) n. fine silk net used for dresses, hats, etc. [fr. *Tulle*, France].

tum·ble (tum'.bl) v.i. to fall heavily; to trip over; to toss from side to side; to turn head over heels; to perform acrobatic tricks; to slump, as prices; v.t. to overturn; to rumple, as bedclothes; to toss about, as contents of drawer; n. act of tumbling; fall; confusion. **—down** a. ramshackle; derelict. **-er** n. one who tumbles; acrobat; kind of pigeon; glass drinking vessel; spring catch of a lock. **tumbling** n. act of falling or turning somersault [O.E. *tumbian*, to dance].

tum·brel, tumbril (tum'.bral) n. cart used for carrying dung; low open cart in which victims of French Revolutionists were conveyed to guillotine [Fr. *tomber*, to fall].

tu·me·fy (tū'.ma.fi) v.t. to cause to swell; v.i. to swell; to develop into a tumor. **tumefaction** n. a swelling; a tumor [L. *tumere*, to swell; *facere*, to make].

tu·mid (tū'.mid) a. swollen; turgid; pompous. **tumescence** n. **tumescent** a. **-ness, tumidity** n. **-ly** adv. [L. *tumere*].

tu·mor (tū'.mer) n. (*Med.*) morbid overgrowth of tissue, sometimes accompanied by swelling. **-ous** a. Also **tumour** [L. *tumere*, to swell].

tu·mult (tū'.mult) n. commotion as of a crowd; violent uproar; mental disturbance. **-uary, -uous** a. confused; uproarious; disturbing. **-uously** *adv.* **-uousness** *n.* [L. *tumultus,* uproar].

tu·mu·lus (tū′·mya·ləs) *n.* artificial burial mound, erected by primitive peoples; barrow. *pl.* **-es, tumuli. tumulous** *a.* [L. fr. *tumere,* to swell].

tun (tun) *n.* large cask; measure of liquid, as for wine, usually equivalent to 252 gallons; *v.t.* to store in casks [O.E. *tunne,* a cask].

tu·na (tōō′·na) *n.* large oceanic food and game fish. [Sp.].

tun·dra (tun′·dra) *n.* one of vast treeless plains of Arctic Circle [Russ. *tundra,* a marsh].

tune (tūn) *n.* melody; rhythmical arrangement of notes and chords in particular key; quality of being in pitch; mood; unison; *v.t.* to adjust to proper pitch; to harmonize; to adapt or make efficient, esp. part of machine; (*Radio*) to adjust circuit to give resonance at desired frequency. **tunable** *a.* **tunableness** *n.* **tunably** *adv.* **-ful** *a.* melodious; harmonious. **-fully** *adv.* **-fulness** *n.* **-less** *a.* without melody; discordant; silent. **-r** *n.* **tuning fork** *n.* steel two-pronged instrument giving specified note when struck. **in tune** (*Fig.*) mentally and emotionally adjusted, as to one's company or environment. **out of tune,** at variance with. **to tune in** (*Radio*) to adjust radio set to desired wavelength [O.Fr. *ton,* a tone].

tung·sten (tung′·stan) *n.* hard grey metallic element used in alloys, special forms of steel, and for filaments in electric lamps [Scand. *tung,* heavy; *sten,* a stone].

tu·nic (tū′·nik) *n.* short-sleeved knee-length garment worn by women and boys in ancient Greece and Rome; short-sleeved eccles. vestment; blouselike outer garment extending to hips [L. *tunica,* undergarment of both sexes].

tun·nel (tun′·al) *n.* subterranean passage; burrow of an animal; *v.t.* and *v.i.* to cut tunnel through; to excavate. **-er** *n.* [O.Fr. *tonne,* tun or cask].

tun·ny (tun′·i·) *n.* edible fish of mackerel family; tuna fish [Gk. *thunnos*].

tur·ban (tur′·ban) *n.* Oriental male headdress comprising long strip of cloth swathed round head or cap; close-fitting cap or scarf headdress worn by women. **-ed** *a.* **-like** *a.* [Turk. *tulbend*].

tur·bid (tur′·bid) *a.* having dregs disturbed; muddy; thick; dense. **-ly** *adv.* **-ness, -ity** *n.* [L. *turbidus,* fr. *turbare,* to disturb].

tur·bine (tur′·bin or ·bīn) *n.* rotary engine driven by steam, hot air, or water striking on curved vanes of wheel, or drum; high speed prime mover used for generating electrical energy. **turbinal, turbinate** *a.* coiled like a spiral. **turbojet** *n.* jet propelled gas turbine. **turboprop,** jet engine in which turbine is coupled to propeller [L. *turbo,* whirl].

tur·bot (tur′·bət) *n.* large flat sea fish [L. *turbo,* a top].

tur·bu·lent (tur′·bya·lənt) *a.* disturbed; in violent commotion; refractory. **-ly** *adv.* **turbulence, turbulency** *n.* [L. *turbare,* to disturb].

tu·reen (tōō·rēn′ or tyoo·rēn′) *n.* large, deep dish with removable cover, for serving soup [Fr. *terrine,* an earthen vessel].

turf (turf) *n.* surface soil containing matted roots, grass, etc.; sod; peat; a race-course. *v.t.* to cover with turf, as lawn. **-like** *a.* **the turf,** track over which horse races are run. **-man** *n.* one interested in horse racing. **-y** *a.* covered with turf [O.E. *turf,* turf].

turgent (tur′·jənt) *a.* (*obs.*) swelling; puffing up like a tumor; pompous; bombastic. **-ly** *adv.* **turgescence, turgescency** *n.* swelling caused by congestion; empty bombast. **turgid** *a.* swollen; distended abnormally; bombastic. **turgidity, turgidness** *n.* **-ly** *adv.* [L. *turgere,* to swell].

Turk (turk) *n.* native of *Turkey*; Ottoman; a fierce person; a Mohammedan. **-ish** *a.* pert. to Turks or Turkey. **-ish bath,** steam or hot air bath after which person is rubbed down, massaged, etc. **-ish towel,** an absorbent towel.

tur·key (tur′·ki·) *n.* large bird, bred for food; guinea fowl. **— trot** *n.* an eccentric ragtime dance [fr. *Turkey*].

tur·mer·ic (tur′·mer·ik) *n.* E. Indian plant; powder prepared from it used as a condiment, dye, medicine [L. *terra merita,* deserving earth].

tur·moil (tur′·moil) *n.* commotion; tumult.

turn (turn) *v.t.* to move round; to cause to revolve; to deflect; to form on lathe; to change direction of; to convert; to upset or nauseate; to blunt; *v.i.* to rotate; to move as on a hinge; to depend; to become giddy, nauseated, or upset; (of tides) to change from ebb to flow or the reverse; to become sour, as milk; *n.* act of turning; change of bend; an action, as *good turn;* action done in rotation with others; short walk; a subtle quality of expression, as *turn of phrase;* crisis. **-about** *n.* merry-go-round; reversal of position, opinion. **-coat** *n.* renegade; one who betrays party or other principles. **-ing** *n.* act of turning; deflection; winding; juncing and two roads or streets; process of shaping and rounding articles with lathe. **-ing point** *n.* decisive moment; crisis. **-key** *n.* one in charge of prison keys; warder. **—out** *n.* act of coming forth; production, as of fac-

tory; number of people at any gathering. **-over** *n.* total sales made by a business in certain period; rate at which employees of factory are replaced by others; tart of pastry folded over a filling of jam, or fruit. **-pike** *n.* **-pike road,** main highway with tollgate. **-spit** *n.* one who turns a spit. **-stile** *n.* revolving gate for controlling admission of people. **-table** *n.* revolving circular platform for turning locomotives on to another line or in opposite direction; revolving disk of a phonograph. **— about** alternately. **to turn down,** to decline, as offer; to reject, as application. **to turn in,** to bend inwards; to hand in; to go to bed [O.E. *tyrnan,* to turn].

turnstile

tur·nip (tur′·nip) *n.* plant of mustard family.

tur·pen·tine (tur′·pən·tīn) *n.* oily liquid extracted by distillation of resin exuded by pine and other coniferous trees [Gk. *terebinthos*].

tur·pi·tude (tur′·pa·tūd) *n.* revolting baseness; lewdness; infamy [L. *turpis,* baese].

tur·quoise (tur′·kwoiz, ·koiz) *n.* bluish-green gem stone [Turkish (stone)].

tur·ret (tur′·it) *n.* small tower on building; revolving gun tower on ship, tank, or aircraft. **-ed** *a.* having turrets [O.Fr. *tourete,* a little tower].

tur·tle (tur′·tl) *n.* marine tortoise with hard shell and limbs like paddles.

tur·tle·dove (tur′·tl·duv) kind of pigeon, noted for its soft cooing and its affection for its mate [L. *turtur,* a dove].

Tus·can (tus′·kən) *a.* pert. to Tuscany in Italy; (*Archit.*) denoting the simplest of the five classical styles in architecture.

tusk (tusk) *n.* the long, protruding side tooth of certain animals such as elephant, wild boar, walrus. **-ed** *a.* **-er** *n.* animal with fully developed tusks. **-y** *a.* **-less** *a.* **-like** *a.* [O.E. *tusc,* tooth].

tus·sle (tus′·l) *n.,* *v.t.* struggle; scuffle.

tus·sock (tus′·ak) *n.* (*Poet.*) clump, tuft, or hillock of growing grass [etym. doubtful].

tut (tut) *interj.* exclamation of irritation.

tu·te·lage (tū′·ta·lij) *n.* guardianship; instruction state or period of being under this. **tutelar, tutelary** *a.* having protection over a person or place; protective [L. *tutela*].

tu·tor (tū′·ter) *n.* (*Law*) one in charge of minor; private teacher; (*Brit.*) university lecturer who directs and supervises studies of undergraduates; *v.t.* to teach; to prepare another for special examination by private coaching; to have guardianship of. **-ial** *a.* pert. to tutor. **-ially** *adv.* **-ing** *n.* **-ship** *n.* [L. *tutor,* a guardian].

tut·ti-frut·ti (tōō′·ti·frōō′·ti) *n.* preserve of fruits; ice cream sundae with fruit, nuts, etc.; ice cream made with mixed fruits [It. = all fruits].

tu·tu (tōō′·tōō) *n.* ballet dancer's skirt [Fr.].

tux·e·do (tuk·sē′·dō) *n.* semiformal dinner jacket [fr. *Tuxedo Park,* country club near New York].

twad·dle (twåd′·l) *n.* inane conversation; non-sensical writing; *v.i.* to talk inanely. **-r** *n.* **twaddling** *n.* twaddle. **twaddly** *a.* silly.

twain (twān) *a., n.* (*Arch.*) two [O.E. *twegin*].

twang (twang) *n.* sharp, rather harsh sound made by tense string sharply plucked; nasalized speech; *v.t.* to pluck tense string of instrument; *v.i.* to speak with a twang [limit.].

tweak (twēk) *v.t.* to twist and pull with sudden jerk; *n.* sharp pinch or jerk [var. of *twitch*].

'twas (twoz) *contr.* of *it was.*

tweed (twēd) *n.* heavy woolen fabric esp. for costumes, coats, suits; *a.* of tweed [fr. mistaken reading of *'tweel'*].

'tween (twēn) *contr.* of *between.* **'tween deck,** between upper and lower decks.

tweez·ers (twē′·zerz) *n. sing.* small pair of pincers, esp. for pulling superfluous hairs.

twelve (twelv)*a.* one more than eleven; two and ten; dozen; *n.* sum of ten and two; symbol representing twelve units, as 12, xii. **twelfth** *a.* next after eleventh; constituting one of twelve equal parts; *n.* one of twelve equal parts. **Twelfth Day,** January 6th, twelfth day after Christmas; Feast of Epiphany. **twelfthly** *adv.* **Twelfth Night,** evening of, or before, Twelfth Day, when special festivities were held. **the Twelve,** twelve Apostles [O.E. *twelf,* twelve].

twen·ty (twen′·ti·) *a.* twice ten; nineteen and one; *n.* number next after nineteen; score; symbol representing twenty units, as 20, xx. **twentieth** *a.* next after nineteenth; *n.* one of twenty equal parts. **-fold** *adv.* twenty times as many [O.E. *twentig*].

'twere (twur) *cont.* of *it were.*

twice (twis) *adv.* two times; doubly [O.E. *twa,* two].

twid·dle (twid′·l) *v.t.* to play with; to twirl idly; *v.i.* to spin round; to trifle with. **-r** *n.* **to twiddle one's thumbs,** to have nothing to do [etym. doubtful].

twig (twig) *n.* small shoot or branch of tree. **-gy** *a.* covered with twigs [O.E. *twig,* branch].

twi·light (twī′·lit) *n.* half-light preceding sunrise or, esp., immediately after sunset; faint, indeterminate light; *a.* pert. to or like twilight. **— sleep,** in obstetrics, modern method of inducing state of partial insensibility in woman in childbirth by use of drug, scopolamine-morphine [lit, 'between-light'; O.E. *twa,* two; *leoht,* light].

twill (twil) *n.* fabric woven with diagonal ribbing; *v.t.* to weave with twill [O.E. *twilic,* two-threaded].

twin (twin) *n.* one of two born at birth; exact counterpart; *a.* being one of two born at birth; consisting of two identical parts; growing in pairs. **-ned** *a.* **— beds** *n.pl.* two single beds of identical size. **—born** *a.* born at the same birth. **— brother, sister** *n.* **—screw** *a.* of a vessel having two propellers on separate shafts [O.E. *twinn,* double].

twine (twin) *n.* cord composed of two or more strangs twisted together; spring; tangle; *v.t.* to twist together; to entwine; to encircle; *v.i.* to wind; to coil spirally, as tendrils of plant; to follow circuitous route. **twining** *a.* winding; coiling [O.E. twin, double-thread].

twinge (twinj) *n.* sudden, acute spasm of pain; pang; *v.t.* (*Dial*) to tweak; to effect momentarily with sudden pain [O.E. *twengan,* to pinch].

twin·kle (twing′·kl) *v.i.* to sparkle; (of eyes) to light up; of feet to move quickly and neatly; *n.* act of twinkling; gleam of amusement in eyes; flicker; quick movement of feet, esp. in dancing;. sparkle. *n.* **twinkling** *n.* twinkle; an instant [O.E. *twinclian,* to sparkle].

twirl (turl) *v.t.* to whirl around; to flourish; to twiddle; *v.i.* to turn round rapidly; *n.* a rapid, rotary motion; a flourish; curl; convolution **-er** *n.* one who or that which twirls; (*Colloq.*) baseball pitcher. [O.E. *thwiri,* a whisk for beating milk].

twist (twist) *v.t.* to contort; to coil spirally; to wind; to encircle; to distort; to form, as cord, from several fibers wound together; *v.i.* to become tangled or distorted; to wriggle; to be united by winding around each other; to coil; to follow a roundabout course; *n.* turning movement; curve; bend; act of entwining; a turn in meaning; a heavy silk thread; small roll of tobacco; **-ed** *a.* **-er** *n.* one who, or that which, twists; swindler. **-ability** *n.* **-able** *a.* **-ingly** *adv.* [O.E. *twist,* rope].

twit (twit) *v.t.* to taunt; to reproach; to tease. *pr.p.* **-ting.** *pa.t.* and *pa.p.* **-ted.** *n.* taunt [O.E. *twiccian*, to pluck].

twitch (twich) *v.t.* to pull suddenly with ~ slight jerk; to snatch; *v.i.* to be suddenly jerked; to contract with sudden spasm, as a muscle; to quiver; *n.* sudden spasmodic contraction of fiber or muscle. **-ing** *n.* [O.E. *twiccian*, to pluck].

twitch-grass (twich'.gras) *n.* prolific weed, couch grass or quitch grass.

twit-ter (twit'.er) *n.* chirping sound; slight trembling of nerves; half-suppressed laugh; *v.i.* to make succession of small light sounds; to chirp; to talk rapidly and nervously; to titter. **-ing** *n.* **-y** *a.* [imit.].

'twixt (twikst) *prep.* contr. of **between.**

Two (tōō) *a.* one and one; *n.* sum of one and one; symbol representing two units, as 2, ii; a pair. **—edged** *a.* having two sharp edges, as a sword; (*Fig.*) ambiguous. **—faced** *a.* having two faces; hypocritical; double-dealing. **-fold** *a.* double; doubly. **—handed** *a.* requiring two hands or two players; ambidextrous. **-penny** (tup'.an.i.) (*Brit.*) *a.* costing two pennies (*Colloq.*) worthless; *n.* kind of ale. **—ply** *a.* having two strands twisted together, two layers, etc. **—seater** *n.* small automobile designed for two people only. **—sided** *a.* having two surfaces or aspects; (of cloth) reversible; (*Fig.*) double-dealing.

ty·coon (tī.kóón') *n.* former title of a Japanese official; head of great business combine; a magnate [Jap. *taikun*, great prince].

tyke (tīk) *n.* a cur; boor; (*Colloq.*) small child [Sc. *tik*, bitch].

tym·pa·num (tim'.pa.nam) *n.* a drum (*Anat.*) cavity of the middle ear; ear drum; (*Archit.*) flat, triangular space between sides of pediment; similar space over door between lintel and arch. *pl.* **-s, tympana. tympanal, tympanic** *a.* like a drum; pert. to middle ear. **tympanist** *n.* one who plays drum or any percussion instrument [Gk. *tumpanon*, a kettle-drum].

type (tīp) *n.* model; pattern; class or group; person or thing representative of group or of certain quality; stamp on either side of a coin; (*Chem.*) compound which has basic composition of other more complex compounds; (*Biol.*) individual specimen representative of species; (*Print.*) metal block on one end of which is raised letter, etc.; such blocks collectively; similar block in typewriter; style or form of printing; *v.t.* to typify; to represent in type; to reproduce by means of typewriter; to classify; *v.i.* to use a typewriter. **typal** *a.* **— cutter** *n.* one who engraves blocks for printing types. **— founder** *n.* one who casts type for printing. **— metal** *n.* alloy of lead, antimony,and tin used for casting type. **-script** *n.* a typewritten document. **-setting** *n.* process or occupation of preparing type for printing. **-writer** *n.* machine with keyboard operated by fingers, which produces printed characters on paper; **typist -writing** *n.* **-written** *a.* **typical** (tip'.a.kal) *a.* pert. to type; symbolic; true bolize; to exemplify. **typing** *n.* act of typing; script typed. **typist** *n.* one who operates typewriter. **typographer** *n.* printer. **typographic, -al** *a.* pert. to printing. **typography** *n.* art of printing; style or mode of printing [Gk. *tupos*, mark of a bowl].

ty·phoid (tī'.foid) *a.* resembling typhus; pert. to typhoid fever; **— fever** *n.* infectious disease characterized by severe diarrhea, profound weakness, and rash. **-al** *a.* [Gk. *tuphos*, fever; *eidos*, form].

ty·phoon (tī.fóón') *n.* cyclonic hurricane oc-

typewriter

curring in China seas. **typhonic** *a.* [Ar. *tufan*].

ty·phus (tī'.fas) *n.* highly contagious disease caused by virus conveyed by body lice and characterized by purplish rash, prostration, and abnormally high temperature. **typhous** *a.* [Gk. *tuphos*, fever].

ty·rant (tī'.rant) *n.* in ancient Greece, usurper; harsh, despotic ruler; any person enforcing his will on others, cruelly and arbitrarily. **tyrannic, -al, tyrannous** (tir'.an.as) *a.* **tyrannically** *adv.* **tyrannously** *adv.* **tyrannicalness** *n.* **tyrannize** *v.i.* to rule tyrannically; to exert authority ruthlessly; *v.t.* to subject to tyrannical authority. **tyrannizer** *n.* **tyrannizingly** *adv.* **tyranny** (tir'.a.nē) *n.* despotic government; cruelly harsh enforcement of authority [Gk. *turannos*, an unconstitutional ruler].

ty·ro (tī'.rō) *n.* beginner; novice. Also **tiro** [L. *tiro*, recruit].

Tzar, Tzarina Same as **Czar, Czarina.**

U

u·biq·ui·ty (ū.bik'.wa.ti.) *n.* existing in all places at same time; omnipresence. **ubiquitous, ubiquitary** *a.* existing or being everywhere. **ubiquitously** *adv.* **ubiquitousness** *n.* omnipresence [L. *ubique*, everywhere].

U-boat (ū'.bōt) *n.* German submarine [Ger. *untersee*, under the sea, and *boat*].

ud·der (ud'.er) *n.* milk gland of certain animals, as cow [O.E. *uder*, udder].

u·dom·e·ter (ū.dàm'.a.ter) *n.* instrument for measuring rainfall. **udometry** *n.* **udometric** *a.* [L.*udus*, moist; *metron*, measure].

ug·ly (ug'.li.) *a.* offensive to the sight; of disagreeable aspect; dangerous, of situation. **uglify** *v.t.* to make ugly. **uglification** *n.* **ugliness** *n.* **uglily** *adv.* [O.N. *uggr*, fear].

u·kase (ū'.kās) *n.* official Russian decree [Russ. *ukaz*, edict].

U·krain·i·an (ū.krā'.ni.an) *n.* citizen of Ukraine in S.W. Russia; Slavic language related to Russian. *a.* pert. to Ukraine.

u·ku·le·le (ū.ka.lā'.li.) *n.* small four-stringed instrument like guitar [Hawaiian].

ul·cer (ul'.ser) *n.* superficial sore discharging pus; (*Fig.*) source of corruption. **-ate** *v.i.* to become ulcerous. **-ated, -ative, -ation** *n.* **-ed** *a.* having ulcers. **-ous** *a.* having ulcers; like an ulcer. **-ously** *adv.* **-ousness** *n.* [L. *ulcus*].

ul·lage (ul'.ij) *n.* amount which cask lacks of being full; loss of wine, grain, etc. by leakage [O.Fr. *eullage*, the filling up of a cask].

ul·na (ul'.na) *n.* the larger of two bones of forearm. *pl.* **-s, ulnae. -r** *a.* [L. *ulna*, elbow].

ul·ster (ul'.ster) *n.* long loose overcoat originally made in *Ulster*, Ireland. **-ed** *a.*

ul·te·ri·or (ul.tir'.i.er) *a.* situated on the farther side; beyond; (of motives) undisclosed; not frankly stated. **-ly** *adv.* [L. *ulterior*, farther].

ul·ti·mate (ul'.ta.mit) *a.* farthest; final; primary; conclusive. **-ly** *adv.* **-ness** *n.* **ultimatum** (ul.ta.mā'.tam) *n.* final proposition; final terms offered as basis of treaty. *pl.* **ultimatums,** or **ultimata. ultima** *n.* last syllable of a word. **ultimo** *a.* in the month preceding current one (*abbrev.* **ult.**) [L. *ultimus*, last].

ul·tra (ul'.tra) *a.* beyond; extreme; in combination words with or without hyphen, as **ultra modern** [L. *ultra*, beyond].

ul·tra·ma·rine (ul.tra.ma.rēn') *a.* situated beyond the sea; *n.* bright blue pigment obtained from powdered lapis lazuli, or produced synthetically [L. *ultra*, beyond; *mare*, the sea.

ul·tra·mon·tane (ul.tra.màn'.tān) *a.* being beyond the mountains, esp. the Alps; used of Italians by those on northern side of Alps, and vice versa; pert. to absolute temporal and spiritual power of Papacy or to party upholding this claim; *n.* advocate of extreme or ultra-papal views. **ultramontanism** *n.* **ultramontanist** *n.*

ul·tra·vi·o·let (ul.tra.vī'.a.lit) *a.* beyond limit of visibility at violet end of the spectrum.

ul·u·lant (ūl'.ya.lant) *a.* howling. **ululate** *v.i.* to howl; to lament. **ululation** *n.* [L.].

um·bel (um'.bal) *n.* (*Bot.*) flower clusters, the stalks of which rise from a common center on main stem, forming a convexed surface above, as in carrot, parsley, etc. **-lar, -late, -d** *a.* having umbels. **-liferous** *a.* bearing umbels. **-liform** *a.* having shape of umbel [L. *umbella*, little shade].

um·ber (um'.ber) *n.* natural earth pigment, yellowish-brown in color when raw, reddish-brown when calcined or burnt [fr. *Umbria*, in Italy].

um·bil·i·cal (um.bil'.i.kal) *a.* pert. to umbilicus or umbilical cord. **— cord** (*Anat.*) fibrous cord joining fetus to placenta. **umbilicus,** the navel **umbiliform** *a.* [L. *umbilicus*].

um·bra (um'.bra) *n.* shadow; (*Astron.*) complete shadow cast by earth or moon in eclipse, as opposed to *penumbra*, partial shadow in eclipse. **-l** *a.* [L. *umbra*, shadow].

um·brage (um'.brij) *n.* (*Poetic*) shadow; feeling of resentment. **umbrageous** *a.*

shady. **umbrageously** *adv.* **to take umbrage,** to feel resentful [L. *umbra*, shadow].

um·brel·la (um.brel'.a) *n.* light-weight circular covering of silk or other material on folding framework of spokes, carried as protection against rain (or sun). **-less** *a.* **-like** *a.* **— stand** *n.* stand for holding umbrellas [It. *ombrella*, dim. of *ombra*, shade].

um·laut (óom'.lout) *n.* term used to denote mutation, e.g., caused by influence of vowel *i* (earlier *j*) on preceeding vowel such as a, o, u; in Modern German this vowel mutation is indicated by diaeresis over vowel, as in Führer (Fuehrer); in English it is seen in plural forms of man (*men*), mouse (*mice*), foot (*feet*). Also called **imutation** [Ger. *um*, about; *laut*, sound].

um·pire (um'.pīr) *n.* person chosen to arbitrate in dispute; impartial person chosen to see that rules of game are properly enforced; referee; *v.t.* and *v.i.* to act as umpire [orig. *numpire*, fr. O.Fr. *nomper*, peerless].

un- *prefix* before nouns, adjectives, and adverbs adding negative force; before verbs, expressing reversal of the action, separation, etc.

un·a·bashed *a.* (abash)
un·a·bat·ed *a.* (abate)
un·a·ble *a.* (able)
un·a·bridged *a.* (abridge)
un·ac·cent·ed *a.* (accent)
un·ac·cept·a·ble *a.* (accept)
un·ac·com·mo·dat·ing *a.* (accommodate)
un·ac·com·pa·nied (un.a.kum'.pa.nēd) *a.* not accompanied; sung or played on instrument without piano, organ, or orchestral accompaniment.
un·ac·count·a·ble *a.* (account)
un·ac·cus·tomed *a.* (accustom)
un·ac·quaint·ed *a.* (acquaint)
un·a·dorned *a.* (adorn)
un·a·dul·ter·at·ed *a.* (adulterate)
un·ad·vised *a.* (advise)
un·af·fect·ed (un.a.fek'.tid) *a.* not affected unmoved; straightforward; sincere. **-ly** *adv.* simply; void of affection.
un·a·fraid *a.* (afraid)
un·aid·ed *a.* (aid)
un·al·loyed *a.* (alloy)
un·al·ter·a·ble (un.awl'.ter.a.bl) *a.* not capable of alteration; fixed; permanent. **-ness** **unalterability** *n.* **unalterably** *adv.* **unaltered** *a.* unchanged.
un·am·bi·tious *a.* (ambition)
u·nan·i·mous (vóo.nan'.a.mas) *a.* all of one

mind; agreed to by all parties. **unanimity** (ū'·na·nim·a·ti) *n.* **-ly** *adv.* **-ness** *n.* [L. *unus*, one; *animus*, mind].

un·an·nealed *a.* (anneal)

un·an·nounced *a.* (announce)

un·an·swer·a·ble *a.* **unanswerability, -ness** *n.* (answer)

un·ap·pre·ci·at·ed *a.* **unappreciative** *a.* (appreciate)

un·ap·proach·a·ble *a.* **-ness** *n.* **unapproachably** *adv.* (approach)

un·arm (un·ärm') *v.t.* to disarm; to render harmless; *v.i.* to lay down arms. **-ed** *a.* defenseless. **-ored** *a.* without weapons; (of ships, etc.) not protected by armor plating.

un·a·shamed *a.* (ashamed)

un·asked *a.* (ask)

un·as·sail·a·ble (un·a·sāl'·a·bl) *a.* not assailable; irrefutable; invincible. **unassailed** *a.*

un·as·sim·i·la·ted *a.* **unassimilable** *a.* **unassimilating** *a.* (assimilate)

un·as·sist·ed *a.* (assist)

un·as·sum·ing (un·a·sòòm'·ing) *a.* not assuming; modest; not overbearing.

un·at·tached (un·a·tacht') *a.* not attached; dangling; not posted to a particular regiment; not married or engaged.

un·at·tain·a·ble *a.* **unattainably** *adv.* (attain)

un·at·tend·ed *a.* **unattending** *a.* **unattentive** *a.* (attend)

un·at·test·ed *a.* (attest)

un·at·trac·tive (un·a·trak'·tiv) *a.* not attractive; repellent; plain; not prepossessing. **-ly** *adv.* **-ness** *n.*

un·au·thor·ized *a.* **unauthoritative** *a.* (authorize)

un·a·vail·ing (un·a·vāl'·ing) *a.* not availing; fruitless; having no result. **unavailability** *n.* **unavailable** *a.* not procurable; not at one's disposal. **-ly** *adv.* fruitlessly.

un·a·void·a·ble *a.* **-ness**, **unavoidability** *n.* **unavoidably** *adv.* **unavoided** *a.* (avoid)

un·a·ware (un·a·wār') *a.* having no knowledge of; *adv.* unawares. **-s** *adv.* unexpectedly; without previous warning.

un·baked *a.* (bake)

un·bal·ance (un·bal'·ans) *v.t.* to upset. **-d** *a.* not balanced; lacking equipoise, or mental stability; not adjusted or equal on credit and debit sides (of ledger). **unbalance** *n.*

un·bar *v.t. and i.* (bar)

un·bear·a·ble (un·ber'·a·bl) *a.* not bearable; intolerable; (of pain) excruciating. **-ness** *n.* **unbearably** *adv.*

un·beat·en *a.* (beat)

un·be·com·ing (un·bi·kum'·ing) *a.* not becoming; not suited to the wearer; (of behavior) immodest; indecorous. **-ly** *adv.*

un·be·fit·ting *a.* (befit)

un·be·known (un·bi·nōn') *a.* not known. **-st** *adv.* without the knowledge of.

un·be·lief *n.* **unbelievability** *n.* **unbelievable** *a.* **unbelieving** *a.* **unbelievingly** *adv.* (believe)

un·belt *v.t.* (belt)

un·bend (un·bend') *v.t.* to free from bend position; to straighten; to relax; to loose, as anchor; *v.i.* to become relaxed; to become more friendly. *pa.t., pa.p.* **bent** *or* **-ed. ing** *a.* not pliable; rigid; (*Fig.*) coldly aloof; resolute. **-ingly** *adv.* **unbent** *a.* straight.

un·bi·ased *v.t.* (bias)

un·bid·den *a.* (bid)

un·bind *v.t.* (bind)

un·bit·ten *a.* (bite)

un·blamed *a.* (blame)

un·bleached *a.* (bleach)

un·blem·ished (un·blem'·isht) *a.* not blemished; faultless; (of character) pure; perfect. **unblemishable** *a.*

un·blessed *or* **unblest** *a.* (Bless)

un·blink·ing *a.* (blink)

un·blush·ing·ly *adv.* (blush)

un·bod·ied (un·bàd'·id) *a.* free from the body; incorporeal.

un·bolt *v.t.* **-ed** *a.* (bolt)

un·bolt·ed (un·bōl'·tid) *a.* (of grain) unsifted; not fastened with a bolt. **unbolt** *v.t.*

un·born (un·bawrn') *a.* not yet born; future, as *unborn generations.*

un·bos·om (un·booz'·am) *v.t.* to disclose freely; to reveal one's intimate longings.

un·bound (un·bound') *a.* not bound; free; without outer binding, as a book; *pa.p., pa.t.* of **unbind. -ed** *a.* illimitable; abundant; irrepressible. **-edly** *adv.*

un·bowed *a.* (bow)

un·break·a·ble *a.* (break)

---

un·bri·dle (un·brī'·dl) *v.t.* to remove the bridle from, as a horse. **-d** *a.* unrestrained; violently passionate.

un·bro·ken (un·brō'·kn) *a.* complete; whole; (of horse) untamed; inviolate; continuous. **-ly** *adv.* **-ness** *n.*

un·buck·le *v.* **-d** *a.* (buckle)

un·bur·den (un·bur'·dn) *v.t.* to relieve of a burden; (*Fig.*) to relieve the mind of anxiety. **-ed** *a.* **-ing** *n.a.*

un·bur·ied *a.* (bury)

un·burned *a.* (burn)

un·busi·ness·like *a.* (business)

un·but·ton *v.t.* (button)

un·cage *v.t.* (cage)

un·cal·cu·la·ted *v.t.* (calculate)

un·called (un·kawld') *a.* not summoned. **uncalled for,** unnecessary or without cause.

un·can·ny (un·kan'·i.) *a.* weird; unearthly. **uncannily** *adv.* **uncanniness** *n.*

un·caused *a.* (cause)

un·ceas·ing *a.* **-ly** *adv.* (cease)

un·cer·e·mo·ni·ous (un·ser·a·mō'·ni·as) *a.* not ceremonious; informal; abrupt. **-ly** *adv.* **-ness** *n.*

un·cer·tain (un·sur'·t(i)n) *a.* not certain; not positively known; unreliable; insecure. **-ly** *adv.* **-ness** *n.* **-ty** *n.* state of being or that which is uncertain; lack of assurance.

un·chain *v.t.* (chain)

un·change·a·ble *a.* **unchangeability, -ness** *n.* **unchangeably** *adv.* **unchanged** *a.* **unchanging** *a.* **unchangingly** *adv.* (change)

un·char·i·ta·ble *a.* **-ness** *n.* **uncharitably** *adv.* (charity)

un·chart·ed (un·chär'·tid) *a.* not shown on a map; unexplored.

un·checked *a.* (check)

un·chris·tian *a.* **-ly** *adv.* (christian)

un·church (un·church') *v.t.* to excommunicate; to deprive of name and status of a church.

un·ci·al (un'·shal) *a.* pert. to a type of rounded script, found in ancient MSS from 4th-9th cents.; *n.* uncial letter or manuscript. **-ly** *adv.* [L. *uncia*, inch; (*lit.*) letters, an inch high].

un·ci·form (un'·si·fawrm) *a.* shaped like a hook. **uncinal, uncinate** *a.* hooked; having hook-like prickles. [L. *uncus*, a hook].

un·cir·cum·cised (un·sur'·kam·sīzd) *a.* not circumcised; Gentile. **uncircumcision** *n.*

un·civ·il *a.* **-ity, ness** *n.* **-ized** *a.* **-ly** *adv.* (civil, civilize)

un·claimed *a.* (claim)

un·clasped *a.* (clasp)

un·clear *a.* **-ed** *a.* (clear)

un·cloud·ed *a.* (cloud)

un·cle (ung'·kl) *n.* brother of one's father or mother; any elderly man; (*Slang*) pawnbroker. [L. *avunculus*, mother's brother].

un·clean (un·klēn') *a.* not clean; filthy; ceremonially unsanctified; obscene. **uncleanliness** *n.* (un·klen'·li·nas). **-ly** (un·klēn'·li·, or un·klen·li··) *a. adv.* **-ness** *n.*

un·clench *v.t.* (clench)

un·clothe *v.t.* **-d** *a.* (clothe)

un·cock (un·kàk') *v.t.* to let down hammer of gun without exploding charge.

un·coil *v.t.* (coil)

un·come·ly (un·kum'·li·) *a.* not comely; unprepossessing; ugly; obscene.

un·com·fort·a·ble *a.* **-ness** *n.* **uncomfortably** *adv.* **uncomforted** *a.* (comfort)

un·com·mer·cial *a.* (commerce)

un·com·mit·ted *a.* (commit)

un·com·mon *a.* **-ly** *adv.* **-ness** *n.* (common)

un·com·mu·ni·ca·tive (un·ka·mū'·na·kā'·tiv) *a.* not communicative; discreet; taciturn. **-ly** *adv.* **-ness** *n.* **uncommunicable** *a.* not capable of being shared or communicated. **uncommunicableness** *n.* **uncommunicated** *a.*

un·com·plain·ing (un·kam·plān'·ing) *a.* not complaining; resigned. **-ly** *adv.* without complaint.

un·com·plet·ed *a.* (complete)

un·com·pli·men·ta·ry *a.* (compliment)

un·com·pro·mis·ing (un·kàm·pra·mī'·zing) *a.* not compromising; making no concession; rigid. **-ly** *adv.*

un·con·cealed *a.* (conceal)

un·con·cern (un·kan·surn') *n.* lack of concern; apathy. **-ed** *a.* not concerned; disinterested; apathetic; not involved. **-edly** *adv.* **-edness** *n.*

un·con·di·tioned (un·kan·dish'·and) *a.* not

---

subject to conditions; absolute; instinctive. **unconditional** *a.* complete; absolute; without reservation. **unconditionally** *adv.* **— reflexes,** the instinctive responses of an animal to external stimuli.

un·con·firmed *a.* (confirm)

un·con·gen·i·al *a.* (congenial)

un·con·nect·ed *a.* (connect)

un·con·quer·a·ble *a.* **unconquerably** *adv.* (conquer)

un·con·scion·a·ble (un·kàn'·shan·a·bl) *a.* beyond reason; unscrupulous; excessive. **-ness** *n.* **unconscionably** *adv.*

un·con·scious (un·kàn'·shas) *a.* not conscious; unaware; deprived of consciousness; involuntary. **-ly** *adv.* **-ness** *n.* state of being insensible. **the unconscious,** in psychoanalysis, part of mind which appears to act without a conscious effort of will.

un·con·sti·tu·tion·al (un·kàn·sti·tū'·shan·al) *a.* not constitutional; contrary to the constitution, as of a society or state. **constitutionality** *n.* **-ly** *adv.*

un·con·strained *a.* **-ly** *adv.* **unconstraint** *n.* (constrain)

un·con·trol·la·ble (un·kan·trōl'·a·bl) *a.* not capable of being controlled; unmanageable; irrepressible. **-ness** *n.* **uncontrollably** *adv.* **uncontrolled** *a.* not controlled; (of prices) not restricted by government regulations. **uncontrolledly** *adv.*

un·con·ven·tion·al (un·kan·ven'·shan·al) *a.* **-ity** *n.* **-ly** *adv.* not conforming to convention, rule or precedent.

un·con·ver·sant *a.* (converse *v.*)

un·con·vert·ed (un·kan·vur'·tid) *a.* not converted; unchanged in heart; heathen; not changed in opinion. **unconversion** *n.* **unconvertible** *a.* not convertible.

un·con·vinced *a.* **unconvincing** *a.* (convince)

un·cooked *a.* (cook)

un·cork *v.t.* (cork)

un·cor·rupt·ed *a.* (corrupt)

un·count·ed *a.* not counted; innumerable.

un·cou·ple (un·kup'·l) *v.t.* to loose, as a dog from a leash; to disjoin, as railway carriages. **-d** *a.* not mated; not joined.

un·couth (un·kòòth') *a.* awkward in manner; strange; unpolished; unseemly. **-ly** *adv.* **-ness** *n.* [O.E. *cuth,* known].

un·cov·e·nant·ed (un·kuv'·a·nan·tid) *a.* not agreed to by covenant.

un·cov·er *v.t.* (cover)

un·crowned *a.* (crown)

unc·tion (ungk'·shan) *n.* act of anointing with oil, as in ceremony of consecration or coronation; (*Med.*) ointment; act of applying ointment; that which soothes; insincere fervor. **unctuosity** *n.* **unctuous** *a.* oily; excessively suave. **unctuously** *adv.* **unctuousness** *n.* **extreme unction,** R.C. rite of anointing the dying [L. *unguere, unctum,* to anoint].

un·cul·ti·va·ble (un·kul'·ti·va·bl) *a.* not capable of being cultivated; waste. **uncultivated** *a.* not cultivated; not tilled; (*Fig.*) undeveloped. **uncultured** *a.* not cultured; not educated; crude.

un·cured *a.* (cure)

un·cut *a.* (cut)

un·damped (un·dampt') *a.* not damped; dry; (*Fig.*) not downhearted or dispirited.

un·dat·ed *a.* (date)

un·daunt·ed *a.* **-ly** *adv.* (daunt)

un·de·ceive (un·di·sēv') *v.t.* to free from deception. **-d** *a.*

un·de·cid·ed (un·di·sī'·did) *a.* not settled; irresolute; vacillating. **undecidable** *a.* not capable of being settled. **-ly** *adv.*

un·de·ci·pher·a·ble *a.* (decipher)

un·de·clared (un·di·klàrd') *a.* not declared; (of taxable goods at customs) not admitted as being in one's possession during customs' examination.

un·de·fend·ed *a.* (defend)

un·de·filed *a.* (defile *v.*)

un·de·fined *a.* **undefinable** *a.* (define)

un·dem·o·crat·ic (un·dem·a·krat'·ik) *a.* not according to the principles of democracy. **undemocratize** *v.t.* to make undemocratic.

un·de·mon·stra·tive *a.* **-ly** *adv.* **-ness** *n.* (demonstrate)

un·de·ni·a·ble *a.* **undeniably** *adv.* (deny)

un·de·nom·i·na·tion·al *a.* (denomination)

un·de·pend·a·ble *a.* **(depend)**
un·der (un'·dẹr) *prep.* below; beneath; subjected to; less than; liable to; included in; in the care of; during the period of; bound by; *adv.* in a lower degree or position; less; *a.* subordinate; lower in rank or degree. **under age,** younger than 21 years [O.E. *under*].
un·der·act (un·dẹr·akt') *v.t.* or *v.i.* to act a part in a play in a colorless, ineffective way.
un·der·arm (un'·dẹr·ärm) *a.n.* under the arm; armpit; *adv.* from below .the shoulder (as a throw); *v.t.* to arm insufficiently. **-ed** *a.*
un·der·bid (un·dẹr·bid') *v.t.* to bid lower than another for a contract, etc.; to make lower bid at bridge than one's cards justify. *pr.p.* **-ding.** *pa.p., pa.t.* **underbid. -der** *n.*
un·der·bred (un·dẹr·bred') *a.* of inferior manners; not thoroughbred.
un·der·brush (un'·dẹr·brush) *n.* undergrowth of shrubs and bushes.

un·der·car·riage (un'·dẹr·kar·ij) *n.* (*Aero.*) landing gear of aircraft.
un·der·charge (un·dẹr·chärj.) *v.t.* to charge less than true price; *n.* price below the real value.
un·der·clothes (un'·dẹr·klō(TH)z) *n.pl.* garments worn below the outer clothing, esp. next the skin; underclothing; lingerie. **underclothed** *a.* **underclothing** *n.*
un·der·cov·er (un'·dẹr·kuv'·ẹr) *a.* (*Colloq.*) secret; used esp. of secret service agents.
un·der·cur·rent (un'·dẹr·kur·ant) *n.* current under surface of main stream, sometimes flowing in a contrary direction; hidden tendency.
un·der·cut (un·dẹr·kut') *v.t.* to cut away from below, as coal seam; to strike from beneath; to sell goods cheaply in order to capture a market or monopoly; (*Golf*) to hit ball so it backspins. *pr.p.* **-ting.** *pa.p., pa.t.* **undercut.** (un'·dẹr·cut) *n.* act of cutting away from below; (*Boxing*) punch from underneath.
un·der·de·vel·op (un·dẹr·di·vel'·ạp) *v.t.* (*Photog.*) to develop insufficiently so that the photographic print is indistinct. **-ed** *a.* not developed physically; (of film) not sufficiently developed.
un·der·dog (un'·dẹr·dawg) *n.* (*Colloq.*) dog which is beaten in fight; person who fares badly in any struggle.
an·der·dose (un·dẹr·dōs') *v.t.* to give an insufficient dose (of medicine) to; (un'·dẹr·dōs) *n.* an insufficient dose.
un·der·es·ti·mate (un·dẹr·es'·tạ·māt) *v.t.* to miscalculate the value of; to rate at too low a figure; *n.* an inadequate valuation.
un·der·ex·posed (un·dẹr·iks·pōzd') *a.* (*Photog.*) insufficiently exposed to the light to impress details on a sensitive surface with clarity of outline. **underexposure** *n.*
un·der·feed (un·dẹr·fēd') *v.t.* to feed insufficiently; to undernourish. **underfed** *a.*
un·der·foot (un·dẹr·foot') *adv.* beneath the feet; *a.* lying under the foot; in subjection.

un·der·gar·ment (un'·dẹr·gär·mant) *n.* a garment worn underneath the outer clothes.
un·der·go (un·dẹr·gō') *v.t.* to bear; to suffer; to sustain; to participate in. *pr.p.* **-ing.** *pa.t.* **underwent.** *pa.p.* **undergone.**
un·der·grad·u·ate (un·dẹr·graj'·ŏŏ·it) *n.* student attending classes for his first degree at a university or college; *a.* pert. to such student or university course.
un·der·ground (un'·dẹr·ground) *a.* under the ground; subterranean; secret; *n.* (*chiefly Brit.*) a subway; (*Fig.*) secret organization or resistance movement; *adv.* below surface of earth; secretly.

underground

un·der·growth (un'·dẹr·grōth) *n.* small trees, shrubs, or plants growing beside taller trees.
un·der·hand (un'·dẹr·hand) *adv.* by secret means; fraudulently; *a.* (*Sports*) served or thrown, as a ball, with hand underneath and an upward swing of the arm from below the waist; sly and dishonorable. **-ed** *a.* **-edly** *adv.* **-edness** *n.*
un·der·hung (un·dẹr·hung') *a.* projecting beyond upper jaw, as lower jaw.
un·der·lay (un·dẹr·lā') *v.t.* to lay underneath; to support by something put below; *n.* something placed under another thing; piece of paper, cardboard, etc. used by printers to raise type plate; floor covering laid underneath a carpet. *pa.p., pa.t.* **underlaid.**
un·der·lie (un·dẹr·lī') *v.t.* to lie underneath; to be the basis of. *pr.p.* **underlying.** *pa.p.* **underlain** or **underlaid.** *pa.t.* **underlay. underlying** *a.* basic; placed beneath; obscure.
un·der·line (un·dẹr·līn') *v.t.* to mark with line below, for emphasis; to emphasize. (un'·dẹr·lin) *n.* **-d** *a.*
un·der·ling (un'·dẹr·ling) *n.* one who holds inferior position; subordinate member of a staff; a weakling.
un·der·manned (un·dẹr·mand') *a.* supplied (as a ship) with too small a crew; having too small a staff.
un·der·mine (un·dẹr·mīn') *v.t.* to excavate for the purpose of mining, blasting, etc.; to erode; to sap, as one's energy; to weaken insidiously.
un·der·neath (un·dẹr·nēth') *adv.* and *prep.* beneath; below; in a lower place.
un·der·nour·ished (un·dẹr·nur'·isht) *a.* insufficiently nourished. **undernourishment** *n.*
un·der·pass (un'·dẹr·pas) *n.* road or passage (for cars, pedestrians) under a highway or railroad.
un·der·pay (un·dẹr·pā') *v.t.* to pay inadequately for the work done; to exploit. *pa.p., pa.t.* **underpaid. -ment** *n.*
un·der·pin·ning (un·dẹr·pin'·ing) *n.* a support; *pl.* the legs.
un·der·priv·i·leged (un·dẹr·priv'·a·lijd) *a.* deficient in the necessities of life because of poverty, discrimination, etc.
un·der·proof (un'·dẹr·prŏŏf) *a.* containing less alcohol than proof spirit.
un·der·rate (un·dẹr·rāt') *v.t.* to rate too low; to underestimate.
un·der·score (un·dẹr·skōr') *v.t.* to underline for emphasis. **-d** *a.*
un·der·sec·re·tar·y (un'·dẹr·sek'·ra·ter·i.) *n.* secretary who ranks below the principal secretary, esp. of government department.
un·der·sell (un·dẹr·sel') *v.t.* to sell more cheaply than another. *pa.p., pa.t.* **undersold. -er** *n.*
un·der·set (un'·dẹr·set) *n.* (*Naut.*) an ocean undercurrent.
un·der·shot (un'·dẹr·shät) *a.* (of mill-wheel) turned by water flowing under; having a protruding lower jaw.
un·der·side (un·dẹr·sīd) *n.* the surface underneath.
un·der·sign (un·dẹr·sin') *v.t.* to write one's name at the foot of or underneath. **-ed** *a.*
un·der·sized (un'·dẹr·sīzd) *a.* smaller than normal size; dwarf. Also **undersize.**
un·der·skirt (un'·dẹr·skurt) *n.* petticoat; skirt worn or placed under another.
un·der·stand (un·dẹr·stand') *v.t.* to comprehend; to grasp the significance of. *pap., pa.t.* **understood. -able** *a.* **-ably** *adv.* **-ing** *n.* **-ingly** *adv.* [O.E. *understandan*].
un·der·state (un·dẹr·stāt') *v.t.* to state less strongly than truth warrants; to minimize deliberately. **-ment** *n.*
un·der·stud·y (un·dẹr·stud·i.) *n.* one ready to substitute for principal actor (or actress) at a moment's notice; *v.t.* to study theatrical part for this purpose.
un·der·take (un·dẹr·tāk') *v.t.* to take upon oneself as a special duty; to agree (to do); to warrant; *v.i.* to be under obligation to do something; (*Colloq.*) to make arrangements for burial. *pa.t.* **undertook.** *pa.p.* **-n. -r** *n.* one who undertakes; one who manages a burial. **undertaking** *n.* project; guarantee.
un·der·tone (un'·dẹr·tōn) *n.* low, subdued tone of voice or color.

un·der·tow (un'·dẹr·tō) *n.* undercurrent or backwash of a wave after it has reached the shore.
un·der·val·ue (un·dẹr·val'·ū) *v.t.* to set too low a price on; to esteem lightly; to underestimate; *n.* an underestimate. **undervaluation** *n.*
un·der·wear (un'·dẹr·wer) *n.* underclothes.
un·der·went (un·dẹr·went') *pa.t.* of **undergo.**
un·der·wood (un'·dẹr·wood) *n.* small trees growing among larger trees.
un·der·world (un'·dẹr·wurld) *n.* the nether regions; Hades; the antipodes; section of community which lives by vice and crime.
un·der·write (un·dẹr·rīt') *v.t.* to write under something else; to subscribe; to append one's signature, as to insurance policy; to undertake to buy shares not bought by the public, and thereby guarantee success of issue of business capital. *pa.t.* **underwrote.** *pa.p.* **underwritten.** *n.*
un·der·wrought (un·dẹr·rawt') *pa.t.* and *pa.p.* of **underwork.**
un·de·served *a.* **undeserving** *a.* **undeservingly** *adv.* **(deserve)**
un·de·sir·a·ble (un·di·zīr'·a·bl) *a.* not desirable; having no appreciable virtues; *n.* person of ill-repute. **undesirability.** **undesirability** *adv.* **undesiring, undesirous** *a.* not desirous.
un·de·ter·mined *a.* **undeterminable** *a.* **undeterminate** *a.* **(determine)**
un·de·terred *a.* **(deter)**
un·de·vel·oped *a.* **(develop)**
un·de·vi·at·ing (un·dē'·vi·ā·ting) *a.* not deviating; resolute in pursuing a straight course; (*Fig.*) resolute of purpose.
un·did (un·did') *pa.t.* of **undo.**
un·dies (un'·dēz) *n.pl.* (*Colloq. abbrev.*) women's underwear.
un·dif·fer·en·ti·at·ed *a.* **(differ)**
un·di·gest·ed *a.* **(digest)**
un·di·lut·ed *a.* **(dilute)**
un·di·min·ished *a.* **(diminish)**
un·dine (un·dēn') *n.* water sprite; [L. *unda*, a wave].
un·di·rect·ed *a.* **(direct)**
un·dis·ci·plined *a.* **(discipline)**
un·dis·crim·i·nat·ing *a.* **(discriminate)**
un·dis·guised *a.* **(disguise)**
un·dis·mayed *a.* **(dismay)**
un·dis·posed *a.* **(dispose)**
un·dis·put·ed *a.* **undisputable** *a.* **undisputableness** *n.* **-ly** *adv.* **(dispute)**
un·dis·solved *a.* **(dissolve)**
un·dis·tin·guished *a.* **distinguishable** *a.* **undistinguishableness** *n.* **(distinguished)**
un·dis·turb·ed *a.* **(disturb)**
un·di·vid·ed *a.* **(divide)**
un·do (un·dŏŏ') *v.t.* to reverse what has been done; to annul; to loose; to unfasten; to damage character of. *pa.t.* **undid.** *pa.p.* **undone. undoer** *n.* **-ing** *n.* act of reversing what has been done; ruin, esp. of reputation. **undone** *a.* ruined; not done; not completed.
un·do·mes·tic *a.* **-ated** *a.* **(domestic)**
un·doubt·ed *a.* **-ly** *adv.* **undoubtably** *adv.* **undoubtful** *a.* **(doubt)**
un·dress (un'·dres) *n.* informal dress; off-duty military uniform. (un·dress') *v.t.* and *i.* **-ed** *a.*
un·due (un·dū') *a.* not yet payable; unjust; immoderate; not befitting the occasion. **-ness** *n.*
un·du·late (un'·dya·lāt) *v.t.* to move up and down like waves; to cause to vibrate; *v.i.* to move up and down; to vibrate; to have wavy edge; (un'·dya·lit) wavy. **undulant** *a.* undulating; wavy. **-ly** *adv.* **undulating** *a.* wavy; having series of rounded ridges and depressions, as surface of landscape. **undulatingly** *adv.* **undulation** *n.* wave; fluctuating motion, as of waves; wave-like contour of stretch of land; series of wavy lines; vibratory motion. **undulatory** *a.* pert. to undulation; moving like a wave; pert. to theory of light which argues that light is transmitted through ether by wave motions. [L. *unda*, a wave].
un·du·ly (un·dŏŏ'·li.) *adv.* unjustly; improperly; excessively.
un·dy·ing *a.* not dying; immortal; everlasting. **-ly** *adv.* **-ness** *n.*
un·earned (un·urnd') *a.* not earned by personal labor. — **income,** income derived from sources other than salary, fees, etc. — **increment,** increased value of property, land, etc. due to circumstances other than owner's expenditure on its upkeep.
un·earth (un·urth') *v.t.* to dig up; to drive as a fox, rabbit, etc. from its burrow; to bring to light. **-liness** *n.* **-ly** *a.* not of this world; supernatural.
un·eas·y (un·ē'·zi.) *a.* anxious; awkward; uncomfortable. **uneasiness** *n.* **uneasily** *adv.* **(ease)**
un·e·co·nom·ic *a.* **(economy)**
un·ed·i·fy·ing *a.* **(edify)**
un·ed·u·cat·ed *a.* **(education)**
un·em·ploy·ment (un·im·ploi'·mant) *n.* state of being unemployed. — **benefit,** money received by unemployed workers according to conditions laid down by insurance regulations. — **insurance,** insurance against periods of unemployment contributed to by workers, employers, etc. **unemployed** *n.a.*
un·end·ing *a.* **unended** *a.* **-ly** *adv.* **(end)**
un·en·dur·a·ble *a.* **(endure)**

un·en·light·ened *a.* (enlighten)
un·e·qual *a.* **-led** *a.* **-ly** *adv.* **-ness** *n.* (equal)
un·e·quiv·o·cal *a.* **-ly** *adv.* (equivocal)
un·er·ring (-ly). *a.* and *adv.* (err)
U·nes·co (ū·nes′·kō) *n.* coined word from initial letters of *United Nations Educational, Scientific and Cultural Organization,* established in November, 1945.
un·es·sen·tial *a.* (essential)
un·e·ven *a.* **-ly** *adv.* (even)
un·e·vent·ful *a.* (event)
un·ex·cep·tion·a·ble *a.* **unexceptional** *a.* (except)
un·ex·e·cut·ed *a.* (execute)
un·ex·pect·ed (un·iks·pek′·tid) *a.* not expected; sudden; without warning. **-ly** *adv.* **-ness** *n.*
un·ex·pired *a.* (expire)
un·ex·plained *a.* (explain)
un·ex·plored *a.* (explore)
un·ex·pressed *a.* (express)
un·ex·tin·guished *a.* (extinguish)
un·ex·tir·pat·ed *a.* (extirpate)
un·fad·a·ble *a.* **unfaded** *a.* **unfading** *a.* (fade)
un·fail·ing (un·fāl′·ing) *a.* not liable to fail; ever loyal; inexhaustible. **-ly** *adv.* **-ness** *n.*
un·fair (un·fār′) *a.* not fair; unjust; prejudiced; contrary to the rules of the game. **-ly** *adv.* **-ness** *n.*
un·faith·ful *a.* **-ly** *adv.* **-ness** *n.* (faith)
un·fal·ter·ing *a.* (falter)
un·fa·mil·iar *a.* **-ity** *n.* **-ly** *adv.* (familiar)
un·fash·ion·a·ble *a.* **-ness** *n.* **unfashionably** *adv.* (fashion)
un·fas·ten *v.t.* **-ed** *a.* (fasten)
un·fath·om·a·ble *a.* **-ness** *n.* **unfathomably** *adv.* **unfathomed** *a.* (fathom)
un·fa·vor·a·ble *a.* (favor)
un·feel·ing (un·fēl′·ing) *a.* void of feeling; callous; unsympathetic. **-ly** *adv.*
un·feigned *a.* **-ly** *adv.* **-ness** *n.* (feign)
un·fet·ter *v.t.* **-ed** *a.* (fetter)
un·fil·i·al *a.* (filial)
un·fin·ished (un·fin′·isht) *a.* not finished; roughly executed; not published. **unfinish** *n.* **unfinishable** *a.*
un·fit *a.* **-ly** *adv.* **-ness** *n.* **-ting** *a.* **-tingly** *adv.* (fit)
un·fledged (un·flejd′) *a.* not yet covered with feathers; immature.
un·fleshed (un·flesht′) *a.* (of sword) not yet used in fighting; not having tasted blood. **unfleshly** *a.* uncorporeal. **unfleshy** *a.* having no flesh.
un·flinch·ing *a.* **-ly** *adv.* (flinch)
un·fold (un·fōld′) *v.t.* to open the folds of; to spread out; to disclose; *v.i.* to expand. **-er** *n.* **-ing** *n.* **-ment** *n.* **-ed** *a.*
un·fore·seen (un·fōr·sēn′) *a.* unexpected. **unforeseeable** *a.* not capable of being foreseen; unpredictable. **-unforeseeing** *n.*
un·for·get·ta·ble *a.* **unforgettably** *adv.* (forget)
un·for·giv·a·ble *a.* **unforgiving** *a.* **unforgivingness** *n.* **unforgotten** *a.* (forgive)
un·formed (un·fawrmd′) *a.* not formed; amorphous; immature.
un·for·tu·nate *a.* **-ly** *adv.* **-ness** *n.* (fortune)
un·found·ed (un·foun′·did) *a.* not based on truth; not established. **-ly** *adv.* **-ness** *n.* (found)
un·fre·quent·ed *a.* **unfrequent** *a.* (frequent)
un·friend·ly *a.* **unfriended** *a.* **unfriendedness** *n.* **unfriendliness** *n.* (friend)
un·frock (un·frák′) *v.t.* to deprive of a frock, esp. to deprive of the status of a monk or priest. **-ed** *a.*
un·fruit·ful (un·frōot′·fạl) *a.* not productive; not profitable.
un·furl (un·furl′) *v.t.* and *i.* to open or spread out.
un·fur·nished *a.* **unfurnish** *v.t.* (furnish)
un·gain·ly (un·gān′·li·) *a.* clumsy; awkward; *adv.* in a clumsy manner. **ungainliness** *n.* [M.E. *ungein,* awkward].
un·gar·nished *a.* (garnish)
un·gen·er·ous *a.* (generous)
un·gen·tle *a.* **-manly** *adv.* (gentle)
un·glaze *v.t.* **-d** *a.* (glaze)
un·god·ly (un·gád′·li·) *a.* not religious; sinful; (*Colloq.*) outrageous(ly). **ungodliness** *n.*
un·gov·ern·a·ble *a.* **-ness** *n.* **ungovernably** *adv.* **ungoverned** *a.* (govern)
un·grace·ful *a.* **-ly** *adv.* **-ness** *n.* (graceful).
un·gra·cious *a.* **-ly** *adv.* (grace)
un·gram·mat·i·cal *a.* **-ly** *adv.* (grammar)
un·grate·ful *a.* **-ly** *adv.* **-ness** *n.* (grateful)
un·ground·ed (un·groun′·did) *a.* having no foundation; false.
un·grudg·ing *a.* **ungrudged** *a.* **-ly** *adv.* (grudge)
un·gual (ung·gwạl) *a.* having nails, hooves, or claws. **ungulate** (ung′·gvạ·lit) *a.* having hoofs, *n.* one of the hoofed mammals [L. *unguis,* a nail].
un·guard·ed *a.* **-ly** *adv.* **-ness** *n.* (guard)
un·guent (ung′·gwạnt) *n.* ointment. **-ary** *a.* pert. to unguents. **unguinous** *a.* oily [L. *unguere,* to anoint].
un·hal·lowed (un·hal′·ōd) *a.* unholy; not consecrated; wicked. **unhallowing** *n.*
un·hamp·ered (hamper)
un·hand (un·hand′) *v.t.* to let go. **-ily** *adv.* awkwardly. **-iness** *n.* **-led** *a.* not handled.

-y *a.* not handy; inconvenient; lacking skill.
un·hap·py *a.* **unhappily** *adv.* **unhappiness** *n.* (happy)
un·harmed *a.* (harm)
un·har·ness *a.* (harness)
un·health·y *a.* **unhealthful** *a.* **unhealthfully** *adv.* **unhealthfulness** *n.* **unhealthily** *adv.* **unhealthiness** *n.* (health)
un·heard (un·hurd′) *a.* not heard; not given hearing. **unheard of,** unprecedented.
un·heed·ed *a.* (heed)
un·hes·i·tat·ing (un·hez′·ạ·tā·ting) *a.* not hesitating; spontaneous; resolute. **-ly** *adv.* without hesitation.
un·hinge (un·hinj′) *v.t.* to take from the hinges; (*Fig.*) to cause mental instability. **-d** *a.* (of the mind) unstable; distraught.
un·ho·ly (un·hō′·li·) *a.* not sacred; (*Colloq.*) dreadful. **unholily** *adv.* **unholiness** *n.* (holy)
un·hon·ored *a.* (honor)
un·hook *v.t.* (hook)
un·horse (un·hawrs′) *v.t.* to throw from a horse; to cause to fall from a horse.
un·hur·ried *a.* (hurry)
un·hurt *a.* **-ful** *a.* (hurt)
un·hy·gi·en·ic (un·hī·ji·en′·ik) *a.* not hygienic; unsanitary; unhealthy.
u·ni-, (ūni) *prefix* denoting one or single [fr. L. *unus,* one].
u·ni·ax·i·al (ū·ni·ak′·si·ạl) *a.* having a single axis; having one direction along which ray of light can travel without bifurcation. **-ly** *adv.*
u·ni·cam·er·al having one legislative chamber.
u·ni·cel·lu·lar (ū·ni·sel′·yạ·ler) *a.* having a single cell; monocellular.
u·ni·corn (ū′·ni·kawrn) *n.* (*Myth.*) horselike animal with a single horn protruding from forehead [L. *unus,* one; *cornu,* horn].

un·i·de·al (un·ī·dē′·ạl) *a.* realistic; prosaic. **-ism** *n.*
u·ni·form (ū′·nạ·fawrm *a.* having always same form; conforming to one pattern; regular; consistent; not varying, as temperature; *n.* official dress, as a livery, etc. **-ed** *a.* wearing uniform. **-ity** *n.* conformity to pattern or standard. **-ly** *adv.* **-ness** *n.* [L. *unus,* one; *forma,* form].
u·ni·fy (ū′·nạ·fi) *v.t.* to make into one; to make uniform. **unifiable** *a.* capable of being made one. **unification** *n.* act of unifying; state of being made one; welding together of separate parts. **unifier** *n.* [L. *unus,* one; *facere,* to make].
u·ni·lat·er·al (ū·ni·lat′·er·ạl) *a.* one-sided; binding one side only, as in party agreement. **-ity** *n.* **-ly** *adv.*
u·ni·loc·u·lar (ū·ni·lạk′·ū·lạr) *a.* having single chamber or cavity.
un·im·ag·i·na·ble (un·i·maj′·i·nạ·bl) *a.* not imaginable; inconceivable. **-ness** *n.* **unimaginably** *adv.* **unimaginative** *a.* not imaginative; dull; uninspired. **unimaginatively** *adv.* **unimaginativeness** *n.* **unimagined** *a.* not imagined.
un·im·paired *a.* (impair)
un·im·peach·a·ble (un·im·pēch′·ạ·bl) *a.* not impeachable; irreproachable; blameless. **-ness,** **unimpeachability** *n.* **unimpeachably** *adv.* **unimpeached** *a.*
un·im·por·tant *a.* **unimportance** *n.* (import)
un·im·proved *a.* (improve)
un·in·flect·ed *a.* (inflect)
un·in·formed (un·in·fawrmd′) *a.* having no accurate information; ignorant; not expert.
un·in·hab·it·able *a.* **uninhabitability** *n.* **uninhabited** *a.* (inhabit)
un·in·jured *a.* (injure)
un·in·spired (inspire)
un·in·sured *a.* (insure)
un·in·tel·li·gent *a.* **unintelligence** *n.* **unintelligently** *adv.* **unintelligibility** *n.* **unintelligible** *a.* **unintelligibleness** *n.* **unintelligibly** *adv.* (intelligent)
un·in·ten·tion·al *a.* **-ly** *adv.* (intent)
un·in·ter·est·ed *a.* **-ly** *adv.* **-ness** *n.* **uninteresting** *a.* **uninterestingly** *adv.* (interest)
un·in·ter·rupt·ed *a.* **-ly** *adv.* (interrupt)
un·in·vit·ed *a.* **uninviting** *a.* **uninvitingly**

adv. (invite)
un·ion (ūn′·yạn) *n.* act of joining two or more things into one; federation; marriage; harmony; combination of administrative bodies for a common purpose; trade union; **-ed** *a.* joined. **-ist** *n.* one who supports union. **Union Jack,** national flag of United Kingdom [Fr. *union,* fr.L. *unus,* one].

Union Jack

u·nip·a·rous (ū·nip′·ạ·rạs) *a.* producing normally just one at a birth; (*Bot.*) having single stem [L. *unus,* one; *parere,* to bring forth].
u·nique (ū·nēk′) *a.* single in kind; having no like or equal; unusual; different. **-ly** *adv.* **-ness** *n.* [L. *unicus,* one].
u·ni·sex·u·al (ū·ni·sek′·shoo·ạl) *a.* of one sex only, as a plant; not hermaphrodite or bisexual. **-ity** *n.* **-ly** *adv.*
u·ni·son (ū′·nạ·sạn) *n.* harmony; concord; (*Mus.*) identity of pitch. **in unison,** with all voices singing the same note at the same time; sounding together; in agreement.
u·nit (ū′·nit) *n.* single thing or person; group regarded as one; standard of measurement; (*Math.*) the least whole number. **-ary** *a.* pert. to unit(s); whole [L. *unus,* one].
U·ni·tar·i·an (ū·ni·ter′·i·an) *n.* one who rejects doctrine of the Trinity and asserts the oneness of God and the teachings of Jesus. **-ism** *n.* [L. *unus,* one].
u·nite (ū·nit′) *v.t.* to join; to make into one; to form a whole; to associate; to cause to adhere; *v.i.* to be joined together; to grow together; to act as one; to harmonize. **united** *a.* joined together; harmonious; unanimous. **unitedly** *adv.* **-r** *n.* **unity** *n.* state of oneness; agreement; coherence; combination of separate parts into connected whole, or of different people with common aim; (*Math.*) any quantity taken as one. **unitive** *a.* **United Nations,** international organization, formed 1942. **United Nations Organization,** international organization set up after *World War 2* with Security Council as chief executive body. *Abbrev.* **UN. United States,** N. Amer. country; federal union of 50 states U.S.A. [L. *unus,* one].
u·ni·va·lent (u·ni·vā′·lạnt) *a.* (*chem.*) having a valence of one; (*Bot.*) unpaired. **univalence, univalency** *n.*
u·ni·valve (ū′·ni·valv) *a.* having only one valve; *n.* a single-shelled mollusk. Also **univalvular** *a.*
u·ni·verse (ū′·ni·vurs) *n.* all created things regarded as a system or whole; the world. **universal** *a.* pert. to universe; embracing all created things; world-wide; general (as opp. of *particular*); *n.* universal proposition; general concept; (in motoring) universal joint. **-ize** *v.t.* to make universal. **-ization** *n.* **Universalism** *n.* theological doctrine of the ultimate salvation of all mankind. **Universalist** *n.* **universalistic** *a.* **-ity** *n.* **— joint** (in motoring device whereby one part of machine has perfect freedom of motion in relation to another. **-ly** *adv.* **-ness** *n.* [L. *unus,* one; *vertere, versum,* to turn].

universal joint

u·ni·ver·si·ty (ū·ni·vur′·sa·ti·) *n.* institution for educating students in higher branches of learning, and having authority to confer degrees [L. *universitas,* a corporation].
un·just *a.* **-ifiable** *a.* **-ifiably** *adv.* **-ly** *adv.* **-ness** *n.* (just)
un·kempt (un·kempt′) *a.* dishevelled; rough [O.E. *un-,* not; *cemban,* to comb].
un·kind (un·kīnd) *a.* not kind, considerate, or sympathetic; cruel. **-liness** *n.* **-ly** *a.* **-ness** *n.* (kind)

un·know·a·ble (un·nō´·ạ·bl) *a.* not capable of being known; *n.* that which is beyond man's power to understand; the absolute. **-ness** *n.* **unknowably** *adv.* **unknowing** *a.* ignorant. **unknowingly** *adv.* **unknown** *a.* not known; incalculable; *n.* unknown quantity; unexplored regions of mind; part of globe as yet unvisited by man.

un·lace *n.* (lace)

un·lament·ed *a.* (lament)

un·latch *v.* (latch)

un·law·ful **-ly** *adv.* **-ness** *n.* (law)

un·learn *v.t.* **-ed** *a.* (learn)

un·leash *v.t.* **-ed** *a.* (leash)

un·leav·ened (un·lev´·ạnd) *a.* not leavened; made without yeast, as *unleavened bread.*

un·less (un·les´) *conj.* except; if not; supposing that; *prep.* except.

un·let·tered (un·let´·ẹrd) *a.* illiterate.

un·li·censed *a.* (license)

un·like (un·līk´) *a.* not like; dissimilar; *prep.* different from; *adv.* in a different way from. **-lihood**, **-ness** *n.* **-ly** *a.* improbable; unpromising; *adv.* improbably. **-liness** *n.*

un·lim·it·ed **-ly** *adv.* (limit)

un·load (un·lōd´) *v.t.* to remove load from; to remove charge from, as gun; to sell out quickly, as stocks, shares, etc. before slump; (*Fig.*) to unburden, as one's mind; *v.i.* to discharge cargo. **-ed** *a.* not containing a charge, as gun; not containing a plate or film, as camera.

un·lock *v.t.* (lock)

un·looked-for (un·lookt´·fawr) *a.* unexpected, unforeseen.

un·loose (un·lóós´) *v.t.* to set free. **-n** *v.t.*

un·lov·a·ble *a.* **unloved** *a.* **unloving** *a.* (love)

un·love·ly *a.* **unloveliness** *n.* (lovely)

un·luck·y *a.* **unluckily** *adv.* **unluckiness** *n.* (lucky)

un·make (un·māk´) *v.t.* to destroy what has been made; to annul; to ruin, destroy; to depose. *pa.p.*, *pa.t.* **unmade. -r** *n.* **unmade** *a.* not made. **unmakable** *a.* **unmaking** *n.*

un·man *v.t.* **—like** *a.* **-liness** *n.* **-ly** *a.* **-ned** *a.* (man)

un·man·age·a·ble *a.* **-ness** *n.* **unmanageably** *adv.* **unmanaged** *a.* (manage)

un·man·ner·ly *a.* **unmannered** *a.* **unmannerliness** *n.* (manner)

un·marked (un·markt´) *a.* without a mark.

un·mar·ried *a.* **unmarriageable** *a.* **unmarriageableness** *n.* (marry)

un·mask *v.t.* **-ed** *a.* (mask)

un·mean·ing (un·mēn´·ing) *a.* without meaning; unintentional; insignificant. **-ly** *adv.* **unmeant** (un·ment´) *a.* not intended; accidental.

un·meas·ured *a.* **unmeasurable** *a.* **unmeasurably** *adv.* (measure)

un·men·tion·a·ble (un·men´·shạn·ạ·bl) *a.* not worthy of mention; not fit to be mentioned. **-ness** *n.* **-s** *n.pl.* facetious synonym for undergarments.

un·mer·ci·ful (un·mur´·si·fạl) *a.* having or showing no mercy; cruel. **-ly** *adv.*

un·mind·ed (un·mīn´·did) *a.* not remembered **unmindful** *a.* forgetful; regardless. **unmindfully** *adv.* **unmindfulness** *n.*

un·mis·tak·a·ble (un·mis·tāk´·ạ·bl) *a.* clear; plain; evident. **unmistakably** *adv.*

un·mit·i·gat·ed (un·mit´·i·gāt·id) *a.* not softened or lessened; absolute; unmodified.

un·mixed *a.* (mix)

un·mo·lest·ed *a.* (molest)

un·moor *v.t.* (moor)

un·mor·al (un·mär´·, un·mawr´·ạl) *a.* not concerned with morality or ethics. **-izing** *a.* not given to reflecting on ethical values. **-ity** *n.* **-ly** *adv.*

un·mount·ed *a.* (mount)

un·moved *a.* **unmovable**, **unmoveable** *a.* **unmoving** *a.* (move)

un·mu·si·cal *a.* **-ity** *n.* **-ly** *adv.* (music)

un·named *a.* (name)

un·nat·u·ral *a.* **-ize** *v.t.* **-ized** *a.* **-ly** *adv.* (natural)

un·nav·i·ga·ble *a.* **unnavigability** *n.* **unnavigated** *a.* (navigate)

un·nec·es·sar·y *a.* **unnecessarily** *adv.* **unnecessariness** *n.* (necessary)

un·nerve (un·nurv´) to deprive of courage, strength; cause to feel weak. *v.t.* **-d** *a.*

un·no·ticed *a.* (notice)

un·num·bered (un·num´·bẹrd) *a.* not counted; innumerable.

un·ob·served *a.* (observe)

un·ob·struct·ed *a.* (obstruct)

un·ob·tru·sive *a.* **-ly** *adv.* **-ness** *n.* (obtrude)

un·oc·cu·pied (un·ak´·yạ·pīd) *a.* not occupied; untenanted; not engaged in work; not under control of troops.

un·of·fi·cial *a.* (official)

un·o·pened *a.* (open)

un·or·gan·ized (un·ȯr´·gạ·nīzd) *a.* without organic structure; having no system or order; not belonging to a labor union.

un·op·posed *a.* (oppose)

un·or·tho·dox *a.* (orthodox)

un·os·ten·ta·tious *a.* **-ly** *adv.* (ostentation)

un·pack (un·pak´) *v.t.* to remove from a pack or trunk; to open by removing packing; *v.i.* to empty contents of. **-ed** *a.* **-er** *n.*

un·paid *a.* (pay)

---

un·pal·at·a·ble *a.* (palate)

un·par·al·leled (un·par´·ạ·leld) *a.* having no equal; unprecedented.

un·par·don·a·ble *a.* **unpardonably** *adv.* **unpardoned** *a.* (pardon)

un·par·lia·men·ta·ry (un·par·lạ·men´·tạ·ri·) *a.* contrary to parliamentary law or usage.

un·per·turbed *a.* **-ness** *n.* (perturb)

un·pick *v.t.* **-ed** *a.* (pick)

un·placed *a.* **unplace** *v.t.* (place)

un·pleas·ant *a.* **-ly** *adv.* **-ness** *n.* **unpleasing** *a.* **unpleasingly** *adv.* **unpleasurable** *a.* (please)

un·pol·ished *a.* (polish)

un·pop·u·lar *a.* **unpopularity** *n.* (popular)

un·prec·e·dent·ed (un·pres·ạ·den´·tid) *a.* without precedent; having no earlier example; novel. **-ly** *adv.*

un·pol·lut·ed *a.* (pollute)

un·pre·dict·a·ble *a.* (predict)

un·pre·med·i·tat·ed *a.* **unpremeditable** *a.* **-ly** *adv.* **-ness**, **unpremeditation** *n.* (premeditate)

un·pre·pared *a.* **-ly** *adv.* **-ness** *n.* (prepare)

un·pre·pos·sess·ing *a.* **unprepossessed** *a.* (prepossess)

un·pre·ten·tious *a.* (pretend)

un·prin·ci·pled *a.* (principle)

un·print·a·ble (un·print´·ạ·bl) *a.* not printable; too shocking to be set down in print.

un·pro·duc·tive *a.* **-ly** *adv.* **-ness** *n.* (product)

un·pro·fes·sion·al (un·prạ·fesh´·ạn·l) *a.* not professional; contrary to professional ethics. **-ly** *adv.* (profess)

un·prof·it·a·ble *a.* **-ness** *n.* **unprofitably** *adv.* (profit)

un·prom·is·ing *a.* (promise)

un·pro·nounce·a·ble *a.* (pronounce)

un·pro·tect·ed *a.* (protect)

un·pro·vid·ed *a.* (provide)

un·pro·voked *a.* (provoke)

un·pruned *a.* (prune v.)

un·pub·lished *a.* (publish)

un·pun·ished *a.* **unpunishable** *a.* (punish)

un·qual·i·fied (un·kwal´·ạ·fīd) *a.* not qualified; not having proper qualifications; not modified; absolute. **unqualifying** *a.*

un·quench·a·ble *a.* (quench)

un·ques·tion·a·ble *a.* **unquestionability, -ness** *n.* **unquestionably** *adv.* **unquestioned** *a.* **unquestioning** *a.* (question)

un·qui·et *a.* (quiet)

un·quote (un·kwōt) *v.t.* and *i.* to end a quotation.

un·rav·el *v.t.* **-ed** *a.* (ravel)

un·read (un·red´) *a.* (of a book) not read; not having gained knowledge by reading. **-able** (un·rēd´·ạ·bl) *a.* not readable—illegible, uninteresting or unsuitable.

un·read·y *a.* **unreadily** *adv.* (ready)

un·re·al (un·rēl´) *a.* not real; insubstantial; illusive. **-izable** *a.* not realizable. **-izableness** *n.* **-ized** *a.* not realized; unfulfilled. **unreality** *n.* want of reality. **-ly** *adv.* **-ity** *n.*

un·rea·son (un·rē´·zn) *n.* lack of reason; irrationality. **-able** *a.* immoderate; impulsive; exorbitant (of prices). **-ableness** *n.* **-ably** *adv.* **-ed** *a.* not logical. **-ing** *a.* irrational.

un·rec·og·nized *a.* **unrecognizable** *a.* **-izably** *adv.* (recognize)

un·re·cord·ed *a.* (record)

un·rec·ti·fied *a.* (rectify)

un·re·fined *a.* (refine)

un·re·gen·er·ate *a.* **unregeneracy, unregeneration** *n.* **-ly** *adv.* (regenerate)

un·re·lat·ed (un·ri·lāt´·id) *a.* not related; having no apparent connection; diverse.

un·re·lent·ing *a.* **-ly** *adv.* (relent)

un·re·li·a·ble *a.* **unreliability, -ness** *n.* (reliable)

un·re·lieved *a.* (relieve)

un·re·mem·bered *a.* (remember)

un·re·mit·ting (un·ri·mit´·ing) *a.* not relaxing; incessant; persistent. **unremitted** *a.* not remitted. **unremittedly, -ly** *adv.*

un·re·proved *a.* (reproof)

un·re·quit·ed *a.* **unrequitable** *a.* **-ly** *adv.* (requite)

un·rest (un·rest´) *n.* want of rest; disquiet; political or social agitation. **-ful** *a.* **-fulness** *n.* **-ing** *a. not resting.* **-ingly** *adv.*

un·re·strained *a.* (restrain)

un·re·strict·ed *a.* (restrict)

un·right·eous *a.* **-ly** *adv.* **-ness** *n.* **unrightful** *a.* **unrightfully** *adv.* **-fulness** *n.* (righteous, right)

un·ripe *a.* **-ned** *a.* **-ness** *n.* (ripe)

un·robe *v.t.* and *v.i.* (robe)

un·ri·valed *a.* (rival)

un·roll *v.* (roll)

un·ruf·fled (un·ruf´·ld) *a.* not ruffled; placid. **unruffle** *v.i.* to become placid.

un·ruled (un·róóld´) *a.* not ruled; ungoverned; (of paper) blank; unrestrained. **unruliness** *n.* state of being unruly. **unruly** *a.* lawless; disobedient.

un·sad·dle *v.* (saddle)

un·safe *a.* **-ly** *adv.* **-ness** *n.* **-ty** *n.* (safe)

un·sale·a·ble *a.* **unsalability** *n.* (sale)

un·san·i·tar·y *a.* (sanitary)

un·sat·is·fac·to·ry *a.* **unsatisfactorily** *adv.* **unsatisfactoriness** *n.* **unsatisfied** *a.* **unsatisfying** *a.* (satisfy)

un·sa·vo·ry *a.* **unsavorily** *adv.* **unsavori-**

---

ness *n.* (savory)

un·say (un·sā´) *v.t.* to retract (what has been said). *p.pa.*, *pa.t.* **unsaid.**

un·scathed (un·skāTHd´) *a.* unharmed; without injury.

un·schooled *a.* not educated. (school)

un·sci·entif·ic *a.* **-ally** *adv.*

un·scram·ble (un·skram´·bl) *v.t.* to decode a secret message; to straighten out.

un·scru·pu·lous (un·skróó´·pyạ·lạs) *a.* not scrupulous; ruthless; having no moral principles. **-ly** *adv.* **-ness** *n.*

un·seal *v.t.* **-ed** *a.* (seal *n.*, *v.t.*)

un·sea·son·a·ble (un·sē´·zạn·ạ·bl) *a.* untimely; out of season. **-ness** *n.* **unseasonably** *adv.* **unseasoned** *a.*

un·seat (un·sēt´) *v.t.* to throw from a horse; to deprive of official seat.

un·seem·li·ness *n.* **unseemly** *a.* and *adv.* (seem)

un·seen *a.* (see)

un·self·con·scious (un·self·kȧn´·shạs) *a.* not self-conscious; natural. **-ly** *adv.* **-ness** *n.*

un·self·ish *a.* **-ly** *adv.* **-ness** *n.* (self)

un·set·tle (un·set´·l) *v.t.* to move or loosen from a fixed position; to disturb mind; to make restless or discontented. **-d** *a.* not settled; changeable, as weather; unpaid, as bills; not allocated; not inhabited. **-dly** *adv.* **-dness**, **-ment** *n.* **unsettling** *a.* disturbing.

un·shack·le *v.t.* **-d** *a.* (shackle)

un·shad·ed *a.* (shade)

un·shak·en *a.* (shake)

un·shav·en *a.* (shave)

un·sheathe *n.* (sheath)

un·shed *a.* (shed)

un·shod (un·shȧd´) *a.* barefoot.

un·sight·ed (un·sī´·tid) *a.* not sighted; not observed; (of gun) without sights; (of shot) aimed blindly. **unsightable** *a.* invisible. **unsightliness** *n.* ugliness. **unsightly** *a.* ugly; revolting to the sight.

un·skill·ful *a.* **-ly** *adv.* **-ness** *n.* **unskilled** *a.* (skill)

un·sling (un·sling´) *v.t.* (*Naut.*) to remove slings from, as from cargo; to take down something which is hanging by sling, as a rifle. *pa.p.*, *pa.t.* **unslung.**

un·smil·ing *a.* **-ly** *adv.* (smile)

un·so·cia·ble *a.* **unsociability, -ness** *n.* **unsociably** *adv.* (sociable)

un·smirched *a.* (smirch)

un·so·lic·it·ed (un·sạ·lis´·i·tid) *a.* not solicited; gratuitous. **unsolicitous** *a.* unconcerned.

un·so·phis·ti·cat·ed (un·sạ·fis´·ti·kāt·id) *a.* not sophisticated; ingenuous; simple. **-ly** *adv.* **-ness, unsophistication** *n.*

un·sound (un·sound´) *a.* imperfect; damaged; decayed; (of the mind) insane; not based on reasoning; fallacious. **-ly** *adv.* **-ness** *n.*

un·speak·a·ble (un·spēk´·ạ·bl) *a.* beyond utterance or description (in good or bad sense); ineffable. **unspeakably** *adv.* **unspeaking** *a.* dumb.

un·spoiled *a.* Also **unspoilt** (spoil)

un·sport·ing (un·spȯr´·ting) *a.* (*Colloq.*) not like sportsman; unfair. **unsportsmanlike** *a.* not in accordance with the rules of fair play.

un·spot·ted *a.* (spot)

un·sprung (un·sprung´) *a.* not fitted with springs, as a vehicle, chair, etc.

un·sta·ble (un·stā´·bl) *a.* unsteady; wavering; not firm; unreliable; (*Chem.*) applied to compounds which readily decompose or change into other compounds. **unstability, -ness** *n.* **unstably** *adv.* (stable *a.*)

un·stained *a.* (stain)

un·stead·y *a.* **unsteadily** *adv.* **unsteadiness** *n.* (steady)

un·stead·fast *a.* **unsteadfastly** *adv.* **unsteadfastness** *n.* (steadfast)

un·stop (un·stȧp´) *v.t.* to open by removing a stopper, as a bottle; to clear away an obstruction; to open organ stops. *pr.p.* **-ping.** *pa.p.*, *pa.t.* **-ped.** *a.* not stopped; having no cork or stopper.

un·strained (un·strānd´) *a.* not strained, as through a filter; (*Fig.*) relaxed; friendly.

un·stuck (un·stuk´) *a.* not glued together.

un·sub·dued *a.* (subdue)

un·sub·stan·tial *a.* (substantial)

un·suc·cess·ful (un·sạk·ses´·fạl) *a.* not succeeding; unfortunate; incomplete. **-ly** *adv.* **-ness** *n.*

un·suit·a·ble *a.* **unsuitability** *n.* **unsuited** *a.*

un·sul·lied *a.* (sully)

unstop

un·sung (un·sung′) a. not sung or spoken; not celebrated.

un·sup·port·ed (un·sa·pōr′·tad) a. not supported; without backing. **unsupportable** a. not supportable; intolerable.

un·sure a. **-ness** n. (**sure**)

un·sur·passed a. (**surpass**)

un·sus·pect·ed a. (**suspect**)

un·sus·pi·cious a. (**suspicious**)

un·sweet·ened a. (**sweeten**)

un·swept a. (**sweep**)

un·swerv·ing a. **-ly** adv. (**swerve**)

un·sym·pa·thet·ic a. **-ally** adv. **unsympathizable** a. **unsympathizing** a. (**sympathy**)

un·taint·ed a. (**taint**)

un·tan·gle v. (**tangle**)

un·tar·nished a. (**tarnish**)

un·taught (un·tawt′) a. pa.p., pa.t. of **unteach**; uneducated; ignorant; natural, without teaching.

un·ten·a·ble a. (**tenable**)

un·thank·ful (un·thangk′·fal) a. ungrateful.

un·tamed a. **untamable** a. (**tame**)

un·think·ing (un·thingk′·ing) a. thoughtless; heedless. **-ly** adv. **unthinkable** a. (**think**)

un·ti·dy a. **untidily** adv. **untidiness** n.

un·tie v.t. **-d** a. (**tie**)

un·til (un·til′) prep. till; to; as far as; as late as; conj. up to the time that; to the degree that.

un·time·ly (un·tim′·li) a. not timely; premature; inopportune. **untimeliness** n.

un·tir·ing a. **untirable** a. **untired** a. **-ly** adv. (**tire** v.)

un·to (un′·tŏŏ) prep. (Poet.) to; until [M.E. und to, up to, as far as].

un·touch·a·ble (un·tuch′·a·bl) a. incapable of being touched; unfit to be touched; out of reach; belonging to non-caste masses of India; n. non-caste Indian whose touch or even shadow was regarded as defiling. **-untouchability** n. **untouched** a.

un·to·ward (un·tōrd′) a. unlucky; inconvenient; hard to manage.

untrained a. (**train**)

un·trav·eled (un·trav′·eld) a. not having traveled; unexplored.

un·tried (un·trid′) pa.p., pa.t. of **try**; not proven, attempted or tested, not tried in court.

un·trimmed a. (**trim**)

un·true (un·trŏŏ′) a. not true; false; disloyal; not conforming to a requisite standard. **-ness** n. **untruly** adv. falsely. **untruth** n. **untruthful** a. dishonest; lying. **untruthfully** adv. **untruthfulness** n.

un·turned a. (**turn**)

un·twist v. (**twist**)

un·tu·tored a. (**tutor**)

un·used (un·ūzd′) a. not used; not accustomed. **unusual** a. not usual; uncommon; strange. **unusually** adv. **unusualness** n.

un·ut·ter·a·ble (un·ut′·er·a·bl) a. unspeakable beyond utterance. **unutterability** n. **unutterably** adv. **unuttered** a. unspoken.

un·var·nished a. (**varnish**)

un·vary·ing a. (**vary**)

un·veil v.t. (**veil**)

un·ver·i·fied a. (**verify**)

un·vexed a. (**vex**)

un·vis·it·ed a. (**visit**)

un·want·ed a. (**want**)

un·war·rant·a·ble (un·war′·ant·a·bl) a. not justifiable; improper. **-ness** n. **unwarrantably** adv. **unwarranted** a. **unwarrantedly** adv. (**warrant**)

un·wary a. **unwarily** adv. **unwariness** n. (**wary**)

un·washed (un·wȧsht′) a. not washed; dirty; not reached by the sea.

un·well (un·wel′) a. ill; ailing.

un·wept (un·wept′) a. not mourned or regretted.

un·whole·some a. **-ly** adv. **-ness** n. (**wholesome**)

un·wield·y a. **unwieldily** adv. **unwieldiness** n. (**wield**)

un·will·ing (un·wil′·ing) a. loath; reluctant. **-ly** adv. **-ness** n. (**will**)

un·wind (un·wind′) v.t. to wind off; to loose what has been wound; to roll into a ball from a skein, as wool, silk, etc.; v.i. to become un-

wound. pa.p., pa.t. **unwound**.

un·wit·ting (un·wit′·ing) a. unawares; not knowing. **-ly** adv.

un·wont·ed (un·wunt′·ad, un·wŏnt′·ad) a. unaccustomed; unusual. **-ly** adv. **-ness** n.

un·work·a·ble a. (**work**)

un·world·ly a. **unworldliness** n. (**worldly**)

un·wor·thy a. **unworthily** adv. **unworthiness** n. (**worthy**)

un·writ·ten (un·rit′·n) a. not written; oral; not expressed in writing. **unwritten Law,** law originating in custom, usage, or court rather than statute.

un·yield·ing (un·yēl′·ding) a. not yielding; stubborn; implacable; not flexible. adv. **-ness** n.

un·yoke v. (**yoke**)

up (up) adv. prep. to or toward a higher place or degree; on high; on one's legs; out of bed; above horizon; in progress; in revolt; as far as; of equal merit or degree; thoroughly well versed in; competent. Also used as a verb intensifier. a. advanced; standing; reaching; tending toward; higher; even with; finished; v.t. and i. to put, left or take up; to raise; to bet more. pr.p. **-ping**. pa.p., pa.t. **-ped**. **up-and-coming,** alert; enterprising.

u·pas (ū′·pas) n. tree of E. Indian islands, yielding sap of deadly poison [Malay = poison].

up·braid (up·brād′) v.t. to reprove severely; to chide; v.i. to voice a reproach. **-ing** n. reproach; a. reproachful [O.E. up, on; bregdan, to braid].

up·bring·ing (up′·bring·ing) n. the process of rearing and training a child; education.

up·coun·try (up′·kun·tri·) adv. inland; a. away from the sea.

up·date (up′·dāt) v.t. bring up-to-date.

up·end (up·end′) v.t. to stand on end.

up·grade (up′·grād) a. adv. uphill; n. incline; v.t. to raise to a higher level.

up·heave (up·hēv′) v.t. to lift up, as heavy weight. **upheaval** n. raising up, as of earth's surface, by volcanic force; (Fig.) any revolutionary change in ideas, etc.

up·held (up·held′) pa.t. and pa.p. of **uphold**.

up·hill (up′·hil) a. going up; laborious; difficult; adv. towards higher level.

up·hold (up·hōld′) v.t. to hold up; to sustain; to approve; to maintain, as verdict in law court. pa.p., pa.t. **upheld**. **-er** n.

up·hol·ster (up·hōl′·ster) v.t. to stuff and cover furniture. **-y** n. craft of stuffing and covering furniture, etc.; material used. **-er** n.

up·keep (up′·kēp) n. maintenance; money required for maintenance, as of a home.

up·land (up′·land) n. high land or region. a. pert. to or situated in higher elevations.

up·lift (up·lift′) v.t. to lift up; to improve conditions of, morally, socially etc.; to exalt. **-er** n. **-ment** n. (up′·lift) n. emotional or religious stimulus; moral and social improvement; a brassiere.

up·on (a·pȧn′) prep. on [O.E. uppon, on].

up·per (up′·er) a. higher in place, rank, or dignity; superior; more recent; n. the part above; (Colloq.) upper berth; n.pl. (Colloq.) upper teeth. **—most. —case** n. (Print.) case containing capital letters. **-cut** n. (Boxing) blow struck upwards inside opponent's guard; v.t. to deliver such blow. **—hand** n. superiority; advantage over another. **uppish** or **uppity** (Colloq.) a. arrogant; affectedly superior in manner or attitude. **uppishly** adv. **uppishness** n. **-most** a. adv. [fr. up].

up·right (up′·rit) a. standing, pointed straight up; honest; adv. in such a position; n. a vertical part.

up·rise (up·riz′) v.i. to rise up; to revolt. pa.p. **-n** (up·ri′·zan). pa.t. **uprose**. **uprising** n. insurrection; revolt; a slope.

up·roar (up′·rōr) n. tumult; violent, noisy disturbance. **-ious** a. **-iously** adv. **-iousness** n. [Dut. oproer].

up·root (up·rŏŏt′) v.t. to tear up by the roots; to eradicate. **-al** n. **-er** n.

up·set (up·set′) v.t. to turn upside down; to knock over; to defeat; to disturb or distress. pr.p. **-ting** pa.p., pa.t. **upset**; (up′·set) n. an overturn; overthrow; confusion; a. disordered; worried; overturned. **— price,** lowest price at which goods will be sold by auction.

up·shot (up′·shȧt) n. final issue; conclusion.

up·side (up′·sid) n. the upper side. **—down** adv. with the upper side underneath; inverted; in disorder.

up·stage (up′·stāj′) a., adv. of or toward rear of stage; v.t. to act on stage so as to minimize another actor.

up·stairs (up·sterz′) adv. in the upper story; on the stairs; a. pert. to upper story; n. upper story.

up·stand·ing (up·stan′·ding) a. erect; honorable.

up·start (up′·stȧrt) n. one who has suddenly risen to wealth, power, or honor; parvenu; v.i. to rise suddenly.

up·stream (up′·strēm) adv. in direction of source (of stream).

up·stroke (up′·strōk) n. the upward line in handwriting; upward stroke.

up·surge (up·surj′) v.t. to surge upwards. (up′·surj) n. welling, as of emotion.

up·sweep (up′·swēp) n. a curve upward; an upswept hair-do.

up·swing (up′·swing) n. a trend upward.

up·thrust (up′·thrust) n. upward thrust.

up·to-date (up′·ta·dāt′) a. modern; most recent; extending up to, present, to, the present time.

up·town (up′·toun) a. pert. to, or in upper part of, town; adv.

up·turn (up·turn′) v.t. to turn up. (up′·turn) n. an upward turn for the better. **-ing** n.

up·ward (up′·werd) a. directed towards a higher place; adv. upwards. **-s**, **-ly** adv. towards higher elevation or number [O.E. upweard, upward].

u·ran·i·nite (yoo·rȧn′·a·nit) n. pitchblende, in which uranium was first found in 1789.

u·ra·nite (yoor′·a·nit) n. an almost transparent ore of uranium. **uranitic** a.

u·ra·ni·um (yoo·rā′·ni·am) n. radio-active metallic element (symbol U), used as an alloy in steel manufacture and in the production of atom bomb. **uranic, uranous** a. [fr. Uranus, the planet].

u·ra·nog·ra·phy (yoor·a·nȧg′·ra·fi·) n. descriptive astronomy. **uranographer, uranographist** n. **uranographic, uranographical** a. **uranometry** n. measurement of heavens; chart of heavens [Gk. ouranos, heaven].

ur·ban (ur′·ban) a. pert. to, or living in, city or town. **urbane** a. refined; suave; courteous. **urbanely** adv. **urbanity** n. **-ize** v.t. to make urban; to bring town conditions and advantages to rural areas. [L. urbs, a city].

ur·chin (ur′·chin) n. sea urchin; (Arch.) hedgehog (Arch.) goblin; mischievous child; a child [L. ericius, hedgehog].

Ur·du (oor·dŏŏ′) n. a language form of Hindustani, mixture of Persian, Arabic, and Hindi [Hind. urdu, camp].

u·re·a (ū′·rē·a) n. crystalline solid, the principle organic constituent of urine [Gk. ouron, urine].

u·re·ter (ū·rē′·ter) n. one of two ducts of kidney conveying urine to bladder. **urethra** n. duct by which urine passes from bladder. pl. **urethrae. urethral** a. [Gk. ouron, urine].

urge (urj) v.t. to press; to drive; to exhort; to stimulate; to solicit earnestly; v.i. to press onward; to make allegations, entreaties, etc. n. act of urging; incentive; irresistible impulse. **-ncy** n. quality of being urgent; compelling necessity; importunity. **-nt** a. calling for immediate attention; clamant; importunate. **-ntly** adv. **-r** n. [L. urgere, to press].

u·rine (ū′·rin) n. yellowish fluid secreted by kidneys, passed through ureters to bladder from which it is discharged through urethra. **uremia** n. toxic condition of the blood caused by insufficient secretion of urine. **uremic** a. **uric** a. pert. to or produced from urine. **urinal** n. vessel into which urine may be discharged; a place for urinating. **urinary** a. pert. to urine. **urinate** v.i. to pass urine. **urination** n. **urinogenital** a. pert. to urinary and genital organs. **urology** n. branch of Med. dealing with urinogenital system. **urologist** n. [Gk. ouron, urine].

urn (urn) n. vase-shaped vessel of pottery or metal with pedestal, and narrow neck, as used for ashes of dead after cremation; vessel of various forms usually fitted with tap, for liquid in bulk, as tea urn. **-al** a. [L. urna].

ur·sine (ur′·sin) a. pert. to or resembling a bear. **ursiform** a. resembling bear in shape [L. ursus, a bear].

us (us) pron. pl. the objective form of **we**.

use (ūz) v.t. to make use of; to employ; to consume or expend (as in material); to practice habitually; to accustom; to treat; v.i. to be accustomed (only in past tense). **use** (ūs) n. act of using or employing for specific purpose; utility; custom; (Law) profit derived

from trust. **usable** *a.* fit for use. **usability** *n.* **usage** *n.* mode of using; treatment; long-established custom. **usance** *n.* usual time allowed for payment of foreign bills of exchange. **-ful** *a.* of use; handy; profitable; serviceable; **-fully** *adv.* **-fulness** *n.* **-less** *a.* of no use; inefficient; futile. **-lessly** *adv.* **-lessness** *n.* **-r** *n.* [L. *uti*, *usus*, to use].
ush·er (ush′·er) *n.* doorkeeper; one who conducts people to seats in church, theater, etc.; official who introduces strangers or walks before person of high rank; *v.t.* to act as usher. **-ette** *n.* girl employed, as in theater to show patrons to seats. **to usher in**, to precede [O. Fr. *ussier*, fr. L. *ostiarius*, a doorkeeper].
us·que·baugh (us′·kwi·baw) *n.* whiskey [Gael. *uisge*, water, *beatha*, life].
u·su·al (ū′·zhoo·al) *a.* customary; ordinary. **-ly** *adv.* **-ness** *n.* [L. *usus*, to use].
u·su·fruct (ū′·za·frukt) *n.* right of using and enjoying produce benefit, or profits of another's property provided that the property remains undamaged. **-uary** *a.* pert. to usufruct; *n.* one who has the use of another's property by usufruct [L. *usus*, use; *fructus*, fruit].
u·surp (ū·surp′, zurp′) *v.t.* to take possession of unlawfully or by force. **-ation** *n.* act of usurping; violent or unlawful seizing of power [L. *usurpare*, to seize].
u·su·ry (ū′·zha·ri·) *n.* charging of exorbitant interest on money lent. **usurer** *n.* money lender who charges exorbitant rates of interest **usurious** *a.* **usuriously** *adv.* **usuriousness** *n.* [L. *usura*, use].
u·ten·sil (ū·ten′·sal) *n.* vessel of any kind which forms part of domestic, esp. kitchen, equipment [L. *utensilis*, fit for use].
u·ter·ine (ū′·ter·in) *a.* pert. to uterus or womb; born of the same mother but by a different father. **uterus** *n.* womb [L. *uterus*].
u·til·i·tar·i·an (ū·til·a·ter′·i·an) *a.* pert. to utility or utilitarianism; of practical use. *n.* one who accepts doctrines of utilitarianism. **-ism** *n.* ethical doctrine, the ultimate aim and criterion of all human actions must be 'the greatest happiness for the greatest number' [L. *utilis*, useful].
u·ti·lize (ū·ta·līz) *v.t.* to put to use; to turn to profit. **utilizable** *a.* **utilization** *n.* **-r** *n.* **utility** *n.* usefulness; quality of being advantageous; *pl.* public services, as gas, electricity, telephone, etc. [L. *utilis*, useful].
ut·most (ut′·mōst) *a.* situated at farthest point or extremity; to highest degree; *n.* most that can be; greatest possible effort [O.E. *utemest*, superb. of *ut*, out].
u·to·pi·a (ū·tō′·pi·a) *n.* any ideal state, constitution, system, or way of life. **-n** *a.* ideally perfect but impracticable; visionary [=nowhere; Gk. *ou*, not; *topos*, place].
u·tri·cle (ū′·tri·kl) *n.* (*Bot.*) little bag or bladder, esp. of aquatic plant; (*Anat.*) a sac in inner ear influencing equilibrium. **utricular, utriculate** *a.* [L. *utriculus*, small bag].
ut·ter (ut′·er) *a.* total; unconditional. **-ly** *adv.* **-ness** *n.* [O.E. *utor*, outer].
ut·ter (ut′·er) *v.t.* to speak; to disclose; to put into circulation. **-able** *a.* **-ableness** *n.* **-ance** *n.* act of speaking; manner of delivering speech; something said; a cry. **-er** *n.* [O.E. *utian*, to put out].
ut·ter·most (ut′·er·mōst) *a.* farthest out; utmost; *n.* the highest degree.
u·vu·la (ū′·vya·la) *n.* fleshy tag suspended from middle of lower border of soft palate. **-r** *a.* [L. *uva*, grape].
ux·o·ri·ous (uk·sōr′·i·as) *a.* foolishly or excessively fond of one's wife. **uxorial** *a.* pert. to wife. **-ly** *adv.* **-ness** *n.* [L. *uxor*, wife].

V

va·cant (vā′·kant) *a.* empty; void; not occupied; unintelligent. **-ly** *adv.* **vacancy** *n.* emptiness; opening; lack of thought; place or post, unfilled. **vacate** (vā′·kāt) *v.t.* to leave empty or unoccupied; to quit possession of; to make void. **vacation** *n.* act of vacating; intermission of stated employment; recess; holidays. **vacational** *a.* **vacationist** *n.* [L. *vacare*, to be empty].
vac·cine (vak·sēn′·, vak′·sēn) *a.* pert. to, or obtained from cows; *n.* virus of cowpox, used in vaccination; any substance used for inoculation against disease. **vaccinate** *v.t.* to inoculate with cowpox, to ward off smallpox or lessen severity of its attack. **vaccination** *n.* act or practice of vaccinating; the inoculation. **vaccinator** *n.* [L. *vacca*, cow].
vac·il·late (vas′·a·lāt) *v.i.* to move to and fro; to waver; to be unsteady; to fluctuate in opinion. **vacillating, vacillatory** *a.* **vacillation** *n.* [L. *vacillare*].
vac·u·um (vak′·yoom) *n.* space devoid of all matter; space from which air, or other gas, has been almost wholly removed, as by air pump. **vacuous** *a.* empty; vacant; expressionless; unintelligent. **-ly** *adv.* **-ness** *n.* **vacuity** (va·kū′·a·ti·) *n.* emptiness; empty space; lack of intelligence. **— cleaner** *n.* apparatus for removing dust from carpets, etc. by suction. **— bottle** *n.* double-walled flask with vacuum between walls. for keeping contents at temperature at which they were inserted. **— tube** used in Radio, TV, and electronic equipment; a sealed tube containing metallic electrodes but (almost) no air or gas. [L. *vacuus*, empty].

vacuum cleaner

va·de·me·cum (vā′·dē·mē′·kam) *n.* small handbook or manual for ready reference [L. =go with me].
vag·a·bond (vag′·a·band) *a.* moving from place to place without settled habitation; wandering; *n.* wanderer or vagrant, having no settled habitation; idle scamp; rascal. **-age ism,** *n.* [L. *vagari*, to wander].
va·ga·ry (vā′·ga·ri·, va·ger′·i·) *n.* whimsical or freakish notion; unexpected action; caprice. **vagarious** *a.* [L. *vagari*, to wander].
va·gi·na (va·jī′·na) *n.* (*Anat.*) canal which leads from uterus to external orifice; (*Bot.*) sheath as of leaf **-l** *a.* [L.].
va·grant (vā′·grant) *a.* wandering from place to place; moving without certain direction; roving; *n.* idle wanderer; vagabond; disorderly person; beggar. **-ly** *adv.* **vagrancy** *n.* [L. *vagari*, to wander].
vague (vāg) *a.* uncertain; indefinite; indistinct; not clearly expressed. **-ly** *adv.* **-ness** *n.* [L. *vagus*, wandering].
vain (vān) *a.* useless; unavailing; fruitless; empty; worthless; conceited; **-ly** *adv.* **-ness** *n.* **vanity** (van′·a·ti·) *n.* conceit; something one is conceited about; worthlessness; dressing table. **vanity case** *n.* lady's small handbag or case, fitted with powder puff, mirror, lipstick, etc. [L. *vanus*, empty].
vain·glo·ry (vān·glō′·ri·) *n.* excessive vanity; boastfulness. **vainglorious** *a.* **vaingloriously** *adv.* **vaingloriousness** *n.* [*vain* and *glory*].
val·ance (val′·ans) *n.* short drapery across the top of a window, bed, etc.; similar facing of wood or metal. **-d** *a.* [O.Fr. *avalant* to hang].
vale (vāl) *n.* valley [L. *vallis*, valley].
val·e·dic·tion (val·a·dik′·shan) *n.* farewell; a bidding farewell. **valedictory** *a.* bidding farewell; suitable for leave-taking; *n.* a valedictory address, esp. by a school valedictorian. **valedictorian** *n.* student in a graduating class with the highest scholastic standing who gives the valedictory at graduation exercises. [L. *valedicere*, to say farewell].
va·lence, va·len·cy (vā′·lans, vā′·lan·si·) *n.* (*Chem.*) the combining power of an element or atom as compared with a hydrogen atom [L. *valere*, to be strong].
Va·len·ci·ennes (va·len(t)·sē·enz′) *n.* rich lace, made orig. at *Valenciennes*, in France.
val·en·tine (val′·an·tin) *n.* sweetheart chosen on *St. Valentine's* day; card containing profession of love, sent on *St. Valentine's* day, Feb. 14th [L. proper name *Valentinus*].
va·le·ri·an (va·lir′·i·an) *n.* flowering herb with strong odor; its root, used as sedative drug [O.Fr. *valeriane*].
val·et (val′·it, val′·ā) *n.* manservant who cares for clothing, etc. of his employer [Fr. *valet*, a groom, Doublet of *varlet*].
val·e·tu·di·nar·i·an (val·a·tū·da·ner′·i·an) *a.* sickly; infirm; solicitous about one's own health; *n.* person of sickly constitution; person disposed to live life of an invalid. **-ism** *n.* **valetudinary** *a.* [L. *valetudo*, health].
Va·hal·la (val·hal′·a) *n.* (*Norse myth.*) hall of immortality where Odin received souls of heroes slain in battle [O.N. *valr*, slain; *holl*, hall].
val·iant (val′·yant) *a.* brave; heroic; courageous; intrepid. **-ly** *adv.* **-ness** *n.* **valiance, valiancy** *n.* valor; courage [L. *valere*, to be strong].

val·id (val′·id) *a.* sound or well-grounded; capable of being justified; (*Law*) legally sound; executed with proper formalities. **-ly** *adv.* **-ate** *v.t.* to make valid; to ratify. **-ation** *n.* **-ness, -ity** *n.* [L. *validus*, strong].
va·lise (va·lēs′) *n.* suitcase [Fr.].

Val·kyr (val′·kir) *n.* (*Norse myth.*) one of Odin's nine handmaidens. who conduct the souls of slain heroes to Valhalla. Also **Valkyrie** (val·wir′·i·) **Valkyria** (val·kir′·ya). **Valkyrian** *a.*
val·ley (val′·i·) *n.* low ground between hills; river basin [L. *vallis*, vale].
val·or (val′·er) *n.* bravery; prowess in war; courage. **-ous** *a.* brave; fearless. **-ously** *adv.* **-ousness** *n.* [L. *valere*. to be strong].
valse (vàls) *n.* waltz, esp. one played as concert piece [Fr.].
val·ue (val′·ū) *n.* worth; utility; importance; estimated worth or valuation; precise significance; equivalent; (*Mus.*) duration of note; *v.t.* to estimate worth of; to hold in respect and admiration; to prize. **-r** *n.* **-less** *a.* **valuable** *a.* precious; worth a good price; worthy; *n.* thing of value (generally *pl.*). **valuableness** *n.* **valuably** *adv.* **valuate** *v.t.* to set value on; to appraise. **valuation** *n.* value estimated or set upon a thing; appraisal. **-d** *a.* **valuator** *n.* [L. *valere*, to be worth].
valve (valv) *n.* device for closing aperture (as in pipe) in order to control flow of fluid, gas, etc. (*Anat.*) structure (as in blood-vessel) which allows flow of fluid in one direction only; (*Zool.*) either of two sections of shell of mollusk; (*Mus.*) device in certain instruments (as horn, trumpet, etc.) for changing tone. **-less, -like** *a.* **valvular** *a.* **-let, valvule** *n.* small valve [L. *valva*, leaf of folding door].
va·moose (va·mōós′) *v.i., t.* (*Slang*) to depart quickly; to leave; to decamp [Sp. *vamos*, let us go].
vamp (vamp) *n.* upper leather of shoe or boot; new patch put on old article; (*Mus.*) improvised accompaniment; *v.t.* to provide (shoe, etc.) with new upper leather; to patch; (*Mus.*) to improvise accompaniment to [Fr. *avant-pied*, front of foot].
vamp (vamp) *n.* (*Slang*) woman who allures and exploits men; adventuress; *v.t.* and *v.i.* (*Slang*) to allure and exploit; to flirt unscrupulously [contr. of *vampire*].
vam·pire (vam′·pir) *n.* reanimated body of dead person who cannot rest quietly in grave, but arises from it at night and sucks blood of sleepers; one who lives by preying on others; extortioner; a vamp. **— bat** *n.* of several species of bat of S. America which sucks blood

of animals. **vampiric, vampirish** a. **vampirism** n. [Fr fr. Serbian *vampir*].

van (van) n. covered wagon or motor truck for goods [contr. of *caravan*].

van (van) n. leaders of a movement. **-guard** n. detachment of troops who march ahead of army [Fr. *avant*, before; *garde*, a guard].

va·na·di·um (va·nā′·di·am) n. a metallic element (the hardest known) used in manufacture of hard steel [fr. *Vanadis*, Scand. goddess].

van·dal (van′·dal) n. one who wantonly damages or destroys property of beauty or value; **-ic** a. **-ism** n. [L. *Vandalus*, Vandau, tribe which ravaged Europe in 5th cent.].

van·dyke (van·dīk′) n. one of the points forming an edge, as of lace, ribbon, etc.; broad collar with deep points of lace as worn in portraits by *Van Dyck*; painting by Van Dyck. — **beard**, pointed beard. — **brown**, dark brown [*Van Dyck*, Flemish painter].

vane (vān) n. a device on a windmill, spire, etc. to show the direction of the wind; a weathercock; the blade of a propeller, of a windmill, etc.; a fin on a bomb to prevent swerving **-d** a. **-less** a. [O.E. *fana*, a banner].

van·guard (van′·gärd) n. See **van** (2).

va·nil·la (va·nil′·a) n. tropical American plant of orchid family; long pod of plant, used as flavoring. **vanillic** a. **vanillin** n. [dim. fr. Sp. *vaina*, sheath].

van·ish (van′·ish) v.i. to pass away; to be lost to view; to disappear; (*Math.*) to become zero. **-er** n. **-ing** a. disappearing. **-ingly** adv. [L. *evanescere*, fr. *vanus*, empty].

van·i·ty. See **vain**.

van·quish (vang′·kwish) v.t. to conquer in battle; to defeat in any contest; to get the better of; **-able** a. **-er** n. [Fr. *vaincre*, fr. L. *vincere*].

van·tage (van′·tij) n. better situation or opportunity; advantage; in tennis, same as 'advantage.' Used esp. in — **ground**, position of advantage [M.E. *avantage*, advantage].

vap·id (vap′·id) a. having lost its life and spirit; flat; insipid; dull. **-ly** adv. **-ness**, **vapidity** n. [L. *vapidus*, state].

va·por (vā′·per) n. any light, cloudy substance which impairs clearness of atmosphere, as mist, fog, smoke, etc.; a substance converted into gaseous state; anything unsubstantial; pl. (*Arch.*) disease of nervous debility; depression; melancholy; v.i. to pass off in vapor; (*Fig.*) to talk idly; to brag. **-ize** v.t. to convert into vapor; v.i. to pass off in vapor. **-izable** a. **-ization** n. **-izer** n. mechanism for splitting liquid into fine particles. **-ish** a. full of vapor; prone to depression. **-ishness** n. **-ous** a. like vapor; unsubstantial; full of fanciful talk. **-ously** adv. **-ousness** n. **-ings** n.pl. boastful talk. **-y** a. full of vapor; depressed [L. *vapor*].

var·i·a·ble (ver′·i·a·bl) a. changeable; capable of being adapted; unsteady or fickle; n. that which is subject to change; symbol that may have infinite number of values; indeterminate quantity; shifting wind. **variably** adv. **-ness** n. **variability** n. (*Biol.*) tendency to vary from average characteristics of species. **variant** a. different; diverse; n. different form or reading. **variance** n. difference that produces controversy; state of discord or disagreement. **variation** (ver′·i·ā′·shan) n. act of varying; alteration; modification; extent to which thing varies; (*Gram.*) change of termination; in magnetism, deviation of magnetic needle from true north; (*Mus.*) repetition of theme or melody with various embellishments and elaborations. **at variance**, not in harmony or agreement [L. *variare*, to change, vary].

var·i·col·ored (ver′·i·kul·erd) a. having various colors.

var·i·cose (var′·i·kōs) a. enlarged or dilated, as veins, esp. in legs [L. *varix*, a dilated vein; fr. *varus*, crooked].

var·ied a. See **vary**.

var·i·e·gate (ver′·i·a·gāt, ver′·i·gāt) v.t. to diversify by patches of different colors; to streak, spot, dapple, etc. **variegation** n. **-d** a. [L. *varius*, various; *agere*, to make].

va·ri·e·ty (va·rī′·a·ti·) n. state of being varied; diversity; collection of different things; many-sidedness; different form of something; subdivision of a species. — **show** n. mixed entertainment, consisting of songs, dances, short sketches, juggling, etc. [L. *varietas*, variety, fr. *varius*, various].

var·i·o·rum (ver·i·ō′·ram, var·i·ō′·ram) n. an edition of a work with notes by various commentators [L. = of various men].

var·i·ous (ver′·i·as, var′·i·as) a. different; diverse; manifold; separate; diversified. **-ly** adv. **-ness** n. [L. *varius*].

var·let (vär′·lit) n. (*Arch.*) page or attendant; scoundrel. **-ry** n. [O.Fr. *varlet*, var. of *vaslet*, fr. L.L. *vassalus*, vassal].

var·nish (vär′·nish) n. clear, resinous liquid laid on work to give it gloss and protection; glossy appearance; outward show; v.t. to lay varnish on; to conceal something with fair appearance **-ed** a. [Fr. *vernis*, varnish].

var·si·ty (vär′·sa·ti·) n. team, usu. athletic, representing a university, school, etc. in competition; a. designating such a team [contr. of *university*].

var·y (ver′·i·, var′·i·) v.t. to change; to make different or modify; to diversify; v.i. to alter, or be altered; to be different; **varied** a. various; diverse; diversified. **varier** n. **-ingly** adv. [L. *variare*, to vary].

vas (vas) n. (*Anat.*) vessel or duct. **-cular** (vas′·kya·lar) a. pert. to vessels or ducts for conveying blood, lymph, sap, etc. **-cuium** n. botanist's collecting box. **-omotor** a. pert. to nerves controlling tension of blood vessels and thus the flow of blood. n.pl. **vasa** [L.].

vase (vās, vāz) n. vessel for flowers or merely for decoration; large sculptured vessel, used as ornament, in gardens, on gateposts, etc. [L. *vas*, vessel].

vas·e·line (vas′·a·lēn) n. brand of petroleum used in ointments, pomades, as lubricant, etc. (*Cap.*) trademark for this [Ger. *Wasser*, water; Gk. *elaion*, oil].

vas·sal (vas′·al) n. one who holds land from superior, and vows fealty and homage to him; dependant; retainer. **-age** n. state of being a vassal [Fr. fr Celt. *gwaz*, servant].

vast (vast) a. of great extent; very spacious; very great in numbers or quantity; n. (*Poet.*) boundless space. **-ly** adv. **-ness** n. **-itude** n. [L. *vastus*, very great].

vat (vat) n. large vessel, tub, for holding liquids [O.E. *foel*, a vessel, cask].

vat·ic (vat′·ik) a. prophetic; oracular. Also **-al** a. **-inal** (va·tis′·i·nal) a. **-inate** (va·tis′·i·nāte) v.t. and i. to prophesy. **-ination** (vat·a·si·nā′·shan) n. [L. *vates*, a prophet].

Vat·i·can (vat′·i·kan) n. palace and official residence of Pope on Vatican Hill (L. *Mons Vaticanus*), in Rome; papal authority.

vaude·ville (vawd′·(a)vil, vōd′·vil) n. stage show with mixed specialty acts; variety show [fr. *Vau de Vire* in Normandy].

vault (vawlt) n. arched roof; room or passage covered with vault, esp. subterranean; cellar; sky; anything resembling a vault; v.t. to cover with arched roof; to form like vault. **-ed** a. arched [L. *volutus*, turned].

vault (vawlt) v.i. to spring or jump with hands resting on something; to leap or spring, as horse; v.t. to spring or jump over; n. such a spring [Fr. *volte*, turn; fr. L. *volutus*].

vaunt (vawnt, vänt) v.t. to boast of; to make vain display of; n. boast; vainglorious display. **-er** n. **-ingly** adv. [O.Fr. *vanter*; fr. L. *vanitas*, vanity].

veal (vēl) n. flesh of a calf killed for the table [O.Fr. *veel*, fr. L. *vitellus*, calf].

vec·tor (vek′·ter) n. (*Math.*) any quantity requiring direction to be stated as well as magnitude in order to define it properly; disease-carrying insect. **vectorial** a. [L. *vehere, vectum*, to convey].

Ve·da (vā′·da) n. most ancient sacred literature of Hindus. **Vedic** a. pert. to the Vedas [Sans. *veda*, knowledge].

ve·dette (va·det′) n. mounted sentinel placed in advance of outposts to give notice of danger [It. *vedetta*, fr. *vedere*, to see, fr. L. *videre*].

veer (vēr) v.t. and v.i. to turn; of wind, to change direction, esp. clockwise; (*Naut.*) to change ship's course; (*Fig.*) to change one's opinion or point of view [Fr. *virer*].

veg·e·ta·ble (vej′·(a)·ta·bl) a. belonging to plants; having nature of plants; n. plant, esp. plant used as food, e.g. potato, carrot, cabbage, bean. **vegetal** a. **vegetarian** (vej·a·ter′·i·an) n. one who abstains from animal flesh and lives on vegetables, eggs, milk, etc.; a. pert. to vegetarianism; consisting of vege-

tables. **vegetarianism** n. **vegetate** v.i. to grow as plant does; to lead idle, unthinking life. **vegetation** n. process of vegetating; vegetable growth; plants in general. **vegetational** a. **vegetative** a. **vegetatively** adv. **vegetativeness** n. [L. *vegetare*, to enliven].

ve·he·ment (vē′·a·mant) a. acting with great force; impetuous; vigorous; passionate. **-ly** adv. **vehemence, vehemency** n. impetuosity; fury; violence; fervor [L. *vehemens*, eager].

ve·hi·cle (vē′·(h)a·kl) n. any means of conveyance (esp. on land) as carriage, etc.; liquid medium in which drugs are taken, or pigments applied; means or medium of expression or communication. **vehicular** (vē·hik′·ya·ler) a. Also **vehiculatory** (L. *vehiculum*, fr. *vehere*, to carry].

veil (vāl) n. piece of thin, gauzy material worn by women to hide or protect face; covering; curtain; disguise; v.t. to cover with veil; to conceal. **-ed** a. **-less** a. **-ing** n. act of covering with veil; material from which veil is made. **to take the veil**, to become a nun [L. *velum*].

vein (vān) n. each of the vessels or tubes which receive blood from capillaries and return it to heart; (loosely) any blood vessel; (*Biol.*) one of the small branching ribs of leaf or of insect's wing; layer of mineral intersecting a stratum of rock; streak or wave of different color appearing in wood, marble, etc.; distinctive tendency; mood or cast of mind; v.t. to mark with veins. **-ed** a. **-less** a. surface. **-ous, -y** a. **venation** n. [L. *vena*].

veld, veldt (felt, velt) n. in S. Africa, open grass country [Dut. *veld*, a field].

vel·lum (vel′·am) n. fine parchment made of skin; paper of similar texture; a. [O.Fr. *velin*, fr. L. *vitulus*, calf].

ve·loc·i·pede (va·lås′·a·pēd) n. a vehicle propelled by the rider, early form of bicycle or tricycle [L. *velox*, swift; *pes*, the foot].

ve·loc·i·ty (va·lås′·a·ti·) n. rate of motion; swiftness; speed; distance traversed in unit time in a given direction [L. *velox*, swift].

ve·lours (va·loor′) n. sing. and pl. fabric resembling velvet or plush. Also **velour** [Fr.].

vel·vet (vel′·vit) n. soft material of silk with thick short pile on one side; a. made of velvet; soft and delicate. **-y** a. soft as velvet. **-een** n. a pile fabric made of cotton, or of silk and cotton mixed [L.L. *vellutum*, fr. L. *villus*, shaggy hair].

ve·nal (vē′·nal) a. to be obtained for money; prepared to take bribes; mercenary. **-ly** adv. **venality** n. quality of being purchaseable [L. *venalis*, fr. *venus*, sale].

ve·nat·ic, ve·nat·i·cal (vi·nat′·ik, ·i·kal) a. relating to hunting. **-ally** adv. [L. *venari*, to hunt].

vend (vend) v.t. to sell; to dispose of by sale. **-ible** a. **-ibly** adv. **-ibility, -ibleness** n. the quality of being saleable. **-or** n. person who sells. **-ue** n. public auction [L. *vendere*].

ven·det·ta (ven·det′·a) n. blood feud, in which it was the duty of the relative of murdered man to avenge his death by killing murderer or relative of murderer; any bitter feud [It. fr. L. *vindicta*, revenge].

ve·neer (va·nēr′) n. thin layer of valuable wood glued to surface of inferior wood; thin coating of finer substance; superficial charm or polish of manner; v.t. to coat or overlay with substance giving superior surface; to disguise with superficial charm. **-ing** n. act of treating with veneer; thin layer used in this process [Fr. *fournir*, to furnish].

ven·er·ate (ven′·a·rāt) v.t. to regard with respect and reverence. **venerator** n. **veneration** n. respect mingled with awe; worship. **venerable** a. worthy of veneration; deserving respect by reason of age, character, etc.; sacred by reason of religious or historical associations, aged. **venerability, venerableness** n. **venerably** adv. [L. *venerari*, to worship].

ve·ne·re·al (va·nir′·i·al) a. pert. to sexual intercourse; arising from sexual intercourse with infected persons [L. *Venus, Veneris*, goddess of Love].

ven·er·y (ven′·a·ri·) n. (*Arch.*) hunting; sports of the chase [L. *venari*, to hunt].

Ve·ne·tian (va·nē′·shan) a. pert. to city of Venice, Italy; n. native, inhabitant of Venice. — **blind**, blind made of thin, horizontal slats, so hung as to overlap each other when closed.

Venetian blind

venge·ance (ven′.jans) *n.* infliction of pain or loss on another in return for injury or offense. **vengeful** *a.* disposed to revenge; vindictive. **vengefully** *adv.* **vengefulness** *n.* [L. *vindicare*, to avenge].

ve·ni·al (vē′.ni.al) *a.* capable of being forgiven; excusable. **-ly** *adv.* **-ness, -ity** *n.* [L. *venialis*, pardonable, fr. *venia*, forgiveness].

ven·i·son (ven′.a.zn) *n.* flesh of the deer [Fr. *vendison*, fr. L. *venari*, to hunt].

ven·om (ven′.am) *n.* poison, esp. that secreted by serpents, bees, etc.; spite; malice. **-ous** *a.* poisonous; spiteful; malicious. **-ously** *adv.* **-ousness** *n.* [L. *veneum*, poison].

ve·nous, ve·nose (vē′.nas) *a.* pert. to veins or the blood in veins. **venosity** *n.* [L. *venosus*, fr. *vena*, vein].

vent (vent) *n.* small opening; outlet; flue or funnel of fireplace; touch hole of gun; utterance; emission; voice; escape; anus of certain lower animals; slit in back of coat; *v.t.* to give opening or outlet to; to let escape; to utter or voice; to publish. **-age, -er** *n.* **-less** *a.* **to give vent to**, to pour forth [Fr. *fendre*, fr. L. *findere*, to cleave].

ven·ti·late (ven′.ta.lāt) *v.t.* to remove foul air from and supply with fresh air; to expose to discussion; to make public. **ventilation** *n.* replacement of stale air by fresh air; free exposure to air; open discussion. **ventilator** *n.* contrivance for keeping air fresh [L. *ventilare*, fr. *ventus*, wind].

ven·tral (ven′.tral) *a.* belonging to belly; abdominal; opp. of *dorsal*; *n.* one of the pair of fins on belly of fish. **ventricle** *n.* (*Anat.* or *Zool.*) small cavity in certain organs, esp. one of chambers of heart. **ventricular** *a.* [L. *ventralis*, fr. *venter*, belly].

ven·tril·o·quism (ven.tril′.a.kwizm) *n.* art of speaking in such a way that words or sounds seem to come from some source other than speaker. Also **ventriloquy**. **ventriloquist** *n.* **ventriloquistic** *a.* **ventriloquize** *v.i.* to practice ventriloquism [L. *venter*, belly; *loqui*, to speak].

ven·ture (ven′.cher) *n.* undertaking of chance or danger; business speculation; *v.t.* to expose to hazard; to risk; *v.i.* to run risk; to dare; to have presumption to. **-r** *n.* **venturous** *a.* daring; risky. **venturously** *adv.* **venturousness** *n.* **-some** *a.* bold; dangerous. **-someness** *n.* [contr. of *adventure*].

ven·ue (ven′.ū) *n.* (*Law*) district in which case is tried; scene of an event [L. *venire*, to come].

ven·ule (ven′.ūl) *n.* small vein.

Ve·nus (vē′.nas) *n.* (*Myth.*) Roman goddess of love and beauty; brightest planet of solar system; beautiful woman [L.].

ve·ra·cious (va.rā′.shas) *a.* truthful; true. **-ly** *adv.* **-ness** *n.* **veracity** (va.ras′.a.ti.) *n.* quality of being truthful; truth; correctness [L. *verax, veracis*, fr. *verus*, true].

ve·ran·da, verandah (va.ran′.da) *n.* open porch or gallery, along side of house, often with roof [Sp. *veranda*, balcony].

verb (vurb) *n.* (*Gram.*) part of speech which expresses action or state of being. **-less** *a.* **-al** *a.* pert. to words; expressed in words, esp. spoken words; literal or word for word; pert. to verb; derived from verb. **-ally** *adv.* **-alize**

v.t. and *v.i.* to put into words; to turn into verb. **-alization** *n.* **-alism** *n.* something expressed orally; over-attention to use of words; empty words. **-alist, -alizer** *n.* **-atim** (ver.bā′.tim) *a.* and *adv.* word for word [L. *verbum*, a word].

ver·be·na (ver.bē′.na) *n.* genus of plants of family Verbenaceae, used in ornamental flower beds. Also called **vervain** [L.].

ver·bi·age (vur′.bi.ij) *n.* excess of words; use of many more words than are necessary; wordiness. **verbose** (ver.bōs′) *a.* prolix; tedious because of excess of words. **verbosely** *adv.* **verboseness, verbosity** (ver.bás′.a.ti.) *n.* [L. *verbum*, a word].

ver·bo·ten (fer.bō′.tan) *a.* forbidden [Ger.].

ver·dant (vur′.dant) *a.* green or fresh; flourishing; ignorant or unsophisticated. **-ly** *adv.* **verdancy** *n.* **verdure** (vur′.jer) *n.* greenness or freshness; green vegetation. **-less** *a.* [O.Fr. *verd*, fr. L. *viridis*, green].

ver·dict (vur′.dikt) *n.* decision of jury in a trial; decision or judgment [O.Fr. *verdit*, fr. L. *vere dictum*, truly said].

ver·di·gris (vur′.di.grēs) *n.* green rust on copper, bronze, etc.; basic acetate of copper, used as pigment, etc. [O.Fr. *verd de Gris*, Greek green].

verge (vurj) *n.* border, or edge; brink; a rod of office; mace of bishop, etc. **-r** *n.* one who carries verge or emblem of authority; caretaker of church [L. *virga*, slender twig].

verge (vurj) *v.i.* to tend; to slope; to border upon [L. *vergere*, to tend towards].

ver·i·fy (ver′.a.fi) *v.t.* to prove to be true; to confirm truth of; **verifier** *n.* **verifiable** *a.* **verifiability** *n.* **verification** *n.* act of verifying or state of being verified; confirmation [L. *verus*, true; *facere*, to make).

ver·i·ly (ver′.i.li.) *adv.* (*Arch.*) truly; certainly.

ver·i·sim·i·lar (ver.a.sim′.a.ler) *a.* having the appearance of truth; probable; likely. **-ly** *adv.* **verisimilitude** *n.* appearance of truth; probability; likelihood [L. *verus*, true; *similis*, like].

ver·i·ta·ble (ver′.a.ta.bl) *a.* actual; genuine. **-ness** *n.* **veritably** *adv.* [L. *veritas*, truth].

ver·i·ty (ver′.a.ti.) *n.* quality of being true; truth; reality [L. *veritas*].

ver·juice (vur′.jóos) *n.* sour juice of crabapples, unripe grapes, etc. used in cooking; sourness of disposition [Fr. *verjus*, fr. L. *viridis*, green; *jus*, juice].

ver·mi- (vur′.mi) *prefix.* fr. L. *vermis*, worm. **-an** *a.* worm-like; pert. to worms. **-celli** (·sel′.i., ·chel′.i.) *n.* paste made from same ingredients as macaroni, and formed into slender worm-like threads. **-cide** *n.* any substance that destroys worms. **-icidal** *a.* **-icular** *a.* pert. to worm; like a worm in shape or movement; vermiculate. **-curarly** *adv.* **-culate** *a.* *v.t.* to ornament in pattern like worm tracks. **-culation** *n.* **-form** *a.* having shape of a worm.

ver·mil·ion (ver.mil′.yan) *n.* prepared red sulfide of mercury; brilliant red color; *v.t.* to color with red. Also **vermeil** [L. *vermiculus*, little worm].

ver·min (vur′.min) *n.* collectively noxious or troublesome small animals or insects, e.g. squirrels, rats, worms, lice, etc.; low contemptible persons. **-ous** *a.* infested by vermin; caused by vermin; tending to breed vermin. **-ously** *adv.* **-ousness** *n.* [L. *vermis*, worm].

ver·mouth, vermuth (ver.móoth′, vur′.mōoth) *n.* cordial of white wine flavored with wormwood, used as aperitif [Ger.].

ver·nac·u·lar (ver.nak′.ya.ler) *a.* belonging to country of one's birth; native (usu. applied only to language or idiom); *n.* native idiom of place; mother tongue; common name for a plant, animal, etc. [L. *vernaculus*, native, fr. *verna*, home-born slave].

ver·nal (vur′.nal) *a.* belonging to, or appearing on, spring; youthful. **-ly** *adv.* — **equinox**, equinox occurring about March 21 [L. *ver*, spring].

ver·ni·er (vur′.ni.er) *n.* short, graduated-scale instrument, for measuring fractional parts [fr. P. *Vernier*, inventor].

Ver·o·nal (ver′.a.nal) *n.* hypnotic or sedative drug [Protected Trade Name].

ve·ron·i·ca (va.rán′.i.ka) *n.* genus of plants, including speedwell [L. *vettonica*, betony].

ver·ru·ca (va.róo′.ka) *n.* wart or wart-like elevation. *pl.* **verrucae** (·sē), **verrucose, verrucous** *a.* **verrucosity** *n.* [L.].

ver·sa·tile (vur′.sa.til) *a.* having aptitude in many subjects; liable to change; capable of moving freely in all directions. **-ly** *adv.* **-ness** *n.* **versatility** *n.* [L. *versatilis*, fr. *versare*, fr. *vertere*, to turn].

verse (vurs) *n.* metrical line containing certain number of feet; metrical arrangement of language; short division of any literary composition; stanza; piece of poetry. **-d** (vurst) *a.* skilled; experienced (foll. by 'in'); practiced. **versicle** *n.* little verse. **versify** (vur′.sa.fi) *v.t.* to turn prose into verse; to express in verse. *v.i.* to make verses. **versification** *n.* **versifier** *n.* [L. *vertere, versum*, to turn].

ver·sion (vur′.zhan) *n.* translation; account from particular point of view. **-al** *a.* [L.

versio, fr. *vertere*, to turn].

vers li·bre (ver′ lē′.br) *n.* free verse [Fr.].

ver·so (vur′.sō) *n.* left-hand page; reverse side of coin or medal [L.].

ver·sus (vur′.sas) *prep.* (*Law, Games*) against; contrasted with [L.].

ver·te·bra (vur′.ta.bra) *n.* one of the small bony segments of spinal column. *pl.* **-e, -i** *a.* pert. to vertebrae or spine. **vertebrate** *a.* having backbone; *n.* vertebrate animal [L.].

ver·tex (vur′.teks) *n.* highest point; summit; top of head; (*Astron.*) zenith; (*Geom.*) angular point of triangle etc. *pl.* **-es, vertices** (vur′.ta.sēz). **vertical** *a.* situated at vertex; directly overhead or in the zenith; upright or perpendicular; *n.* vertical line. **vertically** *adv.* **verticalness** *n.* **verticality** *n.* [L.].

ver·ti·go (vur′.ti.gō) *n.* sensation of whirling or swimming of head, with loss of equilibrium; dizziness. **vertiginous** (ver.tij′.a.nas) *a.* revolving; giddy; causing giddiness. **vertiginously** *adv.* **vertiginousness** *n.* [L. *vertigo*, whirling, fr. *vertere*, to turn].

ver·tu. See **virtu**.

ver·vain (vur′.vān) *n.* plant of genus *Verbena* [L. *verbena*].

verve (vurv) *n.* enthusiasm or vigor; energy; spirit [Fr.].

ver·y (ver′.i.) *a.* true; real; actual; genuine; now used chiefly to emphasize word following. *adv.* in a high degree; extremely. **verily** *adv.* truly [L. *versus*, true].

ves·i·cal (ves′.i.kal) *a.* (*Med.*) pert. to bladder. **vesicant** *a.* tending to raise blisters; *n.* blistering application. **vesicate** *v.t.* to raise blisters on. **vesication** *n.* process of blistering. **vesicle** *n.* small bladder-like structure; blister; cyst. **vesicular** (va.sik′.ya.ler) *a.* pert. to vesicles. **vesiculate, vesiculose, vesiculous** *a.* vesicular **vesiculation** *n.* [L. *vesica*, bladder].

Ves·per (ves′.per) *n.* the evening star, Venus; (*l.c.*) evening; *a.* (*l.c.*) pert. to evening or vespers. **-s** *n.pl.* an evening prayer; evensong; late afternoon or evening service. [L. *vesper*].

ves·pi·ar·y (ves.pi.er′.i.) *n.* paperlike wasps' nest. **vespid** *n.* social wasp or bee [L. *vespa*, wasp].

ves·sel (ves′.al) *n.* utensil for holding either liquids or solids; large ship; (*Anat.*) tube or canal; recipient or means of conveying something [L. *vas*].

vest (vest) *n.* short, sleeveless garment worn under a man's suit coat; undergarment; *v.t.* to clothe; to cover; to put in possession; to endow; to furnish with authority. **-ed** *a.* that cannot be transferred or taken away; robed. **-ment** *n.* ceremonial or official garment. **-ure** *n.* (*Arch.*) clothing. **-ee** *n.* a vest. **—pocket** *a.* relatively small (as a book) [L. *vestis*, garment].

ves·tal (ves′.tal) *a.* chaste; pure. *n.* nun; chaste woman [fr. Rom. Myth. *Vesta*, goddess of the hearth].

ves·ti·bule (ves′.ta.būl) *n.* small room or hall between outer and inner doors at entrance to house or building [L. *vestibulum*, entrance].

ves·tige (ves′.tij) *n.* trace or sign; mark of something that has been; remains; (*Biol.*) trace of some part or organ formerly present in body. **vestigial** *a.* **vestigially** *adv.* [L. *vestigium*, a footprint].

ves·try (ves′.tri.) *n.* room attached to church for holding ecclesiastical vestments, prayer meetings, etc.; committee of parishioners to deal with parochial affairs. **-man** *n.* [L. *vestiarium*, fr. *vestis*, garment].

vet (vet) *n.* (*Colloq. abbrev.*) veterinary surgeon or a veteran.

vetch (vech) *n.* plant of bean family used for fodder [L. *vicia*].

vet·er·an (vet′.er.an) *n.* person who has served a long time; *a.* long practiced [L. *veteranus*, fr. *vetus*, old].

vet·er·i·nar·y (vet′.er.a.ner.i.) *a.* pert. to healing diseases and surgical treatment of domestic animals. **veterinarian** *n.* one skilled in medical and surgical treatment of animals [L. *veterinarius*, pert. to beasts of burden].

ve·to (vē′.tō) *n.* power or right of forbidding. *pl.* **-es.** *v.t.* to withhold assent to; to reject. **-er** *n.* **-less** *a.* [L. *veto*, I forbid].

vex (veks) *v.t.* to make angry; to irritate; to distress. **-ation** *n.* **-atious** *a.* causing vexation; distressing. **-atiously** *adv.* **-atiousness** *n.* **-ed** *a.* [L. *vexare*, to harass].

vi·a (vī′.a, vē′.a) *prep.* by way of [L.].

vi·a·ble (vī′.a.bl) *a.* born alive and sufficiently developed to be able to live; capable of living or growth. **viability** *n.* [L. *vita*, life].

vi·a·duct (vī′.a.dukt) *n.* high bridge or series of arches for carrying road or railway over valley etc. [L. *via*, way; *ducere*, to lead].

vi·al (vī′.al) *n.* small glass bottle; phial; *v.t.* to put into a vial [Gk. *phialē*, shallow bowl].

vi·and (vī′.and) *n.* article of food; chiefly *pl.* food, victuals, provisions [L. *vivenda*, provisions, fr. *vivere*, to live].

vi·at·i·cum (vī.at′.i.kam) *n.* supplies for a journey; Communion or Eucharist given to dying person. *pl.* **-s, viatica** [L. *via*, a way].

vi·brate (vī′.brāt) *v.t.* to move to and fro; to cause to quiver; to measure by vibrations or oscillations; *v.i.* to swing or oscillate; to quiver; to thrill or throb; of sound, to produce quivering effect; to sound tremulous.

vibration *n.* **vibrator** *n.* **vibratory** *a.* vibrating; causing vibration. **vibrant** *a.* vibrating; thrilling or throbbing; powerful. **vibrancy** *n.* **vibrantly** *adv.* [L. *vibrare*, to swing or shake].

viaduct

vi·bur·num (vi·bur′·nam) *n.* any of a group of shrubs of honeysuckle family [L.].

vic·ar (vik′·er) *n.* a deputy; clergyman. **-age** *n.* residence of vicar. **-ial** (vi·ker′·i·al) *a.* pert. to, acting as, vicar. **-ship** *n.*

vi·car·i·ous (vi·kar′·i·as) *a.* delegated, substituted; done or suffered for another. **-ly** *adv.* **-ness** *n.* [L. *vicarius*, deputy].

vice (vis) *n.* depravity or immoral conduct; blemish or defect in character, etc.; failing or bad habit. **vicious** (vish′·as) *a.* depraved; wicked; spiteful; not well broken, as horse. **viciously** *adv.* **viciousness** *n.* **vicious circle**, describes state in which remedy for evil produces second evil, which when remedied in its turn leads back to first [L. *ritium*, blemish, fault].

vice See **vise**.

vice- (vis) *prefix* in words signifying persons, denoting one who acts in place of another, or one who is second in authority, as **vice-ad-miral**, **vice-chairman**, **vice-president**, **vice-principal**, etc. [L. *vice*, in place of].

vice·ge·rent (vis·jir′·ant) *a.* exercising delegated power; *n.* holder of delegated authority [L. *vice*, in place of; *gerere*, to act].

vice·roy (vis′·roi) *n.* governor of country or province who rules as representative of his king; red and black butterfly [L. *vice*, in place of; *roi*, king].

vi·ce ver·sa (vi′·si·ver′·sa) *adv.* the order being reversed; the other way round [L.].

vi·chy·ssoise (vē·shē·swáz′) *n.* thick cream soup of potatoes [Fr.].

vi·cin·i·ty (va·sin·a·ti·) *n.* neighborhood; nearness or proximity. **vicinage** (vis′·n·ij) *n.* neighborhood [L. *vicinus*, near].

vi·sious See **vice**.

vi·cis·si·tude (va·sis′·a·tūd) *n.* regular change or succession; alteration; *pl.* ups and downs of fortune. **vicissitudinary, vicissitudinous** *a.* [L. *vicissitudo*, alteration].

vic·tim (vik′·tim) *n.* living creature sacrificed in performance of religious ceremony; person, or thing, destroyed or sacrificed; person who suffers; dupe or prey. **-ize** *v.t.* to make victim of. **-ization** *n.* **-izer** *n.* [L. *victima*].

vic·tor (vik′·ter) *n.* one who defeats enemy in battle; conqueror; winner in contest. **-y** *n.* defeat of enemy in battle, or of antagonist in contest; conquest; triumph. **-ious** (vik·tōr′·i·as) *a.* having conquered; indicating victory; triumphant; winning. **-iously** *adv.* **-iousness** *n.* [L. *victor*, fr. *vincere* to conquer].

vic·to·ri·a (vik·tōr′·i·a) *n.* low four-wheeled carriage with folding top; early touring car with folding top [fr. Queen *Victoria*].

Vic·to·ri·an (vik·tōr′·i·an) *a.* of or characteristic of time of Queen *Victoria*; prudish; easily shocked; (of style) ornate, flowery.

vic·tro·la (vik·trō′·la) *n.* a phonograph [Trade Mark].

vict·ual (vit′·l) *v.t.* to supply with provisions; *v.i.* to take in provisions. **-s** *n.pl.* (Colloq.) food. **-er** (vit′·ler) *n.* one who supplies provisions. **-ess** *a.* [L. *victualis*, of food].

vi·cu·na (vi·kū′·na) *n.* S. Amer. animal; soft shaggy wool or fabric made from it [Sp.].

vid·e·o (vid′·i·ō) *n.* television; *a.* of picture phase of television (opp. to *audio*) [L. = I see].

vi·dette See **vedette**.

vie (vi) *v.i.* to strive for superiority; to contend. *pr.p.* **vying**. *pa.p.* and *pa.t.* **-d** (vid) [O.Fr. *envier*, to challenge].

view (vū) *n.* sight; inspection by eye or mind; power of seeing; range of sight; what is seen; pictured representation of scene; manner of looking at anything, esp. mental survey; opinion; aim or intention. *v.t.* to see; to look at; to survey mentally; to consider. **-er** *n.* **-less** *a.* — **finder** *n.* device in camera for showing limits of picture. **-point** *n.* attitude or standpoint. **on view**, displayed. **in view of**, taking into consideration [L. *videre*, to see].

vig·il (vij′·il) *n.* staying awake at night, either for religious exercises, or to keep watch; a watch or watching; *pl.* nocturnal devotions. **-ant** *a.* watchful; alert; circumspect. **-ante** (an′·ti·) *n.* a member of an unlawful group which sets itself up to control and punish crime. **-antly** *adv.* **-ance** *n.* wakefulness; watchfulness [L. *vigilia*, a

watch].
vigilia, a watch].

vi·gnette (vin·yet′) *n.* orig. running ornament of leaves or tendrils; small designs used as headings or tail pieces in books; any engraving, woodcut, etc. not enclosed within border; photograph or portrait showing only head or quarter-length likeness against shaded background; short, neat description in words [Fr. dim. of *vigne*, vine].

vig·or (vig′·er) *n.* active strength; capacity for exertion; energy; vitality; forcefulness of style, in writing. **-ous** *a.* full of physical or mental strength; powerful. **-ously** *adv.* **-ousness** *n.* **-oso** *a.* Mus. direction. (Brit.) **vigour** [L.].

vi·king (vī′·king) *n.* Scand. sea rover or pirate who ravaged the northwest coast of Europe (8th–10th cent.) [O.N. *vikingr*].

vile (vil) *a.* mean; worthless; base; depraved; repulsive; shockingly bad. **-ly** *adv.* **-ness** *n.*

vil·i·fy (vil′·a·fi) *v.t.* to speak ill of; to try to degrade by slander; to defame or traduce. **vilifier** *n.* **vilification** *n.* [L. *vilis*, base].

vil·la (vil′·a) *n.* country seat; large suburban residence [L. = a farm-house].

vil·lage (vil′·ij) *n.* assemblage of houses, smaller than town and larger than hamlet; *a.* pert. to village; rustic. **-r** *n.* an inhabitant of a village [L. *villaticus*, of a villa].

vil·lain (vil′·an) *n.* wicked, depraved or criminal person. **-ous** *a.* wicked; vile. **-ously** *adv.* **-ousness** *n.* **-y** *n.* extreme wickedness; an act of great depravity [L.L. *villanus*, farm servant].

vil·la·nelle (vil·a·nel′) *n.* poem of 19 lines on 2 rhymes having 5 three-lined stanzas, followed by one of four lines [It. *villanella*].

vil·lein (vil′·in) *n.* serf who was slave to his lord but free with respect to others. **-age** *n.* serfdom [fr. *villain*].

vil·lus (vil′·as) *n.* one of the small, fine, hair-like processes which cover certain membranes; any of the fine soft hairs covering certain fruits, flowers, or plants. *pl.* **villi** (vil′·i) **villous** *a.* [L. *villus*, shaggy hair].

vim (vim) *n.* force; energy; vigor [L. *vis*, force].

vin·ai·grette (vin·a·gret′) *n.* small box, containing sponge saturated with aromatic vinegar salts, etc.; a savory sauce [Fr. dim. fr. *vinaigre*, vinegar].

vin·ci·ble (vin′·sa·bl) *a.* that may be conquered. **vincibility** *n.* [L. *vincere*].

vin·cu·lum (ving′·kya·lam) *n.* bond of union; (*Alg.*) straight, horizontal mark placed over several members of compound quantity to be treated as one quantity. *pl.* **vincula** [L. = bond, fr. *vincire*, to bind].

vin·di·cate (vin′·da·kāt) *v.t.* to justify; to maintain as true and correct; to clear of suspicion, dishonor, etc. **vindicable** *a.* **vindicability** *n.* **vindication** *n.* justification; defense of statement against denial or doubt. **vindicator** *n.* **vindicatory** *a.* [L. *vindicare*, to claim].

vin·dic·tive (vin·dik′·tiv) *a.* given to revenge; revengeful. **-ly** *adv.* **-ness** *n.* [L. *vindicta*, vengeance].

vine (vin) *n.* woody, climbing plant that produces grapes; any plant which trails or climbs. **vinery** *n.* greenhouse for rearing vines. **-yard** (vin′·yerd) *n.* plantation of grapevines. **vinic** *a.* pert. to, or obtained from, wine; alcoholic. **viniculture** *n.* cultivation of vines. **vinicultural** *a.* **viniculturist** *n.* **vinaceous, vinous** *a.* pert. to, or like, wine [L. *vinea*, vine; *vinum*, wine].

vin·e·gar (vin′·a·ger) *n.* acid liquor obtained from malt, wine, cider, etc. by fermentation, and used as condiment or in pickling. *a.* like vinegar; sour. **-y** *a.* [Fr. *vinaigre*, fr. L. *vinum*, wine; *acer*, sour].

vin·tage (vin′·tij) *n.* gathering of grapes; season's yield of grapes or wine; wine of particular year (Colloq.) any output of a season — **wine**, wine made from grapes of particularly good year [L. *vindemia*, vintage].

vi·nyl (vī′·nil, vin′·il) *n.* man-made plastic material.

vi·ol (vī′·al) *n.* medieval stringed musical instrument like violin but larger. **bass-viol** *n.* predecessor of violoncello. **-ist** *n.* one who plays viol [Fr. *viole*].

vi·o·la (vi·ō′·la) *n.* instrument larger than violin, but smaller than violoncello; alto or tenor violin [It.].

vi·o·la (vī′·ō·la) *n.* (*Bot.*) genus of plants including violet and pansy [L.].

vi·o·late (vī′·a·lāt) *v.t.* to infringe or break a promise; to treat with disrespect; to outrage or rape. **violation** *n.* transgression; profanation; ravishment; infringement. **violative** *a.* **violator** *n.* **violability** *n.* **violable** *a.* [L. *violare*].

vi·o·lence (vī′·a·lans) *n.* force; vehemence; intensity; assault or outrage. **violent** *a.* characterized by physical force, esp. improper force; forcible; furious; passionate. **violently** *adv.* [L. *violare*, fr. *vis*, force].

vi·o·let (vī′·a·lit) *n.* flower of genus Viola, generally of bluish-purple color; color produced by combining blue and red; *a.* bluish or purple [Fr. fr. L. *viola*].

vi·o·lin (vi·a·lin′) *n.* modern musical instrument of viol family, with four strings, played

with bow; fiddle. **-ist** *n.* [It. *violino*].

violet

vi·o·lon·cel·lo (vi·a·lau·chel′·ō) *n.* bass violin, much larger than violin, held between player's knees; usually *abbrev.* **cello**. **violoncellist** *n.* [It. dim. of *violone*].

vi·per (vī′·per) *n.* a venomous snake; malicious person. **-ish** *a.* like a viper. **-ine, -ous** *a.* venomous [L. *vipera*].

vi·ra·go (vi·rā′·gō) *n.* turbulent or scolding woman [L.].

vi·res·cent (vi·res′·ant) *a.* turning green. **virescense** *n.* **viredescent** *a.* **viredity** *n.* greenness, freshness [L. *virescere* fr. *viridis*, green].

vir·gin (vur′·jin) *n.* girl or woman who has not had sexual intercourse; maiden; *a.* without experience of sexual intercourse; unsullied; chaste; fresh; untilled (of land). **-al** *a.* pert. to virgin; maidenly; fresh and pure; *n.* old musical instrument like spinet. **-ity** *n.* **the Virgin**, mother of Christ [L. *virgo, virginis*, maiden].

Vir·gin·ia creep·er (ver·jin′·ya krēp′·er) climbing vine whose leaves turn bright red in autumn. **Virginia reel**, a country dance.

Vir·go (vur′·gō) *n.* (*Astron.*) the Virgin, one of the signs of Zodiac [L. *virgo*, virgin].

vir·gule (vur′·gūl) *n.* short diagonal line (/) between 2 words indicating either may be used [L. *verga*, slender twig].

vir·i·des·cent, viridity See **virescent**.

vir·ile (vir′·il) *a.* pert. to man; masculine; strong; having vigor. **virility** *n.* manliness; power of procreation [L. *vir*, man].

vir·tu (vur·tōō′) *n.* objects of art or antiquity, collectively; taste for objects of art [It. fr. L. *virtus*, excellence].

vir·tu·al (vur′·choo·al) *a.* being in essence or effect, though not in fact; potential. **-ly** *adv.* to all intents and purposes. **-ity** *n.* [L. *virtus*, excellence].

vir·tue (vur′·chōō) *n.* moral excellence; merit; good quality; female chastity; power or efficacy. **virtuous** *a.* upright; dutiful; chaste. **virtuously** *adv.* **virtuousness** *n.* [L. *virtus*, manly excellence].

vir·tu·o·so (vur·chōō·ō′·sō) *n.* one with great knowledge of fine arts; highly skilled musician, painter, etc. *pl.* **-s, virtuosi**. **virtuosity** (vur·chōō·as′·a·ti·) *n.* great technical skill in fine arts, esp. music [It.].

vir·u·lent (vir′·ya·lant) *a.* extremely poisonous; bitter in enmity; malignant; deadly. **-ly** *adv.* **virulence** *n.* acrimony; rancor; malignity; bitterness. **virulency** *n.* **virus** (vī′·ras) *n.* organism causing disease; corrupting influence [L. *virus*, poison].

vi·sa (vē′·za) *n.* official endorsement, as on passport, in proof that document has been examined and found correct, granting entry into that country [Fr. fr. L. *videre, to see*].

vis·age (viz′·ij) *n.* face; countenance; look or appearance. **-d** *a.* [Fr.].

vis·a·vis (vē′·za·vē) *adv.* face to face; *n.* person facing another [Fr. = face to face].

vis·cer·a (vis′·a·ra) *n.pl.* internal organs of body; intestines; entrails. **-l** *a.* [pl. of L. *viscus*].

vis·cid (vis′·id) *a.* glutinous; sticky; tenacious. **-ity** *n.* **viscose** (vis′·kōs) *n.* viscid solution of cellulose, drawn into fibers and used in making rayon, cellophane. **viscous** (vis′·kas) *a.* glutinous; tenacious; thick. **viscosity** *n.* [L. *viscidus*, sticky, fr. *viscum*, birdlime].

vis·count (vī′·kount) *n.* (*fem.* **-ess**) a degree or title of nobility next in rank below earl [L. *vice*, in place of; *comes*, companion].

vise (vis) *n.* device with two jaws that can be brought together with screw, for holding steady anything which needs filing, etc. Also **vice** [Fr. *vis*, a screw].

vise

vis·i·ble (viz′·a·bl) *a.* that can be seen; perceptible; in view. **visibly** *adv.* **visibility** *n.* degree of clarity of atmosphere, esp. for flying [L. *visibilis*, fr. *videre*, to see].

vi·sion (vizh′·an) *n.* act or faculty of seeing external objects; sight; thing seen; imaginary sight; phantom; imaginative insight or foresight. **-ary** *a.* apt to see visions; indulging in fancy or reverie; impractical; existing only in the imagination; *n.* one prone to see visions. **-al** *a.* [L. *visio*, sight, fr. *videre*, to see].

vis·it (viz′·it) *v.t.* to go, or come, to see; to punish; *v.i.* to be a guest; *n.* act of visiting or going to see; stay or sojourn; official or formal inspection. **-ant** *a.* visiting. *n.* one who visits; migratory bird. **-ation** *n.* act of visiting; formal or official inspection; visit of inordinate length; dispensation of divine favor or anger. **-or** *n.* one who visits. **-orial**, **-atorial** *a.* pert. to official visit or visitor **-ing** *n.a.* [L. *visitare*, fr. *videre*, to see].

vi·sor (vī′·zer) *n.* front part of helmet which can be lifted to show face; projecting from brim of cap; similar protective device on car windshield. **-ed** *a.* **-less** *a.* [Fr. *risière*, fr. O.Fr. *vis*, face].

vis·ta (vis′·ta) *n.* view, esp. distant view, as through avenue of trees; mental view [It. fr. L. *videre*, to see].

vis·u·al (viz′·, vizh′·oo·al) *a.* relating to sight; used in seeing; visible. **-ly** *adv.* by sight; with reference to vision. **-ize** *v.t.* to make visual; to call up mental picture of. **-ization** *n.* **-izer** *n.* [L. *visualis*].

vi·tal (vī′·tal) *a.* necessary to or containing life; very necessary. **-s** *n.pl.* essential internal organs, as lungs, heart, brain. **-ly** *adv.* **-ize** *v.t.* to give life to; to lend vigor to. **-ization** *n.* **-ity** *n.* the principle of life; vital force; vigor. — **statistics** data concerning births, deaths, etc. [L. *vitalis*, belonging to life].

vi·ta·min (vī′·ta·min) *n.* any of a group of chemical substances present in various foods and indispensable to health and growth [L. *vita*, life].

vi·ti·ate (vish′·i·āt) *v.t.* to make faulty or impure; to corrupt; to impair; to invalidate. **vitiation** *n.* **vitiator** *n.* [L. *vitium*, vice].

vit·i·cul·ture (vit′·a·kul′·cher) *n.* cultivation of grapevines [L. *vitis*, vine].

vit·re·ous (vit′·ri·as) *a.* pert. to, or resembling, glass; glassy; derived from glass. **-ness** *n.* **vitrescent** *a.* tending to become like glass; capable of being formed into glass. **vitrescence** *n.* **vitric** *a.* [L. *vitrum*, glass].

vit·ri·fy (vit′·ra·fī) *v.t.* to convert into glass or glassy substance; *v.i.* to be converted into glass. **vitrifiable** *a.* **vitrifiability** *n.* **vitrifaction**, **vitrification** *n.* [L. *vitrum*, glass; *facere*, to make].

vit·ri·ol (vit′·ri·al) *n.* sulfuric acid. **-ic** *a.* pert. to, resembling, derived from, vitriol; sarcastic, caustic; bitter. **-ize** *v.* **-ization** *n.* [L. *vitreolus*, of glass].

vi·tu·per·ate (vī·tōō′·pa·rāt) *v.t.* to abuse in words; to revile; to berate. **vituperative** *a.* abusive; scolding. **vituperatively** *adv.* **vituperator** *n.* **vituperation** *n.* [L. *vituperare*, to blame].

vi·va (vē′·va) *interj.* long live [It.].

vi·va·ce (vē·vä′·chi) *adv.* (*Mus.*) with spirit [It.].

vi·va·cious (vī·vā′·shas) *a.* lively; sprightly; animated; having great vitality. **-ly** *adv.* **vivacity** (vi·vas′·a·ti) *n.* liveliness [L. *vivax*, fr. *vivere*, to live].

vi·var·i·um (vi·ver′·i·am) *n.* place for keeping or raising living animals or plants [L.].

vi·va vo·ce (vī′·va vō′·si·) *adv.* orally; *a.* oral [L. = with the living voice].

viv·id (viv′·id) *a.* animated; lively; clear; evoking brilliant images; (of color) bright; glaring. **-ly** *adv.* **-ness** *n.* [L. *vividus*, lively, fr. *vivere*, to live].

viv·i·fy (viv′·a·fī) *v.t.* to imbue with life; to animate; to make vivid. **vivification** *n.* **vivifier** *n.* [L. *vivus*, living; *facere*, to make].

vi·vip·a·rous (vī·vip′·a·ras) *a.* producing young in living state, instead of eggs. **-ly** *adv.* **-ness** *n.* **viviparity** *n.* [L *vivus*, living; *parere*, to give birth].

viv·i·sec·tion (viv·a·sek′·shan) *n.* dissection of, or experimenting on, living animals for purpose of physiological investigations **-al** *a.* **-ist** *n.* [L. *vivus*, alive; *secare*, to cut].

vix·en (vik′·en) *n.* she-fox; cross bad-tempered woman. **-ish** *a.* [O.E. *fyxen*, a she-fox].

vi·zier, **vi·zir** (vi·zir′) *n.* high executive officer in Turkey and other Oriental countries. **-ate**, **-ship** *n.* **-ial** *a.* [Ar. *wazir*].

vo·ca·ble (vō′·ka·bl) *n.* a word esp. with ref. to sound rather than meaning; term [L. *vocabulum*, an appellation].

vo·cab·u·lar·y (vō·kab′·ya·ler·i·) *n.* list of words, usu. arranged in alphabetical order and explained; wordbook; stock of words used by language, class, or individual [L. *vocabulum*, a word].

vo·cal (vō′·kal) *a.* pert. to voice or speech; having voice; uttered by voice; (*Phon.*) sounded; having character of vowel. **-ly** *adv.* **-ize** *v.t.* to make vocal; to utter with voice, and not merely with breath; *v.i.* to make vocal sounds. **-ist** *n.* [L. *vox*, the voice].

vo·ca·tion (vō·kā′·shan) *n.* divine call to religious career; profession, or occupation. **-al** *a.* **-ally** *adv.* [L. *vocare*, to call].

voc·a·tive (vak′·a·tiv) *a.* relating to, used in, calling or address; *n.* (*Gram.*) case used in direct address. [L. *vocare*, to call].

vo·cif·er·ate (vō·sif′·a·rāt) *v.t.* to utter noisily or violently; to bawl; *v.i.* to cry with loud voice. **vociferation** *n.* **vociferator** *n.* **vociferous** *a.* making loud outcry; noisy or clamorous. **vociferously** *adv.* **vociferousness** *n.* [L. *vox, vocis*, the voice; *ferre*, to carry].

vod·ka (vad′·ka) *n.* in Russia and Poland alcoholic liquor distilled from cereals or potatoes [Russ. = little water].

vogue (vōg) *n.* prevailing fashion; mode; style; current usage [Fr.].

voice (vois) *n.* faculty of uttering audible sounds; sound produced by organs of respiration; utterance; quality of utterance; expression of feeling or opinion; vote; share in discussion; (*Gram.*) mode of inflecting verbs to show relation of subject to action, as *active, passive voice*; *v.t.* to give expression to; to announce. **-d** (voist) *a.* furnished with voice or with expression; (*Phon.*) uttered with vocal tone. **-ful** *a.* **-less** *a.* **-lessly** *adv.* **-lessness** *n.* [L. *vox*, voice].

void (void) *a.* empty; being without; not legally binding; *n.* an empty space; *v.t.* to make vacant; to empty out; to make ineffectual or invalid. **-er** *n.* **-ness** *n.* **-able** *a.* **-ance** *n.* act of voiding; state of being void; (*Eccles.*) ejection from benefice [O.Fr. *voit*].

voile (voil, vwäl) *n.* thin cotton, woolen, or silk material [Fr. = veil].

vo·lant (vō′·lant) *a.* borne through the air; capable of flying [L. *volare*, to fly].

Vo·la·puk (vō′·la·pook′) *n.* artificial language invented in 1879 [= world's speech].

vol·a·tile (val′·a·tal) *a.* evaporating quickly; easily passing into a vapor state; fickle; changeable. **volatilize** *v.t.* and *v.i.* to render or become volatile; to cause to pass off in vapor. **volatilizable** *a.* **volatilization** *n.* **volatizer** *n.* **volatility** *n.* [L. *volatilis*, flying].

vol·ca·no (val·kā′·nō) *n.* opening in crust of earth, from which heated solid, liquid, and gaseous matters are ejected. **volcanic** (val·kan′·ik) *a.* **volcanically** *adv.* **volcanicity** [It. fr. L. *Vulcanus*, god of fire, whose forge was supposed to be below Mt. Etna].

vole (vōl) *n.* mouse-like rodent living out-of-doors [Scan. *roll*, field].

vol·i·tant (val′·a·tant) *a.* volant; flying; having power of flight. **volitation** *n.* flight. **volitational** *a.* [L.*volare*, to fly].

vo·li·tion (vō·lish′·an) *n.* act of willing or choosing; exercise of will. **-al** *a.* **-ally** *adv.*

vol·i·tive *a.* [L. *volo, velle*, to be willing].

vol·ley (val′·i·) *n.* discharge of many shots or missiles at one time; missiles so discharged; rapid utterance; (*Tennis*) return of ball before it touches ground; *v.t.* to discharge in a volley; *v.i.* to fly in a volley; to sound together; (*Tennis*) to return ball before it touches ground. **-er** *n.* **-ball** *n.* team game played with ball and net. [L. *volare*, to fly].

volt (vōlt) *n.* practical unit of electro-motive force, being the pressure which causes current of one ampere to flow through resistance of one ohm. **-age** *n.* electro-motive force reckoned in volts. **-aic** *a.* **-meter** *n.* instrument used for measuring electro-motive force in volts [*Volta*, Italian scientist].

volt, volte (vōlt) *n.* in fencing, sudden turn or movement to avoid thrust; gait, or track, made by horse going sideways round center; circle so made [Fr. fr. L. *volvere*, to roll].

volte-face (vawlt·fas′) *n.* turning round; sudden reversal of opinion or direction [Fr.].

vol·u·ble (val′·ya·bl) *a.* having flowing and rapid utterance; fluent in speech; glib. **volubly** *adv.* **-ness**, **volubility** *n.* [L. *volubilis*, fr. *volvere*, to roll].

vol·ume (val′·yam) *n.* formerly, roll or scroll; book; part of a work which is bound; bulk or compass; cubical content; power, fullness of voice or musical tone. **volumetric** *a.* pert. to measurement by volume. **volumetrically** *adv.* **voluminal** *a.* pert. to cubical content. **voluminous** *a.* consisting of many volumes; bulky. **voluminousness** *n.* **voluminosity** *n.* [L. *volumen*, roll or scroll, fr. *volvere*, to roll].

vol·un·tar·y (val′·an·ter·i·) *a.* proceeding from choice or free will; unconstrained; spontaneous; subject to the will; *n.* organ solo played during, or after, church service. **voluntarily** *adv.* **voluntariness** *n.* [L. *voluntas*, will].

vol·un·teer (val·an·tēr′) *n.* one who enters service, esp. military, of his own free will; *a.* serving as a volunteer; composed; pert. to volunteers; *v.t.* to offer or bestow voluntarily; *v.i.* to enter into of or of one's own free will [L. *voluntas*, free will].

vo·lup·tu·ar·y (va·lup′·choo·er·i·) *n.* one addicted to luxurious living or sensual gratification; sensualist; *a.* concerned with, or promoting, sensual pleasure. **voluptuous** *a.* **voluptuously** *adv.* **voluptuousness** *n.* [L. *voluptas*, pleasure].

vo·lute (va·lōōt′) *n.* (*Archit.*) spiral scroll used in Ionic, Corinthian, and Composite capitals; (*Zool.*) tropical spiral shell; *a.* rolled up spiraled. **-d** *a.* **volution** *n.* [L. *volvere*, *volutum*, to roll].

vom·it (vam′·it) *v.t.* to eject from stomach by mouth; to spew or disgorge; *v.i.* to eject contents of stomach by mouth; *n.* matter ejected from stomach. **-er** *n.* **-ive** *a.* **-ory** *a.* provoking vomiting; *n.* emetic; an opening through which matter is discharged [L. *vomere*, to throw up].

voo·doo (vōō′·dōō) *n.* body of primitive rites and practices; one who practices such rites; evil spirit; *a.* belonging to, or connected with, system of voodoo. **-ism** *n.* [Creole Fr. *vandoux*, a sorcerer].

vo·ra·cious (vō·rā′·shas) *a.* greedy in eating; eager to devour; ravenous. **-ly** *adv.* **-ness**, **voracity** (vō·ras′·i·ti·) *n.* [L. *vorax*, greedy to devour].

vor·tex (vawr′·teks) *n.* whirling motion of any fluid, forming depression in center of circle; whirlpool; whirling mass of air, fire, etc. which draws with irresistable power. *pl.* **-es**, **vortices** (vawr′·ti·sēz) **vortical**, **vorticose** *a.* **vortically** *adv.* [L.].

vo·ta·ry (vō′·ta·ri·) *a.* consecrated by vow devoted to any service, study, etc. **votaress** or promise; *n.* one engaged by vow; one *n.(fem.)* [L. *votum*, vow].

vote (vōt) *n.* formal expression of wish, choice, or opinion, of individual, or a body of persons; expression of will by a majority; right to vote; suffrage; what is given or allowed by vote; *v.t.* to declare by general consent; *v.i.* to express one's choice, will, or preference. **-r** *n.* [L. *votum*, vow].

vo·tive (vō′·tiv) *a.* offered or consecrated by vow; given in fulfillment of vow. **-ly** *adv.* **-ness** *n.* [L. *votivus*, promised by vow].

vouch (vouch) *v.t.* to warrant; to attest; to affirm; *v.i.* to bear witness; to be guarantee (for). **-er** *n.* one who bears witness or attests to anything; paper or document that serves to vouch truth of accounts, or to establish facts; receipt [L. *vocare*, to call].

vouch·safe (vouch·sāf′) *v.t.* to condescend to grant or do something; *v.i.* to deign. **-ment** *n.*

vow (vou) *n.* solemn promise made esp. to deity; *v.t.* to consecrate or dedicate by solemn promise; to devote; *v.i.* to make vow or solemn promise [L. *votum*, vow].

vow·el (vou′·al) *n.* any vocal sound (such as *a, e, i, o, u*) produced with least possible friction or hindrance from any organ of speech; letter or character that represents such sound; *a.* pert. to vowel. **-less** *a.* **-ize** *v.* **-ization** *n.* [L. *vocalis*, fr. *vox*, voice].

voy·age (voi′·ij) *n.* journey esp. by sea; *v.i.* to sail or traverse by water. **-r** *n.* one who makes voyage [Fr. fr. L. *viaticum*, traveling money, fr. *via*, way].

Vul·can (vul′·kạn) *n.* (*Myth.*) Roman god of fire and of metal working. **vulcanize** *v.t.* to treat rubber with sulfur at high temperature to increase durability and elasticity. **vulcan·ization** *n.* **vulcanite** *n.* rubber hardened by vulcanizing. **vulcanizable** *a.* **vulcanizer** *n.* [L. *Vulcanus*, god of fire].

vul·gar (vul′·gẹr) *a.* of common people; in common use; coarse or offensive; rude; boorish. **-ly** *adv.* **-ian** *n.* vulgar person, esp. rich and unrefined. **-ize** *v.t.* to make vulgar. **-izer**

n. **-ization** *n.* **-ism** *n.* vulgar expression; grossness of manners. **-ness, vulgarity** *n.* commonness; lack of refinement in manners; coarseness of ideas or language [L. *vulgaris*, fr. *vulgus*, the common people].

vul·ner·a·ble (vul′·nẹr·(ạ)·bl) *a.* capable of being wounded; offering open to criticism; assailable; in contract bridge, denoting side which has won first game in rubber and is subject to increased honors and penalties. **-ness, vulnerability** *n.* **vulnerably** *adv.*

[L. *vulnus*, wound].

vul·pine (vul′·pīn) *a.* pert. to fox; cunning; crafty [L. *vulpes*, fox].

vul·ture (vul′·cher) *n.* large, rapacious bird of prey; rapacious person. **vulturine, vulturish, vulturious** *a.* characteristic of vulture; rapacious [L. *vultur*].

vul·va (vul′·vạ) *n.* fissure in external organ of generation in female [L.].

vy·ing (vī′·ing) *pr.p.* of **vie.**

W

wad (wȧd) *n.* little tuft or bundle; soft mass of loose, fibrous substance, for stuffing, etc., roll of bank notes; *v.t.* to form into wad; to line with wadding; to pad; *pr.p.* **-ding.** *pa.t.* and *pa.p.* **-ded. -ding** *n.* soft material for wads [Scand.].

wad·dle (wȧd′·l) *v.i.* to walk like duck, with short swaying steps; *n.* slow, rocking gait [freq. of *wade*].

wade (wȧd) *v.i.* to walk through something which hampers movement, as water, mud, etc.; to cope with, as accumulation or work; *v.t.* to cross (stream) by wading; *n.* a wading. **-r** *n.* one who wades; long-legged bird, e.g. stork, heron. **-rs** *n.pl.* high waterproof boots [O.E. *wadan*].

wa·di, wa·dy (wȧd′·i·) *n.* channel or stream which is dry except during rainy season [Ar. *wadi*, ravine].

wa·fer (wā′·fẹr) *n.* very thin biscuit; thin disk of unleavened bread, used in Eucharist service of R.C. Church; thin, adhesive disk for sealing letters; *v.t.* to seal or close with wafer. **-y** *a.* [O.Fr. *waufre*].

waf·fle (wȧf′·l) *n.* a thin cake of batter with criss-cross pattern. — **iron** *n.* hinged metal utensil for baking both sides of waffle at once [Dut. *wafel*, a wafer].

waft (wȧft, waft) *v.t.* to impel lightly through water or air; *v.i.* to float gently; *n.* breath or slight current of air or odor; puff. **-ure** *n.* [O.E. *wafian*, to wave].

wag (wag) *v.t.* to cause to move to and fro; *v.i.* to shake; to swing; to vibrate. *pr.p.* **-ging.** *pa.p., pa.t.* **-ged.** *n.* swinging motion, to and fro [O.E. *wagian*].

wag (wag) *n.* droll, witty person; humorist. **-gery** *n.* pleasantry; prank; jocularity. **-gish** *a.* frolicsome; droll. **-gishly** *adv.* **-gishness** *n.* [orig. E. *wag-halter*, one who deserves hanging—jocularly].

wage (wāj) *v.t.* to carry on; *n.* (usu. *pl.*) payment paid for labor or work done; hire; reward; pay [O.Fr. *wagier*].

wa·ger (wā′·jẹr) *n.* something staked on issue of future event or of some disputed point; bet; stake; *v.t.* to bet; to lay wager. **-er** *n.* [O.Fr. *wageure*, fr. Gothic, *wadi*, pledge].

wag·gle (wag′·l) *v.t.* and *v.i.* to move one way and the other; to wag [freq. of *wag*].

wag·on (wag′·ạn) *n.* four-wheeled vehicle or truck, for carrying heavy freight; (*Brit.*) railway freight car. (*Colloq.*) station wagon; police wagon. **-er,** *n.* one who drives wagon. **-ette** *n.* four-wheeled open carriage with two lengthwise seats facing one another behind driver's seat. **-less** *a.* **-load** *n.* [Dut. *wagen*].

wag·tail (wag′·tāl) *n.* bird distinguished by long tail almost constantly in motion.

waif (wāf) *n.* homeless person, esp. neglected child; stray article or animal [Ice. *veif*].

wail (wāl) *v.t.* and *v.i.* to lament (over); to express sorrow audibly; to weep; to bewail; to bemoan; to cry loudly; *n.* loud weeping; great mourning; doleful cry. **-er** *n.* **ing** *n.* **-ingly** *adv.* [O.N. *vaela*].

wain (wān) *n.* (*Poetic*) wagon, esp. in farm use. **wainwright** *n.* wagon maker [O.E. *waegen*].

wain·scot (wān′·skạt) *n.* paneling of wood or other material used as lining for inner walls of building; lower part of a wall; *v.t.* to line with wainscoting. **-ing** *n.* wall paneling material [Low, Ger. *wagenschot*, oak wood].

waist (wāst) *n.* part of human body immediately below ribs and above hips; garment or part of woman's dress covering from neck to waist; middle part of anything; part of upper deck of ship which lies between quarter-deck and forecastle. **-band** *n.* part of dress or trousers which fits round waist [M.E. *waste*, growth, fr. *wax*, to grow].

wait (wāt) *v.t.* to stay for; *v.i.* to stop until arrival of some person or event; to be temporarily postponed; to be expecting; to serve at table; to attend (on); *n.* act, period of waiting. **-er** *n.* one who waits; a man who waits on table; tray. **-ing** *n.* and *a.* **-ing-list** *n.* list of names of those wishing some article, etc. in short supply. **-ing room** *n.* room set aside for use of people waiting in public place, office, etc. **-ress** *n.* female waiter [O.Fr. *waiter*, to lurk]

waive (wāv) *v.t.* to give up claim to; to forgo; (*Law*) to relinquish a right, etc. **-r** *n.* (*Law*) relinquishment, or statement of such [O.N.Fr. *weyver*, to renounce].

wake (wāk) *v.t.* to rouse from sleep; to waken; to excite; to kindle; to provoke; *v.i.* to awaken; to be stirred up or roused to action. *pa.t.* and *pa.p.* **-d** or **woke.** *pr.p.* **waking.** *n.* vigil; act of sitting up overnight with corpse. **-ful** *a.* indisposed to sleep; sleepless; watchful; wary. **-fully** *adv.* **-n** *vt., i.* **-ner** *n.* **waking** *a.* as in *waking hours*, period when one is not asleep [O.E. *wacian*].

wake (wāk) *n.* that part of track immediately astern of ship; air disturbance caused in rear of airplane in flight. **in the wake of,** following behind; in rear of [Dut. *wak*].

wale (wāl) *n.* mark left on flesh by rod or whip; ridge in the weave of a fabric; *v.t.* to mark with wales. **waling** *n.* wale, piece of heavy timber fastened horizontally to tie together boards supporting sides of trench or vertical pieces of jetty [O.E. *walu*].

walk (wawk) *v.t.* to pass through, along, upon; to cause to step slowly; to lead, drive, or ride (horse) at a slow pace; *v.i.* to go on foot; to appear as specter; to conduct oneself; *n.* act of walking; slowest pace of quadruped; characteristic gait or style of walking; path for pedestrians; avenue set with trees; stroll; distance walked over; sphere of life; conduct. **-er** *n.* **-ie-talkie** *n.* portable wireless combined transmitting and receiving set. **-out** *n.* a strike. **—over** *n.* in sporting contests, easy victory. **—on** minor role in a play. **—up** apartment house without an elevator. [O.E. *wealcan*, to roll].

wall (wawl) *n.* structure of brick, stone, etc. serving as fence, side of building, etc.; surface or side; anything resembling a wall; *pl.* fortifications; works for defense; *v.t.* to enclose with wall; to block up with wall. **—board** *n.* lining of various materials for applying to or making walls. **-ed** *a.* provided with walls; fortified. **-flower** *n.* garden plant, with sweet-scented flowers; lady left sitting at dance for lack of partners. **-less** *a.* **-like** *a.* [L. *vallum*].

wal·la·by (wȧl′·a·bi·) *n.* a small kangaroo [Austral. native name].

wal·la·roo (wȧl′·a·rŏŏ′) *n.* large kangaroo [Austral.].

wal·let (wȧl′·it) *n.* folding pocketbook for paper money identification, cards, etc.

wall-eye (wawl′·ī) *n.* variety of fish having large eyes. affection of the eye due to opacity of cornea; an eye turned outward. **-d** *a.* glary-eyed [Scand.].

Wal·loon (wȧ·lŏŏn′) *n.* descendant of ancient Belgae, race of mixed Celtic and Roman stock, now French speaking population of Belgium; their dialect; *a.* of, or pert. to, Walloons [O.Fr. *Wallon*, fr. L. *Gallus*, a Gaul].

wal·lop (wȧl′·ạp) *v.t.* (*Colloq.*) to beat soundly; to strike hard; to stroke or blow. **-ing** *n.* a thrashing; *a.* tremendous; big.

wal·low (wȧl′·ō) *v.i.* to roll about (in mud, etc.); to thrive or revel in filth, vice, luxury, etc. [O.E. *wealwian*, to roll round].

wal·nut (wawl′·nut) *n.* large tree producing rich, dark-brown wood of fine texture; fruit of tree, large nut with crinkled shell [O.E.

wealh, foreign; *knutu,* nut].

walnut

wal·rus (wawl′·ras) *n.* mammal closely related to seal but with down-turned tusks [Dan. *hvalros* = whale-horse].

waltz (wawlts) *n.* ballroom dance in three-four time; music for this dance;*v.i.* to dance a waltz; to skip about, from joy, etc.**-er** *n.* **-ing** *n.* [Ger. *walzer*, fr. *walzen*, to roll].

wam·pum (wȧm′·pạm) *n.* strings of shells, strung like beads, used as money and for ornament by N. American Indians [Native, *wanpanpiak*, string of white shell beads].

wan (wȧn) *a.* having a sickly hue; pale; pallid; ashy; gloomy. **-ly** *adv.* **-ness** *n.* [O.E.].

wand (wȧnd) *n.* long, slender, straight rod; rod used by conjurers or as sign of authority [O.N. *vondr*, switch].

wan·der (wȧn′·dẹr) *v.i.* to ramble; to go astray; to be delirious; to depart from subject. **-er** *n.* **-ing** *a.* rambling; unsettled; *n.* journeying here and there, usually in *pl.* **-ingly** *adv.* **-lust** (wȧn′·dẹr·lust) *n.* urge to wander or travel [O.E. *wandrian*].

wane (wān) *v.i.* to decrease; to fail; *n.* decrease of illuminated part of moon; decline; diminution [O.E. *wanian*, fr. *wan*, wanting].

wan·gle (wang′·gl) *v.t.* (*Colloq.*) to obtain by deception or trickery; *v.i.* to manage with difficulty. **-r** *n.* (*Colloq.*) trickery; artifice.

want (wawnt) *n.* scarcity of what is needed; poverty; *v.t.* to be without; lack; *v.t.* to be without; to lack; to need; to crave; *v.i.* to be lacking; to have need. **-ed** *a.* desired; required; sought after; searched for (by police). **-er** *n.* **-less** *a.* **-ing** *a.* lacking; deficient. *prep.* without; minus. **-s** *n.pl.* requirements [O.N. *vant*].

wan·ton (wawn'.tan) *a.* dissolute; unrestrained; recklessly arrogant, malicious; *n.*; *v.i.* **-ly** *adv.* **-ness** *n.* [M.E. *wantowen*].

wap·i·ti (wàp'.a.ti.) *n.* N. American elk related to red deer [Amer.-Ind.].

war (wawr) *n.* armed conflict between two (groups of) states; state of opposition or hostility; profession of arms; art of war; *v.i.* to make war; to carry on hostilities; to contend. *pr.p.* **-ring.** *pa.t.* and *pa.p.* **-red.** — **cry** *n.* wild whoop or battle cry uttered by attacking troops; slogan. — **dance** *n.* wild dance, among savages, preliminary to entering battle. **-fare** *n.* hostilities. **—head** *n.* explosive cap on missile. **—horse** *n.* charger. **-like** *a.* disposed for war; martial; hostile; **-monger** *n.* advocate of war. **—paint** *n.* special adornment of Indians when on warpath; (*Slang*) full dress or regalia. **-path** *n.* military foray, esp. among Amer. Indians on scalping expedition. **-ship** *n.* vessel equipped for war. Also **man-of-war. civil war,** war between citizens of same country. **cold war,** state of international hostility short of actual warfare [O.N.Fr. *werre*, Fr. *guerre*].

war·ble (wawr'.bl) *v.t.* to sing in quavering manner; to trill; to carol; *v.i.* to sound melodiously; *n.* soft, sweet flow of melody; carol; song. **-r** *n.* one that warbles; bird with pleasant trilling song [O. Fr. *werbler*].

war·ble (wawr'.bl) *n.* hard tumor on back of horse. — **fly,** fly which lays its eggs in skin of cattle, horses, etc.

ward (wawrd) *v.t.* to repel; to turn aside; *n.* division of city; room for patients in hospital; guardianship; minor legally in the care of a guardian; divisions of a prison; custody; district of city or town for purposes of administration, voting, etc. slot in key; defensive movement in fencing, parry. **-en** *n.* civil defense officer; keeper; supervisor of prison. **-er** *n.* watchman; staff of authority. **-robe** *n.* cupboard for holding clothes; wearing apparel in general. **-room** *n.* mess room on liner or battleship for senior officers. **-ship** *n.* office of guardian; state of being under guardian [O.E. *weard*, protection].

ware (wer) *n.* article of merchandise; pottery; usually in combinations as, *earthenware, hardware,* etc.; *pl.* goods for sale; commodities; merchandise. **-house** *n.* storehouse for goods; *v.t.* to store in warehouse [O.E.*waru*].

ware (wer) *a.* aware; cautious; *v.t.* to beware of [A.S. *warian*].

war·i·ly, war·i·ness See **wary**.

warm (wawrm) *a.* having heat in moderate degree; not cold; hearty; lively; of colors, suggesting heat, as red, orange, yellow; excited; passionate; affectionate; *v.t.* to communicate moderate degree of heat to; to excite interest or zeal in; *v.i.* to become moderately heated; to become animated. **-blooded** *a.* of animals with fairly high and constant body-temperature; passionate; generous.**—hearted** *a.* affectionate; kindly disposed; sympathetic. **-ly** *adv.* **-ness, -th** *n.* slight heat; cordiality; heartiness; enthusiasm [O.E.*wearm*].

warn (wawrn) *v.t.* to notify by authority; to caution; to admonish; to put on guard. **-ing** *n.* advance notice of anything; admonition; caution; notice to leave premises, situation, etc.; *a.* cautioning [O.E.*warnian*].

warp (wawrp) *v.t.* to twist permanently out of shape; to bend; to pervert; to draw vessel or heavy object along by means of cable coiled on windlass; *v.i.* to turn, twist, or be twisted; *n.* distortion of wood due to unequal shrinkage in drying; system of spun threads extended lengthwise in loom on which woof is woven; a towing line. **-ed** *a.* twisted by unequal shrinkage; perverted; depraved. **-er** *n.* one who, or that which, warps. **-ing** *n.* [O.E. *weorpan,* to throw, to cast].

war·rant (wàr'., wawr'.ant) *v.t.* to give justification for; to authorize or sanction with assurance of safety; to guarantee to be as represented; to vouch for; to assure; to indemnify against loss; *n.* (*Law*) instrument which warrants or justifies act otherwise not permissible or legal; instrument giving power to arrest offender; authorization; guarantee; naval or military writ inferior to commission. **-able** *a.* **-ably** *adv.* **-ableness** *n.* **-ed** *a.* guaranteed. **-er, -or** *n.* **-y** *n.* security; guarantee. — **officer,** officer in Navy and Army intermediate between non-commissioned and commissioned officer [O.Fr. *varantir*].

war·ren (wawr'.an) *n.* enclosure for breeding rabbits and other game; overcrowded slum [O.Fr. *warenne,* Fr. *garenne*].

war·ri·or (wawr'.i·er) *n.* soldier; fighting man; brave fighter [*war*].

wart (wawrt) *n.* small hard conical excrescence on skin; (*Bot.*) hard, glandular protuberance on plants and trees. — **hog** *n.* African mammal of pig family with large warty protuberances on face. **-y** *a.* [O.E. *wearte*].

war·y (war'.i., wer'.i.) *a.* cautious; heedful; careful; prudent. **warily** *adv.* **wariness** *n.* [*ware*].

was (wuz) *pa.t.* of verb **to be** [O.E. *waes*].

wash (wàsh, wawsh) *v.t.* to free from dirt with water and soap; to tint lightly and thinly; to separate, as gold, by action of water; *v.i.* to perform act of ablution; to cleanse clothes in water; to be washable; *n.* clothes, etc. washed at one time; liquid applied to surface as lotion or coat of paint; flow of body of water; rough water left behind by vessel in motion; marsh or fen; shallow bay or inlet **-able** *a.* **-board** *n.* baseboard; board with a corrugated surface for washing clothes on; board above gunwale of boat to keep waves from washing over. **-er** *n.* one who washes; flat ring of metal, rubber, etc to make a tight joint, distribute pressure from nut or head of bolt, prevent leakage, etc. **-erman, -erwoman** *n.* **-basin, -bowl, -tub** *n.* for washing purposes. **-iness** *n.* state of being washy, weak, or watery. **-ing** *n.* act of one who washes; ablution; clothes washed at one time; *a.* used in, or intended for, washing. **-ing soda,** form of sodium carbonate used in washing. **-out** *n.* cavity in road, etc. caused by action of flood water; (*Colloq.*) failure or fiasco. **-y** *a.* watery; weak; thin; insipid. **-ed out,** exhausted; faded [O.E. *wascan*].

wasp (wàsp, wawsp) *n.* stinging insect like bee with longer body and narrow waist; an ill-natured, irritable person. **-ish** *a.* like wasp; irritable; snappy. **-ishly** *adv.* **-ishness** *n.* **—waisted** *a.* having slender waist [O.E. *waesp, waeps*].

was·sail (wàs'.al) *n.* ancient salutation in drinking of health; celebration or festivity; spiced ale; *v.i.* to carouse; to drink wassail. **-er** *n.* [O.E. *wes hal,* be hale = 'your health'].

waste (wàst) *v.t.* to expend uselessly; to use extravagantly; to squander; to neglect; to lay waste; to spoil; *v.i.* to wear away by degrees; to become worn and emaciated; to decrease; to wither; *a.* lying unused; of no worth; desolate; unproductive; *n.* act of wasting; that which is wasted; refuse; uncultivated country; loss; squandering. **wastage** *n.* loss by use, leakage, or decay. **-basket** *n.* container for waste materials. **-ful** *a.* full of waste; destructive; prodigal; extravagant. **-fully** *adv.* **-fulness** *n.* **-land** *n.* barrenland. — **pipe** *n.* discharge pipe for drainage water. **-r** *n.* **wastrel** *n.* waster; profligate; spendthrift. **to waste away,** to be in state of decline. **to lay waste,** to devastate [O.Fr. *waster;* L. *vastare,* to lay waste].

watch (wach) *n.* state of being on the lookout; close observation; vigil; one who watches; watchman; sentry; city night patrol of earlier times; portable timekeeper for pocket, wrist, etc.; one of the divisions of working day on ship; sailors on duty at the same time; division of the night; *v.t.* to give heed to; to keep in view; to guard; to observe closely; *v.i.* to be vigilant; to be on watch; to keep guard; to be wakeful; to look out (for); to wait (for). **-dog** *n.* guard dog; any watchful guardian. **-er** *n.* **-ful** *a.* vigilant; attentive; cautious. **-fully** *adv.* **-fulness** *n.* **-maker, -making** *n.* **-man** *n.* man who guards premises. **—night,** New Year's Eve. **—word** *n.* password; a slogan; rallying cry [O.E. *waecce*].

wa·ter (waw'.ter, wà'.ter) *n.* transparent, tasteless liquid, substance of rain, rivers, etc.; body of water; river; lake; sea; saliva; tear; urine; serum; transparency of gem; *v.t.* to wet or soak with water; to put water into; to cause animal to drink; to irrigate; to give

cloth wavy appearance; *v.i.* to shed water; to issue as tears; to gather saliva in mouth as symptom of appetite; to take in or obtain water. — **closet** *n.* sanitary convenience flushed by water. **—color** *n.* artist's color ground up with water; painting in this medium. **—colorist** *n.* **-course** *n.* channel worn by running water; canal. **-cress** *n.* aquatic plant with succulent leaves. **-ed** *a.* diluted with water; of silk fabrics upon which wavy pattern has been produced. **-fall** *n.* fall or perpendicular descent of water of river; cascade; cataract. **-fowl** *n.* any aquatic bird with webbed feet and coat of closely packed feathers or down. — **gauge** *n.* instrument for measuring height of water in boiler, etc. **—glass** *n.* mixture of soluable silicates of potash and soda, used in storing eggs or for preserving stone work; glass for drinking water. **-iness** *n.* state of being watery. **-ing place** *n.* a place where water may be obtained. **-ish** *a.* containing too much water; watery; thin. **-less** *a.* **-level** *n.* level formed by surface of still water; leveling instrument in which water is employed. **-lily** *n.* aquatic plant with fragrant flowers and large floating leaves. **—line** *n.* line on hull of ship to which water reaches. **—logged** *a.* saturated or full of water. — **main** *n.* large pipe running under streets, for conveying water. **—man** *n.* man who manages water craft; ferryman. — **mark** *n.* in paper making, faint translucent design stamped in substance of sheet of paper and serving as trademark. **-melon** *n.* large fruit with smooth, dark-green rind and red pulp. — **moccasin** *n.* poisonous semiaquatic pit viper of southern U.S., related to copperhead. — **polo** *n.* ball game played in water. — **power** *n.* power of water used as prime mover. **-proof** *a.* impervious to water; *v.t.* to make impervious to water. **-shed** *n.* area drained by a river. **-spout** *n.* whirlwind over water, producing vortex connecting sea and cloud, resulting in moving gyrating pillar of water; drain carrying rain water down side of building. **-tight** *a.* so fitted as to prevent water escaping or entering. — **tower** *n.* raised tank for water storage. **-way** *n.* fairway for vessels; navigable channel. — **wings** *n.pl.* small rubber floats filled with air to support learners at swimming. **-works** *n.pl.* reservoirs, etc. for the purification, supply and distribution of water; (*Slang*) tears. **-y** *a.* resembling water; thin or transparent, as a liquid. **above water,** financially sound; solvent. **heavy water,** deuterium oxide, differing from ordinary water in its density, boiling-point, and physiological actions. **high (low) water,** highest (lowest) elevation of tide; maximum (minimum) point of success, etc. **mineral water,** water impregnated with mineral matter and possessing specific medicinal properties; artificially aerated water. **in hot water,** involved in trouble. **in low water,** financially embarrassed. **of the first water,** of finest quality. **to hold water,** of statement, to be tenable or correct. **to water down,** to moderate [O.E. *waeter*].

watt (wàt) *n.* unit of power represented by current of one ampere produced by electromotive force of one volt (746 watts = 1 horsepower) [fr. James *Watt,* 1736-1819].

wat·tle (wàt'.l) *n.* fleshy excrescence, usually red, under throat of cock or turkey; one of numerous species of Australian acacia; woven work made of sticks and twigs for roofs, fences, etc. **-d** *a.* [O.E. *watel, watul,* hurdle].

wave (wāv) *n.* waving movement or gesture of hand; advancing ridge or swell on surface of liquid; surge; undulation; unevenness; extended group of attacking troops or planes; rise of enthusiasm, heat, etc.; wavelike style of hair dressing; spatial form of electrical oscillation propagated along conductor or through space; passage of sound or light through space; *pl.* (*Poet.*) the sea; *v.t.* to raise into inequalities of surface; to move to and fro; to give the shape of waves; to brandish; to beckon; *v.i.* to wave one way and the other; to flap; to undulate; to signal. **—band** *n.* range of wave lengths allotted for broadcasting, morse signals, etc. **-d** *a.* undulating. **wavily** *adv.* — **length** *n.* distance between maximum positive points of two successive waves; velocity of wave divided by frequency of oscillations. —let n. ripple. —like a. waviness n. waving a. moving to and fro. wavy a. [O.E. wafian, to brandish]. wa·ver (wā'·vẹr) v.i. to move to and fro; to fluctuate; to vacillate; to tremble; to totter. -er n. -ing n. and a. -ingly adv. [M.E. waveren, to wander about].

wax (waks) n. a fatty acid ester of a monohydric alcohol; an amorphous, yellowish, sticky substance derived from animal and vegetable substances; beeswax; sealing wax, cerumen, waxy secretion of ear; v.t. to smear, rub, or polish with wax. -bill n. name given to several small, seed-eating cage birds. -en a. made of or resembling wax; plastic; impressionable. -er n. -iness n. -ing n. —paper n. paper coated with wax, used for airtight packing. -wing n. hook-billed bird of chatterer family with quills tipped with red hornlike appendages resembling sealing wax. -work n. figure modeled in wax, pl. exhibition of wax figures. -y a. made of or like wax [O.E. weax, beeswax].

wax (waks) v.i. to increase in size; to grow; opposite of wane [O.E. weaxan].

way (wā) n. street; highway; passage; path; lane; route; progress; distance; method; mode; custom; usage; habit; means; plan; desire; momentum; movement of ship through water; state or condition. -bill n. list of passengers or articles carried by vehicle. -farer n. wanderer on foot. -faring a. and n. -lay v.t. to lie or wait in ambush for; pat. and pa.p. -laid. -layer n. -side n. border of road or path. -ward a. adjoining side of road. -ward a. liking one's way; perverse; refractory. -wardly adv. -wardness n. ways and means, methods; resources. by the way, as we proceed; incidentally. right-of-way n. right to use path through private property; such a path. under way, of vessel when moving. to make way, to step aside [O.E. weg].

we (wē) pron. plural form of I; another person, or others, and I [O.E.].

weak (wēk) a. feeble; frail; delicate; fragile; easily influenced; simple; low; faint; thin; watery; diluted; inconclusive; (Gram.) of verb, forming past by addition of d or t. -en v.t. to make weak; v.i. to become weak or less resolute. —minded a. indecisive. —kneed a. irresolute. -liness n. -ling n. feeble person, physically or mentally. -ly adv. -ness n. -er sex, women [O.N. veikr]. weal (wēl) n. streak left on flesh by blow of stick or whip; wale [fr. wale].

weal (wēl) n. (Arch.) prosperity; welfare. the common weal, well-being and general welfare of state or community [O.E. wela].

weald (wēld) n. (Poetic) woodland; open country. [O.E. weald, forest].

wealth (welth) n. riches; affluence; opulence; abundance. -iness n. -y a. [O.E. wela, wellbeing].

wean (wēn) v.t. to discontinue breast-feeding of infant gradually; to detach or alienate. -ling n. newly-weaned infant [O.E. wenian, to accustom].

weap·on (wep'·ạn, wep'·ṇ) n. instrument to fight with [O.E. waepen].

wear (wer) v.t. to carry clothes, decorations and the like, upon the person; to consume or impair by use; to deteriorate by rubbing; v.i. to last or hold out; to be impaired gradually by use or exposure. pat. wore. pa.p. worn. n. act of wearing; impairment from use; style of dress; fashion; article worn. -able a. -er n. -ing a. intended for wearing; exhausting; exhausting to mind and body. -ingapparel n. dress in general. wear and tear, loss or deterioration due to usage. to wear off, to disappear slowly. wear out, become useless [O.E. werian].

wear (wer) v.t., i. to bring ship on the other tack by presenting stern to wind; opposite to tack. pat. wore. pa.p. worn [var. of veer].

wear·y (wir'·i·) a. fatigued; tired; bored; exhausted; tiresome; v.t. to exhaust one's strength or patience; to make weary; v.i. to become weary; to become dissatisfied with. wearily adv. weariless a. tireless. weariness n. wearisome a. tedious; causing annoyance or fatigue. wearisomely adv. wearisomeness n. [O.E. werig].

wea·sel (wē'·zl) n. small, long-bodied, shortlegged, bloodthirsty carnivore [O.E. wesle].

weath·er (weTH'·ẹr) n. combination of all atmospheric phenomena existing at one time in any particular place; v.t. to expose to the air; to season by exposure to air; to sail to windward of; to endure; v.i. to decompose or disintegrate, owing to atmospheric conditions. —beaten a. seasoned, marked, or roughened by continual exposure to rough weather. Weather Bureau (bū·rō') n. meteorological office directed by U.S. Department of Commerce. —chart n. synoptic chart, an outline map on which lines are plotted to indicate areas of similar atmospheric pressure along with other meteorological conditions. —cock n. pivoted vane, commonly in shape of cock, to indicate direction of wind; one who changes his mind repeatedly. — forecast n. prediction of probable future weather conditions based on scientific

data collected by meteorological office. — gauge n. bearing of ship to windward of another. —glass n. instrument to indicate changes in atmospheric pressure; barometer. -ing n. process of decomposing of rocks, wood, etc. exposed to elements. — report, daily report of meteorological conditions. —strip v.t. to fit with weather stripping (strips used to keep out draft around doors, windows). —vane n. weather cock. under the weather, (Colloq.) ill; drunk [O.E. weder].

weave (wēv) v.t. to cross the warp by the woof on loom; to interlace threads, etc.; to construct, to fabricate, as a tale; v.i. to practice weaving; to move from side to side. pat. wove. pa.p. woven. n. style of weaving. -r n. [O.E. wefan].

web (web) n. that which is woven; whole piece of cloth woven in loom; weaver's warp; membrane which unites toes of water fowls; network spun by spider; anything as plot, intrigue, cunningly woven. -bed a. having toes united by membrane of skin. -bing n. strong, hemp fabric woven in narrow strips, used for chairs, etc. -footed a. [O.E. webb].

wed (wed) v.t. to take for husband or wife; to marry; to join closely; to contract matrimony. pr.p. -ding. pat. and pa.p. -ded or wed. -ded a. married; wholly devoted (to art, etc.) -ding n. nuptial ceremony; nuptials; marriage. [O.E. weddian].

wedge (wej) n. piece of wood or metal, tapering to thin edge at fore end, used for splitting, lifting heavy weights, or rendering rigid two parts of structure; anything shaped like wedge; something used for dividing; v.t. to jam; to compress; to force (in); to squeeze (in); to fasten with wedge. -d a. cuneiform or wedge-shaped; jammed tight [O.E. wecg].

Wedg·wood (wej'·wood) n. and a. fine Eng. pottery [fr. Josiah Wedgwood].

wed·lock (wed'·lãk) n. marriage; married state [O.E. wedd, a pledge; lac, a gift].

Wednes·day (wenz'·di·) n. fourth day of week [O.E. Wodnesdaeg, day of Woden, Norse god].

wee (wē) n. small; tiny [M.E. we, wei, bit].

weed (wēd) n. plant growing where it is not desired; sorry, worthless person or animal; (Colloq.) cigar; tobacco; v.t. to free from weeds; to remove (something undesirable). —killer n. preparation for killing weeds. -y a. full of weeds; lanky and weakly. to weed out, to eliminate [O.E. weed].

weed (wēd) n. (Arch.) garment; mourning garb, as of widow (usu. pl.) [O.E. waed].

week (wēk) n. seven successive days, usually Sunday to Sunday. —day n. any day of week except Sunday. —end n. Friday or Saturday to Monday; holiday for this period. -ly a. pert. to a week; happening once a week. n. publication issued weekly; adv. once a week. Holy Week, Passion Week, week preceding Easter Sunday [O.E. wicu].

weep (wēp) v.i. to grieve for by shedding tears; to cry; to drip; to exude water; v.t. to lament; to bewail. pat. and pa.p. wept. -er n. one who weeps; crepe band worn by men at funerals; male professional mourner; mourning sleeve, sash, or veil. -ing a. of trees whose branches droop, as weeping willow. -y a. [O.E. wepan].

wee·vil (wē'·val) n. common name given to thousands of different kinds of small beetles, all distinguished by heads lengthened out to resemble beaks—larvae attack plants and stored grain [O.E. wifel].

weft (weft) n. filling thread carried by shuttle under and over the warp in a weaving loom. Also woof [O.E. wefta].

weigh (wā) v.t. to find weight of; to deliberate or consider carefully; to oppress; to raise (anchor, etc.); v.i. to have weight; to be considered as important; to press hard; to bear heavily (on). -er n. -t n. gravity as property of bodies; heavy mass; object of known mass for weighing; importance; power and influence; v.t. to make more heavy. -tily adv. -tiness n. -ty a. having great weight; important; momentous; forcible. dead weight n. heavy burden [O.E. wegan].

weir (wir) n. fence of stakes set in stream for taking fish; a dam [O.E. wer].

weird (wird) a. unearthly; uncanny; (Colloq.) odd. -ly adv. -ness n. [O.E. wyrd, fate].

welch (welch) v.t., i. (Slang) to welsh. -er n.

wel·come (wel'·kam) a. received gladly; causing gladness; free to enjoy or use; n. kind or hearty reception; v.t. to greet with kindness and pleasure.

weld (weld) v.t. to join pieces of heated, plastic metal by fusion without soldering materials, etc.; to unite closely; n. homogeneous joint between two metals. -er n. [var. of well, to boil up].

wel·fare (wel'·fãr) n. well-doing or wellbeing; prosperity.

well (wel) n. shaft or tube sunk deep in ground to obtain water, oil, etc.; spring; fountain; source; bottom of elevator shaft; cavity or pit below ground level; chamber for catching surplus water or oil; enclosure in hold of fishing vessel, for preservation of fish; v.i. to issue forth in volume, as water [O.E. wella].

well (wel) a. comp. better. superl. best. in

good health; fortunate; comfortable; satisfactory; adv. agreeably; favorably; skillfully; intimately; satisfactorily; soundly; interj. exclamation of surprise, interrogation, resignation, etc. —advised a. prudent; sensible. —appointed a. handsomely furnished or equipped. —balanced a. eminently sane. —being n. welfare. -born a. of good family. —bred a. courteous and refined in manners; of good stock. —favored a. good-looking; pleasing to the eye. —informed a. knowing inner facts; possessing wide range of general knowledge; having considerable knowledge. —meaning a. having good intentions. —nigh adv. nearly; almost. —spoken a. cultured in speech; favorably commented on; speaking easily, fluently, graciously. —timed a. opportune. —to-do a. wealthy. as well as, in addition to; besides. -spring, source of stream, knowledge [O.E. wel].

Welsh, Welch (welsh, welch) a. relating to Wales or its inhabitants; n. language or people of Wales. —man, —woman n. —rabbit, or rarebit, savory dish consisting of melted cheese on toast [O.E. waelise, foreign].

welsh, welch (welsh, welch) v.t. and v.i. (Slang) to cheat by failing to pay a debt or meeting an obligation. -er n. [perh. fr. Ger. welken, to fade].

welt (welt) n. cord around border or seamline of upholstery, etc.; a flat, overlapping seam; narrow strip of leather between upper and sole of shoe; weal; (Colloq.) ridge on flesh from whiplash, etc. v.t. to furnish with welt; (Colloq.) beat soundly. -ed n. -ing n.

wel·ter (wel'·ter) v.i. to roll about; to wallow in slime, blood, etc.; n. confusion; turmoil. -ing a. [O.E. wealt, unsteady].

wel·ter·weight (wel'·ter·wāt) n. in boxing or wrestling, class of contestants weighing between 135lb. and 147lb.; boxer or wrestler of this weight.

wen (wen) n. small superficial tumor or cyst, esp. on scalp. -nish a. [O.E. wenn].

wench (wench) n. girl; maid; (Arch.) lewd woman; v.i. (Arch.) to associate with wenches. (Arch.) -ing n. fornication [O.E. wencel].

wend (wend) v.t. (Arch.) to direct; to betake (one's way); v.i. to go [O.E. wendan, to turn].

went (went) pat. of wend; pat. of go.

wept (wept) pat. and pa.p. of weep.

were (wur) pat. plural, and subjunctive singular and plural, of be [O.E. waeron].

were·wolf, wer·wolf (wir'·woolf) n. human being who, at will, could take form of wolf while retaining human intelligence [O.E. wer, a man; wulf, a wolf].

Wes·ley·an (wes'·li·ạn) n. pert. to Wesley or Wesleyanism. -ism n. Wesleyan Methodism, i.e. religion practiced in methodical manner [John Wesley, (1703-1791)].

west (west) n. point in heavens where sun sets; one of four cardinal points of compass; region of country lying to the west; a. situated in, facing, coming from the west; adv. to the west. —erly a. situated in west; of wind, blowing from west. -ern a. situated in west; coming from west; n. inhabitant of western country or district; film featuring cowboys in western states of U.S. —erner n. native of the west. —ernmost, -most a. farthest to west. —ward a. and adv. toward west. -ward(s) adv. -bound a. going west [O.E.].

wet (wet) a. comp. -ter. superl. -test. containing water; full of moisture; humid; dank; damp; rainy; n. water; moisture; rain; v.t. to make wet; to moisten; pr.p. -ting. pat. wet or ted. -blanket n. a kill-joy. -ness n. —nurse n. woman who suckles child of another. -tish a. humid; damp [O.E. waet].

weth·er (weTH'·er) n. castrated ram [O.E.].

whack (hwak) v.t. to hit, esp. with stick; to beat; (Slang) to share; v.i. to strike with smart blow; n. blow; (Slang) chance; good condition; share. -y a. [fr. thwack].

whale (hwāl) n. large fishlike mammal; (Slang) something huge; v.i. to hunt for whales. -back n. type of freight vessel on Great Lakes in N. America with covered, rounded deck. -boat n. long boat with sharp bow at each end. -bone n. baleen, an elastic, flexible, horny product of jaws of baleen whale. — oil n. lubricating oil extracted from blubber of sperm whale. -r n. man or ship engaged in whaling industry. [O.E. hwael].

whale (hwāl) v.t. (Slang) to thrash. **whaling** n. a thrashing.

wharf (hwawrf) n. structure on bank of navigable waters at which vessels can be loaded or unloaded; quay. pl. **-s, wharves.** v.t. to moor at, or place on, wharf. **-age** n. charge for use of wharf; wharf accommodation. **-inger** (hwawr'.fin.jer) n. one who owns or has charge of wharf [O.E. hwearf].

what (hwät, hwut) pron. interrogative pronoun (used elliptically, in exclamation, or adjectively); relative pronoun, meaning that which (used adjectively); a. which; which kind; conj. that; interj. denoting surprise, anger, confusion, etc.; adv. to what degree? **-ever** pron. anything that; all that. **-soever** pron. whatever [O.E. hwaet].

what·not (hwut'.nät) n. piece of furniture, having shelves for books, bric-a-brac, etc.; indescribable thing.

wheal (hwēl) n. raised spot or ridge on skin due to mosquito bite, hives, etc. [O.E. hwele].

wheat (hwēt) n. edible portion of annual cereal grass providing most important bread food of the world. **-en** a. made of wheat or whole flour [O.E. hwgete].

whee·dle (hwē'.dl) v.t. to cajole; to coax.

wheel (hwēl) n. solid disk or circular frame with spokes. pl. controlling forces; circular frame used for punishing criminals; (Colloq.) bicycle; steering wheel; wheeling movement; v.t. to convey on wheels; to furnish with wheels; v.i. to turn on, or as on, axis; to change direction by pivoting about an end unit, as in marching; to roll forward; to revolve. **-barrow** n. conveyance with a single wheel and two shafts for pushing. **-er** n. one who wheels; maker of wheels; hindmost horse, nearest wheels of carriage. **-house** n. (Naut.) a deckhouse to shelter steersman. **-ing** n. **-wright** n. one who makes and repairs wheels [O.E. hweol].

wheelhouse

wheeze (hwēz) v.i. to breathe audibly and with difficulty; n. the sound or act of wheezing; (Colloq.) joke. **-r** n. **wheezingly** adv. **wheezy** a. **wheezily** adv. **wheeziness** n. [O.N. hvaesa, to hiss].

whelk (hwelk) n. spiral-shelled sea snail used as bait and food [O.E. weoloc].

whelm (hwelm) v.t. to cover completely; to submerge; to overpower.

whelp (hwelp) n. young dog, lion, seal, wolf, etc.; a youth (contemptuously); v.i. and v.t. to bring forth young [O. E. hwelp].

when (hwen) adv. and conj. at what time? at the time that; whereas; at which time. **-ce** adv. and conj. from what place; from what, or which, cause, etc. **-cesoever** adv. and conj. from whatsoever place, source, or cause.**-e'er** or **-ever** adv. and conj. at whatever time. **-soever** adv. and conj. whenever [O.E. hwaenne].

where (hwer) adv. and conj. at what place?; in what circumstances? at or to the place in which. **-abouts** adv. and conj. about where; near what or which place? n. place where one is. **-as** conj. considering that; when in fact. **-at** adv. and conj. at which; at what. **-by** adv. and conj. by which; how. **-fore** adv. for which reason? why? conj. accordingly; in consequence of which; n. the cause. **-in** adv. in which; in which, or what, respect, etc.; in what. **-of** adv. of which; of what. **-on** adv. on which; on what. **-soever** adv. in, or to, whatever place. **-to** adv. to which; to what; to what end. **-upon** adv. upon which; in consequence of which. **-'er, -ver** adv. at whatever place. **-with** adv. with what. **the wherewithal,** the money; the means [O.E. hwaer].

wher·ry (hwer'.i.) n. a light rowboat; skiff. (Brit.) vessel used in fishing; light barge.

---

whet (hwet) v.t. to sharpen by rubbing; to make sharp, keen, or eager; to stir up; n. act of sharpening. pr.p. **-ting.** pa.t. and pa.p. **-ted. -stone** n. fine-grained stone used for sharpening cutlery and tools; sharpener. **-ter** n. [O.E. hwettan].

wheth·er (hweTH'.er) conj. used to introduce the first of two or more alternative clauses, the other(s) being connected by or [O.E.hwaether].

whew (hwū) n. or interj. whistling sound, expressing astonishment, dismay, or pain.

whey (hwā) n. clear liquid left as residue of milk after separation of fat and casein (curd). **-face** n. palefaced person. **-faced** a. **-ey** a. [O.E. hwaeg].

which (hwich) pron. as interrogative, signifying who, or what one, of a number; as relative, used of things; a thing or fact that; whatever. **-ever, -soever** pron., a. whether one or the other [O.E. hwile].

whiff (hwif) n. puff of air, smoke, etc.; an odor; v.t. to throw out in whiffs; to blow; v.i. to emit whiffs, as of smoke [imit.].

whif·fle (hwif'.l) v.t. to disperse, as by a puff; v.i. to veer, as wind; to be fickle[fr. whiff].

Whig (hwig) n. (U.S.) supporter of American Revolution; member of early political party (1834-1955); (Brit.) political party supporting Hanoverian succession but after 1832 replaced by term, 'Liberal'; a. pert. to Whigs.**-gish** a. **-gism** n. [contr. fr. Scots whiggamore].

while (hwil) n. space of time; conj. during time when; as long as; whereas; adv. during which. **whilom** (hwil'.am) adv. (Arch.)formerly; a. former. **to while away,** to pass time (usually idly) [O.E. hwil, time].

whim (hwim) n. passing fancy; caprice; fad. **-sical** a. capricious; freakish; fanciful; quaint. **-sicality** n. fanciful idea; whim. **-sically** adv. **-sicalness** n. **-sy** n. caprice; fancy [O.N. hvima, to have straying eyes].

whim·brel (hwim'.bral) n. bird resembling, but smaller than, curlew [imit.].

whim·per (hwim'.per) v.i. to cry, or utter, with low, fretful, broken voice; n. low peevish, or plaintive cry. **-er** n. **-ing** n.

whin (hwin) n. whinstone; low, coarse evergreen.

whine (hwin) n. drawing, peevish wail; unmanly complaint; v.i. to utter peevish cry; to complain in childish way. n. whining n. **whiningly** adv. **whiny** a. [O.E. hwinan].

whinny (hwin'.i.) v.i. to neigh; n. sound made by horse [O.E. hwinan, to whine].

whin·stone (hwin'.stōn) n. basaltic or hard unstratified rock. Also **whin.**

whip (hwip) v.t. to strike with lash; to flog; to overcast edges of seam, etc.; to bind ends of rope with twine; to snatch or jerk (away); to beat into froth, as cream or eggs; (Colloq.) to defeat decisively; v.i. to start suddenly. pr.p. **-ping.** pa.t. and pa.p. **-ped.** n. lash attached to handle for urging on or correction; legislative manager appointed to ensure fullest possible attendance of members of his party at important debates, etc. **-cord** n. worsted fabric with bold, diagonal ribbing. **— hand** n. hand which holds whip; mastery, upper hand.**-like** a. **-per** n. **-per-snapper** n. n. insignificant person; impertinent young fellow. **-ping** n. flogging. [M.E. whippen].

whip·pet (hwip'.it) n. cross-bred dog of greyhound type, for racing [prop. fr. whip].

whip·poor·will (hwip'.per.wil) n. nocturnal American bird [echoic].

whir (hwur) v.i. to dart, fly, or revolve with buzzing or whizzing noise. pr.p. **-ring.** pa.t. and pa.p. **-red.** n. buzzing or whizzing sound [Dan. hvirre, to twirl].

whirl (hwurl) v.t. to turn round rapidly; to cause to rotate; v.i. to rotate rapidly; to spin; to gyrate; to move very rapidly; n. rapid rotation; anything which whirls; bewilderment. **-igig** n. spinning toy; merry-go-round. **-ing** n. and a. **-pool** n. vortex or circular eddy of water. **-wind** n. forwardmoving column of air revolving rapidly and spirally around low-pressure core [ON. hvirfila, ring].

whish (hwish) v.i. to move with soft, rustling sound; n. such a sound [echoic].

whisk (hwisk) n. rapid, sweeping motion; small bunch of feathers, straw, etc. used for brush; instrument for beating eggs, etc. v.t. to sweep with light, rapid motion or with a whisk. **-er** n. thing that whisks; pl. hair on a man's face; long stiff hairs at side of mouth of cat or other animal. **-ered** a. [Scand. visk, wisp].

whis·key (hwis'.ki.) n. distilled alcoholic

---

liquor made from various grains. Also **whisky** [Gael. uisge beatha, water of life].

whisk

whis·per (hwis'.per) v.t. to utter in low, sibilant tone; to suggest secretly or furtively; v.i. to speak in whispers, under breath; to rustle; n. low, soft, sibilant remark; hint or insinuation. **-er** n. **-ing** n. **-ingly** adv. [O.E. hwisprian].

whist (hwist) n. card game for four players (two a side) [fr. whisk].

whis·tle (hwis'.l) n. sound made by forcing breath through rounded and nearly closed lips; instrument or device for making a similar sound; form of horn; v.i. to make such sound; v.i. and v.t. to render tune by whistling; to signal, by whistling. **-r** n. one who whistles. **whistling** n. [O.E. hwistlian].

whit (hwit) n. smallest part imaginable; bit [O.E. wiht].

white (hwit) a. of the color of snow; light in color; hoary; pale; pure; clean; bright; spotless; (Colloq.) honest; just; n. color of pure snow; albuminous part of an egg; white part of eyeball surrounding iris. **— alloy,** **— metal** n. alloy containing lead or tin, as pewter, resembling silver. **—ant** n. termite. **-bait** n. newly hatched young of sprat, herring, and related fishes, used as table delicacy. **—cap** n. wave with crest of white foam. **—collar** a. of clerical or professional workers. **— corpuscle,** leucocyte. **— elephant,** sacred elephant of Siam; gift entailing bother and expense; object valueless to the owners. **— feather** n. symbol of cowardice. **—fish** n. non-oily food fish. **— flag,** sign of truce or surrender. **— gold** alloyed gold with platinum appearance. **—heat** n. temperature at which substances become incandescent; state of extreme excitement or passion. **—hot** a. **—lead** n. compound of lead carbonate and hydrated oxide of lead, used as base and pigment for paint. **— lie,** harmless fib. **-n** v.t. and v.i. to make or turn white. **-ner** n. **-ening** n. making white. **-ness** n. **— slave,** woman or girl enticed away for purposes of prostitution. **-wash** n. mixture of whiting, water, and size, for coating walls; v.t. to cover with whitewash; to clear reputation of; to conceal errors, faults, etc. **whitish** a. somewhat white [O.E. hwit].

whith·er (hwiTH'.er) (Poetic) adv. to which, or what, place? [O.E. hwider].

whit·ing (hwit'.ing) n. edible seafish; pulverized chalk, for making putty and whitewash [fr. white].

whit·low (hwit'.lō) n. inflammatory sore affecting fingernails; [for whickflaw i.e. quick, sensitive part under fingernail, flaw, crack].

Whit·sun·day (hwit'.sun·di.) n. seventh Sunday after Easter, festival day of Church, kept in commemoration of descent of Holy Ghost. **Whitsun, Whitsuntide,** week containing Whitsunday [so called because newly baptized appeared in white garments].

whit·tle (hwit'.l) v.t. and v.i. to cut off thin slices or shavings with knife; to pare away [O.E. thwitan, to cut].

whiz, whizz (hwiz) v.i. to make hissing sound, as arrow flying through air. pr.p. **-zing.** pa.t. and pa.p. **-zed.** n. violent hissing and humming sound; person or thing regarded as excellent. **-zingly** adv. **-bang** n. (Slang) high-velocity, light shell whose explosion occurs almost immediately after its flight through the air is first heard [imit.].

who (hōō) *pron.* relative or interrogative, referring to persons. **-ever** *pron.* whatever person; any one, without exception. **-m** *pron.* objective case of *who.* **-msoever** *pron.* objective of **-soever** *pron.* any person, without exception. **-se** (hōōz) *pron.* possessive case of *who* or *which.* **-dunit** (hōō·dun′·it) *n.* (*Slang*) a detective story [O.E. *hwa*].

whoa (wō, hwō) *interj.* stop! [var. of ho].

whole (hōl) *a.* entire; complete; not defective or imperfect; unimpaired; healthy; sound; *n.* entire thing; complete system; aggregate; gross; sum; totality. **-hearted** *a.* earnest; sincere. **-heartedly** *adv.* **-heartedness** *n.* **-hog** *n.* completeness; without any reservations. **-ness** *n.* **-sale** *n.* sale of goods in bulk to retailers; *a.* selling or buying in large quantities; extensive; indiscriminate. **-saler** *n.* **-some** *a.* tending to promote health; healthy; nourishing; beneficial. **-someness** *n.* **wholly** *adv.* completely [O.E. *hal*].

whom See **who.**

whoop (hwōōp, hōōp) *n.* loud cry or yell; hoot, as of owl; convulsive intake of air after cough; *v.i.* to utter loud cry; to hoot; to make the sound characteristic of whooping cough. **-ee** *interj.* exclamation of joy or abandonment. **-er** *n.* one who whoops; bird with a loud harsh note. **-ing cough** *n.* infectious disease marked by fits of convulsive coughing, followed by characteristic loud whoop or indrawing of breath. **to make whoopee** (*Slang*) to celebrate uproariously [O.Fr. *houper*, to shout].

whop (hwáp) *v.t.* to beat severely. *pr.p.* **-ping.** *pa.p.*, *pa.t.* **-ped.** **-per** *n.* (*Colloq.*) anything unusually large; monstrous lie. **-ping** *a.* (*Colloq.*) very big [fr. *whip*].

whore (hōr) *n.* harlot; prostitute; *v.i.* to have unlawful sexual intercourse [O.N. *hora*].

whorl (hwurl, hwawrl) *n.* spiral of univalve shell; ring of leaves, petals, fingerprints, etc. **-ed** *a.* [O.E. *hweorfan*, to turn].

whor·tle·ber·ry (hwurt′·ạl·ber·i·) *n.* huckleberry [O.E. *wyrtil*, dim. of *wurt*, wort].

whose (hōōz) *poss.* of *who*, *which*. **whosoever**, **whomsoever** See **who.**

why (hwī) *adv.* and *conj.* for what reason? on which account? wherefore? *interj.* expletive to show surprise, indignation, protest; *n.* reason; cause; motive [O.E. *hwi*].

wick (wik) *n.* cotton cord which draws up oil or wax, as in lamp or candle, to be burned. **-less** *a.* [M.E. *wicke*, fr. O.E. *weoce*].

wick·ed (wik′·id) *a.* addicted to vice; evil; immoral; mischievous. **-ly** *adv.* **-ness** *n.* [M.E. *wikke*, evil].

wick·er (wik′·er) *n.* small flexible twig; wickerwork; withe; *a.* made of pliant twigs. **-work** *n.* basketwork [Cf. O.E. *wican*, to bend].

wick·et (wik′·it) *n.* small door or gate, adjacent to or part of larger door; arch; one of wire arches used in croquet; box-office window [O.Fr. *wiket*].

wide (wid) *a.* broad; spacious; distant; comprehensive; missing the mark; *adv.* to a distance; far; astray; to the fullest extent. **—angle** *a.* of motion picture system using one or more cameras and projectors and a wide curved screen. **-awake** *a.* fully awake. **-ly** *adv.* **-n** *v.t.* to make wide or wider; *v.i.* to grow wide or wider; to expand. **-ness** *n.* width. **-spread** *a.* extending on all sides; diffused; circulating among numerous people. **width** *n.* wideness; breadth. **widthwise** *adv.* [O.E. *wid*].

width See **wide.**

wield (wēld) *v.t.* to use with full command or power; to swing; to handle; to manage; to control. **-able** *a.* **-er** *n.* **-iness** *n.* **-y** *a.* manageable; controllable [O.E. *gewieldan*, to govern].

wie·ner (wē′·ner) *n.* smoked sausage in casing; frankfurter. Also **weenie** [Ger. *Wiener wurst*, Vienna sausage].

wife (wif) *n.* married woman; spouse; (*Colloq.*) woman. *pl.* **wives. -hood** *n.* **-less** *a.* **-less-ness** *n.* without wife; unmarried. **-ly** *a.* as befits a wife [O.E. *wif*].

wig (wig) *n.* artificial covering for head which imitates natural hair. **-ged** *a.* [for *periwig*].

wig·gle (wig′.l) *v.i.* to waggle; to wriggle; *n.* a wriggling motion. **-r** *n.* wiggling thing; mosquito larva. [var. of *waggle*].

wig·wag (wig′·wag) *v.t.* to move back and forth; to signal with flags, etc. *pr.p.* **-ging.** *pa.p.*, *pa.t.* **-ged. -ger** *n.* [fr. *wag*].

wig·wam (wig′·wám) *n.* Amer. Ind. conical shelter [N. Amer. Ind. *Wigiwam*, their dwelling].

wild (wild) *a.* living in state of nature; not domesticated or cultivated; native; savage; turbulent; *n.* uncultivated, uninhabited region. **-cat** *n.* medium-sized, undomesticated feline; experimental oil well; *a.* reckless; financially unsound; highly speculative. **-fire** *n.* anything which burns rapidly or spreads fast; sheet lightning; **—goosechase** *n.* foolish, futile pursuit or enterprise. **-ly** *adv.* **-ness** *n.* **to sow wild oats,** to be given to youthful excesses [O.E. *wilde*].

wil·de·beest (wil′·dạ·bēst) *n.* gnu [Dut.].

wil·der (wil′·der) (*Arch.*) *v.t.* to cause to lose the way; to bewilder [fr. *bewilder*].

wil·der·ness (wil′·der·nạs) *n.* tract of land uncultivated and uninhabited by human beings; waste; desert; state of confusion [O.E. *wildor*, wild animal].

wile (wil) *n.* trick or stratagem practiced for ensnaring or alluring; artifice; lure; ruse; *v.t.* to entice; to pass (time) lazily. **willily** *adv.* **wiliness** *n.* artfulness; guile; cunning. **wily** *a.* [O.E. *wil*].

will (wil) *n.* power of choosing what one will do; volition; determination; discretion; wish; desire; (*Law*) declaration in writing showing how property is to be disposed of after death; *v.t.* to determine by choice; to ordain; to decree; to bequeath; to devise; *v.i.* to exercise act of volition; to choose; to elect; *v.i.* used as an auxiliary, to denote futurity dependent on subject of verb, intention, or insistence. *pa.t.* **would. -able** *a.* **-er** *n.* **-ing** *a.* favorably inclined; minded; disposed; ready. **-ingly** *adv.* readily; gladly. **-ingness** *n.* **— power** *n.* strength of will. **at will,** at pleasure. **with a will,** zealously and heartily [O.E. *willan*].

will·ful (wil′·fạl) *a.* governed by the will without yielding to reason; obstinate; intentional. **-ly** *adv.* **-ness** *n.* [fr. *will*].

will·o'·the·wisp (wil′·ạ·thạ·wisp) *n.* ignis fatuus, flickering, pale-bluish flame seen over marshes; anything deceptive or illusive.

wil·low (wil′·ō) *n.* name of number of trees of genus Salix, having flexible twigs used in weaving; machine for cleaning cotton. **-er** *n.* **— pattern,** design used in decorating chinaware, blue on white ground. **-ware** *n.* china of this pattern. **-y** *a.* abounding in willows; pliant; supple and slender. **weeping willow** *n.* tree with pendent branches [O.E. *welig*].

wil·ly·nil·ly (wil′·i·nil′·i·) *a.* indecisive; *adv.* whether or not [fr. *will I, nill I*].

wilt (wilt) *v.i.* to fade; to droop; to wither; *v.t.* to depress; *n.* weakness; plant disease.

Wil·ton (wil′·tn) *n.* velvet-pile carpet [*Wilton*, town in Wiltshire].

wil·y See **wile.**

wim·ble (wim′·bl) *n.* tool for boring; *v.t.* [O.Fr.].

wim·ple (wim′·pl) *n.* covering for neck, chin and sides of face, still retained by nuns; *v.i.* to ripple; to lie in folds [O.E. *wimpel*].

win (win) *v.t.* to gain by success in competition or contest; to earn; to obtain; to reach, after difficulty; *v.i.* to be victorious; *pr.p.* **-ning.** *pa.p.*, *pa.t.* **won.** *n.* (*Colloq.*) victory, success. **-ner** *n.* **-ning** *n.* act of gaining; *pl.* whatever is won in game or competition; *a.* attractive; charming; victorious. **-ningly** *adv.* [O.E. *winnan*, to strive].

wince (wins) *v.i.* to shrink or flinch, as from blow or pain; *n.* act of wincing. **-r** *n.* [O.Fr. *guinchir*, to shrink].

winch (winch) *n.* hoisting machine; a wheel crank; a windlass [O.E. *wince*, pulley].

Win·ches·ter (win′·ches·ter) *n.* lever action repeating rifle [fr. *maker*].

wind (wind) *n.* air in motion; current of air; gale; breath; power of respiration; flatulence; idle talk; hint or suggestion; (*Naut.*) point of compass; *pl.* wind instruments of orchestra; *v.t.* to follow by scent; to run, ride, or drive till breathless; to rest (horse) that it may recover wind; to expose to wind; *v.t.* (wind) to sound by blowing (horn, etc.). *pa.p.*, *pa.t.* **-ed. -bag** *n.* leather bag, part of bagpipe, filled with wind by mouth; (*Slang*) empty, pompous talker. **-breaker** *n.* a warm sports jacket. **ed** *a.* breathless. **-fall** *n.* anything blown down by wind, as fruit; unexpected legacy or other gain. **-flower** *n.* the anemone. **-ily** *adv.* **-iness** *n.* **— instrument** *n.* musical instrument played by blowing or air pressure. **-jammer** *n.* (*Colloq.*) merchant sailing ship; crew member. **-less** *a.* calm; out of breath. **-mill** *n.* mill worked by action of wind on vanes or sails. **-pipe** *n.* trachea; cartilaginous pipe admitting air to lungs. **-shield** *n.* protection against wind for driver or pilot. **— sock** (or **sleeve**) cone-shaped bag to show direction of wind. **-storm** *n.* **— tunnel** in aviation, tunnel-shaped chamber for making experiments with model aircraft in artificially created atmospheric conditions. **-ward** *n.* point from which wind blows; *a.* facing the wind; *adv.* toward the wind. **-y** *a.* consisting of, exposed to wind; tempestuous; flatulent; empty; **before the wind,** with the wind driving behind. **in the wind,** afoot; astir; in secret preparation. **second wind,** restoration of normal breathing. **to get wind of,** to be secretly informed of [O.E.].

windpipe

wind (wind) *v.t.* to twist around; to coil; to twine, to wrap; to make ready for working by tightening spring; to meander; *v.i.* to twine; to vary from direct course—*pa.t.* and *pa.p.* **wound. -er** *n.* one who, or that which, winds; step, wider at one end than the other. **-ing** *a.* twisting or bending from direct line; sinuous; meandering; *n.* turning; twist. **-ing-sheet** *n.* sheet in which corpse is wrapped. **—up** *n.* conclusion; closing stages; baseball pitcher's preliminary swing of arm before delivery. **to wind up,** to coil up; to bring to conclusion. **wound-up** *a.* highly excited [O.E. *windan*].

wind·lass (wind′·lạs) *n.* form of winch for hoisting or hauling purposes, consisting of horizontal drum with rope or chain, and crank with handle for turning [O.N. *vindill*, winder; *ass*, pole].

win·dow (win′·dō) *n.* opening in wall to admit air and light, usually covered with glass. **— box** *n.* box for growing plants outside window. **— dressing** *n.* effective arrangement of goods in shop window. **— sill** *n.* flat portion of window opening on which window rests [O.N. *vindauga*, wind-eye].

wine (win) *n.* fermented juice of grape; similar liquor made from other fruits; *v.t.* to entertain by serving wine; *v.i.* to drink much wine at a sitting. **—bibber** *n.* one who drinks much wine. **— cellar,** stock of wine. **-press** *n.* apparatus for pressing juice out of grapes. **-ry** place where wine is made [O.E. *win*, fr. L. *vinum*].

wing (wing) *n.* organ of flight; one of two feathered fore limbs of bird; flight; main lifting surface of airplane; extension or section of a building; right or left division of army or fleet; section of team to right or left of center or regular scrimmage line; sidepiece; *pl.* the side parts of a stage; *v.t.* to furnish with wings; to enable to fly or hasten; to wound in wing, arm, or shoulder; *v.i.* to soar on the wing. **-ed** *a.* furnished with wings; wounded in wing; swift. **-less** *a.* **-spread** *n.* distance between tips of outstretched wings of bird or of airplane [O.N. *vaengr*].

wink (wingk) *v.t.* and *v.i.* to close and open eyelids; to blink; to convey hint by flick of eyelid; to twinkle; *n.* act of winking; hint conveyed by winking. **forty winks,** short nap. **to wink at,** to connive at; to pretend not to see [O.E. *wincian*].

win·kle See **periwinkle.**

win·ner, win·ning See **win.**

win·now (win′·ō) *v.t.* to separate grain from chaff by means of wind or current of air; to fan; to separate; to sift; to sort out. **-er** *n.* **-ing** *a.* and *n.* [O.E. *windwian*].

win·some (win′·sạm) *a.* cheerful; charming; attractive. **-ly** *adv.* **-ness** *n.* [O.E. *wynsum*, fr. *wynn*, joy].

win·ter (win′·ter) *n.* fourth season; (*Astron.*) in northern latitudes, period between winter solstice and vernal equinox (22nd Dec.—20th-21st March); any dismal, gloomy time; *a.* wintry; pert. to winter; *v.t.* to keep and feed throughout winter; *v.i.* to pass the winter. **-er** *n.* **-green** *n.* aromatic evergreen plant from which is obtained oil of wintergreen, used in medicine and flavoring. **-ize** *v.t.* ready for winter. **-ly** *adv.* **wintriness** *n.* **wintry** *a.* of or like winter [O.E.].

wipe (wīp) *v.t.* to rub lightly, so as to clean or dry; to remove gently; to clear away; to efface; *n.* act of wiping. **-r** *n.* one who, or that which, wipes; in motoring, automatically operated arm to keep part of windshield free from rain or dust. **wiping** *n.* act of wiping. **to wipe out**, to erase; to destroy utterly [O.E. *wipian*].

wire (wīr) *n.* metal drawn into form of a thread or cord; a length of this; telegraphy; a telegram; string of instrument; a rabbit snare; *v.t.* to bind or stiffen with wire; to pierce with wire; to fence with wire; to install (building) with wires for electric circuit; (*Colloq.*) to telegraph; to snare; *a.* formed of wire. **-d** *a.* **—gauze** *n.* finely woven wire netting. **—haired** *a.* having short, wiry hair. **-less** *a.* without wires; pert. to several devices operated by electromagnetic waves. *n.* wireless telegraphy or telephony; (*Brit.*) a radio; *v.t.* and *v.i.* to communicate by wireless. **-less operator** *n.* one who receives and transmits wireless messages. **— netting** *n.* galvanized wire woven into net. **-photo** *n.* method of sending photographs by means of electric impulses; the photograph so reproduced. **-puller** *n.* one who exercises influence behind scenes, esp. in public affairs. **-r** *n.* one who installs wire. **— tapping** act of tapping telephone wires to get information. **-worm** *n.* larva of various click beetles, very destructive to roots of plants. **wirily** *adv.* **wiriness** *n.* **wiring** *n.* system of electric wires forming circuit. **wiry** *n.* stiff (as hair); lean, sinewy and strong, **a live wire**, wire charged with electricity; enterprising person [O.E. *wir*].

wis·dom (wiz'·dạm) *n.* quality of being wise; knowledge and the capacity to make use of it; judgment. **— tooth** *n.* posterior molar tooth, cut about twentieth year [O.E.].

wise (wīz) *a.* enlightened; sagacious; learned; dictated by wisdom. **-acre** *n.* a foolish know-it-all. **-crack** *n.* concise flippant statement; *v.i.* to utter one. **-ly** *adv.* **-ness** *n.* [O.E. *wis*].

wise (wīz) *n.* way; manner [O.E. *wise*].

wise (wīz) *adv. suffix.* in the way or manner of, arranged like, as in *clockwise*, *likewise*, *crosswise*, etc.

wish (wish) *v.t.* to desire; to long for; to hanker after; to request; *v.i.* to have a desire; to yearn; *n.* expression or object of desire; longing; request. **(ing)-bone** *n.* forked bone of fowl's breast. **-er** *n.* **-ful** *a.* desirous; anxious; longing; wistful. **-fully** *adv.* **-fulness** *n.* [O.E. *wyscan*].

wish·wash (wish'·wàsh) *n.* thin, weak, insipid drink. **-y** *a.* morally weak; watery; diluted [redupl. of *wash*].

wisp (wisp) *n.* twisted handful, usually of hay; whisk or small broom; stray lock of hair. **-like** *a.* **-y** *a.* [M.E. *wisp, wips,* Cf. **wipe**].

wis·te·ri·a (wis·tir'·i·ạ) *n.* hardy climbing leguminous shrub, with blue, purple, white or mauve flower clusters [*Wistar*, Amer. anatomist, 1761-1818].

wist·ful (wist'·fạl) *a.* pensive; sadly contemplative; earnestly longing. **-ly** *adv.* **-ness** *n.* [*var.* of wishful].

wit (wit) *n.* intellect; understanding; (one with) ingenuity in connecting amusingly incongruous ideas; humor; pleasantry; *pl.* mental faculties. **-less** *a.* lacking wit or understanding; silly; stupid. **-lessly** *adv.* in all innocence. **-lessness** *n.* **-ticism** *n.* witty remark. **-tily** *adv.* **-tiness** *n.* **-tingly** *adv.* with foreknowledge or design; knowingly; of set purpose. **-ty** *a.* possessed of wit; amusing. **at one's wits' end**, baffled; perplexed what to do. **to wit**, namely [O.E. *witan*, to know].

wit·an (wit'·ạn) *n.pl.* members of the witenagemot [O.E. *vita*, wise man].

witch (wich) *n.* woman who was supposed to practice sorcery; ugly old woman; hag; crone; *v.t.* to bewitch; to enchant. **-craft** *n.* black art; sorcery; necromancy. **— doctor** *n.* medicine man of a savage tribe. **-ery** *n.* arts of a witch; sorcery. **-hunt** search for, and trial of subversives. **-ing** *a.* fascinating. **-ingly** *adv.* [O.E. *wicca*].

witch haz·el (wich·hā'·zạl) *n.* shrub with yellow flowers and edible seeds; of dried bark and leaves of the tree used, in distilled form, as astringent drug [O.E. *wice*, drooping].

wit·e·na·ge·mot (wit'·a·na·ga·mōt) *n.* national council of England in Anglo-Saxon times [O.E. *vita*, wise man; *gemot*, meeting].

with (wiTH, with) *prep.* in company or possession of; in relation to; against; by means of; denoting association, cause, agency, comparison, immediate sequence, etc. [O.E.].

with·al (wiTH·awl') *adv.* (*Arch.*) besides.

with·draw (wiTH·draw') *v.t.* to take away; to recall; to retract; *v.i.* to go away; to retire; to retreat; to recede. *pa.t.* **withdrew.** *pa.p.* **-n, -al** *n.* **-ment** *n.*

withe (with, wiTH) *n.* tough, flexible twig, esp. willow, reed, or osier. Also **withy.** **withy** *a.* (*Chiefly Brit.*) made of withes; flexible and tough [O.E. *withig*, willow].

with·er (wiTH'·er) *v.t.* to cause to fade and become dry; to blight; to rebuff; *v.i.* to fade; to decay; to languish. **-ing** *a.* **-ingly** *adv.* scathingly; contemptuously [var. of *weather*].

with·ers (wiTH'·erz) *n.pl.* ridge between horse's shoulder blades [O.E. *wither*, resistance].

with·hold (with·hōld') *v.t.* to hold or keep back. *pa.p., pa.t.* **withheld.**

with·in (wiTH·in') *prep.* in the inner or interior part of; in the compass of; *adv.* in the inner part; inwardly; at home.

with·out (wiTH·out') *prep.* on or at the outside of; out of; not within; beyond the limits of; destitute of; exempt from; all but; *adv.* on the outside; out of doors.

with·stand (with·stand') *v.t.* to oppose; to stand against; to resist. *pa.t.* and *pa.p.* **withstood. -er** *n.*

wit·ness (wit'·nis) *n.* testimony; one who, or that which, furnishes evidence or proof; one who has seen or has knowledge of incident; one who attests another person's signature to document; *v.t.* to be witness of or to; *v.i.* to give evidence; to testify. **— stand** *n.* place where witness gives testimony in court of law. **-er** *n.* [O.E. *witnes*, evidence].

wit·ti·cism, wit·ty, etc. See **wit.**

wive (wiv) *v.t.* to provide with or take for a wife; *v.i.* to take a wife [fr. *wife*].

wi·vern (wī'·vern) *n.* (*Her.*) imaginary monster, with two clawed feet, two wings and serpent's tail [O.Fr. *wivre*, viper].

wives (wivz) *pl.* of **wife.**

wiz·ard (wiz'·erd) *n.* one devoted to black art; sorcerer; magician; conjurer; a skillful person; *a.* with magical powers. **-like** *a.* **-ly** *a.* **-ry** *n.* magic [fr. *wise*].

wiz·en, wiz·ened (wiz'·n, wiz'·nd) *a.* dried up; withered [O.E. *wisnian*, to wither].

woad (wōd) *n.* plant yielding blue dye derived from pounded leaves [O.E. *wad*].

wob·ble, wabble (wàb'·l) *v.i.* to rock from side to side; (*Colloq.*) to vacillate; to be hesitant; *n.* rocking; unequal motion. **-r,** *n.* **wobbly, wabbly** *a.* shaky; unsteady.

woe, wo (wō) *n.* grief; heavy calamity; affliction; sorrow. **-begone** *a.* overwhelmed with woe; sorrowful; **-ful** *a.* sorrowful; pitiful; paltry. **-fully** *adv.* [O.E. *wa*].

woke. alt. *pa.t.* of **wake.**

wold (wōld) *n.* wood; open tract of country; low hill [O.E. *veald, wald,* a forest].

wolf (woolf) *n.* carnivorous wild animal, allied to dog; rapacious, cruel person; (*Slang*) lady-killer. *pl.* **wolves** (woolvz). *v.t.* (*Colloq.*) to devour ravenously. **— dog** *n.* animal bred from wolf and dog; large dog for hunting wolves. **-hound** *n.* dog bred for hunting wolves. **-ish** *a.* rapacious, like wolf; voracious; fierce and greedy. **-ishly** *adv.* **-ishness** *n.* [O.E. *wulf*].

wolf·ram·ite (wool'·fram·īt) *n.* the mineral, ferrous tungstate, the chief source of the metal tungsten. Also **wolfram** [Ger.].

wol·ver·ine, wol·ver·ene (wool·va·rēn') *n.* a carnivorous mammal inhabiting northern region; the glutton [fr. *wolf*].

wolves *pl.* of **wolf.**

wo·man (woom'·an) *n.* adult human female; the quality of being a woman. *pl.* **women** (wim'·in). **-hood** *n.* adult stage of women; the qualities of women. **-ish** *a.* like a woman; effeminate. **-ishness** *n.* **-kind, womenkind** *n.* female sex. **-like** *a.* like, or characteristic of, a woman. **-liness** *n.* **-ly** *a.* befitting a mature woman; essentially feminine; *adv.* in manner of a woman [O.E. *wifmann*].

womb (woom) *n.* female organ of conception and gestation; uterus [O.E. *wamb*, belly].

wom·bat (wàm'·bat) *n.* group of Australian and Tasmanian fur-bearing, burrowing marsupial animals [Austral. *womback*].

wo·men (wim'·in) *pl.* of **woman.**

won (wun) *pa.t.* and *pa.p.* of **win.**

won·der (wun'·der) *n.* astonishment; surprise; amazement; admiration; prodigy; miracle; *v.i.* to feel wonder; to marvel; to speculate. **-er** *n.* **-ful** *a.* very fine; remarkable; amazing. **-fully** *adv.* **-fulness** *n.* **-ing** *a.* **-ingly** *adv.* in a wondering and expectant manner. **-land** *n.* land of marvels; fairyland.

wondrous *a.* wonderful. **wondrously** *adv.* **wondrousness** *n.* [O.E. *wundor*].

wont (wawnt, wunt) *a.* accustomed; used; *n.* habit; custom; use; *v.i.* (*Poetic*) to be accustomed. **-ed** *a.* accustomed; habitual; usual. **-edness** [O.E. *gewun*, usual].

won't (wōnt) *v.i.* a contr. of **will not.**

woo (wóò) *v.t.* to make love to; to court; to endeavor to gain (sleep, etc.) **-er** *n.* **-ing** *n.* [O.E. *wogian*].

wood (wood) *n.* (*usu. pl.*) land with trees growing close together; grove; forest; hard, stiffening tissue in stem and branches of tree; timber; wood-wind instrument; *v.t.* to supply with wood; to plant with trees; *v.i.* to take in good. **— alcohol** *n.* methyl alcohol, product of dry distillation of wood, esp. beech and birch. **-bine,** *n.* wild honeysuckle; Virginia creeper. **-chuck,** *n.* small burrowing rodent; ground hog. **— coal** *n.* wood charcoal; lignite or brown coal. **-cock,** *n.* migrant game-bird of snipe family. **-craft** *n.* expert knowledge of woodland conditions; art of making objects of wood. **-cut** *n.* engraving on wood; impression from such engravings. **-cutter** *n.* a woodsman. **-ed** *a.* covered with trees. **-en** *a.* made of wood; expressionless; stiff; stupid.

— engraver *n.* **— engraving** *n.* art or process of cutting design on wood for printing; impression from this; woodcut. **-enhead** *n.* (*Colloq.*) a numbskull; a blockhead. **-enly** *adv.* stiffly. **-enness** *n.* **-enware** *n.* articles of wood. **-iness** *n.* **-land** *n.* and *a.* (of) wooded country. **— louse** *n.* the slater, prolific in damp places, esp. under decaying timber. **-man** *n.* or **-sman.** — **nymph** *n.* goddess of woods, a dryad; a moth. **-pecker** *n.* bird which taps and bores with bill the bark of trees in search of insects. **— pulp** *n.* wood crushed and pulped for paper making. **-sman** *n.* forest dweller; forester; woodcutter. **— sorrel** *n.* perennial herb of geranium order with small white flowers and acid leaves. **-shed** *n.* firewood storage place. **-sy** *a.* like the woods. **-wind** *n.* wooden musical instrument, as flute, oboe, clarinet, bassoon, etc. **-work** *n.* fittings made of wood, esp. interior moldings of a house. **-y** *a.* abounding with trees or wooded growth. **not out of the woods,** still in jeopardy [O.E. *wudu*, forest].

woodbine

woo·er See **woo.**

woof (wóóf) *n.* threads which cross warp in weaving; texture [O.E. *owef*].

woof·er (woof'·er) *n.* large loud-speaker that reproduces low frequency sound waves (opp. of *tweeter*).

wool (wool) *n.* soft, curled hair of sheep, goat, etc.; yarn or cloth of this; **-gathering** *n.* day dreaming. **-(l)en** *n.* cloth made of wool; *pl.* woolen goods; *a.* made of, pert. to, wool. **-liness** *n.* **-ly** *a.* of, or like wool; muddled and confused. **-pack** *n.* a pack of wool; a cumulus cloud resembling a fleecy woolen ball. **dyed-in-the-wool,** become inherent; unchangeable [O.E. *wull*].

word (wurd) *n.* spoken or written sign of idea; term; oral expression; message; order; password; promise; brief remark or observation; *pl.* speech; language, esp. contentious; wordy quarrel; *v.t.* to express in words; to phrase. **-ed** *a.* phrased; expressed. **-ily** *adv.* verbosely; pedantically. **-iness** *n.* verbosity. **-ing** *n.* precise words used; phrasing; phraseology. **-less** *a.* **-ly** *a.* verbose; prolix. **word for word,** literally; verbatim. **by word of mouth,** orally [O.E. *word*].

wore (wōr) *pa.t.* of **wear.**

work (wurk) *n.* exertion of strength; effort directed to an end; employment; toil; labor; occupation; production; achievement; manufacture; that which is produced; (*Phys.*) result of force overcoming resistance over definite distance; *pl.* structures in engineering; manufacturing establishment; good deeds; artistic productions; mechanism of a watch, etc.; fortifications; *v.i.* to exert oneself; to labor; to be employed; to act; to be effective; to have influence (on, upon); *v.t.* to produce or form by labor; to operate; to perform; to effect; to embroider. **-able** *a.* **-aday** *a.* commonplace. **-bag, -basket, -box** *n.* receptacle for holding work implements, esp. for needlework. **—day** *n.* day when work is done; week-day. **-er** *n.* **-house** *n.* house of correction. **-ing** *n.* act of laboring or doing something useful; mode of operation; fermentation; *pl.* a mine as a whole, or a part of it where work is being carried on, e.g. level, etc.; *a.* laboring; fermenting. **-man** *n.* one actually engaged in manual labor; craftsman. **-man-like** *a.* befitting skilled workman; skillful. **-manship** *n.* skill. **-out** *n.* practice; performance; training. **-shop** *n.* place where things are made or repaired; people meeting for intensive study in some field. **to work off,** to get rid of gradually. **to work out,** to solve (problem); to plan in detail; to exhaust (mine, etc.). **to work up,** to excite unduly; to study intensively; to advance [O.E. *weorc*].

world (wurld) *n.* earth and its inhabitants; whole system of things; universe; any planet or star; this life; general affairs of life; society; human race; mankind; great quantity or number. **-liness** *n.* state of being worldly. **-ling** *n.* one who is absorbed in the affairs, interests, or pleasures of this world. **-ly** *a.* relating to the world; engrossed in temporal pursuits; earthly; mundane; carnal; not spiritual. **-ly-wise** *a.* experienced in the ways of people. **—weary, —wearied** *a.*

tired of worldly affairs. —**wide** *a.* extending to every corner of the globe. —**man (woman) of the world**, one with much worldly experience. **old-world** *a.* old-fashioned; quaint. **the New World**, N. and S. America. **the Old World**, Europe, Africa, and Asia [O.E. *weorold*].

worm (wurm) *n.* small, limbless, invertebrate animal with soft, long, and jointed body; spiral thread; small, metal screw that meshes with the teeth of a worm wheel; spiral pipe through which vapor passes in distillation; emblem of corruption, of decay, or remorse; groveling, contemptible fellow; *pl.* disease of digestive organs or intenstines of humans and animals due to parasite worms; *v.i.* to work (oneself) in insidiously; to move along like a worm; *v.t.* to work slowly and secretly; to free from worms. —**drive** *n.* system in which power is communicated by means of worm, through worm wheel. —**eaten** *a.* of wooden furniture, etc., full of holes gnawed by worms; old; antiquated. -**er** *n.* -**less** *a.* -**like** *a.* — **wheel** *n.* cogged wheel whose teeth engage smoothly with coarse threaded screw or worm. -**y** *a.* worm-like; abounding with worms; groveling [O.E. *wyrm*, serpent].

worm·wood (wurm'·wood) *n.* bitter plant, Artemisia, used in making absinthe, vermouth, etc.; bitterness [O.E. *wermod*].

worn (wōrn) *pa.p.* of **wear**. —**out** *a.* no longer serviceable; exhausted; tired.

wor·ry (wur'·i·)*v.t.* to cause anxiety; to torment; to vex; to plague; to tear or mangle with teeth; *v.i.* to feel undue care and anxiety; *n.* mental disturbance due to care and anxiety; trouble; vexation. **worrier** *n.* **worrisome** *a.* causing trouble, anxiety, or worry. -**ing** *a.* [O.E. *wyrgan*, to strangle].

worse (wurs) *a. comp.* of **bad, ill**; more unsatisfactory; of less value; in poorer health; *adv.* in a manner more evil or bad. **worsen** *v.t.* to make worse; to impair; *v.t.* and *i.* to make or become worse; to deteriorate. **worsening** *n.* [O.E. *wyrsa*].

wor·ship (wur'·ship) *n.* religious reverence and homage; act or ceremony of showing reverence; adoration; *v.t.* to adore; to pay divine honors to; *v.i.* to perform religious service; to attend church. -**ful** *a.* -**fully** *adv.* -**fulness** *n.* -**er** *n.* [O.E. *weorthscipe* = worth-ship].

worst (wurst) *a. superl.* of **bad, ill**; most evil; of least value or worth; *adv.* in most inferior manner or degree; *n.* that which is most bad or evil; *v.t.* to get the better of; to defeat [O.E. *wyrst, wyrsta*].

wor·sted (woos'·tid, woor'·stid) *n.* yarn spun from long-fibred wools which are combed, not carded; cloth of this yarn; *a.* made of worsted [*Worstead*, England].

wort (wurt, wawrt) *n.* plant, herb—usually appearing as the last element of a compound term, e.g. *milkwort*, etc. [O.E. *wyrt*].

wort (wurt) *n.* in brewing of beer, liquid portion of mash of malted grain produced during fermenting process before hops and yeast are added; malt extract used as a medium for culture of micro-organisms [O.E. *wyrt*, a plant].

worth (wurth) *n.* quality of thing which renders it valuable or useful; relative excellence of conduct or of character; value, in terms of money; merit; excellence; *a.* equal in value to; meriting; having wealth or estate to the value of. -**ily** *adv.* -**iness** *n.* -**less** *a.* of no worth or value; useless. -**while** *a.* -**lessly** *adv.* -**lessness** *n.* -**y** (wur'THi·) *a.* having worth or excellence; deserving; meritorious; *n.* man of eminent worth; local celebrity. *pl.* **worthies** [E. *weorth*].

wot (wát) (*Arch.*) *v.i.* to know; to be aware [O.E. fr. *witan*, to know].

would (wood) *pa.t.* of **will**; expresses condition, futurity, desire. —**be** *a.* desiring or intending to be.

wound (wound) *pa.t.* and *pa.p.* of **wind**.

wound (wŏŏnd) *n.* injury; cut, stab, bruise, etc.; hurt (to feelings); damage; *v.t.* to hurt by violence; to hurt feelings of; to injure. -**er** *n.* -**less** *a.* [O.E. *wund*].

wove (wōv) *pa.t.* of **weave**. -**n** *pa.p.* of **weave**. — **paper** *n.* paper with no marks of wire as in laid paper.

wow (wou) *interj.* exclamation of astonishment; *n.* (*Slang*) great success.

wrack (rak) *n.* seaweed thrown ashore by waves; shipwreck; ruin. Also **rack** [var. of *wreck*].

wraith (rāth) *n.* apparition of person seen shortly before or after death; specter; ghost. -**like** *a.* [O.N. *vorthr*, guardian].

wran·gle (rang'·gl) *v.i.* to dispute angrily; to bicker; to tend horses; *n.* angry dispute; an argument, *n.* angry disputant; ranch hand who rounds up cattle. -**r** *n.* [M.E. *wranglen*, to dispute].

wrap (rap) *v.t.* to cover by winding or folding something around; to enfold; to envelop; to muffle. *pr.p.* -**ping**. *pa.t., pa.p.* -**ped** (or -**t**) *n.* a loose garment; a covering. -**per** *n.* one who, or that which, wraps; loose dressing-gown worn by women; negligee. -**ping** *n.* wrapping material [earlier *wlap*, etym. uncertain].

wrapt (rapt) *a.* alt. *pa.p., pa.t.* of wrap; rapt; ecstatic; transported.

wrath (rath) *n.* violent anger; indignation; rage; fury. -**ful** *a.* -**fully** *adv.* -**fulness** *n.* [O.E. *wrath*, angry].

wreak (rēk) *v.t.* to inflict (vengeance, etc.) -**er** *n.* [O.E. *wrecan*, to avenge].

wreath (rēth) *n.* circular garland or crown of flowers, leaves, etc. entwined together; chaplet; a similar formation, as of smoke. **wreathe** (rēTH) *v.t.* to surround; to form into a wreath; to wind round; to encircle; *v.i.* to be interwoven or entwined [O.E. *wraeth*, a fillet].

wreck (rek) *n.* destruction of vessel; hulk of wrecked ship; remains of anything destroyed or ruined; desolation; *v.t.* to destroy, as vessel; to bring ruin upon; to upset completely. -**age** *n.* remains of something wrecked. -**er** *n.* one who wrecks; one employed in tearing down buildings, salvaging or recovering cargo from, wreck [O.E. *wraec*, punish].

wren (ren) *n.* tiny song-bird about 4 in. long, with reddish-brown plumage [O.E. *wrenna*].

wrench

wrench (rench) *v.t.* to wrest, twist, or force by violence; to distort; *n.* sudden, violent twist; tool with fixed or adjustable jaws for holding or adjusting nuts, bolts, etc. [O.E. *wrenc*, twist].

wrest (rest) *v.t.* to pull or force away by violence; to extort; to get with difficulty; to twist from its natural meaning; to distort; *n.* violent pulling or twisting [O.E. *wraestan*].

wres·tle (res'·l) *v.i.* to contend by grappling and trying to throw another down; to struggle; to strive (with). -**r** *n.* **wrestling** *n.* sport in which contestants endeavor to throw each other to the ground in accordance with rules [O.E. *wraestlian*, fr. *wraestan*, to twist about].

wretch (rech) *n.* miserable creature; one sunk in vice or degradation; one profoundly unhappy. -**ed** (rech'·id) *a.* very miserable; very poor or mean; despicable. -**edly** *adv.* -**edness** *n.* [O.E. *wraecca*, an outcast].

wrig·gle (rig'·l) *v.i.* to move sinuously, like a worm; to squirm; *v.t.* to cause to wriggle; *n.* act of wriggling; wriggling motion. -**r** *n.* **wriggling** *n.* **wriggly** *a.* [Dut. *wriggelen*, to move].

wright (rīt) *n.* one who fashions articles of wood, metal, etc., as *wheelwright* [O.E. *wyrhta*].

wring (ring) *v.t.* to twist and compress; to turn and strain with violence; to squeeze or press out; to pain; to extort; *v.i.* to turn or twist, as with pain. *pa.t.* and *pa.p.* **wrung**. -**er** *n.* one who wrings; machine for pressing out water from wet clothes, etc. -**ing wet**, absolutely soaking [O.E. *wringan*].

wrin·kle (ring'·kl) *n.* ridge or furrow on surface due to twisting, shrinking, or puckering; crease in skin; fold; corrugation; *v.t.* to make ridges, creases, etc. *v.i.* to shrink into wrinkles. -**ling** *n.* **wrinkly** *a.* [O.E. *wrincle*].

wrin·kle (ring'·kl) *n.* (*Colloq.*) valuable hint; novel method or approval [O.E. *wrenc*, trick].

wrist (rist) *n.* joint connecting the forearm and hand; the carpus. -**band** *n.* part of shirt sleeve covering wrist; elastic band to give support to injured wrist. -**let** *n.* band clasping wrist fairly tightly; bracelet; (*Slang*) handcuff. -**lock** *n.* wrestling hold [O.E.].

writ (rit) *n.* that which is written; in law, mandatory precept issued by a court; **Holy Writ**, the Scriptures [fr. *write*].

write (rīt) *v.t.* to set down or express in letters or words on paper, etc.; to compose, as book, song, etc.; *v.i.* to form characters representing sounds or ideas; to be occupied in writing; to express ideas in writing. *pr.p.* **writing**. *pa.t.* **wrote**. *pa.p.* **written**. -**r** *n.* one who writes; scribe; clerk; author. -**r's cramp** *n.* neurosis of muscles of hand. -**up** *n.* (*Colloq.*) favorable press criticism or report. **writing** *n.* mechanical act of forming characters on paper or any other material; anything written; style of execution or content of what is written; *pl.* literary or musical works; official papers, etc. **written** *a.* expressed in writing. **to write off**, to cancel, as bad debts [O.E. *writan*].

writhe (rīTH) *v.t.* to twist or distort; to turn to and fro; *v.i.* to twist or roll about (as in pain) [A.S. *writhen*, to twist].

writ·ten *pa.p.* of **write**.

wrong (rawng) *a.* not right; incorrect; mistaken; evil; immoral; injurious; unjust; illegal; unsuitable; improper; *n.* harm; evil; injustice; trespass; transgression; error; *adv.* not rightly; erroneously; *v.t.* to treat with injustice; to injure; to impute evil to unjustly. -**doer** *n.* one who injures another; one who breaks law; offender; sinner. -**ful** *a.* -**fully** *adv.* -**fulness** *n.* -**headed** *a.* obstinate; stubborn; perverse. -**headedly** *adv.* -**headedness** *n.* -**ly** *adv.* -**ness** *n.* **in the wrong**, at fault; blameworthy [O.E. *wrang*, injustice].

wrote (rōt) *pa.t.* of **write**.

wroth (rawth) *a.* full of wrath; angry; incensed [fr. *wrath*].

wrought (rawt) *pa.t.* and *pa.p.* of **work**. *a.* hammered into shape, as metal products. —**iron** *n.* purest form of commercial iron, fibrous, ductile, and malleable, prepared by puddling. —**up** *a.* excited; frenzied [O.E. *worhte*, worked].

wrung (rung) *pa.t.* and *pa.p.* of **wring**.

wry (rī) *a.* turned to one side; twisted; distorted; crooked; askew. -**ly** *adv.* -**neck** *n.* condition in which head leans permanently towards shoulders. -**necked** *a.* -**ness** *n.* [O.E. *wrigian*, to twist].

wy·an·dotte (wī'·an·dát) *n.* breed of domestic fowls [name of N. Amer. tribe].

X

xebec

xan·tip·pe (zan.tip′.ē) *n.* a scolding, shrewish woman [*Xantippē*, wife of Socrates].
X chro·mo·some (eks′.krōmạ.sōm) *n.* (*Biol.*) chromosome which determines the sex of the future organism.
xe·bec (zē′.bek) *n.* small three-masted vessel with lateen and square sails, used formerly in the Mediterranean by pirates [Fr. *chebec*].
xe·nog·a·my (zi.någ′.ạ.mi.) *n.* (*Bot.*) cross-fertilization. **xenogamous** *a.* [Gk. *xenos*, stranger; *gamos*, marriage].
xen·o·gen·e·sis (zen.ạ.jen′.ạ.sis) *n.* fancied generation of organism totally unlike parent. **xenogenetic** *a.* [Gk. *xenos*, stranger; *gamos*].
xe·non (zē′.nån) *n.* non-metallic .element belonging to group of rare or inactive gases [Gk. *xenos*, a stranger].
xen·o·pho·bi·a (zen.ạ.fō′.bi.ạ) *n.* fear or hatred of strangers or aliens [Gk. *xenos*, strange; *phobos*, fear].
xe·rog·ra·phy (zē.råg′.rạ.fi.) *n.* a process similar to photography, but not requiring specially sensitized paper or plates, using instead a special photoconductive plate.
X rays (eks′.rāz) *n.pl.* Röntgen rays—electromagnetic rays of very short wave length, capable of penetrating matter opaque to light rays and imprinting on sensitive photographic plate picture of objects; the picture so made. *v.t.* to treat, examine, or photograph with X-rays.
xy·lo·graph (zī′.lạ.graf) *n.* a wood engraving; impression from wood block. **-er** *n.* **-ic a. -ical** *a.* **-y** *n.* the art of wood engraving. [Gk. *xylon*, wood; *graphein*, to write].
xy·loid (zī′.loid) *a.* of the nature of wood; resembling wood; ligneous [Gk. *xylon*, wood].
xy·lol (zī′.lawl) *n.* commercial name for **xylene**, dimethyl benzene—hydrocarbon de-from coal tar used medicinally and as solvent for fats [Gk. *xylon*, wood; L. *oleum*, oil].
xy·lo·phone (zī′.lạ.fōn) *n.* musical instrument consisting of blocks of resonant wood, notes being produced by striking blocks with two small hammers. **xylophonist** *n.* [Gk. *xulon*, wood; *phonē*, a voice].
xy·lo·py·rog·ra·phy (zī.lō.pī.råg′.rạ.fi.) *n.* production of designs in wood by charring with hot iron [Gk. *xulon*, wood; *pur*, fire; *graphein*, to write].
xys·ter (zis′.tẹr) *n.* surgical instrument for scraping bones [Gk. fr. *xuein*, to scrape].

Y

yacht (yát) *n.* light sailing or power-driven vessel, for pleasure or racing; *v.i.* to sail in a yacht. **-ing** *n.* art or act of sailing a yacht; *a.* pert. to yacht. **-sman** *n.* **-smanship** *n.* [Dut. *jagt*].
yah (yå) *interj.* exclamation of derision, defiance or disgust.
yak (yak) *n.* species of ox found in C. Asia, with a hump and long hair [Tibetan, *gyag*].
yam (yam) *n.* tuber of tropical climbing-plant; sweet potato [Port. *inhame*].
yam·mer (yam′.ẹr) *v.i.* (*Colloq.*) to whine; to wail; to shout; complain [O.E. *geomor*, sad].
yank (yangk) *v.t.* and *v.i.* (*Colloq.*) to jerk; to tug; to pull quickly; *n.* quick tug.
Yank (yangk) *n.* (*Slang*) Yankee.
Yan·kee (yang′.kē) *n.* (in U.S.A.) citizen of New England, or of Northern States; (outside U.S.A.) an American; *a.* American. **-domn.**
yap (yap) *v.i.* to yelp; (*Slang*) to chatter incessantly; *n.* yelp. *pr.p.* **-ping.** *pa.p.* and *pa.t.* **-ped** [imit. origin].
yapp (yap) *n.* style of bookbinding in limp leather projecting beyond edges of book [Fr. *Yapp*, the inventor].
yard (yård) *n.* standard measure of length, equal to three feet or thirty-six inches; (*Naut.*) spar set crosswise to mast, for supporting a sail. **-age** *n.* measurement in yards; amount to be measured. **-arm** *n.* either half of a ship's yard. **-stick** *n.* measuring stick 36 inches long; (*Fig.*) standard of measurement [O.E. *gyrd*, a rod].
yard (yård) *n.* grounds surrounding a building; enclosed space used for specific purpose as *brickyard*, a *railroad yard*, etc. [O.E. *geard*, enclosure].
yarn (yårn) *n.* spun thread, esp. for knitting or weaving; thread of rope; (*Colloq.*) imaginative story; *v.i.* to tell a story. [O.E. *gearn*].
yar·row (yar′.ō) *n.* plant having strong odor and pungent taste [O.E. *gearwe*].
yash·mak (yash′.mak) *n.* veil worn by Mohammedan women, covering the face from beneath the eyes down [Ar.].
yat·a·ghan (yat′.ạ.gan) *n.* Turkish dagger, without a guard and usually curved [Turk.]
yaw (yaw) *v.i.* of ship or aircraft, to fail to keep steady course; *n.* act of yawing; temporary deviation from a straight course [O.N. *jaga*, to bend].
yawl (yawl) *n.* small, two-masted sailing boat, with smaller mast at stern; ship's small boat [Dut. *jol*].
yawn (yawn) *v.i.* to open mouth involuntarily through sleepiness, etc.; to gape; *n.* involuntary opening of mouth through sleepiness, etc. a gaping space. **-ing** *a.* gaping [O.E. *geonian*].
yaws (yawz) *n.* tropical contagious disease of the skin, usually chronic; (*Med.*) frambesia [Afr. *yaw*, a raspberry].
y·clept (i.klept′) *a.* (*Arch.*) called [O.E. *clipian*, to call].
ye (yē) *pron.* (*Arch.*) you [O.E. *ge.*].
ye (yē) *a.* an *Arch.* spelling of article **the.**
yea (yā) *n.* yes; *adv.* indeed [O.E. *eag*.].
yean (yēn) *v.t.* and *v.i.* to bring forth young; as sheep or goat. **-ling** *n.* a lamb; kid [O.E. *eanian*].
year (yir) *n.* time taken by one revolution of earth round sun, i.e. about 365¼ days; twelve months; scholastic session in school, university, etc.; *pl.* age; old age. **-ly** *a.* and *adv.* happening every year; annual. **-ling** *n.* young animal, esp. horse, in second year; *a.* being a year old. **-long** *a.* **-book** *n.* reference book of facts and statistics published yearly. **leap year,** year of 366 days, occurring every fourth year. [O.E. *gear*].
yearn (yurn) *v.i.* to seek earnestly: to feel longing or desire; to long for. **-ing** *n.* earnest desire; longing; *a.* desirous. **-ingly** *adv.* [O.E. *gyernan*].
yeast (yēst) *n.* froth that rises on malt liquors during fermentation; frothy yellow fungus growth causing this fermentation, used also in bread making, as leavening agent to raise dough. **-y** *a.* frothy; fermenting. **-cake** *n.* yeast mixed with meal and formed into small cakes for use in baking. [O.E. *gist*].
yegg (yeg) *n.* (*Slang*) criminal.
yell (yel) *v.i.* to cry out in a loud, shrill tone; to scream; to shriek; *n.* a loud, shrill cry.
-ing *n.* [O.E. *gellan*].
yel·low (yel′.ō) *n.* primary color; color of gold, lemons, buttercups, etc.; *a.* of this color; (*Colloq.*) cowardly; mean; despicable; of newspaper, sensational; *v.t.* to make yellow; *v.i.* to become yellow. **-ish** *a.* somewhat yellow. **-ishness** *n.* **-ness** *n.* — **fever** *n.* infectious, tropical disease, characterized by a yellow skin, vomiting, etc. — **jack** *n.* (*Colloq.*) yellow fever; yellow flag flown by ships, etc. in quarantine. — **jacket** *n.* a bright yellow wasp [O.E. *geolu*].
yelp (yelp) *n.* sharp, shrill bark or cry; *v.i.* to utter such a bark or cry. **-er** *n.* [O.E. *gilpan*, to boast].
yen (yen) *n.* (*Colloq.*) longing; urge.
yeo·man (yō′.man) *n.* (*Arch.*) officer of royal household; (*Navy*) petty officer. *pl.* yeomen. **-ly** *a.* **-ry** *n.* yeomen collectively. — **service,** long and faithful service; effective aid [contr. of *young man*].
yes (yes) *interj.* word expressing affirmation or consent. —**man** *n.* servile and obedient supporter [O.E. *gese*].
yes·ter (yes′.tẹr) *a.* (*Arch.*) pert. to yesterday; denoting period of time just past, esp. in compounds, e.g. 'yester-eve.' **-day** *n.* day before today. **-year** *n.* last year [O.E. *geostran*].
yet (yet) *adv.* in addition; at the same time; still; at the present time; now; hitherto; even; *conj.* nevertheless; notwithstanding. **as yet,** up to the present time [O.E. *giet*].
yew (ū) *n.* cone-bearing evergreen tree; its fine-grained wood, formerly used for making bows for archers [O.E. *iw*].
Yid·dish (yid′.ish) *n.* a mixture of dialectal German, Hebrew and Slavic, spoken by Jews; *a.* to or in this language [Ger. *Judisch*, Jewish].
yield (yēld) *v.t.* to produce; to give in return, esp. for labor, investment, etc.; to bring forth; to concede; to surrender; *v.i.* to submit; to comply; to give way; to produce; to bear; *n.* amount produced; return for labor, investment, etc.; profit; crop. **-ing** *a.* **-ingly** *adv.* [O.E. *gieldan* to pay].

yo·del, yo·dle (yō′·dl) v.t. and v.i. to sing or warble, with frequent changes from the natural voice to falsetto tone; n. falsetto warbling. **-er, yodler** n. [Ger. jodeln].

yo·ga (yō′·ga) n. system of Hindu philosophy; strict spiritual discipline practiced to gain control over forces of one's own being, to gain occult powers, but chiefly to attain union with the Deity or Universal Spirit. **yogi** n. one who practices yoga [Sans. = union].

yo·gurt (yō′·goort) n. a thick liquid food made from fermented milk [Turk. yoghurt].

yoicks (yoiks) interj. old fox-hunting cry.

yoke (yōk) n. wooden framework fastened over necks of two oxen, etc. to hold them together, and to which a plough, etc. is attached; anything having shape or use of a yoke; separately cut piece of material in garment, fitting closely over shoulders; bond or tie; emblem of submission, servitude, bondage; couple of animals working together; v.t. to put a yoke on; to couple or join, esp. to unite in marriage; to attach draft animal to vehicle; v.i. to be joined [O.E. geoc].

yo·kel (yō′·kl) n. rustic; country bumpkin.

yolk (yōk, yōlk) n. yellow part of egg. **-less** a. **-y** a. [O.E. geolu, yellow].

yon (yản) (Arch.) a. and adv. yonder. **-der** a. that or those there; adv. at a distance [O.E. geon].

yoke

yore (yōr) n. the past; old times [O.E. geara, fr. gear, year].

York·shire (yawrk′·sher) n. county in north of England. **— pudding,** batter baked in roasting tin along with meat. **— terrier,** small, shaggy terrier, resembling Skye terrier.

you (ū) pron. sing., pl. of second person in nominative or objective case, indicating person or persons addressed; also used indefinitely meaning, one, they, people in general. **your, yours** a. possessive form of you, meaning belonging to you, of you, pert. to you. **yourself**

pron. your own person or self (often used for emphasis or as a reflexive). pl. **yourselves** [O.E. eow, eower].

young (yung) a. not far advanced in growth, life, or existence; not yet old; vigorous; immature; n. offspring of animals. **-ish** a. somewhat young. **-ling** n. young person or animal. **-ster** n. young person or animal; child. **with young,** pregnant [O.E. geong].

youth (yōoth) n. state of being young; life from childhood to manhood; lad or young man; young persons collectively. **-ful** a. possessing youth; pert. to youth; vigorous. **-fully** adv. **-fulness** n. [O.E. geoguth].

yowl (youl) v.i. to howl; n. cry of a dog; long, mournful cry [M.E. yowlen].

yo-yo (yō′·yō) n. toy consisting of flat spool with string wound round in the deep groove in its edge, which when released from hand spins up and down string. [Trade Name].

yuc·ca (yuk′·a) n. genus of lilaceous plants, having tall, handsome flowers [W. Ind. name].

Yu·go·slav (yōó′·gō·slàv) a. pert. to Yugoslavia, the country of the Serbs, Croats, and Slovenes, in the N.W. of the Balkan Peninsula; n. a native of Yugoslavia. Also **Jugo-slav.** [Slav. jug, the south].

yule (yōol) n. feast of Christmas. **-tide** n. season of Christmas. **— log** n. log of wood to burn on the open hearth at Christmas time [O.E. geol].

Z

za·min·dar (za·mĕn·dàr′) n. in India, land-owner paying revenue to government. Also **zemindar** [Pers. = a landowner].

za·ny (zā′·ni·) n. formerly, buffoon who mimicked principal clown; simpleton. a. comical. **-ism** n. [corrupt. of It. Giovanni].

za·re·ba (za·rē′·ba) n. in Sudan, stockade of thorny bushes to protect against enemies and wild animals [Ar. zaribah, an enclosure].

zeal (zēl) n. intense enthusiasm for cause or person; passionate ardor. **zealot** (zel′·at) n. fanatic; enthusiast. **zealotry** n. fanaticism. **zealous** (zel′·as) a. ardent; enthusiastic; earnest. **zealously** adv. **zealousness** n. [Gk. zēlos, ardor].

ze·bec Same as **xebec.**

ze·bra (zē′·bra) n. genus of African quadrupeds of horse family, with tawny coat striped with black [W. Afr.].

ze·brass (zē′·bras) n. offspring of male zebra and she-ass.

ze·bu (zē′·bū) n. the humped Indian ox [Fr.].

zed (zed) n. name for letter z.

ze·na·na (ze·nà′·na) n. women's apartments in Hindu household [Pers. zan, woman].

Zend (zend) n. interpretation of the Avesta, sacred writings of Zoroastrians; Iranian language in which Zend-Avesta is written. **—Avesta** n. sacred writings and commentary thereon (Zend) of Zoroastrians [Pers. Avistak va Zand, text and commentary].

ze·nith (zē′·nith) n. point of heavens directly above observer's head; summit; height of success; acme; climax. **-al** a. [Ar. samt. path].

zeph·yr (zef′·er) n. west wind; gentle breeze; fine, soft woolen fabric [Gk. zephuros, west wind].

zep·pe·lin (zep′·(a)·lin) n. cigar-shaped long-range dirigible [fr. Count Zeppelin, inventor].

ze·ro (zē′·rō) n. nought; cipher; symbol, 0; neutral fixed point from which graduated scale is measured, as on thermometer, barometer, etc.; lowest point. pl. **-s, -es.** v.t. to adjust instrument to a fixed point. **— hour,** precise moment at which military offensive, etc. is timed to begin; crucial moment. **— in,** v.i. to adjust gun fire to a specific point [Ar. cifr. a cipher].

zest (zest) n. relish; fillip; stimulus; keen pleasure. **-ful** a. [O.Fr. zeste, lemon peel].

zeug·ma (zóóg′·ma) n. condensed sentence in which word, such as a verb, is used with two nouns to only one of which it applies. **-tic** a. [Gk. zeugnunai, to yoke].

Zeus (zōos) n. in Greek mythology, chief deity and father of gods and men, his seat being Mt. Olympus [Gk.].

zig·zag (zig′·zag) n. line, with short sharp turns; a. forming zigzag; v.t. and v.i. to form, or move with, short sharp turns. pr.p. **-ging.** pa.p., pa.t. **-ged.** adv. [Ger. zacke, sharp point].

zil·lion (zil′·yan) n. (Colloq.) inconceivably large number [coined word].

zinc (zingk) n. hard bluish-metal used in alloys, esp. brass, and because of its resistance to corrosion, for galvanizing iron; v.t. to coat with zinc. to galvanize. **— alloys** (Met.)

alloys containing percentage of zinc, as brass, etc. **-ic** a. **-iferous** a. containing zinc. **-ify** v.t. **-ograph** n. waxed-zinc engraving plate for etching; print of this. **-ographer** n. **-ographic** a. **-ographical** a. **-ography** n. process of engraving on zinc. **-oid** a. resembling zinc. **-ous** a. pert. to zinc [Ger. Zink, zinc].

zing (zing) n. the high-pitched sound of something moving at great speed; pep [echoic].

zin·ga·ro (tsing′·ga·rō) n. Italian name for Gypsy. fem. **zingara,** pl. **zingari, zingare.**

zin·ni·a (zin′·i·a) n. plant with bright-colored flowers [fr. Zinn, a German botanist].

Zi·on (zī′·an) n. hill in Jerusalem; town of Jerusalem; the Jewish people; Church of God; heaven. **-ism** n. movement among Jews to further the Jewish national state in Palestine. **-ist** n. advocate of Zionism [Heb. tsiyon, a hill].

zip (zip) n. whizzing sound, as of bullet in air; (Slang) energy; v.t. to shut with a zipper; v.i. to move with great speed. pr.p. **-ping.** pa.p., pa.t. **-ped, -per** n. device of interlocking, flexible teeth opened and shut by sliding clip. (Cap.) trademark for this. **-py** a. lively [imit.].

zir·con (zur′·kản) n. silicate of zirconium occurring in crystals; transparent ones used as gems. **zirconium** (zer·kŏn′·i·am) n. metal obtained from zircon, and resembling titanium **-ic** a. [Ar. zargun].

zith·er (ziTH′·er, zith′·er) n. flat, stringed instrument comprising résonance box with strings. Also **zithern. -ist** n. [Ger.].

zlo·ty (zlà′·ti·) n. Polish coin and monetary unit [Pol.].

zo·an·thro·py (zō·an′·thra·pi·) n. form of mental disorder in which man believes himself to be one of the lower animals [Gk. zōon, animal; *anthropos*, man].

zo·di·ac (zō·di·ak) *n.* (*Astron.*) imaginary belt in heavens following path of sun, and divided into twelve equal areas containing twelve constellations, each represented by appropriate symbols, called the *signs of the zodiac*; namely Aries (*Ram*), Taurus (*Bull*), Gemini (*Twins*), Cancer (*Crab*), Leo (*Lion*), Virgo (*Virgin*), Libra (*Balance*), Scorpio (*Scorpion*), Sagittarius (*Archer*), Capricornus (*Goat*), Aquarius (*Water-bearer*), Pisces (*Fishes*); a circular chart representing these signs **-al** *a.* [Gk. *zōdiakos*, fr. *zōon*, animal].

zom·bi, zom·bie (zăm'·bi·) *n.* orig. in Africa, deity of the python; in West Indies, corpse alleged to have been revived by black magic; the power which enters such a body; human being without will or speech but capable of automatic movement; intoxicating drink made with rum [W. African *zumbi*, fetish].

zone (zōn) *n.* girdle; climatic or vegetation belt; one of five belts into which earth is divided by latitude lines, as *frigid zone* of Arctic and Antarctic, *torrid zone* between Tropics of Cancer and Capricorn, *temperate zone* north of Tropic of Cancer and south of Tropic of Capricorn; division of a city, etc., for building or other purposes; *v.t.* to enclose; to divide into zones; to divide country into regional areas. **zonal** *a.* pert. to or divided into zones. **-d** *a.* having zones; distributed regionally. **zonate** *a.* striped [Gk. *zonē*].

zoo (zōō) *n.* zoological garden; place where wild animals are kept for showing.

zo·o (zō'·a) *prefix* (from Greek word *zōon*, animal) used in compound words, such as *zoochemistry, zoogeny*, etc.

zo·o·chem·is·try (zō·a·kem'·is·tri·) *n.* chemistry of constituents of animal body [Gk. *zōon*, animal; and *chemistry*].

zo·o·ge·og·ra·phy (zō·a·jē·àg'·ra·fi·) *n.* science which treats of the regional distribution of animals in the world. **zoogeographer** *n.* **zoogeographic, -al** *a.*

zo·oid (zō'·oid) *a.* resembling an animal; *n.* organism capable of relatively independent existence; a compound organism [Gk. *zōon*, an animal; *eidos*, a form].

zo·ol·a·try (zō·àl'·a·tri·) *n.* animal worship. **zoolater** *n.* **zoolatrous** *a.* [Gk. *zōon*, animal; *latreia*, worship].

zo·ol·o·gy (zō·àl'·a·ji·) *n.* natural history of animals, part of science of biology. **zoological** *a.* **zoologically** *adv.* **zoologist** *n.* one versed in zoology. **zoological gardens, zoo**, park where wild animals are kept for exhibition [Gk. *zōon*, animal; *logos*, discourse].

zoom (zōōm) *n. v.t.* (of prices) to become inflated; (of aircraft) to turn suddenly upwards at sharp angle; to move camera rapidly toward or away from an object which thus appears to move similarly [imit.].

zo·on (zō'·àn) *n.* individual part of compound animal; complete product of fertilized germ. *pl.* **zoa, zoons, -ic** *a.* [Gk. *zōon*, animal].

zo·oph·a·gous (zō·àf'·a·gas) *a.* feeding on animals; carnivorous. Also **zoophagan** [Gk. *zōon*, animal; *phagein*, to eat].

zo·o·phyte (zō'·a·fit) *n.* plant-like animal, such as sponge. **zoophytic, -al** *a.* pert. to zoophytes. **zoophytology** *n.* study of zoophytes [Gk. *zōon*, animal; *phuton*, plant].

zoot suit (zōōt'·sōōt) *n.* flashy type of man's suit, generally with padded shoulders, fitted waist, knee-length jacket and tight trousers.

Zo·ro·as·tri·an (zō·rō·as'·tri·an) *n.* follower of Zoroaster; *a.* pert. to Zoroaster or his religion; **-ism** *n.* ancient Persian religious doctrine taught by Zoroaster, principal feature of which is the recognition of the dual principle of good and evil; religion of the Parsees [fr. L. corrupt. of Persian *Zarathustra*].

zounds (zoundz) (*Arch.*) *interj.* of anger and surprise [corrupt. of *God's wounds*].

zuc·chet·to (zōō·ket'·ō, tsōōk·ket'·ō) *n.* skull cap worn by R.C. ecclesiastics, and differing in color according to rank of wearer. [It. *zucca*, a gourd].

zuc·chi·ni (zōō·kē'·ni·) *n.* a long greenskinned squash [It. dim. of *zucca*, squash].

Zu·lu (zōō'·lōō) *n.* member of Bantu tribe of S. Africa; *a.* pert. to Zulus [Native].

zwie·back (swē'·bak, ·bak, swī'·bak)*n.* a dry crisp bread, usually sweetened, that has been baked, sliced and then toasted [G. = twice baked].

zyme (zīm) *n.* ferment; disease germ. **zymic** *a.* **zymogen** *n.* any substance producing an enzyme. **zymogenesis** *n.* **zymogenic** *a.* **zymoid** *a.* resembling ferment. **zymosis** *n.* fermentation. **zymotic** *a.* pert. to or caused by fermentation. **zymotically** *adv.* **zymotic disease**, infectious or contagious disease caused by germs introduced into body from without [Gk. *zumē*, leaven].

zy·mur·gy (zi'·mur·ji·) *n.* branch of chemistry dealing with fermentation process. [Gr. *zūme* leaven + *-ourgia*, working].